W9-AQP-927

WEBSTER'S DICTIONARY OF SYNONYMS

FIRST EDITION

A Merriam-Webster
REG. U.S. PAT. OFF.

A DICTIONARY

OF

DISCRIMINATED SYNONYMS

WITH ANTONYMS AND

ANALOGOUS AND CONTRASTED WORDS

G. & C. MERRIAM CO., PUBLISHERS
SPRINGFIELD, MASS., U.S.A.

MADE IN THE U.S.A.
GEORGE BANTA PUBLISHING COMPANY, ELECTROTYPERS, PRINTERS, AND BINDERS
THE COLLEGIATE PRESS, MENASHA, WIS., U.S.A.

CONTENTS

PREFACE

The publishers of this book have long felt that there is a widespread need for a work devoted to synonymy that emphasizes discrimination among synonyms and that provides accessory material in the form of word lists of various kinds. For many years there has been great interest in the articles devoted to discussion of synonyms that are included in various general dictionaries of the English language. Those prepared by Dr. John Livingston Lowes for the Merriam-Webster dictionaries from the publication of *Webster's New International Dictionary* in 1909 have proved especially stimulating and have led to numerous requests on the part of consultants of the dictionary that they be issued separately, extended in number and scope, and supplemented with word-finding lists. In recent years these suggestions have been so frequent as to convince the publishers that a book of this sort should be undertaken.

Before the editorial work was begun, a survey was made of all the principal works devoted to treatment of synonyms, both independent publications and dictionaries containing this type of material. As a part of this survey, an intensive study was made of the technique employed by all the leading synonymists and all their differing points of view.

The information thus obtained has been summarized in the form of an essay (pp. vii–xxv). The publishers believe that this, the first definite attempt to survey the problems and issues in the field of English synonymy, will prove not only of interest to readers of this book but of very great value to them by giving them a background against which to set the articles in the present work. The survey provided the present editors with a firm grasp of their complex task, and the making of it is more than justified in the resultant sharpening of the editorial point of view and the consequent enrichment of the work in the discriminating articles in this book.

The core of the present work is the discriminating articles. It is not its purpose to assemble mere word-finding lists for consultants with but a vague notion of the sort of word they seek, but rather to provide consultants with the means of making clear comparisons between words of a common denotation and to enable them to distinguish the differences in implications, connotations, and applications among such words, and to choose for their purposes the precisely suitable word. (Compare the discussion of Roget's aims on pp. xvi–xvii, below.)

In addition to the central core of articles discriminating groups of words, this book provides auxiliary information of three types, in the form of liberal lists of analogous words, antonyms, and contrasted words. These three types are explained on pp. xxxii–xxxiii.

As far as possible, the editors have tried to make this book self-contained. To do this completely, it would of course be necessary to discuss in at least one article of synonymy every word listed as an antonym or in a word-finding list. It is not practicable, perhaps not even desirable, to carry the ideal of a self-contained book to this extreme. In the case of antonyms, those appropriate to an entry have been chosen and exhibited at that entry regardless of whether they are themselves discriminated in the book. This is, however, the only absolute exception. A merely apparent exception, but one readily explained, consists in the use (in the word-finding lists of analogous words and contrasted words) of derivative words or of words related to other words as their negatives or affirmatives. The editors have felt free to use such derivative, negative, and affirmative words when the primitive words or the correlative words are themselves discriminated in some article in the book.

Otherwise, the book is self-contained. Every word discussed in an article of synonymy is entered in its own alphabetical place and is followed by a list of its synonyms, with a reference (by means of an asterisk or a direction introduced by "see") to the entry where the discussion of these listed words is to be found. The words listed as analogous, and those listed as contrasted, are always displayed in groups, each group having a clear reference (asterisk or "see") to the term under which an article of synonymy is to be found.

As the value of illustrative citations (whether made up by the editor and representing common current use, or whether quoted from some author) has long been recognized, the present work provides a wealth of such illustrative material. Besides illustrations already found in the articles of synonymy in *Webster's New International Dictionary, Second Edition*, and numerous additional citations available in our editorial files and in various repositories of citations (such as concordances and books of familiar quotations), a large accumulation of quotations was newly collected for this work. The editorial staff of G. & C. Merriam Company spent many months reading for this special purpose, particularly first-class contemporary writers and well-known books published within the last twenty to thirty years, as well as current periodical literature both American and British. The file of citations resulting from this reading has been of inestimable value, serving not merely as a source for illustrative quotations but as a means of establishing current usage and reflecting recent changes in the implications, connotations, and applications of words.

As the Historical Survey makes clear (pp. xxiii–xxv, below), it is the feeling of the present editors that the work on synonymy done by Dr. Lowes in consultation with the late George Lyman Kittredge marked the highest development of English synonymy up to the present time. They have endeavored to preserve as much of this work as the enlarged scope and aim of the present book would permit. It must be obvious, however, that the increase of the number of words to be subjected to discrimination as synonyms inevitably brings about a regrouping of much of the material treated by Professor Lowes. The present work, then, is by no means a reprint of material from any other Merriam-Webster dictionary.

In its preparation, broad questions of form and policy were determined by the permanent editorial board of G. & C. Merriam Company, consisting of William Allan Neilson (*chairman*), *Editor in Chief of Merriam-Webster Dictionaries, formerly President of Smith College*, Robert C. Munroe, *President of G. & C. Merriam Company*, John P. Bethel, *General Editor of Merriam-Webster Dictionaries*, and Lucius H. Holt, *Managing Editor of Merriam-Webster Dictionaries.*

Every article included in this book was read by Dr. Neilson and Dr. Bethel. All points of disagreement, no matter how minor, were thoroughly canvassed, and each article was subjected to revision before achieving its final form.

The writing of the articles was done chiefly by Miss Rose F. Egan, *Assistant Editor on the permanent editorial staff*, who also prepared the essays that form the larger part of the introductory matter. To her clear analysis and understanding of the purposes of the book and to her skill in dealing with the difficult material of synonymy this work owes much of its quality. By far the largest number of articles were written originally by her. Some were written by the following *Assistant Editors*, Mr. Edward Artin, Miss Elsie Mag (who also gathered the material from which Miss Egan prepared the word-finding lists) and Mr. Hubert P. Kelsey (who wrote many of the articles on scientific terms), and by Dr. Holt and Dr. Bethel; and much valuable information and criticism was supplied by Dr. Everett E. Thompson and Mr. Edward F. Oakes, *Assistant Editors*, and Miss Ervina Foss, *Editorial Assistant.* Certain articles of a technical nature were submitted to the scrutiny of outside consultants, notably articles dealing with terms in law, chemistry, and medicine, which were reviewed by Dr. Roscoe Pound of Harvard University, Dr. Austin M. Patterson, Vice-President of Antioch College, and Dr. Esmond R. Long, Professor of Pathology at the University of Pennsylvania and Director of the Henry Phipps Institute, respectively.

Throughout the editorial work, Miss Egan was assisted by Miss Anne M. Driscoll, *Editorial Assistant*, who had charge of all typing and filing and provided invaluable assistance in many ways. Proofreading of typed copy, including the verification of quotations, was done by Mr. Hubert Roe; proofreading of printers' proofs by Mr. Roe and Miss Driscoll; checking of cross references by Miss Eliane Yelle, Miss Driscoll, and Mr. Roe. The list of authors and sources quoted (see pp. 899 ff.) was compiled by Mr. Roe and Dr. Bethel.

The typesetting and electrotyping were done by The George Banta Publishing Company, of Menasha, Wisconsin, whose staff gave unstinted co-operation and assisted with excellent proofreading.

INTRODUCTORY MATTER

SURVEY OF THE HISTORY OF ENGLISH SYNONYMY

Consultation of a work on synonyms is made easier if the consultant has a reasonable background of the theory and of the technique that have developed since the first English synonymy was published. The following essay is, so far as we know, the first attempt to survey broadly the course of that development from its beginnings to the present. It is not intended to be exhaustive. Some good books have been published which have not been specifically discussed because they have played no essential part in this development or have advanced no new ideas which, by challenging attention or debate, have led to further clarification of the problems involved. The purpose of this article has not been primarily to praise or to denounce, but to lead up to the exposition of principles which have dominated the writing of this book. These principles, we believe, are founded upon the practice of those who have seen and known clearly what could be accomplished by a book of synonyms: there are others who disagree, but we have tried to present their case fairly.

It was not until the second half of the eighteenth century that the first book on synonyms appeared in English. The Rev. John Trusler (1735–1820) was its author, *The Difference between Words Esteemed Synonymous* its title, and 1766 its date. Its source is definitely established. In 1718, the Abbé Gabriel Girard (1677–1748) had published in France *La Justesse de la langue françoise ou les Différentes significations des mots qui passent pour être synonymes*, a work which had great vogue not only in France but also abroad, especially in England. That Trusler's book was based upon it is evidenced not only by the likeness of the titles but also (in the first edition) by an English version of Girard's preface and by the admission in the author's preface that he had translated as much of the articles as was in keeping with the peculiar genius of the English language. The second edition of 1783, however, increases the divergence between the two books: the prefaces are consolidated and the result is given as the work of the author, although many passages from Girard are included without being quoted. There are, too, many new articles dealing with peculiarly British terms, such as those which concern the church and daily life in England; but these, although they represent an enrichment of vocabulary, add little to the originality of the work, which still remains an imitation. A clear-cut distinction which sharply reveals the meanings of synonymous French terms often becomes a forced distinction when applied to English. In fact, Trusler never knew whether it was his aim to point out the "delicate differences between words reputed synonymous" or to give the particular idea of each word "which constitutes its proper and particular character." He claims both aims as one, not realizing that often they are divergent.

The next significant work was the *British Synonymy* of Hester Lynch Piozzi (1741–1821), better known as Mrs. Thrale, the close friend of Dr. Johnson. It first appeared in 1794 and was succeeded by at least two editions, the best known of which was published in Paris in 1804. That it was immediately popular is evident from the testimony of its 1804 editors, who asserted its merits on the ground "of the successive editions it has passed through being the best proof of the estimation in which it is held." That it was not written without a knowledge of Girard's work we know on the authority of these same editors. "So great indeed was the estimation" in which the French work was held, "that in a few years after its publication, an imitation of it appeared in England": presumably the "imitation" was Trusler's.

The editors imply, however, that Mrs. Piozzi's work is something better than had yet been given to the public. "But it was only in the year 1794," they continue, in a tone that implies contempt for the "imitation," "that Mrs. Piozzi (formerly Mrs. Thrale) so well known in the literary world for her different publications, and her intimacy with the learned Dr. Johnson, brought out the work we have now the pleasure of presenting to our Readers, and which is totally grounded on the structure of the English language." Whoever had been the compiler of the "imitation," he had not been subjected in the same measure to the influence of Dr. Johnson, for there are, say the editors in a footnote, "some who are of opinion that divers articles in it [Mrs. Piozzi's book] were drawn up by that great Lexicographer himself."

Despite this intimation of helpfulness from a great source, Mrs. Piozzi's book more often reveals an independence of spirit and a feminine disregard of advice than it does subservience. It is, in fact, never profound: it is full of errors or dubious assertions, and it is often absurdly naïve. More than this, it frequently takes issue with Dr. Johnson or, in a sprightly manner, casts doubt on his judgments. There is the story of the milliner's apprentice who saved her chicken bones to feed a horse. Johnson contended that such an action showed that she was *ignorant*, but Mrs. Piozzi maintained that it proved her *senseless*. "I thought her an ideot [sic]" was, for her, the last word on the matter.

Great as was her respect for Dr. Johnson in his own field, she believed that she also had her field, and that it was incumbent on her to remain within the limits she had set for herself. Her object is very clear. Like Girard and Trusler, she was distinguishing not synonyms (that is, words identical in meaning) but words so similar in meaning as to be "apparently synonymous." The subtitle of her book announces her aim and reveals a further limitation of purpose: "An attempt at regulating the choice of words in familiar conversation." Her preface to the 1794 edition develops these ideas:

> If then to the selection of words in conversation and elegant colloquial language a book may give assistance, the Author. . . . modestly offers her's; persuaded that, while men teach to write with propriety, a woman may at worst be qualified—through long practice—to direct the choice of phrases in familiar talk.

Her book, she modestly claimed, "is intended chiefly for a parlour window" and is "unworthy of a place upon a library shelf," but it may be of help to others "till a more complicated and valuable piece of workmanship be found to further their research." She wished in particular to help those who desired to converse elegantly and to save foreigners from ridiculous mistakes in speech. "If I can in the course of this little work dispel a doubt, or clear up a difficulty to foreigners. . . . I shall have an honour to boast."

For this reason, she could not see that her method of discrimination had much in common with that of the lexicographer and the logician. Theirs was to define: hers was to indicate propriety in the use of words. It was not her intent to establish differences in meaning, but to indicate the fitness of words for use, often depending on "the place in which they should stand" but sometimes depending on their relative fineness, strength, force, or the like. She makes a distinction between the methods of the definer and the methods of the synonymist by giving, first, two examples of definition of the word *fondness*, one from "an eminent logician" and one from Dr. Johnson, and, secondly, by an ideal synonymy in which she reveals the same word's meaning by showing it in use along with similar words. This was not invariably her method, but it illustrates what in the main she was trying to achieve.

> . . . I have before me the definition of *fondness*, given into my hands many years ago by a most eminent logician.
>
> '*Fondness*,' says the Definer, 'is the hasty and injudicious determination of the will towards promoting the present gratification of some particular object.'
>
> '*Fondness*,' in the opinion of Dr. Johnson, 'is rather the hasty and injudicious attribution of excellence, somewhat beyond the power of attainment, to the object of our affection.'
>
> Both these definitions may possibly be included in *fondness;* my own idea of the whole may be found in the following example:
>
> Amintor and Aspasia are models of true *love:* 'tis now seven years since their mutual *passion* was sanctified by marriage; and so little is the lady's *affection* diminished, that she sat up nine nights successively last winter by her husband's bed-side, when he had a malignant fever that frightened relations, friends, servants, all away. Nor can any one allege that her *tenderness* is ill repaid, while we see him gaze upon her features with that *fondness* which is capable of creating charms for itself to admire, and listen to her talk with a fervour of admiration scarce due to the most brilliant genius.
>
> For the rest, 'tis my opinion that men love for the most part with warmer *passion* than women do—at least than English women, and with more transitory *fondness* mingled with that passion. . . .

It was in her simpler versions of this method that she developed a formula that has been followed by many of her successors in the discriminated synonymy—not always felicitously. We shall have opportunity to return to this method later when it becomes an object of attack, and shall call it for the sake of convenience the Piozzi method. At present let examples of her usage suffice:

> To ABANDON, FORSAKE, RELINQUISH, GIVE UP, DESERT, QUIT, LEAVE. . . though at first sight apparently synonymous, conversing does certainly better shew the peculiar appropriation than books, however learned; for. . . familiar talk tells us in half an hour—that a man *forsakes* his mistress, *abandons* all hope of regaining her lost esteem, *relinquishes* his pretensions in favour of another. . . .
>
> We say a lad of an active and *diligent spirit*, or else of an *assiduous temper*, or *sedulous disposition*.
>
> We say that reports are *confirmed*, treaties *ratified*, and affairs *settled*.
>
> A hard question *puzzles* a man, and a variety of choice *perplexes* him: one is *confounded* by a loud and sudden dissonance of sounds or voices in a still night; *embarrassed* by a weight of clothes or valuables, if making escape from fire, thieves, or pursuit. . . .
>
> The gentleman who discharges a gaming debt in preference to that of a tradesman, apparently prefers *honour* to another virtue, *justice*.

It seems a fair statement of her aim to say that she was attempting to indicate and establish idiomatic English. However, in determining such English, she had only two tests to apply: the drawing-room usage of her time, and her own instinct. To literary use, in general, she was indifferent. Therefore her judgments are nearly always subjective and sometimes arbitrary. Moreover, she discounted the great help that discrimination of meanings is to the synonymist. "We must not meantime retard our own progress," she wrote in her preface, "with studied definitions of every quality coming under consideration.... Although the final cause of definition is to fix the true and adequate meaning of words or terms, without knowledge of which we stir not a step in logic; yet *here* we must not suffer ourselves to be so detained, as synonymy has more to do with elegance than truth."

Her judgments are often limited or partial, for they represent her personal feelings or the predilections of her age. Yet, within those limits, she frequently hit upon an exact meaning of a word in a particular sense and gave it life and color. What she seldom saw was that a word might have more meanings than the one which was illustrated (as *honor* in her example of the tradesman) or that a good but narrow instance of use might be taken as idiomatic by her readers (as when by implication *puzzle* suggests a question or problem needing determination, and *perplex* a variety of choices). The danger of her work is not in the falsity of the example, for it is usually true or just, but in its inadequacy in suggesting other instances of good use.

Yet in her refusal to accept her age's theory of definition and in her approach to a concept of good usage, we must recognize an independent spirit. The time was not ripe for a fully developed conception of the differences between logic and lexicography, yet she was somewhat nearer the present conception than some later and cleverer persons, and she had at least a feeling of rightness in the use of language that suggested, even if it did not consciously approach, the later theory of good usage as a test of such rightness. Besides, her book has an engaging quality, often lacking in books of this character, which is not necessarily a sign of the levity with which critics have charged this book, but rather of a spirited challenge to the ideals of a hidebound age.

Mrs. Piozzi's book was followed by William Perry's *Synonymous, Etymological, and Pronouncing English Dictionary*, published in 1805. On its title page and in its preface the editor explicitly offers his work as derived from *The Dictionary* of Samuel Johnson. Perry was the compiler of the better known *Royal Standard English Dictionary* brought out in England in 1775 and in America in 1788.

The *Synonymous Dictionary*, as we shall call the 1805 book, evidently did not achieve the fame or popularity of the *Royal Standard*. Chauncey Goodrich, Noah Webster's son-in-law, referred to it in 1847 in his preface to the royal octavo volume of Webster as "entirely out of print." There is no evidence to show that it passed beyond the first edition. On its title page it is described as "an attempt to synonymise his [Johnson's] Folio Dictionary of the English Language." In its preface Perry claims that it contains "the only synonymous vocabulary ever offered to the public," and that "To the philological, critical, and other interesting observations of the above learned author [Dr. Johnson], we have superadded two exclusive advantages to our publication; the one—as a *synonymous*, the other—as a *pronouncing* nomenclature. The *former* is new and unique..."

The work, he informs us, was begun in 1797, three years, therefore, after the publication of the first edition of Mrs. Piozzi's *British Synonymy*. Yet there is no indication of knowledge of that work nor of the work of Girard; in fact, Perry recognized no predecessor save Johnson. From Johnson, by explicit credit, he extracted his vocabulary and his explanations of meanings. Not so openly, however, did he extract the synonyms themselves: for example, his entry *good* is followed by Johnson's definition of sense 1, but the synonyms are taken from all of Johnson's succeeding twenty-nine senses. Nor does he provide many citations, and these are chiefly in entries at the end of the book; elsewhere, in parentheses, he lists the authors Johnson quoted but not the passages cited.

In addition, he adopted an original method of presenting his material. There were two types of entries, one in lower case and one in capitals. The latter, which he called "radicals," were followed by an exhaustive list; the former were succeeded by a much shorter list, but one word was printed in small capitals to indicate it was the radical. Thus "marches," a lower-case entry, has "borders, limits, confines, BOUNDARIES" as its synonyms: "BOUNDARY," an entry in capitals, has a much longer list which includes "limit, bound, bourn, term, mere, but, abuttal, border, barrier, marches, confines, precinct, line of demarcation, utmost reach or verge of a territory; a landmark, a mere-stone." If, then, one wished all the synonyms of a lower-case entry such as *marches* or *abbreviation*, one must turn to BOUNDARY or ABRIDGMENT, the word entered as the radical.

There are two things to notice here that are important. Perry was not merely greatly extending the traditional definition of *synonym* (as one of two or more words of identical meaning, or of apparently identical meaning) and broadening it to include a group of words which have resemblances in meaning, but he was doing so in what seems to be a misunderstanding of Dr. Johnson's purposes in adding such words to his definitions and in ignorance of what he supplied as a corrective. The fact of the matter is that Johnson was aware of the difficulties of his task, that he was conscious that the part of his work on which "malignity" would "most frequently fasten is the *Explanation* [i.e., the definition]."

> I cannot hope to satisfy those, who are perhaps not inclined to be pleased, since I have not always been able to satisfy myself. To interpret a language by itself is very difficult; many words cannot be explained by synonimes, because the idea signified by them has not more than one appellation; nor by paraphrase, because simple ideas cannot be described.

That was the difficulty. Synonyms would not perfectly satisfy the need when either the word defined had many meanings or when the word defining had more significations than the one intended, for in either case one must be too broad and the other too narrow. Then, too, "simple ideas" (really those involved in simple words such as *be, do, act*) were beyond definition, as Johnson saw it.

> The rigour of interpretative lexicography requires that *the explanation, and the word explained, should be always reciprocal;* this I have always endeavoured but could not always attain. Words are seldom exactly synonimous; a new term was not introduced, but because the former was thought inadequate: names, therefore, have often many ideas, but few ideas have many names. It was then necessary to use the proximate word, for the deficiency of single terms can very seldom be supplied by circumlocution...

So Johnson wrote and so Perry quotes in his preface. But instead of continuing Johnson's statement to its end, Perry broke off with "circumlocution," thereby giving the reader some reason to infer that Johnson thought the method of definition by synonym preferable to that of definition by paraphrase. He had failed to notice, or possibly had deliberately ignored, that this was not in any sense Johnson's meaning, that both methods were faulty, but that there was a remedy for the imperfections of each. Johnson's addition to this last sentence, "nor is the inconvenience great of such mutilated interpretations, because the sense may easily be collected entire from the examples," makes that point clear. Perry may have been obtuse rather than disingenuous when, for the most part, he omits the examples (citations) of Johnson and enters synonyms, which are not, in Johnson's language, "exactly synonymous" but only "proximate words." But he may have known what Dr. Johnson meant, though his explanation is by no means clear:

> We by no means contend, that the whole of the explanations collected under such initial words as...we call Radicals, are all strictly synonymous; neither, on the other hand, can we agree with those who roundly assert, that there are not two words in the whole English language of precisely the same signification; but this we take upon us to say, that we have no less than Dr. Johnson's authority for their selection and disposition as explanatory of their meaning...

Dr. Johnson's example, great as was its authority and prestige at that time, was an unstable prop when his statements were misunderstood. Perry perhaps indirectly rendered a service by raising the issue as to whether the term "synonym" needed redefinition, since it was being broadened in its extension: he may also have done a service in showing to others the values implicit in word-finding lists. But he did not see that he had raised those issues, and what purports to be a dictionary succeeds chiefly in being a word finder.

Between 1805 and 1852 (the latter the date of publication of Roget's *Thesaurus of English Words and Phrases*), several works on synonyms appeared. Some were of the word-finding list type, and among these there was nothing of particular importance. On the other hand, there were as many as five works discriminating synonyms of which at least four stand out for one reason or another: *English Synonymes Discriminated*, by William Taylor (1813), *English Synonymes Explained*, by George Crabb (1816), *English Synonyms Classified and Explained*, by George F. Graham (1846), and *A Selection of English Synonyms*, by Miss Elizabeth Jane Whately (1851). Both Crabb's and Miss Whately's books are still influential and have been reprinted in recent years.

William Taylor (1765–1836), the author of the first of these books, is better known as the translator of Burger's *Lenore*, Lessing's *Nathan the Wise*, and Goethe's *Iphigenia in Tauris*, and as one of the leading promoters of knowledge of contemporary German literature during the romantic era. His *English Synonymes Discriminated* is the result of his studies in German, French, Italian, and other languages and of his conviction that no English work the equal of certain foreign treatises on synonyms had as yet been written. The work is, as a whole, uneven, but a few articles in it are not only better than any others written up to that time but the equal of any that were to be written for over ninety years. A favorite theory of his was that if one is thoroughly grounded in the original meaning of a term, one "can never be at a loss how to employ it in metaphor." Consequently, etymologies became for him an important means of showing this original meaning. They formed not an invariable part of his discrimination but a very useful part when they were needed. Usually, also, he knew when his etymology was grounded on fact and when it was merely hypothetical. His method at its best is exemplified in the article covering *austere*, *severe*, and *rigid*, which we give here in abridged form:

> Austerity (says Blair[1]) relates to the manner of living: severity, of thinking, rigour, of punishing. To austerity is opposed effeminacy; to severity, relaxation; to rigour, clemency. A hermit is austere in his life; a casuist, severe in his decision; a judge, rigorous in his sentence.
>
> In this discrimination there is little exactness. Austerity is applied not only to habit, but to doctrine, and to infliction. Solitary confinement is a severe form of life, and a severe punishment. Rigid observances, rigid opinions, are oftener spoken of than rigid sentences.
>
> A hermit is austere, who lives harshly; is severe who lives solitarily; is rigid who lives unswervingly. A casuist is austere who commands mortification, severe, who forbids conviviality, rigid, whose exactions are unqualified. A judge is austere, who punishes slight transgressions; severe, who punishes to the utmost; rigid, who punishes without respect of persons and circumstances.
>
> Why this? Austerity is an idea of the palate; it means crabbedness....These modes of life which are painful to the moral taste, are called austere....Austerity is opposed to suavity.
>
> Severity is not traced back to the sensible idea in which the word originates. *Se* and *vereor*, to bend down apart, are perhaps the component ideas. The *lying prostrate apart* is not only characteristic of the praying anchoret, and of public penance, but of cruel infliction: and to all these cases severity is accordingly applied ....To severity is opposed remissness.
>
> Rigour is stiffness: rigid means frozen: stiff with cold....To rigour is opposed pliancy.
>
> Religious competition renders sects austere, priests severe, and establishments rigid.

With the exception of *severe* (the ultimate origin of which is still doubtful), the words, in the main, conform to their etymology. *Austere* does originally mean something like "crabbed," and *rigid* means "stiff," though not necessarily "stiff with cold"; also, something that is *austere* is not sweet or suave, and something that is *rigid* is not pliant or flexible. He has caught the essential difference here, and the proper application follows. If Taylor had been able to maintain this method and the penetration it involved, he might have changed the course of synonymizing. But three years later *English Synonymes Explained*, by George Crabb (1778–1851), appeared and caught the public favor. For thirty-seven years, Taylor's book remained unreprinted: then between 1850 and 1876 there were three new editions. For a few years it attracted some attention and then disappeared from favor.

Crabb's book, while still highly regarded by some, meets much adverse criticism from others. In his own day it was thought of generally as the best work available, although Crabb complicated matters somewhat by frequent revisions which changed its character. In his introduction to the first edition, he complained of the lack of a work on English synonyms in which the subject is treated "in a scientific manner adequate to its importance." Englishmen though great in literature and philology had in this field fallen short of the French and Germans who "have had several considerable works on the subject." He did not wish "to depreciate the labors of those who have preceded" him; rather he claimed "to have profited by every thing which has been written in any language upon the subject; and although I always pursued my own train of thought, yet whenever I met with any thing deserving of notice I adopted it, and referred it to the author in a note."

Crabb's *English Synonymes Explained* is both the most laborious and the most ambitious work of its kind. In spirit and objective it is a far remove from Mrs. Piozzi's *British Synonymy*, few as are the years which intervened between their publication. For Mrs. Piozzi represented the old temper where sprightliness, elegance, and ease were paramount, and Crabb the new temper in which the world had grown solemn and serious under the influence of many currents, such as the pressure of momentous events, the influence of Continental, especially German, thinkers, and the spread of all the new ideas spoken of collectively as romanticism. When the best philosophers and philosophic poets of the age were seeking to answer the questions, what is beauty?, what is poetry?, what is art?, what is genius?, and were discriminating the beautiful and the sublime, the naïve and the sentimental, imagination and fancy, the ugly and the grotesque, what synonymist could in conscience say that "synonymy has more to do with elegance than truth"?

Crabb was undoubtedly concerned with truth rather than elegance. He was stimulated by the thinking of his age and, like many persons of his time, responded with joy to the new philosophy that deepened and enriched the concepts of beauty, poetry, and truth. Although he was in no sense a philosopher, he had a smattering of philosophical knowledge, a small philosophical vocabulary, and a deep love of philosophical distinctions. He was also interested in philology as it was understood in his time. In the study of synonyms he found satisfaction of all these interests, all the more so since he had come to regard synonyms not as words of the same meaning, but as "closely allied" words between which there are "nice shades of distinction." Discrimination not only gave him profound intellectual satisfaction: it also afforded him great opportunities. In his introduction he wrote:

> My first object certainly has been to assist the philological inquirer in ascertaining the force and comprehension of the English language; yet I should have thought my work but half completed had I made it a

[1] Hugh Blair, rhetorician, 1718–1800.

mere register of verbal distinctions. While others seize every opportunity unblushingly to avow and zealously to propagate opinions destructive of good order, it would ill become any individual of contrary sentiments to shrink from stating his convictions, when called upon as he seems to be by an occasion like that which has now offered itself.

His justification for "the introduction of morality in a work of science" is very ingenious. In answer to anticipated objections he wrote, "a writer, whose business it was to mark the nice shades of distinction between words closely allied, could not do justice to his subject without entering into all the relations of society, and showing, from the acknowledged sense of many moral and religious terms, what has been the general sense of mankind on many of the most important questions which have agitated the world."

It is not easy to find in Crabb proofs that he was discriminating historical meanings (the interpretation that may be given to his "the acknowledged sense"), but one can readily discover evidence that often he was supporting an older conception he favored rather than a new conception he heartily disliked. A good example of this is found in his discrimination of SOUL and MIND.

There are minute philosophers, who. . .deny that we possess any thing more than what this poor composition of flesh and blood can give us; and yet, methinks, sound philosophy would teach us that we ought to prove the truth of one position, before we assert the falsehood of its opposite; and consequently that if we deny that we have any thing but what is material in us, we ought first to prove that the material is sufficient to produce the reasoning faculty of man. . . . [He continued this line of argument through several sentences.]

But not to lose sight of the distinction drawn between the words *soul* and *mind*, I simply wish to show that the vulgar and the philosophical use of these terms altogether accord, and are both founded on the true nature of things.

Poets and philosophers speak of the *soul* in the same strain as the active and living principle.[2]

Arguments of this character were mostly occasional with Crabb, but the method of discriminating things which the words named or to which they were applied was characteristically infixed. He could not, for instance, mark the distinctions between *finical* and *foppish*, but between a *finical gentleman* and a *foppish gentleman*.

A *finical* gentleman clips his words and screws his body into as small a compass as possible to give himself the air of a delicate person. . . : a *foppish* gentleman seeks by extravagance in the cut of his clothes, and by the tawdriness in their ornaments, to render himself distinguished for finery.

He could not discriminate *beautiful, fine, handsome,* without determining what is *the beautiful, the fine, the handsome.*

The *beautiful* is determined by fixed rules; it admits of no excess or defect; it comprehends regularity, proportion, and a due distribution of colour, and every particular which can engage the attention: the *fine* must be coupled with grandeur, majesty, and strength of figure; it is incompatible with that which is small; a little woman can never be *fine:* the *handsome* is a general assemblage of what is agreeable; it is marked by no particular characteristic, but the absence of all deformity. . . .

Even simple words were so discriminated; each one had an abstract reference which was the test of its right use no matter how little cultivated writers and speakers respected that test.

The *gift* is an act of generosity or condescension; it contributes to the benefit of the receiver: the *present* is an act of kindness, courtesy, or respect; it contributes to the pleasure of the receiver.

What we *abhor* is repugnant to our moral feelings; what we *detest* contradicts our moral principle; what we *abominate* does equal violence to our religious and moral sentiments. . . . Inhumanity and cruelty are objects of *abhorrence;* crimes and injustice of *detestation;* impiety and profanity of *abomination*. . . .

Crabb's habitual attitude to words as names of things, or for what he might have called "true concepts of things," vitiates his entire work. It has made it of negligible value in our time when lexicography has become an independent science with clearly defined objectives and functions, the chief of which is to respect the meanings men have agreed to give words, rather than the notions individuals have concerning the things named or described by those words. His concepts, however interesting, are still subjective and have not been tested to any extent by actual written or spoken language. There are many citations in his work, but the sensitive reader often finds little relevancy between the word as used there and the sense defined. For example, in illustrating the meaning of the "soul" as "the active and living principle" he cites Thomson:

"In bashful coyness or in maiden pride,
The soft return conceal'd, save when it stole
In side-long glances from her downcast eyes,
Or from her swelling *soul* in stifled sighs"

But here *soul* as cited means simply and narrowly the rising emotions and not "the active and living principle."

[2] This paragraph did not appear in the first edition.

His synonymies are, on the whole, hard reading because confused and inconsistent. As a rule, they attempt too much yet do not fully apprehend the greatness of the task and leave the reader without any clear or definite impression or without any remembered distinctions. Also, they excite rebellion in a reader who can give any number of citations to show that Crabb's dogmatic assertions are not justified by usage. Despite these fundamental defects which, with the passage of time and changes in the basic conceptions, have come to be more and more striking, Crabb deserves recognition for some additions to the art of synonymizing. Even these, however, may not be entirely his contributions: a bit here and a bit there may have been done by others. Taylor, for example, gave etymologies when they served his purpose. Moreover, after Crabb the work of perfecting often remained to be done and many others are responsible for deeper insight into the possibilities of the method or the extent to which each possibility is serviceable. The chief contributions are:

1. The addition of an etymology to the article. Much more, however, needed to be known before certain words could be correctly etymologized, and before they could be related to the sense to be defined. In some cases, Crabb's etymologies are "learned" additions to the article, in no way reflecting the words' semantic development.

2. The addition of a statement (usually introductory) as to how far the words are equivalent in meaning. There was an approach to this in the work of Mrs. Piozzi, but it was hardly of the same character. Crabb's method was not only clearer and firmer but was much less subject to idiosyncrasies. Since this was his most enduring contribution, a few examples may be given to illustrate his method.

> **Ingenuity, wit**.... Both these terms imply acuteness of understanding, and differ mostly in the way of displaying themselves....
>
> **Disparage, detract, traduce, depreciate, degrade, decry**....The idea of lowering the value of an object is common to all these words, which differ in the circumstances and object of the action....
>
> **Discernment, penetration, discrimination, judgment**....The first three of these terms do not express different powers, but different modes of the same power; namely the power of seeing intellectually, or exerting the intellectual sight....

In clearness of statement, in pointedness, in "hitting the nail on the head," nearly all of these introductions leave something to be desired. Nevertheless, they are historically important because they represent the first tentative formulation of what has proved to be an important and essential part of the discriminated synonymy at its best.

3. In the arrangement of his word lists Crabb claims to have moved from the most comprehensive to the less comprehensive. In such articles as those discussing **form, ceremony, rite, observance**; and **short, brief, concise, succinct, summary,** the principle is clear, but in others, such as those for **apparel, attire, array**; and **belief, credit, trust, faith**; and **execute, fulfill, perform,** the procedure is not perfectly clear. In general, however, he seems to have had a plan and to have stuck to it when he could.

There are other devices used by Crabb which in later and defter hands proved valuable, but these three are the ones on which he has exerted his powers and with which he had greatest success. That the success was not complete is not entirely his fault. The English language is not a symmetrical language: it was never intended to be prodded into shape by the pen of the lexicographer or of the synonymist. No method is uniformly successful: every method must achieve a degree of fluidity before it can be turned to use. What was eminently true in Crabb's case is still eminently true, but some writers of today have learned to bow to necessity, a lesson which many early synonymists could not learn easily or gracefully.

His book continued to be held in high regard for many decades. In fact, a centennial edition in honor of the first (1816) was published in 1917 in the United States. Its editors' names are not given, but it contains an eloquent introduction by John H. Finley, then Commissioner of Education in New York State, which ends with the sentence: "Long life to Crabb and to that for which his name is as a synonym!"

By this time—that is, particularly between the first edition of Crabb's work and the first edition of Miss Whately's book—keen interest was being displayed in the use of synonyms in education. Several texts suitable for use in the schools were prepared. Not necessarily the best of these, but the most thoughtful and suggestive was *English Synonymes Classified and Explained with Practical Exercises Designed for School and Private Tuition* by George F. Graham. The emphasis in the book is entirely upon discrimination. Since there is no attempt to supply as many synonyms as possible, and every effort to make differences clear, two words only are given in each article. Although this has the effect of making the book seem purely pedagogical, it admits employment of a method of classification which would break down if more words were to be added. It is, therefore, only by courtesy that it can be called a synonymy.

The study of synonyms ought, according to Graham, to begin in the elementary schools. In the hope of making this possible, he divides all pairs of synonyms into five classes marking the relationships of these words. He calls his classes *General and Specific*, *Active and Passive*, *Intensity*, *Positive and Negative*, and *Miscellaneous*. The classification is obviously not clean-cut and the classes not necessarily mutually exclusive. As illustrations of *General and Specific* relationships, he compares *answer* and *reply*, *bravery* and *courage;* as instances of *Active and Passive* relationships, he discriminates *burden* and *load*, and *actual* and *real;* and as examples of *Intensity* in relationships, he considers *agony* and *anguish*, and *intention* and *purpose*. It is needless to say that a rigid classification begets a rigid method of discrimination. Sometimes, it serves to bring out the true distinction between the words, but more often, it serves to confuse them by bending them to suit a set purpose. It is the best example we have had so far of the futility of applying a rigid method to the direct study of anything so nonrigid and living as a language.

Crabb's supremacy as a synonymist seems not to have been seriously threatened by a slight book which appeared in 1851, won general praise, and has been listed in practically every bibliography since that time. This book, usually called "Whately's book on synonyms," has never, so far as we know, been properly esteemed for its own values, nor has its true author ever been adequately recognized. Credit for its authorship is often given to the famous logician Richard Whately (1787–1863), Anglican Archbishop of Dublin; rightly, it belongs to his daughter, Elizabeth Jane Whately. A fairly recent but undated edition from the Boston house of Lathrop, Lee, and Shepard confuses both details of title and authorship by calling it on the title page "English Synonyms Discriminated, by Richard Whately, D.D., Archbishop of Dublin." It has two prefaces, one the editor's preface signed, in the characteristic fashion of Anglican bishops, "Richard Dublin"; the other the preface by the author, which is unsigned.

The editor's preface is very short and abstruse, but pregnant with meaning. The archbishop took occasion to say that "this little work has been carefully revised by me, throughout," and that though "far from presuming to call it perfect, it is, I am confident, very much the best that has appeared on the subject." Some of its readers will acknowledge its value in the "cultivation of correctness and precision in our expressions." There will be those, however [we are paraphrasing, amplifying, and interpreting his very cryptic statements], who are so blinded by their adoption of "the metaphysical theory of *ideas*" that they will regard words as of little importance in themselves, and the ideas named as of great significance. There are others, such as himself, who regard words as "an indispensable instrument of thought, in all cases, where a process of *reasoning* takes place." Words are the symbols which men use in discourse. For the most part they do not name real things, for abstractions, such as the one called "beauty," or the generalized notion, such as the one called "tree," exist nowhere except in the mind and have not reality. Only in particular things can beauty be found: only particular objects which are classed together under the name "tree" exist. Therefore, if words are to serve as convenient instruments of discourse, they must often be regarded as signs not of real things but of notions of things, and must have a fixed and generally accepted content. Otherwise human minds could never come together in discourse. Moreover, actual discourse is often futile because words are loosely or incorrectly used.

The preface by the author, though it avoids all references to philosophy, is in general based on the same premises. The author, as has been said, is the archbishop's daughter Miss E. J. Whately, and the proper title of the book is *A Selection of Synonyms*. To her, as well as to her father, words are, for the most part, the names for human ideas or concepts of things. There may be words which name approximately the same thing but which, because of differences in human points of view, are distinguishable by slight differences in meaning. Synonyms, or as she preferred to call them "pseudo-synonyms," have "sufficient resemblance of meaning to make them liable to be confounded together. And it is in the number and variety of these that...the richness of a language consists. To have two or more words with exactly the same sense, is no proof of copiousness, but simply an inconvenience." A language, in her estimation, should have no more words than it needs, just as a house should have no more chairs or tables than required for convenience.

Differences in meaning she found even in words which denote exactly the same object, act, process, quality, emotion, and the like. Such words often have different connotations. "*Swine's flesh*," she says, is prohibited by the Mosaic Law, for "it is plain that it presents to the mind a gross idea, which *pork* does not." Some words may denote the same thing but their different origins or their varying historical associations give them a distinct character which better fits one than the other for use in certain contexts. In polite phrases such as "May I take the liberty?" the Latin derivative *liberty* is more suitable than the Saxon *freedom*. A heathen or an atheist may be called *just* but not *righteous* because Biblical use of the latter word has narrowed its application. Much more acute is her observation that two words may name the same thing but differ because they regard that thing from opposite points of view. She instances *inference* and *proof*.

> Whoever justly infers, proves; and whoever proves, infers: but the word 'inference' leads the mind from the premises which have been assumed, to the conclusion which follows from them: while the word 'proof' follows a reverse process, and leads the mind from the conclusion to the premises.

In a footnote she referred to Aristotle's admirable parallel between *anger* and *hatred,* but after summing up his distinctions, she added significantly:

> His [Aristotle's] example...has not been followed in this work...because, though the two *passions* may often be confounded together, and mistaken one for the other, the two *words* are not liable to be mistaken; and it is with words that we have now to do.

There, one is forced to comment, is the lexicographer speaking, and not the would-be philosopher who would use definition or discrimination of words as an instrument for the expression of his own ideas.

Here and there in her preface and in her synonymies, without evident plan or intention, Miss Whately advanced ideas which when brought together indicate a conception of the synonymist's function and equipment far beyond any yet presented. Not only was she, in effect if not by design, distinguishing lexicography from philosophy but she was defining and enriching the concept of the ideal synonymy and the ideal synonymist. And she did so by flying in the face of all Crabb's admirers and imitators.

Although she realized the importance per se of the "history of the *derivation* of words," she omitted etymologies "which are generally appended to every group of synonyms as an almost essential part of it." She questioned the value of "this procedure" because it "tends...to confuse the subject it was intended to clear," for "in inquiring into the *actual* and *present* meaning of a word, the consideration of what it *originally* meant may frequently tend to lead us astray." Nevertheless, she made good use of her knowledge of etymology when it helped in the discrimination of words.

> *Contentment* may be classed among those words in the English language which adhere strictly to their etymology. Its root was undoubtedly the verb "to contain," and the substantive and its adjective have not departed from this meaning. A *contented* person does not indulge in fruitless wishes for what is beyond his reach; his desires are limited by what he possesses.
>
> *Satisfaction* implies more: this word has likewise retained the signification of its root, and means that we have obtained all we want; not that our desires are limited, but that they have been gratified. A poor and needy man may be *contented*, but he cannot feel *satisfaction* with his condition.

Her illustrations are many and reveal wide reading, a broad linguistic background, and a deep interest in developments of meaning, in differences in meaning between words of the same origin in different languages (e.g., between the English *defend* and the French *défendre* which means not only to defend but also to forbid), and in English words which have "corresponding origins" yet are "widely different in their significations," such as *substance* (printed as *substantia* in her book), *understanding*, and *hypostasis*. She was interested also in the notions which gave names to things, as " 'Heaven'.... conveyed with it the idea of something *heaved* or *lifted up*....'Coelum'...referred to something hollowed out or vaulted."

> All these variations of meaning...are valuable and curious; but though they may occasionally help us, they must not be allowed to influence our decisions with respect to the significations of words. Our question is, not what *ought* to be, or formerly was, the meaning of a word, but what it *now* is; nor can we be completely guided by quotations from Shakespeare or Milton, or even from Addison or Johnson. Language has undergone such changes, even within the last sixty or seventy years, that many words at that time considered pure, are now obsolete; while others...formerly slang, are now used by our best writers....The standard we shall refer to in the present work, is the sense in which a word is used by the purest writers and most correct speakers of our own days.

Although Miss Whately cannot be said to be the first to discriminate meanings of synonyms, she was, so far as we know, the first in England to make that the avowed aim of a book of synonyms and to realize clearly the distinction between the meaning of a word and the thing or idea for which it stood.

Unfortunately, Miss Whately was not so successful in finding a method of synonymizing as she was in expounding its principles. She had, in theory, thrown off the yoke of Crabb, but in practice, she occasionally submitted to it. Nor had she, any more than Crabb, been able to discard completely or to transform to her own use what has been called the Piozzi method of illustration. Some of the difficulty arises from her use of other writers and from the reviser (her father) who, though sympathetic in principle, did not always agree with the exposition in detail and made many heavy-handed changes. But these sources of difficulty are superficial: the real but unassignable reason probably has its roots in something that lies in temper and lack of experience. Yet, in spite of everything, she made several significant advances, not only in the theory, but in the art of synonymizing. Summed up, they are:

1. The principle that knowledge of meanings and all the background that such knowledge implies (derivations, historical development of senses, usage of purest writers and speakers, especially of one's

own period, the associations that affect connotations, etc.) are indispensable elements of the synonymist's equipment, to be used or discarded as the occasion warrants.

2. The principle that the synonymist goes beyond the definer, in a difference of purpose. It is the function of the one who would define a word to estimate truly the meanings men have agreed should be given to it: it is the function of the synonymist to point out the differences between words with meanings so nearly alike that he gives help not only in their correct use but promotes precision of expression so necessary to the thinker and writer.

3. A clearer conception of the ways in which synonyms differ, such as:

(a) Because of differences in implications.

"Both *obstinacy* and *stubbornness* imply an excessive and vicious perseverance in pursuing our own judgment in opposition to that of others; but to be *obstinate* implies the doing what we ourselves chose. To be *stubborn* denotes rather, not to do what others advise or desire." (Quoted by Miss Whately from Sir James Mackintosh.)

A *trifling* matter is one merely of small importance: a *trivial* matter is a small matter made too much of. The word 'trivial' implies contempt, which 'trifling' does not. By saying, 'He never neglects a *trifling* matter,' we are rather supposed to praise; but in blaming a person for frivolity, we often say, 'He is always engrossed with *trivial* concerns.'

(b) Because of differences in applications.

"*Obstinacy* is generally applied to the superior; *stubbornness* to the inferior... *Obstinacy* refers more to outward acts, and *stubbornness* to disposition." (Quoted by Miss Whately from Sir James Mackintosh.)

Strictly speaking, *expense* should be applied to the purchaser, and *cost* to the thing purchased.... Many persons are tempted to buy articles... because they are not *costly*, forgetting that... these purchases may still be too *expensive*.

Delightful is applied both to the pleasures of the mind and those of the senses: *delicious* only to those of the senses. An excursion, a social circle, a place of abode, may be *delightful;* a perfume, or a fruit, *delicious*.

(c) Because of differences in extension, or range of meaning.

Timid is applied both to the state of mind... in which a person may happen to be at the moment, and to the habitual disposition; *timorous*, only to the disposition. *Timid* is therefore the more extensive term, and comprehends the meanings of *timorous*....

To understand, to comprehend. The former of these verbs is used in a much more extended sense than the latter. Whatever we *comprehend*, we *understand;* but *to understand* is used on many occasions in which *to comprehend* would be inadmissible.... It would be quite correct to say, 'I did not *comprehend* his exposition, or his arguments, although I *understood* the language, and the grammatical import of each sentence.'

(d) Because of differences in association or origin and, therefore, in connotations.

Fatherly, paternal; motherly, maternal... are formed from corresponding roots in Latin and Saxon... the Latin word being the more polite and cold, the Saxon the more hearty and cordial.... We speak of 'a *paternal* government'—'*maternal* duties'; but of 'a *fatherly* kindness of manner'—'a *motherly* tenderness.'

Righteous, just... a Saxon and a Latin term, whose roots exactly correspond in meaning; but they have even more curiously diverged than many other pairs of words. *Righteous* is now exclusively applied to rectitude of conduct drawn from religious principle, while *just* is simply used for moral uprightness. A heathen or atheist may be called *just*, but not *righteous*.

(e) Because of the difference in the point of view from which the same thing is regarded.

Anger is more correctly applied to the inward feeling: *wrath* to the outward manifestation.... We should not speak of the 'anger,' but of the 'wrath' of the elements. We therefore speak of the *wrath* of God, more correctly than of his *anger*. We cannot attribute to Him passions like those of men: we can only describe the external effects which in man would be produced by those passions.

In 1852, the year after Miss Whately's *Selection of Synonyms* was published, appeared the first edition of the *Thesaurus of English Words and Phrases*, by Peter Mark Roget (1779–1869), a book that was to exert very great influence on the development of interest in synonyms and to provoke a new interest in opposite or contrasted terms. The modern consultant of the *Thesaurus*, accustomed to depend on the elaborate index (provided in 1879 by the compiler's son John L. Roget), has little knowledge of the original plan of the book, though it has in no way been disturbed by revisers of the Roget family. But this plan is obviously hard to use and few consultants of the *Thesaurus*, if any, now avail themselves of it. It depends upon a classification of all words into six main categories, those dealing with Abstract Relations, Space, Matter, Intellect, Volition, and Affections, each of which is divided into smaller and appropriate subdivisions until an appropriate heading, such as *Interpretation* or *Lending* gives the clue for the left-hand column of nouns, verbs, adjectives, and adverbs gathered under it and an appropriate heading, such as *Misinterpretation* or *Borrowing*, gives the clue for the right-hand column of nouns, verbs, adjectives, and adverbs that are theoretically opposed or in contrast. But Roget did not call these word lists *Synonyms* and *Antonyms* (the latter word indeed had not yet been coined): his usual name was "Analogous Words" for those in the left-hand column and "Correlative Words" for those in the right-hand column. Despite this, other revisers than those of the Roget family have consistently misinterpreted this volume as a book of synonyms and antonyms and have rearranged it or alphabetized it in the hope of making this clear.

It is, therefore, merely because of its historical connections with the treatment of synonyms and antonyms that this book is of immediate significance to us. Only when it is clear that the book purports to be a supplier of words—technically, a "word finder"—and nothing else, shall we be able to estimate correctly the heresy that has arisen out of its misunderstanding. To reach this end, it is necessary for us to know very clearly just what Roget tried to accomplish by this book and just what he ruled out as extraneous to his purpose.

As early as 1805, Roget realized that what he needed for his own writing was a classified list of words in which he might find not only the right words to express his ideas but words that would help him in clarifying or formulating confused or vague ideas. He found the lists he made so useful to himself that he came to believe that they would prove, if amplified, of great value to others. For nearly fifty years he had this project in mind but only at the age of seventy, after his retirement in 1849 from his position as secretary of the Royal Society of London for the Advancement of Science, was he able to realize it.

He held from the start that what was needed was not a dictionary of synonyms. Roget had in mind a consultant who not only did not know a near word, but who could not even recall a word somewhat similar in meaning to the word desired or who only vaguely apprehended an idea because of the want of the right word or words to help him in formulating it. For example, a geologist who has found a rock, probably hitherto undiscovered, because it fitted into no known classification might be at a loss for the exact terms to describe its peculiar texture. Such a person could hope to find in the section headed "Matter" the concrete adjective he needed (such as *fissile, friable, splintery*, etc.). No word, no phrase, was too narrow in its meaning to serve Roget's purpose, nor too archaic, nor too slangy, nor too erudite. Whether one was writing a technical treatise or a witty essay, a historical novel or a definition for a dictionary, one might hope to discover in this *Thesaurus* the expressions "which are best suited to his purpose and which might not have occurred to him without such assistance." For words, "like 'spirits from the vasty deep'....come not when we call"; "appropriate terms notwithstanding our utmost efforts cannot be conjured up at will."

More than this, Roget did not call the words he selected *synonyms*, when they were of the same part of speech and belonged in the same column. That he understood "synonyms" as denoting words of equivalent meaning is evident in his reference to the discrimination of "apparently synonymous" terms. There can be no question that he thought word-finding lists of synonyms and of "apparently synonymous" terms would be too meager to suit the purposes he had in mind.

As for the discrimination of synonyms, that was entirely foreign to the purpose of his book. He was very explicit about that:

> The investigation of the distinctions to be drawn between words apparently synonymous, forms a separate branch of inquiry, which I have not presumed here to enter upon; for the subject has already occupied the attention of much abler critics than myself, and its complete exhaustion would require the devotion of a whole life. The purpose of this Work, it must be borne in mind, is not to explain the signification of words, but simply to classify and arrange them according to the sense in which they are now used, and which I presume to be already known to the reader. I enter into no inquiry into the changes of meaning they may have undergone in the course of time. I am content to accept them at the value of their present currency, and have no concern with their etymologies, or with the history of their transformations; far less do I venture to thrid [thread] the mazes of the vast labyrinth into which I should be led by any attempt at a general discrimination of synonyms.

It is also important to notice that Roget believed himself without a precursor "in any language." He may have known Perry and many others who worked in the word-finding field before 1852: like other cultivated men he probably knew Crabb and others working on the discrimination of synonyms; but he always thought of himself as doing something quite distinct from both. In fact, he gave his successors many reasons for refusing to believe that his two series of word-supplying lists were synonyms or antonyms, or were capable of discrimination as synonyms or of opposition as antonyms.

Despite that, his purpose was misunderstood and his book misinterpreted. In 1867 appeared a small book called *A Complete Collection of Synonyms and Antonyms*, by the Rev. Charles J. Smith, which gave evidence that here and there men were quietly substituting their judgment of Roget's work for his own. It is true that there is only one sentence in the preface of Smith's book to support this inference, and that concerns the reason why its author has chosen the dictionary method of presenting his material, "from finding that the abstract classifications of words, under certain broad ideas, according to the plan of Dr. Roget, seems invalidated by the necessity, in his well-known Thesaurus, of numberless cross-divisions, and is practically disregarded in favor of the Alphabetical Index." Yet, brief as is that statement, it reveals that he thought his work and Roget's had a common purpose—to give synonyms and their opposites or, to use the word which he now coined, their "antonyms"—and that the difference between the two books was merely a matter of method.

There is no evidence that Smith realized that he was changing the time-honored definition of *synonym*. His chief object in phrasing his definition of *synonym* was to set that term in opposition to *antonym*, which he regarded as its antithesis. Nevertheless, in so doing, he introduced a subtle and important change in the definition. His statement reads as follows:

> Words which agree in expressing one or more characteristic ideas in common [with the entry word] he [i.e., Smith himself] has regarded as Synonyms, those which negative one or more such ideas he has called Antonyms.

The inference that he changed the traditional definition of *synonym* is supported not only by this statement, but also by his method of selecting synonyms. One example must suffice:

> ACCELERATE, *v.t. Ad* and *celer*, quick. To quicken the speed or process of events, objects, or transactions.
> SYN. Quicken. Hasten. Urge. Speed. Expedite. Promote. Despatch. Facilitate.
> ANT. Delay. Obstruct. Impede. Retard. Clog. Hinder. Drag. Shackle.

The important thing to notice about these lists is not their parallelism, nor even how good or bad the synonyms or antonyms are, but that they have been selected according to a new principle. The synonyms are not all closely allied words differing only in minor ways, or words which are essentially alike in meaning, but some, such as *urge* and *promote*, are words which come together only in some part of their meaning, and that not necessarily their essential meaning. Nor are the antonyms necessarily opposed to the essential meaning of *accelerate*. It is quite possible that neither Smith nor anyone else at the time fully realized what a radical change in definition he had made. In his *Synonyms Discriminated*, the work with which four years later (1871) he followed his *Synonyms and Antonyms*, he adhered to the orthodox definition of *synonym*. The later work proved the more popular, and it is probable that the inconspicuousness of *Synonyms and Antonyms* helped to obscure its definition of *synonym*, buried as it was in the preface.

Moreover, in the same year as *Synonyms Discriminated*, appeared another book of undiscriminated synonyms, Richard Soule's *A Dictionary of English Synonymes and Synonymous or Parallel Expressions* (1871), which attracted far more attention than had Smith's *Synonyms and Antonyms*. New editions appeared in rapid succession, and it was revised in 1891 by Professor George H. Howison, and in 1937 by Professor Alfred D. Sheffield.

Although Soule acknowledged help from Roget's *Thesaurus* and a number of other works such as the dictionaries of Webster and Worcester and the books by Crabb, Miss Whately, and others discriminating synonyms, he claims in no particular instance to have followed them strictly or to have been influenced by them in any way. If we judge from the words of Professor Howison, who, nearly twenty years after the first edition, undertook revision at the request of Soule's family, he "found little more to do than to carry out to a greater completeness the lines of Mr. Soule's original design." That Soule's original design was clear and definite and that he saw himself as doing something quite different from Roget, on the one hand, and from Crabb and Miss Whately, on the other, is obvious from what Professor Howison has further to say:

> A perfect manual of that sort is impossible within the compass of a single work of convenient size and arrangement....A work on Synonymes may thus have for its purpose either an alphabetic list of all the more important words in the language, with their various meanings or shades of meaning set down under them, each followed by its appropriate synonymes; or a list of general notions, duly named and properly divided and subdivided, with the words and phrases that belong to the expression of each collected under them as fully as possible; or, again, the collocation of words allied in meaning with subjoined disquisitions on the shades of difference between them. The latter conception has been the prevailing one among English makers of synonymic dictionaries, and is represented by the well-known work of Crabb, as well as by any; the second is that of Roget's Thesaurus; while the first is that of Soule.

Consequently, we are not surprised to find that Soule's definition of *synonym* approaches the orthodox one. True, he gives us no detailed definition, but he does say enough to show that he does not mistake the relation between words of the same part of speech in the left-hand or the right-hand column of Roget (he is obviously not interested in their cross relation), and he does not show any knowledge—much less any interest—in Smith's definition of a synonym as a word which agrees in expressing one or more characteristic ideas in common with a given word. A synonym, he says, has "the same meaning as" the entry word under which it is listed "or a meaning very nearly the same." Within limits, his lists of synonyms are about as good as is possible when they are not submitted to the test of discrimination.

Even though Soule's *Dictionary of Synonyms* has been the model for a great many works issued in imitation of it, some claiming to have improved upon it, it still remains, in both its original and its revised forms, the best dictionary of synonyms that does not provide discriminations. Like Roget's work, within its own limits it has not yet been bettered.

But beyond those limits, both in the realm of books providing discriminating synonymies and in the realm of books providing synonyms and antonyms without discriminations, there has arisen a state of affairs which makes us believe that we are at a point where a stand must be taken if we are to avert chaos in the field. In the forefront of this battle are the American general dictionaries and certain manuals written by men who have been at one time or another members of their staffs.

The general dictionaries have so far been omitted from this survey. Not that they were inactive—for, almost from the start, they were not. A few ventures were merely tentative, such as that in James Barclay's *Complete and Universal Dictionary* issued in England in 1774. This work Chauncey Goodrich (in his preface to Webster's *A Pronouncing and Defining Dictionary*, 1856, an abridgment of the 1828 Webster) notices with the observation that discriminations of "synonymous words" were "first introduced into a general dictionary by Barclay, though in a very imperfect manner." Goodrich also calls attention to the fact that Noah Webster had often successfully used the method of discrimination as part of his definitions. But these attempts do not merit the honor of being the first discriminating synonymies in the general dictionary. No one in fact laid serious claim to their introduction before Joseph Worcester who, in 1855, issued his *Pronouncing, Explanatory, and Synonymous Dictionary*. The slight foundation for the claim is evident from the following typical examples:

> DEFEND....*Syn.—Defend* the innocent; *protect* the weak; *vindicate* those who are unjustly accused; *repel* aggression.
>
> FIGURE....*Syn.*—A fine *figure;* regular *shape;* circular *form;* a carved *statue;* a graven *image.*—A *metaphor* is a *figure* of speech; a lamb is an *emblem* of innocence; the paschal lamb was a *type* of Christ.

One year later (1856), William G. Webster and Chauncey A. Goodrich, the son and son-in-law of Noah Webster, brought out abridged editions of his *American Dictionary* for school, business, and family use. Short discriminating synonymies were introduced, all of them written by Chauncey Goodrich. A few typical illustrations will indicate how much better a title he had than had Worcester to the claim of having introduced such synonymies into a dictionary:

> Things are *adjacent* when they lie near to each other without touching, as *adjacent* fields; *adjoining* when they meet or join at some point, as *adjoining* farms; *contiguous* when they are brought more continuously in contact, as *contiguous* buildings.
>
> *Liveliness* is an habitual feeling of life and interest; *gayety* refers more to a temporary excitement of the animal spirits; *animation* implies a warmth of emotion and a corresponding vividness of expressing it; *vivacity* is a feeling between liveliness and animation, having the permanency of the one and the warmth of the other.

The first serious attempt in a general dictionary at discriminating synonymies on a par with those published by Mrs. Piozzi, Crabb, Miss Whately, and others, came in 1859 with the publication by G. & C. Merriam Co. of a "provisional edition"[3] of Webster as a preparation for the first complete revision (issued in 1864) of the *American Dictionary*. These also were written by Chauncey A. Goodrich (1790–1860), whose articles in the smaller dictionaries of 1856 had been, according to the publishers' preface of 1859, "so highly appreciated by distinguished scholars" that they had prevailed upon him in his capacity as editor of the 1859 edition to add a treatment of synonyms to this book. For some years Goodrich had been engaged on "a distinct work on this subject" and it was the material gathered for this project that was developed and presented in the table of synonyms as part of the "front matter" of the 1859 edition.

These synonymies, with slight changes in phrasing and many additions, served for the two ensuing complete revisions of Merriam-Webster dictionaries, *Webster's Unabridged Dictionary* of 1864 and *Webster's International Dictionary* of 1890, both under the editorship of Noah Porter. In these books, the articles on synonymy, instead of being grouped in the front matter, were distributed through the main vocabulary.

In the publishers' statement in the 1859 edition of the *American Dictionary*, note was made of the great advance in Goodrich's synonymies over those of preceding writers:

---

[3] As stated in the preface to *Webster's Unabridged Dictionary* (1864).

> This is only an application on a broad scale of one mode adopted by Dr. Webster, for giving clearness and precision to his definitions. It is also peculiarly appropriate in a work like this, which aims at great exactness as a defining dictionary; since it affords an opportunity of giving in connection with the leading terms of our language, those nicer discriminations and shades of thought which it is impossible to reach in the way of ordinary definitions.... Unless the distinctive meaning of the several words is previously given, little or no aid is afforded as to their proper use and application, by adducing such passages. This will be seen by turning to such a work as *Platts' Dictionary of English Synonyms*,[4] which is framed chiefly upon this plan. On the first page, we find under the words *abandon, desert, leave*, etc., such examples as these: "Men are *abandoned* by their friends; we *desert* a post or station; *leave* the country," etc. But these words may be equally well interchanged. Men may be *deserted* by their friends; we may *abandon* a post or station, etc. Such examples, therefore, afford no light or guidance as to the proper use of these words. So, if the phrase be given "the officer abandoned his post," the question may arise whether he really *abandoned*, or *deserted*, or *surrendered*, or *left* it. He may have *abandoned* it on the approach of an enemy, or as no longer important to maintain; he may have *deserted* it unworthily or treacherously; he may have *surrendered* it to a superior force; he may have *left* it temporarily.

The criticism clearly shows that the chief defect of the current discriminating synonymy was a defect in method: it was not a defect in the definition of *synonym* or in the selection of synonyms. But in the thirty years following there were signs that Perry's vague conceptions of a synonym, and Smith's freer definition were beginning to enter the minds of synonymists. Neither Perry nor Smith was largely responsible for this change in definition. Roget, because of the enormous popularity of his work, or rather those who misinterpreted Roget's aim, must be considered as originating the trend, and be blamed for it. By 1889, the first evidence of its more general acceptance had made its appearance.

In that year was published the first edition of the *Century Dictionary*, and in 1894 followed Funk and Wagnalls' *Standard Dictionary*. Both were new ventures in dictionary making and had the advantage of being in the limelight. Both followed the initiative of the Merriam-Webster dictionaries and introduced discriminating synonymies as an essential part of their contribution. But neither followed Webster in its adhesion to the traditional definition of *synonym*.

Although the *Century Dictionary* attempted many new things in the way of dictionary making, such as an encyclopedic character and a format of several volumes, it placed little stress on its treatment of synonyms. The writer of these articles, Henry Mitchell Whitney, was the brother of the editor in chief, William Dwight Whitney: his work was given only a four-line notice in the editorial preface:

> Discussions of synonyms treating of about 7000 words...will be found convenient as bringing together statements made in the definitions in various parts of the dictionary, and also as touching in a free way upon many literary aspects of words.

It was probably because of the division of the *Century Dictionary* into several volumes that its editors could entertain the idea that the function of a discriminating synonymy is to assemble definitions of comparable terms from various parts of the dictionary, but such a function, because of its accidental character, has no inherent value. As a matter of fact, Henry M. Whitney, the synonymist of the *Century*, often depended on cross reference to definitions for support or amplification of his statements and, therefore, invalidated the description (quoted above) by William Dwight Whitney in the editorial preface. Nor do his synonymies "touch in a free way upon many literary aspects of words." In the first place, it is not quite clear what is meant by that statement, and, in the second, there is no consistent proof of anything like it in the articles themselves. As a general rule, with the possible exception of Miss Whately, synonymists had not yet felt strongly any difference between the literary and colloquial use of words.

There is not only the lack of a clearly defined policy in the preface, but there is also the lack of one in the synonymies themselves. Yet Henry M. Whitney seems to have had in him the makings of a good synonymist, but to have been suffering from conditions over which he had no control. It may be that his job was too big for one man or for the time set for its completion, and that he had little leisure to think through its problems: it may be that what he considered a good synonymy was not in accord with the opinion of the editor in chief. At any rate, his synonymies vary greatly in method, aim, and accomplishment. The most that can be said is that he was experimenting with different methods and aims and that he never reached definite conclusions as to the superiority of one over the other.

The most vital problem which concerned him was the selection of synonyms. Sometimes he provides a very limited selection, as at **adept**, where he gives only *expert*, leaving out such words as *master, proficient*, and *specialist*, which might well have been treated as synonyms. In other places he gives a much longer and more heterogeneous list, as at **ample**: *ample, copious, plenteous*, spacious, roomy, extensive, extended, wide, capacious, abundant, sufficient, full, enough, unrestricted, plenary, unstinted.

[4] A small work for use in schools, published 1825.

Only the italicized words are discriminated, it is true, but the others are given as synonyms. The average reader may doubt the justification of many of these words as synonyms, though he will readily find a relationship in meaning.

There was good reason for H. M. Whitney's uncertainty, in that around the eighteen-seventies and eighties synonymists were confronted with a problem that had not particularly concerned their predecessors. The demand then was not only for discriminating synonymies but for word-finding lists more or less in the manner of Roget and Soule. Crabb's work was still influential, but was not satisfying those who wanted more words synonymized and more synonyms for each word. Roget was immensely popular but extremely difficult to use, not only because of his classificatory method but because he supplied no definitions. In 1879 a "new and elaborate Index, much more complete than that which was appended to the previous editions" had been added by Roget's son, in the belief that "almost every one who uses the book finds it more convenient to have recourse to the Index first." In this way, the major difficulty, the classificatory system which the elder Roget had pertinaciously believed in, became no longer an obstacle. The other difficulty, the lack of discrimination, was not touched and, in view of Roget's primary purpose, was not likely to be.

As a result, there followed an attempt to provide synonymies which would combine the virtues and value of the discriminating synonymies and yet would deal with word lists that approached in number and variety those of Roget. Henry M. Whitney more or less played with the problem, but James C. Fernald (1838–1918), the editor of synonymies for Funk and Wagnalls' *Standard Dictionary* (1894) and author of a manual, *English Synonyms and Antonyms* (1896), attacked it with vigor and offered what seemed to him a solution.

Fernald and the editors of the *Standard Dictionary* set out to increase markedly the number of synonyms and antonyms at each entry. Hitherto, from two to eight words represented the norm in each of these lists: in the *Standard Dictionary* the average number lies between ten and twenty. First of all, they believed that they were justified in extending the definition of *synonym* to include both words of identical or closely allied meaning (the time-honored definition) and words which agree in some part of their meaning. The definition of *synonym* in the 1894 edition of the *Standard Dictionary* (slightly changed in the current edition) reads:

> A word having the same or almost the same meaning as some other; oftener, one of a number of words that have one or more meanings in common, but that differ either in the range of application of those meanings or in having other senses not held in common; opposed to antonym. . . . Words of this class may often be used interchangeably, but discrimination in their choice is one of the most important characteristics of a good writer.

The discriminating synonymy given at the entry of *synonymous* in the main vocabulary reads:

> *Syn.* alike, correspondent, corresponding, equivalent, identical, interchangeable, like, same, similar, synonymic. In the strictest sense, *synonymous* words scarcely exist; rarely, if ever, are any two words in any language *equivalent* or *identical* in meaning; where a difference in meaning can not easily be shown, a difference in usage commonly exists, so that the words are not *interchangeable*. By *synonymous* words we usually understand words that coincide or nearly coincide in some part of their meaning, and may hence within certain limits be used interchangeably, while outside of those limits they may differ very greatly in meaning and use. It is the office of a work on synonyms to point out these correspondences and differences, that language may have the flexibility that comes from freedom of selection within the common limits, with the perspicuity and precision that result from exact choice of the fittest word to express each shade of meaning outside of the common limits. To consider *synonymous* words *identical* is fatal to accuracy; to forget that they are *similar*, to some extent *equivalent*, and sometimes *interchangeable*, is destructive of freedom and variety.

It is possible that definition and synonymy were designed to avoid provoking criticism from those who adhered to the commonly accepted definition of *synonym* yet at the same time to extend the sense to accord with what was believed to be Roget's practice and to satisfy the demands of those who urged more words. It may be granted that this is a legitimate practice, provided it does not force the issue but represents a genuine change in conception among a large, or even a small, class of those who use the term *synonym*. That the growing demand was for more synonyms cannot be questioned, but that a change in the conception of *synonym* had occurred, from the one that had been in vogue since Crabb's time, may justly be disputed. At any rate, let us see how it affected the *Standard Dictionary's* choice of synonyms. Two lists will illustrate its practice:

> ADEQUATE able, adapted, capable, commensurate, competent, equal, fit, fitted, fitting, qualified, satisfactory, sufficient, suitable.
>
> HARMONY accord, accordance, agreement, amity, concord, concurrence, conformity, congruity, consent, consistency, consonance, symmetry, unanimity, uniformity, union, unison, unity.

The *Standard Dictionary's* definition justifies the selection of such lists of "synonyms." Each is a word which has one or more meanings in common with the introductory word (*adequate* or *harmony*). But if *adequate* means exactly commensurate with the requirements, only *sufficient* and *competent* (in one of its senses) with the addition of *enough* approach it in content. A person may be *adequate* if he is *able, capable, competent* (in another sense), or *qualified;* a person or thing may be *adequate* if he or it is *adapted, fitted,* or *suitable;* a thing may be *adequate* if it is equal to the requirement by being *fit* or *satisfactory:* but in all these cases, he or it may also be more than *adequate* or less than *adequate,* in some way, or the question of adequacy may never arise. *Harmony* in its musical sense may be related to *accord, concord, consonance,* in its aesthetic sense to *symmetry* and other terms not in this list; but what relation there is between it and *amity, uniformity, unanimity, agreement, concurrence, congruity,* etc., except as a cause or result or concomitant, needs to be proved. A word-finding list may consist of terms which, by agreeing in some implications and connotations, overlap, for those lists serve their purpose in helping the user to locate his word. But when the object is discrimination, only those words serve the purpose whose basic likeness can be proved by showing that they have a common denotation as well as not readily discerned differences.

It is true that Fernald found no difficulty here. His clearest expression of the method of discrimination is found in the preface to his *English Synonyms, Antonyms, and Prepositions:*

> The great source of vagueness, error, and perplexity in many discussions of synonyms is, that the writer merely associates stray ideas loosely connected with the different words, sliding from synonym to synonym with no definite point of departure or return, so that a smooth and at first sight pleasing statement really gives the mind no definite resting-place and no sure conclusion. A true discussion of synonyms is definition by comparison, and for this there must be something definite with which to compare. When the standard is settled, approximation or differentiation can be determined with clearness and certainty.

What type of synonymy Fernald was criticizing is not clear. It was probably what may be called "the chain-formula type." When a synonymist had made so poor a selection of synonyms that there could be no common ground, and his list presented an array of associated rather than synonymous terms, he often fell into the habit of giving a series of definitions with a factitious relation. A repetition of a previous word was usually enough to make a connection. This was the defect of certain synonymies into which all writers of articles, good as well as bad, fell at one time or another and is probably the type to which Fernald referred when he described the "easy sliding from synonym to synonym." Yet it is not always bad: when one word carries a general meaning, which serves as a substitute for the common denotation, it is possible to use it with good effect. A short example from *The New Century Dictionary* (1927) must suffice for the good use:

> **Banter** is good humored jesting.... **Raillery** is often sharp, sarcastic banter; **pleasantry,** delicate and pleasant banter; **badinage,** diverting and purposeless banter; **persiflage,** light, frivolous, or flippant banter.

With lists such as Fernald's own it would be impossible to avoid this formula, unchanged. It was necessary for him to find some way of varying "the chain formula" so that he could secure the desired qualities, "unity of the group" and "some point of departure and return." Therefore, he devised the method whereby one word would be selected as the key word and all the other words should be compared or contrasted with it. A good example is afforded by his article at *money:*

> **money. Syn.:** bills, bullion, capital, cash, coin, currency, funds, gold, notes, property, silver, specie. *Money* is the authorized medium of exchange; coined *money* is called *coin* or *specie.* What are termed in England bank-*notes* are in the United States commonly called *bills;* as, five-dollar *bill.* The *notes* of responsible men are readily transferable in commercial circles, but they are not *money;* as, the stock was sold for $500 in *money* and the balance in merchantable paper. *Cash* is *specie* or *money* in hand, or paid in hand; as, the *cash* account; the *cash* price. In the legal sense, *property* is not *money,* and *money* is not *property;* for *property* is that which has inherent value, while *money,* as such, has but representative value, and may or may not have intrinsic value. *Bullion* is either *gold* or *silver* uncoined, or the coined metal considered without reference to its coinage, but simply as merchandise, when its value as *bullion* may be very different from its value as *money.* The word *capital* is used chiefly of accumulated *property* or *money* invested in productive enterprises or available for such investment. Compare PROPERTY; WEALTH.

Nothing could be clearer than that these words are not synonyms in the generally accepted sense. They include names for kinds of money (coin, specie, bills), names of material used for money or, in figurative language, meaning money or wealth (gold, silver), and words denoting things that have some intimate association with money (bullion, property, capital). The article keeps more or less consistently before the reader the relation of these to the key word *money.* The reader is bound to see and understand the distinctions and carry away a unified impression. There can be no quarrel with such articles on the ground of their not giving useful information. It may even be argued that a discrimination of terms that coincide in some part of their meaning may be in itself a valuable thing. But neither justification touches the issue raised by the Fernald synonymies. The ground of valid objection to them is that they offer *as synonyms* many words which even by the loosest of definitions cannot be accepted as such. The point of absurdity is reached at *spontaneous,* where the key word is so important that *voluntary* and *involuntary, free* and *instinctive, automatic* and *impulsive* are included.

By 1909, the date of publication of the next complete revision of the Merriam-Webster dictionaries (the first edition of *Webster's New International Dictionary*), there had been time for consideration of these matters and for a more sober judgment. The Goodrich synonymies clearly needed revision on account of the growth of the language and, partly, because the synonym lists could be enriched. The work was entrusted to John Livingston Lowes (then a professor at Washington University, St. Louis, but later at Harvard University) under the advisory supervision of Professor George Lyman Kittredge of Harvard. They were to deal only with general senses, but a few technical articles written by specialists were to be submitted to them, so as to insure uniformity in manner and method. The articles thus prepared were included in *Webster's New International Dictionary* and reprinted, with minor changes, in *Webster's New International Dictionary, Second Edition* (1934).

Certain points of agreement were established by Lowes and Kittredge early in the course of their partnership. Very early in the writing of these articles Lowes called Kittredge's attention to the Fernald list at *adequate* (see p. xxi, above) and the *Century* list, *adequate, sufficient, enough.*

"Is not the *Century's* list adequate?" he wrote. "I did not notice the test my question affords, but none of the other words in the *Standard's* list can be substituted for 'adequate.' Are they not better distributed among other articles? The longer I study the material, the more strongly I feel that more articles, each discriminating fewer words, are advisable. The longer articles are, as a matter of fact, confusing, and seem to have led often to strained attempts to find a single common factor for words which fall more naturally into several groups. What is your opinion?"

Kittredge answered briefly: "Yes. I agree fully."[5]

Thus, very early it was established that the Webster tradition of discriminating synonyms, which are synonyms in the accepted sense, be followed. Looser synonyms, or closely related words, were still given in the word-finding lists and these also were revised by Lowes, whose interests, however, were concentrated on the articles discriminating synonyms.

By temperament and training, Professor Lowes was especially fitted for the task assigned him. He excels all his predecessors in philosophic grasp and powers of analysis, yet he never confuses synonymizing with philosophizing or moralizing; he outstrips them all in the range of his knowledge of literature and of his contacts with language as the medium of expressing ideas and emotions; great scholar though he is, his work is utterly free of the pedantry, dogmatism, and heaviness that so often mars the work of lesser men. Though not a lexicographer by training or experience, he almost perfectly adapted the art of synonymizing to the science of lexicography, so that whatever can contribute in either to the advantage of the other was brought out in his articles.

It is in the clarification of the differences between terms that are to a large extent equivalent in denotation that Lowes made the greatest advances in the art of synonymizing. Practically every synonymist before him had inklings of the kinds of differences that he saw clearly; many of them, such as Miss Whately, had used the language adopted by him, but no one so fully realized its possibilities. Rambling, persistent missing of the real differences, and constant confusion of the content of the word itself with the concept for which that word stood, were characteristic and prevalent faults of many earlier writers of synonymies. With Lowes, direct attack at each problem became possible and, with it, swift, sure shafts that rarely fail to make the desired cleavage.

It may be said that as a rule he was careful in his synonymies to state the ground of agreement; but sometimes he neglected to do so when the likeness was obvious. But in regard to differences he was extremely particular and rarely departed from the aim he held before him. His most frequently used method may be illustrated by an excerpt from the article at **foretell** in *Webster's New International Dictionary* (1909):

> **Foretell** (*Saxon*) and **predict** (*Latin*) are frequently interchangeable; but *predict* is now commonly used when inference from facts (rather than occult processes) is involved; as, "Some sorcerer. . . had *foretold,* dying, that none of all our blood should know the shadow from the substance" (*Tennyson*); "Mr. Brooke's conclusions were as difficult to *predict* as the weather" (*G. Eliot*); an astronomer *predicts* the return of a comet. **Prophesy** connotes inspired or mysterious knowledge, or great assurance of prediction; as, "ancestral voices *prophesying* war" (*Coleridge*); "Wrinkled benchers often talked of him approvingly, and *prophesied* his rise" (*Tennyson*). **Forecast** connotes conjecture rather than inference; **presage** implies shrewd forecast,

[5] From manuscript notes in the editorial files of G. & C. Merriam Company.

sometimes presentiment or warning; as, "Who shall so *forecast* the years" (*Tennyson*); "I *presage*, unless the country make an alarm, the cause is lost" (*Scott*).... **Forebode**...implies obscure prescience or premonition (esp. of evil); **portend**..., threatening or ominous foretokening; as, "His heart *forebodes* a mystery" (*Tennyson*); "My father put on the countenance which always *portends* a gathering storm" (*Richardson*).

If we supply the common denotation of all these words — "to indicate what will happen," — the difference lies in other ideas involved in their meaning. In each case, this difference forms part of the word's definition, the other part of which will be the common denotation. Indeed, although the dictionary definition may be presented from another point of view, a good and fair definition may be made according to this method. The synonymist, however, should find it the best method when his job is merely to show how far a group of words agree and then to point out their individual differences. Other methods are conceivable, indeed some are necessary in special cases, but as yet no better method has been devised for the general run of synonyms. Miss Whately is largely responsible for it, but Lowes has greatly improved it.

It was (and is), however, impossible always to be equally exact, clear, and direct. This is especially true when the differences are less a matter of meaning than of coloring, as by historical and literary associations, or a matter of idiomatic usage. The difference in coloring or, in other terms, the difference in connotations—is especially difficult, requiring not only great knowledge but fine perceptions, imagination, and taste. Few would dare to attempt to distinguish connotations, but Lowes, whose feeling for these differences is not equaled by any synonymist, is especially successful in their handling. Many of these could not be incorporated in a dictionary definition, but they must be felt if the word is to be used with the accumulated power that has been stored in it. A particularly effective synonymy of this type is to be found at **idiot.**

Idiot, imbecile, fool, simpleton are here compared esp. in their connotations; for technical distinctions, see defs. **Idiot** (a learned word become popular) implies absence, commonly congenital, of intellectual or reasoning powers; it is often less strictly used to characterize one who is felt to have acted with utter stupidity; **imbecile** (less common as a popular term) implies great mental feebleness or (in its looser derogatory sense) entire fatuity; **fool,** the more vigorous word, is wholly popular, and frequently suggests lack of sense or wisdom rather than of brains; from its Biblical use, it still connotes, in elevated style, grave, pitying, or scathing condemnation; in colloquial usage, as a term of contempt, it is strongly offensive; **simpleton** (also wholly popular) implies silliness or (sometimes) unsophisticatedness; it is often used lightly as a term of indulgent contempt; as, "He said you were...a senseless, driveling *idiot*" (*Wycherly*); "What an *idiot* am I, to wait here for a fellow who probably takes a delight in mortifying me" (*Goldsmith*); "custom's *idiot* sway" (*Cowper*); cf. an *idiotic* grin; "The petty passions, the *imbecile* desires..., daily moving her contempt" (*G. Eliot*); "She's a *fool* to stay behind her father" (*Shak.*); "*Fools* rush in where angels fear to tread" (*Pope*); "They look upon persons employing their time in making verses...as *simpletons* easily to be deceived" (*V. Knox*); poor, innocent little *simpleton!* "The 'Great *simpleton!*'...of Mr. Newman, and the 'Thou *fool!*' of the Bible, are something alike; but 'Thou *fool!*' is very grand, and 'Great *simpleton!*' is an atrocity. So too...Shakespeare's 'Poor venomous *fool,* be angry and dispatch!' is in the grand style" (*M. Arnold*)....

Differences in idiomatic usage are oftentimes not a matter that can easily be presented by definition. Many terms in a dictionary are defined almost in the same words, though written by various editors, the only clue to difference consisting in the illustrations. The consultant is often at a loss, because he does not see that these examples may constitute the only uses of the term, or a few such uses, and are not representative of a large number of uses. It was in such cases that the method which we have called (p. viii, above) the Piozzi method (from Mrs. Piozzi, its originator) was first used, but without a full understanding of its dangers and limitations. Lowes avoided this method except where he was dealing with fixed idioms. Then he safeguarded his statement with a parenthetical elimination such as "one *ascends* (not *mounts*) a mountain; one *mounts* (not *ascends*) a horse." The sparing use of this method did not, however, lead to his ignoring the problem presented by such synonyms as are definable in almost identical terms yet are incapable of discrimination in implications and connotations. To get at his method, let us examine parts of certain synonymies where his effectiveness is most apparent:

One **excuses** (either as a superior or as an equal) small faults, minor omissions, or neglects, esp. in social or conventional obligations; one **pardons** (as a superior, or by act of mercy or generosity) serious faults, crimes, or grave offenses, esp. against laws or morals; as, to *excuse* an unintentional oversight, an absence from a required exercise; "*Excuse* my glove" (*Sheridan*); to *pardon* a thief; to *pardon* a theft; "Apollo, *pardon* my great profaneness 'gainst thine oracle" (*Shak.*).

Stop...applies primarily to action, or to that which is thought of as *moving;* **cease** applies also to states and conditions, or to that which is thought of as *being;* as, a train *stops,* but does not *cease;* the noise it makes both *stops* and *ceases;* one's love may *cease,* but scarcely *stop.*

Fast and *rapid* are often used without distinction; but **fast** frequently applies to the moving object, whereas **rapid** is apt to characterize or suggest the movement itself; as, a *fast* horse, a *fast* train, boat; a *rapid* current, gait, progress.

Hateful and *odious* are sometimes used with little distinction. But **hateful** more frequently applies to that which excites actual hatred, **odious,** to that which is excessively disagreeable, or which awakens repugnance; as, "Why shouldn't we hate what is *hateful* in people, and scorn what is mean?" (*Thackeray*)...."There was something more *odious* to him in her friendship than her hatred" (*Thackeray*).

In these discriminations, the original contribution of Lowes is the generalization regarding usage or application. An occasional synonymist before him had experimented with it, but no one before him succeeded. He knows how to guard the expression, never claims too much, and yet, in spite of all the difficulties involved, makes statements that are just and therefore convincing. There seems to have been no inclination on his part to overstate the case. If there must be inexactness, he preferred it on the side of understatement. "This is as much as it is safe to say" was a not infrequent comment of his.[6]

Much more could be said about the interesting technique developed by Lowes. Much more could also be said about other excellences and some defects which characterize his work. But when all is said and done there still remains his superiority as a discriminator, as manifested in his selection of methods according to his material. Whether his synonyms differed in implications, in connotations, or in applications or, more probably, some in one way, some in another, he was seldom at a loss.

Just a word about antonyms. There is no evidence at hand[7] to prove that Lowes was ever asked to enter antonyms in *Webster's New International Dictionary.* He did, however, incorporate a few (though not by that name) in his articles under the general formula of "opposed to...," when the difference between synonyms (usually very general ones) could be apprehended more easily by knowing the term which was the direct opposite of each. He does this several times, as at **base,** where *base* is "opposed to *high-minded,*" *vile* is "opposed to *pure, noble,*" and *mean* is "opposed to *generous, magnanimous.*" It is possible to guess his definition of *antonym,* but no more. The addition of antonyms and the revision of Lowes's word-finding lists were made by an office editor for *Webster's New International Dictionary, Second Edition* (1934).

There is no need to go further in the history of synonymy. Further synonymists[8] there have been, some very good, some not quite so good, and some very bad; but they have all taken sides, either with those who support the traditional definition of *synonym* as one of two or more words having the same essential meaning, or with those who favor its extension to one of two or more words which coincide in some part of their meaning. There has been no compromise: it might even be said that the break has scarcely been noticed. Nevertheless, it is apparent that, unless there be some clarification in definitions, especially of *synonym* and *antonym,* the prevailing popular misunderstanding will increase—with what results no one can estimate. This clarification we propose to undertake in the essays that follow.

It is because we firmly believe in the values implicit in the study of synonyms, antonyms, and word-finding lists (in this book divided into analogous words and contrasted words) that this Dictionary has been written. We hope, therefore, that it not only carries some steps forward the admirable work accomplished by Goodrich and Lowes, but that it removes some sources of confusion or perplexity which have arisen outside of their work. The old defect inherent in synonymies, the overuse of illustration without a sufficient background in differences of implications (which we have called, above, the Piozzi method), has not entirely disappeared from more recent writing, but, at least, the snake was scotched by the publishers' preface of the 1859 edition of *Webster's Dictionary.* In its place has come an uncertainty in the definitions of *synonym* and *antonym* which is even more insidious. In the three essays that follow, we shall, therefore, make clear our own position. In the first of these essays (pp. xxvi–xxviii), we shall define *synonym* briefly, in order to show what effect that definition has had on our choice of words to be discriminated and on the technique of discrimination. In the second (pp. xxviii–xxxii), we shall define *antonym* at length, for the reason that this term has never been clearly examined and that the definitions in the major dictionaries are all at variance with Smith's tentative definition and with the selections of many of his successors. In the third (p. xxxiii), we shall explain our aims and practices with respect to the word-finding lists.

---

[6] In manuscript notes in the editorial files of G. & C. Merriam Company.

[7] That is, in the editorial files of G. & C. Merriam Company.

[8] Some of the best of these are: Francis A. March, sr. and Francis A. March, jr., *Thesaurus Dictionary of the English Language* (Philadelphia, 1902); C. O. Sylvester Mawson, *The Standard Thesaurus of English Words and Phrases, a Dictionary of Synonyms and Antonyms* (New York, 1911); F. Sturges Allen, *Allen's Synonyms and Antonyms* (New York, 1920); A. C. Baugh and P. C. Kitchen, *Synonyms, Antonyms and Discriminations* (included as an appendix in *The New Century Dictionary,* New York, 1927); C. O. Sylvester Mawson, *The Roget Dictionary of Synonyms and Antonyms* (New York, 1931).

SYNONYM: ANALYSIS AND DEFINITION

The chief reason for including in this Introduction an article on synonyms is not to phrase a new definition of that term. It is rather to make a protest as to the loosening of the definition within the last fifty or sixty years and to restate very clearly what we believe to be the true and generally accepted meaning. In addition, we shall show briefly the effect of this definition upon our method.

For approximately one hundred years in the history of English synonymy there was very little real difference of opinion as to what a synonym is, or as to what words should be the material of discrimination. It is true that John Trusler discriminated "words esteemed synonymous," Mrs. Piozzi "words apparently synonymous," and Miss Whately "pseudo-synonyms." Roget, who held that discrimination was foreign to his purpose, claimed that "the investigation of the distinctions to be drawn between words apparently synonymous, forms a separate branch of inquiry." Nevertheless, all four made a distinction between true, or actual, synonyms (that is, words identical in meaning), and the terms which they discriminated or, in the case of Roget, which were discriminable (that is, terms that are so nearly alike that they appear to be synonyms). For all practical purposes, however, the words which were discriminated were not at all different from the "words closely allied" in meaning between which, according to Crabb, it is the business of the synonymist "to mark the nice shades of distinction"; nor is there any clash with Soule's simple definition of a synonym as that which has "the same meaning as" the entry word under which it is listed "or a meaning very nearly the same."

It is also true that these synonymists did not always agree in their choice of synonyms. In part, this was due to some confusion as to the limits of their scope, but mostly it is the result of conditions which still, to a degree, prevail. Some advances have been made in precision, but the truth was and is that there are too many factors entering into the selection of synonyms to make for absolute certainty or perfect accuracy in their choice. But these synonymists were not so far wrong as William Perry, who accepted Johnson's "proximate words" as synonyms and made no distinction between them in reference to sense. The failure of his *Synonymous...Dictionary* may be ascribed to this cause.

The error Perry made has renewed itself, though with slightly more justification. This renewal, also, is initially the result of the misinterpretation of a highly popular work, Roget's *Thesaurus of English Words and Phrases,* and of a belief that Roget presented two lists of terms, those that were alike (*synonyms*) and those that were opposed. It was to give voice to this interpretation that Charles J. Smith coined the word "antonym" for the opposed terms and gave to the world in 1867 his small book *A Complete Collection of Synonyms and Antonyms* (see p. xvii, above). But because he was not following Roget in the arrangement of his material, choosing the dictionary (alphabetical) method rather than the classificatory method, he defined *synonym* (and *antonym*) in such a way that it would apply to Roget's lists (so far as they were of the same part of speech) and to his own. Synonyms are, in Smith's definition, "words which agree in expressing one or more characteristic ideas in common" (with the entered word). It is possible that he believed he was more careful in his selection than Roget. In line with his definition, he gives lists of synonyms such as that at **accelerate,** which are, it is true, less diverse than Roget's, but which are still susceptible of criticism as synonyms. There are, for example, some that are not questionable, such as *speed, quicken,* and *hasten,* but there are others such as *promote, urge, expedite, facilitate,* and *dispatch,* which are open to question. *Accelerate* means to make go faster: so do *speed, hasten,* and *quicken.* But *promote,* for example, stresses aid given in attaining an end, and only occasionally implies to make go faster; *urge* throws the emphasis upon the force that impels rather than upon the result, which usually, but not always, is to make go faster; *expedite* stresses the removal of impediments so that a progress or process is not delayed longer than is necessary or normal, and therefore usually means to make go faster than it might. But in all these three cases, a making go faster may or may not be implied; if implied, this notion is subordinate to the main implication of the word. Agreement "in one or more ideas" is a poor basis for the selection of synonyms, for these may or may not form a part of the essential meaning.

As the demand grew for a large number of synonyms, even agreement in one or more characteristic ideas tended to break down. Twenty-five and more years later, certain synonymists of repute were offering groups of words as synonyms of one word rather than of one another and were not restricting those words to one sense of their key term. For instance, one synonymist of this period gave as the synonyms of **stain,** *blot, color, discolor, disgrace, dishonor, dye, soil, spot, sully, tarnish, tinge, tint.* It is true that not all are discriminated, *blot, disgrace, dishonor, soil, spot, sully, tarnish,* and *tint* being omitted, but even so, they are all given in alphabetical order as synonyms and without explanation. In the list as it stands, some words are synonyms of *stain* in the sense of to discolor, some in the sense of to impart color to or suffuse with color, and some in the sense of to bring reproach upon; but others have only a slight idea in common with *stain* in one of its senses. Such lists are far from rare in the very late nineteenth century or the early twentieth century: to the consultant who seeks another and closer word for the one which occurs to him, they must be hopelessly confusing. They have no value in teaching the precise use of language: their only merit is to indicate some of the words which may be used when one feels the need of a word like *stain* in any of its senses.

It is against a definition so loose as that favored by Smith, or implied by others who went even further, that this book makes a protest. In line with the tradition of the Merriam-Webster dictionaries, we believe that such a definition is destructive of all the values that have come to be recognized in synonyms. We hold that only by a clear return to something like the time-honored definition can we conserve these values and recognize a synonym when we see it. To emphasize this aim, we propose in this Dictionary to restate that definition fully and unequivocally so that none of the loopholes may be left through which some synonymists have escaped, and to tighten the method of discrimination, so that it will be very clear at points where even the best of synonymists have, in the past, unconsciously permitted vagueness.

A synonym, in this Dictionary, will always mean one of two or more words in the English language which have the same or very nearly the same *essential* meaning. This is not a matter of mere likeness in meaning, for words may have some implications (ideas involved in their meaning) in common and yet not be synonymous. It is rather a likeness in denotation, which may be inadequately defined as the meaning which includes all the important implications, but which is more strictly defined as the meaning or signification of a term as expressed in its definition. The denotation must include more than a summary of implications: it must indicate the part of speech and the relations of the ideas involved in a term's meaning. Synonyms, therefore, are only such words as may be defined wholly, or almost wholly, in the same terms. Usually, they are distinguished from one another by an added implication or connotation, or they may differ in their idiomatic use or in their application. They may be, and usually are, interchangeable within limits, but interchangeability is not the final test, since idiomatic usage is often a preventive of that. The only satisfactory test of synonyms is their agreement in denotation. This agreement is seldom so perfect as to make the words absolutely identical in meaning, but it is always so clear that the two or more words which are synonyms can be defined in the same terms up to a certain point.

Consequently, the statement of this common denotation is of the greatest importance. In the discriminating articles in this Dictionary it is, as a general rule, presented in the first sentence, but sometimes when there is need of a preliminary statement it is put in the second sentence. For example, at **nice**, the common denotation of the words to be discriminated (*nice, dainty, fastidious, finical, particular, fussy, squeamish*) is given as "exacting or displaying exacting standards as in selection, judgment, workmanship, or the like"; at **object** (where *object, protest, remonstrate, expostulate, kick* are discriminated) it is "to oppose something such as a course, a procedure, a policy, or a project, especially by making known one's arguments against it"; at **delusion** (where *delusion, illusion, hallucination, mirage* are discriminated) it is "something which is believed to be or accepted as true or real, but which is actually false or unreal." Each of these sentences is so worded that the part of speech of the words discriminated is made clear. For example, the wording is in the form of a definition of an adjective where the words discriminated are adjectives, in the form of a definition of a verb where the words discriminated are verbs. Some of these synonyms have other senses than the one here given, but in each such meaning the word has other synonyms and another common denotation. A distinct attempt, it may be said here, has been made to select synonyms according to their range of meaning. It has not always been possible to do so, since, occasionally, the more general word has no synonyms except more specific words (cf. *let* in the list: *let, allow, permit, suffer, leave*). As a rule, however, a division between words of wide range and words of narrow range of meaning has been made, because it permits a more definite denotation for the narrower terms and makes for closer agreement and fewer differences. It is for this reason that we have separated the general terms for a political or legal agreement (*agreement, accord, understanding*) from those that are very explicit (*contract, bargain, compact, pact, treaty*, etc.), and have separated the general terms *large, big, great* from terms which specify unusual size (*enormous, immense, huge, vast*, etc.) and from terms which imply size and impressiveness (*grand, magnificent, imposing, stately*, etc.). But the difference between groups of synonyms is not always dependent on generality: it often implies a different emphasis or a different combination of implications. There have been many times when it was a serious question whether to add a word as a synonym to one group or to another, the arguments on both sides being of equal cogency. In such cases (as, for example, *hellish* and *fiendish*) the decision has usually depended on many factors, such as basic rather than derived meaning and the fact that, if certain words were treated separately, terms which are synonyms of one, but not of the other, could be added. For many reasons, the problem of selecting synonyms has not been an easy one, but we have always tried to base our judgment upon evidence that was not affected by any personal prejudices or predilections.

Not all the words discriminated in this Dictionary are synonyms. A few articles discuss a group of words that are sometimes wrongly taken as synonyms because they are confused or their actual meanings are misunderstood or because they once had one or more meanings which made them synonymous. In articles discussing such words, the reason for their not being synonyms, whatever it may be, is stated clearly and unambiguously in the first or second sentence of the article. We have added these groups not merely because we believe them useful, but because we believe that they come rightly within the province of the discriminator.

The method of discrimination is not invariable, for every set of synonyms presents its own problems. But, in general, the points of distinction are in: (1) implications — here, mostly minor ideas involved in the meaning of the word; (2) connotations — the ideas which color the word's meaning and are the product of various influences, such as etymology, language of origin, and historical and literary association; (3) applications — the restrictions in a word's use as prescribed by idiom or in accordance with the nature of the other words with which it may be associated, as when an adverb may be used to modify only certain kinds of verbs, or when a verb may take only certain kinds of nouns as its subject or its object. Not all of the words discriminated in a single article differ in only one of these ways, however: some may differ in implications, some in connotations, some in applications, and some in more than one way. For no method adopted by the discriminator should be so artificial as to foster merely theoretical distinctions. The distinctions drawn should be real distinctions based on the evidence of recorded use — and it is such evidence, we cannot too strongly emphasize, that has guided the editors of this Dictionary and has determined the distinctions set forth in its discriminating articles.

ANTONYM: ANALYSIS AND DEFINITION

There are probably few words more generally used with less understanding of their meaning than the word *antonym*. True, all the dictionaries define it, but often in such terms that the definition may be interpreted to include radically different conceptions. Is an antonym theoretically only one word, or, at the most, one of two or three words, which can be opposed to another word in a definite sense or is it any one of several words which may be opposed to it or to a group of synonymous terms? Probably because the latter conception is the easier one it has gained widespread acceptance, but still the dictionary definitions incline to back up the opinion of those who think of an antonym in the abstract as something more specialized and nearer to the former conception.

No one will dispute the right of a person to coin a term that fills a definite need or to give to that term the meaning he desires — provided such definition accords with the term's etymology. Where it does not accord, however, the meaning may fairly be questioned — as in the case of *antonym*. For C. J. Smith who, in his ...*Synonyms and Antonyms* (1867), introduced this term (which, in his own phrasing, "he has ventured, not to coin, but to reissue") adopted it primarily because of its analogy to *synonym* and knew that only by considerable stretching could the meaning he proposed for it be made to approach the meaning of its Greek original. Despite his recognition of this fact, the term seemed to Smith preferable to *counterterm*, though he acknowledged that some persons might still prefer the latter. As for definition, he related *synonym* and *antonym*. "Words," he wrote, "which agree in expressing one or more characteristic ideas in common [that is, with a given term] he has regarded as Synonyms, those which negative one or more such ideas he has called Antonyms."

Therefore, no one is likely to dispute the right of a later investigator to examine anew the meaning of a coined word falsely grounded and vaguely defined that has become established in the language. In fact, there is not only the right but a duty on the part of such an investigator when, as in the case of *antonym*, he finds that there is a great difference between the theory, as manifested in the definition, and the practice, as manifested in selection. There will always be strict constructionists and loose constructionists but, in this case at least, the difference is more apparent than real, for many of the latter have been forced into this position by the practical difficulties confronting them in the selection of antonyms, rather than by indifference to the concept involved.

What we propose to do here, then, is to examine the word *antonym*, to determine the concept it involves, and to state its definition in as clear terms as possible. When we find a term like this used frequently with such qualifying words as *exact* and *true* (the "exact antonym" of this word; the "true antonym"), we must suspect an attempt on the part of men to approximate an ideal.

Modern unabridged dictionaries, without exception, define *antonym* with comparative strictness. It is "a word of opposite meaning" (*Webster's New International Dictionary, Second Edition*), "a term which is the opposite or antithesis of another, a counter-term" (*Oxford English Dictionary*), "a word directly opposed to another in meaning; a counterterm: the opposite of *synonym*" (*Funk and Wagnalls New Standard Dictionary*), "a counterterm; an opposite; an antithetical word: the opposite of *synonym*" (*Century Dictionary*), and "a word that is an opposite in meaning of a particular word" (*New Century Dictionary*). In all of these definitions, the burden is on the word *opposite* or *opposed;* and, it should be added, all differences of opinion as to the criteria for determining antonyms are due to uncertainty as to what is meant by *opposite* or *opposed*. The physical connotations of these words always stand in the way of a strict definition of their abstract senses. How complex is the concept of opposition may be seen from the following analysis of its physical connotations.

Opposition is a relation involved when two things are so placed that: (1) they may be connected by a straight line (straightness as distinguished from obliquity being determined by external conditions such as the lines of a room) drawn from one to another (as, *opposite* windows); (2) they lie at either end of an axis, diameter, or the like (as, *opposite* points on the earth's surface); (3) they are contiguous but reversed in position (as, the *opposite* halves of the globe); (4) they face each other, the distance apart being of no consequence (as, partners stand *opposite*); (5) they depart or diverge from each other (as, to go their *opposite* ways); (6) they work against each other (as, *opposite* forces); (7) they cannot exist together, because they reverse or undo each other (as, the *opposite* processes of growth and decay); (8) they represent the obverse and the reverse (as, the *opposite* faces of a coin).

What this relation is both materially and immaterially and in all instances is, frankly, hard to determine. It is not invariably the confrontation of one with another, for "persons who go their *opposite* ways" and "the *opposite* processes of growth and decay," for example, do not respond to this test; it is hardly complete divergence or difference, for "the *opposite* halves of the globe" and "the *opposite* faces of a coin" represent difference only in one or more particulars, otherwise remaining fundamentally alike; it is still less antagonism or irreconcilability, for there is no hint of either in the *opposite* position of partners in a dance or in *opposite* windows. Although some of these ideas exist as implications distinguishing meanings of the word *opposite*, they do not yield any fundamental meaning which is involved in every sense. One can go no further than to say that *opposite* represents a setting of one thing against another so as to sharpen their differences or to reveal their divergencies.

It will be necessary, therefore, to get at what is meant by "opposite meaning" in another way. First, let us take the words listed as antonyms in the dictionaries and manuals of synonyms and antonyms and see into what classifications they fall. When possible, we shall offer a classification known to logic, but when not possible, we shall form our own, naming it in unambiguous terms.

A large number of words listed as antonyms fall into two well-known logical categories, those of *contradictory terms* (or *contradictories*) and *contrary terms* (or *contraries*).

(1) *Contradictory terms* are so opposed to each other that they are mutually exclusive and admit no possibility between them. If either is true, the other must be false; if either is false, the other must be true. Examples:—A thing is either *perfect* or *imperfect:* no matter how slight or how extensive the imperfection, the fact remains that the thing cannot be called *perfect* if any flaw, blemish, or defect exists. If a person is asked for his opinion, he may *agree* with that of others, or he may *disagree*, or *differ:* it is unimportant whether the disagreement is radical or superficial or the difference concerns a major or a very minor point; he cannot be said to *agree*.

(2) *Contrary terms* are so opposed in meaning that the language admits no greater divergence. They are the true "diametrical opposites." But they must be of, or must apply to things of, the same genus or fundamental kind. Thus, white and black represent the extremes in color, the former, as popularly understood, implying the absorption of all colors and the latter implying the privation of every vestige of color. *Prodigal* and *parsimonious* represent extremes in expenditure (chiefly of money), but *prodigal* implies excessive extravagance and *parsimonious* excessive frugality. *Superiority* and *inferiority* represent extremes judged by a standard of what is good. Between these extremes represented by each of these pairs of examples, there are many words which may more truly describe or designate the person or thing in question.

Other classes are the following:

(3) Many words are listed as antonyms that normally appear in pairs. Some are what the logician calls *relative terms*, pairs of words which indicate such a relationship that one of them cannot be used without suggesting the other; as, *parent* and *child*, *husband* and *wife*, *predecessor* and *successor*, *employee*

and *employer*. Others are *complementary terms* involving, usually, a reciprocal relation or the incompleteness of one unless the other follows; as, *question* and *answer*, *attack* and *defend*, *stimulus* and *response*.

(4) An important class of words sometimes listed in antonymies may be called for want of a better name *reverse terms:* these comprise adjectives or adverbs which signify a quality, or verbs or nouns which signify an act or state, that reverse or undo the quality, act, or state of the other. Although they are neither contradictory nor contrary terms, they present a clear opposition. Their addition is usually justified in this way: if the antonym of *admit* is *reject*, what shall we do with *eject* which implies not the negative, but the reverse of *admit;* if the antonym of *destructive* is *harmless*, must we ignore *constructive*, which goes further and implies either the reverse or the undoing of *destructive?* Many words of the reverse type are often equal in value, sometimes they are even stronger than the first.

(5) There is still a class of words listed as antonyms, which are neither contradictories nor contraries nor reverse terms, which do, however, present a sharp contrast—for example, such pairs as *rich* and *destitute*, *dry* and *moist*, and *keep* and *abandon*. This is one of the most perplexing of classes and one that appears very frequently in antonym lists. Such words may be designated *contrasted terms*. We shall return to them later (see p. xxxi).

(6) The last class of so-called antonyms is very inclusive. Words in this class might be called "loosely contrasted terms," since, when they are presented side by side with the word of which they are given as antonyms, they never fully clash but show a difference in only a small part of their meaning (as, *abstruse* and *superficial*, *frank* and *hypocritical*, *vigilant* and *careless*). For the sake of uniformity, however, we shall call them *incompatibles*, for they usually cannot both at the same time be said of, or applied to, the same person or thing. *Frank* means open and free in one's talk and uninhibited by any restraints, such as fear, whereas *hypocritical* means presenting an appearance of being other, and usually better, than one is; *abstruse* means so remote from the range of ordinary human experience that there is difficulty in comprehension, while *superficial*, in this limited sense, means not penetrating below the surface or exterior so as to unveil what lies behind. So put there is not the slightest sign of a clash in meaning, yet the difference which confuses, though slight, is there, for the person who is called *frank* gives the appearance of sincerity and the person who is called *hypocritical* is adjudged insincere. Similarly, a work that is spoken of as *abstruse* differs from a work that is spoken of as *superficial* in that the one is profound, the other shallow. It is *sincere* and *insincere* (not *frank* and *hypocritical*), and *profound* and *shallow* (not *abstruse* and *superficial*) which clash in meaning. Since this class is based upon a mistake in analysis, it will be eliminated from the discussion.

If, then, we were to make a definition of *antonym* according to the type of word which dictionaries and manuals select as such, it would be phrased something like this: "An antonym is a word that so differs from another word that it represents its contradictory, its contrary, its relative (or counterpart), its complement, its reverse, its contrasted term, or its incompatible in some way or degree."

That this is too inclusive a definition is obvious. No one, it seems fair to state, would define in terms as broad as this the word *antonym* as it is understood in concept; yet everyone who has made it his business to select antonyms is aware of the dangers involved and of the difficulty in avoiding the questionable types. An easygoing attitude is not chiefly responsible for this wide diversity. The English language was clearly not made to measure: it was not devised to show likenesses or differences. The discovery both of words which are closely alike and of words which are sharply different is, for the most part, the product of the need for expressing ideas or of understanding expressed ideas. No mechanical shaping power sets words right before men begin to use them.

It must be remembered that the task of selecting antonyms is imposed upon a living structure, in a desire to know its resources and so far as possible bend it to our needs. The selection not only of antonyms but also of synonyms is similar, at least in aim, to the scientist's classification of animals into orders, families, genera, and species. Both help us in the understanding and mastery of the material involved. When an old system breaks down in its study of the animal world, a new one must arise. None is perfect, but each is a help in bringing within the range of human understanding something that would otherwise be too vast for study and beyond the range of experience of any one man. So we proceed to study synonyms, words which closely resemble each other not in particular ways but in the very heart of their meaning, that we may know them better and use them more wisely, more precisely, more effectively, or the like.

We should like to do the same thing with antonyms. It is good, we feel, to know the exact antonym of a word, for not only will it give us a firmer grasp of the meaning of the word to which it is opposed but inversely, of itself. Is there any test that will help us in discovering such words, that we may be enabled not only to speak and to write more expressively but to have a richer understanding of the pages of men who have known how to express themselves?

There is a word in Smith's definition of *antonym* which may give us the clue, "those [words] which *negative* one or more such ideas he has called Antonyms." In fact, even today, some persons argue that an antonym is "the *exact* negative" of a word. It is not clear just what this is intended to mean. Taken quite literally and expressed in the phraseology of logic an "exact negative" is a word's *contradictory term.* But this is too narrow, as even those who vigorously support this definition must agree. By the terms of its definition, a word's contradictory must be the equivalent in meaning of its *not*-compound. Otherwise the two terms (a word and its contradictory) could not be mutually exclusive. Let us see this in tabular form.

word	*not-compound*	*contradictory*
colored	not-colored	colorless
perfect	not-perfect	imperfect
agree	not-agree	disagree *or* differ

So put, it is obvious that there is no disagreement between the *not*-term and contradictory: in this case the negative and the opposite agree. The trouble comes, however, with the naming of the antonym. As a matter of practical policy, if we accept the "exact negative" as the antonym, we must restrict ourselves to the very few contradictories which have an independent form, and to the very few *in-*, *un-*, *dis-* and similar compounds which are obviously contradictory terms. But if we wish completeness, we must supply antonyms for the vast majority of English words by constructing a *not*-form. That might do in logic, but it would not do when greater knowledge of the English language exists as our clear aim. Moreover, we feel the lack of the clash that gives so much savor to the antonym.

On the other hand, it is clear that the other terms listed as antonyms do not equal the "exact negative." The logical contradictory of *white* (*not-white*) may include any chromatic color or any other achromatic color, yet the contrary, or diametrical opposite, is only *black;* the logical contradictory of *parsimonious* (*not-parsimonious*) may include many terms, such as *liberal, extravagant, prodigal,* yet the contrary, or diametrical opposite, is *prodigal; not-liking* may include both *indifference* and *aversion,* but no one will question that *aversion* is the contrary of *liking.* Even more obvious is the difference between the logical contradictory and the relative or the complementary term, for in this case they neither represent nor include the same thing. *Not-attack,* for example, does not equal *defend; not-husband* is not the equivalent of *wife;* and *not-stimulus* does not in any way approach *response.*

More important than relative and complementary terms (most of which may be doubted, with good reason, to be the antonyms of each other) are the terms which take a reverse as the opposite. While the *not*-term in these cases often equals or includes a word that is called the term's *antonym,* it is never equivalent with what may be called the "reverse antonym." For instance, *not-admit* equals *reject,* but it does not cover the reverse of *admit,* which may be either *eject* or *expel: not-abandon* may include *keep,* but it cannot be interpreted to cover the reverse of *abandon,* which is *reclaim.*

One class of words listed as antonyms remains for our consideration, contrasted terms (see p. xxx, above). As has been said, this class covers a large number of words the listing of which as antonyms puzzles rather than enlightens the reader. It is easy to prove that they cannot be "exact negatives." For example, *keep,* which is often given as the antonym of *abandon,* is not its contradictory, for the logical contradictory (*not-keep*) also includes *sell, lose, give away,* and many other words; *rich* is not the contradictory of *destitute,* for the logical contradictory *not-rich* includes *needy, indigent, poor, comfortable,* and many other terms as well as *destitute.* But this does not get at the heart of the matter and display what is wrong with these terms. Obviously also, they are not contraries, for they do not represent extremes of divergence as do *parsimonious* and *prodigal* or *white* and *black.* What is the matter with them? In answering this question, we shall find the clue to the solution of our problem.

Superficially viewed, these contrasted terms differ sharply in some part, but not in all parts, of their meaning. They do not clash full force. One term covers more ground than the other, or one term is more explicit in its implications than the other. The logician would say that they equal each other neither in extension nor in intension. Put more simply, they differ (1) in their range of application or applicability, one being general, the other specific, or one being more inclusive or less inclusive than the other, and (2) in their depth of meaning — that is, in the number and quality of implications contained in the terms. It is clear that *keep* is more general than *abandon* and that to equal it in generality and at the same time to negative (or, much better, to negate) its implications, *relinquish* would be a better choice: it is clear that *abandon* has more specific implications than are found in *keep,* such as surrender of possession or control and relegation to the mercy of others, and that a word which exactly equates these implications in number and quality, yet, at the same time, negates them, must be the true antonym. There seems to be no term that fills these demands except a "reverse term," one that undoes what has been accomplished by the act of abandoning. That term is *reclaim* in its definite sense of regaining control or possession of something and giving it full care and attention. *Rich* is too broad and general to pair with the very explicit *destitute.* There are many implications in the latter which have no clear parallel in *rich.* Only *poor* could be opposed to *rich* in breadth of extension and in vagueness of intension, because *rich* suggests more possessions than one needs, and *poor* suggests fewer possessions than one requires and so negates in full the meaning of the other. On the other hand, *opulent* could be opposed to *destitute* in narrowness of extension and in explicitness of intension, for *destitute* suggests the miserable condition where one is deprived of all that is needed for bare existence, and *opulent* the felicitous condition where everything that is desired is possessed in abundance. Though *rich* and *poor* come close together (the dividing line being marked by such a word as *comfortable*) and *destitute* and *opulent* are very far apart, being in fact "diametrical opposites," each represents the negation of the other.

In this way, *wet,* because it equals *dry* in range of meaning and negates *dry* in number and quality of implications, is the antonym of *dry,* whereas *damp* and *moist* are merely contrasted terms to *dry; alleviate* for the same reasons is the antonym of *aggravate,* and *mitigate, assuage,* and *allay* are nothing more than contrasted terms; *elevation* in the sense of promotion is the antonym of *degradation* in the sense of demotion, for it contains implications not found in *preferment* or *advancement.*

In selecting antonyms, therefore, one should be on guard to match in range of meaning the word from which one starts, and to negate every one of its implications, so that the opposition is complete. Otherwise the opposing words do not clash full force, one word covering more or less ground than the other or exhibiting differences not apparent in the other. It is for this reason that in this Dictionary we have preferred to give *contrasted words* as distinct from *antonyms,* not denying or ignoring the value of the former in word study, but emphasizing the unique, disciplinary value of the latter.

It is for a similar reason that we have ruled out relative and complementary terms as antonyms of each other. Pairs of words of this class are, it is true, usually matched in extension, but one of the pair seldom negates the intension of the other. Rather they suggest union, convergence, or completion when taken together. *Husband* and *wife, employer* and *employee* are different elements in a combination, which we may call opposites, not in the sense of negating each other, but of fulfilling each other. The same is true of *stimulus* and *response,* of *question* and *answer.* Without the former, the latter could not be: without the latter, the former remains incomplete. An occasional instance, however, remains, such as *attack* and *defend.* Since these come as close to reverse terms as they do to complementary terms, they may be treated as the former.

The foregoing analysis would seem to leave us with three classes as possible antonyms: contradictory, contrary, and reverse terms. It is true that, in general, all antonyms may be fitted into each of these classes. But, as the first two classes are the creation of logicians, who are dealing with symbols rather than with words, they are somewhat too rigid or too artificial for our use. Whether *good* and *bad, right* and *wrong, true* and *false* are contradictories or contraries might be disputed: it is wiser, for our purposes, not to raise this issue. They still remain antonyms according to our tests. So do a large number of more specific terms, which are equated in range of meaning and are negated in their specific implications, such as *extol* and *decry, aboveboard* and *underhand, constant* and *fitful* (as applied to things), *adulation* and *abuse.* The designation "reverse term" may also be dropped now that its purpose in exposition has been served. There are only three tests which should be applied to a word selected as the antonym of another word, and these are stated in the following definition:

An antonym is a word so opposed in meaning to another word, its equal in breadth or range of application, that it negates or nullifies every single one of its implications.

It is this definition that has guided the selection of antonyms in this Dictionary. Not every entry, of course, exhibits an antonym, for there are many words that have no antonym. In some few cases, moreover, we have been unable to supply any word that meets the three tests of the above definition or have been obliged to resort to an approximation. In such cases, we shall always welcome intelligent criticism that may enable us to supply these gaps. But, for the most part, where an antonym is listed, the editors rely upon its self-justification to the consultant who will apply these tests.

THE TREATMENT OF ANTONYMS

A few words should be added to clarify the practice of this Dictionary in regard to antonyms. They form an important part of its make-up; but, as they do not require much space, their significance may be overlooked.

It must be emphasized that each antonym is directly related to its entry word in the special sense in which that word is discriminated. It bears not a loose relation but a very close one to that word, and even though it may also be the antonym of some other word (especially of a synonym of the entry word) it must be judged only by the relation it bears to the entry word with which it is associated.

Sometimes, however, the antonym fits that word only when it is used in a narrowed sense or in a narrow application. This limitation is indicated in a parenthetical phrase with words in italics. Thus, at **abet,** we have as antonym "deter (*with a personal subject*)" and at **actuate,** "deter (*with a motive, fear, etc., as subject*)." A simpler instance is the antonym at **brilliant,** in the sense of *bright,* which reads "subdued (*of light, color, etc.*)."

At other times, the entry word is so inclusive that it takes more than one antonym to cover it. Then some indication is given of the differing collocations in which each antonym appears. Thus, **check,** as a synonym of *restrain,* has for its antonyms "accelerate (*of speed, etc.*): advance (*of movements, plans, hopes, etc.*): release (*of feelings, energies, etc.*)."

A cross reference (introduced by "see") following an antonym is merely an indication of the sense in which it is used. Thus, **close,** as a synonym of *silent* and *reticent,* takes *open* as its antonym, but the sense in which *open* is used here is made clear by the cross reference to FRANK, where the word *open* is discriminated.

ANALOGOUS AND CONTRASTED WORDS

The essential part of this Dictionary consists of the synonyms and their discriminations and of the antonyms of the words thus discriminated. With these, judged from the point of view of one who is interested in the clarification of the differences in meaning between synonyms and in finding their direct opposites, it is a complete work. Yet for those who use this book as a word finder or as a vocabulary builder, there might be something lacking if it went no further. It is in view of the needs of such consultants that we have added lists of *analogous words* and of *contrasted words.*

Some of the analogous words, or terms closely related in meaning, merit the name of "near synonyms," so close are they to the vocabulary entry: some contain much the same implications as the entry word, but the implication that they emphasize is not the same as that expressed in the common denotation of the discriminated group of which the entry word forms a part. Some are more general than the entry word, some more specific; some come together in only a part of their meaning. But in some important particulars they are all like the word under which they are listed.

So, too, with contrasted words, or terms sharply differing in meaning from the entry word. Some are close synonyms of its antonym, but many are opposed to it only in part of their meaning. Through these lists, the consultant who is seeking a word may find exactly the one he needs or the student may discover a useful means of extending his vocabulary.

These aims are made practical and easy of attainment by an additional aid which no work on synonyms has hitherto given the consultant. Terms listed as *analogous words* and *contrasted words* are arranged in groups, all of which are discriminated in this book. Most of the words are themselves directly discriminated, cross reference to the entry where the article is given being made by means of an asterisk or a reference introduced by "see": a few that are not themselves directly discriminated are closely dependent on words that are, as by being their derivatives or inflected forms, or by being their negatives, and are thereby covered by the article to which a clear cross reference is made. Thus, at **amenity** (in the sense of courtesy) the list of analogous words contains: (1) *civility, politeness, courteousness,* plus a cross reference to the article at CIVIL, where *civil, polite, courteous* are discriminated; (2) *graciousness, affability, cordiality, geniality, sociability,* plus a cross reference to GRACIOUS, where *gracious, affable, cordial, genial, sociable* are discriminated. Similarly, among the contrasted words at **banal** are *stimulating* or *stimulative, provoking* or *provocative, exciting, piquing,* which, though not discriminated themselves, are fully covered by the article at PROVOKE, where their corresponding verbs are treated. Through the cross reference, then, the consultant can find the meaning of every term in the word lists, and can sharpen his sense of their differences.

It is perhaps unnecessary to point out that the selection of words in each of these lists is not determined by the group of synonyms, but by the one word at whose entry the list appears. As a result, each vocabulary entry is complete in itself: it has not only its synonyms and antonym or antonyms, but also analogous words which are closely related to it and contrasted words which are sharply opposed to it. It is thus treated as a unit, and all essential information is gathered about it.

EXPLANATORY NOTES

The left-hand column below consists of entries or, usually, parts of entries selected from the main vocabulary to illustrate the principal devices used in this Dictionary. The right-hand column provides explanations of these devices.

adage. *Saying, saw, proverb, maxim, motto, epigram.

1 The vocabulary entry (usually a single word; occasionally a phrase) is printed in heavy-faced type.

aeon *or* **eon.** Age, era, epoch, *period.

2 Alternative forms, chiefly variant spellings, are listed when they are likely to be of value to the consultant.

aerial *or* **aërial,** *adj.* *Airy, ethereal.
aerial *or* **aërial,** *n.* *Antenna.

3 The part of speech is indicated (by means of the commonly accepted abbreviations, printed in italic type) where it is desirable or necessary to do so.

affection.[1] *Feeling, emotion, passion, sentiment.
affection.[2] *Disease, malady, complaint, distemper, ailment.

4 Words identical in spelling and part of speech, but of different etymology, are given separate entries and each entry is numbered with a superior numeral. These numerals are also used in cross references to such entries.

amble, *v.* **1** Rack, single-foot, pace, walk, canter, lope, trot. See under TROT, *n.*
2 *Saunter, stroll.

5 Two or more meanings (or senses) of a single vocabulary entry are clearly separated, and each meaning is numbered with a heavy-faced numeral.

ambush, *n.* **Ambush, ambuscade, ambuscado** agree in meaning a device to entrap the enemy by lying in wait. **Ambush,** however, is also used to designate any act of lying in wait or in concealment as for spying, frightening, obtaining an advantage, or the like; as, "*ambushes* of cutthroats" (*Thackeray*). **Ambuscade** usually implies the legitimate strategic disposition of troops in concealment, but in military use is more often applied to the body of troops or to their position than to the trap. "An *ambuscade* to cut off the convoy" (*Froude*). **Ambuscado** was once more common in English than *ambuscade,* but is now distinctly archaic. "Then dreams he of cutting foreign throats, Of breaches, *ambuscadoes,* Spanish blades" (*Shak.*).

6 The words to be discriminated in an article (see pp. xxvii ff., above) are listed in heavy-faced type at the beginning of the article.
Each word is repeated in heavy-faced type at the point in the article where it is individually discussed.
The meanings or applications of the words discriminated are profusely illustrated by means of familiar examples (often idiomatic or characteristic phrases) or by quotations from named authors or sources. The word illustrated is printed in italic type.
The source of a quotation is also printed in italics. A list of sources quoted is given on pp. 899 ff.

artful. Wily, crafty, cunning, tricky, *sly, foxy.
articulation. **1** Integration, concatenation. See under INTEGRATE, *v.*
2 *Joint, suture.

7 Where there is no discriminating article, the first item under an entry is a list of its synonyms (except as explained on p. xxviii). These synonyms are discriminated from one another in an article in this Dictionary. The place where this article is to be found is indicated by an asterisk prefixed to one of the words in the list or by a reference introduced by the word "see."

ascertain. Determine, *discover, unearth, learn.
Ana. Inquire, query, interrogate, *ask: study, contemplate, weigh, *consider: observe, survey (see SEE).
Con. *Conjecture, surmise, guess: presume, assume (see PRESUPPOSE).

8 Each vocabulary entry is provided (where the facts require or permit) with "finding lists" of two kinds (see p. xxxiii, above): Analogous Words introduced by the label *Ana.* and Contrasted Words introduced by *Con.*
Words given in these finding lists are divided into groups. Each group consists of words discriminated (or related to those discriminated) in a single article.
The groups are separated from one another by colons. Words within each group are separated by commas. The place of entry of the article discussing each group is indicated by an asterisk or a "see" reference (see §7).

ascetic, *adj.* Austere, *severe, stern.
Ant. Luxurious, voluptuous (see SENSUOUS).
assuage. Alleviate, *relieve, mitigate, lighten, allay.
Ant. Exacerbate: intensify.

9 The label *Ant.* introduces the antonym or antonyms of a vocabulary entry.
In the antonym lists, commas are used between words that are synonyms of one another, and colons are used to separate words that do not have such a relationship.
While many of the words listed as antonyms are themselves entered as vocabulary entries and are therefore discussed in the articles in this Dictionary, the selection of antonyms has not been restricted to such words (see pp. xxxii ff., above). For this reason the antonym lists do not as a rule contain references to discriminating articles.

austere. *Severe, stern, ascetic.
Ant. Luscious (*of fruits, etc.*): warm, ardent (*of persons, feelings, etc.*): exuberant (*of style, quality, etc.*).

10 In the lists of Antonyms and, less often, of Analogous Words and Contrasted Words, italic notations in parentheses indicate the limited use or application in which the preceding word is to be taken. See also p. xxxiii.

A DICTIONARY OF DISCRIMINATED SYNONYMS

WITH ANTONYMS

AND ANALOGOUS AND CONTRASTED WORDS

a-. *Un-, non-, in-.

abaft. **Abaft, aft, astern** are nautical terms meaning behind, or to or at the rear (of). *Abaft* and *aft* are applied to objects or their positions in a ship. **Abaft** (opposed to *afore*) commonly suggests position relatively nearer the stern or rear part of the ship; as, his station is *abaft* the foremast; the wave struck her *abaft* the beam. **Aft** (opposed to *forward*) suggests position actually in that part of the ship to the rear of the midship section; as, they went *aft* to hoist the mainsail; a cabin *aft* of the lounge. **Astern** (opposed to *ahead*) now chiefly implies position outside and to the rear of a ship; as, the wake *astern* of a vessel; a brisk breeze *astern*.

Ana. After, rear, back, *posterior, hind, hinder.

Ant. Afore. — *Con.* Ahead, forward, *before.

abandon, *v.* **1** **Abandon, desert, forsake,** though often used interchangeably in the sense of to quit absolutely, are not exact synonyms. **Abandon,** in its strictest use, implies surrender of control or possession and, frequently, the knowledge that the thing abandoned is left to the mercy of someone or something else. "The ghost of grandeur that lingers between the walls of *abandoned* haciendas in New Mexico" (*M. Austin*). "In the frantic rush to escape, the insane had usually been forgotten and *abandoned* to horrible deaths" (*V. Heiser*). **Desert,** in precise usage, commonly implies previous occupation, companionship, or guardianship, and often connotes desolation; in its narrower sense (esp. in **deserter, desertion**) it emphasizes violation of one's duty as guardian or protector, and extreme culpability. "He that takes the forlorn hope in an attack, is often *deserted* by those that should support him" (*Scott*). **Forsake** still often retains its etymological connotation of repudiation; it frequently suggests renunciation; even in its loosest use it commonly stresses the breaking off of an association with someone or something; as, to *forsake* the world and all its pleasures. "She was *forsaken* at the altar" (*Deland*).

Ana. *Discard, cast (away *or* off), scrap, junk: reject, repudiate (see DECLINE).

Ant. Reclaim. — *Con.* Hold, possess, enjoy (see HAVE): shield, safeguard, protect (see DEFEND): redeem, *rescue, save.

2 Surrender, *relinquish, yield, resign, leave.

Ant. Cherish (*hopes, opinions, etc.*): restrain (*oneself*). — *Con.* *Keep, retain: treasure, prize (see APPRECIATE): *maintain, assert, defend: inhibit, bridle, curb (see RESTRAIN).

abandon, *n.* *Unconstraint, spontaneity.

Ana. License, *freedom, liberty: relaxation, laxity *or* laxness, looseness (see LOOSE).

Ant. Self-restraint. — *Con.* Repression, suppression (see SUPPRESS): self-possession, aplomb (see CONFIDENCE): poise (see BALANCE, TACT).

abandoned. **Abandoned, reprobate, profligate, dissolute** fundamentally mean utterly depraved. *Abandoned* and *reprobate* were originally applied to sinners, and to their acts. One is **abandoned** who by his complete surrender to a life of sin seems spiritually lost or morally irreclaimable. "I disdain . . . to paint her as she is, Cruel, *abandoned*, glorying in her shame!" (*Cowper*). One is **reprobate** who is abandoned and therefore rejected—in Calvinism, by God; in more general use, by one's fellows. In its modern weakened sense, *reprobate* implies ostracism by, or exclusion from, a social group for a serious offense against its code. "Don't count on my appearing your friend too openly. . . . remember always that I'm a *reprobate* old clergyman" (*Hugh Walpole*). *Profligate* and *dissolute* convey little, if any, suggestion of divine or social condemnation but both imply complete moral breakdown and self-indulgence to such an extreme that all standards of morality and prudence are disregarded. One is **profligate** who openly and shamelessly flouts all the decencies and wastes his substance in riotous living. "There was no excess which was not encouraged by the ostentatious *profligacy* of the King and his favourite courtiers" (*Macaulay*). One is **dissolute** who has completely thrown off all moral and prudential restraints on the indulgence of his appetites. "Chance spectators, chiefly *dissolute* men and shameless women" (*Wordsworth*).

Ana. Depraved, debauched, perverted, debased (see DEBASE): degenerate, corrupt (see VICIOUS): wanton, lewd, lascivious, libidinous, lecherous (see LICENTIOUS).

Ant. Redeemed, regenerate. — *Con.* Saved, rescued, reclaimed, delivered (see RESCUE).

abase. **Abase, demean, debase, degrade, humble, humiliate** are synonymous when they denote to lower (one) in one's own estimation or in that of others. **Abase** commonly suggests loss of dignity or prestige without necessarily implying permanency in that loss; as, to *abase* the proud. When used reflexively (*abasement* often equals *self-abasement*), it usually connotes humility, abjectness, or a sense of one's inferiority. In this reflexive use, *humble* is often used interchangeably. "Whosoever exalteth himself shall be *abased* [D.V. and R.V. *humbled*]; and he that *humbleth* himself shall be exalted" (*Luke* xiv. 11). **Demean** implies less humility than *abase* but is stronger in its implications of loss of dignity or social standing. "It was . . . Mrs. Sedley's opinion that her son would *demean* himself by a marriage with an artist's daughter" (*Thackeray*). **Debase** emphasizes deterioration in value or quality: it is more often used of things (as, to *debase* the currency), but when used of persons it commonly connotes weakening of moral standards or of the moral character; as, officeholders *debase* themselves by accepting bribes. "How books . . . *debase* The many for the pleasure of those few" (*Wordsworth*). **Degrade** stresses a lowering in plane rather than in rank and often conveys a strong implication of the shamefulness of the condition to which the person (or group or thing) has been reduced. "That she and Charlotte, two spent old women, should be . . . talking to each other of hatred, seemed unimaginably hideous and *degrading*" (*E. Wharton*). Often (esp. in **degradation**) it connotes actual degeneracy or corruption. "It was by that unscrupulous person's liquor her husband had been *degraded*" (*Hardy*). **Humble** is frequently used in place of *degrade* in the sense of demote, when the ignominy of the reduction in rank is emphasized. "We are pleased . . . to see him taken down and humbled" (*Spectator*). When it is employed without any implication of demotion, it often suggests a salutary increase of humility or the realization of one's own littleness or impotence. "It was one of those illnesses from which we turn away our eyes, shuddering and *humbled*" (*Deland*). Occasionally it implies a lowering in station. "In such a man . . . A race illustrious for heroic deeds, *Humbled*, but not *degraded*, may expire" (*Wordsworth*). **Humiliate,** once a close synonym of *humble*, now comes closer to *mortify*, for it stresses chagrin and shame. "When we ask to be *humbled*, we must not recoil from being *humiliated*" (*C. Rossetti*).

Ana. Cringe, truckle, cower, *fawn, toady: grovel (see WALLOW): abash, discomfit, disconcert, *embarrass.

Ant. Exalt: extol (*esp. oneself*). — ***Con.*** Magnify, aggrandize (see EXALT): elevate, *lift, raise: laud, acclaim, *praise.

abash. Discomfit, *embarrass, disconcert, faze, rattle.

Ana. Fluster, flurry, *discompose, perturb, disturb, agitate: chagrin, mortify (see ASHAMED): confound, dumfound, nonplus (see PUZZLE).

Ant. Embolden: reassure. — ***Con.*** Elate, exult (see ELATED).

abate. **1** *Abolish, extinguish, annihilate.

Ana. End, terminate (see CLOSE): *annul, void, avoid, abrogate: cancel, obliterate (see ERASE): *nullify, invalidate.

Ant. Perpetuate. — ***Con.*** *Continue, last, persist, abide.

2 Reduce, diminish, *decrease, lessen.

Ana. Retard, slow, slacken, *delay: *moderate, temper: mitigate, lighten, alleviate (see RELIEVE).

Ant. Augment: accelerate (*pace, speed*): intensify (*hopes, fears, a fever*). — ***Con.*** *Increase, multiply, enlarge: aggravate, heighten, enhance (see INTENSIFY): *speed, quicken, hurry.

3 **Abate, subside, wane, ebb** are synonymous in their extended senses only. All then denote to die down in force or intensity; all imply previous approach to a high point and present movement towards a vanishing point. **Abate,** however, stresses the idea of progressive diminution in intensity; **subside** suggests falling to a low level and cessation of turbulence or agitation; as, the wind is *abating;* the waves are *subsiding.* "The revolutionary spirit has *abated*" (*Grandgent*). "The child's quick temper *subsided* into listlessness under the fierce Italian heat" (*A. Repplier*). **Wane** adds to *abate* the implications of fading or weakening; it tends, therefore, to be predicated of things that have value or excellence as well as force and intensity. "After the first flush of excitement, the interest of doctors, nurses, and patients all began to *wane*" (*V. Heiser*). **Ebb** adds to *abate* the suggestion of recession or of gradual loss; it is idiomatically associated with things subject to fluctuation; as, *ebbing* vitality is often a warning of illness. "There were many, many stages in the *ebbing* of her love for him, but it was always *ebbing*" (*D. H. Lawrence*).

Ana. Dwindle, diminish, *decrease.

Ant. Rise: revive. — ***Con.*** *Increase, augment: *expand, swell, dilate: mount, soar, tower, surge (see RISE).

abatement. *Deduction, rebate, discount.

Ant. Addition. — ***Con.*** Increment, accretion, accession (see ADDITION): increase, augmentation, enlargement (see corresponding verbs at INCREASE).

abbé. *Cleric, clergyman, priest, ecclesiastic.

abbey. *Cloister, convent, nunnery, monastery, priory.

abbreviate. *Shorten, abridge, curtail.

Ana. Reduce, *decrease, lessen: *contract, compress, shrink, condense: attenuate, extenuate (see THIN).

Ant. Elongate, lengthen. — ***Con.*** *Extend, prolong, protract: enlarge, *increase: *expand, amplify, dilate.

abdicate. **Abdicate, renounce, resign, demit** are synonymous when they are used in the sense of to give up formally or definitely as a position of trust, honor, or glory, or its concomitant authority or prerogatives. **Abdicate** is the precise word to use when that which is relinquished involves sovereign or inherent power; it is applied specifically to the act of a monarch who gives up his throne, but in extended use it may also be applied to any act involving surrender of an inherent dignity or claim to preeminence. "The Herr Doktor has a lamentably feeble character. He means to be kind . . . but he *abdicates* his rights [as a parent] and avoids his duties" (*Santayana*). **Renounce** is often used in place of *abdicate* (as, the king *renounced* his throne), especially when sacrifice for a greater end is intentionally implied. So strong is this implication and also that of finality in *renounce* (as here considered: see also ABJURE) that it often, and its derivative **renunciation** commonly, connotes self-denial or surrender for the sake of moral or spiritual discipline. Consequently, in good use, one *renounces* not only a right, a title, an inheritance, but also some desired or desirable possession. "She remains . . . the sort of woman who has *renounced* all happiness for herself and who lives only for a principle" (*T. S. Eliot*). **Resign** is used in reference chiefly to positions held on tenure and formally relinquished. Ordinarily it implies asking permission to leave a position or office before the expiration of a term. **Demit** is chiefly Scottish and may have the force of either *abdicate* or *resign.* It commonly connotes voluntary relinquishment.

Ana. *Relinquish, surrender, abandon, leave.

Ant. Assume: usurp. — ***Con.*** *Take (sense 3): *arrogate, appropriate, confiscate.

abdomen. **Abdomen, belly, stomach, paunch** are often regarded as synonyms, selection being determined merely by the proprieties. It is historically correct to employ any one of them to name the front part of the human trunk below the chest; as, to crawl on one's *abdomen, stomach,* or *belly;* a bulging *abdomen, belly,* or *paunch:* it is also historically correct to use *stomach, belly,* or *paunch* to designate the place where food is digested. In technical usage, **abdomen** refers to the cavity below the diaphragm (and sometimes, above the brim of the pelvis), the structures in that cavity, or the walls (often the front wall) enclosing it; as, a pain in the *abdomen;* an *abdominal* incision or operation. Technically, **stomach** designates the organ in which the earlier processes of digestion take place. **Belly** and **paunch** have no technical standing and they savor of vulgarity; when used in place of *abdomen* they suggest roundness and protuberance; when used in place of *stomach* they are less definitely referred to a particular organ and suggest rather the region where food is digested.

abdominal. Abdominal, ventral, anterior. Abdominal is the adjective corresponding to *abdomen.* **Ventral,** though synonymous with *abdominal* in its primitive sense, is more often employed, as in zoology and anatomy, to imply relationship to the entire front surface of the body (in man) or to the under surface of most vertebrates normally in a horizontal position, such as reptiles, fish, dogs, and horses; as, the *ventral* abdominal wall; the *ventral* scales of a reptile. In anatomy, **anterior** often replaces *ventral* when applied to parts of the human body; as, the *anterior* thoracic nerve.

abduct. Abduct, kidnap are terms commonly employed without distinction as denoting to carry off (a person) surreptitiously for an illegal purpose. In popular usage, **kidnap** is regarded as the more specific term because it commonly connotes seizure and detention for ransom. In law, however, the reverse is true, for the verbs acquire their meanings from the rigid technical definitions of *kidnaping* and *abduction.* **Kidnaping** is the legal term of wider application, implying that a person has been seized by violence or fraud and detained against his will or that of his legal guardian. **Abduction** is the carrying off of a girl (usually one below the legal age of consent), either against her will or with her consent, for the purpose of marriage or defilement. Consequently, in law, *kidnaping* and *abduction,* and *kidnap* and *abduct* can be used interchangeably only when the person carried off is a girl below a fixed age, her seizure and detention are against her will, and the motive is marriage or rape.

Ana. Seduce, entice, *lure, inveigle.

Con. *Rescue, ransom, redeem, deliver.

aberrant. Atypic, *abnormal.

Ana. Divergent, *different, disparate: *irregular, anomalous, unnatural: *exceptional: singular, peculiar, odd, *strange, eccentric.

Ant. True (*to type*). — *Con.* *Usual, wonted, customary: normal, *regular, typical, natural.

aberration. 1 *Deviation, deflection.

Ana. Abnormality, aberrancy (see ABNORMAL): *error, blunder, mistake, slip, lapse: *fault, failing: *variation, mutation: anomaly (see PARADOX).

Ant. Conformity: regularity. — *Con.* Normality (see REGULAR): norm, *average, mean: agreement, correspondence, accord (see corresponding verbs at AGREE).

2 Aberration, derangement, alienation, as here compared, denote mental disorder. **Aberration** may be used to designate any form of mental unsoundness; commonly, however, it names a disorder insufficient to constitute insanity; often, it connotes a temporary mental lapse. **Derangement** may be applied to any functional mental disturbance whether permanent or not. **Alienation,** the strongest word, implies more or less permanence in the condition, the irresponsibility of the individual, and the necessity for his restraint.

Ana. *Insanity, lunacy, mania, dementia: *delusion, hallucination, illusion: *mania, delirium, hysteria, frenzy.

Ant. Soundness (*of mind*).

abet. *Incite, foment, instigate.

Ana. Aid, assist, *help: back (*up*), *support, uphold: co-operate, concur (see UNITE): forward, further, promote (see ADVANCE).

Ant. Deter (*with a personal subject*). — *Con.* *Frustrate, thwart, foil, balk, circumvent.

abettor *or* **abetter.** Accessory, accomplice, *confederate, conspirator.

abeyant. Dormant, quiescent, *latent, potential.

Ana. Deferred, suspended, postponed, stayed, intermitted (see DEFER): suppressed, repressed (see SUPPRESS).

Ant. Operative: active: revived. — *Con.* In progress (see PROGRESS, *n.*): live, dynamic (see ACTIVE): *living, alive, quick: renewed, restored, refreshed (see RENEW).

abhor. Abominate, loathe, detest, *hate.

Ana. *Despise, contemn, scorn: shun, avoid, eschew (see ESCAPE).

Ant. Admire (*persons, their qualities, acts, etc.*): enjoy (*things which are a matter of taste*). — *Con.* *Like, love, relish, dote (on *or* upon): cherish, treasure, prize, value (see APPRECIATE): court, woo, solicit (see INVITE): esteem, respect, regard (see under REGARD, *n.*).

abhorrence. Detestation, loathing, abomination, hatred, hate. See HATE, *v.*

Ana. Distaste, repugnance, repellency (see corresponding adjectives at REPUGNANT): horror, dismay (see FEAR).

Ant. Admiration: enjoyment. — *Con.* Esteem, *regard, respect: liking, relish (see corresponding verbs at LIKE): love, affection, *attachment.

abhorrent. 1 Abominable, *hateful, detestable, odious.

Ana. *Contemptible, despicable, scurvy: *execrable, damnable.

Ant. Admirable: enjoyable. — *Con.* Grateful, agreeable, *pleasant, pleasing, gratifying, welcome: *delightful, delectable.

2 *Repugnant, repellent, obnoxious, distasteful, invidious.

Ana. *Antipathetic: uncongenial, unsympathetic (see INCONSONANT): foreign, alien (see EXTRINSIC).

Ant. Congenial. — *Con.* Attractive, alluring, captivating (see corresponding verbs at ATTRACT): tempting, enticing, seductive (see corresponding verbs at LURE).

abide. 1 *Stay, wait, remain, tarry, linger.

Ana. Dwell, *reside, live, sojourn, lodge: *stick, cleave, cling, adhere.

Ant. Depart. — *Con.* *Go, leave, quit: *move, remove, shift.

2 Endure, last, persist, *continue.

Ana. *Stay, remain, linger: subsist, exist, live (see BE).

Ant. Pass, *v.i.* — *Con.* Flee, fly, *escape: *flit.

3 Endure, *bear, suffer, tolerate, stand, brook.

Ana Submit, *yield, bow, defer: acquiesce (in), accede (to), consent (to) (see ASSENT): accept, *receive, take.

Ant. Resist. — *Con.* Withstand, *oppose, combat: *decline, refuse, spurn: shun, avoid, evade, elude (see ESCAPE).

ability. Ability, capacity, capability are often confused in use, in both their primary and extended senses. **Ability,** in its most general significance, denotes the quality or character of being able (to do, perform, etc.) and is applied chiefly to human beings. **Capacity,** in its fundamental sense, means the power to receive, hold, or absorb something expressed or understood, and is said of persons or things. Thus, it is correct to say "a child's *ability* to learn" but not, "the hall's *ability* to seat 2000 persons"; on the other hand, it is correct to say "a child's mental *capacity* (or *capacity* for learning)" or, "the hall has a seating *capacity* of 2000." In an extended sense, and especially as referred to persons, *ability* suggests actual power, whether native or acquired, whether exercised or not. "He [the curate leaving his first curacy] was intended to take away . . . an *ability* to understand and to sympathize with the commonplace of clerical effort" (*C. Mackenzie*). In its secondary sense, *capacity* still stresses receptiveness, but since the commonly implied reference is to man's intellectual, moral, or spiritual, rather than physical, nature, the implication of receptiveness becomes more explicitly that of responsiveness, susceptibility, aptitude, or the like. *Capacity* therefore suggests potential, as distinguished from actual or, especially, manifest power. This distinction is not only perceptible in good usage but also in English idiom. Thus, *ability* to weep, the *ability* to work, the *ability* to pay, are not respectively identical in meaning with the *capacity* for tears, the *capacity* for work, the *capacity* for payment. The phrases of the first group mean that one can weep (because his tear glands are normal), one can work (because strong, trained, etc.), one can pay (because he has the money): those of the latter group indicate, in the first case, a special sensitiveness to that which is pathetic; in the second case, a readiness to work as hard as is necessary on any or every occasion; in the third case, the qualities of mind and character that promise earning power and imply a recognition of one's obligations. "If Peter had a *capacity* for friendship, these speechless years had made it dumb" (*Deland*). "Had he discovered in himself a *capacity* and a taste for that sort of thing [preaching]?" (*Conrad*). **Capability** is the character in a person (less often, a thing) arising from the possession of the qualities or qualifications necessary to the performance of a certain kind of work or the achievement of a given end; as, to test the *capability* of the ear to distinguish pitches; no applicant will be considered who does not offer proof of *capability*. In a secondary sense, as applied exclusively to persons, *capability* means competence, often special competence. This connotation is usually supplied or enforced by the context.

Ana. *Power, strength, might, force, energy: proficiency, skill, adeptness (see PROFICIENT): aptitude, talent, genius, faculty (see GIFT): competence, qualification (see corresponding adjectives at ABLE).

Ant. Inability, incapacity. — ***Con.*** Impotence, powerlessness, impuissance (see corresponding adjectives at POWERLESS): incompetence, incapability (see corresponding adjectives at INCAPABLE).

abject. *Mean, ignoble, sordid.

Ana. Servile, slavish, menial (see SUBSERVIENT): *miserable, wretched: cringing, truckling, cowering (see FAWN): groveling (see WALLOW): abased, demeaned, humbled, humiliated (see ABASE).

Ant. Exalted (*in rank, state, condition, mood, behavior, etc.*): imperious (*in manner, speech, attitude, etc.*). — ***Con.*** Arrogant, lordly, overbearing, supercilious (see PROUD): domineering, *masterful: aristocratic, patrician (see corresponding nouns at GENTLEMAN).

abjure. **Abjure, renounce, forswear, recant, retract** are synonymous when they agree in meaning to abandon irrevocably and, usually, with solemnity or publicity. Except in the extended senses of *abjure, renounce,* and *forswear*, they all imply the recall of one's word. **Abjure** and **renounce** are scarcely distinguishable when they imply solemn repudiation as of an oath or vow. "He shall, before he is admitted to citizenship, declare on oath in open court that he . . . absolutely and entirely *renounces* and *abjures* all allegiance and fidelity to any foreign prince, potentate, state, or sovereignty" (*U. S. Code*). In their extended senses, however, *abjure* distinctively suggests deliberate rejection or avoidance; *renounce* specifically connotes disclaiming or disowning; as, to *abjure* force; to *renounce* one's principles. "If a man is content to *abjure* wealth and to forego marriage, to live simply without luxuries, he may spend a very dignified gentle life here" (*A. C. Benson*). "Science will never *renounce* the attempt to bring everything under a single system of laws" (*Inge*). **Forswear** often adds to *abjure* (especially in the reflexive use of the verb or in the participial adjective **forsworn**) the suggestion of perjury or of culpable violation of a solemn engagement. "I have sworn to obey the laws, and I cannot *forswear* myself" (*Blackie*). In its chief current use, it often means little more than to swear off. "One is often tempted of the Devil to *forswear* the study of history altogether as the pursuit of the Unknowable" (*Birrell*). **Recant** and **retract** stress the withdrawal of something professed or declared; *recant* always, and *retract* often, implies admission of error. One *recants*, however, something that one has openly professed or taught, as religious or scientific doctrines; one *retracts* something one has written or spoken, as a charge, a promise, an order. "A word informs your brother I *retract* this morning's offer" (*Browning*).

Ana. *Forgo, forbear, eschew: abstain (from), *refrain (from): reject, repudiate, spurn (see DECLINE): abandon, *relinquish.

Ant. Pledge (*allegiance, a vow, etc.*): elect (*a way of life, a means to an end, an end, etc.*). — ***Con.*** Plight, engage (see PROMISE): *choose, select, opt: own, avow, *acknowledge.

☞ *Do not confuse* abjure *with* adjure.

able. **Able, capable, competent, qualified** are close synonyms when they denote having marked power or fitness for work and are used attributively. In their predicative use *able* (followed by *to* and infinitive) and *capable* (followed by *of*) suggest mere possession of ability or capacity without any clear indication of its extent or quality. "They must be *capable* of living the life of the spirit . . . ; they must be *able* to cope intelligently with weighty problems of public policy" (*Grandgent*). In general, *competent* and *qualified* in predicative use suggest mere fitness in the one case and sufficient training in the other; as, a servant *competent* to take full charge. "Headmasters and education authorities want to be able to distinguish between those who are '*qualified*' to teach them [literature and fine arts] and those who are not" (*A. Huxley*). On the other hand, all four words are manifestly richer in implications when (especially in attributive use) they are thought of as characterizing persons or their activities. **Able** then suggests ability markedly above the average; it often connotes power of mastery; it does not exclude the connotation of promise even when the emphasis is on performance. "*Able* boys and girls will . . . submit willingly to severe discipline in order to acquire some coveted knowledge or skill" (*B. Russell*). **Capable,** so used, stresses possession of qualities such as adaptability, resourcefulness, versatility, industry, or efficiency and seldom indicates, apart from its context, the specific ability involved. "Pretty and charming, but stupid . . . because she believes men prefer women to be useless and extravagant; if left to herself she would be a domestic and *capable* person" (*Millay*). **Competent** and **qualified** are seldom used to characterize a person or his activities except in relation to a specific calling; as, a *competent* housekeeper; a *qualified* accountant. *Competent* implies the ability to satisfy capably all the special demands or

requirements of a particular situation, craft, or profession, but it does not necessarily imply, as does *qualified* in its current strict use, compliance with set standards, such as special training and the testing of one's competence at the end of such training; as, a *qualified* accountant. "A *competent* portraitist knows how to imply the profile in the full face" (*A. Huxley*).
Ana. Skilled, skillful, *proficient, expert: efficient, *effective: clever, brilliant, *intelligent, smart.
Ant. Inept (*by nature, training, etc.*): unable (*to do, etc.*). — ***Con.*** *Incapable, incompetent, unqualified: inefficient, *ineffective: mediocre, fair, indifferent (see MEDIUM): maladroit (see AWKWARD).

ablution. *Purification, lustration, purgation, catharsis.
Ana. Cleansing, cleaning (see CLEAN, *v.*).

abnegate. Sacrifice, *forgo, eschew, forbear.
Ana. Renounce, *abdicate: surrender, abandon, *relinquish, waive: abstain (from), *refrain (from).
Ant. Indulge (in). — ***Con.*** Gratify, delight, regale, rejoice, gladden, *please: *satisfy, content.

abnegation. Self-abnegation, *renunciation, self-denial.
Ana. Forgoing (*or* foregoing), forbearance, eschewal (see corresponding verbs at FORGO): abstinence, abstemiousness, continence, *temperance: restraining, curbing, bridling (see RESTRAIN).
Ant. Indulgence, self-indulgence. — ***Con.*** Intemperance, incontinence (see affirmative nouns at TEMPERANCE).

abnormal. **Abnormal, atypic** (*or* **atypical**), **aberrant,** agree in meaning deviating markedly from the rule or standard of its kind. All are terms often used in the sciences, as in biology and psychology, to express nonconformity to type. **Abnormal** frequently connotes strangeness or excess and sometimes, as in *abnormality* or *abnormity*, deformity or monstrosity. "Power when wielded by *abnormal* energy is the most serious of facts" (*H. Adams*). In psychology, as applied to persons, *abnormal* often suggests poorer than normal performance or poorer than normal adjustment to the conditions of life, and is equivalent to *subnormal;* in general use, however, better than normal powers are often implied. "If a boy has *abnormal* mental powers in some direction . . . he may be quite incapable of fitting into a crowd of normal boys" (*B. Russell*). **Atypic** stresses divergence, upward or downward, from that which has been established as the average for anything of its kind or for any person at a particular stage of development; as, *atypical* reactions. When applied to students, it suggests intelligence or achievement below or above the average and therefore requiring special educational treatment. **Aberrant** seldom loses its literal implication of wandering or straying; in the sciences, where it is applied to departures from type, it carries none of the extra connotations of *abnormal* and is less restricted in its reference than *atypic;* as, *aberrant* forms of a botanical species. In general use, it often suggests moral deviation. "Such a choice must argue *Aberrant* senses, or degenerate blood" (*Kingsley*).
Ana. *Irregular, unnatural, anomalous: unusual, unwonted, uncustomary, unaccustomed (see affirmative adjectives at USUAL): *monstrous, prodigious.
Ant. Normal. — ***Con.*** *Regular, typical, natural: ordinary, *common, familiar: *usual, wonted, customary.

abode. Residence, domicile, dwelling, *habitation, house, home.

abolish. **Abolish, annihilate, extinguish, abate** are comparable terms when they mean to make nonexistent. All are found both in general and legal use except *abate* which is now rarely employed except in law. **Abolish** seldom refers to purely physical objects but rather to such things as are the outgrowth of law, custom, human conception, or the conditions of human existence; as, attempts to *abolish* slavery; a proposal to *abolish* the income tax. "No plan will be acceptable unless it *abolishes* poverty" (*Shaw*). **Annihilate** distinctively implies destruction so complete that the (material or immaterial) thing or things involved are wiped out of existence, and cannot be revived in any form. "The possibility of both the creation and *annihilation* of matter" (*Jeans*). **Extinguish** or its related form **extinction** is often interchangeable with *annihilate* (or *annihilation*). It, however, stresses the power of the cause to overwhelm and suppress rather than the finality of the result. "The man whose hopes and fears are all centred upon himself can hardly view death with equanimity, since it *extinguishes* his whole emotional universe" (*B. Russell*).

In law, **abolish** keeps close to its general sense of to make nonexistent; **annihilate** is sometimes used as an emphatic substitute for *abolish.* "The appointment cannot be *annihilated*" (*Ch. Just. Marshall*). **Extinguish** implies destruction of a right or obligation by some act, decision, or the like, which nullifies it or makes it void. **Abate** implies termination, especially by a legal decision; as, to *abate* a nuisance; to *abate* an action or writ.
Ana. Extirpate, eradicate, wipe out, *exterminate: obliterate, efface, blot out, expunge (see ERASE): negate, *nullify, annul, abrogate.
Ant. Establish. — ***Con.*** *Found, institute: *bear, produce, turn out: create, discover, *invent.

abominable. Detestable, *hateful, odious, abhorrent.
Ana. *Execrable, damnable, accursed, cursed: scurvy, despicable, *contemptible, sorry: loathsome, repulsive, revolting, repugnant, *offensive: horrid, *horrible.
Ant. Laudable (*practices, habits, customs, etc.*): enjoyable, delightful. — ***Con.*** Pleasing, *pleasant, gratifying: commendable, applaudable (see corresponding verbs at COMMEND): attractive, charming, enchanting (see under ATTRACT).

abominate. Loathe, detest, abhor, *hate.
Ana. *Despise, contemn, scorn, disdain: *execrate, objurgate, curse, damn.
Ant. Esteem: enjoy. — ***Con.*** Admire, respect, regard (see under REGARD, *n.*): relish, *like, love, dote (on *or* upon).

abomination. **1** Abhorrence, detestation, loathing, hatred, hate. See HATE, *v.*
Ana. Scorn, despite, contempt, disdain (see under DESPISE): execration, objurgation (see corresponding verbs at EXECRATE).
Ant. Esteem: enjoyment. — ***Con.*** Admiration, respect, *regard: relish, gusto, zest, *taste.
2 Abomination, anathema, bugbear, bête noire agree in meaning a person or thing from which one shrinks with intense dislike. That which is an **abomination** (in older idiom, without the article) provokes loathing, disgust, and extreme displeasure. "Lying lips are *abomination* to the Lord: but they that deal truly are his delight" (*Proverbs* xii. 22). "Everything was to be slick, which was Marvin's term of approbation; but not too slick, which was his *abomination*" (*M. Austin*). That which is **anathema** (or *an anathema*) to one is banned from one's presence, dismissed from one's mind, or the like, as something odious or beyond the pale. The word in this sense is always reminiscent of St. Paul's use: "If any man love not the Lord Jesus Christ, let him be *Anathema*" (*1 Corinthians* xvi. 22). "They [new writers] were as welcome to him as they were *anathema* to most editors of that day" (*A. Repplier*). "All plays are *anathema* to him, and he even disapproves of dancing bears" (*Quiller-Couch*). That which is a **bugbear** to one is something one anticipates encountering with detestation and dread and therefore

tries to evade or avoid; often, but not invariably, the word connotes an imaginary basis for one's fears. "What is the dire necessity and 'iron' law under which men groan? Truly, most gratuitously invented *bugbears*" (*T. H. Huxley*). "But to the world no *bugbear* is so great, As want of figure, and a small estate" (*Pope*). That which is one's **bête noire** (the English translation *black beast* is very rarely used) is one's pet aversion, a person or thing one habitually or particularly avoids, often with superstitious fear. "Truth . . . the breath of the poet, the vision of the artist and prophet, the quarry of the scientist . . . the toy of the careless, the *bête noire* of the politician" (*Forum*). "It was the *bête noire* of Clerk Gum's life, Mrs. Jones" (*Mrs. H. Wood*).

Ana. Plague, pest, annoyance (see corresponding verbs at WORRY): aversion, *antipathy.

Ant. Joy. — *Con.* Delight, *pleasure, delectation: gratification, regalement (see corresponding verbs at PLEASE).

aboriginal. Indigenous, autochthonous, *native.

Ana. Primitive, primordial, primeval, pristine (see PRIMARY): savage, barbarous, *barbarian, barbaric.

Con. Sequent, successive (see CONSECUTIVE): advanced, progressive (see LIBERAL; PROGRESS, *v.*): civilized, cultured (see corresponding nouns at CIVILIZATION).

aborigine. Native, indigene, autochthon, endemic. See NATIVE, *adj.*

abortion. **Abortion, miscarriage** denote the premature expulsion of a fetus before it is capable of living independently. **Abortion,** esp. in law, connotes purposeful and therefore criminal induction of the process in order to avoid childbearing. In medicine, however, *abortion* sometimes denotes the expulsion of the human fetus through any cause during the first sixteen weeks of pregnancy. **Miscarriage,** in general use, differs from *abortion* in suggesting a natural expulsion rather than one produced artificially. In medicine, *miscarriage* is technically used of any expulsion of the fetus occurring after the first sixteen weeks, and before the fetus is capable of living independently.

abortive. Fruitless, vain, *futile, bootless.

Ana. *Immature, unmatured, unripe: inchoate, unformed (see FORMLESS): ineffectual, *ineffective, inefficacious: unfortunate, unlucky (see affirmative adjectives at LUCKY).

Ant. Consummated. — *Con.* Completed, concluded (see CLOSE, *v.*): finished, accomplished, *consummate: effectual, *effective, efficacious.

abound. Superabound, overflow, *teem, swarm.

Ana. Predominate, preponderate (see corresponding adjectives at DOMINANT).

Ant. Fail, fall short. — *Con.* Want, *lack, need, require: scant, skimp, scrimp (see corresponding adjectives at MEAGER).

about. 1 **About, around, round** are often used interchangeably in their comparable prepositional and adverbial senses but not without slight changes in meaning in nearly every case. Thus, when it is said of the earth that it revolves "*around* the sun," the circularity of its orbit and the central position of the sun are more clearly implied than if "*about* the sun" were the chosen expression. When "*around* the sun" is changed to "*round* the sun," the orbit is less definitely suggested than motion in a circular direction and repeated passage through a circuit. Throngs may crowd *about* a man whose back is to a wall, but not *around* or *round* him until he can be surrounded on all sides. To travel *about* the world is to journey hither and thither over much of the earth's surface; to travel *around* or *round* the world is to cover the circumference of the globe in one's journeyings and end one's travels where one has begun them.

In America, **around** is often used colloquially in senses better covered by **about**; as, to travel *around* the country; he weighs *around* 200 pounds. It is often used also where the British prefer **round,** especially when a circuit including a succession of persons or places, or a ring formation, or an encompassing limit, is to be implied; as, there were not enough cigars to go *around* (Brit. *round*).

2 **About, concerning, regarding, respecting, anent** are synonymous prepositions when they take an object that names something which is the subject of talk, thought, interest, or the like. **About** is usually interchangeable with any of the others without marked loss of meaning, but it alone may follow its object as well as precede it; as, to talk *about* many things; there is nothing to complain *about.* **Concerning** is more meaningful because it often retains its verbal implications of affecting and influencing; as, to make laws *concerning* public welfare. *Regarding* and *respecting* commonly suggest little more than *about:* in very precise use, however, **regarding** is appropriate when its object names the goal or center of attention or thought; as, they avoided all discussion *regarding* the scandal; **respecting** is felicitously employed when selectiveness or specification is to be implied; as, he had nothing to say *respecting* Spain. "There's no outwitting you *respecting* him" (*Browning*). **Anent** comes very close to *respecting,* but it is now rather pedantic.

above. **Above, over** are synonymous prepositions when they indicate elevation in position. They seldom imply contact between that which is higher and that which is lower; as a rule, they allow an interval. *Over* and *above* differ in that *over* implies verticality, while *above* may or may not. Thus, the entire second story of a building is *above,* but only a small part of it is directly *over,* one who stands on the ground floor. Between the figurative senses analogous relations hold. *Over* and *above* agree in the idea of superiority, but differ in the immediacy of reference. Thus, the rank of ambassador is *above* that of minister, but the British ambassador is not *over* the Chinese minister; he stands in that relation to his own subordinates only. Similarly, *above* and *over* indicate a relationship of excess; as, his strength is *above* the average; we now have *over* half the amount required; we shall not be tempted *above* our power to resist. *Above* only, however, implies transcendence. "One there is, *above* all others, Well deserves the name of Friend; His is love beyond a brother's" (*J. Newton*).

Ant. Below.

aboveboard. *Straightforward, forthright.

Ana. Open, *frank, candid: honest, *upright, scrupulous: *fair, impartial, just: ingenuous, unsophisticated, artless (see NATURAL).

Ant. Underhand, underhanded. — *Con.* Furtive, covert, surreptitious, *secret, clandestine: *dishonest, deceitful, mendacious: *crooked, devious.

abracadabra. *Gibberish, hocus-pocus, mummery.

Ana. *Magic, sorcery, thaumaturgy: amulet, charm, periapt (see FETISH).

Con. Sense, *meaning, significance, import.

abrade. **Abrade, excoriate, chafe, fret, gall** come into comparison chiefly when they are referred to injuries of the skin, but they are also comparable to an extent in some of their more extended applications. **Abrade,** which means to wear off the surface of something by rubbing or scraping, may be used wherever that result is attained consciously, as by grinding, filing, or polishing, or accidentally by friction; as, an abrasive is a substance used in *abrading,* smoothing, or polishing a surface; the steel plates of the ship's side were *abraded* in the collision. In medical use, *abrade* implies the scraping off of skin or mucous membrane in patches and shreds. **Excoriate** in medicine often equals *abrade*, but it sometimes implies a corrosive rather than an abrasive agent as the cause of the injury. *Chafe* and *fret* come close to *abrade* in denoting to injure a surface by friction. Distinctively, they usually imply prolonged friction that causes wear or, in the case of the skin, irritation rather than loss of cuticle. **Chafe** is often used in reference to ropes or yarn, but is more commonly used in connection with slight inflammations of the skin; as, woolen garments *chafe* some skins. **Fret** adds to *chafe* so strong a suggestion of annoyance or disturbance that the implication of physical irritation is often blurred; as, high collars *fret* him (that is, annoy him by chafing his skin). In reference to other substances, *fret* retains its etymological implication of eating and sometimes suggests erosion; as, the dripping water *fretted* a channel in the stone. **Gall,** now chiefly used with reference to persons and animals, implies a superficial flesh wound or a blister induced by friction; as, a saddle too long worn *galls* a horse's back.

abrasion. *Erosion, attrition, corrosion.

abridge. *Shorten, curtail, abbreviate, retrench.
Ana. Condense, *contract, compress, shrink: *cut, slash: *limit, restrict: reduce, diminish, *decrease.
Ant. Expand: extend. — *Con.* Amplify, swell, distend (see EXPAND): lengthen, elongate, prolong, protract (see EXTEND): enlarge, augment, *increase.

abridgment. **Abridgment, abstract, brief, synopsis, conspectus, epitome** are terms denoting a condensation of a larger work or of an extended treatment. **Abridgment** implies reduction in compass with the retention of relative completeness; it is widely applied, but seldom without further specification except in reference to dictionaries or similar works. An **abstract** is a condensation of a treatise or of a proposed treatment, summarizing its essential points; it is seldom thought of as attaining independent worth. A **brief** is an abstract stating concisely a case or an argument, especially in law. A **synopsis** or **conspectus** is a presentation of the salient points of a treatise (sometimes a subject) in so concise and orderly a fashion that the whole treatment (or subject) may be apprehended at a glance. An **epitome** is the briefest possible condensation, giving a complex whole in miniature, often in such fashion as to acquire value of its own.
Ana. Digest, précis, *compendium, sketch, syllabus.
Ant. Expansion. — *Con.* Paraphrase (see TRANSLATION): *development.

abrogate. 1 *Annul, avoid, vacate, quash, void.
Ana. *Abolish, extinguish, abate.
Ant. Institute (*by enacting, decreeing, etc.*). — *Con.* *Ratify, confirm: establish, *found.
2 *Nullify, annul, negate, invalidate.
Ana. *Abolish, annihilate, extinguish: *destroy, demolish: *ruin, wreck: cancel, obliterate, blot out (see ERASE).
Ant. Establish, fix (*a right, a character, a quality, a custom, etc.*). — *Con.* Settle, firm (see SET): uphold, *support.

abrupt. 1 *Steep, precipitous, sheer.
Ana. Perpendicular, *vertical, plumb.
Ant. Sloping. — *Con.* *Level, flat, plain, plane, even, smooth: slanting, inclined (see SLANT, *v.*).
2 Sudden, *precipitate, headlong, impetuous, hasty.
Ana. Quick, speedy (see FAST): hurried, hastened (see HASTEN): unceremonious (see *ceremonious* under CEREMONIAL): curt, brusque (see BLUFF).
Ant. Deliberate, leisurely. — *Con.* *Slow, dilatory, laggard: easy, *comfortable, restful, reposeful.

abscess. **Abscess, ulcer, canker, canker sore** denote sores formed by the disintegration of tissue. An **abscess** is a collection of pus having its beginning in the depths of the tissues, usually resulting from bacterial infection; it may or may not break through to a surface. An **ulcer** is an open, and, often, pus-discharging sore on the surface of the skin or of an organ, or on any of the mucous membranes. It is commonly caused by bacterial or parasitic infection, faulty nutrition of a part, or chemical action; thus, a peptic *ulcer* is caused by the action of the gastric juice on the walls of the stomach or intestine. **Canker** denotes a corroding or sloughing ulcer, but now usually refers to a spreading ulcer or collection of ulcers in or about the mouth. A **canker sore** is a small ulcer affecting chiefly the lips and mouth, and is caused by digestive derangements.

abscond. Decamp, flee, fly, *escape.
Ana. Depart, leave, quit, *go, scram, clear out.
Ant. Give (*oneself*) up. — *Con.* *Stay, wait, remain, abide: confess, *acknowledge.

absence. *Lack, privation, defect, want.
Ana. *Need, necessity, exigency: deficiency (see corresponding adjective at DEFICIENT): destitution (see corresponding adjective at DEVOID): void, vacuum (see HOLE).
Ant. Presence. — *Con.* Abundance, copiousness, plenty (see corresponding adjectives at PLENTIFUL): sufficiency, adequacy, competence, enough (see corresponding adjectives at SUFFICIENT).

absent, *adj.* Preoccupied, *abstracted, absent-minded, distrait, distraught.
Ana. Engrossed, absorbed, *intent, rapt: heedless, inadvertent (see CARELESS): oblivious, unmindful, *forgetful.
Ant. Attentive. — *Con.* *Thoughtful, considerate: attending, listening, hearkening (see ATTEND).

absent-minded. Absent, *abstracted, preoccupied, distrait, distraught.
Ana. Inattentive, thoughtless, inconsiderate (see affirmative adjectives at ATTENTIVE): heedless, inadvertent (see CARELESS): unobserving, unseeing, unperceiving, unnoticing (see affirmative verbs at SEE).
Ant. Wide-awake. — *Con.* *Watchful, alert, vigilant: *attentive.

absolute. 1 *Pure, simple, sheer.
Ana. *Perfect, whole, entire: *real, true: *abstract, ideal: *consummate, finished.
Ant. Mixed, qualified. — *Con.* Incomplete (see affirmative adjective at FULL): imperfect, unentire, unintact (see affirmative adjectives at PERFECT).
2 **Absolute, autocratic** (*or* **autocratical**), **arbitrary, despotic** (*or* **despotical**), **tyrannical, tyrannous** denote in common exercising power or authority without external restraint. **Absolute** does not of itself add any further implication to this general denotation. It is restricted in application chiefly to words for authority or for one in authority; as, an *absolute* monarch; *absolute* control. "The power of the lawyers was not *absolute* . . . . The King by exceptional action could compel them to do his will" (*Belloc*). **Autocratic** implies assumption or exercise of absolute power or authority; though it is not necessarily opprobrious, it often connotes egotistical consciousness of power and haughty imposition of one's own will. "Let the Emperor turn his nominal sovereignty into a real central and *autocratic* power" (*Belloc*). **Arbitrary** implies the exercise, usually the abuse, of power in accord with one's opinion of the moment, free of such reasoned guides as constitution and laws which make for consistent and reasonably predictable action. "All the constitutional safeguards of English freedom were swept away. *Arbitrary* taxation, *arbitrary* legislation, *arbitrary*

imprisonment were powers claimed without dispute and unsparingly used by the Crown" (*J. R. Green*). **Despotic** and **tyrannical** are stronger than *autocratic; despotic* implying the arbitrary and imperious exercise of absolute power or control, and *tyrannical*, the abuse of such power or control (frequently through harshness, oppression, or severity). "The simplest form of government is *despotism*, where all the inferior orbs of power are moved merely by the will of the Supreme" (*Burke*). "How could I have borne to become the slave of her *tyrannical* humors?" (*Burney*). "The [school] master, I fear, must be something of a *despot* at the risk of his becoming something like a *tyrant*" (*Scott*). **Tyrannous** is more frequently used of things than of persons. "A . . . skeptical smile, of all expressions the most *tyrannous* over a susceptible mind" (*G. Eliot*).

Ana. *Totalitarian, authoritarian: *dictatorial, magisterial: domineering, imperious, *masterful.

Ant. Restrained: limited. — ***Con.*** Circumscribed, restricted (see LIMIT, *v.*): irresponsible, unanswerable, unamenable (see affirmative adjectives at RESPONSIBLE).

3 *Ultimate, categorical.

Ana. Ideal, transcendent, transcendental (see ABSTRACT): independent, autonomous, *free, sovereign: *infinite, eternal, boundless.

Ant. Conditioned. — ***Con.*** Relative, *dependent, conditional, contingent, adjective: circumscribed, limited, restricted (see LIMIT, *v.*).

☞ Very frequently in loose use *absolute* (and still more, *absolutely*) suggests no more than one of the simple ideas involved in any of the complex meanings of the word. For example, *absolute* is often regarded as an exact synonym of *unqualified* (an *absolute* denial), or *unconditional* (an *absolute* gift), or *complete* (*absolute* indifference), or *positive* (*absolute* proof). Moreover, in loose use, the prime implication of *absolute* in its rich senses—detachment from that which conditions or determines—is lost or obscured.

absolution. *Pardon, indulgence, amnesty.

Ana. Forgiveness, remission (see corresponding verbs at EXCUSE).

Ant. Condemnation: reservation (*as defined in canon law*). — ***Con.*** Censure, reprobation, reprehension (see corresponding verbs at CENSURE).

absolve. 1 Exonerate, acquit, *exculpate, vindicate.

Ana. Pardon, forgive, remit (see EXCUSE): release, *free, discharge.

Ant. Hold to (*a promise, an obligation, etc.*): charge (*with a sin, the blame, the responsibility, etc.*). — ***Con.*** Blame (see CRITICIZE): *sentence, condemn, doom: *punish, discipline, chasten.

2 *Confess, shrive, remit.

absorb. 1 Absorb, imbibe, assimilate agree in denoting to take (something) in so as to become imbued with it or to make it a part of one's being. The original meaning of **absorb,** to swallow up (both literally and figuratively), has been maintained in spite of the development of a later and more common sense, to soak up (both literally and figuratively). When the former idea is stressed, *absorb* implies the loss of identity of that taken in; as, the trust *absorbed* three small corporations. "In England . . . the aristocracy are subordinate to the middle class, which is gradually *absorbing* and destroying them" (*T. S. Eliot*). When soaking up is implied, *absorb* often suggests enrichment of the recipient; as, the roots of plants *absorb* moisture. "An adult reader with trained habits of attention and concentration will *absorb* the contents of a book with . . . speed and retentiveness" (*C. W. Eliot*). In its literal sense, **imbibe** usually implies drinking or inhaling; as, to *imbibe* intoxicating liquors; to *imbibe* fresh air. However, *imbibe,* like *absorb,* often connotes soaking up; as, the ground *imbibes* (or *absorbs*) moisture. In its figurative sense, *imbibe,* like *absorb,* implies a process of learning, but it often carries the suggestions that the process has been unconscious and that the effect has been noticeable or profound. "The pupils *imbibe* no respect for intellectual values at home, and find none among their school-fellows" (*Inge*). "Egdon was her Hades, and since coming there she had *imbibed* much of what was dark in its tone" (*Hardy*). **Assimilate** implies not only absorption, but also the conversion of what is absorbed into the substance of the assimilating body. In its strict sense, it applies esp. to physiological processes; as, food is *assimilated* and converted into organic tissue. In its figurative use, it often suggests lasting enrichment without loss of integrity or unity. "Poets . . . who *assimilate* a number of influences and construct an original speech from them" (*Day Lewis*). Sometimes it stresses completeness of fusion and consequent loss of identity; as, races incapable of *assimilation*.

Ana. *Soak, saturate, impregnate: *receive, take: incorporate, embody (see IDENTIFY).

Ant. Exude, give out. — ***Con.*** *Eject, expel: *throw (off), cast (off *or* out).

2 Engross, *monopolize, consume.

Ana. Fix, *fasten: rivet, *secure: immerse, submerge (see DIP).

Ant. Dissipate (*time, attention, energies, etc.*). — ***Con.*** *Scatter, disperse, dispel: *deplete, drain, exhaust.

absorbed. *Intent, engrossed, rapt.

Ana. Immersed (see DIP): riveted (see SECURE, *v.*): fixed, fastened (see FASTEN).

Ant. Distracted. — ***Con.*** Absent, absent-minded, distraught, distrait, *abstracted: wandering, straying, rambling (see WANDER).

abstain. *Refrain, forbear.

Ana. *Forgo, eschew, abnegate: *decline, refuse, spurn, reject: desist (*from*) (see STOP).

Ant. Indulge. — ***Con.*** Pamper (see INDULGE): *satiate, sate, surfeit, cloy, gorge, glut: gratify, regale (see PLEASE).

abstemiousness. Abstinence, *temperance, sobriety, continence.

Ana. Self-denial, self-abnegation (see RENUNCIATION): asceticism, austerity (see corresponding adjectives at SEVERE).

Ant. Gluttony. — ***Con.*** Greed, rapacity (see CUPIDITY): epicurism (cf. EPICURE).

abstinence. *Temperance, continence, abstemiousness, sobriety.

Ana. Forbearance, refrainment (see corresponding verbs at REFRAIN): forgoing, eschewal, abnegation (see corresponding verbs at FORGO): *renunciation, self-denial, self-abnegation.

Ant. Self-indulgence. — ***Con.*** Greediness, covetousness, graspingness, acquisitiveness (see corresponding adjectives at COVETOUS): satisfying, contenting (see SATISFY): gorging, sating, surfeiting (see SATIATE).

abstract, *adj.* **Abstract, ideal, transcendent, transcendental** are, in strict use, closely analogous rather than synonymous terms. The difference in meaning between *abstract* and *ideal* is not apparent when they are applied to things which are admirable in actuality as well as in idea, as a virtue, some qualities, some attributes; as, *abstract* (or *ideal*) justice; *ideal* (or *abstract*) morality. When, however, they are applied to the name of a species or type known through actually existing representatives, they reveal their fundamental differences in meaning; as, *abstract* man (or, man in the *abstract*); *ideal* man. For **abstract** implies the formulation of the idea by *abstrac-*

tion, a logical process in which the mind selects the characters common to every known member of a species or every known instance of a quality and builds up a conception (technically, a *concept*) which describes no one actually existing thing or instance, but covers all things of the same kind or marked by the given quality. "To shed tears over *abstract* justice and generosity, beauty, etc., and never to know these qualities when you meet them" (*W. James*). "Poetic theory is almost invariably an *abstraction* from poetic practice" (*Day Lewis*). **Ideal** may or may not imply abstraction; very often it suggests the exercise of imagination, or the adding and the elimination of characteristics, as the mind seeks a conception of a thing in its perfection. "Plato, in the construction of his *ideal* republic, is thinking . . . of the symmetry and beauty of the whole" (*G. L. Dickinson*). In general, therefore, *abstract* connotes apartness from reality and, often, lack of specific application to actual things. "Algebra . . . is more *abstract* than geometry" (*B. Russell*). On the other hand, *ideal* very frequently connotes superiority to reality or, less often, fancifulness, and, at times, untruth. "That lofty order of minds who pant after the *ideal* . . . [whose] emotions are of too exquisite a character to find fit objects among their everyday fellow-men" (*G. Eliot*). **Transcendent** and **transcendental,** though often used as though they are equivalents of *ideal*, actually imply existence beyond experience and lack of correspondence to reality as known through the senses. Thus, in careful use, *transcendent* (or *transcendental*) beauty is not the perfection of the beauty that is known, but a supersensual beauty which has no parallel in experience and which cannot be apprehended through any likeness in actuality. "The idea that God is *transcendent* . . . exalted above the world . . . is yielding to the idea of God as immanent in his creation" (*A. V. G. Allen*). In Kant's philosophy they are distinguished. That which is *transcendent* is both beyond experience and beyond human knowledge; that which is *transcendental* is beyond experience yet knowable, because the mind possesses knowledge not derived from experience but inherent in its own constitution and essential to its understanding of experience. Thus, space and time, in Kant's philosophy, are *transcendental* ideas.

Ana. *Universal, general, generic: specific (see SPECIAL): *ultimate, absolute, categorical.

Ant. Concrete. — *Con.* Practical (see PRACTICABLE): actual, *real: *material, physical, corporeal, objective, phenomenal.

abstract, *n.* Brief, synopsis, epitome, *abridgment, conspectus.

Ana. Sketch, précis, aperçu, *compendium, digest.

Ant. Amplification. — *Con.* Expansion, dilation (see corresponding verbs at EXPAND): enlargement (see corresponding verbs at INCREASE).

abstract, *v.* Prescind, *detach, disengage.

Ana. Withdraw, *remove, draw: *separate, part, divorce, divide: purloin, filch, *steal.

Ant. Insert, introduce. — *Con.* Interpolate, insinuate, interpose (see INTRODUCE): *replace.

abstracted. Abstracted, preoccupied, absent, absent-minded, distrait, distraught are comparable when they mean inattentive to that which presently claims or demands consideration. **Abstracted** implies absorption of the mind in something other than one's surroundings, and often suggests reflection on weighty matters. "Then he sat and thought . . . in the concentrated, *abstracted* way he has . . . almost forgetting my presence" (*R. Macaulay*). **Preoccupied** implies unreadiness for any new demands on one's attention because one is already busy with other thoughts or occupations. "Edna was so *preoccupied* with misgivings as to whether he wanted to marry her that she had never faced squarely the more important problem of whether she wanted to marry him" (*M. A. Barnes*). **Absent** stresses inability to fix the mind on present concerns; it often connotes mental wandering rather than concentration on other things. "Sir Joshua . . . was quite *absent* all the day, not knowing a word that was said to him" (*Burney*). **Absent-minded** implies that the mind is fixed elsewhere: it suggests abstractedness or preoccupation more than absentness; as, he *absent-mindedly* put the lighted end of the cigar in his mouth. It often implies a mental habit rather than a present mood; as, the *absent-minded* professor. **Distrait,** a French word now naturalized in English, implies dispersal of the powers of attention and inability to concentrate. It may describe a temperament or a mood; as, she has been noticeably *distrait* since her illness. **Distraught** also suggests inability to concentrate but it always implies an agitated state of mind caused by worry or perplexity. "O, if I wake, shall I not be *distraught*, Environed with all these hideous fears?" (*Shak.*).

Ana. *Intent, engrossed: oblivious, unmindful (see FORGETFUL): ignoring, overlooking, disregarding (see NEGLECT, *v.*).

Ant. Alert. — *Con.* Wide-awake, vigilant, *watchful: attentive, *thoughtful, considerate: observant, noting, noticing, seeing (see corresponding verbs at SEE).

abstruse. *Recondite, occult, esoteric.

Ana. *Complex, complicated, intricate, knotty: *abstract, ideal: enigmatic, cryptic, dark, *obscure.

Ant. Obvious, plain. — *Con.* *Evident, manifest, clear, palpable: *easy, simple, facile: *clear, perspicuous, lucid.

absurd. Silly, preposterous, *foolish.

Ana. Ludicrous, ridiculous, *laughable, droll, funny, comic: *irrational, unreasonable: asinine, silly, fatuous, *simple.

Ant. Rational, sensible. — *Con.* Reasonable (see RATIONAL): *wise, sane, judicious, prudent: *logical.

abundant. Copious, ample, *plentiful, plenteous.

Ana. Abounding, teeming, overflowing, superabounding (see TEEM): *profuse, lavish, luxuriant, lush, exuberant.

Ant. Scarce. — *Con.* *Infrequent, rare, uncommon: *meager, scant, scanty, skimpy, exiguous, sparse: *deficient.

abuse, *v.* **Abuse, misuse, mistreat, maltreat, ill-treat, outrage** all denote to use or treat a person or thing improperly or wrongfully. *Abuse* and *misuse* are capable of wider use than the others for they do not invariably imply either deliberateness or wantonness. "My dear Vicar, I can't *abuse* your generosity to that extent. You're doing more than enough for me already" (*C. Mackenzie*). "It turns a man's stomach t'hear the Scripture *misused* i' that way" (*G. Eliot*). **Abuse,** however, commonly suggests perversion of the ends for which something was intended. "The constitution leaves them [the states] this right in the confidence that they will not *abuse* it" (*Ch. Just. Marshall*). "In the heyday of Capitalism, when . . . no laws had been made to limit its *abuse*" (*Shaw*). Sometimes it implies excess in use that injures or impairs; as, to *abuse* one's strength. **Misuse,** by contrast with *abuse*, emphasizes the actual mistreatment or misapplication rather than its results. "Who *misuses* a dog would *misuse* a child—they cannot speak for themselves" (*Tennyson*). "Artful *misuse* of the confidence of others" (*J. Martineau*). **Mistreat, maltreat,** and **ill-treat** usually imply a fault or an evil motive in the agent, such as meanness, culpable ignorance, or spitefulness. "Many more patients die from being *mistreated* for consumption than from consumption itself" (*Lytton*). "The metre, though a well-known English critic has *maltreated* it of late, is a very fine one" (*Saintsbury*). "His deliberate *maltreatment* of another man's soul resulted in the loss of his own moral free-will" (*J. Hawthorne*). "*Ill-treatment* of animals was especially tormenting to him" (*G. Bradford*). **Outrage** implies abuse so violent or extreme in its nature as to exceed all bounds. "This interview *outrages* all decency" (*Broome*). "Wherever there is war there is misery and *outrage*" (*Cowper*).

Ana. Hurt, *injure, harm, damage, impair, mar, spoil: *wrong, persecute, oppress: pervert, corrupt, *debase, debauch, vitiate.

Ant. Respect, honor. — *Con.* Esteem (see corresponding noun at REGARD): *revere, venerate, reverence: *commend, applaud, compliment: cherish, treasure, prize (see APPRECIATE).

abuse, *n.* **Abuse, vituperation, invective, obloquy, scurrility, billingsgate** agree in denoting vehemently expressed condemnation or disapproval. **Abuse,** the most general term, implies the anger of the speaker and stresses the offensiveness of the language. "The extended vocabulary of barrack-room *abuse*" (*Kipling*). "Those thunderous comminations, that jeering and *abuse* which make Milton's prose such lively reading" (*A. Huxley*). In a weakened sense it now often implies hardly more than expression of personal disapproval or displeasure. "The word ['rhetoric'] is merely a vague term of *abuse* for any style that is bad" (*T. S. Eliot*). **Vituperation** suggests the overwhelming of someone or something with a torrent of abuse. "The daily vollies of that great French master of *vituperation*, Léon Daudet" (*T. S. Eliot*). **Invective** implies vehemence and bitterness in attack or denunciation, and (often in distinction from *abuse*) connotes a command of language and skill in making one's points. It is the precise term when the attack is public and made in a good cause. "*John Bull* stopped at nothing in the way of insult; but its blazing audacity of *invective* never degenerated into dull abuse" (*A. Repplier*). **Obloquy** suggests defamation and consequent disgrace. "Those who . . . stood by me in the teeth of *obloquy*, taunt and open sneer" (*Wilde*). **Scurrility** stresses coarseness or indecency of language and emphasizes the quality of the abuse rather than the attack in itself. "He was . . . interrupted in his defence by ribaldry and *scurrility* from the judgment seat" (*Macaulay*). **Billingsgate** stresses more strongly than any of the other words the offensiveness, often foulness or obscenity, of the language of an attack. "The more I humbled myself the more he stormed . . . provoking me with scandalous names that I could not put up with; so that I gave a loose to my passion, [and] returned his *billingsgate*" (*Smollett*).

Ana. Aspersion, reflection, stricture, *animadversion: reviling, railing, rating, berating (see SCOLD, *v.*): vilification, malignment (see corresponding verbs at MALIGN).

Ant. Adulation. — *Con.* Praise, laudation, acclaim (see corresponding verbs at PRAISE): *encomium, panegyric, eulogy: commendation, applause, compliment (see corresponding verbs at COMMEND).

abusive. Abusive, opprobrious, vituperative, contumelious, scurrilous, scurrile (*or* **scurril**) apply chiefly to language or utterances, and to persons as they employ such language: in such use, the words agree in meaning coarse, insulting, and contemptuous in character or utterance. **Abusive** means little more than this; as, *abusive* language; an *abusive* master; *abusive* satire. All the other terms carry specific and distinctive implications. **Opprobrious** suggests the imputation of disgraceful actions or of shameful conduct: it implies not only abusiveness but also severe, often unjust, condemnation. "This party . . . has generally mentioned [the allies] under *opprobrious* appellations, and in such terms of contempt or execration as never had been heard" (*Burke*). **Vituperative** implies indulgence in a stream of abusive, insulting, or opprobrious language, especially in attacking an opponent; as, the *vituperative* controversialists of the seventeenth century; "*vituperative* . . . editors" (*Carlyle*); "to restrain this employment of *vituperative* language" (*J. S. Mill*). **Contumelious** adds to *opprobrious* the implications of insolence and extreme disrespect and usually connotes the bitter humiliation of its victim; as, "With scoffs and scorns and *contumelious* taunts" (*Shak.*); "Curving a *contumelious* lip, [he] gorgonized me from head to foot with a stony British stare" (*Tennyson*); "I . . . expose a chain of causes and effects that Roosevelt himself, if he were alive, would denounce as grossly *contumelious* to his native purity of spirit—and perhaps in all honesty" (*Mencken*). **Scurrilous** or, now less often, **scurrile** or **scurril,** often approaches *vituperative* in suggesting attack and abuse, but it always implies gross, vulgar, often obscenely ribald, language; as, "They never fail to attack the passengers with all kinds of *scurrilous*, abusive, and indecent terms" (*Fielding*); "May plaister his clean name with *scurrilous* rhymes!" (*Tennyson*); "What outcries and lewd laughter, *scurril* gibe" (*Browning*).

Ana. Insulting, affronting, offending, outraging (see OFFEND): aspersing, maligning, vilifying (see MALIGN).

Ant. Complimentary: respectful. — *Con.* Flattering (see COMPLIMENT, *v.*): panegyrical, eulogistic (see corresponding nouns at ENCOMIUM): praising, lauding, extolling, acclaiming (see PRAISE, *v.*).

abutment. Pier, *buttress.

abutting. Contiguous, adjoining, *adjacent, tangent, conterminous, juxtaposed.

Ana. *Close, near, nigh, near by: joining, connecting (see JOIN): *nearest, next: impinging (cf. *impingement* under IMPACT).

Con. Detached, disengaged (see DETACH): disconnected, disjoined, disassociated (see affirmative verbs at JOIN).

abysm. *Gulf, chasm, abyss.

abysmal. *Deep, profound.

Ana. Illimitable, *infinite.

Con. *Superficial, shallow.

abyss. *Gulf, chasm, abysm.

abyssal. Bathysmal, bathybic, pelagic, oceanic, marine (see AQUATIC).

academic. 1 Scholastic, *pedantic, bookish.

Ana. *Dry, arid: erudite, scholarly, *learned.

Con. Unlettered, uneducated, untaught, unlearned, illiterate, *ignorant.

2 *Theoretical, speculative.

academy. Academy, seminary, institute, college, lycée, gymnasium are here compared as types of secondary schools and not in their other applications. In general, but not without exceptions, the first three represent American usage; the last three, respectively, British, French, and German. **Academy** was originally applied to a type of school established in the early republic to educate youth not planning to enter a university yet wishing to go further than was possible in the lower schools. Many of these old foundations still exist, some as public high schools, some as private schools, and are still called *academies;* as, Rome Free *Academy;* Phillips Exeter *Academy*. Newer schools using the designation *academy* are for the most part private; as, Friends *Academy*. **Seminary,** in its early English use with reference to a secondary school, was a designation (often a supposedly refined designation) of a private school, especially one for young ladies. It is now nearly obsolete in England but is still found in the United States in the names of some finishing schools for girls and of some private denominational schools for both sexes; as, Wyoming *Seminary*. **Institute** is even more variable in its application. It is especially applied to technical schools and military schools (as, Virginia Military *Institute*), though some of the former are now or were originally of collegiate rank; as, Pratt *Institute*. **College,** as used in reference to secondary schools, is found only in the names of a few mostly ancient English public schools (as, Eton *College*, Winchester *College*) or of similar schools in the British dominions and colonies; as, Upper Canada *College*. *Collège* is also used in the name of some secondary schools in France, but **lycée** is the designation of the type of government-controlled school, with a seven-year course ending with the baccalaureate and preparing for the university, for St. Cyr (the military school) or for one of the great technical schools. The German **gymnasium** has a nine-year course and corresponds roughly to the American secondary school and the first two years of college, as understood in the United States. *Lycée* and *gymnasium* are also used of similar schools in other European countries.

accede. Acquiesce, *assent, consent, agree, subscribe.
Ana. Concur, co-operate (see UNITE): *yield, submit, defer, relent: allow, permit, *let.
Ant. Demur. — *Con.* *Decline, refuse, reject, spurn: shy, stickle, stick, strain, balk (see DEMUR): *object, protest, kick: *oppose, resist, withstand.

accelerate. *Speed, quicken, hurry, hasten, precipitate.
Ana. Forward, further, *advance, promote: drive, impel (see MOVE).
Ant. Decelerate: retard. — *Con.* *Delay, slow, slacken: impede, obstruct, block, *hinder: *hamper, clog.

accent, *n.* **1** Stress, accentuation, *emphasis.
Ana. Beat, pulse, throb, pulsation (see corresponding verbs at PULSATE): *rhythm, cadence, meter.
2 Intonation, *inflection.
Ana. Pronunciation, enunciation, articulation (see corresponding verbs at PRONOUNCE).

accentuation. Accent, stress, *emphasis.
Ana. *Rhythm, cadence, meter: pronunciation, enunciation, articulation (see corresponding verbs at PRONOUNCE).
Ant. Inaccentuation. — *Con.* Evenness, steadiness, uniformity (see corresponding adjectives at STEADY).

accept. *Receive, admit, take.
Ana. *Adopt, embrace, espouse: acquiesce (in), *assent (to), agree (to), subscribe (to).
Ant. Reject. — *Con.* *Decline, refuse, repudiate, spurn: disavow, disown, disacknowledge (see affirmative verbs at ACKNOWLEDGE): *deny, contradict, negative: ignore, disregard (see NEGLECT).

acceptance. **Acceptance, acceptation** have both at one time or another carried the meanings: the act or fact of accepting, or the state of being accepted. Present good usage, however, restricts their denotations. **Acceptance** only is used to denote the act of accepting ("A blind *acceptance* of authority"—*Inge*) or the state of one who accepts something, especially something inevitable or inescapable ("All settled back into a sad sort of *acceptance* of the situation"—*Deland*). Both *acceptance* and *acceptation* may be used to denote the state of being accepted, or especially, of being approved or believed. "Metrical forms are conventional, and therefore rest . . . on *acceptance*" (*Lowes*). "This is a faithful saying, and worthy of all *acceptation*" (*1 Timothy* i. 15). **Acceptation** tends, however, to confine itself to denoting the sense in which a word or expression is generally received. "Not . . . a cultivated man in the ordinary *acceptation* of the words" (*C. W. Eliot*).

acceptation. **1** *Meaning, sense, signification, significance, import.
2 *Acceptance.

access. **1** Ingress, *entrance, entree, entry.
Ana. Approaching *or* approach, nearing (see APPROACH, *v.*): *admittance, admission: *way, route, passage: *door, portal, gate, gateway.
Ant. Outlet. — *Con.* Departure, withdrawal, retirement (see corresponding verbs at GO): retreat, recession (see corresponding verbs at RECEDE).
2 Accession, attack, *fit, paroxysm, spasm, convulsion.
Ana. Onset, onslaught, assault (see ATTACK): seizure, clutch, taking (see corresponding verbs at TAKE): twinge, *pain, stitch, pang, throe.

accession. **1** *Addition, accretion, increment.
Ant. Discard.
2 Access, attack, *fit, paroxysm, spasm, convulsion.
Ana. See those at ACCESS, 2.

accessory *or* **accessary,** *adj.* Contributory, *auxiliary, subsidiary, adjuvant, ancillary, subservient.
Ana. Secondary, collateral, tributary, succursal, *subordinate: concomitant, concurrent, coincident (see CONTEMPORARY): incidental, adventitious (see ACCIDENTAL).
Ant. Constituent, integral: principal (*in law*). — *Con.* *Inherent, intrinsic, constitutional, ingrained: essential, indispensable, requisite, *needful, necessary: fundamental, vital, cardinal (see ESSENTIAL).

accessory, *n.* **1** Appurtenance, adjunct, *appendage.
Ana. Concomitant, *accompaniment: *addition, accretion, increment.
2 Accomplice, abettor, *confederate, conspirator.
Ant. Principal.

accident. **1** *Quality, character, attribute, property.
Ana. Mark, *sign, note, badge, token, symptom: characteristic, peculiarity (see corresponding adjectives at CHARACTERISTIC).
Ant. Substance (*in philosophy*).
2 *Chance, hazard, luck, fortune, hap.
Ana. Contingency, fortuity *or* fortuitousness, adventitiousness (see corresponding adjectives at ACCIDENTAL).
Ant. Design, intent. — *Con.* Calculation, circumspection (see corresponding adjectives at CAUTIOUS): *plan, plot, project, scheme: *intention, purpose.
3 **Accident, casualty, mishap** are synonyms when they designate chance or a chance event bringing injury or loss. **Accident** is broadest in its application, being used of events that involve persons or things, or injuries or losses, serious or slight; as, he was crippled by the *accident;* a railway *accident;* owing to an *accident* to the machines, one department was closed down; *accidental* spilling of ink. **Casualty** commonly implies destruction, especially of life. "The martlet [=the martin, a bird], Builds in the weather on the outward wall, Even in the force and road of *casualty*" (*Shak.*). *Casualty* is now chiefly applied to an individual whose death, serious injury, or even desertion, constitutes a loss to a military (or similar) force engaged in hazardous activities; as, the regiment suffered heavy *casualties*. As applied to insurance, *accident* and *casualty* are usually distinguished: *accident insurance* is a provision against injury to oneself through accident; *casualty insurance* is a provision for indemnification, especially for damages incurred through one's liability for injury or loss to others. **Mishap,** as a rule, is applied only to slight accidents, especially those involving disappointment or frustration; as, a day seldom passes without one *mishap* or another.
Ana. *Disaster, catastrophe: mischance, *misfortune.

accidental. **Accidental, casual, fortuitous, contingent, incidental, adventitious.** The last five of these words are synonyms of *accidental* but not always of one another. For **accidental** denotes simply either happening by chance (as, an *accidental* meeting) or not of the real or essential nature of a thing (as, the essential and the *accidental* values of a college education). *Casual, fortuitous,* and *contingent* come into comparison with *accidental* in the first of these senses; *incidental* and *adventitious,* chiefly in its second sense. **Casual** so strongly stresses absence of prearrangement or premeditation that it tends to obscure the implication of chance; as, a *casual* discovery. "It was no *casual* re-encounter. He had been enticed into the place . . . with some sinister and perhaps deadly purpose" (*Froude*). As applied to persons, their actions, their clothes, and the like, it often implies heedlessness or indifference. "This strange landscape, which seemed so dull to the *casual* view" (*C. Rourke*). "[The rector] had been very *casual* about visiting his parishioners" (*C. Mackenzie*). Sometimes it is the appearance of carelessness or nonchalance, and not the reality, that is suggested. "This sense of an audience made him deliberately *casual* in his bearing" (*H. G. Wells*). **Fortuitous** so strongly implies chance that it sometimes connotes the absence, or seeming absence, of a cause. "The good frame of the universe was not the product of chance or *fortuitous* concourse of particles of matter" (*M. Hale*). **Contingent,** as here compared, always implies both possibility and uncertainty, the former because that which is so described may come about, the latter because the outcome is unpredictable owing to the possible operation of chance, of unseen causes, or of the possible influence of unforeseen events. *Contingent* is therefore always applied to what may come; as, the *contingent* advantages of a new law are to be distinguished from those that are immediate and certain; to prepare for all *contingencies.* **Incidental** may or may not imply chance: it often suggests a real, and it may be, a designed relationship, but one which is secondary and nonessential; thus, an *incidental* advantage of a college education may have been foreseen or sought after, but it is not regarded as of first importance; the *incidental* expenses of housekeeping must be provided for in one's budget, but they cannot be enumerated under any of the usual headings. "The Irish question is only *incidental* to the larger question" (*J. R. Lowell*). *Incidental* sometimes implies contingency that amounts to a strong probability; as, ills *incidental* to old age; loss of morale is *incidental* to poverty. **Adventitious** conveys no necessary suggestion of chance but it does imply a lack of essential relationship. That which is *adventitious* is that which does not belong to the original and intrinsic nature of a thing but has been added. "In works of imagination and sentiment . . . metre is but *adventitious* to composition" (*Wordsworth*).

Ana. Haphazard, *random, hit-or-miss, chance: unintended, undesigned, unpurposed (see affirmative verbs at INTEND): contingent, *dependent, adjective, conditional.

Ant. Planned: essential. — *Con.* Intended, designed, purposed (see INTEND): plotted, projected, schemed (see corresponding verbs under PLAN, *n.*): *inherent, constitutional, intrinsic, ingrained: *innate, inborn.

acclaim, *v.* Extol, laud, *praise, eulogize.

Ana. *Applaud, cheer, root, huzza: *exalt, magnify: glorify, honor (see corresponding nouns at FAME).

Ant. Vituperate. — *Con.* Revile, berate, rate (see SCOLD): *execrate, objurgate, damn: denounce, censure, reprobate (see CRITICIZE).

acclaim, *n.* Acclamation, *applause, plaudits.

Ana. Homage, *honor, reverence: renown, glory, éclat (see FAME): huzza, hurrah, cheer (see corresponding verbs at APPLAUD).

Ant. Vituperation. — *Con.* Obloquy, *abuse, invective: condemnation, denunciation, reprobation, censure (see corresponding verbs at CRITICIZE).

acclamation. Acclaim, *applause, plaudits.

Ana., Ant., Con. See those at ACCLAIM, *n.*

acclimate. Acclimatize, *harden, inure, season.

Ana. Accustom, *habituate: *adapt, adjust, conform.

acclimatize. Acclimate, *harden, inure, season.

Ana. See ACCLIMATE.

acclivity. Slope, *slant, grade, gradient, incline, inclination.

Ana. Ascent, *ascension: elevation, *height, altitude.

Ant. Declivity. — *Con.* Descent (see corresponding verb at DESCEND): decline, declension (see DETERIORATION).

accommodate. **1** Adjust, *adapt, conform, reconcile.

Ana. *Yield, submit, bow, defer: modify, *change, alter, vary: temper, attemper, *moderate, qualify.

Ant. Constrain. — *Con.* *Estrange, alienate.

2 *Oblige, favor.

Ana. *Help, aid, assist: gratify, gladden, *please: *indulge, humor.

Ant. Incommode. — *Con.* *Inconvenience, discommode, trouble: annoy, harass, harry, *worry: vex, irk (see ANNOY).

3 Hold, *contain.

Ana. Lodge, house, board, shelter, *harbor, entertain: take (in), *receive, admit.

accompaniment. **Accompaniment, concomitant** denote in common something attendant upon, or found in association with, another thing. Both may imply addition, but they vary chiefly in the kind of relationship connoted between the principal and the attendant things. **Accompaniment** often suggests enhancement by the addition of something appropriate; as, the piano *accompaniment* for a violin solo; the usual *accompaniments* of a turkey dinner; fame is not always the *accompaniment* of success. Sometimes, it so stresses concurrence or coincidence that a lack of causal connection is suggested. "A Roman sedition was the all but invariable *accompaniment* of a Roman coronation" (*Bryce*). **Concomitant,** by contrast, conveys the idea of customary or necessary association. It does not as a rule need the qualifying words "invariable," "essential," "inevitable" which so often precede it, for it implies in itself the qualities attributed by these words; as, disruption of routine is the *concomitant* of illnesses in a staff; unemployment is the *concomitant* of a financial panic. "Reproach is a *concomitant* to greatness" (*Addison*).

accompany. **Accompany, attend, conduct, escort, convoy, chaperon** agree in meaning to go or be together with; they differ chiefly in their implications as to the nature or purpose of the association. **Accompany** implies companionship (its etymological notion) or closeness of association and, often, with a personal subject, equality of status; as, rain *accompanied* by wind; "the light-headedness which *accompanies* fever" (*Kipling*); to *accompany* a friend. **Attend** commonly implies the subordinate or inferior status of the accompanying person or thing; as, the prince was *attended* (rather than *accompanied*) by an equerry, a secretary, and a courier. "The physical sensation that *attends* it [an emotion]" (*Lowes*). Sometimes it suggests a service or courtesy. "The General *attended* her himself to the street door" (*Austen*). Sometimes it connotes following or coming in the wake of someone or something. "A train of mourning friends *attend* his pall" (*Gray*). "The Nemesis that *attends* upon human pride" (*G. L. Dickinson*). **Conduct** usually retains its etymological implication of guidance, even when the subject is impersonal; as, to *conduct* a blind man across the street; to *conduct* sightseers through a museum; the pipe *conducts* water from a trough. Occasionally, the emphasis is not on guidance but on conveyance or transmission; as, metals that *conduct* heat. **Escort** and **convoy** add to *accompany* the implication of protection. In contemporary use both words and their corresponding nouns often suggest the use of an armed force as a guard, but there is a tendency to prefer *escort* when persons, and *convoy* when things, are protected. Also, *escort* is more often used for journeys on land and *convoy* for journeys by sea; as, soldiers *escorted* the caravan through the desert; a cruiser *convoyed* the freighter (or troop ship) through the submarine zone. *Escort,* however, often suggests (as *convoy* in current good English no longer suggests) attending as a courtesy or honor; as, three battleships *escorted* the visiting potentate's ship into the harbor; to *escort* a lady to her home after a party. **Chaperon** suggests propriety, or sometimes, supervision as the motive of the one who accompanies; in ordinary use, it implies the presence of an older woman as the protector of a young girl at a public place or affair or in mixed company; as, she is younger than you, and therefore cannot *chaperon* you.

Ana. Associate (with), link (with), combine (with), *join (to): *guide, lead, pilot.

Con. Forsake, desert, *abandon: leave, quit, withdraw (see GO).

accomplice. *Confederate, accessory, abettor, conspirator.

accomplish. Achieve, effect, fulfill, discharge, execute, *perform.

Ana. Complete, finish, conclude (see CLOSE): consummate (see corresponding adjective at CONSUMMATE): implement, *enforce.

Ant. Undo. — *Con.* Thwart, *frustrate, foil, circumvent: defeat, beat, lick (see CONQUER): *nullify, annul, negate.

accomplished. Finished, *consummate.

Ana. *Proficient, skillful, skilled, adept, expert: *versatile, many-sided, all-round.

accomplishment. Attainment, *acquirement, acquisition.

Ana. *Art, skill, craft: proficiency, adeptness, expertness (see corresponding adjectives at PROFICIENT).

accord, *v.* **1** Comport, *agree, harmonize, correspond, tally, conform, square, jibe.

Ana. Concur, coincide (see AGREE): blend, fuse, merge, coalesce (see MIX): cohere, adhere (see STICK).

Ant. Conflict. — *Con.* Clash, collide, jar (see corresponding nouns at IMPACT): differ (from), *differ (with): contrast, *compare.

2 *Grant, vouchsafe, concede, award.

Ana. Deign, condescend (see STOOP): bestow, present, confer, *give.

Ant. Withhold. — *Con.* *Deny, gainsay: refuse (see DECLINE): hold back, detain, reserve (see KEEP).

accord, *n.* **1** Concord, consonance, *harmony.

Ana. Agreement, acquiescence, consent (see corresponding verbs at ASSENT): union, solidarity, *unity: sympathy, affinity, *attraction.

Ant. Dissension, strife: antagonism. — *Con.* *Discord, conflict, variance, contention: antipathy, animosity, hostility (see ENMITY).

2 *Agreement, understanding.

Ana. Pact, compact, treaty, entente, concordat (see CONTRACT).

accordingly. So, consequently, *therefore, hence, then.

accost. *Address, greet, hail, salute.

Ana. *Speak (to), talk (with), converse (with): affront, *offend, insult.

Con. Avoid, shun, elude, evade, *escape: ignore, slight, overlook (see NEGLECT).

accouchement. Delivery, labor, travail, *childbirth, parturition.

account, *v.* **1** *Consider, deem, regard, reckon.

Ana. Regard, esteem (see under REGARD, *n.*): rate, appraise, evaluate, assess, *estimate.

Con. Underrate, underestimate, undervalue (see primitive verbs at ESTIMATE): disregard, disesteem (see affirmative verbs under REGARD, *n.*).

2 In form **account for.** *Explain, justify, rationalize.

Ana. *Answer (for): expound, elucidate, interpret (see EXPLAIN).

account, *n.* **1 Account, statement, bill** are comparable in their commercial senses when they denote a record of charges or credits. An **account** is a running record or detailed reckoning of charges incurred or of debits and credits; as, no entries have been made in this *account* for a long time; to balance *accounts* monthly. A **statement** is the record of an account, rendered either on demand or periodically. A **bill** gives the amount due for, or an itemized list of, purchases made, services rendered, etc., and always implies notice that payment is due; it may be submitted periodically or at the time of transaction; as, a dentist's or a grocer's *bill;* to receipt a *bill.*

2 *Use, service, advantage, profit, avail.

Ana. Benefit (see corresponding verb at BENEFIT): usefulness, utility (see USE): *worth, value.

Con. Futility, vanity, fruitlessness, bootlessness (see corresponding adjectives at FUTILE): unimportance, inconsequence, insignificance (see affirmative nouns at IMPORTANCE).

3 Account, report, chronicle, version, story, as here compared, denote a statement of actual events or conditions or of purported occurrences or conditions. An **account** is an oral or written, detailed, often firsthand statement. "Lord Mountfalcon asked for an *account* of her passage over to the island; receiving distressingly full particulars" (*Meredith*). A **report** is an account, usually of something witnessed or investigated, given by one person to another (often a superior); as, spies send in their *reports* in cipher; the secretary gave a verbatim *report* of the conference. A **chronicle,** in its nontechnical sense, is a detailed and extended account or report of events in their order of occurrence. "No more yet of this [Prospero's experiences after being shipwrecked]; For 'tis a *chronicle* of day by day, not a relation for a breakfast" (*Shak.*). A **version** or **story** is a statement of purported facts. *Version* always, and *story* often, implies contrast with another statement of the same events, and, usually, difference in details. But whereas *version* commonly implies honest difference of detail or of interpretation owing to limitations in each point of view, *story* often implies actual or suspected falsification (which may, however, be meant to amuse and not to deceive; as, a "tall" *story*); as, the Democratic and the Republican *version* of the state of the nation; the witness had been primed to tell a different *story;* he returned after a week's absence with a *story* of having been held captive by kidnapers.

accountable. *Responsible, answerable, amenable, liable.

Ant. Unaccountable. — *Con.* *Absolute, autocratic, despotic, tyrannical, arbitrary: irresponsible, inamenable, unanswerable (see affirmative adjectives at RESPONSIBLE).

accountant. Auditor, *bookkeeper.

accouter *or* **accoutre.** Equip, arm, outfit, *furnish, appoint.

Ana. Array, attire, *clothe, dress, vest, invest: deck, *adorn, embellish, decorate.

Con. *Strip, divest, dismantle.

accredit. 1 Certify, *approve, endorse, sanction.

Ana. Recommend, *commend: vouch for, attest, *certify.

Con. Reject, repudiate (see DECLINE): *disapprove, deprecate.
2 Commission, *authorize, license.
3 Credit, charge, assign, *ascribe, attribute, impute.
Ana. Attach, *fasten: connect, link, associate (see JOIN).

accretion. *Addition, increment, accession.
Ana. Adjunct, *appendage: adhesion, cohesion (see corresponding verbs at STICK): increase, augmentation, enlargement (see corresponding verbs at INCREASE).
Con. Attrition, *erosion: diminution, dwindling, decrease (see corresponding verbs at DECREASE).

accrue. Redound, contribute, *conduce.
Ana. Gain, win, earn (see GET): collect, *gather: *increase, augment, multiply, enlarge.
Con. *Decrease, lessen, dwindle, diminish: *abate, subside, wane, ebb.

accumulate. Accumulate, amass, hoard agree, in their literal and figurative senses, in denoting to bring together so as to make a store or great quantity. **Accumulate** implies a piling up by a series of increases rather than by a single complete act; it is applicable to almost anything that may increase in amount; as, unused books *accumulate* dust; a rolling stone *accumulates* force; he *accumulated* a fortune in his lifetime. "True poetry, however simple it may appear on the surface, *accumulates* meaning every time it is read" (*Day Lewis*). **Amass** refers usually, but not always, to things that are regarded as valuable, such as money or treasures; as, to *amass* a fortune in a business venture; to *amass* a stock of information. It frequently implies more imposing results and more rapid action than *accumulate.* "The triumvirs . . . had *amassed* from confiscations enough to furnish the sinews of war" (*Buchan*). **Hoard** always implies storing up, and frequently, concealment of that stored; as, squirrels *hoard* nuts for the winter months. Frequently, *hoard* implies greed and, when used of money, avarice; as, a miser is one who *hoards* gold.
Ana. *Gather, collect: *heap, pile, stack.
Ant. Dissipate. — *Con.* *Scatter, disperse, dispel: diminish, lessen, *decrease: *distribute, dispense, deal, dole.

accumulative. *Cumulative, summative, additive.
Ana. Aggregative, conglomerative (see corresponding nouns at AGGREGATE): multiplicative, augmentative (see corresponding verbs at INCREASE).
Con. Dissipating, dispelling, dispersing, scattering (see SCATTER): disintegrating, crumbling, decomposing (see DECAY, *v.*).

accurate. *Correct, exact, precise, nice, right.
Ana. True, veracious (see corresponding nouns at TRUTH): *impeccable, errorless, flawless, faultless: punctilious, meticulous, *careful.
Ant. Inaccurate. — *Con.* *Careless, heedless, inadvertent: *slipshod, slovenly: fallacious (see corresponding noun at FALLACY).

accursed. Damnable, cursed, *execrable.
Ana. Abominable, odious, *hateful, abhorrent, detestable: revolting, repulsive, loathsome, *offensive, repugnant.
Ant. Blessed. — *Con.* Admirable, estimable (see corresponding nouns at REGARD): *holy, sacred, divine: *honorable, honorary.

accuse. Accuse, charge, incriminate, criminate, indict, impeach, arraign denote in common to declare a person guilty of a fault or offense. **Accuse** is commonly immediate and personal, and often suggests directness or sharpness of imputation or censure; **charge** retains much of its primary implication of something laid upon one, and frequently connotes seriousness in the offense and formality in the declaration; as, to *accuse* a bystander of attempting to pick one's pocket (an *accusation* which may become a formal *charge* before a magistrate); to *accuse* a man of cheating (as an offense which one personally resents); to *charge* a man with cheating (as an infraction of the laws of the game). **Incriminate** and **criminate** denote to charge with crime or serious offense. "It would be wrong to *incriminate* the Order of S. Francis by any suspicion" (*Symonds*). "We must begin in self-justification . . . by *criminating* those whom we mean to destroy" (*M. Keatinge*). **Indict** adds to *charge* the implications of a formal consideration of the evidence, as in law, by a grand jury, or in extended use, by a person or persons acting in the role of jury, and of a decision that the accused person should be called to trial or to an accounting; as, the jury refused to *indict* the men accused of arson. "I am not . . . bringing an *indictment* against vers libre" (*Lowes*). **Impeach** implies, legally, a charge of malfeasance in office formally brought against a public officer by a branch of the government constitutionally authorized to bring such charges; as, the House of Representatives *impeached* President Andrew Johnson of high crimes and misdemeanors. In nontechnical language, *impeach* implies a direct charge which demands an answer. " 'You buy your loves.' . . . he did not plead verbally against the *impeachment*" (*Meredith*). To **arraign,** in law, is to call or bring a prisoner before a court to answer to the charge of an indictment; figuratively, it often preserves its legal implication, and means to call a person or thing to account before the bar of reason, taste, or the like; as, the indicted men will be *arraigned* next week; the relief projects were severely *arraigned* in an editorial. "I was carried down to the Sessions house, where I was *arraigned*" (*Defoe*).
Ana. Denounce, blame, reprobate, censure, *criticize.
Ant. Exculpate. — *Con.* Exonerate, vindicate, acquit, absolve (see EXCULPATE).

accustom. *Habituate, familiarize, addict.
Ana. *Adapt, accommodate, adjust: *harden, inure, season, acclimatize.
Ant. Disaccustom. — *Con.* Alienate, wean, *estrange.

accustomed. Wonted, customary, habitual, *usual.
Ana. Natural, normal, *regular, typical: *common, ordinary, familiar.
Ant. Unaccustomed. — *Con.* *Strange, singular, peculiar, odd, queer, erratic: *infrequent, uncommon, rare, occasional.

acerbity. *Acrimony, asperity.
Ana. Sourness, acidity, tartness (see corresponding adjectives at SOUR): crabbedness, surliness, dourness, saturninity (see corresponding adjectives at SULLEN): bitterness, acridity (see corresponding adjectives at BITTER): harshness, roughness (see corresponding adjectives at ROUGH).
Ant. Mellowness. — *Con.* Gentleness, mildness, blandness (see corresponding adjectives at SOFT): amiableness, good nature, complaisance (see corresponding adjectives at AMIABLE).

ache, *n.* *Pain, pang, throe, twinge, stitch.
Ana. *Distress, suffering, agony, misery: anguish, heartache (see SORROW): hurt, *injury: torment, torture, rack (see corresponding verbs at AFFLICT).
Con. Relief, alleviation, assuagement, mitigation (see corresponding verbs at RELIEVE): ease, comfort (see REST).

achieve. 1 Accomplish, effect, *perform, fulfill, execute, discharge.
Ana. Complete, finish, conclude (see CLOSE): surmount, overcome, *conquer.

Ant. Fail (*to do something*), fail (in). — *Con.* *Begin, commence, start.
2 Attain, *reach, gain, compass.
Ana. Win, secure, obtain, acquire, earn, *get: *realize, actualize: *come (to), arrive (at).
Ant. Miss (*getting or attaining*). — *Con.* Deviate (from), depart (from), *swerve (from): *escape, avoid, elude, shun.

achievement. *Feat, exploit.
Ana. Deed, act, *action: *victory, conquest, triumph: consummation, accomplishment (see corresponding adjectives at CONSUMMATE).
Ant. Failure. — *Con.* Negligence, *neglect: omission, slighting (see corresponding verbs at NEGLECT): defeat, vanquishment, beating, licking (see corresponding verbs at CONQUER).

achromatic. *Colorless, uncolored.
Ana. *Neutral, negative.
Ant. Chromatic. — *Con.* Colored, tinted, tinged (see corresponding nouns at COLOR).

acid, *adj.* Acidulous, tart, *sour, dry.
Ana. Acrid, *bitter: hard (see ALCOHOLIC): *sharp: *astringent.
Ant. Bland: sweet: alkaline. — *Con.* *Suave, smooth: mild, *soft, gentle: basic (see ALKALINE).

acidulous. Acid, tart, *sour, dry.
Ana. *Astringent: *sharp: *pungent, piquant: biting, cutting (see INCISIVE).
Ant. Saccharine. — *Con.* Mellow, ripe (see MATURE): bland, mild, *soft: *suave, smooth, urbane.

acknowledge. 1 **Acknowledge, admit, own, avow, confess** are synonymous when they mean basically to disclose something against one's will or inclination. All usually imply some sort of pressure, as that of the law or of conscience, leading to the disclosure. **Acknowledge** implies the making public of one's knowledge of something which has been, or might have been, kept back or concealed; as, to *acknowledge* a secret marriage, one's faults, one's ignorance. "She did at last extort from her father an *acknowledgment* that the horses were engaged" (*Austen*). **Admit,** with less suggestion of possible concealment, stresses reluctance to grant or concede, and refers rather to facts than to their implications; to *admit* a charge may involve merely the granting of the fact alleged, not necessarily (as frequently with *acknowledge*) the acceptance of the point of view which the charge implies. "We . . . were brought up never to *admit* that there was anything the matter with Howie except that he wasn't very well, or that he was a little backward" (*M. Austin*). **Own** is less formal than *acknowledge*, and regards the thing acknowledged in its relation to oneself; as, to *own* oneself at a loss; to *own* to forty years. "When a man *owns* himself to have been in an error, he does but tell you in other words that he is wiser than he was" (*Pope*). **Avow,** which in both of its senses implies an open or bold declaration, as here compared usually implies assertion in the face of hostility; as, to *avow* one's participation in a movement. "We who practice it [physics] scarcely dare *avow* ourselves as physicists in any group of laymen" (*Karl K. Darrow*). **Confess** usually applies to what one feels to be wrong; as, to *confess* a crime; to *confess* one's sins: but it is often used with no such implication, suggesting merely deference to the opinion of others; as, I am not, I *confess*, convinced.
Ana. Disclose, divulge, *reveal: *grant, concede, allow: publish, *declare, proclaim.
Ant. Deny. — *Con.* Conceal, *hide, secrete: disavow, disown (see affirmative verbs at ACKNOWLEDGE): gainsay, contradict, impugn, negative (see DENY).
2 **Acknowledge, recognize** agree in meaning to take cognizance of in some way, usually in a way dictated by custom or convention and implying acceptance or assent. **Acknowledge** is found in certain idioms where the concrete method of taking notice is not stated but connoted; as, to *acknowledge* a letter (that is, to send a note of its receipt); to *acknowledge* a gift (that is, to send a message indicating the receipt and acceptance of the gift and one's gratitude); to *acknowledge* an introduction (that is, to respond to it by a bow, a greeting, or the like). In freer expression, *acknowledge* usually implies definite or formal acceptance, as of a principle as binding or of a claim as rightful or of a person as ruler; as, he *acknowledged* the obligation of a son to support his aged parents. "In Italy during the fourteenth and fifteenth centuries there were two *acknowledged* sources of political power: the Empire and the Church" (*A. Huxley*). **Recognize,** though often used interchangeably with *acknowledge*, suggests more strongly authoritative sanction or full admission as to a given or implied status, or suggests actual and manifest, as contrasted with formal or merely verbal, acceptance; as, they *acknowledged* the part he had played in their success, but they refused to *recognize* it suitably; in 1918, England, France, and the United States *recognized* Czechoslovakia as an independent state. "The ladies never acted so well as when they were in the presence of a fact which they *acknowledged* but did not *recognize*" (*Meredith*). *Recognize* sometimes implies, as *acknowledge* never does, full realization or comprehension. "Courts . . . have been . . . slow to *recognize* that statutes . . . may imply a policy different from that of the common law" (*Justice Holmes*). "Some interval . . . between the real advent of the new state of things and the . . . full *recognition* of that state of things" (*Belloc*).
Ana. Accept, *receive: notice, note, remark (see SEE): respond, reply, *answer.
Ant. Ignore. — *Con.* Disregard, slight, *neglect: repudiate, spurn, reject (see DECLINE).

acme. Apex, zenith, culmination, climax, *summit, peak, apogee, pinnacle, meridian.

acoustic, acoustical. *Auditory, audile.

acquaint. *Inform, apprise, advise, notify, advertise.
Ana. Tell, *reveal, disclose, divulge: *teach, instruct, educate, school: familiarize, accustom, *habituate.
Con. Conceal, *hide: withhold, reserve, hold back (*information*) (see KEEP).

acquaintance. *Friend, intimate, confidant.
Ana. *Associate, companion, comrade, crony.
Con. *Stranger, outsider.

acquiesce. Consent, agree, *assent, accede, subscribe.
Ana. Accept, *receive: conform, *adapt, adjust, accommodate, reconcile (*oneself*): *yield, submit, bow: concur, coincide (see AGREE).
Ant. Object. — *Con.* Protest, remonstrate, kick (see OBJECT): *demur, stickle, stick, shy, balk: differ (from), *differ (with).

acquiescence. Compliance, resignation. See under COMPLIANT.
Ana. Deference, obeisance (see HONOR): submissiveness (see corresponding adjective at TAME).
Ant. Rebelliousness *or* rebellion. — *Con.* Insubordination, contumaciousness (see corresponding adjectives at INSUBORDINATE).

acquiescent. Resigned, *compliant.
Ana. Submissive (see TAME): yielding, submitting, deferring, bowing, relenting (see YIELD).
Ant. Rebellious. — *Con.* Contumacious, *insubordinate: protesting, objecting, kicking, remonstrating (see OBJECT, *v.*): resisting, opposing, combating (see OPPOSE).

acquire. Obtain, *get, gain, win, earn, secure, procure.

Ana. Attain, achieve, compass, *reach: annex, *add, superadd: *buy, purchase: *take, seize, snatch, grab.
Ant. Forfeit. — *Con.* Alienate, alien, *transfer, convey: *relinquish, surrender, abandon, yield.

acquirement. **Acquirement, acquisition, attainment, accomplishment** come into comparison when they denote a power or skill that is the fruit of exertion or effort; in this sense, they are very often used in the plural. **Acquirement** implies achievement as a result of continued endeavor and self-cultivation rather than of natural gifts or talent. "A woman of considerable information and literature; *acquirements* not common amongst . . . ladies" (*Edgeworth*). **Acquisition** adds to *acquirement* (in specific and general senses) the implications that the thing acquired is an addition or gain and that the endeavor to acquire has been characterized by avidity, sometimes even by cupidity. "Accumulations of knowledge . . . in excess of his present mental energy. His *acquisitions* interfere with his judgment" (*S. M. Crothers*). As applied to an acquired power or skill, *acquisition* usually stresses, as *acquirement* does not, the inherent value of that power or skill; as, absolute disinterestedness is a rare *acquisition,* even in historians. "No philosopher would resign his mental *acquisitions* for the purchase of any terrestrial good" (*Peacock*). **Attainment** commonly refers to distinguished achievements as in the arts, in statesmanship, in science; it suggests fully developed talent or talents; as, artists of high *attainments;* remarkable literary *attainments.* "Men that count it a great *attainment* to be able to talk much" (*Glanvill*). **Accomplishment** refers to any acquired power or grace such as may make for agreeable social intercourse. "My new *accomplishment* of dancing" (*C. Churchill*). "We found that even for Men of Science this neat clean carving of words was a very necessary *accomplishment*" (*Quiller-Couch*). "He was distinguished not only by solid acquirements, but by elegant *accomplishments*" (*G. Smith*).
Ana. Achievement (see FEAT): *addition, accretion.
Con. *Lack, want, defect, privation.

acquisition. *Acquirement, attainment, accomplishment.
Ana. *Addition, accession, accretion, increment: *possessions, belongings, means, assets: *gift, genius, talent, aptitude: *art, skill, cunning.

acquisitive. Grasping, avaricious, greedy, *covetous.
Ana. Avid, *eager, keen, athirst: possessing *or* possessive, owning, enjoying (see corresponding verbs at HAVE).
Ant. Sacrificing, abnegating. — *Con.* Forgoing, forbearing, eschewing (see FORGO): self-denying, renunciative (see corresponding nouns at RENUNCIATION).

acquit. **1** Absolve, exonerate, vindicate, *exculpate.
Ana. Discharge, *free, release, liberate: *excuse, pardon, forgive, remit.
Ant. Convict. — *Con.* Condemn, *sentence, doom, proscribe, damn, attaint: denounce, blame (see CRITICIZE).
2 Quit, *behave, conduct, demean, deport, comport.
Ana. *Act, behave, work, operate, react.
Con. Misbehave, misconduct, misdemean (see primitive verbs at BEHAVE).

acrid. **1** *Bitter.
Ana. *Pungent, piquant: *astringent: biting (see INCISIVE): *offensive, repugnant, loathsome.
Ant. Savory. — *Con.* *Palatable, sapid, saporous, toothsome, tasty: fragrant, *odorous, aromatic, balmy: delicious, delectable, luscious, *delightful.
2 *Caustic, mordant, mordacious, scathing.
Ana. *Sharp, keen: surly, crabbed, morose (see SULLEN): malevolent, malign, spiteful, *malicious: virulent, venomous, *poisonous.
Ant. Benign, kindly. — *Con.* *Suave, urbane, bland, smooth, politic.

acrimonious. *Angry, irate, indignant, wrathful, mad.
Ana. Testy, splenetic, choleric, *irascible, cranky, cross: rancorous, hostile, antagonistic (see corresponding nouns at ENMITY): quarrelsome, contentious, *belligerent.
Ant. Irenic, peaceable. — *Con.* Good-natured, good-tempered, good-humored (see corresponding noun phrases at GOOD NATURE): *kind, kindly, benign, benignant.

acrimony. **Acrimony, acerbity, asperity** agree in denoting temper or language marked by irritation or some degree of anger or resentment. **Acrimony** implies bitterness or ill will and also greater stinging or blistering power in what is said than the others; as, the controversial writings of the seventeenth century are notorious for their *acrimony.* "We all know how easy it is to . . . defend a pet theory with *acrimony*" (*Quiller-Couch*). **Acerbity** implies sourness as well as bitterness, sometimes as shown in words or mood, but more often as manifested in a morose, embittered nature. "The judge's smile seemed to operate on her *acerbity* of heart like sunshine upon vinegar, making it ten times sourer" (*N. Hawthorne*). Often it suggests crabbedness. "The Milton of religious and political controversy . . . is not seldom disfigured by want of amenity, by *acerbity*" (*Arnold*). **Asperity** now retains its etymological implications of harshness and roughness chiefly in reference to style. "Each of these metres . . . is strange and arresting . . . . their *asperities* tend, with repetition, to pass into beauties" (*Quiller-Couch*). In general use, *asperity* stresses quickness of temper or sharpness of resentment but it rarely, if ever, suggests bitterness. "Mrs. Bennet . . . assured him with some *asperity* that they were very well able to keep a good cook" (*Austen*).
Ana. Bitterness (see corresponding adjective at BITTER): ill will, malignity, spite, spleen, *malice, malevolence: rancor, animus, animosity, antipathy (see ENMITY).
Ant. Suavity. — *Con.* Urbanity, diplomacy (see corresponding adjectives at SUAVE): courtesy, civility, politeness (see corresponding adjectives at CIVIL).

acropolis. Citadel, *fort, fortress, stronghold, fastness.

across. **Across, crosswise** (*or* **crossways**), **athwart** are synonymous when they mean so as to intersect the length of something. *Across* and *athwart* may be used as prepositions as well as adverbs but carry the same implications in either part of speech. **Across** usually implies extension or passage from one side to the other; as, this board will not go *across;* he could not get *across* (the river) that night. **Crosswise** stresses intersection at right angles and usually, but not invariably, suggests a horizontal direction; as, the stripes run *crosswise;* the defect lies *crosswise* to the grain of the wood. **Athwart** commonly, but not always, implies obliquity of direction or intersection at an acute angle; as, the tree fell *athwart* the road; on the slopes, the shadows lie *athwart;* in some weaves, the filling threads run *athwart* those of the warp.

Figuratively, especially with reference to plans, purposes, hopes, and the like, these words are not always synonymous because they retain and stress their distinguishing implications. **Across** (colloquial in this use) often implies fulfillment; as, he was able to get his point *across* to his audience. **Crosswise** implies contrariety and, therefore, frustration; as, everything goes *crosswise* with us tonight. **Athwart** (somewhat archaic in this use) suggests perverseness and distortion, and is now usually replaced by *awry.* "And quite *athwart* Goes all decorum" (*Shak.*).

act, *n.* **1** *Action, deed.

Ana. Performance, accomplishment, achievement (see corresponding verbs at PERFORM): *feat, exploit.
2 Statute, law, *bill.

act, *v.* **1 Act, behave, work, operate, function, react** are comparable when used with reference to the way in which a person or thing does what is expected or responds to external influences or circumstances. **Act** is not only the most general word of this group but also the most general of all English intransitive verbs except those which assert being, a state of being, or relation (*be, exist, belong, etc.*). *Act* is therefore used largely in interrogative sentences when knowledge of the specific nature of the action is sought or in declarative sentences with a qualifying adverb, adverbial phrase, or adjective complement; as, how did the child *act* when you called him?; he *acted* as if he were about to cry; he *acted* frightened; how should this powder *act* when mixed with water? It seems to me to *act* strangely; this medicine *acts* as a poison to some persons. **Behave,** in its earliest and still most common use, applies chiefly to persons and their conduct with reference to a standard of what is right or proper or decorous. "One must keep one's contracts, and *behave* as persons of honour and breeding should *behave*" (*R. Macaulay*). However, under the influence of physics and psychology, *behave* more and more tends to approach *act* in generality; as, to study how steel *behaves* under stress or how the thyroid gland *behaves* during emotional excitement. "Two men may *behave* like a crowd . . . when their emotions are engaged" (*Conrad*). **Work, operate, function** agree in meaning to act in the way that is natural or intended. "The Swiss clock had long since ceased to *work*" (*Bennett*). "But she had not thought. Her brain would not *operate*" (*Bennett*). "Sound organs *functioning* vigorously all the time" (*Conrad*). In distinction from one another, *work* may, especially when qualified, suggest success or effectiveness; *operate* stresses efficient activity rather than achievement except when followed by *on* or *upon; function* always implies activity with reference to the accomplishment of the end or office for which a thing exists or is designed. "The fact that a theory has actually *worked* is a better recommendation for its soundness than any amount of ingenious dialectic" (*A. Huxley*). "The revolutionary spirit, ceasing to *operate* in politics" (*Macaulay*). "His sanguine temper, and fearlessness of mind, *operated* very differently on her" (*Austen*). "Consciousness ceases altogether at death, when the brain no longer *functions*" (*Grant Allen*). "Rules of the game which must be observed, if society is to *function* at all" (*Galsworthy*). **React,** a word of rapidly shifting implications, is often used as though it were a close synonym of the preceding words, especially of *act* or *behave*. "How . . . he would have acted—or you, I believe, would say *reacted*" (*F. M. Ford*). In discriminating use, it always suggests recoil or rebound; often more narrowly, but still consistently, it implies reciprocal or counteractive influence, or a reverse effect; as, home and the school *react* [that is, act reciprocally] on each other. "Whilst most people's minds succumb to inculcation and environment, a few *react* [that is, behave in the contrary fashion] vigorously: honest and decent people coming from thievish slums, and sceptics and realists from country parsonages" (*Shaw*). As a result of use in chemistry and psychology, *react* now often implies a favorable or desired response; as, children *react* [that is, act as desired, in response] to kind treatment.
2 Act, play, impersonate, personate are synonyms when they mean to assume the appearance or role of another person or character. **Act,** nearly always, and **play,** usually, imply feigning for theatrical representation; as, to *act* Hamlet; to *play* the melancholy Dane. Even the idiom "to *play* one's part" has a theatrical origin and still connotes performance and a contribution to an ensemble. Whether **impersonate** and **personate** (now increasingly rare) imply simulation for the sake of theatrical representation or for deception can be gathered only from the context; as, an actor who *impersonates* women; he was arrested for *impersonating* a clergyman. **Personate** does not imply fraud, however, when it suggests representation, or standing for someone. "The donors . . . are identified with, and *personated* by, the trustees" (*Ch. Just. Marshall*).

acting, *adj.* *Temporary, supply, ad interim, provisional.

action. 1 Action, act, deed agree in designating something done or effected. **Action** refers primarily to the process of acting; **act** and **deed,** to the result, the thing done. An *action* is usually regarded as occupying some time, and involving more than one step; an *act* is more frequently thought of as momentary or instantaneous, and as individual; as, the rescue of a shipwrecked crew is a heroic *action;* the launching of the lifeboat, a brave *act;* a course of *action,* the springs of *action;* an *act* of vengeance, caught in the *act*. But the distinction cannot always be made. In the plural, *action* has frequently an ethical connotation, and is loosely synonymous with *conduct*. "By him [the Lord] *actions* are weighed" (*1 Samuel* ii. 3). "Only the *actions* of the just Smell sweet and blossom in their dust" (*Shirley*). *Deed* refers to a thing as done; it invariably presupposes intelligence and responsibility in the agent, and therefore often connotes, as *act* does not (except where it is a translation of the Latin *actum*) illustriousness or achievement. "The *deed* is worthy doing" (*Shak.*). "What, are my *deeds* forgot?" (*Shak.*). "Little, nameless, unremembered *acts* Of kindness and of love" (*Wordsworth*). *Deed* is frequently opposed to *word,* as *act* to *thought*. "I'll endeavour *deeds* to match these *words*" (*Shak.*). "Be great in *act,* as you have been in *thought*" (*Shak.*). "Give thy thoughts no tongue, Nor any unproportion'd thought his *act*" (*Shak.*).
Ana. *Process, proceeding, procedure: performance, execution, fulfillment (see corresponding verbs at PERFORM): activity, operation, work, behavior, reaction (see corresponding verbs at ACT).
2 Cause, case, *suit, lawsuit.
3 *Battle, engagement, push.
Ana. Combat, conflict, fight, fray, affray, *contest: *encounter, skirmish, brush.

activate. 1 Energize, *vitalize.
Ana. Animate, vivify, *quicken, enliven: *stir, rouse, arouse, rally, awaken.
Ant. Arrest.
2 Activate, actuate, motivate are sometimes confused when used with reference to persons and the motives which govern their actions. They are not synonyms, however, because they carry divergent denotations. Some external influence or agent, rather than a motive or desire, **activates** a person or thing when it supplies an effective stimulus to activity; the motive, or, at least, a latent desire, for such activity being commonly presupposed. "Kapteyn's work . . . was not final, but it . . . . attracted and *activated* others" (*G. W. Gray*). A motive, a principle, a desire, or the like, **actuates** a person (not an action or undertaking) when it governs or determines his actions; as, the desire for conquest *actuated* the explorers of the sixteenth century. "In suggesting . . . [another's] name to Moxon-Hughes he had been *actuated* by good will" (*C. Mackenzie*). A dramatist, a novelist, or the like, **motivates** the actions of his characters or the incidents of his plot when he supplies the motives for each; as, the novelist failed to *motivate* adequately his hero's surrender

to temptation. Also, an objective, a desire, a passion, or the like, *motivates*, or gives the underlying motive of an action or undertaking; as, the desire for conquest *motivated* the explorations of the sixteenth century; ambition *motivated* Macbeth's murder of Duncan.

Ana. Stimulate, *provoke, excite, galvanize: spur, goad, induce (see corresponding nouns at MOTIVE): *incite, instigate, foment, abet: drive, impel, *move.

Ant. Restrain, inhibit. — *Con.* Curb, check, bridle (see RESTRAIN): thwart, foil, baffle, balk, *frustrate.

active. **Active, operative, dynamic, live** are synonymous when they mean at work or in effective action. Some of their distinctions in implications are observable when they are applied to the same things; as, *active, operative, dynamic, live* principles; an *active, operative, dynamic, live* sense of duty. Other distinctions are evident only when their widely varying ranges of application are indicated. **Active,** in general, may be employed wherever the others are applicable, but it is also capable of being used where none of the others would be appropriate. It may qualify anything that shows its nature or its existence in acts, in action, or in work; as, an *active* volcano; an *active* brain; *active* sympathy: it is applicable to anything which can be worked, operated, manipulated, wielded, or the like; as, an *active* pen; an *active* fan; an *active* bond on the market. It is also applicable to an agent, an operator, an instrument, or a means, and to that which is accomplished by any such agency; as, an *active* enforcer of the law or *active* enforcement of the law; an *active* propagandist or *active* propaganda; an *active* seeker of truth or an *active* search for truth. *Active* may imply little more action or movement or exertion than shows a state that is not death, rest, or inertness; as, his pulse is low, but his heart is still *active:* it may, and usually does, imply vigor and energy in action or movement; as, an *active* market; an *active* writer; the *active* stage of a disease. Often it suggests causation or activation; as, the *active* principle in a soporific. In contrast with *active,* **operative** is applicable only to things that have a capacity for acting, working, or effecting ends (as a principle, a motive, an emotion), or for being put into operation (as laws); as, when strict ethical principles are *operative* in society, men may expect the millennium; the rule has been *operative* since January first. In contrast with *active,* however, *operative* usually is weaker in its implication of effectiveness; thus, one's sense of duty is *operative* when it in any degree influences one's thoughts or actions; it is *active* when it serves as a spur to action or is the determinant of one's actions. **Dynamic** stresses the realization of that which is potential in a thing: it therefore often connotes release of great energy and consequent forcefulness; thus, a *dynamic* personality is one that exhibits great power and exerts a great influence; love is a *dynamic* emotion when it sweeps away all that would obstruct its movement. **Live,** in the figurative sense in which it is here considered, is also applicable to persons, personalities, principles, laws, emotions, and motives. It stresses vitality and modernity more than forcibleness and, when used of persons, intelligent awareness of present conditions or needs and progressiveness more than effectiveness. "Steve had in him the making of a *live* man of affairs" (*S. Anderson*). "Remy de Gourmont . . . a powerfully *live* thinker" (*H. Ellis*).

Ana. *Agile, nimble, brisk: alert, wide-awake (see WATCHFUL): *busy, industrious, assiduous, diligent: energetic, strenuous, *vigorous.

Ant. Inactive. — *Con.* Quiescent, *latent, dormant: inert, idle, supine, passive (see INACTIVE): *lazy, indolent, slothful.

actor. **Actor, player, performer, mummer, mime, Thespian, impersonator, trouper** denote in common one who, for the entertainment or edification of an audience, takes part in an exhibition simulating happenings in real life. An **actor** is one who makes a profession of taking part in such exhibitions on the stage or in motion pictures; as, an ambition to be an *actor.* A **player** is one who acts in a stage play, whether professionally or for the nonce. "All the world's a stage, And all the men and women merely *players*" (*Shak.*). **Performer** is a wider term than the others of this group: it may refer to one who appears on the stage or in motion pictures, a dancer, musician, circus acrobat, etc. It emphasizes actual participation in an exhibition before an audience. "In theatrical speaking, if the *performer* is not exactly proper and graceful, he is utterly ridiculous" (*Steele*). A **mummer** is a disguised merrymaker who goes about especially at Christmas time and entertains chiefly by means of dumb show. The term and practice are chiefly British. *Mummer* is sometimes loosely or contemptuously used for an actor, as in George Moore's novel *A Mummer's Wife.* **Mime** is in modern use a term of no very definite application, being applied to various kinds of performances (often dancing) which tell a story by actions rather than by speech. It may be equivalent to *pantomime;* as, Charlie Chaplin is a *mime.* **Thespian** is a mock-heroic term for a stage player, sometimes specifically for a tragedian. An **impersonator** is one who imitates actual persons, in speech, actions, appearance (as, an *impersonator* of Theodore Roosevelt), or one who enacts a particular dramatic role (as, an *impersonator* of Hamlet). A **trouper** is a member of a group, esp. a traveling group, of actors staging a play or repertory of plays. The term often connotes the seasoning, or the sense of obligation to audience and fellow actors, that characterizes an experienced actor. "No real *trouper* while conscious will ever confess himself too sick to go on" (*E. Ferber*).

actual. *Real, true.

Ana. *Material, physical, phenomenal, objective: concrete, particular (see SPECIAL).

Ant. Ideal: imaginary. — *Con.* *Abstract, transcendent, transcendental: spiritual, divine (see HOLY): *theoretical, speculative, academic: fabulous, *fictitious, mythical.

actuality. *Existence, being.

Ana. Reality, truth (see corresponding adjectives at REAL): realization, actualization, materialization, externalization, incarnation (see corresponding verbs at REALIZE): attainment, achievement (see corresponding verbs at REACH).

Ant. Potentiality, possibility. — *Con.* Abstraction, ideality, transcendence (see corresponding adjectives at ABSTRACT).

actualize. *Realize, embody, incarnate, externalize, objectify, materialize, substantiate, substantialize, hypostatize, reify.

actuate. 1 *Move, drive, impel.

Ana. Stimulate, *provoke, excite, galvanize, quicken: *stir, rouse, arouse: energize, activate, *vitalize.

2 *Activate, motivate.

Ana. Influence, *affect, sway: *incline, dispose, predispose: *induce, prevail on *or* upon.

Ant. Deter (*with a motive, fear, etc., as subject*). — *Con.* *Hinder, impede, bar: *restrain, inhibit, curb, check.

acumen. Penetration, *discernment, insight, perception, discrimination, divination, clairvoyance.

Ana. Shrewdness, sagacity, perspicacity, astuteness (see corresponding adjectives at SHREWD): sharpness, keenness, acuteness (see corresponding adjectives at SHARP).

Ant. Obtuseness. — *Con.* Dullness, stupidity, denseness (see corresponding adjectives at STUPID): blindness, purblindness (see corresponding adjectives at BLIND).

acute. 1 *Sharp, keen.

Ana. *Incisive, trenchant, cutting: penetrating, piercing (see ENTER).

Ant. Obtuse. — *Con.* *Dull, blunt: *stupid, dull, crass, dense.

2 **Acute, critical, crucial** are synonyms when they are applied to times, situations, problems, and the like, and mean full of uncertainty or of menace to the future of those concerned. **Acute** suggests intensification, as of unfavorable symptoms or conditions, or of conflicting emotions, to the culminating or breaking point; as, the controversy has reached its *acute* stage; the situation in Europe in 1914 did not become *acute* until the end of June. **Critical,** in its richest significance, adds to *acute* the implications of certain imminent change, of concomitant suspense, and of decisiveness in the outcome; sometimes, the last of these implications is stressed at the expense of the others; as, the *critical* point in a disease; Gettysburg was the *critical* battle of the Civil War. **Crucial,** in loose use, stresses perils or hardships and often means little more than *trying;* as, it was a *crucial* experience. In discriminating use it always implies a crossing or dividing of the ways and suggests a test or trial involving the determination, not of an issue or outcome, but of a course or direction; thus, a *critical* experiment is one which determines the success or failure of a scientific investigation; a *crucial* experiment is one that determines the future course or line to be taken by the investigator. "The children were . . . in the *crucial* stage of adolescence" (*D. H. Lawrence*).

Ana. Culminating, climactic (see corresponding nouns at SUMMIT): *dangerous, hazardous, precarious, perilous: menacing, threatening (see THREATEN): intensified, aggravated (see INTENSIFY).

adage. *Saying, saw, proverb, maxim, motto, epigram, aphorism, apothegm.

adamant *or* **adamantine.** Obdurate, inexorable, *inflexible.

Ana. Unyielding, unsubmitting (see affirmative verbs at YIELD): immovable, immobile (see affirmative adjectives at MOVABLE): *grim, implacable, unrelenting.

Ant. Yielding. — *Con.* Submissive, subdued (see TAME): obliging, complaisant (see AMIABLE): relenting, submitting, capitulating (see YIELD).

adapt. Adapt, adjust, accommodate, conform, reconcile agree in denoting to bring into correspondence. To **adapt** (*to*) is to fit or suit to something; it distinctively implies modification to meet new conditions, frequently with the added suggestion of pliability or readiness. "He knew how to *adapt* himself. To one correspondent he is gay . . . . To another he is gravely reflective" (*A. Huxley*). To **adjust** (*to*) is to bring into as close and exact correspondence or harmony as exists between the parts of a mechanism; in contrast with *adapt,* it suggests less of flexibility or tact in the agent and more of ingenuity or calculation. "He must divine what men would welcome and shun what men might resent. He must delicately mould and *adjust* the popular will to his own" (*Buchan*). **Accommodate** (*to*) is used in preference to *adjust* when there exists a somewhat marked variance or discrepancy between the objects brought into (often merely superficial, sometimes temporary) agreement or harmony. "Man is no lawgiver to nature, he is an absorber. She it is who stands firm; he it is who must *accommodate* himself" (*W. James*). *Accommodate* is used in preference to *adapt* when yielding or compromise is to be suggested; as, she is a very *accommodating* person. "They *accommodate* their counsels to his inclination" (*Addison*). To **conform** (*to*) is to bring into harmony or accordance with a pattern, example, or principle. "The Liberal . . . does not wish to have to *conform* himself to any programme or policy" (*Inge*). In current English the reflexive *to conform oneself* is comparatively rare, its place being taken usually by the intransitive *conform* (for other intransitive sense see AGREE). "This officer [secretary of state], as his duties were prescribed by that act, is to *conform* precisely to the will of the president. He is the mere organ by whom that will is communicated" (*Ch. Just. Marshall*). Partly because of the association of this word with compulsory legislation regarding religious observances it often implies compliance or, at times, slavish acceptance. "Mark Twain . . . had *conformed* to a moral régime in which the profoundest of his instincts could not function" (*Van W. Brooks*). To **reconcile** (*with, to*) is to demonstrate to one's own or another's satisfaction the fundamental consistency or congruity of things that are, or seem to be, incompatible. "Mrs. Ballintin's confidence in her own capacity to *reconcile* conflicting portraits of herself" (*M. Austin*). "The great men among the ancients understood how to *reconcile* manual labor with affairs of state" (*Locke*). In reflexive use, *reconcile* adds to *adapt* the implication of resignation or of submission; as, to *reconcile* oneself to a lonely existence or to the loss of one's fortune.

Ana. Temper, attemper, qualify (see MODERATE): acclimatize, acclimate, inure (see HARDEN).

Ant. Unfit.

adaptable. Pliant, ductile, *plastic, pliable, malleable.

Ana. Tractable, amenable (see OBEDIENT): supple, flexible, resilient, *elastic.

Ant. Inadaptable, unadaptable. — *Con.* Intractable, refractory (see UNRULY): unaccommodating, nonconforming, irreconcilable (see affirmative verbs at ADAPT).

adaptation. *Variation, modification, mutation.

add. 1 **Add, sum, total, figure, cast, foot** are synonyms when they are followed (usually, but not in every case necessarily) by *up* and mean to find or represent the amount reached by putting together arithmetically a series of numbers or quantities. **Add** is both the common and the technical word; it usually implies strict adherence to the traditional arithmetical process. Even in its somewhat rare figurative use it implies a similar operation. "She could not understand Constance's state of mind. Certainly she could not claim to have '*added up*' Constance yet" (*Bennett*). **Sum** stresses the result attained rather than the method followed. This is especially clear in its tendency to escape its literal significance. Thus, one seldom hears today "to *sum up* the votes in an election"; the commoner expression is "to *sum up* the results of an election." In figurative use, *sum up* implies a gathering together in small compass for the production of a single telling effect; thus, a lawyer *sums up* when he presents in brief and logical form the evidence that has been given in his client's favor. "I *summed up* all systems in a phrase and all existence in an epigram" (*Wilde*). "In this knowledge [of the relative values of things], and in the use made of it, is *summed up* the whole conduct of life" (*Inge*). **Total** (often without *up*) tends to replace *sum up* in the literal sense; as, to *total* (*up*) the liabilities of a defunct corporation. Sometimes it means to reach the sum or number of; as, street accidents in 1938 *totaled* 162. *Figure, cast,* and *foot* are felt to be somewhat colloquial in comparison with the preceding words: at least, their connotations are more homely; **figure** usually suggests the mere labor of addition (as, to *figure* the costs of operating an automobile); **cast** often implies ready reckoning as in mental arithmetic, though commonly used only in the phrase "to *cast* (or *cast up*) an account"; **foot** usually connotes bookkeeping and totals at the bottom of each column of figures (as, the statements have not yet been *footed* up).

2 Add, append, annex, subjoin, superadd. Add, the most general of these words, means to join one thing to another thing or to a group, series, or combination of other things so as to increase the original unit in numbers, size, amount, or the like; as, to *add* ten books to ones' library; please *add* these items to my order; to *add* eggs to a batter; she always *adds* spice to the conversation. One **appends** when one adds something that is supplemental and accessory (literally, hangs from it) and does not form an integral part of the principal thing; as, to *append* notes to a book; to *append* a seal to a document. One **annexes** when one adds something that becomes part of the original whole yet bears, usually, a subordinate or subsidiary relation to it, or suffers loss of identity in the merging; as, to *annex* a codicil to a will; to *annex* conquered territory to the kingdom. One **subjoins** when one adds something under another thing, or, especially, to what has already been said or written; as, to *subjoin* a postscript to a letter; to *subjoin* additional matter in an appendix. One **superadds** when one adds something to that which is complete in itself or already at its maximum; as, the phrase "to paint the lily" means to *superadd* decoration to that which in itself is superlatively decorative; the horrors of pestilence *superadded* to the horrors of war.

Ana. *Fasten, attach, affix: augment, enlarge, *increase.

Ant. Subtract, deduct. — *Con.* Lessen, *decrease, diminish, reduce: abstract, *detach, prescind.

addendum *or* (*pl.*) **addenda.** Supplement, *appendix.

addict, *v.* *Habituate, accustom, familiarize.

Ana. *Incline, dispose, predispose, bias: devote, apply, address, *direct.

Ant. Wean. — *Con.* Alienate, *estrange: *detach, disengage: disincline, indispose (see affirmative verbs at INCLINE).

addict, *n.* **Addict, votary, devotee, habitué, fiend, fan,** as here compared, designate a person who by habit and strong inclination indulges in something or the pursuit of something. **Addict** implies excessive and continuous indulgence, usually in harmful, but sometimes in harmless, things; as, a drug *addict;* a detective-story *addict.* **Votary** and **devotee** retain some of the implications of their religious senses such as enthusiasm, often amounting to fanaticism, and zeal. They rarely suggest attachment to that which is degrading or debasing but they do not invariably imply attachment to that which is uplifting; as, a *votary* of science; a *devotee* of vegetarianism. "Any worthy object of study, pursued disinterestedly . . . does not permit its *votary* to be very seriously narrowed by his zeal" (*Inge*). "Ye *devotees* to your adored employ [pursuit of worldly pleasures]" (*Cowper*). **Habitué** always implies frequent attendance at a place but it commonly also connotes habitual indulgence in a pleasure; thus, a *habitué* of the theater is a *devotee* of the drama; a *habitué* of a gambling house is a gambling *addict.* **Fiend** and **fan** are not literary terms; the latter is still regarded as slang. *Fiend* implies even greater excess than *addict* or even greater fanaticism than *votary* or *devotee;* as, a dope *fiend;* a golf *fiend;* when used of devotees of games, contests of wit, or the like, it often also connotes extraordinary skill; as, a *fiend* at mathematics. *Fan* adds to *habitué* the implication of ardent enthusiasm; as, a baseball *fan.* It suggests even more than *votary* or *devotee* naïve admiration or partisanship; as, a Roosevelt *fan;* an actor's *fan* mail.

addition. Addition, accretion, increment, accession, in the sense in which they are here compared, agree in denoting a thing that serves to increase another in size, amount, or content. **Addition** implies union with something already existing as a whole or as a unit; as, he built an *addition* to his house in 1900; no *addition* was made to the collection for five years. "The office boy, a recent *addition* to the staff, was busy with the copying press" (*Arch. Marshall*). Sometimes improvement rather than increase is stressed; as, the paintings were an *addition* to the room. **Accretion** implies attachment from the outside; it may be used of the process as well as of the thing added; as, a rolled snowball grows by *accretion.* The word often suggests additions made to an original body over a considerable period of time. "The professional historian, whose aim is exact truth, should brush aside the glittering *accretions* of fiction that have encrusted it" (*Grandgent*). Nearly always it implies the addition of unessential or alien matter. "All progress in literary style lies in the heroic resolve to cast aside *accretions* and exuberances" (*H. Ellis*). **Increment** usually implies addition bit by bit in consecutive or serial order; as, teachers' salaries are raised by annual *increments.* "The movement [free verse] is . . . one more wave in the endless ebb and flow of action and reaction, the infinitesimal *increments* of which we call Progress" (*Lowes*). Sometimes it signifies increase in value; as, an unearned *increment* in the value of land resulting from social progress or increase in population. **Accession** denotes something acquired that constitutes an addition to contents, holdings, or possessions; as, recent *accessions* to a library or a museum (that is, new books, new paintings, or the like). "The greatest *accession* of positive knowledge has come in our own time" (*Inge*).

additive. Summative, *cumulative, accumulative.

Ana. Aggregative, conglomerative, agglomerative (see corresponding nouns at AGGREGATE): constituent, component, elemental (see corresponding nouns at ELEMENT).

addle. Muddle, bemuddle, *confuse, fuddle, befuddle.

Ana. Confound, dumfound, nonplus, bewilder (see PUZZLE): amaze, flabbergast, astound (see SURPRISE): fluster, flurry, agitate, upset (see DISCOMPOSE).

Ant. Refresh (*mentally*). — *Con.* *Quicken, enliven, vivify, animate.

address, *v.* **1** *Direct, devote, apply.

Ana. Bend, turn (see CURVE): appeal, pray, sue, plead (see under PRAYER): aim, point, level (see DIRECT).

2 Address, accost, greet, salute, hail agree in meaning to speak to (sometimes, to write or to make a sign to) a person in recognition or in order to obtain recognition. **Address** usually implies formality and an ulterior purpose; it also frequently suggests length of speech or communication; as, to *address* prayers to God or a petition to Congress; how does one *address* a governor? "It was Franklin, the thick chief mate, who was *addressing* him" (*Conrad*). *Address* once carried more often than now the suggestion of courting or wooing. "Poor Edward O'Connor was not allowed to *address* Fanny" (*Lover*). **Accost** adds to *address* the idea of speaking first or without being introduced; it always implies absence of formality but it often suggests boldness or sometimes, evil intent; as, he *accosted* a passer-by and asked for money. "The women . . . were *accosted* by two men who wanted to walk with them" (*S. Anderson*). **Greet** usually implies friendliness, good will, or cordiality; it is the precise word when welcoming is to be suggested; as, the whole town appeared at the station to *greet* them. "My lord, the Mayor of London comes to *greet* you" (*Shak.*). **Salute** commonly stresses ceremoniousness or observance of courtesies demanded by custom. "The wife of his brother . . . must be *saluted* every day; but his paternal and maternal kinswomen need only be *greeted* on his return from a journey" (*Sir W. Jones*). "Then I *salute* you with this kingly title: Long live Richard, England's royal king" (*Shak.*). Specifically, *salute* applies to formal or prescribed acts of recognition; as, the soldier *saluted* his superior officer; the president was *saluted* with 21 guns. **Hail** implies heartiness, joyousness, and often noisiness. "He smiled and nodded and *saluted*, To those who *hailed* him, as it suited" (*Masefield*). It often stresses the idea of calling out, especially from a distance; as, to *hail* a cab; to *hail* a friend.

Ana. *Speak (to), talk (to), converse (with): court, woo (see INVITE).

address, *n.* **1** *Tact, savoir-faire, poise.

Ana. Dexterity, facility, ease, *readiness: adroitness, cleverness (see corresponding adjectives at CLEVER): graciousness, affability (see corresponding adjectives at GRACIOUS): suavity, urbanity, diplomacy (see corresponding adjectives at SUAVE).

Ant. Maladroitness, gaucherie. — *Con.* Awkwardness, clumsiness, ineptness (see corresponding adjectives at AWKWARD): boorishness, churlishness (see corresponding adjectives under BOOR).

2 *Speech, oration, harangue, allocution, lecture, prelection, talk, sermon, homily.

adduce. **Adduce, advance, allege, cite** are often used interchangeably in the meaning to bring forward by way of explanation, proof, illustration, or the like. Actually, however, they are clearly distinguishable in their implications and in their idiomatic associations. One **adduces** facts, evidence, instances, passages, reasons, arguments, when one presents these in support of a contention. "The psychologist W. H. R. Rivers *adduced* evidence which has led him to believe that the natives of that unfortunate archipelago [Melanesia] are dying out" (*T. S. Eliot*). "I will not *adduce* poets of admitted eminence—Mr. Watson, for instance, or Mr. Yeats—to prove my case" (*Quiller-Couch*). One **advances,** or puts forward, something that is in itself contentious, as a theory, a proposal, a claim, an argument, when one presents it for acceptance or consideration; as, a writer recently *advanced* the prediction that modern methods of warfare will bring about the depopulation of large cities. "Half a century later when the Bourbon claim to the Spanish succession is *advanced*" (*Belloc*). **Allege,** because of confused derivation, has two leading senses not quite sharply distinguished from each other. In the first sense, one *alleges* something when one asserts positively or under oath that it is true and capable of proof; as, the state *alleges* that the indicted man is guilty of conspiracy. "They [Australians in 1916] *alleged* we were avoiding the risks of war while reaping the financial benefits of neutrality" (*V. Heiser*). In law, *allege* usually means to state in an *allegation*, or formal recital of what a party undertakes to prove. "It seems to me a miscarriage of justice to sustain liability . . . until the facts have been heard which the petitioner *alleged*" (*Justice Holmes*). In the other sense, one *alleges* something when one adduces it as the reason, ground, excuse, or the like, of an action, decision, or position that is, or may be, questioned; as, he refused to be surety on his friend's bond, *alleging* a resolve never to be a bondsman after one unfortunate experience. In both cases, the use of *allege* implies a measure of doubt of that which is asserted; its participial adjective *alleged*, especially, often serves as a disclaimer of responsibility for the assertion; as, an *alleged* miracle; the *alleged* thief. "Some of the *alleged* reasons for changing our coinage" (*Bagehot*). One **cites** only that which is concrete and specific, as a passage from a book or a definite instance, when one adduces it in support of a contention; thus, one *cites*, or quotes, a passage to give an authority; one *cites* an instance that serves as a precedent or illustration; one *cites* definite facts in support of a generalization. "The very real difficulties of modern physical science originate, in large degree, in the facts just *cited*" (*Jeans*).

Ana. *Exemplify, illustrate: *remark, comment, commentate, animadvert.

adept, *n.* *Expert, wizard, artiste, dab, dabster, artist, virtuoso.

Ant. Bungler. — *Con.* Dabbler, tyro, *amateur, dilettante: apprentice, *novice, probationer.

adept, *adj.* *Proficient, skilled, skillful, expert.

Ana. *Conversant, versed: efficient, *effective: *dexterous, adroit, deft, feat: competent, *able, capable, qualified.

Ant. Inadept, inept: bungling. — *Con.* Amateurish, dabbling, dilettantist (see corresponding nouns at AMATEUR): *awkward, clumsy, maladroit.

adequate. *Sufficient, enough, competent.

Ana. *Fit, suitable, meet, appropriate, proper: requisite, *needful, essential: *due, condign.

Ant. Inadequate. — *Con.* *Deficient, defective: scant, scanty, *meager, exiguous: abundant, copious, plenteous, *plentiful.

adhere. *Stick, cohere, cling, cleave.

Ana. *Fasten, attach, affix: glue, *cement, agglutinate: unite, link, combine, *join.

Con. *Separate, part, sever, divide: *detach, disengage: disunite, disjoin (see affirmative verbs at JOIN).

adherence. **Adherence, adhesion** are usually distinguished in current good use. In spite of exceptions, the tendency prevails to use **adherence** when mental or moral attachment, and **adhesion** when physical attachment, is implied; as, they gave their *adherence* (in older idiom, gave in their *adhesion*) to the cause of reform; the *adhesion* of iron to a magnet or of lung tissues to the pleura. Sometimes, however, *adhesion* is used in place of *adherence* when the writer feels that the physical connotations of the former will add emphasis. "The iron force of *adhesion* to the old routine" (*Arnold*).

Ant. Inadherence, nonadherence.

adherent. *Follower, disciple, partisan, satellite, henchman, sectary.

Ana. Supporter, upholder, backer, champion (see corresponding verbs at SUPPORT).

Ant. Renegade. — *Con.* Apostate, recreant (see RENEGADE): deserter, forsaker (see corresponding verbs at ABANDON): adversary, *opponent, antagonist.

adhesion. *Adherence.

Ant. Nonadhesion, inadhesion.

adhesive. **Adhesive, gluey, glutinous, mucilaginous, gummy, sticky** describe the quality of a substance that adheres to any surface with which it comes in contact. **Adhesive** is applied to any substance, whether in a fluid state or not, that is capable of acquiring this quality when softened by heat or by moisture; as, an *adhesive* paste; an *adhesive* plaster; "good *adhesive* mud" (*G. Eliot*). As a noun, *adhesive* is the general term used for any substance uniting surfaces, such as glue (hence, **gluey** and **glutinous**), mucilage (*U. S.*) or gum (*Brit.*) (hence, **mucilaginous, gummy**), cement, and the like. **Sticky** is colloquial and usually describes that which is adhesive (often unpleasantly adhesive) because of weather conditions, imperfect drying, or the like; as, *sticky* candy; varnish becomes *sticky* in hot weather.

adiaphorous. Indifferent, *neutral, negative.

Ana. Unimportant, insignificant, inconsequent (see affirmative nouns at IMPORTANCE): unnecessary, nonessential (see affirmative adjectives at NEEDFUL).

Ant. Obligatory, compulsory. — ***Con.*** Essential, necessary (see NEEDFUL): important, significant (see corresponding nouns at IMPORTANCE).

adieu. Adios, *good-by, farewell, Godspeed, au revoir, auf Wiedersehen, bon voyage.

ad interim. *Temporary, provisional, acting, supply.

Ant. Permanent.

adios. Adieu, *good-by, farewell, Godspeed, au revoir, auf Wiedersehen, bon voyage.

adipose, *n.* **Adipose, marrow, suet, tallow, lard** designate various forms of animal fat. **Adipose,** or the more common *adipose tissue,* may denote the type of membranous tissue in which a greasy semisolid substance called *fat* (see FAT) is stored in the animal body, but it is more often applied to such tissue with its accumulation of fat. **Marrow** designates the soft substance which fills the cavities of most bones. Because in the long bones it contains about 95 per cent of fat, *marrow* is often used, especially figuratively, as though it were akin to *fat.* All the other words designate fat derived from the animal body. **Suet** is the hard adipose tissue around the kidney or loins of beef or mutton. When the suet or other adipose tissue of beef and mutton is melted and clarified, it forms a very hard, white, tasteless substance called **tallow.** The corresponding adipose tissue in hogs when rendered and clarified forms a somewhat soft, buttery, white substance called **lard.**

adjacent. Adjacent, adjoining, contiguous, abutting, tangent, conterminous, juxtaposed agree in meaning being in close proximity. **Adjacent** does not always imply actual contact but it does not admit of anything of the same kind between; thus, *adjacent* lots are in contact, but *adjacent* houses may or may not be. "It is not likely that pure accident caused three *adjacent* windows to take a Spanish tone" (*H. Adams*). Objects are **adjoining** when they meet and touch at some line or point of junction; as, *adjoining* estates; *adjoining* rooms. **Contiguous** adds to *adjoining* the implication of meeting and touching on one side or a considerable part of one side; as, streets lined with rows of *contiguous* houses. It may be used figuratively of events as well as of objects. "*Adjacent* events need not be *contiguous;* just as there may be stretches of a string which are not occupied by beads, so the child may experience uneventful periods of time" (*Jeans*). **Abutting** is usually applied to that which borders on, or is in contact with, something else, often with the implication of the termination of one thing by the other; as, land *abutting* on the road. "The Bettersworth yard *abutted* on the Allingham's for the space of one woodshed and a horse-chestnut tree" (*M. Austin*). **Tangent** implies contact at a single point; its use is chiefly geometrical; as, a line *tangent* to a curve; *tangent* circles. Objects are **conterminous** which border on each other or have a common boundary. "Defending the side of Germany *conterminous* to France" (*Lecky*). *Conterminous* applies also to things having the same bounds, limits, or ends; as, the civil and the ecclesiastical parishes in England are sometimes, but not always, *conterminous.* Things are **juxtaposed** when they are placed side by side, especially so as to permit comparison or contrast; as, *juxtaposed* styles of writing; *juxtaposed* ideas; when colors are *juxtaposed,* they become affected in hue.

Ana. *Nearest, next: successive, *consecutive: joining, connecting (see JOIN, *v.*).

Ant. Nonadjacent. — ***Con.*** *Distant, removed, remote: separated, parted (see SEPARATE, *v.*).

adjective, *adj.* *Dependent, relative, conditional, contingent.

Ant. Substantive (*in law and in logic*): self-sufficient. — ***Con.*** Independent, autonomous, *free: derived (from) or derivative, sprung (from), stemmed (from) (see corresponding verbs at SPRING).

adjoining, *adj.* *Adjacent, contiguous, abutting, tangent, conterminous, juxtaposed.

Ana. Joined, connected (see JOIN, *v.*): attached (see FASTEN).

Ant. Detached, disjoined. — ***Con.*** Removed, *distant, remote, far.

adjourn. Adjourn, prorogue, dissolve are used of public bodies when they suspend business. When a deliberative body **adjourns,** it merely suspends (usually for a brief period) its deliberations, which at the next meeting may be resumed where they ended, except for something to the contrary in its rules of procedure; when the crown or its representative **prorogues** a parliament or other legislative body in Great Britain or her colonies, the session is ended, and all bills not enacted are quashed, and can be taken up only as new business at its subsequent session; when a deliberative body **dissolves** itself or is *dissolved* (as, a parliament *dissolved* by the crown), it entirely ceases to exist as it is then constituted, and cannot have any further meeting or session until after an election.

Ana. Suspend, stay, postpone, *defer.

Ant. Convene. — ***Con.*** *Summon, convoke, call: *begin, commence, start.

adjudge. Adjudicate, *judge, arbitrate.

Ana. Rule, *decide, determine, settle: award, accord, *grant: *allot, assign.

adjudicate. Adjudge, *judge, arbitrate.

Ana. Determine, settle, rule (see DECIDE).

adjunct, *n.* *Appendage, appurtenance, accessory.

Ana. *Addition, accretion: appanage (see RIGHT): attachment, affix, fixture (see corresponding verbs at FASTEN).

adjure. Conjure, entreat, *beg, beseech, implore, importune, supplicate.

Ana. Pray, plead (with), appeal (to) (see under PRAYER): request, *ask: bid, enjoin, charge, *command.

☞ *Do not confuse* adjure *with* abjure.

adjust. 1 Adjust, regulate, fix are often used interchangeably in the sense to set right, or to rights. **Adjust** always implies modification to meet a need. In general, one *adjusts* a thing or things when by some change one brings it into its exact or proper position or condition or them into their right relationship; thus, one *adjusts* a telescope when one changes the distance between its eyepiece and its object glass so as to bring it into focus; one *adjusts* the temperature of a house when one changes the setting of a thermostat. Specifically, *adjust* also often implies rectification or correction; as, to *adjust* an error in an account; to *adjust* a loose screw in a machine; to *adjust* spectacles that are not properly centered: frequently it implies straightening out or settling; as, to *adjust* one's affairs before going on a journey; to *adjust* a difficulty with a neighbor; to *adjust* a claim for insurance. **Regulate,** on the other hand, usually implies the maintenance of something in a desired condition. One *regulates* a mechanism, a device, an organ, or the like when one uses (or serves as) the means to make it work or operate regularly, uniformly, or accurately; thus, one *regulates* a clock when one adjusts its mechanism so that it will keep accurate time; some drugs *regulate* the beat of the heart by slowing it up, others by hastening it, until its rate of speed is normal. One also *regulates* that which is produced or effected by a mechanism, an organ, etc., when one uses the means to keep it at a fixed or uniform rate, degree, or the like; thus, one *regulates* the temperature of one's house when one sets a thermostat at the desired mark and keeps it there. **Fix,** as a synonym of these words, is colloquial and an Americanism. It is often used

where *adjust* or *regulate* would be more explicit and effective; as, the optician will *fix* her glasses; please *fix* the clock; he will *fix* up matters for us. In distinctive use it implies restoration to good order or a state of repair; as, to *fix* one's hair; these shoes are not worth *fixing*.
Ana. Rectify, *correct: trim, steady, *stabilize, balance: *order, arrange: align, *line, range.
Ant. Derange. — *Con.* Disarrange, *disorder, disturb: upset, *discompose.
2 *Adapt, accommodate, conform, reconcile.
Ana. *Harmonize, attune: correspond, conform, accord, square (see AGREE).
Ant. Disadjust.

adjutant, *n.* *Assistant, coadjutor, aide, aide-de-camp, helper.

adjuvant, *adj.* *Auxiliary, contributory, ancillary, accessory, subsidiary, subservient.
Ana. Aiding, helping, assisting (see AID, *v.*): supporting, upholding, backing (see SUPPORT, *v.*): *effective, efficient, efficacious, effectual.
Ant. Counteractive. — *Con.* Neutralizing, negativing (see NEUTRALIZE): obstructing, hindering, impeding (see HINDER, *v.*).

administer. **1** **Administer, dispense** come into comparison because they are used in certain idiomatic phrases, similar in wording but not always equivalent in meaning, such as to *administer* justice or to *dispense* justice; to *administer* a medicine or to *dispense* medicine (or medicines); to *administer* a sacrament or to *dispense* the Sacrament. Historically, these words have a common basic meaning, to act in the capacity of a steward, or by extension, of one who is entrusted with the right use of possessions or of power belonging to another. They diverged in meaning, however, in that *administer* implied management and the carrying out of the wishes or the will of the master and *dispense* implied meting out or just distribution to individuals. These divergent implications are now often transferred, with the result that it is difficult to distinguish their meanings, especially when the object of the verb is an abstraction, such as justice or charity. "The citizens disliked the rule of William [the Conqueror] on account of the strict justice which he *administered*" (*Freeman*). " 'These be the sort,'—she took a fine judicial tone . . . . 'These be the sort to *dispense* justice. They know the land and the customs of the land' " (*Kipling*). In reference to a sacrament, the two words were early used interchangeably. Now, "to *administer* a sacrament" means to perform the rites and duties prescribed for its proper observance; thus, a layman may in a case of necessity *administer* baptism; a priest *administers* the sacrament of penance when he hears a penitent's confession and grants him absolution. In good modern English, the minister does not *dispense* a sacrament, but only "the Sacrament," that is, the bread and wine of the Eucharist, or the Lord's Supper: this implies distribution and is, therefore, close to the original sense of the word. *Administer*, however, because it has acquired the implication of distribution, is also used in this latter collocation. In modern English, the two words when used in reference to medicine are precisely distinguished. One *administers* a medicine who gives the prescribed dose directly to the patient; one *dispenses* medicines who compounds them according to the prescription of the physician. In this use, *dispense* retains its etymological implication of weighing and measuring. Thus, also, one *administers* a blow, a rebuke, advice, or the like, when he deals it out directly to the individual. *Dispense*, in similar phrases, however, retains its implication of distribution; thus, one *dispenses* advice when he metes it out to those who in his opinion need it; one *dispenses* alms when he manages their distribution.
2 *Execute.
Ana. Direct, *conduct, manage, control.

administration. *Government.

administrative. Executive. See under EXECUTE, 2.

administrator, *fem.* **administratrix, administratress.** Executive, executor. See under EXECUTE, 2.

admiration. **1** *Wonder, wonderment, amaze, amazement.
Ana. Astonishment, surprise (see corresponding verbs at SURPRISE): awe, fear, *reverence: rapture, transport, *ecstasy.
Con. Indifference, unconcern, aloofness (see corresponding adjectives at INDIFFERENT): boredom, *tedium, ennui.
2 Esteem, respect, *regard.
Ana. Appreciation, cherishment (see corresponding verbs at APPRECIATE): liking, loving, enjoying (see LIKE): adoration, veneration, reverence, worship (see under REVERE).
Ant. Abhorrence. — *Con.* Loathing, detestation, hate, hatred (see under HATE, *v.*).

admire. Esteem, respect, regard. See under REGARD, *n.*
Ana. *Appreciate, value, prize, cherish: *revere, reverence, venerate, adore, worship.
Ant. Abhor. — *Con.* *Hate, loathe, abominate, detest: *despise, contemn, scorn, disdain.

admission. *Admittance.

admit. **1** *Receive, accept, take.
Ana. Allow, permit, suffer (see LET): *harbor, entertain, shelter, lodge, house.
Ant. Eject, expel. — *Con.* *Exclude, debar, shut out: bar, obstruct, block, *hinder.
2 *Acknowledge, own, confess, avow.
Ana. Concede, *grant, allow: *assent (to), acquiesce (in), agree (with), subscribe (to): divulge, disclose, *reveal.
Ant. Gainsay: disdain. — *Con.* *Deny, contradict, negative.
3 *Enter, introduce.
Ana. Induct, *initiate, install: *introduce, insert, interject, interpose.
Ant. Exclude. — *Con.* Debar, shut out (see EXCLUDE): withdraw, *remove: expel, *eject, oust.

admittance. **Admittance, admission.** In present usage **admittance** is mostly confined to the literal sense of allowing one to enter a locality or building; as, no *admittance; admittance* to the grounds. **Admission** has acquired the figurative sense of admitting to rights, privileges, standing, membership; as, *admission* of a person to the church or to the best society, or of new words into the language. When entrance into a building or a locality carries with it certain privileges, *admission* rather than *admittance* is used; as, *admission* to a theater; the *admission* of aliens into a country.

admixture. **1** *Mixture, composite, blend, compound, amalgam.
2 **Admixture, alloy, adulterant** are comparable when they denote an added ingredient that destroys the purity or genuineness of a substance. **Admixture** suggests the addition of the foreign or the nonessential; as, pure Indian without any *admixture* of white blood; love with an *admixture* of selfishness. "In the Oration of Aspasia . . . you hear her claim that . . . 'ours is the land of pure Hellenes, free from *admixture*' " (*Quiller-Couch*). **Alloy,** as here compared, derives, from its literal application to a baser substance added to a precious metal to give it hardness, its figurative implication of the addition of that which detracts from the value or perfection of a thing. "There's no fortune so good, but it has its *alloy*" (*Bacon*).

"He had his *alloy*, like other people, of ambition and selfishness" (*R. Macaulay*). **Adulterant,** both literally and figuratively, implies the addition of that which debases or impairs a thing without markedly affecting its appearance. Consequently, it usually implies the intent to deceive; as, paraffin is used as an *adulterant* of wax; piety without any *adulterant* of hypocrisy.

Ana. *Addition, accretion: *touch, suggestion, streak, dash, spice, tinge, smack, shade: infusion, suffusion, leaven (see corresponding verbs at INFUSE).

admonish. Chide, *reprove, reproach, rebuke, reprimand.

Ana. *Warn, forewarn, caution: counsel, advise (see under ADVICE, *n.*): *criticize, reprehend, reprobate.

Ant. Commend. — *Con.* *Approve: applaud, compliment (see COMMEND).

ado. Fuss, pother, flurry, bustle, *stir.

Ana. Trouble, pains, exertion, *effort.

Con. Quietness, stillness, silence (see corresponding adjectives at STILL): calm, serenity, tranquillity (see corresponding adjectives at CALM).

adolescence. *Youth, puberty, pubescence.

Ant. Senescence.

adopt. Adopt, embrace, espouse come into comparison when they mean to make one's own that which in some fashion one owes to another. One **adopts** something of which one is not the begetter, author, or the like, or which is not one's own naturally; as, to *adopt* the style of Swinburne; to *adopt* the British pronunciation of a word. "The Ralstons gave up old customs reluctantly, but once they had *adopted* a new one they found it impossible to understand why everyone else did not immediately do likewise" (*E. Wharton*). One **embraces** that which, figuratively, one takes to one's bosom: in looser use it implies merely willingness to accept, in richer use it suggests eager or joyful acceptance; as, to *embrace* an opportunity; to *embrace* Christianity. "She *embraced* with ardour the fantastic ideal of the cleaning up of England" (*R. Macaulay*). One **espouses** that to which one attaches oneself as closely as to a wife, giving it support, or sharing the same fortunes and participating in the same experiences; as, to *espouse* a friend's quarrel. "Those who . . . *espouse* the cause of free literature" (*Galsworthy*).

Ana. Appropriate, *arrogate, usurp: *assume, affect.

Ant. Repudiate: discard. — *Con.* Reject, spurn (see DECLINE): renounce, forswear, *abjure.

adoration. Worship, veneration, reverence. See under REVERE, *v.*

Ana. *Honor, homage, obeisance: praise, laud, extolling (see corresponding verbs at PRAISE).

Ant. Blasphemy. — *Con.* Execration, cursing (see corresponding verbs at EXECRATE): *profanation, desecration, sacrilege.

adore. 1 Worship, venerate, *revere, reverence.

Ana. Laud, *praise, extol: *exalt, magnify.

Ant. Blaspheme. — *Con.* *Execrate, curse.

2 Adore, worship, idolize are here compared only in their nonreligious senses and as meaning to love or admire excessively. **Adore** commonly implies emotional surrender to the charms or attractions of that which is loved or admired; it often connotes extreme adulation, if the object of love is a person. "Several women of thirty or thereabouts *adored* him—before it is good for youth to be *adored*" (*H. G. Wells*). **Worship** usually implies more extravagant admiration or more servile attentions than *adore;* it also commonly connotes an awareness of one's own inferiority or of one's distance from the object of one's love; as, hero *worshipers;* he *worships* his wife (cf. he *worships* the ground she walks on). **Idolize** often implies absurdly excessive admiration or doting love; sometimes, however, it comes very close to *adore;* as, a spoiled child is usually one that has been *idolized* by his parents.

Ana. Love, dote on *or* upon (see LIKE): admire, esteem (see under REGARD, *n.*).

Ant. Detest. — *Con.* *Hate, loathe, abhor, abominate: *despise, scorn, contemn, disdain.

adorn. Adorn, decorate, ornament, embellish, beautify, deck, bedeck, garnish agree in meaning to enhance the appearance of something, usually by additions. These words, especially the first five, are often used interchangeably; certain distinctions, however, are apparent in the work of good writers, especially when the subject of the verb is the thing that enhances rather than the agent or enhancer. That which **adorns** not only serves to heighten the beauty of its background or setting, but also is beautiful in itself. *Adorn* is now more often used of immaterial than of material things. "Her modest looks the cottage might *adorn*, Sweet as the primrose peeps beneath the thorn" (*Goldsmith*). "The most elevated rank, instead of giving her consequence, would be *adorned* by her" (*Austen*). That which **decorates** is that which relieves the plainness or monotony of a background by contributing beauty of color or design to it; as, the walls are yet to be *decorated;* well-arranged trees *decorate* a lawn; to use inlaying as a chair *decoration.* That which **ornaments** is an adjunct or an accessory which sets off a thing to advantage. "Whose bridle was *ornamented* with silver bells" (*Scott*). *Ornament,* especially the noun, is often used figuratively. "The royal navy of England hath ever been its greatest defence and *ornament*" (*Blackstone*). **Embellish** more often suggests the act of an agent than the effect of a thing. One *embellishes* who modifies his material, especially by adding adventitious, sometimes gaudy or fictitious, ornament for the sake of effect; as, to *embellish* one's style with imagery. *Embellish* often suggests disregard for truth; as, a highly *embellished* account of a battle. That which **beautifies** (or one *beautifies* who) either enhances the beauty of something or counterbalances its plainness or ugliness. "The eternal orbs that *beautify* the night" (*Shelley*). "And there, by fresh hopes *beautified*, Stood He . . . our youngest, fairest flower!" (*Wordsworth*). That which **decks** or **bedecks** is something (or one *decks* or *bedecks* who adds something) which contributes to the gaiety, splendor, or, especially in the case of *bedeck*, showiness of appearance; as, to *bedeck* oneself with jewels. "*Decking* with liquid pearl the bladed grass" (*Shak.*). "He likes to *deck* out his little person in splendor and fine colors" (*Thackeray*). One **garnishes** something when one decks it out with something bright and attractive, as the final touch in preparation for use or service. "And when he cometh [to his house], he findeth it swept and *garnished*" (*Luke* xi. 25). The word is now used chiefly in cookery; as, to *garnish* a broiled fish with lemon slices and chopped parsley.

Ana. Enhance, heighten, *intensify.

Ant. Disfigure. — *Con.* *Deface, disfeature: mar, spoil, impair, *injure: *deform, distort, contort.

adroit. 1 *Dexterous, deft, feat, handy.

Ana. *Agile, nimble: expert, adept, skillful, skilled, *proficient: effortless, smooth, facile, *easy.

Ant. Maladroit. — *Con.* Clumsy, *awkward, inept.

2 *Clever, cunning, ingenious.

Ana. *Shrewd, astute, perspicacious: *intelligent, quick-witted, smart: artful, crafty (see SLY).

Ant. Stolid. — *Con.* *Impassive, apathetic, phlegmatic: *stupid, dull, dense.

adulation. Flattery, *compliment.

Ana. Praise, laud, extollation (see corresponding verbs at PRAISE): *applause, acclaim: fulsomeness, unctuousness (see corresponding adjectives at FULSOME).

Ant. Abuse. — *Con.* Obloquy, vituperation (see ABUSE): censure, condemnation, reprobation, criticism (see corresponding verbs at CRITICIZE).

adult, *adj.* *Mature, grown-up, matured, ripe, mellow, full-fledged.
Ana. Developed, ripened, aged (see MATURE, *v.*).
Ant. Juvenile: puerile. — *Con.* *Youthful, boyish, virgin, virginal, maiden: adolescent, pubescent (see corresponding nouns at YOUTH).

adulterant, *n.* *Admixture, alloy.

adulterate. **Adulterate, sophisticate, load, weight, doctor, deacon** agree in meaning to alter fraudulently, especially for profit. **Adulterate,** the usual and technical term, especially when used with reference to foodstuffs and drugs, implies either the admixture of ingredients of similar appearance to increase the bulk, or of a harmful substance as a preservative or as a restorer or improver of appearance; as, to *adulterate* maple sirup with beet sugar sirup. "Lime juice *adulterated* with five percent sulphuric acid, jellies with formaldehyde, peas with copper" (*V. Heiser*). In its extended use, *adulterate* always implies spuriousness or loss of purity; such implications come out strongly in *unadulterated,* which is the equivalent of *pure* and *sheer* in their hyperbolic senses; as, that book is *unadulterated* trash. **Sophisticate,** though now comparatively rare, is almost exactly identical in meaning with *adulterate,* but it is used chiefly of expensive liquors, oils, and the like. **Load** implies the admixture of something to add weight (as, to *load* sugar) or specifically, of a substance, such as barite, to a fabric to make it heavier (as, to *load* silk). **Weight** is used interchangeably with *load* in the specific sense. **Doctor** and **deacon** are purely colloquial terms which always imply tampering, sometimes by adulteration, but more often by alterations or falsifications which give an illusion of genuineness, of superior quality, or of great value; as, to *doctor* liquor; to *doctor* accounts; to *deacon* fruit (by placing the best specimens at the top of the container).
Ana. *Debase, vitiate, corrupt: pollute, defile, taint (see CONTAMINATE).
Ant. Refine (*wine, sugar, oil, etc.*). — *Con.* *Improve, better.

adultery. **Adultery, fornication, incest** designate forms of illicit sexual intercourse which are clearly distinguished in legal use, both civil and ecclesiastical. **Adultery** implies unfaithfulness to one's spouse, and therefore can be applied only to sexual intercourse on the part of a married man with a woman other than his wife, or of a married woman with a man other than her husband. **Fornication** designates sexual intercourse on the part of an unmarried person; thus, in commerce between a married and an unmarried person, the former is guilty of *adultery* and the latter of *fornication.* **Incest** designates sexual intercourse between persons so closely related that their marriage is prohibited by church or state, and usually by both.
Ana. Unfaithfulness, inconstancy, untrueness (see affirmative adjectives at FAITHFUL): infidelity, disloyalty (see affirmative nouns at FIDELITY).

adumbrate. *Suggest, shadow.
Ana. Symbolize, typify, emblematize (see corresponding nouns at SYMBOL): signify, denote, *mean.

adumbration. Shadow, umbra, penumbra, *shade, umbrage.
Ana. *Symbol, type, emblem: *sign, token, symptom, note: hint, suggestion, intimation (see corresponding verbs at SUGGEST).
Ant. Revelation. — *Con.* Disclosure, revealing, divulging, discovering (see corresponding verbs at REVEAL).

advance, *v.* **1 Advance, promote, forward, further.** All of these words by derivation mean to move or put ahead, but they come most closely into comparison in their transitive senses when they imply help in moving or putting ahead. **Advance** still retains its etymological sense, though its use is confined largely to certain idiomatic phrases; as, the army was *advancing* (moving ahead to its goal or, if a definite point of view is implied, approaching) at a rapid pace; he *advanced* a step (moved a step ahead or nearer); "a row of girls . . . each with slippered foot well *advanced* [put forward]" (*Deland*); the date of opening has been *advanced* (put ahead, or nearer in time, as opposed to *postponed*). In its richer transitive meaning, *advance* usually implies effective assistance, as in hastening a process (the warm rains greatly *advanced* the spring crops), as in bringing about a desired end (the pact should *advance* peace among nations), as in exalting or elevating a person, especially in rank or in power ("Ahasuerus . . . *advanced* him . . . above all the princes" —*Esther* iii. 1). **Promote** commonly stresses the assistance more than its effect. However, the implication of moving ahead is dominant when the word means to advance in grade or rank, especially in a predetermined order; thus, to *promote* a pupil is, provided there is no further qualification, to advance him to the next grade in school; to *promote* a member of a college faculty is, with the same proviso, to advance him to the next rank in his profession. When the dominant implication is assistance, *promote* may suggest open backing or support, especially when the subject names a person. "The objects for which a corporation is created are universally such as the government wishes to *promote*" (*Ch. Just. Marshall*). It may, especially when the subject names a person, his influence, or his acts, imply actual advance by encouraging or fostering. "Christian mystics, whose influence for good, both in *promoting* personal piety and in *advancing* the Kingdom of God upon earth" (*Inge*). It may, when said of a thing, such as a practice, a policy, a habit, imply subservience to an end that may not be intended. "The habit of regarding the language of poetry as something dissociated from personal emotion . . . was *promoted* by the writing of Greek and Latin verse in school" (*Babbitt*). In one or two collocations only, **forward** does not imply assistance; as, to *forward* a shipment by express; please *forward* all letters during my absence. In its more common sense, *forward* is often not clearly distinguishable from *advance,* except that it is seldom, if ever, used with reference to persons. "Marie de Médicis had *advanced* Marillac by marrying him to one of her maids of honor . . . yet . . . she only *forwarded* the marriage because she wanted to do the girl a favour" (*Belloc*). **Further,** less than any other word in this group, implies movement ahead and, perhaps more than any other, emphasizes the assistance given, especially in the removing of obstacles, either to a person in an undertaking or to the project he undertakes, the cause he espouses, or the like. "Her sole object . . . was to *further* him, not as an artist but as a popular success" (*Van W. Brooks*). "Bodies like the French Academy have such power for *promoting* it [genius], that the general *advance* of the human spirit is perhaps, on the whole, rather *furthered* than impeded by their existence" (*Arnold*).
Ana. *Help, aid, assist: hasten, accelerate, quicken, *speed: elevate, raise, *lift.
Ant. Retard: check. — *Con.* *Hinder, impede: *restrain, curb: *arrest: *delay, slow.

2 Advance, progress, both as intransitive verbs and as nouns, agree in meaning to move (or movement) forward in space, in time, or in approach to a material or ideal objective. In current good usage they are often employed interchangeably; however, there are instances in which one is preferable to the other. **Advance** only may be used when a concrete instance is signified; though one may say that at a given time science made no *advance* (or *progress*), one must say that there were no *advances* (not *progresses*) in science at that time. *Advance* is preferable to *progress* when the context implies, literally or figuratively, movement ahead such as that of an army marching to its objective, the distance traveled, or the rate of traveling. "There are some . . . who picture to themselves Religion as retreating . . . before the victorious *advance* of science" (*Inge*). "In the eighteenth century they [physicists] *advanced* a long way" (*Karl K. Darrow*). "It [the Constitution] does not forbid the cautious *advance*, step by step . . . [characteristic] of English legislation" (*Justice Holmes*). **Progress** usually carries, literally or figuratively, implications derived from earlier meanings of a process, a circuit, or a cycle, and so is preferable to *advance* when the movement forward involves these implications, as by suggesting a normal course, growth, or development; as, the trial is *progressing*. "Moon . . . begins . . . her rosy *progress*" (*Milton*). "[Summer] oft, delighted, stops to trace The *progress* of the spiky blade" (*Burns*). In its richest meaning the word does not lose these implications, but it carries additional connotations, largely as a result of its connection with theories of evolution. Sometimes, it stresses development through a series of steps or stages, each marking a definite change. "It would be . . . a dull world that developed without break of continuity; it would surely be a mad world that *progressed* by leaps alone" (*Lowes*). "The *progress* of an artist is a continual self-sacrifice, a continual extinction of personality" (*T. S. Eliot*). *Progress* is the preferable word when development with improvement is implied. "It [a certain trend in poetry] may prove . . . to be nothing more than a localized and temporary disturbance of the general *progress* of poetry" (*Day Lewis*).

Ana. Develop, *mature: *intensify, heighten.

Ant. Recede. — ***Con.*** Retreat, retrograde (see RECEDE): retire, withdraw (see GO).

3 *Adduce, allege, cite.

Ana. *Offer, present, proffer: propose (see corresponding noun at PROPOSAL): broach, *express, air.

advance, *n.* **1** Progress (see under ADVANCE, *v.*, 2).

Ana. *Development, evolution: improvement, betterment (see corresponding verbs at IMPROVE).

Ant. Recession, retrogression. — ***Con.*** Retrograding, retreating (see RECEDE).

2 *Overture, approach, tender, bid.

Ana. *Proposal, proposition: offer, proffer (see corresponding verbs at OFFER).

advanced. **1** Forward, precocious, *premature, untimely.

Ant. Backward. — ***Con.*** Retrogressive, retrograde, regressive (see BACKWARD).

2 Radical, *liberal, progressive, left.

Ana. Daring, temerarious, venturous, venturesome, *adventurous.

Ant. Conservative.

advancement. **Advancement, preferment, promotion, elevation** are here compared as designating the act of raising a person in grade, rank, or dignity, or the honor that comes to one who is so raised. **Advancement** is the general term of widest application; as, to lose all hope of *advancement*. **Preferment,** especially in older use, often comes close to *advancement*. "'Tis the curse of service, *Preferment* goes by letter and affection, And not by old gradation, where each second Stood heir to the first" (*Shak.*). As a rule, however, it implies choice, especially from a series of candidates or possibilities. "Who for *preferments* at a court would wait, Where every gudgeon's nibbling at the bait?" (*Otway*). It is now used principally of ecclesiastical and high civil appointments, especially in England. **Promotion,** usually but not invariably, implies gradation, or raising according to a fixed plan, often involving the passing of tests or the meeting of qualifications. It is the specific word in education to designate the end-of-the-term advance of pupils to a higher grade, or in any field where members of a force or staff are given positions of higher rank with increased remuneration. **Elevation** is applicable only when the advancement carries marked increase in honor or dignity; as, the prime minister's *elevation* to the peerage; the bishop's *elevation* to the cardinalate. "The many men of talent who owed their *elevation* to Wolsey" (*Froude*).

Ant. Degradation: reduction (*in rank or status*).

advantage. **1** **Advantage, handicap, allowance, odds, edge** agree in denoting a factor or set of factors in a competition or rivalry giving one person or side a position of superiority to the other. **Advantage** is the general term, and implies superiority of any kind. "The adult, with trained powers, has an immense *advantage* over the child in the acquisition of information" (*C. W. Eliot*). A **handicap** is an artificial advantage assigned by an umpire to an inferior competitor. Thus, in golf, the *handicap* assigned a player is often the difference between the average of a certain number of his best scores and par for the course; for instance, if the player's best-score average is 78 and par is 75, the *handicap* is 3, and in a *handicap* match the player deducts three strokes from his total score. But *handicap* often (virtually always in extended use) means the exact opposite: an artificial disadvantage imposed on a superior competitor. An **allowance** is an advantageous handicap stated as a deduction of some sort. Thus in horse racing an *allowance* is a deduction from the weight that the rules require a horse to carry, granted to a horse considered to be at a disadvantage. **Odds** usually implies a material advantage, as in strength, numbers, or resources. It is often used of such an advantage possessed by the opposite side. "The overwhelming *odds* it [the double-barrel gun] affords the sportsman over bird and animal" (*Jefferies*). "The peculiarly British quality . . . of sticking out against *odds*" (*Contemp. Rev.*). *Advantage* is often stated as a difference, *odds* as a ratio; as, one boxer has an *advantage* of ten pounds in weight; one army has *odds* of two to one over the other. *Odds* may also denote an equalizing concession made to an inferior competitor; it then differs from *handicap* and *allowance* in that the concession is made by the superior competitor, and not assigned by a third party. "Each side feels that it cannot allow any *odds* to the other" (*Bryce*). **Edge** is a corruption of the card term *age* (the right belonging to the player to the left of the dealer to have the last say); but the idea of a last say is not a necessary nor even a common implication in the extended sense of *edge*, which is little more than a slang equivalent of *advantage* or *odds*. "Here we have the *edge* on our rivals, not only because of our superior location, but also because we are reputedly reckless about reducing prices" (*Publishers' Weekly*).

Ana. Pre-eminence, superlativeness (see corresponding adjectives at SUPREME): *supremacy, ascendancy.

Ant. Disadvantage: handicap (*in extended sense*). — ***Con.*** *Obstacle, obstruction, impediment, bar.

2 *Use, service, account, profit, avail.

Ana. Improvement, betterment (see corresponding verbs at IMPROVE): enhancement, heightening (see corresponding verbs at INTENSIFY): benefit (see corresponding verb at BENEFIT).

Ant. Detriment. — *Con.* Harm, hurt, damage, *injury.
advantageous. *Beneficial, profitable.
Ana. *Expedient, advisable: useful, utilitarian (see corresponding nouns at USE).
Ant. Disadvantageous. — *Con.* Detrimental, deleterious (see PERNICIOUS): harmful, hurtful, injurious (see corresponding nouns at INJURY).
advenient. *Adventitious, supervenient, adventive.
Ana. Acquired (see GET): external, outside (see OUTER).
Ant. Constitutional.
advent. *Arrival.
Ana. Coming, arriving (see COME): approaching, nearing (see APPROACH, *v.*): appearing, emerging (see APPEAR).
Ant. Leaving, passing.
adventitious. 1 *Accidental, incidental, fortuitous, casual, contingent.
Ana. Acquired (see GET): accessory, subservient (see AUXILIARY).
Ant. Inherent. — *Con.* Constitutional, essential, intrinsic, ingrained (see INHERENT): *innate, inborn, inbred.
2 Adventitious, adventive, advenient, supervenient agree in meaning added from without or occurring as a result of external causes. That is **adventitious** which does not belong to a thing naturally, normally, or historically. "It is important that we distinguish between borrowed, *adventitious* energy in verse, and its natural energy" (*Day Lewis*). In the sciences, *adventitious* and **adventive** sometimes suggest abnormality; thus, an *adventitious* root is one arising at any point of the stem other than a normal point of origin; an *adventive* crater is one on the flanks of a volcanic cone. Both words are used, especially in botany, for sporadic growths of something neither native nor naturalized; as, an *adventive* weed. *Advenient* and *supervenient* have acquired new importance through their use in very modern philosophy and psychology. That is **advenient** to a thing (especially to the mind) which comes to it as the result purely of external causes. The word is used especially to distinguish that element in a sense impression or an apprehension which is wholly external, from that which is the result of the constitution of the sense organ or the mind. "Admittedly *advenient* to us is electro-magnetic influence; but color is referred to the thing by projicience" (*Lloyd Morgan*). That is **supervenient** which occurs unexpectedly or without known cause. In modern philosophical (as distinguished from biological) theories of evolution it implies emergence of that which is unpredictable and completely novel. "Later in evolutionary sequence life emerges . . . with *supervenient* vital relations hitherto not in being" (*Lloyd Morgan*).
Ana. *Abnormal, aberrant, atypic: unnatural, anomalous, *irregular: derived, stemmed (see SPRING, *v.*).
Ant. Natural, normal.
adventive. Advenient, *adventitious, supervenient.
Ana. & *Ant.* See those at ADVENTITIOUS, 2.
adventure. Adventure, enterprise, emprise (*or* **emprize**), **quest** come into comparison mainly when they denote an undertaking, an exploit, or an experience involving hazards and requiring boldness. **Adventure** so stresses the excitement or thrills associated with the encountering of risks or hardships that the word is applicable either to the event or to its emotional effect; as, to seek *adventures* (the experiences) for *adventure's* (the emotional effect's) sake. In modern usage, *adventure* tends to emphasize the pleasurable excitement induced by newness and strangeness, as much as that induced by perils or difficulties. "The thirst for *adventure* . . . a war, a crusade, a gold mine, a new country, speak to the imagination and offer . . . play to the confined powers" (*Emerson*). "Why fear death? Death is only a beautiful *adventure*" (*C. Frohman*). **Enterprise,** in its richer as well as in its thinner sense, is always applied to an undertaking (rather than an experience) or to the spirit required for such an undertaking. As distinguished from *adventure,* it implies arduousness in the undertaking, and initiative, resourcefulness, and sustained energy in the one who carries it through. "Ripe for exploits and mighty *enterprises*" (*Shak.*). "Fresh news is got only by *enterprise* and expense" (*Justice Holmes*). "The nurse of manly sentiment and heroic *enterprise* is gone" (*Burke*). **Emprise** and **quest** are archaic words now used only in poetry or elevated prose. Both suggest days of chivalry and romantic adventure. *Emprise* distinctively connotes deeds of gallantry and daring. "What course were best to take in this hot bold *emprize*" (*Spenser*). *Quest* implies a search or pursuit, always of that which is elusive, often of that which is unattainable; as, the *quest* of the Holy Grail. Only *emprise,* however, is used of the spirit as well as the undertaking. "I love thy courage yet, and bold *emprise*" (*Milton*).
Ana. Exploit, *feat, achievement: hazard, peril, risk (see DANGER).
adventurous. Adventurous, venturous, venturesome, daring, daredevil, rash, reckless, temerarious, foolhardy denote in common courting danger, or exposing oneself to danger in a greater degree than is required for courage. One is **adventurous** who is inclined to adventure; the word may or may not imply indiscretion or imprudence in incurring risk or hazard. "A mind active, ambitious, and *adventurous* . . . always aspiring" (*Johnson*). "*Adventurous* boys . . . climbed, shouting and laughing, over the rafters" (*S. Anderson*). One is **venturous** who is inclined to take chances; **venturesome** (often interchangeable with *venturous*) frequently implies an excessive tendency in that direction. "Every corner Among these rocks, and every hollow place That *venturous* foot could reach" (*Wordsworth*). "In 1919 Alcock and Brown undertook the first and highly *venturesome* crossing of the Atlantic by air" (*Manchester Guardian*). **Daring** heightens the implication of fearlessness. "A *daring* pilot in extremity, pleased with the danger, when the waves went high" (*Dryden*). **Daredevil** implies ostentation in daring and is often specifically applied to stunts performed for hire as a public spectacle or to their performers; as, a *daredevil* act, acrobat, or aviator. **Rash** implies imprudent hastiness or boldness in word or action; **reckless,** utter heedlessness or carelessness of consequences. "We must detain him . . . . If we do not I am convinced Austin will do something *rash* that he will for ever repent" (*Meredith*). "A *recklessness* which made her almost indifferent whether she sank or swam" (*Trollope*). **Temerarious** (the adjective is much rarer than its noun *temerity*) implies such recklessness as induces one to attempt something that stands but slight chance of success. "The King was one of the first that entred [the breach], choosing rather to be thought *temerarious* than timorous" (*Speed*). One is **foolhardy** who is foolishly daring or reckless. "If any yet be so *foolhardy* to expose themselves to vain jeopardy" (*Bp. Butler*).
Ana. Audacious, bold, intrepid, doughty (see BRAVE): aspiring, panting (see AIM, *v.*): *ambitious, emulous.
Ant. Unadventurous: cautious.
adversary. *Opponent, antagonist.
Ana. Assailant, attacker, assaulter (see corresponding verbs at ATTACK): *enemy, foe: competitor, rival (see corresponding verbs at RIVAL).
Ant. Ally. — *Con.* Colleague, *partner: supporter, champion, backer, upholder (see under SUPPORT, *v.*).

adverse. **1** **Adverse, antagonistic, counter, counteractive** agree in meaning so opposed as to cause interference, often harmful or fatal interference. All four may be applied to one thing that comes into conflict with another; as, an *adverse* policy; an *antagonistic* associate; a *counter* attack; a *counteractive* agency. Only *antagonistic, counter,* and, occasionally, *counteractive* are used to express mutual or reciprocal opposition; as, *antagonistic* principles; *counter* currents; *counteractive* poisons. Thus, one says that the ship was delayed by *adverse* winds (that is, by one head wind after another) or that the trade winds are *counter* winds (that is, winds coming from opposite points of the compass). Despite their common ground of meaning, each of these four words has distinct implications which limit its applicability and greatly increase its expressiveness. **Adverse** conveys so strongly the idea of unfavorable or unpropitious opposition that it often means harmful or fatal; as, *adverse* criticism; *adverse* fortune; a spirit *adverse* to the existence of democracy. **Antagonistic** commonly, but not invariably, implies hostility and also, when mutual opposition is suggested, incompatibility or even irreconcilability; as, neighboring races are often *antagonistic;* some sociologists believe that the welfare of the individual and the welfare of society are *antagonistic* aims. In its technical use, *antagonistic* often connotes the play of opposing things or forces that makes them nullify or neutralize each other; as, *antagonistic* reflexes. **Counter,** which usually denotes acting, moving, or proceeding from the opposite side (or sides) does not necessarily connote hostility, but it does imply inevitable contact, with either resulting conflict or tension; as, whirlpools are usually caused by *counter* currents in a stream; the *counter* influences of authority and freedom in shaping the character of youth. **Counteractive,** on the other hand, invariably implies the destruction or nullification of the thing or things opposed; as, prescribing physicians must know the *counteractive* effects of certain medicines on others; in the training of delinquents, a bad influence is dealt with by the introduction of a *counteractive* good influence.

Ana. Harmful, hurtful, injurious (see corresponding nouns at INJURY): hindering, impeding, obstructing (see corresponding verbs at HINDER): detrimental, deleterious, *pernicious: fatal, *deadly.

Ant. Propitious. — ***Con.*** Auspicious, *favorable, benign: *beneficial, advantageous.

2 **Adverse, averse** are actually contrasted rather than synonymous terms, though they are occasionally (now rarely) used as though similar in meaning. Etymologically, *adverse* means "turned to," and *averse* "turned from." Consequently, in botany they are used to distinguish contrasted types of leaves. In current literary use, **adverse** implies opposition that interferes and is applied to the thing that stands in the way of one's progress or success; as, the leader would tolerate no *adverse* opinions among his followers. **Averse** implies repugnance in the person opposed to a thing, rather than a quality in the thing which is opposed; as, the leader is *averse* to (British, *averse from*) all independence of opinion among his followers. However, they are sometimes used as synonyms by good writers with only this distinction, that *adverse* is chiefly referred to opinion or intention and *averse* to feeling and inclination. "I . . . hope that our periodical judges will not be very *adverse* to me, and that perhaps they may even favour me" (*Cowper*). "The writer of critical studies . . . has to mediate between the author whom he loves and the public, who are certainly indifferent and frequently *averse*" (*Stevenson*).

adversity. *Misfortune, mischance.

Ana. *Trial, tribulation, affliction: *distress, misery, suffering: *poverty, privation, indigence, destitution.

Ant. Prosperity. — ***Con.*** Felicity, *happiness, bliss: ease, comfort (see REST): wealth, affluence, opulence, richness (see corresponding adjectives at RICH).

advert. **1** **Advert, revert** are sometimes confused because of a similar basic meaning when they are used in reference to discourse or contemplation. **Advert** denotes to turn from the point, topic, or incident under consideration in order to take up another. In modern usage, it sometimes suggests an unconscious or an illogical break in the chain of thought, but in highly discriminating use, it still retains the verb's primary implication of heeding or taking notice. "We are but too apt to consider things in the state in which we find them, without sufficiently *adverting* to the causes by which they have been produced" (*Burke*). "The distinction . . . will be rendered more apparent by *adverting* to that provision in the second section . . . of the constitution" (*Ch. Just. Marshall*). **Revert** adds to *advert* the implication of return (either consciously or unconsciously) to a point or topic already discussed or previously in one's mind. "He now drops this idea, and *reverts* to his reasoning on death" (*Goldsmith*).

2 *Refer, allude.

Ana. Remark, notice, note, observe (see SEE).

Con. Ignore, disregard, overlook, *neglect.

advertise. **1** Notify, *inform, apprise, advise, acquaint.

Ana. *Warn, forewarn, caution: *reveal, disclose, divulge, tell.

2 Publish, announce, proclaim, broadcast, promulgate, *declare.

Ana. Report, recount, *relate: *communicate, impart.

Con. *Suppress, repress: conceal, *hide, bury.

advertisement. Publication, announcement, broadcasting, proclamation, promulgation, declaration. See under DECLARE.

Ana. *Publicity, ballyhoo, promotion, propaganda.

advice. **1** **Advice, counsel** and their corresponding verbs **advise, counsel,** agree in denoting recommendation (or to make a recommendation) as to a decision or a course of conduct. **Advice** and **advise** imply real or pretended knowledge or experience, often professional or technical, on the part of the one who advises, and may apply to any of the affairs of life; as, *advice* (or, to *advise*) regarding the choice of books, the conduct of a business, the care of poultry; legal or medical *advice*. **Counsel** often stresses the fruit of wisdom or deliberation, and presupposes weightier occasions than *advice*, or more authority or a closer personal relationship in the one who counsels; as, "I do in friendship *counsel* you To leave this place" (*Shak.*); to seek *counsel* in an emergency, in affairs of state. The noun sometimes suggests instruction or advice of a lofty or ideal character; as, the Christian *counsel* of perfection.

Ana. Admonition (see corresponding verb at REPROVE): warning, forewarning, cautioning (see WARN): instruction, teaching (see corresponding verbs at TEACH).

2 Intelligence, *news, tidings.

advisable. *Expedient, politic.

Ana. Prudent, *wise, sensible: *beneficial, advantageous, profitable: practical, *practicable.

Ant. Inadvisable.

advise. **1** Counsel (see under ADVICE, 1).

Ana. Admonish (see REPROVE): *warn, forewarn, caution: *induce, persuade.

Con. Consult, *confer, advise.

2 Consult, *confer, commune, parley, treat, negotiate.

Ana. *Discuss, debate, argue: converse, talk (over) (see SPEAK): deliberate (see THINK).

Con. Counsel (see under ADVISE, 1).
3 Notify, *inform, apprise, acquaint, advertise.
Ana. Tell, disclose, *reveal: *communicate (with), impart (to).

advised. *Deliberate, considered, premeditated, designed, studied.

advocate, *n.* **1** *Lawyer, counselor, barrister, counsel, procurator, proctor, attorney, solicitor.
2 Supporter, champion, upholder, backer. See under SUPPORT, *v.*
Ana. Defender, vindicator, justifier (see corresponding verbs at MAINTAIN): espouser (see corresponding verb at ADOPT): *sponsor, backer: promoter (see corresponding verb at ADVANCE).
Con. *Opponent, antagonist, adversary: assailant, attacker (see corresponding verbs at ATTACK): impugner, traverser (see corresponding verbs at DENY).

advocate, *v.* *Support, uphold, champion, back.
Ana. Defend, justify, vindicate, *maintain: espouse (see ADOPT): promote, forward, *advance.
Ant. Impugn. — *Con.* Assail, *attack: combat, *oppose.

aeon *or* **eon.** Age, era, epoch, *period.

aeonian *or* **eonian.** *Secular, centuried, agelong, diuturnal.
Ana. Eternal, illimitable (see INFINITE): *everlasting, endless: perpetual, perdurable, *lasting.

aerate. Aerate, ventilate, oxygenate, carbonate. Aerate is the general term and interchangeable in certain phrases with any of the others; the last three are specific terms which are not (except in one instance) interchangeable with each other. **Aerate** means to supply or impregnate with air or to expose to the action of air. It frequently implies a mechanical process; as, to *aerate* soil by plowing; to *aerate* water from a reservoir by spraying it into the air so as to remove a flat taste; to *aerate* sewage by agitation in fresh air so that bacterial action will decompose it. It sometimes, however, implies a natural process; as, when through fresh air that is inhaled, the blood is *aerated* in the lungs. **Ventilate** is the term commonly used when the introduction of air, especially in large quantities, with the object of purifying, freshening, or cooling, is implied; as, to *ventilate* a room by opening windows or by mechanical means; to *ventilate* an engine by means of holes in its covering. It may be used interchangeably with *aerate* when applied to the blood, but *aerate* suggests rather the exposure to air and *ventilate* the resulting purification. More exact than either for this process is **oxygenate,** since it is the oxygen in the air that is required by the blood. Technically, *aerate* and **carbonate** are not synonyms, for the latter means to impregnate with a gas or carbon dioxide. *Aerate* (or especially *aerated*) is, however, used in certain designations, such as *aerated* water or *aerated* bread, where *carbonated* would correctly describe the process. Carbon dioxide was once called "fixed air," and in appearance water and bread impregnated with it suggest the presence of air. As applied to water, however, *aerated* is distinguishable from *carbonated,* the former being applied almost exclusively to artificially charged waters, the latter being used also of those naturally impregnated with carbon dioxide (as, *carbonated* springs).

aerial *or* **aërial,** *adj.* *Airy, ethereal.
Ana. Immaterial, incorporeal (see MATERIAL): impalpable, *imperceptible, imponderable: *subtle, subtile.

aerial *or* **aërial,** *n.* *Antenna.

aeronautics *or* **aëronautics. Aeronautics** (*or* **aëronautics), aviation, avigation** have to do with the operation of aircraft: *aeronautics* and *avigation* with the operation of any kind of aircraft, *aviation* with the operation of heavier-than-air aircraft. **Aeronautics** is primarily a science (as, an *aeronautical* engineer; well versed in *aeronautics*), **aviation** an art or practice (as, a man of long experience in *aviation*). **Avigation,** a more recent term coined on the analogy of *navigation,* is the science or art of directing aircraft from point to point through determination of position, course, etc., by methods similar to those of navigation, as by use of the principles of astronomy and geometry, recognition of landmarks, etc.

aerostat *or* **aërostat. Aerostat** (*or* **aërostat), balloon, airship, dirigible, zeppelin, blimp** denote a lighter-than-air aircraft. An **aerostat** is any such craft. A **balloon** is an aerostat, usually spherical, without means of propulsion (other than air currents) and without means of steering. **Airship** and **dirigible** are in careful use interchangeable terms for an elongated motor-propelled aerostat, rigid, semirigid, or nonrigid, having steering apparatus. *Dirigible,* however, is the more definite term, *airship* being sometimes loosely used for any kind of aircraft. **Zeppelin,** originally a name for any of the large rigid dirigibles built by Count von Zeppelin and, later, by the Luftschiffbau-Zeppelin, is now often applied in English to any such dirigible of German make, sometimes to any such dirigible, wherever made. A **blimp** is a small nonrigid dirigible.

aesthete *or* **esthete. Aesthete** (*or* **esthete), dilettante, virtuoso, connoisseur** are comparable because all designate a person conspicuous for his enjoyment and appreciation of the beautiful, the exquisite, or the choice. **Aesthete** implies highly developed sensibilities, with acute delight in beauty of color, line, sound, texture, and the like, and violent distaste for the ugly, shapeless, and discordant. "No woman could walk down the street without risk of having her hat torn off . . . by some *aesthete* who happened to think it unbecoming" (*Shaw*). "That mystical synthetic sense, of which the modern *aesthete* dreams,—the sense that 'sees, hears, tastes, smells, touches, all in one' " (*Babbitt*). Because *aesthete* was originally applied to one of a small group of artists and writers around 1880 who won notoriety on account of their affectations, as in dress, and their emphasis upon decorative beauty, the term often carries derogatory connotations, such as absurdity, extravagance, decadence, namby-pambiness, and the like. "He [Maecenas] had all the foibles of the *aesthete*" (*Buchan*). **Dilettante** originally and still stresses the attitude of the lover of art as distinguished from that of the creative artist. Through its application to amateurs who were neither thoroughly familiar with the technique of their particular form of art nor seriously seeking for mastery, it acquired connotations of desultoriness, dabbling, and superficiality. At present, though still often used in an uncomplimentary sense (as, he is a mere *dilettante*), there is a strong tendency among good writers to stress its original implication, and to apply it to one who pursues an art or studies it merely for his own delight. "He would always be by nature a contemplative and a *dilettante;* but he had had high things to contemplate, great things to delight in" (*E. Wharton*). "A generalization with which I find myself (with all the diffidence of an unlearned *dilettante*) disagreeing" (*A. Huxley*). **Virtuoso,** a term now chiefly in historical use in the sense in which it is here considered, was applied originally (around 1700) to a collector of interesting things such as old coins, butterflies, curios, and the like. Later, it was limited to a collector of articles of virtu, and especially of beautiful antiques. It has also acquired various depreciatory connotations such as faddishness, trifling, and the like, which the word rarely carries in modern historical use. "In the retrospect we can see that some of these *virtuosi* were on the way to become serious antiquaries" (*Babbitt*). **Connoisseur,** like *dilettante,* implies high appreciation of that which is beautiful in art; unlike it, it implies profound knowledge and a trained taste. Because of the latter implication, *connoisseur* is applied not only to one who knows a work of art when he sees it but also to one who recognizes superiority in foods, wines, and the like. Therefore the word often comes close to *epicure* in its meaning. Like *virtuoso,* which it has practically supplanted, it is also applied to collectors of beautiful things. "Supposing also that the material of his Apologia was . . . defunct . . . who but a few discerning *connoisseurs* of style would ever read that book now or a century hence?" (*T. S. Eliot*). "He has found time to make himself a *connoisseur* of porcelains, one of the most esoteric of collector's hobbies" (*V. Heiser*).

aesthetic *or* **esthetic.** *Artistic.

Ant. Unaesthetic *or* unesthetic.

afeard *or* **afeared.** *Afraid, aghast.

Ana., Ant., Con. See those at AFRAID, 1.

affable. *Gracious, cordial, genial, sociable.

Ana. Courteous, polite (see CIVIL): open, candid, *frank: *amiable, obliging, complaisant: *talkative, loquacious: *suave, urbane.

Ant. Reserved. — *Con.* Uncommunicative, taciturn, reticent, *silent: curt, brusque (see BLUFF): surly, glum, crabbed (see SULLEN).

affair. 1 **Affair, business, concern, matter, thing** come into comparison only when they are little more than vague or general terms meaning something done or dealt with, or to be done or dealt with. Some (rarely all) are used interchangeably in certain similar collocations even by good writers; as, it is his own *affair, business, concern;* public and private *affairs, concerns, matters, business;* it is a sorry *affair, business, matter, thing; affairs, matters, things* are in good condition. However, a degree of precision is possible, for each word carries distinctive implications which are not always obscured. **Affair** suggests action or performance; it often implies a process, an operation, a proceeding, an undertaking, a transaction. "Seeing a book through the press is a laborious and time-wasting *affair*" (*T. H. Huxley*). In the plural it often denotes transactions of great importance, such as those involved in the management of finances or in the carrying on of diplomatic negotiations; as, men of *affairs.* "He had married a rich woman and administered her *affairs.* He was not supposed . . . to have any *affairs* of his own" (*M. Austin*). **Business,** as here compared, usually stresses duty or office; sometimes it suggests an imposed task. "Because a Thing is every Body's *Business,* it is no Body's *Business*" (*Steele*). "The flight of his imagination is very swift: the following of it often a breathless *business*" (*Day Lewis*). **Concern** suggests personal or direct relationship: it often implies an important bearing on one's welfare, success, or the like; thus, it is not my *concern* (that is, it has no bearing on my interests, welfare, etc.). "The simplest way out of the difficulty was to do nothing and dismiss the matter as no *concern* of theirs" (*Conrad*). Sometimes, *concern* is preferred to *affair* when that which requires attention involves a degree of anxiety or solicitude; as, the *concerns* of state. **Matter** usually is more objective as well as more vague than the preceding words. It generally refers to something that is merely an object of consideration or that is to be dealt with; as, he will attend to these *matters* very soon; this is still a *matter* of dispute. "Never insist without carrying the *matter* through" (*B. Russell*). " 'They order,' said I, 'this *matter* better in France' " (*Sterne*). **Thing** is even more indefinite than *matter* and is often intentionally used when there is a desire to be vague or inexplicit; as, he promised that *things* would be better in the future; first *things* should come first; *things* political. "More *things* are wrought by prayer Than this world dreams of" (*Tennyson*). "These *things* are managed so well in France" (*Harte*).

2 Affaire, *amour, intrigue, liaison.

affaire. Affair, *amour, intrigue, liaison.

affect.[1] Simulate, *assume, pretend, feign, counterfeit, sham.

Ana. Posture, attitudinize, pose (see under POSTURE, *n.*).

affect.[2] 1 **Affect, influence, touch, impress, strike, sway** are more or less closely synonymous when they mean to produce or to have an effect upon a person or upon a thing capable of a reaction. **Affect** always presupposes a stimulus powerful enough to evoke a response or elicit a reaction. "Our ear-drums are *affected* by ten octaves, at most, out of the endless range of sounds" (*Jeans*). "Even changes of season *affect* the townsman very little" (*A. Huxley*). Very often, in addition, *affect* implies a definite alteration or modification. " 'I am afraid, Mr. Darcy . . . . that this adventure has rather *affected* your admiration of her fine eyes' " (*Austen*). When the object of the verb is a person, an intellectual or emotional effect is usually implied; as, such poetry *affects* one as trite and meaningless; the sight *affected* her to tears; he was in no way *affected* by their misery. **Influence** always presupposes an agent or agency that moves a person or thing in some way or to some degree from his or its course, or effects changes in his or its nature, character, or behavior; as, the judge was never *influenced* in his decisions by his sympathies or prejudices; the body *influences* the mind and the mind the body. "The Society of Friends had been *influenced* by Quietism, and adversely *affected* by the paralysing rationalism of the reigns of the first two Georges" (*Inge*). Sometimes, the implication of inducing, or inciting, or persuading, or even bribing, is strong. "Monomaniacs, having first persuaded themselves, contrive to *influence* their neighbors" (*Meredith*). **Touch,** as here compared, frequently equals *affect,* but it often carries a more vivid suggestion of close contact or of the force of an impact, and therefore variously connotes stirring, arousing, harming, and the like. "He was for the first time powerfully *touched* by the presence of a woman" (*S. Anderson*). "Did . . . [ancient Greek religion] *touch* the conscience as well as the imagination and intellect?" (*G. L. Dickinson*). "I do not wish to do anything which may *touch* your credit" (*Hardy*). *Touch,* most often, but *impress* and *strike* always, imply a mental or emotional effect. **Impress** usually stresses the depth and the lastingness of the effect, for that which impresses is commonly that which is remembered or remarked or is worth remembering or remarking; as, only one of the speeches that evening *impressed* him. "The men he wanted to *impress* were only amused" (*S. Anderson*). **Strike** is often felt to be more colloquial than *impress* and less rich in its suggestions; as, the sight *struck* him speechless with awe (or *impressed* him); a hat that *struck* her fancy. However, *strike* connotes suddenness or sharpness of response rather than depth of impression; it may even carry a hint of a swift passing; as, the remark *struck* him as extremely acute. "Such sweet neglect more taketh me Than all the adulteries of art: They *strike* mine eyes, but not my heart" (*B. Jonson*). **Sway** (as here compared: see also SWING), which basically means to influence, differs from the latter word in always implying both the pressure or control of some force that is either not resisted or is in itself irresistible, and resulting change or fluctuation in the character, the opinions, etc., of the person or persons concerned; as, "the notion . . . of capricious deities, *swayed* by human passions and desires, was incompatible

with the idea of fixed law" (*G. L. Dickinson*); "Other conditions than those of classroom have *swayed* him [the pupil] for good or evil" (*H. Suzzallo*); "he is *swayed* by fashion, by suggestion, by transient moods" (*Mencken*).
Ana. *Move, actuate, drive, impel: pierce, penetrate (see ENTER): *thrill, electrify.
2 *Concern.
3 Affect, effect are often a source of difficulty because both verbs imply the production of an effect and take as their corresponding noun the same word, *effect*. **Affect,** the verb (see AFFECT, 1) distinctively implies the action or operation of an agency rather than of an agent: it, therefore, means to influence; as, moisture *affects* steel; high prices *affect* our pocketbooks; the climate has *affected* his health; he [that is, his personality] *affects* me unpleasantly. **Effect,** the verb (see PERFORM), implies the achievement of an end in view, and therefore requires as its subject in the active voice an intelligent agent or the means he uses to attain his end: it therefore means to bring about; as, the prisoners *effected* their escape; the new system of accounting will *effect* a reduction in costs. Since the noun *effect* may be applied to any result whether brought about unconsciously or consciously, it serves equally well whether it names that which results from the influence of one thing upon another or from directed effort.

affectation. *Pose, air, mannerism.
Ana. *Pretense, pretension: pretentiousness, ostentation, pompousness (see corresponding adjectives at SHOWY).
Ant. Artlessness. — ***Con.*** Naturalness, simplicity, ingenuousness, naïveté, unsophistication (see corresponding adjectives at NATURAL).

affecting, *adj.* Touching, *moving, pathetic, poignant, impressive.
Ana. Stirring, rousing, rallying (see STIR, *v.*): distressing, troubling (see TROUBLE, *v.*): *pitiful, piteous, pitiable.

affection.[1] **1** *Feeling, emotion, passion, sentiment.
Ana. Propensity, *leaning, penchant: *predilection, bias: inclination, disposition (see corresponding verbs at INCLINE).
Ant. Antipathy. — ***Con.*** Aversion (see ANTIPATHY): *hate, hatred.
2 Love, *attachment.
Ana. Devotion, piety, *fidelity: liking, doting on, enjoying (see LIKE, *v.*): tenderness, warmth, sympathy (see corresponding adjectives at TENDER).
Ant. Coldness. — ***Con.*** Coolness, frigidity (see corresponding adjectives at COLD): hate, detestation, hatred, abhorrence (see under HATE, *v.*).

affection.[2] *Disease, malady, complaint, distemper, ailment.
Ana. Attack, access, paroxysm (see FIT): sickness, illness (see corresponding adjectives at SICK): disorder, derangement (see corresponding verbs at DISORDER).

affectionate. *Loving, devoted, fond, doting.
Ana. Ardent, fervent, passionate (see IMPASSIONED): *tender, sympathetic, warm.
Ant. Cold: undemonstrative. — ***Con.*** Apathetic, *impassive, stolid.

affiance, *n.* *Engagement, betrothal, espousal, sponsalia.

affidavit. Deposition, testimony, *evidence.

affiliated. Allied, *related, kindred, cognate.
Ana. Dependent, succursal, *subordinate.
Ant. Unaffiliated. — ***Con.*** Independent, *free, autonomous.

affinity. **1** *Kinship, consanguinity, cognation, agnation, enation.
Ana. Relation *or* relationship, connection (see corresponding verbs at JOIN).
2 *Attraction, sympathy.
Ant. Diffinity. — ***Con.*** Repugnance, repellency *or* repulsion, abhorrence (see corresponding adjectives at REPUGNANT): *antipathy, aversion.
3 Resemblance, *likeness, similarity, similitude, analogy.
Ana. Agreement, conformity, correspondence, accord (see corresponding verbs at AGREE).

affirm. **1** Aver, avow, protest, avouch, declare, *assert, warrant, predicate.
Ana. Asseverate, *swear, depose: attest, *certify, vouch for, witness: state (see RELATE).
Ant. Deny. — ***Con.*** Contradict, negative, traverse, gainsay (see DENY): dispute, debate (see DISCUSS).
2 *Swear, asseverate, depose, depone, testify.

affirmative. **Affirmative, positive** cause difficulties in their extended use, since each term has *negative* for its opposite and since both words may qualify identical or similar nouns. The distinctions are not clearly fixed, but tendencies in good usage may be noted. In general, **affirmative** implies denial as its opposite, and **positive,** negation, or the absence of truth, reality, or actuality. That which is not *affirmative* may be destructive; that which is not *positive* may be null or nugatory. Hence, an *affirmative* philosophy either affirms accepted principles or establishes new ones, and so is opposed to *negative* philosophies such as skepticism and nihilism. A *positive* philosophy (this often equals *positivism*) deduces its principles from that which is evident to the senses or is from the commonsense point of view regarded as real and factual. Metaphysics is from the positivist's point of view a *negative* philosophy. An investigation has an *affirmative* result when it confirms the hypothesis of the investigator; it has a *positive* result if something definite is discovered, whether the result proves or disproves the hypothesis. A person may be said to exercise an *affirmative* influence when he strengthens or improves that which exists or develops something better to take its place; he may be said to exert a *positive* influence when he affects others in definite, concrete ways. A defeatist may exert a very *positive* influence which cannot be described as *affirmative;* an optimist's attitude is *affirmative,* but it often fails to exert a *positive* influence.
Ana. *Effective, effectual, efficacious.
Ant. Negative. — ***Con.*** Destroying, demolishing (see DESTROY): abolishing, annihilating, extinguishing (see ABOLISH).

affix, *v.* *Fasten, attach, fix.
Ana. Append, *add, subjoin, annex: *stick, adhere: glue, *cement.
Ant. Detach. — ***Con.*** Disengage (see DETACH): *remove, withdraw.

afflatus. *Inspiration, enthusiasm, fury, furor, frenzy.

afflict. **Afflict, try, torment, torture, rack, grill** agree in meaning to inflict upon a person something which he finds hard to bear. Anything or anyone that causes pain, disability, suffering, acute annoyance, irritation, or embarrassment, may be said to **afflict** a person; as, he is *afflicted* with heart disease; blindness *afflicts* many aged persons; she is *afflicted* with shyness. "O, how this discord doth *afflict* my soul" (*Shak.*). "He who *afflicts* me knows what I can bear" (*Wordsworth*). Any affliction or any person or thing that imposes a strain upon one's physical or spiritual powers of endurance or tests one's stamina or self-control may be said to **try** a person, his body, his soul, his character, or the like; as, a *trying* situation; his *trying* temper. "The great heat of the sun and the heat of hard labour . . . *try* the body and weaken the digestion" (*R. Jefferies*). Any affliction or any person or thing that persecutes and causes continued or repeated acute suffering or annoyance may be said to **torment** one; as, recurrent stomach pains *torment* him; he is *tormented* by his suspicions; bullies *torment* smaller boys; the horses are *tormented* by flies. "I wish you would not talk like this, papa. You are only *tormenting* me, and *tormenting* yourself" (*Conrad*). Any affliction or any person or thing that severely torments one physically or mentally and causes pain or suffering under which one writhes may be said to **torture** one; as, to *torture* prisoners of war. "An idea of what a pulsating sciatica can do in the way of *torturing* its victim" (*Bennett*). "The unseen grief That swells with silence in the *tortured* soul" (*Shak.*). Any person or, especially, any thing (often a painful emotion or disease) that pulls or seems to pull one this way and that beyond endurance and in a manner suggestive of the excruciating straining and wrenching of the body on the rack, an ancient instrument of torture, may be said to **rack** a person; as, *racked* with pain; he is *racked* by doubts of his friend's loyalty; to be *racked* by demands from every quarter; "Vaunting aloud, but *racked* with deep despair" (*Milton*); "How on earth can you *rack* and harry . . . a man for his losings, when you are fond of his wife, and live in the same station with him?" (*Kipling*). Any thing (especially intense heat) or any person (especially a severe cross-examiner) that causes one to suffer tortures suggestive of being broiled over a fire may be said to **grill** one; as, a *grilling* hot day; the sun *grills* one today; every witness for the defense left the stand exhausted after having been *grilled* by the prosecuting attorney; the detectives *grilled* the suspects.

Ana. *Worry, annoy, harass, harry, plague, pester: vex, bother, irk (see ANNOY): distress, *trouble, ail.

Ant. Comfort. — *Con.* Console, solace (see COMFORT): delight, gladden, rejoice, *please.

affliction. Visitation, *trial, tribulation, cross.

Ana. Adversity, *misfortune, mischance: *distress, suffering, misery, agony: anguish, *sorrow, grief, woe.

Ant. Solace, consolation. — *Con.* Relief, assuagement, alleviation (see corresponding verbs at RELIEVE): joy, delight, *pleasure.

affluent. Wealthy, *rich, opulent.

Ana. Possessing, owning, holding, having, enjoying (see HAVE): acquisitive (see COVETOUS).

Ant. Impecunious: straitened. — *Con.* Indigent, penurious, destitute, poor (see corresponding nouns at POVERTY): impoverished, bankrupt (see DEPLETE).

afford. 1 *Manage, contrive.

2 *Give, confer, bestow, present, donate.

Ana. *Offer, proffer: *furnish: *grant, accord.

Ant. Deny (*something one wants, asks, hopes for, etc.*). — *Con.* Withhold, hold back (see KEEP): refuse, *decline.

affranchise. Enfranchise, liberate, emancipate, manumit, *free, release, deliver, discharge.

Ant. Enslave.

affray, *v.* *Frighten, fright, affright, scare, alarm, terrify, terrorize, startle.

Ana., Ant., Con. See those at AFFRIGHT.

affray, *n.* Fray, fight, combat, conflict, *contest.

Ana. *Brawl, row, fracas, melee, rumpus: *encounter, skirmish, brush: dispute, *argument, controversy.

affright, *v.* *Frighten, fright, affray, scare, alarm, terrify, terrorize, startle.

Ana. Daunt, horrify, appall, *dismay: cow, *intimidate, bulldoze: confound, bewilder (see PUZZLE).

Ant. Nerve, embolden. — *Con.* Animate, fire, inspire (see INFORM).

affront, *v.* *Offend, outrage, insult.

Ana. Slight, ignore, *neglect: nettle, peeve, provoke, *irritate.

Ant. Gratify (*by an attention*). — *Con.* Humor, *indulge, pamper: flatter, compliment (see corresponding nouns at COMPLIMENT).

affront, *n.* **Affront, insult, indignity** agree in denoting a speech or an action having for its intention or effect the dishonoring of a person, a cause, an institution, or the like. An **affront** is a designed, usually an open, mark of disrespect; as, an *affront* to the flag. "An old *affront* will stir the heart Through years of rankling pain" (*Ingelow*). An **insult** is a personal attack, either by words or actions, meant to humiliate or degrade. "A gifted Labour member . . . says that it [a pensions bill] is the most brutal *insult* ever flung in the face of the poor" (*C. E. Montague*). An **indignity** is an outrage upon one's personal dignity. "Whom I beseech To give me ample satisfaction For these deep shames and great *indignities*" (*Shak.*).

Ana. Slighting, ignoring, overlooking, neglecting (see NEGLECT, *v.*): offending, outraging (see OFFEND, *v.*): impudence, brazenness (see corresponding adjectives at SHAMELESS).

Ant. Gratification. — *Con.* Deference, *honor, homage: adulation, *compliment, flattery.

afore. Forward, ahead, *before.

Ant. Abaft. — *Con.* Aft, astern (see ABAFT).

afraid. 1 **Afraid, afeard** (*or* **afeared**), **aghast** agree in meaning manifestly or visibly frightened. Usually, but not necessarily, they are used without qualification; they are rarely, if ever correctly, found in the attributive position. **Afraid,** and its archaic form **afeard,** connote signs of fright such as shrinking, trembling, or shuddering. "And when the disciples heard it, they fell on their face, and were sore *afraid*" (*Matthew* xvii. 6). "Be not *afeard;* the isle is full of noises" (*Shak.*). **Aghast** always implies amazement and its signs, such as stupefaction or loss of power to speak or act; it usually also connotes horror, and then becomes a much stronger word than *afraid.* "'*Afraid*' was the word, wasn't it? . . . I should have said, *aghast;* you exhibited every symptom of one labouring under uncontrollable fear" (*Borrow*).

Ana. Shuddering, trembling, quaking (see SHAKE, *v.*): terrified, frightened, affrighted, alarmed (see FRIGHTEN): dismayed, horrified, appalled (see DISMAY).

Ant. Undaunted. — *Con.* Intrepid, dauntless (see BRAVE).

2 *Fearful, apprehensive.

Ana. Alarmed, scared (see FRIGHTEN): timorous, *timid.

Ant. Unafraid: sanguine. — *Con.* *Cool, composed, imperturbable, collected: *confident, assured, sure.

afresh. Anew, *again, encore, anon.

aft. *Abaft, astern.

Ana. *After, behind: rear, back, *posterior, hind.

Ant. Fore. — *Con.* *Before, afore, ahead, forward.

after, *prep., adj., adv.* **After, behind** are synonymous adverbs, prepositions, and adjectives when they mean following upon, especially in place or in time. They are rarely interchangeable, however, without a loss of precision. With reference to place, **after** usually implies order of movement or sequence, and characteristically goes with verbs or nouns implying motion; as, the faculty marched in pairs, one *after* another. So used, *after* not only conveys no suggestion of precedence in order of following, but it may, by stressing pursuit, even obscure its common implication of succession; thus, to run *after* a person is to attempt to overtake him. When, as often happens, *after* is used with verbs of rest, the implication of movement or sequence is rarely lost but, rather, is transferred to the object or is to be gathered from the context; thus, one stays *after* the others (who have left); one calls *after* a person (who is walking ahead); one looks *after* the children of a friend (who is away, ill, or the like). In the same connection, **behind** characteristically implies a position at the back of something at rest; as, the chair is *behind* the door; the men seated themselves *behind* the women; the garden is *behind* the house. When, however, the reference is to something moving, *behind* usually adds the implications of delay, lagging, or immobility; thus, to run *behind* another is to be outstripped; to be left *behind* is to be outstripped or to remain when others have departed.

With reference to time, *after* is in far more frequent use than *behind* and is the required choice when only subsequence is implied; as, who ruled *after* James I?; *after* one o'clock, no one may leave the room. When *behind* is used in this connection, it usually implies a time when someone or something is due according to a schedule, a system, a normal order of progression, or the like. Consequently it implies variously lateness, backwardness, falling in arrears, etc.; as, you are two hours *behind;* she is *behind* her years; to get *behind* financially.

Ana. *Abaft, aft, astern.

Ant. Before. — ***Con.*** Forward, ahead, afore (see BEFORE).

after, *adj.* Hinder, hind, rear, *posterior, back.

Con. *Preceding, antecedent, prior.

aftereffect. *Effect, consequence, result, aftermath, sequel, outcome, upshot, issue, event.

aftermath. Sequel, consequence, result, aftereffect, *effect, issue, outcome, upshot, event.

again. Again, anew, afresh, anon, encore agree in meaning once more or another time. In ordinary use, **again** adds nothing to this definition; as, tell him *again.* "I shall not look upon his like *again*" (*Shak.*). It so strongly implies repetition, however, that phrases such as "*again* and *again,*" "over and *again,*" mean repeatedly or continually, especially at intervals. Sometimes, *again* implies return, as in response or reaction; as, he is himself *again.* "No mystery at all: you loved, Were loved *again*" (*Browning*). **Anew** and **afresh** both imply repetition without loss of vitality, energy, freshness, or the like. *Anew* often suggests a new form or fashion; as, to begin life *anew.* "As one defeated batsman after another . . . sank into his deck-chair, I deplored *anew* the absence of national pride" (*E. V. Lucas*). *Afresh* usually connotes a revival of interest, energy, or the like. "In *The Moonstone* these devices succeed, every time, in stimulating our interest *afresh*" (*T. S. Eliot*). "Packed up her slender belongings and sought for employment *afresh*" (*Kipling*). **Anon** is a synonym of *again* only in certain collocations such as "ever and *anon*" (which approaches "again and again" but often suggests less regularity in repetition) or as the second in a pair of correlatives, such as *now* . . . *anon,* or *sometimes* . . . *anon.* "Came ever and *anon* a breath-like sound" (*Wordsworth*). "On hill sometimes, *anon* in shady vale" (*Milton*). **Encore,** which is French for *again,* is used in English as an interjection, especially as a call to a singer, an instrumentalist, or the like, to repeat his performance.

against. Against, versus, con agree in meaning in opposition to (something). **Against** is the most widely applicable of these terms, for it may indicate opposition of any sort, such as contrariety, incompatibility, conflict, hostility, competition, counteractivity, etc.; as, your conclusion is *against* reason; action *against* the law; man *against* nature; one's reason *against* one's desires; speakers for and *against* a proposal; to swim *against* a current; to play *against* a stronger team. **Versus** (often used in abbreviated form *v.* or *vs.*) usually implies personal opposition, as between parties to a lawsuit or teams in a match or contest; as, the suit of Brown *versus* Jones; the Cubs *versus* the Giants; it may, however, be used in reference to alternative policies, methods, solutions, etc., set up for consideration; as, preparedness *versus* disarmament. **Con** (which occurs chiefly as an adverb equaling a prepositional phrase of which the object is suppressed) is seldom, if ever, used without its correlative *pro* (in favor of). It implies opposition in argument, or support of the negative side; as, they argued the measure pro and *con.*

Ant. For.

age, *n.* **1 Age, senility, senescence, senilism, dotage** are comparable when they denote the period in one's life when one is old in years and declining physically or mentally (or both). **Age** is now usually replaced by *old age* except in literary use. "*Age* cannot wither her" (*Shak.*). "A youth of labour with an *age* of ease" (*Goldsmith*). "*Age,* I make light of it, Fear not the sight of it" (*T. W. Higginson*). **Senility** adds to *age* the implication of decay, especially of mental decay. "A rheumy old man, crumpled together . . . his mind gone down the road to *senility*" (*E. M. Roberts*). **Senescence** designates the period or the process of the decline which results in senility or old age; it is in the life of the individual the antithesis of youth or adolescence; **senilism** is the medical term for premature senescence or senility. **Dotage,** even more than *senility,* implies childishness or imbecility and thus indirectly heightens the suggestion of extreme old age. "Old Daniel begins; he stops short—and his eye, Through the lost look of *dotage,* is cunning and sly" (*Wordsworth*).

Ant. Youth.

2 Age, majority are synonymous when they denote the time of life when one attains one's full civil rights and becomes independent of guardianship. **Age,** in this sense, is to be found chiefly in idiomatic expressions such as to come of *age;* he is under *age* (or, not yet of *age*). In other contexts, *full age* or *legal age* is the usual designation. In most English-speaking countries this age is fixed by common law for both men and women at twenty-one years, but in some States of the United States full age is fixed for women at eighteen years. In many other countries twenty-five years is the accepted full age. **Majority** is the customary legal term for the status of one who is of age; as, he will attain his *majority* next year.

Ant. Nonage. — ***Con.*** *Infancy, minority.

3 *Period, era, epoch, aeon.

age, *v.* *Mature, ripen, develop.

aged. Aged, old, elderly, superannuated, when applied to persons, agree in meaning far advanced in years. **Aged** implies extreme old age with signs of feebleness or, sometimes, senility. "The *aged* creature came, shuffling along with ivory-headed wand" (*Keats*). **Old** stresses the years of one's life, but in itself carries no connotations of marked decline. "A man, *old,* wrinkled, faded, wither'd" (*Shak.*). **Elderly** implies that the prime of life has been passed. "When you see me again I shall be an old man—that was a slip, I meant to say 'elderly' " (*J. R. Lowell*). **Superannuated** indicates that one has been retired or pensioned because of having reached a certain age (varying in different callings); as, *superannuated* teachers; *superannuated* judges. Sometimes the word implies merely that one has passed the years of usefulness, and so by extension it is applied to things as well as to persons.

Ana. *Senile, doting, doddering: infirm, feeble, decrepit (see WEAK).

Ant. Youthful. — ***Con.*** Juvenile, puerile, boyish, virgin, virginal, maiden (see YOUTHFUL).

agelong. *Secular, centuried, aeonian, diuturnal.

Ana. Perpetual, constant, *continual, continuous: enduring, abiding, lasting, persisting (see CONTINUE).

Ant. Short-lived: momentary. — ***Con.*** *Transient,

ephemeral, fleeting, evanescent, transitory, passing: *brief, short: *temporary, temporal.

agency. *Means, agent, instrumentality, instrument, medium, vehicle, channel, organ.
Ana. *Cause, determinant, antecedent: operation, action, working (see corresponding verbs at ACT): activity (see corresponding adjective ACTIVE): machinery, apparatus, gear, *equipment.

agenda. *Program, schedule, timetable.

agent, *n.* **1** *Means, instrument, agency, instrumentality, medium, vehicle, organ, channel.
Ana. Actor, operator, worker (see corresponding verbs at ACT): activator, energizer (see corresponding verbs at VITALIZE): performer, executor *or* executive (see corresponding verbs at PERFORM).
Ant. Patient.

2 Agent, factor, attorney, deputy, proxy are here compared mainly in their general senses, in which they agree in meaning one who performs the duties of or transacts business for another, but with some reference to their differences in specific application. **Agent** is very general and may be used to express this idea in any context where a specific term is not required; distinctively, however, it often implies the activity of a go-between; as, ambassadors, ministers, emissaries, nuncios are diplomatic *agents* of their governments or sovereigns. "The heads of departments are the political or confidential *agents* of the executive" (*Ch. Just. Marshall*). "Let every eye negotiate for itself And trust no *agent*" (*Shak.*). **Factor** was once a near equivalent of *agent*, differing from it chiefly in implying delegated authority to act. "Some . . . of us . . . have mingled sums To buy a present for the emperor; Which I, the *factor* for the rest, have done In France" (*Shak.*). In present use *factor* is chiefly employed as a designation for a landlord's agent (see STEWARD) or for a commission merchant on a large scale who is delegated either to buy or to sell for his clients; as, a wool *factor;* a flour *factor*. It is also used specifically to name the official in charge of one of the Hudson's Bay Company's trading posts. **Attorney,** now chiefly used as a designation for a professional legal agent (see LAWYER), once was applied to one who performed the personal offices of another who was absent, incapacitated, or unqualified for the work. "I will attend my husband, be his nurse . . . for it is my office, And will have no *attorney* but myself" (*Shak.*). This sense still survives in English but in a narrower application to a person legally delegated to transact certain specified business for another who is absent or otherwise disqualified. Such a person is often called (in distinction from an attorney at law) a "private attorney" or an "attorney in fact," and the power delegated him is called "power of attorney." **Deputy** always implies the delegation of some or all of the powers of a superior, such as a sovereign, a chief executive in a department of government, or the like. Almost always, also, it connotes responsibility to the person whose powers are deputed, rather than to the state, the people, or the like; thus, the governor general of Canada or Australia may appoint *deputies* to exercise his powers or functions locally or temporarily; a vicar general is a *deputy* of a bishop. **Proxy** implies a substitution of persons when a promise or pledge is solemnly made or a vote, as at a stockholders' meeting, is to be cast. In a marriage service, a *proxy* for the bride or groom, or in the baptismal service, a *proxy* for a godparent, merely utters the promises in the name of the absent person, the latter assuming the obligation of fulfilling them.
Ant. Principal: ordinary (*in ecclesiastical use*).

3 Oeconomus, factor, *steward, reeve, seneschal, majordomo.

Ant. Lord: master.

agglomerate *or* **agglomeration.** Conglomerate, conglomeration, *aggregate, aggregation.
Ana. Combination, association (see corresponding verbs at JOIN): accumulation (see corresponding verb ACCUMULATE): *heap, pile, mass.

agglutinate, *v.* *Cement, glue.
Ana. Cohere, *stick, adhere, cling.
Con. *Separate, part, divide.

aggrandize. *Exalt, magnify.
Ana. Heighten, enhance, aggravate, *intensify: elevate, raise, *lift, boost.
Ant. Belittle. — *Con.* Minimize, depreciate, disparage, *decry, detract from, derogate from.

aggravate. 1 Heighten, *intensify, enhance.
Ana. Magnify, aggrandize (see EXALT): augment, *increase, multiply, enlarge.
Ant. Alleviate. — *Con.* Lighten, mitigate, allay (see RELIEVE): *palliate, extenuate: lessen, reduce, diminish, abate (see DECREASE).

2 Exasperate, *irritate, provoke, roil, peeve, nettle.
Ana. Perturb, upset, disturb (see DISCOMPOSE): vex, irk, *annoy: *anger, incense, infuriate.
Ant. Appease. — *Con.* *Pacify, placate, mollify: tranquilize, calm (see corresponding adjectives at CALM).

aggregate, *n.* **1** *Sum, total, whole, number, amount, quantity.
Ant. Individual: particular.

2 Aggregate, aggregation, conglomerate, conglomeration, agglomerate, agglomeration agree in denoting a mass formed by parts or particles that are not merged into each other. **Aggregate** and **aggregation** always imply the formation of a whole but without the blending or the organic union of its constituents; thus, sandstone is a natural *aggregate* of several minerals such as quartz and feldspar; concrete is an artificial *aggregate* consisting of crushed rock, sand, and cement. "We have no communities. Our villages even are apt, rather, to be *aggregations*" (*Brownell*). **Conglomerate** and **conglomeration** emphasize the heterogeneousness of the components and often suggest their assemblage from a wide variety of sources; sometimes either is applied to a heap of things, sometimes to an aggregate in which the parts are clearly distinguishable. "Pantheism is generally a *conglomerate* of animism, poetical fancy, and mysticism" (*Inge*). "That *conglomeration* of men we call a nation" (*H. P. Liddon*). **Agglomerate** and **agglomeration** in general use seldom imply coherence of parts; they suggest either a huddling together or, more often, a fortuitous association. "A mere *agglomeration* of different races, without national unity, national aims" (*W. H. Page*). In geology, *agglomerate* designates a rock aggregate composed of irregularly shaped fragments scattered by volcanic explosions as distinguished from *conglomerate*, an aggregate composed of rounded, waterworn stones.
Ana. Union, *unity, integrity: unification, consolidation (see corresponding verbs at COMPACT): complex, *system, organism, network.
Ant. Constituent.

aggregation. *Aggregate, conglomerate, conglomeration, agglomerate, agglomeration.
Ana. & *Ant.* See those at AGGREGATE, 2.

aggression. *Attack, offense, offensive.
Ana. *Invasion, incursion, irruption, raid, inroad.
Ant. Resistance.

aggressive. 1 Attacking, offensive. See primitive nouns at ATTACK.
Ana. Invading, encroaching, trespassing. See TRESPASS, *v.*
Ant. Resisting: repelling.

2 Aggressive, militant, assertive, self-assertive, pushing are here compared as applied to persons, their dispositions, their acts, and the like, and as meaning conspicuously or obtrusively active or energetic. **Aggressive** implies a disposition to assume or maintain leadership or domination, sometimes by bullying, sometimes by indifference to others' rights, but more often, in current use, by self-confident and forceful prosecution of one's ends. "The captain [spoke] in . . . an *aggressive* tone" (*Conrad*). "To protect themselves against a too *aggressive* prosecution of the women's business" (*Shaw*). "If a man is wanted for any kind of job—mayor, floor-walker, professor, or secretary of a peace conference—he must be '*aggressive*' " (*Grandgent*). **Militant,** like *aggressive,* implies a fighting disposition, but unlike it, seldom conveys a suggestion of self-seeking. In modern nontechnical use, *militant* usually implies extreme devotion to some cause, movement, or institution, and energetic and, often, self-sacrificing prosecution of its ends; as, *militant* feminists; a *militant* church or churchman. "The cause of reform slowly went on gaining adherents—most of them . . . of the acquiescent rather than the *militant* type" (*Grandgent*). **Assertive** stresses self-confidence and boldness in action or, especially, in the expression of one's opinions. It often implies a determined attempt to make oneself or one's influence felt. "Somewhat too diffident, not *assertive* enough" (*Bennett*). "The soap maker, an *assertive* positive man" (*S. Anderson*). **Self-assertive** usually adds to *assertive* the implication of bumptiousness or undue forwardness; as, *self-assertiveness* is incompatible with co-operativeness. **Pushing,** when used without any intent to depreciate, comes very close to *aggressive* in the current sense of the latter; however, the word is more commonly a derogatory epithet and implies, variously, officiousness, social climbing, or offensive intrusiveness. "Mrs. Erlynne, a *pushing* nobody" (*Wilde*). "An energetic, *pushing* youth, already intent on getting on in the world" (*S. Anderson*).

Ana. Energetic, strenuous, *vigorous: *masterful, domineering, imperious: fighting, combating *or* combative (see corresponding nouns at CONTEST).

aggrieve. *Wrong, oppress, persecute.

Ana. *Afflict, try, torment: harass, harry, plague, annoy, *worry: *injure, hurt, harm.

Ant. Rejoice. — *Con.* Gladden, delight, *please: *benefit, profit.

aghast. *Afraid, afeard.

Ana. Appalled, horrified (see DISMAY, *v.*): terrified, startled, frightened (see FRIGHTEN): astounded, amazed (see SURPRISE, *v.*).

Ant. Unmoved: apathetic. — *Con.* *Impassive, stolid, phlegmatic.

agile. Agile, nimble, brisk, spry agree in meaning acting or moving with quickness and alacrity. **Agile** implies dexterity and ease in the management of one's limbs or, by extension, one's wits; as, *agile* as a monkey. "Managing their spears with incredible *agility*" (*Evelyn*). "A development . . . of thought which requires considerable *agility* on the part of the reader" (*T. S. Eliot*). **Nimble** suggests surpassing lightness and swiftness of movement or action, and often implies a darting here and there; as, *nimble* as a squirrel; "Madame Defarge knitted with *nimble* fingers" (*Dickens*). "She ran ahead of his thoughts like *nimble* fire" (*Meredith*). **Brisk** implies liveliness, animation, or vigor of movement; as, a *brisk* canter; a *brisk* walking pace. "To have *brisk* and intelligent talk" (*A. C. Benson*). "*Brisk* and lively rhythm" (*A. Huxley*). It is sometimes applied to things that do not move, but are invigorating, exhilarating, or the like; as, a *brisk* day; a *brisk* reply. "She walked *briskly* in the *brisk* air" (*G. Eliot*). **Spry** (more colloquial than the others) stresses alacrity arising from vigor or health; it, however, is frequently applied to those from whom alacrity or briskness of movement is not to be expected; as, the old lady is as *spry* as a cricket; she is down one day, and up and *spry* the next.

Ana. *Dexterous, adroit, deft, feat: quick, fleet, speedy (see FAST): limber, lithesome, *supple: *lively, sprightly.

Ant. Torpid. — *Con.* *Lethargic, sluggish, comatose, stuporous: inert, *inactive, passive, supine.

agitate. 1 *Shake, rock, convulse.

Ana. *Stir, rouse, arouse: *move, actuate, drive, impel.

Ant. Quiet, lull, still.

2 Perturb, *discompose, upset, fluster, flurry, disturb, disquiet.

Ana. *Irritate, provoke, roil, exasperate, peeve: *worry, harass, plague: *annoy, vex, irk, bother.

Ant. Calm, tranquilize. — *Con.* *Pacify, placate, appease, mollify.

3 Argue, dispute, debate, *discuss.

Ana. Controvert (see DISPROVE): assail, *attack: revolve, *consider: air, ventilate, broach (see EXPRESS).

agnation. Consanguinity, cognation, enation, *kinship, affinity.

agnostic, *n.* **1** *Atheist, deist, freethinker, unbeliever, infidel.

2 Skeptic (see corresponding adjective SKEPTIC).

agnosticism. Skepticism (see under SKEPTIC, *adj*).

ago. *Since.

agog. A-tiptoe, *eager, keen, anxious, avid, athirst.

Ana. Excited, galvanized, stimulated (see PROVOKE): roused, aroused, stirred (see STIR, *v.*): *impatient, restive, feverish, hectic.

Ant. Aloof. — *Con.* *Indifferent, unconcerned, incurious, detached: uninterested, *disinterested.

agonize. *Writhe, squirm.

Ana. Suffer, endure, *bear: torment, rack, torture, *afflict.

agonizing. *Excruciating, racking.

Ana. Torturing, tormenting, racking (see AFFLICT): *intense, vehement.

Con. *Comfortable, easy, restful, reposeful: comforting, solacing, consoling (see COMFORT).

agony. Suffering, passion, *distress, misery, dolor.

Ana. Pang, throe, ache, *pain, twinge: *trial, tribulation, affliction, visitation.

Con. *Rest, repose, ease, comfort: solace, consolation (see corresponding verbs at COMFORT): relief, assuagement, mitigation (see corresponding verbs at RELIEVE).

agrarian. Agrarian, agricultural are sometimes confused because they carry common implications and are used to qualify like terms; as, an *agrarian* or an *agricultural* society; an *agrarian* or an *agricultural* crisis; an *agrarian* or an *agricultural* policy. Both terms have reference to land, the conditions under which it is held, and its profitable use. **Agrarian,** however, stresses the economic or political issues involved in the ownership of land, in the conditions of tenancy, and in the right of the individual to the profits of his labor on the land; **agricultural** stresses rather the successful and profitable use of land for the production of crops and the breeding of animals; thus, *agrarian* crises were frequent in Ireland in the eighteenth and nineteenth centuries when the issue of tenant rights became acute; *agricultural* crises are likely to occur when overproduction and a restriction of markets coincide. When, however, agricultural interests are at stake and political action is held to be necessary, a party formed to promote these ends may be called an *agrarian* rather than an *agricultural* party, and a measure advocated an *agrarian* rather than an *agricultural* measure.

agree. 1 *Assent, accede, consent, acquiesce, subscribe.
Ana. *Grant, concede, allow: accept, *receive: admit, *acknowledge.
Ant. Protest (*against*): differ (*with*). — *Con.* *Object, kick, expostulate, remonstrate: *demur, balk, jib: *oppose, resist, withstand.

2 **Agree, concur, coincide** are comparable when they mean to come into, or to be in, harmony regarding a matter of opinion, a policy, or the like. **Agree** implies unison in thought or a complete accord: even if the context suggests previous discussion, the word usually indicates that argument is ended; as, this is a point upon which all persons *agree*. "If two of you shall *agree* on earth as touching any thing that they shall ask, it shall be done" (*Matthew* xviii. 19). **Concur** usually implies reference to a specific or definite agreement, particularly one arrived at by a vote or expression of opinion and made the basis of future action, the starting point of a discussion, or the like. "I will presume that Mr. Murry and myself can *agree* that for our purpose these counters [terms] are adequate, and *concur* in disregarding [objections to them]" (*T. S. Eliot*). **Coincide** implies an agreement amounting to complete identity of opinion. Only occasionally, however, in current use do persons *coincide;* more frequently opinions, judgments, wishes, and the like *coincide*. "Whether we *coincide* or not in this doctrine" (*Lyell*). "I had hoped that our sentiments *coincided*" (*Austen*). More often, especially in current use, *coincide* implies an agreement in time of occurrence (far less often an agreement in place occupied) and therefore frequently stresses synchronousness of events; as, the fall of Granada and the discovery of America *coincided* (see *coincident* under CONTEMPORARY).
Ana. *Unite, co-operate: conspire, collude (see CONNIVE).
Ant. Differ: disagree. — *Con.* *Contend, fight, battle: dispute, argue, debate (see DISCUSS): quarrel, wrangle, squabble, bicker (see under QUARREL, *n.*).

3 **Agree, square, conform, accord, comport, harmonize, correspond, tally, jibe** (*or* **gibe**) come into comparison when they mean to exist or go together without conflict or incongruity. One thing **agrees** with another when their comparison or association reveals no discrepancy, no inequality, no untoward effects, or the like; as, the conclusion *agrees* with the evidence; the two accounts *agree* in every particular; pronouns must *agree* with their antecedents in person, number, and gender; the climate does not *agree* with him. One thing **squares** with another when there is exact, almost mathematically exact, agreement between the two; as, to force facts to *square* with one's theory. "No works shall find acceptance . . . That *square* not truly with the Scripture plan" (*Cowper*). One thing **conforms** to or with another when there is likeness or agreement in form, in nature, or in essential character. "A rule to which experience must *conform*" (*Whewell*). "My views of conduct . . . *conform* with what seem to me the implications of my beliefs" (*T. S. Eliot*). One thing **accords** with another when there is perfect fitness in the relation or association as in character, spirit, quality, or tone; as, the speaker's remarks did not *accord* with the sentiments of those who listened to him. "False tints [of rouged women] too well *accorded* with the glare" (*Wordsworth*). One thing **comports** with another when the former measures up to the standard set by the latter or when there is no obvious disparity between the two. In contrast with each other, *accord* usually stresses positive congruity; *comport*, lack of incongruity; as, manners that *comport* with one's social station. "How ill this dullness doth *comport* with greatness" (*Beaumont & Fletcher*). One thing **harmonizes** with another when, in spite of their real and, often, marked differences, their combination or juxtaposition produces an agreeable or aesthetic effect. "From the waves, sound . . . broke forth *Harmonising* with solitude" (*Shelley*). "With that luxuriant tropical nature, its green clouds and illusive aerial spaces . . . they [monkeys] *harmonised* well in language, appearance and motions" (*Hudson*). One thing **corresponds** to (or with) another when, however far apart or however close the two things may be, they belong together because they match each other, or complement each other, or answer to each other. Sometimes, *correspond* implies agreement; as, fulfillment seldom *corresponds* to anticipation. "I should never *correspond* to your pattern of a lady" (*G. Eliot*). Sometimes it implies an analogous relation; as, the bird's wing *corresponds* to the human arm. Sometimes it implies commensurateness. "Incomes do not always *correspond* with the efforts or skill that appear to be involved" (*J. A. Hobson*). One thing **tallies** with another when the correspondence is so close that they either, as in very discriminating use, complement each other or agree with each other. "Pain and pleasure no more *tally* in our sense than red and green" (*Browning*). **Jibe** is a colloquial word much used in the United States as equivalent to *agree*, or sometimes to *harmonize*, and sometimes to *accord;* as, his actions do not *jibe* with his words.
Ant. Differ (*from*). — *Con.* Negative, counteract, *neutralize: negate, *nullify.

agreeable. Grateful, pleasing, *pleasant, gratifying, welcome.
Ana. *Comfortable, easy, restful, reposeful: *delightful, delectable: attractive, charming, alluring (see under ATTRACT).
Ant. Disagreeable. — *Con.* *Repugnant, repellent, obnoxious, distasteful: *hateful, abhorrent, abominable, odious: *offensive, loathsome, repulsive.

agreement. Agreement, accord, understanding are here compared in their political and legal uses. They agree in designating a settlement reached by parties to a dispute or engaged in negotiations. All these terms imply concurrence as to what should be done or not done; all imply reconciliation of differences. **Agreement** is the most positive word; it usually implies a final settlement of terms. An *agreement* may or may not be put into writing, as in the form of a contract, concordat, or treaty; it may or may not be accompanied by a consideration. In English law, it is not legally binding until it is in writing or is accompanied by a consideration. An **accord** is, in controversies between governments, an informal agreement; use of this term often implies that all details have not yet been settled or that the terms of the agreement are not yet ready for publication, but that the conditions necessary to a final agreement have been fulfilled. In law, an *accord* is an agreement between the parties concerned in a case where satisfaction for an injury is demanded. The execution of such an accord bars further litigation. An **understanding** is the least binding of accepted settlements. If the term is used to denote the final stage in a negotiation or in settlement of a dispute, it implies the existence of definite engagements or the exchange of promises, and dependence on the honor of the parties to the agreement for the keeping of such engagements or promises.
Ana. Pact, entente, concordat, convention, cartel (see CONTRACT).

agrestic. Rustic, bucolic, geoponic, georgic, *rural, pastoral, Arcadian.

agricultural. *Agrarian.

agriculture. Agriculture, farming, husbandry agree in

meaning the science or the business of raising plants and animals useful to man. **Agriculture** is by far the most comprehensive of these terms; in common with *farming* and *husbandry*, it implies the cultivation of the soil, the production and harvesting of crops, the care and breeding of livestock; it includes in addition other pursuits that may or may not be connected with farming and husbandry, such as horticulture, forestry, dairying, sugar making, beekeeping, and the like; specifically it stresses knowledge of the chemical constituents of soils in relation to crop production (**agrology**), the scientific management of soil so as to promote crop production (**agronomy**), and the conversion of farm products such as milk, hides, etc., into manufactured products, on the farm or in close relation to it (**agrotechny**). **Farming,** the term in common use, has never lost its emphasis on land devoted to the production of crops or animals for the market; it may imply small or extensive holdings, but it usually suggests the inclusion of tilled land bearing crops, of pasture land for cattle, of meadowland for hay, and the like. **Husbandry,** an old English word seldom used in this sense outside of the British Isles except in a literary context, usually suggests small holdings, and production for the use of a household or community rather than for a distant market. It often suggests more varied employments than farming, such as dairying, beekeeping, etc., and it often, in general use, denotes management of one's affairs, especially with respect to thrift (as, good *husbandry;* bad *husbandry*).

agrology. See AGRICULTURE.

agronomy. See AGRICULTURE.

agrotechny. See AGRICULTURE.

ahead. Forward, *before, afore.
Ant. Behind. — *Con.* *After: *abaft, aft, astern.

aid, *v.* *Help, assist.
Ana. *Support, uphold, back: *relieve, lighten, alleviate, mitigate: abet (see INCITE).
Ant. Injure. — *Con.* Harm, hurt, damage (see INJURE): *hinder, impede, block.

aid, *n.* Help, assistance. See under HELP, *v.*
Ana. Relief, assuagement, alleviation, mitigation (see corresponding verbs at RELIEVE): *remedy, cure, medicine: support, backing (see corresponding verbs at SUPPORT).
Ant. Impediment. — *Con.* *Obstacle, bar, obstruction: restraint, curb, check (see corresponding verbs at RESTRAIN).

aide *or* **aid.** *Assistant, adjutant, aide-de-camp, coadjutor, helper.

aide-de-camp. Aide, adjutant, *assistant.

aigrette. *Egret.

ail, *v.* *Trouble, distress.
Ana. *Afflict, try: *annoy, vex, irk, bother.
Con. *Comfort, solace, console: *relieve, assuage, alleviate, mitigate.

ailment. Affection, malady, *disease, complaint, distemper.

aim, *v.* **1** Point, *direct, level, train, lay.
Ana. Turn, bend, *curve, twist.

2 Aim, aspire, pant often convey the same meaning, to have as a controlling desire something beyond one's present power of attainment. **Aim** stresses a clearly defined end toward which one's efforts are directed or which one holds before one as a goal to be reached through endeavor or striving. "Men *aiming* to advance in life with glory" (*Hardy*). "Christianity *aims* at nothing less than absolute truth" (*Inge*). "Get honour, and keep honour free from flaw, *Aim* at still higher honour" (*Browning*). **Aspire,** especially when followed by an infinitive, often adds little to *aim* except the suggestion of ambition. "Those who do not *aspire* to be scholars" (*S. M. Crothers*). "*Aspiring* to be the leader of a nation of third-rate men" (*Mencken*). However, when used with a sense of its distinctive values, it implies urgency of longing for something that is high, often too high for attainment. "Since first my thirsting soul *aspired* to know The secrets of their wondrous world" (*Shelley*). "What I *aspired* to be, And was not, comforts me: A brute I might have been, but would not sink i' the scale" (*Browning*). **Pant** comes into comparison with the other words only in its extended sense of Biblical origin. "As the hart *panteth* after the water brooks, so *panteth* my soul after thee, O God" (*Psalms* xlii. 1). Even more than *aspire* it stresses the fervor of the desire and the remoteness of that which is desired. Sometimes it connotes urgent unsatisfied thirst. "More happy, happy love! For ever warm and still to be enjoy'd, For ever *panting*, and for ever young" (*Keats*). Sometimes, especially in modern use, it suggests not the gasps of one thirsting, but of one toiling upward. "[The] Brave, and Good, and Wise, For their high guerdon not in vain have *panted!*" (*Wordsworth*).
Ana. *Intend, purpose, propose, design: *attempt, essay, endeavor, try.

aim, *n.* End, goal, objective, purpose, *intention, object, intent, design.
Ana. Aspiration, *ambition: *effort, exertion, pains, trouble.

air, *n.* **1 Air, atmosphere, ether, ozone. Air,** the ordinary term, designates the invisible mixture of gases which surrounds the earth. More narrowly, it denotes an impalpable respirable substance essential to life (as, the *air* we breathe), or that substance mixed with or contaminated by other substances (as, perfumed *air;* smoky *air*), or that substance regarded as the medium which transmits sound or through which birds and the like fly. **Atmosphere** designates the layers of air which form the envelope of the earth or a similar gaseous envelope of any celestial body; as, the *atmosphere* of Mars; more loosely, it is applied to the portion of air which permeates a particular place; as, the heated *atmosphere* of a room. **Ether,** except in its technical senses a rhetorical word, usually suggests either more rarefied air than that found in the earth's immediate atmosphere or an element like air, but far more delicate or subtle, which fills the upper regions or interstellar space. In physics, *ether* designates a hypothetical medium for the transmission of transverse waves which is characterized by continuity and extreme tenuity and which permeates all space, even intra-atomic space. **Ozone** is strictly a form of oxygen obtained not only from the upper levels of the air but from other sources, and used commercially as a sterilizer, a purifier, and a bleach. In popular use, it is applied to air that is markedly pure and has a pungent refreshing odor.

2 *Pose, affectation, mannerism.
Ana. Mien, manner, *bearing, port, presence, front: ostentation, pomp, pretentiousness, show (see corresponding adjectives at SHOWY): *art, artifice, craft.

3 *Melody, air, tune.

air, *v.* Ventilate, vent, utter, voice, *express, broach.
Ana. *Reveal, disclose, divulge, tell, discover: publish, proclaim, broadcast, *declare.
Con. *Hide, conceal: *suppress, repress.

airport. Airport, airdrome (*or* **aerodrome, aërodrome**), **air field, flying field, landing field** denote a place where aircraft may land in safety. **Airport** implies a well-marked and lighted place, either on land or water, providing facilities for sheltering passengers, handling cargo, supplying fuel, making repairs, and housing aircraft. **Airdrome** (*or, Brit.,* **aerodrome**) is practically synonymous with *airport* and is being replaced by it. **Air field** in strict usage is applied only to the part of an airport where aircraft land or take off. A **flying field** is a field with a graded portion for taking off and landing, and an area free of tall trees and other obstructions, for flying operations, often involving the instruction of pilots. A **landing field** is merely one of the level fields suitable for landings, spaced at regular intervals along an airway and often provided with special lights.

airship. *Aerostat, dirigible, zeppelin, blimp, balloon.

airy. Airy, aerial (*or* **aërial**), **ethereal** are here compared in their figurative senses. Though all three mean as light and insubstantial as air, they are distinguishable in discriminating use. **Airy** seldom suggests a transcendent quality; in its widest sense it implies little more than immateriality. "The poet's pen . . . gives to *airy* nothing a local habitation and a name" (*Shak.*). When applied to persons, their words, their manners, it often, in colloquial use, implies affectation of grandeur, or "putting on airs"; as, as her *airiness* increased, her admirers decreased: in better established English it implies merely an affectation of nonchalance. " 'It is all the same,' said the spy, *airily*, but discomfited too" (*Dickens*). When applied to motion or to movements it suggests buoyancy. "E'en the slight harebell raised its head, Elastic from her *airy* tread" (*Scott*). **Aerial,** in its figurative sense, is now found chiefly in poetry. In discriminating use, it commonly connotes impalpability, extraordinary delicacy, or elusiveness, and is applied to things rather than to persons. "Mountains . . . fair of aspect, with *aerial* softness clad" (*Wordsworth*). "The *aërial* hue Of fountain-gazing roses" (*Shelley*). "Fine and *aërial* distinctions" (*Milman*). **Ethereal,** as in its primary sense, implies not the atmosphere surrounding the earth, but the rarefied air once believed to fill the heavenly regions. Hence, it almost invariably imputes a celestial or supramundane character to the person or thing it qualifies. Sometimes it suggests an unearthly translucency. "Fire . . . without heat, flickering a red gold flame . . . *ethereal* and insubstantial" (*V. Woolf*). "[hair] So . . . *ethereal* in appearance with its cloud colours, that . . . even . . . the most beautiful golden shades . . . seemed heavy and dull and dead-looking by comparison" (*Hudson*). Sometimes, especially when referred to persons, their words, or their thoughts, it suggests disembodied spirit or apartness from material interests; as, the *ethereal* quality of Shelley's poetry. "At times he [Joubert] tends to fall into excessive subtlety, to be too vaporous and *ethereal*" (*Babbitt*).

Ana. Tenuous, rare, *thin: delicate, dainty, exquisite (see CHOICE): light, volatile, frivolous (see corresponding nouns at LIGHTNESS).

Ant. Substantial. — ***Con.*** *Massive, massy, bulky, monumental: *material, corporeal, physical: solid, hard, *firm.

aisle. *Passage, passageway, ambulatory, corridor.

akin. *Similar, alike, like, analogous, comparable, parallel, homogeneous, uniform, identical.

Ana. *Related, kindred, cognate, allied: corresponding, agreeing, harmonizing, according, conforming (see AGREE).

Ant. Alien. — ***Con.*** Foreign, extraneous (see EXTRINSIC): divergent, disparate, *different.

alacrity. *Celerity, legerity.

Ana. Eagerness, avidity, anxiety (see corresponding adjectives at EAGER): quickness, promptness, readiness (see corresponding adjectives at QUICK): agility, nimbleness, briskness (see corresponding adjectives at AGILE): expedition, dispatch, *haste.

Ant. Languor. — ***Con.*** *Lethargy, torpidity, stupor: impassiveness, apathy, stolidity (see under IMPASSIVE): indifference, unconcern, aloofness (see corresponding adjectives at INDIFFERENT).

alarm, *n.* **1 Alarm, alarum, tocsin, alert** agree in meaning a signal that serves as a call to action or to be on guard, especially in a time of imminent danger. **Alarm,** once specifically a call to arms, is now used of any signal that arouses to activity not only troops, but firemen, policemen, workers, or the like; it always suggests a sound such as a cry or cries, a peal or pealing of a bell, a beating of drums, or a siren; as, to sound a fire *alarm;* the dog's barking gave the *alarm.* "Better dwell in the midst of *alarms,* Than reign in this horrible place" (*Cowper*). **Alarum,** a variant of *alarm,* is now chiefly archaic or poetic, except in its occasional application to the mechanism or apparatus that sounds an alarm. **Tocsin** is either an alarm sounded by bells, usually from the belfry of a church, or, more often, the bell or bells sounding an alarm. "The loud *tocsin* tolled their last *alarm*" (*Campbell*). **Alert,** a military term for a signal to be on guard and ready for an attack, is now chiefly used of a warning, as by a siren, of an imminent gas or bomb attack and serves as an order to equip oneself with a gas mask; as, to sound an *alert.*

2 Fright, *fear, panic, terror, horror, dismay, dread, consternation, trepidation.

Ana. Frightening, scaring, startling (see FRIGHTEN): agitation, perturbation, upset (see corresponding verbs at DISCOMPOSE).

Ant. Assurance: composure. — ***Con.*** Calmness, tranquillity, serenity (see corresponding adjectives at CALM): self-possession, self-assurance (see CONFIDENCE): *equanimity, sang-froid.

alarm, *v.* *Frighten, fright, scare, startle, terrify, affright, terrorize, affray.

Ana. Appall, daunt, horrify, *dismay: *surprise, astound, amaze, astonish.

Ant. Assure: relieve. — ***Con.*** *Comfort, solace, console.

alarum. *Alarm, tocsin, alert.

albeit. Although, *though.

alchemy. *Magic, thaumaturgy, wizardry, sorcery, witchery, witchcraft.

alcoholic, *adj.* **Alcoholic, spirituous, ardent, hard, strong** are comparable when they are used in reference to beverages and denote containing ethyl alcohol. **Alcoholic,** the most general of these terms, does not indicate the amount of alcohol present or whether it has been obtained by fermentation or by distillation; as, beer, wine, and whisky are *alcoholic* beverages. **Spirituous** signifies the presence of alcohol as the result of distillation and suggests a comparatively high proportion of it; as, brandy is a *spirituous* liquor distilled from wine. **Ardent,** now used only in the phrase *ardent spirits,* adds to *spirituous* the suggestion of the burning sensation experienced upon drinking beverages such as brandy, rum, whisky, having a high alcoholic content. **Hard** (in this meaning, an Americanism) also is very close to *spirituous* in meaning and is commonly used in the phrase *hard liquor,* which is distinguished from soft beverages and from light wines, beer, and other beverages of comparatively low alcoholic content. *Hard* cider is cider that has two to eight per cent of alcohol as the result of fermentation. **Strong** is sometimes equivalent to *alcoholic;* usually, however, it implies a comparatively high alcoholic content; as, *strong* beer, *strong* drink, *strong* liquor. *Hard* and *strong* are most suggestive of power to intoxicate.

alcoholic, *n.* *Drunkard, inebriate, dipsomaniac, sot, soak, toper, tosspot, tippler.

alcove. *Recess, nook, cubicle, carrell, carol, embrasure, bay, niche.

ale. *Beer, stout, porter, lager, bock.
alert, *adj.* **1** *Watchful, wide-awake, vigilant.
Ana. *Agile, nimble, brisk: wary, circumspect, *cautious.
Ant. Supine. — *Con.* Heedless, *careless: unconcerned, aloof, detached, *indifferent.
2 Clever, *intelligent, smart, bright, quick-witted, brilliant, knowing.
Ana. *Sharp, keen, acute: *quick, ready, prompt, apt: *shrewd, perspicacious.
Ant. Slow (*mentally*). — *Con.* *Languid, lackadaisical, listless: *lethargic, sluggish: *stupid, dull, dense.
alert, *n.* *Alarm, alarum, tocsin.
alfresco. *Outdoor, open-air, plein-air.
alias, *n.* *Pseudonym, nom de guerre, allonym, incognito, nom de plume, pen name.
alibi, *n.* Excuse, pretext, plea, *apology, apologia.
Ana. Explanation, justification, rationalization (see corresponding verbs at EXPLAIN).
alien, *adj.* Foreign, extraneous, *extrinsic.
Ana. External, exterior, outside (see corresponding adjectives at OUTER): adventitious, incidental, *accidental: *repugnant, repellent, abhorrent: incompatible, incongruous, *inconsonant.
Ant. Akin: assimilable. — *Con.* *Relevant, material, pertinent, germane: compatible, *consonant, congruous, congenial: kindred, cognate, *related.
alien, *v.* Alienate, *transfer, convey, deed.
alien, *n.* Foreigner, *stranger, outlander, outsider, immigrant, émigré.
Ant. Citizen. — *Con.* Subject, national (see CITIZEN): native, aborigine (see under NATIVE, *adj.*).
alienate. **1** Alien, *transfer, convey, deed.
2 *Estrange, disaffect, wean.
Ana. Convert, proselyte, proselytize (see corresponding nouns at CONVERT): *separate, part, sever, sunder, divorce.
Ant. Unite: reunite. — *Con.* Reconcile, conform, accommodate, adjust, *adapt: associate, link, *join.
alienation. Derangement, *aberration.
Ana. *Insanity, lunacy, mania, dementia: imbecility, idiocy, moronity (see primitive nouns at FOOL).
alienist. Psychiatrist, psychopathologist, *neurologist, psychotherapist, psychoanalyst.
alight, *v.* **1** *Descend, dismount.
Con. Mount, *ascend, scale, climb.
2 Alight, light, land, perch, roost come into comparison when they mean to come to rest after, or as after, a flight, a descent, or a fall. **Alight** suggests previous movement through the air or open space, as of a flying bird or a floating snowflake; as, skylarks *alight* on the ground. "The sun paused ere it should *alight*" (*Shelley*). **Light,** sometimes the equivalent of *alight,* more often presupposes a falling or jumping than flying or floating, and sometimes merely a wandering or roving; as, he sprang from the roof and *lighted* on his feet; her eyes finally *lighted* on the object of her search. Sometimes it implies random or chance hitting or meeting. "You could not *light* upon a sweeter thing" (*Tennyson*). **Land,** as here considered, derives its implications from its literal application to a boat docking or an airplane grounding. Though often used interchangeably with *light,* it is distinguishable in precise use, where it connotes arrival at a destination, and sometimes, though not invariably, driving force or power; as, the airplane *landed* in a swamp; he fell headlong and *landed* on his face; his blow *landed* in the spot he aimed at; he has *landed* where he hoped, in an executive position. **Perch** and **roost,** in literal use, imply alighting of birds, but *perch* suggests settling on something elevated to which the claws may cling, as a pole, a bar, or a twig; and *roost,* the settling for rest or sleep especially of domestic fowls on the perches and in the shelters prepared for them. Therefore, in extended use, *perch* often implies elevation of position and tenuousness of grasp or hold. "Twenty or more [rooks] *perched* aloft, cawing and conversing comfortably" (*Jefferies*). "A lofty perpendicular cliff . . . with a castle . . . *perched* on the distant top" (*Lucas*). **Roost,** when used of persons, often suggests a position like that of roosting fowls (as, boys *roosting* on the rail of a fence) or is a vulgar synonym for *sleep* or *go to bed;* as, it is time for all of us to *roost* (or go to *roost*).
Con. *Rise, arise, soar, ascend, rocket.
align *or* **aline.** *Line, range, array.
Ana. *Order, arrange, marshal: regulate, fix, *adjust.
Con. *Disorder, disarrange, derange, unsettle.
alike. Like, *similar, identical, homogeneous, uniform, akin, analogous, comparable, parallel.
Ana. *Same, selfsame, equivalent, identical.
Ant. Different. — *Con.* *Distinct, separate: *different, divergent, diverse, disparate, various.
aliment. *Food, pabulum, nutriment, nourishment, sustenance, pap.
Con. *Poison, venom, bane.
alive. **1** *Living, quick, animated, animate, vital.
Ana. *Active, dynamic, live, operative: *lively, vivacious, sprightly: being, existing (see BE).
Ant. Dead, defunct. — *Con.* Lifeless, inanimate, deceased (see DEAD): inert, *inactive: torpid, comatose (see LETHARGIC).
2 *Aware, awake, sensible, cognizant, conscious.
Ana. Alert, wideawake, vigilant, *watchful: *intelligent, knowing, quick-witted.
Ant. Blind (*to*): anesthetic (*to*). — *Con.* *Indifferent, unconcerned, aloof: insensitive, *insensible, impassible.
alkahest. *Solvent, dissolvent, resolvent, menstruum.
alkaline. Alkaline, basic are closely related but not synonymous terms that are often confused. Both terms are opposites or correlatives of the adjective *acid,* but **alkaline** suggests the characteristic properties of bases or alkalies, as neutralizing acids, turning litmus paper blue, etc.; as, *alkaline* taste, *alkaline* solution, *alkaline* earth. **Basic** pertains more directly to the bases themselves, implying their composition; as, *basic* salt, *basic* dye, *basic* rock. Sodium bicarbonate is an *acid* salt (the opposite of a *basic* salt) but it has an *alkaline* reaction because sodium hydroxide is a very strong *base* and carbonic acid is a very weak *acid.*
all, *adj.* **1** *Whole, entire, total, gross.
Ana. Complete, plenary, *full.
Ant. Part (*of*). — *Con.* *Some, any.
2 All, every, each, when applied to the individuals of a group, imply inclusion of the entire membership and admit no exceptions. **All** is applied to the aggregate of individuals and implies consideration of it as a unit without regard to the individuals as distinct persons or things; as, *all* men are mortal; *all* books are written to be read but not *all* books are worth reading. **Every** is applied to any of the individuals comprising the group, regarded not as a concrete person or thing, but as the type or representative of the entire membership; as, *every* man is mortal; *every* book that is published should be worth reading. **Each** is applied to any or every individual of the group, but unlike *every* it implies reference to him or to it as a distinct, recognizable, and, therefore, concrete person or thing; as, he knows *each* person in the society; *each* book on this shelf is worth reading; *each* person in this club must pay his share of the expense.
Ant. No.

allay. *Relieve, alleviate, lighten, assuage, mitigate.
Ana. Abate, lessen, *decrease, diminish: mollify, *pacify, appease: *moderate, temper, attemper.
Ant. Intensify. — *Con.* *Provoke, excite, stimulate: *stir, rouse, arouse: aggravate, enhance (see INTENSIFY).
allée. Alley, mall, *avenue.
allege. *Adduce, cite, advance.
Ana. Affirm, *assert, declare, avouch, avow: *swear, asseverate, depose, depone: recite, recount, rehearse, state (see RELATE).
Ant. Contravene: (*in law*) traverse. — *Con.* *Deny, contradict, gainsay, negative, impugn: *disprove, refute, rebut, controvert.
allegiance. 1 **Allegiance, homage, fealty** are here compared primarily as terms referring to the relationship between a vassal and his lord. They are not synonymous words for they do not bear a common denotation. **Allegiance** originally denoted the duty or the obligation of a vassal to his lord or sovereign or the subject relationship which such an obligation entailed. It implied that in return for land and protection the vassal promised service in war and at court, obedience to the lord's will in certain matters, and fidelity. In modern use, *allegiance* has not changed its denotation except in regard to the status of the principals. Instead of "vassal" one now speaks of "subject" or "citizen," and instead of "lord" one speaks of "sovereign" or "government." Also, the subject or citizen, in general, owes obedience to the law and accepts the obligations to pay taxes and to render military service, when called upon, in return for the maintenance of order within the state and the protection of his rights as an individual at home and abroad. **Homage** (see also HONOR) designates the act or ceremony in which a vassal, on assuming tenancy, publicly declared his allegiance to his lord. Homage was done not only by the first to take possession but by each heir in his turn. **Fealty** (see also FIDELITY) primarily denotes the oath (sometimes called *oath of fealty*) taken by the vassal to be faithful to his lord. Like homage it was demanded not only of the first holder of a fief but of each succeeding one; the doing of homage was the first and the swearing of fealty was the second of the steps in the process of entering into the full possession of a fief.
2 Fealty, loyalty, *fidelity, devotion, piety.
Ana. Faithfulness, steadfastness, constancy, stanchness (see corresponding adjectives at FAITHFUL): obeisance, deference, homage, *honor: obedience (see corresponding adjective OBEDIENT): *obligation, duty.
Ant. Treachery: treason. — *Con.* Traitorousness, perfidy, faithlessness, disloyalty (see corresponding adjectives at FAITHLESS): disaffection, alienation (see corresponding verbs at ESTRANGE).
allegorical. **Allegorical, allegoristic** tend to be clearly distinguished in modern scholarly use. **Allegorical** is preferable when the intent is to describe something as being (or as belonging to something that is) an allegory obviously and intentionally; as, an *allegorical* poem; *allegorical* characters; the *allegorical* meaning of *Pilgrim's Progress*. **Allegoristic** is preferable when the intent is to imply allegorizing, or the turning of a work into an allegory or the regarding of a thing as having allegorical significance but not allegorical intention; as, *allegoristic* interpretation of Scriptures; *allegoristic* criticism of Vergil's *Aeneid;* the *allegoristic* method of studying poetry; the *allegoristic* treatment of animals in the medieval bestiaries.
allegoristic. *Allegorical.
allegory. 1 **Allegory, symbolism** are here compared as designating methods of representation in art. Both characteristically aim to represent concretely that which is abstract or for some other reason unrepresentable. **Allegory** is applied to a form of representation found not only in literature but also in painting and sculpture, especially decorative painting and sculpture. It evokes a dual interest, one in the story, scene, or characters presented, and the other in the ideas they convey or the significance they bear; it demands not only aesthetic enjoyment but intellectual interpretation. The incidents, scenes, or characters may be historical or fictitious or fabulous, but if the artist has given that which is historical an added meaning or has invented his material to convey an idea or truth, he has employed *allegory*. **Symbolism** is applied to a form of representation used not only in literature, painting and sculpture but also in music, architecture, ceremonial, pageantry, and the like. It implies an attempt to represent that which by its very nature is incapable of representation because immaterial, ideal, or spiritual. Originally, *symbolism* denoted representation by an accepted sign or symbol (see SYMBOL, 2); thus, in painting and sculpture, the divinity of Jesus was represented by a nimbus enclosing a cross, and sainthood by a simple nimbus usually enclosing rays. In modern use, *symbolism* also implies artistic imitation and invention, not as an end in itself, but as a means of suggesting that which eludes representation or, sometimes, that which is not directly representable for some reason, such as defiance of the generally accepted moral code. Thus, a poet employs *symbolism* when his images, his rhythms, his words, evoke ideas or emotions that escape analysis; a painter employs *symbolism* when he uses arrangements of colors and of lines not to represent definite objects but to suggest something that is impalpable or intangible; a novelist or dramatist employs *symbolism* when his novel or play carries more than its surface meaning or offers hints of an underlying significance. Especially in literature, *symbolism* is not always clearly distinguishable from *allegory*. The latter term, however, implies organization and a pattern in which the characters, incidents, and setting serve as symbols.
2 **Allegory, parable, myth, fable, apologue** are here compared only as literary forms that typically tell a story for the sake of presenting a truth or of enforcing a moral. An **allegory** always veils its true meaning (its underlying, or allegorical, sense) by leaving that to be deduced from the story it tells (the outward, or literal, sense). Its characters and incidents are therefore either figurative or typical; they serve as a bait to the consideration of dull or unpleasant truths, as in Bunyan's *Pilgrim's Progress*, or as a graded approach to the apprehension of ideas too difficult for the ordinary man, as in Dante's *Divine Comedy*, or as a cloak for an attack on persons or for an exposure of vices and follies, as in parts of Spenser's *Faerie Queene*. When the allegory is very short and simple and narrates or describes a familiar occurrence in nature or life that by analogy conveys a spiritual truth, it is called a **parable.** The term is specifically applied to the brief allegories used by Jesus in his sermons, such as the one likening the kingdom of heaven to the growth of a mustard seed. **Myth** (sometimes for the sake of distinction called **Platonic myth**) is applied to a type of brief allegory used especially by Plato in expounding a difficult philosophical conception. Such myths are, as a rule, invented and their characters and incidents are purely imaginary. In a **fable** or **apologue** (the latter the more bookish term) the moral is usually clearly stated at the end. Its characters are animals or inanimate things that by talking and acting as human beings reflect the weaknesses and follies of men.
allergy. *Susceptibility, hypersensitivity, anaphylaxis.
Ant. Immunity: anergy (*in technical use*).
alleviate. *Relieve, lighten, assuage, mitigate, allay.

Ana. *Moderate, temper, attemper: lessen, reduce, diminish, *decrease: remedy, *cure.
Ant. Aggravate. — *Con.* *Intensify, heighten: *provoke, excite, stimulate: arouse, awaken, rouse, *stir.

alley. 1 Allée, mall, *avenue.
2 Alleyway, byway, lane, roadway, *road, street, thoroughfare.

alleyway. Alley, byway, lane, roadway, *road, street, thoroughfare.

alliance. **Alliance, league, coalition, fusion, confederacy, confederation, federation** agree in the idea of combination, chiefly political, for a common object. **Alliance** applies particularly to a joining of interests on the part of families (by marriage) or of states (by compact or treaty): it is also less formally used of a connection, for mutual benefit, between other bodies, organized or not; as, an *alliance* between two royal houses; a defensive *alliance;* the *alliance* between Czechoslovakia, Yugoslavia, and Rumania; an *alliance* between producers and consumers. **League,** often used without distinction from *alliance,* commonly suggests a more formal compact or more definite object, and may frequently (unlike *alliance*) be taken in a bad sense; as, the Solemn *League* and Covenant; to be in *league* with the powers of darkness. **Coalition** refers to a temporary alliance of otherwise opposing interests, parties, or factions; as, "Mr. Fox, and his famous *coalition* with Lord North" (*Gibbon*); a *coalition* ministry. **Fusion** is a coalition of political parties for the purpose of defeating another party in an election; as, a *fusion* of Republicans and independent Democrats in New York City opposed the Tammany Democratic ticket. **Confederacy** and **confederation,** in their political sense, apply specif. to a union by compact or treaty of independent states under a government to which powers are delegated for dealing primarily with common external relations; as, the Southern *Confederacy;* the Articles of *Confederation;* the German *Confederation.* **Federation** in its broad sense includes any union under the terms of a league or covenant; but specif. it designates a sovereign state, a city, etc., especially one formed by the union of other states, etc., with a central general government and several local governments; as, the *Federation* of Labor or of the British Empire; in the strictest sense, the United States of America constitutes a *federation.* "*Federation* was the name given to the scheme for blending the Five Towns into one town" (*Bennett*).

allied. *Related, cognate, kindred, affiliated.
Ana. Akin, homogeneous, parallel, *similar: linked, associated, united, connected (see JOIN): co-operating, uniting, conjoining (see UNITE).
Ant. Unallied. — *Con.* Alien, foreign, extraneous (see EXTRINSIC): *different, divergent, diverse, various, disparate.

alligator. *Crocodile, cayman.

allocate. *Allot, assign, apportion.
Ana. *Distribute, dispense, divide, deal, dole: *grant, accord, award.
Con. Withhold, detain, retain, hold back, *keep.

allocution. *Speech, address, sermon, oration, homily, talk, lecture, harangue, prelection.

allonym. *Pseudonym, alias, nom de guerre, pen name, nom de plume, incognito.

allot. **Allot, assign, apportion, allocate** agree in meaning to give as one's share, portion, or the like. **Allot** implies more or less arbitrary or haphazard selection and, unless qualified, conveys no suggestion of a fair or equal distribution; as, to *allot* oneself an hour a day for exercise; to *allot* 500 square feet to an exhibitor. "He had been *allotted* a small sitting-room" (*C. Mackenzie*). "Brutus and Cassius . . . were *allotted* the minor governments of Crete and Cyrene" (*Buchan*). **Assign** stresses authoritative and, usually, fixed allotment; it too carries no hint of an even division. "This original and supreme will [that of the people] organizes the government, and *assigns* to different departments their respective powers" (*Ch. Just. Marshall*). "In the beginning, Father Jove . . . *assigned* [the day] to work, the night to rest . . . But little by little business began to encroach on the time *allotted* to rest" (*S. M. Crothers*). **Apportion,** on the other hand, implies a principle of fair division, sometimes of equivalence in sharing, but more often of a proportionate distribution; as, after each decennial census, Congress *apportions* the number of representatives to be elected by each state. "His guardians had *apportioned* to him an allowance . . . adequate to his position" (*Disraeli*). **Allocate** is used chiefly in reference to money, property, territory, powers, and the like, and suggests definite appropriation to a particular person or group or dedication to a particular use; as, to *allocate* a sum of money for the construction of a bridge; the districts of Czechoslovakia *allocated* to Germany by the Munich Agreement. "The whole subtle question of the *allocation* of powers under the Constitution" (*North American Review*).
Ana. Divide, dispense, *distribute, deal, dole: *give, bestow.
Con. *Keep, retain, withhold, detain, hold back: confiscate, appropriate, *arrogate.

allow. 1 Permit, suffer, *let, leave.
Ana. Tolerate, endure, stand, brook (see BEAR): accede, acquiesce (see ASSENT): *yield, submit, defer.
Ant. Inhibit. — *Con.* *Forbid, prohibit, enjoin: *prevent, avert, ward off.
2 *Grant, concede.
Ana. Admit, *acknowledge, confess: acquiesce (in), accede (to), *assent (to).
Ant. Disallow. — *Con.* Reject, refuse (see DECLINE): *disapprove, deprecate: *deny, gainsay, contradict, traverse.

allowance. 1 *Ration, dole, pittance.
Ana. Allotment, apportionment, assignment (see corresponding verbs at ALLOT): share (see corresponding verb SHARE): grant, *appropriation, subsidy.
2 **Allowance, concession** come into comparison when they signify a change made by way of compromise or adjustment. **Allowance** usually implies a modification or variation of a requirement, a standard, etc., made for a good reason, such as probable contingencies or mitigating circumstances; as, to make *allowance* for the current in steering; to make *allowance* for a person's inexperience; to make *allowance* for wear through friction in designing the parts of a machine. "If business imposes its restraints and its silences and impediments, Mr. Darnay as a young gentleman of generosity knows how to make *allowance* for that circumstance" (*Dickens*). **Concession** implies that the change has been made reluctantly and usually as a favor or indulgence; as, they would make no *concession* to a candidate's youth and inexperience. "The sole *concession* to leisure allowed me out of the year was one month on a farm" (*V. Heiser*). "Any *concession* to fashion was, they felt, unbecoming to their age" (*V. Sackville-West*).
Ana. Adjustment, accommodation, adaptation (see corresponding verbs at ADAPT): modification, variation (see under CHANGE, *v.*).
3 *Advantage, handicap, odds, edge.

alloy. *Admixture, adulterant.

all-round *or* **all-around.** *Versatile, many-sided.
Ana. Complete, *full: apt, ready, *quick.

allude. *Refer, advert.
Ana. *Suggest, imply, hint, intimate.

allure, *v.* *Attract, captivate, charm, fascinate, take, enchant, bewitch.
Ana. *Lure, entice, seduce: *invite, solicit, woo, court: beguile, delude (see DECEIVE).
Ant. Repugn (*Rare*), repel. — *Con.* Alienate, *estrange, disaffect, wean: shun, avoid, elude, eschew (see ESCAPE).

alluring. Attractive, charming, fascinating, bewitching, enchanting, captivating, taking. See under ATTRACT, *v.*
Ana. Lovely, fair, *beautiful, pretty, bonny: seductive, enticing, tempting, luring (see corresponding verbs at LURE): beguiling, delusive (see corresponding verbs at DECEIVE).
Ant. Repulsive. — *Con.* *Offensive, loathsome, repugnant, revolting: repellent, abhorrent, distasteful, obnoxious (see REPUGNANT).

allusion. See corresponding verb at REFER.

allusive. See corresponding verb at REFER.

alluvium *or* **alluvion.** *Wash, drift, diluvium, silt.

ally. Colleague, *partner, copartner, confederate.
Ana. *Associate, comrade, companion: supporter, upholder, backer (see under SUPPORT, *v.*): co-operator (see corresponding verb at UNITE).
Ant. Adversary. — *Con.* *Enemy, foe: competitor, rival (see corresponding verbs at RIVAL): *opponent, antagonist.

almighty. *Omnipotent.
Ana. *Infinite, eternal, uncircumscribed: potent, puissant, *powerful.

almost. *Nearly, approximately, well-nigh.
☞ *Do not confuse* almost *with* most.

alms. Benefaction, contribution, *donation.
Ana. *Charity, philanthropy: dole, pittance, allowance, *ration.

alone, *adj.* **1 Alone, solitary, lonely, lonesome, lone, forlorn, lorn, desolate** agree in denoting apart from others; by oneself or itself. **Alone** lays stress upon the objective fact of being entirely by oneself; **solitary** connotes a sense of isolation or remoteness. "*Alone, alone,* all, all *alone, Alone* on a wide wide sea" (*Coleridge*). "A mind forever voyaging through strange seas of thought, *alone*" (*Wordsworth*). "The notice . . . has been delayed . . . till I am indifferent, and cannot enjoy it; till I am *solitary,* and cannot impart it" (*Johnson*). "I am to be left . . . with Dora only. That will be rather *solitary.* However, I never am and never can be *alone*" (*T. E. Brown*). "All is bright, and clear, and still, Round the *solitary* hill" (*Shelley*). One is **lonely** who feels oneself alone and longs for companionship; the word also applies to places which are unfrequented; **lonesome** heightens the implication of dreariness; **lone** is chiefly poetical. "I wandered *lonely* as a cloud" (*Wordsworth*). "This soul hath been Alone on a wide wide sea: So *lonely* 'twas, that God himself Scarce seemed there to be" (*Coleridge*). "Like one that on a *lonesome road* Doth walk in fear and dread" (*Coleridge*). "A dismal and *lonesome* old woman" (*N. Hawthorne*). "Her life is *lone;* he sits apart" (*Tennyson*). One is **forlorn** who is woebegone and listless because of separation from what is dear to him (usually from persons or a person); a place is *forlorn* that is remote, uninhabited, uncultivated, and dreary. "There is nothing so bad as parting with one's friends. One seems so *forlorn* without them" (*Austen*). "Repair me with thy presence, Silvia; Thou gentle nymph, cherish thy *forlorn* swain!" (*Shak.*). "The fascination of the Polar continent . . . is the fascination of the unknown, the limitlessly rigorous, the terrible and the *forlorn*" (*Times Lit. Sup.*). **Lorn** differs from *forlorn* in that it is chiefly literary, is not often used of places, and often specifically implies lovelorn. "I weep as I wander, *lorn* and lone, Through the coral caves where the mermaids roam, And all but me have the comforts of home" (*N. Y. Sun*). "Where was *lorn* Urania When Adonais died?" (*Shelley*). **Desolate** intensifies the implications of *forlorn,* implying a more irreparable loss, a more poignant grief, as disconsolateness because of desertion or bereavement (as, a widow *forlorn* because her only child is away at school; a widow *desolate* on the death of an only child). As applied to places, *desolate* often implies barrenness, dilapidation, ruination, etc. "I cry in my sleep where is he! I demand of Heaven, will he not come to deliver me! No answer. Ah Monsieur . . . I send my *desolate* cry across the sea" (*Dickens*). "Little town, thy streets for evermore Will silent be; and not a soul to tell Why thou art *desolate,* can e'er return" (*Keats*).
Ana. *Single, sole, lone, unique: deserted, abandoned, forsaken (see ABANDON): isolated, secluded (see corresponding nouns at SOLITUDE).
Ant. Accompanied. — *Con.* Attended, escorted, convoyed, chaperoned (see ACCOMPANY): aided, assisted, helped (see HELP).
2 Alone, *adj.* & *adv.* *Only.

aloof. *Indifferent, detached, disinterested, unconcerned, incurious.
Ana. Disdainful, haughty, arrogant, *proud: uninterested, *disinterested: cool, *cold: reserved, reticent, *silent.
Ant. Familiar, close. — *Con.* Friendly, neighborly (see AMICABLE): intimate, confidential, chummy (see FAMILIAR).

alp. Peak, *mountain, mount.

alphabetize. Classify, pigeonhole, *assort, sort.
Ana. *Order, arrange, systematize, methodize.

also. Also, too, likewise, besides, moreover, furthermore agree in meaning in addition, and are used when joining (not necessarily in the same sentence) one proposition or consideration to another. **Also** adds to a statement something that may be affirmed equally with what precedes. "That where I am, there ye may be also" (*John* xiv. 3). "Every simile ought not only to be well adapted to the subject, but *also* to include every excellence of description" (*Goldsmith*). **Too** is less formal than *also,* and adds with a lighter touch. "Like Twilight's, *too,* her dusky hair" (*Wordsworth*). "I can like now, and admire you *too,* sir" (*Thackeray*). **Likewise** is more formal and slightly more explicit than *also;* it sometimes, but no longer necessarily, implies specific likeness or connection between the ideas which it unites. "Have I not seen—ye *likewise* may have seen" (*Wordsworth*). "Greek, was your ambition *likewise* doomed to failure?" (*Browning*). The last three words introduce a statement which must be taken into consideration along with that which precedes. **Besides** usually introduces a statement that strengthens what has been said; as, his project is an excellent one; *besides,* it is likely to help a great many persons. **Moreover** is more emphatic than *besides,* and often serves as a transitional word between sentences: it often implies that the stronger of two considerations is yet to be presented; as, the mountain was steep and rugged; *moreover,* its sides were coated with ice. **Furthermore** is sometimes the most formal of these words; its chief use, however, is in a chain of additions where either *besides* or *moreover* has (or where both have) already been used; as, he is well-liked; *moreover,* he is absolutely dependable; *furthermore,* there is no one who can take his place.

altar. Altar, shrine, tabernacle, chantry are sometimes confused when applied to structures used in Christian ceremonies. An **altar** is a tablelike structure used in celebrating the Eucharist. It is indispensable to the celebration of Mass, or, in the Eastern churches, to the celebration of the Divine Liturgy. It is also found in many Protestant churches. A **shrine** is a structure before which devotions to a saint or sacred personage are carried on. Originally, a shrine was a cofferlike or tomblike structure containing the relics of the saint; now it is more often a statue in a niche or on a pedestal, or an altar surmounted by a statue. As an altar, the latter may be used in the celebration of the Eucharist; as a shrine of a particular saint, the term implies that prayers said before it invoke his intercession. A **tabernacle,** as here compared, is a boxlike structure placed at the center of an altar to receive the unconsumed consecrated bread and wine. **Chantry,** originally applied to an endowment for masses for the soul of a dead person or persons, is also applied to an altar endowed for the same purpose.

alter. *Change, vary, modify.
Ana. Adjust, accommodate, *adapt: qualify, temper, attemper (see MODERATE): *transform, metamorphose, convert.
Ant. Fix. — *Con.* *Set, settle, establish: preserve, conserve (see SAVE): *continue, last, endure, abide, persist.

alteration. Change, variation, modification. See under CHANGE, *v.*
Ana. Adjustment, adaptation, accommodation (see corresponding verbs at ADAPT): transformation, metamorphosis, conversion (see under TRANSFORM).
Ant. Fixation: fixity. — *Con.* Permanence, stability, perdurability (see corresponding adjectives at LASTING): continuance, endurance, persistence (see corresponding verbs at CONTINUE).

alterative. *Restorative.

altercate, *v.* Quarrel, wrangle, squabble, bicker, spat, tiff. See under QUARREL, *n.*
Ana. Fight, *contend, battle, war: dispute, debate, agitate (see DISCUSS).
Ant. Concur. — *Con.* *Agree, coincide: conform, reconcile, accommodate, *adapt.

altercation. *Quarrel, wrangle, squabble, bickering, spat, tiff.
Ana. Fight, conflict, combat, *contest: *discord, dissension, contention, variance, strife: controversy, dispute, *argument.
Ant. Concurrence: accord. — *Con.* Agreement, coincidence (see corresponding verbs at AGREE): *harmony, concord, consonance.

alternate, *adj.* *Intermittent, recurrent, periodic.
Ana. Alternating, rotating (see ALTERNATE, *v.*): *reciprocal, correspondent, complementary.
Ant. Consecutive. — *Con.* Successive, sequent (see CONSECUTIVE).

alternate, *n.* *Substitute, supply, understudy, double, stand-in, pinch hitter, locum tenens.

alternate, *v.* *Rotate.
Ana. Recur, *return, revert: oscillate, fluctuate, sway, waver (see SWING).
Con. *Follow, succeed.

alternation. Vicissitude, *change, mutation, permutation.
Ana. Rotation (see corresponding verb ROTATE): oscillation, fluctuation, wavering (see corresponding verbs at SWING): turning, revolving, rotating, wheeling (see TURN, *v.*): recurrence, return, reversion (see under RETURN, *v.*).

alternative. Option, *choice, preference, selection, election.

although. *Though, albeit.

altitude. *Height, elevation, stature.
Ana. Highness, tallness, loftiness (see corresponding adjectives at HIGH): *summit, peak, apex.
Con. Depth, profundity (see corresponding adjectives at DEEP).

altruistic. Benevolent, *charitable, humanitarian, philanthropic.
Ana. Self-abnegating, self-denying (see corresponding nouns at RENUNCIATION): generous, bountiful, *liberal.
Ant. Egoistic. — *Con.* Egotistic, self-loving, self-esteeming, conceited (see corresponding nouns at CONCEIT): self-indulging, self-pampering (see primitive verbs at INDULGE).

always. *Forever, ever, aye, evermore, forevermore.

amalgam. *Mixture, admixture, compound, blend, composite.

amalgamate. Blend, commingle, merge, coalesce, fuse, *mix, mingle.
Ana. Combine, unite, link, associate, *join: consolidate, unify, *compact.
Con. Disintegrate, crumble, decompose (see DECAY): disperse, dissipate, *scatter: *separate, part, divide.

amalgamation. *Consolidation, merger.

amanuensis. Scrivener, scribe, *secretary, stenographer, typist.

amaranthine. Fadeless, deathless, unfading, *immortal, undying.
Ana. *Everlasting, endless, never-ending: eternal (see INFINITE): *lasting, perdurable, perpetual.

amass. *Accumulate, hoard.
Ana. Collect, *gather, assemble: *heap, pile, mass, stack.
Ant. Distribute. — *Con.* Dissipate, *scatter, disperse: dispense, divide, deal, dole (see DISTRIBUTE).

amateur. **Amateur, dilettante, dabbler, tyro** (*or* **tiro**) come into comparison when they denote a person who follows a pursuit without showing proficiency or a professional purpose. Originally, **amateur** denoted (and still occasionally denotes) one who has a taste or liking for something rather than an expert knowledge of it: in this sense it is distinguished from *connoisseur;* as, an *amateur* of cameos; "[speaking] in his quality of an *amateur* of dogs" (*Bennett*). In current use, *amateur* is commonly applied to a person whose participation in an activity requiring skill is due to a personal rather than a professional interest. It usually, but not invariably, also implies a lack of mastery. This latter implication is not found in sports, where a technical distinction between an *amateur* (one who competes without remuneration) and a *professional* (one who competes for reward) prevails. In other use the word is opposed to *expert* and *adept,* as well as *professional.* Sometimes it suggests lack of experience or apprenticeship; as, "every artist was first an *amateur*" (*Emerson*): sometimes it connotes indulgence in a particular pursuit as a pastime or as an avocation. "How could an *amateur* venture out and make an exhibition of himself after such splendid rowing!" (*Jefferies*). Very often, especially in contrast to *expert* or *adept,* it connotes superficiality, bungling, indifference to professional standards, or the like. "It is beginning to be hinted that we are a nation of *amateurs*" (*Rosebery*). "The third Earl of Shaftesbury . . . illustrated this unsystematic method of thinking. He was an *amateur,* an aristocratic *amateur,* careless of consistency" (*H. Ellis*). **Dilettante** was originally and is now again applied to an amateur (in the early underogatory sense of that word) in the fine arts (see AESTHETE). Like *amateur* it acquired depreciatory connotations, but its original implication of a genuine liking and taste for the pursuit has not been lost. It stresses enjoyment rather than effort, a frittering rather than a concentration of one's energies, and, sometimes, the point of view of the aesthete. "The *dilettante* lives an easy, butterfly life, knowing nothing of . . . toil and labor" (*Osler*). "We continue to respect the erudite mind, and to decry the appreciative spirit as amateurish and *dilettante*" (*A. C. Benson*). **Dabbler** also implies a lack of serious purpose, but it suggests desultory habits of work and lack of persistence. "Your *dabblers* in metaphysics are the most dangerous creatures breathing" (*A. Tucker*). "The certainty of touch which marks the difference between an artist and the *dabbler* . . . can come only after patient study" (*B. Wendell*). **Tyro,** though originally applied to a young soldier just recruited, and later to a beginner, especially a young one, now does not necessarily imply youth; it does, however, suggest comparable inexperience or audacity with resulting incompetence or crudeness. "It may be fancy on the part of a *tyro* in music to suggest that a change from poetry to prose occurs when Beethoven introduces in the last movement of the Choral Symphony . . . a subject in words" (*S. Alexander*). " 'A noble theme!' the *tyro* cried, And straightway scribbled off a sonnet. 'A noble theme,' the poet sighed, 'I am not fit to write upon it' " (*C. Wells*).

Ana. *Novice, apprentice, probationer.

Ant. Professional: expert. — *Con.* Adept, wizard, dab, dabster, virtuoso (see EXPERT).

amative. Amorous, amatory, *erotic.

amatory. *Erotic, aphrodisiac, amative, amorous.

amaze, *v.* Astound, flabbergast, astonish, *surprise.

Ana. Dumfound, bewilder, confound, nonplus (see PUZZLE): impress, touch, strike, *affect.

amaze, *n.* Amazement, *wonder, wonderment, admiration.

Ana. Bewilderment, dumfounding, confounding, mystification (see corresponding verbs at PUZZLE).

amazement. Amaze, *wonder, wonderment, admiration.

Ana. See those at AMAZE, *n.*

amazon. *Virago, termagant.

ambassador *or* **embassador. Ambassador** (*or* **embassador**), **legate, nuncio, minister, envoy, internuncio** are here compared only in their technical senses with reference to their order of precedence as fixed by international regulations. All designate a diplomatic agent serving his sovereign or government in a foreign country. *Ambassador, legate,* and *nuncio* designate a diplomatic agent of the first rank who, as the official representative of his sovereign or chief executive, has access to the sovereign or chief executive of the country in which he serves and is entitled to the same honors as would be accorded to the head of the government were he present in person. An **ambassador** is almost always a resident agent, though sometimes the term is applied to one who goes on a special mission as the chief executive's diplomatic agent. In this case he may be called an **ambassador-at-large.** The comparable diplomatic agents of the pope are called **legate** and **nuncio,** the difference between them being that a legate goes on a special mission and is clothed with authority to act in the name of the pope, and a nuncio serves as the accredited resident ambassador of the Holy See at a foreign court or seat of government. **Minister** is applicable to a diplomatic agent of the second and of the third rank. As an agent of the second rank, he may also be called an **envoy,** for his full title is **envoy extraordinary and minister plenipotentiary.** Though he also carries letters (letters of credence) to the sovereign or chief magistrate of the state to which he is sent, asking credit for what he says or does in the name of the head of his own government, he is not entitled to the same honors as an ambassador. **Internuncio** is the designation of the papal diplomatic agent of the second rank equivalent to an envoy extraordinary or minister plenipotentiary. An agent of the third rank, called more fully **minister resident,** transacts diplomatic business for his government in a foreign country but is not empowered to represent its sovereign or chief executive.

ambiguity. Ambiguity, equivocation, tergiversation, amphibology, amphibologism, double-entendre (*or* **double entente**), are comparable when they denote expression or, usually, an expression, that is capable of more than one interpretation. **Ambiguity** is referable to any expression that admits of two (sometimes more) interpretations; commonly, however, it suggests the use of a word or phrase, rather than a construction, that may be taken in either of two senses. "Where no *ambiguity* arises, the word polygon may be used to refer either to the broken line, or to the part of the plane inclosed by it" (*R. R. Smith,* "Beginners' Geometry," 1931). *Ambiguity* does not in itself suggest intentional lack of explicitness; when that idea is to be conveyed or when an attempt to mislead or (less often) an indifference to accuracy in statement is to be suggested, **equivocation** is the preferable word. "The first cardinal sin from the logician's standpoint is *equivocation.* Thus Hobbes has declared that 'in all discourses wherein one man pretends to instruct or convince another, he should use the same word constantly in the same sense' " (*The Kenyon Review*). "*Equivocation* is half-way to lying" (*Penn*). But *equivocation* often specifically implies the use of a word that is important to the argument or thought in another sense than that one in which it has been already employed, either because the writer or speaker is himself confused or because he wishes to confuse those whom he is addressing. **Tergiversation,** a less common word, stresses a shifting of senses, especially of a word or words important to one's argument. It always implies evasion and looseness of thought; sometimes it connotes intentional subterfuge, and often, in current use, a low standard of intellectual honesty. "Humanism depends very heavily, I believe, upon the *tergiversations* of the word 'human'; and in general, upon implying clear and distinct philosophic ideas which are never there" (*T. S. Eliot*). **Amphibology** and **amphibologism,** terms used chiefly (though now rarely) in logic, imply ambiguity arising from a grammatical construction which can be made to say two divergent things; thus, in "there is no army in existence that our army can overcome" there is an *amphibology,* or *amphibologism,* for "that" and "our army" may be construed respectively as subject and as object of "can overcome" or vice versa. **Double-entendre** (literally, double meaning), a French phrase used more often in an English context than its idiomatic French equivalent **double entente** (literally, double manner of being understood), designates an intentional ambiguity where an expression is used because of its twofold meaning, its obvious sense being a cover for a subtle implication, especially a stinging or an indelicate implication. "Sometimes with these Parliamentary comedies, the humour lay in a kind of *double entendre,* using the phrase in an innocent sense" (*Manchester Guardian*).

Ant. Lucidity: explicitness. — *Con.* Clearness, perspicuousness (see corresponding adjectives at CLEAR): definiteness, specificity, expressness (see corresponding adjectives at EXPLICIT).

ambiguous. Equivocal, cryptic, enigmatic, vague, *obscure, dark.

Ana. Dubious, *doubtful, questionable.

Ant. Explicit. — *Con.* Lucid, perspicuous, *clear: express, definite, specific, categorical (see EXPLICIT).

ambit. Compass, *circumference, perimeter, periphery, circuit.

ambition. Ambition, aspiration, pretension agree in meaning strong desire for advancement. **Ambition** has personal advancement or preferment as its end: it may be praiseworthy: it is sometimes inordinate; as, *ambition* for fame; *ambition* to hold office; *ambition* to acquire wealth; "Vaulting *ambition*, which o'erleaps itself" (*Shak.*). **Aspiration** implies as its object something felt to be above one, the striving after which is uplifting or ennobling; as, *aspiration* after knowledge, excellence, holiness; "That spirit of his In *aspiration* lifts him from the earth" (*Shak.*). *Aspiration*, however, is sometimes used (esp. in the plural) in a derogatory sense of ambition which is felt to be unwarranted or presumptuous; as, his *aspirations* must be nipped in the bud. **Pretension** (see also CLAIM, PRETENSE) was once preferred to *aspiration* in this latter sense, for it etymologically carries a hint of presumptuousness and, therefore, of lack of real claim to the powers which fulfillment of the ambition or aspiration requires. "They are always looked upon, either as neglected, or discontented because their *pretensions* have failed" (*Lady M. W. Montagu*). In current use, the term is rare in this sense (see also CLAIM) but it does occur, and usually implies less driving power than *ambition* or *aspiration* and, often, the guidance of mere desire rather than the possession of the necessary gifts. "It was the undergraduate literary club, whose membership included all nice boys with literary *pretensions*" (*J. P. Marquand*).

Ana. Urge, yen, lust, *desire: eagerness, avidity, keenness, anxiety (see corresponding adjectives at EAGER): spur, goad, incentive, *motive.

Con. Contentment, satisfaction (see corresponding verbs at SATISFY): resignation, *patience: indolence, faineance, sloth (see corresponding adjectives at LAZY).

ambitious. 1 Ambitious, emulous agree in meaning extremely desirous of something that will give one power, fame, success, riches, or the like. **Ambitious** usually implies inordinate, sometimes presumptuous, eagerness to advance oneself or to attain something beyond one's present reach; it often, in addition, connotes aggressiveness in the pursuit of one's ends. "The noble Brutus Hath told you Caesar was *ambitious:* If it were so, it was a grievous fault" (*Shak.*). **Emulous** stresses the desire to equal or surpass another or all others; in older use, it often implied envy or covetousness, but in modern use it suggests rivalry or the spirit of competition. "Men of pedigree . . . *Emulous* always of the nearest place To any throne, except the throne of grace" (*Cowper*).

Ana. *Eager, avid, anxious, keen: aspiring, panting, aiming (see AIM, *v.*): daring, venturous, venturesome, *adventurous.

Ant. Unambitious. — ***Con.*** Apathetic, phlegmatic, stolid (see IMPASSIVE): indolent, fainéant, slothful, *lazy.

2 Ambitious, pretentious, utopian come into comparison when they are applied to plans, designs, programs, policies, and the like, and mean straining or exceeding the capacity of their authors or executants. That is **ambitious** which is either so far beyond what can with certainty be accomplished that its realization or execution is doubtful or which, if realized, is accomplished only by excessive effort or by testing one's powers to the utmost; as, "The philosopher has the *ambitious* aim of unifying, or harmonising, these points of view" (*Inge*); his last novel was his most *ambitious* and, possibly, his best. That is **pretentious** which so far exceeds one's powers or resources that any attempt to carry it out reveals one's inadequacy, inexperience, lack of sufficient skill, or the like; in this sense it often, but not necessarily, implies ostentation; as, the program was too *pretentious* for so young a violinist. That is **utopian** which is utterly impracticable or unattainable under present (or sometimes, any) conditions. *Utopian*, if it does not suggest an idealistic approach, invariably implies indifference to actualities; as, *utopian* schemes for the eradication of poverty; the reformers started out with an *ambitious* program which its critics called *utopian;* time has shown that it was too *pretentious*.

Ana. Audacious, bold (see BRAVE): daring, venturous, temerarious (see ADVENTUROUS): ostentatious, *showy.

Ant. Modest. — ***Con.*** Lowly, *humble: *moderate, temperate.

amble, *v.* **1** Rack, single-foot, pace, walk, canter, lope, trot. See under TROT, *n.*

2 *Saunter, stroll.

Ana. Loiter, dawdle (see DELAY): meander, ramble, roam (see WANDER).

amble, *n.* Rack, single-foot, pace, walk, canter, lope, *trot, gallop.

ambrosia. Ambrosia, nectar, manna, amrita (*or* **amreeta**) are sometimes confused in their metaphorical senses because their literal meanings are not definitely understood. In general, each denotes a divine or miraculous food or drink. **Ambrosia,** literally the food of the Olympian gods, has come to mean food fit for the gods; it and its derivative **ambrosial** are applicable chiefly to foods that give exquisite pleasure and are delectable not only to the palate but to the eye and the nostrils; as, "divine *ambrosial* fruits" (*Milton*); "but he upon *ambrosia* daily fed, That grew in Eden" (*G. Fletcher*). **Nectar,** on the other hand, is literally the drink of the Olympian gods; in precise use, it and its derivatives **nectared, nectarean, nectareous** are applicable only to that which is, literally or figuratively sipped, sucked, or imbibed with ecstatic enjoyment because of its surpassing sweetness and bouquet. "I [am] as rich in having such a jewel As twenty seas, if all their sand were pearl, The water *nectar* and the rocks pure gold" (*Shak.*). "The juice *nectareous*" (*Pope*). "That gall-drop we require lest *nectar* cloy" (*Browning*). **Manna,** literally the food rained from Heaven in the form of flakes for the sustenance of the Children of Israel during their journey through the wilderness, is metaphorically applied to that which is given to nourish or refresh body, mind, or spirit. "Fair ladies, you drop *manna* in the way Of starved people" (*Shak.*). **Amrita,** a Hindu word akin to *ambrosia*, in its figurative use in English poetry is often equivalent to *nectar*. However, in either use, it suggests a revivifying or immortalizing power more often than delectableness. "The divine *Amrita* tree, That blesses heaven's inhabitants With fruits of immortality" (*T. Moore*). "Wide-petaled plants that boldly drink Th'*Amreeta* of the sky" (*E. B. Browning*).

ambrosial. Nectared, nectarean, nectareous. See under AMBROSIA.

Ana. Delectable, delicious, luscious, *delightful.

ambulant. Ambulatory, peripatetic, *itinerant, nomadic, vagrant.

Ant. Bed-ridden (*of patients*).

ambulatory, *adj.* Ambulant, peripatetic, *itinerant, nomadic, vagrant.

ambulatory, *n.* *Passage, passageway, aisle, gallery, cloister, arcade, hall, hallway.

ambuscade. Ambuscado, *ambush.

ambuscado. Ambuscade, *ambush.

ambush, *n.* **Ambush, ambuscade, ambuscado** agree in meaning a device to entrap the enemy by lying in wait under cover for an opportune moment to make a surprise attack. **Ambush,** however, is also used to designate any act of lying in wait or in concealment as for spying, frightening, obtaining an advantage, or the like; it sometimes connotes unfairness or cowardliness; as, "*ambushes* of cutthroats" (*Thackeray*). "When he was a boy he had

. . . once, at their festival time . . . spied on the Pecos men . . . . He had lain in *ambush* for two nights on the mountain" (*Cather*). **Ambuscade** usually implies the legitimate strategic disposition of troops in concealment, but in military use is more often applied to the body of troops or to their position than to the trap. "The knights and gentlemen volunteered for an *ambuscade* to cut off the convoy" (*Froude*). "Fear'd In every wavering brake an *ambuscade*" (*Tennyson*). **Ambuscado** was once more common in English than *ambuscade*, but is now distinctly archaic. "Then dreams he of cutting foreign throats, Of breaches, *ambuscadoes*, Spanish blades" (*Shak.*).

Ana. Trap, snare,* lure: *attack, onset, onslaught, assault.

ambush, *v.* *Surprise, waylay.

Ana. *Attack, assault, assail: trap, entrap, snare, ensnare, nab, capture, *catch.

ameliorate. *Improve, better, help.

Ana. Amend, remedy, reform, rectify, *correct: mitigate, alleviate, *relieve, lighten.

Ant. Worsen: deteriorate (*v.t.*). — ***Con.*** *Injure, harm, hurt, damage, impair, mar, spoil: *intensify, aggravate.

amenable. 1 Answerable, liable, accountable, *responsible.

Ana. Open, subject, *liable: *subordinate, dependent, subject.

Ant. Independent (*of*): autonomous. — ***Con.*** Autocratic, arbitrary, *absolute: *free, autonomic, autarchic.

2 Tractable, *obedient, docile, biddable.

Ana. Pliant, adaptable, pliable (see PLASTIC): responsive (see TENDER): sensitive, open (see LIABLE): submissive, *tame, subdued.

Ant. Recalcitrant, refractory. — ***Con.*** Intractable, *unruly, ungovernable, headstrong: truculent, *fierce: *obstinate, stubborn, mulish.

amend. Reform, *correct, rectify, revise, emend, remedy, redress.

Ana. *Improve, better, ameliorate: *mend, repair: elevate, raise, *lift.

Ant. Debase: impair. — ***Con.*** Corrupt, vitiate, deprave, debauch, pervert (see DEBASE): *injure, mar, spoil, damage, harm, hurt.

amends. Redress, *reparation, indemnity, restitution.

Ana. Compensation, recompense, requital (see corresponding verbs at PAY): atonement, expiation (see under EXPIATE).

amenity. 1 Amenity, luxury, pleasance are synonymous when they agree in denoting a thing (an object, a feature, a quality, an experience) that gives refined or exquisite pleasure or is exceedingly grateful to the mind or senses. **Amenity,** in precise use, implies a delightful mildness, gentleness, or softness, especially in contrast to an uncomfortable or distressing harshness, roughness, crudeness, or the like; thus, many English go to the Riviera in the winter because of the *amenity* of its climate; *amenities* of modern automobile travel such as broad, smooth highways and scenic routes. "The *amenity* of a fine day in its decline surrounded me with a beneficent, a calming influence" (*Conrad*). **Luxury,** as here compared, stresses keen, often voluptuous, enjoyment and unalloyed gratification of the mind or senses, usually, even if not always, without any hint of opulence in the thing enjoyed or sensuality in the pleasure. "And learn the *luxury* of doing good" (*Goldsmith*). "Mark decided to walk back by the road . . . instead of indulging himself in the *luxury* of once more rejoicing in the solitude of the green lanes" (*C. Mackenzie*). "A dressing-room with a marble bath that made cleanliness a *luxury* instead of one of the sternest of the virtues" (*Shaw*). **Pleasance** is now chiefly poetic; it often emphasizes delight in beauty, especially in the beauty of nature, but it invariably implies enjoyable sensations. "With *pleasaunce* of the breathing fields yfed" (*Spenser*). "Thence thro' the garden I was drawn— A realm of *pleasance*" (*Tennyson*). "And searched the garden's little length Some new *pleasaunce* to find; And there some yellow daffodils, and jasmine hanging high, Did rest the tired eye" (*E. W. Tennant*).

Ana. *Pleasure, delight, joy, enjoyment: ease, comfort, relaxation (see REST): mildness, softness, blandness, lenity *or* leniency, gentleness (see corresponding adjectives at SOFT).

Ant. Rigor. — ***Con.*** Harshness, roughness, ruggedness (see corresponding adjectives at ROUGH): disagreeableness, unpleasantness (see affirmative adjectives at PLEASANT): hardship, *difficulty, vicissitude.

2 *Courtesy, comity, attention, gallantry.

Ana. Civility, politeness, courteousness (see corresponding adjectives at CIVIL): graciousness, affability, cordiality, geniality, sociability (see corresponding adjectives at GRACIOUS): *form, convention, convenance: ceremony, formality (see FORM).

Ant. Acerbity, asperity: rudeness. — ***Con.*** Glumness, moroseness, crabbedness, surliness (see corresponding adjectives at SULLEN): *acrimony: *affront, insult, indignity: discourtesy, incivility, impoliteness (see corresponding adjectives at RUDE).

amerce. Fine, mulct, sconce, *penalize.

amercement. Fine (see under PENALIZE).

amiable. 1 *Lovable.

Ana. Attractive, alluring, charming, taking (see under ATTRACT): *pleasant, pleasing, agreeable.

Ant. Unpleasant, displeasing. — ***Con.*** Distasteful, repellent, obnoxious, *repugnant: *offensive, loathsome.

2 Amiable, good-natured, obliging, complaisant bear in common the meaning having or manifesting the desire or disposition to please. All may refer either to moods or to temperaments. **Amiable** usually implies friendliness, affability, kindliness, and other qualities that inspire liking. "From what he said of Miss Darcy, I was thoroughly prepared to see a proud, reserved, disagreeable girl. Yet he . . . . must know that she was as *amiable* and unpretending as we have found her" (*Austen*). Often, however, the word suggests little more than a sweet temper. "She lacked *amiability;* as her mother said, she was 'touchy' " (*Bennett*). Occasionally it additionally connotes lack of firmness or strength. "She suddenly married a poor, good-for-nothing, *amiable* fellow, an artist" (*Deland*). **Good-natured** not only implies a disposition to please but to be pleased; consequently it often connotes undue compliance or indifference to imposition. "He was too *goodnatured* a man to behave harshly" (*Macaulay*). "When he [a child's natural father] is good-natured and not too poor he will often pay her [the mother] more than he is legally obliged to" (*Shaw*). **Obliging** stresses a readiness to be helpful, sometimes, but far from frequently, as a sign of amiability. "Keppel had a sweet and *obliging* temper" (*Macaulay*). "Perfect civility and *obligingness* I certainly did receive from the Virginian, only not a word of fellowship" (*O. Wister*). **Complaisant,** because of its frequent confusion with *complacent,* has either lost or obscured some of its leading implications in undiscriminating modern use. When employed with a feeling for its historic values, it implies a courteous, or sometimes, a merely amiable, desire to please or to be agreeable. " 'We mustn't forget the Ring . . . Mrs. Berry!' . . . [She] was only prevented by natural *complaisance* from shouting: 'Oh, drat ye! And your Ring' " (*Meredith*).

Ana. *Gracious, cordial, affable, genial: warmhearted, warm, responsive, *tender: kindly, *kind, benignant, benign.

Ant. Unamiable: surly. — *Con.* Ungracious, *rude, ill-mannered, discourteous, impolite: *sullen, glum, morose, crabbed, dour.

amicable. **Amicable, neighborly** (*or* **neighbourly**), **friendly** come into comparison when they are applied to the attitudes, acts, words, etc., of persons, communities, and states that have intercourse with each other, and when they mean marked by or exhibiting good will or absence of antagonism. **Amicable** frequently implies little more than that the parties concerned are not disposed to quarrel or are at peace with each other; as, an *amicable* adjustment; an *amicable* suit. "The boys parted *amicably*" (*Meredith*). "The sometimes *amicable* processes of bargaining between a federation of employers and a trade union" (*J. A. Hobson*). **Neighborly** sometimes suggests good will and kindliness, and a disposition to live on good terms with those with whom one must associate because of their proximity; as, she is a *neighborly* soul; Jones thought it was not *neighborly* of Mrs. White to refuse to lend him her lawn mower. Very often, however, because of connotations acquired from scriptural uses of *neighbor*, especially in the parable of the Good Samaritan ("Which now of these three . . . was *neighbour* unto him that fell among the thieves?"—*Luke* x. 36) it implies the duty of helpfulness and the spirit of fellowship. "He hath a *neighbourly* charity in him" (*Shak.*). "He in a very *neighbourly* manner admonished me" (*Swift*). **Friendly** is more positive in its implications of cordiality than either of the others and, also, often suggests warmth of feeling; as, a *friendly* nod; a *friendly* (cf. a *neighborly*) call; a *friendly* state; their relations are *friendly*.

Ana. Peaceful, *pacific, peaceable: harmonious, concordant, accordant (see corresponding nouns at HARMONY): *social, gregarious, co-operative, hospitable.

Ant. Antagonistic. — *Con.* Quarrelsome, contentious, *belligerent, bellicose, pugnacious: hostile, antipathetic (see corresponding nouns at ENMITY).

amidst *or* **amid.** *Among.

amiss. **Amiss, astray** are not often used interchangeably but they carry in common the meaning wrong, or otherwise than intended. **Amiss,** which etymologically implies failure, as of an arrow, to reach the mark aimed at, now frequently suggests a shortcoming or defect, as by failure to reach a standard, an expectation, a definite conclusion, the point of being useful, or the like; as, his shafts of wit went *amiss;* she seemed unconcerned, as though nothing had happened *amiss;* no information came *amiss* to him. Sometimes, *amiss* suggests a divergence from the normal or usual order. "Whether his general health had been previously at all *amiss*" (*Dickens*). " 'What's *amiss* in the Square?' . . . . 'Just now I saw a man running along Wedgewood Street' " (*Bennett*). **Astray** emphasizes wandering from a predetermined path or the right way or course; it usually suggests moral or intellectual errancy. "Lest in temptation's path ye gang *astray*" (*Burns*). "In many an hour when judgment goes *astray*" (*Wordsworth*).

Ana. *Wrong *or* wrongly, bad *or* badly.

Ant. Aright, right.

amity. *Friendship, comity, good will.

Ana. *Harmony, concord, accord: amicableness, neighborliness, friendliness (see corresponding adjectives at AMICABLE).

Ant. Enmity. — *Con.* Hostility, animosity, antipathy, antagonism (see ENMITY): *discord, strife, contention, dissension, conflict, variance.

ammunition. Artillery, munitions, *armament, ordnance, arms.

amnesty. *Pardon, absolution, indulgence.

among *or* **amongst.** **1** **Among** (*or* **amongst**), **amidst** (*or* **amid**) agree in denoting surrounded or encompassed by. **Among,** however, implies a mingling or intermixture with distinct or separable objects; as, "A certain man . . . fell *among* thieves" (*Luke* x. 30); a minister should live *among* the people he serves. Hence it is regularly followed by a plural or a collective noun. **Amidst** literally means in the midst or middle of, hence that which surrounds may or may not consist of distinct or separable objects; as, "to the lonely inn, '*mid* the rocks" (*Arnold*); "She stood in tears *amid* the alien corn" (*Keats*); "*amidst* the splendor and festivity of a court" (*Macaulay*). When both *among* and *amidst* are applicable to the same objects, *among* regards them in their individual, *amidst* in their collective, aspect. Thus Milton describes the seraph Abdiel as "*among* the faithless, faithful only he," having in mind the other angels as individual rebels; but when he adds, "From *amidst* them forth he passed," he is thinking of the angels rather as a collective body.

2 *Between, betwixt.

amoral. Nonmoral, unmoral, *immoral.

amorous. Amative, *erotic, amatory.

Ana. Passionate, fervid, ardent, *impassioned: *enamored, infatuated: lustful, lascivious (see LICENTIOUS).

Ant. Frigid. — *Con.* *Indifferent, aloof, detached: *cold, cool: *impassive, apathetic.

amorphous. Shapeless, unformed, inchoate, *formless, chaotic.

Ana. Unorganized, unordered, unsystematized (see affirmative verbs at ORDER): unshaped, unformed (see affirmative verbs at MAKE).

Ant. Morphous.

amount, *n.* *Sum, total, quantity, number, aggregate, whole.

amour. **Amour, liaison, intrigue, affair, affaire** are synonyms when they denote an instance of illicit love. **Amour** is particularly applied to the illicit attachment of persons in high life; it stresses passion as the motivating force and therefore often connotes transience. **Liaison** implies duration, but not necessarily permanence, in the attachment; it is commonly used to designate the relation between a man and his mistress. **Intrigue** emphasizes the clandestine element in the relation and is often closer to *amour* than to *liaison* in its other implications. **Affair** and its French equivalent **affaire** often suggest equivocal, even if not definitely illicit, relations; however, the English word is often used without any imputation of evil.

amour-propre. Self-esteem, self-love, egoism, egotism, *conceit.

Ana. *Pride, vanity, vainglory: complacency, self-complacency, smugness, self-satisfaction (see corresponding adjectives at COMPLACENT).

amphibologism. Amphibology, *ambiguity, equivocation, tergiversation, double-entendre, double entente.

amphibology. Amphibologism, *ambiguity, equivocation, tergiversation, double-entendre, double entente.

ample. **1** *Spacious, capacious, commodious.

Ana. Expanded, distended, swelled *or* swollen, inflated (see EXPAND): *large, big, great.

Ant. Meager: circumscribed. — *Con.* Limited, restricted, confined (see LIMIT, *v.*): contracted, compressed, condensed, shrunken (see CONTRACT, *v.*): scant, skimpy, exiguous, spare (see MEAGER).

2 Abundant, *plentiful, plenteous, copious.

Ana. *Liberal, generous, handsome, bountiful: *profuse, lavish, prodigal: *sufficient, enough, adequate.

Ant. Scanty, meager. — *Con.* Skimpy, scrimpy (see MEAGER): insufficient, inadequate (see affirmative adjectives at SUFFICIENT): *stingy, niggardly.

amplify. *Expand, swell, distend, dilate, inflate.
Ana. Develop (see MATURE): enlarge, augment (see INCREASE).
Ant. Abridge, condense. — *Con.* *Shorten, abbreviate: *contract, compress.

amplitude. *Expanse, spread, stretch.
Ana. Largeness, bigness, greatness (see corresponding adjectives at LARGE): spaciousness, commodiousness, capaciousness (see corresponding adjectives at SPACIOUS): magnitude, extent, *size: *bulk, mass, volume.
Ant. Straitness: limitation. — *Con.* Narrowness (see corresponding adjective at NARROW): restriction, circumscription (see corresponding verbs at LIMIT).

amrita *or* **amreeta.** *Ambrosia, nectar, manna.

amulet. Periapt, charm, talisman, *fetish.

amuse. **Amuse, divert, entertain, recreate** are synonyms when they mean to cause or enable one to pass one's time in pleasant or agreeable occupations. Their corresponding derivative nouns **amusement, diversion, entertainment, recreation** are also synonyms denoting such an occupation or its effect. Although these words are used more or less interchangeably they are fundamentally different in implications. **Amuse** and **amusement** stress the engagement of one's attention, especially during hours of leisure, in that which keeps one interested or engrossed. They do not necessarily imply play or sport; nevertheless, especially apart from a context, the words often suggest light, purposeless, trivial, or laughter-provoking pastimes. "What he wanted was to be *amused*, to get through the twenty-four hours pleasantly, without sitting down to dry business" (*Macaulay*). "I don't write because I've got things to say . . . . I write because it *amuses* me" (*R. Macaulay*). "We may speculate, for *amusement*, whether it would not have been beneficial . . . to Britain in particular, to have had a more continuous religious history" (*T. S. Eliot*). **Divert** and **diversion,** on the other hand, stress the distraction of the attention from that which is occupying it, as routine interests, worry, or the like, and its capture by something different, especially by something that enlivens or promotes gaiety. "After the novelty of their surroundings had ceased to attract and *divert* the lepers, they often became homesick" (*V. Heiser*). "'It is all very well to reduce the drama to "*amusement*." . . . I believe that the drama has something else to do except to *divert* us' " (*T. S. Eliot*). **Entertain** and **entertainment,** because of their etymological implications of receiving and holding, commonly imply the activities of others to provide amusement or diversion. The words therefore suggest more or less formal expedients or more or less formal circumstances, which are usually implied in the context; as, Mrs. Brown will *entertain* the Burtons over the weekend; radio *entertainers;* a church *entertainment.* "*Entertainment* is what schoolboys are now led to expect . . . ; they are disappointed if the school is not a hall of unbroken *amusement*" (*Grandgent*). **Recreate** and the far more common **recreation** usually imply a change of occupation or an indulgence in diversions for the sake of relaxation or refreshment of body or mind. "The Lord Chancellor was *recreating* himself, after a long stretch of arduous business, with a journey in Scotland" (*H. Martineau*). "Just to sit in the Sun, to bask like an animal in its heat—this is one of my country *recreations*" (*L. P. Smith*).
Ana. Engross, absorb (see MONOPOLIZE): beguile, *while, wile: enliven, *quicken, animate: *thrill, electrify.
Ant. Bore. — *Con.* *Tire, weary, fatigue: *depress, oppress: irk, vex, *annoy.

amusement. Diversion, entertainment, recreation. See under AMUSE, *v.*
Ana. Engrossment, absorption (see corresponding verbs at MONOPOLIZE): play, sport, *fun, jest: disporting, frolicking, rollicking, romping (see PLAY, *v.*): jollity, *mirth.
Ant. Boredom. — *Con.* *Tedium, ennui: languidness, listlessness, spiritlessness (see corresponding adjectives at LANGUID): languor, *lethargy.

anachronism. **1 Anachronism, metachronism, parachronism, prochronism** denote an error in timing an event or detail, especially in historical writing. **Anachronism,** which is the most common of these words, implies a misplacing of an event or detail that belongs to an earlier or a later time than the one under consideration (see article 2, below). Sometimes it specifically implies antedating, but more often it is used in reference to any mistake in chronology. **Metachronism** (which is now rare and often ambiguous) and **parachronism** designate an anachronism that involves giving a later than the true date; **prochronism,** an anachronism in which an earlier than the true date is indicated.

2 Anachronism, solecism are occasionally used interchangeably as meaning something that does not properly belong to the setting or background in which it is placed and that is incongruous with it. **Anachronism,** in precise use, always implies a mistake in associating things which do not belong to the same time or age; thus, an automobile in a story of American Civil War times would be an *anachronism* because automobiles did not come into use until late in the nineteenth century; a Chippendale chair is an *anachronism* in a Jacobean room because the Jacobean style of furniture belongs to the seventeenth century and the Chippendale style was originated at the end of the eighteenth century. When applied to something that does exist at the time under consideration, *anachronism* implies that the thing is behind the times or antiquated and useless. "It [the Roman Senate] became more and more a dignified *anachronism* . . . with no inherent power of initiation or resistance" (*Buchan*). **Solecism,** on the other hand, implies lack of concord or consonance in the association of things that do not properly (that is, according to the proprieties, the decencies, the conventions, or the like) belong together; thus, one who in affectation introduces foreign words into English speech commits a *solecism* in language; a curtsy is a *solecism* (or an *anachronism*) in a modern American drawing room; by eighteenth-century standards, Shakespeare was guilty of a *solecism* when he introduced the comic porter scene into the tragedy of Macbeth. "I feel certain that a *solecism* of this kind—the introduction into a particular rite of features not sanctioned by the texts—would have seemed a shocking thing to . . . so accurate a scholar" (*L. P. Smith*).

anaesthetic. Variant of ANESTHETIC.

anagogical *or* **anagogic.** *Mystical, mystic, cabalistic.
Ana. Allegorical, symbolical (see corresponding nouns at ALLEGORY): *allegorical, allegoristic: occult, esoteric, *recondite.

analgesic. *Anodyne, anesthetic.
Ant. Irritant.

analogous. Comparable, parallel, *similar, like, alike, akin, identical, uniform, homogeneous.
Ana. Correspondent, convertible (see RECIPROCAL): kindred, *related, allied, cognate.

analogue. Counterpart, *parallel, correlate.

analogy. **1** *Likeness, similitude, resemblance, similarity, affinity.

2 Analogy, simile, metaphor agree in designating a comparison between things essentially or generically different, but strikingly alike in one or more pertinent aspects. **Analogy,** in nontechnical use, is the general term, since the simile and the metaphor are kinds of analogies: it is, however, usually restricted in its application to a comparison which brings out the analogy (for this sense see LIKENESS) between two things for the sake of elucidating something hard to understand; thus, God cannot be described except by *analogy;* the socialist, arguing for a co-operative economy, used as an *analogy* a colony of ants. A **simile** is an imaginative analogy, used largely for the sake of literary effect, as by carrying over the emotion aroused by one image or idea to the other with which it is compared. A simile is often brief but it characteristically indicates, as by the use of *like, as, so,* etc., that comparison is intended. Good examples of similes are: "As cold waters to a thirsty soul, so is good news from a far country" (*Proverbs* xxv. 25); "The feeling of unhappiness . . . covered him as water covers a log" (*Kipling*). A **metaphor** differs from a simile in not stating explicitly that it is an analogy: it therefore imaginatively identifies one object with another, and ascribes to the first one or more of the qualities of the second, or invests the former with emotional or imaginative associations attached to the latter. Good examples of metaphor are: "The spirit of man is the candle of the Lord" (*Proverbs* xx. 27); "Life's but a walking shadow, a poor player That struts and frets his hour upon the stage And then is heard no more" (*Shak.*).

analysis. Resolution, dissection, anatomy, breakdown. See under ANALYZE.

Ana. Separation, division (see corresponding verbs at SEPARATE): disintegration, decomposition (see corresponding verbs at DECAY).

Ant. Synthesis. — *Con.* Uniting *or* union, combining *or* combination (see corresponding verbs at JOIN): integration, concatenation (see under INTEGRATE).

analytical *or* **analytic.** Subtle, *logical.

Ana. Acute, keen, *sharp: profound, *deep: penetrating, piercing (see ENTER): organizing, ordering, marshaling (see ORDER, *v.*).

Ant. Creative, inventive, constructive.

analyze *or* **analyse. Analyze** (*or* **analyse**), **resolve, dissect, anatomize, break down** come into comparison when they mean to divide a complex whole or unit into its component parts or constituent elements. When their corresponding nouns (**analysis, resolution, dissection, anatomy, breakdown**) denote such a division, they are similarly applied and are distinguishable by the same implications. **Analyze** and **analysis,** as a rule, presuppose a personal agent and stress division for the sake of determining a thing's true nature or the inner relationship of its parts; as, to *analyze* a sentence, or the plot of a novel, or a sound, or a sensation, or a motive, or a situation; Liebig, by *analyzing* foodstuffs of every kind, came to the conclusion that the principal elements of food are proteins, fats, and carbohydrates; "the final *analysis* of material objects into electrons and protons" (*Inge*). Sometimes these words specifically suggest an intent to discover or uncover qualities, causes, effects, motives, possibilities, or the like, often as a basis for action or for a judgment; as, to *analyze* a mental complex; to *analyze* a person's behavior; to *analyze* the condition of a business; to *analyze* the potential market for cotton. "I could not then so far *analyse* all that is roughly lumped together as 'religion' as to disentangle the essential from the accidental" (*H. Ellis*). Often, especially in chemistry and its allied sciences, the words imply close examination as for detecting impurities or the quantity or quality of each of the constituent elements; as, to *analyze* a city's water supply; to *analyze* an ore; to *analyze* a hypothesis. **Resolve** and **resolution** may, but commonly do not, imply a personal agent; they therefore seldom suggest more than the actual division or separation into elements or parts. "Star-clusters . . . so distant that even in telescopes of great power they could not be *resolved*" (*J. N. Lockyer*). "Oxygen and hydrogen, into which the water is being *resolved* by the [electric] current" (*Karl K. Darrow*). "When each one of them [gusts] raced past, the sound of its progress *resolved* [that is, resolved itself] into . . . . treble, tenor, and bass notes" (*Hardy*). Sometimes, especially in medicine, *resolve* implies a breaking up or disintegration, and usually, as a consequence, a dissipation or scattering; as, to *resolve* a tumor; "crystallised beyond change, not to be disintegrated by time . . . nor *resolved* by any alchemy" (*Hudson*). **Dissect** and **dissection** stress the actual and visible separation of parts; literally, one *dissects*, or cuts into sections, an animal or a plant so that its physical structure can be studied; in extended or figurative use, one *dissects* something when one takes it to pieces and offers it for examination from every angle and in every detail, pleasant or unpleasant. "We *dissect* The senseless body, and why not the mind? . . . the mind of man, upturned, Is in all natures a strange spectacle; In some a hideous one" (*Wordsworth*). "The student who is willing . . . to discipline his mind by the patient correlation of facts and the fearless *dissection* of theories" (*H. Baerlein*). "When you . . . *dissect* the Odyssey, what amazing artifice is found under that apparently straightforward tale!" (*Quiller-Couch*). **Anatomize** and **anatomy** are close synonyms of *dissect* and *dissection* but are now comparatively infrequent in use. They usually emphasize critical study of minute detail or the laying bare of that which is hidden from sight. "Then let them *anatomize* Regan; see what breeds about her heart. Is there any cause in nature that makes these hard hearts?" (*Shak.*). "Such an unripping, such an *Anatomie* of the shiest, and tenderest particular truths" (*Milton*). **Break down** and **breakdown** are used chiefly with reference to financial reports, statements, estimates, and the like, or to substances separated by chemical agents. In both fields, these words imply reduction to simpler parts or divisions. Thus, the annual report of a company's financial position, giving a general statement of assets and liabilities, with yearly income and profit and loss account, may be followed by a *breakdown* showing the status, earnings, etc., of each of the several departments of the business; a consolidated balance sheet is often accompanied by a *breakdown* giving a detailed statement for each of the main items involved. In chemistry, division into simpler substances (rather than division into elements) is implied; thus, proteins are *broken down* by enzymes into amino acids.

Ana. *Separate, divide, part: classify, pigeonhole, *assort.

Ant. Compose, compound: construct. — *Con.* *Integrate, concatenate, articulate.

anaphylaxis. Hypersensitivity, hypersensitiveness, *susceptibility, allergy.

anarchic *or* **anarchical.** Anarchistic, anarchist. See under ANARCHY, 1.

anarchism. *Anarchy.

anarchist. Nihilist (see COLLECTIVIST).

anarchistic *or* **anarchist.** Anarchic, anarchical. See under ANARCHY, 1.

Ant. Authoritarian.

anarchy. 1 Anarchy, anarchism overlap in their implications but are not synonyms because of differing denotations. **Anarchy** denotes a state or condition of society where there is no law or order or, by extension, where there is complete disorder: **anarchism** denotes a theory that government is an evil because it imposes limitations upon the freedom of the individual; as, when the city fell, *anarchy* prevailed; nihilism is a form of *anarchism.* The same distinctions extend to their respective adjectives **anarchic** (*or* **anarchical**) and **anarchistic** (*or* **anarchist**); as, *anarchic* influences; *anarchic* conditions; *anarchistic* influences; *anarchistic* doctrines.

2 Anarchy, chaos, lawlessness denote in common absence, suspension, breakdown, or widespread defiance of, government, law, and order. **Anarchy** is the total absence or suspension of government. "Beginning . . . with an energy that inspired without shattering the forms of discipline and law, it [the Athenian democracy] dissolved by degrees this coherent whole into an *anarchy* of individual wills" (*G. L. Dickinson*). **Chaos** is the utter negation of order; as, "a process calculated to reduce the orderly life of our complicated societies to *chaos*" (*A. Huxley*). **Lawlessness** signifies rather a prevalent or habitual disregard of law and order than their absence or suspension. When *anarchy* and *lawlessness* (or their adjectives) are used of actions rather than of a state of things, there is often little distinction of meaning. "The hydrogen atom was not conforming to the canons of the classical music of physics, and yet it was not *anarchic* in the least, for . . . it was flawlessly obeying the laws of a different music" (*Karl K. Darrow*). "Illusion is not *lawless.* It is a world apart, if you please, but within it are its own necessities, which exact inexorable adherence to their mandates" (*Lowes*). Cf. CONFUSION, REBELLION.

Ant. Order: discipline.

anathema. 1 *Excommunication, interdict.

2 *Abomination, bête noire, bugbear.

3 *Curse, malediction, malison, imprecation.

Ana. Denunciation, condemnation, reprobation, censure (see corresponding verbs at CRITICIZE).

anathematize. Ban, curse, damn, *execrate, objurgate.

Ana. Denounce, condemn, censure, reprobate (see CRITICIZE): proscribe, *sentence.

anatomize. Dissect, *analyze, resolve, break down.

Ana. Divide, *separate, part.

anatomy. 1 Dissection, analysis, resolution, breakdown. See under ANALYZE.

2 *Structure, skeleton, framework.

ancestor. Ancestor, progenitor, forefather, forebear (*or* **forbear**) are close synonyms meaning a person from whom one is descended. **Ancestor,** especially in genealogical and in historical use, implies lineal descent through one's father or mother; as, he had three *ancestors* who were judges. It is, however, seldom applied to a grandparent except humorously. In less precise use, *ancestor* (especially in the plural) may imply kinship through collaterals or through race. "The gentleman will please remember that when his half-civilized *ancestors* were hunting the wild boar in Silesia, mine were princes of the earth" (*J. Benjamin*). *Ancestor* often, but not invariably, suggests knowledge of identities and family pride in them as persons; as, *ancestor* worship; they had plenty of money, but apparently no *ancestors.* **Progenitor** differs from *ancestor* chiefly in its connotations rather than in its implications. It does not exclude parents or grandparents; in itself, as apart from its context, it carries no hint of family or racial feeling, and it often suggests a reference to heredity or the transmission of characters. "Do as your great *progenitors* have done, And, by their virtues, prove yourself their son" (*Dryden*). "Men resemble their contemporaries even more than their *progenitors*" (*Emerson*). Whenever an evolution is suggested, *ancestor* and *progenitor* may be used of living things (plants and animals) or of developing things (such as races, social castes, literary or artistic forms); they then often denote a species or group from which a later or a presently existing species or group has been derived; thus, the dinosaur has been mistakenly regarded as the *ancestor* of the bird. *Progenitor,* even more than *ancestor,* names that which is believed to be the ultimate source or root; as, "he sang of the nuptials of Janus and Comesena, *progenitors* of the Italian people" (*Quiller-Couch*). **Forefather** is used less often than *ancestor* in historical writing but is probably more common in poetic and in colloquial use, especially when simplicity of life, or strength of family feeling, or persistence of a family in one locality is connoted. "Each in his narrow cell for ever laid, The rude *Forefathers* of the hamlet sleep" (*Gray*). "Think of your *forefathers!* Think of your posterity!" (*J. Q. Adams*). **Forebear** is not only less rich in its implications than *forefather,* but it is also less connotative of sentiment; as, the land had been owned by his *forebears* for generations; his *forebears* came from Scotland around 1800.

Ant. Descendent.

ancestry. Ancestry, lineage, pedigree are often used interchangeably as meaning either one's progenitors collectively or their quality or character as a whole. The words, however, are clearly distinguishable. **Ancestry,** in its most precise use, evokes the image of a family tree with its increase in branchings and ramifications by geometrical progression the further it ascends; as, only brothers and sisters have a common *ancestry.* However, in looser but still good use *ancestry* often suggests one's progenitors in general, known or unknown, a cause of pride often, but sometimes of indifference or of shame; as, no one is responsible for his *ancestry,* but one's ancestors are (or one's *ancestry* is) to a certain extent responsible for one's qualities; a snob judges a person by his *ancestry.* **Lineage** stresses descent in a line; it evokes therefore the image of a list of the persons who in order of generation are descended from a single ancestor; thus, the evangelist Matthew traced the *lineage* of Jesus by each step from Abraham down (see *Matthew* i. 1 ff.); any group of persons who can trace their derivation from (or back to) a common ancestor are of the same *lineage,* although their *ancestry* may be widely different. For this reason, *lineage* is often used as the equivalent of *race.* "Though of a *lineage* once abhorred" (*Wordsworth*). **Pedigree** is even more definite in its suggestions, for it implies a known and recorded ancestry. In commonest usage, to have a *pedigree* is to have a distinguished or notable ancestry, and to have a long *pedigree* is to have an ancient as well as distinguished ancestry; as, "Who proud of *Pedigree,* is poor of Purse" (*Pope*); "The deference due To a man of *pedigree*" (*W. S. Gilbert*). The term is applied to the ancestry of persons, and to that of animals and plants propagated under controlled conditions.

Ant. Descendants: posterity.

anchor, *v.* **1 Anchor, moor,** in nautical use, agree in meaning to fix a boat or ship securely in place. In general, *anchor* stresses the means by which a boat is held in position; *moor,* the effect, or the securing. Therefore, **anchor** commonly implies the use of a weight, especially one with flukes or hooks, which is attached to the boat by a chain or rope and dropped overboard until it is firmly grounded in the soil beneath; as, "Whilst our pinnace *anchors* in the Downs" (*Shak.*). **Moor,** on the other hand, except in technical use as applied to a vessel secured offshore or in open water, does not suggest a specific means of holding the boat in place. A vessel may be *moored* by anchoring it or by attaching it to a wharf or jetty or to an anchored buoy by means of cables. In its restricted nautical sense, however, it implies the use of two anchors (usually connected by a swivel to prevent interlocking of their cables) which fix the vessel so securely that it cannot ride as freely as a vessel held by a single anchor. Often, but not necessarily, *anchor* suggests a brief stop, and *moor* a comparatively lengthy one; as, battleships from all countries were *moored* in the Hudson during the tercentenary celebration.

2 Moor, *secure, rivet.

Ana. *Fasten, attach, fix, affix.

anchorite *or* **anchoret.** Hermit, eremite, *recluse, cenobite.

Ana. *Ascetic, mystic: *religious, monk, friar.

ancient. *Old, venerable, antediluvian, antique, antiquated, archaic, obsolete.

Ana. *Secular, centuried, agelong, aeonian, diuturnal: primeval, pristine, primal, primordial (see PRIMARY).

Ant. Modern. — *Con.* *New, newfashioned, newfangled, fresh, novel, neoteric, modernistic: current, *prevailing.

ancillary. *Auxiliary, contributory, subsidiary, adjuvant, subservient, accessory.

Ana. Assisting, aiding, helping (see HELP, *v.*): secondary, *subordinate, succursal: supplementary, complementary (see corresponding nouns at COMPLEMENT).

androgynous. *Bisexual, hermaphrodite, hermaphroditic, epicene.

anecdote. *Story, tale, yarn, narrative.

Ana. Incident, episode, event, *occurrence: narration, relation, recital (see corresponding verbs at RELATE).

anele. *Anoint, chrism.

anemic *or* **anaemic.** Bloodless, *pale.

Ant. Full-blooded: florid.

anent. Concerning, regarding, respecting, *about.

anesthetic *or* **anaesthetic,** *adj.* Insensitive, *insensible, impassible.

Ana. *Dull, obtuse: *impassive, apathetic, stolid: impervious, impermeable, impenetrable, *impassable.

Ant. Alive. — *Con.* *Aware, awake, conscious, cognizant: responsive (see TENDER).

anesthetic *or* **anaesthetic,** *n.* *Anodyne, analgesic.

Ant. Stimulant.

anew. Afresh, *again, anon, encore.

anfractuous. Tortuous, *winding, serpentine, sinuous, flexuous.

Ana. Complicated, intricate, involved, *complex: circuitous, roundabout, *indirect.

Ant. Undeviating. — *Con.* Simple, *easy, smooth: straightforward, forthright.

angel. 1 Angel, archangel, cherub, seraph are here compared as denoting, literally or figuratively, one of a category of celestial beings whose existence is inferred mainly from various Biblical references to them as attendants on the Supreme Being or as intermediaries between him and men. The applications and connotations of these words have been greatly affected by the representations of these beings in art and literature, by additions mainly from apocryphal and cabalistic sources, and by the notion of a celestial hierarchy, or of nine orders of celestial beings, developed in the early Middle Ages. In this hierarchic arrangement, *angels* stand lowest, *archangels* next; above them in ascending order are *thrones, dominations, virtues, powers, principalities* (names gleaned from Scriptures), *cherubim,* and *seraphim.* In ordinary use, **angel** is the inclusive term, though it calls up a distinctive image (always more or less dependent on the individual's religious and cultural background), most commonly that of a radiant, winged youth. "O, speak again, bright *angel!* for thou art As glorious . . . As is a winged messenger of heaven . . . When he . . . sails upon the bosom of the air" (*Shak.*). Very often, the word suggests a disembodied spirit, an ethereal being akin to man but far surpassing him in intuitive power, in refinement of feeling, and in delicacy of perception; as, "Thou hast made him [man] a little lower than the *angels*" (*Psalms* viii. 5); "Tears, such as *angels* weep" (*Milton*). "Unless you can love, as the *angels* may, with the breadth of heaven betwixt you . . . Oh, never call it loving" (*E. B. Browning*). Sometimes the emphasis is on function, particularly that of guiding or guarding (the guardian *angel*) or of ministering in time of sorrow or need. "Some *angel* guide my pencil, while I draw, What nothing less than *angel* can exceed" (*Young*). "O woman! . . . When pain and anguish wring the brow, A ministering *angel* thou!" (*Scott*). **Archangel** seldom, if ever, carries the homelier, human connotations which are so often attached to *angel;* the word commonly evokes the image of a knightly or princely being of unrivaled splendor and brilliance (often indicated in art by raiment or armor). *Archangels* are the warriors or ambassadors of heaven. They are usually known by name: Michael, who contended with the devil (*Jude* 9); Gabriel, the angel of the Annunciation; Raphael, the companion of Tobias; and several others from apocryphal sources. In Milton, who is responsible for many of the connotations of this term in English use, the word is also a designation of Lucifer and other leaders of the fallen angels. "His [Lucifer's] form had not yet lost All her original brightness, nor appeared Less than *Archangel* ruined, and the excess Of glory obscured" (*Milton*). "[Coleridge] an *archangel* a little damaged" (*Lamb*). In modern use, **cherub** evokes an image of a head with a child's face, intent eyes, and shoulder wings; this figure is common in ecclesiastical decoration and in paintings, especially of the Madonna, where the cherubs' eyes are fixed on the infant Jesus. Though the word is often used in the Bible (frequently, in the Authorized Version, in a corrupt plural *cherubims*), it is in most passages definitely not applied to an angel; in those where it has been interpreted as so applying, the emphasis is upon nearness to the throne of God (or mercy seat) and upon the face and wings. Consequently, in the celestial hierarchy, the cherub whose gaze is fixed on God excels all other celestial beings in knowledge. *Cherub,* therefore, as applied to an angel, stresses watching and contemplation; cherubs may soar, but they do so within range of the beatific vision. "Him that yon soars on golden wing . . . The *Cherub* Contemplation" (*Milton*). "He [a dead child] seemed a *cherub* who had lost his way And wandered hither . . . 'twas most meet . . . That he should . . . stand before his God" (*J. R. Lowell*). **Seraph** derives its implications from its one Biblical source (*Isaiah* vi.) and from its being the designation in the celestial hierarchy of the spirit closest to God and excelling all others in love. In the vision of Isaiah (verse 2), each seraph "had six wings; with twain he covered his face, and with twain he covered his feet, and with twain he did fly." It also was a seraph who took a coal of fire from the altar and touched the lips of Isaiah, a symbol of divine inspiration. In literary use, the word lacks the concrete implications of the other terms, for no clear image seems to have become associated with it. It is not wanting in connotations, however, of transcendent glory, ecstatic love, and mystical aspiration. "As the rapt *Seraph* that adores and burns" (*Pope*). "We loved . . . With a love that the wingèd *seraphs* of Heaven Coveted her and me" (*Poe*). "The *Seraph's* face . . . All radiant with the glory and the calm Of having looked upon the front of God" (*J. R. Lowell*).

2 Backer, *sponsor, patron, surety, guarantor.

anger, *n.* **Anger, ire, rage, fury, indignation, wrath** agree in denoting the emotional excitement induced by intense displeasure. **Anger,** the generic term of this group, names merely the emotional reaction; the word in itself suggests no definite degree of intensity and carries no necessary implication of outward manifestation; as, to conceal one's *anger;* easily aroused to *anger;* self-destroying *anger.* "He saw the calf, and the dancing: and Moses' *anger* waxed hot" (*Exodus* xxxii. 19). **Ire,** which is now regarded as literary or affected, suggests greater intensity than *anger* unqualified, and usually, but not necessarily, a display of that feeling in looks, acts, or words. "Belinda burns with more than mortal *ire*" (*Pope*). " 'Then, my lad, ye've come to tall [tell] me a lie!' Farmer Blaize looked straight at the boy, undismayed by the dark flush of *ire* he had kindled" (*Meredith*). **Rage** adds to *anger* the implications of lost self-control and of violent boiling over of feeling; it often connotes variously a sense of frustration, or temporary derangement of the mind, or determination to get revenge; as, "terrible and impotent *rage*" (*Wilde*); "blind with *rage* she miss'd the plank" (*Tennyson*). "His first hot *anger* against the beast had changed into a cold *rage:* at all costs now he must get it" (*S. Cloete*). **Fury** is overmastering destructive rage verging on madness. "What *fury* drove us into saying the stupid, intolerant, denunciatory things we said?" (*L. P. Smith*). "The war against physical evil, like every other war, must not be conducted with such *fury* as to render men incapable of the arts of peace" (*B. Russell*). **Indignation** implies depth and intensity of anger, often righteous or generous anger, aroused by that which one considers mean, shameful, or otherwise unworthy of a man or men. "Whose souls No honest *indignation* ever urged To elevated daring" (*Shelley*). "The question now placed before society . . . is this: Is man an ape or an angel? I, my lord, I am on the side of the angels. I repudiate with *indignation* and abhorrence those new fangled theories" (*Disraeli*). **Wrath** may imply either rage or indignation as its emotional basis, but in addition to either of these, it also often implies a grievance and a desire or intent to avenge or punish, or to get revenge. "Let not the sun go down upon your *wrath*" (*Ephesians* iv. 26). "Nursing her *wrath* to keep it warm" (*Burns*). "In describing external effects, which seem like those produced by anger, the word 'wrath' is always used. We should not speak of the 'anger' but of the 'wrath' of the elements. We therefore speak of 'the *wrath* of God,' more correctly than of his *anger.* We cannot attribute to Him passions like those of men: we can only describe the external effects which in men would be produced by those passions" (*E. J. Whately*).

Ana. *Acrimony, asperity: exasperation, irritation, provocation (see corresponding verbs at IRRITATE).

Ant. Pleasure, gratification: forbearance. — ***Con.*** *Patience, longanimity, long-suffering: forgiveness, condonation, pardon (see corresponding verbs at EXCUSE): indulgence, clemency, leniency (see under FORBEARING).

anger, *v.* **Anger, incense, enrage, infuriate, madden.** All these verbs carry in common with **anger,** their general term, the denotation to make angry (see ANGRY) or to rouse to anger (see ANGER, *n.*). "Laugh then at any, but at Fools or Foes; These you but *anger,* and you mend not those" (*Pope*). **Incense** implies hotness of anger, especially as provoked by that which is excessively irritating and offensive. "Mr. Critchlow, aged and unaccustomed to interference, had to render accounts of his trusteeship to this young man, and was *incensed*" (*Bennett*). "Magistrates and populace were *incensed* at a refusal of customary marks of courtesy and respect for the laws" (*Inge*). **Enrage** suggests a violent display of wrath or fury. "I pray you, speak not . . . Question *enrages* him" (*Shak.*). **Infuriate** implies a sense of being outraged, or, in weaker use, of being exasperated beyond endurance. "How it *infuriates* a bigot, when he is forced to drag into the light his dark convictions!" (*L. P. Smith*). "His colleagues and his subordinates had been alternately delighted and *infuriated* by his assumed reluctance to deal with any practical question" (*V. Sackville-West*). **Madden** is often not distinguishable from *infuriate.* "Can it be fancied that Deity ever vindictively Made in his image a mannikin merely to *madden* it?" (*Poe*). At other times it implies merely excessive annoyance or vexation; as, *maddening* delays.

Ana. *Offend, outrage, affront: exasperate, provoke, *irritate, nettle, roil: vex, *annoy, irk.

Ant. Please, gratify: pacify. — ***Con.*** Placate, mollify, appease, propitiate (see PACIFY): rejoice, delight, gladden, tickle (see PLEASE).

angle, *v.* *Fish.

angle, *n.* **1** *Corner.

2 *Point of view, viewpoint, standpoint, slant.

Ana. Attitude, *position, stand.

3 Aspect, facet, side, *phase.

Ana. *Item, detail, particular.

Anglican. *English, British, Anglo-Saxon.

Anglo-Saxon. *English, Anglican, British.

angry. Angry, irate, indignant, wrathful, acrimonious, mad agree in meaning feeling or showing displeasure with passion or in a bad temper. **Angry** is applied to persons or their moods, acts, looks, or words; it is also applied to animals (as, an *angry* bull) and by extension, because of some of its implications, to things (as, an *angry* boil; an *angry* sky). In reference to persons, it implies both emotional and physical excitement, usually, but not necessarily, exhibited as by an inflamed countenance or inflamed words or by threatening looks or speeches. "The king is *angry:* see, he bites the lip" (*Shak.*). "The adultress! What a theme for *angry* verse!" (*Cowper*). **Irate** is applied only to persons or their looks, acts, or words; it often suggests greater exhibition of feeling than *angry* and, as a rule, implies loss of self-control. "Ah, Sir, none the less, contain you, nor wax *irate!*" (*Browning*). Sometimes it is used half humorously to suggest the disparity between the emotion and its exciting cause. "Refractory children, over whom Mr. Spratt . . . exercised an *irate* surveillance" (*G. Eliot*). **Indignant,** in contrast with *irate,* suggests righteousness in the anger and sufficiency of provocation. Often, its use imputes injustice or indignity to that which arouses anger. "Let the sword speak what the *indignant* tongue Disdains to brand thee with" (*Shelley*). **Wrathful** is capable of being used where *irate* or *indignant* would be more explicit. However, it usually connotes more justification of the anger than *irate* and more vehemence in its expression than *indignant.* " 'Why did they lie to me?' the young man *wrathfully* exclaimed" (*Meredith*). **Acrimonious,** though sometimes still applied to a person's temper or mood, is chiefly used to characterize intercourse and utterances. It invariably adds to *angry* the implication of irreconcilable difference of opinion and consequent bitterness of feeling that may or may not be shown in criminations and recriminations. "The dispute [over the Maine-New Brunswick boundaries] dragged on, becoming progressively more *acrimonious,* for another eleven years" (*A. Huxley*). **Mad** (see INSANE), though once in good use, is now colloquial or dialectal for *angry.*

Ana. *Impassioned, passionate: angered, incensed, enraged, infuriated, maddened (see corresponding verbs at ANGER): offended, outraged, affronted (see corresponding verbs at OFFEND).

Ant. Good-tempered. — ***Con.*** *Amiable, good-natured, complaisant, obliging: *pleasant, agreeable.

anguish. Woe, heartache, grief, *sorrow, dole, regret.

Ana. *Distress, suffering, dolor, misery, agony: worry, anxiety (see CARE): *pain, pang, throe, ache: torture,

torment, affliction (see corresponding verbs at AFFLICT).
Ant. Relief. — *Con.* Comfort, solace, consolation (see corresponding verbs at COMFORT): assuagement, alleviation, mitigation (see corresponding verbs at RELIEVE): *ecstasy, rapture, transport.

angular. Gaunt, rawboned, lank, lanky, *lean, spare, scrawny, skinny.
Ana. *Thin, slender, slim: *awkward, clumsy: cadaverous, *haggard.
Ant. Rotund. — *Con.* Plump, chubby, *fleshy, stout, portly.

anile. *Senile, doting, doted, doddering, doddered.
Ana. *Aged, old, superannuated: ancient, venerable (see OLD): effeminate, womanish (see FEMALE): decadent, declining, deteriorating (see corresponding nouns at DETERIORATION).
Ant. Virginal, virgin. — *Con.* Maiden, *youthful, juvenile.

animadversion. **Animadversion, stricture, aspersion, reflection** are comparable when they denote a remark or statement that is an adverse criticism. **Animadversion,** as here narrowly considered (see *animadvert* at REMARK) implies as its motive deep-seated prejudice or ill will or a tendency to carp or cavil; as, given to *animadversions* on the clergy. "Maty's *animadversions* hurt me more. In part they appeared to me unjust, and in part ill-natured" (*Cowper*). **Stricture** always implies censure, which may be either ill-natured or judicious; as, "foreign *strictures* on the dress, looks, and behavior of the English abroad" (*Arnold*). "The lash of the merciless Porson . . . [whose] *strictures* are founded in argument, enriched with learning, and enlivened with wit" (*Gibbon*). **Aspersion** imputes a slanderous character to the criticism. "Who by *aspersions* throw a stone At th' head of others, hit their own" (*Herbert*). "At Cambridge (they tell me) while you speak very well, you write less expertly . . . . you will not set the *aspersion* down to me" (*Quiller-Couch*). **Reflection** often, but not invariably, implies indirect aspersion or a defamatory imputation which may be inferred from what has been said. "He cannot restrain himself from *reflections* on kings and priests when he is most contending for them" (*Hallam*).
Ana. Criticism, reprehension, censure (see corresponding verbs at CRITICIZE): observation, comment, *remark: captiousness, faultfinding, caviling, carping, censoriousness (see corresponding adjectives at CRITICAL).
Ant. Commendation. — *Con.* Praise, laudation, extollation, acclaim (see corresponding verbs at PRAISE): *approbation, approval.

animadvert. Comment, commentate, *remark.
Ana. *Criticize, reprehend, censure, reprobate: deprecate, *disapprove: depreciate, disparage, *decry.
Con. Ignore, disregard, overlook (see NEGLECT): *commend, applaud, compliment.

animal, *n.* **Animal, brute, beast** are synonyms only when they denote a creature lower than man but like him in possessing senses, instincts, and appetites. **Animal** sometimes carries no further implications. "Physiological experiment on *animals* is justifiable for real investigation, but not for mere damnable and detestable curiosity" (*Darwin*). Very often, however, the word specifically implies a difference from, rather than a likeness to, man; it may be the lack of reasoning powers, or it may be the control of instincts and appetites by biological laws rather than by a will. "No *animal* . . . Obeys its like: with strength all rule began, The stoutest awes the pasture . . . nicer power Man needs To rule him than is bred of bone and thew" (*Browning*). **Brute** stresses the absence of faculties or powers that are distinctive marks of a human being's superiority, such as speech, intellect, self-control, sensibility, and the like. It is therefore especially effective in ironical use. "Below my window goes the cattle train, And stands for hours along the river park, Fear, cold, exhaustion, hunger, thirst, and pain; Dumb *brutes* we call them" (*C. P. Gilman*). **Beast** is applied chiefly to quadrupeds; except for this distinction, it is often not clearly distinguishable from *animal;* as, painters of *beasts;* the *beasts* of the field; "like the bat, they are neither bird nor *beast*" (*Marryat*). *Beast,* however, when used in distinction to *man,* may imply a closer likeness than *brute* (which stresses the difference), because it is applied to animals just below man in the scale of creatures. "When he is best, he is a little worse than a man, and when he is worst, he is little better than a *beast*" (*Shak.*).

When applied figuratively to human beings, *animal* either throws the emphasis on purely physical qualities or implies the ascendancy of the physical nature over the rational and spiritual nature; *brute* implies extreme dullness, or insensibility to others' pain or suffering, or uncontrollable passion; *beast* suggests surrender to one's lower nature or sensual indulgence unworthy of a man; thus, one may speak of a prize fighter as a superb *animal,* of an imbecile as a mere *animal,* of a cruel husband as a *brute,* of a stupid powerful athlete as a great hulking *brute,* and of a drunkard as making a *beast* of himself. Both *animal* and *beast* are also, in modern usage, applied to man's lower nature, often regarded as a relic from an earlier stage in the evolution of the species. "His fleshly desires were strong, and he was unmerciful to the *animal* in himself" (*M. K. Bradby*). "Man . . . The herald of a higher race . . . Move upward, working out the *beast,* And let the ape and tiger die" (*Tennyson*).

animal, *adj.* *Carnal, fleshly, animalistic, sensual.
Ana. Physical, corporeal, *bodily: bestial, brutal (see corresponding nouns at ANIMAL).
Ant. Rational. — *Con.* Intellectual, *mental, psychic: spiritual (see HOLY).

animalism. *Animality.
Ana. Sensualism, voluptuousness (see corresponding adjectives at SENSUOUS): lustfulness, lasciviousness, lecherousness (see corresponding adjectives at LICENTIOUS).

animalistic. Sensual, *carnal, fleshly, animal.
Ana Sensual, voluptuous, *sensuous: lustful, lascivious, libidinous, lecherous (see LICENTIOUS).

animality. **Animality, animalism** are not always clearly distinguished when they are used to denote animal nature, character, or springs of action on a man or in men. Good writers, however, tend to prefer **animality** when they wish a word that suggests likenesses between men and animals rather than differences, and **animalism** when they wish one which carries in addition all the derogatory implications of *sensuality* or *sensualism.* "He disliked union with a woman whom he had never seen; moreover, when he did see her, she disappointed him, and he begat his first child in mere *animality*" (*E. M. Forster*). "Puritanism was a natural and necessary revolt . . . against that Naturalism which threatened to end in sheer *animalism*" (*Kingsley*).
Ana Virility, maleness, masculinity (see corresponding adjectives at MALE).

animate, *v.* **1** *Quicken, vivify, enliven.
Ana. *Vitalize, activate, energize.
2 *Inform, inspire, fire.
Ana. Motivate, actuate, *activate: *move, drive, impel, actuate: *stir, rouse, arouse.
Ant. Inhibit. — *Con.* *Restrain, curb, check: *frustrate, thwart.

animate, *adj.* *Living, quick, alive, animated, vital.

Ana. Physical, corporeal, *bodily: animal, *carnal, fleshly.
Ant. Inanimate. — *Con.* Lifeless, *dead.
animated. 1 Alive, *living, animate, quick, vital.
Ana. *Active, live, dynamic: vitalized, energized, activated (see VITALIZE).
Ant. Inert. — *Con.* *Inactive, passive: lifeless, inanimate, *dead.
2 *Lively, vivacious, sprightly, gay.
Ana. Buoyant, volatile, effervescent (see ELASTIC): *agile, brisk, spry, nimble: *spirited, high-spirited.
Ant. Depressed, dejected. — *Con.* *Languid, listless, spiritless, enervated: *lethargic, torpid, comatose.
animosity. Animus, rancor, *enmity, hostility, antipathy, antagonism.
Ana. Hatred, hate, detestation, abhorrence (see under HATE, *v.*): vindictiveness, revengefulness, vengefulness (see corresponding adjectives at VINDICTIVE): *malice, malevolence, ill will, spite.
Ant. Good will. — *Con.* *Friendship, amity, comity: friendliness, neighborliness, amicableness (see corresponding adjectives at AMICABLE).
animus. Animosity, rancor, *enmity, hostility, antipathy, antagonism.
Ana. Ill will, spite, spleen, grudge (see MALICE): prejudice, bias (see PREDILECTION).
Ant. Favor. — *Con.* Good will, countenance (see FAVOR): *predilection, partiality: sympathy, empathy (see PITY).
annals. Chronicle, *history.
anneal. *Temper.
annex, *v.* *Add, append, subjoin, superadd.
Ana. *Join, unite, connect, link, associate: attach, affix, *fasten.
Con. *Detach, disengage, abstract: divorce, *separate, part.
annex, *n.* **Annex, dependence, extension, wing, ell** designate an addition to the main (and, often, the original) building. An **annex** may or may not be attached to the main building; it may even not be adjacent to it. When used of an addition to a hotel, an office building, or the like, it usually implies a provision for expanded business and, therefore, the same management. **Dependence** is rare in English, but is sometimes found as a translation of *dependance,* which is the French term covering a hotel annex. An **extension** is always attached to the main or central building; when it projects from the central building and is connected with it at only one point it is called a **wing**; when it extends at right angles from one end of the building it is called an **ell.**
Ana. *Addition, increment, accretion.
annihilate. Extinguish, *abolish, abate.
Ana. Obliterate, efface, expunge, blot out, cancel, *erase: extirpate, *exterminate, eradicate, wipe out.
Con. Create, *invent, discover: *make, form, fashion, forge, shape: *renew, restore.
anniversary, *adj.* *Annual, yearly.
annotate. **Annotate, gloss** (*or, Obs.,* **gloze** *or* **glose**) and their corresponding nouns **annotation, gloss,** agree in meaning, as verbs, to add or append comment, or as nouns, an added or appended comment, intended to be helpful in interpreting a passage or text. One **annotates** a text, a literary work, or the like, when one furnishes it with critical, historical, or explanatory notes (as footnotes, marginal notes, or notes in an appendix); as, to *annotate* the works of Milton; an *annotated* edition of Shakespeare's sonnets. The subject of an annotation may be any word, passage, or detail which is capable of being explained to the advantage of the reader or student. In its strict sense, one **glosses** a word or phrase which is obscure in meaning because foreign, obsolete, rare, or the like, by providing its definition, as in a marginal or interlinear note (see *glossary* under DICTIONARY), or one *glosses* a text when one supplies definitions of its difficult words and phrases. "Hereunto have I added a certain *glosse* . . . for thexposition of old wordes, and harder phrases; which maner of *glosing* . . . wil seeme straunge and rare in our tongue" (*E. K.* in Epistle prefacing Spenser's *Shepherd's Calendar*). The word acquired (possibly by confusion with *gloss,* to give a luster to) a derogatory implication of perversion or sophistication of meaning which is still sometimes found. "Preaching the people for profit of the belly, And *glosing* the Gospel as them good liked" (*Piers Plowman*).
Ana. Elucidate, interpret, construe, *explain, expound: comment, commentate, *remark.
annotation. Gloss (see under ANNOTATE).
Ana. Commentary, comment, observation, note, *remark.
announce. Publish, proclaim, *declare, promulgate, advertise, broadcast.
Ana. Disclose, *reveal, divulge, tell: *communicate, impart.
Con. *Suppress, repress: conceal, *hide, bury: withhold, hold back, reserve (see KEEP).
announcement. Publication, proclamation, declaration, promulgation, advertisement, broadcasting. See under DECLARE.
annoy, *v.* 1 **Annoy, vex, irk, bother** agree in meaning to disturb and nervously upset a person. **Annoy** stresses loss of equanimity or patience, as a result of being forced to endure that which one finds obnoxious or offensive, or merely displeasing. It seldom implies more than a temporary disturbance or display of nerves. "Richard's absence *annoyed* him. The youth was vivacious, and his enthusiasm good fun" (*Meredith*). "It was . . . his lack of the ghost of a notion what any one else was feeling that *annoyed* her, had always *annoyed* her" (*V. Woolf*). **Vex** usually implies greater provocation and a stronger disturbance than *annoy;* it often connotes a degree of anger but at other times it suggests deep perplexity or some worry; as, "faulty translation that so *vexes* teachers" (*Grandgent*); to *vex* one's mind with insoluble problems. "Mr. Darcy's behaviour astonished and *vexed* her. 'Why, if he came only to be silent, grave, and indifferent,' said she, 'did he come at all?' " (*Austen*). "Such petty details as now *vexed* the brooding soul of the old gentlewoman" (*N. Hawthorne*). **Irk** emphasizes difficulty in enduring and resulting weariness of spirit; it is most often used in reference to that which persists or recurs annoyingly; as, "The speed and the clatter *irk* me" (*Kipling*); "the over-iterated becomes the monotonous, and the monotonous *irks* and bores" (*Lowes*). **Bother** stresses interference with one's comfort or peace of mind; sometimes in addition it implies bewilderment or mystification or, on the other hand, worry and anxiety. "I can't be *bothered* to consider Jane any more" (*R. Macaulay*). "They were a good, stupid, earnest couple and very much *bothered* [by something]" (*Conrad*).
Ana. *Irritate, nettle, aggravate, exasperate, roil: perturb, disturb, upset, agitate (see DISCOMPOSE).
Ant. Soothe. — *Con.* *Comfort, solace, console: *please, gratify, tickle.
2 *Worry, pester, plague, tantalize, tease, harass, harry.
Ana. Fret, chafe (see ABRADE): badger, hector, heckle, chevy (*or* chivy, chivvy), *bait: trouble, molest (see INCONVENIENCE).
Con. *Neglect, ignore, overlook: mollify, appease (see PACIFY).

annual, *adj.* **Annual, yearly, anniversary** are synonyms only when they mean occurring or recurring once a year; as, *annual, yearly,* or *anniversary* celebrations; an *annual, yearly,* or *anniversary* periodical. **Annual** and **yearly** may mean also, as *anniversary* does not, covering or taking a whole year; as, the *annual,* or *yearly,* output, supply, income, cost; the *annual,* or *yearly,* revolution of the sun. *Annual* may, however, as *yearly* does not, mean lasting one year only; as, an *annual* plant; an *annual* Parliament. **Anniversary,** the most restricted of these terms, always implies a connection with a definite day of the year, which is annually commemorated because the date is associated with a significant event in the life of a person (such as a birth or a wedding) or in the history of a nation (such as a liberation or a victory) or of an organization, or the like; thus, an *anniversary* celebration is an annual celebration on (or near) the date of a memorable occurrence; an *anniversary* periodical is one that comes out annually to commemorate a significant event and the date of its occurrence.

Ant. Perennial (*especially of plants*).

annul. 1 *Nullify, negate, invalidate, abrogate.

Ana. *Neutralize, negative, counteract: cancel, efface, obliterate, blot out, *erase: annihilate, *abolish, extinguish.

2 **Annul, abrogate, void, avoid, vacate, quash** are terms chiefly in legal (but not always in technical) use meaning to deprive of validity, force, or authority. Though varying little in denotation, these words are not always interchangeable, their proper selection being dependent on the character or status of the invalidating agent and on the character of the thing invalidated. **Annul** is the most general term, applicable to anything that may be adjudged invalid or void, as a right, a marriage, a charter, a statute. It implies the exercise of competent legal authority. "Had parliament, immediately after the emanation of this charter . . . *annulled* the instrument . . . the perfidy of the transaction would have been universally acknowledged" (*Ch. Just. Marshall*). To **abrogate** is the act of one having force and authority, and often, but far from always, legal jurisdiction. A ruler, an arbiter, as well as a court, may *abrogate* something previously effective, as a law, a treaty, or a convention, and in effect or in intent abolish it. "We are not . . . called upon to *abrogate* the standards of values that are fixed, not by you and not by me, but by . . . time" (*Lowes*). **Void,** the verb, is not a technical term in law, but the adjective *void* is. That is *void* which has no legal validity; a will is *void* (or incapable of confirmation or ratification) when made by an insane person; a contract that is *void* is no contract in the view of the law. It is the insanity of the testator that *voids* his will, not the act of a court. To **avoid** is to adjudge invalid. Thus, a will with defects in the instrument is not necessarily void, but it may be voidable, or capable of being either confirmed or *avoided* by legal decision. Only competent legal authority can **vacate,** or make ineffectual or invalid, something that previously was effectual or valid; as, to *vacate* proceedings after the discovery of fraud; to *vacate* a grant of crown property. **Quash** is a strictly legal term applied chiefly to indictments thrown out of court as defective.

annular. *Round, circular, orbicular.

anodyne. 1 **Anodyne, analgesic, anesthetic** are not often interchangeable, although they agree in denoting something used to relieve pain. **Anodyne,** the oldest, most inclusive, and least scientific of these terms, is also the most widely applicable. It covers drugs (as paregoric), medicinal preparations used internally or externally (as a narcotic, a liniment, a plaster) and various therapeutic measures such as hot or cold applications and electricity, which relieve pain by lessening the sensibility of the nerves or by dulling the brain. **Analgesic** is a more scientific term than *anodyne* and is narrower in its application, usually being applied to any substance the chief clinical use of which is to induce a loss of sensibility to pain. Analgesics relieve either by interfering with the conduction of impulses in nerves or by dulling the brain. They may, like aspirin, be taken internally, or like a salve for burns, be applied externally. **Anesthetic** is applied to any substance or agent that produces total insensibility not only to pain but also to all other sensations in either a part (a *local anesthetic*) or in the whole body (*general anesthetic*). Local anesthetics include cold applications and injections of drugs. General anesthetics include substances to be inhaled, such as ether and chloroform, as well as drugs to be injected. Anesthetics are used not only to destroy suffering from pain but also to prevent suffering during surgical procedures.

2 **Anodyne, opiate, narcotic, nepenthe** come into comparison in their figurative senses when they mean something used to dull or deaden one's senses or one's sensibility. **Anodyne** is frequently used as the opposite of *stimulant;* it suggests something that allays excitement or mitigates mental distress by inducing forgetfulness or oblivion. "This kind of religion cannot be anything better than an *anodyne;* but an *anodyne* is unfortunately just what many people want from their religion" (*Inge*). " 'I used to imagine reading was meant to be a stimulant. Out here [at the front during the World War] it has to be an *anodyne*' " (*H. G. Wells*). **Opiate** usually is applied to something that induces a dream state and a delusion of happiness; it also commonly suggests indifference to actual evils and a false sense of security, well-being, or the like, with consequent stilting of all disturbing thoughts. "[The delights of harmony] lenient as soft *opiates* to the mind, Leave vice and folly unsubdued behind" (*Cowper*). "No military swagger of my mind, Can smother from myself the wrong I've done him,— Without design, indeed,—yet it is so,— And *opiate* for the conscience have I none" (*Keats*). **Narcotic** implies a putting to sleep or into a stupor; in figurative use, it suggests merely a pleasant drowsiness which overcomes one and has a lulling effect on mind and body. "But, for the unquiet heart and brain, A use in measured language lies; The sad mechanic exercise, Like dull *narcotics,* numbing pain" (*Tennyson*). **Nepenthe,** the designation of a legendary opiate (possibly narcotic) of the ancient Greeks, is used by English poets variously and without a clear conception of whether it was a potion or a drug or whether it induced complete insensibility to pain and sorrow or a forgetfulness of them. Usually, however, it implies a substitution of something sweet and pleasurable for something painful. "After the fiery stimulants, compounded of brimstone and bigotry, offered by the polemic theologians, the gentle sedative of Montaigne's conversation comes like a draft of *nepenthe*" (*Preserved Smith*).

Ana. Emollient, demulcent, *balm, salve.

Ant. Stimulant: irritant.

anoint. 1 *Oil, inunct, cream, grease, pomade, pomatum, lubricate.

2 **Anoint, chrism, anele** agree in meaning to smear ceremonially, especially in the administration of a sacrament, with oil or with chrism (a consecrated oil mixed usually with balm, or with balm and spices). **Anoint** is now the only one of these words in general use. Anointing is a part of the ritual of baptism, confirmation, holy orders, and extreme unction, and of the coronation of sovereigns. When used colloquially without qualification (as, he was *anointed* today) it implies the administration of the sacrament of extreme unction to a dying person.

The phrase "one of the Lord's *anointed*" is commonly applied to a king, especially to one who has been anointed at his coronation; it is also occasionally used of a priest who has been anointed with chrism in the sacrament of holy orders. **Chrism,** which denotes to anoint with chrism (that is, consecrated oil), is now rarely found; as, a *chrismed* child (that is, a baptized or confirmed child). **Anele** is archaic; though etymologically it is the equivalent of *anoint*, it is used chiefly (now exclusively) in reference to the sacrament of extreme unction. "Cut off even in . . . my sin, Unhousel'd, disappointed, *unaneled*" (*Shak.*).

anomalous. *Irregular, unnatural.
Ana. *Abnormal, aberrant, atypic: *monstrous, prodigious: singular, unique, peculiar, *strange.
Con. Normal, natural, *regular, typical: *usual, wonted, accustomed, customary.

anomaly. *Paradox, antinomy.

anon. **1** *Directly, immediately, forthwith, straightway, at once, right away, instantly, instantaneously.
2 *Again, encore, anew, afresh.

answer, *n.* Reply, replication, response, rejoinder, retort. See under ANSWER, *v.*, 1.
Ana. Defense, vindication, justification (see corresponding verbs at MAINTAIN): refutation, rebuttal (see corresponding verbs at DISPROVE).
Con. Question, query, inquiry, interrogation (see corresponding verbs at ASK): summoning *or* summons, call (see corresponding verbs at SUMMON).

answer, *v.* **1 Answer, respond, reply, rejoin, retort** and their corresponding nouns **answer, response, reply** (or, in law, **replication**), **rejoinder, retort** agree in meaning to say or write, or sometimes, to do, something (or that which is said, written, or done) in return, as to a question, a call, a request, a charge, or the like. One **answers,** or makes an **answer** to, the question, call, etc., or the person or thing questioning, calling, etc., when one gives the attention or service demanded by one's situation or office or required by courtesy; as, to *answer* a query, a letter; to *answer* the telephone, the doorbell. In specific collocations, the words carry more definite implications; thus, to *answer* an accusation is to give a detailed, and sometimes, by suggestion, a successful, defense; to have the *answers* to all the problems is to have their correct solutions. "Hobart . . . . could talk; he could assert; produce opinions and information, but he couldn't meet or *answer* arguments" (*R. Macaulay*). One **responds,** or makes a **response,** to a person who endeavors to elicit an answer or to a thing which serves as a stimulus, when one reacts, often spontaneously and usually without resistance, to the influence; as, to *respond* immediately to an appeal for help; an unsatisfactory *response* to a call for recruits; when she smiled, even strangers *responded.* "Is it true that antiquated legal ideas prevent government from *responding* effectively to the demands which modern society makes upon it?" (*Frankfurter*). "A trustful affectionate disposition . . . creates the *response* which it expects" (*B. Russell*). *Respond* and *response* are used in preference to *answer* and *reply* when they refer to the set answers to supplications, as in a litany, or to questions, as in a catechism. "He *answered* by a deep, gravely accented: 'Thanks, I will,' as though it were a *response* in church" (*Conrad*). One **replies,** or makes a **reply,** as to a question, charge, argument, or salute (or to a questioner, an accuser, etc.) when one answers so as to cover the same ground (etymologically, *reply* means "fold back") as the question, charge, etc.; thus, one may *answer* a letter by merely acknowledging its receipt, but one *replies* to it (in precise usage) only when one answers all its questions or touches on all points requiring attention; an *answer* to a salute is uncertain in its nature if no details are given; a *reply* to a salute usually indicates that the salute has been returned in kind and spirit. Often, *reply* is equivalent to *answer back*, as by echoing, protesting, or, when the question is rhetorical, by agreeing. "The nymph exulting fills with shouts the sky; The walls, the woods, and long canals *reply*" (*Pope*). "Theirs not to make *reply* Theirs not to reason why, Theirs but to do and die" (*Tennyson*). " 'Who is here so vile that will not love his country? If any, speak; for him have I offended. I pause for a *reply.*' 'None, Brutus, none' " (*Shak.*). One **rejoins,** or makes a **rejoinder,** in the original senses of these words, when one answers a reply. "The assembly took the governor's reply . . . into consideration, and prepared a suitable *rejoinder*" (*Franklin*). In current English, the words are chiefly used in literary dialogue to indicate the speaker and often serve to vary the expression; however, in discriminating use, they often indicate an answer to an unspoken question or to an objection. " 'What are you writing?' the Baronet inquired testily of Adrian, after a pause. . . . 'Do I disturb you, Sir?' *rejoined* Adrian" (*Meredith*). "To an abstract objection an abstract *rejoinder* suffices" (*W. James*). One **retorts,** or makes a **retort,** to an explicit or implicit charge, criticism, attack, or the like, when one responds with an answer that is in effect a retaliation, or a counter charge, criticism, or attack. "It amused me . . . to read the interview and learn that I had . . . uttered a number of trenchant sayings upon female novelists. But the amusement changed to dismay when the ladies began to *retort*" (*Quiller-Couch*).

In law, especially in pleading, *answer, replication* (or *reply*), and *rejoinder* are technical terms. *Answer* is not uniformly used in all English-speaking countries, but in general it is applied to the plea (often including a demurrer) of the defendant in response to the plaintiff's or complainant's allegation; thus, where there is a statute covering the situation, a judgment by default may be entered if no *answer* is filed. *Replication*, or in Scots law, *reply*, is applied to the plaintiff's or complainant's response to the defendant's *answer*. **Rejoinder** designates the defendant's response to a replication.
Ana. *Acknowledge, recognize: *disprove, refute, rebut: defend, justify, vindicate, *maintain.
Con. Question, *ask, interrogate, query, inquire, quiz: *summon, call.
2 Meet, *satisfy, fulfill.

answerable. *Responsible, accountable, amenable, liable.
Ana. Obliged, constrained, compelled (see FORCE, *v.*): subject, *subordinate.

Antaean. *Enormous, immense, huge, vast, gigantic, giant, gigantean, colossal, mammoth, elephantine, titanic, herculean, Cyclopean, Gargantuan, Brobdingnagian.

antagonism. Antipathy, *enmity, hostility, animosity, rancor, animus.
Ana. Opposition, resistance, withstanding (see corresponding verbs at OPPOSE): strife, conflict, variance, dissension, contention, *discord.
Ant. Accord: comity. — *Con.* *Agreement, understanding: concord, *harmony, consonance.

antagonist. *Opponent, adversary.
Ana. Foe, *enemy: rival, competitor (see corresponding verbs at RIVAL): assailant, attacker (see corresponding verbs at ATTACK).
Ant. Supporter. — *Con.* Ally, *partner, colleague.

antagonistic. Counteractive, counter, *adverse.
Ana. Opposing, resisting, withstanding (see corresponding verbs at OPPOSE): incompatible, discordant,

*inconsonant: hostile (see corresponding noun at ENMITY): *antipathetic, averse.
Ant. Favoring, favorable.
Con. Propitious, auspicious, benign (see FAVORABLE): advantageous, *beneficial.

antagonize. *Oppose, combat, resist, withstand.
Ana. *Attack, assail, assault: *offend, outrage, affront, insult: *incite, foment, instigate.
Ant. Conciliate. — *Con.* *Pacify, placate, propitiate, mollify, appease.

ante. Blind, stake, pot, *bet, wager.

antecedent, *adj.* *Preceding, precedent, foregoing, previous, prior, former, anterior.
Ant. Subsequent: consequent.

antecedent, *n.* *Cause, determinant, reason, occasion.
Ana. Precursor, *forerunner: progenitor, forebear (see ANCESTOR).
Ant. Consequence. — *Con.* *Effect, result, issue, sequel, aftereffect, aftermath, outcome, upshot.

antechamber. Anteroom, vestibule, foyer, lobby, hall, *entry, entryway, narthex.

antediluvian. Ancient, antiquated, obsolete, antique, venerable, archaic, *old.
Ana. Primordial, primeval, primal, pristine (see PRIMARY): *early.

antenna. **Antenna, aerial** (*or* **aërial**). **Antenna** is used in radio to designate that part (consisting of conductive material in the form of wire, a rod, ball, tower, or the like) of an apparatus used for radiating radio waves into, or for receiving radio waves from, space. Since the most conspicuous part of an antenna was an elevated (aerial) horizontal wire or wires, **aerial** has come to be used interchangeably with *antenna.* In strict scientific usage, however, *aerial* is restricted to the elevated portion of the conductors used for the reception or transmission of radio waves; as, the *aerial* and the lead-in of an antenna system. Formerly, *antenna* was used to designate the part used for reception and *aerial* the part for transmitting, but today *antenna* is used for either one; as, transmitting *antenna,* receiving *antenna.*

anterior, *adj.* **1** *Preceding, precedent, previous, prior, foregoing, antecedent, former.
Ant. Posterior. — *Con.* Rear, hind, back, hinder, after (see POSTERIOR).
2 Ventral, *abdominal.

anteroom. Antechamber, vestibule, hall, foyer, lobby, *entry, entryway, narthex.

anthem. *Hymn, laud, psalm, canticle, antiphon, canon.

anthology. **Anthology, garland, florilegium, treasury, thesaurus, corpus, chrestomathy, chapbook** are here compared only as designating a literary miscellany, especially one published in book form. **Anthology,** literally a "gathering of flowers," was originally applied to a collection of epigrams, choice passages, and the like; now it is the usual designation of any collection of literary works, poems or prose writings, or both, representative of an age, a national literature, a literary type, or the like; as, an *anthology* of contemporary American essays; an *anthology* of sonnets. **Garland** and **florilegium** are more or less poetic equivalents of *anthology,* though they sometimes suggest selection of choice passages rather than of complete works, and reference to a particular theme, occasion, or the like. "In the reign of James I. they [ballads] began to be collected into little Miscellanies, under the name of *Garlands*" (*Percy*). "We have made but a small *florilegium* from Mr. Hazlitt's remarkable volumes" (*J. R. Lowell*). Both words are found chiefly in titles of old collections of poetic passages or works. **Treasury** is more common in modern titles of poetic anthologies, but it distinctively suggests selection of complete poems that are the treasures, or the poems worth preserving, rather than representative specimens, of their age or literature; as, Francis T. Palgrave's "Golden *Treasury* of English Songs and Lyrics." **Thesaurus** is more often used, especially in titles, of a collection, or storehouse, of words (as, Roget's "*Thesaurus* of English Words and Phrases") than of writings, but it is occasionally employed in the latter sense by writers and speakers to denote an omnium gatherum, where the principle of selection plays no part and the assemblage of all the writings is the aim; as, Child's "English and Scottish Popular Ballads" is a *thesaurus,* not an anthology. The technical term, however, for a collection including all the writings on a subject, or by a given author, school, or the like, is **corpus** "Though we have a few [early English lyrics], they have not been collected . . . into a *corpus,* and the total does not appear to be very large" (*Saintsbury*). A **chrestomathy** is a collection, usually of extracts from the work of a representative author or group of authors; its purpose is not so much to give pleasure as to provide material for study, as in learning a language. "A general course in Russian Literature in connection with the reading of a historical *chrestomathy*" (*Yale Univ. Catalogue,* 1900). **Chapbook** is mainly a collector's designation of a type of literary miscellany, containing a collection of ballads, tracts, popular tales, or the like, sold by peddlers (or "chapmen").

anthropoid. **Anthropoid, anthropomorphous, anthropomorphic** agree in meaning like man or a human being. They are, however, not interchangeable. **Anthropoid** is exclusively applied to animals that bear close physical likenesses to man; as, the *anthropoid* apes. **Anthropomorphous** is applicable to anything that may be likened to man in form, appearance, qualities, or characters; as, *anthropomorphous* natural formations; *anthropomorphous* idols or deities. **Anthropomorphic,** the adjectival form of *anthropomorphism,* or the ascription of human characters to beings not human, especially to the Supreme Being, is applied not only to beings so conceived, but to the conceptions, and the like; as, the *anthropomorphic* God of Milton's "Paradise Lost"; *anthropomorphic* religions.

anthropology. **Anthropology, ethnology, archaeology** (*or* **archeology**) are clearly distinguishable sciences, but they are often confused by laymen because the investigations of scholars in these fields are largely (though in the case of the first two far from exclusively) concerned with ancient or primitive races. **Anthropology** (in the modern sense of that word) is a general term covering many sciences which deal with the physical and cultural evolution of the human species from prehistoric times to the present. One very important branch of anthropology is **ethnology,** which is concerned with the origin, development, geographical distribution, and distinguishing characters of the human races. **Archaeology** is rather a branch of history than of anthropology but since its field is the investigation of prehistoric and ancient cultures and civilizations and a study of their remains (fossil human relics, implements, artifacts, monuments, etc.), it supplies the material evidence which gives anthropologists and ethnologists some of the data from which they may draw their conclusions.

anthropomorphic. Anthropomorphous, *anthropoid.

anthropomorphous. Anthropomorphic, *anthropoid.

antic, *adj.* Grotesque, bizarre, *fantastic.
Ana. Preposterous, absurd, *foolish: ludicrous, ridiculous, comic, comical, farcical, *laughable.
Con. *Serious, solemn, grave, sedate: sensible, prudent, *wise: conventional, formal (see CEREMONIAL).

antic, *n.* **1** Monkeyshine, caper, *prank, dido.

Ana. *Trick, wile, artifice: *caprice, freak, vagary, whim: gambol, frolic, romp (see under PLAY, *v.*).
2 Clown, buffoon, zany, merry-andrew, *fool, jester, comic, stooge, comedian, pantaloon.

anticipate. 1 Forestall, *prevent.
Ana. Introduce, *enter: *foretell, forecast, presage: *frustrate, thwart, balk.
Ant. Consummate. — ***Con.*** Finish, complete, terminate, *close.
2 Apprehend, *foresee, foreknow, divine.
Ana. *Foretell, forecast, prognosticate: foretaste (see corresponding noun at PROSPECT): look for, await, *expect.

anticipation. Foretaste, *prospect, outlook.
Ana. Foreseeing, foreknowing (see FORESEE): presentiment, foreboding, *apprehension: forecast, prophecy, prediction, presage (see corresponding verbs at FORETELL): conceiving, envisioning, imagining (see THINK).
Ant. Retrospect. — ***Con.*** Recollection, reminiscence, remembrance, *memory: realization, actualization (see corresponding verbs at REALIZE).

antidote. *Corrective, check, control.
Ana. Counteractive, neutralizer (see corresponding verbs at NEUTRALIZE): nullifier, negator, annuller (see corresponding verbs at NULLIFY): *remedy, medicine, physic.

antinomy. *Paradox, anomaly.
Ana. Opposite, contradictory, contrary, antithesis (see under OPPOSITE, *adj.*): contradiction, denial (see corresponding verbs at DENY): conflict, variance, *discord.

antipasto. *Appetizer, hors d'oeuvre, smörgåsbord.

antipathetic. **Antipathetic, unsympathetic, averse** are often used as if they were synonyms. They are, however, not interchangeable if employed in the senses sanctioned by the best usage. In very discriminating use, **antipathetic** is applied only to things (or to persons objectively considered) which are disagreeable, distasteful, uncongenial, abhorrent, or repellent. "The whole place and everything about it was *antipathetic* to her" (*Trollope*). "Settlers to whom this formula was *antipathetic* were asked to go elsewhere" (*A. Repplier*). "Ushering in the year with a series of calls on the most remote and the most personally *antipathetic* of our innumerable relations" (*A. Huxley*). In loose and dubiously correct use, the word is applied to persons (or groups of persons) as though it were the antonym of *sympathetic;* in the attributive position, it is definitely objectionable (as, an *antipathetic* doctor), but in the predicate position it is, at least, countenanced, especially when it implies animosity and not merely the absence of sympathy; as, "these nations are *antipathetic* and cannot unite" (*Harper's Mag.*). In this illustration, however, the addition of "to each other" after *antipathetic* would (probably) not alter the writer's meaning but would both clarify it and improve his English. **Unsympathetic,** on the other hand, is with rare exceptions applied to persons (or to things personified or thought of as expressing personal feeling) and suggests an attitude of indifference or insensitiveness or the absence of a response to an appeal to one's interest or emotions; as, an *unsympathetic* nurse; an *unsympathetic* review of a new book. **Averse** (for synonyms in this sense see DISINCLINED) is closer to *unsympathetic* than to *antipathetic* in that it suggests the spirit in which a person meets something objective rather than the effect of a thing upon a person. However, *averse* implies not merely a lack of response, but a definite turning away, and consequently either avoidance or rejection; as, to be *averse* to a suggestion; to be *averse* from exercise on a hot day. Thus, a man may be *unsympathetic* by nature yet not be *averse* to helping the worthy poor; the undeserving he would confine to institutions, for shiftlessness is utterly *antipathetic* to him. In general, it may be said that one is *averse* to (or from) anything which is *antipathetic* to one.
Ana. Repellent, *repugnant, distasteful, abhorrent, obnoxious: *offensive, loathsome, repulsive, revolting.
Ant. Congenial. — ***Con.*** Attractive, alluring, charming (see under ATTRACT): sympathetic, compatible, *consonant: agreeable, grateful, gratifying, pleasing, *pleasant.

antipathy. 1 Antagonism, *enmity, hostility, animosity, rancor, animus.
Ana. Repugnance, abhorrence, repellency, distaste (see corresponding adjectives at REPUGNANT): avoidance, evasion, eschewal, escape (see corresponding verbs at ESCAPE).
Ant. Taste (*for*): affection (*for*). — ***Con.*** *Attraction, sympathy: *predilection, partiality, prepossession: *attachment, love.
2 Antipathy, aversion are closer synonyms than their corresponding adjectives when they denote the state of mind created by that which is antipathetic to one. **Antipathy** distinctively implies an emotional state, often a settled emotion, which prevents reconciliation or contact, or which, more often, definitely implies hostility (see ENMITY). **Aversion,** on the other hand, suggests a predisposition, or an unwillingness to meet, encounter, or entertain, which shows itself in avoidance or rejection rather than in hatred; thus, one has an *antipathy* to cats who is violently repelled by them and drives them from one's presence; one has an *aversion* to cats who merely avoids contact with them.
Ana., Ant., Con. See those at ANTIPATHY, 1.

antiphon. Psalm, canticle, canon, *hymn, anthem, laud.

antipodal, antipodean. Antithetical, contrary, *opposite, contradictory, antonymous.

antipodes, antipode. Antithesis, contrary, opposite, contradictory, antonym. See under OPPOSITE, *adj.*

antiquated. Archaic, obsolete, antediluvian, antique, *old, ancient, venerable.
Ana. Superannuated, *aged.
Ant. Modernistic: modish. — ***Con.*** Modern, newfashioned, novel, newfangled, *new: *stylish, fashionable, smart.

antique. Ancient, *old, venerable, antiquated, antediluvian, obsolete, archaic.
Ant. Modern: current.

antisepsis. See under STERILE.

antiseptic, *adj.* **1** Germicidal, bactericidal, disinfectant. See under ANTISEPTIC, *n.*
2 *Sterile, aseptic.

antiseptic, *n.* **Antiseptic, germicide, bactericide, disinfectant, bacteriophage, phage, antitoxin** agree in denoting an agent that interferes with the growth and activity of microorganisms. An **antiseptic** is an agent that prevents or arrests the growth and activity of microorganisms, especially disease germs, without necessarily killing them. The word is most commonly applied to substances, such as solutions of alcohol, bichloride of mercury, boric acid, or iodine, that are mild enough to be used on living tissue. The word **germicide** is used of an agent that kills microorganisms, or, in its specific sense, disease germs. It is commonly applied to strong chemicals which cannot safely be used on living tissues, and to heat, sunlight, and the like. A **bactericide** is a germicide that destroys all kinds of bacteria (but does not necessarily kill bacterial spores). A **disinfectant** is a germicide, usually a chemical, used to kill disease germs and other harmful microorganisms in sources of infection, such as drains, sick rooms, clothing, bedding, laboratories, and stables. *Disinfectant* is sometimes applied to any of certain substances, such as chloride of lime, which destroy disagreeable odors by interfering with the activity of the bacteria causing putrefaction. The same distinctions hold for the corresponding adjectives **antiseptic, germicidal, bactericidal, disinfectant. Bacteriophage** (or its shortened form **phage**) and **antitoxin** differ from the preceding terms in applying to substances produced in a living body and effective in destroying disease germs or in counteracting the poison or toxin they create. *Bacteriophage* applies specifically to a bacteria-destroying agent normally found in the intestinal tract of those recovering from a bacterial disease, and in blood, urine, pus, and the like. *Antitoxin* applies specifically to a substance produced in the body of a human being or animal which is effective in counteracting the toxin developed by an infectious disease. In ordinary use, however, the term designates a substance produced in the body of an animal, such as a horse, by the injection of the toxin of diphtheria and used in the treatment of persons suffering from that disease.

antisocial. Asocial, *unsocial, nonsocial.
Ana. Anarchic, anarchistic, anarchist (see under ANARCHY): misanthropic, pessimistic, *cynical.
Ant. Social.

antithesis. 1 Contrast, *comparison, parallel, collation.
2 Opposite, antipodes, contradictory, contrary, antonym. See under OPPOSITE, *adj.*

antithetical *or* **antithetic.** *Opposite, contrary, contradictory, antonymous.

antitoxin. Bacteriophage, bactericide, germicide, *antiseptic, disinfectant.

antitype. Ectype (see PROTOTYPE).
Ant. Type (*in sense covered at* SYMBOL, 2).

antonym. Opposite, contradictory, contrary, antithesis, antipodes. See under OPPOSITE, *adj.*

antonymous. *Opposite, contradictory, contrary, antithetical, antipodal.

anxiety. Worry, *care, concern, solicitude.
Ana. *Distress, suffering, misery: *fear, dread, alarm, panic: *apprehension, foreboding, misgiving: doubt, *uncertainty, mistrust.
Ant. Security. — *Con.* *Certainty, assurance, certitude: *confidence, self-possession, aplomb: composure, *equanimity, sang-froid.

anxious. 1 Worried, concerned, solicitous, careful. See under CARE, *n.*
Ana. *Fearful, apprehensive, afraid: uneasy, jittery, *impatient: perturbed, agitated, upset (see corresponding verbs at DISCOMPOSE).
Ant. Composed. — *Con.* *Cool, unruffled, imperturbable, collected: *confident, assured, sanguine, sure.
2 *Eager, keen, agog, a-tiptoe, avid.
Ana. Desiring *or* desirous, wishing *or* wishful, craving (see corresponding verbs at DESIRE): yearning, longing, pining (see LONG, *v.*).
Ant. Loath. — *Con.* Reluctant, hesitant, *disinclined, indisposed, averse.

any, *adj.* *Some.

apache. *Ruffian, thug, Mohock, gangster, desperado.

apartment. 1 Flat, tenement, chambers, *room(s), lodgings, quarters, diggings, digs.
2 *Room, chamber.

apathetic. Phlegmatic, stolid, *impassive, stoic.
Ana. Insensitive, impassible, *insensible, anesthetic: callous, *hardened: unaffected, untouched, unimpressed (see affirmative verbs at AFFECT): listless, spiritless, *languid.
Ant. Alert (sense 1): aghast. — *Con.* Stirred, roused, aroused, awakened (see STIR, *v.*): vigilant, *watchful, wide-awake.

apathy. Phlegm, stolidity, impassivity, impassiveness, stoicism. See under IMPASSIVE.
Ana. Inertness, inactivity, passiveness, supineness (see corresponding adjectives at INACTIVE): indifference, unconcern, aloofness, detachment (see corresponding adjectives at INDIFFERENT): *lethargy, torpidity, torpor.
Ant. Zeal: enthusiasm. — *Con.* Ardor, fervor, *passion: anxiety, concern, solicitude (see CARE, *n.*).

ape, *v.* *Copy, imitate, mimic, mock.
Ana. *Caricature, burlesque: emulate, *rival.

aperçu. Sketch, précis, survey, digest, pandect, *compendium, syllabus.
Ana. Epitome, brief, abstract, *abridgment.

aperient, aperitive. *Physic, laxative, purgative, cathartic, purge.

apéritif. *Appetizer.

aperture. **Aperture, interstice, orifice** are general terms denoting an opening allowing passage through or in and out. **Aperture** is applied especially to any opening in a thing that otherwise presents a solid or closed surface or structure; it may be applied to an opening that is a flaw, such as a crack or cleft, or to one that is structurally essential; as, daylight filtered through small *apertures* in the dungeon's outside wall; windows are *apertures* to admit light and air; the *aperture* of a camera; pores are minute *apertures* in the skin through which moisture is exuded and absorbed. **Interstice** is applied to any unfilled space, or gap, or interval, especially in a fabric (in its widest sense), or in a mass. It is especially applicable to any of the openings in something that is loose in texture, coarse-grained, layered, piled up, and the like; as, the *interstices* between the stones of the wall were not filled with mortar; a mesh is one of the *interstices* in a fish net, a wire screen or sieve, or the like. *Interstice* is also used of time, in the sense of an empty interval; as, "What . . . do they do . . . in all the mysterious *interstices* of their lives?" (*L. P. Smith*). **Orifice** (now chiefly in technical or literary use) is applied to any opening that serves chiefly as a mouth or as a vent; as, the *orifice* of the bladder; the *orifice* of a chimney; the *orifice* of a wound. "Horror . . . when Mongibello belches forth from all its *orifices* its sulphureous fires" (*Borrow*).
Ana. Perforation, puncture, bore, prick (see corresponding verbs at PERFORATE): *hole, hollow, cavity: slit, slash, cut (see corresponding verbs at CUT).

apex. 1 **Apex, vertex** are so often used interchangeably with reference to the tip or top point of a cone, a pyramid, a conic section, or the like, that a fundamental difference in implications is often ignored. **Apex** has particular reference to the sharpness or angularity of the point or tip; it may or may not in its literal application to things imply that this is the highest point; thus, the *apex* of the heart is its lower and pointed end; the *apex* of a lung is its upper cone-shaped end. *Apex* may also refer to the converging point of two lines whether they extend in a vertical plane or not; as, the *apex* of a leaf; the *apex*, or crest, of a vein in a mine. **Vertex,** as a rule and apart from some technical senses in mathematics, implies a base (real or assumed) and therefore a top or highest point. This implication is retained when the word is applied to concrete things; thus, the *vertex* of the head or of the skull is the highest point, or the upper end of its axis; *vertex* in astronomy is the zenith either with reference to the observer or to the particular body under observation.
2 Peak, *summit, culmination, pinnacle, climax, acme, meridian, zenith, apogee.

aphorism. Apothegm, epigram, *saying, saw, maxim, adage, proverb, motto.

aphrodisiac *or* **aphrodisiacal.** *Erotic, amatory, amorous.

Ant. Anaphrodisiac.

apiece. *Each, severally, individually, respectively.

aplomb. Assurance, self-assurance, self-possession, *confidence, self-confidence.

Ana. Coolness, collectedness, nonchalance, imperturbability (see corresponding adjectives at COOL): *equanimity, composure, sang-froid: poise, savoir-faire (see TACT).

Ant. Shyness. — *Con.* Embarrassment, discomfiture (see corresponding verbs at EMBARRASS): confusion, befuddlement (see corresponding verbs at CONFUSE): perplexity, bewilderment, distraction (see corresponding verbs at PUZZLE).

apocalypse. Vision, *revelation, prophecy.

☞ *Do not confuse* apocalypse *with* apocrypha.

apocalyptic *or* **apocalyptical.** See under REVELATION.

Ana. Visionary, *imaginary, chimerical, quixotic: *mysterious, arcane, inscrutable: mystic, *mystical, anagogical: grandiose, magnificent, august, *grand.

apocrypha. **Apocrypha, pseudepigrapha** denote certain Jewish and early Christian writings of doubtful authenticity or authority. **Apocrypha** is the general term for all such writings, especially for those which have not been admitted into the canons of the Old and New Testaments. The term, however, in general and in specifically Protestant use, is applied narrowly (written with a capital letter) to a group of books or of parts of books which belong to the Old Testament in the Vulgate (the standard Latin version of the Roman Catholic Church) and were rejected by the Protestant reformers because not found in the Hebrew. These books had been and still are admitted as canonical books in the Roman Catholic versions on the ground that they are found in the Septuagint, the Greek version of the Old Testament, and quoted in the New Testament. They are, however, distinguished in Roman Catholic use from the books found in the Hebrew by the designation *deuterocanonical books* (that is, books of a second, or later, canon). **Pseudepigrapha,** in its more common meaning, designates as a group a large number of Jewish and Christian writings attributed to various Biblical characters but held to be spurious or of doubtful authenticity. Protestants, as a rule, use this term in preference to *apocrypha* for Jewish writings of this description which Roman Catholics, also as a rule, call the "Old Testament *apocrypha*." All Christian works of this character are called New Testament *apocrypha* by both Protestants and Catholics.

☞ *Do not confuse* apocrypha *with* apocalypse.

apocryphal. Mythical, *fictitious, legendary, fabulous.

Ana. Questionable, dubious, *doubtful.

Con. Genuine, *authentic, veritable, bona fide.

apodictic *or* **apodeictic, apodictical** *or* **apodeictical.** Necessary, inevitable, *certain.

Ana. Proved, demonstrated, tried, tested (see PROVE).

Ant. Indemonstrable.

apogee. Climax, peak, culmination, apex, acme, meridian, zenith, *summit, pinnacle.

Ant. Perigee.

apologetic *or* **apologetical.** *Controversial, polemic, polemical.

Ana. Explanatory *or* explaining, expounding, interpretative *or* interpreting, elucidating (see corresponding verbs at EXPLAIN): defending, justifying, vindicating (see MAINTAIN).

apologia. *Apology, excuse, plea, alibi, pretext.

Ana. Defense, justification, vindication (see corresponding verbs at MAINTAIN): interpretation, elucidation, explanation (see corresponding verbs at EXPLAIN).

apologue. Fable, *allegory, parable, myth.

apology. **Apology, apologia, excuse, plea, pretext, alibi** come into comparison when they denote the reason or reasons offered in explanation or defense of an act, a policy, a view, or the like. In modern, especially popular, use **apology** implies that one has been, at least apparently, in the wrong; it suggests either a defense that brings forward palliating circumstances, or a frank acknowledgment of error, with an expression of regret, by way of reparation. " 'Pardon us the interruption Of thy devotion . . .'—'My lord, there needs no such *apology*' " (*Shak.*). In its older sense, still used by discriminating writers, it implies no admission of guilt or error but a desire to make clear the grounds for some course, belief, or the like, that appears wrong to others; as, Sidney's "*Apologie* for Poetrie"; "*Apologies* for various . . . doctrines of the faith" (*Newman*). **Apologia** is now often used in English in place of *apology* in this latter sense. "Basil de Selincourt's *apologia* for Ruskin in the Contemporary Review" (*The Nation*). "Viscount Grey of Fallodon . . . the other day delivered an *apologia* for democracy" (*N. Y. Times*). **Excuse** always implies an intent to remove or avoid blame, as for a neglect of duty, a failure to accomplish an end, or a violation of a rule, a law, a custom. " 'Achilles will not to the field tomorrow' —'What's his *excuse?*' " (*Shak.*). "We have forty million reasons for failure, but not a single *excuse!*" (*Kipling*). "His pride . . . does not offend me so much as pride often does, because there is an *excuse* for it" (*Austen*). **Plea** stresses argument or appeal to others for understanding or sympathy. "Old Hepzibah's scowl could no longer vindicate itself entirely on the *plea* of nearsightedness" (*N. Hawthorne*). "He mumbled something about not having a license [for hunting], and was putting that in for a *plea* against the expedition" (*Meredith*). **Pretext** invariably suggests subterfuge and the offering of one reason or motive in place of the true one. "He made my health a *pretext* for taking all the heavy chores, long after I was as well as he was" (*Cather*). **Alibi** (literally, *elsewhere*) in law designates a plea of having been in another place at the time a crime was committed. In its broader colloquial use, it implies a desire to shift blame or to evade punishment. It commonly connotes plausibility rather than truth in the excuse offered. "We lie to ourselves, in order that we may still have the *excuse* of ignorance, the *alibi* of stupidity and incomprehension, possessing which we can continue with a good conscience to commit and tolerate . . . crimes" (*A. Huxley*).

Ana. Defense, justification, vindication (see corresponding verbs at MAINTAIN): extenuation, palliation, glozing, whitewashing (see corresponding verbs at PALLIATE): amends, *reparation.

apoplexy. Stroke, shock. See PARALYSIS.

apostasy. Desertion, *defection.

apostate, *n.* *Renegade, pervert, turncoat, recreant, backslider.

Ana. Deserter, forsaker, abandoner (see corresponding verbs at ABANDON): *heretic, schismatic, dissenter, nonconformist.

Con. *Convert, proselyte.

apostle. **1** *Disciple, evangelist.

2 *Missionary, evangelist, revivalist.

apothecary. Pharmacist, pharmaceutist, *druggist, chemist.

apothegm. Aphorism, epigram, *saying, saw, maxim, adage, proverb, motto.

apotheosis. Sublimation, *paragon, phoenix, nonpareil, nonesuch.

appall *or* **appal.** Horrify, *dismay, daunt.
Ana. Terrify, affright, *frighten: confound, dumfound, bewilder (see PUZZLE).
Ant. Nerve, embolden. — *Con.* Energize, *vitalize, activate: *comfort, solace, console.

appalling. *Fearful, dreadful, terrible, horrible, frightful, shocking, awful, terrific, horrific.
Ana. Dismaying, horrifying, daunting (see DISMAY, *v.*): bewildering, dumfounding, confounding (see PUZZLE, *v.*).
Ant. Reassuring.

appanage *or* **apanage.** Prerogative, perquisite, birthright, *right.

apparatus. 1 *Equipment, gear, tackle, outfit, paraphernalia, machinery, matériel.
Ana. Tool, *implement, utensil, instrument: network, *system, scheme.
2 *Machine, appliance, engine.
Ana. *Device, contrivance, contraption, gadget.

apparel, *v.* *Clothe, attire, tire, dress, array, robe, vest, invest.
Ana. Outfit, accouter, appoint, equip (see FURNISH).
Ant. Divest. — *Con.* *Strip, bare, dismantle, denude.

apparel, *n.* *Clothes, clothing, dress, attire, tire, raiment, vesture, array.

apparent. 1 *Evident, manifest, patent, distinct, obvious, palpable, plain, clear.
Ana. Discernible, noticeable (see corresponding verbs at SEE): *perceptible, ponderable, tangible, appreciable.
Ant. Unintelligible. — *Con.* *Obscure, dark, enigmatic, vague, ambiguous, cryptic.
2 Apparent, illusory, seeming, ostensible agree in meaning not really or actually that which it appears to be. That is **apparent** which, however evident it may be from the point of view of the unaided senses, is not borne out by scientific investigation or by a knowledge of all the facts or circumstances; as, the *apparent* size of the sun; "the *apparent* loss of weight of a body immersed in water" (*Karl K. Darrow*). "I am anxious to leaven our *apparent*, for it is really more *apparent* than real, our *apparent* worldliness" (*C. Mackenzie*). That is **illusory** which is the result of a false impression and acquires a character or appearance other than that found in the real thing, or which seems to exist when it is actually nonexistent. The deception may be the result of one's sense limitations, as in an optical illusion, or of a misleading appearance assumed by something else, as in certain natural phenomena (a mirage or will o' the wisp), or of one's own state of mind which colors or alters the objective reality, or of the strong stimulation of the imagination, as by a work of art, that causes one to accept as real that which is purely imaginary; as, lengthwise stripes give an *illusory* height to the figure; *illusory* pools of water on a highway; a lover often attributes an *illusory* beauty to his beloved. "The beautiful is in a certain sense *illusory*, or rather contains an element of illusion" (*S. Alexander*). That is **seeming** which is so like the reality in appearance that it may be mistaken for it. *Seeming* usually implies a character in the thing observed rather than, as the two preceding words, a defect of observation. Often, but not invariably, it suggests an intent to deceive or delude. "Miss Wilmot's reception [of him] was mixed with *seeming* neglect, and yet I could perceive she acted a studied part" (*Goldsmith*). "The whole of Burns's song has an air of straight dealing . . . but these *seeming* simplicities are craftily charged . . . with secondary purposes, ulterior intimations" (*C. E. Montague*). That is **ostensible** which is explicitly declared, professed, or avowed (as an aim or motive), or which has the outward marks of the character ascribed to it, yet which, by implication, may not be its true aim, or motive, or character; thus, when one says that the *ostensible* purpose of a naval review is the celebration of a national holiday, one implies that there may be another, deeper, and more significant purpose not revealed, such as mobilization for war. "Natives from independent and feudatory courts whose *ostensible* business was the repair of broken necklaces . . . but whose real end seemed to be to raise money for angry Maharanees or young Rajahs" (*Kipling*).
Ana. *False, wrong: deceptive, delusory, delusive, *misleading: specious, credible, *plausible.
Ant. Real. — *Con.* Actual, true (see REAL): intrinsic, *inherent, essential.

apparition. Apparition, phantasm, phantom, wraith, fetch, ghost, spirit, specter, shade, revenant, spook, haunt (*or* **hant**) agree in meaning a visible but immaterial appearance of a person or thing, especially a likeness of a dead person or of a person or thing that is not physically present. **Apparition, phantasm, phantom** all stress the illusory character of that which appears to the sight, but *apparition* often connotes suddenness or unexpectedness of coming, *phantasm* the workings of a disordered or overexcited imagination, and *phantom* a dreamlike character and form without substance, or shape without body or mass. "[Enter the ghost of Caesar] . . . I think it is the weakness of mine eyes That shapes this monstrous *apparition*" (*Shak.*). "Horrible forms, What and who are ye? Never yet there came *Phantasms* so foul thro' monster-teeming Hell" (*Shelley*). "So live and laugh, nor be dismayed As one by one the *phantoms* go" (*E. A. Robinson*). **Wraith** and **fetch** specifically denote an apparition of a living person that appears to a friend or relative and portends the former's death, but both are also used of an apparition of a dead person. "She was uncertain if it were the gypsy or her *wraith*" (*Scott*). "The Earl of Cornwall met the *fetch* of his friend William Rufus" (*E. B. Tylor*). *Wraith*, especially in extended use, stresses the insubstantial and evanescent character of the apparition. "O hollow *wraith* of dying fame, Fade wholly, while the soul exults" (*Tennyson*). The remaining words in their literal senses all denote an apparition of a dead person. **Ghost** and **spirit** are the familiar and general terms for a disembodied soul; **specter** (not necessarily human) connotes more of the mysterious or terrifying. "*Ghosts*, wandering here and there, Troop home to churchyards" (*Shak.*). "I am thy father's *spirit*, Doom'd for a certain term to walk the night" (*Shak.*). "Grisly *spectres*, which the Fiend had raised" (*Milton*). "Lo! when the service was ended, a form appeared on the threshold . . . Why does the bridegroom start and stare at the strange *apparition?* . . . Is it a *phantom* of air . . . ? Is it a *ghost* from the grave . . . ?" (*Longfellow*). **Shade** (a somewhat literary word, commonly with classical reference) usually connotes impalpability but it stresses personality rather than mode of appearance; as, "mighty heroes' more majestic *shades*" (*Dryden*); " 'How once we lov'd, remember still, Till you are dust like me' 'Dear *Shade!* I will' " (*Pope*). **Revenant,** when it denotes a ghost, carries none of the implications of the other terms for a disembodied spirit except the return from the grave; it is therefore used often in straight prose or where a term without emotional connotations is desirable. "Thus, our *revenant* from a hundred years ago would find us occupied yet with measuring intensities of force" (*Karl K. Darrow*). "I felt for a queer moment of hallucination more of a *ghost* than the *ghost* I had come to visit—a *revenant* out of a rowdy present into the more stately epoch" (*L. P. Smith*). **Spook** is now a humorous and colloquial term something like *specter* in its suggestion of a terrifying character. **Haunt** or **hant** is a dialectal term common in some parts of the United States for *ghost,* especially for one that frequently revisits a spot or house.

Ana. Illusion, *delusion, hallucination.

appeal, *v.* Plead, pray, sue, petition. See under PRAYER.

Ana. Implore, *beg, beseech, entreat, supplicate: solicit, request, *ask.

Con. *Demand, exact, claim: protest, kick, *object.

appeal, *n.* Plea, *prayer, petition, suit.

Ana. Entreating *or* entreaty, beseeching, supplicating *or* supplication, imploring (see corresponding verbs at BEG): soliciting *or* solicitation, requesting *or* request, asking (see corresponding verbs at ASK).

Con. Demanding *or* demand, exacting *or* exaction, claim (see corresponding verbs at DEMAND): protesting *or* protest, objecting *or* objection, kicking (see corresponding verbs at OBJECT).

appear. 1 Appear, loom, emerge carry basically the same meaning: to come out into view. Actually, however, they are only rarely interchangeable. **Appear** is weakest in its implication of a definite, physical background or a source; consequently it sometimes means merely to become visible or to become apparent (see EVIDENT); as, one by one the stars *appeared* in the sky; nothing *appears* in the testimony to cause suspicion of another's guilt. Sometimes it means to present oneself in public in a particular capacity or to be presented or given out to the public; as, Lawyer Blank *appeared* as counsel for the defendant; Booth *appeared* nightly as Hamlet for the last two weeks of his run; the new biography of Lincoln will *appear* next month; weeklies usually *appear* on Thursday or Friday. **Loom** seems to have been used originally of ships appearing on the horizon, but later acquired the meaning of appearing as through a mist or haze. "A smear of . . . lead-coloured paint had been laid on to obliterate Henchard's name, though its letters dimly *loomed* through like ships in a fog" (*Hardy*). "Between the bed and the ottoman . . . the cot *loomed* in the shadows" (*Bennett*). Because things seen in a fog are often magnified by their indistinct outlines, *loom,* especially when followed in figurative use by *large, great,* etc., or when followed by *up,* suggests apparent, and sometimes appalling, magnitude. "Some mornings it [a mesa] would *loom* up above the dark river like a blazing volcanic mountain" (*Cather*). "That which *loomed* immense to fancy low before my reason lies" (*Browning*). **Emerge** definitely implies a coming out into the open from something that envelops: the word therefore presupposes a period or condition of concealment, obscurity, gestation, insignificance, or the like; as, the sun *emerged* from the clouds; after a long hunt for him, we saw him *emerging* from the crowd. "That part of northern Ohio where the Bentley farms lay had begun to *emerge* from pioneer life" (*S. Anderson*). "Lord Sligo *emerges* from this account as an able and conscientious administrator" (*Times Lit. Sup.*).

Ana. *Come, arrive: issue, emanate, rise, arise, *spring.

Ant. Disappear: vanish. — *Con.* Depart, retire, withdraw, *go, leave.

2 *Seem, look.

appearance. Appearance, look, aspect, semblance are here considered primarily as general terms denoting the outward show presented by a person or thing. **Appearance** often carries no additional implications; as, "Judge not according to the *appearance*" (*John* vii. 24); "In drawing, represent the *appearances* of things, never what you know the things to be" (*Ruskin*). The word, however, frequently implies an apparent, as opposed to an actual or genuine, character and therefore often connotes hypocrisy, dissembling, pretense, or the like, when used of persons or of their acts and works. "To be able to tyrannize effectively they needed the title and *appearance* of constitutional authority" (*A. Huxley*). "They spent their lives trying to keep up *appearances,* and to make his salary do more than it could" (*Cather*). In its general application, **look** is often indistinguishable from *appearance,* except that it more often occurs in the plural; as, never judge a thing merely by its *looks.* They are not interchangeable, however, in all instances. When a personal impression or a judgment is implied, *appearance* is the precise word. "Aristotle . . . while admitting that Plato's scheme has a plausible *appearance* of philanthropy, maintains that it is inapplicable to the facts of human nature" (*G. L. Dickinson*). When the emphasis is upon concrete details, such as of color, shape, expression, observable to everybody, *look* is the proper choice; as, he had the *look* of a man who works indoors and takes little exercise. " 'I choose my friends for their good *looks,* my acquaintances for their good characters, and my enemies for their good intellects' " (*Wilde*). Specifically *look* is often applied to a person's expression, as manifest in one's face or posture. "She had a *look* about her That I wish I could forget— The *look* of a scared thing Sitting in a net!" (*Millay*). **Aspect,** like *look,* stresses the features of a person or thing, but when applied to persons, it usually distinctively suggests the characteristic or habitual appearance and expression, especially facial expression; as, "Not risking a landing because of the fierce *aspect* of the natives" (*V. Heiser*); "he was a very handsome man, of a commanding *aspect*" (*Austen*). *Aspect* often specifically implies reference to all the features that give a distinguishing appearance to a place at a definite moment, an age, a particular situation, or the like. "The *aspect* of affairs was very alarming" (*Dickens*). "Fifty years from now, it may be, the olive tree will almost have disappeared from southern France, and Provence will wear another *aspect*" (*A. Huxley*). **Semblance** comes into comparison with the other words of this group because it basically implies outward seeming, without necessarily suggesting a false appearance. Nevertheless, it is rarely used in this sense without an expressed or implied contrast between the outward appearance and the inner reality. "Thou, whose exterior *semblance* doth belie Thy Soul's immensity" (*Wordsworth*). Consequently, the word frequently implies a false appearance or a counterfeit of the truth. "It was also a snuff-box that brought about the only *semblance* of reconciliation that ever occurred" (*Lucas*). Sometimes, however, the word stresses the likeness of the thing to something else, without suggesting deceptiveness in the appearance. "A piked road that even then had begun to take on the *semblance* of a street" (*S. Anderson*).

appease. *Pacify, placate, mollify, propitiate, conciliate.

Ana. Assuage, alleviate, mitigate, lighten, *relieve: *palliate, extenuate: *satisfy, content.

Ant. Exasperate, aggravate. — *Con.* Perturb, upset, disturb, *discompose: vex, irk, *annoy, bother: *anger, incense, enrage, infuriate.

appellation. *Name, title, designation, denomination, style.

append. *Add, subjoin, annex, superadd.

Ana. Affix, attach, *fasten.

Con. *Detach, disengage: curtail (see SHORTEN).

appendage. Appendage, appurtenance, accessory, adjunct agree in designating something regarded as additional, and at the same time as subsidiary, to another object. **Appendage** implies a certain closeness of attachment or connection, yet often stresses (esp. when used of a person), even to mild contempt, the idea of subordination; as, the caudal *appendage;* the smaller borough is a mere *appendage* of the larger. "Those graceful and useless *appendages,* called Directors" (*Scott*). **Appurtenance** is applied to something that belongs to the principal object, or goes with it customarily, yet is not an integral part of it, as the barns, outhouses, gardens, etc., on a piece of land, or the permanent fixtures in a building. "The bed itself, with all *appurtenances* of palliasse, mattresses, etc." (*Barham*). **Accessory** is applied usually to that which is dispensable yet contributes to the appearance, usefulness, comfort, convenience, or the like, of the principal thing; as, automobile *accessories;* costume *accessories.* **Adjunct** is applied to that which is or may be added or joined to the principal thing without becoming an essential part of it. "In the great age of Louis XIV, it [the ballet] became an established institution, still an *adjunct* of opera" (*H. Ellis*). "Metre and rhyme are not mere *adjuncts* of poetry" (*S. Alexander*).

appendix. Appendix, addendum *or* (*pl.*) **addenda, supplement** come into comparison when they designate additional matter subjoined to a book. **Appendix** is used of appended material which contributes, by way of illustration, amplification, citation of documents, etc., to the effectiveness of a treatment that is still relatively complete in itself. **Addendum** and **supplement,** however, agree in implying that the additional matter is essential to completeness of treatment, but differ in that *addendum* suggests greater brevity and is frequently used of material added to supply omissions, while *supplement* implies larger compass, and is often applied to material added after some lapse of time, often as a separate publication, to embody later information. When the additional matter of an addendum is a list, as of words or items, the plural *addenda* is often used instead of *addendum.*

apperception. Assimilation, identification, *recognition.

appertain. Pertain, belong, relate, *bear, apply.

appetence *or* **appetency.** Appetite, *desire, concupiscence, lust, passion, urge, yen.

Ana., Con. See those at APPETITE.

appetite. Appetence, *desire, concupiscence, lust, passion, urge, yen.

Ana. Hungering *or* hunger, thirsting *or* thirst, yearning, longing (see corresponding verbs at LONG): craving, wishing, coveting (see DESIRE, *v.*): impulse, spring, *motive: *cupidity, greed.

Con. Abnegation, self-abnegation, self-denial, *renunciation: asceticism (see under ASCETIC, *n.*): repugnance, distaste (see corresponding adjectives at REPUGNANT).

appetizer. Appetizer, hors d'oeuvre, antipasto, smörgåsbord, apéritif. Appetizer is the comprehensive term denoting any food or drink served in advance of a meal as a whet to the appetite. In American use, *appetizer* is a generic term including cocktails and any savory tidbit served before going to the table, or a first course, such as of oysters, clams, a fruit cocktail, or a canapé served at the table. **Hors d'oeuvre,** a French term widely current in English-speaking countries in place of *appetizer,* may be used of any savory, salt, smoked, tart, or uncooked food served with cocktails or as a first course at table. Its more common plural form, *hors d'oeuvres,* generally suggests a tray of such foods from which one selects what pleases one's taste. The typical hors d'oeuvres include small sausages, small molds of potted or jellied meats, sliced salt meats, sardines, anchovies, herrings, crevettes, canapés, olives, radishes, tomatoes, fresh fruits such as figs and melon, and the like. Sometimes hot foods are added, such as small patties or snails in a sauce. Fresh butter is a characteristic French addition. **Antipasto** designates an Italian collection of cold appetizers, usually served as an essential first course of a complete dinner and on an individual plate. *Antipasto* characteristically, but not invariably, includes salami, anchovy, sliced ham, sliced tomatoes, celery, radishes, and olives on a bed of lettuce. **Smörgåsbord,** the comparable Swedish term, is now used widely in the United States for a collection of appetizers similar to hors d'oeuvres, but characteristically displayed on a table or sideboard, and presenting a more extensive variety of cold and hot dishes. *Smörgåsbord* is preferable to *hors d'oeuvres* as a designation when there is a wider choice of dishes and an emphasis on heartier foods (not tidbits) such as smoked salmon, cheese, hard-boiled eggs, the heavier sausages, and the like. Fish in various forms (pickled, smoked, paste, etc.) usually predominates in smörgåsbord. An **apéritif** is a small drink of liquor (vermouth, sherry, and the like) taken shortly before lunch or dinner for the purpose of, or under the pretext of, stimulating the appetite. In somewhat loose use, the meaning of this word has been at times extended to be equivalent to *appetizer,* but in France, where the term originated, it is used of liquor alone.

appetizing. *Palatable, relishing, tasty, toothsome, flavorsome, savory, sapid, saporous.

Ant. Nauseating.

applaud. 1 Applaud, cheer, hurrah, huzza, root agree in meaning to demonstrate one's feeling, especially one's approbation or joy, audibly and enthusiastically. **Applaud** specifically and usually implies hand clapping; as, it is not the custom to *applaud* preachers; the audiences at grand opera are asked to *applaud* only at the end of an act or scene; each graduate was *applauded* as he came up to receive his diploma. **Cheer** suggests shouting, usually of meaningless words such as rah-rah-rah, hip-hip-hooray, or of a set form of words adopted by a school, college or organization as its own; in one very modern use, it implies organized rather than spontaneous effort, and includes singing as well as shouting. *Cheer* differs from *applaud* also in its purpose, which is chiefly that of encouraging or inspiriting individuals or a team going into or taking part in a competition or contest; often, however, it suggests jubilation aroused by a successful play or a brilliant feat. **Hurrah** and **huzza** also suggest shouting, but they emphasize the shouting of these particular words in unison and as an expression particularly of triumph and exultation, as over a military or political victory. The words are now less used in speech than formerly. **Root,** which is peculiarly American slang, may imply cheering or applauding, but it stresses encouragement as the motive. Consequently, in extended use, it implies strong partisanship and vocal public championship of that which one favors; as, to *root* for a candidate; to *root* for one's home team or one's town's advantages.

Ana. Acclaim, extol (see PRAISE).

Ant. Hiss: boo. — *Con.* Deride, taunt, *ridicule, mock.

2 *Commend, compliment, recommend.

Ana. *Praise, eulogize, laud: *approve, endorse, sanction.

Ant. Disparage: criticize. — *Con.* *Decry, depreciate, belittle: censure, reprobate (see CRITICIZE): *disapprove, deprecate.

applause. Applause, acclamation, acclaim, plaudits agree, both in their concrete and abstract senses, in denoting public expression of approbation. **Applause** usually suggests loudness or liveliness of demonstration, and often carries its literal implication of clapping hands; as, she waited until the *applause* died down; round after round of *applause* greeted him. However, it may be used to designate any other noisy or emphatic expression of approval, such as stamping of feet, cheering, or waving of flags. "*Applause* rang out from a hundred thousand throats" (*Froude*). "Caps, hands, and tongues, *applaud* it to the clouds" (*Shak.*). **Acclamation** adds to *applause* the implications of eagerness, enthusiasm, and, often, unanimity of assent: it often retains its etymological implication of crying out; as, he was nominated to the office by *acclamation;* that is, without a ballot, and, usually, with emphatically voiced approval; his speech was received with *acclamation.* **Acclaim** is more poetic than *acclamation,* though often interchanged with the latter; it sometimes carries implications of loftier deeds and more enduring esteem than *acclamation;* as, the heroes were hailed with *acclaim;* his poetry met with universal *acclaim.* **Plaudits** (the singular form is rare), though literally equal to *applause,* may suggest polite or gracious, rather than demonstrative, expressions of approval. "The colonel bowed and smiled with very pleasant good-nature at our *plaudits*" (*Thackeray*).

Ana. Cheering *or* cheers, hurrahing *or* hurrahs, huzzaing *or* huzzas, rooting (see corresponding verbs at APPLAUD).

Ant. Hisses: boos. — *Con.* Deriding *or* derision, taunting *or* taunts, ridiculing *or* ridicule, twitting, mocking (see corresponding verbs at RIDICULE).

appliance. 1 Tool, *implement, instrument, utensil.

Ana. Accessory, adjunct (see APPENDAGE): *device, contrivance, gadget.

2 Apparatus, *machine, engine.

applicable. *Relevant, pertinent, apposite, apropos, germane, material.

Ana. *Fit, suitable, appropriate, apt, felicitous, happy, meet, fitting, proper.

Ant. Inapplicable. — *Con* *Impertinent: inept, *awkward.

applicant. Aspirant, *candidate.

application. Concentration, *attention, study.

Ana. Intentness, engrossment, absorption (see corresponding adjectives at INTENT): toil, grind, drudgery (see WORK): sedulousness, assiduousness, industriousness *or* industry, diligence (see corresponding adjectives at BUSY).

Ant. Indolence. — *Con.* Abstractedness *or* abstraction, absent-mindedness (see corresponding adjectives at ABSTRACTED): laziness, slothfulness, faineance (see corresponding adjectives at LAZY).

appliqué, *v.* *Overlay, superpose, superimpose.

Ana. Ornament, *adorn, decorate: affix, attach, *fasten.

apply. 1 *Use, employ, utilize, avail oneself of.

2 Devote, *direct, address.

Ana. Attend, mind, *tend: addict, accustom, *habituate: toil, labor, work, grind (see corresponding nouns at WORK).

Con. *Neglect, slight: divert (see AMUSE).

3 Go, turn, *resort, refer.

Ana. Appeal, petition (see under PRAYER): *beg, beseech, implore, supplicate.

4 *Bear, relate, pertain, appertain.

appoint. 1 Name, *designate, nominate, elect.

Ana. *Choose, select, pick, single out: commission, *authorize, accredit.

Con. *Dismiss, discharge, cashier.

2 *Furnish, equip, accouter, outfit, arm.

Ana. Garnish, beautify, embellish, bedeck, deck (see ADORN): array, vest, invest (see CLOTHE).

Con. Dismantle, divest, denude, *strip.

appointed. Destined, *prescribed.

Ana. Allotted, assigned (see ALLOT): forecast, foretold, predicted (see FORECAST, *v.*): determined, decided, settled (see DECIDE).

appointment. *Engagement, rendezvous, tryst, assignation, date.

apportion. 1 Allocate, *allot, assign.

Ana. *Distribute, divide, dispense, deal, dole: *share, participate, partake.

Con. *Gather, collect, assemble: consolidate, concentrate, *compact.

2 Apportion, portion, parcel, ration, prorate agree in meaning to divide something carefully and distribute it among a number. **Apportion** suggests division on a just, fair, or equitable basis; it does not, however, imply equality in the divisions or in the persons or things affected by the distribution; as, to *apportion* one's time among various employments; to *apportion* the residue of an estate according to the terms of a will; "to *apportion* the judicial power between the supreme and inferior courts" (*Ch. Just. Marshall*). **Portion** (often with *out*) commonly, but not necessarily, suggests division into shares; as, to *portion* out the leftovers from a banquet to the servants; the country was *portioned* out among the petty chiefs. **Parcel** (commonly with *out*) does not always imply immediate distribution, but it does imply division for the sake of ultimate distribution among purchasers, heirs, etc.; it is the preferred word when that which is divided is cut into pieces or lots or is distributed in small amounts. "It could be *parceled* out into lots fifty by one hundred feet at five hundred dollars per lot" (*Dreiser*). "[In the seventeenth century] colonies were estates to be exploited for the benefit of the home merchants, and the world was *parceled* out among privileged companies" (*J. H. Randall, jr.*). **Ration** usually implies authoritative allowance and an equal division of necessities (fuel, food, clothing, and the like) according to some principle such as that of adequacy, sufficiency, or dietary variety, or, when the available supply is limited or scanty, that of fairness to all; as, to *ration* the food for horses; it was found necessary to *ration* coal, flour, and sugar in the United States during the World War; the drinking water was *rationed* during the prolonged voyage. **Prorate** (chiefly U. S.) implies proportional division (sometimes proportional assessment) for the sake of fairness to those concerned: it may imply an authoritative decision, as by a legislature, or an agreement among those concerned; as, to *prorate* employment among the workers during slack seasons; to *prorate* the annual production of oil by the various companies; to *prorate* overhead expenses among the various departments of a company.

Ana. *Grant, accord, award: *give, bestow: *separate, divide, part.

apposite. Pertinent, germane, *relevant, apropos, applicable, material.

Ana. Felicitous, happy, apt, appropriate, suitable, *fit, fitting: pat, timely opportune, *seasonable.

Ant. Inapposite, inapt. — *Con.* *Impertinent: *awkward, inept: casual, hit-or-miss, haphazard, *random.

appraise *or* **apprize.** Value, *estimate, evaluate, assay, rate, assess.

Ana. *Judge, adjudge: determine, ascertain, *discover: inspect, examine, *scrutinize, audit.

appraising. See under ESTIMATE, *v.*

appreciable. *Perceptible, sensible, ponderable, palpable, tangible.

Ana. Apparent, *evident: discernible, noticeable (see corresponding verbs at SEE).

Ant. Inappreciable. — *Con.* Impalpable, imponderable, *imperceptible, intangible, insensible.

appreciate. 1 Comprehend, *understand.

Ana. Appraise, value, rate, *estimate, evaluate: *judge, adjudge: *apprehend, comprehend.

Ant. Depreciate. — *Con.* Disparage, derogate from, detract from, belittle, *decry.

2 Appreciate, value, prize, treasure, cherish come into

comparison when they mean to hold in high estimation. One **appreciates** that which one understands sufficiently to admire critically, or to enjoy with discrimination of its values, especially its aesthetic values; as, relatively few persons are able to *appreciate* the fugues of John Sebastian Bach; "he liked to . . . have his talent as a whittler *appreciated*" (*S. Anderson*). In loose use, *appreciate* does not always carry this strong implication of intelligent admiration, but stresses rather a response such as warm approval, keen enjoyment, or gratitude; as, "Those who are just beginning to *appreciate* the idea" (*C. Mackenzie*); "Nature actually made him ache, he *appreciated* it so" (*Galsworthy*); "children easily *appreciate* justice" (*B. Russell*). One **values** that which one rates highly or as worth more than other persons or things; as, to *value* honor more than life; there is nothing he *values* so much as the respect of his children. "Suddenly Gard was smitten by the tragedy of plain women; to be *valued*, but not loved" (*M. Austin*). One **prizes** that which one values highly, especially as a possession, and takes deep pride in or sets great store by; as, "The good we never miss we rarely *prize*" (*Cowper*); "We loved the man, and *prized* his work" (*Tennyson*). One **treasures** that which one keeps safe from danger of being lost or stolen, especially, but not invariably, because one regards it as precious, or attaches great sentimental value to it; as, she *treasures* every memento of her youth; those who *value* money because it makes them independent are the reverse of those who *treasure* every penny they acquire and become slaves to their avarice. When used in reference to persons, *treasure* implies a clinging to more often than appreciation or love. "Pay me no homage, Mario,—but if it be I have your friendship, I shall *treasure* it" (*Millay*). **Cherish** (etymologically, to hold dear) may often be used interchangeably with *prize* and *treasure;* the word, however, carries a stronger implication of love or affection for what is cherished and often suggests closer, more intimate association or attentions. "*Cherish* a few books only, and those few chosen not for their fame in the world but wholly for the pleasure that they give you" (*C. E. Montague*). "He was a man who *cherished* his friends. He liked to call at the Bishop's house to advise him about the care of his young orchard, or to leave a bottle of home-made cherry brandy for Father Joseph" (*Cather*).

Ana. *Criticize (also see CRITICISM): admire, esteem, respect, regard (see under REGARD, *n.*): enjoy, *like, relish.

Ant. Despise. — ***Con.*** Contemn, scorn, disdain (see DESPISE): depreciate, disparage, *decry.

apprehend. **1** *Arrest, detain, attach.

Ana. Seize, *take: capture, *catch, cop, nab.

Con. Release, discharge, liberate, *free.

2 Apprehend, comprehend and their derivative nouns **apprehension** and **comprehension** are clearly distinguished in psychological use. The verbs carry in common the meaning to lay hold of something with the mind so as to know it. **Apprehend** and **apprehension,** however, do not imply attainment of full knowledge or of complete understanding, but only a glimpsing of the nature, meaning, or significance of that which is the object of thought; **comprehend** (see also UNDERSTAND) and **comprehension** imply an understanding of the object of thought in its entire compass and extent. *Apprehend* may suggest a single act of the mind, and *comprehend* a complex and laborious process, but this distinction is not so essential as that between imperfect and perfect understanding; thus, one *apprehends* many things which one can never *comprehend,* such as infinity or beauty; one *apprehends* many things as a child, such as mother love, which one does not *comprehend* until late in life. "Who shall say how quickly the babe *apprehends* the relation between the causative howl and its effect, the demanded ministration?" (*Grandgent*). "The thirteenth century which cared little to *comprehend* anything except the incomprehensible" (*H. Adams*).

Ana. *Understand, appreciate: grasp, *take (in): perceive, observe, notice, note (see SEE).

3 Divine, anticipate, *foresee, foreknow.

Ana. Fear, dread (see corresponding nouns at FEAR): forecast, predict, forebode, *foretell.

apprehension. **1** Arrest, detention, attachment. See under ARREST, *v.*

Ana. Seizing *or* seizure, taking (see corresponding verbs at TAKE): capturing *or* capture, catching, copping, nabbing (see corresponding verbs at CATCH).

Con. Releasing *or* release, discharging *or* discharge, liberation (see corresponding verbs at FREE).

2 Comprehension (see under APPREHEND, 2).

Ana. Understanding, appreciation (see corresponding verbs at UNDERSTAND): perceiving *or* perception, observing *or* observation, noticing *or* notice, noting (see corresponding verbs at SEE).

3 Apprehension, foreboding, misgiving, presentiment are here compared as meaning fear (or an instance of it) that something is going wrong or will go wrong. **Apprehension** usually implies fear that obsesses the mind and keeps one anxious and worried; as, to be under *apprehension* concerning a child's health. "The relapse you have described . . . was not quite unforeseen by its subject . . . . You have no idea how such an *apprehension* weighs on the sufferer's mind" (*Dickens*). **Foreboding,** in precise use, designates oppressive anticipatory fear, often superstitious, unreasoning, or inadequately defined fear; thus, one may relieve a person's *apprehensions,* yet find it hard to dispel his *forebodings.* "There was a sadness and constraint about all persons that day, which filled Mr. Esmond with gloomy *forebodings*" (*Thackeray*). **Misgiving** suggests uneasiness and mistrust rather than anxiety or dread; it is often applied to sudden fears, such as a suspicion that one is making a mistake, a doubt of one's capacity to accomplish what one has undertaken, or a disturbing loss of courage. "In the midst of my anecdote a sudden *misgiving* chilled me—had I told them about this Goat before?" (*L. P. Smith*). "His self-confidence had given place to a *misgiving* that he had been making a fool of himself" (*Shaw*). **Presentiment** always implies a vague feeling or a dim, almost mystical, perception of something (not necessarily unpleasant) that seems bound to happen; however, because it commonly (but not invariably) suggests an element of anticipatory fear, and, in many cases, of foreboding, it comes into comparison with the other words of this group. "The delicious repose of the soul . . . had been shaken . . . and alarmed with dim *presentiment*" (*G. Eliot*).

Ana. *Fear, dread, alarm, panic: worry, anxiety, *care.

Ant. Confidence. — ***Con.*** *Trust, faith: assurance, self-possession (see CONFIDENCE): *equanimity, sangfroid, composure.

apprehensive. *Fearful, afraid.

Ana. Anxious, worried, solicitous (see under CARE, *n.*): nervous, uneasy, jittery (see IMPATIENT).

Ant. Confident. — ***Con.*** Assured, sanguine, sure (see CONFIDENT): unruffled, imperturbable, composed, *cool, nonchalant.

apprentice. *Novice, novitiate, probationer, postulant, neophyte.

Ana. Beginner, starter (see corresponding verbs at BEGIN): tyro, *amateur.

Con. *Expert, adept, wizard.

apprise *or* **apprize.** *Inform, advise, notify, acquaint, advertise.

Ana. Tell, *reveal, disclose, divulge, discover, betray: publish, proclaim, *declare, announce.

apprize. Variant of APPRAISE.

approach, *v.* **1 Approach, near, approximate** agree in meaning to come or draw close (to). **Approach** is by far the widest in its range of application. Very often, it implies a coming close in space; as, he left the group and *approached* us; the storm was *approaching.* Often also, it suggests a drawing close in time; as, it was *approaching* three o'clock; the day of the wedding *approached.* Sometimes it is closeness in order of thought or in an intellectual relation, such as likeness or identification, that is implied; as, her interest in others sometimes *approaches* intrusiveness; students are expected to *approach* the standard set for them by their teachers; many words of distinctly different origin gradually *approach* each other in meaning. Often, especially in current use, though the word retains its implication of coming close, it also implies actual or imminent contact; thus, to *approach* a man with a proposal is actually to make advances to him; to *approach* a topic with reluctance is actually to enter upon a discussion of it. Hence, *approach* often stresses the manner or method of beginning, especially one calculated to evoke the response or effect desired; as, he did not know how to *approach* the subject. "Every problem in painting was to Leonardo a problem in science, every problem in physics he *approached* in the spirit of the artist" (*H. Ellis*). In a still more specific sense, when used in reference to persons, *approach* suggests advances made by the agent for some ulterior motive such as diplomatic negotiation, solicitation, or bribery; as, the committee awaited a favorable opportunity to *approach* the governor concerning his candidacy; the attorney for the prosecution declared that two jurors had been *approached* during the trial. **Near** is interchangeable with *approach* only when used in reference to persons or things that draw close in space or time. The word, because of its simplicity and familiarity, is sometimes preferred to *approach* in poetry: nevertheless, it is not as frequent in speech as might be expected, the expressions "get near" and "come near" often being used in preference. "The lark could scarce get out his notes for joy . . . as he *near'd* His happy home, the ground" (*Tennyson*). "The echoed hoof *nearing* the distant shore" (*Wordsworth*). "As the time of the birth of our Lord *neared*" (*Pusey*). **Approximate,** on the other hand, is interchangeable with *approach* chiefly in reference to things which come close to each other in some intellectual relation, as the actual to the ideal, the material to the spiritual, one idea or entity to another, etc.; as, results that *approximate* perfection. "For law, at any given moment, even under the most favorable conditions, cannot do more than *approximate* to its own ideal" (*G. L. Dickinson*). "The plastic arts of painting and sculpture are most art when they *approximate* to music" (*S. Alexander*). *Approximate* is specifically used in reference to a sum, an amount, a quantity, or the like, that approaches, but does not necessarily equal, a given sum, amount, etc.; as, a tablespoonful *approximates* three teaspoonfuls; their fund now *approximates* $5000.

Ana. Accost, *address: *begin, commence, initiate: consult, *confer, advise, negotiate.

Con. Avoid, elude, shun, evade, *escape: *refrain, abstain, forbear: retreat, *recede: withdraw, retire, depart, leave, *go.

2 Touch, equal, *match, rival.

Con. Diverge, deviate (see SWERVE).

approach, *n.* *Overture, advance, tender, bid.

Ana. Attempt, endeavor, essay, try (see under ATTEMPT, *v.*).

Ant. Repulse.

approbation. Approbation, approval are both derived from the same root as *approve* and are therefore closely related in meaning. **Approbation,** the older word, once carried all the meanings usually found in nouns (derived from verbs) ending in *-tion,* such as the act of approving or the state or fact of being approved: in current English, however, it is not so inclusive or so widely applicable. It now stresses admiration or high favor and is applied either to actual expressions of such feeling or to the state of mind of the person or persons whose favorable opinion is manifest; as, his speech won general *approbation;* terms of *approbation;* to feel pleasure in the *approbation* of his superiors; disapprobation and *approbation,* when socialized, exert a powerful influence over legislators and legislation. **Approval** requires qualification by words such as *warm, hearty,* or *enthusiastic* to be interchangeable with *approbation,* especially when the latter term denotes expression of favor. For *approval,* in itself, implies no greater favor than that involved in giving full consent with no reservations, or in sanctioning. It therefore is applied especially to the formal act of approving or to a formal statement such as a permission, an endorsement, or a confirmation; as, no interscholastic games are to be played without the *approval* of the principal; the president gave his *approval* to the proposed legislation in yesterday's conference with reporters. " 'Ho!' said Dr. Lavendar, 'boys don't wait for their parson's *approval* to debate!' " (*Deland*).

Ana. Admiration, esteem, respect, *regard: *applause, acclaim, acclamation, plaudits.

Ant. Disapprobation. — *Con.* Odium, opprobrium, disrepute (see DISGRACE): hatred, detestation, abhorrence (see under HATE, *v.*): censuring *or* censure, condemning *or* condemnation, reprehension (see corresponding verbs at CRITICIZE).

appropriate, *adj.* Fitting, proper, *fit, suitable, apt, meet, happy, felicitous.

Ana. Apposite, pertinent, germane, *relevant: pat, timely, *seasonable, opportune.

Ant. Inappropriate. — *Con.* Wrong, *false: incongruous, incompatible, *inconsonant.

appropriate, *v.* Pre-empt, *arrogate, confiscate, usurp.

Ana. *Take, seize, grab: annex, *add: embezzle, peculate, *defalcate.

appropriation. Appropriation, grant, subvention, subsidy agree in meaning money or property given or set apart by an authorized body for a predetermined use by others. **Appropriation** is the comprehensive term used in government, business, or any institution controlling large sums of money, for the amount formally and officially allotted to any one of its departments, projects, services, or beneficiaries, in advance of the expenditure of that money; as, every department must keep within its *appropriation;* since the *appropriations* bill just signed by the president carries no *appropriation* for the new bridge, it is obvious that construction will not begin this year. **Grant** (sometimes, to distinguish it from more general senses of *grant,* called *grant-in-aid*), as a rule, applies to a gift made by a government or by a corporation, such as an educational or charitable foundation, to a beneficiary on the condition that certain terms be accepted or certain engagements fulfilled. The beneficiary may be a specific institution, a corporation, or even an individual; the gift may be a sum of money, but when the government is the benefactor, it is often a tract of land or a valuable franchise; thus, *grants* of land (*land grants*) from the federal government were made to various railroads building new lines and to various colleges and universities providing agricultural and industrial courses in the mid-nineteenth century; the Rockefeller Foundation makes *grants* chiefly to institutions engaged in health and medical research. **Subvention** is more restricted than *grant* since it always implies pecuniary aid, especially to a person or institution in straits; it now more often applies to a grant-in-aid to an artistic, literary, or scientific undertaking than a commercial one; as, opera in many places is possible only because of a *subvention; subventioned* research (that is, research supported by a subvention). **Subsidy** applies to a grant made to an individual or a company to enable him (or it) to carry on some work regarded as advantageous to the public but not, for one reason or another, self-supporting. *Subvention* is often preferred when the grant is made by an educational or charitable foundation or similar agency; *subsidy*, when it is made by the government; thus, the Carnegie Corporation makes *subventions* to libraries and educational institutions; the British government provides *subsidies* for mail-carrying vessels.

approval. *Approbation.

Ana. Commending *or* commendation, applauding *or* applause, compliment (see corresponding verbs at COMMEND): endorsing *or* endorsement, sanction (see corresponding verbs at APPROVE).

Ant. Disapproval. — *Con.* Criticizing *or* criticism, reprehension, censure (see corresponding verbs at CRITICIZE); disparagement, depreciation, derogation (see corresponding verbs at DECRY).

approve. Approve, endorse (*or* **indorse**), **sanction, accredit, certify** agree in meaning to have or to express a favorable opinion of. **Approve** often means no more than this. "Daring them . . . to *approve* her conduct" (*Conrad*). Sometimes, however, it suggests esteem or admiration. "Jane secretly *approved* his discernment" (*R. Macaulay*). **Endorse** adds to *approve* the implication of backing or supporting, as by an explicit statement: it is therefore used chiefly in reference to things requiring promotion or publicity; as, to *endorse* a person's candidacy; to *endorse* the platform of a new political party; to *endorse* an advertised article. **Sanction** not only implies approval but also authorization; as, the school dances were *sanctioned* by the board of education. The agent (or one that sanctions) may be not only a person or group, but anything which provides a standard by which something can be approved and authorized or disapproved and discountenanced; as, proposed laws not *sanctioned* by public opinion; some churches permit divorce, but do not *sanction* remarriage. "These statements are *sanctioned* by common sense" (*J. Gilbert*). "The introduction into a particular rite of features not *sanctioned* by the texts" (*L. P. Smith*). **Accredit** and **certify** now usually imply official endorsement and conformity with certain standards. Their selection is dependent on idiom rather than on distinctions in meaning; as, an *accredited* herd of dairy cattle; *certified* milk; an *accredited* school or college; a *certified* teacher; a *certified* public accountant. *Accredited*, however, is sometimes used generally, as implying public approval or general acceptance. "If any . . . break away from *accredited* custom" (*Inge*). "Sages so fully *accredited* as Mr. Bertrand Russell" (*C. E. Montague*).

Ana. *Commend, applaud, compliment: *ratify, confirm.

Ant. Disapprove. — *Con.* Reject, refuse, repudiate, spurn (see DECLINE): condemn, reprehend, *criticize.

approximate, *v.* *Approach, near.

approximately. *Nearly, almost, well-nigh.

Ant. Precisely, exactly.

appurtenance. Accessory, adjunct, *appendage.

Ana. Belonging, possession, effect (see POSSESSIONS): furnishing *or* furniture, equipment, appointment (see corresponding verbs at FURNISH).

apropos *or* **à propos.** Apposite, pertinent, *relevant, germane, applicable, material.

Ana. Pat, timely, opportune, *seasonable: appropriate, fitting, *fit, suitable, apt, proper, meet, happy.

Ant. Unapropos.

apt. 1 Happy, felicitous, appropriate, fitting, *fit, suitable, meet, proper.

Ana. Apposite, pertinent, *relevant, apropos: pat, timely, opportune (see SEASONABLE): telling, convincing (see VALID): right, nice, precise, exact (see CORRECT).

Ant. Inapt, inept. — *Con.* *Awkward, maladroit: wrong, *false.

2 Apt, likely, liable are often confused in use, even by good writers, when followed by *to* and the infinitive. The correct choice is often difficult, but their differences in meaning are clear and offer the safest guide in selection. **Apt** implies an inherent or habitual tendency such as an inclination, bent, predisposition; it refers to the past and the present as much as, if not more than, to the future; it applies commonly to persons, but may apply to things that show a tendency or drift. "You are just a little *apt* to let yourself be a slave to that house of yours" (*Bennett*). "The upper circles . . . are *apt* to favor a pronunciation derived . . . from that which prevailed in England" (*Grandgent*). "Long poems are always *apt* to drop in places into what is only not called prose because it is metrical" (*S. Alexander*). **Likely** stresses probability; it refers in time to the future and therefore has its place in predictions; as, he is *likely* to succeed; the wedding is *likely* to cost her parents more than they can afford; it is *likely* to rain tomorrow. " 'How now! is Jack Cade slain?' 'No, my lord, nor *likely* to be slain; for they have won the bridge' " (*Shak.*). **Liable** (as here considered: see also LIABLE, RESPONSIBLE) implies exposure to a risk or danger; it suggests a chance rather than a probability and is therefore often used in warnings, in cautions, or in the expression of fears; as, children who play in the street are *liable* to be injured or killed by automobiles (*likely* might be used here if the chances are so great as to amount to a probability); drivers must remember that cars are *liable* to skid on wet roads; anyone who disobeys this rule is *liable* to be punished severely. Thus, a person who is *apt* to lose his head under stress knows that he is *likely* to fail when he is put to a test and therefore forms the habit of avoiding situations in which he is *liable* to encounter difficulties.

Ana. Inclined, disposed, predisposed (see INCLINE, *v.*): prone, *liable.

Con. Averse, *disinclined, indisposed, loath.

3 *Quick, prompt, ready.

Ana. Clever, smart, bright, *intelligent, quick-witted, alert: gifted, talented (see corresponding nouns at GIFT).

Con. *Slow, laggard: *lethargic, sluggish: *stupid, dull, dense, crass.

aptitude. Bent, turn, talent, faculty, *gift, knack, genius.

Ana. *Taste, gusto, zest: propensity, *leaning, penchant, flair.

Ant. Inaptitude.

aquatic. Aquatic, lacustrine (*or* **lacustrian**), **lacuscular, fluvial, fluviatile, marine, oceanic, thalassic, neritic, pelagic, abyssal, bathysmal, bathybic** imply reference to water, especially to a body of water, but all of them except *aquatic* are highly specific in their applications and all, as here compared, more or less technical terms in the geographical and biological sciences and in geology. **Aquatic** may imply a habitat in water, but as applied to animals and plants it often means living in (but not necessarily submerged by) water, or on the water, or around a body of water. It is specifically applicable to any plant that has its roots in water or in a mud bottom, such as the water hyacinth and the water lily. It is also applicable to any animal that frequents the water, especially to any swimming bird or fowl, such as a gull or a duck. A frog is more often described as an amphibious animal but, as compared to a toad, its habits may be said to be *aquatic*. **Lacustrine** implies reference only to a lake; its use is chiefly in biogeography; as, *lacustrine* shells; *lacustrine* fauna and flora. It is also used by geologists (as, *lacustrine* deposits) and by archaeologists (as, the *lacustrine* period, a prehistoric period when dwellings were erected over lakes). **Lacuscular** implies reference to a pool or small lake; as, *lacuscular* vegetation. **Fluvial** and **fluviatile** are specific terms suggesting the action or operation or influence of flowing water. They imply reference, therefore, to streams, and especially to rivers, and are far more often used in the geographical sciences and in geology than in the biological sciences; as, *fluvial* ice; a *fluvial* plain is one made by *fluvial* deposits. "The river is, itself, a powerful agent of direct denudation—*fluviatile* denudation, as it is sometimes termed" (*T. H. Huxley*). In reference to salt water, **marine** (see also MARINE) is the comprehensive term, applicable not only to things that pertain to the open ocean, but to those that pertain to bays, harbors, salt marshes, salt ponds, and the like. When specific reference to the open ocean or to mid ocean is intended, **oceanic** is the preferred word; thus, *marine* shells; *marine* vegetation; *marine* deposits; *oceanic* fauna; *oceanic* currents; *oceanic* storms. When reference is to seas, gulfs, or the like, as distinguished from the ocean, **thalassic** is often the term preferred especially by historians; as, a *thalassic* empire. These terms, however, are not so definitely restricted and therefore so precise as the succeeding technical terms, which usually name definite zones of the ocean. **Neritic** is referable only to the belt or region of shallow water surrounding the coast; **pelagic**, which in general use implies definitely the open sea or the high seas (as, *pelagic* sealing), in its stricter biogeographical application has reference in its extent only to the realm of the open ocean enclosed by the neritic zone and in its depth only to so much of the water covering that expanse as is penetrable by light. Below the pelagic zone in the deepest part of the ocean lies the *abyssal* zone, where no plant life exists and animals are carnivorous and are usually blind or luminescent. To things that pertain to this zone **abyssal, bathysmal,** or **bathybic** are applicable.

Arab. Arabic, *Arabian.

Arabian, *adj.* **Arabian, Arab, Arabic** are not, in general, applicable to the same things and are, consequently, often misused. **Arabian** is used chiefly with reference to a place, *Arabia*, the large peninsula in southwestern Asia which includes the modern kingdom of Saudi Arabia. Thus, one speaks of the *Arabian* peninsula, desert, kingdoms, flora, fauna, caravans, rugs, history, etc. **Arab** is used chiefly with reference to a people (the *Arabs*), either the pure Semites who still dwell in Arabia, or their descendants of mixed blood who are common in northern, eastern, and central Africa, in Madagascar, India, and the Malay Archipelago, and in some parts of Syria and Persia. The word, therefore, often implies characteristics or habits associated with Arabs, such as a nomadic life, equestrian skill, or Mohammedan practices; as, *Arab* customs; *Arab* descent; *Arab* bazaars; *Arab* harems; *Arab* horses. **Arabic,** however, refers usually to a language (*Arabic*), originally the language of the Arabs, but now the prevailing speech of several countries whose inhabitants are not exclusively Arab in origin, such as Palestine, Syria, Iraq, Egypt, and northern Africa; as, the *Arabic* language, literature, liturgy. Since the written language (the spoken language has many dialectal forms) conforms to the classical standards set by the Koran and is that of an important literature which flourished in western Asia, northern Africa, and Spain between A.D. 750 and 1250, the term *Arabic* is also applicable to a culture or to any manifestations of that culture; as, *Arabic* architecture, philosophers; *Arabic* numerals.

Arabic. Arab, *Arabian.

arbiter. *Judge, arbitrator, umpire, referee.

arbitrary. Autocratic, *absolute, despotic, tyrannical, tyrannous.

Ana. *Dictatorial, authoritarian, magisterial, magistral, oracular: domineering, *masterful, imperious, peremptory, imperative.

Ant. Legitimate. — *Con.* *Lawful, legal, licit.

arbitrate. Adjudicate, adjudge, *judge.

Ana. Mediate, intervene (see INTERPOSE): *decide, determine, settle: conciliate, placate, appease (see PACIFY).

arbitrator. *Judge, referee, arbiter, umpire.

arc. *Curve, arch, bow.

arcade. 1 Arcature, *colonnade, portico, peristyle.
2 Gallery, cloister, ambulatory, *passage, passageway.

Arcadian. Pastoral, bucolic, georgic, rustic, *rural, agrestic, geoponic.

arcane. *Mysterious, inscrutable.

Ana. Occult, esoteric, *recondite: cabalistic, anagogical, mystic, *mystical.

arcature. Arcade, *colonnade.

arch, *n.* *Curve, bow, arc.

arch, *adj.* *Saucy, pert.

Ana. Roguish, waggish, impish, mischievous, *playful: mocking, deriding *or* derisive, twitting (see corresponding verbs at RIDICULE): *disarming, ingratiating, insinuating.

archaeology *or* **archeology.** *Anthropology, ethnology.

archaic. Obsolete, antiquated, antique, *old, ancient, antediluvian, venerable.

Ant. Up-to-date. — *Con.* Fresh, novel, *new, newfangled, newfashioned, modern, modernistic: fashionable, modish (see STYLISH).

archangel. *Angel, cherub, seraph.

archbishop. Metropolitan, *bishop, ordinary, primate.

archetype. *Prototype, ectype.

architect. *Artist, artificer, artisan.

architectonic, *adj.* Architectural (see under ARCHITECTURE).

architectonic *or* **architectonics,** *n.* *Architecture.

architectural. Architectonic (see under ARCHITECTURE).

architecture. **Architecture, architectonic** (*or* **architectonics**) and their corresponding adjectives **architectural** and **architectonic** are often not distinguishable, but in current use they tend to diverge, if not in their meanings, at least in their emphasis. The nouns agree in meaning the science of planning and building structures, such as churches, houses, bridges, and ships, involving problems of artistic design, engineering, and adaptation to the ends in view. In modern popular use, **architecture,** and hence **architectural,** often suggest that artistry or beauty in design is the end and goal of the architect; in technical use they stress design as the result of attention to practical as well as artistic ends, and imply that the profession is both a science and an art. **Architectonic,** or more often **architectonics,** and its corresponding adjective **architectonic,** place the emphasis on constructive skill; they suggest attention to the framework, skeleton, or supporting structure, sometimes without reference to the details necessary for the completion or elaboration of the structure; thus, when one speaks of Chartres Cathedral as a triumph of *architecture*, one calls attention to its beauty of design and ornamentation; but when one speaks of it as a triumph of *architectonics*, one calls attention to it as a great work of engineering where the supporting parts of pillars, props, and ribs are united so as to form a stone skeleton capable of carrying the enormous weight of stone roof and high towers, yet permitting many windows in its enclosing walls. *Architectonic* and its adjective are far more common in extended use than *architecture* and *architectural*, for the latter seldom escape their suggestions of building with stone, wood, steel, or other material. *Architectonic*, on the other hand, often is referable to a system of ideas or philosophy, or to a work of art, especially to an epic or a poetic drama, where there is not only perfect articulation of parts, but their combination into an integral or organic whole. "In Boccaccio and Dante he [Chaucer] found for the first time among his moderns *architectonic* powers which in the case of Dante were supreme" (*Lowes*).

archive. **1** In plural form **archives.** Library, *museum, treasury, thesaurus, gallery.
2 *Document, record, muniment, monument.

arctic. Frigid, freezing, icy, gelid, glacial, *cold, chilly, frosty, cool.
Ant. Torrid.

ardent. **1** Passionate, fervid, perfervid, fervent, *impassioned.
Ana. *Intense, vehement: enthusiastic, zealous (see corresponding nouns at PASSION): *eager, avid, keen: glowing, flaming (see BLAZE, *v.*).
Ant. Cool. — *Con.* *Cold, frigid: composed, imperturbable, nonchalant (see COOL): dispassionate, impartial (see FAIR): apathetic, *impassive, phlegmatic.
2 *Alcoholic, spirituous, hard, strong.

ardor *or* **ardour.** Fervor, enthusiasm, zeal, *passion.
Ana. Excitement, stimulation, quickening, galvanizing (see corresponding verbs at PROVOKE): eagerness, avidity (see corresponding adjectives at EAGER): zest, gusto (see TASTE).
Ant. Coolness: indifference. — *Con.* Unconcernedness *or* unconcern, aloofness, detachment, disinterestedness (see corresponding adjectives at INDIFFERENT): listlessness, languidness *or* languor, lackadaisicality (see corresponding adjectives at LANGUID).

arduous. *Hard, difficult.
Ana. Laborious, toilsome (see corresponding nouns at WORK): exhausting, wearying *or* wearisome, tiring, fatiguing (see corresponding verbs at TIRE): *onerous, exacting, oppressive.
Ant. Light, facile. — *Con.* *Easy, simple, effortless, smooth.

area. **1** **Area, tract, region, zone, belt** agree in meaning an extent of space (especially of ground or surface) that is distinguishable from its surroundings in appearance or in certain distinctive features. **Area** still carries its original implication of clearly marked bounds, but it may be used with reference to a space defined on a map or chart as well as to one the limits of which are actually visible; as, an oasis is a green or fertile *area* in a desert; there are vast uncultivated *areas* even in the most populous of the states. "Two colors—aspen and evergreen, not intermingled but lying in solid *areas* of light and dark" (*Cather*). **Tract,** on the other hand, stresses extent rather than limits; it is therefore preferred to *area* in designating a space that might otherwise be described as an expanse, or is thought of as widespread or far stretching and uniform in character. "Beyond the *area* of small farms lay larger *tracts* that were immensely productive" (*S. Anderson*). "Panley Common, viewed from the back windows of Moncrief House, is a *tract* of grass, furze and rushes, stretching away to the western horizon" (*Shaw*). *Tract* is often used in an extended sense, in reference to anything that has extent or duration; as, "wide *tracts* of life" (*Day Lewis*); "a large *tract* of unwritten history" (*T. S. Eliot*). **Region,** as here compared, always suggests reference to some definite place or locality, as on the earth's surface, in the atmosphere, or in the human body, distinguished from other localities by certain features or by being subject to a particular condition, influence, or the like; as, the upper *region* of the air; the Finger Lake *region* of central New York State; what *region* of the brain is the seat of consciousness? " 'Is this the *region*, this the soil, the clime,' Said then the lost Archangel, 'this the seat That we must change for Heaven?' " (*Milton*). **Zone,** in precise use, is referred to an area or region that looks like a circle or an encircling band, especially on a map or chart; as, the torrid, arctic, and temperate *zones;* the parcel post *zones;* the pelagic *zone* of the ocean; the tree *zone* of a high mountain. In looser use, it is often applied to a region that suggests a band or strip and is distinctly set off from its environs by some peculiarity of feature; as, the firing *zone* of a battlefield; the business *zones* of a city; the wheat *zone* of Russia. "That milky way Which nightly as a circling *zone* thou seest Powdered with stars" (*Milton*). **Belt** is a synonym of *zone*, but is more frequent in colloquial or journalistic English than in literary or scientific English; as, the cotton *belt* of the United States.
Ana. *Locality, district: *expanse, stretch.
2 Extent, *size, dimensions, magnitude, volume.

arena. **Arena, circus, lists, ring, cockpit, court, field, gridiron, diamond, rink** denote in common an area or place in which a contest or combat is held, usually in the presence of spectators. **Arena** (meaning literally, in Latin, *sand*) designated originally the oval area (usually covered with sand to absorb the blood), in the central part of an ancient Roman amphitheater, in which gladiatorial combats, combats between beasts or between gladiators and beasts, and mock sea fights were held. In modern use *arena* is often applied to a large indoor space, surrounded by seats for spectators, in which various kinds of athletic contests or exhibitions of animals (as ice hockey games or horse shows) are held, or to the entire structure. A **circus,** in ancient Rome, was a level oblong space surrounded on three sides by tiers of seats, divided lengthwise through the middle by a barrier, and used chiefly for chariot races. The name *circus* (meaning literally *circle* or *ring*) referred to the circuit which the racing chariots made around the middle barrier. In modern use a *circus* is typically an oblong area of ground or turf surrounded by tiers of seats and enclosed by a large tent in which wild animals, feats of horsemanship, acrobatic performances, etc., are exhibited, in from one to three rings placed in the enclosure, by an itinerant company. **Lists** were the barriers of a field, and by extension the field itself, on which mounted combatants contended with lances or spears in the days of knighthood and chivalry. A **ring** is a comparatively small rope-enclosed platform or plot of ground, originally, as the name indicates, circular, but now often square, usually (in the case of boxing and wrestling) covered with a pad or cushion, in which boxing or wrestling bouts are held or in which acts are performed in a circus. A **cockpit** is a pit or enclosure for cockfights. A **court** is a space, primarily quadrangular, on which various games are played with a ball, as tennis, rackets, squash, and handball. Not all of these necessarily have seats for spectators. A *court* may or may not be enclosed (on all sides or on three sides) and may or may not have a roof or ceiling. A **field** is an area, usually outdoors and frequently enclosed, for baseball, cricket, football, lacrosse, and certain other athletic contests; as used of the area on which a track-and-field meet is held, *field* is applied to that part of the area, usually enclosed by the racing track, on which are contested all events (as jumping, vaulting, weight throwing) other than the running, hurdling, and walking races. **Gridiron** is a colloquial term for a field on which American or Canadian Rugby football is played. A **diamond** is, properly, the infield of a baseball field, or sometimes, by loose extension, the entire field. A **rink** is a smooth and level extent of ice, sometimes enclosed, for skating (often specifically for hockey or curling), or by extension, an area of turf for bowling or of planking for roller skating. A rink is not necessarily surrounded by seats for spectators.

Arena, lists, ring, cockpit often have figurative senses which derive from the literal senses here treated. **Arena** is used for any place of public contest or exertion, or for any sphere of action. "To the schoolboys it [the world] is an *arena*, a risky place, where, however, fortune favours the brave" (*Times Lit. Sup.*). **Lists** is most felicitously made the scene of charging, impetuous contest; in the common expression *to enter the lists*, it emphasizes the courage, foolhardiness, or other motive that prompts one to risk contest, controversy, etc. "[Let] the spirit Range in free battle *lists*" (*Kingsley*). "Dagon hath presumed, Me overthrown, to enter *lists* with God" (*Milton*). **Ring** is especially used of a political contest; as, another man has thrown his hat into the *ring* (i.e., announced himself as a candidate: from the practice of throwing one's hat into the ring, in boxing, etc., to announce one's readiness to contend). A **cockpit** is a region that has been the scene of many conflicts, especially military. "She [Italy] was wearied by the long years when she had been the *cockpit* of war" (*Buchan*).

argosy. Ship, vessel, craft, *boat.
Ana. *Fleet, squadron, armada, flotilla.

argot. Cant, jargon, slang, *dialect, patter, lingo, vernacular, patois.

argue. 1 Debate, dispute, agitate, *discuss.
Ana. *Prove, demonstrate: *disprove, refute, rebut, controvert: expostulate, protest, *object, remonstrate.
2 Bespeak, prove, attest, betoken, *indicate.
Ana. *Show, manifest, evidence, demonstrate, evince: imply, *suggest, intimate.

argument. 1 Proof, *reason, ground.
Ana. Proving, demonstrating *or* demonstration (see corresponding verbs at PROVE): disproving *or* disproof, refuting *or* refutation, rebutting *or* rebuttal (see corresponding verbs at DISPROVE).
2 Argument, dispute, controversy come into comparison when they mean a vigorous, often heated, discussion of a moot question. **Argument** stresses the appeal to the mind, and the use of evidence and reasoning to support one's claims; it implies the hope of each side to prove its case and to convince its opponents. "If Winthrop had not by force of *argument* . . . obtained the lifting of duties from goods sent to England . . . the Boston colony would have been bankrupt" (*A. Repplier*). **Dispute** fundamentally implies the contradiction of something maintained by another and therefore a challenge to argument; as, the decrees of a dictator are not subject to *dispute*. When applied to a verbal contention, *dispute* suggests not only a challenger and one challenged, but an effort on the part of each to get the upper hand. Hence it often implies more or less anger or disturbance of the peace. "A *dispute* begun in jest . . . is continued by the desire of conquest, till vanity kindles into rage, and opposition rankles into enmity" (*Johnson*). " 'You dislike an *argument*, and want to silence this.' 'Perhaps I do. *Arguments* are too much like *disputes*' " (*Austen*). **Controversy** emphasizes a profound difference of opinion, not so often between persons as between parties; the term is applied chiefly to debates over issues of importance or of widespread interest, involving two or more religions, governments, schools of thought, political parties, or the like, and carried on mainly by writings addressed to the public or by speeches on public platforms; as, the Arian *controversy;* the Shakespeare-Bacon *controversy*. "When a thing ceases to be a subject of *controversy*, it ceases to be a subject of interest" (*Hazlitt*).
Ana. *Argumentation, disputation, debate: controverting, refuting, rebutting (see DISPROVE): contention, dissension (see DISCORD).
3 Theme, *subject, matter, subject matter, topic, text, motive, leitmotiv.

argumentation. Argumentation, disputation, debate, forensic, dialectic come into comparison when they mean the act or art of argument or an exercise of one's powers of argument. In contrast with *argument, dispute, controversy* (see ARGUMENT, 2) they stress formality and a more or less disciplinary intention. **Argumentation** is the designation given to a form of discourse the aim of which is to prove or disprove propositions, or to an oral or written exercise having such proof or disproof for its end; as, a course in exposition and *argumentation;* the next theme will be an *argumentation*. **Disputation** and **debate** both imply the handling of a proposition with the intent to sustain one's position not only by advancing arguments in its support, but by attacking the position of one's opponent and by defending one's own from his attacks. *Disputation*, however, is more often applied to a formal exercise common in medieval universities, and still found in some modern universities, in which a thesis is tested by the ability of its proponent or defender to sustain it in the face of severe critical attack; *debate*, to a two-sided contest between persons or teams which is governed by strict rules of procedure and in which the victory goes to the person or team regarded by the appointed judges as manifesting the greater ability. **Forensic,** in its academic use (chiefly in the United States), is commonly applied to an argumentative exercise intended to convince its readers or hearers; the word suggests emphasis on the qualities of successful legal argument, such as the ability to marshal evidence, to make telling points, to persuade as well as to convince. **Dialectic** is a term more common among philosophers than in general or academic use. It is, however, applied to a method of reasoning, the aim of which is to reach the truth by the correct application of the rules of logic, or, less often, to argument or argumentation that observes what its writer believes to be the laws of reasoning. "Newman's masterly English, and his competent, if not supreme, *dialectic*" (*Saintsbury*).
Ana. *Argument, dispute, controversy.

arid. *Dry.
Ana. Barren, infertile, *sterile, unfruitful: *bare, bald, barren: desiccated, dehydrated, parched (see DRY).
Ant. Moist: verdant: quick (sense 1). — *Con.* *Wet, damp, dank, humid: *living, alive, vital: lush, luxuriant (see PROFUSE): *fertile, fruitful, fecund.

arise. 1 *Rise, ascend, mount, soar, levitate, surge, tower, rocket.
Ana. *Lift, raise, elevate, rear.
Ant. Recline: slump.
2 Rise, *spring, originate, derive, flow, issue, emanate, proceed, stem.

Ana. Emerge, *appear, loom: *begin, commence, start: ensue, succeed, *follow.

aristocracy. 1 Plutocracy, *oligarchy.

2 **Aristocracy, nobility, gentry, county, gentlefolk, elite, society** are here compared as meaning a body of persons who constitute a socially superior caste. **Aristocracy** often refers to an ideally superior caste, and therefore does not invariably apply to a fixed or definite group of persons. "There is a natural *aristocracy* among men. The grounds of this are virtue and talents" (*Jefferson*). Usually the term connotes superiority in birth, breeding, and social station and is applicable to all those persons generally recognized as first in family and in personal importance. "He comes of the Brahmin caste of New England. This is the harmless, inoffensive, untitled *aristocracy*" (*Holmes*). However, in countries where there is a privileged and titled class, the **nobility,** *aristocracy* is often used to designate the same group with this difference in implication: that *nobility* stresses rank inferior to that of royalty, but superior to that of all other classes, and *aristocracy* stresses the possession of power over the people through ownership of land and through long-established and generally acknowledged superiority. "The word 'cousin' in the mouth or from the pen of a royalty signified a recognition of rank superior to *nobility*" (*Belloc*). "The distinguishing characteristic of an *aristocracy* is the enjoyment of privileges which are not communicable to other citizens simply by anything they can themselves do to obtain them" (*Hallam*). However, *nobility* in British use does not include titled commoners such as baronets and knights. These latter are thought of as members of the *aristocracy*. **Gentry** and **county** are distinctively British terms applied to a class, usually a leisured class, who by birth and breeding can be described as gentlemen (in the technical sense) and ladies, but who are without hereditary title and are classed as commoners. In British use, *gentry* refers to a class in rank just below the nobility but often having in its membership persons of equally high birth or breeding. *County,* however, carries a suggestion of an association of the family with the county, or section, and usually, the ownership of an estate in the country; as, the *gentry* and the *nobility* were on friendliest terms; the newcomers were slow in being accepted by the *county*. "The advantage claimed for this plan is that it provides us with a *gentry*: that is, with a class of rich people able to cultivate themselves by an expensive education" (*Shaw*). " 'I am sure,' said Mrs. Rochford, 'the *county* will like far better to see you there than Mrs. Russell Penton' " (*Mrs. Oliphant*). **Gentlefolk** is in both British and American use; in the former it is often nearly equivalent to *gentry;* in American and in some British use it is applicable to those persons who are marked as apart by their gentleness of breeding or habituation to the refinements of life and living rather than by their definite social status or long pedigrees. "Oh, Sir, you would not talk thus, if you knew What life is this of ours . . . You *gentlefolk* have got Warm chambers to your wish" (*Wordsworth*). **Elite,** which literally means the chosen, is referable not to a social rank, but to those members of any group or class who stand out as its flower, or the ones most frequently sought after; as, the *elite* of the nobility; "few others of the mathematical *elite*" (*Karl K. Darrow*). When used without qualification, *elite* usually means the group regarded as the highest, especially as judged by social or cultural standards. "It is the business of the college to produce an *elite*—superior men" (*North American Review*). **Society,** as here compared, is applied to that portion of a community which marks itself apart as a leisured class, much given to formal entertainments, fashionable sports, and other pursuits characteristic of an active social life. "*Society* is now one polish'd horde, Form'd of two mighty tribes, the Bores and Bored" (*Byron*). "There are only about four hundred people in New York *Society*" (*Ward McAllister*).

Ant. People, proletariat.

aristocrat. Patrician, *gentleman.

Ant. Commoner (*i.e., one of the common people*).

ark. Refuge, *shelter, retreat, sanctuary, asylum, cover.

arm, *n.*[1] Might, puissance, *power, force, energy, strength.

Ana. Auxiliary, subsidiary (see corresponding adjectives at AUXILIARY): executor, executive, administrator (see under EXECUTE).

arm, *n.*[2] *Weapon.

arm, *v.* Accouter, outfit, equip, *furnish, appoint.

Ant. Disarm.

armada. *Fleet, squadron, flotilla.

armament. Armament, munitions, arms, ordnance, artillery, ammunition are here compared as used in modern warfare. They are not all synonyms of one another, but they are frequently confused. In general they mean material used in military and naval (including air) operations. **Armament** is by far the most inclusive term, for it comprehends everything that must be considered in determining a nation's military strength, such as trained soldiers, sailors, and fliers, land fortifications, battleships and all other war vessels, including transports, submarines, destroyers, and the like, aircraft, guns, provisions, equipment, available man power, resources, etc. **Munitions** is far less inclusive; it comprehends materials only, or supplies of war, including military equipment of all kinds, especially all weapons of attack and defense and the missiles, projectiles, propellants, and the like, necessary for their use. **Arms** (see also WEAPON) is less definite in its application than either of the preceding words, but in general, when used as an inclusive term, it covers whatever weapons soldiers or sailors need in actual fighting, such as cannon, guns, rifles, pistols, swords, and bayonets. **Ordnance** is used in two senses, the more general of which is probably the less common. In that sense, the term includes not only everything which is covered by *arms*, but every other weapon of attack or defense, such as tanks, and everything needed for the equipment and use of these weapons, such as mounts, carriages, projectiles, and missiles, or for their manufacture or repair, such as tools and machinery. In the United States Navy, *ordnance* also includes torpedoes, submarine mines, range finders, armor, and the like. More narrowly, and more commonly also, *ordnance* is a comprehensive term for all kinds of heavy firearms, especially those discharged from mounts, such as cannon, guns, howitzers, and mortars. **Artillery** is a close synonym of *ordnance* in this latter sense, but it suggests actual warfare and therefore implies group service in the management of mounted firearms. The term sometimes comprehends not only ordnance but also the mounts, ammunition, and the like, essential to the work of that branch of the army dealing with the operation of heavy guns (also called the *artillery*). **Ammunition,** though once used as a general term nearly equal to *munitions*, is now restricted in its application to the projectiles used in warfare, such as bullets, shells, grenades, bombs, and their necessary propellants, detonators, fuses, and primers.

Ana. *Weapon, arm: *fleet, squadron, armada, flotilla: *fort, fortress, citadel, stronghold: *bulwark, breastwork, rampart, barbette, bastion, parapet.

armistice. *Truce.

armory *or* **armoury. Armory** (*or* **armoury**), **arsenal,**

magazine are here compared chiefly in their technical military senses. **Armory** once carried the meanings now associated with *arsenal* and *magazine*, but in current use, especially in the United States, it has commonly two applications: one, a public building in which troops, such as those belonging to the National Guard, have their headquarters, drill rooms, and the like; the other, an establishment under government control for the manufacture of arms, such as rifles, pistols, bayonets, and swords. **Arsenal** is correctly applied to a government establishment for the manufacture, storage, and issue of arms, ammunition, and the like: in popular nontechnical use, especially in figurative use, the word usually suggests a store of, or a storehouse for, weapons and ammunition; as, "Weapons from the *arsenal* of poetic satire" (*H. Reed*); to make America the *arsenal* of the democracies. **Magazine** is strictly applied to a storehouse for all sorts of military and naval supplies, including arms, ammunition, provisions, and the like. In extended use, it often more narrowly suggests a storehouse for ammunition, especially for explosives; as, a powder *magazine*. "As when high Jove his sharp artillery forms, And opes his cloudy *magazine* of storms" (*Pope*). "An educated man stands, as it were, in the midst of a boundless *arsenal* and *magazine*, filled with all the weapons and engines which man's skill has been able to devise from the earliest time" (*Carlyle*). In extended but correct use, *magazine* is applied to a supply chamber, as one in a gun for cartridges, one in a camera for films, one in a typesetting machine for matrices, or the like.

arms. Ordnance, artillery, munitions, *armament, ammunition.
Ana. *Weapon, arm.

army. Host, legion, *multitude.
Ana. Throng, press, crush, *crowd, mob, rout, horde.

aroma. Odor, scent, *smell.
Ana. *Fragrance, perfume, redolence, incense, bouquet: savor (see TASTE).
Ant. Stink, stench. — *Con.* Stinkingness, rankness, malodorousness (see corresponding adjectives at MALODOROUS).

aromatic. Balmy, redolent, fragrant, *odorous.
Ana. Spicy, *pungent, piquant: savory (see PALATABLE).
Ant. Acrid (*of odors*). — *Con.* *Malodorous, fetid, musty, fusty, noisome, rank, putrid.

around. Round, *about.

arouse. Rouse, awaken, waken, *stir, rally.
Ana. *Wake, awake: stimulate, quicken, galvanize, excite, *provoke: electrify, *thrill: inflame, kindle, enkindle, fire (see LIGHT): *move, drive, impel.
Ant. Quiet, calm. — *Con.* Allay, assuage, alleviate, mitigate, *relieve: *pacify, mollify, placate.

arraign. Charge, *accuse, impeach, indict, incriminate, criminate.
Ana. *Summon, cite: try, test (see PROVE).
Con. *Answer, rejoin, reply, respond: acquit, exonerate, *exculpate, absolve, vindicate: defend, justify (see MAINTAIN).

arrange. 1 *Order, marshal, organize, systematize, methodize.
Ana. Dispose (see corresponding noun DISPOSAL): *line, range, array, align: *assort, classify, alphabetize, pigeonhole, sort.
Ant. Derange, disarrange. — *Con.* *Disorder, disorganize, unsettle, disturb: disperse, *scatter.
2 *Negotiate, concert.
Ana. *Manage, contrive: plan, design, scheme, project (see under PLAN, *n.*).

arrant. Out-and-out, *outright, unmitigated.

array, *v.* 1 *Line, range, align.
Ana. Marshal, arrange, *order.
Ant. Disarray.
2 *Clothe, apparel, attire, tire, robe, dress, vest, invest.

array, *n.* 1 *Display, parade, pomp.
Ana. Showing *or* show, exhibiting *or* exhibition, exposing *or* exposition (see corresponding verbs at SHOW): arranging *or* arrangement, marshaling (see corresponding verbs at ARRANGE): disposition (see DISPOSAL).
2 Raiment, apparel, attire, tire, vesture, *clothes, clothing, dress.

arrear *or* **arrears.** Arrearage, *debt, indebtedness, debit, obligation, liability.

arrearage. Arrear, *debt, indebtedness, debit, obligation, liability.

arrest, *n.* Apprehension, detention, attachment. See under ARREST, *v.*
Ana. Seizing *or* seizure, taking (see corresponding verbs at TAKE): capturing *or* capture, catching, copping, nabbing (see corresponding verbs at CATCH).
Con. Liberation, discharging *or* discharge, releasing *or* release (see corresponding verbs at FREE).

arrest, *v.* 1 **Arrest, check, interrupt** come into comparison when they mean to stop in mid-course. **Arrest** implies a holding fixed in the midst of movement, development, or progress, and also, usually, a prevention of further advance until someone or something effects a release; as, to *arrest* the progress of a disease; a tree *arrested* the aviator's fall; discouragement sometimes *arrests* a child's development; books that *arrest* attention. **Check** (see also RESTRAIN) suggests suddenness and force in stopping, as though bringing to a halt sharply or with a jerk; as, the entrance of the teacher *checked* the disturbance in the schoolroom; he *checked* himself just as he was about to blurt out his indignation. "He caught her by the arm as she ran past and . . . without trying to *check* her, simply darted in with her and up the stairs" (*Conrad*). **Interrupt** stresses a breaking in and a consequent stopping, but it carries no clear suggestion that continuation is impossible or improbable; as, to *interrupt* a lecture with a question; their talk was *interrupted* by the arrival of visitors; he was discouragingly *interrupted* at the point when ideas and words were flowing freely.
Ana. *Interpose, intervene, interfere: *delay, detain, retard: *frustrate, thwart, balk.
Ant. Activate: quicken. — *Con.* *Vitalize, energize: *stir (up), rouse, arouse, awaken.
2 **Arrest, apprehend, attach, detain** are here compared only as meaning to seize and hold under restraint or in custody by authority of the law. The same likenesses and differences in meaning are manifest in the comparable use of **arrest, apprehension, attachment, detention.** **Arrest** (verb or noun) is the most widely used of these words for the seizing of a person and holding him in custody. It refers both to civil cases where a person is placed under restraint, and to criminal cases, where **apprehend** and **apprehension** are also used; thus, one *arrests* a person for debt, but one *apprehends* a thief; witnesses are under *arrest;* to demand the *apprehension* of the rioters. As a matter of fact, laymen seldom use *arrest* except in the sense of *apprehend,* for it carries connotations which make its use objectionable in reference to witnesses or even suspects. *Arrest* is now not used with reference to the seizure and holding of property and chattels except in admiralty courts and in Scots law; as, to *arrest* a vessel. The words commonly used when property is seized and held, as for payment of a debt, are **attach** and **attachment;** as, to *attach* the accounts of a firm suspected of falsification of income tax reports. *Attach* and *attachment* are used in reference to persons chiefly when the

intent is to make them appear in court, as to answer for contempt or to serve as a witness. **Detain** and **detention** usually imply holding in custody for inquiry, inspection, or the like. They are not strictly legal terms but are often used when there is the desire to avoid the stigma associated with the word *arrest;* as, the health officers *detained* the ship; to *detain* a suspect or a witness.

Ana. Seize, *take: *catch, capture, cop, nab: *imprison, incarcerate, jail.

Con. Discharge, release, liberate, *free.

arresting. Striking, remarkable, *noticeable, outstanding, salient, signal, prominent, conspicuous.

Ana. Impressive, *moving, touching, affecting, poignant: fascinating, taking, attractive, enchanting (see under ATTRACT).

Con. *Common, ordinary, familiar: hackneyed, stereotyped, *trite.

arride. Delight, tickle, regale, gratify, *please, gladden, rejoice.

Ana. *Amuse, divert, entertain: beguile, wile, *while.

Con. Irk, bother, vex, *annoy: *tire, weary.

arrival. **Arrival, advent** denote in common the reaching of a destination. **Arrival** commonly implies precedent movement; as, the *arrival* and departure of trains; the morning of my *arrival.* **Advent** is sometimes applied to an important, or even momentous, arrival; as, to look forward to the *advent* of the Messiah. Except when it connotes birth, it usually stresses appearance on the scene more than expected coming or reaching the end of a journey. "With the *advent* of an attractive young woman [life] took on acknowledged connotations of interest" (*M. Austin*).

Ana. Coming (see COME): appearing *or* appearance, emerging *or* emergence (see corresponding verbs at APPEAR).

Ant. Departure. — *Con.* Going, leaving, withdrawing *or* withdrawal (see corresponding verbs at GO).

arrive. *Come.

Ant. Depart. — *Con.* *Go, leave, withdraw, retire.

arrogant. *Proud, haughty, lordly, insolent, overbearing, supercilious, disdainful.

Ana. Imperious, domineering, *masterful, peremptory, imperative: pretentious, pompous, ostentatious (see SHOWY).

Ant. Meek: unassuming. — *Con.* *Humble, modest, lowly: yielding, submitting *or* submissive, deferring *or* deferential (see corresponding verbs at YIELD).

arrogate, *v.* **Arrogate, usurp, pre-empt, appropriate, confiscate** agree in meaning to seize or assume something by more or less high-handed methods. **Arrogate** (commonly, but not invariably, followed by *to* and a reflexive pronoun) implies an unwarranted claim, usually an insolent or presumptuous claim, to that which one assumes, frequently to the exclusion of others. "By *arrogating* to himself too much, he was in danger of losing that degree of estimation to which he was entitled" (*Johnson*). "He *arrogated* to himself the right of deciding dogmatically what was orthodox doctrine" (*Macaulay*). "The exploitation of the tourists was a monopoly which the most active of the children had *arrogated,* by force and cunning, to themselves" (*A. Huxley*). **Usurp** stresses unlawful or wrongful intrusion of oneself into the place of another (usually a person; by extension, a thing) that by law, custom, natural right, or the like, is in possession, and the seizure for oneself of his (or its) territory, power, authority, prerogatives, or rights; as, to *usurp* a throne; the dictator *usurped* the powers not only of the king but of the parliament. "Literature, or culture, tended with Arnold to *usurp* the place of Religion" (*T. S. Eliot*). **Pre-empt** implies beforehandedness in taking something desired by others and keeping it in one's own possession. Historically, it implies the right to purchase or acquire (land, property, or the like) before others, and, usually, on more favorable terms: this implication is now sometimes found in discriminating figurative use. "Prose has *pre-empted* a lion's share of the territory once held, either in sovereignty or on equal terms, by poetry" (*Lowes*). In current use, it more often suggests arrogation or usurpation than lawful methods such as purchase, and is therefore not fully accepted as literary English; as, when the townspeople arrived they found that the visitors had *pre-empted* all the parking places; the best of the slogans suggested had already been *pre-empted* by a rival manufacturer. In the game of bridge, to *pre-empt,* or to make a *pre-emptive* bid, is to make a declaration that is aimed at shutting out shifts by the partner or bids by the adversaries. **Appropriate** now more often suggests conversion to one's own use than, as originally, a setting apart for a particular or peculiar use. However, the latter implication is often retained; as, Congress *appropriated* three million dollars for flood control (see APPROPRIATION). The word now usually suggests an acquiring for oneself or an annexing, sometimes by lawful, sometimes by unlawful, means; as, growing plants *appropriate* whatever elements they need from the soil and the air; a plagiarist *appropriates* the ideas of others. "If we could by any means *appropriate* to our use some of the extraordinary digestive power that a boa constrictor has" (*Meredith*). **Confiscate** implies seizure, as of others' property or goods, through the exercise of one's authority: it does not, however, like *appropriate,* suggest conversion to one's own use, though that may or may not follow; as, the teacher *confiscated* all packages of chewing gum; the police *confiscated* the cached liquor. "If miners, or any other sort of workers, find that the local authorities will *confiscate* the incomes of the ratepayers to feed them when they are idle, their incentive to pay their way by their labor will be . . . perceptibly slackened" (*Shaw*).

Ana. Seize, *take, grab: *take, assume.

Ant. Renounce: yield. — *Con.* *Relinquish, surrender, cede, resign.

arsenal. *Armory, magazine.

art, *n.* **1 Art, skill, cunning, artifice, craft** come into comparison when they mean the faculty of performing or executing that which is planned or devised. **Art** is not actually a comprehensive term, but is so variable in its implications that it is interchangeable with any one of the others and capable of carrying its specific implications; hence, the last four words are synonyms of *art,* but they are not always closely synonymous with each other and may even, at times, be used in distinction from each other. The earliest and still common implications of *art* are those which are now associated specifically with **skill:** technical knowledge, and proficiency or expertness in its exercise or practical application. "True ease in writing comes from *art,* not chance, As those move easiest who have learn'd to dance" (*Pope*). "'Tis hard to say, if greater want of *skill* Appear in writing or in judging ill" (*Pope*). Both words are also used concretely with these implications. "There's a great *art* in doing these things properly. I have often had to carry off a man of fourteen stone, resting him all the time as if he was in bed" (*Shaw*). "Able boys and girls will . . . submit willingly to severe discipline in order to acquire some coveted . . . *skill*" (*B. Russell*). *Art* also, at times, comes close to **cunning** (as here compared: see also DECEIT), especially in the older underogatory, and now archaic, sense of that word, where it adds to *skill* such implications as great or recondite knowledge, inventive or creative power, and capacity for perfection in execution. This sense prevails especially

in the phrase "a work of *art*," once often called "a work of *cunning*." In the following citations either word may be substituted for the other without change of meaning. "High-ribbed vault . . . With perfect *cunning* framed" (*Wordsworth*). "Praised be the *Art* whose subtle power could stay Yon cloud, and fix it in that glorious shape" (*Wordsworth*). *Art* also may be used interchangeably with **artifice** (as here compared: see also TRICK) when the latter stresses skill and intelligence (or obedience to rules) in contriving, devising, or constructing, and suggests lack of creative power. In this sense both *art* and *artifice* in their emphasis on mechanical skill imply a contrast with power derived from nature or inspiration. "Flowers worthy of Paradise, which not nice *Art* In beds and curious knots, but Nature boon Poured forth profuse on hill" (*Milton*). "When you come to dissect the *Odyssey*, what amazing *artifice* is found under that apparently straightforward tale" (*Quiller-Couch*). *Art* and **craft** (see also TRADE) were once close synonyms but now tend to become contrasted terms. Both words still imply ingenuity and subtlety in workmanship; both may suggest, but *art* less often suggests, trickery or guile in the attainment of one's ends; as, a gold bracelet made with the *craft* (or *art*) of a Benvenuto Cellini. "*Craft*, where strength doth fail, And piece the lion with the fox's tail" (*J. Wilson*). "The lion's skin too short, you know . . . Was lengthened by the fox's tail; And *art* supplies, where strength may fail" (*Unknown*). Both words, as here considered, are also affected by their use as designations of pursuits (for the discrimination of *art* and *craft* in this sense, see TRADE), *craft* tending to be applied to a lower kind of skill or inventive power revealing itself in the mastery of materials or technique, and in effects that can be analyzed and imitated, and *art* to a higher creative power capable of expressing a personal vision and of achieving results which defy analysis and imitation; thus, an artist may demonstrate his *craft* in painting sunlight but he manifests his *art* in painting a scene that conveys his feeling to the spectator.
2 Craft, handicraft, profession, *trade.
3 Art, science are comparable when they designate a branch of learning. **Art** (especially as it is found today in the phrases: the liberal *arts*, bachelor of *arts*, master of *arts*) historically refers to one of the fundamental branches of learning regarded as necessary to every educated person and serving as an instrument for his advancement in knowledge not only generally but specifically in his professional studies. In the Middle Ages, the liberal arts were grammar, logic, rhetoric, arithmetic, geometry, music, and astronomy; with these as a foundation, a student was ready to proceed with his studies in philosophy, theology, law, or the like. In modern times, the liberal arts, as interpreted by various colleges giving arts degrees, are the disciplinary or instrumental branches of learning, as distinguished from those that are technical or professional in their character; or, often, the cultural, as distinguished from the vocational, studies. **Science** was also used in the late Middle Ages and the Renaissance of a branch of learning. It was not identical with *art*, however, because it was not restricted to studies giving the rudiments or providing the apparatus for further study, but was applied to any branch of learning that was a recognized subject of study. "I do present you with a man of mine, Cunning in music and the mathematics, To instruct her fully in those *sciences*" (*Shak.*). "A gentleman of Tyre; my name, Pericles; My education been in *arts* and arms" (*Shak.*).

Since the nineteenth century, especially in reference to departments of knowledge or courses given in schools, colleges, and universities, these words show a wider divergence in implications and applications and a tendency (especially in the plural forms) to be used as generic terms. On the one hand, *art* is applied to those courses which have for their end teaching students to make or do something that requires skill and a knowledge of technique, and also, usually, special gifts such as inventiveness, taste, or ingenuity; as, the manual *arts;* the fine *art* of painting; instruction in the *arts* of design. On the other hand, *science* is applied only to such courses (or generally, to all such courses or studies) as deal with the gathering and classification of facts, the drawing of correct inferences from them, and the establishment of verifiable general laws; as, the *science* of physics, of botany, of economics; to major in *science;* teachers of *science*. Still other distinctions are drawn between the two, when *art* or *science* refers not so much to a branch of learning as to a pursuit for which one is prepared by the study of an art or science; thus, questions arise as to whether architecture is an *art* or a *science*, that is, (1) whether its essential demands of the architect are inventiveness, taste, and technical skill, or a knowledge of the principles of physics, of engineering, and of other related sciences; (2) whether the end to be served is to give aesthetic pleasure or to produce something useful. "Hence rhetoric was for Rome both an *art* and a *science* . . . . It had obvious utilitarian value, and its materials were not only exact logical concepts, but the sonorous words and the noble rhythms which were the glory of their tongue" (*Buchan*).

artefact. Variant of ARTIFACT.

artery. Route, course, *way, passage, pass.
Ana. *Road, highway, highroad, roadway, thoroughfare, parkway, drive.

artful. Wily, crafty, cunning, tricky, *sly, foxy.
Ana. Adroit, *dexterous: politic, diplomatic, smooth, *suave: ingratiating, insinuating (see DISARMING).
Ant. Artless. — *Con.* Simple, *natural, ingenuous, unsophisticated, naïve: candid, open, *frank.

article, *n.* **1** Clause, plank, count, *paragraph, verse.
2 *Thing, object.
Ana. *Item, detail, particular.
3 *Essay, paper, theme, composition.

articled. Indentured, *bound, bond.

articulate, *adj.* **1** *Also* **articulated.** Integrated, concatenated. See under INTEGRATE.
Ana. United, joined, connected, linked, related (see JOIN): organized, systematized, methodized, ordered (see ORDER, *v.*).
Con. Dissected, anatomized, resolved, analyzed (see ANALYZE): separate, *distinct, discrete.
2 *Vocal, oral.
Ana. Distinct, clear (see EVIDENT): uttered, voiced (see EXPRESS, *v.*).
Ant. Inarticulate, dumb.
3 *Vocal, fluent, eloquent, voluble, glib.
Ana. Expressing, voicing, uttering, venting (see EXPRESS, *v.*): *expressive, meaningful, significant: voluble, *talkative.
Ant. Inarticulate, dumb.

articulate, *v.* **1** *Integrate, concatenate.
Ana. Unite, *join, connect, link, relate: organize, systematize, methodize, *order.
Con. Dissect, anatomize, resolve, *analyze: *separate, part, divide.
2 Enunciate, *pronounce.

articulation. **1** Integration, concatenation. See under INTEGRATE, *v.*
Ana. Organization, systematizing, methodizing (see corresponding verbs at ORDER): *system, organism, economy, scheme, complex.

2 *Joint, suture.

artifact *or* **artefact.** Product, *work, production, opus.

artifice. 1 *Art, cunning, craft, skill.

Ana. Ingeniousness *or* ingenuity, cleverness, adroitness (see corresponding adjectives at CLEVER): adeptness, proficiency, expertness (see corresponding adjectives at PROFICIENT).

2 *Trick, ruse, wile, stratagem, maneuver, feint.

Ana. *Deception, chicanery, chicane, trickery: *deceit, guile, duplicity, dissimulation.

Con. *Means, instrument, instrumentality, vehicle, channel: *device, contrivance: expedient, shift, makeshift (see RESOURCE).

artificer. Artisan, *artist, architect.

Ana. Craftsman, handicraftsman, mechanic, workman (see WORKER).

artificial. Artificial, factitious, synthetic, ersatz come into comparison because they mean not brought into being by nature but by human art, effort, or some process of manufacture. They are not often interchangeable, however, because of differences in some of their implications and in their range of application. **Artificial** is far more extensively used than the others. It may be applied to anything that is not produced by natural conditions but is, in a sense, a human creation; as, "most of the inequalities in the existing world are *artificial*" (*B. Russell*); the family is a *natural* society, the state is an *artificial* society; in law, a corporation, an institution, or the like, that may be the subject of rights or duties, is called an *artificial person*, in distinction from a human being, who is a *natural person*. *Artificial* is also applicable to something that has its counterpart in nature and is, therefore, an imitation or likeness; thus, *natural* heat emanates from the sun, from warm-blooded bodies, or the like, but *artificial* heat comes from burning fuel or electricity; *natural* ice is produced by the freezing of water in temperatures below 32° Fahrenheit, *artificial* ice is produced by chemical and physical means. The word is also applied to things which imitate the appearance of something that is found in nature, and in some cases serve the same purposes, but which are otherwise described as false, or not genuine; as, *artificial* flowers, leather, or gems. *Artificial* is also applicable to persons, their acts, utterances, and the like; it then implies lack of naturalness or spontaneity and often connotes affectation, conventionality, formalism, or the like. "Set him [a Frenchman] to write poetry, he is limited, *artificial*, and impotent; set him to write prose, he is free, natural, and effective" (*Arnold*). "The strained *artificial* romanticism of Kotzebue's lugubrious dramas" (*J. W. Krutch*). **Factitious** is applied largely to intangible things such as emotions, states of mind, situations, relations, reasons, which are not naturally caused or are not the product of real circumstances, but are manufactured (that is, "got up," "trumped up," "worked up," "cooked up," or the like) for one's own ends or purposes; as, to create a *factitious* demand for shares of a given stock; the vogue was short-lived because *factitious*. "His trick of doing nothing with an air, His salon manners and society smile, Were but skin-deep, *factitious*" (*W. Watson*). "They stood for Parliament and played the game of politics upon *factitious* issues" (*H. G. Wells*). **Synthetic,** as here compared, is applicable to any manufactured substance that is made either by a chemical combination of natural substances (as, a *synthetic* perfume) or by chemical treatment of one natural substance so that it acquires the appearance and characteristics of another and may be used in place of it; thus, *synthetic* silk is made by the chemical treatment of cellulose; a *synthetic* rubber is made by the polymerization of chloroprene. *Synthetic* is often preferred to *artificial* in distinguishing products that are derived by chemical combination or treatment from natural products of the same class or kind; thus, one may speak of rayon as an *artificial* silk or as a *synthetic* fabric, or of oleomargarine as *artificial* butter or as a *synthetic* foodstuff. This use is especially favored when the synthetic article has qualities, virtues, or uses not characteristic of the thing it originally imitates. However, the content and application of the word are still in a process of fluctuation. **Ersatz** (a German word meaning primarily replacement, and secondarily an artificial substitute for a natural product) is now frequently used in English as a synonym of *artificial* or *synthetic* always, however, with the implication of use as a substitute; it is used chiefly with the name of a natural product (as, *ersatz* coffee, *ersatz* butter, *ersatz* wool) thereby implying imitation and inferiority and, often, suggesting a base or disagreeable origin. "The search for *Ersatz* . . . materials was unceasing. Sugar from sawdust; flour from potato meal; gasoline from wood and coal" (*J. Gunther*).

Ana. Fabricated, manufactured, fashioned (see MAKE, *v.*): simulated, feigned, counterfeited *or* counterfeit (see corresponding verbs at ASSUME).

Ant. Natural. — *Con.* Genuine, veritable, bona fide, *authentic: *real, true, actual.

artillery. Ordnance, *armament, munitions, arms, ammunition.

artisan. 1 Artificer, *artist, architect.

2 Mechanic, workman, workingman, *worker, operative, craftsman, handicraftsman, hand, laborer, roustabout.

artist. 1 Artist, artificer, artisan, architect are here compared chiefly as meaning one who makes something beautiful or useful (or both). In their larger senses (which are sometimes their original rather than their extended senses) the words are often confused; in their current specific applications only some of them are a source of difficulty. The earliest and the abiding implication of **artist** is skill or proficiency (see *artist* under EXPERT); it was in Shakespeare's time, and later, applied to anyone who made or did things requiring learning and skill; thus, a teacher, a philosopher, a physician, a scientist, an alchemist, or a craftsman was then called an *artist*. "The wise and fool, the *artist* and unread" (*Shak.*). "I will give you more directions concerning fishing; for I would fain make you an *Artist*" (*Walton*). Gradually, however, the word became associated with those whose aim is to produce something which gives pleasure, first with musicians, dancers, actors, and the like, and later with poets, painters, and sculptors. The two ideas of skill and the aim to give pleasure were combined, so that since the early nineteenth century, *artist* (when it does not mean specifically a painter) is usually applied to a gifted person who works in the fine arts, and especially to one who reveals his skill, taste, and power to create beautiful things. "Of the faults of Scott as an *artist* it is not very necessary to speak" (*Chesterton*). "The counsels of Marcus Aurelius . . . are more fit for a moralist than for an *artist*" (*Conrad*). **Artificer,** the oldest of these words in English (antedating *artist* by nearly two centuries), still retains its earliest meaning of one who makes something by means of art and skill. Originally it was applied especially to mechanics. "I saw a smith stand with his hammer, thus. . . With open mouth swallowing a tailor's news . . . Another lean unwash'd *artificer* Cuts off his tale" (*Shak.*). Around 1600, the idea of art or skill in devising became involved in its meaning, so that it came to imply more in the way of inventiveness than is usually ascribed to mechanics. In current English it suggests craftsmanship and is applied especially to those who work in some plastic substance such as silver or gold, which permits the exercise of skill, taste, and ingenuity in contrivance. "A fine cook and *artificer* of strange English dishes" (*Bennett*). "The teacher has been only one of the *artificers* in the making of this changing personality [the school child]" (*H. Suzzallo*). In Shakespeare's time **artisan** was applied to the practitioner of any art (especially industrial art), chiefly, in distinction from an artist, one highly proficient in his art (especially an art requiring taste and learning). "The Germans . . . are better *Artisans* than *Artists;* better at handy-crafts then [than] at headcraft" (*J. Colgrave*). This difference between *artisan* and *artist* widened as *artist* came to imply a love of the beautiful and the power to create or produce beautiful things and became restricted in its application to a worker in the fine arts. In current use, *artisan* is a general term almost equal to *workman,* and names one engaged in a craft, a handicraft, a trade, or the like; it comprehends in its range *mechanic, artificer, craftsman, machinist,* and similar terms. In extended use, it is still often contrasted with *artist,* the latter now implying imaginative power and a passion for perfection, the former mere mechanical industry. "Free verse is not yet out of the experimental stage, and the *artists* who practice it have still the *artisans* in their own craft to reckon with" (*Lowes*). **Architect** has never lost its etymological implication of a master builder, though it has come to stress more the designing of that which is to be built than actual participation in its erection. Specifically it designates a person whose profession it is to plan buildings or structures in detail and to exercise supervision over their construction in order to see that the design is executed in every particular. In extended use, the word usually implies the power to conceive a thing as a whole and in detail in advance of its coming into being, as well as to control its execution. It is often applied to the Creator (as, "the *Architect,*" "the great *Architect,*" "the grand *Architect*"). Although it comes close to *artist* in its implications of imaginative power and constructive ability, it differs from the former in its greater emphasis upon design than upon execution. "The hasty multitude Admiring entered [the newly erected palace of Satan]; and the work some praise, And some the *architect*" (*Milton*). "The poet is an *artificer* by profession, an *architect* experimenting with a variety of materials, concerned with . . . new designs" (*Day Lewis*).

Ana. Craftsman, workman (see WORKER): creator, *maker: *writer, composer, author.

2 Artiste, virtuoso, *expert, adept, wizard, dab, dabster.

artiste. Artist, virtuoso, adept, *expert, dab, dabster, wizard.

artistic. **Artistic, aesthetic** (*or* **esthetic**) are often understood as equivalent terms, especially when used in such collocations as the *artistic,* or *aesthetic,* temperament; *artistic,* or *aesthetic,* satisfaction; *artistic,* or *aesthetic,* standards or values; for *artistic,* or *aesthetic,* reasons. In precise use, they are very carefully distinguished. In general, **artistic** stresses the point of view of the artist, or of one who actually produces a work of art, who thinks in terms of technique, of the relationship of details to the design of the whole, of the effects to be gained, and who, therefore, regards beauty as a thing that results from his attention to these matters and that is his creation. By extension, *artistic* also may imply the point of view of one who studies or judges art objectively from the artist's angle. On the other hand, **aesthetic** stresses the point of view of one who contemplates a finished work of art or beauty that exists, and thinks in terms of the effect it has upon him and especially of the sensations it stimulates and the feelings it excites. Strictly, the *artistic* temperament shows itself in an urge to fashion or to express, and to create out of materials, or of words, or of sounds, the beautiful thing that the artist designs or conceives: the *aesthetic* temperament shows itself in responsiveness to beauty wherever it is found, and by contrast, in aversion to that which is ugly. *Artistic* satisfaction is the gratification that comes to one who can look at a work of art (his own or another's) and call it good: *aesthetic* satisfaction is the content that accompanies the enjoyment of beauty for its own sake and independently of all other considerations. For *aesthetic,* largely because of its connection with *aesthetics,* the branch of philosophy or of psychology dealing with beauty, usually implies a distinction between that which is beautiful and that which is moral, or useful, or merely pleasing. *Artistic* standards are, therefore, the tests of perfection in a work of art which artists and critics have accepted: *aesthetic* standards are the criteria (usually subjective) which have been set up by aestheticians or by the individual to enable one to distinguish that which is beautiful from that which is merely pleasing or gratifying.

artless. *Natural, simple, ingenuous, naïve, unsophisticated, unaffected.

Ana. *Spontaneous, impulsive: candid, open, plain, *frank: *straightforward, aboveboard, forthright.

Ant. Artful: affected. — *Con.* *Sly, cunning, wily: designing (see INTEND).

as. Since, *because, for, inasmuch as.

ascend. **1** *Rise, arise, mount, soar, tower, rocket, levitate, surge.

Ana. Elevate, raise, rear, *lift: *advance, progress.

Ant. Descend.

2 **Ascend, mount, climb, scale** agree in meaning to move upward to or toward the top of (something). **Ascend** is the most colorless of these terms, for it implies little more than progressive upward movement; as, to *ascend* a mountain or hill; the car rapidly *ascended* the steep grade. It may, however, be specifically used of movement along a river in the direction of its source; as, the Amazon can be *ascended* by seagoing ships 2300 miles. **Mount** almost invariably implies getting up on something above the level of the ground and is therefore preferred to *ascend* in some collocations; thus, one *mounts* (better than *ascends*) a platform or a scaffold but one may *ascend* (or *mount*) a throne; one *mounts* (not *ascends*) a horse. **Climb** usually suggests effort and ascent by the use of various means, such as the hands and feet or, in the case of vehicles, of gears or extra power; as, to *climb* a tree, a pole, the social ladder. "To *climb* steep hills Requires slow pace at first" (*Shak.*). **Scale** adds to *climb* not only the suggestion of progression by steps but that of great difficulty; it is referable therefore to feats of climbing; as, to *scale* a wall, a precipice. "A ladder quaintly made of cords . . . Would serve to *scale* another Hero's tower" (*Shak.*).

Ant. Descend.

ascendancy *or* **ascendency.** *Supremacy.

Ana. Dominance, predominance (see corresponding adjectives at DOMINANT): command, sway, dominion, control, *power, authority: sovereignty (see corresponding adjective at FREE).

ascension. **Ascension, ascent** are often used in distinction from each other when they denote the act of moving upward or the movement upward. **Ascension** in modern precise use occurs chiefly where there is no implication of effort or difficulty in rising, and where there is, usually, the suggestion of movement activated by some property in the thing which ascends; as, a balloon *ascension.* The chief use is religious, however, and in one restricted reference; as, the *Ascension* of Jesus (or Our Lord) into heaven. The phrase "the Ascension of the Virgin Mary" occurs, but is regarded as incorrect, "Assumption" (a taking up) being the technical term. **Ascent,** on the other hand, is preferred when there is any implication of effort or of a human agent or operator; as, during their *ascent* of the mountain; the scientists effected an *ascent* to the stratosphere; her rapid *ascent* in the social scale; to make an *ascent* of three miles in an airplane. These distinctions are not always observed, however, for *ascension* is increasingly rare except in religious and some astronomical use, and *ascent* is employed, even by good writers, in all collocations where *ascension* is sometimes preferred or is traditionally used.

ascent. *Ascension.

ascertain. Determine, *discover, unearth, learn.

Ana. Inquire, query, interrogate, *ask: study, contemplate, weigh, *consider: observe, survey (see SEE).

Con. *Conjecture, surmise, guess: presume, assume (see PRESUPPOSE).

ascetic, *adj.* Austere, *severe, stern.

Ana. Disciplined, trained, schooled (see TEACH): self-denying, self-abnegating (see corresponding nouns at RENUNCIATION): abstaining *or* abstinent, forbearing (see corresponding verbs at REFRAIN): abstemious (see corresponding noun at TEMPERANCE).

Ant. Luxurious, voluptuous (see SENSUOUS). — *Con.* *Sensuous, sensual, epicurean, sybaritic: dissolute, *abandoned.

ascetic, *n.* **Ascetic, mystic** and their derivative nouns **asceticism, mysticism** are not synonyms but are not always clearly distinguished, partly because of overlapping implications but largely because the first two are often applicable to the same person. Historically many of the great mystics have been ascetics. But **ascetic** suggests an austere mode of life in which everything that does not contribute to, or may interfere with, the end in view (usually spiritual, sometimes intellectual, perfection) is sacrificed, and certain acts, such as fasting and mortification in the religious life, are practiced not for their own sake but for their disciplinary effect, especially in strengthening one's powers of contemplation. **Mystic,** on the other hand, suggests the possession of a power, such as a high capacity for contemplation, or of an "inner light," by means of which one overpasses the limits of human reason and by a kind of spiritual sight comes to a knowledge of that which is divine or supernatural. *Ascetic* and *mystic*, therefore, when applied to the same person, regard him from different points of view; the former implies that he practices austerities believed favorable to spiritual contemplation; the latter, that he has had the mystical experiences that are the end of contemplation. But the two terms do not necessarily imply each other; *ascetic*, even when applied to those who aim at spiritual perfection, does not connote attainment of mystical knowledge; *mystic*, on the other hand, does not invariably imply a connection with an ascetic life. Although **asceticism** and **mysticism** may denote doctrines or practices, their chief differences are apparent when they denote the theory upon which such doctrines and practices are based. *Asceticism* often designates the theory that abstinence from otherwise lawful acts or pleasures and the practice of austerities are conducive to spiritual and intellectual perfection; *mysticism*, the theory that immediate knowledge of God or ultimate reality is attainable through a faculty that transcends the reason and makes no use of ordinary human perceptive or ratiocinative powers. "One is sometimes tempted to think that to approve *mysticism* is to preach *asceticism*. Certainly many *mystics* have been *ascetic*. But that has been the accident of their philosophy, and not the essence of their religion" (*H. Ellis*).

Ana. Anchorite, hermit, eremite, cenobite (see RECLUSE): monk, friar, nun, *religious.

Ant. Bon vivant. —*Con.* *Epicure, gourmet, gourmand, glutton: sensualist, voluptuary, Sybarite (see corresponding adjectives at SENSUOUS).

asceticism. Mysticism (see under ASCETIC, *n.*).

ascribe. Ascribe, attribute, impute, assign, refer, credit, accredit, charge are synonymous when they mean to lay something (creditable, discreditable, or neutral) to the account of a person or thing. The first four of these words are often used interchangeably without marked loss, but their distinctions in discriminating use are here emphasized. One **ascribes** *to* a person or thing something which is not outwardly apparent but which may be inferred or conjectured, such as a motive, a feeling, an opinion, or a value. "Whatever else might be in her head, it was . . . neither love, nor romance, nor any of the emotions usually *ascribed* to the young" (*V. Sackville-West*). Also, one *ascribes* something whose origin is unknown or disputed *to* that which is conjectured to be its source, cause, or author; as, a poem formerly *ascribed* to Chaucer. "That conceit always *ascribed* to a lack of intelligence" (*Brownell*). One **attributes** *to* a person or thing something believed, usually on good grounds, to belong to it or to be appropriate to it, such as a quality, a character, or a value, or something for which that person or thing is judged to be responsible or accountable. "If he disclaimed the virtues *attributed* to him he should only accentuate his embarrassment" (*C. Mackenzie*). "A combination . . . might have *attributed* to it . . . the character of a monopoly merely by virtue of its size" (*Justice Holmes*). "The counter-reformation, and the collapse of Protestantism in France, must be largely *attributed* to Jesuit efforts" (*B. Russell*). One **imputes** when one so definitely ascribes something *to* a person or, less often, a thing, that the ascription is impressed on (etymologically, "thought into") that person or thing. For this reason, *impute* commonly, but not invariably, implies accusation and, often, its resulting stigma. "How dare you, sir, *impute* such monstrous intentions to me?" (*Shaw*). One **assigns** something *to* a person or thing when one deliberately attributes a character, a value, an origin, or the like which definitely places or fixes that person or thing, as in the class to which he or it belongs, under a certain description, at the date when it occurred, or the like. "More than one rejoinder declared that the importance I here *assigned* to criticism was excessive" (*Arnold*). "He concluded that they [poems of disputed authorship] must be *assigned* to Vaughan" (*Quiller-Couch*). Also, one *assigns* a reason *for* something when one definitely fixes or states the ground, excuse, or motive for that thing; as, it is impossible to *assign* any reason for his failure. Sometimes, *assign* suggests allegation, but this connotation is usually derived from the context. "Whatever reason of discontent the farmers may *assign*, the true cause is this" (*Coleridge*). One **refers** a thing (rarely a person) *to* the class to which it belongs or to its origin when, after tracing it back, one assigns it to its proper category or to its ultimate cause or source; as, the aurora borealis is commonly *referred* to the class of electric phenomena. "I am convinced that at least one-half of their bad manners may be *referred* to their education" (*Quiller-Couch*). One **credits** someone *with* something, or something *to* someone, when one ascribes the thing to some person or thing as its author, its agent, its source, or its explanation. "People *credited* Moriarty's queerness of manner and moody ways to the solitude" (*Kipling*). Sometimes, *credit* suggests unwarranted belief. "Aunty Rosa had *credited* him in the past with petty cunning and stratagem that had never entered into his head" (*Kipling*). One **accredits** a person or, rarely, a thing *with* something said or done, when one accepts him as the author or agent or it as the cause or motive, thereby tasking him or it with responsibility. "Mr. Bright himself was *accredited* with having said that his own effort to arouse a reforming spirit . . . was like flogging a dead horse" (*J. McCarthy*). One **charges** something *on* (or *upon*) a person or thing when one fixes the responsibility for a fault, crime, evil, or the like on him or it. "Crimes as base as any *charged* on me?" (*Cowper*).

Ana. Attach, *fasten, affix: *conjecture, surmise, guess: allege, advance, *adduce, cite.

asepsis. See under STERILE.

aseptic, *adj.* *Sterile, antiseptic.

asexualize. *Sterilize, castrate, spay, geld, emasculate, mutilate, caponize.

ash. *Ashes, cinders, embers, clinkers.

ashamed. **Ashamed, mortified, chagrined** agree in meaning acutely or manifestly conscious of embarrassment and humiliation. One is **ashamed** whose embarrassment and humiliation are mixed sometimes with a sense of guilt, and always with the awareness of being discredited or disgraced by one's own or, vicariously, another's, shameful or indecorous act, behavior, situation, or the like. "He sees he has nothing to be *ashamed* of in you—rather everything to be proud of" (*Meredith*). "Suddenly Joe began to cry. He was *ashamed* and did not want his wife to see" (*S. Anderson*). One is also *ashamed* who by anticipating such feelings is reluctant or unwilling to do something that seems shameful. "What shall I do? for my lord taketh away from me the stewardship: I cannot dig; to beg I am *ashamed*" (*Luke* xvi. 3). One is **mortified** whose embarrassment and humiliation are mixed with a strong sense of being put in a false or disagreeable light and who suffers more because of loss of esteem or a hurt to his own pride than because of the shameful or indecorous character of the act, behavior, or situation; as, he professed not to be *ashamed* of his conduct, but he was *mortified* when his parents learned of it. " 'Don't spare him; let the university expel him! . . . Let Robert be *ashamed*, if you would save his soul alive!' . . . Robert was sullen and *mortified*, but, alas, not *ashamed*" (*M. Deland*). One is **chagrined** whose embarrassment and humiliation are accompanied by vexation or annoyance. "Tony, somewhat *chagrined* at his mistake, said he should like to see the other pictures" (*Arch. Marshall*). "I was as much *chagrined* as they were flabbergasted by this involuntary outbreak" (*L. P. Smith*).

Ana. Embarrassed, discomfited, abashed (see EMBARRASS): humiliated, humbled, abased (see ABASE): abject, *mean: contrite, penitent, repentant (see corresponding nouns at PENITENCE).

Ant. Proud. — ***Con.*** Vain, vainglorious (see under PRIDE, *n.*): arrogant, overbearing (see PROUD).

ashen. Ashy, livid, pallid, wan, *pale.

Ana. *Ghastly, grim, macabre: blanched, bleached, decolorized (see WHITEN).

ashes. **Ashes, ash, cinders, clinkers, embers** are comparable when they mean the remains of combustible material after it has been destroyed by fire. **Ashes,** in precise use, implies perfect combustion and a powdery residue consisting only of incombustible and thoroughly disintegrated mineral or earthy substances; as, wood *ashes* are used as a fertilizer; the house and its furnishings were reduced to *ashes*. **Ash** differs from *ashes* only in suggesting a solid mass, not yet disintegrated; as, the *ash* of a cigar; soda *ash*. **Cinders,** in careful use, carries the implication of either incomplete or imperfect combustion and is applied to a residue, usually of a coal fire, consisting of coarse particles which, if the combustion is incomplete, are capable of further burning, but without flame (as, to sift the *ashes* from the *cinders*), or which, if combustion is imperfect, are more precisely called small **clinkers.** A *clinker* is a fused or vitrified stony mass such as is formed in burning impure coal or in smelting metals containing impurities, or is ejected from a volcano; thus, *cinders* which are composed mainly of small *clinkers* are often used for surfacing paths, driveways, and tracks (cf. a *cinder* track). **Embers** is applied to the still glowing or still smoldering remains of a fire just before it is reduced to ashes or cinders.

ashy. Ashen, livid, pallid, wan, *pale.

Ana. See those at ASHEN.

asinine. *Simple, fatuous, silly, foolish.

Ana. *Stupid, crass, dumb, dense, dull: puerile (see YOUTHFUL): *irrational, unreasonable.

Ant. Sensible, judicious. — ***Con.*** *Wise, sane, prudent, sapient, sage: *intelligent, clever, knowing, smart: *rational, reasonable.

ask. **1 Ask, question, interrogate, query, inquire** (*or* **enquire**), **speer** (*or* **speir, spier**), **catechize, quiz, examine** agree in meaning to address a person in an attempt to elicit information. **Ask** is the general or colorless term for putting a question; as, *ask* and you will find; to *ask* the price of an article; *ask* your brother if he will join us. "None of them [certain philosophers] understood how to *ask* the question which they were trying to answer" (*H. Ellis*). **Question** usually suggests asking one question after another, as in teaching, in examining a witness or a candidate, or the like; as, to *question* a suspect at length; Socrates preferred *questioning* his disciples to lecturing them. **Interrogate** stresses formal or systematic questioning. "They examined many witnesses . . . whom they *interrogated*, not only upon the express words of the statute, but upon all . . . collateral or presumptive circumstances" (*Bp. Burnet*). **Query** is often formal or bookish for *ask*, but it may be used without a suggestion of either formality or bookishness when it strongly implies a desire for authoritative information or the resolution of a doubt; as, "Should not one *query* whether he had not those proofs in his hands antecedent to the cabinet?" (*Walpole*). In current use, the word is specifically a proofreader's term. "If the copy is not perfectly clear, or if you have reason to doubt its correctness, look up the point or *query* it to the publisher's editor . . . Do not *query* a misspelled word in ordinary text . . . Never *query* style to the author" (*Manual of Style, U. of Chicago Press*). **Inquire** has for its fundamental implication a search for the facts or the truth; only when it distinctly implies in addition to such an intention the asking of a question or questions does it come into comparison with the other words of this group; as, to *inquire* the best route to New York City; to *inquire* when the public library would be open. "It was soon evident that this was the reddleman who had *inquired* for her" (*Hardy*). **Speer,** which is chiefly a Scottish and North of England term, comes very close to *inquire*, with its dual implication of a search and the asking of questions. It does not, however, as often suggest an investigation as does *inquire*, and frequently it connotes curiosity as the motive. "*Speer* as little about him as he does about you" (*Scott*). **Catechize** adds to *interrogate* the suggestion of an aim to elicit a certain kind of answer. Often the answers expected are definite statements of doctrine already phrased in a catechism (a book supplying questions and answers concerning the doctrines of a church); as, to *catechize* a candidate for the ministry. In extended use, however, there is often the implication of a desire to lead the person who is questioned into making answers that are self-condemnatory or that will reveal his weaknesses; as, it was their policy to *catechize* every candidate for a doctor's degree at the beginning of his advanced studies. **Quiz** is a colloquial term frequently used in American colleges; it implies a careful, often a thoroughgoing, interrogation of a class to determine how well a series of lectures or a course of reading has been understood and assimilated. **Examine,** in the special sense in which it is here considered (for leading sense, see SCRUTINIZE), implies interrogation or catechizing for the purpose of drawing answers that indicate how much or how little a person knows, as from students when their fitness for promotion is to be decided, or from candidates for a position when it is necessary to determine the extent of their preparation and the adequacy of their training, or from those giving testimony in a trial, or when the lawyers on each side try to elicit information of value to their clients; as, the students in this course are *examined* at the end of the year; no candidate for a civil service position is considered until he has been *examined* with all other candidates and given a satisfactory rating; it took the whole day to *examine* and to *cross-examine* the principal witness.

Con. Reply, *answer, respond, rejoin, retort.

2 Ask, request, solicit agree in meaning to seek to obtain by making one's wants or desires known. **Ask,** in this as well as in its primary sense, implies expectation of a response, often an affirmative response; as, I am going to *ask* a favor of you; he *asked* the close attention of all his audience; to *ask* the citizens for their full co-operation. **Request,** by its suggestion of greater courtesy and formality in the manner of asking, is preferable to *ask* when one feels that what one wants may not be granted, either for lack of power or means or of interest on the other side, or when one wishes to be exceedingly polite or ingratiating; as, to *request* a loan; to *request* the presence of a person at a reception (the formula for a formal invitation); to *request* an opportunity to present one's opinions. **Solicit** belongs with this group rather than with that discriminated at BEG, because it now seldom implies earnest entreaty or urging; its most common suggestion in present-day use is that of calling attention to one's wants and desires in the hope of having them satisfied; thus, a merchant *solicits* trade by means of letters, or handbills, or advertisements in journals; a magazine *solicits* subscriptions when it sends an agent (a solicitor) to interview possible subscribers.

Ana. Appeal, petition, plead, pray, sue (see under PRAYER): *address, accost.

Con. *Get, obtain, acquire, secure: *decline, refuse, spurn: *deny, gainsay.

askance. Askew, *awry.

Ana. Mistrustfully, distrustfully (see corresponding verbs at DISTRUST): enviously, jealously (see corresponding adjectives at ENVIOUS).

Ant. Straightforwardly, directly.

askew. *Awry, askance.

Ana. Crookedly, obliquely (see corresponding adjectives at CROOKED).

Ant. Straight.

asocial. *Unsocial, antisocial, nonsocial.

Ant. Social.

aspect. 1 Look, *appearance, semblance.

Ana. *Face, countenance, visage: *bearing, mien, carriage, port, presence.

2 Exposure, *frontage.

Ana. Outlook, *prospect.

3 *Phase, side, facet, angle.

Ana. Angle, slant, *point of view, standpoint, viewpoint.

asperity. *Acrimony, acerbity.

Ana. Sharpness, keenness (see corresponding adjectives at SHARP): causticity, mordancy (see corresponding adjectives at CAUSTIC): snappishness, waspishness, irritability (see corresponding adjectives at IRRITABLE).

Ant. Amenity. — *Con.* *Courtesy, gallantry, comity: suavity, urbanity, blandness (see corresponding adjectives at SUAVE).

asperse, *v.* 1 *Sprinkle, besprinkle, spatter, bespatter, splash.

2 Vilify, *malign, traduce, calumniate, slander, defame, libel.

Ana. Disparage, depreciate, derogate from, detract from, *decry: revile, vituperate (see SCOLD): defile (see CONTAMINATE).

Con. *Praise, extol, laud, acclaim, eulogize: *commend, applaud, compliment.

aspersion. Reflection, *animadversion, stricture.

Ana. *Libel, lampoon, pasquinade, squib, skit: *abuse, vituperation, invective, obloquy: *detraction, backbiting, calumny, slander, scandal.

Con. Praise, laudation, extollation, eulogizing *or* eulogy (see corresponding verbs at PRAISE): *applause, acclaim, acclamation, plaudits: commendation, complimenting *or* compliment (see corresponding verbs at COMMEND).

aspirant. *Candidate, applicant, nominee.

aspiration. *Ambition, pretension.

Ana. Aim, goal, objective (see INTENTION): *desire, passion, lust, yen.

aspire. *Aim, pant.

Ana. Crave, covet, *desire: *long, yearn, hunger, thirst, pine.

Con. *Stoop, condescend, deign: grovel, *wallow.

assail. Bombard, *attack, assault, storm.

Ana. Beset (see INFEST): belabor, pummel, buffet, pound, *beat.

assassin. Assassin, cutthroat, gunman, trigger man, finger man, bravo designate a murderer, or one who can be hired to murder, in cold blood. **Assassin,** etymologically a hashish eater, was originally applied to one of an order of Mohammedans who were employed during the Crusades and later to murder Christians and who were sent forth under the influence of this drug. The term in all of its uses stresses secrecy and treachery in operation; as, like *assassins*, these destructive animals do their work in the dark. It is now chiefly applied to murderers of important personages; as, tyrants always live in dread of *assassins;* revolutions breed *assassins. Cutthroat* and *gunman* designate professional and, usually, hireling murderers. **Cutthroat** is now chiefly literary (or merely figurative) because daggers and knives are no longer the weapons usually employed by such criminals, but the word still commonly suggests the brutal methods of a ruffian. "Thou [the hired murderer of Banquo] art the best o' the *cut-throats*" (*Shak.*). "I am a soldier, sir, and not a *cut-throat*" (*Froude*). **Gunman,** in current use, is applied chiefly to a gangster, especially to one engaged in a robbery and supplied with firearms, or to a murderer by occupation who, under the orders of a leader or employer, shoots to kill. Since the term is also applied to a person who aids the killer in accomplishing his aim, **trigger man** is often used, in underworld slang, in place of *gunman* for the actual murderer, and **finger man** for the assistant who points out the intended victim. **Bravo** was the term common in the seventeenth and eighteenth centuries for a type of brutal ruffian; the term usually implied his availability for hire as a murderer. It is now chiefly historical or literary. "The hired *bravos* who defend The tyrant's throne" (*Shelley*).

Ana. Murderer, slayer, killer, assassinator (see corresponding verbs at KILL).

assassinate. Murder, *kill, slay, dispatch, execute.

assault, *n.* *Attack, onslaught, onset.

Ana. Assailing, bombarding *or* bombardment, storming *or* storm (see corresponding verbs at ATTACK): *invasion, incursion, raid.

assault, *v.* Storm, *attack, bombard, assail.

Ana. Smite, slug, *strike: *beat, pound, buffet, pummel.

Con. Resist, withstand, *oppose, combat: *defend, protect, shield, guard.

assay, *n.* Essay, attempt, try, endeavor, striving, struggle. See under ATTEMPT, *v.*

Ana. *Effort, exertion: trial, test, proof (see under PROVE).

assay, *v.* **1** Essay, *attempt, try, endeavor, strive, struggle.

Ana. *Aim, aspire: *begin, commence, start.

2 Assess, evaluate, *estimate, appraise, value, rate.

Ana. *Analyze, resolve: *calculate, compute, reckon: *prove, test, try, demonstrate.

assemblage. **1** Assembly, collection, congregation, gathering. See under GATHER.

Ana. *Aggregate, aggregation: *crowd, throng, horde, crush, press: *flock, drove, herd, pack, swarm.

2 Assemblage, assembly are not always interchangeable in concrete use (that is, when they denote that which is assembled). **Assemblage** may be used freely in reference either to persons or to things (as, an *assemblage* of farmers from every section of the state; an *assemblage* of the city's manufactured products for exhibition); it may imply a unit that is a collection of individuals of the same general kind, or one that is a whole formed by the union of miscellaneous things (as, an *assemblage* of logs; an automobile is an *assemblage* of various distinct parts); it may be applied to something that can be seen as a unit or whole or that can be conceived as such. "We have just been picturing nature as an *assemblage* of particles set in a framework of space and time" (*Jeans*). **Assembly,** on the other hand, was until recently restricted in its application to a group of persons who gather together in a given place, usually for the purpose of acting in concert or of social enjoyment, or, in a more specific sense, in order to serve as a deliberative or legislative body; as, the mayor decided to call an *assembly* of the citizens; the New York State *Assembly.* There is a tendency now to use *assembly* instead of *assemblage* of a structure, or machine, or part of a machine, that is formed by the union of different parts; as, a hub *assembly.*

Ana. See those at ASSEMBLAGE, 1.

assemble. Congregate, collect, *gather.

Ana. Convene, convoke, muster (see SUMMON): combine, associate, unite (see JOIN).

Ant. Disperse. — *Con.* *Scatter, dissipate, dispel: *distribute, dispense, divide, deal, dole.

assembly. **1** Assemblage, congregation, gathering, collection. See under GATHER.

Ana. *Company, party, troop, band: *crowd, throng, crush, press: *convention, convocation, congress, synod, conference, council.

2 *Assemblage.

Ana. See those at ASSEMBLY, 1.

assent, *v.* **Assent, consent, accede, acquiesce, agree, subscribe** and their corresponding nouns, express in common the idea of concurrence with what someone else has stated or proposed. **Assent** implies primarily an act of the understanding and applies to opinions or propositions. "One was convinced and believed and *assented*" (*D. Webster*). "Whatever is expressed with art—whether it be a lover's despair or a metaphysical theory—pierces the mind and compels *assent* and acceptance" (*A. Huxley*). **Consent** involves the will or the feelings and indicates compliance with what is requested or desired. A lady may *assent* to a gentleman's opinion on the weather, but if he makes a proposal of marriage he must await her *consent.* "If a thing has been practiced for two hundred years by common *consent,* it will need a strong case for the Fourteenth Amendment to affect it" (*Justice Holmes*). Neither *assent* nor *consent* necessarily implies approval; as, one sometimes *assents* against his better judgment. **Accede** implies a yielding, either of one's adherence (as to a cause) or of one's assent (as to a statement or proposal). "Potidaea had already *acceded* to the confederacy" (*Thirlwall*). "Mr. Bennet could have no hesitation in *acceding* to the proposal before him" (*Austen*). **Acquiesce** implies tacit acceptance or forbearance of opposition. "No organism *acquiesces* in its own destruction" (*Mencken*). **Agree** may or may not imply previous difference of opinion, but it very often carries an implication of this and also of previous discussion, negotiation, or attempts at persuasion; as, he reluctantly *agreed* that his son be allowed to choose his own college; he finally *agreed* to the proposal. "Post, my lord, to France; *Agree* to any covenants" (*Shak.*). **Subscribe** denotes assent but it implies in addition hearty approval; as here compared, it seldom implies signing one's name in token of assent, but it does connote a willingness to go on record. "No one would *subscribe* at present to the Kantian doctrine, that mathematics derive their validity from their applicability to sensible experience" (*S. Alexander*).

Ana. Accept, *receive: *adopt, embrace, espouse: believe, credit (see corresponding nouns at BELIEF).

Ant. Dissent. — *Con.* *Deny, gainsay, impugn: reject, spurn, refuse (see DECLINE): *object, protest.

assert. **1 Assert, declare, affirm, aver, protest, avouch, avow, predicate, warrant,** as here compared, agree in meaning to state positively either in anticipation of denial or objection or in the face of it. **Assert** implies absence of proof: it usually ascribes to the speaker or writer either assurance of the grounds for his statement or such confidence in his opinions as to make him indifferent to evidence. "That rigid sect which *asserts* that all real science is precise measurement" (*H. Ellis*). "Hobart . . . . could talk; he could *assert* . . . but he couldn't meet or answer arguments" (*R. Macaulay*). **Declare** (see also DECLARE) adds to *assert* the implication of open or public statement. "They do not, for the most part . . . *declare* . . . that no war can ever be right" (*Inge*). "Some one had seen Steve Hunter shot down in the street and had *declared* the harness maker had done it" (*S. Anderson*). **Affirm** implies conviction of truth and willingness to stand by one's statement because it is supported by evidence, one's experience, faith, or the like. "Yet, with the evidence before us . . . we cannot *affirm* that this is the later play" (*T. S. Eliot*). "These things I will that thou *affirm* constantly (*Titus* iii. 8). **Aver** suggests complete confidence and certainty of truth. "For all *averred,* I had killed the bird" (*Coleridge*). **Protest** (see also OBJECT) stresses emphasis in affirmation, especially in the face of doubt or contradiction. "I here *protest,* in sight of heaven . . . I am clear" (*Shak.*). "He *protested* that, except Lady Catherine and her daughter, he had never seen a more elegant woman" (*Austen*). **Avouch** usually imputes authority or personal knowledge to the one who makes a positive statement. "His own deposition, as three Cardinals *avouched* that he had made it before them" (*C. M. Yonge*). **Avow,** now somewhat rare in this sense, implies open and emphatic declaration and personal responsibility for the statement. "We affirm and *avow* that the very meanest translation of the Bible in English . . . containeth the word of God" (*Bible: Preface to A.V.*, 1611). **Predicate,** though once often and still occasionally used as a close synonym of the preceding words, is now chiefly a term of logic implying the affirmation of something as a quality, a property, or an attribute of a thing, especially of a thing as a member of its class, species, or genus; as, to *predicate* sweetness of sugar, or whiteness of snow; to *predicate* intelligence of human beings; "logic works by *predicating* of the single instance what is true of all its kind" (*W. James*). In somewhat looser use, the term implies the affirmation of a quality, property, or attribute which can be regarded as evidently or permanently a possession of the individual person or thing described. "There was nothing to be *predicated* of him in general: he was but a bundle of incongruities, most of them unattractive, and, in combination, futile" (*Belloc*). Because that which is predicated of a thing is accepted as true and forms a postulate for one's reasoning regarding that thing, the word *predicate* is now often used, especially in the United States, in the sense of to ground or to base (as, success *predicated* on efficiency). Such a meaning, though found in writers like Charles Sumner and J. R. Lowell, has not been generally approved. **Warrant,** in the sense here considered (see also JUSTIFY, 3), is now found chiefly in colloquial use; it carries a strong implication of assurance or positiveness, sometimes suggesting little or no fear that one will be doubted or contradicted, and at other times connoting one's personal guarantee; as, I *warrant* that's just what will happen; "[My neck is] as smooth as silk, I *warrant* ye" (*L'Estrange*); "cheap-jacks who sell at dockyard gates a pill *warranted* to cure measles, toothache and rupture" (*C. E. Montague*).

Ana. Allege, advance, cite, *adduce: asseverate, affirm, *swear, depose.

Ant. Deny: controvert. — ***Con.*** Gainsay, contradict, negative, traverse, contravene (see DENY): *disprove, refute, rebut, confute.

2 Vindicate, justify, *maintain, defend.

Ana. Proclaim, *declare, publish, advertise: *express, voice, utter.

assertive. Self-assertive, *aggressive, pushing, militant.

Ana. Positive, *affirmative: blatant, clamorous, *vociferous: cocksure, certain, *sure, positive: *confident, assured, sanguine.

Ant. Retiring: acquiescent. — ***Con.*** *Shy, bashful, diffident, modest: docile, *obedient, amenable, biddable.

assess. Assay, appraise, value, evaluate, *estimate, rate.

Ana. *Calculate, compute, reckon.

assessment. Levy, *tax, rate, duty, impost, toll, tithe, teind, cess, customs, excise, tribute, tariff.

asset. 1 In plural form **assets.** Resources, means, *possessions, effects, belongings.

Ant. Liabilities.

2 *Credit.

Ant. Handicap.

asseverate. *Swear, affirm, depose, depone, testify.

Ana. *Assert, declare, affirm, aver, protest, avow, avouch.

assiduous. Sedulous, diligent, industrious, *busy.

Ana. *Indefatigable, tireless, untiring, unwearied.

Ant. Desultory. — ***Con.*** *Random, haphazard, casual, hit-or-miss, happy-go-lucky: *lazy, slothful, indolent, fainéant: remiss, lax, slack (see NEGLIGENT).

assign. 1 *Allot, allocate, apportion.

Ana. Fix, *set, establish, settle: *distribute, deal, dole, dispense.

2 Refer, *ascribe, attribute, impute, credit, accredit, charge.

Ana. Attach, *fasten, affix: relate, link, associate (see JOIN): pigeonhole, classify (see ASSORT).

3 *Prescribe, define.

Ana. Determine, settle, *decide: consign, relegate, *commit, entrust.

assignation. Rendezvous, tryst, date, *engagement, appointment.

assignment. *Task, stint, duty, job, chore, chare.

assimilate. 1 *Identify, incorporate, embody.

Ana. *Change, alter, modify, vary: *transform, metamorphose, transmute: blend, fuse, merge, commingle, *mix.

2 *Absorb, imbibe.

Ana. Engross, absorb, *monopolize: *adopt, embrace, espouse: *infuse, imbue, ingrain, suffuse, inoculate, leaven.

assimilation. Apperception, identification, *recognition.

assist. *Help, aid.

Ana. Support, uphold, back, *champion: profit, avail, *benefit: attend, *accompany, escort: co-operate, concur (see UNITE).

Ant. Hamper: impede. — ***Con.*** *Hinder, obstruct, block: trammel, clog, fetter (see HAMPER): *prevent, forestall.

assistance. Help, aid. See under HELP, *v.*

Ana. Service, advantage, profit, avail, *use: supporting, upholding, backing (see SUPPORT, *v.*): subsidy, grant, subvention, *appropriation: co-operation, concurrence (see corresponding verbs at UNITE).

Ant. Impediment: obstruction.

assistant, *n.* **Assistant, helper, coadjutor, adjutant, aide** (*or* **aid**)**, aide-de-camp** are here compared as designations of persons who take over part of the duties of another, especially in a subordinate capacity. **Assistant** is applicable to any person who meets this description, regardless of the status of his work; as, a baker's *assistant;* a bishop's *assistant;* a superintendent's *assistant.* **Helper** often implies apprenticeship in a trade or the status of an unskilled laborer; as, a bricklayer's *helper.* Sometimes, it is euphemistic; thus, a mother's *helper* often performs the duties of a nursemaid. **Coadjutor,** in its general use, usually implies equivalence except in authority; it is chiefly applied to a co-worker. "He [Octavian] no longer stood alone; the companions of his youth [Agrippa and Maecenas] had become in the full sense his *coadjutors*" (*Buchan*). In specific use, it names or is applied to a bishop who serves as an assistant to the bishop having jurisdiction over a diocese. Especially in Roman Catholic and Protestant Episcopal use it implies the right of succession. **Adjutant,** now rare in its general sense, is applied almost exclusively to a staff officer in charge of the personnel division of a military command, and responsible for all records, reports, correspondence, orders (except combat orders), and the like. **Aide** and **aide-de-camp** designate a military or naval officer who personally attends a general or a sovereign, a president or a governor, often as an escort but sometimes with definitely prescribed duties.

associate, *v.* Connect, relate, link, *join, combine, unite.

Ana. Merge, mingle, *mix, blend, amalgamate, coalesce: organize (see ORDER, *v.*).

Con. Alienate, *estrange: *separate, part, divorce, sever, sunder, divide.

associate, *n.* **Associate, companion, comrade, crony, chum, pal, buddy** are here compared as meaning a person in company with whom one is found. **Associate** is the general term, referable to anyone whose company one enjoys or tolerates more or less regularly and usually on terms of equality, because of a business, social, fraternal, or similar connection, or because of a community of interests or aims; as, a person is known by his *associates;*

his *associates* included all the prominent young men of the town. "He became a leader of fashion. Then, to the visible embarrassment of his young *associates*, he suddenly tired of it all" (*Day Lewis*). **Companion** is referable only to a person who actually accompanies or attends one; a person who walks along the street with one or who sits with one at a restaurant table or in a Pullman section may be called a *companion* for the time being even if one has never seen him before and never sees him afterwards. However, the word often implies more habitual association and closer personal relationship than *associate;* as, his wife was his lifelong *companion*. "He no longer stood alone; the *companions* of his youth had become in the full sense his coadjutors" (*Buchan*). "He was her darling brother, her beloved *companion* in adventure" (*R. Macaulay*). Sometimes the association is not the result of friendship or of relationship but of a business arrangement; as, the old lady sought a competent paid *companion*. **Comrade** always implies association in a common calling or pursuit, and more or less familiarity in companionship; as, *comrades* in arms; school *comrades*. Commonly, however, it connotes more sentiment than either *associate* or *companion*, even though that sentiment is sometimes no more than a sense of shared fortunes or experiences, or a consciousness of having worked or played together. "Return to her . . . ? No, rather I abjure all roofs, and choose . . . To be a *comrade* with the wolf and owl" (*Shak.*). "Which weep the *comrade* of my choice . . . The human-hearted man I loved" (*Tennyson*). The word is also used as a term of address for a member of one's party or faction by communists and others. **Crony** was originally a term of university and school slang in England for one's most intimate friend and companion. It is now seldom used of a young person, though often applied to an older person who was one's intimate friend in school days or with whom one has been on intimate terms for a very long time; as, an old *crony* of his turned up after a long absence from England; the two old ladies are great *cronies*. **Chum** (regarded as colloquial) and **pal** (regarded as slang) are applied to one's most intimate friend or associate who is also one's close companion or comrade. *Chum*, which is a contraction of *chamber fellow*, was originally applied to one's roommate at school or college; although that implication is no longer always carried by the word, *chum* usually suggests constant companionship and intimacy; as, they have been *chums* since boyhood. **Pal** often carries a suggestion of helpfulness or of partnership in work or recreation; as, one does not double-cross a *pal*. **Buddy,** originally a diminutive or pet name for *brother*, was used by American soldiers during the World War as a slang term for a soldier comrade or, loosely, for any fellow soldier, then by extension as a general slang term equivalent in meaning to *chum*. The last three terms (especially *chum* and *buddy*) are applied, in loose American slang usage, especially as terms of address, to casual acquaintances or even strangers; as, a man passing by called to him "Look out, *buddy*."

Ana. *Partner, colleague, ally, confederate: accomplice, abettor, accessory (see CONFEDERATE): *assistant, helper, coadjutor, aide.

Con. Antagonist, adversary, *opponent: *enemy, foe: rival, competitor (see corresponding verbs at RIVAL).

association. Association, society, club, order are comprehensive terms which agree in denoting a body of persons who unite in the pursuit of a common aim or object. **Association** is in general used of an organization which is inclusive in its membership, excluding only those whose personal affiliations, interests, and needs are different from those of the typical member, or, if the object of the organization is service of some sort, those who do not belong to the business, the industry, or the profession served; as, the Young Men's Christian *Association;* the Modern Language *Association;* the National *Association* of Manufacturers. **Society** is often used interchangeably with *association*, but it tends to suggest a more restricted aim, a closer union of members, and their more active participation, and, sometimes, a narrower field of choice of membership; as, the Christian Endeavor *Society; Society* for the Prevention of Cruelty to Animals; a missionary *society;* a secret *society;* the Philological *Society; Society* for Ethical Culture. **Club** usually suggests such privacy that admission to membership is only through election and invitation; it often also implies quarters for the meeting and entertainment of members, and therefore is applied to the buildings or rooms as well as to the organization; as, going to the country *club* to play golf; Rotary *clubs;* a political *club;* a bridge *club;* most large cities have a university *club*. **Order** is now applied chiefly to a society whose members have common aims and accept common obligations, such as those of working together in brotherly union and of practicing certain virtues; as, a religious *order;* a fraternal *order*. In modern societies, *order* in the legal name usually, but not necessarily, suggests in addition a ritual, a uniform, and honorary distinctions; as, the Independent *Order* of Odd Fellows; the Benevolent and Protective *Order* of Elks.

assoil. Archaic form of *absolve*. For synonyms, see CONFESS, EXCULPATE.

assort. Assort, sort, classify, alphabetize, pigeonhole, agree in meaning to arrange in systematic order or according to some definite method of arrangement or distribution. **Assort** (see also *assorted* under MISCELLANEOUS) implies division into groups, as of like things or of things intended for the same purpose or destination; as, to *assort* the contents of an attic; to *assort* one's papers. When used in reference to homogeneous material, *assort* usually implies grading, as according to size, condition, value, or the like; as, to *assort* oranges for the market; to *assort* one's books before an auction. Often, additionally, it implies selection, either of that to be eliminated or of that to be chosen or preserved. "The company indeed was perfectly *assorted*, since all the members belonged to the little inner group of people who, during the long New York season, disported themselves together daily and nightly" (*E. Wharton*). **Sort** usually equals *assort*, but is often preferred to it when the latter would seem too literary or too technical; as, to *sort* mail; to *sort* stockings; to *sort* yarns. Frequently, especially with out, *sort* implies culling or selection even more than arrangement. "He *sorted* and *re-sorted* his cargo, always finding a more necessary article for which a less necessary had to be discarded" (*Cather*). **Classify** is more often used of things that fall into intellectual categories than of those which can be physically grouped. It usually implies a division into types, genera, species, or the like, and an arrangement for convenience in dealing with material that cannot be assembled or that is not before one; as, to *classify* bodies of water; to *classify* poems as epic, lyric, and dramatic; to *classify* languages according to the way in which words are formed. **Alphabetize** is used only of material which lends itself to arrangement according to the letters of the alphabet or to some filing scheme; thus, letters may be *alphabetized* under their writers' names; papers may be *alphabetized* by subject or topic; one must *assort* one's papers before *alphabetizing* them. **Pigeonhole** is a picturesque term suggesting an arrangement of small compartments as in a writing desk or of boxes in a post office, each compartment being a receptacle for one group of letters or papers that are sorted or classified. In extended use, the word implies the ability to put each of a number of things in its right class or category; thus, one who *pigeonholes* the wild flowers he meets on a day's walk assigns each to its proper classification or is able to give it its proper specific or generic name; one *pigeonholes* every bit of information that comes to him who files it away in his memory properly labeled and in its right place with relation to the rest of his knowledge.

Ana. Arrange, methodize, systematize, *order.

Con. *Mix, mingle, commingle: derange, disarrange, disorganize, *disorder.

assorted. *Miscellaneous, heterogeneous, motley, promiscuous.

Ana. Diverse, *different, various, disparate, divergent: selected, picked, chosen, preferred (see CHOOSE): mixed, mingled (see MIX).

Ant. Jumbled. — ***Con.*** Like, *similar, identical, uniform.

assortment. See corresponding adjective *assorted* at MISCELLANEOUS.

Ana. *Mixture, blend, compound: combining *or* combination, associating *or* association, uniting *or* union (see corresponding verbs at JOIN).

Ant. Jumble, hodgepodge.

assuage. Alleviate, *relieve, mitigate, lighten, allay.

Ana. Temper, *moderate, attemper: *comfort, solace, console: mollify, placate, appease, *pacify.

Ant. Exacerbate: intensify. — ***Con.*** Kindle, enkindle, inflame (see LIGHT, *v.*): aggravate, heighten (see INTENSIFY): *increase, augment.

assume. 1 *Take.

Ana. Accept, *receive: *arrogate, pre-empt, usurp: vest, invest, *clothe.

2 Assume, affect, pretend, simulate, feign, counterfeit, sham agree in meaning to put on false or deceptive appearances. **Assume** often implies a pardonable motive rather than an intent to deceive. "It sometimes happens that by *assuming* an air of cheerfulness we become cheerful in reality" (*Cowper*). To **affect** is to make a show of possessing or using, usually for effect, sometimes because of one's liking for it; as, to *affect* plainness of speech. "To *affect* a gesture, an opinion, a phrase, because it is the rage with a large number of persons" (*Hazlitt*). "Jones had really that taste for humour which others *affect*" (*Fielding*). **Pretend** implies overt profession of what is false; as, "that *pretended* liking called politeness" (*L. P. Smith*); to *pretend* to be insane. To **simulate** is to assume the appearance or characteristics of something else by imitating its signs; as, to *simulate* insanity. **Feign** implies more invention than *pretend*, less specific imitation of life than *simulate;* as, to *feign* madness (by a fictitious representation). "I grow angry and I curse them, and they *feign* penitence, but behind my back I know they call me a toothless old ape" (*Kipling*). But *feign* and *simulate* are often interchangeable. **Counterfeit** implies the highest degree of verisimilitude of any of the words in this group. "Are you not mad indeed? or do you but *counterfeit?*" (*Shak.*). "There was never *counterfeit* of passion came so near the life of passion" (*Shak.*). **Sham** always implies feigning with an intent to deceive; it usually connotes deception so obvious that it fools only the gullible; as, to *sham* sickness; to *sham* sleeping. "'E's all 'ot sand an' ginger when alive, An' 'e's generally *shammin'* when 'e's dead" (*Kipling*).

Ana. Dissemble, *disguise, cloak, mask.

3 *Presuppose, postulate, presume, premise, posit.

Ana. *Conjecture, surmise: *grant, concede, allow: *assert, affirm, aver, predicate.

assumption. Presupposition, postulate, position, presumption, premise. See under PRESUPPOSE.

Ana. *Hypothesis, theory: *principle, fundamental, axiom, theorem: conjecture, surmise (see under CONJECTURE, *v.*).

assurance. 1 *Insurance.

2 Certitude, *certainty, conviction.

Ana. *Belief, faith, credence, credit: *trust, confidence, reliance, dependence: positiveness, sureness, cocksureness (see corresponding adjectives at SURE).

Ant. Mistrust: dubiousness. — ***Con.*** Doubt, *uncertainty, skepticism, suspicion: disbelief, *unbelief, incredulity.

3 Self-assurance, *confidence, self-confidence, self-possession, aplomb.

Ana. Sang-froid, composure, *equanimity: sureness, sanguineness (see corresponding adjectives at CONFIDENT): mettle, resolution, spirit, *courage, tenacity: effrontery, *temerity, nerve.

Ant. Diffidence: alarm. — ***Con.*** Timorousness, timidity (see corresponding adjectives at TIMID): shyness, bashfulness, modesty (see corresponding adjectives at SHY).

assure. Insure, *ensure, secure.

Ant. Alarm. — ***Con.*** *Frighten, scare, fright, terrify: abash, discomfit, *embarrass: *intimidate, cow.

assured. *Confident, sanguine, sure.

Ana. Fearless, unapprehensive, unafraid (see affirmative adjectives at FEARFUL): *cool, composed, unruffled, imperturbable, collected: *reliant, self-reliant.

Ant. Abashed: timorous. — ***Con.*** Discomfited, embarrassed, rattled, disconcerted (see EMBARRASS): *fearful, apprehensive, afraid: hesitant, reluctant (see DISINCLINED).

astern. *Abaft, aft.

Ana. After, hind, rear, back (see POSTERIOR).

Ant. Ahead. — ***Con.*** *Before, afore, forward.

astonish. *Surprise, astound, amaze, flabbergast.

Ana. Nonplus, dumfound, bewilder, confound (see PUZZLE): impress, strike, touch, *affect.

astound. *Surprise, astonish, amaze, flabbergast.

Ana. Dumfound, confound, nonplus, bewilder (see PUZZLE): startle, affright, alarm, terrify (see FRIGHTEN).

astral. *Starry, stellar, sidereal.

astray. *Amiss.

astringent, *adj.* **Astringent, constringent, styptic** come into comparison when they mean having the quality of contracting or shrinking organic tissue or matter. **Astringent,** the most inclusive term, is applicable to any of several agents used in the treatment of mucous membranes and other surfaces to dry up secretions, arrest discharges, contract the ends of blood vessels, or, in cosmetics, to tighten the pores; as, tannin is an *astringent* substance used in medicine; an *astringent* lotion. **Constringent** occurs infrequently in comparison with *astringent;* it usually suggests a stiffening effect rather than a drying up; thus, timothy is said to have a *constringent* property which keeps horses from becoming flabby; the *constringent* effect of severe cold. **Styptic** was once frequently, but is now seldom, used as an equivalent of *astringent;* it is now commonly restricted in its application to an astringent agent used in arresting bleeding; as, to apply a *styptic* colloid to a cut; a *styptic* pencil (a stick of some styptic substance used in treating small cuts, such as those made in shaving).

astute. *Shrewd, perspicacious, sagacious.

Ana. *Sharp, keen, acute: discreet, prudent, foresighted (see under PRUDENCE): knowing, *intelligent, clever, smart: wily, crafty, cunning, *sly.

Ant. Gullible. — ***Con.*** Ingenuous, naïve, simple, unsophisticated (see NATURAL): candid, open, plain, *frank: forthright, *straightforward, aboveboard.

asylum. *Shelter, refuge, retreat, sanctuary, ark, cover.

at. 1 **At, in, on** cause difficulty when used in phrases giving the place or locality of an action. When reference to the interior of any place is made prominent, **in** is used; when a place is regarded as a mere local point, **at** is more commonly employed; when the direction is indicated, **on** is sometimes used in place of *at;* as, to look for a book *in* the library; to meet a friend *at* the library; sit *on* my right; the town lies *on* the east coast. "He appointed regular meetings of the States of England twice a year *in* London" (*Hume*); "An English king was crowned *at* Paris" (*Macaulay*). *In* is commonly employed before the names of countries or districts and *at* before names of institutions, public offices, business houses, etc.; as, *in* America; *in* the South; Milton was educated *at* Christ's College; *at* the customhouse; *at* the jeweler's. With names of towns and cities the use of *in* or *at* is usually determined according as the place designated is regarded respectively (1) as an including area or scene, especially with an implication of destination or permanence of occupancy, or of having familiar associations for the speaker, or (2) merely as a point, as along a journey or course, on a map or plan, or at a remove from the speaker; as, on our way to visit *in* Troy we lunched *at* Albany; after a stopover *at* Chicago, we arrived *in* Sioux Falls on Friday; a man born here *in* Zenith is consul *at* Hong Kong. In giving a town address we say *at* 141 Wood Street, *in* Springfield. In giving the street without the number, *in* is preferred in Great Britain, *on* in the United States; as, he lives *in* (or *on*) Riverside Avenue.
2 **At, in, on** are clearly distinguishable when used to introduce a phrase giving the time of an action. When reference is to time by the clock, or to a point of time registered by a clock, **at** is commonly used; as, *at* two o'clock; promptly *at* the hour appointed; *at* three minutes to six. When the reference is not to a point but to a period in the course of which an action occurs, **in** is the correct preposition; as, at two o'clock *in* the afternoon; September 1st *in* the year 1939; *in* the month of May. When the reference is to a particular day in the course of which something occurs, **on** is used; as, *on* July fourth there will be a celebration; it happened *on* a Sunday. *On* is sometimes used also with reference to a point of time with which there is, or should be, coincidence; as, be here *on* the hour; he is always *on* the dot.

atavism. *Reversion, throwback.

atavistic. Reversionary, reversive. See under REVERSION.

atheist. **Atheist, agnostic, deist, freethinker, unbeliever, infidel** designate a person who rejects some or all of the essential doctrines of religion, such as the existence of God. An **atheist** is one who denies the existence of God; an **agnostic** (see also under SKEPTIC) is one who withholds belief (though he does not deny the possible existence of a supreme being) because he does not know and is unwilling to accept as proof the evidence of revelation and spiritual experience; a **deist**, in the historical sense, is one who rejects the conception of a supreme being as ruler and guide of men and the universe, but still believes in a god who is the creator and the final judge of men. Since deism was tantamount to a denial of revelation and supernaturalism, *deist* has often been used as though it were the equivalent of *atheist.* The other terms are words whose application depends on the point of view of the person using them; usually, they imply reproach. **Freethinker** suggests loss of faith and the rejection of any or all of the tenets of revealed religion in favor of what seems rational or credible. **Unbeliever** is more negative than *freethinker,* because it carries no implication of a substitute for faith. **Infidel**, once a highly contumelious term, is now rarely used with such value except in historical narratives. Rather, it tends to become a designation applied by Christians to an adherent of any of the great world religions (especially Mohammedanism) that do not accept the Christian (and usually, the Jewish) conception of God, and thereby to be distinguishable from *heathen* and *pagan.* In Roman Catholic canon law, it is a very inclusive term designating any unbaptized person and covering such extremes as a heathen and an unbaptized Protestant. From the Mohammedan point of view, especially as presented in English fiction and poetry, *infidel* often means a Christian.
Ant. Theist.

athirst. Avid, *eager, keen, anxious, a-tiptoe, agog.
Ana. Thirsting, hungering, pining, yearning, longing (see LONG, *v.*): craving, coveting *or* covetous, desiring *or* desirous (see corresponding verbs at DESIRE).
Con. *Indifferent, unconcerned, incurious, aloof: *languid, lackadaisical, listless: apathetic, *impassive.

athlete. **Athlete, gymnast** agree in denoting a person skilled in the performance of physical exercises requiring agility, powers of endurance, and, often, muscular strength. **Athlete** also implies the status of a contender in games or in sports involving a contest, whether outdoor or indoor; thus, college *athletes* are the students who participate in college football, baseball, basketball, and other games, or who belong to the track team. A **gymnast** is one who is skilled, whether as participator or as teacher, in gymnastics; that is, bodily exercises, which may or may not involve competition, performed in a gymnasium, often with the aid of apparatus, for the development of nimbleness, strength, and control in the use of the body. "Leaping back a yard . . . with the speed and security of a trained *gymnast*" (*Stevenson*).

athletic. *Muscular, husky, sinewy, brawny, burly.
Ana. *Strong, stalwart, sturdy: lusty, *vigorous, strenuous, energetic.
Con. Frail, fragile, *weak.

athletics. **Athletics, sports, games** agree in denoting physical activities engaged in as for exercise or play. **Athletics** is a collective term (not used in the singular) for exercises for the performance of which one acquires and maintains agility, skill, stamina, etc., by regular and systematic training and practice, usually with the aim of competing, singly or as a member of a team, with others similarly trained, whether for pleasure, to keep the body in trim, to win honor for oneself, one's team, college, club, etc., or to earn a livelihood; as, college football, basketball, hockey, baseball, rowing, and tennis, and professional baseball, hockey, football, and tennis, are forms of *athletics.* **Sports** are forms of physical activity, usually outdoor, that afford pleasure or diversion. The term may be used in the singular for any of the various forms of athletics, inasmuch as, whatever the main purpose of athletic activity may be, a certain amount of pleasure is usually derived; as, football, basketball, hockey, baseball, rowing, and tennis are perhaps the most popular *sports* with those who go out for *athletics* in college; major-league baseball is a professional *sport.* The idea of training to develop agility, skill, stamina, etc., prominent in *athletics,* is frequently wanting in *sports,* which may involve so little exertion (as fishing) or be engaged in for so short a period or so infrequently as not to require it; thus, an impromptu baseball game between two pick-up teams falls under the head of *sport,* but hardly of *athletics.* So also the idea of competition, usually present in *athletics,* is frequently wanting in *sports;* as, noncompetitive skating, skiing, canoeing, and swimming are *sports.* The term is wider than *athletics,* including such activities as hunting and fishing (in which the pleasure derives from pursuit of quarry). Since sports contests are often an object of interest to others, the term *sports* is also applied to contests which provide amusement or diversion for spectators as well as, or rather than, contestants; hence, horse racing, dog racing, bull fighting, cock fighting, and bear baiting are *sports*. "We . . . have every source of amusement open to us, and yet follow these cruel *sports*" (*W. Windham*). **Games** (as here compared: for singular see FUN) are athletic or sports contests, usually those which are of a somewhat artificial nature and therefore require more extensive rules than such contests as rowing, boxing, wrestling, and skiing. Thus, practically all forms of competition that center around a ball or similar object are called *games*, as baseball, football, hockey, golf, tennis, and polo. Although the plural *games* is sometimes applied collectively in titles to a competition (now usually called *meet*) consisting chiefly or only of track-and-field events (as, Olympic *games*, Nemean *games*), the singular *game* is applied to none or few of the individual events of such a competition.

athwart. Crosswise, crossways, *across.

a-tiptoe. *Eager, avid, keen, agog, athirst, anxious.

Ana. Alert, *watchful, vigilant: ready, *quick, prompt: tense, taut (see TIGHT).

Con. Nonchalant, *cool, composed: *calm, tranquil, serene.

atmosphere. 1 *Air, ether, ozone.

2 Atmosphere, feeling, feel, savor (*or* **savour**), **tone, aura** come into comparison when they denote an intangible and, usually, unanalyzable quality or aggregate of qualities which gives something an individual and distinctly recognizable character. **Atmosphere** is used chiefly in reference to places, to groups of persons, or to periods of time that have a definite identity. It frequently denotes a character that accrues to something or that pervades it as a whole and determines the impression it produces on those who come within the range of its influence; thus, a place that has no *atmosphere* is by implication a place that leaves no clear impression of its difference from other places of the same type or kind; a poet who re-creates the *atmosphere* of the Middle Ages is one who by implication gives a true and vivid impression of the life of that time. But *atmosphere* may also denote an environment (regarded as a sum total of physical, social, intellectual, and spiritual conditions) that not only produces a distinct impression but exerts a definite influence on the state of mind, habits of work, views, and the like, of those who are encompassed by it. "Genius can only breathe freely in an *atmosphere* of freedom" (*J. S. Mill*). "Any judge who has sat with juries knows that . . . they are extremely likely to be impregnated by the environing *atmosphere*" (*Justice Holmes*). **Feeling,** as here compared (see also FEELING, SENSATION), may refer either to the character one ascribes to something when one has a clear and unified impression of its distinctive qualities or atmosphere, or to the aesthetic effect of a work of art which not only represents a thing but re-creates its atmosphere or conveys the impression the artist seeks to produce. "Most of those who have educated themselves in the technique of painting are city-bred, and can never have the *feeling* of the country, however fond they may be of it" (*Jefferies*). "They bring the notion of the thing described to the mind, they do not bring the *feeling* of it to the imagination" (*Arnold*). **Feel,** although it occurs in the works of good writers, is commonly regarded as colloquial or informal. It may be used interchangeably with *feeling* (as, to describe or paint a scene so that one gives another the *feel* of it), but it may also be substituted for *atmosphere*, especially when the quality of a thing is known through frequent experience or intimate knowledge. "The factory had a homely *feel*" (*D. H. Lawrence*). "The sensitive reader may discover in them, also, something of the quality and '*feel*' of Shakespeare's own poetry" (*Day Lewis*). **Savor** differs from *feel* not only in being a more literary or a less homely word, but in connoting an epicurean enjoyment of that which has an atmosphere or of the sensations it evokes. "A healthy craving for the sap and *savour* of a more personal, national art" (*Binyon*). "Carrying on his life at Hilbury as if nothing had happened to change all the *savour* of it" (*Arch. Marshall*). "The exactness which Miss Lowell loved is nowhere more remarkable than in her sense of the *savour* and '*feel*' of words" (*Lowes*). "It is in moments like this of waiting and hushed suspense that one tastes most fully the *savour* of life" (*L. P. Smith*). **Tone** is a character associated with the thing itself as its inner spirit, its tenor, its prevailing quality, rather than with the impression it produces or the influence it exerts; thus, one may praise a community for its high moral *tone* yet find its *atmosphere* somewhat depressing. Nevertheless, a *tone* is thought of as a character that may be imparted or acquired and, therefore, as one capable of exerting an influence. "She was rather afraid of the self-possession of the Morels, father and all. [but] She took their *tone* . . . . It was a cool, clear atmosphere, where everyone was himself" (*D. H. Lawrence*). "A furious attack [on Poe] by Rufus W. Griswold . . . set the *tone* of native criticism for years" (*Mencken*). **Aura** (etymologically, a breeze) is a highly poetic word used chiefly in reference to persons who seem to be enveloped by an ethereal spirit which is an emanation of their inner life or of their secret thoughts; by extension, it is also used of things that are invested with a mysterious quality or character; as, in their company, he was always conscious of an *aura* of disapproval. "There was about her the *aura*, the glow, the roseate exhalation that surrounds the woman in love" (*E. Ferber*). "Throughout the Middle Ages the Taunus and the Harz had about them an *aura* of the uncanny as the last haunt of the primeval gods" (*Buchan*).

Ana. *Quality, character, property: peculiarity, individuality, characteristic (see corresponding adjectives at CHARACTERISTIC): *impression, impress.

atom. 1 *Particle, molecule, corpuscle.

2 *Particle, bit, mite, smitch, smidgen, jot, tittle, iota, whit.

Ana. Smack, spice, dash, suspicion, soupçon, *touch, suggestion, tincture, tinge, shade.

at once. *Directly, immediately, instantly, forthwith, straightway, right away, anon, instantaneously.

atone, atone for. *Expiate.

Ana. Compensate (*for*), *pay (*for*): propitiate, conciliate, appease (see PACIFY).

atonement. Expiation (see under EXPIATE).

Ana. Compensating *or* compensation, offsetting (see corresponding verbs at COMPENSATE): conciliation, propitiation, appeasement (see corresponding verbs at PACIFY): *reparation, amends.

atrabilious, atrabiliar. Hypochondriac, *melancholic, melancholy.

Ana. Morose, glum, saturnine, crabbed, *sullen: *despondent, hopeless, forlorn: depressed, dejected, gloomy (see corresponding nouns at SADNESS).

Ant. Blithe. — *Con.* *Merry, jocund, jovial, jolly: *glad, happy, cheerful, lighthearted, joyful, joyous.

atrocious. Heinous, monstrous, *outrageous.

Ana. *Flagrant, gross, rank, glaring: nefarious, flagitious, infamous, iniquitous, *vicious: barbarous, savage, barbaric, *barbarian.

Ant. Humane: noble (see MORAL). — *Con.* Righteous, virtuous (see MORAL): *gentle, genteel.

atrophy, *v.* *Stunt, stultify.
Ant. Vitalize.

attach. 1 *Arrest, apprehend, detain.
Ana. Seize, *take, grab: capture, *catch, nab, cop.
Con. Release, discharge, deliver, *free.
2 *Fasten, affix, fix.
Ana. *Join, link, unite, connect: annex, *add, append: *tie, bind.
Ant. Detach. — *Con.* Disengage (see DETACH): disencumber, disentangle, disembarrass (see EXTRICATE): sever, sunder, divorce, part, *separate.

attachment. 1 Arrest, apprehension, detention. See under ARREST, *v.*
2 **Attachment, affection, love** denote the feeling which animates a person who is genuinely fond of someone or something. **Attachment** and **affection** differ in that *affection* usually has for its object a sentient being, whereas that of *attachment* may be even an inanimate thing; as, an *attachment* to one's profession, to a house in which one has lived. *Attachment* implies strong liking, devotion, or loyalty; *affection,* rather warmth and tenderness of sentiment. "A profound *attachment* to the King as king" (*Belloc*). "It cannot show lack of *attachment* to the principles of the Constitution that she thinks it can be improved" (*Justice Holmes*). "Between him [Horace] and Augustus there was a strong *affection*" (*Buchan*). *Affection* and **love** differ in that *affection* implies a feeling more settled and regulated, less intense or ardent, than *love,* which alone of the three may connote passion. Thus to one's friends any one of the three terms may be applicable; to the members of one's own family, *love* or *affection,* but usually not *attachment;* to God, *love* (in the sense of reverent devotion), but not *affection* or *attachment;* to one's country, *love,* especially if ardent patriotism is implied, *affection,* if the emphasis is upon genuine but not blind devotion, *attachment,* if allegiance and loyalty are definitely connoted.
Ana. Fondness, devotedness (see corresponding adjectives at LOVING): devotion, piety, fealty, *fidelity, allegiance.
Ant. Aversion. — *Con.* *Antipathy: estrangement, alienation, disaffection (see corresponding verbs at ESTRANGE).

attack, *v.* **Attack, assail, assault, bombard, storm** come into comparison not only in their military but also in their extended senses. All carry as their basic meaning to make a more or less violent onset upon. **Attack,** which is etymologically related to *attach,* originally connoted a fastening upon something, as a beast of prey fastens upon its victim. It now implies aggression or aggressiveness in all its senses and usually the initiative in entering into an engagement or struggle, as with a person or thing that is opposed or that one intends to conquer; as, to plan to *attack* the enemy at dawn; to *attack* the position of one's opponents in a debate; to *attack* a problem in engineering. "They lack the courage to *attack* their other studies with the vigor requisite to success" (*Grandgent*). "It had become increasingly apparent that the logical method of eradicating disease was to *attack* it at its source" (*V. Heiser*). **Assail** etymologically connotes a jumping upon, but in modern use it suggests the action of one who would conquer by force of repeated blows rather than by brute strength. Its chief distinction from *attack* is in this suggestion of repetition of blows, strokes, shots, thrusts, or other means of breaking down resistance; as, to *assail* an enemy with shells; to *assail* with reproaches; *assailed* by temptations. "Property interests . . . *assailed* by attempts to put industry upon a more reasonable and more equitable footing" (*J. A. Hobson*). "Old pains keep on gnawing at your heart, old desires . . . old dreams, *assailing* you" (*Conrad*). **Assault,** which also etymologically connotes a jumping upon, now always implies close contact or a direct confrontation; in contrast with *assail,* it suggests the use of brute strength and an attempt to overpower by suddenness and violence of onslaught; as, to *assault* a person with a club; to *assault* a stronghold on all sides. "My ending is despair, Unless I be relieved by prayer, Which pierces so that it *assaults* Mercy itself" (*Shak.*). "A universal hubbub wild Of stunning sounds . . . *assaults* his ear" (*Milton*). **Bombard** literally means to assail (as a town, a fortress, an army) continuously and devastatingly with bombs or shells; as, the advancing German army in 1914 expected to *bombard* Paris and bring a quick end to the war. In extended use, it is, in its stronger implication of importunity or of continuous pestering, distinguishable from *assail;* as, "He [Octavius] *bombarded* Cicero with letters asking for advice" (*Buchan*); the reporters *bombarded* the district attorney with questions. **Storm,** as here considered, means to assault with the violence, rush, and effectiveness of a sudden and devastating storm or wind; in literal and extended use it connotes an attempt to sweep from its path every obstacle to a victory. "Several of their bravest officers were shot down in the act of *storming* the fortress" (*Irving*). "Who think to *storm* the world by dint of merit" (*Burns*).
Ana. Fight, *contend, battle, war, cope: beset, overrun (see INFEST): *surprise, waylay, ambush.
Con. *Defend, shield, guard, protect: resist, withstand, *oppose, combat.

attack, *n.* 1 **Attack, assault, onslaught, onset** come into comparison when they denote an attempt made on another or on others to injure, destroy, defame, or the like. An **attack** (for military and allied senses see ATTACK, *v.*) may be upon the person or it may be upon the character, the reputation, the writings, or the like, of a person or persons; it often suggests animosity or definite enmity as its cause, but it may imply motives as various as wanton cruelty, partisan feeling, or a critical intention; as, the victim of a cowardly *attack* by ruffians; the speech was a severe *attack* upon the policies of the administration; the book was the object of *attacks* from all sides; an unprovoked *attack* upon the fairness of the court. **Assault,** in general use, implies more violence, more malice or viciousness, and often the infliction of greater damage or less reparable damage than *attack.* However, an *assault* upon the person is legally an apparently violent attempt, or a willful offer with force or violence, to injure or hurt that person physically. When the hurt has been inflicted the precise legal term for the act is *assault and battery.* Rape is sometimes specifically called an *assault,* but this usage of *assault* is chiefly euphemistic. In military language an *assault* is sometimes distinguished from an *attack* upon the enemy, the former term being applied only to the last phase of an *attack,* or offensive movement, when the aggressors close upon their opponents and the issue is determined. In general use, however, *assault* and *attack* are not clearly distinguishable except in emphasis; thus, an *assault* upon a person's character suggests violent emotion, such as hatred or vindictiveness; an *attack* upon a person's character may or may not imply strong feeling as its motive. "The two men [Matthew Arnold and F. H. Bradley] fought . . . in spite of Bradley's *assault* upon Arnold, for the same causes" (*T. S. Eliot*). "The passage . . . shows how alarmed a Hegelian may be by an *assault* upon the authority of science" (*Inge*). **Onslaught** suggests a vigorous and destructive method of attack; it usually implies an attempt to overwhelm as by force of momentum or of numbers or by the fury of the assault; as, the defenders, taken by surprise, were unable to repel the *onslaught;* no play can withstand such an *onslaught* from the critics. "He sees I am no man to take rebuff . . . . Quick to the *onslaught,* out sword, cut and thrust!" (*Browning*). **Onset** is applicable not only to the first furious rush that initiates an attack (an offensive movement, an act of aggression, a fit of illness, or the like), but to any such succeeding rush that marks a renewal of vigor in the attack; as, at the *onset,* the twelfth regiment bore the brunt of the attack; a pause in the fighting gave the officers time to rally their scattered troops and to prepare for a fresh *onset* from the enemy. "At every *onset* of the gale convulsive sounds came from the branches" (*Hardy*).

Ana. Push, action, *battle: striking, hitting, smiting, slugging (see STRIKE): *criticism, condemnation, denouncing *or* denunciation (see corresponding verbs at CRITICIZE).

Con. Defending *or* defense, vindication, justification (see corresponding verbs at MAINTAIN): resistance, opposition (see corresponding verbs at OPPOSE).

2 Attack, aggression, offense (*or* **offence**), **offensive** and their corresponding adjectives **attacking, aggressive, offensive** come into comparison when they denote or describe action in a struggle for supremacy which must be met with defense or by means of defenses. The terms are used not only of military operations but of competitive games, exhibitions of skill, as in fencing and swordplay, and the like. **Attack** always implies the initiation of action; commonly, also, it suggests an attempt to catch the enemy or opposition off guard and therefore connotes suddenness, and often violence, of onset. "The first raiding *attack* was . . . repulsed with heavy losses" (*H. G. Wells*). **Aggression,** which also commonly implies initiation of hostile action, stresses rather a lack of provocation and a desire for conquest or domination. *Attack* is applicable to any movement or action in a series of operations, *aggression* is applied chiefly to a war or to a type of fighting that involves invasion or encroachment on another's territory; it usually further connotes a determination to maintain the advantage of the attacking side; as, pledged never to fight in a war of *aggression.* "The business of government is to check *aggression* only" (*Adam Smith*). "An *aggressive* war, as distinguished from mere plundering inroads" (*Freeman*). **Offense** and (in the sense here considered) the more common **offensive** characterize the position or the methods of the attacking side. The noun is interchangeable with *attack* only when the latter word does not refer to a concrete action; as, methods of *attack* (or *offense*) and of defense; weapons of *offense,* or *offensive* weapons; a war of *offense* (not *attack*); to be ready for an *attack* (not an *offense*). Both words are distinguishable from *aggression* and *aggressive,* which in many ways they closely resemble, by their absence of suggestion of any motive or aim other than that of a desire for supremacy; thus, an *aggressively* fought battle is one in which each side struggles to maintain the upper hand. **Offensive,** as a noun, is commonly a substantive use of the adjective; thus, to take the *offensive* is to carry on *offensive* operations; to maintain the *offensive* is to succeed in holding an *offensive* position. Sometimes, however, it closely approaches *attack* in meaning; as, the *offensive* began at 10 a.m.

3 *Fit, access, accession, paroxysm, spasm, convulsion.

attacking, *adj.* Aggressive, offensive. See under ATTACK, *n.*

attain. *Reach, compass, gain, achieve.

Ana. *Come (to), arrive (at): win, acquire, secure, obtain, *get: accomplish, effect (see PERFORM).

attainment. Accomplishment, *acquirement, acquisition.

attaint, *v.* **1** Proscribe, condemn, *sentence, damn, doom.

Ana. *Banish, exile, transport: execute, dispatch, *kill, slay.

2 Taint, pollute, defile, *contaminate.

attemper. Temper, *moderate, qualify.

Ana. *Palliate, extenuate: mitigate, alleviate, lighten, assuage, *relieve.

Ant. Intensify. — *Con.* Heighten, aggravate, enhance (see INTENSIFY): augment, *increase.

attempt, *v.* **Attempt, try, endeavor** (*or* **endeavour**), **essay, assay, strive, struggle** are here compared as verbs meaning to make an effort to do something that may or may not be successful and as nouns (the single exception in form being **striving**) meaning the effort made to accomplish such an end. **Attempt,** in precise use, always implies an actual beginning of, or venturing upon, that which one hopes to accomplish or carry through; it often, but not invariably, suggests failure; as, to form a plan and yet make no *attempt* to execute it; the troops were driven back when they *attempted* to break through the enemy's line; after many *attempts* to construct a flying machine, the Wright brothers succeeded; nothing *attempted,* nothing gained. In several idiomatic expressions *attempt* also implies the end in view; thus, to *attempt* the king's life is to make an effort to assassinate him; to make an *attempt* on a fortress is to attack it; to *attempt* a person (now archaic) is to make an effort to tempt, seduce, move, or bribe that person. "It made the laughter of an afternoon That Vivien should *attempt* the blameless king" (*Tennyson*). **Try** is often thought of as a simpler and more colloquial word than *attempt;* in discriminating use, however, the two terms are distinguishable by subtle differences in meaning. *Try,* in such use, seldom loses the implication found in nearly all of its leading senses: that of effort or experiment directed toward the end of ascertaining a fact or of testing or proving a thing. This implication is especially apparent in some idiomatic phrases such as: to *try* a window (that is, to attempt to open it so as to find out if it is fastened); to *try* one's hand at something (that is, to attempt to do something new to test one's ability or aptitude); to *try* one's luck with the horses (that is, to bet on horse races in the hope of proving one's luck). In freer use, *try* often carries the same implication but not quite so obviously; nevertheless, it is the preferable word when effort or experiment or testing are stressed rather than a venturing upon or undertaking; as, to *try* to find which of two methods is the better; to make a *try* at solving the problem; to succeed at the first *try.* "Freedom in thought, the liberty to *try* and err, the right to be his own man" (*Mencken*). **Endeavor** heightens the implication of exertion and should be avoided as too strong when likelihood of success is implied; as, I shall *try* (better than *endeavor*) to make time for a game of tennis tomorrow; "she walked up and down the room *endeavouring* to compose herself" (*Austen*); "the Good, which is the goal of all moral *endeavour*" (*Inge*); "In Arnold's phrases the first step for every aspirant to culture is to *endeavor* to see things as they are, or 'to learn, in short, the will of God'" (*C. W. Eliot*). "We all *endeavour,* as Spinoza says, to persist in our own being; and that *endeavour* is, he adds, the very essence of our existence" (*L. P. Smith*). **Essay** and the now less common **assay** both imply that the thing to be accomplished is especially difficult; otherwise they combine the foremost implications of *attempt* (that is, making a beginning) by suggesting a tentative effort, and of *try* (that is, experiment) by suggesting the testing of a thing's feasibility. "Sculpture which attempted to unite repose and action, the 'far off' and the familiar, in a way which Phidias and Donatello were too prudent to *essay*" (*Brownell*). "Till I have brought him to his wits again, Or lose my labour in *assaying* it" (*Shak.*). "[Literary] conventions frequently take their rise . . . from the faulty *essays* of an early and as yet undeveloped technique" (*Lowes*). The last terms of this group, **strive** and **struggle,** not only carry heightened implications of difficulty and of correspondingly greater exertion, but also connote greater opposition to be overcome. *Strive* and *striving* suggest persistent endeavor to surmount obstacles created by one's weaknesses, one's lack of experience, the height of one's ambitions, the power of resisting forces, or the like; as, to *strive* to overcome a bad habit; a *striving* to reach the top of one's class; "*Strive*, my son, when you represent the People, to provide for their education" (*Meredith*); "sick of self and tired of vainly *striving*" (*W. James*); "the bitter, desperate *striving* unto death of the oppressed race" (*R. Macaulay*). **Struggle** literally and figuratively implies straining or stretching that suggests a tussle, a wrestling, or an effort to extricate oneself from that which impedes or fetters one; as, to *struggle* to free oneself from attackers; a *struggle* to reach the shore. So strong at times is this implication that the word loses or nearly loses its implication of endeavor; as, "He clambered over half-visible rocks, fell over prostrate trees, sank into deep holes and *struggled* out" (*Cather*); "The *struggle* between two strong-willed women to control one weak-willed man is the usual motive of the French drama in the nineteenth century" (*H. Adams*).

Ana. *Begin, commence, start, initiate, inaugurate.

Ant. Succeed. — *Con.* Accomplish, achieve, effect, fulfill, execute, *perform: attain, compass, *reach, gain.

attempt, *n.* Endeavor, essay, assay, try, striving, struggle. See under ATTEMPT, *v.*

Ana. Experiment (see EXPERIENCE): trial, test (see under PROVE): beginning, commencement, starting *or* start, initiation (see corresponding verbs at BEGIN).

attend. 1 Listen, list, hearken, hark, *hear.

Con. Ignore, disregard, *neglect, slight.

2 *Tend, mind, watch.

Ana. *Nurse, foster, nurture, cherish: supervise, oversee (see corresponding nouns at OVERSIGHT).

3 Escort, *accompany, chaperon, convoy.

attention. 1 **Attention, study, concentration, application** come into comparison when they mean the direct focusing of the mind on something, especially on something to be learned, worked out, accomplished, or the like. **Attention** is applicable to the faculty or power as well as to the act; as, to fix one's *attention* on something; noises that distract one's *attention;* this requires *attention;* "if we had to think about breathing or digesting . . . we should have no *attention* to spare for anything else" (*Shaw*); "every awareness is the simple form of *attention*" (*S. Alexander*). Since the word does not carry any implications descriptive of the quality or nature of the power or the act or of the length of the latter's duration, it usually requires qualifying words or phrases; as, close *attention;* trained habits of *attention;* a few moments' *attention.* **Study,** on the other hand, stresses continuity and closeness of attention; it usually also implies an aim such as the acquisition of knowledge, or the analysis of something that is complex or confusing, or the working out of a plan, as for action, or of a design, as for a book; as, the president said that he would not comment upon the proposal until he had given it further *study.* "Of making many books there is no end; and much *study* is a weariness of the flesh" (*Ecclesiastes* xii. 12). **Concentration** emphasizes the centering of the attention on one thing to the exclusion of everything else; as, amazing powers of *concentration.* "The learning to read poetry takes as much patience and *concentration* as the learning to write it" (*Day Lewis*). **Application** usually suggests persistence in fixing one's attention, and diligence and assiduity in the performance of all that is required; it suggests therefore a virtue won by effort and sheer force of will rather than, as *concentration*, a power that has its origin in one's temperament or is the result of profound interest as much, if not more, than of directed effort or training. "*Application* for ever so short a time kills me" (*Lamb*). "Louise won the disfavor of . . . Mary and Harriet by her *application* to her studies in school" (*S. Anderson*).

Ana. Diligence, assiduity, sedulousness, industriousness (see corresponding adjectives at BUSY).

Ant. Inattention. — *Con.* Preoccupation, abstraction, absent-mindedness (see corresponding adjectives at ABSTRACTED).

2 *Courtesy, gallantry, amenity, comity.

Ana. Courting *or* court, wooing (see corresponding verbs at INVITE): deference, homage, *honor, reverence: solicitude (see CARE).

Con. Neglect, *negligence: indifference, aloofness, unconcernedness *or* unconcern (see corresponding adjectives at INDIFFERENT): rudeness, discourteousness *or* discourtesy, impoliteness (see corresponding adjectives at RUDE).

attentive. *Thoughtful, considerate.

Ana. Courteous, polite, gallant, chivalrous, *civil: solicitous, concerned (see under CARE, *n.*).

Ant. Inattentive: neglectful. — *Con.* *Indifferent, unconcerned, aloof: *negligent, remiss: heedless, thoughtless, *careless.

attenuate, *v.* *Thin, rarefy, dilute, extenuate.

Ana. *Weaken, sap: reduce, lessen (see DECREASE): dissipate (see SCATTER): *contract, shrink, constrict, deflate.

Ant. Enlarge: dilate: enrich. — *Con.* *Expand, amplify, swell, distend, inflate: *increase, augment.

attest. 1 Witness, *certify, vouch for.

Ana. Testify, depose, depone, affirm, *swear, asseverate: *confirm, corroborate, substantiate, verify.

Con. *Disprove, controvert, refute, confute: *deny, contradict, gainsay.

2 Argue, prove, bespeak, *indicate, betoken.

Ana. Demonstrate, test (see PROVE): *confirm, authenticate, substantiate.

Ant. Belie. — *Con.* *Misrepresent.

attire, *v.* *Clothe, apparel, array, tire, dress, robe, invest, vest.

Ana. Accouter, appoint, equip, outfit, arm (see FURNISH).

Ant. Divest. — *Con.* *Strip, bare, denude, dismantle.

attire, *n.* *Clothes, clothing, tire, apparel, raiment, dress, vesture, array.

attitude. 1 *Posture, pose.

Ana. Mien, *bearing, carriage, manner, port, presence, demeanor.

2 *Position, stand.

Ana. *Point of view, angle, slant, standpoint, viewpoint: bias, prepossession, prejudice, *predilection.

attitudinize. Posture, pose. See under POSTURE, *n.*

Ana. Affect, pretend, *assume, feign, simulate, counterfeit, sham.

attorney. 1 *Agent, deputy, proxy, factor.

Ana. *Substitute, supply, alternate.

2 *Lawyer, solicitor, proctor, procurator, counselor, barrister, counsel, advocate.

attract, *v.* **Attract, allure, charm, fascinate, bewitch, enchant, captivate, take** agree in meaning to draw another by exerting an irresistible or compelling influence over him. The same distinctions in implications and connotations are observable in the adjectival forms of these words, **attractive, alluring, charming, fascinating, bewitching, enchanting, captivating, taking. Attract** always implies a drawing of one thing to another either because of material or immaterial qualities or properties in the agent (such as magnetism) or because of an affinity in the one attracted for that which draws it or a susceptibility to its influence; as, a magnet *attracts* iron; positive electricity *attracts* negative; a store of honey *attracts* a bear; a stimulating new book *attracts* attention. "Milton, in whom there was so much to repel Goethe rather than to *attract* him" (*Arnold*). When used in reference to persons of different sexes, it commonly also suggests the arousing of strong admiration or the awakening of love or desire in the person attracted. "Talking, in that beautiful voice which made everything she said sound like a caress, to Papa, who had begun to be *attracted* rather against his will" (*V. Woolf*). **Allure** implies not only attraction but enticement by that which is fair, pleasing, seductive, or the like. It may, like *lure*, suggest enticement into evil or danger, but in modern use this is not as often connoted as in the past, though the implication of a siren's attraction is always conveyed. "Ancient fables of men *allured* by beautiful forms and melodious voices to destruction" (*Hudson*). More often the stress is on the overcoming of resistance or indifference by the use of winning methods, such as delicate flattery or the enhancement of one's charms, or by the bait of a pleasant prospect; as, an *alluring* advertisement of a summer resort; she did not naturally attract men, but she became accomplished in *alluring* them; the prospect of an interesting, vivid life *allures* many young women to the big cities. "Young children should rather be *allured* to learning by gentleness and love, than compelled to learning by beating and fear" (*Ascham*). **Charm** implies a power in the agent to cast a spell (literal or figurative) over the person or thing affected, thereby holding the latter under the agent's power or compelling him (or it) to do the agent's will. "Only his daughter had the power of *charming* this black brooding from his mind" (*Dickens*). In its commonest use, *charm* implies a power to evoke or attract admiration, but it usually heightens that implication by retaining the suggestion of casting a spell over the senses or, far more often, over the mind. "There was a grace about him which *charmed*, and a hint of latent power which impressed" (*Buchan*). "Cyril, having taken a fancy to his brilliant aunt [Sophia], had tried to *charm* her as he seldom or never tried to *charm* his mother. Cyril and Sophia had dazzled and conquered each other" (*Bennett*). **Fascinate,** like *charm*, implies the casting of a spell, but in precise or discriminating use, it usually suggests the ineffectiveness of resistance, or a person's enslavement or being at the mercy of one that fascinates. "Blandishments will not *fascinate* us, nor will threats of a 'halter' intimidate. For, under God, we are determined that . . . we will die free men" (*Jos. Quincy*). "Personality . . . so *fascinating* that . . . it would absorb my whole nature, my whole soul, my very art itself" (*Wilde*). **Bewitch** and **enchant** likewise imply the exertion of a magical influence; the former, in its literal sense, suggesting witchcraft, and the latter, sorcery (see MAGIC), but these implications are often either exceedingly weak or actually lost. *Bewitch*, in its commonest sense, implies the exertion of a power of fascination that causes another to succumb to one's charms or allurements and to be under one's thrall. *Enchant*, on the other hand, usually suggests a power to evoke joy or rapture or ecstatic admiration in the person fascinated; as, he is *enchanted* by the young lady's beauty; he is *bewitched* by her charms. "Heavens grant that Warwick's words *bewitch* him not!" (*Shak.*). "Sophia enjoyed the intimacy with Constance. As for Constance, she was *enchanted*" (*Bennett*). "There was in Mary [Queen of Scots] 'some *enchantment* whereby men are *bewitched*' " (*J. R. Green*). **Captivate** is the weakest of these words in its suggestion of an irresistible influence or attraction. It implies a capturing of the fancy or feelings, and a holding them in thrall for the time being, but it carries no suggestion of prolonged influence or of enslavement; as, the child *captivates* everyone with his sunny smile; "just the hero to *captivate* a romantic girl" (*Irving*). **Take,** which in early use was often employed in the sense of to charm by casting a spell over (as, "Then [Christmas Eve] no planets strike, No fairy *takes*, nor witch hath power to charm"—*Shak.*), now frequently occurs in the extended senses of *attract, fascinate*, and *captivate;* in fact, the word is sometimes preferred when the literal implications of these terms might obscure the meaning; as, he hadn't been particularly *taken* with the girl; "He stared at her from doorways . . . as she went about with her partners; and the more he stared, the more *taken* was he" (*Kipling*); he has a very *taking* smile.

Ana. *Invite, solicit, court: entice, *lure, tempt, seduce: *catch, capture.

Ant. Repel. — ***Con.*** *Offend, affront, outrage, insult.

attraction. Attraction, affinity, sympathy are comparable in their abstract senses when they denote the relationship between persons or things that are involuntarily or naturally drawn together and exert, to some degree, an influence over each other. **Attraction** implies the possession by one person or thing of a quality or qualities that have the power to pull another person or thing so that the latter moves toward the former or, in the case of things, is drawn into contact with it or cleaves to it. *Attraction*, however, also implies the existence in the thing attracted of susceptibility to the influence of that which attracts; in the case of persons it may be a natural inclination for, or a predisposition to, or an innate liking of, that which attracts; in the case of things, a tendency to unite or combine with it. This natural or constitutional susceptibility is called **affinity.** In very precise use, therefore, *affinity* is the complement of *attraction* and not its synonym; thus, *attraction* is the force whereby a magnet draws iron to it, but iron is one of the few metals that have an *affinity* for the magnet; chemistry has a powerful *attraction* for minds that have an *affinity* for it. "He [Marcus Aurelius] too yearns as they do for something unattained by him. What an *affinity* for Christianity had this persecutor of the Christians!" (*Arnold*). The words are interchangeable only when used of persons and things that are mutually attracted or have a reciprocal affinity for each other: even in these cases, however, the fundamental distinction in meaning prevails; as, two persons who have an *attraction* (or an *affinity*) for each other; atoms remain in combination in a substance because of their *affinity* (or *attraction*) for each other; it is not by chance that in physics, the science concerned with energy, *attraction* is the word used in reference to atomic cohesion, and that in chemistry, the science concerned with the composition of substances, *affinity* is the technical term. **Sympathy,** as here considered, stresses not so much the drawing together of persons or things (though that is usually inferable) as their reciprocal influence or their susceptibility to the same influences. When used in reference to things, it commonly implies interaction; as, the tides rise and fall in *sympathy* with the moon; there is close *sympathy* between the heart and the lungs. When used in reference to persons, *sympathy* usually connotes spiritual affinity, or compatibility in tastes, interests, aims, etc. "Union of hearts, not hands, does marriage make, And *sympathy* of mind keeps love awake" (*Aaron Hill*).

attractive. Alluring, charming, fascinating, bewitching, enchanting, captivating, taking. See under ATTRACT.
Ana. Lovely, fair, *beautiful, bonny, pretty, comely: luring, enticing, tempting, seductive (see corresponding verbs at LURE).
Ant. Repellent: forbidding. — *Con.* *Repugnant, abhorrent, distasteful, obnoxious: *offensive, repulsive, revolting, loathsome.

attribute, *v.* *Ascribe, impute, assign, credit, accredit, refer, charge.
Ana. *Fasten, attach, fix: predicate (see ASSERT): blame (see CRITICIZE): *accuse, charge.

attribute, *n.* **1** *Quality, property, character, accident.
2 Emblem, *symbol, type.
Ana. *Sign, mark, token, badge, note: *character, symbol, sign.

attrition. **1** Contrition, repentance, *penitence, remorse, compunction.
Ana. Regret, *sorrow, grief, anguish.
2 Abrasion, *erosion, corrosion.
Ana. Disintegration, crumbling, decomposition (see corresponding verbs at DECAY).
Ant. Accretion.

attune. Tune, *harmonize.
Ana. Adapt, adjust, accommodate, reconcile, conform: accord, *agree, harmonize: attemper, temper (see MODERATE): balance, counterbalance, *compensate.
Con. Alienate, *estrange, wean.

atypic *or* **atypical.** *Abnormal, aberrant.
Ana. *Irregular, anomalous, unnatural: divergent, *different: deviating, departing (see SWERVE, *v.*): *exceptional.
Ant. Typical: representative. — *Con.* Ordinary, *common, familiar: *usual, customary.

auction, *v.* *Sell, vend, barter, trade.

audacious. Bold, intrepid, courageous, *brave, valiant, valorous, doughty, undaunted, dauntless.
Ana. Daring, daredevil, reckless, venturous, venturesome, *adventurous, rash, foolhardy, temerarious: brazen, brash, *shameless.
Ant. Circumspect. — *Con.* *Cautious, wary, chary, calculating: prudent, sane, judicious, *wise: *cowardly, craven, pusillanimous.

audacity. *Temerity, hardihood, effrontery, nerve, cheek, gall.
Ana. Intrepidity, boldness, courageousness (see corresponding adjectives at BRAVE): daring, daredeviltry, recklessness, rashness, foolhardiness (see corresponding adjectives at ADVENTUROUS): *courage, mettle, spirit: brazenness *or* brass (see corresponding adjective at SHAMELESS).
Ant. Circumspection. — *Con.* Caution, wariness, calculation (see under CAUTIOUS): timidity, timorousness (see corresponding adjectives at TIMID): fearfulness, apprehensiveness (see corresponding adjectives at FEARFUL).

audible. *Aural, auricular.
Ant. Inaudible.

audience. **1** *Hearing, audition.
2 Public, *following, clientele, clientage.
Ana. Fans, devotees, votaries (see singular nouns at ADDICT).

audile. *Auditory, acoustic, acoustical.

audit, *n.* Examination, inspection, scrutiny, scanning. See under SCRUTINIZE.
Ana. Check, *corrective, control: investigation, probe, *inquiry.

audit, *v.* Examine, inspect, *scrutinize, scan.

audition. *Hearing, audience.

auditor. *Bookkeeper, accountant.
Ana. Examiner, inspector, scrutinizer (see corresponding verbs at SCRUTINIZE): verifier, authenticator (see corresponding verbs at CONFIRM).

auditory. **Auditory, audile, acoustic, acoustical** agree in meaning of or relating to the hearing of sounds. **Auditory** often stresses hearing more than sound; as, the *auditory* (not *acoustic*) powers of a dog; the *auditory* (not *acoustic*) sensitivity of an individual's organs of hearing. **Audile,** a term coined to correspond to *tactile, motile, visile,* etc., is more often used in psychology than in physiology, and is applied chiefly to sounds as heard (as, *audile* images) or to persons who recall most easily that which they have heard (as, the *audile* type of mentality). **Acoustic,** on the other hand, emphasizes sound with reference to its capacity for being heard or the conditions under which it is heard; as, the *acoustic* quality of a person's voice; the *acoustic* properties of a hall. Both words are used in anatomy with little distinction, except that some human anatomists prefer *acoustic;* as, the *auditory,* or *acoustic,* nerve; the *auditory,* or *acoustic,* area of the brain. **Acoustical** is often interchangeable with *acoustic.* When, however, direct reference to the science of acoustics is intended, the former is the correct word; as, *acoustical* engineering.

auf Wiedersehen. Au revoir, farewell, Godspeed, adieu, adios, *good-by, bon voyage.

aught, *n.* Ought, naught, nought, *cipher, zero.

augment. *Increase, enlarge, multiply.
Ana. *Intensify, aggravate, enhance, heighten: swell, *expand, amplify, dilate.
Ant. Abate (sense 2). — *Con.* Reduce, diminish, *decrease, lessen, dwindle: curtail, abridge, *shorten.

augur. Prognosticate, presage, portend, forebode, prophesy, forecast, *foretell, predict.
Ana. Betoken, *indicate, bespeak, argue: apprehend, anticipate, divine, foreknow, *foresee.

augury. Omen, portent, presage, prognostic, *foretoken.
Ana. *Sign, symptom, token, note, badge, mark: precursor, *forerunner, harbinger, herald.
Con. Fulfillment, accomplishment, effecting *or* effect (see corresponding verbs at PERFORM): realization, actualization, materialization (see corresponding verbs at REALIZE).

august. Majestic, imposing, stately, noble, grandiose, *grand, magnificent.
Ana. Impressive, *moving: *splendid, sublime, superb: awful, *fearful.
Ant. Unimpressive: unimposing.

aura. *Atmosphere, feeling, feel, savor, tone.

aural. **Aural, auricular, audible** agree in meaning heard, or perceived by the ear. They are, however, not often interchangeable. **Aural** is applicable to any sensation, impression, or the like, which affects the ears rather than the nose (nasal) or the eyes (ocular or visual) or the nerve ends (muscular); as, insensitiveness to *aural* stimuli; to prefer the *aural* to the visual method in learning a language. **Auricular** is applicable not only to that which is heard, as distinguished from that which is read, but also especially to that which is communicated privately and is addressed to the ear of a particular person; thus, *auricular confession* is used of the private confession of sins to a priest, as distinguished from open confession before a congregation. "You shall . . . by an *auricular* assurance have your satisfaction" (*Shak.*). **Audible** is applicable only to sounds, voices, conversation, etc., which are heard, as distinguished from those which are not heard because too faint, too low, uttered in a whisper, or the like; as, "his voice being distinctly *audible* in the street" (*Hardy*).

aureate, *adj.* Euphuistic, flowery, *rhetorical, grandiloquent, magniloquent, bombastic.
Ana. *Ornate, florid, flamboyant, rococo, baroque.
Ant. Austere (*in style*).

aureole *or* **aureola.** Glory, nimbus, *halo.
Ana. Effulgence, radiance (see corresponding adjectives at BRIGHT).

au revoir. Auf Wiedersehen, *good-by, farewell, Godspeed, adieu, adios, bon voyage.

auricular. *Aural, audible.

auspicious. *Favorable, propitious, benign.
Ana. *Lucky, fortunate, happy, providential: *hopeful, roseate: indicating *or* indicative, betokening (see corresponding verbs at INDICATE).
Ant. Inauspicious: ill-omened. — *Con.* *Sinister, baleful, malign, malefic: *adverse, antagonistic, counter: *ominous, portentous, unpropitious, fateful.

austere. *Severe, stern, ascetic.
Ana. Bald, *bare: unembellished, unadorned, unornamented, undecorated (see affirmative verbs at ADORN): dispassionate (see FAIR): rigorous, strict (see RIGID): grave, *serious, sober, earnest.
Ant. Luscious (*of fruits, etc.*): warm, ardent (*of persons, feelings, etc.*): exuberant (*of style, quality, etc.*). — *Con.* Lush, prodigal, *profuse: clement, lenient, indulgent (see FORBEARING): grandiloquent, magniloquent, aureate, flowery, *rhetorical: *impassioned, passionate, fervid, fervent.

autarchic *or* **autarchical.** Autarkic, autonomous, autonomic, independent, *free, sovereign.

autarchy. Autarky, autonomy, independence, freedom, sovereignty. See under FREE, *adj.*

autarkic *or* **autarkical.** Autarchic, autonomous, autonomic, independent, *free, sovereign.

autarky. Autarchy, autonomy, independence, freedom, sovereignty. See under FREE, *adj.*

authentic. Authentic, genuine, veritable, bona fide agree in the sense of being exactly what the thing in question is said to be or professes to be. The prevailing sense of **authentic** is authoritative, trustworthy, with the implication of actuality, or accordance with fact; as, "confirmed both by legend and *authentic* record" (*Froude*); an *authentic* description of the Great Fire of London. The prevailing sense of **genuine** is real, true (see REAL), often with the implication of descent, without admixture, from an original stock, or of correspondence, without adulteration, to the natural or original product called by that name; as, *genuine* maple sirup; a *genuine* Russian wolfhound; this is real merino, the *genuine* article. Often the stress is on sincerity, or lack of factitiousness; as, *genuine* piety; "true simplicity and *genuine* pathos" (*Wordsworth*). Both terms are used—*genuine* more frequently than *authentic*—as opposed to *spurious, counterfeit, apocryphal;* as, "Let them contrast their own fantastical personages . . . with the *authentic* rustics of Burns" (*Jeffrey*); "What is *genuine* knowledge, and what is its counterfeit" (*Newman*). The 18th-century distinction between the two terms, as applied to documents—"A *genuine* book, is that which was written by the person whose name it bears, as the author of it. An *authentic* book, is that which relates matters of fact, as they really happened" (*R. Watson*)—while still often observed, is becoming obliterated in present usage. However, it is idiomatic to say of a work such as a portrait, "this is an *authentic* portrait of George Washington" (that is, it was painted from life) and "this is a *genuine* Gilbert Stuart portrait of Washington" (that is, it is properly ascribed to Gilbert Stuart, the painter). **Veritable,** in precise use, always implies a correspondence with truth; it is seldom used without a suggestion of asseveration or of affirmation of belief. "I who am now talking . . . am the *veritable* Socrates" (*Blackie*). "Though Christ be the *veritable* Son of God" (*Quiller-Couch*). In looser use, it is applied to words or phrases used figuratively or hyperbolically, as an assertion of the justice of the designation or of its truth in essentials; as, his fits of passion are *veritable* hurricanes; he is a *veritable* fool. **Bona fide,** though often used as though it were the equivalent of *genuine* or *authentic*, is properly applied when good faith or sincerity is in question; as, a *bona fide* sale of securities; a *bona fide* bid for a piece of property.
Ana. Authoritative, authoritarian, oracular (see DICTATORIAL): *reliable, trustworthy, dependable: *correct, right, exact: true, *real, actual.
Ant. Spurious. — *Con.* *Fictitious, apocryphal, fabulous, mythical, legendary: *false, wrong: deceptive, *misleading, delusive, delusory: *supposed, supposititious, putative, hypothetical.

authenticate. Validate, verify, *confirm, substantiate, corroborate.
Ana. Certify, accredit, endorse, *approve: *prove, try, test, demonstrate: avouch, warrant (see ASSERT).
Ant. Impugn. — *Con.* *Deny, gainsay, contradict, traverse, negative, contravene: reject, repudiate, spurn (see DECLINE).

author. 1 *Maker, creator.
2 *Writer, composer.

authoritarian. 1 Authoritative, dogmatic, *dictatorial, magisterial, magistral, doctrinaire, oracular.
Ana. Despotic, autocratic, arbitrary, tyrannical, tyrannous, *absolute: domineering, imperious, *masterful.
Ant. Liberal, libertarian: anarchistic, anarchic.
2 *Totalitarian.

authoritative. Magisterial, magistral, authoritarian, oracular, dogmatic, *dictatorial, doctrinaire.
Ana. Authorized, accredited (see AUTHORIZE): certified, endorsed, approved (see APPROVE): *authentic, bona fide, genuine: *masterful, imperative, peremptory.
Ant. Questionable: servile. — *Con.* *Doubtful, dubious: meek, modest, *humble.

authority. 1 *Power, jurisdiction, command, control, dominion, sway.
Ana. Ascendancy, *supremacy: government, ruling *or* rule (see corresponding verbs at GOVERN).
2 *Influence, weight, credit, prestige.
Ana. Exemplar, ideal, standard, pattern, *model, example: *expert, adept, artist: connoisseur, virtuoso, *aesthete.

authorize. Authorize, commission, accredit, license (*or* **licence**) denote in common to invest with power or the right to act. One **authorizes** a person to act for oneself when he is given the necessary legal right or power, with or without instructions of a specific character. Often, discretionary powers are implied; as, to *authorize* a friend to make an answer to an attack on one's character; our clerks are *authorized* to receive contributions for the Red Cross. One **commissions** a person when one not only authorizes but instructs him to perform a definite duty or office. "I am *commissioned* to make you an offer which I have told him . . . you would not accept" (*Gray*). Specifically, *commission* may imply appointment as one's business agent, as in buying, selling, or supplying goods, or it may suggest an order to do a certain kind of work, especially work of a professional or artistic nature; as, to *commission* an artist to paint portraits of one's family. In military and naval use, it implies the conferring of

rank and authority on officers above a certain rank. One **accredits** a person when one sends him, invested with authority and possessed of the proper credentials, as a representative, delegate, ambassador, or the like; as, John Hay was *accredited* to the Court of St. James's. "The sovereign to whom I am *accredited*" (*Motley*). One **licenses** a person (or, sometimes, a business, a trade, a craft) when one grants formal legal permission to act in a certain capacity (or to carry on a certain business, trade, or craft); as, to *license* teachers; to *license* medical school graduates to practice medicine. *License* sometimes stresses permission so strongly that the implication of authorization is obscured and that of regulation substituted; as, to *license* beggars; to *license* a firm to sell liquor.
Ana. Empower, *enable: permit, allow, *let.
Con. Enjoin, *forbid, prohibit, interdict.

autochthon, *n.* Native, aborigine, indigene. See under NATIVE, *adj.*
Con. Foreigner, alien, *stranger.

autochthonous *or* **autochthonal, autochthonic.** Indigenous, *native, aboriginal, endemic.
Ant. Naturalized.
Con. Foreign, alien, extraneous, *extrinsic.

autocratic *or* **autocratical.** Arbitrary, *absolute, despotic, tyrannical, tyrannous.
Ana. *Dictatorial, magisterial, magistral: authoritarian, *totalitarian: *masterful, domineering, imperious: overbearing, arrogant (see PROUD).
Con. Yielding, deferring, submitting, capitulating (see YIELD, *v.*): tolerant, lenient, *forbearing, indulgent.

autogenous. Endogenous, spontaneous, *automatic.

automatic, *adj.* **1 Automatic, spontaneous, autogenous, endogenous,** as here compared, are not close synonyms, but they agree in meaning brought into being or action by an internal, as opposed to an external, agency. **Automatic** has historically been subjected to various changes in meaning and has only within recent generations acquired stable senses. Originally, it was used to describe a thing that was self-acting or self-activated because it contained the principle of motion within itself. "In the universe, nothing can be said to be *automatic*" (*Sir H. Davy*). Now, in the sense here considered, it is applied to machines and mechanical contrivances which, after certain conditions have been fulfilled, continue to operate indefinitely without human supervision or until the conditions have materially changed; thus, an *automatic* firearm is so constructed that after the first round is exploded the force of the recoil or gas pressure loads and fires round after round until the ammunition is exhausted or the trigger is released; a thermostat is an *automatic* device which maintains the temperature of artificially heated rooms by operating the appropriate parts of a furnace when the temperature exceeds or falls below the point at which it is set. **Spontaneous** (see also SPONTANEOUS) is applicable not so much to objective things as to processes, particularly natural processes, thought of as originating without external agency or, more often in noncontroversial use, without human agency; thus, *spontaneous* generation implies origin of living directly from nonliving matter; *spontaneous* combustion implies a generation of heat through chemical changes in matter causing it to burn; a *spontaneous* growth refers to vegetation produced neither from humanly sown seed nor from plantings. *Autogenous* and *endogenous* are used chiefly in the biological sciences. **Autogenous** usually stresses origin within the same individual as contrasted with origin in another; as, an *autogenous* bone graft; an *autogenous* infection; *autogenous* vaccines. **Endogenous** emphasizes origin within the organism as contrasted with external origin (*exogenous* origin); as, the *endogenous* toxins of bacteria; tuberculosis of *endogenous* origin; the *endogenous* causes of cancer.
2 Mechanical, instinctive, *spontaneous, impulsive.
Ana. Trained, disciplined, schooled, instructed (see TEACH): prompt, *quick, ready.
Con. Deliberate, *voluntary, intentional.

autonomic. Autonomous, independent, sovereign, *free, autarchic, autarkic.

autonomous. Autonomic, independent, sovereign, *free, autarchic, autarkic.

autonomy. Independence, freedom, sovereignty, autarky, autarchy. See under FREE, *adj.*

auxiliary. Auxiliary, subsidiary, accessory (*or* **accessary**), **contributory, subservient, ancillary, adjuvant** agree in meaning supplying aid or support. **Auxiliary** may or may not imply subordinate rank or position; as, an *auxiliary* organization; an *auxiliary* bishop. "The conclusion that the humanistic point of view is *auxiliary* to and dependent upon the religious point of view" (*T. S. Eliot*). It now often suggests something in reserve; as, an *auxiliary* motor (in a sailboat). **Subsidiary** once had in English its etymological notion of a reserve supply; as, *subsidiary* forces. "A *subsidiary* fund always at hand to be mortgaged in aid of any other doubtful fund" (*Adam Smith*). In present use, however, *subsidiary* stresses subordinate or inferior status or capacity, often to the obscuring, even loss, of the notion of supplying aid; as, *subsidiary* streams (that is, tributaries); a *subsidiary* company (one controlled by another company that holds a majority of the shares of its stock). **Accessory** stresses so strongly the mere fact of association or accompaniment that in many applications the notion of assistance or support is obscured or even lost; as, *accessory* sounds in music; an *accessory* mineral (one present in a rock but not an essential constituent); cf. automobile *accessories*. A person *accessory* to a crime (for example, the hirer of an assassin or a receiver of stolen goods) need not actively participate in its commission (see also *accessory*, n., under CONFEDERATE). **Contributory** stresses the assistance rather than the subordinate status of the assistant and usually implies the effecting of an end or result; as, resentment against the unjust tax was one of the *contributory* causes of the revolt; *contributory* negligence (negligence on the part of an injured person contributing to the production of the injury). **Subservient** usually stresses the subordinate nature of the assistance. "A catastrophe to which every incident should be *subservient*" (*Crabbe*). It also stresses the importance or usefulness of the end it serves and, often also, the nature of its motive, such as commendable self-subordination or a sense of order and due relation; as, "He has uniformly made his talents *subservient* to the best interests of humanity" (*Coleridge*); "those features of a work of art which by themselves would be unattractive or repulsive, like an 'ugly' face, but in the work are *subservient* to the total effect and may even heighten its beauty" (*S. Alexander*). **Ancillary** preserves to some extent, even in present use, its etymological association with maidservant (Latin *ancilla*) and more than the other terms stresses the intimacy of the assistance. "Does it not follow that some practice in the deft use of words, with its correspondent defining of thought, may well be *ancillary* even to the study of natural science in a university?" (*Quiller-Couch*). **Adjuvant** differs from *auxiliary*, its closest synonym, in attributing greater importance, or more noticeable effectiveness, or a more definite influence, to the thing so qualified; thus, an *adjuvant* ingredient in a prescription often modifies the major ingredient so as to aid significantly the latter's action or to make it

effective; as, "used as *adjuvant* respiratory organs" (*R. B. Todd*).
Ana. *Subordinate, succursal, secondary, tributary: supporting, upholding, backing (see SUPPORT, *v.*): helping, aiding, assisting (see HELP, *v.*): supplementary, complementary (see corresponding nouns at COMPLEMENT).

avail, *v.* **1** *Benefit, profit, bestead, boot.
Ana. Meet, answer, *satisfy, fulfill: *help, aid.
Con. Harm, hurt, *injure, damage.
2 In form **avail oneself of.** Utilize, employ, *use, apply.
Con. *Abuse, misuse: *neglect, ignore, slight, overlook: reject, refuse, spurn (see DECLINE).

avail, *n.* *Use, service, account, advantage, profit.

avant-propos. Preface, foreword, proem, *introduction, prologue, induction, prelude, prolegomenon, exordium, preamble, prolusion, protasis, overture.

avarice. Greed, *cupidity, rapacity.
Ana. Avariciousness, covetousness, acquisitiveness (see corresponding adjectives at COVETOUS): stinginess, niggardliness, miserliness, parsimoniousness (see corresponding adjectives at STINGY).
Ant. Prodigality. — *Con.* Extravagance (see corresponding adjective at EXCESSIVE): liberality, generosity, munificence, bountifulness (see corresponding adjectives at LIBERAL).

avaricious. *Covetous, acquisitive, grasping, greedy.
Ana. Miserly, close, close-fisted, parsimonious, *stingy.
Ant. Generous. — *Con.* *Liberal, bountiful, munificent: lavish, prodigal (see PROFUSE).

avenge. Avenge, revenge agree in meaning to inflict punishment on a person who has wronged oneself or another. Once close synonyms, these verbs are now increasingly divergent in implications. One may *avenge* or *revenge* (a person who is wronged), but **avenge** is the preferred word when that person is another than oneself and one is motivated by a desire to vindicate him or to serve the ends of justice. *Avenge* may also be used when the person injured is oneself and one is thought of as visiting just or merited punishment on the wrongdoer. In either case the word is often followed by *on, upon,* or the archaic *of* (the wrongdoer). "*Avenge,* O Lord, thy slaughtered saints" (*Milton*). "I swear on my knees, on these stones, to *avenge* you on Foulon" (*Dickens*). "He had *avenged* himself on them by havoc such as England had never before seen" (*Macaulay*). On the other hand, one **revenges** oneself, now almost never another, when one inflicts injury *on* or *upon* (or, archaic, *of*) an offender in a desire to exact satisfaction *for* his offense. *Revenge* may imply a desire for vindication or an aim to serve the ends of justice, but more often it suggests a desire to get even, to pay back in kind or degree, and therefore variously connotes malice, spite, an unwillingness to forgive, or the like. "The hope of *revenging* himself on me was a strong inducement" (*Austen*). "Monti at least *revenged* himself of Pius for placing him below Metastasio" (*J. C. Hobhouse*). "He saw that his true policy was not to *revenge* himself by executions and confiscations" (*Stubbs*). Also, one may either *avenge* or *revenge* (a wrong, injury, or the like) but *avenge* now usually implies that the end is just retribution whether the activity is in one's own or another's behalf, whereas *revenge* implies that the end is retaliation and the compelling spirit of the act hatred or bitterness; as, Orestes *revenged* his father's murder by killing the murderess, his mother, but the gods *avenged* his matricide by driving him mad.
Ana. Requite, recompense, compensate, *pay (back): vindicate, defend, justify (see MAINTAIN): *punish, chasten, chastise.
Con. Forbear, *refrain, abstain: remit, pardon, forgive (see EXCUSE).

avenue. 1 *Road, street, boulevard, terrace, drive, parkway, roadway, highway, highroad, thoroughfare.
2 Avenue, alley, allée, mall designate a shaded walk or road, especially in a park or on an estate. **Avenue** is applied to an approach which leads to a house or building at a distance from the gate and which is lined on both sides by tall trees; **alley,** to a narrow walk bordered by shrubs or trees, as one through a garden or a grove. **Allée,** the French equivalent, is sometimes preferred to *alley* to avoid confusion; it is, however, specifically applied to an alley where the trees or shrubs are twice as high as the width of the path. **Mall** is applied to a public promenade, often, especially originally, tree lined, and used frequently but not invariably as a proper name.

aver. Declare, avouch, avow, affirm, *assert, protest.
Ana. Asseverate, testify, *swear: *maintain, defend, justify.
Ant. Deny. — *Con.* Gainsay, negative, contradict, traverse (see DENY).

average, *n.* **Average, mean, median, norm, par** agree in denoting something, usually a number, a quantity, a condition, or the like, that represents a middle point between extremes. Of these words **average, mean, median** and **par** are also used as adjectives. Except in extended use, **average** is an arithmetical term applied to a quotient obtained by dividing a sum total by another figure or quantity. When the figures or quantities added up are unequal in value, the divisor is the number of items involved, and the quotient represents the figure or quantity each would be if all were alike; thus, the *average* of 10, 12, 14, 16, 18, 20 is 15 (that is, 90÷6). Such averages are computed to give one a fair estimate of a group, a series, or the like, in which there are inequalities; as, his *average* (that is, the *average* of his ratings) for his high school course was 82; the *average* of the apple pickers (that is, the *average* quantity of apples picked) was 25 bushels a day. When, especially in sports, the sum total represents the number of chances taken or of opportunities offered or provided, the quotient, or *average,* is obtained by dividing the number of successes, or successful performances, by this sum total. Such an average is expressed as a percentage (often more accurately, as a permillage) and gives a fair estimate of a player's performance and a basis for comparison with others; thus, a baseball fielder who handles a total of 1114 chances and makes 6 errors, has a fielding *average* of .9946 (that is, 1108÷1114); a baseball batter who is credited with 633 appearances at bat and has made 254 hits has a batting *average* of .401 (that is, 254÷633). A similar method is used in estimating probabilities, such as the chances of death for a person between given ages and the length of the period between recurrences of an unpredictable phenomenon; thus, the *average* of mortality for persons of a given age is computed from statistics of deaths at that age and of the population group consisting of persons of that age. In extended use, *average* is applied not to a number but to a concept of what is the typical or ordinary person or thing of its kind (see also *average,* under MEDIUM); as, the boy is above the *average* for his age and background; the play is below the season's *average* in dramatic interest. **Mean,** in its earliest use in English, named a condition, quality, intensity, rate, or the like, that is midway between two extremes. This meaning still prevails, but it is found chiefly in idiomatic phrases such as "the golden *mean,*" "the happy *mean*" implying moderation and avoidance both of blamable excess and of blamable deficiency; as, to observe a happy *mean* between abjectness and arrogance or between effusiveness and reserve. "He that holds fast the golden *mean,* And lives contentedly between The little and the great"

(*Cowper:* transl. of Horace). In its mathematical use, *mean* is more general than *average* (for which another name is *arithmetical mean*): it covers also the *geometric mean,* that is, the square root of the product of two numbers or quantities (or the *n*th root of the product of *n* quantities); thus, 10 is the *arithmetical mean* (or *average*) of 4, 16, while 8 is the *geometric mean* of 4, 16. In computing the mean of temperatures, only the averages of the highest and of the lowest readings during the given period are considered. The average of the highest readings of a thermometer each day for a month is known as the *mean maximum temperature;* of the lowest readings, as the *mean minimum temperature.* These two figures are averaged to give the *mean temperature* for the month. **Median,** in the sense here considered, as in all its senses, refers to a midway point in position: in statistics it names the figure or quantity which represents the point at which there are as many instances below as there are above it; thus, the *average* of a group of 5 workers earning respectively 3, 4, 5, 8, and 10 dollars a day is six dollars a day, whereas the *median* for the same group is five dollars, because one half of them earn less than five dollars a day and one half more. When, however, the figure is the same for some members of the group, the median is derived by taking into account two factors, the figure for each member of the series, and the number of members coming under each of these figures. Thus, if the scores of a class of fifteen are 4, 6, 8, 8, 8, 8, 9, 9, 9, 9, 9, 9, 10, 10, 10, the *median* score is 9 (the eighth figure in the series). **Norm** etymologically suggests a rule for guidance or, by extension, a definite pattern to be followed: it has come also to denote, especially in scientific fields, such as psychology and sociology, the average (sometimes the mathematically computed average, sometimes the estimated average) of performance or achievement of a group, class, category, or the like, which is set up as the standard for, or as the minimum of accomplishment by, the entire membership of the group; thus, a course of study for a certain grade is based upon whatever is the accepted *norm* for children of the age, experience, and background commonly found in that grade. "Crime is merely a name for the most obvious, extreme, and directly dangerous forms of . . . departure from the *norm* in manners and customs" (*H. Ellis*). "It is everything to have acquired and to possess such a *norm* of Poetry within us that we know whether or not what he wrote was Poetry" (*Quiller-Couch*). **Par,** which in the sense here considered is more common in British than in American use, usually refers to an average for an individual and not, as *norm,* to the average for a group. In the United States, as in Great Britain, it often refers to an individual person's average in health, accomplishment, or the like; as, I feel below *par* (that is, below my average in health) today; this theme is above *par* for that student (that is, above his average theme in quality). In British use, however, *par* may be employed in reference to an average in amount (as, the *par* of crop production for a given farm) or in barometric pressure (as, the *par* for this particular level), or the like.

Ant. Maximum: minimum.

average, *adj.* **1** Mean, median, par. See under AVERAGE, *n.*

2 Middling, *medium, indifferent, fair, moderate, mediocre, second-rate.

Ana. *Common, ordinary, familiar: *usual, customary.

Ant. Exceptional: extraordinary. — *Con.* Outstanding, prominent, conspicuous, *noticeable: superlative, *supreme, surpassing, pre-eminent.

averse. 1 *Disinclined, indisposed, loath, reluctant, hesitant.

Ana. Recoiling, shrinking, flinching, quailing (see RECOIL, *v.*): uncongenial, unsympathetic (see INCONSONANT): balky, *contrary, perverse.

Ant. Avid (*of* or *for*): athirst (*for*).

2 Unsympathetic, *antipathetic.

3 *Adverse.

aversion. *Antipathy.

Ana. Repugnance, repellency, abhorrence, distaste *or* distastefulness (see corresponding adjectives at REPUGNANT): horror, dread, *fear.

Ant. Predilection: penchant. — *Con.* Partiality, bias, prejudice (see PREDILECTION): *leaning, propensity, flair.

avert. 1 *Turn, deflect, sheer, divert.

Ana. Bend, twist, *curve: shift, remove, transfer, *move.

2 Ward off, *prevent, obviate, preclude.

Ana. *Escape, avoid, shun, eschew, evade, elude: forestall, anticipate (see PREVENT): *frustrate, balk, thwart, foil.

aviation. *Aeronautics, avigation.

avid. *Eager, keen, anxious, agog, a-tiptoe, athirst.

Ana. Desiring *or* desirous, craving, coveting *or* covetous (see corresponding verbs at DESIRE): longing, yearning, pining, hankering, hungering, thirsting (see LONG, *v.*).

Ant. Indifferent: averse. — *Con.* Indisposed, *disinclined, loath: aloof, disinterested (see INDIFFERENT): listless, *languid: apathetic, *impassive.

avigation. *Aeronautics, aviation.

avocation. *Vocation.

Ana. Diversion, amusement, recreation (see under AMUSE).

avoid. 1 Void, vacate, quash, abrogate, *annul.

Ana. Invalidate, *nullify, negate: cancel, *erase.

2 *Escape, shun, eschew, evade, elude.

Ana. Avert, ward off, *prevent, obviate: forestall, anticipate (see PREVENT): flee, fly (see ESCAPE).

Ant. Face: meet. — *Con.* *Incur, contract, catch: court, solicit, *invite.

avouch. Aver, affirm, avow, declare, *assert, protest, warrant, predicate.

Ana. Testify, depose, depone, asseverate, *swear: *confirm, corroborate.

Con. Gainsay, contradict, *deny, negative, traverse, impugn.

avow. 1 Affirm, declare, aver, avouch, warrant, *assert, protest, predicate.

Ana. *Maintain, defend, vindicate: testify, asseverate, *swear.

2 Own, *acknowledge, confess, admit.

Ana. Proclaim, *declare, publish, announce: *reveal, discover, disclose, divulge, tell.

Ant. Disavow. — *Con.* Repudiate, reject, refuse (see DECLINE, *v.*): *deny, gainsay, negative, contradict.

await. Look for, *expect, hope, look.

Ana. Wait, abide, *stay.

Ant. Despair (of).

awake, *adj.* *Aware, alive, cognizant, conscious, sensible.

Ana. Alert, vigilant, *watchful: roused, aroused, stirred (*up*), awakened (see STIR).

Con. *Sleepy, drowsy, somnolent, slumberous: *inactive, inert, supine.

awake, *v.* *Wake, awaken, waken.

Ana. Excite, stimulate, quicken, galvanize (see PROVOKE): rouse, arouse, *stir.

awaken. 1 Waken, awake, *wake.

2 Waken, rouse, arouse, *stir, rally.

Ana. Excite, galvanize, quicken, stimulate, *provoke:

kindle, enkindle, fire, inflame (see LIGHT): elicit, evoke (see EDUCE).

Ant. Subdue. — *Con.* *Arrest, check: *frustrate, thwart, baffle, balk, foil.

award, *v.* *Grant, accord, vouchsafe, concede.

Ana. Bestow, confer, present, *give: assign, *allot, apportion, allocate: adjudicate, adjudge, *judge, arbitrate.

award, *n.* Prize, *premium, reward, guerdon, meed, bonus, bounty.

aware. **Aware, cognizant, conscious, sensible, alive, awake** agree in meaning having knowledge of something, especially of something that for some reason is not obvious or apparent to all. One is **aware** of something through information or, especially, through one's own vigilance in observing or in drawing inferences from what one sees, hears, feels, or the like. "Few, so far as I am *aware,* now claim the free speech to call a knave a knave" (*T. S. Eliot*). "Mr. Potter would not . . . have been worthy of his reputation had he not been *aware* . . . of the existence of this League. Journalists have to be *aware* of such things" (*R. Macaulay*). "It is only through imagination that men become *aware* of what the world might be" (*B. Russell*). One is **cognizant** of something who has had it called to his attention or has become aware of it through his own powers of observation; in careful use the word commonly implies first-hand or certain knowledge; as, he is not, as yet, fully *cognizant* of the facts. "If the Saints in bliss Be *cognizant* of aught that passeth here" (*Southey*). One is **conscious** of something that he sees, hears, feels, or otherwise apprehends, when he allows it to enter his mind so that, at the very least, he recognizes its existence or, at the most, he fixes his attention on it; thus, one may or may not be *conscious* of his heartbeat, or of someone passing through the room. "He stood there motionless and in wonder, dimly *conscious* that Hallward was speaking to him" (*Wilde*). "To be happy or miserable without being *conscious* of it seems to me utterly inconsistent and impossible" (*Locke*). "Lifelong short-sightedness . . . of which he has never ceased to be *conscious*" (*H. Ellis*). One is **sensible** of something who through feeling or a sixth sense realizes its existence. "She was disturbing him extremely . . . but he was much too *sensible* of her goodwill to wound her feelings by telling her so" (*C. Mackenzie*). "Even he was *sensible* of the decorous atmosphere" (*Joyce*). One is **alive** to something who is acutely susceptible to its influence or sensible of its existence. "The Spring Finds thee not less *alive* to her sweet force Than yonder upstarts" (*Cowper*). "They were fully *alive* to the danger of thwarting Barbara" (*Galsworthy*). One is **awake** to something who is aroused to it or on the alert for developments; as, the country is not *awake* to the potential evils of a strict censorship.

Ana. *Sure, certain, positive: informed, acquainted, apprised (see INFORM).

Ant. Unaware. — *Con.* *Insensible, insensitive, impassible, anesthetic: *ignorant, nescient.

awe, *n.* Fear, *reverence.

Ana. Respect, esteem, *regard: *wonder, wonderment, admiration, amaze, amazement.

Con. Contempt, scorn, disdain, despite (see under DESPISE): insolence, superciliousness, arrogance (see corresponding adjectives at PROUD).

awful. *Fearful, dreadful, frightful, terrible, horrible, shocking, appalling, terrific, horrific.

Ana. Impressive, *moving: solemn, *serious, grave: imposing, august, majestic (see GRAND): sublime, superb, *splendid: *ominous, portentous.

awkward. **Awkward, clumsy, maladroit, inept, gauche** come into comparison when they mean not adapted by constitution or character to act, operate, or achieve the intended or desired ends with ease, fitness, or grace. *Awkward* and *clumsy* are by far the widest of these terms in their range of application. **Awkward** (etymologically, wrong in direction) in many of its applications involves the idea of unfitness for easy handling or dexterous management. It may suggest unhandiness or inconvenience; as, an *awkward* tool; an *awkward* arrangement of controls. It may suggest embarrassment or discomfiture; as, an *awkward* situation; an *awkward* silence; an *awkward* meeting. "How earnestly did she then wish that her former opinions had been more reasonable, her expressions more moderate! It would have spared her from explanations . . . which it was exceedingly *awkward* to give" (*Austen*). When applied to persons, their build, their movements, their manners, or the like, *awkward* usually implies a lack of ease or grace and often suggests muscular in-co-ordination or deficiency in poise; thus, an *awkward* gait implies lack of muscular control; an *awkward* greeting implies want of tact or address; so, an *awkward* dancer; an *awkward* gesture; an *awkward* response; "His [Tiberius's] manners were *awkward* and unconciliatory" (*Buchan*). "Somehow these two could not talk. Constance perceived that Sophia was impeded by the same *awkwardness* as herself" (*Bennett*). **Clumsy** (etymologically, benumbed) stresses stiffness or heaviness with consequent want of flexibility or dexterity. The word is often applied to that which is so constructed or contrived as to be lumbering or ponderous; as, a boy of *clumsy* build; a bear is the most *clumsy* of animals; a *clumsy* style; *clumsy* boots. "When a great writer, like Carlyle or Browning, creates a speech of his own which is too *clumsy* to be flexible and too heavy to be intimate" (*H. Ellis*). Sometimes the word also implies unwieldiness; as, "a great play in spite of . . . the *clumsy* machinery of the plot" (*T. S. Eliot*). More often, however, and especially when applied to persons and their acts, it implies a lack of expertness or adroitness in manipulation, often with a suggestion of bungling; as, "the *clumsy* attempts of governments or other social bodies to interfere . . . will only make matters worse!" (*J. A. Hobson*); "he was a *clumsy* dissector because of his injury" (*H. G. Wells*). The next two words, *maladroit* and *inept,* imply awkwardness or clumsiness in managing that which requires mental or social dexterity, and are applicable only to persons and their acts or utterances. **Maladroit** implies a lack of tact or of skill in avoiding difficult situations in human intercourse, or a capacity for making things awkward; for this reason it is often opposed to *politic* or *diplomatic* in their extended senses; as, a *maladroit* reply to a letter; a *maladroit* remark. "It was more correct to 'break' a piece of bad news to a person by means of a (possibly *maladroit* and unfeeling) messenger" (*Thackeray*). **Inept** stresses inappropriateness or lack of aptness, especially in a person's acts or utterances; often, in addition, it carries a suggestion of futility or absurdity; thus, a remark may be *inept* because it is so out of keeping with the topic under discussion as to seem pointless and yet at the same time be *maladroit* because it gives an awkward turn to the conversation. "If these two noticed Angel's growing social *ineptness,* he noticed their growing mental limitations" (*Hardy*). "He [Henry James] is . . . the sharp-eyed and penetrating critic for whom . . . . this extraordinary and extraordinarily *inept* society has in fancied security unwittingly been waiting" (*Brownell*). **Gauche** (etymologically, left-handed) suggests a lack of social graces that makes for clumsiness or ineptness: it may imply also shyness, inexperience, or ill-breeding. "This journey

. . . tended to reduce my shy, taciturn, and somewhat *gauche* manner" (*G. G. Scott*).
Ana. *Stiff, wooden, rigid: embarrassing, discomfiting, disconcerting (see EMBARRASS).
Ant. Handy, deft: graceful. — *Con.* Adroit, *dexterous, feat: skillful, adept, *proficient: *easy, simple, facile, effortless.

awry. Awry, askew, askance agree in meaning deviating from a straight line or direction when used in their original literal senses. In their current extended senses, they all imply divergence from that which is straight or straightforward, direct, symmetrical, or orderly, but they are seldom applicable to the same things. **Awry** carries a strong implication of disorderliness, of disarrangement, or of confusion; as, the blinds all hang *awry;* everything in the kitchen was *awry;* their plans went *awry.* **Askew** stresses crookedness or distortion. It implies that the thing so described is set at a wrong angle, is twisted out of its proper position, goes off in the wrong direction, or the like; as, every chair in this room is *askew;* since the hurricane many of the trees are *askew;* the seam in the front of your skirt runs *askew.* **Askance** is used chiefly in the set phrases "to look (eye, view) *askance*"; in early use the word meant sidelong or sidewise; in current use, the phrase, not the word, is important, and it means to look at with mistrust, suspicion, disfavor, jealousy, or the like. "Aside the Devil turned For envy; yet with jealous leer malign Eyed them *askance*" (*Milton*). "Both . . . were viewed *askance* by authority" (*Gladstone*).

axiom. *Principle, fundamental, law, theorem.

aye. *Forever, ever, always, evermore, forevermore.

B

babble, *v.* Gabble, jabber, prattle, chatter, patter, prate, gibber, gab, *chat.
Ana. *Gossip, blab, tattle: converse, talk, *speak.

babel. Hubbub, racket, *din, uproar, hullabaloo, pandemonium.
Ana. Clamorousness *or* clamor, vociferousness (see corresponding adjectives at VOCIFEROUS): *confusion, disorder.
Con. Stillness, quietness *or* quiet, silentness *or* silence, noiselessness (see corresponding adjectives at STILL).

baby, *v.* Mollycoddle, humor, pamper, *indulge, spoil.

bacillus. Bacterium, pathogen, virus, *germ, microbe.

back, *v.* **1** *Support, uphold, champion, advocate.
Ana. Assist, aid, *help: favor, accommodate, *oblige: abet (see INCITE).
Con. *Weaken, undermine, disable, cripple: subvert, upset (see OVERTURN): *oppose, resist, combat.
2 Retrograde, crawfish, *recede, retreat, retract.
Con. *Advance, progress.

back, *adj.* *Posterior, rear, hind, hinder, after.
Ant. Front.

backbiting, *n.* *Detraction, slander, scandal, calumny.
Ana. Aspersion, *animadversion, reflection, stricture: *abuse, invective, obloquy, vituperation: vilifying *or* vilification, defaming *or* defamation (see corresponding verbs at MALIGN).
Ant. Vindication (see corresponding verb at MAINTAIN). — *Con.* *Compliment, flattery, adulation: praising *or* praise, eulogizing *or* eulogy, extolling *or* extollation (see corresponding verbs at PRAISE).

backbone. 1 *Spine, vertebrae, chine.
2 Grit, guts, sand, *fortitude, pluck.
Ana. *Courage, resolution, tenacity, mettle, spirit: courageousness, intrepidity, dauntlessness, valiancy (see corresponding adjectives at BRAVE): nerve, *temerity, hardihood.
Ant. Spinelessness. — *Con.* Cowardliness *or* cowardice, pusillanimousness *or* pusillanimity (see corresponding adjectives at COWARDLY).

backdrop. *Background, setting, milieu, mise-en-scène, environment.

backer. 1 Supporter, upholder, champion, advocate. See under SUPPORT, *v.*
2 *Sponsor, surety, guarantor, patron, angel.

background. Background, setting, environment, milieu, mise-en-scène, backdrop come into comparison when they are used in reference to human beings and their actions as found in real life or as represented in art, and denote the place, time, circumstances, and conditions in which those persons live or carry on their activities. However, they vary widely in their derivations and are not always interchangeable. **Background,** the oldest of these words in the sense here considered, was first used with reference to a dramatic performance and to the back and usually dimly lighted part of the stage, as distinguished from the better-lighted foreground where the main action usually took place; as, "Ranger retires to the *background*" (*Wycherley*); "Elvira walks about pensively in the *background*" (*Sheridan*). Later, it was used in reference to paintings, engravings, and the like, and applied to that part of a picture which seems most remote from the spectator and against which the figures or principal objects represented seem to be projected; as, many of the Renaissance painters preferred a natural *background,* such as mountain peaks and blue sky, others preferred an architectural *background,* such as a group of buildings or an interior. Both of these uses are still common, but the term's applicability has been widely extended to cover that which lies behind anything (such as a historical event, a movement, a career, or a phase of a person's or a people's development) that is capable of being seen in perspective or that may be viewed in its relation to its surroundings or the influences that have determined it in whole or in part; as, to know a person well one needs to know his *background;* students of English literature must have as *background* a knowledge of English history. "Landscape is treated as an accessory to human life and a *background* to human events" (*Binyon*). "The Latin of the Vulgate and the Offices has been a *background* giving depth and, as the painters say, 'value' to nine-tenths of our serious writing" (*Quiller-Couch*). **Setting** also derives its basic implications from the arts, originally from the jewelers' art, where the term is still used of the framework of precious metal in which a gem is mounted, and later from the dramaturgists' art, where it is used of the framework, in the way of scenic paintings, furniture, and the like, which indicates to the spectator the surroundings in which the action of a play takes place. Hence, *setting* is preferred to *background* as a designation of that element in a novel, a play, or other literary representation of human life, which is distinguished from the plot and the characters, and which is the author's imaginative reconstruction of the time, place, and conditions in which his characters live and act. When used in reference to real life, *setting* commonly connotes the standpoint of one who looks at human beings and their activities as though they were dramatic or literary representations. "What a social *setting* it was, that little world into which Mark Twain was born! It was drab, it was tragic" (*Van W. Brooks*). **Environment,** which came into common use early in the nineteenth century, was at first hardly distinguishable from the much older word *environs*, or the surroundings (usually natural surroundings) of a town, a body of water, or the like. "The *environment* of this loch put me in mind of Grasmere" (*Blackie*). However, after the theory of evolution was definitely propounded in the mid-century, *environment* came to be applied to all the external conditions which affect the life and development of an organism. When the human species and the factors influencing its development became a matter of widespread interest, the term acquired new implications. Consequently, when used in reference to persons, *environment* suggests not only natural surroundings but social conditions, and implies their importance as factors in the physical, mental, and moral development of the species or the individual or as formative influences; as, "the *environment* which produced Jonathan Edwards and Cotton Mather" (*Brownell*); "They were, perhaps, too far advanced for their time and *environment*" (*Cather*). When the formative influences in a person's development are the result of heredity or nature, *background* is the preferred term; when they are the product of his surroundings or his nurture, *environment* is the proper choice; thus, one may say that, although it is impossible to change a child's *background*, he will turn out well if brought up in a different *environment*. **Milieu,** a French word now naturalized in English, carries none of the scientific implications of *environment*, yet it also means surroundings and is used chiefly in reference to the physical and social surroundings of a person or group of persons. It is preferred to *environment* when there is the intent to evoke a clear picture or to suggest the specific character or atmosphere of such surroundings; it may be used in reference to imagined as well as to actual persons, and therefore is often interchangeable with *setting;* as, "A duplicate of the village in which Mark Twain had grown up, the *milieu* of Huck Finn and Tom Sawyer" (*Van W. Brooks*); "His chief object...is not to make an isolated study of this or that *milieu*, or to describe a particular social sphere" (*Athenaeum*). "A Chicago journal...treating of courtship, apostrophizes...'the turned-down light, the single chair,' but it would be idle to pretend that the *milieu* thus briefly characterized is congenial to all of us" (*Brownell*). **Mise-en-scène,** also a French term in increasing use in English, is the equivalent of *setting*, especially as referred to a theatrical performance. However, its stronger suggestion of the use of properties to achieve a given atmosphere or theatrical effect is the reason for its preference by some writers when the reference is not specifically to a dramatic performance, or even to invented scenes. "In 'The Scarlet Letter' how truly in the spirit of art is the *mise-en-scène* presented.... The material investiture of the story is presented...by the reserved, fastidious hand of an artist, not by the gaudy fingers of a showman or the mechanical industry of a department-store window-dresser" (*Cather*). **Backdrop,** literally a drop curtain at the rear of the stage which provides the decorative or realistic background for the action of a play and brings players and their movements into relief, is now increasingly common in an extended sense as a substitute for *background*, or *setting*, or *milieu*, when there is the intent to stress pictorial effect rather than social influence or spiritual significance. "In *Imperial City*.... Against the multi-towered *backdrop* of New York he [Elmer Rice] has pictured...the passions and hopes, the dreams and desolations...of...seven million souls" (*Atlantic Monthly*).

backslide, *v.* Relapse, recidivate, *lapse.
Ana. Revert, *return: deteriorate, degenerate, decline (see corresponding nouns at DETERIORATION): *recede, retreat, retrograde.

backslider. *Renegade, renegado, apostate, recreant, turncoat, pervert.

backsliding, *n.* Relapse, recidivation, recidivism, lapse. See under LAPSE, *v.*
Ana. Retrogressiveness *or* retrogression, retrogradation (see corresponding adjectives at BACKWARD): abandoning, deserting, forsaking (see ABANDON).

backstairs *or* **backstair,** *adj.* Privy, clandestine, furtive, covert, *secret, surreptitious, stealthy, underhand, underhanded.

backward, *adj.* **Backward, retrograde, retrogressive, regressive** all involve the idea of not moving or going ahead, or forward, or in advance. Only when applied to motion or a movement does **backward** imply the reverse of forward motion; as, a *backward* thrust of a hand; the *backward* swimming of a crayfish. Its commonest implication is failure to move ahead; in this sense it is chiefly applied to human beings who do not or cannot progress or develop with others of their age, kind, or class, or to persons or things that hold back or are held back from doing that which is normal or to be expected; thus, a child who is unable to keep up with others of his age in school because of some degree of mental deficiency, or because his normal mental development has been retarded, is described as *backward;* a person who holds back from expressing his appreciation, or in urging his candidacy for a position, because of shyness or self-distrust, is also describable as *backward* in doing the thing expected; when cold weather and frosts delay the development of vegetation beyond the normal or usual time, the season may be called *backward*. "Anthropology has come to mean chiefly the study of the *backward* races" (*Inge*). **Retrograde** is not only applicable to backward motion and backward movement but also to any moving or seemingly moving thing that proceeds in a direction which is contrary to the direction usually followed by things of its kind; as, the *retrograde* motion of a wheel; a *retrograde* planet (that is, a planet seemingly moving from east to west). It is also applicable to a process, such as the evolution of a species when it passes through stages in the order contrary to that which is normal and progressive; thus, some species of animal life that show indications of development in the direction of simpler and less specialized forms are said to manifest *retrograde* evolution. *Retrograde,* when applied to races, peoples, institutions, movements, and the like, differs from *backward* in implying decline or degeneration; thus, a *backward* race is one that does not progress; a *retrograde* race is one that is relapsing into barbarism or sinking into an inferior state. **Retrogressive** always implies diametric opposition to *progressive*. Like *retrograde*, and unlike *backward*, it implies movement in the direction that is the reverse of forward; unlike *retrograde*, however, it is seldom applied to physical movement; thus, one speaks of a *retrograde* (but not a *retrogressive* glacier), but one would speak of a *retrogressive* (not a *retrograde*) inquiry when such an inquiry leads the investigator from that which is near to that which is remote. *Retrogressive* is usually the preferred term when the reverse of improvement or betterment is implied; as, a *retrogressive* policy; objections were made to the proposed legislation on the ground of its probable *retrogressive* effect. **Regressive** carries a stronger implication of going backward by steps or degrees and often, also, a weaker implication of failure to progress or move ahead than any of the others. Consequently, it is often the preferred term when a colorless or uncolored statement of fact is intended; thus, when one infers the cause from the effect, or a principle from a number of facts, he is said to follow a *regressive* process of reasoning; the process of growing old may be described as a *retrograde* development when the emphasis is on its backward direction, as a *retrogressive* development when the stress is on the reversing of progress, and as a *regressive* development when the intent is to indicate that it is marked by an inversion of order in its stages; a *regressive* loss of memory implies that the most recent memories disappear first and the earliest linger longest.

Ana. Laggard, dilatory, *slow: *stupid, dull, dense: *lethargic, sluggish: *abnormal, atypic, atypical.

Ant. Advanced. — ***Con.*** Civilized, cultured (see corresponding nouns at CIVILIZATION): cultivated, cultured, refined (see corresponding nouns at CULTURE): educated, instructed (see TEACH).

bactericidal, *adj.* Germicidal, antiseptic, disinfectant. See under ANTISEPTIC, *n.*

bactericide. Germicide, *antiseptic, disinfectant, bacteriophage, phage, antitoxin.

bacteriophage, phage. Antitoxin, bactericide, germicide, *antiseptic, disinfectant.

bacterium. Usually in plural form **bacteria.** *Germ, microbe, bacillus, pathogen, virus.

bad. 1 **Bad, evil, ill, wicked, naughty** are synonymous when they mean not meeting with the approval of the ethical consciousness. **Bad** ranges in implication from the utmost moral reprehensibility to a force so weakened that it is interchangeable with *naughty* (see below), or is even applied to animals; as, "Almost as *bad*, good mother, As kill a king, and marry with his brother" (*Shak.*); "Young people...are often corrupted by *bad* books" (*J. Fordyce*); Johnnie's been a *bad* boy today: he's emptied the cooky jar; *Bad* dog! you've torn up my scarf! **Evil,** a stronger term than *bad* often is, is not often applied, in present usage, to persons, and frequently has a more or less sinister or baleful connotation; as, *evil* deeds, an *evil* life, the *evil* eye. "He knew nothing bad about him, but he felt something *evil*" (*Cather*). **Ill,** as a synonym for *evil,* occurs in modern usage chiefly in a few combinations, such as *ill* will, *ill* temper, *ill* nature. Its chief use is adverbial; as, *ill* disposed. **Wicked** implies the actual contravention or violation of moral law; as, "God is angry with the *wicked* every day" (*Psalms* vii. 11); *wicked* designs. It is sometimes used with weakened, even jocular, force. "You are the *wickedest* witty person I know" (*Lytton*). **Naughty** was once serious ("A most vile flagitious man, a sorry and *naughty* governor as could be"—*Barrow*) but is now trivial in its application. Most commonly it implies mischievousness on the part of a child too young to have any or a very lively sense of right and wrong. "Charles never was a *naughty* boy. He never robbed birds' nests, or smoked behind the barn, or played marbles on Sunday" (*Deland*). Sometimes it expresses charitable censure of a person of responsible age who has done wrong, or is applied to what is amusingly risqué. "It was only one *naughty* woman out of the world. The clergyman of the parish didn't refuse to give her decent burial" (*Meredith*). "Euphrosyne...had neglected the study of the lives of the saints, and turned her attention to the *naughty* reading in the Greek classics" (*G. Finlay*).

Ana. Iniquitous, *vicious, villainous: *base, low, vile: *immoral, unmoral, amoral.

Ant. Good. — ***Con.*** Righteous, virtuous, *moral, ethical, noble.

2 **Bad, poor, wrong** come into comparison only in their most general senses when they mean not measuring up to a standard of what is satisfactory. **Bad** (as opposed to *good*) implies a failure to meet one's approval; it may or may not imply positive condemnation, but it always suggests that the thing so described falls below the mark or is not up to what one would call good; as, he is a *bad* correspondent; her handwriting is very *bad;* it's a *bad* day for a long walk. In richer use it often also implies positive harmfulness; as, a *bad* light for the eyes; *bad* food for the young; a *bad* book for a depressed person; a *bad* environment; it is *bad* for her to live alone. Sometimes it suggests corruption, pollution, or the like; as, this meat is *bad; bad* air; *bad* water. Often also it may suggest unpleasantness in any degree, in this sense ranging from that which is merely displeasing to that which is offensive, or painful, or a cause of unhappiness; as, it leaves a *bad* taste in the mouth; to have *bad* news; a *bad* prospect; he always comforted himself when things were *bad* by thinking how much worse they might have been. **Poor** (also as opposed to *good*) also implies a failure to reach a satisfactory point, but it usually imputes to the thing so described a deficiency in amount or in returns, or a lack of a quality or qualities essential to excellence; thus, a *poor* crop is one that is relatively scanty; *poor* land is wanting in fertility; a *poor* book may be devoid of interest or artistic quality; a *poor* carpenter is one lacking in skill; so, business was *poor* this year; a *poor* dancer; *poor* bread; a *poor* return for one's effort. **Wrong** (as opposed to *right*) in all of its senses (see FALSE) implies a failure to conform to a strict standard: as here compared, it suggests deviation from a standard of what is satisfactory or, more specifically, fit, appropriate, proper, orderly, or the like; as, I know that something is *wrong* with this suit; do not make a *wrong* choice in selecting your profession; to hang a picture in the *wrong* light; there is nothing *wrong* in this arrangement of the furniture.

Ant. Good. — ***Con.*** Excellent, perfect, meritorious (see corresponding nouns at EXCELLENCE): right (see GOOD).

badge. *Sign, token, mark, note, symptom.

badger, *v.* *Bait, hound, chevy, hector, ride, heckle.

Ana. *Annoy, vex, bother, irk: harass, harry, *worry, pester, plague, tease.

badinage. Badinage, persiflage, raillery agree in denoting a kind of banter. **Badinage** is applied to banter that is playful and delicate, **persiflage** to that which is derisive but not cutting, and **raillery** to that which is keen and often sarcastic in its ridicule. "Love...permits itself even gentle mocking and friendly *badinage*" (*Mrs. H. Ward*). "I have the fresh and charming letter she wrote to her husband on the occasion...with a trace of gay *persiflage* of all the old people at Sudbury and their meeting-house" (*H. Ellis*). "A company in which you have been galled by the *raillery* of some wag by profession" (*J. Beresford*).

Ana. Bantering *or* banter, chaffing, rallying, kidding, joshing, jollying (see corresponding verbs at BANTER): *fun, game, jest, sport.

badlands. *Waste, desert, wilderness.

baffle. Balk, circumvent, outwit, foil, thwart, *frustrate.

Ana. *Puzzle, mystify, confound, dumfound: discomfit, rattle, faze, *embarrass, disconcert: *confuse, addle, muddle, bemuddle: *hamper, fetter, hog-tie: *hinder, impede, obstruct, block.

bag, *n.* **Bag, sack, pouch** are general terms denoting a container made of a flexible material such as paper, cloth, or leather, and open or opening at the top. **Bag** is the widest in its range of application for it is referable to anything that comes under this general description and is used to hold something; as, a money *bag;* a traveling *bag;* a paper *bag;* a trapper's *bag;* a saddle*bag;* a mail *bag.* It is also referable to such a container and its contents; as, a *bag* of flour; a *bag* of money; a *bag* of game. **Sack** is usually more restricted in its application than *bag:* within these limits, however, the terms are interchangeable. For *sack* commonly suggests oblong shape, a coarse material and, often, crude workmanship; as, a gunny *sack;* a paper *sack;* flour *sacks.* It is probably more often used than *bag* when it refers to containers and their contents being stored, marketed, transported, or the like; as, to deliver 1000 *sacks* of grain; *sacks* of potatoes; to sell coal in *sacks.* **Pouch** is applied chiefly to a small bag which is carried on the person or in the hand and which serves as a substitute for a pocket. In current use, it specifically designates a bag or sack that is opened or closed by means of a gathering string, zipper, or the like; as, a tobacco *pouch;* a *pouch* for bullets; a *pouch*-shaped handbag; a mail *pouch.*

bag, *v.* Capture, trap, snare, entrap, ensnare, *catch, nab, cop.

baggage, *n.* **1 Baggage, luggage, impedimenta** come into comparison as denoting the trunks, valises, etc., containing personal effects, carried by one who is traveling, or transported for him in a railway train or other conveyance (as in a baggage car, a luggage van). **Baggage** is the usual term in the United States and in Canada, and **luggage** in Great Britain. However, *baggage* is occasionally used in Great Britain in its older sense of army equipment that is being moved (in a baggage, or supply, train), and *luggage* is coming into common use in the United States as a collective term for trunks, valises, suitcases, and the like, thought of as merchandise, and not as filled containers of personal property. **Impedimenta** is used humorously in all English-speaking countries for baggage or luggage regarded as an encumbrance; it is, however, the technical military term for *baggage* as the entire equipment of a moving army.

2 Minx, hussy, *wench.

bail, *n.* Bond, surety, security, *guarantee, guaranty.

bail *or* **bale,** *v.* Lade, *dip, ladle, scoop, spoon, dish.

bailiff. 1 Agent, factor, *steward, reeve, seneschal, major-domo, oeconomus.

2 Constable, catchpole, officer, *policeman, bobby, peeler, copper, cop, bull.

bailiwick. Province, domain, territory, *field, sphere.

bait, *n.* *Lure, snare, trap, decoy.

Ana. Allurement, attraction (see corresponding verbs at ATTRACT): enticement, temptation (see corresponding verbs at LURE).

bait, *v.* **Bait, badger, heckle, hector, chevy** (*also* **chivy** *or* **chivvy**), **hound, ride** agree in meaning to torment or harass another person by efforts to break him down. **Bait** derives its implications from its original and still frequent reference to the action of dogs set on to bite and worry an animal such as a chained bear, boar, or bull. Both in this and in extended use it suggests wanton cruelty or malicious delight in persecution. "A stone post ...to which the oxen had formerly been tied for *baiting* with dogs to make them tender before they were killed in the adjoining shambles" (*Hardy*). "The diversion of *baiting* an author has the sanction of all ages" (*Johnson*). **Badger** is more specific than *bait.* Literally it means to bait a badger that has been trapped in a hole or barrel and can neither escape nor adequately defend himself from attack; in extended use as referred to persons, it implies pestering or persecuting that drives the victim into a hopelessly confused or frenzied state of mind; as, to *badger* a witness being cross-examined. "I'm so pressed and *badgered,* I don't know where to turn" (*Thackeray*). **Heckle** implies persistent questioning of a speaker (as a candidate for election, or a legislator discussing a bill before the house, or a person advocating or condemning a movement or cause) and an attempt to bring out his weaknesses or to destroy the effect of his argument. In current use it carries a weaker implication of catechizing than formerly, and suggests an intent to harass and confuse a speaker by frequent interruptions and by inconvenient or embarrassing questions; as, the advocates of any unpopular cause must learn to endure *heckling;* British legislators are more accustomed than American legislators to being *heckled.* **Hector** always carries a suggestion of bullying, but its original implication of brutality or intimidation has grown increasingly weaker and the implication of spirit-breaking scolding or of maddening domineering treatment has taken its place. "We are...not to be *hectored,* and bullied, and beat into compliance" (*Fielding*). "They had hard times when they were little...and were *hectored* and worried when they ought to have been taking some comfort" (*H. B. Stowe*). "Mrs. Morel shifted in her chair, angry with him [her son] for his *hectoring*" (*D. H. Lawrence*). **Chevy** (a predominantly English word) and **hound** both stress relentless chasing and pursuing. *Chevy,* however, often also suggests teasing or annoying past the endurance of the victim (as, he was so *chevied* by the older boys that he ran away from school), and *hound* implies persistent and long-continued persecution till the tormentor's end is achieved or the victim acknowledges himself defeated; as, he was *hounded* by reporters until he made his stand known. "Grandfather had been *hounded* out of his congregation because he couldn't hold her to their standards of behavior for a minister's wife" (*M. Austin*). **Ride** often carries a step further its earlier meaning of to ride hard or exhaust, so that it not only suggests reference to a horse or idea, but also to a person. In such use, which is chiefly colloquial, it implies persistent goading, pricking, or spurring, as by criticism, ridicule, or onerous impositions; as, a hard taskmaster *rides* those who serve him; he was *ridden* so hard by the coach that he was no longer fit to remain on the team.

Ana. *Worry, annoy, harass, harry: torment, rack, torture, try, *afflict.

bake, *v.* **1 Bake, roast, broil, grill, barbecue** come into comparison as meaning to cook by exposure to dry heat. **Bake** implies cooking in an oven or a similar enclosure with heated sides or walls so that the surfaces of the food are browned or toasted and the inside is thoroughly cooked but not hardened; as, to *bake* a cake, a fish, a pie, sausages, beans, a custard, a soufflé. *Bake* is also used of batters or soft mixtures that are quickly cooked on a hot griddle, usually without fat, and turned as soon as brown on one side; as, to *bake* pancakes or scones. **Roast** originally implied and still often implies exposure to an open fire or flame or other form of radiant heat; as, to *roast* chicken on a spit; to *roast* ears of corn. However, it now more often implies oven cooking, but at a heat intense enough to cook the surfaces so quickly that the juices are in part imprisoned and the natural flavor is retained; it often also connotes basting with the juices that have escaped; hence, it is more often used of meats than *bake,* which usually connotes more or less drying of the insides; as, to *roast* beef or lamb. It is also used of foods susceptible of being cooked in a bed of hot ashes, sand, stones, and the like, such as potatoes or apples. *Roast* is idiomatically used of coffee berries, chestnuts, and the like, which are cooked quickly, often in revolving ovens, so as to bring out flavors not apparent in their green state. **Broil** implies exposure to fire, as to hot coals, a flame, or other form of radiant heat, or rapid cooking on a grill or gridiron, so as to give very brown surfaces and juicy insides. The word is occasionally used without connoting use of radiant heat but these instances are few and commonly imply the use of a very hot, often red-hot, griddle or spider. *Broil* is used chiefly in reference to meats, fish, and the like, that come in slices, steaks, or slabs; as, to *broil* a chop or chicken in preference to frying it; to *broil* tomatoes; to broil mushrooms. **Grill** (as here compared: see AFFLICT), a close synonym of *broil*, is now often preferred to *broil* in modern use when it is the intention to imply cooking over hot coals on a grill or gridiron; as, to *grill* a steak; to *grill* a cutlet. **Barbecue** usually suggests roasting or grilling of an entire carcass or of a large portion or large pieces of it before an open fire, on a gridiron or revolving spit, or in a trench: in modern use basting with a highly seasoned sauce made with vinegar is also usually implied; as, to *barbecue* a hog or an ox.

2 Parch, *dry, desiccate, dehydrate.

balance, *n.* **1 Balance, scale** (*or* **scales**) come into comparison when they mean a device for weighing ponderable things. **Balance** usually suggests the primitive instrument with a beam or lever supported exactly in the middle, and carrying at either end a suspended dish or pan (a scale), each of which is exactly the same weight as the other. When a weight is put into one pan, the other rises and is not again brought to its normal horizontal position until something that is of equal weight is put into it. The forms of balances have changed much in the course of time, but whatever form is indicated by the word, the term implies an equalization of a pull on one side and a pull on the other, with resulting equilibrium and rest. **Scale** (etymologically, a cup or bowl), or the more frequent **scales,** though originally applied to the pan (or pans) of a balance, and later to the balance itself, is now more often used of an apparatus for discovering the exact weight of a thing (rather than for finding its equivalent in weight). This apparatus usually has only one dish, pan, or, for larger things, platform, in or on which the thing to be weighed is placed. In some cases, it has a visible beam which is inscribed with a graduated scale (see SCALE, *n.*) of weights, and which drops slightly when a sliding weight, or poise, drawn across it reaches the figure which shows the exact weight. In other forms no mechanism is visible, the weight of that on the platform or in the pan being indicated by a hand pointing to a figure on a dial. Since both of these types of instrument are in common use today, **scales** is now more often employed than *balance* except in their extended senses. When the idea of weighing or evaluating one thing in terms of another is emphasized, *balance* is the preferred word; when that of determining the exact value or importance of a thing or the exact point as in a course, development, or the like, where there is neither excess nor deficiency or where the odds are for or against a thing, or where change occurs and an issue is determined, *scale* or *scales* is the preferred word. This is evident in idiomatic expressions; as, he was weighed in the *balance* (not *scales*) and found wanting (compare the original: "Thou art weighed in the *balances*, and art found wanting."—*Daniel* v. 27); that one word was sufficient to turn the *scale* (or *scales:* but not *balance*) in his favor. "Poetic Justice, with her lifted *scale*, Where, in nice *balance*, truth with gold she weighs, And solid pudding against empty praise" (*Pope*). "Let none presume to measure the irregularities of Michael Angelo or Socrates by village *scales*" (*Emerson*).

2 Balance, equilibrium, equipoise, poise, tension come into comparison when they denote the stability or the efficiency which results from the equalization or the exact adjustment of two or more opposing or opposite forces affecting a thing. **Balance** implies a state in which no one part, element, factor, or influence overweights another or is out of due proportion to the others. It therefore suggests a steadiness or well-being that is usually not outwardly evident until a disturbance occurs, as by a maladjustment of weight or energy or by a change in the due proportions; thus, a man loses his *balance* and falls when by slipping on the ice his weight is shifted and his legs no longer support him; one's mental *balance* depends not only on not allowing one's emotions or imagination to get the better of one's reason, but also on one's ability to keep all three powers working effectively in co-operation with each other; a *balance* of power is said to exist among neighboring nations or groups of allied nations when no one nation or group is decidedly stronger (especially in a military sense) than any of the others. "Can we spoil the *balance* [between negative and positive electricities]? Indeed we can! That is precisely what we are doing by rubbing amber on cloth. We rub some of the negative electrons out of the cloth and into the amber" (*Karl K. Darrow*). **Equilibrium** is often used interchangeably with *balance* when the latter implies equality in weight or energy of forces that exert a pull on each other. *Equilibrium*, however, has a different range of application and is often more restricted in its implications. Except when it denotes a mental characteristic it commonly suggests a mechanically produced or producible, rather than an organic or inherent, property which is dependent either on a thing's shape or construction with reference to its resistance to pressure, strain, or stress, or on a thing's support with reference to its center of gravity or to conditions in its supporting medium (air, water, etc.). The term also implies, as *balance* does not, a tendency to return to the original position after a disturbance or displacement, or the extent to which this tendency exists; hence, when displacement is suggested, *stable equilibrium* implies power of recovery, *unstable equilibrium*, the tendency to move further from its original position, and *neutral equilibrium*, the remaining in equilibrium despite a change of position. Thus, a naval architect must give thought in designing to the ship's *equilibrium* (that is, not only to its ability to move on even keel through the water, but also to its ability to regain its position when buffeted by heavy seas); a flying airplane maintains its *equilibrium* so long as there is fuel to propel it and there is sufficient support from the pressure of air or wind against its wings; a knife may be held aloft by some slight support, such as a pencil, without losing its *equilibrium* if its center of gravity rests on the support. **Equipoise** usually implies either perfection of balance or stability of equilibrium; as, in a properly constructed girder there are two strains, tension and compression, which, because of their *equipoise*, offset each other; in an ideal democracy, the executive, legislative, and judicial powers are held in *equipoise*. "By Art alone can true harmony in human affairs be fostered, true Proportion revealed, and true *Equipoise* preserved" (*Galsworthy*). "There is here [in Marvell's poetry] an *equipoise*, a balance and proportion of tones, which, while it cannot raise Marvell to the level of Dryden or Milton, extorts an approval which these poets do not receive from us" (*T. S. Eliot*). **Poise,** as here compared (see also TACT), is a shortening of the phrase *equal* or *even poise*, which denoted equality of poise (that is, of weight, which is a pull downward) of two opposed or different things. In current use, *equipoise* names the quality characteristic of something which maintains its equilibrium or balance, and *poise* names the state (often temporary) or the appearance of perfect equilibrium or balance. *Poise* therefore often suggests suspension, or seeming suspension, of motion or effort; as, the *poise* of a gull in its flight. "The Central Powers, which hold the lasting Orbs [the celestial bodies] in their just *Poize*" (*Shaftesbury*). "No trepidation...should imperil from its *poise* The ball o' the world" (*Browning*). *Poise* is also preferable to *equipoise* when mental equilibrium is implied and the emphasis is upon the state of mind rather than on the mental characteristic. "Dreadful things should not be known to young people until they are old enough to face them with a certain *poise*" (*B. Russell*). **Tension** in this, its least common sense, as in its other sense (see STRESS, 1), implies strain—either a pull from both ends or outward pressure in every direction. It comes into comparison with words of this group only when it implies such equality in the force of the pulls or outward pressures that there is tautness without danger of breaking apart or there is expansion to the limit without undue strain at any one point. Oftentimes *tension*, when it is used with these implications, is modified by *proper*, *due*, or a similar word; however, it is employed with increasing frequency without such a qualifier with the same meaning; as, the warp threads on the loom must be held in *tension;* in a healthy living cell, the cell wall is in a state of *tension*. In extended use, *tension* is often employed in reference to a mental or spiritual condition in which opposing or opposite powers, or qualities, or moods, are not only balanced but have full play. *Tension* in this sense implies far more vitality, tone, and energy than *balance*. "The youthful intellect is thus held in full *tension*, and its developing energy directed into all sorts of new channels" (*H. Ellis*). "In letting the whole physical system lose tone for lack of the *tension* which gayety imparts" (*Brownell*). "Faraday's first great characteristic was his trust in facts, and his second his imagination.... it was because...they were held together in vital *tension* that he became so potent an instrument of research into Nature's secrets" (*H. Ellis*).

3 *Symmetry, proportion, harmony.

4 *Remainder, rest, residue, residuum, leavings, remnant, remains, relics.

balance, *v.* **1** Counterpoise, counterbalance, *compensate, countervail, offset.

Ana. Attune, *harmonize, tune: correspond, accord, square, *agree.

2 Poise, ballast, trim, *stabilize, steady.

Ana. Settle, firm, *set: waver, sway, oscillate, fluctuate (see SWING): rock, *shake.

Con. *Overturn, upset, capsize: *tip, tilt, cant, careen, list, heel.

balcony. Balcony, gallery, loggia, veranda (*or* **verandah**), **piazza, porch, portico, stoop** are here compared as denoting a platform, usually with a balustrade, extending from an outside wall of a building and serving either a decorative or utilitarian purpose, or both. The words are not commonly used with precision, and some historically incorrect applications are now so firmly established in various localities that they have been accepted as good, though not the best, usage. It is the intent of this article only to indicate the applications which meet approval on historical and architectural grounds, so far as these can be determined. **Balcony** is applicable to any such structure, large or small, which is unroofed, supported by brackets, corbels, consoles, or the like, and enclosed by a balustrade or railing; thus, a *balcony* may be outside a window or a door, or it may extend along the front or side, or part of the front or side of a building. The term usually implies elevation. **Gallery** here, as in all of its senses (see PASSAGE, MUSEUM), connotes length and narrowness. It may be applied to a long narrow balcony extending along an outer wall, but it is also applied to a similar structure that has a roof upheld by pillars or columns and is supported on projecting members such as brackets, or on a foundation as of stone, bricks, or wood. *Gallery*, unlike *balcony*, does not invariably suggest openness on three sides; a gallery may be in a wall's recess and open only at the front. **Loggia,** in technical architectural use, is applied only to a balcony or a covered gallery that is an integral part of a building's design or an essential decorative feature. In current nontechnical use, it is applied chiefly to such a structure in a magnificent or pretentious house, which is used for out-of-door living in mild or warm weather, whether or not it is technically describable as a balcony or gallery. The approved term for a covered out-of-door structure attached to a house, open to the air except on one or two sides, often protected by screens or lattices, and used as though it were a living room, is **veranda.** Except in certain localities, this term carries none of the definite implications of shape, construction, placing, or the like, which are so strong in nearly all the other words of this group but it commonly suggests openness, airiness, and suitability for out-of-door living. **Piazza** is often loosely applied, especially in the English-speaking parts of the Western Hemisphere, to a veranda. Historically, the word means an open square in a city, often one surrounded by important buildings, such as in European cities a church, a hall of justice, a palace, and the like. **Porch** is also used loosely in place of *veranda;* in strict use, however, a porch is a roofed entrance to a building more or less open at the sides, but designed chiefly for the protection from the weather of those who are entering or leaving a building. Such porches are characteristic of some of the older churches in Great Britain, France, and other European countries, their place often being taken in modern churches by vestibules (in some localities called *porches*); they are also common in house construction, especially in countries having rainy or wintry seasons; thus, a front, side, or back *porch* leads to a front, side, or back door. Because *porch* in *sun porch* and *sleeping porch* does not imply entrance from without, these structures are by some preferably called *verandas*. **Portico,** like *porch*, suggests a structure before an entrance; the term, however, is applied chiefly to a gallerylike colonnade which fronts a building in a classic style of architecture and which serves chiefly as an ambulatory. **Stoop,** which is of Dutch origin, was originally used in and around New York City and is now used elsewhere to designate a small porch, flanked by seats or benches, at the entrance to a house; it is now also applied to any platform, at the entrance to a house, which one ascends by a step or two, or more often by a flight of steps (as in houses having a high basement); as, rows of brownstone houses with high *stoops*.

bald. *Bare, barren, naked, nude.

Ana. Austere, *severe: unembellished, unadorned, unornamented (see affirmative verbs at ADORN): *colorless, uncolored.

Con. *Ornate, florid.

bale, *n.*[1] *Evil, ill.

Ana. Harm, hurt, *injury, mischief, damage: woe, dole, anguish, *sorrow, grief: *disaster, calamity: misery, *distress, dolor.

Ant. Bliss. — *Con.* *Happiness, felicity, beatitude, blessedness: joy, *pleasure, delight.

bale, *n.*[2] *Bundle, package, pack, fardel, parcel, bunch, packet.

bale, *v.* Variant of BAIL, *v.*

baleful. Malefic, malign, *sinister.

Ana. Threatening, menacing (see THREATEN): *ominous, portentous, fateful: hellish, *infernal: diabolical, *fiendish, devilish.

Ant. Beneficent. — *Con.* *Beneficial, advantageous: salutary, wholesome, *healthful: benign, *favorable, propitious, auspicious.

balk, *v.* **1** *Frustrate, thwart, foil, baffle, circumvent, outwit.

Ana. Defeat, beat, lick, *conquer, overcome: block, obstruct, impede, *hinder: *prevent, forestall.

Ant. Forward. — *Con.* Further, promote, *advance: abet (see INCITE): assist, aid, *help: *support, uphold, back.

2 Jib, shy, boggle, stickle, scruple, *demur, strain, stick.

Ana. *Hesitate, falter, waver: refuse, *decline: shrink, flinch, quail, *recoil.

Con. *Yield, submit, capitulate, succumb, relent.

balky. *Contrary, restive, perverse, froward, wayward.

Ana. Hesitant, reluctant, averse, loath, *disinclined, indisposed: *obstinate, stubborn, mulish: refractory, recalcitrant, *unruly.

Con. Amenable, docile, tractable, *obedient, biddable: submissive, subdued, *tame.

ball, *n.* *Sphere, globe, orb.

ballast, *v.* *Stabilize, steady, balance, trim, poise.

balloon, *n.* *Aerostat, blimp, dirigible, airship, zeppelin.

ballot, *n.* Vote, *suffrage, franchise.

ballyhoo, *n.* *Publicity, promotion, propaganda.

Ana. Advertisement, broadcasting (see under DECLARE).

balm. Balm, salve, emollient, demulcent come into comparison chiefly in their figurative and extended senses rather than in their literal senses, though in the latter they all come under the description of remedies that ease pain and soothe. A **balm** literally is an aromatic preparation, especially one that cools and refreshes as well as soothes. Hence, in its extended sense, the word is applied to that which delights, refreshes, or comforts almost in the same degree that it relieves. "Sleep...sore labour's bath, *Balm* of hurt minds" (*Shak.*). "We are denied the one thing that might heal us and keep us, that might bring *balm* to the bruised heart" (*Wilde*). A **salve** is a waxy or greasy substance applied to sores or wounds, especially (and always in older medical use) to cover and protect them and keep them from becoming painful or inflamed. Figuratively, the term is applied to anything laid on to quiet disturbance, prevent an outbreak or outburst of feeling, or the like. " 'When mamma asks I will tell,' was the *salve* that he laid upon his conscience" (*Kipling*). "All your processes of election, your so-called democratic apparatus, are only a blind to the inquiring, a sop to the hungry, a *salve* to the pride of the rebellious" (*Galsworthy*). An **emollient** is a preparation applied to the skin and mucous membranes that are dry, harsh, irritated, and the like, in order to soothe, soften, or sometimes relax, the tissues. Figuratively, it is more often used as an adjective than as a substantive, and it frequently adds to the implication of soothing a hint of enervation. "For the business of poetry...is to set up a sweet denial of the harsh facts that confront all of us—to soothe us in our agonies with *emollient* words" (*Mencken*). A **demulcent** is an oily or mucilaginous substance used on abraded or inflamed mucous membranes as a protective film and a soothing agency. It is not so frequent as the others in figurative use, even as an adjective, but has sometimes been thought of as a counteractant or a salve to acrimony; thus, one who "pours oil on troubled waters" in a controversy may be said to exert a *demulcent* influence.

Ana. Comfort, solace, consolation (see corresponding verbs at COMFORT): refreshing *or* refreshment, renewing *or* renewal, rejuvenation (see corresponding verbs at RENEW).

Ant. Irritant.

balmy. 1 Aromatic, fragrant, *odorous, redolent.

Ana. Refreshing, restoring, rejuvenating (see RENEW): pleasing, grateful, welcome, *pleasant.

Ant. Rank, noisome. — *Con.* *Malodorous, fetid, stinking, fusty, musty, putrid.

2 *Soft, gentle, bland, mild, lenient.

Ana. Agreeable, *pleasant, gratifying, grateful: gladdening, delighting, rejoicing, regaling (see PLEASE): assuaging, allaying, lightening, relieving (see RELIEVE): salubrious, salutary (see HEALTHFUL).

Con. *Intense, vehement: vexing, bothering *or* bothersome, irking *or* irksome, annoying (see corresponding verbs at ANNOY).

bamboozle. Trick, hoodwink, *dupe, gull, hoax, befool.

Ana. Delude, *deceive, beguile, mislead: outwit, circumvent (see FRUSTRATE): defraud, cozen, overreach, *cheat, swindle.

ban, *v.* **1** Anathematize, curse, damn, objurgate, *execrate.

Ana. Denounce, condemn, reprobate, censure (see CRITICIZE): *disapprove, deprecate: *malign, asperse, vilify.

Ant. Bless. — *Con.* Extol, laud, *praise, acclaim: applaud, *commend.

2 Prohibit, *forbid, interdict, inhibit, enjoin.

Ana. Bar, block, *hinder: *prevent, preclude: *exclude, debar, rule out.

Con. Allow, permit, suffer, *let: tolerate, abide, suffer (see BEAR).

banal. Flat, jejune, inane, vapid, wishy-washy, *insipid.

Ana. *Trite, hackneyed: *simple, fatuous, silly, asinine: commonplace, platitudinous, bromidic (see corresponding nouns at COMMONPLACE).

Ant. Original: recherché. — *Con.* Fresh, *new, novel: pithy, terse, succinct (see CONCISE): stimulating *or* stimulative, provoking *or* provocative, exciting, piquing (see corresponding verbs at PROVOKE).

band, *n.* **1** *Bond, tie.

Ana. Connection, link, joining (see corresponding verbs at JOIN): *joint, articulation, suture.

2 *Strip, stripe, ribbon, fillet.

3 Troop, troupe, *company, party.

Ana. Coterie, clique, *set, circle: horde, mob, *crowd: society, club, *association, order.

bandit. *Brigand, highwayman, footpad, marauder.

bandy, *v.* *Exchange, interchange, swap.

bane. *Poison, venom, virus, toxin.

baneful. *Pernicious, noxious, deleterious, detrimental.

Ana. Harmful, injurious, mischievous, hurtful (see corresponding nouns at INJURY): malign, *sinister, baleful: *poisonous, venomous, toxic.

Ant. Beneficial. — *Con.* Advantageous, profitable (see BENEFICIAL): salutary, wholesome, *healthful.

banish. Banish, exile, expatriate, ostracize, deport, transport, extradite agree in denoting to remove by authority or force from a country, state, or sovereignty. To **banish** is to compel, by public edict or sentence, to leave a country (which may or may not be one's own) either permanently or for a fixed time, and with or without restriction to a given place. To **exile** is to banish or cause to remove under constraint from one's own country; it may connote either expulsion by formal sentence or decree or the compulsion of circumstances and an enforced absence, or sometimes, prolonged voluntary absence. Thus, Russians and foreigners alike may be *banished* from Russia, but only Russians *exiled* to Siberia; Dante was *banished* from his native Florence because of political troubles, but he *exiled* himself for the rest of his life as a protest against conditions there. **Expatriate** differs from *exile* sometimes in its implication of loss of citizenship in one's own country (as, to *expatriate* Jews from Germany), oftener in its implication of voluntary exile or naturalization in another country (as, Henry James *expatriated* himself). *Exile* often suggests a possibility of return with full rights to one's own country; *expatriate*, however, may imply, but often does not, the exclusion of that possibility. To **ostracize,** historically, was to banish temporarily and by popular vote from any one of certain cities in ancient Greece a person considered dangerous to the state. The term is now chiefly used in an extended sense which implies not expatriation, but a forced exclusion, by common consent, from recognition or acceptance by society; the society implied is usually, but not invariably, that which is comprised of the social circle or group of social circles leading a life marked by leisure and devotion to pleasure and fashionable sports; as, since his downfall, he has been completely *ostracized*. To **deport** is to send a person out of a country of which he is not a citizen, either because his presence is considered inimical to the public welfare or because he has not lawfully entered that country. It often, but not necessarily, implies return to the country of which the deported person is a citizen or subject, or from which he has emigrated, especially if he is without funds to go where he chooses. To **transport,** as here compared, is to banish to a penal colony or the like a person convicted of a crime; as, convicts were *transported* to Australia. To **extradite** is to deport an alleged criminal at the request of the sovereignty or state having jurisdiction to try the charge; as, the United States refused to *extradite* certain persons on the ground that they were allegedly guilty of political offenses which are not *extraditable;* the escaped prisoner was *extradited* by the State of Illinois at the request of the State of Georgia.

Ana. *Eject, expel, oust: *exclude, debar, eliminate, shut out.

Con. Admit, *receive, accept: *harbor, shelter, entertain: protect, shield (see DEFEND).

bank, *n.* **1** Embankment, terrace, *mound, dune, tumulus, barrow.

2 *Shoal, bar, reef.

3 *Shore, ripa, strand, coast, beach, foreshore, littoral.

4 Mass, heap, pile, stack, shock, **cock.** See under HEAP, *v.*

Ana. *Aggregate, aggregation, conglomerate, conglomeration: assemblage, assembly, collection, gathering (see under GATHER).

bank, *v.*[1] Mass, *heap, pile, stack, shock, cock.

Ana. Collect, assemble, *gather.

Con. *Scatter, disperse.

bank, *v.*[2] *Rely, count, reckon, trust, depend.

bankrupt, *adj.* Insolvent (see under INSOLVENCY).

bankrupt, *v.* Impoverish, exhaust, *deplete, drain.

Ana. Denude, *strip, bare: sap, cripple, disable, undermine (see WEAKEN).

bankruptcy. Failure, *insolvency, receivership, suspension.

banner, *n.* *Flag, standard, ensign, color, streamer, pennant, pennon, jack.

banner, *adj.* Pre-eminent, incomparable, superlative, surpassing, peerless, *supreme, transcendent.

Ana. Paramount, *dominant, predominant, sovereign: outstanding, salient, signal (see NOTICEABLE).

banquet, *n.* **Banquet, dinner** are here compared only with reference to the propriety of their use in designating an elaborate meal (usually an evening meal) for the entertainment of guests, the members of an association, or the like. The choice of *banquet* in designating such a meal has frequently been criticized, the preference being given to *dinner*. Not only current good use but good usage in the past justifies the employing of **banquet** when there is the intent to suggest the sumptuousness of the meal, the magnificence of its setting, and often, the ceremonial character of the entertainment. Only in some American use is it thought of as a dinner held in a more or less public place, such as a hotel or an auditorium, and followed by speechmaking. "This is the feast that I have bid her to, And this the *banquet* she shall surfeit on" (*Shak.*). "Royal Maud...greets most noble Glocester from her heart, Intreating him, his captains, and brave knights, To grace a *banquet*" (*Keats*). "Grandees who give *banquets* worthy Jove" (*Browning*). Because of its historical implications, *banquet* is now used with propriety only as a descriptive term. **Dinner** is the preferred designation, especially in invitations and in colorless reference to such an affair; as, the president and his wife plan to give several state *dinners* (not *banquets*) this season; he is in great demand as a speaker at public *dinners;* the annual *dinner* of the Chamber of Commerce.

banshee. Shee, faery, *fairy, fay, goblin.

banter, *v.* **Banter, chaff, rally, quiz, kid, rag, guy, rib, josh, jolly** agree in denoting to make fun of good-naturedly. The same distinctions in implications and connotations are found in their corresponding nouns. Typical methods of such funmaking are: reminding one of an actual fault, foible, failure, shortcoming, etc. (sometimes indirectly by bestowal of exaggerated praise obviously remote from the truth); playful imputation of undeserved success; attempting to dupe a person into believing what is untrue (esp., absurdly untrue) in order that one may laugh at his gullibility. **Banter** is the generic term, and may usually be substituted for any of the others, though not without loss of specificness. " 'Why didn't you get tipsy, Sir? Don't you ever intoxicate yourself but at lawful marriages?...' Ripton endured his *bantering* that he might hang about Richard" (*Meredith*). To **chaff** is to nettle with rough banter. "Have you ever been stuck with a horse?...What I resent is the *chaff* that follows, especially from the boy who stuck me" (*Kipling*). **Rally** implies greater keenness and sarcasm, and frequently a poking fun at matters so private as to cause extreme embarrassment or resentment. "He loved his mistress....no one dared...*rally* him on his weakness" (*Shaw*). To **quiz** is usually to banter by asking puzzling or embarrassing questions. "Attacked by the older students...with all sorts of *quizzing* questions" (*C. C. Felton*). **Kid** (slang) is frequently as general in meaning as *banter*. "He [Édouard Herriot] is very fond of placing his hand on his heart and declaiming about his warm virtues. He gets a lot of *kidding* for it" (*John Gunther*). More often than perhaps any other word in this group, however, it specifically implies an attempt at good-natured imposition on one's gullibility; thus, "No *kidding?*" is a common way of asking "Are you serious?" of one who has made a statement that sounds incredible. "She says he's going to do a portrait of her. I think he's *kidding* her" (*Harper's Mag.*). Used with a reflexive pronoun, *kid* implies a shutting one's eyes to the truth; as, if you think you can avoid hard work and long hours and yet write something memorable, you are just *kidding* yourself. To **rag** (slang) is to banter repeatedly or persistently and, often, annoyingly to the victim. "I won't *rag* you any more, if you'll tell me one thing" (*M. Sinclair*). "Baiting Penhale became a fashionable pastime....the small boys took up the *ragging*" (*C. Garstin*). **Guy** (colloq.) implies public, vociferous, often concerted, often merciless but nevertheless good-natured, banter. "If you heard all that gang *guyin'* me you'd think 'twas somethin' " (*J. C. Lincoln*). **Rib** (slang) implies bantering under conditions which make it impossible or inadvisable for the butt to retort or defend himself, and also often implies assumed identity, often specifically the enactment of a role, on the part of the ribber; as, high government officials are *ribbed* in the skits presented yearly before the Gridiron Club in Washington. "Tamara Geva [actress] *ribs* her fellow Russians as the temperamental ballerina who introduces her equals as her 'supporting cast' " (*Time*). **Josh** (slang, U. S.) and esp. **jolly** (colloq.) imply transparent good humor in the funmaker. *Josh* usually implies homeliness and unsophistication. "By the conclusion, in Gunch's renowned humorous vein, he was enchanted.... 'I've heard your business has been kind of under the eye of the gov'ment since you stole the tail of Eathorne Park and sold it!' 'Oh, you're a great little *josher*, Verg' " (*Sinc. Lewis*). *Jolly* often implies an ulterior aim, such as putting the person bantered into good humor so that he will grant a favor; as, he was a good salesman who *jollied* his customers, but not too obviously.

Ana. Twit, rally, deride, *ridicule.

baptize. **Baptize, christen** agree in meaning to make one a Christian or to admit one to a Christian communion by a ceremony in which water is poured or sprinkled on the head or in which the body is immersed in water. **Baptize** is the precise term for this ceremony because it implies both the rite and its ends. The term may also be used in reference to infants and adults. **Christen** is the popular word (originally meaning to convert to Christianity or to make a Christian by baptizing), but for several centuries it has so emphasized the giving of a name, which is in some churches a part of the ceremony of baptism, that it now is used at times without any reference to the religious ceremony and even with reference to inanimate objects which are formally named, often with a ceremony analogous to that of baptism; thus, "the baby has not yet been *christened*" may mean either "not yet baptized" or "not yet named," though both are commonly implied; to *christen* a ship is to perform the ceremony of breaking a bottle of wine or other liquid against its sides while pronouncing its name.

bar, *n.* **1 Bar, barrier, barricade** agree in meaning something which hinders or obstructs. As here compared, both **bar** and **barrier** apply to that which prevents free communication or passage; more specifically, in their literal uses, *bar* frequently suggests ingress or egress, *barrier*, rather advance, progress, or attack, as that to which the obstacle is opposed; as, the *bars* of a prison, of a gate; a harbor *bar;* a mountain *barrier;* to erect dikes as a *barrier* against the sea; a *barrier* reef. "Religious myths may come to be a *bar* to progress in science" (*Inge*). "A perpetual and impassable *barrier*...between the white race and the one which they had reduced to slavery" (*Ch. Just. Taney*). *Barrier* usually implies greater magnitude or extent than *bar*. **Barricade** is rarely used except in the sense of an obstruction thrown across a street or way to check a hostile advance; as, the fighting at the *barricades* in Paris during the Commune (March–May, 1871).

2 *Obstacle, obstruction, impediment, snag.

Ana. Hindrance, block, dam (see corresponding verbs at HINDER): *difficulty, hardship, vicissitude.

Ant. Advantage. — ***Con.*** Odds, edge (see ADVANTAGE): help, aid, assistance (see under HELP, *v.*).

3 *Shoal, bank, reef.

bar, *v.* Obstruct, block, dam, impede (see HINDER).

Ana. Shut out, debar, *exclude: *prevent, preclude, obviate: *forbid, prohibit, interdict: *close, shut.

Ant. Admit: open. — ***Con.*** Accept, *receive, take.

barbarian, *n.* *Obscurantist, Philistine.

barbarian, *adj.* **Barbarian, barbarous, barbaric, savage** denote in common uncivilized, or characteristic of uncivilized peoples. **Barbarian** expresses little more than the opposite of *civilized*. "She [Rome] saw her glories star by star expire, And up the steep, *Barbarian* monarchs ride" (*Byron*). "Without what we call our debt to Greece we should have neither our religion nor our philosophy nor our science nor our literature nor our education nor our politics. We should be mere *barbarians*" (*Inge*). The noun *barbarian* is sometimes used in the sense of one whose manners are so rude as to suggest those of an uncivilized person. "He'll grow up a *barbarian*, with no manners!" (*Deland*). See *barbarian*, n. at OBSCURANTIST. **Barbarous** is frequently used in the sense of *barbarian*, without further implication; as, "Civilized ages inherit the human nature which was victorious in *barbarous* ages" (*Bagehot*). It may also express the harsh and brutal side of uncivilized life; as, *barbarous* warfare. **Barbaric** refers to the crudeness of taste and fondness for gorgeous display characteristic of uncivilized peoples. "Or where the gorgeous East with richest hand Showers on her kings *barbaric* pearl and gold" (*Milton*). "The whole world seems to be growing increasingly *barbaric* in this matter of symmetry. I have actually heard the epithet beautiful applied to skyscrapers" (*Babbitt*). **Savage** comes into comparison with both *barbarian* and *barbarous*, but it usually suggests a more primitive state and less evidence of organizing power than *barbarian*, and it characteristically implies greater harshness or fierceness than *barbarous*. "The impossibility of reducing a huge, educated population to the spiritual homogeneity of a *savage* tribe" (*A. Huxley*). "With the disappearance of this distinction [between combatants and noncombatants] war becomes pure *savagery*" (*Inge*).

Ant. Civilized.

barbaric. *Barbarian, savage, barbarous.

Ana. *Showy, ostentatious: florid, *ornate, flamboyant: *gaudy, garish, flashy, meretricious.

Ant. Restrained: refined: subdued.

barbarism. 1 Barbarism, barbarity are frequently confused. **Barbarism** is used chiefly of a state of society or of a culture that may be described as *barbarian*, or as neither savage and crude nor civilized and highly refined. "Outside civilisation the divorce [between science and mysticism] is not found; the savage mystic is also the savage man of science, the priest and the doctor are one. It is so also for the most part in *barbarism*" (*H. Ellis*). "The human race...is as yet only a little bit civilized and...in time of serious trouble...has a very strong tendency to stampede back into *barbarism*" (*Lippmann*). **Barbarity** is used chiefly in reference to a temper or to practices that may be described as barbarous, or uncivilized, brutal, and inhumane; as, *barbarity* seldom equaled by the fiercest of savages; "to mitigate the *barbarity* of the criminal law" (*Inge*). Sometimes, however, *barbarity* denotes a taste that is barbaric; as, "the supposed influence of Seneca on the *barbarity* of Elizabethan tragedy" (*T. S. Eliot*).

Ant. Civilization. — ***Con.*** *Culture, cultivation, refinement.

2 Impropriety, *solecism.

barbarity. *Barbarism.
Ana. Barbarousness, savagery, ferociousness *or* ferocity, cruelty, inhumanity (see corresponding adjectives at FIERCE).
Ant. Humaneness. — *Con.* Gentleness, mildness, lenity *or* leniency (see corresponding adjectives at SOFT).

barbarous. **1** Savage, barbaric, *barbarian.
Ana. *Rough, harsh: untutored, untaught, uneducated, illiterate, *ignorant: *rude, rough, crude.
Ant. Civilized: humane.
2 Savage, inhuman, ferocious, *fierce, cruel, fell, truculent.
Ana. Pitiless, ruthless, uncompassionate (see corresponding nouns at PITY): atrocious, monstrous, *outrageous.
Ant. Clement. — *Con.* Merciful, *forbearing, tolerant, lenient: *tender, compassionate, sympathetic: humane, humanitarian, benevolent (see CHARITABLE).

barbecue, *v.* *Bake, roast, broil, grill.

barbette. Parapet, bastion, breastwork, *bulwark, rampart.

bard, *n.* *Poet, scop, trouvère, scald, minstrel, gleeman, jongleur, troubadour, minnesinger, rhymer, rhymester, versifier, poetaster.

bare, *adj.* **1 Bare, naked, nude, bald, barren** come into comparison when they mean destitute or divested of the naturally or conventionally appropriate covering or clothing. **Bare** strongly suggests the removal, or often the rejection, of that which is additional, superfluous, dispensable, acquired, or the like; thus, a *bare* head is one without a hat (especially under circumstances where hats are usually worn); *bare* legs suggest lack of socks or stockings; *bare* trees have lost all their leaves; to take one's *bare* word for a thing is not to ask for anything more, such as confirmation or documentary proof; a *bare* room has no furniture or, more often, only such furniture as is indispensable. "The *bare* statement that 'art is useless' is so vague as to be really meaningless, if not inaccurate and misleading" (*H. Ellis*). **Naked** suggests absence of all covering, especially in the way of protective or ornamental covering. When used with regard to persons, and implying absence of clothing, the word is not uniform in its pictorial and emotional evocations; it may suggest many conditions, such as a state of nature and of physical beauty, a state of destitution and of pitiful suffering, a state of privacy and of admirable modesty or purity, a state of shameful publicity or of wanton exhibitionism. "Eve...in *naked* beauty more adorned, More lovely, than Pandora, whom the gods Endowed with all their gifts" (*Milton*). "Poor *naked* wretches, wheresoe'er you are, That bide the pelting of this pitiless storm" (*Shak.*). " 'But prove me [Godiva] what it is I would not do.' And from a heart as rough as Esau's hand, He answer'd 'Ride you *naked* thro' the town' " (*Tennyson*). In extended use, therefore, *naked* is preferred to *bare* when the emphasis is on revelation or exposure, or on the power of revealing or exposing something as it is in its severe outlines or structure, in its plain truth or without disguise, or in its hidden weakness or strength; as, "Craft must have clothes, but truth loves to go *naked*" (*T. Fuller* [1654–1734]); "the *naked* boughs of winter" (*Binyon*); "It is not asked that poetry should offer *naked* argument" (*Day Lewis*); "the power of striking out, in a few *naked*, simple words, a picture which is ineffaceable" (*Lowes*). **Nude** and *naked* are very close synonyms when they are used in reference to persons, but *nude*, because of its association with the representation of undraped figures in art, tends to suggest little more than the absence of covering and to be comparatively a colorless word with little extended use and with few, if any, significant and distinctive implications. Because of its unequivocal meaning, *nude* is preferred to *naked* when the mere fact of being without clothing is indicated and there is no intent to convey an aesthetic or ethical implication; as, the three *nude* statues in the exhibition; the residents of the houses along the river objected to *nude* swimmers. **Bald** implies absence of a natural covering, originally, and still chiefly, of the hair of the head or, by extension, of foliage, of feathers, or the like. Etymologically, however, the word suggests the conspicuous whiteness of a bald man's head and its lack of color as well as of its natural growth; it is therefore often applied to something white or gray at the top whether it is devoid of its natural covering or not; thus, the *bald* eagle is the common eagle after it has reached an age when its head and neck feathers are white; a *bald* tree is one that no longer bears leaves at its top; a *bald* mountain is one whose peak, usually rocky peak, is bare of vegetation. In extended use, *bald* implies austere or colorless bareness, and a conspicuous absence of qualities that might add charm, vividness, interest, or the like; thus, a *bare* style is one that indicates economy of means or a meagerness of ornament; a *naked* style is one that disguises nothing and shows not the slightest obscurity or hesitancy in presenting the thought; a *bald* style is bare and plain to the point of severity. "His [Wordsworth's] expression may often be called *bald*...; but it is *bald* as the bare mountain tops are *bald*, with a *baldness* which is full of grandeur" (*Arnold*). "He was determined to put the case *baldly*, without vain recrimination or excuse" (*E. Wharton*). **Barren,** in this as well as in its more common sense (see STERILE, 1), implies a lack of fertility or productive power. As a synonym of the other words here discussed, it implies an absence of natural or appropriate covering that is the outward sign of impoverishment, impotency, or aridity; hence, *barren* lands are not only absolutely bare, but they are waste, desolate lands incapable of producing vegetation; a *barren* style is the style of a person who has not the mind, heart, or imagination to give his style any signs of life or vitality, any coloring of fancy, or the like; so, a *barren* life; "*barren* theoretic talk" (*C. E. Montague*); "the bright and *barren* stars" (*R. Macaulay*).
Ana. Stripped, divested, denuded (see STRIP, *v.*): unclothed, undressed, unrobed (see affirmative verbs at CLOTHE).
Ant. Covered.
2 *Mere.

bare, *v.* Denude, divest, *strip, dismantle.
Ant. Cover. — *Con.* *Clothe, dress, apparel, robe, attire: *disguise, cloak, mask, dissemble.

barefaced. Brazen, *shameless, brash, impudent.
Ana. Open, plain, *frank, candid: indecent, unseemly, *indecorous.
Ant. Furtive. — *Con.* Covert, surreptitious, stealthy, *secret.

barely. Scarcely, *hardly.

bargain, *n.* *Contract, compact, pact, indenture, mise.

barge, *n.* Termagant, scold, shrew, vixen, *virago, amazon.

bark, *n.* *Skin, rind, peel, hide, pelt, fell.

baroque, *adj.* *Ornate, florid, rococo, flamboyant.

barren. **1** *Sterile, unfruitful, infertile, impotent.
Ant. Fecund. — *Con.* *Fertile, prolific, fruitful.
2 Bald, *bare, naked, nude.
Ana. Arid, *dry: desolate, forlorn (see ALONE): impoverished, exhausted, depleted (see DEPLETE): austere, *severe, stern.
Con. Luxuriant, lush, *profuse: opulent, *luxurious, sumptuous.

barricade, *n.* Barrier, *bar.
barrier, *n.* Barricade, *bar.
barrister. *Lawyer, counselor, counsel, advocate, attorney, solicitor, proctor, procurator.
barrow. Tumulus, *mound, bank, dune, embankment, terrace.
barter, *v.* Trade, vend, *sell, auction.
Ana. Swap, *exchange, interchange, bandy.
basal. Basic, underlying, *fundamental, substratal, substrative, radical.
base, *n.* **Base, basis, foundation, ground, groundwork** agree in meaning something on which another thing is reared or built or by which it is supported or fixed in place. **Base,** in earliest use, was applied to the lowest part, or bottom, of something and carried no strong implication of purpose as a support or prop (as, at the *base* of a tree or a mountain); the term soon acquired specific reference to a broad bottom or to a substructure on which a thing rests (or seems to rest) for support, or by which it is kept upright or stable; as, the *base* of a pyramid; the *base* of a pillar; the *base* of a lamp; the *base* of a triangle; "The Great War shook civilisation to its *base*" (*Inge*). In its sense development the word often failed to stress a literal underlying, and so came to apply to something which serves either as a starting point of a development, an operation, or a process (as, a *base* of operations; a submarine *base*) or as the essential ingredient of a compound (as, lanolin is the *base* of many cosmetics; dynamite often has an absorbent *base* such as sawdust). **Basis,** like *base* (its close synonym historically) may be used in reference to something that underlies and supports or to something that serves as a starting point; the term, however, is rarely applied to a physical or material thing; thus, one may speak of the *base* (but not the *basis*) of a monument, or of the *basis* (not the *base*) for a certain belief; so, implicit trust is the *basis* of a lasting friendship; to phrase certain questions as a *basis* for discussion; "Tradition forms a *basis* for the acquiring of literary taste" (*Day Lewis*); "Darwinism.... cannot be made the *basis* of a philosophy" (*Inge*). **Foundation,** in precise use, usually implies, as *base* or *basis* sometimes do not imply, solidity in that which underlies and supports, and fixity or stability in that which is erected on that support; thus, a house always has a *base* even if it rests directly on the ground, but may properly be said to have a *foundation* only when it rests on a substructure, such as a wall of stones or bricks, lining an excavation and usually rising above the surface of the ground. A report may be said to have its *basis* (not *foundation*) in speculation, but a report that is said to be without *foundation* has no *basis* in fact. "Let me pry loose old walls; Let me lift and loosen old *foundations*" (*Sandburg*). "As the happiness of the people is the sole end of government, so the consent of the people is the only *foundation* of it" (*John Adams*). "How firm a *foundation*, ye saints of the Lord, Is laid for your faith in His excellent Word!" (*Old Hymn*). **Ground,** in the sense here considered, implies something solid or firm beneath, or a substratum comparable to the earth or ground in its firmness and capacity for support; the term is therefore applied to a material, a substance, a surface, or the like, upon which another thing is built or against which it is displayed; thus, a piece of net may serve as a *ground* upon which a pattern is worked in lacemaking; before a decorative design is applied to a wall, the *ground*, or wall surface, must be treated and colored so that it will take the pattern and display it properly (see also *ground* under REASON). **Groundwork** is applied not to a substratum, but to a substructure; like *foundation*, the term suggests something built up before the superstructure is erected, but unlike *foundation*, it is used chiefly in a figurative sense; as, early training is the *groundwork* of good habits; to lay a *groundwork* in college for one's professional studies. "The *groundwork* of all happiness is health" (*Hunt*).
Ant. Top. — *Con.* *Summit, peak, apex.
base, *adj.* **Base, low, vile** agree in meaning contemptible because beneath what is expected of the average man. That is **base** which excites indignation because devoid of all nobility or even of humanity; the term usually implies the setting (as through cowardice or avarice) of self-interest ahead of duty to others. "He is not Talbot's blood, That *basely* fled when noble Talbot stood" (*Shak.*). "Peace had brought only the shabby, dispiriting spectacle of Versailles, with its *base* greeds and timidities" (*C. E. Montague*). That is **low** which outrages one's sense of what is decent or proper even for the most ignorant of men. The term, when implying moral contemptibility, often suggests a taking advantage of a person who is helpless or not in a position to defend himself, as by cunning, deceit, or other devious practice; as, no one thought he could be *low* enough to steal a nickel from a blind beggar's cup. "Whenever a dramatist wished to introduce intrigue, chicanery, or other dirty work, his *dramatis personae* included a *low* attorney" (*Law Times*). *Low* also is often used of persons, thoughts, language, actions, etc., that strongly offend one's sense of propriety; as, a *low* mind; "snot" is a *low* word. "They were *low*, those sensual feelings; they were ignoble" (*A. Huxley*). That is **vile** which is inexpressibly base or low; the word often implies disgusting foulness or depravity. "It was *vile* indeed to unaccustomed and unhardened senses. Every little habitation...left its own heap of refuse on its own landing, besides flinging other refuse from its own windows" (*Dickens*). "A place where every *vileness* of cruelty and lust was practised" (*Cather*). "The *vilest* epithet in the English language" (*Freeman*).
Ana. *Mean, ignoble, abject, sordid: *bad, evil, ill, wicked: ignominious, infamous, disgraceful (see corresponding nouns at DISGRACE).
Ant. Noble. — *Con.* *Moral, ethical, virtuous, righteous: honorable, *upright, honest, just.
bashful. *Shy, diffident, modest, coy.
Ana. Shrinking, recoiling (see RECOIL, *v.*): timorous, *timid: embarrassed, abashed (see EMBARRASS).
Ant. Forward: brazen. — *Con.* Brash, barefaced, impudent, *shameless: bold, intrepid (see BRAVE).
basic. **1** Basal, *fundamental, underlying, substratal, substrative, radical.
Ana. Principal, capital, *chief, main: primordial, *primary.
Ant. Top: peak (*wage, price, etc.*).
2 *Alkaline.
basis. *Base, foundation, ground, groundwork.
Ana. *Principle, fundamental, axiom, law, theorem: premise, postulate, presupposition, presumption, assumption (see under PRESUPPOSE).
baste, *v.* *Beat, pummel, thrash, thresh, buffet, pound, belabor.
Ana. Chastise, castigate, *punish, discipline.
bastion. Breastwork, barbette, parapet, *bulwark, rampart.
bathos. *Pathos, poignancy.
Ana. Sentimentality, sentimentalism (see SENTIMENT): mawkishness, maudlinism, soppiness, mushiness (see corresponding adjectives at SENTIMENTAL).
bathybic. Bathysmal, abyssal, pelagic, neritic, marine, oceanic, thalassic, *aquatic, lacustrine, lacuscular, fluvial, fluviatile.

bathysmal. Bathybic, abyssal, pelagic, neritic, marine, oceanic, thalassic, *aquatic, lacustrine, lacuscular, fluvial, fluviatile.

batter, *v.* Mangle, *maim, mutilate, cripple.
Ana. *Beat, pound, pummel, thrash, buffet, belabor, baste.

battle, *n.* **Battle, engagement, action, push** agree in denoting a hostile meeting between opposing military forces. **Battle** is commonly used of a general and prolonged combat, and is distinguished, therefore, from *skirmish, brush,* etc. (see ENCOUNTER). **Engagement** stresses the actual encountering of forces, and may be applied to either a general encounter, as between entire armies, or a minor encounter, as between subdivisions or outposts. **Action** is often employed today in place of *battle* or *engagement* when the stress is on the idea of active, frequently sharp, offensive and defensive operations; as, to clear the warship's decks for *action;* Gustavus Adolphus, King of Sweden, was killed in *action* at Lützen, 1632; a brisk *action* between scouting patrols. "How many gentlemen have you lost in this *action?*" (*Shak.*). **Push,** a slang term, is applied to a strongly organized offensive action in which large numbers of troops participate.
Ana. *Encounter, skirmish, brush: *attack, assault, onslaught, onset: combat, conflict, fight, *contest.

battle, *v.* War, fight, *contend, cope.
Ana. Combat, *oppose, resist, withstand: *attack, assail, assault, bombard: kick, protest, *object.

bawl out. Rate, berate, tonguelash, upbraid, *scold, wig, rail, revile, vituperate.
Ana. Reprimand, rebuke, reproach, *reprove, chide: censure, denounce, condemn, reprehend, reprobate (see CRITICIZE).

bay, *n.* Embrasure, *recess, alcove, nook, niche, cubicle, carrell, carol.

be, *v.* **Be, exist, live, subsist** come into comparison only when they mean to have actuality or reality. **Be** (not considered here as a copula, or a verb expressing a relation between subject and predicate terms) applies to whatever has any place in the realm of things describable as real in a material or immaterial sense (see REAL); only its context makes clear whether it asserts physical or spiritual reality. "To *be,* or not to *be:* that is the question" (*Shak.*). "I think, therefore I *am*" (*transl. from Descartes*). "Whatever *is,* is right" (*Pope*). "To *be,* contents his natural desire" (*Pope*). **Exist** adds to *be* the implication of continuance in time; it also commonly implies a place in the realm of things which are describable as entities or as having independent, objective (though not necessarily sensible) being. "A fact which has *existed* cannot be made never to have *existed*" (*Ch. Just. Marshall*). "Everybody saw the drawings of the temples. strange walls and columns, but nobody believed these things *existed*" (*Stark Young*). **Live,** in its primary sense, implies existence in the realm of things which have the character called *life,* or the inner power manifest in plants and animals to maintain existence for a term, to grow, to perform natural functions, to reproduce their kind, and the like; as, many men *live* to be threescore and ten; plants cannot *live* without moisture; whatever *lives* must have sustenance. *Live,* however, is often used in an extended sense, as applied to immaterial entities, ideas, and the like; in this use, it often carries a suggestion of qualities associated with life, such as persistent existence, vigor, activity, and development; as, his name will *live* as long as his country *lives;* poems that *live;* a *living* church. **Subsist** may be used in place of *be,* or *exist,* or *live,* because it may imply the kind of reality or actuality connoted by one of those terms, but it always additionally suggests a relation to or dependence on something; thus, a thing that *subsists* by itself (or is *self-subsistent*) is not dependent on anything outside of itself and is independent and self-contained; an idea *subsists,* or maintains its existence, only so long as it appeals to the mind of thinking men. "Those secret distributions without which the body cannot *subsist* in its vigor" (*Addison*). In current philosophical use, *subsist* is used often in reference to purely mental conceptions, and implies logical validity or the character of being true or logically conceivable. " 'The round square does not *subsist*' is just as true as 'the present King of France does not *exist*' " (*B. Russell*).

beach, *n.* Strand, coast, foreshore, *shore, bank, ripa, littoral.

beachcomber. Comber, breaker, roller, billow, *wave, undulation, ripple.

beak. *Bill, nib.

beam, *n.* *Ray.
Ana. Flash, gleam, glint, scintillation, coruscation (see corresponding verbs at FLASH).

beaming, *adj.* Beamy, radiant, refulgent, effulgent, *bright, brilliant, luminous, lustrous, lambent, lucent.
Ana. Flashing, gleaming, glittering, glistening, glinting, sparkling, coruscating, scintillating (see FLASH, *v.*): glowing, flaming (see BLAZE, *v.*).

beamy. Beaming, radiant, refulgent, effulgent, brilliant, *bright, luminous, lustrous, lambent, lucent.
Ana. See those at BEAMING.

bear, *v.* **1** *Carry, convey, transport, transmit.
Ana. *Move, remove, shift, transfer: hold, *contain.
2 Bear, produce, yield, turn out come into comparison when they mean to bring forth as products. **Bear** usually implies a giving birth to offspring or a bringing of fruit to maturity, though it may be used somewhat figuratively in reference to something which tends to reproduce itself or to aid reproduction, such as the earth, a seed, money, or the like; as, she *bore* three children; the apple trees *bear* (i.e., bear fruit) every year; the soil is not rich enough to *bear* crops; the seed he sowed *bore* fruit; the deposit *bears* a low interest. **Produce** is far wider in its range of application, for it, unlike *bear,* carries no clear implication of a carrying during a period of development prior to the bringing forth; hence, it may be used in the widest sense of bring forth as by human or natural agency (as, he *produced* the book for his friends' inspection; nobody could *produce* the desired witness) and, as here especially considered, in the narrow sense of bringing forth as issue of one's body, one's mind, one's imagination, or as an output of labor or effort; as, it is necessary for the colleges to *produce* straight thinkers; the tree will *produce* no fruit this year; the plantation *produces* a vast amount of cotton; the factory *produces* more shoes than ever; Raphael *produced* an unusual number of widely known paintings; he feels he can never *produce* another book as good as the one he has just written; the glands *produce* secretions. "A plough is useful because it breaks up the ground. But breaking up the ground is...merely useful because it enables seed to be sown. This is useful because it *produces* grain, which is useful because it *produces* bread" (*B. Russell*). **Yield** (as here compared: see also RELINQUISH, YIELD) fundamentally implies a giving out, as of something within the confines of a thing or within one's power of production: it therefore stresses the outcome, result, return, reward, or the like, and not the previous effort or endurance; as, "The utmost care could not always secure the most valuable fruits. The pinery [i.e., a pineapple hothouse] had *yielded* only one hundred in the last year" (*Austen*); (cf. the annual *yield* of a field, orchard, tree, etc.); "two

kinds of classics...those that *yield* their meaning at the first encounter and those that we have to discover by effort and insight" (*Van W. Brooks*); "The discovery of ...its [calcium carbide's] reaction with ordinary water to *yield* a highly flammable gas, acetylene" (*A. C. Morrison*). **Turn out,** like *yield,* stresses the outcome or result, but it always implies previous labor or effort; as, the company promises to *turn out* 300 airplanes a month; "the main object is to *turn out* good Englishmen" (*Inge*).

Ana. Reproduce, propagate, breed, *generate.

3 Bear, suffer, endure, abide, tolerate, stand, brook, agree in denoting to sustain something trying or painful. **Bear** and **suffer** are also synonyms in their more comprehensive denotation to sustain whatever is imposed; as, this theory will *bear* examination; the stone *suffers* no alteration in a colder climate. Both verbs, however, are more often used in their specific senses because of their customary reference, in the case of *bear,* to things that are heavy or difficult, or, in the case of *suffer,* to things that are painful or injurious. *Bear* suggests more the power to sustain than the manner in which something is sustained; as, water as hot as one can *bear* it; to *bear* the brunt of battle; to *bear* affliction. *Suffer* more often implies acceptance of infliction than it implies patience or courage in bearing; as, to *suffer* fools gladly. "Authority...like that of a captain of a football team, which is *suffered* voluntarily in order to achieve a common purpose" (*B. Russell*). **Endure** and **abide,** in precise use, refer to long-continued trials or sufferings borne without giving in. *Endure* usually connotes stamina or firmness of mind; *abide,* patience and submission. "I am able now, methinks.... To *endure* more miseries and greater far" (*Shak.*). "What fates impose, that men must needs *abide*" (*Shak.*). **Tolerate** and **stand** (the more colloquial term) imply overcoming one's own resistance to that which is distasteful or antagonistic. *Tolerate* often connotes failure to resist through indifference or, sometimes, through a desire for peace or harmony; as, to *tolerate* differences in opinion. "Archer's New York *tolerated* hypocrisy in private relations; but in business matters it exacted...impeccable honesty" (*E. Wharton*). *Stand* is often used in place of *bear,* but distinctively it implies the ability to keep from flinching; as, he can *stand* teasing; he *stood* the attack well. **Brook,** now rather literary and chiefly in negative constructions, implies self-assertion and defiance. "Restraint she will not *brook*" (*Milton*). The other verbs are also used commonly in negative clauses but with weakened emphasis; as, I cannot *bear* him, *suffer* him, *endure* him. In such constructions, *bear* (with the negative) commonly implies dislike, *suffer* rejection, *endure* intolerance, *abide* impatience, *tolerate* contempt, and *stand* repugnance.

Ana. Accept, *receive: *take, assume: *afflict, try, torment, torture.

4 Bear, relate, pertain, appertain, belong, apply come into comparison in their intransitive use when they mean to have a connection, especially a logical connection. One thing **bears** *on* or *upon* another thing when the former touches so directly upon the latter thing (usually something in question) as to carry appreciable weight in its solution or in the understanding of issues it involves; as, to ignore all facts except those that *bear* upon this particular case; this situation *bears* directly upon the question under discussion. One thing **relates** *to* another thing when the former has some connection with the latter which permits, or more often, requires, them to be considered together with reference to their effect upon each other. The connection implied is usually closer in the intransitive than in the transitive verb (see JOIN), being commonly one of dependence or interdependence; as, in an organism each part *relates* to every other part; to show how the demand *relates* to the supply; an incident *relates* to the plot; a detail in a painting *relates* to the design of the whole. "The duties of the citizen, as he [T. Roosevelt] understood them, *related* not only to acts, but also to thoughts" (*Mencken*). One thing **pertains** or **appertains** to another when the former has any connection with the latter that permits their association in practice or thought. Both of these words are more widely applicable than *bear* and *relate,* for they cover not only the connections specifically implied in those words but others, such as those close connections implied by *belong,* and those remote connections implied by *have to do with;* thus, the things that *pertain* to happiness are all the things that can be thought of as causing happiness, contributing to it, preventing it, affecting its quality, and the like; moral philosophy is the branch of philosophy that deals with all problems *pertaining* to morals or ethics. *Pertain* more often implies a necessary connection or a very close relation than the more formal *appertain,* which commonly suggests an incidental or acquired connection; as, "a...faithful high priest in things *pertaining* to God" (*Hebrews* ii. 17); "It *appertaineth* to the discipline of the church, that enquiry be made of evil Ministers" (*Bk. of Com. Prayer*); "the crown And all wide-stretched honours that *pertain* By custom and the ordinance of times Unto the crown of France" (*Shak.*); "To that simple object *appertains* a story" (*Wordsworth*). One thing **belongs** *to* another thing when the former is a part or element without which the latter can not exist, function, have its true character or being, or the like. In this widest sense, a thing that *belongs* is a property, an attribute, a duty, a proper concern, or the like; as, "the Government of the United States....does not possess all the powers which usually *belong* to the sovereignty of a nation" (*Ch. Just. Taney*); "Nor does value *belong* to what concerns man only" (*S. Alexander*); "this comparative slightness [of Chinese and Japanese paintings] *belongs*...to the character of the medium and the fragility of the material employed" (*Binyon*). But *belong* also may be used of things as they pertain to persons, then implying possession (as, the watch *belongs* to James; this land *belongs* to the government) or, in colloquial use, of persons with reference to their qualifications for fitting into a group, especially a social group (as, "She's smart and jolly and everything, but she just doesn't *belong*"—*E. Ferber*). One thing **applies** *to* another thing when the former (a law, a principle, a rule, a theory, a general term) covers the latter (a specific instance), usually also explaining, interpreting, or describing it or having some clear bearing upon it. "The rules of addition *apply* to our debts as rigorously as to our assets" (*W. James*). "He really was the one child to whom the 'spare-the-rod' precept did not *apply*—he was naturally good" (*Deland*).

Ana. *Concern, affect: touch, influence, *affect: weigh (see DEPRESS).

bearing, *n.* **Bearing, deportment, demeanor** (*or* **demeanour), mien, manner, carriage, port, presence, front** come into comparison when they denote the way in which, or the quality by which, a person outwardly manifests his personality and breeding. **Bearing** is the most general of these words for it may imply reference to a person's mental attitude to others, his conduct in society, or, especially in current use, his characteristic posture or way of holding himself. "If 'twere so, She could not sway her house, command her followers... With such a smooth, discreet and stable *bearing*" (*Shak.*). "Verinder's *bearing* toward strangers is apt to be brutal"

(*Quiller-Couch*). " 'You should have seen him as a young man,' she cried...drawing herself up to imitate her husband's once handsome *bearing*" (*D. H. Lawrence*). **Deportment** applies especially to a person's actions in their relations to the external, often conventional, amenities of life; it so strongly suggests the influence of breeding or training that in current educational use it often means little more than *behavior;* as, lessons in *deportment;* the boy was rated 90 in *deportment.* "There is [now] little, in dress and outward *deportment,* to distinguish a Quaker from other people" (*Inge*). **Demeanor** applies rather to one's attitude as shown in one's behavior in the presence of others. "His *demeanor* in public was still, silent, almost sepulchral. He looked habitually upon the ground when he conversed, was chary of speech, embarrassed" (*Motley*). "The child who has been treated wisely and kindly has a frank look in the eyes, and a fearless *demeanour* even with strangers" (*B. Russell*). **Mien** implies reference both to bearing and demeanor; it is now chiefly a literary term. "For truth has such a face and such a *mien,* As to be lov'd needs only to be seen" (*Dryden*). "In his *deportment,* shape, and *mien,* appeared Elysian beauty, melancholy grace" (*Wordsworth*). **Manner,** as here compared (see METHOD), denotes characteristic or customary mode of acting, with special reference to a person's attitude, gesture, or address; as, I do not like his *manner;* he soon learned that he must change his *manner* if he would have friends; "the smooth *manner* of the spy" (*Dickens*). Usually in the plural, but sometimes in the singular, *manner* suggests reference to the outward signs of conformity to the conventions of polite intercourse, and, at times, denotes the deportment characteristic of the best society; as, he has no *manners;* to the *manner* born. "We country persons can have no *manner* at all" (*Goldsmith*). "Outward...looks, *manners,* accomplishments" (*Arnold*). **Carriage** narrowly implies reference to a person's bearing physically, or the way in which he holds himself, especially while standing or walking. "His *carriage,* conversation, and deportment combined aristocratic hauteur with...sarcastic wit" (*Symonds*). "A superb health in their [country women's] *carriage* princesses could not obtain" (*Jefferies*). **Port** was once a close synonym of *bearing* and *carriage;* it is now a literary term and is more specific than either, for it implies reference to physique, especially, through long association with adjectives such as *majestic, regal, proud,* etc., to a stately or dignified physique. "Pride in their *port,* defiance in their eye, I see the lords of humankind pass by" (*Goldsmith*). "People with a dignity of *port,* an amplitude of back, an emphasis of vocabulary" (*L. P. Smith*). **Presence** is more explicit than *bearing,* for it denotes a person's bearing with reference to its power to impress his personality on others or to attract their attention, interest, or admiration; as, "A graceful *presence* bespeaks acceptance" (*J. Collier*). "In mature life he [George Fox] became 'a bulky person,' with strong health and a commanding *presence*" (*Inge*). "Mr. Potter; a small, bird-like person, of no *presence*" (*R. Macaulay*). "Gossips...said, to distinguish them, that Henrietta Maria had a *port,* and Melchisedec a *Presence*.... By a *Port,* one may understand them to indicate something unsympathetically impressive; whereas a *Presence* would seem to be a thing that directs the most affable appeal to our poor human weaknesses. His Majesty King George IV., for instance, possessed a *Port;* Beau Brummel[l] wielded a *Presence*" (*Meredith*). **Front,** which is a more or less colloquial term, is applicable to a bearing that represents nothing deeper than a person's outward appearance or aspect, or the way he consciously presents his personality to others. "One sometimes feels that it is only with a *front* of brass and a lip of scorn that one can get through the day at all" (*Wilde*). The term usually suggests an assumed demeanor, often, specifically, an assumed dignity of manner, but only in some use does it connote pretense for the sake of giving a favorable impression; as, he is all *front;* many are impressed more by *front* than by deeper qualities of character.

Ana. *Posture, attitude, pose: *behavior, conduct: attitude, stand, *position: poise, address (see TACT).

beast. Brute, *animal.

beat, *v.* **1 Beat, pound, pummel, thrash, thresh, buffet, baste, belabor** (*or* **belabour**) come into comparison when they mean to strike repeatedly. **Beat,** the usual and general word of this group, often implies no more than the simple action with one's hands, or, sometimes, with one's arms or legs or feet, or with an implement, especially one devised for a certain purpose. The purpose is usually suggested by the object beaten, even when the manner of beating or the kind of implement used is not specifically stated; as, to *beat* a rug (i.e., with an implement, which, when so used, forces the dust out of the rug); to *beat* one's breast (by implication, with one's hands in sorrow or anguish); to *beat* a child (i.e., to punish by spanking or by raining blows upon him); to *beat* the ground (by implication, to strike the ground repeatedly, often rhythmically or restlessly, with one's foot or feet). **Pound** in earliest use implied beating with a pestle or the like to crush or reduce to a pulp or powder: this sense still occurs, though the method is no longer the most common one. In current English the term usually implies heavier, more damaging blows than *beat:* it may suggest repeated striking by a heavy hammer, strong doubled fists, the hoofs of horses, bombs, shells, and the like, and it often also suggests rhythmical, loud and heavy sounds; as, "The big boys who sit at the tables *pound* them and cheer" (*T. Hughes*); "the hoofs of the horses *pounding* on the bridge" (*S. Anderson*); his heart was *pounding;* he *pounded* the door (or on the door) in an effort to rouse the sleeping family; night after night the port was *pounded* by bombs. **Pummel** implies the beating of a person with one's fists: although it does not suggest as heavy blows as *pound,* it carries a stronger suggestion of continuous raining of blows and, often, of the infliction of injury, than *beat;* as, "a desire to *pummel* and wring the nose of the aforesaid Stiggins" (*Dickens*); "with Dick fastened on him, *pummelling* away most unmercifully" (*Lover*). **Thrash** and **thresh** in their earliest and still current senses mean to separate the grain, as of wheat, from the husks and straw by beating: the methods by which this was accomplished have changed through the ages, but the most important was striking with a flail. Consequently, *thrash* usually (for *thresh,* and not *thrash,* tends to retain the original meaning), means to strike repeatedly in a manner suggestive of strokes with a flail. When that which is thrashed is a person, the word usually implies a flogging with a stick or whip; when it is a thing, the word suggests motions and, sometimes, an implement comparable to those used in such flogging; as, to *thrash* a hedge with one's cane in order to drive out the rabbits; so poor a boxer that he spent much of his time *thrashing* the air with his arms; in the crawl stroke a swimmer's legs move up and down, *thrashing* the water. **Buffet** implies a repeated striking with or as if with an open hand: it therefore suggests a slapping, rather than a pounding, and in extended use is employed chiefly with reference to that which dashes against the face or the body in the manner of a slap, or which one fights as if by slapping; as, "the two hands of Madame Defarge *buffeted* and tore her face" (*Dickens*); *buffeted* by high waves; to *buffet* the waves which assail one. **Baste** implies a sound vigorous thrashing with any weapon (including the tongue); as, to *baste* an employee for his negligence; "I took a broom, and *basted* her, till she cried extremely" (*Pepys*). **Belabor** implies a prolonged and mighty basting or buffeting; as, "He saw Virago Nell belabour, With Dick's own staff his peaceful neighbour" (*Swift*).

Ana. Slug, clout, swat, punch, *strike, hit, smite, slap, box, cuff.

2 Defeat, lick, *conquer, vanquish, subdue, subjugate, reduce, overcome, surmount, overthrow, rout.

Ana. Surpass, excel, outstrip (see EXCEED): confound, nonplus (see PUZZLE).

3 *Pulsate, throb, pulse, palpitate.

Ana. Quiver, quaver, quake (see SHAKE): vibrate, oscillate, fluctuate, pendulate (see SWING).

beat, *n.* Pulsation, pulse, throb, palpitation. See under PULSATE.

Ana. Accent, accentuation, stress (see EMPHASIS): *rhythm, cadence.

beatitude. Blessedness, bliss, felicity, *happiness.

Ana. Rapture, *ecstasy, transport: joy, fruition, enjoyment, *pleasure.

Ant. Despair: dolor. — *Con.* Tribulation, affliction, *trial, cross: anguish, woe, *sorrow, grief: suffering, agony, misery, *distress.

beau, *n.* *Fop, exquisite, élégant, dandy, coxcomb, dude, macaroni, buck, spark, swell, nob, toff.

beau ideal *or* **beau idéal.** Ideal, exemplar, pattern, *model, example, mirror, paradigm, standard.

beauteous. Pulchritudinous, fair, good-looking, handsome, pretty, comely, bonny, lovely, *beautiful.

Ana. Alluring, attractive, fascinating, charming (see under ATTRACT).

beautiful, *adj.* **Beautiful, lovely, handsome, pretty, bonny, comely, fair, beauteous, pulchritudinous, good looking** come into comparison when they express one's judgment of a person or a thing that one perceives or contemplates with sensuous or aesthetic pleasure. Although they differ widely not only in their implications and connotations but also in their range of reference, they carry in common the meaning very pleasing or delightful to look upon. Of all these adjectives, **beautiful** is usually the richest in significance: since the abstraction it represents (*the beautiful*) has been for many centuries the subject of discussion by philosophers, artists, and aestheticians, its content in a particular context often depends upon the speaker's or writer's cultural background, his chosen philosophy, or, in some cases, his own peculiar definition. In general, however, both in learned and in ordinary use, *beautiful* is applied to that which excites the keenest pleasure, not only of the senses but also, through the medium of the senses, of mind and soul. It commonly also suggests an approach to, or a realization of, perfection, often specifically the imagined perfection associated with one's conception of an ideal. That is why *beautiful* is applicable not only to things that are directly perceived by the senses (as, a *beautiful* woman; a *beautiful* scene; the *beautiful* "Winged Victory"; an exquisitely *beautiful* painting) but to things that are actually mental constructions formed in the mind through the instrumentality of language, as a result of inferences from certain outward manifestations, or the like (as, a *beautiful* poem; a *beautiful* thought; a *beautiful* character). **Lovely,** like *beautiful,* usually suggests a more than sensuous pleasure, but it implies keen emotional delight rather than profound intellectual or spiritual pleasure. It is applied therefore to that which is so pleasant to look upon, to hear, to smell, or to touch that the person affected dwells delightedly, almost amorously, upon it or the sensations it produces. "Why ever wast thou *lovely* in my eyes?" (*Shak.*). "In after years... thy mind shall be a mansion for all *lovely* forms" (*Wordsworth*). "A thing of beauty is a joy for ever: Its *loveliness* increases" (*Keats*). "A sailing ship—that *loveliest* of human creations" (*H. Ellis*). **Handsome,** on the other hand, carries little connotation of emotional or spiritual pleasure; it implies rather a judgment of approval occasioned by that which is pleasant to look upon because it conforms to one's conception of what is perfect in form and detail or in perfect taste, and pleasing because of its due proportions, symmetry, elegance, or the like. It is applied chiefly to that which can be regarded unemotionally and with detachment; thus, a man is usually described as *handsome* rather than *beautiful;* a woman who is described as *handsome,* rather than as *beautiful* or *lovely* is, by implication, one whose appearance aesthetically satisfies the observer but does not markedly stir his deeper feelings; so, a *handsome* dress; a *handsome* house; a *handsome* table. " 'They say I'm *handsome.*' 'You're *lovely,* Bella!' She drank in his homage" (*Meredith*). **Pretty,** in contrast to *handsome,* is applied largely to that which pleases by its delicacy, grace, charm, or the like, rather than by its perfection or elegance of form or style. It is seldom used to describe that which is large or impressive; consequently it often connotes diminutiveness, daintiness, exquisiteness, or the like; as, a group of *pretty* girls; a very *pretty* child; a *pretty* cottage. *Pretty* is often used depreciatively to suggest mere pleasingness of appearance and the absence of qualities that make for beauty, grandeur, or strength; as, a *pretty* poem; a *pretty* view. **Bonny,** though often employed as a close synonym of *pretty* by persons other than those who use it colloquially (as in Scotland and some parts of England), carries few of the connotations of the latter adjective. Usually, it implies approbation of a person's or thing's looks, but it may also imply sweetness, simplicity, healthiness, plumpness, and the like; as, a *bonny* baby. "Eh, Miss Baines, I haven't seen ye for over thirty years...and you're looking *bonny*" (*Bennett*). **Comely** was once a term of high praise when applied to persons, especially to ladies, of exalted station, and connoted rarity, delicacy, or distinction in beauty. In more recent use, the term is applied to persons of all classes and implies an opposition to that which is homely and plain rather than to that which is crude or ugly. The word suggests a measure of good looks or physical attractiveness but it carries few, if any, distinguishing connotations except of good proportions and wholesomeness of aspect; as, a *comely* barmaid; the *comeliest* women in the club. "Sarah Drew might be rather called *comely* than *beautiful*" (*Gay*). "Jack was so *comely,* so pleasant, so jolly" (*C. Dibdin*). "Once a moorland Helen, and still *comely* as a blood horse and healthy as the hill wind" (*Stevenson*). **Fair** applies especially to that which gives delight because of the purity, the flawlessness, or the freshness of its beauty. "Fair as a star, when only one Is shining in the sky" (*Wordsworth*). "*Fairer* than the lily, than the wild white cherry: *Fair* as in image my seraph love appears... *Fair* as in the flesh she swims to me on tears" (*Meredith*). **Beauteous** was once used in poetry and elevated prose in place of *beautiful;* at present it occurs chiefly in humorous or journalistic prose where it often carries a suggestion of derogation or implies an emphasis on mere physical attractiveness; as, *beauteous* candidates for the title of "Miss America"; a *beauteous* platinum blonde. Even in poetical and dignified use it often carries a stronger implication of opulence of charms than *beautiful.* "How *beauteous* mankind is! O brave new world, That has such people in't!" (*Shak.*). "It is a *beauteous* evening, calm and free" (*Wordsworth*). **Pulchritudinous,** a term first used in the early twentieth century, is sometimes employed humorously or disparagingly with much the same implications as *beauteous;* it is even more often used to describe persons who are strikingly good-looking, but who are not properly described as *beautiful, lovely, handsome,* or *fair,* because of the specific connotations of those terms; as, the *pulchritudinous* women of Arles; *pulchritudinous* chorus girls. **Good-looking** is a less expressive word than *handsome* or *pretty,* but is often used as a close synonym; as, the children of that family are all *good-looking.*

Ana. *Splendid, resplendent, glorious, sublime, superb: exquisite, elegant, *choice.

Ant. Ugly. — ***Con.*** Repulsive, repugnant, revolting, *offensive.

beautify. Embellish, deck, bedeck, *adorn, ornament, decorate, garnish.

Ana. Enhance, heighten (see INTENSIFY): primp, prink, prank, *preen, prune, doll up, perk up.

Ant. Uglify. — ***Con.*** *Deface, disfigure, disfeature: *deform, distort, contort: mar, spoil, *injure, damage.

because. **Because, for, since, as, inasmuch as** are the chief causal conjunctions in English. **Because** assigns a cause or reason immediately and explicitly; as, I hid myself, *because* [=for the express reason that, or as caused to do so by the fact that] I was afraid; he must have passed this way, *because* [=owing to the specific fact that] there is no other road; cf., he must have passed this way, *because* [=as is directly proved by the fact that] his footprints are here. **For,** in modern usage, is a particle of less immediate reference than *because;* it regards the statement to which it is subjoined as relatively independent, and proceeds to adduce for it some ground, reason, evidence, proof, explanation, or justification; as, I hid myself, *for* [=as I may add by way of explanation] I was afraid; he must have passed this way, *for* [=as you may readily see] here are his footprints; I like him, *for* [=I ask, in justification of the fact] who can help it? **Since** (originally denoting sequence in time) is less formal and more incidental than *because;* **as** assigns a reason even more casually than *since;* each of them frequently begins its sentence; as, *Since* (or *As*) I was afraid, I hid myself; I will come, *since* you ask me; *As* I knew him to be out of town, I did not call. **Inasmuch as** assigns a reason in a somewhat concessive or qualified fashion; as, *Inasmuch as* [=in view of, or considering, the fact that] I was afraid, I hid myself; I am ready to accept your proposal, *inasmuch as* [=seeing that] I believe it is the best you can offer.

bedeck. Deck, garnish, embellish, beautify, decorate, ornament, *adorn.

Ana. Doll up, primp, prink, prank, *preen, prune.

beer. **Beer, lager, bock, ale, stout, porter** denote in common a fermented liquor brewed from malt (and sometimes malt substitutes), hops, water, and yeast (and sometimes sugar). **Beer** in its widest sense denotes any kind of malt liquor; often, however, especially in the United States, it is equivalent to **lager** (or **lager beer**), which is a malt liquor made by bottom fermentation (a slow fermentation in which the yeast cells collect at the bottom of the liquid) and stored for several months before being marketed. **Bock (beer)** is a dark, less bitter kind of lager, having a higher content of alcohol and of extract (soluble constituents exclusive of alcohol and carbon dioxide), brewed in the winter and drunk in the spring. **Ale** is a malt liquor made by top fermentation (a rapid fermentation in which the yeast cells are carried to the top of the liquid) and marketed soon after fermentation takes place. In England, where lager beer is rarely produced, *ale* and *beer* are usually interchangeable terms. **Stout** differs from ale in having a dark color imparted by an admixture of roasted or charred malt, and, usually, in having a higher content of alcohol and extract. **Porter** is weak stout.

befall. Betide, occur, *happen, hap, chance, transpire.

befool. Trick, hoax, hoodwink, *dupe, gull, bamboozle.

Ana. *Cheat, cozen, overreach: *deceive, delude, beguile, mislead: blandish, cajole, wheedle, *coax.

before. **Before, afore, ahead, forward** are comparable when they mean in advance, especially in place or in time. **Before,** as an adverb, is now more commonly used in reference to time than to place. Its most frequent implication is previousness or priority; as, I have heard that *before;* the *before*-mentioned facts. "Not dead, but gone *before*" (*S. Rogers*). "Dreams no mortal ever dared to dream *before*" (*Poe*). Sometimes, however, it implies futurity. "We look *before* and after, And pine for what is not" (*Shelley*). This use is not a contradiction of the temporal sense, but a figurative application of the adverb in its less frequent meaning of in front or in the van. "Thou art so far *before* That swiftest wing of recompense is slow To overtake thee" (*Shak.*). **Afore** is obsolete in literary English except as an archaism or a dialectal form; it is, however, found in nautical language, to indicate a position relatively nearer the prow of the vessel and so is opposed to *abaft.* Though it occurs as an adverb, it, like *before,* is vastly more frequent as a preposition when it implies place; as, the sailors sleep *afore* (or more often, *afore the mast*). **Ahead** and **forward** are the commonest adverbs indicating position in advance or in front of something and have practically supplanted *before; ahead,* however, usually implies a position outside of a thing, often a moving thing, and *forward* frequently implies a front position in the thing itself. Thus, to send a group of scouts *ahead* implies their detachment from an advancing body of troops; to send a company *forward* usually means to send them to a position nearer the front or in the van of a regiment. In nautical language, *ahead* (opposed to *astern*) indicates a position or direction in front of and outside of the ship (as, breakers *ahead;* a sail *ahead;* full speed *ahead*); *forward* (opposed to *aft*), a position in front of the midships section of the vessel; as, the guns were placed *forward.* The same distinction is often found in figurative use; thus, one looks *ahead* who can foresee the remote consequences of a decision and ignore the immediate results; one looks *forward* who anticipates something likely or bound to occur. "No longer *forward* nor behind I look in hope or fear" (*Whittier*). There is no difference between *ahead* and *forward* in reference to mechanisms which can be reversed or the opposite, except as determined by usage; thus, the more common expressions are to set a clock *ahead* and to drive an engine *forward. Forward* is rarely used in reference to time except in its sense of onward (see ONWARD); *ahead* frequently is. Like *before,* it commonly implies previousness, but it may also, when there is an implication of position, imply the opposite. Thus, if the hour in mind is one o'clock, "to set the clock an hour *ahead*" means to set it so that it indicates two o'clock, and "to arrive an hour *ahead*" means to arrive at twelve o'clock.

Ant. After. — ***Con.*** Behind (see AFTER): *abaft, aft, astern.

beforehand. *Early, betimes, soon.

Ant. Behindhand.

befuddle. Fuddle, addle, bemuddle, muddle, *confuse.

Ana. Bewilder, distract, confound, perplex (see PUZZLE):

intoxicate, inebriate (see corresponding adjectives at DRUNK).

Ant. Clarify, clear.

beg. **Beg, entreat, beseech, implore, supplicate, adjure, conjure, importune** agree in meaning to ask or request urgently. **Beg** suggests earnestness or insistence, especially in asking a favor. "Why, boy, before I left, you were constantly *begging* to see Town" (*Meredith*). **Entreat** implies an attempt to persuade or to overcome resistance in another, especially by ingratiating oneself. "He was accustomed to command, not to *entreat*" (*Cather*). **Beseech** implies great eagerness and often anxiety or solicitude. "She *besought* him, for his Soul's sake, to speak the truth" (*Kipling*). **Implore,** often used interchangeably with *beseech,* at times suggests even greater urgency in the plea or more manifest anguish. "The last look of my dear mother's eyes, which *implored* me to have mercy" (*Dickens*). **Supplicate** adds to *entreat* the suggestion of fervent prayer or of a prayerful attitude. "I have attempted, one by one, the lords... with *supplication* prone and father's tears, to accept of ransom for my son" (*Milton*). **Adjure,** when it retains its full historical significance, implies an injunction as well as a plea, and is strengthened by the expressed or implied invocation of something sacred. "I *adjure* thee by the living God, that thou tell us whether thou be the Christ" (*Matthew* xxvi. 63). In its thinner modern sense, *adjure* often connotes peremptoriness. "So E company ...doubled for the dear life, and in the rear toiled the perspiring sergeant, *adjuring* it to double yet faster" (*Kipling*). **Conjure,** historically a close synonym of *adjure,* is not often distinguishable from it. "I *conjure* thee to leave me and be gone" (*Shak.*). It is rarer in current English than *adjure,* but is preferred when a humorous warning is to be conveyed; as, do not forget your promise, I *conjure* you. **Importune** commonly suggests repeated attempts to break down resistance, and often, as a result, connotes annoying pertinacity; as, his father would not listen to *importuning.*

Ana. Solicit, request, *ask: plead, pray, petition, sue (see under PRAYER): *demand, exact.

beget. Get, *generate, sire, procreate, engender, breed, propagate, reproduce.

Ana. *Bear, produce, yield.

beggarly. Cheap, scurvy, sorry, *contemptible, despicable, pitiable.

Ana. Paltry, measly, *petty, trifling: *mean, abject, sordid.

begin, *v.* **Begin, commence, start, initiate, inaugurate** come into comparison when they mean to set something going or in progress or to take the first step or steps in a course, process, or operation. *Begin, commence,* and *start* are also used intransitively, with the activity, work, instrument, or the like, as the subject, in the sense of to get going or in progress; as, he *began* the letter; play *begins* when the whistle blows; to *start* a race; the race *starts* at ten. **Begin** (implying opposition to *end*) and **commence** (implying opposition to *conclude*) are identical in meaning; the former is often preferred because less formal than the latter; as, to *begin* work; the lecture *began* with an apology; well *begun* is half done. "Things never *began* with Mr. Borthrop Trumbull; they always *commenced*" (*G. Eliot*). Traditional good usage, however, supports the choice of *commence* in reference to court proceedings, religious or other ceremonies, military operations, and the like; as, to *commence* a lawsuit; divine service *commences* promptly at eleven; war was declared in 1939, but operations on a large scale did not *commence* at once. **Start** is often used as though it also were identical in meaning with *begin* and *commence;* the term, however, carries implications which distinguish it sharply from the other words. *Start* implies opposition to *stop:* it therefore suggests a setting out from a particular point, as on a journey, a race, or a course, often, but not necessarily, after inaction or waiting; as, the horses are ready to *start* (that is, to *begin* the race); the children like to see the train *start* (that is, set out from the station at which it has stopped); conversation *started* and stopped, and after an embarrassing pause, *started* again. *Start* also frequently takes as its subject, not the person or agency that begins a process or course, but the one that causes, enables, or permits him or it to begin; as, his father *started* him in business; he quickly *started* the engine working by pressing a button (cf. self-*starter;* an elevator or train *starter*). **Initiate** (see also INITIATE) suggests reference to the first step or steps in a process and carries no implication of an end or ending; it often suggests an opposition to *carry on, continue,* or *maintain;* thus, a person *initiates* (better than *begins* or *starts* except in informal speech) a custom or practice when he is its originator; a diplomat *initiates* negotiations between the government he represents and another when he takes the first step or steps leading to future discussions in which he may or may not take part, but he *begins* negotiations on behalf of his government when he enters into actual discussions which in the natural course of events, will end only when there is agreement or hopeless disagreement. "Taft had to make himself popular as a necessary incident to *initiating* a civil government [in the Philippines]" (*V. Heiser*). **Inaugurate,** in the sense here considered, retains, from its more frequent sense of to induct into office (see INITIATE), a hint of a ceremonial beginning. Often it is an inflated term for *begin* or *commence;* as, the Curies *inaugurated* a new era in science by their discovery of radium; to *inaugurate* proceedings on behalf of the heirs. The word sometimes takes as its subject the act, action, or incident that serves as the first step in a course, procedure, or the like; as, the discovery of radium *inaugurated* a new era in science. "Prayers and scripture *inaugurated* the official day" (*H. G. Wells*).

Ana. *Found, institute, establish, organize: introduce, admit, *enter: originate, derive, *spring, arise, rise.

Ant. End. — *Con.* *Close, terminate, conclude, finish, complete: *stop, cease, quit, discontinue, desist: achieve, accomplish, effect, fulfill (see PERFORM).

begrudge. *Covet, envy, grudge.

beguile. 1 Delude, *deceive, mislead, betray, double-cross.

Ana. *Dupe, gull, befool, trick, hoax, hoodwink, bamboozle: cajole, wheedle, blandish, *coax: *cheat, cozen: *lure, entice, seduce.

2 *While, wile, beguile, fleet.

Ana. Divert, *amuse, entertain: *comfort, solace: *speed, hasten, hurry.

behave. **Behave, conduct, demean, deport, comport, acquit, quit** come into comparison when they are used reflexively meaning to cause or to allow oneself to act or to do something in a way that evokes comment. *Demean, deport, comport,* and *quit* are now used less often than formerly and have a bookish or archaic flavor. One **behaves** oneself when one's actions meet a standard, usually a standard of what is proper or decorous; as, these children know how to *behave* themselves. "Those that *behaved* themselves manfully" (*2 Maccabees* ii. 21). One **conducts** oneself in a specified way when one's action on a particular occasion or one's behavior in some experience shows the extent of one's power to direct or control oneself; as, the soldiers *conducted* themselves bravely throughout the grilling shellfire; he knew how to *conduct* himself in an emergency. One **demeans** oneself in a given manner when one's conduct, one's bearing, one's mien, or one's attitude to others answers the given description. "They have *demeaned* themselves Like men born to renown by life or death" (*Shak.*). "It shall be my earnest endeavor to *demean* myself with grateful respect towards her Ladyship" (*Austen*). One **deports** oneself in a specified way when one's behavior shows how far one conforms to the rules of discipline, the conventions of one's group, or the accepted proprieties. "Dido and Æneas, in the 'Roman d'Eneas,' *deport* themselves in accordance with the strictest canons of courtly love" (*Lowes*). One **comports** oneself when one conducts oneself to the extent specified, the measure being what is expected or required of a person in one's class, one's position, or the like; as, he has not yet learned how to *comport* himself in good society. One **acquits,** or (*archaic*) **quits,** oneself *well, admirably,* or the like, when one conducts oneself so as to win approval or to meet expectations. "A border action in which the Dogra companies of the Loodhiana Sikhs had *acquitted* themselves well" (*Kipling*). "*Quit* you like men" (*1 Corinthians* xvi. 13).

Ana. Bear, *carry: manage, control, direct (see CONDUCT).

Ant. Misbehave.

2 *Act, react, operate, work, function.

behavior *or* **behaviour.** **Behavior** (*or* **behaviour**), **conduct, deportment** are here compared only as denoting one's actions in general or on a particular occasion, so far as they serve as a basis of another's judgment of one's character, temperament, mood, manners, morals, or the like. **Behavior** may be used in reference to any human being regardless of age, state of development, social standing, or the like, for it may or may not imply consciousness of what one is doing. *Behavior* may be thought of as instinctive or as voluntary, as a spontaneous expression of one's personality or character, or as the result of training or breeding. "The captain's *behaviour* to his wife and to his wife's father....was as if they had been a pair of not very congenial passengers" (*Conrad*). "Courageous *behaviour* is easier for a man who fails to apprehend dangers" (*B. Russell*). "Grandfather had been hounded out of his congregation because he couldn't hold her to their standards of *behavior* for a minister's wife" (*M. Austin*). Since *behavior* is increasingly used in the various sciences in reference to animals and substances, the term as referred to human beings tends in present usage to become more and more sharply differentiated from **conduct** than in the past. The latter term has always, in discriminating use, carried a hint of moral responsibility, but since *behavior* does not rule out this suggestion, the words have often been used interchangeably. In current good speech and writing they are frequently distinguished; as, to dismiss a person because of his *conduct* (better than *behavior* because it implies violation of principles); what do you mean by such *conduct* (better than *behavior*)?; "No animal's *behaviour* is controlled by moral principles. Generally speaking, they do not rise from *behaviour* to *conduct*" (*J. S. Clarke*). **Deportment** (see also BEARING) is often used of behavior as taught or as the result of discipline; its strongest implication is that of degree of conformity to the accepted code of good manners or the conventions governing one's relations to one's fellows, one's superiors, or one's inferiors; as, children held up as models of *deportment;* his old-fashioned *deportment* marked him out from others.

Ana. Demeanor, mien, manner, carriage, deportment, *bearing: *action, act, deed.

behest, *n.* Bidding, dictate, injunction, *command, order, mandate.

Ana. Precept, rule, *law: request, solicitation (see corresponding verbs at ASK).

behind. *After.

Ant. Ahead.

behindhand. *Tardy, late, overdue.

Ana. Dilatory, laggard, *slow: delayed, retarded, detained (see DELAY, *v.*).

Ant. Beforehand. — *Con.* *Early, soon, betimes: punctual (see CAREFUL): *quick, prompt.

behold. *See, view, survey, observe, descry, espy, notice, perceive, discern, remark, note, contemplate.

Ana. Watch, look, *see: regard, *consider.

beholder. Onlooker, looker-on, observer, witness, eyewitness, *spectator, bystander, kibitzer.

being. *Existence, actuality.

Ana. Personality, individuality, character (see DISPOSITION).

Ant. Becoming: nonbeing.

belabor *or* **belabour.** *Beat, pound, pummel, thrash, thresh, buffet, baste.

Ana. *Strike, hit, smite, slug, clout, swat, punch, box, cuff, slap.

belie. *Misrepresent.

Ana. Contradict, contravene, negative (see DENY): controvert, *disprove.

Ant. Attest. — *Con.* *Reveal, discover, disclose: bespeak, betoken, argue, *indicate, prove.

belief. **1** **Belief, faith, credence, credit** come into comparison when they mean the act of one who assents intellectually to something proposed or offered for acceptance as true, or the state of mind of one who so assents. **Belief** is less restricted in its application than the other terms, for it may or may not imply certitude or certainty in the one who assents; it may even suggest nothing more than his mere mental acceptance; as, his conclusions are beyond *belief;* the theory merits *belief; belief* in God; nothing could shake his *belief* in the Bible as the word of God. "Hope is the *belief,* more or less strong, that joy will come" (*Sydney Smith*). "*Belief* consists in accepting the affirmations of the soul; unbelief, in denying them" (*Emerson*). **Faith** implies full assent of the mind, and therefore certitude, but it adds to this a strong implication of complete trust or confidence in the divinity, the institution, the person, or the like, that proposes something or offers itself for belief and confidence. Consequently, although *belief* may represent the mind's act or state when something is assented to, regardless of whether it is or is not fully supported by evidence, *faith,* in discriminating usage, represents the mind's act or state only when something is assented to on grounds other than merely those of the evidence of one's senses or of conclusions entirely supported by reason. "*Faith* is the substance of things hoped for, the evidence of things not seen" (*Hebrews* xi. 1). "To believe only possibilities is not *faith,* but mere philosophy" (*Browne*). "Such tales, whether false or true, were heard by our ancestors with eagerness and *faith*" (*Macaulay*). "He's still touchingly full of *faith,* even after all that has happened, in a new heaven and a new earth" (*R. Macaulay*). In theological use, *faith* is variously defined, but the older implications are retained in general use. In current English, *faith* often carries a strong suggestion of credulity or overreadiness to accept authority; as, he takes everything on *faith.* **Credence** stresses mere intellectual assent, without implying weak or strong grounds for belief and without suggesting credulity or its absence. Consequently, it is seldom used in reference to religious or philosophical doctrines and is commonly employed in reference to reports, rumors, opinions, and the like. "There is no superstition too absurd to find *credence* in modern England" (*Inge*). "We are not now concerned with the finality or extent of truth in this judgment. The point is that it gained a widespread *credence* among the cultured class in Europe" (*Day Lewis*). **Credit** (as here compared: see also INFLUENCE) carries a weaker implication than any of the preceding words of certitude or of acceptance as a result of conviction: often, it specifically suggests as its ground a reputation for truth in the person who offers something for acceptance; as, anything he will tell you about the circumstances is entitled to *credit;* I can give no *credit* to the gossip she retails.

Ana. Certitude, assurance, *certainty, conviction: assenting *or* assent, acquiescing *or* acquiescence (see corresponding verbs at ASSENT).

Ant. Unbelief, disbelief. — ***Con.*** Incredulity (see UNBELIEF): skepticism, agnosticism (see under SKEPTIC): *uncertainty, doubt, mistrust.

2 Conviction, persuasion, view, *opinion, sentiment.

Ana. *Doctrine, dogma, tenet: *principle, fundamental: conclusion, judgment (see under INFER).

believable. Credible, *plausible, colorable, specious.

Ana. *Probable, possible, likely.

Ant. Unbelievable. — ***Con.*** Fabulous, mythical (see FICTITIOUS): *doubtful, dubious, questionable.

belittle. Depreciate, disparage, derogate from, detract from, minimize, *decry.

Ana. Underestimate, undervalue, underrate (see affirmative verbs at ESTIMATE): diminish, reduce, lessen, *decrease.

Ant. Aggrandize, magnify. — ***Con.*** *Exalt: heighten, *intensify, enhance, aggravate: vaunt, gasconade, brag, *boast, crow.

belles-lettres. *Literature, letters, the humanities.

bellicose. *Belligerent, pugnacious, contentious, litigious, quarrelsome.

Ana. Militant, *aggressive, assertive: antagonizing *or* antagonistic, combating *or* combative (see corresponding verbs at OPPOSE): rebellious, factious, seditious, mutinous (see INSUBORDINATE).

Ant. Pacific: amicable. — ***Con.*** Peaceful, pacifist, peaceable (see PACIFIC).

belligerent, *adj.* **Belligerent, bellicose, pugnacious, quarrelsome, contentious, litigious** agree in meaning having or taking an aggressive or fighting attitude. **Belligerent** usually implies actual engagement in hostilities; as, the *belligerent* powers in the World War; to define a nation's status as not neutral yet not *belligerent.* When applied to a tone, speech, gesture, or the like, the term implies an actively hostile mood or warlike temper; as, a *belligerent* reply to a diplomatic note. **Bellicose** applies usually to a state of mind or temper; it suggests a desire or readiness to fight or, sometimes, a disposition to stir up a fight; as, a *bellicose* tribe; an intoxicated man in a *bellicose* mood; an editorial in a *bellicose* vein. **Pugnacious** differs from *bellicose* (which is sometimes given a semihumorous or mock-heroic turn) in applying more commonly to disposition or character; it does not, however, convey the impression of pettiness or ill nature, or of readiness to fight without genuine cause, so frequently implied in **quarrelsome.** "The Scotch are certainly a most *pugnacious* people; their whole history proves it" (*Borrow*). "Soon every father-bird and mother Grew *quarrelsome,* and pecked each other" (*Cowper*). "On the days they worked they were good-natured and cheerful...on our idle days they were mutinous and *quarrelsome*" (*Franklin*). **Contentious** frequently suggests a certain perversity of temper and wearisome persistence in dispute. "A continual dropping in a very rainy day and a *contentious* woman are alike" (*Proverbs* xxvii. 15). **Litigious** is now commonly confined to fondness for legal contention; as, a *litigious* client. "He was apparently a lawyer, 'clerk in the King's Bench,'...with chambers in Fleet Street, himself most *litigious,* and not always strictly scrupulous" (*H. Ellis*).

Ana. Hostile, antagonistic (see corresponding nouns at ENMITY): fighting, warring, battling, contending (see CONTEND): warlike, *martial.

Ant. Friendly. — ***Con.*** Neighborly, *amicable: *neutral, indifferent.

belly. *Abdomen, paunch, stomach.

belong. Pertain, appertain, relate, apply, *bear.

belongings. *Possessions, effects, means, resources, assets.

below. Below, under, beneath, underneath, in their literal senses, agree in meaning in a lower position relatively to some other object or place. **Below** (opposed to *above*) applies to that which is anywhere in a lower plane than the object of reference; **under** (opposed to *over*), to that which is below in a relatively vertical line: it sometimes implies actual covering; as, *below* sea level, the valley far *below* us; *under* a tree, *under* the bed; to hide one's light *under* a bushel; the Whirlpool Rapids are *below,* the Cave of the Winds is *under,* Niagara Falls; the whole visible landscape is *below,* but only a small portion of it *under,* an observer in a balloon. **Beneath** is an equivalent of both *below* and, especially, *under;* as, "heaven above, or...the earth *beneath*" (*Exodus* xx. 4); "*beneath* the spreading tree" (*Goldsmith*). **Underneath** is often employed in place of *under* or *beneath.* It is, however, the preferred term when there is the intent to imply complete or nearly complete concealment; as, mines *underneath* the city; garments worn *underneath* a dress. In their figurative senses, *below* and *under* agree in expressing inferiority, but differ (like *above* and *over*) in the immediacy of the relation expressed; thus, one officer may be *below* another in rank, without being *under* him in immediate subordination. Similarly, with reference to deficiency, *below* is commonly used in general, *under* in more specific, relations; as, *below* the standard or average; *under* six years of age. *Beneath* frequently suggests social, moral, or general inferiority; as, to marry *beneath* one, *beneath* one's notice, *beneath* contempt. *Underneath* suggests not inferiority, but something underlying and not indicated clearly by that which is outwardly manifest; as, *underneath* his ingratiating manner, one felt a sinister intention; there is something *underneath* this announcement, I am sure.

Ant. Above. — ***Con.*** Over (see ABOVE).

belt. Zone, *area, tract, region.

bemoan. Bewail, lament, *deplore.

Ana. *Grieve, mourn, sorrow.

Ant. Exult.

bemuddle. Muddle, *confuse, addle, fuddle, befuddle.

Ana. Mystify, perplex, *puzzle, bewilder, distract: bother, vex, irk, *annoy: flounder, *wallow.

bend, *v.* Turn, *curve, twist.

Ana. Contort, *deform: deflect, divert (see TURN).

Ant. Straighten.

beneath. Underneath, under, *below.

Ant. Above, over.

benediction. *Blessing, benison.

Ant. Malediction. — ***Con.*** *Curse, malison, anathema, imprecation.

benefaction. *Donation, contribution, alms.

Ana. *Gift, present, largess, boon: endowment (see corresponding verb at DOWER): grant, subvention (see APPROPRIATION): *charity, philanthropy.

beneficial. Beneficial, advantageous, profitable are ap-

plied to that which brings good or gain. **Beneficial** refers to that which promotes health or well-being; **advantageous,** to that which more directly conduces to relative superiority or subserves a desirable end; **profitable,** to that which yields useful or lucrative returns; as, a climate *beneficial* to rheumatism; "measures...*beneficial* to the kingdom" (*J. R. Green*); the enemy were in an *advantageous* position on the hill; "you see...how swift and *advantageous* a harbinger it [a good reputation] is, wherever one goes" (*Chesterfield*); a *profitable* study, investment.
Ana. Salutary, *healthful, wholesome: *favorable, benign, propitious.
Ant. Harmful: detrimental. — *Con.* *Pernicious, deleterious, baneful, noxious.

benefit, *v.* **Benefit, profit, avail, boot, bestead** (*or* **bested**) agree in meaning to do good or to be of advantage to someone. *Benefit* and *profit* also come together in meaning to gain or derive advantage from something. **Benefit** usually implies personal betterment or improvement, as of one's physical, intellectual, moral, or spiritual condition, but it may suggest enrichment or a furtherance of one's ends; as, a summer at the seashore *benefits* the entire family; he will *benefit* more from two years of travel than from two years of college; the expansion of the city's industries *benefits* everyone indirectly. **Profit** carries a strong implication of gain, especially, but not invariably, material gain. It is, therefore, preferred when an increase or yield, as opposed to a decrease or loss, in one's wealth, one's power, one's knowledge, or the like is to be suggested; as, he always *profits* (not *benefits*, unless one wishes to imply a salutary effect) by the misfortunes of others; no one *benefits* from a war except those who seek to *profit* by it; it will *profit* you as a congressman to pay more attention to your constituency's wishes. "What is a man *profited*, if he shall gain the whole world, and lose his own soul?" (*Matthew* xvi. 26). "Do we not lose something...when we hurry by and disregard what does not seem to *profit* our own existence?" (*Binyon*). *Avail, boot, bestead* all have an archaic and literary flavor that makes them rare in speech except in historical novels or in sermons or orations. **Avail** stresses efficacy. "Ah wretched shepherd, what *avails* thy art, To cure thy lambs, but not to heal thy heart!" (*Pope*). "Say not the struggle nought availeth, The labour and the wounds are vain" (*Clough*). **Boot** is used chiefly in rhetorical questions and in negative assertions; in highly discriminating use it implies something "to boot" as in compensation for loss or deficiency, or in reward for effort. "Nor *boots* it me to say I honour him, If he suspect I may dishonour him" (*Shak.*). "Alas! what *boots* it with uncessant care To tend the homely, slighted, shepherd's trade, And strictly meditate the thankless Muse?" (*Milton*). **Bestead** usually implies relief or sustenance, as in distress or need. "Hence, vain deluding Joys, The brood of Folly without father bred! How little you *bested*, Or fill the fixèd mind with all your toys!" (*Milton*).
Ana. Better, *improve, ameliorate: *help, assist, aid.
Ant. Harm. — *Con.* *Injure, hurt, damage, impair.

benevolent. *Charitable, philanthropic, humanitarian, humane, altruistic.
Ana. Benign, benignant, kindly, *kind: generous, *liberal, bountiful: obliging, complaisant, *amiable.
Ant. Malevolent. — *Con.* *Malicious, malignant, malign, spiteful: *stingy, close, miserly, curmudgeonly.

benign. **1** Benignant, kindly, *kind.
Ana. *Gracious, genial, cordial, affable: sympathetic, *tender, compassionate: *suave, urbane, bland.
Ant. Malign. — *Con.* Malignant, malevolent, *malicious, spiteful: *caustic, acrid, mordant, mordacious.
2 Auspicious, *favorable, propitious.
Ana. Fortunate, happy, providential, *lucky: gentle, mild (see SOFT): benevolent, humane, *charitable: merciful, clement, *forbearing.
Ant. Malign. — *Con.* *Sinister, baleful, malefic: threatening, menacing (see THREATEN).

benignant. Benign, *kind, kindly.
Ana. Benevolent, humane, *charitable, humanitarian, philanthropic: *gracious, affable: compassionate, *tender, sympathetic.
Ant. Malignant. — *Con.* Malevolent, spiteful, *malicious: merciless, unrelenting, implacable, relentless, *grim.

benison. *Blessing, benediction.
Ant. Malison. — *Con.* *Curse, imprecation, malediction, anathema.

bent, *n.* Turn, talent, aptitude, knack, *gift, faculty, genius.
Ana. Propensity, penchant, *leaning, proclivity, flair: *predilection, bias, prepossession, prejudice, partiality: capacity, *ability, capability.
Con. Disinclination, indisposition, reluctance (see corresponding adjectives at DISINCLINED): aversion, *antipathy.

berate. Rate, tonguelash, upbraid, jaw, bawl out, *scold, wig, rail, revile, vituperate.
Ana. Censure, denounce, condemn, reprehend, reprobate, *criticize: rebuke, reprimand, reproach, *reprove, chide.

berth. Billet, post, job, situation, *position, place, office, capacity.

beseech. Entreat, implore, supplicate, *beg, importune, adjure, conjure.
Ana. Pray, petition, sue, plead, appeal (see under PRAYER).

beset. Overrun, *infest.
Ana. *Worry, annoy, harass, harry, pester, plague: assail, *attack, assault.
Con. Resist, withstand, combat, *oppose.

beside. **Beside, besides** in earlier English use often were interchangeable. In present usage, **beside** is employed, with rare exceptions (such as, he is *beside* himself with fear), only as a preposition in a local sense, meaning by the side of; as, he stood *beside* her; the house *beside* the river. On the other hand, **besides** has now almost entirely replaced *beside* as a preposition in the sense of other than, as a preposition in the sense of in addition to (as, he received other gifts *besides* the watch), and as an adverb in the senses of otherwise and moreover (see ALSO).

besides, *adv.* Moreover, furthermore, *also, too, likewise.

besides, *adv. & prep.* *Beside.

besotted. Infatuated, *fond, insensate.
Ana. Fatuous, asinine, foolish, silly, *simple: *drunk, drunken, intoxicated, inebriated: *stupid, dull, dense, crass.
Con. Sensible, sane, *wise, judicious, prudent: *rational, reasonable: sober, *serious, earnest.

bespatter. Spatter, *sprinkle, besprinkle, asperse, splash.

bespeak. Betoken, attest, *indicate, argue, prove.
Ana. Manifest, evidence, *show, evince, demonstrate: imply, hint, *suggest.

besprinkle. *Sprinkle, asperse, spatter, bespatter, splash.

bestead *or* **bested,** *v.* Profit, *benefit, avail, boot.

bestow. Confer, present, donate, *give, afford.

Ana. *Distribute, dispense, divide: *grant, award.

bet, *n.* **Bet, wager, stake, pot, blind, ante** denote in common something of value, usually money, risked in the confidence or hope that something is true or will turn out in a certain way, something else of value being risked by at least one other party in support of an opposing confidence or hope. **Bet** and **wager** are used with little distinction of meaning either of what is risked or of the act of risking it. **Stake** implies money or valuables bet and actually produced, for example, entrusted to a neutral party (stakeholder), or placed in the pot in a card game. By extension, a stake is anything, material or nonmaterial, that one stands in jeopardy of losing. "And will probably always have the largest commercial *stake* in the African continent" (*Livingstone*). "With my most affectionate wishes for Dr. Johnson's recovery, in which his friends...have so deep a *stake*" (*Sir A. Dick*). **Pot,** in British use, often means a large bet; as, to put the *pot* on at cards. A **blind** is a compulsory stake, usually a predetermined small percentage of the betting limit, which the age (that is, player at dealer's left) puts into the pot before the deal, in draw poker. Among draw poker players who use the blind, an **ante** is a stake which each player who wishes to continue a particular hand puts up after he has seen his original five cards but before he draws other cards. Often, however, in stud poker, in draw poker when, as is often the case, the blind is not used, and in other games, as blackjack, the ante is a compulsory stake (in poker, of predetermined amount) put up by each player before the cards are seen. By extension, an ante is a price which must be paid before something desired can be obtained, or one of several payments made to a joint venture; as, Jones is asking only $5000 for the house; I'm afraid that if I don't buy right away, he'll raise the *ante;* the captain collected an *ante* of fifty cents from each member of the team.

bête noire. *Abomination, bugbear, anathema.

bethink. Recollect, remind, *remember, recall, reminisce, mind.

betide. Befall, hap, *happen, chance, occur, transpire.

betimes. *Early, soon, beforehand.
Ant. Unseasonably, inopportunely.

betoken. Bespeak, attest, *indicate, argue, prove.
Ana. Presage, augur, portend, forebode (see FORETELL): import, signify, denote, *mean: evidence, manifest, *show, evince, demonstrate.

betray. **1** Mislead, delude, *deceive, beguile, double-cross.
Ana. Trap, entrap, snare, ensnare (see CATCH): *dupe, trick, befool, hoodwink, gull.
2 Discover, *reveal, disclose, divulge, tell.
Ana. Manifest, evidence, evince, *show, demonstrate: attest, betoken, bespeak, argue, *indicate.
Con. Shield, guard, safeguard, protect, *defend.

betrothal. *Engagement, affiance, espousal, sponsalia.

better, *v.* *Improve, ameliorate, help.
Ana. *Correct, amend, reform, rectify, remedy, redress: enhance (see INTENSIFY).
Ant. Worsen. — *Con.* Impair, mar, harm, damage, *injure: *debase, vitiate, corrupt.

between. **Between, betwixt, among** come into comparison when they take as object two or more persons or things and indicate their relation in position, in a distribution, in participation, and the like. **Between,** and its archaic form **betwixt,** in their literal senses apply to only two objects; as, *between* Scylla and Charybdis; *between* two fires. When this word is used of more than two objects, it brings them severally and individually into the relation expressed; as, a treaty *between* three powers; the three survivors had but one pair of shoes *between* them; "I hope that *between* public business, improving studies, and domestic pleasures, neither melancholy nor caprice will find any place for entrance" (*Johnson*). **Among** always implies more than two objects, which it brings less definitely into the relation expressed; as, *among* so many candidates one must find a good one; *among* the survivors were two boys; "Five barley loaves, and two small fishes: but what are they *among* so many?" (*John* vi. 9).

betwixt. *Between, among.

bevy, *n.* *Flock, drove, pack, herd, covey, gaggle, flight, swarm, shoal, school.

bewail. Lament, *deplore, bemoan.
Ana. Sorrow, *grieve, mourn: wail, weep, *cry.
Ant. Rejoice.

bewilder. Mystify, perplex, distract, *puzzle, confound, nonplus, dumfound.
Ana. *Confuse, addle, fuddle, muddle: fluster, flurry, perturb, agitate, upset (see DISCOMPOSE): baffle, foil (see FRUSTRATE).

bewitch. Enchant, captivate, fascinate, take, charm, allure, *attract.
Ana. *Thrill, electrify: delight, *please: infatuate, enamor (see corresponding adjectives at ENAMORED).

bewitching. Enchanting, captivating, fascinating, taking, charming, alluring, attractive. See under ATTRACT.

bewray. Betray, *reveal, discover, disclose, divulge, tell.
Ana. & *Con.* See those at BETRAY, 2.

bias, *n.* Prejudice, prepossession, partiality, *predilection.
Ana. Slant, standpoint, *point of view, viewpoint, angle: *leaning, propensity: inclining *or* inclination, predisposition, disposition (see corresponding verbs at INCLINE).
Con. Fairness, justness, impartiality, dispassionateness (see corresponding adjectives at FAIR).

bias, *v.* *Incline, dispose, predispose.
Ana. Sway, influence, *affect, impress.

bicker. Squabble, spat, tiff, quarrel, wrangle, altercate, See under QUARREL, *n.*
Ana. *Contend, fight, battle, war.

bickering. Spat, tiff, squabble, *quarrel, wrangle, altercation.
Ana. *Discord, contention, dissension, strife, conflict.

bid, *v.* **1** *Command, order, enjoin, direct, instruct, charge.
Ana. *Summon, call, cite.
Ant. Forbid. — *Con.* Prohibit, enjoin, interdict, inhibit (see FORBID).
2 *Invite, solicit, court, woo.
Ana. *Ask, request.

bid, *n.* Tender, *overture, advance, approach.
Ana. Offering *or* offer, proffering *or* proffer (see corresponding verbs at OFFER): *proposal, proposition: inviting *or* invitation, soliciting *or* solicitation (see corresponding verbs at INVITE).

biddable. Docile, amenable, tractable, *obedient.
Ana. *Compliant, acquiescent: obliging, complaisant, good-natured, *amiable: submissive, *tame.
Ant. Willful. — *Con.* Intractable, refractory, recalcitrant, headstrong, ungovernable, *unruly: *obstinate, stubborn, stiffnecked, mulish.

bidding. Behest, *command, order, injunction, mandate, dictate.
Ana. Direction, instruction (see corresponding verbs at COMMAND): summoning *or* summons, calling *or* call, citing *or* citation (see corresponding verbs at SUMMON).

big. *Large, great.
Ana. *Grand, magnificent, imposing, grandiose, majestic, august: huge, immense, *enormous, gigantic, colossal.
Ant. Little. — *Con.* *Small, diminutive, wee, tiny, petite, minute, microscopic, miniature.

bigot. Fanatic, *enthusiast, zealot.

bill, *n.*[1] **Bill, beak, nib** (*or* **neb**) denote in common the horny bipartite projection that serves a bird for jaws. In ornithology, **bill** and **beak** are used without distinction of meaning. *Bill* is decidedly more often used by American zoologists. *Beak,* if not more common than *bill* among British zoologists, at least occurs very frequently in their writings. In popular usage, *bill* is the usual term when the projection is flattened, or long and slender; as, the *bill* of a duck or swan, of a hummingbird, crane, heron, sandpiper, or snipe. *Beak* is associated with striking or tearing, and is the usual term for a projection, characteristic especially of birds of prey, in which the tip of the upper mandible has a sharp downward curvature and, usually, overhangs the lower mandible; as, the *beak* of an eagle, vulture, or hawk. "Although the kite soar with unbloodied *beak*" (*Shak.*). *Beak* is more often used than *bill* for a conical projection having a basal circumference large in proportion to the length; as, the *beak* of a cardinal bird or hawfinch (cf. the term *grosbeak* often applied to either of these birds). A projection not of any of the extreme types mentioned above is called either *bill* or *beak,* though *bill* appears to be commoner in England, and is certainly much commoner in the United States; as, the *bill* (less often *beak*) of a sparrow, swallow, jay, or robin. "In his *bill* An olive-leaf he [the dove] brings" (*Milton*). **Nib,** meaning bill, or beak, now occurs chiefly in dialect or poetry or in an extended sense; as, the *nib* of a pen.

bill, *n.*[2] **1 Bill, act, statute, law** are frequently confused when used to designate a legislative measure. **Bill** is properly applied only to the draft of a measure submitted to a legislature for its acceptance or rejection. The other terms are properly applied only to bills which have been passed. In actual use, they are practically identical. Strictly, however, a bill becomes an **act** when it is passed and duly signed by an executive officer; an act becomes a **statute** when it is legally effective and a part of the written law of the state; a statute is one kind of **law** (for fuller discrimination, see LAW).
2 Statement, *account.

billet. Berth, post, job, situation, *position, place, office, capacity.

billingsgate. Scurrility, vituperation, *abuse, invective, obloquy.

billow, *n.* *Wave, breaker, roller, comber, beachcomber, undulation, ripple.

bind. *Tie.
Ana. *Fasten, attach: *join, link, unite, connect.
Ant. Loose: unbind.

biological, *n.* *Drug, simple, medicinal, pharmaceutical.

birthright. **1** *Right, appanage, prerogative, privilege, perquisite.
2 Patrimony, *heritage, inheritance.

bisexual, *adj.* **Bisexual, hermaphrodite, hermaphroditic, androgynous, epicene** agree in meaning combining male and female functions, characters, or qualities in the same individual. **Bisexual** usually (but not invariably) suggests normal or functional coexistence of the reproductive organs of both sexes in the same individual; it is employed chiefly in botany and in zoology; thus, most garden plants are *bisexual* in that they have both male and female organs in the same flower; some invertebrate organisms such as certain mollusks and worms are described as *bisexual* because each individual elaborates both male and female germ cells, and is adapted, in some cases, for self-impregnation; in others, for mutual impregnation; and in still others, for serving as male or as female to another organism of the same species. In the instances cited, **hermaphrodite** or **hermaphroditic** may also be used, though usage varies somewhat in the individual biological sciences. However, since the term is also applied to human beings or other vertebrates in which there is an abnormal combination of sex organs, or more often, an ambiguity of sex owing to such a combination with imperfect development of the organs, the word may, as *bisexual* seldom does, connote monstrosity. In general, as opposed to technical, use, **androgynous** stresses the union of the characters or qualities of the two sexes, is applicable chiefly to persons, their acts, their words, their clothes, etc., and conveys no suggestion of abnormality. "The truth is, a great mind must be *androgynous*" (*Coleridge*). In botany, however, *androgynous* is distinguishable from *bisexual* and *hermaphroditic* in being applied to plants that carry male and female flowers in the same cluster, or inflorescence. **Epicene** was originally applied to Greek and Latin words invariable in gender but applicable to either the male or the female of the species; thus, the Greek *bous,* which can be translated according to the context bull, ox, or cow, is an *epicene* noun. In literary use, *epicene* often implies ambiguity in sex, or sexlessness; thus, *epicene* garments may belong to either a man or a woman. *Epicene,* when applied to a man or his qualities, often suggests effeminacy or womanishness; as, *epicene* interests; "*epicene* Reforms of this or that" (*E. L. Masters*).

bishop, *n.* **Bishop, archbishop, metropolitan, primate, ordinary** are not always clearly distinguished as used in some churches, especially in the Roman Catholic Church and the Church of England. A bishop, in the Roman Catholic, Orthodox, and Anglican churches, is an ecclesiastic who has been consecrated for his office (in Anglican Churches, who has received the highest of Holy Orders), who is regarded by his church as a successor of the apostles and the inheritor of their powers and authority, who is the head of a diocese, and who is responsible for his episcopal actions only to that authority which is specifically designated by his church as a whole. Thus, the bishop of Rome, who is also the pope, is the only bishop of the Roman Catholic Church now having jurisdiction over other bishops. An **archbishop,** so far as the powers given at consecration are concerned, is no higher than a bishop; he has for his see an important diocese (an archdiocese). In the Roman Catholic Church he is usually the presiding bishop of a province or a group of dioceses but has no authority to interfere in the government of any of the suffragan dioceses. His powers are chiefly those that are the prerogative of his precedence, dignity, and leadership. In the Church of England, he is the head of one of the two most important dioceses from the historical point of view, Canterbury and York. He takes precedence over other bishops and may give them counsel, but he has no jurisdiction over them, except where the law provides for an appeal to the archbishop from the decision of a diocesan bishop. A **metropolitan,** historically, was the bishop of the chief city or diocese of a province (in this instance, a geographical province) who, in the early church, had some jurisdiction over other bishops in that province. In modern use, the term is applicable to any archbishop who is the head of a province, or group of dioceses. The term is used in the Orthodox Church where, in essential features, it is equivalent to *archbishop,* but implies jurisdiction over the suffragan dioceses. A **primate,** historically, was a bishop who had jurisdiction over all the bishops in a province, a group of provinces, or a nation, serving as a vicar of the Holy See. The bishops of such dioceses today are usually called *primates,* but in the Roman Catholic Church the title is largely honorary. Thus, England has two primates for the Church of England, the archbishop of Canterbury, who specifically is designated **Primate of All England,** and the archbishop of York, whose title is **Primate of England.** In Ireland, there are four primates, two for the Roman Catholic Church and two for the Church of Ireland. In each group, the archbishop of Armagh is called **Primate of All Ireland,** and the archbishop of Dublin, **Primate of Ireland.** An **ordinary,** in ecclesiastical use and in the phrase *the ordinary of a diocese,* is the person who has immediate or original jurisdiction in his own right in a diocese, and who has judicial power in all ecclesiastical cases. Since the bishop of a diocese possesses such jurisdiction, the ordinary of a diocese is, except in extraordinary circumstances, its bishop (or archbishop). If there is an auxiliary or suffragan bishop in the diocese, he is not the ordinary, except where the powers have been deputed to him. In case of a vacancy in a see, the temporary ordinary is usually the administrator of the diocese or the vicar-general, or, in the Church of England, the archbishop of the province.

bit. *Particle, mite, smitch, smidgen, whit, atom, iota, jot, tittle.
Ana. Piece, fragment, detail, fraction, *part, portion.

biting. Cutting, crisp, trenchant, *incisive, clear-cut.
Ana. *Caustic, mordant, mordacious, acrid: *pungent, poignant, piquant, racy.

bitter. **Bitter, acrid** are applied to things that have an unpleasant taste (also smell, in the case of *acrid*) that is neither sweet nor bland yet seldom distinctly acid or stinging. **Bitter** is traditionally associated with the repellent taste of wormwood, quinine, and aloes, but it is also used to describe the taste of beer, unsweetened chocolate, and the rind of citrus fruits. That which is *bitter* usually lacks the pleasant tang and freshness of pure acids such as lemon juice. **Acrid** implies bitterness in taste that has an astringent or irritating effect on the mucous membranes, such as the taste of choke cherries or of alum. It is also applied to that which is bitter and salty (sometimes in general, sometimes in chemical, sense), as perspiration. An *acrid* smell is a penetrating, suffocating, repugnant odor. It is especially associated with certain fumes, such as those emanating from burning sulphur or with certain noxious vapors, such as those of a heavy London fog.
Ana. *Sour, acid, acidulous, tart: *astringent, constringent: *pungent, piquant.
Ant. Delicious. — *Con.* Delectable, luscious, *delightful.

bizarre. Grotesque, *fantastic, antic.
Ana. Outlandish, erratic, eccentric, *strange, singular, odd, queer, curious: extravagant, extreme (see EXCESSIVE).
Ant. Chaste: subdued.

blab. Tattle, *gossip.
Ana. Babble, gabble, chatter, prate, *chat: divulge, disclose, betray (see REVEAL).

blackball, *v.* Debar, shut out, *exclude, eliminate, rule out, disbar, suspend.
Con. Admit, accept, *receive.

blame, *v.* Reprehend, reprobate, condemn, denounce, censure, *criticize.
Ana. *Accuse, charge, indict, impeach: impute, attribute, *ascribe: implicate, *involve.
Con. Exonerate, vindicate, *exculpate, absolve, acquit: *excuse, remit, forgive.

blame, *n.* **Blame, culpability, guilt, fault** come into comparison when they mean responsibility for misdeed or delinquency. **Blame** is a term of shifting denotations, sometimes, for example, meaning the reprehension, criticism, or censure of those who find fault or judge one's work or acts (as, "I have never desired praise...I have been indifferent to, if not indeed contemptuous of, *blame*"—*H. Ellis*), or sometimes, though now less often, a charge or accusation of some fault, misdeed, or delinquency (as, "fear of incurring *blame* in Wiltstoken for wantonly opposing her daughter's obvious interests"—*Shaw*). In all its other senses, as well as the one here considered, it implies also that the person criticized or accused is held responsible for the misdeed or delinquency in question. When the term denotes responsibility for wrongdoing or delinquency, it also implies the meriting of reproof, censure, or the appropriate penalty; as, to take on oneself all the *blame* for a project's failure; they tried to shift the *blame* for their defeat. Often, the term means ultimate rather than immediate responsibility; as, "The *blame* [for backwardness in American education] has sometimes been put, and with some justice, upon our migratory habits and upon the heterogeneous character of our population" (*Grandgent*). **Culpability** is a much simpler term than *blame,* for it usually means little more or no more than the fact or the state of being responsible for any act or condition that may be described as wrong, harmful, or injurious; as, they could not prove his *culpability* for the accident; "As if the estrangement between them had come of any *culpability* of hers" (*Dickens*). **Guilt,** which originally denoted a crime or sin, in its current senses usually retains an implication of a connection with misdeeds of a grave or serious character from the moral and social points of view. Also, it usually implies a deserving of severe punishment (such as condemnation, loss of freedom or, in the case of sin, loss of salvation) or of a definite legal penalty (such as a fine, imprisonment, or death). Therefore, when the term denotes responsibility for a crime or sin, it also carries implications of need of proof before punishment can be determined or forgiveness granted; as, though she was strongly suspected of murder, her *guilt* was not established until after her death; since he admitted his *guilt,* he saved the state the cost of a trial; to confess one's sins is to acknowledge one's *guilt* for those sins. **Fault** (as here considered: see also FAULT, 1) is often used in place of *culpability* as a simpler word; as, the *fault* is her parents', not the child's; "The *fault,* dear Brutus, is not in our stars, But in ourselves, that we are underlings" (*Shak.*); "That you are thus, the *fault* is mine" (*Wordsworth*).
Ana. Responsibility, accountability, answerability (see corresponding adjectives at RESPONSIBLE): censure, condemnation, denunciation, reprehension (see corresponding verbs at CRITICIZE).
Con. Commendation, compliment (see corresponding verbs at COMMEND): *applause, acclaim, plaudits, acclamation.

blameworthy. **Blameworthy, guilty, culpable** come into comparison in the sense of deserving reproach and punishment for a sinful or criminal act, practice, or condition. A person or his act or work is **blameworthy** that deserves blame or criticism and must suffer or receive reproach, censure, or even more severe punishment. "Thee [England] therefore still, *blameworthy* as thou art ... Thee I account still happy, and the chief Among the nations, seeing thou art free" (*Cowper*). A person is **guilty** who is justly chargeable with responsibility for a delinquency, crime, or sin, either in his own knowledge or in that of others, by his confession or by proof (often legal proof) of his responsibility: the term may stress either the fact that guilt has been proved or the fact or the fear of resulting punishment; as, the defendant was found *guilty;* "Suspicion always haunts the *guilty* mind; The thief doth fear each bush an officer" (*Shak.*); "Let no *guilty* man escape, if it can be avoided" (*U. S. Grant*). Often, the term suggests merely a state of mind, such as a consciousness that one has committed a sin or a crime, or a fear that one is justly suspected of wrongdoing or of a misdeed; as, a *guilty* conscience; "there is no use in making the refractory child feel *guilty*" (*B. Russell*). A person is **culpable** in an older and now rare sense of the word who has been found guilty (as, "I pray you all, Proceed no straiter 'gainst our Uncle Gloucester Than from true evidence... He be approved [i.e., proved] in practice *culpable*"—*Shak.*) or, in the now more common sense, has been shown to be blameworthy and open to severe censure or condemnation (as, "prove the pair not *culpable,* Free as unborn babe from connivance at, Participation in, their daughter's fault"—*Browning*). The term is also applicable to a blameworthy act, condition, practice, or the like, for which one is responsible or which leads to an accident, crime, etc.; as, *culpable* ignorance; *culpable* neglect; *culpable* disregard of others' safety.

Ant. Blameless. — ***Con.*** Faultless, *impeccable, flawless.

blanch, *v.* *Whiten, bleach, decolorize, etiolate.

bland, *adj.* **1** Smooth, *suave, urbane, diplomatic, politic.

Ana. Benign, benignant, *kind, kindly: *amiable, complaisant, obliging, good-natured: sleek, unctuous (see FULSOME).

Ant. Brusque. — ***Con.*** *Bluff, blunt, gruff, curt, crusty.

2 Mild, gentle, *soft, balmy, lenient.

Ana. *Neutral, indifferent: *temperate, moderate: *insipid, flat, vapid, wishy-washy.

Ant. *Pungent, piquant: savory, tasty (see PALATABLE). — ***Con.*** Stimulating, exciting, quickening (see PROVOKE): thrilling, electrifying (see THRILL, *v.*).

blandish. Wheedle, cajole, *coax.

Ana. Allure, charm, bewitch, captivate (see ATTRACT): *lure, entice, seduce: beguile, delude (see DECEIVE).

Con. Constrain, oblige, coerce, compel, *force: drive, impel (see MOVE): *intimidate, cow, bulldoze, browbeat, bully.

blank, *adj.* Void, *empty, vacant, vacuous.

Ana. *Bare, barren: *clean.

Con. *Expressive, meaningful, significant, pregnant.

blasphemous. *Impious, profane, sacrilegious.

Ana. Cursing, damning, execrating, anathematizing, objurgating (see EXECRATE): *irreligious, ungodly, godless.

Ant. Reverent.

blasphemy. **1 Blasphemy, profanity, swearing, cursing** are here compared only as meaning impious or irreverent speech. **Blasphemy,** the strongest term (for its looser use, see PROFANATION), applies strictly to any intentional or malicious utterance in which the Supreme Being is defied or offered indignity; as such it is regarded as a serious sin in theology and as a crime at the common law. "Genuine *blasphemy,* genuine in spirit and not purely verbal, is the product of partial belief, and is as impossible to the complete atheist as to the perfect Christian" (*T. S. Eliot*). **Profanity** has a wider range, and includes all irreverent reference to holy things; it is particularly applied to speech in which the names of God, Jesus, and the Virgin Mary are used lightly and irreverently, and often coarsely, especially in giving vent to rage or passion in oaths, curses, and imprecations. "He [Mark Twain] had what one might call a preliminary recourse in his *profanity,* those 'scorching, singeing blasts' he was always directing at his companions" (*Van W. Brooks*). **Swearing** and **cursing,** as here considered, are forms of profanity, the former stressing indulgence in profane and often meaningless oaths; the latter, indulgence in profane curses or imprecations, as by calling on God to damn or punish the object of one's wrath or hatred. "Among labourers and others, that ungodly custom of *swearing* is too frequently heard, to the dishonour of God and contempt of authority" (*Sir C. Wren*). "Why, what an ass am I!... That I...must...unpack my heart with words, And fall a-*cursing*" (*Shak.*).

Ana. Insult, *affront, indignity: scurrility, vituperation (see ABUSE, *n.*).

Ant. Adoration. — ***Con.*** Worship, reverence, veneration (see under REVERE): *blessing, benediction, benison.

2 *Profanation, desecration, sacrilege.

Ana. Debasement, corruption, perversion (see corresponding verbs at DEBASE): misrepresentation, falsehood, untruth, *lie.

blast, *n.* Gust, gale, *wind, breeze, flaw, zephyr, hurricane, whirlwind, cyclone, typhoon, tornado, waterspout, twister.

blatant. Clamorous, *vociferous, strident, boisterous, obstreperous.

Ana. Assertive, self-assertive, pushing, *aggressive, militant: *vocal, articulate, voluble, glib: vulgar, *coarse, gross.

Ant. Decorous: reserved. — ***Con.*** *Silent, uncommunicative, reticent, taciturn: subdued, *tame: discreet, prudent (see under PRUDENCE).

blaze, *n.* Flare, flame, glare, glow. See under BLAZE, *v.*

Ana. Firing *or* fire, kindling, enkindling, igniting *or* ignition (see corresponding verbs at LIGHT): effulgence, refulgence, radiance, brilliance *or* brilliancy (see corresponding adjectives at BRIGHT).

blaze, *v.* **Blaze, flame, flare, glare, glow** are here compared both as verbs meaning to burn or appear to burn brightly and as nouns denoting a brightly burning light or fire. **Blaze** implies great activity in burning, the thorough kindling of the burning substance or material, and the radiation of intense light and, often, heat; as, the *blazing* noonday sun; "in one of these [clefts] a pine-fire was soon *blazing*" (*J. Tyndall*); "A few withered dry sticks, with which they made a *blaze*" (*Defoe*); "her eyes *blazing* in her white face" (*Stevenson*). **Flame** suggests a darting tongue or tongues of fire, formed by rapidly burning gas or vapor; it therefore often connotes less steadiness than *blaze* and sometimes less heat and light; as, the burning house was soon a mass of *flames;* the torches *flamed* in the wind; the dry fuel soon burst into *flame;* "dimmed hope's newly kindled *flame*" (*Shelley*). **Flare** implies flame or flames, especially a flame darting up suddenly against a dark background or from a dying fire; as, "torches that guttered and *flared*" (*Hewlett*). "He...lighted a cigarette and then remembered that the *flare* of the match could probably be seen from the station" (*S. Anderson*). **Glare** (see also GAZE) emphasizes the emission or reflection of bright light; it sometimes connotes an almost unendurable brilliancy; as, "dazed by the lantern *glare*" (*Kipling*); the snow *glares* in the sunlight; the *glare* of a forest fire in the sky; "He [Dante]...lets the fire *glare* on the sullen face for a moment, and it sears itself into the memory forever" (*J. R. Lowell*). "His [Augustus's] days were passed in the *glare* of publicity" (*Buchan*). **Glow** also stresses the emission of light, but it suggests an absence of flame and therefore connotes steadiness, intensity, radiance without effulgence, and often, warmth and duration; as, the *glow* of coals; "her fine effect of *glowing* from within as a lamp glows" (*M. Austin*). "The fire that burned within him, that *glowed* with so strange and marvellous a radiance in almost all he wrote" (*A. Huxley*).

Ana. *Illuminate, illumine, light, illume: *burn: *flash, gleam, glance, spark.

bleach, *v.* *Whiten, etiolate, decolorize, blanch.

Ant. Dye.

blemish, *n.* **Blemish, defect, flaw** agree in denoting an imperfection. **Blemish** applies to what is external or superficial, such as a spot or a stain, as marring or disfiguring the appearance of an object; as, "on their sustaining garments not a *blemish*" (*Shak.*); "a lamb without *blemish* and without spot" (*1 Peter* i. 19); a reputation without a *blemish.* **Defect** implies the lack or want (which may or may not appear superficially) of something which is essential to completeness or perfection; as, a *defect* in the mechanism; a *defect* in the organs of vision; the *defects* of this poem are not obvious; a *defect* in an argument. A **flaw** is a defect in continuity or cohesion, such as a break, a crack, or a fissure; as, a *flaw* in a crystal; "Or some frail China jar receive a *flaw*" (*Pope*); "My love to thee is sound, sans crack or *flaw*" (*Shak.*); a *flaw* (or *defect*) in his character. "Style is not a sheet of glass in which the only thing that matters is the absence of *flaws*" (*H. Ellis*).

Ana. Blot, stain, *stigma: tainting *or* taint, pollution, defilement (see corresponding verbs at CONTAMINATE): *fault, failing, frailty: *lack, want, privation.

Ant. Immaculateness. — *Con.* Purity, simplicity (see corresponding adjectives at PURE): cleanness, cleanliness (see corresponding adjectives at CLEAN): clearness, transparency, pellucidness (see corresponding adjectives at CLEAR).

blench. Quail, shrink, *recoil, flinch, wince.

Ana. Evade, elude, avoid, shun, eschew, *escape: tremble, quiver, shudder, quake, *shake.

Con. *Bear, suffer, endure, abide, stand.

blend, *v.* Fuse, *mix, merge, coalesce, mingle, commingle, amalgamate.

Ana. Combine, unite (see JOIN): *integrate: consolidate, unify, *compact.

Ant. Resolve. — *Con.* *Analyze, break down: *separate, part, divorce: decompose, disintegrate (see DECAY).

blend, *n.* *Mixture, admixture, compound, composite, amalgam.

blessed. *Holy, sacred, divine, spiritual, religious.

Ant. Accursed.

blessedness. Beatitude, bliss, *happiness, felicity.

Ana. Enjoyment, fruition, joy, *pleasure.

Ant. Misery, dolor. — *Con.* Suffering, *distress, agony: woe, dole, anguish, *sorrow, grief.

blessing, *n.* **Blessing, benediction, benison** are not always clearly distinguished when they denote the religious act or ceremony in which a person, often a clergyman, blesses someone or something. The chief distinction between *blessing* and *benediction* is that *blessing* carries both of the major meanings of the verb *bless; benediction* carries but one of them. Consequently, a **blessing** may take the form of (1) a prayer of consecration or dedication of something to religious uses or of offering something to God (as, the *blessing* of a bell; a *blessing* [of food] before meals), (2) a prayer invoking God to give happiness (usually spiritual happiness) to someone, or to guard him from harm (as, "calling down a *blessing* on his head" [*Tennyson*]; none of the children left home to seek their fortune without their father's *blessing*). In some churches, especially the Roman Catholic Church, each of these prayers also includes the making of the sign of the cross over the person or thing blessed. **Benediction,** on the other hand, applies only to a prayer or ceremony invoking a blessing or blessings upon a person or persons. In this sense, it may be used interchangeably with *blessing*. However, it is the customary term for certain ceremonial blessings of an audience or congregation, such as the concluding prayer at a public assembly, or the service, in some Christian churches, known more fully as the *Benediction of the Blessed Sacrament,* in which the Eucharistic Host is exhibited in a monstrance that is moved by the officiating priest so as to make the sign of the cross over the congregation. **Benison** is now archaic for *benediction* or *blessing* in the sense of benediction; it has no currency in ecclesiastical use and is found chiefly in poetry and literary prose; as, "God's *benison* go with you" (*Shak.*); "I have slept sound under such a *benison*" (*Scott*).

Ant. Curse. — *Con.* Imprecation, malediction, malison, anathema (see CURSE).

blimp. Balloon, airship, *aerostat, dirigible, zeppelin.

blind, *adj.* **Blind, sightless, purblind** come into comparison because they mean or have meant lacking the power to see or to discriminate objects. **Blind** still is used to imply absence or deprivation of the power of vision, either by congenital defect or as a result of disease or of an injury to the organs of vision; as, Milton was *blind* when he wrote *Paradise Lost;* "if the *blind* lead the *blind,* both shall fall into the ditch" (*Matthew* xv. 14). In current English it is as often employed in a figurative sense, especially as implying a lack of the mental, moral, or spiritual vision essential to the perception or discernment of that which actually exists or that which is really true. "His divine power hath given unto us all things that pertain unto life and godliness.... But he that lacketh these things is *blind*" (*2 Peter* i. 3–9). "Human nature is weak, and I am not a *blind* woman to insist that he is perfect" (*Hardy*). *Blind* is also applicable to things devoid of intelligence or of ability to know whither they are moving or tending (as, *blind* agencies; "*blind,* mechanical forces of society"—*Wilde*), or to acts, emotions, attitudes, and the like, which are the result of or which produce mental, moral, or spiritual blindness (as, *blind* terror; a *blind* acceptance of authority), or to spaces, structures, and the like, that are so dark or obscure or obstructed that one cannot see through, into, or around them (as, "air...*blind* with snow"—*Cather*); a *blind* wall; a *blind* alley; a *blind* corner. **Sightless** is sometimes the preferred term when total blindness is implied; as, the *sightless* Homer; "his letter talks of a disjointed thumb, a contusion on the hip, and a *sightless* eye" (*Lucas*). The term may also be used in place of *blind* when impenetrability to the vision is implied; usually, however, it applies to that which is actually invisible, though its existence is otherwise known; as, "Drown'd in yonder living blue The lark becomes a *sightless* song" (*Tennyson*). **Purblind** in literal use has long been obsolete in the sense of totally blind (as, "*Purblind* Argus, all eyes and no sight"—*Shak.*), but it still occasionally occurs in the sense of nearly blind, or without sight enough to do one's work or make one's way successfully. For a long time the term was applied to those whose sight was dimmed through age or disease; as, "Old Nanon the cook, *purblind,* stone-deaf, and all but imbecile" (*M. E. Braddon*). In current use, *purblind* is chiefly used in a figurative sense, implying the imperfection, sometimes the absence, of mental, moral, or spiritual vision, and usually connoting obtuseness or short-sightedness that comes from ignorance, stupidity, indifference, or the like; as, "the intolerable narrowness and the *purblind* conscience of the society" (*G. Eliot*); "the moral *purblindness* that accompanies all economic activities" (*J. A. Hobson*).

Con. Seeing, perceiving, discerning, noticing, noting (see SEE): *aware, alive, conscious, sensible, cognizant, awake.

blind, *n.* Stake, pot, ante, *bet, wager.

blink, *v.* *Wink.

Ana. Ignore, disregard, overlook, slight, *neglect: evade, elude, avoid, shun (see ESCAPE).

Con. *See, note, notice, observe, remark.

bliss. Beatitude, blessedness, felicity, *happiness.

Ana. Enjoyment, joy, delectation, fruition, *pleasure: rapture, *ecstasy, transport.

Ant. Anguish: bale. — *Con.* Misery, suffering, *distress, agony, dolor: woe, dole, *sorrow, grief: gloom, dejection, melancholy, *sadness.

blithe. Jocund, *merry, jovial, jolly.

Ana. Gay, *lively, animated, vivacious, sprightly: joyful, joyous, lighthearted, *glad, happy, cheerful: buoyant, effervescent, volatile (see ELASTIC).

Ant. Morose: atrabilious. — *Con.* Sad, depressed, dejected, gloomy (see corresponding nouns at SADNESS): *sullen, glum, dour, saturnine: *melancholic, melancholy.

bloc. Party, *combination, faction, ring, combine, cabal, junto.

block, *v.* Obstruct, bar, dam, impede, *hinder.

Ana. Check, *arrest, interrupt: *hamper, clog, trammel: prohibit, *forbid, inhibit: *frustrate, thwart, foil: *prevent, forestall.

Con. *Advance, forward, further, promote.

blockade, *n.* **Blockade, siege** are here compared as denoting an attempt of a belligerent force to break down the resistance of the enemy by preventing egress or ingress of men or entrance of supplies over a considerable period of time. **Blockade** (etymologically, a blocking or obstructing) is used commonly, but not invariably, of an attempt made to close a port, harbor, or coast, especially by effectively investing it with warships, and in recent years with mines, so that fresh supplies of food, fuel, ammunition, and the like, are cut off from the enemy; as, to run a *blockade;* to raise a *blockade;* the allied *blockade* of the North Sea avenues to the German coast during the World War. **Siege** (etymologically, a sitting down) is applied chiefly to a military (as opposed to a naval) attempt. The term implies investment, commonly with troops, on all sides of a fortified place (often a metropolis). It also suggests, as *blockade* does not, frequent assaults by the besieging forces, as efforts to compel surrender; as, the *Siege* of Paris (Franco-Prussian War, 1870–71); the *Siege* of Vicksburg (1863 in the American Civil War).

bloodless. Anemic, *pale.

Ana. *Colorless, uncolored: wishy-washy, vapid, inane (see INSIPID).

Ant. Sanguine: plethoric. — *Con.* Vital, alive, *living: vivid, *graphic: *vigorous, lusty, nervous.

bloody. **Bloody, sanguinary, sanguine, sanguineous, gory** come into comparison when they mean affected by or involving the shedding of blood. **Bloody** may be used in place of any of the succeeding words, but it specifically and distinctively applies to that which is covered with blood or is of the nature of blood; as, a *bloody* knife, wound, sweat. **Sanguinary** usually, and *bloody* also when a simpler, more forcible word is desired, apply to that which is attended by, or bent upon, bloodshed; as, a *sanguinary* conflict, disposition, code; a *bloody* battle. **Sanguine** and **sanguineous** are, as here considered, used chiefly in a literary context in place of either of the preceding words, or specifically, implying a literal or figurative association with bleeding or bloodthirstiness, or the color of blood. "To find his way through the *sanguine* labyrinth of passion through which he was wandering" (*Wilde*). "His passion, cruel grown, took on a hue Fierce and *sanguineous*" (*Keats*). **Gory** sometimes suggests clotted blood, but more often it suggests a profusion of blood that testifies to slaughter; as, a *gory* blade; "never shake Thy *gory* locks at me" (*Shak.*); "Mad Ambition's *gory* hand" (*Burns*).

bloomer. *Error, mistake, blunder, bull, howler, boner, slip, lapse, faux pas, floater.

blot, *n.* *Stigma, brand, stain.

Ana. Taint, defilement, pollution (see corresponding verbs at CONTAMINATE): *blemish, flaw, defect: shame, *disgrace, ignominy, obloquy.

blot, *v.* In form **blot out.** Delete, dele, obliterate, expunge, *erase, cancel, efface.

Ana. *Abolish, annihilate, extinguish: wipe out, *exterminate, extirpate.

Con. Preserve, *save, conserve: imprint, print, impress, stamp (see corresponding nouns at IMPRESSION).

blowzy. Frowzy, *slatternly, dowdy.

Ana. Flashy, tawdry, *gaudy, garish: slovenly, sloppy, unkempt, *slipshod: florid, flamboyant (see ORNATE): vulgar, *coarse.

Ant. Smart, spruce: dainty. — *Con.* *Neat, tidy, trim, trig: fastidious, particular, *nice.

blubber, *v.* *Cry, weep, wail, keen, whimper.

bluejacket. *Mariner, sailor, seaman, tar, gob, matlow, rating.

blueprint, *v.* *Sketch, draft, trace, plot, diagram, delineate, outline.

blueprint, *n.* Sketch, draft, tracing, plot, diagram, delineation, outline. See under SKETCH, *v.*

blues. Dejection, depression, melancholy, gloom, dumps, vapors, *sadness.

bluff, *adj.* **Bluff, blunt, brusque, curt, crusty, gruff** agree in meaning abrupt and unceremonious in speech or manner. **Bluff,** the only term of the group used in a complimentary sense, connotes outspokenness, rough good nature, and unconventionality which bespeak a sincerity that scorns the forms of politeness; as, "*bluff* King Hal" (*Scott*); *bluff* honesty; a *bluff* sea captain. "The old gentleman was burly and *bluff*, very kind and generous, but passionate" (*Crabb Robinson*). **Blunt** (see also DULL) implies such directness and plain-speaking as to suggest lack of consideration for the feelings of others, and some disregard for the amenities of life; as, a *blunt* reply; *blunt* manners; " 'That dog does smell,' said Lily, *bluntly*" (*Bennett*). "One always feels that he [Charles Whibley] is ready to say *bluntly* what every one else is afraid to say" (*T. S. Eliot*). **Brusque** suggests a certain (real or apparent) sharpness of manner and ungraciousness of speech; as, a *brusque* refusal. "I was nettled by her *brusque* manner of asserting her folly" (*Conrad*). "He [Augustus] could be trusted to deal fairly with opponents, and there was a *brusque* kindliness even in his reproofs" (*Buchan*). **Curt** implies disconcerting shortness, or rude conciseness; as, a *curt* answer, nod. "Octavia ...felt it to be her duty to join him [her husband, Antony], but a *curt* message from him bade her return at once to Rome" (*Buchan*). **Crusty** (literally, having a hard crust) implies a forbidding exterior and a manner marked by asperity or acerbity that sometimes belies real kindness of heart; as, a *crusty* bachelor; "He was a *crusty* old fellow, as close as a vise" (*N. Hawthorne*); "An old English gentleman, of great probity, some understanding, and very considerable *crustiness*" (*Irving*). **Gruff** carries a stronger implication of (real or seeming) surliness and roughness than *crusty* and distinctively suggests curt and hoarse or guttural utterance; as, "*Gruff*, disagreeable, sarcastic remarks" (*Thackeray*).

Ana. Hearty, *sincere: plain, open, *frank, candid: abrupt, *precipitate.

Ant. Suave, smooth. — *Con.* Urbane, diplomatic, bland (see SUAVE): courteous, courtly, gallant, polite, *civil.

blunder, *n.* Mistake, *error, bull, howler, boner, bloomer, slip, lapse, faux pas, floater.

Ana. *Fault, failing, frailty, vice: *anachronism, solecism: aberration, *deviation: transgression, violation, *breach.

blunt. 1 *Dull, obtuse.

Ant. Keen, sharp. — *Con.* Acute (see SHARP): penetrating, piercing, probing (see ENTER).

2 Brusque, curt, *bluff, gruff, crusty.

Ana. Plain, candid, *frank: *rude, discourteous, ungracious, uncivil, impolite: *forthright, downright.

Ant. Tactful: subtle. — *Con.* Diplomatic, politic, smooth, *suave, urbane.

blurb. Puff, review, critique, *criticism.

board, *v.* House, lodge, *harbor, shelter, entertain.

Ana. *Feed, nourish.

boast, *v.* **Boast, brag, vaunt, crow, gasconade** agree in meaning to give vent in speech to one's pride in oneself (or one's family, one's connections, one's race, one's accomplishments, or the like). *Boast* and *vaunt* are often used transitively as well as intransitively; the other words are chiefly intransitive in current good use. **Boast** is the general term; it may or may not carry a suggestion of contempt, or impute exaggeration, ostentation, vaingloriousness, or the like, to the boaster; as, "what folly then To *boast* what arms can do!" (*Milton*); "The wretch... Abhors the craft he *boasted* of before" (*Cowper*); "And these dull swine of Thebes *boast* their descent" (*Shelley*); "He was childishly anxious to *boast* that he had walked the whole of the six or seven miles" (*C. Mackenzie*). **Brag** is more colloquial than *boast*, and carries a stronger implication of exaggeration and conceit; it often also implies glorying in one's superiority, or in what one can do as well as in what one is, or has, or has done. " 'Why, what are you?' 'One, sir, that for his love dares yet do more Than you have heard him *brag* to you he will' " (*Shak.*). "That we may *brag* we hae a lass, There's nane again sae bonie" (*Burns*). **Vaunt** is more literary than either of the preceding terms; it usually connotes more pomp and bombast than *boast* and less crudeness or naïveté than *brag*. "Charity [in *R. V.*, love] *vaunteth* not itself, is not puffed up" (*1 Corinthians* xiii. 4). "And ye *vaunted* your fathomless power, and ye flaunted your iron pride" (*Kipling*). **Crow** (a colloquial term) usually implies exultant boasting or especially blatant bragging, in a manner suggestive of the triumphal crowing of a cock; as, the Blues were wont to *crow* over any team that met defeat at their hands; to *crow* over one's success in a competition. **Gasconade** (literally, to boast as the Gascons, a proverbially boastful people, do), the least common of these terms, implies habitual or extravagant self-vaunting. "The English reproach the French with gasconade, but they never *gasconaded* as the English do now" (*J. Q. Adams*).

Ana. Flaunt, parade (see SHOW): *pride, plume, pique, preen: *exalt, magnify, aggrandize.

Ant. Depreciate (*oneself, one's accomplishments*). — *Con.* *Decry, disparage, belittle, minimize: deprecate (see DISAPPROVE).

boat. **Boat, vessel, ship, craft, argosy** come into comparison when they denote a floating structure designed to carry persons or goods over water. **Boat** is used as a general designation of such a structure only in extended use. Originally it was, and it still is, applicable chiefly to a small, typically open structure (such as might have been constructed by hollowing out and shaping the trunk of a tree) operated by oars, paddles, or poles (as a rowboat, a canoe, or a punt) or by sails or a power mechanism (as, a sail*boat*, a motor*boat*). **Vessel** etymologically suggests a purpose as well as a form, the term, in general, applying to anything hollowed out so as to serve as a receptacle. Hence, *vessel* is commonly preferred when the containing and transporting of goods and persons is stressed; it is applied chiefly to large boats, especially seagoing boats, in the business of carrying passengers or freight or serving as a base of operations at sea, as in fishing or in war; as, steam *vessels;* a fleet of war *vessels* including dreadnoughts, cruisers, destroyers, and submarines; fishing *vessels;* a line owning fifty *vessels.* **Ship** is the preferred term for the large seagoing vessel, especially when its navigation rather than its business is emphasized; as, a sailing *ship;* a steam*ship;* a battle*ship;* the captain stands by his *ship* (not *vessel*) or is the last to leave his *ship. Ship* also suggests more personality, more romance, and more beauty than the other words and therefore is far more common in poetry and in figurative use. "Sailing, Like a stately *ship* ... Sails filled, and streamers waving" (*Milton*). "O Captain! my Captain! our fearful trip is done! The *ship* has weather'd every wrack, the prize we sought is won" (*Whitman*). **Craft** may be used as a singular or collective noun and is now applicable to any type of boat or ship that plies the water. Originally it was found only in the phrase *small craft*, and was applied to smaller vessels, especially to those in the service of ships, such as lighters, tugs, and fireboats, or to those forming part of a navy or fleet. The word has now nearly displaced the phrase, and although it is often used in the sense of *small craft*, it tends to become a comprehensive term covering all kinds of boats and vessels; as, the harbor is filled with *craft.* As a singular, *craft* unqualified is often a vague and general term. "For me, my *craft* is sailing on, Through mists to-day, clear seas anon" (*J. K. Bangs*). However, for that very reason, *craft* is often, when it is qualified, a better choice than *boat, ship*, or *vessel;* as, a huge, lumbering *craft.* "For she is such a smart little *craft*" (*W. S. Gilbert*). **Argosy,** though it actually designates an old type of merchant vessel sailing the Mediterranean, is now a poetic or literary term for *ship* or *vessel* or, more rarely, for a fleet of ships. Usually it carries one or more of the poetic connotations of *ship*, but it also implies the transportation of treasures. "Venetian merchants with deep-laden *argosies*" (*Longfellow*).

bobby. *Policeman, officer, constable, peeler, copper, cop, bailiff, catchpole, gendarme, bull.

bock. *Beer, lager, ale, stout, porter.

bodily. **Bodily, physical, corporeal, corporal, somatic** are comparable when used narrowly and mean of or pertaining to the human body. **Bodily** suggests opposition to *mental* or *intellectual;* as, so engrossed in thought as to be unaware of his *bodily* needs; he has never known *bodily* pain. "*Bodily* illness is more easy to bear than mental" (*Dickens*). **Physical** (for more inclusive use, see MATERIAL), though often used interchangeably with *bodily*, does not carry so strong a suggestion of organic structure as the latter; thus, *bodily* suffering implies some disturbance within the organism or, if external, some stimulus directly affecting the organism; *physical* suffering may also mean this, but often it is vaguer and less explicit in its implications or reference; as, *bodily* pains induced by *physical* exhaustion; a sense of *physical* well-being is often the result of freedom from *bodily* ailments. **Corporeal** refers more specifically to the substance or matter of which the body is composed; like *physical* it has a more inclusive sense (see MATERIAL) but when used with reference to the human body, it implies an opposition to *immaterial* or to *spiritual* as applied to substance or nature; as, most Protestants do not believe in the *corporeal* presence of Jesus in the consecrated bread and wine. "Until, the breath of this *corporeal* frame... Almost suspended, we are laid asleep In body, and become a living soul" (*Wordsworth*). **Corporal,** originally synonymous with *bodily* in all its senses (as, "*corporal* soundness"—*Shak.;* "*corporal* servitude"—*Milton*), in present usage applies almost exclusively to things that have for their object an effect (painful or otherwise) upon the body; as, *corporal* works of mercy (that is, the seven duties of a Christian to others, so far as they affect the body, such as "to feed the hungry" and "to clothe the naked"); *corporal* (never *corporeal*) punishment; "He publicly professed his resolution of a violent and *corporal* revenge" (*Johnson*). **Somatic,** because of its freedom from theological and poetic connotations, is now preferred to *bodily* and *corporeal* by physiologists, psychologists, and the like, with an implied opposition to *psychical;* as, *somatic* reactions to a stimulus; a *somatic* disturbance; *somatic* behavior.

Ana. *Carnal, fleshly, animal, sensual.

Con. *Mental, psychic, intellectual: spiritual (see HOLY).

body. **Body, corpse, carcass** (*or* **carcase**), **cadaver, stiff** are terms used to denote the physical organism of a man or animal (especially one of the larger animals). **Body** refers to the animal organism, living or dead, but its commonest use is in reference to man, then often implying an opposition to *mind* or *soul;* as, "absent in *body*, but present in spirit" (*1 Corinthians* v. 3); men take great care of their *bodies;* they removed the *body* to a morgue. **Corpse** and **carcass** (of man and beast respectively) refer to the dead body; as, "Make a ring about the *corpse* of Caesar" (*Shak.*); "There was a swarm of bees and honey in the *carcase* of the lion" (*Judges* xiv. 8). *Carcass* is also used as a term of contempt for the human body, dead or alive; as, "On the bleak shore now lies th' abandoned king, A headless *carcass*, and a nameless thing" (*Dryden*); "to pamper his own *carcass*" (*South*). **Cadaver** (but cf. *cadaverous* at HAGGARD), and the slang term **stiff** apply to a corpse used for the purpose of dissection in a laboratory. In humorous use, *cadaver* is sometimes applied to living men, suggesting the appearance of a skeleton.

Con. *Soul, spirit: *mind, intellect, psyche, intelligence.

boggle, *v.* Stickle, stick, strain, scruple, *demur, balk, jib, shy.

Ana. *Object, protest, kick, remonstrate, expostulate: *recoil, shrink, flinch, wince, blench, quail.

Ant. Subscribe (*to*). — *Con.* Acquiesce, accede, *assent, agree: accept, admit, *receive.

boisterous. Obstreperous, clamorous, blatant, *vociferous, strident.

Ana. Sporting, disporting, rollicking, frolicking, gamboling (see under PLAY, *v.*): *unruly, ungovernable: *indecorous, unseemly.

Con. Quiet, noiseless, *still: peaceful, *calm, tranquil, serene, placid: staid, sedate, *serious, sober.

bold. Audacious, intrepid, dauntless, undaunted, *brave, courageous, valiant, valorous, doughty.

Ana. Daring, reckless, venturous, venturesome, *adventurous, daredevil, rash, foolhardy, temerarious: mettlesome, *spirited: fearless, unapprehensive, unafraid (see affirmative adjectives at FEARFUL).

Ant. Cowardly. — *Con.* *Timid, timorous: pusillanimous, craven, dastardly, recreant (see COWARDLY): quailing, flinching, shrinking, recoiling (see RECOIL).

Bolshevist. Communist, socialist, *collectivist, nihilist, anarchist.

bolt, *v.* Winnow, screen, *sift, sieve, riddle.

bombard. Assail, storm, assault, *attack.

bombast, *n.* **Bombast, rhapsody, rant, fustian, rodomontade** are all terms designating a kind of high-flown high-sounding speech or writing. All of them are derogatory in some degree; some of them are frankly contemptuous. **Bombast** does not necessarily connote emptiness of thought, but it always implies inflation, or a grandiosity or impressiveness in language and style which so outruns the thought that the attention is distracted from the matter and concentrated upon the manner of expression. When used in description rather than in censure, *bombast* often additionally suggests a soaring eloquence or a kind of oratorical grandeur, such as is found in Marlowe's *Tamburlaine the Great* or is characteristic of Elizabethan drama in comparison with modern realistic drama; when used in depreciation, it suggests padding, windiness, verbosity, "tall talking," and the like. "To outbrave better pens with the swelling *bombast* of a bragging blank verse" (*Nash*). "Their eloquence is all *bombast*" (*Kingsley*). "It [the verse of Jonson's *Volpone*] looks like mere 'rhetoric,' certainly not 'deeds and language such as men do use.' It appears to us [at first consideration], in fact, forced and flagitious *bombast*" (*T. S. Eliot*). **Rhapsody,** like *bombast*, may be scarcely or obviously derogatory. It designates a kind of ecstatic or effusive utterance or writing in which the language or style is governed by the feelings rather than by logical thought. It may, at one extreme, suggest inspired utterance as in rapture or, at the other, an almost maudlin loquaciousness. "O then my breast Should warble airs, whose *rhapsodies* should feast The ears of seraphims" (*Quarles*). "After some wild and vehement *rhapsodies*...he was easily persuaded to retire" (*G. P. R. James*). In learned use, however, it is often applied to a kind of writing that has no perceptible argument and is seemingly incoherent, yet moves, by a kind of logic of its own, from one expression of feeling or one image to another. "The poem [Hopkins's *The Leaden Echo and the Golden Echo*] must be read aloud, and with an unprejudiced intellect, for it is a sustained sensual *rhapsody;* something for which our acquaintance with civilized poetry leaves us unprepared" (*Day Lewis*). **Rant** and **fustian,** on the other hand, are definitely terms of derogation. Both are applicable to bombast and rhapsody at their worst, but *rant* stresses its extravagance or violence of expression or utterance, and *fustian* the banality of its quality or the preposterousness of its character. "Spend all the powers Of *rant* and *rhapsody* in virtue's praise; Be most sublimely good, verbosely grand, And with poetic trappings grace thy prose, Till it outmantle all the pride of verse" (*Cowper*). "He, whose *fustian's* so sublimely bad, It is not poetry but prose run mad" (*Pope*). "Romantic *fustian;* which may be defined as the enormous disproportion between emotion and the outer object or incident on which it expends itself. Victor Hugo abounds in *fustian* of this kind" (*Babbitt*). **Rodomontade** is applied especially to the rant of the braggart, of the demagogue, or of anyone given to bluster and magniloquence. "Until the general public can no longer be stampeded by *rodomontade* into actions

contrary to self-interest no less than to common humanity, all sane advances towards true democracy will be very difficult" (*Survey Graphic*).
Ana. Grandiloquence, magniloquence, rhetoric (see corresponding adjectives at RHETORICAL): inflatedness, turgidity, tumidity, flatulence (see corresponding adjectives at INFLATED).
Con. Temperateness *or* temperance, soberness *or* sobriety, unimpassionedness (see corresponding adjectives at SOBER): dispassionateness, justness (see corresponding adjectives at FAIR).

bombastic. Grandiloquent, magniloquent, *rhetorical, aureate, flowery, euphuistic.
Ana. *Inflated, turgid, tumid: verbose, diffuse, *wordy: eloquent, voluble, fluent, articulate, *vocal.
Con. Temperate, unimpassioned, *sober: *sincere: unaffected, *natural, simple, artless: dispassionate, just, impartial, *fair.

bona fide. *Authentic, genuine, veritable.
Ana. True, *real, actual: *reliable, dependable, trustworthy: pure, *absolute, simple, sheer.
Ant. Counterfeit, bogus. — *Con.* Simulated, feigned, pretended, affected, shammed, assumed (see ASSUME).

bond, *adj.* *Bound, indentured, articled.
Ant. Free. — *Con.* Emancipated, manumitted, liberated, freed (see FREE, *v.*): independent (see FREE, *adj.*).

bond, *n.* **1 Bond, band, tie** are here considered as comprehensive terms which denote something which serves to bind or bring two or more things firmly together, and which differ from each other not only in implications but in their specific applications. **Bond** still often carries its original implication of restraint upon the freedom of the individual. In early use it was applied to any restraining device, such as a rope, a chain, a fetter, or a manacle which prevented a prisoner from escaping; in figurative use, it is still applicable to anything that interferes with one's liberty and holds one down; as, it has been said that only the dying man is free, for death breaks every *bond*. But *bond* also was applied early in its history to something that connects or brings together two individuals (persons or things), or all the individuals comprising a group or mass, into a stable union. In this sense the term may and often does refer to a connection that is primarily spiritual; occasionally, especially when the plural is used, there is also a hint of restraint or constraint; as, the *bond* (or *bonds*) of marriage; the *bond* of faith; the *bond* of fellowship; the *bonds* of a common tradition. "The religion of the Greeks [was]...the *bond* of their political life" (*G. L. Dickinson*). But the term is also used in reference to a connection that is purely material, especially by bricklayers, slaters, and others. In each trade where the term is used, it means a way of arranging the individual bricks, slates, blocks, or the like, so that the vertical joinings do not follow a straight line and the points of strain are precisely distributed, thereby producing a compact, thoroughly integrated wall or structure; thus, in bricklaying, the term "English *bond*" designates a way of arranging bricks in alternate rows so that the face of the wall presents one row in which the bricks are laid lengthwise, and a second row in which they are laid endwise, and so on. **Band** also in its history has carried some of these senses of *bond*, for in Middle English *bond* was a variant form of *band* when used in reference to something that restrains or something that unites. These uses of *band* are now largely archaic; as, to unite in the *bands* of marriage. On the other hand, *band*, which has a very complicated etymology, its meanings being derived not from one but from several sources, acquired the meaning of a strip of material (for its synonyms in this sense see STRIP). Therefore, when *band* now retains its earliest implications of a restraint, a fastening, a connection, it usually also implies something material in the form of a flat and narrow piece of material, sometimes one that is perfectly straight but often one that is rounded and forms a hoop, ring, or the like; thus, a *band* around the hair is worn to confine the hair and may be a ribbon with ends tied together, a metallic hoop or half-hoop, or the like; an endless strip of rubber or elastic material is called a rubber *band;* a hooplike piece which holds together two parts of a structure, such as the barrel and stock of a gun, two sections of a pillar, or the like, is called a *band;* also, a straight member of a wall, such as a continuous molding, a frieze, a strip of brickwork in a different pattern, often serves not only as an ornament but also as a union or connection between two sections of the wall or structure, and is therefore called in architecture a *band.* **Tie** was originally applied to a bond or band (for fastening or restraining) which was of a flexible substance, such as a rope, cord, or string, and could be secured by knotting the loose ends together or one end to the thing fastened and the other to its support. Consequently, in its extended and figurative use, *tie* tends to suggest a less integral union and often more flexibility in the connection than *bond*, which it otherwise closely resembles; thus, one breaks the *bond* of friendship but one severs the *tie* of friendship; the *ties* of blood suggest the pull exerted by blood relationship, but the *bond* of blood suggests an obligation or a duty. *Tie*, as applied to specific fastenings or connections, is used chiefly when the object of the connection is not, as in *bond*, to form into an integral unit or, as in *band*, to keep closely united or together, but to bring together two things that are affected by common forces so that when they are subjected to strain or tension they will not spread, pull apart, or the like; thus, the transverse bars on which rails rest and which serve to keep the rails equidistant from each other are in the United States called *ties* (in Great Britain *sleepers*); a beam, a post, a rod, or any piece which connects two parts or sides of a structure, such as the ribs of a vessel, the two sides of a pointed arch, and serves to brace and stay the whole, is called a *tie*. "The *tie* between the Dagonets, the du Lacs of Maryland, and their aristocratic Cornish kinsfolk, the Trevennas, had always remained close and cordial" (*E. Wharton*).
2 Surety, security, bail, *guarantee, guaranty.

bondage. *Servitude, slavery.
Ana. Serfdom, thralldom, peonage, helotry (see primitive nouns at SERF).

bondman, bondsman. Slave, bondslave, thrall, *serf, Helot, peon, villein, vassal.

bondslave. Slave, *serf, thrall, bondsman, bondman, peon, Helot, villein, vassal.

boner. Blunder, mistake, *error, howler, bull, bloomer, slip, lapse, faux pas, floater.

bonny. Comely, pretty, good-looking, fair, lovely, *beautiful, handsome, beauteous, pulchritudinous.
Ana. Pleasing, agreeable, *pleasant: attractive, taking, charming, captivating (see under ATTRACT).
Ant. Homely.

bonus. Bounty, *premium, reward, guerdon, award, prize, meed.

bon vivant. Gastronome, gastronomer, gourmet, gourmand, *epicure, glutton.
Ant. Ascetic.

bon voyage. *Good-by, farewell, Godspeed, adieu, au revoir, auf Wiedersehen, adios.

bookish. Academic, scholastic, *pedantic.

bookkeeper. **Bookkeeper, accountant, auditor.** A **bookkeeper** keeps a regular, concise, and accurate record of business transactions by making the proper entries in the various books of account for that purpose. An **accountant** is a person skilled in the art of bookkeeping and may be employed either to organize and set up a system of records suitable to the needs of a particular organization or to investigate and report upon the financial condition of an organization by a study and analysis of its books of record. An **auditor** is an examiner who checks and verifies the financial records of an organization to see that these records correctly represent its condition.

boon. Favor, *gift, present, gratuity, largess, fairing.
Ana. Benefaction, *donation, contribution: *blessing, benediction.
Ant. Calamity. — *Con.* *Misfortune, mischance: *trial, cross, tribulation, affliction.

boor. **Boor, churl, lout, clown, clodhopper, bumpkin** come into comparison as meaning an uncouth, ungainly fellow. Most of these words were applied originally to one of the lowest class of rustics or countrymen, but in present usage they imply reference to breeding, manners, and appearance oftener than to social status. The same distinctions in connotations and implications are apparent in the adjectives derived from the first four of these nouns, **boorish, churlish, loutish, clownish. Boor,** literally a peasant, implies an opposition to *gentleman;* originally, the contrast implied was in reference to social status; in current usage, the contrast is between characteristics, *boor* suggesting qualities that are the reverse of the good breeding and fineness of feeling now commonly implied by the term *gentleman.* As a rule, *boor* and **boorish** imply variously rudeness of manner, insensitiveness, lack of ceremony, or unwillingness to be agreeable in the presence of others. "Love makes gentlemen even of *boors,* whether noble or villain, is the constant moral of mediaeval story" (*H. Adams*). "Comparing...a polished rascal with a *boorish* good man" (*H. B. Stowe*). **Churl** which originally meant *man* in the sense of *husband,* and somewhat later simply a free man without rank and therefore not of gentle, noble, or royal birth, has retained in modern usage this suggestion of low birth and, often, of independence of spirit, especially in one's attitude to social superiors. This latter implication is far more common in the adjective **churlish,** which characteristically implies surliness, irresponsiveness, or ungraciousness. "[He] warns all whom it concerns, from King to *churl*" (*J. Morley*). "By what magic was it that this divine sweet creature could be allied with that old *churl!*" (*Meredith*). "Who are the present tenants? I hear that they object to the dairymaids and men crossing the elm vista.... It seems *churlish,* Lydia" (*Shaw*). "When she rebelled he disclosed the merest hint of his sullen-*churlish* side, and she at once yielded" (*Bennett*). **Lout** and **loutish** apply especially to hulky youths or men and usually suggest stupidity, clumsiness, and sometimes, abjectness of bearing or demeanor. Both words are terms of contempt frequently applied to idlers or loafers of particularly unprepossessing appearance. "It was inevitable that the older boys should become mischievous *louts;* they bullied and tormented and corrupted the younger boys because there was nothing else to do" (*H. G. Wells*). **Clown,** as here compared (see also FOOL, 2), and **clownish** applied originally, like *boor* and *boorish,* to a countryman, especially to one who works the soil, but their connotations are closer to those of *lout* and *loutish.* Instead of stupidity, however, the terms often connote ignorance or simplicity and instead of hulkiness they suggest the ungainliness of a person whose body and movements reveal hard plodding labor. "The *clown,* the child of nature, without guile" (*Cowper*). When used in reference to those who are not countrymen, the terms still imply general uncouthness and awkwardness, and often, by association with the other sense of *clown,* a propensity for absurd antics. "He was the sort of boy that becomes a *clown* and a *lout* as soon as he is not understood, or feels himself held cheap" (*D. H. Lawrence*). **Clodhopper** distinctively suggests the frame and the heavy movements generally associated with plowmen, but is not restricted in application to rustics; **bumpkin** implies a loutishness suggestive of unfamiliarity with city ways and manners; as, she indignantly referred to her partner in the dance as a *clodhopper;* "bashful country *bumpkins*" (*Irving*).
Ant. Gentleman.

boorish. Churlish, loutish, clownish. See under BOOR.
Ana. *Awkward, clumsy, maladroit, inept: *rude, discourteous, ungracious, uncivil, impolite, ill-mannered.
Ant. Gentlemanly. — *Con.* *Gentle, genteel: *suave, urbane, smooth: courteous, courtly, gallant, polite, *civil.

boost, *v.* *Lift, raise, elevate, hoist, rear, heave.
Ana. *Exalt, aggrandize: heighten, enhance (see INTENSIFY): mount, soar, levitate, surge, ascend, *rise.

boot, *v.* *Benefit, profit, avail, bestead.

bootless. Fruitless, *futile, vain, abortive.
Ana. Idle, empty, hollow, nugatory, *vain, otiose.
Con. *Beneficial, advantageous, profitable.

bootlicker, bootlick. Sycophant, toady, lickspit, hanger-on, *parasite, favorite, leech, sponge.

booty. *Spoil, loot, plunder, pillage, prize, swag.

border, *n.* **1 Border, margin, verge, edge, rim, brim, brink** agree in meaning the line or relatively narrow space which marks a (or the) limit or outermost bound of something. A **border** (see also BOUNDARY) is that part of a surface which is just within its boundary line; it is sometimes the boundary line itself; as, the *border* of a rug, of a flower bed; "I had at last reached the *border* of the forest" (*Hudson*). **Margin** denotes a border of definite width, or distinguished in some way from the remaining surface; it also applies to the space immediately contiguous to a body of water; as, the *margin* of a page; the *margin* of a lake or river. "They wandered onward till they reached the nether *margin* of the heath, where it became marshy, and merged in moorland" (*Hardy*). **Verge** applies chiefly in literal use to the line (sometimes to a very narrow space within that line) which sharply marks the limit or termination of a thing, such as a surface or an expanse; as, "The sky was clear from *verge* to *verge*" (*Hardy*); "the child...was balanced on the very *verge* [of the roof]" (*Jefferies*). *Verge* in figurative use is frequently applied to the extreme limit of something. "It is not enough that a statute goes to the *verge* of constitutional power. We must be able to see clearly that it goes beyond that power" (*Justice Holmes*). Sometimes, however, it refers to what is on the far (rather than the near) side of that line; as, he is on the *verge* of ruin or of suicide. An **edge** is a sharply defined terminating line made by the converging of two surfaces, as of a blade, a dish, a plank, a box, or the like. In strict use, *edge* often implies sharpness (as opposed to bluntness) and therefore power to cut; as, "A tool with a fine *edge* may do mischief" (*Godwin*); put an *edge* on this knife. It is this implication that comes out strongest in figurative use, where it often suggests asperity, trenchancy, keenness, and the like; as, there was an *edge* in his tone; "the *edge* had gone from his spirit, and he shrank from the long, toilsome road in front of him" (*Buchan*). **Rim** usually applies to the verge or edge of something circular or curving; as, the *rim* of the moon; the *rim* of a bucket, the *rim* of a wheel. **Brim** applies to the inner side of the rim of a hollow vessel (as, fill the pot to the *brim*) or to the topmost line of the basin of a river, lake, or other body of water (as, the river has risen to the *brim*). **Brink** denotes the edge of something steep; as, the *brink* of a precipice; on the *brink* of the grave; the river's *brink* (which differs from the river's *brim* in stressing the abruptness of the bank or shore rather than the close approach of the water to the basin's rim).

Ana. *Limit, bound, confine, end.

Con. Inside, interior (see corresponding adjectives at INNER).

2 *Boundary, march, frontier.

bore, *v.* *Perforate, drill, puncture, punch, prick.

Ana. Penetrate, pierce, *enter.

boredom. *Tedium, ennui, doldrums.

Ant. Amusement. — *Con.* Diversion, entertainment, recreation (see under AMUSE).

bother, *v.* Vex, *annoy, irk.

Ana. *Worry, harass, harry, pester, tease, tantalize: interfere, *meddle, tamper: *puzzle, perplex, distract: molest, trouble, *inconvenience, incommode, discommode.

Ant. Comfort. — *Con.* Solace, console (see COMFORT): appease, placate, *pacify, mollify, propitiate.

bough. Branch, limb, *shoot.

boulevard. Avenue, street, *road, roadway, highway, highroad, parkway, drive, terrace, thoroughfare.

bounce, *v.* *Dismiss, sack, fire, discharge, cashier, drop.

bound, *n.* *Limit, confine, end, term, bourn.

Ana. *Boundary, border, frontier, march: *border, verge, edge.

bound, *v.* *Skip, ricochet, hop, curvet, lope, lollop.

Ana. Dart, skim, scud (see FLY): *rebound, recoil, resile.

bound, *adj.* **Bound, bond, indentured, articled** are synonyms when they mean obliged to serve a master or in a clearly defined capacity for a certain number of years by the terms of a contract or mutual agreement. **Bound** not only stresses the obligation, but it also often connotes a condition of or approaching servitude. It frequently implies the status of an apprentice, that is, one obliged to serve a master for an agreed term in return for being taught a trade, a craft, an art, or a profession. It may, however, imply the status of an unskilled laborer, such as a domestic servant, who agrees to serve, as in a distant colony, in return for transportation, keep, and, in some instances, a wage; as, he emigrated from England to the American colonies as a *bound* servant. When the condition of servitude is emphasized, and service without a wage is implied, **bond** (placed before the noun) is often used in place of *bound;* as, *bond* servants; *bond*slaves. **Indentured** implies apprenticeship and emphasizes the fact that the agreement is in writing, has been executed in duplicate, and has legal validity. Usually it carries the implication of fairness and equity to both parties to the agreement; as, a tailor's *indentured* employees; a solicitor's *indentured* clerk. Sometimes, especially in reference to an apprentice in a law office, **articled** is preferred to *indentured,* though there seems to be no clear distinction between the two; as, he started out as an *articled* clerk in an attorney's office.

boundary. Boundary, border, march, frontier come into comparison when they mean a territorial dividing line, especially one between two states or countries. **Boundary** implies a fixed geographical limit so clearly ascertained and charted, and so definitely indicated by a line on maps, that its exact location is known and observed by parties on either side; as, he stood at the *boundary,* one foot in Massachusetts and the other in Connecticut; the president of the United States and the governor-general of Canada met at the *boundary* between the two countries; the *boundary* between France and Germany has shifted several times in the course of 150 years; so, in figurative use, "the arts have each their *boundaries*" (*Binyon*). **Border** (see also BORDER) is often used in place of *boundary,* but historically it is an older term, and seldom carries the connotations of exactness of location or of clear definition so strong in the latter term. Because of the use of *border* in reference to the entire district on both sides of the boundary between England and Scotland (called, especially by the Scots, *The Border*), the scene of many conflicts between the two peoples, the term now suggests the territory adjoining a boundary on both sides; as, *border* raids; fighting along the Mexican *border;* a strongly fortified *border.* **March,** which is now a historical or archaic term, is even less explicit in its connotations of exact location than *border.* It is never interchangeable with *boundary* because it does not suggest a clear dividing line, but rather a district in which lie the more or less debatable limits of each country's territory. Historically, it has been used chiefly by the English in reference to the borders between England and Wales, and England and Scotland. "He craved a fair permission to depart, And there defend his *marches*" (*Tennyson*). **Frontier,** etymologically the part of one country that fronts an adjoining country, is correctly applicable in this sense only to one side of a boundary or of a border; thus, one does not in very precise use say the *frontier* between France and Italy, but France's Italian *frontier* or Italy's French *frontier. Frontier,* in the United States, came to be associated with the imaginary or theoretical line marking the outmost bound of settled territory, a line that was constantly being advanced as the population increased and territory, especially to the west and south, became colonized. Consequently, in American use, a *frontier* is thought of as a shifting line, capable of being advanced or pushed forward by those willing to pioneer in unsettled territory or to venture beyond the lands already explored; as, in 1860 the American *frontier* was a line approximately corresponding to the present western boundaries of Minnesota and Iowa, and one drawn southward through the center of Kansas down through the middle of Texas; in 1940, the American *frontier* has practically disappeared. *Frontier,* in this sense, is now common in figurative use in reference to the advance of knowledge. "The *frontiers* of knowledge [are] being pushed farther into the unknown in the fields of the infinitely great (astronomy) and of the infinitely small (microscopy)" (*A. C. Morrison*).

Ana. *Limit, bound, confine, end, bourn: *border, verge, edge.

boundless. *Infinite, uncircumscribed, illimitable, eternal, sempiternal.

Ana. Vast, immense, *enormous: *monstrous, prodigious, tremendous, stupendous.

Con. Circumscribed, limited, confined, restricted (see LIMIT, *v.*).

bountiful. Generous, munificent, *liberal, handsome.

Ana. *Charitable, philanthropic, benevolent: prodigal, lavish (see PROFUSE).

Ant. Niggardly. — *Con.* *Stingy, parsimonious, penurious, close, miserly: avaricious, *covetous, greedy, grasping: frugal, *sparing, economical.

bounty. Award, reward, meed, guerdon, prize, *premium, bonus.

Ana. Gratuity, largess, *gift, boon: grant, subvention, subsidy (see APPROPRIATION).

bouquet. Scent, perfume, *fragrance, redolence, incense.
Ana. Odor, aroma, *smell, scent.

bourn *or* **bourne.** Bound, confine, end, term, *limit.
Ana. Verge, edge, *border, rim, brim: aim, end, goal, objective (see INTENTION).

bow, *v.* Defer, *yield, submit, capitulate, succumb, relent, cave in.

bow, *n.* Arc, arch, *curve.

bowels. Compassion, commiseration, *pity, ruth, condolence, sympathy, empathy.

box, *v.* Smite, cuff, swat, clout, punch, *strike, hit, slug, slap.

boyish. *Youthful, juvenile, puerile, maiden, virgin, virginal.

brace, *n.* *Couple, pair, yoke.

brag, *v.* *Boast, vaunt, crow, gasconade.
Ana. Plume, pique, *pride, preen: flaunt, parade (see SHOW).
Ant. Apologize (*for a shortcoming, defect, etc.*). — *Con.* Extenuate, *palliate, whitewash, gloze, gloss.

braid, *v.* Plait, *weave, knit, crochet, tat.

brain, brains. *Mind, intellect, intelligence, wit, wits, psyche, soul.

branch, *n.* Limb, bough, *shoot.

brand, *n.* *Stigma, blot, stain.
Ana. Sear, burn, scorch (see corresponding verbs at BURN): tainting *or* taint, defilement (see corresponding verbs at CONTAMINATE): *blemish, defect, flaw.

brandish. Flourish, *swing, wave, thrash.
Ana. Wield, swing, *handle, manipulate, ply: flaunt, parade, display, exhibit, *show.

brash, *adj.* Brazen, barefaced, impudent, *shameless.
Ana. Bold, audacious (see BRAVE): temerarious, rash, reckless (see ADVENTUROUS): impetuous, headlong, abrupt, *precipitate: intrusive, officious, *impertinent.
Ant. Wary. — *Con.* *Cautious, chary, circumspect: *timid, timorous: reserved (see SILENT): discreet (see under PRUDENCE).

bravado. *Bravery, bravura.
Ana. Pompousness, pretentiousness, ostentatiousness *or* ostentation (see corresponding adjectives at SHOWY): *display, parade, pomp: vainglory, vanity, *pride: gasconading, vaunting, bragging, boasting (see BOAST): strutting, swaggering (see STRUT).
Ant. Diffidence, modesty.

brave, *adj.* **1 Brave, courageous, bold, audacious, dauntless, undaunted, intrepid, valiant, valorous, doughty** come into comparison in the sense of having or showing fearlessness in meeting that which is dangerous, difficult, or unknown. **Brave** usually implies resolution and self-control in meeting, without flinching, a situation that inspires fear, rather than a temperamental liking for danger. "The *brave* man is not he who feels no fear ... But he, whose noble soul its fear subdues, And *bravely* dares the danger nature shrinks from" (*J. Baillie*). **Courageous** stresses stoutheartedness and firmness of temper: it therefore implies either a temperamental readiness to encounter dangers or difficulties that test one's spirit or resolution, or an ability in the face of actual danger or difficulty to do what is required of one; as, few were *courageous* enough to answer the call for volunteer rescuers; *courageous* in telling the truth. "A man is *courageous* when he does things which others might fail to do owing to fear" (*B. Russell*). "His mother was so strong, so *courageous*, the only strong and *courageous* influence he [Mark Twain] knew" (*Van W. Brooks*). **Bold** implies either a temperamental liking for danger or a willingness to court danger or to dare the unknown, especially when something important is at stake. There is nearly always in *bold* a connotation of pushing forward without hesitation, sometimes courageously, always daringly, sometimes presumptuously, and sometimes defiantly; as, only a *bold* man would beard the lion in his den; "What makes robbers *bold* but too much lenity?" (*Shak.*); "penalties...not immediate enough nor real enough to deter a *bold* child" (*Shaw*). **Audacious,** in contrast with *bold*, gives greater emphasis to the idea of recklessness or imprudence in daring, and when it implies presumptuousness, usually adds a suggestion of effrontery. "This seems a fairly obvious notion, as I write it down in the spring of 1936; but in the spring of 1926 it was *audacious*" (*Karl K. Darrow*). "The compound insolence of this amused the Strong Man, and...he listened to the proposals of the *audacious* Tarrion" (*Kipling*). **Dauntless** and **undaunted** imply such boldness and fearlessness that, in the case of the first, one cannot be intimidated, cowed, discouraged, or subdued, or, in the case of the second, one has either come out uncowed, undefeated, or unsubdued from a violent struggle or great dangers or hardships, or has shown no fear in the anticipation of such struggle, dangers, or hardships; as, "Helen Keller...the product of a miracle of human love and *dauntless* patience" (*Times Lit. Sup.*); "To war they follow their *undaunted* King" (*Dryden*). **Intrepid** etymologically implies complete absence of fear: it is often so used, especially in its derivative noun *intrepidity;* the adjective, however, commonly stresses dauntlessness and the capacity for meeting courageously and enduring with fortitude whatever happens; as, an *intrepid* explorer or pioneer; the *intrepid* prosecutor of graft. **Valiant** originally implied conspicuous physical strength or the might of a hero: it now stresses heroic courage and fortitude, not only in meeting danger but sometimes in achieving one's ends; as, "the *valiant* champions of new ideals" (*S. Alexander*); "Against all these...forces the critic and historian must make a *valiant* struggle" (*L. P. Smith*). "Cowards die many times before their deaths; The *valiant* never taste of death but once" (*Shak.*). **Valorous** differs from *valiant* chiefly in its weaker implication of fortitude and in its stronger suggestion of illustriousness. Though not limited in their applications, *valorous* more often qualifies accomplishments, and *valiant* qualifies persons or their exertions; as, "*valorous* feats of arms" (*Caxton*); the *valorous* deeds of the *valiant* defenders of Troy; "The whole universe will acknowledge those *valorous* efforts" (*Wellington*); "I, therefore, made him of our Table Round ... One of our noblest, our most *valorous*" (*Tennyson*). **Doughty** adds to *valiant* the implication of formidableness: it is now seldom used except when an archaic flavor or a burlesque effect is desired; as, the *doughty* deeds of *doughty* knights of old; a *doughty* critic. "Its heroes [those of the heroic age] were *doughty* men to whom diabolic visitors were no more unusual than angelic ones" (*J. W. Krutch*).
Ana. Daring, venturous, venturesome, daredevil, *adventurous: heroic, gallant (see corresponding nouns at HEROISM): plucky, gritty (see corresponding nouns at FORTITUDE).
Ant. Craven. — *Con.* *Cowardly, pusillanimous, poltroon, recreant: *timid, timorous: shrinking, flinching, blenching (see RECOIL, *v.*).
2 *Stylish, braw, smart, fashionable, modish, dapper, dashing, spruce, natty, chic, nifty, nobby, posh, toffish.

bravery. Bravery, bravado, bravura are here compared only as meaning a dashing or showy style or manner. All three words in this sense bear little relation to the adjective *brave* in its sense of courageous (see BRAVE), but come closer to the implications of its secondary sense: marked by fine show or display. In such use, **bravery** refers chiefly to dress, trappings, furnishings, or the like, and implies splendor or gorgeousness, or a showy, dandyish appearance. "The Queen's three thousand robes were rivaled in their *bravery* by the slashed velvets, the ruffs, the jeweled purpoints of the courtiers around her" (*J. R. Green*). "In the *bravery* of light gloves, buff waistcoats, feathers, and frocks" (*Galsworthy*). **Bravado** has reference to the manner and spirit of a person rather than to his appearance; it implies swaggering, defiance, daring, and usually, an affected display of outward signs of power and wealth or of courage. "In those days she was completely reckless; did the most idiotic things out of *bravado*" (*V. Woolf*). "When he spent money furiously, he did it with *bravado*, too conscious of grandeur and too conscious of the difficulties of acquiring that which he threw away" (*Bennett*) **Bravura** has reference chiefly to style of singing, playing, painting, and the like; it connotes spirit, brilliancy, or dash of execution, but often carries a suggestion of pretentiousness rather than power. In music, the term is often applied to a type of composition intended for bravura performance. "Listening to a lady amateur skylark it up and down through the finest *bravura* of Rossini or Mozart" (*Irving*). The word is, however, used of other arts than those of music or painting. "Occasionally he writes in simplicity as well as sincerity, without labored linguistic *bravuras*" (*The Nation*).

Ana. Stylishness *or* style, fashionableness *or* fashion, smartness, dashingness *or* dash, modishness (see corresponding adjectives at STYLISH): ostentatiousness *or* ostentation, showiness *or* show (see corresponding adjectives at SHOWY): parade, array, pomp, *display.

bravo. *Assassin, cutthroat, gunman, trigger man, finger man.

Ana. *Ruffian, thug, Mohock, desperado, gangster, apache.

bravura. *Bravery, bravado.

braw. Brave, *stylish, dashing, dapper, fashionable, modish, smart, chic, spruce, natty, nifty, nobby, posh, toffish.

brawl, *n.* **Brawl, broil, fracas, melee, row, rumpus, scrap** are here compared as meaning a noisy fight or quarrel. **Brawl** implies angry contentions, blows, and a noisy racket; it usually suggests participation by several persons; as, a family *brawl* that kept the neighbors awake; a drunken *brawl;* street *brawls.* **Broil** stresses disorder, confusion, and turmoil among the combatants more than the disturbance they cause others. The term may be used contemptuously in place of *war, conflict,* or *controversy* (as, "plunging us in all the *broils* of the European nations"—*Jefferson*), but it is more often used of a violent fight or quarrel where the issues are not clear or significant or where the opposing parties are not clearly distinguished, "O, how this discord doth afflict my soul!.... Who should study to prefer a peace, If holy churchmen take delight in *broils?*" (*Shak.*). "But village mirth breeds contests, *broils,* and blows" (*Shelley*). **Fracas** is applicable to any noisy quarrel, especially to one that leads to blows; the term does not suggest as much vulgarity or as many participants as *brawl,* but it may imply as much noise and excitement. "There was suddenly a *fracas,* and one of them clenched his fists and hit another full in the face" (*Lucas*). **Melee** is still, as originally, applied chiefly to a more or less disorganized hand-to-hand conflict, especially between soldiers, or to a dispute which resembles such a combat in disorderliness or in violation of parliamentary rules. "Lacey's pistol was in his hand, David's sword was gripped tight as they rushed upon the *mêlée.* Lacey's pistol snapped, and an Arab fell" (*G. Parker*). However, in current use, the emphasis is increasingly on confusion and mix-up, and often the implication of combat or contention is weakened or lost. "The calmness of the platform was transformed into a *mêlée.* Little Constance found herself left on the fringe of a physically agitated crowd which was apparently trying to scale a precipice surmounted by windows and doors" (*Bennett*). **Row** is a colloquial term applicable to any fight, whether a quarrel, a squabble, or a dispute, that is so public or so noisy as to attract attention; as, the school bully kicks up a *row* every time he forces himself into a game; there is no sense in making a *row* when you are not properly served, for it ends only in making all the waiters hate you. **Rumpus,** also a colloquial term, suggests even greater agitation and disturbance than *row,* for it usually connotes an uproar. "You incur my serious displeasure if you move one inch in this contemptible *rumpus*" (*Scott*). **Scrap** is a slang term; originally, it seems, a boxer's term, applicable to any fight or fracas. It usually suggests a physical tussle but often, in ordinary use, it implies little more than a noisy, sharp quarrel; as, the boys are good friends but they have many a *scrap.*

Ana. Conflict, fight, fray, affray (see CONTEST): contention, dissension, strife, *discord: wrangle, altercation, *quarrel, squabble: uproar, racket, *din, hubbub.

brawny. *Muscular, burly, husky, sinewy, athletic.

Ana. Stalwart, *strong, sturdy, stout, tough: *fleshy.

Ant. Scrawny. — ***Con.*** Lanky, lank, gaunt, rawboned, *lean, spare, skinny: *thin, slender, slight, slim.

brazen. *Shameless, brash, impudent.

Ana. Callous, *hardened, indurated: insolent, arrogant (see PROUD): temerarious, rash, reckless (see ADVENTUROUS): bold, audacious (see BRAVE).

Ant. Bashful. — ***Con.*** *Shy, diffident, modest, coy: *timid, timorous: stealthy, surreptitious, underhand, *secret.

breach, *n.* **Breach, infraction, violation, transgression, trespass, infringement, contravention** are here compared as denoting the act or the offense of one who fails to keep the law or to do what the law, one's duty, or an obligation requires. **Breach** (etymologically, a break) occurs rarely by itself, except in phrases such as "a law more honored in the *breach* than in the observance." The word is usually followed by *of* and a noun or pronoun which indicates the thing which is broken or not kept; as, a *breach* of discipline; his action constitutes a *breach* of faith; he was found guilty of a *breach* of the peace (i.e., of noisy, disorderly, or annoying conduct); to be sued for *breach* of promise or *breach* of contract. **Infraction** is now more often used than *breach* (except in certain time-honored idioms) for any breaking of a law or obligation; as, an *infraction* of the school rules; an *infraction* of a treaty; an *infraction* of canon law. "We have scrutinized the case, but cannot say that it shows an *infraction* of rights under the Constitution of the United States" (*Justice Holmes*). **Violation** adds to *breach* and *infraction* the implication of flagrant disregard of the law or of the rights of others and often suggests the exercise of force or violence; thus, the *violation* of a treaty suggests positive, often aggressive and injurious, action rather than a mere failure to keep one's engagements; so, a *violation* of military discipline; the police interference was a *violation* of the right to free assembly. "When more of the people's sustenance is exacted through the form of taxation than is necessary to meet the just obligations of Government ...such exaction becomes ruthless extortion and a *violation* of the fundamental principles of a free Government" (*G. Cleveland*). **Transgression** (etymologically, a stepping across) is applied to any act that goes beyond the limits prescribed by a law, rule, order, or the like; often the term is used specifically of an infraction of the moral law or of one of the commandments; as, "for sin is the *transgression* of the law" (*1 John* iii. 4); " 'I was forgetting,' she said. 'I am forbidden tea.'...She looked at the cup, tremendously tempted.... An occasional *transgression* could not harm her" (*Bennett*). **Trespass** also implies, etymologically, an overstepping of prescribed bounds, but it carries in addition a strong implication of encroachment upon the rights, the comfort, or the property of others. In Scriptural and religious use, a *trespass* is particularly an offense against God or one's neighbor; as, "If ye forgive not men their *trespasses*, neither will your Father forgive your *trespasses*" (*Matthew* vi. 15). In law, a *trespass* is an unlawful act, involving force or violence, committed against the person, the property, or the rights of another; thus, the passing through another's premises against his wish or without his invitation constitutes a *trespass;* a burglar who is frightened away before he actually enters a house is liable to arrest for *trespass*. **Infringement** is sometimes used as though it were identical in meaning with *infraction;* as, an *infringement* of the law; an *infringement* of a treaty. In current use, however, it implies trespass more often than violation, and therefore is the idiomatic term when trespass involving an encroachment upon a legally protected right or privilege is implied; thus, the unauthorized manufacture of something which has been patented constitutes an *infringement* of a patent; the unauthorized reproduction and sale of matter already copyrighted by a publisher or by an author, engraver, photographer, or the like constitutes an *infringement* of the copyright; so, an *infringement* upon the rights of property owners; an *infringement* on the liberty of the American people. **Contravention** applies specifically to a going contrary to the intent of the law or to an act in defiance of what is regarded as right, lawful, obligatory, or the like; as, "Warrants in *contravention* of the acts of Parliament" (*Macaulay*); "if there is in a work of art a *contravention* of nature" (*Lowes*).

Ant. Observance.

bread *or* **bread and butter.** Sustenance, *living, livelihood, subsistence, maintenance, support, keep.

break, *n.* Chance, *opportunity, occasion, time, tide, hint.

breakdown, *n.* Analysis, resolution, dissection, anatomy. See under ANALYZE.

break down. *Analyze, resolve, dissect, anatomize.

Con. Concatenate, articulate, *integrate.

breaker. Billow, *wave, roller, comber, beachcomber, undulation, ripple.

breastwork. *Bulwark, bastion, parapet, barbette, rampart.

breed, *v.* *Generate, engender, propagate, reproduce, procreate, beget, sire, get.

breeding. Cultivation, *culture, refinement.

Ana. *Tact, address, poise, savoir-faire: *courtesy, amenity, gallantry: grace, dignity, *elegance.

Ant. Vulgarity. — *Con.* Boorishness, churlishness (see primitive nouns at BOOR): grossness, coarseness (see corresponding adjectives at COARSE): rudeness, discourteousness *or* discourtesy, ungraciousness (see corresponding adjectives at RUDE).

breeze. *Wind, gust, flaw, zephyr, blast, gale, whirlwind, cyclone, typhoon, tornado, waterspout, twister.

bridle, *v.* **1** Check, curb, *restrain, snaffle, inhibit.

Ana. Repress, *suppress: *govern, rule: control, direct, manage (see CONDUCT).

Ant. Vent. — *Con.* *Express, utter, air, voice, ventilate.

2 Bristle, ruffle, *strut, swagger.

Ana. Posture, attitudinize, pose (see under POSTURE, *n.*): plume, preen, pique, *pride.

Con. Grovel, *wallow: cringe, cower (see FAWN): wince, flinch (see RECOIL).

brief, *adj.* **Brief, short** are the most comprehensive adjectives in English meaning not long. **Brief** refers primarily to duration; **short,** to either duration or linear extent; as, a *brief* interview, discourse; a *short* sermon, time, distance; *short* legs or grass. As applied to duration, *brief* and *short* are sometimes complete synonyms (as, a *brief*, or a *short*, battle). But *short* frequently (not always) suggests incompleteness, curtailment, or sudden stoppage; *brief* sometimes (but not always) implies condensation; as, he cut his speech *short;* he made his speech as *brief* as possible. As applied to linear extent, *brief* is chiefly humorous and means extremely short; as, a *brief* skirt.

Ana. *Transient, fleeting, passing, momentary, short-lived: *concise, terse, succinct, laconic, pithy: compacted *or* compact, concentrated (see corresponding verbs at COMPACT): shortened, abbreviated, abridged, curtailed (see SHORTEN).

Ant. Prolonged, protracted. — *Con.* Lengthened *or* lengthy, extended *or* extensive, elongated (see corresponding verbs at EXTEND).

brief, *n.* Abstract, epitome, *abridgment, synopsis, conspectus.

brigand, *n.* **Brigand, bandit, highwayman, footpad, marauder** come into comparison as more or less literary (sometimes journalistic) terms denoting a person who roves about in search of plunder. **Brigand** was originally applied to one of a class of lightly armed foot soldiers, many of whom exercised their wartime right of pillage and plundering in times of peace. Later, it was applied to any of the armed rovers who, working singly or in bands, infested lonely places, especially the mountainous districts of the Mediterranean countries, and robbed travelers or held them for ransom. In current extended use, it is applied to any armed robber who preys on travelers or defenseless persons, especially in unpopulated or sparsely populated sections of a country. "François, with his belt, sabre, and pistols, had much the aspect of a Greek *brigand*" (*B. Taylor*). In current newspaper use, *brigand* is often applied to any person who, in effect, preys upon the weak and defenseless, by unscrupulous use of wealth or power. Strictly, a **bandit** is an outlaw or proscribed person; in actual use, however, the word is applied to any of an organized band or gang of outlawed, lawless, or hunted men who infest certain districts, especially remote districts, indulging not only in terrorism and brigandage but also in other lawless acts and depredations. In current newspaper use, *bandit* is often employed as the equivalent of *gangster* (as, the bank was held up by armed *bandits*). *Brigand* and *bandit* overlap in implications, but they differ widely in their historical connotations. A **highwayman** is a robber who roves over a highway or post road waylaying carriages and stagecoaches and forcing their occupants to surrender their valuables. In strict use, a *highwayman* is commonly distinguished from a **footpad,** the former term being applied to a highway robber on horseback, the latter to a highway robber on foot. **Marauder** is usually applied to a plunderer or robber whose method is incursion or raid rather than waylaying or ambushing; it often connotes the lawless actions of vagabonds, nomads, undisciplined soldiers, or camp followers; as, the inhabitants of the Scottish Border in the late Middle Ages were at the mercy of English *marauders; marauders* descended on the caravan by night and carried away everything of value; the *marauder* who had visited the henhouse nightly turned out to be a fox.

Ana. Gangster, desperado, *ruffian.

bright, *adj.* **1 Bright, brilliant, radiant, luminous, lustrous, effulgent, refulgent, beaming, beamy, lambent, lucent** come into comparison when they mean actually or seemingly shining or glowing with light. **Bright** implies an opposition to *dim* or *dull;* it applies chiefly to things that vary in the degree in which they shed light or are pervaded by light, according to circumstances; thus, when used in reference to a fire, burning coals, or the like, it suggests a good draft and flames; when used in reference to a day, it implies lack of clouds, fog, smoke, or other obstacles to the passage of sunlight; so, a *bright* sky; a *bright* star; a *bright* sword; *bright* eyes; a *bright* color. **Brilliant** (see also INTELLIGENT) implies conspicuous or intense brightness; it also often connotes scintillating or flashing light; as, a well-cut diamond is the most *brilliant* of gems; the sun is too *brilliant* for the human eye; a *brilliant* smile; "Madame Olenska's face grew *brilliant* with pleasure" (*E. Wharton*). "What one saw when one looked about was that *brilliant* blue world of stinging air and moving cloud" (*Cather*). **Radiant,** in contrast with *bright* and *brilliant,* stresses the emission or seeming emission of rays of light; it suggests, therefore, a property or power possessed by a thing rather than a quality ascribed to it because of its effect on the vision; thus, a celestial body is properly described as *radiant* only when it emits rays of light; a planet, no matter how bright it appears to the eye, is preferably described as *bright* or *brilliant* because it shines by reflected light. "Virtue could see to do what Virtue would By her own *radiant* light, though sun and moon Were in the flat sea sunk" (*Milton*). The term, however, is used loosely, but still correctly, of anything that seems to give out light in the manner of the sun or a star. "In warlike armour drest, Golden, all *radiant!*" (*Shelley*). " 'Just bagged a splendid bird!' *radiant* Richard informed him" (*Meredith*). **Luminous,** like *radiant,* suggests emission of light, but unlike it, seldom implies the sending forth of rays; also, it is applicable to anything that shines by reflected light or that shines (brightly or dimly) in the dark because of some chemical, physiological, or other cause; as, all celestial bodies are *luminous,* but only self-*luminous* bodies (stars in the strict astronomical sense) are also *radiant;* phosphorus is a *luminous* substance. As applied to color or to colored things, the term implies more than *bright* for it usually suggests a jewel-like quality (as, the *luminous* green of the emerald) or iridescence. "The blue off Nantucket is not the miracle of *luminous,* translucent color off Sardinia" (*Lowes*). "He [Audubon] painted a tall sandhill crane...finding a posture that displayed the rich *luminous* gray feathers" (*C. Rourke*). As applied to ideas or their expression, the term implies crystallike clearness and the absence of all obscurity; as, a *luminous* treatment of a subject; "A *luminous* statement" (*Brougham*). **Lustrous** is applied only to an object (often an opaque object) whose surface reflects light; it therefore seldom implies pervading light, but rather a brilliant or iridescent sheen or gloss; as, the *lustrous* brass of a burnished lamp; the *lustrous* surface of an enameled vase; *lustrous* satin. **Effulgent** implies excessive radiance; it is often used as an intensive of *radiant,* especially in the looser senses of the latter term; as, an *effulgent* smile; her *effulgent* beauty. **Refulgent** etymologically suggests light cast back; the term, in very precise use, implies brilliant reflected light or a radiance emanating from something not seen; as, a *refulgent* crystal chandelier. "We gazed, in silence hushed, with eyes intent On the *refulgent* spectacle [of rays of light shooting up from the sunken sun]" (*Wordsworth*). **Beaming** and **beamy** (the rarer and poetical form) literally imply emission of a beam or beams (see *beam* under RAY). "The...rising moon, Fair *beaming,* and streaming Her silver light the boughs amang" (*Burns*); "*beamy* radiance" (*Wordsworth*). In commonest use, however, as applied to looks or expression, *beaming* suggests a display (often a naïve display) of happiness, satisfaction, or the like; as, the *beaming* eyes of children greeting Santa Claus; "broad *beaming* smile" (*G. Eliot*). **Lambent** is applied to a thing, such as a flame or a luminous body, which throws a play of light over an object or surface without rendering it brilliant or lustrous. "The *lambent* flame of genius....lights up the universe" (*Hazlitt*); "*lambent* lightning-fire" (*Shelley*). Often, *lambent* suggests the emission of soft gleams of light. "Kind, quiet, near-sighted eyes, which his round spectacles magnified into *lambent* moons" (*M. Deland*). **Lucent,** a highly poetical or literary adjective, approaches *luminous* or, less often, *lustrous,* in its meaning: it is usually applied to that which is transfigured by light from the sun, a fire, or the like; as, "the *lucent* fume of the city's smoke rising up [in the early morning sky]" (*C. Mackenzie*); "Till every particle glowed... And slowly seemed to turn To *lucent* amber" (*W. W. Gibson*).

Ana. Illuminated, illumined, lighted, lightened, enlightened (see ILLUMINATE): flashing, gleaming, glistening, sparkling (see FLASH, *v.*): glowing, flaming (see BLAZE, *v.*).

Ant. Dull: dim. — ***Con.*** Dusky, murky, gloomy, *dark, obscure, dusk, darkling, opaque: *colorless, uncolored: *pale, pallid, ashen, livid.

2 Smart, quick-witted, brilliant, clever, *intelligent, knowing, alert.

Ana. *Sharp, keen, acute: *quick, ready, prompt, apt: precocious, advanced (see PREMATURE).

Ant. Dense, dull (*mentally*). — ***Con.*** *Stupid, crass, dumb: *lethargic, sluggish: phlegmatic, stolid, *impassive.

brilliant. 1 Radiant, luminous, *bright, effulgent, lustrous, refulgent, beaming, beamy, lambent, lucent.

Ana. Flashing, scintillating, sparkling, gleaming, glittering, coruscating (see FLASH, *v.*): blazing, flaming, flaring, glowing (see BLAZE, *v.*).

Ant. Subdued (*of light, color, etc.*). — ***Con.*** Gloomy, murky, obscure, dim, dusky (see DARK).

2 *Intelligent, clever, bright, smart, alert, quick-witted, knowing.

Ana. Erudite, *learned, scholarly, polymathic: sage, sapient, *wise.

Ant. Crass. — ***Con.*** *Stupid, dull, dense, dumb.

brim. Rim, edge, brink, *border, verge, margin.

bring. Bring, take, fetch are not synonyms, but in the sense of to convey from one place to another they are often misused. **Bring** implies carrying, leading, or transporting from a distance to the point where the speaker or agent is or will be; **take** a carrying, leading, or conducting to a point away from the one where the speaker or agent is or will be; thus, a mother asks her boy setting out for school to *take* a note to the teacher and to *bring* home a reply; a farmer *takes* his cattle to the market and *brings* back a supply of sugar, flour, and fresh meat. **Fetch** implies going to a place where something is to be found, getting it, and bringing it back to the starting point; as, please *fetch* me a chair from the next room; I shall *fetch* whatever you need. "He called to her, and said, *Fetch* me, I pray thee, a little water in a vessel, that I may drink. And as she was going to *fetch* it, he called to her, and said, *Bring* me, I pray thee, a

morsel of bread in thine hand" (*1 Kings* xvii. 10, 11).
Ana. Bear, *carry, convey: obtain, procure, *get.
Ant. Withdraw, remove.

brink. Verge, edge, *border, rim, margin.
Ana. *Limit, bound, end, confine, bourn: *shore, strand, coast.

brisk. Nimble, *agile, spry.
Ana. *Fast, quick, rapid, fleet, swift, speedy: ready, prompt, *quick: dynamic, live, *active.
Ant. Sluggish. — *Con.* *Lethargic, torpid, comatose: *lazy, indolent, slothful, fainéant: *inactive, inert, idle.

bristle, *v.* Bridle, ruffle, *strut, swagger.
Ana. Preen, plume, *pride, pique: evince, manifest, *show, evidence: flaunt, parade, display, exhibit (see SHOW).
Con. Conceal, *hide, bury.

British. *English, Anglican, Anglo-Saxon.

brittle. Crisp, *fragile, frangible, short, friable.
Ana. *Hardened, indurated.
Ant. Supple. — *Con.* *Elastic, resilient, springy, flexible: tough, tenacious, *strong, stout.

broach, *v.* Voice, utter, *express, vent, air, ventilate.
Ana. *Reveal, disclose, divulge: *introduce, interject, interpose.

broad, *adj.* **Broad, wide, deep** come into comparison chiefly when they mean measuring so much (inches, feet, meters, etc.) horizontally. **Broad, wide,** and often, **deep** (see also DEEP) apply to surfaces or areas as measured from side to side. *Broad* and *wide,* however, suggest a measurement from one side to the other of a surface, when the length is the same as the height; as, a picture two feet *wide;* a screen five feet *broad. Broad* and *wide* always, and *deep* only in some instances, may be used of surfaces that spread away from one; thus, a river may be a half mile *wide* or *broad* (but not *deep,* which would here refer only to vertical distance) at a given point, but a flower border may be four feet *wide, broad,* or preferably, *deep.* When a plot of ground or similar area is measured, *broad* or, especially, *wide* is used of the distance from one side to the other and *deep* of that from front line to back line; as, the lot is 33 feet *wide* and 100 feet *deep. Broad* and *wide* are frequently interchangeable when used descriptively to mean having relatively great extent across or from side to side; as, a *broad* or *wide* street, ribbon, margin. But *broad* commonly applies only to surfaces or areas as such; as, a *broad* leaf, a *broad*-headed tack, *broad*-shouldered. *Wide* applies also to apertures, or to that which (literally or figuratively) opens or spreads. *Wide,* therefore, is the preferred term when the emphasis is upon the distance between limits rather than on the extent of the intervening surface; as, a *wide* wound; a *wide* opening; a *wide* view. *Deep,* in similar descriptive use, when it carries an implication only of horizontal extent, is applicable only to something that has great extent backward as from an opening or from the front; as, a *deep* forest; a *deep* cavern; a *deep* lot.
Ana. Extended *or* extensive (see EXTEND): *spacious, capacious, commodious, ample: vast, immense (see ENORMOUS): expanded, dilated (see EXPAND).
Ant. Narrow. — *Con.* Strait (see NARROW): confined, circumscribed, limited, restricted (see LIMIT, *v.*).

broadcast, *v.* Promulgate, publish, advertise, announce, *declare, proclaim.

broadcasting. Promulgation, publication, advertisement, announcement, declaration, proclamation. See under DECLARE.

Brobdingnag'an. *Enormous, immense, huge, vast, gigantic, giant, gigantean, colossal, mammoth, elephantine, titanic, herculean, Cyclopean, Antaean, Gargantuan.
Ant. Lilliputian.

broil, *v.* Grill, barbecue, *bake, roast.

broil, *n.* Fracas, melee, row, *brawl, rumpus, scrap.
Ana. Fray, affray, fight, conflict, combat, *contest: altercation, wrangle, *quarrel: *contention, strife, dissension, conflict (see DISCORD).

bromide. Cliché, platitude, truism, *commonplace.

brook, *v.* Stand, abide, *bear, tolerate, suffer, endure.

browbeat. Bulldoze, bully, *intimidate, cow.
Ana. Terrorize, terrify, *frighten, scare.
Con. *Coax, cajole, wheedle, blandish.

brownie *or* **browny.** Gnome, dwarf, puck, *fairy, faery, fay, elf, sprite, pixy, goblin, nix, shee, leprechaun, banshee.

brume. *Haze, mist, fog, smog.

brunt, *n.* *Impact, impingement, jar, jolt, collision, clash, shock, concussion, percussion.
Ana. Strain, *stress, pressure, tension: burden, *load.

brush, *n.* Skirmish, *encounter.
Ana. *Contest, conflict, combat, fight, fray: engagement, action, *battle, push: *attack, assault, onset, onslaught.

brusque. Curt, blunt, gruff, *bluff, crusty.
Ana. Ungracious, *rude, impolite, uncivil, discourteous: *rough, harsh.
Ant. Unctuous: bland. — *Con.* *Suave, urbane, smooth: *gracious, cordial, affable, genial: courteous, gallant, polite, *civil.

brute, *n.* Beast, *animal.

buck, *n.* Dude, swell, macaroni, spark, *fop, dandy, beau, nob, toff, exquisite, élégant.

bucolic. Georgic, pastoral, *rural, rustic, Arcadian, agrestic, geoponic.
Ana. Boorish, loutish, clownish, churlish (see under BOOR): *natural, simple, naïve, ingenuous.
Ant. Urbane.

buddy. Chum, pal, comrade, crony, companion, *associate.

buff, *v.* *Polish, shine, burnish, furbish.

buffet, *v.* Baste, pummel, *beat, pound, belabor, thrash, thresh.
Ana. *Strike, smite, hit, slap, slug: batter (see MAIM).

buffoon. Clown, antic, zany, *fool, jester, merry-andrew, pantaloon, harlequin, comedian, comic, stooge.

bugbear. Bête noire, *abomination, anathema.

building, *n.* **Building, edifice, structure, fabric, pile** come into comparison when they mean a construction of wood, brick, stone, or the like, intended to house a family, a business, an institution, or the like. **Building** is the common, and in most cases the adequate, term; as, "the *buildings* of the temple" (*Matthew* xxiv. 1). **Edifice** usually applies to large and elegant buildings only; as, "Should I go to church And see the holy *edifice* of stone. . . ?" (*Shak.*). **Structure** retains more frequently than the others the sense of something constructed, often in a particular way; as, a tumble-down *structure;* a modern steel *structure.* Like *edifice, structure* is often used of buildings of some size or magnificence; as, "many a towered *structure* high" (*Milton*). **Fabric,** which is now archaic in this sense, implies architectural design. Consequently, the term is applied chiefly to great edifices, especially to Norman and Gothic cathedrals or other buildings of similar construction; as, "The august *fabriq* of Christ Church" (*Evelyn*); "The ruinous *fabric* was very rich in the interior" (*Dickens*). In current use, especially in Great Britain, *fabric* denotes the construction and maintenance of the church building; as, contributions for the *fabric*. **Pile** is usually a literary, but sometimes a humorous, term for a very large building (or, sometimes, a mass of buildings), especially one of stone: it usually suggests a palace, a cathedral, a government building, or the like; as, "Philip testified his joy ...by raising the magnificent *pile* of the Escorial" (*Prescott*).

bulge, *n.* Protuberance, *projection, protrusion.
Con. Cavity, hollow, *hole, pocket.

bulk, *n.* **Bulk, mass, volume** come into comparison when they mean an aggregate, accumulation, assemblage, or the like, that forms a body or unit. **Bulk** is applied mainly to an object that is inordinately large or heavy (as, "the *bulk* Of ancient minster"—*Wordsworth*) and, often, more or less shapeless or unshapely. "On the living sea rolls an inanimate *bulk*" (*Shelley*). "A blue night set with stars, the *bulk* of the solitary mesas cutting into the firmament" (*Cather*). "Dr. Lanskell sank his gouty *bulk* into the armchair behind his desk" (*E. Wharton*). **Mass** is applied mainly to something (not necessarily a concrete object) built up by the piling or gathering together of things of the same kind, so that they cohere and have a real or apparent unity; as, the towering *mass* of the Jungfrau [the mountain]. "Pieces of obsolete science, imprisoned...in the solid *mass* of a religious creed" (*Inge*). "The *mass* [that is, of people] never comes up to the standard of its best member, but on the contrary degrades itself to a level with the lowest" (*Thoreau*). **Volume** usually applies to that which flows, rolls, or the like, and is therefore without outline, and often continuous in extent; as, a tremendous *volume* of water; a *volume* of gas poured into the room. "It [the voice] rose through progressive gradations of sweetness and power, until its *volume* seemed to envelop her" (*N. Hawthorne*). These three terms also come into comparison when they designate the quantity or amount. But *the bulk* and *the mass* mean the greater part or a large majority of something objective. "Some must know medicine, but for *the bulk* of mankind it is sufficient to have an elementary knowledge of physiology and hygiene" (*B. Russell*). "*The* great *mass* of the articles on which impost is paid is foreign luxuries" (*Jefferson*). **Volume,** on the other hand, denotes the total amount or quantity, especially of something subject to seasonal, periodic, or other fluctuations; as, the *volume* of travel increases greatly in the vacation season; to enlarge the *volume* of the currency; the *volume* of business in certain lines has decreased since the beginning of the war.
Ana. *Form, figure, shape.

bulky. *Massive, massy, monumental, substantial.
Ana. Huge, gigantic, colossal, mammoth, elephantine, *enormous: corpulent, obese, portly, *fleshy: burly, husky (see MUSCULAR).
Con. Petite, diminutive, *small, little.

bull, *n.*[1] Blunder, howler, boner, bloomer, mistake, *error, slip, lapse, faux pas.

bull, *n.*[2] *Policeman, officer, constable, bobby, peeler, copper, cop, bailiff, catchpole, gendarme.

bulldoze. Bully, browbeat, *intimidate, cow.
Ana. *Threaten, menace: terrorize, terrify, *frighten: *worry, harass, harry.
Con. Cajole, wheedle, blandish, *coax.

bullheaded. Pigheaded, stiffnecked, stubborn, mulish, *obstinate, dogged, pertinacious.

bully, *v.* Bulldoze, browbeat, *intimidate, cow.
Ana. Torment, grill, rack, torture (see AFFLICT): *threaten, menace: terrorize, terrify, *frighten, scare.
Ant. Coax. — *Con.* Wheedle, cajole, blandish (see COAX): *lure, entice, inveigle, decoy.

bulwark, *n.* **Bulwark, breastwork, rampart, parapet, barbette, bastion** come into comparison when they denote a structure above the ground that forms part of a fortification and is specifically intended for purposes of defense. **Bulwark** is the most general and the least technical of these terms. It is or has been applied to various types of structures, such as a wall intended to keep out an enemy, or a structure of logs, earth, stones, or the like, from behind which the defenders can safely attack besiegers or an assaulting force, and to a breakwater or sea wall. In current use it is chiefly figurative, being applied to any person or any thing regarded as a firm, steadfast, or powerful defense or defender; as, "He stood, the *bulwark* of the Grecian band" (*Pope*). "A mighty fortress is our God, A *bulwark* never failing" (*Luther, transl. by F. H. Hedge*). "The support of the State governments in all their rights, as the most competent administrations for our domestic concerns, and the surest *bulwarks* against anti-republican tendencies" (*Jefferson*). "Britannia needs no *bulwarks*, No towers along the steep; Her march is o'er the mountain waves, Her home is on the deep" (*Campbell*). **Breastwork** applies chiefly to a structure of earth or the like, which is often hastily thrown up and is usually only a few feet in height, and behind which defenders may crouch or stand so as to fire their guns from a concealed position; as, "the mud *breastworks* had long been levelled with the earth" (*Irving*). **Rampart** and **parapet** are the common technical terms, especially when fortifications of the type that prevailed before the World War are under consideration. In this sense a *rampart* is an embankment round a place, often, especially in old castles, built inside the moat and rising high enough to conceal the forces lying behind it, yet broad enough on its top level to permit the movement of men and of guns when they are needed in action. A parapet, in contrast with a rampart, is a structure rising above the top level of a rampart and serving as a breastwork for those aiming and firing guns and as a bulwark against the missiles of the enemy. But, in less technical use, *rampart* is applied to any wall or to any elevation or level on which defenders may operate when in action, or which may be thought of as suitable for such action, and *parapet* is applied to any structure resembling a parapet of a fortification, such as a low wall, a balustrade, or the like. "Art thou [Nineveh] better than populous No [=Thebes], that was situate among the rivers, that had the waters round about it, whose *rampart* was the sea...?" (*Nahum* iii. 8). "On a summer's day Wolstanbury Hill is an island in sunshine; you may lie on the grassy *rampart*, high up in the most delicate air" (*Jefferies*). "The terrace surrounded with a stone *parapet* in front of the house" (*G. Eliot*). **Barbette** applies to a part of a fortification that is typically a platform behind a parapet on which guns are mounted so that when fired, their missiles fly over the parapet. *Barbette* is also applicable to a similar arrangement on a warship, when the guns are mounted so that their armor, or *barbette*, protects the loading platform. The term is chiefly found in phrases such as "*barbette* guns" or "guns mounted in *barbette*." **Bastion** applies to a projection extending from the main wall of a fortification: typically, a bastion is a four-sided projection ending in an acute angle and providing a means whereby the enemy may be covered in several directions and the fortification protected from at least four angles. In figurative use, *bastion* differs little from *rampart* except in carrying a stronger suggestion of attack than of defense. "They build each other up ... As *bastions* set point blank against God's will" (*Cowper*).
Ana. Stronghold, fortress, *fort, citadel.

bum, *n.* *Vagabond, vagrant, tramp, hobo, truant, stiff, swagman, sundowner.

Ana. Sot, toper, *drunkard, inebriate, alcoholic, soak.

bumpkin. Clodhopper, clown, lout, *boor, churl.

bunch, *n.* *Bundle, bale, parcel, pack, fardel, package, packet.

Ana. Collection, assemblage, gathering (see under GATHER): quantity, number, aggregate (see SUM).

bundle, *n.* **Bundle, bunch, bale, parcel, pack, fardel, package, packet** denote a thing or things done up for storage, sale, or carriage. A **bundle** is a collection of articles bound or rolled together, often loosely; as, a *bundle* of papers, of kindling wood, of groceries; a *bundle* for the laundry; a *bundle* of old clothes. A **bunch** is a collection of things, usually of the same sort, fastened closely together in orderly fashion; as, a *bunch* of violets, of radishes, of asparagus, of keys. **Bale,** originally any large bundle of goods bound up for storage or transportation, now applies to one composed of materials such as rags, hay, straw, cotton, wool, and the like, which are closely pressed together so as to form a mass, usually rectangular, tightly bound with stout cord or wire, and, often, wrapped in paper, burlap, or the like. Because there is in various localities a uniform size for a bale of a certain commodity, the word often also implies an average or approximate weight; thus, in the United States a *bale* of cotton weighs approximately 500 lbs., and in Brazil and Peru, 250 lbs. **Parcel,** as here considered (see also PART), no longer carries its original implication of a number of things detached from a larger group or whole and bound together; it now implies a state of being wrapped and tied and a small or moderate size, and it carries no suggestion of the number or kind of things so wrapped and tied; as, a shopping bag for *parcels;* loaded down with *parcels;* to send *parcels* through the mail. **Pack** now implies more careful and more compact arrangement than *bundle;* specifically, it denotes a conveniently packed bundle of goods or supplies that is carried on the back, as by a peddler, by a soldier on the march, or by a boy scout on an expedition. **Fardel,** now archaic or dialect, sometimes comes close to *pack* in its meaning and sometimes to *bundle.* It tends, however, to imply, more than either of these terms, either a burdensome or a miscellaneous character, and is often used figuratively. "Who would *fardels* bear, To grunt and sweat under a weary life...?" (*Shak.*). "A *fardel* of never-ending misery and suspense" (*Marryat*). A **package** is specifically something packed (as in a box or receptacle of moderate size, or in a compact bundle), especially for convenience in sale or transportation; as, an express *package;* a *package* of envelopes; candy in the original *package; package* goods. A **packet** is a small package or parcel; as, especially, a *packet* of letters or dispatches.

Ana. Collection, assemblage, gathering (see under GATHER): *bag, sack.

buoyant. Volatile, expansive, resilient, effervescent, *elastic.

Ana. *Spirited, high-spirited, mettlesome, gingery: *lively, vivacious, animated, sprightly: jocund, blithe, *merry: optimistic, *hopeful.

Ant. Depressed, dejected. — *Con.* Doleful, lugubrious, *melancholy: *sullen, morose, glum, dour: *despondent, despairing, hopeless, forlorn.

burden, *n.* *Load, cargo, freight, lading.

burdensome. Oppressive, *onerous, exacting.

Ana. *Heavy, ponderous, cumbersome, cumbrous, weighty: *irksome, wearisome: fatiguing, exhausting, fagging, tiring (see TIRE): arduous, *hard, difficult.

Ant. Light. — *Con.* *Easy, facile, simple, smooth, effortless.

burglar. Larcener, thief, robber. See under THEFT.

Ana. Stealer, pilferer, filcher, purloiner (see corresponding verbs at STEAL): plunderer, looter, rifler (see corresponding verbs at ROB).

burglarize. *Rob, plunder, thieve, rifle, loot.

Ana. *Steal, pilfer, filch, purloin, lift, pinch, snitch, cop, swipe: sack, pillage, *ravage, despoil.

burglary. *Theft, larceny, robbery.

burlesque, *v.* Caricature, parody, travesty. See under CARICATURE, *n.*

Ana. Mimic, ape, mock, imitate, *copy: *ridicule, deride.

burlesque, *n.* *Caricature, parody, travesty.

Ana. Mimicry, mockery, imitation (see corresponding verbs at COPY): *fun, jest, sport, game: satire, sarcasm, humor, *wit: derision, ridicule (see corresponding verbs at RIDICULE).

burly. Husky, *muscular, brawny, athletic, sinewy.

Ana. Corpulent, *fleshy, portly: bulky, substantial, *massive: *vigorous, lusty: *powerful, forceful, potent.

Ant. Lanky, lank. — *Con.* *Lean, spare, gaunt, rawboned, angular, scrawny, skinny.

burn, *v.* **Burn, scorch, char, sear, singe,** as here compared, agree in meaning to injure by exposure to fire or intense heat. **Burn** is the most comprehensive of these terms, for it is applicable regardless of the extensiveness or the slightness of the injury, or of whether fire or heat is the destructive agency; as, the cake was *burned* to a crisp in the oven; only the lower edge of his coat was *burned* by the flames; the grass was badly *burned* by the sun; the child's hand was *burned* by touching the hot stove; to *burn* steel in forging. *Burn* is also applicable when a similar injury or similar effects are produced by another agency; as, to *burn* plants by using too strong a fertilizer; a sharp wind *burns* the face. **Scorch** implies superficial burning that changes the color (especially to brown or black) or texture of something; as, to *scorch* a dress in ironing it; the paint of the house was badly *scorched* by the flames from the grass fire. **Char** usually implies complete carbonization (or reduction to coal) by fire; as, *charred* wood; to *char* coffee berries in roasting them; the lower parts of the rafters were *charred* in the fire. **Sear,** in literal use, applies only to the burning or scorching of animal tissues by fire or intense heat; specifically, it is used of cauterizing a wound, of branding an animal, and of quickly browning the outside of roasting or broiling meats so that they will retain their juices in later and slower cooking; as, to *sear* a wound; to *sear* beef as the first step in roasting it. **Singe** strictly implies a very superficial burning (as, the fire next door merely *singed* our house); sometimes such burning is intentional, as when the short hairs or bristles covering a carcass being prepared for the market or for cooking are quickly destroyed by a flame; as, to *singe* the ends of one's hair to prevent their breaking; to *singe* a chicken before broiling it.

Ana. Kindle, enkindle, fire, ignite, inflame, *light: *blaze, flame, glow.

burnish. *Polish, shine, buff, furbish.

bursal. Fiscal, *financial, monetary, pecuniary.

bury. Secrete, cache, *hide, conceal, screen, ensconce.

Con. Expose, display, parade, flaunt, exhibit, *show: unearth, *discover, ascertain, learn, determine.

business, *n.* **1** *Work, occupation, pursuit, calling, métier, employment.

Ana. *Trade, craft, handicraft, art, profession.

2 *Affair, concern, matter, thing.

Ana. *Function, office, duty, province: *task, job, assignment, chore, stint.

3 Business, commerce, trade, industry, traffic are here compared chiefly in their most inclusive senses in which they denote one of those forms or branches of human endeavor which have for their objective the supplying of commodities. **Business,** as here compared, specifically applies to the combined activities of all those who are engaged in the barter, purchase, or sale of commodities of any sort, either in wholesale or retail transactions, or in financial transactions connected with them: in this sense, *business* is thought of as the combined activities of merchants, bankers, and the like, as opposed to those of agriculturists, manufacturers, and others whose immediate end is production. The term, however, is also used to include the activities of producers as well as of merchants and bankers, and also of those engaged in the transportation of goods, since all these have for their ultimate aims the supplying of commodities and the increase of private wealth; as, there should be no conflict between government and *business; business* is greatly depressed throughout the world; *business* is improving everywhere. **Commerce** and **trade,** on the other hand, apply to the activities of those who are engaged in the exchange of commodities, especially such exchange as involves transactions on a large scale and the transportation of goods from place to place. The words are often used interchangeably (as, foreign *commerce* [or *trade*] has been much affected by the war); but in general *commerce* is preferred when different countries or states are involved, when transportation is across seas or by sea, and when the dealings are not only in merchandise, but also in money, bills of exchange, and the like, and *trade,* when different business organizations in the same country are involved or when the dealings are in merchandise; as, laws regulating interstate *commerce;* ships engaged in *commerce* with the West Indies; a slump in the sale of automobiles has adversely affected the *trade* between the manufacturers and the steel companies; "free *trade*" designates a policy of permitting entry of natural and manufactured products from foreign countries without duties or tariff restrictions. In the United States, the Interstate Commerce Commission regulates common carriers of all kinds (rail, water, motor) engaged in interstate transportation of passengers or goods; the Federal Trade Commission was created to prevent use of unfair methods of competition in interstate commerce and to investigate trade conditions in and with foreign countries. **Industry** applies chiefly to the activities of those who are engaged in production, especially in the processing of natural products, the manufacture of artificial products, the erection of buildings and other structures, on so large a scale that problems of capital and labor are involved. The term may be used generally to include all activities covered by this definition; as, the replacing of hand tools by machines has revolutionized *industry.* It may also be used more narrowly of any branch of industry as determined by the thing produced; as, the sugar *industry* (that is, all the business organizations devoted to the manufacture of sugar); the steel *industry;* the automobile *industry;* the building *industry.* **Traffic,** in the sense here considered (see also BUSINESS, 4; INTERCOURSE), applies to the activities of those who are engaged in the operation of public carriers, such as vessels, railroads, bus lines, and systems of trucking, and who are, therefore, primarily responsible for the transportation not only of commodities and articles of manufacture but also of persons from one part of a country or of the world to another; as, the *traffic* interests were also represented at the conference.

4 Business, trade, traffic are here compared in a narrow sense, in which they agree in meaning the pursuit or occupation of a person or group of persons engaged in the buying and selling of commodities for profit. **Business** was formerly more often used in the United States than in Great Britain in this restricted meaning, **trade** being once the usual but now the literary term in the latter country, especially for the carrying on of mercantile or commercial transactions in a store or shop; thus, when an American says "Jones has decided to engage in *business,*" he often means that Jones has decided to open a store or shop, or, as a Briton might put it, "Jones has decided to go into *trade.*" But the American may mean that Jones plans to engage in some mercantile or commercial enterprise. "Every *trade*...is a *business,* but every *business* is not a *trade.* To answer that description, it must be conducted by buying and selling, which the *business* of keeping a lunatic asylum is not" (*Baron Denman*). **Traffic** (see also BUSINESS, 3; INTERCOURSE) is now used chiefly when something underhand or venal is implied; as, to engage in *traffic* in narcotics, or in liquor, or in votes; "Engaged in a low, clandestine *traffick,* prohibited by the laws of the country" (*Burke*); the white-slave *traffic.*

Ana. Selling, vending, trading, auctioning, bartering, (see SELL, *v.*).

bustle, *n.* Flurry, *stir, ado, fuss, pother.

Ana. *Business, commerce, trade, industry, traffic: movement, *motion: hubbub, racket, babel, *din.

Con. Inactivity, idleness, inertness, passiveness, supineness (see corresponding adjectives at INACTIVE).

busy. Busy, industrious, diligent, assiduous, sedulous agree in meaning actively engaged or occupied in work, in accomplishing a purpose or intention, or the like. **Busy** may imply nothing more than that the person or thing referred to is not idle, that is, that he is at work or that it is in use; as, the doctor is *busy* just now; the telephone is *busy.* In British and often in American use *engaged* is preferred to *busy* in this sense. In attributive use and some predicative use, *busy* usually implies habitual or temporary engrossment in activity or the appearance of such engrossment; as, the *busy* bee; a *busy* gossip; a *busy* life. "Nowhere so *busy* a man as he there was [original text, *nas*], And yet he seemed *busier* than he was" (*Chaucer*). **Industrious** applies to one who is characteristically attentive to his business or work: it implies habitual devotion to labor. "The nation [France] is at once the most *industrious* and the least industrial of the great nations" (*Brownell*). **Diligent** (of narrower range than *industrious*) implies earnest application to some specific object or pursuit; one may be *diligent* in seeking some favorite end without being in general *industrious.* "It is this conviction [that success in life depends on the power to think] which converts a listless undergraduate into a *diligent* student of law or medicine" (*C. W. Eliot*). **Assiduous** implies studied and unremitting, **sedulous** implies painstaking and persevering, application to a business or enterprise; as, to acquire the power to speak French fluently by *assiduous* practice; an *assiduous* nurse; a *sedulous,* but not brilliant, student; to attempt to gain one's ends by *sedulous* flattery. "He on her side played his part of supporter, councillor and friend with an *assiduity* sometimes comic. He even learned to play the lute that he might please her" (*Belloc*). "I read with *sedulous* accuracy...the metrical romances" (*Coleridge*). "She would never fail in *sedulous* attention to his wants" (*M. Wilkins*).

Ana. Engrossed, absorbed, *intent: working, toiling, laboring, travailing (see corresponding nouns at WORK).

Ant. Idle: unoccupied. — *Con.* *Inactive, inert, passive: indolent, slothful, *lazy: slack, relaxed (see LOOSE).

but. **But, however, still, nevertheless, yet** are here compared as adversative terms; that is, as terms whose use implies that what follows in some degree opposes or contradicts that which precedes. **But** marks the opposition without emphasizing it; as, This is not winter, *but* it is almost as cold. **However** is weaker, and throws the opposition into the background: for this reason it is often used parenthetically; as, This is not winter: it is, *however,* almost as cold. *However* also introduces a final decision or conclusion; as, the truth, *however,* has not yet fully come out—that is, such is the speaker's conclusion in view of the whole case. **Still,** like *nevertheless* and *yet,* states more strongly an adversative conclusion, implying a concession in what precedes; as, It is true that winter is over: *still,* it is almost as cold. **Nevertheless** implies that even if the concession be fully made, it has no real bearing on the question or is not really decisive; as, To be sure, it is no longer winter: *nevertheless,* it is quite cold; Say what you will, we must *nevertheless* go forward. **Yet** implies that, however extreme the concession may be, the consequence naturally to be expected does not follow; as, It is well on in May, *yet* it is almost as cold as midwinter. "Though he slay me, *yet* will I trust in him" (*Job* xiii. 15).

butchery. Slaughter, *massacre, carnage, pogrom.
Ana. Murdering *or* murder, slaying, killing (see corresponding verbs at KILL).

butt, *v.* In form **butt in.** *Intrude, obtrude, interlope.
Ana. Interfere, *meddle, intermeddle: *interpose, intervene, interfere, mediate, intercede.
Con. Withdraw, retire, clear out (see GO): *refrain, abstain, forbear.

buttress. **Buttress, pier, abutment** are technical terms used in architecture for auxiliary structures designed to serve as a prop, shore, or support for the wall of a building. A **buttress** is a structure, as of masonry, projecting from and supporting a wall, often designed especially for receiving and carrying the outward pressure, or thrust, exerted on the wall by the weight of an arch or vault. In a *flying buttress,* the pressure or thrust is carried over an open space by a rigid bar resting against a masonry structure (the *pier*). A **pier** is a thickened piece of masonry designed to stiffen a wall. A pier may be built as a part of the wall, or it may be a detached mass, used as the vertical part of a flying buttress, carrying the thrust of a masonry bar or rod extending between it and the wall. An **abutment** is the particular section of either a buttress or a pier which actually receives the pressure or thrust exerted by the weight of an arch or vault.
In bridgebuilding, an **abutment** is the support at either extreme end of the structure, or, by extension, the anchorage of the cables for an extension bridge; a **pier** is any intermediate support between the ends of a bridge.

buy. **Buy, purchase** agree in meaning to acquire something by paying (usually money) for it. The words are often used interchangeably without loss. **Buy,** however, is the homelier and (often) the more emphatic word and it usually stresses getting what one wants for a price; **purchase,** on the other hand, frequently implies a transaction of some dignity or importance and negotiations or other efforts to obtain it; as, to *buy* eggs; to *purchase* a steam yacht; "Peace, how oft, how dearly *bought*" (*Pope*); "Thou hast thought that the gift of God may be *purchased* with money" (*Acts* viii. 20). Whereas *buy* may almost always be substituted for *purchase* without disadvantage, the use of *purchase* instead of *buy* often weakens the effect or strikes a jarring note.
Ana. Obtain, acquire, procure, *get: *pay, compensate, remunerate.
Con. *Sell, vend, auction.

by. **By, through, with** come into comparison only as prepositions followed by a word or phrase naming the agent, means, or instrument. **By** is followed commonly by the agent or causative agency; as, a wall built *by* the Romans; a novel *by* Scott; destroyed *by* fire; devoured *by* wolves; blessed *by* a priest; inflamed *by* the jibes of officers; impressed *by* the evidence; awakened *by* dreaming of fire. **Through,** as here compared, as well as in its primary sense, implies intermediacy; it is followed by the name of the person or thing that serves as the medium or the means by which one gains one's end, produces some effect, or the like; as, to speak *through* an interpreter; to procure a rare book *through* a friend; to express ideas *through* words; to acquire a position *through* influence; an opportunity lost *through* indecision. **With,** on the other hand, is often followed by the name of the instrument which accompanies the action; as, to write *with* a pen; to eat *with* a fork; to defend oneself *with* a stick; "He was torn to pieces *with* a bear: this avouches the shepherd's son" (*Shak.*). It may, however, take for its object something not consciously used as an instrument, but serving as the instrumentality by which an effect is produced; as, he amused the crowd *with* his anecdotes; do not kill us *with* kindness.

bystander. Onlooker, looker-on, witness, eyewitness, *spectator, observer, beholder.

byway. *Road, roadway, street, thoroughfare, lane, alley, alleyway.

C

cabal. **1** Intrigue, conspiracy, complot, machination, *plot, frame-up.
2 Combine, junto, bloc, faction, ring, *combination, party.

cabalistic *or* **cabalistical.** Anagogical, mystic, *mystical.
Ana. Occult, esoteric, *recondite, abstruse: cryptic, enigmatic, *obscure: arcane, *mysterious.
Con. Plain, clear, obvious, manifest, *evident, palpable, apparent.

cabinetmaker. *Carpenter, joiner, framer.

cache, *v.* Secrete, bury, *hide, conceal, ensconce, screen.
Con. Expose, exhibit, display, *show: unearth, *discover.

cadaver. Corpse, stiff, *body, carcass.

cadaverous. Wasted, pinched, *haggard, worn, careworn.
Ana. Gaunt, skinny, scrawny, angular, rawboned, lank, lanky, *lean, spare.
Ant. Plump, stout. — *Con.* Fleshy, fat, corpulent, obese, portly, rotund.

cadence. *Rhythm, meter.

Ana. Accentuation, accent, stress, *emphasis: beat, pulse, throb, pulsation (see corresponding verbs under PULSATE).

cajole. Wheedle, blandish, *coax.

Ana. Entice, inveigle, seduce, decoy, *lure: beguile, delude, *deceive: tease, tantalize (see WORRY).

Con. Browbeat, bully, bulldoze, cow, *intimidate: constrain, oblige, compel, coerce, *force.

calamity. *Disaster, catastrophe, cataclysm.

Ana. *Accident, casualty, mishap: *misfortune, mischance, adversity: tribulation, visitation, affliction, *trial, cross: ruin, wreck (see corresponding verbs at RUIN).

Ant. Boon. — *Con.* Fortune, luck (see CHANCE): favor, *gift: benefaction (see DONATION): *blessing, benediction.

calculate. **Calculate, compute, estimate, reckon** agree in meaning to determine something (such as cost, speed, quantity, etc.) by mathematical or arithmetical processes. **Calculate** is the preferred term when highly intricate or elaborate processes are followed and when the result arrived at is, because of the great difficulties involved, more or less problematical; as, to *calculate* the velocity of light, the distance between the sun and the earth, or the number of atoms in a cubic centimeter of hydrogen. **Compute** is preferred where the data are given or the actual figures involved are known and at hand, and not arrived at indirectly; it therefore commonly implies the use of simple arithmetical processes; as, to *compute* the interest due, the area of a farm for sale, or the cost of running a business during a given year. **Estimate** carries so strong an implication from its more common sense (see ESTIMATE) of an evaluation based on one's experience and good judgment, that even when, as here compared, it implies careful calculation or computation, it still connotes a result that is not necessarily exact, but approximates the exact result: for he who *estimates* deals with data or figures that are to some extent unsatisfactory. Hence, *estimate* is preferred to *calculate* and *compute* when the cost of a piece of work to be done is computed at present prices; thus, a contractor's bid on a projected building is based on its *estimated* cost to him; a printer *estimates* a printing job when he names the price he will probably ask for doing it. **Reckon** is now used more or less colloquially in place of *compute.* It often connotes simpler mathematical processes, especially such as can be carried on in one's head or aided by the use of counters, and the like; as, to *reckon* the cost of a trip to the city; to *reckon* the number of eggs laid by the hens during the month.

Ana. Weigh, revolve, study, *consider: *ponder, ruminate: determine, ascertain, *discover.

Con. Guess, *conjecture, surmise.

calculating. Circumspect, *cautious, wary, chary.

Ana. *Deliberate, designed, considered, studied, premeditated: designing, scheming, plotting (see corresponding verbs under PLAN, *n.*): wily, crafty, artful, cunning, *sly.

Ant. Reckless, rash. — *Con.* Foolhardy, daring, temerarious, venturous, venturesome, *adventurous: improvident, imprudent, indiscreet (see affirmative adjectives at PRUDENT).

calculation. Circumspection, caution, wariness, chariness. See under CAUTIOUS.

Ana. *Prudence, forethought, foresight, providence, discretion: *care, concern, solicitude: astuteness, perspicacity, sagacity, shrewdness (see corresponding adjectives at SHREWD).

Ant. Recklessness, rashness.

call, *v.* *Summon, cite, convoke, convene, muster.

Ana. Assemble, *gather, collect: *invite, bid.

call, *n.* *Visit, visitation.

caller. *Visitor, visitant, guest.

calling. Occupation, pursuit, métier, business, *work, employment.

Ana. *Vocation, avocation: profession, *trade, craft, art, handicraft.

callous. *Hardened, indurated.

Ana. Tough, tenacious, stout, *strong: *firm, solid, hard: *inflexible, adamant, obdurate, inexorable: insensitive, impassible, *insensible, anesthetic.

Ant. Tender. — *Con.* *Soft, lenient, gentle: yielding, submitting, relenting (see YIELD): compassionate, responsive, sympathetic (see TENDER): sensitive, susceptible, open, exposed, subject, *liable.

callow. Green, crude, raw, *rude, rough.

Ana. Puerile, boyish, juvenile, *youthful: naïve, ingenuous, simple, unsophisticated, artless, *natural: adolescent, pubescent (see corresponding nouns at YOUTH).

Ant. Full-fledged, grown-up. — *Con.* *Mature, adult, matured.

calm, *adj.* **Calm, tranquil, serene, placid, peaceful, halcyon** agree in meaning quiet and free from all that disturbs or excites. **Calm,** primarily applied to sea or weather, usually conveys an implicit contrast with its opposite, *stormy,* and suggests freedom, real or assumed, from agitation of whatever sort; as, "a season of *calm* weather" (*Wordsworth*); "As men for ever temp'rate, *calm,* and wise" (*Pope*). **Tranquil** implies a more settled composure, a more inherent quiet, than *calm,* with less suggestion of previous agitation overcome; as, "Farewell the *tranquil* mind! farewell content!" (*Shak.*); "the *tranquil* beauty of Greek sculpture" (*FitzGerald*). **Serene** suggests a lofty and unclouded tranquillity; as, "regions mild of calm and *serene* air, Above the smoke and stir of this dim spot Which men call Earth" (*Milton*); "the *serene* satisfaction of certitude" (*Newman*). **Placid** connotes lack of excitement and suggests an unruffled and equable aspect or temper, even, sometimes, in derogatory use, a kind of bovinity; as, "to confirm by *placid* silences the fact that the wine had been good" (*H. James*); "the *placid* common sense of Franklin" (*J. R. Lowell*); she is as *placid* as a cow. **Peaceful,** as here compared (see also PACIFIC), implies repose, or the attainment of undisturbed tranquillity; as, "I am grown *peaceful* as old age tonight" (*Browning*). **Halcyon,** etymologically calm as the legendary "halcyon days" (fourteen days around the winter solstice), when the halcyon, or kingfisher, traditionally nests on the sea, now implies an almost magic or golden calmness, especially of weather or of spirit. "Soft blue stone, the colour of robins' eggs, or of the sea on *halcyon* days of summer" (*Cather*).

Ana. *Still, quiet, stilly, noiseless: *pacific, peaceable: *impassive, stoic: unruffled, composed, collected, imperturbable, *cool.

Ant. Stormy: agitated. — *Con.* Shaken, rocked, convulsed (see SHAKE): disturbed, perturbed, discomposed, upset (see DISCOMPOSE).

calumniate. Defame, slander, asperse, traduce, *malign, vilify, libel.

Ana. Revile, vituperate (see SCOLD): *decry, derogate from, detract from, belittle, disparage.

Ant. Eulogize: vindicate. — *Con.* Extol, laud, *praise, acclaim: defend, justify (see MAINTAIN).

calumny. Slander, *detraction, backbiting, scandal.

Ana. Aspersion, reflection, *animadversion, stricture: defaming *or* defamation, maligning, traducing, vilifying *or* vilification, libeling *or* libel (see MALIGN, *v.*).

Ant. Eulogy: vindication. — *Con.* *Encomium, panegyric, tribute: *compliment, adulation, flattery.

can, *v.* **Can, may** are often confused in use. In its commonest sense **can** expresses ability, whether physical or mental; as, he *can* climb this pole; he is but four, but he *can* read; he will do it, if he possibly *can;* "When Duty whispers low, Thou must, the youth replies, I *can*" (*Emerson*). But *can* may imply ability that is granted, as by God, the will of the people, or the like. "The law does all that is needed when it does all that it *can*" (*Justice Holmes*). **May** fundamentally expresses not ability, but possibility; as, he *may* go if the day is pleasant; you *may* be right. Therefore when the possibility depends for its fulfillment on the permission or sanction of another, *may* is the correct term; as, I shall call tomorrow if I *may;* you *may* go, if you wish; "*May* we take your coach to town?" (*Thackeray*). The use of *can* for *may* in asking permission is incorrect, but in denying permission *cannot* is common.

cancel. Efface, obliterate, expunge, delete, dele, *erase, blot out.

Ana. Invalidate, annul, *nullify: void, *annul, abrogate: *deface, disfigure: *neutralize, counteract, negative.

Con. Confirm, *ratify: *enforce, implement.

cancer. *Tumor.

Ana. Canker, canker sore, *abscess, ulcer.

candid. Open, *frank, plain.

Ana. Truthful, veracious (see corresponding nouns at TRUTH): *fair, dispassionate, impartial, unbiased, just: *sincere: honest, scrupulous, *upright.

Ant. Evasive. — *Con.* *Dishonest, deceitful, lying, mendacious, untruthful.

candidate. Candidate, aspirant, nominee, applicant are the chief words in English to denote one who seeks an office, honor, position, or the like. **Candidate** is applied not only to a seeker, but to one who is put forward by others or is considered as a possibility by those whose function it is to make a choice. It implies therefore an examination of qualifications and is applicable wherever selection is dependent upon others' judgment of one's fitness; as, the Republican *candidate* for governor; *candidates* for the degree of doctor of philosophy; *candidates* for holy orders. Since the word often implies previous training or grooming for a position or honor, it is sometimes used more widely of a person whose career is such that he seems headed for a certain place or end; as, a grafter is a *candidate* for prison. **Aspirant** definitely implies that one seeks an office, honor, post, promotion, or the like, because of one's own desire or decision; it therefore often connotes ambition or laudable efforts to improve one's state or condition. "The preliminary physical examination [for entrance into the Marine Hospital Service] was so rigid that twelve *aspirants* were promptly ruled out" (*V. Heiser*). "In [Matthew] Arnold's phrases the first step for every *aspirant* to culture is to endeavor to see things as they are" (*C. W. Eliot*). **Nominee** is applied to a candidate for office who has been chosen to represent a party or a faction in a coming election, or who has been proposed as the (sometimes an) appropriate person to fill a particular office and whose election therefore is recommended. **Applicant** is applied to one who definitely or formally submits himself as a possibility for a post or position. It is often used interchangeably with *candidate* when personal solicitation is implied in the latter, but unlike *candidate*, it conveys no suggestion of consideration by those who make the selection; as, to weed out *applicants* without experience. "There are plenty of unemployed sempstresses and laborers starving for a job, each of them trying to induce you to give it to her or him rather than to the next *applicant*" (*Shaw*).

canker, canker sore. *Abscess, ulcer.

canon. **1** *Law, precept, regulation, rule, statute, ordinance.

Ana. *Principle, fundamental, axiom: criterion, *standard, yardstick, touchstone, gauge.

2 *List, roster, rota, register, roll, inventory, table, catalogue, schedule.

3 *Hymn, laud, psalm, canticle, antiphon, anthem.

cant, *v.* *Tip, tilt, careen, heel, list.

Ana. *Throw, cast, fling, pitch, toss: incline, lean, slope, *slant: *turn, deflect, divert.

cant, *n.* **1** Jargon, argot, *dialect, lingo, patter, vernacular, slang, patois.

Ana. Phraseology, vocabulary, diction, *language: idiom, speech (see LANGUAGE).

2 Canting, *hypocrisy, sanctimony, Pharisaism.

canter, *n.* Gallop, run, lope, *trot, pace, single-foot, walk, rack, amble.

canter, *v.* Gallop, run, lope, trot, pace, single-foot, walk, rack, amble. See under TROT, *n.*

canticle. *Hymn, laud, psalm, antiphon, anthem, canon.

canting, *n.* Cant, *hypocrisy, sanctimony, Pharisaism.

canting, *adj.* Hypocritical, sanctimonious, pharisaical. See under HYPOCRISY.

capability. *Ability, capacity.

Ana. Competence, qualification *or* qualifications (see corresponding adjectives at ABLE): proficiency, adeptness, expertness, skillfulness (see corresponding adjectives at PROFICIENT): *art, skill, cunning.

Ant. Incapability, incompetence. — *Con.* *Inability, disability.

capable. Competent, qualified, *able.

Ana. Efficient, *effective, effectual, efficacious.

Ant. Incapable. — *Con.* Incompetent, unqualified (see INCAPABLE).

capacious. *Spacious, commodious, ample.

Ana. *Broad, wide: extended *or* extensive (see corresponding verb EXTEND): expanded *or* expansive (see corresponding verb EXPAND).

Ant. Exiguous (*of quarters, spaces, containers, etc.*). — *Con.* Circumscribed, limited, confined, restricted (see LIMIT, *v.*).

capacity. **1** *Ability, capability.

Ana. Amplitude, *expanse, spread: extent, magnitude, *size, volume: aptitude, *gift, faculty, talent, bent, turn, knack.

Ant. Incapacity. — *Con.* Powerlessness, impotence, impuissance (see corresponding adjectives at POWERLESS).

2 *Position, place, post, office, situation, job, berth, billet.

Ana. Duty, office, *function, province.

caper, *n.* *Prank, monkeyshine, antic, dido.

Ana. Gamboling *or* gambol, rollicking *or* rollick, romping *or* romp, frolicking *or* frolic (see corresponding nouns under PLAY, *v.*): skipping *or* skip, hopping *or* hop, bounding *or* bound (see corresponding verbs at SKIP).

capital, *adj.* *Chief, principal, main, leading, foremost.

Ana. *Primary, primordial, primal: *fundamental, basic, radical, underlying: cardinal, vital, *essential.

capitulate. Submit, *yield, succumb, relent, defer, bow, cave in.

Ana. Surrender, abandon, waive, cede (see RELINQUISH).

capitulation. *Surrender, submission.

Ana. Yielding, relenting, succumbing, caving in (see YIELD): *truce, armistice.

caponize. *Sterilize, asexualize, castrate, spay, emasculate, mutilate, geld.

caprice. **Caprice, freak, whim, whimsey** (*or* **whimsy**), **vagary, crotchet** agree in denoting a more or less irrational and arbitrary fancy or notion. **Caprice** emphasizes the lack of apparent motivation and implies a certain willfulness or wantonness. "They...without reason or judgment, beyond the *caprice* of their good pleasure, threw down the image from its pedestal" (*Byron*). "The restraint which ordinary persons...are able to impose on their *caprices*" (*Froude*). **Freak** suggests an impulsive, seemingly causeless, change of mind, like that of a child or a lunatic; as, "a light word flung in the air, a mere *freak* of perverse child's temper" (*Thackeray*); "Follow this way or that, as the *freak* takes you" (*Stevenson*); "a thousand Puckish *freaks*" (*J. R. Green*). **Whim** and **whimsey** suggest not so much a sudden as a quaint, fantastic, or humorous turn or inclination, but *whim* often stresses capriciousness, and *whimsey* fancifulness. "A young lady of some birth and fortune...who had strange *whims* of fasting" (*G. Eliot*). "Less mad the wildest *whimsey* we can frame, Than ev'n that passion [one's ruling passion], if it has no aim" (*Pope*). **Vagary** suggests still more strongly the erratic, extravagant, or irresponsible character of the notion or fancy; as, "Straight they changed their minds, Flew off, and into strange *vagaries* fell" (*Milton*); "A great force of critical opinion controlling a learned man's *vagaries*, and keeping him straight" (*Arnold*). **Crotchet** implies even more perversity of temper or more indifference to right reason than *vagary*; it often is applied to a capriciously heretical opinion on some (frequently) unimportant or trivial point; as, "It is a note of the provincial spirit not to hold ideas of this kind a little more easily, to be devoured by them, to suffer them to become *crotchets*" (*Arnold*). "You have no opinions, Lydia. The impracticable *crotchets* you are fond of airing are not recognized in England as sane political convictions" (*Shaw*).

Ana. Humor, *mood, temper, vein: notion, *idea: impulse (see MOTIVE): irrationality, unreasonableness (see corresponding adjectives at IRRATIONAL): perverseness, contrariness (see corresponding adjectives at CONTRARY).

Con. Intent, purpose, *intention, design: project, scheme, *plan: deciding *or* decision, determining *or* determination, resolving *or* resolution (see corresponding verbs at DECIDE).

capricious. Mercurial, unstable, *inconstant, fickle.

Ana. *Changeable, changeful, protean, variable: moody, humorsome (see corresponding nouns at MOOD): volatile, effervescent (see ELASTIC).

Ant. Steadfast. — *Con.* Constant, resolute, stanch, loyal, *faithful: *steady, constant.

capsize, *v.* Upset, *overturn, overset, overthrow, subvert.

Ana. *Tip, careen, heel, cant, tilt, list.

captain, *n.* Commander, master, *chief, leader, head, chieftain.

captious. Caviling, carping, *critical, hypercritical, faultfinding, censorious.

Ana. *Contrary, perverse: exacting, demanding (see DEMAND, *v.*): peevish, petulant, snappish, *irritable: testy, techy, choleric, *irascible.

Ant. Appreciative. — *Con.* Reasonable, *rational: judicious, *wise, sensible.

captivate. Fascinate, bewitch, enchant, charm, take, allure, *attract.

Ana. Delight, *please, gratify: win, gain (see GET).

Ant. Repulse.

captivating. Fascinating, bewitching, enchanting, charming, taking, alluring, attractive. See under ATTRACT.

Ana. Pleasing, *pleasant, agreeable, grateful: *delightful, delectable: lovely, bonny, fair, *beautiful.

Ant. Repulsive. — *Con.* Repellent, *repugnant, distasteful, obnoxious: *offensive, loathsome, revolting.

captive, *n.* *Prisoner, convict.

capture, *v.* *Catch, nab, cop, trap, snare, entrap, ensnare, bag.

Ana. Seize, *take, grab, grasp, clutch, snatch: *arrest, apprehend.

Con. Release, *free, liberate: surrender, yield, *relinquish.

carbonate, *v.* *Aerate, ventilate, oxygenate.

Ant. Decarbonate.

carbon copy *or* **carbon.** Copy, duplicate, transcript, *reproduction, facsimile, replica.

carcass. Corpse, cadaver, stiff, *body.

cardinal, *adj.* Vital, *essential, fundamental.

Ana. Requisite, necessary, indispensable, *needful: radical, *fundamental, basic: capital, principal, *chief, main, leading: important, significant, momentous (see corresponding nouns at IMPORTANCE).

Ant. Negligible.

care, *n.* **Care, concern, solicitude, anxiety, worry** agree in meaning a state of mind in which one is engrossed and more or less troubled by an affair or affairs, either one's own or another's, or in meaning an affair that engrosses and troubles one. The same distinctions in implications and connotations are evident in their corresponding adjectives (**careful, concerned, solicitous, anxious, worried**) when they mean engrossed and troubled by an affair or affairs. **Care** and **careful** (which is archaic in this sense) imply preoccupation and oppression of mind, because of heavy responsibilities or disquieting fears or apprehensions; as, "the king...most sovereign slave of *care*" (*Thoreau*); her face was worn with *care*. "She was free...to go where she liked and do what she liked. She had no responsibilities, no *cares*" (*Bennett*). "Be *careful* for nothing; but in every thing...let your requests be made known unto God" (*Philippians* iv. 6). **Concern** and **concerned** stress absence of indifference, but they also imply a greater or less degree of care, because of one's interest, affection, respect, or the like; as, his child's future was his greatest *concern*. "Your friends, Señora, would feel less *concern* for your safety if you kept them [valuables] farther from your person" (*M. Austin*). "It was quite characteristic of the state of mind of England in the summer of 1914 that Mr. Britling should be mightily *concerned* about the conflict in Ireland, and almost deliberately negligent of the possibility of a war with Germany" (*H. G. Wells*). **Solicitude** and **solicitous** imply profound concern; sometimes they connote extreme apprehensiveness, but more often they suggest thoughtfulness for another's welfare, well-being, success, or the like, or almost hovering attentiveness in another's misfortune. "They...tended the wounded man with the gentlest *solicitude*" (*Dickens*). "'I do hope baby will not wake,' was her chief *solicitude*" (*Meredith*). "They...were as *solicitous* to see it through for me as though I had been an only child among a lot of maiden aunts" (*M. Austin*). The last two pairs of words in this group imply far more agitation and depression than the first three. **Anxiety** and **anxious** stress the anguish of fear coupled with uncertainty or of the anticipation of impending misfortune, disaster, or the like. "Poor Miss Maria! she was *anxious*, no doubt...over money matters. 'Ladies ought not to have such *anxieties*,' thought Mr. Ezra" (*Deland*). "The child's inner life is often a turmoil of terrors and *anxieties* of which his parents know almost nothing" (*Inge*). **Worry** and **worried** usually suggest more mental activity (often futile activity) than *anxiety* and *anxious* or more fretting or stewing over problems, or situations, or persons that are a cause of solicitude or anxiety. "He thought that now all the *worries* were over, that there was nothing before him but duties" (*Conrad*). "*Worried*...by the need for keeping up their social positions" (*Shaw*).

Ana. Trouble, pains, *effort, exertion: disquieting *or* disquiet, perturbing *or* perturbation, discomposing *or* discomposure (see corresponding verbs at DISCOMPOSE): vigilance, watchfulness, alertness (see corresponding adjectives at WATCHFUL).

careen, *v.* Heel, cant, *tip, list, tilt.

Ana. Incline, slope, *slant, lean: *overturn, overset, capsize, upset.

Con. Balance, ballast, trim, *stabilize, steady.

careful. 1 Solicitous, anxious, worried, concerned. See under CARE, *n.*

Ana. Disquieted, perturbed, discomposed, disturbed, upset (see DISCOMPOSE): troubled, distressed (see TROUBLE, *v.*): *watchful, vigilant, alert.

2 Careful, meticulous, scrupulous, punctilious, punctual come into comparison only in their basic sense of showing or revealing close attention to details, or care in execution or performance. **Careful** implies great concern for the persons or things in one's charge, or for the way in which one's duties or tasks are performed. With regard to the former, the term implies solicitude or watchfulness (as, a *careful* mother; a *careful* nurse; a *careful* workman; a *careful* spender of money); with regard to the latter, it usually implies painstaking efforts, thoroughness, cautiousness in avoiding errors, a desire for perfection, or the like (as, a *careful* piece of work; a *careful* examination by the doctor; a *careful* mapping out of the plan of battle). All of the other words mean exceedingly careful, but they vary in their implications of the motives which inspire such carefulness and, to a less extent, in regard to the objects of attention. **Meticulous,** in very precise use, implies the prompting of fear: it usually suggests timorousness lest one make the slightest error or fall short of a high standard and therefore, in addition, it implies extreme fussiness or fastidiousness in attention to details; as, "Mr. Prufrock...like most converts, *meticulous* over points of ritual" (*Day Lewis*); "He [Augustus] took desperate risks, but only after *meticulous* calculation" (*Buchan*). "There were men who ploughed clumsily...leaving banks of land untouched...but Hendrik was not one of these, his work was *meticulous*" (*S. Cloete*). **Scrupulous,** as here compared (see also UPRIGHT), implies the promptings of conscience, not only of one's moral conscience, but of one's sense of what is right and wrong in fact, in logic, in aesthetics, and the like; it therefore also implies strict or painstaking adherence to what one knows to be true, correct, exact, or the like; as, *scrupulous* fairness of statement; *scrupulous* observation of details. "Bradley, like Aristotle, is distinguished by his *scrupulous* respect for words, that their meaning should be neither vague nor exaggerated" (*T. S. Eliot*). **Punctilious,** on the other hand, implies knowledge of the fine points of law, etiquette, ceremony, morality, and the like, and usually connotes excessive or obvious attention to the details or minutiae of these. "I am sorry...to see you so *punctilious* as to stand upon answers, and never to come near me till I have regularly left my name at your door" (*Gray*). "The *punctilious* gods who judged them according to the principles laid down in some celestial Book of Etiquette" (*J. W. Krutch*). **Punctual,** in earlier and now comparatively rare use, came close to *punctilious* in its stress on attention to the fine points of a law or code: the term, however, carried a much stronger implication than *punctilious* of emphasis on their observance and a weaker implication of concentration upon the minutiae; as, "We are not altogether so *punctual* as the French, in observing the lawes of comedy" (*Dryden*); "His *punctual* discharge of his duties" (*Froude*). In current use, the term implies almost perfection in one's adherence to appointed times as for engagements, in following a schedule, or the like, and so usually means punctiliously prompt; as, "I made Mr. Middleditch *punctual* before he died, though when he married me he was known far and wide as a man who could not be up to time" (*C. Mackenzie*); "*Punctual*, commonplace, keeping all appointments, as I go my round" (*L. P. Smith*).

Ana. *Cautious, circumspect, wary: provident, foresighted, prudent (see under PRUDENCE): accurate, precise, nice, exact (see CORRECT): studied, *deliberate.

Ant. Careless. — ***Con.*** Heedless, thoughtless, inadvertent (see CARELESS): neglectful, *negligent, lax, slack, remiss.

careless, *adj.* **Careless, heedless, thoughtless, inadvertent** come into comparison as meaning showing lack of concern or attention. **Careless** often implies the absence of cares such as responsibilities or worries; it then usually connotes casualness, spontaneity, lightheartedness, or the like, and carries little or no suggestion of culpability. "Her *careless* refinement of manner was so different from the studied dignity and anxious courtesy of the actor-manager" (*Shaw*). "He presented to the world the appearance of a *careless* and hospitable millionaire strolling into his own drawing-room with the detachment of an invited guest" (*E. Wharton*). Often, however, the term implies a more or less culpable indifference, which at its best is the product of independence or of concentration on other and more important things (as, "I was strangely bold and *careless* of danger then"—*Hudson*) and at its worst is the result of laziness or negligence, and manifests itself in blameworthy lack of pains or thought (as, a *careless* bookkeeper; a *careless* piece of work; *careless* errors). **Heedless** also implies indifference, but it stresses inattentiveness, or a failure to see, observe, take note of, or remark, rather than laziness or negligence; the term often, but not invariably, also connotes light-mindedness, frivolousness, or flightiness. "Heaps of flies...fell dead....Their decease made no impression on the other flies out promenading....Curious to consider how *heedless* flies are!" (*Dickens*). "Discreetly *heedless*, thanks to her long association with nobleness in art, to the leaps and bounds of fashion" (*H. James*). **Thoughtless** frequently emphasizes lack of reflection or of forethought. "Ah, how unjust to Nature and himself Is *thoughtless*, thankless, inconsistent man!" (*Young*). More frequently, especially in current use, it suggests lack of thoughtfulness, or consideration for others. "Now and then, however, he is horribly *thoughtless*, and seems to take a real delight in giving me pain" (*Wilde*). **Inadvertent** usually implies heedlessness; the term, however, is now rarely applied to persons or their minds, but is used in qualifying their acts, especially those which are mistakes, errors, or blunders, that are the result of heedlessness or inattention resulting from concentration on other things and that arise, therefore, neither from ignorance nor from intention; as, an *inadvertent* wakening of a person who is asleep; an *inadvertent* error in spelling or in pronunciation.

Ana. *Negligent, neglectful, lax, slack, remiss: casual, desultory, haphazard, *random, hit-or-miss, happy-go-lucky.

Ant. Careful. — ***Con.*** Meticulous, scrupulous, punctilious, punctual (see CAREFUL): accurate, precise, exact, nice (see CORRECT).

caress, *v.* **Caress, fondle, pet, cuddle, dandle** agree in meaning to manifest affection or love by touching, handling, or the like. **Caress** implies an expression of tender interest or of affection, ordinarily without undue familiarity, such as by soft stroking or patting. "Soothing with a touch the wild thing's fright...*caressed* it into peace with light, kind palms" (*Sir E. Arnold*). "The little Isaac...leans...against his father's knee...while Abraham's left hand quiets him and *caresses* the boy's face" (*H. Adams*). **Fondle** implies doting fondness, and frequently lack of dignity; it usually suggests attentions more obvious and less gentle than caressing, such as hugging, kissing, and the like; as, to *fondle* a baby (or a lap dog); "flattering, amorous *fondling*, to...melt her guardless heart" (*W. J. Mickle*). "She [Elizabeth]...*fondled* her 'sweet Robin,' Lord Leicester, in the face of the court" (*J. R. Green*). **Pet,** in its broadest sense, implies special attentions and indulgences, including more or less fondling; as, the *petted* child of the family. In current colloquial use, however, the term often stresses flirtatious or amorous fondling, and sometimes suggests undue or improper familiarity; as, a *petting* party. **Cuddle** chiefly suggests the action of a mother or nurse in drawing a child close to her breast to keep it warm, happy, and quiet. "Little boys...who have kind mammas to *cuddle* them" (*Kingsley*). The term is used figuratively to suggest any attentions which imply a desire to protect and keep warm and contented. "Temple seems...to have been coaxed, and warmed, and *cuddled* by the people round about him" (*Thackeray*). **Dandle** suggests playful handling of a child as by moving him up and down lightly on one's knee; as, the mother *cuddles*, but the father *dandles*, their little boy. In its extended use, *dandle* usually implies toying with, especially in a playful but pampering manner. "No man or nation ever was *dandled* into greatness" (*G. Smith*).

Ana. *Trifle, toy, dally, flirt, coquet: cherish, *nurse.

careworn. Worn, *haggard, pinched, wasted, cadaverous.

Ana. Troubled, distressed (see TROUBLE, *v.*): *lean, gaunt, scrawny, skinny: exhausted, fagged, jaded, tuckered (see TIRE, *v.*).

Ant. Carefree.

cargo. Burden, *load, freight, lading.

caricature, *n.* **Caricature, burlesque, parody, travesty** come into comparison not only as nouns meaning a grotesque or bizarre imitation of something but also as verbs meaning to make such an imitation. **Caricature** implies ludicrous exaggeration or distortion (often, but far from exclusively, pictorial) of the characteristic or peculiar features of a person, a group, a people, or the like, for the sake of satire or ridicule; as, cartoonists who *caricature* prominent politicians. "That propensity to *caricature* which tempts clever writers...to transform into objects of derision the venerated Great" (*L. P. Smith*). "If you compare any satiric 'character' of Pope with one of Dryden, you will see that the method and intention are widely divergent. When Pope alters, he diminishes....His portrait of Addison, for example... depends upon...the apparent determination not to exaggerate. The genius of Pope is not for *caricature*" (*T. S. Eliot*). **Burlesque** implies mimicry (especially of words or actions in the theater) that arouses laughter. The term usually also suggests distortion for the sake of the comic effect, as by treating a trifling subject in mock-heroic vein, or by giving to a serious subject a frivolous or laughable turn; as, in *Don Quixote*, Cervantes *burlesques* the old romances of chivalry. "*Burlesque* is... of two kinds; the first represents mean persons in the accoutrements of heroes; the other describes great persons acting and speaking like the basest among the people" (*Spectator*). **Parody** implies the employment in the treatment of a ludicrous or mean or trivial subject of the exact style (especially in its mannerisms) of some serious and (usually) well-known composition or writer; **travesty,** on the other hand, implies that the subject remains unchanged, but that the style is made extravagant or absurd. "Their idea was to write a number of *parodies* in the manner of the most popular poets of the day" (*Percy Fitzgerald*). "[In *MacFlecknoe*] Dryden's method ...is something very near to *parody;* he applies vocabulary, images, and ceremony which arouse epic associations of grandeur, to make an enemy helplessly ridiculous" (*T. S. Eliot*). "To apply that manner and that rhythm to Homer's incidents, is not to imitate Homer, but to *travesty* him" (*Arnold*). Figuratively, *parody* may be applied to any feeble or inappropriate attempt at imitation; *travesty,* to any ironically grotesque suggestion or resemblance; as, "a certain *parody* of devotion" (*Stevenson*); "The house! What a *travesty* of a home!" (*Lucas*).

Ana. Satire, humor, sarcasm (see WIT): grotesqueness, fantasticality, bizarreness (see corresponding adjectives at FANTASTIC): lampoon, *libel, skit, squib, pasquinade.

caricature, *v.* Burlesque, parody, travesty. See under CARICATURE, *n.*

Ana. Mimic, mock, ape, imitate, *copy: distort, *deform: simulate, counterfeit (see ASSUME): *ridicule, deride.

carnage. Slaughter, butchery, *massacre, pogrom.

carnal. **Carnal, fleshly, sensual, animal, animalistic** come into comparison when they are used in reference to human beings, their acts, works, desires, and the like, and mean having or manifesting a physical rather than an intellectual or spiritual character or origin. Both **carnal** and **fleshly** imply a connection with the body or flesh, especially when thought of as distinct from the soul. In earliest usage and sometimes now in certain idiomatic phrases, *carnal* does not in itself imply condemnation; often it is a purely descriptive or classificatory term; thus, in some of the older psychologies, hunger and thirst were called *carnal* appetites and the hunger for knowledge and the thirst for happiness, spiritual or intellectual appetites, but all were regarded as capable either of abuse and misdirection or of being ordered to good ends. "*Carnal* knowledge" is as neutral in its implications as its more modern near-equivalent "sexual intercourse." In later usage, the word acquired its now common derogatory implications of a connection with man's lower nature and an absence of a positive spiritual or moral character; as, "the passion of Giovanni and Annabella...hardly rises above the purely *carnal* infatuation" (*T. S. Eliot*); "an age grossly *carnal* in its pleasures" (*Wilde*). **Fleshly,** though it implies a connection with the flesh, thought of as man's lower nature, is not so suggestive of condemnation as *carnal;* as, "his *fleshly* desires were strong" (*M. K. Bradby*); "The godly dame, who *fleshly* failings damns" (*Pope*). In another sense, current since the middle of the nineteenth century when the term was used in describing a group ("The *Fleshly* School") of poets, including Swinburne, Morris, and Rossetti, *fleshly* is applied to artists and poets or their work to indicate emphasis on the evocation of sensations, usually delightful sensations. **Sensual** also implies a connection with sensations, but it further implies an indulgence in bodily sensation for its own sake rather than for an aesthetic end. "His feet and hands were always cold and there was for him an almost *sensual* satisfaction to be had from just lying perfectly still... and letting the hot sun beat down on him" (*S. Anderson*). Very often in modern use, the word carries implications of grossness or bestiality, and not merely, as in the case of *carnal*, of an absence of higher qualities. "A sloping meaty jaw, and large discolored buck-teeth which showed unpleasantly in a mouth...always half open.... that gave his face its *sensual*, sly, and ugly look" (*T. Wolfe*). **Animal** implies a connection with man's physical nature as distinguished chiefly from his rational nature. In good modern use it more and more rarely implies an intent to depreciate. "Under this head come all the *animal* activities of men, eating and drinking, maternal devotion or ordinary maternal care" (*S. Alexander*). "The state in his view is not merely the convenient machinery that raises a man above his *animal* wants" (*G. L. Dickinson*). "He taught the boy boxing, and shooting, and...superintended the direction of his *animal* vigour" (*Meredith*). When there is the intent to imply sensuality, **animalistic** is now sometimes preferred, but the word is still comparatively rare.

Ana. Physical, *bodily, corporeal, corporal, somatic: *sensuous: gross, *coarse, vulgar, obscene: *earthly, earthy, worldy, mundane: lustful, lewd, wanton, lascivious (see LICENTIOUS).

Ant. Spiritual: intellectual. — *Con.* *Moral, ethical, virtuous, noble, righteous: ethereal, aerial (see AIRY): pure, *chaste, modest, decent.

carol. Carrell, cubicle, bay, *recess, alcove, nook, niche, embrasure.

carpenter, *n.* **Carpenter, joiner, cabinetmaker** *or* **cabinetworker, framer** are here compared as designating a man who works in wood. In English usage, **carpenter** is specifically applied to the ordinary worker in wood; **joiner,** to the worker in hard wood, or in soft wood when delicate work is required; **cabinetmaker,** to a joiner for fine work. In Scotland, *joiner* is the general term, *carpenter* not being in use. In the United States, *joiner* is rarely used; *carpenter* denotes the worker in wood for ordinary requirements, both the job workman who puts up shelves, hangs doors, etc., and also the structural woodworker engaged in the general erection of buildings; **framer** (which is used also of workers in steel and the like) denotes the workman who handles the constructional parts, such as the heavy timber of floors, roofs, and partitions; *cabinetmaker*, or the alternative **cabinetworker,** the workman, especially in hard wood, who does fine work (such as on cabinets, furniture, etc.) requiring special skill in fitting of parts, in finishing surfaces, and in elegance of detail.

carping, *adj.* Caviling, faultfinding, captious, *critical, hypercritical, censorious.

Ana. Blaming, reprehending, reprobating, criticizing (see CRITICIZE): upbraiding, jawing, railing (see SCOLD): depreciating *or* depreciative, disparaging, decrying (see corresponding verbs at DECRY).

Ant. Fulsome. — *Con.* Commending *or* commendatory, applauding, complimenting (see corresponding verbs at COMMEND): praising, lauding, extolling (see PRAISE, *v.*): approving, endorsing (see APPROVE).

carrell. Carol, cubicle, bay, *recess, alcove, nook, niche, embrasure.

carriage. *Bearing, port, presence, mien, deportment, demeanor, manner, front.

Ana. *Posture, pose, attitude: *behavior, conduct: poise, address, savoir-faire, *tact.

carry, *v.* **Carry, bear, convey, transport, transmit** come into comparison when they mean to be, or to serve as, the agent or the means whereby something (or someone) is moved from one place to another. **Carry** originally and still often implies the use of a cart or carriage (now a train, ship, automobile, airplane, or the like: cf. the phrase *common carrier*) but it may imply a personal agent or a beast of burden or some natural or artificial passage, such as an artery or a pipe; as, the ship *carries* a heavy cargo; airplanes *carry* mail; to *carry* passengers; to *carry* news; please *carry* the basket to the house; the arteries *carry* the blood from the heart to the various parts of the body. **Bear,** in literal use, stresses the support of the weight of that which is being moved; in its extended senses, even though actual weight may not be implied, *bear* is preferred to *carry* when effort is suggested, or the importance or the significance of that which is carried is to be connoted; as, "Let four captains *Bear* Hamlet, like a soldier, to the stage" (*Shak.*); "over his head was *born* a rich canopy" (*Johnson*); then came the envoys *bearing* rich gifts; to come *bearing* good news. **Convey** is now more often used than *carry* of things that move continuously or in the mass or that pass through natural or artificial channels or mediums; as, an apparatus for *conveying* dirt from an excavation to the vehicles removing it (cf. a belt *conveyer*); freight cars (or in British use, goods wagons) for *conveying* coal from the mines to the various cities and towns; to build pipe lines to *convey* natural gas from one section to another; language *conveys* thought. **Transport** is used in place of *carry* or *convey* when the stress is on the movement of persons or goods from one place to another, as in vessels or in railway trains; as, to *transport* troops from Great Britain to France (cf. ships used as troop *transports*); California and Florida orange growers *transport* their produce to all parts of the country. "Most modern well-to-do Englishmen and Americans, if they were *transported* by magic into the Age of Elizabeth, would wish themselves back in the modern world" (*B. Russell*). **Transmit** emphasizes the causative power in an agent or instrument; it implies either an actual sending by some means of conveyance or transportation (as, the telegraph company *transmits* messages to all parts of the world; the steamship company will *transmit* your baggage whenever it receives the word) or the power or the property of permitting passage through or from one place to another (as, glass *transmits* light; metals *transmit* electricity).

Ana. Take, *bring, fetch: *move, remove, shift, transfer: drive, *ride.

cartel. **1** Compact, pact, convention, *contract, bargain, covenant, concordat, treaty, entente, indenture, mise.

2 Pool, syndicate, corner, *monopoly, trust.

Ana. Combine, *combination: *consolidation, merger, amalgamation.

carve. *Cut, slit, hew, chop, slash.

Ana. Shape, fashion, form (see MAKE): *separate, divide, part.

case. **1** *Instance, illustration, example, specimen, sample.

Ana. *Occurrence, event, incident, episode, circumstance: situation, condition, *state.

2 Cause, action, *suit, lawsuit.

casement. *Window, dormer, oriel.

cash, *n.* Currency, *money, legal tender, specie, coin, coinage.

cashier, *v.* *Dismiss, discharge, fire, sack, bounce, drop.

Ana. *Eject, expel, oust: eliminate, disbar, *exclude, suspend.

Con. Hire, *employ: engage (see PROMISE): elect, appoint, *designate, name.

cast, *v.* **1** *Throw, fling, hurl, pitch, toss, sling.

Ana. *Direct, aim, point, level, train, lay: *scatter, disperse.

2 *Discard, shed, molt, exuviate, slough, scrap, junk.

Ana. *Relinquish, abandon, yield, surrender, leave: repudiate, reject (see DECLINE): *dismiss, drop.

3 Figure, foot, *add, sum, total.
Ana. Compute, *calculate, reckon.

castigate, *v.* Chastise, *punish, chasten, discipline, correct.
Ana. *Beat, baste, thrash, pummel, belabor: berate, tonguelash, rate, upbraid, wig, rail (see SCOLD): *penalize, fine, amerce, mulct, sconce.

castrate. *Sterilize, asexualize, spay, emasculate, mutilate, geld, caponize.

casual. **1** *Accidental, incidental, adventitious, contingent, fortuitous.
Ana. Unpremeditated (see EXTEMPORANEOUS): *indifferent, unconcerned, incurious: *negligent, slack, lax, remiss: inadvertent, *careless, heedless.
Con. Intentional, *voluntary: premeditated, *deliberate, studied, considered, advised, designed: *careful, meticulous, punctilious, scrupulous.
2 Desultory, *random, haphazard, chancy, hit-or-miss, happy-go-lucky.
Ana. Offhand, impromptu, improvised, *extemporaneous, extempore: *spontaneous, impulsive: unmethodical, unsystematic (see affirmative adjectives at ORDERLY).
Ant. Deliberate. — *Con.* Formal, conventional, ceremonious (see CEREMONIAL).

casualty. *Accident, mishap.
Ana. *Disaster, calamity, catastrophe, cataclysm: *misfortune, mischance.

casuistical. Sophistical, fallacious, paralogistic. See under FALLACY.
Ana. *Plausible, specious: tortuous (see WINDING): oblique, devious, *crooked: *misleading, delusive, deceptive, delusory: *subtle, subtile.
Con. Sound, cogent, convincing, *valid.

casuistry. Sophistry, sophism, *fallacy, paralogism.

cataclysm. Catastrophe, *disaster, calamity.
Ana. Convulsing *or* convulsion, rocking, shaking, agitation (see corresponding verbs at SHAKE): revolution (see REBELLION): *misfortune, mischance.

catalogue, *n.* *List, inventory, table, schedule, register, roll, roster, rota, canon.

catastrophe. *Disaster, calamity, cataclysm.
Ana. Closing *or* close, concluding *or* conclusion, ending *or* end, termination, finishing *or* finish (see corresponding verbs at CLOSE): outcome, sequel, issue, aftermath, result, *effect: culmination, climax (see SUMMIT): *trial, tribulation, visitation: defeating *or* defeat, overthrowing *or* overthrow, routing *or* rout (see corresponding verbs at CONQUER).
Con. *Victory, triumph.

catch, *v.* **1** **Catch, capture, nab, cop, trap, snare, entrap, ensnare, bag** come into comparison as meaning to get into one's possession or under one's control either by taking or seizing or by means of skill, craft, or trickery. **Catch,** the ordinary and general term of this group, distinctively implies that the thing laid hold of has been in flight, in concealment, in constant movement, or the like, and that possession has been gained only by pursuit, force, strategy, or surprise, or by means of a device or accident which brings it within one's reach physically, ocularly, mentally, or the like; as, after several days' search, the detectives *caught* the murderer; he was not able to *catch* the man who snatched his purse; to *catch* fish; to *catch* a ball; to *catch* a pupil cheating in an examination; "his eyes *caught* the skirt of her dress" (*Dickens*); he did not *catch* the words they spoke; "that other aspect of truth which the scientist strives to *catch* and fix" (*Lowes*). Sometimes, the power of laying hold of is ascribed not to a person, his vision or other sense, his mind, heart, or imagination, but to the thing which draws to itself his attention, his eye, his fancy, etc.; as, "The fact *caught* her interest, just as sometimes a point in a wide dull landscape *catches* the eye" (*Deland*); "It may have seemed to Augustus an easy way of filling his treasury, and it *caught* the imagination of the Roman poets" (*Buchan*). **Capture** implies heavier odds than does *catch*, such as greater opposition or difficulty or more competition, with the result that possession suggests an overcoming or spells a victory; as, to *capture* a stronghold of the enemy; to *capture* a company of retreating soldiers; "he was making plans...to *capture* the banking of the country" (*Belloc*); "No artist can set out to *capture* charm; he will toil all the night and take nothing" (*A. C. Benson*). **Nab** and *cop* (both colloquial, the latter the more slangy term) imply a catching by means of which one is brought into custody, literally or figuratively; as, the boy was *nabbed* (or *copped*) by the police while stealing; "Ay, by my soul, you have *nabbed* me cleverly" (*Richardson*). **Cop, trap, snare, entrap,** and **ensnare** imply catching by a device which holds that which is caught in a position that is fraught with danger or difficulty, or from which escape is difficult or impossible. Literally, *trap* and *snare* imply the use of a trap or snare (see LURE, *n.*) but *entrap* and *ensnare* suggest trickery in capture more often than the use of an actual trap or snare: all four terms, both literally and figuratively, impute craft to the catcher and unwariness or lack of caution to the one that is caught. Distinctively, *trap* and *entrap* suggest a being held in a position where one is at the mercy of the captor and his designs, and *snare* and *ensnare* a being held so that the more one struggles the more desperate becomes one's situation; as, to *trap* an animal; to *snare* a bird; to *trap* a detachment of soldiers; "Themselves in bloody toils were *snared*" (*Scott*); to *entrap* wild elephants for use in a circus; to *entrap* a person into making a dangerous admission; "Let these *Ensnare* the wretched in the toils of law" (*Thomson*). **Bag** carries a double implication of catching (as game, specimens, etc.) and of putting them in a bag; as, he *bagged* several rare butterflies within the last month; to *bag* pheasants. So strong is the implication of catching and killing game in this use, that the word is often employed without suggestion of putting in a bag; as, they *bagged* three bears on their last hunting expedition.
Ana. Seize, *take, grasp, grab, clutch, snatch: apprehend, *arrest.
Ant. Miss.
2 *Incur, contract.

catching. Contagious, *infectious, communicable.

catchpole *or* **catchpoll.** Bailiff, constable, officer, *policeman, bobby, peeler, copper, cop, bull, gendarme.

catechism. *Creed, confession, symbol.
Ana. *Doctrine, dogma, tenet: belief, conviction, persuasion, view, *opinion.

catechize. Interrogate, quiz, examine, question, *ask, query, inquire, speer.

categorical. **1** *Ultimate, absolute.
Con. Hypothetical, conjectural, supposititious (see SUPPOSED): conditional, contingent, relative, *dependent.
2 Express, definite, *explicit, specific.
Ana. Positive, certain, *sure: *forthright, downright.
Con. Ambiguous, equivocal, vague, cryptic, enigmatic, *obscure: dubious, *doubtful, questionable, problematic.

cater, *v.* **Cater, purvey, pander** come into comparison when they mean to furnish a person or persons with that which satisfies his appetite or desires. **Cater** literally implies the provision of what is needed in the way of food and drink. "He that doth the ravens feed, Yea, providently *caters* for the sparrow" (*Shak.*). In modern use, however, the term more often implies provision of food and drink ready for the table; as, to *cater* for dinners, weddings, and receptions. In extended use, *cater* often implies the provision of something that appeals to another and often lower appetite; as, "He rarely *caters* for the populace of the theatre by such indecencies" (*Hallam*); "*Catering* to the national taste and vanity" (*Thackeray*). Often, especially when followed by *to*, the term implies a certain subserviency to popular standards or uncultivated tastes; as, to *cater* to the public demand for the sensational, the entertaining, the sentimental. **Purvey** usually suggests the provision of food, but sometimes of other material necessities such as lodgings and clothes. In contrast with *cater*, however, it suggests service as a source of supply, either as an agent through whom what is wanted may be found or as a merchant who sells the needed articles; as, merchants who *purveyed* to the troops during the Seven Years' War. In figurative use, especially when followed by *for* or, much less often, *to*, *purvey* implies the provision of whatever is needed to satisfy, delight, or indulge. "This for his lust insatiably *purveys*" (*Ken*). **Pander,** which etymologically means to supply someone with one that gratifies his lust, in its more frequent extended use implies a purveying of that which will gratify desires and passions which are degrading or base; it frequently connotes servility or truckling; as, to *pander* to depraved appetites; to *pander* to morbid tendencies; to *pander* to a venal official.

Ana. *Furnish, equip, appoint, accouter: pamper, *indulge, humor: *satisfy, content.

catharsis. Purgation, *purification, ablution, lustration.

cathartic. Purge, purgative, *physic, laxative, aperient.

catholic, *adj.* *Universal, ecumenical, cosmopolitan, cosmic.

Ana. *Whole, entire, total: all-round, many-sided, *versatile: prevalent, *prevailing, current.

Ant. Parochial: provincial. — ***Con.*** *Narrow, strait: bigoted, fanatic, enthusiastic (see corresponding nouns at ENTHUSIAST).

cause, *n.* **1 Cause, determinant, antecedent, reason, occasion** are here compared as denoting that which in whole or in part produces an effect or result. **Cause** is applicable to any circumstance, condition, event, force, or the like, that contributes to the production of an effect, or to any combination of circumstances, conditions, events, etc., that inevitably or necessarily brings about a result; as, one of the *causes* of the French Revolution was the bankruptcy of the government; every effect must have an adequate *cause;* what was the *cause* of this outbreak? "Water and soil pollution are the root *causes* of mortality in the tropics" (*V. Heiser*). *Cause* is sometimes loosely used of the agent whose activities are instrumental in bearing consequences (as, he is the *cause* of all our troubles) or of the motive which prompts one to action (as, he claimed to have just *cause* for his attack). A **determinant** is a circumstance, factor, element, quality, motive, or the like, that by itself or in combination with other circumstances, factors, etc., conditions, or fixes the nature of, a result, especially of a product or outcome; thus, environment is an important *determinant* of character; the ideals and the character of citizens are the final *determinants* of their form of government. " 'Imponderables,' which in philosophy as in politics are the most important factors of experience and *determinants* of action" (*Inge*). "Strength of organisation, shelter from foreign or other distant competition, command of markets in key industries—these...are the main direct *determinants* of wage-rates" (*J. A. Hobson*). **Antecedent,** as here considered, is applicable to any person or thing (often an object, sometimes a circumstance, condition, or event) that is responsible, usually in part, for a later existing person or thing, as by being one of its progenitors, precursors, or predeterminants. "It is certainly true that these twelfth-century windows...had no *antecedent*, and no fit succession" (*H. Adams*). "The *antecedents* of emperor-worship lay far back in history" (*Buchan*). "Insisting...that whatever happens could be explained simply and adequately if we knew its natural *antecedents*" (*Inge*). **Reason** is interchangeable with *cause* only as meaning specifically a traceable or explainable cause; it always implies therefore, as *cause* does not necessarily, that the effect is known or has actually been brought about. "There was a *reason* for Mark Twain's pessimism, a *reason* for that chagrin....That bitterness of his was the effect of a certain miscarriage in his creative life, a balked personality, an arrested development" (*Van W. Brooks*). **Occasion** applies to any situation or to any person, place, or event which provides a situation that, either directly or indirectly, serves to set in motion causes already existing or to translate them into acts; thus, the *cause* of a war may be a deep-rooted enmity between two peoples, the *occasion* of it, a relatively unimportant incident, such as the murder of a citizen of one country within the confines of the other; an *occasion* of sin may be a visit to a place, such as a saloon or public house, where the real *cause*, a propensity to drink, is not resisted.

Ana. *Motive, spring, incentive, inducement, spur, goad, impulse: motivation, activation, actuation (see corresponding verbs at ACTIVATE): agent, agency (see MEANS): *origin, root, source, prime mover.

Con. *Effect, result, consequence, outcome, issue.

2 *Suit, lawsuit, action, cause, case.

caustic. Caustic, mordant, mordacious, acrid, scathing come into comparison in their secondary senses when they mean stingingly incisive. **Caustic** usually implies a biting wit, a ready tongue or pen, and the power to drive disagreeable truths home. " 'I really do not know what to do with my books,' he said, and looked round for sympathy. 'Why not read them?' said a...*caustic* Fellow opposite" (*A. C. Benson*). **Mordant** is not always clearly distinguishable from *caustic*. In distinctive use, however, it suggests greater blighting power or deadlier effectiveness in the thrusts of wit; as, the *mordant* humor of G. B. Shaw. "Absolute master of a *mordant* pen" (*Lowes*). "Other aspects of American society were *mordantly* analyzed" (*Forum*). **Mordacious,** now comparatively rare, equals *mordant* in implications but is more often applied to persons or their qualities. "Grand-duke and taxes were synonimes, according to this *mordacious* lexicographer!"(*I. D'Israeli*). **Acrid** adds to *caustic* the implications of bitterness and, often, malevolence. "Most satirists are indeed a public scourge.... Their *acrid* temper turns...the milk of their good purpose all to curd" (*Cowper*). **Scathing** retains its etymological implication of injuring chiefly in its suggestion of a deliberate intent to scorch or blister. It seldom implies, as the other words of this group often imply, insensitiveness or maliciousness, and it often connotes both righteous indignation and fierce and withering severity; as, *scathing* censure or satire; a *scathing* exposure of graft.

Ana. Biting, cutting, *incisive, trenchant: *bitter: *sharp, keen, acute: *sarcastic, satirical, ironical.

Ant. Genial: lenient (*in strict sense*). — ***Con.*** *Suave, urbane, bland, diplomatic: *gracious, cordial: gentle, mild (see SOFT).

caution, *n.* Circumspection, wariness, chariness, calculation. See under CAUTIOUS.

Ana. Watchfulness, vigilance, alertness (see corresponding adjectives at WATCHFUL): *prudence, providence, foresight, forethought, discretion.

Ant. Temerity: adventurousness. — ***Con.*** Audacity, hardihood, nerve (see TEMERITY): rashness, recklessness, foolhardiness, daring, daredeviltry (see corresponding adjectives at ADVENTUROUS).

caution, *v.* *Warn, forewarn.

Ana. Admonish (see REPROVE): counsel, advise (see under ADVICE).

cautious. Cautious, circumspect, wary, chary, calculating agree in meaning prudently attentive to the dangers one may encounter or the risks one may face, or revealing such attentiveness. The same differences in implications and connotations are apparent in the nouns **caution, circumspection, wariness, chariness, calculation** when they denote the quality of the character or the mental processes of one who is so attentive. **Cautious** and **caution** usually imply both the prompting of fear, especially of fear of failure or of harm to oneself or others, and the exercise of forethought in planning, or of prudence in proceeding, so that the dangers of failure or the risks of disaster may be avoided or minimized; as, the troops advanced with great *caution;* a *cautious* investor. "For the most part, he generalizes with a sobriety and a *caution* worthy of the highest praise" (*A. Huxley*). "The old man, *cautious* in all his movements, always acting as if surrounded by invisible spies, delayed setting out until an hour after dark" (*Hudson*). **Circumspect** and **circumspection** (etymologically, looking all around) frequently, but not invariably, imply less fear than *cautious* and *caution;* commonly, however, they suggest the exercise of great prudence and discretion, especially in making decisions or in acting, and the surveying of all possible consequences, lest moral, social, business, or political harm may inadvertently occur. "And in all things that I have said unto you be *circumspect*" (*Exodus* xxiii. 13). "The...*circumspection* with which it [the U. S. Supreme Court] approaches the consideration of such questions" (*Ch. Just. Marshall*). **Wary** and **wariness** usually carry a far stronger suggestion of suspiciousness than *cautious* and *caution* and sometimes, as a result, connote less well-grounded fear. Often, also, the terms imply alertness in watching out for difficulties or dangers, or cunning in escaping them. "They...had a *wary* eye for all gregarious assemblages of people, and turned out of their road to avoid any very excited group of talkers" (*Dickens*). "A subtle diplomacy and *wary* tactics would be necessary" (*Bennett*). "Our domestic dogs are descended from wolves...they may not have gained in cunning, and may have lost in *waryness*" (*Darwin*). **Chary** and **chariness** imply the cautiousness of those who are careful of what they have or what they can give, say, do, or the like, and proceed with great reserve or discretion. "I am *chary* of admitting native differences between the sexes, but I think that girls are less prone than boys to punish oddity by serious physical cruelty" (*B. Russell*). "Nature favored our understanding in this case, but as a rule she is *chary* of such favors" (*Karl K. Darrow*). "There was no fastidious over-refined *chariness* in the use of that name" (*F. W. Robertson*). **Calculating** and **calculation** imply the caution of one who carefully and deliberately plans the way to attain his end (often, but not invariably, a selfish end) taking into account every possible danger and the way in which it can be met. "Some day the American boy's outlook upon the future may be as clear and *calculating* as that of his European brother" (*Grandgent*). "Only in regard to la France do they [the French] permit themselves illusions. Only here does sentiment triumph freely and completely over *calculation*" (*Brownell*). The suggestion of selfish prudence that disregards the cruelty of the means, provided the end is attained, is often so strong in these words that the implication of cautiousness is lost and that of cold-hearted scheming or of deliberate cruelty takes its place. "The terrible men are the men who do everything in cold blood, icily, with *calculation*" (*Hearn*).

Ana. *Watchful, vigilant, alert: prudent, provident, foresighted, forethoughted, discreet (see under PRUDENCE): heedful, careful (see negative adjectives at CARELESS).

Ant. Adventurous, temerarious. — ***Con.*** Venturous, venturesome, daring, rash, reckless, foolhardy (see ADVENTUROUS): *precipitate, impetuous, headlong.

cave in. Succumb, submit, *yield, capitulate, relent, defer, bow.

caviling, *adj.* Captious, faultfinding, censorious, carping, *critical, hypercritical.

Ana. Exacting, demanding (see DEMAND): *contrary, perverse: objecting, protesting, expostulating, kicking (see OBJECT).

Con. Accommodating, obliging, favoring (see OBLIGE): complaisant, *amiable, good-natured: conciliating, pacifying, mollifying, appeasing (see PACIFY).

cavity. Hollow, *hole, pocket, void, vacuum.

Con. Bulge, protuberance, protrusion, *projection.

cayman. Alligator, *crocodile.

cease. *Stop, quit, discontinue, desist.

Ana. End, terminate, *close, conclude, finish: stay, suspend, intermit (see DEFER).

Con. *Spring, arise, rise, originate: *begin, commence, start, initiate, inaugurate: *extend, prolong, protract: *continue, persist.

cede. Surrender, abandon, waive, resign, yield, *relinquish, leave.

Ana. *Grant, concede, award, accord, vouchsafe.

Con. Withhold, hold back, retain (see KEEP).

celebrate. Commemorate, solemnize, observe, *keep.

celebrated. Renowned, noted, *famous, famed, distinguished, eminent, illustrious, notorious.

Ana. Prominent, conspicuous, outstanding, signal (see NOTICEABLE).

Ant. Obscure (*of persons, achievements, etc.*).

celebrity. *Fame, renown, glory, honor, éclat, reputation, repute, notoriety.

Ana. Prominence, conspicuousness (see corresponding adjectives at NOTICEABLE).

Ant. Obscurity.

celerity. Celerity, alacrity, legerity are comparable when they are used in reference to human beings and denote quickness in movement or action. **Celerity** stresses speed in moving, or especially in accomplishing work. "The dinner...was dispatched with uncommon *celerity*" (*Peacock*). "She could, when she chose, work with astonishing *celerity*" (*Bennett*). **Alacrity** emphasizes promptness in response more than swiftness in movement, though the latter is usually implied. " 'You must wait till she sends for you—' and she winced a little at the *alacrity* of his acceptance" (*E. Wharton*). Very often also, it connotes eagerness or cheerful readiness. "France, where *alacrity* of service counted for more than the service itself" (*Hewlett*). "Working away at his subject with the *alacrity*...of a man...fulfilling the very office...for which nature had designed him" (*L. P. Smith*). **Legerity,** a less common word than the others, refers more to the quality than to the rate of speed, and implies nimbleness and ease; as, to cover the ground with the *legerity* of a trained runner. "When the mind is quick'ned...The organs...newly move, With...fresh *legerity*" (*Shak.*).

Ana. Expedition, dispatch, speed, hurry, *haste: quickness, rapidity, swiftness, fleetness (see corresponding adjectives at FAST): velocity, *speed: agility, briskness, nimbleness (see corresponding adjectives at AGILE).

Ant. Leisureliness. — *Con.* Slowness, deliberateness *or* deliberation, dilatoriness (see corresponding adjectives at SLOW): *lethargy, languor.

celestial, *adj.* **Celestial, heavenly, empyrean** (*or* **empyreal**) agree in meaning of, in, or from heaven or the heavens. **Celestial** (opposed to *terrestrial*) may refer either to the visible heavens (that is, the region surrounding the earth and seemingly enclosed by the sky) or to the religious conception of heaven or the heavens (that is, in Christian use, the abode of God, the angels, and the blessed dead); thus, a *celestial* globe is one on whose surface the stars, planets, comets, nebulae, etc., are depicted; a *celestial* body is a star, planet, or other aggregation of matter that forms a unit for astronomical study; a *celestial* visitant is an angel or other spirit from the spiritual heaven; *celestial* bliss is the happiness enjoyed by the souls in heaven. But *celestial* may also be used in reference to pagan conceptions of the abode of the gods; as, "That's a brave god, and bears *celestial* liquor" (*Shak.*); "*Celestial* Venus haunts Idalia's groves" (*Pope*). **Heavenly,** although it is applicable, especially in nontechnical use, to the visible heavens (as, "*heavenly* bodies"—*Bacon*) or to pagan conceptions of Olympus, or other abodes of the gods (as, "the immortal Sun, Who, borne by *heavenly* steeds his race doth run"—*Shelley*), is far more often applied to heaven as conceived by Jews and Christians and is apt, therefore, to suggest spiritual qualities; as, "your *heavenly* Father" (*Matthew* vi. 14); "They desire a better country, that is, an *heavenly*" (*Hebrews* xi. 16); "I thought that Liberty and Heaven To *heavenly* souls had been all one" (*Milton*). **Empyrean** suggests association with the empyrean, either as thought of in ancient and medieval cosmology as the highest celestial sphere, a region of light or fire (as, "From the Courts of the *Empyrean* dome Came forth ...a fiery car"—*Praed*) or, more often, as conceived by various theologians and poets as the highest of the spiritual heavens, where God is and reigns in spiritual light and fire (as, "Into the Heaven of Heavens I have presumed ...and drawn *empyreal* air"—*Milton*). The words, however, are chiefly poetic, and often somewhat vague as to which idea is in the poet's mind.

Ana. Ethereal, aerial, *airy: divine, spiritual, *holy.

Ant. Terrestrial. — *Con.* *Earthly, mundane, earthy, terrene, worldly, sublunary, mortal: *infernal, hellish, chthonian.

cement, *v.* **Cement, glue, agglutinate,** though synonymous in their literal senses are, in discriminating use, precisely differentiated in their extended senses. All three carry the meaning to cause to unite or stick together by or as if by the use of an adhesive or binder. **Cement,** literally, implies the use of a plastic substance, which by hardening holds things together firmly and indissolubly. "The molten matter...*cements* the loose ashes and cinders into a compact mass" (*T. H. Huxley*). Figuratively, it implies a solid grounding or a stiffening and fixing; as, the marriage of the English queen and the Spanish king was expected to *cement* the relations between the two countries. "The great writers of our own age are... forerunners of some unimagined change in our social condition or the opinions which *cement* it" (*Shelley*). **Glue,** literally, implies the use of some sticky or viscous substance that causes things to adhere; as, to *glue* two pieces of wood together: figuratively, however, it seldom connotes union but rather a fastening of one thing upon another, often with a suggestion of unpleasant effects; as, his eye was *glued* to the keyhole. "As a ferret in a blind burrow might *glue* himself comfortably to the neck of a rabbit" (*Kipling*). **Agglutinate** is now seldom found in its strictly literal sense implying the presence of a viscous substance that causes things to cohere. In its extended use, it commonly implies a natural or an innate tendency to cluster or stick together; as, a substance in the blood, such as an antibody, may *agglutinate* certain harmful bacteria; in some languages, words are commonly formed by *agglutination,* or the running together of primitive words into compounds.

Ana. *Join, unite, combine: *stick, adhere, cohere.

cenobite *or* **coenobite.** *Recluse, eremite, hermit, anchorite.

Ana. Monk, friar, *religious, nun.

cenobitic, cenobitical *or* **coenobitic, coenobitical.** *Monastic, monachal, monkish.

censorious. Faultfinding, *critical, hypercritical, captious, carping, caviling.

Ana. Reproaching *or* reproachful, chiding (see corresponding verbs at REPROVE): condemning *or* condemnatory, denouncing *or* denunciatory, reprehending (see corresponding verbs at CRITICIZE).

Ant. Eulogistic. — *Con.* Praising, extolling, lauding *or* laudatory, acclaiming *or* acclamatory (see corresponding verbs at PRAISE): complimenting *or* complimentary, flattering, adulatory (see corresponding nouns at COMPLIMENT).

censure, *v.* *Criticize, reprehend, blame, condemn, denounce, reprobate.

Ana. Reprimand, rebuke, reproach, *reprove: upbraid, berate, tonguelash (see SCOLD).

Ant. Commend. — *Con.* Applaud, compliment, recommend (see COMMEND): eulogize, laud, *praise.

center, *n.* **Center** (*or* **centre**), **middle, midst, core, hub, omphalos, focus, nucleus, heart** are here compared as meaning the point, spot, or portion of a thing which literally or figuratively is comparable to a point around which a circle is described. Literally, **center** approximates more or less closely its strict geometrical sense as the point within a circle or sphere that is equidistant from every other point on the circumference or is the average distance from the exterior points of a body or figure; as, the *center* of a circle, of a table, of a target, of a ball, of a lake, of the earth. Figuratively, *center* applies to anything or to any part of a thing which suggests a geometrical center, as being the point around which everything else rotates or revolves (as, "each airy thought revolved Round a substantial *centre*"—*Wordsworth*) or at which all lines, as of activity, converge (as, "Draw to one point, and to one *centre* bring Beast, Man, or Angel, Servant, Lord, or King"—*Pope*) or from which every line, branch, or the like, radiates (as, a railroad *center;* a power *center*) or which lies midway between extremes (thus, especially in Europe, a party of moderate views, neither conservative [the right] nor radical [the left] is often called the *center*). Literally, **middle** is less precise than *center,* and suggests a space rather than a point; it is the part of an object which surrounds the center; thus, the *middle* of a room is the central portion of it. "They have what they call a central depôt here, because it's the *middle* of England" (*Bennett*). *Middle,* unlike *center,* also applies to that which has duration (as, the *middle* of the night), and to merely linear extension (as, the *middle* of the road). Figuratively, *middle* applies chiefly to that which lies between the beginning and end, as of a process, a course, a piece of work, or the like; as, he was stopped in the *middle* of his speech; a play should have a beginning, *middle,* and end. **Midst** is often used in place of *middle* for a point or spot well within a group or number of enveloping persons or objects, or figuratively, of things such as duties, affairs, burdens, and the like, that surround or beset one; however, it seldom occurs except in a prepositional phrase introduced by *in, into, from, out of*, and the like; as, he stood in the *midst* of a crowd; he penetrated into the *midst* of the forest; "Sense of right, Uppermost in the *midst* of fiercest strife" (*Wordsworth*). **Core,** literally the portion of a fruit of the apple family which lies at its center and is made up of papery or leathery envelopes containing seeds, is by extension applied to anything that similarly lies at the center of a thing, and that resembles an apple core, as in being unconsumed or unused (thus, the unburnt portion of a coal or of a lump of lime is called a *core*), or in forming a firm central mass in a growth (as, the *core* of a boil), or in having a different character from that which surrounds or encloses it (thus, a corncob, in Australian use, is the *core* of an ear of Indian corn; in cabinetmaking soft wood on which veneers are glued is called a *core*), or more often, especially in figurative use, as in being the very center of a thing's life, significance, power, or the like. "I will wear him In my heart's *core*, ay, in my heart of heart" (*Shak.*). "My own dim life should teach me this, That life shall live for evermore, Else earth is darkness at the *core*" (*Tennyson*). "The Romans...proved rebellious to the idea that living is an art; yet it may well be that they still retained that idea at the *core* of their morality" (*H. Ellis*). **Hub,** literally the central and usually solid part of a wheel from which the spokes radiate and which rotates on (or with) the axle, is figuratively and often humorously applied to any place, person, or thing on which all other places, persons, or things depend for their life, activity, ideas, progress, or the like. "Boston State-house is the *hub* of the solar system" (*Holmes*). "Listen! John A. Logan is the Head Center, the *Hub*, the King Pin, the Main Spring...of the...plot by which partisanship was installed in the Commission" (*N. Y. Herald-Tribune*). **Omphalos,** literally a navel, is less frequently used than *hub* in much the same figurative sense. "Bideford Bridge ...is the very *omphalos*, cynosure, and soul, around which the town [of Bideford]...has organised itself" (*Kingsley*). **Focus,** etymologically a hearth, or fireplace, is applicable to any point of convergence or concentration, or in less precise use, of emanation; thus, the point at which rays of light meet after reflection or refraction is called a *focus*; a person to whom all eyes are turned is the *focus* of attention. "It [Antioch] was...a place of exchange for the merchandise of East and West, the nearest point to the Euphrates, and the *focus* of a network of trade routes" (*Buchan*). "We may say...that they [the arts and the sciences] all emanate from the same *focus*" (*H. Ellis*). **Nucleus,** literally the kernel, or the innermost part, of a nut or seed, applies in its extended senses to the vital and usually small and stable center of a larger mass, about which matter is gathered or concentrated, or to which accretions are made; as, the *nucleus* of a cell; the *nucleus* of an atom or of an assemblage of atoms; a small but good collection of books as a *nucleus* for his library. "[D. H. Lawrence] unable to recreate a satisfactory social group from the *nucleus* of his own individuality" (*Day Lewis*). **Heart,** like the organ from which it derives its figurative implications, applies to a place or thing that lies well within a region, a system, or the like, and which, usually, constitutes the source of life and power of the entire region or system; as, "exploits done in the *heart* of France" (*Shak.*); "Rome was the *heart*...of the empire...and on its well-being hung the future of the civilized world" (*Buchan*). "His proposals for making that Sunday School...the *heart* and *focus* of the parochial life" (*C. Mackenzie*).

Con. *Circumference, periphery, perimeter, compass: bounds, confines, limits (see singular nouns at LIMIT).

centuried. *Secular, agelong, aeonian, diuturnal.

Ana. *Lasting, perdurable, durable, stable, permanent, perpetual: established, settled, fixed (see SET).

cerebral. *Mental, intellectual, psychic, intelligent.

ceremonial, *adj.* **Ceremonial, ceremonious, formal, conventional, solemn** come into comparison when they mean characterized or marked by attention to the forms, details, etc., prescribed as right, proper, or requisite. Both **ceremonial** and **ceremonious** imply strict attention to what is prescribed by the etiquette or tradition of the court or of polite society, by the ritual of a church, or by the formalities of the law for an occasion, a ceremony, a procedure, or the like. But in present usage *ceremonial* applies only to things that in themselves are ceremonies or form an essential part of a ceremony or follow a set and elaborate procedure; as, the new ambassador made a *ceremonial* call on the president; "*ceremonial* observances and outward show" (*Hallam*); "the crisp, *ceremonial* laurel wreath of the Roman conqueror" (*Pater*). *Ceremonious* applies to things that are attended with ceremony (frequently elaborate or impressive), or to persons who are addicted (or to acts which show addiction) to a punctilious observance of formalities; as, "Let us take a *ceremonious* leave" (*Shak.*); "[He] repeated the responses very audibly, evincing that kind of *ceremonious* devotion punctually observed by a gentleman of the old school" (*Irving*); "the *ceremonious* extinguishing of the candles" (*L. P. Smith*). **Formal,** as synonymous with *ceremonial*, suggests set form or procedure rather than external ceremonies; as, a *formal* call (cf. *ceremonial* call); *formal* dress. As synonymous with *ceremonious*, *formal* suggests stiffness, restraint, decorousness, rather than impressive dignity or punctiliousness. "The fatigue and slavery of maintaining a ceremonial, more stiff, *formal*, and oppressive than the etiquette of a German elector" (*Smollett*). "The habits of the family...may be termed *formal*, and old-fashioned by such visitors as claim to be the pink of the mode" (*Scott*). **Conventional** applies to that which is in accord with or governed by the recognized, frequently artificial, conventions or standards; it connotes lack of originality or independence; as, a *conventional* expression of regret; the *conventional* white tie with men's full evening dress; a highly *conventional* person; "the discord...between *conventionality* and originality" (*C. Waldstein*). **Solemn,** as here compared, is used only in relation to religious observances or services and to certain acts the conduct of which is prescribed by law. The term implies, usually, strict attention to every detail that is prescribed or allowed by the ritual of the church or by the formalities of the law; thus, a *solemn* Mass is one in which the full liturgy is followed; a *solemn* feast is one celebrated not only by the full liturgy but by other ceremonial observances such as processions, pageants, and the like; a *solemn* war is one that begins with a formal declaration of war; so, the probate of a will in *solemn* (as distinguished from *common*) form.

Ana. Liturgical, ritualistic (see corresponding nouns at FORM).

ceremonial, *n.* Ceremony, ritual, rite, liturgy, *form.

ceremonious. *Ceremonial, formal, solemn, conventional.

Ana. Impressive, *moving: *decorous, seemly, proper, comme il faut: stately, imposing, majestic, grandiose (see GRAND).

Ant. Unceremonious, informal.

ceremony. Ceremonial, ritual, liturgy, rite, *form, formality.

certain, *adj.* **1** Positive, *sure, cocksure.
Ana. *Confident, assured, sanguine.
Ant. Uncertain. — ***Con.*** *Doubtful, dubious, questionable.
2 Certain, inevitable, necessary, apodictic (*or* **apodictical, apodeictic, apodeictical**) come into comparison only when they mean bound to follow in obedience to the laws of nature or of thought. That is **certain** which does not admit of being described as probable, even in the highest conceivable degree, and which, therefore, is beyond question or dispute; as, death is the only future event we can regard as *certain;* "it is *certain* that effects must have a cause" (*Bp. Butler*). That is **inevitable** (see also INEVITABLE) which is what it must be (sometimes should be) according to the unchangeable laws of nature, laws of logic, laws of beauty, and the like. In this sense *inevitable* often carries no suggestion of unavoidability, its etymological implication, but stresses finality, as in truth or rightness, or an ultimate character, such as perfection. "The results obtained in an actual experiment ....seem nonsensical...when we picture light as bullets, but perfectly natural and *inevitable* when we picture it as waves" (*Jeans*). "The design is, indeed, so happy, so right, that it seems *inevitable;* the design is the story and the story is the design" (*Cather*). That is **necessary** which is logically or naturally inevitable and which cannot be denied without resulting contradiction or frustration. "Most of the distinctions of law are distinctions of degree. If the States had any power it was assumed that they had all power and that the *necessary* alternative was to deny it altogether" (*Justice Holmes*). "His [Shakespeare's] plays are the *necessary* expression of his mind and character, not the *necessary* conditions of his existence"(*Inge*). That is **apodictic** which is logically necessary or the logical necessity of which can be demonstrated; as, *apodictic* truths; "the *apodictic* certainty belonging to mathematical conclusions" (*G. H. Lewes*).
Ant. Probable: supposed. — ***Con.*** Possible, likely (see PROBABLE): precarious (see DANGEROUS).

certainty. Certainty, certitude, assurance, conviction are here compared only as denoting a state of mind in which one is free from doubt. **Certainty** and **certitude** both imply the absence of all doubt as to the truth of something; they are not always distinguishable in use, although philosophers and psychologists have often tried to distinguish the states of mind which they designate. The psychological differentiation of *certainty* as the state of mind induced by that of which there is objectively, as well as subjectively, not the slightest question, from *certitude,* as the state of mind of one whose faith or belief is so strong that it resists all attack, has indubitably affected the meanings and the use of these terms by careful writers and speakers; as, to know something with scientific *certainty;* some philosophies tend to destroy man's *certainty* of his own existence; one has *certainty* of nothing in the future, even that the sun will rise tomorrow, but that does not weaken one's *certitude* that the world will go on indefinitely. "*Certitude* is not the test of *certainty.* We have been cocksure of many things that were not so" (*Justice Holmes*). In looser use, however, *certitude* usually suggests deeper roots for one's freedom from doubt than *certainty,* or less likelihood of a change of belief. "Robert did so well in the lawyer's office that by-and-by his...assurance came back to him, his old intelligent *certainty* of ability" (*Deland*). "One thing, however, we feel with irresistible *certitude,* that Mark Twain's fate was once for all decided there" (*Van W. Brooks*). **Assurance** (see also CONFIDENCE, 2) stresses sureness and confidence rather than certainty; the grounds of such sureness are not objective proofs or the evidence of one's senses, for that of which one has assurance is usually something that is indemonstrable or is yet to happen; the word usually suggests implicit reliance on oneself (one's powers, one's intuitions, one's methods, etc.) or complete trust in another (as one's source of information, one's supporter, one's sovereign, God). "I'll make *assurance* double sure, And take a bond of fate" (*Shak.*). "Faith is the *assurance* of things hoped for" (*Hebrews* xi. 1, *R.V.*). "Rather, it might be said that he [Emerson] went beyond hope to the *assurance* of present happiness" (*P. E. More*). **Conviction** usually, but not invariably, implies previous doubt or uncertainty. It involves the idea of *certitude,* but is not its equivalent, for *certitude* may or may not imply a rational basis for one's freedom from doubt, and *conviction,* in careful use (but see also OPINION), commonly does. It differs from *certainty* in stressing one's subjective reaction to evidence rather than the objective validity of the evidence itself. *Conviction* is therefore commonly applied to the state of mind of one who has been, or is in the process of being, convinced. "Rational assent [to the dogmas of Christianity] may arrive late, intellectual *conviction* may come slowly, but they come inevitably without violence to honesty and nature" (*T. S. Eliot*). "She does not wish me to go unless with a full *conviction* that she is right" (*Conrad*).
Ana. *Belief, faith, credence: proof, demonstration (see under PROVE).
Ant. Uncertainty. — ***Con.*** Doubt, skepticism, mistrust (see UNCERTAINTY).

certify. 1 Certify, attest, witness, vouch for come into comparison when they mean to testify to the truth or genuineness of something. **Certify** usually implies a statement in writing, especially one that carries one's signature or seal or both, or one that is legally executed; thus, a *certified* check carries the guarantee of a bank that the signature is genuine and that there are sufficient funds on deposit to meet it; a certificate of a school is a document in which the proper authorities *certify* that the holder has met the requirements of a course or the school and has passed a final examination. "They said their chemists...could *certify* on their honor that their extract contained no salicylic acid" (*V. Heiser*). **Attest** (see also INDICATE) implies oral or written testimony from a person in a position to know the facts, usually but not invariably given under oath or on one's word of honor; thus, when one says that something is well *attested,* one implies that there is sufficient documentary or oral testimony from competent persons to warrant its acceptance. "The pleader...had witness ready to *attest*... that every article was true" (*Swift*). "But of the Mediaeval university the lawlessness, though well *attested,* can scarcely be conceived" (*Quiller-Couch*). In current legal use, *attest* is used chiefly in reference to the official authentication of a document, such as a will, a deed, a record, or to the guaranteeing of the genuineness of a signature, to a statement or oath, or the like, by a notary public, a commissioner of deeds, or the like. "An *attested* copy of the marriage record" (*Cather*). **Witness** as here compared implies attestation, but not necessarily official or notarial attestation, of a signature of a statement, a will, a bond, or the like, by one who has seen that signature actually made and who subscribes his own name to the document as evidence of its genuineness; as, he called in two of his servants to *witness* the signature to his will. **Vouch for** now rarely implies official or legal proof, which the other words in this group so often do imply, but it suggests that the one who testifies is a competent authority or a reliable person who will stand behind his affirmation and support it further if necessary. "*For* the

exactness of this story [of a purported miracle] in all its details, Bishop James of Voragio could not have *vouched*, nor did it greatly matter. What he could *vouch for* was the relation of intimacy and confidence between his people and the Queen of Heaven" (*H. Adams*).
Ana. Testify, depose, depone, asseverate, affirm, *swear: avouch, avow, aver, *assert.
2 Endorse, accredit, *approve, sanction.
Ana. Vouch for (see CERTIFY): *authorize, commission, license.
Con. Reject, repudiate, refuse (see DECLINE).

certitude. *Certainty, assurance, conviction.
Ana. *Belief, faith, credence, credit: sureness, positiveness, cocksureness (see corresponding adjectives at SURE).
Ant. Doubt. — *Con.* *Uncertainty, skepticism, mistrust.

cess. Rate, *tax, levy, assessment, excise, impost, customs, duty, toll, tariff, tribute, tithe, teind.

chafe. Fret, gall, *abrade, excoriate.

chaff, *v.* *Banter, rally, kid, rag, guy, jolly, rib, josh, quiz.
Ana. Tease, tantalize, *worry: *ridicule, deride, twit, taunt.

chagrined. Mortified, *ashamed.
Ana. Discomfited, abashed, embarrassed, disconcerted (see EMBARRASS): humiliated (see ABASE): discomposed, perturbed, upset (see DISCOMPOSE).

chain, *n.* Series, train, string, set, sequence, suit, suite, *succession, progression.

chamber. **1** *Room, apartment.
2 In plural form **chambers.** *Rooms, lodgings, quarters, diggings, digs, apartment, flat, tenement.

champion, *n.* **1** Vanquisher, *victor, winner, conqueror.
2 Backer, advocate, upholder, supporter. See under SUPPORT, *v.*

champion, *v.* Back, advocate, uphold, *support.
Ana. *Contend (for), fight (for), battle (for): espouse (see ADOPT): defend, justify, vindicate, *maintain: aid, assist, *help.
Ant. Combat. — *Con.* *Oppose, resist, withstand: condemn, denounce (see CRITICIZE).

chance, *n.* **1 Chance, accident, fortune, luck, hap, hazard,** as here compared, agree in designating that which happens without an apparent or determinable cause or as a result of unpredictable forces. **Chance** serves often as a general name for the incalculable and fortuitous element in human existence and in nature and is usually opposed to *law* (see PRINCIPLE). "It is incorrect to say that any phenomenon is produced by *chance;* but we may say that two or more phenomena are conjoined by *chance*...meaning that they are in no way related by causation" (*J. S. Mill*). In nontechnical use, *chance* seldom loses implications derived from its early association with the casting of dice or lots and the selection of one out of many possibilities by this means. Consequently, it may mean determination by irrational, uncontrollable forces; as, to leave things to *chance:* it may mean degree of probability; as, his *chance* of success is one in ten: it may mean one possibility of success among many possibilities of failure; as, he is always willing to take a *chance.* **Accident** is interchangeable with *chance* only when a particular event or situation is in mind; as, it happened by *accident* (or, by *chance*). It differs from *chance* mainly in its emphasis on lack of intention. "Buildings are not grouped like that by pure *accident*" (*Cather*). "The extension of her [Rome's] boundaries had been achieved rather by *accident* than by design" (*Buchan*). **Fortune,** owing to its historical connection with the ancient Roman goddess of chance, Fortuna, often designates the hypothetical cause of that which happens fortuitously; as, *fortune* favored him in his first attempt. It also often suggests qualities ascribed to the goddess, such as variability, fickleness, and malignity. "I may conquer *fortune's* spite By living low, where *fortune* cannot hurt me" (*Shak.*). "Vicissitudes of *fortune*" (*Gibbon*). *Fortune* is also applied to the issue or outcome of an undertaking the success of which is problematical; as, the *fortunes* of the chase. "Now heaven send thee good *fortune!*" (*Shak.*). **Luck** differs from *fortune* chiefly in its connotations. It not only lacks the dignity accruing to *fortune* through the latter's mythological associations, but it is somewhat debased by its association, etymologically and in continued use, with gambling. Because of its colloquial quality, it is preferable in contexts where *fortune* would seem bookish; as, bad *luck* followed him all his days; it was just our *luck* to miss that train; the fisherman had good *luck* today. *Luck* unqualified can, however, imply success or a happy outcome, as *fortune* unqualified rarely does; as, I wish you *luck;* he had *luck* in all his adventures. **Hap** commonly denotes that which (or something which) falls to one's lot; as, throughout their lives they had known good *hap* and evil *hap*. Even when personified, it differs from *luck* and *fortune* in implying actual occurrence; as, as *hap* would have it, I missed the train (cf. if *fortune* [not *hap*] permits me to catch the train). **Hazard,** which originally denoted a game of dice in which the chances are complicated by arbitrary rules, is now often used in place of *accident*, especially when there is the traceable but not predictable influence of existing conditions or of concomitant circumstances. "Men and women danced together, women danced together, men danced together, as *hazard* had brought them together" (*Dickens*). "The choice [of examples] has been determined more by the *hazards* of my recent reading than by anything else" (*A. Huxley*).
Ana. Contingency, emergency, pass, *juncture, exigency.
Ant. Law (see PRINCIPLE). — *Con.* Inevitableness *or* inevitability, necessariness *or* necessity, certainty (see corresponding adjectives at CERTAIN).
2 *Opportunity, occasion, break, time, tide.
Ana. Possibility, likelihood, probability (see corresponding adjectives at PROBABLE): *prospect, outlook, foretaste, anticipation.

chance, *v.* *Happen, hap, befall, betide, occur, transpire.

chance, *adj.* *Random, haphazard, chancy, casual, desultory, hit-or-miss, happy-go-lucky.

chancy. Haphazard, chance, hit-or-miss, happy-go-lucky, *random, casual, desultory.

change, *v.* **Change, alter, vary, modify** (and their corresponding nouns **change, alteration, variation, modification**), agree in denoting to make or become different (or in denoting a difference effected). **Change** implies either an essential difference, even a loss of identity, or the substitution of one thing for another. "Can the Ethiopian *change* his skin, or the leopard his spots?" (*Jeremiah* xiii. 23). "And Earth be *changed* to Heaven, and Heaven to Earth" (*Milton*). **Alter** stresses difference in some particular respect, as in form or detail, without implying loss of identity; as, one may *alter* a coat without *changing* its style. "The whole existing order must be, if ever so slightly, *altered*" (*T. S. Eliot*). "External circumstances may *change* catastrophically, as during a war; or gradually, as when means of production are *altered*" (*A. Huxley*). The two words are, however, frequently interchangeable. **Vary** frequently implies a difference or a series of differences due to shifting, diversification, growth, etc.; as, the temperature *varies* greatly during the day; to *vary* one's diet. "Any intelligent effort to *vary* or improve the effect" (*H. Adams*). Sometimes it implies a deviation from the normal, the conventional, the usual, etc. "The voice of a town-crier, *varied* by a bitter accentuation and satiric sing-song tone" (*Meredith*). "This is not a proceeding which may be *varied*...but is a precise course...to be strictly pursued" (*Ch. Just. Marshall*). **Modify,** when used with a full sense of its historic meaning, suggests, now more often than implies, a difference that limits or restricts; thus, an adjective is said to *modify* a noun because it definitely reduces the range of application of that noun, as *old* in "old men" and *red* in "a red rose." Oftentimes it implies moderation, as of severity, or toning down, as of excess. "In London, in Vienna...traffic rules were *modified* to let him [Mark Twain] pass in the street" (*Van W. Brooks*). "Sophia was at first set down as overbearing. But in a few days this view was *modified*" (*Bennett*). In looser, but still correct, usage it often suggests minor changes or absence of radical changes. "History shows you men whose master-touch Not so much *modifies* as makes anew" (*Browning*).

Ana. *Transform, metamorphose, transmute, convert, transmogrify: *exchange, interchange: fluctuate, oscillate (see SWING, *v.*).

Con. Settle, *set, establish, fix: endure, abide, *continue, persist.

change, *n.* **1** Alteration, variation, modification. See under CHANGE, *v.*

Ana. *Variety, diversity: divergence, *deviation, aberration.

Ant. Uniformity: monotony.

2 Change, mutation, permutation, vicissitude, alternation come into comparison especially in their concrete senses. **Change,** the inclusive term, denotes not only any variation, alteration, or modification in a thing, as in its form, substance, or aspect, but also any substitution of one thing for another; as, he could detect no *change* in her when they met again; the body undergoes *changes* during puberty; a *change* of season; a *change* of clothes often makes a *change* in one's appearance. *Mutation* and *permutation* are applied to a change within a thing or in a combination of things regarded as a whole or unit. **Mutation** stresses lack of permanence or stability; in older use it was applied to variations or alterations that are expected only because they are inherent in the nature of things, but are otherwise fortuitous or unaccountable. "O world! But that thy strange *mutations* make us hate thee, Life would not yield to age" (*Shak.*). In modern use, these latter implications have been much affected by the theory of evolution; the term often connotes suddenness and unpredictableness, but seldom implies impossibility of explanation; often also it implies orderly change. "So far as reality means experienceable reality, both it and the truths men gain about it are everlastingly in process of *mutation—mutation* towards a definite goal, it may be" (*W. James*). **Permutation** implies transposition within a group or combination of things without change in the constituent elements or parts of that group or combination. It is now used largely in reference to a change in position within a group of digits, letters, and the like; as, the 26 letters of the alphabet are capable of endless combinations and *permutations*. In literary use, however, it implies a rearrangement of constituent elements that effects a change in relations, emphasis, or significance, and so gives a new form to what is substantially the same material. "Conventions beget conventions, to be sure, and their ramifications and *permutations* are endless" (*Lowes*). "[Pater's] *permutation* of Arnold's view of life" (*T. S. Eliot*). **Vicissitude** implies a change so great as to seem a substitution for, or a reversal of, what has been. Sometimes, it is applied to such changes as occur in natural succession or from one extreme to another. "Nature indeed vouchsafes for our delight The sweet *vicissitudes* of day and night" (*Cowper*). "Like walking in a wood where there is...a constant *vicissitude* of light and shade" (*J. R. Lowell*). More often, it is applied to a sweeping and unpredictable change that overturns what has been, and so has the character of a revolution or an upheaval. "The place and the object gave ample scope for moralising on the *vicissitudes* of fortune, which spares neither man nor the proudest of his works, which buries empires and cities in a common grave" (*Gibbon*). This implication of reverse is now so strong that the original implication of succession in turn is gradually disappearing (see DIFFICULTY). **Alternation,** though derived from the verb *alternate* (see ROTATE, 2) and therefore often limited to succession of two things in turn, is now used, as *vicissitude* once was, of two or more things; as, the *alternation* of the seasons.

Ana. Metamorphosis, transformation, conversion, transmutation, transmogrification (see under TRANSFORM): substitute, surrogate, shift (see RESOURCE).

changeable. Changeable, changeful, variable, mutable, protean come into comparison as meaning having or showing a marked capacity for changes or a marked tendency to alter itself or be altered under the slightest provocation. **Changeable,** the ordinary and most comprehensive term of this group, usually suggests this capacity or tendency as a characteristic or property that is the result of inconstancy, fickleness, an unsettled state, a ready responsiveness to certain influences, a roving habit, or the like; as, *changeable* weather; " 'young men especially...are so amazingly *changeable* [i.e., in their affections or interests]' " (*Austen*); a *changeable* disposition; a *changeable* silk (that is, one that seems to change its color with each change of position or point of view. **Changeful** is not only a more poetic term than *changeable* but it throws greater stress on the fact of changing frequently rather than on the underlying characteristic or property which manifests itself in such changes; as, "The *changeful* April day" (*Southey*); "His course had been *changeful*" (*Motley*); "He felt that life was *changeful*, fluid, active, and that to allow it to be stereotyped into any form was death" (*Wilde*); "All your charms more *changeful* than the tide" (*Millay*). **Variable** carries an implication of subjection to frequent and, often, deeper changes than either of the preceding words: it stresses shifting or fluctuation as a characteristic or property and, therefore, usually connotes uncertainty or unpredictability; as, a region of *variable* winds; "Man himself was a *variable*, mixed and transitory creature; he could not escape the law of his own being" (*L. P. Smith*); "the methods of statistics are so *variable* and uncertain...that it is never possible to be sure that one is operating with figures of equal weight" (*H. Ellis*); "The ends which individual works of art attempt to achieve are...diverse, and the means...[employed] seem almost infinitely *variable*" (*J. W. Krutch*). **Mutable** also implies subjection to change, but it suggests an opposition to *unchanging, fixed,* or *permanent*, and therefore is less often applied to that which is fluctuating and variable than to that which, in living, growing, developing, or the like, exhibits changes due to progression or retrogression or to external influences or conditions over which the thing affected has no control; as, "my lord, you know what Virgil sings, Woman is various and most *mutable*" (*Tennyson*); "Our valuation of poetry...depends upon several considerations, upon the permanent and upon the *mutable* and transitory" (*T. S. Eliot*); "All that gladdens, saddens, maddens us men and women on this brief and *mutable*

traject [i.e., passage, or course of existence]" (*Quiller-Couch*). **Protean** suggests a capacity for assuming many different forms or shapes, in the manner of the god Proteus, without loss of identity: the term therefore implies changeability with respect to outer manifestations rather than inner character or nature; as, an amoeba is a *protean* animalcule; the *protean* genius of Shakespeare; "For poetry is *protean* in its moods and dispositions, and its diction changes with its bents and its occasions" (*Lowes*).
Ana. Unstable, *inconstant, mercurial, capricious, fickle: mobile, *movable, motile.
Ant. Stable: unchangeable. — ***Con.*** Set, fixed, settled, established (see SET, *v.*): unceasing, *everlasting: enduring, abiding, persisting *or* persistent (see corresponding verbs at CONTINUE).

changeful. *Changeable, variable, protean, mutable.
Ana. Fluid (see under LIQUID, *n.*): *active, dynamic, live: progressing, advancing (see ADVANCE, *v.*): declining, deteriorating, degenerating (see corresponding nouns at DETERIORATION).
Ant. Changeless: stereotyped. — ***Con.*** Constant, uniform, *steady: stable, *lasting, durable, perdurable.

channel. **1** Passage, *strait, straits, narrows, sound.
2 Vehicle, *means, instrument, instrumentality, organ, agency, agent.

chantry. *Altar, tabernacle, shrine.

chaos. **1** *Confusion, disorder, disarray, jumble, clutter, pie, snarl, muddle.
Ant. System. — ***Con.*** Ordering *or* order, organization, (see corresponding verbs at ORDER): organism, scheme (see SYSTEM).
2 *Anarchy, lawlessness.

chaotic. *Formless, unformed, shapeless, inchoate, amorphous.
Ant. Orderly. — ***Con.*** Systematic, methodical (see ORDERLY): ordered, organized, systematized, arranged (see ORDER, *v.*).

chapbook. *Anthology, garland, florilegium, treasury, thesaurus, corpus, chrestomathy.

chaperon, *v.* *Accompany, attend, escort, convoy, conduct.
Ana. Protect, shield, guard, safeguard (see DEFEND).

char, *v.* *Burn, scorch, sear, singe.

char, *n.* Variant of CHARE.

character, *n.* **1 Character, symbol, sign, mark, note** are here compared only in the specific sense of an arbitrary or conventional device that is used in writing and in printing, but is neither a word nor a phrase nor a picture. **Character** (etymologically something engraved) always suggests the generally accepted form or shape of such a device; it is applicable to any letter of an alphabet, to any digit in arithmetical notation, to any note in musical notation, or to any single and simple figure or diagram which is the conventional representation of something, such as a comma (,), a direction to delete (ϑ), a minute in degree (′), an indication of G clef in music (𝄞), or the like. **Symbol** is often used interchangeably with *character* in this sense; in precise use, however, it is employed when the meaning or significance of the character rather than its shape is stressed; thus, one would say that for each letter in the English alphabet there are four *characters*, two (small letter and capital) for writing and two (lower-case and capital) for printing; each letter of an alphabet is a *symbol* for a speech sound; the *character* ? is the *symbol* used to indicate that a question has been asked. However, *symbol* and *character* are not always interchangeable, for single characters may be symbols for different things; thus, the *character* X is the twenty-fourth letter of the English alphabet, and a *symbol* for the sound associated with that letter, but it is also a *symbol* for an unknown quantity in algebra, for the number ten in Roman notation, etc. *Symbol* is also sometimes extended to other devices than those strictly called *characters*, such as abbreviations (as, O is the *symbol* for oxygen), as diagrams or schematic figures (as, ⊛ is the *symbol* for full moon in calendars), or as more or less arbitrary arrangements of numerals, letters, or other characters (as, 12mo, or 12°, is the *symbol* for duodecimo). **Sign,** like *symbol,* stresses the meaning rather than the form of the device; unlike *symbol,* however, it is seldom interchangeable with *character,* either because it may be a complicated device involving many characters, or because it is less arbitrary and actually suggests through its shape or form the thing which it signifies. There is a tendency therefore to prefer *sign* to *symbol* when the device is complicated or in its form gives a hint of what it represents, either because it is a schematic representation of the thing (as, ⊛ is the *sign* for full moon; ᑎ is a highway *sign* for double right curves; △ is in botany the *sign* for an evergreen tree, many of which are conifers) or because it has figurative associations with the idea represented (as, →, an arrow, or *sign* indicating direction; Ω, a horseshoe, or *sign* of good luck). *Sign,* however, is used idiomatically of characters indicating a mathematical operation (as, the plus *sign* [+]; the minus *sign* [−]), and of those indicating one of the twelve divisions of the Zodiac (♈ is the *sign* of Aries, the Ram). **Mark** comes closer to *character* than *symbol* or *sign,* because it carries little, if any, suggestion of reference to an idea. It is the ordinary designation of any of various characters that are used to make clear the meaning of a passage but that add nothing to that meaning (as, punctuation *marks,* such as the comma [,] or the question *mark* [?]) or that indicate to the eye how words should be pronounced (as, pronunciation *marks* such as the acute accent [´] or the cedilla c [ç]; diacritical *marks* such as ¨ over the vowel a). In music, *sign* and *mark* are sometimes used interchangeably, but more often conventionally in given phrases; thus, 𝆒 is called either the crescendo *mark* or *sign; :S:* is called the repeat *sign* and 𝄇 the repeat *marks;* the arrangement of sharps and flats after a clef is called the *sign* of the key (or technically, *key signature*). **Note,** as here compared, is now used chiefly in reference to any of the characters which in written or printed music indicate by their shape the relative duration of a tone, and by their position on a staff, the pitch of a tone; as, ♩ is a quarter *note;* the first *note* on the staff is *b,* and the second is *d. Note* is sometimes used in place of *mark,* especially for a punctuation mark that indicates an inflection or tone; as, ? is a *note* of interrogation. This use is not now as common as formerly.
2 *Quality, property, attribute, accident.
Ana. Characteristic, peculiarity, distinctiveness *or* distinction, individuality (see corresponding adjectives at CHARACTERISTIC).
3 Individuality, personality, complexion, temperament, temper, *disposition.
Ana. *Mind, intellect, soul, intelligence: *soul, spirit: *courage, mettle, spirit, resolution.
4 Nature, description, *type, kind, ilk, sort, stripe, kidney.

characteristic, *adj.* **Characteristic, individual, peculiar, distinctive** come into comparison when they mean indicating or revealing the special quality or qualities of a particular person or thing or, less often, of a particular group of persons or things. **Characteristic** stresses the indication or revelation not only of that which is essential or typical, but of that which distinguishes and serves to identify the person, the thing, or the group: the word, however, fixes the attention on the thing considered more as it is in itself than as it seems in contrast or relation to other things; as, he answered with *characteristic* courtesy; "It was *characteristic* of the relationship between these two that, in all the pleadings and protests of the poor deferred lover, Sally never made the offer of convention and custom to release him" (*Deland*); "A fertile oasis possesses a *characteristic* colour scheme of its own" (*A. Huxley*). **Individual** (as here considered: see also SPECIAL) not only implies a reference to a particular person or thing but also places much more stress on a quality or qualities that distinguish him or it from all other members of the same class or kind than does *characteristic:* it therefore usually applies to something that indicates or reveals a personality or a nature that is different from all others; as, "That singularly *individual* voice of Tom's—mature, confident, seldom varying in pitch, but full of slight, very moving modulations" (*Cather*). **Peculiar** (as here compared: see also STRANGE) comes close to *individual* in this latter sense, for it usually implies a reference to a person or thing as he or it is in himself or itself and as differentiated from all others of the same kind. It may, however, apply to a class, such as a sex, a race, a people, or the like. In this use, the term does not, as in its more common derived sense, necessarily carry any hint of strangeness or oddness: rather it suggests private and undisputed possession, as of a quality, a character, an emotion, or a significance; as, "a grief that was private and *peculiar*" (*Meredith*); "a drowsy fervour of manner and tone which was quite *peculiar* to her" (*Hardy*). "In these aspects... of his work we pretend to find what is *individual*, what is the *peculiar* essence of the man" (*T. S. Eliot*). "It is the pattern [of word arrangement] that gives to this meaning its *peculiar* quality and intensity" (*A. Huxley*). **Distinctive** implies the possession of an individuality or peculiarity that marks the thing so described as apart from all others of its class or type and often, therefore, as worthy of special recognition or praise. "It is this... *distinctive* vision of the world as a whole which seems to give Leonardo that marvellous flair for detecting vital mechanism in every field" (*H. Ellis*). "It is...the exquisite craftsmanship...that has given to free verse, alike in England and America, its most *distinctive* qualities" (*Lowes*).

Ana. *Special, especial, specific, particular: typical, natural, normal, *regular.

chare *or* **char.** Chore, job, *task, duty, stint, assignment.

charge, *v.* **1** Direct, instruct, bid, enjoin, *command, order.

Ana. Request, solicit, *ask: adjure, conjure (see BEG).

2 *Accuse, incriminate, criminate, indict, impeach, arraign.

Ana. Denounce, blame, censure, condemn (see CRITICIZE).

Ant. Absolve. — *Con.* *Exculpate, exonerate, vindicate, acquit: pardon, remit, forgive, *excuse.

3 *Ascribe, attribute, impute, assign, refer, credit, accredit.

Ana. *Fasten, attach, fix, affix: *join, connect, link.

charge, *n.* *Price, cost, expense.

Ana. Levy, *tax, assessment, rate, impost, tariff, toll.

chariness. Circumspection, caution, wariness, calculation. See under CAUTIOUS.

Ana. *Prudence, providence, discretion, foresight, forethought.

charitable. **Charitable, benevolent, humane, humanitarian, philanthropic, altruistic** are comparable when they mean having or showing interest in the welfare of others. **Charitable,** in modern use, stresses either active generosity to the poor or leniency and mercifulness in one's judgments of others, but in each case it usually retains, in some degree, the implications that were emphasized in its early use of fraternal love or of compassion as the animating spirit behind the gift or the judgment. "Generous and *charitable*, prompt to serve" (*Wordsworth*). "Mrs. Hawthorne had been rude...to a friend of his, but that friend, so much more *charitable* and really good than she was, had made excuses for her" (*Arch. Marshall*). **Benevolent** also stresses an inner compulsion, such as native kindliness, a desire to do good, or an interest in others' happiness and well-being. In contrast with *charitable*, however, it more often suggests an innate disposition than an inculcated virtue; as, his intentions are *benevolent*. "Old Dimple with his *benevolent* smile" (*H. G. Wells*). "My mother...always employed in *benevolent* actions while she uttered uncharitable words" (*E. Wharton*). "The administrator of the future must be the servant of free citizens, not the *benevolent* ruler of admiring subjects" (*B. Russell*). **Humane** implies tenderness and compassion, sometimes as qualities of one's temperament, but sometimes as qualifications of enlightened and sensitive human beings; it is referable chiefly, but not exclusively, to methods, policies, and the like, affecting the welfare of others; as, *humane* treatment of prisoners or of animals. "With reasonable men, I will reason; with *humane* men I will plead; but to tyrants I will give no quarter, nor waste arguments where they will certainly be lost" (*W. L. Garrison*). **Humanitarian** suggests an interest in the welfare or well-being of masses of men more than of the individual. In early use it often connoted sentimentality or evasion of actual contact with misery. "Pecksniff presents himself as a *humanitarian* philosopher" (*A. W. Ward*). "The most mischievous men of our day are our conceited political economists and our ultra *humanitarians*" (*A. Baring*). In present use, it seldom carries such connotations, for it is now most often applied to the acts and policies of institutions, rulers, governments, and the like. "Health should be regarded from the economic as well as from the *humanitarian* viewpoint. To be without it [is] to be without earning power" (*V. Heiser*). **Philanthropic** also suggests interest in humanity rather than in the individual, but it now commonly implies, as *humanitarian* does not, the giving of money on a large scale to organized charities, to endow institutions for human advancement or social service, or the like, or the dedication of one's fortune and efforts to humanitarian causes; as, *philanthropic* millionaires; a *philanthropic* foundation. **Altruistic** presupposes the guidance of an ethical principle: that the interests of others should be exalted above those of self; it, therefore, usually implies the absence of selfishness and, often, indifference to one's own welfare or interests; as, *altruistic* motives; an *altruistic* physician.

Ana. Generous, *liberal, bountiful, munificent: merciful, *forbearing, lenient, clement, tolerant: *tender, compassionate, warmhearted, sympathetic.

Ant. Uncharitable. — *Con.* Merciless, relentless, implacable (see GRIM): *stingy, close, closefisted, parsimonious, niggardly, cheeseparing, curmudgeonly.

charity. 1 *Mercy, clemency, grace, lenity.

Ana. Love, affection, *attachment: benevolence, humaneness, altruism (see corresponding adjectives at CHARITABLE): benignness *or* benignity, benignancy, kindness, kindliness (see corresponding adjectives at KIND): generousness *or* generosity, liberalness *or*

liberality, bountifulness *or* bounty (see corresponding adjectives at LIBERAL): good will, amity, *friendship.
Ant. Malice, ill will. — *Con.* Malevolence, malignity, spite, spleen (see MALICE).
2 Charity, philanthropy come into comparison in several of their meanings. Both words denote basically a love for one's fellow men and a disposition to help those who are in need. But **charity** in this sense tends to suggest a Christian virtue and the will to help, as well as the deed, whenever the occasion arises; as, "Alas for the rarity Of Christian *charity* Under the sun!" (*Hood*); "Melt not in an acid sect The Christian pearl of *charity*" (*Whittier*). **Philanthropy** in this sense is much vaguer because it usually implies a love of mankind and a disposition to help the community or one's fellow men rather than the individual; as, "This *philanthropy*...is every where manifest in our author" (*Dryden*). Consequently, in current use there is a tendency to think of charity as benevolence manifested especially, but not exclusively, in public or private provision for the relief of the poor, and of philanthropy as benevolence manifested in efforts to promote the welfare or wellbeing of one's fellow men; thus, out of *charity* one provides for the support of a destitute orphan; out of *philanthropy* one sends a large gift of money to an educational institution. "In benevolence, they excel in *charity*, which alleviates individual suffering, rather than in *philanthropy*, which deals with large masses and is more frequently employed in preventing than in allaying calamity" (*Lecky*). The terms also may be applied to that which is done or to that which is given out of charity or philanthropy, or to the institution or cause which is the object of the benefaction; as, "The cold *philanthropies*, the ostentatious public *charities*...he exposed with utter and relentless scorn" (*Wilde*); many *charities* and many *philanthropies* were aided by him during his lifetime.

charlatan. Mountebank, quack, empiric, *impostor, faker.
Ana. Humbug, fraud, cheat, fake (see IMPOSTURE): pretender, feigner, counterfeiter (see corresponding verbs at ASSUME).

charm, *n.* Talisman, amulet, periapt, *fetish.

charm, *v.* Fascinate, allure, captivate, take, enchant, bewitch, *attract.
Ana. Delight, rejoice, *please, gratify.
Ant. Disgust.

charming. Fascinating, alluring, captivating, taking, enchanting, bewitching, attractive. See under ATTRACT, *v.*
Ana. *Delightful, delectable, delicious: pleasing, agreeable, grateful, *pleasant.
Ant. Forbidding.

chart, *n.* **Chart, map, graph** come into comparison as nouns meaning a graphic and explanatory representation, usually on a plane surface, by means of lines, dots, colors, and the like, of something incapable of pictorial representation (because too large, too detailed, too abstract, or the like), and as verbs meaning to make such a representation of something. **Chart** now is the most inclusive term of this group, for it implies the aim to make clear to the mind, through the eye, not only, as originally, the relative geographical positions of certain places on, and certain features of, the earth's surface or of a part of it, but a course, a development, a route, a scheme, or the like; as, a temperature *chart;* a magnetic *chart;* a historical *chart;* stock-market *charts;* to *chart* the course of an aviator's flight; to *chart* the fluctuations in the price of steel. However, *chart* also specifically implies a graphic representation of a body of water or of a portion of it, made for the use of navigators and indicating nearby or adjacent land, the depth at various points, dangers to be avoided, and the like; as, the United States Coast Survey *charts;* the British Admiralty *charts;* an un*charted* rock. **Map** usually implies such a representation of the earth's surface or of a part of it that shows, according to some given scale or projection, the relative position and size of cities, towns, villages, counties, states, provinces, or countries, as well as the shape and proportionate extent of bodies of water, mountain ranges, coasts, and other natural features; as, a *map* of Europe; a *map* of China; to *map* a newly explored country. It may, however, be used in reference to a representation of the celestial sphere; as, a *map* (or *chart*) of the northern heavens. **Graph** applies specifically to a chart or diagram in which two variable factors (for example, the prices of a commodity and the times at which these varying prices were asked) are so represented as to indicate their interrelationship. The usual method of preparing a graph is to locate, by means of their coordinates, and mark (on a paper or other surface) a series of points and often to join them with a curve or a series of straight lines; as, a *graph* of a patient's fever; to *graph* the course of business since 1929.
Ana. *Plan, plot, scheme, design, project.

chart, *v.* Map, graph. See CHART, *n.*
Ana. See those at CHART, *n.*

charter, *v.* *Hire, let, lease, rent.

chary. *Cautious, circumspect, wary, calculating.
Ana. Prudent, discreet, provident (see under PRUDENCE): *sparing, economical, frugal, thrifty: reluctant, hesitant, loath, *disinclined.

chase, *v.* *Follow, pursue, trail, tag, tail.
Con. Flee, fly, *escape: elude, evade, *escape: *abandon, forsake, desert.

chasm. *Gulf, abyss, abysm.

chaste, *adj.* **Chaste, pure, modest, decent** come into comparison when they mean free from all taint of that which is lewd or salacious. **Chaste** fundamentally implies an opposition to *immoral* in the restricted sense of that word in which it connotes lustfulness and licentiousness. The term therefore suggests a refraining from all acts, thoughts, etc., that incite desire or are not in accordance with one's virginity or one's marriage vows (as, "strew me over With maiden flowers, that all the world may know I was a *chaste* wife to my grave"—*Shak.*): in current use, it particularly stresses restraint and an avoidance of that which would defile or make unclean not only the love of man and woman but of anything that needs to be free from that which cheapens, debases, or makes vulgar; as, a *chaste* style; the *chaste* beauty of a work of art. "One of the most striking characteristics of a man who is really in love, is that his conversation is *chaste*. He is willing to analyze sentiment, but not sensation" (*Dimnet*). **Pure** differs from *chaste* mainly in its suggestion of freedom from all taint of evil thought or immoral desires: it implies innocence and absence of temptation rather than, as *chaste* implies, control over one's impulses and actions; as, "Come, pensive nun, devout and *pure*" (*Milton*); "Blessed are the *pure* in heart: for they shall see God" (*Matthew* v. 8); "My strength is as the strength of ten, Because my heart is *pure*" (*Tennyson*). **Modest** and **decent** are frequent in this sense as applied, especially in current use, to behavior and to dress as outward manifestations of an inward chastity or purity. *Modest* usually also implies an absence of brazenness, boldness, or other characteristics unbefitting one who is by nature chaste or pure; *decent*, a due concern for what is regarded as seemly or proper (see also DECOROUS); as, "Fair, sweet, and *modest* maid forgive my thoughts" (*Beaumont & Fletcher*); "That women adorn themselves in *modest* apparel, with shamefacedness and sobriety" (*1 Timothy* ii. 9); *decent* men leading *decent* lives; "a paper *decent* people don't see" (*R. Macaulay*); "Sex must be treated from the first as natural, delightful and *decent*" (*B. Russell*).

Ana. Virtuous, *moral, righteous, ethical: *faithful, true, constant, loyal, leal: austere, *severe.

Ant. Lewd, wanton, immoral (*of persons, actions, etc.*): bizarre (*of style, effect, etc.*). — *Con.* Obscene, gross, *coarse, vulgar, ribald: *licentious, lustful, lascivious, lecherous: *fantastic, grotesque.

chasten. Discipline, correct, *punish, chastise, castigate.

Ana. Humble, humiliate, *abase: try, *afflict: test, try, *prove.

Ant. Pamper, mollycoddle. — *Con.* *Indulge, humor, baby, spoil.

chastise. *Punish, discipline, correct, castigate, chasten.

Ana. *Beat, thrash, pummel, baste, belabor.

chat, *v.* **Chat, gab, chatter, patter, prate, prattle, babble, gabble, jabber, gibber** agree in denoting to emit a loose and ready flow of inconsequential talk. To **chat** is to talk in light, easy, and pleasant fashion. "In easy mirth we *chatted* o'er The trifles of the day before" (*W. Whitehead*). To **gab** is to talk trivia glibly and long, often tiresomely. "[He] came in to tea and sat there *gabbing* till ten o'clock" (*Jane W. Carlyle*). To **chatter** is to talk aimlessly, incessantly, and (often) with great rapidity. "It was she who *chattered, chattered,* on their walks, while... he dropped a gentle word now and then" (*Conrad*). To **patter** is to speak or repeat rapidly or hurriedly and mechanically and mumblingly, as a barker or puller-in in order to drum up or hold a crowd, a conjurer in order to divert attention from the manner in which he performs his tricks, or a person who has attained considerable facility in speaking a foreign language or a technical jargon. "The *patter* of thimbleriggers at a county fair" (*D. Canfield*). To **prate** is to talk idly and boastfully. "A *prating* fool shall fall" (*Proverbs* x. 8). The word is often specifically used in reproach implying platitudinous or fulsome boasting or a readiness to talk at length about things of which the speaker is really ignorant or has only superficial knowledge. "We may *prate* of democracy, but actually a poor child in England has little more hope than had the son of an Athenian slave to be emancipated into that intellectual freedom of which great writings are born" (*Quiller-Couch*). To **prattle** is to talk artlessly and freely, like a child. "We are...charmed with the pretty *prattle* of children" (*Sidney*). **Babble, gabble, jabber,** and **gibber** agree in suggesting volubility, together with inarticulateness, unintelligibility, or incoherence. **Babble** is especially associated with babies; **gabble,** with geese; **jabber,** with monkeys; **gibber,** with ghosts, apes, idiots, or lunatics. "I *babbled* for you, as babies for the moon" (*Tennyson*). "I... *gabble* like a goose amidst the swanlike quire" (*Dryden*). "The monkey-mimics rush discordant in; 'Twas chatt'ring, grinning, mouthing, *jabb'ring* all" (*Pope*). "The sheeted dead Did squeak and *gibber* in the Roman streets" (*Shak.*).

Ana. Converse, talk, *speak: *gossip.

chatter, *v.* *Chat, gab, patter, prate, babble, gabble, jabber, gibber.

Ana. See those at CHAT.

cheap. Beggarly, pitiable, sorry, *contemptible, despicable, scurvy.

Ana. *Mean, ignoble, sordid, abject: paltry, *petty, measly, trifling: meretricious, tawdry (see GAUDY): low, *base, vile: poor, *bad, wrong.

Ant. Noble.

cheat, *n.* Fraud, fake, deceit, deception, *imposture, counterfeit, sham, humbug, simulacrum.

Ana. Hoaxing *or* hoax, bamboozling *or* bamboozlement (see corresponding verbs at DUPE): *deception, trickery, chicanery, chicane: charlatan, quack, mountebank, faker, *impostor: swindler, defrauder, cozener (see corresponding verbs at CHEAT).

cheat, *v.* **Cheat, cozen, defraud, swindle, overreach** agree in meaning to obtain something (usually money or valuables) from, or an advantage over, another by dishonesty and trickery. **Cheat** suggests deceit and, usually, tricks that escape or are intended to escape the observation of others; as, to *cheat* at cards (or in an examination); "she and her husband had *cheated* every one with whom they had dealings" (*S. Anderson*). "He is not *cheated* who knows he is being *cheated*" (*Coke*). **Cozen,** a term of somewhat archaic flavor, implies more artfulness or craft and often more allurements than *cheat;* it usually suggests the victim's loss of something of value to him whether of real worth or not; as, soldiers *cozened* of their pay by clever girls. "Cousins, indeed; and by their uncle *cozen'd* Of comfort, kingdom, kindred, freedom, life" (*Shak.*). " 'I fought With tooth and nail to save my niche [for his tomb in the cathedral], ye know: —Old Gandolf *cozened* me, despite my care' " (*Browning*). **Defraud** always implies depriving another of that which is his by right, as by taking it from him or by withholding it; the word, however, implies misleading statements or deliberate perversion of the truth more often than it implies craft, artfulness, or wiles; as, to *defraud* a widow of a piece of property; the stockholders held that they had been *defrauded* by those who reorganized the company. "Thou shalt not *defraud* thy neighbor, neither rob him" (*Leviticus* xix. 13). **Swindle** implies either gross cheating or defrauding, especially by imposture or by gaining the victim's confidence; it usually implies the obtaining of money, or something quickly or easily convertible into money, by false pretenses; as, the forger *swindled* the merchants of the city out of large sums of money. "The despised Chinese, who were cuffed and maltreated and *swindled* by the Californians" (*Van W. Brooks*). **Overreach,** as here compared, always implies getting the better of a person with whom one is dealing or negotiating, or bargaining by unfair or dishonest means; often it implies cheating or defrauding or swindling. "He never made any bargain without *overreaching* (or, in the vulgar phrase, *cheating*) the person with whom he dealt" (*Fielding*).

Ana. *Dupe, gull, hoax, hoodwink, bamboozle, trick, befool: *deceive, delude, beguile, double-cross, mislead.

check, *n.* *Corrective, control, antidote.

Ana. *Oversight, supervision, surveillance.

check, *v.* **1** *Arrest, interrupt.

Ana. Stay, suspend (see DEFER): *stop, cease, discontinue, desist: repress, *suppress: *frustrate, thwart, foil, circumvent: stultify, *stunt.

2 Bridle, curb, snaffle, *restrain, inhibit.

Ana. *Hinder, impede, obstruct, block: *prevent, preclude, obviate: baffle, balk (see FRUSTRATE): control, manage (see CONDUCT, *v.*).

Ant. Accelerate (*of speed, etc.*): advance (*of movements, plans, hopes, etc.*): release (*of feelings, energies, etc.*).

cheek. Nerve, effrontery, hardihood, gall, *temerity, audacity.

Ana. Boldness, intrepidity (see corresponding adjectives at BRAVE): impudence, brazenness, shamelessness, brashness (see corresponding adjectives at SHAMELESS).

Ant. Diffidence. — *Con.* Shyness, modesty, bashfulness (see corresponding adjectives at SHY): timorousness, timidity (see corresponding adjectives at TIMID): reservedness *or* reserve, reticence (see corresponding adjectives at SILENT).

cheer, *v.* Hurrah, huzza, root, *applaud.

Ana. Acclaim, laud, *praise.
Con. Deride, mock, *ridicule, taunt.

cheerful. Lighthearted, joyful, joyous, *glad, happy.
Ana. Jolly, jovial, *merry, blithe, jocund: mirthful, gleeful (see corresponding nouns at MIRTH): gay, vivacious, *lively, animated.
Ant. Glum, gloomy. — *Con.* *Sullen, saturnine, dour, morose: dejected, depressed, melancholy, sad (see corresponding nouns at SADNESS): doleful, lugubrious, rueful (see MELANCHOLY).

cheeseparing. *Stingy, close, closefisted, tight, tightfisted, niggardly, curmudgeonly, penny-pinching, parsimonious, penurious, miserly.

chemist. *Druggist, apothecary, pharmacist, pharmaceutist.

cherish. **1** Prize, treasure, value, *appreciate.
Ana. Love, enjoy, *like: esteem, respect, regard (see under REGARD, *n.*): *revere, venerate, reverence: protect, *defend, shield, safeguard, guard.
Ant. Neglect. — *Con.* Ignore, overlook, slight, disregard, forget (see NEGLECT): desert, forsake (see ABANDON).
2 Foster, *nurse, nurture, cultivate.
Ana. Preserve, conserve, *save: *harbor, shelter, entertain.
Ant. Abandon. — *Con.* Repudiate, scorn, reject (see DECLINE, *v.*): contemn, *despise, disdain.

cherub. *Angel, seraph, archangel.

chevy *or* **chivy** *or* **chivvy,** *v.* *Bait, badger, heckle, hector, hound, ride.
Ana. *Worry, annoy, harry, harass, tease: chase, pursue, trail, *follow: torment, try, *afflict.

chic, *adj.* Smart, natty, fashionable, modish, *stylish, dashing, dapper, spruce, nifty, nobby, posh, toffish, brave, braw.

chicane, chicanery. Trickery, double-dealing, *deception, subterfuge, fraud.
Ana. Artifice, stratagem, maneuver, ruse, feint, *trick, wile: intrigue, machination, *plot: underhandedness, furtiveness, surreptitiousness (see corresponding adjectives at SECRET).
Con. Straightforwardness, forthrightness (see corresponding adjectives at STRAIGHTFORWARD): *honesty, integrity, probity, honor.

chide. Reproach, *reprove, rebuke, reprimand, admonish.
Ana. *Criticize, reprehend, censure, blame, condemn, denounce: *scold, upbraid, rate, berate.
Ant. Commend. — *Con.* Applaud, compliment (see COMMEND): *praise, laud, extol.

chief, *n.* **Chief, chieftain, head, headman, leader, master** come into comparison when they mean the person in whom resides authority or ruling power, but they differ in their applications and associations. **Chief** is the most comprehensive of these terms, being applicable as a general term to anyone from an absolute monarch to one's immediate superior (as, the *chief* of a court of inquisition was called the grand inquisitor; the chargé d'affaires reports daily to his *chief*). Usually, however, the term is applied specifically to one who is supreme in power or authority over a tribe or clan (as, an Indian *chief*), or to the superior officer in a civil department (as, the fire *chief;* the *chief* of police), or to one who is vested with authority and power to act by the organization over which he presides (as, the chairmen of the national committees of the leading political parties are virtually party *chiefs*). The phrase *in chief* is often added to a title, held by two or more, to indicate the one who is the first in authority; as, commander *in chief;* editor *in chief.* **Chieftain** has never obtained the generality of *chief,* and still usually carries implications derived from its early and still leading application to the chief of a tribe, a clan, or of any primitive, savage, or barbaric group; as, the *chieftain's* plaid; "Prevailing upon the Crow [an Indian tribe] *chieftain* to return him his horses" (*Irving*); a robber *chieftain.* **Head,** though seemingly as comprehensive as *chief,* is applied most frequently to the person of a group who serves as its chief executive or on whose shoulders the responsibility finally rests; as, the *head* of the family; the *head* of a school; the British prime minister is actually the *head* of the government; the *head* of a department. **Headman** comes close to *chieftain* in that it usually applies to the person who serves as the chief of his tribe, village, or the like: the term, even more than *chieftain,* implies a condition of savagery or barbarism. **Leader** implies headship, sometimes of a nation or people but more often of a party, a society, or an organized body as for singing, playing, or the like. The term usually implies a capacity for guidance, direction, or, especially in current use, for the assumption of full control and of winning the support of those under one; as, "A *leader* is one who has the power to induce other people to follow him" (*S. M. Crothers*); the *leader* of an orchestra; the *leader* of the opposition in the British parliament. **Master,** on the other hand, applies to a head who has another or others under him subject to his direction or control and necessarily obedient to his will: the term stresses his authority rather than his capacity for guidance. In general use, the term is applied as a designation to an employer of servants, the head of a school or of a class, or the like. It is also applied generally to anyone who exerts great and controlling influence over others or who is regarded as one to be followed or obeyed. In this sense, it is used by many Christians in reference to Jesus. The chief specific use of *master* is as the title of the person in command of a merchant vessel. The common designation of such a person as *captain* is colloquial rather than technical.
Ana Governor, ruler (see corresponding verbs at GOVERN).
Con. *Follower, disciple, henchman, adherent, satellite: vassal, thrall, *serf, slave.

chief, *adj.* **Chief, principal, main, leading, foremost, capital** agree in meaning first in importance or in standing. **Chief** is applicable to the person that serves as the head of his class, group, order, or the like, or to the thing that stands out as above all the rest of its class or kind in rank, importance, dignity, or the like; the term therefore usually implies the subordination of all others; as, the *chief* justice of the supreme court; the president of a republic is its *chief* magistrate; the cathedral is the *chief* church of a diocese; the *chief* topic of conversation; the *chief* concern of a mother. **Principal** is applicable to that which is the first in order of power or importance, and so is applied chiefly to the person to whom is given direction, control, or government of others or to the thing (or person thought of as a thing) that, because of its size, its position, its intrinsic importance, or the like, precedes all others of its class or kind; as, the *principal* dancer in a ballet; the *principal* keeper in a prison; the *principal* gate to the grounds of an institution; the *principal* streets of a city; the *principal* witness against the accused. **Main** (etymologically: strong, powerful) is applicable in strict use to that thing (often the part, unit, or the like, of a large or extensive thing) that excels all the others of its class or kind in size, potency, importance, or the like; as, the *main* line of a railroad; the *main* street of a small city; the *main*land; "words have been used so long as the *main* channel for communication"

(*Day Lewis*); "The literary critic...will yet find, like the historian, his *main* subject-matter in the past" (*L. P. Smith*). **Leading**, like *principal*, implies precedence, but it often distinctively implies, in addition, a capacity or fitness for drawing others, for guiding them, or for giving a particular quality or character to a movement; as, the *leading* men of the city; the *leading* actor in a play; "he had been the *leading* counsel for the seven Bishops" (*Macaulay*); the *leading* automobile in a procession. "Another *leading* object in education for efficiency is the cultivation of the critical discernment of beauty and excellence in things and in words and thoughts, in nature and in human nature" (*C. W. Eliot*). **Foremost** differs from *leading*, which it otherwise closely resembles, in its stronger implication of being first in an advance or progressive movement; it is preferable for that reason whenever there is a suggestion of the person's or thing's having forged ahead to that position. "One of us, That struck the *foremost* man [Julius Caesar] of all this world" (*Shak.*). "The poor dog, in life the firmest friend, The first to welcome, *foremost* to defend" (*Byron*). **Capital** is applicable to a thing that stands at the head of its class or kind because of its importance, its significance, its seriousness, or the like; as, a *capital* plan; his *capital* offense was that he had omitted to mention her at all; thus, the seven *capital* sins (more often called "deadly sins") are the most important sins theologically, not because they are the worst sins, but because they lead to other sins and are fatal to spiritual progress. "With a little managing...she would have gained every point as easily as she had gained the *capital* one of taking the foundling baby under her wing" (*E. Wharton*).

Ana. *Dominant, paramount, sovereign, predominant, preponderant, preponderating: *primary, prime: *supreme, pre-eminent.

Ant. Subordinate. — *Con.* Secondary, dependent, subject (see SUBORDINATE): subservient, ancillary, subsidiary, *auxiliary.

chieftain. *Chief, head, leader, commander, captain, master.

childbirth. **Childbirth, parturition, delivery, labor, travail, accouchement** are often used interchangeably to denote the act of giving birth to young. **Childbirth** is used in both technical and nontechnical language and refers to human beings only. **Parturition,** a scientific term for the act of giving birth to young, often specifically designates the final step in the process beginning with conception, continuing through gestation, or pregnancy, and ending with the expulsion of the young. **Delivery,** though often equal to *parturition*, may be used by preference to stress obstetric operation; as, a normal *delivery; delivery* by Caesarean section. However, *delivery* is often applied to the process more correctly designated by **labor;** that is, the course of events starting with the initial pains and concluding with the expulsion of the afterbirth. *Labor* suggests both the pangs and the muscular efforts involved in the process. *Labor* and *travail* are often used synonymously, but **travail** is a nonscientific term having poetic and archaic connotations, and suggesting the discomfort and pain incident to childbirth. **Accouchement** is occasionally used in scientific language to denote *delivery;* though not common in general use, it is sometimes chosen when a polite and dignified word seems desirable; as, the *accouchement* of the queen.

childish. *Childlike.

Ana. Puerile, boyish, *youthful: *simple, foolish, silly, fatuous, asinine.

Ant. Mature, grown-up. — *Con.* Adult, matured (see MATURE): manly, manful, virile, manlike (see MALE): womanly, womanlike (see FEMALE).

childlike. **Childlike, childish** agree in meaning having or showing the manner, spirit, or disposition of a child. Both are applicable to adolescents and to adults as well as to children. **Childlike,** however, usually suggests those qualities of childhood which are worthy of admiration or emulation, such as innocence, simplicity, or straightforwardness; **childish** suggests its less pleasing and less admirable characteristics, such as helplessness, peevishness, or undeveloped mentality; as, "The *childlike*, grave-eyed earnestness with which Dorothea said anything was irresistible" (*G. Eliot*); "The same thought which clothed in English seems *childish*, and even foolish, assumes a different air in Latin" (*Cowper*). "The quality of their poetry seems to fall into line with the simple, direct, *childlike* quality which all observers note in the Chinese themselves" (*H. Ellis*). "To lose sight of such distinctions is to show one's self, not *childlike*, but *childish*" (*Babbitt*).

Ana. Naïve, unsophisticated, ingenuous, artless (see NATURAL): docile, *obedient, tractable, biddable.

chilly. Cool, *cold, frosty, frigid, freezing, gelid, icy, glacial, arctic.

Ant. Balmy.

chimerical. Fantastic, fanciful, visionary, *imaginary, quixotic.

Ana. Utopian, *ambitious, pretentious: illusory, *apparent: delusive, delusory, *misleading, deceptive: fabulous, mythical (see FICTITIOUS): preposterous, absurd (see FOOLISH).

Ant. Feasible. — *Con.* *Possible, practicable: reasonable, *rational: sensible, sane, *wise, prudent.

chine. Backbone, *spine, vertebrae.

chipper. Perky, jaunty, *debonair, cocky.

Ana. Sprightly, *lively, animated, vivacious, gay: nimble, brisk, spry, *agile.

Ant. Languid (*physically and mentally*). — *Con.* *Inactive, inert, idle: *lethargic, sluggish, torpid: languorous, listless, spiritless (see LANGUID).

chivalrous. Gallant, courtly, courteous, polite, *civil.

Ana. *Gentle, genteel: *spirited, mettlesome, high-spirited: *disinterested.

Ant. Churlish. — *Con.* *Rude, ungracious, discourteous: boorish, loutish, clownish (see corresponding nouns at BOOR).

chivvy *or* **chivy.** Variants of CHEVY.

choice, *n.* **Choice, option, alternative, preference, selection, election** come into comparison when they mean the act or opportunity of choosing or the thing chosen. **Choice** usually implies the right or the privilege to choose freely from a number of persons, things, courses, etc.; as, take your *choice* of rooms; he had no *choice* in the determination of his profession; everyone admires his *choice*, for she is a very attractive young woman. **Option** stresses power to choose, especially as granted by a person (group, or the like) in whom that power is normally vested to another person (or the like), who is usually the one immediately affected by the choice; as, the state constitution gives local *option* to the cities and towns in the matter of granting or withholding licenses for the sale of intoxicants; the court sentenced the convicted speeder to one month's imprisonment with the *option* of a fine; the students have no *option* in the matter of vacations. In business transactions, an *option* is usually purchased and enables one to hold, for a certain length of time, property he is considering buying, at the end of which time he promises to pay the price agreed upon or to return it to its original owner; as, to acquire an *option* on a tract of land; buying and selling *options* on the Stock Exchange. **Alternative,** in precise usage, stresses restriction of choice between two mutually exclusive things, usually two propositions, theories, courses, policies, or the like. Commonly, it implies that all other propositions, courses, etc., are ruled out by force of circumstances (as, the *alternatives* before the country were peace with dishonor or war with honor), or by unconquerable personal aversion (as, the only *alternative* to liberty, in Patrick Henry's estimation, was death), or by logical necessity. "If the States had any power it was assumed that they had all power and that the necessary *alternative* was to deny it altogether" (*Justice Holmes*). *Alternative,* however, is often loosely used of more than two possible choices. **Preference** emphasizes the guidance of one's choice by one's bias or predilections or by one's judgment of values or of desirability; as, he was promised his *preference;* he said he had no *preference* and would wait until others had declared their *preferences.* **Selection** implies a wide range of choice and the need of discrimination or taste in choosing; as, he was commended for his *selection* of books; she did not have time for a careful *selection.* **Election** adds to *selection* the implication of an end or purpose which necessitates the exercise of judgment; as, the students will make their *election* of courses (or *elections*) before returning to college; the doctrine of predestination holds that men are destined to heaven or hell by divine *election.*

choice, *adj.* **Choice, exquisite, elegant, recherché, rare, dainty, delicate** come into comparison when they mean having qualities that appeal to a person of fine or highly refined taste. **Choice** stresses pre-eminence in quality or kind rather than careful selection of the best, although the latter may or may not be connoted; consequently, the word usually suggests an appeal to a highly cultivated and discriminating taste; as, "The *choice* and master spirits of this age" (*Shak.*); "a rich collection of the *choice* things of all times" (*Pater*); "When education in America began, it was intended for the fit and was designed to produce a *choice* type" (*Grandgent*). **Exquisite** (etymologically, sought out), as here compared, implies consummate perfection in workmanship, in choice, in quality, or in impression produced—a perfection so fine and unobtrusive that it attracts only the most sensitive and fastidious; as, "He [Horace] paints with *exquisite* art the charm of the deep country and the lure of the simple life" (*Buchan*); "Poetry of the most evanescent type, so tenuous in thought and feeling that only the most *exquisite* diction can justify its perpetuation in cold print" (*Grandgent*); "Angels, supporting, saluting, and incensing the Virgin and Child with singular grace and *exquisite* feeling" (*H. Adams*). **Elegant** also etymologically implies selection, but in most discriminating use it differs widely from *exquisite;* strictly, it implies either an impressive richness or grandeur restrained by fine taste, or grace and dignity characterized by a noble simplicity. "Whoever wishes to attain an English style...*elegant* but not ostentatious, must give his days and nights to the volumes of Addison" (*Johnson*). "To live content with small means; to seek *elegance* rather than luxury, and refinement rather than fashion" (*W. E. Channing*). "Don Manuel Chavez, the handsomest man of the company, very *elegant* in velvet and broadcloth" (*Cather*). **Recherché,** a French word now naturalized in English, like the preceding terms implies care in selection; it often suggests a studied exquisiteness or elegance; as, "might put the *recherché* taste of a finished Parisian milliner to the blush of inferiority" (*Lady S. Morgan*); "giving long and *recherché* dinners" (*Saintsbury*). Very frequently, however, it implies a search for the novel or fresh as well as the choice; hence, it often carries a connotation of artificiality or of straining for effect. "The word 'devastating'.... was [at first] thought to be *recherché;* the discerning reader is likely to call it affected" (*J. W. Beach*). **Rare,** as here considered, derives from its ordinary senses (see INFREQUENT, THIN) connotations of uncommonness and of a fineness associated with the rarefied air of the upper regions; nevertheless, its major implication is distinction in merit or excellence or a superlative quality; as, "an exquisite perception of things beautiful and *rare*" (*A. C. Benson*); "he [W. H. Hudson] is, of living writers that I read, the *rarest* spirit" (*Galsworthy*). **Dainty** (see also NICE, 1) once meant much the same as *choice,* but was somewhat more restricted in its application, being used chiefly to describe things which give delight to the fastidious taste, especially to the eye, and often also the palate; as, "As at English feasts... The *daintiest* last, to make the end most sweet" (*Shak.*); "Her house is *elegant* and her table *dainty*" (*Johnson*). At times, however, the term has also implied smallness and exquisiteness; this is, in current use, an almost invariable implication of the term; as, "those *dainty* limbs, which Nature lent For gentle usage and soft delicacy" (*Milton*); "a *dainty* bower" (*Herbert*); "Steps *dainty* as those of a French dancing-master" (*Meredith*). **Delicate,** like *dainty,* implies exquisiteness and an appeal to a fastidious taste; however, it ascribes fineness, subtlety, and often fragility, to the thing rather than smallness, and it implies an appeal not only to the eye or palate, but to any of the other senses or to the mind or spirit; as, "the more *delicate* perfume of the pink-flowering thorn" (*Wilde*); "high up in the most *delicate* air—Grecian air, pellucid" (*Jefferies*). "I have, alas! only the words we all use to paint commoner, coarser things, and no means to represent all the exquisite details, all the *delicate* lights, and shades" (*Hudson*). "An irony so quiet, so *delicate,* that many readers never notice it is there...or mistake it for naïveté" (*J. B. Priestley*).

Ana. Pre-eminent, surpassing, peerless, incomparable, *supreme, superlative: picked, handpicked, selected, culled, chosen (see CHOOSE).

Ant. Indifferent (see MEDIUM). — ***Con.*** Mediocre, second-rate, middling, fair, average, *medium: *common, ordinary.

choleric. Splenetic, testy, techy, *irascible, touchy, cranky, cross.

Ana. *Irritable, fractious, huffy, querulous, petulant, peevish: *angry, acrimonious, wrathful, indignant, mad, irate: fiery, peppery, spunky (see SPIRITED): captious, carping, faultfinding (see CRITICAL).

Ant. Placid: imperturbable. — ***Con.*** *Calm, tranquil, serene: *cool, composed, nonchalant.

choose. Choose, select, elect, opt, pick, cull, hand-pick, prefer, single out come into comparison when they mean to fix upon one (or more) of a number of things as the one (or ones) to be taken, accepted, adopted, or the like, or to make such a determination. **Choose** commonly implies a decision of the judgment and the actual taking or adoption of that which is fixed upon; as, "that he may know to refuse the evil, and *choose* the good" (*Isaiah* vii. 15); "between them...we can see little to *choose*" (*H. Adams*). "The disinterested search for truth is certainly one of the highest and noblest careers that a man can *choose*" (*Inge*). **Select** usually implies a wide range of choice, and discrimination or discernment of values in making one's choice or choices; as, "one particular nation to *select* from all the rest" (*Milton*); "Pythagoras... established religious brotherhoods of carefully *selected* candidates" (*H. Ellis*). "His [Hemingway's] temperament was *selecting* the instances he should narrate, his mind *selecting* the words to employ" (*F. M. Ford*). **Elect** often implies a deliberate choice, especially between alternatives, or a careful selection of some out of many possibilities (usually persons); ordinarily, it carries a stronger implication of the rejection of that or those not chosen than either of the preceding words; as, to *elect* a president; "I *elected* to remain" (*Hudson*); according to the doctrine of predestination, God *elects* those who are to be saved. "Will it not look a little odd...when you have so many devoted children, that you should *elect* to live alone?" (*V. Sackville-West*). **Opt** implies an election between alternatives, often specifically, in the case of inhabitants of territory transferred by treaty, between retaining one's former citizenship or acquiring citizenship in the new state; as, to *opt* to remain a British subject; to *opt* for French rather than German citizenship. **Pick** implies a careful selection, often on personal grounds; **cull,** a nice or fastidious choice; as, "Geraint, dismounting, *pick'd* the lance that pleased him best" (*Tennyson*); to *pick* an all-star team from the players in the city; to *pick* a winner. "[Gray] had exquisite felicity of choice; his dictionary had no vulgar word in it, no harsh one, but all *culled* from the luckiest moods of poets" (*J. R. Lowell*). **Hand-pick,** in its extended sense, implies careful selection for a definite end or purpose; as, a *hand-picked* staff of assistants: it sometimes implies improper motives or corrupt ends; as, to *hand-pick* a jury. **Prefer** implies choice that indicates what one favors or desires; it does not, however, always carry an implication of taking or adopting what one chooses or of getting one's choice; as, to *prefer* the blue dress to the brown one; "certain colours were *preferred*...for reasons of association and tradition" (*Binyon*); "Don't explain ....It's enough if you tell him that I *preferred* to marry Gard" (*M. Austin*). **Single out** implies choice or election of an individual person or thing from a number. "[Julius Caesar] had *singled* him [Octavius] *out* as his successor" (*Buchan*).

Ana. *Adopt, espouse, embrace: *desire, wish, crave.

Ant. Reject: eschew. — *Con.* *Forgo, forbear, abnegate: refuse, *decline, spurn, repudiate.

chop, *v.* Hew, *cut, slit, slash, carve.

Ana. Split, cleave, rive (see TEAR, *v.*).

chore. Chare, job, duty, *task, stint, assignment.

Ana. *Work, occupation, employment, business.

chow. *Food, victuals, eats, grub, viands, provisions, provender, fodder, forage.

chrestomathy. *Anthology, garland, florilegium, treasury, thesaurus, corpus, chapbook.

chrism. *Anoint, anele.

christen. *Baptize.

chroma. *Color, hue, tinge, shade, tint.

chronic. *Inveterate, confirmed, deep-seated, deep-rooted.

Ana. Established, fixed, settled (see SET): *hardened, indurated, callous.

Ant. Acute (*of illness*).

chronicle. **1** *History, annals.

2 *Account, story, report, version.

Ana. Narration, recital, recountal (see corresponding verbs at RELATE).

chthonian. *Infernal, Hadean, Stygian, hellish, Tartarean.

chubby. Rotund, plump, fat, *fleshy, stout, portly, corpulent, obese.

Ana. Chunky, stubby, dumpy, squat (see THICK).

Ant. Slim.

chum, *n.* Comrade, pal, buddy, crony, companion, *associate.

Ana. Intimate, confidant, *friend.

chummy. Intimate, close, thick, confidential, *familiar.

chunky. Thickset, squat, dumpy, stubby, stocky, *thick.

Ana. Rotund, chubby (see FLESHY).

church. *Religion, denomination, sect, communion, creed, faith, cult, persuasion.

churl, *n.* *Boor, lout, clown, clodhopper, bumpkin.

Ana. Villein, vassal (see SERF).

Ant. *Gentleman, aristocrat.

churlish. Boorish, loutish, clownish. See under BOOR.

Ana. Ungracious, ill-mannered, discourteous, *rude, uncivil, impolite: curt, blunt, brusque, gruff, crusty (see BLUFF): surly, dour (see SULLEN).

Ant. Courtly. — *Con.* *Civil, polite, courteous, gallant: urbane, *suave, diplomatic, bland, politic, smooth.

cinders. *Ashes, clinkers, embers, ash.

cipher, *n.* **Cipher, zero, naught, nought, aught, ought** are the common designations of the character 0 in Arabic notation. **Cipher** more often refers to the symbol than to the quantity or magnitude (or absence of such) which it represents; **zero,** in the United States, is probably the commoner designation of the symbol than *cipher*, but it is the preferred term in general use for the absence of quantity or magnitude denoted by the symbol; it therefore often means "nothing," or "absolutely nothing"; as, if you place three *ciphers* (or *zeros*) after 1000, your number becomes 1,000,000; 25 multiplied by *zero* (not *cipher* or *the cipher*) brings *zero* as its result. *Zero* is also used of an arbitrary point of division, as in a scale of temperatures, where all below is regarded as minus. **Naught** and **nought,** etymologically related words, are close synonyms of *cipher*, but they are rarely, if ever, now used in technical language. **Aught** and **ought** as synonyms of *naught* and *nought* arose from an error in printing or writing; thus, *a naught* became *an aught*, and the use of the decapitated forms became common. Such use, however, is now regarded as erroneous. "It was said ...that all Cambridge scholars call the cipher *aught* and all Oxford scholars call it *nought*" (*Edgeworth*).

circle, *n.* *Set, coterie, clique.

Ana. Friends, acquaintances, intimates (see singular nouns at FRIEND): associates, companions, comrades, pals (see singular nouns at ASSOCIATE).

circle, *v.* Revolve, rotate, *turn, gyrate, wheel, spin, whirl, twirl, eddy, swirl, pirouette.

circuit. Compass, ambit, *circumference, perimeter, periphery.

Ana. Route, course, *way: tour, *journey.

circuitous. Roundabout, *indirect.

Ana. *Winding, serpentine, sinuous, tortuous, flexuous, anfractuous: *crooked, devious.

Ant. Straight.

circular, *adj.* *Round, annular, discoid, orbicular, spherical, globular.

Ant. Linear.

circumference. **Circumference, perimeter, periphery, circuit, compass, ambit** come into comparison because all in their literal senses denote a continuous line enclosing an area or space. They differ, however, in the extent to which they retain this literal meaning and in the number and character of their acquired implications and connotations. In modern use, only the first two words keep very close to their literal senses, for both are technical terms in geometry. Precisely, **circumference** designates either the line that describes a circle or an ellipse, or the length of such a line; in extended use, however, it is applied to the line bounding any area thought of as circular or elliptical or to the surface of anything thought of as spherical. "Nature set from centre to *circumference*" (*Milton*). "And guard the wide *circumference* around" (*Pope*). **Perimeter** is more comprehensive than *circumference* for it includes not only the line that bounds any circular figure or area, but also the broken line that encloses any polygon (including triangle, square, etc.); moreover it may designate the whole outer boundary of a body, especially a more or less spherical body; as, the *perimeter* of a hexagon; the *perimeter* of the globe. **Periphery** is sometimes interchangeable with *perimeter* but it is less frequently used in a technical than in an extended sense. More often than any other word in this group is it referred to the actual edge, or border, or boundaries of something concrete; as, the sections of an orange extend from the center to the *periphery* (that is, the rind); we had just time enough to explore the *periphery* (the encircling shore) of the island; the *periphery* (the wall) of a blood vessel. Occasionally it suggests limits which cannot be exceeded; as, stimuli beyond the *periphery* of consciousness. **Circuit** is now rarely used in its literal sense but has become so tied up with the idea of a journey round the periphery of something that the two ideas are fused; as, the hour hand of a clock covers its *circuit* every twelve hours; "He [Augustus] also completed the great *circuit* of coast highways; in...Gaul...the roads radiated outward from a centre, while in Spain the importance lay in the *periphery*" (*Buchan*). On the other hand, **compass** and its near equivalent **ambit** (a more bookish word) usually refer to the area or space within the enclosing line, or the ground that figuratively might be covered by the leg of a compass describing such a line. "Within thy crown, Whose *compass* is no bigger than thy head" (*Shak.*). "And, with a touch, shift the stupendous clouds Through the whole *compass* of the sky" (*Wordsworth*). "Within the *ambit* of the ancient kingdom of Burgundy" (*F. Palgrave*). "Homer, who comes neither within my map nor within the *ambit* of the Tripos" (*Quiller-Couch*).

Ana. *Outline, contour: *boundary, border.

circumlocution. Periphrasis, pleonasm, *verbiage, redundancy, tautology.

Ana. Prolixity, diffuseness, wordiness, verbosity (see corresponding adjectives at WORDY).

Con. Compactness (see corresponding adjective at CLOSE): conciseness *or* concision, terseness, succinctness, pithiness (see corresponding adjectives at CONCISE).

circumscribe. Confine, *limit, restrict.

Ana. *Restrain, inhibit, curb, check: *hamper, trammel, fetter.

Ant. Expand, dilate. — *Con.* Distend, amplify, inflate, swell (see EXPAND): enlarge (see INCREASE, *v.*).

circumspect, *adj.* *Cautious, wary, calculating, chary.

Ana. *Careful, punctilious, punctual, meticulous, scrupulous: vigilant, *watchful, alert.

Ant. Audacious. — *Con.* Venturous, venturesome, rash, reckless, daring, daredevil, foolhardy, *adventurous: bold (see BRAVE): heedless, *careless.

circumspection. Caution, wariness, calculation, chariness. See under CAUTIOUS.

Ana. Carefulness *or* care, punctiliousness, punctuality, meticulosity, scrupulousness (see corresponding adjectives at CAREFUL): discretion, forethought, foresight, providence, *prudence.

Ant. Audacity. — *Con.* Venturousness, venturesomeness, rashness, recklessness, daring, daredeviltry, foolhardiness (see corresponding adjectives at ADVENTUROUS): boldness (see corresponding adjective at BRAVE): heedlessness, carelessness (see corresponding adjectives at CARELESS).

circumstance. *Occurrence, event, incident, episode.

Ana. *Item, detail, particular: factor, constituent, component, *element.

circumstantial. **Circumstantial, minute, particular, particularized, detailed, itemized** come into comparison when they mean dealing with a matter point by point. **Circumstantial** applies especially to accounts of events or to narratives, but it is applicable also to the persons who recount or narrate, to their memories, and the like. The term implies full and precise reference to the incidents or circumstances attending an event; as, a *circumstantial* account of the battle has not yet been written; Audubon's story of the rattlesnake chasing the squirrel is too *circumstantial* to have been invented; "My memory is exact and *circumstantial*" (*Dickens*). **Minute,** in addition, applies to investigations, researches, inspections, descriptions, and the like; it stresses interest in every detail, no matter how trivial or insignificant outwardly. It therefore usually connotes exhaustiveness or meticulous exactness; as, "a division in the tapestry so artfully constructed as to defy the *minutest* inspection" (*Austen*); "a reporter as faithful as he was *minute*" (*H. Martineau*); "he prolonged the flower-picking process by *minute* and critical choice" (*Deland*); "Plato...in the Laws...provides for the state a perfect jungle of *minute* regulations" (*Buchan*). **Particular,** which is rare in this sense in current English, differs little from *circumstantial* except in being applicable also to descriptions, lists, and the like; it may therefore imply attention to every feature or item rather than to every incident or circumstance; as, a *particular* description of every musical instrument in the collection. "It is as *particular* as the four-sheet maps from which it is taken" (*Jefferson*). "I think my self obliged to be very *particular* in this relation, lest my veracity should be suspected" (*Swift*). **Particularized** now usually replaces *particular* as applied to narratives, descriptions, lists, and the like; it is, however, not used of those who so narrate, describe, or list, but it may be applied to the circumstances, features, and items that they present; as, Scott's *particularized* descriptions of his characters; the *particularized* facts and phenomena considered in an astronomical treatise. **Detailed** applies to any circumstantial or minute account, description, study, representation (as in a painting), or the like; it implies, however, abundance of, rather than exhaustiveness in, detail; as, "Perera in the sixteenth century...presents a *detailed* picture of Chinese life" (*H. Ellis*); "the *detailed* study of history should be supplemented by brilliant outlines" (*B. Russell*). **Itemized** implies complete enumeration of details, especially of those that indicate the separate purchases, separate credits, and the like, in a mercantile account, or of those that indicate the articles or groups of articles in the possession of a person or business, as in an inventory; as, an *itemized* bill; an *itemized* list of his expenditures. The term is also applicable to descriptions, narratives, and the like which, in addition to being particularized, have something of the formality of an inventory; as, an *itemized* description of a room.

Ana. Precise, nice, exact, accurate (see CORRECT): *full, complete, replete.

Ant. Abridged: summary. — *Con.* Succinct, terse, laconic, *concise, pithy, compendious: shortened, abbreviated, curtailed (see SHORTEN).

circumvent. Outwit, baffle, balk, *frustrate, thwart, foil.

Ana. Forestall, anticipate, *prevent: evade, *escape, elude, avoid: trick, befool, hoodwink, *dupe.

Ant. Conform to (*laws, orders, etc.*): co-operate with (*persons, etc.*). — *Con.* Promote, further, *advance, forward: abet (see INCITE).

circus. *Arena, ring, lists, cockpit, court, field, gridiron, diamond, rink.

citadel. Stronghold, fortress, *fort, acropolis, fastness.

citation. *Encomium, eulogy, tribute, panegyric.
Ana. Commendation, recommendation, complimenting *or* compliment (see corresponding verbs at COMMEND): award, guerdon, reward (see PREMIUM).

cite, *v.* **1** *Summon, call, convoke, convene, muster.
Ana. Bid, *invite: *arrest, detain, apprehend: *praise, extol, eulogize, laud, acclaim: award, accord (see GRANT).
2 *Quote, repeat.
3 *Adduce, advance, allege.
Ana. Enumerate, tell, *count, number: recount, recite, narrate, rehearse (see RELATE).

citizen. **1** *Inhabitant, resident, denizen.
Con. *Stranger, outsider.
2 Citizen, subject, national are compared here only as denoting a person who is regarded as a member of a sovereign state, entitled to its protection, and subject to its laws. **Citizen,** which is far more common in the United States than in the British Commonwealth of Nations, implies *alien* as its opposite. It is applicable to any native or naturalized person, regardless of sex or age, who owes allegiance to a government and is entitled to its protection of his life, liberty, and property, at home or abroad. Ordinarily, as in the United States, citizenship does not imply possession of all political rights, such as the right to vote. *Citizen* often implies allegiance to a government in which the sovereign power (theoretically or absolutely) is retained by the people; it is usually the preferred term in designating those persons in a republic whose status is not that of aliens; as, American *citizens* living in Mexico. "All persons born or naturalized in the United States, and subject to the jurisdiction thereof, are *citizens* of the United States and of the State wherein they reside" (*U. S. Const.*). **Subject** is applicable to any person, no matter where he resides, who by right of birth or naturalization owes allegiance to a personal sovereign, such as a monarch or ruler. *Subject* is the preferred term in the British Commonwealth of Nations, largely for historical reasons, in spite of the limitations on the power of the sovereign, and in spite of the representative form of government in Great Britain and in its dominions; as, British *subjects* living in the United States; the millions of *subjects* of King George. The term is also applicable to any person residing in territory governed by another state that has gained power over it by force of arms or by conquest, whether the sovereign power in that state is vested in a person or in the people; as, some Poles are German *subjects*, some are Russian *subjects*. **National** belongs with this group of terms in spite of its shifting significance and more or less conflicting implications. It is applicable chiefly to any of a body of persons of the same nation or people living in a country other than the one in which they have, or, sometimes, have had, the status of citizen or subject. In diplomatic use, the term is often applied to one's fellow-countrymen; as, the consul in each of the large cities is responsible for protecting the rights of his own *nationals*. Still other denotations, not so common, have come into recent use. Chief among these is the definition of a *national* as anyone who has been born in the territory of a given government, even though he now resides in another country, either as an alien or, by naturalization, as a citizen or subject of that country; as, some European governments claim authority over their *nationals* in North and South America. There is also a tendency to prefer *national* to *subject* or *citizen* in some countries where the sovereign power is not clearly vested in a monarch or ruler or in the people, or where theories of racism prevail. In some use, especially in international law, *national* is applied to anyone entitled to the protection of a government, regardless of whether his status is that of citizen or not; in this sense, the Filipinos are *nationals* of the United States. In France, a person who enjoys full civil and political privileges is called a *citizen* (*citoyen*); one who owes allegiance to the French government is called a *national* (*national*).
Ant. Alien. — *Con.* Foreigner (see STRANGER).

civil, *adj.* **Civil, polite, courteous, courtly, gallant, chivalrous** are here compared as applied to persons, their words and acts when in intercourse with others, and as meaning observant of the forms required by good breeding. **Civil,** in present usage, commonly suggests the bare fulfillment of the ordinary requirements of social intercourse; it frequently implies little more than forbearance from rudeness. "I was never more surprized than by his behaviour to us. It was more than *civil;* it was really attentive" (*Austen*). "This man...cut short one of our party, and addressed a silly remark to Spencer.... Spencer's answer was *civil*, but brief and not inviting" (*J. Fiske*). **Polite,** while sometimes suggesting a merely perfunctory attitude, is more positive than *civil;* it commonly implies thoughtfulness for the feelings of others, united with polish of manners and address. "Nothing was ever so serene as his countenance, so unembarrassed as his manner, so *polite* as his whole demeanour" (*Landor*). "The Bishop seldom questioned Jacinto about his thoughts or beliefs. He didn't think it *polite*" (*Cather*). **Courteous** implies more considerate and dignified, **courtly,** more highbred, stately, and ceremonious, observance of due civilities; as, "The indulgence that a half-learnt speech [i.e., of a foreigner speaking French] Wins from the *courteous*" (*Wordsworth*); "Be *courteous* to all, but intimate with few" (*G. Washington*); "his great-uncle, a *courtly* and stately old gentleman" (*Symonds*); "He did not seem to know much about them, but made his effect of a *courtly* host with what he did know" (*Arch. Marshall*). **Gallant** and **chivalrous,** as here compared, imply courteous attentiveness to women. But *gallant* suggests spirited and dashing or ornate and florid expressions of courtesy; *chivalrous*, high-minded, disinterested, sometimes self-sacrificing, attentions. "The General attended her himself to the street door, saying everything *gallant*...admiring the elasticity of her walk, which corresponded exactly with the spirit of her dancing" (*Austen*). "The qualities...of surface chivalry and *gallant* attentiveness in her brilliant American friend had for a moment seemed to reveal a lack in me" (*H. Ellis*). "Nothing can beat a true woman for a clear vision of reality; I would say a cynical vision if I were not afraid of wounding your *chivalrous* feelings" (*Conrad*). "With what *chivalrous* accents would he address...those witty and wise women of old worlds" (*L. P. Smith*).
Ana. Complaisant, obliging, *amiable: *gracious, affable, cordial: politic, diplomatic, bland, urbane, *suave.
Ant. Uncivil, rude. — *Con.* Churlish, boorish, loutish (see under BOOR): ill-mannered, impolite, discourteous, ungracious (see RUDE).

civilization. **Civilization, culture** are here compared only as meaning the particular state or stage of advancement in which a race, a people, a nation, a specific class, or an integrated group of these finds itself at a given period. **Civilization** always implies a definite advance from a state of barbarism; often it suggests the absence of all signs of barbarism, or a divorce from all the ways of living, all the beliefs, all the conditions that distinguish a primitive from a civilized society. "The *civilization* of France has been for centuries, and is still, the central and dominating *civilization* of Europe" (*L. P. Smith*). "This mesa had once been like a bee-hive; it was full of little cliff-hung villages, it had been the home of a powerful tribe [of Indians], a particular *civilization*" (*Cather*). **Culture** (see also CULTURE), on the other hand, suggests rather the complex of attainments, beliefs, customs, traditions, and the like, which form the background of a particular people or group, which distinguishes them from all other peoples or groups, and which gives their particular civilization, no matter how little or how far advanced, its peculiar quality or character. "Greece for our purposes means not a race, but a *culture*, a language and literature, and still more an attitude towards life, which for us begins with Homer, and persists, with many changes but no breaks, till the closing of the Athenian lecture-rooms by Justinian" (*Inge*). "It would no doubt have been more satisfactory to select a people like the Fijians rather than the Lifuans, for they represented a more robust and accomplished form of a rather similar *culture*, but their *culture* has receded into the past" (*H. Ellis*).

Ana. Cultivation, *culture, breeding, refinement.

Ant. Barbarism. — *Con.* Barbarity (see BARBARISM): barbarousness, savagery (see corresponding adjectives at BARBAROUS).

claim, *v.* *Demand, exact, require.

Ana. *Maintain, assert, defend, vindicate, justify: allege, *adduce, advance.

Ant. Disclaim: renounce. — *Con.* Disavow, disown, disacknowledge (see affirmative verbs at ACKNOWLEDGE): reject, repudiate, refuse (see DECLINE, *v.*): concede, allow, *grant: waive, cede, *relinquish: *forgo, abnegate.

claim, *n.* **Claim, title, pretension, pretense** (*or* **pretence**) come into comparison when they denote an actual or alleged right to demand something as one's possession, quality, power, prerogative, or the like. **Claim** carries the strongest implication of a demand for recognition of any of these terms: only the context can indicate whether that demand is regarded as justifiable or not or whether the right is actually asserted by the person or persons involved; as, though the house was legally the daughter's, the father, as the one who had paid for it and had taken care of all taxes and insurance, had a moral *claim* to live there the rest of his life; intelligent persons cannot accept the *claims* made for many patent medicines; he advanced no *claim* to be counted as a man of science; "The Tractarians were driven to formulate a theory of the Church...which should justify the exclusive *claim* of Anglicanism to be the Church of Christ in these islands" (*Inge*); "it is to be hoped that its [the book's] *claim* to possess a real and special interest of its own has been established by the extracts already given" (*Day Lewis*). *Claim* also occurs in a more concrete sense as denoting the property, possession, or the like for which one sets up a claim; as, to stake out a *claim*. **Title** (see also NAME), on the other hand, distinctively imputes validity or justice to the claim, or its substantiation in law or in reason; as, his distinguished success as the governor of a great state gives him a *title* to our support of his candidacy for president; "Many of the people who masquerade under the name of 'men of science' have no sort of *title* to that name" (*H. Ellis*). "[Augustus] had the consulship, the chief magistracy, and most of the powers of a tribune....these three offices gave him a *title* to remodel the state" (*Buchan*). **Pretension** (see also PRETENSE, AMBITION) is sometimes used in place of *claim* (as, "gifts and excellences to which Wordsworth can make no *pretension*"—*Arnold*) and less often, in place of *title* (as, "The courtier, the trader, and the scholar, should all have an equal *pretension* to the denomination of a gentleman"—*Steele*). Very often, however, *pretension* connotes a lack of warrant or a weakness in the claim and may or may not attribute to it a measure of hypocrisy or deceit; as, "This court disclaims all *pretensions* to such a power" (*Ch. Just. Marshall*); "His *pretension*, deftly circulated by press-agents, was that he was a man of brilliant and polished mind" (*Mencken*). **Pretense** is now rarely employed in the sense of *claim* (for more common sense see PRETENSE), but it was of frequent occurrence in the past. Usually, the term applies to an asserted claim (as, "Marlborough calmly and politely showed that the *pretence* was unreasonable"—*Macaulay*), but it may apply to a claim that is tacitly made because one is assumed by another to be something that one is not or to have a right that one does not actually possess; as, she knew that she was in the house under false *pretenses*, for her host and hostess had warmly welcomed her as a daughter of old friends of the same name.

Ana. Assertion, affirmation, protestation, declaration (see corresponding verbs at ASSERT): *right, prerogative, birthright, privilege.

clairvoyance. Insight, divination, *discernment, penetration, perception, discrimination, acumen.

Ana. Intuition, understanding (see REASON, *n.*): intelligence, *mind, intellect.

Ant. Denseness *or* density (*of mind*). — *Con.* Stupidity, dullness, crassness (see corresponding adjectives at STUPID).

clamorous. *Vociferous, blatant, strident, boisterous, obstreperous.

Ana. Importuning *or* importunate, begging, imploring, adjuring (see corresponding verbs at BEG): *vocal, articulate, voluble, eloquent: protesting, expostulating, remonstrating (see OBJECT, *v.*).

Ant. Taciturn. — *Con.* *Silent, reserved, uncommunicative, close-lipped: *still, noiseless, quiet.

clan. *Tribe, sib, horde, sept.

clandestine. *Secret, covert, surreptitious, privy, furtive, underhand, underhanded, stealthy, backstairs.

Ana. Concealed, hidden (see HIDE): *sly, artful, foxy: illicit, illegitimate (see affirmative adjectives at LAWFUL).

Ant. Open. — *Con.* Aboveboard, *straightforward, forthright: obvious, manifest, *evident, clear, patent.

clash, *n.* Collision, *impact, impingement, shock, concussion, percussion, jar, jolt, brunt.

Ana. Conflict, strife, *discord: noise, *sound: incompatibility, incongruousness, discordance (see corresponding adjectives at INCONSONANT).

Con. Concord, accord, consonance, *harmony.

classify. Alphabetize, pigeonhole, *assort, sort.

Ana. *Order, arrange, systematize, methodize, marshal.

clause. *Paragraph, verse, article, plank, count.

clean, *adj.* **Clean, cleanly** are often confused. **Clean** is applied to a person or thing that is actually free from dirt; **cleanly** to a person (or animal) whose habit or tendency is to be clean; thus, one who is *cleanly*, though not always able to keep *clean*, will never remain dirty by choice. "An ant is a very *cleanly* insect" (*Addison*).

Ana. Cleaned, cleansed (see CLEAN, *v.*): pure, decent, *chaste.

Ant. Dirty. — *Con.* Filthy, foul, nasty, squalid (see DIRTY).

clean, *v.* **Clean, cleanse** agree in meaning to remove soil, dirt, or the like, from someone or something. **Clean** is the word in common and literal use for the removal of soil, dirt, litter, or the like, as by washing, sweeping, and dusting or clearing away; as, to *clean* a dress, or a room, or the yard. **Cleanse** may be used in place of *clean* when the reference is to garments and the like that are washed in water or gasoline, or from which spots or stains have been removed by gasoline, ether, or other solvent; as, a freshly *cleansed* dress; dyeing and *cleansing*. It is used preferably to *clean* when foul matter is removed as by purging; as, to *cleanse* the bowels. But *cleanse* has acquired the more elevated and figurative senses associated with purification of any sort. "Wash me throughly from mine iniquity, and *cleanse* me from my sin" (*Psalms* li. 2.) "With some sweet oblivious antidote *Cleanse* the stuff'd bosom" (*Shak.*). "The air was purer for the *cleansing* rain" (*G. Macdonald*).

Ant. Soil.

cleanly, *adj.* *Clean.

Ana. Spick-and-span, *neat, tidy, trim, snug: *orderly: dainty, fastidious, fussy, *nice.

Ant. Uncleanly. — ***Con.*** Slovenly, unkempt, sloppy, *slipshod.

cleanse. *Clean.

Ana. *Sterilize, disinfect, sanitize.

Ant. Defile, besmirch.

clear, *adj.* **1 Clear, transparent, translucent, lucid, pellucid, diaphanous, limpid** come into comparison when they mean having the property of being literally or figuratively seen through. That is **clear,** as here compared, which is free from all impediments to the vision such as clouds, mist, or haze (as, *clear* air, a *clear* day), or from muddiness, cloudiness, or turbidity (as, *clear* water, *clear* glass, *clear* crystals), or figuratively, from obscurity, vagueness, or indistinctness of any sort (as, *clear* thinking, a *clear* mind, a *clear* style [for this sense see CLEAR, 2]; "a *clear* vision of reality"—*Conrad; clear* tones). That is **transparent** which is so very clear that objects (or figuratively, what lies beyond) can be easily seen through it. "The water...is as *transparent* as the air, so that the stones and sand at the bottom seem, as it were, trembling in the light of noonday" (*Shelley*). "An ingenuous, *transparent* life was disclosed [by the changes on her face]; as if the flow of her existence could be seen passing within her" (*Hardy*). "Nor...is it [Bergson's style] always so clear as to be *transparent*" (*H. Ellis*). "Rushing away from the discussion on the *transparent* pretence of quieting the dog" (*Conrad*). That is **translucent** which admits the passage of light through it but which, especially in current usage, does not permit a clear sight of what lies beyond; as, frosted glass is *translucent;* "under the glassy, cool, *translucent* wave" (*Milton*); "the blue off Nantucket is not the miracle of luminous, *translucent* color off Sardinia" (*Lowes*); "*translucent* phrases, which mirror...the woodland lights and shadows" (*L. P. Smith*). That is **lucid,** as here compared (for application to expression see CLEAR, 2), which is both transparent and luminous; this use is now chiefly literary. "Gods, who haunt The *lucid* interspace of world and world Where never creeps a cloud, or moves a wind" (*Tennyson*). "The thought [of Dante] may be obscure, but the word is *lucid*, or rather *translucent*" (*T. S. Eliot*). That is **pellucid** which is clear as crystal; as, "more *pellucid* streams, An ampler ether, a diviner air" (*Wordsworth*); "you may lie on the grassy rampart, high up in the most delicate air—Grecian air, *pellucid*" (*Jefferies*); "[Goldsmith's] *pellucid* simplicity" (*F. Harrison*). That is **diaphanous** which is so delicate and gossamerlike in texture that it is almost transparent or is actually translucent; as, a *diaphanous* veil; a *diaphanous* cloud; "I like *diaphanous* illusions, with the shapes of things as they are showing not too faintly through them" (*L. P. Smith*). "In her flowery loveliness, she looked *diaphanous*, ethereal" (*Hewlett*). That is **limpid** which has the soft clearness of or as of pure water; as, "a...rill of *limpid* water" (*Wordsworth*); "The whole atmosphere has a luminous serenity, a *limpid* clearness" (*Mrs. H. Ward*); "that...simple, *limpid* style which is the supreme style of all" (*Arnold*); "Archer's New York...in business matters...exacted a *limpid* and impeccable honesty" (*E. Wharton*).

Ana. *Bright, luminous: *liquid: *pure, sheer.

Ant. Turbid (*of air, days, water, etc.*): confused (*of minds, thoughts, etc.*). — ***Con.*** Dim, obscure, murky, dusk, dusky, gloomy (see DARK): muddy, roiled, roily (see TURBID): muddled, bemuddled, addled, fuddled, befuddled (see CONFUSE).

2 Clear, perspicuous, lucid are here compared as used in reference to qualities of thought or style and as meaning quickly and easily understood. **Clear** implies freedom from obscurity, ambiguity, or the danger of being misunderstood; as, " 'Many are called;' there is a *clear* truth: 'Few are chosen;' there is an obscure truth" (*Arnold*); "Few, *clear*, definite, and calm as stars were the words [T. H. Huxley] spoke" (*B. Waugh*). **Perspicuous** lays more stress than *clear* upon the medium of expression regarded for itself; it frequently connotes a certain simplicity and elegance of style; as, "Extreme conciseness of expression, yet pure, *perspicuous*, and musical, is one of the grand beauties of lyric poetry" (*Gray*); "We may still borrow descriptive power from Tacitus, dignified *perspicuity* from Livy" (*Sydney Smith*). **Lucid** especially implies clearness of order or arrangement; as, "He [Macaulay] thought little of recasting a chapter in order to obtain a more *lucid* arrangement" (*G. O. Trevelyan*). "His [T. H. Huxley's] descriptions of the most complicated organic structures are astonishingly *lucid*" (*A. Huxley*).

Ana. Express, *explicit, definite: *graphic, vivid: clear-cut, *incisive, trenchant.

Ant. Unintelligible: abstruse. — ***Con.*** Vague, *obscure, ambiguous, equivocal, cryptic, enigmatic: turgid, tumid (see INFLATED): *recondite, occult, esoteric.

3 Manifest, *evident, obvious, distinct, apparent, patent, palpable, plain.

Con. *Doubtful, dubious, questionable, problematic.

clear-cut. Trenchant, *incisive, cutting, biting, crisp.

Ana. Distinct, plain, clear, manifest, *evident: definite, *explicit, express: precise, exact, nice (see CORRECT).

Con. Confused, muddled, bemuddled (see CONFUSE): hazy, misty, fogged (see corresponding nouns at HAZE).

clear out, clear off. Withdraw, retire, scram, quit, depart, *go, leave.

Ana. *Escape, flee, fly, decamp, abscond: desert, *abandon, forsake.

cleave.[1] Cling, *stick, adhere, cohere.

Ana. *Fasten, attach, fix, affix: unite, *join, associate, link, combine.

Ant. Part. — ***Con.*** *Separate, divorce, divide, sever, sunder: *detach, disengage: *estrange, alienate.

cleave.[2] Split, rive, rend, *tear, rip.

Ana. *Separate, divide, sever, sunder, part, divorce: *cut, hew, chop, slit.

Con. *Join, unite, link: attach, *fasten.

clemency. 1 Lenity, *mercy, charity, grace.

Ana. Compassion, *pity, commiseration, sympathy, ruth: gentleness, mildness (see corresponding adjectives at SOFT): fairness, equitableness, justness (see corresponding adjectives at FAIR).

Ant. Harshness. — ***Con.*** Severity, sternness, austerity (see corresponding adjectives at SEVERE): rigorousness, strictness, rigidity (see corresponding adjectives at RIGID): inflexibility, obduracy, inexorableness (see corresponding adjectives at INFLEXIBLE).

2 Mercifulness, leniency, indulgence, forbearance, tolerance. See under FORBEARING.
Ana., Ant., & *Con.* See CLEMENCY, 1.

clement. Merciful, lenient, indulgent, *forbearing, tolerant.
Ana. Compassionate, *tender, sympathetic: benign, benignant, kindly, *kind: humane, benevolent, *charitable.
Ant. Harsh: barbarous (*treatment of enemies, offenders, etc.*). — *Con.* *Severe, stern, austere: *rigid, rigorous, strict, stringent: implacable, merciless, relentless, unrelenting, *grim.

clergyman. *Cleric, ecclesiastic, priest, abbé.

cleric. **Cleric, clergyman, priest, ecclesiastic, abbé,** all of which designate a churchman in orders, are often used loosely and without an understanding of their distinguishing implications. **Cleric** is the most comprehensive, though not the most common, of these terms. It may be applied to any man who has passed through the rite of tonsure, or shaving of the head, which symbolizes his acceptance as a candidate for orders in the Roman Catholic and Eastern churches. However, it is often used as the equivalent of **clergyman,** which, properly distinguished from *cleric,* implies the taking of the highest of holy orders, that of priesthood. *Clergyman,* therefore, is equivalent to **priest,** or an ordained minister of churches recognizing holy orders, such as the Anglican, Roman Catholic, and Orthodox churches. In England, *clergyman* is often restricted in its application to a priest of the Church of England; in the United States, it is commonly used to designate any ordained minister. **Ecclesiastic** also equals *priest* in denotation, but in actual use it so often connotes administrative rather than distinctively priestly functions that it tends to be applied narrowly to those priests in whom governmental powers are vested, such as rectors, bishops, and archbishops. **Abbé** comes closer to *cleric* than any of the others; though it commonly implies ordination to the priesthood (of the Roman Catholic Church) it does not necessarily do so, and has often been applied to clerics who never have been admitted to holy orders but who wear the soutane, or cassock.

clever. **1** *Intelligent, quick-witted, brilliant, bright, smart, alert, knowing.
Ana. *Quick, apt, ready, prompt: *versatile, all-round, many-sided: capable, competent, *able: *sharp, keen, acute.
Ant. Dull (*mentally*). — *Con.* *Stupid, dense, crass: *simple, foolish, fatuous, asinine.
2 **Clever, adroit, cunning, ingenious** come into comparison when they mean having or showing a high degree of practical intelligence, or of skill in contrivance. **Clever,** as here considered, often carries its etymological implication of physical dexterity, but it usually stresses its much later won implication of mental quickness or resourcefulness. "I became so *clever* with the gloves that Ned matched me against a light-weight" (*Shaw*). "But Jane's mother had been too *clever* for him....she had come to the dinner-table primed to do just that thing" (*M. Austin*). Often, it implies native aptitude or a knack. "A...pond in the middle of the garden, into which Tranquilino, *clever* with water, like all Mexicans, had piped a stream" (*Cather*). **Adroit** usually suggests greater shrewdness and astuteness than *clever,* and often implies the skillful (sometimes, the crafty) use of expedients to attain one's ends in the face of difficulties. "The *adroit* William Penn...found means to stand well at the court of the persecuting James the Second" (*C. E. Montague*). "The whole tendency of French instruction has been... to conceal the obstacles [to learning the language] so *adroitly* that the learner shall never be aware of them" (*Grandgent*). **Cunning,** in the more complimentary of its literary senses, still retains its etymological implications of learning and expert knowledge. Originally applied to philosophers and the like, it is now chiefly applied to craftsmen or artists whose work exhibits a high degree of constructive or creative skill. "He knew how...to construct a plot, he was *cunning* in his manipulation of stage effects" (*T. S. Eliot*). "Every speech in it [any great tragedy] has to be *cunningly* calculated" (*C. E. Montague*). **Ingenious** retains only a trace of its earliest implication, a high degree of intellectuality. In current use it stresses inventive power or skill in discovery; sometimes it implies brilliancy of mind, sometimes little more than cleverness. "Powerful and *ingenious* minds... may, by a course of...refined and metaphysical reasoning...explain away the constitution of our country" (*Ch. Just. Marshall*). "A gigantic tent...*ingeniously* constructed without poles or ropes" (*Hardy*).
Ana. *Dexterous, deft, feat, handy: nimble, *agile: *proficient, skillful, skilled, adept, expert.
Con. Inept, maladroit, *awkward, clumsy, gauche: *slow, laggard, dilatory.

cliché. Platitude, truism, *commonplace, bromide.

clientele, clientage. *Following, public, audience.

climate. **Climate, clime** are no longer synonyms in the best current usage. **Climate** applies to the normal or characteristic weather conditions over a very long period in a particular locality or region; it implies consideration of both the extremes and the mean of temperatures and wind velocities, the amount and the frequency of precipitation, and the like; as, the mild *climate* of the French Mediterranean coast. "Is not their *climate* foggy, raw and dull?" (*Shak.*). **Clime** is a poetic or elevated term for a region, especially for one having a definitely marked climate or for one characterized by a markedly prevailing type of weather; as, "cold northern *climes*" (*Pope*); "In *climes* beyond the solar road" (*Gray*).

climax, *n.* Culmination, peak, apex, acme, zenith, apogee, *summit, pinnacle, meridian.

climb, *v.* *Ascend, mount, scale.
Ant. Descend.

clime. *Climate.
Ana. Region, zone (see AREA).

cling. Cleave, *stick, adhere, cohere.
Ana. Depend, *rely, trust, count, bank, reckon: attach, affix, *fasten: *hang, dangle, suspend.
Con. Desert, forsake, *abandon: *relinquish, leave, resign, yield.

clinkers. Cinders, *ashes, ash, embers.

clique. *Set, circle, coterie.
Ana. Party, faction, bloc, ring, junto, combine, *combination.

cloak, *v.* Mask, *disguise, dissemble.
Ana. Conceal, *hide, screen.
Ant. Uncloak. — *Con.* *Reveal, disclose, discover, betray.

clodhopper. Bumpkin, *boor, lout, clown, churl.

clog, *v.* Fetter, hog-tie, shackle, manacle, *hamper, trammel.
Ana. Impede, obstruct, *hinder, block: balk, baffle, *frustrate: check, curb, snaffle (see RESTRAIN).
Ant. Expedite, facilitate. — *Con.* *Free, liberate, release: forward, further, *advance, promote.

cloister, *n.* **1** **Cloister, monastery, nunnery, convent, abbey, priory.** **Cloister** and **convent** are general terms, denoting a place of retirement from the world for members of a religious community; they properly apply to houses for recluses of either sex. *Cloister* stresses the idea of seclusion from the world; *convent*, of community of living. A **monastery** is, strictly speaking, a cloister for monks; in actual use it is often applied to any convent for men (occasionally for women) who combine the cloistered life with that of a teacher, preacher, or the like. **Nunnery,** the older word for a cloister for nuns, is now being displaced by *convent*, in a restricted sense. A monastery or nunnery governed by an abbot or an abbess is called an **abbey;** by a prior or prioress, a **priory.** A priory is subordinate in rank to, but often independent of, an abbey.

2 Arcade, *passage, passageway, ambulatory, gallery, corridor, aisle, hall, hallway.

close, *adj.* **1** Also *adv.* **Close, near, nigh, near by** (*or* **near-by**) come into comparison both as adjectives and as adverbs when they mean not far, as in place, time, or relationship, from the point, relation, etc., that is indicated or understood. **Close** (as here compared: see also CLOSE, *adj.*, 2) commonly implies so slight a difference that the two things (sometimes persons) under consideration may be said literally or figuratively to be almost in contact if the difference is in distance, or almost coincident if the difference is in time, or of the immediate family if the difference is in relationship, or very like the original if the difference is in a copy; as, the houses on this street are *close* together; *close* relatives; *close* friends; to hold one *close* to one's breast; "the more accurately we use words the *closer* definition we shall give to our thoughts" (*Quiller-Couch*); a *close* shave; to give *close* attention to a problem; a *close* translation of a passage. **Near** may be used in place of *close* (as, *near* houses; events that come *near* to each other; *near* relatives) but it carries a much less explicit suggestion of contiguousness or adjacency and may be used of persons or things that, though not far off as in place, time, relationship, or the like, are not almost in contact, almost coincident, of the immediate family, or the like; as, come *near* where I can see you; a *near* concern of all of us; "the *nearer* the church, the farther from God" (*Old Proverb*). *Near* also is often applied to things copied, imitated, translated, or the like, that bear some resemblances to the original: the term may or may not be used in depreciation; as, *near* beer; a *near* translation; *near* silk; *near*-leather upholstery. **Nigh** is now dialectal or archaic or poetic in the sense of *near*. As an adverb it, even more often than *near*, is followed by *to, unto, about, on, upon;* as, "he was sick *nigh* unto death" (*Philippians* ii. 27); "This change had brought them *nigher* to each other" (*Cooper*); he lives *nigh* abouts; "Now the day is over, night is drawing *nigh*" (*Baring-Gould*). As an adjective, it differs little from *near* except in sometimes being given preference in the comparative and superlative degrees to *nearer* and *nearest;* as, "[He] seized the *nighest* ship" (*W. Morris*); "The *nigher* and the safer road to Liege" (*Scott*). **Near by** is now chiefly an Americanism for near in distance or close at hand; as, *near-by* towns; the *near-by* houses; there is no hotel *near by*. In the sense of near in amount or number, it is a Scotticism; as, they made 400 miles or *near by* in one day's drive.

Figuratively, in their adjectival forms, all of these words except *near by* imply a degree of parsimony. **Close** usually suggests niggardliness or stinginess, sometimes miserliness (as, "He was *close* in small matters of money" —*Trollope*); **near** often carries a stronger suggestion of cautiousness or care in the expenditure of money (as, her early experience with poverty made her *near* all her life; "his neighbours called him '*near*'" (*G. Eliot*). **Nigh** is now rarely used in this sense except in dialectal language.

Ana. Adjoining, *adjacent, contiguous, abutting: *related, kindred.

Ant. Remote *or* remotely. — ***Con.*** *Distant, removed, far, faraway, far-off.

2 Close, dense, compact, thick come into comparison when they mean having its parts, particles, atoms, or the like, massed tightly together. **Close** may apply to the texture or weave of something; as, a paper of fine, *close* texture; a cloth of *close* weave. More often, however, the term applies to something that is made up of a number of single things pressed or seemingly pressed together; thus, he writes a *close* hand (that is, each letter in his handwriting is very near to its neighbor); the troops fought in *close* formation. Figuratively, especially as applied to literary expression, it implies a compression of what is to be said into the fewest and most telling words possible. "The greatest beauty of speech [is] to be *close* and intelligible" (*Steele*). "It is a relief to turn back to the austere, *close* language of *Everyman*" (*T. S. Eliot*). **Dense** applies to an aggregate, or to a mass in which the arrangement of parts or particles is exceedingly close, or to matter of any kind in which the constituent particles are very closely set together; as, *dense* clouds; a *dense* forest; a *densely* populated district; a *dense* star; a *dense* flower spike; *dense* air. In its figurative use, the term commonly implies impenetrability; as, a *dense* mind; *dense* stupidity; "*dense* silence" (*S. Anderson*). **Compact** suggests close and firm union or consolidation of parts, especially within a small compass; it often also implies neat or effective arrangement; as, "With much less compass of muscle than his foe, that which he had was more seasoned, firm and *compact*" (*Lytton*). "Small, *compact*, homogeneous communities such as the Greek city state or Elizabethan England" (*Day Lewis*). **Thick** (as here compared: see THICK) usually applies to that which is condensed or is made up of abundant and concentrated parts; as, "Make the gruel *thick* and slab" (*Shak.*); a *thick* swarm of bees; a *thick* grove; a *thick* head of hair.

Ana. Compressed, condensed, constricted (see CONTRACT, *v.*): concentrated, compacted (see COMPACT, *v.*).

Ant. Open. — ***Con.*** Scattered, dispersed (see SCATTER): expanded (see EXPAND).

3 Close-lipped, close-mouthed, tight-lipped, secretive, reserved, taciturn, reticent, uncommunicative, *silent.

Ant. Open (see FRANK). — ***Con.*** *Frank, candid, plain: garrulous, loquacious, *talkative, voluble.

4 Intimate, confidential, chummy, thick, *familiar.

Ant. Aloof.

5 Closefisted, tight, tightfisted, niggardly, parsimonious, penurious, *stingy, cheeseparing, penny-pinching.

Ana. *Sparing, economical, frugal, thrifty.

Ant. Liberal. — ***Con.*** Generous, bountiful (see LIBERAL): lavish, prodigal (see PROFUSE).

close, *v.* **1 Close, shut** are very close synonyms in the sense of to stop or fill in an opening by means of a door, a gate, a lid, or cover of any kind and are often used as though they are indistinguishable in meaning. Actually, they are distinguishable not only in nuances of meaning, but also in idiomatic use for in certain phrases established usage shows a preference for one rather than the other. **Close** is the more general of these two terms, usually implying both the act of stopping an opening and the result produced by such an act but stressing exclusion of those who would enter or pass through. **Shut** stresses the act or process and the means employed in this process: it not only carries a more emphatic implication or a more vivid suggestion of drawing a door, gate, lid, window, or the like, into a position which closes the opening, but it often also evokes an image of drawing a bar or a bolt, of locking, or other means of fastening securely; hence, in very precise use, to *close* a door or gate is merely to draw it into a position which bars entrance or egress until it is again opened; to *shut* a door or gate is to push or pull it into the position where it is closed. But one *closes* (not *shuts*) an opening or a gap or one *closes* (not *shuts*) a park or a church to the public, because in neither case is the use of a door, gate, or other means of exclusion clearly or definitely implied. On the other hand, in idiomatic use *shut*, especially when followed by *up*, *out*, *against*, and the like, carries a stronger and often a more direct and emphatic suggestion than *close* of the interposition of a barrier or obstacle (often an immaterial one) that effectually prevents ingress or egress; as, he found every road to the accomplishment of his desires *shut* against him; he *shut* his eyes to everything he did not wish to see (cf. to *close* one's eyes in death); he was warned to *shut* his mouth.

Ana. *Exclude, debar: block, bar, dam (see HINDER).

Ant. Open.

2 **Close, end, conclude, finish, complete, terminate** come into comparison as transitive verbs meaning to bring something to a stopping point or to its limit, or, with the exception of *complete*, as intransitive verbs meaning to come to that point. **Close** usually has latent in it the idea of action upon that which may be regarded as in some sense *open* (see CLOSE, *v.*, 1); as, to *close* an account (or a debate, or a subscription list); "As many lines *close* in the dial's center" (*Shak.*); "Recall those nights that *clos'd* thy toilsome days" (*Pope*); "Over! the sweet summer *closes*" (*Tennyson*). **End** conveys a stronger sense of finality; it frequently has implicit reference to a progress or development which is thought of as having been carried through; as, "The harvest is past, the summer is *ended*, and we are not saved" (*Jeremiah* viii. 20); "All's Well that *Ends* Well" (*Shak.*); to *end* one's life; to *end* one's labors upon a book. **Conclude** is a more formal term, and applies particularly to transactions, proceedings, or writings that have a formal or special close; as, to *conclude* one's speech with a peroration; to *conclude* a meeting with a benediction. "I shall *conclude* this essay upon laughter with observing that the metaphor of laughing...runs through all languages" (*Spectator*). **Finish** implies that what one set out to do is done; often, therefore, it connotes the completion of the final act in a process of elaboration, such as polishing or perfecting (the "last" or "*finishing* touch"); as, "I have *finished* the work which thou gavest me to do" (*John* xvii. 4); "It wants but seventeen lines of having an end, I don't say of being *finished*" (*Gray*). **Complete** implies the removal of all deficiencies or a finishing of all that has been attempted; as, "When Blondel paused about the middle, the king began the remainder, and *completed* it" (*T. Warton*); to *complete* their education in Europe. "Art partly *completes* what Nature is herself sometimes unable to bring to perfection" (*H. Ellis*). "He [Augustus] may well have thought that his days would be few on earth, and that it would be foolish to put his hand to a task which he could not *complete*" (*Buchan*). **Terminate** implies the setting of a limit in time or space; as, "Ben Lomond *terminates* the view" (*D. Wordsworth*); "My philosophic walks were soon *terminated* by a shady bench" (*Gibbon*); "He had never seen the instrument that was to *terminate* his life" (*Dickens*); hostilities *terminate* at sundown.

Ana. *Stop, cease, quit, desist.

Con. *Begin, commence, start, inaugurate, initiate.

closefisted. *Stingy, close, tight, tightfisted, niggardly, parsimonious, penurious, miserly, curmudgeonly, cheeseparing, penny-pinching.

Ana., Ant., & *Con.* See those at CLOSE, *adj.*, 5.

close-lipped. Close, close-mouthed, uncommunicative, taciturn, reserved, reticent, secretive, *silent, tight-lipped.

Ant. & *Con.* See those at CLOSE, *adj.*, 3.

close-mouthed. Close, close-lipped, tight-lipped, reticent, reserved, uncommunicative, *silent, taciturn, secretive.

Ant. & *Con.* See those at CLOSE, *adj.*, 3.

clothe. Clothe, attire, tire, dress, apparel, array, robe, vest, invest. Clothe, the least specific of these terms, means to cover or, sometimes, to provide that which will cover (one's body or that which is bare) with or as with garments; as, to *clothe* oneself; to *clothe* the child warmly; to *clothe* one's thoughts in words. The other words convey the same meaning but each one adds to it distinctive implications and connotations. **Attire** and its archaic form **tire** suggest more careful process than *clothe*, with the result that the words savor of formality and therefore are avoided except when the context requires that note. "He said it was for the honour of the Service that he *attired* himself so elaborately; but those who knew him best said that it was just personal vanity" (*Kipling*). *Tire* is found chiefly in historical novels and in reference to ladies of high degree. **Dress** is far less formal than *attire* and much richer in its connotations than *clothe*. It often suggests care in the choice and arrangement of clothes and sometimes, especially in **dress up**, preening and prinking; as, to *dress* the children for school or for a party; every afternoon she *dresses up* and goes out; *dressed up* in one's Sunday clothes; to *dress up* as Cleopatra. *Dress*, especially in its intransitive or reflexive forms, often implies a change of clothes to those that are appropriate for a special occasion; thus, to *dress* for dinner implies a change into dinner or evening clothes; I shall not have time to *dress* (that is, to change into suitable clothes for the particular occasion). The idea of decking or adorning is frequently associated with the word, especially in its extended senses; as, to *dress* the hair with flowers; to *dress* the table for dinner. "Yet shall thy grave with rising flow'rs be *dressed* (*Pope*). **Apparel** and **array** are now chiefly literary words, used when there is the intent to connote splendor, elegance, or gorgeousness in that with which a person or thing is clothed. "And she had a garment of divers colours upon her: for with such robes were the king's daughters... *apparelled*" (*2 Samuel* xiii. 18). "A time when meadow, grove, and stream... To me did seem *Apparelled* in celestial light" (*Wordsworth*). "Consider the lilies of the field, how they grow; they toil not, neither do they spin: And yet I say unto you, That even Solomon in all his glory was not *arrayed* like one of these" (*Matthew* vi. 28, 29). "I rode with him to court, And there the Queen *array'd* me like the sun" (*Tennyson*). **Robe, vest, invest** imply a formal clothing with the garments belonging to one's office, profession, rank, or the like. *Robe* suggests the enveloping apparel worn by a king, queen, or noble on state occasions, by a judge or a professor when the conventions of his office demand it, by a bishop or other high ecclesiastic when formally but not liturgically attired. *Vest*, once used in place of *robe*, is now rare except in a specific sense, to clothe in liturgical vestments, such as the alb, chasuble, and the like. "The altar and the *vested* priest" (*Milton*). **Invest,** especially in historical and in liturgical use, implies clothing (a king, a bishop, etc.) with the robes and other insignia of his dignity for the first time as a part of the ceremony of a consecration, installation, or the like; as, to *invest* a king with his crown; to *invest* an archbishop with the pallium and other archiepiscopal insignia. Since in such use the insignia of one's office are merely the outward signs of one's power or authority, *invest* also implies the formal clothing with such power (see INITIATE, 2). In their extended senses, **robe** usually connotes envelopment (as, "*Robed* in the long night of her deep hair"—*Tennyson*), **vest** suggests the addition of something that enhances (as, "It was my fortune scarcely to have seen... The face of one, who... Was *vested* with attention or respect Through claims of wealth or blood"—*Wordsworth*), **invest,** which now occurs far more commonly in its figurative than in its literal sense, implies endowment with a new character, dignity, beauty, or the like (as, "The Indian mode of *investing* all things with a personal aspect and a mystical apprehension of unseen powers"—*M. Austin;* "In this art...we do not find animals *invested* with a false reflection of human sentiment"—*Binyon*).

Ant. Unclothe. — *Con.* *Strip, divest, dismantle.

clothes. **Clothes, clothing, dress, attire, tire, apparel, raiment, vesture, array** come into comparison when they denote a person's garments considered collectively. **Clothes** and **clothing** are general words which do not necessarily suggest a wearer or personal owner, but sometimes a manufacturer or a merchant; as, evening *clothes;* summer *clothing* for men; her *clothes* are always immaculate; each child has ample *clothing.* **Dress,** as here compared, is used with reference only to a wearer's outer clothes; it is not only far less inclusive than *clothes* and *clothing,* but less concrete in its suggestions, except when qualified; as, both men and women are expected to wear full *dress;* the actors will be costumed in the *dress* of the period of each play. "A man of sense carefully avoids any particular character in his *dress*" (*Chesterfield*). **Attire** and its archaic equivalent **tire** usually stress the appearance or the total impression produced by one's clothes; *attire,* therefore, is rarely used colloquially with reference to one's own clothes, except in affectation or humorously; when applied to another person's, it is, as a rule, qualified; as, "let thy *attire* be comely but not costly" (*Lyly*); "her artless manners, and her neat *attire*" (*Cowper*); "Our speech, our colour, and our strange *attire*" (*Pope*); "the dandy's *attire*" (*Meredith*). **Apparel** (often specifically *wearing apparel*) carries a weaker suggestion of the effect produced and a stronger implication of a collection or assemblage of clothes than *attire,* which otherwise it closely resembles in meaning; therefore, one says an article of *apparel* (rather than *attire*) and the richness of her *attire* (rather than *apparel*); a blue serge suit, a grey shirt, a blue and red necktie, a gray homburg, and black shoes and gloves comprised his *apparel.* "The *apparel* oft proclaims the man" (*Shak.*). **Raiment** is a more or less literary term that is nearly as comprehensive as *clothes* for it includes everything that is worn for decency, comfort, and adornment, and therefore suggests reference to undergarments as well as to outer garments; as, to bring a change of *raiment* with one. When the quality or the texture of the clothing is to be indicated, *raiment* is the appropriate word; as, fine *raiment;* the coarse *raiment* of a penitent pilgrim. "But what went ye out for to see? A man clothed in soft *raiment?* behold, they that wear soft clothing are in kings' houses" (*Matthew* xi. 8). **Vesture** also is a formal and poetic word, similar in its denotation to *apparel,* but different in its connotations, for it usually connotes flowing robes, ceremonial attire, or the like, and suggests little reference to everyday existence or current fashion. Oftentimes even its collective implication is not clear, and the word becomes very shadowy and vague in its reference to a concrete thing. "And he saw the Blessed Vision Of our Lord, with light Elysian Like a *vesture* wrapped around him" (*Longfellow*). "The rustling of your *vesture* through my dreams" (*E. B. Browning*). **Array** is rarely found outside of poetry or rhetorical prose as a close synonym of *attire.* To the latter term it adds suggestions of splendor or of gorgeousness in appearance; as, "Set not thy sweet heart on proud *array*" (*Shak.*). "The wasting moth ne'er spoil'd my best *array;* The cause was this, I wore it every day" (*Pope*).

clothing. *Clothes, dress, attire, tire, apparel, raiment, vesture, array.

clout, *v.* Hit, *strike, smite, slug, punch, box, cuff, slap, swat.

Ana. *Beat, pummel, thrash, baste, belabor.

clown. 1 *Boor, clodhopper, lout, bumpkin, churl.

Ana. Simpleton, natural (see FOOL).

2 *Fool, jester, antic, buffoon, zany, merry-andrew, pantaloon, harlequin, comedian, comic, stooge.

clownish. Loutish, boorish, churlish. See under BOOR.

Ana. *Awkward, clumsy, gauche: *rude, rough, raw, green.

Ant. Urbane. — *Con.* *Suave, bland, smooth, politic.

cloy, *v.* *Satiate, sate, surfeit, pall, glut, gorge, surcharge.

Ant. Whet. — *Con.* Stimulate, pique, excite, *provoke.

club. Society, *association, order.

clumsy. *Awkward, gauche, maladroit, inept.

Ana. *Rude, rough, green, callow: loutish, clownish, boorish (see under BOOR): *stiff, wooden, tense, rigid.

Ant. Dexterous, adroit: facile. — *Con.* Deft, feat (see DEXTEROUS): graceful, dignified, elegant (see corresponding nouns at ELEGANCE): *elastic, resilient, flexible, supple, springy: *easy, effortless, smooth.

clutch, *v.* Grasp, grab, *take, seize, snatch.

Ana. Capture, *catch, nab, cop: hold, *have, possess, own.

clutter, *n.* *Confusion, disorder, disarray, jumble, chaos, muddle, pie, snarl.

coadjutor. *Assistant, helper, adjutant, aide, aide-de-camp.

coalesce. Merge, fuse, blend, mingle, commingle, *mix, amalgamate.

Ana. *Compact, consolidate, concentrate, unify: *contract, condense, compress: cohere, adhere, *stick, cleave, cling: mass (see HEAP).

Con. Disintegrate, crumble, decompose (see DECAY): *separate, part, divide: dissolve, deliquesce (see LIQUEFY): dissipate, disperse (see SCATTER).

coalition. Fusion, confederacy, confederation, federation, *alliance, league.

coarse. **Coarse, vulgar, gross, obscene, ribald** come into comparison when applied to persons, their language, or behavior, and mean offensive to a person of good taste or moral principles. **Coarse** is opposed to *fine,* not only literally with reference to fiber, texture, structure, but also figuratively, as here considered, with reference to quality of mind, spirit, manners, words, and the like; it implies roughness, rudeness, crudeness, or the like; as, "Whose laughs are hearty, tho' his jests are *coarse*" (*Pope*); "What is fine within thee growing *coarse* to sympathize with clay" (*Tennyson*). "Some of the royal family were as *coarse* as the king was delicate in manners" (*H. Adams*). **Vulgar,** as here compared (see COMMON, 3), is, except perhaps with respect to language, a stronger term; it suggests that which is offensive to good taste or decency, frequently with the added implication of boorishness or ill breeding; as, "Caliban is *coarse* enough, but surely he is not *vulgar*" (*Hazlitt*); "Burns is often *coarse,* but never *vulgar*" (*Byron*); "How finely is the true Shakespearean scene contrasted with Dryden's *vulgar* alteration of it...displaying nothing but indelicacy without passion" (*Coleridge*); "The Have-nots demand a place in the sun, or in more *vulgar* language, a share in the loot" (*A. Huxley*). **Gross** (see RANK, 3) is opposed to *fine* in the sense of delicate, subtle, ethereal; it implies either a material, as contrasted to a spiritual, quality, or a bestiality unworthy of man; as, "the *grosser* forms of pleasure" (*E. Wharton*); *gross* habits of eating. "Caliban...is all earth, all condensed and *gross* in feelings and images" (*Coleridge*); "Thou art mated with a clown, And the *grossness* of his nature will have weight to drag thee down" (*Tennyson*); "My anger and disgust at his *gross* earthy egoism had vanished" (*Hudson*). **Obscene** stresses more strongly the idea of loathsome indecency or nastiness; as, an *obscene* allusion; "The jest unclean of link-boys vile, and watermen *obscene*" (*Pope*); "The rabble of Comus...reeling in *obscene* dances" (*Macaulay*). **Ribald** suggests vulgarity, often impropriety or indecency, such as provokes the laughter of people who are not too fastidious; as, "a *ribald* folk-song about fleas in straw" (*Lowes*); "their backs...shaking with the loose laughter which punctuates a *ribald* description" (*M. Austin*).

Ana. Rough, crude, *rude, raw, green, callow: *rank, rampant: boorish, loutish, clownish (see under BOOR).

Ant. Fine: refined. — *Con.* Delicate, dainty, exquisite, *choice: cultivated, cultured (see corresponding nouns at CULTURE): *gentle, genteel.

coast, *n.* *Shore, ripa, strand, beach, bank, foreshore, littoral.

coast, *v.* Toboggan, *slide, glide, slip, skid, glissade, slither.

coax. **Coax, cajole, wheedle, blandish** agree in meaning to use ingratiating art in persuading or attempting to persuade. **Coax** implies gentle, persistent efforts to induce another or to draw what is desired out of another; in earlier use, it implied coddling, fondling, caressing, flattery, and the like (as, "in a *coaxing* voice, suited to a nurse soothing a baby"—*Burney*), but in current English it more often suggests artful pleading or teasing in an attempt to gain one's ends. "Little by little, he *coaxed* some of the men whom the measure concerned most intimately to give in their views" (*Kipling*). "One... who can linger over and taste a phrase, *coaxing* its flavor to the palate as if it were an old wine" (*W. V. Moody*). "His [Donne's] skill in *coaxing*...the attention of the variable human mind to Divine objects" (*T. S. Eliot*). **Cajole,** in earlier use, stressed deceit, as by flattering, making specious promises, and the like. "They...should be treated as they themselves treat fools, this is, be *cajoled* with praises" (*Pope*). In current use, it often implies enticing or alluring and suggests beguilement rather than duplicity. "I wish Good Fairies were a little more active. They seem to be *cajoled* into security by the happiness of their favourites" (*Meredith*). "I think a vein of sentiment...induced me to take the journey, and to *cajole* a reluctant friend into accompanying me" (*A. Repplier*). **Wheedle** suggests more strongly than *cajole* the use of soft words, artful flattery, or seductive appeal; as, "she could *wheedle* the soul out of a saint" (*Hewlett*); "he had *wheedled* the Abeyta woman out of her geraniums, and left her pleased with herself for surrendering them" (*M. Austin*). **Blandish** implies less artfulness than *wheedle*, and more open flattery and a more apparent desire to win over by charming or alluring. "Would the *blandishing* enchanter still weave his spells around me" (*Dickens*).

Ana. *Induce, persuade, prevail on *or* upon: tease, pester (see WORRY): inveigle, entice, tempt, *lure.

Ant. Bully. — *Con.* Bulldoze, browbeat, *intimidate, cow: *threaten, menace: compel, coerce, oblige, *force, constrain.

cock, *n.* Stack, shock, pile, heap, mass, bank. See under HEAP, *v.*

cock, *v.* Stack, shock, pile, *heap, mass, bank.

Ana. *Gather, collect, assemble.

Con. *Scatter, disperse.

cockpit. Ring, *arena, circus, lists, court, field, gridiron, diamond, rink.

cocksure. Positive, certain, *sure.

Ana. *Confident, assured, sanguine: pompous, pretentious (see SHOWY): *decided, decisive.

Ant. Dubious, doubtful. — *Con.* Modest, diffident (see SHY).

cocky. Jaunty, perky, *debonair, chipper.

Ana. Conceited, egotistic, egoistic (see corresponding nouns at CONCEIT): arrogant, overbearing, supercilious, disdainful, insolent, *proud: dashing, dapper, spruce, natty (see STYLISH).

coenobite. Variant of CENOBITE.

coenobitic, coenobitical. Variants of CENOBITIC.

coerce. Compel, *force, constrain, oblige.

Ana. *Intimidate, bulldoze, bully, browbeat, cow: *threaten, menace: drive, impel (see MOVE): terrorize (see FRIGHTEN).

Con. *Induce, persuade, prevail on *or* upon: *coax, cajole, wheedle, blandish: *lure, entice, tempt, seduce, inveigle.

coercion. Compulsion, *force, violence, duress, constraint, restraint.

Ana. *Power, might, puissance, strength: intimidation, bulldozing, bullying, browbeating (see corresponding verbs at INTIMIDATE): threatening *or* threat, menacing *or* menace (see corresponding verbs at THREATEN).

coeval. Synchronous, concurrent, simultaneous, coincident, concomitant, *contemporary, contemporaneous.

cogent. Convincing, telling, *valid, sound.

Ana. Forceful, forcible, potent, *powerful, puissant: compelling, constraining (see FORCE, *v.*): inducing, persuading *or* persuasive (see corresponding verbs at INDUCE): proving, demonstrating (see PROVE): *effective, effectual.

cogitate. *Think, reflect, deliberate, reason, speculate.

Ana. *Ponder, ruminate, meditate, muse: *consider, revolve, excogitate, weigh, contemplate, study: *think, conceive, imagine, envisage, envision.

cognate. *Related, allied, kindred, affiliated.

Ana. Akin, alike, identical, *similar: common, generic, general, *universal.

Ant. Various. — *Con.* Diverse, *different, divergent, disparate.

cognation. Consanguinity, *kinship, affinity, agnation, enation.

cognizant *or* **cognisant.** *Aware, conscious, sensible, alive, awake.

Ana. *Conversant, versed: informed, acquainted, apprised (see INFORM).

Ant. Ignorant. — *Con.* *Insensible, insensitive, impassible, anesthetic: ignoring, overlooking, slighting, neglecting (see NEGLECT): oblivious, unmindful, *forgetful.

cohere. *Stick, adhere, cleave, cling.

Ana. Coalesce, fuse, merge, blend (see MIX): *cement, glue, agglutinate: *fasten, attach, affix: *join, combine, unite, connect, associate.

Con. *Detach, disengage: disentangle, untangle, disembarrass (see EXTRICATE).

coherence. **Coherence** (*or* **coherency**), **cohesion** agree in meaning the quality or character of a whole all of whose parts cohere, or stick together. **Coherence** (or the less frequent **coherency**) usually implies a unity of immaterial or intangible things, such as the points of an argument, the details of a picture, the incidents, characters, and setting of a story, or of material or objective things that are bound into unity by a spiritual, intellectual, or aesthetic relationship as through their clear sequence or their harmony with each other; it therefore commonly connotes an integrity which makes the whole and the relationship of its parts clear and manifest. "To treat the subject with the clearness and *coherence* of which it is susceptible" (*Wordsworth*). "Is there or is there not a spiritual *coherence* in Christianity, or is it only a gathering of laws and precepts, with no inherent connected spiritual philosophy?" (*Galsworthy*). "Scientific work... may indeed possess the appearance of beauty, because of the inner *coherence* which it shares with fine art" (*S. Alexander*). "No more *coherence* than the scattered jangle of bells in the town below" (*Quiller-Couch*). **Cohesion** more often implies a unity of material things held together by a physical substance such as cement, mortar, glue, or the like, or by a physical force such as attraction or affinity. "A house stands and holds together by the natural properties, the weight and *cohesion* of the materials which compose it" (*T. H. Huxley*). "What am I, Life? A thing of watery salt Held in *cohesion* by unresting cells Which work they know not why, which never halt" (*Masefield*). *Cohesion* may also be used of either material or immaterial things when the emphasis is on the process by which things cohere rather than on the resulting unity; as, a state composed of discordant races incapable of *cohesion*.

Ana. *Unity, integrity, solidarity, union: clearness, perspicuousness, lucidity (see corresponding adjectives at CLEAR).

Ant. Incoherence.

cohesion. *Coherence.

Ana. Unification, consolidation, concentration, compacting (see corresponding verbs at COMPACT): coalescence, fusing *or* fusion, blending *or* blend, merging (see corresponding verbs at MIX): cementing, gluing, agglutination (see corresponding verbs at CEMENT).

Con. Disintegration, decomposition, crumbling (see corresponding verbs at DECAY): dissolution, deliquescence (see corresponding verbs at LIQUEFY).

coin, *n.* Coinage, currency, specie, tender, cash, *money.

coinage. Coin, currency, cash, species, legal tender, *money.

coincide. Concur, *agree.

Ana. Accord, correspond, jibe, harmonize, tally (see AGREE): *match, equal.

Ant. Differ (*from*). — ***Con.*** Diverge (see SWERVE).

coincident. Synchronous, simultaneous, concurrent, concomitant, coeval, contemporaneous, *contemporary.

cold. **Cold, cool, chilly, frosty, frigid, freezing, gelid, icy, glacial, arctic** agree in meaning having a temperature below that which is normal or comfortable. **Cold** is the general term, often implying nothing more than the absence of heat; as, a *cold* day; a *cold* hand; *cold* meat. Occasionally, however, it also connotes discomfort; as, a *cold* room; a *cold* wind. **Cool** suggests moderate coldness, sometimes refreshing (as, a *cool* breeze; a *cool* hand on one's brow; a *cool* drink), but sometimes disagreeable, especially when hotness or warmth is desirable (as, *cool* soup; a *cool* radiator). **Chilly** implies coldness that makes one shiver; as, a *chilly* morning; a *chilly* room. **Frosty** implies coldness that makes one tingle or that causes vegetation to droop and die; as, a *frosty* night; *frosty* clearness. **Frigid** and **freezing** both imply temperatures below 32° Fahrenheit, but *frigid* stresses the intensity of the cold (as, a *frigid* climate; *frigid* weather) and *freezing* its congealing effect on man, vegetation, water, and the like (as, a *freezing* wind; a *freezing* temperature). **Gelid** in strict use equals *freezing*, but it is chiefly a literary word applicable to anything that is frozen or is indicative of freezing temperatures; as, a *gelid* mass; a *gelid* moon; "while sea-born gales their *gelid* wings expand" (*Goldsmith*). **Icy,** when used to indicate a kind of coldness, implies frigidity so great as to be painful and cutting; it is applicable chiefly to winds, storms, and the like; as, an *icy* rain; an *icy* northeast wind. **Glacial** is now rare in literal use in the sense of *icy;* it is mainly employed in reference to a geological period (a *glacial* epoch), especially one known as the Pleistocene epoch, during which much of the northern parts of North America, Europe, and Asia were covered with ice (as, *glacial* soil; *glacial* boulders). **Arctic** is the strongest of these words in its suggestion of intense coldness. It connotes the frigidity of the polar regions and is a hyperbolic rather than an exact term; as, a winter notable for its *arctic* temperatures.

When applied to persons, their temperaments, their acts and words, and their responses to stimuli, these words are also marked by differences in implications. **Cold** suggests absence of feeling or emotion, or less than normal human sympathy, friendliness, sensitiveness, or the like; as, his plea left us *cold; cold* words; he treated us with *cold* justice; "*cold* philanthropies" (*Wilde*). "Their *cold* intelligence, their stereotyped, unremitting industry repel me" (*L. P. Smith*). "Okio [a Japanese painter], in spite of his unerring eye and his incomparable cunning of hand, was of too *cold* a temperament to infuse a powerful current of life into the old tradition" (*Binyon*). **Cool** stresses control over one's feelings or emotions, and therefore absence of excitement or agitation. It may specifically connote composure, detachment, deliberativeness, or indifference. "This wonder, that when near her he should be *cool* and composed, and when away from her wrapped in a tempest of desires" (*Meredith*). "Both [Horace and Augustus] looked at life with a *cool* realism which was not allowed to become cynical" (*Buchan*). **Chilly, frosty,** and **freezing** usually stress the effect of another's coldness: *chilly* connotes a depressing or repressive influence; as, a *chilly* greeting, a *chilly* reception; *frosty* connotes a checking or restraining of advances; as, a *frosty* smile or manner; *freezing* connotes a blighting or repelling; as, a *freezing* reply to a letter, "many...had been repelled by his *freezing* looks" (*Macaulay*). **Frigid** emphasizes such deficiency of natural feeling as is abnormal or repellent; it is specifically applicable to persons who are sexually passionless and averse to sexual intercourse, but it is often applied to things which are not, but by their nature should be, impassioned or infused with feeling or warmth; as, *frigid* verse; a *frigid* religion; *frigid* hospitality. **Gelid** usually stresses the power to benumb (as, a *gelid* fear); **icy,** the power to cut and stab (as, an *icy* stare). **Glacial** suggests the total lack of vitality or animation; as, "such *glacial* metres" (*Longfellow*); "his manner more *glacial* and sepulchral than ever" (*Motley*). **Arctic** frequently adds to *frigid* a connotation of remoteness from all that is human or referable to humanity; as, "exact and *arctic* justice" (*Mencken*).

Ant. Hot.

collate. *Compare, contrast.

collateral, *adj.* *Subordinate, secondary, dependent, succursal, subject, tributary.

Ana. *Related, allied, kindred, cognate: correlative, complementary, correspondent, *reciprocal.

collation. *Comparison, parallel, contrast, antithesis.

Ana. Corroboration, verification, confirmation, authentication (see corresponding verbs at CONFIRM): emending *or* emendation, revising *or* revision, correcting *or* correction (see corresponding verbs at CORRECT).

colleague. *Partner, copartner, ally, confederate.

Ana. *Associate, companion, comrade.

collect. *Gather, assemble, congregate.
Ana. Mass, *heap, pile: *accumulate, amass, hoard: consolidate, concentrate, *compact.
Ant. Disperse: distribute. — *Con.* *Scatter, dissipate, dispel: dispense, divide, deal, dole (see DISTRIBUTE): *separate, part, sever, sunder: *assort, sort.

collected. Composed, *cool, unruffled, imperturbable, nonchalant.
Ana. *Calm, placid, tranquil, serene: quiet, *still: assured, *confident, sure, sanguine: *complacent, smug, self-satisfied.
Ant. Distracted, distraught. — *Con.* Agitated, perturbed, upset, disturbed, flustered, flurried (see DISCOMPOSE).

collection. Assemblage, assembly, gathering, congregation. See under GATHER, *v.*
Ana. Heap, pile, mass, stack (see under HEAP, *v.*): accumulation, hoarding *or* hoard (see corresponding verbs at ACCUMULATE).

collectivist. **Collectivist, socialist, communist, Bolshevist, nihilist, anarchist** come into comparison as names applied to persons who oppose the system of capitalist control of industry. The **collectivist** advocates common ownership of the means of production, distribution, and exchange. The term **socialist** has been variously used. As often used it is indistinguishable from *collectivist.* Broadly, the *socialist* advocates a less unequal distribution of income, to be attained through governmental ownership, or some measure of governmental control, of the means of production. The *state socialist,* for instance, would utilize existing forms of government to equalize income and opportunity, as by graduated taxation, compulsory insurance, and by state administration of industries, public utilities, common carriers, etc. The *Marxian socialist* believes that capitalism and profit should be abolished, and that this can be accomplished only through the attainment of political power by the proletariat. **Communist,** in the usual sense of the word, denotes an extreme Marxian socialist, who would abolish by force private property as well as profit. **Bolshevist,** originally a term for a member of the communist wing of the Social Democratic party in Russia, is often loosely used as an equivalent of *communist.* The **nihilist** [from L. *nihil,* nothing] believes that conditions in the social organization are so bad as to make destruction desirable for its own sake, independent of any constructive program or possibility. "It is because 'nothing' as it exists at present finds favour in their eyes that they have been called '*Nihilists*' " (*Nineteenth Century*). The **anarchist** demands emancipation from all law, moral as well as economic and political, outside the individual. At best, anarchism stands for a society made orderly by good manners rather than by law, in which each person produces according to his powers and receives according to his needs. At worst, it stands for a terroristic resistance to all present government and social order.

college. Institute, lycée, gymnasium, *academy, seminary.

collision. *Impact, impingement, clash, shock, concussion, percussion, jar, jolt, brunt.
Ana. Striking, hitting (see STRIKE, *v.*): wrecking *or* wreck, ruining *or* ruin, dilapidation (see corresponding verbs at WRECK): demolishment, destruction (see corresponding verbs at DESTROY).

collocation. *Phrase, locution, expression, idiom.

collude. Conspire, *connive.
Ana. Plot, scheme (see under PLAN, *n.*): concur, coincide, *agree: co-operate, concur, *unite, combine.

collusion. Conspiracy, connivance. See under CONNIVE.
Ana. *Agreement, accord, understanding: intrigue, conspiracy, *plot, machination.

colonnade. **Colonnade, arcade, arcature, portico, peristyle** are here discriminated as those terms are used in architecture. A **colonnade** is a row of columns (typically on the outside of a building) spaced at regular intervals and carrying an architrave or horizontal member lying directly across their capitals, so that the opening between each pair of columns is square-topped. *Colonnade* is usually applied not only to the columns, but to the entire structure, consisting of columns, roof, pavement, etc., or to the space which they enclose. Strictly, the word is used only in reference to classical architecture. An **arcade** is a long series of arches with their supporting columns and piers, together with the other members that complete the structure as an architectural feature. An arcade may be either inside or outside of a building; it may be a purely decorative feature or a means of admitting light and air. In the former case, the spaces between the arches and piers may be filled in (sometimes providing niches for statues); this type of arcade is called strictly an **arcature.** In the latter case, an arcade may take the place of an outer wall as of a gallery or cloister. Strictly, *arcade* is used of types of architecture in which the arch is an essential feature, such as the late Romanesque and the Gothic. **Portico** and **peristyle** are used in reference to architectural features employing the colonnade. When the colonnade extends across (or nearly across) one side of a building and serves as an entrance, it is called a *portico;* when it is continued so as to extend along three or, usually, all four sides of a building, it is called a *peristyle.*

colony. *Possession, dependency, dominion, protectorate, mandate, territory.

color, *n.* **1 Color** (*or* **colour**), **chroma, hue, shade, tint, tinge** come into comparison when they mean a property or attribute of a visible thing that is recognizable only when rays of light fall upon the thing and that is distinct from its shape, size, or other property apparent in dusk. **Color** is the ordinary term and, in careful use, the only generic term of this group. It may apply to the quality of blood which one describes as redness, of grass as greenness, of snow as whiteness, or of ebony as blackness, or to the optical sensation which one experiences when one sees these things respectively as red, green, white, and black. It may refer to any of the bands, called colors, of the spectrum, or to any of the variations by or as if by combination of one or more of these with another or with white, black, or gray; as, "Walden is blue at one time and green at another....Lying between the earth and the heavens, it partakes of the *color* of both" (*Thoreau*). *Color* is also specifically applicable to the attribute of things seen as red, yellow, blue, orange, green, purple, or the like (sometimes called *chromatic colors*), as distinct from the attribute of things seen as black, white, or gray (sometimes called *achromatic colors*); as, to give a white house touches of *color* by painting the window sashes and shutters green. In this sense of *color,* especially when there is no reference to concrete things, the scientist often prefers **chroma. Hue,** in poetry or elevated prose, is often synonymous with *color;* as, "As brown in *hue* As hazel nuts and sweeter than the kernels" (*Shak.*). More specifically, *hue* suggests some modification of color; as, "Their shining green has changed to a less vivid *hue;* they are taking bluish tones here and there" (*Hearn*). In scientific use, *hue* is often applied to the second of the three attributes of a chromatic color, which are: (1) *brilliance,* or its degree of correspondence to the grays as they move from low, that is from black, which has zero brilliance, to high, that is to white, which has the greatest brilliance; (2) *hue*, or its susceptibility of being classed as red, yellow, blue, or the like; (3) *saturation*, or its distinctness or vividness of hue. Thus, olive, the color, may be described as the color of the pickled green olive, or as a color yellowish-green in *hue*, of low brilliance, and low saturation; pink may be described as red in *hue*, of high brilliance, and low saturation. The remaining words of this group have not been generally adopted by scientists and as a result they sometimes fluctuate in meaning. **Shade** (literally, comparative darkness) is often used in the sense of one of the gradations of a color, especially as its hue is affected by its brilliance; as, to seek a darker *shade* of blue (i.e., a blue that is lower in brilliance because nearer to dark gray or black); a brighter *shade* of green (i.e., one higher in brilliance and saturation) is desirable; various *shades* of gray; "The dark ultramarine of the west turns a *shade* paler" (*J. C. Van Dyke*). **Tint** (etymologically, a dyeing or dipping in color) is also used as meaning a gradation of color in respect to brilliance, but it always suggests hue, and is commonly used in reference to light colors (or colors of high brilliance) that seem to be given by a light or delicate touching; thus, what are often called "pastel *colors*" or, less properly, "pastel *shades*," are, in precise use, *tints*. The term is not infrequently used in contrast to *shade*, especially when the latter word connotes comparative darkness or dullness (or low brilliance); as, "the flags by the shore were turning brown; a *tint* of yellow was creeping up the rushes" (*Jefferies*); "colours as pure and delicate as the *tints* of early morning" (*Cather*); "The sprays of bloom which adorn it [a tree] are merely another *shade* of the red earth walls, and its fibrous trunk is full of gold and lavender *tints*" (*Cather*). **Tinge** implies more of interfusion or stain than *tint;* as, "Autumn bold, With universal *tinge* of sober gold" (*Keats*); "The water...imparts to the body of one bathing in it a yellowish *tinge*" (*Thoreau*).

Nearly all of these terms carry extended meanings derived from or related to the senses previously considered. **Color** usually suggests an outward character or aspect, such as may be changed by circumstances (as, "Your love for him has changed its *colour* since you have found him not to be the saint you thought him"—*Hardy;* "it had been an essentially aristocratic movement.... But...it took on a strongly democratic *color*"—*Mencken*) or may be imparted to a thing to brighten and vivify it (as, "people talk of matters which I had believed to be worn threadbare by use, and yet communicate a rich *colour*...to them"—*A. C. Benson*). **Hue** is less often used figuratively than *color:* it usually suggests a character rather than an aspect, but it does not necessarily imply an ingrained character; as, that is a question of another *hue* (or *color*); "Our mental *hue* depends... completely on the social atmosphere in which we move" (*H. Smith*). **Tint** applies to a character that is not dominant but imparted as if by contact or influence; as, "Our inborn spirits have a *tint* of thee" (*Byron*). **Shade** and **tinge** are used figuratively in the sense of *trace, touch, trifle* (for this sense, see TOUCH); as, a *shade* less cordial than usual; a *tinge* of sadness, or of regret.

2 *Flag, ensign, standard, banner, streamer, pennant, pennon, jack.

colorable *or* **colourable.** *Plausible, credible, believable, specious.

Ana. Convincing, telling, cogent, sound, *valid.

colorless. **Colorless, uncolored, achromatic** mean without color. In exact use, however, they are not interchangeable. **Colorless** is applied to that which is transparent (as, water is a *colorless* liquid), or to that which is bleached, blanched, or pallid (as, *colorless* leaves, *colorless* cheeks and lips). **Uncolored** is applied to that which is left in its natural state or is not dyed or stained (as, *uncolored* pongee) or to objects which have not been touched or touched up with color (as, an *uncolored* photograph; *uncolored* cheeks and lips). **Achromatic** is applied to that which is free from any of the hues in the spectrum or from any hues formed by combinations of these, or which gives images which are free from extraneous colors produced by refraction; as, an *achromatic* color; an *achromatic* telescope. Thus, a color (in its inclusive sense) may be *chromatic* or *achromatic:* if the former, it has a hue; if the latter, it has not, and is, therefore, white, black, or a pure gray.

Ana. *Pale, pallid, ashen, wan: whitened, blanched, bleached, decolorized (see WHITEN).

Ant. Colorful.

colossal. Gigantic, giant, gigantean, mammoth, elephantine, titanic, immense, huge, *enormous, vast, herculean, Cyclopean, Antaean, Gargantuan, Brobdingnagian.

Ana. Monumental, stupendous, tremendous, prodigious, *monstrous.

column. *Pillar, pilaster.

comatose. Torpid, stuporous, sluggish, *lethargic.

Ana. *Languid, languorous, listless, languishing: phlegmatic, *impassive: *insensible, anesthetic, impassible: inert, passive, supine (see INACTIVE).

Ant. Awake.

combat, *v.* *Oppose, resist, withstand, antagonize.

Ana. Cope, fight, *contend, battle, war: *attack, assail, assault, bombard, storm.

Ant. Champion: defend. — *Con.* Protect, shield, guard (see DEFEND): *support, uphold, advocate: *maintain, justify, vindicate.

combat, *n.* Conflict, fight, *contest, affray, fray.

Ana. *Battle, engagement, action, push: *encounter, skirmish, brush: controversy, dispute, *argument: contention, strife, conflict, *discord.

comber. Breaker, beachcomber, roller, billow, undulation, ripple, *wave.

combination. **Combination, combine, party, bloc, faction, ring, cabal, junto** agree in denoting a union, either of individuals or of organized interests, for mutual support in obtaining common political or private ends. **Combination** is the most comprehensive of these terms, being applicable to any such union, whether a trust, an alliance, or simply an association for the purpose of urging demands or resisting claims; as, a *combination* of coal consumers against an increase in prices; a *combination* of railroads to maintain existing rates. **Combine** is a colloquialism, especially in the United States, for *combination;* as, the coal *combine*. A **party** is a number of persons united in support of some opinion, cause, or principle; it usually implies a similar body in opposition, especially when used in reference to a political organization built up to continue the action and policies of government through election of its candidates to office; as, in the United States, there are usually only two strong *parties;* the Labor *party* in England. "He who draws his pen for one *party* must expect to make enemies of the other" (*Dryden*). "Who [Burke], born for the universe, narrowed his mind, And to *party* gave up what was meant for mankind" (*Goldsmith*). **Bloc** commonly implies a combination, of persons or groups who otherwise differ in party or in interests, for the sake of achieving a common, and often temporary, end; thus, in France and in Italy, a *bloc* is a combination of members of two or more political parties; in the United States, a *bloc* is a combination not of parties but of members of different parties who have a common end; as, the agricultural, or farm, *bloc* formed in the Congress of the United States in 1921 by members from the agricultural states wishing to secure legislation helpful to their constituents. **Faction** (cf. *factious* at INSUBORDINATE) frequently suggests a smaller body than *party*, and commonly implies selfish ends and the use of unscrupulous or turbulent means. "So several *factions* from this first ferment Work up to foam and threat the government" (*Dryden*). "The Whigs and Tories in Rome, Athens, and Jerusalem never forgot national points with more zeal, to attend to private *faction*, than we have lately" (*Walpole*). **Ring** is applicable to an exclusive (often more or less secret) combination for a selfish, and often corrupt, purpose, such as the control of the market, of political patronage, and the like; as, the Tweed *Ring* was in control of New York City politics for six years. A **cabal** is a small and secret combination seeking private or sinister ends by scheming or intrigue. "Mr. Philips [said] that I was entered into a *cabal* with Dean Swift and others to write against the Whig interest" (*Pope*). **Junto** (a corruption of the Spanish *junta*, meaning "council," or "assembly") oftener than *cabal* suggests intrigue for party or political, as well as for private, ends; as, the Essex *Junto* of the War of 1812, which became the exponent of New England Federalism; the Cuban *junto* of 1898.

Ana. *Monopoly, corner, pool, cartel, syndicate, trust.

combine, *v.* **1** Unite, associate, link, *join, connect, relate.

Ana. *Mix, mingle, commingle, blend, fuse, amalgamate: consolidate, unify (see COMPACT, *v.*).

Ant. Separate. — ***Con.*** Part, divide, sever, sunder, divorce (see SEPARATE): *detach, disengage.

2 *Unite, co-operate, concur, conjoin.

Ana. Coalesce, merge (see MIX): conspire, collude, *connive: coincide, *agree, concur.

combine, *n.* *Combination, party, bloc, faction, ring, cabal, junto.

Ana. See those at COMBINATION.

come. Come, arrive are comparable because both basically mean to get to one point from another more or less distant in space, time, relation, development, or the like. *Come to* and *arrive at* are synonyms of *reach* and, with exceptions, of its synonyms (see REACH); as, to *come to* (or *arrive at*) the end of a journey; to *come to* (or *arrive at*) a decision; what are we *coming to* (or *arriving at*)? **Come** is Anglo-Saxon in its origin, is one of the elementary intransitive verbs of motion, always implying movement toward, and may be used wherever such movement, whether actual or apparent, whether physical or spiritual, is implied. **Arrive,** on the other hand, is derived from Old French, and in modern use is very much affected by its earliest sense, to come to shore; that is, to land or disembark. *Come,* therefore, may be used with or without the implication that the destination is reached; *arrive* consistently carries that implication; as, I can see them *coming;* they will *arrive* at three o'clock; he has *come* (or *arrived*). When used in reference to things that move or progress without an agent or agency, as because of some law of nature or in obedience to some inner law or principle, *come* is usually preferable unless a definite end or termination or, often, fulfillment, as of expectation, is suggested; thus, the days *come* and go; at last the day of departure *arrived;* the longed-for breeze was slow in *coming* but when it *arrived* it brought joy to all; success never *comes* to those who await it idly; it usually *arrives* only after years of patient endeavor. *Come* often suggests or requires statement of a source or place from which a thing has issued; *arrive,* on the other hand, often suggests or requires a statement of an end, a goal, or a climax to a progress or development; as, the family *comes* from peasant stock; the family *arrived* socially when the grandfather of the present baron was elevated to the peerage. In such cases, *come* and *arrive* are not interchangeable for the former is loosely synonymous with *issue, emanate, originate, arise,* and the like, and the latter with *succeed, triumph,* or when followed by *at,* with *acquire,* and the like.

Ana. *Approach, near: rise, arise, *spring, proceed, emanate, issue, stem.

Ant. Go. — ***Con.*** Leave, depart, quit, withdraw, retire (see GO).

comedian (*fem.* **comedienne**). Comic, *fool, jester, clown, stooge, buffoon, zany, merry-andrew, pantaloon, harlequin, antic.

comely, *adj.* Fair, pretty, bonny, handsome, lovely, *beautiful, good-looking, beauteous, pulchritudinous.

Ant. Homely.

comestibles. Provisions, viands, victuals, *food, provender, fodder, forage.

comfort, *v.* **Comfort, console, solace** come into comparison as meaning to give or offer a person help or assistance in relieving his suffering or sorrow. **Comfort,** the homelier, more intimate word, suggests relief afforded by imparting positive cheer, hope, or strength, as well as by the lessening of pain; as, "He hath sent me... to *comfort* all that mourn" (*Isaiah* lxi. 1–2); a mother *comforts* her sobbing child. "But there was about him a certain reserve, and she dared not *comfort* him, not even speak softly to him" (*D. H. Lawrence*). **Console,** the more formal term, emphasizes rather the alleviation of grief or the mitigation of the sense of loss than the communication of pleasure; it frequently implies some definite source of relief; as, the presence of his friend *consoled* him; to *console* oneself by philosophic reflections. "If you really want to *console* me, teach me rather to forget what has happened" (*Wilde*). **Solace** frequently suggests relief from weariness, despondency, chagrin, loneliness, dullness, or the like, rather than from grief or pain, and often, specifically, a lift of the spirits; and the source of that relief is more commonly things than persons; as, to *solace* oneself with books; "The same [lips] that oft in childhood *solaced* me ... 'Grieve not, my child, chase all thy fears away!' " (*Cowper*); "She was not really *solaced* by Religion" (*Meredith*).

Ana. Delight, gladden, rejoice, *please: *relieve, assuage, mitigate, alleviate: refresh, restore (see RENEW).

Ant. Afflict: bother. — ***Con.*** *Distress, trouble: torment, torture, try (see AFFLICT): vex, *annoy, irk.

comfort, *n.* Ease, *rest, repose, relaxation, leisure.

Ana. Contentedness *or* content, satisfaction (see corresponding adjectives under SATISFY, *v.*): enjoyment, joy, fruition, *pleasure: relief, assuagement, alleviation (see corresponding verbs at RELIEVE).

Ant. Discomfort. — ***Con.*** *Distress, suffering, misery.

comfortable. Comfortable, cozy (*or* **cosy**), **snug, easy, restful, reposeful** come into comparison when they mean enjoying or providing conditions or circumstances which make for one's contentment and security. **Comfortable** usually implies the absence of that which gives trouble, pain, or distress in any degree or of any kind to the body or mind (as, a *comfortable* chair or bed; a *comfortable* room both in summer and in winter; he is never *comfortable* except in his own home; "a makeshift arrangement not altogether agreeable or *comfortable* for either of us"—*H. Ellis*), but it often applies to persons or things that encourage in one serenity of mind, tranquillity, a sense of well-being, complacency, or the like (as, the family was left in *comfortable* circumstances; a *comfortable,* motherly woman; "although Darwin may have held this *comfortable* opinion [that history is development towards a goal], it is no part of his system"—*Inge*). **Cozy** suggests comfortableness derived from warmth, shelter, ease, friendliness, and the like; as, a *cozy* fire; a *cozy* armchair; to close all the windows and doors so as to make the house *cozy;* "the *cosy* talk by the fireside" (*J. R. Green*); "He made as if to change his *cosy* position, but reconsidered, and deferred it" (*Meredith*). **Snug** (as here considered: see also NEAT) suggests the state or the frame of mind of one who has as much room, or responsibility, or freedom, or money, or the like, as is essential to one's well-being, but no more than one actually needs to keep one cozy, content, or secure: the term usually connotes comfort such as is associated with small but comfortable quarters as distinguished from those that are spacious, or with a quiet, restricted, but pleasant way of life as distinguished from one where there is little time for one's own interests or where one is driven by ambitions or restlessness: often, specifically, the term suggests protection from the elements, and warmth and dryness, as contributions to one's comfort; as, "There is hardly to be found upon the earth, I suppose, so *snug* a creature as an Englishman by his fireside in the winter" (*Cowper*); "All the gipsies and showmen...lay *snug* within their carts and tents" (*Hardy*); "Arnold the heartbroken outcast from the *snug* household of faith, wearying in spiritual wastes of sand and thorns" (*C. E. Montague*). **Easy** (as here considered: see also EASY, 2) implies relief from all that makes for discomfort or hardships, with the result that one is happy or free from care, anxiety, trouble, doubt, or the like; as, to be in *easy* circumstances for the first time in his life; she could now enjoy herself with an *easy* conscience; "People of the right sort are never *easy* until they get things straight" (*Shaw*); "Mrs. Struthers's *easy* Sunday hospitality" (*E. Wharton*). **Restful** and the somewhat less common **reposeful** usually suggest a state of mind of one who is comfortable, cozy, or easy, as well as relaxed, or a character in a thing that induces such a state of mind; as, "It's *restful* to arrive at a decision, and *restful* just to think about New Hampshire" (*Frost*); "A *restful,* friendly room, fitted to the uses of gentle life" (*M. Austin*); "An attractive expression of *reposeful* friendliness pervaded his whole appearance" (*G. Macdonald*).

Ana. Comforting, consoling, solacing (see COMFORT, *v.*): content *or* contented, satisfied (see under SATISFY): grateful, welcome, agreeable, gratifying (see PLEASANT).

Ant. Uncomfortable: miserable. — ***Con.*** Wretched (see MISERABLE): distressing, troubling (see TROUBLE, *v.*): annoying, vexing, irking, bothering (see ANNOY).

comic, *adj.* Comical, *laughable, farcical, funny, droll, risible, ludicrous, ridiculous.

Ana. Diverting, amusing, entertaining (see AMUSE): *witty, humorous, facetious: grotesque, antic, *fantastic.

Ant. Tragic. — ***Con.*** *Serious, solemn, grave, sober: pathetic, touching, poignant, *moving, affecting.

comic, *n.* Comedian, *fool, jester, clown, buffoon, stooge, antic, zany, merry-andrew, pantaloon, harlequin.

comical. Comic, farcical, ludicrous, ridiculous, *laughable, risible, droll; funny.

Ana. Absurd, silly, *foolish: jocular, jocose, humorous (see WITTY): waggish, impish, roguish, sportive (see PLAYFUL): deriding *or* derisive, ridiculing, mocking (see corresponding verbs at RIDICULE).

Ant. Pathetic. — ***Con.*** *Melancholy, doleful, lugubrious, dolorous: *moving, poignant, touching, affecting.

comity. 1 *Courtesy, amenity, attention, gallantry.

Ana. Civility, politeness, courteousness (see corresponding adjectives at CIVIL): graciousness, cordiality, geniality, sociableness, affability (see corresponding adjectives at GRACIOUS): suavity, urbanity (see corresponding adjectives at SUAVE): *intercourse, commerce, dealings.

Ant. Dissension: antagonism. — ***Con.*** Rancor, animosity, animus, antipathy, *enmity, hostility: conflict, strife, *discord, variance, contention.

2 Amity, good will, *friendship.

Ana. *Association, society: companionship, comradeship (see primitive nouns at ASSOCIATE): concord, accord, *harmony.

command, *v.* **Command, order, bid, enjoin, direct, instruct, charge,** as here compared, mean to issue orders to someone to give, get, or do something. **Command** and **order** agree in stressing the idea of authority, *command* implying its more formal and official exercise, *order,* its more peremptory, sometimes even arbitrary, exercise; as, a king, a military officer, the captain of a ship, *commands;* a landowner *orders* a trespasser off his premises; one is apt to resent being *ordered,* except by those who have a right to *command.* But *order* is used of a physician with no such connotation; as, the doctor *ordered* outdoor exercise. **Bid** in this sense is somewhat archaic or literary, except when it is colloquial; it usually implies ordering or commanding (often with a suggestion of peremptoriness) directly and by speech; as, she *bade* him be seated. "He seized him by the collar and sternly *bade* him cease making a fool of himself" (*Shaw*). **Enjoin, direct,** and **instruct** are all less imperative than *command* or *order* but they all connote expectation of obedience. *Enjoin* adds to the idea of authority the implication of pressing admonition; *direct* and *instruct* suggest rather business, official, or diplomatic relations, *direct* being perhaps the more mandatory, *instruct* the more formal, of the two; as, a parent *enjoins* his children to be quiet; the church *enjoins* certain duties; the editor *directed* his secretary to admit no callers during a conference; to *instruct* an assistant to gather certain information. "St. Peter... *enjoins* us to be ready always to give an answer to every man that asks us a reason for the faith that is in us" (*Lowes*). "Why otherwise does it [the Constitution of the United States] *direct* the judges to take an oath to support it?" (*Ch. Just. Marshall*). "Marvin [the architect] was *instructed* to secure a Saint Joseph for the garden" (*M. Austin*). **Charge,** a more or less bookish term, implies not only enjoining but the imposition of a task as a duty; as, his mother *charged* him to look out for his little brother; "Mrs. Yeobright gave him the money-bags, *charged* him to go to Mistover" (*Hardy*).

Ana. Control, manage, *conduct, direct: exact, *demand, require: *force, compel, coerce, constrain, oblige.

Ant. Comply, obey.

command, *n.* **1 Command, order, injunction, bidding, behest, mandate, dictate** agree in meaning a direction, that must or should be obeyed, to do or not do something. **Command** imputes to the person who issues the directions either unquestioned authority (as, the *commands* of a general) or complete control of a situation (as, at the *command* of the intruder, he held up his hands). The term usually connotes either peremptoriness or imperativeness; as, at the *command* of his father, he returned to the house; every request of hers he interpreted as a *command.* **Order** is not always clearly distinguishable from *command;* it is, however, the preferred word for directions to subordinates that are instructions as well as commands; in such use it commonly implies explicitness in detail; as, the troops were awaiting *orders* from headquarters; in response to the principal's *order,* the pupils maintained silence while passing through the

corridors. **Injunction** carries a weaker implication of imperativeness than the preceding words, except in legal use, where it is applied to a court order commanding a person to do, or more often, to refrain from doing, something on the penalty of being adjudged guilty of contempt of court. In general use, the word commonly stresses admonition without losing the implication of expected or demanded obedience; as, "The high *injunction* not to taste that fruit" (*Milton*); she carefully obeyed the *injunctions* laid upon her by her physician. "They went off to play tennis ...with *injunctions* from Mrs. Hawthorne not to be late for dinner" (*Arch. Marshall*). **Bidding** usually implies the status of master or parent in the person who issues the orders, and therefore stresses expected obedience or the fact of being obeyed; as, "thousands at his [God's] *bidding* speed" (*Milton*). "Whatever Godwine did he did at the *bidding* of his lord" (*Freeman*). **Behest** is a distinctly literary term, equivalent to *bidding* in its implications; as, "to do his master's high *behest*" (*Scott*); "not to disobey her lord's *behest*" (*Tennyson*). **Mandate** (see also MANDATE, 2) carries the strongest implication of imperativeness of all of these words, for it denotes a command or order issued by a very high, often the highest, authority. It has or has had specific applications, such as an order from a superior court or official to an inferior one or from a Roman emperor to the commander of his military forces. In current use, it is often applied to something inexorably demanded, as by the exigencies of the situation, rather than actually or verbally commanded; as, he accepted the nomination, believing that his huge majority indicated a *mandate* from his party. "It was a bold step, for he [Augustus] had no legal military command, and no *mandate* from Senate or people" (*Buchan*). "Poe's doctrine of brevity, as a *mandate* laid upon poetry by the inflexible nature of things" (*Lowes*). *Mandate* also specifically applies to any order or commission granted by the League of Nations to one of its member nations to establish a responsible government over a colony or territory that belonged to Germany before the Treaty of Versailles. **Dictate** etymologically denotes a command given orally, but it is now rarely used literally. "He...received his suggestions, and bowed to his *dictates*" (*Meredith*). In commonest use, it denotes a command or authoritative judgment figuratively uttered by an inner voice such as that of the conscience or formulated in a principle or law. "The government which has a right to do an act, and has imposed on it the duty of performing that act, must, according to the *dictates* of reason, be allowed to select the means" (*Ch. Just. Marshall*). "A suspicion that... the Moral Law speaks in equivocal tones to those who listen most scrupulously for its *dictates*" (*L. P. Smith*).
Ana. Direction, instruction, charging *or* charge (see corresponding verbs at COMMAND): precept, ordinance, *law, statute, canon, rule.
2 Control, authority, *power, jurisdiction, sway, dominion.
Ana. Ascendancy, *supremacy: sovereignty (see FREE, *adj.*).

commander. Captain, master, *chief, chieftain, head, leader.

comme il faut. Proper, seemly, *decorous, decent, nice, demure.
Ana. Conventional, formal, ceremonious, *ceremonial: fitting, appropriate, meet, *fit.
Con. Unseemly, improper, *indecorous, indecent, unbecoming, indelicate.

commemorate, *v.* Celebrate, observe, *keep, solemnize.

commence. *Begin, start, initiate, inaugurate.
Ana. Institute, *found, organize, establish.
Con. Finish, complete, conclude, terminate, end, *close.

commend. **Commend, recommend, applaud, compliment** come into comparison when they mean to voice or otherwise manifest to others one's warm approval. **Commend** usually implies judicious or restrained praise, but it suggests as its motive a desire to call attention to the merits of a person or a thing; as, the police commissioners publicly *commended* the officers who made the arrest. "His wife seriously *commended* Mr. Collins for having spoken so sensibly" (*Austen*). "It is always dangerous and impertinent to *commend* a poem for anything but its poetry" (*Day Lewis*). **Recommend** adds to *commend* the implication of offering that which is praised for acceptance, use, or employment by another; as, the physician *recommended* the treatment of bruises with alternating cold and hot applications; his present employers highly *recommended* him to his prospective employers. **Applaud** implies an enthusiastic expression of approval; it commonly, but not necessarily, suggests approval by a large number of persons or by the public; as, the president was *applauded* for his closing of all banks in the crisis of March, 1933. "Everybody *applauded* the mayor's proposed entertainment, especially when it became known that he meant to pay for it all himself" (*Hardy*). **Compliment** stresses either courtesy in the commendation or, sometimes, flattery in the manner or words of praise; as, the visitors to the convention *complimented* the townspeople on the arrangements made for their comfort. " 'Marvellous cognac this, madame!' It was the first time it had ever been so *complimented*, and Madame Defarge knew enough of its antecedents to know better" (*Dickens*).
Ana. *Praise, laud, extol, eulogize, acclaim.
Ant. Censure: admonish. — *Con.* *Criticize, reprehend, reprobate, blame: *reprove, reproach, rebuke, reprimand, chide.

commensurable. Commensurate, proportionable, proportionate, *proportional.
Ana. Equivalent, equal, identical, tantamount (see SAME): *reciprocal, correspondent.
Ant. Incommensurable.

commensurate. Commensurable, proportionate, *proportional, proportionable.
Ana. Adequate, *sufficient, enough: corresponding *or* correspondent, according *or* accordant, squaring, conforming (see corresponding verbs at AGREE): balancing, counterbalancing, compensating, offsetting (see COMPENSATE).
Ant. Incommensurate.

comment, *n.* Commentary, *remark, observation, note, obiter dictum, descant.
Ana. Interpreting *or* interpretation, elucidation, explication, expounding *or* exposition, explaining *or* explanation (see corresponding verbs at EXPLAIN): annotation, gloss (see under ANNOTATE).

comment, *v.* Commentate, *remark, animadvert.
Ana. Interpret, elucidate, expound, *explain, construe, explicate: *annotate, gloss: *criticize: illustrate, *exemplify.

commentary. Comment, *remark, observation, note, obiter dictum, descant.
Ana. See those at COMMENT, *n.*

commentate, *v.* Comment, *remark, animadvert.
Ana. See those at COMMENT, *v.*

commentator. See under *commentate* at REMARK, *v.*

commerce. 1 Trade, *business, industry, traffic.
2 Traffic, *intercourse, dealings, communication, communion, commune, conversation, converse, correspondence.

commercial, *adj.* **Commercial, mercantile** come into comparison when they mean of, relating to, or dealing with the supplying of commodities. **Commercial** is the more widely applicable term: it may be used in reference to anything which has to do with the buying or selling of commodities for profit, with their transportation, and sometimes, even, with their production, or with business affairs in general; thus, a *commercial* transaction is any piece of business involving a buyer and seller of goods or property that is for the financial benefit of the seller; *commercial* law deals with all matters that have reference to business, such as contracts, negotiable papers, liens, payment of debts, partnerships, etc.; a *commercial* attaché is, in the United States, an officer of the Department of Commerce attached by the Department of State to an embassy or legation in a country where trade is important; a *commercial* traveler (the regular British term, and the once-common American term, now often replaced by "traveling salesman") is a person employed to travel, to display the goods or products of a business that engages in selling, and to take orders for them; the term *commercial* fertilizer is applied to a prepared product, as distinguished from *natural* fertilizer. Also, *commercial* is used to describe anything which has for its aim financial profit or is guided by the methods or practices of business; as, the *commercial* theater; *commercial* aviation; *commercial* sports; *commercial* radio programs (i.e., programs paid for by advertisers). **Mercantile** is often used interchangeably with *commercial* with little, sometimes no, difference in meaning; thus, a *mercantile* transaction is not ordinarily distinguishable from a *commercial* transaction, nor *mercantile* law from *commercial* law. The term, however, often suggests actual buying and selling (the occupation of a merchant) rather than commerce in general, including production and transportation, and is, therefore, more restricted in its application; thus, a *commercial* house is a business or company engaged in foreign or domestic commerce; a *mercantile* house is a business (now usually a wholesale business) engaged in merchandizing; "*mercantile* career" is more explicit or less ambiguous than "*commercial* career"; so, a *mercantile* agent; a *mercantile* establishment. When used in an extended sense, it commonly implies an opposition to some other thing of the same general character; thus, a *mercantile* marine (or merchant marine) consists of the privately owned and commercially operated ships of a country as distinct from those that are publicly owned, or the navy.

commingle. Mingle, blend, *mix, merge, coalesce, fuse, amalgamate.

Ana. Combine, unite, associate (see JOIN): *integrate.

commiseration. Compassion, *pity, condolence, sympathy, ruth, empathy, bowels.

Ana. Compassionateness, tenderness, warmheartedness (see corresponding adjectives at TENDER): mercifulness, clemency (see under FORBEARING): lamenting *or* lamentation, bewailing, bemoaning (see corresponding verbs at DEPLORE): pitifulness, piteousness, pitiableness (see corresponding adjectives at PITIFUL).

Ant. Ruthlessness, pitilessness.

commission, *v.* *Authorize, accredit, license.

Ana. Appoint, *designate, name, nominate: empower, *enable: instruct, enjoin, charge, bid, order, *command.

commit, *v.* **Commit, entrust** (*or* **intrust**), **confide, consign, relegate** come into comparison when they mean to assign to a person or place for some definite end or purpose, such as custody or safekeeping. **Commit** is the widest term; it may express merely the general idea of delivering into another's charge (as, to *commit* the management of an estate to an agent), or it may have the special sense of a transfer to a superior power, to a place of custody, or the like; as, "Into thine hand I *commit* my spirit" (*Psalm* xxxi. 5); "We therefore *commit* his body to the ground; earth to earth, ashes to ashes, dust to dust" (*Book of Common Prayer*); to *commit* a person to prison; to *commit* one's thoughts to paper. To **entrust** is to commit with trust and confidence; to **confide** is to entrust with entire reliance and assurance; as, to *entrust* one with a secret, with the care of a child; to *confide* to a friend the execution of one's dying wish. "A government, *entrusted* with such ample powers...must also be *entrusted* with ample means for their execution" (*Ch. Just. Marshall*). "The right of naturalization was therefore, with one accord, surrendered by the States, and *confided* to the Federal Government" (*Ch. Just. Taney*). **Consign** implies a more formal act, and frequently suggests such transfer or delivery as removes its object from one's immediate control; as, to *consign* goods to an agent for sale; "The family mansion had been *consigned* to the charge of a kinsman, who was allowed to make it his home for the time being" (*N. Hawthorne*); "He must now...*consign* him to a living tomb again" (*N. Hawthorne*). To **relegate** is to consign to some particular class, position, or sphere, usually with the implication of setting aside or getting rid of; as, "[Man] is *relegated* to his place in a classification" (*J. H. Newman*). "He supposed that he had disappointed the Bishop and that he was being *relegated* into the limbo of moderately satisfactory young parsons" (*C. Mackenzie*).

Ana. Transfer, shift, remove, *move: assign, *allot.

commodious. Capacious, *spacious, ample.

Ana. *Comfortable: *large, big, great: *broad, wide, deep.

Con. Circumscribed, confined, limited, restricted (see LIMIT, *v.*): *narrow, strait: inconvenient, incommodious (see corresponding verbs at INCONVENIENCE).

common, *adj.* **1** *Universal, general, generic.

Ana. Shared, partaken, participated (see SHARE, *v.*): joined *or* joint, united, connected, associated (see corresponding verbs at JOIN): merged, blended, amalgamated (see MIX).

Ant. Individual.

2 Mutual, *reciprocal.

Ana. & *Ant.* See those at COMMON, 1.

3 Common, ordinary, familiar, popular, vulgar come into comparison when they mean being in kind or having the character of that which is generally or usually seen, known, used, thought, or the like. **Common,** as here compared, implies the lack of distinguishing, conspicuous, or exceptional qualities; positively, it suggests usualness, everyday character or quality, or frequency of occurrence; as, the *common* people; a *common* soldier; the *common* chickweed; a *common* error; he lacks *common* honesty (or decency). "For *common* men and women two or three of the *common* loves will suffice—the love of family and home, of school and church, of mountain and sea" (*C. W. Eliot*). Often the term also connotes inferiority, coarseness, lack of breeding, or low station; as, the *common* herd; of *common* clay; he is hopelessly *common.* **Ordinary** expresses more definitely accordance with the regular order or run of things; as, "the *ordinary* intercourse of man with man" (*J. H. Newman*); "It's not like *ordinary* photographs. There's something special about it" (*Bennett*). It commonly implies qualities not above, frequently below, the average; as, "Choice word and measured phrase, above the reach Of *ordinary* men" (*Wordsworth*); "Let others expatiate on trivial objects, *ordinary* characters, and uninteresting events" (*Landor*). As a term of depreciation, *ordinary* is similar to but less contemptuous than *common;* as, a very *ordinary*-looking (cf. *common*-looking) person; his ability is no more than *ordinary*. **Familiar** stresses the fact of being generally known and easily recognized because of its frequency of occurrence or one's constant association with it rather than because of its lack of distinguishing qualities; as, "the tyranny of *familiar* surroundings over the imagination" (*B. Russell*); "To remind you of what is so *familiar* as to be frequently forgotten" (*Frankfurter*). "The doctrine of Einstein, which sweeps away axioms so *familiar* to us that they seem obvious truths, and substitutes others which seem absurd because they are *unfamiliar*" (*H. Ellis*). **Popular** and **vulgar** (see also COARSE), as here compared, imply commonness that arises from use or acceptance by or prevalence among the vast majority of persons, often specifically among the common people of a country, an age, or the like; as, *popular* fallacies; the *vulgar* tongue; *Vulgar* Latin. In current use, *popular* more often stresses the implication of widespread prevalence, currency, favor, or the like, among the people than does *vulgar*, which even in this sense often carries derogatory connotations such as of inferiority, coarseness, and the like; as, a *popular* song; "dancing...of all the arts... most associated in the *popular* mind with pleasure" (*H. Ellis*); "this mode of interpreting Scripture is fatal to the *vulgar* notion of its verbal inspiration" (*Arnold*); "a *popular* instead of an accurate and legal conception of what the word 'monopolize' in the statute means" (*Justice Holmes*); "We were reluctant to expose those silent and beautiful places to *vulgar* curiosity" (*Cather*).

Ana. Prevalent, *prevailing, rife, current: *usual, customary: *plentiful, abundant, ample.

Ant. Uncommon: exceptional. — *Con.* Rare, *infrequent, occasional: singular, unique, peculiar, odd, *strange.

commonplace, *n.* **Commonplace, platitude, truism, bromide, cliché** agree in meaning an idea or expression lacking in originality or freshness. A **commonplace** is a stock idea or expression which is frequently little more than the obvious, conventional, and easy thing to think or say on a given subject. "The machinery as well as the characters of those novels became the *commonplaces* of later romancers" (*Sir W. Raleigh*, d. 1922). "The mediaeval lover...was not unlikely, in his panegyric of his lady, to identify her with a panther. It was a *commonplace* of compliment" (*Lowes*). **Platitude** adds to *commonplace* the suggestions of flatness or triteness and often, utterance with an air of importance or novelty. "What is that sentimental *platitude* of somebody's... about the sun being to flowers what art is to life?" (*Hewlett*). "Traditional schoolbook *platitudes* and campaign slogans" (*Frankfurter*). A **truism** is a self-evident truth; it differs from an axiom (see *axiom* at PRINCIPLE) in frequently implying a somewhat superfluous insistence upon the obvious; as, Pope's palpable *truism* "The proper study of mankind is man." "It is a *truism* that a sound society makes for sound individuals" (*Day Lewis*). **Bromide** (a slang term) applies to any commonplace, platitude, or truism that strikes the listener or reader as especially dull or hackneyed and often, as an evidence of its maker's low-grade mentality; as, "Despite the silly old *bromide* [nobody loves a fat man], the fat man is more often than not the best loved of men" (*McClure's Mag.*). **Cliché** applies to any expression which when new was fresh and full of meaning, but which by constant iteration has become not only dull but hackneyed and stereotyped; as, "The *cliché* is merely the sometime novel, that has been loved not wisely but too well" (*Lowes*).

Ana. Expression, *phrase, collocation, idiom, locution: banality, jejuneness, inanity, wishy-washiness (see corresponding adjectives at INSIPID): triteness, threadbareness (see corresponding adjectives at TRITE).

common sense. See SENSE, 2.

commune, *v.* *Confer, consult, advise, parley, treat, negotiate.

Ana. Converse, talk, *speak: *discuss, debate, argue.

commune, *n.* Communion, *intercourse, commerce, traffic, converse, dealings, communication, conversation, correspondence.

Ana. See those at COMMUNION, 1.

communicable. *Infectious, contagious, catching.

communicate. Communicate, impart agree in meaning to convey or transfer something (now always something neither tangible nor concrete) such as information, qualities, or the like; they differ chiefly in emphasis, *communicate* stressing the result, *impart*, rather the process, of the transfer. To **communicate** (the more general term) is to make common to both parties or objects involved the knowledge or quality conveyed; to **impart** is to share with another what is regarded as primarily one's own; as, the sky *communicated* its color to the sea; his courage *communicated* itself to his men; the smoke *imparted* its odor to his clothes; to *impart* one's knowledge or skill to others. "I wonder do we ever succeed really in *communicating* our thoughts to one another" (*Shaw*). "You are worth to society the happiness you are capable of *imparting*" (*J. G. Holland*).

Ana. Acquaint, apprise, *inform, advise, notify: tell, disclose, *reveal, divulge, discover: convey, *transfer.

Con. Conceal, *hide: *suppress, repress: withhold, hold back, reserve (see KEEP).

communication. *Intercourse, commerce, traffic, dealings, conversation, converse, correspondence, communion, commune.

Ana. Exchanging *or* exchange, interchanging *or* interchange (see corresponding verbs at EXCHANGE): conversing, talking (see SPEAK): *news, tidings, advice, intelligence.

communion. 1 Commune, *intercourse, commerce, traffic, converse, dealings, communication, conversation, correspondence.

Ana. Empathy, sympathy (see PITY, *n.*): mysticism (see under ASCETIC): contemplation (see corresponding verb at CONSIDER): *ecstasy, rapture, transport.

2 *Religion, denomination, faith, church, creed, sect, cult, persuasion.

communist. Bolshevist, socialist, *collectivist, nihilist, anarchist.

compact, *adj.* Dense, *close, thick.

Ana. Compressed, condensed, contracted (see CONTRACT, *v.*): concentrated, consolidated, compacted (see COMPACT, *v.*): solid, *firm, hard: *tight.

Con. *Loose, slack: diffuse, prolix, verbose, *wordy: tenuous, rare, *thin.

compact, *v.* **Compact, consolidate, unify, concentrate** agree in meaning to bring or gather together the parts, particles, elements, or units of a thing so as to form a close mass or an integral whole. **Compact** stresses the process more than the effect. It usually suggests a packing or pressing together of many things so as to form a closely arranged mass or a dense substance, and may be used in reference both to material and immaterial things: sometimes, it carries so strong an implication of solid formation or construction that it fundamentally means to build firmly or to strengthen; as, heat and lack of rain have *compacted* the soil; to *compact* matted fibers of wool and hair into felt by rolling and pressing; "Sweet spring ... A box where sweets *compacted* lie" (*Herbert*). **Consolidate** implies a merging or uniting, often in an exceedingly close union, of previously distinct but, usually, homogeneous or complementary things. The term may take as its object a whole, such as a nation, a people, or an empire, or such as a substance or material, and may imply a process which promotes the binding together of the parts, elements, individuals, and the like, so that solidarity or solidity is achieved; as, war tends to *consolidate* a people; "They believed that the Church was the only force which could *consolidate* the nation and check fissiparous tendencies" (*Inge*); rolling and cooling *consolidated* the newly laid asphalt into a firm smooth pavement. But *consolidate* can also take as its objects the parts, elements, individuals, groups, etc., which have been brought together in close union; as, "these organizations worked independently, and subsequently they were partially *consolidated*" (*V. Heiser*); "Two marriages with the Dutch Vandergraves had *consolidated* these qualities of thrift and handsome living" (*E. Wharton*). **Unify** implies a union of heterogeneous or homogeneous parts, elements, individuals, or the like, that results in the making or producing of a thing that has oneness and integrity and that stands by itself as a thing apart: the term does not, however, carry as strong an implication of solidarity as does *consolidate* but, on the other hand, it places stress on the integration of parts so that each does its appointed work or serves its own purpose to the benefit not only of itself but of the whole; thus, a dramatist *unifies* (not *consolidates*) the play he composes; after a civil war, the task of the government is to *unify* (rather than *consolidate*) a nation; the imagination of a great poet *unifies* a mass of images and impressions; the Homeric poems may have been originally a collection of narrative poems, but it seems likely that one person *unified* them. **Concentrate** usually carries the implication of bringing together a number of things that are scattered or diffused and of massing them around a point or center; as, to *concentrate* troops at places where an attack is expected; to *concentrate* one's efforts on a single piece of work; "The science of that age was all divination, clairvoyance...seeking in an instant of vision to *concentrate* a thousand experiences" (*Pater*). In a figurative extension of this sense, *concentrate* often implies the fixing of the mind or attention on one thing so that all distracting objects or thoughts are eliminated; as, her excitement made her unable to *concentrate* on the task. A similar implication of eliminating that which weakens, dilutes, or adulterates, is found in scientific and technical use; thus, the chemist *concentrates* a solution by evaporating the solvent; a miner *concentrates* ores (i.e., separates the base from the precious metals) by a machine or by washing.

Ana. Compress, condense, *contract: bind, *tie: unite, combine (see JOIN): knit, *weave.

Con. Dissipate, disperse, *scatter: *separate, part, divide.

compact, *n.* Pact, entente, convention, covenant, concordat, treaty, cartel, *contract, bargain, indenture, mise.

companion, *n.* Comrade, *associate, chum, pal, buddy, crony.

Ana. *Friend, confidant, intimate, acquaintance: *partner, colleague: attendant, escort, chaperon (see corresponding verbs at ACCOMPANY).

companionable. *Social, co-operative, convivial, gregarious, hospitable.

Ana. Friendly, neighborly, *amicable: *amiable, obliging, complaisant, good-natured: sociable, affable, *gracious, cordial.

Con. Uncongenial, unsympathetic (see INCONSONANT): reserved, taciturn, uncommunicative (see SILENT).

company, *n.* **Company, party, band, troop, troupe** come into comparison when they denote a group of persons who are associated in a joint endeavor or who are assembled for a common end. **Company** is the general term for either a temporary assemblage or a permanent association of individuals who join forces. "The glorious *company* of the apostles" (*Bk. of Com. Prayer*). "The right to enter every other State whenever they pleased, singly or in *companies*" (*Ch. Just. Taney*). A **party** is a company assembled temporarily for a common purpose; as, a search *party;* a dinner *party;* "a *party* of visitors from the country" (*Shaw*). A **band** is a company united by a common tie or purpose; the term implies closer organization and a less casual coming together than does *company;* as, the robbers worked in *bands;* a *band* of musicians. "That small, transfigured *band*...whose one bond is, that all have been unspotted by the world" (*Arnold*). A **troop** is a company or band that works or acts together in close formation or in unanimity; the term frequently suggests a throng or multitude; as, "*troops* of friends" (*Shak.*); "There entertain him all the Saints above, In solemn *troops*, and sweet societies" (*Milton*). In specific use, *troop* is applied to a band of soldiers, or in the plural *troops*, to soldiers collectively; as, "Farewell the plumed *troop*, and the big wars" (*Shak.*); the British *troops*. When the reference is to a company of performers (especially on the stage) **troupe** is the preferred spelling; as, a circus *troupe*.

Ana. *Set, circle, coterie, clique: *association, society, club, order: *crowd, throng, mob, horde.

comparable. Analogous, akin, parallel, *similar, like, alike, identical, homogeneous, uniform.

Ant. Disparate. — *Con.* *Different, divergent, diverse, various.

compare, *v.* **Compare, contrast, collate** agree in meaning to set two or more things side by side in order to show likenesses and differences. **Compare** implies as an aim the showing of relative values or excellences, or a bringing out of characteristic qualities, whether they are similar or divergent; **contrast** implies as the aim an attempt to emphasize their differences; as, one may *compare* the movement of the *Odyssey* with that of the *Aeneid* to arrive at their distinctive qualities; one may thereupon *contrast* the buoyancy and rapidity of the one with the stateliness and dignity of the other. One object is *compared with* another, as above: it is *compared to* another when it is formally represented, on the basis of a real or (frequently) imagined similarity, as like it; as, Pope *compares* Homer *with* (not *to*) Vergil; he *compares* Homer *to* (not *with*) the Nile, pouring out his riches with a boundless overflow, Vergil *to* (not *with*) a river in its banks, with a gentle and constant stream. **Collate** suggests a minute or critical comparison in order to note points of agreement and divergence; it applies especially to the minute comparison of books and manuscripts containing different versions of the same work for the sake of ascertaining or establishing the correct text. "He has visited all Europe...not to collect medals, or *collate* manuscripts: but...to *compare* and *collate* the distresses of all men in all countries" (*Burke*).

Ana. *Match, equal, approach, touch, rival.

comparison. Comparison, contrast, antithesis, collation, parallel, as here compared, agree in meaning a setting of things side by side so as to discover or exhibit their likenesses and differences, especially their generic likenesses and differences. **Comparison** is often used more or less loosely as the comprehensive term; in precise use it is preferred when the differences are obvious, and an intent to lay bare resemblances and similarities for the sake of expounding or judging is implied; as, despite the fact that Bolshevism and Fascism are antagonistic ideologies, there is ground for a *comparison* between them; students who make a *comparison* of Shakespeare's *Hamlet* and the play which was its source acquire intimate knowledge of the great dramatist's indebtedness to others. Because measuring one thing in terms of another is usually implied by *comparison*, the word often imputes an offensive character either to the association (as in the *comparison* of "the colonel's lady" and "Judy O'Grady") or to the judgment; as, "*comparisons* are odious"; a tactful person never makes *comparisons;* he will lose nothing by the *comparison.* **Contrast** is the preferable term when one wishes to imply an intent to distinguish or discriminate things which are so much alike that their differences are not obvious; as, the correct use of close synonyms can be shown only by *contrast.* "The parallelism and succession [of Bismarck and Richelieu] are apparent. But the *contrast* also must be noted; the *contrast* in character and the *contrast* in the respective advantages and disadvantages which aided and hindered them" (*Belloc*). *Contrast* often also suggests an aesthetic rather than an expository aim, or an artistic effect gained by the exhibition of startling differences. "In physical appearance that *contrast* is glaring....the square, full blooded, blunt face of the one, the pointed chin and finely cut, pale features of the other" (*Belloc*). **Antithesis** also implies contrast for the sake of revealing startling differences, but it distinctively suggests such opposition in the things contrasted that they either represent extremes or negate each other. The word may imply an expository intent; it then presupposes that the true nature of one thing is fully understood only when it is presented as opposed to that which is unlike it in every particular. "The philosophy of fascism and the philosophy of democracy are...irreconcilable....the true *antithesis* [is] not that between fascism and communism which have much in common [but between] Democracy and fascism...opposed ways of life with contradictory standards of value" (*N. Y. Herald Tribune*). **Collation** and **parallel** denote a kind of comparison for the purpose of revealing both likenesses and differences. Both imply a close study and, usually, a specific aim. *Collation* denotes a comparison of different versions, accounts, editions, texts, manuscripts, etc., of the same thing, for the purpose of verification, co-ordination, correction, selection of the original, or the like; as, to make a *collation* of the Scriptural accounts of the Resurrection. "Of these [corrupt passages in Shakespeare] the restoration is only to be attempted by *collation* of copies or sagacity of conjecture" (*Johnson*). *Parallel* usually denotes a minute comparison of passages, articles, works, etc., which are believed to have a different origin, in order to detect correspondences, or of accounts, records, stories told at different times, etc., which ought to agree, in order to detect discrepancies; thus, by what is often called "the deadly *parallel*," a comparison of two articles may reveal such correspondences in language and thought as to give ground for a charge of plagiarism, or a comparison of testimony given by the same witness on two occasions may reveal discrepancies that make him liable to arrest for perjury.

Ana. *Likeness, similarity, resemblance, analogy, similitude, affinity: *parallel, counterpart, analogue, correlate.

compass, *n.* **1** *Circumference, perimeter, periphery, circuit, ambit.

Ana. Area, extent, magnitude, *size: *field, sphere, domain.

2 Sweep, scope, *range, reach, radius, gamut, ken, purview, horizon, orbit.

Ana. Circumscription, limitation, restriction (see corresponding verbs at LIMIT): limits, bounds, confines (see singular nouns at LIMIT).

compass, *v.* Gain, attain, achieve, *reach.

Ana. Effect, fulfill, accomplish, *perform: complete, finish (see CLOSE, *v.*).

compassion. *Pity, commiseration, ruth, sympathy, empathy, bowels, condolence.

Ana. Tenderness, compassionateness, responsiveness, warmheartedness (see corresponding adjectives at TENDER): *mercy, charity, grace, lenity, clemency.

Con. Indifference, aloofness, unconcern (see corresponding adjectives at INDIFFERENT): mercilessness, relentlessness, implacability (see corresponding adjectives at GRIM).

compassionate. *Tender, sympathetic, warmhearted, warm, responsive.

Ana. *Pitiful, piteous: merciful, *forbearing, clement, lenient: humane, benevolent, *charitable.

Con. Merciless, unrelenting, relentless, implacable, *grim: obdurate, inexorable, *inflexible, adamant.

compatible. Congruous, *consonant, consistent, congenial, sympathetic.

Ana. Suitable, appropriate, proper, meet, fitting, *fit: harmonizing, corresponding *or* correspondent, according *or* accordant (see corresponding verbs at AGREE): harmonious (see corresponding noun HARMONY).

Ant. Incompatible. — ***Con.*** Incongruous, *inconsonant, inconsistent, uncongenial, discordant, discrepant: *adverse, antagonistic, counter.

compel. *Force, coerce, constrain, oblige.

Ana. Impel, drive, *move: *command, order, enjoin.

Con. Prevail on *or* upon, *induce, persuade: *coax, cajole, wheedle, blandish.

compendious. Summary, pithy, succinct, *concise, terse, laconic.

Ana. *Compact, close: condensed, contracted (see CONTRACT, *v.*): abridged, abbreviated, shortened (see SHORTEN).

Con. Amplified, expanded, inflated (see EXPAND): *full, complete: diffuse, prolix (see WORDY).

compendium. **Compendium, syllabus, digest, pandect, survey, sketch, précis, aperçu** come into comparison when they mean a treatment of a subject or of a topic in brief compass. Unlike the terms discriminated at ABRIDGMENT, these words do not stress condensation of a previous work, though that implication is at times found in some of them. **Compendium** applies to a work which gathers together and presents in brief form (either in outline form or in discursive writing) all the facts, principles, or other details essential to a general or comprehensive knowledge of the subject: the term is used chiefly in reference to a work in which its author or authors compile in orderly and intelligible form information gathered from others and not obtained by independent investigation or research; as, a *compendium* of economics for the use of the business man; "Mr. Lengyel's 'Turkey' is in the nature of a *compendium* of Turkish history" (*N. Y. Herald Tribune*). **Syllabus** applies mainly to a series of headings, points, propositions, concise statements of the substance of courses to be given or of lectures to be delivered, or the like, which give the material necessary for a view of the whole and an understanding of its drift or pattern; as, a *syllabus* of college courses; a *syllabus* of forum lectures; the "*Syllabus* of [Pope] Pius X" is a table of 65 propositions advanced by Modernists and condemned by him as erroneous. **Digest** applies to a body of information gathered from many sources and arranged and classified so that it may be made accessible. The term applies chiefly to a compilation of legal rules, statutes, decisions, opinions, and the like, alphabetically arranged and fully indexed; as, a *digest* of Roman law; a *digest* of Jewish law. *Digest* also is used to designate an abstract in outline or essay form giving briefly the substance of something heard or read; as, the professor asked his students to write a *digest* of the lecture to which they had just listened. In current use, the term is often employed in titles of magazines that give abridgments of articles from recent issues of other magazines or of recently issued books; as, "The Reader's *Digest*." **Pandect,** which is used chiefly in the plural, is the equivalent of *digest* as applied to a compilation of laws, but it is used chiefly of the monumental digest of Civil, or Roman, law (the *Pandects* or *Digest*) compiled under the authority of the Emperor Justinian in the sixth century A.D. **Survey** applies to any brief but comprehensive presentation of a subject or topic, especially one that is to be treated later in detail, so that those who hear it or read it will have a view of the whole, of its leading features, and of their relation to each other as in time, space, or importance; as, he devoted his first lecture on the Middle Ages to a *survey* of that period; the course will give you a *survey* of English literature. The remaining terms of this group suggest reduction to an extremely brief compass. **Sketch** (as here considered: see also under SKETCH, *v.*) suggests slighter and, often, more tentative treatment than *survey;* as, to submit a *sketch* of the proposed book. **Précis** (etymologically, a French adjective meaning *concise*) applies to any brief clear-cut statement of essential facts, points, details, or the like: in school use, it applies to a concise restatement, not an outline, made by a student in part in his own words, often as an exercise in composition, of the main ideas of a lecture, chapter, poem, text assigned for collateral reading, or the like, preserving usually the order, emphasis, and tone of the original. In general use, the term may apply to an abstract (see this term at ABRIDGMENT); but, as it does not necessarily imply condensation of a book or treatment, it is preferred to *abstract* when the matter presented constitutes a report, such as a report of events sent by a diplomatic agent to his department of state during a crisis in the affairs of the government to which he is accredited, or a very short description of an important occurrence, or the like; as, "I know she goes in for giving a rapid *précis* of all her guests" (*Wilde*). **Aperçu** applies to a sketch that ignores details and gives only enough to give a quick impression of the whole; as, "it is one of the most memorable of the striking *aperçus* which abound in Plato" (*J. S. Mill*).

Ana. Conspectus, epitome, brief, abstract (see ABRIDGMENT).

compensate, *v.* **1 Compensate, countervail, balance, offset, counterbalance, counterpoise** agree in meaning to make up for that which is excessive, deficient, harmful, or the like, in something else, or to undo the good or evil, benefit or harm, or the like, of something else. One thing **compensates** another, or *for* another (or a person *compensates* a thing for which he is responsible) when the former makes amends for, or supplies a recompense for, whatever has been lost or suffered through the latter; as, "a dramatist like Tourneur can *compensate* his defects by the intensity of his virtues" (*T. S. Eliot*); "He has missed a training in criticism, in analysis, in open-mindedness ...which no other training can *compensate*" (*H. Ellis*); "No other qualities, however brilliant, can *compensate* for the absence of this quality [truthfulness] in a teacher" (*C. W. Eliot*); "the relief of seeing Lanning 'settled' would more than *compensate* for the...drawbacks of the marriage" (*E. Wharton*). One thing **countervails** another, or *against* another, when the former is sufficiently strong, powerful, efficient, or the like, to counteract the influence exerted or the harm or damage done by the latter or suffered in consequence of it; as, "For nought against their wills might *countervail*" (*Spenser*); "So shall my credit *countervail* your shame" (*Browning*); "Admitting losses, are there *countervailing* gains?" (*Lowes*). "The fact...shall, in the absence of strong *countervailing* testimony, be deemed conclusive evidence" (*Lincoln*). A *countervailing* duty is a special and additional tax placed on an import that for some reason or other could otherwise be sold more cheaply than the same article produced at home. One thing **balances** another, or two (sometimes more) things *balance* (or *balance* each other), when both (or all) things are so adjusted that they are equal or properly proportioned, as in numbers, quantity, size, importance, or effectiveness, and the combination is harmonious because no one outweighs the other or others or can exert a harmful influence on the whole; as, in sentencing prisoners, the judge *balanced* justice and mercy; in the healthy human body the salt intake and the salt loss through excretion *balance*. "The general tendency to the degradation or dissipation of energy is *balanced*...by a building-up process in the cell and in the organism" (*Inge*). "That, like a ground in painting, *balances* All hues and forms, combining with one tone Whatever lights or shades are on it thrown" (*Bridges*). One thing **offsets** another (this and the following terms have no intransitive use) when the former, as the exact opposite of the latter and its equal in importance, in effectiveness, in power, in numbers, or the like, neutralizes the latter's good or evil effect, gain or loss, benefit or harm; as, his loss of thousands of votes from his own party was *offset* by his gain in independent votes; the disadvantages of the plan are sufficient to *offset* its clear advantages. "The benefits of favorable climatic environment are oftentimes more than *offset* by the inconveniences of travel, loneliness, and homesickness" (*V. Heiser*). One thing **counterbalances** another when the former serves or is intended to serve to offset an excess, a deficiency, an evil, or the like, in the latter, or, in very precise use, when the former acts as a corrective of any tendency in the latter to loss of equilibrium or proper balance, especially when it, or one of its parts, is subjected to undue pressure, strain, or tension; as, a heavy weight suspended on a cable which is attached to an elevator and passes over a pulley at the top of the shaft serves to *counterbalance* the increased load when the elevator carries passengers or freight; mine hoists are often operated by the *counterbalancing* of an ascending and a descending car. One thing **counterpoises** another when the former provides the equivalent of the latter in weight or value (physical, spiritual, artistic, or the like), and insures the balance of the whole. "They [the boats] were like scales, in which the weight on one side must be *counterpoised* by a weight in the other" (*Jefferies*). "The new tower [of Chartres Cathedral] is a little wanting in repose for a tower whose business is to *counterpoise* the very classic lines of the old one" (*H. Adams*).

Ana. Counteract, *neutralize, negative: *nullify, negate, annul, abrogate, invalidate: *complement, supplement: correspond, square, tally, jibe, *agree.

2 Remunerate, *pay, recompense, requite, repay, reimburse, satisfy, indemnify.

competent. 1 Capable, qualified, *able.

Ana. *Proficient, skillful, skilled, adept, expert: efficient, *effective.

Ant. Incompetent. — ***Con.*** *Incapable, unqualified: inefficient, *ineffective.

2 Adequate, *sufficient, enough.
Ana. *Needful, necessary, requisite: *fit, suitable, meet.
Con. *Meager, scanty, scant, exiguous: *excessive, inordinate, immoderate, exorbitant.

compete with. Vie with, *rival, emulate.
Ana. Cope, *contend, fight: *match, rival, approach, equal, touch.

complacent. **Complacent, self-complacent, self-satisfied, smug, priggish** come into comparison as meaning feeling or showing satisfaction especially in one's own possessions, attainments, accomplishments, or the like. **Complacent** implies that a feeling of pleasure accompanies this satisfaction: it may suggest merely a sense of well-being that comes from having no complaint to make or, at the other extreme, it may imply gloating over the success of something for which one is in some way or in some degree responsible; as, "Mrs. Baines laughed with the *complacent* ease of obesity" (*Bennett*); " 'Nothing in my brain I bring'—he seems to hymn with a pious and *complacent* humility his freedom from intellectual baggage" (*C. E. Montague*); "She glanced *complacently* at the French wall-paper that reproduced a watered silk" (*E. Wharton*); "I viewed the peaceful scene *complacently*, proud of the way I had managed the whole affair" (*V. Heiser*). Although *complacent* usually suggests an attitude toward oneself, it does not carry that implication so clearly that there is left no room for doubt. For this reason, **self-complacent** or **self-satisfied** is often preferred when an unequivocal or an unambiguous word is desired: *self-satisfied* always, and *self-complacent* usually, carries a strong implication either of a comparison made between oneself and others to the great disadvantage of the others, or of a feeling that one can rise no higher. "All nature may be represented as groaning and travailing to produce at last her consummate masterpiece, our noble selves. There is a certain provincialism about this last assumption, characteristic of a *self-complacent* age" (*Inge*). "No bandit fierce, no tyrant mad with pride, No cavern'd hermit, rests *self-satisfy'd* (*Pope*). **Smug** now usually implies a habitual self-satisfaction that arouses in some degree dislike or contempt: in its earliest sense, now rare if not obsolete, it suggested neatness or trimness of appearance, especially but not exclusively of those who are self-respecting or belong to the so-called "respectable" classes. In current use, the term often implies both self-satisfaction and conscious respectability and, less often, it additionally connotes either narrowness or provinciality or a degree of Pharisaism; as, "his worldwide sympathy...with everything but the *smug* commonplace" (*Birrell*); "a *smug*...quality...had crept into that stern piety" (*K. L. Bates*); "Those late Georgian days which were the *smuggest* known to fame" (*A. Repplier*). **Priggish,** like *smug*, is difficult to confine to any one sense or to any constant emphasis on certain implications. In current use, however, it commonly connotes either self-satisfaction, self-sufficiency, or self-righteousness, and it usually also suggests either a more or less conscious assumption of one's own superiority or an obvious effort to live up to what one considers one's high principles or one's high ideals; as, a serious, earnest lad who gave many the impression that he was *priggish;* "Already, in the *Essays* [of Matthew Arnold], Culture begins to seem a little more *priggish*...and a little more anaemic" (*T. S. Eliot*).
Ana. Self-assured, self-confident, self-possessed, assured, confident (see corresponding nouns at CONFIDENCE): conceited, egotistic, egoistic (see corresponding nouns at CONCEIT): *proud, vain, vainglorious (see under PRIDE, *n.*).
Con. *Humble, modest: diffident, *shy.
☞ *Do not confuse* complacent *with* complaisant.

complaint. Ailment, *disease, affection, malady, distemper.

complaisant. Obliging, good-natured, *amiable.
Ana. Affable, genial, cordial, *gracious: courteous, courtly, gallant, polite, *civil: *suave, urbane, politic, diplomatic, smooth, bland: agreeable, *pleasant, pleasing.
Ant. Contrary, perverse. — *Con.* Disagreeable, unpleasant (see affirmative adjectives at PLEASANT): uncongenial, unsympathetic (see INCONSONANT): *cold, chilly, frigid.
☞ *Do not confuse* complaisant *with* complacent.

complement, *n.* **Complement, supplement** come into comparison both as nouns meaning one thing that makes up for a want or deficiency in another thing and as verbs meaning to supply that which is needed to make up for this want or deficiency. **Complement,** as here considered, implies a completing: it may suggest such a relation between two things or two groups of things that if they are put together they form a whole, or the full number, amount, or quantity necessary for a given purpose; thus, a grammatical *complement* is a word or phrase which must be added to a predicate if the latter is to make a definite assertion, as, for example, *well* in "he feels *well*," *free* in "to set him *free*," *of no use* in "it proved *of no use*"; you need two more chairs to *complement* those you already have in the room. However, the term even more often suggests such disparity in two things that what is supplied by either one is lacking in the other, with the result that their actual or theoretical combination gives a completeness that constitutes or approaches perfection; as, Norman refinement and flexibility are the *complement*, in the English vocabulary, of its Saxon homeliness and strength; "No adequate conception of the pictorial art of Asia can be attained without taking account of these wonderful works [of Japanese figure painting], *complementing*, as they do, the philosophic and poetic art which culminated in the Chinese painting of the Sung era" (*Binyon*). "Shakespeare gives the greatest width of human passion; Dante the greatest altitude and greatest depth. They *complement* each other" (*T. S. Eliot*). **Supplement** implies an addition to something relatively complete, but capable of improvement, enrichment, enhancement, or the like, by such an addition; thus, a *supplement* to a newspaper (often, a "book *supplement*," or a "literary *supplement*") is an additional section which enriches the character of the issue. Usually, the term means exactly this; as, a year of foreign travel is an excellent *supplement* to a college education; to *supplement* a work with an index; "the detailed study of history should be *supplemented* by brilliant outlines" (*B. Russell*). Sometimes, however, the term carries the implication of needless addition (as, "[of the Orphic and other mysteries in ancient Rome] their real weakness lay in the fact that they were *supplements*, something tacked on to life, and involved no new vision of the universe"—*Buchan*); sometimes, on the other hand, it comes pretty close to *complement* in suggesting essential differences (often in more than two things) and a need of combination if perfection is to be attained (as, "A complete philosophy would find room for all [physics, history, religion with their different valuations of experience] and would show how they *supplement* each other" (*Inge*).
Ana. Counterpart, correlate, *parallel.

complement, *v.* Supplement (see under COMPLEMENT, *n.*).
Ana. Complete, finish, *close.

complementary, complemental. *Reciprocal, correlative, correspondent, convertible.
Ana. Complementing, supplementing (see corresponding verbs under COMPLEMENT, *n.*): completing, finishing (see CLOSE, *v.*): related, associated (see JOIN).
Con. *Different, diverse, divergent, disparate: *inconsonant, incompatible, incongruous, inconsistent.

complete, *adj.* *Full, plenary, replete.
Ana. Entire, *whole, total, all: *perfect, intact, whole, entire.
Ant. Incomplete.

complete, *v.* Finish, conclude, *close, end, terminate.
Ana. Effect, fulfill, achieve, execute, accomplish, *perform, discharge.
Con. Initiate, inaugurate, start, *begin, commence.

complex, *adj.* **Complex, complicated, intricate, involved, knotty** agree in meaning having parts or elements that are more or less confusingly interrelated. That is **complex** which is made up of so many different interrelated or interacting parts or elements that it requires deep study or expert knowledge to deal with it; as, the *complex* mechanism of a watch; "Our general failure to grasp the need of knowledge and thought in mastering the *complex* modern world" (*B. Russell*). That is **complicated** which is so complex that it is exceedingly difficult to understand, solve, explain, or the like; as, a *complicated* problem in mathematics. "His [T. H. Huxley's] descriptions of the most *complicated* organic structures are astonishingly lucid" (*A. Huxley*). That is **intricate** which, because of the interwinding or interlacing of its parts, is perplexing or hard to follow out; as, the *intricate* tracery of an arabesque. "Nature utilizes the sunshine, the air and the earth as raw materials for creating myriad perfumes, but so *intricate* are her processes...that man cannot follow precisely in her footsteps" (*A. C. Morrison*). That is **involved** in which the parts are, or are thought of as, intertwined, or that return in some fashion upon themselves; the term, therefore, in reference especially to financial affairs, implies extreme complication or disorder; as, the *involved* patterns of sailors' or heraldic knots; an *involved* sentence or argument. "At his death ...[her husband] had left his affairs dreadfully *involved*" (*Austen*). "Public issues are so large and so *involved* that it is only a few who can hope to have any adequate comprehension of them" (*G. L. Dickinson*). That is **knotty** which is not only complicated but is so full of perplexities, difficulties, entanglements, or the like, that understanding or solving seems almost impossible. "That brings up at last the *knotty* question, what is enough?" (*Shaw*). The same object may often be regarded from more than one of the above points of view; as, a sailor's knot may be *intricate* and *complicated*, as well as *involved;* a network of railroad tracks may be *complicated* as well as *intricate*, though not *involved*.
Ana. Mixed, mingled, blended, merged, fused, amalgamated (see MIX): composite, compound (see corresponding nouns at MIXTURE).
Ant. Simple (see PURE).

complex, *n.* *System, scheme, network, organism, economy.
Ant. Component. — *Con.* Member, *part, portion, piece: constituent, integrant, *element, factor: *item particular, detail.

complexion. Temperament, temper, *disposition, character, personality, individuality.
Ana. Humor (see WIT): *mood, humor, vein, temper: nature, kind, *type, sort.

compliance. Acquiescence, resignation. See under COMPLIANT.
Ana. Obedience, docility, amenableness, tractableness (see corresponding adjectives at OBEDIENT): submitting *or* submission, yielding, deferring *or* deference (see corresponding verbs at YIELD).
Ant. Frowardness. — *Con.* Obstinacy, stubbornness (see corresponding adjectives at OBSTINATE).

compliant. Compliant, acquiescent, resigned, and their corresponding nouns **compliance, acquiescence, resignation,** are synonymous only when used in reference to a person, a mood, or a disposition that manifests acceptance, as of another's will or of that which is disagreeable or hard to endure. **Compliant** always suggests a flexibility or lack of firmness in mood or temper, and frequently implies readiness to accept meekly and without question; as, educational methods that make children *compliant;* a naturally *compliant* race. **Acquiescent** implies acceptance without protest or rebellion; it often also connotes a temperamental lack of self-assertiveness. "The cause of reform slowly went on gaining adherents—most of them ...of the *acquiescent* rather than the militant type" (*Grandgent*). **Resigned** usually presupposes a disposition or a temper neither compliant nor acquiescent and implies deliberate, but not necessarily happy, acceptance and resolute forbearance from repining. "He had become *resigned* to her perpetual lamentation" (*Meredith*). "*Resignation* to inevitable evils is the duty of us all" (*Austen*).
Ana. *Obedient, amenable, tractable, docile: submissive, *tame, subdued: accommodating, conforming, adapting *or* adaptable (see corresponding verbs at ADAPT).
Ant. Froward. — *Con.* *Contrary, perverse, balky, restive, wayward: refractory, recalcitrant, *unruly, ungovernable, intractable, willful, headstrong.

complicated. Intricate, involved, *complex, knotty.
Ana. Difficult, arduous, *hard: abstruse, *recondite: perplexing, puzzling, mystifying (see PUZZLE, *v.*).
Ant. Simple (see EASY). — *Con.* *Easy, facile, light.

compliment, *n.* **Compliment, flattery, adulation** agree in denoting praise addressed directly to a person. A **compliment** is a courteous expression of commendation, and may be either sincere or merely formal. "In the noble dedication...to the Duchess of Ormond we have an example of Dryden's most polished and magnificent style in elaborate personal *compliment*" (*Gosse*). **Flattery** implies insincerity in compliment or a play upon self-love or vanity by means of artful or obsequious praise. "When one is flagging, a little praise (if it can be had genuine and unadulterated by *flattery*)...is a cordial" (*Scott*). "It is better to leave genuine praise unspoken than to expose yourself to the suspicion of *flattery*" (*Shaw*). **Adulation** adds to *flattery* the implications of servility or fulsomeness. "He fascinated others into believing him a superior being; feasted his self-esteem on their *adulation* until it swelled to monstrous proportions" (*A. Huxley*).
Ana. *Encomium, tribute, panegyric, eulogy: praise, lauding *or* laudation, extolling *or* extollation (see corresponding verbs at PRAISE).
Ant. Taunt. — *Con.* *Affront, insult, indignity: depreciation, disparagement (see corresponding verbs at DECRY): criticism, censure, reprehension, reprobation, denunciation (see corresponding verbs at CRITICIZE).

compliment, *v.* *Commend, applaud, recommend.
Ana. *Praise, laud, extol, eulogize, acclaim.
Con. *Criticize, censure, reprehend, condemn, denounce: *decry, depreciate, disparage.

complot. Conspiracy, *plot, intrigue, machination, cabal, frame-up.
Ana. See those at CONSPIRACY, 2.

component. Constituent, ingredient, *element, integrant, factor.

Ana. Member, *part, detail, portion, piece: *item, particular.
Ant. Composite: complex. — ***Con.*** *Mixture, compound, blend, admixture, amalgam.

comport. **1** Acquit, quit, demean, *behave, conduct, deport.
2 Accord, conform, *agree, square, harmonize, correspond, tally, jibe.

compose. Compose, consist of, consist in, comprise, constitute are confused rather than synonymous terms. All involve the idea of making up or forming a complex whole, but they vary greatly in the subjects which they take when the verb is used in the active voice and in the sense (sometimes the voice) of "form" or "make up" that is expressed in the term. **Compose,** the most generally useful of these words, has two major senses. The first and most common sense is to form, fashion, or construct by putting together two or more things so as to produce a new and unified thing. In this sense, the term no longer, except in the passive forms, implies construction out of material or objective substances (as, "Were it a casque *composed* by Vulcan's skill, My sword should bite it"—*Shak.;* concrete is *composed* of cement, sand, and gravel mixed with water): the emphasis is now on intellectual labor and the term often connotes exercise of imagination and taste (as, to *compose* a novel or a sonata; he is at work *composing* his sermon). In its second major sense, and the one most closely relating it to the other terms in this group, *compose* takes a plural subject (sometimes a collective noun) and means to go together to form or make up the thing named by the object; as, "See worlds on worlds *compose* one universe" (*Pope*); "the people who *compose* these [American] Indian political communities have always been treated as foreigners" (*Ch. Just. Taney*); "a principle which so entirely pervades the constitution, is so intermixed with the materials which *compose* it" (*Ch. Just. Marshall*). The passive in this sense is often indistinguishable from that of the first sense, except that it more often suggests analysis than construction; as, "the elements of which human nature is *composed*" (*G. L. Dickinson*). *Consist* (etymologically, to stand still or firm) comes into comparison with the other verbs (which are transitive) only in its forms **consist of** and **consist in.** The former is equal in its meaning to the passive of *compose* and, sometimes, like the latter word, implies previous construction or formation and sometimes only existence and capacity for analysis, and not a bringing into being; as, concrete *consists of* cement, sand, and gravel, mixed with water; "your army, which doth most *consist Of* war-mark'd footmen" (*Shak.*); coke *consists* mainly *of* carbon; his estate *consists of* several pieces of real property and of a very large amount of personal property; "Newton imagined light to *consist of* particles darted out from luminous bodies" (*J. Tyndall*). *Consist in,* on the other hand, means to have something lying in it, residing in it, or inhering in it, as its essential nature, substance, foundation, or cause; as, "pretty much all law *consists in* forbidding men to do some things they want to do" (*Justice Holmes*); "It is *in* the failure to grasp this that the human tragedy has often *consisted*" (*H. Ellis*); "There is a large part of critical writing which *consists in* 'interpreting' an author, a work" (*T. S. Eliot*). **Comprise** (which is etymologically a doublet of *comprehend,* to grasp, to seize) is no longer a close synonym of *comprehend* (see under UNDERSTAND, INCLUDE, APPREHEND), although in precise use it usually carries some of the implications of *comprehend.* In its currently leading senses, *comprise* is a synonym either of *compose* (in the sense of to go together to make up a thing) or of *consist of.* Whether the subject is a plural noun naming the parts, elements, factors, etc., or a singular noun naming the whole made up of such parts, elements, factors, etc., *comprise* in careful use always differs from *compose* and *consist of* in carrying no suggestion or little suggestion of things put together and an obvious implication of an inclusion in, or a covering by, or a taking in by the whole that is designated; as, the district *comprises* three counties and part of a fourth; "If one short volume could *comprise* All that was witty, learned, and wise" (*Swift*); "It was these last words that proved to Joseph that the ringlets and bracelets did not *comprise* the whole of this young man's soul" (*G. Moore*); "It is music that moulds the manners and customs that are *comprised* under ceremony" (*H. Ellis*); "In the case of stories...reread in later years, my present recollection *comprises* only what lingers from the first reading" (*Grandgent*). **Constitute,** as here considered, may be used either with a singular or a plural subject in the sense of to go into the construction, makeup, nature, or character of a thing as its (or one of its) components or constituents; as, "the greater number of the couples *constituting* New York society" (*E. Wharton*); "flogging on weekdays and sermons on Sundays do not *constitute* the ideal technique for the production of virtue" (*B. Russell*); "that mysterious remoteness which *constituted* half her fascination" (*Galsworthy*).
Ana. *Make, fabricate, fashion, form: create, *invent.

composed. Collected, *cool, unruffled, imperturbable, nonchalant.
Ana. Quiet, *still: serene, placid, tranquil, *calm: sedate, staid, *serious: repressed, suppressed (see SUPPRESS).
Ant. Discomposed: anxious. — ***Con.*** Agitated, perturbed, upset, disquieted, flustered, flurried (see DISCOMPOSE): worried, concerned (see under CARE, *n.*).

composer. *Writer, author.
Ana. *Maker, creator, author: *artist, artificer.

composite. Admixture, blend, compound, amalgam, *mixture.
Ana. Composition, constitution (see corresponding verbs at COMPOSE): combining *or* combination, uniting *or* union (see corresponding verbs at JOIN).

composition. Theme, paper, article, *essay.

composure. *Equanimity, sang-froid, phlegm.
Ana. Coolness, collectedness, imperturbability, nonchalance (see corresponding adjectives at COOL): self-possession, aplomb (see CONFIDENCE): placidity, serenity, calmness (see corresponding adjectives at CALM).
Ant. Discomposure, perturbation. — ***Con.*** Agitation, disquieting *or* disquiet, flustering *or* fluster (see corresponding verbs at DISCOMPOSE): alarm, consternation, terror, *fear, panic: discomfiture, embarrassment (see corresponding verbs at EMBARRASS).

compound, *n.* *Mixture, amalgam, composite, admixture, blend.
Ana. Combining *or* combination, uniting *or* union (see corresponding verbs at JOIN): coalescence, fusing *or* fusion, merging *or* merger (see corresponding verbs at MIX).
Ant. Element (*in science*).

comprehend. **1** *Understand, appreciate.
Ana. Seize, grasp (see TAKE): conceive, envisage, envision (see THINK).
2 *Apprehend.
Ana. See those at COMPREHEND, 1.
3 Embrace, involve, *include, imply, implicate, subsume.

Ana. Comprise, constitute (see COMPOSE): *contain, hold: classify, pigeonhole (see ASSORT).

comprehension. Apprehension. See under APPREHEND.

Ana. Understanding, appreciating *or* appreciation (see corresponding verbs at UNDERSTAND): *knowledge, science, learning, erudition.

compress, *v.* Constrict, deflate, *contract, condense, shrink.

Ana. *Compact, concentrate, consolidate: bind, *tie.

Ant. Stretch: spread. — *Con.* *Expand, dilate, distend, swell, inflate: disperse, *scatter, dissipate.

comprise. *Compose, consist of, constitute, consist in.

Ana. Comprehend, embrace, *include: *contain, hold.

compulsion. Coercion, constraint, duress, *force, violence, restraint.

Ana. Impelling *or* impulsion, driving *or* drive (see corresponding verbs at MOVE): pressure, *stress: necessity, exigency, *need.

Con. Persuasion, inducement (see corresponding verbs at INDUCE): *choice, option, election, preference.

compunction. 1 Remorse, *penitence, repentance, contrition, attrition.

Ana. Regret, *sorrow: conscientiousness, scrupulousness *or* scrupulosity (see corresponding adjectives at UPRIGHT).

2 Scruple, demur, *qualm.

Ana. *Hesitation, hesitancy: reluctance, disinclination (see corresponding adjectives at DISINCLINED).

compute. *Calculate, reckon, estimate.

Ana. *Count, enumerate, number: sum, total, figure, cast, *add.

comrade. *Associate, companion, crony, chum, pal, buddy.

Ana. *Friend, intimate, confidant: colleague, *partner, confederate, ally.

con. *Against, versus.

Ant. Pro.

conation. *Will, volition.

Ana. *Effort, exertion: *action, act: *choice, selection, option.

concatenate, *v.* Articulate, *integrate.

Ana. Link, connect, relate, unite, combine, *join, associate: fuse, blend, merge, coalesce (see MIX): organize, systematize (see ORDER, *v.*).

Con. Break down, resolve, *analyze, dissect.

concatenated. Articulated, integrated. See under INTEGRATE, *v.*

Ana. *Cumulative, accumulative, additive: linked, connected, united, related (see JOIN): organized, systematized (see ORDER, *v.*).

concatenation. Articulation, integration. See under INTEGRATE, *v.*

Ana. Sequence, *succession, chain, train.

conceal. *Hide, screen, secrete, bury, cache, ensconce.

Ana. Cloak, mask, *disguise, dissemble.

Ant. Reveal. — *Con.* Disclose, discover, divulge, betray (see REVEAL): expose, exhibit, display, *show, parade, flaunt: manifest, evidence, *show, evince.

concede. 1 *Grant, allow.

Ana. Admit, *acknowledge: waive, cede (see RELINQUISH).

Ant. Dispute. — *Con.* Argue, debate, *discuss, agitate.

2 *Grant, vouchsafe, accord, award.

Ana. *Yield, submit: surrender, resign, cede, *relinquish.

Ant. Deny (*something to somebody*). — *Con.* Refuse (see DECLINE).

conceit. **Conceit, egotism, egoism, self-esteem, self-love, amour-propre** agree in meaning an attitude of regarding oneself with favor. **Conceit** implies a conviction of one's superiority in one or more lines of achievement or an overweeningly favorable opinion of one's powers or accomplishments. It often, but not necessarily, connotes a failure to see oneself truly, or an offensive, bumptious manner. "To have lost the godlike *conceit* that we may do what we will, and not to have acquired a homely zest for doing what we can, shows a...mind that...forswears compromise" (*Hardy*). "*Conceit* may puff a man up, but never prop him up" (*Ruskin*). **Egotism** (hence also *egotist*) stresses the tendency to make oneself, one's thoughts, one's deeds, etc., the object of others' notice, as by making them the leading topic of conversation or by attracting attention to them in any way. "He [Samuel Butler] was...an *egotist* bitten with self-distrust, concealing his wounds in self-assertion and his hesitancies in an external aggressiveness" (*S. P. Sherman*). The word may or may not imply contempt for others' interests or opinions. "A man and a boy of ten are perhaps better company than a man and a boy of fifteen. There's so much less *egotism* between them" (*H. G. Wells*). **Egoism** (hence also *egoist*) emphasizes concentration on oneself, one's interests, one's needs, or the like. It seldom suggests a tendency to display oneself or to attract attention to oneself; but it commonly implies self-interest, especially as opposed to altruism, or interest in others, as the inner spring of one's acts or as the measure by which all things are judged. "She preferred to be herself, with the *egoism* of women!" (*Meredith*). "Mrs. Fyne brushed them [appeals to her compassion] aside, with the semi-conscious *egoism* of all safe, established existences" (*Conrad*). **Self-esteem** implies a proper and balanced pride in oneself. "Ofttimes nothing profits more Than *self-esteem,* grounded on just and right" (*Milton*). "Love, Hope, and *Self-esteem,* like clouds depart And come, for some uncertain moments lent" (*Shelley*). **Self-love** usually implies an abnormal regard for oneself that excludes all other interests or affections. On the other hand, it occasionally designates that degree of love for oneself or interest in one's well-being which is the proper and necessary complement of one's love for others. "But 'tis not easy with a mind like ours... To bid the pleadings of Self-love be still" (*Cowper*). "*Self-love* but serves the virtuous mind to wake, As the small pebble stirs the peaceful lake.... Friends, parent, neighbour, first it will embrace; His country next; and next all human race" (*Pope*). **Amour-propre,** which is the French equivalent for *self-love,* in English use (possibly because of a misinterpretation of *propre*) comes closer to *self-esteem,* for it stresses pride, usually pardonable pride, in oneself. It is therefore used when the idea of sensitiveness to others' opinions is indicated. "The *amour propre* of the French people had been outraged" (*Holt & Chilton*). "She flattered his *amour propre* by asking that from his generosity, which she could have taken as a right" (*C. Reade*).

Ana. *Pride, vanity, vainglory: arrogance, superciliousness, insolence (see corresponding adjectives at PROUD): complacency, smugness, priggishness (see corresponding adjectives at COMPLACENT).

Ant. Humility. — *Con.* Humbleness, modesty, meekness, lowliness (see corresponding adjectives at HUMBLE): diffidence, shyness, bashfulness (see corresponding adjectives at SHY).

conceive. *Think, imagine, fancy, realize, envisage, envision.

Ana. *Consider, revolve, excogitate: speculate, cogitate, *think: *ponder, ruminate, meditate.

concentrate, *v.* *Compact, consolidate, unify.

Ana. *Gather, collect, assemble: mass, *heap, pile:

fix, *fasten, attach: engross, *monopolize, absorb.
Ant. Dissipate. — *Con.* Disperse, dispel, *scatter: dilute, *thin, attenuate, extenuate, rarefy: *distribute, divide, dispense, deal.

concentration. Application, *attention, study.
Ana. Intentness, raptness, engrossment, absorption (see corresponding adjectives at INTENT).
Ant. Distraction.

concept. *Idea, conception, notion, thought, impression.
Con. Percept, image, *sensation.

conception. Concept, *idea, thought, notion, impression.
Ana. *Opinion, view, belief, conviction, persuasion, sentiment: theory, *hypothesis.

concern, *v.* **Concern, affect** are sometimes confused. **Concern** implies the bearing or influence, **affect,** the direct operation or action, of one thing on another; as, a piece of legislation may *concern* (that is, have to do with, have reference or relation to) certain vested interests without *affecting* them (that is, producing an effect upon them, changing them in any way).
Ana. *Bear, pertain, appertain, apply, relate, belong: influence, sway, *affect, touch.

concern, *n.* **1** *Affair, business, matter, thing.
2 Solicitude, *care, anxiety, worry.
Ana. Thoughtfulness, considerateness *or* consideration, attentiveness *or* attention (see corresponding adjectives at THOUGHTFUL).
Ant. Unconcern. — *Con.* Indifference, aloofness, incuriousness, disinterestedness (see corresponding adjectives at INDIFFERENT).

concerned. Solicitous, careful, anxious, worried. See under CARE, *n.*
Ana. Engrossed, absorbed, *intent: impressed, affected, influenced, touched (see AFFECT, *v.*): troubled, distressed (see TROUBLE, *v.*).
Ant. Unconcerned. — *Con.* *Indifferent, incurious, aloof, detached: uninterested, *disinterested: *negligent, neglectful, remiss.

concerning. Regarding, respecting, *about, anent.

concert, *v.* *Negotiate, arrange.
Ana. *Discuss, debate, argue: concur, co-operate, *unite, conjoin, combine: conspire, collude, *connive.

concession. *Allowance.
Ana. Favor, boon, *gift: indulgence, leniency, tolerance, forbearance (see under FORBEARING).

conciliate. *Pacify, appease, placate, propitiate, mollify.
Ana. Arbitrate, adjudicate (see JUDGE, *v.*): mediate, intervene (see INTERPOSE): persuade, prevail on *or* upon (see INDUCE): calm, tranquilize (see corresponding adjectives at CALM): adjust, accommodate, reconcile, *adapt.
Ant. Antagonize. — *Con.* *Estrange, alienate, disaffect: *provoke, excite, stimulate, pique: *incite, foment.

concise. **Concise, terse, succinct, laconic, summary, pithy, compendious** agree in meaning briefly stated or presented or given to or manifesting brevity in statement or expression. A person is **concise** who speaks or writes briefly: a thing is *concise* that is brief because all superfluities have been removed and all elaboration avoided; as, a *concise* report; "I hadn't known Jane spoke so well. She has a clever, coherent way of making her points, and is *concise* in reply if questioned" (*R. Macaulay*). A thing (now rarely a person) is **terse** that is both concise and finished: the word implies both pointedness and elegance; as, "pure, *terse*, elegant Latin" (*John Edwards*); "His [Dante's] verse...has the *terseness* and edge of steel" (*J. R. Lowell*); a *terse* style; "And where [other than in the poetry of Pope], in fine, in all our English verse, A style more trenchant and a sense more *terse?*" (*Dobson*); "it is a relief to come to a diction that is frequently crisp, and incisive, and *terse*" (*Lowes*). A person or thing is **succinct** that compresses or is marked by compression into the smallest possible space: the term suggests great compactness and the use of no more words than are necessary; as, a *succinct* writer; "A strict and *succinct* style is that, where you can take away nothing without loss, and that loss to be manifest" (*B. Jonson*); "Dryden imported a trimmer and *succincter* dress" (*Landor*); "A book must have a title, and to-day it must have a *succinct* title; therefore this book appears as *Richelieu*" (*Belloc*). A person or thing is **laconic** that is characterized by such succinctness as to seem curt, brusque, unperturbed, mystifying, or the like; as, "This *laconic* fool makes brevity ridiculous" (*Davenant*); "I cannot exactly say with Caesar, 'Veni, vidi, vici': however, the most important part of his *laconic* account of success applies to my present situation" (*Byron*); "[Diary entries] Bare and *laconic;* yet those first days had been crammed...with feelings, ideas, and discoveries" (*Jan Struther*). A thing (rarely, if ever, a person in this sense) is **summary** that presents only the bare outlines or the main points without details; as, a *summary* account of the year's events under a few main headings: the term often suggests almost rude curtness or extreme generality; as, "the terms I use here are exceedingly *summary.* You may interpret the word 'salvation' in any way you like" (*W. James*); "her diary and her letters continued to be mainly the swift and *summary* record of crowded and delightful days" (*H. Ellis*). A thing (less often a person) is **pithy** that is not only terse or succinct but full of substance and meaning, and therefore especially forcible or telling; as, *pithy* epigrams; "In all these particulars [he] was very short but *pithy*" (*Addison*); "the displacement of the long-drawn-out epic similes by...*pithy* and *succinct* comparisons" (*Lowes*); "His speech was blacksmith-sparked and *pithy*" (*Masefield*). That is **compendious** which is concise, summary, and weighted with matter: it is applied to a type of treatment that distinguishes the typical compendium; as, a *compendious* account of the Reformation; a *compendious* style; "The *compendious* scholarly words which save so much trouble" (*T. E. Brown*).
Ana. Condensed, compressed (see CONTRACT, *v.*): compacted, concentrated (see COMPACT, *v.*): abridged, abbreviated, shortened (see SHORTEN): *brief, short.
Ant. Redundant. — *Con.* Prolix, diffuse, verbose, *wordy.

conclude. **1** *Close, finish, terminate, end, complete.
Ant. Open. — *Con.* Commence, *begin, start, initiate, inaugurate.
2 Judge, gather, *infer, deduce.
Ana. Reason, speculate (see THINK): *conjecture, surmise, guess.

concluding, *adj.* *Last, final, terminal, latest, ultimate, extreme.
Ana. Closing, terminating, ending, finishing, completing (see CLOSE, *v.*).
Ant. Opening. — *Con.* Beginning, commencing, starting, initiating *or* initial, inaugurating *or* inaugural (see corresponding verbs at BEGIN).

conclusion. Judgment, deduction, inference. See under INFER.

conclusive. **Conclusive, decisive, determinative, definitive** come into comparison when they mean having or manifesting qualities that bring something to a finish or end. **Conclusive** applies most frequently to an argument, evidence, reasoning, or the like, that is irrefutable or so convincing that it compels certainty or certitude and puts an end to all question or debate concerning a matter; as, the proof that the signature was not forged gives *conclusive* evidence of the authenticity of the will. "There is one very convincing text which so strongly supports the tradition that it seems *conclusive*" (*Belloc*). **Decisive** (as here considered: see also DECIDED) applies mainly to acts, events, influences, arguments, and the like, that put an end to fighting, to a controversy or competition, to vacillation, to uncertainty, to indefiniteness of course, or the like: it often comes close in meaning to *critical;* as, the *decisive* battle of the war had not yet been fought; "The *decisive* word about Lessing [in the controversy regarding Lessing's claim to fame] was really uttered by Goethe: We may, he said, have another intelligence like Lessing, but we shall wait long before seeing another such character" (*Babbitt*). **Determinative** applies especially to decisions, judgments, operative causes, influences, and the like, which put an end to uncertainty, wavering, fluctuation, etc., and serve to give a fixed direction, goal, or character to a life, a course, a movement, etc.; as, "Incidents...*determinative* of their course" (*I. Taylor*); the *determinative* cause of the country's decision to take part in the war; the *determinative* influence in shaping his career. **Definitive,** which is often opposed to *tentative* and, sometimes, to *provisional,* applies to anything which is put forth as final and as serving to make further questioning, dispute, uncertainty, or experiment needless, or to put an end to an unsettled state or condition where temporary measures have been necessary; as, the decisions of the Supreme Court of the United States are *definitive;* a *definitive* treaty; a *definitive* edition of an author's work (i.e., one that claims to have said the last word on all textual problems). "Not until there is a settled and *definitive* world order can there be such a thing as a settled and *definitive* version of human history" (*A. Huxley*). "Jefferson in these dawning days of his power....is ineffably happy over the triumph of his principles and the *definitive* acceptance of his political philosophy" (*C. G. Bowers*).

Ana. Convincing, telling, cogent (see VALID): *certain, inevitable, necessary, apodictic.

Ant. Inconclusive. — ***Con.*** *Doubtful, dubious, questionable, problematic: *theoretical, speculative, academic: *plausible, credible, specious.

concomitant, *adj.* Coincident, concurrent, synchronous, simultaneous, contemporaneous, *contemporary, coeval.

Ana. Attending *or* attendant, accompanying (see corresponding verbs at ACCOMPANY): associated, connected, related, linked (see JOIN).

Con. Antecedent, *preceding, foregoing, previous, precedent: following, succeeding, ensuing (see FOLLOW).

concomitant, *n.* *Accompaniment.

concord. *Harmony, consonance, accord.

Ana. Agreement, concurrence, coincidence (see corresponding verbs at AGREE): peacefulness *or* peace, tranquillity, serenity, placidity, calmness (see corresponding adjectives at CALM): amity, comity, good will, *friendship.

Ant. Discord. — ***Con.*** Strife, conflict, dissension, contention, variance (see DISCORD): dissonance, discordance (see under DISSONANT).

concordat. Covenant, compact, pact, treaty, entente, convention, cartel, *contract, bargain, indenture, mise.

concrete, *adj.* Specific, particular, individual, *special, especial, respective.

Ana. Tangible, palpable, *perceptible, sensible: *material, physical, corporeal, objective.

Ant. Abstract. — ***Con.*** Ideal, transcendental, transcendent (see ABSTRACT): intangible, impalpable, *imperceptible, insensible: general, generic, *universal.

concupiscence. *Desire, appetite, appetence, lust, passion, urge, yen.

Ana. Longing, yearning, pining, hungering *or* hunger, thirsting *or* thirst (see corresponding verbs at LONG): coveting, craving (see DESIRE, *v.*).

Con. *Will, volition.

concur. **1** Conjoin, *unite, combine, co-operate.

Ana. Accord, harmonize, *agree, jibe: *conduce, contribute, redound.

2 *Agree, coincide.

Ana. Consent, *assent, accede, acquiesce, agree: collude, conspire, *connive.

Ant. Contend: altercate. — ***Con.*** Fight, battle, war (see CONTEND): quarrel, wrangle (see under QUARREL, *n.*): dispute, debate, argue (see DISCUSS).

concurrent. Coincident, simultaneous, synchronous, concomitant, contemporaneous, *contemporary, coeval.

concussion. Shock, percussion, *impact, impingement, collision, clash, jar, jolt, brunt.

Ana. Beating, pounding, buffeting (see BEAT, *v.*): striking, smiting, swatting, slapping (see STRIKE, *v.*).

condemn. **1** Denounce, censure, blame, reprobate, reprehend, *criticize.

Ana. *Judge, adjudge: *decry, belittle, depreciate, disparage: *disapprove, deprecate.

Con. *Commend, applaud, compliment: *praise, laud, extol, acclaim, eulogize: condone, *excuse, pardon, forgive.

2 *Sentence, doom, damn, proscribe, attaint.

Con. *Free, release, liberate, discharge: acquit, absolve, exonerate, *exculpate, vindicate: *rescue, redeem, save, deliver.

condense. *Contract, shrink, compress, constrict, deflate.

Ana. Abridge, abbreviate, *shorten, curtail: reduce, diminish, *decrease: *compact, concentrate, consolidate.

Ant. Amplify (*a speech, article, etc.*). — ***Con.*** *Expand, swell, distend, dilate, inflate.

condescend. *Stoop, deign.

Ana. Favor, accommodate, *oblige: vouchsafe, concede, *grant.

Ant. Presume.

condign. *Due, rightful.

Ana. Just, equitable, *fair: merited, deserved (see corresponding nouns at DUE).

condition, *n.* *State, situation, mode, posture, status, estate.

Ana. Circumstance, *occurrence, event: occasion, antecedent, *cause: *phase, aspect, side, facet, angle.

conditional. *Dependent, contingent, relative, adjective.

Ana. Problematical, questionable (see DOUBTFUL): *provisional, tentative: subject, prone, *liable, open: *accidental, fortuitous, incidental.

Ant. Unconditional.

condolence. Sympathy, *pity, commiseration, compassion, ruth, empathy, bowels.

Ana. Consoling *or* consolation, solacing *or* solace, comforting (see corresponding verbs at COMFORT).

Con. Felicitation, congratulation (see corresponding verbs at FELICITATE).

condone. *Excuse, forgive, pardon, remit.

Ana. Disregard, overlook, forget, ignore (see NEGLECT, *v.*): *exculpate, absolve, acquit.

Con. *Punish, chastise, discipline, castigate, correct: condemn, denounce, censure, reprobate, reprehend (see CRITICIZE): *disapprove, deprecate.

conduce. Conduce, contribute, redound, accrue are not close synonyms but they bear in common the meaning to serve as an effective aid or impetus. Only that which in itself tends toward a certain result or has a capacity for furthering some aim can **conduce** or lead to an end, usually an inevitable or desired end. "The people have an original right to establish...such principles as...shall most *conduce* to their own happiness" (*Ch. Just. Marshall*). "To divert interest from the poet to the poetry... would *conduce* to a juster estimation of actual poetry, good and bad" (*T. S. Eliot*). Only that which with other agencies effects a result can **contribute,** or share in leading, to an end or consequence; as, low wages and high prices *contributed* to popular discontent. Only that which has consequences which in turn affect the agent or those with whom he is associated can **redound,** or flow back, to his or their advantage or disadvantage, or credit or discredit. "Seekers often make mistakes, and I wish mine to *redound* to my own discredit only, and not to touch Oxford" (*Arnold*). Only that which in itself represents or effects a gain can **accrue,** or come by way of increase, to one for one's profit or advantage; as, advantages *accruing* to society from the freedom of the press. "A trifling percentage of this value *accruing* to the inventor...may make him a millionaire" (*J. A. Hobson*).

Ana. Further, promote, forward, *advance: *help, aid, assist: lead, *guide: effect, accomplish, achieve, fulfill (see PERFORM).

Ant. Ward (*off*). — ***Con.*** *Prevent, preclude, obviate, avert: *hinder, impede, obstruct, block: *arrest, interrupt, check: interfere (see INTERPOSE).

conduct, *n.* *Behavior, deportment.

Ana. Act, deed, *action: demeanor, mien, deportment, manner, *bearing.

conduct, *v.* **1** Escort, convoy, *accompany, attend, chaperon.

Ana. *Guide, lead: convey, transmit, *carry.

2 Conduct, manage, control, direct come into comparison when they mean to use one's skill, authority, or other powers in order to lead, guide, command, or dominate persons or things. **Conduct** may imply the act of an agent who is both the leader and the person responsible for the acts and achievements of a group having a common end or goal (as, to *conduct* an orchestra; the minister *conducts* the prayer meetings; "the men who actually *conduct* and order the industry of the country"—*Shaw*), but often the idea of leadership is lost or obscured, and the stress is placed on a carrying on by all or by many of the participants (as, "Debates, *conducted* seriously with a view to ascertaining the truth, could be of great value" —*B. Russell;* "it was judged desirable for him to see how affairs were *conducted* in the United States"—*V. Heiser*). **Manage,** which literally means to train a horse so that it can be ridden or driven with ease or grace, in its now ordinary sense usually implies the handling, manipulating, or maneuvering of a person or persons or a thing or things so as to bring about a response or submission to one's wishes or attempts to use, guide, lead, or command (as, he *manages* the sailboat admirably; he cannot *manage* himself, so how can he be expected to *manage* others; to *manage* a refractory child; "the boy...could not yet *manage* his 'r's' and 'th's' aright"—*Kipling;* "the first condition for an artist in glass is to know how to *manage* blue"—*Viollet-le-Duc, transl. by H. Adams;* "[the prince's] choice of [dancing] partners, which seemed so spontaneous, was often *managed*"—*V. Heiser*). But *manage* is also often used to imply the action of one who is in authority and charged with the handling of groups of employees, or of all the details of a business or industry or of one of its departments, or of any complex or intricate system or organization; as, he *manages* a theater; to *manage* the financial affairs of the company; to *manage* a chain of restaurants. **Control** originally meant to check one thing by another, especially one register or account by a duplicate register or account. This sense is now comparatively rare except in science (thus, a *controlled* experiment is one that is checked or verified by counter or parallel experiments) but the idea of keeping within the bounds of what is correct, essential, proper, or the like, still prevails, with the result that the term usually implies a regulation or a restraining by getting or keeping the upper hand; as, "no attempt was made...to *control* by public authority the production and distribution of wealth" (*G. L. Dickinson*); "in order to make its highways most useful, the business traffic upon them must be *controlled*" (*Justice Holmes*); "the capitalist system...became a sort of blind monster which neither we nor the capitalists could *control*" (*Shaw*); "It was apparently regarded as impossible to root out bad desires; all we could do was to *control* them" (*B. Russell*). Sometimes, however, *control* implies little more than domination or the complete subjection of the dominated person or thing to one's will; as, he has learned to *control* himself (or his emotions); "The struggle between two strong-willed women to *control* one weak-willed man is the usual motive of the French drama in the nineteenth century" (*H. Adams*). **Direct** (as here considered: see also COMMAND; DIRECT, 1; DIRECT, 2) implies a regulation of the activities, as of a group of persons, or of the course or courses which they follow: it carries no suggestion of a desire or aim to dominate, but of an intent or purpose to keep the persons or things involved straight, well organized, or properly administered; as, the president and trustees *direct* the affairs of the institution; the architect *directed* the building of the bank; the principal *directs* the teachers, pupils, and janitors who make up the organization of his school.

Ana. Supervise, oversee (see corresponding nouns at OVERSIGHT): *govern, rule: engineer, pilot, steer, lead (see GUIDE, *v.*): operate, work, function (see ACT, *v.*).

3 Demean, deport, *behave, comport, acquit, quit.

confederacy, confederation. Federation, coalition, fusion, *alliance, league.

confederate, *n.* **1** *Partner, copartner, colleague, ally.

Ana., Ant., & ***Con.*** See those at ALLY.

2 Confederate, conspirator, accessory (*or* **accessary**), **abettor** (*or* **abetter**), **accomplice.** As used in law these words all convey the idea of complicity or common guilt in a wrongful act. **Confederate** is the general term applied to any person who in conjunction with others intentionally contributes to the commission of an unlawful act, whether the act be a crime or a civil injury, as a tort. For civil joint wrongdoers the specific term is **conspirator.** An **accessory** is neither the chief actor (*principal*) in an offense nor a person present at its performance, but one who accedes to or becomes involved in its guilt, by some act either previous or subsequent, as of instigating, encouraging, aiding, or concealing, etc. In treason or misdemeanors no distinction is made between an accessory and a principal. An **abettor** is one who is actually or constructively present at the commission of the deed and contributes to it by moral or physical force. An **accomplice** is one who with criminal intent participates in the commission of an offense, whether as principal, abettor, or accessory. Legal usage does not recognize the distinction made by laymen between *principal* and *accomplice.*

confer. 1 Bestow, present, *give, donate, afford.

Ana. Accord, award, vouchsafe, *grant.

2 Confer, commune, consult, advise, parley, treat,

negotiate are synonyms when they are used intransitively and bear the meaning to carry on a conversation or discussion, especially in order to reach a decision or settlement. Their derivative nouns of action also manifest the same likenesses and differences in meaning. **Confer** implies comparison of views or opinions, and, as a rule, equality in those participating in the discussion, or *conference;* as, the executives *confer* weekly about important business affairs. "The Dauphin and his train Approacheth, to *confer* about some matter" (*Shak.*). **Commune,** once a close synonym of *confer,* now is rare in this sense. "We were *communing* on important matters" (*Walpole*). In current use, it implies spiritual intercourse (or *communion*), as in prayer or meditation, or in a close union of minds and spirits. "There, sitting on the ground, the two [mother and child] would *commune* with each other by the hour" (*Hudson*). **Consult** adds to *confer* the implication of seeking or taking counsel; as, the president will not make his reply to the ambassador until he has *consulted* with the cabinet; the doctors will hold a *consultation* tomorrow. **Advise** often is not clearly distinguishable from *consult,* except that it is more suitable for use regarding personal matters on which one seeks advice; as, before he makes his decision, he will *advise* with his friends. *Parley, treat,* and *negotiate* all imply conference for the sake of settling differences or of coming to an agreement on terms. **Parley** stresses the talk involving the discussion of terms. "They are at hand, To *parley* or to fight" (*Shak.*). **Treat** adds to *parley* the implication either of a common will to adjust differences or of the need of diplomacy; as, the warring nations were ready to *treat* for peace. **Negotiate** implies compromise or bargaining; as, after the preliminaries were over, they proceeded to *negotiate;* a treaty is usually an agreement reached by *negotiation.*

Ana. Converse, talk, *speak: *discuss, debate, argue.

conference. Convocation, council, synod, *convention, congress.

confess. **1** Avow, *acknowledge, admit, own.

Ana. *Grant, concede, allow: disclose, divulge, *reveal, discover: *declare, proclaim, publish.

Ant. Renounce (*one's beliefs, principles, etc.*).

2 Confess, shrive, absolve, remit are often misused in their technical religious senses. All of them imply as agent (and, therefore, take as subject in the active voice) a priest performing his sacerdotal function as confessor in the sacrament of penance. A priest **confesses,** or **shrives,** when he listens to a penitent's avowal (or *confession*) of sins and when, if assured of the latter's contrition and desire for amendment, he pronounces the forgiveness of these sins. *Shrive* is now found only in literary use; *confess,* because of its more common application to the act of the penitent, is often avoided except in its derivative form *confessor,* which is always used of the priest. A priest **absolves** when as the final act in confessing, or shriving, he pronounces *absolution,* or the words imparting forgiveness of sins. **Remit** (see also EXCUSE) takes only *sin* or *sins* for its object; *to remit sin(s)* is an elliptical expression meaning to remit the eternal punishment merited by a person for his sins. In the doctrine of churches accepting sacramental confession, the real agent (*remitter*) is Christ, and the priest serves as his instrument. Remission of sins is therefore the effect of absolution.

confession. *Creed, symbol, catechism.

confidant. Intimate, *friend, acquaintance.

Ana. Comrade, crony, chum, pal, companion (see ASSOCIATE, *n.*).

confide. Entrust, *commit, consign, relegate.

Ana. Bestow, present, *give: *grant, vouchsafe, accord, award.

confidence. **1** *Trust, reliance, dependence, faith.

Ana. Certitude, assurance, conviction, *certainty: credence, credit, *belief, faith.

Ant. Doubt: apprehension. — *Con.* *Distrust, mistrust: despair, hopelessness (see under DESPONDENT).

2 Confidence, self-confidence, assurance, self-assurance, self-possession, aplomb come into comparison as denoting either a state of mind free from diffidence, misgivings, or embarrassment, or the easy, cool, or collected bearing or behavior resulting from this attitude. **Confidence** stresses faith in oneself and in one's powers; it does not as a rule imply conceit nor preclude the suggestions of support from external agencies or influences or of modest recognition of that assistance. "Far better that the task should be entrusted to one who had ...a sincere *confidence* in his power of dealing with the difficulties of the situation" (*A. C. Benson*). "The *confidence* that springs from complete mastery of his subject" (*Grandgent*). When self-sufficiency is connoted, **self-confidence** is preferable to *confidence;* as, "he has the *self-confidence* of one who has made money" (*Shaw*); "in extreme youth one has to be second-hand...one lacks *self-confidence*" (*R. Macaulay*). **Assurance** is distinguishable from *confidence* only by its far stronger implication of certainty and its frequent suggestion of arrogance; thus, one meets a situation with *confidence* when one's belief in one's powers is strong, but with *assurance* when one never questions the outcome or the rightness of what one is saying or doing. "There was indeed in the personality of that little old lady the tremendous force of accumulated decision—the inherited *assurance* of one whose prestige had never been questioned" (*Galsworthy*). "No experience so far served to reveal the whole offensiveness of the man's *assurance*" (*M. Austin*). **Self-assurance** is often preferred to *assurance* when the attitude, bearing, or behavior are obtruded on one's attention; as, his *self-assurance* has been a bar to his getting a good position. **Self-possession** implies that ease or coolness arising from command over one's powers; it connotes, usually, controlled but not repressed emotions and actions, or speech free from flurry and appropriate to the situation. "She was rather afraid of the *self-possession* of the Morels, father and all....It was a cool, clear atmosphere, where everyone was himself, and in harmony" (*D. H. Lawrence*). **Aplomb** describes the behavior or, less often, the bearing, of one whose assurance (real or assumed) or self-assurance is conspicuously, but not necessarily disagreeably, manifest; as, "ignoring with admirable *aplomb* the fact that we are tardy" (*Lowes*). "It is native personality, and that alone, that endows a man to stand before presidents and generals...with *aplomb*" (*Whitman*).

Ana. *Courage, resolution, mettle, spirit, tenacity: self-reliance, reliance (see corresponding adjectives at RELIANT).

Ant. Diffidence. — *Con.* Modesty, bashfulness, shyness (see corresponding adjectives at SHY): misgiving, *apprehension.

confident. **Confident, assured, sanguine, sure** are here compared only as applied to a person, or to his temperament, looks, manner, acts, utterances, and the like, and as meaning not inhibited by doubts, fears, or a sense of inferiority. **Confident** may or may not imply a strong belief in oneself or one's powers, but it nearly always implies freedom from fear of failure, frustration, or attack and, as a corollary, certitude of success, fulfillment, or approval. As a rule, it is not a depreciative term, and often is complimentary; as, his voice was manly and *confident;* "the happy and joyous temper, which characterizes a fresh and *confident* faith" (*Inge*). "Do you grapple the task that comes your way With a *confident*, easy mind?" (*E. Guest*). **Assured** suggests the absence of any question in one's mind as to whether one is right or wrong, secure or insecure in one's position, likely to fail or to succeed, and the like; it may also imply certitude of one's rightness, security, success, but this is not one of its consistent or emphatic implications; as, "talking with *assured* authority about places we have not visited, plays we have not seen" (*Lucas*); "the *assured* gaze of one who is accustomed to homage" (*Bennett*); "she had the casual, *assured* way of speaking" (*T. Wolfe*). **Sanguine** implies a greater measure of optimism than *confident*, sometimes suggesting this as a weakness rather than as a virtue; it often also connotes other qualities suggestive of vigorous health, such as cheerfulness, ardor, or the like. "Mr. Britling's thoughts were quick and *sanguine* and his actions even more eager than his thoughts" (*H. G. Wells*). "If the Liberals expect quick results, they are too *sanguine*, for the love of truth is not very common" (*Inge*). "*Sanguine* and very susceptible to flattery, Haydon was always ready to believe that the smallest stroke of good fortune must be the herald of complete success" (*A. Huxley*). **Sure** implies that one's freedom from doubts or fears is the consequence of certainty or of complete confidence in one's skill, rather than of temperament or health. The word also often connotes a steady and disciplined mind, mental or emotional stability, or unfailing accuracy; as, a *sure* scholar; a *sure* craftsman; a *sure* thinker; "As he is slow he is *sure*" (*Steele*). *Sure* is applicable also to any part of the body equipped to do a certain kind of work under the control of the brain, or to the work itself; thus, a *sure* hand works with unfaltering skill and accuracy; *sure* feet pick their way fearlessly over slippery rocks; a *sure* eye is necessary for a *sure* aim; hence, a pianist's *sureness* of touch; "the *sure* rhythm of their tiny moccasined feet" (*Cather*).

Ana. Courageous, intrepid, *brave, bold, dauntless, undaunted, valiant: positive, certain, *sure: self-reliant, *reliant.

Ant. Apprehensive: diffident. — ***Con.*** *Fearful, afraid: nervous, uneasy, jittery (see IMPATIENT): *shy, bashful, modest: dubious, *doubtful.

confidential. Close, intimate, *familiar, chummy, thick.

Ana. Privy, *secret: trusty, tried, trustworthy (see RELIABLE).

configuration. Conformation, figure, shape, *form, Gestalt.

Ana. *Outline, contour, silhouette, profile, skyline.

confine, *n.* Bound, bourn, *limit, end, term.

Ana. *Boundary, border, frontier, march: verge, edge, *border: *circumference, periphery, compass.

confine, *v.* Circumscribe, *limit, restrict.

Ana. Bind, *tie: *restrain, curb, inhibit, check: *hamper, trammel, fetter, shackle, hog-tie, manacle: *imprison, incarcerate, immure, intern, jail.

confirm. 1 *Ratify.

Ana. *Assent (to), consent (to), acquiesce (in), accede (to), subscribe (to): validate (see CONFIRM, 2): sanction, *approve, endorse.

Con. Reject, refuse, *decline.

2 Confirm, corroborate, substantiate, verify, authenticate, validate agree in meaning to attest to the truth, genuineness, accuracy, or validity of something. *Confirm* and *corroborate* are both used in reference to that which is doubtful or not yet proved. **Confirm,** however, usually implies the resolving of all doubts, as by an authoritative statement or by indisputable facts; as, the president *confirmed* the rumor of Bryan's appointment as secretary of state; his failure to pay his debts *confirmed* their suspicion that he was not to be trusted. "It was expectation exquisitely gratified, superabundantly *confirmed*" (*H. James*). **Corroborate** suggests particularly the strengthening of one statement or piece of evidence by another; as, the bystanders *corroborated* his story. "Having considered the evidence given by the plays themselves ...let us now inquire what *corroboration* can be gained from other testimony" (*Johnson*). **Substantiate** presupposes something to be demonstrated or proved and implies the offering of evidence sufficient to sustain the contention or to create a strong presumption in its favor; as, they were able to *substantiate* their claim to the property when the long-lost deed was found; Darwin spent nearly a lifetime in gathering evidence to *substantiate* his theory of the origin of species. **Verify** has for its distinctive implication the established correspondence of the actual facts or details to those that are given in an account, a statement, or the like. When that which is in question is a suspicion, a fear, a probability, or the like, it can be *verified* only in the result, event, or fulfillment; as, the prediction of a severe storm was *verified* in every detail. "It [faith] begins as a resolution to stand or fall by the noblest hypothesis...; but it is *verified* progressively as we go on" (*Inge*). In its more common current sense, *verify* implies a deliberate effort to establish the accuracy or truth of something by putting it to a test such as a comparison with ascertainable facts, an original, or a series of control experiments; as, to *verify* all the citations in a book; statements of accounts due are not sent out until they are *verified;* the careful scientist *verifies* every step in an experiment; "I do not think that they [my opinions] are such as can either be *verified* or refuted by scholars" (*T. S. Eliot*). **Authenticate** presupposes question of a thing's genuineness or validity, and therefore implies a demonstration of either of these by one in a position to know or to determine, such as an expert or the proper authority; as, the collector refused to purchase the manuscript until it had been *authenticated* by experts; the bank *authenticated* the signatures on the note. **Validate** is now more often used than *authenticate* when applied to legal papers requiring an official signature or seal before becoming valid; as, to *validate* a passport or a contract. It is, however, also used when the soundness of a judgment, of a belief, of a policy, or the like, is in question; as, "the expansion of demand which alone can *validate* the policy" (*J. A. Hobson*); he *validated* his conclusion when he demonstrated that his facts and his reasoning were correct in every detail. *Validate* is also used in reference to the election of a candidate for office when all the returns are in and the result is officially confirmed; as, the mayor's election will not be *validated* until there has been a recount of the votes.

Ana. *Support, uphold, back: vouch for, attest, *certify.

Ant. Contradict. — ***Con.*** Gainsay, *deny, traverse, impugn, contravene, negative: confute, refute, controvert, *disprove.

confirmed. *Inveterate, chronic, deep-seated, deep-rooted.

Ana. Established, fixed, set, settled, firmed (see SET, *v.*): *hardened, indurated, callous.

confiscate. Appropriate, *arrogate, usurp, pre-empt.

Ana. Seize, *take, grab: condemn, attaint, proscribe (see SENTENCE, *v.*).

conflict, *n.* **1** Combat, fight, *contest, affray, fray.

Ana. Engagement, *battle, action: *encounter, skirmish, brush: controversy, dispute, *argument.

2 Strife, contention, dissension, variance, *discord.

Ana. Clash, collision, impingement, *impact: antagonism, hostility, *enmity: incompatibility, incongruousness, inconsistency, inconsonance, discordance (see corresponding adjectives at INCONSONANT).
Ant. Harmony. — *Con.* Consonance, concord, accord (see HARMONY): comity, amity, *friendship: compatibility, congruity (see corresponding adjectives at CONSONANT).

conform. 1 *Adapt, adjust, accommodate, reconcile.
Ana. *Harmonize, tune, attune: *assent, accede, acquiesce: accept, *receive.
2 *Agree, accord, comport, harmonize, correspond, square, tally, jibe.
Ant. Diverge. — *Con.* *Differ.

conformation. Configuration, *form, shape, figure, Gestalt.
Ana. *Structure, anatomy, framework, skeleton.

confound. 1 Dumfound, nonplus, bewilder, mystify, *puzzle, perplex, distract.
Ana. Flabbergast, amaze, astound, astonish, *surprise: discomfit, faze, rattle, abash, *embarrass, disconcert.
2 Confuse, *mistake.
Ana. Muddle, addle, *confuse: *mix, mingle.
Ant. Distinguish, discriminate.

confuse. 1 **Confuse, muddle, bemuddle, addle, fuddle, befuddle** agree in meaning to throw one out mentally so that one cannot think clearly or act intelligently. **Confuse** usually implies intense embarrassment or bewilderment. " 'Come down, Lily. You've got to go through with it.' The young woman, delicately *confused* and blushing, obeyed" (*Bennett*). "You *confuse* me, and how can I transact business if I am *confused?* Let us be clear-headed" (*Dickens*). **Muddle** (literally, to make muddy) and **bemuddle,** in present use often connote floundering in deep waters. In earlier use, *muddle* frequently suggested stupefaction, as by drink. Both usually imply blundering, aimless, but not necessarily unsuccessful, attempts to deal with ideas, situations, or tasks beyond one's powers of analysis or one's capacity; as, subjects so abstruse as to *muddle* (or *bemuddle*) the brains of all but exceptional students. "We have *muddled* through so often that we have come half to believe in a providence which watches over unintelligent virtue" (*Inge*). **Addle** (literally of an egg, to make rotten and infertile) suggests staleness or emptiness of mind and resulting mental impotence. "I have *addled* my head with writing all day" (*Dickens*). **Fuddle** and the more common **befuddle** imply tippling or indulgence in a drug that clouds the mind and makes one's thinking and speech absurdly incoherent; as, Shakespeare's Falstaff is most amusing when he is completely *befuddled.*
Ana. Confound, bewilder, mystify, perplex, *puzzle: discomfit, disconcert, faze, rattle (see EMBARRASS): fluster, flurry (see DISCOMPOSE).
Ant. Enlighten.
2 *Mistake, confound.
Ant. Differentiate.

confusion. **Confusion, disorder, chaos, disarray, jumble, clutter, pie, snarl, muddle** come into comparison when they mean the state or a condition in which things are not in their right places or arranged in their right relations to each other, or an instance of such a state or condition. **Confusion** suggests such mixing or mingling as obliterates clear demarcation or distinction; **disorder** implies lack, more frequently disturbance or breach, of due order or arrangement; as, his desk was in *confusion* (that is, with objects of all sorts mixed together), in *disorder* (that is, with objects deranged or thrown out of place); mental *confusion* (an inability to perceive distinctly or to understand even simple ideas), mental *disorder* (derangement of functions). " 'Mid the misery and *confusion* Of an unjust war" (*Shelley*). "Cowardice has succeeded to courage, *disorder* to discipline" (*G. L. Dickinson*). **Chaos** suggests the absolute, or sometimes hopeless, confusion associated with the ancient Greek conception of Chaos, the unorganized state of primordial matter before the creation of distinct and orderly forms; the term therefore usually implies lack of organization rather than derangement. "A work where nothing's just or fit; One glaring *chaos* and wild heap of wit" (*Pope*). "The Essays of Montaigne...a *chaos* indeed, but a *chaos* swarming with germs of evolution" (*J. R. Lowell*). **Disarray,** more even than *disorder*, implies disarrangement; it is therefore preferable when the breaking up of order or discipline is to be suggested. "The *disarray* into which society had been thrown by this deplorable affair made their presence in town more necessary than ever" (*E. Wharton*). **Jumble** implies the mixing of incongruous things with resulting confusion; as, "The house they lived in...was a heterogeneous architectural *jumble*" (*Meredith*). "A vulgar Darwinism which is exactly the *jumble* of Naturalism with pieces of other and incompatible philosophies" (*Inge*). **Clutter,** which is now chiefly dialectal in British use, is still accepted by good American speakers and writers; it implies confusion and crowding, and often suggests a disagreeable or more or less messy state. "Lord, what a mess This set is in! If there's one thing I hate Above everything else... It's *clutter*" (*Millay*). **Pie,** literally a printer's term applied to a confusion or disarrangement of type, is by extension applied to any disarrangement of things that should be in a set order or in right relations to each other if they are to work or attain their ends; as, his finances are all in *pie;* "To make *pie* of the European arrangements for securing peace" (*Spectator*). **Snarl,** literally applied to a tangle of hairs, threads, and the like, implies confusion and entanglement; it therefore suggests great difficulty in unraveling and ordering; as, his affairs are in a *snarl.* **Muddle** also implies confusion and entanglement, but in addition it suggests the influence of bungling and a more or less hopeless condition. "We both grub on in a *muddle*" (*Dickens*). "Hitherto...the world's been confused and poor, a thorough *muddle;* there's never been a real planned education for people" (*H. G. Wells*).
Ana. Derangement, disarrangement, disorganization, disturbance (see corresponding verbs at DISORDER): *din, babel, pandemonium, hullabaloo: *anarchy, lawlessness.
Con. Ordering *or* order, systematization, organization (see corresponding verbs at ORDER): system, *method.

confute. Controvert, refute, *disprove, rebut.

congenial. *Consonant, consistent, compatible, congruous, sympathetic.
Ana. Companionable, co-operative, *social: sociable, genial, cordial, *gracious, affable: pleasing, *pleasant, agreeable.
Ant. Uncongenial: antipathetic (*of persons*): abhorrent (*of tasks, duties, etc.*).

congenital. Inborn, *innate, hereditary, inherited, inbred.
Ana. *Inherent, constitutional, ingrained: *native.
Con. Acquired (see GET): *accidental, adventitious.

conglomerate, conglomeration. Agglomerate, agglomeration, *aggregate, aggregation.
Ana. Mass, heap, pile, stack (see under HEAP, *v.*): accumulation, amassment, hoarding *or* hoard (see corresponding verbs at ACCUMULATE).

congratulate. *Felicitate.
Con. Console, solace, *comfort: commiserate, condole (with), pity (see corresponding nouns at PITY).

congregate. *Gather, assemble, collect.
Ana. Convoke, convene, *summon, muster: swarm, *teem.
Ant. Disperse.

congregation. Assembly, assemblage, gathering, collection. See under GATHER, *v.*
Ana. Audience, *following, public: *crowd, throng, press, crush.

congress. Council, convocation, *convention, synod, conference.
Ana. Assembly, assemblage, gathering, congregation (see under GATHER): *association, order, society.

congruous. Compatible, congenial, *consonant, sympathetic, consistent.
Ana. Harmonizing *or* harmonious, according *or* accordant, corresponding *or* correspondent, agreeing *or* agreeable (see corresponding verbs at AGREE): seemly, proper, comme il faut (see DECOROUS): meet, appropriate, fitting, *fit.
Ant. Incongruous. — *Con.* Incompatible, uncongenial, *inconsonant, discordant, discrepant.

conjectural. Hypothetical, suppositious, *supposed, supposititious, reputed, putative.
Ana. Presumed, assumed, postulated (see PRESUPPOSE): *theoretical, speculative: alleged (see ADDUCE).
Con. Proved, demonstrated (see PROVE).

conjecture, *v.* **Conjecture, surmise, guess** come into comparison both as verbs, meaning to draw an inference from slight evidence, and as nouns, denoting an inference based upon such evidence. **Conjecture** implies formation of an opinion or judgment upon what is recognized as insufficient evidence; as, "We saw below us...a hut, which we *conjectured* to be a bark hut" (*D. Wordsworth*); "Mysteries which must explain themselves are not worth the loss of time which a *conjecture* about them takes up" (*Sterne*). **Surmise** implies still slighter evidence, and exercise of the imagination or indulgence in suspicion; as, "What thoughts he had beseems not me to say, Though some *surmise* he went to fast and pray" (*Dryden*); "Just how long the small multiplied impressions will take to break into *surmise*...nobody can tell" (*Quiller-Couch*). **Guess,** in current best usage, implies a hitting upon (or to attempt to hit upon), either at random or from insufficient, uncertain, or ambiguous evidence; as, "You would never *guess* from meeting them that anyone would pay them for their ideas" (*R. Macaulay*). "My daughter Lucie is...such a mystery to me; I can make no *guess* at the state of her heart" (*Dickens*). The use of *guess* in the sense of *think, believe,* or *suppose,* although sanctioned by older usage (as, "Of twenty yeer of age he was, I *gesse*"—*Chaucer*), is now merely colloquial; when employed (as frequently in the United States) with reference to a fact or purpose about which there is no uncertainty, it is a vulgarism; as, I *guess* I'll go to bed.
Ana. *Infer, gather, conclude, judge, deduce: speculate, reason, *think: imagine, fancy, conceive (see THINK).
Con. Ascertain, determine, learn, *discover: *prove, demonstrate, test, try.

conjecture, *n.* Surmise, guess. See under CONJECTURE, *v.*
Ana. Theory, *hypothesis: *opinion, view, belief, sentiment: inference, deduction, conclusion, judgment (see under INFER).
Ant. Fact.

conjoin. Combine, *unite, concur, co-operate.

conjugal. *Matrimonial, marital, connubial, nuptial, hymeneal.
Ant. Single.

conjure. Adjure, implore, supplicate, beseech, *beg, entreat, importune.
Ana. Plead, appeal, pray, sue. See under PRAYER.

connect. *Join, link, associate, relate, unite, combine.
Ana. Attach, *fasten, affix: articulate, concatenate, *integrate: *cement, glue, agglutinate.
Ant. Disconnect. — *Con.* Sever, sunder, divorce, *separate, part, divide: *detach, disengage.

connivance. Collusion, conspiracy. See under CONNIVE.
Ana. Intrigue, machination, conspiracy, *plot, frame-up, cabal.

connive. Connive, collude, conspire are not interchangeable synonyms, but they come into comparison because they mean to take part by a secret understanding or agreement in furthering something, typically something that is evil or injurious. The same distinctions in implications and connotations are evident in their corresponding nouns **connivance, collusion, conspiracy. Connive** (etymologically, to wink) and **connivance** imply a shutting of one's eyes or a feigned ignorance of what is being or is about to be perpetrated, thereby giving tacit permission to the actual perpetrators or actual encouragement of an unlawful, criminal, or otherwise reprehensible act; as, "the early persecutions [of Christians] were like Russian 'pogroms,' instigated or *connived* at by the government" (*Inge*); "In presence of his ladylove...and certainly with her *connivance,* he was unmercifully thrashed" (*Stevenson*); "All the traditions of honour and probity in which she had been brought up forbade her to *connive* at such a plan" (*E. Wharton*). **Collude** (etymologically, to play with) and **collusion** imply acting with another privily and underhandedly to trick a third person or party into giving what cannot be rightfully gained, or to frustrate his (or its) plans or ends; as, cross-examination of witnesses tended to prove that the defendant *colluded* with the plaintiff in an attempt to win a verdict for high damages; the divorce was obtained by the *collusion* of the husband with his wife; "a blundering world, in *collusion* with a prejudiced philosophy" (*Pater*). **Conspire** (etymologically, to blow or breathe together; hence, to agree) and **conspiracy** differ from the preceding terms in usually (though not invariably) suggesting the action not of one person or party but of two or more; also, *conspire* and *conspiracy* may be used figuratively of impersonal agencies; as, Brutus and Cassius *conspired* to murder Caesar; "And when they [Joseph's brethren] saw him afar off...they *conspired* against him to slay him" (*Genesis* xxxvii. 18); "Princes *conspire* against me" (*Lytton*); "the accidents and *conspiracies* which had led to his being defeated three times in the ring" (*Shaw*); "the historical circumstances of recent years have *conspired* to intensify nationalism" (*A. Huxley*).
Ana. Abet, instigate, *incite, foment: *wink, blink.

connoisseur. Virtuoso, dilettante, *aesthete.
Ana. *Epicure, gourmet, bon vivant: *expert, adept.
Con. *Amateur, tyro, dabbler.

connotation. Denotation (see under DENOTE).
Ana. Suggestion, implication, intimation (see corresponding verbs at SUGGEST): evoking *or* evocation (see corresponding verb at EDUCE): import, signification, *meaning, significance, sense.

connote. *Denote.
Ana. *Suggest, imply, intimate, hint: *express, voice, utter: import, signify, *mean, denote.

connubial. Conjugal, *matrimonial, marital, nuptial, hymeneal.

conquer. Conquer, vanquish, defeat, beat, lick, subdue, subjugate, reduce, overcome, surmount, overthrow, rout

agree in meaning to get the better of or to bring under one's power by the exertion of force or strategy. **Conquer** usually implies the gaining possession or mastery of something (less frequently of someone), **vanquish,** the complete overpowering or discomfiture of someone (less frequently of something); as, to *conquer* a difficulty; to *vanquish* an opponent in debate; "We *conquered* France, but felt our captive's charms" (*Pope*); "a Roman by a Roman valiantly *vanquished*" (*Shak.*). *Vanquish* is more likely than *conquer* to refer to a single engagement. "Miss Goff is a celebrated lawn-tennis player. She *vanquished* the Australian champion last year" (*Shaw*). **Defeat** does not imply the finality of *vanquish;* it may even imply no more than a temporary checking or frustrating; as, "But though *defeated,* the Cotton States were not *vanquished*" (*Westminster Rev.*); "Two factions, each intent not merely on *defeating* the other, but on excluding it altogether from political rights" (*G. L. Dickinson*). **Beat** is a somewhat colloquial term for *defeat,* but it often carries the connotation of finality so obvious in *vanquish.* "The Russo-Japanese war...furnishes another proof of the saying that Russia is always *defeated* but never *beaten*" (*The Spectator,* 1913). **Lick,** a slang term, suggests a thorough and humiliating beating; as, to *lick* the opposing team. **Subdue** implies not only a defeating but a suppressing, or often, a compulsion to submission; as, "the tumults and disorders of the Great Rebellion had hardly been *subdued*" (*T. S. Eliot*); "the desire to meet and *subdue* it [skepticism]...was the motive of his [Plato's] philosophy" (*G. L. Dickinson*). **Subjugate** implies as a result complete subjection, as under a yoke; as, "The line of distinction between the...free and the *subjugated* races" (*Ch. Just. Taney*). "Austria making the murder of the Archduke a pretext for *subjugating* Serbia" (*Shaw*). **Reduce,** as here compared (see DECREASE), often implies a bringing to capitulation or surrender; it applies especially to a beleaguered town or fortress; as, "*reduced* a province under Roman yoke" (*Milton*). The term, however, often implies subjugation, especially a gradual one. "The difficulty of their country made it necessary to *reduce* them step by step" (*Buchan*). **Overcome** and **surmount** suggest a conquering of someone or something that confronts one and must be (in the case of *overcome*) overpowered or (in the case of *surmount*) exceeded or surpassed, as in power, force, skill, or the like; as, "Where there is an enemy to be *overcome* [by school children], let it be matter rather than other human beings" (*B. Russell*); to *overcome* one's fears; to *surmount* an obstacle; "This crisis will be *surmounted* if the Church has the faith and courage...to face it candidly" (*Inge*). Both **overthrow** and **rout** imply disaster as well as defeat, *overthrow* often implying destruction, and *rout,* flight and complete dispersion. "They are not *overthrown* by revolutionists. They collapse first, and then the revolutionists take charge of affairs" (*W. Lippmann*). "A small English force...sufficed to *rout* the disorderly levies" (*J. R. Green*).

Ana. *Frustrate, thwart, foil, circumvent, outwit, baffle, balk.

Con. Surrender, submit, capitulate (see corresponding nouns at SURRENDER): *yield, succumb, bow, cave in.

conqueror. Vanquisher, *victor, winner, champion.

conquest. *Victory, triumph.

Ana. Subjugation, subdual, defeating *or* defeat, overthrowing *or* overthrow, routing *or* rout (see corresponding verbs at CONQUER).

consanguinity. *Kinship, affinity, cognation, agnation, enation.

conscientious. Scrupulous, honorable, honest, *upright, just.

Ana. Righteous, virtuous, ethical, *moral: strict, *rigid: particular, fastidious, finical, *nice: meticulous, punctilious, *careful.

Ant. Unconscientious, unscrupulous. — ***Con.*** Slack, lax, remiss, *negligent, neglectful: *careless, heedless, thoughtless.

conscious. Sensible, *aware, cognizant, alive, awake.

Ana. Attending *or* attentive, minding *or* mindful, watching (see corresponding verbs at TEND): *watchful, alert, vigilant: perceiving, noticing, noting, remarking, observing (see SEE).

Ant. Unconscious. — ***Con.*** Ignoring, overlooking, disregarding (see NEGLECT, *v.*): *forgetful, unmindful, oblivious.

consecrate. Hallow, dedicate, *devote.

Con. Desecrate, profane (see corresponding nouns at DESECRATION): defile, pollute (see CONTAMINATE).

consecutive. **Consecutive, successive, sequent, sequential, serial, discrete** are not all synonyms of one another, but, as here considered, they agree in meaning following one after the other in order. **Consecutive** and **successive** apply to objects which follow one another without interruption or break. But *consecutive* is somewhat more emphatic, stressing the immediacy of the succession, the regularity or fixedness of the order, and the close connection as in time, space, logic, etc., of the units; *successive* is applicable to things that follow regardless of differences in duration, extent, or the like, or the length of the interval between the units; as, it rained four *consecutive* days; a group of ten *consecutive* numbers; three *successive* (not *consecutive*) leap years; the *successive* strokes of a piston; his last five *successive* books are of higher quality than any of his first five. *Consecutive* is also applicable to a person or to thought that manifests logical sequence; as, "*consecutive* thinking absolutely requires personal initiative" (*C. W. Eliot*). **Sequent** and **sequential** apply to an arrangement or to things (sometimes a thing) following a sequence, such as a causal, logical, or chronological sequence, or some settled order; as, the events of the narrative do not follow in *sequent* order; "The galleys Have sent a dozen *sequent* messengers This very night at one another's heels" (*Shak.*); changes which proceed with *sequential* regularity. **Serial,** when used in the sense here considered, always implies that the thing or things so qualified form a series or will appear as a series: it therefore suggests likeness or uniformity in the units and, usually, a prearranged order, especially in time or space; as, the fifth of the *serial* concerts; the story will first be published *serially* (that is, in successive installments in a periodical); from the publisher's point of view, mystery stories make good *serial* narratives. **Discrete** (as here considered: see also DISTINCT) comes into comparison with the other terms only when it applies to a number of things that follow each other in time or space or are massed together. In this sense, it stresses discontinuousness, and the distinctness or separateness of each unit; thus, a "*discrete* series" in mathematics is a series in which every element, except the first, has a predecessor, and every element, except the last, has a successor. "The trend of all but the best current poetry is away from the *consecutive* [i.e., from chronological or logical order] and towards the *discrete* [i.e., towards an arrangement where there is no connection between the details or units]. I have read volumes of recent verse in which little fragment after little fragment is dropped into the receptive mind" (*Lowes*).

Ana. Following, succeeding, ensuing (see FOLLOW): continuous, *continual, incessant: coherent (see corresponding noun COHERENCE): *logical.

Ant. Inconsecutive, unconsecutive. — *Con.* Alternate, *intermittent, recurrent, periodic: desultory, *random, haphazard, hit-or-miss.

consent, *v.* *Assent, accede, acquiesce, agree, subscribe.
Ana. *Yield, submit, defer, relent: permit, allow, *let: *approve, sanction: concur (see AGREE).
Ant. Dissent. — *Con.* Refuse, *decline: *disapprove, deprecate: *demur, balk, stick, stickle, strain.

consequence. 1 Result, *effect, aftereffect, aftermath, issue, outcome, event, upshot, sequel.
Ant. Antecedent. — *Con.* *Cause, determinant, reason, occasion: *origin, source, root.
2 *Importance, moment, weight, significance, import.
Ana. Necessity, *need, exigency: *worth, value: renown, honor, reputation, repute, *fame: eminence, illustriousness, distinction (see corresponding adjectives at FAMOUS).

consequently. *Therefore, hence, then, accordingly, so.

conserve, *v.* Preserve, *save.
Ana. Protect, shield, safeguard, guard, *defend.
Ant. Waste, squander.

conserves. See under SAVE, *v.*

consider. 1 **Consider, study, contemplate, weigh, revolve, excogitate** come into comparison chiefly as transitive verbs meaning to fix the mind for a time on something in order to increase one's knowledge or understanding of it or to solve a problem involved in it. **Consider** often suggests little more than an applying of one's mind (as, a proposal so unreasonable that one does not need to *consider* it), but sometimes it also carries a restricting implication such as that of a definite point of view (as, "In the last paragraphs we have *considered* science as a steadily advancing army of ascertained facts"—*Inge*), or as that of thinking over (as, the publishers told him they would *consider* his book; "marriage is an action too freely practised and too seldom adequately *considered*"—*R. Macaulay*), or as that of casting about in order to reach a suitable conclusion, opinion, decision, or the like (as, "Her father *considered* a little before he answered"—*Dickens*). **Study** implies greater mental concentration than *consider;* usually, it also suggests more care for the details or minutiae and more of an effort to comprehend fully or to learn all the possibilities, applications, variations, or the like; as, the president said that the bill must be *studied* before he reached a decision regarding the signing or vetoing of it; a work of architecture that deserves to be *studied* closely; to *study* a patient's reactions to the new treatment for pneumonia. "I like very naturally to think that I am being read; but the idea that I am being *studied* fills me, after the first outburst of laughter, with a deepening gloom" (*A. Huxley*). "Bryce, who had *studied* the matter ...thoroughly, was wont to insist...[that] the smallest democracies...stand highest in the scale" (*H. Ellis*). **Contemplate** (as here compared: see also SEE) implies, like *meditate* (see under PONDER), the focusing of one's attention upon a thing and a close dwelling upon it: the term, however, does not always carry a clear implication of the purpose or result. When the object on which the mind rests is a plan, a project, an imaginative conception, or the like, the word usually suggests its formulation in detail or its enjoyment as envisioned; as, "Henchard bent and kissed her cheek. The moment and the act he had *contemplated* for weeks with a thrill of pleasure" (*Hardy*); "the poet 'has an idea,' and in the course of *contemplating* it he draws up from his subconscious a string of associated ideas and images" (*Day Lewis*). When the object contemplated lies outside the mind and has either material or immaterial existence, the term suggests an attempt to increase one's knowledge and comprehension of it through meditation upon it or through stimulating the activity of a higher mental power such as intuition; as, "Nature is beautiful only to the mind which is prepared to apprehend her beauty, to *contemplate* her for her own sake apart from the practical delight she brings" (*S. Alexander*); "the opinion... widely held, that while science, by a deliberate abstraction, *contemplates* a world of facts without values, religion *contemplates* values apart from facts" (*Inge*). **Weigh** (cf. PONDER), in the extended sense here considered, implies evaluation of something, usually of one thing in respect to another and relevant thing or things: it suggests an attempt to get at the truth by balancing counterclaims, contradictory data, conflicting evidence, and the like. "In teaching the young to think hard, any subject will answer. The problem is to get them to *weigh* evidence, draw accurate inferences...and form judgments" (*C. W. Eliot*); "As the great Morgagni had said much earlier, it is not enough to count, we must evaluate; 'observations are not to be numbered, they are to be *weighed*'" (*H. Ellis*). **Revolve** implies a consideration by mentally turning over and over a problem, a question, a plan, or the like, so that all its aspects or phases are taken into account; as, he knew that he must *revolve* the matter before he could decide how to deal with it; "Should he write to his son? For a time he *revolved* a long, tactful letter in his mind" (*H. G. Wells*). **Excogitate,** a now rare word usually replaced by *think out,* implies the application of the mind to something so that one may find the solution of the problems involved; as, "In style, to *consider* what ought to be written, and after what manner, he must first think and *excogitate* his matter" (*B. Jonson*); to *excogitate* a plan whereby poverty may be relieved without unduly burdening the taxpayers.
Ana. *Ponder, meditate, ruminate, muse: reflect, cogitate, *think, reason, speculate: inspect, examine, *scrutinize, scan.
Con. Ignore, *neglect, overlook, disregard, slight.
2 **Consider, regard, account, reckon, deem,** denote in common to hold the view or opinion that someone or something is as described or designated. They are commonly used interchangeably without attention to their fine shadings of meaning. **Consider,** in discriminating use, suggests a conclusion reached through reflection; as, he *considers* exercise a waste of energy; some persons *consider* poor relief an incentive to laziness. **Regard,** in exact use, does not lose its primary implication of looking upon. Sometimes, it suggests a judgment based on appearances. "I was...plainly *regarded* as a possible purchaser" (*L. P. Smith*). Often, it implies a point of view, sometimes merely personal, sometimes partisan. "The regulations of the state were not *regarded* by the Greeks—as they are apt to be by modern men—as so many vexatious, if necessary, restraints on individual liberty" (*G. L. Dickinson*). "A church...which *regarded* all dissentients as rebels and traitors" (*Inge*). **Account** and **reckon** retain their etymological implications of counting or calculating: they are most precisely employed when they imply evaluation, differentiation, or the like; as, these trees were not *accounted* (or *reckoned*) of much value. "I *account* the justice which is grounded on utility to be the...most sacred and binding part of all morality" (*J. S. Mill*). **Deem** is now chiefly literary. It is often used as the equivalent of *consider,* but it distinctively stresses judgment rather than reflection. "Behind the economic problem lies a psychological or ethical problem, that of getting persons to recognise truths which they *deem* it to their interest to avoid" (*J. A. Hobson*). "The first time he [Don Quixote] made a

helmet, he tested its capacity for resisting blows, and battered it out of shape; next time he did not test it, but '*deemed*' it to be a very good helmet" (*B. Russell*).

Ana. *Think, conceive, imagine, fancy: judge, gather, *infer, conclude.

considerate. *Thoughtful, attentive.

Ana. Kindly, *kind: *tender, sympathetic, warmhearted, compassionate: obliging, complaisant, *amiable.

Ant. Inconsiderate. — *Con.* *Forgetful, unmindful, oblivious: *careless, heedless, thoughtless.

considered. *Deliberate, premeditated, advised, designed, studied.

Ana. Intentional, *voluntary, willful: planned, projected, schemed (see corresponding verbs under PLAN, *n.*).

Ant. Unconsidered. — *Con.* *Precipitate, impetuous, headlong: impulsive, *spontaneous, instinctive.

consign. *Commit, entrust, confide, relegate.

Ana. Transfer, *move, remove, shift: assign, allocate, *allot: resign, surrender, yield (see RELINQUISH).

consistent. Congruous, *consonant, compatible, congenial, sympathetic.

Ana. Conforming *or* conformable, tallying, jibing, squaring (see corresponding verbs at AGREE): matching, equalling (see MATCH, *v.*): identical, alike, *similar, like.

Ant. Inconsistent. — *Con.* Discrepant, discordant, incongruous, *inconsonant, incompatible: contradictory, contrary, *opposite, antithetical.

consist. 1 In form **consist of.** Consist in, comprise, *compose, constitute.

Ana. *Include, comprehend, embrace, involve: *contain, hold.

2 In form **consist in.** Consist of, comprise, *compose, constitute.

console, *v.* *Comfort, solace.

Ana. Assuage, alleviate, mitigate, *relieve, allay: calm, tranquilize (see corresponding adjectives at CALM): *satisfy, content.

Con. *Trouble, distress: *discompose, disturb, perturb, agitate, upset, disquiet.

consolidate. *Compact, unify, concentrate.

Ana. *Integrate, articulate, concatenate: amalgamate, merge, fuse, blend (see MIX): condense, compress (see CONTRACT, *v.*): *weave, knit.

Con. Dissolve, melt, *liquefy: *separate, sever, sunder, part: *distribute, dispense, divide: dissipate, *scatter, disperse.

consolidation. Consolidation, merger, amalgamation are here compared as terms denoting a union of two or more corporations. **Consolidation** is often used loosely as a general term; strictly, however, it implies the fusion of the companies or corporations, with dissolution of their separate corporate identities and transference of their combined assets, franchises, good will, etc., to a single corporate unit, often under an entirely new name. **Merger,** in its technical sense, is a form of consolidation in which the assets, franchises, good will, etc., of one or more companies or corporations are transferred to, or merged into, one of the units without change in the name of the absorbing unit. In a merger, additional shares of stock are issued by the absorbing company or corporation to replace on an agreed basis the shares of the units absorbed. **Amalgamation** is often loosely or generally used of any form of consolidation or merger. It may be applied narrowly to a consolidation in which a new corporation with an entirely new name and corporate identity results. In British use, however, it is more commonly applied to a union of the merger type. These technical distinctions are observed only in precise use and have not (with the possible exception of *merger*) been clearly established.

Ant. Dissolution.

consonance. *Harmony, concord, accord.

Ana. Agreement, conformity, correspondence (see corresponding verbs at AGREE): concurrence, coincidence (see corresponding verbs at AGREE): compatibility, congruity (see corresponding adjectives at CONSONANT).

Ant. Dissonance (*in music*): discord. — *Con.* Inconsonance, discordance, incompatibility, incongruity, discrepancy (see corresponding adjectives at INCONSONANT).

consonant, *adj.* **Consonant, consistent, compatible, congruous, congenial, sympathetic** come into comparison when they mean in agreement with one another or agreeable one to the other. **Consonant** (now usually followed by *with*, rarely by *to*) implies agreement with a concurrent circumstance or situation, or conformity to an accepted standard, or harmony between two things that must come into contact or comparison with each other: the term suggests absence of discord; as, "She...first sounded their inclinations, with which her sentiments were always strictly *consonant*" (*Fielding*); "Fijians possessed a physical endurance *consonant* with their great stature" (*V. Heiser*); "it is...more *consonant* with the Puritan temper to abolish a practice than to elevate it and clear away abuses" (*Quiller-Couch*); "to pursue callings more *consonant* with Buddha's teaching" (*Binyon*); "Nature has no ends *consonant* with...the desires of man which would make it possible for him to accord himself to her" (*J. W. Krutch*). **Consistent** (often followed by *with* but sometimes used attributively) suggests such agreement or harmony between things or between the details of the same thing as implies the negation of contradiction; as, "That their letters should be as kind as was *consistent* with proper maidenly pride" (*De Quincy*); "Congress...may require that they [contracts for public works] shall be carried out only in a way *consistent* with its views of public policy" (*Justice Holmes*); "No one has yet imagined a *consistent* picture of what the electron and proton really are" (*Jeans*). **Compatible** (often followed by *with*) implies a capacity for existing or coming together without disagreement, discord, disharmony, or the like: the term does not necessarily suggest positive agreement or harmony, but it does imply the absence of such conflict between two (or more) things as would make their association or combination impossible; as "With all the eagerness *compatible* with...elegance, Sir Walter and his two ladies stepped forward to meet her" (*Austen*); "To combine, in the highest measure in which they are *compatible*, the two elements of refinement and manliness" (*Froude*); "Many bad qualities are of course *compatible* with vitality—for example, those of a healthy tiger. And many of the best qualities are *compatible* with its absence" (*B. Russell*). **Congruous** (sometimes followed by *to* or *with*) implies more positive agreement or harmony than *compatible* does: ordinarily it implies the fitness, suitability, or appropriateness of one thing to another so that their association or combination, no matter how much they are in contrast, produces a pleasing or, at least, a not disagreeable impression; as, the *congruous* furnishings of a room; "Not *congruous* to the nature of epic poetry" (*H. Blair*); "Thoughts *congruous* to the nature of their subject" (*Cowper*). The negative form *incongruous* is currently far more common than *congruous*. **Congenial** (sometimes followed by *to*) is most often used of persons or things that are in such harmony with the taste of a person that they afford him pleasure, or delight, or satisfaction; as, a *congenial* companion; "a pair of not very *congenial* passengers" (*Conrad*); "the reticence and understatement of the method made it specially *congenial* [to the Chinese]" (*Binyon*); "[Hobbes's] theory of government is *congenial* to that type of person who is conservative from prudence but revolutionary in his dreams" (*T. S. Eliot*). Occasionally, however, *congenial* is used of things in the sense of wholly and satisfyingly congruous; as, "all such introduced ideas are *congenial* to the subject" (*S. Alexander*); "statement, overstatement and understatement in letters. Given a *congenial* context, every one of them is right" (*C. E. Montague*). **Sympathetic** (as here compared: see also TENDER), like *congenial*, usually suggests qualities in the person or thing so described that make him or it in agreement with another person's likings or tastes but, in contrast with *congenial*, it suggests a more subtle appeal and, often, a less hearty acceptance; as, "every author who is '*sympathetic*' to them" (*Bradley*); "To my generation...he [Matthew Arnold] was a more *sympathetic* prose writer than Carlyle or Ruskin" (*T. S. Eliot*); "an air of rather self-conscious bravado [in myself] which...was a little repellent to one or two who loved me and my work... and was not *sympathetic* to my own most genuine tastes" (*H. Ellis*).

Ana. Conforming *or* conformable, harmonizing *or* harmonious, agreeing *or* agreeable, according *or* accordant (see corresponding verbs at AGREE): concurring *or* concurrent, coinciding *or* coincident (see corresponding verbs at AGREE).

Ant. Inconsonant: dissonant (*in music*). — ***Con.*** Discordant, discrepant, inconsistent, incompatible, incongruous (see INCONSONANT).

conspectus. Synopsis, epitome, *abridgment, abstract, brief.

Ana. *Compendium, syllabus, digest, survey, sketch, précis, aperçu.

conspicuous. Prominent, salient, signal, *noticeable, remarkable, striking, arresting, outstanding.

Ana. Patent, manifest, *evident, distinct, obvious: eminent, distinguished, celebrated, illustrious, notorious (see FAMOUS).

Ant. Inconspicuous. — ***Con.*** *Common, ordinary: *obscure, vague: lowly, *humble, modest: hidden, concealed (see HIDE): *secret, covert, privy.

conspiracy. **1** Collusion, connivance. See under CONNIVE.

Ana. *Combination, combine, ring, cabal, junto, faction.

2 Complot, cabal, intrigue, machination, *plot, frame-up.

Ana. *Sedition, treason: treacherousness *or* treachery, perfidiousness *or* perfidy, disloyalty, faithlessness, falseness *or* falsity (see corresponding adjectives at FAITHLESS).

conspirator. *Confederate, accessory, accomplice, abettor.

conspire. *Connive, collude.

Ana. *Unite, combine, conjoin, concur, co-operate: plot, scheme (see under PLAN, *n.*): *conduce, contribute.

constable. Officer, *policeman, catchpole, bobby, peeler, copper, cop, bull, bailiff.

constant, *adj.* **1** *Faithful, true, loyal, leal, stanch, steadfast, resolute.

Ana. Abiding, enduring, persisting *or* persistent, lasting (see corresponding verbs at CONTINUE): dependable, trustworthy, *reliable, trusty, tried.

Ant. Inconstant, fickle. — ***Con.*** Unstable, capricious, mercurial (see INCONSTANT): disloyal, *faithless, false, perfidious.

2 *Steady, uniform, even, equable.

Ana. Established, settled, set, fixed (see SET, *v.*): invariable, immutable, unchangeable (see affirmative adjectives at CHANGEABLE): *regular, normal, typical, natural.

Ant. Variable. — ***Con.*** *Changeable, changeful, mutable, protean: fluctuating, wavering (see SWING).

3 *Continual, incessant, continuous, perpetual, perennial.

Ana. Persisting *or* persistent, persevering (see corresponding verbs at PERSEVERE): pertinacious, dogged, *obstinate, stubborn: chronic, confirmed, *inveterate.

Ant. Fitful. — ***Con.*** *Intermittent, alternate: spasmodic (see FITFUL): occasional, sporadic, *infrequent.

consternation. Panic, terror, alarm, fright, *fear, dread, dismay, horror, trepidation.

Ana. Confusion, muddlement *or* muddle, bemuddlement (see corresponding verbs at CONFUSE): bewilderment, distraction, perplexity (see corresponding verbs at PUZZLE): agitation, perturbation (see corresponding verbs at DISCOMPOSE).

Con. Sang-froid, composure, *equanimity, phlegm: aplomb, self-possession (see CONFIDENCE).

constituent, *n.* Component, *element, ingredient, integrant, factor.

Ana. *Part, portion, piece, detail, member: *item, particular.

Ant. Whole, aggregate. — ***Con.*** *System, complex, organism, economy: composite, compound, blend, amalgam (see MIXTURE).

constitute. *Compose, comprise, consist in, consist of.

Ana. Form, *make, fashion, shape, fabricate, forge.

constitutional, *adj.* *Inherent, intrinsic, essential, ingrained.

Ana. Congenital, *innate, inborn: *native: natural, normal (see REGULAR): *characteristic, individual, peculiar.

Ant. Advenient. — ***Con.*** *Accidental, adventitious, fortuitous: unnatural, *irregular, anomalous: foreign, alien, extraneous, *extrinsic.

constrain. Oblige, coerce, compel, *force.

Ana. Impel, drive, *move, actuate: require, exact, *demand.

constraint. Compulsion, coercion, duress, restraint, *force, violence.

Ana. Suppression, repression (see corresponding verbs at SUPPRESS): impelling *or* impulsion, driving *or* drive (see corresponding verbs at MOVE): goad, spur, *motive, spring: *obligation, duty.

constrict. Compress, *contract, shrink, condense, deflate.

Ana. *Tie, bind: restrict, confine, circumscribe, *limit: *restrain, curb, snaffle.

Con. *Expand, dilate, distend, swell, inflate: enlarge, *increase.

constringent, *adj.* *Astringent, styptic.

constructive. *Implicit, virtual.

Ana. Inferential, illative, ratiocinative (see under INFERENCE): implied, involved (see INCLUDE).

Ant. Manifest. — ***Con.*** Express, *explicit, definite: *evident, patent, obvious.

construe, *v.* Explicate, elucidate, interpret, expound, *explain.

Ana. *Analyze, resolve, break down, anatomize, dissect: *understand, comprehend, appreciate.

construe, *n.* *Translation, version, paraphrase, metaphrase.

consuetude. Custom, usage, use, wont, practice, *habit, habitude.

Ant. Desuetude.

consult. *Confer, advise, parley, commune, treat, negotiate.

Ana. *Discuss, debate: deliberate, cogitate (see THINK): counsel, advise (see under ADVICE).

consume. Engross, absorb, *monopolize.

consummate, *adj.* **Consummate, finished, accomplished** agree in meaning brought to completion or perfection. Their distinctions lie chiefly in the degree of perfection, in the means by which this perfection is attained, and, at times, in their application: for *consummate* and *finished* apply to persons or to things; *accomplished*, as a rule, to persons only. That is **consummate** which attains the highest possible point or degree of perfection or which possesses the highest possible qualities, whether natural or acquired; as, *consummate* wisdom or skill; *consummate* happiness; a *consummate* hypocrite. "The little band held the post with *consummate* tenacity" (*Motley*). "A man of perfect and *consummate* virtue" (*Addison*). "Pope...is...one of the most *consummate* craftsmen who ever dealt in words" (*Lowes*). That which is **finished** manifests such care and exquisiteness in performance or workmanship that nothing additional is required to perfect it or to increase its technical excellence; as, a *finished* gentleman is always courteous; *finished* actors usually give *finished* performances. "The most *finished* bat [i.e., batsman] of his day" (*A. J. Balfour*). One is **accomplished** who is distinguished for his skill, his versatility, and his finesse; the word often suggests mastery in whatever is attempted; as, an *accomplished* musician; an *accomplished* villain. "They...are more *accomplished* and ingenious in this sort of rationalizing than Arnold was" (*T. S. Eliot*). *Accomplished* sometimes implies merely the acquirement of social arts and graces, or accomplishments; as, *accomplished* young ladies (cf. ACQUIREMENT).

Ana. *Perfect, whole, entire, intact: complete, *full: flawless, *impeccable, faultless: *supreme, superlative, transcendent, peerless, surpassing.

Ant. Crude. — *Con.* Rough, *rude, callow, green, raw: primitive, primeval (see PRIMARY): defective, *deficient.

contagion. *Infection.

contagious. *Infectious, communicable, catching.

Ana. Toxic, pestilential, pestilent, virulent, mephitic, miasmal, miasmatic (see POISONOUS).

contagium. See under INFECTION.

contain. **Contain, hold, accommodate** denote in common to have, or be capable of having, within. To **contain** is to have within, or as an element, fraction, or part; to **hold** is to have the capacity to contain or to retain; as, the bookcase *contains* (that is, actually has in it) fifty volumes, but *holds* (that is, is capable of containing) a hundred; a bushel *contains* (not *holds*) four pecks; a bushel basket *holds* (not *contains*) a bushel; these boxes *contain* apples; the compound *contains* iron, which it *holds* in solution; his philosophy *contains* some elements of truth. "Of Plato himself we know nothing...that could not be *held* in a single sentence" (*H. Ellis*). But the distinction between *hold* and *contain* is often inconsiderable or disregarded. To **accommodate** is to hold without crowding and inconvenience; as, thirty passengers were crowded into a bus built to *accommodate* twenty; the parking lot *accommodates* fifty cars. "The earth can *accommodate* its present population more comfortably than it does or ever did" (*Shaw*). This is sometimes an attendant implication of *accommodate* (see OBLIGE, 2) as used of the provision of lodgings; as, the hotel was unable to *accommodate* all who applied for rooms.

Ana. *Receive, admit, take: *harbor, shelter, lodge, house.

contaminate. **Contaminate, taint, attaint, pollute, defile** agree in meaning to debase by rendering impure or unclean. **Contaminate** implies the presence or the influence of something external which by entering into or by coming in contact with a thing destroys or may destroy the latter's purity; as, the city's water supply was in danger of being *contaminated* by surface drainage; Mrs. Brown refused to allow her children to play with other children for fear their manners and morals might be *contaminated;* the *contamination* of air in a mine by gases. **Taint** differs from *contaminate* in stressing the effect rather than the cause; that which is *contaminated* has been touched by or mixed with that which will debase or corrupt; that which is *tainted* is no longer pure, clean, unspoiled, or the like, but is in some measure or degree sullied or stained, or is in process of corruption or decay; as, *tainted* meat. "His unkindness may defeat my life, But never *taint* my love" (*Shak.*). "Woman! above all women glorified, Our *tainted* nature's solitary boast" (*Wordsworth*). "The Claudii, brilliant, unaccountable, *tainted* with some deep congenital madness" (*Buchan*). By an etymological confusion with *taint*, the now rare *attaint* acquired many of the implications of the former term and became its close synonym: in some uses, however, it has retained from its primary sense of to sentence to outlawry or death (see SENTENCE) a hint of sullying the purity of one's name or the honor of one's family or line by actual or imputed nefarious crimes. "Wherein a good name hath bin wrongfully *attainted*" (*Milton*). "No breath of calumny ever *attainted* the personal purity of Savonarola" (*Milman*). **Pollute** implies that the process which begins with contamination is complete and manifest and that what was literally or figuratively pure and clean has lost its clearness or fairness and has become muddy, or filthy, or poisoned. "The nuisance set forth in the bill was one which would be of international importance—a visible change of a great river from a pure stream into a *polluted* and poisoned ditch" (*Justice Holmes*). *Pollute*, in discriminating use, is the preferred term when the reference is to something that ideally is clean, clear, or bright; as, to *pollute* the minds of children by obscenities; to keep one's honor *unpolluted*. **Defile** strongly implies befouling of that which ought to be clean, pure, or held sacred. It, therefore, usually suggests violation, profanation, or desecration, and is highly opprobrious in its connotations. "An evil bird that *defiles* his own nest" (*Latimer*). "For out of the heart proceed evil thoughts, murders, adulteries, fornications, thefts, false witness, blasphemies: These are the things which *defile* a man" (*Matthew* xv. 19–20). "Scenes such as these, 'tis his [the hunter's] supreme delight To fill with riot, and *defile* with blood" (*Cowper*).

Ana. *Debase, vitiate, corrupt, deprave: impair, spoil, *injure, harm.

contemn. *Despise, disdain, scorn, scout.

Ana. Repudiate, reject (see DECLINE): slight, *neglect, disregard: flout, *scoff, jeer.

Con. Venerate, *revere, reverence: respect, esteem, admire, regard (see under REGARD, *n.*).

contemplate. **1** Study, *consider, weigh, revolve, excogitate.

Ana. *Ponder, meditate, muse, ruminate: reflect, cogitate, speculate, *think.

2 Observe, survey, notice, remark, note, perceive, discern, *see, view, behold, descry, espy.

Ana. *Scrutinize, inspect, examine, scan.

contemplative. Meditative, reflective, *thoughtful, speculative, pensive.

Ana. *Intent, rapt, engrossed, absorbed: musing, ruminating, pondering (see PONDER): reflecting, cogitating, reasoning, thinking (see THINK).

contemporaneous. *Contemporary, coeval, synchronous, simultaneous, coincident, concomitant, concurrent.

Con. *Preceding, antecedent, previous, prior, foregoing: following, ensuing, succeeding (see FOLLOW).

contemporary, *adj.* **Contemporary, contemporaneous, coeval, synchronous, simultaneous, coincident, concomitant, concurrent** come into comparison when they mean existing, living, or occurring at the same time. In **contemporary** and **contemporaneous** (of which *contemporary* is applied more frequently to persons, *contemporaneous* to events), the time regarding which agreement is implied is known only through the context; as, Shakespeare was *contemporary* with Cervantes, who died in the same month; Shelley's last year was *contemporaneous* with Matthew Arnold's first; the reign of Louis XIV was *contemporaneous* with the Commonwealth in England, as also with the Restoration and the revolution of 1688; a recent history of the 15th century based on *contemporary* accounts. *Contemporary*, but not *contemporaneous*, may imply reference to the present; it then means of the same time as that of the speaker or writer; as, "we are not without *contemporary* talent" (*E. Wharton*); "most *contemporary* novels Jane found very bad" (*R. Macaulay*). **Coeval** usually implies contemporaneousness for a long, or at a remote, period or time; as, "Every one knows that the Roman Catholic religion is at least *coeval* with most of the governments where it prevails" (*Burke*); "The theory requires that these *coeval* stars should be of nearly the same mass and brightness" (*Eddington*). **Synchronous** implies an exact correspondence between the (usually brief) periods of time involved; **simultaneous** more frequently denotes agreement in the same point or instant of time; as, two pendulums so adjusted that their movements are *synchronous;* the two shots were *simultaneous.* "French speech has run a similar and almost *synchronous* course with English" (*H. Ellis*). "It was proposed that there should be *simultaneous* insurrections in London...and at Newcastle" (*Macaulay*). **Coincident** applies to events that are regarded as falling or happening (sometimes in a notable or singular manner) at the same time; as, the discovery of America was almost *coincident* with the capture of Granada; his sudden departure was suspiciously *coincident* with the stranger's arrival. **Concomitant** carries so strong an implication of attendance or association that it often imputes a subordinate character; however, only when it implies coincidence or synchronousness is it truly a synonym of the other words; as, the *concomitant* circumstances of this event cannot be ignored. "As the beauty of the body always accompanies the health of it, so certainly is decency *concomitant* to virtue" (*Spectator*). **Concurrent** adds to *synchronous* the implication of parallelism or agreement in length of existence, in quality or character, or the like; as, *concurrent* terms in prison; the *concurrent* operation of many machines.

Ana. Living, existing, subsisting (see BE).

Con. See those at CONTEMPORANEOUS.

contempt. Despite, disdain, scorn. See under DESPISE, *v.*

Ana. Abhorrence, detestation, loathing, hatred, hate (see under HATE, *v.*): aversion, *antipathy: repugnance, distaste (see corresponding adjectives at REPUGNANT).

Ant. Respect. — *Con.* Esteem, admiration, *regard: *reverence, awe, fear.

contemptible, *adj.* **Contemptible, despicable, pitiable, sorry, scurvy, cheap, beggarly** come into comparison when they mean arousing or deserving scorn or disdain. **Contemptible** applies to that which inspires such scorn or disdain for any reason, as for being insignificant, or mean, or vile, or utterly base. "There is no vice or folly ...which, by ill management, makes so *contemptible* a figure [as vanity]" (*Swift*). "Why mayn't they [women] do what men do?...I hate that *contemptible* narrow-mindedness" (*Meredith*). "The one disgraceful, unpardonable, and to all time *contemptible* action of my life was to allow myself to appeal to society for help and protection" (*Wilde*). **Despicable** is a stronger term, and frequently implies keen and scornful, sometimes indignant, disapprobation. "I know none so *despicable* as those who despise others" (*Fielding*). "The immorality of James's Court was hardly more *despicable* than the imbecility of his government" (*J. R. Green*). **Pitiable,** as here compared (see also PITEOUS), implies the inspiring of pity mixed with contempt; as, a *pitiable* show of weakness; a *pitiable* attempt at reform. **Sorry** is often used interchangeably with *pitiable* without marked loss; however, the word often distinctively implies contemptible or ridiculous inadequacy, wretchedness, or sordidness; as, *sorry* accommodations for the travelers; "mounted...upon a lean, *sorry*, jack-ass of a horse" (*Sterne*); "thus...ideals die; not in the conventional pageantry of honoured death, but *sorrily*, ignobly, while one's head is turned" (*Bennett*). **Scurvy** (etymologically covered with scurf or scabs) implies extreme despicability and meanness and the arousing of disgust as well as scornful contempt; as, a *scurvy* trick; a *scurvy* impostor. "What difference betwixt This Rome and ours... between That *scurvy* dumb-show and this pageant sheen...?" (*Browning*). **Cheap** often implies contemptibility that results from undue familiarity or accessibility. "Had I so lavish of my presence been ... So stale and *cheap* to vulgar company" (*Shak.*). More often, however, *cheap* and **beggarly** imply contemptible pettiness, *cheap* by falling far below the standard of what is worthy, *beggarly* by its remoteness from that which is adequate; as, *cheap* politics; "a *cheap* and nasty life" (*Shaw*); "About his shelves A *beggarly* account of empty boxes" (*Shak.*); a *beggarly* exhibition; a *beggarly* wage.

Ana. Detestable, abominable, abhorrent, odious, *hateful: vile, low, *base: abject, *mean, sordid, ignoble.

Ant. Admirable, estimable: formidable. — *Con.* *Splendid, sublime, glorious, superb.

contend. Contend, cope, fight, battle, war come into comparison when they mean to strive in opposition to someone or something. **Contend,** the most general of these words, always implies a desire or an effort to overcome that which is opposed, but it may imply rivalry rather than animosity, the use of argument rather than the exercise of physical strength or skill or the employment of weapons, a nonhuman rather than a human antagonist, and the like; as, "Although Mrs. Smith and Stephen were always *contending*, they were never at enmity" (*Hardy*); "the river was stronger than I, and my arms could not for many hours *contend* with the Thames" (*Jefferies*); "since they had left the Española country behind them, they had *contended* first with wind and sand-storms, and now with cold" (*Cather*); "The Manichean theory of a good and an evil spirit *contending* on nearly equal terms in the arena" (*Inge*). **Cope** (followed by *with*) implies contending (often struggling with a problem) successfully or on equal terms: because of this added implication, *cope* is often used in negative (or, in effect, negative) statements to imply the impossibility of success and in affirmative statements to suggest victory or triumph; as, "Do not imagine that you can *cope* with me in a knowledge of Julias and Louisas" (*Austen*); "Once he had the subject chosen, he could *cope* with nature singlehanded, and make every stroke a triumph" (*Stevenson*); "The burden of the mystery, the weight of all this incorrigible world...was really more than I could *cope* with" (*L. P. Smith*); "It is a good thing to make pupils feel that their education is fitting them to *cope* with matters about which the world is excited" (*B. Russell*). **Fight** in its earliest and still most common sense implies a struggle involving physical strength or prowess, originally between men (whether with the fists or with weapons) and later also between animals; as, "*Fight*, gentlemen of England! *fight*, bold yeomen!" (*Shak.*); a dog that will *fight* other dogs larger than himself. In extended use, *fight* differs from *contend* not so much in its range of application (for both may imply other than a human adversary) as in its stress on a rigorous effort to achieve one's ends, and in its suggestion of a struggle against odds or great difficulties; as, to *fight* for the defeat of a bill; to *fight* for breath; to *fight* against a growing evil. **Battle** and **war** are more picturesque or more poetic terms than *fight:* they are used chiefly in a figurative sense, the first to suggest a continuous assailing or attacking of the enemy or other method characteristic of open battle, and the second to suggest the noise, fury, or tumult of war; as, he found he must *battle* his way to success; "[I] Sometimes a patriot, active in debate, Mix with the world, and *battle* for the State" (*Pope*); "Who loved, who suffer'd countless ills, Who *battled* for the True, the Just" (*Tennyson*); "He *wars* with darkling Powers (I *war* with a darkling sea)" (*Kipling*).

Ana. Quarrel, wrangle, altercate, squabble (see under QUARREL, *n.*): resist, combat, withstand, *oppose: compete with, vie with, *rival.

content, contented. Satisfied (see under SATISFY).

Ana. Gratified, pleased (see PLEASE): sated, satiated, cloyed, surfeited (see SATIATE): replete (see FULL).

content, *v.* *Satisfy.

Ana. Gratify, *please: sate, *satiate, surfeit, cloy.

Con. Tantalize, tease (see WORRY): pique, stimulate, *provoke, excite.

contention. Dissension, variance, strife, *discord, conflict.

Ana. *Quarrel, wrangle, altercation, squabble: controversy, dispute, *argument: contending, fighting, warring (see CONTEND).

Con. Agreement, concurrence, coincidence (see corresponding verbs at AGREE): *harmony, accord, concord, consonance.

contentious. Quarrelsome, bellicose, litigious, *belligerent, pugnacious.

Ana. *Contrary, perverse, froward: captious, faultfinding, caviling, carping (see CRITICAL): *aggressive, militant.

Ant. Peaceable. — *Con.* *Pacific, peaceful, irenic: serene, tranquil, *calm: *amiable, good-natured, complaisant, obliging.

conterminous. Contiguous, abutting, adjoining, *adjacent, tangent, juxtaposed.

contest, *n.* **Contest, conflict, combat, fight, affray, fray** agree in denoting a battle between opposing forces for supremacy, for possessions, or the like. **Contest** is the broadest term; originally it referred merely to strife in argument but it is now applicable to any struggle, whether friendly or hostile, for a common object, that involves a test of ability, strength, endurance, or strategic skill; as, a swimming *contest;* a *contest* of wits. "What mighty *contests* rise from trivial things" (*Pope*). **Conflict** always implies discord and warfare (literal or figurative); it also suggests a closer engagement than *contest.* "Arms on armor clashing brayed...dire was the noise of *conflict*" (*Milton*). Figuratively, *conflict* frequently denotes a struggle (often spiritual or mental) between opposing principles or forces. "There is [in a Shakespearean tragedy] an outward *conflict* of persons and groups, there is also a *conflict* of forces in the hero's soul" (*Bradley*). **Combat** is less commonly used in a figurative sense (as, a *combat* against despair): it implies an encounter, especially an armed encounter, between two (individuals, parties, or forces), frequently for the determination of a dispute. "Let these have a day appointed them for a single *combat* in convenient place" (*Shak.*). **Fight** usually implies a hand-to-hand conflict and therefore emphasizes the individual participants. It ranges in dignity from a spiritual struggle (as, "Fight the good *fight* of faith" —*1 Timothy* vi. 12) to actual fisticuffs; as, a prize *fight.* **Affray** commonly refers to a tumultuous disturbance, such as a street fight between mobs or factions, that inspires terror. Legally, an affray is a fight that disturbs the public peace; in literary use the word is often applied to an unseemly or acrimonious dispute; as, "the suppressing of riots and *affrays*" (*Burke*); "days of European crises, diplomatic *affrays*, hecatombic accidents" (*C. E. Montague*); "some bloody *affray* between scholars" (*Quiller-Couch*). **Fray** is now chiefly either a literary term, often with more dignified connotations than *affray* of which it is otherwise a very close synonym, or it is, in colloquial use, a humorous or hyperbolical substitute for *contest, game,* etc. " 'Where are the vile beginners of this *fray?*' 'O noble prince, I can discover all The unlucky manage of this fatal brawl' " (*Shak.*).

Ana. *Encounter, skirmish, brush: competition, emulation, rivalry (see corresponding verbs at RIVAL): *battle, engagement, action, push.

contiguous. Adjoining, abutting, conterminous, *adjacent, tangent, juxtaposed.

Ana. *Nearest, next: *close, near, nigh, near by.

continence. *Temperance, abstemiousness, sobriety, abstinence.

Ana. Chasteness *or* chastity, purity (see corresponding adjectives at CHASTE): moderateness *or* moderation, temperateness (see corresponding adjectives at MODERATE).

Ant. Incontinence. — *Con.* Lecherousness, lustfulness, lewdness, lasciviousness, licentiousness, wantonness (see corresponding adjectives at LICENTIOUS): excessiveness, inordinateness (see corresponding adjectives at EXCESSIVE).

continent, *adj.* Temperate, unimpassioned, *sober.

Ana. Restrained, bridled, curbed, inhibited (see RESTRAIN): decent, *chaste, pure: self-denying, self-abnegating (see corresponding nouns under RENUNCIATION).

Ant. Incontinent.

contingency. Emergency, exigency, pinch, *juncture, pass, strait, crisis.

Ana. Chance, break, *opportunity, occasion, time, tide.

contingent. **1** *Accidental, fortuitous, casual, incidental, adventitious.

Ana. Possible, *probable, likely: unforeseen *or* unforeseeable, unanticipated *or* unanticipable (see affirmative verbs at FORESEE).

Con. Inevitable, necessary, *certain.

2 Conditional, *dependent, relative, adjective.

Ana. Subject, *liable, open, exposed, incident.

Con. Absolute, *ultimate, categorical.

continual. **Continual, continuous, constant, incessant, perpetual, perennial** are here compared as meaning characterized by continued occurrence or recurrence over a relatively long period of time. **Continual** implies a close or unceasing succession or recurrence; **continuous,** an uninterrupted continuity or union, of objects, events, parts, or the like; as, to ensure a *continual* supply of provisions at regular intervals; "a *continuous* series" (*De Quincey*); "*continual* and regular impulses of pleasurable surprise from the metrical arrangement" (*Wordsworth*); "Analytic studies are *continuous,* and not to be pursued by fits and starts, or fragmentary efforts" (*De Quincey*); "The *continual* suggestion of the landscape... entering...into the texture of *continuous* intelligent narration" (*Stevenson*). As applied to objects in the singular, *continual* also stresses frequently the idea of going on indefinitely (though not without interruptions) in time, rather than (like *continuous*) that of unbroken connection or substance; thus, "*continual* industry" (*Stevenson*) implies that one is always at it; "*continuous* labor" (*Hazlitt*), that the work itself is performed at a stretch; so, "He that is of a merry heart hath a *continual* feast" (*Proverbs* xv. 15); "That dull and *continuous* burden of the sea heard inland before or after a great storm" (*J. R. Lowell*). *Continuous* refers to both time and space, *continual* only to time; as, a *continuous* (not *continual*) expanse; a *continual* (or *continuous*) noise; "Humanism has been sporadic, but Christianity *continuous*" (*T. S. Eliot*). **Constant,** as here compared, implies uniform, steady, or persistent occurrence or recurrence; it usually connotes lack of change or variation in character, degree, or the like; as, *constant* interruptions; the *constant* throbbing of the engine; "Such a career meant *constant* toil" (*Buchan*). **Incessant** implies ceaseless or uninterrupted activity; **perpetual** (as here compared: see LASTING) unfailing repetition or lasting duration; as, "an *incessant* cough" (*Cowper*); "*perpetual* colds" (*Cowper*); "the most delightful little girl in the world chattering *incessantly*" (*FitzGerald*); "the *perpetual* fuel of controversy" (*J. H. Newman*). **Perennial** carries the implication of existence over an indeterminate number of years; in older use this idea was stressed and that of exhaustlessness was often connoted; as, "the *perennial* beauty and heroism of the homeliest human nature" (*J. R. Lowell*); "the *perennial* feeling of silent worship" (*Carlyle*). In current use, probably because of the application of the term to plants that die down to the roots and spring up again seasonally over a number of years, *perennial* often implies continual recurrence or constant renewal; as, "revolt is *perennial*" (*Lowes*); "the *perennial* question of the relation between 'ought' and 'is,' of obligation and fact" (*S. Alexander*).

Ana. Unceasing, endless, never-ending, interminable, *everlasting: eternal (see INFINITE): *lasting, permanent, perdurable.

Ant. Intermittent. — *Con.* Recurrent, periodic, alternate (see INTERMITTENT): *fitful, spasmodic.

continuance. *Continuation, continuity.

Ana. Endurance, persistence, lasting (see corresponding verbs at CONTINUE): perseverance, persistence (see corresponding verbs at PERSEVERE): remaining, staying, tarrying (see STAY).

continuation. Continuation, continuance, continuity are often confused, especially when meaning the quality, the act, or the state of continuing or of being continued or an instance revealing such a quality, action, or state. **Continuation** suggests prolongation or resumption; as, the *continuation* of a line, a story; "It's the *continuation* of a philosophic plan" (*Meredith*). "The boy from a good classical school finds that his college Latin, Greek, and mathematics are the natural *continuation* of what he has already acquired" (*Grandgent*). **Continuance** implies duration, perseverance, or stay; as, "eleven years' *continuance*" (*Shak.*); "patient *continuance* in well doing" (*Romans* ii. 7); our *continuance* in the city depends on our boy's health; "the idleness and vice of many years *continuance*" (*Austen*). **Continuity** stresses uninterrupted or unbroken connection, sequence, or extent; as, the *continuity* of a series, a surface, a discourse; *continuity* of attention; "the entire breach of *continuity* in your history made by the Revolution" (*Arnold*). "Space and time are thus vehicles of *continuity* by which the world's parts hang together" (*W. James*). In the technical language of those engaged in making motion pictures or in radio broadcasting, *continuity* denotes that which is written in advance (such as the scenario of a motion picture or the lines to be spoken in a radio broadcast) as provision for perfection in sequence and in timing of the performance.

Ana. Extending *or* extension, prolonging *or* prolongation, protracting *or* protraction (see corresponding verbs at EXTEND).

Ant. Cessation.

continue. Continue, last, endure, abide, persist agree in meaning to remain indefinitely in existence or in a given condition or course. **Continue** distinctively refers to the process, and stresses its lack of an end rather than the duration of, or the qualities involved in, that process. Often, in addition, it suggests an unbroken course. "What a man is as an end perishes when he dies; what he produces as a means *continues* to the end of time" (*B. Russell*). **Last,** and especially its derivative **lasting,** when unqualified usually stress length of existence passing that which is normal or expected. "The anger of slow, mild, loving people has a *lasting* quality" (*Deland*). When qualified, *last* often loses this distinctive implication; as, the refrigerator is guaranteed to *last* five years; the tire *lasted* only three months. **Endure** adds to *last* the implication of resistance, especially to destructive forces or agencies. "For living things, who suffer pain, May not *endure* till time can bring them ease" (*Amy Lowell*). "An art...which *endured*...until man changed his attitude toward the universe" (*H. Adams*). **Abide,** and its derivative **abiding,** imply stability or constancy, especially in opposition to mutability or impermanence. "Tho' much is taken, much *abides*" (*Tennyson*). **Persist** adds to *continue* the implication of outlasting the appointed or normal time; it often also connotes recurrence, especially in sporadic instances. "...an attitude towards life, which...*persists*, with many changes but no breaks, till the closing of the Athenian lecture-rooms by Justinian" (*Inge*).

Ana. Remain, *stay: survive, *outlive, outlast.

Con. *Arrest, interrupt, check: *stop, cease, desist, quit, discontinue: suspend, stay, intermit, *defer, postpone.

continuity. *Continuation, continuance.

Ana. *Succession, sequence, chain, train, progression.

Con. Intermittence, recurrence, alternation, periodicity (see corresponding adjectives at INTERMITTENT): fitfulness (see corresponding adjective at FITFUL).

continuous. Constant, perpetual, perennial, *continual, incessant.

Ana. Connected, related, linked (see JOIN): successive, *consecutive, sequent, serial: *steady, constant, uniform.

Ant. Interrupted. — *Con.* *Intermittent, recurrent, periodic, alternate.

contort. Distort, gnarl, warp, *deform.

Ana. Twist, bend, turn, *curve.

contour. *Outline, silhouette, sky line, profile.

Ana. Configuration, shape, *form, conformation, figure.

contract, *n.* **Contract, bargain, compact, pact, treaty, entente, convention, cartel, covenant, concordat, indenture, mise** designate an agreement reached after negotiation and ending in an exchange of promises between the parties concerned. **Contract** applies especially but not exclusively to a formal written agreement, often of a business nature, couched in such explicit terms as to be enforceable at law. "A regular *contract* to the above effect was drawn up by a lawyer, and signed and sealed in the presence of witnesses" (*N. Hawthorne*). **Bargain** applies especially to an agreement regarding purchase and sale; as, this *bargain* provides for an exchange of so much American wheat and cotton for so much British rubber and tin. A **compact** is an earnest or solemn exchange of promises, sometimes between state or political groups and often between persons. A compact may be unwritten or undocumented, the only assurance of its execution being the trust which each party places in the word of honor of the other or others. The word is used when a keen sense of the obligation which it imposes is assumed of each of the parties. " 'Men and women... marry and promise loyalty to some one person. They can keep that *compact* and yet not shut themselves away from other men and other women' " (*R. Macaulay*). "Let us make a *compact*. I shall do everything to please you, and you must promise to do everything to please me" (*Hudson*). "The National Assembly, inspired by Thiers's patriotism, adopted...the '*Compact* of Bordeaux,' whereby it was agreed that political differences should be put aside in order to carry through expeditiously the work of reconstruction" (*J. S. Schapiro*). **Pact,** as used of an agreement between persons or groups is usually interchangeable with *compact;* but, except in certain stereotyped expressions (as, suicide *pact*, an agreement between two persons to commit suicide), *pact* is much rarer than *compact* for an agreement between persons. "The *Pact* of Corfu was a constitutional *pact* wherein leaders of the southern Slavs agreed to join in a unitary kingdom" (*The Nation*). Since the World War, especially, helped perhaps by the popularity with newspaper headline writers which its brevity won for it, *pact* has been used with increasing frequency in the (often unofficial) title of agreements between states; in this use it is frequently interchanged with **treaty,** which is the generic term for an agreement between states, made by negotiation or diplomacy; as, the Lateran *Pact* or *Treaty* (establishing Vatican City); the Locarno *Pact* or *Treaty;* a nonaggression *pact* or *treaty;* a trade *pact*, a commercial *treaty*. *Treaty*, and never *pact*, however, is the term for an agreement establishing peace after a period of armed hostility; as, the *Treaty* of Versailles. **Entente** is the French word for *understanding;* as used in English, it is often short for *entente cordiale*, a cordial or amicable agreement between nations in regard to their foreign affairs, as a promise of joint military action in case of aggression against any adherent to the entente; as, the Triple *Entente* (between France, Great Britain, and Russia). An *entente* may or may not be set forth in a published document; in fact, it may not be in writing at all: it may be based simply on an exchange of promises between heads of government, or may be merely a state of mind of the peoples concerned. "Captain Lindbergh is busily occupied in establishing an exceedingly cordial *entente* between France and the United States" (*Springfield* [Mass.] *Union*). The word is also used of an understanding between groups, as between economic competitors. "The signing of the steel *entente*...by the producers of Germany, France, Belgium, Luxemburg, and the Saar marked another step in the effort of these continental countries to coordinate their production and sales to avoid cutthroat competition" (*U. S. Daily*). **Convention,** in current use, is usually an agreement which is either less formal or more specific than a treaty: it may be an agreement between several states regulating matters affecting all of them, such as postage, copyright, the conduct of war, etc., or an agreement between commanders of armies in respect to military operations. "The *conventions* for suspending hostilities agreed upon by me with Marshals Soult and Suchet" (*Wellington*). A **cartel** (see also MONOPOLY) is a written agreement or convention between opposing nations as, in view of or during war, for the regulation of intercourse between them. Cartels provide for the treatment and exchange of prisoners, for postal and telegraphic communication, for the mode of reception of bearers of flags of truce, for the treatment of the wounded, etc. **Covenant** has special reference to a sworn or solemn engagement to uphold or defend a faith, a principle, or the like; as, the Scottish National *Covenant* of 1638 (a covenant to support Presbyterianism), the *Covenant* of the League of Nations. "I do set my bow in the cloud, and it shall be for a token of a *covenant* between me and the earth" (*Genesis* ix. 13). **Concordat** usually applies to an agreement between the pope and a secular government for regulating the relations between church and state; as, the *Concordat* of Worms, an agreement with Germany (1122) regulating investiture of bishops and abbots. Less often, the term is used for any agreement regulating ecclesiastical matters. "The prospect of a union of the Protestant Episcopal church and the Presbyterian Church...which a *concordat* proposed a year ago" (*Springfield* [Mass.] *Republican*). An **indenture** is an agreement in writing between two or more parties, whereof each party has usually a counterpart or duplicate. Such agreements were originally executed in duplicate, the parts being indented by a notched cut or line either by laying them together and cutting them, or, when written on the same piece of parchment, by cutting them apart along a notched line so that the two papers or parchments corresponded to each other. Specifically, the word is used (especially in the plural) for a contract by which an apprentice is bound to a master, or a servant to service in a colony, etc. **Mise** implies a determination of expenses, and a settlement of these by agreement; as, the *mise* of Amiens (1264) between King Henry III of England and the rebelling barons.

contract, *v.* **1** Pledge, covenant, engage, *promise, plight.

2 Catch, *incur.

Con. *Escape, avoid, evade, elude, shun, eschew: avert, ward off, *prevent.

3 Contract, shrink, condense, compress, constrict, deflate agree in denoting to decrease in bulk, volume, or content, but they vary widely in their suggestion as to how this decrease is effected and what consequences it has. **Contract** means to draw together the sides or the particles of, especially by a force from within, with a consequent reduction in compass or a compacting of the mass; as, the heart, by *contracting* and dilating rhythmically, keeps up the circulation of the blood; molten iron *contracts* as it cools. **Shrink** means to contract (literally or figuratively) so as to fall short of its original length, bulk, or volume; as, to *shrink* cloth; his assets have *shrunk;* apples often *shrink* before rotting. **Condense** denotes reduction, usually of something more or less homogeneous, to greater compactness without material loss of content; as, to *condense* a gas to a liquid; to *condense* a speech into a few paragraphs. **Compress,** which also means to reduce to a compact state, differs from *condense* in that it connotes a pressing (often, a squeezing) of something formless or diffused into definite shape or into a small compass; as, to *compress* air; to *compress* cotton into bales; to *compress* the events of a lifetime into a play taking three hours to present. **Constrict** means to make narrow or smaller in diameter either by contraction or by squeezing; as, the pores of certain bodies are *constricted* under the influence of cold; the throat is *constricted* by too tight a collar. **Deflate** means to cause to shrink by exhausting of gas, air, or figuratively, of something insubstantial; as, to *deflate* a balloon; to *deflate* a wild rumor or an undeserved reputation.

Ana. Dwindle, diminish, *decrease, reduce.
Ant. Expand. — *Con.* Dilate, swell, distend, inflate (see EXPAND).

contradict. *Deny, gainsay, negative, contravene, traverse, impugn.
Ana. *Dispute (see DISCUSS): controvert, *disprove, refute, confute: belie (see MISREPRESENT).
Ant. Confirm. — *Con.* Corroborate, verify, authenticate, substantiate (see CONFIRM).

contradictory, *adj.* Contrary, antithetical, *opposite, antonymous, antipodal.
Ana. Negating, nullifying (see NULLIFY): counter, counteractive, antagonistic, *adverse.
Con. Agreeing, squaring, tallying, jibing (see AGREE).

contradictory, *n.* Contrary, antithesis, opposite, antonym, antipodes. See under OPPOSITE, *adj.*
Ana. *Converse, reverse.

contraption. Gadget, *device, contrivance.
Ana. Appliance, tool, instrument, *implement, utensil: *machine, engine, apparatus: expedient, makeshift (see RESOURCE).

contrary, *adj.* **1** Antithetical, *opposite, contradictory, antonymous, antipodal.
Ana. Divergent, disparate, *different: counter, antagonistic, *adverse: negating, nullifying (see NULLIFY).
2 Contrary, perverse, restive, balky, froward, wayward come into comparison when they mean given to opposing wishes, commands, conditions, circumstances, and the like. A person is **contrary** who by nature or disposition is so self-willed that he cannot or will not accept dictation or advice (as, she is the most *contrary* child I have ever seen) or who vigorously objects to any arrangements or plans made by others (as, "They've been in your way all these years, and you've always complained of them, so don't be *contrary*, sir"—*Cather*). A person (or, by extension, one of his acts, utterances, or desires) is **perverse** who by temperament or disposition, or sometimes by physical constitution or moral character, runs counter to what is right, true, correct, in keeping with human nature, or the like, especially as determined by the moral law, by custom, or by the law of nature or the state. Sometimes, like *contrary*, the term suggests obstinate willfulness, but even then it usually carries a stronger suggestion of wrongheadedness; as, "*Perverse* disputings of men of corrupt minds, and destitute of the truth" (*1 Timothy* vi. 5); "They will not be resolute and firm, but *perverse* and obstinate" (*Burke*). More often, however, the term suggests defiance of or disobedience to the law, especially the moral law or the established proprieties; as, "she knows how to manage *perverse* children" (*H. Adams*); "The poet's sense of responsibility to nothing but his own inner voice, is perhaps his only way of preserving poetic integrity against the influences of a *perverse* generation" (*Day Lewis*). In current use, *perverse* sometimes suggests perversion, or a sexual maladjustment that reveals itself in aberrant or abnormal desires or acts. "The presence of a small minority of abnormal or *perverse* persons...affords no excuse for restricting the liberty of the many to the standard of the few" (*H. Ellis*) "The last *perverse* whim which has taken possession of the debauchee" (*J. W. Krutch*). A person is **restive** (in the strict sense in which it is here considered: see also RESTLESS) who obstinately refuses to obey the commands or the will of another: the term may imply inaction or a turning in another direction (as, " 'This Parliament—We'll summon it...I'll care For everything....' 'If they prove *restive*...' 'I shall be with you' "—*Browning*) but more often it suggests intractability or unruliness (as, "Your colonies become suspicious, *restive*, and untractable"—*Burke*). A person or, more often, an animal such as a horse is **balky** when he or it stops short and refuses to go further, as in the desired direction or in the performance of something undertaken; as, the horse never proved *balky* until he reached the foot of a steep hill; a child often becomes *balky* when he is asked to solve a problem beyond his powers. A person (often a child) is **froward** who is so contrary or so prone to disobedience that he will not comply with the most reasonable of requests or suggestions: the term usually suggests a characteristic rather than an occasional or a justifiable reaction. "All the words of my mouth are in righteousness; there is nothing *froward* or perverse in them" (*Proverbs* viii. 8). "I never entered on disobedience without having settled with myself that the fun of it would be worth the pains, scorned repentance, and endured correction with a philosophy which got me the reputation of being a hardened and *froward* child" (*M. Austin*). A person is **wayward** who is so perverse that he is incapable of government by those in authority over him and therefore goes his own way, however wanton, capricious, or depraved it may be; as, an institution for *wayward* girls; "I have been wild and *wayward*, but you'll forgive me now" (*Tennyson*). Things that are erratic or follow no clear law or principle are also describable as *wayward;* as, *wayward* fancies; *wayward* opinions.
Ana. Refractory, recalcitrant, intractable, headstrong, *unruly: contumacious, rebellious, *insubordinate.
Ant. Good-natured, complaisant. — *Con.* *Amiable, obliging: *compliant, acquiescent: amenable, tractable (see OBEDIENT).

contrary, *n.* Antithesis, opposite, contradictory, antonym, antipodes. See under OPPOSITE, *adj.*
Ana. *Converse, reverse.

contrast, *v.* *Compare, collate.

contrast, *n.* *Comparison, collation, parallel, antithesis.
Ana. Distinction, difference, divergence, *dissimilarity, unlikeness: conflict, *discord.

contravene. *Deny, contradict, traverse, impugn, negative.
Ana. *Oppose, combat, resist: controvert, *disprove: transgress, violate (see corresponding nouns at BREACH): *trespass, encroach, infringe.
Ant. Uphold (*law, principle, etc.*): allege (*right, claim, privilege*).

contravention. Trespass, transgression, violation, infringement, *breach, infraction.
Ana. *Offense, vice, sin, crime.
Con. Compliance, acquiescence (see under COMPLIANT).

contribute. *Conduce, redound, accrue.
Ana. Concur, co-operate, combine, *unite: *help, aid, assist: promote, further, forward, *advance.

contribution. *Donation, benefaction, alms.
Ana. Grant, subvention, subsidy, *appropriation: *gift, present, largess, boon.

contributory. *Auxiliary, ancillary, adjuvant, subservient, accessory.
Ana. Concurring, co-operating (see UNITE): helping *or* helpful, aiding, assisting *or* assistant (see corresponding verbs at HELP).

contrition. Attrition, repentance, *penitence, compunction, remorse.
Ana. *Sorrow, grief, regret: confessing *or* confession, shriving *or* shrift, absolving *or* absolution, remitting *or* remission (see corresponding verbs at CONFESS).

contrivance. *Device, gadget, contraption.
Ana. Invention, creation, discovery (see corresponding verbs at INVENT): *implement, tool, instrument, appliance, utensil: *machine, engine, apparatus.

contrive. *Manage, afford.
Ana. Plan, plot, scheme, design (see under PLAN, *n.*).

control, *v.* Direct, manage, *conduct.
Ana. *Govern, rule: regulate, *adjust: *guide, lead, pilot, engineer, steer: *restrain, curb, check.

control, *n.* **1** Command, dominion, authority, *power, jurisdiction, sway.
Ana. Ascendancy, *supremacy: might, puissance, *power, force: management, direction (see corresponding verbs at CONDUCT).
Con. Mutiny, revolt, *rebellion.
2 *Corrective, check, antidote.
Ana. Regulation, *law, ordinance, rule, precept, statute, canon: experiment, *experience.

controversial. Controversial, eristic, polemic, polemical, apologetic (*or* **apologetical**) come into comparison when they mean disputatious in character or intent. **Controversial,** like all the other words in this group, is applicable to writings and speeches involving disputation, and to the tone or temper of the disputants, but it does not as expressly indicate the method or the purpose as some of the others; as, the *controversial* writings of Theodore Roosevelt; his object in this article is didactic rather than *controversial.* When specifically applied to subjects, questions, issues, proposals, and the like, *controversial* is richer in its implications and suggests provocativeness, violent difference of opinion, and sometimes the activities of propagandists; as, *controversial* subjects should be avoided in drawing-room conversation; to exclude *controversial* matter from the radio. "Boys and girls ought to be encouraged to take an interest in current *controversial* questions of importance.... and...to read all sides in such controversies, not only the orthodox side" (*B. Russell*). **Eristic** (the least frequent of these words) stresses the method of disputation more than its purpose or its subject matter; it often specifically implies sophistry, quibbling, captiousness, or attention to details rather than to the larger issues involved. "He fought the combat syllogistic With... skill and art *eristic*" (*T. Moore*). **Polemic** and **polemical** both emphasize the spirit and the methods of combat, or of ardent defense of one's beliefs or views, or especially of the doctrines of one's religious faith. Usually the words imply the intent to refute errors or to make converts but because of their association with violent religious controversies they have acquired unpleasant connotations of contentiousness, rancor in argument, and intemperance in attack; as, the discussion took on a *polemic* tone; the *polemical* style of Milton's treatises on divorce. "After the fiery stimulants, compounded of brimstone and bigotry, offered by the *polemic* theologians, the gentle sedative of Montaigne's conversation comes like a draft of nepenthe" (*Preserved Smith*). **Apologetic,** also, suggests partisanship, and the defense of one's beliefs, especially of one's religious beliefs. But it often implies an expository rather than an argumentative method, and stresses the clearing up of misunderstandings by an appeal to reason rather than the refutation of errors on the other side or the indication of agreements between both sides. "It was also stipulated [by the editor] that the essays should not be directly *apologetic* in tendency. The book is neither a defence of Christianity nor a criticism of it" (*Inge*).
Ana. Disputed *or* disputable, debated *or* debatable, argued (see corresponding verbs at DISCUSS): argumentative, disputatious (see corresponding nouns at ARGUMENTATION).

controversy. Dispute, *argument.
Ana. Contention, dissension (see DISCORD): disputation, *argumentation, forensic, debate.

controvert, *v.* Rebut, refute, *disprove, confute.
Ana. Contravene, traverse, impugn, *deny, gainsay: *oppose, combat: dispute, debate, agitate, argue, *discuss.
Ant. Assert. — *Con.* Defend, justify, *maintain, vindicate.

contumacious. Rebellious, *insubordinate, mutinous, seditious, factious.
Ana. *Contrary, perverse, froward: refractory, recalcitrant, intractable, ungovernable, *unruly, headstrong.
Ant. Obedient. — *Con.* *Compliant, acquiescent, resigned: amenable, tractable, docile (see OBEDIENT).

contumelious. *Abusive, opprobrious, vituperative, scurrilous, scurrile, scurril.
Ana. Insolent, overbearing, arrogant, disdainful (see PROUD): humiliating, demeaning, debasing, abasing (see ABASE): flouting, scoffing, jeering, sneering (see SCOFF).
Ant. Obsequious. — *Con.* Complimenting *or* complimentary, commending *or* commendatory, applauding (see corresponding verbs at COMMEND).

conundrum. Puzzle, riddle, enigma, problem, *mystery.

convenance. Convention, usage, *form.

convene. Convoke, muster, *summon, call, cite.
Ana. *Gather, congregate, assemble, collect.
Ant. Adjourn. — *Con.* Disperse, *scatter: dissolve, prorogue (see ADJOURN): dismiss, *eject.

convent. *Cloister, nunnery, monastery, abbey, priory.

convention. 1 Convention, convocation, conference, congress, council, synod are the most general terms in English use designating a body of representatives, executives, or the like, called together for deliberation and action on the affairs of a larger body. In American use, **convention** is the most general of these terms, usually implying little more than a meeting of representatives for a common and definitely stated purpose or purposes. It is the ordinary term for an annual or periodic meeting of representatives from all the branches of an association or organization within a given area, such as a county, a state, or a nation, for the purpose of transacting business and electing officers; as, the state *convention* of the American Legion; the annual *convention* of the National Education Association. It is also applied to a meeting of elected representatives of a political party in the nation or a state to nominate candidates for a coming election and to frame a party platform; as, in 1940, the Democratic *convention* was held in Chicago, the Republican *convention* in Philadelphia. A meeting of elected representatives to frame a new constitution or to amend an old constitution for one of the states of the United States is called a constitutional *convention.* In British use, the term is even more general, for it equals *assembly:* when applied to any gathering of representatives in the American sense, it usually suggests a more or less informal character. The preferred terms in British use are **convocation** (especially for a formal assembly of the clergy of a province of the Church of England or their representatives [as, the *Convocation* of the Province of Canterbury; the *Convocation* of the Province of York] or for a deliberative or advisory body composed of all or some of the graduates of one of the universities) and **conference** for formal and, often, periodic meetings of representatives of an organization or association (as, the annual *conference* of the National Union of Teachers; an international monetary *conference*). But *conference* is used for an annual assembly of Methodist ministers, as of a given district (sometimes also called a *conference*), for the transaction of ecclesiastical business, or an assembly of representatives or committees from the various branches of a legislative body for consultation or adjustments of legislation, or, in a more general sense, for any assembly of representatives or executives of an organization or corporation whose chief purposes are to consult, deliberate, and decide. **Congress,** because of its use as a designation of the body which exercises legislative power in a country, especially in the United States, is not so common in general use as formerly. It still applies, however, to any formal assembly or large body gathered in formal assembly to discuss and decide questions of great significance: the term usually imputes an exalted character to the representatives who make up that body and, therefore, is used especially of a conference of princes, envoys, deputies, or the like; as, a pan-American *congress;* an international *congress* in the interest of peace, the Congress of Vienna readjusted territories and governments after the Napoleonic wars. The term is also applied to any extremely large assembly or body composed not of appointed or elective representatives but of voluntary attendants from far and near who meet for a common purpose; as, a Eucharistic *congress.* **Council** is applicable to a body, small or large, assembled for consultation, deliberation, and decision or advice. It is the historical term for any of the great bodies of ecclesiastics convened to legislate on matters of doctrine, discipline, morals, or law affecting the Christian church or, since the Reformation, the Roman Catholic Church; thus, the great *councils,* such as the Nicene Council, convoked from the entire church, are called ecumenical *councils;* a *council* convoked and presided over by a bishop and composed of the clergy of his diocese is called, in the Roman Catholic and some other churches, a diocesan *council.* In Protestant churches where *council* is used, it applies to a deliberative and advisory rather than a legislative body. *Council* is also specifically applied both to a smaller advisory group, such as one (termed executive *council*) that advises the executive of a nation or state (as, specifically, the king's privy *council* in Great Britain, a governor's *council* in some states of the United States, the executive *council* in some British colonies) and to a legislative body of a city, borough, county, or the like; as, a city *council* (sometimes, common *council*); a county *council.* **Synod,** which in general denotes an ecclesiastical council, is used largely by Protestant and Orthodox denominations, with, however, great variations in application; thus, the holy *synod* of an Orthodox church, such as the Russian or Greek Orthodox churches, is its governing body; in Presbyterian, Lutheran, and Dutch (and other) Reformed churches, it is a governing or advisory body having only the powers and jurisdiction granted it by the congregations which send members or delegates to it: in the Protestant Episcopal Church, a synod is a provincial assembly of bishops and elected clerical and lay diocesan representatives.

Ana. Assembly, assemblage, congregation, gathering (see under GATHER).

2 Entente, compact, pact, treaty, covenant, cartel, concordat, *contract, bargain, indenture, mise.

Ana. *Agreement, accord, understanding.

3 *Form, convenance, usage.

Ana. Custom, practice, consuetude (see HABIT): canon, precept, rule, *law: etiquette, propriety, *decorum.

conventional. Formal, ceremonious, *ceremonial, solemn.

Ana. *Decorous, proper, comme il faut, seemly, decent: *correct, right, precise.

Ant. Unconventional. — *Con.* *Negligent, slack, lax, remiss: *natural, simple, unsophisticated, ingenuous, naïve, artless.

conversant. **Conversant, versed** come into comparison because they agree in meaning being familiar with something: they are seldom, if ever, found in attributive use. **Conversant** (usually followed by *with*) implies a familiarity with a subject, a field of knowledge, the writings on that subject or in that field, or the like, that comes from long association, long experience, frequent intercourse, or many dealings with them; as, "Those men who are most *conversant* with American affairs" (*J. Bright*); "Like Walpole...he was thoroughly *conversant* with questions of finance" (*Lecky*); "The Pilgrim's Progress is known not only to everyone who is *conversant* with the other writings of the period, but to thousands, the world around, who never heard of...[Bacon's] Essays" (*Lowes*). **Versed** (followed by *in*), though often used interchangeably with *conversant,* in discriminating use carries not only an implication of familiarity with something, but of skill, adeptness, proficiency, or the like, as in an art or a profession; thus, to be *versed* in law (but, to be *conversant* with the laws of all European countries); to be *versed* in medicine (but, to be *conversant* with all the new methods of treating pneumonia). Because of this added implication, *versed* is often used in combination; as, well-*versed;* ill-*versed;* poorly *versed.* "I don't think him [Leigh Hunt] deeply *versed* in life" (*Byron*).

Ana. Intimate, *familiar: informed, acquainted (see INFORM): *learned, erudite: adept, *proficient, skilled, expert, skillful.

Ant. Ignorant.

conversation, converse. Communion, commune, communication, *intercourse, commerce, traffic, dealings, correspondence.

Ana. Conversing, talking *or* talk, speaking *or* speech (see corresponding verbs at SPEAK).

converse, *v.* Talk, *speak.

Ana. *Express, voice, broach, air, ventilate, vent, utter: *chat, chatter, gabble: *gossip, tattle: *discourse, descant, expatiate, dilate.

converse, *n.*[1] See CONVERSATION.

converse, *n.*[2] **Converse, obverse, reverse** are frequently confused when they mean that which is the opposite of another thing. **Converse** applies chiefly to statements or to propositions; because it etymologically connotes a turning about, in strict use it implies an interchange or transposition of the important terms; as, the *converse* of "None but the brave deserves the fair" is "None but the fair deserves the brave." *Converse* is not to be confused with *contradictory* (see under OPPOSITE, *adj.*); thus, the *contradictory* of "None but the brave deserves the fair" would be "All but the brave deserve the fair." So long as the important terms are transposed, one proposition is the *converse* of another whether or not it is its opposite. "The feeling that society needs protection against the individual rather than the *converse*" (*Brownell*). **Obverse** and **reverse** are specifically applied to the two faces of a coin, medal, etc.; *obverse* applying to the one containing the head or principal inscription, *reverse* to the other. More generally, *obverse* refers to the more, *reverse* to the less, apparent or intentionally conspicuous side or face of anything (or, in colloquial language, *obverse* to the right, *reverse* to the wrong, side or face) as, "Looking at the fair tapestry of Life, with its royal and even sacred figures, he dwells not on the *obverse* alone, but here chiefly on the *reverse;* and indeed turns out the rough seams, tatters, and manifold thrums of that unsightly wrong side" (*Carlyle*).

Ana. Opposite, contrary, antithesis, contradictory (see under OPPOSITE, *adj.*).

conversion. Transformation, metamorphosis, transmutation, transmogrification, transfiguration. See under TRANSFORM.

convert, *v.* *Transform, metamorphose, transmute, transmogrify, transfigure.

Ana. Manufacture, fabricate, forge, *make: apply, utilize, employ, *use.

convert, *n.* **Convert, proselyte** are synonyms only in their applicability to the same person. Both denote a person who has embraced another creed, opinion, or doctrine than the one he has previously accepted or adhered to. **Convert** is commonly used in a good sense, implying a sincere and voluntary change of belief: it is, therefore, the designation preferred by the church, the party, or the school of thought of which such a person becomes a new member. *Convert* is also applied to a person who undergoes the religious experience called *conversion,* or a turning from a life of sin or indifference to one guided by religious (specifically, Christian) principles and motives. **Proselyte** was originally applied to any convert to another religion: it is still used in reference to a convert to Judaism who manifests his sincerity and fidelity by strict adherence to religious laws and practices. In general use, however, the term always suggests a being won over, usually by an apostle, a missionary, or a zealot, but, sometimes, by another with less praiseworthy motives; as, "Ye compass sea and land to make one *proselyte*" (*Matthew* xxiii. 15). *Proselyte* is often, but not invariably, the designation preferred by the members of a church for one formerly of their number who has been converted to another faith. The term is also applied to any person won over to a party, a cause, or a way of life in which he has formerly expressed disbelief; as, "You agree with the rest of the married world in a propensity to make *proselytes*" (*Shenstone*).
Ana. Neophyte, *novice.
Con. Apostate, *renegade, pervert, backslider, recreant, turncoat.

convertible. *Reciprocal, correspondent, correlative, complementary.
Ana. Interchangeable, exchangeable (see corresponding verbs at EXCHANGE).

convey. 1 Transport, *carry, transmit, bear.
Ana. *Move, remove, shift, transfer: take, fetch, *bring.
2 *Transfer, deed, alienate, alien.
Ana. Consign, *commit, relegate: *sell, vend, trade, auction, barter.

convict, *n.* *Prisoner, captive.

conviction. 1 Assurance, certitude, *certainty.
Ana. Faith, *belief, credence, credit: *creed, confession, symbol.
Con. Doubt, *uncertainty, dubiety, dubiosity, skepticism: disbelief, *unbelief, incredulity.
2 Belief, persuasion, *opinion, view, sentiment.
Ana. Tenet, dogma, *doctrine: judgment, conclusion (see under INFER).

convincing. Telling, cogent, *valid, sound.
Ana. Proving, demonstrating (see PROVE): persuading *or* persuasive, inducing (see corresponding verbs at INDUCE): forceful, forcible, potent, *powerful.

convivial. Companionable, *social, gregarious, hospitable, co-operative.
Ana. Sociable, genial, cordial, affable, *gracious: gay, *lively, vivacious: *merry, jocund, jolly, jovial: hilarious, mirthful (see corresponding nouns at MIRTH).
Ant. Taciturn: staid. — *Con.* Reserved, reticent, *silent: *serious, sober, grave, sedate, solemn: asocial, *unsocial.

convocation. *Convention, conference, congress, council, synod.
Ana. Assembly, assemblage, congregation, gathering (see under GATHER).

convoke. Convene, muster, *summon, call, cite.
Ana. Assemble, *gather, congregate, collect: *invite bid.
Ant. Prorogue, dissolve. — *Con.* *Adjourn: disperse, *scatter.

convoy, *v.* Escort, conduct, *accompany, attend, chaperon.
Ana. Protect, shield, guard, safeguard, *defend: *guide, lead, pilot.

convulse. Rock, *shake, agitate.
Ana. *Discompose, disturb, disquiet, perturb.

convulsion. Spasm, paroxysm, *fit, attack, access, accession.

convulsive. Spasmodic, *fitful.
Con. *Steady, uniform, even, equable, constant.

cool. 1 Chilly, *cold, frosty, frigid, freezing, gelid, icy, glacial, arctic.
Ant. Warm.
2 Cool, composed, collected, unruffled, imperturbable, nonchalant come into comparison when applied to persons, their manners, appearance, temper, or acts, in the sense of showing or seeming to show freedom from agitation or excitement. **Cool** basically implies such self-control that no hint is given of any emotion or motive that might warm, inflame, excite, or impassion. Specifically, it may further imply detachment or dispassionateness (as, "Modest youth, with *cool* reflection crown'd"—*Pope;* "My work, I am often told, is *cool* and serene, entirely reasonable and free of passion"—*H. Ellis*), or calm courage in assault or under attack (as, soldiers *cool* under fire), or deliberateness or determination in gaining one's ends (as, "The coquette [Queen Elizabeth] of the presence chamber became the *coolest* and hardest of politicians at the council board"—*J. R. Green*), or calm assurance or effrontery (as, "It is the *cool* manner in which the whole is done that annoys you"—*Hazlitt*), or actual or seeming indifference (as, a *cool* lover). **Composed** implies the freedom from signs of agitation or excitement that is characteristic of a decorous, sedate temperament or is the result of self-discipline; as, "In her *composed,* schooled manner she despised and disliked both father and daughter exceedingly" (*Conrad*); "She was *composed* without bravado, contrite without sanctimoniousness" (*A. Repplier*); "She was pale, and looked as if she hadn't slept, but *composed,* as she always is" (*R. Macaulay*). **Collected** stresses a concentration of the mind or spirit with resulting elimination of all distractions: otherwise it differs little from *composed;* as, "Be *collected:* No more amazement" (*Shak.*); "The most *collected* spectator" (*Arnold*); "Mrs. Hawthorne wore her *collected* Sunday expression, and Tony knew that she did not allow them to talk of mundane affairs on these expeditions to and from church" (*Arch. Marshall*). **Unruffled** implies coolness, placidity, and often, poise, in the midst of excitement or when there is cause for agitation; as, while others fretted and fumed, he remained *unruffled;* "Her mind was *unruffled* by the spiritual problems which were vexing the minds around her" (*J. R. Green*). **Imperturbable** implies such coolness and assurance that one cannot be abashed, annoyed, disconcerted, alarmed, or otherwise disturbed: it usually implies a temperamental rather than an acquired frame of mind; as, "Franklin's *imperturbable* common sense" (*Arnold*); "Gautier, working *imperturbably* in the midst of the clatter of printing presses" (*Lowes*); "a very good-looking, rosy little man with . . . a soft voice and a manner of *imperturbable* urbanity" (*H. G. Wells*). **Nonchalant** stresses an easy coolness of manner, or casualness that suggests, rather than necessarily implies, indifference or unconcern: it often connotes lightheartedness or off-handedness; as, "God . . . knows, if he is not as indifferent to mortals as the *nonchalant* deities of Lucretius" (*Byron*); "Dallying with a cigar, which he smoked *nonchalantly* as he sang" (*T. E. Brown*); "He walked in a *nonchalant* fashion" (*D. H. Lawrence*).

Ana. *Calm, tranquil, serene, placid: detached, aloof, *indifferent: *impassive, stoic, phlegmatic.
Ant. Ardent: agitated. — *Con.* Fervid, fervent, passionate, perfervid, *impassioned: perturbed, discomposed, disturbed, upset, flustered, flurried (see DISCOMPOSE).

co-operate. Conjoin, *unite, combine.
Ana. Coincide, *agree, concur: conspire, collude, *connive.
Ant. Counteract. — *Con.* *Neutralize, negative: *nullify, negate, annul.

co-operative. *Social, companionable, gregarious, convivial, hospitable.
Ana. Sociable, cordial, genial, affable, *gracious: helping *or* helpful, aiding, assisting (see corresponding verbs at HELP).
Ant. Un-co-operative. — *Con.* *Unsocial, asocial.

cop, *v.* **1** *Catch, capture, nab, trap, snare, entrap, ensnare, bag.
Ana. Grab, seize, *take, snatch, clutch, grasp.
2 *Steal, filch, pinch, snitch, swipe, lift, pilfer, purloin.

cop, *n.* *Policeman, officer, copper, bull, bobby, peeler, constable, catchpole, gendarme.

copartner. *Partner, colleague, ally, confederate.
Ana. *Associate, companion, comrade.

cope. *Contend, fight, battle, war.
Ana. Compete with, vie with, *rival, emulate: *oppose, combat, resist, withstand.

copious. *Plentiful, abundant, ample, plenteous.
Ana. *Profuse, lavish, exuberant, prodigal, luxuriant, lush.
Ant. Meager. — *Con.* Scanty, scant, scrimpy, sparse, exiguous, spare (see MEAGER): *thin, slight, tenuous, slim, slender.

copper. *Policeman, officer, cop, bull, bobby, peeler, constable, catchpole, gendarme.

copy, *n.* *Reproduction, duplicate, carbon, carbon copy, transcript, facsimile, replica.
Ana. Counterpart, *parallel: imprint, print, *impression, impress: *image, simulacrum, effigy.
Ant. Original. — *Con.* Archetype, *prototype.

copy, *v.* **Copy, imitate, mimic, ape, mock** agree in meaning to make something like an already existing thing in form, appearance, obvious or salient characteristics, or the like. **Copy** implies duplication of an original and thereby as close a resemblance as is possible under the circumstances; as, to *copy* a letter; to *copy* Da Vinci's "Mona Lisa"; to *copy* the clothes of a great designer. **Imitate** stresses following something as a pattern or model; it does not therefore preclude variations from the original; thus, a writer who *imitates* Keats may merely re-echo enough of that poet's rhythms, images, or sentiments to produce poetry reminiscent of Keats. *Imitate* may imply emulation (as, to *imitate* the example of one's elders): it may imply representation in another medium (as, art *imitates* nature; the dramatist *imitates* life; the music *imitates* a storm): it may imply simulation (as, fabrics that *imitate* leather). **Mimic** usually implies an exact copying, especially of a person's movements, gestures, voice, mannerisms, etc., sometimes for the sake of making sport of them, but often with the intention of giving a lifelike representation of them. "'This is disgraceful,' said Maisie, *mimicking* Mrs. Jennett's tone" (*Kipling*). "I am sure I repeat her words, though I cannot *mimic* either the voice or air with which they were spoken" (*Fielding*). The word sometimes suggests a counterfeiting clever enough to seem real; it therefore often implies the skill of an actor. "I might *mimic* a passion that I do not feel, but I cannot *mimic* one that burns me like fire" (*Wilde*). **Ape** also implies close copying, sometimes in the spirit of mimicry, but often also in the spirit of emulating that which one admires. "The stout, tall captain...becomes their pattern, upon whom they fix their whole attention, and *ape* all his tricks" (*Cowper*). **Mock** commonly adds to *mimic* the implication of a derisive intent. It often distinctively suggests immediate repetition of the words or actions mimicked; as, to *mock* one's teacher; "the babbling echo *mocks* the hounds" (*Shak.*); "her shadow still Glower'd about... As though... to *mock* behind her back" (*Keats*).
Ant. Originate.

coquet, *v.* Flirt, *trifle, dally, toy.

cordial. Genial, affable, *gracious, sociable.
Ana. Warm, warmhearted, responsive, sympathetic, *tender: *sincere, heartfelt, hearty, wholehearted.
Con. Cool, *cold, frosty, frigid: *indifferent, aloof, detached, disinterested: reserved, taciturn, *silent.

core, *n.* *Center, middle, midst, hub, focus, nucleus, heart, omphalos.

corner. **1** **Corner, angle** denote in common the space included between converging surfaces or lines. In common usage, **corner** applies to the space included or the projection formed by the convergence of the actual two or three sides or edges of a material structure; as, the *corner* of a box, a table, a room, a house; a street *corner;* a chimney *corner;* to drive into a *corner.* **Angle** has usually the more technical sense of the space included between, or the degree of inclination of, two converging lines or planes; as, a right *angle;* the *angle* of the faces of a crystal; the walls forming the *corner* met at an obtuse *angle. Angle* is also used in the sense of a sharp projection; as, "We rub each other's *angles* down" (*Tennyson*); compare "I hit my head against the sharp *corner* of the table."
Ana. Edge, verge, *border.
2 Pool, *monopoly, syndicate, trust, cartel.

corporal, *adj.* Corporeal, *bodily, physical, somatic.
Ana. Fleshly, *carnal, animal, sensual.

corporeal. **1** *Material, physical, sensible, phenomenal, objective.
Ana. Actual, *real: tangible, palpable, ponderable, *perceptible.
Ant. Incorporeal. — *Con.* Intangible, impalpable, *imperceptible, insensible, imponderable.
2 *Bodily, physical, corporal, somatic.
Ana. See those at CORPORAL.

corpse. Carcass, cadaver, *body, stiff.
Ana. Remains, relics (see REMAINDER).

corpulent. *Fleshy, portly, fat, stout, obese, rotund, plump, chubby.
Ana. Burly, husky, brawny, *muscular: thickset, chunky, stubby, dumpy (see THICK).
Ant: Spare. — *Con.* *Lean, gaunt, rawboned, angular, lanky, lank, skinny, scrawny: slender, slim, slight, *thin.

corpus. Thesaurus, treasury, *anthology, chrestomathy, chapbook, garland, florilegium.

corpuscle. *Particle, atom, molecule.

correct, *v.* **1** **Correct, rectify, emend, remedy, redress, amend, reform, revise** agree in meaning to set or make right that which is wrong. One **corrects** that which is inaccurate, untrue, or imperfect, or that which contains errors, faults, or defects, when one by substitutions brings it into conformity with a standard or rule of accuracy, truth, or perfection; as, to *correct* one's mistakes in pronunciation; to *correct* printers' proofs. "It [appellate jurisdiction]...*corrects* the proceedings in a cause already instituted" (*Ch. Just. Marshall*). Also, one *corrects* a person when one points out his errors or faults for disciplinary purposes (see also PUNISH). "She's been with me such a long time....She takes liberties. I've *corrected* her once or twice" (*Bennett*). One thing *corrects* another thing when the former serves to counteract or neutralize the bad effect of the latter; as, alkaline tablets that *correct* stomach acidity; his head *corrects* his heart in the choice of friends. One **rectifies** something which requires straightening out or ordering because it deviates from the rule or standard of what is right, just, equitable, properly controlled or directed, or the like; as, to *rectify* a mistake in an account; to *rectify* an error of judgment; to *rectify* mischief one has done. "Reason is here no guide, but still a guard: 'Tis hers to *rectify*, not overthrow, And treat this passion [one's ruling passion] more as friend than foe" (*Pope*). One **emends** a thing when one frees it from error or defects; specifically one, as an editor, *emends* a corrupt text when one replaces doubtful readings with others that are judged to be closer to the original or to the intention of the author; as, the eighteenth-century editors of Shakespeare freely *emended* the texts of his plays. One **remedies** that which is a source of evil or harm when one makes such corrections as will either bring about its eradication or restore that which is harmed to a normal, sound, or prosperous condition; as, to *remedy* an abuse of a privilege; to *remedy* the maldistribution of relief; to *remedy* a social evil. One **redresses** something which involves unfairness, injustice, or lack of proper balance in any way; the word usually suggests reparation or compensation. "There is no calamity which right words will not begin to *redress*" (*Emerson*). "The Church looked to charity, not to legislation, to *redress* social wrongs" (*Inge*). "The balance [of electricities] is *redressed* by a mass migration of the electrons out of the overpopulated substance" (*Karl K. Darrow*). One **amends** something when one makes such corrections or changes in it that it is bettered or raised to a much higher standard; as, to *amend* one's ways; to *amend* one's life. "Laws that are not repealed are *amended* and *amended*" (*Shaw*). One **reforms** something when one makes drastic changes in it in an attempt to eliminate imperfections; the word usually implies a new form or character; as, to *reform* the church. "The fact is that the world does not care to be *reformed*....This makes the way of the improver hard" (*S. M. Crothers*). One **revises** something when one looks it over to discover where it requires correction or amendment and makes the necessary changes; as, to *revise* a book before its second printing; to *revise* a state constitution. "There can be no doubt as to the jurisdiction of this court to *revise* the judgment of a Circuit Court" (*Ch. Just. Taney*).

Ana. *Improve, better, ameliorate: offset, *compensate, countervail, counterbalance, balance: *neutralize, counteract: *adjust, regulate, fix: *reprove, reprimand, admonish, chide.

Con. Impair, spoil, mar, *injure, damage, harm, hurt: aggravate, *intensify.

2 Discipline, *punish, chastise, chasten, castigate.

Con. *Indulge, pamper, spoil, humor, baby: condone, *excuse.

correct, *adj.* **Correct, accurate, exact, precise, nice, right** agree in meaning conforming to standard, fact, or truth. **Correct,** the most colorless term, implies scarcely more than freedom from fault or error, as judged by some (usually) conventional or acknowledged standard; as, *correct* dress, style, deportment. "A supposed center of *correct* information, *correct* judgment, *correct* taste" (*Arnold*). "Sedley's valet, the most solemn and *correct* of gentlemen" (*Thackeray*). **Accurate** implies, more positively, fidelity to fact or truth attained by the exercise of care; as, an *accurate* investigation, statement, observer. "A reasonably *accurate* and refined use of the mother-tongue" (*C. W. Eliot*). **Exact** emphasizes the strictness or rigor of the agreement, which neither exceeds nor falls short of the fact, standard, or truth; as, an *exact* likeness; the *exact* value; his *exact* words. "The acquisition of *exact* knowledge...is essential to every kind of excellence" (*B. Russell*). **Precise** stresses rather sharpness of definition or delimitation, or scrupulous exactness; as, the *precise* meaning of a word. "*Precise* statements of principles" (*A. C. Benson*). "She did not ...understand...the *precise* nature of what she was doing" (*Conrad*). **Nice,** as here compared, implies great, occasionally excessive, precision and delicacy, as in discrimination, adjustment, or the like; as, a *nice* calculation, distinction, point of law. "Overbalance the *nice* adjustment on either side of the scale, and loss is the inevitable result" (*Lowes*). "This method [of calculating longitude], though theoretically possible, is not sufficiently *nice* to be of practical value" (*Preserved Smith*). **Right** (as here compared: see also GOOD) stresses an absence of deviation from and, therefore, a strict accordance with the facts, the truth, or the standard. Often, it is so close in meaning to *correct*, that it is only in collocations where the latter's stress on freedom from error or fault is set up against *right's* emphasis on strict accordance with the facts, truth, or a standard that one can determine which word is preferable; thus, an answer to a problem in arithmetic may be said to be either *correct* or *right;* she knows the *right* (or *correct*) use of "each" and "every"; a *correct* (not *right*) gentleman; the *right* (not *correct*) people were invited; though he gave an assumed name the police know his *right* (better than *correct*) name.

Ana. *Impeccable, faultless, flawless: punctilious, punctual, scrupulous, meticulous, *careful.

Ant. Incorrect. — ***Con.*** *False, wrong: fallacious, casuistical (see under FALLACY).

corrective, *n.* **Corrective, control, check, antidote** are here compared only in their extended senses where they agree in denoting something which serves to keep another thing in its desired place or condition. **Corrective** is applied to any agency or influence which keeps true a thing that is subject to aberration or deviation, or which rectifies or remedies any departure in it from truth, soundness, health, or the like. "The sight of the product [of our work] put to its full uses....is the best *corrective* to our blunders" (*H. Suzzallo*). "[Louis MacNeice's] work should be a salutary *corrective* to the sometimes facile optimism and mass-hypnotized rhetoric of the revolutionary poets" (*Day Lewis*). **Control** is applied to any predetermined device, rule, agency, or the like, which sets a guard upon a person or thing so as to prevent his (or its) overpassing prescribed limits or so as to enable him or it to be discovered if in error; thus, the Constitution of the United States sets up various *controls* for the three branches of government, such as the veto power of the president; a scientific investigator sets up a *control* for an experiment when he provides a means (usually a similar experiment identical in all but one factor) for testing the accuracy of his findings. **Check** is applied to anything which affords a means of securing or insuring accuracy, uniformity in quality, or the maintenance of a standard; as, duplicate records are kept by different clerks as a *check* upon each other; by means of state-wide examinations of pupils, the regents keep a *check* on the efficiency of the schools. **Antidote,** literally a remedy that counteracts a poison, implies that the harm has been done and that a corrective which will neutralize or nullify these effects is necessary. "There is no *antidote* against the opium of Time" (*Browne*). "The whole truth is the best *antidote* to falsehoods which are dangerous chiefly because they are half-truths" (*Coleridge*).

correlate, *n.* *Parallel, analogue, counterpart.

correlative, *adj.* Correspondent, complementary, *reciprocal, convertible.

correspond. *Agree, square, accord, tally, jibe, harmonize, conform.

Ana. Approach, touch, *match, rival, equal.

correspondence. *Intercourse, communication, conversation, converse, communion, commune, commerce, traffic, dealings.

correspondent, *adj.* Correlative, complementary, *reciprocal, convertible.

Ana. *Similar, analogous, like, parallel, comparable.

corridor. Passageway, *passage, hall, hallway, gallery, arcade, cloister, aisle, ambulatory.

corroborate. *Confirm, substantiate, verify, authenticate, validate.

Ana. Attest, vouch for, *certify: *support, uphold, back.

Con. Invalidate, negate, *nullify.

corrosion. *Erosion, attrition, abrasion.

corrupt, *adj.* **1** Also **corrupted.** Debased, vitiated, depraved, perverted. See under DEBASE.

Ana. *Abandoned, dissolute, profligate, reprobate.

Con. *Upright, honorable, honest, just, conscientious, scrupulous: virtuous, righteous, *moral, ethical, noble.

2 Iniquitous, nefarious, flagitious, infamous, *vicious, villainous, degenerate.

Ana. *Crooked, devious, oblique: venal, *mercenary: *base, low, vile: *pernicious, noxious, deleterious, detrimental, baneful: degraded, abased (see ABASE).

corrupt, *v.* Deprave, debauch, pervert, *debase.

Ana. Degrade, debase, *abase: *ruin, wreck: pollute, defile, *contaminate.

Con. Reform, amend, *correct.

coruscate. *Flash, gleam, scintillate, glance, glint, sparkle, glitter, glisten, glimmer, shimmer, twinkle, glister, spark.

cosmic. *Universal, catholic, ecumenical, cosmopolitan.

Con. *Earthly, terrestrial, terrene, mundane, worldly.

cosmopolitan, *adj.* Catholic, *universal, ecumenical, cosmic.

Con. *Liberal, progressive: all-round, many-sided, *versatile.

Ant. Provincial: insular: parochial.

cosmos. Universe, macrocosm, *earth, world.

cost, *n.* Expense, *price, charge.

costly, *adj.* **Costly, expensive, dear, valuable, precious, invaluable, priceless** agree in meaning having a high value or valuation, especially in terms of money. *Costly, expensive, dear* refer to the expenditure or sacrifice involved in obtaining or procuring a thing. **Costly** applies to that which costs much: it usually implies sumptuousness, rarity, fine workmanship, or the like; as, their home is filled with *costly* furniture; "I took a *costly* jewel from my neck, A heart it was, bound in with diamonds" (*Shak.*). **Expensive** applies chiefly to that which is high-priced, especially with the implication of a cost beyond the thing's value or the buyer's means; as, an *expensive* suit of clothes; "The father...was unable to give the child as *expensive* an education as he had desired" (*Froude*). Both *costly* and *expensive* may be applied to that which involves great losses or is a drain upon one's resources, not only in money but in time, effort, or the like; as, a *costly* (or *expensive*) error; *costly* litigation; a *costly* (but not, usually, when lives are concerned, *expensive*) victory. "The rat is *expensive* to get rid of, but even more *expensive* to maintain" (*V. Heiser*). **Dear,** as here compared (opposed to *cheap*), commonly suggests a high, often an exorbitant, price or excessive cost: usually it implies a relation to other factors than the intrinsic worth of a thing; as, "butter is cheap when it is plentiful, and *dear* when it is scarce" (*Shaw*); "if she took it into her head to live in the *dearest* hotel in England" (*Bennett*); "relatively high wages of building labour bring *dearer* housing" (*J. A. Hobson*). **Valuable,** when applied to things which have monetary value, usually suggests the price they will bring in a sale or exchange; as, the most *valuable* dog in the kennel; he stores away all his *valuable* effects when he goes on a tour; a *valuable* piece of property. *Valuable,* however, often suggests worth that is not measured in material goods, but in usefulness, serviceableness, advantageousness, or the like; as, a *valuable* citizen; the most *valuable* course in one's college career; a *valuable* piece of evidence; "Food is *valuable* to the animal and moisture to the plant" (*S. Alexander*); "Beauty which is humanly *valuable* but biologically useless" (*J. W. Krutch*). **Precious** etymologically comes closer in meaning to *costly* than to *valuable* of which it is now a very close synonym. But it carries a heightened implication of worth and often applies to something or someone whose value can scarcely be computed in terms of money; as, "*precious* friends" (*Shak.*); "[Wisdom] is more *precious* than rubies" (*Proverbs* iii. 15); "To any one who has ever looked on the face of a dead child or parent the mere fact that matter could have taken for a time that *precious* form, ought to make matter sacred ever after" (*W. James*); "And these two things, judgment and imagination, are, with knowledge itself, the most *precious* results of well directed schooling" (*Grandgent*). When applied to a thing of monetary value, *precious* usually means that it is one of the rarest and most costly of the class that is named; as, *precious* stones; "an alabaster box of very *precious* ointment" (*Matthew* xxvi. 7), but it may mean that the thing so described is too scarce (and therefore, often, too expensive) to use freely or generally (as, be careful of the butter; it's too *precious* to waste). **Invaluable** and **priceless** literally imply worth that cannot be estimated in any terms. They are sometimes used when *precious* is actually meant but would seem not quite in keeping for one reason or another; as, an *invaluable* servant; a *priceless* jewel. Therefore their use tends to be hyperbolical and often, especially in the case of *priceless,* loosely intensive; as, I've just heard a *priceless* story; isn't that dress *priceless?*

Ana. Exorbitant, extravagant, *excessive: sumptuous, *luxurious, opulent.

Ant. Cheap. — *Con.* Beggarly, sorry, scurvy, *contemptible: poor, *bad.

coterie. Circle, *set, clique.

couch, *v.* *Lurk, skulk, slink, sneak.

Ana. *Hide, conceal, screen, secrete, ensconce.

couchant. Recumbent, reclining, dormant, supine, *prone, prostrate.

council. Conference, synod, convocation, congress, *convention.

Ana. Assembly, assemblage, gathering, congregation (see under GATHER).

☞ *Do not confuse* council *with* counsel.

counsel, *n.* **1** *Advice.

Ana. Admonishing *or* admonition, chiding, reproaching *or* reproach (see corresponding verbs at REPROVE): warning, forewarning, cautioning *or* caution (see corresponding verbs at WARN): precept, rule (see LAW).

☞ *Do not confuse* counsel *with* council.

2 *Lawyer, counselor, barrister, advocate, attorney, solicitor, proctor, procurator.

counsel, *v.* Advise (see under ADVICE).
Ana. Admonish, chide (see REPROVE): *warn, forewarn, caution: remonstrate, expostulate (see OBJECT, *v.*): instruct, direct (see COMMAND, *v.*).

counselor. *Lawyer, barrister, counsel, advocate, attorney, solicitor, proctor, procurator.

count, *v.* 1 **Count, tell, enumerate, number** come into comparison when they mean to ascertain the total of units in a collection by noting one after another or one group after another. **Count** is often employed in a more or less extended sense, but in strict literal use it implies computation of a total by assigning to each unit or each group of units as noted its proper numeral in succession, such as one, two, three, etc., or three, six, nine, etc.; as, they were *counting* the books one by one when he told them it would be quicker to *count* them by fives. "As many as thirty bonfires could be *counted* within the whole bounds of the district" (*Hardy*). **Tell,** which is now archaic or dialectal in this sense, was once commoner than *count,* but usually it carried the implication of counting one by one; as, the shepherd *tells* his sheep. "Thou shalt have as many dolours for thy daughters as thou canst *tell* in a year" (*Shak.*). "He *telleth* the number of the stars" (*Psalms* cxlvii. 4). **Enumerate** implies a listing or mentioning of each one in a series not only that their total may be ascertained, but that they may be individually known or specified; thus, to *enumerate* the population of a city is not merely to count it but to get a record of every individual's name, address, occupation, and the like; so, to *enumerate* the powers of the supreme court; to *enumerate* the species of plants found on an island; to *enumerate* the various dishes served at a dinner. **Number,** as here compared, is somewhat literary or archaic for either *count* or *enumerate;* in some uses also it carries a suggestion of allotment or limit; as, the days of every man are *numbered;* to *number* the flowers of the field; "But even the very hairs of your head are all *numbered*" (*Luke* xii. 7); "His hosts of blind and unresisting dupes The despot *numbers*" (*Shelley*).
Ana. *Calculate, compute, reckon, estimate: *add, sum, figure, total, cast, foot.
2 *Rely, depend, bank, trust, reckon.

count, *n.* *Paragraph, verse, article, clause, plank.

countenance, *n.* 1 *Face, visage, physiognomy, mug, puss.
2 *Favor, good will.
Ana. Supporting *or* support, backing, upholding (see corresponding verbs at SUPPORT): *approbation, approval.
Ant. Disapproval, disapprobation. — *Con.* Ill will, malevolence, malignity, spite, *malice.

counter. Antagonistic, counteractive, *adverse.
Ana. Contrary, *opposite, antithetical, antipodal, antonymous, contradictory: hostile, inimical (see corresponding nouns at ENMITY).

counteract. *Neutralize, negative.
Ana. *Correct, rectify: offset, counterbalance, countervail, counterpoise, balance, *compensate.
Ant. Co-operate. — *Con.* Conjoin, concur, *unite, combine.

counteractive. Counter, *adverse, antagonistic.
Ana. Countervailing, counterbalancing, counterpoising, compensating, offsetting, balancing (see COMPENSATE): correcting (see CORRECT, *v.*, 1): neutralizing (see NEUTRALIZE).

counterbalance, *v.* Offset, *compensate, countervail, balance, counterpoise.
Ana. *Stabilize, steady, poise: *correct (sense 1).
Con. *Overturn, upset, capsize, overset.

counterfeit, *n.* Fraud, sham, fake, *imposture, cheat, humbug, deceit, deception, simulacrum.
Ana. *Reproduction, copy, facsimile.

counterfeit, *v.* Feign, sham, simulate, pretend, *assume, affect.
Ana. *Copy, imitate, mimic, ape: dissemble, *disguise.

counterpart. Correlate, *parallel, analogue.
Ana. *Complement, supplement: duplicate, copy, facsimile, replica, *reproduction.
Con. Antithesis, opposite, contradictory. See under OPPOSITE, *adj.*

counterpoise, *v.* Balance, countervail, counterbalance, *compensate, offset.
Ana. Poise, *stabilize, steady, balance, ballast, trim.
Con. Upset, capsize, *overturn, overset.

countervail, *v.* Offset, balance, *compensate, counterbalance, counterpoise.
Ana. *Correct (sense 1): counteract, *neutralize, negative: overcome, surmount (see CONQUER): foil, thwart, *frustrate.

county. Gentry, *aristocracy, gentlefolk, elite, nobility, society.

coup d'oeil. Glimpse, glance, peep, peek, *look, sight, view.

couple, *n.* **Couple, pair, brace, yoke** agree in meaning two things of the same kind. **Couple** applies to two things of the same sort, regarded as in some way associated, but not necessarily (except in the case of a married or betrothed pair) matched or belonging together; it frequently means no more than *two;* as, "Make me a *couple* of cakes" (*2 Samuel* xiii. 6); "a *couple* of short-legged hens" (*Shak.*); a *couple* of hours or dollars. **Pair,** in modern usage, applies to two things that belong or are used together, frequently so that one is useless or defective without the other; it also applies to a single object composed of two corresponding or complementary parts; as, "one *pair* of English legs" (*Shak.*); "a *pair* of gloves" (*Pope*); "wedded *pair*" (*Milton*); "a *pair* of shears" (*Shak.*); a *pair* of trousers, spectacles, compasses, tongs; a matched *pair* of carriage horses. **Brace** commonly applies to a couple of certain birds or animals (as, a *brace* of pheasants, ducks, greyhounds); occasionally, to a couple of inanimate objects (as, a *brace* of pistols); rarely, to persons, with contemptuous or humorous connotation (as, "a *brace* of dukes"—*Goldsmith*). **Yoke** applies to two animals linked together; it is used of persons only in contempt; as, "plowing with twelve *yoke* of oxen" (*1 Kings* xix. 19); "a *yoke* of his discarded men" (*Shak.*).

courage, *n.* **Courage, mettle, spirit, resolution, tenacity** come into comparison when they mean a quality of mind or temperament which makes one resist temptation to give way in the face of opposition, danger, or hardship. **Courage** (in its earliest English senses, either the heart regarded as the seat of feeling and thought, or what is in one's heart) stresses firmness of mind or purpose and a casting aside of fear (for *courage* meaning *courageousness,* see *courageous* under BRAVE): it implies a summoning of all one's powers in order that one's desires or ends may be achieved; as, a reformer must have the *courage* of his convictions; "But screw your *courage* to the sticking place, And we'll not fail" (*Shak.*); "the unconquerable will... And *courage* never to submit or yield" (*Milton*). **Mettle** (which seems to have some etymological relation to *metal,* in the sense of a substance capable of being tempered) suggests an ingrained or characteristic capacity for meeting strain or stress in a manner suggestive of a finely tempered sword blade; as, the challenge put him on his *mettle*. It often implies resiliency, ardor, fearlessness, fortitude, gallantry, or other qualities associated less with physical strength than with mental or spiritual vigor. "Now I see there's *mettle* in thee, and even from this instant do build on thee a better opinion than ever before" (*Shak.*). "Doing one's bit, putting one's shoulder to the wheel, proving the *mettle* of the women of England, certainly had its agreeable side" (*R. Macaulay*). **Spirit**, like *mettle*, refers to a temperamental quality, but unlike the latter word, it suggests something far more volatile or fragile. It implies an ability to hold one's own, or to assert oneself or one's principles, or to keep up one's morale when opposed, interfered with, frustrated, tempted, or the like. "I do not think I can forgive you entirely, even now—it is too much for a woman of any *spirit* to quite overlook" (*Hardy*). "To quit a comrade on the road, and return home without him: these are tricks which no boy of *spirit* would be guilty of" (*Meredith*). "Successive crop failures had broken the *spirit* of the farmers" (*Cather*). **Resolution**, like *courage*, implies firmness of mind and purpose, but it stresses determination to achieve one's ends in spite of opposition or interference of men or of circumstances rather than a casting aside of fear of danger or a dread of hardship. "Good-humoured-looking on the whole, but implacable-looking, too; evidently a man of a strong *resolution* and a set purpose; a man not desirable to be met rushing down a narrow pass with a gulf on either side, for nothing would turn the man" (*Dickens*). "He saw that England was saved a hundred years ago by the high *spirit* and proud *resolution* of a real aristocracy" (*Inge*). **Tenacity** adds to *resolution* the implications of stubborn persistence and of unwillingness to acknowledge defeat; as, the *tenacity* of the bulldog breed. "This is not to say that the French lack *tenacity*....Having determined upon a thing, the French character tends to exceed in its pursuit, and, while fighting for it, to hold out to the death" (*Belloc*).

Ana. Bravery, boldness, audacity, dauntlessness, intrepidity, doughtiness (see corresponding adjectives at BRAVE): valor, *heroism, gallantry: *fortitude, grit, pluck, guts, backbone, sand.

Ant. Cowardice. — *Con.* Pusillanimousness *or* pusillanimity, cowardliness, poltroonery (see corresponding adjectives at COWARDLY): timorousness, timidity (see corresponding adjectives at TIMID).

courageous. *Brave, bold, valiant, valorous, dauntless, undaunted, audacious, intrepid.

Ana. Mettlesome, *spirited, high-spirited, fiery: resolute, stanch (see FAITHFUL): stout, tenacious, *strong.

Ant. Pusillanimous. — *Con.* *Fearful, apprehensive, afraid: *timid, timorous: *cowardly, craven, poltroon, recreant, dastardly.

course, *n.* *Way, route, passage, pass, artery.

Ana. Circuit, ambit (see CIRCUMFERENCE): orbit, scope (see RANGE, *n.*): drift, trend, current, *tendency: procedure, *process.

court, *n.* Field, *arena, circus, lists, ring, cockpit, gridiron, diamond, rink.

court, *v.* *Invite, woo, bid, solicit.

Ana. Allure, *attract, captivate, charm, take: toady, truckle, *fawn, cringe.

courteous. Polite, *civil, courtly, gallant, chivalrous.

Ana. *Gracious, affable, cordial: *suave, urbane, politic, diplomatic: considerate, *thoughtful, attentive: obliging, complaisant (see AMIABLE).

Ant. Discourteous. — *Con.* *Rude, impolite, uncivil, ill-mannered, ungracious: curt, brusque, gruff, blunt (see BLUFF): insolent, supercilious, overbearing (see PROUD).

courtesy. **Courtesy, amenity, attention, gallantry, comity** come into comparison when they denote a manner or an act which promotes agreeable or pleasant intercourse. **Courtesy** suggests consideration for others or deference to their rank, sex, age, or the like; it usually implies good, or even exquisite, breeding and acquired graces but, especially in modern use, it sometimes connotes innate gentleness or instinctive politeness rather than social training. "The beauty of an inherited *courtesy* ...of a thousand little ceremonies flowering out of the most ordinary relations and observances of life" (*Binyon*). "Rising to receive him...with all the engaging graces and *courtesies* of life" (*Dickens*). **Amenity** implies a disposition to make easy and pleasant the approach to, or the continuance of, delightful social relations; when used concretely it may be applied not only to words or acts but to pursuits, interests, or the like, that bring men into rapport. "He [Joubert] was...a charming letter-writer; above all, an excellent and delightful talker. The gaiety and *amenity* of his natural disposition were inexhaustible" (*Arnold*). "Stopping now and then to exchange *amenities* with fellow-strollers" (*R. Macaulay*). "Would she be interested to read it? Might he send it to her? Joan's chaperon...put no bar upon these *amenities*" (*H. G. Wells*). **Attention** implies a singling out of a particular person for special favor or consideration, or as the recipient of courtesies manifesting one's admiration or love (as in courting); as, the elder son is paying *attention* to his chum's sister. "A well-bred man...takes care that his *attentions* for [*to*, in modern idiom] you be not troublesome" (*Chesterfield*). "She loved her children, but did not unduly spoil them or turn their heads with injudicious *attentions*" (*R. Macaulay*). **Gallantry** stresses devoted attention, sometimes amorous attention, to a lady or to ladies; it also often connotes ingratiating personal qualities such as ease of address, a dashing style, or a polished manner. " 'Now despise me if you dare.' 'Indeed I do not dare.' Elizabeth, having rather expected to affront him, was amazed at his *gallantry*" (*Austen*). "Cashel, in a business-like manner, and without the slightest air of *gallantry*, expertly lifted her and placed her on her feet" (*Shaw*). **Comity** is now increasingly rare in its older sense of courtesy, especially among friends or equals. "*Comity* and Affability are the Ornaments of Converse" (*Rules of Civility*, 1673). "It is the rule of mere *comity*...to agree where you can" (*Emerson*). In modern use it is applied chiefly to the interchange of courtesies between states (as of the United States) or between nations, such as the recognition within their own boundaries of the laws and institutions of the others. "Gave him no rights or privileges in other States beyond those secured to him by the laws of nations and the *comity* of States" (*Ch. Just. Taney*).

Ana. Graciousness, cordiality, affability, geniality (see corresponding adjectives at GRACIOUS): politeness, courteousness, courtliness, chivalrousness *or* chivalry, civility (see corresponding adjectives at CIVIL): considerateness *or* consideration, attentiveness, thoughtfulness (see corresponding adjectives at THOUGHTFUL).

Ant. Discourtesy. — *Con.* Churlishness, boorishness (see primitive nouns under BOOR): rudeness, impoliteness, ungraciousness, incivility (see corresponding adjectives at RUDE).

courtly. Courteous, gallant, chivalrous, polite, *civil.

Ana. Ceremonious, formal, conventional, *ceremonial: elegant, dignified, graceful (see corresponding nouns at ELEGANCE): finished, *consummate.

Ant. Churlish. — *Con.* Ungracious, discourteous, ill-mannered, impolite, *rude, uncivil: *coarse, vulgar, gross: boorish, loutish (see under BOOR).

covenant, *n.* Compact, pact, concordat, treaty, entente, convention, cartel, *contract, bargain, indenture, mise.
Ana. *Agreement, accord, understanding.

covenant, *v.* Pledge, engage, *promise, plight, contract.
Ana. *Agree, concur, coincide: *unite, combine, conjoin, co-operate.

cover, *n.* *Shelter, retreat, refuge, asylum, sanctuary, ark.
Ana. Hiding *or* hiding place, concealment, screening *or* screen (see corresponding verbs at HIDE): safety, security (see corresponding adjectives at SAFE).
Ant. Exposure.

covert. *Secret, clandestine, surreptitious, underhand, underhanded, privy, backstairs, stealthy, furtive.
Ana. Hidden, concealed, screened (see HIDE): disguised, dissembled, masked, cloaked (see DISGUISE, *v.*).
Ant. Overt. — *Con.* Open, plain, candid, *frank: plain, clear, manifest, patent, *evident, obvious.

covet. 1 Covet, envy, grudge, begrudge are not synonymous terms but they are sometimes confused because all carry the implication of a selfish desire to have something for one's own enjoyment or possession. To **covet** (for fuller treatment see DESIRE) is to long inordinately for something which belongs to another; as, to *covet* a neighbor's piece of property because of its fine view; to **envy** is to regard another with more or less chagrin, repining, jealousy, or hatred because he possesses something one covets or feels should have come to oneself; as, to *envy* a person his good fortune or his promotion; to **grudge** or **begrudge** implies reluctance or hesitation (often, but not necessarily, through selfishness, meanness, or stinginess) in giving another that which he (or it) ought to have because it is his (or its) due or need; as, "Surely you wouldn't *grudge* the poor old man Some humble way to save his self-respect" (*Frost*); to *begrudge* every penny given to one's child (or to a charity or spent on cabs); to *grudge* every moment spent on a disagreeable but necessary task.
2 Crave, *desire, wish, want.
Ana. Yearn (for), *long (for), pine (for), hanker (for), thirst (for), hunger (for): pant (after), aspire (to be, to know, etc.), *aim (at).
Ant. Renounce (*something desirable*). — *Con.* Resign, *relinquish, yield, surrender: *abjure, forswear: *decline, refuse, reject.

covetous. Covetous, greedy, acquisitive, grasping, avaricious agree in meaning having or manifesting a strong desire for possessions, especially material possessions. **Covetous** always implies inordinateness of desire; very often, with allusion to the last (or, in Roman Catholic use, last two) of the Ten Commandments, it implies longing for that which is rightfully another's. "*Covetous* of Shakespeare's beauty" (*Cowper*). It is, however, used with derogatory intent or effect only when envy is implied or wrongful means of acquiring possession are suggested. "Is not thy kindness subtle, *covetous* ...Expecting in return twenty for one?" (*Shak.*) **Greedy** emphasizes absence of restraint in desire; it is a censorious term only when the object of longing is evil in itself or in immoderation, or cannot be possessed without harm to oneself or to others; as, *greedy* for knowledge; *greedy* for gold. "Exploitation [of provinces] by *greedy* proconsuls" (*Buchan*). "The Elizabethans...with their artistic *greediness*...for every sort of effect" (*T. S. Eliot*). **Acquisitive** implies not only eagerness to possess but the capacity for acquiring and retaining that which is desired. Thus, an *acquisitive* mind is not only greedy for knowledge but is capable of absorbing it in large amounts; the *acquisitive* classes of society not only covet possessions but have the means whereby they can constantly add to their possessions. **Grasping** always implies eagerness and capacity to acquire wealth of any sort and invariably implies selfishness, and often suggests use of wrongful or unfair means. "People who are hard, *grasping*...and always ready to take advantage of their neighbors, become very rich" (*Shaw*). **Avaricious** also implies eagerness and capacity to acquire wealth, but especially a form of wealth, such as money, which can be hoarded. It, more than any of the others, emphasizes extreme stinginess. "An unremitting, *avaricious* thrift" (*Wordsworth*).
Ana. *Envious, jealous: desirous, concupiscent, lustful (see corresponding nouns at DESIRE): avid, athirst, *eager: rapacious, ravening, gluttonous, ravenous, *voracious.
Con. Self-denying, self-abnegating (see corresponding nouns at RENUNCIATION): renouncing, abjuring, forswearing (see ABJURE).

covey. *Flock, herd, drove, pack, bevy, gaggle, flight, swarm, shoal, school.

cow, *v.* *Intimidate, browbeat, bulldoze, bully.
Ana. *Frighten, terrorize, terrify: daunt, *dismay, appall: abash, discomfit, rattle, faze, disconcert, *embarrass.
Con. Animate, *quicken, vivify, enliven: cringe, cower, *fawn.

cowardly, *adj.* **Cowardly, pusillanimous, poltroon, craven, dastardly, recreant** agree in meaning excessively timid or timorous. **Cowardly,** the most general term, implies a weak or ignoble, **pusillanimous,** a mean-spirited and contemptible, lack of courage; as, "He... plac'd behind With purpose to relieve and follow them, *Cowardly* fled, not having struck one stroke" (*Shak.*); "*Cowardly* dogs! ye will not aid me then?" (*Shelley*); "I lived in a continual, indefinite, pining fear; tremulous, *pusillanimous,* apprehensive of I knew not what" (*Carlyle*); "having no 'materialized' class above it, it [American vulgarity] is not obsequious and *pusillanimous*" (*Brownell*). **Poltroon, craven,** and **dastardly** are terms of extreme opprobrium. *Poltroon* (more frequently a noun) implies arrant cowardice; *craven,* abject pusillanimity; *dastardly,* especially the cowardly or skulking execution of an outrageous or malicious design; as, a *poltroon* surrender; a *craven* fear of death; a *dastardly* assassination; a *dastardly* stab in the back. **Recreant** implies cowardly submission, especially under a threat; in current use, it often implies apostasy or faithlessness; as, "Thou wear a lion's hide! doff it for shame, And hang a calf's-skin on those *recreant* limbs" (*Shak.*); "Yield thyself *recreant,* villain, or thou diest" (*T. Heywood*); "It is the breath of this spirit that pours through the 'Areopagitica' as through a trumpet, sounding the charge against whatever is base and *recreant*" (*J. R. Lowell*).
Ana. *Timid, timorous: cowed, intimidated, browbeaten, bullied, bulldozed (see INTIMIDATE): afraid, *fearful, apprehensive.
Ant. Bold. — *Con.* *Brave, courageous, valorous, valiant, audacious, intrepid, doughty, dauntless: *adventurous, daring, venturous, venturesome.

cower. Cringe, truckle, *fawn, toady.
Ana. Shrink, quail, flinch, blench, wince, *recoil.
Con. Cow, bully, bulldoze, browbeat, *intimidate: *strut, swagger, bristle.

coxcomb. *Fop, dandy, beau, exquisite, élégant, dude, macaroni, buck, spark, swell, nob, toff.

coy. Bashful, *shy, diffident, modest.
Ana. Demure, nice, proper, seemly, *decorous, decent: aloof, detached (see INDIFFERENT): *cautious, wary, chary.

Ant. Pert. — *Con.* *Saucy, arch: brazen, brash, impudent (see SHAMELESS).

cozen. *Cheat, defraud, swindle, overreach.
Ana. *Dupe, bamboozle, gull, trick, hoax, hoodwink, befool: delude, beguile, *deceive, mislead.

cozy *or* **cosy.** *Comfortable, snug, easy, restful, reposeful.
Ana. Sheltering, harboring, housing, lodging (see HARBOR, *v.*): *safe, secure: contenting, satisfying (see SATISFY).
Con. *Miserable, wretched.

crabbed. *Sullen, surly, glum, morose, gloomy, sulky, saturnine, dour.
Ana. Crusty, gruff, brusque, blunt (see BLUFF): testy, choleric, cranky, cross, splenetic, *irascible: snappish, huffy, *irritable.
Con. *Amiable, good-natured, obliging, complaisant: kindly, *kind, benign, benignant: *pleasant, agreeable: genial, affable, *gracious.

crack, *n.* Wisecrack, witticism, *jest, joke, jape, quip, gag.

craft. 1 Skill, cunning, *art, artifice.
Ana. Adeptness, expertness, proficiency (see corresponding adjectives at PROFICIENT): ingeniousness *or* ingenuity, cleverness (see corresponding adjectives at CLEVER): competence, capability (see corresponding adjectives at ABLE): efficiency (see corresponding adjective at EFFECTIVE).
2 *Trade, handicraft, art, profession.
Ana. Occupation, employment, pursuit, métier, *work.
3 *Boat, ship, vessel, argosy.

craftsman. Handicraftsman, mechanic, artisan, *worker, workman, workingman, laborer, navvy, hand, operative, roustabout.

crafty. Tricky, *sly, cunning, foxy, wily, artful.
Ana. Adroit, *clever, cunning: *shrewd, astute: *sharp, keen, acute.
Con. *Stupid, dull, dense, crass, dumb: obtuse, *dull.

cranky. Cross, choleric, splenetic, testy, *irascible, techy, touchy.
Ana. *Irritable, fractious, peevish, petulant, snappish: *contrary, perverse, froward: *impatient, nervous, jittery.
Con. *Calm, tranquil, serene, placid: good-natured, *amiable, obliging, complaisant.

crass, *adj.* Dense, *stupid, dull, dumb.
Ana. Obtuse, *dull: crude, raw, *rude, rough.
Ant. Brilliant. — *Con.* *Intelligent, clever, alert, quick-witted, bright, smart.

crave. Covet, *desire, wish, want.
Ana. *Long, hanker, yearn, pine, hunger, thirst.
Ant. Spurn. — *Con.* Reject, repudiate, refuse, *decline: abhor, abominate, detest, loathe, *hate: *despise, contemn, scorn, disdain.

craven. *Cowardly, pusillanimous, poltroon, dastardly, recreant.
Ana. Afraid, *fearful, apprehensive: terrified, frightened, scared (see FRIGHTEN): *timid, timorous.
Ant. Brave. — *Con.* Courageous, bold, valorous, valiant, intrepid, dauntless, undaunted, audacious (see BRAVE): *adventurous, venturous, venturesome, daring: mettlesome, *spirited, high-spirited.

crawfish, *v.* *Recede, retreat, retrograde, retract, back.

crawl, *v.* *Creep.

craze. Vogue, fad, rage, *fashion, style, mode, dernier cri, cry.

crazy, crazed. *Insane, mad, demented, lunatic, maniac, deranged, wood, non compos mentis.

Con. *Rational, reasonable: sane, sensible, *wise, sapient.

cream, *v.* Grease, pomade, pomatum, *oil, lubricate, anoint, inunct.

create. *Invent, discover.
Ana. *Make, form, fashion, shape, forge: design, plan, scheme (see under PLAN, *n.*).

creator. *Maker, author.
Ana. *Artist, architect, artificer: composer, *writer, author.

credence. Credit, *belief, faith.
Ana. Conviction, assurance, certitude, *certainty: accepting *or* acceptance, admitting *or* admission, receiving *or* reception (see corresponding verbs at RECEIVE): assenting *or* assent, acquiescing *or* acquiescence (see corresponding verbs at ASSENT): reliance, confidence, *trust, faith.
Con. Doubt, *uncertainty, skepticism: mistrust, *distrust: disbelief, *unbelief, incredulity.

credible. Believable, *plausible, colorable, specious.
Ana. *Probable, likely, possible: reasonable, *rational: trustworthy, *reliable, dependable.
Ant. Incredible. — *Con.* Fabulous, mythical, apocryphal, *fictitious: dubious, *doubtful, questionable.

credit, *n.* **1** *Belief, faith, credence, credit.
Ana. Reliance, *trust, confidence, faith: assurance, certitude, conviction, *certainty.
Con. *Unbelief, disbelief, incredulity: *distrust, mistrust: doubt, *uncertainty.
2 Prestige, authority, *influence, weight.
Ana. Reputation, repute, *fame, renown: authority, *power, sway.
Ant. Discredit. — *Con.* Opprobrium, obloquy, ignominy, disrepute (see DISGRACE).
3 Credit, asset come into comparison when they mean a person or a thing that enhances another. Someone or something is a **credit** *to* another when he or it is a source of honor or of increase in good repute; as, the boy is a *credit* to his school; his integrity is a *credit* to his upbringing. Someone or something is an **asset** *to* another when he or it adds to the usefulness, the worth, the advantages, the attractiveness, or the like, of another; as, the new teacher is an *asset* to the school; his knowledge of how to deal with people made him an *asset* to his employer.

credit, *v.* Accredit, *ascribe, assign, attribute, impute, refer, charge.

creed. 1 Creed, confession, symbol, catechism come into comparison when they mean an authoritative summary of the beliefs and doctines of a church. **Creed,** the usual and ordinary term, applies chiefly to one of the three brief summaries of Christian belief known as the Apostle's *Creed,* the Nicene *Creed,* and the Athanasian *Creed,* but it is also applicable to any brief formulation of beliefs of a congregation, a particular denomination, or the like, or, by extension, of an individual, a party, a profession, or of any group that for any reason wishes to make known the principles to which it or its membership adheres; as, "The League of Nations was to the peace-wishers as his *creed* is to the Christian" (*R. Macaulay*). **Confession** (more fully, *confession of faith*) applies strictly to one of the authoritative statements of the doctrines of one of the churches established after the Reformation; thus, the earliest of these, the Augsburg *Confession* (1530) presented the doctrines taught by Luther and Melanchthon and became the chief creed of the Lutheran Church; the Westminster *Confession* (1646) is the authoritative statement of the beliefs of English-speaking Presbyterian churches. **Symbol,** in the sense of *creed*, was derived from a Latin sense of *symbolum* traceable to the second century after Christ when "The Creed" (the Apostles' Creed) was accepted as the sign or mark of a Christian. This sense now occurs chiefly in theology when the term is applied to a creed or a confession. "The Nicene Creed, the great *symbol* in which the divinity of Christ is asserted and defined" (*C. Hazard*). **Catechism** applies specifically to an authoritative presentation of the doctrines of a church in the form of question and answer, used in the instruction of members or prospective members of that church; thus, the Roman *Catechism*, a manual intended primarily for parish priests, was published by Pope Pius V in 1566; the Geneva *Catechism* of 1536 gives the doctrines of Calvinism; the Anglican *Catechism* (1549, 1604) provides instruction for a member of the Anglican Communion seeking to be confirmed by the bishop; the Westminster Larger *Catechism* and Shorter *Catechism*, prepared by the Westminster Assembly 1647, are used (the latter especially) by Presbyterian churches.

Ana. Tenet, dogma, *doctrine.

2 Faith, persuasion, *religion, denomination, sect, cult, communion, church.

creep, *v.* **Creep, crawl** agree in meaning to move slowly along the ground or floor in a prone or crouching position. In their literal senses, they were once interchangeable but, in current good English, **creep** is more often used of quadrupeds or of human beings who move on all fours and proceed slowly, or stealthily, or silently (as, a baby usually *creeps* before it walks; "Crouching down...in a corner...he made out the three fishermen *creeping* through some rank grass"—*Dickens*) and **crawl** of serpents, snakes, worms, etc., that move by drawing the body along the ground or a surface, or of human beings who imitate such movement (as, when she saw the snake *crawling* along the path, she screamed; slugs *crawled* along the stems and leaves of the plant; he was so badly injured that he could only *crawl* to the open door). Figuratively, both words often imply intolerable slowness; as, "To-morrow, and to-morrow, and to-morrow, *Creeps* in this petty pace from day to day" (*Shak.*); "That sad, disappointing, disillusioning...war *crawled* through that bitter winter of defeat" (*R. Macaulay*). Both often imply a slow movement of a person, especially into another's favor or into a given status or position, but *creep* usually suggests stealthy and insinuating methods (as, "But *creep* along the hedge-bottoms, an' thou'll be a bishop yet"—*Tennyson;* "these northerners [barbarian tribes]....were steadily *creeping* nearer [the frontiers of the Roman empire]"—*Buchan;* "even in later and more enlightened times, the study of Literature has *crept* its way into official Cambridge"—*Quiller-Couch*) and *crawl*, procedure by abjectness, servility, cringing, or groveling (as, "Cranmer... Hath *crawl'd* into the favour of the king"—*Shak.;* "pomp-fed king... art thou not the veriest slave that e'er *Crawled* on the loathing earth?"—*Shelley*). Both also imply a sensation such as might be produced by lice, fleas, or other human or animal parasites, but *creep* suggests a shivering, nervous reaction, and *crawl*, a feeling of loathing or intense repugnance; as, "Something in their countenances that made my flesh *creep* with a horror I cannot express" (*Swift*); my flesh *crawls* at the sight of such dirty, unkempt children.

crime. *Offense, vice, sin, scandal.

Ana. *Fault, failing, frailty, foible, vice.

Con. Virtue, *excellence, merit, perfection.

criminate. Incriminate, indict, impeach, *accuse, charge, arraign.

Ana. *Involve, implicate.

Con. Absolve, acquit, *exculpate, exonerate, vindicate.

cringe. Cower, truckle, *fawn, toady.

Ana. *Recoil, quail, flinch, blench, wince: bow, cave in, *yield, submit, defer.

cripple, *v.* **1** *Maim, mutilate, batter, mangle.

Ana. *Injure, hurt.

2 Disable, *weaken, enfeeble, debilitate, undermine, sap.

Ana. Damage, harm, impair, mar. See INJURE.

crisis. Exigency, emergency, pinch, *juncture, pass, contingency, strait.

crisp. 1 Brittle, short, friable, *fragile, frangible.

Con. *Limp, flabby, flaccid.

2 Clear-cut, cutting, *incisive, trenchant, biting.

Ana. Terse, pithy, laconic, succinct, *concise: piquing, stimulating, provoking *or* provocative (see corresponding verbs at PROVOKE).

criterion. *Standard, touchstone, yardstick, gauge.

Ana. Test, proof, trial, demonstration (see under PROVE): *principle, axiom, law: judging *or* judgment, adjudgment, adjudication (see corresponding verbs at JUDGE).

critic. Variant of CRITIQUE.

critical. 1 Critical, hypercritical, faultfinding, captious, caviling, carping, censorious agree in meaning exhibiting the spirit of one who detects and points out faults or defects. **Critical,** when applied to persons who judge and to their judgments, not only may, but in very precise use does, imply an effort to see a thing clearly and truly so that not only the good in it may be distinguished from the bad and the perfect from the imperfect, but also that it as a whole may be fairly judged or valued. "In the garden he prolonged the flower-picking process by minute and *critical* choice" (*Deland*). "A tête-à-tête with a man of similar tastes, who is just and yet sympathetic, *critical* yet appreciative...is a high intellectual pleasure" (*A. C. Benson*). In less precise but nevertheless good use, *critical* commonly implies a keen awareness of faults or imperfections with, often, the suggestion of loss of fairness in judgment. "The attitude of Euripides towards the popular religion is...clearly and frankly *critical*" (*G. L. Dickinson*). "The vast audience [at a beheading] ...was wont to be exceedingly *critical.* Bungling work drew down upon the headsman the execrations of the mob, and not infrequently placed his own life in danger" (*A. Repplier*). When this loss of balance is implied, or when the judge's undue awareness of defects and overemphasis of them is to be suggested, very precise writers often prefer **hypercritical** to *critical;* as, the audience that night was, as the actors soon knew, *hypercritical.* "He was...exceedingly difficult to please, not...because he was *hypercritical* and exacting, but because he was indifferent" (*Bennett*). **Faultfinding** is the direct, somewhat colloquial term, sometimes taking the place of *critical*, sometimes of *hypercritical*, but usually suggesting less background, less experience, or less fastidiousness than either; it is therefore frequently used when an unreasonably exacting or a querulous temperament is also to be suggested; as, the continually *faultfinding* reviewer of books; a *faultfinding* parent. **Captious** implies a readiness, usually a temperamental readiness, to detect trivial faults or to take exceptions on slight grounds, because one is either unduly exacting or perversely hard to please. "Is it *captious* to say that, when Manoah's locks are called 'white as down,' whiteness is no characteristic of down?" (*Landor*). "The body [the Roman Senate] had lost corporate vitality...; its members....were inclined to be *captious* and childish, and to shirk their duties" (*Buchan*). **Caviling** usually implies a captious disposition but stresses the habit or act of raising picayune or petty objections; as, *caviling* legislators who delay the passage of a bill. "The most *cavilling* mind must applaud their devoted sense of duty" (*N. P. Willis*). **Carping,** far more than *hypercritical* or *fault-finding*, implies ill-natured or perverse picking of flaws, and often in addition suggests undue emphasis upon them as blameworthy. "And to that end we wish'd your lordship here, To avoid the *carping* censures of the world" (*Shak.*). "That *carping* spirit in which she had been wont to judge of his actions" (*Trollope*). **Censorious** implies a disposition or a tendency to be both severely critical and condemnatory of that which one criticizes. "Such is the mode of these *censorious* days, The art is lost of knowing how to praise" (*J. Sheffield*). "French morality differs fundamentally from our own. But this is only all the more reason for replacing *censoriousness* by candor in any consideration of it" (*Brownell*).

Ana. Judicious (see WISE): *judicial: fastidious, finical, particular, *nice, fussy, squeamish: discriminating, discerning, penetrating (see corresponding nouns at DISCERNMENT): understanding, comprehending, appreciating (see UNDERSTAND).

Ant. Uncritical. — ***Con.*** *Superficial, shallow, cursory.

2 Crucial, *acute.

Ana. Decisive, determinative, *conclusive: momentous, consequential, weighty, significant, important (see corresponding nouns at IMPORTANCE).

criticism. Criticism, critique (*or* **critic**), **review, blurb, puff** are here compared only as meaning an essay or other discourse written (sometimes, delivered as a lecture) for the purpose of presenting one's conclusions after having examined a work of art or, especially, of literature. None of these terms has a clearly established meaning but, in general, each can be distinguished from the others with reference to its leading implications and its place in usage. **Criticism** is of all these terms the word of best repute, as preferred by the best writers and speakers and as carrying no derogatory connotations. The proper aim and the content of a criticism have never been definitely fixed, and are still subjects of controversy, but the term usually implies an author who is expected to have expert knowledge in his field, a clear definition of his standards of judgment, and an intent to evaluate the work under consideration; as, to read every *criticism* of a new play the day following its first performance. *Criticism* is even more often applied to the art, craft, or collective writings of such writers or speakers than to the individual article; as, "this feeling, that contemporary judgments are apt to turn out a little ludicrous... has converted much *criticism* of late from judgment pronounced into impression recorded" (*Galsworthy*). Because of this tendency to restrict the use of *criticism* to its general sense, **critique** (often spelled *critic* or *critick* in its use earlier than the mid-eighteenth century) is often preferred as a designation of a critical essay, especially of one dealing with a literary work. The use of this term has not been so common within the last half century as it was during much of the nineteenth century, so that currently it is often avoided as an affectation; as, Jeffrey's *critiques* in the *Edinburgh Review*. **Review** (often specifically *book review*) is now the common designation of a more or less informal critical essay dealing particularly with new or recent books. The term is frequently preferred by newspaper and magazine critics as a more modest designation of their articles than *criticism* or *critique*, and as permitting less profound or exhaustive treatment or as requiring a personal rather than a final judgment of the merits and faults of the work. *Review*, in present use, generally suggests literary criticism of a less pretentious kind, giving in general a summary of a book's contents and the impressions it produces on the reviewer; as, the Sunday editions of many newspapers have a supplement devoted to book *reviews*. **Blurb,** a word coined by Gelett Burgess to designate a short, fulsome, critical essay, is now applied chiefly to a publisher's description of a work printed usually on the jacket of a book for the purposes of advertisement. "As a term of reprobation for fulsomeness on the 'jackets,' or dust-cloaks, of new books, '*blurb*' is a peach of the first order" (*C. E. Montague*). **Puff,** a word common in the eighteenth century for any unduly flattering account of a book, play, or the like, such as appeared in bills of a play or in journals, carried many of the connotations of *blurb*. In current use, it often applies to a review that seems animated by a desire to promote the sale of a book or the success of a play, regardless of its real merits, or to one that is markedly uncritical in its flattering comments.

criticize. Criticize, reprehend, blame, censure, reprobate, condemn, denounce come into comparison when they mean to find fault with someone or something openly, often publicly, and with varying degrees of severity. **Criticize,** in its strict etymological sense, does not carry fault-finding as its invariable, or even major, implication: rather it suggests a discernment of the merits and faults of a person or thing. "Know well each ancient's [classic poet's] proper character; His fable, subject, scope in ev'ry page; Religion, country, genius of his age: Without all these at once before your eyes, Cavil you may, but never *criticize*" (*Pope*). In ordinary use, however, the word does commonly imply an unfavorable judgment or a pointing out of faults and is probably the term most frequently used to express this idea; as, to *criticize* a play severely; averse to being *criticized;* to avoid *criticizing* a person's errors in speech. "It is foolish...to *criticize* an author for what he has failed to achieve" (*A. Huxley*). The current phrase "to *criticize* constructively (or destructively)" is confusing because the verb is ordinarily used in the second of these senses. Even if it is clear that the first, or strict, sense is intended, either adverb is incongruous because evaluation, not correction, is implied by the verb. In neither meaning does *criticize* imply suggestion of remedies. **Reprehend,** in earlier use, came closer to *reprove* and its synonyms (see REPROVE) than to *criticize;* in present-day English it takes a person as an object far less often than one of his faults, errors, sins, or the like. In such use, it not only explicitly suggests the approach of a critic, and his disapproval, but implies a more or less severe rebuke. "Why are the [dramatic] asides ridiculous, which Mr. Archer *reprehends* in *A Woman Killed with Kindness?* Because they are not a convention, but a subterfuge" (*T. S. Eliot*). "The thing to be *reprehended* is the confusing misuse of the word 'verse' " (*Grandgent*). **Blame** fundamentally implies speaking in dispraise of a person or thing rather than in his or its favor; in general, it also suggests the mental approach of a critic or detector of faults, who assumes that he has the knowledge or the competency to judge. "Some judge of authors' names, not works, and then Nor praise nor *blame* the writings, but the men" (*Pope*). "Heine...cared quite as much as his brethren [brother poets]...whether people praised his verses or *blamed* them" (*Arnold*). "Aristotle, while *blaming* the man who is unduly passionate, *blames* equally the man who is insensitive" (*G. L. Dickinson*). In colloquial use and, to an extent, in literary use, *blame* does not imply so strong an opposition to *praise;* often it suggests an imputation or accusation of wrongdoing (as, one cannot *blame* starving children who steal food) or of guilt (as, there is no one to *blame* [idiomatic for *to be blamed,* that is, to be held guilty] but yourself). Sometimes, *blame* connotes ultimate responsibility rather than actual guiltiness and then may take a thing as well as a person for its object. "I would not have you so uncritical as to *blame* the Church or its clergy for what happened" (*Quiller-Couch*). "The drug-fiend will get drugs somewhere: if he finds his poppy and mandragora in poetry, you must *blame* his habit, not the poet" (*Day Lewis*). Since *blame* no longer invariably implies the reverse of commendation, **censure** is usually preferred to *blame* as the antonym of *praise.* The word carries a stronger suggestion of authority or competence in the critic or judge than does *blame,* as well as a clearer connotation of reprehension or, sometimes, of a reprimand; as, the judge *censured* the jury for their failure to render a verdict on the evidence; the official was not dismissed until after he had more than once been severely *censured* for his mistakes of judgment. "I lose my patience, and I own it too, When works are *censur'd,* not as bad but new" (*Pope*). "It is not one writer's business to *censure* others. A writer should expound other writers or let them alone" (*F. M. Ford*). **Reprobate** is often used loosely as though it were a close synonym of *reproach* or *rebuke.* "'I put it to you, miss,' she continued, as if mildly *reprobating* some want of principle on Lydia's part" (*Shaw*). In discriminating use, however, it implies not only strong disapproval and, usually, vigorous censure, but also a rejection or a refusal to countenance. "He *reprobated* what he termed the heresies of his nephew" (*Irving*). "That wanton eye so *reprobated* by the Founder of our Faith" (*L. P. Smith*). "Those who...*reprobate* what has been technically termed the post-habited prefix" (*H. Ellis*). **Condemn** carries even stronger judicial connotations than *censure,* for it implies a final decision or a definitive judgment; it commonly also suggests an untempered judgment which is wholly unfavorable and merciless. "*Condemn* the fault, and not the actor of it? Why, every fault's *condemn'd* ere it be done" (*Shak.*). "The freedom with which Dr. Johnson *condemns* whatever he disapproves, is astonishing" (*Burney*). "It is wise to be cautious in *condemning* views and systems which are now out of fashion" (*Inge*). **Denounce** adds to *condemn* the implication of public declaration or proclamation. "In all ages, priests and monks have *denounced* the growing vices of society" (*H. Adams*). "Nothing... makes one so popular as to be the moral *denouncer* of what everybody else *denounces*" (*Van W. Brooks*).

Ana. Inspect, examine, *scrutinize, scan: *judge, adjudge: appraise, evaluate, assess (see ESTIMATE).

critique *or* **critic.** *Criticism, review, blurb, puff.

crochet, *v.* Knit, *weave, plait, braid, tat.

crocodile. Crocodile, alligator, cayman denote large long-tailed lizardlike reptiles, with a tough skin stiffened with small bony plates and horny scales, that belong to the same family (Crocodilidae) but to different genera. In strict usage **crocodile** is applied only to a reptile of the genus *Crocodilus.* However, the term has been extended to apply to any reptile of the family Crocodilidae or order Crocodilia. True crocodiles occur in the waters of tropical Africa, Asia, Australia, and America. In some localities they are dangerous to man, being much more aggressive and vicious than alligators. **Alligator** is applied correctly to any of several aquatic reptiles of the genus *Alligator* or allied genera. These reptiles have a shorter and broader snout than the crocodiles, and the large teeth of the lower jaw shut into pits in the upper jaw, instead of into marginal notches. True alligators occur only in the warmer parts of America, except for one species found in China. In many places crocodiles are popularly called *alligators.* **Cayman** is applied to any of several tropical American alligators differing from typical alligators chiefly in having the ventral armor composed of overlapping scales (scutes).

crony. Comrade, chum, companion, *associate, pal, buddy.

Ana. Intimate, *friend, confidant.

crooked. Crooked, devious, oblique agree in meaning not straight or straightforward. **Crooked** literally implies the presence of curves, turns, or bends; as, a *crooked* back; a *crooked* road; the *crooked* trunk of a tree. Figuratively, it implies fraudulence, cheating, graft, or other practices involving marked departures from rectitude; as, *crooked* dealings; a *crooked* politician; *crooked* policies; "They are a perverse and *crooked* generation" (*Deuteronomy* xxxii. 5). **Devious,** both literally and figuratively, implies departure from a direct, appointed, regular, or fixed course, and hence suggests wandering or errancy, and often, but not invariably, circuitousness. "We sought with relief the empty roads of the fens, and, by *devious* routes, wound our way between golden buttercups and brown cattle" (*Lucas*). "He went by *devious* ways, a little proud of himself for knowing the short cuts, through a building used as a thoroughfare from one street to another, through what had once been the churchyard of an ancient church" (*Arch. Marshall*). The term as applied to persons and their acts or practices usually implies unreliability and often trickiness or shiftiness; as, the *devious* policies of the administration; "he had been a *devious* rascal" (*Bennett*); "The marks of the thoroughbred were simply not there. The man was blatant, crude, overly confidential, *devious*" (*Mencken*). **Oblique** literally implies a departure from the perpendicular or horizontal direction, or a slanting course; as, an *oblique* tower; an *oblique* sunbeam. Figuratively, the term suggests indirection, or lack of perfect straightforwardness; as, an *oblique* glance; an *oblique* reference; an *oblique* accusation; "All censure of a man's self is *oblique* praise" (*Johnson*). "'He shouldn't have done it, of course....And he meant to pay the money back. I don't see anything so very wicked in that,' she would sigh, with that singular moral *obliquity* which in money matters seems to belong to feminine love" (*Deland*).

Ana. *Awry, askew: twisted, bended *or* bent, turned (see corresponding verbs at CURVE): distorted, contorted, deformed, warped, gnarled (see DEFORM): tortuous, anfractuous, *winding: corrupt, nefarious, iniquitous, *vicious: stealthy, furtive, underhand (see SECRET).

Ant. Straight. — ***Con.*** *Straightforward, aboveboard, forthright: *upright, honest, scrupulous, conscientious, honorable, just.

cross, *n.* *Trial, tribulation, affliction, visitation.

cross, *adj.* Cranky, testy, techy, touchy, choleric, splenetic, *irascible.

Ana. Captious, carping, caviling, faultfinding (see CRITICAL): *irritable, fractious, peevish, petulant, snappish, waspish, querulous.

Con. Good-humored, good-tempered, good-natured (see GOOD NATURE).

crosswise, crossways. *Across, athwart.

crotchet. Whim, *caprice, vagary, freak, whimsey.

crow, *v.* *Boast, brag, vaunt, gasconade.

crowd, *n.* **Crowd, throng, press, crush, mob, rout, horde** come into comparison when they mean a more or less closely assembled multitude; usually, but far from always, of persons. **Crowd,** etymologically and in discriminating use, implies a close gathering and pressing together; as, "the *crowd* came pouring out with a vehemence that nearly took him off his legs" (*Dickens*). Especially in current use, *crowd* often implies a merging of the individuality of the units into that of the mass; as, to study the psychology of *crowds;* "no one in European art has rivalled Keion in the mastery of *crowds* of men each individually alive yet swept along by a common animating impulse, whether the raging passion of the victors or the panic of the routed" (*Binyon*); "A number of individuals gather together for one purpose, and you get not a number of individuals, but a *crowd*" (*R. Macaulay*). **Throng** varies so little in meaning from *crowd* that the two words are often used interchangeably without loss. *Throng* sometimes carries the stronger implication of movement and of pushing and the weaker implication of density; as, a *crowd* jammed the hall; *throngs* circulating through the streets. "So they went northward...past droves and droves of camels, armies of camp followers, and legions of laden mules, the *throng* thickening day by day" (*Kipling*). **Press** (which is now an archaic term) differs from *throng* in being more often applied to a concentrated mass in which movement is difficult because of the numbers, but otherwise it also suggests pushing or pressing forward; as, "They could not come nigh unto him for the *press*" (*Mark* ii. 4). **Crush** carries a stronger implication than either *crowd* or *throng* of compactness of the group, of offering difficulty to one who wishes to make his way through it, or of causing discomfort to one who is part of it. "The *crush* was terrific for that time of day...for the street was blocked" (*V. Woolf*). Specifically, *crush* applies to an overcrowded reception; as, "Two months ago I went to a *crush* at Lady Brandon's" (*Wilde*). **Mob** strictly applies to a crowd or throng made up of the rabble and bent on the accomplishment of riotous or destructive acts; as, the citizens were terrorized for weeks by *mobs;* "A *mob*...which pulled down all our prisons" (*Burke*). In extended use, especially in the United States and in Australia, *mob* is employed as an intensive of *crowd,* sometimes implying more disorganization (as, it is the tendency of a large crowd to become a *mob*), sometimes denoting merely an extremely large crowd (as, you could scarcely call it a *crowd;* it was a *mob*). In theatrical and cinematic use, *mob* applies to any large and manifestly agitated crowd of persons that has to be directed as a unit to achieve the proper or the intended effects. **Rout** (originally, a great company) applies to an especially disorderly or tumultuous mob, particularly to one made up of the lowest, the most disreputable, or the most lawless classes; as, "a hireling *rout* scraped together from the dregs of the people" (*Milton*). "The world should soon have clearance.... from such a *rout* as now so vilely Handles you.... Wait until the *mob,* now masters, willy-nilly are Servants as they should be" (*Browning*). **Horde** as here compared (see also TRIBE) usually, though not necessarily, applies to an assemblage or to a multitude massed together. It is sometimes preferred to *crowd, throng, mob,* or *rout* when a contemptuous term is desired, especially one that suggests the rude, rough, savage character of the individuals who constitute the multitude or mass; as, *hordes* of small boys roving through the streets; the *horde* of excursionists took possession of the beach.

Ana. *Multitude, army, host, legion.

crucial. Critical, *acute.

Ana. Threatening, menacing (see THREATEN): trying, afflicting, torturing *or* torturous (see corresponding verbs at AFFLICT).

crude. *Rude, rough, raw, callow, green.

Ana. Primitive, primeval (see PRIMARY): *immature, unmatured, unfledged: *coarse, vulgar, gross.

Ant. Consummate, finished. — *Con.* Cultivated, refined, cultured (see corresponding nouns at CULTURE): *mature, mellow, adult: matured, developed, ripened (see MATURE, *v.*).

cruel. Inhuman, fell, *fierce, truculent, ferocious, barbarous, savage.

Ana. Atrocious, *outrageous, monstrous, heinous: brutal, bestial (see corresponding nouns at ANIMAL): merciless, relentless, implacable, *grim.

Ant. Pitiful. — *Con.* Compassionate, *tender, sympathetic: merciful, clement, *forbearing, lenient: humane (see CHARITABLE).

cruise, *n.* Voyage, tour, trip, *journey, jaunt, excursion, expedition, pilgrimage.

crumble. Disintegrate, decompose, *decay, rot, putrefy, spoil.

crush, *n.* Press, throng, *crowd, horde, mob, rout.

Ana. *Multitude, army, legion, host.

crusty. Brusque, gruff, blunt, curt, *bluff.

Ana. Snappish, waspish, huffish, *irritable: choleric, splenetic, cranky, testy, *irascible: crabbed, surly, saturnine, dour (see SULLEN).

cry, *v.* **Cry, weep, wail, keen, whimper, blubber** agree in meaning to show one's grief, pain, or distress by tears and utterances, usually inarticulate utterances. **Cry** and **weep** (the first the homelier, the second the more formal, term) are frequently interchanged. *Cry* is more apt to stress the audible lamentation, *weep,* the shedding of tears; as, "If you hear a child *cry* in the night, you must call to the nurse" (*Shak.*); "*Weep* not, sweet queen; for trickling tears are vain" (*Shak.*); "*Wept* unseen, unheeded *cried*" (*Millay*). **Wail** usually implies a giving vent to one's grief without restraint, in mournful and often long-drawn-out cries, moans, and lamentations; as, " 'Where is my father, and my mother, nurse?' '*Weeping* and *wailing* over Tybalt's corse' " (*Shak.*); "Hear him, o'erwhelmed with sorrow, yet rejoice; No womanish or *wailing* grief has part" (*Cowper*); "Soon as she ... saw the life-blood flow ... *wailing* loud She clasped him" (*Shelley*). **Keen** (an Irish term) implies the wailing lamentations or dirges of a professional mourner. "*Keen* [means] Hideous, dismal wailing or howling practised in Ireland among the humbler classes in token of grief, at funerals, and on hearing news of a death or other calamity" (*H. C. Wyld*). **Whimper** implies low, whining, broken cries such as those made by a baby or puppy; as, *whimpering* in fright. **Blubber** implies scalding, disfiguring tears and noisy, broken utterances, such as those of a child who cannot have his way; as, he always *blubbers* until those who oppose him give in to him.

Ana. Lament, bewail, bemoan, *deplore: sob, moan, *sigh, groan.

cry, *n.* Vogue, rage, *fashion, style, mode, fad, craze, dernier cri.

cryptic. Enigmatic, *obscure, dark, vague, ambiguous, equivocal.

Ana. Puzzling, perplexing, mystifying (see PUZZLE, *v.*): occult, esoteric, *recondite: *mysterious, arcane.

cubicle. Carrell, carol, nook, alcove, *recess, niche, embrasure, bay.

cuddle. Fondle, dandle, pet, *caress.

cuff, *v.* Slap, swat, clout, *strike, hit, smite, slug, punch, box.

cull, *v.* Pick, hand-pick, single out, *choose, select, elect, opt, prefer.

culmination. Peak, climax, apex, acme, *summit, pinnacle, meridian, zenith, apogee.

culpability. *Blame, guilt, fault.

Ana. Responsibility, accountability (see corresponding adjectives at RESPONSIBLE).

culpable. Guilty, *blameworthy.

Ana. *Responsible, accountable, answerable, amenable, liable.

cult. Sect, denomination, *religion, communion, faith, creed, persuasion, church.

cultivate. Nurture, *nurse, foster, cherish.
Ana. *Develop, mature, ripen: raise, rear (see LIFT): educate, train, instruct, *teach: *improve, better, ameliorate.
Con. *Stunt, stultify, atrophy: *neglect, ignore, disregard, slight.

cultivation. Breeding, *culture, refinement.

culture, *n.* **1 Culture, cultivation, breeding, refinement** come into comparison only when they denote a quality of a person or group of persons which distinguishes him (or them) as superior even in polite society. **Culture** is probably the vaguest of these terms, but in general it implies a high degree of enlightenment that has been acquired by intercourse with what is best in the civilized life of many ages and lands; in addition, it usually suggests fineness of taste, delicacy of perception, and gracious urbanity of manners; as, a man of *culture.* "*Culture,* the acquainting ourselves with the best that has been known and said in the world" (*Arnold*). **Cultivation** is often preferred to *culture* by discriminating writers and speakers because it suggests the continuous pursuit of culture, and the self-discipline which accompanies such pursuit, rather than its achievement, and is therefore more modest and often more appropriate; as, he has found many persons of *cultivation* in the city to which he has recently moved. "Gratitude is a fruit of great *cultivation;* you do not find it among gross people" (*Johnson*). **Breeding** implies such training or lifelong experience in courtesy and the amenities of gracious living that one is never at a loss how to act or what to say; moreover, the word often suggests poise, tact, an ability to come forward or to retire at will or at need, and other social qualities which mark one out even among one's social equals. "I am a gentleman of blood and *breeding*" (*Shak.*). "As men of *breeding,* sometimes men of wit, T'avoid great errors, must the less commit" (*Pope*). "Politely learned, and of a gentle race, Good *breeding* and good sense gave all a grace" (*Cowper*). **Refinement** implies not only the absence (often the eradication) of all that is gross, vulgar, or merely common, but also the presence of fineness of feeling, delicacy of perception or understanding, and fastidiousness. "That marvellous bold touch of his, that had the true *refinement* and perfect delicacy that in art, at any rate, comes only from strength" (*Wilde*). "He had true *refinement;* he couldn't help thinking of others, whatever he did" (*Galsworthy*).
2 *Civilization.

cumbersome, cumbrous. Ponderous, *heavy, weighty, hefty.
Ana. Burdensome, *onerous: *awkward, clumsy: *irksome, wearisome, tiresome.
Con. Compact, *close: *easy, light, facile.

cumulative. Cumulative, accumulative, additive, summative are synonymous only when used in the meaning increasing or produced by the addition of like or assimilable things. But they carry common implications, even when they differ in denotation. That is **cumulative** which is constantly increasing or is capable of constant increase in size, amount, power, severity, or the like, by successive additions, successive accretions, or successive repetitions, as of an experience; thus, the *cumulative* effect of a drug may be harmful even though the immediate effect of each dose has, apparently, been beneficial; terror is *cumulative* because one fear tends to inspire another. That is **accumulative** which is constantly increasing in amount or bulk through successive additions or which has reached its sum total or magnitude through many such additions. "The art of nations is to be *accumulative*...the work of living men not superseding, but building itself upon the work of the past" (*Ruskin*). "Such persons cannot understand the force of *accumulative* proof" (*Whately*). *Cumulative* is now used more often than *accumulative,* especially where increasing severity, enhancement in influence or power, and the like, are to be suggested. That is **additive** which is of such a nature that it is capable either of assimilation to or incorporation in something else or of growth by additions. An *additive* detail, element, factor, or the like, is one that has such affinity for another thing that it becomes a constituent part of that thing; thus, red, green, and blue-violet are the *additive* colors and are used in color photography because they blend to form any color. "This new hypothesis assigns to the atom properties which are in no way inconsistent with the inverse-square attraction of its electrons and protons; rather they are *additive* to it" (*Jeans*). An *additive* whole is not an organism complete in itself but an aggregate or extensible magnitude. "This pluralistic view, of a world of *additive* constitution, is one that pragmatism is unable to rule out from serious consideration" (*W. James*). That is **summative** (a relatively uncommon word), which is capable of association or combination with other things so as to produce a sum total, such as an additive whole or a cumulative effect; as, the *summative* action of bacteria. "If the student could not add up his achievements, if there was nothing *summative* in his education" (*Educational Review*).
Ana. Accumulated, amassed (see ACCUMULATE): multiplying, increasing, augmenting (see INCREASE).
Con. Dissipated, dispersed, scattered (see SCATTER).

cunning, *adj.* **1** Ingenious, *clever, adroit.
Ana. Skillful, skilled, adept, *proficient, expert.
2 Crafty, tricky, artful, *sly, foxy, wily.
Ana. Devious, oblique, *crooked: *sharp, acute, keen: *shrewd, astute: knowing, smart (see INTELLIGENT).
Ant. Ingenuous. — *Con.* Artless, unsophisticated, naïve (see NATURAL).

cunning, *n.* **1** Skill, *art, craft, artifice.
Ana. Dexterousness *or* dexterity, adroitness, deftness, featness (see corresponding adjectives at DEXTEROUS): proficiency, adeptness, expertness (see corresponding adjectives at PROFICIENT): ingeniousness *or* ingenuity, cleverness (see corresponding adjectives at CLEVER).
2 Guile, *deceit, duplicity, dissimulation.
Ana. Craftiness, wiliness, trickiness *or* trickery, artfulness, slyness (see corresponding adjectives at SLY): stratagem, ruse, maneuver, feint, *trick, wile.
Ant. Ingenuousness.

cupidity. Cupidity, greed, rapacity, avarice come into comparison as meaning inordinate desire for wealth or possessions. **Cupidity** stresses the intensity and compelling nature of the desire, and often suggests covetousness as well; as, the sight of so much wealth aroused his *cupidity.* "[Horace]...sings the praises...of Rome—Rome destined to unite the severed countries of the world, provided...she...curbed her own *cupidity:* 'Riches the hardy soldiers must despise, And look on gold with undesiring eyes'" (*A. Repplier*). **Greed,** more than *cupidity,* implies a controlling passion; it suggests not strong but inordinate desire and it commonly connotes meanness as well as covetousness. "Decent, honest, fawsont [seemly] folk, Are riven out baith root an' branch, Some rascal's pridefu' *greed* to quench" (*Burns*). **Rapacity** implies actual seizing or snatching not only of that which excites cupidity but of anything that will satisfy one's greed for money or property; hence, it often suggests extortion, plunder, or oppressive exactions of any kind; as, the *rapacity* of the conquerors knew no bounds; "the woman's greed and *rapacity*...disgusted me" (*Thackeray*). **Avarice,** although it involves the idea of cupidity and often carries a strong suggestion of rapacity, stresses that of miserliness, and implies both an unwillingness to let go whatever wealth or property one has acquired and an insatiable greed for more. "Such A stanchless *avarice* that, were I king, I should cut off the nobles for their lands, Desire his jewels and this other's house: And my more-having would be as a sauce To make me hunger more" (*Shak.*).

Ana. Covetousness, avariciousness, greediness, acquisitiveness (see corresponding adjectives at COVETOUS): avidity, eagerness (see corresponding adjectives at EAGER): lust, concupiscence, *desire.

curb, *v.* Check, bridle, snaffle, *restrain, inhibit.

Ana. Repress, *suppress: shackle, manacle, fetter, *hamper, hog-tie: thwart, foil, balk, *frustrate.

Ant. Spur. — *Con.* *Indulge, pamper, humor.

cure, *n.* *Remedy, medicine, medicament, specific, physic.

cure, *v.* **Cure, heal, remedy** agree in meaning to rectify a morbid or unhealthy condition, especially by or as if by medication or other treatment. **Cure** and **heal,** in their literal senses, apply to both wounds and diseases, and are frequently interchanged; as, "Pierced to the soul with slander's venom'd spear, The which no balm can *cure*" (*Shak.*). "Physician, *heal* thyself" (*Luke* iv. 23). In current usage, however, they tend to be differentiated in such applications, *cure* more frequently implying restoration to health after disease, *heal* implying restoration to soundness of an affected part after a wound or lesion; as, the treatment failed to *cure* him (or to *cure* his eczema); the salve will *heal* slight burns; "His fever...might *cure* him of his tendency to epilepsy" (*Byron*); "Where I will *heal* me of my grievous wound" (*Tennyson*). Figuratively, a similar distinction often holds; as, to *cure* (not *heal*) mistrust; to *heal* (not *cure*) a breach between friends. "If you can compass it, do *cure* the younger girls of running after the officers" (*Austen*). "We are denied the one thing that might *heal* us...that might bring balm to the bruised heart, and peace to the soul in pain" (*Wilde*). **Remedy,** in its now comparatively rare literal use, implies reference to a morbid condition of body or mind, whether it affects one's physical or mental health or causes local or occasional discomfort, and suggests the use of any means of correction or relief, such as medication, surgery, rest, exercise, or the like; as, a prolonged stay in a dry climate and much rest *remedied* his tubercular condition; "Who...may likeliest *remedy* The stricken mind" (*Southey*). Figuratively (see also CORRECT, *v.*, 1), *remedy* is often used in reference to evil conditions corrected, relieved, or counteracted by any means; as, to *remedy* an abuse; "[This mockery] 'tis partly my own fault, Which death or absence soon shall *remedy*" (*Shak.*).

curious. 1 Curious, inquisitive, prying, snoopy, nosy (*or* **nosey**) are here compared as meaning interested in finding out, or in a search for, facts that are not one's personal concern. **Curious** may or may not imply objectionable qualities such as intrusiveness or impertinence, but it always suggests an eager desire to learn, especially to learn how or why things have happened or are happening; as, children are naturally *curious* about almost everything; *curious* onlookers were held back by the police; she did not wish to seem *curious* about her neighbor's affairs; "a Latin poet whose reputation [for bombast] would deter any reader but the most *curious*" (*T. S. Eliot*); "Edgar was a rationalist, who was *curious*, and had a sort of scientific interest in life" (*D. H. Lawrence*). **Inquisitive** implies habitual and impertinent curiosity and, usually, suggests the asking of many questions regarding something secret or unrevealed; as, "In me [Delilah], but incident to all our sex, Curiosity, *inquisitive*, importune Of secrets" (*Milton*); "They grew *inquisitive* after my name and character" (*Spectator*). **Prying** adds to *curious* and *inquisitive* the implications of busy meddling and of officiousness; as, "a *prying* old woman" (*J. Hawthorne*); "the world might guess it; and I will not bare my soul to their shallow *prying* eyes" (*Wilde*). **Snoopy** and **nosy** are somewhat vulgar colloquialisms, highly expressive of contempt. *Snoopy* adds to *prying* suggestions of slyness or sneaking; as, a *snoopy* legal investigator; everyone felt that she was *snoopy* and soon refused to welcome her as a visitor. *Nosy* suggests the methods of a dog pursuing a scent, and implies a desire to discover the ins and outs of every situation that arouses one's curiosity; as, a *nosy*, disagreeable child. In British use, a nosy person is often called a "*nosy Parker.*"

Ana. Meddling, intermeddling, interfering, tampering (see MEDDLE): scrutinizing, inspecting, examining (see SCRUTINIZE): intrusive, meddlesome, *impertinent.

Ant. Incurious: uninterested. — *Con.* *Indifferent, aloof, detached, unconcerned: apathetic, stolid, *impassive, phlegmatic.

2 Singular, *strange, peculiar, unique, odd, queer, quaint, outlandish, eccentric, erratic.

curmudgeonly. Miserly, *stingy, close, closefisted, tight, tightfisted, niggardly, parsimonious, penurious, cheeseparing, penny-pinching.

Ana. *Mean, ignoble: surly, crabbed (see SULLEN).

Con. Generous, *liberal, handsome, bountiful.

currency. Cash, *money, legal tender, specie, coin, coinage.

current, *adj.* *Prevailing, prevalent, rife.

Ana. General, *universal, common: popular, ordinary, familiar, *common: *usual, customary.

Ant. Antique, antiquated (*of fashions, etc.*): obsolete (*of words, expressions, etc.*).

current, *n.* **1** Stream, *flow, flood, tide, flux.

2 Drift, trend, *tendency, tenor.

Ana. Movement, *motion: course, route, *way: progress, advance (see under ADVANCE, *v.*): progression, *progress.

curse, *n.* **Curse, imprecation, malediction, malison, anathema** come into comparison when they denote a denunciation that conveys a wish or threat of evil. **Curse** (opposed to *blessing*) usually implies a call upon God or a supernatural power to visit punishment or disaster upon a person; in dignified use, it commonly presupposes a profound sense of injury and a plea to a divine avenger for justice. No other word in this group suggested so strongly, in earlier times, the certainty of the threatened evil. "The untented woundings of a father's *curse* Pierce every sense about thee!" (*Shak.*). "An orphan's *curse* would drag to Hell A spirit from on high" (*Coleridge*). **Imprecation** also implies an invocation of evil or calamity, but it often suggests wrath rather than a sense of injury, and a desire for revenge rather than for justice, as its provocations. "With *imprecations* thus he fill'd the air, And angry Neptune heard the unrighteous prayer" (*Pope*). Both *curse* and *imprecation*, in current use, are applied to profane swearing involving blasphemy, but, again, the latter is weaker in its implications than the former. **Malediction** (opposed to *benediction*) and its archaic form **malison** are applied chiefly to bitter reproaches or denunciations publicly proclaimed and bringing disgrace or ignominy to their object. "My name... To all posterity may stand defamed, with *malediction* mentioned" (*Milton*). "Cleopatra has long ago passed beyond the libels with which her reputation was blackened by a terrified Rome—even the *maledictions* of great poets" (*Buchan*). "My *malison* light... On them that drink and dinna pay" (*A. Ramsay*). **Anathema,** as here compared, denotes a solemn, authoritative (especially, in older use, ecclesiastical), and usually, by implication, violent denunciation invoking a curse upon a person or thing. "The Pope...has condemned the slave trade—but no more heed is paid to his *anathema* than to the passing wind" (*Gladstone*). "The robust *anathemas* of Ritson, Percy, and Warton" (*Lowes*). Though often employed in this sense as though it were a technical ecclesiastical term (as, the pope hurled *anathemas* at Luther), the word acquired the denotation of *curse* only in post-Reformation times; in ecclesiastical use, the word is found (1) in the dogmatic canons of various councils, where the formula regarding the ipso facto excommunication of heretics is commonly phrased: "If anyone says [the heretical proposition follows], let him be *anathema*" (that is, excluded from communion with the Church; see ABOMINATION); (2) as the designation of the severest form of excommunication (see EXCOMMUNICATION).

Ana. Execration, objurgation (see corresponding verbs at EXECRATE): profanity, *blasphemy, swearing.

Ant. Blessing. — *Con.* Benediction, benison (see BLESSING).

curse, *v.* Damn, ban, anathematize, *execrate, objurgate.

Ana. Condemn, denounce, reprobate (see CRITICIZE): blaspheme, swear (see corresponding nouns at BLASPHEMY).

Ant. Bless.

cursed. Accursed, damnable, *execrable.

Ana., *Ant.*, & *Con.* See those at ACCURSED.

cursing. Profanity, swearing, *blasphemy.

Ana. *Curse, imprecation, malediction, malison, anathema: execration, objurgation (see corresponding verbs at EXECRATE).

cursory. *Superficial, shallow, uncritical.

Ana. Hasty, speedy, quick, rapid, swift, *fast: *brief, short: casual, desultory, *random, haphazard.

Ant. Painstaking. — *Con.* Meticulous, *careful, scrupulous, punctilious.

curt. Brusque, blunt, crusty, gruff, *bluff.

Ana. Laconic, terse, summary, *concise: *brief, short: snappish, waspish, *irritable: peremptory, imperious (see MASTERFUL).

Ant. Voluble.

curtail. *Shorten, abbreviate, abridge, retrench.

Ana. Reduce, *decrease, lessen: *cut, slash.

Ant. Protract, prolong. — *Con.* *Extend, lengthen, elongate.

curve, *n.* **Curve, arc, bow, arch** agree in meaning a line or something which follows a line that is neither straight nor angular, but rounded. **Curve** is the general term and the most widely applicable. It may be used in reference to any line, edge, outline, turn, formation that describes a part of a circle, ellipse, or the like (or a combination of parts of different circles); as, the *curve* of a ship's side; the deep *curve* of the back of a wing chair; a serpentine *curve*. "The *curve* of the greyhound is not only the line of beauty, but a line which suggests motion" (*Jefferies*). **Arc** is used chiefly in geometry to denote any part or section of the circumference of a circle; it is applied concretely only to a limited number of things, such as, formerly, to the rainbow, and now chiefly, to the luminous glow which under some conditions spans a break in an electric circuit; as, an *arc* lamp. **Bow,** unlike the preceding words, has never been in geometrical use: it has always designated concrete things that are curved, and, especially in modern use, it has drawn its implications from its reference to the archer's bow with its long, gradually curving strip of wood that may be bent almost into a U. Hence, many things which resemble an archer's bent bow are figuratively described by that term or are so designated; as, the *bows* of spectacles; an ox *bow*; *bow*legs. "The moon, like to a silver *bow*, New-bent in heaven" (*Shak.*). **Arch,** which was originally equivalent to *arc* in denotation (though not in etymology), is now chiefly applied to a supporting structure built up of wedge-shaped pieces of stone or other substance in such a way that they form a round arch (typically a semicircular curve with a keystone at the apex) or a pointed arch (typically two opposite curves with a joint at the apex), and provide an opening underneath as for a window, a door, or a passageway. Hence, *arch* is applied to any similarly curved structures; as, the *arch* of the eyebrow; the *arch* of the foot; an *arch* formed by meeting tree tops.

Ana. Circuit, compass, ambit, *circumference.

curve, *v.* **Curve, bend, turn, twist** come into comparison when they mean to swerve or cause to swerve (sometimes figuratively) from a straight line or a normal direction. **Curve** is the word of widest application, its single restricting implication being that the line followed is, at least approximately, an arc of a circle or an ellipse; as, to *curve* the top of an arch; to *curve* a road; to *curve* a ball in pitching it. **Bend** usually implies reference to something normally straight that is neither completely rigid nor completely flexible but that yields to force or efforts to curve; as, to *bend* a lead pipe; to *bend* a strip of wood to form a bow; to *bend* one's knee; to *bend* one's back over one's work; to *bend* one's mind to the accomplishment of a task; "He *bends* figures and cycles so readily to his will that he finds no difficulty in proving that when there is a marked increase in sunspots there is a rise in the temperature in Southern France" (*W. Kaempffert*). In reference to material things, **turn** is much less often used than *bend*: in only a few instances are the terms interchangeable (as, to *turn* a lead pipe) but idiomatically one *turns* (not *bends*) the edge of a razor; one *turns* (not *bends*) one's ankle when one's foot is caught by an obstruction. *Turn* may be employed, as *bend* may not, in reference to materials that can be folded together (as, to *turn* the top of a sheet over the blanket) or to materials that are curved in the process of construction (as, to *turn* the heel of a stocking; to *turn* a new road to the right). **Twist** carries a stronger implication than *bend* of the influence of an irresistible force and often, though not always, suggests a wrenching out of shape rather than a giving of a desired shape; as, the shaft was *twisted* beyond the point of safety; he *twisted* her wrist until she could have screamed with pain; hands *twisted* by hard work and old age.

Ana. Deflect, divert, *turn: *swerve, veer, deviate.

curvet, *v.* *Skip, bound, hop, lope, lollop, ricochet.

custom, *n.* Usage, habitude, *habit, practice, consuetude, use, wont.

Ana. Convention, *form, usage, convenance: rule, precept, canon, *law.

customary. *Usual, wonted, accustomed, habitual.

Ana. *Regular, normal, typical, natural: *prevailing, prevalent, current: familiar, ordinary, *common: general, *universal.

Ant. Occasional. — *Con.* *Infrequent, uncommon, rare, sporadic: *exceptional.

customs. Duty, impost, excise, tariff, toll, *tax, levy, assessment, rate, tribute, tithe, teind, cess.

cut, *v.* **Cut, hew, chop, carve, slit, slash** agree in meaning to penetrate so as to divide something by means of a tool or instrument with a sharp blade, such as a knife, ax, or sword. **Cut** is by far the most comprehensive term, for it is not only interchangeable with any other word in the group but also with any of a large number of verbs that suggest use of a specific instrument (as, *knife, shear, reap, mow*), or dividing in a certain way (as, *mince, shred*), or an operation having a definite end (as, *prune, lop, amputate*), or the like. Often it requires an adverb to describe the process or purpose more clearly; as, to *cut* down a tree; to *cut* off dead branches; to *cut* up a carcass of beef; to *cut* out a paper doll. Its figurative uses are many: usually it implies a result similar to one produced by cutting, such as separation or isolation (as, to *cut* off a member of the family; she is *cut* off from all her friends) or stabbing or hurting (as, the remark *cut* her to the heart). **Hew** is not only more restricted in its application than *cut* but it carries far more explicit implications both in literal and figurative use. It usually suggests the use of a tool such as an ax or a sword which must be swung with great force, though it may imply the use of a sharp tool, like a chisel in the cutting and shaping of stone or rock; as, "*Hew* them to pieces, hack their bones asunder" (*Shak.*); rough-*hewn* stones; "And now also the axe is laid unto the root of the trees: every tree...which bringeth not forth good fruit is *hewn* down, and cast into the fire" (*Luke* iii. 9); "There's a divinity that shapes our ends, Rough-*hew* them how we will" (*Shak.*). **Chop** implies a cleaving or dividing by a quick, heavy blow or blows of an ax, a cleaver, a hatchet, or similar tool or, more often, a dividing into pieces by repeated blows of this character; as, to *chop* off branches of a tree; to *chop* wood (i.e., to divide the trunk or branches of a tree into pieces suitable for firewood); to *chop* meat (i.e., to divide a piece of meat into small pieces by means of a butcher's cleaver or other tool). **Carve** was in earliest use almost as comprehensive a term as *cut* now is, but in the course of its development it has come to be restricted to two types of cutting: one which requires the use of a sharp knife or chisel and has for its end the artistic shaping, fashioning, or adornment of a material such as stone, ivory, or wood (as, a sculptor *carves* a statue out of marble; the back and legs of the chair were elaborately *carved;* an exquisite ivory box *carved* with figures); the other which requires a sharp knife and has for its end the cutting up, often the slicing, of meat at table in pieces suitable for serving (as, to *carve* a roast of beef; the head of the family *carves* the turkey). **Slit** implies the making of a lengthwise cut: except that it suggests the use of a sharp clean-cutting instrument such as scissors, a scalpel, a sword, knife, or the like, it carries no clear connotations as to the extent of the cut in depth or in length; as, the surgeon *slit* the abdominal wall in front of the appendix; the long skirt was *slit* to the knee; to *slit* a sealed envelope. **Slash** also implies a lengthwise cut, but usually suggests a sweeping, random stroke with a sharp sword, knife, tomahawk, or the like, that inflicts a deep and very long cut or wound: very frequently it connotes repeated cuts and, often, furious or rough-and-tumble fighting; as, few emerged alive from that battle who were not *slashed;* the trunk of nearly every tree was *slashed* by the rowdies.
Ana. Split, cleave, rive (see TEAR): sever, sunder (see SEPARATE, *v.*): curtail (see SHORTEN).

cutthroat. *Assassin, gunman, trigger man, finger man, bravo.

cutting. *Incisive, trenchant, clear-cut, biting, crisp.
Ana. *Sharp, keen, acute: piercing, penetrating, probing (see ENTER).

cyclone. Whirlwind, hurricane, typhoon, tornado, *wind, gale, twister, breeze, gust, blast, flaw, zephyr, waterspout.

Cyclopean. Gigantic, giant, gigantean, colossal, herculean, *enormous, immense, huge, vast, mammoth, elephantine, titanic, Antaean, Gargantuan, Brobdingnagian.

cynical. **Cynical, misanthropic** (*or* **misanthropical**), **pessimistic, misogynic** (*or* **misogynical**), **misogynous** come into comparison only as meaning deeply, often contemptuously, distrustful. **Cynical** implies a sneering disbelief in sincerity and rectitude. "The ease with which she [Queen Elizabeth] asserted or denied whatever suited her purpose was only equaled by the *cynical* indifference with which she met the exposure of her lies" (*J. R. Green*). "But people are nowadays so *cynical*—they sneer at everything that makes life worth living" (*L. P. Smith*). **Misanthropic** implies a rooted dislike and distrust of one's fellow men and aversion to their society; as, Swift was a man of an unhappy, *misanthropic* state of mind; "He...view'd them not with *misanthropic* hate" (*Byron*). **Pessimistic** suggests a distrustful and gloomy view of things in general; as, the *pessimistic* philosophy of Schopenhauer. "Our doctor....was...of kindly heart, though of violent speech...and of *pessimistic* temperament" (*H. Ellis*). **Misogynic** (or the rarer **misogynous**) implies a deep-seated aversion to, and a profound distrust of, women; as, "his *mysogynic* soul" (*Meredith*); a *misogynic* old bachelor.
Ana. Sneering, girding, flouting, scoffing (see SCOFF): captious, caviling, carping, censorious, *critical: disbelieving, unbelieving (see corresponding nouns at UNBELIEF).
Con. *Hopeful, optimistic, roseate.

D

dab, *n.* Dabster, adept, *expert, wizard, artist, artiste, virtuoso.
Con. Dabbler, tyro, *amateur, dilettante.

dabbler. Tyro, *amateur, dilettante.
Con. Dab, dabster, adept, *expert, wizard, artist.

dabster. Dab, adept, *expert, wizard, artist, artiste, virtuoso.
Con. See those at DAB.

daemon. *Demon, devil, fiend.

daily. **Daily, diurnal, quotidian** agree in meaning of each or every day. **Daily** is used with reference to the ordinary concerns of life; as, *daily* wants, cares; the *daily* newspaper. Sometimes, however, it implies an opposition to *nightly;* as, "the *daily* anodyne, and nightly draught" (*Pope*). **Diurnal** is commonly either astronomical (with special reference to the movements of the heavenly bodies) or poetic in its use; as, the *diurnal* revolution of the earth; "Rolled round in earth's *diurnal* course" (*Wordsworth*). *Diurnal* also implies opposition to *nocturnal;* as, the *diurnal* and *nocturnal* offices of the monks. **Quotidian**

adds to *daily* the implication of recurrence each day (as, a *quotidian* fever). In current usage, it often also suggests a commonplace, routine, or everyday character or quality; as, "That quality of strangeness which puts a new light on all *quotidian* occupations" (*Bennett*); "he [Mark Twain] has found in *quotidian* interests and affections and appetites so complete an escape from the labors and the struggles of the creative spirit" (*Van W. Brooks*).

Con. *Nightly, nocturnal: periodic, alternate, recurrent, *intermittent: occasional, *infrequent, sporadic.

dainty. 1 Delicate, exquisite, *choice, elegant, recherché, rare.

Ana. Petite, diminutive, little, *small: pretty, bonny, fair, lovely, *beautiful: *delightful, delectable, delicious.

Ant. Gross. — *Con.* *Coarse, vulgar: *common, ordinary.

2 Fastidious, finical, *nice, particular, fussy, squeamish, pernickety.

Ana. *Careful, meticulous, punctilious, scrupulous: discriminating, discerning (see corresponding nouns at DISCERNMENT).

dally. 1 Flirt, coquet, toy, *trifle.

Ana. *Play, sport, frolic, gambol: *caress, fondle, pet.

2 Dawdle, dillydally, procrastinate, *delay, lag, loiter.

Ana. Linger, tarry (see STAY): *hesitate, vacillate, falter, waver.

Con. Hurry, hasten, *speed.

dam, *v.* Bar, block, obstruct, *hinder, impede.

Ana. Clog, *hamper, trammel, shackle, fetter, hog-tie: *suppress, repress.

Con. *Advance, forward: *express, vent, utter, air.

damage, *n.* Harm, *injury, hurt, mischief.

Ana. Impairment, marring (see corresponding verbs at INJURE): ruining, dilapidation, wrecking (see corresponding verbs at RUIN): detrimentality *or* detriment, deleteriousness (see corresponding adjectives at PERNICIOUS).

Con. Improvement, betterment (see corresponding verbs at IMPROVE): benefiting *or* benefit, profiting *or* profit (see BENEFIT, *v.*): advantage, service, *use.

damage, *v.* Harm, *injure, impair, mar, hurt, spoil.

Ana. *Ruin, dilapidate, wreck: *deface, disfigure, defeature: *abuse, misuse, mistreat, ill-treat, maltreat, outrage.

Con. *Improve, better, ameliorate: *benefit, profit, avail: repair, *mend.

damn, *v.* 1 Doom, condemn, *sentence, attaint, proscribe.

Ana. *Judge, adjudge: *punish, castigate, discipline.

Ant. Save (*from eternal punishment*). — *Con.* Redeem, ransom, *rescue, deliver.

2 Curse, *execrate, anathematize, ban, objurgate.

Ana. Denounce, condemn (see CRITICIZE): revile, vituperate (see SCOLD).

damnable. Accursed, cursed, *execrable.

Ana. Atrocious, *outrageous, monstrous, heinous: *hateful, abominable, detestable, odious, abhorrent.

Con. Admirable, estimable (see corresponding verbs at REGARD, *n.*): laudable, praiseworthy (see corresponding verbs at PRAISE).

damp, *adj.* Moist, dank, humid, *wet.

Con. *Dry, arid.

dandle. Cuddle, pet, fondle, *caress.

Ana. *Trifle, toy, dally: *play, sport, disport: *handle, swing.

dandy, *n.* *Fop, beau, coxcomb, exquisite, élégant, dude, macaroni, buck, spark, swell, nob, toff.

Ant. Sloven.

danger, *n.* **Danger, peril, jeopardy, hazard, risk** agree in meaning either the state or fact of being threatened with loss of life or property, or with serious injury to one's health, morals, or the like, or the cause or source of such a threat. **Danger** is the general term, and implies contingent evil in prospect, but not necessarily impending or inescapable; as, "To win renown Even in the jaws of *danger* and of death" (*Shak.*); "Where one *danger*'s near, The more remote, tho' greater, disappear" (*Cowley*); "A frame of adamant, a soul of fire, No *dangers* fright him" (*Johnson*). **Peril** usually carries a stronger implication of imminence than *danger* and suggests even greater cause for fear and a much higher degree of probability of loss or injury; as "In *perils* of waters, in *perils* of robbers... in *perils* in the city, in *perils* in the wilderness, in *perils* in the sea" (*2 Corinthians* xi. 26); "He [Augustus] lived in constant *peril*" (*Buchan*); "the *perils* which threaten civilisation" (*H. Ellis*). **Jeopardy** implies exposure to extreme or dangerous chances; as, "Why stand we in *jeopardy* every hour?" (*1 Corinthians* xv. 30). The term is much used in law in reference to persons accused of serious offenses, being tried in court, and therefore exposed to the danger of conviction and punishment. "Nor shall any person be subject for the same offense to be twice put in *jeopardy* of life or limb" (*U. S. Constitution*). "It seems to me that logically and rationally a man cannot be said to be more than once in *jeopardy* in the same cause, however often he may be tried" (*Justice Holmes*). **Hazard** implies danger from something fortuitous or beyond one's control; it is not so strong a term as *jeopardy;* as, "The amusements...of most of us are full of *hazard* and precariousness" (*Froude*); "There would have been no triumph in success, had there been no *hazard* of failure" (*J. H. Newman*); "Travel on the thoroughfares of Manila was not without its *hazards*" (*V. Heiser*). **Risk,** more frequently than *hazard,* implies a voluntary taking of doubtful or adverse chances; as, " 'No chance of opulence,' he said, 'is worth the *risk* of a competence' " (*Scott*); "No adventure daunted her and *risks* stimulated her" (*H. Ellis*).

Ana. Threatening *or* threat, menacing *or* menace (see corresponding verbs at THREATEN): precariousness (see corresponding adjective at DANGEROUS): emergency, exigency, pass (see JUNCTURE).

Ant. Security. — *Con.* Safety (see corresponding adjective SAFE): immunity, *exemption: safeguarding *or* safeguard, guarding *or* guard, protection, defending *or* defense, shielding *or* shield (see corresponding verbs at DEFEND).

dangerous. Dangerous, hazardous, precarious, perilous, jeopardous, risky are here compared more because they are often used interchangeably without warrant than because they are close synonyms. However, some are actually synonyms and all carry the meaning attended by or involving the possibility of loss, evil, injury, harm, or the like. **Dangerous** applies to persons or to things that should be or are avoided or that should be or are treated with exceeding care because contact with them or use of them is unsafe and exposes one at least to danger; as, a *dangerous* weapon; a *dangerous* occupation; a *dangerous* practice; a *dangerous* doctrine; conditions *dangerous* to health; a *dangerous* person; "The child discovers that grown-ups lie to him, and that it is *dangerous* to tell them the truth" (*B. Russell*). **Hazardous** carries a far stronger implication of dependence on chance than *dangerous* carries: it is often the preferred term when the chances of loss, death, severe injury, or the like, are comparatively great; thus, a *hazardous* occupation (especially in insurance) is one in which the worker must run very great risks of accident or loss of life; a *hazardous* enterprise is one which has as many (if not more) chances of failing as of succeeding. "No one should be deluded into believing that we can ever have completely assured lives. Living is a *hazardous* business at the best" (*C. C. Furnas*). **Precarious** is often used incorrectly where *dangerous* or even *hazardous* would be the far better word. The basic meaning of this word is *uncertain* or *insecure:* therefore, it may be used without any implication of threatened danger or of possible hazards; thus, in strict use, a *precarious* tenure of office is one that is not fixed but is dependent on the will or pleasure of one's superiors; *precarious* health is uncertain health, rather than a physical condition threatening death; a *precarious* occupation is one that may be neither dangerous nor hazardous, but that is uncertain as in its tenure or in its remunerativeness; so, "Whoever supposes that Lady Austen's fortune is *precarious* is mistaken....It is...perfectly safe" (*Cowper*); "A National Church in the early Caroline sense depended upon the *precarious* harmony of the King, a strong Archbishop, and a strong First Minister" (*T. S. Eliot*). Nevertheless, especially in current use, the term often carries also an implication of attendance by danger or hazards: this use is by many regarded as questionable unless the stress is on insecurity or uncertainty; thus, a *precarious* hold or footing is one that is so insecure that it involves danger; so, "the *precarious* track through the morass" (*Scott*); "keeping a *precarious* and vital balance, like a man walking on high on a tight rope" (*C. E. Montague*); "We had to scramble *precariously* on the slopes of crumbling banks" (*A. Huxley*). **Perilous** carries a stronger implication of the immediacy of a threatened evil than *dangerous;* as, "After all their intolerable toils, the sounding tumult of battle, and *perilous* sea-paths, resting there...amid the epitaphs and allegorical figures of their tombs" (*L. P. Smith*); "We all know how *perilous* it is to suggest to the modern woman that she has any 'sphere'" (*Babbitt*). **Jeopardous** applies strictly to that in which the chances of great evil, such as of loss, serious injury, death, or the like, are about equal to the chances of good, such as success, profits, safety, or the like: the term, therefore, usually connotes exposure to the worst as well as the possibility of the best; as, it is a *jeopardous* venture to start a new business in these times; he felt that he was in a *jeopardous* situation, but hoped that all would turn out well. **Risky** comes close to *perilous* in suggesting high possibility of harm, but it is usually, though far from invariably, applied to that which a person does, or accepts, or carries on voluntarily and often with knowledge of the perils or risks to which it exposes him; as, to undertake a *risky* job; to make a *risky* investment; that was a *risky* stroke in tennis.

Ana. Unsafe, insecure (see affirmative adjectives at SAFE): chancy, chance, haphazard, *random, hit-or-miss.

Ant. Safe, secure.

dangle. Suspend, *hang, sling.

Ana. Oscillate, sway, pendulate, fluctuate (see SWING): *swing, wave.

dank. Damp, humid, moist, *wet.

Ana. Soaked, saturated, sogged *or* soggy, sopped *or* soppy, drenched (see corresponding verbs at SOAK).

dapper. Spruce, dashing, natty, nifty, nobby, *stylish, fashionable, modish, smart, chic, posh, toffish, brave, braw.

daredevil, *adj.* Daring, rash, reckless, foolhardy, temerarious, venturesome, venturous, *adventurous.

Ana. & *Con.* See those at DARING.

daring. Rash, reckless, daredevil, foolhardy, temerarious, venturesome, venturous, *adventurous.

Ana. Bold, intrepid, audacious (see BRAVE).

Con. *Timid, timorous: *cowardly, pusillanimous, craven: *cautious, wary, circumspect, chary: prudent, sensible, sane, *wise, judicious.

dark, *adj.* **1 Dark, dim, dusky, dusk, darkling, obscure, murky, opaque, gloomy** come into comparison when they mean partly or wholly destitute of light. **Dark,** the ordinary word and the most general of these terms, implies a lack of the illumination necessary to enable one to see or to identify what is before him. It may imply lack of natural illumination, as by the sun or moon (as, a *dark* forest; a *dark* night), or of artificial illumination as by gas or electricity (as, a *dark* room), or a lack of immaterial light, such as cheerfulness (as, a *dark* mood; a *dark* countenance), moral or spiritual light (as, a *dark* deed), or lack of brilliance—that is, the quality of lightness in color (as, a *dark* blue). **Dim** suggests just so much darkness that the things before one cannot be seen clearly or in their distinct or characteristic outlines: the term, therefore, so often suggests a degree of luminosity that it is even more often applied to the source of illumination (as, the light has grown *dim; dim* stars), or to a thing seen indistinctly (as, he could just make out *dim* figures in the distance; "Even to himself that past experience had become *dim*"—*G. Eliot*), or to a usually bright thing that is dulled or softened ("a...*dim* and tender red"—*Hudson;* "a *dim* image of their glorious vitality"—*J. W. Krutch*), than it is to a place or time that is nearly dark ("scrambled over to join the other ghosts out on the *dim* common"—*Galsworthy;* "the hazy light...reminded him of the *dim* distances of his own...country"—*S. Anderson*). *Dim* is also applied to eyes, sight, etc., to suggest a loss of keenness of vision; as, eyes *dim* with tears; *dim* eyesight. **Dusky** and the now far less common **dusk** suggest the halfway state between light and dark characteristic of twilight: like *dim* they imply faintness of light, but unlike that word, they definitely connote grayness and an approach to darkness; as, *dusky* winter evenings; the *dusky* windowless loft; *dusky* clouds; "rich as moths from *dusk* cocoons" (*Tennyson*). **Darkling,** originally and still often an adverb, is a literary term, close to *dark* in its implications, but carrying a stronger suggestion of blackness, mysteriousness, or uncanniness; as, "He wars with *darkling* Powers (I war with a *darkling* sea)" (*Kipling*); "the dock like a sheet of *darkling* glass" (*Conrad*); "under the shadow of the *darkling* cloud the house seemed bare and cold" (*M. Austin*). **Obscure** is now more often used in its extended senses (see OBSCURE) than in its literal sense, but it is still employed when there is a suggestion of darkening by covering, concealment, overshadowing, or the like, that deprives a thing of its lightness, brightness, or luster; as, "*Obscurest* night involved the sky" (*Cowper*); *obscure* stars; an *obscure* corner of the attic; *obscure* men and women. **Murky** originally implied and still sometimes implies intense darkness, or a darkness in which things are not even faintly visible; as, " 'Hell is *murky!*' " (*Shak.*). In current use, the term more often suggests a thick, heavy darkness suggestive of smoke-laden fogs or of air filled with mist and dust; as, "an atmosphere *murky* with sand" (*Cather*); "as if its [London's] low sky were the roof of a cave, and its *murky* day a light such as one reads of in countries beneath the earth" (*L. P. Smith*). In some use, *murky* implies an opposition to *transparent* and *translucent,* but commonly the specific term in this sense is **opaque;** thus, an *opaque* liquid is one through which rays of light do not pass; a *murky* liquid is so muddy or turbid that it is *opaque.* **Gloomy** (as here considered: see also SULLEN) implies imperfect illumination owing to causes that interfere seriously with the radiation of light, such as dense clouds, or the heavy shade of many closely set trees: in addition, it often connotes pervading cheerlessness; as, the day was especially *gloomy* for June; the *gloomiest* part of the forest; the room was *gloomy* and depressing with only a dim light from a small candle.

Ant. Light. — ***Con.*** *Bright, brilliant, radiant, luminous: illumined, illuminated, enlightened, lighted (see corresponding verbs at ILLUMINATE).

2 *Obscure, vague, enigmatic, cryptic, ambiguous, equivocal.

Ana. Abstruse, occult, *recondite, esoteric: *mystical, mystic, anagogical, cabalistic: intricate, complicated, knotty, *complex.

Ant. Lucid. — ***Con.*** *Clear, perspicuous: simple, *easy, light, facile.

darkling. Dim, dusk, dusky, *dark, obscure, murky, opaque, gloomy.

Ana. Uncanny, *weird, eerie: *mysterious, inscrutable, arcane.

dart, *v.* *Fly, scud, skim, float, shoot, sail.

Ana. *Speed, precipitate, hasten, hurry.

dash, *n.* *Touch, suggestion, suspicion, soupçon, tincture, tinge, shade, smack, spice, vein, strain, streak.

dashing. Smart, *stylish, fashionable, modish, chic, dapper, spruce, natty, nifty, nobby, posh, toffish, brave, braw.

dastardly. Poltroon, craven, *cowardly, pusillanimous, recreant.

Ana. Sneaking *or* sneaky, skulking, slinking, lurking (see LURK): *sinister, malign: furtive, stealthy, underhand, underhanded (see SECRET).

Ant. Gallant: valiant. — ***Con.*** *Brave, courageous, bold, intrepid, doughty, dauntless, valorous.

date, *n.* *Engagement, rendezvous, tryst, appointment, assignation.

daunt. Appall, *dismay, horrify.

Ana. Cow, *intimidate, browbeat: discomfit, disconcert, faze (see EMBARRASS): foil, thwart, baffle (see FRUSTRATE): *frighten, alarm, scare, terrify.

Con. Rally, rouse, arouse, *stir, waken, awaken: impel, drive, *move, actuate: activate, *vitalize, energize.

dauntless. Undaunted, intrepid, valiant, valorous, doughty, *brave, courageous, bold, audacious.

Ana. Indomitable, unconquerable, *invincible: heroic, gallant (see corresponding nouns at HEROISM).

Ant. Poltroon. — ***Con.*** *Cowardly, pusillanimous, craven, dastardly: *fearful, afraid, apprehensive.

dawdle. *Delay, procrastinate, loiter, lag, dally, dillydally.

Ana. Linger, tarry, wait, *stay: *trifle, toy, dally: *play, sport, disport.

Con. *Stir, rally, rouse, arouse: hurry, hasten, *speed.

daydream, *n.* Dream, *fancy, fantasy, phantasy, phantasm, vision, nightmare.

Ana. Imagining *or* imagination, conceiving *or* conception, fancying (see corresponding verbs at FANCY): illusion, *delusion, hallucination.

deacon, *v.* Doctor, *adulterate, sophisticate, load, weight.

Ana. Tamper, *meddle: alter, vary, modify, *change.

dead, *adj.* **Dead, defunct, deceased, departed, late, lifeless, inanimate** come into comparison especially in their literal senses since all mean devoid of life. **Dead** applies strictly to anyone or to anything that has been deprived of life, and has therefore ceased to grow or to function; as, a *dead* person; a *dead* animal; a *dead* tree; every plant in the garden is *dead* as a result of the intensely severe winter. But *dead* is also applicable to things which have not had life in the literal sense of that word, but have existed for a time and have been used or accepted or have proved effective, influential, or the like; thus, a *dead* language is no longer in use by any people; a *dead* belief no longer has any acceptance; a *dead* journal no longer is printed and circulated; a *dead* issue or question no longer arouses interest or debate. Figuratively, the term implies lack or loss of sensation, consciousness, feeling, activity, energy, or any of the qualities associated with life; as, *dead* fingers; a *dead* engine; a *dead* cigar; the *dead* season in a business. "Breathes there the man, with soul so *dead*, Who never to himself hath said, This is my own, my native land?" (*Scott*). **Defunct** differs little in its literal sense from *dead*, except in the fact that it is somewhat bookish, and, therefore, used chiefly in grandiose or humorous speech or writing. "Charlotte had entered society in her mother's turned garments, and shod with satin sandals handed down from a *defunct* aunt" (*E. Wharton*). The term is more often applied to a thing that by failure, dissolution, or the like, has ceased to function or to operate; as, a *defunct* newspaper; a *defunct* corporation. **Deceased,** except in rare humorous use, applies only to a person, and especially to one who has died comparatively recently or who, though dead, is at the moment under consideration: the use, however, is largely legal or euphemistic; as, laws prohibiting the marriage of a man with his *deceased* wife's sister; the legal heirs of the *deceased* millionaire were never found. **Departed** is even more euphemistic or formal (especially in religious use) than *deceased;* as, to pray for the souls of *departed* relatives and friends. **Late** is often used in place of *deceased* or *departed* when there is a strong implication of a recent death or of one affecting the relations or status of a living person, a going institution, or the like. Ordinarily, it is applied only to a person who was the one preceding the present in the same relationship or status; as, John Harrison, son of Mrs. J. G. Brown and the *late* Mr. Harrison; the *late* chairman of the board of directors; the *late* master of the house. **Lifeless,** unlike the preceding words, does not necessarily imply deprivation of life for it is applicable not only to that which is literally dead or defunct but also to that which never had life or is incapable of life. In comparison with *dead*, however, *lifeless* stresses the absence (sometimes, when loss of consciousness is implied, the apparent absence) of life; thus, a *dead* person; a *lifeless* body; when the day of his expected return came, he was *dead;* "There in the twilight cold and grey, *Lifeless*, but beautiful, he lay" (*Longfellow*). In its extended use, *lifeless* is especially applicable to things (far less often to persons) that have not or never have had vitality, power, or spirit; as, a *lifeless* color; a *lifeless* poem; she has been *lifeless* since her recovery from a prolonged illness; "dull *lifeless* mechanical systems that treat people as if they were things" (*Wilde*). "Monochrome is a starved and *lifeless* term to express the marvellous range and subtlety of tones of which...the preparation...known as Chinese ink is capable" (*Binyon*). **Inanimate** is more consistently used than *lifeless* in describing that which never had life; it is the preferred term when a contrast between that which is devoid of life and that which possesses life is expressed or implied; as, "objects which consist of *inanimate* matter" (*Jeans*); "a transition...from the inorganic to the organic, from the *inanimate* to the living" (*Inge*); "harnessing *inanimate* power to carry us and our burdens" (*C. C. Furnas*). But *inanimate* is also applicable in extended use to that which is spiritless, inactive, or not lively, and therefore dull; as, an *inanimate* style or sermon; an *inanimate* stock market.

Ant. Alive. — ***Con.*** *Living, quick.

deadly, *adj.* **1 Deadly, mortal, fatal, lethal** come into comparison when they mean causing or causative of death. **Deadly** does not in current usage always imply certainty of death, but an extremely high degree of probability; the term therefore applies to anything that is bound or extremely likely to cause death; thus, a *deadly* disease is one that usually destroys life (as, tuberculosis is no longer a *deadly* disease); a *deadly* weapon is one that is almost certain to inflict death when used with skill or precision; the seven *deadly* sins in theology are those sins which must be avoided because when committed they are certain to be the source of other sins and therefore are destructive of spiritual life and progress. "Two brave vessels matched in *deadly* fight, And fighting to the death" (*Wordsworth*). "Poisons more *deadly* than a mad dog's tooth" (*Shak.*). **Mortal,** as here compared, implies that death has occurred; the term therefore is applicable only to that which actually, and often immediately, has caused death; thus, a *mortal* disease is one that causes a person or many persons to die (as, in his case, tuberculosis was a *mortal* disease); his wound was *mortal* (that is, he died as a result of it); a *mortal* sin (in contrast with a *deadly* sin) is a grievous sin deliberately committed and actually inflicting spiritual death. *Deadly* applies to the instrument that deals the wound, blow, or the like, that proves mortal; as, a *deadly* lance; a *mortal* stab. **Fatal** stresses inevitability, and applies to that which will result in, or has actually resulted in, death, destruction, or disaster. The term is often used in place of *mortal* as applied to wounds, blows, illnesses, and the like, especially when some time has intervened between the wounding or sickening and the dying. *Fatal* rather than *mortal* is used in predictions; as, to remove him to the hospital would be *fatal;* "at her age...it [diabetes] was not speedily or necessarily *fatal*" (*H. Ellis*); "I will not repeat your words...because the consequences to you would certainly be *fatal*" (*H. Adams*). **Lethal** applies only to that which by its very nature is bound to cause death or which exists for the purpose of destroying life; as, a *lethal* dose of morphine; a *lethal* poison (or gas); a *lethal* chamber (that is, a room for the execution of those condemned to death); a *lethal* weapon. All of these terms except *lethal* may be used in a lighter sense not implying physical or spiritual death, but something dreaded or greatly feared; thus, a *deadly* shaft of irony causes complete discomfiture; *mortal* terror always suggests extreme terror, but only occasionally the terror of losing one's life; a *fatal* error or a *fatal* slip may imply the destruction of one's plans or hopes, rather than of one's life.

Ana. Destroying *or* destructive (see DESTROY): killing, slaying (see KILL, *v.*): malignant, malign (see MALICIOUS): baneful, *pernicious: toxic, virulent, *poisonous, pestilential, pestilent: ruinous (see corresponding verb RUIN).

2 Deadly, deathly are no longer synonyms but they are frequently confused. In strict use, **deadly** applies to that which is bound or extremely likely to cause death (see DEADLY, 1); in one of its extended senses, it applies to that which is so implacable or virulent, or so relentless, that it can result only in death, destruction, ruin, or the like; as, a *deadly* enmity existed between them; the two railroads are engaged in a *deadly* conflict over rates. In loose use, *deadly* often implies an extreme of something (as, *deadly* monotony; why are you in such *deadly* haste?), often a disgusting extreme of some depressing or spirit-destroying quality; as, the city is *deadly* in summer. **Deathly** applies only to that which suggests the appearance or the presence of death; as, his *deathly* pallor; the *deathly* stillness of the place.

deal, *v.* *Distribute, divide, dispense, dole.

Ana. Apportion, *allot, assign, allocate: *share, participate, partake.

Con. Collect, *gather, assemble: *receive, take: *keep, retain, withhold, hold back, detain, reserve.

dealings. *Intercourse, commerce, traffic, communication, communion, commune, conversation, converse, correspondence.

dear. Expensive, *costly, precious, valuable, invaluable, priceless.

Ana. Exorbitant, *excessive, extravagant, inordinate.

Ant. Cheap.

death. Death, decease, demise, passing agree in denoting the end or the ending of life. **Death** is the general word for the termination of every form of existence, of plants and animals as well as of men; **decease** and **demise** apply only to human beings, except in figurative use. *Decease* is the legal term or, in ordinary use, a slightly euphemistic or rhetorical term for death. *Demise* in common usage is a grandiloquent term for death. "Considered as a *demise*, old Featherstone's *death* assumed a merely legal aspect" (*G. Eliot*). **Passing** is a euphemism for the death of a person.

Ant. Life.

deathless. *Immortal, undying, unfading, fadeless, amaranthine.

Ana. *Everlasting, endless, never-ending: eternal (see INFINITE): enduring, abiding, persisting (see CONTINUE).

Con. Ephemeral, *transient, transitory, evanescent, passing.

deathly. *Deadly.

Ana. *Ghastly, macabre, gruesome, grisly.

Ant. Lifelike.

debar. *Exclude, blackball, disbar, suspend, shut out, eliminate, rule out.

Ana. Preclude, obviate, *prevent: *forbid, prohibit, ban, interdict.

Con. *Invite, court, woo, solicit, bid: permit, allow *let.

debase. 1 Debase, vitiate, deprave, corrupt, debauch, pervert come into comparison as meaning to cause a person or thing to become impaired and lowered in quality or character, especially in moral character or influence. The same distinctions in implications and connotations are also evident in the adjectives (usually participial adjectives) corresponding to the verbs, **debased, vitiated, depraved, corrupted** (but more often, **corrupt**), **debauched, perverted. Debase** (as here considered: see also ABASE) and **debased** imply a loss of worth, value, or dignity and are applicable, therefore, to a great number of things; as, plays that *debase* the taste of the people; a *debased* coinage. "The life-and-death struggle with Hannibal...had permanently *debased* the Roman temper and left in it a core of hard inhumanity" (*Buchan*). "Success permits him to see how those he has converted distort and *debase*...his teaching" (*A. Huxley*). "The fine old [English] language which has been slowly perfected for centuries, and which is now being... *debased* by the rubbishy newspapers which form almost the sole reading of the majority" (*Inge*). **Vitiate** and **vitiated** imply impairment through the introduction of a fault, a defect, or anything that destroys the purity, validity, or effectiveness of a thing; as, a style *vitiated* by exaggeration; "inappropriate and badly chosen words *vitiate* thought" (*A. Huxley*); "Alceste's [one of Moliere's characters] sincerity is *vitiated* by its unreasonableness" (*S. Alexander*); the *vitiated* air of a crowded hall; "Party jealousies *vitiated* the whole [Spanish loyalist] military organization" (*Times Lit. Sup.*); "a final decree... *vitiated* [i.e., invalidated] by the judge's assumption that he was bound by the master's findings of fact" (*Justice Holmes*). **Deprave** and **depraved** now usually imply pronounced moral deterioration; thus, a person who has a *debased* literary taste cannot enjoy that which is really good or beautiful if it lacks external qualities to which he is accustomed; a person with a *depraved* literary taste finds satisfaction only in that which is wholly or partly obscene or prurient; "The belief that a witch was a person who leagued herself with the Devil to defy God and *deprave* man" (*The Spectator*, 1890). **Corrupt** (both verb and adjective: for the latter see also VICIOUS) and **corrupted** imply a loss of soundness, purity, integrity, or the like, through forces or influences that break down, pollute, or destroy: the terms are applicable to things which are subject to decay, disintegration, or irreparable contamination of any sort; as, "Lay not up for yourselves treasures upon earth, where moth and rust doth *corrupt*" (*Matthew* vi. 19); "we must not So stain our judgement, or *corrupt* our hope" (*Shak.*); "the idea of beauty has been *corrupted* by those who would make it purely impressionistic or expressive" (*Babbitt*); "Our schools teach the morality of feudalism *corrupted* by commercialism" (*Shaw*). Often also, the terms imply seduction, bribery, or the like, as leading to a moral breakdown or to an immoral act; as, men who make a business of *corrupting* young girls; they were not able to *corrupt* the new legislators; *corrupted* courts. **Debauch** and **debauched** imply a demoralizing and depraving through corrupting influences such as a life of pleasure, ease, or sensual indulgence: they suggest the weakening, more often than the loss, of such qualities as loyalty to one's allegiance or duties, fitness for responsibility or high endeavor, and moral purity or integrity, and they often also connote dissoluteness or profligacy; as, "To betray their master and *debauch* his army" (*James Mill*); to *debauch* a woman; "the Duke of Anjou...was thrust forward to be the figurehead of it [a plot against Richelieu] and the gay, *debauched*, quite inconsequent lad was managed like a puppet" (*Belloc*). **Pervert** and **perverted** imply a twisting or distorting of something (sometimes someone) from what it is in fact or in its true nature, so as to debase it completely or make it incapable of proper or correct application; thus, to *pervert* the meaning of a text is to twist that meaning in interpreting it so that it will serve one's own ends or seem to prove one's thesis; to *pervert* the facts in a case is to give a distorted and, usually, personally advantageous view of them; to *pervert* the ends of nature is to use one's appetites or natural desires for other ends than those which are normal and in accordance with nature; so, "subjugation of the eternal to the temporal in a *perverted* set of values" (*Times Lit. Sup.*); "these nothings which...people are so prone to start a row about, and nurse into hatred from an idle sense of wrong, from *perverted* ambition" (*Conrad*); "The truth to him....is not only not to be spoken at all times, but it is now and then to be *perverted*" (*Brownell*).

Ana. Defile, pollute, taint, *contaminate: *adulterate, sophisticate, load, weight, doctor, deacon: impair, spoil, mar, damage, harm, *injure.

Ant. Elevate (*taste, character, etc.*): amend (*morals, way of life, etc.*). — ***Con.*** Enhance, heighten (see INTENSIFY): raise, *lift: *improve, better, ameliorate.

2 Degrade, demean, *abase, humble, humiliate.

Ana. *Weaken, undermine, sap, enfeeble, debilitate, cripple, disable.

Con. *Vitalize, energize, activate: vivify, enliven, *quicken: *renew, restore, refresh, rejuvenate.

debased. Vitiated, depraved, corrupted, debauched, perverted. See under DEBASE, 1.

Ana. Deteriorated, degenerated *or* degenerate, decadent (see corresponding nouns at DETERIORATION).

Con. Improved, bettered, ameliorated (see IMPROVE): raised, elevated, lifted (see LIFT, *v.*).

debate, *v.* Dispute, argue, *discuss, agitate.

Ana. *Contend, fight, battle, war: wrangle, altercate, quarrel (see under QUARREL, *n.*): controvert, refute, confute, rebut, *disprove: *prove, demonstrate.

Con. *Grant, allow, concede.

debate, *n.* Disputation, forensic, *argumentation, dialectic.

Ana. Controversy, *argument, dispute: contention, dissension (see DISCORD).

debauch. Corrupt, deprave, pervert, *debase, vitiate.

Ana. *Injure, harm, damage, spoil, mar: seduce, inveigle, decoy, tempt, *lure: pollute, defile, taint (see CONTAMINATE).

debauched. Corrupted, depraved, perverted, debased, vitiated. See under DEBASE.

Ana. Dissolute, reprobate, *abandoned, profligate: *licentious, libertine, lascivious, libidinous, lecherous, lewd, wanton.

debilitate. Enfeeble, *weaken, undermine, sap, cripple, disable.

Ana. Impair, *injure, damage, harm, hurt, mar, spoil.

Ant. Invigorate. — ***Con.*** Energize, *vitalize: *renew, restore, rejuvenate, refresh.

debit. Indebtedness, liability, *debt, obligation, arrear, arrearage.

Ant. Credit.

debonair. Debonair (*or, rarely,* **debonaire**), **jaunty, perky, cocky, chipper** are not close synonyms, but they come into comparison in their basic meaning, that is, distinguished by a gay, sprightly manner and well-set-up appearance. **Debonair** still carries implications derived from its earliest sense of gentle or gracious, of a manner or bearing characteristic of persons of high birth and fine breeding: it carries not the slightest suggestion of priggishness, affectation, or of coxcombry, but rather connotes an easy graciousness, a lightness of heart, a distinguished but not obtrusive grace of bearing, that are inherent rather than acquired; as, "In spite of his gay and *debonair* manner, he looked old" (*Edgeworth*); "his frank *debonair* manner, his charming boyish smile, and the infinite grace of that wonderful youth that seemed never to leave him" (*Wilde*); "Bodies trained and tuned to the perfect pitch, Eager, blithe, *debonair*, from head to heel Aglow and alive in every pulse" (*W. W. Gibson*). **Jaunty** suggests the manner or bearing of one who has consciously acquired sprightliness, ease, spruceness, dignity of bearing, or the like. It may suggest long training and discipline (as, "He had the spare, alert, and *jaunty* figure that one often finds in army men, an almost professional military quality that somehow seemed to set his figure upon a horse as if he had grown there"—*T. Wolfe*), or complacent airiness or affectation (as, "an indescribable air of *jaunty* impudence"—*Dickens;* "The ladies have a *jaunty* walk"—*Livingstone*). **Perky** and **cocky** suggest a ridiculous jauntiness or a preposterous affectation of debonairness considering one's stature, station in life, or the like. *Perky* usually stresses self-assertiveness or a bold putting forward of oneself or of one's charms, opinions, good points, or the like, so as to attract attention (as, "the *perky* Roman patrician, strutting the Forum ere manhood scarce attained, spouting the stale wisdom of middle age"—*Harper's Mag.*); *cocky* emphasizes an assumed arrogance or dash that attracts unfavorable attention (as, "This might have been all very well...if the *cocky* major had had plenty of money"—*Surtees;* "The little old man was so *cocky*. He went along up the cobblestone street like a banty rooster"—*S. Anderson*). **Chipper,** a colloquialism apparently of British origin, but now chiefly used in the United States, carries implications of jauntiness, nimbleness, sprightliness, and good health: it often suggests the lightness and ease of movement of a small bird such as the wren or lark; as, "As bloomin' as a rose, and as *chipper* as a canary bird" (*T. C. Haliburton*); "Sim's ben to college, and he's pretty smart and *chipper*" (*H. B. Stowe*); "I, a woman of seventy, and only a trifle gray,— I, who am smart and *chipper*, for all the years I've told" (*W. Carleton*).

Ana. *Gentle, genteel: *gracious, affable, genial, cordial: elegant, graceful, dignified (see corresponding nouns at ELEGANCE): sprightly, gay, *lively: lithe, lithesome, lissome (see SUPPLE).

Con. *Awkward, clumsy, gauche, maladroit, inept: stolid, *impassive, phlegmatic.

debt. **Debt, indebtedness, obligation, liability, debit, arrear** (*or* **arrears**), **arrearage** come into comparison when they mean something, most often a sum of money, that is owed another. **Debt** usually implies that the amount is owed in return for goods, property, services, or the like, and can be definitely computed, or if something other than money is owed, that it equals in value if not in kind the thing sold, the service given, or the like; as, to incur a heavy *debt* for services; to pay one's social *debts;* this *debt* is now due; an action (a legal action) in *debt;* the firm has no *debts* at present. **Indebtedness** is applied either to the total amount owed one's creditors or a single creditor; as, the *indebtedness* of the city exceeds the legal limit; his *indebtedness* to his father fell just short of a thousand dollars. **Obligation,** which is chiefly a legal term in this sense, implies a formal agreement to pay a certain amount or to do something, or an acknowledgment of such a promise, such as a contract or a bond; thus, a contractor's *obligations* may be less than his *debts.* **Liability** is an accountant's term used chiefly in reference to general balance sheets of a company or corporation and is the opposite of *asset.* It is also used of individuals in bankruptcy actions. Technically, it applies to any amount (or what purports to be its equivalent) which constitutes an item of indebtedness. Liabilities include accounts payable, accrued interest, taxes, obligations such as notes, bonds, and debentures, and even capital stock. **Debit** is also a term in accounting for any item shown on the left side of an account; it usually designates a purchase and its price, and is opposed to *credit,* or any entry on the right side (that is, for an article returned or an amount paid on account). **Arrear,** or its more common plural **arrears,** and the less frequent **arrearage,** usually imply that some of a debt, but not all, has been paid, but they always imply that the amount owed is overdue; as, to pay off the *arrears* (or *arrearage*) of one's rent; the servants found it difficult to obtain the *arrears* (or *arrearage*) of their wages.

decadence. Decline, declension, *deterioration, degeneration, devolution.

Ana. Retrogressiveness *or* retrogression, regressiveness *or* regression *or* regress, retrograding *or* retrogradation (see corresponding adjectives at BACKWARD).

Ant. Rise: flourishing. — ***Con.*** Advance, progress (see under ADVANCE, *v.*): *progress, progression.

decamp. *Escape, flee, fly, abscond.

Ana. Depart, clear out, scram, quit, leave, *go: elude, evade, *escape, shun, avoid.

decay, *v.* **Decay, decompose, rot, putrefy, spoil, disintegrate, crumble** come into comparison as meaning to undergo or, in some cases, to cause something to undergo destructive dissolution. **Decay** implies change, commonly a natural and gradual change, from a state of soundness or perfection; it may or may not suggest the certainty of complete destruction; as, too many sweets cause the teeth to *decay;* "Infirmity, that *decays* the wise" (*Shak.*); "As winter fruits grow mild ere they *decay* (*Pope*). "Nor shall I discuss the causes why science *decayed* and died under the Roman Empire" (*Inge*). **Decompose** stresses the idea of breaking down, either by separation into constituent parts or elements or, more or less euphemistically, of animal and vegetable matter, by corruption; as, "whenever molecules combine or *decompose* or atoms change partners, it is chemistry" (*C. C. Furnas*); "The action of bacteria in *decomposing* the organic products contained and forming gases useful for power and heat" (*A. C. Morrison*); the odor of *decomposing* meats. **Rot** implies decay and corruption, usually of or as if of animal or vegetable matter; the term may or may not imply offensiveness or foulness; figuratively, it differs from *decay* in stressing stagnation or corruption rather than decline; as, "The...little pitted speck in garner'd fruit, That *rotting* inward slowly moulders all" (*Tennyson*); "Blossoms...which fall before they wither rather than cling *rotting* to the stalk" (*Binyon*); "There shall they *rot*, Ambition's honour'd fools!" (*Byron*). **Putrefy** not only suggests the rotting of or as if of animal matter, but also suggests and even stresses its extreme offensiveness to sight and smell; as, corpses *putrefying* on the sun-drenched battlefields; *putrefying* carcasses. **Spoil** (see also INJURE) is often used in place of *decay, rot,* or *putrefy* when foodstuffs, especially in the home or the market, are referred to; as, roasted pork *spoils* quickly if not kept in a refrigerator. **Disintegrate** implies either a breaking down or a breaking apart so that the wholeness or integrity of the thing or the cohesiveness of its particles is destroyed or is in process of destruction; as, the London atmosphere tends to *disintegrate* bricks. "Rutherford and Soddy found that radio-active substances *disintegrate* in a way they described as 'spontaneous'—the rate of decay cannot be expedited or retarded by any known physical process" (*Jeans*). "The other great civilisations with which it was once contemporary have passed away or been *disintegrated* and transformed" (*H. Ellis*). **Crumble** implies disintegration of (or, in figurative use, as if of) a substance that breaks into fine particles; as, to *crumble* a piece of bread with one's fingers. "Winter rains had washed and washed against its...old bricks until the plaster between them had *crumbled*" (*Deland*). "Great periods of human culture which flourished at their height just as the substructure *crumbled*" (*J. W. Krutch*).

Ana. *Weaken, undermine, sap, debilitate, enfeeble: taint, *contaminate, defile, pollute: dilapidate, *ruin, wreck: dissolve, deliquesce (see LIQUEFY).

decease. *Death, demise, passing.

deceased. Departed, late, *dead, defunct, lifeless, inanimate.

deceit. 1 **Deceit, duplicity, dissimulation, cunning, guile** come into comparison when they mean the quality, the habit, the act, or the practice of imposing upon the credulity of others by dishonesty, fraud, or trickery. **Deceit** usually implies the intent to mislead or delude; otherwise, it is the most comprehensive of these terms, for it may imply deliberate misrepresentation or falsification, the assumption of a false appearance, the use of fraud or trickery or craft, or the like; as, addicted to *deceit;* "The fox barks not when he would steal the lamb No, no, my sovereign; Gloucester is a man Unsounded yet and full of deep *deceit*" (*Shak.*); "No! There my husband never used *deceit*" (*Browning*). **Duplicity** commonly implies double-dealing or bad faith; usually it suggests a pretense of feeling one way and an acting under the influence of another and opposite feeling. "I should disdain myself as much as I do him, were I capable of such *duplicity* as to flatter a man whom I scorn and despise" (*Burney*). Occasionally, however, the word does not imply intentional deceit, but the appearance of it arising out of a complexity of motives or a lack of singlemindedness. "It was chiefly that the simplicity and openness of their lives brought out for him the *duplicity* that lay at the bottom of ours" (*M. Austin*). **Dissimulation** implies deceit by concealing what one truly is, or what one actually feels, and therefore often, but not invariably, suggests duplicity. "Archer looked at her perplexedly, wondering if it were lightness or *dissimulation* that enabled her to touch so easily on the past at the very moment when she was risking her reputation in order to break with it" (*E. Wharton*). "The levity of Hamlet, his repetition of phrase, his puns, are not part of a deliberate plan of *dissimulation*, but a form of emotional relief" (*T. S. Eliot*). **Cunning,** as here compared, implies deceit by the use of trickery, wiles, or stratagems; it often connotes a perverted intelligence and almost vicious shrewdness in attaining one's end. "Surely the continual habit of *dissimulation* is but a weak and sluggish *cunning*, and not greatly politic" (*Bacon*). "He ...had come to the belief that I was incapable of the *cunning* and *duplicity* they practised....to deceive with lies and false seeming was their faculty and not mine" (*Hudson*). **Guile** carries an even stronger implication of lack of obviousness in the arts practiced or tricks used than does *cunning;* in very strict use, it carries a strong implication of insidiousness or treacherousness. "We now return To claim our just inheritance of old ...by what best way, Whether of open war or covert *guile*, We now debate" (*Milton*). "But Father Vaillant had been plunged into the midst of a great industrial expansion, where *guile* and trickery and honorable ambition all struggled together" (*Cather*). The word has, however, so long been used in phrases such as "without *guile*," "devoid of *guile*," and the like, that it now often is used in a very much weaker sense than *cunning*, sometimes implying little more than artfulness or the use of wiles. "Her heart innocent of the most pardonable *guile*" (*Conrad*). "There is a note of unconscious *guile*, the *guile* of the peasant, of the sophisticated small boy, in the letter he [Mark Twain] wrote to Andrew Lang" (*Van W. Brooks*).

Ana. *Deception, fraud, trickery, double-dealing, chicane, chicanery, subterfuge: craft, artifice (see ART): cheating, cozening, defrauding, overreaching (see CHEAT, *v.*).

Con. Honesty, uprightness, scrupulousness (see corresponding adjectives at UPRIGHT): openness, candidness *or* candor, frankness (see corresponding adjectives at FRANK): straightforwardness, forthrightness (see corresponding adjectives at STRAIGHTFORWARD).

2 *Imposture, cheat, fraud, sham, fake, deception, counterfeit, humbug, simulacrum.

Ana. Ruse, wile, *trick, feint, stratagem, maneuver, artifice.

deceitful. *Dishonest, mendacious, lying, untruthful.

Ana. Crafty, tricky, wily, foxy, cunning, *sly, artful: underhand, underhanded, stealthy, furtive, clandestine (see SECRET): *crooked, devious, oblique: delusory, deceptive, delusive, *misleading.

Ant. Trustworthy. — ***Con.*** *Reliable, dependable, trusty.

deceive. Deceive, mislead, delude, beguile, betray, double-cross come into comparison when they mean to lead astray or into evil or to frustrate by underhandedness or craft. A person or thing **deceives** one when he or it leads one to take something false as true, something nonexistent as real, something counterfeit as genuine, something injurious as helpful, or the like: the term usually implies either an imposing upon a person an idea or belief that contributes to his ignorance, bewilderment, or helplessness, or a deliberate ensnaring or entrapping for the agent's own, and usually evil, ends; as, " 'No woman's safe with him.' 'Ah, but he hasn't *deceived* me, Mrs. Berry. He has not pretended he was good' " (*Meredith*); "A person who first sub-consciously *deceives* himself and then imagines that he is being virtuous and truthful" (*B. Russell*). A person or thing **misleads** one when he, often by intention, or it, by the mistake of the person misled, causes one to follow a wrong path, way, or course, or to fall into error; as, to be *misled* by a confusing traffic signal; "We never find them *misled* into the conception that such gifts [of fortune] are an end in themselves" (*G. L. Dickinson*); "Nor is there any safeguard against the nations being *misled* and *deceived* by their governments into sanctioning another great war" (*Inge*). A person or thing **deludes** one when he or it deceives or misleads so completely that one is made a fool of or becomes incapable of distinguishing the false from the true; as, "I began to wonder whether I, like the spider that chased the shadow, had been *deluded*, and had seemed to hear a sound that was not a sound" (*Hudson*); "Did he, did all the people who said they didn't mind things, know that they really did? Or were they indeed *deluded?*" (*R. Macaulay*). A person or, less often, a thing, **beguiles** one when by some subtle and, usually, agreeable or alluring devices he (or it) misleads, deceives, or deludes one; as, "the male propensity to be *beguiled*" (*M. Austin*); "I recalled some of the Indian beliefs, especially that of the...man-devouring monster who is said to *beguile* his victims into the dark forest by mimicking the human voice" (*Hudson*). A person or thing **betrays** one when he or it by deception or by treachery delivers one into the hands of his enemy or puts him in a dangerous or false position; as, "Verily I say unto you, that one of you shall *betray* me" (*Matthew* xxvi. 21); "Knowing that nature never did *betray* The heart that loved her" (*Wordsworth*); "So, times past all number *deceived* by false shows, *Deceiving* we cumber the road of our foes, For this is our virtue: to track and *betray*" (*Kipling*). A person **double-crosses** another when, by double-dealing or duplicity, he deceives him or, more often, betrays him; as, it takes a friend to *double-cross* a friend; Blank said he had been *double-crossed* by his partner.

Ana. *Cheat, cozen, defraud, overreach: outwit, circumvent (see FRUSTRATE): *dupe, gull, befool, trick, hoax, hoodwink, bamboozle.

Ant. Undeceive: enlighten.

decency. *Decorum, propriety, dignity, etiquette.

Ana. Seemliness, decorousness (see corresponding adjectives at DECOROUS): fitness, suitability, fittingness, appropriateness (see corresponding adjectives at FIT).

decent. 1 *Decorous, seemly, proper, comme il faut, nice, demure.

Ana. Fitting, *fit, appropriate, suitable, meet: conventional, formal, ceremonious (see CEREMONIAL).

Con. *Awkward, gauche, inept, maladroit, clumsy: crude, rough, *rude.

2 Modest, pure, *chaste.

Ana. Virtuous, *moral, ethical, noble: pleasing, grateful, welcome, agreeable, *pleasant.

Ant. Indecent: obscene. — ***Con.*** Lewd, lascivious, wanton, libertine, *licentious: ribald, gross, *coarse, vulgar: dissolute, profligate, reprobate, *abandoned.

deception. 1 Deception, fraud, double-dealing, subterfuge, trickery, chicane, chicanery come into comparison as meaning the act or practice of, or the means used by, one who deliberately deceives in order to accomplish his ends. **Deception** may or may not imply blameworthiness, for it may be used not only of cheating, swindling, tricking, and the like, but also of many arts or games in which the object is illusion or mystification; as, to be given to *deception;* he is incapable of *deception;* "There is, as the conjurers say, no *deception* about this tale" (*Kipling*); magicians are adepts in *deception. Deception* also may be used in the passive sense for the state of being deceived; as, to fall into *deception;* "Hee is surely greedy of delusion, and will hardly avoide *deception*" (*Browne*). **Fraud,** on the other hand, except in humorous use, always implies guilt, often criminality, in act or practice. Distinctively, it usually suggests the perversion of the truth for the sake of persuading someone to surrender some valuable possession, a legal right, or the like; as, the elder brother gained control of the property by *fraud;* he will never stoop to *fraud,* no matter how much he desires to enrich himself. The term, however, may suggest any act or practice involving concealment of truth, the violation of trust and confidence, or the nonperformance of contracted acts, by which one (such as an agent, an attorney, an executor, an employer, or an employee) gains against conscience an advantage over the other party to the injury of the latter; as, according to one legal decision "silence where necessity requires speech may sometimes constitute *fraud.*" "I think that obtaining money by *fraud* may be made a crime as well as murder or theft; that a false representation, expressed or implied at the time of making a contract of labor, that one intends to perform it and thereby obtaining an advance, may be declared a case of fraudulently obtaining money" (*Justice Holmes*). **Double-dealing** usually implies duplicity in character and in actions, for it frequently suggests an act that in its essence is contrary to one's professed attitude. "In Berlin our fanatical anti-monarchist [Mark Twain]...having been...invited to dine at the Kaiser's right hand...proceeds to tell the world...how incomparable the German Empire is.... Yet it was not hypocrisy, this...*double-dealing*" (*Van W. Brooks*). However, the term often implies secret treating with each of two opposed persons or groups as though one were friendly to that person or group and inimical to the other. "Saville...by his *double-dealing* with the King and the Scots, proved himself a political traitor" (*I. D'Israeli*). **Subterfuge** usually applies to an act or a practice which is the means by which one deceives others and accomplishes an end, in precise use always a cowardly end such as escaping censure or attack, evading performance of a duty or a provision of the law, or avoiding the force of an argument or meeting a difficulty. "By a miserable *subterfuge,* they hope to render this proposition safe by rendering it nugatory" (*Burke*). "Frauds By forgery, by *subterfuge* of law" (*Cowper*). In looser use, the term applies to any deceptive artifice by which one gains an end. "Men resorted to various *subterfuges* to get a satisfactory look without rudely betraying their intention" (*Shaw*). **Trickery,** usually a collective term, implies acts or practices that are intended to dupe or befool others; it often, but far from always, implies moral turpitude and then connotes fraud, double-dealing, and the like. "We rely not upon management or *trickery,* but upon our own hearts and hands" (*Jowett*). "I swear I have no heart To be your Queen. To reign is restless fence, Tierce, quart, and *trickery*" (*Tennyson*). **Chicane** and **chicanery** imply petty or paltry trickery and often subterfuge, especially, but not exclusively, in legal proceedings; as, "To wrest from them by force, or shuffle from them by *chicane*" (*Burke*); "Many scenes of London intrigues and complex *chicanery*" (*De Quincey*); "Making a tremendous fight [to maintain his hold on the presidency], chiefly by *chicane*—whooping for peace while preparing for war, playing mob fear against mob fear" (*Mencken*).

Ana. *Deceit, duplicity, dissimulation, cunning, guile: cheating, cozening, defrauding, overreaching (see CHEAT): duping, gulling, hoaxing, hoodwinking, bamboozling, befooling (see DUPE).

2 *Imposture, cheat, fraud, sham, fake, humbug, counterfeit, deceit, simulacrum.

Ana. Illusion, *delusion, hallucination, mirage.

deceptive. *Misleading, delusory, delusive.

Ana. Specious, *plausible, colorable: *false, wrong.

Con. Genuine, *authentic, veritable, bona fide: true, *real, actual.

decide. Decide, determine, settle, rule, resolve come into comparison when they mean to come, or, less often, to force to come, to a conclusion. **Decide** (etymologically, to cut off) presupposes previous consideration of a matter causing doubt, wavering, debate, or controversy and implies the arriving at a more or less logical conclusion that brings doubt, debate, etc., to an end: the word may take as its subject the person or persons arriving at such a conclusion or the thing or things that bring them to the conclusion; as, "The time for deliberation has then passed. He has *decided*" (*Ch. Just. Marshall*); "This exordium, and Miss Pross's two hands in quite agonised entreaty clasping his, *decided* Mr. Cruncher" (*Dickens*); "the...mistress of the household referred to her whether we should have another round or go in to supper. Of course, she always *decided* as she supposed the hostess wished" (*Jefferies*); "It was Sophia's list slippers which had finally *decided* Amy to drop the mask of deference" (*Bennett*). **Determine** (as here considered: see also DISCOVER, 2) originally meant to set limits or bounds to: when, in more recent use, the term means basically to decide, this implication of fixing definitely something or other so that its identity, its character, its scope, its direction, or the like, is clear and beyond doubt, distinguishes it from *decide;* thus, one *decides* to give a dinner party but *determines* the guests to be invited; a legislature *decides* that the state constitution should be revised and appoints a committee with power to *determine* what changes shall be made; a snub *decides* a person never again to recognize the offender when he meets him; but the way in which a newly introduced person greets a sensitive man *determines* the extent to which the latter will make advances when he again meets that person. Also, in a slightly different sense, *determine* implies the arrival at a conclusion that either is a fixed and unalterable purpose or intention (as, "Can you weep [i.e., move by weeping] Fate from its *determined* purpose?"—*Middleton;* "She was...obviously tormented by shyness, but as obviously *determined* to conquer it"—*C. Mackenzie*), or is the inevitable result, outcome, or end of what precedes (as, "What we notice *determines* what we do; what we do again *determines* what we experience"—*W. James;* "Their civilization was one of 'city-states,' not of kingdoms and empires; and their whole political outlook was necessarily *determined* by this condition"—*G. L. Dickinson*). **Settle** implies the arrival at a conclusion, often a mental or logical conclusion, but sometimes a termination for which no individual is responsible, that brings to an end all doubt, all wavering, all dispute, and the like; as, the Supreme Court of the United States has power to *settle* all questions of law; "Time has *settled* few or none of the essential points of dispute" (*H. Adams*); death *settled* all their problems. **Rule** (as here considered: see also GOVERN) implies a decision or determination by authority, especially by the authority of the court; as, the judge *ruled* that the question was inadmissible. **Resolve** implies an expressed or clear decision or determination to do or refrain from doing something; as, to *resolve* to get up earlier in the mornings; to *resolve* to give up smoking. "He was *resolved* to win through to fortune, but he must first discover his tools" (*Buchan*).

Ana. Conclude, judge, gather (see INFER): *judge, adjudge, adjudicate.

Con. Vacillate, waver, *hesitate, falter.

decided. Decided, decisive are often confused, especially when they mean positive and leaving no room for doubt, uncertainty, or further discussion. In this sense, the words are applied chiefly, but not exclusively, to persons, their natures, their utterances or manner of utterance, their opinions, choices, and the like. **Decided** implies an opposition to that which is undetermined, indefinite, and neither this nor that; thus, a *decided* blue raises no question of its greenness, blackness, or the like; a *decided* success so far overpasses the line between success and failure that no one can question its favorable termination; a *decided* answer leaves no doubt of a person's wishes, intentions, or the like. When applied to a person's character, expression, movements, and the like, *decided* suggests qualities (often outward signs of qualities) such as determination, resolution, lack of all hesitation or vacillation, and the like; as, the mother was a *decided* person to whose will everyone in the family submitted; he has very *decided* opinions; "I see too many ways of saying things; a more *decided* mind hits on the right way at once" (*Mrs. H. Ward*); "Then with a *decided* step she turned toward home" (*E. Wharton*). **Decisive,** on the other hand, implies an opposition to that which is unsettled, uncertain, or wavering between this and that (for this sense as applied to things see CONCLUSIVE). When used in reference to persons it implies one's ability or one's intent to settle, or success in settling, a controverted matter once and for all; as, "This was enough to determine Sir Thomas, and a *decisive* 'Then so it shall be' closed that stage of the business" (*Austen*); "She stood up and surveyed herself in the pier-glass. The *decisive* expression of her great florid face satisfied her" (*Joyce*).

Ana. *Definite, definitive: determined, resolved (see DECIDE): positive, cocksure, certain, *sure: categorical, *explicit, express.

Con. Dubious, *doubtful, questionable, problematic.

decision. Decision, determination are here compared as denoting strength of mind or character that reveals itself in a power to get or have one's way. **Decision** often implies both decidedness and decisiveness (see DECIDED) but it usually stresses a power or habit of promptly and definitely making up one's mind when circumstances demand it: it is often imputed as a quality to those who have long and ably exercised authority, but it is also ascribable to one who has great force of personality; as, "You find the *decision* of the great soldier perpetually appearing in the career of this sickly indomitable man [Richelieu]" (*Belloc*); "There was...in the personality of that little old lady the tremendous force of accumulated *decision*—the inherited assurance of one whose prestige had never been questioned" (*Galsworthy*); "Within his face Courage and power had their place, Rough energy, *decision*, force" (*Masefield*). **Determination** often implies dogged adherence to a settled purpose, but as here especially considered, it emphasizes force of will great enough to carry one through difficulties and hardships without weakening and to impress others with its power or irresistibility. "Into his handsome face, the bitter waters of captivity had worn; but, he covered up their tracks with a *determination* so strong, that he held the mastery of them, even in his sleep" (*Dickens*). "His will, so long lying fallow, was overborne by her *determination*" (*Conrad*).

Ana. Certitude, assurance, conviction, *certainty: self-confidence, self-assurance, self-possession, *confidence, aplomb: imperiousness, imperativeness, masterfulness (see corresponding adjectives at MASTERFUL).

Ant. Indecision. — ***Con.*** *Uncertainty, dubiety, dubiosity, doubt, skepticism.

decisive. 1 *Conclusive, determinative, definitive.

Ana. Critical, crucial, *acute: momentous, significant, consequential, important (see corresponding nouns at IMPORTANCE).

Ant. Indecisive.

2 *Decided.

Ana. Peremptory, imperative, *masterful, imperious: certain, *sure, positive, cocksure: resolute, steadfast (see FAITHFUL).

Ant. Irresolute. — ***Con.*** Wavering, fluctuating (see SWING): hesitant, reluctant (see DISINCLINED).

deck, *v.* Bedeck, *adorn, decorate, ornament, garnish, embellish, beautify.

Ana. Array, apparel, attire, dress, *clothe: primp, prank, *preen, prune, doll up, perk up.

declaration. Announcement, publication, advertisement, proclamation, promulgation, broadcasting. See under DECLARE, 1.

declare. 1 Declare, announce, publish, advertise, proclaim, promulgate, broadcast (and their corresponding nouns **declaration, announcement, publication, advertisement, proclamation, promulgation, broadcasting**) agree in denoting to make known (or, a making known) openly or publicly. To **declare** is to make known explicitly or plainly, and usually, in a formal manner. "If Lord Wolseley should *declare* his preference for a republic..." (*Brownell*). "The law...*declares* all such marriages absolutely null and void" (*Ch. Just. Taney*). To **announce** is to declare, esp. for the first time, something presumed to be of interest or intended to satisfy curiosity; as, to *announce* a discovery, one's candidacy for office, the winners in a contest, a forthcoming book. To **publish** is to make public, now commonly through the medium of print. "He was...exercising great self-denial, for he was longing to *publish* his prosperous love" (*Austen*). "There were no newspapers to *publish* every mystery" (*C. G. Leland*). To **advertise** is to call public attention to by repeated or widely circulated statements. In its general sense, it often connotes unpleasant publicity or extravagance in statement. "An issue which *advertised* me...throughout the Church as a supporter of heresy" (*W. Lawrence*). "[Baudelaire] had...the misfortune to be...extravagantly *advertised* by Swinburne" (*T. S. Eliot*). In its specific sense, as implying publicity for the sake of gaining patronage or support for an article of merchandise, it implies the use of the press, the radio, handbills, or the like; so used, it is devoid of unfavorable connotation; as, to *advertise* a particular make of automobile or brand of cigarettes. To **proclaim** is to announce orally (sometimes by means of other sound, as that of a trumpet) and loudly in a public place; by extension, to give wide publicity to, often insistently, proudly, boldly, defiantly, or the like. "A lie is as much a lie, when it is whispered, as when it is *proclaimed* at the market-cross" (*Wollaston*). " 'You *proclaim* in the face of Hellas that you are a Sophist' " (*Jowett* [*Plato*]). To **promulgate** is to make known to all concerned something that has binding force (as a law of the realm or a dogma of the church) or something for which adherents are sought (as a theory or doctrine). "The Doctrine of the Immaculate Conception was *promulgated* in December 1854" (*A. Robertson*). "That for the training of the young one subject is just as good as another...is surely...an amazing doctrine to *promulgate*" (*Grandgent*). To **broadcast** is to make known in all directions over a large area, now commonly by means of radio. "The doctrine of missionary zeal...has been *broad-cast* over Christendom" (*I. Taylor*, 1829). "The largest...wireless station that can *broadcast* to the world" (*Daily Mail*).

Ana. *Inform, apprise, acquaint, advise, notify: impart, *communicate: *reveal, disclose, discover, divulge.

2 *Assert, affirm, aver, avouch, avow, protest, predicate, warrant.

Ana. *Express, voice, utter, vent, broach, air, ventilate.

Con. *Suppress, repress: *hide, conceal.

declension. Decline, decadence, *deterioration, degeneration, devolution.

Ana. Decaying *or* decay, disintegration, crumbling (see corresponding verbs at DECAY): retrogressiveness *or* retrogression, regressiveness *or* regression (see corresponding adjectives at BACKWARD).

Con. Ascent, *ascension: rising *or* rise (see corresponding verb RISE): advance, progress (see under ADVANCE, *v.*): *progress, progression.

decline, *v.* **Decline, refuse, reject, repudiate, spurn** are comparable when they mean to turn away something or someone by not consenting to accept, receive, or consider it or him. **Decline** is the most courteous of these terms; it is therefore used chiefly in respect to invitations, offers as of help, services, or the like; as, to *decline* an invitation to dinner; "she *declined* the chair the Judge pushed toward her" (*Cather*). "I am very sensible of the honour of your proposals, but it is impossible for me to do otherwise than *decline* them" (*Austen*). **Refuse** is more positive, often implying decisiveness, even ungraciousness; as, "Meats by the law unclean... young Daniel could *refuse*" (*Milton*); "The employers *refused* to 'recognize' the unions" (*Shaw*). *Refuse*, however, may imply, as *decline* does not, the denial of something expected or asked for; as, to *refuse* one permission or help. "Mark knew that Mrs. Pluepott only lived to receive visitors, and he had not the heart to *refuse* her the pleasure of a few minutes" (*C. Mackenzie*). **Reject** stresses a throwing away, a discarding, or abandoning; it implies a refusal to have anything to do with a person or thing; as, "those who accepted the offer and those who *rejected* it" (*C. E. Montague*); "Plotinus definitely *rejects* the notion that beauty is only symmetry" (*H. Ellis*); "common sense, *rejecting* with scorn all that can be called mysticism" (*Inge*). **Repudiate** etymologically implies a casting off, originally and still sometimes of a wife whom one refuses any longer to recognize or accept; it now usually connotes either a disowning or a rejection with scorn as untrue, unauthorized, unworthy of acceptance, or the like; as, to *repudiate* a son; the state has *repudiated* its debts; to *repudiate* a religious doctrine or a scientific theory. "I do not see how the United States could accept the contract and *repudiate* the consequence" (*Justice Holmes*). "It is the law of nature that the strong shall rule; a law which everyone recognizes in fact, though everyone *repudiates* it in theory" (*G. L. Dickinson*). **Spurn** (etymologically, to kick against; hence, to kick out) carries even a stronger implication of disdain or contempt in rejection than *repudiate;* as, "the proposals which she had proudly *spurned* only four months ago" (*Austen*). "He would be *spurned* out of doors with a kick" (*J. C. Snaith*). "Must *spurn* all ease, all hindering love, All which could hold or bind" (*Amy Lowell*).

Ana. *Demur, balk, shy, boggle, jib, stick, stickle, scruple.

Ant. Accept. — ***Con.*** Take, *receive: consent, *assent, acquiesce, accede.

decline, *n.* Declension, decadence, *deterioration, degeneration, devolution.

Ana. & ***Con.*** See those at DECLENSION.

declivity. Slope, incline, inclination, *slant, grade, gradient.

Ant. Acclivity.

decolorize, decolorate. Blanch, bleach, etiolate, *whiten.

decompose. *Decay, rot, putrefy, spoil, disintegrate, crumble.

Ana. Dissolve, deliquesce, *liquefy, melt.

decorate. Ornament, embellish, beautify, *adorn, deck, bedeck, garnish.

Ana. Enhance, heighten, *intensify: prank, prink, primp, doll up (see PREEN).

decorous. Decorous, decent, seemly, proper, nice, comme il faut, demure come into comparison when applied to persons, their utterances, and their behavior, and mean conforming to or being in accordance with the accepted standard of what is right or fitting or is regarded as good form. That is **decorous** which is marked by decorum, or the observance of the proprieties; the term usually implies a dignified, sometimes ceremonious, sometimes prim, formality; as, "the *decorous* platitudes of the last century" (*J. R. Lowell*); "done something strange and extravagant and broken the monotony of a *decorous* age" (*Emerson*); "On Sunday mornings the whole school went to church; in the afternoon it had a *decorous* walk" (*H. G. Wells*). That is **decent** (in its now somewhat archaic sense; for other sense, see CHASTE), which keeps within the bounds of what is appropriate or fitting to its kind or class, not only from the points of view of morality or social propriety but also from those of good taste or the exigencies of a situation. "To praise a man's self [oneself], cannot be *decent*, except it be in rare cases" (*Bacon*). "Expression is the dress of thought, and still Appears more *decent*, as more suitable" (*Pope*). "He cast only one glance at the dead face on the pillow, which Dolly had smoothed with *decent* care" (*G. Eliot*). That is **seemly** which is not only decorous or decent, but also pleasing to the eye, ear, or mind of the observer; as, "To make a *seemly* answer" (*Shak.*); a *seemly* display of enthusiasm. "It was not *seemly* that one so old should go out of his way to see beauty, especially in a woman" (*Galsworthy*). That is **proper** which is exactly what it should be according to the ethical or social standards or conventions of any class. "Henchard's creed was that *proper* young girls wrote ladies'-hand—nay, he believed that bristling characters were as innate and inseparable a part of refined womanhood as sex itself" (*Hardy*). "A few pages back I was expressing a *proper* diffidence about any conclusions in view, and here I am, almost shouting in favour of one" (*C. E. Montague*). That is **nice** (see also NICE, 1; CORRECT) which satisfies a more or less fastidious taste in behavior, manners, speech, or the like; as, his conduct is not always so *nice;* "It is not enough for the knight of romance that you agree that his lady is a very *nice* girl" (*Justice Holmes*). "The undergraduate literary club, whose membership included all *nice* boys with literary pretensions" (*J. P. Marquand*). That is **comme il faut** (a French phrase, much used in English, meaning "as it ought to be") which is proper from the point of view of polite society or of well-bred persons. "But it never can have been *comme il faut* in any age or nation for a man of note...to be constantly asking for money" (*Macaulay*). **Demure,** in current English, no longer stresses decorousness and staidness of demeanor or behavior. This, however, is the sense carried by the word as used by many of the classic English writers; as, "Come, pensive Nun, devout and pure, Sober, steadfast, and *demure*" (*Milton*). In present-day use, *demure* usually suggests a decorously modest appearance, and often connotes the assumption or the more or less deliberate acquirement of that appearance; as, "received by bustling male assistants...instead of by *demure* anaemic virgins" (*Bennett*); "lowering her glance unexpectedly till her dark eyelashes seemed to rest against her white cheeks she presented a perfectly *demure* aspect" (*Conrad*).

Ana. Formal, conventional, ceremonious, *ceremonial: dignified, elegant (see corresponding nouns at ELEGANCE).

Ant. Indecorous: blatant.

decorticate. *Skin, peel, pare, flay.

decorum. Decorum, decency, propriety, dignity, etiquette come into comparison either when they mean a code (in some cases, an article of a code) of rules respecting what is right, fitting, or honorable, especially in conduct or behavior or, more often, when they mean the quality or character of rightness, fitness, or honorableness in conduct, behavior, and the like, resulting from the observance of such a code. The first three words, though still often used in the senses here considered, have a slightly literary or archaic flavor: the last two are the most common in current speech. Both *decorum* and *decency* imply that the code is based upon the nature of things or the circumstances which attend them, and therefore the rules which it embodies have their basis in nature or sound reason. In current use, **decorum** especially suggests a code of rigid rules or laws governing the conduct or behavior of civilized men under given or understood conditions; as, "If gentlemen of that profession [the army] were at least obliged to some external *decorum* in their conduct" (*Swift*); "that continual breach of...*decorum* which, in exposing his wife to the contempt of her own children, was so highly reprehensible" (*Austen*); "he enjoyed a distinguished reputation for the excellence of his sermons, for the conduct of his diocese..., and for the *decorum* and devotion of his private life" (*T. S. Eliot*). The term may, however, suggest (as it did from the mid-sixteenth to the mid-eighteenth century, when the terms denoted a code of laws founded on nature, reason, and the practice of the ancients, and declaring what is seemly and becoming in dramatic, poetic, and other art) a literary or artistic beauty based on order, moderation, and a high degree of intelligibility; as, "that *decorum* and orderliness without which all written speech must be ineffective and obscure" (*H. Ellis*). **Decency** in current colloquial use often stresses a freedom from immodesty or obscenity (as, *decency* in dress; *decency* in conduct), but in the earlier sense of the word still followed by discriminating writers it implies a seemliness or appropriateness that is based upon the right relation of one thing to another, such as that of a person to his profession, or rank, or condition in life, or of a thing with reference to its use or end; as, *decency* of worship; "for himself, Father Joseph was scarcely acquisitive to the point of *decency.* He owned nothing in the world but his mule, Contento" (*Cather*); "There are those...for whom St. Paul's [in London], in comparison with St. Peter's [in Rome], is not lacking in *decency*" (*T. S. Eliot*); "And there were May [his wife], and habit, and honour, and all the old *decencies* that he and his people had always believed in" (*E. Wharton*). **Propriety** stresses conformity to a standard of what is proper or correct. When used in reference to language, it implies a regard for the established meanings of words, and a refusal to accept what is novel, or not in accordance with a word's etymology or historical development in senses, or not countenanced by good usage; as, the severe *propriety* of his diction. More often, however, the word implies a rigid code of rules respecting conduct or manners, laid down as correct, proper, and essential by the class (or a class) that regards itself as having the right or the privilege of dictating such rules and of enforcing them, especially in society; as, "My whole life has been at variance with *propriety,* not to say *decency*" (*Byron*); "In the reign of James I the conduct of ladies and gentlemen was not marked by the same prim *propriety* as in the reign of the highly respectable Victoria" (*H. Ellis*); "With characteristic independence she had made her reception rooms upstairs and established herself (in flagrant violation of all the New York *proprieties*) on the ground floor of her house" (*E. Wharton*). Although in this sense *propriety* is often used ironically or humorously, the word is sometimes preferred to *decency* when merely seemly or fitting correctness (and not conformity to convention) is implied; as, "the *propriety* and necessity of preventing interference with the course of justice" (*Justice Holmes*). **Dignity** (as here compared: see also ELEGANCE) seldom, if ever, applies directly to a code or a rule but it does often apply to a state of being that arises from obedience to what one, or one's class, or one's profession, regards as elevated, noble, or in full accordance with one's rank, status, or position: in the senses here considered, it implies governance by a code or by forces which often correspond to the decencies or proprieties; as, to keep one's *dignity;* to lose one's *dignity;* not in accord with the *dignity* of man as a son of God; "I had half a mind to save my *dignity* by telling him that..." (*Conrad*). "It is of the essence of real *dignity* to be self-sustained, and no man's *dignity* can be asserted without being impaired" (*H. Taylor*). **Etiquette** is now the usual term (in place of "the proprieties") for the code of manners and behavior governing one's conduct in society or in a particular milieu, such as a court or legislature, or, often in place of *propriety,* for the conventional observance of these rules; as, trained in the *etiquette* of a formal presentation at court; unaware of the *etiquette* governing the setting of a table for a formal dinner; "The pompous *etiquette* of the court" (*Prescott*). "Augustus had kept to the strict constitutional *etiquette,* indicating his preference but leaving the choice of his successor to the Senate" (*Buchan*).

Ana. Formality, conventionality, ceremoniousness, solemnity (see corresponding adjectives at CEREMONIAL): *form, convention, convenance, usage.

Ant. Indecorum: license.

decoy, *n.* *Lure, bait, snare, trap.

decoy, *v.* *Lure, entice, inveigle, tempt, seduce.

Ana. Snare, ensnare, trap, entrap, capture, *catch, cop, nab, bag: beguile, delude, *deceive, mislead.

decrease, *v.* **Decrease, lessen, diminish, reduce, abate, dwindle** agree in denoting to make or grow less, but they are not always interchangeable. *Dwindle* is almost never used transitively; *diminish* is used as an intransitive verb less frequently than *dwindle; reduce* is used intransitively only in specialized senses; as, the doctor ordered him to *reduce.* **Decrease** and **lessen,** the most general of these words, are often employed in place of any of the others. Nevertheless, *decrease* is precisely and felicitously used only when it retains, even in the transitive, its etymological implication of the process of growing less, and suggests progressive decline; as, forces that *decrease* the population (that is, cause it to grow less); his temperature *decreases;* his fears *decreased* as dawn approached. **Diminish** is the more precise word when the ideas of taking away (or subtraction) by an agent and of resultant perceptible loss are to be emphasized; as, their funds were greatly *diminished* by their extravagance. "His sense of personal initiative is cultivated instead of being *diminished*" (*B. Russell*). **Reduce** adds to *diminish* the implication of bringing down, or lowering; it suggests more than any of the others the operation of a personal agent; as, to *reduce* the time needed for an operation; prices were *reduced* to below cost; to *reduce* budget estimates drastically. *Reduce* also is applicable to lowering in rank, status, or condition; as, to *reduce* a lieutenant to the ranks; "...suddenly *reduced* from riches to absolute penury" (*Conrad*). **Abate** differs from *diminish* and *reduce* in its presupposition of something excessive, as in force, intensity, or amount, and in its strong implication of moderation or, especially, when referred to taxes or imposts, of deduction. "Unconsciously the boy *abated* his stride so that the old man could keep up with him" (*M. Austin*). **Dwindle,** like *decrease*, implies progressive lessening, but is more often applied to things capable of growing visibly smaller. It specifically connotes approach to a vanishing point. "Hull down—hull down and under —she *dwindles* to a speck" (*Kipling*).

Ana. Curtail, *shorten, retrench, abridge, abbreviate: *contract, shrink.

Ant. Increase. — *Con.* Augment, multiply, enlarge (see INCREASE): *extend, protract, prolong, lengthen, elongate: *expand, amplify, swell, dilate, distend.

decrepit. Infirm, feeble, *weak, frail, fragile.

Ana. Worn, wasted, *haggard: *aged, superannuated, old: tottering, quavering, shaking (see SHAKE).

Ant. Sturdy. — *Con.* *Strong, stalwart, stout, tough, tenacious: *vigorous, lusty, energetic.

decry. Decry, depreciate, disparage, derogate from, detract from, belittle, minimize agree in meaning to write, speak, or otherwise indicate one's feeling in regard to something in such a way as to reveal one's low opinion of it. **Decry** implies open or public condemnation or censure with the intent to discredit or run down someone or something. "There seems almost a general wish of *decrying* the capacity and undervaluing the labor of the novelist" (*Austen*). "You've had a Western education... but you're *decrying* everything Western science has contributed to the world" (*V. Heiser*). **Depreciate** implies a representation of a person or thing as of smaller worth than that usually ascribed to it. "To prove that the Americans ought not to be free, we are obliged to *depreciate* the value of freedom itself" (*Burke*). "He seems to me to *depreciate* Shakespeare for the wrong reasons" (*T. S. Eliot*). **Disparage** implies depreciation by more subtle methods, such as slighting or invidious reference or faint praise; as, "The critic...is generally *disparaged* as an artist who has failed" (*L. P. Smith*); "cities [such as Boston, Philadelphia]...which they [Americans] sometimes pretended to *disparage*, but of which they were secretly and inordinately proud" (*A. Repplier*). **Derogate from** and **detract from** stress the idea of taking away, positively and injuriously, especially from reputation or merit; *derogate from* may be used with an impersonal subject only, *detract from* with either a personal or an impersonal subject. "A few instances of inaccuracy or mediocrity can never *derogate from* the superlative merit of Homer and Vergil" (*Goldsmith*). "Far am I from *detracting from* the merit of some gentlemen...on that occasion" (*Burke*). "The advocates of pure poetry are apt to take the line that any admixture of logical, of 'prose' meaning *detracts from* the value of a poem" (*Day Lewis*). **Belittle** and **minimize** both imply depreciation, but *belittle* suggests an effort to make a thing contemptibly small, and *minimize* to reduce it to a minimum or to make it seem, sometimes disparagingly, as small as possible; as, he was inclined to *belittle* the assistance he had received from others; he *minimized* the dangers of the task. "Let there be no *belittling* of such qualities as Archer's—his coherent thinking, his sense of the worth of order and workmanship" (*C. E. Montague*). " 'Don't think that I am trying to *minimize* your excellent work among the hop pickers this year,' he told his curate" (*C. Mackenzie*).

Ana. *Disapprove, deprecate: *criticize, denounce, reprehend, censure, reprobate, condemn.

Ant. Extol. — *Con.* Acclaim, laud, eulogize, *praise: *exalt, magnify.

dedicate. Consecrate, hallow, *devote.

Ana. Devote, *direct, address, apply.

deduce. *Infer, gather, conclude, judge.

Ana. Reason, cogitate, *think, speculate.

deduction. 1 Deduction, abatement, rebate, discount are comparable when they mean an amount subtracted from a gross sum. **Deduction,** the most general term, is interchangeable with any of the others, but not without loss in precision. **Abatement** is a deduction from a levied tax or impost; as, an *abatement* of the duties levied at the customhouse; **rebate** is an amount deducted and returned after payment, either in adjustment of an overcharge or to gain a competitive advantage; as, a *rebate* on an income tax; a *rebate* on an insurance premium. **Discount** is a deduction from an amount owed or price asked in consideration of a cash or prompt payment; as, this bill is subject to 2 per cent *discount* if paid within thirty days; also, it is an advance deduction of the amount of interest payable on a loan or note from the time the loan is made or the note purchased until the due date; as, the bank credited his account with the proceeds of the note less the *discount*.

2 Inference, conclusion, judgment. See under INFER.

3 Deduction, induction and their corresponding adjectives **deductive, inductive** are here compared only as used in logic as meaning (or in the case of the adjectives, as designating) forms of reasoning. **Deduction** and **deductive** imply reasoning from premises, or propositions antecedently proved or assumed as true or certain, and procedure from the general or universal to a particular conclusion; thus, the conclusion that one must die someday is based on the premises that all men are mortal and that one is a man; therefore one infers by *deduction*, or *deductive reasoning*, that one must necessarily be mortal. **Induction** and **inductive** imply reasoning from particular facts to a conclusion that is general or universal in its nature. In its simplest form, *induction* implies a knowledge of every particular and a generalization from these; thus, the conclusion that all of a certain man's books have red bindings is reached by *induction*, or *inductive reasoning*, when one has surveyed his library and has found no exception to this rule. In its more complicated forms, since knowledge of every particular is usually impossible, *induction* often implies the use of postulates or assumptions which are generally accepted (such as the uniformity of nature), more or less tentative conclusions, and constant observation and experiment and re-examination of the evidence. In this sense, many of the laws of nature stated in the various sciences are derived by *induction*, but when these laws are used as premises and become the bases for further inferences, the reasoning becomes *deductive*.

deductive. Inductive (see under DEDUCTION, 3).

Ana. Inferential, ratiocinative, illative (see under INFERENCE).

deed, *n.* *Action, act.

Ana. Exploit, *feat, achievement.

deed, *v.* *Transfer, convey, alienate, alien.

deem. *Consider, regard, account, reckon.

Ana. Conclude, gather, *infer.

deep. **1 Deep, profound, abysmal.** *Deep* and *profound* in their literal senses denote extended either downward from a surface (actual or assumed) or, less often, backward or inward from the front or outer part. **Deep** is the most general term; as, a *deep* pond, ravine, well. Figuratively, as applied to persons or to mental states or processes, *deep* implies the presence, or a necessity for the exercise, of penetration or subtlety, sometimes of craft; as, a *deep* politician; *deep* plots. "A little knowledge often estranges men from religion, a *deeper* knowledge brings them back to it" (*Inge*). **Profound** in its literal sense connotes exceedingly great depth, but is now rare in this use. "A gulf *profound* as that Serbonian bog... where armies whole have sunk" (*Milton*). "Canyons more *profound* than our deepest mountain gorges" (*Cather*). Figuratively, *profound* implies the presence or need of thoroughness; as, a *profound* thinker; a *profound* treatise. As expressing intensity, *profound* is commonly stronger than *deep*. "Motherhood, this queer, sensuous, cherishing love....an emotion more *profound* than most" (*R. Macaulay*). **Abysmal** in its literal sense carries over the idea of *abyss*, infinite depth, and implies fathomless distance downward, backward, or inward from a surface (real or assumed). "Not much happens to starlight in its long passage through the *abysmal* depths of interstellar space" (*P. W. Merrill*). Figuratively, *abysmal* implies measureless degree and is used only with words denoting a lack or want of something; as, *abysmal* ignorance; *abysmal* darkness. "Plays of an *abysmal* foolishness" (*Van W. Brooks*).

Con. Shallow, *superficial: flat, plane, plain, *level.

2 *Broad, wide.

deep-rooted. Deep-seated, chronic, confirmed, *inveterate.

Ana. Established, fixed, set, settled. See SET, *v.*

Con. Eradicated, extirpated, uprooted, wiped out. See EXTERMINATE.

deep-seated. Chronic, deep-rooted, confirmed, *inveterate.

Ana. Ingrained, constitutional, *inherent: profound, *deep.

deface. **Deface, disfigure, disfeature, defeature** come into comparison as meaning to mar the appearance of a thing. **Deface** usually suggests a marring (literally or figuratively) of the face or external appearance of anything: it frequently implies the effacement, obliteration, or removal of some part or detail; as, "Earth has yet a little gilding left, not quite rubbed off, dishonored, and *defaced*" (*Hazlitt*); "a door *defaced* by innumerable incised inscriptions" (*Shaw*); "Bad poets *deface* what they take [from others], and good poets make it into something better" (*T. S. Eliot*). **Disfigure,** as applied to a surface, implies deeper or more permanent injury than *deface:* as applied to figure or conformation, it frequently suggests such impairing of beauty or attractiveness as results from other than structural injury; as, a book *disfigured* by many serious faults; "The smallpox...fell foul of poor little Oliver's face...and left him scarred and *disfigured* for his life" (*Thackeray*); "where trees, *disfigured* by no gaudy lanterns, offered the refreshment of their darkness and serenity" (*Galsworthy*). **Disfeature** and the rarer **defeature** suggest the marring, as by distortion, deformation, or eradication, not only of features of the human face but of those of a landscape, a view, a formation, or the like, that depends for its effectiveness on outlines, contours, or diversity of elevations; as, grief *disfeatured* her usually beautiful face; a hillside *disfeatured* by great gashes in its surface, from quarrying operations; "Ruined *defeatured* shapes of beauty" (*Lytton*); "The prey of pale *disfeaturing* death" (*John Todhunter*).

Ana. *Injure, damage, mar: *deform, distort, contort: mutilate, batter, mangle (see MAIM).

defalcate. **Defalcate, peculate, embezzle** come into comparison as meaning to steal or purloin money or valuables committed to one's care or custody. The same distinctions in implications and connotations are apparent in the corresponding nouns **defalcation, peculation, embezzlement. Defalcate** (usually an intransitive verb), and the far more common **defalcation,** in the narrow senses in which they are here considered, usually but not invariably imply a breach of trust: they always suggest a shortage in one's accounts or a failure to turn over money or property to those to whom it belongs. The term may or may not connote the misappropriation of the funds or property involved in such a shortage or failure, or its diversion to one's own use; as, under the present management, three of the bank's tellers have *defalcated;* owing to the *defalcation* of the treasurer of the company, the business passes temporarily into the hands of a receiver. *Defalcation* less often denotes the act or fact of defalcating than the amount of shortage in one's accounts; as, they estimate the cashier's *defalcations* as $50,000. **Peculate** (either transitive or intransitive) and **peculation,** especially in later and modern use, definitely imply a stealing of money or property that belongs to another and is under one's control for a longer or shorter time. In current English, the term commonly suggests graft, or the use for his own purposes of public money by an official who has access to it; as, "The people... accused them of having *peculated* the public money" (*Southey*); "Marlborough was dismissed from his command, charged with *peculation,* and condemned" (*J. R. Green*). **Embezzle** (a transitive verb which may be used absolutely) and **embezzlement** may imply either defalcation or peculation; however, they carry a far stronger suggestion of the fraudulent misuse, through misappropriation or careless dissipation, of funds definitely entrusted to one's care and not merely passing through one's hands; thus, in very strict legal use, the treasurer of a corporation may be said to *embezzle* funds when he diverts corporation funds to his own use; an executor of an estate may be said to be guilty of *embezzlement* when he uses trust funds for his own ends rather than for those dictated by the testator of the will. *Embezzle* and *embezzlement* distinctively imply that the money or property has been consigned to one in trust at the wish or with the consent of the owner; therefore, they suggest criminality not in the acquisition but in the use for oneself of what belongs to another.

Ana. *Steal, purloin, pilfer, filch: *rob, loot, rifle, plunder: abscond, decamp (see ESCAPE).

defalcation. Peculation, embezzlement. See under DEFALCATE.

Ana. *Theft, larceny, robbery.

defame. Vilify, calumniate, *malign, traduce, asperse, slander, libel.

Ana. Vituperate, revile (see SCOLD): *decry, disparage, detract from, derogate from.

Con. *Praise, laud, eulogize, extol, acclaim.

defeat, *v.* Beat, *conquer, vanquish, lick, subdue, subjugate, reduce, overcome, surmount, overthrow, rout.

Ana. *Frustrate, thwart, foil, baffle, balk, circumvent, outwit.

Con. *Yield, submit, capitulate, succumb, cave in, bow, defer.

defeature. Variant of DISFEATURE.

defect. **1** Want, *lack, absence, privation.

Ana. Deficiency, defectiveness (see corresponding adjectives at DEFICIENT): *need, necessity, exigency.

Con. Sufficiency, adequacy, competency (see corresponding adjectives at SUFFICIENT).
2 Flaw, *blemish.
Ana. *Fault, failing, frailty, foible.
Con. *Excellence, perfection, virtue, merit.

defection. **Defection, desertion, apostasy** agree in meaning an abandonment that involves the breaking of a moral or legal bond or tie and that is highly culpable from the point of view of the person, cause, or party abandoned. **Defection** emphasizes both the fact of one's falling away and the loss that is sustained by one's failure to adhere to one's allegiance; in itself as apart from the context it commonly gives no certain indication of motive, though at times disaffection or loss of confidence is connoted; as, the *defections* from the majority party were so numerous as to cause the first defeat in generations; "the higher we stand, the baser our *defection*" (*Bridges*). "The news of the *defection* of Lepidus caused the Senate to declare him a public enemy" (*Buchan*). **Desertion,** in the specific sense here considered, presupposes an oath of allegiance or a duty or an obligation to guard, protect, or support, the violation of which constitutes a crime or a distinctly blameworthy act. It also suggests a base motive, such as cowardly fear or a desire to shirk; as, the penalty for *desertion* from an army in time of war is usually death; many persons considered Wordsworth's *defection* from the liberal cause a *desertion.* **Apostasy** implies a repudiation of something one has formerly and voluntarily professed; it connotes therefore a retreat, as in weakness, from a position or stand one has taken. The term is used chiefly with reference to a repudiation of religious beliefs, but it is employed with equal correctness when moral, philosophical, or other principles are involved. "When Raphael ...had forewarned Adam, by dire example, to beware *Apostasy*" (*Milton*). " 'Marriage is to me *apostasy*...sale of my birthright, shameful surrender' " (*Shaw*). "But my political *apostasy* [from the Republican party after the Civil War]...was attended with no diminution of reverence for that great citizen army that defended and saved the Union" (*M. Nicholson*).
Ana. Disaffection, alienation, estrangement (see corresponding verbs at ESTRANGE): abandonment, forsaking (see corresponding verbs at ABANDON).
Con. Faithfulness, loyalty, constancy (see corresponding adjectives at FAITHFUL): allegiance, *fidelity, fealty.

defective. *Deficient.
Ana. Impaired, damaged, injured, marred (see INJURE): vitiated, corrupted, debased (see under DEBASE): deranged, disordered (see DISORDER).
Ant. Intact. — *Con.* *Perfect, entire, whole: complete, *full, plenary: sound, *healthy.

defend. 1 **Defend, protect, shield, guard, safeguard** come into comparison when they mean to keep secure from danger or against attack. **Defend** implies the use of means to ward off that which actually threatens or to repel that which actually attacks; as, to raise a large army to *defend* the country from aggression; guns used in *defending* the explorers against hostile incursions of the natives. **Protect** etymologically implies a covering, especially a frontal, but sometimes an overhead, covering, that serves as a bar to the admission or impact of that which may injure or destroy; as, to *protect* one's estate from intruders by a high wall; to *protect* one's eyes from the sun by dark glasses; to *protect* one's family by ample insurance; to *protect* tobacco plants by a tentlike cheesecloth screen. **Shield** differs from *protect* sometimes in its figurative suggestion of the use of something like the medieval warrior's shield, but more often in much more strongly connoting imminent danger or actual attack or protective intervention; as, "Heavens *shield* Lysander, if they mean a fray!" (*Shak.*); "I... That *shielded* all her life from harm" (*Tennyson*). "I could scarcely believe that she would wish to *shield* her husband's murderer, if he were that" (*R. Macaulay*). **Guard** implies a standing watch over for the sake of defense, as at an entrance or exit or as in a circle or ring around a person or place; it usually connotes vigilance; as, the entrances to the palace are well *guarded;* the president is always *guarded* by secret service men; the inmates of a fortress are *defended* by its guns, *protected* by its walls, and *guarded* by sentries against surprise. **Safeguard,** much more strongly than any of the preceding words, implies use of protective measures where merely potential danger exists; as, to *safeguard* children who play on the streets; to *safeguard* our shores from attack. "In all this he was more than worldly-wise. He was *safeguarding* his own self-respect" (*A. Repplier*).
Ana. Ward off, avert, *prevent: *oppose, resist, withstand: fight, battle, war, *contend, cope.
Ant. Combat: attack. — *Con.* Assault, assail, bombard, storm (see ATTACK): submit, cave in, *yield, capitulate.
2 Assert, *maintain, justify, vindicate.
Ana. Voice, vent, utter, *express, air: *explain, account for, justify, rationalize: *support, champion, uphold, back.

defer.[1] **Defer, postpone, intermit, suspend, stay** agree in meaning to cause a delay in an action, activity, or proceeding. **Defer** suggests little more than a putting off till a later time: ordinarily it implies an intentional delaying (as, to *defer* a discussion of a proposal until more members are present; to *defer* payment on a note; he *deferred* giving his son needed advice until he found the boy in a less refractory mood) but it may imply a delay in fulfillment, attainment, fruition, etc., that is occasioned by conditions beyond one's control (as, "Hope *deferred* maketh the heart sick"—*Proverbs* xiii. 12). **Postpone** implies an intentional deferring, commonly until a definite time (except in the euphemistic *to postpone indefinitely*, which often actually implies the calling off of an event); as, to *postpone* a meeting for a week; her dentist was willing to *postpone* her appointment until Saturday; "I think that we had better *postpone* our look round the church until after lunch" (*C. Mackenzie*). **Intermit** implies a stopping for a time, usually as a measure of relief, but sometimes merely as a break in a course or proceeding; as, "Pray to the gods to *intermit* the plague" (*Shak.*); "When seriously urged to *intermit* his application [to study], and allow himself a holiday" (*M. Pattison*). **Suspend** also implies a stopping for a time, but for any one of various reasons, such as diversion of one's interest (as, "Eleanor's work was *suspended* while she gazed with increasing astonishment" —*Austen*), an order or a condition prohibiting continuation or demanding an intermitting (as, to *suspend* publication; to *suspend* trolley service during the parade; "Henchard gave orders that the proceedings were to be *suspended*"—*Hardy*), or a legislative, executive, or judicial decision (as, "Congress has authorized the President to *suspend* the operation of a statute"—*Justice Holmes;* to *suspend* the sentence of a convicted person), or a desire to wait for more evidence or information (as, to *suspend* one's judgment of a person charged with a crime). **Stay** implies the interposition of an obstacle to something that is in progress: it may suggest bringing it to a complete stop, but more often it suggests an intermitting or suspending or a slackening of pace; as, "two spectators started forward, but she *stayed* them with a motion of her hand" (*Dickens*); "they couldn't *stay* the flow of her ideas by reminding her how much the alteration would cost" (*M. Austin*); "When his [man's] mind fails to *stay* the pace set by its inventions, madness must ensue" (*Day Lewis*).

Ana. *Delay, retard, slow: *adjourn.

Con. Hasten, hurry, *speed, accelerate.

defer.[2] Bow, *yield, submit, cave in, capitulate, succumb, relent.

Ana. Accede, acquiesce, *assent, agree: conform, accommodate, *adapt, adjust: truckle, *fawn, cringe.

deference. Reverence, homage, *honor, obeisance.

Ana. Veneration, worship, adoration (see under REVERE): respect, esteem, admiration, *regard.

Ant. Disrespect. — *Con.* Disdain, scorn, contempt, despite (see under DESPISE).

deficient, *adj.* **Deficient, defective** agree in meaning showing lack of something necessary. The words are still sometimes used interchangeably even though in current good usage they tend to diverge in their meanings. **Deficient** is the preferred term when there is an intent to imply a falling short in the amount, quantity, force, or the like, considered essential to adequacy or sufficiency; **defective** is the preferred term when there is the intent to imply some definite fault, injury, flaw, or the like, that impairs the completeness or efficiency of a thing; thus, a person is said to be *deficient* in courage when he has not sufficient courage to meet his difficulties; he is said to be mentally *deficient* when he has not sufficient intelligence to enable him to take care of himself; he is said to be mentally *defective* (or a mental *defective*) when some fault or defect in his nervous or cerebral organism is apparent and he lacks the ability to think coherently, to speak intelligibly, or to co-ordinate his muscles; he suffers from *defective* hearing when by disease or injury the organ of hearing is impaired; so, *deficient* sympathies; a *deficient* supply of food; a *defective* crystal; a *defective* mechanism.

Ana. *Meager, scanty, scant, sparse, exiguous: scarce, rare, *infrequent, uncommon.

Ant. Sufficient, adequate: excessive. — *Con.* Competent, enough (see SUFFICIENT): *plentiful, plenteous, ample, abundant: *excessive, inordinate, immoderate, extravagant.

defile. Pollute, taint, *contaminate, attaint.

Ana. *Debase, vitiate, deprave, corrupt, pervert, debauch: profane, desecrate (see corresponding nouns at PROFANATION).

Ant. Cleanse: purify. — *Con.* Hallow, consecrate (see DEVOTE).

define, *v.* *Prescribe, assign.

Ana. *Limit, circumscribe: fix, *set, establish.

Con. *Mix, merge, mingle: *mistake, confuse, confound.

definite. **1** **Definite, definitive** are sometimes confused. That is **definite** (see also EXPLICIT) which has limits so clearly fixed or defined or so unambiguously stated that there can be no doubt concerning the scope or the meaning of that which is so qualified; as, he has very *definite* opinions on the matter; *definite* accomplishments; appointments are made for *definite* periods of time. That is **definitive** (for fuller treatment see CONCLUSIVE) which fixes or settles something else and therefore is final or decisive; as, a *definitive* statement of a doctrine; a *definitive* judicial decision by the highest court of the land. "This joint effort of church and crown indeed is *definitely* traceable from the time of Charlemagne...and it found its culmination under Louis XIV., when the nobles were *definitively* conquered by the crown and the Reformation by the church" (*Brownell*).

Ana. Defined, prescribed, assigned (see PRESCRIBE): limited, restricted, circumscribed (see LIMIT, *v.*): determined, settled, decided (see DECIDE).

Ant. Vague: loose. — *Con.* *Obscure, ambiguous, equivocal.

2 *Explicit, express, specific, categorical.

Ana. Clear, plain, distinct (see EVIDENT): *full, complete: downright, *forthright: precise, exact (see CORRECT, *adj.*): concrete (see SPECIAL): clear-cut, *incisive.

Ant. Indefinite: equivocal. — *Con.* *Doubtful, dubious, questionable.

definitive. **1** Determinative, decisive, *conclusive.

Ana. Settling, deciding, determining (see DECIDE): final, concluding, *last, terminal, ultimate.

Ant. Tentative, provisional. — *Con.* *Temporary, temporal: experimental (see corresponding noun at EXPERIENCE).

2 *Definite.

Ana., Ant., & *Con.* See those at DEFINITIVE, 1.

deflate. Compress, shrink, *contract, condense, constrict.

Ana. Reduce, *decrease, lessen: exhaust, *deplete, drain: puncture, prick (see PERFORATE): attenuate, extenuate (see THIN).

Ant. Inflate. — *Con.* Distend, *expand, dilate, swell.

deflect. *Turn, divert, avert, sheer.

Ana. Deviate, depart, diverge, *swerve, veer, digress: bend, *curve, twist.

deflection *or* **deflexion.** *Deviation, aberration, divergence.

Ana. Bending, curving, turning, twisting (see CURVE): swerving *or* swerve, veering *or* veer, departing *or* departure (see corresponding verbs at SWERVE).

deform. **Deform, distort, contort, warp, gnarl** come into comparison when they mean to mar or spoil a person's or thing's appearance, character, true nature, development, or the like, by or as if by twisting. **Deform** is the least specific of these terms in its implications: sometimes, it carries no significance other than that expressed in the first sentence above; sometimes, however, it suggests a loss of some particular excellence or essential such as comeliness, perfection of line, attractiveness, or the like; as, "Soul-killing witches that *deform* the body" (*Shak.*); "To *deform* thy gentle brow with frowns" (*Rowe*); "I suspect Mr. Babbitt at times of an instinctive dread of organized religion, a dread that it should cramp and *deform* the free operations of his own mind" (*T. S. Eliot*); "with the best intentions in the world, Mr. Imam is incessantly at work to *deform* and degrade the content of poetry" (*Times Lit. Sup.*). **Distort** usually carries a clear implication of twisting or wresting away from or out of the natural, regular, or true shape, posture, or direction: the term, however, is used not only in reference to physical or material things, but also in reference to minds, judgments, facts, statements, etc., that may be twisted by conditions, circumstances, or, when a personal agent is involved, by a dominating purpose or intent; as, "*Distorted* as a living thing by pain" (*Wilde*); "the upward slant of the candle-light *distorted* Mary Adeline's mild features, twisting them into a frightened grin" (*E. Wharton*); "there is an element of truth in what you say, grossly as you may *distort* it to gratify your malicious humor" (*Shaw*); "some accident of immediate overwhelming interest which appeals to the feelings and *distorts* the judgment" (*Justice Holmes*). **Contort** implies a more involved or continuous twisting together or upon itself: it, therefore, both in literal and figurative use, differs from *distort* in suggesting a grotesque or a painful effect rather than a departure from the natural, the true, or the normal; as, "That most perverse of scowls *contorting* her brow" (*N. Hawthorne*); "the baby's face muscles *contorted* in a manner that only Mammy Clo could have interpreted as an expression of merriment" (*R. Bradford*); "One generation of fearless women could transform the world, by bringing into it a generation of fearless children, not *contorted* into unnatural shapes, but straight and candid, generous, affectionate, and free" (*B. Russell*). **Warp** literally implies a twisting, or bending, or drawing out of a flat plane, by some force such as drying and shrinking (as, the covers of the book are *warped;* the back of the chair is *warped*), but in its common extended use the term implies the operation of any force that twists or wrests a thing so as to give it a bias, a wrong slant, an abnormal direction, a distorted significance, or the like; as, cares have *warped* her mind; *warped* views or opinions; "So they [trees] slowly come to full growth, until *warped*, stunted, or risen to fair and gracious height, they stand open to all the winds" (*Galsworthy*). "To cut me off from all natural and unconstrained relations with the rest of my fellow creatures would narrow and *warp* me if I submitted to it" (*Shaw*). "I'm sure you are disinterested . . . but, frankly, I think your judgment has been *warped* by events" (*Cather*). **Gnarl** in literal use chiefly refers to the roots or trunk of an old tree, sometimes twisted and contorted or, in the case of the trunk, covered with large knots or protuberances. In application to things such as human hands, human bodies, and the like, the term suggests the contortions and deformations characteristic of old age or a rheumatic condition but sometimes produced by heavy work or constant exposure to winds and sun (as, *gnarled* and weather-beaten sailors; "his drawn bayonet in his large *gnarled* hand"—*H. T. Cockburn*): in reference to minds, souls, dispositions, and the like, it suggests extreme or settled contrariness, ingrained unreasonable prejudices, or intense acerbity (as, "Even the shrewd and bitter, *Gnarled* by the old world's greed" —*V. Lindsay*).

Ana. *Maim, cripple, mutilate, mangle, batter: disfigure, *deface: *injure, mar, damage, impair.

defraud. Swindle, overreach, *cheat, cozen.

Ana. Trick, bamboozle, hoax, gull, *dupe, befool: outwit, circumvent, foil (see FRUSTRATE).

deft. Feat, *dexterous, adroit, handy.

Ana. Nimble, *agile, brisk: *quick, ready, apt, prompt: skillful, skilled, adept, *proficient: sure, assured, *confident.

Ant. Awkward. — *Con.* Clumsy, maladroit, inept, gauche (see AWKWARD).

defunct. Deceased, departed, late, *dead, lifeless, inanimate.

Ant. Alive: live.

degenerate, *adj.* Corrupt, infamous, *vicious, villainous, iniquitous, nefarious, flagitious.

Ana. Degraded, demeaned (see ABASE): debased, depraved, debauched, perverted (see DEBASE): dissolute, *abandoned, reprobate, profligate.

degeneration. Devolution, decadence, *deterioration, decline, declension.

Ana. Retrogressiveness *or* retrogression, regressiveness *or* regression (see corresponding adjectives at BACKWARD): debasement, degradation (see corresponding verbs at ABASE).

degrade. Debase, demean, humble, *abase, humiliate.

Ana. *Debase, deprave, debauch, pervert, corrupt, vitiate.

Ant. Uplift. — *Con.* *Exalt, magnify, aggrandize.

dehydrate, *v.* Desiccate, *dry, parch, bake.

deign. Condescend, *stoop.

Ana. Vouchsafe, accord, concede, *grant, award.

deist. Freethinker, *atheist, agnostic, unbeliever, infidel.

dejection. Depression, melancholy, melancholia, gloom, *sadness, blues, dumps, vapors.

Ana. Despondency, hopelessness, forlornness, despair, desperation (see under DESPONDENT).

Ant. Exhilaration.

delay, *v.* **1 Delay, retard, slow, slacken, detain** are not always close synonyms but they carry the same basic meaning: to make someone or something behind in his or its schedule or usual rate of movement or progress. **Delay** implies the operation, usually the interference, of something that keeps back or impedes, especially from completion or arrival at a set or given time; as, a train is *delayed;* "A plague upon that villain Somerset, That thus *delays* my promised supply" (*Shak.*). **Retard** applies especially to motion, movement, or progress, and implies something which causes it to reduce its speed; as, to *retard* the swing of a pendulum, the revolution of a wheel; the snow *retards* our progress; children *retarded* in development. "Mental evolution has perhaps *retarded* the progress of physical changes" (*Inge*). "The rate of decay [of radioactive substances] cannot be expedited or *retarded* by any known physical process" (*Jeans*). **Slow** (usually followed by *up* or *down*) and **slacken** also imply a reduction in speed or rate of progress, but *slow* often specifically implies deliberation or intention; *slacken*, an easing, or letting up, or a relaxation of some sort; as, the engineer *slowed* down the train as he approached the city; the doctor administered digitalis to *slow* up his pulse; he *slackened* his pace to a walk; "having never *slackened* her . . . search for your father" (*Dickens*). **Detain** (see also ARREST, 2) implies a being held back beyond an appointed time, often with resulting delay in arrival or departure or in accomplishment of what one has in mind; as, "I had been *detained* by unexpected business in the neighborhood" (*Conrad*); "Tell him that as I have a headache I won't *detain* him today" (*Hardy*). "You will not thank me for *detaining* you from the bewitching converse of that young lady" (*Austen*).

Ana. Impede, obstruct, *hinder, block: *defer, postpone, stay, suspend, intermit.

Ant. Expedite: hasten. — *Con.* *Speed, hasten, hurry, accelerate, quicken, precipitate.

2 Delay, procrastinate, lag, loiter, dawdle, dally, dillydally agree in meaning to move or act slowly so that progress is hindered or work remains undone or unfinished. **Delay** (for transitive sense see DELAY, 1) usually carries an implication of putting off, as one's departure, one's initiation of an action or activity, one's accomplishment of necessary work, or the like; as, when he had his instructions, he did not *delay* an instant. "Wind of the sunny south! oh still *delay*, In the gay woods and in the golden air" (*Bryant*). "Time and again were we warned of the dykes, time and again we *delayed*" (*Kipling*). **Procrastinate** implies blameworthy or inexcusable delay, such as that caused through laziness, indifference, hesitation, or the habit of putting off until tomorrow what should be done today. "The less one has to do, the less time one finds to do it in. One yawns, one *procrastinates*, one can do it when one will, and therefore one seldom does it at all" (*Chesterfield*). "A timid, unsystematick, *procrastinating* ministry" (*Burke*). **Lag** implies a failure to maintain a speed or pace, either as set by and therefore in comparison with that of another (as, after an hour's brisk walk, two of the hikers *lagged* behind the rest; "It was a time of great men, but our learning and scholarship *lagged* far behind those of Germany"—*Inge*) or as necessary to the accomplishment of an end or the attainment of a goal (as, "military preparation does *lag* at a shameful rate"—*Carlyle;* the production of certain parts necessary for airplanes is *lagging*). **Loiter** implies delay while in progress, commonly while one is walking but sometimes while one is trying to accomplish a piece of work: it also suggests lingering or aimless sauntering, lagging, or the like. "Very little remained to be done. Catherine had not *loitered;* she was almost dressed, and her packing almost finished" (*Austen*). "The caravan has to go on; to *loiter* at any distance behind is to court extinction" (*C. E. Montague*). "The children sauntered down Sloane Street, *loitering* at the closed shop windows, clinking their shillings in their pockets" (*R. Macaulay*). **Dawdle** carries a slighter implication of delay in progress (especially in walking) than *loiter* but an even stronger connotation of idleness, aimlessness, or of a wandering mind; consequently, it usually implies a wasting of time or a taking of more time than is warranted; as, to *dawdle* through four years of college; the new servant *dawdles* over her work; "I did not hurry the rest of the way home; but neither did I *dawdle*" (*V. Heiser*). **Dally** and, now more often, **dillydally** imply dawdling, but they often also suggest wasting time in trifling, pottering, or foolish employments, or in hesitation or vacillation; as, "[He postponed] his return till the next day. Lucy was his. It was...sweet to *dally* with the delight of seeing her" (*Meredith*); "lest when he find me *dallying* along...he may hurry ahead" (*Irving*); "What you do, sir, do; don't stand *dilly-dallying*" (*Richardson*); "There is no time to *dilly-dally* in our work" (*Stevenson*).

Ana. Linger, tarry, wait (see STAY): *hesitate, falter, vacillate, waver.

Ant. Hasten, hurry.

dele. Delete, cancel, efface, obliterate, blot out, expunge, *erase.

Ana. See those at DELETE.

delectable. *Delightful, delicious, luscious.

Ana. Gratifying, grateful, agreeable, pleasing, welcome, *pleasant: exquisite, rare, delicate, dainty, *choice: *palatable, savory, sapid, saporous, toothsome.

Con. *Offensive, repulsive, revolting, loathsome: repellent, *repugnant, distasteful, abhorrent, obnoxious.

delectation. Enjoyment, delight, *pleasure, joy, fruition.

Ana. Amusement, diversion, entertainment (see under AMUSE): gratifying *or* gratification, regaling *or* regalement (see corresponding verbs at PLEASE).

delete. Dele, cancel, efface, obliterate, blot out, expunge, *erase.

Ana. Eliminate, *exclude, rule out: omit (see NEGLECT, *v.*).

deleterious. Detrimental, *pernicious, baneful, noxious.

Ana. Injuring *or* injurious, harming *or* harmful, hurting *or* hurtful (see corresponding verbs at INJURE): destroying *or* destructive (see corresponding verb DESTROY): ruining *or* ruinous (see corresponding verb RUIN).

Ant. Salutary. — ***Con.*** *Beneficial, advantageous, profitable: wholesome, *healthful, healthy.

deliberate, *adj.* **1** Willful, intentional, *voluntary, willing.

Ana. Purposed, intended (see INTEND): conscious, cognizant, *aware: mortal, *deadly.

Ant. Impulsive. — ***Con.*** Inadvertent, *careless, heedless, thoughtless.

2 Deliberate, considered, advised, premeditated, designed, studied come into comparison when applied to a person's acts, words, or accomplishments and agree in meaning thought out in advance. **Deliberate** implies full awareness of the nature of what one says or does, and, in very precise use, a careful and unhurried calculation of the intended effect or of the probable consequences; as, a *deliberate* lie; a *deliberate* snub. "Poe's consummate and *deliberate* technique" (*Lowes*). "The *deliberate* insertion into a lyrical context of pieces of slang and 'prosaic' words" (*Day Lewis*). "The tone of most comment, whether casual or *deliberate,* implies that ineptitude and inadequacy are the chief characteristics of government" (*Frankfurter*). **Considered,** unlike *deliberate,* which it closely resembles in meaning, is seldom applied to questionable acts or practices; it suggests careful study from all angles rather than calculation, and often, therefore, connotes soundness or maturity of judgment; as, there was no time for a *considered* reply; the committee had before it many half-baked and a few *considered* proposals. **Advised** is seldom used in its adjectival form (except in combination, as ill-*advised*), but its adverbial derivative *advisedly* is commonly selected by those who wish a word to carry the implications of *considered* (which has no adverb). Derived from an obsolete meaning of the verb *advise,* "to think through" (found also in *advisement,* which is equivalent to *consideration*), both adjective and adverb sometimes distinctively suggest an awareness of objections; as, he told them he used the offending word *advisedly;* everything in this difficult situation has been done *advisedly.* **Premeditated** emphasizes forethought and planning but often falls far short of *deliberate* in implying careful calculation and awareness of consequences. It is applied chiefly, but not exclusively, to offenses which are heinous if not the result of impulse or passion; as, a *premeditated* murder; a *premeditated* insult. **Designed** and its adverb *designedly* are often applied to that which has the appearance of being accidental, spontaneous, or natural, but which is actually the result of intention; as, the *designed* failure of a project. "Useless to seek to know whether he has been for years overlooked, or always *designedly* held prisoner" (*Dickens*). **Studied** is applied chiefly to effects gained or qualities achieved as a result of painstaking effort or careful attention to detail; it connotes absence of spontaneity; as, a *studied* performance of a Beethoven symphony. "The *studied* dignity and anxious courtesy of the actor-manager" (*Shaw*). It is also applied to offensive acts, committed with cool deliberation and with attention to its probable effect; as, to treat the opposition with *studied* discourtesy.

Ana. Planned, schemed, projected (see corresponding verbs under PLAN, *n.*): calculated (see CALCULATE): *careful, meticulous, scrupulous.

Ant. Casual. — ***Con.*** Haphazard, *random, hit-or-miss, desultory, happy-go-lucky, chance, chancy.

3 Leisurely, *slow, dilatory, laggard.

Ana. *Cautious, circumspect, wary, chary, calculating: *cool, collected, composed, imperturbable.

Ant. Precipitate, abrupt. — ***Con.*** Impetuous, headlong, sudden, hasty (see PRECIPITATE).

deliberate, *v.* Reflect, cogitate, *think, reason, speculate.

Ana. *Ponder, meditate, ruminate, muse.

delicate. Exquisite, dainty, rare, *choice, recherché, elegant.

Ana. Delectable, *delightful, delicious: *soft, gentle, mild, lenient, balmy: ethereal, *airy, aerial.

Ant. Gross. — ***Con.*** *Coarse, vulgar: rank, rancid, *malodorous.

delicious. Delectable, luscious, *delightful.

Ana. *Palatable, sapid, saporous, savory, toothsome, appetizing: delicate, dainty, exquisite, *choice, rare.

Ant. Bitter. — ***Con.*** Distasteful, obnoxious, *repugnant, repellent: *insipid, vapid, flat, wishy-washy, inane, jejune, banal.

delight, *n.* *Pleasure, delectation, enjoyment, joy, fruition.
Ana. Glee, *mirth, jollity, hilarity: rapture, transport, *ecstasy: satisfaction, contentment (see corresponding verbs at SATISFY).
Ant. Disappointment: discontent.

delight, *v.* Gratify, *please, rejoice, gladden, tickle, arride, regale.
Ana. *Satisfy, content: divert, *amuse, entertain: charm, enchant, fascinate, allure, *attract, take.
Ant. Distress: bore. — *Con.* *Trouble: *afflict, try: *grieve: *annoy, vex, irk, bother.

delightful. **Delightful, delicious, delectable, luscious** agree in meaning extremely pleasing or gratifying to one's senses or aesthetic taste. **Delightful,** the least restricted in its application of these words, is referable to anything that affords keen, lively pleasure and stirs the emotions agreeably, whether the direct appeal is to the mind, the heart, or the senses; as, a *delightful* prospect; a *delightful* talk; a *delightful* companion. "My ears were never better fed With such *delightful* pleasing harmony" (*Shak.*). "The experience of overcoming fear is extraordinarily *delightful*" (*B. Russell*). **Delicious,** in current colloquial usage, commonly refers to sensuous pleasures, especially those of taste and smell (as, *delicious* food, fragrance, sense of warmth), but in literary usage the term is applicable to anything which is so delightful that one dwells upon it with sensuous gratification; as, "her gestures *delicious* in their modest and sensitive grace" (*Bennett*); "I am not staying here, but with the Blenkers, in their *delicious* solitude at Portsmouth" (*E. Wharton*); "There are people whose society I find *delicious*" (*L. P. Smith*). **Delectable** is used chiefly in poetry or elevated prose; in its implications it is often indistinguishable from *delightful*, and especially from *delicious*, though it often suggests more refined or discriminating enjoyment; as, "The trees of God, *Delectable* both to behold and taste" (*Milton*); a *delectable* tale; the *delectable* fragrance of freesia. The term is more often used than either *delightful* or *delicious* with a humorous or ironical connotation; as, "the spoken word of some *delectable* Sarah Gamp" (*C. E. Montague*). **Luscious** adds to *delicious* an implication of richness as of flavor, of fragrance, of coloring, of sound, and the like; specifically, as applied to fruits, it suggests flavor and juiciness; as, *luscious* peaches; *luscious* roses; *luscious* music. Like *delectable* it is often used humorously or ironically, but it then in addition commonly implies extravagance, exaggeration, or more specifically, voluptuousness; as, *luscious* passages of description; "those Don Juans, those melting beauties...those *luscious* adventuresses" (*A. Huxley*).
Ana. Enchanting, charming, fascinating, taking, alluring, attractive (see under ATTRACT): lovely, fair, *beautiful: ineffable (see UNUTTERABLE).
Ant. Distressing: boring: horrid. — *Con.* *Miserable, wretched: distasteful, obnoxious, repellent, *repugnant.

delineate. Trace, outline, *sketch, diagram, draft, plot, blueprint.
Ana. Describe, *relate: design, plan (see under PLAN, *n.*).

delineation. Tracing, outline, sketch, diagram, plot, blueprint. See under SKETCH, *v.*
Ana. Map, *chart, graph: design, *plan.

deliquesce. *Liquefy, melt, dissolve, fuse, thaw.
Ana. *Decay, decompose, disintegrate.

delirium. Frenzy, hysteria, *mania.

deliver. 1 *Free, release, liberate, discharge, emancipate, manumit, enfranchise, affranchise.
Ana. *Escape, elude, evade: *extricate, disencumber, disentangle: voice, utter, vent, *express.
Con. Confine, circumscribe, restrict, *limit.
2 *Rescue, redeem, save, ransom, reclaim.
Con. *Imprison, incarcerate, jail, immure, intern: *catch, capture, nab, cop, trap, snare, entrap, ensnare.

deliverance. **Deliverance, delivery** are distinguished in current good use. **Deliverance** more commonly refers to the state or fact of being delivered, or of being freed from, restraint, captivity, peril, or the like. "We have... *deliverance* found Unlooked for, life preserved and peace restored" (*Cowper*). "It [Independence Day] ought to be commemorated as the day of *deliverance*" (*John Adams*). **Delivery** applies more commonly to the act of delivering from restraint, captivity, peril, or the like; as, the *delivery* of the prisoners in the Bastille; to effect the *delivery* of a captive (see also CHILDBIRTH). "He...swore, with sobs, That he would labor my *delivery*" (*Shak.*). *Delivery*, but not *deliverance*, is used when the transfer or conveyance of something is implied; as, the store promises prompt *delivery* of purchases; trucks for the *delivery* of mail; the *delivery* of a fort to the conquerors.
Ana. Freedom, independence, autonomy (see under FREE, *adj.*): *freedom, liberty, license: redeeming *or* redemption, rescuing *or* rescue, reclaiming *or* reclamation, saving *or* salvation (see corresponding verbs at RESCUE).

delivery. 1 *Deliverance.
Ana. Releasing *or* release, liberating *or* liberation, freeing (see corresponding verbs at FREE): conveying *or* conveyance, transmitting *or* transmission, transporting *or* transportation, carrying *or* carriage (see corresponding verbs at CARRY): voicing, venting, utterance, expression (see corresponding verbs at EXPRESS).
2 Accouchement, *childbirth, parturition, labor, travail.

delude. Beguile, *deceive, mislead, betray, double-cross.
Ana. *Dupe, gull, hoodwink, befool, bamboozle, hoax, trick: *cheat, cozen, overreach.
Ant. Enlighten.

delusion. **Delusion, illusion, hallucination, mirage** come into comparison when they denote something which is believed to be or is accepted as being true or real, but which is actually false or unreal. **Delusion,** in general, implies self-deception or deception by others; it may connote a disordered state of mind, extreme gullibility, or merely an inability to distinguish between what only seems to be, and what actually is, true or real; as, to suffer from *delusions* of persecution. "He recovered consciousness slowly, unwilling to let go of a pleasing *delusion* that he was in Rome" (*Cather*). "Old Nuflo, lately so miserable, now happy in his *delusions*" (*Hudson*). "She laboured under the *delusion* that the constitution and social condition of her country were...on the upward plane" (*R. Macaulay*). **Illusion** seldom implies mental derangement or even the inability to distinguish between the true and the false; rather it implies an ascription of truth or reality to that which only seems to be true or real, as to the eyes (as, an optical *illusion*), or to the imagination (as, artistic *illusion*), or to one's mind as influenced by one's feelings or sentiments (as, a lover's *illusions*). "During a quake, when I used to...observe the houses swaying toward one another, I would have the *illusion* that they were actually bumping heads" (*V. Heiser*). "Nature, we know, first taught the architect to produce by long colonnades the *illusion* of distance" (*Hudson*). "If you have built up an immunity against the *illusion* that you know the whole truth" (*Lippmann*). **Hallucination** implies the perception of objects or, less often, of conditions, which have no reality but are merely the product of disordered nerves, of mental derangement, of delirium tremens, or the like; as, the burglar in her room was only a *hallucination;* to suffer from the *hallucination* that one is being pursued. **Mirage**

comes into comparison with the preceding terms only in its extended sense. Literally, it denotes an optical illusion whereby, owing to atmospheric conditions, something that is not actually present at the point where it is observed, and often is not even within the range of one's vision, is seen, not in its reality but in its (usually inverted or distorted) reflection; thus, a seeming pool of water on a highway on a hot day is a *mirage* in which, across a stratum of hot air, the traveler sees a reflection of the sky on the pavement. In its extended sense, *mirage* usually applies to a vision, dream, hope, or the like, which one takes as a guide, not realizing that it is merely an illusion. "This hope to find your people...is a *mirage*, a *delusion*, which will lead to destruction if you will not abandon it" (*Hudson*).

Ana. *Deception, trickery, chicane, chicanery, subterfuge: *imposture, simulacrum, counterfeit, cheat, fraud, sham, fake, humbug, deceit: fantasy, vision, dream, daydream, *fancy.

delusive, delusory. Deceptive, *misleading.

Ana. Fantastic, chimerical, visionary, *imaginary, fanciful, quixotic: fallacious, sophistical, casuistical (see under FALLACY): illusory, seeming, ostensible, *apparent.

☞ *Do not confuse* delusive *with* elusive *and* illusive, *or* delusory *with* illusory.

delve. *Dig, spade, grub, excavate, exhume, disinter.

demand, *v.* **Demand, claim, require, exact** come into comparison not as close synonyms but as carrying in common the basic meaning to ask or call for something as due or as necessary, or as strongly desired. **Demand** carries a strong implication of peremptoriness or insistency; if the subject is a person (or sometimes an expression of his will, such as a law), it usually implies that he possesses, or believes he possesses, the right or the authority not only to issue a peremptory request but also to expect its being regarded as a command; as, the physician *demanded* payment of his bill; the court *demands* fair treatment of the accused by the prosecutor; the father *demanded* knowledge of what had occurred during his absence from home. "Can he [the keeper of a public record] refuse a copy thereof to a person *demanding* it on the terms prescribed by law?" (*Ch. Just. Marshall*). "Instincts which the conventions of good manners and the imperatives of morality *demand* that they should repress" (*A. Huxley*). If the subject of the verb is a thing, the verb implies the call of necessity, of imperative need, or the like; as, "the fire that the cool evenings of early spring *demanded*" (*M. Austin*); "The mind and body of a child *demand* a great deal of play" (*B. Russell*); "He is best in his plays when dealing with situations which do not *demand* great emotional concentration" (*T. S. Eliot*). **Claim** implies a demanding either the delivery or concession of something due one as one's own, one's right, one's prerogative, or the like, or the admission or recognition of something which one asserts or affirms; thus, one who *claims* a piece of property *demands* its delivery to him as his own; one who *claims* that he has solved a problem *demands* recognition of the truth of his assertion. "Surely I divide your grief, and may I not *claim* your confidence?" (*Meredith*). "There is no right to freedom or life. But each man does *claim* such freedom" (*S. Alexander*). "Scientific men, and many others who cannot *claim* to be men of science" (*Inge*). "I am not *claiming* a direct influence of Rousseau upon Wagner" (*Babbitt*). **Require** is often used interchangeably with *demand*, but in precise English it usually distinctively implies imperativeness such as arises from inner necessity (as, "consecutive thinking absolutely *requires* personal initiative"—*C. W. Eliot*), or the compulsion of law or regulation (as, to *require* that every member of the bank's staff be bonded), or the exigencies of the situation (as, "I shall not go away till you have given me the assurance I *require*"—*Austen*). **Exact** implies not only demanding something but getting that which one demands; as, to *exact* payment of overdue rent; to *exact* a promise from a friend. "She...kept a keen eye on her Court, and *exacted* prompt and willing obedience from king and archbishops" (*H. Adams*). "Some [occupations] *exact* little of the mind, but much of the eye" (*Grandgent*).

Ana. Request, *ask, solicit: order, *command, charge enjoin, direct, bid: call, *summon, cite.

Con. Waive, resign, *relinquish: concede, allow, *grant.

demean.[1] *Abase, degrade, debase, humble, humiliate.

Con. Heighten, enhance (see INTENSIFY): *exalt, magnify, aggrandize.

demean.[2] Deport, comport, *behave, conduct, acquit, quit.

Ana. *Carry, bear (*as reflexive verbs*).

Ant. Misdemean.

demeanor *or* **demeanour.** Deportment, *bearing, mien, manner, carriage, port, presence, front.

Ana. *Behavior, conduct, deportment: *posture, attitude, pose: air, mannerism, *pose, affectation.

demented. *Insane, mad, crazy, crazed, deranged, lunatic, maniac, wood, non compos mentis.

Ana. *Irrational, unreasonable: delirious, hysterical, frenzied (see corresponding nouns at MANIA).

Ant. Rational.

dementia. *Insanity, lunacy, mania, psychosis.

Ana. *Mania, delirium, hysteria, frenzy.

demise. *Death, decease, passing.

demit. *Abdicate, resign, renounce.

Ana., Ant., & Con. See those at ABDICATE.

demolish. *Destroy, raze.

Ana. Wreck, *ruin, wrack, dilapidate: devastate, *ravage, waste, sack.

Ant. Construct.

demon, *n.* **Demon, daemon, devil, fiend** have all been used to designate an evil spirit that leads human beings astray, and have therefore been employed even by good writers without discrimination. Both **demon** and **daemon** go back etymologically to a Greek word [*daimōn*] meaning a spirit or inferior divinity. In some Greek writings the term is used without clear distinction from *god*. Both Jewish and early Christian writers used this Greek word in the sense of *idol, false god*, or *unclean spirit*, and were more or less responsible for its confusion with another Greek word [*diabolos*, the slanderer] which properly applies to the Devil, or the tempter of man and adversary of God. In good current use, *demon* consistently applies to an evil spirit (or in extended use, an evil person) that seeks the ruin of men's souls. *Daemon* has for centuries been used as a variant spelling of *demon*. During this time, however, it was also employed by learned men in a sense closer to that of the Greek original or to another allied word [*daimonion*] which means a tutelary spirit, sometimes thought of as attendant upon the individual, sometimes as indwelling in him. In recent precise use, this distinction has been sharpened, so that *demon* is now employed by careful writers only in its derived sense of an evil spirit, and *daemon* in one of its historical senses or in the derived sense of genius, or inner controlling spirit supplying driving energy or creative power. "O Antony, stay not by his side: Thy *daemon* [First Folio spelling], that's thy spirit which keeps thee, is Noble, courageous, high, unmatchable, Where Caesar's is not" (*Shak.*). "If that same *demon* [First Folio *Daemon*] that hath gull'd thee thus Should with his lion gait walk the whole world, He might return... And tell the legions 'I can never win A soul so easy as that Englishman's'" (*Shak.*). "The *Demon* of Discord, with her sooty wings, had breathed her influence upon our counsels" (*Smollett*). "When your *Daemon* is in charge, do not try to think consciously. Drift, wait, and obey" (*Kipling*). **Devil** in earliest usage applied to the spirit of evil or the tempter of men, as conceived in Jewish and Christian theology, and usually called Satan, but sometimes called by any one of a number of names such as Lucifer, Beelzebub, Mephistopheles, the Prince of Darkness, or, colloquially, the Old Boy, the Old One, Old Harry, Old Nick, Old Poker, Old Scratch, and Scottish, Clootie, or Old Clootie. Though properly capitalized and applied to one being (as, to sell one's soul to the *Devil*), the term was used by some Biblical translators (especially those who made the Authorized Version) as the equivalent of the Greek *daimon* (or the Latin *daemon*) and so occurs without a capital as an equivalent of *demon* or in the sense of an unclean indwelling spirit; as, to cast out *devils;* possessed by a *devil;* pursued by *devils.* **Fiend** (etymologically, an enemy or foe) was in early use applied (as was the word *enemy* itself) to the Devil, conceived as the archenemy of mankind: it was also applied to any evil spirit, or demon, conceived of as maliciously plotting or bringing about the ruin of men. With this word especially, but far from exclusively, are associated many of the characteristics or outward aspects of the Devil or of devils as conceived by the popular mind; as, "Inflam'd with rage like *fiends* in hell" (*J. Wesley*); "a frightful *fiend* Doth close behind him tread" (*Coleridge*).

Ant. Angel. — ***Con.*** Archangel, cherub, seraph (see ANGEL).

demoniac, demoniacal, demonic. Diabolic, diabolical, *fiendish, devilish.

Ana. Hellish, *infernal: crazed, crazy, maniac, *insane: inspired, fired (see INFORM).

Con. *Celestial, heavenly.

demonstrate. 1 Manifest, evince, *show, evidence.

Ana. *Reveal, disclose, discover, betray, bewray: display, exhibit, parade, flaunt, expose, *show.

Con. *Hide, conceal, secrete: dissemble, cloak, mask, *disguise.

2 *Prove, try, test.

Ana. *Argue, debate (see DISCUSS): substantiate, verify, authenticate, *confirm, corroborate, validate.

demonstration. Proof, trial, test. See under PROVE.

Ana. Substantiation, confirming *or* confirmation, corroboration, verification (see corresponding verbs at CONFIRM): experiment, *experience.

demulcent. Emollient, *balm, salve.

demur, *v.* **Demur, scruple, balk, jib** (*or* **gib**), **shy, boggle, stick, stickle, strain** are comparable when they mean to hesitate or show reluctance because of difficulties in the way. One **demurs** *to* (or *at,* rarely *on*) something when one raises objections to it, casts doubt upon it, or takes exception to it, thereby interposing obstacles which delay action, procedure, decision, or the like; as, many an opportunity is lost by *demurring.* In older use, the stress was on delay, as it still is in the term *demurrage.* "Notwithstanding he hoped that matters would have been long since brought to an issue, the fair one still *demurs*" (*Spectator*). In modern use, the emphasis is commonly on objection, as it is also in the legal term *demurrer.* "Jerry ...proposed that...we stretch a point by going to supper at Reeves's. Sarah and I *demurred* as women will at such a proposal from a man whose family exigencies are known to them" (*M. Austin*). "It would seem hazardous to *demur* to a proposition which is so widely accepted" (*S. Alexander*). One **scruples** *to do* something (or, now rarely, *at* something) when one is reluctant because one's conscience bothers or because one is doubtful of the propriety, expediency, or morality of the action; the word is increasingly common in a negative construction; as, to *scruple* to accept any gift that might seem a bribe; "he does not *scruple* to ask the most abominable things of you" (*Meredith*). "Greece and in particular Athens was overrun by philosophers, who...did not *scruple* to question the foundations of social and moral obligation" (*G. L. Dickinson*). One **balks** (oftentimes *at* something) when one stops short and obstinately refuses to go further in one's course because one has reached the limit of one's strength, one's courage, one's credulity, one's tolerance, or the like; as, the horse *balked* at the leap; he never *balks* at any task no matter how difficult it is. "There is the opposite case of the man who yields his poetic faith too readily, who does not *balk* at any improbability" (*Babbitt*). "One rather *balks* at the idea of synthetic roughage—excelsior, wood chips, or whatever may be at hand" (*C. C. Furnas*). One **jibs,** or less often, **gibs** (oftentimes *at* something) when one balks like a horse and backs away or out. "I had settled to finish the review, when, behold...I *jibb'd*" (*Scott*). "When Charnacé spoke of stopping the Polish war, he [Brandenburg] was all in favour, but he *jibbed* at alliance with the Catholic League" (*Belloc*). "His soldiers, many of whom had served with Antony, *jibbed* at the attack on their old leader" (*Buchan*). One **shies** *at, away from, off from* something when, like a suddenly frightened horse, one recoils in alarm, or distaste, or suspicion and is unable to proceed, act, and the like; as, to *shy* at the sight of blood. "These turns of speech may as yet be called slang; but they have the old virtue in them; you see the old temperament of the race still evincing itself; still *shying* away from the long abstract word" (*C. E. Montague*). One **boggles** *at, over, about* something from which one by temperament, instinct, or training shies away. In addition, *boggle* often implies scrupling or fussing. "When a native begins perjury he perjures himself thoroughly. He does not *boggle* over details" (*Kipling*). "We [lovers of poetry] do not *balk* at the sea-wave washing the rim of the sun, which we know it does not do, any more than we *boggle* at blackberries that are red when they are green" (*Lowes*). "It [pleasure at election to certain societies at Harvard] was in the essence a snobbish pleasure; why should I *boggle* at the word?" (*L. P. Smith*). One **sticks** *at* something to which one demurs because of scruples, especially scruples of conscience; the term is used chiefly in the phrase "he *sticks* at nothing," which is another way of saying he is absolutely unscrupulous. One **stickles** *at, about, over* something to which one demurs or raises objections because it is offensive, distasteful, contrary to one's principles, or the like; as, the purist *stickles* at using clipped words such as gas for gasoline, phone for telephone, exam for examination; there is no time in a serious emergency to *stickle* over means if they achieve the desired ends. One **strains** *at* something (sometimes *to do* something) when one demurs to it as beyond one's power to believe, accept, understand, do, or the like. This usage is chiefly dependent on the scriptural passage "Ye blind guides, which *strain* at [D.V. & R.V. *strain out*] a gnat, and swallow a camel" (*Matthew* xxiii. 24). In extended use, the object of *at* or of *to do* is commonly something which might without real difficulty be believed, accepted, understood, done, or the like; as, persons who *strain* at the truth yet accept every wild rumor without question. "I do not *strain* at the position,— It is familiar,—but at the author's drift" (*Shak.*).

Ana. *Hesitate, falter, vacillate, waver: *oppose, resist, combat: *object, remonstrate: *disapprove, deprecate.
Ant. Accede. — *Con.* Accept, admit, *receive, take: acquiesce, agree, *assent, consent, subscribe.

demur, *n.* *Qualm, compunction, scruple.
Ana. *Hesitation, hesitancy: reluctance, loathness, aversion, disinclination (see corresponding adjectives at DISINCLINED): objection, remonstrance (see corresponding verbs at OBJECT).
Con. Readiness, promptness, quickness (see corresponding adjectives at QUICK).

demure. Proper, nice, *decorous, decent, seemly, comme il faut.
Ana. Grave, solemn, *serious, sedate, staid, earnest, sober: modest, coy, diffident, bashful, *shy.
Ant. Jaunty. — *Con.* Brazen, brash, impudent, *shameless, barefaced: wanton, mischievous, impish, roguish (see PLAYFUL).

denizen. *Inhabitant, resident, citizen.

denomination. 1 *Name, designation, appellation, title, style.
2 Sect, communion, *religion, faith, creed, cult, persuasion, church.

denotation. Connotation (see under DENOTE).
Ana. *Meaning, signification, significance, sense, acceptation, import.

denote. 1 Signify, *mean, import.
Ana. Betoken, bespeak, *indicate, attest, argue, prove: *intend, mean: *suggest, imply, hint, intimate, insinuate.
2 **Denote, connote** and their corresponding nouns **denotation, connotation** bear a complementary rather than a synonymous relation to each other. Taken together, the verbs as used in reference to terms equal *mean* (see MEAN, *v.*, 2). Taken singly, a term **denotes** that which is expressed in its definition, as in a noun the thing which it names, in a verb the act or state which is affirmed (thus, "plant" *denotes* a living thing which is rooted, usually, in the earth); a term **connotes** any or all of the ideas or emotions that are added to it and cling to it, often as a result of experience but sometimes as a result of something extraneous, such as a great poet's effective use of the term, or its constant association with another term or idea, or a connection between it and some historical event; thus, "home" *denotes* the place where one lives with one's family, but it *connotes* comforts, intimacy, and privacy. What a term *denotes* (or the *denotation* of a term) can be definitely fixed; what a term *connotes* (or its *connotation*) often depends upon the background of the person using it. "I have used the term 'post-war poets' to *denote* those who did not begin to write verse till after the war" (*Day Lewis*). "There is no word that has more sinister and terrible *connotations* in our snobbish society than the word promiscuity" (*Shaw*).

In logic, *denote* and *connote*, though still complementary and still predicated of terms, carry very different implications. They are dependent on two highly technical terms, both collective nouns, *denotation* and *connotation*. A term *denotes* (or bears as *denotation*) the entire number of things or instances covered by it; as, "plant" *denotes* the aggregate of all things that come under the definition of that word; the *denotation* of "plant" is far more inclusive than the *denotation* of "shrub." A term *connotes* (or bears as *connotation*) the sum total of the qualities or characteristics that are implied by it and are necessarily or commonly associated with it; as, "plant" *connotes* (or bears as *connotation*) life, growth and decay, lack of power of locomotion, and, commonly, roots and cellular structure invested with a cellulose wall.

☞ *In this book* denote *and* connote, denotation *and* connotation, *are used with the meanings discussed in the first paragraph above, unless otherwise specified.*

denounce. Condemn, censure, reprobate, reprehend, blame, *criticize.
Ana. *Accuse, charge, arraign, impeach, incriminate, criminate, indict: *decry, disparage, depreciate: revile, vituperate (see SCOLD).
Ant. Eulogize. — *Con.* *Commend, applaud, compliment, recommend: *praise, extol, laud, acclaim.

dense. 1 Compact, *close, thick.
Ana. Consolidated, concentrated, compacted (see COMPACT, *v.*): compressed, condensed (see CONTRACT, *v.*): massed, heaped, piled, stacked (see HEAP, *v.*).
Ant. Sparse (*of population, forests, etc.*): tenuous (*of clouds, air, masses, etc.*). — *Con.* Scattered, dispersed, dissipated (see SCATTER): *thin, rare: *meager, scanty, scant, exiguous.
2 Crass, *stupid, dull, dumb.
Ana. Obtuse, *dull: stolid, phlegmatic, *impassive.
Ant. Subtle: bright. — *Con.* *Intelligent, brilliant, clever, alert, quick-witted.

dent, *n.* **Dent, dint, indentation, indenture, nick, notch** agree in meaning a depression or recess made by or as if by a blow or incision. *Dent* and *dint* apply chiefly to surfaces; *indentation, nick,* and *notch* more frequently to edges. **Dent** and **dint** (the latter now chiefly literary and more expressive of violence in impact) refer to a depression made, especially in metal, by a blow; as, a *dent* in a teakettle; a *dent* in an automobile fender; "Every *dint* a sword had beaten in it [a shield]" (*Tennyson*). An **indentation** or, less often, an **indenture,** is a toothlike or angular recess or incision made by nature or by artifice; as, the *indentations* of a leaf, of a coastline; through *indentations*, the beginnings of the paragraphs are indicated; "This noble lake...spreads...around the *indentures* and promontories of a fair and fertile land" (*Scott*). **Nick** and **notch** carry a stronger implication of the removal of a part than *indentation; nick* usually suggests a slighter indentation (often the result of accidental chipping or breaking) than *notch*, which commonly implies deliberate cutting; as, a *nick* in a teacup, in a knife blade; the *notch* of an arrow; to cut *notches* in a stick.
Con. *Projection, protuberance, bulge, protrusion.

denude. Bare, *strip, divest, dismantle.
Ant. Clothe.

deny. **Deny, gainsay, contradict, negative, traverse, impugn, contravene** come into comparison as meaning, when they refer to an act, to declare something untrue, untenable, or unworthy of consideration or, when they refer to a condition, to go counter to that which is true or to the facts as they are. **Deny** (etymologically, to say no) commonly implies a refusal, usually an outspoken refusal, to accept as true (as, to *deny* the report that the British ambassador has resigned; "He is no vulgar and stupid cynic who *denies* the existence...of any feelings higher than the merely physical"—*A. Huxley*), or to grant or concede (as, to *deny* citizenship to certain applicants; to *deny* a request for more books; "For he's a jolly good fellow, which nobody can *deny!*"), or to own or acknowledge the existence or the claims of (as, "the necessities of his own life...not any longer to be *denied*" —*M. Austin;* "It would seem that I was *denying* God"—*Meredith*). In the reflexive form, *deny* usually implies abstinence or renunciation often, but not necessarily, for religious or moral reasons; as, she *denied* herself all luxuries; to *deny* oneself to visitors; he resolved to *deny* himself the pleasure of smoking (cf. self-*denial*). **Gainsay** (etymologically, to say against) is now chiefly a literary term: it implies opposition, usually by way of disputing the truth of what another has said; as, facts which cannot be *gainsaid;* "But she's a fine woman—that nobody can *gainsay*" (*Meredith*); "His mother, whom he could not *gainsay*, was unconsciously but inflexibly set against his genius" (*Van W. Brooks*). **Contradict** (also, etymologically, to say or speak against) differs from *gainsay* not only in usually implying a more open or a flatter denial of the truth of an assertion, but also in commonly suggesting that the contrary is true or that the statement is utterly devoid of truth; thus, "to *contradict* a rumor" is a stronger expression than "to *deny* a rumor"; one may *contradict* (never in this sense *deny*) a person, whereas one may *deny* or *contradict* (the stronger term) an assertion of his. "A report which highly incensed Mrs. Bennet, and which she never failed to *contradict* as a most scandalous falsehood" (*Austen*). " 'Nobody *contradicts* me now,' wrote Queen Victoria after her husband's death, 'and the salt has gone out of my life.' " (*H. Ellis*). *Contradict* is also used without implication of a spoken or written denial: it then suggests that an assertion, a doctrine, a teaching, or the like, runs counter to something else, and therefore it cannot be true (as, "All the protestations of the employers that they would be ruined by the Factory Acts were *contradicted* by experience"—*Shaw*) or if it be true, the other must be false, or vice versa (as, "they insisted on teaching and enforcing an ideal that *contradicted* the realities"—*H. Adams*). **Negative** is usually a much milder term than those which precede: often it implies merely a refusal to assent to a suggestion, a proposition, a nomination, a bill, or the like; as, the senate *negatived* the proposed taxation; "after a polite request that Elizabeth would lead the way, which the other as politely...*negatived*" (*Austen*); "Beaufort stood, hat in hand, saying something which his companion seemed to *negative*" (*E. Wharton*). When the idea of going counter to is uppermost, *negative* usually implies disproof; as, "The omission or infrequency of such recitals does not *negative* the existence of miracles" (*W. Paley*). **Traverse,** as here considered, is chiefly a legal term implying a formal denial, especially of the truth of an allegation (as, to *traverse* a fact as alleged) or of the justice of an indictment (as, to *traverse* an indictment). **Impugn** (etymologically, to attack or assail) retains its basic implication so markedly that it carries the strongest suggestion of any of these terms of directly disputing or questioning or of forcefully contradicting (a statement, proposition, etc., or, less often, a person): it sometimes connotes prolonged argument in an attempt to refute or confute; as, "The idealists... took up the challenge, but their reply was to disparage the significance, and even to *impugn* the reality, of the world as known to science" (*Inge*); " 'The morality of our Restoration drama cannot be *impugned.* It assumes orthodox Christian morality, and laughs (in its comedy) at human nature for not living up to it' " (*T. S. Eliot*); "No one cares to *impugn* a fool; no one dares to *impugn* a captain of industry" (*Van W. Brooks*). **Contravene** (etymologically, to come against), in the sense here considered, carries a weaker implication of intentional opposition or running counter to, but a stronger implication of coming into conflict with, than any of the preceding terms: when it implies what in effect amounts to a denial or a contradiction it often, but not always, suggests an inherent and often unforeseen incompatibility between what is said, taught, or, in law, done, and things as they are; as, "A proposition...not likely to be *contravened*" (*Southey*); "the public force will be brought to bear upon those who do things said to *contravene* it [a legal right]" (*Justice Holmes*); "he [Mark Twain] could not strike out in any direction without wounding his wife or his friends, without *contravening* some loyalty that had become sacred to him" (*Van W. Brooks*).

Ana. *Decline, refuse, reject, repudiate: controvert, refute, rebut, confute, *disprove.

Ant. Concede. — ***Con.*** Aver, affirm, *assert: *acknowledge.

depart. **1** Leave, withdraw, retire, *go, quit, scram, clear out.

Ant. Arrive: remain, abide. — ***Con.*** *Stay, tarry, linger, wait: *come.

2 Digress, deviate, *swerve, diverge, veer.

Ana. Forsake, *abandon, desert: reject, repudiate (see DECLINE, *v.*): *discard, cast.

departed. Deceased, late, *dead, defunct, lifeless, inanimate.

depend. *Rely, trust, count, reckon, bank.

Ana. Lean, incline (see SLANT, *v.*).

dependable. *Reliable, trustworthy, trusty, tried.

Ana. Sure, assured, *confident: *responsible: authoritative (see DICTATORIAL): stanch, steadfast, constant, *faithful.

Con. *Doubtful, questionable, dubious: capricious, fickle, unstable, *inconstant, mercurial.

dependence. **1** Reliance, *trust, confidence, faith.

2 *Annex, extension, wing, ell.

dependency. *Possession, colony, protectorate, territory, dominion, mandate.

dependent, *adj.* **1 Dependent, contingent, conditional, relative, adjective** are close synonyms when they mean having its existence or nature determined by something else. All of these terms are used in philosophy, some in law, but only the first four are found (often with a weakening of the sense) in general use. That is **dependent** which cannot exist or come into existence by itself. In philosophy, and often in ordinary language, nothing escapes this description except that which is, in the strict sense of each of these words, absolute, infinite, or original. "We are all *dependent* on one another, every soul of us on earth" (*Shaw*). That is **contingent** which takes its character from something that already exists or may exist, and which, therefore, is limited or qualified by something extraneous or is incapable of existence apart from it; as, one's conception of love is *contingent* both on experience and on the nature of the experience. "If propriety should die, there could be no impropriety, inasmuch as the continuance of the latter is wholly *contingent* on the presence of the former" (*Grandgent*). That is **conditional** which depends for its realization, fulfillment, execution, expression, or the like, on what may or may not occur or on the performance or observance of certain terms or conditions. *Conditional* and *contingent* are often interchangeable but the former is preferred when eventualities are in the power of the human will; as, the pardon is *conditional* (better than *contingent*) on his behavior during probation. "There is not between women that fund of at least *conditional* loyalty which men may depend on in their dealings with each other" (*Conrad*). That is **relative** which cannot be known, considered, or determined apart from its reference to something else and which, therefore, is affected by the limitations, the instability, the imperfections, and the like, of the other thing; as, market values are always *relative* to the demand. "The idea of civilisation is *relative* ...any community and any age has its own civilisation and its own ideals of civilisation" (*H. Ellis*). That is **adjective** (chiefly in legal and technical use) which is not self-sufficient or self-contained but depends on something else for its fullness of existence or effectiveness; thus, *adjective* law (as opposed to *substantive* law) has nothing

to do with the conceptions of justice, rights, and obligations, but only with legal procedure; an *adjective* color, in dyeing, is one that requires the addition of a substance to fix it. "The women were treated on both sides as *adjective* beings" (*Grote*).
Ana. Subject, *liable, open, exposed, susceptible.
Ant. Absolute: infinite: original. — *Con.* *Ultimate, categorical: uncircumscribed, boundless, eternal, illimitable (see INFINITE): underived (see affirmative verb at SPRING).
2 Subject, tributary, *subordinate, succursal, secondary, collateral.
Ana. Relying (*on*), depending (*on*), trusting (*in* or *to*), reckoning (*on*), counting (*on*) (see RELY): subsidiary, subservient, *auxiliary: abased, humbled, debased (see ABASE).
Ant. Independent. — *Con.* *Self-reliant, reliant.

deplete, *v.* **Deplete, drain, exhaust, impoverish, bankrupt** are comparable especially in their extended senses when they mean to deprive a thing in whole or in part of that which is essential or necessary to its existence or potency. **Deplete** is often used as though it implied merely a reduction in numbers, in quantity, or the like; discriminating writers and speakers, however, employ it only when they wish to suggest the potential harm of such a reduction or the impossibility of restoring what has been lost before such consequences are evident; thus, bloodletting *depletes* the system, not only by reducing the quantity of blood but by depriving the system of elements essential to its vitality and vigor; an epidemic may be said to *deplete* an army when it reduces the army not only in size but in effective strength, especially at a time when that strength is needed. "He would have us fill up our *depleted* curriculum with subjects whose worth has not even been tried" (*Grandgent*). **Drain** is also a word subject to undiscriminating use; when precisely employed it retains its earliest implications of slow withdrawal of liquid as by straining, seepage, suction, or the like, until the substance which is drained becomes dry or the container which holds the liquid is emptied. Hence, in extended use, *drain* connotes a gradual depletion and ultimate deprivation of that which is figuratively the lifeblood of a thing or the sine qua non of its existence or well-being; as, the Thirty Years' War (1618–1648) nearly *drained* Germany of men and materials; the writer has treated this theme so many times that he has *drained* it of all interest to himself or his readers. "Their country's wealth our mightier misers *drain*" (*Pope*). **Exhaust,** as here compared (see also TIRE), is very close to *drain* in its extended sense but it stresses emptying or evacuation rather than disastrous depletion. That which is exhausted, such as the essential ingredients of a substance, the full possibilities of a subject for treatment, the nutritive elements of a soil, or the contents of a mine, although it deprives the substance, subject, soil, or mine of further value or possible use, is not itself useless but, more often than not, useful in another form; thus, one *exhausts* a subject who treats it so fully that nothing more can be said about it; one (in humorous use) *exhausts* the English language when he leaves no word that might express his idea unused; molasses is *exhausted* when no further sugar can be extracted from it. "The theme of mother and child has proved a theme which no age has ever *exhausted* or ever will *exhaust*" (*Binyon*). **Impoverish** implies a depletion or a draining of something as essential to a thing as money or its equivalent is to a human being; it stresses the deprivation of qualities essential to a thing's strength, richness, or productiveness; as, to *impoverish* the blood by too meager a diet; to *impoverish* the soil by planting year after year crops that are gross feeders; to *impoverish* one's mind by reading only light books. **Bankrupt** stresses such impoverishment of a thing that it is destitute of qualities essential to its continued existence or productiveness; it connotes a complete or imminent collapse or breaking down; as, to argue that science by inattention to immaterial phenomena is *bankrupting* itself. "Dainty bits Make rich the ribs, but *bankrupt* quite the wits" (*Shak.*).
Ana. Undermine, sap, debilitate, *weaken, enfeeble, cripple, disable: reduce, diminish, *decrease, lessen.
Con. Augment, *increase, enlarge.

deplore. Deplore, lament, bewail, bemoan agree in meaning to manifest grief or sorrow for something. All carry an implication of weeping or crying, but in modern usage this is more or less figurative. **Deplore** implies keen and profound regret, especially for that which is regarded as irreparable, calamitous, or destructive of something good or worth keeping; as, "Ev'n rival wits did Voiture's death *deplore*" (*Pope*); to *deplore* a quarrel between friends; "they *deplore* the divorce between the language as spoken and the language as written" (*T. S. Eliot*). **Lament** commonly implies a strong or demonstrative expression of sorrow; it suggests mourning rather than regret but it seldom, in current use, implies actual tears, cries, or wails. It does, however, in contrast to *deplore*, usually imply utterance, sometimes passionate, sometimes fulsome. "Yet I *lament* what long has ceased to be" (*Shelley*). "He made the newly returned actress a tempting offer, instigating some journalist friends of his at the same time to *lament* over the decay of the grand school of acting" (*Shaw*). **Bewail** and **bemoan** imply poignant sorrow finding an outlet in words or cries, *bewail* commonly suggesting the louder, *bemoan*, the more lugubrious, expression of grief or, often in current more or less humorous use, of a grievance or a complaint. "The valet *bewailing* the loss of his wages" (*S. Alexander*). "Even at the time when our prose speech was as near to perfection as it is ever likely to be, its critics were *bemoaning* its corruption" (*H. Ellis*). "And all wept, and *bewailed* her" (*Luke* viii. 52). "The silver swans her hapless fate *bemoan*, In notes more sad than when they sing their own" (*Pope*).
Ana. Deprecate, *disapprove: *grieve, mourn, sorrow: weep, wail, *cry.
Con. Vaunt, crow, *boast, brag.

depone. Depose, *swear, affirm, testify, asseverate.

deport. 1 Demean, comport, *behave, conduct, acquit, quit.
Ana. & *Ant.* See those at DEMEAN.
2 Transport, *banish, exile, expatriate, ostracize, extradite.

deportment. 1 *Behavior, conduct.
Ana. See those at BEHAVIOR.
2 Demeanor, *bearing, mien, carriage, manner, port, presence, front.
Ana. *Form, formality, ceremony, ceremonial, ritual: *culture, cultivation, breeding, refinement: dignity, grace, *elegance.

depose. Depone, testify, *swear, affirm, asseverate.

deposition. Affidavit, testimony, *evidence.

depot. *Station.

depravation. *Depravity.
Ana. Debasing, degrading (see ABASE): corrupting *or* corruption, vitiating *or* vitiation, perverting *or* perversion, debauching (see corresponding verbs at DEBASE): impairing *or* impairment, injuring, harming (see corresponding verbs at INJURE).
Con. Improvement, betterment, amelioration (see corresponding verbs at IMPROVE).

deprave. *Debase, vitiate, corrupt, debauch, pervert.
Ana. Defile, pollute, taint, *contaminate: *injure, impair, damage, spoil.
Con. *Improve, better, ameliorate: *exalt, magnify.

depraved. Debased, vitiated, corrupted, corrupt, debauched, perverted. See under DEBASE.
Ana. Dissolute, *abandoned, reprobate, profligate: degenerate, infamous, villainous, *vicious: degraded, debased (see ABASE).

depravity. **Depravity, depravation** agree in denoting a depraving, or reducing to a degraded or degenerate state. **Depravity** commonly applies to the state of being, **depravation,** to the act or process of making or becoming, depraved or degenerate. *Depravity* also commonly implies a degraded moral condition; as, "Lamenting the *depravity* of this degenerate age" (*Peacock*); "the *depravity* of the Valois" (*H. Adams*). *Depravation,* on the other hand, may imply marked deterioration of any sort; as, *depravation* of language, of instincts, of the blood. "If this be improvement, truly I know not what can be called a *depravation* of society" (*Burke*).
Ana. Degeneration, devolution, *deterioration, decadence, decline, declension: baseness, lowness, vileness (see corresponding adjectives at BASE): *disgrace, shame, infamy, ignominy.
Con. Honor, *honesty, integrity, probity: virtue, rectitude, morality, *goodness.

deprecate. *Disapprove.
Ana. *Deplore, lament, bewail, bemoan: reprobate, reprehend, condemn (see CRITICIZE).
Ant. Endorse. — *Con.* *Approve, sanction: *commend, applaud.
☞ *Do not confuse* deprecate *with* depreciate.

depreciate. *Decry, disparage, derogate from, detract from, belittle, minimize.
Ana. Underestimate, undervalue, underrate (see primitive verbs at ESTIMATE): asperse, *malign.
Ant. Appreciate. — *Con.* Prize, cherish, treasure, value (see APPRECIATE): *understand, comprehend.
☞ *Do not confuse* depreciate *with* deprecate.

depress. **Depress, weigh down** (*or* **weigh on,** *or* **upon**), **oppress** come into comparison as meaning to put such pressure or such a load upon a thing (sometimes, a person) as to cause it (or him) to sink under the weight. **Depress,** in all its senses, implies a lowering of something by the exertion of pressure or by an overburdening; in current use, however, it most commonly implies either a lowering of spirits as by physical or mental causes (as, "The long dull evenings in these dull lodgings when one is weary with work *depress* one sadly"—*J. R. Green;* "The mere volume of work was enough to crush the most diligent of rulers and *depress* the most vital"—*Buchan;* "he was *depressed* by his failure"—*S. Anderson*) or a lowering of bodily vigor or the power of certain organs to function, as by a drug, a disease, an external condition, or the like (as, the drug aconite *depresses* heart action). In reference to other things, such as the stock market, the prices asked for a certain commodity, a social or cultural state, *depress* often, as a result of its more common uses, suggests a lowering in activity, intensity, vigor, or the like; as, the first effect of the World War was greatly to *depress* the prices of stocks; the wheat market is *depressed* by the existence of a large surplus. "To *depress* the culture of the minority below the point at which a full understanding of poetry becomes possible" (*Day Lewis*). **Weigh,** with *down, on,* or *upon,* carries a weaker implication of the result, or lowering, than *depress* but a stronger implication of the difficulty or burdens imposed upon a person or thing; as, he is *weighed down* with cares; the responsibility *weighs* heavily *upon* him; "Forget him, my precious. Don't let any prince *weigh on* your little mind" (*R. Macaulay*). Like *weigh down,* etc., **oppress** stresses the burden which is borne or is imposed and, like *depress,* the consequent ill effects, such as the lowering of spirits or of power to function, or in its more common sense (see WRONG), a trampling down, a harassing, or a subjection to heavy penalties; as, "The weary world of waters between us *oppresses* the imagination" (*Lamb*); "the butler, *oppressed* by the heat...was in a state of abstraction bordering on slumber" (*Shaw*); she is so *oppressed* by fear that she may lose her mind.
Ana. Distress, *trouble, ail: *afflict, try, torment: *tire, weary, fatigue, exhaust, fag, jade, tucker.
Ant. Elate: cheer. — *Con.* Gladden, rejoice, delight, gratify, *please.

depression. Dejection, gloom, blues, dumps, *sadness, melancholy, melancholia, vapors.
Ana. Despondency, forlornness, hopelessness, despair, desperation (see under DESPONDENT): doldrums, boredom, ennui, *tedium.
Ant. Buoyancy. — *Con.* Elation, exultation (see corresponding adjectives at ELATED): cheerfulness, lightheartedness, gladness, joyousness (see corresponding adjectives at GLAD): *mirth, hilarity, glee.

deputy. Attorney, *agent, factor, proxy.
Ana. Substitute, surrogate (see RESOURCE).

deracinate. Uproot, eradicate, extirpate, *exterminate, wipe out.
Ana. *Abolish, extinguish, annihilate, abate: *destroy, demolish.

derange. Disarrange, unsettle, *disorder, disturb, disorganize.
Ana. Upset, *discompose, perturb: discommode, incommode, *inconvenience.
Ant. Arrange (*a scheme, plan, system, etc.*): adjust.

deranged. Demented, non compos mentis, crazed, crazy, *insane, mad, lunatic, maniac, wood.

derangement. *Aberration, alienation.

deride. *Ridicule, mock, taunt, twit, rally.
Ana. *Scoff, jeer, gibe, flout, sneer, gird, fleer: chaff, *banter, kid, rag, jolly, guy, rib.

derive. Originate, arise, rise, *spring, emanate, issue, stem, flow, proceed.

dernier cri. *Fashion, style, mode, vogue, fad, rage, craze, cry.

derogate from. Disparage, detract from, belittle, minimize, depreciate, *decry.
Ana. Reduce, lessen, *decrease, diminish.
Con. Enhance, heighten, *intensify.

descant, *n.* Observation, comment, *remark, note, commentary, obiter dictum.

descant, *v.* *Discourse, expatiate, dilate.

descend. **Descend, dismount, alight** are synonyms only when they mean to get or come down from a height. One **descends** when one climbs down a slope, as of a hill or mountain, a ladder, a step or a stair, a wall, a tree, or the like; one **dismounts,** in modern English, only when one gets down from a horse (or, by extension, from a bicycle) or dislodges another person from a horse; one **alights** (only in intransitive use) when one dismounts with a spring or descends, especially with lightness or grace, from a vehicle, such as a carriage or an airplane.
Ant. Ascend, climb.

describe. *Relate, narrate, state, report, rehearse, recite, recount.
Ana. Delineate, *sketch, outline.

description. Kind, sort, *type, character, nature, stripe, kidney, ilk.

descry. Espy, *see, behold, observe, notice, remark, note, perceive, discern, view, survey, contemplate.

desecration. *Profanation, sacrilege, blasphemy.

Ana. Defilement, pollution (see corresponding verbs at CONTAMINATE).

Con. *Purification, lustration, purgation, ablution.

desert, *n.*[1] *Due, merit.

Ana. Meed, guerdon, reward (see PREMIUM): punishment, chastisement, chastening, disciplining *or* discipline (see corresponding verbs at PUNISH).

desert, *n.*[2] *Waste, badlands, wilderness.

desert, *v.* Forsake, *abandon.

Ana. Leave, quit, depart, clear out, scram (see GO).

Ant. Stick to, cleave to.

desertion. *Defection, apostasy.

Ana. Recreancy, dastardliness, cowardliness *or* cowardice, cravenness, poltroonery (see corresponding adjectives at COWARDLY): perfidiousness *or* perfidy, treacherousness *or* treachery, disloyalty, faithlessness (see corresponding adjectives at FAITHLESS).

desiccate, *v.* *Dry, dehydrate, parch, bake.

design, *v.* **1** Mean, *intend, propose, purpose.

Ana. *Aim, aspire: destine, appoint (see corresponding adjectives at PRESCRIBED).

2 Plan, plot, scheme, project. See under PLAN, *n.*

Ana. *Sketch, outline, diagram, delineate, blueprint, draft: *invent, create.

Con. Execute, fulfill, effect, accomplish, achieve, *perform.

design, *n.* **1** *Plan, plot, scheme, project.

Ana. Delineation, sketch, draft, outline, tracing, diagram (see under SKETCH, *v.*): conception, *idea.

Con. Execution, fulfillment, accomplishment, achievement, performance (see corresponding verbs at PERFORM).

2 *Intention, intent, purpose, aim, end, object, objective, goal.

Ana. *Will, volition, conation: deliberation, reflection, thinking *or* thought (see corresponding verbs at THINK): intrigue, machination, *plot.

Ant. Accident. — *Con.* Impulse (see MOTIVE).

3 *Figure, pattern, motif, device.

designate. **Designate, name, nominate, elect, appoint** are here compared only in the sense to declare a person as one's choice for incumbency of an office, position benefice, or the like. **Designate** implies selection by the person or body having the power to choose an incumbent or to detail a person to a certain post; it often connotes selection well in advance of incumbency; as, Harold contended that he had been *designated* by Edward the Confessor as the latter's successor to the English throne; a clergyman who has been *designated* by the proper ecclesiastical authority as the incumbent of an episcopacy is usually called bishop-*designate* until he has been consecrated or has been installed. **Name** varies little in meaning from *designate* except that it stresses announcement rather than selection; it is more informal, however, and is usually preferred when the reference is to a political or government office within the gift of an executive or of an executive body; as, the mayor has not yet *named* the commissioner of public safety; only one member of the incoming president's cabinet remains to be *named,* the secretary of war. **Nominate,** though etymologically the equivalent of *name,* is now rarely used as its equivalent in meaning. "The House of Commons was crowded with members *nominated* by the Royal Council" (*J. R. Green*). Commonly, it implies merely the presentation of the name of one's choice for an office for the approval of, or rejection by, others who have the final say; thus, a person from the floor at a convention may *nominate* his choice for a particular office; a state convention of a political party meets to *nominate* the party's candidates for governor, lieutenant governor, and the like. *Nominate* is not always used in place of *name* (though strictly correct) when the executive's choice must be confirmed by a body having that power; as, the president has not yet decided whom he will *nominate* to fill the vacancy in the Supreme Court. **Elect,** as distinguished from *nominate,* implies a final selection, as by the electorate, from the candidates who have been previously nominated; as, the Democratic candidates for the state offices were all *elected;* not one person on the nominating committee's slate was *elected* at today's meeting. **Appoint** always implies that the selection is determined without a general vote (usually a vote of an electorate) and represents the choice of the person or the body in whom such power is legally vested. *Appoint* may be used even when confirmation, as by the U. S. Senate, or, as in Massachusetts, by the governor's council, has been necessary to make the designation valid; as, three justices of the Supreme Court have been *appointed* by the president within twelve months. "He [the president] shall *nominate,* and by and with the Advice and Consent of the Senate, shall *appoint* Ambassadors, other public Ministers and Consuls, Judges of the supreme Court" (*U. S. Const.*).

Ana. *Choose, select, single out, opt, pick.

designation. *Name, denomination, appellation, title, style.

Ana. Identification, *recognition: classification, pigeonholing *or* pigeonhole (see corresponding verbs at ASSORT).

designed. Premeditated, *deliberate, considered, advised, studied.

Ana. Intentional, *voluntary, willful, deliberate, willing: purposed, intended (see INTEND): resolved, determined, decided (see DECIDE).

Ant. Accidental. — *Con.* Fortuitous, casual (see ACCIDENTAL): *spontaneous, impulsive: natural, normal, *regular, typical.

desire, *v.* **Desire, wish, want, crave, covet** agree in meaning to have a longing for something. **Desire,** in its most effective use, emphasizes strength and ardor of feeling, **wish,** especially in poetic language, often connotes longing for the unattainable. "*Wishing* me like to one more rich in hope, Featured like him, like him with friends possess'd, *Desiring* this man's art and that man's scope" (*Shak.*). *Desire,* however, often implies intention or aim more than yearning and often, therefore, connotes striving or the need for striving. "The painter whose predominant aim is moral instruction and edification almost always fails of the effect he *desires*" (*Binyon*). " 'If you *desire* faith—then you've faith enough' " (*Browning*). *Desire* is sometimes used in place of *wish,* but only when greater formality is sought; as, to *desire* (or *wish,* or *wish for*) happiness in one's marriage. **Want** (see also LACK) was long regarded as colloquial and not to be used in place of *wish* unless need or lack is implied; as, "Not what we *wish,* but what we *want*" (*J. Merrick*); "Man *wants* but little here below, Nor *wants* that little long" (*Goldsmith*). Now, however, it is frequently used in place of *wish,* especially when the latter is felt to be slightly more formal than the object or the context requires; as, Senator Smith does not *want* (or *wish*) renomination; they *want* (or *wish*) to leave early; do you *want* (or *wish*) tea or coffee? **Crave** carries a stronger implication of the impulsion of physical or mental appetite or need than the preceding terms; it may definitely imply unsatisfied or ungratified hunger, thirst, love, ambition, or the like; as, to *crave* fresh fruits; to *crave* exercise; to *crave* a college education; to *crave* peace in one's old age; "for every grief, Each suffering, I *craved* relief" (*Millay*). **Covet** implies inordinate and eager or passionate longing, often, but now far from commonly, for something which belongs to another. In the last case, it often implies envy of the person who possesses that which is longed for. "Thou shalt not *covet* thy neighbour's house, thou shalt not *covet* thy neighbour's wife" (*Exodus* xx. 17). "I have sometimes thought of rechristening our house The Hotel of the Four Seasons, and thereby releasing its true name (The Haven) to a friend who *covets* it for his own" (*Quiller-Couch*). "Her invitations came to be *coveted* by people who were desirous of moving in good society" (*Shaw*).

Ana. *Long, yearn, hanker, pine, hunger, thirst: aspire, pant, *aim.

Con. Abhor, abominate, loathe, detest, *hate: spurn, repudiate, reject, refuse, *decline.

desire, *n.* **Desire, appetite, appetence** (*or* **appetency**), **concupiscence, lust, passion, urge, yen** are here compared primarily as meaning a longing for something regarded as essential to one's well-being or happiness, but most of them are also considered secondarily as meaning an impulse originating in a man's nature and driving him toward the object or the experience which promises him enjoyment or satisfaction in its attainment. **Desire** is capable of the widest application for it may be used of every conceivable longing that stirs one emotionally, whether that longing originates in man's animal or in his spiritual nature, whether it is natural and normal or unnatural and perverted, whether it is generally regarded as low or high in the scale of moral or spiritual values; as, the *desire* for food; the *desire* for an education; a *desire* for change; the *desire* for peace; "his physical *desire* to sit in the sun and do nothing" (*S. Anderson*); "the keen *desire*...to pay their debts" (*A. Repplier*); "nothing dies harder than the *desire* to think well of oneself" (*T. S. Eliot*). It is, however, used specifically to denote sexual longing, but it does not always convey derogatory connotations when so restricted in meaning. "Like the flesh of animals distended by fear or *desire*" (*Cather*). *Desire* is often used in contrast (commonly an implicit contrast) to *will* or *volition*, for in itself it carries no implication of a determination or effort to possess or attain. "She had the *desire* to do something which she objected to doing" (*Bennett*). "Guiltless even of a *desire* for any private possession or advantage of their own" (*G. L. Dickinson*). **Appetite** is almost as extensive in its range of application as *desire*, and it invariably implies an imperative demand for satisfaction. It is specifically applied to the longings which arise out of man's animal nature: hunger, thirst, and sexual desire, which may be thwarted only by circumstances beyond one's control or by deliberate self-control; as, a slave to his *appetite* for drink; the child is losing his *appetite* (that is, for food); to impose restraints upon one's physical *appetites*. In extended use, the word is applied to equally exacting longings which drive one to their satisfaction, whether they originate in one's nature or are acquired; as, man's distinguishing characteristic is the *appetite* for happiness; an insatiable *appetite* for news; "almost pathological in his *appetite* for activity" (*Mencken*); the world has no *appetite* for further fighting. **Appetence** and **appetency** are somewhat literary substitutes for *appetite;* they are sometimes preferred when the stimulation of appetite is connoted. "Bred only and completed to the taste Of lustful *appetence*, to sing, to dance, To dress, and troll the tongue, and roll the eye" (*Milton*). "The eyes of drinking men when they smell liquor, bright with *appetence*" (*M. Austin*). The next two words (*concupiscence* and *lust*) are here considered only in their older and broader senses. **Concupiscence,** which is now rare in other than philosophic use in this sense, is nearly equivalent to *desire* in the abstract, except that it stresses delight or pleasure as its end and implies even more strongly a distinction from *will.* **Lust** combines the specific denotation of *desire* as a longing that stirs emotion and that of *appetite* as a longing that exacts satisfaction; often, but not invariably, it implies domination by the emotion or insatiability of the appetite. "Jansen...utterly condemned, as abominable *concupiscence*, not only sensuality (the *lust* of the flesh) but scientific curiosity (the *lust* of knowing) and ambition (the *lust* of power)" (*Preserved Smith*). "Whose ruling passion was the *lust* of praise" (*Pope*). **Passion** is applied to any intense and preoccupying emotion which gives one's mind its particular bent or which serves as an outlet for and gives direction to one's energies. Though it comes close to *lust* in suggesting the energizing of desire by the vehemence of the emotions, *passion* is the better choice when personal predilection is implied; as, he, too, knew the *lust* (better than *passion*) for power; his work reveals a *passion* (better than *lust*) for perfection. "Avarice, he assured them, was the one *passion* that grew stronger and sweeter in old age. He had the *lust* for money as Martinez had for women" (*Cather*). "The dream, the ambition, the *passion* of Mr. Raycie's life was (as his son knew) to found a Family" (*E. Wharton*). **Urge,** which originally meant a force or motive which drives one to action, now often means a strong, persistent, and compelling desire that has its origin in one's physical nature or one's peculiar temperament. The word is sometimes applied to the physical appetites (the sexual appetite is often called "the biological *urge*"), but it is more often used of a desire so strong and insistent that it must be satisfied or a sense of frustration ensues; as, an *urge* to travel; an *urge* to marry. **Yen** is a slang term for a particularly urgent desire or craving; as, a *yen* for fresh fruit; a *yen* for release from routine.

Ana. Longing, yearning, hankering, pining, hungering *or* hunger, thirsting *or* thirst (see corresponding verbs at LONG): *cupidity, greed, avarice, rapacity.

Ant. Distaste. — ***Con.*** Repugnance, repellency *or* repulsion, abhorrence (see corresponding adjectives at REPUGNANT).

desist. Discontinue, cease, *stop, quit.

Ana. *Refrain, abstain, forbear: *relinquish, yield, abandon, resign.

Ant. Persist. — ***Con.*** *Continue: *persevere.

desolate. Forlorn, lorn, lonesome, lone, solitary, lonely, *alone.

Ana. Deserted, forsaken, abandoned (see ABANDON): *miserable, wretched.

Con. Cheerful, lighthearted, joyful, joyous, happy, *glad.

despair, *n.* Hopelessness, desperation, despondency, forlornness. See under DESPONDENT, *adj.*

Ana. Dejection, melancholy, *sadness, gloom, depression.

Ant. Hope: optimism: beatitude. — ***Con.*** Exultancy *or* exultation, elatedness *or* elation (see corresponding adjectives at ELATED): rapture, transport, *ecstasy.

despairing, *adj.* Hopeless, desperate, *despondent, forlorn.

Ana. Melancholy, *melancholic, atrabilious: pessimistic, misanthropic, *cynical: depressed, weighed down (see DEPRESS).

Ant. Hopeful. — ***Con.*** Optimistic, roseate, rose-colored (see HOPEFUL): *elated, elate, exultant: sanguine, *confident, assured, sure.

despatch. Variant of DISPATCH.
desperado. *Ruffian, thug, gangster, Mohock, apache.
Ana. *Assassin, cutthroat, bravo.
desperate. Hopeless, despairing, *despondent, forlorn.
Ana. Reckless, rash, foolhardy, venturous, venturesome, temerarious (see ADVENTUROUS): *precipitate, headlong: thwarted, foiled, frustrated, outwitted, circumvented, baffled, balked (see FRUSTRATE).
Con. *Cool, collected, composed, nonchalant: sanguine, assured, *confident, sure.
desperation. Hopelessness, despair, despondency, forlornness. See under DESPONDENT, *adj.*
Ana. Fury, frenzy (see INSPIRATION): grit, pluck, guts, sand, *fortitude: recklessness, rashness, foolhardiness (see corresponding adjectives at ADVENTUROUS): *temerity, audacity.
Con. *Confidence, assurance, aplomb: *equanimity, composure, sang-froid, phlegm.
despicable. *Contemptible, pitiable, sorry, scurvy, cheap, beggarly.
Ana. *Base, low, vile: ignominious, infamous, disgraceful (see corresponding nouns at DISGRACE): ignoble, *mean, abject, sordid.
Ant. Praiseworthy, laudable.
despise. **Despise, contemn, scorn, disdain, scout** come into comparison as meaning to regard a person or thing as beneath one's notice or as unworthy of one's attention or interest. The same differences in implications and connotations are observable in the corresponding nouns **despite, contempt, scorn, disdain** when they denote such an attitude toward, or such treatment of, a person or thing. **Despise** and **despite** (the latter now literary) may imply any emotional reaction from strong disfavor to loathing, but in precise use it always stresses a looking down upon a thing and its evaluation as mean, petty, weak, worthless, or the like. "He must learn, however, to *despise* petty adversaries. No good sportsman ought to shoot at crows" (*Scott*). "Bird and beast *despised* my snares, which took me so many waking hours at night to invent" (*Hudson*). "Receive thy friend, who, scorning flight, Goes to meet danger with *despite*" (*Longfellow*). **Contemn** (now bookish) and **contempt** imply even a harsher judgment than *despise* or *despite*, for the latter pair may connote mere derision, whereas the former pair (especially *contempt*) usually suggest vehement, though not necessarily vocal, condemnation of the person or thing as low, vile, ignominious, or the like; as, "I *contemn* their low images of love" (*Steele*); "his own early drawings of moss-roses and picturesque castles—things that he now mercilessly *contemned*" (*Bennett*); "I was on fire with the same anger, dislike, and *contempt* that burned in Hobart towards me" (*R. Macaulay*); "It was to proclaim their utter *contempt* for the public and popular conceptions of art, that the Dadaists launched into a series of outrageous practical jokes" (*Day Lewis*). **Scorn** implies quick, indignant, or profound contempt; as, "Instructed from her early years to *scorn* the art of female tears" (*Swift*); "I knew he'd *scorn* me. He hates frumps" (*Meredith*); "Voltaire, with his quick intellectual *scorn* and eager malice of the brain" (*E. Dowden*); "Common sense, rejecting with *scorn* all that can be called mysticism" (*Inge*). **Disdain** suggests a visible manifestation of pride and arrogance (sometimes unwarrantable) or aversion to what is base; as, "A great mind *disdains* to hold anything by courtesy" (*Johnson*); "His *disdain* of affectation and prudery was magnificent" (*Mencken*). **Scout** stresses not only derision but a refusal to consider the person or thing concerned as of any value, efficacy, or truth. It therefore suggests rejection or dismissal. "Many great philosophers have not only been *scouted* while they were living, but forgotten as soon as they were dead" (*Hazlitt*). "Alice would have *scouted*... any suggestion that her parent was more selfish than saintly" (*Shaw*).
Ana. Abominate, loathe, abhor, detest, *hate: spurn, repudiate (see DECLINE).
Ant. Appreciate. — *Con.* Admire, esteem, respect (see under REGARD, *n.*): value, prize, cherish, treasure (see APPRECIATE).
despite, *n.* **1** Spite, ill will, malevolence, spleen, grudge, *malice, malignity.
Ana. Contempt, scorn, disdain (see under DESPISE): abhorrence, loathing, detestation, abomination, hatred, hate (see under HATE, *v.*).
Ant. Appreciation: regard. — *Con.* Admiration, esteem, respect (see REGARD, *n.*): *reverence, awe, fear.
2 Contempt, scorn, disdain. See under DESPISE.
despite, *prep.* In spite of, *notwithstanding.
despiteful. Spiteful, despiteous, malevolent, *malicious, malignant, malign.
Ana. Contemptuous, scornful, disdainful (see corresponding nouns under DESPISE): *envious, jealous: *vindictive, revengeful, vengeful.
Con. Kindly, *kind, benignant, benign.
despiteous *or* **dispiteous.** Despiteful, spiteful, wanton, *malicious, malevolent, malignant, malign.
Ana. Merciless, implacable, *grim, relentless, unrelenting: pitiless, ruthless (see corresponding nouns at PITY).
Con. Benevolent, humane, *charitable.
despoil. *Ravage, devastate, waste, sack, pillage, spoliate.
Ana. Plunder, *rob, rifle, loot: *strip, bare, denude.
despondency, despond. Despair, desperation, hopelessness, forlornness. See under DESPONDENT, *adj.*
Ana. Dejection, depression, melancholy, melancholia, *sadness, blues, dumps.
Ant. Lightheartedness. — *Con.* Elatedness *or* elation, exultancy *or* exultation (see corresponding adjectives at ELATED): cheerfulness, gladness, happiness, joyfulness, joyousness (see corresponding adjectives at GLAD).
despondent, *adj.* **Despondent, despairing, desperate, hopeless, forlorn** come into comparison as meaning having lost all, or practically all, hope. The same distinctions in implications and connotations are to be found in their corresponding nouns **despondency** (*or* **despond**), **despair, desperation, hopelessness, forlornness** when they denote the state or feeling of a person who has lost hope. **Despondent** and **despondency** (or **despond,** which occurs rarely, and chiefly in Bunyan's phrase "slough of *despond*") imply disheartenment or deep dejection arising out of a conviction that there is no longer any justification of hope or that further efforts are useless; as, a *despondent* youth; a *despondent* lover. "Whenever...the repressed spirit of the artist...perceived...the full extent of its débâcle, Mark Twain was filled with a *despondent* desire, a momentary purpose even, to stop writing altogether" (*Van W. Brooks*). "We Poets in our youth begin in gladness; But thereof come in the end *despondency* and madness" (*Wordsworth*). "England, they said, was wont to take her defeats without *despondency*, and her victories without elation" (*A. Repplier*). **Despairing** and **despair** imply sometimes the passing of hope, sometimes the utter loss of hope and, often, but not necessarily, accompanying despondency. "[Matthew Arnold's] *despairing* appeal to the democracy when his jeremiads evoked no response from the upper class...or from the middle class" (*Inge*). "To fortify ourselves against the ultimate disaster—which is *despair*" (*Times Lit. Sup.*). "A...*despair* of her ever understanding either the terms of a contract or the

nature of working conditions" (*M. Austin*). **Desperate** and **desperation** imply despair, but not the cessation of effort: rather, they often suggest violence, recklessness, or the like, as a last resource, especially in the face of defeat or frustration. "The bitter, *desperate* striving unto death of the oppressed race, the damned *desperation* of the rebel" (*R. Macaulay*). "A *desperate* determination that nothing should interfere with her marriage with Hugh had taken possession of her. 'If necessary I'll ride the man down,' she thought" (*S. Anderson*). "He was fighting a fight of *desperation*, and knew it" (*Meredith*). "Not knowing...how near my pursuer might be, I turned in *desperation* to meet him" (*Hudson*). **Hopeless** and **hopelessness** imply both the complete loss of hope and the cessation of effort; as, the *hopeless* look in the faces of the doomed men. The words do not necessarily suggest despondency, dejection, or gloom, for sometimes they imply acceptance or resignation. " 'Why should you say such desperate things?' 'No, they are not desperate. They are only *hopeless*' " (*Hardy*). "Not that Dr. Lavendar was *hopeless;* he was never *hopeless* of anybody...but he was wise; so he was deeply discouraged" (*Deland*). **Forlorn** (see also ALONE, 1) and **forlornness** stress utter hopelessness: they derive this sense from the phrase *forlorn hope* (etymologically, a lost band or troop) which in early use denoted a party of soldiers or others sent out to do a piece of work—such as beginning an attack—which, whatever the ultimate result might be, was certain to lead them to death or capture. Consequently, they differ from *hopeless* and *hopelessness* in implying hopelessness even in the act of undertaking something because its failure is all but certain; as, "[We] sit down in a *forlorn* scepticism" (*Berkeley*); "Poor prince, *forlorn* he steps... and proud in his despair" (*Keats*). *Desperate, hopeless,* and *forlorn* and their corresponding nouns are applicable not only to men, their moods, words, and the like, but to the things which make men despairing or hopeless; as, *desperate* straits; the *hopeless* situation of a beleaguered garrison; "*desperate* grime and greasiness" (*Wm. McFee*); "all the high ardour and imaginative force which the Celt has ever thrown into a *forlorn* and failing cause" (*Cyril Robinson*); "The leaders of *forlorn* hopes are never found among men with dismal minds. There must be a natural resiliency of temper which makes them enjoy *desperate* ventures" (*S. M. Crothers*).

Ana. Grieving, mourning, sorrowing (see GRIEVE): depressed, dejected, melancholy, sad (see corresponding nouns at SADNESS).

Ant. Lighthearted. — ***Con.*** *Elated, elate, exultant: cheerful, joyful, joyous, happy, *glad: buoyant, volatile, resilient, *elastic.

despotic, despotical. Tyrannical, tyrannous, arbitrary, autocratic, *absolute.

Ana. Domineering, imperious, *masterful, imperative: *dictatorial, authoritarian, magisterial.

destined. *Prescribed, appointed.

Ana. Intended, purposed, designed (see INTEND): *inevitable, ineluctable, inescapable, unavoidable.

destiny. *Fate, lot, doom, portion.

Ana. *End, termination, terminus, ending: goal, objective (see INTENTION): *vocation.

destitute. *Devoid, void.

Ana. Lacking, wanting (see LACK, *v.*): *deficient: *empty: barren, *bare: depleted, drained, exhausted, bankrupted *or* bankrupt (see corresponding verbs at DEPLETE).

Con. *Full, replete, complete.

destitution. Want, indigence, *poverty, penury, privation.

Ana. *Need, necessity, exigency: *lack, absence, want, privation: adversity, *misfortune: straits (see JUNCTURE).

Ant. Opulence.

destroy. **Destroy, demolish, raze** come into comparison as meaning to pull or tear down. **Destroy,** which etymologically means to unbuild (the reverse of to *construct*), is now so general in its application that it may imply the operation of any force that wrecks, kills, annihilates, or the like; as, to *destroy* a building, a paper, a nest of caterpillars; to *destroy* life, affection, one's influence. In very precise use, however, its opposition to *construct* is usually apparent. "It is proverbially easier to *destroy* than to construct" (*T. S. Eliot*). "Very few established institutions, governments and constitutions...are ever *destroyed* by their enemies until they have been corrupted and weakened by their friends" (*Lippmann*). **Demolish** implies a pulling or smashing to pieces; when used in reference to buildings or other structures of wood, stone, steel, and the like, it implies complete wreckage and often a heap of ruins; as, houses *demolished* by a hurricane; the automobile was *demolished* in a collision with the train. Figuratively, the term implies the destruction of all coherency or integrity in a thing and, consequently, of all its usefulness; as, to *demolish* an opponent's argument. "People are inclined to believe that what Bradley did was to *demolish* the logic of Mill and the psychology of Bain" (*T. S. Eliot*). **Raze** implies a bringing to the level of the ground; it may or may not imply an orderly process with no destruction of usable parts; thus, several buildings were *razed* to make room for the new city hall; the village was *razed* to the ground by a disastrous fire. In extended use, the term implies obliteration or effacement, more, however, with reference to the etymological implication of scraping than the acquired sense of pulling or tearing down. "Canst thou not minister to a mind diseased ... *Raze* out the written troubles of the brain...?" (*Shak.*).

Ana. *Ruin, wreck, wrack, dilapidate: *abolish, extinguish, annihilate: *ravage, devastate, sack.

Con. *Found, establish, institute, organize: *make, form, shape, fashion, fabricate, forge, manufacture: preserve, conserve, *save.

desultory. Casual, hit-or-miss, haphazard, *random, happy-go-lucky, chance, chancy.

Ana. *Fitful, spasmodic: unsystematic, unmethodical, disorderly (see affirmative adjectives at ORDERLY): capricious, mercurial, *inconstant, fickle.

Ant. Assiduous (*study, search, or other activity*): methodical (*something designed, planned, constructed, etc.*).

detach. **Detach, disengage, abstract, prescind** come into comparison when they mean to remove one thing from another (or others) with which it is in union or association. One **detaches** something when one breaks (literally or figuratively) a connection, a tie, or a bond and thereby isolates it or makes it independent; as, to *detach* sheets from a loose-leaf book; to *detach* a ship from a fleet; to *detach* oneself from one's prejudices. "It was as if the bonfire-makers [on a distant hill at night] were... *detached* from and independent of the dark stretches below" (*Hardy*). One **disengages** something that is held by or involved with something else and thereby sets it free; as, she *disengaged* her hand; to *disengage* gears from each other; it is hard for the mind to *disengage* itself from depressing thoughts. "I could not rest satisfied until I...had *disengaged*...[Wordsworth's] good work from the inferior work joined with it, and had placed before the public the body of his good work by itself" (*Arnold*). One **abstracts** something by withdrawing it from the place where it belongs or by separating it from a mass of like things so as to put it in another place or another relation; as, to *abstract* papers from a file; to *abstract* (in this case often with implications of furtiveness and theft) eggs from a nest or money from a till; to *abstract* the essential points from an argument (usually with the implication of making an abridgment); to *abstract* one's attention from one's surroundings (especially so as to concentrate it on something else). *Abstract* in its intransitive sense means to perform the logical process of abstraction (see ABSTRACT, *adj.*). **Prescind,** unlike the other words, is used only of abstractions, and is therefore found chiefly in philosophical writing. One *prescinds* who by an act of the mind separates one idea or notion from all others with which it is usually involved, so that it can be examined in itself; as, few can consider happiness *prescinded* from pleasure and self-indulgence; the philosophical notion of force, *prescinded* from matter and gravity.

Ana. *Separate, part, sever, sunder, divorce: disjoin, disconnect, disunite (see affirmative verbs at JOIN).

Ant. Attach, affix. — ***Con.*** *Fasten, fix: *tie, bind: *unite, combine, conjoin.

detached. Aloof, disinterested, *indifferent, unconcerned, incurious.

Ana. Impartial, dispassionate, objective, unbiased, *fair: altruistic (see CHARITABLE).

Ant. Interested: selfish. — ***Con.*** *Mercenary: concerned (see under CARE).

detail, *n.* **1** *Item, particular.

Con. *Structure, framework, anatomy, skeleton: whole, aggregate, total, *sum: mass, *bulk: design, scheme, *plan, plot.

2 *Part, portion, piece, parcel, member, division, segment, sector, fraction, fragment.

detailed. Itemized, particularized, *circumstantial, minute, particular.

Ana. *Full, complete, replete: copious, abundant (see PLENTIFUL): exhausting *or* exhaustive (see corresponding verb at DEPLETE).

detain. **1** *Arrest, apprehend, attach.

Ana. *Catch, capture, nab, cop: seize, *take: *imprison, incarcerate, intern, jail.

2 Withhold, hold back, keep back, reserve, *keep.

3 *Delay, retard, slow, slacken.

Ana. Curb, check, *restrain, inhibit: *arrest, interrupt: *defer, suspend, stay.

Con. *Advance, promote, forward, further. *speed, hasten, hurry.

detention. Arrest, apprehension, attachment. See under ARREST, *v.*

Ana. Imprisonment, internment, incarceration (see corresponding verbs at IMPRISON).

deterioration. Deterioration, degeneration, devolution, decadence, decline, declension are here compared as meaning either the process of falling from a higher to a lower level or the state of a thing when such a falling has occurred. **Deterioration** is the least specific of these terms and applies to any process or condition in which there are signs of impairment in quality, in character, in value, or the like; as, chemicals that reduce the *deterioration* of rubber in aging; the *deterioration* of his memory is marked in recent years. "Man the tool-maker has made 'inanimate instruments'...do his manual work for him; he is now trying to make them do his mental work....The price may be the progressive *deterioration* of our faculties" (*Inge*). **Degeneration** usually implies retrogression, or a return to a simpler or more primitive state or condition; when used in reference to plants, animals, or any of their organs, it often suggests physical changes in structure, but it may imply a progressive deterioration owing to a morbid condition; as, the sea squirt in its adult stage evidences *degeneration* through the loss of the vertebrate characters apparent in its larval stage; fatty *degeneration* of the heart. When applied to men in groups or as individuals, or to states, empires, and the like, it suggests physical, intellectual, and often moral degradation and a reversion toward (but not necessarily to) barbarism or, in the case of individuals, bestiality; as, the *degeneration* of the American Indians confined to reservations; the *degeneration* of the ancient Roman Empire. In scientific language, **devolution** usually takes the place of *degeneration* (as, the *devolution* of the sea squirt) but in general use it carries even a stronger implication of opposition to *evolution*. "The process of human evolution is nothing more than a process of sifting, and where that sifting ceases evolution ceases, becomes, indeed, *devolution*" (*H. Ellis*). **Decadence** presupposes a previous maturing and usually a high degree of excellence; it implies that the falling takes place after a thing (such as a people, a literature or other form of art, a branch of knowledge) has reached the peak of its development. "There seems to be no more pronounced mark of the *decadence* of a people and its literature than a servile and rigid subserviency to rule" (*H. Ellis*). "Hanbridge had already...robbed Bursley of two-thirds of its retail trade—as witness the steady *decadence* of the Square!" (*Bennett*). **Decline** is often interchangeable with *decadence* because it, too, suggests a falling after the peak has been reached in power, prosperity, excellence, or the like. It, however, usually suggests more momentum, more obvious evidences of deterioration, and less hope of a return to the earlier state; as, the rise and *decline* of the imperial power; he is in the *decline* of life. "The association so often noted between the flowering of the intellect and the *decline* of national vigor" (*J. W. Krutch*). **Declension** differs from *decline* only in connoting less precipitancy or a slower or more gradual falling toward extinction or destruction. "The love that cheers life's latest stage ... Preserved by virtue from *declension*" (*Cowper*). "The moral change, the sad *declension* from the ancient proud spirit...was painfully depressing" (*Bennett*).

Ana. Impairment, spoiling (see corresponding verbs at INJURE): decaying *or* decay, decomposition, disintegration, rotting, crumbling (see corresponding verbs at DECAY): debasement, degradation (see corresponding verbs at ABASE).

Ant. Improvement, amelioration.

determinant. Antecedent, *cause, reason, occasion.

Ana. Factor (see ELEMENT): *influence, weight, authority.

determination. *Decision.

Ana. Decidedness, decisiveness (see corresponding adjectives at DECIDED): resolution, tenacity, mettle, spirit, *courage: backbone, grit, pluck, guts, sand, *fortitude: doggedness, pertinaciousness *or* pertinacity, stubbornness (see corresponding adjectives at OBSTINATE).

determinative. *Conclusive, decisive, definitive

Ana. Determining, deciding, settling (see DECIDE): influencing, affecting (see AFFECT): shaping, fashioning, forming *or* formative (see corresponding verbs at MAKE).

Con. *Ineffective, ineffectual, inefficacious, inefficient.

determine. **1** Settle, rule, *decide, resolve.

Ana. Fix, *set, establish: dispose, predispose, *incline, bias: drive, impel, *move, actuate: *induce, persuade.

2 Ascertain, *discover, unearth, learn.

detest. *Hate, abhor, abominate, loathe.

Ana. *Despise, contemn, scorn, disdain: spurn, repudiate, reject (see DECLINE, *v.*).

Ant. Adore (sense 2). — ***Con.*** Love, *like, dote on *or* upon, fancy, relish: cherish, prize, treasure, value, *appreciate.

detestable. Odious, *hateful, abominable, abhorrent.
Ana. *Contemptible, despicable, sorry, scurvy: atrocious, *outrageous, monstrous, heinous: *execrable, damnable, accursed.

detestation. Hate, hatred, abomination, abhorrence, loathing. See under HATE, *v.*
Ana. *Antipathy, aversion: despite, contempt, scorn, disdain (see under DESPISE).
Con. Admiration, esteem, respect, *regard: love, affection, *attachment: tolerance, indulgence, forbearance (see under FORBEARING).

detract from. Belittle, minimize, disparage, derogate from, *decry, depreciate.
Ana. Asperse, *malign, traduce, defame, vilify, calumniate, slander, libel: reduce, lessen, diminish, *decrease.
Con. Enhance, heighten, *intensify: magnify, aggrandize, *exalt.

detraction. **Detraction, backbiting, calumny, slander, scandal** come into comparison when they denote either the offense of one who defames another or casts aspersions upon him, or that which is uttered by way of defamation or aspersion. **Detraction** stresses the injurious effect of what is said and the loss through it of something precious to the person affected, such as loss of the esteem of others, or loss of his credit, of his deserts, or even of his good name. "Bring candid eyes unto the perusal of men's works, and let not...*detraction* blast well-intended labors" (*Browne*). "To listen to *detraction* is as much an act of *detraction* as to speak it" (*Manning*). **Backbiting** imputes both furtiveness and spitefulness to the one who asperses or defames; it suggests an unfair, mean, and cowardly attack when the victim is absent and unable to defend himself. "Refrain your tongue from *backbiting:* for there is no word so secret, that shall go for nought" (*Wisdom of Solomon* i. 11). "Face-flatterer and *backbiter* are the same" (*Tennyson*). **Calumny** stresses malicious misrepresentation; it therefore implies that the detractor is a liar and that his intent is to blacken another's name. "Be thou as chaste as ice, as pure as snow, thou shalt not escape *calumny*" (*Shak.*). "*Calumny* differs from most other injuries in this dreadful circumstance: he who commits it can never repair it" (*Johnson*). "To persevere in one's duty and be silent is the best answer to *calumny*" (*Washington*). **Slander** (for legal use, see TRADUCE) stresses the dissemination of calumnies, especially those of a highly defamatory character; thus, a person who is given to *calumny* is prone to malicious misrepresentation of the acts, the motives, or the character of others; a person who is given to *slander* is one who repeats (not necessarily originates) calumnies or defamatory reports without ascertaining, or with complete indifference to, their truth or falsehood; so, a man lays himself open to an action for *slander* if, however well-founded his suspicions, he calls a man a thief when sufficient evidence is lacking. "Who spake no *slander*, no, nor listen'd to it" (*Tennyson*). **Scandal,** as here compared (see OFFENSE, DISGRACE), usually suggests the activity of a gossip, especially of an idle, irresponsible gossip (a scandalmonger), who gives information of any shocking details, often true, that reflect discredit on another or that tend to tarnish or blacken his reputation; as, it is difficult for a man to remain long in public life untouched by *scandal.* "Her tea she sweetens, as she sips, with *scandal*" (*S. Rogers*).
Ana. *Injury, damage, harm, hurt: *injustice, injury, wrong, tort: defaming *or* defamation, aspersion, maligning, traducing, slandering *or* slander, calumniation, vilification, libeling *or* libel (see corresponding verbs at MALIGN).

detrimental. Deleterious, noxious, *pernicious, baneful.
Ana. Harming *or* harmful, hurting *or* hurtful, injuring *or* injurious, damaging, impairing (see corresponding verbs at INJURE).
Ant. Beneficial. — ***Con.*** Advantageous, profitable (see BENEFICIAL): helping *or* helpful, aiding (see corresponding verbs at HELP).

devastate. Waste, *ravage, sack, pillage, despoil, spoliate.
Ana. *Destroy, demolish, raze: *ruin, wreck: plunder, loot, *rob, rifle.

develop. *Mature, ripen, age.
Ana. *Advance, progress: *expand, dilate.
Con. *Wither, shrivel, rivel, wizen.

development. **Development, evolution** come into comparison when they mean growth from a lower to a higher state. **Development,** however, which etymologically implies an unfolding, in all of its senses stresses the bringing out of the hidden or latent possibilities in a thing, chiefly through growth and therefore through a series of natural stages (as, the *development* of a seed into a plant; the *development* of a human being from the embryo), but also through the exercise of human energy, ingenuity, art, or the like (as, the *development* of an industry, of a tract of land, of a photographic negative, of an argument). **Evolution,** on the other hand, etymologically implies an unrolling, and stresses an orderly succession of events or of living things, each growing out of that which precedes, yet marked by changes which transform it and give it a particular identity and usually (especially in regard to organisms or organs), a more elaborate and more complex character; as, the *evolution* of species; the *evolution* of the drama. Consequently, *development* should be used when the emphasis is on the realization of the full possibilities of a particular thing through natural or artificial means, and *evolution* when the stress is placed on the transformations which occur in a type, class, or order of things, the individual instances of which retain a likeness to the parent but manifest striking differences, especially in the direction of complexity and progress. "The Aristotelian canon that the 'nature' of a thing must be sought in its completed *development*, its final form" (*Inge*). "No, 'revolution' is not the proper word! What is happening in modern physics is a tremendously rapid *evolution*" (*Karl K. Darrow*).
Con. Decline, declension, decadence, devolution, *deterioration, degeneration.

deviate. Digress, diverge, *swerve, veer, depart.
Ana. Deflect, *turn, divert, avert, sheer: stray, *wander, rove.

deviation. **Deviation, aberration, divergence** (*or* **divergency**), **deflection** (*or* **deflexion**) in both their literal and their figurative senses agree in denoting departure (or an instance of departure) from a straight course or procedure or from a norm or standard. **Deviation,** the term of widest application, almost invariably requires qualification or a context to complete its meaning; as, no *deviation* from traditional methods was permitted; there were many *deviations* from fact in his account; the road proceeds without *deviation* for two miles. **Aberration** adds to *deviation* definite implications of error, fault, or abnormality, and therefore has highly technical significations in some of the sciences. In general use, it commonly implies transgression of the moral law or the social code, and is often used euphemistically for a reprehensible act or reprehensible behavior; as, the *aberrations* of his youth had long been forgotten. **Divergence** is sometimes used interchangeably with *deviation*, but ordinarily it denotes deviation of two (or more) things which from a common meeting point proceed in different directions; as, an angle is formed by the *divergence* of two lines; at no point in the discussion was there *divergence* of opinion on this question. **Deflection** adds to *deviation* the implication of bending or curving; as, the *deflection* of rays of light passing through a prism.

device. 1 **Device, contrivance, gadget, contraption** come into comparison when they mean something (usually but not always of a mechanical character) which is invented as a means of doing a particular piece of work or of effecting a given end. **Device** is the most widely applicable of these terms; it may be used of a thing that serves as a tool or instrument or as an effective part of a machine, especially one which shows some ingenuity in invention (as, a *device* for controlling the speed of a car; he invented various kitchen *devices* such as one for whipping cream and one for hulling strawberries), of any artifice or stratagem concocted as a means of accomplishing one's end (as, her *device* for keeping the children quiet; "he will...entrap thee by some treacherous *device*"—*Shak.*), and of any pattern or design that shows the play of fancy, especially of one that proves useful to the less inventive (as, a common literary *device;* "that old stale and dull *device* [in painting] of a rustic bridge spanning a shallow stream"—*Jefferies*). **Contrivance** stresses skill and dexterity in the adaptation of means (especially the means at hand) to an end; it often is used, however, with a suggestion of contempt; as, a *contrivance* for frightening birds that would eat his corn; "All sorts of *contrivances* for saving more time and labour" (*Shaw*); "He would look at none of the *contrivances* for his comfort" (*Conrad*). **Gadget,** originally a slang term, but now more or less accepted as good colloquial English, once denoted any device for which one did not know the name: now it applies to any small and novel device, especially one in the nature of an accessory or of an appliance, which adds to a person's comfort, convenience, or pleasure; as, their new car has all the latest *gadgets;* the cook refuses to use any of the *gadgets* we bought for her. **Contraption,** also a colloquial term, is more depreciative than *gadget;* also, it usually suggests a clumsy contrivance rather than an ingenious invention; as, he has rigged up a *contraption* which he calls a radio.

Ana. Instrument, tool, *implement, appliance, utensil: apparatus, *machine, engine: expedient, *resource, shift, makeshift, resort: invention, creation (see corresponding verbs at INVENT): artifice, ruse, *trick.

2 *Figure, design, motif, pattern.

Ana. *Symbol, emblem, attribute, type.

devil. *Demon, fiend, daemon.

devilish. Diabolical, diabolic, *fiendish, demoniacal, demoniac, demonic.

Ana. *Infernal, hellish: nefarious, iniquitous, villainous, *vicious.

Ant. Angelic.

devious. *Crooked, oblique.

Ana. Deviating, diverging, digressing (see SWERVE): aberrant, *abnormal: tricky, crafty, artful, cunning, foxy, *sly.

Ant. Straightforward. — *Con.* Downright, *forthright.

devoid. **Devoid, void, destitute** come into comparison when they are followed by *of* and mean showing entire want or lack. **Devoid** stresses the absence or the nonpossession of a particular quality, character, tendency, or the like; as, "I was not *devoid* of capacity or application" (*Gibbon*); "they will steal from you before your very face, so *devoid* are they of all shame" (*Hudson*); "a human being *devoid* of hope is the most terrible object in the world" (*V. Heiser*). **Void** (see also EMPTY, 1) usually implies freedom from the slightest trace, vestige, tinge, or taint of something; as, a man *void* of honor; "A conscience *void* of offence" (*Acts* xxiv. 16); "A drama which, with all its preoccupation with sex, is really *void* of sexual interest" (*Shaw*). **Destitute** stresses deprivation or privation; it therefore is seldom used with reference to that which is evil or undesirable; as, "A domestic life *destitute* of any hallowing charm" (*G. Eliot*); "Men of genius...wholly *destitute* of any proper sense of form" (*J. R. Lowell*); "No woman...so totally *destitute* of the sentiment of religion" (*J. R. Green*).

Ana. Barren, *bare: lacking, wanting (see LACK, *v.*): *empty.

devolution. Decadence, decline, declension, *deterioration, degeneration.

Ana. Retrogressiveness *or* retrogression, regressiveness *or* regression (see corresponding adjectives at BACKWARD): receding *or* recession, retrograding *or* retrogradation (see corresponding verbs at RECEDE).

Ant. Evolution. — *Con.* *Development: *progress, progression.

devote. 1 **Devote, dedicate, consecrate, hallow** come into comparison as meaning to set apart something (sometimes some one) for a particular use or end. **Devote** etymologically implies a vow, but in its present somewhat extended sense it often implies a giving up or setting apart because of motives almost as impelling as those that demand a vow; as, to *devote* one's full time to the care of the unfortunate; for days a group of men *devoted* themselves to the search for the lost child. "Eloquence, erudition, and philosophy...were humbly *devoted* to the service of religion" (*Gibbon*). **Dedicate** implies solemn and exclusive devotion and often a ceremonial setting apart for a serious and often a sacred use; as, to *dedicate* a church; "I will *dedicate* all the actions of my life to that one end" (*Belloc*). "I had *devoted* the labour of my whole life, and had *dedicated* my intellect...to the slow and elaborate toil of constructing one single work" (*De Quincey*). **Consecrate** etymologically implies the giving of a sacred or exalted character; in strictest use, it implies rites, such as those by which a building is set apart (often in perpetuity, especially in distinction from *dedicate*) for the service or worship of God (as, to *consecrate* a church), or by which a bishop or king is elevated to his throne (as, kings of England are *consecrated* in Westminster Abbey), or by which ground is set apart as a burial place of the dead (as, to *consecrate* a cemetery). In an extended sense, however, *consecrate* does not imply such rites, but it carries a stronger connotation of almost religious devotion than *dedicate*. "A night of memories and of sighs I *consecrate* to thee" (*Landor*). **Hallow** is the stronger term, partly because of its use in the Lord's Prayer ("Our Father which art in heaven, *Hallowed* be thy name"—*Matthew* vi. 9) and because it often implies an ascription of intrinsic sanctity. "But in a larger sense we cannot *dedicate*, we cannot *consecrate*, we cannot *hallow* this ground" (*Lincoln*).

Ana. *Commit, consign, confide, entrust: assign, *allot: *sentence, doom.

2 Apply, *direct, address.

Ana. Endeavor, strive, struggle, try, *attempt.

devoted. *Loving, affectionate, fond, doting.

Ana. *Faithful, loyal, leal, true, constant: attentive, considerate, *thoughtful.

devotee. Votary, *addict, habitué, fiend, fan.

Ana. *Enthusiast, zealot, fanatic.

devotion. Loyalty, fealty, *fidelity, piety, allegiance.

Ana. Fervor, ardor, zeal, enthusiasm, *passion: love, affection, *attachment: dedication, consecration (see corresponding verbs at DEVOTE).

devout. **Devout, pious, religious, pietistic, sanctimonious** are here compared as applying mainly to persons, their acts, and their words, and as meaning showing fervor and reverence in the practice of religion. **Devout** stresses an attitude of mind or a feeling that leads one to frequent, though not necessarily outwardly evident, prayer, to solemn and reverent attention in public worship, and to strong attachment to the exercises and observances of religion; as, "A *devout* man, and one that feared God" (*Acts* x. 2); "All those various 'offices' which, in Pontifical, Missal, and Breviary, *devout* imagination had elaborated from age to age" (*Pater*). **Pious** emphasizes rather the faithful and dutiful performance of one's religious obligations; although often used interchangeably with *devout* it tends, even in nonderogatory use, to suggest outward acts which imply faithfulness and fervor rather than, as does *devout*, an attitude or feeling which can only be inferred; as, *pious* churchmen; *pious* regularity in church attendance. "Our whole duty is made up of but three things: that a man live soberly with respect to himself; righteously with respect to his neighbor; and *piously* with respect to God" (*J. Sharp*). The term often, however, carries a hint of depreciation, sometimes of hypocrisy. "The saying that we are members one of another is not a mere *pious* formula to be repeated in church without any meaning" (*Shaw*). Cf. *pious fraud* under IMPOSTURE. **Religious** may, and usually does, imply both devoutness and piety, but it stresses faith in a God or gods, and adherence to a way of life believed in consonance with that faith. "A man may be moral without being *religious*, but he cannot be *religious* without being moral" (*F. W. H. Myers*). "He [the Roman general who carried images of his gods] did it because...he was *religious*, and his gods must go with him" (*Quiller-Couch*). **Pietistic** is commonly more derogatory than *pious;* historically, it implies an insistence on the emotional aspects rather than on the intellectual aspects of religion; as, "An emotional person with *pietistic* inclinations that nearly carried him over at different times to the Plymouth Brethren" (*H. G. Wells*). In current use, the historical association is largely forgotten and the term is applied to that which the speaker or writer regards as sentimentally or affectedly pious; as, *pietistic* practices; a *pietistic* discourse. **Sanctimonious** has in current use entirely lost its original implication of a holy or sacred character; now it implies a pretension to or appearance of holiness or piety; as, a *sanctimonious* hypocrite like Mr. Pecksniff; *sanctimonious* phrases. Often, it connotes a hypocritical aloofness or superiority of manner. "If it only takes Some of the *sanctimonious* conceit Out of one of those pious scalawags" (*Frost*).

Ana. Fervent, fervid, ardent (see IMPASSIONED): worshiping, adoring, venerating (see REVERE).

dexterity. Facility, ease, *readiness.

Ana. Dexterousness, adroitness, deftness, featness (see corresponding adjectives at DEXTEROUS); expertness, adeptness, skillfulness, proficiency (see corresponding adjectives at PROFICIENT).

Ant. Clumsiness. — ***Con.*** Awkwardness, ineptness *or* ineptitude, maladroitness (see corresponding adjectives at AWKWARD).

dexterous. **Dexterous** (*or* **dextrous**), **adroit, deft, feat, handy** agree in meaning having or showing readiness and skill in the use of one's hands, limbs, or body. By extension, the first three may also imply physical or mental readiness or skill. **Dexterous** implies expertness with consequent facility and agility in manipulation or movement. "With a couple of *dexterous* turns of the wrist, [he] pegged the bird on its back with outstretched wings" (*Kipling*). **Adroit** is gradually being displaced by *dexterous* in its physical sense. It is still occasionally used, however, with reference to feats of manual skill requiring resourcefulness or artfulness; thus, an *adroit* fencer or an *adroit* magician is, by implication, not only *dexterous* in his manipulations, but able to cope quickly and without bungling with every situation that arises. "A daring but consummately *adroit* transference of conventions" (*Lowes*). **Deft** stresses lightness, neatness, and sureness of touch or handling; as, a *deft* watch repairer. "When he was about to salt his tea, she *deftly* substituted the sugar bowl" (*Atlantic Monthly*). "The delicacy...and the *deftness*, and the crystalline quality of the verse of China and Japan" (*Lowes*). **Feat,** now a bookish word, comes close to *deft;* in very precise use, however, it adds the connotation of grace, or beauty in movement. " 'She dances *featly*.' 'So she does any thing' " (*Shak.*). **Handy** usually implies lack of training but a degree of skill in doing small jobs of carpentry, plumbing, repairing, etc.; it is sometimes applied to a jack-of-all-trades; as, a *handy* man.

Ana. Nimble, *agile: skilled, skillful, expert, adept, *proficient: *easy, effortless, smooth, facile.

Ant. Clumsy. — ***Con.*** *Awkward, maladroit, inept, gauche.

diabolical, diabolic. Devilish, *fiendish, demoniacal, demoniac, demonic.

Ana. & ***Ant.*** See those at DEVILISH.

diagram, *v.* Outline, plot, blueprint, draft, trace, *sketch, delineate.

Ana. Design, plan, plot, scheme. See under PLAN, *n.*

diagram, *n.* Outline, draft, tracing, sketch, delineation, plot, blueprint. See under SKETCH, *v.*

Ana. Design, *plan, plot, scheme.

dialect, *n.* **1** **Dialect, vernacular, patois, lingo, jargon, cant, argot, patter, slang** are here compared as denoting a form of language or a style of speech which varies from that accepted as the literary standard. **Dialect,** as here compared (see also LANGUAGE, 1), is applied ordinarily to a form of a language that is confined to a locality or to a group, that differs from the standard form of the same language in peculiarities of vocabulary, pronunciation, usage, morphology, and the like, and that persists for generations or even centuries. It may represent an independent development from the same origin as the standard form (as, the Sussex *dialect*) or a survival (as, the *dialect* of the Kentucky mountaineers). The term is often, in spite of some philological opposition, applied to a corruption of the standard language (as, the Gullah *dialect*, a corrupted English used by descendants of African Negroes living chiefly along the coast of South Carolina and Georgia). "A Babylonish *dialect* Which learned pedants much affect" (*Butler*). **Vernacular** (usually *the vernacular*) has several applications, though it always denotes the form of language spoken by the people in contrast with that employed by learned or literary men. In the Middle Ages, when the language of the church, of the universities, and of learned writings was Latin, the vernacular was the native language of the people, whatever it might be in the locality in question; as, to translate the Bible into the *vernacular*. "Freeman ...laments...that the first Christian missionaries from Rome did not teach their converts to pray and give praise in the *vernacular*" (*Quiller-Couch*). When a contrast with the literary language rather than with Latin is implied, *the vernacular* is an underogatory designation for the spoken language, that is, for the language that represents the speech of the people as a whole, that is colloquial but not necessarily vulgar, and is marked chiefly by the spontaneous choice of familiar, often native (as opposed to exotic), words and phrases. "Pope...

is absolute master of the raciest, most familiar, most cogent and telling elements of the *vernacular*" (*Lowes*). In current use, *vernacular* often implies a contrast with scientific nomenclature; as, the botanical and the *vernacular* names for flowers. **Patois,** a French word adopted in English, is often used as if it were the equivalent of *dialect*. It tends, however, to be restricted, especially in North America, to designating a form of speech used by the uneducated people in a bilingual section or country; the word often specifically refers to the hybrid language (English, and French Canadian) spoken in some parts of Canada. **Lingo** is a term of contempt applied to any language that is not easily or readily understood. It is applicable to a strange foreign language, a dialect, a patois, or to the peculiar speech of any class, cult, or the like. "I have often warned you not to talk the court gibberish to me. I tell you, I don't understand the *lingo*" (*Fielding*). **Jargon,** which originally meant the twittering or chattering of birds, and later was applied to any unintelligible or meaningless speech (as in a foreign tongue or a patois) suggestive of such chattering, is now used chiefly in reference to the technical or esoteric language of a subject, a class, a profession, or a cult, often, but not always, from the point of view of one unfamiliar with it and confused or baffled by it. "Cockets, and dockets, and drawbacks, and other *jargon* words of the customhouse" (*Swift*). "Whitman...has a somewhat vulgar inclination for technical talk and the *jargon* of philosophy" (*Stevenson*). **Cant,** which is etymologically related to *chant*, seems to have been applied first to the whining speech of beggars; in later times, it has been applied variously, as to the secret language of gypsies and thieves, to the technical language of a trade or profession, and to the peculiar phraseology of a religious sect or of its preachers. From the last of these applications, not only has a new sense been developed (see HYPOCRISY), but a new connotation has been derived for the word in the sense here considered. For *cant*, when referred to the peculiar language of a subject or profession usually suggests the hackneyed use of set words or phrases, often in a specialized or "off" sense; *cant*, therefore, does not usually imply unintelligibility; thus, the language of sports writers is a *cant* (not a *jargon*); the scientific nomenclature used by physicians in official reports may be called medical *jargon* (not *cant*) by those who do not understand it; a person who repeatedly calls an investigation a "probe," a large book a "tome," a preacher a "parson," his wife "my better half," and the like, may be said to be given to *cant*. **Argot** is applicable chiefly to the cant of the underworld, originally to that of Paris; it is now sometimes used of any form of peculiar language adopted by a clique, a set, or other closely knit group. **Patter** always implies rapid voluble speech, such as is characteristic of a circus barker or of a faker selling wares, or is found half-recited, half-sung as a farcical act on the stage or in a musical comedy. In extended use it usually also implies a cant; as, the *patter* of an auctioneer; the *patter* of a clown. **Slang** does not as often denote a form of language or a type of speech as it does a class of recently coined words or phrases or the type of word which belongs to that class; as, in the *slang* of college students a drudge is a "greasy grind"; the difference between American *slang* and British *slang*. *Slang* implies comparatively recent invention, the appeal of the words or phrases to popular fancy because of their aptness, picturesqueness, grotesqueness, or humorousness, and either an ephemeral character or, if the words or phrases persist in use, their nonacceptance by the authorities as a permanent addition to the language; thus, "to escape with the skin of one's teeth" sounds like *slang*, but it is not so designated because it is derived from the Authorized Version of the Bible (*Job* xix. 20).

2 *Language, tongue, speech, idiom.

dialectic. *Argumentation, disputation, debate, forensic.

diamond. *Arena, circus, lists, ring, cockpit, court, field, gridiron, rink.

diaphanous. Limpid, pellucid, transparent, translucent, *clear, lucid.

dictate, *n.* Behest, bidding, injunction, *command, order, mandate.

Ana. *Law, rule, precept, canon, ordinance, statute, regulation.

dictatorial. **Dictatorial, magisterial, magistral, authoritative, authoritarian, dogmatic** (*or* **dogmatical**), **doctrinaire, oracular** come into comparison in the sense of imposing or having the manner or disposition of one who would impose his will or his opinions upon others. Etymologically, **dictatorial** implies the powers of a dictator (historically, a person, often a military man, in whom supreme or absolute power is vested during an emergency), but it has acquired so strong an implication of the assumption of such power that it now often stresses autocratic or highhanded methods and a domineering, overbearing temper. "A captain who has been entrusted with *dictatorial* power" (*Macaulay*). "He is... very learned, very *dictatorial*, very knock-me-down" (*M. R. Mitford*). "He [Dryden] has nothing of the unpleasant *dictatorial* manner of Temple" (*Gosse*). **Magisterial** and the now comparatively rare **magistral** derive their chief implications from their etymological reference to a magistrate or, more often, to a schoolmaster. They seldom imply an assumption of power, highhandedness, or a bad temper, but they do suggest excessive use or display of the powers or prerogatives associated with the offices of a magistrate or schoolmaster, such as in controlling and disciplining or in enforcing the acceptance of one's opinions. "We are not *magisterial* in opinions, nor...obtrude our notions on any man" (*Browne*). "It will not do to say *magisterially:* 'Take the child away!' I suspect that even exhortation is superfluous" (*Lowes*). *Magisterial* is now also applied to opinions, ideas, and the like, which are so deeply impressed on the mind, especially the popular mind, that they cannot easily be eradicated. "The 'possible,' as something less than the actual and more than the wholly unreal, is another of these *magisterial* notions of common sense" (*W. James*). **Authoritative** may or may not carry derogatory connotations. More often than not, it implies exercise of acknowledged power, such as that of "the authorities," or the person or persons having the power to exact obedience, to make final decisions, or to authorize something, or of "an authority," a person competent because of his official status, learning, or experience to present the facts or to give an opinion that has weight; as, the majority opinion of the supreme court has the effect of an *authoritative* decision; an *authoritative* statement from the secretary of the treasury regarding the national finances; an *authoritative* body of scientists; an *authoritative* book on economics. When *authoritative* implies an assumption of such power, it more often suggests a manner, an attitude, or the like, than an arbitrary exercise of power; as, he always took an *authoritative* tone in stating his views. "That self-possession and *authoritativeness* of voice and carriage which belonged to a man who thought of superiors as remote existences" (*G. Eliot*). **Authoritarian** is used chiefly in reference to states or governments (for this use see TOTALITARIAN), to churches, to bodies, persons, or their policies or attitudes. As here compared, it implies

assumption of one's own (or another's) power to exact obedience or of the right to determine what others should believe or do; often it suggests an opposition to *liberal* or *libertarian* and sometimes to *anarchic* or *anarchistic;* as, an *authoritarian* church; an *authoritarian* economic policy; an *authoritarian* system of education; the *authoritarian* type of mind. "The decline of *authoritarian* control and the rapid changes in our ways of living have made changes in our education imperative" (*Christian Century*). **Dogmatic,** as here compared, implies the attitude of an authoritative or authoritarian teacher or preacher and the laying down of principles or dogmas as true and beyond dispute. "Art is never *dogmatic;* holds no brief for itself—you may take it or you may leave it" (*Galsworthy*). "Now physics is, or should be, un*dogmatic;* mathematics is, and must be, *dogmatic.* No mathematician is infallible; he may make mistakes; but he must not hedge. Even in this age which dislikes dogma, there is no demand for an un*dogmatic* edition of Euclid" (*Eddington*). In depreciative use, *dogmatic* implies an assertive (sometimes an arrogant) attitude that discourages, if it does not inhibit, debate. "Mr. Raycie made no pretence to book-learning....But on matters of art he was *dogmatic* and explicit, prepared to justify his opinions" (*E. Wharton*). **Doctrinaire** usually, but not invariably, implies a dogmatic disposition; it usually suggests an opposition to *practical,* for it emphasizes a disposition to be guided by one's theories or the doctrines of one's school of thought in teaching, in framing laws, or in policies or decisions, especially those affecting others. "The rationalist mind...is of a *doctrinaire* and authoritative complexion: the phrase 'must be' is ever on its lips" (*W. James*). "The most profound contribution to political thought in America, namely, the *Federalist,* was not the work of *doctrinaire* thinkers but of men of affairs" (*Frankfurter*). **Oracular,** with its implied reference to an ancient oracle (a priest or priestess through whom the gods or a god made a revelation), suggests the possession of hidden knowledge and the manner of one who delivers his opinions or views in cryptic phrases or with pompous dogmatism. "What really annoys him is that [anyone]...should take a gnomic and *oracular* tone in place of trying to be ingratiating, whimsical, and entertaining" (*J. C. Powys*).
Ana. *Masterful, domineering, imperative, imperious, peremptory: despotic, tyrannical, arbitrary, autocratic, *absolute.

diction. *Language, vocabulary, phraseology, phrasing, style.
Ana. Speech, tongue, idiom, *language: enunciation, pronunciation, articulation (see corresponding verbs at PRONOUNCE).

dictionary, *n.* **Dictionary, onomasticon, gazetteer, synonymicon, lexicon, wordbook, glossary** come into comparison as denoting a work of reference which embodies an alphabetized vocabulary with definitions or explanations of each term. **Dictionary** is now the usual term for a book which gives not only the words that belong to a language (or in an abridged dictionary, the most important and most common words of a language) but also their meanings, their accepted spelling or spellings, their pronunciation, etymology, and the like; as, Webster's New International *Dictionary* of the English Language. It is also the general term applied to a book that embodies an alphabetized list of names with explanatory information or that presents an alphabetized list of terms with their synonyms; as, a *dictionary* of proper names, formerly often called by the now learned word **onomasticon**; a biographical *dictionary;* a geographical *dictionary,* now commonly called a **gazetteer;** a *dictionary* of synonyms, also, though rarely, called a **synonymicon.** The term is also applied to a book that lists and defines terms used in a particular field or department of knowledge; as, a chemical *dictionary;* a *dictionary* of the fine arts. **Lexicon,** though often used interchangeably with *dictionary,* especially as a name for the type (as, "In the *lexicon* of youth...there is no such word As—fail!"—*Lytton*), is especially applied to a dictionary of an ancient language such as Greek, Hebrew, Sanskrit, or the like, originally with definitions in Latin but now usually in the vernacular. Consequently, *lexicon* is often, but not invariably, the preferred designation of a dictionary that interprets words of one language in terms of another; as, a Latin-English *lexicon;* an English-French *lexicon.* Both in general and in technical use, the term often specifies a dictionary for students of any language, any science, or the like. **Wordbook** is often preferred when the distinctive vocabulary of a class, the people of a locality, or other restricted group is presented with definitions; as, "The Sailor's *Word-Book*" by W. H. Smyth. **Glossary** applies to a book or, more often, to an appendix to a book, containing a list of words so ancient, so unusual, so abstruse, so technical, or the like, that they need to be glossed (see *gloss* under ANNOTATE), or defined for the benefit of the ordinary reader; as, this collection of Burns's poems has an adequate *glossary;* few can read Chaucer without the aid of a *glossary;* a *glossary* of medical terms.

didder, *v.* *Shake, tremble, quake, dither, shimmy, totter, quiver, shiver, shudder, quaver, wobble, teeter.
Ana. Vibrate, sway, fluctuate, oscillate, waver, pendulate (see SWING).

dido. *Prank, caper, antic, monkeyshine.

differ. 1 In form **differ from.** Differ with (see DIFFER, 2).
Ana. Disagree, dissent (see affirmative verbs at ASSENT): diverge, deviate, depart (see SWERVE).
Ant. Concur, coincide.

2 In form **differ with. Differ with, differ from** are not always clearly distinguished. To express mere divergence of opinion, both **differ with** and **differ from** may be used, though in current good use *differ with* tends to be preferred; as, "I *differ with* the honorable gentleman on that point" (*Brougham*); "I do not rashly *differ from* so great a grammarian" (*Cowper*). When, however, to the implication of disagreement in opinion is added a hint of dispute or contention, *differ with* is the preferred phrase. "I have *differed with* the President...on many questions of great general interest and importance" (*D. Webster*). To express unlikeness between persons or things *differ from* alone is used; as, the twins *differ from* one another in appearance; "Day *differs from* day in respect of the importance of the public events they bring forth" (*C. E. Montague*); "how widely the world as known to science *differs from* the final analysis of material objects into electrons and protons" (*Inge*).
Ana. Disagree, dissent (see affirmative verbs at ASSENT): *contend, cope, battle, fight: *oppose, combat, withstand, resist.
Ant. Concur, agree.

difference. Unlikeness, *dissimilarity, divergence, distinction.
Ana. Discrepantness *or* discrepancy, inconsistency, inconsonance, discordance (see corresponding adjectives at INCONSONANT): variation, modification (see under CHANGE, *v.*): disparity, diversity (see corresponding adjectives at DIFFERENT).
Ant. Resemblance. — *Con.* Similarity, *likeness, similitude, analogy, affinity.

different. Different, diverse, divergent, disparate,

various come into comparison only when they are used to qualify plural nouns and mean not identical or alike in kind or character. **Different** often implies little more than distinctness or separateness; as, four *different* persons told me the same story. Sometimes, however, it implies contrast or contrariness; as, they approached the subject from *different* points of view. **Diverse** is stronger, and implies marked difference and decided contrast; as, "I obtained from three cultivated Englishmen at *different* times three *diverse* pronunciations of a single word" (*J. R. Lowell*); "The isolation of the Church of England causes distress to all Anglicans, but the remedies suggested are very *diverse*" (*Inge*). **Divergent** implies a movement away from each other and usually connotes the impossibility of an ultimate meeting, combination, reconciliation, or the like; as, they took *divergent* paths; "he was bothered very much by *divergent* strands in his own intellectual composition" (*H. G. Wells*); "A great part of the quarrel between science and religion arises from *divergent* opinions...about what it [the world] will be" (*Inge*). **Disparate** implies absolute or essential difference, often as between incongruous or incompatible things or ideas; as, "two divergent, yet not wholly *disparate* emotions" (*F. W. H. Myers*); "For if men are so *diverse*, not less *disparate* are the many men who keep discordant company within each one of us" (*Pater*). **Various** (see also MANY) commonly lays stress on the number of sorts or kinds; as, "in *various* shapes of Parsons, Critics, Beaus" (*Pope*); "An exuberant energy which displayed itself in *various* fields" (*H. Ellis*).

Ana. *Distinct, separate, several: *single, particular: various, sundry, divers (see MANY).

Ant. Identical, alike, same. — ***Con.*** *Similar, like, uniform, akin, analogous, comparable.

difficult. *Hard, arduous.

Ana. Perplexing, puzzling, mystifying (see PUZZLE): intricate, involved, complicated, *complex, knotty: *obscure, enigmatic, cryptic: exacting, *onerous, burdensome.

Ant. Simple. — ***Con.*** *Easy, facile, light, effortless, smooth: *clear, perspicuous, lucid.

difficulty. **Difficulty, hardship, rigor** (*or* **rigour**), **vicissitude** are here compared as general terms that are synonyms only when they mean something which demands effort and endurance if it is to be overcome or one's end achieved. **Difficulty,** the most widely applicable of these terms, applies to any condition, situation, experience, or task which presents a problem extremely hard to solve or which is seemingly beyond one's ability to suffer or surmount: the term does not imply insolubility or insurmountability or even intolerableness but it does suggest the need of skill and perseverance or patience; as, "the wise gods have put *difficulty* between man and everything that is worth having" (*J. R. Lowell*); "Ten thousand *difficulties* do not make one doubt, as I understand the subject; *difficulty* and doubt are incommensurate" (*Newman*); "the simplest way out of the *difficulty* was to do nothing and dismiss the matter as no concern of theirs" (*Conrad*). **Hardship** stresses suffering, toil, privation, or the like, that is almost beyond endurance or is extremely hard to bear: the term does not necessarily imply any effort to overcome or any patience in enduring (as, "Men to much misery and *hardship* born"—*Milton;* the *hardships* of life in a slum area), but in current use, it is so frequently applied to the suffering, toil, and privation encountered in an attempt to accomplish an end, that it often comes very close to *difficulty* in its implications; as, "The search for truth ....makes men and women content to undergo *hardships* and to brave perils" (*C. W. Eliot*); "they had practically overcome the worst *hardships* that primitive man had to fear" (*Cather*). **Rigor,** in the sense in which it is here considered, usually applies to a hardship that is imposed upon one, sometimes by oneself as through asceticism or ambition, but more often by an austere religion, a tyrannical government or other power, a trying climate, an extremely exacting enterprise or undertaking, or the like; as, "to undergo much pain, many *hardships*, and other *rigours*" (*Bp. Burnet*); the *rigors* of an explorer's life; "A vast deal of sympathy has been lavished upon the Puritan settlers because of the *rigours* of their religion" (*A. Repplier*); the *rigors* of an arctic winter. **Vicissitude** (as here considered: for stricter sense, see CHANGE, *n.*, 2) applies to a difficulty or hardship incident to one's life, especially as it is subjected to influences beyond one's powers of foresight or control, or to a rigor incident especially to a career or way of life one has chosen: oftentimes, the word may be intended to imply alternations of fortune, but this implication is so obscured by the context that the term actually suggests reference to something that demands effort and endurance if it is to be overcome; as, "the fierce *vicissitudes* of deadly combat" (*Lecky*); "it is the work he performed during these years, often in illness, danger, and *vicissitudes*, that should earn him particular gratitude from his Church" (*T. S. Eliot*).

Ana. *Obstacle, impediment, snag, obstruction: *predicament, dilemma, quandary, plight, scrape, fix, jam, pickle: pinch, strait, emergency, exigency, pass (see JUNCTURE).

diffident. Modest, bashful, *shy, coy.

Ana. Shrinking, flinching, blenching (see RECOIL): hesitant, reluctant (see DISINCLINED): timorous, *timid.

Ant. Confident. — ***Con.*** Assured, sure, sanguine (see CONFIDENT): self-confident, self-assured, self-possessed (see corresponding nouns at CONFIDENCE): brash, brazen, impudent, *shameless.

diffuse. Prolix, redundant, verbose, *wordy.

Ana. *Profuse, lavish, exuberant: desultory, casual, *random: copious (see PLENTIFUL): *loose, relaxed, slack, lax.

Ant. Succinct. — ***Con.*** *Concise, terse, laconic, pithy, summary: compact, *close.

dig, *v.* **Dig, delve, spade, grub, excavate, exhume, disinter** come into comparison when they mean to use a spade or similar utensil in breaking up the ground to a point much below the surface and in turning or removing the earth so broken up. **Dig,** the common and usual word both in literary and colloquial use, originally implied, and in some use still implies, a loosening of the earth around or under something so as to bring it to the surface; as, to *dig* in the ruins of Pompeii; to *dig* for gold; to *dig* up roots embedded in the earth. **Delve,** which is now archaic in its literal sense, more regularly implies the use of a spade (the implement) or, in its more common extended sense, of efforts comparable to the use of a spade, than does *dig:* it also carries a stronger connotation of laboriousness and depth of penetration and usually, but not invariably, the work of a farmer or gardener, or of one who cultivates an interest or follows a hobby; as, "When Adam *delve*, and Eve span, Who was then the gentleman?" (*Old Proverb*); "a smug and spectacled best scholar, spending...time *delving* among the chronicles...in the reading-room of the British Museum" (*R. Macaulay*). *Dig* and **spade** have taken the place of *delve* in its literal sense and may imply all the operations necessary to manual (as opposed to mechanical) preparation of soil for planting of any vegetables or flowers or for the harvesting of root crops; as, to *dig* a garden; to *dig* (or *spade*) up potatoes; to *dig* in (or *spade* in) fertilizer. In extended and figurative use, *dig* may imply a result comparable to that obtained by spading (as, "[The ants] *dug* deeper and deeper to deposit their eggs"—*Goldsmith*), or a bringing to the surface or out of concealment (as, to *dig* up a man's past), or prolonged laborious effort as in study or research (as, "Laurie '*dug*' to some purpose that year, for he graduated with honor"—*L. M. Alcott*). **Grub** strictly implies a more superficial digging, such as that done in clearing ground for agricultural use or in breaking up and turning the topsoil, but in current use, it carries so strong a suggestion of laborious, dirty, and often, back-breaking work in a garden or farm that in literal use it seldom connotes actual digging and, frequently, as in extended use, not even work on the ground but some equally dirty and grueling labor; as, "Both the parlormaid and her employer...if they are fond of flowers...will *grub* in a garden all day...without considering the dirt involved ...in the least derogatory to their dignity" (*Shaw*); "*Grubbing* among Roman remains and relics" (*A. Lang*). **Excavate** suggests making a hollow in or through something such as the ground, a mass of rock, a mountainside, by or as if by means of a spade or shovel or a machine which performs the operations of spading and shoveling; as, to *excavate* the ground for a foundation wall and cellar; to *excavate* a tomb; to *excavate* a tunnel; archaeologists engaged in *excavating* the site of an ancient city. **Exhume** implies a digging or excavating that has for its aim or result the removal of something buried beneath the surface of the ground; as, to *exhume* all the bodies buried in an old cemetery; the archaeologist *exhumed* a particularly fine piece of sculpture. **Disinter** usually implies the exhuming of that which has been buried by human hands; as, he was permitted to *disinter* the remains of his parents and transfer them to the new cemetery; when the suspicion that he had been murdered grew rife, the coroner ordered his body to be *disinterred*.

Ana. Pierce, penetrate, probe, *enter.

digest, *n.* *Compendium, syllabus, pandect, survey, sketch, précis, aperçu.

Ana. Collection, assemblage, gathering (see under GATHER): *abridgment, conspectus, abstract, brief, synopsis, epitome.

digging *or* **dig.** In plural form **diggings** *or* **digs.** Chambers, quarters, lodgings, *rooms, apartment, flat, tenement.

dignity. 1 *Decorum, decency, propriety, etiquette.

Ana. *Excellence, virtue, merit, perfection: nobleness *or* nobility, morality, ethicalness *or* ethics (see corresponding adjectives at MORAL).

2 *Elegance, grace.

Ana. *Worth, value: beautifulness *or* beauty, loveliness, comeliness (see corresponding adjectives at BEAUTIFUL): grandness *or* grandeur, magnificence, stateliness, nobleness *or* nobility, majesticness *or* majesty, augustness (see corresponding adjectives at GRAND).

digress. Deviate, diverge, depart, *swerve, veer.

Ana. *Wander, stray.

digression. **Digression, episode, excursus, divagation** come into comparison when they denote a departure from the main course of development, especially of a narrative, a drama, an exposition, or the like. **Digression** applies to any deviation, especially one at the expense of unity of effect, from the main subject of a discourse; it may or may not suggest intention or design. "In this long *digression* which I was accidentally led into, as in all my *digressions*..., there is...an excellence seldom looked for...in a *digression*...; though...I fly off from what I am about, as far, and as often too, as any writer in Great Britain, yet I constantly take care...that my main business does not stand still in my absence" (*Sterne*). **Episode** (see also OCCURRENCE) usually, but not invariably, applies to an incidental narrative which, though separable from the main subject, arises naturally from it; sometimes an episode is definitely a purposeful digression for some end such as giving variety to the narration, heightening the illusion of reality, or elucidating a motive; thus, in *Paradise Lost*, Raphael's account of the war in heaven is in this sense an *episode* because it breaks the chronological order of the poem and reverts to events which occurred prior to those told in the first book. "Descriptive poetry...may be interspersed with dramatic *episodes*" (*S. Alexander*). *Episode* is used not only of a literary work but of any form of art, or of a life, in reference to something that seems apart from the main subject or course of a thing. "Delight in the virginal beauty of fresh blossoms, in the dewy green of water-meadows...is evident in numberless pictures of the earlier schools of Europe; but there these amenities of nature are but an *episode*" (*Binyon*). "Miss Dix's biographer, Dr. Tiffany, considers her war work an *episode*, not equal in quality to her life-work" (*Dict. Amer. Biog.*). **Excursus** applies to an avowed and usually formal digression elucidating at some length an incidental point. "This started an ethnological *excursus* on swineherds, and drew from Pinecoffin long tables showing the proportion per thousand of the caste in the Derajat" (*Kipling*). **Divagation** is often used in preference to *digression* when aimless wandering from the main course or inattentiveness to logic is implied. "Froissart's style of poetry invites the widest...liberty of *divagation*, of dragging in anything that really interested him" (*Saintsbury*).

dilapidate. *Ruin, wrack, wreck.

Ana. *Decay, disintegrate, crumble, decompose: *neglect, ignore, disregard, forget, slight, overlook.

Con. Repair, rebuild, *mend: *renew, restore, renovate, rejuvenate.

dilate. 1 *Discourse, expatiate, descant.

Ana. *Relate, recount, rehearse, recite, narrate, describe: expound, *explain: *discuss, argue.

2 *Expand, distend, swell, amplify, inflate.

Ana. Enlarge, *increase, augment: *extend, protract, prolong, lengthen: widen, broaden (see corresponding adjectives at BROAD).

Ant. Constrict: circumscribe: attenuate. — *Con.* *Contract, shrink, compress, condense.

dilatory. *Slow, laggard, deliberate, leisurely.

Ana. Procrastinating, delaying, dawdling, dallying, dillydallying (see DELAY): *negligent, neglectful, lax, slack, remiss.

Ant. Diligent. — *Con.* *Busy, assiduous, sedulous, industrious: *quick, prompt, ready.

dilemma. *Predicament, quandary, plight, scrape, fix, jam, pickle.

Ana. Perplexity, bewilderment, mystification (see corresponding verbs at PUZZLE): *difficulty, vicissitude.

dilettante. 1 *Amateur, dabbler, tyro.

Con. Artist, *expert, adept.

2 *Aesthete, connoisseur, virtuoso.

Con. *Artist, artificer, architect: *writer, composer, author: craftsman, workman (see WORKER).

diligent. Assiduous, sedulous, industrious, *busy.

Ana. Persevering, persisting *or* persistent (see corresponding verbs at PERSEVERE): *indefatigable, tireless, untiring, unwearied, unflagging.

Ant. Dilatory. — *Con.* *Slow, laggard, deliberate, leisurely: desultory, casual, happy-go-lucky (see RANDOM).

dillydally. Dally, dawdle, procrastinate, *delay, lag, loiter.

Ana. *Trifle, toy: *play, sport: linger, tarry (see STAY).
Con. Hurry, hasten, *speed.

dilute, *v.* Attenuate, *thin, rarefy.
Ana. Temper, attemper, *moderate, qualify: *weaken, enfeeble: dissolve, *liquefy, deliquesce: *adulterate, sophisticate.
Ant. Condense: concentrate (*in chemistry, esp. in past participial form*).

diluvium. Drift, *wash, alluvium, alluvion, silt.

dim, *adj.* Dusk, dusky, *dark, darkling, obscure, murky, opaque, gloomy.
Ant. Bright: distinct. — *Con.* Brilliant, radiant, luminous, effulgent (see BRIGHT): manifest, patent, *evident, plain, clear.

dimensions. Extent, *size, area, magnitude, volume.

diminish. Reduce, *decrease, lessen, abate, dwindle.
Ana. Wane, ebb, *abate, subside: *moderate, temper, attemper: lighten, alleviate, mitigate (see RELIEVE): attenuate, extenuate (see THIN).
Con. Enlarge, augment, *increase: *extend: *intensify, enhance, heighten, aggravate.

diminutive, *adj.* Little, *small, wee, tiny, minute, miniature.
Con. *Large, big, great: *enormous, immense, huge, vast, colossal, mammoth.

din, *n.* **Din, uproar, pandemonium, hullabaloo, babel, hubbub, racket** agree in meaning a disturbing or confusing welter of sounds or a scene or situation marked by such a welter of sounds. **Din** emphasizes the pain suffered by the ears and the completely distracting effect of the noise as a whole; it now often, but not invariably, suggests prolonged and deafening clangor or insistent ear-splitting metallic sounds; as, the *din* of a machine shop; to escape the *din* of heavy traffic; the *din* of a New Year's Eve party. "Think you a little *din* can daunt mine ears?.... Have I not heard great ordnance in the field, And heaven's artillery thunder in the skies? Have I not in a pitched battle heard Loud 'larums, neighing steeds, and trumpets' clang?" (*Shak.*). **Uproar** and **pandemonium** both imply tumult or wild disorder, usually in a crowd of persons, but often among wild animals or in the elements; when the reference is to men, *uproar* usually suggests the clamor of a multitude vociferously, sometimes riotously, protesting, arguing, defying, or the like, and *pandemonium*, the din produced when a group or crowd usually under discipline breaks bounds and runs riot or becomes uncontrollably boisterous; as, the suggestion threw the assemblage into an *uproar; pandemonium* followed the announcement of the armistice. "Draw not the sword; 'twould make an *uproar*, Duke, You would not hear the end of" (*Keats*). "The modern parent... does not want a fictitious Sabbath calm while he is watching, succeeded by *pandemonium* as soon as he turns his back" (*B. Russell*). **Hullabaloo** is often interchangeable with *din* or *uproar*, especially in a construction following *make* (as, to *make* a *din*, an *uproar*, or a *hullabaloo*), but it seldom carries the suggestions of piercing, ear-splitting noise or of vociferation and turmoil which are respectively so strong in *din* and *uproar*. When it refers to a welter of sounds, it suggests great excitement and an interruption of peace or quiet; as, the *hullabaloo* made by hunters and hounds in the chase; the children are making a great *hullabaloo* at their party. When it refers to a situation, it suggests a storm of protest, an outburst of passion or wrath, a torrent of comment or sensational gossip, or the like; as, the project was not again brought before the public until the *hullabaloo* about it had died down; the lavish wedding made a great *hullabaloo*. **Babel,** with its implied reference to *Genesis* xi. 9, stresses the confusion of vocal sounds resulting either from their multiplicity and variety, or from differences in tongues; as, the *babel* of a polyglot assembly or of a busy market; unable to endure the *babel* of a crowded reception. **Hubbub** denotes the confusing mixture of sounds characteristic of activities and business; it implies incessant movement or bustle rather than turmoil; as, a sound heard above the *hubbub* of the city streets. "Strollers on the common could hear, at certain hours, a *hubbub* of voices and racing footsteps from within the boundary wall" (*Shaw*). **Racket,** like *din*, stresses the psychological effect of noises more than their character or origin. It implies, however, annoyance or disturbance rather than pain and distraction, and is applicable to any combination of sounds or any scene that strikes one as excessively or inordinately noisy. "We wanted quiet, not *racket*" (*Steele*). "Something like forty feet of chain and wire-rope, mixed up with a few heavy iron blocks, had crashed down from aloft on the poop with a terrifying *racket*" (*Conrad*).
Ana. Clamorousness *or* clamor, stridency, boisterousness, blatancy (see corresponding adjectives at VOCIFEROUS): clash, percussion (see IMPACT).
Ant. Quiet.

dinner. *Banquet.

dint. *Dent, indentation, indenture, nick, notch.
Con. See those at DENT.

dip, *v.* **1 Dip, immerse, submerge, duck, souse, dunk** are here compared as meaning to plunge a person or thing into, or as into, water or other liquid. **Dip,** as here compared, implies a momentary or partial plunging into a liquid, or figuratively, a slight or cursory entrance into a subject; as, "The priest shall *dip* his finger in the blood" (*Leviticus* iv. 6); to *dip* a dress in cleansing fluid; to *dip* into a book. **Immerse** implies that the person or thing is covered by the water or other liquid, or figuratively, buried or engrossed in something; as, to *immerse* the persons being baptized; to *immerse* a dress in boiling dye for several minutes; to *immerse* oneself in thought; "I am at present wholly *immersed* in country business" (*Addison*). **Submerge** implies complete and often prolonged immersion, or a covering by water as in an inundation; as, to *submerge* a submarine (or, the submarine *submerged*); several houses were completely *submerged* by the flood; figuratively, even more often than literally, it suggests a being overwhelmed, or sometimes, overpowered and rendered helpless (as, "the last and most violent religious rebellion against the French Crown... seemed likely to *submerge* that monarchy"—*Belloc*) or a sinking to the lowest state, grade, status, or the like (as, "Almost unheard of for such a girl to enter into relations with a man of that *submerged* class"—*Mencken*). **Duck** implies a sudden plunging (usually of a person) into water and an almost immediate withdrawal. "I say, *duck* her in the loch, and then we will see whether she is witch or not" (*Scott*). **Souse** adds to *duck* the suggestion of more prolonged immersion and often of a thorough soaking; as, the boy was *soused* before he was freed from his captors; to *souse* offenders; "a blazing caldron in which Beelzebub is *sousing* the damned" (*Arnold*). In its earliest and still current sense, *souse* implies steeping of meat, fish, or the like, in a pickle or tart liquid for the sake of preserving and flavoring it; as, *soused* mackerel. In figurative use, *souse* therefore often implies not only immersion but a being saturated or, in the case of liquor drinking, a becoming intoxicated; as, he came home night after night thoroughly *soused;* to *souse* oneself in a subject that interests one. **Dunk,** originally a dialect term in German-settled parts of the United States but now in general use, means to dip and soak something, as bread or a doughnut, or the like, in coffee, tea, or milk before eating it. In extended applications, it is equivalent to *duck* or *immerse* (cf. the name *Dunkers*, applied to the German Baptist Brethren, a religious denomination practicing trine immersion).

2 Dip, lade, bail (*or, less correctly*, **bale**), **scoop, ladle, spoon, dish** are here compared as meaning to remove a liquid, a fluid, or a friable or soft substance from a container by means of an implement, usually a vessel with a handle. In this sense they are often followed by *up* or *out*. **Dip** suggests literally or figuratively the process of plunging the utensil (usually called a *dipper*) into the substance and lifting it out full or nearly full; it is the preferred word when the labor involved is to be implied or the action is described; as, to *dip* water from a boiler; to *dip* out the milk from a can; to *dip* into one's memory for facts one has nearly forgotten. **Lade** usually adds to *dip* the suggestion of emptying a container or removing its contents; it is used chiefly in industry or in laborious operations; as, having no pump, they were compelled to *lade* out the water from the well; to *lade* ale wort into the tun tub; to *lade* out smelted silver into molds for casting. **Bail** is used chiefly in reference to boats in which water has accumulated or is accumulating; like *lade*, it implies emptying or an attempt to empty, but it suggests the use of a vessel (sometimes any available vessel) such as a pail, a bucket (formerly called a *bail*), a basin, or the like; as, to *bail* the water out of a rowboat. "By the help of a small bucket and our hats we *bailed* her [a boat] out" (*R. H. Dana, jr.*). *Scoop, ladle, spoon* throw the emphasis on the kind of implement employed in an operation consisting usually of dipping, conveying, and pouring. **Scoop** suggests a shovellike implement, often a small kitchen utensil for dipping out flour, sugar, or the like, or for gouging out pieces of a soft substance, such as cheese, and frequently for a much larger and heavier implement used in digging or excavating operations, or in the removal of a heap of things from one place to another; as, to *scoop* out three cups of sugar; to *scoop* up the catch of fish into barrels. **Ladle** implies the use of a ladle, or long-handled implement with a bowl-shaped end and often a pouring lip; it is especially used of substances which are liable to be spilled; as, to *ladle* soup; to *ladle* out the punch; to *ladle* out the melted tar. The term sometimes implies the use of a mechanical device for conveying liquid from one container from which it has been dipped to another into which it is poured. **Spoon** implies the use of a spoon of any size, but especially a tablespoon, when the service of food to another's plate is also implied; as, the girl who *spoons* up vegetables in the cafeteria; to *spoon* out food to the baby. **Dish** implies transference to the individual plate or dish of the portion of food that is ladled or spooned or otherwise lifted; as, to *dish* out the vegetables; to *dish* up the ice cream.

diplomatic. Politic, smooth, bland, *suave, urbane.

Ana. Astute, *shrewd: courteous, courtly, polite (see CIVIL): artful, wily, crafty (see SLY): tactful, poised (see corresponding nouns at TACT).

dipsomaniac. Alcoholic, inebriate, *drunkard, sot, soak, toper, tosspot, tippler.

direct, *v.* **1 Direct, address, devote, apply** are synonymous when used reflexively meaning to turn or bend one's attention, one's energies, or the like, to something. They are less closely related but still often synonymous in other constructions when they mean to turn, bend, or point (as one's attention, one's thoughts, one's efforts) to a certain object or objective. Between **direct** and **address** there is often very little perceptible difference. One *directs* or *addresses* oneself to a task, or to one's work, or to the study of a problem. One *directs* or *addresses* one's attention to a certain thing, one's remarks to a given person, one's book to a special type of reader. Also, one *directs* or *addresses* a letter when one writes on the envelope the name of the recipient and the place of delivery. In general, however, modern usage shows a tendency to prefer *direct* when an intent or aim is implied or indicated and *address* when an appeal to the mind or feelings is expressed or understood; as, the Democratic members *directed* their energies to the defeat of the measure; a demagogue *addresses* his arguments to the least intelligent in his audience. "Mrs. Yeobright...sat by the breakfast-table...her eyes listlessly *directed* towards the open door" (*Hardy*). "Those to whom it [propaganda] is *addressed*" (*A. Huxley*). **Devote** often adds to *direct* and *address* the implication of persistence. One *devotes* oneself to a task, a work, the study of a problem, or one *devotes* one's energies to the prosecution of a work, when one resolutely continues at the task, work, etc., to which one has directed or addressed oneself. Quite as often, and in distinction from the other words, *devote* implies dedication or setting apart for a certain end or use; as, to *devote* oneself to the public good; to *devote* one's leisure to charity. "Small farms *devoted* to fruit and berry raising" (*S. Anderson*). **Apply** distinctively suggests concentration. One *applies* oneself to a task, to one's work, or the like, when one gives one's entire attention to that to which one has directed or addressed oneself. In modern English idiom, *apply oneself* and *apply one's mind* often equal "concentrate" or "give one's entire attention"; as, he learned early to *apply himself;* an anxious person cannot *apply his mind* to the task in hand. Sometimes *apply* comes very close to *direct* and *address*, with, however, the additional implication of employment. "That they may sample several kinds of knowledge... and have a chance to determine wisely in what direction their own individual mental powers can be best *applied*" (*C. W. Eliot*).

Ana. Turn, bend (see CURVE): *set, fix, settle: endeavor, strive, try, *attempt.

Con. Divert, deflect, *turn: digress, diverge, deviate, *swerve.

2 Direct, aim, point, level, train, lay are synonyms only when they mean to turn something toward its appointed or intended mark or goal. One **directs** something or someone *to* its (or his) destination or objective when one heads it (or him) toward the proper course or guides it (or him) along that course; as, to *direct* one's eyes to the door; to *direct* a stranger to the railroad station; to *direct* a searchlight to the opposite shore. " 'Tis Heav'n each Passion sends, And diff'rent men *directs* to diff'rent ends" (*Pope*). One **aims** a weapon or something used as a weapon when one by careful calculation or estimation of counterinfluences turns it toward the exact spot or the object one designs to hit; as, to *aim* a pistol at a burglar; to *aim* a blow at a man's stomach; to *aim* a law at tax evaders. One **points** something *at* (sometimes *to*) a person or thing when one turns its point or tip to the spot one wishes to indicate or to penetrate, puncture, or the like; as, to *point* one's finger at one's choice; to *point* a sword at an opponent's breast; to *point* a boat to shore; she felt all eyes were *pointed* at her. One **levels** a weapon (esp. a spear, a lance, a rifle, etc.) or something which serves as a weapon *at* (or *against*) something when one brings it to the position or line (often a horizontal position or line) where it will do its most deadly or most effective work; as, to *level* a spear at a foe; to *level* a rifle at a deer; to *level* a charge against the mine owners. "Like an arrow shot From a well-experienc'd archer hits the mark His eye doth *level* at" (*Shak.*). One **trains** or **lays** a gun, a cannon, or the like, when one sets it in position and pointed directly at its mark; as, when the smoke screen dissipated, the cruiser discovered the enemy's cannon *trained* on it; the distinguished visitors could go nowhere without finding a battery of cameras *trained* upon them; to *lay* a gun for a shot.

Ana. Steer, pilot, *guide, lead, engineer.

Ant. Misdirect.

3 Manage, control, *conduct.

Ana. *Govern, rule: lead, *guide: administer, *execute.

4 *Command, order, bid, enjoin, instruct, charge.

Ana. *Prescribe, assign, define.

direct, *adj.* **Direct, immediate,** as applied to relations and as meaning marked by the absence of interruption (as between the cause and the effect, the source and the issue, the beginning and the end), though frequently used with little distinction, often retain their etymological connotations. **Direct** suggests unbroken connection between one and the other or a straight bearing of one upon the other; **immediate** suggests the absence of any intervening medium or influence; thus, *direct* knowledge is knowledge gained firsthand, but *immediate* knowledge is that attained by intuition or insight rather than through inference from facts or premises; *direct* contact stresses the bearing of one thing upon the other, but *immediate* contact implies the coherence or cohesion of one and the other; *direct* descent implies descent in a straight line from an ancestor; one's *immediate* family is composed of those who are the nearest in relation only, or one's father, mother, brothers, and sisters; a *direct* cause leads straight to its effect, but an *immediate* cause (which may or may not be the *direct* cause) is the one which serves as the last link in a chain of causes and brings about the result.

directly. Directly, immediately, instantly, instantaneously, forthwith, straightway (*or* **straightaway**), **right away, at once, anon** come into comparison when they mean without delay or loss of time. **Directly,** like **immediately,** implies the absence of any intervening time; as, Do it *directly, immediately.* In modern usage, however, *directly* (cf. the similar development of *presently*) has acquired the sense of "soon, before long"; as, I am coming *directly.* **Instantly** retains the implication of absolutely immediate sequence; as, answer me *instantly;* the report followed *instantly* upon the flash. **Instantaneously** implies the imperceptibility of the interval of time between the beginning and end of an action or process; as, light passes *instantaneously* through the earth's atmosphere; "Clare had *instantaneously* consented to accept Mr. John Todhunter as lord of her days" (*Meredith*). **Forthwith** implies less quickness than *instantly,* but nevertheless it connotes dispatch. "*Immediately* there fell from his eyes as it had been scales: and he received sight *forthwith*" (*Acts* ix. 18). **Straightway** (or the less common **straightaway,** both now rather literary or archaic) and the American colloquialism **right away** differ little from *directly* or *immediately;* as, "And *straightway* the damsel arose, and walked" (*Mark* v. 42); come *right away.* **At once,** like *instantly,* suggests not the slightest loss of time; as, come to me *at once.* **Anon** is now obsolete or archaic for *at once;* as, "Tel me *anon,* withouten wordes mo" (*Chaucer*).

dirigible. Airship, zeppelin, *aerostat, balloon, blimp.

dirty, *adj.* **Dirty, filthy, foul, nasty, squalid** agree in meaning conspicuously unclean or impure. **Dirty** is the general term for that which is sullied or defiled with dirt of any kind; as, *dirty* hands; *dirty* linen; *dirty* streets. **Filthy** is a much stronger term than *dirty* in its suggestion of offensiveness; it usually also suggests dirt which besmears or clutters up rather than that which merely soils; as, his clothes are *filthy;* a *filthy* hovel; a *filthy* street. **Foul** carries a still stronger implication of revolting offensiveness; etymologically, it implies an accumulation of that which is rotten, putrid, or stinking; as, a *foul* sewer; a *foul* dungeon; a *foul* pond. In somewhat extended use, it comes nearer to *loathsome* or *disgusting;* as, a *foul* smell; a *foul* sight. **Nasty,** which originally was not clearly distinguishable from *foul,* now applies chiefly to that which is repugnant to a person who is fastidious about cleanliness, sweetness, freshness of appearance, or the like; as, a *nasty* ship; a *nasty* odor; the care of pigs is *nasty* work. In British colloquial usage *nasty* has been softened to a mere synonym for "objectionable, disagreeable" (as, *nasty* weather; a *nasty* fall; a *nasty* temper; to be *nasty* to someone); in the United States it was formerly tabooed in polite speech in the sense of *foul,* and is now used with increasing frequency in its British sense. **Squalid** adds to the idea of dirtiness or filth that of extreme slovenliness or neglect; as, *squalid* poverty; "The East, so *squalid* and splendid, so pestilent and so poetic" (*E. Wharton*).

In their extended use, all of these terms may imply moral uncleanness or baseness, or obscenity. **Dirty,** however, stresses meanness or despicability (as, "The creature's at his *dirty* work again"—*Pope*); **filthy** and **foul** imply disgusting obscenity, *filthy* stressing the presence of obscenity, and *foul,* its hateful ugliness (as, *filthy* talk; a *foul* jest); **nasty** implies extreme offensiveness or unpleasantness (as, a *nasty* mind; "he hated it as a gentleman hates to hear a *nasty* story"—*E. E. Hale*); **squalid** implies sordidness as well as baseness (as, "the *squalid* scenes and situations through which Thackeray portrays the malign motives and unclean soul of Becky Sharp"—*C. W. Eliot*). The first four terms also apply to weather, meaning the opposite of that which is clear, thereby implying rainy, snowy, stormy, or foggy weather. Otherwise, they are distinguishable only by the degree in which they express disgust or distaste.

Ant. Clean.

disability. *Inability.

disable. Cripple, undermine, *weaken, enfeeble, debilitate, sap.

Ana. *Injure, damage, harm, hurt, impair, mar, spoil: *maim, mutilate, mangle, batter: *ruin, wreck, wrack.

Ant. Rehabilitate (*a disabled person*).

disaffect. Alienate, *estrange, wean.

Ana. Upset, agitate, *discompose, disquiet, disturb: sever, sunder, divorce (see SEPARATE).

Ant. Win (*men to a cause, allegiance, etc.*).

disapprove. Disapprove, deprecate agree in meaning to feel or to express an objection to or condemnation of a person or thing. **Disapprove** implies an attitude of dislike or distaste on any good grounds (social, ethical, intellectual, or the like) and an unwillingness to accept or to praise; the word may or may not, however, connote rejection or the expression of condemnation. "Gard loved his sister, but there were times when he wished for a way of making her understand how thoroughly he *disapproved* of her" (*M. Austin*). "[D. H.] Lawrence *disapproved* of too much knowledge, on the score that it diminished men's sense of wonder" (*A. Huxley*). **Deprecate,** as compared with *disapprove,* stresses the implication of regret, frequently profound, occasionally diffident or apologetic; as, "Shaping the plays to modern taste by the very excisions which scholars will most *deprecate*" (*FitzGerald*); "Wallace earnestly *deprecates* the modern tendency to disparage reason" (*Inge*); "There is nothing I more *deprecate* than the use of the Fourteenth Amendment...to prevent the making of social experiments" (*Justice Holmes*).

Ana. Reprehend, reprobate, censure, *criticize: *decry, disparage.

Ant. Approve. — ***Con.*** *Commend, recommend, applaud, compliment: endorse, sanction (see APPROVE).

disarming. **Disarming, ingratiating, insinuating, insinuative** come into comparison as meaning winning or designed to win another's favor or interest in spite of his disinclination or indifference. **Disarming** usually implies actual or potential anger, hostility, or opposition in the person to be won, and some quality such as innocence, candor, humility, or the like, in the person who wins, that allays or prevents irritation; as, though his words were critical, his smile was *disarming.* " 'I have brought Richard's wife, Sir,' he said with a pleased, perfectly uncalculating, countenance, that was *disarming*" (*Meredith*). **Ingratiating** carries a stronger implication of design than *disarming;* it often suggests a sedulous, sometimes even a servile or fawning, attempt to please or to win favor or attention; as, "What really annoys him is that any...heretic should take a gnomic and oracular tone in place of trying to be *ingratiating,* whimsical, and entertaining" (*J. C. Powys*); "her manner is quiet and *ingratiating* and a little too agreeable; she speaks a little too gently" (*G. Bottomley*). **Insinuating** and **insinuative** distinctly imply subtlety and suavity in winning favor or confidence; they often, however, carry a strong implication of artfulness, *insinuating,* in particular, sometimes strongly suggesting wiliness in flattery. "I cannot flatter and speak fair, Smile in men's faces ... But thus...simple truth must be abused By silken, sly, *insinuating* Jacks" (*Shak.*). "Englishmen of honourable name, distinguished appearance, and *insinuating* address" (*Macaulay*). "Craftily and *insinuatively* introduced by the subtlety of Satan" (*Evelyn*).

Ana. Mollifying, conciliating, propitiating, placating, appeasing, pacifying (see PACIFY).

Con. Irritating, nettling, exasperating, provoking *or* provocative (see corresponding verbs at IRRITATE): infuriating, maddening, enraging (see ANGER, *v.*).

disarrange. Derange, disorganize, *disorder, unsettle, disturb.

Ana. *Misplace, mislay: displace, *replace: upset, *overturn.

Ant. Arrange. — ***Con.*** *Order, systematize, methodize.

disarray. Disorder, chaos, *confusion, jumble, clutter, pie, snarl, muddle.

Con. *Method, system: ordering *or* order, arrangement, marshaling, organization (see corresponding verbs at ORDER).

disaster. **Disaster, calamity, catastrophe, cataclysm** come into comparison when they denote an event or situation that is regarded as a terrible misfortune. A **disaster** is an unforeseen mischance or misadventure (such as a shipwreck, a fatal railroad accident, the failure of a great enterprise) which happens, either through culpable lack of foresight or through adverse external agency, and brings with it destruction, as of life and property, or ruin, as of projects, careers, great hopes, and the like. **Calamity** is a grievous misfortune, particularly one which involves a great or far-reaching personal or, especially, public loss, or which produces profound, often widespread, distress; as, the rout at Bull Run was a *disaster* for the North; the assassination of President Lincoln, a *calamity;* the wreck of the "Don Juan" was a *disaster;* as involving the loss of Shelley, it was a *calamity.* "We have heard of his decision.... It is a *disaster*—for me a *calamity*" (*Galsworthy*). **Catastrophe** (properly a denouement of any sort) is here compared in the sense of a disastrous conclusion; in strict use, it emphasizes the idea of finality; as, the captain's folly hastened the *catastrophe.* "What had become of them [the inhabitants of a deserted village]? What *catastrophe* had overwhelmed them?" (*Cather*). **Cataclysm** (etymologically a deluge, hence, in geology, any violent convulsion involving profound geological changes) is often used figuratively, especially of an event or situation that brings with it an overwhelming of the old order or a violent social or political upheaval. "In the general upheaval of doctrine...during the Reformation *cataclysm*" (*J. H. Blunt*). "A thought so imperishably phrased that it sums up not only the *cataclysm* of a world, but also the stoic and indomitable temper that endures it" (*Lowes*).

Ana. Mishap, *accident, casualty: adversity, *misfortune, mischance.

disbar. Shut out, eliminate, rule out, suspend, debar, *exclude, blackball.

disbelief. *Unbelief, incredulity.

Ana. Atheism, deism (cf. nouns at ATHEIST): skepticism, agnosticism (see under SKEPTIC): rejection, repudiation, spurning (see corresponding verbs at DECLINE).

Ant. Belief. — ***Con.*** Faith, credence, credit (see BELIEF).

discard, *v.* **Discard, cast, shed, molt, exuviate, slough, scrap, junk** are synonymous verbs when they mean to get rid of as of no further use, value, or service. **Discard** literally implies the getting rid of a card or cards from one's hand in any of several games of cards, usually because they are worthless or can be replaced by better cards: in its more common extended sense, it implies a getting rid of something which one can no longer use to advantage or which has become a burden, an annoyance, an interference, or the like; as, "he sorted and re-sorted his cargo, always finding a more necessary article for which a less necessary had to be *discarded*" (*Cather*); "modern research, which *discards* obsolete hypotheses without scruple or sentiment" (*Inge*); "in portrait-painting, where a painter *discards* many trivial points of exactness, in order to heighten the truth of a few fundamentals" (*C. E. Montague*). **Cast** (as here considered: see also THROW) may imply a seasonal process such as the throwing off of skin by a reptile or, now less often, the loss of hair or teeth by an animal or of leaves by a tree (as, "Creatures that *cast* their skin are, the snake, the viper"—*Bacon*), but, especially when followed by *off, away,* or *out,* it more frequently implies a discarding, a rejection, a discharging, a repudiation, or the like (as, *cast*off clothes; "the state ... Cannot with safety *cast* him"—*Shak.;* "His wife was *casting* him off, half regretfully, but relentlessly"—*D. H. Lawrence*). **Shed** is now the ordinary, general term for the seasonal or periodic casting of skin, hair, leaves, and the like (as, deciduous trees *shed* their leaves every autumn; male deer *shed* their antlers annually; it is warm enough to *shed* one's overcoat). The term is also used to imply a throwing off or discarding of anything that is a burden to carry, that represents a past stage in one's development, or the like; as, "statesmen may try to *shed* their responsibility by treating the situation as a natural phenomenon" (*J. A. Hobson*); "Jane...was acquiring new subtleties, complexities, and comprehensions, and *shedding* crudities" (*R. Macaulay*). **Molt** is the specific term for the periodic shedding of feathers, skin, shells, hair, and horns by various animals such as birds, reptiles, crustaceans, and stags, and the growth of new feathers, shells, etc.: in general use, however, it more often suggests a process of a change in plumage including the shedding of feathers and their renewal; as, "The eagle when he *moults* is sickly" (*Carlyle*); while hens are *molting* they do not lay eggs. In an extended sense, *molt,* even more often than *shed,* implies change, flux, or transition; as, "England is *moulting.* Opinions...are...in a state of flux" (*G. Smith*). **Exuviate** (a technical term), like *molt,* may be used generally of shedding any covering, but commonly it implies the casting off of a shell; as, "The young crayfish *exuviate* two or three times in the course of the first year" (*T. H. Huxley*). **Slough** implies the shedding of skin, such as that periodically shed by a snake or other reptile or, especially in intransitive use, such as that which forms on the surface of a sore or wound; as, the snake often *sloughs* its skin in mid-September; the scab is *sloughing* off from the sore. The term is also common in extended use in the sense of to discard or throw off that which has become objectionable, burdensome, or the like; as, to *slough* a bad habit; "This talented author has *sloughed* off most of her more irritating sentimentalities" (*Times Lit. Sup.*). The last two words, *scrap* and *junk*, have literal reference to the throwing away of fragments, parts, or pieces that are useless to the owner or can no longer be used by him. **Scrap** suggests a discarding as rubbish or refuse, but it may carry an implication of some use to another, such as a processor or a dealer in parts or accessories; as, to *scrap* out-of-date machinery (cf. *scrap* iron); to *scrap* a plan as impractical; all the old ideas of combat had to be *scrapped;* "The English language that Shakespeare was born to had used up and *scrapped* a good deal of the English of Chaucer" (*C. E. Montague*). **Junk,** a slang term, differs little from *scrap* except in stressing a throwing away and in carrying little implication of value to a second-hand dealer or to a processor of waste; as, to *junk* all their old furniture before moving into their new home.

Ana. *Abandon, forsake, desert: reject, repudiate, spurn (see DECLINE, *v.*): dismiss, *eject, oust.

Con. *Adopt, embrace, espouse: utilize, employ, *use: retain, *keep, hold back.

discern. Perceive, descry, observe, notice, remark, note, espy, behold, *see, view, survey, contemplate.

Ana. *Discover, ascertain: divine, apprehend, anticipate, *foresee: pierce, penetrate, probe (see ENTER).

discernment. **Discernment, discrimination, perception, penetration, insight, acumen, divination, clairvoyance** are comparable when they denote keen intellectual vision. All imply power to see below the surface and to understand that which is not evident to the average mind. **Discernment** stresses accuracy, as in reading character or motives or in appreciation of art. "She [Marie de Médicis] had not had the *discernment* to discover the calibre of this young favourite" (*Belloc*). **Discrimination** emphasizes the power to distinguish and select the excellent, the appropriate, the true. "There was a time when schools attempted...to cultivate *discrimination* and to furnish the material on which selection can be founded" (*Grandgent*). **Perception** implies quick discernment and delicate feeling. "[He] was of a temperament to feel keenly the presence of subtleties; a man of clumsier *perceptions* would not have felt as he did" (*G. Eliot*). **Penetration** implies a searching mind and power to enter deeply into something beyond the reach of the senses. "It did not require any great *penetration* to discover that what they wished was that their letters should be as kind as was consistent with proper maidenly pride" (*De Quincey*). **Insight** emphasizes depth, or understanding sympathy, of discernment. "You have lived long, and got much experience, but not *insight*—not that inner vision that sees further than the eyes" (*Hudson*). **Acumen** suggests characteristic penetration and keenness and soundness of judgment. "A paradox which your natural *acumen*, sharpened by habits of logical attention, will enable you to reconcile in a moment" (*Cowper*). **Divination** is instinctive insight; **clairvoyance,** preternaturally clear or acute perception, esp. of what is not ordinarily discernible. "By some secret *divination*...she guessed all his wants, and supplied them" (*Carlyle*). "With the *clairvoyance* of a genuine love, she had pierced the mystery that had so long embarrassed Frank" (*Stevenson*).

Ana. Intuition, understanding, *reason: perspicaciousness *or* perspicacity, sagaciousness *or* sagacity, shrewdness, astuteness (see corresponding adjectives at SHREWD).

Con. Stupidity, dullness, density, crassness (see corresponding adjectives at STUPID): blindness (see corresponding adjective BLIND).

discharge, *v.* **1** *Free, release, liberate, deliver, emancipate, manumit, enfranchise, affranchise.

Ana. *Eject, expel, oust, dismiss: eliminate, *exclude.

2 *Dismiss, cashier, sack, fire, bounce, drop.

Ana. Displace, supplant, supersede, *replace.

3 *Perform, execute, accomplish, achieve, effect, fulfill.

Ana. Finish, complete, *close, end, terminate.

disciple. **1** Pupil, *scholar, student.

2 Adherent, *follower, henchman, satellite, sectary, partisan.

Ana. Votary, devotee (see ADDICT, *n.*): *enthusiast, zealot, fanatic.

3 **Disciple, apostle, evangelist** come into comparison when they denote one of the followers and close associates of Jesus in his lifetime. **Disciple,** the most comprehensive term, may be applied to anyone who comes under this description. In actual use, however, the term is far more restricted in its reference, for it commonly designates any one of those persons chosen by Jesus to assist him in his labors of preaching and converting, such as one of twelve (also called an *apostle*) or one of seventy (*Luke* x. 1, *A.V.*) or seventy-two (*Luke* x. 1, *D.V.*). When *disciple* is used in distinction from *apostle,* it commonly refers to one of the latter group. **Apostle** strictly designates one of the twelve who were the closest associates of Jesus, who were commissioned by him to go and to preach to all nations, on whom the Holy Ghost descended after his ascension (*Acts* ii), and who carried on his work after his death. In this strict sense, the term is applied not only to one of the original twelve, but also to Matthias, who was chosen after the defection of Judas, and to Paul, who was always regarded as the equal of the twelve in office and dignity. An **evangelist** (as here compared) is one of the four writers of the gospels included in the New Testament (Matthew, Mark, Luke, and John). Of these, Matthew and John are commonly identified as the apostles of the same name.

discipline, *v.* **1** Train, educate, *teach, instruct, school.

Ana. Lead, *guide: control, manage, direct, *conduct: drill, exercise, *practice.

2 *Punish, chastise, castigate, chasten, correct.

Ana. Subdue, overcome, reduce, subjugate (see CONQUER): *restrain, curb, bridle, check, snaffle, inhibit.

disclose. *Reveal, divulge, tell, discover, betray, bewray.

Ana. Confess, admit, own, *acknowledge, avow: *declare, proclaim, announce, publish, broadcast, advertise.

Con. Conceal, *hide: cloak, mask, dissemble, *disguise.

discoid, discoidal. *Round, circular, annular, spherical, globular, orbicular.

discomfit. Disconcert, *embarrass, faze, abash, rattle.

Ana. *Annoy, vex, irk, bother: perturb, *discompose, agitate, upset, disturb: check, *arrest, interrupt.

discommode. Incommode, *inconvenience, trouble, molest.

Ana. Disturb, perturb, upset, fluster, flurry, *discompose: vex, irk, bother (see ANNOY).

discompose. **Discompose, disquiet, disturb, perturb,**

agitate, upset, fluster, flurry are synonymous when they mean to excite one so as to destroy one's capacity for clear or collected thought or prompt action. **Discompose** is sometimes only slightly more suggestive of mental confusion than *disconcert* or *discomfit;* usually, however, it implies greater emotional stress and an actual loss of self-control or self-confidence. "He was still *discomposed* by the girl's bitter and sudden retort. It had cast a gloom over him" (*Joyce*). **Disquiet** stresses the loss, not of composure, but of something far deeper, such as one's sense of security or of well-being, or one's peace of mind. "Why art thou cast down, O my soul? and why art thou *disquieted* within me?" (*Psalms* xlii. 11). "He was indubitably not happy at bottom, restless and *disquieted,* his *disquietude* sometimes amounting to agony" (*Arnold*). **Disturb,** unlike the preceding words, carries no implication of a loss of one's balance or of an excess of emotion; usually it implies marked interference with one's mental processes that is caused by worry, perplexity, disappointment, interruption, or the like. "Constance and Amy were profoundly *disturbed* by the prospective dissolution of a bond which dated from the seventies" (*Bennett*). "Nothing is more *disturbing* than the upsetting of a preconceived idea" (*Conrad*). **Perturb** implies deep disturbance and unsettlement of mind; it usually connotes a cause for disquietude or alarm. "In this *perturbed* state of mind, with thoughts that could rest on nothing, she walked on" (*Austen*). **Agitate** emphasizes the loss of calmness and self-control and implies obvious signs of nervous or emotional excitement. It does not, however, always suggest distress of mind or a cause of worry. "Miss Clara was so *agitated* that she was incoherent" (*Deland*). "Growing more and more irritated, more and more *agitated*" (*V. Woolf*). "[She] burst into tears. For it was a happiness that *agitated* rather than soothed her" (*S. M. Crothers*). **Upset,** like *agitate,* implies a nervous reaction, but it usually presupposes a cause that brings one disappointment, or distress, or sorrow. "They wouldn't have believed they could be so *upset* by a hurt woodpecker" (*Cather*). **Fluster,** in its earlier sense and still in occasional use, carries a suggestion of the excitement and confusion induced by drinking intoxicants (as, "*flustered* with new wine"—*Tennyson*) but in current use it commonly suggests the agitation, bewilderment, and sometimes fright, induced by sudden, and often unexpected, demands, commands, needs, or the like. "The aged housekeeper was no less *flustered* and hurried in obeying the numerous...commands of her mistress" (*Scott*). "Scared with threats of jail and halter... that *fluster'd* his poor...wits" (*Tennyson*). **Flurry** suggests the excitement, commotion, and confusion induced by great haste or alarm; as, they reached the station, hot and *flurried,* just as the train pulled out; "Thoughts, with their attendant visions, which...*flurried* her too much to leave her any power of observation" (*Austen*).

Ana. Discomfit, disconcert, rattle, faze, *embarrass: vex, irk, bother, *annoy: *worry, harass, plague, pester.

Con. Appease, *pacify, conciliate, mollify, placate, propitiate.

disconcert. Rattle, faze, discomfit, *embarrass, abash.

Ana. Bewilder, nonplus, perplex, *puzzle: *discompose, fluster, flurry, disturb, perturb.

discontinue. Desist, cease, *stop, quit.

Ana. Suspend, intermit, stay (see DEFER): *arrest, check, interrupt.

Ant. Continue.

discord, *n.* **Discord, strife, conflict, contention, dissension, variance** are here compared as meaning a state or condition marked by disagreement and lack of harmony, or the acts or circumstances which manifest such a state or condition. **Discord** implies not only a want of harmony or of concord between persons or between things but also, usually, a positive clashing which manifests itself in personal relations by quarreling, factiousness, antagonism, and the like, in relations between sounds by a resulting dissonance or cacophony, and in relations between other things that are incongruous or incompatible by creating unpleasant impressions or mental disturbance. "They were firm and understanding friends. I know of but one approach to *discord* in their relations" (*A. Repplier*). "In this state of enlightenment there is no more *discord* between the will, the intellect, and the feelings, and the objects of our reverence" (*Inge*). "The seeker after truth...must disclaim responsibility for the way in which his discoveries fit into the general scheme of things. For the moment they may seem to produce *discord* rather than harmony" (*S. M. Crothers*). **Strife** throws the emphasis on a struggle for superiority rather than on the incongruity or incompatibility of the persons or things that disagree: commonly, it applies to relations between persons, but when used in reference to things, it is nearly always figurative. Also, the term may imply any of widely different motives for the struggle, such as rivalry, emulation, difference in opinion, disagreement, deep antagonism, or violent hostility; as, "domestic fury and fierce civil *strife*" (*Shak.*); "Yet live in hatred, enmity, and *strife* Among themselves" (*Milton*); "I strove with none, for none was worth my *strife*" (*Landor*); "a face in which a strange *strife* of wishes, for and against, was apparent" (*Hardy*); "The crowd swells, Laughing and pushing toward the quays in friendly *strife*" (*Amy Lowell*). **Conflict** (as here considered: see also CONTEST) implies a clashing and a struggle, but it stresses not the aim or end but the process, usually connoting a series of ups and downs, or the uncertainty of the outcome, or the trials, difficulties, or torments it involves. In this sense the term may apply to battles, wars, etc., but usually it applies to a mental, moral, or spiritual state of a person or group of persons, or to its outward manifestations; as, "pale With *conflict* of contending hopes and fears" (*Cowper*). "Who, if he be called upon to face Some awful moment to which Heaven has joined Great issues, good or bad for human kind ...through the heat of *conflict,* keeps the law In calmness made" (*Wordsworth*). "No more for him [Lincoln] life's stormy *conflicts*" (*Whitman*). The term is also used in a milder sense to imply an incompatibility between, or the impossibility of reconciling, two things which come together, as at the same time or upon the one person; as, a *conflict* of engagements; a *conflict* of duties. **Contention** may be, but now seldom is, used in place of *strife* in any of the senses of the latter word: in current good English, following scriptural use it applies chiefly to strife that manifests itself in quarreling, disputing, controversy, and the like: it may even be applied to a condition of affairs marked by altercations or brawls. "Cast out the scorner, and *contention* shall go out; yea, *strife* and reproach shall cease" (*Proverbs* xxii. 10). "Let the long *contention* cease! Geese are swans, and swans are geese, Let them have it how they will" (*Arnold*). **Dissension** may imply discord or strife between persons or parties, but it lays greater stress on a breach between those persons or parties than do any of the preceding words; thus, to say that there is *dissension* in a church or political party is to imply that it is broken up into contentious or discordant factions. "France, torn by religious *dissensions,* was never a formidable opponent" (*Macaulay*). "He [Richelieu] left the seeds of philosophic *dissension* vigorous in French soil" (*Belloc*). **Variance** usually implies a clash between persons or things owing to a difference in opinion, character, nature,

or the like, that makes for discord, conflict, or strife. The term also often suggests apparent or actual incompatibility or impossibility of reconciliation; as, "to remain at *variance* with his wife seemed to him....almost a disaster" (*Conrad*); "ascertained facts, with which religious tradition is often at *variance*" (*Inge*); "religious doubters who vaguely feel that their faith is at *variance* with science" (*H. Ellis*).
Ana. Discordance, dissonance (see under DISSONANT): incompatibility, incongruity, inconsonance, inconsistency, uncongeniality, discrepancy (see corresponding adjectives at INCONSONANT): antagonism, hostility, *enmity, rancor, animosity, antipathy.
Con. *Harmony, consonance, accord.

discordance. Dissonance (see under DISSONANT).

discordant. 1 *Inconsonant, incongruous, uncongenial, unsympathetic, incompatible, inconsistent, discrepant.
Con. *Consonant, congruous, congenial, sympathetic, compatible: harmonizing *or* harmonious, according *or* accordant, agreeing (see corresponding verbs at AGREE).
2 *Dissonant.

discount. *Deduction, rebate, abatement.

discourse, *v.* **Discourse, expatiate, dilate, descant** come into comparison as meaning to talk (sometimes write) more or less formally and at length upon a subject. **Discourse** frequently implies the manner or attitude of the lecturer, the monologist, the preacher, or the like; it often suggests detailed or logical and sometimes profound, witty, or brilliant discussion; as, "Jonson is a real figure—our imagination plays about him *discoursing* at the Mermaid, or laying down the law to Drummond of Hawthornden" (*T. S. Eliot*); "We talk in the bosom of our family in a way different from that in which we *discourse* on state occasions" (*Lowes*). **Expatiate** (etymologically, to spread out) implies ranging without restraint or, sometimes, wandering at will over a subject; it connotes more copiousness than *discourse* and often, therefore, carries a hint of long-windedness; as, "We will *expatiate* freely over the wide and varied field before us" (*Landor*); "the promoter of the raffle...was *expatiating* upon the value of the fabric as material for a summer dress" (*Hardy*). **Dilate** implies a discoursing that enlarges the possibilities of a subject, as by dwelling on each small detail; as, "She proceeded to *dilate* upon the perfections of Miss Nickleby" (*Dickens*); "those joys on which Stevenson *dilates* in that famous little essay in '*Virginibus Puerisque*'" (*Quiller-Couch*). **Descant** (originally, a melody or counterpoint sung above the plain song of the tenor, which was the first attempt at part music) stresses free comment, but it often also connotes delight or pleasure in this free expression of one's opinions, observations, or the like; as, "To praise his stable, and *descant* upon his claret and cookery" (*Goldsmith*); "he *descanted* to his heart's content on his favorite topic of the [prize] ring" (*Shaw*).
Ana. *Discuss, argue, dispute: converse, talk, *speak: lecture, harangue, orate, sermonize (see corresponding nouns at SPEECH).

discourteous. Impolite, uncivil, ungracious, *rude, ill-mannered.
Ana. Brusque, curt, crusty, gruff, blunt (see BLUFF): boorish, churlish (see under BOOR).
Ant. Courteous. — *Con.* *Civil, polite, courtly, gallant, chivalrous.

discover. 1 *Reveal, disclose, divulge, betray, bewray.
Ana. Impart, *communicate: *declare, announce, publish, advertise, proclaim.
2 **Discover, ascertain, determine, unearth, learn** come into comparison when they mean to find out something which was not previously known to one. **Discover** may presuppose investigation or exploration: on the other hand, it may presuppose accident. But it always implies that the thing existed, either actually or potentially, in fact or in principle, but had not been hitherto seen or known, or brought into view, action, use, or actual existence; as, to *discover* an island, a planet, electricity, a new field for industry; to *discover* a new writer, the true character of a friend, the uses of a weed; to *discover* the laws of heredity, the process of refining gold. "Those rules of old *discovered*, not devis'd" (*Pope*). **Ascertain** seldom, if ever, implies accidental discovery: it usually presupposes an awareness of one's ignorance or uncertainty, and conscious efforts, such as study, investigation, observation, and experiment, directed to the end of finding the truth or of discovering the facts. "Old paintings were compared to *ascertain* the dresses of the period" (*Shaw*). "Scientific experiment has *ascertained* how many trials are needed by a rat [in finding his way through a maze]" (*Grandgent*). **Determine** (as here compared: see also DECIDE) differs from *ascertain* only in its greater emphasis upon the intent to establish the facts or the truth or to decide a dispute or controversy. Its use is chiefly, but not exclusively, legal and scientific; as, experts were called to *determine* the presence or absence of poison in the vital organs; if the site of his birthplace can be *determined*, the memorial will be erected there; to *determine* the local reaction when ragweed pollen is injected beneath the skin. **Unearth,** which literally means to exhume, is more often used in its figurative sense of to bring to light or out into the open something that has been hidden, forgotten, lost, or is exceedingly difficult to trace. Frequently it also suggests intensive or prolonged investigation preceding discovery; as, to *unearth* old records; to *unearth* the evidence necessary for a conviction. **Learn,** in this sense as well as in its more usual meaning, implies acquirement of knowledge; as here compared, it commonly suggests little or no effort on the part of the one who discovers; as, it was only today that I *learned* his name. "Judy *learned* that the ayah must be left behind" (*Kipling*). "They have not yet even *learnt* that 'science' is not the accumulation of knowledge... but the active organization of knowledge" (*H. Ellis*).
Ana. Discern, observe, perceive, espy (see SEE).
3 *Invent, create.

discreet. Prudent, forethoughted, foresighted, provident. See under PRUDENCE.
Ana. *Cautious, circumspect, wary: politic, diplomatic (see SUAVE).
Ant. Indiscreet. — *Con.* Rash, reckless, temerarious, foolhardy (see ADVENTUROUS): foolish, fatuous, asinine, *simple.

discrepant. Inconsistent, *inconsonant, discordant, incompatible, incongruous, uncongenial, unsympathetic.
Ana. Divergent, disparate, *different, diverse.
Ant. Identical (*as accounts, explanations*). — *Con.* Agreeing, squaring, conforming, corresponding, jibing, tallying (see AGREE): uniform, parallel, alike, like, *similar.

discrete. 1 Separate, *distinct, several.
Ana. Individual, distinctive, peculiar (see CHARACTERISTIC).
Con. Blended, merged, fused, mingled (see MIX).
2 Successive, sequent, *consecutive, serial, sequential.
Ana. Disjoined, disconnected, dissociated (see affirmative verbs at JOIN).
Con. Related, linked, associated, united (see JOIN).

discretion. *Prudence, forethought, foresight, providence.
Ana. Caution, circumspection, wariness (see under

CAUTIOUS): judgment, *sense, wisdom, gumption.
Ant. Indiscretion. — *Con.* Foolishness, fatuousness, asininity, simplicity (see corresponding adjectives at SIMPLE): rashness, recklessness, foolhardiness (see corresponding adjectives at ADVENTUROUS).

discrimination. Penetration, insight, *discernment, perception, acumen, divination, clairvoyance.
Ana. Wisdom, judgment, *sense: subtlety, logicalness *or* logic (see corresponding adjectives at LOGICAL).
Con. Crassness, density, dullness, stupidity (see corresponding adjectives at STUPID).

discuss. Discuss, argue, debate, dispute, agitate agree in meaning to discourse about something in order to arrive at the truth or to convince others. **Discuss** implies an attempt to sift or examine, especially by presenting considerations pro and con; it often suggests an interchange of opinion for the sake of clarifying issues and testing the strength of each side. "Hobart couldn't *discuss.* He could talk; he could assert...but he couldn't meet or answer arguments" (*R. Macaulay*). **Argue** usually implies conviction and the adducing of evidence or reasons in support of one's cause or position. "Agrippa advised a republican restoration and Maecenas *argued* for a principate" (*Buchan*). **Debate** stresses formal or public argument between opposing parties, or (sometimes) deliberation with oneself. "They had gathered a wise council to them of every realm, that did *debate* this business" (*Shak.*). "Enid...*debating* his command of silence given...held commune with herself" (*Tennyson*). **Dispute,** in the sense of *discuss* or *debate,* is somewhat archaic. "[Paul] spake boldly for the space of three months, *disputing* and persuading the things concerning the kingdom of God" (*Acts* xix. 8). It now ordinarily implies contentious or heated argument. **Agitate** stresses both vigorous argument and a practical objective; it usually implies active propaganda and a determination to bring about a change. "When workers working ten hours a day *agitate* for an eight-hour day, what they really want is...sixteen hours off duty instead of fourteen" (*Shaw*). "If you really expect success, *agitate, agitate, agitate*" (*H. W. Paget*).
Ana. *Explain, expound, interpret, elucidate, explicate: *discourse, expatiate, dilate, descant.

disdain, *v.* Scorn, scout, *despise, contemn.
Ana. Spurn, repudiate, reject (see DECLINE, *v.*).
Ant. Favor: admit. — *Con.* Accept, *receive, take: *acknowledge, own.

disdain, *n.* Scorn, despite, contempt. See under DESPISE.
Ana. Aversion, *antipathy: insolence, superciliousness, arrogance (see corresponding adjectives at PROUD).
Con. *Regard, admiration, respect, esteem: *reverence, awe, fear.

disdainful. Supercilious, overbearing, insolent, arrogant, lordly, *proud, haughty.
Ana. Spurning, repudiating, rejecting (see DECLINE, *v.*): scorning, despising, contemning, scouting (see DESPISE): averse, *antipathetic, unsympathetic.
Con. Obliging, complaisant, *amiable: considerate, attentive, *thoughtful.

disease, *n.* **Disease, affection, ailment, malady, complaint, distemper,** as here compared, designate a physical disorder, especially one which causes illness or loss of health. **Disease** implies derangement or disturbance of vital functions either in the body or organism as a whole, or in one of its organs or parts, traceable to a cause such as a parasite, a toxin, or a diet deficiency; as, his suffering is caused by the wound and not by *disease.* Specifically, as used in names of physical disorders, it implies that the special symptoms and, often, the causes, are known; as, Bright's *disease;* contagious *diseases; diseases* of the heart; plant *diseases.* **Affection** is seldom, if ever, used absolutely, for the term implies an attack upon a particular part or organ; it therefore requires a qualifying or complementary word or phrase; as, an *affection* of the liver; pulmonary *affections.* **Ailment** is rarely used except in reference to human beings; it is more often applied to chronic than to acute diseases; though it implies sickness or debility, it does not in itself connote seriousness; as, the minor *ailments* of the aged; he suffers from a grave *ailment.* **Malady,** like *ailment,* is applied chiefly to human diseases which cause illness or suffering, but unlike the latter word it often names a serious and deep-seated organic affection or a possibly fatal acute disease. "Addison's disease, a *malady* which was nearly always fatal until steps were taken to supply the missing hormone" (*C. C. Furnas*). **Complaint** distinctively suggests the invalid's point of view. It is applied chiefly to affections of the stomach, the bowels (as, summer *complaint*), the heart, etc., which involve spells or attacks of pain. "To the proper temperament a congenial *complaint*...is...a source of agreeable emotions" (*C. E. Montague*). **Distemper,** once applied to human ailments, is now, with rare exceptions, used only of animals. It serves either as an inclusive term covering certain infectious diseases or specifically as the name for a serious, often fatal, contagious catarrhal disease which affects dogs, or as an alternative name for strangles, an infectious febrile disease of horses.

Figuratively, certain of these terms also come into comparison, especially as applied to mental, spiritual, or similar disorders. **Disease** usually connotes manifest derangement requiring remedies or a cure; as, *diseases* of the body politic. "This strange *disease* of modern life, with its sick hurry, its divided aims" (*Arnold*). **Ailment** implies something wrong that makes for unsoundness, weakness, or loss of well-being. "A bodily disease... may, after all, be but a symptom of some *ailment* in the spiritual part" (*N. Hawthorne*). **Malady,** especially as contrasted with *disease,* implies a deep-seated morbid condition or unwholesome abnormality. "How would they be troubled by this beauty, into which the soul with all its *maladies* had passed" (*Pater*). **Distemper** takes its figurative implications from its earlier reference to human ailments considered as the result of disturbed "humors" and stresses a lack of balance or of a sense of proportion. "To seek of God more than we well can find, Argues a strong *distemper* of the mind" (*Herrick*).

disembarrass. Disencumber, disentangle, untangle, *extricate.
Ana. Release, *free, liberate: *relieve: disengage, *detach.
Con. *Hamper, trammel, clog, fetter, shackle.

disencumber. Disembarrass, disentangle, untangle, *extricate.
Ana. *Relieve, alleviate, lighten: disengage, *detach: liberate, release, *free.
Con. *Depress, weigh (on *or* upon), oppress: *hamper, fetter, shackle, manacle, trammel, clog.

disengage. *Detach, abstract, prescind.
Ana. Disembarrass, disencumber, disentangle, untangle, *extricate: release, liberate, *free: disconnect, disjoin, dissociate, disunite (see affirmative verbs at JOIN).
Ant. Engage (*one part, one thing, etc., with another*). — *Con.* Involve, *include, embrace, comprehend, imply, implicate: link, associate, connect, unite, *join.

disentangle. Untangle, *extricate, disembarrass, disencumber.
Ana. Disengage, *detach: *separate, part, sever, sunder: *free, release, liberate.
Ant. Entangle.

disfeature, defeature. Disfigure, *deface.
Ana., Ant., & *Con.* See those at DISFIGURE.

disfigure. Disfeature, *deface.
Ana. Mangle, batter, *maim, mutilate: *deform, distort, contort, gnarl, warp: *injure, damage, mar, impair.
Ant. Adorn. — *Con.* Embellish, beautify (see ADORN).

disgrace, *n.* **Disgrace, dishonor** (*or* **dishonour**), **disrepute, shame, infamy, ignominy, opprobrium, obloquy, odium, scandal** are here compared as meaning the state, condition, character, or less often the cause, of suffering disesteem and of enduring reproach or severe censure. **Disgrace** in its weakest and earliest, yet most precise, sense implies a loss of the favor or esteem one has enjoyed; as, Queen Elizabeth's favorites were constantly in danger of *disgrace* if they offended her in the slightest degree. "He was shut up in an attic...and forbidden to speak to his sisters, who were told that he was in *disgrace*" (*B. Russell*). The term, however, often implies complete humiliation and, sometimes, ostracism. "You may find yourself at any moment summoned to serve on a jury and make decisions involving the *disgrace* or vindication...of your fellowcreatures" (*Shaw*). **Dishonor** may often be employed in place of *disgrace*, but in very discriminating use it suggests a previous condition of being honored or of having a high sense of honor; it therefore may imply the loss of the honor that one has enjoyed or the loss of one's self-respect or self-esteem; as, to prefer death to *dishonor;* "But now mischance hath trod my title down, And with *dishonor* laid me on the ground" (*Shak.*). "The shackles of an old love straiten'd him, His honour rooted in *dishonour* stood, And faith unfaithful kept him falsely true" (*Tennyson*). **Disrepute** stresses either the loss of one's good name or the attribution of a bad name or reputation; as, the actions of certain of its guests have brought the hotel into *disrepute;* the *disrepute* into which this once famous name has now fallen. **Shame** implies particularly humiliating disgrace or disrepute such as is caused by an illicit union, illegitimate birth, inferior blood, relationship to a traitor or criminal, commission of a crime, or the like; as, to live in *shame;* a child of *shame.* " 'Is it not...a pity to live no better life?' 'God knows it is a *shame!'* " (*Dickens*). "If mixture of blood be a *shame,* we [the British] have purchased at the price of that *shame* the glory of catholicism" (*Quiller-Couch*). **Infamy,** etymologically the antithesis of *fame* or *glory,* usually implies notoriety as well as exceeding shame. "Men who prefer any load of *infamy,* however great, to any pressure of taxation, however light" (*Sydney Smith*). "I have come, not from obscurity into the momentary notoriety of crime, but from a sort of eternity of fame to a sort of eternity of *infamy*" (*Wilde*). **Ignominy,** more than *infamy*—which in some ways it closely resembles, stresses the almost unendurable contemptibility or despicability of the disgrace or its cause; as, "The *ignominy* [horsewhipping] he had been compelled to submit to" (*Meredith*); "Was she now to endure the *ignominy* of his abandoning her?" (*D. H. Lawrence*); "The *ignominy* of returning to Spain, having accomplished nothing, became more obvious the more it was considered" (*Froude*). **Opprobrium** adds to *disgrace* the implication of being severely reproached or condemned; as, the *opprobrium* which often attaches itself to the term "politician." "Spain...has been plundered and oppressed, and the *opprobrium* lights on the robbers, not on the robbed" (*Buckle*). "The name 'educator,' for many intelligent people, has become a term of *opprobrium*" (*Grandgent*). **Obloquy** (see also ABUSE, *n.*) adds to *disgrace* the implication of being abused or vilified; as, "And undergo the perpetual *obloquy* of having lost a Kingdom" (*Clarendon*). "He [Mark Twain] never thought of publishing them ['Tom Sawyer' and 'Huckleberry Finn'] anonymously, as he published 'Joan' at first, lest it ['Joan of Arc'] should suffer from the *obloquy* of a pen-name that had been compromised by so many dubious ventures" (*Van W. Brooks*). **Odium** applies to the disgrace or the opprobrium that is attached to the fact or state of being an object of widespread or universal hatred or intense dislike; as, "Whatever *odium* or loss her manoeuvres incurred she [Queen Elizabeth] flung upon her counselors" (*J. R. Green*); "As a preliminary Augustus...revised the senatorial roll. This was always an invidious task....in the end he was compelled to make the nominations himself and face the *odium*" (*Buchan*); "Many materialists...seek to eliminate the *odium* attaching to the word materialism, and even to eliminate the word itself" (*W. James*). **Scandal** (as here compared: see also OFFENSE, 3; DETRACTION) applies to the disgrace or shame that is attached to any act, practice, condition, or the like, which arouses severe censure, creates objectionable gossip, or reflects on the competency, the intelligence, or the morals of those who are associated or involved; as, the fall of the bridge was a *scandal* both to the engineers and to the officials responsible for its construction; "It was that spring that...Miss Jane Jay, to the *scandal* and grief of her sisters, made up her mind not to go to church any more" (*Deland*). "A sinful man—why Mrs. Caroline expected nothing better: but a sinful woman—Oh! that was a *scandal,* a *shame!*" (*Meredith*).
Ana. Degradation, debasement, abasement, humbling, humiliation (see corresponding verbs at ABASE): *stigma, brand, blot, stain.
Ant. Respect, esteem. — *Con.* Admiration, *regard: *reverence, awe, fear: honor, repute, glory, renown, *fame.

disguise, *v.* **Disguise, cloak, mask, dissemble,** as here compared, agree in meaning to assume a dress, an appearance, or an expression that conceals one's identity, intention, true feeling, or the like. **Disguise,** which etymologically implies an alteration in one's dress, now frequently retains that implication with the added suggestion either of concealment of identity or of the assumption (as on the stage) of another identity; as, to escape captivity *disguised* as a woman; they *disguise* themselves as Turks for a joke. The term, however, may take for its object a feeling, an intention, a motive, or the like, when one's words, one's expression, or one's acts imply a contrary feeling, intention, etc.; as, "I *disguised* my impatience and suspicion of him and waited" (*Hudson*). "However we may *disguise* it by veiling words we do not and cannot carry out the distinction between legislative and executive action with mathematical precision" (*Justice Holmes*). **Cloak** implies the assumption of something which covers and conceals identity or nature in the manner of a long heavy loose cloak or wrap; as, the appearance of good will *cloaked* a sinister intention; "Wife-worship *cloaks* a secret shame" (*Tennyson*). **Mask** implies a disguise comparable to that of a mask, or a covering for the face or head, which prevents recognition of a thing's true character, quality, presence, or the like; as, icy spots *masked* by newly fallen snow; to *mask* troops by secreting them in trenches. "*Masking* with a smile The vain regrets that in their hearts arose" (*W. Morris*). **Dissemble,** which is used as often as an intransitive as a transitive verb, stresses simulation for the purpose of deceiving as well as disguising; it, therefore, is the preferred term when actual deception is achieved. "Ross bears, or *dissembles,* his disappointment better than I expected of him" (*Gray*). "The Scripture moveth us...to acknowledge and confess our manifold

sins and wickedness; and that we should not *dissemble* nor *cloke* them before the face of Almighty God" (*Bk. of Com. Prayer*).
Ana. Conceal, *hide: *misrepresent, belie: *assume, pretend, feign, counterfeit, sham, simulate, affect.
Con. Expose, exhibit, display, parade, flaunt (see SHOW, *v.*): *reveal, disclose, discover, betray, bewray.

dish, *v.* Ladle, spoon, *dip, lade, bail, scoop.

dishonest. Dishonest, deceitful, mendacious, lying, untruthful come into comparison especially when applied to persons, their utterances, and their acts, and mean lacking in honesty and unworthy of trust or belief. **Dishonest** may imply the act or the habit of willfully perverting the truth, but it also may suggest the act or habit of stealing, cheating, or defrauding; as, a *dishonest* statement; a *dishonest* merchant or employee or lawyer or historian. **Deceitful** usually implies the intent to mislead or to impose upon another in order to keep that one from knowing the truth, especially as to one's real nature or one's actual purpose or intention, or the true character of what is offered, given, sold, or the like; it therefore usually suggests a false or specious appearance, indulgence in falsehoods, or cheating, defrauding, or double-dealing; as, *deceitful* propaganda; *deceitful* children; a *deceitful* statement. **Mendacious,** a literary rather than colloquial term, differs little from **lying,** the ordinary, direct, unequivocal word, except in being used more often, when applied to persons, to suggest the habit of telling lies rather than, as the latter, the act of telling a lie; thus, one preferably describes a person as *mendacious* when his character is in mind and as *lying* when the untruth of something he has said or written is in mind; as, a child who relates fanciful experiences is not *mendacious* but unduly imaginative; a *lying* boy is easily detected, especially if he is by nature honest. "[The pagan ages] were not *mendacious* and distracted, but in their own poor way true and sane!" (*Carlyle*). "Silly newspapers and magazines for the circulation of *lying* advertisements" (*Shaw*). **Untruthful** is often used in place of *mendacious* or *lying* as a slightly less brutal word; however, the term distinctively implies lack of correspondence between what is said or what is represented, and the facts of the case or the reality, and is therefore more often applied to statements, accounts, reports, descriptions, and the like; as, an *untruthful* account of the incident; the artist's representation of the scene at Versailles was *untruthful* in many of its details.
Ana. *Crooked, devious, oblique: false, *faithless, perfidious: cheating, cozening, defrauding, swindling (see CHEAT, *v.*).
Ant. Honest. — ***Con.*** *Upright, honorable, scrupulous, conscientious, just: *straightforward, forthright, aboveboard: candid, open, *frank, plain.

dishonor *or* **dishonour,** *n.* *Disgrace, disrepute, shame, infamy, ignominy, opprobrium, obloquy, odium, scandal.
Ana. Humiliation, humbling, debasement, degradation, abasement (see corresponding verbs at ABASE): *stigma, brand, blot, stain.
Ant. Honor. — ***Con.*** Glory, renown, repute, *fame: reverence, veneration (see under REVERE): prestige, *influence, credit, authority, weight: esteem, respect, *regard, admiration.

disinclined, *adj.* **Disinclined, indisposed, hesitant, reluctant, loath** (*or* **loth**), **averse** agree in meaning manifesting neither the will nor the desire to do or to have anything to do with the thing that is indicated or understood. One is **disinclined** *to* (sometimes *for* or *to do*) something for which one has no natural bent or no present taste or inclination, or which meets one's disapproval. "I should not be *disinclined* to go to London, did I know anybody there" (*Richardson*). "Mr. Lorry and Defarge were rather *disinclined* to this course, and in favour of one of them remaining" (*Dickens*). "Now, when it has become a sort of fashion to exalt the spiritual qualities of the Chinese above those of other peoples, one may well feel *disinclined* to admit any interest in China" (*H. Ellis*). One is **indisposed** *to* or *to do* something when one's attitude is not favorable or is actually hostile or unsympathetic. "Unfit to rule and *indisposed* to please" (*Crabbe*). "Yeobright...was *indisposed* to take part in the feasting and dancing.... 'I wish I could be there without dashing your spirits,' he said. 'But I might be too much like the skull at the banquet' " (*Hardy*). One is **hesitant** *to do* (or *in doing*, or *about doing*) something who holds back through fear, distaste, disinclination, irresolution, or the like; as, she was *hesitant* to accept the invitation; *hesitant* in seeking advice; a *hesitant* suitor; to feel *hesitancy* about applying for a position. One is **reluctant** *to do* something who is not only hesitant but unwilling. "I was simply persuading a frightened and *reluctant* girl to do the straight and decent and difficult thing" (*R. Macaulay*). "People were *reluctant* to charge a dead man with an offense from which he could not clear himself" (*E. Wharton*). "We were *reluctant* to expose those silent and beautiful places to vulgar curiosity" (*Cather*). *Reluctant* is also applied directly to the thing which is done reluctantly or to a thing which by extension seems reluctant; as, "giving *reluctant* consent to publication" (*R. A. Cram*); "the constant strain of bringing back a *reluctant* and bored attention" (*B. Russell*); "they wring from the *reluctant* soil food enough to keep...alive" (*A. Repplier*). One is **loath** *to do* that which one is hesitant about doing because it is not in harmony with one's likes or dislikes, one's tastes or distastes, or one's sympathies or antipathies; thus, a tender person may be *loath* to punish a refractory child but a strict disciplinarian would be *loath* to allow that child to go unpunished; one may be *loath* to believe a well-founded report that discredits a friend yet *loath* to disbelieve a rumor that confirms one's bad opinion of a person. One is **averse** *to* something (or frequently, in British use, *from* something) when one turns away from it because one finds it distasteful or repugnant; as, to be *averse* to all advice from others; to be *averse* to dissension in one's family; to be *averse* to eating in public places. "His impulses were generous, trustful, *averse* from cruelty" (*J. R. Green*).
Ana. *Antipathetic, unsympathetic: opposing, resisting (see OPPOSE): balking, shying, boggling, sticking, stickling (see DEMUR): objecting, protesting (see OBJECT, *v.*).
Con. *Eager, avid, keen, anxious: inclined, disposed, predisposed (see INCLINE, *v.*).

disinfect. *Sterilize, sanitize, fumigate.
Ant. Infect.

disinfectant, *adj.* Antiseptic, germicidal, bactericidal. See under ANTISEPTIC, *n.*

disinfectant, *n.* *Antiseptic, germicide, bactericide.

disintegrate. Crumble, decompose, *decay, rot, putrefy, spoil.
Ana. Dissolve, deliquesce (see LIQUEFY): *scatter, disperse, dissipate: break down, resolve, *analyze, dissect.
Ant. Integrate. — ***Con.*** Articulate, concatenate (see INTEGRATE): fuse, blend, merge, coalesce (see MIX): unite, combine, link, associate, *join, connect.

disinter. Exhume, excavate, *dig, delve, spade, grub.
Ana. Unearth, *discover.

Ant. Inter. — *Con.* Bury, secrete, cache, conceal, *hide.

disinterested. 1 Detached, aloof, unconcerned, *indifferent, incurious.
Ana. Dispassionate, unbiased, impartial, *fair, just: *neutral, negative.
Ant. Interested: prejudiced, biased.
2 **Disinterested, uninterested,** though often used interchangeably in the past, are now, as a rule, sharply distinguished in meaning. Both words are compounds of negative prefixes and of *interested*, the adjective, and both carry the meanings of not having an interest in and of not interested (the past participle). The latter was the earlier sense of *disinterested*, and the former of *uninterested*. In present good use, these meanings are reversed. **Disinterested** now implies a lack of personal concern, not only of selfish motives or thought of advantage, but also of bias, predilection, or prejudice. **Uninterested,** which now means not having the mind or feelings engaged, suggests inattentiveness, apathy, or indifference. Thus, a *disinterested* witness is one that either has no personal interest in the outcome of a trial or is able to put aside such interest and give impartial testimony; an *uninterested* witness is bored and unresponsive to attempts to elicit testimony. When a problem is up for discussion, a *disinterested* person refuses to allow any ulterior considerations to affect his judgment; an *uninterested* person maintains an attitude of indifference or refuses to participate in the discussion.

disloyal. *Faithless, false, perfidious, traitorous, treacherous.
Ana. Disaffected, estranged, alienated (see ESTRANGE): recreant (see COWARDLY): *inconstant, fickle, unstable.
Ant. Loyal. — *Con.* *Faithful, constant, leal, true, stanch, steadfast, resolute.

dismantle. Divest, *strip, denude, bare.
Con. *Furnish, equip, outfit, appoint.

dismay, *v.* **Dismay, appall** (*or* **appal**), **horrify, daunt** agree in meaning to unnerve and arrest in action by arousing fear, apprehension, or strong aversion. The meanings of most of these words have undergone emasculation in the course of time, so that in current use they seldom imply as overpowering fear, apprehension, or aversion as in older usage. **Dismay** implies a loss of power to proceed either because the prospect is terrifying or disheartening, or, more often in modern use, because one is balked and perplexed or at a loss how to deal with the situation. "Be not afraid nor *dismayed* by reason of this great multitude; for the battle is not yours, but God's. To-morrow go ye down against them" (*2 Chronicles* xx. 15–16). "Here was an opponent that more than once puzzled Roosevelt, and in the end flatly *dismayed* him" (*Mencken*). **Appall,** in its most forceful use, implies an overwhelming and paralyzing dread or terror; as, the sight *appalled* the stoutest hearts. " 'Are you a man?' 'Ay, and a bold one, that dare look on that Which might *appal* the devil' " (*Shak.*). In weaker modern use, the word usually implies the sense of impotence aroused when one is confronted by something that perturbs, confounds, or shocks, yet is beyond one's power to alter; as, an *appalling* waste of human life; *appalling* statistics. "The unpunctuality of the Orient...is *appalling* to those who come freshly from a land of fixed meal-times and regular train services" (*A. Huxley*). **Horrify** still often emphasizes a reaction of horror or of shuddering revulsion from that which is ghastly or hideously offensive. "To developed sensibilities the facts of war are revolting and *horrifying*" (*A. Huxley*). "This theme—a man ready to prostitute his sister as payment for a debt of honour—is too grotesque even to *horrify* us" (*T. S. Eliot*). In its weakened sense, *horrify* comes close to *shock* in meaning and implies momentary agitation occasioned by a surprising breach of the proprieties or decencies; as, they were *horrified* by his playing golf on Sunday; *horrifyingly* bad manners. **Daunt** presupposes an attempt to do something that requires courage and implies therefore a stoppage by someone or something that cows or subdues. "He had come back [from Russia] because he had been completely *daunted* by what he had found Over There ....he looked not only *daunted* but dunted; the Revolution...had been something against which self-assertion had been of no avail" (*M. Austin*). *Daunt* often occurs in negative constructions; as, nothing can *daunt* the man whose last concern is for his own safety.
Ana. Perplex, confound, bewilder, nonplus, dumfound, mystify, *puzzle: disconcert, rattle, faze, abash, discomfit, *embarrass: alarm, *frighten, terrify.
Ant. Cheer. — *Con.* Assure, secure, *ensure: pique, quicken, stimulate, galvanize, excite, *provoke.

dismay, *n.* Alarm, consternation, panic, *fear, dread, fright, terror, horror, trepidation.
Ana. Perturbing *or* perturbation, agitation, disquieting *or* disquietude, discomposing *or* discomposure, upsetting *or* upset (see corresponding verbs at DISCOMPOSE): *apprehension, foreboding.
Con. *Confidence, assurance, aplomb, self-possession: *courage, mettle, spirit, resolution.

dismiss. 1 **Dismiss, discharge, cashier, sack, fire, bounce, drop** come into comparison when they mean to let go from one's employ or service. **Dismiss** etymologically implies a giving permission to go; as, "he *dismissed* the assembly" (*Acts* xix. 41). When used in the sense here considered, it carries apart from the context no suggestion of the reason for the act and is, therefore, often preferred as the softer or as the more comprehensive term; as, with the let-up in business, thousands of employees were *dismissed;* the new governor *dismissed* the staff that served his predecessor and appointed members of his own party in their places; to *dismiss* a servant. **Discharge** is usually a harsher term, implying dismissal for cause and little, or commonly no, likelihood of being called back; as, to *discharge* an employee for insubordination; she has the habit of *discharging* her servants without notice: only in military and court use does it, when unqualified, carry no implication of dissatisfaction on the part of the employer; as, the enlisted man will be *discharged* after three years' service; the three convicted soldiers were dishonorably *discharged;* the judge *discharged* the jury with thanks. **Cashier** implies a summary or ignominious discharge from a position of trust or from a position that is high in the scale; as, to *cashier* a suspected official; "Many a duteous and knee-crooking knave, That... Wears out his time, much like his master's ass, For nought but provender, and when he's old, *cashier'd*" (*Shak.*); "the few sentimental fanatics who...proceeded upon the assumption that academic freedom was yet inviolable, and so got themselves *cashiered*" (*Mencken*). **Sack, fire,** and **bounce** are all colloquial synonyms of *discharge: sack* stresses a being discarded, or thrown out of employ (as, he was *sacked* after long years of service), *fire* stresses a dismissal as sudden and peremptory as the action of firing a gun (as, he *fired* his clerk one day in a fit of anger, but the next day he called him back), and *bounce* stresses a discharge that suggests, rather than implies, a kicking out (as, he *bounced* the boy after one day of unsatisfactory service). **Drop** is a common colloquial synonym of *dismiss* and equally colorless; as, in off seasons, all part-time employees are *dropped.*
Con. Hire, *employ.

2 *Eject, oust, expel, evict.
Ana. *Discard, cast, shed, slough: spurn, repudiate, reject, refuse (see DECLINE, *v.*): scorn, scout (see DESPISE).
Con. Accept, *receive, admit: entertain, *harbor.

dismissal. **Dismissal, dismission** agree in meaning the act of dismissing or the state of being dismissed. **Dismissal** in recent usage has almost displaced the older and regularly formed **dismission** in all its senses; however, *dismission* is still sometimes preferred when a formal discharge or expulsion is implied; as, the *dismissal* of a congregation; "A preoccupied nod and a perfunctory salutation which was in truth a *dismissal*" (*Stevenson*); "to be punished by *dismission* from the public service" (*Macaulay*); "More than 200 of the 230 voting... members of the church voted for his [Jonathan Edwards's] *dismission*" (*Dict. Amer. Biog.*).
Ana. Dispersion, scattering (see corresponding verbs at SCATTER): releasing, liberating, freeing (see FREE, *v.*).
Con. Convening, convoking, mustering (see SUMMON).

dismission. *Dismissal.
Ana. Discharging *or* discharge, sacking, firing, cashiering (see corresponding verbs at DISMISS): expelling *or* expulsion, ejection, ousting, eviction (see corresponding verbs at EJECT).
☞ *Do not confuse* dismission *with* demission *or* dimission.

dismount. Alight, *descend.
Ant. Mount.

disorder, *n.* *Confusion, disarray, clutter, jumble, chaos, pie, snarl, muddle.
Ana. Derangement, disarrangement, disorganization, disturbance, unsettlement (see corresponding verbs at DISORDER): *anarchy, chaos, lawlessness.
Ant. Order. — *Con.* Arrangement, organization, methodization, systematization (see corresponding verbs at ORDER): system, *method.

disorder, *v.* **Disorder, derange, disarrange, disorganize, unsettle, disturb** come into comparison when they mean to undo the fixed or proper order of something. **Disorder,** the least explicit of these terms in its further implications, is commonly used in reference to that which depends for its proper functioning or effectiveness upon being properly ordered (see ORDER, *v.*, 1) or in good order or array; as, "tresses all *disordered*" (*Milton*); too rich a diet will *disorder* his digestive system. **Derange** implies a throwing out of proper arrangement the parts, or an important part, of something in which all the parts or elements are ordered with reference to each other or are so carefully adjusted or so closely related to each other that they work together as a unit. The term usually carries a strong implication of resulting confusion or a destruction of normal or healthy conditions; as, war *deranges* the life of a nation; fear has *deranged* his mind; by *deranging* that part of the plan, you have made the whole scheme useless. **Disarrange,** on the other hand, often implies little more than the changing of a fixed or a perfect order or arrangement, and may carry no suggestion of confusion; as, "She...would not let his chamber be *disarranged* just at present" (*H. Martineau*); one glance told him that someone had *disarranged* the papers on his desk; they must now arrange their books, so *disarranged* by the woman who had house cleaned their library. **Disorganize** implies usually the destruction of order and functioning in a body or whole all the parts of which have an organic connection with each other or have been so ordered with reference to each other that what affects one part affects every other part: the term therefore usually suggests a disordering that runs through an entire body, or system, or the like, and breaks it up, or seriously impedes or impairs its functioning; as, blitzkrieg methods *disorganize* the internal communications of the enemy's country; "The Whigs...though defeated, disheartened, and *disorganized*, did not yield without an effort" (*Macaulay*). "He meant to stay two nights, but was knocked down by rheumatic fever, and for six weeks *disorganized* Polder's establishment, stopped Polder's work, and nearly died in Polder's bedroom" (*Kipling*). **Unsettle** literally implies a loosening of that which is fixed in position, or a moving of it from its rightful place to another: when used in reference to a body, a system, an organism, or the like, it also implies a disordering or disarrangement that causes instability, unrest, inability to concentrate, or the like; as, to *unsettle* the government by frequent and violent disagreements among the legislators; these constant rumors keep one *unsettled;* to *unsettle* the beliefs of the people; his mind has become *unsettled.* **Disturb** (as here compared: see also DISCOMPOSE) usually implies a force or combination of forces that unsettles or disarranges; frequently it also suggests an interruption or interference that affects a settled or orderly course, plan, growth, or the like; as, the attraction of planets *disturbs* the course of comets; "regulation....produces a uniform whole, which is as much *disturbed* and *deranged* by changing what the regulating power designs to leave untouched, as that on which it has operated" (*Ch. Just. Marshall*); "the warps and strains of civilised life...seem to *disturb* the wholesome balance of even the humblest elements of the possessive and aesthetic instincts" (*H. Ellis*).
Ant. Order. — *Con.* Arrange, marshal, organize, methodize, systematize (see ORDER, *v.*): array, align, range, *line: regulate, *adjust, fix.

disorganize. Disturb, unsettle, *disorder, derange, disarrange.
Ant. Organize. — *Con.* Systematize, methodize, arrange, marshal, *order.

disparage. *Decry, depreciate, derogate from, detract from, belittle, minimize.
Ana. Asperse, *malign, traduce, defame, slander, libel: deprecate, *disapprove.
Ant. Applaud. — *Con.* *Praise, laud, extol, eulogize, acclaim: *commend, compliment: *exalt, magnify, aggrandize.

disparate. Diverse, divergent, *different, various.
Ana. *Inconsonant, incompatible, incongruous, discrepant, discordant, inconsistent: *distinct, separate.
Ant. Comparable, analogous. — *Con.* *Similar, like, homogeneous, parallel.

dispassionate. Unbiased, impartial, objective, uncolored, *fair, just, equitable.
Ana. Disinterested, detached, aloof, *indifferent: *cool, collected, composed: candid, open, *frank.
Ant. Passionate: intemperate.

dispatch *or* **despatch,** *v.* *Kill, slay, murder, assassinate, execute.

dispatch *or* **despatch,** *n.* **1** Speed, expedition, *haste, hurry.
Ana. *Celerity, alacrity, legerity: quickness, fleetness, swiftness, rapidity (see corresponding adjectives at FAST): diligence (see corresponding adjective at BUSY).
Ant. Delay.
2 Message, note, *letter, epistle, report, memorandum, missive.

dispel. Dissipate, disperse, *scatter.
Ana. Expel, *eject, oust, dismiss: disintegrate, crumble (see DECAY).
Con. *Accumulate, amass: *gather, collect, assemble.

dispense. **1** *Distribute, divide, deal, dole.
Ana. *Allot, assign, apportion, allocate: portion, parcel, ration, prorate, *apportion.

2 *Administer.

disperse. *Scatter, dissipate, dispel.

Ana. *Separate, part, divide: *dismiss, discharge.

Ant. Assemble, congregate (*persons*): collect (*things*). — *Con.* *Summon, convoke, convene, muster, cite, call.

dispiteous. Variant of DESPITEOUS.

displace. Supplant, *replace, supersede.

Ana. Transpose, *reverse, invert: shift, remove, transfer, *move: derange, disarrange, *disorder: *eject, oust, expel, dismiss.

display, *v.* Exhibit, *show, expose, parade, flaunt.

Ana. Manifest, evidence, evince, demonstrate, *show: *reveal, disclose, discover.

Con. *Disguise, cloak, mask, dissemble: *hide, conceal, secrete.

display, *n.* **Display, parade, array, pomp** are here compared only as denoting a striking or spectacular show or exhibition for the sake of effect. **Display** commonly suggests a spreading out or an unfolding of that which is usually concealed, or visible only in the mass or in individual instances, so that the observer is impressed, as by the extent, the detail, the beauty, or the lavishness of what is revealed to him; as, a *display* of meteors; a parvenu's *display* of wealth; a nation's *display* of power. "The piece of Dryden's which is...the most sustained *display* of surprise after surprise of wit...is *MacFlecknoe*" (*T. S. Eliot*). **Parade** implies ostentatious or flaunting exhibition; *display* may or may not suggest a conscious endeavor to impress, but *parade* invariably, in correct use, implies such an intention. "To see Lydia, with anxious *parade*, walk up to her mother's right hand, and hear her say to her eldest sister, 'Ah, Jane, I take your place now...because I am a married woman'" (*Austen*). "Mr. Cruncher could not be restrained from making rather an ostentatious *parade* of his liberality" (*Dickens*). "He died, as erring man should die, Without *display*, without *parade*" (*Byron*). **Array** stresses order, numerousness, and brilliancy in display; it usually suggests an impression such as might be produced by marshaled ranks of armed soldiers and therefore may be used of displays that strike one as beautiful, or as terrible, or as merely astonishing; as, an *array* of tulips; an *array* of silver on a sideboard; "the terrible *array* of evils around us and dangers in front of us" (*Shaw*). "Clouds ... Each lost in each, that marvellous *array* Of temple, palace, citadel" (*Wordsworth*). **Pomp** stresses ceremonial grandeur or splendor. It was once often, but is now rarely, used of a pageant or solemn procession, but it still suggests an outward spectacular show of magnificence or glory. "It [Independence Day] ought to be solemnized with *pomp* and *parade*, with...bonfires, and illuminations" (*John Adams*). "Pride, *pomp* and circumstance of glorious war!" (*Shak.*). "Lo, all our *pomp* of yesterday Is one with Nineveh and Tyre!" (*Kipling*).

Ana. Ostentatiousness *or* ostentation, pretentiousness *or* pretension, showiness *or* show, pompousness (see corresponding adjectives at SHOWY).

disport, *n.* Sport, play, frolic, rollick, romp, gambol. See under PLAY, *v.*

Ana. Recreation, diversion, amusement, entertainment (see under AMUSE): merriment, jollity (see corresponding adjectives at MERRY).

disport, *v.* Sport, *play, frolic, rollick, romp, gambol.

Ana. Divert, *amuse, recreate, entertain.

disposal. **Disposal, disposition** are frequently used without clear distinction when they mean the act or the power of disposing of something. However, when the emphasis is upon what shall be done with money, property, possessions, or the like, **disposal** tends to imply a getting rid of, as by selling, giving away, assigning to others, destroying, or the like, and **disposition,** a proper or orderly distribution or utilization; as, the *disposal* (not *disposition*) of her jewels seemed necessary; the *disposition* (not *disposal* unless sale or the like is implied) of the intestate's property has been agreed upon by the heirs; incinerators used for the *disposal* of garbage. "I am happy that the speedy *disposal* of the pictures will enable you...to settle this unpleasant affair" (*M. R. Mitford*). "The donors have stipulated for the future *disposition* ...of those funds" (*Ch. Just. Marshall*). When the idea of arrangement or ordering or of making arrangements is stressed, *disposition*, rather than *disposal*, is employed by good writers. "While the *disposition* of the branches is unsymmetrical, balance is maintained" (*Binyon*). "A deserter had informed Octavian of the general plan... and he made his *dispositions* accordingly" (*Buchan*). The idiomatic phrases *at one's disposal* and *at* (or *in*) *one's disposition* differ in that though both imply a placing under one's control, the former suggests use as one sees fit and the latter, subjection to one's direction, arrangement, or command; as, they put their summer home at the *disposal* of the bridal couple; "[He] had at his *disposition* no inconsiderable sums of money" (*Trench*).

Ana. Selling *or* sale, auctioning *or* auction, trading *or* trade, vending, bartering (see corresponding verbs at SELL): destroying *or* destruction, demolishing *or* demolition (see corresponding verbs at DESTROY).

dispose. Predispose, bias, *incline.

Ana. Influence, *affect, sway.

disposition. 1 *Disposal.

Ana. Administering *or* administration, dispensing *or* dispensation (see corresponding verbs at ADMINISTER): management, direction, controlling *or* control, conducting *or* conduct (see corresponding verbs at CONDUCT): arrangement, ordering (see corresponding verbs at ORDER).

2 **Disposition, temperament, temper, complexion, character, personality, individuality** come into comparison when they mean the prevailing and dominant quality or qualities which distinguish or identify a person or group. **Disposition** applies to the predominating bent or constitutional habit of one's mind or spirit. "She...is always cheerful and sweet-tempered....This *disposition* in her is the more comfortable, because it is not the humor of the day, a sudden flash of benevolence and good spirits" (*Cowper*). "Ages of fierceness have overlaid what is naturally kindly in the *dispositions* of ordinary men and women" (*B. Russell*). **Temperament** applies to the sum total of characteristics that are innate or inherent and the result of one's physical, nervous, and mental organization; as, a nervous, bilious *temperament;* "I verily believe that nor you, nor any man of poetical *temperament*, can avoid a strong passion of some kind" (*Byron*). "Shall I ever be cheerful again, happy again? Yes. And soon. For I know my *temperament*" (*Twain*). **Temper,** as here compared, was once a close synonym of *temperament;* in current English, possibly through the influence of the verb *temper* (see TEMPER, *v.*, 1), it implies a combination of all the qualities, especially those acquired through experience, which determine the way one (not only a person, but a people, an age, or the like) meets the situations, difficulties, or problems that confront one. "There was a general confidence in her [Elizabeth's] instinctive knowledge of the national *temper*" (*J. R. Green*). "The leaders of forlorn hopes are never found among men with dismal minds. There must be a natural resiliency of *temper* which makes them enjoy desperate ventures" (*S. M. Crothers*). **Complexion,** as here compared, originally referred to temperament regarded as

the result of the physical, rather than the nervous or mental, constitution (the four "humors" and their proportions). "Or else his *complexion* is so courageous that he may not forbear" (*Chaucer*). The physiological implications of this earlier sense are no longer accepted, but the term still implies something fundamentally distinctive that determines the impression one produces on others. "The rationalist mind...is of a doctrinaire and authoritative *complexion:* the phrase 'must be' is ever on its lips" (*W. James*). **Character** applies to the aggregate of qualities, especially moral qualities, which distinguish an individual at any one time in his development, though constantly tending to become more or less fixed, and which must be taken as a whole into consideration in any ethical judgment of him; as, he is a man of good *character;* in his youth, his *character* was weak and unstable. "That inexorable law of human souls that we prepare ourselves for sudden deeds by the reiterated choice of good or evil that determines *character*" (*G. Eliot*). Oftentimes, *character* means such an aggregate of qualities brought to a high state of moral excellence by right principles and right choices and by the rejection of all that weakens or debases. "When we say of such and such a man that he has...*character*, we generally mean that he has disciplined his temperament, his disposition, into strict obedience to the behests of duty" (*Brownell*). **Personality** also applies to the aggregate of qualities which distinguish an individual, but the term differs from *character* in that it implies his being distinguished as a person rather than as a moral being. In general, personality may be said to be revealed in unconscious as well as in conscious acts or movements, in physical and emotional as well as in mental and moral behavior, and especially, in a person's relations to others; thus, one may know very little about the *character* of an acquaintance, yet have a very definite idea of his *personality*. Therefore, *personality* is qualified not as good, bad, or the like, but by an adjective implying the extent to which it pleases, displeases, or otherwise impresses the observer. "There was a pious and good man, but an utterly negligible *personality*" (*C. Mackenzie*). "The mere presence of *personality* in a work of art is not sufficient, because the *personality* revealed may be lacking in charm" (*A. C. Benson*). Hence, *personality* often distinctively means personal magnetism or charm. "*Personality* is not something that can be sought; it is a radiance that is diffused spontaneously" (*H. Ellis*). **Individuality,** as here compared, implies a personality that distinguishes one from all others; often, it connotes the power of impressing one's personality on others; as, he is a man of marked *individuality;* she has no *individuality;* "Sophia quietened her by sheer force of *individuality*" (*Bennett*).

disprove. Disprove, refute, confute, rebut, controvert come into comparison as meaning to show or attempt to show by argument that a statement, a claim, or the like, is not true. **Disprove** stresses the success of an argument in showing the falsity, erroneousness, invalidity, or the like, of that which is attacked; as, he could not *disprove* the major contention of his opponents, but he could show that they had not proved it; "I speak not to *disprove* what Brutus spoke, But here I am to speak what I do know" (*Shak.*). **Refute** stresses the method more than the effect of argument in disproof: it therefore is preferred to *disprove* when one wishes to convey implications of the adducing of evidence, of a bringing forward of witnesses, experts, or authorities, and of close reasoning: it connotes a gathering of forces and an elaboration of arguments not present in *disprove;* as, "With respect to that other, more weighty accusation, of having injured Mr. Wickham, I can only *refute* it by laying before you the whole of his connection with my family" (*Austen*); "There is great force in this argument, and the Court is not satisfied that it has been *refuted*" (*Ch. Just. Marshall*). **Confute** emphasizes a destruction of arguments or a reducing to silence of opponents by clearly revealing the falsity or the untenability of the points which have been made: the term usually implies refutation, but it may also suggest methods such as raillery, denunciation, sarcasm, or the like; as, "Satan stood ...*confuted* and convinced Of his weak arguing and fallacious drift" (*Milton*); "Elijah...*confuted* the prophets of Baal in precisely that way, with...bitter mockery of their god when he failed to send down fire from heaven" (*Shaw*). **Rebut** differs from *refute*, its closest synonym, in suggesting greater formality of method, such as that used in organized debate or in courts of law. Although its aim is disproof of an opponent's contentions, the term does not necessarily imply the achievement of one's end, but it does suggest the offering of argument, evidence, or testimony that contradicts argument, evidence, or testimony given in support of the other side; as, at the end of the formal arguments, each member of the debating team was allowed three minutes for *rebutting* the arguments of his opponents; "The Tractarians were driven to formulate a theory of the Church...which should justify the exclusive claim of Anglicanism to be the Church of Christ in these islands, while *rebutting* the arguments of Rome" (*Inge*). **Controvert** usually carries a dual implication, that of denying or contradicting a statement, proposition, or doctrine, or a set of these, and of refuting or attempting to refute it. It does not necessarily suggest disproof but it does connote a valiant effort to achieve that end; as, "This doctrine has been *controverted;* it is, however, very ably defended by Mr. Hargrave" (*W. Cruise*); "I am glad that this year we are assembled not to *controvert* the opinions of others, nor even to defend ourselves" (*Inge*).

Ana. Negative, traverse, impugn, contravene (see DENY).

Ant. Prove, demonstrate.

disputation. Debate, forensic, *argumentation, dialectic.

Ana. *Argument, dispute, controversy.

dispute, *v.* Argue, debate, *discuss, agitate.

Ana. See those at DEBATE.

Ant. Concede. — *Con.* *Grant, allow.

dispute, *n.* *Argument, controversy.

Ana. *Argumentation, disputation, debate, forensic, dialectic: contention, dissension, strife, *discord, conflict.

disquiet. *Discompose, disturb, agitate, perturb, upset, fluster, flurry.

Ana. *Annoy, vex, irk, bother: *worry, harass, harry: *trouble, distress.

Ant. Tranquilize, soothe.

disregard, *v.* Ignore, overlook, slight, forget, *neglect.

Con. Attend, mind, watch, *tend: observe, notice, note, remark (see SEE).

disrepute, *n.* *Disgrace, dishonor, shame, infamy, ignominy, opprobrium, obloquy, odium, scandal.

Ant. Repute. — *Con.* *Fame, reputation, renown, honor, glory.

dissect. Anatomize, *analyze, break down, resolve.

Ana. *Scrutinize, examine, inspect: pierce, penetrate, probe (see ENTER).

dissection. Anatomy, breakdown, analysis, resolution. See under ANALYZE.

dissemble. Mask, cloak, *disguise.

Ana. Simulate, feign, counterfeit, sham, pretend, *assume, affect.

Ant. Betray. — *Con.* *Reveal, disclose, discover, bewray: *show, manifest, evidence, evince, demonstrate.

dissension. Variance, strife, conflict, contention, *discord.

Ana. Altercation, wrangle, *quarrel, bickering: *argument, dispute, controversy.

Ant. Accord (sense 1): comity (sense 2). — *Con.* *Harmony, concord, consonance: *friendship, good will, amity.

dissenter. Nonconformist, sectarian, sectary, schismatic, *heretic.

dissimilarity. Dissimilarity, unlikeness, difference, divergence (*or* **divergency**), **distinction** come into comparison when they mean lack of agreement or correspondence (or an instance of such lack of agreement or correspondence) in appearance, in qualities, in nature, etc., brought out by a comparison of two or more things. **Dissimilarity** and **unlikeness,** the most general terms in this group, are often used interchangeably without loss, but when there is little basis for comparison and the contrast is obvious, *dissimilarity* is usually preferred by discriminating writers and speakers (as, the effectiveness of a metaphor depends, in part, on the *dissimilarity* of the things which are compared): on the other hand, when the things contrasted are of the same species, genus, or other category, and there are fundamental likenesses between them, *unlikeness* is commonly the preferred term (as, the *unlikeness* between these violets is obvious only to an expert; "But he was rich where I was poor, And he supplied my want the more As his *unlikeness* fitted mine"—*Tennyson*). **Difference** suggests notice of a quality, feature, or the like, which marks one thing as apart from another. The term may imply want of resemblance in one or more particulars (as, to note the *differences* between the first poems of Keats and those written after he had achieved mastery of his art; there are both resemblances and *differences* in the designs of these two cathedrals), or want of identity (as, "*Difference* of opinion is the one crime which kings never forgive"—*Emerson;* "*Difference* of religion breeds more quarrels than *difference* of politics"—*W. Phillips*), or a disagreement or cause of disagreement which separates individuals or makes them hostile to each other (as, there have been *differences* between them for some time). **Divergence,** when used in the sense here considered, applies to a difference between things (sometimes persons) having the same origin, the same ends, the same background, or the like, or belonging to the same type or class: in this sense, there is usually an implication of a difference that makes for cleavage or increasing unlikeness; as, "An illustration of the *divergences* between countries both highly democratic" (*Bryce*); "the greatest *divergence* in the educational value of studies is due to the varying degree to which they require concentration, judgment, observation, and imagination" (*Grandgent*). **Distinction** usually implies want of resemblance in detail, especially in some minute or not obvious detail: it therefore commonly applies to a difference that is brought out by close observation, study, analysis, or the like, or that marks the line of division between two like things; as, to point out the *distinction* in meaning between two close synonyms; a hair-splitting *distinction* between "original" and "creative" writing. "Apprehend the vital *distinction* between religion and criticism" (*Arnold*). "So intoxicated with dreams of fortune that he had lost all sense of the *distinction* between reality and illusion" (*Van W. Brooks*). "This is not a *distinction* without a *difference.* It is not like the affair of 'an old hat cocked' and 'a cocked old hat'... but there is a *difference* here in the nature of things" (*Sterne*).

Ana. Difference, diversity, disparity (see corresponding adjectives at DIFFERENT): discrepancy, discordance, inconsonance (see corresponding adjectives at INCONSONANT).

Ant. Similarity. — *Con.* *Likeness, resemblance, similitude: correspondence, agreement, conformity (see corresponding verbs at AGREE).

dissimulation. 1 Duplicity, *deceit, cunning, guile.

Ana. Dissembling, cloaking, masking, disguising (see DISGUISE): hiding, concealing, secreting (see HIDE): pretending *or* pretense, feigning, shamming (see corresponding verbs at ASSUME): *hypocrisy, Pharisaism, sanctimony.

Con. Candidness *or* candor, openness (see corresponding adjectives at FRANK): sincerity (see corresponding adjective SINCERE).

2 *Simulation.

Ana. & *Con.* See those at DISSIMULATION, 1.

dissipate. Dispel, disperse, *scatter.

Ana. Disintegrate, crumble (see DECAY): *separate, part, divide: dissolve, deliquesce, melt (see LIQUEFY).

Ant. Accumulate (*possessions, wealth, a mass of things*): absorb (*one's energies, one's attention, etc.*): concentrate (*one's thoughts, powers, efforts*).

dissolute. Profligate, reprobate, *abandoned.

Ana. *Licentious, libertine, wanton, lewd: inebriate, inebriated, intoxicated, drunken, *drunk: debauched, depraved, corrupt, debased, perverted (see under DEBASE).

dissolve. 1 *Liquefy, deliquesce, melt, fuse, thaw.

Ana. Disintegrate, crumble (see DECAY).

2 *Adjourn, prorogue.

Ana. Terminate, end, *close.

Con. *Summon, convoke, convene, call.

dissolvent. *Solvent, resolvent, menstruum, alkahest.

dissonance. Discordance (see under DISSONANT).

dissonant. Dissonant, discordant and their corresponding nouns **dissonance** and **discordance** come into comparison when they mean (in the case of the adjectives) not in harmony with one another or with something else or (in the case of the nouns) the lack of such harmony. **Dissonant** and **dissonance** are used chiefly with regard to sounds, especially musical tones. Originally, both stressed the harshness or unmelodiousness of a single sound or tone or of a combination of sounds or tones; as, "Hanno would fain have assuaged their fury, but he knew not how; for he less understood their *dissonant* loud noises, than they did his oration" (*Raleigh* [d. 1618]). Now, they imply a combination of inharmonious musical tones that causes a quick succession of beats and produces an unrestful but not necessarily displeasing effect that is usually resolved by an ensuing consonance. The terms therefore in such use commonly suggest artistic intention rather than artistic failure. "Hitherto the foundation of all music was consonance, with *dissonance* freely admitted; the new system is founded on *dissonance,* with consonance as a rare and not very welcome guest" (*Baker's Biog. Dict. of Musicians*). **Discordant** and **discordance** differ from *dissonant* and *dissonance* in suggesting combinations of inharmonious tones that produce a jarring and highly disagreeable effect. "*Dissonant* tones are related, organized, musical; *discordant* tones (discords) are unrelated, unorganized, unmusical" (*K. W. Gehrkens*). In their general application, *dissonant* and *dissonance* commonly imply the disagreement of one thing with another; *discordant* and *discordance* commonly imply mutual variance or incongruity; as, opinions *dissonant* from truth; *discordant* views; the meeting was in

confusion because of *discordant* opinions. "The smooth manner of the spy, curiously in *dissonance* with his ostentatiously rough dress" (*Dickens*). "They were in *discordance* with each other, from the first" (*Newman*).
Ana. *Inconsonant.
Ant. Consonant. — *Con.* Harmonizing *or* harmonious, agreeing, according *or* accordant (see corresponding verbs at AGREE).

distant. **Distant, far, faraway, far-off, remote, removed** agree in meaning not near or close, but separated by an obvious interval, especially in space or in time. **Distant** carries a stronger reference to the length of the interval (whether long or short) than the other terms; only when it directly qualifies a noun does it necessarily imply that the interval is markedly long; as, a book held six inches *distant* from the eyes; the sun is about 93,000,000 miles *distant* from the earth; a *distant* city; a *distant* prospect; at a *distant* date. "I do not ask to see The *distant* scene,—one step enough for me" (*Newman*). **Far,** except for the possible reference to a short distance involved in the question "How *far?*", applies (as adverb as well as adjective) only to what is a long way off; as, "[He] took his journey into a *far* country" (*Luke* xv. 13); to take a *far* view; "As *far* as the east is from the west" (*Psalms* ciii. 12); "Across the hills, and *far* away Beyond their utmost purple rim" (*Tennyson*). **Faraway** and **far-off** not only mean extremely far, but they are preferred when distance in time is specifically implied; as, "*far-away* ancestors" (*G. Eliot*); "Old, unhappy, *far-off* things, And battles long ago" (*Wordsworth*); however, both may suggest distance in space; as, "a cheer that started the echo in a *far-away* hill" (*Stevenson*); "the *far-off* places in which he had been wandering" (*Dickens*). **Remote** suggests a far removal, especially from something regarded as a center or vantage ground, such as one's present location, one's point of view, one's time, or the like; as, "some forlorn and naked hermitage, *Remote* from all the pleasures of the world" (*Shak.*); "the sands Of a *remote* and lonely shore" (*Shelley*); "Dunstan, whose nature it was to care more for immediate annoyances than for *remote* consequences" (*G. Eliot*). **Removed,** which is commonly a predicative adjective, carries a stronger implication of separateness and distinction than *remote;* it therefore usually implies a contrast between two things apart not only in space or in time but in character or quality; as, an age far *removed* from the present age in its accomplishments and ideals; he sought a retreat *removed* from all centers of population.

Figuratively, *distant* implies slightness of connection or aloofness of manner; as, a *distant* resemblance; a *distant* nod, reception: *remote* imputes to the thing so described a foreign or alien character or an inaccessible nature; as, "I told Oliver about your modern monastery; but the thing is too *remote* from his experience to have any interest for him" (*Santayana*); "The captain of a ship at sea is a *remote*, inaccessible creature...alone of his kind, depending on nobody" (*Conrad*): *removed* stresses difference, often a diametrical or antithetical difference; as, "To Queen Scheherazade the dream might have seemed not far *removed* from commonplace" (*Hardy*); he accepted the nomination for considerations entirely *removed* from those influencing the average candidate.
Con. Near, *close, nigh, near-by.

distasteful. Obnoxious, *repugnant, repellent, abhorrent, invidious.
Ana. *Hateful, odious, detestable, abominable: *offensive, loathsome, repulsive, repugnant, revolting.
Ant. Agreeable: palatable. — *Con.* *Pleasant, pleasing, gratifying, grateful, welcome: delectable, *delightful, delicious.

distemper. Complaint, *disease, malady, ailment, affection.

distend. Swell, dilate, *expand, inflate, amplify.
Ana. Enlarge, *increase, augment: *extend, lengthen.
Ant. Constrict. — *Con.* *Contract, shrink, compress, condense, deflate.

distinct. 1 **Distinct, separate, several, discrete** come into comparison when used in reference to two or more things (sometimes persons) and in the sense of not individually the same. **Distinct** always implies a capacity for being distinguished by the eye or by the mind as apart from the other or others, sometimes in space or in time, but more often in character, nature, or identity; as, I see three *distinct* objects in the distance, but I cannot identify them; the novel has two related, but nevertheless *distinct*, plots; "There has been endless discussion whether we have a *distinct* faculty for the knowledge of God" (*Inge*); "for him the work of literature is not *distinct* or separable from its author" (*L. P. Smith*). **Separate** (as here considered: see also SINGLE) is often used interchangeably with *distinct* and often in combination with it, as if one strengthened the other; as, "the power...is given in two *separate* and *distinct* sections of the constitution" (*Ch. Just. Marshall*); "these two characteristics were not *separate* and *distinct*....they were held together in vital tension" (*H. Ellis*). But *separate* stresses, as *distinct* does not, the lack of a connection between the things considered, usually by reason of the distance in space or time or the difference in identity of the things in question; thus, a drama with two *separate* plots is not the same as one with two *distinct* plots, for the former expression implies no connection (or, often, merely a factitious connection) between the plots, and the latter suggests only that they can be distinguished. "I can agree with Eliot's statement that 'the more perfect the artist, the more completely *separate* in him will be the man who suffers and the mind which creates,' but it must be realized that '*separate*' means '*distinct*,' and not 'unconnected' " (*Day Lewis*); "the reestablishment of ethics and esthetics as *separate* and autonomous realms" (*J. W. Krutch*). *Separate* is also often used in preference to *distinct* when an opposition to *common*, *shared*, or the like, is implied; as, please give us *separate* (not *distinct*) rooms; the children had *separate* toys and *separate* books. **Several** (as here considered: see also MANY) is now archaic in this sense, but it occurs frequently in the work of the great English writers of the past. The term implies an existence, a character, a status, or a location separate or distinct from that of the others. Unlike *respective* (see SPECIAL), which it sometimes resembles, it may modify a singular noun, especially when "each" precedes, as well as a plural noun; as, "conduct These knights unto their *several* lodgings" (*Shak.*); "Each individual seeks a *sev'ral* goal" (*Pope*). **Discrete,** even more than *separate*, implies that the individuals are not the same and are not connected: it is, however, often more precise than *separate* because it stresses numerical distinctness (that is, distinctness as individuals) rather than difference in kind, nature, goal, or the like; thus, *discrete* things may be exactly the same in appearance, nature, or value, but they are not selfsame and are physically disconnected; so, "The books on a shelf are not merely *discrete*" (*Bosanquet*); "According to which [Einstein's theory of light quanta] all radiation consisted of *discrete* bullet-like units" (*Jeans*). "[The phage] has been identified as existing in *discrete* units, that is, it is a particle like granulated sugar and not a continuum like molasses" (*C. C. Furnas*).
Ana. Individual, distinctive, peculiar (see CHARACTERISTIC): *single, sole, separate, particular: particular,

individual, *special, especial, concrete, respective: *different, diverse, disparate, divergent.

Con. *Same, selfsame, identical.

2 *Evident, manifest, patent, obvious, apparent, palpable, plain, clear.

Ana. Defined, prescribed (see PRESCRIBE): *explicit, definite, express, specific, categorical: perspicuous, *clear, lucid: clear-cut, *incisive, trenchant.

Ant. Indistinct: nebulous. — *Con.* Vague, *obscure, dark, enigmatic, cryptic.

distinction. Difference, divergence, *dissimilarity, unlikeness.

Ant. Resemblance. — *Con.* *Likeness, similarity, analogy, similitude, affinity.

distinctive. Peculiar, individual, *characteristic.

Ana. *Special, particular, specific, especial: unique, particular, separate, *single: *distinct, separate, several, discrete.

Ant. Typical. — *Con.* *Common, ordinary, familiar, popular, vulgar: *similar, like, alike, identical, comparable, parallel, analogous: *same, equivalent, equal: generic, general, *universal.

distinguished. Eminent, illustrious, renowned, noted, celebrated, *famous, famed, notorious.

Ana. Outstanding, prominent, remarkable, conspicuous (see NOTICEABLE).

Ant. Commonplace.

distort. Contort, warp, gnarl, *deform.

Ana. Twist, bend, turn, *curve: disfigure, disfeature, *deface: *injure, damage, mar, impair: misinterpret, misconstrue (see affirmative verbs at EXPLAIN).

distract. Bewilder, nonplus, confound, dumfound, mystify, perplex, *puzzle.

Ana. *Confuse, muddle, bemuddle, addle, fuddle, befuddle: baffle, balk (see FRUSTRATE): agitate, upset, fluster, flurry, perturb, *discompose.

Ant. Collect (*one's thoughts, one's powers, etc.*).

distrait. Distraught, absent-minded, absent, *abstracted, preoccupied.

Ana., Ant., & *Con.* See those at DISTRAUGHT.

distraught. Distrait, absent-minded, absent, *abstracted, preoccupied.

Ana. Distracted, bewildered, nonplused (see PUZZLE, *v.*): muddled, addled, confused (see CONFUSE): agitated, perturbed, discomposed, flustered (see DISCOMPOSE).

Ant. Collected. — *Con.* *Cool, composed, unruffled, imperturbable, nonchalant.

distress, *n.* **Distress, suffering, misery, agony, dolor** (*or* **dolour**), **passion** agree in denoting the state of one that is in sore trouble or in pain of mind or body. **Distress,** in precise use, commonly implies conditions or circumstances that cause physical or mental stress or strain; usually also it connotes the possibility of relief or the need of assistance. "To pity *distress* is human; to relieve it is Godlike" (*Horace Mann*). The word is applicable to things as well as to persons; thus, a ship in *distress* is helpless and in peril because of some untoward circumstances such as a breakdown in machinery or the loss of necessary equipment; a community's *distress* may be the result of a disaster or any event bringing devastation with it or imposing extreme hardships on the people. When used to designate a mental state, *distress* usually implies the stress or strain of fear, anxiety, shame, or the like. "The original shock and *distress* that were caused by the first serious work of scholars on the Bible" (*C. E. Montague*). "It had evidently been a great *distress* to him, to have the days of his imprisonment recalled" (*Dickens*). **Suffering** is used especially in reference to human beings; often it implies conscious awareness of pain or distress and conscious endurance. "Extreme sensibility to physical *suffering*...characterises modern civilisation" (*Inge*). Therefore, it often comes close to *trial, tribulation,* and *cross* in its suggestions of merit won through acceptance. "I know no one...better prepared by habitual *suffering* to receive and enjoy felicity" (*Austen*). "Our present joys are sweeter for past pain; To love and Heaven by *suffering* we attain" (*G. Granville*). **Misery** stresses the unhappy or wretched conditions attending distress or suffering; it often connotes sordidness, or dolefulness, or abjectness, or the like. "For bleak, unadulterated *misery* that dâk-bungalow was the worst...I had ever set foot in" (*Kipling*). "She had...cheated and shamed herself...exchanged content for *misery* and pride for humiliation" (*Bennett*). **Agony** suggests suffering so intense that both body and mind are involved in a struggle to endure the unbearable. "His mood was often like a fiend, and rose And drove him into wastes and solitudes For *agony*" (*Tennyson*). **Dolor,** which is now archaic or poetic, is applicable chiefly to mental suffering that involves sorrow or intense anxiety. "Spending his daies in *dolour* and despaire" (*Spenser*). **Passion** is now rarely used in this sense except in reference to the events beginning with the agony of Jesus in the garden at Gethsemane and culminating in his crucifixion. Sometimes it is restricted to the crucifixion and its attendant agony.

Ana. Affliction, *trial, tribulation: *sorrow, grief, anguish, woe: straits, pass, pinch, exigency (see JUNCTURE): hardship, *difficulty, rigor, vicissitude: *pain, pang, ache.

Con. Comforting *or* comfort, solacing *or* solace, consolation (see corresponding verbs at COMFORT): alleviation, assuagement, mitigation, allaying, relieving *or* relief (see corresponding verbs at RELIEVE).

distress, *v.* *Trouble, ail.

Ana. *Afflict, try, torment, torture, rack, grill: *worry, annoy, harass, harry, plague, pester: *depress, oppress, weigh (on *or* upon).

Con. *Comfort, console, solace: *help, aid, assist: *relieve, alleviate, lighten, mitigate, assuage, allay.

distribute. Distribute, dispense, divide, deal, dole come into comparison when they mean to give as his share to each of many or to all within expressed or implied limits, or, less often, to one of many. **Distribute** basically implies an apportioning among many by separation of something into parts, units, or amounts, and by assigning each part, unit, or amount to the proper person or place: beyond this, it may imply any of several immediate purposes; thus, to *distribute* one's possessions among one's heirs is to give (by will, usually) each of those heirs such a part or portion of one's estate as one deems proper; to *distribute* handbills is to pass them out one by one to individuals or to leave them one by one at the entrances to houses or to apartments; to *distribute* one's guests at a huge reception is to cause them to separate into smaller groups throughout one's home or grounds; to *distribute* fertilizer is to spread or scatter it over a garden or piece of cultivated land; to *distribute* profits among employees is to give each one some part or portion of them; to *distribute* type is to return each piece of used type to its proper compartment in a case; to *distribute* the burdens in an emergency is to give each person affected his due share of extra work or responsibility. "The old habit of centralizing a strain at one point, and then dividing and subdividing it, and *distributing* it on visible lines of support to a visible foundation" (*H. Adams*). "All modern societies aim...to *distribute* impartially to all the burdens and advantages of the state" (*G. L. Dickinson*). **Dispense** (as here compared:

see also ADMINISTER, 1) differs from *distribute* in rarely implying a spreading out that affects a large number or a separation that reduces the size or amount of each part or portion: it does, however, usually suggest the giving of a carefully weighed or measured portion to each of a group as a right or as due, or as accordant to need; as, to *dispense* alms to the needy; "If every just man that now pines with want Had but a moderate and beseeming share ... Nature's full blessings would be well-*dispensed*" (*Milton*); "Let us... Receive whatever good 'tis given thee to *dispense*" (*Wordsworth*). **Divide** (as here compared: see also SEPARATE) stresses the separation of a whole into parts but it implies as the purpose of that separation a dispensing of those parts to, or a sharing of them by, each of a group, especially of persons, of communities, of institutions, or the like: the term usually implies, if the context gives no further information, that the parts are equal; as, he *divided* the residue among three charities; the three partners *divide* the profits of the business, the size of each share depending on the size of the partner's investment; he claimed that his confederates would not *divide* the booty fairly; "Of the rent, a large proportion was *divided* among the country gentlemen" (*Macaulay*). **Deal** (usually followed by *out*) in its earliest use stressed the division of something into shares or portions (as, "Ye shall *deal* among you their spoil and cattle"—*Joshua* viii. 2 [Coverdale edition]) but in its later and still current sense, it emphasizes the delivery of something piece by piece, or in suitable portions, to those who have a right to expect it; as, to *deal* the cards for a game of bridge; to *deal* out equipment and supplies to each soldier; "the king's pages...move through the crowd...*dealing* out water all round" (*Arnold*). Often, the term carries no suggestion of distribution, and means little more than to give or deliver; as, he *dealt* his opponent a blow; " 'Now give the ticket to Umballa.' The babu scowled and *dealt* the proper ticket" (*Kipling*). **Dole** (also frequently followed by *out*) originally and still often implies a dispensing of alms to the needy (as, to *dole* out daily one thousand loaves of bread), but since in this sense it usually suggests a carefully measured portion, it now often suggests scantiness or niggardliness in the amount dispensed and does not necessarily suggest a charitable intent; as, "This comfort...she *doled* out to him in daily portions" (*Fielding*); "I can accept what is given in love and affection to me, but I could not accept what is *doled* out grudgingly or with conditions" (*Wilde*).

Ana. Apportion, *allot, allocate, assign: ration, portion, parcel, prorate, *apportion: *administer, dispense.

Ant. Collect (*supplies, etc.*): amass (*wealth, a fortune, etc.*). — ***Con.*** *Gather, assemble: *accumulate, hoard.

district. *Locality, vicinage, vicinity, neighborhood.

Ana. *Area, tract, region, zone, belt: section, sector, division, parcel (see PART, *n.*): *field, province, territory, sphere.

distrust, *v.* **Distrust, mistrust** come into comparison both as verbs meaning to lack trust or confidence in someone or something, and as nouns denoting such a lack of trust or confidence. **Distrust,** however, implies far more certitude that something is wrong than *mistrust;* often it suggests conviction of another's guilt, treachery, weakness, or the like. "Octavius had imbibed sufficient philosophy to *distrust* the sword as a cure for all ills" (*Buchan*). "The same *distrust* and horror of the unnatural forms into which life for the majority of people is being forced" (*Day Lewis*). **Mistrust** suggests domination by suspicion and, usually, fear. "He took me into a place so wild that a man less accustomed to these things might have *mistrusted* and feared for his life" (*Cather*). "Something...roused in him a suspicion that in the near future he was not going to have matters quite so much his own way. However, he concealed his *mistrust* as well as he could" (*C. Mackenzie*).

Con. *Rely, trust, depend, count, bank, reckon: confide, entrust, *commit, consign.

distrust, *n.* Mistrust (see under DISTRUST, *v.*).

Ana. Doubt, *uncertainty, dubiety, dubiosity, suspicion: *apprehension, foreboding, misgiving, presentiment.

Con. Confidence, *trust, reliance, dependence, faith.

disturb. 1 Unsettle, derange, *disorder, disarrange, disorganize.

Ana. Displace, *replace: shift, remove, *move: *arrest, interrupt, check: *meddle, intermeddle, interfere, tamper.

Con. Settle, *set, fix, establish: regulate, *adjust: *order, arrange, organize, systematize.

2 *Discompose, perturb, upset, disquiet, agitate, fluster, flurry.

Ana. *Frighten, alarm, terrify, scare: perplex, *puzzle, bewilder, distract: discomfit, rattle, faze, disconcert (see EMBARRASS): discommode, incommode, trouble, *inconvenience, molest.

dither, *v.* Didder, *shake, tremble, quake, quiver, shiver, quaver, wobble, teeter, shimmy, shudder, totter.

Ana. See those at DIDDER.

diurnal. *Daily, quotidian.

Con. See those at DAILY.

diuturnal. *Secular, centuried, agelong, aeonian.

Ana. Eternal, *infinite: *everlasting, endless.

divagation. *Digression, episode, excursus.

diverge. *Swerve, veer, deviate, depart, digress.

Ana. Differ from (see DIFFER): divide, part, *separate.

Ant. Converge (*as paths, roads, times, etc.*): conform (*as customs, habits, practices, etc.*).

divergence *or* **divergency. 1** *Deviation, deflection, aberration.

Ana. Division, separation, parting (see corresponding verbs at SEPARATE): differing from, differing with (see DIFFER).

Ant. Convergence. — ***Con.*** Agreement, concurrence, coincidence (see corresponding verbs at AGREE).

2 Difference, *dissimilarity, unlikeness, distinction.

Ana. Diversity, *variety.

Ant. Conformity, correspondence. — ***Con.*** Consonance, accord, *harmony, concord.

divergent. *Different, diverse, disparate, various.

Ana. *Opposite, contradictory, contrary, antithetical.

Ant. Convergent. — ***Con.*** *Similar, like, parallel, identical, uniform.

divers. *Many, several, sundry, various, numerous, manifold, multifold, multifarious.

diverse. *Different, divergent, disparate, various.

Ana. Contrasted *or* contrasting (see corresponding verb at COMPARE): contrary, *opposite, contradictory: *distinct, separate.

Ant. Identical, selfsame. — ***Con.*** *Same, equivalent, equal.

diversion. Amusement, recreation, entertainment. See under AMUSE, *v.*

Ana. *Play, sport, disport (see under PLAY, *v.*): levity, frivolity (see LIGHTNESS).

diversity. *Variety.

Ana. Divergence, difference, *dissimilarity, unlikeness, distinction: multifariousness, manifoldness (see corresponding adjectives at MANY).

Ant. Uniformity: identity.

divert. 1 *Turn, deflect, avert, sheer.

Ana. Bend, *curve, turn, twist: deviate, digress,

diverge, *swerve, veer: *change, alter, modify.
Con. Fix, *set, settle: absorb, engross, *monopolize.
2 *Amuse, entertain, recreate.
Ana. Beguile, *while, wile, fleet: regale, delight, gladden, tickle, arride, *please.
Con. *Tire, weary, fatigue, exhaust, jade, fag.

divest. *Strip, denude, bare, dismantle.
Ant. Invest, vest (*in robes of office, with power or authority, etc.*): apparel, clothe.

divide, *v.* 1 *Separate, part, sever, sunder, divorce.
Ana. Cleave, split, rend, rive (see TEAR): *cut, carve, chop.
Ant. Unite.
2 *Distribute, dispense, deal, dole.
Ana. *Apportion, portion, prorate, ration, parcel: *share, participate, partake: *allot, assign, allocate.

divination. Clairvoyance, penetration, insight, acumen, *discernment, discrimination, perception.
Ana. Intuition, understanding (see REASON).

divine, *adj.* *Holy, sacred, spiritual, religious, blessed.

divine, *v.* *Foresee, foreknow, apprehend, anticipate.
Ana. Discern, perceive, descry (see SEE): predict, prophesy, prognosticate, presage (see FORETELL)

division. Section, segment, sector, *part, portion, piece, detail, member, fraction, fragment, parcel.

divorce, *v.* *Separate, sever, sunder, part, divide.
Ana. Dissolve (see LIQUEFY): alienate, *estrange, wean, disaffect.

divulge. Tell, disclose, *reveal, betray, bewray, discover.
Ana. Impart, *communicate: announce, *declare, publish, advertise, proclaim: blab, tattle, *gossip.

doat. Variant of DOTE.

docile. *Obedient, biddable, tractable, amenable.
Ana. *Compliant, acquiescent: pliant, pliable, adaptable (see PLASTIC): yielding, submitting *or* submissive (see corresponding verbs at YIELD).
Ant. Indocile: unruly, ungovernable. — *Con.* Intractable, refractory, recalcitrant, willful, headstrong (see UNRULY): stubborn, *obstinate.

doctor, *v.* *Adulterate, sophisticate, load, weight, deacon.

doctrinaire. Dogmatic, magisterial, magistral, oracular, *dictatorial, authoritative, authoritarian.

doctrine. **Doctrine, dogma, tenet** are synonymous only when they agree in meaning a principle (usually one of a series or of a body of principles) accepted as authoritative by members of a church, a school of philosophers, a branch of science, or the like. **Doctrine** is often used in a much less restricted sense to denote a formulated theory that is supported by evidence, backed by authority, and proposed for acceptance; as, the *doctrine* of evolution; Einstein's *doctrine* of relativity. In the narrower sense in which the word is here considered, *doctrine* retains its etymological implication of authoritative teaching, but it presupposes acceptance by a body of believers or adherents; as, a catechism of Christian *doctrines* (or *doctrine*). "A...mathematical *doctrine* of waves which nowadays has almost come to dominate... physics" (*Karl K. Darrow*). **Dogma** also stresses authoritative teaching but unlike *doctrine* it seldom, if ever, implies proposal for acceptance. A dogma is not advanced as reasonable and worthy of acceptance, but laid down as true and beyond dispute; as, the *dogmas* of a church are usually stated in a creed or confession; in 1870, Pope Pius IX defined the *dogma* of papal infallibility. In extended use, *dogma* (or especially its derivative *dogmatic*) often connotes insistence, sometimes arrogant insistence, on authority or imposition by authority; as, the *dogma* that the king can do no wrong. **Tenet** emphasizes acceptance and belief rather than teaching. It is therefore thought of as a principle held or adhered to, and implies a body of adherents; as, the *tenets* of modern Socialism are not in every instance identical with the *doctrines* of Karl Marx.
Ana. Teaching, instruction (see corresponding verbs at TEACH): *creed, confession, symbol, catechism: *principle, fundamental.

document. 1 **Document, monument, muniment, record, archive** are here compared as denoting something preserved and serving as evidence, as of an event or a situation, or of the thought of its time. **Document,** except in extended use, commonly designates anything written or printed, such as a letter, a charter, a deed, a will, or a book, or anything carrying an inscription, such as a coin, a tombstone, or a medal, that has value as evidence because of its contemporaneousness. "While the poor little affairs of obscure, industrious men of letters are made the subject of intensive research, the far more romantic, thrilling and illuminating *documents* about the seekers and makers of great fortunes, are neither gathered nor cherished" (*H. G. Wells*). " 'The Waste Land' seems to me chiefly important as a social *document.* It gives an authentic impression of the mentality of educated people in the psychological slump that took place immediately after the war" (*Day Lewis*). **Monument** is applicable to anything that serves as a memorial of the past; it may be applied to a written document. "All our *monuments* [surviving legal documents] bear a strong evidence to this change [in the laws]" (*Burke*). However, it is more often applied to any building, work of art, or other relic of the past, especially one that serves as a reminder of a country's greatness, a nation's triumphs in war, a period's accomplishments in art, or the like; as, the French government has taken over many of the ancient cathedrals in order to preserve them as public *monuments.* "The English Church has no literary *monument* equal to that of Dante, no intellectual *monument* equal to that of St. Thomas, no devotional *monument* equal to that of St. John of the Cross" (*T. S. Eliot*). **Muniment,** which is sometimes confused with *monument,* is the most restricted in meaning of these words, for it is correctly applied only to certain written documents, chiefly title deeds, charters, etc., which are preserved as evidence of ownership, and can be used in the defense of one's claims. The word is now found chiefly in historical writing, especially in combinations such as *muniment* chest. "The *muniment*-room of a Catholic family in Lancashire" (*Buchan*). **Record** implies the intent to preserve as evidence of something; it therefore names something (either an item, or in a collective sense, all the items) written down so that exact knowledge of what has occurred will be perpetuated; as, to keep a *record* of a conversation; the *records* of the trial were destroyed in a fire; "there was no *record*...of any prisoner with those initials" (*Dickens*). "It is not only the right, but it is the judicial duty of the court, to examine the whole case as presented by the *record*" (*Ch. Just. Taney*). **Archive** (see also MUSEUM) implies preservation, sometimes, but far from invariably, with the intent to provide material for future use by historians or scholars; it is applicable to any document, record, or muniment that is so kept, especially throughout a long period. Its more common plural form **archives** suggests a miscellaneous accumulation, rather than a carefully selected collection, of papers; as, the *archives* of the Vatican are now accessible to scholars. "The *archives* of every city" (*Dryden*). "Some rotten *archive,* rummaged out of some seldom-explored press" (*Lamb*).
Ana. *Evidence, testimony.
2 Instrument, *paper.

doddering, doddered. *Senile, anile, doting, doted.
Ana. Infirm, decrepit, feeble (see WEAK): *aged, superannuated.
Ant. Spry.

dogged. *Obstinate, pertinacious, mulish, stubborn, stiffnecked, pigheaded, bullheaded.
Ana. Determined, resolved, decided (see DECIDE): tenacious (see STRONG): persevering, persistent (see corresponding verbs at PERSEVERE): resolute, steadfast (see FAITHFUL).
Ant. Faltering.

dogma. *Doctrine, tenet.
Ana. Belief, conviction, persuasion, view (see OPINION): *creed, confession, catechism, symbol: *principle, fundamental.

dogmatic, dogmatical. Magisterial, magistral, doctrinaire, oracular, *dictatorial, authoritative, authoritarian.
Ana. Peremptory, *masterful, imperative, imperious, domineering.

doldrums. Boredom, ennui, *tedium.
Ana. Dejection, depression, gloom, blues, dumps (see SADNESS).
Ant. Spirits, high spirits.

dole, *n.*[1] Anguish, woe, *sorrow, grief, heartache, regret.
Ana. Dolor, agony, passion, suffering, *distress, misery: tribulation, affliction, *trial.

dole, *n.*[2] Allowance, pittance, *ration.
Ana. Apportioning *or* apportionment, parceling *or* parcel, portioning *or* portion (see corresponding verbs at APPORTION): sharing *or* share (see corresponding verb SHARE).

dole, *v.* Dispense, deal, *distribute, divide.
Ana. *Apportion, ration, portion, parcel, prorate: bestow, confer, present, *give.

doleful. Lugubrious, dolorous, *melancholy, plaintive, rueful.
Ana. Mourning *or* mournful, sorrowing *or* sorrowful, grieving (see corresponding verbs at GRIEVE): piteous, *pitiful.
Ant. Cheerful, cheery.

doll up. *Preen, primp, prink, prank, prune, perk up.

dolor *or* **dolour.** Agony, suffering, passion, *distress, misery.
Ana. Anguish, woe, dole, *sorrow, grief: tribulation, *trial, affliction, cross, visitation.
Ant. Beatitude, blessedness.

dolorous. Doleful, *melancholy, plaintive, lugubrious, rueful.
Ana. & *Ant.* See those at DOLEFUL.

domain. Sphere, province, *field, territory, bailiwick.
Ana. *Area, region, zone: district, *locality: jurisdiction, dominion (see POWER).

domicile. Residence, abode, home, house, *habitation, dwelling.

dominant. **Dominant, predominant, paramount, preponderant, preponderating, sovereign** agree in meaning superior to all others in power, influence, position, or the like. That is **dominant** which is thought of as (especially figuratively) ruling or commanding, or as uppermost; as, the *dominant* race; "The idea of beauty and of a human nature perfect on all its sides, which is the *dominant* idea of poetry" (*Arnold*). That is **predominant** which is for the time being in the ascendant or exerts the most marked influence; as, "The power of...modifying a series of thoughts by some one *predominant* thought or feeling" (*Coleridge*); "A variety of subjects...in which no particular one is *predominant*" (*Cowper*); "The painter whose *predominant* aim is moral instruction" (*Binyon*). That is **paramount** which has pre-eminence or supremacy in importance, order, rank, or jurisdiction; as, "Hengist, wishing to become *paramount* in southern Britain" (*Borrow*); "Men to whom forms are of *paramount* importance" (*N. Hawthorne*). "According as one or other of these [modes of entertaining propositions] is *paramount* within him, a man is a skeptic...a philosopher...or...a believer....Many minds of course there are, which are not under the *predominant* influence of any one of the three" (*Newman*). That is **preponderant** or **preponderating** which outweighs or overbalances every other thing of its kind as in power, influence, or force: these terms are commonly used without clear distinction in meaning, but *preponderating* sometimes suggests active operation (as, the *preponderating* tendency), and *preponderant* the actual effect (as, for several years, this political party has been the *preponderant* party in the affairs of the nation; the *preponderant* influence of a group of banks). That is **sovereign** (as here considered: see also FREE) to which every other comparable thing is subordinate, inferior, or of lower value: the term therefore imputes unquestioned supremacy to the thing so described; as, the *Sovereign* Ruler of the universe; the *sovereign* power in the United States of America is vested in the people; to seek the *sovereign* good; a *sovereign* remedy; "Wearing...an amulet *Sovereign* against all passion" (*Browning*).
Ana. *Prevailing, prevalent: pre-eminent, *supreme, transcendent, surpassing: outstanding, salient, signal (see NOTICEABLE): governing, ruling (see GOVERN).
Ant. Subordinate.

domineering. *Masterful, imperious, imperative, peremptory.
Ana. Arrogant, overbearing, lordly, insolent (see PROUD): magisterial, magistral, *dictatorial, authoritative.
Ant. Subservient. — *Con.* Obsequious, servile (see SUBSERVIENT).

dominion. **1** Control, command, sway, authority, jurisdiction, *power.
Ana. Ascendancy, *supremacy: sovereignty (see under FREE, *adj.*).
2 *Possession, dependency, territory, colony, protectorate, mandate.

donate. Present, bestow, *give, confer, afford.
Ana. *Grant, accord, award.

donation. **Donation, benefaction, contribution, alms** are comparable when they denote a gift of money or its equivalent for a charitable, philanthropic, or similar object. **Donation,** though often used loosely for any such gift, is in discriminating usage applied only to a gift of substantial value, presented more or less publicly, and usually without reference to other givers or gifts. Originally, the word denoted the act or right of presenting something at the disposal of a powerful person, such as a king, a lord, or a patron; in modern times the word more often designates the thing presented, but careful writers and speakers still remember that it implies wealth and power in the giver; as, the endowment funds of the great universities are increased mainly by *donations* and bequests; a list of the Rockefeller *donations*. **Benefaction** is often used in place of *donation*, especially when there is the intent to compliment the donor and to imply his benevolence or the beneficence of his gift. The latter, however, is the basic implication and the word may be correctly used of any benefit conferred or received whether it has money value or not; as, her *benefactions* are remembered by many philanthropic agencies; her example was a *benefaction*. "Sometimes give your services [as a physician] for nothing, calling to mind a previous *benefaction* or present satisfaction" (*Precepts of Hippocrates*). **Contribution** implies participation in giving; when used in the sense here considered, it is applicable to small as well as large amounts of money; it is the modest term which one may apply to his own gift, though others may rightly call it a *donation* or *benefaction;* as, please accept my *contribution* to the endowment fund of your institution; a community chest *contribution.* **Alms,** the oldest of these words in English, is somewhat archaic. It now always implies the aim of relieving poverty; in the older use it also implied the fulfillment of a religious obligation or a practical manifestation of the virtue of charity. "The gift without the giver is bare; Who gives himself with his *alms* feeds three, —Himself, his hungering neighbor, and me [Christ]" (*J. R. Lowell*). In more modern use, it often is applied to the petty sums given beggars or paupers. "Though poor And forced to live on *alms*" (*Wordsworth*). "Scorning an *alms*" (*Tennyson*).

Ana. Grant, subvention, *appropriation, subsidy.

doom, *n.* *Fate, destiny, lot, portion.

doom, *v.* Damn, condemn, *sentence, attaint, proscribe.

Ana. Destine, appoint, prescribe (see corresponding adjectives at PRESCRIBED).

door. Door, gate, portal, postern, doorway, gateway are here compared chiefly as meaning an entrance to a place. **Door,** in literal use, applies chiefly to the movable and usually swinging barrier which is set in the opening which serves as an entrance to a building or to any room or apartment in a building; as, an oak *door;* the front *door* of a house; sometimes, *door* is used also of the opening; as, the children came running through the *door.* **Gate,** in literal use, applies often to an opening in a wall, fence, or other enclosure, especially one surrounding a tract of land in which a building or group of buildings is located, but it more commonly implies reference not only to the opening but to the movable and often swinging barrier (especially one made of a grating or open frame, or a heavy or rough structure) set in it and closed or opened at will; as, the north *gate* to the campus; he is now opening the garden *gate.* **Portal** applies usually to an elaborate and stately door or gate, with its surrounding framework, if any; as, the *portal* to the temple; the knights were admitted through the *portal* to the palace. **Postern** applies to a private or retired door or gate, such as one at the back of a castle or fortress. **Doorway** and **gateway** apply not so much to the structure as to the passage when a door (in the case of *doorway*) or a gate (in the case of *gateway*) is opened for ingress or egress; as, to stand in the *doorway* awaiting the postman; the automobiles passed through the *gateway* in constant succession.

In their literary, and usually figurative, use, these words are still more sharply distinguished. **Door** usually applies to that which provides opportunity to enter or withdraw or makes possible an entrance or exit; as, "The love of books, the golden key That opens the enchanted *door*" (*A. Lang*); "I know death hath ten thousand several *doors* For men to take their exit" (*J. Webster*). **Gate** differs from *door* chiefly in its connotations of facility in admission or of entrance into that which constitutes a wide, or even infinite, expanse; as, "What sweet contentments doth the soul enjoy by the senses! They are the *gates* and windows of its knowledge" (*W. Drummond*); "Their lot Forbad [the dead in the country churchyard] to wade through slaughter to a throne, And shut the *gates* of mercy on mankind" (*Gray*). **Portal** often carries similar connotations, but it usually applies to a definite place or thing which is itself splendid or magnificent and through which something, such as the sun at rising and at setting, is admitted or allowed exit; as, "Heaven, That opened wide her blazing *portals*" (*Milton*); "Since your name will grow with time . . . have I made the name A golden *portal* to my rhyme" (*Tennyson*). **Postern,** on the other hand, implies inconspicuousness or, in some contexts, a hidden means of entrance or escape. "It finds a readier way to our sympathy through a *postern* which we cannot help leaving sometimes on the latch, than through the ceremonious *portal* of classical prescription" (*J. R. Lowell*). **Gateway** is usually preferred to **doorway** in figurative use because it more strongly suggests a passage through which entrance is gained to that which is desirable or difficult; as, "Yea, the *gateway* [the Panama Canal] shall be free Unto all, from sea to sea" (*J. J. Roche*).

Ana. *Entrance, entry, entree, ingress, access.

doorway. *Door, portal, postern, gate, gateway.

dormant. 1 Quiescent, *latent, abeyant, potential.

Ana. *Inactive, inert, passive, idle.

Ant. Active, live.

2 Couchant, *prone, recumbent, reclining, supine, prostrate.

dormer, *n.* *Window, casement, oriel.

dotage. Senility, *age, senescence, senilism.

Ant. Infancy.

dote (*or* **doat**) **on** *or* **upon.** Love, relish, enjoy, fancy, *like.

Ant. Loathe. — *Con.* Abhor, abominate, detest, *hate: *despise, contemn, scorn.

doting. 1 Also **doted.** Doddering, *senile, anile.

Ana. See those at DODDERING.

2 Fond, devoted, *loving, affectionate.

Ana. Infatuated, *enamored: fatuous, foolish, silly, asinine, *simple.

double, *n.* Understudy, stand-in, *substitute, supply, locum tenens, alternate, pinch hitter.

double-cross. Delude, betray, beguile, *deceive, mislead.

double-dealing, *n.* Chicanery, chicane, trickery, *deception, fraud, subterfuge.

Ana. Duplicity, dissimulation, *deceit, guile, cunning.

double-entendre, double entente. Equivocation, *ambiguity, tergiversation, amphibology, amphibologism.

doubt, *n.* *Uncertainty, skepticism, suspicion, mistrust, dubiety, dubiosity.

Ana. Dubiousness, doubtfulness, questionableness (see corresponding adjectives at DOUBTFUL): incredulity, *unbelief, disbelief.

Ant. Certitude: confidence. — *Con.* *Certainty, conviction, assurance: *trust, reliance, dependence, faith.

doubtful. Doubtful, dubious, problematical (*or* **problematic**), **questionable** are here compared in the sense, in which they are applied to things (sometimes persons), of not affording one certainty of its (or his) worth, soundness, or the like. *Doubtful* and *dubious* are sometimes used with little distinction not only in this sense, but as applied to the person who is uncertain. **Doubtful,** however, is commonly so positive in its implication of uncertainty as almost to impute worthlessness, dishonesty, invalidity, or the like, to the thing in question; **dubious** stresses suspicion, mistrust, or hesitation in accepting, believing, following, choosing, or the like; thus, a man of *doubtful* repute is by implication more distrusted than one of *dubious* repute; to be *doubtful* of the outcome of a project is by implication to have better grounds for fearing its failure than to be *dubious* about it, for the latter may imply mere vague suspicions and fears and little evidence; so, a *doubtful* or a *dubious* prospect; a *dubious* transaction; a *doubtful* title to an estate; *dubious* friends. "Whispers and glances were interchanged, accompanied by shrugs and *dubious* shakes of the head" (*Irving*). **Problematical** is the only one of the terms here considered that is free from a suggestion of a moral judgment or suspicion: it is especially applicable to things whose existence, meaning, fulfillment, realization, is very uncertain, sometimes so uncertain that the probabilities of truth and of falsehood, or of success and of failure, or the like, are nearly equal. "*Problematical* points, of which, either side may be true...should not extinguish particular charity towards one another" (*Donne*). "The very existence of any such individual [Homer]...is more than *problematic*" (*Coleridge*). "Excellent acoustics, always so *problematic* a quality in halls built for the hearing of music" (*E. Wharton*). **Questionable** may imply little more than the existence of doubt respecting the thing so qualified; as, the legality of this action is *questionable;* a *questionable* theory. In its commonest use, however, *questionable* is euphemistic, or was originally euphemistic, for *immoral, low, improper, rude, unsound, untrue,* or the like: the term implies suspicions so well grounded as to be accepted as facts but, nevertheless, not to be asserted except in a guarded statement; thus, to say that a man is a *questionable* character is to cast a reflection on his honesty or morality; *questionable* dealings suggest underhandedness and dishonesty; so, women of *questionable* virtue. "The propriety of Lydia's manners was at least *questionable*" (*Shaw*). "The illustration is *questionable*, but the notion implied may be sound" (*S. Alexander*).

Ana. Distrusting *or* distrustful, mistrusting *or* mistrustful (see corresponding verbs at DISTRUST): *fearful, apprehensive, afraid.

Ant. Cocksure, positive.

doughty. Intrepid, valiant, valorous, *brave, courageous, bold, audacious, dauntless, undaunted.

Ana. *Formidable, redoubtable: venturous, venturesome, *adventurous, daring.

dour. Saturnine, glum, gloomy, *sullen, morose, surly, sulky, crabbed.

Ana. *Severe, stern, austere: rigorous, strict, *rigid: *grim, implacable.

dowdy. *Slatternly, frowzy, blowzy.

Ana. Slovenly, *slipshod, unkempt, sloppy.

Ant. Smart (*in dress, appearance*). — ***Con.*** Fashionable, *stylish, modish, chic: flashy, *gaudy, garish.

dower, *v.* **Dower, endow, endue** come into comparison as meaning to furnish or provide with a gift. **Dower** literally implies the provision of the dowry which a woman brings to a husband in marriage; as, a well-*dowered* bride. In its extended sense, *dower* implies the bestowal of any gift, talent, or the like; as, poets *dowered* with genius; Nature had *dowered* her with beauty. **Endow,** in the earliest of its English senses, implied the bestowing of money or property on a person or institution for its support or maintenance. This sense still prevails; as, "With all my worldly goods I thee *endow*" (*Anglican Marriage Service*); to erect and *endow* a hospital; a large bequest sufficient to *endow* the new college. **Endue** (etymologically a different word from *endow*) in the earliest of its current senses means to clothe or invest with something, such as a garment, a dignity, a right, a possession, or the like; as, "a loose gown...such as elderly gentlemen loved to *endue* themselves with" (*N. Hawthorne*); "to make him a citizen of the United States, and *endue* him with the full rights of citizenship" (*Ch. Just. Taney*); "A new and penetrating light descends on the spectacle, *enduing* men and things with a seeming transparency" (*Hardy*). But *endue* early in its history became confused with *endow* and *dower;* as, "And Leah said, God hath *endued* me with a good dowry" (*Genesis* xxx. 20). This confusion with the literal senses is now rare, but the confusion of *endue* with *endow* in its extended sense of to bestow upon one a faculty, power, or other spiritual or mental gift, has continued so that it is difficult to trace any differences in meaning between the two words. But *endow* in very precise use usually implies a permanent enriching, and *endue* an investing or clothing (either temporarily or permanently) with a specific quality or character; as, "those who are the most richly *endowed* by nature, and accomplished by their own industry" (*Spectator*); "For learning *endueth* men's minds with a true sense of the frailty of their persons...and the dignity of their soul and vocation" (*Bacon*); "finer faculties with which the continued process of evolution may yet *endow* the race" (*C. E. Montague*); "The [French] Revolution awakened it [French democracy] into consciousness...and *endued* it with efficient force" (*Brownell*).

Ana. *Furnish, equip, outfit, appoint, accouter.

downright, *adj.* Also *adv.* *Forthright.

Ana. Blunt, *bluff, brusque, curt: candid, plain, open, *frank: *straightforward, aboveboard.

Con. Devious, oblique, *crooked.

draft *or* **draught,** *n.* Outline, diagram, sketch, delineation, tracing, plot, blueprint. See under SKETCH, *v.*

draft *or* **draught,** *v.* Outline, diagram, *sketch, delineate, trace, plot, blueprint.

drag, *v.* Draw, *pull, haul, hale, tug, tow.

Con. *Push, shove, thrust, propel: drive, impel, *move.

drain, *v.* *Deplete, exhaust, impoverish, bankrupt.

Ana. Sap, undermine, debilitate, *weaken.

dramatic. Dramatic, theatrical, dramaturgic (*or* **dramaturgical), melodramatic, histrionic** are not close synonyms although all imply special reference to plays as produced by actors and actresses or to the effects which are produced by acted plays. **Dramatic,** when it denotes something more than relationship to the drama as written or as produced (as, a *dramatic* critic; a *dramatic* performance) implies an effect or a combination of effects appropriate to the drama or a representation of a drama, such as a stirring of the imagination and emotions by vivid and expressive action, speech, and gesture, or by the exciting complications of a plot; as, the *dramatic* appeal of a great orator; "the *dramatic* story-telling... of incidents which have a sympathetic hero" (*B. Russell*). "An idyll of Theocritus...is today as much alive as the most *dramatic* passages of the 'Iliad'—stirs the reader's feeling quite as much" (*Cather*). **Theatrical,** when it denotes something more than relationship to the theater (as, a *theatrical* office; a *theatrical* agent), implies effects appropriate to the theater as the place where plays are produced, and to the demands which its limitations, its conventions, and, often, its need of financial success, make both upon a play and its performance; the term therefore usually implies a marked degree of artificiality or conventionality, a direct and sometimes a blatant appeal to the senses and emotions, and often an overdoing or exaggeration in gesture, in speech, in action, and the like; as, "The situations [in Wilkie Collins's *The New Magdalen*] are in the most effective sense *theatrical*, without being in the profounder sense *dramatic*" (*T. S. Eliot*); "He had already learned that with this people religion was necessarily *theatrical*" (*Cather*). **Dramaturgic** is now often used in place of *theatrical* when the more or less derogatory connotations of that word are to be avoided and the emphasis is upon those elements in a play which fit it for representation in a theater; as, poetic plays are often lacking in *dramaturgic* quality; a play that is said to be "good theater" is both *dramatic* and *dramaturgic* in its character. **Melodramatic** implies a manner characteristic of the sensational and usually sentimental melodrama; the term commonly connotes exaggerated emotionalism or inappropriate theatricalism; as, to make a *melodramatic* speech; to employ *melodramatic* gestures. **Histrionic,** etymologically of or characteristic of actors, is more limited than *theatrical* for it implies reference to the tones of voice, gestures, movements, and appearance characteristic of actors, especially in older times before realism was attempted in dramatic performances; as, "Good looks are more desired than *histrionic* skill" (*Shaw*); "A tall, *histrionic*, dark man with a tossing mane" (*S. E. White*).

dramaturgic, dramaturgical. Theatrical, *dramatic, histrionic, melodramatic.

draught. Variant of DRAFT.

draw, *v.* **1** Drag, *pull, tug, tow, haul, hale.
Ana. *Bring, fetch: *attract, allure: *lure, entice: extract, elicit, evoke, *educe.
Con. See those at DRAG.
2 *Remove, withdraw.

dread, *n.* *Fear, horror, terror, fright, alarm, trepidation, panic, consternation, dismay.
Ana. *Apprehension, foreboding, misgiving, presentiment: timidity, timorousness (see corresponding adjectives at TIMID).

dreadful. Horrible, horrific, appalling, *fearful, awful, frightful, terrible, terrific, shocking.

dream, *n.* *Fancy, fantasy, phantasy, phantasm, vision, daydream, nightmare.
Ana. *Delusion, illusion, hallucination.

drench. *Soak, saturate, sog, sop, steep, impregnate, ret, waterlog.
Ana. *Permeate, pervade, penetrate, impenetrate.

dress, *v.* *Clothe, attire, tire, apparel, array, invest, robe, vest.
Ana. *Preen, prune, primp, prank, prink, doll up.
Ant. Undress.

dress, *n.* *Clothes, clothing, attire, tire, apparel, raiment, vesture, array.

drift, *n.* **1** Trend, *tendency, current, tenor.
Ana. *Flow, stream, current: movement, *motion: progression, *progress: *intention, purpose, end, objective, goal, intent, aim.
2 *Wash, diluvium, alluvium, alluvion, silt.

drill, *v.* **1** Bore, *perforate, punch, puncture, prick.
Ana. Pierce, penetrate, *enter, probe.
2 *Practice, exercise.
Ana. Train, discipline, *teach, instruct, school: *habituate, accustom, familiarize.

drill, *n.* Practice, exercise (see under PRACTICE, *v.*).

drive, *v.* **1** Impel, *move, actuate.
Ana. *Push, shove, propel: compel, *force, coerce: *incite, instigate.
Con. *Restrain, curb, snaffle, check, inhibit: lead, *guide, pilot, steer.
2 *Ride.

drive, *n.* **1** Ride (see under RIDE, *v.*).
2 *Road, roadway, highway, highroad, street, avenue, boulevard, terrace, parkway, thoroughfare, byway, lane, alley, alleyway.

droll. *Laughable, comic, comical, risible, funny, ludicrous, ridiculous, farcical.
Ana. Amusing, diverting, entertaining (see AMUSE): absurd, preposterous (see FOOLISH): humorous, *witty, facetious.

drop, *v.* *Dismiss, discharge, cashier, sack, fire, bounce.

drove, *n.* Herd, *flock, pack, bevy, covey, gaggle, flight, swarm, shoal, school.

drowsy. *Sleepy, somnolent, slumberous.
Ana. Comatose, stuporous, *lethargic, sluggish, torpid.
Con. Alert, vigilant, *watchful: *active, live, dynamic: animated, *lively, vivacious.

drudgery. Toil, travail, labor, *work, swink, grind.
Ana. Exertion, *effort, pains, trouble.

drug, *n.* **Drug, medicinal, pharmaceutical, biological, simple** come into comparison when they denote a substance used by itself or in a mixture with other substances as a medicine or medicament or in the diagnosis, prevention, or mitigation of disease. **Drug** is the ordinary comprehensive term in both general and professional use for any such substance, whether of vegetable, animal, or mineral origin, or produced synthetically. The term is referable to a wide variety of substances, as, for example, spermaceti (a waxy solid obtained from the oil of the sperm whale and used in making ointments), pepsin (a preparation derived from the stomachs of certain animals and used as a digestive), belladonna (the dried roots and leaves of the plant of that name used in relieving pain or in dilating the pupils of the eye), cascara sagrada (the dried bark of the California buckthorn used as a laxative), sulphur (a mineral used in medicine to induce perspiration, to promote the healing of lesions, etc.), and aspirin (a compound produced synthetically used in relieving pain and in reducing fever). Since *drug* is also specifically used to designate any habit-forming narcotic, and since some substances such as spermaceti and sulphur have other uses than in the preparation of medicines and medicaments, **medicinal** is often preferred to *drug*, especially in commerce, in manufacture, and in law, where indication of the ultimate use of the substance is for one reason or another desirable; as, exports of *medicinals* to China; *medicinals* are not contraband. **Pharmaceutical** is also often preferred to *drug* by pharmacists and manufacturers, especially as a designation of drugs which are commercially refined or prepared or synthetically manufactured, such as quinine, cod liver oil, and aspirin. The term is also used to distinguish medicinals, or strictly therapeutic substances, from other substances of similar origin or composition; as, *pharmaceuticals*, dyes, and cosmetics. **Biological** is the increasingly frequent designation for any of certain therapeutic products such as insulin, adrenaline, or thyroxine, derived from substances produced by living organisms. **Simple** is the archaic designation for any vegetable drug, such as dried roots, leaves, bark, or the like, used in compounding medicines or medicaments. It is also applied to a medicinal product made from one ingredient.
Ana. Medicine, medicament, *remedy, physic, specific, cure.

druggist, *n.* **Druggist, pharmacist, pharmaceutist, apothecary, chemist** agree in denoting one who deals in medicinal drugs. **Druggist,** the broadest of these terms, commonly designates the owner or operator of a store or wholesale house selling drugs or medicinal preparations. It is also loosely applied, instead of the precise terms **pharmacist** or **pharmaceutist,** to denote one who is skilled in compounding drugs and dispensing medicines prescribed by a physician. *Pharmacist* and *pharmaceutist* specifically imply, as *druggist* does not, special training in pharmacy, licensing following a test of one's qualifications, and professional standing. **Apothecary,** in early English use, was distinguished from *druggist*, the latter term then designating one who sold what are now called "crude drugs," herbs, roots, and other ingredients of medicines, and the former, one who compounded these ingredients or made them up into medicines. In somewhat later English use, an apothecary was a subordinate medical practitioner who prescribed as well as dispensed medicines. The term was employed until recently in the United States as a designation of a practitioner of pharmacy. In England, **chemist** is the popular or commercial equivalent of *druggist.*

drunk, *adj.* **Drunk, drunken, intoxicated, inebriate, inebriated, tipsy, tight** come into comparison when they mean conspicuously under the influence of liquor. **Drunk** and **drunken** are the plain-spoken, direct, and inclusive terms; as, *drunk* as a fiddler; *drunk* as a lord; dead *drunk;* "I have seen Sheridan *drunk,* too, with all the world; but his intoxication was that of Bacchus, and Porson's that of Silenus" (*Byron*). *Drunk* and *drunken* differ in that *drunk* is commonly used predicatively, while *drunken* is chiefly attributive; as, "They reel to and fro, and stagger like a *drunken* man" (*Psalms* cvii. 27). *Drunken* frequently suggests habitual drinking to excess; it also applies to whatever pertains to or proceeds from intoxication; as, "Stephano, my *drunken* butler" (*Shak.*); "a *drunken* sleep" (*Shak.*); a *drunken* brawl. **Intoxicated** may be exactly synonymous with *drunk,* though it is generally felt to be a less offensive term and has thus come to be applied to a person but slightly under the influence of liquor. "My friend requested me to add, that he was firmly persuaded you were *intoxicated* during a portion of the evening, and possibly unconscious of the extent of the insult you were guilty of" (*Dickens*). **Inebriate** (now rare except in figurative use) and **inebriated** imply such a state of intoxication that exhilaration or undue excitement (sometimes, however, stupefaction) results; as, *inebriated* revelers. All these words are used in a figurative sense as implying excess of emotion; as, *drunk* with joy; "*Drunk* with divine enthusiasm" (*Shelley*); "Even a man like Novalis...could find no better name for him [Spinoza] than a *Gott trunkner Mann*—a God *intoxicated* man" (*Froude*); "the rush of men *Inebriate* with rage" (*Shelley*); "a sweet *inebriated* ecstasy" (*Crashaw*). **Tipsy** implies a degree of intoxication that deprives one of muscular control, or, sometimes, of mental control; **tight,** a slang term, usually implies obvious intoxication, but does not suggest loss of power over one's muscles. There are many slang terms that imply intoxication: most of them, such as *spiflicated* (or *spifflicated*), *soused, lit,* and *blotto* are strong in their implications, suggesting loss of powers of locomotion, recognition, speech, and the like.

Ana. Fuddled, befuddled, bemuddled, confused (see CONFUSE): maudlin, soppy (see SENTIMENTAL).

Ant. Sober.

drunkard. Drunkard, inebriate, alcoholic, dipsomaniac, sot, soak, toper, tosspot, tippler designate one who drinks to excess. **Drunkard,** the common word, implies frequency of intoxication; **inebriate,** a habitually intoxicated condition; **alcoholic,** a more or less impaired body or mind; **dipsomaniac,** a morbid, uncontrollable, sometimes periodical, sometimes constant, craving for strong drink. **Sot** suggests dissoluteness and utter degradation; **soak,** a slang term, extreme dissipation. **Toper, tosspot, tippler** all imply habits of drinking: **toper** suggests the habitué of taverns or saloons and drinking with treating crowds; **tosspot** evokes the image of heavy drinking, and often also connotes conviviality; **tippler** carries the idea of light but constant and, often, secret drinking.

Ant. Teetotaler.

drunken. *Drunk, intoxicated, inebriate, inebriated, tipsy, tight.

Ana. & *Ant.* See those at DRUNK.

dry, *adj.* **1 Dry, arid** agree in meaning devoid of moisture. **Dry** may suggest freedom from moisture, often noticeable moisture, as merely a characteristic or as a desirable state (as, a *dry* climate; *dry* clothing; *dry* land; *dry* provisions; *dry* floors); it may suggest deficiency of moisture, or the lack of normal or necessary moisture (as, *dry* soil; a *dry* summer; *dry* berries); it may suggest exhaustion or dissipation of water or other liquid (as, a *dry* fountain pen; a *dry* pond; a *dry* well; *dry* bones). **Arid** always implies destitution or deprivation of moisture and therefore extreme, not relative, dryness. In its chief applications to regions or territory, it suggests waste or desert land; as, the *arid* sections of the southwestern United States; *arid* plains; an *arid* condition of soil. In humorous use, both *dry* and *arid* sometimes imply a ban upon intoxicating liquors, but *dry* connotes the difficulty; *arid,* the impossibility, of procuring them; as, the *dry* era between 1920 and 1933; an *arid* town. In extended use, as applied to subjects, books, sermons, etc., *dry* suggests the lack of qualities which compel one's interest or one's attention; as, the course is *dry* but useful; "his [the businessman's] work is not necessarily *dry:* modern businesses tend to become...interesting and important" (*Shaw*). *Arid,* on the other hand, connotes absence of all qualities which mark the thing so qualified as worthwhile, fruitful, or significant; as, an *arid* treatise on poetry; a particularly *arid* discussion of poverty and its causes. As applied to persons, their manner, their words, and the like, *dry* implies a loss of normal (often youthful) human warmth, freshness, responsiveness, or enthusiasm; *arid,* an absence of these qualities or an incapacity for them. "His [Herbert Spencer's] *dry* schoolmaster temperament, the hurdy-gurdy monotony of him" (*W. James*). "Some *arid* matron made her rounds at dawn sniffing, peering, causing blue-nosed maids to scour" (*V. Woolf*). Specifically, *dry* often suggests the repression of feeling for the sake of outwardly appearing aloof or imperturbed; as, a *dry* joker; comments which did not seem to be censures because uttered in a *dry* tone of voice. *Arid,* on the other hand, often connotes a deadening of feeling, especially as shown by a loss of fervor or hope. "The flower of virtue and love blooming in an *arid* and desolate heart" (*A. C. Benson*). "If Shakespeare himself ever had that 'dark period'...it was at least no darkness like that bleak and *arid* despair which sometimes settles over modern spirits" (*J. W. Krutch*).

Ana. Barren, *bare, bald: dehydrated, desiccated, dried, parched, baked (see DRY, *v.*): drained, depleted, exhausted, impoverished (see DEPLETE): sapped (see WEAKEN).

Ant. Wet. — *Con.* Damp, moist, humid, dank (see WET): *tender, sympathetic, warm, responsive: exuberant, lush, luxuriant, prodigal, *profuse.

2 *Sour, acid, acidulous, tart.

Ant. Sweet (*wine*).

dry, *v.* **Dry, desiccate, dehydrate, bake, parch** come into comparison as meaning to treat or to affect so as to deprive of moisture. **Dry** is the comprehensive word which may be used without regard to the process naturally taking place or artificially brought about, such as evaporation (to *dry* apples; clothes *dried* in the wind), draining (to *dry* up a ditch; to *dry* up a suppurating wound), absorption (the ink has not *dried;* to *dry* dishes with a towel), solidification (linseed oil added to paint makes it *dry* more quickly), or firing (to *dry* bricks in a kiln). **Desiccate** is narrower in its range of reference for it implies a complete deprivation of moisture, especially of vital juices, and often therefore, in its common extended use, a withering or shriveling. Literally, it is chiefly applicable to animal and vegetable products preserved by thoroughly drying and sometimes shredding, mincing, or pulverizing; as, *desiccated* fish, coconut (meat), eggs. Figuratively, it is applied chiefly to persons, to their attitudes, activities, expression, and the like, which have lost all their spiritual or emotional freshness or vitality. "Analysis is *desiccating* and takes the bloom off things" (*Babbitt*). "They were all...living on the edge of their nerves, a harsh, angular, *desiccated* existence" (*Van W. Brooks*). **Dehydrate** suggests extraction or elimination of water, or, in chemistry, of hydrogen and oxygen in the proportion to form water; it is now often preferred to *desiccate*, of which it is a close synonym, when the reference is to foods, because it conveys no unpleasant connotations; as, to *dehydrate* phosphoric acid, salt, natural gas, vegetables. **Bake,** as here compared (see BAKE, 1), implies not only dehydrating by means of heat or firing, but a hardening or caking of that which is dried; as, sun-*baked* earth; to *bake* bricks. **Parch** stresses the destroying effect of drying by intense heat or drought; it is preferred to *bake*, therefore, when the restoration of the proper amount of water is necessary or highly desirable; as, *parched* fields; a *parched* throat.

Ana. Drain, *deplete, exhaust: *wither, shrivel, rivel, wizen.

Ant. Moisten, wet.

dubiety. *Uncertainty, dubiosity, doubt, skepticism, suspicion, mistrust.

Ana. *Hesitation, hesitancy: wavering, vacillation, faltering (see corresponding verbs at HESITATE).

Ant. Decision. — *Con.* *Certainty, certitude, assurance, conviction: decisiveness, decidedness (see corresponding adjectives at DECIDED).

dubiosity. Dubiety, *uncertainty, doubt, skepticism, suspicion, mistrust.

Ana. Confusion, muddlement, addlement (see corresponding verbs at CONFUSE): wavering, vacillation, faltering, hesitation (see corresponding verbs at HESITATE).

Ant. Decidedness. — *Con.* *Decision, determination: assurance, certitude, *certainty: cocksureness, positiveness (see corresponding adjectives at SURE).

dubious. *Doubtful, questionable, problematical.

Ana. Suspicious, skeptical, mistrustful, uncertain (see corresponding nouns at UNCERTAINTY): hesitant, reluctant, *disinclined.

Ant. Cocksure (*state of mind, opinion, etc.*): reliable (*of things in general*): trustworthy (*of persons*). — *Con.* Dependable, trusty, tried (see RELIABLE): *sure, certain, positive.

duck, *v.* *Dip, immerse, submerge, souse, dunk.

ductile. *Plastic, pliable, pliant, malleable, adaptable.

Ana. Tractable, amenable (see OBEDIENT): responsive (see TENDER): yielding, submitting (see YIELD): fluid, *liquid: flexible, *elastic, resilient.

Con. Refractory, intractable (see UNRULY): rigid, *stiff, inflexible: obdurate, *inflexible, adamant.

dude. *Fop, dandy, beau, coxcomb, exquisite, élégant, macaroni, buck, spark, swell, nob, toff.

dudgeon. Umbrage, huff, pique, resentment, *offense.

Ana. *Anger, indignation, wrath, rage, fury, ire: temper, humor, *mood.

due, *adj.* **Due, rightful, condign** come into comparison when they mean being in accordance with what is just and appropriate. **Due,** which literally means owed or owing as a debt (not, however, as in current finance, a debt payable because of terms agreed upon in advance), carries in the senses here considered a strong implication that the thing so described is grounded upon an obligation, duty, or debt which should not or cannot be ignored; thus, one who takes *due* precautions uses the care that is required by his obligation to look out for his own or for others' safety or well-being; one who has a *due* sense of another person's rights accords to that person all that belongs to him by natural or moral right; one who has *due* respect for the law observes the individual laws as the duty of a responsible citizen. Oftentimes, the term implies little more than an accordance with that which is right, or reasonable, or necessary; as, "the *due* relation of one thing with another" (*Galsworthy*); "Your *due* and proper portion" (*Meredith*); "many non-commissioned officers have a firm belief that without a *due* admixture of curses, an order is inaudible to a private" (*C. E. Montague*). **Rightful** carries a much stronger and more consistently involved implication than *due* of a ground in right and justice, and usually suggests a moral or legal claim; as, the *rightful* heir to the estate; the *rightful* claimant to the crown could not be determined; to possess the *rightful* authority. **Condign** applies to that which is distinctly deserved or merited and, usually, which neither exceeds nor falls below one's deserts or merits: the term since the end of the seventeenth century has been applied chiefly to punishment, often with the implication of severity (as, "He had been brought to *condign* punishment as a traitor"—*Macaulay*), but there is no other reason etymologically or historically why it should not be applied in its general sense. " 'Speak you this in my praise, master?' 'In thy *condign* praise' " (*Shak.*). "Capriciously...the word *condign* is used only in connection with the word *punishment*....These and other words, if unlocked from their absurd imprisonment, would become extensively useful. We should say, for instance, '*condign* honours,' '*condign* reward,' '*condign* treatment' " (*De Quincey*).

Ana. Appropriate, meet, suitable, *fit, fitting, proper: right, *good: just, *fair, equitable.

Con. *Excessive, inordinate, immoderate, extravagant, exorbitant: *deficient.

due, *n.* **Due, desert, merit** come into comparison when they mean that which is justly owed to a person (sometimes a thing), especially as a recompense or compensation. **Due** usually implies a legal or moral right on the part of the person or thing that makes the claim or is in a position to make the claim; it usually suggests, however, a determination of what is owed by strict justice; as, "More is thy *due* than more than all can pay" (*Shak.*). "Carve to all but just enough, Let them neither starve nor stuff, And that you may have your *due*, Let your neighbor carve for you" (*Swift*). **Desert** (often in plural **deserts**) suggests not a legal right but a moral right based upon what one actually deserves, whether it be a reward or a penalty. " 'My lord, I will use them according to their *desert*.' 'God's bodykins, man, much better: use every man after his *desert*, and who should 'scape whipping?' " (*Shak.*). "You have deprived the best years of his life of that independence which was no less his *due* than his *desert*" (*Austen*). "Any Federal officer, regardless of his *deserts*, has much prestige" (*V. Heiser*). **Merit** is a somewhat complex term, often shifting in its major implication, but as here compared (see also EXCELLENCE) commonly implying a deserving either of reward or punishment on the ground of what has been accomplished, or of commendation, esteem, acceptance, or the like, on the ground of intrinsic, and usually excellent, qualities; as, "No tribute can be paid to them which exceeds their *merit*" (*Ch. Just. Marshall*); to treat every case on its *merits;* " 'As a pilgrim to the Holy Places I acquire *merit*' " (*Kipling*).

Ana. Compensation, recompensing *or* recompense, requital, repayment, satisfaction, payment (see corresponding verbs at PAY): retribution, *retaliation, reprisal, vengeance, revenge: reward, meed, guerdon (see PREMIUM).

dull, *adj.* **1** *Stupid, dumb, dense, crass.

Ana. *Lethargic, sluggish, stuporous, comatose: phlegmatic, stolid, *impassive, apathetic: *backward: retarded (see DELAY, *v.*).

Ant. Clever, bright. — ***Con.*** *Intelligent, alert, quick-witted, smart, brilliant, knowing.

2 Dull, blunt, obtuse come into comparison in many senses where they mean the reverse of *sharp, keen,* and *acute.* The words of the group under consideration do not necessarily find their antonyms among the group of words which are in general their opposites, because of a lack of parallelism in distinctive implications and connotations. As used of things, especially of tools, instruments, and the like, **dull** refers to either an edge or a point that has lost its sharpness by use (as, a *dull* knife; a *dull* razor; a *dull* pencil); **blunt** refers to an edge or point that is through use, nature, or intention, not sharp or keen (as, use the *blunt* side of the knife in prying; an ax is a *blunt* instrument as compared with a razor, but its edge should not be allowed to become *blunt* [or *dull*] through use); **obtuse** applies only to a point or to the shape of something whose sides converge at an angle that is broader than a right angle (as, the *obtuse* apex of some wings; an *obtuse* leaf). In their extended senses, **dull** (see also STUPID) is the most widely applicable and the richest as well as the most variable in its connotations. It implies, in general, the lack or the loss of that which gives keenness, zest, pungency, poignancy, intensity, interest, or the like; as, a *dull* pain; a *dull* red; a *dull* mood; *dull* conversation; a *dull* market; *dull* anger; a *dull* book. **Blunt** (see BLUFF for application to manners and utterances) usually implies a lack of edge or point (in the figurative senses of these words). Often, it refers to a person's powers of perception or to his sensibilities, which normally should be sharp or keen. "She [Shakespeare's Emilia]...is *blunt* in perception and feeling, and quite destitute of imagination" (*Bradley*). "To the age of twelve...all my emotions were wholesomely undeveloped and *blunt,* never at any point exasperated into acute sensibility" (*H. Ellis*). Less often, it applies to contrasts, critical judgments, and the like, requiring sharp distinction or differentiation. "Matthew Arnold distinguishes far too *bluntly,* it seems to me, between the two activities [creation and criticism]" (*T. S. Eliot*). **Obtuse** suggests such bluntness of perception or sensibilities as makes one insensitive to emotions or ideas; as, an *obtuse* audience; *obtuse* understanding; "*obtuseness* of moral sense" (*J. R. Lowell*); "obstinate *obtuseness* in regard to one...of the fine arts" (*De Quincey*).

Ant. Sharp (*edge, point, etc.*): poignant (*sensation, feeling, reaction, etc.*): lively (*action or activity*).

dumb, *adj.* **1 Dumb, mute, speechless, inarticulate** agree in meaning lacking the power to speak. **Dumb** and **mute** are often used interchangeably, but when used in distinction from each other, *dumb* implies an incapacity for speech, as in the case of brute animals and inanimate objects or of human beings whose organs of speech are defective; *mute* implies an inability to speak, owing to one's never having heard speech sounds, especially as in the case of one who is deaf congenitally or has lost his hearing before being old enough to reproduce heard sounds; thus, persons once called deaf and dumb are usually deaf-mutes who have healthy speech organs and can be trained to speak through the senses of sight and touch; so, "*dumb* idols" (*Habakkuk* ii. 18); "*dumb* stones whereon to vent their rage" (*Arnold*); a *mute* child. When used of persons who are normally able to speak, *dumb* (see also STUPID) usually suggests deprivation of the power to speak; *mute* stresses a compelling cause for keeping or maintaining silence; as, "Deep shame had struck me *dumb*" (*Shak.*); "how terrible is that *dumb* grief which has never learned to moan" (*Galsworthy*); "All sat *mute,* Pondering the danger with deep thoughts" (*Milton*); "some *mute* inglorious Milton" (*Gray*). **Speechless** commonly implies momentary deprivation of the power of speech; as, struck *speechless* with terror. **Inarticulate** implies either lack of the power to speak at all (as, "the *inarticulate* people of the dead"—*Shelley;* "the *inarticulate* hungers of the heart"—*S. P. Sherman*), or, especially, inability to speak intelligibly or clearly, usually on account of some powerful emotion, but sometimes because of lack of power to express one's thoughts or feelings; as, *inarticulate* with rage; "[He] stood looking down on her in *inarticulate* despair" (*E. Wharton*).

2 Dull, *stupid, dense, crass.

Ana. & ***Con.*** See those at DULL, 1.

Ant. Articulate (sense 3).

dumfound *or* **dumbfound.** Confound, nonplus, bewilder, distract, mystify, perplex, *puzzle.

Ana. Astound, flabbergast, amaze, astonish, *surprise: *confuse, muddle, addle, fuddle: disconcert, rattle, faze, discomfit (see EMBARRASS).

dumps. Dejection, gloom, blues, depression, melancholy, melancholia, vapors, *sadness.

Ana. Despondency, forlornness, hopelessness, despair (see under DESPONDENT): doldrums, ennui, boredom, *tedium.

dumpy. Chunky, stubby, stocky, thickset, squat, *thick.

dune. *Mound, bank, embankment, terrace, tumulus, barrow.

dunk, *v.* *Dip, immerse, souse, submerge, duck.

Ana. *Soak, saturate, sop.

dupe, *v.* **Dupe, gull, befool, trick, hoax, hoodwink, bamboozle** agree in meaning to delude a person by underhand means or for one's own ends. **Dupe** suggests unwariness or unsuspiciousness on the part of the person or persons deluded and the acceptance of what is false as true, what is counterfeit as genuine, what is worthless as valuable, or the like; as, the public is easily *duped* by extravagant claims in advertising; he was so soft-hearted that he was constantly being *duped* into helping impostors. "William had too much sense to be *duped*" (*Macaulay*). **Gull** implies great credulousness or a disposition that lends itself to one's being easily imposed upon or made a laughing stock of. "For Monsieur Malvolio, let me alone with him: if I do not *gull* him into a nayword, and make him a common recreation, do not think I have wit enough to lie straight in my bed" (*Shak.*). "If the world will be *gulled,* let it be *gulled*" (*Burton*). "*Gull* who may, they will be *gulled!* They will not look nor think" (*Browning*). **Befool** stresses the effect on the victim, that of being made a fool of in his own eyes or in those of others; it does not so strongly suggest a temperamental weakness in the victim as the preceding words, nor so clearly imply an intent to delude on the part of the agent, as most of the words that follow; as, to confess themselves *befooled* by the candidate, his personable appearance, and his promises. "This term [moral sense] was long a stumbling-block in the eyes of innocent philosophic critics, too easily *befooled* by words" (*H. Ellis*). **Trick** implies the intent to delude on the part of the agent by means of a stratagem, a ruse, or wiles, or by fraud; it always suggests the intent to deceive, but it does not necessarily imply a base end. It may, for example, imply illusion as the end; as, a skillful dramatist *tricks* the spectators into accepting the impossible as probable; a magician's success depends upon his ability to *trick* his audience. It more often suggests deliberate misleading and the use of cunning or craft; as, pills are coated with sugar or chocolate in order to *trick* children into taking them; he was *tricked* out of his savings by the promises of large returns on an investment; the people felt that they had been *tricked* into approval of the project. **Hoax,** in strict use, implies indulgence in tricking as a sport or for the purpose of proving how gullible a person or persons can be when a skillful imposture or fabrication is presented to them; in looser use, it more often suggests a fraud intended to deceive even the most skeptical and oftentimes, also, to work for one's own profit or personal advantage; as, the American public was successfully *hoaxed* by the Cardiff giant; did Mark Twain intend to *hoax* people by his "Personal Recollections of Joan of Arc," published without his name and as the work of one of her contemporaries? **Hoodwink** connotes either a deliberate confusing intended to blind the mind of another to the truth, or, less often, self-delusion arising from one's inability to distinguish the false from the true; as, he will not be *hoodwinked* by sentimental platitudes into doing things that are against right reason; "to *hoodwink* everybody by pretending to conform" (*Cabell*); "Some to the fascination of a name Surrender judgment *hoodwinked*" (*Cowper*). **Bamboozle** usually implies the use of cajolery, or humbug, or illusion, or the like; the word is often used interchangeably with *trick, hoax,* or *hoodwink,* but it is less definite or fixed in its implications; as, to be *bamboozled* into a belief that he was a great man. "What Oriental tomfoolery is *bamboozling* you?" (*Newman*).

Ana. *Deceive, beguile, delude, mislead, double-cross, betray: *cheat, cozen, defraud, overreach: outwit, baffle, circumvent (see FRUSTRATE).

duplicate, *n.* *Reproduction, facsimile, copy, carbon copy, transcript, replica.

Ana. Counterpart, *parallel, analogue.

duplicity. *Deceit, dissimulation, cunning, guile.

Ana. Double-dealing, chicanery, chicane, trickery, *deception, fraud, subterfuge: treacherousness *or* treachery, perfidiousness *or* perfidy, faithlessness (see corresponding adjectives at FAITHLESS).

Con. Straightforwardness, forthrightness (see corresponding adjectives at STRAIGHTFORWARD).

durable. *Lasting, perdurable, permanent, stable, perpetual.

Ana. Enduring, abiding, persisting (see CONTINUE): *strong, stout, tenacious.

Con. Fragile, frail, feeble, *weak: *transient, transitory, fleeting, ephemeral, fugitive.

duress. Constraint, coercion, compulsion, violence, *force, restraint.

dusk, *adj.* Dusky, dim, darkling, *dark, obscure, murky, gloomy, opaque.

dusky. 1 Dusk, dim, *dark, darkling, obscure, murky, gloomy, opaque.

2 **Dusky, swarthy, tawny** *or* **tawney** come into comparison as meaning dark and dull. **Dusky** is the most general term; it applies to that which is somewhat dark yet not black, and void of light or color; as, "*dusky* vapours of the night" (*Shak.*); "twilight groves and *dusky* caves" (*Pope*); a *dusky* complexion. **Swarthy** and **tawny** stress darkness and dullness of hue or color only; *swarthy* implies a shade verging on brownness or blackness, *tawny* suggests a shade characteristically brown, but sometimes a yellowish-brown or tan; as, "a *swarthy* Ethiope" (*Shak.*); "the *swarthy* Moors" (*Pope*); "*tawny* Tartar" (*Shak.*); "your orange-*tawny* beard" (*Shak.*). When applied to the human complexion directly, *swarthy* is now usually preferred to *tawny,* even though dark brownness is not suggested; as, "The face was saturnine and *swarthy*" (*Wilde*).

duty. 1 *Obligation.

Ana. Responsibility, accountability, amenability, answerability, liability (see corresponding adjectives at RESPONSIBLE).

2 Office, *function, province.

Ana. Concern, business, *affair.

3 *Task, job, chare, chore, assignment, stint.

Ana. *Work, métier, business, employment, occupation, calling: *trade, craft, art, profession.

4 Customs, impost, tariff, *tax, levy, excise, assessment, rate, toll, tribute, tithe, teind, cess.

dwarf, *n.* 1 **Dwarf, pygmy, midget, manikin** (*or* **mannikin**), **homunculus** (*or* **homuncle, homuncule**), **runt** come into comparison when they mean a person of diminutive size. **Dwarf** is the general term not only for a human being but for any animal or plant that is far below the normal size of the species: often, but not necessarily, the term suggests stunted development. "His [the fool's] value was trebled in the eyes of the king by the fact of his being also a *dwarf* and a cripple" (*Poe*). **Pygmy,** in earliest use, was applied to one of a race (or races) of fabled dwarfs mentioned by Homer and others, and now is applied especially to one of a dwarf people found in central Africa. The term carries a stronger connotation of diminutiveness and a weaker suggestion of arrested development than *dwarf;* when used generally in reference to a person, it often implies tininess (often relative tininess), sometimes in body but more often in intellect. "To him all the men I ever knew were *pygmies.* He was an intellectual giant" (*Byron*). **Midget** stresses abnormal diminutiveness but, unlike *dwarf,* carries little suggestion of malformation or deformity; the term is applied usually to a tiny but otherwise shapely person exhibited in a circus or employed in place of a child in theatrical performances; as, P. T. Barnum's famous *midget,* Tom Thumb. **Manikin** is often applied contemptuously not only to a dwarf but to any human being who for one reason or another seems despicably small or weak. "Can it be fancied that Deity ever vindictively Made in his image a *mannikin* merely to madden it?" (*Poe*). **Homunculus** usually suggests even greater diminutiveness and often greater perfection in form than *midget:* it is the specific term for an exceedingly small artificial human being such as was supposedly developed by Paracelsus, a famous Renaissance alchemist; it is also applied, as a technical term, to the human fetus. **Runt,** usually a contemptuous designation, applies to a dwarf or undersized person, especially to one who is conspicuously puny or undeveloped or, occasionally, to one who is thick as well as short. "I always did admire a good, sizable, stout man. I hate a *runt*" (*McClure's Mag.*). The term is also applied to an animal, especially a domestic animal, small of its kind; and, dialectally in the United States, it is applied specifically to the undersized one of a litter, as of pigs.

2 Gnome, pixy, sprite, elf, *fairy, faery, fay, brownie, puck, goblin, nix, leprechaun, shee, banshee.

dwell. *Reside, live, lodge, sojourn, stay, put up, stop.

dwelling. Residence, abode, domicile, home, house, *habitation.

dwindle. Diminish, lessen, *decrease, reduce, abate.

Ana. Wane, ebb, *abate, subside: attenuate, extenuate, *thin: *moderate: disappear (see affirmative verb at APPEAR, 1).

dynamic. Live, *active, operative.

Ana. Potent, forceful, forcible, *powerful: *intense, vehement: vitalizing, energizing, activating (see VITALIZE).

E

each, *adj.* Every, *all.

each, *adv.* **Each, apiece, severally, individually, respectively** come into comparison when they mean for (or to, or by) every one of the many, or several, persons or things comprising a group. All imply distribution. **Each** and **apiece** (the more colloquial term) usually connote equality in the amount or value of that distributed, unless the context indicates otherwise; as, he gave the five children a dollar *each* (or *apiece*); the students have a bedroom and study *apiece* (or *each*). **Severally** stresses the apartness of each of the persons and things involved, but at the same time often, especially in legal use, implies that each of them is favored, bound, guilty, responsible, or the like, in the same degree as the group as a whole; thus, to try a group of conspirators *severally* is to try them not jointly, or together, but one at a time, and usually on the identical charge; to be bound jointly and *severally* is to be under obligation as a group and singly as individuals, damages being recoverable from all or from any member of the group. **Individually,** like *severally,* implies a distinction between each member of the group but it goes further in not suggesting equality in responsibility, favor, disfavor, or the like; thus, to try a group of conspirators *individually* is to try each one on a specific charge, usually on the assumption that they are not equally guilty; to greet each member of a visiting delegation *individually* is to greet him separately and personally. **Respectively** is used only when the persons or things involved in the distribution follow a given order and that which is distributed goes to each in the same order; as, he gave John, James, and Edward ten dollars, five dollars, and three dollars, *respectively;* the suites of offices 101, 102, 103 are assigned *respectively* to the president, the treasurer, and the secretary of the company.

eager. Eager, avid, keen, anxious, agog, a-tiptoe, athirst agree in meaning actuated by a strong and urgent desire or interest. **Eager** implies ardor and, often, enthusiasm; it frequently also connotes impatience. "It is not a life for fiery and dominant natures, *eager* to conquer" (*A. C. Benson*). "His [Southey's] *eagerness* admits of no doubt or delay" (*Hazlitt*). **Avid** adds to *eager* the implication of greed or of unbounded desire. "A too *avid* thirst for pleasure" (*G. W. Russell*). "Cultivated, excitable, *avid* of new things" (*Buchan*). **Keen** suggests intensity of interest and quick responsiveness in action. "Boys in white flannels—all *keen* as mustard, and each occupied with his own game, and playing it to the best of his powers" (*Quiller-Couch*). "Tories who are as *keen* on State interference with everything and everybody as the Socialists" (*Shaw*). **Anxious** emphasizes fear lest one's desires be frustrated or one's hopes not realized; it often additionally connotes insistence or perseverance in making one's desires known. "Visibly *anxious* that his wife should be on easy terms with us all" (*A. Repplier*). "Schoolmasters may be pathetically *anxious* to guide boys right, and to guard them from evil" (*A. C. Benson*). **Agog** and **a-tiptoe** are picturesque words, the first of which suggests the excitement and bustle attending something interesting about to be begun or an event eagerly awaited; the second, the alertness and readiness to spring into action of one poised on tiptoe, eager to dart forth at a signal. "Six precious souls, and all *agog* To dash through thick and thin" (*Cowper*). "It was disquieting news, and the ordnance branch of our navy, we may be sure, is *a-tiptoe*" (*The Nation*). **Athirst** implies yearning or longing more vividly than the others; it seldom connotes readiness for action. "I that for ever feel *athirst* for glory" (*Keats*). "*Athirst* for the beauty of the beyond" (*Binyon*).

Ana. Desiring, coveting, craving (see corresponding verbs at DESIRE): longing, yearning, hungering, thirsting (see corresponding verbs at LONG): *impatient, restless, restive.

Ant. Listless. — ***Con.*** *Indifferent, unconcerned, incurious, aloof: uninterested (see DISINTERESTED): apathetic, *impassive, stolid.

early, *adv.* **Early, soon, beforehand, betimes** carry in common the meaning of at, or nearly at, a given point of time or around the beginning of a specified or implied period of time. **Early** is used chiefly, but not exclusively, in reference to a period of time (such as a day, a lifetime, an age, a term) and in dating a happening with reference to the beginning of that period. In such use, it implies occurrence shortly after the time at which the period is set to begin or is regarded as beginning; as, crocuses blossomed *early* this spring; migrations took place *early* in the Middle Ages. "*Early* to bed and *early* to rise, Makes a man healthy, wealthy, and wise" (*Franklin*). "Voltaire perceived very *early* in life that to be needy was to be dependent" (*J. Morley*). Sometimes, especially when the reference is to a point of time, *early* may mean in advance of the time set or expected, or of the usual time; thus, a person who arrives *early* at a meeting and leaves *early,* comes slightly before (sometimes just at) the time set, or noticeably ahead of the others, and leaves before the gathering breaks up; winter came *early* (that is, ahead of scheduled or normal time) this year. **Soon** usually refers to a definite point of time, such as the present or the beginning of a period, a process, a course, or the like, but it commonly implies occurrence after the moment in mind; thus, when a physician tells a patient to come *early,* he by implication asks that patient to come in advance of the time set for the beginning of his office hours so that the patient may be attended to *soon,* or shortly after the office hours begin; on the other hand, when he asks a patient to come *soon,* he by implication requests another visit shortly after the present one. But *soon* carries not only the implication of subsequence to a specified or implied point of time, but also, even more strongly, that of quickness or promptness or lack of delay; as, I called, and he *soon* appeared; the absconder was apprehended *soon* after his disappearance; I hope you will find your ring very *soon. Soon,* however, is sometimes used in place of *early,* though commonly with greater emphasis on promptness, in poetry, in some idiomatic expressions, and in the comparative and superlative degrees; as, "Late and *soon,* Getting and spending, we lay waste our powers" (*Wordsworth*); must you go so *soon?;* excuse my not writing *sooner;* "The spirit... may know How *soonest* to accomplish the great end" (*Shelley*). **Beforehand** sometimes implies a time in advance of that set or expected or customary; as, he promised to be here *beforehand.* More often, however, it refers to a time in advance of a possible, probable, or certain occurrence, and it then usually implies anticipation or anticipatory measures; as, if one knows a thing *beforehand* one can be prepared; to be *beforehand* in dealing with an enemy; to pay a debt *beforehand* (that is, in advance of when it is due or, sometimes, incurred). **Betimes** (now somewhat bookish) has been used in the past in place of both *early* and *soon.* "Not to be a-bed after midnight is to be up *betimes*" (*Shak.*). "He tires *betimes* that spurs too fast" (*Shak.*). In current usage, it implies occurrence at the proper or due time, and therefore stresses seasonableness. That which happens *betimes* is neither too early nor too late; as, to know the art of giving advice *betimes;* because he had learned his lesson *betimes,* he was able to give perfect satisfaction afterwards.

Ant. Late.

earn. Win, gain, acquire, secure, *get, obtain, procure.

Ana. Work, toil, labor, travail (see corresponding nouns at WORK): achieve, attain, gain, *reach.

earnest, *adj.* *Serious, solemn, grave, sober, sedate, staid.

Ana. Zealous, enthusiastic, passionate (see corresponding nouns at PASSION): diligent, *busy, industrious, assiduous, sedulous: *sincere, wholehearted, whole-souled.

Ant. Frivolous. — *Con.* Volatile, effervescent, buoyant, *elastic: flippant, flighty, light (see corresponding nouns at LIGHTNESS).

earnest, *n.* Token, *pledge, pawn, hostage, gage.

earth, *n.* **Earth, world, universe, cosmos, macrocosm** come into comparison when they mean the entire area or extent of space in which man thinks of himself and of his fellow men as living and acting. **Earth** applies, however, only to part of that which he knows by sight or by faith to exist; the term usually suggests a distinction between the sphere or globe called astronomically the earth, which he knows to be composed of land and water, and the bodies which he sees in the heavens (as, "this goodly frame, the *earth*"—*Shak.;* "Land is part of *Earth's* surface which stands at a given time above sea level"—*R. Lord*). It may, however, imply a distinction from heaven and hell (as, "Thy will be done in *earth,* as it is in heaven" —*Matthew* vi. 10; "The infinite loftiness of Mary's nature, among the things of *earth,* and above the clamour of kings"—*H. Adams*). **World** is a far less definite term than *earth.* When applied to a physical entity, it usually denotes all that illimitable area which to man's senses, at least, includes not only the earth and other planets, but all the space surrounding the earth and all the bodies contained within it (as, "It is not accident that wherever we point the telescope...wherever we look with the microscope there we find beauty. It beats in through every nook and cranny of the mighty *world*"—*R. Jones*): to persons who accept the account of creation in Genesis the term denotes the entire system that was brought into being by the word of God; as, God made the *world;* to expect the destruction of the *world.* The term, nevertheless, is often used as equivalent to *earth,* the globe; as, a trip around the *world;* he wanted to visit every corner of the *world.* As applied to an immaterial entity, *world* may imply the sum total of all the inhabitants of earth and of their interests and concerns (as, all the *world* loves a lover; the *world* was one in desiring peace), or that section or part of this larger world which comes within the knowledge of the individual (as, man's relation to the *world* about him; his family and his business comprised his *world*), or the section or part of the larger world which is devoted to secular, as distinct from religious or spiritual, concerns (as, to retire from the *world;* the *world,* the flesh, and the devil; "The *world* is too much with us"—*Wordsworth*). **Universe,** in its most precise sense, denotes the entire system of created things (or of physical phenomena), regarded as a unit both in its organization and in its operation; as, ancient and medieval astronomers regarded the earth as the fixed center of the *universe;* the astronomers of today teach that the *universe* is finite, but that it is constantly expanding. *Universe,* however, often is more loosely used in reference to an entire system of phenomenal things as that system appears to the limited vision of the typical man or of the individual; as, "From the *universe* as we see it both the Glory of God and the Glory of Man have departed" (*J. W. Krutch*); "He inhabited a different *universe* from that of common men" (*A. Huxley*). **Cosmos,** because of its opposition to *chaos,* carries a stronger implication of order and harmony in operation than *universe,* which it otherwise closely resembles in meaning. "Were it not for the indwelling reason the world would be a chaos and not a *cosmos*" (*Blackie*). **Macrocosm** applies to the universe thought of as a great whole characterized by perfect organic unity exhibited elsewhere only in the small whole, the individual man or *microcosm;* as, "The microcosm repeats the *macrocosm*" (*T. H. Huxley*).

earthly. Earthly, terrestrial, terrene, earthy, mundane, worldly, mortal, sublunary come into comparison when they mean of, belonging to, or characteristic of, the earth. **Earthly** is used chiefly in opposition to *heavenly;* as, *earthly* love; an (or the) *earthly* paradise. "If I have told you *earthly* things, and ye believe not, how shall ye believe, if I tell you of heavenly things?" (*John* iii. 12). "A peace above all *earthly* dignities, A still and quiet conscience" (*Shak.*). **Terrestrial** is sometimes used in place of *earthly* as a more sonorous term; frequently, however, it implies an opposition to *celestial* rather than to *heavenly* (see CELESTIAL); as, a *terrestrial* globe; a *terrestrial* telescope; less often, it implies a distinction of earth from the other planets (as, *terrestrial* magnetism; "Whose vision is cosmic, not *terrestrial*"—*Lowes*), or more specifically in astronomy, a distinction of certain planets assumed to be like the earth from others assumed to be unlike the earth (thus, the *terrestrial* planets are Earth, Mars, Venus, and Mercury). "There are also celestial bodies, and bodies *terrestrial:* but the glory of the celestial is one, and the glory of the *terrestrial* is another" (*1 Corinthians* xv. 40). "When from under this *terrestrial* ball He fires the proud tops of the eastern pines" (*Shak.*). *Terrestrial* in some use suggests land as a habitat, rather than water (or, sometimes, trees); as, *terrestrial* serpents; *terrestrial* plants. **Terrene** is now rare except in poetry; it may be used in place of *earthly* especially when it suggests an opposition to that which is spiritual (as, "Its [the principle of beauty's] body of poetry, as the body of man, Is but a *terrene* form"—*G. Bottomley*), but it may also be used in place of *terrestrial* in any of the given senses (as, "all such *terrene* dross"—*T. Heywood;* "Substances entirely *terrene*"—*Goldsmith*). **Earthy,** in the historical development of its senses, has stressed a connection with the earth as soil rather than the earth as the abode of men (as, an *earthy* smell); therefore, even when it comes close to *earthly* in its meaning, it carries a stronger implication of grossness of substance or of material interests than the latter word, and is opposed more to *spiritual* than to *heavenly;* as, "The first man [Adam] is of the earth, *earthy:* the second man is the Lord from heaven" (*1 Corinthians* xv. 47). "My anger and disgust at his gross *earthy* egoism had vanished" (*Hudson*). "With much *earthy* dross in her, she [Cleopatra] was yet pre-eminently a creature of 'fire and air' " (*Buchan*). **Mundane** and **worldly** both imply a relationship to the world thought of as the affairs, concerns, and activities of human beings, especially as they are concentrated on practical ends, on immediate pleasures, and the like. *Mundane* specifically suggests an opposition to that which is eternal and stresses transitoriness or impermanence; as, *mundane* glory; "There I quaff the elixir and sweet essence of *mundane* triumph" (*L. P. Smith*). "Tony knew that she did not allow them to talk of *mundane* affairs on these expeditions to and from church" (*Arch. Marshall*).

Worldly, which is applied chiefly to persons and their interests, specifically implies indifference to things of the spirit and concentration on that which satisfies one's love of success, one's desire for pleasure, one's self-esteem, and the like. "The obvious thing to say of her was that she was *worldly;* cared too much for rank and society and getting on in the world" (*V. Woolf*). **Mortal** (see also DEADLY, 1) comes into comparison with these other terms when it suggests a relationship to the earth or world as the dwelling place of human beings; it therefore sometimes takes the place of *earthly*, without necessarily suggesting a lack of connection with heaven, or of *terrestrial*, without necessarily suggesting a lack of connection with the celestial regions; as, "a moment of brilliance making *mortal* fields elysian" (*Day Lewis*). **Sublunary** (etymologically, under the moon) is a distinctly literary or poetic term variously interchangeable with *earthly, mundane*, and *terrestrial*. "All things *sublunary* are subject to change" (*Dryden*). "What then would matter the quakes and *sublunary* conflicts of this negligible earth?" (*L. P. Smith*).

Ana. Temporal, *profane, secular: temporal (see TEMPORARY): *material, physical, corporeal.

Con. *Celestial, heavenly, empyrean: spiritual, divine (see HOLY).

earthy. Mundane, worldly, *earthly, terrestrial, terrene, mortal, sublunary.

Ana. *Material, physical, corporeal: fleshy, *carnal, sensual: gross, *coarse.

ease, *n.* **1** Comfort, relaxation, *rest, repose, leisure.

Ana. Inactivity, idleness, inertness, passiveness, supineness (see corresponding adjectives at INACTIVE): tranquillity, serenity, placidity, calmness, peacefulness (see corresponding adjectives at CALM).

Con. Toil, travail, *work, labor: *distress, suffering, misery.

2 Facility, dexterity, *readiness.

Ana. Effortlessness, smoothness, easiness (see corresponding adjectives at EASY): grace (see ELEGANCE): expertness, adeptness, skillfulness, proficiency (see corresponding adjectives at PROFICIENT): deftness, featness, adroitness (see corresponding adjectives at DEXTEROUS).

Ant. Effort. — *Con.* Exertion, pains, trouble (see EFFORT): awkwardness, clumsiness, ineptness, maladroitness (see corresponding adjectives at AWKWARD).

easy, *adj.* **1** *Comfortable, reposeful, restful, cozy, snug.

Ana. *Soft, lenient, gentle: commodious, *spacious: *calm, tranquil, serene, placid: unconstrained, spontaneous (see corresponding nouns at UNCONSTRAINT).

Ant. Disquieting *or* disquieted. — *Con.* Disturbed, perturbed, agitated, upset, discomposed (see DISCOMPOSE): anxious, worried, concerned (see corresponding nouns at CARE).

2 Easy, facile, simple, light, effortless, smooth come into comparison as meaning not involving undue effort or difficulty in doing, making, giving, understanding, or the like. **Easy** is applicable both to persons and things that make demands, especially for physical or mental effort, or that impose a task upon a person, and to the acts or activities involved in satisfying such demands or in accomplishing such a task; as, the book was *easy* to read; I would like some more *easy* reading; our teacher was *easy* today; her assignment for tomorrow is short and *easy;* an *easy* riddle; an *easy* solution of the riddle; the place is *easy* to reach; the place is within *easy* reach of the city; it will not be *easy* for him to understand your breaking of your promise. "Take my yoke upon you, and learn of me....For my yoke is *easy*, and my burden is light" (*Matthew* xi. 29–30). "I have been a dreamer and an artist, a great dreamer, for that is *easy*, not a great artist, for that is hard" (*H. Ellis*). **Facile** was once and to some extent is still used as a very close synonym of *easy;* as, "having won...his *facile* victory" (*Froude*); "The *facile* modes of measurement which we now employ" (*Tyndall*). But it now chiefly applies to that which comes, or moves, or works, or gains its ends seemingly without effort or at call: it therefore is often used in derogation implying lack of constraint or restraint, undue haste, dexterity rather than meticulousness, fluency with shallowness, or the like; as, a writer's *facile* pen; a woman's *facile* tears; "I am not concerned with... offering any *facile* solution for so complex a problem" (*T. S. Eliot*); "she was a prey to shoddy, *facile* emotions and moods, none of which had power to impel her to any action" (*R. Macaulay*). **Simple,** as here compared, stresses ease in apprehending or understanding: it implies freedom from complication, intricacy, elaboration, or other involvements which render a thing difficult to see through; as, problems in arithmetic too *simple* to hold the interest of pupils of that age; "true poetry, however *simple* it may appear on the surface, accumulates meaning every time it is read" (*Day Lewis*); "Don't do religious people the injustice of believing that anything is *simpler* or *easier* for them [than for others]; it's more difficult, since life is more exacting" (*R. Macaulay*). **Light** implies an opposition to *heavy* in nearly all of its senses, but in the one here considered it suggests freedom from burdensomeness, or from exactions that make undue or difficult demands on one; as, a *light* task; his work is very *light; light* reading; a *light* lunch (i.e., a lunch that is easily digested); *light* punishment; *light* taxes (i.e., taxes easy to pay). **Effortless,** though it carries many of the connotations characteristic of *facile*, suggests the appearance of ease rather than actual absence of effort: oftentimes, therefore, it implies mastery, skill, artistry, or the like, and the attainment of such perfection that the movements or technique seem to involve no strain; as, the *effortless* dancing of a Pavlova; "even the swallows...glided in an *effortless* way through the busy air" (*Jefferies*); a natural, *effortless* style. **Smooth** suggests an absence of, or the removal of, all difficulties or obstacles that makes a course, a career, or the like, easy to follow or to pursue; as, the car speeded along over the *smooth* road; to make a son's way *smooth* for him by providing him with a good post in one's own business.

Ant. Hard. — *Con.* Difficult, arduous (see HARD): exacting, *onerous, burdensome, oppressive.

eats. *Food, victuals, grub, chow, viands, provisions, provender, fodder, forage.

ebb, *v.* Subside, *abate, wane.

Ana. Dwindle, diminish, *decrease, lessen: *recede, retrograde, retreat.

Ant. Flow (*as the tide*). — *Con.* *Advance, progress: *rise, mount, ascend.

ebullition. Ebullition, effervescence, fermentation, ferment are here compared in their extended senses as meaning a state of agitation or excitement or the exhibition in words or acts of such a state. **Ebullition,** literally the act, process, or state of boiling or bubbling up or over, suggests a comparably sudden and forcible rising to the surface of a feeling or emotion, so that it overflows and pours itself forth lavishly or unrestrainedly; as, "Sensitive to tone and manner as he was, his *ebullition* of paternal feeling was frozen" (*Meredith*); "impetuous love-letters, fervid with the *ebullitions* of unmoderated feeling, are apt to pall upon the unenamoured reader" (*L. P. Smith*). **Effervescence,** literally the noisy bubbling and hissing as of carbonated waters when gas is released, or the foaming and frothing as of seething liquors, suggests a comparable excitement or exaltation of spirits manifesting itself while the mood lasts in irrepressible lightness, gaiety, exhilaration, or volubility; as, "The wild *effervescence* of his mood—which had... impelled him to talk from the mere necessity of giving vent to this bubbling-up gush of ideas—had entirely subsided" (*N. Hawthorne*); "Things didn't settle down; as embodied in Bill Gracy they continued in a state of *effervescence*" (*E. Wharton*). **Fermentation** and **ferment** literally denote an activity within a liquid such as cider or new wine, or within a substance such as dough mixed with yeast, that often manifests itself in effervescence or ebullition and that results in a chemical transformation of substance, as of cider into vinegar or into an alcoholic drink, or of dough into a light porous mass inflated with carbon dioxide. In figurative use, these words suggest a comparable activity or condition marked by internal commotion or great unrest; as, a *ferment* of ideas; "The cynical view is congenial to certain moods, and is so little inconsistent with original nobleness of mind, that it is not seldom the acetous *fermentation* of it" (*J. R. Lowell*). *Ferment* is now more often used than *fermentation* in a sense which usually applies to a condition that involves a painful or disturbing transition from old to new, or from a condition lower in the scale to one that is higher. "The imagination of a boy is healthy, and the mature imagination of a man is healthy; but there is a space of life between, in which the soul is in a *ferment*, the character undecided" (*Keats*). "The nation at this time was seething with new life; it was a time of spiritual as well as of political *ferment*" (*Inge*).

Ana. Agitation, convulsion, shaking, rocking (see corresponding verbs at SHAKE): excitement, stimulation (see corresponding verbs at PROVOKE): exuberance, lavishness, profuseness *or* profusion, luxuriantness *or* luxuriance (see corresponding adjectives at PROFUSE).

eccentric. Erratic, odd, queer, peculiar, *strange, singular, unique, quaint, outlandish, curious.

Ana. *Abnormal, atypic, aberrant: *irregular, anomalous, unnatural: *exceptional, exceptionable: *fantastic, bizarre, grotesque.

Con. *Common, ordinary, familiar: *usual, customary, habitual: normal, natural, typical, *regular.

eccentricity. **Eccentricity, idiosyncrasy** are not always clearly distinguished when they denote an act, a practice, a characteristic, or the like, that impresses the observer as strange or singular. **Eccentricity** (cf. STRANGE) emphasizes the idea of divergence from the usual or customary; **idiosyncrasy** implies a following of one's peculiar temperament or bent, especially in trait, trick, or habit; the former, therefore, often suggests mental aberration; the latter, strong individuality and independence of action. "Jennie's *eccentricity*, her possibly uncanny deviation from the ordinary ways of life" (*M. Wilkins*). "Letters to Native Princes, telling them...to refrain from kidnapping women, or filling offenders with pounded red pepper, and *eccentricities* of that kind" (*Kipling*). "This decided love of the slope, or bank above the wall, rather than below it, is one of Turner's most marked *idiosyncrasies*" (*Ruskin*). "What I learned of mathematics and science has been...of great intrinsic value, as affording subjects of contemplation and reflection, and touchstones of truth in a deceitful world. This is, of course, in part a personal *idiosyncrasy*" (*B. Russell*).

Ana. *Deviation, aberration, divergence: peculiarity, oddity, queerness, singularity (see corresponding adjectives at STRANGE): freak, vagary, crotchet, *caprice, whim, whimsey.

ecclesiastic, *n.* Clergyman, *cleric, priest, abbé.

éclat. Renown, glory, celebrity, notoriety, repute, reputation, *fame, honor.

Ana. Prominence, conspicuousness, remarkableness, noticeableness (see corresponding adjectives at NOTICEABLE): notedness *or* note, illustriousness *or* luster, eminence (see corresponding adjectives at FAMOUS).

economical. Frugal, thrifty, *sparing.

Ana. Prudent, provident (see under PRUDENCE): close, cheeseparing, parsimonious, penurious (see STINGY).

Ant. Extravagant. — ***Con.*** Lavish, prodigal, exuberant, *profuse.

economy. *System, scheme, organism, network, complex.

Ana. Organization, institution, establishment, foundation (see corresponding verbs at FOUND).

ecstasy, *n.* **Ecstasy, rapture, transport** agree in denoting a feeling or a state of intense, sometimes excessive or extreme, mental exaltation. **Ecstasy** in its earlier sense, and in the meaning now found chiefly in religious and poetical writings, implies a trancelike state in which consciousness of one's surroundings is lost and the mind is intent either on that which it contemplates, as in the case of the mystic, or on that which it conceives and creates, as in the case of the inspired poet or artist; as, "Like a mad prophet in an *ecstasy*" (*Dryden*). "Anthems clear, As may with sweetness, through mine ear, Dissolve me into *ecstasies*, And bring all Heaven before mine eyes" (*Milton*). In later and now general use, the term implies overmastering, entrancing joy or other emotion that exalts the mind and overcomes the senses. "Men in whom the manual exercise of combat seems to light a wonderful fire in the blood. To them battle brings *ecstasy*. They are ravished above pain and fear" (*C. E. Montague*). "She loved him with an acute, painful *ecstasy* that made her dizzy and blinded her to all the world besides" (*R. Macaulay*). **Rapture** etymologically implies a state of being seized; in its early religious use, *rapture* differed from *ecstasy* in implying a lifting of the mind or soul out of itself by divine power, so that it might see things beyond the reach of human vision; thus, the experiences narrated by the Apostle Paul (*2 Corinthians* xii. 2–4) of being caught up to the third heaven are in this sense (still occasionally found in theology, mystical writings, and poetry) *raptures*. In its chief current sense, *rapture* merely implies intense bliss or beatitude with or without the connotation of accompanying ecstasy, or loss of perception of everything else; as, "I drank it in, in a speechless *rapture*" (*Twain*). "As a child I first read Pope's Homer with a *rapture* which no subsequent work could ever afford" (*Byron*). "She burned again with the same *ecstasy*, the same exaltation. How fine it had been, to live in that state of *rapture!*" (*V. Sackville-West*). **Transport** (etymologically, a carrying across) applies to any violent or powerful emotion that lifts one out of oneself and, usually, provokes enthusiastic or vehement expression; as, "I mean to... support with an even temper, and without any violent *transports*...a sudden gust of prosperity" (*Fielding*); "*transports* of rage" (*Austen*); "What a *transport* of enthusiasm!" (*Landor*). "In art, as in poetry, there are the *transports* which lift the artist out of...himself" (*Pater*).

Ana. Bliss, beatitude, blessedness, felicity, *happiness: joy, delectation, delight, *pleasure: *inspiration, enthusiasm, fury, frenzy, afflatus.

ectype. Antitype, archetype, *prototype.

ecumenical *or* **oecumenical.** *Universal, catholic, cosmopolitan, cosmic.

Ant. Provincial: diocesan.

eddy, *v.* Rotate, gyrate, circle, spin, whirl, revolve, *turn, twirl, wheel, swirl, pirouette.

edge, *n.* **1** Verge, rim, brink, margin, *border, brim.
Ana. *Limit, end, bound, confine: *circumference, periphery, compass.
2 Odds, *advantage, handicap, allowance.

edifice, *n.* Structure, fabric, pile, *building.

educate. Train, discipline, school, *teach, instruct.

educe. **Educe, evoke, elicit, extract, extort** agree in meaning to bring or draw out that which is hidden, latent, reserved, or the like. **Educe** commonly implies the development and outward manifestation of something potential or latent. "Gray, with the qualities of mind and soul of a genuine poet....could not fully *educe* and enjoy them" (*Arnold*). **Evoke** (etymologically, to call out) originally suggested the voice or the words of a magician compelling spirits to leave the other world or the dead to arise from their graves; as, to *evoke* a demon; to *evoke* the ghost of one's father. In current use, the term implies the operation of a powerful agency that produces an effect instantly or that serves as a stimulus in arousing an emotion, a passion, or an interest; as, "the delight which growing flowers and blossoming trees *evoke*" (*Binyon*); "it is useless to obtrude moral ideas [upon children] at an age at which they can *evoke* no response" (*B. Russell*). "All harmonies...are latent in the complex mechanism of an organ, but a master's hand is necessary to *evoke* them" (*Lowes*). **Elicit** usually implies pains, trouble, or skill, in drawing something forth or out; it often implies resistance either in the person or thing that is the object of effort; as, to *elicit* important information from a witness by cross-examination. "It is the trouble we take over our children that *elicits* the stronger forms of parental affection" (*B. Russell*). **Extract** implies (literally or figuratively) pressure, suction, or similar agency; as, to *extract* the juice of an orange; to *extract* a tooth; "to *extract* all the dramatic value possible from the situation" (*T. S. Eliot*). "He had not that faculty of *extracting* the essence from a heap of statements" (*Dickens*). "To make the comparison at all was...to return to it often, to brood upon it, to *extract* from it the last dregs of its interest" (*H. James*). **Extort** implies (literally or figuratively) a wringing or wresting, especially from one who is reluctant or resisting; as, to *extort* money from one's relatives; to *extort* a promise. "She did at last *extort* from her father an acknowledgment that the horses were engaged" (*Austen*). "The Christians *extorted* the admiration of their fellow countrymen by the courage with which they...consoled the last hours of the sufferers" (*Lecky*).
Ana. Draw, drag (see PULL): produce, *bear, yield, turn out: *summon, call.

eerie *or* **eery.** *Weird, uncanny.
Ana. *Fantastic, bizarre, grotesque: *mysterious, inscrutable, arcane: *fearful, awful, dreadful, horrific: *strange, odd, queer, curious, peculiar.

efface. Obliterate, *erase, expunge, blot out, delete, dele, cancel.
Ana. Remove, *move, shift: eradicate, extirpate, wipe out (see EXTERMINATE): eliminate, *exclude, rule out.

effect, *n.* **1** **Effect, consequence, result, aftereffect, event, aftermath, issue, outcome, upshot, sequel** agree in denoting any condition, situation, occurrence, or the like, traceable to a cause or combination of causes. **Effect** is the direct correlative of *cause;* it names only those factors in a complex situation or those occurrences that of necessity follow a cause and that may be definitely attributed to its operation. "[These] qualities...of the Athenians, were partly the cause and partly the *effect* of their political constitution" (*G. L. Dickinson*). **Consequence** implies a more remote and looser connection with a cause than *effect* does; it names any condition, situation, or event that may be traced back to an original cause through a more or less complicated chain of causes and effects; as, never during his life was he to escape the *consequences* of his youthful mistake; the *consequences* of a war are felt by succeeding generations. **Result,** though often employed as the equivalent of *effect,* is in very precise use applied chiefly to the effect that terminates the operation of a cause; as, the *result* of an election; his death was the *result* of accident. The result is not always immediate; it may be the last in a series of effects directly traceable to a given cause. Thus, the *effect* of a blow on the head may be concussion of the brain; the *consequence,* shattered health; the *result,* the retirement of the injured man from active business. When an effect in turn serves as a cause and produces a secondary effect, that is often called an **aftereffect;** as, some drugs are avoided because of their harmful *aftereffects.* When the effect of a deliberate action, speech, choice, or the like, could not be foreseen or was affected by conditions beyond human control, that which actually resulted is called **event.** "In that case [where a ship's captain's decision was followed by disaster] great weight is given to his determination and the matter is to be judged on the facts as they appeared then and not merely in the light of the *event*" (*Justice Holmes*). **Aftermath** (literally, a second crop of grass following a mowing of the first) is in current English often applied to belated consequences which appear after the effects (esp. the disastrous effects) seem to have passed; as, every great war has its *aftermath.* All the other words in the group here discriminated are more or less figurative substitutes for *result.* **Issue** adds to *result* the implication of exit, as from difficulties; it therefore usually designates a result that is a solution or a resolution. "What is the final ending? The *issue,* can we know?" (*V. Lindsay*). " 'God has been very good to let me live to see a happy *issue* to those old wrongs' " (*Cather*). **Outcome** implies less finality than *issue* but often stresses the visibility or tangibility of the result. "Naturalism is ...a jejune and self-contradictory philosophy. Its *outcome* is not to leave religion alone, but to destroy it" (*Inge*). **Upshot** adds to *result* the suggestion of a climax or of an inescapable conclusion; as, the *upshot* of the situation was that he assumed entire control. "The *upshot* of the effort [to achieve originality in writing]... is a more or less violent straining after the unusual" (*Lowes*). **Sequel** is applied to a result that follows as a logical consequence but usually occurs after an interval; as, the *sequel* of a marriage of persons so mismated is easily foreseen.
Ant. Cause. — *Con.* Determinant, antecedent, reason, occasion (see CAUSE): basis, ground, *base, foundation, groundwork.
2 In plural form **effects.** *Possessions, belongings, means, resources, assets.

effect, *v.* **1** Accomplish, achieve, *perform, execute, discharge, fulfill.
Ana. *Reach, attain, achieve, compass, gain: finish, complete, conclude, end, terminate, *close: implement, *enforce: *realize, actualize.
2 *Affect.

effective. **Effective, effectual, efficient, efficacious** are frequently confused because all mean producing or capable of producing a result or results. **Effective** emphasizes the actual production of an effect or the power to produce a given effect whenever in active use, exercise, force, or the like; as, *effective* thinking; an *effective* speaker; an *effective* rebuke; the law becomes *effective* on a given date; *effective* capital. "Set him to write poetry, he is limited, artificial, and impotent...to write prose, he is free, natural, and *effective*" (*Arnold*). "Research chemists... are actively investigating to learn why particular materials are *effective* and to make them more so" (*A. C. Morrison*). **Effectual** suggests the accomplishment of the result that is desired or the fulfillment of a purpose or intention, so that the term frequently becomes synonymous with "decisive, final," and looks backward rather than forward; as, an *effectual* measure; an *effectual* refutation, retort; "His recommendation was *effectual*, and I was...chosen" (*Gibbon*); "A certain shyness... prevented Michael Henchard from following up the investigation with the loud hue-and-cry such a pursuit demanded to render it *effectual*" (*Hardy*). **Efficient** applies to that which is actively operative and produces its result through the exercise of energy (as, an *efficient* cause), or more often in current use, through the exercise of skill, pains, vigilance, and the like (so that it often becomes synonymous with *capable, competent* and is applied especially, but not invariably, to persons who have given proof of their power or skill; as, an *efficient* officer, workman. "He [Augustus] gave her [Rome] an *efficient* police and a vigilant fire brigade" (*Buchan*). "The further back we can project our vision, the more comprehensive, the more thorough, the more *efficient* is that knowledge" (*Grandgent*). **Efficacious** implies the possession of the quality or virtue that gives a thing (more often than a person) the potency or power that makes it effective; as, quinine is *efficacious* in cases of malaria; "[The influence of Dr. Arnold] to this day is *efficacious* in moulding upper-class Englishmen" (*B. Russell*).

Ana. Forceful, forcible, potent, *powerful: producing *or* productive, bearing, turning out (see corresponding verbs at BEAR): telling, cogent, convincing (see VALID): operative, *active, dynamic.

Ant. Ineffective: futile (*thinking, treatment, action, etc.*). — ***Con.*** Vain, fruitless, bootless, abortive (see FUTILE): nugatory, idle, otiose, *vain, empty, hollow.

effectual. *Effective, efficacious, efficient.

Ana. Effecting, accomplishing, achieving, fulfilling (see corresponding verbs at PERFORM): operative, dynamic, *active: decisive, determinative, *conclusive.

Ant. Ineffectual: fruitless. — ***Con.*** *Futile, vain, bootless, abortive.

effeminate, *adj.* Womanish, womanlike, womanly, feminine, *female, ladylike.

Ana. Emasculated, enervated, unmanned (see UNNERVE): epicene (see BISEXUAL): *soft, mild, gentle, lenient, bland: pampered, indulged, humored, mollycoddled (see INDULGE).

Ant. Virile.

effervescence. *Ebullition, fermentation, ferment.

Ana. Volatility, buoyancy, expansiveness, resiliency, elasticity (see corresponding adjectives at ELASTIC): frivolity, levity, *lightness, flippancy, flightiness: froth, *foam, yeast.

Con. Staidness, sedateness, soberness, gravity, seriousness (see corresponding adjectives at SERIOUS).

effervescent. Volatile, buoyant, expansive, resilient, *elastic.

Ana. *Lively, vivacious, sprightly, gay, animated: hilarious, jolly, gleeful, mirthful (see corresponding nouns at MIRTH).

Ant. Subdued.

efficacious. Effectual, *effective, efficient.

Ana. Potent, *powerful, puissant: cogent, telling, sound, convincing (see VALID).

Ant. Inefficacious: powerless.

efficient. *Effective, effectual, efficacious.

Ana. Competent, qualified, *able, capable: expert, skillful, skilled, *proficient, adept.

Ant. Inefficient.

effigy. Simulacrum, *image, statue, icon, portrait, photograph, mask.

effort. Effort, exertion, pains, trouble agree in meaning the active use or expenditure of physical or mental power in producing a desired result. **Effort** may suggest a single action or continued activity but it usually implies consciousness that one is making an attempt, or sometimes, even, is toiling or straining to achieve one's end; as, to make a final supreme *effort;* "the constant *effort* of the dreamer to attain his ideal" (*H. Adams*); "Utterly absorbed in the writing of a private letter—how you lose count of time and have no sense of disagreeable *effort*" (*C. E. Montague*). **Exertion** in general stresses the active, often vigorous, exercise of any power or faculty; as, the continued *exertion* of memory; wearied by over*exertion;* "A...man, capable of close application of mind, and great *exertion* of body" (*Dickens*). Often, however, especially when not followed by of, *exertion* means a laborious effort. "His [an acrobat's] work was done with remarkable grace, but with *exertions* which it was painful to witness; for he had but one leg, and had to use a crutch" (*Deland*). **Pains** implies toilsome or solicitous effort; **trouble** implies exertion that inconveniences or incommodes. "Those luckless brains That ... Indite much metre with much *pains*" (*Cowper*). "The Indians had exhaustless patience; upon their blankets and belts and ceremonial robes they lavished their skill and *pains*" (*Cather*). "Is twenty hundred kisses such a *trouble?*" (*Shak.*). " 'I feel that I am beginning to get a grip of the people....' 'I should hope so, after the amount of time and *trouble* you've taken' " (*C. Mackenzie*).

Ana. *Work, labor, toil, travail: energy, force, *power, might, puissance: endeavor, essay, assay (see under ATTEMPT, *v.*).

Ant. Ease.

effortless. *Easy, smooth, facile, simple, light.

Ana. *Proficient, skilled, skillful, expert, adept.

Ant. Painstaking.

effrontery. *Temerity, audacity, hardihood, nerve, cheek, gall.

Ana. Impudence, brazenness, brashness (see corresponding adjectives at SHAMELESS): impertinence, intrusiveness, officiousness (see corresponding adjectives at IMPERTINENT).

effulgent. Radiant, luminous, brilliant, *bright, lustrous, refulgent, beaming, beamy, lambent, lucent.

Ana. Flaming, blazing, glowing, flaring (see BLAZE, *v.*): flashing, gleaming (see FLASH, *v.*): resplendent, *splendid, glorious.

Con. Murky, gloomy, *dark, dim, obscure, dusk, dusky.

egoism. Egotism, *conceit, amour-propre, self-love, self-esteem.

Ana. Self-confidence, self-assurance, self-possession (see CONFIDENCE): self-reliance (see corresponding adjective at RELIANT): self-satisfaction, self-complacency, complacency, smugness, priggishness (see corresponding adjectives at COMPLACENT).

Ant. Altruism. — ***Con.*** Humility, meekness, modesty, lowliness (see corresponding adjectives at HUMBLE).

egotism. Egoism, *conceit, self-love, amour-propre, self-esteem.

Ana. Vanity, vainglory, *pride: boasting *or* boastfulness, vaunting *or* vauntfulness, gasconading (see corresponding verbs at BOAST): pluming, piquing, priding, preening (see PRIDE, *v.*).

Ant. Modesty. — ***Con.*** Humility, meekness, lowliness (see corresponding adjectives at HUMBLE): diffidence, bashfulness, shyness (see corresponding adjectives at SHY).

egret. **Egret, aigrette** designate one of certain herons bearing silky plumes on the lower back during the breeding season. These plumes have been much used as a headdress or hat trimming, and are obtained only by killing the bird. **Egret** is now the more common term in use for the bird, **aigrette** for the plume as an article of millinery. The latter word is also applied to any similar, and usually artificial, plume or tuft worn as a headdress or hat trimming.

eikon. Variant of ICON.

eirenic, eirenical. Variants of IRENIC, IRENICAL.

eject, *v.* **Eject, expel, oust, evict, dismiss** agree in meaning to force or thrust something or someone out. **Eject,** although it is the comprehensive term of this group and is often interchangeable with any of the others, carries the strongest implication of throwing out from within. So emphatic is this suggestion that the term covers actions so far apart as those implied by *dislodge, disgorge, vomit, emit, discharge,* and many other terms; as, the volcano *ejected* lava for three days in succession; to *eject* an intruder from one's house; the chimney *ejected* flames rather than smoke. **Expel** stresses a thrusting out or a driving away: it therefore more regularly implies the use of voluntary force or compulsion than does *eject* (as, the stomach *ejects* [not *expels*] substances it cannot digest; the cigarette smoker *expels* [often clearer than *ejects*] smoke through the nose), and indicates more clearly than *eject* an intent to get rid of for all time (as, to *expel* a student from college; "a curse ...in his blood...which no life of purity could *expel*"—*Meredith;* "Octavian...forbade the practice of certain eastern cults, and *expelled* from Rome Greek and Asiatic magicians"—*Buchan*). **Oust** implies a removal, dispossession, or the like, by the power of the law or, in more general use, by the exercise of force or by the compulsion of necessity; as, "Farmers were *ousted* of their leases made by tenants in tail [i.e., owners by right of entail]" (*Blackstone*); "in America...a new set of officials *oust* the old ones whenever the Opposition *ousts* the Government" (*Shaw*); "insidious attempts to disparage the findings of Reason, or to *oust* it from its proper province" (*Inge*). **Evict** (etymologically, to overcome completely) derives the sense here considered from its legal sense, which is to recover by legal process or by virtue of a superior title some property to which one has a clear or a proved right or claim; as, "If A. gives in exchange three acres to B. for other three acres, and afterwards one acre is *evicted* from B....the whole exchange is defeated" (*W. Cruise*). Since such recovery implies an ousting of one who has not a clear right or a proved claim, *evict* has come to mean to turn out of house or home (especially a tenant who has fallen behind in payment of rent) by legal or equally effective process; as, after not paying their rent for six months, they were *evicted* by the sheriff; all the residents of the valley were *evicted* by the flood. **Dismiss** (for the sense of to let go from employ, see DISMISS) stresses a getting rid of something such as a legal case by rejecting a claim or prayer and refusing it further consideration (as, "this court reversed the judgment given in favor of the defendant, and remanded the case with directions to *dismiss* it"—*Ch. Just. Taney*), or a fear, a grudge, a hatred, etc., by ejecting it from the mind or thoughts (as, "I declare to you...that I have long *dismissed* it from my mind"—*Dickens*), or an unwelcome subject, duty, prospect, etc., by taking adequate measures to ensure its no longer annoying or confronting one (as, "exercising the privilege of old age to *dismiss* peremptorily any subject [of conversation]"—*L. P. Smith;* "the Judge was sharply angry...because he found himself unable to *dismiss* the whole thing by packing the child off"—*Deland*).

Ana. *Exclude, eliminate, shut out, rule out, debar, disbar: *dismiss, discharge, cashier, fire, sack: *discard, cast, shed: reject, repudiate, spurn (see DECLINE).

Ant. Admit (sense 1).

elastic, *adj.* **1 Elastic, resilient, springy, flexible, supple** come into comparison when they mean able to endure strain (such as extension, compression, twisting, bending, or other distortion) without being permanently affected or injured. *Elastic* and *resilient* are both general and scientific terms; the scientific senses are later and are in part derived from the earlier meanings. **Elastic,** in popular use, is applied chiefly to substances or materials that are easy to stretch or expand and that quickly recover their shape or size when the pressure is removed; as, a rubber band is *elastic; elastic* cord for hats; a toy balloon is an *elastic* bag which can be blown up greatly beyond its original size. In scientific use, *elastic* is applicable to any solid that may be changed in volume or shape, or to any fluid (gas or liquid) that may be changed in volume, when in the course of the deformation of such a solid or fluid internal forces arise which tend to make it recover its original volume or shape once the deforming force or forces are removed. The term in such use describes a property which a substance possesses up to the point (the *elastic limit*) beyond which it cannot be deformed without permanent injury; thus, a steel ball possesses *elasticity;* one may test the comparative *elastic* properties of natural and of synthetic rubber. **Resilient,** in popular use, is applicable to anything which springs back into place or into shape, especially after compression; thus, rising bread dough is said to be *resilient* because it quickly recovers from a deforming pressure by the hand; a tree's branch may be described as *resilient* when it snaps back into its former position once a pull is released. Scientifically, *resilient* is not the equivalent of *elastic,* but it may be used as its counterpart; *elastic* stresses the capacity for deformation without permanent injury, *resilient* the capacity for recovering shape or position after strain or pressure has been removed; so, when an *elastic* substance is stretched or compressed, it shows itself *resilient;* as arteries gradually lose their *elasticity* with age, to the same extent their *resiliency* is impaired. **Springy** is a popular term often used in place of *elastic* or *resilient* but actually a compound of the two because it implies both the ease with which a thing yields to pressure or strain and the quickness of its return; as, to walk on *springy* turf; firm, *springy* muscles; "A laughing school-boy... Riding the *springy* branches of an elm" (*Keats*). **Flexible** is applicable to anything that can be bent or turned without breaking: the term may or may not imply resiliency, or quick recovery of shape; as, lead pipe is *flexible* and may be bent into shape; a *flexible* young tree often endures a heavy windstorm better than a rigid, fully developed one; "*flexible* and gracious as the willow" (*Binyon*). **Supple** applies to things which are, in general, not as solid or firm in structure as some which may be described as *flexible;* it also implies ease in bending, twisting, folding, or the like, but it suggests resistance to breaks, cracks, or other signs of injury; as, *supple* silks; *supple* muscles; a *supple* leather. "Mere manual labour stiffens the limbs, gymnastic exercises render them *supple*" (*Jefferies*).

In extended use, these words often carry the implications of their literal senses. **Elastic** stresses ease in stretching or expanding beyond the normal or appointed limits; as, an *elastic* conscience; "some principles there must be, however *elastic*" (*Buchan*); an *elastic* term. **Resilient** implies a tendency to rebound or recover quickly health, spirits, etc., especially after subjection to stress or strain (see ELASTIC, 2); as, a *resilient* constitution. **Springy,** which is less common in extended use, may suggest youth, freshness, or buoyancy; as, a *springy* step. **Flexible** implies an adaptable or accommodating quality or, when applied to persons, pliancy or tractability; as, a *flexible* scheme; a *flexible* term; a *flexible* arrangement. "His [John Wesley's] mind became more *flexible* with age" (*S. M. Crothers*). **Supple,** in its extended use, is applied chiefly to persons or their utterances. Sometimes it suggests little more than flexibility: at other times, it implies obsequiousness or complaisance, or a show of these with what is actually astute mastery of a situation. "In...Bismarck, the *supple* spirit is hidden under an external directness and rough assertion" (*Belloc*).

Ana. Pliable, pliant, ductile, *plastic, malleable: limber, lithe, *supple.

Ant. Rigid (*of bodies*). — ***Con.*** *Stiff, inflexible, tense.

2 Elastic, expansive, resilient, buoyant, volatile, effervescent come into comparison only in their secondary senses when referred to persons, their temperaments, moods, acts, words, and the like, and mean showing ease or readiness in the stimulation of spirit, especially of high spirits. **Elastic** implies an incapacity for being kept down in spirits; specifically, it may suggest an ability to recover quickly from a state of depression (as, "those *elastic* spirits...had borne up against defeat"—*Macaulay*), or a tendency to moods of exaltation, elation, optimism, or the like (as, "There are times when one's vitality is too high to be clouded, too *elastic* to stay down"—*Cather*). "Not an *elastic* or optimistic nature—on the contrary, rigid and circumscribed, depressed by a melancholy temperament" (*Symonds*). **Expansive,** in current use, implies exaltation of spirit that tends to make a person unusually genial, communicative, sociable, or the like. In psychiatry, it often suggests additionally a delusion of greatness or a morbid sense of well-being, but these connotations are rare in general use. "She had an *expansive* temperament, a brilliant personality, a widely sympathetic disposition, troops of friends" (*H. Ellis*). **Resilient** implies a quick rebounding, or springing back to an original state after having been subjected to strain or stress; the word usually implies a return to normal good spirits, which may or may not be what are called high spirits; as, he was as *resilient* as ever, one day utterly exhausted, and the next day ready for fresh labors. "Evidently her *resilient* strength was going; she could no longer react normally to the refreshment of food" (*H. Ellis*). **Buoyant** (etymologically, having the power to rise or float) implies such lightness or vivacity of heart or spirits as is either incapable of depression or that readily shakes it off. "No such immaterial burden could depress that *buoyant*-hearted young gentleman for many hours together" (*G. Eliot*). "His *buoyant* spirits were continually breaking out in troublesome frolics" (*Prescott*). **Volatile** (etymologically, having the power to fly) implies diametrical opposition to all that is serious, sedate, or settled; it therefore suggests lightness, levity, or excessive buoyancy of spirits, and often flightiness or instability; as, "as giddy and *volatile* as ever" (*Swift*). "He [Leonardo] seemed to them [his contemporaries] so *volatile* and unstable. He was an enigma to which they never secured the key" (*H. Ellis*). **Effervescent** (etymologically, having the power to bubble and hiss like fermenting liquors) in its extended use implies liveliness, often boisterousness of spirits: it often suggests the effect of release after restraint and even more than *buoyant* implies the impossibility of suppression so long as the mood or temper lasts.

Ana. *Elated, elate, exultant: *spirited, high-spirited, mettlesome: *lively, vivacious, sprightly, animated, gay.

Ant. Depressed. — ***Con.*** Dejected, gloomy, melancholy, sad, blue (see corresponding nouns at SADNESS): flaccid, *limp.

elated *or* **elate. Elated, elate, exultant** agree in meaning feeling or manifesting great joy. **Elated** commonly suggests a certain excitement or exaltation of spirit, following upon success, good fortune, high praise, or the like; it frequently connotes undue self-satisfaction; as, "Keen anglers with unusual spoil *elated*" (*Wordsworth*). "I have found American writers, of world-wide reputation, strangely solicitous about the opinions of quite obscure British critics, and *elated* or depressed by their judgments" (*Thackeray*). Compare: "I felt no little *elation* at having now so happily established an acquaintance of which I had been so long ambitious" (*Boswell*). **Elate** is poetical or elevated for *elated;* as, "He walks As if he trod upon the heads of men: He looks *elate*" (*Shelley*). **Exultant** emphasizes rather the outward expression of triumph or joy; as, "Shouts *exultant* echo to the skies" (*P. Whitehead*); "he was *exultant* and could not conceal his delight" (*S. Anderson*); "that fierce *exultation* in carnage with which the war poetry of so many nations ...is crimsoned" (*Froude*).

Ana. Rapturous, transported, ecstatic (see corresponding nouns at ECSTASY): joyous, joyful (see GLAD): high-spirited, *spirited.

Ant. Dejected. — ***Con.*** Depressed, melancholy, blue, gloomy, sad (see corresponding nouns at SADNESS): humiliated, humbled, abased (see ABASE): chagrined, mortified, *ashamed.

elderly. Old, *aged, superannuated.

Ant. Youthful.

elect, *adj.* Picked, *select, exclusive.

Ana. *Choice, exquisite, rare: selected, preferred, chosen, singled out (see CHOOSE): redeemed, saved, delivered (see RESCUE, *v.*).

Ant. Reprobate (*in theology*). — ***Con.*** Rejected, repudiated, spurned, refused (see DECLINE, *v.*): scorned, disdained (see DESPISE): doomed, damned (see SENTENCE, *v.*).

elect, *v.* **1** Select, pick, prefer, single out, opt, *choose, cull, hand-pick.

Ana. *Decide, determine, settle, resolve: conclude, judge (see INFER): *receive, accept, admit, take.

Ant. Abjure. — ***Con.*** Reject, spurn, repudiate, refuse, *decline: dismiss, *eject, oust, expel.

2 *Designate, name, nominate, appoint.

election. Selection, option, *choice, preference, alternative.

Ana. Deciding *or* decision, determining *or* determination, settling *or* settlement (see corresponding verbs at DECIDE).

electrify. *Thrill, enthuse.

Ana. Galvanize, excite, stimulate, quicken, *provoke: *stir, rouse, arouse, rally.

elegance. Elegance, grace, dignity come into comparison only when they denote an impressive beauty or comeliness. **Elegance** is used in reference to persons chiefly when their grooming, their clothes, and the way they wear them are specifically considered; it then often implies fashionableness and good taste, but it stresses perfection of detail and exquisiteness (sometimes, over-exquisiteness) as in materials, lines, ornamentation, and the like; as, the *elegance* in dress of a Beau Brummell.

When used in reference to things, such as the furnishings of a home, the details of a dinner, a literary style, the term also implies the perfection and propriety in detail that indicate excellence of taste, a nice selective instinct, and often, but far from always, a restrained luxuriousness. "A very pretty sitting-room, lately fitted up with greater *elegance* and lightness than the apartments below" (*Austen*). "A cultivated man should express himself by tongue or pen with some accuracy and *elegance*" (*C. W. Eliot*). **Grace,** as here compared, is more commonly applied to that which is inward and native than to that which is outward and acquired, especially when used in reference to persons; it always suggests a quality, or a harmonious combination of qualities, that gives aesthetic pleasure through a natural or simple beauty such as is shown in suppleness or rhythm of movement, in clean-flowing lines or contours, or in spontaneity and felicitousness of manner, mood, expression, style, or the like; as, "a behavior so full of *grace* and sweetness, such easy motions, with an air so majestic, yet free from stiffness or affectation" (*Lady M. W. Montagu*). "The effect upon the observer of this exquisite little edifice...was of an unparagoned lightness and *grace*" (*C. Mackenzie*). "She took the congratulations of her rivals and of the rest of the company with the simplicity that was her crowning *grace*" (*E. Wharton*). **Dignity** applies to that which compels respect and honor. The term often suggests stateliness, majesty, elevation of character or style, or the like, as the compelling cause; as, "the qualifications which frequently invest the façade of a prison with far more *dignity* than is found in the façade of a palace double its size" (*Hardy*); "There was a *dignity* in his Client, an impressiveness in his speech, that silenced remonstrating Reason" (*Meredith*); "Those who are just beginning to appreciate the idea of lending greater *dignity* to the worship of Almighty God" (*C. Mackenzie*). Very frequently, however, in current use, the term suggests the compulsion of intrinsic worth or merit, apart from any superficial characteristics that give it external beauty or comeliness; as, the *dignity* of work; the *dignity* of motherhood. "It matters not how trivial the occupation, if the man or woman [in a painting] be wholly given to it, there will be a natural compelling *dignity* in the figure" (*Binyon*).

Ana. Beautifulness *or* beauty, handsomeness, comeliness (see corresponding adjectives at BEAUTIFUL): fastidiousness, niceness *or* nicety, daintiness (see corresponding adjectives at NICE): perfection, *excellence: *taste (sense 2).

elegant, *adj.* Exquisite, *choice, recherché, rare, dainty, delicate.

Ana. Majestic, stately, noble, august, *grand: *beautiful, handsome: fastidious, *nice: *consummate, finished: sumptuous, *luxurious, opulent.

Con. Crude, *rude, rough: ostentatious, *showy, pretentious: bizarre, grotesque, *fantastic.

élégant, *fem.* **élégante,** *n.* Exquisite, *fop, dandy, beau, coxcomb, dude, macaroni, buck, spark, swell, nob, toff.

element. Element, component, constituent, ingredient, integrant, factor come into comparison when they mean one of the parts, substances, principles, or the like, which comprise a compound or complex thing. **Element** is, except in its specific sense in science, the most widely applicable of these terms, being referable both to material and immaterial and to tangible and intangible things; as, the native and foreign *elements* in English; words are the *elements* of a sentence; the basic *element* of his character. "His life was gentle, and the *elements* So mix'd in him that Nature might stand up And say to all the world 'This was a man!'" (*Shak.*). Always in its scientific sense, often in its general sense, the term implies irreducible simplicity, or, if applied to a substance, incapacity for separation into simpler substances; thus, gold, silver, carbon, lead are among the chemical *elements*, or ultimate building units of matter; so, to analyze the *elements* of a situation; various substances are made of the same *elements* in different proportions. **Component** and **constituent** are often used interchangeably for any of the substances (whether elements or compounds) which enter into the makeup of a mixed thing, or for any of the principles or qualities which comprise an intangible composite. *Component,* however, stresses the separate identity or distinguishable character of the substance; *constituent* stresses its essential and formative character; as, copper and zinc are the *components* of brass; hydrogen and oxygen are the *constituents* of water; the *components* of the typical novel are its plot, its characters, and its setting; to break a ray of light into the colors which are its *constituents;* the hazardous *components* of burning oil; the *constituents* of a perfume. **Ingredient** applies literally to any of the substances or materials which when combined form a particular mixture such as a drink, a medicine, a food, an alloy, an amalgam; as, the *ingredients* of a cocktail (or of a cough medicine or of a cake); iron and carbon are the *ingredients* of steel. The term, however, is widely used figuratively of any component or constituent that can be thought of as added or as left out. "In this transaction every *ingredient* of a complete and legitimate contract is to be found" (*Ch. Just. Marshall*). **Integrant** (which is somewhat rare) applies only to a component, constituent, or ingredient which is essential to the whole; thus, not all the *ingredients* of a cake are *integrants,* for some are added merely to improve the taste; the *integrants* of blood. **Factor** is only loosely synonymous with the words of this group, *constituent* being its nearest synonym. Moreover the term is applicable only to a constituent, element, component, part, or member that has effective force enabling the whole substance, movement, organization, system, or the like, to perform a certain kind of work, or helping it in the production of a definite result. "God....is not one of the *factors* for which science has to account" (*Inge*). "Various *factors* entered the inception of the American enterprise" (*H. Ellis*). "The word 'vitamins' was coined to designate these essential food *factors*" (*A. C. Morrison*).

Ana. *Principle, fundamental: *part, portion, member: *item, detail, particular.

Ant. Compound (*in science*): composite. — ***Con.*** Mass, *bulk, volume: aggregate, whole, total, *sum.

elemental. *Elementary.

Ana. *Ultimate, categorical, absolute: *primary, prime, primordial.

elementary. Elementary, elemental are often confused. That is **elementary** which pertains to rudiments or beginnings; that is **elemental** which pertains to the elements, especially to the ultimate constituents or forces; as, an *elementary* treatise; an *elementary* knowledge of physics; an *elementary* virtue; an *elementary* school; the *elemental* sounds of language; an *elemental* substance; "they...busied themselves with the *elemental,* enduring things: sex, fatherhood, work" (*R. Macaulay*).

Ana. Basic, *fundamental, substratal: primal, *primary.

Ant. Advanced.

elephantine. *Enormous, huge, gigantic, giant, gigantean, colossal, mammoth, immense, vast, titanic, herculean, Cyclopean, Antaean, Gargantuan, Brobdingnagian.

elevate. *Lift, raise, rear, hoist, heave, boost.

Ana. *Exalt, aggrandize, magnify: heighten, enhance (see INTENSIFY): *rise, mount, ascend, tower, soar, rocket.

Ant. Lower. — *Con.* *Abase, debase, degrade, demean, humble.

elevation. 1 Altitude, *height, stature.

Ana. *Ascension, ascent.

2 Promotion, *advancement, preferment.

Ana. Exaltation, aggrandizement (see corresponding verbs at EXALT).

Ant. Degradation.

elf. *Fairy, fay, sprite, faery, pixy, gnome, dwarf, goblin, brownie, puck, nix, shee, leprechaun, banshee.

elicit, *v.* Evoke, *educe, extract, extort.

Ana. Draw, drag, *pull: *bring, fetch.

eliminate. Rule out, *exclude, debar, blackball, disbar, suspend, shut out.

Ana. *Eject, oust, dismiss, expel, evict: eradicate, extirpate, *exterminate, uproot, wipe out: expunge, *erase, delete, efface: winnow (see SIFT).

elite. Society, *aristocracy, nobility, gentry, county, gentlefolk.

Ant. Rabble.

ell. Wing, extension, *annex, dependence.

elocution. **Elocution, oratory, eloquence** are comparable only when they mean the art or the power of speaking impressively, especially in public, or the manifestation of such art or power. In current use, **elocution** applies, more frequently than either of the other terms, to the art of public speaking, whether it concerns the delivery of one's own or another's words. The term is now used chiefly in reference to a subject of study or of a course in a curriculum which stresses good speech, intonation, gesture, and other graces of delivery, rather than the content of what is uttered; as, a teacher of *elocution;* a prolonged study of *elocution.* "As she had never learnt *elocution,* practised speakers were puzzled at her method of voice production and its success" (*H. Ellis*). In older use, *elocution* implied a graceful, correct, or sometimes mellifluous, manner of speaking; as, "You have a natural, fluent, and unforced *elocution*" (*Burke*); "When he speaks, what *elocution* flows!" (*Pope*). In current use, the term is frequently used derogatorily with implications of artifice or of emphasis on sound rather than on sense. "Wherefore waste our *elocution* On impossible solution?" (*W. S. Gilbert*). **Oratory,** in early use, as still often in current use, applies to the art of delivering public addresses. In this sense, it implies emphasis upon the composition of effective speeches as well as upon their effective delivery, and therefore suggests attention to persuasive argument, telling exposition, and to all the means whereby auditors may be moved or swayed; as, "that part of *oratory,* which relates to the moving of passions" (*Swift*). The term is more often used, however, of the art as manifested or as practiced by public speakers, sometimes with approval, but frequently with the intent to depreciate its effectiveness, sincerity, or the like; as, the usual fourth of July political *oratory.* "*Oratory* is the power of beating down your adversary's arguments, and putting better in their place" (*Johnson*). "The Chadband style of *oratory* is widely received and much admired" (*Dickens*). **Eloquence** (etymologically, a speaking out) stresses the power of expressing one's thoughts and feelings with fluency and force. In older use, it emphasized rhetorical skill as well as actual or seeming loftiness of thought and expression; as, "With great wisdom and grave *eloquence*" (*Spenser*); "Talking and *eloquence* are not the same: to speak and to speak well, are two things" (*B. Jonson*); "The poetry of western nations is chiefly rhetoric—*eloquence* in metre" (*Santayana*). In current use, it implies impassioned, moving utterance and is applicable to that which is written as well as to that which is spoken; as, "The deep soul-moving sense Of religious *eloquence*" (*Wordsworth*); "His *eloquence* was irresistibly impressive" (*Grote*); "She had no flights of *eloquence*" (*H. Ellis*).

elongate. Lengthen, *extend, prolong, protract.

Ant. Abbreviate, shorten. — *Con.* Abridge, curtail, retrench (see SHORTEN): shrink, compress, *contract.

eloquence. *Elocution, oratory.

eloquent. 1 Articulate, voluble, *vocal, fluent, glib.

Ana. *Impassioned, passionate, fervid, perfervid, ardent, fervent: expressing, voicing, venting, uttering (see EXPRESS, *v.*): forceful, forcible, potent, *powerful.

2 *Expressive, significant, meaningful, pregnant, sententious.

Ana. Revealing, disclosing, telling, betraying (see REVEAL): impressive, *moving, poignant, touching, affecting.

elucidate. Interpret, construe, expound, *explain, explicate.

Ana. Illustrate, *exemplify: demonstrate, *prove.

elude. *Escape, evade, avoid, shun, eschew.

Ana. Thwart, foil, outwit, circumvent, baffle (see FRUSTRATE): flee, fly, *escape.

Con. *Follow, pursue, chase, trail, tag, tail.

emanate. Issue, proceed, *spring, rise, arise, originate, derive, flow, stem.

Ana. Emerge, loom, *appear: *begin, commence, start, initiate.

emancipate. Manumit, enfranchise, affranchise, *free, liberate, release, deliver, discharge.

emasculate. 1 *Sterilize, asexualize, castrate, spay, mutilate, geld, caponize.

2 Enervate, unman, *unnerve.

Ana. *Weaken, enfeeble, debilitate, sap, undermine.

Con. Energize, *vitalize.

embankment. Bank, dune, *mound, terrace, tumulus, barrow.

embarrass. **Embarrass, discomfit, abash, disconcert, rattle, faze** (*or* **phase, fease, feeze**) are commonly employed as though they were exact synonyms meaning merely to balk by confusing or confounding. Actually, in discriminating use, each one of these words is capable of expressing nice and distinctive shades of meaning. **Embarrass** characteristically implies some influence which impedes freedom of thought, speech, or action and may be used with reference not only to persons but also to the things they plan or desire to do. "A course of legislation ...which...*embarrassed* all transactions between individuals, by dispensing with a faithful performance of engagements" (*Ch. Just. Marshall*). When said of persons it commonly implies, and often stresses, resulting uneasiness or constraint. "He had, he knew, a sort of charm —it *embarrassed* him even to admit it" (*M. Austin*). **Discomfit** still retains in good writers its etymological implication of being put to rout. It has, however, lost all military connotations, though a contest such as a battle of wits is often implied. "The idea of Mr. Slope's *discomfiture* [at failure to receive expected promotion] formed no small part of the Archdeacon's pleasure" (*Trollope*). If is often loosely and not warrantably used as though it meant to make uncomfortable. **Abash** presupposes self-confidence or self-possession and implies a check (usually a sudden check) to that mood by some influence that awakens shyness, a conviction of error or inferiority, or now, by confusion with *abase,* of shame. "A man whom no denial, no scorn could *abash*" (*Fielding*). "Delia [was]...*abashed* by the base motives she found herself attributing to Charlotte" (*E. Wharton*). **Disconcert,** like *embarrass,* may be used in reference to actions and plans, but it is more frequently referred to persons. In either case, it implies an upsetting or derangement; in the latter, it suggests temporary loss of equanimity or of assurance. "When she saw him there came that flicker of fun into her eyes that was so *disconcerting* to Mr. Ezra" (*Deland*). **Rattle** (a colloquial word) more than *disconcert* stresses the emotional agitation accompanying the upset and implies, therefore, a complete disorganization of one's mental processes; as, the jeering *rattled* the team and caused them to play badly. **Faze** is an Americanism that has many variant forms which are mostly British and originally different in meaning. It is commonly found in negative expressions, where it comes close to *disconcert,* but sometimes carries the implications of *abash* and *rattle;* as, neither rebuffs nor threats *faze* him in the least.

Ana. *Discompose, disturb, perturb, fluster, flurry: bewilder, nonplus, perplex (see PUZZLE): *trouble, distress: vex, *annoy, bother, irk: impede, obstruct, block, *hinder: *hamper, fetter, shackle, hog-tie.

Ant. Relieve (*persons*): facilitate (*plans, projects, etc.*).

embassador. Variant of AMBASSADOR.

embellish. Beautify, deck, bedeck, garnish, *adorn, decorate, ornament.

Ana. Enhance, heighten, *intensify: apparel, array (see CLOTHE).

Con. Denude, *strip, bare, divest.

embers. *Ashes, ash, cinders, clinkers.

embezzle. Peculate, *defalcate.

Ana. *Steal, purloin, filch, pilfer, lift: *rob, loot, plunder, rifle: appropriate, *arrogate, confiscate.

embezzlement. Peculation, defalcation. See under DEFALCATE.

Ana. *Theft, larceny, robbery.

emblem. Attribute, *symbol, type.

Ana. Device, motif, design, *figure, pattern: *sign, mark, token, badge.

embody. **1** Incarnate, materialize, externalize, objectify, *realize, actualize, substantiate, substantialize, hypostatize, reify.

Ana. Invest, *clothe: illustrate, *exemplify: manifest, demonstrate, evidence, evince, *show.

Ant. Disembody.

2 Incorporate, assimilate, *identify.

Ana. *Add, annex, superadd, append: *introduce, insert, interpolate, interject: comprehend, *include, embrace, involve, imply.

embrace, *v.* **1** *Adopt, espouse.

Ana. Assume, *take: accept, *receive: seize, grasp, *take.

Ant. Spurn. — ***Con.*** Reject, refuse, repudiate, *decline: scorn, disdain (see DESPISE).

2 Comprehend, *include, involve, imply, implicate, subsume.

Ana. *Contain, hold, accommodate: comprise, *compose: embody, incorporate (see IDENTIFY).

Con. *Exclude, rule out, shut out, debar, eliminate.

embrasure. Bay, nook, alcove, *recess, niche, cubicle, carrell, carol.

emend. *Correct, rectify, revise, amend, remedy, redress, reform.

Ana. *Mend, repair, remodel: *improve, better, ameliorate.

Ant. Corrupt (*a text, passage, etc.*).

emerge. *Appear, loom.

Ana. Issue, emanate, *spring, flow, arise, rise, proceed, stem, derive, originate.

emergency. Exigency, contingency, crisis, pass, *juncture, pinch, strait.

Ana. Situation, condition, posture, *state: *difficulty, vicissitude.

emigrant. **Emigrant, immigrant** are here compared only as denoting a person who leaves one country in order to settle in another. **Emigrant** (so also **emigrate** and **emigration**) is used with reference to the country from which, **immigrant** (so also **immigrate** and **immigration**) is used with reference to the country into which, migration is made. The former marks the going out from a country; the latter, the entrance into a country; as, a large crowd of Italian *emigrants* boarded the ship at Naples; Ireland lost heavily through *emigration* in the middle of the nineteenth century; "Our surplus cottage children *emigrate* to Australia and Canada or migrate into the towns" (*H. G. Wells*); Scandinavian *immigrants* settled large parts of the Middle Western United States; *immigration* from Europe has greatly decreased in the United States since a quota has been established for each country.

emigrate. Immigrate (see under EMIGRANT).

emigration. Immigration (see under EMIGRANT).

émigré. Immigrant, alien, foreigner, outlander, outsider, *stranger.

eminent. Illustrious, distinguished, noted, renowned, celebrated, *famous, famed, notorious.

Ana. Signal, outstanding, prominent, remarkable, conspicuous, *noticeable.

emissary, *n.* **Emissary, spy, secret-service agent, secret agent, scout, intelligencer** are here compared as denoting a person who secretly gathers information concerning the movements or plans of opponents, enemies, or the like. An **emissary** is an agent (in past usage, one who works in secret) appointed to detect the schemes of an opposing party or to influence their councils, or both; as, "By buzzing *emissaries* fills the ears Of listening crowds with jealousies and fears" (*Dryden*); "I am endeavouring to get this information by *emissaries*" (*Wellington*). The word is now less frequently used in a bad sense and often is applied to a diplomatic agent sent on a special mission; as, an *emissary* came from that government to negotiate the purchase of certain islands. A **spy** is properly one who enters an enemy's camp or territories in disguise, to obtain information; the term is usually one of opprobrium; as, "Ye are *spies;* to see the nakedness of the land ye are come" (*Genesis* xlii. 9); "His *spies* were everywhere, mingling with the suspected and insinuating themselves into their confidence" (*Prescott*). In current use, the terms **secret-service agent** or **secret agent** are often preferred to *spy,* but they (especially the first term) are also applicable to any agent who does detective work for the government, as in relation to counterfeiters, treasonable activities, and the like. A **scout,** as here compared, is a soldier sent out without disguise, usually at some hazard, to gain information; the word is not used in a derogatory sense; as, "As when a *scout,* Through dark and desert ways with peril gone All night... Obtains the brow of some high-climbing hill" (*Milton*). "The captain...continued to maintain the most vigilant precautions; throwing out *scouts* in the advance, and on every rising ground" (*Irving*). An **intelligencer** may be an emissary or spy, or he may be a secret agent whose chief aim is to gather and supply information that may be useful to his government in any way. "He has no diplomatic character whatever, but is to receive eight thousand livres a year, as an *intelligencer*" (*Jefferson*).

Ana. Envoy, *ambassador, legate, nuncio, minister: *agent, deputy, attorney.

emollient, *n.* Demulcent, *balm, salve.

Ant. Irritant.

emolument. Stipend, salary, fee, *wage, pay, hire, screw.
Ana. Compensation, remuneration, recompensing *or* recompense (see corresponding verbs at PAY): reward, meed, guerdon (see PREMIUM).

emotion. *Feeling, affection, passion, sentiment.

empathy. Sympathy, *pity, compassion, commiseration, ruth, condolence, bowels.
Ana. *Imagination, fancy, fantasy: appreciation, understanding, comprehension (see UNDERSTAND).

emphasis. Emphasis, stress, accent, accentuation agree in denoting exerted force by which one thing stands out conspicuously among other things; they also often designate the effect produced or the means used in gaining this effect. **Emphasis** implies effort to bring out that which is significant or important; as, he puts the *emphasis* on discipline in his teaching; an effective orator knows how to be sparing in his use of *emphasis.* Sometimes, it also suggests vigor or intensity of feeling. "Any one, however ignorant, can feel the sustained dignity of the sculptor's work, which is asserted with all the *emphasis* he could put into it" (*H. Adams*). **Stress,** though often used interchangeably with *emphasis,* is distinguishable from it both in some of its implications and in its association with particular arts, where it has acquired specific meanings. In most skillful use, it rarely loses its original implication of weight that causes pressure or strain, though this is often merely suggested. "'I wouldn't lay too much *stress* on what you have been telling me,' I observed quietly" (*Conrad*). "The rule of 'plainness' on which the Society [of Friends] still lays *stress*" (*Inge*). At times, *stress* strongly implies urgency or insistency. "Jane secretly approved his discernment. But all she said was, with her cool lack of *stress,* 'It's not so bad'" (*R. Macaulay*). In phonetics and prosody, *stress* is the general term referring to the prominence given to certain syllables or words by force of utterance. It may be used whether this prominence is attained, as in English, by tone emphasis or relative loudness, or, as in Greek and Latin, by the relatively longer time taken in utterance. It may also be used of the natural emphasis on certain words in a sentence. It may even suggest degree of emphasis. "Each syllable [was] given its due *stress*" (*E. Wharton*). **Accent** always implies contrast for the sake of effect, very frequently, an aesthetic effect. *Accent* carries no connotation of weight, but it strongly suggests relief, in both senses, that of relieving monotony, and that of bringing out sharply, or into relief; as, the room was quiet and neutral in coloring, but it was given *accent* by bowls of bright flowers. "It [the nurse's story] meandered...Tony had sometimes become...impatient over it, and insisted upon a sharper *accent,* in one or other of the little happenings" (*Arch. Marshall*). In prosody, accent is the form of stress characteristic of English verse, akin to the beat in music and involving force in utterance. In English phonetics, *accent* and *stress* are commonly used interchangeably. Since force of utterance (*stress*) is the principal means by which a syllable, a word, or a group of words is accented, or brought into sharp contrast with the others, one may speak of the syllabic *accent* or *stress,* word *accent* or *stress,* or the like. **Accentuation,** though close to *accent* (except in technical senses) often goes beyond it in its emphasis on increased conspicuousness; it also often suggests disagreeableness in the contrast. "The great length of his figure and his arms was *accentuated* by the wavering uncertain light" (*S. Anderson*).

empiric, *n.* Quack, charlatan, mountebank, faker, *impostor.
Ana. Tyro, dabbler, *amateur, dilettante.
Ant. Specialist.

employ, *v.* **1** *Use, utilize, apply, avail oneself of.
Ana. *Practice, exercise, drill: engross, absorb, *monopolize: *choose, select, pick.
2 Employ, hire are here compared not as synonyms, but as terms commonly confused in the sense of to engage a person's services. **Employ** (see also USE) implies use of a person's services, as in an industrial, clerical, or professional capacity; as, the company *employs* (that is, has in its employ) ten stenographers; the factory *employs* 1000 men. Thus, it is perfectly good English to say that a charitable organization *employs* only volunteer workers. **Hire** (see also HIRE) stresses the act of engaging the services of a person for compensation; as, ten additional men were *hired* this morning; it is the employment manager's business to *hire* and fire; he was *hired* to do repairing only.
Ana. Engage (see PROMISE).

employment. *Work, occupation, business, métier, calling, pursuit.
Ana. *Trade, craft, handicraft, art, profession.

empower. *Enable.
Ana. *Authorize, commission, accredit, license: train, instruct, discipline, *teach: endow, endue (see DOWER).
Con. Debar, disbar, shut out, rule out, *exclude.

emprise *or* **emprize.** Enterprise, *adventure, quest.
Ana. *Feat, exploit, achievement.

empty, *adj.* **1 Empty, vacant, blank, void, vacuous** agree in meaning lacking the person(s) or thing(s) it (the noun qualified) may or should contain or hold. That is **empty** which has nothing in it; that is **vacant** which is without an occupant, incumbent, tenant, inmate, or the person or thing it appropriately contains; as, an *empty* (never *vacant*) bucket, bottle, purse, stomach; *empty*-handed; a *vacant* (not *empty*) see, pastorate, professorship, apartment, office, post. When qualifying the same nouns, the words usually suggest distinctly different ideas; thus, an *empty* house has neither furniture nor occupants; a *vacant* house is without inmates and presumably for rent or for sale; an *empty* chair has no one sitting in it at the time; a *vacant* chair is one that has lost its usual occupant by death or other cause; an *empty* space has nothing in it; a *vacant* space is one left to be filled with that which is appropriate. "[It] enabled him to fill a place which would else have been *vacant*" (*N. Hawthorne*). That (especially a surface) is **blank** which is free from writing or marks of any kind, or which has vacant spaces that are left to be filled in; as, a *blank* page, a *blank* application. The last two words are now comparatively rare in their literal senses. However, they (especially *void,* followed by *of*) are still occasionally found. That is **void** which is absolutely empty so far as the senses can discover; as, a conscience *void* of offense; "Sandy wilderness, all black and *void*" (*Wordsworth*); "The *void,* hollow, universal air" (*Shelley*). That is **vacuous** which is void or which encloses a vacuum; as, the *vacuous* glove of an incandescent lamp.

Figuratively, the same distinctions hold; thus, an *empty* mind is destitute of worthwhile ideas or knowledge; a *vacant* mind lacks its usual occupant, the soul or intellect; a *blank* look is without expression; a person is said to be *void* of learning or of common sense when not the slightest evidence of either one can be detected; a *vacuous* mind, look, or expression reveals inanity rather than emptiness. "*Empty* heads console with *empty* sound" (*Pope*). "The loud laugh that spoke the *vacant* mind" (*Goldsmith*). "His eyes had that *blank* fixed gaze ...that babies' eyes have" (*Wilkins*). "It is dull and *void* as a work of art" (*C. E. Montague*). "In later years, some of Everett's pupils, seeing how *vacuous* his career had

been, wondered that he had so beguiled their minds" (*Van W. Brooks*).
Ana. *Devoid, destitute, void: *bare, barren: exhausted, drained, depleted (see DEPLETE).
Ant. Full. — *Con.* Replete, complete (see FULL).
2 Idle, hollow, *vain, nugatory, otiose.
Ana. Inane, *insipid, vapid, flat, jejune, banal: trifling, trivial, paltry, *petty: fruitless, *futile, vain, bootless.
Con. *Real, true, actual: significant, meaningful, pregnant (see EXPRESSIVE): *genuine, authentic, veritable, bona fide.

empyrean *or* **empyreal.** *Celestial, heavenly.

emulate. *Rival, compete with, vie with.
Ana. Imitate, *copy, ape: *match, equal, approach, touch.

emulous. *Ambitious.
Ana. Aspiring, aiming, panting (see AIM, *v.*): *eager, avid, keen, anxious, athirst, agog.

enable. **Enable, empower** come into comparison as meaning to make one able to do something. In ordinary usage, **enable** implies provision of the means or opportunity; **empower,** the granting of the power or the delegation of the authority, to do something; as, an income *enabling* one to live with dignity; a letter *empowering* one to act in another's behalf; "To give to the Cathedral fund a sum sufficient to *enable* Father Latour to carry out his purpose" (*Cather*); the president was *empowered* by Congress to conscript men for military service.
Ana. Permit, allow, *let.
Con. *Forbid, prohibit, inhibit: *prevent, preclude.

enamored *or* **enamoured. Enamored** (*or* **enamoured**), **infatuated** are very frequently used interchangeably, though with a loss in precision, in the sense of being passionately in love. **Enamored** usually, but not necessarily, connotes complete absorption in the passion. "Elizabeth-Jane...did not fail to perceive that her father...and Donald Farfrae became more desperately *enamoured* of her friend every day" (*Hardy*). **Infatuated,** when applied to lovers and their acts, carries all the implications of *enamored* but does not, in careful usage, surrender the implications of its primary sense (see FOND, 1), blind folly and unreasoning ardor. "You Scythrop Glowry, of Nightmare Abbey...*infatuated* with such a dancing...thoughtless, careless...thing as Marionetta" (*Peacock*).
Ana. Bewitched, captivated, fascinated (see ATTRACT): fond, devoted, doting, *loving.

enation. Consanguinity, *kinship, affinity, cognation, agnation.

enchant. Charm, captivate, allure, take, fascinate, bewitch, *attract.
Ana. Delight, rejoice, gladden, gratify, *please.
Ant. Disenchant.

enchanting. Charming, captivating, alluring, taking, fascinating, bewitching, attractive. See under ATTRACT.
Ana. *Delightful, delectable: *pleasant, pleasing, grateful, gratifying.
Con. Repulsive, repugnant, revolting, loathsome, *offensive: distasteful, obnoxious, repellent, abhorrent, *repugnant.

encomium. Encomium, eulogy, panegyric, tribute, citation agree in denoting a more or less formal and public expression of praise. **Encomium** implies enthusiasm or warmth in praising a thing or, now more often, a person; as, "*Encomium* in old time was poet's work" (*Cowper*); "the *encomiums* by my friend pronounced On humble life" (*Wordsworth*); "Lady Blandish's *encomiums* of her behaviour and her beauty annoyed him" (*Meredith*). **Eulogy** implies a more studied form than *encomium;* as a rule it applies to a speech (or writing) extolling the virtues and the services of a person; the term is especially and specifically applied to a funeral oration or sermon of this character. "Great minds should only criticize the great who have passed beyond the reach of *eulogy* or fault-finding" (*A. Lang*). "I would rather have a plain coffin without a flower, a funeral without a *eulogy,* than a life without...love and sympathy" (*G. W. Childs*). **Panegyric** carries a far stronger implication of elaborate, high-flown, often poetical or rhetorical, compliment than any of the preceding terms but it does not now emphasize publicity as much as it once did. "But verse, alas! your Majesty disdains; And I'm not us'd to *panegyric* strains" (*Pope*). "All *panegyrics* are mingled with an infusion of poppy" (*Swift*). **Tribute** applies not only to spoken or written praise but to any act or situation which can be construed as taking its place; thus, Mrs. M. R. S. Andrews calls her story of the silence which followed Lincoln's delivery of the Gettysburg Oration, "The Perfect *Tribute.*" "No *tribute* can be paid to them which exceeds their merit" (*Ch. Just. Marshall*). "I am appointed sole executor, a confidence I appreciate as a *tribute* to my lifelong friendship" (*H. G. Wells*). **Citation** is used, chiefly in the United States, in designating either the formal eulogy accompanying the awarding of an honorary degree or the specific mention of a person in military service in an order or dispatch; as, the *citations* at the 1940 commencement were written by the president of the university; the lieutenant holds ten *citations* for bravery in action.
Ana. Lauding *or* laudation, extolling *or* extollation, praising *or* praise (see corresponding verbs at PRAISE): plaudits, *applause, acclaim, acclamation: commending *or* commendation, complimenting *or* compliment (see corresponding verbs at COMMEND).
Con. Invective, *abuse, vituperation, obloquy.

encore. *Again, anew, afresh, anon.

encounter, *n.* **Encounter, skirmish, brush.** In their military senses, an **encounter** is a hostile meeting, often unexpected; a **skirmish,** a slight and desultory, often preliminary, *encounter,* commonly between light detachments of troops; a **brush,** a short but brisk skirmish. All three words are used of other than military contests; as, a sharp *encounter* of wits; a *skirmish* preliminary to a political campaign; a *brush* between opposing legal counsel.
Ana. *Battle, engagement: *contest, combat, conflict, fight, fray: clash, collision, *impact, impingement.

encroach. *Trespass, trench, entrench, infringe, invade.
Ana. *Enter, penetrate, pierce, probe: *intrude, butt in, obtrude, interlope: interfere, intervene, *interpose.

end, *n.* **1** *Limit, bound, term, bourn, confine.
Ana. *Extreme, extremity.
2 End, termination, ending, terminus come into comparison as opposed to *beginning* or *starting point* and as meaning the point or line beyond which a thing does not or cannot go, as in time or space or magnitude. **End** is not only the ordinary but also the most inclusive of these terms and it may be used of the final limit in nearly every possible application, such as in time (as, the *end* of the world; the *end* of a period; at the *end* of his life), or in space (as, the *end* of the road; the boy at the *end* of the line; the *end* of the peninsula), or in various other ways, such as in movement or action, in magnitude, in range of possibility, in extent of influence, etc. (as, the *end* of his journey; we have reached the *end* of the book; there is no *end* to his energy; the work approaches its *end;* to put an *end* to his capers. **Termination** and **ending** apply especially to the end in time or, less often, in

space, of something that is brought to a close for any one of several reasons, such as having a set term or bounds or predetermined limits, or by being complete, finished, futile, or the like; as, the *termination* of a lease; the *termination* of the period agreed upon; the *termination* of a search; a fair beginning but a bad *ending;* "The maiden sang As if her song could have no *ending*" (*Wordsworth*). **Terminus** applies to the end (often in clear opposition to *starting point*) to which a person or a thing moves or progresses. The term usually suggests spatial relations and often indicates a definite point or place; as, the *terminus* of his tour; New York is the *terminus* of several important railroads; an airway *terminus;* "the object is the starting-point, not the *terminus,* of an act of perception" (*Jeans*).
Ana. Closing *or* close, concluding *or* conclusion, finishing *or* finish, completion (see corresponding verbs at CLOSE): culmination, climax (see SUMMIT): term, bound, bourn, *limit.
Ant. Beginning. — *Con.* Inception, *origin, source, root.
3 Objective, goal, aim, object, *intention, intent, purpose, design.
Ana. Destiny, *fate, lot, doom, portion: *function, office, duty.
end, *v.* *Close, conclude, terminate, finish, complete.
Ant. Begin. — *Con.* Commence, start, initiate, inaugurate (see BEGIN): originate, derive, arise, rise, *spring.
endeavor *or* **endeavour,** *n.* Essay, assay, striving, struggle, attempt, try. See under ATTEMPT, *v.*
Ana. Toil, labor, travail, *work: *effort, exertion, pains, trouble.
endeavor *or* **endeavour,** *v.* *Attempt, try, essay, assay, strive, struggle.
Ana. Apply, devote, *direct, address: determine, resolve, *decide.
endemic, *adj.* Indigenous, *native, autochthonous, aboriginal.
Ant. Exotic: pandemic (*in medicine*). — *Con.* Foreign, alien, extraneous, *extrinsic.
endemic, *n.* Indigene, native, autochthon, aborigine. See under NATIVE, *adj.*
ending, *n.* *End, termination, terminus.
Ana., Ant., & *Con.* See those at END, *n.,* 2.
endless. Interminable, *everlasting, unceasing, never-ending.
Ana. *Lasting, perdurable, perpetual, permanent: eternal, illimitable, boundless, *infinite: *immortal, deathless, undying.
Con. Transitory, *transient, fugitive, passing, short-lived, ephemeral, evanescent.
endogenous. Autogenous, spontaneous, *automatic.
Ant. Exogenous.
endorse *or* **indorse.** *Approve, sanction, accredit, certify.
Ana. Vouch for, attest, *certify, witness: *commend, recommend: *support, uphold, champion, back, advocate.
Con. *Disapprove, deprecate: condemn, denounce, reprobate, reprehend, censure, *criticize: reject, repudiate, spurn (see DECLINE).
endow. *Dower, endue.
Ana. Bestow, confer (see GIVE): *grant, award, accord: empower, *enable: *furnish, equip.
Con. Denude, *strip, divest, bare: despoil, spoliate, *ravage: exhaust, drain, *deplete, impoverish.
endue. Endow, *dower.
Ana. *Clothe, invest, vest: *furnish, equip, outfit, accouter: bestow, confer (see GIVE).
Con. See those at ENDOW.
endure. 1 *Continue, last, abide, persist.
Ana. Survive, outlast, *outlive: *stay, remain, wait, linger, tarry, abide.
Ant. Perish. — *Con.* Disintegrate, crumble, *decay.
2 Abide, tolerate, suffer, *bear, stand, brook.
Ana. Accept, *receive, take: submit, *yield.
Con. Reject, refuse, *decline, spurn, repudiate.
enemy. Enemy, foe agree in denoting a person or body of persons that is hostile or that manifests hostility to another. **Enemy** (etymologically, one who is unfriendly, or not a friend) usually stresses antagonism that arises from a cherished hatred or a desire to harm or destroy, but it may suggest nothing much more than active or evident dislike, or a habit of preying upon; as, a man with many friends and no *enemies;* the anarchist is the *enemy* of government; the woodpecker is the natural *enemy* of insects that infest the bark of trees; "Let the teacher appear always the ally of the pupil, not his natural *enemy*" (*B. Russell*). **Foe,** on the other hand, implies active warfare, either literally or figuratively; as, he is the *foe* of all reform measures; "[Samuel] Daniel, in his dedication of *Cleopatra* to the Countess of Pembroke, declared himself the *foe* of 'Gross Barbarism' " (*T. S. Eliot*); "Give me the avowed, the erect, the manly *foe,* Bold I can meet,—perhaps may turn his blow!" (*G. Canning*). When, however, the reference is to the nation or group of nations with whom a country (or the like) is at war, *enemy* is now preferred, *foe* being used in this sense chiefly in poetry or rhetorical prose; as, "We have met the *enemy,* and they are ours" (*O. H. Perry*); "Whispering with white lips—'The *foe*! They come! they come!' " (*Byron*).
Ana. *Opponent, adversary, antagonist: rival, competitor (see corresponding verbs at RIVAL).
Con. *Friend: ally, *partner, confederate, colleague: adherent, *follower, partisan.
energetic. *Vigorous, strenuous, lusty, nervous.
Ana. Forceful, forcible, *powerful, potent: *active, dynamic, live: *busy, industrious, diligent: *strong, stout, sturdy, stalwart, tough, tenacious.
Ant. Lethargic. — *Con.* *Languid, enervated, spiritless, listless: phlegmatic, apathetic, stolid, *impassive: sluggish, stuporous (see LETHARGIC): indolent, slothful, *lazy.
energize. *Vitalize, activate.
Ana. Stimulate, quicken, galvanize, excite (see PROVOKE): *stir, arouse, rouse, rally.
Con. Enervate, emasculate (see UNNERVE): *weaken, enfeeble, debilitate.
energy. Force, *power, strength, might, puissance, arm.
Ana. Dynamism, activity, operativeness *or* operation (see corresponding adjectives at ACTIVE): momentum, impetus, *speed, velocity, headway.
Ant. Inertia (*in nonscientific use*). — *Con.* Weakness, feebleness, decrepitude (see corresponding adjectives at WEAK): powerlessness, impotence, impuissance (see corresponding adjectives at POWERLESS).
enervate. *Unnerve, emasculate, unman.
Ana. *Weaken, enfeeble, debilitate, undermine, sap, disable: *abase, demean, debase, degrade: exhaust, jade, fatigue, *tire, weary.
Ant. Harden, inure. — *Con.* Energize, *vitalize, activate: galvanize, stimulate, quicken (see PROVOKE).
enervated. Languishing, *languid, languorous, lackadaisical, spiritless, listless.
Ana. Decadent, degenerated, deteriorated (see corresponding nouns at DETERIORATION): enfeebled, debilitated, weakened (see WEAKEN).

Con. Hardened, inured, seasoned (see HARDEN): stout, sturdy, tough, tenacious, *strong, stalwart: *vigorous, lusty, energetic, strenuous.

enfeeble. *Weaken, debilitate, sap, undermine, cripple, disable.

Ana. Impair, mar, harm, *injure: enervate, emasculate, *unnerve, unman.

Ant. Fortify.

enforce. **Enforce, implement** come into comparison when they mean to put something into effect or operation. **Enforce,** in the sense here considered, is used chiefly in reference to laws or statutes. The term suggests the exercise of executive rather than legislative power, or the use of the authority and the means given the magistrates, police, etc., to maintain order and security in the community; as, the governor decided to *enforce* certain blue laws which had long been ignored, as a means of calling attention to them and of arousing a demand for their repeal; to *enforce* traffic laws and regulations strictly. But *enforce* is also used in reference to agreements, rights, ends, and the like, which have legal sanction or a legal character and require the compulsory powers of the government or of the courts to ensure their fulfillment or their protection in case of violation; as, "Congress, as incident to its power to authorize and *enforce* contracts for public works" (*Justice Holmes*); "There was no legal process by which a citizen could *enforce* his rights against the state" (*Buchan*); "A government cannot inquire into religious conviction, but it can *enforce* conformity and outward respect for the forms of worship as 'by law established' " (*Inge*). **Implement,** which came into English use around 1800 in the sense of to fulfill or carry into effect a contract, an agreement, a promise, or the like, has seen rapid development in its implications since that time and especially since early in the third decade of the twentieth century, and its leading connotations are now fairly clear. *Implement* usually suggests reference to bills or acts which have been passed, proposals or projects which have been accepted, policies which have been adopted, and the like, and implies the performance of the acts that definitely carry them into effect or ensure their being put into operation. What these acts are varies according to the nature of the thing considered; thus, an agreement to reduce armaments is not *implemented* until the countries concerned have definitely determined the extent to which each one will destroy old armaments, the lowered rate at which it will make needed replacements, and the penalties which will accompany failure to observe the pledge; "equality of status" which was granted by the Imperial Conference of 1926 to the dominions of the British Commonwealth of Nations, was not *implemented* until the Statute of Westminster was passed by Parliament in 1931 repealing certain laws incompatible with this status and granting certain powers essential to its maintenance; an act providing for a greatly increased army and navy is not *implemented* until the necessary money is appropriated.

Ana. *Execute, administer: execute, fulfill, discharge, *perform: compel, constrain, oblige, *force.

Ant. Relax (*discipline, rules, demands, etc.*). — ***Con.*** Ignore, forget, disregard, *neglect.

enfranchise. Affranchise, emancipate, manumit, *free, release, liberate, deliver, discharge.

engage. Pledge, plight, *promise, covenant, contract.

Ana. Bind, *tie: agree, accede, acquiesce, *assent, consent, subscribe: hire, *employ.

engagement. 1 **Engagement, affiance, betrothal, espousal, sponsalia,** as here compared, mean an agreement between a man and woman to marry each other. **Engagement,** the ordinary term, implies merely a mutual pledge and carries no suggestion of a formal contract. **Affiance,** now rare as a noun (more frequent as a verb, especially as the participial adjective *affianced*) adds to *engagement* the implication of a formal announcement or of public acknowledgment. It may or may not imply the existence of a contract. **Betrothal,** even in loose use, stresses the act of plighting troth; in strict use, it suggests not only the act, but a ceremony in which the pledge is passed. Commonly also, in this stricter sense, it implies a formal contract regarding dowry and dower. **Espousal,** originally and in commonest current use, designates the act or ceremony of marriage. However, it is sometimes applied to the betrothal ceremony. This usage seems to have grown out of confusion with **sponsalia,** the term in canon law for a formal contractual marriage agreement. *Espousal,* in this sense, or *sponsalia,* in Roman Catholic usage, implies a contractual relationship which constitutes an impediment to the marriage of either party to another person and which makes such a marriage illegal, though not void.

Ana. Promising *or* promise, plighting, pledging *or* pledge, covenanting *or* covenant, contracting *or* contract (see corresponding verbs at PROMISE).

2 **Engagement, appointment, rendezvous, tryst, assignation, date** agree in meaning a promise or an agreement to be in a specified place at a specified time, usually for a specified or understood purpose. **Engagement** is the general term usable in place of any of the others; as, he has no business *engagements* for the rest of the week; an *engagement* to play golf at four o'clock; the lecturer can make no more *engagements* for the season. **Appointment** is applied chiefly to an engagement with a person who because of the exigencies of his office, his profession, or his position in life must keep a calendar and apportion his time carefully among those who wish to consult him professionally or confer with him; as, the governor sees visitors only by *appointment;* the doctor's secretary said it was impossible to make an *appointment* before Thursday of the following week. **Rendezvous** more often designates a place agreed upon for the meeting of persons, often a group of persons (as, the old soldiers made the town hall their *rendezvous*), than an engagement to meet. This latter sense, however, is now more frequently found because the word was so used in Alan Seeger's poem written during the World War, "I have a *rendezvous* with Death" ("At some disputed barricade ....When Spring trips north again this year, And I to my pledged word am true, I shall not fail that *rendezvous*"). As a consequence, *rendezvous* now usually connotes a pledge or covenant (often an implicit one) to meet something or someone that cannot be escaped without violation of one's honor. "This generation of Americans has a *rendezvous* with destiny" (*F. D. Roosevelt*). **Tryst** is now chiefly poetic; like *rendezvous,* it may designate the place of meeting (which, however, is more often termed **trysting place**) as well as the agreement to meet at a certain place, but the latter is the commoner denotation of *tryst;* as, a lovers' *tryst;* to keep their *tryst* in the wood. "Vivien, like the tenderest-hearted maid That ever bided *tryst* at village stile" (*Tennyson*). **Assignation** now usually denotes a lovers' tryst, but it commonly conveys a suggestion of an illicit love or of a clandestine meeting. **Date** is colloquial for *engagement,* and is used especially of casual engagements between friends or of an agreed meeting between a young man and young woman.

3 *Battle, action, push.

Ana. *Encounter, skirmish, brush: *contest, conflict, combat, fight.

engender. *Generate, breed, beget, get, sire, procreate, propagate, reproduce.
Ana. Produce, *bear, yield: *provoke, excite, stimulate, quicken: rouse, arouse (see STIR).
engine. *Machine, apparatus, appliance.
engineer, *v.* *Guide, pilot, lead, steer.
Ana. Manage, direct, *conduct, control.
English, *adj.* **English, British, Anglo-Saxon, Anglican.** Only the first two of these terms are frequently confused, but all of them are sometimes used carelessly. **English** suggests primarily a racial difference; it implies reference to the people who inhabit England, especially in contrast to those (the Scots and the Welsh) who inhabit other parts of the island called Great Britain (or Britain for short). Thus, the *English* language is not only the tongue of this people, but it was developed in that part of Great Britain inhabited by them. Consequently, whenever anything is thought of as the peculiar possession or contribution of the people of England, *English* is the required adjective; as, *English* traditions; *English* blood; *English* customs; an *English* Christmas; *English* common law; *English* fair play. **British,** as applied to a people, suggests reference primarily (especially in historical writing) to the race which inhabited Great Britain prior to the invasions of Low Germans in the fifth and sixth centuries; it is, however, used frequently with reference to the people of Great Britain or of the United Kingdom, and less often, but in a generic sense, of any person of English, Scottish, Welsh, or Irish descent living in any part of the British Empire whether inside or outside the British Isles; as, any subject of *British* descent. "She didn't look *British,* she looked like a foreigner, a Hungarian or something like that" (*Maugham*). More often, however, *British* suggests a political reference, or implies connection with a political unit, the British Empire, or especially, the United Kingdom of Great Britain and Northern Ireland (or, prior to 1922, Great Britain and Ireland); as, *British* subjects; *British* dominions, colonies; the *British* sovereign, constitution, parliament (*English* only when the emphasis is on its origin); the *British* prime minister. These, however, are the precise uses of *British;* in looser usage *English* is often employed where *British* would be the exact term. **Anglo-Saxon,** a much misused term, in discriminating use always implies reference either to the people which in England was formed by the consolidation of the Low German invaders, Danes, and native Celts (the original British) after the sixth century, or to the language brought into England by these invaders and developed by Anglo-Saxons; as, the *Anglo-Saxon* heptarchy; *Anglo-Saxon* (as distinguished from Celtic, Danish, Norman, etc.) elements in the *English* language. In loose modern usage, the term often implies English or British birth or ancestry, especially when free from admixture; as, of *Anglo-Saxon* stock: in still looser use, it implies the predominance of persons of British ancestry; as, the *Anglo-Saxon* nations. **Anglican** is very occasionally used in place of *English;* its chief application, however, is to the Established Church of England, or to the communion (*Anglican* Communion) or loose federation of churches, including the Church of England and those churches in other countries (such as the Protestant Episcopal Church in the United States) which are offshoots of the former and follow, in general, its doctrines, discipline, and ritual; as, *Anglican* services; *Anglican* preachers.
engrain. Variant of INGRAIN.
engross. *Monopolize, absorb, consume.
Ana. Utilize, employ, *use, apply: control, manage (see CONDUCT).
Con. Distract, bewilder (see PUZZLE): dissipate, *scatter, disperse.
engrossed. Absorbed, *intent, rapt.
Ana. Monopolized, consumed (see MONOPOLIZE): fixed, set, settled (see SET, *v.*): *busy, industrious, diligent, sedulous, assiduous.
Con. Distracted, bewildered (see PUZZLE, *v.*): distraught, distrait (see ABSTRACTED): *uninterested, disinterested: *indifferent, unconcerned, detached.
enhance. Heighten, *intensify, aggravate.
Ana. *Lift, elevate, raise: *exalt, magnify, aggrandize: augment, *increase: *adorn, embellish, beautify.
Con. Diminish, reduce, lessen, *decrease: attenuate, extenuate, *thin: belittle, minimize, depreciate, detract from (see DECRY).
enigma. Riddle, puzzle, conundrum, *mystery, problem.
enigmatic. Cryptic, *obscure, dark, vague, ambiguous, equivocal.
Ana. Puzzling, perplexing, mystifying, bewildering (see PUZZLE, *v.*): abstruse, occult, esoteric, *recondite: dubious, problematic, *doubtful.
Ant. Explicit. — *Con.* Express, specific, definite (see EXPLICIT): *clear, perspicuous, lucid: plain, candid, open, *frank.
enjoin. **1** Direct, order, *command, bid, instruct, charge.
Ana. Prescribe, appoint (see participial adjectives at PRESCRIBED): advise, counsel (see under ADVICE): admonish (see REPROVE): *warn, forewarn, caution.
2 Interdict, prohibit, *forbid, inhibit, ban.
Ana. Debar, shut out, rule out (see EXCLUDE): bar, *hinder, impede.
Con. Permit, allow, *let, suffer.
enjoy. **1** *Like, love, relish, fancy, dote on *or* upon.
Ana. Delight, rejoice, gratify, gladden, regale, tickle, arride, *please.
Ant. Loathe, abhor, abominate. — *Con.* *Hate, detest: *despise, contemn, scorn.
2 Possess, own, *have, hold.
enjoyment. Delight, *pleasure, joy, delectation, fruition.
Ana. Delighting, rejoicing, gratifying, regaling, gladdening, pleasing (see PLEASE): *happiness, felicity, bliss, beatitude: zest, relish, gusto, *taste.
Ant. Abhorrence. — *Con.* Aversion, *antipathy: distastefulness *or* distaste, repugnance, repellency *or* repulsion (see corresponding adjectives at REPUGNANT).
enkindle. Kindle, ignite, fire, inflame, *light.
Ana. & *Ant.* See those at KINDLE.
enlarge. *Increase, augment, multiply.
Ana. *Extend, lengthen, elongate, prolong, protract: amplify, *expand, distend, dilate, inflate: magnify, aggrandize (see EXALT).
Con. *Thin, attenuate, extenuate: abridge, abbreviate, *shorten, curtail, retrench: compress, shrink, *contract, condense: *compact, concentrate.
enlighten. Illustrate, *illuminate, illumine, illume, light, lighten.
Ana. Educate, instruct, train, *teach, school: *inform, apprise, acquaint, advise.
Ant. Confuse, muddle. — *Con.* Mystify, perplex, *puzzle, bewilder: bemuddle, addle, fuddle (see CONFUSE).
enliven. Animate, *quicken, vivify.
Ana. Refresh, *renew, restore, rejuvenate: stimulate, excite, quicken, galvanize, *provoke: entertain, recreate, divert, *amuse: inspire, fire, *inform, animate.
Ant. Deaden: subdue. — *Con.* *Depress, oppress, weigh down, on, *or* upon.

enmity. **Enmity, hostility, antipathy, antagonism, animosity, rancor** (*or* **rancour**), **animus** agree in meaning intense deep-seated dislike or ill will or a manifestation of that feeling. **Enmity** implies more than the absence of amity or a friendly spirit; it suggests positive hatred which may or may not be dormant or concealed. "I will put *enmity* between thee and the woman" (*Genesis* iii. 15). "Angry friendship is sometimes as bad as calm *enmity*" (*Burke*). **Hostility,** on the other hand, suggests active and usually, but not necessarily, open enmity manifesting itself, as in warfare, in violent attacks, in ostracism, and the like. "The unremitting *hostility* with which...[these poems] have each and all been opposed" (*Wordsworth*). "If we could read the secret history of our enemies, we should find in each man's life sorrow and suffering enough to disarm all *hostility*" (*Longfellow*). **Antipathy** and **antagonism** usually imply a temperamental or constitutional basis for one's hatred or dislike. *Antipathy* suggests aversion or repugnance, and often, in consequence, avoidance or repulsion of the person or thing hated. "Inveterate *antipathies* against particular nations and passionate attachments for others should be excluded" (*Washington*). "Mark...found it so hard to conceal his *antipathy* that he could not understand...[why] Dayrell went out of his way to cultivate his society" (*C. Mackenzie*). *Antagonism* stresses the clash of temperaments and the quickness with which hostilities are provoked or the spirit of resistance is aroused; as, Karl Marx believed that the *hostility* of one nation to another will come to an end when the *antagonism* between classes within these nations vanishes. "Some note of viceregal authority must have lingered in her voice for the caretaker's *antagonism* changed to a sort of bedraggled obsequiousness" (*V. Sackville-West*). **Animosity** and **rancor** denote emotions of such intensity or violence that they may, if not given release, provide the ground for active hostility. *Animosity* usually suggests anger, vindictiveness, and sometimes, a desire, if not an intent, to destroy that which one hates. "The Bishop had let the parish alone, giving their *animosity* plenty of time to cool" (*Cather*). "Her hatred of the idea of it was intensified into a violent *animosity*" (*Bennett*). *Rancor* stresses bitterness and ill will amounting to malevolence; it often implies a grudge or grievance. " 'Tis not my speeches that you do mislike, But 'tis my presence that doth trouble ye. *Rancour* will out: proud prelate, in thy face, I see thy fury" (*Shak.*). **Animus** suggests less emotional violence than *animosity*, but it implies more definitely a prejudice or ill will that seeks to find expression. "There was no mistaking his intentions; he had transferred his *animus* to me, convinced I was to blame for his rejection" (*V. Heiser*).

Ana. Hate, hatred, detestation, abhorrence, loathing (see under HATE, *v.*): aversion (see ANTIPATHY): malignity, ill will, malevolence, *malice.

Ant. Amity. — ***Con.*** Friendliness, amicability (see corresponding adjectives at AMICABLE): *friendship, comity, good will.

ennui. Doldrums, boredom, *tedium.

Ana. Depression, dejection, dumps, blues, vapors, melancholy, *sadness: listlessness, languidness, languorousness *or* languor, spiritlessness (see corresponding adjectives at LANGUID): satiation *or* satiety, surfeiting *or* surfeit, cloying (see corresponding verbs at SATIATE).

enormity. **Enormity, enormousness** are usually distinguished in good current usage, even though both mean the state or the quality of being enormous. **Enormity** applies preferably to the state or quality of exceeding all bounds in wickedness or evil, and therefore of being abnormally, monstrously, or outrageously evil. "Newson...failed to perceive the *enormity* of Henchard's crime" (*Hardy*). "The sensation of standing there...and wishing her dead, was so strange, so fascinating and overmastering, that its *enormity* did not immediately strike him" (*E. Wharton*). **Enormousness** applies to the state or quality of exceeding all other things of its kind in size or amount; as, the *enormousness* of a whale; the *enormousness* of the cost of war; the *enormousness* of Greater New York; the *enormousness* of a candidate's majority in an election. *Enormity*, but not *enormousness*, may also be used as an instance of that which is characterized by enormity, or monstrous wickedness; as, the *enormities* of which Caligula was guilty.

Ana. Outrageousness, atrociousness *or* atrocity, heinousness, monstrousness (see corresponding adjectives at OUTRAGEOUS): flagrancy, grossness, rankness (see corresponding adjectives at FLAGRANT).

enormous. **Enormous, immense, huge, vast, gigantic, giant, gigantean, colossal, mammoth, elephantine, titanic, herculean, Cyclopean, Antaean, Gargantuan, Brobdingnagian** (*or, incorrectly,* **Brobdignagian**) come into comparison as meaning exceedingly or excessively large. **Enormous** suggests an exceeding of all bounds and therefore abnormality not only in size or amount but in degree (specifically of wickedness); as, *enormous* rocks; *enormous* herds; *enormous* expenditures; an *enormous* appetite; an *enormous* change; to take *enormous* delight in something; *enormous* wickedness; *enormous* crimes. **Immense** etymologically implies immeasurableness, but in current use it more often suggests a size, amount, degree, or the like, which exceeds ordinary measurements or standards; it therefore often means extremely large without suggesting abnormality or monstrousness; as, an *immense* plain; *immense* clouds; "the world of today ...in its *immense* variety" (*C. W. Eliot*); the *immense* influence of a book. **Huge** commonly suggests immensity of bulk, **vast** suggests immensity of extent; as, a *huge* mass of earth; a *vast* expanse of the sky; "*huge* overdressed dowagers" (*Wilde*); a *vast* expanse of bosom. In the extended senses of the terms, these distinctions do not always hold but careful writers and speakers usually prefer *huge* when the emphasis is on the greatness of a person's (or thing's) capacity (as, his *huge* enjoyment of a tour; a *huge* eater) and *vast* when the emphasis is on a thing's range, scope, or variety, as well as extent (as, *vast* knowledge; his *vast* interests; the *vast* number of his activities). **Gigantic** implies comparison (literally or figuratively) with the size, the prowess, or the activities of a giant or one who has exceeded normal human limits in size and in strength; as, a *gigantic* man; *gigantic* efforts; "a *gigantic* rose-tree" (*L. P. Smith*); "if this is our object, we must confess that our [academic] instruction is a *gigantic* failure" (*Grandgent*). **Giant, gigantean** are often used in place of *gigantic*, the ordinary word in best usage. **Colossal** implies comparison (literally or figuratively) with a statue of enormous height and size (such as the Colossus of Rhodes, a statue of Apollo, 120 feet in height) and therefore suggests stupendousness or incredibility; as, "the *colossal* speed of 15,000 miles a second" (*Jeans*); "physics is building *colossal* high-voltage engines for invading the recesses of the atoms" (*Karl K. Darrow*); "wars have now become so *colossal* that every woman's husband, father, son, brother, or sweetheart, if young and strong enough to carry a rifle, must go to the trenches" (*Shaw*). **Mammoth** and **elephantine** suggest the hugeness characteristic of, or a ponderousness appropriate to, the mammoth (an extinct and very large elephant), and the elephant; as, a *mammoth* ox; a *mammoth* rock; the *Mammoth* Cave in Kentucky; an *elephantine* tread; "he was no sooner stretched in bed, than he seemed to be of an *enormous* size; all his limbs—his nose, his mouth, his toes—were *elephantine!*" (*Meredith*). All the other terms imply the enormousness or the hugeness of certain mythical or fictitious personages: **titanic,** that of the Titans, or the primeval Greek gods, conceived of as colossal in size and earth-shaking in power (as, a *titanic* effort; a *titanic* ship; "Eight million volts, or four million, or even a single million—these are *titanic* voltages!"—*Karl K. Darrow*); **herculean,** that of the Greek hero Hercules, noted for his gigantic strength and prowess (as, a *herculean* task; "he swallowed at one *gigantic* gulp, and out of the same *herculean* jug"—*Mencken*); **Cyclopean,** that of a mythical race of giants of great brute strength and capacity for heavy work (as, a *Cyclopean* engine); **Antaean,** that of Antaeus, the mythical Libyan giant and wrestler, son of Gaea (the goddess Earth), whose strength was renewed when he touched his mother earth (as, *Antaean* powers; *Antaean* strength); **Gargantuan,** that of Gargantua, the gigantic king with an enormous appetite who is the hero of the satirical romance (usually called *Gargantua*) by Rabelais (as, a *Gargantuan* pudding; a *Gargantuan* voice; a *Gargantuan* appetite); **Brobdingnagian,** that of the inhabitants of the mythical country of Brobdingnag (in Swift's *Gulliver's Travels*), where each man is "as tall as an ordinary spire steeple" (as, "a bran-new *brobdignagian* hotel"—*Disraeli*).

Ana. Prodigious, stupendous, tremendous, *monstrous, monumental: inordinate, exorbitant, *excessive, extravagant.

enormousness. *Enormity.

Ana. Immenseness *or* immensity, hugeness, vastness (see corresponding adjectives at ENORMOUS): tremendousness, prodigiousness, stupendousness, monstrousness, (see corresponding adjectives at MONSTROUS).

enough. *Sufficient, adequate, competent.

Ana. Satisfying, contenting (see SATISFY): ample, plenteous, *plentiful.

Con. *Meager, scanty, scant, skimpy, exiguous: *deficient.

enquire. Variant of INQUIRE.

enquiry. Variant of INQUIRY.

enrage. Infuriate, madden, incense, *anger.

Ana. Exasperate, provoke, aggravate, roil (see IRRITATE).

Ant. Placate. — *Con.* *Pacify, appease, mollify, propitiate, conciliate.

ensconce. Screen, secrete, *hide, conceal, cache, bury.

Ana. Shield, guard, safeguard, protect, *defend: shelter, lodge (see HARBOR).

Con. Expose, exhibit, display, *show.

ensign. *Flag, standard, banner, color, streamer, pennant, pennon, jack.

ensnare. Snare, entrap, trap, bag, *catch, capture, nab, cop.

Ana. *Lure, entice, inveigle, decoy.

ensue. *Follow, succeed, supervene.

Ana. Issue, emanate, proceed, stem, *spring, derive, originate, rise, arise: pursue, *follow, chase.

ensure. **Ensure, insure, assure, secure** come into comparison because they all carry as their underlying meaning to make a person or thing sure. **Ensure** and **insure** are practically variant forms when they mean to make one thing sure, certain, or inevitable as the consequence, result, or sequel of another. *Ensure,* however, is generally preferred by good writers and speakers; as, this medicine will *ensure* (or *insure*) his recovery; to take precautions that will *ensure* (or *insure*) the safety of passengers. "That to read poetry is a gentlemanly occupation is not a very high class motive for reading it, but it *insured* poetry against neglect" (*Day Lewis*). "The child crept to the edge, and was balanced on the very verge. To call to it, to touch it, would have *insured* its destruction" (*Jefferies*). Both words may also take a personal object (seldom a personal subject except in the technical sense of *insure*), but the preferred word, when the implication is that of making a person sure by removing all doubt, or suspense, or uncertainty from his mind, is **assure;** thus, a certain financial arrangement may *ensure* a fixed income to a person for a long period, or it may *assure* him of a fixed income for that time. For *assure* usually means to impart certainty or, when the subject of the verb is a person, to impart one's own conviction or subjective certitude. "I dare *assure* thee that no enemy Shall ever take alive the noble Brutus" (*Shak.*). "What your father needs is to be *assured* that your change of plans is going to make you happy" (*M. Austin*). *Insure* (but no longer *ensure*) and *assure* are closely related in their technical sense of to indemnify (a person) against loss by a contingent event (see INSURANCE), but *insure* is now the common and general term even in Great Britain where *assure* was once frequently used specifically in reference to life insurance. **Secure** implies the performance of an act, the taking of a measure, or the existence of a condition that ensures the safety of a person or of a thing, or his or its protection against contingencies; as, "how to *secure* the lady from surprisal" (*Milton*); "lock the door to *secure* us from interruption" (*Dickens*); "[the cultivated Greek needed] a competence, to *secure* him against sordid cares, health, to *ensure* his physical excellence" (*G. L. Dickinson*). Specifically, one *secures* a debt, or a note, or any financial obligation when one provides the means whereby the creditor will be protected from loss in the event of the debtor's default.

entente. Treaty, pact, compact, covenant, concordat, convention, cartel, *contract, bargain, indenture, mise.

enter. **1 Enter, penetrate, pierce, probe,** as here compared, agree in meaning to make way into something so as to reach (at least) the interior. **Enter** (see also ENTER, 2) is the most comprehensive of these words and the least explicit in its implications. When the word takes a person for its subject, it often means little more than to go in or to go into (as, he *entered* the house; the women *entered* the dining room), but sometimes it also suggests the beginning of a course of study, a career, or the like (as, to *enter* college; to *enter* Parliament; "to *enter* the highest finance"—*Belloc*). When *enter* takes a thing for its subject, it implies a making way through some medium, sometimes a dense, sometimes a resisting, medium; as, the rain could not *enter* the frozen earth; the bullet *entered* the body near the heart; such an idea never *entered* his mind. **Penetrate** (see also PERMEATE) carries a far stronger implication than *enter* of an impelling force or of a compelling power that makes for entrance (as, "the salt rain...*penetrates* the thickest coat"—*Jefferies*): it also more often suggests resistance in the medium (as, "Frémont had tried to *penetrate* the Colorado Rockies"—*Cather;* his sight could not *penetrate* the darkness) and it may imply either a reaching the center or a passing through and an issuing on the further side (as, to *penetrate* the depths of a forest; armor plate so thick that no cannon ball can *penetrate* it). *Penetrate,* especially as an intransitive verb, often specifically takes as its subject something that is intangible or at least not objective but that has (in affirmative expressions) the power of making its way through; as, the influence of Christianity has *penetrated* to the ends of the earth; a *penetrating* odor; a *penetrating* voice. Often also, as distinguished from the other terms, *penetrate* suggests the use of a keen mind, or the exercise of powers of intuition or discernment in the understanding of the abstruse or mysterious; as, "We cannot *penetrate* the mind of the Absolute" (*Inge*); "in seeking to *penetrate* the essential character of European art" (*Binyon*); "Aunty Rosa could *penetrate* certain kinds of hypocrisy, but not all" (*Kipling*). **Pierce** in the earliest of its English senses implies a running through with a sharp-pointed instrument such as a sword, a spear, a knife, or the like; as, "they *pierced* both plate and mail" (*Spenser*); to *pierce* his opponent with a sword. In all of its extended senses it carries a far stronger implication than *penetrate* of something that stabs or runs through, or of something that cuts into the very center or through to the further side; as, to feel the *piercing* cold in every nerve; "A passion like a sword-blade That *pierced* me thro' and thro'" (*V. Lindsay*); "How was one to *pierce* such hidebound complacency?" (*C. Mackenzie*). Often, the term imputes great poignancy or aesthetic effectiveness far beyond what is usual to the thing that pierces; as, "The remembrance of all that made life dear *pierced* me to the core" (*Hudson*); "Whatever is expressed with art—whether it be a lover's despair or a metaphysical theory—*pierces* the mind and compels assent and acceptance" (*A. Huxley*). **Probe** derives its implications from the earliest of its senses, to use a probe (i.e., a long slender instrument used by surgeons in exploring wounds, cavities, and the like, for the sake of ascertaining their depth, their condition, or their contents). In its extended senses it implies penetration so far as circumstances allow or so far as one's powers or skills permit and it usually suggests an exploratory or investigatory aim; as, "The bog or peat was ascertained, on *probing* it with an instrument, to be at least fifteen feet thick" (*Lyell*); "*Probe* my quick core, and sound my depth" (*C. Rossetti*); "the only one...with whom he cared to *probe* into things a little deeper than the average level of club and chop-house banter" (*E. Wharton*). In one of its current senses, *probe* means little more than to investigate thoroughly as by questioning those in a position to know facts; as, "A rascally calumny, which I was determined to *probe* to the bottom" (*Scott*).

Ana. Invade, entrench, *trespass, encroach: *intrude, butt in: *begin, commence, start.

Ant. Issue from.

2 Enter, introduce, admit are synonymous only when they mean to cause or permit to go in or get in. **Enter,** in its causative sense, is used chiefly in idiomatic phrases, though occasionally it is employed in the sense to drive or force in; as, he could not *enter* the wedge between the layers of rock. In idiomatic use, it commonly implies writing down, as in a list, a roll, a catalogue, or a record, but in some of these phrases it also connotes the observance of other formalities; thus, to *enter* a word in a dictionary is to list it in alphabetical order and define its meaning; to *enter* one's son at a private school is to send in his name as a candidate for admission; to *enter* a judgment is to put it upon record in the proper legal form and order. **Introduce** is often preferred to *enter* when it implies insertion. "The painter who was *introducing* a tree into his landscape" (*H. Ellis*). "When a bit of finely filiated platinum is *introduced* into a chamber containing oxygen and sulphur dioxide" (*T. S. Eliot*). "Aunt Harriet...*introduced* herself through the doorway ...into the interior of the vehicle" (*Bennett*). It is the precise word when used of things not native and brought into a country or locality for the first time; as, plants *introduced* into America by the colonists. Sometimes, its use connotes an alien character in that whose entrance is effected; as, to *introduce* one's own ideas into the interpretation of a poem. **Admit,** as here compared, usually means let in; it may imply a human agent; as, the maid *admitted* the callers to the drawing room: more often, however, it is predicated of a means; as, small windows *admit* light to the cell.

Ana. Insert, interpolate, intercalate, insinuate, *introduce.

enterprise, *n.* *Adventure, emprise, quest.

Ana. Exploit, *feat, achievement: struggle, striving, endeavor, essay, attempt (see under ATTEMPT, *v.*).

entertain. 1 *Harbor, shelter, lodge, house, board.

Ana. *Receive, admit: cultivate, cherish, foster (see NURSE): *feed, nourish.

2 Divert, *amuse, recreate.

Ana. *Please, delight, gratify, rejoice, gladden, regale: beguile, *while, wile.

entertainment. Diversion, amusement, recreation. See under AMUSE.

Ana. *Feast, fete, fiesta, festival: *banquet, dinner: play, sport, disport (see under PLAY, *v.*).

enthuse. *Thrill, electrify.

enthusiasm. 1 *Inspiration, afflatus, fury, furor, frenzy.

Ana. *Ecstasy, rapture, transport: fanaticism, zealotry, bigotry (see corresponding nouns at FANATIC).

2 Fervor, ardor, *passion, zeal.

Ant. Apathy. — ***Con.*** Impassivity, phlegm, stolidity (see under IMPASSIVE): unconcern, detachment, aloofness, indifference (see corresponding adjectives at INDIFFERENT).

enthusiast, *n.* **Enthusiast, fanatic, zealot, bigot,** as here compared, denote a person who manifests excessive ardor, fervor, or devotion in his attachment to some cause, party, church, or the like. Although **enthusiast** in current general use commonly denotes a person of keen and ardent interests, and carries either favorable or unfavorable connotations, such as mental or spiritual vitality or a subordination of judgment to enthusiasm, its strict etymological sense still obtains in historical works and is the more common in literature up to the nineteenth century. In that sense, the term applies particularly to a preacher, a member of a religious sect, or, sometimes, a poet, who claims to be immediately inspired or who outwardly manifests signs (such as rapture, madness, intense emotionalism) associated with divine inspiration or possession by a god. In the seventeenth and eighteenth centuries particularly, the term was usually one of contempt applied to a member of one of the new evangelical sects such as Anabaptists; as, "the visions, voices, revelations of the *enthusiast*" (*Glanvill*). "Harmonic twang!... Such as from lab'ring lungs th'*enthusiast* blows" (*Pope*). "She [the Roman Catholic Church] thoroughly understands what no other Church has ever understood, how to deal with *enthusiasts*" (*Macaulay*). **Fanatic,** like *enthusiast* in this restricted sense, also carries a hint of madness or irrationality. In contrast to *enthusiast*, however, the term suggests extreme, monomaniac devotion and a concentration of attention, sometimes on the end to be gained but, possibly more often, on the chosen means to one's end, regardless of the real value of that end. *Fanatic*, therefore, in distinction from *enthusiast*, connotes determination, often silent determination, and an uncompromising temper; as, the murderer of Lincoln was, according to one theory, a *fanatic;* anarchism tends to produce *fanatics*. "This creature Man, who in his own selfish affairs is a coward to the backbone, will fight for an idea like a hero. He may be abject as a citizen; but he is dangerous as a *fanatic*" (*Shaw*). **Zealot** often implies fanaticism, it always sug-

gests ardent devotion, but it distinctively emphasizes vehement activity in the service of one's cause, party, or church. It may or may not connote blinding partisanship but it usually suggests jealous vigilance in protecting one's beliefs or institutions. "For modes of faith let graceless *zealots* fight" (*Pope*). "A furious *zealot* may think he does God service by persecuting one of a different sect" (*J. Gilpin*). **Bigot** implies obstinate, often blind, devotion to one's own (especially religious) beliefs or opinions; as compared with *fanatic* and *zealot*, the term implies dogged intolerance and contempt for those who do not agree rather than enthusiasm or zeal; as, "the hell that *bigots* frame to punish those who err" (*Shelley*); "Not that the modern *bigot* is any more tolerant or less cruel than her ancestors" (*Shaw*).
Ana. Devotee, votary, *addict, fiend.

entice. *Lure, inveigle, decoy, tempt, seduce.
Ana. Snare, ensnare, trap, entrap (see CATCH): cajole, blandish, *coax, wheedle.
Ant. Scare. — *Con.* *Frighten, alarm, terrify, fright.

entire. 1 *Whole, total, all, gross.
Ana. Complete, *full, plenary.
Ant. Partial.
2 *Perfect, whole, intact.
Ana. Integrated, concatenated (see under INTEGRATE, *v.*): unified, consolidated, compacted (see COMPACT, *v.*).
Ant. Impaired.

entrance. **Entrance, entry, entree, ingress, access,** in the sense in which they are here considered, agree in meaning the act, fact, or privilege of going in or coming in. All but *entree* also carry the denotation of a way or means of entering. Their differences are largely in their applications and in their connotations. **Entrance** is the widest in its range of application and the thinnest in its specific implications; it fits in with nearly every context; as, to await the *entrance* of the king, of a wedding party, of the jury; a twenty-five cent ticket gives you *entrance* to this exhibit; the *entrance* is through a gate or a hole in the fence. **Entry,** by comparison, often but not always imputes a formal or ceremonial character to the act of entering. "The trumpet will announce the Nuncio's *entry*" (*Browning*). When used with reference to a place where one enters, it usually signifies a door, a gate, a portico, or now commonly, a vestibule or entrance hall; as, the postman throws the letters in the *entry*. "I hear a knocking At the south *entry*" (*Shak.*). It has almost completely yielded its meaning of the privilege or right of entrance to **entree.** The latter word, however, is usually restricted in its application and suggests exclusiveness in those admitting, or distinction or social gifts in those admitted. "My mother's introductions had procured me the *entree* of the best French houses" (*Lytton*). **Ingress,** because of legal use, carries more than any of the others the implication either of permission to enter or of encroachment; as, his deed gives him use of the path with free *ingress* and egress. "We pardon it; and for your *ingress* here Upon the skirt and fringe of our fair land" (*Tennyson*). When used concretely it more often suggests a natural passageway than an architectural structure; as, a narrow gap is the only *ingress* to the valley. **Access,** like *ingress*, implies admission where barriers are imposed, but they may be of many kinds: social, legal, personal, etc., as well as natural. "He is here at the door and importunes *access* to you" (*Shak.*). *Access* is distinguished from the other words of this group by its emphasis on approach rather than on entrance; as, explorers still find the North Pole difficult of *access*, in spite of their use of airplanes; the *access* to the harbor was through a long narrow channel.
Ant. Exit.

entrap. Trap, snare, ensnare, bag, *catch, capture, nab, cop.
Ana. Seize, *take, clutch: *lure, inveigle, decoy, entice.

entreat. *Beg, beseech, implore, supplicate, importune, adjure, conjure.
Ana. *Ask, request, solicit: pray, appeal, plead, petition, sue (see under PRAYER).

entree. *Entrance, entry, ingress, access.
Ana. Admission, *admittance.

entrench *or* **intrench.** Trench, encroach, *trespass, infringe, invade.
Ana. *Monopolize, engross, consume, absorb: *interpose, interfere, intervene.

entrust *or* **intrust.** Confide, *commit, consign, relegate.
Ana. *Allot, assign, allocate: *rely, trust, depend, count, bank, reckon.

entreat. *Beg, beseech, implore, supplicate, importune, adjure, conjure.
Ana. *Ask, request, solicit: pray, appeal, plead, petition, sue (see corresponding nouns at PRAYER).

entry. 1 *Entrance, entree, ingress, access.
Ana. *Door, doorway, gate, gateway, portal, postern.
2 **Entry, entryway, hall, vestibule, narthex, foyer, anteroom, antechamber, lobby** agree in denoting a room leading to the interior of a building or of a special apartment or suite. **Entry, entryway,** and **hall** are the most common terms for a room or way through which one passes after entering a building from out of doors or after entering an apartment from a public corridor. *Entry* and *entryway* are sometimes distinguished from *hall*, especially in the United States and in reference to residences, when there are two rooms or ways that come under this description. The small space between an outer and an inner door in which one waits until one's ring or knock is answered is then termed an *entry*, or *entryway;* the room or passage to which one is admitted is called, in contradistinction, a *hall*. **Vestibule** is often used in a general sense, but it is more commonly applied to a large space serving as a passageway or waiting room between the outside door or doors of a building and the doors leading to the interior (often an auditorium); as, the bridal party waited in the *vestibule* of the church. The vestibule of a church is sometimes technically called a **narthex**; the vestibule of a theater and of some pretentious apartment buildings is often called a **foyer.** The latter term is also often applied to a large hall or reception room at the entrance to a luxurious apartment. An **anteroom** and an **antechamber** are rooms in which callers, clients, and the like, wait until admitted to an apartment, an office, or private quarters. *Antechamber*, in distinction from *anteroom*, carries connotations of a regal or official setting, and often of regal splendor. A large open space on the ground floor of a hotel or a capitol building, which serves not only as a vestibule and as an anteroom but also as a place where the guests of the hotel or the members of a legislative body in session may confer with others, is called a **lobby.** Though the word in American use commonly suggests an entrance room, in British use it may suggest an anteroom or a corridor; thus, *lobby* in reference to the British House of Commons may designate either a large room for the public outside the legislative chamber or one of two corridors (*division lobbies*) to which the members retire to vote when the house divides.

entryway. *Entry, hall, vestibule, narthex, foyer, lobby, anteroom, antechamber.

enumerate. *Count, tell, number.
Ana. Compute, *calculate, reckon: *add, sum, total, figure: rehearse, recount, recite (see RELATE).

enunciate. *Pronounce, articulate.

envious. **Envious, jealous** are not close synonyms but they come into comparison because both carry as their basic meaning that of grudging another's possession of something desirable. But **envious** stresses a coveting of that which belongs to another, such as riches, possessions, or attainments, or of that which has come to another, such as success or good fortune; in its strictest, but not now most common sense, it implies either a gnawing, often a malicious, desire to deprive one of that which gives him gratification, or a spiteful delight in his dispossession or loss of it; as, "Still in thy right hand carry gentle peace, To silence *envious* tongues" (*Shak.*). "Here and there along the course wherein we hoped to glide Some *envious* hand has sprinkled ashes just to spoil our slide" (*Eugene Field*). Frequently, however, the stress is on coveting, rather than on a desire to injure; as, we are all *envious* of your good fortune. **Jealous** often stresses intolerance of any rival for the possession of a thing which one regards as peculiarly one's own or on the winning of which one has set one's heart, but sometimes it merely implies intensely zealous efforts to maintain that which one possesses. The term often is used without derogation; as, "Thou shalt have no other gods before me....for I the Lord thy God am a *jealous* God" (*Exodus* xx. 3–5); "proud of their calling, conscious of their duty, and *jealous* of their honour" (*Galsworthy*). However, the term often carries a strong implication of distrust, suspicion, enviousness, or sometimes, anger; as, a *jealous* wife; "he was *jealous* of Carson's fame as an Indian-fighter" (*Cather*); stabbed by a *jealous* lover.
Ana. *Covetous, grasping, greedy: grudging, coveting, envying (see COVET): malign, malignant, spiteful, *malicious, malevolent.
Con. Generous, *liberal, bountiful: kindly, *kind, benign, benignant.

environment. *Background, setting, milieu, backdrop, mise-en-scène.

envision, envisage. Conceive, imagine, *think, realize, fancy.
Ana. View, behold, survey, contemplate (see SEE): objectify, externalize, materialize, *realize.

envoy. *Ambassador, legate, minister, nuncio, internuncio.

envy, *v.* *Covet, grudge, begrudge.
Ana. *Long, pine, hanker, yearn.

eon. Variant of AEON.

eonian. Variant of AEONIAN.

ephemeral. *Transient, transitory, passing, fugitive, fleeting, evanescent, momentary, short-lived.
Ana. *Daily, diurnal: *brief, short.

epicene. Hermaphrodite, hermaphroditic, *bisexual, androgynous.
Ana. Effeminate, womanish (see FEMALE, *adj.*).

epicure. **Epicure, gourmet, gourmand, glutton, bon vivant, gastronome, gastronomer** come into comparison as meaning one who takes pleasure in eating and drinking. An **epicure,** in modern usage, is one who is choice and fastidious while at the same time voluptuous, in enjoyment of food and drink; the term is also applied to a connoisseur in any art the enjoyment of which suggests both feasting and delicacy of taste. "I am become a perfect *epicure* in reading; plain beef or solid mutton will never do" (*Goldsmith*). A **gourmet** is a connoisseur in delicate viands, liquors, wines, and the like; the term carries as its distinctive connotation the savoring as of each morsel of food or sip of wine, and the power to distinguish delicate differences in flavor or quality; as, "the most finished *gourmet* of my acquaintance" (*Thackeray*). **Gourmand** implies less fastidiousness and less discernment than *gourmet,* but it suggests a hearty interest in good food and drink rather than, as **glutton,** greedy and voracious eating and drinking; as, "I dare say, their table is always good, for the Landgrave is a *gourmand*" (*Chesterfield*); "Youth is a *gourmand* when it cannot be a *gourmet*" (*McClure's Mag.*). "It would be difficult to determine whether they were most to be distinguished as *gluttons* or *epicures;* for they were, at once, dainty and voracious, understood the right and the wrong of every dish, and alike emptied the one and the other" (*Burney*). **Bon vivant** (literally, a good liver), a French phrase much used in English, differs little from *gourmand* except in its stronger connotation of a lively or spirited enjoyment of the pleasures of the table, especially in the company of others; as, "The Major was somewhat of a *bon-vivant,* and his wine was excellent" (*Scott*); "he was also a *bon-vivant,* a diner-out, and a story-teller" (*Fraser's Mag.*). **Gastronome** and the rarer **gastronomer** are equivalents of *epicure* though far less frequently used than that term. "A conversation on the mysteries of the table, which...a modern *gastronome* might have listened to with pleasure" (*Scott*).
Ana. Connoisseur, *aesthete, dilettante.

epicurean. Sybaritic, luxurious, *sensuous, sensual, voluptuous.
Ana. Fastidious, dainty, *nice, particular.
Ant. Gross (*taste, life, habits, etc.*).

epigram. Aphorism, apothegm, *saying, saw, maxim, adage, proverb, motto.

episode. 1 *Digression, divagation, excursus.
Ana. *Deviation, divergence, deflection: departing *or* departure (see corresponding verb at SWERVE).
2 Incident, event, *occurrence, circumstance.

epistle. *Letter, missive, note, message, dispatch, report, memorandum.

epitome. Conspectus, synopsis, *abridgment, abstract, brief.
Ana. Précis, aperçu, sketch, digest, *compendium.

epoch. Era, age, *period, aeon.

equable. Even, constant, *steady, uniform.
Ana. Regular, *orderly, methodical, systematic: invariable, immutable, unchangeable (see affirmative adjectives at CHANGEABLE): *same, equal, equivalent.
Ant. Variable, changeable. — *Con.* Fluctuating, wavering (see SWING): *fitful, spasmodic.

equal, *adj.* Equivalent, *same, very, identical, identic, tantamount.
Ana. Equable, even, uniform (see STEADY): like, alike (see SIMILAR): proportionate, commensurate (see PROPORTIONAL).
Ant. Unequal. — *Con.* *Different, diverse, disparate, various, divergent.

equal, *v.* *Match, rival, approach, touch.
Ana. *Compare: square, accord, tally, correspond, *agree.

equanimity. **Equanimity, composure, sang-froid, phlegm** agree in meaning the mental temper of one who is self-possessed or not easily disturbed or perturbed. **Equanimity** suggests either a proper mental balance or a constitutionally equable temper; it therefore may imply a delicate adjustment of one's emotional and mental powers that is liable to disturbance only under great strain, or a settled attitude of mind which repels all that disturbs; as, "His placidity of demeanor...arose from ...the *equanimity* of a cold disposition rather than of one well ordered by discipline" (*Trollope*); "it was some time before Wildeve recovered his *equanimity*" (*Hardy*); "Stoicism teaches men...to accept with proud *equa-*

nimity the misfortunes of life" (*Inge*). **Composure** commonly implies the conquest of mental agitation or disturbance, but it may imply a temperamental freedom from agitation; as, "His passions tamed and all at his control, How perfect the *composure* of his soul!" (*Cowper*); "There was his son lying all but dead, and the man was still unconvinced of the folly he has been guilty of. I could hardly bear the sight of his *composure*" (*Meredith*). **Sang-froid** (a French term meaning cold blood) implies great coolness and steadiness, especially under strain; as, "no being ever stood in a pedagogue's presence with more perfect *sang froid*" (*Disraeli*); "at all these [gambling games] she won and lost, with the same equable *sangfroid*" (*R. Macaulay*). **Phlegm** suggests an apathy of mind or sluggishness of temperament that results from a physical condition rather than from discipline or self-control; it therefore suggests even greater imperturbability and insensitiveness than any of the preceding terms; as, soldiers with *phlegm* stand war better than all others; "the patience of the people was creditable to their *phlegm*" (*Meredith*).

Ana. Poise, equipoise, *balance, equilibrium: self-possession, self-assurance, aplomb (see CONFIDENCE): tranquillity, serenity, placidity, calmness (see corresponding adjectives at CALM).

Con. Discomposure, agitation, disquieting *or* disquiet, perturbing *or* perturbation, disturbance (see corresponding verbs at DISCOMPOSE).

equilibrium. Equipoise, poise, *balance, tension.

Ana. Stableness *or* stability (see corresponding adjective at LASTING): stabilization, steadying (see corresponding verbs at STABILIZE): counterbalancing *or* counterbalance, counterpoising *or* counterpoise (see corresponding verbs at COMPENSATE).

equip. *Furnish, outfit, appoint, accouter, arm.

Con. Divest, dismantle, denude, *strip: despoil, spoliate, *ravage.

equipment. **Equipment, apparatus, machinery, paraphernalia, outfit, tackle, gear, matériel** (*or* **material**) are comparable when they mean all the things that are used in a given work or are useful in effecting a given end. **Equipment** usually, but not invariably, covers everything needed for efficient operation or efficient service, except the personnel; thus, the *equipment* for a polar expedition would include not only the vessels, instruments, and implements required, but also the sleds, dogs, clothing, food, medicines, and the like; the *equipment* for any industry includes its buildings, machines, tools, and the like; the *equipment*, of furnishings, utensils, supplies, etc., provided for beginning housekeeping. Sometimes, but not often, *equipment* is more limited in its application; thus, in railroading, it covers only the rolling stock and not the roadbed and stations. In extended use *equipment* is also employed in reference to persons and covers the qualities and skills necessary to their efficiency or competency in a given kind of work. "Knowledge, penetration, seriousness, sentiment, humor, Gray had them all; he had the *equipment* and endowment for the office of poet" (*Arnold*). "A health officer needed more than technical training....it appeared that diplomacy should constitute a major part of his *equipment*" (*V. Heiser*). **Apparatus,** in its literal and collective sense, usually covers only the instruments, tools, machines, and appliances used in a given craft or profession or in a specific operation; thus, the *apparatus* of a dentist includes all the mechanical and electrical devices he uses in his professional work; the *apparatus* of a laboratory, as distinguished from its equipment, consists of all the mechanical requisites for carrying on operations or experiments. When used in reference to persons or employments not requiring mechanical devices, *apparatus* denotes all the external aids useful in prosecuting a particular kind of work; thus, the *apparatus* of a scholar in Old English includes all the reference books, texts, glossaries, bibliographies, and the like, that he finds essential to or helpful in his investigations. "Formal lectures, with an appalling *apparatus* of specimens, charts, and wall pictures" (*Grandgent*). **Machinery,** as a collective term, derives its implications more from its early application to the material contrivances or devices by which an end is effected, especially on the stage and in the production of a play, than from its later and more common application to the power-driven apparatus which effects certain kinds of work by transmitting and modifying force and motion. The term therefore covers all the devices, means, or agencies which permit a thing to function (as an organism, a government, an institution, a law) or which enable it to accomplish its ends (as a movement, a political party, propaganda). "The physiological *machinery* of the body is so adjusted that great variations of atmospheric temperature can be supported without detriment" (*V. Heiser*). "Public meetings, harangues, resolutions, and the rest of the modern *machinery* of agitation had not yet come into fashion" (*Macaulay*). "If the peoples wanted war, no *machinery* could prevent them from having it" (*Inge*). **Paraphernalia** usually suggests a collection of the miscellaneous articles or belongings that constitute the usual accompaniments (often the necessary equipment) of a person or group of persons in a particular employment, activity, or the like; as, the *paraphernalia* of a circus; the *paraphernalia* of a tourist. "Little piles of wheels, strips of unworked iron and steel, blocks of wood, the *paraphernalia* of the inventor's trade" (*S. Anderson*). The word frequently carries a slightly contemptuous connotation such as that associated with trash, trumpery, fripperies; as, to clear a boy's room of all its *paraphernalia.* **Outfit** is sometimes interchangeable with *equipment,* but it has a slightly more colloquial flavor and is preferred when the latter term might seem pretentious; as, a camper's *outfit;* a gambler's *outfit.* It often specifically suggests wearing apparel and other necessities for a journey, a school year, a new employment, or the like; as, a bride's *outfit;* a college girl's *outfit;* a soldier's *outfit.* **Tackle** is also a more colloquial term than *apparatus,* which otherwise it closely resembles; as, fishing *tackle.* **Gear** is variously used, sometimes approaching *equipment* (as, "You've got a good six hours to get your *gear* together"—*Conrad*), sometimes *apparatus* (as, sportsman's *gear*), sometimes *outfit,* or *wearing apparel* (as, "servants...ready in waiting at Pathankote with a change of *gear*"—*Kipling*). It is also occasionally the most general of these terms and equivalent to one's belongings collectively. "They are all, as far as worldly *gear* is concerned, much poorer than I" (*Shaw*). **Matériel,** a French word now naturalized in English, or its English equivalent **material** (somewhat rare in this use), is used in industry and in military affairs as a comprehensive and unambiguous term that covers everything but the personnel; that is, buildings, furnishings, apparatus, and supplies.

equipoise. Equilibrium, poise, *balance, tension.

equitable. *Fair, just, impartial, unbiased, dispassionate, uncolored, objective.

Ana. *Proportional, proportionate, proportionable, commensurate, commensurable: equal, equivalent, *same, identical.

Ant. Inequitable, unfair. — *Con.* Unreasonable, *irrational.

equity. *Justice.

equivalent, *adj.* Equal, *same, identical, identic, selfsame, very, tantamount.
Ana. Like, alike, comparable, parallel, uniform (see SIMILAR): proportionate, commensurate (see PROPORTIONAL): *reciprocal, correspondent, convertible.
Ant. Different. — *Con.* Disparate, diverse, divergent, various (see DIFFERENT): discrepant, discordant, *inconsonant, incompatible.

equivocal. Ambiguous, *obscure, dark, vague, enigmatic, cryptic.
Ana. Dubious, questionable, *doubtful.
Ant. Unequivocal. — *Con.* *Explicit, express, definite, specific, categorical: perspicuous, lucid, *clear.

equivocate. Prevaricate, *lie, palter, fib.
Ana. *Deceive, mislead, delude: evade, elude, *escape.

equivocation. *Ambiguity, tergiversation, double-entendre, amphibology, amphibologism.
Ana. Prevarication, lying *or* lie, paltering, fibbing *or* fib (see corresponding verbs at LIE): duplicity, dissimulation, *deceit.

era. Age, epoch, *period, aeon.

eradicate. Uproot, deracinate, extirpate, *exterminate, wipe out.
Ana. *Abolish, annihilate, extinguish, abate: *destroy, demolish, raze: obliterate, efface, *erase, blot out.
Con. *Set, fix, establish, firm, settle: *implant, inculcate, inseminate, instill, infix: propagate, engender, breed, *generate.

erase. **Erase, expunge, cancel, efface, obliterate, blot out, delete, dele** agree in meaning to strike out something so that it no longer has effect or existence. **Erase,** in its literal sense, implies a scraping or rubbing out of something that is written, engraved, or painted; as, to *erase* a word or a line of an inscription. In its extended sense, *erase* often refers to something that has been eradicated, as if by scraping or rubbing out, after it has impressed or imprinted itself on the memory of a man or on the memories of men, or has become part of an unwritten record. "Have a few years totally *erased* me from your memory?" (*Gray*). "The old boyhood notion...that a town and a people could remake him and *erase* from his body the marks of what he thought of as his inferior birth" (*S. Anderson*). **Expunge** (etymologically, to mark for erasure by pricks or dots set above or below) has in English use, possibly through confusion with *sponge*, come to imply so thoroughgoing an erasure that the thing affected is wiped out completely. "A woman's history, you know: certain chapters *expunged*" (*Meredith*). "The most primitive ways of thinking may not yet be wholly *expunged*" (*W. James*). **Cancel** (etymologically, to strike out something written by marking it with crossing lines suggestive of latticework) was in earliest use applied chiefly to legal documents such as deeds, indentures, wills, and the like, which were rendered null or invalid by so marking them or by tearing or otherwise defacing them. Consequently, *cancel* in its far more common extended sense implies some action that renders a thing null, invalid, or worthless, or rules it out of existence. Sometimes it implies a legal annulling (as, to *cancel* a contract or a writ); sometimes, a revoking or rescinding (as, to *cancel* an order); sometimes, a neutralization, as of one thing by its opposite (as, "The later kindness...may *cancel* a greater previous wrong"—*Jowett*). In legal, postal, and philatelic use, to *cancel* is to mark a stamp so as to indicate that it has served its purpose and to prevent its re-use. Such cancellation was made at first merely with pen and ink (*pen cancellation*), later with obliterators of many devices, and now usually by machine in the form of parallel lines. **Efface,** more strongly than *erase*, implies the complete removal of something impressed or imprinted on a surface; as, constant use gradually *effaces* the figures and letters on a coin; to *efface* the offensive murals in a public building. As a result, in its extended use, *efface* often implies destruction of every visible or sensible sign of a thing's existence. "While nations have *effaced* Nations, and Death has gathered to his fold Long lines of mighty Kings" (*Wordsworth*). "The attempt to *efface* the boundaries between prose and verse" (*Lowes*). Oftentimes, especially in reflexive use, it implies an attempt to make inconspicuous or vague; as, to *efface* oneself in the company of others. **Obliterate** and **blot out** both literally imply rendering a thing undecipherable by smearing it, as with ink, or with something which hides its existence; as, "A smear of decisive lead-coloured paint had been laid on to *obliterate* Henchard's name" (*Hardy*); to *blot out* a passage in a manuscript. Both words are more often used, however, with the implication of the removal of every trace of a thing's existence; as, the falling snow rapidly *obliterated* all signs of approaching spring; "A successful love...*obliterated* all other failures" (*J. W. Krutch*). "Then rose the Seed of Chaos, and of Night, To *blot out* Order, and extinguish Light" (*Pope*). **Delete** and the corresponding cant term of printers, **dele,** both imply marking something in a manuscript or proof for omission from the text that is to be published or distributed. "Whenever you feel an impulse to perpetrate a piece of exceptionally fine writing, obey it—wholeheartedly—and *delete* it before sending your manuscript to press" (*Quiller-Couch*). But *delete*, which etymologically means to destroy, and once carried that meaning in English, now also often suggests eradication or elimination by the exercise of arbitrary power; as, the censor *deleted* all the interesting parts of the letter.
Ana. *Remove, draw, withdraw: annul, *nullify, negate: *abolish, extinguish.
Con. Imprint, impress, print, stamp (see corresponding nouns at IMPRESSION).

eremite. Hermit, anchorite, *recluse, cenobite.

eristic. *Controversial, polemic, polemical, apologetic.

erosion. **Erosion, corrosion, abrasion, attrition** are often confused because of overlapping implications. **Erosion** and **corrosion** imply a gradual wearing away or disintegration; *erosion*, usually by a mechanical process such as friction; *corrosion*, by a chemical process such as rusting. However, they are at times used interchangeably. **Abrasion** (see ABRADE), like *erosion*, implies a wearing away by friction, but it is applied to surfaces only and it usually suggests a more restricted area of effectiveness; as, the *erosion* of a hillside by running water; the *abrasion* of coins by ordinary handling; the *abrasion* of teeth in chewing. **Attrition** implies wearing down by abrasion or a process like abrasion, but it usually connotes action so prolonged that disintegration or, figuratively, exhaustion is the result; as, sand is often formed by the *attrition* of pebbles in a stream. "He [Tiberius] broke the enemy by the only methods possible—starvation, *attrition*, and a slow, deadly scientific envelopment" (*Buchan*).

erotic. **Erotic, amatory, amorous, amative, aphrodisiac** (*or* **aphrodisiacal**) are not always clearly distinguished in use. All involve the idea of love for the opposite sex but they are not interchangeable because of differences in denotation as well as in implications. **Erotic,** though the strongest in its suggestions of love as a violent passion or as a physical appetite, is rarely applied to persons; its chief use is in characterizing or classifying emotions, motives, themes in art, and the like; as, *erotic* love; *erotic* tendencies; *erotic* music; an *erotic* poet is a writer of *erotic* poetry. "It was the persuasion that the deprivation was final that obsessed him with *erotic* imaginations

....almost to the verge of madness" (*H. G. Wells*). **Amatory** is a synonym of *erotic*, but far weaker in its suggestion of sexual desire; it sometimes connotes little more than ardent admiration; thus, one might more correctly describe the youthful love poems of Tennyson as *amatory* than as *erotic* poetry. "Sir Lucius...has been deluded into thinking that some *amatory* letters received by him from Mrs. Malaprop are from Lydia" (*Sir Paul Harvey*). **Amorous** is applied chiefly to persons, their words, or their acts, especially when they are falling in love or are making love. "Came many a tiptoe, *amorous* cavalier, And back retir'd...her heart was otherwhere" (*Keats*). "Yielded, with coy submission, modest pride, And sweet, reluctant, *amorous* delay" (*Milton*). The word often suggests ripeness or eagerness for love. "A prince I was, blue-eyed, and fair in face, Of temper *amorous*, as is the first of May" (*Tennyson*). In this sense it is also applied to animals; as, "While falling, recalling, The *amorous* thrush concludes his sang" (*Burns*). **Amative** implies merely a disposition to fall in love, or a propensity for loving; it is chiefly used in describing temperaments or in analyzing character; as, he is not normally *amative*. **Aphrodisiac,** once applied chiefly to drugs, is now applied also to writings, music, works of art, and the like, that arouse or tend to arouse sexual desire; as, "the laboured unreserve of *aphrodisiac* novels and plays" (*C. E. Montague*); "three men...played upon a violin, a 'cello and a guitar some of T. P.'s most seductive and *aphrodisiacal* compositions" (*American Mercury*).

Ana. Passionate, *impassioned, fervid, perfervid, ardent, fervent: *carnal, fleshly, sensual.

erratic. Eccentric, odd, queer, *strange, singular, peculiar, unique, quaint, outlandish, curious.

Ana. Aberrant, *abnormal, atypical: *irregular, unnatural, anomalous: capricious, fickle, mercurial, *inconstant.

Con. Normal, *regular, typical, natural: *usual, customary, wonted, habitual: *common, ordinary, familiar: conventional, formal (see CEREMONIAL): *decorous, decent, seemly, proper.

error. Error, mistake, blunder, slip, lapse, faux pas, bull, howler, boner, bloomer, floater come into comparison when they denote anything such as an act, statement, or belief that involves a departure from what is, or what is generally held to be, true, right, or proper. **Error** etymologically implies deviation; it suggests culpability but not necessarily carelessness or intention, for it implies a guide to be followed such as a record or manuscript (as, a historical *error;* a typographical *error*), or a rule or set of rules (as, an *error* in addition; an *error* in reasoning), or a principle, law, accepted code, or the like (as, an *error* in conduct, a grammatical *error*). "Those who, with sincerity and generosity, fight and fall in an evil cause, posterity can only compassionate as victims of a generous but fatal *error*" (*Scott*). **Mistake** implies misconception, misunderstanding, a wrong but not always blameworthy judgment, or inadvertence; it expresses less severe criticism than *error;* as, he made a serious *mistake* when he chose the law as his profession; a child makes many *mistakes* in spelling when he strictly follows the phonetic method. "There is a medium between truth and falsehood, and (I believe) the word *mistake* expresses it exactly. I will therefore say that you were mistaken" (*Cowper*). **Blunder** is harsher than *mistake* or *error;* it commonly implies ignorance or stupidity, sometimes blameworthiness. "We usually call our *blunders mistakes*, and our friends style our *mistakes blunders*" (*H. B. Wheatley*). "One's translation [of a medieval poem] is sure to be full of gross *blunders*, but the supreme *blunder* is that of translating at all when one is trying to catch not a fact but a feeling" (*H. Adams*). **Slip** carries a stronger implication of inadvertence or accident than *mistake*, and often, in addition, connotes triviality; as, the wrong date on the check was a *slip* of the pen; "a social *slip* which makes us feel hot all over" (*L. P. Smith*). Often, especially when it implies a transgression of the moral law, the word is used euphemistically or ironically. "Let Christian's *slips* before he came hither ...be a warning to those that come after" (*Bunyan*). "People...don't send for him [the minister] every time they make a slight moral *slip*,—tell a lie, for instance, or smuggle a silk dress through the custom-house" (*Holmes*). **Lapse,** though sometimes used interchangeably with *slip*, stresses forgetfulness, weakness, or inattention more than accident; thus, one says a *lapse* of memory or a *slip* of the pen, but not vice versa. "You gave natives bits to copy under all possible threats against *lapses* of accuracy" (*M. Austin*). When used in reference to a moral transgression, it carries a weaker implication of triviality than *slip* and a stronger one of a fall from grace, one's own standards, or the like. "For all his...*lapses*, there was in him a real nobility, an even ascetic firmness and purity of character" (*H. Ellis*). **Faux pas** (literally, a false step), a French phrase in frequent English use, once was applied to a serious moral lapse, especially one that is a cause of scandal. "The road of vertue, in which I have trod thus long, and never made one Trip, not one *faux pas*" (*Congreve*). In current use, the phrase is often applied to a mistake in etiquette; as, she was carefully instructed so that there was no danger of her making a *faux pas* when she was presented at the Court of St. James's. **Bull** and **howler** apply to ridiculous blunders. *Bull* (often *Irish bull*, because regarded by some persons as characteristically Irish) implies a combination of utterly incongruous ideas in a statement that at first sight or hearing appears reasonable, as, for example: He remarked that it was hereditary in his family not to have children. *Howler* implies ignorance or confusion of ideas and is applied chiefly to gross and ludicrous errors in information tests or in scholastic examinations; as, a printed collection of schoolboy *howlers*. **Boner, bloomer,** and, in British use, **floater** are all slang terms applied chiefly to gross or stupid blunders; as, to pull (i.e., make) a *boner;* "you are making the *bloomer* of a lifetime" (*P. G. Wodehouse*); "She...made what she called...a *floater*" (*A. Huxley*).

errorless. Flawless, faultless, *impeccable.

Ana. *Correct, accurate, exact, precise, right, nice.

ersatz, *adj.* *Artificial, synthetic, factitious.

erudite. *Learned, polymathic, scholarly.

erudition. Learning, scholarship, *knowledge, science, information, lore.

escape, *v.* **1 Escape, flee, fly, decamp, abscond** agree in meaning to run away, especially from that which limits one's freedom or threatens one's well-being. **Escape** so stresses the idea of eluding confinement or restraint that it very often conveys no suggestion of wrongdoing or of danger. "One of the most powerful motives that attract people to science and art is the longing to *escape* from everyday life" (*H. Ellis*). "The cactus, which had *escaped* from a decorative garden bed and now covers virtually thousands of acres" (*V. Heiser*). **Flee** implies haste and often abruptness in the departure; as, there was evidence that the burglars had been frightened and had *fled*. It often, but not always, connotes disappearance, especially when used figuratively of things; as, the mists *fled* before the rising sun. By etymological confusion, **fly** has long been used as a variant of *flee*. However, its use is restricted in idiomatic English to the present tense where it is commonly preferred to *flee*. "*Fly*, father, *fly!* for all your friends are *fled*" (*Shak.*). **Decamp** usually suggests a sudden departure to elude discovery or arrest; it commonly carries a disparaging, sometimes a humorous, connotation. "Having imparted my situation to my companion, she found it high time for us to *decamp*" (*Smollett*). **Abscond** adds to *decamp* the distinctive implications of clandestine withdrawal and concealment to avoid the consequences of fraudulent action. "He had the appearance of a bankrupt tradesman *absconding*" (*Meredith*).

Con. *Follow, chase, pursue, trail, tag.

2 Escape, avoid, evade, elude, shun, eschew, as they are here compared, agree in meaning to get away or to keep away from that which one does not wish to incur, to suffer, to encounter, or the like. **Escape** when referred to persons (sometimes to animals) usually implies a threat to their liberty or well-being; in this sense it may or may not imply running away from, or even an effort to miss that which threatens, but it does suggest the latter's imminence or likelihood; as, to *escape* suspicion or discovery; to *escape* the family tendency to tuberculosis; to *escape* annoyance; to *escape* a blow by dodging it; few fish can *escape* this net. When referred to things, especially to inanimate or even to intangible things, *escape* is largely figurative and connotes something comparable to a net which holds and confines, yet permits passage through it; as, details which *escape* the mind; "nothing *escaped* the kind eyes" (*Deland*); "The exquisite beauty of this passage, even in translation, will *escape* no lover of poetry" (*G. L. Dickinson*). **Avoid,** in contrast with *escape*, suggests a keeping clear of that which one does not wish to risk or knows to be a source of danger, rather than a getting away from that which actually threatens; thus, one may *escape* suspicion by *avoiding* persons or places that are being watched; one may *avoid* all known sources of contagion, yet not *escape* infection. "He kept himself somewhat aloof, seeming to *avoid* notice rather than to court it" (*Arnold*). *Avoid,* however, is often used interchangeably with *escape;* it is the preferred word when a danger is averted by forethought, prudence, or caution. "Mother and son *avoided* an open rupture by never referring to their differences" (*Santayana*). "By pooling our difficulties, we may at least *avoid* the failures which come from conceiving the problems of government to be simpler than they are" (*Frankfurter*). **Evade** implies escape or the intent to escape, but it also commonly suggests avoidance by the use of adroit, ingenious, or, sometimes, underhand means; thus, one *evades* suspicion who escapes it by spreading rumors that throw others off the scent; one *evades* a question one does not wish to answer by seeming not to hear it. "The exacting life of the sea has this advantage over the life of the earth, that its claims are simple and cannot be *evaded*" (*Conrad*). "'I have a horror of the men who *evaded* service during the war'" (*R. Macaulay*). **Elude** comes closer to *escape* than to *avoid,* but stresses a slippery or baffling quality in the thing which gets away or cannot be captured. "Whose secret presence, through creation's veins running quicksilverlike, *eludes* your pains" (*FitzGerald*). "For are we not all fated to pursue ideals which seem eternally to *elude* us" (*L. P. Smith*). *Elude,* however, is sometimes used in place of *evade* when there is a strong suggestion of shiftiness or unreliability or of the use of stratagems; as, she is adept in *eluding* her obligations; in the game of hide-and-seek the players try to *elude* discovery by the one seeking their hiding places. **Shun** differs from *avoid* chiefly in its added implication of an abhorrence or aversion that is sometimes temperamental in its origin, but oftentimes rational and dictated by one's conscience, one's experience, or one's sense of prudence; as, "[lepers] *shunned* and rebuffed by the world" (*V. Heiser*); "to *shun* for his health the pleasures of the table" (*Quiller-Couch*). "Thus have I *shunn'd* the fire for fear of burning" (*Shak.*). "I used to live entirely for pleasure. I *shunned* suffering and sorrow of every kind" (*Wilde*). **Eschew,** up to the eighteenth century, was a close synonym of *avoid;* as, "What cannot be *eschew'd* must be embraced" (*Shak.*). It now admits the implication of avoidance only when the idea of keeping clear of for moral or prudential reasons (see FORGO) is stressed. "Observers...thought that capitalists would *eschew* all connection with what must necessarily be a losing concern" (*Macaulay*).

Con. *Incur, contract, catch: *bear, endure, suffer, tolerate, abide.

eschew, *v.* **1** Shun, elude, avoid, evade, *escape.

Ant. Choose. — *Con.* *Adopt, embrace, espouse: *incur, contract, catch: *take, assume.

2 Forbear, *forgo, abnegate, sacrifice.

Ana. Abstain, *refrain, forbear.

escort, *v.* Conduct, convoy, chaperon, *accompany, attend.

Ana. Protect, shield, guard, safeguard, *defend: lead, *guide, pilot, steer.

esoteric. Occult, *recondite, abstruse.

Ana. Mystic, *mystical, anagogical, cabalistic: arcane, *mysterious.

especial. *Special, specific, particular, individual, respective, concrete.

Ana. Pre-eminent, surpassing, *supreme: paramount, *dominant, predominant, preponderant, sovereign: *exceptional.

espousal. 1 Usually **espousals.** Spousal, *marriage, matrimony, nuptials, wedding, wedlock.

2 Betrothal, sponsalia, *engagement, affiance.

espouse. Embrace, *adopt.

Ana. Assume, *take: *support, uphold, advocate, champion, back.

Con. Renounce, *abjure, forswear: forsake, *abandon, desert.

espy. Descry, behold, *see, perceive, discern, notice, remark, note, observe, survey, view, contemplate.

essay, *v.* Endeavor, assay, strive, struggle, *attempt, try.

Ana. Work, labor, toil, travail (see corresponding nouns at WORK).

essay, *n.* **1** Endeavor, assay, striving, struggle, attempt, try. See under ATTEMPT, *v.*

Ana. *Effort, exertion, trouble, pains: toil, labor, *work, travail.

2 Essay, article, paper, theme, composition are here compared as denoting a relatively brief discourse written for others' reading or consideration. **Essay** is the only one of these terms which suggests a literary character or is included in classifications of literary types. As here considered, it may designate any writing that attempts to cover a subject briefly, competently, and interestingly, whether the attempt is successful or not, and whether it is intended for publication or for submission to a teacher or others for criticism. In such usage, an essay is often distinguished from a short story or an argument, and though use of the word does not debar the introduction of a narrative or argumentative method, it typically has an expository or descriptive aim. **Article,** in careful use, always carries the implication found in all senses of this word: that of membership in a whole without sacrifice of distinctness and individuality. Therefore *article* is correctly applicable only to one of the separate, but in itself complete, writings which make up a single issue of a journal or a magazine or a book, such as an encyclopedia or a history written by different persons; as, have you read the *article* on the prospects of war in today's newspaper?; a writer of *articles* for magazines; the encyclopedia's *article* at "carpet" will furnish you information concerning Oriental rugs. **Paper** is applied to a writing, chiefly an informative writing, that is intended for reading, as at a meeting of a club or a learned society, or for publication, as in a scientific or learned journal, or as a college exercise, especially in a nonliterary course; as, the most interesting *paper* on the program of the Woman's Club was one on the history of dolls. **Theme** and **composition,** as here considered, are applied to writings that are school exercises and submitted for criticism. Although they are seldom distinguished in their use, except that *theme* is more often employed in colleges and high schools, and *composition* in the lower schools, there is a real difference in the implications of the words. *Theme*, strictly, implies the development and elaboration of a definite subject; its tests are chiefly adequacy, or its completeness of treatment within limitations, and readability, or its power to interest those who read it and impress its points on their minds. *Composition*, on the other hand, implies organization of details, facts, ideas, or the like (sometimes of sentences and paragraphs), so that the result is a unified and clear piece of writing.

essential, *adj.* **1** *Inherent, intrinsic, constitutional, ingrained.

Ana. *Innate, inborn, inbred, congenital: *inner, inward: elemental (see ELEMENTARY): *characteristic, individual, peculiar, distinctive.

Ant. Accidental. — *Con.* Adventitious, fortuitous, incidental (see ACCIDENTAL): contingent, *dependent, conditional, adjective.

2 Essential, fundamental, vital, cardinal agree in meaning so important as to be indispensable. That is **essential,** in the strictest sense of the word, which belongs to the very nature or essence of a thing and which therefore cannot be removed without destroying the thing itself or its distinguishing character, efficacy, or the like; as, the *essential* doctrines of Christianity; the *essential* ingredient in a medicine; "both historically and *essentially*, the French revolutionary spirit means devotion to reason" (*Brownell*). That is **fundamental** upon which everything else in a system, institution, or the like, is built up, by which the whole is supported, or from which each addition is derived, and without which, therefore, the whole construction would topple down. "Certainly all those who have framed written constitutions contemplate them as forming the *fundamental* and paramount law of the nation" (*Ch. Just. Marshall*). "The power of concentrated attention as the *fundamental* source of the prodigious productiveness of great workers" (*C. W. Eliot*). That is **vital** which is as necessary to a thing's existence, continued vigor, efficiency, or the like, as food, drink, health, and the like, are to living things; as, a question the solution of which is *vital* to human happiness; the *vital* interests of a people; the capture of the fortified town was *vital* to the invaders. That is **cardinal** upon which something turns or hinges or actively depends; thus, the *cardinal* virtues (prudence, fortitude, temperance, justice, and sometimes, patience and humility) are not, in Christian theology, the highest virtues (which are the Christian virtues faith, hope, and charity), but they are fundamental and without them moral progress would be impossible; so, the *cardinal* arguments in a brief; the *cardinal* defects in a character. "*Cardinal* events are not to be forgotten" (*De Quincey*). "I repeat this sentence, with emphasis on its *cardinal* words" (*Karl K. Darrow*).

Ana. Basic, basal, underlying, *fundamental, substratal: principal, foremost, capital, *chief, main, leading: prime, *primary, primal.

Con. *Subordinate, secondary, dependent: *auxiliary, subsidiary, accessory, contributory, subservient.

3 Indispensable, requisite, necessary, *needful.

Ana. Required, needed, wanted (see LACK, *v.*).

Ant. Nonessential.

establish. 1 *Set, settle, fix, firm.

Ana. *Implant, infix, inculcate, instill: *secure, rivet, anchor, moor.

Ant. Uproot (*a tree, a habit, a practice, etc.*): abrogate (*a right, a privilege, a quality, etc.*). — *Con.* Eradicate, extirpate, wipe out, *exterminate.

2 *Found, institute, organize.

Ana. Start, inaugurate, *begin, commence, initiate.

Ant. Abolish (*a society, an institution, etc.*).

estate. Status, *state, condition, situation, mode, posture.

esteem, *v.* Respect, admire, regard. See under REGARD, *n.*

Ana. Prize, value, *appreciate, treasure, cherish: *revere, reverence, venerate.

Ant. Abominate. — *Con.* Abhor, loathe, *hate, detest: contemn, *despise, scorn, disdain.

esteem, *n.* Respect, admiration, *regard.

Ana. *Honor, homage, reverence, deference, obeisance: veneration, reverence, worship, adoration (see corresponding verbs at REVERE).

Ant. Abomination: contempt. — *Con.* Despite, scorn, disdain (see under DESPISE): abhorrence, loathing, hatred, hate, detestation (see under HATE, *v.*).

esthete. Variant of AESTHETE.

esthetic. Variant of AESTHETIC.

estimate, *v.* **1 Estimate, appraise** (*or* **apprize**), **evaluate, value, rate, assess, assay** are here compared only as meaning to judge a thing with respect to its worth. **Estimate,** as here considered, usually implies a personal judgment (sometimes, but far from always, a reasoned judgment) which, whether considered or casual, is by the nature of the case neither thoroughly objective nor definitive. "In *estimating* him [Byron] and ranking him we have to strike a balance between the gain which accrues to his poetry...from his superiority, and the loss which accrues to it from his defects" (*Arnold*). "To *estimate* the Frenchwoman's moral nature with any approach to adequacy it is necessary...to avoid viewing her from an Anglo-Saxon standpoint" (*Brownell*). "Mr. Brownell says that he did not care enough about his friends to discriminate between them, which was the reason he *estimated* Alcott so highly" (*A. Repplier*). **Appraise** implies the intent to fix definitely and in the capacity of an expert the monetary worth of the thing in question, such as the price it ought to bring in the market if sold, or in case of its loss by fire, theft, etc., the monetary compensation due its owner from the insuring company; as, to *appraise* the decedent's real estate; to *appraise* a fire loss. In extended use, *appraise,* in contrast to *estimate*, implies an intent to give a final, an accurate, or an expert judgment of a thing's worth; *estimate*, therefore, is often preferred by persons speaking of their own judgments because *appraise* seems presumptuous or pretentious. "It is not my business to *appraise* [Ernest Hemingway].... A writer should expound other writers or let them alone" (*F. M. Ford*). "This difficulty of *appraising* literature absolutely inheres in your study of it from the beginning" (*Quiller-Couch*). The participial adjective **appraising** is often used to

qualify *eye, glance, look,* etc.; it then suggests close, critical inspection or scrutiny; as, "addressing him with a watchful *appraising* stare of his prominent black eyes" (*Conrad*); "the monumental and encyclopaedic critic is to be regarded with a carefully *appraising* eye" (*T. S. Eliot*). **Evaluate,** like *appraise,* suggests an intent to arrive at a mathematically correct judgment; it seldom suggests, however, an attempt to determine a thing's monetary worth, but rather to find its equivalent in other and more familiar terms; as, by marks in numbers or in letters a teacher *evaluates* a student's work; many persons find it impossible to *evaluate* a work of art except in terms of morals. **Value,** as here compared (see APPRECIATE, 2), comes very close to *appraise* in that it also implies an intent to determine or fix the market price, but differs from *appraise* in that it carries no implication of an authoritative or expert judgment and must depend on the context to make that point if it is essential; thus, the appraiser *valued* at $10,000 condemned property which had already been *valued* by the owner at $15,000 and by the city at $8000; experts were called in to *value* (or *appraise*) the gems which the alleged smuggler had *valued* (not *appraised*) at $1000. In extended use and in reference to things not marketable, *value* is most often found with a negative or with a restrictive word such as *only;* as, he *values* his life not a penny; he *values* success only as a steppingstone. **Rate** often adds to *estimate* the implication of fixing in a scale of values; as, to *rate* one profession above another in usefulness; to *rate* one person's qualifications as superior to another's. "We English are capable of *rating* him far more correctly if we knew him better" (*Arnold*). **Assess** and **assay,** very specific terms literally, are rapidly coming into use in extended senses which make them synonyms of the other words in this group. *Assess* literally implies valuing for the sake of determining the tax to be levied; in extended use, it implies a determining of the exact value or extent of a thing prior to judging it, to using it as the ground for a decision, or the like. "The task of defining that influence or of exactly *assessing* its amount is one of extraordinary difficulty" (*A. Huxley*). "His [Augustus's] mind...had been working back upon the long record of his people, and striving to *assess* the many elements upon which Rome's future depended" (*Buchan*). *Assay,* which literally implies chemical analysis for the sake of determining a substance's (usually, a metal's) quality, quantity, or value, in extended use implies a critical analysis for the sake of measuring, weighing, and appraising. "To *assay* ...changes which the great reformers within and without the Catholic Church accomplished" (*J. H. Randall, jr.*).
Ana. *Judge, adjudge, adjudicate: determine, *discover, ascertain: settle, *decide, determine.
2 Reckon, *calculate, compute.
Ana. Figure, cast, sum (see ADD): *count, enumerate: *conjecture, surmise, guess.

estrange. **Estrange, alienate, disaffect, wean** agree in meaning to cause one to break a bond or tie, as of affection or loyalty. **Estrange** always implies separation or divorcement with consequent indifference or hostility; **alienate** may or may not suggest actual separation, but it does imply loss of affection or interest, withdrawal of support, or the like, and often connotes a diversion of that affection, interest, etc., to another object. "A little knowledge often *estranges* men from religion, a deeper knowledge brings them back to it" (*Inge*). "I don't want [by ritualistic innovations] to *alienate* those who are just beginning to appreciate the idea of lending greater dignity to the worship of Almighty God" (*C. Mackenzie*). *Estrange* is preferable when the indifference or hostility is mutual, *alienate* when the blame can be fixed on one person or party or on a third person or party; as, Mr. and Mrs. Brown have been *estranged* for a year, but she *alienated* him by her extravagance (or, his affections were *alienated* by another woman). **Disaffect** is more often used with reference to groups from whom loyalty is expected or demanded; it stresses the effects of alienation without separation, such as unrest, discontent, or rebellion; as, the workers were *disaffected* by paid agitators. "To *disaffect* and discontent his majesty's late army" (*Clarendon*). **Wean** implies separation from that which has a strong hold on one or on which one depends as a nursling on its mother. Unlike the other words, it often suggests merit rather than fault in the person who breaks the bond; as, to *wean* a person from a bad habit. "To *wean* your minds from hankering after false Germanic standards" (*Quiller-Couch*).
Ana. *Separate, part, divide, sunder, sever, divorce.
Ant. Reconcile. — ***Con.*** Conciliate, propitiate, appease, *pacify: unite, *join, link.

eternal. Sempiternal, *infinite, boundless, illimitable, uncircumscribed.
Ana. *Everlasting, endless, never-ending, unceasing, interminable: *lasting, perdurable, perpetual, permanent: *immortal, deathless, undying: diuturnal, aeonian, agelong, *secular.
Ant. Mortal.

ether. Atmosphere, *air, ozone.

ethereal. *Airy, aerial.
Ana. *Celestial, heavenly, empyrean: tenuous, rare, *thin.
Ant. Substantial.

ethical. *Moral, righteous, virtuous, noble.
Ant. Unethical. — ***Con.*** Iniquitous, nefarious, flagitious (see VICIOUS): unbecoming, improper, unseemly, *indecorous, indecent.

ethnic, *adj.* Pagan, heathen, Gentile, paynim. See under PAGAN, *n.*

ethnic, *n.* *Pagan, heathen, Gentile, paynim.

ethnology. *Anthropology, archaeology.

etiolate, *v.* Decolorize, blanch, bleach, *whiten.

etiquette. Propriety, *decorum, decency, dignity.
Ana. Manner, deportment, demeanor, mien, *bearing.

eulogize. Extol, acclaim, laud, *praise.
Ana. *Exalt, magnify, aggrandize: *commend, applaud, compliment.
Ant. Calumniate, vilify. — ***Con.*** *Malign, traduce, asperse, defame, slander, libel.

eulogy. *Encomium, panegyric, tribute, citation.
Ana. *Compliment, flattery, adulation: lauding *or* laudation, extolling *or* extollation, praising *or* praise (see corresponding verbs at PRAISE).
Ant. Calumny: tirade. — ***Con.*** *Abuse, invective, obloquy.

euphuistic. Flowery, aureate, grandiloquent, *rhetorical, magniloquent, bombastic.

evade. Elude, avoid, *escape, shun, eschew.
Ana. Flee, fly, *escape: thwart, foil, circumvent, outwit (see FRUSTRATE).

evaluate. Appraise, value, rate, assess, assay, *estimate.
Ana. *Judge, adjudge: *criticize.

evanescent. Ephemeral, passing, fugitive, fleeting, *transient, transitory, momentary, short-lived.

evangelist. **1** Apostle, *disciple.
2 Revivalist, *missionary, apostle.

even, *adj.* **1** Smooth, *level, flat, plane, plain, flush.
Ant. Uneven. — ***Con.*** Curving, turning, bending, twisting (see CURVE, *v.*): waving *or* wavy, undulating *or* undulatory, rippling (see corresponding verbs at WAVE): *crooked, devious: rugged, *rough, scabrous, harsh.

2 Uniform, equable, *steady, constant.
Ana. *Same, equal, identical: continuous, constant, incessant, *continual.
Con. *Irregular: varying, changing (see CHANGE, *v.*): fluctuating, wavering, undulating (see SWING, *v.*).

event. 1 Incident, *occurrence, episode, circumstance.
Ana. *Action, act, deed: exploit, *feat, achievement: *chance, accident, fortune: happening, befalling, transpiring (see HAPPEN).
2 *Effect, consequence, result, aftereffect, aftermath, issue, outcome, upshot, sequel.

eventual. Ultimate, concluding, terminal, final, *last, latest, extreme.
Ana. Ensuing, succeeding (see FOLLOW): terminating, closing, ending (see CLOSE, *v.*).

ever. *Forever, always, aye, evermore, forevermore.
Ant. Never.

everlasting, *adj.* **Everlasting, endless, interminable, unceasing, never-ending** are here compared as meaning continuing on and on without end. Unlike *infinite, eternal,* and similar words (see INFINITE), these terms do not presuppose the absence of a beginning and therefore usually have reference only to continued extent or duration. However, **everlasting** is often used interchangeably with *eternal,* differing from it only in placing more stress on the fact of enduring throughout time than on the quality of being independent of time or of all similar human limitations; as, "The *eternal* God is thy refuge, and underneath are the *everlasting* arms" (*Deuteronomy* xxxiii. 27); "And these shall go away into *everlasting* punishment: but the righteous into life *eternal*" (*Matthew* xxv. 46). Therefore, in serious use, *everlasting,* rather than *eternal,* is applied to material things or earthly conditions which endure, or seem to endure, forever; as, "See Cromwell damn'd to *everlasting* fame" (*Pope*); *everlasting* flowers; "These mighty gates of *everlasting* rock" (*De Quincey*). In lighter use, the term is little more than a hyperbolical term expressing loss of patience or extreme boredom; as, these *everlasting* headaches; his *everlasting* stupidity. **Endless** is applicable not only to things which continue in time but also in extent: the word is used literally (as implying no end) chiefly when a circular form or construction is implied (as, an *endless* belt): usually it implies no known or apparent or determinable end; as, an *endless* chain of letters; an *endless* road through the mountains; "There has been *endless* discussion whether we have a distinct faculty for the knowledge of God" (*Inge*); "*endless* masses of hills on three sides, *endless* weald or valley on the fourth" (*Jefferies*). **Interminable,** like *endless,* is rarely used in its literal sense of incapable of being brought to an end or termination: rather it applies to something so prolonged or protracted that it is exceedingly wearisome or exhausts one's patience; as, "the weeks were *interminable* and papa and mamma were clean forgotten" (*Kipling*); "the [fiddler's] air was now that one...which...best conveys the idea of the *interminable*—the celebrated 'Devil's Dream'" (*Hardy*). **Unceasing** and **never-ending,** like *interminable,* suggest undue prolonging or protracting, but they emphasize the extraordinary capacity for going on and on rather than the psychological effect produced (usually on others) by long-continuing activity or continual recurrence; as, *unceasing* effort; *never-ending* pursuit of an ideal; a *never-ending* hate; "Jules de Goncourt...died from the mental exhaustion of his *unceasing* struggle to attain an objective style adequate to express the subtle texture of the world as he saw it" (*H. Ellis*).
Ana. Eternal, boundless, *infinite: *lasting, perdurable, perpetual: *immortal, deathless, undying, amaranthine.
Ant. Transitory. — *Con.* *Transient, passing, fleeting, fugitive, ephemeral, evanescent, momentary, short-lived.

evermore. Always, aye, forevermore, *forever, ever.

every. Each, *all.

evict. *Eject, oust, expel, dismiss.
Ana. *Exclude, eliminate, shut out: reject, repudiate, spurn (see DECLINE): *dismiss, fire, cashier, discharge.

evidence, *n.* **Evidence, testimony, deposition, affidavit** are, in their legal senses, closely related but not synonymous terms. The last three designate forms of **evidence,** or material submitted to a competent legal tribunal as a means of ascertaining where the truth lies in a question of fact. *Evidence* also implies the intention of the side offering the material to use it as a basis for inference and argument and, therefore, as a medium of proof. **Testimony** is the evidence offered by persons who are alleged to be in a position to know the facts, such as eyewitnesses or experts. It always implies declaration under oath or affirmation, usually on the stand in open court. Testimony does not necessarily constitute evidence for the side that calls the witness, for that depends upon various things, such as inferences that may be drawn from it favorable to the opposition or the effect that cross-examination has upon it. **Deposition,** though still occasionally used interchangeably with *testimony,* is more properly used in a restricted sense to designate a form of testimony given orally in response to questioning by competent officers (usually in advance of court proceedings), taken down in writing, and sworn to or properly affirmed. **Affidavit** covers any written declaration made upon solemn oath before a recognized magistrate or officer. An affidavit may or may not be used as testimony, but when so used, it is as a rule because a witness cannot take the stand. An affidavit submitted as testimony is properly (but not invariably) distinguished from a deposition. When used specifically and in contrast with *deposition, affidavit* always implies that the declaration has been obtained by one side to the dispute and that there has been no cross-examination.

evidence, *v.* Evince, manifest, demonstrate, *show.
Ana. *Reveal, disclose, betray, divulge: display, exhibit, expose, *show: prove, *indicate, betoken, attest, bespeak.

evident. **Evident, manifest, patent, distinct, obvious, apparent, palpable, plain, clear** come into comparison when they mean readily perceived or apprehended. **Evident** implies the existence of visible signs, all of which point to the one conclusion; it may be applied to something which is beyond the range of the senses, such as another person's state of mind, a hidden condition, or an imminent event, but which can be inferred from the outward indications; as, her *evident* delight in the gift; it is *evident* that he has reached the end of his resources; the *evident* breakdown of the negotiations for peace. **Manifest** implies an outward revelation or expression or an open exhibition; it is applied as a rule to something which is displayed so clearly that its recognition seemingly involves no inference. "His joy in the prospect of departure from the Five Towns, from her... was more *manifest* than she could bear" (*Bennett*). "Where the work of such a master [as Milton] is at its best, the greatness of his spirit is most greatly *manifest*" (*L. P. Smith*). **Patent,** as here compared, implies an opposition to that which is imperceptible or obscure but existent; it therefore is applied to things which are not invariably or as a class evident or manifest, such as a cause, an effect, a mistake, an imperfection, etc.; as, the seller is required by law to disclose to the buyer latent as well as *patent* defects in the article sold. "A man is... in jeopardy even when the error is *patent* on the face of the record, as when he is tried on a defective indictment" (*Justice Holmes*). "Three very *patent* reasons for the comparatively slow advance of our children" (*Grandgent*). **Distinct** (as here compared: see also DISTINCT) implies such sharpness of outline or of definition that the thing requires no effort of the eyes to see or discern (as, *distinct* features; his handwriting is unusually *distinct*), or of the ears to hear or interpret (as, *distinct* utterance; *distinct* enunciation), or of the mind to apprehend or comprehend without confusion (as, the course of his reasoning is not only *evident*, it is *distinct;* he gave a *distinct* account of everything that occurred). **Obvious** stresses ease in discovery (sometimes, ease in accounting for) and often connotes conspicuousness in that which is discovered, or little need of perspicacity in the discoverer: it is therefore often applied to something not successfully concealed, or something crudely manifest. "*Obvious* heirs he had none, any more than he had *obvious* progenitors" (*V. Sackville-West*). "Nonsense, Percy. It is perfectly *obvious.* He used to be attracted by Clare, and now he is attracted by Jane" (*R. Macaulay*). "The avidity with which he surrendered himself to her perfectly *obvious* methods" (*M. Austin*). "Acting on the conviction of Mr. Justice Holmes that 'at this time we need education in the *obvious* more than investigation of the obscure'" (*Frankfurter*). **Apparent,** as here compared (see APPARENT, 2), is often so close to *evident* in meaning that the two words are difficult to distinguish. But *evident* usually implies inference directly from visible signs or effects, and *apparent* from evidence plus more or less elaborate reasoning: therefore *apparent* in precise use is applied to that which is apprehended through an induction, a deduction, or a similar course of reasoning; as, the absurdity of their contention is *apparent* (better than *evident*) to one who knows the effects produced by the same causes in the past. "As experience accumulated it gradually became *apparent* that the oils of any of the trees of the [same] family...were equally efficacious" (*V. Heiser*). "'The true science of metaphysics,' he [Joubert] says, 'consists...in rendering sensible that which is abstract; *apparent* that which is hidden'" (*Arnold*). **Palpable** (see also PERCEPTIBLE) implies perceptibility through another sense than that of sight; it therefore is applied to something that is felt, or heard, or smelled, or realized through some other avenue of knowledge such as a sixth sense. "'Tis probable that thou hast never lived, And *palpable* that thou hast never loved" (*R. Garnett*). "We hate poetry that has a *palpable* design upon us" (*Keats*). **Plain** and **clear** are less literary and more colloquial terms than the others here discriminated. They are both applied to something that is immediately apprehended or unmistakably understood, *plain* implying familiarity or distinctness or a lack of intricacy or complexity, and *clear* an absence of that which confuses or muddles the mind or which obscures the issues; as, "a *plain* answer to a direct question" (*S. M. Crothers*). "I was treated with...deference, and ...*plainly* regarded as a possible purchaser" (*L. P. Smith*). "Yes, that makes much which was dark quite *clear* to me" (*Galsworthy*). "Proof as sharp and *clear* as anything which is known" (*Karl K. Darrow*).

Ana. *Perceptible, sensible, palpable, tangible, appreciable, ponderable: conspicuous, prominent, *noticeable.

evil, *adj.* *Bad, ill, wicked, naughty.

Ana. *Base, low, vile: iniquitous, nefarious, flagitious, *vicious, villainous, infamous: *pernicious, baneful: *execrable, damnable.

Ant. Exemplary: salutary.

evil, *n.* **Evil, ill, bale** come into comparison when they mean whatever is harmful or disastrous to morals or well-being. **Evil** is the ordinary term capable of use in any context and referable not only to deeds and practices actually indulged in or to conditions actually suffered (as, to lead a life of *evil;* prostitution is known as the social *evil;* the *evils* of war; to correct the *evils* in a system of government) but also to motivating desires or actuating causes of such deeds, practices, or conditions (as, think no *evil; evil* [the deed or condition] comes of *evil* [the cause]; to shun *evil* [temptations, or places of temptation]), and to their harmful effects or consequences (as, "The *evil* that men do lives after them"—*Shak.;* "*Evils* which our own misdeeds have wrought"—*Milton*). *Evil* is also the term in general use for the abstract conception of whatever is the reverse of good, especially of the morally good, or as a designation of anything that is thought of as the reverse of a blessing; as, to be able to distinguish good from *evil;* the origin of *evil;* St. Francis of Assisi accounted poverty a blessing rather than an *evil.* "*Evil* no nature hath; the loss of good Is that which gives to sin a livelihood" (*Herrick*). "*Evil* is not a quality of things as such. It is a quality of our relation to them" (*Lippmann*). Although **ill,** like *evil,* may imply an antithesis to *good,* it is seldom used to designate the abstraction except in a poetic context and in direct contrast to *good.* "O, yet we trust that somehow good Will be the final goal of *ill*" (*Tennyson*). Also, it is now rare in the sense of moral evil, although it occurred frequently in that sense up to the eighteenth century. "To do aught good never will be our task, But ever to do *ill* our sole delight As being the contrary to His high will Whom we resist" (*Milton*). In present use, as in the past, *ill* is applied chiefly to whatever is distressing, painful, injurious, and the like, and is more often used in reference to what is actually suffered or endured than to what may be inflicted or imposed on one. "And makes us rather bear those *ills* we have Than fly to others that we know not of?" (*Shak.*). "They could never in such a Utopian State feel any other *ills* than those which arise from bodily sickness" (*Hume*). "There mark what *ills* the scholar's life assail,— Toil, envy, want, the patron, and the jail" (*Johnson*). "Servitude, the worst of *ills*" (*Cowper*). **Bale,** a poetic word even in the late Middle Ages and in the Renaissance, was rare until toward the end of the eighteenth century when it was revived by romantic poets. It usually implies an opposition to *bliss* and carries less explicit but more doleful connotations than either *evil* or *ill,* such as of woe, pain, misery, and desolation; as, "Bring us *bale* and bitter sorrowings" (*Spenser*); "tidings of *bale* she brought" (*Bryant*).

Ant. Good.

evince. Manifest, evidence, demonstrate, *show.

Ana. Betoken, *indicate, attest, prove, argue, bespeak: display, exhibit, expose, *show: disclose, *reveal, discover, betray.

Con. *Suppress, repress: *hide, conceal.

evoke. Elicit, *educe, extract, extort.

Ana. *Provoke, excite, stimulate: arouse, rouse, rally, awaken, waken, *stir.

evolution. *Development.

exact, *adj.* Accurate, *correct, right, precise, nice.

Ana. *Careful, meticulous, scrupulous, punctilious: agreeing, squaring, tallying, jibing, conforming (see AGREE).

exact, *v.* Require, *demand, claim.

Ana. *Ask, request, solicit: compel, *force, constrain, coerce, oblige.

exacting, *adj.* *Onerous, burdensome, oppressive.

Ana. *Severe, stern: *rigid, rigorous, strict, stringent: arduous, difficult, *hard.

Ant. Easy: lenient.

exalt. **Exalt, magnify, aggrandize** are here compared chiefly as used in modern English and as meaning to increase in importance or in prestige. *Exalt* and *magnify* also come into comparison in their now archaic sense of to extol or to glorify. "O *magnify* the Lord with me, and let us *exalt* his name together" (*Psalms* xxxiv. 3). In present use, **exalt** retains its etymological implication of lifting up but, as here narrowly considered, emphasizes a raising in a scale of values without necessarily affecting the quality of the thing raised. Therefore, one *exalts* something above another or at the expense of another. "Rousseau's readiness to *exalt* spontaneity even at the expense of rationality" (*Babbitt*). "There is a valid reason for not preventing games, but...not...for *exalting* them into a leading position in the school curriculum" (*B. Russell*). **Magnify** stresses increase in size; it now commonly suggests an agency (such as an optical device) which affects the vision and causes enlargement of actual or apparent size, or one (such as a vivid imagination) which affects the judgment and leads to exaggeration. "Kind, quiet, near-sighted eyes, which his round spectacles *magnified* into lambent moons" (*Deland*). "The public opinion which...*magnifies* patriotism into a religion" (*Brownell*). **Aggrandize** emphasizes increase in greatness or mightiness; it implies efforts, usually selfish efforts, directed to the attainment of power, authority, or worldly eminence. "If we *aggrandize* ourselves at the expense of the Mahrattas" (*Wellington*). "Have we a satisfaction in *aggrandizing* our families...?" (*Fielding*).
Ana. Elevate, raise, *lift: heighten, enhance, *intensify: extol, laud, *praise.
Ant. Abase. — *Con.* Demean, debase, degrade, humble, humiliate (see ABASE): disparage, depreciate, detract from, derogate from, *decry, belittle, minimize.

examination. Inspection, scrutiny, scanning, audit. See under SCRUTINIZE, *v.*
Ana. Questioning, interrogation, inquiry, catechism, quizzing *or* quiz (see corresponding verbs at ASK).

examine. 1 Inspect, *scrutinize, scan, audit.
Ana. *Analyze, dissect, anatomize, resolve: contemplate, observe, survey, view, notice, note (see SEE).
2 Question, interrogate, quiz, catechize, *ask, query, inquire, speer.
Ana. Penetrate, probe (see ENTER): test, try (see PROVE).

example. 1 Sample, specimen, *instance, case, illustration.
Con. Anomaly, *paradox.
2 *Model, exemplar, pattern, paradigm, ideal, beau ideal, standard, mirror.
Ana. Archetype, *prototype: *paragon, sublimation, apotheosis.
Con. Precept, rule, *law.

exasperate. Provoke, nettle, *irritate, aggravate, roil, peeve.
Ana. Vex, *annoy, irk, bother: *anger, incense, enrage, madden, infuriate.
Ant. Mollify. — *Con.* *Pacify, placate, appease, propitiate, conciliate.

excavate. *Dig, delve, exhume, disinter, spade, grub.

exceed. **Exceed, surpass, transcend, excel, outdo, outstrip** agree in meaning to go or to be beyond a stated or implied limit, measure, or degree. **Exceed** may imply an overpassing of a limit set by one's right, power, authority, jurisdiction, or the like (as, this task *exceeds* his ability; he has *exceeded* his authority in allowing such use of our land), or by prescription, as in time, space, or the like (as, they were penalized if they *exceeded* the allotted time by even one day). The term may also imply superiority in size, amount, degree, number, or the like, according to a given standard or measure; as, "My wrath shall far *exceed* the love I ever bore" (*Shak.*); "Though the pleasures of London *exceed* In number the days of the year" (*Cowper*). **Surpass** is often used in place of *exceed*, especially when superiority to a given standard or measure is implied; as, the reality *surpassed* (or *exceeded*) our expectations. When the intent is to imply superiority in quality, as in virtue, in merit, or in skill, rather than in quantity or extent, *surpass* is to be preferred to *exceed;* as, the poem is not *surpassed* in English literature for sheer beauty of sound; he *surpasses* all others in keenness of mind. **Transcend** carries so strong an implication of rising across or above a limit or measure that, although it is sometimes used in place of *exceed* (as, "its limits [the powers of the government] are not to be *transcended*"—*Ch. Just. Marshall*) and often in place of *surpass* (as, "this sorrow *transcending* all sorrows"—*Hudson*), it is the precise term to use when a higher than human or earthly limit, standard, or measure is implied; as, "A point of view *transcending* the purely human outlook on the universe" (*Binyon*); "In the rather sloppy Socialism which pervades this document there is nothing which seems to *transcend* the limits of unaided human intelligence" (*Inge*). **Excel** definitely implies pre-eminence in accomplishment, achievement, attainment, or the like; if no standard of comparison is indicated, that is, when the verb is used intransitively, it suggests superiority to all (as, he *excelled* in the painting of miniatures); if one is indicated, it differs little from *surpass* or *transcend* (as, "Love divine, all love *excelling*"—*C. Wesley;* he *excelled* his friends in archery). "During their seminary years he had easily *surpassed* his friend in scholarship, but he always realized that Joseph *excelled* him in the fervor of his faith" (*Cather*). **Outdo** is a more colloquial term than *excel* or *surpass*, but it is often preferred when there is the intent to connote the breaking of a previously established record; as, "He hath in this action *outdone* his former deeds doubly" (*Shak.*); "The waves beside them danced; but they [the daffodils] *Outdid* the sparkling waves in glee" (*Wordsworth*). **Outstrip** is often preferred to *excel* or *surpass* when one wishes to suggest a race, a competition, or a similar strenuous effort to get ahead; as, he would not allow anyone to *outstrip* him in zeal; to *outstrip* another candidate in the power to win votes.

excel. Surpass, transcend, *exceed, outdo, outstrip.

excellence. **Excellence, merit, virtue, perfection** are here compared as meaning a quality or feature of a person or thing that gives him or it especial worth or value. **Excellence** applies to any quality or feature in which the person or thing excels or surpasses all others: since the term carries no implication that he or it is without fault, defect, or blemish, it is often qualified by a word such as *particular, specific, distinctive*, or the like; as, the particular *excellence* of this cake is its lightness and of that cake its richness; "The great *excellence* of the eastern tableland was...in pasture and in forest" (*Dean Stanley*); "The artisan, for example, ranks...lower than the professional man; but no one maintains that he is...incapable by nature...of the characteristic *excellence* of man" (*G. L. Dickinson*). **Merit** (as here considered: see also DUE) may be used interchangeably with *excellence*, but it typically carries no suggestion of a surpassing quality: rather, it applies to a quality or feature that has evident worth or value or is highly commendable. It is used chiefly in critical estimates in which good points (*merits*) are displayed against bad points (*defects* or *faults*); as, "Mr. Wright's version of the Iliad, repeating in the main the *merits* and defects of Cowper's version" (*Arnold*); "Seneca had as much to do with its [the early Elizabethan drama's] *merits* and its progress as with its faults and its delays" (*T. S. Eliot*); "The faculty of discerning and using conspicuous *merit* in other people distinguishes the most successful administrators, rulers, and men of business" (*C. W. Eliot*). **Virtue,** because of the long association of the term with moral goodness (for this sense see GOODNESS) is, in current use, chiefly applied to a moral excellence or a conspicuous merit of character; as, "[They] have no vices...one is inclined to ask whether, when the right path is so easy to them, they really have any *virtues*" (*H. Ellis*); "reverence for age and authority, even for law, has disappeared; and in the train of these have gone the *virtues* they engendered and nurtured" (*G. L. Dickinson*). But the term still often applies to the quality, feature, or the like, that is the source of a person's or thing's peculiar or distinctive strength, power, or efficacy; as, the special *virtue* of a newly discovered remedy for pneumonia; "that unsparing impartiality which is his [Hallam's] most distinguishing *virtue*" (*Macaulay*); "An aristocracy, if it is to survive, needs certain *virtues;* these were to be imparted at school" (*B. Russell*). **Perfection,** in the sense here considered as well as in its abstract sense of faultlessness ("Faultily faultless, icily regular, splendidly null, Dead *perfection*, no more"—*Tennyson*) suggests an attainment of the ideal. It, therefore, is usually found in less restrained writing or speech than the other terms when it applies to an excellence in the highest degree; as, "But eyes, and ears, and ev'ry thought, Were with his sweet *perfections* caught" (*Spenser*); "What tongue can her *perfections* tell?" (*Sidney*).

Ana. Value, *worth: property, *quality, character.

Ant. Fault. — ***Con.*** *Blemish, defect, flaw: failing, frailty, foible, vice (see FAULT).

exceptionable. *Exceptional.

Ana. *Offensive, repugnant, loathsome, repulsive, revolting: repellent, distasteful, obnoxious, invidious, *repugnant.

Ant. Unexceptionable: exemplary. — ***Con.*** Pleasing, agreeable, gratifying, *pleasant, grateful, welcome.

exceptional. **Exceptional, exceptionable,** although not synonyms, are liable to confusion. That is **exceptional** which is itself an exception, and so is out of the ordinary, being either extraordinary or unusual; as, this is an *exceptional* opportunity; "the bath was habitual in the twelfth century and *exceptional* at the Renaissance" (*H. Adams*). That is **exceptionable** (cf. the commoner *unexceptionable*) to which exception may be taken (that is, to which an objection may be made), and which is therefore displeasing or offensive to others; as, *exceptionable* conduct; there was nothing *exceptionable* in his comment.

Ana. Outstanding, remarkable, *noticeable, conspicuous, prominent, salient, signal: rare, *infrequent, uncommon, scarce: singular, unique, *strange: anomalous, *irregular.

Ant. Common (sense 3): average. — ***Con.*** Ordinary, familiar, popular, vulgar (see COMMON).

excerpt, *n.* *Extract, pericope.

excess, *n.* **Excess, superfluity, surplus, surplusage, overplus** agree in denoting that which goes beyond a limit or bound. **Excess** applies to that which exceeds any limit, measure, bound, or the like (as, "In measure rein thy joy; scant this *excess*"—*Shak.;* "the proper point between sufficiency and *excess*"—*H. James;* "I think poetry should surprise by a fine *excess*"—*Keats*); often it specifically implies intemperance, immoderation, or the like (as, "early *excesses* the frame will recover from"—*Meredith;* "restrain the *excesses* of the possessive instinct"—*H. Ellis*). **Superfluity** applies to an excess of money, clothes, possessions, or the like, that is above or beyond what is needed or desired; as, "the inventory of thy shirts, as, one for *superfluity*, and another for use!" (*Shak.*); "Her *superfluity* the poor supplies" (*Cowper*); "I succumb easily to anyone who asks me to buy *superfluities* and luxuries" (*A. Huxley*). **Surplus** applies to the amount or quantity of something that remains when all that has been needed has been used, spent, sold, or the like, or when all debts have been paid; as, his salary was so small that there was no *surplus* for investment; the problem is how to dispose of the large *surplus* in this year's cotton crop; the company divided its *surplus* (that is, the amount of income in excess of fixed charges and dividends) among its shareholders and employees. **Surplusage** may be used in place of *surplus*, but good writers and speakers employ the term when they wish to imply wasteful or useless excess; as, "the subsequent part of the section is mere *surplusage*, is entirely without meaning, if such is to be the construction" (*Ch. Just. Marshall*); "Say what you have to say...with no *surplusage*" (*Pater*). **Overplus** is often used in place of *surplus*, but it less often implies a remainder than an addition to what is needed; as, "the *overplus* of a great fortune" (*Addison*); there was no *overplus* in the proceeds this year.

Ana. Lavishness, prodigality, profuseness *or* profusion, luxuriance, exuberance (see corresponding adjectives at PROFUSE): inordinateness, immoderation, extravagance (see corresponding adjectives at EXCESSIVE).

Ant. Deficiency: dearth, paucity. — ***Con.*** Meagerness, scantiness, scantness, exiguousness (see corresponding adjectives at MEAGER).

excessive. **Excessive, immoderate, inordinate, extravagant, exorbitant, extreme** come into comparison as meaning characterized by going beyond or above its proper, just, or right limit. **Excessive** implies an amount, quantity, extent, or the like, too great to be just, reasonable, endurable, or the like; as, to attach an *excessive* importance to attendance at every lecture of a course; the *excessive* heat of a midsummer afternoon; "*Excessive* lenity and indulgence are ultimately *excessive* rigor" (*Knox*). **Immoderate** is often used interchangeably with *excessive* (as, *immoderate* heat), but in precise use, it distinctively implies lack of restraint, especially in the feelings or their expression; as, *immoderate* zeal; *immoderate* laughter. **Inordinate** (etymologically, disordered) implies an exceeding of the bounds or limits prescribed by authority or dictated by good judgment; as, "The great difficulty of living content is the cherishing of *inordinate* and unreasonable expectations" (*T. E. Brown*); "I am always staggered...by the *inordinate* snobbery of the English press" (*A. Huxley*); "the parent ....will be *inordinately* pleased by the child's cleverness and exasperated by his stupidity" (*B. Russell*). **Extravagant** (etymologically, wandering outside the bounds) often adds to *excessive* or *immoderate* the implications of wildness, lawlessness, or indifference to restraints such as of truth, decency, prudence, or the like; as, *extravagant* praise; "[he] went off in a second *extravagant* roar of laughter" (*Hudson*). "Could it be the intention of those who gave this power, to say that....a case arising under the constitution should be decided without examining the instrument under which it arises? This is too *extravagant* to be maintained" (*Ch. Just. Marshall*). The term often specifically implies prodigality in expenditure; as, "She was rapacious of money, *extravagant* to excess" (*Fielding*). **Exorbitant** (etymologically, going out of the track, or usual course) implies excessiveness marked by a departure from that which is the customary or established amount or degree; it often but not always connotes extortion or excessive demands on the part of the agent, or the infliction of hardships on the person affected; as, "The legislature...imposed an *exorbitant* security for their appearance" (*Gibbon*); "a resolution to contract none of the *exorbitant* desires by which others are enslaved" (*Spectator*); "The men who worked in the brick-kilns lived in this settlement, and paid an *exorbitant* rent to the Judge" (*Deland*). **Extreme,** as here compared (see also LAST, *adj.*), implies an excessiveness or extravagance that seems to reach the end of that which is possible; it is often hyperbolical in actual use; as, the result gave him *extreme* satisfaction; "the *extreme* oddness of existence is what reconciles me to it" (*L. P. Smith*); "The most *extreme*...statement of such an attitude would be: nothing is poetry which can be formulated in prose" (*Day Lewis*).

Ana. *Superfluous, surplus, supernumerary, extra, spare: *intense, vehement: redundant (see WORDY).

Ant. Deficient. — ***Con.*** *Meager, scanty, scant, skimpy, exiguous, sparse.

exchange, *v.* **Exchange, interchange, bandy, swap** agree in meaning to give a thing to another in return for another thing from him. **Exchange** may imply a disposing of one thing for another, by or as by the methods of bartering or trading (see SELL); as, to *exchange* horses; the hostile forces *exchanged* prisoners of war; to *exchange* one's farm products for manufactured goods. Sometimes the term specifically implies a substitution, such as a change of a first purchase for something else (as, wedding presents are often *exchanged* by the bride at the store where the givers purchased them; to *exchange* a palace for a cell), or an alternation of things by two, sometimes more, persons (as, to *exchange* letters; to *exchange* a few words with each other). **Interchange** is rarely used in place of *exchange* except when alternation, as in reciprocal giving and receiving, is implied, often with the connotation of a continuous succession; as, the townspeople and the summer residents *interchanged* courtesies with each other; "There were repeated cheerings and salutations *interchanged* between the shore and the ship" (*Irving*). **Bandy,** from its earliest sense in English, implies a tossing or beating to and fro as, or in the same manner as, a tennis ball. Hence, the term is often used in place of *interchange* when vigorous, rapid, and more or less prolonged action is implied; as, "to *bandy* hasty words" (*Shak.*); to *bandy* compliments. Often, however, *bandy* implies heated or active discussion or a passing of information from one to another; as, "Your name is... frequently *bandied* at table among us" (*Irving*); "The stories they invent...and *bandy* from mouth to mouth!" (*Dickens*). **Swap** (a colloquial term used in both Great Britain and America) commonly implies the exchange of one thing for another of the same species, and is therefore usually followed by a plural object; as, to *swap* horses; to *swap* knives; to *swap* stories.

Ana. Barter, trade (see SELL).

excise, *n.* Impost, *tax, levy, assessment, rate, customs, duty, toll, tariff, tribute, tithe, teind, cess.

excite. *Provoke, stimulate, pique, quicken, galvanize.

Ana. *Stir, rouse, arouse, rally, waken, awaken: agitate, disturb, perturb, *discompose, disquiet: animate, inspire, fire (see INFORM).

Ant. Soothe, quiet (*persons*): allay (*fears, anxiety, etc.*).

exclude. Exclude, debar, blackball, eliminate, rule out, shut out, disbar, suspend agree in meaning to prevent someone or something from forming part of something else as a member, a constituent, a factor, or the like. **Exclude** (etymologically, to shut out) implies in strict use a keeping out of what is already outside; it therefore suggests a prevention of entrance or admission; as, to *exclude* light from a room by closing the shutters; to *exclude* a subject from consideration; to *exclude* a class from certain privileges. **Debar** implies the existence of a barrier (literal or figurative) which is effectual in excluding someone or something on the outside from entering into a group, body, or system, from enjoying certain privileges, powers, or prerogatives, or from doing what those not so restrained do naturally or easily; as, a high wall *debarred* boys from entering; poor health *debars* him from society. "The qualifications demanded...would be likely to *debar* 99 per cent of the secondary school instructors in America" (*Grandgent*). "The Japanese designer was *debarred* by instinct and tradition from using the resources of texture and of light and shade" (*Binyon*). **Blackball** strictly implies exclusion from a club or society by vote of its members (originally by putting a black ball into a ballot box). "He was very nearly *black-balled* at a West End club of which his birth and social position fully entitled him to become a member" (*Wilde*). The term has some extended use, but it usually implies a deliberate (though not necessarily a voted) decision to exclude a person from one's coterie, clique, set, or the like. **Eliminate** differs from the preceding words in implying a getting rid of, or a removal of what is already in, especially as a constituent element or part; as, to *eliminate* a quantity from an equation, a subject from a curriculum; to *eliminate* a poison from the system. "It is always wise to *eliminate* the personal equation from our judgments of literature" (*J. R. Lowell*). "In most poets there is an intermittent conflict between the poetic self and the rest of the man; and it is by reconciling the two, not by *eliminating* the one, that they can reach their full stature" (*Day Lewis*). **Rule out** may imply either exclusion or elimination, but it usually suggests a formal or authoritative decision; as, to *rule* a horse *out* of a race; to *rule out* certain candidates for a position. **Shut out** may imply exclusion of something by preventing its entrance or admission (as, close the windows to *shut out* the rain) or, in sports use, to prevent from scoring (as, the home team was *shut out* in the second game). **Disbar** (often confused with *debar*) implies the elimination by a legal process of a lawyer (attorney, counselor, or barrister) from the group of those already admitted to practice, thereby depriving him for cause of his status and privileges. **Suspend** implies the elimination of a person who is a member of a staff, a body, or other organization, or a student at a school or college, often for a definite, sometimes for an indefinite, period of time and, usually, because of some offense or serious infraction of the rules: the term seldom, if ever, implies that the case is closed or that readmission is impossible; as, to *suspend* ten members of a club for nonpayment of dues. "There was but one course: to *suspend* the man from the exercise of all priestly functions" (*Cather*).

Ana. *Hinder, bar, block: preclude, obviate, ward off, *prevent: *banish, exile, ostracize, deport.

Ant. Admit (*persons*): include (*things*). — ***Con.*** Comprehend, embrace, involve (see INCLUDE).

exclusive. *Select, elect, picked.

Ana. Excluding, eliminating, debarring, shutting out, ruling out (see EXCLUDE): *narrow, strait: aristocratic, patrician (see corresponding nouns at GENTLEMAN): *gentle, genteel.

Ant. Inclusive. — ***Con.*** Catholic, cosmopolitan, *universal: *common, ordinary, familiar, popular, vulgar.

excogitate. Revolve, weigh, *consider, study, contemplate.

Ana. *Ponder, meditate, ruminate, muse: cogitate, reflect, deliberate, speculate, *think.

excommunication. Excommunication, anathema, interdict are here compared only in their technical ecclesiastical meanings, especially in historic Christian use, and as denoting a punishment for one's offense or offenses by suspension of the privileges of membership in the Church. **Excommunication** always implies ejection from the Church as a communicant (but not always as a worshiper) and denial of the sacraments for as long as one is unrepentant and refuses to make atonement. It does not, except when qualified by *major* (*major excommunication*), imply public censure or ceremonial expulsion. **Anathema,** as a term implying ecclesiastical censure or an ecclesiastical ban, antedates Christianity. "Neither shalt thou bring any thing of the idol into thy house, lest thou become an *anathema* [*Authorized Version*, 'a cursed thing'] like it" (*Douay Version, Deuteronomy* vii. 26). These connotations of a ban and the curse of God were carried over into Christian use and the word, when it came to mean a kind of excommunication, was eventually applied to the severest form of major excommunication, one involving a solemn promulgation of the expulsion by the pope, a denunciation of the offender as a thing accursed, and his condemnation to Hell unless repentant. **Interdict** does not imply excommunication or loss of church membership; it is a form of censure or of punishment whereby a group, as a state, a community, or a diocese, or, sometimes, a person, suffers the deprivation of divine worship, of the Sacraments, or of the right to Christian burial, etc., through papal or episcopal prohibition of them for a stated or indefinite term.

Ana. Ejection, expelling *or* expulsion, ousting, dismissal (see corresponding verbs at EJECT).

excoriate. *Abrade, chafe, fret, gall.

Ana. *Injure, hurt, damage, mar, impair: flay, *skin, peel: *abuse, maltreat, outrage: tonguelash, berate, upbraid, revile, *scold: *execrate, objurgate, curse, damn.

excruciating. Excruciating, agonizing, racking agree in meaning intensely and, usually, unbearably painful. All are commonly used as strong intensives and applied to pain, suffering, torture, and the like. When used to qualify other things, they mean causing intense pain or suffering. **Excruciating** carries strong suggestions of acute physical torture or of exquisitely painful sensation; as, the *excruciating* pains of cancer; *excruciating* engines of torture; *excruciating* noises. **Agonizing** stresses anguish of mind even when it strongly implies physical suffering. "An *agonising* spasm of pain—a memento mori—shot through me and passed away" (*W. J. Locke*). "Lives there a man so firm, who, while his heart Feels all the bitter horror of his crime, Can reason down its *agonizing* throbs" (*Burns*). **Racking** suggests sensations of pulling and straining and tearing comparable to those suffered by a person on the rack; as, *racking* pains in the chest; a *racking* headache; *racking* doubts.

Ana. Torturing, tormenting, racking, grilling (see AFFLICT): *intense, vehement.

exculpate. Exculpate, absolve, exonerate, acquit, vindicate agree in meaning to free from a charge or burden. **Exculpate** implies simply a clearing from blame, especially in a matter of small importance; as, to *exculpate* oneself from a charge of inconsistency. **Absolve** implies a release, often a formal release, either from obligations or responsibilities that bind the conscience, or from the consequences or penalties of their violation; as, to *absolve* one from blame or responsibility; to *absolve* a person from a promise. **Exonerate** implies relief, often in a moral sense, from what is regarded as a load or burden. "It [exemption of a judge's salary from taxation] seems to me no reason for *exonerating* him from the ordinary duties of a citizen" (*Justice Holmes*). In general, *exonerate* more frequently suggests such relief from a definite charge that not even the suspicion of wrongdoing remains; as, to *exonerate* a person charged with theft. **Acquit** implies a decision in one's favor with reference to a specific charge; as, to *acquit* of all participation in a crime. "You do *acquit* me then of anything wrong? You are convinced that I never meant to deceive your brother...?" (*Jane Austen*). **Vindicate,** unlike the preceding words, may have reference to things as well as to persons that have been subjected to attack, suspicion, censure, ridicule, or the like. As here compared (see also MAINTAIN), it implies a clearing through proof of the injustice or the unfairness of such criticism or blame, and the exoneration of the person or the justification of the thing. "Time has *vindicated* the prudence of the Griffiths, the Daffies, and the Pears [early large-scale advertisers]" (*C. E. Montague*). "You may find yourself...summoned to serve on a jury and make decisions involving the disgrace or *vindication*, the imprisonment or freedom, the life or death of your fellowcreatures" (*Shaw*).

Ana. Justify, *explain, rationalize: *excuse, condone, pardon, forgive, remit.

Ant. Inculpate: accuse. — ***Con.*** Blame, denounce, reprehend, reprobate, censure (see CRITICIZE): charge, arraign, indict, criminate, incriminate, impeach (see ACCUSE).

excursion. Trip, jaunt, tour, cruise, *journey, voyage, expedition, pilgrimage.

Ana. Ride, drive (see under RIDE, *v.*).

excursus. Divagation, *digression, episode.

excuse, *v.* **Excuse, condone, pardon, forgive, remit** agree in meaning not to exact punishment or redress for (an offense) or from (an offender). In polite use, *excuse, pardon*, and *forgive* usually suggest a hope that one is not annoyed. Both **excuse** and **condone** imply an overlooking or passing over, either without censure or without adequate punishment; in careful use, one *excuses* faults, omissions, or neglects, especially in social or conventional obligations, or the person committing them (as, please *excuse* my interruption; "In her heart she did not at all justify or *excuse* Cyril"—*Bennett*), and one *condones* grave offenses such as a breach of the moral code or a violation of law (as, "We *condone* everything in this country—private treason, falsehood, flattery, cruelty at home, roguery, and double-dealing"—*Thackeray;* "Slavery struck no deep roots in New England soil, perhaps because the nobler half of the New England conscience never *condoned* it"—*A. Repplier*). **Pardon** (opposed to *punish*) and **forgive** (opposed to *condemn*) are often employed interchangeably, but in strict usage they are differentiated. One *pardons* when one frees from the penalty due for an offense or refrains from exacting punishment for it (as, to *pardon* ten prisoners at Christmas; will you *pardon* my intrusion?; "it became necessary ...to fly for our lives....We could not look to be *pardoned*"—*Hudson*); one *forgives* when one gives up not only any claim to requital or retribution, but also any resentment or desire for revenge (as, "To err is human, to *forgive*, divine"—*Pope;* "The wrath... is past...and I, Lo, I *forgive* thee, as Eternal God *Forgives!*"—*Tennyson*). **Remit** is a synonym only in the idiomatic phrase *to remit sins*, in which it means to free from the punishment due for one's sins.

Ana. Justify, *explain, account for, rationalize: acquit, vindicate, *exculpate, absolve, exonerate, vindicate: *palliate, extenuate, gloze, gloss, whitewash.

Ant. Punish. — ***Con.*** Censure, reprobate, reprehend, blame, *criticize: chastise, castigate, discipline, chasten, correct (see PUNISH).

excuse, *n.* Plea, pretext, *apology, apologia, alibi.

Ana. Explanation, justification, rationalization (see corresponding verbs at EXPLAIN): palliation, extenuation, whitewashing, glossing (see corresponding verbs at PALLIATE).

execrable. **Execrable, damnable, accursed, cursed** agree in meaning so odious as to excite profanity. In actual use they vary little, if any, in force and only slightly in implications. Good usage, to a certain extent, however, limits their applications. **Execrable** is applied chiefly to that which is bad beyond description; as, *execrable* taste; *execrable* poetry or music; an *execrable* performance of Hamlet. **Damnable** and **accursed** are applied most often either to persons, their acts and their vices, or to things that excite righteous indignation and strong condemnation. "Unless that man in there is to be given a chance of expiation in another life, then capital punishment is a *damnable* horror" (*C. Mackenzie*). "*Accursed* tower! *accursed* fatal hand That hath contrived this woful tragedy!" (*Shak.*). **Cursed** varies in dignity, sometimes being applied to that which merely excites profanity and sometimes to that which in itself is worthy of imprecation. "Merciful powers, Restrain in me the *cursed* thoughts that nature Gives way to in repose!" (*Shak.*).

Ana. *Outrageous, atrocious, heinous, monstrous: *base, low, vile: loathsome, revolting, repulsive, *offensive, repugnant.

execrate. **Execrate, curse, damn, ban, anathematize, objurgate** agree in meaning to denounce violently and indignantly. **Execrate** implies intense loathing or hatred and, usually, a fury of passion; as, "they *execrate*... their lot" (*Cowper*); to *execrate* the men who were responsible for their misery; it often suggests acts as well as words which give an outlet to these emotions. "For a little while he [Antony] was *execrated* in Rome; his statues were overthrown, and his name was blotted from the records" (*Buchan*). **Curse** in earlier use often implied an invocation to the Supreme Being to visit deserved punishment upon a person or to afflict him for his sins. "He that withholdeth corn, the people shall *curse* him: but blessing shall be upon the head of him that selleth it" (*Proverbs* xi. 26). In more modern use, *curse* and **damn** (see also SENTENCE) do not markedly differ in meaning. Both usually imply angry denunciation by blasphemous oaths or profane imprecations. "I heard my brother *damn* the coachman, and *curse* the maids" (*Defoe*). *Curse* and **ban** were not clearly distinguished in earlier use, for both implied an invocation that was the opposite of a blessing or benediction. In modern literary use *ban*, more often than *curse*, is used as the opposite of *bless*, and often is associated with it. It implies any attitude from strong (usually vocal) disapproval to violent execration. "Ever she blessed the old and *banned* the new" (*W. Morris*). **Anathematize** implies solemn denunciation, as of an evil, a heresy (not necessarily religious), an injustice, or the like. It is used chiefly in reference to the impassioned denunciations of preachers, moralists, and the like; as, to *anathematize* the violation of a treaty; to *anathematize* graft in politics. **Objurgate** differs from *execrate* chiefly in implying less fury or passion; it often suggests the denunciations of an extremist or of a savage critic; as, cranks are people who *objurgate* everything that displeases them personally. "His [Theodore Roosevelt's] *objurgations*...surely accomplished nothing; the hyphenate [hyphenated American] of 1915 is still a hyphenate in his heart" (*Mencken*).

Ana. Denounce, condemn, reprobate, censure, reprehend (see CRITICIZE): revile, berate, rate (see SCOLD).

Con. *Commend, applaud, compliment, recommend: *praise, laud, extol, acclaim, eulogize.

execute. **1** Effect, fulfill, discharge, *perform, accomplish, achieve.

Ana. Complete, finish, conclude, *close: *realize, actualize, externalize, objectify.

2 **Execute, administer,** and their derivative adjectives, esp. **executive, administrative,** and nouns, esp. **executive, executor** (*feminine* **executrix,** *rarely* **executress**), **administrator** (*feminine* **administratrix** *or* **administratress**) are often confused not only because of overlapping meanings but also because they are employed in reference to similar, and often identical, spheres of activity, acts, or powers. They are, however, only occasionally interchangeable, partly because of distinct technical meanings and partly because idiom determines their choice. In discriminating use, both verbs (and usually their derivatives) always imply vested authority or deputed powers, and therefore suggest a source of that authority or power or a prior determination of what is to be done. They come closest in meaning when used of one who governs in obedience to the will of the people, and whose function it is to see that the laws made by the people's representatives are enforced. **Execute,** in such a context, stresses the carrying out or into effect of that which has been determined by a legislature; **administer** always implies management and therefore stresses rather the actual exercise of the powers given by law and the performance of executive duties; thus, the president is sworn to *execute* the laws of his country, but he often finds difficulty in *administering* them to the satisfaction of all. Idiom permits us to say that the president *executes* (not *administers*) the will of the people, and that he *administers* (not *executes*) his office competently, or the affairs of the country to the admiration of all. "I invite consideration of the...demands citizens make upon government, [and] the instruments by which these demands are *executed*" (*Frankfurter*). "The Senate [of ancient Rome], with the twin tasks of *administering* an empire and curbing the new democracy, failed in both" (*Buchan*). *Executive* and *administrator* also reveal similar differences in implications but they are commonly distinct in application. **Executive** is applied to a person who is the responsible head of a government, or an institution, or a business, or of one of its departments; **administrator** is applied to one charged with the management of something; as, the Secretary of the Treasury is the *administrator* of the finances of the United States. Sometimes, *administrator* is applied to one in temporary control; thus, an ad interim pastor or rector is called an *administrator* of the parish in some churches; in some British colonies, the colonial secretary serves as acting governor under the title of *Administrator*.

Execute and *administer* carry the same fundamental implications when applied to settling the affairs of an estate; thus, one *executes* (not *administers*) the provisions of a will; one *administers* (not *executes*) the estate of a deceased person (sometimes of an incompetent or of a bankrupt). This difference is commonly manifest in *executor* and *administrator*. **Executor** is applied only to one appointed by the maker of a will to see that the provisions of his will are carried out; **administrator** is applicable to an *executor*, but is strictly used as a designation of a person legally appointed to settle the estate of one who has died without leaving a will.

Ana. *Enforce, implement: *govern, rule.

3 *Kill, dispatch, slay, murder, assassinate.

executive, *adj.* Administrative (see under EXECUTE, 2).

executive, *n.* Executor, administrator. See under EXECUTE, 2.

executor (*fem.* **executrix,** *rarely* **executress**). Administrator (see under EXECUTE, 2).

exemplar. Pattern, ideal, beau ideal, example, *model, mirror, standard, paradigm.

Ana. Archetype, *prototype: apotheosis, *paragon, phoenix, nonpareil, nonesuch, sublimation: type, *symbol.

exemplify. **Exemplify, illustrate** come into comparison when they mean to use, as a writer or speaker, concrete instances or cases to make clear that which is difficult, abstract, general, or remote from experience, or to serve, as an instance, case, or the like, in achieving that end. **Exemplify** implies the use of examples for clarification of a general or abstract statement, or as aid in revealing the truth of a proposition or assertion; as, a good preacher usually *exemplifies* each point that he seeks to impress upon his congregation; "the notes of Coleridge [on Massinger] *exemplify* Coleridge's fragmentary and fine perceptions" (*T. S. Eliot*); "Each, in his way, *exemplifies* the peril that besets a highly gifted poetic nature" (*Lowes*). **Illustrate** implies the use not only of concrete examples but also sometimes of pictures or sketches, and the intent not only to clarify but to make vivid or real that which is being explained or to drive home most effectively a point that is being made; as, the textbook is adequately *illustrated* with photographs and diagrams; "I will *illustrate* the word a little further" (*J. R. Lowell*); "The assertion...leans for support...upon the truth conveyed in those words of Cicero, and wonderfully *illustrates* and confirms them" (*Arnold*). "The world was no more made to serve us by *illustrating* our philosophy than we were made to serve the world by licking its boots" (*Santayana*).

exemption. **Exemption, immunity** come into comparison as meaning the act or fact of freeing, or the state of being free or freed, from something burdensome, disagreeable, painful, or the like. **Exemption** is more restricted in its meaning for it applies usually to a release from some legal (or similarly imposed) obligation or burden to which all others in the same circumstances (not similarly freed) are liable; as, married men with families may apply for *exemption* from military service; "[They] have no vices, but they buy that *exemption* at a price, for one is inclined to ask whether...they really have any virtues" (*H. Ellis*). **Immunity** covers all cases for which an exemption may be given or obtained, but the term carries so strong an implication of privilege and of freedom from certain common restrictions that it is often used in reference to persons or classes of persons especially favored by the law or by nature; as, "entitled to the rights of a citizen, and clothed with all the rights and *immunities* which the Constitution and laws of the State attached to that character" (*Ch. Just. Taney*); "the question of the *immunities* of the clergy had been publicly raised" (*Froude*); "the man of creative imagination pays a ghastly price for all his superiorities and *immunities*" (*Mencken*). In current specific use, *immunity* implies a physical power to resist disease (commonly, a particular disease), or particularly to resist infecting microorganisms or their products; as, to build up *immunity* (or an *immunity*) to diphtheria; "he may...after long years of exposure to plague...even develop a certain *immunity*" (*V. Heiser*).

exercise, *v.* *Practice, drill.
Ana. *Use, employ, utilize: display, exhibit, *show: wield, ply, manipulate, *handle.

exercise, *n.* *Practice, drill. See under PRACTICE, *v.*
Ana. *Action, act, deed: using *or* use, employment, utilization, application (see corresponding verbs at USE): operation, functioning, behavior (see corresponding verbs at ACT).

exertion. *Effort, pains, trouble.
Ana. Labor, toil, travail, *work, grind, drudgery: struggle, striving, endeavor (see under ATTEMPT, *v.*).

Con. Relaxation, *rest, repose, leisure, ease: inactivity, inertness *or* inertia, idleness (see corresponding adjectives at INACTIVE).

exhaust, *v.* **1** Drain, *deplete, impoverish, bankrupt.
Ana. Sap, undermine, *weaken: consume, absorb, engross, *monopolize: dissipate, disperse, dispel, *scatter.
Con. Conserve, preserve, *save: restore, redintegrate (see RENEW).
2 Fatigue, jade, weary, *tire, fag, tucker.
Ana. *Unnerve, enervate, emasculate: disable, cripple, debilitate, enfeeble, *weaken.
Con. Refresh, restore, rejuvenate, *renew: vivify, *quicken, animate, enliven.

exhibit, *v.* Display, expose, *show, parade, flaunt.
Ana. *Reveal, disclose, discover, divulge: *show, manifest, evidence, evince, demonstrate.
Con. *Suppress, repress: *hide, conceal, secrete, bury.

exhibit, *n.* *Exhibition, show, exposition, fair.

exhibition. **Exhibition, show, exhibit, exposition, fair** are here compared only in a very specific sense as meaning a public display of objects of interest. **Exhibition** and (less often in formal use, except in art circles; but commonly as a colloquialism) **show** are applicable to any such display of objects of art, manufacture, commerce, or the like, or to any display by pupils, members, associates, or the like, of their prowess or skill in gymnastics, oratory, music, or the like; as, the annual *exhibition* of the Academy of Fine Arts; an *exhibition* of Navaho blankets; the one-man *show* of paintings at the D... Galleries; a gymnastic *exhibition;* a cattle *show.* In law, *exhibition* is applied to any such public display from which the exhibitor or exhibitors hope to make a profit and for which they must obtain a license. An **exhibit** is an object or collection displayed in an *exhibition;* as, the English *exhibit* at the World's Fair. In law, *exhibit* refers only to a document or a material object produced in court or before an examiner and properly identified for use as evidence. **Exposition** is now the technical term for a very large exhibition, especially one involving the participation of many states, countries, or the like; as, the World's Columbian *Exposition* at Chicago in 1893; the annual Canadian National *Exposition* at Toronto; the annual Eastern States *Exposition* at West Springfield, Massachusetts. **Fair** applies usually (though far from invariably; as, for example, a world's *fair*) to a small exhibition of wares, produce, stock, and the like, sometimes for the promotion of sales, sometimes in competition for prizes for excellence; as, street *fairs* in Paris; a county *fair.*

exhume. Disinter, excavate, *dig, delve, grub, spade.
Ana. Unearth, *discover.
Ant. Bury. — *Con.* Secrete, cache, conceal, *hide.

exigency. **1** Pass, emergency, pinch, strait, crisis, contingency, *juncture.
Ana. *Difficulty, vicissitude, rigor, hardship: *predicament, plight, fix, quandary, dilemma, jam, pickle, scrape.
2 Necessity, *need.
Ana. Demanding *or* demand, requirement, exacting *or* exaction, claiming *or* claim (see corresponding verbs at DEMAND): compulsion, coercion, constraint, duress (see FORCE, *n.*).

exiguous. *Meager, scant, scanty, skimpy, scrimpy, spare, sparse.
Ana. Diminutive, tiny, *small, little: tenuous, slender, slight, *thin: limited, restricted, confined (see LIMIT, *v.*).
Ant. Capacious, ample.

exile, *v.* *Banish, expatriate, ostracize, deport, transport, extradite.

Ana. Proscribe, attaint, condemn (see SENTENCE): expel, *eject, oust.

exist. *Be, live, subsist.

existence. Existence, being, actuality are closely allied in meaning but not always interchangeable. **Existence** is the inclusive term which designates the state or condition of anything regarded as occurring in space or time, as distinct and apart from all other things, and as having a nature or substance of its own; as, customs that have recently come into *existence;* a mathematical point has no real *existence;* wars that threaten the *existence* of civilization; his misfortunes have *existence* only in his imagination. The opposite of *existence* is its complete negation *nonexistence.* **Being,** when it denotes existence, adds varying implications: sometimes it implies life, consciousness, or personality; as, "In him we live, and move, and have our *being*" (*Acts* xvii. 28); sometimes it implies fullness or completeness of existence and absence of imperfection; as, "Everything else is in a state of becoming, God is in a state of *Being*" (*F. W. Robertson*); sometimes it suggests the complex of qualities or characteristics that constitute the nature of a person or a personified thing. "All the forces of his *being* were massed behind one imperious resolve" (*Buchan*). **Actuality,** as a synonym of *existence,* stresses realization or attainment; in discriminating use, it usually implies opposition to *possibility* or *potentiality;* as, ambition is the spur that makes dreams come into *actuality.* "Risks which have been seized upon as *actualities* when they have been merely potentialities" (*T. S. Eliot*).

Ana. *State, condition, situation, status, estate: subsisting *or* subsistence, living *or* life (see corresponding verbs at BE).

Ant. Nonexistence.

exonerate. Acquit, vindicate, absolve, *exculpate.

Ana. *Relieve, lighten, alleviate: *excuse, remit.

Ant. Charge (*a person with a task, a duty, a crime, etc.*).

exorbitant. Inordinate, extravagant, *excessive, immoderate, extreme.

Ana. *Onerous, burdensome, oppressive, exacting: greedy, grasping, *covetous: extorting *or* extortionate (see corresponding verb at EDUCE).

Ant. Just (*price, charge, etc.*). — *Con.* *Fair, equitable: reasonable, *rational.

exordium. Preamble, preface, *introduction, foreword, prologue, prelude, overture, prolegomenon, proem, prolusion, protasis, avant-propos.

expand. Expand, amplify, swell, distend, inflate, dilate agree in meaning to increase or to cause to increase in size, bulk, or volume. **Expand** is the most inclusive term in this group, and may often be used interchangeably with any of the others. It distinctively implies enlargement by opening out, unfolding, spreading, or the like, and may be used when the enlarging force is either internal or external; as, tulips *expand* in the sun; the flag *expanded* in the breeze; to *expand* a sponge by soaking it in water; to *expand* tires by introducing air; to *expand* one's chest by breathing exercises; their business is *expanding.* **Amplify** implies extension of that which is inadequate and, often, not clear, as by filling out with details or by magnifying the volume; as, to *amplify* a statement; devices for *amplifying* sounds. "They [the Modernists] don't claim that the Divine revelation has been supplanted or even added to, but that it has been *amplified*" (*C. Mackenzie*). "The author follows the Vulgate narrative closely...but *amplifies* and embroiders" (*Saintsbury*). **Swell** implies expansion, often abnormal expansion, beyond a thing's original circumference or normal limits; as, warm spring rains cause the leaf buds to *swell;* the river is *swelling;* his hand is *swollen;* gifts to *swell* the endowment fund. Often it implies increase in intensity, force, volume, or the like; as, "the laughter *swelled* to hooting" (*Galsworthy*). "Caesar's ambition, Which *swell'd* so much that it did almost stretch The sides o' the world" (*Shak.*). Often, both in literal and figurative use, it implies puffing up or puffing out, to the point of bursting; as, *swollen* veins; his heart *swelled* with pride (or with indignation). **Distend** always implies swelling caused by pressure from within forcing extension outward in all possible directions. Sometimes it presupposes previous collapse; as, a rubber bag *distends* when filled with water; sails *distended* by the wind: sometimes it implies an exceeding of the normal bounds; as, a stomach *distended* by gas; "like the flesh of animals *distended* by fear or desire" (*Cather*). **Inflate** usually implies distention by artificial means, as by the introduction of gas or air or, figuratively, by puffing up with something as insubstantial or as easily dissipated as gas or air; as, to *inflate* a balloon; to *inflate* values; to *inflate* the currency; an *inflated* idea of one's own importance. "Poems...so *inflated* with metaphor, that they may be compared to the gaudy bubbles blown up from a solution of soap" (*Goldsmith*). **Dilate** implies expansion in diameter; it therefore suggests a widening out of something circular rather than a puffing up of something globular or spherical. "As round a pebble into water thrown *dilates* a ring of light" (*Longfellow*). "Half-frighted, with *dilated* eyes" (*Tennyson*). "Some stirring experience...may swiftly *dilate* your field of consciousness" (*C. E. Montague*).

Ana. Enlarge, *increase, augment: *extend, protract, prolong.

Ant. Contract: abridge (*a book, article, etc.*): circumscribe (*a range, a scope, a power, etc.*).

expanse. Expanse, amplitude, spread, stretch are comparable when they denote an area or range of considerable or conspicuous extent. **Expanse** is applied chiefly to vast areas, open to view and usually uniform in character; as, "pure as the *expanse* of Heaven" (*Milton*); "Thy mariners explore the wide *expanse*" (*Cowper*); "great *expanse* of country spread around and below" (*D. H. Lawrence*). **Amplitude** is more often applied to that which is relatively vast in its proportions or range; it additionally implies fullness, abundance, or sometimes complexity; as, "people with a dignity of port, an *amplitude* of back" (*L. P. Smith*); "she went forth into the *amplitude* of tanned wild [the heath]" (*Hardy*); "an immense, leisurely, true novel...with a Tolstoyan or Proustian *amplitude*" (*L. P. Smith*). **Spread** is applied to an expanse thought of as drawn out in all directions; as, "the water...a ripply *spread* of sun and sea" (*Browning*); "a trackless *spread* of moor" (*Blackmore*); "under the immense *spread* of the starry heavens" (*Stevenson*). **Stretch** is applied to an expanse thought of especially with reference to its extent in one of its two dimensions, which one usually being indicated in the context; as, the beach was a wide (or narrow) *stretch* of sand; a *stretch* of farmland extending as far as the distant mountains; "the great *stretches* of fields that lay beside the road" (*S. Anderson*).

Ana. *Range, reach, scope, compass, sweep, orbit: domain, territory, sphere, *field.

expansive. *Elastic, resilient, buoyant, volatile, effervescent.

Ana. Exuberant, luxuriant, lavish, prodigal (see PROFUSE): generous, *liberal, bountiful: *elated, elate, exultant: exalted, magnified, aggrandized (see EXALT).

Ant. Tense: reserved. — *Con.* *Stiff, inflexible, rigid: stern, austere, *severe: taciturn, *silent, reticent.

expatiate. *Discourse, descant, dilate.

Ana. *Speak, talk, converse: *expand, amplify: *discuss, argue, dispute: expound, *explain: *relate, narrate, recount, recite, rehearse.

expatriate, *v.* Exile, *banish, ostracize, deport, transport, extradite.

Ant. Repatriate.

expect. **Expect, hope, look, look for, await** come into comparison because they agree in meaning to have something in mind as more or less certain to happen or come about. They vary, however, so greatly in their implications and in their constructions that they are seldom interchangeable. **Expect** usually implies a high degree of certainty, but it also involves the idea of anticipation, as by making preparations or by envisioning what will happen, or what one will find, or what emotions one will feel; as, he told his mother not to *expect* him for dinner; she had reason to *expect* that the trip would be exciting. "He seems to require and *expect* goodness in his species as we do a sweet taste in grapes and China oranges" (*B. Mandeville*). "What can you *expect* of a girl who was allowed to wear black satin at her coming-out ball?" (*E. Wharton*). **Hope** implies entertainment of the idea that one may expect what one desires or longs for; although it seldom implies certitude, it usually connotes confidence and often, especially in religious use, it implies profound assurance; as, he dared not *hope* that he would succeed in his venture, for he feared disappointment. "Wherefore gird up the loins of your mind, be sober, and *hope* to the end for the grace that is to be brought unto you at the revelation of Jesus Christ" (*1 Peter* i. 13). "He can never *expect*, he can never even reasonably *hope*, that reason will ever hold in leash the emotions" (*H. Ellis*). **Look** (usually followed by *to* with an infinitive and sometimes also by *to* with a personal object) is less literary than *expect;* it often also suggests more strongly than *expect* a counting upon or a freedom from doubt; as, they *look* to profit by their investment; they *looked* to their son to help them in their old age. **Look for,** on the other hand, does not imply as much assurance; it suggests rather an attitude of expectancy and watchfulness; as, they are *looking for* news in the next post; there is no use *looking for* their return tonight. **Await** often adds to *look for* the implication of being ready mentally (sometimes physically) for the event; it also suggests waiting, often patient waiting; as, we *await* your reply with interest; the two armies are eager for action, each *awaiting* an attack by the other. "I...had known it would happen to me, and now it was there with all the strangeness and dark mystery of an *awaited* thing" (*T. Wolfe*). *Await* also differs from the other words in this group in its capacity for taking as subject the thing expected and as object the person who is expecting; as, good fortune *awaits* you; death *awaits* all men.

Ana. *Foresee, foreknow, anticipate, apprehend, divine.

Ant. Despair of.

expectorate. *Spit.

expedient, *adj.* **Expedient, politic, advisable** are comparable when they are used to imply a choice, as of course, action, or method, and to mean dictated by practical wisdom, or by motives of prudence. That is **expedient** from which definite and, usually, immediate advantages accrue. Originally and still occasionally, the word and its derivatives carry no trace of a derogatory implication. "It is *expedient* for you that I go away: for if I go not away, the Comforter will not come unto you; but if I depart, I will send him unto you" (*John* xvi. 7). "The old man believed that the whip of shame and pain could drive her...into an appreciation of the *expediency* of morality" (*Deland*). In its sense development, *expedient* came to imply determination by immediate conditions and, hence, to mean necessary or suitable under present circumstances. "There shall be appointed...such number of...justices of the peace as the president of the United States shall, from time to time, think *expedient*" (*Ch. Just. Marshall*). As a result, *expedient* now commonly implies opportuneness (sometimes with a hint of time-serving) as well as advantageousness; as, they decided that it was not *expedient* (that is, neither opportune nor of advantage) to interfere now. Very frequently also, it connotes an ulterior motive such as self-interest. "It [civilization] was all founded on social *expediency*, on primitive laws to protect inheritance, to safeguard property" (*R. Macaulay*). Consequently, *expedient* is often opposed to *right*, the former suggesting a choice determined by temporal ends, the latter one determined by ethical principles. "Too fond of the right to pursue the *expedient*" (*Goldsmith*). That is **politic** which is the judicious course, action, or method from the practical point of view. Though often used interchangeably with *expedient*, *politic* in discriminating use is applied to choices involving tactics, or the effective handling of persons, and *expedient* to choices involving strategy, or the gaining of objectives; as, the move was a *politic* one, for it served to win friends to the cause and to placate its enemies. "Community of race...is mainly a *politic* fiction, at least in countries of European civilization, in which the races are inextricably mixed up" (*Encyc. Brit., 12th Ed.*). Like *expedient*, however, *politic* often implies material motives. "The question with me is... whether it is not your interest to make them [the American colonists] happy....Is a *politic* act the worse for being a generous one?" (*Burke*). That is **advisable** which is expedient in the original, underogatory sense of that word. *Advisable* has now nearly lost its original derivative sense, and is preferred by writers or speakers who wish to avoid any of the unpleasant implications of *expedient*, or sometimes, of *politic*. "I don't think that it's altogether *advisable* to mention Dickens in a sermon.... Some people might be offended at mentioning a novelist in church" (*C. Mackenzie*).

Ana. Advantageous, *beneficial, profitable: useful, utilitarian (see corresponding nouns at USE): *seasonable, opportune, timely, well-timed: feasible, practicable, *possible.

Ant. Inexpedient. — *Con.* Detrimental, deleterious (see PERNICIOUS): harming *or* harmful, hurting *or* hurtful, injuring *or* injurious (see corresponding verbs at INJURE): *futile, vain, fruitless.

expedient, *n.* *Resource, resort, shift, makeshift, stopgap, substitute, surrogate.

Ana. *Device, contrivance, contraption: *means, agency, instrument, instrumentality, medium.

expedition. 1 Dispatch, speed, *haste, hurry.

Ana. *Celerity, legerity, alacrity: agility, nimbleness, briskness (see corresponding adjectives at AGILE).

Ant. Procrastination. — *Con.* Delaying *or* delay, retarding *or* retardation, slowing, slackening (see corresponding verbs at DELAY).

2 *Journey, voyage, tour, trip, jaunt, excursion, cruise, pilgrimage.

expeditious. Speedy, swift, *fast, rapid, fleet, quick, hasty.

Ana. Efficient, *effective, efficacious, effectual: brisk, *agile, nimble: *quick, ready, prompt.

Ant. Sluggish. — *Con.* Inefficient, *ineffective, inefficacious, ineffectual: *slow, dilatory, leisurely, laggard, deliberate.

expel. *Eject, oust, dismiss, evict.

Ana. *Banish, exile, ostracize: *dismiss, discharge,

cashier, fire: *discard, cast: *exclude, shut out, eliminate.
Ant. Admit (sense 1).

expense. Cost, *price, charge.

expensive. *Costly, dear, valuable, precious, invaluable, priceless.
Ana. Exorbitant, extravagant, *excessive, immoderate.
Ant. Inexpensive.

experience, *n.* **Experience, experiment** are now rarely, if ever, synonymous terms but they are so closely associated in meaning that they are sometimes confused. Both terms denote a practical as opposed to a speculative way of finding out about a thing (or, often, a person) facts that are not obvious or outwardly evident. **Experience** implies direct personal knowledge through immediate observation, actual practice, or conscious subjection, as to an emotional or mental state or condition: it especially implies knowledge which comes as a result of one's normal way of life, one's particular environment, or one's character or training. *Experience* is applicable not only to an individual's way of finding out facts, but to a group's way, as that of a class, a people, a race, or the like. "She knew by prevision what most women learn only by *experience:* she had mentally walked round love, told the towers thereof, considered its palaces; and concluded that love was but a doleful joy" (*Hardy*). "In the case of my own boy, and presumably in other cases too, the *experience* of overcoming fear is extraordinarily delightful" (*B. Russell*). "A colouring harmony obtained by the aid of a long *experience* in the effects of light on translucent surfaces" (*Viollet-le-Duc, transl. by H. Adams*). "I feared that Mr. Powell's want of *experience* would stand in his way of appreciating the unusual" (*Conrad*). **Experiment,** on the other hand, implies the performance of an action or operation or the submission of a person (often oneself) or of a thing to a test which has for its end or aim proof or disproof (as of a theory or hypothesis), the showing by trial that a thing will or will not work or accomplish what is claimed for it, or the establishment, verification, or illustration of a general truth such as a scientific law: thus, one may consciously drink too much liquor either to have an *experience* (not *experiment*) of the release from care which is said to accompany a certain degree of intoxication, or to make an *experiment* (not *experience*) of the truth of that theory; some peoples try democracy as an *experiment* and later accept it or reject it on the ground of their *experience.* "Faith begins as an *experiment,* and ends as an *experience.* It begins as a resolution to stand or fall by the noblest hypothesis, as Frederic Myers says; but it is verified progressively as we go on" (*Inge*).

experiment, *n.* *Experience.
Ana. Trying *or* trial, testing *or* test, proving *or* proof, demonstrating *or* demonstration (see under PROVE).

expert, *adj.* *Proficient, adept, skilled, skillful.
Ana. Practiced, drilled (see PRACTICE, *v.*): trained, schooled (see TEACH): *dexterous, deft, feat, adroit.
Ant. Amateurish. — *Con.* Inept, maladroit, *awkward, clumsy.

expert, *n.* **Expert, adept, artist, artiste, virtuoso, wizard, dab, dabster** come into comparison only when they designate a person who shows mastery in a subject, an art, or a profession, or who reveals extraordinary skill in execution, performance, or technique. **Expert** always implies successful experience, broad knowledge of one's subject, and distinguished achievements; it is applied specifically to one who is recognized as an authority in his field; as, an *expert* in city planning; a handwriting *expert.* "This problem in triangulation was extremely difficult, and an *expert* in geodesy was brought from the United States" (*V. Heiser*). **Adept,** originally applied to an alchemist who claimed to have discovered "the great secret" of transmutation of base into precious metals, still, in discriminating use, connotes understanding of the mysteries of some art or craft or penetration into secrets beyond the reach of exact science. "Thou art an *adept* in the difficult lore Of Greek and Frank philosophy" (*Shelley*). It tends, in modern use, to imply subtlety or ingenuity; as, he is an *adept* in intrigue; he is an *adept* at evasion. **Artist,** as it comes into comparison with the other words of this group, stresses extraordinary skill in execution, or in giving outward form to that which the mind conceives. Much more than any other word in this group it stresses the incentives to skill in performance, such as a passion for perfection in workmanship, a loving attention to detail, a feeling for the material in which one works. "The good craftsman...becomes an *artist* in so far as he treats his materials also for themselves...and is perpetually besieged by dreams of beauty in his work" (*S. Alexander*). "And it came to pass that after a time the *artist* was forgotten, but the work lived" (*O. Schreiner*). **Artiste** was taken over from the French, during the nineteenth century, when *artist* tended to become restricted in its application to painters and sculptors. It was originally applied to actors, singers, and dancers; now it is often, more or less humorously, also applied to workers in crafts where adeptness and taste are indispensable to distinguished achievement; as, that milliner is an *artiste.* **Virtuoso,** though often close to *artist* in meaning, stresses the outward display of great technical skill or brilliance in execution, rather than the inner passion for perfection or beauty. It is applied chiefly, though far from exclusively, to performers on musical instruments, especially to pianists, violinists, and violoncellists; as, the compositions of Liszt are the delight of *virtuosi.* "This precise evocation of forms and colors by the great *virtuosos* of description" (*Babbitt*). **Wizard,** a colloquial term, may be used in place of any of the preceding words: it is often hyperbolic, however, and suggests the achievement of wonders or of the impossible; as, Steinmetz was regarded as the *wizard* among investigators of electricity. **Dab** and **dabster** are British terms implying great proficiency or expertness. The former, originally a schoolboy term, is found in works of good writers, but the latter is chiefly in dialectal use. "I wish to show I am a *dab* in history" (*Thackeray*).
Ant. Amateur. — *Con.* Tyro, dabbler, dilettante (see AMATEUR): *novice, apprentice, probationer.

expiate, *v.* **Expiate, atone** (*or* **atone for**) agree in meaning to make or give satisfaction for an offense, a sin, a crime, or the like. The same distinctions in implications and connotations are observable in their derivative nouns **expiation** and **atonement. Expiate** and **expiation** imply an attempt to undo the wrong one has done, by suffering the penalty, by doing penance, or by making reparation or redress. "Let me here, As I deserve, pay on my punishment, And *expiate,* if possible, my crime" (*Milton*). "Unless that man in there is to be given a chance of *expiation* in another life, then capital punishment is a damnable horror" (*C. Mackenzie*). **Atone** and **atonement** have been greatly colored in their meanings by theological controversies concerning *the Atonement,* or the redemptive end, for which Christ, as God, became man, and suffered and died on the cross. The original meaning of the verb in English was to "make one," by reconciling persons at odds with each other. "I was glad I did *atone* my countryman and you" (*Shak.*). By extension, it also meant to compose or settle differences, an altercation, or the like. "The constable is called to *atone* the broil" (*J. Heywood*). Consequently the implication of reconciliation became mixed with and sometimes subordinated to other implications such as appeasement, propitiation, or reparation. **Atonement,** as a theological term with various interpretations, sometimes stresses one or more of these implications to the exclusion of the others. In current general use, however, *atone* (usually *atone for*) and *atonement* emphasize a restoration, through some compensation, of a balance that has been lost. When the reference is to an offense, sin, crime, or the like, the words usually imply expiation, but they stress the rendering of satisfaction for the evil that has been done by acts that are good or meritorious; thus, one *expiates* a sin by doing penance for it, but one *atones* for it by leading a good life afterwards. "She hated herself for this movement of envy...and tried to *atone* for it by a softened manner and a more anxious regard for Charlotte's feelings" (*E. Wharton*). But not only an offense, but also a deficiency or a default may be *atoned for* by an excess of something else that is equally desirable. "For those who kneel beside us At altars not Thine own, Who lack the lights that guide us, Lord, let their faith *atone!*" (*Kipling*).

Ana. Redress, remedy, rectify, *correct, amend: redeem, deliver, save (see RESCUE).

expiation. Atonement (see under EXPIATE, *v.*).

Ana. *Penitence, repentance, contrition: *trial, tribulation, cross, visitation.

explain. 1 **Explain, expound, explicate, elucidate, interpret, construe** come into comparison when they mean to make oneself or another understand the meaning of something. To **explain,** the most general term, is to make plain or intelligible to another or others something not known or clearly understood; as, to *explain* to a boy the mechanism of an engine; the teacher explained the meanings of the new words in the poem. **Expound** implies careful, elaborate, often learned setting forth of a subject in such a way as to explain it, as in a lecture, a book, a treatise, or the like; as, a clergyman *expounding* a Biblical text; to *expound* a point of law. "Sir A. Eddington in two masterly chapters...*expounds* the law of gravitation" (*S. Alexander*); to *expound* the duties of the citizen. **Explicate** (literally, to unfold), a somewhat learned term, adds to *expound* the idea of development or detailed analysis; as, "the mind of a doctor of the Church who could...*explicate* the meaning of a dogma" (*T. S. Eliot*); "the *explication* of our Saviour's parables" (*Atterbury*). **Elucidate** implies a throwing light upon a subject, a work, a passage, or the like, especially by clear or luminous exposition or illustration; as, to *elucidate* an obscure passage; "the simplicity of the case can be addled...when the object is to addle and not to *elucidate*" (*Shaw*). **Interpret** implies the making clear to oneself or to another the meaning of something which presents more than intellectual difficulties (such as a poem, a dream, an abstraction, a work in a foreign language) and requires special knowledge, imagination, sympathy, or the like, in the person who would understand it or make it understood; as, "I have tried in this all too hasty sketch to *interpret*...the indwelling spirit and ideal of the art of the Far East" (*Binyon*); "Love... [as] the initiation into the higher life....was not invented but *interpreted* by Plato" (*G. L. Dickinson*); "an inscription which no one could understand or rightly *interpret*" (*Hudson*). **Construe** is preferred to *interpret* when the difficulties are textual, either because of the strangeness of the language (such as by being foreign, ancient, dialectal, technical, or the like) or because of ambiguities or equivocations in it. It therefore may suggest either translation involving careful analysis of grammatical structure (as, to *construe* ten lines of Vergil) or a highly individual or particular interpretation; as, "The phrase 'every common carrier engaged in trade or commerce' may be *construed* to mean 'while engaged in trade or commerce' without violence to the habits of English speech" (*Justice Holmes*); "somehow or other, [he] had *construed* the ordinarily polite terms of his letter of engagement into a belief that the Directors had chosen him on account of his special and brilliant talents" (*Kipling*).

Ana. *Analyze, resolve, dissect, anatomize, break down: *discuss, argue, dispute: *exemplify, illustrate.

2 **Explain, account for, justify, rationalize** are synonymous when they mean to give or tell the cause, reason, nature, or significance of something obscure or questionable. One **explains** what is hard to understand, as that which is mysterious in its origin or nature, or lacks an apparent or sufficient cause, or is full of inconsistencies. "These sciences [mathematics and physics] have not succeeded in *explaining* the phenomena of life" (*Inge*). "This...study of Napoleon, which, while free from all desire to defend or admire, yet seems to *explain* Napoleon" (*H. Ellis*). *Explain* often implies an attempt to excuse or to set oneself right with others. "One can do almost anything...if one does not attempt to *explain* it" (*E. Wharton*). One **accounts for** something, rather than *explains* it, when one feels that it is incumbent on one to give an explanation. This sense of *account for* arises out of an earlier one meaning to render an account of something one has to answer for; as, to *account for* money entrusted to one's care; to *account for* the use of one's time or opportunities. In careful English this implication of responsibility is strong in *account for* as here considered. "We [certain philosophers] fail, we are told, to *account for* the world. Well, the world is a solid fact, which we have to accept, not to *account for*" (*Inge*). "Going about her business as if nothing had happened that needed to be *accounted for*" (*E. Wharton*). One **justifies** oneself or another when one explains certain acts or behavior in an attempt to free oneself or another from blame. It may or may not imply consciousness of guilt or a definite accusation. "Powell...began to *justify* himself. 'I couldn't stop him,' he whispered shakily. 'He was too quick for me' " (*Conrad*). "So far is he from feeling the pangs of conscience that he constantly *justifies* his act" (*G. L. Dickinson*). "In her heart she did not at all *justify* or excuse Cyril" (*Bennett*). One **rationalizes** that which is or seems to be contrary to reason when one attempts an explanation that is in accord with scientific principles or with reality as known to the senses; as, to *rationalize* the Greek myths; to *rationalize* the Genesis story of creation. In very modern use, *rationalize* often comes close to *justify* without, however, so strong an implication of blame and with the added implication of self-deception and, at times, of hypocrisy. "In other countries the plutocracy has often produced men of reflective and analytical habit, eager to *rationalize* its instincts" (*Mencken*). "Propaganda...is influential only when it is a *rationalization* of the...prejudices or interests of those to whom it is addressed" (*A. Huxley*).

Ana. *Excuse, condone: *exculpate, exonerate, acquit, absolve.

explicate, *v.* *Explain, expound, elucidate, interpret, construe.

explicit. **Explicit, express, specific, definite, categorical** are here compared chiefly as applied to statements, utterances, language, and the like, and as meaning perfectly clear in significance or reference. That is **explicit** which is stated so plainly and distinctly that nothing is left to be inferred or to cause difficulty by being vague, equivocal, or ambiguous; as, *explicit* directions or promises; "to give an *explicit* and determinate account of what is meant by [the principle of utility]" (*Bentham*). That is **express** which is both explicit and is uttered or expressed with directness, pointedness, or force; as, an *express* prohibition or understanding; *express* testimony. "The defendant should be enjoined from publishing news obtained from the Associated Press for—hours after publication by the plaintiff unless it gives *express* credit to the Associated Press; the number of hours...to be settled by the District Court" (*Justice Holmes*). That is **specific** which is perfectly precise in its reference to a particular thing or in its statement of the details covered or comprehended; as, in addition he made two *specific* criticisms of the school, one dealing with its lack of a playground, the other with the defective ventilation of certain rooms; a command should always be *specific* (that is, it should specify all details). That is **definite** which leaves no doubt either as to its reference or to its details (and therefore is *specific*) or as to what is excluded; *definite*, far more than *specific*, suggests precise and determinate limitations; as, he was asked to make a *definite* statement concerning the young man's prospects with the company. Actually, *specific* and *definite* are often used interchangeably without loss; but careful writers and speakers usually prefer *specific* when they wish to stress particularization of reference or specification of details, and *definite* when they wish to emphasize clear limitations; thus, a colonel's command to a scout may be *specific* and yet not perfectly *definite* if, for example, it leaves the scout in doubt as to what he should do when circumstances become extremely dangerous or the possibility of escape is being cut off. **Categorical** (see also ULTIMATE, 2) implies explicitness without the least suggestion of a qualification or condition; thus, a *categorical* answer is demanded of a person testifying in court when he is compelled to answer yes or no; a *categorical* denial is a denial that is complete and contains not the slightest reservations. "It is perilous to make *categorical* assertions" (*Lowes*).

Ana. Precise, exact, accurate (see CORRECT): *clear, lucid, perspicuous.

Ant. Ambiguous. — ***Con.*** Equivocal, vague, enigmatic, cryptic, dark, *obscure: *implicit, virtual, constructive.

exploit, *n.* *Feat, achievement.

Ana. Act, deed, *action: *adventure, enterprise, emprise, quest.

expose. Display, exhibit, *show, parade, flaunt.

Ana. *Reveal, disclose, discover, divulge: demonstrate, evince, manifest, evidence, *show: air, ventilate, vent, voice, utter, *express: publish, advertise, proclaim, broadcast, *declare.

exposé, *n.* Exposure, *exposition.

exposed. Open, *liable, subject, prone, susceptible, sensitive, incident.

Ana. Threatened, menaced (see THREATEN).

Con. Protected, shielded, guarded, safeguarded, defended (see DEFEND).

exposition. 1 Fair, *exhibition, exhibit, show.

2 Exposition, exposure, exposé come into comparison when they mean a setting forth or laying open of a thing or things hitherto not known or fully understood. **Exposition** often implies a display of something such as wares, manufactures, a collection of rarities, antiquities, or the like (for this sense see EXHIBITION); even more often, it implies a setting forth of that which is necessary for the elucidation or explanation of something such as a theory, a dogma, the law (as, "You know the law, your *exposition* Hath been most sound"—*Shak.*) or the events or situations preceding a story or play (as, the first quarter of the first act is devoted to the *exposition*). In a more general sense, especially in academic use, *exposition* applies to that type of writing which has explanation for its end or aim, and is thereby distinguished from other types the object of which is to describe, to narrate, or, by argument, to prove a contention. **Exposure** (see also FRONTAGE) is now preferred to *exposition* as a term implying a laying (someone or something) bare or open, especially (but not invariably) to detrimental or injurious influences or to reprobation, contempt, or severe censure; as, fabrics faded by *exposure* to the sun; *exposure* to a contagious disease; the *exposure* of a candidate's unsavory past; the *exposure* of a person's motives. *Exposure* is the correct term for the time during which a sensitive surface, such as that of a photographic film, is laid open to the influence of light; as, an *exposure* of two seconds. **Exposé** is often used in place of *exposure* for a revealing (usually a formal or deliberate revealing) of something that is discreditable to a person or group; as, an *exposé* of an allegedly charitable association; an *exposé* of a judge's graft.

expostulate. Remonstrate, protest, *object, kick.

Ana. *Oppose, resist, combat: argue, debate, dispute, *discuss.

exposure. 1 *Frontage, aspect.

Ana. *Prospect, outlook.

2 Exposé, *exposition.

Ant. Cover: covering. — ***Con.*** *Shelter, refuge, asylum, retreat.

expound. *Explain, explicate, elucidate, interpret, construe.

Ana. Dissect, anatomize, break down, *analyze, resolve: illustrate, *exemplify.

express, *adj.* *Explicit, definite, specific, categorical.

Ana. Expressed, voiced, uttered (see EXPRESS, *v.*): lucid, *clear, perspicuous: distinct, plain (see EVIDENT): precise, exact, accurate (see CORRECT).

Con. *Implicit, constructive, virtual: vague, *obscure, cryptic, enigmatic, ambiguous, equivocal.

express, *v.* **Express, vent, utter, voice, broach, air, ventilate** come into comparison when they mean to let out what one feels or thinks. **Express,** the most comprehensive of these words, implies an impulse to reveal not only one's thoughts or feelings, but also one's experiences, one's imaginative conceptions, one's personality, or the like; it implies revelation not only in words but also in gestures, in action, in dress, in what one makes or produces, especially as works of art. "Once again I have to *express* surprise and satisfaction" (*Lucas*). "In speaking or writing we have an obligation to put ourselves into the hearer's or reader's place....To *express* ourselves is a very small part of the business" (*Quiller-Couch*). "There were so many different moods and impressions that he wished to *express* in verse" (*Joyce*). **Vent** stresses an inner compulsion to expression, such as a pent-up emotion that seeks an outlet or a powerful passion that cannot be controlled; as, he *vented* his spleen in libelous caricatures. "His heart's his mouth: What his breast forges, that his tongue must *vent*" (*Shak.*). "By means of ferocious jokes...he [Mark Twain] could *vent* his hatred of pioneer life and all its conditions" (*Van W. Brooks*). **Utter** stresses the use of voice; it does not, however, always imply speech; as, to *utter* a yell; to *utter* one's relief by sobbing. When speech is implied, the context often suggests a reason for secrecy as well as for revelation. "He was caught up into paradise, and heard unspeakable words, which it is not lawful for a man to *utter*" (*2 Corinthians* xii. 4). "Begin by encouraging him to *utter* freely even his most shocking thoughts" (*B. Russell*). **Voice** does not necessarily imply vocal utterance, but it invariably suggests expression in words. "I revelled in being able to *voice* my opinions without being regarded as a dangerous lunatic" (*C. Mackenzie*). Very often *voice* suggests that the writer or speaker serves as a mouthpiece; as, the editorial *voices* the universal longing for peace; one, bolder than the rest, *voiced* their disapproval of the proposal. **Broach** stresses mention for the first time, especially of something long thought over and awaiting an opportune moment for disclosure; as, the mayor did not *broach* the project until he felt that public opinion was in its favor. **Air** implies exposure, often in the desire to parade one's views, sometimes in the hope of attracting attention or sympathy; as, to *air* one's opinions of the government; to *air* a grievance. **Ventilate** implies exposure also, but usually suggests a desire to get at the truth as by discovering the real issues or by weighing the evidence pro and con; it often means to investigate freely, openly, and thoroughly. "The question [the future of literature] has thus been *ventilated* from every point of view" (*Times Lit. Sup.*).

Ana. *Speak, talk: *pronounce, articulate, enunciate: *reveal, disclose, divulge, tell: *declare, proclaim, announce.

Ant. Imply. — ***Con.*** Hint, intimate, *suggest, insinuate.

expression. *Phrase, locution, collocation, idiom.

expressive. Expressive, eloquent, significant, meaningful, pregnant, sententious, as here compared, agree in meaning clearly conveying or manifesting a thought, idea, or feeling, or a combination of these. That is **expressive** which vividly or strikingly represents the thoughts, feelings, or ideas which it intends to convey or which inform or animate it: the term is applicable not only to language but to works of art or, in the case of music, drama, and the like, to their performance, and to looks, features, inarticulate sounds, and the like; as, a forcible and *expressive* word; an *expressive* face; "he laid great stress on the painting of the eyes, as the most *expressive* and dominating feature" (*Binyon*). "A growing emphasis on the element [in beauty] that is described by such epithets as vital, characteristic, picturesque, individual,—in short, on the element that may be summed up by the epithet *expressive*" (*Babbitt*). That is **eloquent** (as here considered: see also VOCAL, 2) which "speaks louder than words," and reveals with even greater or more impressive force one's thoughts, ideas, or feelings (as, "There was a burst of applause, and a deep silence which was even more *eloquent* than the applause"—*Hardy;* "I could scarcely remove my eyes from her *eloquent* countenance: I seemed to read in it relief and gladness mingled with surprise and something like vexation"—*Hudson*), or which gives a definite and clear suggestion of a condition, situation, character, or the like (as, "a tremulous little man, in greenish-black broadcloth, *eloquent* of continued depression in some village retail trade"—*Quiller-Couch;* "a sidewalk *eloquent* of official neglect"—*Brownell*). *Eloquent* is also applicable to words, style, and the like, when a power to arouse deep feeling or to evoke images or ideas charged with emotion is implied; as, words *eloquent* of feeling; a simple but deeply *eloquent* style. That is **significant** which is not empty of ideas, thoughts, purpose, or the like, but conveys a meaning to the auditor, observer, reader, or the like. The term sometimes is applied to words that express a clearly ascertainable idea as distinguished from those words that merely express a relation or a connection, such as prepositions, conjunctions, etc. (as, "his honoured client had a meaning and so deep it was, so subtle, that no wonder he experienced a difficulty in giving it fitly *significant* words"—*Meredith;* "those who lay down that every sentence must end on a *significant* word, never on a preposition"—*H. Ellis*), or to works of art or literature that similarly express a clearly ascertainable idea (such as a moral, a lesson, a thesis) as distinguished from works that exist purely for their beauty or perfection of form and have no obvious purpose or import (as, art-for-art's-sake men deny that any work of art is necessarily *significant;* many persons find it difficult to enjoy poems such as Coleridge's "Kubla Khan" that are not *significant*). More often, *significant* applies to looks, gestures, acts, or the like, that suggest a covert or hidden meaning or intention; as, "By many *significant* looks and silent entreaties, did she endeavour to prevent such a proof of complaisance" (*Austen*); "she could not feel that there was anything *significant* in his attentions" (*Deland*). That is **meaningful** which is significant in the sense just defined: the term, however, is often preferred when nothing more than the presence of meaning or intention is implied and any hint of importance or of momentousness (implications sometimes associated with *significant* in the sense here considered) would be confusing; as, of two close synonyms one word may be more *meaningful* (i.e., richer in connotations) than the other; "it was a...*meaningful* smile" (*G. Macdonald*). That is **pregnant** (literally, heavy with young, as a mother) which conveys its meaning with richness or with weightiness, and often with extreme conciseness or power. "It is pretty and graceful, but how different from the grave and *pregnant* strokes of Maurice's pencil" (*Arnold*). "The *pregnant* maxim of Bacon that the right question is the half of knowledge" (*H. Ellis*). "He had no talent for revealing a character or resuming the significance of an episode in a single *pregnant* phrase" (*Maugham*). That is **sententious** which is full of significance: when applied, as is usual, to expressions, the word connotes the force and the pithiness of an aphorism; as, "*sententious* and oracular brevity" (*Gibbon*); "*sententious* maxims" (*T. S. Eliot*). In current use, the term often connotes platitudinousness or triteness; as, " 'Contentment breeds Happiness'... a proposition...*sententious*, sedate, obviously true" (*Quiller-Couch*).

Ana. Revealing *or* revelatory, disclosing, divulging (see corresponding verbs at REVEAL): *graphic, vivid, picturesque, pictorial: suggesting *or* suggestive, adumbrating, shadowing (see corresponding verbs at SUGGEST).

Con. *Stiff, wooden, rigid, tense, stark: stern, austere, *severe: inane, jejune, flat, banal, vapid, *insipid: vacuous, *empty.

expunge. *Erase, cancel, efface, obliterate, blot out, delete, dele.

Ana. Wipe out, eradicate, extirpate (see EXTERMINATE).

exquisite, *adj.* *Choice, recherché, rare, dainty, delicate, elegant.

Ana. Precious, valuable, priceless, *costly: *consummate, finished: flawless, *impeccable, faultless: *perfect, intact, whole, entire.

exquisite, *n.* *Fop, élégant, coxcomb, beau, dandy, dude, macaroni, buck, spark, swell, nob, toff.

extemporaneous, extemporary. Extemporaneous, extempore, extemporary, improvised, impromptu, offhand, unpremeditated agree in meaning composed, concocted, devised, or done at the moment rather than beforehand. **Extemporaneous** (now, in general use, the most common of the three words), **extempore** (more often used adverbially) and **extemporary** apply to something that is necessitated by the occasion or situation, such as a speech, a prayer, or a song, or in older and now rare use, something which must be hastily constructed, prepared, or produced; as, an *extemporaneous* oration;

an *extempore* sermon; an *extemporary* altar; "*extemporary* government" (*Johnson*). The terms, however, as applied to discourse, often suggest advance knowledge or thought and imply little more than the absence of a written record of what one intends to say; as, he is one of the best *extemporaneous* speakers of our time; *extempore* prayers are preferred in some churches as more likely to be sincere and fervent. **Improvised** stresses the absence of foreknowledge of what is to be accomplished and therefore the composing, concocting, devising, or constructing of something without advance thought or preparation and often without the necessary tools, instruments, or other equipment; as, an *improvised* musical accompaniment; an *improvised* pantomime; an *improvised* bed for the night in the open; "When an emergency came an army had to be *improvised*" (*Buchan*). **Impromptu** stresses the immediate response to a need or suggestion and the spontaneous character of that which is composed, concocted, or the like, on the spur of the moment; as, an *impromptu* speech or reply; an *impromptu* picnic; an *impromptu* dance. **Offhand** (also an adverb) carries so much stronger an implication of casualness, carelessness, or indifference than any of the preceding terms, that at times it loses its suggestion of an impromptu character and means little more than *curt* or *brusque;* as, an *offhand* comment; an *offhand* salute; an *offhand* manner of dealing with strangers. **Unpremeditated** emphasizes less strongly than *extemporaneous* and *impromptu* the immediate stimulus of an occasion but it usually suggests some strong, often suddenly provoked, emotion which drives one to composition, to action, or the like; as, "[the skylark] That from heaven, or near it, Pourest thy full heart In profuse strains of *unpremeditated* art" (*Shelley*); *unpremeditated* murder.

Ana. *Spontaneous, impulsive: ready, prompt, apt, *quick.

Con. Planned, designed, projected, schemed (see verbs under PLAN, *n.*): *deliberate, considered, studied, advised, premeditated: formal, ceremonious, *ceremonial, conventional.

extempore. *Extemporaneous, extemporary, improvised, impromptu, offhand, unpremeditated.

Ana. & *Con.* See those at EXTEMPORANEOUS.

extend. **Extend, lengthen, elongate, prolong, protract** all agree in meaning to draw out or add to so as to increase in length. Both **extend** and **lengthen** (opposed to *shorten*) connote an increase of length either in space or in time but *extend* is also used figuratively to connote increase in range as of kinds, of influence, of applicability, and the like; as, to *extend* (or *lengthen*) a road; to *extend* (or *lengthen*) one's stay; to *extend* (not *lengthen*) one's privileges, a monarch's power, a word's meaning. **Elongate** (usually opposed to *abbreviate*) denotes to increase in spatial length and has wider technical than general use; as, fibers *elongated* by stretching. **Prolong** (opposed to *cut short, arrest*) means to extend in duration beyond usual or normal limits; as, to *prolong* one's childhood; to *prolong* the process of digestion; exercise *prolongs* life. **Protract** (opposed to *curtail*) adds to the denotation of *prolong* the connotations of indefiniteness, needlessness, or boredom; as, a *protracted* debate or visit.

Ana. *Increase, enlarge, augment: *expand, amplify, distend, dilate.

Ant. Abridge, shorten. — *Con.* Abbreviate, curtail, retrench (see SHORTEN): *contract, shrink, condense.

extension. Wing, ell, *annex, dependence.

extent. *Size, dimensions, area, magnitude, volume.

Ana. *Range, scope, compass, sweep, reach, radius: stretch, spread, amplitude, *expanse.

extenuate, *v.* **1** Attenuate, *thin, dilute, rarefy.

Ana. Diminish, lessen, reduce, *decrease: *weaken, enfeeble, debilitate: *moderate, temper, attemper, qualify.

Ant. Intensify. — *Con.* Aggravate, heighten, enhance (see INTENSIFY).

2 *Palliate, gloze, gloss, whitewash, whiten.

Ana. Condone, *excuse: rationalize, *explain, justify.

exterior, *adj.* *Outer, external, outward, outside.

Ana. *Extrinsic, extraneous, foreign, alien.

Ant. Interior. — *Con.* *Inner, inward, internal, inside, intestine: intrinsic, *inherent, ingrained.

exterminate. **Exterminate, extirpate, eradicate, uproot, deracinate, wipe out** come into comparison in their secondary senses in which they mean to effect the destruction or abolition of something. **Exterminate** (etymologically, to expel or banish from the bounds or limits) implies utter extinction; it therefore in current use usually, but not invariably, implies a killing off; as, efforts to *exterminate* certain pests such as mosquitoes, rats, and ragweed have not yet been successful; "the tribe [of Indians] had been *exterminated*, not here in their stronghold, but in their summer camp...across the river" (*Cather*). **Extirpate** (literally, to pluck up a plant by the stem and root so as to cause its death) implies extinction as of a race, or family, or species, or growth, but it may carry a less immediate implication of killing off than *extermination* carries, by suggesting the destruction or removal of the means whereby a thing is propagated rather than the destruction of all the individuals involved; thus, a tribe might be *extirpated* (or *exterminated*) by a famine; a heresy is often *extirpated* (rather than *exterminated*) by the removal of the leaders from a position of influence; a vice cannot easily be *extirpated* so long as the conditions which promote it remain in existence. **Eradicate** (literally, to pluck out by the roots) stresses the driving out or elimination of something that has taken root or has established itself; as, diphtheria has been nearly but not completely *eradicated* from the United States; it is difficult to *eradicate* popular superstitions; "he must gradually *eradicate* his settled conviction that the Italians and the French are wrong" (*Grandgent*). **Uproot** (which literally means the same as *eradicate*) differs from the latter word chiefly in being more definitely figurative and in suggesting forcible and violent methods similar to those of a tempest that tears trees out by their roots; as, "Hands...red with guiltless blood ...*uprooting* every germ Of truth" (*Shelley*); "end forthwith The ruin of a life *uprooted* thus" (*Browning*); refugees from the peoples *uprooted* by war. **Deracinate** varies little from *uproot* in meaning but is far less common in use. "Frights, changes, horrors, Divert and crack, rend and *deracinate* The unity and married calm of states Quite from their fixture!" (*Shak.*). "He fascinated the young Anderson's intellect and *deracinated* certain convictions" (*W. R. Benét*). **Wipe out** (literally, to rub out by erasing) often implies extermination (as, the entire battery was *wiped out* by shell fire) but it equally often suggests a canceling or obliterating as by payment, retaliation, exhaustion of supply, or the like (as, to *wipe out* a debt; to *wipe out* an old score; to *wipe out* a disgrace; the fall in share prices *wiped out* his margin).

Ana. *Abolish, extinguish, annihilate, abate: obliterate, efface, expunge, blot out, *erase: *destroy, demolish, raze.

external, *adj.* *Outer, exterior, outward, outside.

Ana. *Extrinsic, extraneous, foreign, alien.

Ant. Internal. — *Con.* Interior, intestine, *inner, inward, inside: intrinsic, ingrained, *inherent.

externalize. Materialize, actualize, *realize, embody,

incarnate, objectify, substantiate, substantialize, hypostatize, reify.

extinguish. *Abolish, annihilate, abate.

Ana. Extirpate, *exterminate, eradicate, uproot, wipe out: obliterate, efface, blot out, expunge, *erase: *suppress, repress.

extirpate. *Exterminate, eradicate, uproot, deracinate, wipe out.

Ana. Extinguish, *abolish, annihilate: obliterate, efface, expunge, *erase, blot out: *destroy, demolish, raze.

Con. Propagate, *generate, engender, breed.

extol. Laud, *praise, eulogize, acclaim.

Ana. Applaud, *commend, compliment: *exalt, magnify, aggrandize.

Ant. Decry: abase (*oneself*). — *Con.* Depreciate, disparage, detract from, derogate from, belittle, minimize (see DECRY): denounce, condemn, censure, reprobate, reprehend, *criticize.

extort. Extract, *educe, elicit, evoke.

Ana. Draw, drag, *pull: compel, *force, constrain, oblige, coerce: exact, *demand, require.

extra, *adj.* Supernumerary, spare, surplus, *superfluous.

extract, *v.* Extort, elicit, *educe, evoke.

Ana. Draw, *pull, drag: *demand, require, exact: obtain, procure, gain, win, acquire, *get.

extract, *n.* **Extract, excerpt, pericope** agree in denoting a passage transcribed or quoted from a book or document. **Extract** is the general term referring to any such passage regardless of the principle of its selection or its further use; as, *extracts* for citation are copied by the typists as indicated to them by the readers; he makes many *extracts* from every book he reads. **Excerpt** differs from *extract* in implying careful selection for a definite purpose that is commonly indicated in the context; as, to back up his points by *excerpts* from the authoritative writers on the subject; *excerpts* from his letters were entered as evidence. **Pericope** applies generally to any passage to which attention is specifically called. In its most common use, however, it applies specifically to the passage excerpted from Scriptures to be read in a religious service such as the Mass, or to be used as a text by the preacher; as, the *pericope* of the day was taken from the Gospel of St. John.

extradite. Deport, transport, expatriate, *banish, exile, ostracize.

Ana. Surrender, *relinquish, yield, resign.

extraneous. *Extrinsic, foreign, alien.

Ana. External, exterior, outside, *outer, outward: adventitious, *accidental, incidental.

Ant. Relevant: essential (sense 1). — *Con.* Intrinsic, *inherent, ingrained, constitutional: intestine, internal, *inner, inside, interior, inward: pertinent, germane, material (see RELEVANT).

extravagant. Inordinate, immoderate, *excessive, exorbitant, extreme.

Ana. Preposterous, absurd, *foolish, silly: *profuse, prodigal, lavish, exuberant.

Ant. Restrained. — *Con.* Frugal, *sparing, economical.

extreme, *adj.* **1** *Last, final, terminal, latest, concluding, eventual, ultimate.

2 Exorbitant, inordinate, *excessive, immoderate, extravagant.

extreme, *n.* **Extreme, extremity** come into comparison when they mean the utmost limit or degree of something. **Extreme,** however, usually applies to either of two limits which are diametrically opposed, or are as far removed from each other as possible; as, a climate where *extremes* of heat and cold are unknown; " 'Twixt two *extremes* of passion, joy and grief" (*Shak.*); "my tendency is to unite *extremes* rather than to go between them" (*H. Ellis*). The term may, however, when used with a verb of motion or one suggesting movement, imply a definite direction and therefore denote the utmost limit or degree in that direction; as, he always goes to an *extreme* (sometimes, "goes to *extremes*"); he is always dressed in the *extreme* of fashion. **Extremity,** on the other hand, usually implies the utmost removal from that which is reasonable, sane, safe, tolerable, endurable, or the like; as, the *extremity* of their opinions; "an *extremity* of caution" (*H. G. Wells*); an *extremity* of suffering. Often the term applies concretely to the state or condition of one in extreme pain, grief, anxiety, suffering, poverty, or the like; as, "The queen's in labor, They say, in great *extremity*" (*Shak.*); "those...who succour heroic minds in their worst *extremities*" (*L. P. Smith*).

Ana. Antithesis, antipodes, contrary. See under OPPOSITE, *adj.*

extremity. *Extreme.

Ana. *Limit, bound, bourn, end, confine, term.

extricate, *v.* **Extricate, disentangle, untangle, disencumber, disembarrass** come into comparison as meaning to free or release from that which binds or holds one back. **Extricate,** the most widely useful of these words, implies a situation in which a person is (or persons are) so entangled in difficulties, perplexities, or the like, or so restrained from free action or free movements, that great force or ingenuity is required to bring about his (or their) release; as, the fly was not able to *extricate* itself from the spider's web; to *extricate* oneself from financial difficulties; his friends succeeded in *extricating* him from a very awkward predicament; to *extricate* one's car from the mud into which its wheels had sunk. **Disentangle,** which is etymologically akin to *extricate* in meaning, adheres far more closely than the latter word to its literal sense of to free from that which entangles; also, it is used typically of things, rather than of persons, and therefore seldom, if ever, involves the ideas of difficulty or perplexity except for the person who seeks to free the thing entangled or to unravel that which is intricately complicated; as, to *disentangle* a strand from a twisted skein; "[Seneca] is a dramatist...whom the whole of Europe in the Renaissance delighted to honour. It is obviously a task of some difficulty to *disentangle* him from his reputation" (*T. S. Eliot*); "I could not then so far analyse all that is roughly lumped together as 'religion' as to *disentangle* the essential from the accidental" (*H. Ellis*). **Untangle** is sometimes used, especially in colloquial English, in place of *disentangle* with much the same implications; as, to *untangle* one's foot from a vine in which it is caught. **Disencumber** implies a freeing from that which weighs down, clogs, or imposes a very heavy burden; as, "He can call a spade a spade, and knows how to *disencumber* ideas of their wordy frippery" (*G. Eliot*); "the trees, laden heavily with their new and humid leaves, were now suffering more damage than during the highest winds of winter, when the boughs are specially *disencumbered* to do battle with the storm" (*Hardy*). **Disembarrass** implies a release from that which embarrasses as by impeding, hampering, or hindering; as, before going to the tennis court, she *disembarrassed* herself of her long, clinging dress and put on a loose shirt and shorts; "to *disembarrass* himself of his companion" (*Scott*); "I have never been able...to *disembarrass* my head of the most wonderful vision that ever took possession of any man's" (*Landor*).

Ana. Disengage, *detach, abstract: liberate, release, *free: *rescue, deliver.

Con. *Hamper, fetter, trammel, shackle, clog, hog-tie, manacle: impede, obstruct, *hinder, block.

extrinsic. **Extrinsic, extraneous, foreign, alien** are comparable when they mean external to a thing (sometimes a person), its true nature, or its original character. **Extrinsic** applies to that which is distinctly outside the thing in question or is derived from something apart from it; thus, a ring may have *extrinsic* value because of sentimental or historical associations; *extrinsic* influences, such as chance or the assistance of friends, may help a man to succeed. "[Those] who would persuade us ...that style is something *extrinsic* to the subject, a kind of ornamentation laid on" (*Quiller-Couch*). **Extraneous,** though often used interchangeably with *extrinsic,* applies chiefly to that which is introduced from outside and may or may not be capable of becoming an integral part of the thing; as, to advance arguments *extraneous* to the real issue; water is rarely pure and free from *extraneous* matter. "Style...is not—can never be—*extraneous* ornament" (*Quiller-Couch*). "Whatever we gain comprehension of, we seize upon and assimilate into our own being...; that which had been *extraneous* is become a part of ourselves" (*H. B. Alexander*). **Foreign** applies to that which is so different from the thing under consideration that it is either inadmissible because repellent or, if admitted, incapable of becoming identified with it, assimilated by it, or related to it; as, much coal contains *foreign* matter; inflammation caused by a *foreign* body in the stomach. "The mysticism so *foreign* to the French mind and temper" (*Brownell*). "Look round our World .... Nothing is *foreign:* Parts relate to whole...; All serv'd, all serving: nothing stands alone" (*Pope*). **Alien** applies to that which is so foreign that it can never be made an inherent or an integral part of a thing. The word often suggests repugnance or at least incompatibility or irreconcilableness. "A voluptuous devotionality ...totally *alien* to the austerity and penetrating sincerity of the Gospel" (*Inge*). "He would often adopt certain modes of thought that he knew to be really *alien* to his nature" (*Wilde*).

Ana. External, *outer, outside, exterior, outward: acquired, gained, earned (see GET).

Ant. Intrinsic. — *Con.* Internal, *inner, inside, inward, interior, intestine: *real, actual, true.

exuberant. Lavish, *profuse, prodigal, luxuriant, lush.

Ana. Prolific, *fertile, fruitful, fecund: *vigorous, lusty, energetic, nervous: rampant, *rank: copious (see PLENTIFUL).

Ant. Austere: sterile.

exultant. *Elated, elate.

Ana. Joyous, joyful, *glad: ecstatic, rapturous, transported (see corresponding nouns at ECSTASY).

exuviate. *Discard, cast, shed, molt, slough, scrap, junk.

eyewitness. Witness, onlooker, looker-on, *spectator, observer, beholder, bystander, kibitzer.

F

fable. 1 *Fiction, fabrication, figment.
2 Myth, parable, *allegory, apologue.

fabric. *Building, edifice, structure, pile.

fabricate. *Make, fashion, forge, form, shape, manufacture.

Ana. *Invent, create: produce, turn out (see BEAR): devise, contrive (see corresponding nouns at DEVICE).

fabrication. *Fiction, figment, fable.

Ana. Invention, creation (see corresponding verbs at INVENT): art, craft, handicraft (see TRADE): *work, product, production, opus, artifact.

fabulous. *Fictitious, mythical, legendary, apocryphal.

Ana. Astonishing, amazing, astounding (see SURPRISE, *v.*): extravagant, inordinate (see EXCESSIVE): *monstrous, prodigious, stupendous.

Con. Credible, believable, colorable (see PLAUSIBLE): veritable, genuine, *authentic.

face, *n.* **Face, countenance, visage, physiognomy, mug, puss** agree in denoting the front part of a human (sometimes animal) head including the mouth, nose, eyes, forehead, and cheeks. **Face** is the simple and direct word, applicable either to one's own or another's; as, your *face* is dirty; she struck him in the *face;* "To feel the fog in my throat, The mist in my *face*" (*Browning*); "Was this [Helen of Troy's] the *face* that launched a thousand ships and burnt the topless towers of Ilium?" (*Marlowe*). **Countenance** applies especially to the face as it reveals one's mood, character, changing emotions, or the like, to others; as, a benign *countenance;* "his *face* was not the cheerful *countenance* of yesterday" (*Cather*); his *countenance* changed when he heard the news; "Something feminine—not effeminate, mind—is discoverable in the *countenances* of all men of genius" (*Coleridge*). In the phrases "to keep in *countenance*" (that is, to maintain one's composure) and "to put out of *countenance*" (that is, to lose one's composure or cause one to lose it) the term denotes the facial expression as it appears normally when one is composed. Sometimes the word is used in place of *face* when a formal term is desired; as, "That vile representation of the royal *countenance*" (*Swift*). Both *face* and *countenance* may be used in personifications when the outward aspect or appearance of anything is denoted; as, "startling transformations in the outward *face* of society are taking place under our very eyes" (*Frankfurter*); "Beholding the bright *countenance* of truth in the quiet and still air of delightful studies" (*Milton*). **Visage** is a more literary term than the preceding words; it often suggests attention to the shape and proportions of the face, but sometimes to the impression it gives or the changes in mood which it reflects; as, "black hair; complexion dark; generally, rather handsome *visage*" (*Dickens*); "his *visage* all agrin as at a wake" (*Tennyson*). **Physiognomy** is the preferred word when the reference is to the contours of the face, the shape of the features, and the characteristic expression as indicative of race, character, temperament, or the like; as, he has the *physiognomy* of a Pole, of an ascetic; "Nor is there in the *physiognomy* of the people the slightest indication of the Gaul" (*Landor*). Figuratively, the term is applicable to the significant or sharply defined aspect of things; as, "[it] is not exactly one of those styles which have a *physiognomy*...which stamp an indelible impression of him [their author] on the reader's mind" (*Arnold*); "the changing yet abiding *physiognomy* of earth and sky" (*Lowes*). **Mug,** although it dates from around 1800 and is used humorously by many good writers, is still regarded as slang; usually, but not invariably, it carries a suggestion of an ugly, but not necessarily displeasing, physiognomy; as, "I found

A. Tennyson in chambers at Lincoln's Inn: and recreated myself with a sight of his fine old *mug*" (*E. Fitzgerald*); "Among all the ugly *mugs* of the world we see now and then a face made after the divine pattern" (*L. P. Smith*). **Puss,** a term of Irish origin, and now slang (as, she has a sour *puss;* slap him in the *puss*) or dialectal, sometimes denotes a facial expression such as of anger or pouting; as, "Wipe that *puss* off your face" (*American Mercury*); but it more often denotes the physiognomy; as, "it had the head of a bear, the very head and *puss* of a bear" (*Lady Gregory*).

facet. Aspect, side, angle, *phase.

facetious. Humorous, jocose, jocular, *witty.
Ana. Jesting, joking, quipping, wisecracking (see corresponding nouns at JEST): jolly, jovial, jocund, *merry, blithe: comical, comic, droll, funny, ludicrous, *laughable.
Ant. Lugubrious. — *Con.* Grave, solemn, *serious, sober, sedate, staid.

facile. *Easy, smooth, light, simple, effortless.
Ana. Adroit, deft, *dexterous, feat: fluent, voluble, glib (see VOCAL): *superficial, shallow, uncritical, cursory.
Ant. Arduous (*with reference to the thing accomplished*): constrained, clumsy (*with reference to the agent or his method*).

facility. Ease, dexterity, *readiness.
Ana. Spontaneity, *unconstraint, abandon: address, poise, *tact: lightness, effortlessness, smoothness (see corresponding adjectives at EASY).
Con. Ineptness, clumsiness, awkwardness, maladroitness (see corresponding adjectives at AWKWARD): stiffness, rigidity, woodenness (see corresponding adjectives at STIFF): *effort, exertion, pains: *difficulty, hardship.

facsimile. Copy, carbon copy, *reproduction, duplicate, replica, transcript.

faction. Bloc, party, *combination, combine, ring, cabal, junto.
Ana. Clique, *set, coterie, circle.

factious. Contumacious, seditious, mutinous, rebellious, *insubordinate.
Ana. Contending, fighting, warring (see CONTEND): contentious, quarrelsome, litigious (see BELLIGERENT): disaffected, estranged, alienated (see ESTRANGE).
Ant. Co-operative. — *Con.* Companionable, gregarious, *social: *compliant, acquiescent: loyal, leal, true, *faithful.

factitious. *Artificial, synthetic, ersatz.
Ana. Manufactured, fabricated (see MAKE, *v.*): forced, compelled, constrained (see FORCE, *v.*): simulated, feigned, counterfeited, shammed, pretended, affected, assumed (see ASSUME).
Ant. Bona fide, veritable. — *Con.* *Authentic, genuine: *natural, simple, artless, naïve, unsophisticated.
☞ *Do not confuse* factitious *with* fictitious.

factor. **1** *Agent, attorney, deputy, proxy.
2 Agent, bailiff, *steward, reeve, seneschal, major-domo, oeconomus.
3 Constituent, *element, component, integrant, ingredient.
Ana. Determinant, *cause, antecedent: *influence: agency, agent, instrument, instrumentality, *means.

faculty. **1** *Power, function.
2 *Gift, aptitude, knack, bent, turn, genius, talent.
Ana. *Ability, capacity, capability: property, *quality: penchant, flair, propensity, proclivity, *leaning: *predilection.

fad. Vogue, *fashion, style, rage, craze, mode, dernier cri, cry.
Ana. Whim, whimsey, *caprice, vagary.

fadeless. Unfading, amaranthine, *immortal, deathless, undying.
Ana. *Everlasting, never-ending: *lasting, perdurable, perpetual, permanent.

faery. *Fairy, fay, sprite, elf, shee, banshee, leprechaun, pixy, gnome, dwarf, goblin, brownie, puck, nix.

fag, *v.* Exhaust, jade, fatigue, *tire, weary, tucker.

failing, *n.* Frailty, foible, *fault, vice.
Ana. *Blemish, flaw, defect: weakness, infirmity (see corresponding adjectives at WEAK).
Ant. Perfection (*in concrete sense*). — *Con.* *Excellence, merit, virtue.

failure. *Insolvency, bankruptcy, receivership, suspension.

fainéant, *adj.* Indolent, slothful, *lazy.
Ana. Supine, passive, *inactive, inert, idle: apathetic, *impassive, phlegmatic: *lethargic, sluggish: languorous, lackadaisical, *languid.

fair, *adj.* **1** Comely, lovely, *beautiful, pretty, bonny, handsome, beauteous, pulchritudinous, good-looking.
Ana. Delicate, dainty, exquisite (see CHOICE): charming, attractive, enchanting (see under ATTRACT): pure, *chaste.
Ant. Foul: ill-favored.

2 Fair, just, equitable, impartial, unbiased, dispassionate, uncolored, objective come into comparison when they are applied to judgments or to judges or to acts resulting from or involving a judgment and mean free from undue or improper influence. **Fair,** the most general term, implies the disposition or the intention to regard other persons or things without reference to one's own interests, feelings, or prejudices, often even to the point of conceding every reasonable claim of the weaker side or of giving oneself or the stronger side no undue advantage; as, a *fair* distribution of one's estate; a *fair* decision; *fair* play. "When we consider how helpless a partridge is...it does seem *fairer* that the gunner should have but one chance at the bird" (*Jefferies*). "I am being *fair* to both sides...I don't feel I can quite condemn it [socialism] wholesale" (*R. Macaulay*). **Just** implies no divergence from the standard or measure of that which has been determined or is accepted as right, true, lawful, or the like, and dealings that are exactly in accordance with those determinations, no matter what one's personal inclinations or interests may be or what considerations in favor of the person or thing judged may be adduced; as, a *just* judge; "every transgression and disobedience received a *just* recompence" (*Hebrews* ii. 2). "Some *juster* prince perhaps had... safe restored me to my native land" (*Pope*). "How much easier it is to be generous than *just*" (*Junius*). "To divert interest from the poet to the poetry...would conduce to a *juster* estimation of actual poetry, good and bad" (*T. S. Eliot*). **Equitable** implies a freer and less rigid standard than *just,* often, but not invariably, that which guides a court of equity as distinguished from a court of law and which provides relief where rigid adherence to the law would make for unfairness (as, he has an *equitable* claim to the property); more often, however, it implies fair and equal treatment of all concerned; as, "a form of society which will provide for an *equitable* distribution of...riches" (*J. W. Krutch*); "it depended wholly on their [the Roman governors'] individual characters whether their terms of office were *equitable* or oppressive" (*Buchan*). **Impartial** implies absence of favor for, or absence of prejudice against, one person, party, or side, more than the other; as, an *impartial* tribunal, judgment, summing up of evidence. **Unbiased** expresses even more strongly the absence of all prejudice or prepossession, and a disposition to be fair to all; as, an *unbiased* history; to give an *unbiased* opinion or testimony. **Dispassionate** implies freedom from the influence of passion or strong feeling, often also implying great temperateness or even coldness in judgment; as, a *dispassionate* judgment, inquiry, critic, observer. **Uncolored** (see also COLORLESS) implies freedom from all influences that would affect the truth or accuracy of an account, a statement, or a judgment, such as personal feeling, a desire to embellish, or the like; as, an *uncolored* story of a battle; an *uncolored* record of one's experiences; a statement of facts, *uncolored* by personal prejudice. **Objective** implies a tendency to view events or phenomena as apart from oneself and therefore to be judged as they are (or were) in fact and without reference to one's personal feelings, prejudices, opinions, or the like; as, "Nor must we be content with a lazy scepticism, which regards *objective* truth as unattainable" (*B. Russell*); "Even so far stand the great...*objective* writers above all who appeal to you by parade of personality or private sentiment" (*Quiller-Couch*); "The simplicity and practical cast of his [Xenophon's] mind made him a good *objective* reporter of the Socratic conversations" (*J. R. Smith*).

Ana. Disinterested, detached (see INDIFFERENT): reasonable, *rational.

Ant. Unfair. — *Con.* Partial, prepossessed, biased, prejudiced (see corresponding nouns at PREDILECTION).

3 Average, *medium, middling, mediocre, second-rate, moderate, indifferent.

Ana. Ordinary, *common.

Con. *Good, right: *bad, poor, wrong.

fair, *n.* Exposition, *exhibition, show, exhibit.

fairing. Gratuity, largess, *gift, present, favor, boon.

fairy. Fairy, faery, fay, elf, sprite, pixy (*or* **pixie**), **gnome, dwarf, goblin, brownie** (*or* **browny**), **puck, nix** (*or, in feminine form,* **nixie**), **shee, leprechaun, banshee** come into comparison as denoting a legendary supernatural being, chiefly in medieval and modern folklore, capable of assuming a human form and of entering into relations with men for their weal or woe. **Fairy** is the general term for one of this class, but with many writers the term implies a specific kind of being. In its concrete sense, *fairy* applies mainly to either of two types: one who assumes the form of a marvelously beautiful woman and lures men to her abode where they are held enchanted and unable to return to earth; the other who is sometimes masculine but more often feminine, who is extremely diminutive in size, and who, usually, is a creature of lightness and grace possessing magical powers. By some writers the former is distinguished as the Celtic, the latter as the Teutonic, fairy but this classification often breaks down owing to the variety of conceptions that prevail and their intermingling. Also, Shakespeare and Charles Perrault, a Frenchman, are often given credit for the second and more common conception of a fairy. Under the influence of the *Faerie Queene,* the spelling **faery** has come to connote existence in an unreal, romantic, and visionary world such as one associates with Spenser's poem or with the so-called Celtic fairy; as, "O blessèd Bird! the earth we pace Again appears to be An unsubstantial, *faery* place; That is fit home for Thee!" (*Wordsworth*); "Magic casements, opening on the foam Of perilous seas, in *faery* [changed by Keats from an original *fairy*] lands forlorn" (*Keats*). **Fay,** a more or less poetic term for *fairy,* often, but far from invariably, suggests reference to the diminutive fairy; as, "*fays* shall haunt the green" (*Collins*). **Elf** is historically the correct term in English for the so-called Teutonic fairy; the term also carries a stronger implication than *fairy* of sportiveness, of helpfulness or harmfulness (often malicious, but still more often mischievous), of soullessness, and of eeriness in the places which they haunt or inhabit; as, "Ye tiny *elves* that guiltless sport" (*Burns*); "The horns of *Elf*land faintly blowing!" (*Tennyson*). **Sprite** is used as an equivalent of *elf* when its ethereal quality or its soullessness is especially to be suggested; as, a mischievous *sprite;* "that shrewd and knavish *sprite* Call'd Robin Goodfellow" (*Shak.*); "she was a *sprite* rather than a human spirit, fastidiousness with her took the place of morality" (*H. Ellis*). **Pixy,** originally a dialectal term for *fairy* or *elf,* especially in southwestern England, retains in its extended use its early implications of a being that delights in misleading or annoying human beings or is extremely sportive or gay; thus, a person who fell into a state of mental bewilderment was said to be *pixy*-led; a *pixy* ring (now commonly called a *fairy* ring) is a circular fungus growth in a lawn or meadow where pixies are supposed to dance in the moonlight. **Gnome** and **dwarf** designate a sprite (usually conceived of as masculine, misshapen, and extremely ugly) who dwells below the surface of the earth and has guard of metals and minerals or is a skilled artificer of weapons and the like. When his power to terrify or injure men is emphasized he is sometimes called a **goblin;** when he is thought of as man's helper who performs in secrecy at night heavy work, such as churning, threshing, and sweeping, he is often called a **brownie;** when both mischievous and helpful characteristics are implied, **puck** is often employed, but in nearly every case *goblin, brownie,* and *puck* carry few of the very specific implications usually found in *gnome* or *dwarf;* as, "Swift on his sooty pinions flits the *gnome*" (*Pope*); Snow White took refuge with kindly *dwarfs;* "the *Gobble-uns*'ll [the *goblins* will] git you Ef you don't watch out" (*J. W. Riley*); "The *Brownie* formed a class of beings, distinct in habit and disposition from the freakish and mischievous *elves*" (*Scott*); "As I am an honest *Puck* ... We will make amends ere long" (*Shak.*). **Nix** (or, feminine, **nixie**) designates a water sprite similar to a merman or mermaid; as, "If a *pixie,* seek thy ring; If a *nixie,* seek thy spring" (*Scott*). **Shee** and **leprechaun** are in Celtic folklore the equivalents respectively of *fairy* and of *gnome,* but *shee* often carries stronger implication of rare appearance to the human sight than *fairy,* and *leprechaun* one of greater elusiveness and trickery than *gnome.* **Banshee** applies to a female shee who is heard keening or wailing near a house, as a warning of an approaching death in the family.

faith. 1 *Belief, credence, credit.

Ana. Assurance, conviction, *certainty, certitude: assenting *or* assent, acquiescence, agreement (see corresponding verbs at ASSENT).

Ant. Doubt. — *Con.* *Uncertainty, skepticism, dubiety, dubiosity: *unbelief, disbelief, incredulity.

2 Dependence, reliance, confidence, *trust.

Ana. Assurance, certitude (see CERTAINTY).

Con. Incredulity, *unbelief, disbelief: mistrust, suspicion, *uncertainty, doubt: misgiving, *apprehension.

3 Creed, *religion, persuasion, church, denomination, sect, cult, communion.

Ana. Tenets, dogmas, doctrines (see singular nouns at DOCTRINE).

faithful, *adj.* **Faithful, loyal, leal, true, constant, stanch** (*or* **staunch**), **steadfast** (*or* **stedfast**), **resolute** come into comparison as meaning firm in adherence to the person, the country, the cause, or the like, to whom or to which one is bound by duty or promise. **Faithful** in its now most common sense implies firm and unswerving adherence to a person or thing to whom or to which one is united by some tie such as marriage, friendship, political allegiance, gratitude, or honor, or to the oath, pledge, promise, or the like made when one has accepted a position, an office, an obligation, or the like; as, a *faithful* husband is *faithful* to his marriage vows; a *faithful* public servant is *faithful* to his oath of office. "[Cleopatra] was *faithful* to the main policy of her life, the restoration of Egypt to the position which it had held under the first Ptolemies" (*Buchan*). The term is also used when only firm adherence to actuality or reality as in representation or portrayal is implied: it then comes close to *accurate* or *exact* in meaning; as, the photograph is a *faithful* likeness; a *faithful* description of village life. **Loyal** implies faithfulness to one's plighted troth or continued allegiance to the leader, the country, the institution, the principles, or the like, to which one feels oneself morally bound: the term suggests not only adherence but an unwillingness to be tempted from that adherence; as, most of the subjects remained *loyal* to their sovereign; "Your wife, my lord; your true And *loyal* wife" (*Shak.*); "We [French Canadians] are *loyal* because we are free" (*Laurier*); " 'I've been *loyal* to Arch Gunnard for a long time now,' Lonnie said, 'I'd hate to haul off and leave him like that' " (*Erskine Caldwell*). **Leal,** a much older word in English than *loyal*, has been practically displaced by the latter term except in poetic and in Scottish use. Nevertheless, the word has a value of its own which is not quite that of *loyal*, but nearer to that of *true* (or sometimes to *tried and true*). In the sense in which **true** is here considered (see also REAL), there is a strong implication of steadiness in one's allegiance, devotion, fidelity, or the like, which suggests utter dependability and no fear of a change. These connotations are also strong in *leal;* as, "I'm wearin' awa' To the land o' the *leal* [i.e., Heaven]" (*C. Nairne*); "Honest Allan Cunningham...a *leal* and *true* Scotsman" (*Scott*); "Thou, Scotland's son, that would'st be *leal* and *true*" (*Blackie*). **Constant** also stresses firmness or steadiness in attachment, devotion, or the like, but it carries a weaker implication of strict adherence to one's vows, pledges, obligations, and the like. Consequently, it often implies a state of mind that is the opposite of fickleness rather than a course of action that is the opposite of unfaithfulness and disloyalty. "Even Rochester, utterly bad and ignoble, was not only a poet and a wit but a *loyal* husband (*constant* if not *faithful*)" (*A. Repplier*). "I never knew a pair of lovers More *constant* than those two" (*Millay*). **Stanch** carries far more strongly than *loyal* an implication of one's unwillingness to be turned aside from those to whom one owes allegiance, to whom one has pledged one's troth, or to an institution, such as a church or political party, to which by conviction one belongs. From its earliest and still current sense of watertight and sound, as applied to a ship, it suggests an inherent imperviousness to all suggestions or influences that would weaken one's loyalty or steadiness in faith; as, a *stanch* believer; a *stanch* Republican; a *stanch* adherent of the Stuarts; "*staunch* fidelity to law and order" (*C. E. Montague*). "He was *stanch*, however, to church and king" (*Irving*). "You, who from a girl have had a strong mind and a *staunch* heart" (*Dickens*). **Steadfast** so stresses unwavering or unswerving adherence that the term is applicable not only to persons but to things that maintain a steady course or an unchanging quality or character (as, "Which hope we have as an anchor of the soul, both sure and *stedfast*"—*Hebrews* vi. 19; "the blue, the *steadfast*, the blazing summer sky"—*V. Woolf*). However, its most usual application is to persons or their attachments (as, "Therefore, my beloved brethren, be ye *stedfast*, unmoveable"—*1 Corinthians* xv. 58; "If love...survives through all sorrow, and remains *steadfast* with us through all changes"—*Thackeray;* "Narrow of vision but *steadfast* to principles"—*A. Repplier*). **Resolute** implies steadfastness and, often, stanchness, but it throws the emphasis upon a determination which cannot be broken down, and often suggests firm adherence to one's own purposes or ends rather than to those of others; as, "not ...*resolute* and firm, but perverse and obstinate" (*Burke*); "she sat there *resolute* and ready for responsibility" (*Conrad*). "The *resolute* abstinence [of Chinese and Japanese painters] from cast shadows, as a method of giving relief, is partly to be explained by the desire not to be seduced into mere imitative resemblance" (*Binyon*).

Ana. Devoted, *loving, affectionate: tried, trustworthy, *reliable, dependable.

Ant. Faithless. — ***Con.*** Disloyal, false, perfidious, traitorous, treacherous (see FAITHLESS): fickle, *inconstant, unstable.

faithless. Faithless, false, disloyal, traitorous, treacherous, perfidious agree in meaning untrue to a person or institution that has a right to expect one's fidelity or allegiance. **Faithless** applies to any person, utterance, or act that in any degree implies a breach of a vow, a pledge, a sworn obligation, allegiance, or the like. Although often used interchangeably with the strongest of the terms here discriminated, then implying a betrayal of a person or cause, it is also capable of implying untrustworthiness, unreliability, or loss or neglect of an opportunity to prove one's devotion or faith; as, "And hopeless, comfortless, I'll mourn A *faithless* woman's broken vow" (*Burns*); "*Faithless* alike in friendship and in love" (*Cowper*); "The remnant... Have been abandoned by their *faithless* allies" (*Shelley*). **False,** as here considered, differs from *faithless* in its greater emphasis upon a failure to be true, or constant in one's devotion or adherence, to someone or something which has a claim upon one than upon a breach of a vow, pledge, sworn obligation, or the like: however, it may, like *faithless*, carry varying connotations with respect to the gravity or heinousness of that failure; as, a *false* friend; "Never was Plantagenet *False* of his word" (*Marlowe*); "we hope that we can give a reason for the faith that is in us without being *false* to the strictest obligations of intellectual honesty" (*Inge*); "the conception of a lordly splendid destiny for the human race, to which we are *false* when we revert to wars and other atavistic follies" (*B. Russell*). **Disloyal** implies lack of faithfulness in thought, in words, or in actions, to one's friend, superior, sovereign, party, country, or the like; as, to be *disloyal* to one's school; a *disloyal* subject. "Good party people think such openmindedness *disloyal;* but in politics there should be no loyalty except to the public good" (*Shaw*). **Traitorous** implies either actual treason or a serious betrayal of trust or confidence; as, a *traitorous* general; a *traitorous* act; a *traitorous* breach of confidence. **Treacherous** is of wider application than *traitorous:* as used of persons it implies readiness, or a disposition, to betray trust or confidence (as, a *treacherous* spy; a *treacherous* friend): as used of things it suggests aptness to allure to peril or disaster by false or delusive appearances; as, *treacherous* sands; "the *treacherous* Ocean" (*Shelley*); "Up steep crags, and over *treacherous* morasses, he moved... easily" (*Macaulay*). **Perfidious** (which etymologically implies the reverse of *faithful*) is a more contemptuous term than *treacherous* for it implies baseness or vileness as well as an incapacity for faithfulness in the person concerned; as, a *perfidious* violation of a treaty; *perfidious* dealings. "Spain...to lavish her resources and her blood in furtherance of the designs of a *perfidious* ally" (*Southey*).

Ana. *Inconstant, unstable, fickle, capricious: wavering,

fluctuating (see SWING, *v.*): *changeable, changeful.
Ant. Faithful. — *Con.* Loyal, leal, true, stanch, steadfast, resolute, constant (see FAITHFUL).

fake, *n.* Sham, humbug, counterfeit, simulacrum, *imposture, cheat, fraud, deceit, deception.

faker. *Impostor, mountebank, charlatan, empiric, quack.
Ana. Defrauder, cheater *or* cheat, swindler, cozener (see corresponding verbs at CHEAT).

fallacious. Sophistical, casuistical, paralogistic. See under FALLACY.
Ana. *Irrational, unreasonable: *misleading, deceptive, delusive, delusory: equivocal, ambiguous (see OBSCURE).
Ant. Sound, valid.

fallacy. Fallacy, sophism, sophistry, casuistry, paralogism are here compared as meaning unsound and misleading reasoning or line of argument. The same distinctions in implications and connotations are distinguishable in the corresponding adjectives **fallacious, sophistical, casuistical, paralogistic. Fallacy** and **fallacious,** in specific logical use, imply an error or flaw in reasoning that vitiates an entire argument; thus, a syllogism in which one argues from some accidental character as though it were essential and necessary [as, The food you buy, you eat; you buy raw meat; therefore you eat raw meat] contains a *fallacy* or is *fallacious.* "The many *fallacies* that lurk in the generality and equivocal nature of the terms 'inadequate representation' " (*Burke*). In more general use, *fallacy* and *fallacious* apply to any conception, belief, theory, or the like, that is erroneous and logically untenable, whether it has been arrived at by reasoning or by conjecture, or has been taken over from others; as, "The arguments of the *Federalist* are intended to prove the *fallacy* of these apprehensions" (*Ch. Just. Marshall*); "the separatist *fallacy,* the belief that what may be good for any must be good for all" (*J. A. Hobson*); "like a well-wrought but *fallacious* theory" (*S. Alexander*). **Sophism** and **sophistry** and **sophistical** imply, as *fallacy* and *fallacious* do not necessarily imply, either the intent to mislead or deceive by fallacious arguments, or indifference to the correctness of one's reasoning provided one's words carry conviction; the terms, therefore, often connote confusingly subtle, equivocal, or specious reasoning. *Sophism,* however, applies usually to a specific argument of this character, *sophistry* often, but far from invariably, to the type of reasoning employing sophisms; as, "skilled to plead, with a superficial but plausible set of *sophisms,* in favour of...contempt of virtue" (*Shelley*); "the juggle of *sophistry*" (*Coleridge*); "This evil is...inexcusable by any *sophistry* that the cleverest landlord can devise" (*Shaw*); "in the end he [Hobbes in his theory of the will] lands himself in *sophistries*" (*T. S. Eliot*); "Rousseau does not often indulge in such an unblushing *sophism*" (*Babbitt*); "the *sophistical* plea that matter is more important than manner" (*C. E. Montague*). **Casuistry** and **casuistical** imply sophistry only in their extended and now more common senses. In their earlier (and still current) senses both have reference to the science that deals with cases of conscience, or the determination of what is right and wrong in particular cases where there is justifiable uncertainty; as, "we now have to lay the foundation of a new *casuistry,* no longer theological and Christian, but naturalistic and scientific" (*H. Ellis*). In their extended use, both terms now usually imply sophistical and often tortuous reasoning in reference to moral, theological, and legal problems; as, "Those who hold that a lie is always wrong have to supplement this view by a great deal of *casuistry*" (*B. Russell*); *casuistical* hairsplitting. **Paralogism** and **paralogistic** are technical terms of logic, applicable chiefly to any formal fallacy especially in syllogistic reasoning; as, "He is here guilty of a gross *paralogism*" (*Hume*); "We made no appeal even to Theism: which it would...have been grossly *paralogistic* to do, since we are maintaining Freewill as a premise towards the establishment of Theism" (*W. G. Ward*).

false, *adj.* **1 False, wrong** are here compared as general terms meaning not in conformity with that which is true or right. **False,** in all of its senses, is colored by its etymological implication of deceit: the implication of deceiving or of being deceived is strong when the term implies a contrariety between what is said, thought, concluded, or the like, and the facts or reality; as, *false* statements; "Thou shalt not bear *false* witness against thy neighbour" (*Exodus* xx. 16); "whether it [a poet's awareness of the process of poetic creation] is a genuine insight into the workings of his own mind or only a *false* explanation of them" (*Day Lewis*); "You can take a chess-board as black squares on a white ground, or as white squares on a black ground, and neither conception is a *false* one" (*W. James*). An intent to deceive or a deceptive appearance is implied when the term connotes an opposition to that which is real or genuine or authentic; as, *false* tears; *false* pearls; a *false* check; dressed in *false* colors; a *false* arch (i.e., an architectural member which simulates an arch in appearance but does not have the structure or serve the function of a true arch). The term is applied in vernacular names of plants to a species related to, resembling, or having properties similar to another species that commonly bears the unqualified vernacular; as, the pinkster flower is sometimes called *false* honeysuckle. Even when the word stresses faithlessness (for this sense see FAITHLESS) there is usually a hint of a deceptive appearance of faithfulness or loyalty or of self-deception in one's failure to be true; as, so far as outward appearances went, one could not believe him to be a *false* friend. Only in the sense of incorrect or erroneous (as, a *false* note; a *false* policy) is this implication obscured, though there is often a suggestion of being deceived into believing that the thing so described is true or right. **Wrong,** on the other hand, is colored in all of its senses by its etymological implication of wryness or crookedness: in general, it implies a turning from the standard of that which is true, right (especially morally right), correct, or the like, to that which is its reverse. In comparison with *false, wrong* is simple and forthright in its meaning; thus, a *wrong* conception is one that is the reverse of the truth but a *false* conception is not only *wrong* but the result of one's being deceived or of one's intent to deceive; a *wrong* answer to a question is merely an erroneous answer but a *false* answer to a question is one that is both erroneous and mendacious; *wrong* principles of conduct are the reverse of ethically right principles but *false* principles of conduct are not only wrong but are bound to lead astray those who accept them; so, to give a person *wrong* advice (cf. *false* advice); a lie is always *wrong* (not *false,* because the implication of falsity is in the word "lie"); there is something *wrong* about his appearance (but, there is something *false* in his courtesy); he may be *wrong* in his opinions, but he is not *false* to his country in trying to impress them upon others.
Ana. *Misleading, deceptive, delusive, delusory: fallacious, sophistical (see under FALLACY): mendacious, deceitful, *dishonest, untruthful: factitious (see ARTIFICIAL).
Ant. True. — *Con.* *Real, actual: veritable, *authentic, genuine, bona fide: veracious, truthful (see corresponding nouns at TRUTH).

2 Perfidious, disloyal, traitorous, treacherous, *faithless.
Ana. Recreant, apostate, renegade, backsliding (see corresponding nouns at RENEGADE): *inconstant, unstable: *crooked, devious.
Ant. True, leal. — *Con.* Stanch, steadfast, loyal, *faithful, constant, resolute.

falsehood. Untruth, *lie, fib, misrepresentation, story.
Ant. Truth (*in concrete sense*).

falter, *v.* Waver, vacillate, *hesitate.
Ana. Flinch, blench, *recoil, quail, shrink: fluctuate, oscillate, *swing: *shake, tremble, quake, shudder.
Con. *Persevere, persist: resolve, determine, *decide.

fame, *n.* **Fame, renown, honor** (*or* **honour**), **glory, celebrity, reputation, repute, notoriety, éclat** come into comparison when they mean the character or state of being widely known by name for one's deeds, and often, one's achievements. **Fame** is the most inclusive and, in some ways, the least explicit of these terms, for it may be used in place of any of the others, but it gives no clear suggestion of how far the knowledge of one's name extends, of the reasons for it, or of the creditableness of those reasons: although the term often implies longevity, and usually implies a cause or causes to one's credit, it does not invariably carry these favorable implications; as, to acquire some *fame* for his inventions; his *fame* was short-lived; "*Fame* is the spur that the clear spirit doth raise ... To scorn delights and live laborious days" (*Milton*); "*Fame* ... that second life in others' breath" (*Pope*); "Popularity is neither *fame* nor greatness" (*Hazlitt*); "*Fame* is the thirst of youth" (*Byron*). **Renown** implies widespread fame and widespread acclamation for great achievements as in war, in government, in science, in art, or the like; as, "Those other two equalled with me in fate, So were I equalled with them in *renown*" (*Milton*); "Niten's paintings are prized, but it is as a swordsman that he won supreme *renown*" (*Binyon*). **Honor** (as here compared: see also HONOR, 2; HONESTY) implies a measure of fame, as in a section, a country, a continent, or the civilized world, but it also invariably implies that the knowledge of one's achievements has earned for one profound esteem or deep reverence; as, "Length of days is in her right hand; and in her left hand riches and *honor*" (*Proverbs* iii. 16); "one must learn to give *honour* where *honour* is due, to bow down...before all spirits that are noble" (*A. C. Benson*). **Glory** usually suggests renown, but always it implies a position where attention is fixed on one's brilliancy of achievement and the accompaniment of enthusiastic praise or of high honor; as, "The paths of *glory* lead but to the grave" (*Gray*); "To be recognized...as a master...in one's own line of intellectual or spiritual activity, is indeed *glory*" (*Arnold*). "No keener hunter after *glory* breathes. He loves it in his knights more than himself; They prove to him his work" (*Tennyson*). **Celebrity** is often used in place of *fame* when the widespread laudation of one's name and accomplishments in one's own time is implied: the term usually carries a stronger implication of famousness and of popularity than it does of deep-seated or long-lived admiration and esteem. "The lonely precursor of German philosophy, he [Spinoza] still shines when the light of his successors is fading away; they had *celebrity*, Spinoza has *fame*" (*Arnold*). **Reputation** often denotes nothing more than the character of a person or place, not as it really is, but as it is conceived to be by those who know of him or of it (as, he has a good *reputation* in the community; it is a shame to injure a man's *reputation*), but in the sense in which it is here particularly considered, the term implies a measure of fame, often, but not necessarily for creditable reasons; as, his *reputation* for wit was country-wide; a painter of growing *reputation;* "The purest treasure mortal times afford Is spotless *reputation*" (*Shak.*). **Repute** is sometimes used interchangeably with *reputation* in either sense; as, "only a general of *repute* could get recruits" (*Buchan*). More often, however, *repute* suggests a relation that is closer to *honor* than to *fame,* and denotes rather the degree of esteem accorded to a person or thing than the measure of fame it acquires; as, the book has no little *repute* among the best critics; his work is held in high *repute;* he won a great deal of *repute* (not *reputation*) for his bravery. **Notoriety** implies nothing more than public knowledge of a person or deed with the result that it is much discussed or serves as a nine-day wonder: it usually, however, suggests a meretricious fame, and imputes sensationalism to the person or thing that wins such repute; as, he achieved *notoriety* as the author of a most salacious novel; "Everybody of any consequence or *notoriety* in Bath was well known by name to Mrs. Smith" (*Austen*); "that brilliant, extravagant, careless Reverend Doctor Dodd who acquired some *fame* and much *notoriety* as an eloquent preacher, the skilful editor of the *Beauties of Shakespeare*..., and a forger" (*H. Ellis*). **Éclat,** a French word meaning explosion, now naturalized in English, is used in place of *renown* or of *notoriety.* To either idea is added the connotation of great brilliancy or display but when the basic meaning is renown, illustriousness is especially suggested (as, "Consider what lustre and *éclat* it will give you...to be the best scholar, of a gentleman, in England"—*Chesterfield*), and when it is notoriety, flashiness or ostentation is usually implied (as, "his success in such a pursuit would give a ridiculous *éclat* to the whole affair"—*Scott*).
Ana. Acclaim, acclamation, *applause: recognizing *or* recognition, acknowledgment (see corresponding verbs at ACKNOWLEDGE): eminence, distinction, illustriousness (see corresponding adjectives at FAMOUS).
Ant. Infamy: obscurity. — *Con.* Ignominy, obloquy, *disgrace, dishonor, odium, opprobrium, disrepute, shame.

famed. *Famous, renowned, noted, celebrated, notorious, distinguished, eminent, illustrious.
Ant. Obscure.

familiar. 1 **Familiar, intimate, close, confidential, chummy, thick** are here compared as meaning near to one another because of constant or frequent association, shared interests and activities, or common sympathies, or, when applied to words, acts, etc., indicative of such nearness. **Familiar** suggests relations or manifestations characteristic of or similar to those of a family, where long-continued intercourse makes for freedom, informality, ease of address, and the taking of liberties; consequently *familiar* may apply to the relations, words, acts, etc., of persons actually in such a situation, and to the attitude, style of speaking or writing, etc., of persons who assume the freedom and ease of address of those who are; as, he was *familiar* with only a few of his classmates, but these were undoubtedly the most gifted men in his class; *familiar* essays; "Time and intercourse have made us *familiar*" (*S. Johnson*); "[Goldsmith's style] so equable, so easy without being unduly *familiar*" (*J. R. Lowell*); "The *familiar,* if not rude, tone in which people addressed her" (*N. Hawthorne*); "She was a fearless and *familiar* little thing, who asked disconcerting questions" (*E. Wharton*). **Intimate** suggests relations characteristic of those who are in close contact with one another as through ties of blood, of friendship, or of common interests or aspirations, and who have opened their hearts or their minds to such a degree that they deeply know and understand one another; as, "The *intimate* political relation subsisting between the President of the United States and the heads of departments, necessarily renders any legal investigation of the acts of one of those high officers peculiarly...delicate" (*Ch. Just. Marshall*); "They establish and maintain...more *intimate* and confiding relations with us" (*J. R. Lowell*); "though Farfrae must have so far forgiven him as to have no objection to...him as a father-in-law, *intimate* they could never be" (*Hardy*). *Intimate* may also apply to a connection between a person and a thing, especially something he says, does, wears, or the like: it then implies a very close relation between that thing and his inmost thoughts or feelings or his life in the privacy of his home; as, official receptions were few, but small, *intimate* teas were frequent in the governor's home; "the indecency of publishing *intimate* letters...[such as] the love-letters of the Brownings" (*H. Ellis*); "her eyes, lively, laughing, *intimate*, nearly always a little mocking" (*Cather*); "a shirt-sleeved populace moved through them [the streets] with the *intimate* abandon of boarders going down the passage to the bathroom" (*E. Wharton*). As applied directly or indirectly to knowledge, *intimate* differs from *familiar* not only in idiom but also in implying not merely acquaintance but close or deep study; thus, he has an *intimate* knowledge of the situation; he is *familiar* with the facts pertaining to the situation; he is *familiar* with the poem in question; he has an *intimate* knowledge of the poem in question. **Close** is often used in place of *intimate* when one wishes to imply an attachment drawing persons together in such a way as to suggest the exclusion of others or a very strong bond of affection between them; as, *close* friends; a *close* friendship; "Seeing them so tender and so *close*" (*Tennyson*). **Confidential** implies a relationship based upon mutual trust or confidence or upon a willingness (often, but not necessarily, a mutual willingness) to confide one's hopes, thoughts, feelings, and the like, to the other; as, "The growing harmony and *confidential* friendship which daily manifest themselves between their Majesties" (*Chatham*); "he slipped his arm through his father's with a *confidential* pressure" (*E. Wharton*). **Chummy** and **thick** are both colloquial terms with a somewhat vulgar flavor. The former implies a kind of easy intimacy that prevails between chums (see *chum* under ASSOCIATE); as, the two boys were not long in camp before they became *chummy*. **Thick** differs from *close* in stressing constant association more than the strength of the attachment: the word may imply both (as, the two friends are now as *thick* as thieves), but often it carries a sinister suggestion; as, "how long have you been so *thick* with Dunsey that you must collogue with him to embezzle my money?" (*G. Eliot*).

Ana. Friendly, neighborly, *amicable: sociable, cordial, genial, affable, *gracious: easy, *comfortable, cozy, snug: intrusive, obtrusive, officious, *impertinent.

Ant. Aloof. — *Con.* *Indifferent, detached, unconcerned, incurious: formal, conventional, ceremonious, *ceremonial.

2 Ordinary, *common, popular, vulgar.

Ana. *Usual, wonted, accustomed, customary, habitual.

Ant. Unfamiliar: strange. — *Con.* Novel, newfangled, new-fashioned, *new: rare, uncommon, *infrequent: fantastic, chimerical (see IMAGINARY).

familiarize. Accustom, *habituate, addict.

Ana. Inure, season, acclimatize, acclimate, *harden: *adapt, accommodate, adjust.

Con. Wean, alienate, *estrange.

famous. **Famous, famed, renowned, celebrated, noted, notorious, distinguished, eminent, illustrious** come into comparison as meaning known far and wide among men. **Famous** and **famed** apply chiefly to men, events, and things that are much talked of or are widely or popularly known throughout a section, a country, a continent, or the like; in current English, they (especially *famous*) also imply good repute or a favorable reputation. Among discriminating writers and speakers these terms are applied without qualification only to those persons or things who are still so known or who were so known in the time under consideration; as, the once *famous* poems of Owen Meredith; he is the *famous* American aviator. "Some of our most *famous* physicians have had to struggle pitiably against insufficient means until they were forty or fifty" (*Shaw*). "Among the romanticists... Schleiermacher was the most *famous* theologian" (*Inge*). "A corpulent, jolly fellow, *famed* for humor" (*N. Hawthorne*). **Renowned,** in strict use, implies more glory or honor and more widespread acclamation than either of the preceding words; it is, however, often employed as a stronger or more emphatic term than *famous* with little actual difference in meaning, except for a suggestion of greater longevity of fame. "Royal kings... *Renowned* for their deeds... For Christian service and true chivalry" (*Shak.*). "Those far-*renowned* brides of ancient song" (*Tennyson*). **Celebrated** stresses reception of popular or public notice or attention and frequent mention, especially in print; often, but far from always, it also suggests public admiration or popular honor; as, the *celebrated* kidnapping of Charley Ross; the most *celebrated* of the cases pending before the Supreme Court; Benjamin Franklin's *celebrated* kite; the greatest, but the least *celebrated*, general in the war. **Noted** also implies the reception of public attention, but it often suggests more discernment or discrimination on the part of the public than does *celebrated* or imputes more distinction to the person or thing that is singled out for such attention. "He is the most *noted*, and most deserving man, in the whole profession of chirurgery" (*Pope*). "His two children were both daughters, one *noted* for her prettiness, the other for her cleverness" (*H. Ellis*). **Notorious** stresses the fact of being widely known or recognized for certain acts, certain conditions, or certain qualities; now it commonly, but not exclusively, imputes evil to those acts, conditions, or qualities, or qualifies words or phrases that denote an evil or bad person, act, quality, or the like; as, "the city's most *notorious* malefactor" (*Lucas*); "men of *notoriously* loose lives" (*R. Macaulay*); "his fine library was *notorious*" (*Bennett*). "The inconsistencies of Herbert Spencer's Agnosticism are by this time *notorious*" (*Inge*). "The courage and efficiency of Spartan troops were *notorious*" (*G. L. Dickinson*). **Distinguished** stresses the facts of being differentiated from all other persons or things of its kind because of his or its excellence or superiority, and of being widely and publicly recognized for these qualities; as, "[Henry Adams's] *Mont-Saint-Michel and Chartres* is one of the most *distinguished* contributions to literature...America thus far has produced" (*R. A. Cram*); "meetings with *distinguished* and interesting people" (*H. Ellis*); "She had the most *distinguished* house in New York" (*E. Wharton*). **Eminent** adds to *distinguished* an implication of even greater conspicuousness for excellence or other outstanding qualities; it is applicable therefore chiefly to those persons or things that are recognized as topping all others of their kind; as, the age produced no *eminent* writers; "many *eminent* men of science have been bad mathematicians" (*B. Russell*). "*Eminent* manifestations of this magical power of poetry are very rare and very precious" (*Arnold*). **Illustrious** carries a far stronger implication of renown than *eminent;* it also imputes to the thing so described a gloriousness or splendor that

increases its prestige or influence; as, the *illustrious* deeds of great heroes; "his right noble mind, *illustrious* virtue" (*Shak.*); "Boast the pure blood of an *illustrious* race" (*Pope*).
Ant. Obscure.

fan, *n.* Devotee, votary, *addict, habitué, fiend.

fanatic, *n.* Bigot, *enthusiast, zealot.

fanciful. *Imaginary, visionary, fantastic, chimerical, quixotic.
Ana. *Fictitious, fabulous, mythical, apocryphal, legendary: bizarre, grotesque, *fantastic: preposterous, absurd (see FOOLISH): *false, wrong.
Ant. Realistic. — ***Con.*** Matter-of-fact, *prosaic: truthful, veracious (see corresponding nouns at TRUTH).

fancy, *n.* **1** *Imagination, fantasy, phantasy.
Ant. Experience.
2 Fancy, fantasy, phantasy, phantasm, vision, dream, daydream, nightmare come into comparison when they denote a vivid idea or image, or a series of such ideas or images, present in the mind but having no concrete or objective reality. **Fancy** (see also IMAGINATION) is applicable to anything which is conceived by the imagination, whether it recombines the elements of reality or is pure invention. " 'Let us sit quiet, and hear the echoes about which you have your theory.' 'Not a theory; it was a *fancy*' " (*Dickens*). "Surely this great Chamber... did not exist at all but as a gigantic *fancy* of his own" (*Galsworthy*). **Fantasy** applies to a fancy (often to an organized series of fancies presented in writing, painting, or other form of art) that is the product of an unrestrained, and often unlicensed, imagination having no ties with actuality; as, Shakespeare's "Midsummer Night's Dream" is a pure *fantasy*. "A thousand *fantasies* Begin to throng into my memory, Of calling shapes, and beckoning shadows dire, And airy tongues that syllable men's names" (*Milton*). **Phantasy,** though often used (especially in the past) in place of *fantasy*, both as the power of free inventive imagination and as a product of that power, now in very precise use, is preferred in the psychological sense of the image-making power in general (whether the image is the result of sense perception or of the imagination) or of a product of that power. "It [the writing of love poems by the impotent and of sagas of the chase and war by the physically deficient] is the well-attested psychological law of compensation in *phantasy*" (*Day Lewis*); the *phantasies* created by the reading of *Kubla Khan*. **Phantasm** may be applied either to a phantasy, the mental image (as, "Figures...of which the description had produced in you no *phantasm*"—*Jer. Taylor*), or to a fantasy, especially to one that is hallucinatory; as, the *phantasms* of a disordered mind. **Vision** often implies an imagining but it as frequently implies a seeing or a revelation. Specifically, however, the term is applied to that which the mind sees clearly or concretely, as if revealed to it by a supernatural or mysterious power (see REVELATION), or as if by a kind of spiritual sight or intuition, or as if seen in a dream, and therefore often suggests a sight of something that is actually spiritual in essence or is beyond the range or power of the eyes (or mind) to grasp as a whole; as, "A whole life ...devoted to the patient pursuit of a single *vision* seen in youth" (*C. W. Eliot*); "She tried to dismiss the *vision*" (*Hardy*); "Each word's...power of touching springs in the mind and of initiating *visions*" (*C. E. Montague*); "He [Rousseau] then asserts [his conception] to be a true *vision* of the life of primitive man" (*Babbitt*). **Dream** is the general term for the ideas or images present to the mind in sleep; as, "Thus have I had thee, as a *dream* doth flatter, In sleep a king, but waking no such matter" (*Shak.*); "Your old men shall dream *dreams*, your young men shall see *visions*" (*Joel* ii. 28). Figuratively, *dream* (then often specifically called a **daydream**) suggests vague or idle, commonly happy, imaginings of future events or of nonexistent things; as, "childhood's sunny *dream*" (*Shelley*); "The chymist's golden *dream*" (*Cowper*); "*dreams* of the ideal" (*Whitman*); a busy person has no time for *daydreams*. **Nightmare** applies to any frightful and oppressive dream which occurs in sleep or, by extension, to any vision (or, sometimes, actual experience) which inspires terror or which cannot easily be shaken off. "How many of our *daydreams* would darken into *nightmares*, were there a danger of their coming true!" (*L. P. Smith*).
Ana. Figment, fabrication, fable, *fiction: notion, conception, *idea, concept.
Ant. Reality (*in concrete sense*).

fancy, *v.* **1** Dote on *or* upon, *like, love, enjoy, relish.
Ana. *Approve, endorse, sanction.
Con. *Disapprove, deprecate.
2 Imagine, conceive, envisage, envision, realize, *think.
Ana. *Conjecture, surmise, guess.

fang. *Tooth, tusk.

fantastic *or* **fantastical.** **1** Chimerical, visionary, fanciful, *imaginary, quixotic.
Ana. Extravagant, extreme (see EXCESSIVE): incredible, unbelievable, implausible (see affirmative adjectives at PLAUSIBLE): preposterous, absurd (see FOOLISH): *irrational, unreasonable: delusory, delusive, deceptive, *misleading.
Con. Familiar, ordinary, *common: *usual, customary.
2 Fantastic (*or* **fantastical**), **bizarre, grotesque, antic** come into comparison when they are used to describe works of art, effects produced by nature or art, ideas, and the like, and mean conceived or made, or as if conceived or made, without reference to reality, truth, or common sense. **Fantastic** stresses the exercise of unrestrained imagination or unlicensed fancy. It therefore variously connotes absurd extravagance in conception, remoteness from reality, or merely ingenuity in devising. "This theory [of God as the soul of the universe]...will to many seem *fantastic*. There is something absurd in the idea that a vast aggregation of incandescent gas must have a soul of a dignity proportioned to its bulk" (*Inge*). "To the child, they [Bluebeard and Jack the Giant Killer] are purely *fantastic*, and he never connects them with the real world in any way" (*B. Russell*). "He wove *fantastic* stories of the hunting-bridle" (*Kipling*). **Bizarre** is applied to that which is unduly, often sensationally, strange or queer; it suggests the use of violent contrasts as in color, in sound, in emotional effects, or of strikingly incongruous combinations, such as the tragic and the comic, the horrible and the tender, and the like. "The love of energy and beauty, of distinction in passion [in the work of the romanticists], tended naturally to become a little *bizarre*.... Are we in the Inferno?—we are tempted to ask, wondering at something malign in so much beauty" (*Pater*). "The spectacle [of New York City from shipboard] enthralled him by its convincing vigor for all its *bizarreness*" (*R. Grant*). **Grotesque** emphasizes the distortion of the natural to the point either of comic absurdity or of aesthetically effective ugliness. Originally, and still technically, the word is applied to a type of painting or sculpture, of ancient Roman origin, which serves a decorative rather than a pictorial purpose and which employs natural details (animals, men, flowers, foliage, etc.) and conventional designs and figures (scrolls, garlands, satyrs, etc.) in unnatural combinations. Later, the word was used also to describe the comic exaggerations or distortions of human and animal figures in the sculptured decorations of Gothic architecture,

especially of gargoyles; it is from this association that the adjective in general use derives its leading implications of ridiculous ugliness or ludicrous caricature. "[The camel's] *grotesque* head waving about in dumb protest to the blows which often fell on his neck" (*M. Hoffman*). "She differed from other comedians. There was nothing about her of the *grotesque;* none of her comic appeal was due to exaggeration" (*T. S. Eliot*). Sometimes, however, the word suggests an absurdly irrational combination of incompatibles. "The attempts...to dress up the Labour movement as a return to the Palestinian Gospel, are little short of *grotesque*" (*Inge*). **Antic,** which is now rare in other than literary use, was originally indistinguishable from *grotesque;* later, it came to stress ludicrousness or buffoonery more than unnaturalness or irrationality. "He came running to me...making a many *antic* gesture" (*Defoe*). "There was something in him [Maecenas] of the *antic* and the *grotesque.* He had all the foibles of the aesthete and the foppishness of the petit maître" (*Buchan*).

Ana. Imagined, fancied, conceived (see THINK): externalized, objectified (see REALIZE): ingenious, adroit, *clever: eccentric, erratic, singular, *strange, odd, queer.

fantasy. 1 Fancy, *imagination, phantasy.

Ana. Imagining, fancying, conceiving, envisioning (see THINK): externalizing, objectifying (see REALIZE).

2 *Fancy, phantasy, phantasm, vision, dream, daydream, nightmare.

Ana. *Delusion, illusion, hallucination: vagary, *caprice, whimsey, whim, freak: grotesquerie, bizarrerie (see corresponding adjectives at FANTASTIC).

far, faraway, *or* **far-off.** *Distant, remote, removed.

Ant. Near, nigh, near-by.

farcical. Comical, comic, ludicrous, *laughable, ridiculous, risible, droll, funny.

fardel, *n.* Pack, *bundle, bunch, bale, parcel, package, packet.

Ana. Burden, *load.

farewell. *Good-by, Godspeed, adieu, au revoir, auf Wiedersehen, bon voyage, adios.

farming. *Agriculture, husbandry.

farther. **Farther, further** are often used without distinction, even by good writers. Etymologically they are different words, **farther** being the comparative of *far,* and **further,** in its adverbial form (as an adjective, it is without a positive), being the comparative of *fore* or *forth.* At any rate, *farther* etymologically implies a greater distance from a given point in space (sometimes, in time); *further* etymologically implies onwardness or an advance or an addition, as in movement or progression, not only in space, but in time, quantity, degree, or the like; thus, the *farther* (rather than the *further*) tree; Germany is *farther* (not *further*) from the United States than England; to move *farther* (better than *further*) away from the city; no *further* (better than *farther*) steps are necessary; the incident happened *farther* (better than *further*) back than I can remember; "circumstances such as the present...render *further* [not *farther*] reserve unnecessary" (*Shaw*). In spite of this fundamental distinction in meaning, there are many occasions where it is difficult to make a choice, since the ideas of distance from a given point and of advance in movement are both implied. In such cases, either word may be used; as, "To go *further* and fare worse" (*Old Proverb*); "My ponies are tired, and I have *further* [or *farther*] to go" (*Hardy*); "as we climb higher, we can see *further* [or *farther*]" (*Inge*); " 'What!...was Pat ever in France?' 'Indeed he was,' cries mine host; and Pat adds, 'Ay, and *farther* [or *further*]' " (*Lover*).

fascinate. Charm, bewitch, enchant, captivate, take, allure, *attract.

Ana. Influence, impress, *affect, sway, strike, touch: delight, rejoice, gladden, *please.

fascinating. Charming, bewitching, enchanting, captivating, taking, alluring, attractive. See under ATTRACT.

Ana. *Delightful, delectable: luring, enticing, seducing *or* seductive, tempting (see corresponding verbs at LURE).

Con. *Repugnant, repellent, distasteful, obnoxious, abhorrent.

fashion, *n.* 1 Manner, way, *method, mode, system.

Ana. Practice, *habit, custom, usage, wont.

2 **Fashion, style, mode, vogue, fad, rage, craze, dernier cri, cry,** come into comparison as denoting a way of dressing, of furnishing and decorating rooms, of dancing, of behaving, or the like, that is generally accepted at a given time by those who wish to follow the trend or to be regarded as up-to-date. **Fashion** (etymologically, a making) is thought of in general as the current conventional usage or custom which is determined by polite society or by those who are regarded as the leaders in their world (not only the social, but the intellectual, the literary, the artistic, or similar world); as, the dictates of *fashion;* to follow the *fashion;* "Nowhere...is *fashion* so exacting, not only in dress and demeanor, but in plastic art itself" (*Brownell*); "[Augustus] took the view...that externals count for much, since they sway opinion, and opinion sways *fashion,* and *fashion* is reflected in conduct" (*Buchan*). *Fashion* is also applicable to the particular thing (type of dress, furniture, behavior, subject in literature or art, etc.) which is dictated by fashions; as, "this poem [T. S. Eliot's *The Waste Land*]...provided ...the fake-progressive with a new *fashion*" (*Day Lewis*); it is the latest *fashion* in hats. **Style,** in this as in its other senses (see LANGUAGE, 2; NAME; cf. STYLISH), implies a manner or way that is distinctive; it therefore, as here compared, suggests the elegant or distinguished manner or way of dressing, furnishing, living, and the like, characteristic of those who have wealth and taste, rather than, as *fashion,* the manner or way of dressing, etc., which they determine for themselves and others; as, to live in *style;* judging from the *style* they keep, they are both wealthy and cultivated; their clothes, their homes, their tables, their cars have that mysterious quality called "*style.*" However, *style* is often used in place of *fashion;* as, this year's *styles* in automobile bodies; the dress is in the latest *style;* his coat is out of *style.* **Mode,** especially in the phrase "the *mode*" and partly as a result of its connection with the French term *la mode,* suggests the peak of fashion or the fashion of the moment among those who cultivate elegance in dress, behavior, interests, and the like; as, "The easy, apathetic graces of the man of the *mode*" (*Macaulay*); "That summer Russian refugees were greatly the *mode*" (*R. Macaulay*). **Vogue** stresses the prevalence or wide acceptance of the fashion and its obvious popularity; as, "the slender, undeveloped figure then very much in *vogue*" (*Cather*); "The word *morale,* in italics, had a great *vogue* at the time of the War" (*C. E. Montague*); "Yet I am told that the *vogue* of the sermon is passing" (*Quiller-Couch*). *Fad, rage, craze, dernier cri* all apply to an extremely short-lived fashion. **Fad** stresses caprice in acceptance and in dropping; as, "Many people are inclined to see in the popularity of this new subject a mere university *fad*" (*Babbitt*); "A *fashion* is not in France the mere '*fad*' it is in England and with us" (*Brownell*). **Rage** and **craze** imply short-lived and often senseless enthusiasm; as, "Mr. Prufrock fitted in very well with his wife's social circle, and was quite the *rage*" (*Day Lewis*); "Why this *craze* for transmitting ideas by means of marks on

paper?" (*R. Macaulay*). **Dernier cri** (a French phrase meaning the latest cry) or its English equivalent **cry** (especially in "*all the cry*") applies to that which is the very latest thing in fashion; as, a woman whose clothes are always the *dernier cri;* "The spirit of the times is an indiscriminate passion for the *dernier cri*" (*J. W. Beach*); open-toed shoes were all the *cry* at the moment.

Ana. Trend, current, drift, *tendency: convention, *form, usage.

fashion, *v.* Form, shape, *make, fabricate, manufacture, forge.

Ana. Devise, contrive (see corresponding nouns at DEVICE): design, plan, plot (see under PLAN, *n.*): produce, turn out (see BEAR).

fashionable. *Stylish, modish, smart, chic, dapper, dashing, spruce, natty, nifty, nobby, posh, toffish, brave, braw.

Ant. Unfashionable: old-fashioned.

fast. **Fast, rapid, swift, fleet, quick, speedy, hasty, expeditious** come into comparison as meaning moving, proceeding, or acting with great celerity. *Fast* and *rapid* are often used without distinction; but **fast** frequently applies to the moving object, and emphasizes the way in which it covers ground, whereas **rapid** is apt to characterize the movement itself and often to suggest its astonishing rate of speed; as, a *fast* horse; a *fast* train; a *fast* boat; a *rapid* current; a *rapid* gait; *rapid* progress; a *fast* worker; *rapid* work. **Swift** suggests great rapidity, frequently coupled with ease, or facility of movement; **fleet** (commonly poetical or journalistic) connotes lightness or nimbleness as well as extreme fastness or rapidity; as, *fleet*-footed, or *fleet* of foot; "*Fleeter* than arrows, bullets, wind, thought, *swifter* things" (*Shak.*); "more *swift* than swallow shears the liquid sky" (*Spenser*). "How *fleet* is a glance of the mind! Compared with the speed of its flight, The tempest itself lags behind, And the *swift*-winged arrows of light" (*Cowper*). **Quick,** as here compared (see QUICK, 3; LIVING), applies especially to that which happens promptly or which occupies but little time; it suggests alacrity or celerity, especially in action, rather than velocity of movement; as, *quick* thinking saved him from the trap; "Thy drugs are *quick.* Thus with a kiss I die" (*Shak.*); "slow to resolve, but in performance *quick*" (*Dryden*). **Speedy,** when applied to persons or their motions or activities, implies extreme quickness and often hurry or haste; when applied to things and their motion or movement, it also often suggests velocity; in general, it is opposed to *dilatory;* **hasty,** as here compared, suggests hurry or precipitation rather than speed and often connotes carelessness, inattention, nervousness, or the like; as, "No mode sufficiently *speedy* of obtaining money had ever occurred to me" (*De Quincey*); to hope for their *speedy* return; "Be *speedy,* darkness" (*Keats*); "Make *speediest* preparation for the journey!" (*Shelley*); a *hasty* departure; to snatch a *hasty* meal; work that was too *hasty* to be satisfactory. **Expeditious** adds to *quick* or *speedy* the implication of efficiency; it therefore implies the absence of waste, bungling, and undue haste; as, *expeditious* movements of troops; an *expeditious* means of accomplishing an end. "There is no *expeditious* road To pack and label men for God, And save them by the barrel-load" (*F. Thompson*).

Ant. Slow.

fasten. **Fasten, fix, attach, affix** agree in meaning to make something stay firmly in place or in an assigned place. All but *fix* (and that sometimes) imply a uniting or joining of one thing to another or of two things together. **Fasten** commonly implies an attempt to keep a thing from moving, as by tying, binding, nailing, or cementing it to something else, or by means of some mechanical device such as a lock, a screw, a hook and eye; as, to *fasten* a horse to a post; to *fasten* down the lid of a box; to *fasten* a calendar to a wall; to *fasten* a door; to *fasten* a dress. **Fix** implies an attempt to keep something from falling down or from losing hold; it suggests operations such as driving in or implanting deeply; as, to *fix* a stake in the ground; unless their roots are deeply *fixed,* plants will not be strong. It is now more common in its extended than in its literal sense, but the implications remain the same; as, to *fix* a face in one's memory; to *fix* certain facts in one's mind; to *fix* a color in a fabric by use of a mordant. In some phrases where *fasten* and *fix* are used interchangeably, there is a distinction in meaning which is subtle but justified by discriminating use. To *fix* one's affections on someone connotes concentration and fidelity; to *fasten* one's affections on someone may, and often does, suggest covetousness or an attempt to hold in thrall. To *fix* the blame upon a person implies solid grounds for the accusation; to *fasten* the blame upon someone often suggests factitious grounds or selfish motives. "His heart is *fixed,* trusting in the Lord" (*Psalms* cxii. 7). "Society wanted to do what it pleased; all disliked the laws which Church and State were trying to *fasten* on them" (*H. Adams*). **Attach** stresses connection or union in order to keep things together or to prevent their separation; it usually implies therefore a bond, link, or tie (literally or figuratively); as, the lid is *attached* to the box by hinges; to *attach* loose sheets by means of a staple; the collar bone is *attached* to the shoulder blade at one end and to the breastbone at the other; he *attached* himself to the cause in his youth; odium was *attached* to his name; to *attach* a condition to a promise. **Affix** usually implies imposition of one thing upon another. Originally it connoted any of several means, as nailing, impressing, or the like; as, to *affix* a seal to a document. "Felton *affixed* this bull to the gates of the bishop of London's palace" (*Hallam*). Now, however, it usually suggests either attachment, as by paste, gum, or mucilage (as, to *affix* a stamp to an envelope) or subscription, as of a name to a document. "He's old enough to *affix* his signature to an instrument" (*Meredith*).

Ana. *Secure, rivet, moor, anchor: *join, connect, link, unite: adhere, cleave, cling, *stick, cohere: bind, *tie.

Ant. Unfasten: loosen, loose. — *Con.* *Separate, part, sever, sunder, divorce, divide.

fastidious. Finical, particular, fussy, *nice, dainty, squeamish, pernickety.

Ana. Exacting, demanding (see DEMAND, *v.*): *critical, hypercritical, captious: *careful, meticulous, punctilious, scrupulous.

Con. *Negligent, remiss, neglectful, slack, lax: uncritical, cursory (see SUPERFICIAL).

fastness. Stronghold, *fort, fortress, citadel, acropolis.

fat, *adj.* *Fleshy, stout, portly, plump, corpulent, obese, rotund, chubby.

Ant. Lean. — *Con.* Spare, lank, lanky, skinny, gaunt, scrawny, rawboned, angular (see LEAN): *thin, slender, slim, slight.

fat, *n.* Grease, *oil, wax.

fatal. Mortal, *deadly, lethal.

Ana. Killing, slaying (see KILL, *v.*): destroying *or* destructive (see corresponding verb DESTROY): baneful, *pernicious.

fate, *n.* **Fate, destiny, lot, portion, doom** come into comparison when they denote the state, condition, or end which is decreed for one by a higher power. **Fate** presupposes a determining agent or agency such as one of the ancient goddesses (called Fates), the Supreme Being, the law of necessity, or the like; the term, therefore, usually suggests inevitability and, sometimes, immutability (except in its increasingly frequent weakened use; as, to decide a bill's *fate* today). "He either fears his *fate* too much, Or his deserts are small, That dares not put it to the touch To gain or lose it all" (*Montrose*). "Let us, then, be up and doing, With a heart for any *fate*" (*Longfellow*). **Destiny,** in precise use, implies an irrevocable determination or appointment, as by the will of the gods or of God; even in this sense, however, it carries little or no suggestion of something to be feared; on the contrary, it may even imply a great or noble state or end; as, "the conception of a lordly splendid *destiny* for the human race" (*B. Russell*); "Lawrence was... unescapably an artist...there were moments when he wanted to escape from his *destiny*" (*A. Huxley*). Often, *destiny* is more loosely applied to that which one envisions as his end or goal; sometimes, however, with the implication (often slight) that it is the will of God. "I see them [an extinct Indian tribe] here, isolated, cut off from other tribes, working out their *destiny*" (*Cather*). **Lot** and **portion** carry a stronger implication of distribution in the decreeing of one's fate; *lot*, however, stressing blind chance, by or as if by determination through the casting of lots, and *portion*, the more or less fair apportioning of good and evil; as, "It was her unhappy *lot* to be made more wretched by the only affection which she could not suspect" (*Conrad*); "With whom would she be willing to exchange *lots?*" (*Bennett*); "So has my *portion* been meted out to me; and...I have...been able to comprehend some of the lessons hidden in the heart of pain" (*Wilde*). **Doom,** more than any of these words, implies a final, usually an unhappy or calamitous, award or fate; as, "With the sea approaches lost, her [La Rochelle's] *doom* was certain" (*Belloc*). "Involution is as much a law of nature as evolution. There is no escape from this *doom*" (*Inge*).

Ana. Issue, outcome, upshot, consequence, result, *effect: *end, ending, termination.

fateful. *Ominous, portentous, inauspicious, unpropitious.

Ana. Momentous, significant, important (see corresponding nouns at IMPORTANCE): decisive, determinative, *conclusive: crucial, critical, *acute.

fatherly. Paternal, *parental.

fatigue, *v.* Exhaust, jade, *tire, weary, fag, tucker.

Ana. *Deplete, drain: debilitate, disable, *weaken.

Ant. Rest. — ***Con.*** Refresh, restore, rejuvenate, *renew: *relieve, assuage.

fatuous. Asinine, silly, foolish, *simple.

Ana. Idiotic, imbecile, moronic (see corresponding nouns at FOOL): *fond, infatuated, besotted, insensate.

Ant. Sensible. — ***Con.*** Sane, prudent, judicious, *wise, sage, sapient.

fault, *n.* **1 Fault, failing, frailty, foible, vice** come into comparison when they mean an imperfection in character or an ingrained moral weakness. **Fault** implies failure, but not necessarily serious or even culpable failure, to attain the standard of moral perfection in disposition, deed, habit, or the like; as, to have many virtues and few *faults;* "He is all *fault* who hath no *fault* at all" (*Tennyson*); "Our modern appreciativeness is often only the amiable aspect of a *fault*—an undue tolerance for indeterminate enthusiasms and vapid emotionalism" (*Babbitt*). **Failing** is even less censorious than *fault*, for it usually implies a shortcoming, often a weakness of character for which one is not entirely responsible or of which one may not be aware; as, "Pride...is a very common *failing,* I believe" (*Austen*); "A knowledge of his family *failings* will help one man in economising his estate" (*Quiller-Couch*). **Frailty** often implies a weakness in character which makes one prone to fall when tempted; as, "God knows our *frailty*, pities our weakness" (*Locke*). The term therefore often denotes a pardonable or a petty fault; as, "a purely human *frailty*, like a fondness for detective stories" (*Lowes*). **Foible** denotes a harmless, sometimes an amiable, sometimes a temperamental, weakness or failing; as, "I can bear very well to hear my *foibles* exposed, though not my *faults*" (*Shenstone*); "He [Maecenas] had all the *foibles* of the aesthete" (*Buchan*). **Vice** (opposed to *virtue*) is stronger than *fault* and *failing* in its suggestion of violation of the moral law or of giving offense to the moral senses of others, but, as here compared (see also OFFENSE, 3), it does not necessarily imply corruptness or deliberate defiance of the law but is rather a general term attributable to any imperfection or weakness of character. "Knowledge...of all the virtues and *vices*, tastes and dislikes of all the people" (*Galsworthy*). "She had been proud. She was criminally proud. That was her *vice*" (*Bennett*). "As Professor Whitehead has lately said, the intolerant use of abstractions is the major *vice* of the intellect" (*Inge*).

Ana. Weakness, infirmity (see corresponding adjectives at WEAK): flaw, defect, *blemish.

Ant. Merit. — ***Con.*** *Excellence, virtue, perfection.

2 *Blame, culpability, guilt.

Ana. Responsibility, answerability, accountability (see corresponding adjectives at RESPONSIBLE): sin, *offense, crime.

faultfinding, *adj.* Captious, caviling, carping, censorious, hypercritical, *critical.

Ana. Exacting, demanding, requiring (see DEMAND, *v.*): fussy, particular, finical, pernickety (see NICE).

Con. Appreciating *or* appreciative, valuing, prizing, cherishing (see corresponding verbs at APPRECIATE): approving, endorsing (see APPROVE).

faultless. *Impeccable, flawless, errorless.

Ana. *Correct, right, nice, accurate, exact, precise: *perfect, intact, entire, whole.

Ant. Faulty.

faux pas. Blunder, slip, *error, mistake, lapse, bull, howler, boner, bloomer, floater.

favor *or* **favour,** *n.* **1 Favor** (*or* **favour**), **good will, countenance** come into comparison when they denote the attitude of mind of one who is disposed to be friendly and helpful. **Favor** not only implies the absence of all hostility or opposition but it definitely suggests either an active interest and a willingness to give assistance or support (as, "the new...ecclesiastic...woos the *favour* of the Labour party"—*Inge*), or an approval or sanction (as, "The conception of morality as an art...seems now again to be finding *favour* in men's eyes"—*H. Ellis*), or obvious partiality (as, "[the phenomena of life and character] set down without fear, *favour*, or prejudice" —*Galsworthy*). **Good will** (see also FRIENDSHIP) is more positive in its implication of deep and abiding friendliness, but except in its legal and business sense (that is, as denoting the salable asset of a business whose custom or patronage depends on one's reputation for, or on favor won by, the quality of one's merchandise or product, the promptitude with which one fills orders, and the like) the term stresses heartiness of affection for, or zeal for the welfare of, another more than an attitude of interest, approval, or partiality toward him or his projects; as, "Thou art not ignorant what dear *good will* I bear unto the banish'd Valentine" (*Shak.*); "We often made feasts for each other, where *good will* outweighed the frugal luxury" (*Shelley*). Nevertheless, the term is often used without clear distinction from *favor*. "Though his looks did not please her, his name was a passport to her *goodwill*, and she thought with sincere compassion of his approaching disappointment" (*Austen*). **Countenance** emphasizes an attitude of approval or a willingness to favor, but it does not necessarily involve reference to more than the appearance of friendliness; as, "Is there one sentence in the constitution which gives *countenance* to this rule?" (*Ch. Just. Marshall*); "to lend no *countenance* to such adulation" (*Macaulay*); "Else I withdraw favour and *countenance* From you" (*Tennyson*).

Ana. *Predilection, partiality, prepossession, bias, prejudice: *regard, respect, esteem, admiration: approving *or* approval, sanctioning *or* sanction, endorsement (see corresponding verbs at APPROVE).

Ant. Animus. — ***Con.*** Ill will, *malice, malevolence, malignity: antipathy, animosity, *enmity, hostility, rancor.

2 Boon, largess, *gift, present, gratuity, fairing.

Ana. Token, *pledge, earnest: concession, *allowance: *honor, homage, deference: benefaction, *donation, contribution.

favor, *v.* Accommodate, *oblige.

Ana. *Help, aid, assist: *indulge, pamper, humor: *benefit, profit.

Con. Foil, thwart, baffle, circumvent, *frustrate: *inconvenience, incommode, discommode.

favorable *or* **favourable.** **Favorable** (*or* **favourable**), **benign, auspicious, propitious,** as here compared, agree in meaning of good omen, or presaging a happy or successful outcome. **Favorable** implies that the persons or circumstances involved tend to assist one in attaining one's ends—persons, by being kindly disposed or actually helpful, and circumstances, by being distinctly advantageous or encouraging; as, to lend a *favorable* ear to a request; it was feared that many of the small countries were *favorable* to the enemy; a *favorable* breeze; "a hot dry summer, *favourable* to contemplative life out of doors" (*Conrad*). **Benign** (see also KIND) derives its connotations largely, but not entirely, from its application in astrology to the aspect of the stars at a given moment, such as the time of a person's birth or of his beginning a project. It is applicable chiefly to someone or to something that has power to make or mar one's fortunes by his or its aspect, and that is thought of as looking down with favor on one, or of presenting a favorable countenance to one. "So shall the World go on, To good malignant, to bad men *benign*" (*Milton*). "Thy form *benign*, O Goddess [Adversity], wear, Thy milder influence impart" (*Gray*). "On whose birth *benign* planets have certainly smiled" (*C. Brontë*). "They [my poems] will co-operate with the *benign* tendencies in human nature and society...in making men wiser, better, and happier" (*Wordsworth*). **Auspicious,** from its etymological reference to the *auspices*, the signs observed by an augur (see under FORETELL), is applicable to anything that is marked by favorable signs or is in itself regarded as a good omen; as, an *auspicious* beginning of what proved to be a great career. "For sure the milder planets did combine on thy *auspicious* horoscope to shine" (*Dryden*). "Pay the boy...he brought *auspicious* news" (*Kipling*). **Propitious,** although it carries no etymological reference to any of the occult sciences, does suggest such an allusion far more strongly than *favorable*, but not quite so explicitly as *benign* or *auspicious;* it is therefore preferred to *favorable* when such a connotation is desired; as, if the fates are *propitious*, there is no doubt of his success; they looked upon the present moment as *propitious* for starting their project.

Ana. Advantageous, *beneficial, profitable: salutary, wholesome, *healthful: benignant, kindly, *kind: conducing *or* conducive, contributing *or* contributory (see corresponding verbs at CONDUCE).

Ant. Unfavorable: antagonistic.

favorite *or* **favourite,** *n.* Sycophant, toady, lickspit, *parasite, hanger-on, leech, sponge.

fawn, *v.* **Fawn, toady, truckle, cringe, cower** are synonyms when they mean to act or behave with abjectness in the presence of a superior. **Fawn** (literally, of a dog, to show delight and affection by crouching and wagging its tail) in its extended sense implies a courting of favor by servile flattery, exaggerated deference, or other acts of a sycophant. "They *fawn* on the proud feet that spurn them lying low" (*Shelley*). "Courtiers who *fawn* on a master while they betray him" (*Macaulay*). **Toady** (literally, to play the toady, or toadeater, a mountebank's boy who allegedly ate toads so that his master might show his skill in expelling their [supposed] poison) carries a strong implication of a menial as well as of a fawning attitude in an attempt to ingratiate oneself; often also it suggests the close following as of a parasite; as, *toadying* to the rich boys in his school; her generosity encouraged *toadying* among her neighbors. **Truckle** (literally, to take a subordinate or inferior position reminiscent of a truckle bed, which is pushed under a large bed when not in use) always implies subordination of self or submission of one's desires, judgments, or the like, to those of a superior. "Everybody must defer.... A nation must wait upon her decision, a Dean and Chapter *truckle* to her wishes" (*V. Sackville-West*). "She must not expect to be allowed to dictate....There are people who will always *truckle* to those who have money" (*Arch. Marshall*). **Cringe** (literally, to shrink in fear) implies obsequious bowing or crouching as if in awe or fear; it usually connotes abject abasement; as, "We are sneaking and bowing and *cringing* on the one hand, or bullying and scorning on the other" (*Thackeray*); "She [Jenny Lind] is very humble and careless of self. 'My poor, humble self'...is often on her lips; but she never *cringes* or loses dignity" (*Symonds*). **Cower** always implies abject fear, often cowardly fear, especially in the presence of those who tyrannize or domineer. "The whole family *cowered* under Lady Kew's eyes and nose, and she ruled by force of them" (*Thackeray*). "Having found...every incentive to *cower* and *cringe* and hedge, and no incentive...to stand upright as a man" (*Van W. Brooks*).

Ana. Blandish, cajole, wheedle, *coax: defer, bow, cave in, *yield, submit: court, woo, *invite.

Ant. Domineer.

fay. *Fairy, faery, elf, sprite, pixy, gnome, dwarf, goblin, brownie, puck, nix, shee, leprechaun, banshee.

faze *or* **phase, fease, feeze.** Disconcert, discomfit, rattle, *embarrass, abash.

Ana. Nonplus, confound, dumfound, perplex, mystify, *puzzle: *confuse, muddle: fluster, flurry, perturb, *discompose.

fealty. 1 *Allegiance, homage.

2 *Fidelity, loyalty, devotion, allegiance, piety.

Ana. Faithfulness *or* faith, lealty, trueness *or* truth, constancy, stanchness, steadfastness (see corresponding adjectives at FAITHFUL): *obligation, duty.

Ant. Perfidy. — ***Con.*** Perfidiousness, treacherousness *or* treachery, traitorousness, faithlessness, disloyalty, falseness (see corresponding adjectives at FAITHLESS).

fear, *n.* **1** **Fear, dread, fright, alarm, dismay, consternation, panic, terror, horror, trepidation** denote the painful agitation which overcomes one in the anticipation or in the presence of danger. **Fear** is the most general term; like **dread,** it implies apprehension and anxiety, but it also frequently suggests a loss of courage amounting to cowardice. "*Fear* came upon me, and trembling" (*Job* iv. 14). "He [Dr. Johnson] had, indeed, an awful *dread* of death, or rather 'of something after death' " (*Boswell*). "Do you know what *fear* is? Not ordinary *fear* of insult, injury or death, but abject, quivering *dread* of something that you cannot see" (*Kipling*). **Fright** implies the shock of sudden, startling, and commonly short-lived fear; **alarm** suggests the fright which is awakened by sudden awareness of imminent danger. "She had taken *fright* at our behaviour and turned to the captain pitifully" (*Conrad*). "Thou wast born amid the din of arms, And sucked a breast that panted with *alarms*" (*Cowper*). **Dismay** implies deprivation of spirit, courage, or initiative, esp. by an alarming or disconcerting prospect. "The storm prevails, the rampart yields a way, Bursts the wild cry of horror and *dismay!*" (*Campbell*). **Consternation** heightens the implication of prostration or confusion of the faculties. " 'Tis easy to believe, though not to describe, the *consternation* they were all in" (*Defoe*). **Panic** is overmastering and unreasoning, often groundless, fear or fright. "A blockhead, who was in a perpetual *panic* lest I should expose his ignorance" (*De Quincey*). **Terror** suggests the extremity of consternation or (often violent) dread. "The *terror* by night" (*Psalms* xci. 5). "Frozen with *terror*" (*Beckford*). "Soul-chilling *terror*" (*Shelley*). **Horror** adds the implication of shuddering abhorrence or aversion, for it usually connotes a sight, rather than a premonition, which causes fear. "The *horror* of supernatural darkness" (*Pater*). "Fierce thrills of delighted *horror*" (*F. W. Farrar*). "What is *terror* in poetry is *horror* in prose" (*Landor*). **Trepidation** adds to *dread* the implication of timidity, especially timidity as manifested by trembling or by marked hesitation. "The Stubland aunts were not the ladies to receive a solicitor's letter calmly. They were thrown into a state of extreme *trepidation*" (*H. G. Wells*). "I take up with some *trepidation* the subject of programme music" (*Babbitt*).

Ana. *Apprehension, foreboding, misgiving, presentiment: anxiety, worry, concern (see CARE): cowardliness, pusillanimity, cravenness (see corresponding adjectives at COWARDLY).

Ant. Fearlessness. — ***Con.*** Boldness, bravery, intrepidity, valiancy (see corresponding adjectives at BRAVE): *courage, mettle, spirit, resolution: *confidence, assurance, aplomb.

2 Awe, *reverence.

Ana. Veneration, worship, adoration (see under REVERE): admiration, *wonder, amazement: respect, esteem (see REGARD, *n.*).

Ant. Contempt.

fearful. **1 Fearful, apprehensive, afraid** are synonymous when they are followed by *of, that, lest*, or the like, and mean inspired or moved by fear or fears. *Afraid* is never, *fearful* and *apprehensive* are infrequently, used attributively in this sense. **Fearful** carries no suggestion of a formidable cause of fear; it often connotes timorousness, a predisposition to worry, or an active imagination; as, the child is *fearful* of loud noises; they were *fearful* that a storm would prevent their excursion. "It [the American intelligentsia] is timorous and *fearful* of challenge" (*Mencken*). **Apprehensive** suggests a state of mind rather than a temperament and, usually, genuine grounds for fear. It always implies a presentiment or anticipation of evil, of danger, or the like; as, in July 1914, all civilized peoples were *apprehensive* of war. "[The invaders] had driven before them into Italy whole troops of...provincials, less *apprehensive* of servitude than of famine" (*Gibbon*). **Afraid** may or may not imply sufficient motivation of fears, but it usually connotes weakness or cowardice. As here compared, it always implies inhibition of action or utterance. "The trained reason is disinterested and fearless. It is not *afraid* of public opinion" (*Inge*).

Ana. *Timid, timorous: anxious, worried, concerned (see under CARE, *n.*): hesitant, reluctant, *disinclined.

Ant. Fearless: intrepid. — ***Con.*** Bold, audacious, *brave, courageous, dauntless, valiant.

2 Fearful, awful, dreadful, frightful, terrible, terrific, horrible, horrific, shocking, appalling are not here stressed as synonyms, for in loose use they are frequently employed as if they were nearly equivalent in meaning or as if they were more frequently interchangeable than good use permits. All of these words, and especially their adverbs, are found in colloquial use as intensives, meaning little more than *extreme(ly)*. Among writers who use words with precision, however, each one has a definite and distinct value when applied to a thing that stimulates an emotion in which fear or horror is in some degree an element. That is **fearful** which makes one afraid or alarmed. In literary use and in precise speech, the word usually implies a deep and painful emotion and a loss of courage in the face of possible or imminent danger. "All torment, trouble, wonder and amazement Inhabits here: some heavenly power guide us Out of this *fearful* country!" (*Shak.*). "A sight too *fearful* for the feel of fear" (*Keats*). In less precise English, *fearful* may not imply apprehension of danger, but if its use is acceptable it should at least imply that the thing so qualified is a cause of disquiet; as, the *fearful* tenacity of a memory; a *fearfully* distressing (not a *fearfully* interesting) situation. That is **awful** which impresses one so profoundly that one acts or feels as if under a spell or in the grip of its influence. In richest use, it often implies an emotion such as reverential fear or an overpowering awareness of might, majesty, sublimity, or the like. "And wring the *awful* sceptre from his fist" (*Shak.*). "God of our fathers... Beneath whose *awful* Hand we hold Dominion over palm and pine" (*Kipling*). "Men living among the glooms and broken lights of the primeval forest, hearing strange noises in the tree-tops when the thunder crashed, and *awful* voices in the wind" (*Buchan*). "She entered... the drawing-room in which New York's most chosen company was somewhat *awfully* assembled" (*E. Wharton*). In somewhat weakened but still correct use, *awful* may be applied to qualities, conditions, and the like, which are unduly weighted with significance or which strike one forcibly as far above or beyond the normal; as, "No tribunal can approach such a question without a deep sense...of the *awful* responsibility involved in its decision" (*Ch. Just. Marshall*); "a moment of *awful* silence before the questions began" (*Deland*); "suddenly, with the *awful* clarity and singleness of purpose of the innocent and intelligent, she believed in Captain Remson" (*Wm. McFee*). That is **dreadful** from which one shrinks in shuddering fear, or in loathing; as, the *dreadful* prospect of another world war; cancer is a *dreadful* disease. "She felt her two hands taken, and heard a kind voice. Could it be possible it belonged to the *dreadful* father of her husband?" (*Meredith*). "*Dreadful* things should not be known to young people until they are old enough to face them with a certain poise" (*B. Russell*). In looser, but still good, use *dreadful* is applicable to something from which one shrinks as disagreeable or as unpleasant to contemplate or endure; as, a *dreadful* necessity. "Wouldn't it be *dreadful* to produce that effect on people!" (*L. P. Smith*). That is **frightful** which, for the moment at least, paralyzes one with fear or throws one into great alarm or consternation; as, a *frightful* sound broke the quiet of the night; a *frightful* tornado. "The Ghost of a Lady...a scar on her forehead, and a bloody handkerchief at her breast, *frightful* to behold!" (*Mere-*

dith). *Frightful* is now often employed even by good writers without any implication of fright; however, in discriminating use, it imputes to the thing so qualified a capacity for startling the observer by its enormity, its outrageousness, or the like; as, a *frightful* disregard of decency; a *frightful* scandal; "This *frightful* condition of internal strain and instability" (*Shaw*). "The labour of sifting, combining, constructing, expunging, correcting, testing: this *frightful* toil is as much critical as creative" (*T. S. Eliot*). That is **terrible** which causes or is capable of causing extreme and agitating fear or which both induces fright or alarm and prolongs and intensifies it. "Millions of voices arose. The clamor became *terrible*, and confused the minds of all men" (*S. Anderson*). "One of those *terrible* women produced now and then by the Roman stock, unsexed, implacable, filled with an insane lust of power" (*Buchan*). "I have never read a more *terrible* exposure of human weakness—of universal human weakness—than the last great speech of Othello" (*T. S. Eliot*). "A human being devoid of hope is the most *terrible* object in the world" (*V. Heiser*). When the word carries no implication of terrifying, or of capacity for terrifying, it usually, in discriminating use, suggests that the thing so described is almost unendurable in its excess of force, power, or similar potency, or too painful to be borne without alleviation or mitigation. "Knowledge ....is no longer thought to be a secret, precious, rather *terrible* possession" (*A. C. Benson*). "An evil passion may give great physical and intellectual powers a *terrible* efficiency" (*C. W. Eliot*). "Sainte-Beuve believed that the truth is always *terrible*" (*L. P. Smith*). That is **terrific** which is by its size, appearance, potency, or the like, fitted or intended to inspire terror; as, "eyes And hairy mane *terrific*" (*Milton*); to assume a *terrific* expression. "One little tool...transforms the spark [of electricity] from a form too brief and bright and *terrific* to be intelligible into one of the most tractable and lucid of the phenomena...of Nature" (*Karl K. Darrow*). In more recent use, *terrific* is preferred to *terrible* when there is an implication of release of stored-up energy, physical, emotional, or intellectual, and of its stunning effect; as, a *terrific* (better than *terrible*) explosion; a *terrific* outburst of rage. "The most admired single phrase that Shakespeare ever wrote—Ripeness is all.... derives a *terrific* and pure dramatic impact from its context" (*Day Lewis*). That is **horrible** the sight of which induces not only fear or terror but also loathing and aversion; thus, a *fearful* precipice may not be *horrible;* in the practice of the ancient Greek dramatists, murder on the stage was avoided as *horrible*. "Now that wars are between nations, no longer between governments or armies, they have become far more *horrible*" (*Inge*). *Horrible*, like the other words, may be used in a weaker sense; in such cases it seldom suggests horror, but it does suggest hatefulness or hideousness; as, a *horrible* suspicion arose in his mind; a *horribly* shrill voice; a *horrible* taste. *Horrible* emphasizes the effect produced on a person, **horrific** the possession of qualities or properties fitted or intended to produce that effect; as, "that *horrific* yarn 'The Body-Snatcher'" (*C. E. Montague*). "His yearning for the *horrific*, the revolting, the transcendent mystery of whatever is not 'nice'" (*Times Lit. Sup.*). That is **shocking** which startles or is capable of startling because it is contrary to one's expectations, one's standards of good taste, one's moral sense, or the like; as, to like to tell *shocking* stories; to find a *shocking* change in a person's appearance. "The treatment should begin by encouraging him to utter freely even his most *shocking* thoughts" (*B. Russell*). Oftentimes in extended use, *shocking* does not imply a capacity for startling so much as a blamable or reprehensible character. "'It is *shocking* of me, but I have to laugh when people are pompous and absurd'" (*R. Macaulay*). "A solecism of this kind... would have seemed a *shocking* thing to...so accurate a scholar" (*L. P. Smith*). That is **appalling** which strikes one with dismay as well as with terror or horror. "Her overthrow would have been the most *appalling* disaster the Western world had ever known" (*H. Adams*). "The defectives are *appallingly* prolific" (*Shaw*). In looser but correct use, *appalling* often comes close to *amazing* but carries a stronger suggestion of dumfounding than of surprising; as, his *appalling* quickness of mind; an *appalling* suggestion.

Ana. Frightening, terrifying, alarming (see FRIGHTEN): *formidable, redoubtable: *ghastly, gruesome, grisly, grim, macabre, lurid: *sinister, baleful, malign: sublime (see SPLENDID).

fease. Variant of FAZE.

feasible. *Possible, practicable.

Ana. Practical, *practicable: advisable, *expedient, politic: advantageous, *beneficial, profitable: suitable, appropriate, fitting, *fit.

Ant. Unfeasible, infeasible: chimerical (*schemes, projects, suggestions, etc.*). — ***Con.*** Fantastic, visionary, quixotic (see IMAGINARY): utopian, *ambitious, pretentious.

feast, *n.* **Feast, festival, fete** (*or* **fête**), **fiesta** come into comparison in more than one sense, but especially in those of a day or period set apart as a time of rejoicing, or a celebration or observance characteristic of such an occasion. **Feast** bore both of these senses in early English use and continues to bear them. But *feast* as denoting a day or period set apart (universally or nationally or locally) for rejoicing refers commonly to one set apart for religious ceremonies of a solemn and joyful character, commemorating some important event (thus, the Jewish *feast* of Passover commemorates the sparing of the first-born of the Israelites in Egypt [*Exodus* xii]; Easter, or the *feast* of the Resurrection, commemorates the rising of Christ from the dead), or to one set apart for celebrating the day in the church calendar assigned to a saint under whose patronage a country or parish is placed (as, "To keep our great St. George's *feast* withal" —*Shak.*). Since *feast* in this sense is opposed to *fast* (which properly applies to a day or period of abstinence from food and from gaieties; thus, Yom Kippur is a strict *fast* day among Jews) the term often implies celebration not only by pomp and ceremony, but by popular sports and revels, such as games, pageants, plays, bonfires, dances, eating and drinking, and the like; as, "Corpus Christi Day, the greatest *feast* in the year" (*Gray*). *Feast* in the other of its earliest and still common senses denotes an unusually abundant or sumptuous meal, especially one that is provided for the enjoyment of those celebrating an occasion, not only a religious feast, but a marriage, a betrothal, a victory, an assumption of a crown or title, an anniversary, or the like; as, "To share our marriage *feast* and nuptial mirth" (*Keats*). Often, the word in this sense loses all suggestion of the celebration of an occasion and stresses, in figurative as well as in literal use, the delight or gratification induced by the food (or other pleasure) provided; as, she has so excellent a cook that every one of her dinners is a *feast;* "The *feast* of reason and the flow of soul" (*Pope*). **Festival** in early use was the adjective corresponding to the noun *feast*, rather than a substantive (thus, "a *festival* day" was a feast in the religious sense; "a high-*festival* day" was an important feast, such as Christmas or Easter, celebrated with special pomp and ceremony). After the Reformation, however, the word *festival* was accepted as a substantive, often equivalent to *feast* in its implications, but tending more and more to denote a time of civil or popular rather than of religious rejoicing and to impute a carnival rather than a religious character to its celebration; thus, in religious use, Christmas is called "the *Feast* of the Nativity," but in popular use is more commonly called "the Christmas *festival*"; so, the great national *festival* in the United States is Independence Day and in France, Bastille Day; a harvest *festival*. In the other sense of *feast, festival* is not used. But it has another common use of its own, to denote a series of concerts (or of other entertainments) provided at regularly recurring periods for the enjoyment of those interested; as, the city's annual music *festival*. **Fete,** or its French form **fête,** though the French equivalent of *feast*, came into English use in the eighteenth century to denote an entertainment of a sumptuous character, usually, but not necessarily, one provided for one's social equals, given out of doors (then sometimes specifically called *fête champêtre*) or on a body of water, and involving pageantry or other spectacular performances; as, a lawn *fete* or garden *fete* for charitable purposes; "the most splendid and elegant *fête* that was perhaps ever given" (*Gibbon*); "anxious to give the ladies of the imperial Harem a fete on the Black Sea" (*T. Hope*); "a gorgeous night *fête*" (*Manchester Guardian*). **Fiesta,** the Spanish word for *feast*, is much used in the states adjacent to Mexico, not only for any religious feast but especially for a saint's day, and the popular celebrating of it. The term is also used in English to designate a characteristic Spanish celebration of a feast day in Spain or any Spanish-speaking country.

Ana. Celebration, commemoration, observance, solemnization (see corresponding verbs at KEEP): rejoicing, regaling *or* regalement (see corresponding verbs at PLEASE): entertainment, diversion, amusement, recreation (see under AMUSE): dinner, *banquet.

Ant. Fast (*in religious use*).

feat, *n.* **Feat, exploit, achievement** agree in denoting a remarkable deed or performance. **Feat,** in modern usage, commonly suggests an act of strength or dexterity; an **exploit** is an adventurous, heroic, or brilliant feat; **achievement** emphasizes the idea of distinguished endeavor, commonly in the face of difficulty or opposition; all are occasionally used humorously or ironically; as, "Sleights of art and *feats* of strength went round" (*Goldsmith*); *feats* of daring; "I must retreat into the invalided corps and tell them of my former *exploits*, which may very likely pass for lies" (*Scott*); "Great is the rumor of this dreadful knight, and his *achievements* of no less account" (*Shak.*); *achievements* of science.

Ana. Deed, act, *action: triumph, conquest, *victory: emprise, enterprise, *adventure, quest.

feat, *adj.* Deft, adroit, *dexterous, handy.

Ana. *Agile, nimble, brisk, spry: skillful, skilled, *proficient, adept, expert: *easy, effortless, facile, smooth.

Con. *Awkward, clumsy, maladroit, inept, gauche.

fecund. Fruitful, prolific, *fertile.

Ana. Bearing, producing, yielding (see BEAR): breeding, propagating, reproducing, generating (see GENERATE).

Ant. Barren. — *Con.* *Sterile, unfruitful, infertile, impotent.

fecundity. Fruitfulness, prolificacy, fertility. See under FERTILE.

Ana. Producing *or* productiveness (see corresponding verb at BEAR): profuseness *or* profusion, luxuriance, lavishness, prodigality, lushness, exuberance (see corresponding adjectives at PROFUSE).

Ant. Barrenness.

federation. Confederacy, confederation, coalition, fusion, *alliance.

fee. Stipend, emolument, salary, *wage, pay, hire, screw.

Ana. Remuneration, compensation, requital (see corresponding verbs at PAY): charge, *price, cost, expense.

feeble. *Weak, infirm, decrepit, frail, fragile.

Ana. Unnerved, enervated, emasculated, unmanned (see UNNERVE): debilitated, weakened, enfeebled, disabled, crippled (see WEAKEN): doddering, *senile, anile, doting: *powerless, impotent, impuissant.

Ant. Robust. — *Con.* *Strong, sturdy, stout, stalwart: *vigorous, lusty, energetic: hale, *healthy.

feed, *v.* **Feed, nourish, pasture, graze,** come into comparison when they mean to provide the food that one needs or desires. **Feed** is the comprehensive term applicable not only to persons and animals, but also to plants and, by extension, to anything (such as a furnace) that consumes something (such as fuel), or requires something external for its sustenance; as, to *feed* the baby; to *feed* a family of ten on fifty dollars a week; to *feed* the cattle; to use bone meal to *feed* the chrysanthemums; to *feed* a furnace with coal. "Hugh's growing vanity was *fed* by the thought that Clara was interested in him" (*S. Anderson*). "The press exploits for its benefit human silliness and ignorance and vulgarity and sensationalism, and, in exploiting it, *feeds* it" (*R. Macaulay*). In American but not in British use, *feed* sometimes takes for its object the thing that is fed; as, to *feed* oats to the horses; to *feed* coal to the furnace; "He has been *feeding* bread and butter to the dog" (*Kate D. Wiggin*). **Nourish** implies feeding with food that is essential to a person's, or by extension a thing's, growth, health, well-being, or the like. Etymologically, it implies the giving of mother's milk to the suckling child or offspring, but this use is now very rare, *nurse* now being the preferred word. "I do so wish she would not see fit to sit down and *nourish* her baby in my poor old bachelor drawing-room" (*H. G. Wells*). In idiomatic English, *nourish* more often takes as its subject the thing that serves as a sustaining or a building-up food than the person who provides such food; as, milk, eggs, and meat *nourish* the bodies of fast-growing boys and girls; "the humid prairie heat, so *nourishing* to wheat and corn, so exhausting to human beings" (*Cather*); "Freedom *nourishes* self-respect" (*W. E. Channing*); "His zeal seemed *nourished* By failure and by fall" (*Whittier*). **Pasture** (etymologically, to feed) was, in very early use, applied chiefly to animals but very rarely to human beings. Somewhat later it was restricted, except in humorous use, to cattle, sheep, or other domestic animals fed on grass; as, "Unwont with heards to watch, or *pasture* sheepe" (*Spenser*). **Graze** is often preferred specifically to *pasture* when the emphasis is on the use of growing grass for food; as, "a field or two to *graze* his cows" (*Swift*); to *graze* one's cow on the common.

Ana. *Nurse, nurture, foster, cherish: support, sustain, maintain (see corresponding nouns at LIVING).

Ant. Starve.

feel, *n.* Feeling, *atmosphere, savor, tone, aura.

Ana. See those at FEELING, 3.

feeling, *n.* **1** Sensibility, *sensation, sense.

Ana. Reacting *or* reaction, behaving *or* behavior (see corresponding verbs at ACT): responsiveness (see corresponding adjective at TENDER): sensitiveness, susceptibility (see corresponding adjectives at LIABLE).

2 Feeling, affection, emotion, sentiment, passion. Feeling, the general term, denotes any partly mental and partly physical, but not sensory, response (or the state that results) that is characterized by pleasure or pain, attraction or repulsion, or the like. Unless it is qualified or a clue is given in the context, *feeling* gives no indication of the nature, the quality, or the intensity of the response. "Whatever *feelings* were in Sophia's heart, tenderness was not among them" (*Bennett*). "A *feeling* of sadness and longing" (*Longfellow*). Often, *feeling* implies a contrast with *judgment* and connotes lack of thought. "Her humanity was a *feeling*, not a principle" (*H. Mackenzie*). **Affection,** once used technically for *feeling*, is now applied mainly to such feelings as are also inclinations or likings; the word therefore sometimes suggests desire or striving. "The heart...we are, by foolish custom...impelled to call the seat of the *affections*" (*R. Macaulay*). "That serene and blessed mood, In which the *affections* gently lead us on" (*Wordsworth*). **Emotion,** the preferred term in modern psychology because it suggests the physical as well as the mental reaction, usually carries in nontechnical use a stronger implication of excitement or agitation than does *feeling*. "Eagerness for *emotion* and adventure" (*Sydney Smith*). "Means of exciting religious *emotion*" (*Ruskin*). "A sensation of strength, inspired by mighty *emotion*" (*G. Eliot*). **Sentiment** connotes a larger intellectual element in the feeling than any of the others; it often is applied specifically to an emotion inspired by an idea. "Filling the soul with *sentiments* august — The beautiful, the brave, the holy, and the just!" (*Wordsworth*). Commonly the word suggests refined, sometimes romantic, occasionally affected or artificial, feeling; as, "that moral *sentiment* which exists in every human breast" (*G. Bancroft*); "His opinions are more the result of conviction than of *sentiment*" (*J. R. Lowell*); Sterne has been called a man overflowing with *sentiment* on paper, but devoid of real *feeling*. **Passion** suggests powerful or controlling emotion; it, far more than *affection*, implies urgency of desire for possession, revenge, or the like. "Hark! how the sacred calm, that breathes about, bids every fierce tumultuous *passion* cease" (*Gray*). "The ruling *passion*, be it what it will, the ruling *passion* conquers reason still" (*Pope*).

Ana. Impressing *or* impression, touching, affecting *or* affection (see corresponding verbs at AFFECT, *v.*, 1): *mood, humor, temper, vein.

3 Feel, *atmosphere, savor, tone, aura.

Ana. *Impression, impress, imprint: peculiarity, individuality, characteristic (see corresponding adjectives at CHARACTERISTIC): *quality, property, character, attribute.

feeze. Variant of FAZE.

feign. Simulate, counterfeit, sham, pretend, affect, *assume.

Ana. Fabricate, manufacture, forge (see MAKE): dissemble, *disguise, cloak, mask.

feint, *n.* Artifice, wile, ruse, stratagem, maneuver, *trick.

Ana. *Pretense, pretension, make-believe, make-belief: hoaxing *or* hoax, hoodwinking, befooling (see corresponding verbs at DUPE): resort, expedient, shift (see RESOURCE).

felicitate. Felicitate, congratulate agree in meaning to express one's pleasure in the joy, success, elevation, or prospects of another. **Felicitate** is not only the more formal term, but it carries a stronger implication that the person who felicitates regards the other as very happy or wishes him happiness; as, to *felicitate* the parents upon the birth of a child; to *felicitate* His Majesty upon his coronation. **Congratulate** is the more common and often more intimate term; it usually implies that the congratulator regards the other as a person to whom good fortune has come or on whom fortune smiles; thus, it is "good form" to *congratulate* a bridegroom and to *felicitate* a bride; so, to *congratulate* a friend on his promotion; to *congratulate* oneself that one has escaped a trying situation.

felicitous. Happy, apt, fitting, appropriate, *fit, suitable, meet, proper.

Ana. Telling, convincing (see VALID): pat, timely, opportune, *seasonable, well-timed: apposite, pertinent, *relevant.

Ant. Infelicitous: inept, maladroit. — ***Con.*** *Awkward, clumsy, gauche: unfortunate, unhappy, unlucky (see affirmative adjectives at LUCKY).

felicity. *Happiness, bliss, beatitude, blessedness.

Ana. Rapture, transport, *ecstasy: joy, delight, delectation, *pleasure, fruition.

Ant. Misery.

fell, *n.* Pelt, hide, *skin, rind, bark, peel.

fell, *adj.* Cruel, inhuman, savage, barbarous, ferocious, *fierce, truculent.

Ana. Baleful, malign, malefic, *sinister: pitiless, ruthless (see corresponding nouns at PITY): relentless, unrelenting, merciless, *grim, implacable.

female, *n.* **Female, woman, lady** are here compared as meaning a person (especially an adult) who belongs to the sex that is the counterpart of man, or the male of the human species. **Female** (the correlative of *male*) emphasizes the idea of sex; it applies not only to human beings but also to animals and plants. Its employment as a synonym for *woman* was once frequent among good writers (as, "three smart-looking *females*"—*Austen;* "to please the *females* of our modest age"—*Byron*), but this use is now frowned upon as derogatory or contemptuous, except in strictly scientific or statistical use. The term, in such use, may be employed to designate any person of the female sex, whether infant, child, adolescent, or adult; as, the city's population included 12,115 males and 15,386 *females*. As compared with **woman** (the correlative of *man*), which emphasizes the essential qualities of the adult female, **lady** (the correlative of *gentleman*) connotes rather the externals of social position or refinement. *Woman* is now preferred by many persons of fastidious taste whenever the reference is to the person merely as a person (as, the country expects the help of its *women;* the following *women* assisted in receiving the guests; a *woman* of culture; a sales*woman;* working*women;* society *women*). *Lady*, on the other hand, is preferred when exalted social position, gentle breeding, or refinement and delicacy are definitely implied; as, "Alfonso XI at his death left one legitimate son...and five bastards by a *lady* of Seville, Doña Leonor de Guzmán" (*Cambridge Medieval History*); "Miss Nancy...had the essential attributes of a *lady*—high veracity, delicate honor in her dealings, deference to others, and refined personal habits" (*G. Eliot*). The term, nevertheless, is frequently used as a mere courteous synonym for *woman* (as, Please allow these *ladies* to pass; may I speak to the *lady* of the house?), but its indiscriminate substitution for *woman* (as in wash*lady*, sales*lady*) is disapproved both in America and in Great Britain; as, "I admit that our abuse of the word is villainous. I know of an orator who once said...that 'The *ladies* were last at the cross and first at the tomb'!"—*J. R. Lowell;* we once had "seminaries for young *ladies*" but now we have "*women's* colleges."

female, *adj.* **Female, feminine, womanly, womanlike, womanish, effeminate, ladylike** come into comparison as meaning of, characteristic of, or like a female of the species (especially the human species). **Female** (opposed to *male*) applies to animals and plants as well as to human beings, and always suggests sex; as, "the *female* bee" (*Milton*); "the *female* ivy" (*Shak.*); *female* children. **Feminine** (opposed to *masculine*) alone of these words may imply grammatical gender (as, *feminine* nouns and pronouns), but it characteristically applies to features, lines, qualities, and the like, which belong to women rather than to men; it has now practically displaced all except the more strictly physiological senses of *female;* as, "Her heavenly form Angelic, but more soft and *feminine*" (*Milton*); "the domestic virtues, which are especially *feminine*" (*Lecky*). **Womanly** (often opposed to *girlish* or, from another point of view, to *manly*) is used to qualify anything which evidences the qualities of a fully and usually roundly developed woman (as, *womanly* virtues); it often specifically suggests qualities which especially befit a woman by reason of her sex or her functions as a wife and mother, such as tenderness, sympathy, moral strength, fortitude, and the like, or the absence of mannish qualities such as aggressiveness; as, "'Twas just a *womanly* presence, an influence unexprest" (*J. R. Lowell*); "All will spy in thy face A blushing, *womanly*, discovering grace" (*Donne*). **Womanlike** (opposed to *manlike*) is more apt to suggest characteristically feminine faults or foibles; as, "*Womanlike*, taking revenge too deep for a transient wrong Done but in thought to your beauty" (*Tennyson*). **Womanish** (compare *mannish, childish*) is a term of contempt, especially when applied to that which should be virile or masculine; as, "Art thou a man? thy form cries out thou art: Thy tears are *womanish*" (*Shak.*); "*womanish* or wailing grief" (*Cowper*). **Effeminate** emphasizes the idea of unmanly delicacy, luxuriousness, or enervation; as, "A woman impudent and mannish grown Is not more loathed than an *effeminate* man In time of action" (*Shak.*); "an *effeminate* and unmanly foppery" (*R. Hurd*); "Something *feminine*—not *effeminate*, mind—is discoverable in the countenances of all men of genius" (*Coleridge*). **Ladylike** is frequently used sarcastically, especially of men, to imply a dainty and finical affectation of the proprieties (as, "fops at all corners, *lady-like* in mien"—*Cowper*). The term is also applicable to girls and to women or to their conduct, habits, or manners, in such use suggesting conformity to any standard implied by the term *lady;* as, "Your daughter may be better paid, better dressed, more gently spoken, more *ladylike* than you were in the old mill" (*Shaw*).

Ant. Male. — *Con.* Masculine, manly, manlike, manful, mannish, virile (see MALE).

feminine. *Female, womanly, womanish, ladylike, womanlike, effeminate.

Ant. Masculine. — *Con.* *Male, manly, mannish, virile, manlike, manful.

ferment, *n.* Fermentation, *ebullition, effervescence.

Ana. Leavening *or* leaven (see corresponding verb at INFUSE): transformation, metamorphosis (see under TRANSFORM): *change, mutation, vicissitude: change, alteration, modification, variation (see under CHANGE, *v.*).

fermentation. Ferment, *ebullition, effervescence.

Ana. Leavening *or* leaven (see corresponding verb at INFUSE): agitation, disturbance, perturbation (see corresponding verbs at DISCOMPOSE): excitement, stimulation, quickening (see corresponding verbs at PROVOKE).

ferocious. *Fierce, truculent, barbarous, savage, inhuman, cruel, fell.

Ana. Infuriated, maddened, enraged (see corresponding verbs at ANGER): rapacious, *voracious, ravening, ravenous: relentless, implacable, merciless, *grim.

Con. *Tame, subdued, submissive.

fertile. Fertile, fecund, fruitful, prolific agree in meaning having or manifesting (literally or figuratively) the power to produce fruit (that is, grains, vegetables, cotton, flax, the so-called fruits, etc.) or offspring. The same distinctions in implications and connotations are observable in their corresponding nouns **fertility, fecundity, fruitfulness, prolificacy** (also **prolificity** or **prolificness**—all three being comparatively rare terms in general use). **Fertile** (opposed to *sterile, infertile*) applies particularly to that in which seeds take root and grow or may take root and grow because it contains the elements essential to their life and development; as, *fertile* soil; the *fertility* of alluvial land. Consequently, the term often applies to that which is exceedingly productive in that it serves as a soil in which ideas take root and thrive; as, a *fertile* mind; "In the heath's barrenness to the farmer lay its *fertility* to the historian" (*Hardy*). "In him [Dr. Johnson] were united a most logical head with a most *fertile* imagination" (*Boswell*). The term is also applicable to anything which has in itself the elements essential to its growth and development into a living thing (as, a *fertile* egg; a *fertile* seed; hence, a *fertile* idea or conception) or (especially in scientific use) to any person, any animal, or any pair, that is able to produce normal living young (as, a *fertile* husband; a *fertile* couple). **Fecund** (opposed to *barren*) applies especially to that which actually yields in abundance or with rapidity fruits, offspring, or by extension, projects, inventions, works of art, or the like; thus, one speaks of the *fecundity* of a mother if one wishes to imply that she has a large family, but of her *fertility* if the intent is to indicate that she is not sterile; so, by extension, a *fecund* (rather than a *fertile*) inventive genius; a *fecund* printing press. "If you had been born a Dumas—I am speaking of *fecundity*...and of nothing else...and could rattle off a romance in a fortnight" (*Quiller-Couch*). **Fruitful** may be used in place of *fecund* (preferably in the case of trees, plants, and the like) and in the place of *fertile* (in reference to soil or land), but it may also be applied to anything that promotes fertility or fecundity; as, a *fruitful* tree; soil made *fruitful* by cultivation; a *fruitful* rain. Consequently, in its extended sense, it is applicable to anything that bears results, especially useful or profitable results, of almost any kind; as, "the time has always come, and the season is never unripe, for the announcement of the *fruitful* idea" (*J. Morley*); "the enormously *fruitful* discovery [of Pythagoras] that pitch of sound depends upon the length of the vibrating chord" (*H. Ellis*); "Darwinism...is a *fruitful* theory of the means by which nature works" (*Inge*); "The poet...is apt to lack the detachment which alone makes *fruitful* criticism possible" (*Lowes*). **Prolific** is often interchangeable with *fecund*, especially in the literal senses of both words, but it often suggests even greater rapidity in reproduction and is therefore more frequently used than the latter term in disparagement or derogation, especially when applied to types, races, species, or the like; as, guinea pigs are *prolific;* "the starling is so *prolific* that the flocks become immense" (*Jefferies*); "uncultivated, defective people....are appallingly *prolific*" (*Shaw*); "the flabby pseudo-religions in which the modern world is so *prolific*" (*J. W. Krutch*).

Ana. Producing, bearing, yielding (see BEAR): inventing *or* inventive, creating *or* creative (see corresponding verbs at INVENT): quickening, stimulating, provoking, exciting, galvanizing (see PROVOKE).

Ant. Infertile, sterile. — *Con.* Barren, impotent, unfruitful (see STERILE).

fertility. Fruitfulness, fecundity, prolificacy. See under FERTILE.

Ant. Infertility, sterility. — *Con.* Impotence *or* impotency, barrenness, unfruitfulness (see corresponding adjectives at STERILE).

fervent. Ardent, fervid, perfervid, *impassioned, passionate.

Ana. *Devout, pious, religious: warm, warmhearted, *tender, responsive: *sincere, wholehearted, heartfelt, hearty, whole-souled, unfeigned: *intense, vehement.
Con. Cool, *cold, chilly, frigid: apathetic, *impassive, phlegmatic.

fervid. Fervent, ardent, perfervid, *impassioned, passionate.
Ana. *Intense, vehement: earnest, *serious, solemn: *sincere, heartfelt, hearty, wholehearted, whole-souled.
Con. Collected, composed, *cool, imperturbable, nonchalant: *indifferent, aloof, detached, unconcerned.

fervor *or* **fervour.** Ardor, enthusiasm, *passion, zeal.
Ana. Devoutness, piousness *or* piety (see corresponding adjectives at DEVOUT): earnestness, seriousness, solemnity (see corresponding adjectives at SERIOUS): sincerity, heartiness, wholeheartedness (see corresponding adjectives at SINCERE).

festival. *Feast, fete, fiesta.

fetch, *v.* *Bring, take.
Ana. *Get, obtain, procure: transfer, shift, *move, remove: convey, transport, transmit, *carry, bear.

fetch, *n.* Wraith, ghost, spirit, specter, shade, revenant, *apparition, phantasm, phantom, spook, haunt.

fete *or* **fête,** *n.* *Feast, festival, fiesta.

fetid *or* **foetid.** Noisome, *malodorous, stinking, putrid, rank, rancid, fusty, musty.
Ana. Foul, nasty (see DIRTY): *offensive, loathsome, repulsive, repugnant, revolting.
Ant. Fragrant. — *Con.* *Odorous, aromatic, redolent, balmy.

fetish. **Fetish, talisman, charm, amulet, periapt** come into comparison when they designate an object believed to be endowed with the virtue of averting evil or of bringing good fortune. **Fetish** is applied to any object, either natural (as a snake, an animal's tooth or claw) or artificial (as a piece of carved wood or bone) which is held sacred in the belief that a supernatural spirit has entered into it and invested it with the power to bring success, luck, and freedom from evil to its owner or worshiper. In its literal sense, the word is always connected with the religion of savage or barbarous peoples. Figuratively, it is applied to anything which is unreasonably or irrationally regarded as sacred or sacrosanct; as, to make a *fetish* of the Constitution. "The mediocre was repellent to them; cant and sentiment made them sick; they made a *fetish* of hard truth" (*R. Macaulay*). **Talisman,** unlike *fetish*, presupposes a degree of enlightenment, a knowledge of astrology and other occult sciences, and a belief in magical powers. Strictly, it is applied to a cut, incised, or engraved figure or image of a heavenly constellation or planet or to its sign, or to a gem, a piece of metal, or the like, so cut, incised, or engraved. By virtue of this representation it is supposed to be endowed with the same occult influence as that which it represents. "He had stolen from Henry...a *Talisman*, which rendered its wearer invulnerable" (*Stubbs*). Figuratively, it is applied to any object that exerts a magical, extraordinary, and usually happy, influence. "The little circle of the schoolboy's copper coin...had proven a *talisman*, fragrant with good, and deserving to be set in gold and worn next her heart" (*N. Hawthorne*). "The mere touch of a leaf was a *talisman* to bring me under the enchantment" (*Jefferies*). "There is no *talisman* in the word 'parent' which can generate miracles of affection" (*S. Butler*). **Charm,** in its precise use, applies to anything that works a spell repelling evil spirits or influence or attracting favorable ones. It may be used in reference to an incantation, a word, or a form of words, as well as to an object that possesses this power; thus, fetishes and talismans were often carried as *charms*. "The gallant little Abruzzi cob was decorated with...a panoply of *charms* against the evil eye" (*C. Mackenzie*). In its figurative application to a quality in persons or in things it connotes a power to attract or allure that is suggestive of spell-working; as, she has great *charm;* did you not feel the *charm* of the painting? **Amulet** is usually applied to anything worn or carried on the person because of its magical power to preserve one in danger or to protect one from evil, especially from disease. "The French traveller Coudreau...expressly states that 'collars made of jaguars' or bush-hogs' teeth, worn round the neck by small children, are *amulets* intended to protect them, when they grow bigger, against the attack of ferocious beasts'" (*Karsten*). In its rare figurative use, it still implies protection. "Righteousness will give you love...but it will not give you an invincible *amulet* against misfortune" (*F. W. Farrar*). **Periapt,** a learned term, is a comprehensive designation, including not only amulets worn because of their reputed magical influence, but any similar objects, such as asafetida bags, carried on the person and credited with physical influences or effects that are not borne out by science.

fetter, *v.* Shackle, *hamper, trammel, clog, manacle, hog-tie.
Ana. *Hinder, impede, obstruct, block, bar, dam: *restrain, curb, snaffle, check: baffle, balk, thwart, foil, *frustrate: bind, *tie.
Con. *Free, liberate, release: *extricate, disencumber, disembarrass, disentangle, untangle: disengage, *detach.

feverish. Nervous, restless, restive, uneasy, fidgety, *impatient, skittish, jumpy, jittery, unquiet.
Ana. Agitated, perturbed, disturbed, flustered, flurried (see DISCOMPOSE): excited, stimulated, quickened, galvanized (see PROVOKE).
Con. Nonchalant, unruffled, collected, composed, *cool: *calm, serene, tranquil.

fewer. *Less, lesser, smaller.

fib, *n.* Untruth, falsehood, *lie, misrepresentation, story.

fib, *v.* Equivocate, palter, *lie, prevaricate.

fickle. *Inconstant, unstable, capricious, mercurial.
Ana. *Changeable, changeful, variable, protean: *fitful, spasmodic: light, light-minded, frivolous, flighty, volatile (see corresponding nouns at LIGHTNESS).
Ant. Constant, true. — *Con.* *Faithful, leal, loyal, stanch, steadfast.

fiction. **Fiction, figment, fabrication, fable** are here compared as meaning a story, an account, an explanation, a conception, or the like, which is an invention of the human mind. **Fiction** so strongly implies the use of the imagination that it serves as the class name for all prose or poetic writings which deal with imagined characters and situations (or with actual characters or situations with less concern for the historicity of the details than for the telling of an interesting, coherent story). In the sense here particularly considered, a *fiction* is something that is made up without reference to (often in some defiance of) fact, or reality, or truth, for any one of several motives, such as to avoid telling an unpleasant or inconvenient truth (as, "Adrian....was at a loss what to invent to detain him, beyond the stale *fiction* that his father was coming tomorrow"—*Meredith*), or to describe or explain someone or something about whom or which practically nothing is known (as, "Karl Joël... spent fifteen of the best years of his life over the Xenophontic Socrates, to discover that the figure was just as much a *fiction* as the Platonic Socrates"—*H. Ellis*), or to impose upon others an interpretation or an assumption that serves one's own ends or that satisfies the unthinking because of its accord with outward appearances (as, "the notion that a business is clothed with a public interest and has been devoted to the public use is little more than a *fiction* intended to beautify what is disagreeable to the sufferers"—*Justice Holmes;* "Few of the usual *fictions* on which society rested had ever required such defiance of facts"—*H. Adams*), or, especially in legal or scientific use, to provide a convenient assumption or method whereby one can deal with that which is beyond the range of rational or objective proof (as, "The Linnaean and similar classificatory systems are *fictions* ...having their value simply as pictures, as forms of representation"—*H. Ellis*). *Fiction* may apply to something which appears to be true, or is believed to be in accordance with a higher form of truth (such as "poetic truth," "philosophical truth," "spiritual truth"), or with the demands of reason when they come into conflict with fact, or the world as apprehended by the senses: *figment* and *fabrication,* on the other hand, carry no implication of justification and usually suggest a defiance of truth of any kind or degree. **Figment** usually suggests the operation of fancy or of unlicensed imagination and neglect of fact; as, "The rude, unvarnished gibes with which he demolished every *figment* of defence" (*Stevenson*); "This is all a *figment* of your imagination" (*Stevenson*). "A sense of unreality was creeping over him. Surely this great Chamber [the House of Commons]... did not exist at all but as a gigantic fancy of his own! And all these figures were *figments* of his brain!" (*Galsworthy*). **Fabrication,** in the specific sense here considered, applies to something that is made up with artifice and, usually though not invariably, with the intent to deceive; consequently, it is often used of a fiction that is a deliberate and complete falsehood; as, the common account of his disappearance is a *fabrication;* the legend, though some of its details are obviously fictitious, cannot be dismissed as a pure *fabrication.* **Fable** (as here compared: see also ALLEGORY, 2) applies to a fictitious narrative that is obviously unconcerned with fact, usually because it deals with events or situations that are marvelous, impossible, preposterous, or otherwise incredible; as, "if we may take the story of Job for a history, not a *fable*" (*Defoe*); "nothing but whispered suspicions, old wives' tales, *fables* invented by men who had nothing to do but loaf in the drug-store and make up stories" (*S. Anderson*).

Ana. *Narrative, story, tale, anecdote, yarn: *novel, romance.

fictitious. **Fictitious, fabulous, legendary, mythical, apocryphal** agree in meaning having the character of that which is invented or imagined as opposed to that which is true or genuine. Although all these words are more or less affected by the nouns derived from the same root (*fiction, fable, legend, myth, apocrypha*), their fundamental implications come, as a rule, from the root and not from the denotation of the noun. **Fictitious** commonly implies fabrication and, therefore, more often suggests artificiality or contrivance than intent to deceive or deliberate falsification; as, *fictitious* characters and events belong in a novel or romance, but not in a history; many authors prefer to assume a *fictitious* name. In an extended sense *fictitious* definitely connotes falseness when applied to value, worth, significance, or the like, and suggests its determination by other than the right standards; as, the furore created by this incident gives it a *fictitious* importance; in booms and in panics the market value of a sound security is often *fictitious.* **Fabulous** stresses the marvelousness or incredibility of that which is so described; only at times, however, does the adjective imply a thing's impossibility or nonexistence; as, for a year the company paid *fabulous* dividends; his letters gave accounts of *fabulous* exploits; *fabulous* sea monsters. **Legendary** usually suggests popular tradition and popular susceptibility to elaboration of details or distortion of historical facts as the basis for a thing's fictitious or fabulous character; as, the *legendary* deeds of William Tell; the *legendary* wealth of the Aztecs; the Tarquins, *legendary* kings of ancient Rome. **Mythical,** like *legendary,* usually presupposes the working of the popular imagination, but it distinctively implies a purely fanciful explanation of facts, or the creation of purely imaginary beings, events, etc. Therefore, *mythical* in its wider modern use is nearly equivalent to *imaginary,* and implies nonexistence; as, the *mythical* beings called nymphs; Mrs. Harris, Sairey Gamp's friend in Dickens's "Martin Chuzzlewit," is a *mythical* character. **Apocryphal** implies a mysterious or extremely dubious source or origin; in modern use it sometimes suggests merely the lack of authenticity, sometimes spuriousness. "We know them [some of the Elizabethans] unmistakably through their own writings...and by a few anecdotes of the kind which, even when *apocryphal,* remain as evidence of the personal impression that such men must have made upon their contemporaries" (*T. S. Eliot*). "It is not possible to attach much weight to the Sanson memoirs—they are so plainly *apocryphal*" (*A. Repplier*).

☞ *Do not confuse* fictitious *with* factitious.

Ana. Invented, created (see INVENT): *imaginary, fanciful, fantastic: fabricated, fashioned (see MAKE).

Ant. Historical. — ***Con.*** *Real, true, actual: *authentic, veritable: veracious, truthful, verisimilitudinous *or* verisimilar (see corresponding nouns at TRUTH).

fidelity. **Fidelity, allegiance, fealty, loyalty, devotion, piety** agree in denoting faithfulness to that to which one is bound by a pledge or duty. **Fidelity** implies strict adherence to that which is a matter of faith or of keeping faith; it presupposes an obligation, sometimes natural, sometimes imposed as a trust, sometimes voluntarily accepted or chosen; as, *fidelity* to one's word; *fidelity* in the performance of one's duties; *fidelity* to one's friends. Sometimes, even when unqualified, it implies marital faithfulness. "With close *fidelity* and love unfeigned To keep the matrimonial bond unstained" (*Cowper*). Sometimes it implies faithfulness to the original as in representation, portrayal, quotation, etc. "The Russian ....finds relief to his sensitiveness in letting his perceptions have perfectly free play, and in recording their reports with perfect *fidelity*" (*Arnold*). **Allegiance** implies adherence to something objective which one serves or follows as a vassal his lord and which demands unswerving fidelity when conflicting obligations dispute its pre-eminence; as, secret societies that exact the *allegiance* of every member. "But he [the critic] owes no *allegiance* to anything but to Truth; all other *fidelities* he must disregard when that is in question" (*L. P. Smith*). **Fealty,** like *allegiance,* implies a supreme obligation to be faithful, but unlike the latter, it stresses the compelling power of one's sense of duty or of consciousness of one's pledged word. "When I do forget The least of these unspeakable deserts, Romans, forget your *fealty* to me" (*Shak.*). "The extent to which we are accurate in our thoughts, words, and deeds is a rough measure of our *fealty* to truth" (*P. B. Ballard*). **Loyalty** implies more emotion and closer personal attachment than either *fidelity* or *fealty;* it usually connotes steadfastness, sometimes in the face of attempts to alienate one's affections or of a temptation to ignore or renounce one's obligation. "I will follow thee, To the last gasp, with truth and *loyalty*" (*Shak.*). Unlike *fidelity, loyalty* is not invariably regarded as a virtue, especially when personal feeling rather than principle determines it. "[Oxford] home of lost causes, and forsaken beliefs, and unpopular names, and impossible *loyalties!*" (*Arnold*). "Indeed, in public life it is generally considered a kind of treachery to change, because people value what they call *loyalty* above truth" (*A. C. Benson*). **Devotion** stresses zeal in service often amounting to self-dedication; it usually also implies ardent attachment. "He set out to prove the loyalty of his nature by *devotion* to the Queen who had advanced him (*Belloc*). "There is...something outside of the artist to which he owes *allegiance*, a *devotion* to which he must surrender and sacrifice himself" (*T. S. Eliot*). **Piety** emphasizes fidelity to obligations regarded as natural or fundamental, such as reverence for one's parents (filial *piety*), one's race, one's traditions, one's country, or one's God, and observance of all the duties which such reverence requires; thus, filial *piety* inspires respect for the wishes of parents; religious *piety* (usually, just "*piety*") is manifest in faithful and reverent worship. "Having matured in the surroundings and under the special conditions of sea life, I have a special *piety* toward that form of my past....I have tried with an almost filial regard to render the vibration of life in the great world of waters" (*Conrad*).

Ana. Faithfulness, constancy, lealty, stanchness, steadfastness (see corresponding adjectives at FAITHFUL).

Ant. Faithlessness: perfidy. — ***Con.*** Falseness *or* falsity, disloyalty, treacherousness *or* treachery, traitorousness, perfidiousness (see corresponding adjectives at FAITHLESS).

fidgety. Restless, restive, uneasy, skittish, jumpy, jittery, *impatient, nervous, unquiet, feverish, hectic.

field. 1 Gridiron, diamond, *arena, circus, lists, ring, cockpit, court, rink.

2 **Field, domain, province, sphere, territory, bailiwick** come into comparison in their extended senses when they denote the limits in which a person, an institution, a department of knowledge, of art, or of human endeavor appropriately or necessarily confines his or its activity or influence and outside of which by implication he or it may not or should not go. **Field** implies restriction by choice or by necessity but it seldom suggests permanent limitation; thus, a European war narrows the *field* of commerce for neutral American nations; he chose the development of industries in the South as his *field* of investigation; "The philosopher and the practical man ...each is in his own *field*, supreme" (*Buckle*). **Domain** is used chiefly, but not exclusively, in reference to departments of knowledge, of art, and of human endeavor viewed abstractly; it implies exclusive possession and control of a clearly defined field, and a title to regard all outside interference or all intrusion into that field as trespass or invasion; as, the *domain* of science; the *domain* of the spiritual. "What is the difference between the legitimate music of verse and the music it attains by trespassing on the *domain* of a sister art?" (*Babbitt*). "Those who believe in the reality of a world of the spirit —the poet, the artist, the mystic—are at one in believing that there are other *domains* than that of physics" (*Jeans*). **Province** is used in reference not only to the sciences, arts, etc., each of which may be said to have its own domain, but also to any person or institution that because of his or its office, aims, special character, or the like, can be said to have jurisdiction, competence, power, or influence within clearly defined limits; as, it is within the *province* of a parent rather than of a teacher to discipline a pupil for misconduct out of school; it is often stated that art goes beyond its *province* when it attempts to teach morals. "From Tokyo I went to Peiping, where the China Medical Board was already at work. Its activities did not fall within my *province* [as an expert on sanitation], but I was frequently consulted" (*V. Heiser*). *Province* is also used figuratively in the sense of function (see also FUNCTION, *n.*, 1) and in the sense of a part of a larger domain. "I should like the reader to accept engineering as a *province* of physics: so that the feats of the one may serve as credentials for the discoveries of the other" (*Karl K. Darrow*). **Sphere,** even more than *domain*, throws emphasis on clear circumscription of limits; it therefore suggests apartness rather than fundamental differences, and carries no hint of danger of trespass or interference. "The aesthetic and ethical *spheres*...were never sharply distinguished by the Greeks" (*G. L. Dickinson*). "In the *sphere* of morals we must often be content to wait until our activity is completed to appreciate its beauty or its ugliness" (*H. Ellis*). "In the life of a man whose circumstances and talents are not very exceptional there should be a large *sphere* where what is vaguely termed 'herd instinct' dominates, and a small *sphere* into which it does not penetrate" (*B. Russell*). **Territory** comes very close to *domain* in implying a field possessed and controlled and regarded as one's own; it does not, however, carry the implications so strong in *domain* of rightful ownership, of sovereignty, and of the title to inviolability; it may even suggest that the field has been usurped or taken over by the science, art, activity, etc., in question. "Prose has pre-empted a lion's share of the *territory* once held, either in sovereignty or on equal terms, by poetry" (*Lowes*). "If passage-ways connect the *domain* of physics with the *domains* of life or of spirit, physics ought in time to discover these passage-ways, for they start from her own *territory*" (*Jeans*). **Bailiwick,** literally the jurisdiction of a bailiff (see POLICEMAN), is increasingly used during recent years in an extended and humorous sense in reference to an individual and the special and limited province or domain in which he may or does exercise authority. It often also carries a connotation of petty yet despotic display of power; as, a politician whose influence does not extend beyond his own *bailiwick;* he will not get along with others until he learns to keep within his own *bailiwick*. "We may neither be angry nor gay in the presence of the moon, nor may we dare to think in her *bailiwick*" (*J. Stephens*).

Ana. Limits, bounds, confines (see singular nouns at LIMIT): extent, area, *size, magnitude.

fiend. 1 *Demon, devil, daemon.

2 *Addict, votary, devotee, habitué, fan.

fiendish. Fiendish, devilish, diabolical, diabolic, demoniacal, demoniac, demonic come into comparison when they mean having or manifesting the qualities associated with infernal or hellish beings called devils, demons, and fiends. **Fiendish** commonly implies excessive cruelty or malignity; as, *fiendish* tortures; "the *fiendish* joy that illumined his usually stolid countenance sent a sudden disgust and horror through me" (*Hudson*). **Devilish** frequently suggests abnormal wickedness of whatever sort (as, *devilish* orgies; *devilish* treachery), but it often also suggests superhuman or Satanic ingenuity or craft, capacity for destruction, or the like (as, "[Leonardo da Vinci] showed no compunction in planning *devilish* engines of military destruction"—*H. Ellis*). The term is often loosely used as an intensive with a coarsely humorous connotation; as, "*devilish* good dinner" (*Dickens*). **Diabolical** often (and sometimes *devilish*) connotes colder and more calculating malevolence than *fiendish;* as, *diabolical* cruelty; *diabolical* ingenuity; a *diabolical* sneer; "People suffering from the paranoia of persecution often imagine that they are the victims of a *diabolical* secret society" (*A. Huxley*). **Diabolic** is often used interchangeably with *diabolical*, and vice versa, but the former term is preferred by careful writers when the reference is to devils as individuals of a given character or origin rather than to their malign qualities; as, "the difference between the angelic and the *diabolic* temperament" (*Shaw*); "[The heroic age's] heroes were doughty men to whom *diabolic* visitors were no more unusual than angelic ones" (*J. W. Krutch*). **Demoniacal** frequently suggests frenzy or excesses, as of one "possessed"; as, *demoniacal* strength; *demoniacal* laughter. **Demoniac** and **demonic,** though sometimes synonymous with *demoniacal,* more frequently suggest in recent usage (chiefly under the influence of Goethe) the inexplicable or superhuman element in life, or especially, in genius (in this sense the preferred word and spelling is now *daemonic* [see *daemon* under DEMON]); as, "In the solidest kingdom of routine and the senses, he [Goethe] showed the lurking *demonic* power" (*Emerson*); "the rapt, *demonic* features of the Magic Muse" (*Hewlett*).

Ana. Hellish, *infernal: malign, malefic, baleful, *sinister: malignant, malevolent, *malicious.

fierce. Fierce, truculent, ferocious, barbarous, savage, inhuman, cruel, fell come into comparison when they mean displaying fury or malignity in looks or in actions. **Fierce,** as here compared, is applied largely to men or to beasts that inspire terror because of their menacing aspect or their unrestrained fury in attack. "The other Shape...black it stood as night, *Fierce* as ten Furies, terrible as Hell, And shook a dreadful dart" (*Milton*). "No bandit *fierce,* no tyrant mad with pride" (*Pope*). **Truculent,** though it implies fierceness, especially of aspect, suggests the intent to inspire terror or to threaten rather than the achievement of that intention. Consequently, it often implies a bullying attitude or pose. It is applied chiefly, but not exclusively, to persons, groups of persons, and nations; as, a group of *truculent* schoolboys. "He [Carlyle's 'Hero'] must...worry them toward the fold like a *truculent* sheep dog" (*J. R. Lowell*). "The America that [Theodore] Roosevelt dreamed of was always a sort of swollen Prussia, *truculent* without and regimented within" (*Mencken*). **Ferocious** not only connotes extreme fierceness but it implies actions suggestive of a wild beast on a rampage or in an attack on its prey; it therefore usually implies unrestrained violence, extreme fury, and wanton brutality; as, a *ferocious* attack on the enemy; to take a *ferocious* revenge; a particularly *ferocious* dog. **Barbarous** (see also BARBARIAN) in its extended sense applies only to civilized persons or their actions; it implies a harshness, a brutality, and often, a ferocity possible among primitive or uncivilized men but unworthy of human beings in an advanced state of culture; as, "the *barbarous* pleasures of the chase" (*J. Morley*); *barbarous* treatment of prisoners; *barbarous* methods of warfare. **Savage** (see also BARBARIAN) implies an absence of the restraints imposed by civilization or of the inhibitions characteristic of civilized man when dealing with those whom he hates or fears or when filled with rage, lust, or other violent passion; as, a *savage* desire for revenge; *savage* punishment of a disobedient child; a *savage* criticism of a book; "the *savage* wars of religion" (*Inge*). **Inhuman** is even stronger than *savage,* for it suggests not so much undue violence or lack of restraint as absence of all feeling that normally characterizes a human being: on the one hand it may suggest bestiality or wanton brutality, or on the other hand it may imply absence of all capacity for love, kindness, or pity; as, an *inhuman* mother; "Thy deed, *inhuman* and unnatural" (*Shak.*). "Man's *inhumanity* to man Makes countless thousands mourn!" (*Burns*). **Cruel** implies an inhuman indifference to the suffering of others and even a positive pleasure in witnessing it or in inflicting it. "Her mouth *crueler* than a tiger's, colder than a snake's, and beautiful beyond a woman's" (*Swinburne*). "As *cruel* as a schoolboy ere he grows To pity" (*Tennyson*). **Fell,** now rhetorical or poetic, connotes dire or baleful cruelty. "Unsex me here, And fill me from the crown to the toe top-full Of direst *cruelty!* ...Stop up the access and passage to remorse, That no compunctious visitings of nature Shake my *fell* purpose" (*Shak.*).

Ana. Menacing, threatening (see THREATEN): infuriated, maddened, enraged (see corresponding verbs at ANGER): ravening, ravenous, rapacious, *voracious: *fearful, terrible, horrible, horrific.

Ant. Tame: mild.

fiery. *Spirited, high-spirited, peppery, gingery, mettlesome, spunky.

Ana. Impetuous, *precipitate, headlong: passionate, perfervid, ardent, *impassioned, fervid: vehement, *intense.

fiesta. Fete, *feast, festival.

fight, *n.* Combat, fray, affray, conflict, *contest.

Ana. Struggle, striving (see under ATTEMPT, *v.*): strife, contention, conflict, dissension, *discord, variance.

fight, *v.* Battle, war, *contend, cope.

Ana. Struggle, strive (see ATTEMPT): dispute, debate (see DISCUSS): wrangle, squabble, quarrel, altercate (see under QUARREL, *n.*).

figment. Fabrication, fable, *fiction.

Ana. *Fancy, fantasy, dream, daydream, nightmare: invention, creation (see corresponding verbs at INVENT).

figure, *n.* **1** *Form, shape, configuration, conformation, Gestalt.

Ana. *Outline, contour, profile, silhouette: *character, symbol, sign, mark.

2 Figure, pattern, design, motif, device come into comparison when they mean a unit in a decorative composition, in an ornamented textile or fabric, or the like, consisting of a representation of a natural, conventionalized, or imaginary shape or a combination of such representations. **Figure** commonly refers to a small, simple unit which is repeated or is one of those repeated over an entire surface. A figure may be either one of the outlines commonly associated with geometry (*geometrical figures*) such as triangles, diamonds, pentagons, circles, and the like, or such an outline filled in with color, lines, or a representation of another kind: it may, however, be a natural or conventionalized leaf, flower, animal, or the like; as, an Oriental rug with geometrical *figures* in blue and red; a silk print with a small *figure;* the wallpaper has a well-spaced *figure* of a spray of rosebuds; "Carved with *figures* strange and sweet, All made out of the carver's brain" (*Coleridge*). **Pattern** may be used in place of *figure* (as, "arranged in a series of simple and pleasing *patterns*—diamonds, quincunxes, hexagons"—*A. Huxley*) but *figure* is not interchangeable with the more inclusive senses of *pattern.* The latter term is applicable not only to the simplest repeated unit, or figure, or to a larger repeated unit involving several related figures, but also to the whole plan of decoration or adornment (as, the *pattern* of a lace tablecloth; the *pattern* of a rug). Also, *pattern* may be used of other things than those which are visible, objective works of art and craftsmanship, but which nevertheless can be viewed or studied as having diverse parts or elements brought together so as to present an intelligible and distinctive whole; as, the true *pattern* of the campaign revealed itself after the first week; "when he said *pattern,* he did not mean the *pattern* on a wall paper; he meant the *pattern* of life" (*V. Sackville-West*); "as skepticism grows, the *pattern* of human conduct inevitably changes" (*J. W. Krutch*); "The nearness of friends in those days, the familiar, unchanging streets, the convivial clubs, the constant companionship helped to knit the strands of life into a close and well-defined *pattern*" (*A. Repplier*). **Design** (as here considered: see also PLAN, INTENTION) is not always clearly distinguishable from the sense in which it is considered at PLAN, for both stress the disposition of details with the result that a pattern is produced: as here considered, however, *design* emphasizes drawing and arrangement and attention to line and the handling of figures and colors: it often specifically denotes a single unit (figure or pattern) which reveals these qualities; as, "Branches and leaves were disposed, not as combinations of colour in mass, but as *designs* in line" (*Binyon*); "Your golden filaments in fair *design* Across my duller fibre" (*Millay*). **Motif** (for fuller consideration, see SUBJECT, 2) is frequently used in the decorative arts for a figure or a design which stands out not necessarily as the only one, but as the leading one which gives the distinctive character of the whole; as, in lace for ecclesiastical use a sheaf of wheat is often the *motif* of the pattern. **Device** applies usually to a figure that bears no likeness to anything in nature but is the result of imagination or fancy. Unlike the other terms (as here considered), it does not exclusively apply to a decorative unit, though it occurs frequently in that application; as, "Set in the close-grained wood Were quaint *devices; Patterns* in ambers, And in the clouded green of jades" (*Amy Lowell*).

figure, *v.* Cast, *add, sum, total, foot.
Ana. Compute, *calculate, reckon, estimate: *count, enumerate, number.

filch, *v.* Purloin, lift, pilfer, *steal, pinch, snitch, swipe, cop.
Ana. Snatch, grab, *take, seize, grasp: *rob, plunder, loot, rifle, thieve.

fillet, *n.* *Strip, band, ribbon, stripe.

filthy. *Dirty, foul, squalid, nasty.
Ana. Slovenly, unkempt, sloppy, *slipshod: *offensive, loathsome, repulsive, revolting.
Ant. Neat, spick-and-span. — *Con.* Cleaned, cleansed (see CLEAN, *v.*): *clean, cleanly: tidy, trim, trig, shipshape (see NEAT).

final. Terminal, concluding, *last, latest, ultimate, extreme, eventual.
Ana. Closing, ending, terminating (see CLOSE, *v.*): decisive, determinative, *conclusive, definitive.

financial. Financial, monetary, pecuniary, fiscal, bursal come into comparison as meaning of or relating to the possession, the making, or the expenditure of money. **Financial** implies a relation to money matters in general, especially as conducted on a large scale; as, the *financial* concerns of the company are attended to by the treasurer; the *financial* position of the bank is sound; the *financial* interests of the country; the city is in *financial* difficulties. **Monetary** implies a much more direct reference to money as such, and therefore often connotes the coinage, distribution, circulation, or the like, of money; as, the *monetary* unit; the *monetary* systems of Europe; the *monetary* standard; *monetary* gifts. **Pecuniary** suggests a reference to the practical uses of money; it is often, but not exclusively, employed in preference to *financial* when money matters that are personal or on a small scale are being considered; as, to ask for *pecuniary* aid; he is always in *pecuniary* difficulties; he works only for *pecuniary* motives. Both **fiscal** and the less frequent **bursal** imply reference to the financial affairs of a state, a sovereign, a corporation, an institution, or the like, whose concerns with revenue and expenditures are managed by a treasurer (or bursar) or treasury department; as, the *fiscal* year in the United States ends on June 30; a *fiscal* officer of the crown; the *bursal* year of a college.

fine, *n.* Amercement (see under PENALIZE).

fine, *v.* *Penalize, amerce, mulct, sconce.

finger man. Gunman, trigger man, *assassin, cutthroat, bravo.

finical *or* **finicking** *or* **finicky.** Particular, fussy, fastidious, *nice, dainty, squeamish, pernickety.
Ana. Exacting, demanding (see DEMAND, *v.*): captious, carping, hypercritical, *critical: dapper, spruce, natty (see STYLISH): meticulous, punctilious, *careful: conscientious, scrupulous (see UPRIGHT).
Con. *Slipshod, sloppy, slovenly: *slatternly, dowdy, blowzy, frowzy.

finish, *v.* Complete, conclude, *close, end, terminate.
Ana. Achieve, accomplish, effect, fulfill (see PERFORM): *polish, burnish, furbish, shine.

finished. *Consummate, accomplished.
Ana. *Perfect, entire, intact, whole: refined, cultivated, cultured (see corresponding nouns at CULTURE): *suave, urbane, smooth: elegant, exquisite (see CHOICE).
Ant. Crude. — *Con.* *Rude, rough, raw, callow, green.

fire, *v.* **1** Kindle, enkindle, ignite, inflame, *light.
Ana. *Burn, scorch, char: *blaze, flame, flare, glare, glow: *illuminate, lighten.
2 Animate, inspire, *inform.
Ana. Excite, *provoke, stimulate, galvanize: *thrill, electrify: *stir, rouse, arouse: enliven, *quicken, vivify.
Ant. Daunt. — *Con.* *Dismay, appall.
3 Discharge, *dismiss, cashier, sack, bounce, drop.
Ana. *Eject, oust, expel: *discard.

firearms. See under WEAPON.

firm, *adj.* **Firm, hard, solid** are here compared chiefly as meaning having a texture or consistency that markedly resists deformation by external force. **Firm** (opposed to *loose, flabby*) suggests such closeness or compactness of texture, or a consistency so heavy or substantial, that the substance or material quickly returns to shape or is difficult to pull, distort, cut, or the like; as, a *firm* cloth; *firm* muscles or flesh; *firm* jellies; *firm* ground. **Hard** (opposed to *soft;* see HARD, 3) implies impenetrability or relatively complete resistance to pressure, tension, or the like; but unlike *firm, hard* rarely implies elasticity; as, *hard* as adamant; *hard* as steel; *hard* ice. **Solid,** as opposed to *fluid,* implies such density and coherence in the mass as enable a thing to maintain a fixed form in spite of external deforming forces (as, *solid* substances; *solid* mineral matter); as opposed to *flimsy,* the term implies a structure or construction that renders a thing sound, strong, or stable (as, *solid* furniture; a *solid* foundation; "the bungalow was a very *solid* one"—*Kipling*); as opposed to *hollow,* it implies the absence of empty spaces within the structure or mass and, usually, the same or similar density and hardness of material throughout; as, a *solid* rubber tire; a *solid* wall.

Figuratively, **firm** implies stability, fixedness, or resolution (as, a *firm* purpose; a *firm* belief; to guide with a *firm* hand); **hard** implies obduracy or lack of feeling (as, a *hard* master; a *hard* bargain; "She was *firm,* but she was not *hard*"—*Arch. Marshall*); **solid** usually implies substantiality or genuineness (as, a *solid* meal; *solid* facts; *solid* virtues; *solid* attainments) but it may imply absolute reliability or seriousness of purpose (as, *solid* bankers or banks; a *solid* character; a *solid* book) or unbroken continuity as in time, group feeling or opinion, or the like (as, to put in a *solid* week on a piece of work; the *solid* vote of the members).
Ana. Compact, *close, dense, thick: tough, tenacious, *strong: *stiff, rigid, inflexible.
Ant. Loose, flabby. — *Con.* Flaccid, *limp, loppy, flimsy, sleazy.

firm, *v.* *Set, settle, fix, establish.
Ana. *Implant, infix, inculcate: *secure, anchor, moor, rivet.

fiscal. *Financial, bursal, monetary, pecuniary.

fish, *v.* **Fish, angle** agree in meaning to attempt to catch fish; in the case of **fish,** with any kind of apparatus, and as a sport or an occupation; in the case of **angle** (chiefly literary, except in the derivative *angler*), with hook, bait, line, and (usually) rod, and as a sport. Both words are used, without perceptible distinction, in the figurative sense to seek to obtain or win by artifice; as, to *fish* for a compliment. "Modesty is the only sure bait, when you *angle* for praise" (*Chesterfield*). "The first woman who *fishes* for him, hooks him" (*Thackeray*). "She knew her distance and did *angle* for me, Madding my eagerness with her restraint" (*Shak.*).

fit, *adj.* **Fit, suitable, meet, proper, appropriate, fitting, apt, happy, felicitous** are comparable when they mean right with respect to the nature, condition, circumstances, or use of the thing qualified. That is **fit** which is adapted or adaptable to the end in view, the use proposed, or the work to be done; as, food *fit* for a king. "But when to mischief mortals bend their will, How soon they find *fit* instruments of ill!" (*Pope*). "Never even in the most perfect days of my development as an artist could I have found words *fit* to bear so august a burden" (*Wilde*). Sometimes, in addition, *fit* connotes competence or the possession of the required qualifications; as, men *fit* to command; he is not a *fit* father for his children; they do not know what the boy is *fit* for. "And *fit* audience find, though few" (*Milton*). Other times it suggests readiness, as in condition, state of health, mood, inclination, or the like; as, the vessel is now *fit* for service; he played tennis to keep *fit;* "he...keeps you standing till you are *fit* to sink" (*Newman*). That is **suitable** which answers the requirements or demands of the occasion, the circumstances, the conditions, and the like, or suggests no incongruity with them; as, that is not a *suitable* costume for this season of the year; behavior *suitable* to one's age and station in life. "A Cambridge don pronounced a *suitable* epitaph [on Paley's *Evidences*] when he said that Paley had the merit of reducing Christianity to a form eminently fitted for examination purposes" (*Inge*). In discriminating use, that is **meet** which is not only suitable but nicely adapted to the particular situation, need, circumstances, or the like; the word usually suggests rightness or justness rather than an absence of incongruity; thus, a punishment of a childish offense may be *suitable* if it is in accord with the years and mentality of the child, but it may not be described as *meet* unless it suggests due proportion between the offense and its penalty. "It is very *meet,* right, and our bounden duty, that we should at all times and in all places, give thanks unto thee, O Lord" (*Bk. of Com. Prayer*). "Those common phrases which it is peculiarly *meet* to call counters ....have become so common to use because so *fit* to use" (*H. Ellis*). That is **proper** (see also DECOROUS) which belongs to a thing by nature, by custom, by right reason, or on any justifiable grounds; as, water is the *proper* element for fish; the *proper* observance of Memorial Day; the article brought but half its *proper* price. When, as often happens, fitness or suitability is stressed rather than natural or rightful association, *proper* then implies determination of fitness or suitability by right reason or good judgment. "The *proper* study of mankind is man" (*Pope*). "[According to Aristotle] the thing to aim at is to be angry 'on the *proper* occasions and with the *proper* people in the *proper* manner and for the *proper* length of time' " (*G. L. Dickinson*). That is **appropriate** which is so eminently fit or suitable that it seems to belong peculiarly or distinctively to the person or thing with which it is associated, sometimes giving him or it a distinguishing grace or charm through its very congruity. "An excitement in which we can discriminate two sorts of elements, the passions *appropriate* to the subject and the passion *proper* to the artist" (*S. Alexander*). "The eighteenth-century gentleman spoke with a refined accent, quoted the classics on *appropriate* occasions" (*B. Russell*). "We have agreed that our writing should be *appropriate*...that it should rise and fall with the subject, be grave where that is serious, where it is light not afraid of what Stevenson...calls 'a little judicious levity' " (*Quiller-Couch*). That is **fitting** which is in harmony with the spirit, the tone, the mood, the purpose, or the like; "news *fitting* to the night, Black, fearful, comfortless and horrible" (*Shak.*). "And made a *fitting* song, of words but few, Somewhat his woeful heart to make more light" (*Wordsworth*). That is **apt** (as here considered: see also APT, 2; QUICK, 3) which is nicely fitted by its nature or construction to attain the end desired, to accomplish the purpose in view, or to achieve the results contemplated. "It was recognized that while one style was suited to one set of themes, another was *apter* for another set" (*Binyon*). "Fourier...invented a mathematical process which was not only *suitable* for handling his problem, but proved to be so universally *apt* that there is hardly a field of science or of engineering which it has not penetrated" (*Karl K. Darrow*). "Before we can consider the *aptness* of political ideas or the adequacy of political machinery" (*Frankfurter*). That is **happy** (as here compared: see also GLAD, LUCKY) which is singularly appropriate and apt, and therefore brilliantly successful or effective considered in its relation to the situation, the conditions, or other important factors; as, a *happy* choice of words, nicely expressing the subtlety of his thought; "I never saw such *happy* manners!—so much ease, with such perfect good-breeding!" (*Austen*); "whether a composite language like the English is not a *happier* instrument of expression than a homogeneous one like the German" (*Coleridge*). That is **felicitous** which is most opportunely, tellingly, or gracefully happy; as, "I do not like mottoes but where they are singularly *felicitous*" (*Lamb*); "some of the most *felicitous* turns of thought and phrase in poetry are the result of a flash of inspiration under the happy [i.e., fortunate] guidance of a rhyme" (*Lowes*); "let us inquire...whether the relation of the figures to each other and of groups to the space they occupy is a *felicitous* one" (*Binyon*).
Ana. Adapted *or* adaptable, adjusted *or* adjustable, conformed *or* conformable (see corresponding verbs at ADAPT): qualified, capable, *able, competent.
Ant. Unfit.

fit, *n.* **Fit, attack, access, accession, paroxysm, spasm, convulsion** come into comparison when they denote a sudden seizure or spell resulting from an abnormal condition of body or mind. The last three are too specific in their technical medical senses to be synonyms of the others (except of *fit* in its narrower significations), but in their extended senses they are frequently closely parallel. **Fit** is often used narrowly: sometimes to designate a sudden stroke which manifests a disease such as epilepsy and apoplexy and which is characterized by conditions such as violent muscular contractions and unconsciousness; as, to fall in a *fit;* sometimes to designate a period in which there is a marked increase of a physical disturbance characteristic of a disease; as, hysteria often reveals itself in *fits* of alternate laughing and weeping. In its wider application, *fit* still may imply suddenness and violence, but it emphasizes temporariness; as, a *fit* of "the blues"; he works only by *fits* and starts. Occasionally, it suggests nothing more than the unusual and passing character of the condition, and is applied to things as well as to persons; as, to enjoy a *fit* of laziness; a *fit* of bad weather. **Attack** always implies a sudden and often violent onslaught, but carries no suggestion of length of duration; as, frequent *attacks* of pain; an *attack* of melancholy; a prolonged *attack* of bronchitis. **Access** and **accession,** though often interchangeable with *attack*, distinctively imply the initiation of an attack or fit and often come close in meaning to *outbreak* or *outburst*. "Now and then an *access* of...sudden fury...would lay hold on a man" (*Kipling*). "One of his sudden sharp *accessions* of impatience at the leisurely motions of the Trujillo boy" (*M. Austin*). Occasionally, they also connote intensification, as of a mood or state of mind, to the point where control is lost or nearly lost. "Her evident, but inexplicable, *access* of misery" (*G. Meredith*). In their technical medical senses, *paroxysm, spasm,* and *convulsion* are sudden and usually short attacks, especially characteristic of certain diseases. The distinguishing marks of a **paroxysm** are intensification of a symptom, such as coughing, and recurrence of attacks; those of **spasm** are sudden involuntary muscular contraction, in some cases producing rigidity of the body or constriction of a passage and in others producing alternate contractions and relaxations of the muscles; those of **convulsion** are of repeated spasms of the latter kind affecting the whole or a large part of the body and producing violent contortions of the muscles and distortion of features. The implications of these technical senses are usually carried over into the figurative senses. *Paroxysm* commonly occurs in the plural and suggests recurrent, violent attacks; as, the girls went into *paroxysms* of laughter; throughout the night, he suffered *paroxysms* of fear. *Spasm*, especially when used of emotional disturbances, often implies possession by something that for a moment grips and paralyzes. "She could scarcely even look at the wall without a *spasm* of fear" (*Bennett*). When used in the plural, it usually suggests the more or less rapid alternation of contrasting moods or states of mind; as, he worked only by *spasms* (or, *spasmodically*). *Convulsion* implies definite physical effects accompanying the mood or state of mind, and closely resembling those symptomatic of disease. "The ragged crew actually laughed at me...some of them literally throwing themselves down on the ground in *convulsions* of unholy mirth" (*Kipling*).

Ana. Stroke, shock (see PARALYSIS).

fitful. **Fitful, spasmodic, convulsive** come into comparison only when they mean lacking steadiness or regularity as in course, movement, succession of acts or efforts, or the like. **Fitful** stresses variability and intermittency: it implies an irregular succession characterized by fits and starts; as, "After life's *fitful* fever he sleeps well" (*Shak.*); "the *fitful* gloom and sudden lambencies of the room by firelight" (*De Quincey*); "a *fitful*, undecided rain" (*Kipling*); "a *fitful* wind swept the cheerless waste" (*Conrad*). **Spasmodic** implies fitfulness, but it further suggests marked alternations, as of violent activity and inactivity, or of great effort and of negligible effort, or of zeal or enthusiasm and lack of interest: it therefore implies, even more than *fitful*, an opposition to that which is sustained at a high pitch; as, *spasmodic* efforts to reform municipal government; *spasmodic* energy; *spasmodic* industry; "I think Beethoven is rather *spasmodically*, than sustainedly, grand" (*FitzGerald*). A school of nineteenth-century English authors (notably Bailey, the author of "Festus," and Sydney Dobell) has been called the "*spasmodic* school" in allusion to frequent attempts to reach heights of expression that show by contrast the banality of other passages. **Convulsive** differs from the preceding terms in not implying intermittency, and in stressing unsteadiness, strain (often overstrain), and the lack of regular rhythm which is the sign of control, especially of muscular, mental, or spiritual control; as, a *convulsive* rise and fall of the breast; the *convulsive* movement of the earth characteristic of an earthquake.

Ana. *Intermittent, periodic, recurrent: desultory, hit-or-miss, *random, haphazard.

Ant. Constant (sense 2). — *Con.* *Steady, uniform, even, equable: regular, methodical, systematic, *orderly.

fitting, *adj.* Appropriate, proper, meet, suitable, *fit, apt, happy, felicitous.

Ana. *Relevant, pertinent, germane, apposite, apropos: seemly, *decorous, decent, proper, comme il faut: congruous, *consonant: harmonious, concordant, accordant (see corresponding nouns at HARMONY).

Ant. Unfitting.

fix, *v.* **1** *Set, settle, establish, firm.

Ana. *Stabilize, steady: determine, *decide, rule, settle: *prescribe, define.

Ant. Alter: abrogate (*a custom, rule, law, etc.*). — *Con.* Modify, *change, vary: supplant, supersede, displace, *replace.

2 *Fasten, attach, affix.

Ana. *Implant, infix, instill, inculcate: *secure, rivet, anchor, moor.

Con. Eradicate, uproot, extirpate (see EXTERMINATE): upset, *overturn, overthrow, subvert.

3 *Adjust, regulate.

Ana. Repair, *mend, patch, rebuild, remodel: *correct, rectify, revise, amend, emend.

Con. Derange, disarrange, disorganize, unsettle, *disorder.

fix, *n.* *Predicament, plight, dilemma, quandary, scrape, jam, pickle.

flabbergast. Amaze, astound, astonish, *surprise.

Ana. Dumfound, confound, bewilder, nonplus, perplex (see PUZZLE): disconcert, rattle, faze, discomfit (see EMBARRASS).

flabby. Flaccid, loppy, *limp, flimsy, sleazy.

Ana. *Loose, relaxed, slack, lax: *soft: yielding, caving in (see YIELD, *v.*): *powerless, impotent: spiritless, listless, enervated, *languid.

Ant. Firm. — *Con.* Hard, solid (see FIRM): *tight, taut, tense: tough, tenacious, sturdy, *strong: plucky, gritty (see corresponding nouns at FORTITUDE).

flaccid. Flabby, loppy, *limp, flimsy, sleazy.

Ana. Slack, relaxed, lax, *loose: unnerved, enervated, emasculated (see UNNERVE): weakened, debilitated, enfeebled, sapped (see WEAKEN).

Ant. Resilient. — *Con.* *Elastic, springy, flexible, supple: limber, lithe (see SUPPLE): *vigorous, energetic, lusty, nervous.

flag, *n.* **Flag, ensign, standard, banner, color** (*or* **colour**), **streamer, pennant** (*or* **pendant**), **pennon, jack** are not always clearly distinguished. **Flag,** the comprehensive term, is applied to any piece of cloth that typically, but not invariably, is rectangular, is attached to a staff, halyard, or line, and carries an arrangement of colors, an emblematic figure or figures, or a motto. The purpose of a flag is primarily to serve as a sign or symbol of a nation, a branch of the service, an organization, an office, or the like, but it may also serve as a signal, as in military or naval operations, or in giving information, as of a weather change or the approach of a train; as, the *flag* of England; the admiral's *flag;* a *flag* of truce; a trainman's *flag.* **Ensign** is applied chiefly to a flag that indicates nationality, and specifically to one flown by ships at sea; as, the Stars and Stripes is the national *ensign* of the United States; of the three *ensigns* of Great Britain, the white *ensign* is flown by ships of the Royal Navy, by naval barracks, etc., the red *ensign* by British merchant vessels, and the blue *ensign* by certain vessels commanded by officers of the Royal Naval Reserve and by certain classes of government vessels not part of the navy. **Standard** and **banner** are now more or less literary terms for the flag of a country, a party, a religious, civic, or patriotic organization, or the like, thought of as a rallying point or as something to be followed. *Standard* especially suggests the former because the term originally designated and still often designates a flag or a sculptured figure raised on a pole so as to be a gathering point for all who belong under it. "As armies at the call Of trumpet... Troop to the *standard*" (*Milton*). *Banner* was earliest applied to a flag (often hung downward from a crosspiece instead of flying from a staff) of an emperor, king, lord, or the like. Banners were flown from windows or doors, or carried aloft at the head of a procession, such as of troops marching to war. "Hang out our *banners* on the outward walls; The cry is still 'They come' " (*Shak.*). "Terrible as an army with *banners*" (*Song of Solomon* vi. 4). **Color** (most frequently found in the plural **colors**) applies generally to any national flag or ensign but specifically to the flag of a particular regiment or battalion of infantry, artillery, or engineers (that of the cavalry being called a *standard*); the word commonly suggests military, sometimes naval, activity, as in mobilization (as, to call to the *colors*), in ceremonial exercises (as, to hoist the *colors*, to troop the *colors*), or in capture or conquest (as, "The British *colors* were planted on the summit of the breach"—*Wellington*). The last four terms here discriminated are even more specific and definite in their implications than those already considered. **Streamer** applies to any flag that floats in the wind but it usually suggests a long, ribbonlike flag carried at the masthead of a government vessel in commission; **pennant,** and in British naval use, **pendant** (pronounced like *pennant*), apply to a streamer that is long, narrow, and tapering. *Pennant*, however, is even more often used to denote a narrow flag, typically triangular, which is flown by ships, which is used in signaling and in decorating, or which is exhibited, as by a baseball club, as a sign of championship. **Pennon,** the earliest spelling for a flag that suggests a wing, was applied originally to a small streamer attached to a lance or to the top of a helmet, especially of a knight bachelor in the Middle Ages. It is now used instead of *color* in designating the flag of a lancer regiment. **Jack** denotes a small oblong flag which is hoisted on a staff at the bow or bowsprit cap of a ship or is used in signaling. In Great Britain and in the United States, the *jack* carries the same design as that carried by the upper left-hand section of the national ensign; thus, the British *jack* (specifically the *union jack*) displays three crosses, the cross of St. George, the cross of St. Andrew, the cross of St. Patrick, and symbolizes the union of England, Scotland, and Ireland; the American *jack* has a blue field with white stars equal in number to the states comprising the United States.

flagitious. Nefarious, infamous, iniquitous, villainous, *vicious, corrupt, degenerate.

Ana. Scandalous, criminal, sinful (see corresponding nouns at OFFENSE): shameful, disgraceful (see corresponding nouns at DISGRACE): *flagrant, gross, glaring.

flagrant. Flagrant, glaring, gross, rank come into comparison as intensives, often derogatory intensives, meaning conspicuously or outstandingly bad, unpleasant, or the like. **Flagrant** (etymologically, flaming) now usually applies to offenses, transgressions, or errors which are so bad that they cannot escape notice or be condoned; as, his treatise is marked by several *flagrant* errors; a *flagrant* abuse of the executive power; *flagrant* injustice; "open and *flagrant* mutiny" (*Kipling*); "in *flagrant* violation of all the New York proprieties" (*E. Wharton*). **Glaring** carries an even stronger implication of obtrusiveness than *flagrant:* the term is often applied to that which is so evident or so conspicuous that it inflicts pain upon the observer, such as too vivid a color, too harsh a light, an error which stares one in the face, or the like; as, a *glaring* fault in a design; a *glaring* inconsistency in his argument; his second novel is in *glaring* contrast to his first novel; "This evil is so *glaring*, so inexcusable" (*Shaw*). **Gross** (as here compared: see also COARSE; WHOLE, 2) is even more derogatory than *flagrant* or *glaring* because it suggests a magnitude or degree of badness that is beyond all bounds and wholly inexcusable or unpardonable: however, the term is not so often referred to evil acts or serious offenses as it is to human attitudes, qualities, or faults that merit severe condemnation; as, *gross* carelessness; *gross* stupidity; *gross* superstition; "Elizabethan and Jacobean poetry ....had serious defects, even *gross* faults" (*T. S. Eliot*); "The hero is as *gross* an imposture as the heroine" (*Shaw*). **Rank** (as here compared: see also RANK, 1) applies chiefly, though far from exclusively, to nouns that are terms of reproach: it implies that the person or thing described by such a term is extremely, utterly, or violently that which he (or it) is declared to be; as, "O, my offence is *rank*, it smells to heaven" (*Shak.*); "till she looked less of a *rank* lunatic" (*Meredith*); "A powerfully prayerful Highland regiment, officered by *rank* Presbyterians" (*Kipling*); *rank* heresy; *rank* nonsense; it would be *rank* madness to attempt such a journey in this weather.

Ana. Heinous, *outrageous, atrocious, monstrous: conspicuous, outstanding, *noticeable: notorious (see FAMOUS): nefarious, flagitious, infamous (see VICIOUS).

flamboyant. *Ornate, florid, rococo, baroque.

Ana. Luxuriant, exuberant (see PROFUSE): resplendent, gorgeous, glorious, *splendid: dashing, brave (see STYLISH): ostentatious, *showy, pretentious: flashy, *gaudy.

flame, *n.* Blaze, flare, glare, glow. See under BLAZE, *v.*

Ana. Effulgence, radiance, brilliance *or* brilliancy, refulgence, luminosity, brightness (see corresponding adjectives at BRIGHT): ardor, fervor, *passion: flashing, coruscation, gleaming, scintillation (see corresponding verbs at FLASH).

flame, *v.* *Blaze, flare, glare, glow.

Ana. *Flash, gleam, glance, glint, coruscate: *burn: fire, ignite, kindle, *light.

flare, *v.* Glare, flame, *blaze, glow.

Ana. Dart, shoot (see FLY): flutter, flicker (see FLIT): rise, arise, *spring: *flash, glance, glint, coruscate, scintillate: kindle, *light, fire.

Ant. Gutter out.

flare, *n.* Glare, flame, blaze, glow. See under BLAZE, *v.*

Ana. Rising *or* rise, surging *or* surge, towering (see corresponding verbs at RISE): darting *or* dart, shooting (see corresponding verbs at FLY): flashing *or* flash, coruscation, scintillation (see corresponding verbs at FLASH).

flash, *v.* **Flash, gleam, glance, glint, sparkle, glitter, glisten, scintillate, coruscate, glimmer, shimmer, twinkle, glister, spark** agree in meaning to shoot forth light in rays, sparks, or the like. **Flash** implies a sudden and transient outburst of light or a sudden display of something that brilliantly reflects light or seems lighted up; as, "The headlights....*flashed* into barnyards where fowls slept" (*S. Anderson*); "*Flash'd* all their sabres bare" (*Tennyson*); "his *flashing* eyes, his floating hair" (*Coleridge*). **Gleam** commonly implies a ray which shines through an intervening medium, or against a background of relative darkness; as, "I see the lights of the village *Gleam* through the rain and mist" (*Longfellow*); "a light *gleamed* through the chinks in the wall" (*Dickens*); "His dislike of me *gleamed* in his blue eyes and in his supercilious, cold smile" (*R. Macaulay*). **Glance** implies darting or obliquely reflected light; **glint** implies quickly glancing or gleaming light; as, "Besides the *glancing* tears...some diamonds...*glanced* on the bride's hand" (*Dickens*); "An insane light *glanced* in her heavy black eyes" (*H. B. Stowe*); "Specks of sail that *glinted* in the sunlight far at sea" (*Dickens*); "when the first sunshine through their dewdrops *glints*" (*J. R. Lowell*); "the large brass scales near the flour-bins *glinted*" (*Bennett*). **Sparkle** suggests quick, bright, brief, and innumerable small flashes of light; **glitter** connotes greater brilliancy or showiness than *sparkle*, sometimes with the implication of something sinister; as, "The fireflies...*sparkled* most vividly in the darkest places" (*Irving*); "the *sparkling* waves" (*Wordsworth*); "everything *sparkled* like a garden after a shower" (*Cather*); eyes *sparkling* with amusement; eyes *glittering* with greed; "He holds him with his *glittering* eye" (*Coleridge*); "little black eyes which *glittered* like jet" (*Scott*); "*glittering* rings" (*Irving*); "the yellow flower...caught it [the ray of sunshine], and *glittered* like a topaz" (*Deland*). **Glisten** implies a more or less subdued sparkle, glitter, or gleaming that suggests a lustrous shining quality; as, dew *glistening* in the soft morning light; "snowy mountains *glistening* through a summer atmosphere" (*Irving*); "eyes *glistening* with heavenly tears" (*Carlyle*). **Scintillate,** in strict use, implies the emission of sparks in a constant steady stream; **coruscate** the emission of a brilliant flash or succession of flashes; both words are used figuratively as well as literally; as, a night so clear that the stars seem to *scintillate;* "the others [poetic verses] *coruscate* like brilliant pyrotechnics—and go out" (*Lowes*); "*scintillations* of...genius" (*V. Knox*); "*coruscating* wit" (*Carlyle*). **Glimmer** suggests faint and wavering sparkling or flashing; **shimmer** suggests soft, tremulous, and lustrous sparkling or flashing; as, "Now fades the *glimmering* landscape on the sight" (*Gray*); "Whiles all the night, through fog smoke white, *Glimmered* the white moonshine" (*Coleridge*); "The young leafage *shimmered* like a veil of golden gauze" (*Hewlett*); "Everything about her *shimmered* and *glimmered* softly, as if her dress had been woven out of candle-beams" (*E. Wharton*). **Twinkle** suggests a soft and intermittent glimmering; as, "*Twinkle, twinkle,* little star ... like a diamond in the sky" (*J. & A. Taylor*); "[sunbeams] *twinkled* on the glass and silver of the sideboard" (*Cather*); "he looked at her and his eyes *twinkled*" (*S. Anderson*). **Glister,** now found only in archaic or dialectal use, was once a common and very close synonym of *sparkle* and *glisten.* In modern use, however, its place is often taken by *glitter;* as, "All that *glisters* is not gold" (*Shak.*). **Spark,** meaning to emit a spark or sparks, sometimes of light, more often of fire (as, some woods *spark* in burning; to make a flint *spark*), is now chiefly in technical electrical use with reference to the emission of the spark or sparks which produce light, induce fuel combustion, or the like; as, in spite of the pouring rain, the plugs of the motor *sparked* at once and the plane soared away.

Ana. Shoot, dart (see FLY): *rise, surge, tower, rocket: *blaze, flame, flare, glare, glow.

flash, *n.* Trice, second, *instant, moment, minute, jiffy, twinkling, twinkle, split second.

flashy. Garish, *gaudy, tawdry, meretricious.
Ana. *Showy, pretentious, ostentatious: flamboyant, *ornate, florid: glittering, flashing, sparkling (see FLASH, *v.*).
Con. Dowdy, *slatternly: smart, chic, modish (see STYLISH): simple, *natural, unaffected.

flat, *adj.* **1** *Level, plane, plain, even, smooth, flush.
Con. *Rough, rugged, uneven, scabrous.
2 Vapid, *insipid, jejune, banal, wishy-washy, inane.
Con. Piquant, *pungent, poignant, racy, spicy: flavorsome, savory, sapid, saporous, tasty, *palatable: zestful (see corresponding noun at TASTE).

flat, *n.* Apartment, tenement, *rooms, lodgings, chambers, quarters, diggings, digs.

flattery. Adulation, *compliment.
Ana. Blandishment, cajolery (see corresponding verbs at COAX): fawning, toadying, truckling (see FAWN, *v.*): eulogy, panegyric, *encomium: homage, obeisance, deference (see HONOR).

flatulent. *Inflated, tumid, turgid.
Ana. Empty, hollow, *vain: *superficial, shallow: bombastic, grandiloquent, magniloquent, *rhetorical.
Con. Weighty (see HEAVY): pithy, compendious, summary (see CONCISE): cogent, telling, convincing (see VALID): forcible, forceful, potent (see POWERFUL).

flaunt. Parade, expose, display, exhibit, *show.
Ana. *Boast, brag, vaunt, gasconade: *reveal, disclose, discover, divulge: advertise, publish, broadcast, proclaim, *declare.
Con. Cloak, mask, *disguise, dissemble: conceal, *hide, screen, secrete, bury.

flavor *or* **flavour,** *n.* *Taste, sapidity, savor, tang, relish, smack.

flavorsome. Toothsome, tasty, savory, sapid, saporous, relishing, *palatable, appetizing.
Con. *Insipid, vapid, flat, wishy-washy: bland, mild (see SOFT).

flaw, *n.*[1] Defect, *blemish.
Ana. *Fracture, rupture: cleaving *or* cleavage, riving, splitting *or* split, rending *or* rent, ripping *or* rip, tearing *or* tear (see corresponding verbs at TEAR).

flaw, *n.*[2] Blast, gust, *wind, breeze, gale, hurricane, whirlwind, typhoon, tornado, waterspout, twister, cyclone, zephyr.

flawless. Faultless, *impeccable, errorless.
Ana. Intact, entire, whole, *perfect: *correct, accurate, precise, right, nice, exact.
Con. Defective, *deficient: marred, impaired, damaged, injured (see INJURE): fallacious (see under FALLACY).

flay, *v.* *Skin, decorticate, peel, pare.
Ana. *Abrade, excoriate, chafe: grill, rack, torture, torment, *afflict: chastise, castigate, *punish.

flee. Fly, *escape, decamp, abscond.
Ana. Evade, elude, avoid, *escape.

fleer, *v.* *Scoff, jeer, gibe, gird, sneer, flout.
Ana. Deride, mock, *ridicule: grin, *smile, smirk.

fleet, *v.* *While, wile, beguile.
Ana. *Speed, hasten, hurry, quicken, accelerate.

fleet, *adj.* Swift, rapid, *fast, quick, speedy, hasty, expeditious.
Ana. *Agile, brisk, nimble, spry: darting, skimming, scudding, flying (see FLY, *v.*).
Con. Deliberate, leisurely, laggard, dilatory, *slow.

fleet, *n.* **Fleet, squadron, armada, flotilla** are here compared chiefly with reference to their naval and nautical use, where they name a body of ships operating under a single command. *Fleet* and *squadron* are technical terms in naval use. **Fleet** is applied either to all the ships or vessels of any type that comprise the navy of a country and are under the control of the chief naval officer (as, The United States *Fleet*) or to one of its largest units (such as the battle *fleet* of the United States Navy), which is provided with battleships and attendant vessels such as destroyers, submarines, aircraft and aircraft carriers, and the like, necessary for warfare. A **squadron** is a smaller unit of a fleet, consisting of one or more divisions, or groups of four or more vessels, usually of the same type; it is used especially of such a unit detached from a fleet, under the command of a flag officer, and assigned for special duty. In general nautical and extended use, *fleet* suggests a large group of ships, boats, airplanes, trucks, or the like, moving together or belonging to the same owner or company; *squadron*, an organized body, such as of airplanes, moving in formation, or as of persons, operating according to the direction of a commanding officer. **Armada** is not a technical term, but one with historical (the Spanish *Armada*) and literary associations. It is a close synonym of *fleet*, especially of *battle fleet*, for it usually suggests equipment for fighting. It is also applied to a fleet or a squadron of airplanes. **Flotilla**, in current use, is applied most commonly to a fleet of small vessels; as, the *flotilla* of the Yacht Club; a *flotilla* of destroyers. "On the road to Mandalay, Where the old *Flotilla* lay" (*Kipling*). However, it sometimes occurs in its etymological sense of a small fleet, with reference to the number, and not to the size, of the vessels that comprise it, and as such has some naval use as a near equivalent of *squadron*.

fleeting. Evanescent, fugitive, passing, transitory, *transient, ephemeral, momentary, short-lived.

Ant. Lasting.

fleshly. *Carnal, sensual, animal, animalistic.

Ana. Physical, *bodily, corporeal, corporal, somatic: *sensuous, sensual, voluptuous, luxurious, sybaritic, epicurean.

Con. *Moral, ethical, noble, virtuous: spiritual, divine, religious (see HOLY): intellectual, psychic, *mental.

fleshy. Fleshy, fat, stout, portly, plump, rotund, chubby, corpulent, obese agree in meaning thick in body because of the presence of superfluous flesh or adipose tissue. **Fleshy** and **fat** are not clearly discriminated in use, although, strictly, *fleshy* implies overabundance of flesh, or muscular tissue; *fat*, of adipose tissue; when, however, a derogatory connotation is intended, *fat* is usually preferred; as, a *fleshy*, jolly man; a dowdy *fat* woman. **Stout** implies a thickset, bulky figure or build; **portly** adds to *stout* the implication of a more or less dignified and imposing appearance; as, "a very *stout*, puffy man, in buckskins and Hessian boots" (*Thackeray*); "one very *stout* gentleman, whose body and legs looked like half a gigantic roll of flannel, elevated on a couple of inflated pillowcases" (*Dickens*); "a large *portly* figure...the very beau ideal of an old abbot" (*Jane W. Carlyle*); "an elderly gentleman, large and *portly*, and of remarkably dignified demeanor" (*N. Hawthorne*). **Plump** implies a more or less pleasing fullness of figure, and well-rounded curves; as, the *plump* goddesses of Renaissance paintings; she became *plump* at forty. **Rotund** suggests the shape of a sphere; it often, in addition, connotes shortness or squatness. "This pink-faced *rotund* specimen of prosperity" (*G. Eliot*). **Chubby** applies chiefly to children or to very short persons who are otherwise describable as *rotund;* as, a *chubby* cherub of a baby. **Corpulent** and **obese** imply a disfiguring excess of flesh or of fat. "Mrs. Byron...was a short and *corpulent* person and rolled considerably in her gait" (*T. Moore*). "A woman of robust frame, square shouldered...and though *stout*, not *obese*" (*C. Brontë*).

Ana. *Muscular, brawny, burly, husky.

Ant. Skinny, scrawny. — *Con.* *Lean, lank, lanky, gaunt, rawboned, angular, spare: *thin, slim, slender, slight.

flexible. *Elastic, supple, resilient, springy.

Ana. Pliable, pliant, malleable, ductile, *plastic: tractable (see OBEDIENT): limber, lithe, *supple.

Ant. Inflexible. — *Con.* *Stiff, rigid, wooden: tough, tenacious (see STRONG): brittle, crisp, frangible, *fragile: *hardened, indurated, callous.

flexuous. *Winding, sinuous, serpentine, tortuous, anfractuous.

flicker, *v.* Flutter, *flit, flitter, hover.

Ana. Waver, vibrate, oscillate, fluctuate, *swing: flare, flame, glare, *blaze: *flash, gleam, glance, glint, coruscate, shimmer: quiver, quaver, tremble (see SHAKE).

flight. *Flock, herd, drove, pack, bevy, covey, gaggle, swarm, shoal, school.

flightiness. Light-mindedness, volatility, levity, *lightness, frivolity, flippancy.

Ana. Capriciousness, unstableness *or* instability, fickleness, mercurialness, inconstancy (see corresponding adjectives at INCONSTANT): effervescence, buoyancy, elasticity (see corresponding adjectives at ELASTIC): liveliness, gaiety, sprightliness (see corresponding adjectives at LIVELY).

Ant. Steadiness: steadfastness. — *Con.* Constancy, equableness (see corresponding adjectives at STEADY): seriousness, staidness, sedateness, earnestness (see corresponding adjectives at SERIOUS).

flimsy, *adj.* Sleazy, *limp, loppy, flaccid, flabby.

Ana. *Thin, slight, tenuous: *loose, slack: *weak, feeble.

Con. Stout, sturdy, *strong: *heavy, weighty.

flinch. *Recoil, shrink, wince, blench, quail.

Ana. Falter, *hesitate, vacillate: evade, elude, shun, eschew, avoid, *escape: withdraw, retire (see GO): retreat, *recede.

fling, *v.* Hurl, *throw, sling, toss, cast, pitch.

Ana. Thrust, shove, propel, *push: impel, drive, *move.

flippancy. Levity, *lightness, light-mindedness, frivolity, volatility, flightiness.

Ana. Sauciness, pertness, archness (see corresponding adjectives at SAUCY): impishness, waggishness, roguishness, mischievousness, playfulness (see corresponding adjectives at PLAYFUL).

Ant. Seriousness. — *Con.* Earnestness, gravity, solemnity, soberness (see corresponding adjectives at SERIOUS).

flirt, *v.* Coquet, dally, *trifle, toy.

Ana. *Play, sport, disport: *caress, fondle, pet.

flit, *v.* **Flit, flutter, flitter, flicker, hover,** in their current use (but not always for etymological reasons), suggest the movements of a bird or other flying or floating thing and so carry in common the meaning to move in a manner like or reminiscent of such movements. **Flit** implies a light and swift passing from place to place or point to point; as, the birds *flitted* from tree to tree; "the talk *flitting* from one subject to another and never dropping so long as the meal lasts" (*Arnold*); "[he] seemed to pass the whole of his life *flitting* in and out of bedrooms" (*Bennett*); "Clare Potter, flushed and gallantly gay, *flitting* about from person to person" (*R. Macaulay*). **Flutter** implies the movement of a bird rapidly flapping its wings, the restless flitting of a moth about a light, or the like; it commonly implies unsteadiness and agitation; as, "Till she felt the heart within her fall and *flutter* tremulously" (*Tennyson*); "always the rarest [thoughts], those freaked with azure and the deepest crimson, *flutter* away beyond my reach" (*L. P. Smith*); "a little dark shadow *fluttered* from the wall across the floor....it was a bunch of woman's hair" (*Cather*); "her eyes...timidly *fluttering* over the depths of his" (*Meredith*). **Flitter** implies the lightness and quickness of movement suggested by *flit* but usually also suggests the uneasiness or uncertainty connoted by *flutter;* as, the poor silly *flittering* woman; children *flittering* here and there. **Flicker** (once common of birds, now chiefly of light flame) implies a light fluttering or, more often, a fitfully wavering movement; as, "translucent *flickering* wings between the sun and me" (*Stevenson*); "Thou small flame, Which, as a dying pulse rises and falls, Still *flickerest* up and down" (*Shelley*); "Fireflies *flicker* in the tops of trees" (*Amy Lowell*). **Hover** implies a hanging suspended over something like a bird maintaining its position in the air by an even, usually slow, movement of the wings; the word frequently connotes irresolution, sometimes menace, sometimes solicitude; as, vultures *hovering* over a battlefield; "Behold him perched in ecstasies, Yet seeming still to *hover*" (*Wordsworth*); "Your servant...has been *hovering* about us and looking at you anxiously for some minutes" (*Shaw*).

Ana. *Fly, dart, skim, float, scud.

flitter, *v.* *Flit, flutter, flicker, hover.

Ana. *Fly, dart, skim: quiver, quaver, teeter (see SHAKE).

float, *v.* *Fly, skim, sail, dart, scud, shoot.

Ana. Glide, *slide, slip: *flit, hover, flitter.

floater. Bloomer, *error, mistake, blunder, slip, lapse, bull, howler, boner.

flock, *n.* **Flock, herd, drove, pack, bevy, covey, gaggle, flight, swarm, shoal, school** are here compared as meaning a number of persons (sometimes things) assembled together or moving together. Their applications and their implications are derived from their literal reference to particular animals. **Flock** (literally chiefly of birds, wild or domestic, sheep, and goats) suggests a large company or crowd, or in religious use, a congregation; it often connotes care or guidance but sometimes, merely large numbers; as, "Feed the *flock* of God" (*1 Peter* v. 2); "*flocks* of friends" (*Shak.*). **Herd** (literally chiefly of sheep, cattle, or other hoofed animals massed together, or of whales, seals, etc.), **drove** (literally chiefly of sheep, cattle, or swine driven in a body), and **pack** (literally chiefly of hounds and wolves, especially when they are hunting game or food), are terms of derogation or contempt. *Herd* is applied to the masses of people; as, "the common *herd*" (*Shak.*); "the vulgar *herd*" (*Pope*); "What the people but a *herd* confused, A miscellaneous rabble" (*Milton*). *Drove* often connotes a threatening approach; as, "Not one of all the *drove* should touch me: swine!" (*Tennyson*). *Pack* often carries a hint of craft or rapacity and may be applied to a group pursuing its ends relentlessly; as, "Thou... art confederate with a damned *pack*" (*Shak.*); "I'll be revenged on the whole *pack* of you" (*Shak.*). **Bevy** (literally of quails, roes, larks) and less frequently **covey** (literally of partridges) are applied especially to a group of girls or women; as, "a *bevy* of fair women" (*Milton*). **Gaggle** (literally of geese when on the water), now chiefly a dialectal term, is sometimes used as an uncomplimentary term for a group of women. **Flight** (literally of any birds that fly together in large numbers, as when migrating) applies to any group thought of as flying or flitting together in close formation; as, a *flight* of airplanes (a military formation of from 3 to 6 airplanes). "Good night, sweet prince; And *flights* of Angels sing thee to thy rest!" (*Shak.*). "A *flight* of purchasable fair women always at command" (*Pater*). **Swarm** (literally of insects, especially in motion) and **shoal** (literally of fish and aquatic animals) connote thronging numbers; as, "this *swarm* of fair advantages" (*Shak.*); "the *swarm* of female whisperers" (*Tennyson*); "thin airy *shoals* of visionary ghosts" (*Pope*); "crowds that stream from yawning doors, and *shoals* of pucker'd faces" (*Tennyson*). **School,** interchangeable with *shoal* in its literal application (to fish and aquatic animals) and often also applied to other animals, is less frequently applied to persons.

Ana. *Crowd, throng, press, horde, mob.

flood, *n.* *Flow, stream, current, tide, flux.

Ana. *Excess, superfluity, surplus: irruption, incursion, *invasion: *wave, surge.

florid. *Ornate, flamboyant, rococo, baroque.

Ana. Aureate, flowery, euphuistic, grandiloquent, magniloquent, *rhetorical, bombastic: sumptuous, *luxurious, opulent: *showy, ostentatious, pompous, pretentious.

Ant. Chaste (*in style, decoration, etc.*). — *Con.* Bald, barren, *bare: matter-of-fact, *prosaic.

florilegium. Garland, *anthology, treasury, thesaurus, corpus, chrestomathy, chapbook.

flotilla. *Fleet, squadron, armada.

flounder, *v.* *Wallow, welter, grovel.

Ana. Struggle, strive (see ATTEMPT): toil, labor, travail (see corresponding nouns at WORK): muddle, addle, *confuse.

flourish, *v.* Brandish, *swing, wave, thrash.

Ana. Wield, manipulate, ply, *handle: flaunt, display, exhibit, *show.

flout, *v.* *Scoff, jeer, gibe, fleer, gird, sneer.

Ana. Scout, scorn, *despise, contemn, disdain: spurn, repudiate (see DECLINE): deride, *ridicule, mock.

Ant. Revere. — *Con.* Regard, respect, esteem, admire (see under REGARD, *n.*).

flow, *v.* Issue, emanate, proceed, stem, derive, *spring, arise, rise, originate.

Ana. Emerge, *appear, loom: start, *begin, commence.

flow, *n.* **Flow, stream, current, flood, tide, flux** are here compared as meaning anything issuing or moving in a manner like or suggestive of running water. **Flow** may apply to the issuing or moving mass or to the kind of motion which characterizes it, but in either case, it implies the type of motion characteristic of the movement of a fluid, such as a liquid or gas: the term may suggest either a gentle or a rapid pace, and either a copious or a meager supply, but it always implies an unbroken continuity of the particles or parts; as, the *flow* of his ideas exceeded his capacity for setting them down in writing; she expressed herself in a *flow* of words; there is no great *flow* of gas into the pipes today; "the thought of never ceasing life as it expresses itself in the *flow* of the seasons" (*S. Anderson*); "She would tell you what she thought about the world and its ways in a *flow* of racy comment" (*R. Macaulay*). **Stream** implies a flow characteristic of a body of water such as a river, or of a quantity of water pouring forth from a source or outlet (such as a fountain, a faucet, a spigot, a tap), either of which maintains the same direction throughout its entire length. The term places emphasis more upon the quantity or the volume, the extent or the duration, and the constant succession and change of its particles, than upon the type of motion which characterizes it; as, "they [people going about their business] passed us...in an unsmiling sombre *stream*" (*Conrad*); for weeks after the surrender a *stream* of refugees crossed the country's border; "Music, acting, poetry proceed in the one mighty *stream;* sculpture, painting, all the arts of design, in the other" (*H. Ellis*); novelists who present their characters not in action, but through the *stream* of consciousness [i.e., the unbroken succession of thoughts which reflect one's experiences] of each. **Current** (as here compared: see also TENDENCY) differs from *stream* in laying greater stress on the direction or course of the movement implied and in carrying stronger suggestions of its force or velocity; thus, *streams* (not *currents*) of people passed him in either direction but he was finally caught by the *current* (not *stream*) of those moving south; so, he could not maintain his position against the *current* of opposition; *currents* of cold air swept in from the north. **Flood** is often used in place of *flow* or *stream* when one wishes to imply extreme copiousness in the supply or to attribute to it an overwhelming or torrential power; as, "Never came reformation in a *flood*, With such a heady *currance* [current], scouring faults" (*Shak.*); "It is not, he then feels with a sudden *flood* of emotion, that America is home, but that home is America" (*Brownell*); "This poem called forth *floods* of abuse" (*Day Lewis*). **Tide** applies to something that flows or courses like an ocean tide and suggests either an alternation of directions (as, "swayed by the sweeping of the *tides* of air"—*Bryant*) or a power to suck one into its course by the force of its outward or inward pull (as, "Stanley was caught in the *tide* of war fervour"—*R. Macaulay*). **Flux** far more than *stream* stresses the unceasing change in the parts, particles, or elements and, sometimes, direction of that which flows (as, "For this and that way swings The *flux* of mortal things, Though moving inly to one far-set goal"—*Arnold;* "how idle is it to commiserate them [the French] for their instability, when not stability but *flux* is their ideal!"—*Brownell*): often specifically it applies to the outward aspect or appearance which is constantly changing in contrast to its real and abiding nature (as, "to distinguish between the transient, unsatisfying *flux* of things, and the permanent, satisfying reality which lies behind it"—*Inge*).

Ana. *Succession, progression, series, sequence: continuity, *continuation, continuance.

flowery. Aureate, grandiloquent, magniloquent, *rhetorical, euphuistic, bombastic.

Ana. Florid, *ornate, flamboyant: *inflated, tumid, turgid: *wordy, verbose, redundant, prolix, diffuse.

fluctuate. Oscillate, *swing, sway, vibrate, pendulate, waver, undulate.

Ana. Alternate, *rotate: waver, vacillate (see HESITATE).

Con. Fix, *set, establish, settle: resolve, determine, *decide.

fluent. Eloquent, voluble, glib, articulate, *vocal.

Ana. Facile, effortless, smooth, *easy: *quick, prompt, ready, apt.

Con. Stuttering, stammering (see STAMMER, *v.*): fettered, hampered, trammeled (see HAMPER, *v.*).

fluid, *adj.* *Liquid.

Ana. Liquefied, melted, fused, dissolved, deliquesced *or* deliquescent (see corresponding verbs at LIQUEFY).

fluid, *n.* Liquid (see under LIQUID, *adj.*).

Ant. Solid.

flurry, *n.* Bustle, fuss, ado, *stir, pother.

Ana. Perturbation, agitation, disturbance, discomposure (see DISCOMPOSE): *haste, hurry, speed.

flurry, *v.* Fluster, agitate, perturb, disturb, *discompose, disquiet.

Ana. Bewilder, distract, perplex (see PUZZLE): quicken, excite, galvanize, stimulate, *provoke.

flush, *adj.* Even, *level, flat, plane, plain, smooth.

fluster, *v.* Upset, agitate, perturb, flurry, disturb, *discompose, disquiet.

Ana. Bewilder, distract, confound, nonplus, mystify, perplex, *puzzle: rattle, faze, disconcert, discomfit (see EMBARRASS): *confuse, muddle, addle, fuddle.

flutter, *v.* Flitter, flicker, *flit, hover.

Ana. *Shake, tremble, quiver, quaver, wobble: beat, throb, *pulsate, palpitate: fluctuate, vibrate, oscillate, *swing.

fluvial *or* **fluviatile.** *Aquatic, lacustrine, lacuscular, marine, oceanic, thalassic, neritic, pelagic, abyssal, bathysmal, bathybic.

flux. *Flow, current, tide, stream, flood.

Ana. Swinging *or* swing, fluctuation, oscillation, wavering, swaying *or* sway (see corresponding verbs at SWING): shifting, moving (see MOVE, *v.*): *motion, movement, stir.

fly, *v.* **1 Fly, dart, float, skim, scud, shoot, sail** are not synonymous terms in their literal senses, but they come into comparison in their extended senses when they mean to pass, or less often, to cause to pass, lightly or quickly over a surface or above a surface. **Fly** (as here compared: see also ESCAPE, 1) literally implies the aid of wings and is therefore used strictly of winged insects, of birds, of airplanes, and the like, but figuratively it may be used to imply any movement through or as through the air that suggests similar swift passage, buoyancy, lack of impediments, or the like; as, "Swift *fly* the years" (*Pope*); "Saw the snowy whirlwind *fly*" (*Gray*); "And kindling murmurs *flew*" (*Shelley*); "Thy loose hair in the light wind *flying*" (*Shelley*). **Dart** literally implies the use of a dart, or of a pointed weapon such as a lance or a javelin that is hurled with great speed and directness from the hand, or an aimed arrow propelled from a bow. In its figurative intransitive sense, the term implies any movement that is as suddenly initiated and as straight and as swift in its course; as, "Hawks regularly beat along the furze, *darting* on a finch now and then" (*Jefferies*); "He caught her by the arm as she ran past and...without trying to check her, simply *darted* in with her and up the stairs, causing no end of consternation" (*Conrad*); "[stars] *darting* about our galaxy with speeds that range up to 200 miles per second" (*P. W. Merrill*). **Float** in its literal sense suggests movement along or upon the surface of water by someone or something that is buoyed up, such as a boat, a swimmer resting, or the like. In its extended use, it implies a similar buoyant and seemingly effortless gliding as through the air or along a liquid surface; as, "I wandered lonely as a cloud That *floats* on high o'er vales and hills" (*Wordsworth*); "a bright bird which sings divinely as it *floats* about from one place to another" (*L. P. Smith*). **Skim,** which is used as often transitively as intransitively, derives its implications in its more common extended senses from its earliest sense of to remove a film from the surface of a liquid, such as scum from boiling sirup or cream from milk, by means of a spoon or the like. In its figurative use, it implies a passing lightly and swiftly over the surface of something, sometimes darting into it, sometimes floating above it: often, it suggests a mere touching of the surface; as, "Some lightly o'er the current *skim*" (*Gray*); "Down the road *skims* an eave swallow, swift as an arrow" (*Jefferies*); "she had *skimmed* gracefully over life's surface like a swallow, dipping her pretty wings in the shallows...or like a bee, sipping and tasting each flower" (*R. Macaulay*); "What I mean by reading is not *skimming*... but reading again and again, in all sorts of moods" (*C. E. Montague*). **Scud** implies light, rapid movement such as that of a hare pursued by hounds, or of a sailboat driven over the surface of the water by a high wind, or of clouds driven by an approaching hurricane: often, also, it connotes swiftness so great that the surface is barely touched by the speeding object; as, the boat *scuds* before the wind; "the *scudding* rain which drives in gusts over the...great shining river" (*Thackeray*); "Crisp foam-flakes *scud* along the level sand" (*Tennyson*). **Shoot** literally suggests the speed and directness of motion characteristic of a bullet or other missile propelled by a gun or the like: it differs from *dart*, its nearest synonym, in throwing less emphasis upon the suddenness of start and, often, in more definitely suggesting continuous or extended movement; as, "The lambent lightnings *shoot* Across the sky" (*Thomson*); the automobile *shot* around the corner. **Sail** literally implies the smooth and gliding movement of a sailing vessel: it differs from its nearest synonym *float* in more frequently implying power, ostentation (as if of spread sails), directness of course, or the like; as, "Hope...set free from earth ... On steady wing *sails* through the immense abyss" (*Cowper*); "Till over down and over dale All night the shining vapor *sail* And pass the silent-lighted town" (*Tennyson*). "But who is this?... Female of sex it seems— That, so bedecked, ornate, and gay, Comes this way *sailing*" (*Milton*).

Ana. *Flit, flutter, flitter, flicker, hover: soar, mount, *rise, arise, ascend: glide, *slide, slip.

2 Flee, *escape, decamp, abscond.

flying field. *Airport, airdrome, air field, landing field.

foam, *n.* **Foam, froth, spume, scum, lather, suds, yeast** come into comparison when they denote a white or light-colored bubbly substance such as that which gathers on the top of some liquids when they are agitated. **Foam** is the most comprehensive of these terms but is not interchangeable with all; it always implies an aggregation of small bubbles such as arises on the top of a fermenting liquor or an effervescing or boiling liquid, or on the surface of the sea when agitated by high winds or covered with breaking waves; the term is also applicable to a similar substance formed in the mouth or on the skin of some animals (or persons) in a rage, in great excitement, or suffering from intense heat; as, the *foam* on beer or on an ice-cream soda; "The rider from the château, and the horse in a *foam*, clattered away through the village" (*Dickens*). Of all these words, *foam* commonly has the most pleasant and elevated associations, usually connoting in poetry whiteness, delicacy, and grace; as, "Idalian Aphrodite beautiful, Fresh as the *foam*" (*Tennyson*). **Froth** is applicable to any foam, but it carries a far stronger implication, both in its literal and in its figurative use, of insubstantiality, worthlessness, or (when there is direct or indirect reference to persons or animals) of mad excitement than *foam* carries; as, your glass of beer is half *froth; froth* forming at the mouth of a mad dog; his speech had no logical substance, being mostly *froth;* "in all the *froth* and ferment between capital and labor" (*C. C. Furnas*). **Spume,** etymologically cognate with *foam,* is still applicable where *foam* or *froth* might also be employed; as, "They dart forth polypus-antennae, To blister with their poison *spume* The wanderer" (*Shelley*). However, especially since around 1800, the term is chiefly used to denote the foam arising on an agitated body of water; as, "all the billows green Toss'd up the silver *spume* against the clouds" (*Keats*); "as when a sand-bar breaks in clotted *spume* and spray" (*Kipling*). **Scum** also, in its earliest sense, equaled *foam* and *froth* but it was long ago distinctively applied to the film that rises on boiling liquids, especially those containing meats, vegetables, or fruits (as, the *scum* on boiling currant juice), or to a similar film which forms on molten metals (as, the *scum*, or scoria, of iron) or on the surface of a stagnant pool or like body of water (as, the ditch is covered with a green *scum*). Since scum is usually removed from the broth of meats and the like, or from the molten mass of metal, and is discarded, or is regarded as a sign of foulness in stagnant water, the term, especially in extended use and as applied to a class or body of persons, usually connotes worthlessness, vileness, or the like; as, men and women who are the *scum* of the earth. **Lather** and **suds** both apply in current use to the foam produced by agitating water impregnated with soap. *Lather*, however, usually suggests a less frothy condition than *suds* and a heavier aggregation of small soapy bubbles; as, hard water does not produce a good *lather* for shaving. *Suds*, on the other hand, often denotes water so covered with a soapy foam that it is usable for laundering clothes; as, the laundress likes the soap because it gives her plenty of *suds;* soak the cloth in hot *suds. Lather,* however, rather than *suds*, is the preferred term when the foam induced by intense sweating or emotional excitement is denoted (as, a hard-ridden horse working up a *lather;* he was in a *lather* of rage); *suds* is the preferred term when the reference is to something that suggests the appearance of suds in a laundry tub or washing machine (as, "another [medicine-man] whips up a mixture of water and meal into frothy *suds* symbolic of clouds"—*J. G. Frazer*). **Yeast,** in its earliest and still common sense, applies to a substance composed of an aggregate of small cells of sac fungi that arises on the top of, or sinks as a sediment in, malt worts, fruit juices, and other saccharine liquids, and that induces fermentation in them. It is this substance that is used as a leavening agent in bread. But because yeast often appears as a froth on liquids and is accompanied by fermentation, the term is, in extended use, applied to a similar froth, foam, or spume, especially that appearing on the surface of an agitated sea; as, "The ship... swallowed with *yeast* and *froth*" (*Shak.*); "They melt into thy *yeast* of waves" (*Byron*).

focus, *n.* Heart, nucleus, core, *center, middle, midst, hub, omphalos.

fodder. Forage, *food, provender, provisions, comestibles, victuals, viands, grub, eats, chow.

foe. *Enemy.

Ana. Antagonist, *opponent, adversary: assailant, attacker (see corresponding verbs at ATTACK): rival, competitor (see corresponding verbs at RIVAL).

Ant. Friend. — *Con.* Ally, colleague, confederate, *partner: *associate, comrade, companion.

foetid. Variant of FETID.

fog. *Haze, smog, mist, brume.

foible. Failing, *fault, frailty, vice.

Ana. Weakness, infirmity (see corresponding adjectives at WEAK): defect, flaw, *blemish: aberration, *deviation.

foil, *v.* Thwart, *frustrate, circumvent, balk, baffle, outwit.

Ana. Discomfit, *embarrass, disconcert, faze, rattle: curb, check, snaffle, *restrain, inhibit.

Con. *Advance, further, forward, promote: abet, foment, *incite, instigate.

follow, *v.* **1 Follow, succeed, ensue, supervene** agree in meaning to come after someone or, more often, something. Although all of these verbs occur as transitives and intransitives, *ensue* and *supervene* are most commonly intransitive verbs. **Follow** is the general term, for it may imply a coming after in time, in sequence, in pursuit (see FOLLOW, 2), in logic, in understanding, or the like; as, the singing of "America" by the audience will *follow* the introductory prayer; Queen Victoria *followed* William IV as British sovereign. "The driving force in education should be the pupil's wish to learn, not the master's authority; but it does not *follow* that education should be soft and easy and pleasant at every stage"

(*B. Russell*). " 'She converses somewhat rapidly...at times I find it difficult to—' 'To *follow* her? Oh, well, one would get used to that' " (*Deland*). **Succeed** commonly implies an order, by which a certain or given person or thing comes after another, as has been determined by descent, inheritance, election, rank, or the like; as, son *succeeded* father as head of the business for many generations; the eldest son *succeeds* to the title; the person who will *succeed* the late congressman will be appointed by the governor of the state. *Succeed* is often used when the idea of a fixed order is lost, but it still usually retains the idea of taking the place of someone or something; as, "The link dissolves, each seeks a fresh embrace, Another love *succeeds*, another race" (*Pope*); "the anxieties of common life began soon to *succeed* to the alarms of romance" (*Austen*). **Ensue** usually implies some logical connection or the operation of some principle of sequences such as that of necessity; as, "That such a consequence...should *ensue*...was far enough from my thoughts" (*Austen*); "When his [man's] mind fails to stay the pace set by its [civilization's] inventions, madness must *ensue*" (*Day Lewis*). But *ensue* in somewhat archaic transitive use carries a strong implication of seeking after, rather than of coming after because of necessity; as, "Seek peace, and *ensue* it" (*1 Peter* iii. 11); "to seek health, and *ensue* beauty" (*Galsworthy*). **Supervene** suggests the following of something added or conjoined, and often unforeseen or unpredictable; as, "Two worlds, two antagonistic ideals, here in evidence before him. Could a third condition *supervene*, to mend their discord?" (*Pater*); "it was not acute rheumatism, but a *supervening* pericarditis that...killed her" (*Bennett*); "it is in the philosophy that *supervened* upon the popular creed...that we shall find the highest...reaches of their thought" (*G. L. Dickinson*).

2 Follow, pursue, chase, trail, tag, tail come into comparison as meaning to go immediately or shortly after someone or something. **Follow** is the comprehensive term; it usually implies the lead or, sometimes, guidance of someone or something; as, the detective *followed* the boys to their hiding place; hangers-on who *follow* the circus; "the vengeance that *follows* crime" (*G. L. Dickinson*); to *follow* up a clue; to *follow* a calling or trade. "He should not desire to steer his own course, but *follow* the line that the talk happens to take" (*A. C. Benson*). "What was it that made men *follow* Oliver Cromwell?" (*S. M. Crothers*). **Pursue** in its earliest English sense implies a following as an enemy or hunter; as, to *pursue* a fox; *pursuing* rebels in flight; to *pursue* happiness. The term therefore usually suggests an attempt to overtake, to reach, or to attain, and commonly in its extended senses, even when the implications of hostility or of a desire to capture are absent, it connotes eagerness, persistence, or inflexibility of purpose in following one's thoughts, ends, or desires; as, "Ye who...*pursue* with eagerness the phantoms of hope" (*Johnson*); "Thrice happy man! enabled to *pursue* What all so wish, but want the pow'r to do!" (*Pope*); "*pursuing* the game of high ambition with a masterly coolness" (*Buchan*); to *pursue* the career of a diplomat. **Chase** implies fast pursuit in order to, or as if to, catch a fleeing object or to drive away or turn to flight an oncoming thing; as, to *chase* the fleeing thieves; the boys *chased* the intruder out of the school yard; "We were *chased* by two pirates, who soon overtook us" (*Swift*). "If to dance all night, and dress all day ...*chas'd* old-age away ...who would learn one earthly thing of use?" (*Pope*). **Trail** implies a following in one's tracks; as, to *trail* a fugitive to his hiding place; to *trail* a lost child to the edge of a creek. **Tag** (a colloquial term) and **tail** (a slang term) imply close following, often with the implication of watching or observing every movement; as, she refused to have anyone *tagging* after her every time she went out for a walk; he employed detectives to *tail* the suspected man.

Ana. Attend, *accompany, convoy: *copy, imitate, ape: *practice, exercise.

Ant. Precede (*in order*): forsake (*a teacher or his teachings*). — ***Con.*** Lead, *guide, pilot, steer: elude, evade, *escape: desert, *abandon.

follower. Follower, adherent, disciple, sectary, partisan, henchman, satellite. Follower is the inclusive term, denoting a person who attaches himself to the person or opinions of another; as, the *followers* of Jesus; the *followers* of Karl Marx. Its synonyms divide themselves into two groups, the first three designating a follower through choice or conviction and the last three a follower in whom personal devotion overshadows or eclipses the critical faculty. **Adherent** connotes closer and more persistent attachment than *follower;* it may be used without any implication of the personality of the teacher or leader; as, a doctrine that gained many *adherents;* the candidate lost many *adherents* when he announced his views on reform. **Disciple** always presupposes a master or teacher and implies personal, often devoted, adherence to his views or doctrines. "We go to him [Matthew Arnold] for refreshment and for the companionship of a kindred point of view to our own, but not as *disciples*" (*T. S. Eliot*). **Sectary** etymologically means *follower*, but is now rare in this sense or is so affected by its more common meaning (see HERETIC) that it usually implies the acceptance of the doctrines of a religious teacher or body; as, *sectaries* of Mohammed. **Partisan** invariably suggests such devotion to the person or opinions of another or to a party, a creed, a school of thought, that there is incapacity for seeing from any other point of view. It often, therefore, connotes bigotry or prejudice. "Laura was always a passionate *partisan* of her young brother" (*M. Austin*). "A few *partisans* argued for him [Poe]" (*Mencken*). **Henchman** is commonly applied to a subservient follower of a political leader or "boss"; in extended use, it connotes abject submission to the will of a dominating and, usually, unscrupulous leader or group. "The catspaw of corrupt functionaries and the *henchmen* of ambitious humbugs" (*Shaw*). **Satellite,** more than any of the others, suggests devotion to the person of the leader and constant obsequious attendance on him. "Boswell was...made happy by an introduction to Johnson, of whom he became the obsequious *satellite*" (*Irving*).

Ana. Devotee, votary, *addict, habitué, fiend, fan: *parasite, sycophant, toady: *scholar, disciple, pupil.

Ant. Leader.

following, *n.* **Following, clientele, clientage, public, audience** come into comparison when they denote the body of persons who attach themselves to another as his disciples, patrons, admirers, or the like. **Following** is the most comprehensive term, applicable to any group that follows either literally, as a train or retinue, or figuratively, and in a collective sense, as the adherents of a leader, the disciples of a philosopher, the customers of a salesman, the admirers of a young woman, or an actor's "fans." "Such a man, with a great name in the country and a strong *following* in Parliament" (*Macaulay*). "He [the critic] unconsciously enrolls a *following* of like-minded persons" (*C. E. Montague*). **Clientele,** or more rarely **clientage,** is now chiefly used of the persons, collectively, who habitually resort for services to a professional man, such as a lawyer or physician, or who give their patronage to a business establishment such as a hotel, a restaurant, or a shop; as, Dr. Doe counts in his *clientele* all the leading families in the town; summer hotels usually send out circulars to their *clientele* in the spring. **Public** is applied chiefly to the following attracted by a person such as an author, a lecturer, or an actor, by interest in his work, or to that of any establishment or institution the success of which is determined by its attracting the support of such a following; as, the actress declared that her aim was to please her *public;* the author increased his *public* as each new book appeared. "The *public* for which masterpieces are intended is not on this earth" (*T. Wilder*). **Audience** is applicable to a following that listens (literally or figuratively) with attention to what a person has to say whenever he addresses them in a speech, a book, or the like. "Still govern thou my song, Urania, and fit *audience* find, though few" (*Milton*). "The stricken poet of Recanati had no country, for an Italy in his day did not exist, he had no *audience,* no celebrity" (*Arnold*). In literal use *audience,* rather than *spectators* (see SPECTATOR), is the correct term for designating the body of persons attending a lecture, a play, a concert, or the like, because they are there primarily to hear, only secondarily to see; as, the *audience* at the opera packed the house.

foment. Abet, *incite, instigate.

Ana. Goad, spur (see corresponding nouns at MOTIVE): stimulate, quicken, excite, galvanize, *provoke: nurture, *nurse, foster, cultivate.

Ant. Quell. — *Con.* *Suppress, repress: check, curb, *restrain.

fond, *adj.* 1 **Fond, infatuated** (*or* **infatuate**), **besotted, insensate** come into comparison when they mean made blindly or stupidly foolish, as by passion, drink, or the like. **Fond,** in literary use, implies a judgment misled by credulity, undue optimism, excessive affection, or the like; as, Cowper's characterization of the *Biographia Britannica:* "Oh, *fond* attempt to give a deathless lot To names ignoble, born to be forgot!"; "Grant I may never prove so *fond,* To trust man on his oath or bond" (*Shak.*). **Infatuated** (and the now archaic **infatuate**) implies a weakening, rather than the absence, of judgment, especially under the influence of violent passion or unreasoning emotion; it is therefore correctly applied to the acts or qualities of men from whom sagacity or self-control might have been expected. "What the *infatuated* ministry may do, I know not; but our *infatuated* House of Commons...have begun a new war in America" (*Burke*). "Your people are so short-sighted, so jealous and selfish, and so curiously *infatuated* with things that are not...good" (*Jefferies*). **Besotted** adds to *infatuated* the implications of a stupefying or intoxicating influence that destroys the capacity to think clearly and, sometimes, makes its victim disgusting or repulsive; as, men *besotted* by drink; "Are these So far *besotted* that they fail to see This fair wife-worship cloaks a secret shame?" (*Tennyson*). **Insensate** conveys the idea of feeling and judgment lost under the influence of passions such as hatred, desire for revenge, greed, and the like; the term is also applicable to the passion; as, *insensate* rage. "The *insensate* mob Uttered a cry of triumph" (*Shelley*). "Projects the most *insensate* [were] formed" (*Sir A. Alison*).

Ana. Foolish, silly, fatuous, asinine, *simple: *stupid, dumb.

2 Devoted, affectionate, *loving, doting.

Ana. *Enamored, infatuated: *tender, sympathetic, warm, responsive: ardent, passionate, *impassioned.

Con. *Indifferent, unconcerned, aloof.

fondle. Pet, *caress, cuddle, dandle.

food. 1 **Food, victuals, viands, provisions, comestibles, provender, fodder, forage, grub, eats, chow** are here compared as meaning raw or cooked substances that are eaten, digested, and assimilated by human beings or animals. **Food** is the most general of these terms applicable to all substances which satisfy hunger and build up or repair waste in the body of men or animals; it is sometimes distinguished from *drink*—that is, liquids that satisfy thirst; as, to conserve a nation's supply of *food;* refrigerators that keep *food* fresh; there was no lack of *food* or drink during their sojourn on the island. *Victuals* and *viands* (the singular form of the latter still occurs) are both words which came into English during the fourteenth century as designations of food for human beings, especially food that is prepared and ready for eating. **Victuals** (sometimes, in representing dialect or to obtain a humorous effect, spelled **vittles**), however, is now largely dialectal and colloquial, being avoided in standard language except where a racy or pungent word is desired for realistic or humorous effect; as, "I worked hard enough to earn my passage and my *victuals*" (*Shaw*); "when I bear in mind how elegantly we eat our *victuals*" (*L. P. Smith*). **Viands,** on the other hand, savors of bookishness or affectation and, although common enough in the nineteenth century and earlier, now seldom occurs in good colloquial or written English except where daintiness, rarity, or an especially fine quality is to be suggested; as, "all the dainties and *viands* that could be wanted for a feast" (*Wilde*); "He dashed the wine on the earth and scattered about the other *viands*" (*Milman*). **Provisions** applies to food in general, as offered for sale in a market or kept in store as supplies; as, we always go to the Blank Market for our *provisions;* there were not enough *provisions* in the hotel to care for the weekend influx of guests. **Comestibles,** which stresses edibility, is now found chiefly in affected or humorous use for *victuals* or *provisions;* as, "He resolved upon having a strong reinforcement of *comestibles*" (*T. Hook*). **Provender,** in earliest English use, and still in straight precise use, applies to food, such as hay, oats, or corn for horses, mules, asses, and the like; as, "they must be dieted like mules And have their *provender* tied to their mouths" (*Shak.*). In extended and usually humorous or ironical use, *provender* may equal *provisions, victuals,* or *food;* as, "bread and meat, wine, and hot coffee. Monsieur Defarge put this *provender*...on the shoemaker's bench" (*Dickens*); **Fodder** and **forage** are both applied to food for domestic animals such as cattle, but *fodder* (which was originally a close synonym of *food*) now usually denotes the food such as hay, grains, silage, etc., provided for stall feeding, and *forage,* the food gained by grazing, browsing, rooting, or the like; as, the *fodder* is stored and ground in a silo; "A herb like a broad flat thistle supplied the buffaloes...drink as well as *forage*" (*Defoe*). But *forage* is also used in much the same sense as *provender.* **Grub, eats, chow** are all low slang terms for *food,* suggesting hunger or pleasure in eating, but not otherwise easily distinguishable.

2 **Food, aliment, pabulum, nutriment, nourishment, sustenance, pap** are synonymous only when they denote material which feeds and supports the body or organism or, by extension, the mind or the soul. **Food** is referable to anything which enters the system, is assimilated by it, and contributes to its life, its growth, or its power for work; as, moisture and substances in the soil provide *food* for plants; muscle-building *foods;* mineral oil does not fatten since it is not a *food.* **Aliment** and **pabulum** are now chiefly literary or bookish words, especially in their primary senses; in figurative use they are relatively common. They are not always distinguishable from each other, but *aliment* is more often applied to that which nourishes, or which promotes growth, and *pabulum* to

that which serves as an article (sometimes as the substance) of one's diet, especially mental diet; as, "For the ...*aliment* of the natural body...God hath given meat" (*Donne*); many motion pictures provide poor *pabulum* for the adolescent mind. "The *aliments* Nurturing our nobler part, the mind, thought, dreams, Passions, and aims...at length are made Our mind itself" (*Lytton*). "It is notorious that they [detective stories] are the favorite *pabulum* of college professors, kings, queens, presidents, and 'heavy' intellectuals everywhere" (*Michigan Alumnus Quarterly Review*). **Nutriment** and **nourishment** are applied to food necessary for one's growth and health or to the effect of such food or foods; however, *nutriment* is more often applied to that which is actually assimilated or assimilable; *nourishment*, to the food itself; as, the infant received very little *nutriment* from its mother's milk; he was persuaded to take some *nourishment*. **Sustenance,** when it is applied to food, is preferable to *nutriment* (of which it is a close synonym) when the maintenance or support of life rather than the upbuilding of the body or mind is stressed; as, the farm barely provided *sustenance* for the family. "The blossoms of Beaumont and Fletcher's imagination draw no *sustenance* from the soil, but are cut and slightly withered flowers stuck into sand" (*T. S. Eliot*). **Pap,** applied literally to a soft food for infants and invalids, is found chiefly in contemptuous or ironical use, and applies in its extended sense to nourishment for body, or especially for mind, that is as slight, as diluted, and as innocuous as infant pap; as, college courses that are mere intellectual *pap;* a preacher whose sermons are nothing more than *pap*.

fool, *n.* **1 Fool, idiot, imbecile, moron, simpleton, natural** are often used interchangeably in the extended sense of one who lacks sense or good judgment, but in precise (in some cases in technical) use they denote one who is mentally deficient in a clearly marked degree. **Fool,** the most general and probably the oldest of these words, has been applied in the past to anyone who suffers from mental derangement as well as to anyone afflicted with mental deficiency. It implies the lack or the loss of understanding and reason or the absence of signs of the powers which when exercised and developed make for intelligence and wisdom. From its Biblical use, the term still connotes, in elevated style, grave, pitying, or scathing condemnation (as, "The *fool* hath said in his heart, There is no God"—*Psalms* xiv. 1; "For ye suffer *fools* gladly seeing ye yourselves are wise"—*2 Corinthians* xi. 19; "*Fools* rush in where angels fear to tread"—*Pope*); in colloquial usage, as a term of contempt, it is strongly offensive (as, "Who marries one like me but a *fool?*...I could not marry a *fool*. The man I marry I must respect"—*Meredith;* "he was simply an irresponsible and thoughtless *fool*"—*Bennett*). *Idiot, imbecile, moron* are technical designations of a person who is mentally deficient (as opposed to one who is mentally deranged). All imply lack of intelligence to such a degree as to disqualify the person for living and working on a parity with others. **Idiot** designates a mentally deficient person who is incapable of connected speech or of avoiding the common dangers of life and who requires constant care and attention; **imbecile** designates one who is incapable of earning a living but who can be educated to a point where he is capable of attending to the simplest of his wants or of recognizing and avoiding the most ordinary dangers; **moron** (a much misused term) applies to one who has sufficient intelligence to learn a simple trade but who requires constant supervision in his work and recreation. "In Massachusetts, which may be taken as typical of the rest of the country, an *idiot* has only about $\frac{1}{3}$ as much chance of living to be ten years of age as a normal being. *Imbeciles* are slightly better, for they have $\frac{2}{5}$ as much chance. *Morons* have about $\frac{7}{8}$ as much chance" (*C. C. Furnas*). In precise nontechnical use, these terms usually follow the psychiatric classification, *idiot* implying utter feeblemindedness (as, "he said you were...a senseless, drivelling *idiot*"—*Wycherley;* "April Comes like an *idiot*, babbling and strewing flowers"—*Millay*), *imbecile* implying half-wittedness or emptymindedness (as, "What if suddenly everyone were to... discover that she was an *imbecile*, with a quite vacant, unhinged mind?"—*R. Macaulay*), *moron* implying intelligence of the lowest grade and general stupidity (as, "It is possible that while we are governed by high-grade '*morons*' there will be no practical recognition of the dangers which threaten us"—*Inge*). **Simpleton** (a popular, rather than a technical, term) implies silliness or, sometimes, lack of sophistication; it is often used lightly as a term of indulgent contempt; as, "They look upon persons employing their time in making verses...as *simpletons* easily to be deceived" (*V. Knox*); poor, innocent little *simpleton!* **Natural,** which is now comparatively rare in this sense, came into English use in the sixteenth century as a term designating any congenitally feeble-minded person; as, "the minds of *naturals*" (*Locke*); "I own the man is not a *natural;* he has a very quick sense, though very slow understanding" (*Steele*).

2 Fool, jester, clown, antic, buffoon, zany, merry-andrew, pantaloon, harlequin, comedian (*fem.* **comedienne**), **comic, stooge** come into comparison when they denote a person or a character whose business it is to make others laugh. **Fool** in literary use, as in the plays of Shakespeare, is never completely dissociated from another sense of the word in which witlessness or a degree of lunacy is implied. The designation is applied both to a court retainer who amuses his lord or to any person who constantly, often unintentionally, provokes laughter, but in both cases (typically), though the fool by appearance seems a simpleton, his words are evocative not only of laughter but usually also of thought. " 'Who is with him [King Lear]?' 'None but the *fool;* who labours to out-jest His heart-struck injuries' " (*Shak.*). "Let me play the *fool:* With mirth and laughter let old wrinkles come" (*Shak.*). **Jester** as a designation is chiefly applied to the fool who attends a king, a prince, or other personage. The word suggests his function and dress (motley, cap and bells, bauble) rather than, as *fool*, his personality, and the emphasis is upon a gift for raillery or, often, repartee. "He is the prince's *jester:* a very dull fool" (*Shak.*). **Clown** was once (especially in Shakespeare's plays) used interchangeably with the preceding words, but in general, its range of application was far more extensive and it carried distinctive connotations. It was a common designation of the character who provides comic relief in a play; sometimes he is a court fool, but more often a servant or a peasant, who by his boorishness, his ignorance, his blunders, and the like, creates amusement among his superiors. "Let those that play your *clowns* speak no more than is set down for them; for there be of them that will themselves laugh, to set on some quantity of barren spectators to laugh too" (*Shak.*). In recent use, however, the clown is the stock comic character of the pantomime and the circus, who by his makeup (typically all white—face, sugarloaf hat, loose tunic-breeches—with red spots), movements, and acts creates laughter. **Antic** was the older designation of this type of character, especially in the Renaissance dumb shows where the fun was dependent purely on the performer's grotesqueness of appearance, postures, and the like. **Buffoon** implies a more vulgar appeal than *fool* or *clown* and resort to tricks, practical jokes, mimicry, and sometimes bawdy behavior or talk. "Falstaff the cheerful companion, the loud *buffoon*" (*Johnson*). **Zany** and **merry-andrew** are close equivalents of *buffoon*, but they are properly applied to servants of mountebanks or quacks who provided additional amusement for the crowds their masters gathered about them. In modern literary use, *zany* often is contemptuous for *fool* or *simpleton* (as, "The printers are awful *zanies*, they print erasures and corrections too"—*Tennyson*); it is still occasionally applied to one who serves as a laughingstock. "We are the *zanies* of sorrow. We are *clowns* whose hearts are broken" (*Wilde*). **Pantaloon** and **harlequin** designate stock characters in the old popular Italian comedy who aided or abetted the clown in his funmaking. They now are found in pantomime and in the puppet show. The pantaloon is an old and often mean dotard who wears spectacles, slippers, and a tight-fitting combination of trousers and stockings; the harlequin is his servant, a droll youth who typically wears a striped parti-colored suit and carries a light sword of lath. The remaining terms are common in current use and suggest reference to the legitimate theater, vaudeville, burlesque, the motion pictures, and the radio. **Comedian** (or, feminine, **comedienne**) is the comprehensive term applicable to any actor or entertainer who provides amusement by what he says or does, whether his methods and aims be those of high comedy or of low comedy; as, Ada Rehan was probably greater as a *comedienne* than as a tragedienne; slapstick *comedians*. **Comic** specifically implies buffoonery or clowning, and is especially applied to the jokesters of the radio and the slapstick comedians of the motion pictures; as, Charlie Chaplin was one of the great *comics* of the silent motion pictures. **Stooge**, like *merry-andrew*, implies subordination to another funmaker, and often the character of a laughingstock, but the resemblance ends there. The function of a stooge is either to heckle or bait his principal (usually from a seat in the audience) and so feed him lines, or to provide a second and different kind of amusement by his reactions, usually stupid reactions, to his principal's witticisms.

foolhardy. Temerarious, daring, daredevil, rash, reckless, *adventurous, venturous, venturesome.
Ana. Bold, audacious (see BRAVE): headlong, *precipitate, impetuous.
Ant. Wary. — *Con.* *Cautious, circumspect, calculating.

foolish. 1 *Simple, silly, fatuous, asinine.
Ana. Idiotic, imbecilic, moronic (see corresponding nouns at FOOL).
Con. *Intelligent, clever, quick-witted, bright, smart.
2 Foolish, silly, absurd, preposterous, as here compared, imply a judgment of a person, his acts, behavior, utterances, and the like, and agree in meaning ridiculous because not exhibiting good sense. That is **foolish** which does not commend itself to the judgment of others as wise, or sensible, or judicious; as, a *foolish* investment. "Courageous behaviour is easier for a man who fails to apprehend dangers, but such courage may often be *foolish*" (*B. Russell*). That is **silly** which seems witless, pointless, or futile; as, a *silly* dispute; a *silly* sacrifice. "The way she cheats herself [at patience]—it's too *silly!*" (*Bennett*). That is **absurd** which is inconsistent with accepted ideas, common sense, or sound reason; it is applied, therefore, to ideas and projects considered impersonally, as well as to persons and their acts. "The *absurd*...dogma that the king can do no wrong" (*Shaw*). That is **preposterous** which, according to its derivation, puts the cart before the horse and is, therefore, glaringly absurd. "If a man cannot see a church, it is *preposterous* to take his opinion about its altar-piece or painted window" (*T. H. Huxley*). In somewhat looser use, that is *preposterous* which is ridiculously out of keeping with character, situation, or the like. "He put on his *preposterous* old flowered cashmere dressing-gown" (*Deland*).
Ana. Ridiculous, ludicrous, *laughable.
Ant. Sensible. — *Con.* *Wise, sane, judicious, prudent, sage, sapient.

foot, *v.* Figure, cast, *add, sum, total.

footpad. Highwayman, *brigand, bandit, marauder.

fop, *n.* **Fop, dandy, beau, coxcomb, exquisite, élégant** (*or* **élégante**), **dude, macaroni, buck, spark, swell, nob, toff** come into comparison as denoting a person who is conspicuously fashionable or elegant in dress or manners. **Fop** (etymologically, a fool) was early applied to a person who made a foolish pretense of wit, learning, skill, or the like, but this sense yielded to one still earlier in its origin, with the result that *fop* is now applied to a person who is preposterously concerned with fashionableness, elegance, and refinement, not only in respect to dress and manners but in respect to anything, such as literary or artistic taste, that marks the courtier or gentleman of a polite age such as prevailed in England between 1688 and 1750; as, "True *fops* help nature's work, and go to school To file and finish God Almighty's fool" (*Dryden*); "Nature made ev'ry *fop* to plague his brother, Just as one beauty mortifies another" (*Pope*); "His tightened waist, his stiff stock...denoted the military *fop*" (*Disraeli*). **Dandy,** which had its origin (in the sense here considered) around 1800, carries a weaker implication of affectation and overrefinement than *fop* and a stronger suggestion of concern for stylish or striking apparel and a spruce or dapper appearance; as, "That he [Thomas Moore] had the tastes of a *dandy*, we learn from a letter of the time describing his 'smart white hat, kid gloves, brown frock coat, yellow cassimere waistcoat, gray duck trousers, and blue silk handkerchief carelessly secured in front by a silver pin'" (*T. Walsh*); "I amused myself with being...a *dandy*, a man of fashion" (*Wilde*). **Beau,** which in this sense is the counterpart of *belle*, was often used in the eighteenth century in place of *fop*, especially when a word without the implication of absurdity or fatuousness was desired. It was usually applied to what came later to be called a *ladies' man*, and suggests as much attention to details of personal appearance as does *fop;* as, "Why round our [i.e., the Beauties'] coaches crowd the white-glov'd *Beaux?*" (*Pope*); "A *beau* is one who, with the nicest care, In parted locks divides his curling hair; One who with balm and cinnamon smells sweet" (*C. A. Elton*). **Coxcomb,** like *fop*, in early use designated a pretentious fool and, like it, became applicable to a beau, as a term of contempt. However, *coxcomb* retains its earlier implications so clearly that it often stresses fatuousness and pretentiousness as much as, if not more than, foppishness; as, "Of all the fools that pride can boast, A *coxcomb* claims distinction most" (*Gay*); "the young *coxcombs* of the Life Guards" (*Emerson*). **Exquisite** was much used in the nineteenth century as a designation of a dandy who manifested the extreme delicacy and refinement of taste characteristic of a fop. "The particular styles...he affected had their marked influence on the young *exquisites* of the Mayfair balls and Pall Mall club windows" (*Wilde*). **Élégant** or, more often, the feminine **élégante** (both often written without accents) was frequent around 1800 in the sense of a person of fashion and elegance; as, "Would you...know the fashionable dress of a Parisian *elegante?*" (*Edgeworth*). **Dude** is an Americanism applying to a dandy or exquisite: in common use, however, the term applies chiefly to a man who makes himself conspicuously different in dress or manners from the ordinary man: it is therefore the rough man's term for the carefully dressed and groomed man, the quiet gentleman's term for the obvious dandy, a Western American's term for an Easterner or a city-bred man; as, her father told her he would not allow her to marry a *dude;* the boys jeer at every young man wearing a high hat and call him a "*dude*"; "They were all mountain-wise, range-broken men, picked...for diplomacy in handling *dudes*" (*Scribner's*). **Macaroni** (spelled variously) is now a historical term applying to one of a class of fops in the eighteenth century who looked down upon British manners and customs as vulgar, and who affected Continental fashions in dress, manners, diet, and the like; as, "He wore his hair...in the fashion which I remember to have seen in caricatures of what were termed, in my young days, *Maccaronies*" (*Lamb*). **Buck** applies usually to a dashing fellow, a dandy in dress, but not conspicuously, or necessarily, a gentleman in manners; as, "The dashing young *buck,* driving his own equipage" (*Irving*); "I remember you a *buck* of *bucks* when that coat first came out to Calcutta" (*Thackeray*). **Spark,** an older term in English than *beau,* carries much the same implications: it is, however, applicable to a man of any age who manifests interest in parading his good points; as, "These *sparks* with awkward vanity display What the fine gentleman wore yesterday" (*Pope*); "Thus Mr. Povey came out in his true colours as a blood, a blade, and a gay *spark*" (*Bennett*). **Swell, nob, toff** are all colloquial or slang terms applying to one who by his dress and bearing makes it evident that he is a person of fashion. *Swell* originally applied to any fashionably or stylishly clad person, without regard to class or social station, but it is often currently applied to one who belongs to the highest social ranks; as, "I never was a gentleman—only a *swell*" (*Marryat*); "though not what they themselves call great *swells,* they have the manners and appearance and speech and habits of the capitalist class, [and] are described as gentlemen" (*Shaw*). *Nob* and *toff* are British slang terms applied to one who is, as judged by his dress, his manners, or bearing, an aristocrat, or a person of social distinction; as, "The little waiter...began to think Ferdinand was not such a *nob* as he had imagined" (*Disraeli*).

for, *conj.* *Because, since, as, inasmuch as.

forage, *n.* Fodder, provender, *food, provisions, comestibles, victuals, viands, grub, eats, chow.

forbear. 1 *Forgo, abnegate, eschew, sacrifice.

Ana. *Restrain, curb, bridle, inhibit: avoid, *escape, evade, shun: desist (*from*), cease (see STOP).

2 *Refrain, abstain.

Ana. Suffer, tolerate, endure, *bear.

forbearance. 1 Long-suffering, *patience, longanimity, resignation.

Ana. & *Ant.* See those at FORBEARANCE, 2.

2 Tolerance, clemency, mercifulness, leniency, indulgence. See under FORBEARING, *adj.*

Ana. *Patience, long-suffering, longanimity: *mercy, lenity, grace, charity.

Ant. Vindictiveness: anger.

forbearing. **Forbearing, tolerant, clement, merciful, lenient, indulgent** agree in meaning disinclined by nature, disposition, or circumstances to be severe or rigorous. The same differences in implications and connotations are observable in their corresponding nouns **forbearance, tolerance, clemency, mercifulness, leniency** (*or* **lenience**), **indulgence. Forbearing** and **forbearance** imply patience under provocation and deliberate abstention from judging harshly, exacting punishment, seeking vengeance or revenge, or the like. "Madame Beck was...*forbearing* with all the world" (*C. Brontë*). "He thought of old days: of his father's *forbearance,* his own wilfulness" (*Meredith*). **Tolerant** and **tolerance** imply both a freedom from bias or bigotry and a liberal attitude to opinions other than one's own (especially to religious, philosophical, and political doctrines) that forbid severity or rigor in judging others who hold such opinions or doctrines or the imposition of any restrictions upon their freedom to think as they will. "[Anatole] France, as usual, professed a very *tolerant* attitude. One must gratify whatever tastes one has and seek whatever happiness one may be able to find" (*J. W. Krutch*). "Of all kinds of human energy, Art is surely the most free, the least parochial; and demands of us an essential *tolerance* of all its forms" (*Galsworthy*). **Clement** and **clemency** (see also MERCY) suggest a temperament or nature that is mild and gentle, especially in judging offenders, and is slow to exact their punishment if a pardon or forgiveness will satisfy the purpose; as, a *clement* ruler; a judge known far and wide for his *clemency.* "He [Octavian] was *clement* whenever he could be *clement* with safety, and he began to pardon the proscribed" (*Buchan*). **Merciful** and **mercifulness** imply both compassionate and forbearing treatment, especially of those who have offended or of those who merit severity or are defenseless against it. "I will be *merciful* to their unrighteousness" (*Hebrews* viii. 12). "Good my lord, be good to me; your honor is accounted a *merciful* man" (*Shak.*). **Lenient** (see also SOFT) and **leniency** differ from *clement* in suggesting usually, but not invariably, softness rather than gentleness of temper, and a relaxation of discipline or rigor; as, a *lenient* teacher (or parent). "I would ask you, dearest, to be...very *lenient* on his faults when he is not by" (*Dickens*). "She could not show the slightest *leniency* towards the romantic impulses of her elder daughter" (*Bennett*). **Indulgent** and **indulgence** usually imply compliancy as well as leniency; they therefore often suggest a willingness to pamper or favor (see INDULGE). As here compared, however, they imply, even more strongly than *lenient* and *leniency,* concessions made out of charity or the exercise of clemency in the treatment of those who offend or who are under one's government or control. "Neither Fox nor the [early] Christian martyrs [all of whom refused customary marks of courtesy and respect for the laws] made it easy for their judges to be *indulgent*" (*Inge*). "Simple-hearted kindly New York, on whose larger charity she [an unhappy wife suspected of adultery] had apparently counted, was precisely the place where she could least hope for *indulgence*" (*E. Wharton*).

Ana. Gentle, mild (see SOFT): patient, long-suffering, longanimous (see corresponding nouns at PATIENCE).

Ant. Unrelenting. — *Con.* Implacable, merciless, relentless, *grim: *impatient, nervous, restive.

forbid. **Forbid, prohibit, enjoin, interdict, inhibit, ban** agree in meaning to debar a person from using, doing, entering, or the like, or to order something not be used, done, entered, or the like. **Forbid** (the Saxon term) is the more direct and familiar, **prohibit** (the Latin term), the more formal or official; they do not widely differ in their essential implications for they both imply the exercise of authority or the existence of conditions which prevent with similar imperativeness. However, *forbid* carries so strong a connotation of expected obedience that it is preferred when the order is that of a parent, a master, an employer, a physician, or the like; as, to *forbid* a child to leave the house; smoking is *forbidden* on these premises. "Suffer the little children to come unto me, and *forbid* them not" (*Mark* x. 14). "The whole attraction of such knowledge consists in the fact that it is *forbidden*" (*B. Russell*). When circumstances absolutely debar, *forbid* is also preferred; as, his health *forbade* the use of tobacco. *Prohibit* has been used for so long in reference to laws, statutes, regulations, and the like, that it tends to connote a less despotic exercise of authority and restraints imposed for the good of all or for the sake of orderly procedure; as, to *prohibit* the manufacture and sale of intoxicating liquors; to *prohibit*, by international agreement, the bombing of cities; to *prohibit* the indiscriminate use of fireworks. "The powers not delegated to the United States by the Constitution, nor *prohibited* by it to the States" (*U. S. Const.*). **Enjoin** (see also COMMAND) is a legal term implying a judicial order forbidding something under penalty. "By the decision of the Court the defendant should be *enjoined* from publishing news obtained from the Associated Press for—[a certain number of] hours after publication by the plaintiff" (*Justice Holmes*). **Interdict** implies prohibition by authority, usually civil or ecclesiastical authority, commonly for a given time and for a salutary purpose, such as the maintenance of neutrality, the prevention of the spread of disease, or as an exemplary punishment; as, to *interdict* trade with belligerents; to *interdict* the importation of certain kinds of barberries in wheat-growing states; to *interdict* the administration of the sacraments in a rebellious diocese. "Sunday...until two o'clock, was a solemn interval, during which all the usual books and plays were *interdicted*" (*M. Austin*). **Inhibit,** in strict use, implies the imposition of restraints or restrictions that amount to prohibitions, not only by authority but also by the exigencies of the time or situation. "A clause was...inserted which *inhibited* the Bank from advancing money to the Crown without authority from Parliament" (*Macaulay*). "The peril that besets a highly gifted poetic nature, when at bad moments thought *inhibits* imagination" (*Lowes*). In modern psychological use *inhibit* suggests the restraints imposed by one's conscience, one's training, or one's philosophy, which cause one to suppress certain thoughts or desires before they can find full expression; as, "Stoicism teaches men...to *inhibit* the emotion of pity" (*Inge*). "He is *inhibited*, he *inhibits* himself, even from seeking on his own account that vital experience which is the stuff of the creative life" (*Van W. Brooks*). **Ban** carries with it an implication not only of civil or ecclesiastical prohibition, but a strong connotation of condemnation or disapproval; as, to *ban* all obscene magazines; to *ban* profane language.

Ana. Debar, rule out, *exclude: preclude, obviate, *prevent: *prevent, forestall.

Ant. Permit: bid. — ***Con.*** *Let, allow, suffer: *authorize, license: *approve, sanction, endorse: order, *command, enjoin.

force, *n.* **1** *Power, energy, strength, might, puissance, arm.

Ana. *Stress, strain, pressure, tension, shear, thrust, torsion: *speed, velocity, momentum, impetus, headway.

2 Force, violence, compulsion, coercion, duress, constraint, restraint, as here compared, denote the exercise or the exertion of power in order to impose one's will on a person or to have one's will with a thing. *Force* and *violence* regularly but not invariably apply to physical powers used upon either persons or things; *compulsion, coercion, duress, constraint, restraint* apply to either physical or moral power used upon personal agents only (except in certain figurative uses)—*compulsion, coercion,* and *duress* usually implying exercise of such power upon others than oneself, *constraint* or *restraint* upon oneself or others. **Force** (see POWER, 1) applies to any exercise of physical strength or of power comparable to physical strength by means of which an agent imposes his will upon another against that person's will or causes a thing to move as desired in spite of its resistance; as, "Rude fishermen... By *force* took Dromio" (*Shak.*); "To work in close design, by fraud or guile, What *force* effected not" (*Milton*); to move a huge boulder by main *force;* "the sceptical criticism that 'justice' is merely another name for *force*" (*G. L. Dickinson*). **Violence** is often used in place of *force*, then commonly implying an even greater display of power or fury and often connoting the infliction of injury or cruelty; as, "They will by *violence* tear him from your palace" (*Shak.*); "the rest of the party kept off the crowd by mingled persuasion and *violence*" (*Shaw*). As a result of the meaning of the term in law, and of other senses, *violence* often implies a violation of another's legal rights or property (thus, to enter a house by *violence* is to enter it as a burglar by breaking and forcing) or a profanation of someone or something entitled to respect, observance, security, or the like; as, "do *violence* to no man" (*Luke* iii. 14); "all these many and varied powers had been acquired without doing *violence* to republican sentiment" (*Buchan*); "The phrase 'every common carrier engaged in trade or commerce' may be construed to mean 'while engaged in trade or commerce' without *violence* to the habits of English speech" (*Justice Holmes*). **Compulsion** and, still more, **coercion** imply the application, usually by some active agent, of physical force or of moral pressure, or the exercise of one's authority in order to control the action of a voluntary agent and to make him obedient to one's will; as, "I would give no man a reason upon *compulsion*" (*Shak.*); *coercion* by threat or intimidation; "masterpieces I read under *compulsion* without the faintest interest" (*B. Russell*); "solutions forced upon a most practical mind by the stern *compulsion* of facts" (*Buchan*); "In the submissive way of one long accustomed to obey under *coercion*" (*Dickens*). **Duress,** which is chiefly a legal term, implies compulsion to do or forbear some act by means that are illegal, such as by imprisonment, or threats to imprison, or by some other form of violence. In more general use, however, *duress* implies compulsion or coercion through fear of a penalty that will or may be exacted; as, "Ordinary clergymen subscribe them [the Thirty-nine Articles] under *duress* because they cannot otherwise obtain ordination" (*Shaw*). **Constraint** and **restraint** may imply the exercise of physical or moral power either by an active agent or by the force of circumstances; *constraint* sometimes implies an urging or driving to action, but more frequently implies its forcible restriction or confinement, whereas *restraint* suggests its actual hindrance or curbing; as, "The...lion...roar'd With sharp *constraint* of hunger" (*Shak.*); "I will confess...without *constraint*" (*Shak.*); "Obligation [to do one's duty] is felt by the good man, whereas the bad one feels *constraint*" (*S. Alexander*); "Absolute liberty is absence of *restraint;* responsibility is *restraint;* therefore, the ideally free individual is responsible only to himself" (*H. Adams*); "The absence of exuberance on his part, and the *restraint* I put upon myself, lend an element of dignity to our intercourse" (*A. Repplier*); "The emotion...was the deeper and the sweeter for the *restraint* that he had put upon himself" (*Arch. Marshall*).

Ana. Intensity, vehemence (see corresponding adjectives at INTENSE): *effort, exertion, pains, trouble.

force, *v.* **Force, compel, coerce, constrain, oblige** agree in meaning to make a person or thing yield to the will of a person or to the strength or power of a thing. **Force,** the ordinary and most general word in this group, in all of its senses implies the exertion of strength, typically physical strength, or the working of something analogous in moving power or effectiveness to such strength, such as natural or logical necessity. Usually, the verb is followed by an infinitive, such as *to do, to move, to go,* or *to act,* or by a prepositional phrase introduced by *into, to, from, through, out, upon,* or the like; as, to *force* slaves to labor; to *force* food upon a child; he said hunger *forced* him to steal the food; his conscience *forced* him into repaying what he had stolen; to *force* oneself to smile; the man could not be *forced* from the position he had taken. Sometimes, however, the term takes a simple object, naming only the person forced or the thing brought about by force: then the verb carries additional implications which are often apparent only to those who know its idiomatic use in the particular phrase; thus, to *force* a woman is to rape her; to *force* a door is to break it open; to *force* laughter (or a smile or tears, etc.) is to make oneself laugh (or smile or cry, etc.) against one's will; to *force* bulbs is to hasten their development by artificial means; to *force* a word is to make it carry more significance than it can bear by reason of its accepted meaning; so, *forced* language; a *forced* style. **Compel** differs from *force* chiefly in typically requiring a personal object: any other type of object such as a reaction or response (as, she always *compels* admiration; an argument that *compels* assent) or a concrete thing (as, "such a breeze *Compell'd* thy canvas"—*Tennyson*) is possible only in figurative or poetic language when the specific connotations of *compel,* such as the exertion of irresistible power or force or a victory over resistance, are to be carried by the verb. In its typical use, *compel* commonly implies the exercise of authority, the exertion of great effort or driving force, or the impossibility for one reason or another of doing anything else; as, "[They] submit because they are *compelled;* but they would resist, and finally resist effectively, if they were not cowards" (*Shaw*); "We see nothing in the Constitution that *compels* the Government to sit by while a food supply is cut off and the protectors of our forest and our crops are destroyed" (*Justice Holmes*); "There is no possible method of *compelling* a child to feel sympathy or affection" (*B. Russell*); "The westering sun at length *compelled* me to quit the wood" (*Hudson*). **Coerce** suggests far more severity in the methods employed than *compel* does: commonly it connotes the exertion of violence or duress, or the use of means such as threats, intimidation, and the like; as, "There are more ways of *coercing* a man than by pointing a gun at his head" (*Inge*); "Charles the First signed his own death warrant when he undertook to *coerce* that stubborn will [of Londoners]" (*A. Repplier*). **Constrain** (etymologically, to draw tight) stresses far more than does *compel,* its closest synonym, the force exerted by that which presses or binds: it usually suggests the influence of restrictions, self-imposed or placed upon one by force, by nature, by necessity, by circumstances, or the like, that compel one to do a stated or implied thing, live a stated or implied way, think certain thoughts, or the like; as, "the love of Christ *constraineth* us" (*2 Corinthians* v. 14); "I describe everything exactly as it took place, *constraining* my mind not to wander from the task" (*Dickens*); "causes which he loathed in his heart but which he was *constrained* to consider just" (*Van W. Brooks*); "tied him to the wall, where he was *constrained* to stay till a kind passer-by released him" (*Galsworthy*). **Oblige** usually implies the constraint of necessity, sometimes physical necessity (as, "a sharp pain *obliged* him to close his eyelids quickly"—*Hardy*), but equally often moral or intellectual necessity (as, he is *obliged,* in conscience, to undo the harm he has done to a man's good name; "Even the so-called laws of nature are only instruments to be used....we are not *obliged* to believe them"—*Inge*). The term also is used with reference to any person or thing which is regarded as authoritative, or as having the right to determine one's course or acts; as, "the discipline of their great School... *obliges* them to bring up a weekly essay to their tutor" (*Quiller-Couch*); "the convention which *obliged* a satirist to be scathing" (*Inge*).

Ana. Impel, drive, *move: *command, order, enjoin: exact, *demand, require.

forceful. *Powerful, potent, forcible, puissant.

Ana. Compelling, constraining (see FORCE, *v.*): virile, manful (see MALE): cogent, telling, convincing (see VALID): *effective, efficient.

Ant. Feeble. — ***Con.*** *Weak, infirm, decrepit, frail.

forcible. Forceful, *powerful, potent, puissant.

Ana. Vehement, *intense: energetic, strenuous, *vigorous: *aggressive, militant, assertive, self-assertive: coercing *or* coercive (see corresponding verb at FORCE).

forebear *or* **forbear.** Forefather, progenitor, *ancestor.

forebode. Portend, presage, augur, prognosticate, *foretell, predict, forecast, prophesy.

Ana. Betoken, bespeak, *indicate: import, signify (see MEAN): fear, dread (see corresponding nouns at FEAR).

foreboding, *n.* Misgiving, presentiment, *apprehension.

Ana. *Foretoken, presage, omen, portent, augury, prognostic: forewarning, warning (see WARN).

forecast, *v.* Predict, *foretell, prophesy, prognosticate, augur, presage, portend, forebode.

Ana. *Foresee, foreknow, anticipate, apprehend, divine: surmise, *conjecture, guess: *infer, gather, conclude.

forefather. Forebear, progenitor, *ancestor.

forego. Variant of FORGO.

foregoing, *adj.* Antecedent, *preceding, precedent, previous, prior, former, anterior.

Ant. Following.

foreign. Alien, extraneous, *extrinsic.

Ana. External, outside, *outer: *inconsonant, inconsistent, incongruous, incompatible: *repugnant, repellent, obnoxious, distasteful: adventitious, *accidental.

Ant. Germane. — ***Con.*** *Relevant, pertinent, material, apposite, apropos, applicable: akin, alike, homogeneous, uniform (see SIMILAR).

foreigner. Alien, *stranger, outlander, outsider, immigrant, émigré.

foreknow. Divine, *foresee, anticipate, apprehend.

Ana. *Foretell, predict, forecast, prophesy, prognosticate: *infer, gather, conclude.

foremost. Leading, *chief, principal, main, capital.

forensic, *n.* Debate, disputation, *argumentation, dialectic.

forerunner. **Forerunner, precursor, harbinger, herald** are synonymous terms only when they denote someone or something that comes before another person or thing and in some way indicates his (or its) future appearance. **Forerunner** literally denotes a messenger that runs before a king, prince, lord, or the like, to warn others of his approach; as, "There is a *forerunner* come from... the Prince of Morocco, who brings word the prince his master will be here to-night" (*Shak.*). In extended use, the term is applicable to anything that serves as a sign, presage, prognostic, or the like, of something to follow; as, a coma is often the *forerunner* of death; a black sky and a sudden squall are the usual *forerunners* of a thunderstorm. **Precursor** (etymologically, forerunner) in its earliest English use was applied to John the Baptist, who preceded Jesus and prepared the way for his teachings. The word therefore in very careful use commonly carries an implication of making ready or of paving the way for the success or accomplishments of another person or thing, rather than, as *forerunner*, serving as an announcement or prediction of what is to come; as, "the medieval sects which Dr. Rufus Jones describes as *precursors* of Quakerism" (*Inge*); "Kepler, more than any man, was the *precursor* of Newton" (*H. Ellis*); "it is important to realize that a long period of [scientific analysis]...was an essential *precursor* of the present period of synthesis which has been so fruitful of good to mankind" (*A. C. Morrison*). **Harbinger** literally denotes one who goes before, especially to provide lodgings for his lord or master; as, "I'll be myself the *harbinger* and make joyful The hearing of my wife with your approach" (*Shak.*). The term is now used chiefly in a figurative sense, sometimes applying to a person or thing that announces something which is coming and for which one must be prepared (as, "Make all our trumpets speak; give them all breath, Those clamorous *harbingers* of blood and death"—*Shak.*), sometimes applying to something which goes before to provide a place of rest (as, "Drawing near her death, she sent most pious thoughts as *harbingers* to heaven"—*Fuller*). **Herald** literally denotes one who makes a solemn and stately proclamation or announcement as of war or peace, the birth of an heir to the throne, or the like; in careful figurative use, it is applied only to something which similarly announces or proclaims; as, "It was the lark, the *herald* of the morn" (*Shak.*); "He [the cock] is the sun's brave *herald*, That, ringing his blithe horn, Calls round a world dew-pearled The heavenly airs of morn" (*K. Tynan*).

Ana. Anticipator (see corresponding verb at PREVENT): announcer *or* announcement, advertiser *or* advertisement (see corresponding verbs at DECLARE): portent, prognostic, omen, *foretoken, presage, augury: forewarning, warning (see WARN).

foresee. Foresee, foreknow, divine, apprehend, anticipate agree in meaning to know something will happen or come into existence in advance of its occurrence or advent or that something exists before it is manifested or expressed. **Foresee** apart from its context gives no hint of how this knowledge is derived, whether through presentiment, inspiration, one's ability to draw inferences, or the like. "It's certainly unwise to admit any sort of responsibility for our actions, whose consequences we are never able to *foresee*" (*Conrad*). "Nobody can *foresee* how the necessary restriction of the population will be effected" (*Shaw*). "[Lincoln] the kindly-earnest, brave, *foreseeing* man" (*J. R. Lowell*). **Foreknow** usually, but not invariably, implies supernatural powers or the assistance of supernatural powers, as through revelation. "If thou [ghost of Hamlet's father] art privy to thy country's fate, Which, happily, *foreknowing* may avoid, O, speak!" (*Shak.*). "They themselves decreed, Their own revolt, not I [God]. If I *foreknew*, *Foreknowledge* had no influence on their fault" (*Milton*). **Divine,** as here compared, is not always clearly distinguishable from *foresee*, but it often suggests a gift or a special power, or sometimes unusual sagacity or discernment. "To Rima has been given this quickness of mind and power to *divine* distant things" (*Hudson*). "In all the years of his traveling to and fro through Europe he [Mark Twain] *divined* hardly one of the social tendencies that had so spectacular a dénouement within four years of his death" (*Van W. Brooks*). **Apprehend** conveys less of a sense of the certainty of that which is foreseen than any of the preceding words, but it carries a far stronger implication of the emotional effects of advance knowledge. In general, where one *apprehends* an evil, one is filled with fear, anxiety, or dread. "They agree with me in *apprehending* that this false step in one daughter will be injurious to the fortunes of all the others" (*Austen*). "Almost every evening he saw Lucy. The inexperienced little wife *apprehended* no harm in his visits" (*Meredith*). **Anticipate** is a far more complex term than any of its synonyms. Thus, a critic may *foresee* the verdict of posterity on a literary work, but he *anticipates* it only when he formulates a judgment which is either accepted by posterity or is pronounced by it as though the verdict were new. One may *foreknow* one's destiny or *apprehend* a danger, but one *anticipates* one's destiny or a danger only when, through the appropriate advance enjoyment or suffering, one also has a foretaste of that destiny or that danger. One may *divine* a friend's wish in advance of its expression, but one *anticipates* it only when one also gratifies it in advance of its expression. The use of *anticipate* as an alternative to *expect* is not generally approved; its use in the sense of to look forward to (something expected) with a foretaste of the pleasure or pain it promises is, on the other hand, generally countenanced. "'Pleasure not known beforehand is half wasted; to *anticipate* it is to double it'" (*Hardy*).

Ana. Forecast, predict, *foretell, prophesy, prognosticate: perceive, discern, descry, espy (see SEE).

foreshore. Beach, strand, *shore, ripa, coast, littoral.

foresight. Forethought, providence, discretion, *prudence.

Ana. Sagacity, perspicacity, shrewdness, astuteness (see corresponding adjectives at SHREWD): acumen, clairvoyance, *discernment, divination, perception.

Ant. Hindsight.

foresighted. Forethoughted, provident, discreet, prudent. See under PRUDENCE.

Ana. Sagacious, perspicacious, *shrewd, astute: *intelligent, alert, quick-witted, brilliant, knowing: *wise, judicious, sage, sapient.

Ant. Hindsighted.

forestall. *Prevent, anticipate.

Ana. Ward off, avert, *prevent, preclude, obviate: *frustrate, thwart, foil, circumvent.

Con. Court, woo, *invite: further, forward, *advance, promote.

foretaste, *n.* Anticipation, *prospect, outlook.

Ana. Realization, actualization (see corresponding verbs at REALIZE): token, earnest, *pledge: presentiment, foreboding (see APPREHENSION).

Con. Fruition, enjoyment (see PLEASURE): attainment, achievement (see corresponding verbs at REACH).

foretell. Foretell, predict, forecast, prophesy, prognosticate, augur, presage, portend, forebode agree in meaning to tell something before it happens through special knowledge or occult power. **Foretell** and **predict** are frequently interchangeable; but *foretell* stresses the announcement of coming events and does not, apart from a context, indicate the nature of the agent's power or the source of his information. "Some sorcerer...had *foretold*, dying, that none of all our blood should know the shadow from the substance" (*Tennyson*). "The marvelous exactness by which eclipses are *foretold*" (*Karl K. Darrow*). *Predict* now commonly implies inference from facts or accepted laws of nature; it often connotes scientific accuracy in foretelling; as, "Mr. Brooke's conclusions were as difficult to *predict* as the weather" (*G. Eliot*); an astronomer *predicts* the return of a comet. "The infant...has need of reassurance, and it will be happier if everything...seems to happen according to invariable laws, so as to be *predictable*" (*B. Russell*). **Forecast,** in its older and now uncommon sense, implies taking forethought of the future as by anticipation, conjecture of possible eventualities, provision for one's needs, and the like. "Seeking me, who then Safe to the rock of Etham was retired— Not flying, but *forecasting* in what place To set upon them" (*Milton*). "A prudent builder should *forecast* How long the stuff is like to last" (*Swift*). In current use, it implies prediction, but it still retains the implication of anticipated eventualities; as, to *forecast* the weather; since hurricanes have been *forecast*, losses in life and property have dwindled. **Prophesy,** as here compared, either connotes inspired or mystic knowledge or implies great assurance in prediction; as, "ancestral voices *prophesying* war" (*Coleridge*); "Wrinkled benchers often talked of him approvingly, and *prophesied* his rise" (*Tennyson*). **Prognosticate** implies prediction based upon signs or symptoms; as, a skillful physician can *prognosticate* the course of most diseases. "For the last three hundred years the relation of Church to State has been constantly undergoing change....I am not concerned with *prognosticating* their future relations" (*T. S. Eliot*). *Prognosticate* and all the yet undiscriminated words of this group also come into comparison in a second sense, that of to betoken or foreshow future events or conditions. "Everything seems to *prognosticate* a hard winter" (*W. Cobbett*). **Augur,** in its strict sense, implies divination by an *augur*, an official diviner in ancient Rome, who, by interpreting signs and omens, especially those pertaining to the flight of birds, was able to announce whether conditions were favorable or unfavorable for a given project. In its extended sense, the word implies a divining or a foreshadowing of something pleasant or unpleasant, often but by no means invariably through interpretation of signs. "The morrow brought a very sober-looking morning...Catherine *augured* from it everything most favourable to her wishes" (*Austen*). "An unloved brother, of whom worse things had been *augured*" (*G. Eliot*). "Late had he heard, in prophet's dream, The fatal Ben-Shie's boding scream ... The thunderbolt had split the pine,— All *augured* ill to Alpine's line" (*Scott*). **Presage** and **portend** more often imply foreshowing than foretelling, though both senses are found. Both also, in precise use, suggest occult power or an ability to interpret signs and omens as a basis for prediction, but *presage* may be used of neutral or of favorable as well as unfavorable prognostications, whereas *portend* always suggests a threat of evil or disaster. "Lands he could measure, terms and tides *presage*" (*Goldsmith*). "The yellow and vapoury sunset...had *presaged* change" (*Hardy*). "Some great misfortune to *portend*, No enemy can match a friend" (*Swift*). "Had it not been written... that his sign in the high heavens *portended* war?" (*Kipling*). **Forebode** implies unfavorable prognostication based upon premonitions, presentiments, dreams, or the like; as, "His heart *forebodes* a mystery" (*Tennyson*); he was oppressed by a *foreboding* of evil.

Ana. Divine, foreknow, *foresee, anticipate, apprehend: announce, *declare, proclaim: *reveal, divulge, disclose, discover: forewarn, *warn.

forethought. Foresight, providence, discretion, *prudence.

Ana. Premeditatedness *or* premeditation, deliberateness *or* deliberation (see corresponding verbs at DELIBERATE): wisdom, judgment, *sense, gumption.

forethoughted. Foresighted, provident, discreet, prudent. See under PRUDENCE.

Ana. *Cautious, circumspect, wary, calculating: *deliberate, premeditated, considered, advised, studied.

foretoken, *n.* **Foretoken, presage, prognostic, omen, augury, portent** are here compared as meaning an event, a phenomenon, a condition, or the like, that serves as a sign of future happenings. **Foretoken,** the general term, is applicable to anything observable which may be the basis of a prediction or forecast; as, the usual *foretokens* of a thunder storm, intense sultriness, a heavily overcast sky, and suddenly arising winds; in June, 1914, there were few *foretokens* of war. **Presage** is applied chiefly to foretokens which inspire emotions such as fear or hope, dread or longing, confidence or despair, or the like, and therefore give rise to presentiments rather than serve as a basis for prediction. "Three times, while crossing the ocean, he sees a lunar rainbow, and each time he takes it as a *presage* of good fortune" (*Van W. Brooks*). **Prognostic** applies to any advance indication or symptom from which a skilled person can infer what is coming; it is now much used in medicine of any symptom useful to a physician in predicting the course or the termination of an illness. "*Prognostics* do not always prove prophecies, at least the wisest prophets make sure of the event first" (*Walpole*). "*Prognostics* are those circumstances on which a prognosis is based" (*A. Flint*). **Omen** is applicable chiefly to any extraordinary event or circumstance which one feels, especially under the influence of superstition, to be a promise of something to come. "Nay I have had some *omens:* I got out of bed backwards too this morning, without premeditation; pretty good that too; but then I stumbled coming down stairs, and met a weasel; bad *omens* those: some bad, some good, our lives are checquer'd" (*Congreve*). Consequently, an event of ill *omen* or of good *omen* is one that is felt to be a presage of ill or of good. **Augury** and *omen* are often interchangeable but *augury* is applicable to ordinary as well as to phenomenal circumstances, and it usually suggests discernment rather than superstition in determining whether it presages good or evil; as, achievements that he regarded as *auguries* (not *omens*) of a successful career for his son; a black cat crossing her path was to her a fearful *omen* (not *augury*). "I had felt there was a mysterious meaning in that moment, and in that flight of dim-seen birds an *augury* of ill-*omen* for my life" (*L. P. Smith*). **Portent** is applicable chiefly to prodigies or marvels such as an eclipse, a comet, an earthquake, or something comparable, which are interpreted as forewarnings or supernatural intimations of evil to come. "What plagues and what *portents!* what mutiny! What raging of the sea! shaking of earth! Commotion in the winds!" (*Shak.*). "Why gnaw you [Othello] so your nether lip? Some bloody passion shakes your very frame: These are *portents;* but yet I [Desdemona] hope, I hope, They do not point on me" (*Shak.*).

Ana. *Sign, symptom, token, mark, badge, note: *forerunner, harbinger, precursor, herald.

forever *or* **for ever. Forever** (*or*, *Brit.*, **for ever**), **ever, always, aye, evermore, forevermore** (*or*, *Brit.*, **for evermore**) agree in meaning for all time. They are often used interchangeably without loss, but when a nice shade of meaning is to be expressed, there is usually a first choice. When one wishes a term that means perpetually or eternally and without intermission, **forever** is the precise choice; as, I shall think of you *forever* with affection. "*For ever* piping songs *for ever* new" (*Keats*). *Forever* also, in ironic use, can imply, as *perpetually* and *eternally* often do, incessancy or persistency; as, these children are *forever* asking questions. When one wishes a word that means invariably and in every instance, past, present, or future, **ever,** though often regarded as archaic, is the explicit term; as, ostracism is *ever* the consequence of defiance of the proprieties; traitors are *ever* without honor in their own country. When one wishes to imply intermission yet perpetual recurrence, **always** is the proper choice; as, I shall *always* (not *forever* or *ever*) think of you when I return to this place; he is *always* disappointed when he counts confidently on success. **Aye** is archaic and dialectal, usually for *always*, but sometimes for *forever*. "And *ay* the ale was growing better" (*Burns*). When a word, especially an emphatic poetic or literary word, is sought to imply eternity, especially with reference to the future, **evermore** or **forevermore** meets one's needs; as, he will *evermore* regret the course he took; he will be happy *forevermore*. *Evermore* is more often found in quasi-substantive use in the phrase *for evermore*, which equals *forevermore*. "And, little town, thy streets *for evermore* Will silent be" (*Keats*).

forevermore *or, Brit.*, **for evermore.** Evermore, *forever, ever, always, aye.

forewarn. *Warn, caution.

Ana. Notify, advise, apprise, *inform: admonish (see REPROVE): advise, counsel (see under ADVICE).

foreword. Preface, prolegomenon, proem, exordium, *introduction, prologue, prelude, overture, preamble, prolusion, protasis, avant-propos.

forge, *v.* Fabricate, fashion, manufacture, form, shape, *make.

Ana. *Beat, pound: produce, turn out (see BEAR): counterfeit, simulate (see ASSUME): *copy, imitate.

forget. Overlook, ignore, disregard, *neglect, omit, slight.

Ant. Remember. — *Con.* Recollect, recall, bethink, mind (see REMEMBER).

forgetful. **Forgetful, oblivious, unmindful** come into comparison as meaning losing or letting go from one's mind something once known or learned. **Forgetful** usually implies a propensity not to remember, or a defective memory; as, "Bear with me, good boy, I am much *forgetful*" (*Shak.*); she is growing *forgetful*. Sometimes, however, it implies a not keeping in mind something which should be remembered: it then connotes negligence or heedlessness rather than a poor memory; as, one should not be *forgetful* of his social obligations; "Be not *forgetful* to entertain strangers" (*Hebrews* xiii. 2). **Oblivious** in careful use stresses forgetfulness, but it rarely suggests a poor memory. Rather, it suggests a failure to remember, either because one has been robbed of remembrance by conditions beyond one's control (as, the accident rendered him for a few hours *oblivious* of all that weighed upon his mind), or because one has deliberately put something out of one's mind (as, a government *oblivious* of the rights of the governed), or because one has considered something too slight or trivial to note and remember it (as, a people so long unused to aggression as to be *oblivious* of its dangers). In looser use, often regarded as erroneous use, *oblivious* is employed without a clear connotation of forgetfulness, and in a sense close to *unconscious, unaware, insensible,* and the like; as, walking along whistling, *oblivious* of the passing crowds; "*oblivious* of the laws and conditions of trespass" (*Meredith*). *Oblivious* is sometimes used attributively and without a succeeding *of* or *to* in the sense of causing oblivion; as, "She lay in deep, *oblivious* slumber" (*Longfellow*). **Unmindful** is a close synonym of *forgetful* in the sense of not keeping in mind, but it may imply a deliberate consignment to oblivion as well as inattention, heedlessness, or negligence; as, a mother, solicitous of the health of every member of her family, but *unmindful* of her own; "Every person was willing to save himself, *unmindful* of others" (*Goldsmith*); "For at her silver voice came Death and Life, *Unmindful* each of their accustomed strife" (*Shelley*).

Ana. Remiss, *negligent, neglectful, lax, slack: heedless, thoughtless, *careless.

Con. Conscious, *aware, cognizant, sensible, alive, awake: *thoughtful, considerate, attentive.

forgive. Pardon, remit, *excuse, condone.

Ana. Absolve, *exculpate, acquit, exonerate, vindicate: *confess, shrive, absolve, remit.

forgo, *also* **forego.** **Forgo** (*or* **forego**), **forbear, abnegate, eschew, sacrifice** come into comparison when they denote to deny oneself something for the sake of an end. One **forgoes** for the sake of policy, expediency, the welfare of others, or the like, something already enjoyed or indulged in, or within reach. "He agreed...to *forgo* all remuneration until his apprenticeship was completed" (*Van W. Brooks*). Often it implies surrender or abandonment. "By substituting rhythm alone for the fusion of rhythm and metre in one, it [free verse] has *foregone* the great harmonic, orchestral effects of the older verse" (*Lowes*). One **forbears,** through motives of prudence, charity, or the like, doing or saying something one wishes to do or say. *Forbear* usually implies self-restraint. "Although...I do not get much help from general propositions in a case of this sort, I cannot *forbear* quoting what seems to me applicable here" (*Justice Holmes*). One **abnegates** what is intrinsically good but not consistent with one's aims, principles, or limitations. "To treat English poetry [in teaching literature] as though it had died with Tennyson...is to *abnegate* high hope for the sake of a barren convenience" (*Quiller-Couch*). In its narrower and more common signification, *abnegate* implies renunciation or self-effacement, but this distinction is not as commonly maintained in the verb as in the derivative noun *abnegation*. One **eschews** (as here compared: see ESCAPE, 2) something tempting, formerly because it was to be avoided on moral or aesthetic grounds, but now, more often, because abstention or self-restraint is necessary for the achievement of a more significant desire or end. "To work within these strict limits, *eschewing* all the helps to illusion that modelling and shadow give, was doubtless an exercise of incomparable service to the artist" (*Binyon*). One **sacrifices** something highly desirable, or in itself of great value, for the sake of a person, ideal, or end dearer to one than the thing (sometimes person) involved: the term typically, but not invariably, connotes renunciation and self-denial and a religious or ethical motive comparable to that of self-immolation; as, to *sacrifice* a college education for the sake of supporting one's mother; to *sacrifice* one's life in defense of one's country. "I do not mean that the well-to-do should...*forego* educational opportunities which...are not open to all. To do that would be to *sacrifice* civilization to justice" (*B. Russell*).

Ana. Waive, *relinquish, surrender, abandon: renounce, resign, *abdicate.

forlorn. **1** Lorn, lone, desolate, lonesome, lonely, *alone, solitary.

Ana. Separated, parted, divorced, severed, sundered (see SEPARATE, *v.*): forsaken, deserted, abandoned (see ABANDON, *v.*): wretched, *miserable: depressed, weighed down, oppressed (see DEPRESS).

2 Hopeless, *despondent, despairing, desperate.

Ana. Pessimistic, *cynical: *futile, vain, fruitless.

Con. *Elastic, resilient, buoyant, expansive, volatile: *elated, elate, exultant: optimistic, *hopeful, roseate, rose-colored.

forlornness. Hopelessness, despondency, despair, desperation. See under DESPONDENT.

Ana. Dejection, depression, gloom, melancholy, blues, dumps, *sadness.

form, *n.* **1** **Form, figure, shape, conformation, configuration, Gestalt** come into comparison when they denote the disposition or arrangement of content that gives a particular aspect or appearance to a thing as distinguished from the substance of which that thing is made.

Form is not only the most widely applicable of these terms, but it is also the least definitely fixed in its meaning, largely because of its being assigned various denotations in philosophy and aesthetics and because of its frequent use in reference to literature, music, and thought, where more is involved than the disposition or arrangement of content as perceived by the senses. In general, however, *form* more than any of the other words implies reference to internal structure and disposition of details as well as to boundary lines, and suggests unity in the whole; as, "The earth was without *form*, and void" (*Genesis* i. 2); "In a perfect example of either art [painting or poetry] this subject-matter is fused with the *form*, so that we cannot dissolve them from one another" (*Binyon*); "You might go in for building....you've got a feeling for *form*" (*M. Austin*). **Figure,** as here compared, applies usually to the form as determined by the lines which bound or enclose a thing (as, "Flowers have all exquisite *figures*"—*Bacon;* the woman has a beautiful *figure*); in current use, however, the term usually suggests the lines (sometimes the visible form) characteristic of the kind, type, or species (as, to paint Christ under the *figure* of a lamb; because of the darkness it was hard to say whether the person had the *figure* of a man or of a woman) or the lines which follow a more or less conventional pattern rather than represent something actual (as, to cut *figures* on the ice in skating; to decorate the border with *figures* of scrolls, circles, crescents, and the like; a rug design in geometrical *figures*). **Shape,** like *figure,* suggests reference to the boundary lines, but it carries a stronger implication of a mass or of a body than does *figure* and is therefore precisely applicable only to that which is shown in its bulk rather than in its lines; thus, one draws the *figure* (not *shape*) of a circle or a triangle, but one forms a mass of clay in the *shape* (better than *figure*) of a ball or of a man; "the colour of his beard, the *shape* of his leg" (*Shak.*). Often, but not invariably, *shape* applies to the outlines that have been given to a mass as by molding, carving, pressure, or the like; as, "Brooke is a very good fellow, but pulpy; he will run into any mould, but he won't keep *shape*" (*G. Eliot*); "It is the business of the sensitive artist in life to accept his own nature as it is, not to try to force it into another *shape*" (*A. Huxley*). *Form, figure,* and *shape* are also used in reference to the bodies of living creatures, especially of men and women. *Form* is perhaps the most shadowy of these terms: it is applied chiefly to persons or animals identified but not clearly seen or noted in detail; as, "the reddleman watched his *form* as it diminished to a speck on the road" (*Hardy*); "busy *forms* bent over intolerable tasks, whizzing wheels, dark gleaming machinery" (*A. C. Benson*). *Figure* usually suggests closer vision than *form* and some perception of details, but stresses lines, carriage, posture, or the like; as, "here and there a *figure*...leaned on the rail" (*Conrad*); "they watched her white *figure* drifting along the edge of the grove" (*Cather*). *Shape* differs little from *figure* except in its clearer suggestion of flesh and body; as, "Some human *shapes* appearing mysteriously, as if they had sprung up from the dark ground" (*Conrad*); "And the shade under the ash-trees became deserted, save by the tall dark *figure* of a man, and a woman's white *shape*" (*Galsworthy*). **Conformation** stresses the structure of something composed or fashioned of a number of related or carefully adjusted parts: it carries only a slight suggestion of reference to the outer lines or shape; as, the *conformation* of the vocal organs; the *conformation* of the engine is most intricate. **Configuration** emphasizes the disposition or arrangement of parts that are different in size, elevation, shape, and the like, especially over an extent of space or territory; thus, the *configuration* of a county is represented in a relief map of that county; "the remarkable *configuration* of the Atlantic sea-bed" (*T. H. Huxley*); "in every province there was a network of roads following the *configuration* of the country" (*Buchan*). *Configuration* is also used as a translation of the German term **Gestalt,** literally, a form which derives its significance not from the various and varying parts or elements which comprise it, but from the pattern they assume when combined so as to be interrelated and integrated. The term is used chiefly in psychology, in reference to physical, biological, and psychological phenomena which affect or manifest the psychical life of the individual; thus, a man's personality may be studied as a *Gestalt*.

Ana. Contour, *outline, profile, silhouette: *structure, anatomy, framework, skeleton: organism, *system, economy, scheme.

2 Form, formality, ceremony, ceremonial, rite, ritual, liturgy come into comparison when they mean an established or fixed method of procedure, especially as enjoined by law, the customs of social intercourse, the church, or the like. **Form** is the comprehensive term applicable to any recognized way of doing things in accordance with rule or prescription; as, the *forms* of polite society; in due *form;* "the occasional exercise of a beautiful *form* of worship" (*Irving*). *Form* often implies show without substance or suggests an outward shell devoid of its life, or spirit; as, "The rest... Will deem in...specious *forms* Religion satisfied" (*Milton*). "For who would keep an ancient *form* Thro' which the spirit breathes no more?" (*Tennyson*). **Formality** applies narrowly only to some procedure required by law, custom, etiquette, or the like, that is more or less conventional or perfunctory in its character. "There was now and then the *formality* of saying a lesson" (*Lamb*). "Mr. Critchlow entered without any *formalities,* as usual" (*Bennett*). The term often implies endless details or red tape. "Outland was delayed by the *formalities* of securing his patent" (*Cather*). **Ceremony** is more specific than *form,* and implies certain outward acts, usually of an impressive or dignified character, associated with some religious, public, or state occasion, or, collectively, with a church, a court, or the like; as, the marriage *ceremony;* the *ceremonies* attending the coronation of a king. *Ceremony* also applies to the conventional usages of civility; as, "The appurtenance of welcome is...*ceremony*" (*Shak.*); to stand on *ceremony.* "The beauty of an inherited courtesy of manners, of a thousand little *ceremonies* flowering out of the most ordinary relations and observances of life" (*Binyon*). **Ceremonial** is occasionally used in place of *ceremony* in its concrete applications; in very precise use, however, it is a collective noun applied to an entire system of ceremonies prescribed by a court, a church, or the like. "The gorgeous *ceremonial* of the Burgundian court" (*Prescott*). The last three terms of this group refer primarily to religious ceremonies, and only secondarily, or in somewhat loose use, to the ceremonies or forms of civil life. Strictly, a **rite** is the form prescribed by a church or other organization (such as that of Freemasons) for conducting one of its ceremonies or, in the case of a church, for administering one of its sacraments, giving not only the words to be uttered, but the acts to be performed; as, the marriage *rite* of the Church of England; the *rite* for the ordination of priests; the *rite* of initiation; Jewish funeral *rites.* Strictly, **ritual** is, in effect, a collective noun applied either to all the rites that make up an elaborate religious service or to all the rites or all the ceremonies of a particular church, religion, or organization; it is, however, applicable to a rite when that represents the one form in use in the specific religion or body; as, the *ritual* of the Roman Catholic Church is in Latin except in certain Uniat churches; sacrifices, dances, mimetic games, processions, and the like, formed part of the *ritual* of primitive and polytheistic religions; the *ritual* of Freemasonry. Consequently, in extended use, *rite* and *ritual* both refer to the customary or established order of procedure for conducting not only a ceremony of any sort or a series of ceremonial acts, but formalities or forms of any kind. "On Saturday [he] went conscientiously through all the *rites* appertaining to a week-end at Highbank" (*E. Wharton*). "He knew well enough how it would be at the Hondo; the black-shawled women sitting against the wall, the *ritual* of bereavement, impressive in its poverty" (*M. Austin*). **Liturgy** (etymologically, the public worship of God) in historical and still current use applies to the Eucharistic service, especially that of the Orthodox and the Uniat churches (specifically called "Divine *Liturgy*" in many of these) and of the Roman Catholic Church (specifically called the "Mass" in the Latin Church). In the Anglican Communion, *liturgy* applies to the Book of Common Prayer, the service book of that church. In looser use, it is applied to any strictly religious rite or ritual, but this is confusing because *rite* and *ritual* stress the form to be followed and *liturgy* the complete service as followed in a given church; thus, the Roman *rite* is now generally followed in the *liturgy* of that branch of the Roman Catholic Church called the Latin Church. "He [Henry VIII] insisted on...the maintenance of full *ritual* in the *liturgy*" (*Belloc*).

Ana. Proceeding, procedure, *process: practice, usage, custom, *habit: rule, regulation, precept, *law, canon: *method, mode: *decorum, propriety, etiquette.

3 Form, usage, convention, convenance are here compared in one of their senses. For they are synonyms only when they mean a set or accepted way of doing (sometimes of saying or expressing) something. **Form** is the most widely applicable of these words. It may be used in reference to a mode of behavior, a method of procedure, or a technique, prescribed or approved as correct; as, to teach *form* in swimming or dancing. "Mr. Collins made his declaration [of love] in *form*" (*Austen*). It is referable to any sphere of activity where correctness or uniformity of method or manner is held essential, as in the arts, in worship, in society, and the like; as, a well-bred person knows the *forms* of social intercourse. In extended use, *form* often denotes manner or style as tested by the prescribed or approved form; as, his *form* in swimming is excellent. "Nothing could be worse '*form*'...than any display of temper in a public place" (*E. Wharton*). Sometimes it implies rigidity or lack of spontaneity; as, given to *forms* and ceremonies: sometimes it suggests superficiality, insincerity, or emptiness, and is opposed to *spirit* or *essence;* as, his apology was a mere *form* of words. **Usage** implies the sanction of precedent or tradition rather than authority; it is often used to designate a form preserved because it gives distinction or honor to a class, a profession, or the like; as, to follow the *usages* of the Church of England. "[He] bowed to social *usage*, dressed the dress, And decorated to the fit degree His person" (*Browning*). **Convention** is often used in place of *form*, especially in reference to social behavior. The lines of demarcation between these words are not always clear in use, but they can be clearly drawn if attention is centered on the primary implication in *convention:* namely, agreement, usually tacit agreement. In its most general significance, a *convention* is any set way of doing or expressing a thing that is accepted generally and without question; as, the plus and minus signs are *conventions* of arithmetic; the lifting of the hat in greeting to a lady is a modern social *convention*. Sometimes even principles, rules, or laws are called *conventions* when the writer wishes to emphasize the point that their sanction lies in their universal acceptance and not in their rational validity. However, in practical affairs, a *convention* is usually a practice or a device that is universally accepted as an easy, useful, or expedient means to an end. In many cases, conventions may be artificial or absurd, yet pass without question because generally accepted. Thus, the soliloquy was a *convention* of the drama until its truth to life was questioned; a room with three walls is a *convention* of the theater. **Convenance** (still usually regarded as a loan word and given a French pronunciation) is referred only to social conventions, especially to those which are regarded as essential to propriety or decorum; as, to observe the *convenances* of courtship.

form, *v.* *Make, shape, fashion, fabricate, manufacture, forge.

Ana. Devise, contrive (see corresponding nouns at DEVICE): *invent, create: produce, turn out (see BEAR): design, project, scheme, plan, plot (see under PLAN, *n.*): organize, *found, establish.

formal. Conventional, ceremonious, *ceremonial, solemn.

Ana. Systematic, methodical, *orderly, regular: *decorous, proper, comme il faut, seemly.

Ant. Informal.

formality. *Form, ceremony, ceremonial, rite, liturgy, ritual.

Ana. Convention, convenance, usage, *form: practice, custom, *habit, consuetude, use, wont.

former. Prior, previous, *preceding, antecedent, precedent, foregoing, anterior.

Ant. Latter. — ***Con.*** Following, succeeding, ensuing, supervening (see FOLLOW).

formidable. Formidable, redoubtable come into comparison as meaning of such a character as to inspire fear or awe. Both words are now often used humorously or ironically. That is **formidable** which strikes one as exceedingly difficult to meet, attack, resist, overthrow, or the like, and therefore arouses apprehensions of defeat or failure or a sense of helplessness; as, a *formidable* fortress or battleship; a *formidable* opponent; a *formidable* undertaking, requiring experience, skill, and tenacity; "He owed a good deal in the town, but his debts of honour were still more *formidable*" (*Austen*); "The naturalist arguments against a spiritualistic interpretation of nature are certainly *formidable*" (*Inge*). In lighter use, *formidable* is applied to persons or things that strike one aghast by their size, elaborateness, power, fixity, or the like; as, a *formidable* dowager looking at him through her lorgnette; "those *formidable* editions of the later Renaissance, where a slender rivulet of text is almost lost in the wide expanse of commentary" (*Babbitt*). That is **redoubtable** which fills one with fear, dread, awe, deep respect or, by comparison, with a sense of one's own insignificance or powerlessness; as, "Revers'd that spear, *redoubtable* in war" (*Burns*); "Master of mine, learned, *redoubtable*" (*Browning*). In lighter use, *redoubtable* usually carries a stronger suggestion of irony than does *formidable*. "If history belie not this *redoubtable* Swede, he was a rival worthy of the windy and inflated commander of Fort Casimir...'weighing upwards of four hundred pounds,' a huge feeder, and bouser in proportion" (*Irving*).

Ana. *Fearful, awful, terrible, dreadful: threatening, menacing (see THREATEN): indomitable, *invincible, unconquerable: intrepid, dauntless, doughty (see BRAVE).

Ant. Contemptible.

formless. **Formless, unformed, shapeless, chaotic, inchoate, amorphous** are comparable when they mean having no definite or recognizable form. That is **formless** which is so fluid or so shifting in its outlines, structure, or character that it does not assume, or is incapable of assuming, a fixed or determinate form; as, "The rising World of waters... Won from the void and *formless* Infinite" (*Milton*); "Sprang from the billows of the *formless* flood" (*Shelley*); a *formless* fear. That is **unformed** which (as here compared) has existence but has not yet attained the form or character proper to it when it has reached the height of its possible growth or development; as, an *unformed* girl of twelve; an *unformed* mind; an *unformed* genius. Oftentimes it suggests crudeness or callousness. "Very clever in some ways—and very *unformed*—childish almost—in others" (*Mrs. H. Ward*). That is **shapeless** which lacks the clear-cut outline or contour that is regarded as proper to a thing or essential to its beauty; as, a *shapeless* old woman; to beat a silver dish into a *shapeless* mass. "The Iliad is a well-knit epic and the story of Beowulf a *shapeless* monstrosity" (*Quiller-Couch*).

The last three words of this group are not strictly synonyms, because their implications are very different; however, they (especially *chaotic* and *inchoate*) are sometimes confused, and in current use they roughly correspond respectively to *formless*, *unformed*, and *shapeless*. That is **chaotic** which is formless because it is unorganized and its constituent elements are not arranged so that each is clearly distinguishable and its relation to each of the others and to the whole clearly apparent. "[The hypothesis] that the present solar system gradually condensed into its present state from a *chaotic* mass of nebulous material" (*Tait & Stewart*). "The difference [between classicism and romanticism] seems to me rather the difference between the complete and the fragmentary, the adult and the immature, the orderly and the *chaotic*" (*T. S. Eliot*). That is **inchoate** which is unformed because it as yet exists only in its rudiments and awaits perfection, completeness, or fullness of realization. "This...act [the signature of a commission]...necessarily excludes the idea of its being, so far as respects the appointment, an *inchoate* and incomplete transaction" (*Ch. Just. Marshall*). "The undifferentiated, *inchoate* religious sense is thus intensified and fixed [by emotional or orgiastic worship], to the great and lasting injury of the spiritual life" (*Inge*). That is **amorphous** which is shapeless because it has or assumes no clearly or sharply defined outline or structure or because it presents no recognizable design or pattern; as, opals occur in *amorphous* masses. "The [political] groups were *amorphous*, without sharp edges" (*Galsworthy*). "Sentimentality is at its worst in verse, when emotion flows over a theme, vague, and hazy, and *amorphous*" (*Lowes*).

Ana. Fluid, *liquid: rough, raw, crude, *rude.

fornication. *Adultery, incest.

forsake. Desert, *abandon.

Ana. Repudiate, spurn, reject (see DECLINE): *abdicate, renounce, resign: quit, leave (see GO).

Ant. Return to: revert to.

forswear. **1** *Abjure, renounce, recant, retract.

Ana. *Abandon, desert, forsake: repudiate, spurn, reject (see DECLINE): *deny, contravene, traverse, gainsay.

2 *Perjure.

fort. **Fort, fortress, citadel, acropolis, stronghold, fastness** denote in common a structure or place offering resistance to a hostile force. A **fort** is an enclosed, fortified structure occupied by troops. A **fortress** is a large fort of strong construction intended for long-term occupancy, as on the border of a hostile country. A **citadel** (literally, "little city") is a fortification, usually one on an eminence, that protects a city or keeps it in subjection. **Acropolis** (literally, "upper city") is usually restricted to the elevated citadel of an ancient Greek city, particularly that of Athens. A **stronghold** is a strongly fortified place whose resistance to attack or siege affords protection to its occupants. "Here...a famous robber had his *stronghold*" (*L. Ritchie*). A **fastness** is a place whose inaccessibility or remoteness makes for security. It may or may not be fortified. "A strong and almost inaccessible *fastness*" (*H. H. Wilson*).

Fort, fortress, citadel, stronghold, fastness are often used figuratively. A **fort** is something that by its very nature resists attack. "Oft breaking down the pales and *forts* of reason" (*Shak.*). A **fortress** is something that gives a feeling of security. "My Rock and *Fortress* is the Lord" (*J. Wesley*). **Citadel** and **stronghold** are very similar in their figurative uses, both being applied to a place where (or, sometimes, to a class or group in which) something prevails or persists in spite of attacks or encroachment. "The very head quarters, the very *citadel* of smuggling, the Isle of Man" (*Burke*). "The scientific world has been the very *citadel* of stupidity and cruelty" (*Shaw*). "The South of Somersetshire, one of the *strong holds*...of the Anglo-Saxon dialect" (*J. Jennings*). **Fastness** characteristically suggests impenetrability or inaccessibility. "In the impregnable *fastness* of his great rich nature he [the Roman] defies us" (*J. R. Lowell*).

forth. Forward, *onward.

forthright, *adj.* **1** Also *adv.* **Forthright, downright** come into comparison because they agree in their basic sense of moving or in the habit of moving straight to the mark. **Forthright** (see also STRAIGHTFORWARD) applies to that which gets its effect by a straight thrust in front of one as if of a sword driven by the arm of one person into the breast of another: it therefore usually connotes dexterity, directness, straightforwardness, or a deadly effectiveness; as, "Reach the good man your hand, my girl: *forthright* from the shoulder, like a brave boxer" (*Meredith*); "the home thrust of a *forthright* word" (*J. R. Lowell*); "The practical, *forthright*, non-argumentative turn of his mind" (*F. W. Farrar*). **Downright,** on the other hand, suggests a falling down or descending with the straightness and swiftness of one who leaps from a cliff or of a weapon that delivers a crushing blow. The word, therefore, usually implies overwhelming force rather than dexterity, and concern for the effect produced rather than the point reached: often, in addition, when applied to persons or things it connotes plainness, bluntness, flatfootedness, or an out-and-out quality; as, "He... Shot to the black abyss, and plung'd *downright*" (*Pope*); "sculling against a swift current is work—*downright* work" (*Jefferies*); "'You seem a pretty... *downright* sort of a young woman'" (*Shaw*); "A baby. What a coarse, *downright* word for the little creature" (*R. Macaulay*).

Ana. *Bluff, blunt, brusque: candid, open, plain, *frank.

2 *Straightforward, aboveboard.

Ana. Honest, *upright, conscientious, just, honorable.

Ant. Furtive. — *Con.* *Secret, covert, stealthy, surreptitious, underhand: mendacious, *dishonest, untruthful, deceitful.

forthwith. Straightway, at once, *directly, immediately, instantly, instantaneously, anon, right away.

fortitude. **Fortitude, grit, backbone, pluck, guts, sand** agree in denoting a quality of character combining courage and staying power. **Fortitude** stresses strength of mind and firmness of purpose; it implies endurance, often prolonged endurance, of physical or mental hardships or suffering without giving way under the strain. "The man's courage is loved by the woman, whose *fortitude* again is coveted by the man" (*Coleridge*). "For years he led a life of unremitting physical toil and mental anxiety combined with miserable health—no small test of *fortitude*" (*Buchan*). **Grit** also implies strength and firmness of mind, but it stresses an incapacity for being downed by difficulties or hardships, and usually also suggests both a willingness to suffer privation and pain necessary to the attainment of one's ends and the fortitude to bear them; as, it is *grit* that tells in the long run. "Instances of men rising from the lower ranks of society into the most highly remunerated positions in the business world are sufficiently numerous to support the belief that brains and *grit* can always 'make good' " (*J. A. Hobson*). **Backbone** emphasizes resoluteness of character; it implies either the ability to stand up in the face of opposition for one's principles or one's chosen objectives, or determination and independence that require no support from without; as, in spite of all his gifts, he did not have the *backbone* necessary to a good statesman; when mob hysteria prevails, then if ever, *backbone* is needed in our legislators; "in Constance's opinion she lacked *backbone*, or *grit*, or independence of spirit" (*Bennett*). **Pluck** and **guts,** in the sense in which they are here considered, have a similar primary meaning; both literally denote the viscera, or entrails, of animals, but *pluck* is used especially of those that are edible, such as the heart, liver, and lungs, and *guts* of those that form the contents of the abdominal cavity, especially the stomach and the intestines. *Pluck*, in the derived sense, was first a prize fighter's word implying stoutness of heart and gameness in fighting, especially against odds. "If a fellow knows how to box, they always say he has science but no *pluck*. If he doesn't know his right hand from his left, they say that he isn't clever but that he is full of game" (*Shaw*). This implication of a willingness to fight or continue fighting against odds is found when the word is used with precision; thus, it is *pluck* that keeps a sick person at work; it is *pluck* that keeps soldiers from retreating in the face of disaster. "The energy, *fortitude*, and dogged perseverance that we technically style *pluck*" (*Lytton*). "Decay of English spirit, decay of manly *pluck*" (*Thackeray*). *Guts*, which is usually considered vulgar although expressive (therefore sometimes humorously replaced by *intestinal fortitude*), stresses possession of stamina or the physical and mental vigor essential both to facing that which repels or frightens one, and to stomaching, or putting up with, the hardships it imposes; as, he hasn't the *guts* to be a successful surgeon; they used men with *guts* for the East African missions. **Sand,** which is regarded as slang but not as vulgar, comes close to *grit* in its meaning, but since it often carries a suggestion of pluck or of the ability to fight against odds, it does not so strongly as *grit* connote triumph over difficulties. "No more pride than a tramp, no more *sand* than a rabbit" (*Twain*).

Ana. *Courage, mettle, spirit, resolution, tenacity: bravery, courageousness, intrepidity, dauntlessness, valorousness (see corresponding adjectives at BRAVE).

Ant. Pusillanimity. — *Con.* Cowardliness *or* cowardice, cravenness, poltroonery (see corresponding adjectives at COWARDLY): timidity, timorousness (see corresponding adjectives at TIMID).

fortress. *Fort, citadel, acropolis, stronghold, fastness.

fortuitous. *Accidental, contingent, casual, incidental, adventitious.

Ana. *Random, haphazard, chance, chancy, hit-or-miss.

Con. Activated, actuated, motivated (see ACTIVATE): planned, projected, designed, schemed, plotted (see verbs under PLAN, *n.*).

fortunate. *Lucky, providential, happy.

Ana. Auspicious, propitious, *favorable, benign: advantageous, *beneficial, profitable: felicitous, happy (see FIT, *adj.*).

Ant. Unfortunate: disastrous. — *Con.* *Sinister, baleful, malign, malefic.

fortune. *Chance, accident, luck, hap, hazard.

Ana. *Fate, destiny, lot, portion, doom: *opportunity, occasion, break, time, tide.

Con. *Misfortune, mischance, adversity: design, intent, *intention.

forward, *adj.* Advanced, *premature, untimely, precocious.

Ant. Backward. — *Con.* Retrograde, retrogressive, regressive (see BACKWARD).

forward, *adv.* **1** Ahead, afore, *before.

Ant. Backward.

2 Forth, *onward.

Ant. Backward.

forward, *v.* *Advance, promote, further.

Ana. *Speed, accelerate, quicken, hasten: *help, aid, assist: *support, uphold, back, champion.

Ant. Hinder: balk. — *Con.* Impede, obstruct, bar, block (see HINDER): *frustrate, thwart, baffle, outwit, foil, circumvent.

foster, *v.* *Nurse, nurture, cherish, cultivate.

Ana. *Support, uphold, back, champion: *harbor, shelter, entertain, lodge, house: promote, further, forward, *advance: favor, accommodate, *oblige.

Con. *Oppose, combat, resist, withstand: curb, snaffle, inhibit, *restrain: *forbid, prohibit, interdict, ban.

foul. Filthy, *dirty, nasty, squalid.

Ana. Putrid, stinking, fetid, noisome, *malodorous: *offensive, revolting, repulsive, loathsome: obscene, gross, vulgar, *coarse.

Ant. Fair: undefiled.

found, *v.* **Found, establish, institute, organize** are here compared as meaning to set going or to bring into existence something such as a business, a colony, an institution, or the like. **Found** implies nothing more than a taking of the first steps or measures to bring into existence something that requires building up. Just what these steps and measures are vary in usage: in very precise use, however, a person who provides the funds for a new educational institution may be said to have *founded* it, and those who first devised the project and won his support may also be said to have *founded* it. On the other hand, those who took the next steps, such as the choice of a site, the erection of buildings on that site, and the selection of the staff of administration and teaching, are also often listed among those who have *founded* it, though such use occasionally meets objection: however, *found* invariably implies the very earliest acts leading to the existence of something; as, to *found* a parish in a new section of a city; the Pilgrims in 1620 *founded* Plymouth Colony in what is now the State of Massachusetts; a school of philosophy *founded* by Plato. **Establish** (as here considered: see also SET) is often employed in the sense of *found:* in strict use, however, it implies not only the laying of the foundations but also a bringing into enduring existence; thus, Brook Farm was *founded* (not *established*, because its existence was short) by George Ripley and others as an experiment in communistic living; Vassar College was not *established* until some years after the date of its *founding*. "The... Sisters of Loretto, who came to *found* the Academy of

Our Lady of Light. The school was now well *established*" (*Cather*). **Institute** stresses an origination or an introduction: like *found*, it implies the taking of the first steps and like *establish*, the actual bringing into existence, but it differs from both words in its far wider range of application and in being referable to things which do not have a continuous life or a permanent existence, such as a new game or a course of lectures; as, to *institute* a new society; to *institute* a new method of accountancy; to *institute* an inquiry into an official's conduct of his office. **Organize** (as here compared: see also ORDER, *v.*, 1) may or may not imply founding but it usually implies the taking of the steps whereby a business, an institution, a government, or the like, is set up so that it functions properly, with its departments clearly distinguished and governed by a responsible head, and with a supervisory staff responsible for the working of the whole as a unit; as, Smith College was *founded* by Sophia Smith but was *organized* by its first president and board of trustees; the company sent him to Shanghai to *organize* its new branch there.

Ana. *Begin, commence, start, initiate, inaugurate: form, fashion (see MAKE).

Con. Uproot, eradicate, deracinate, extirpate, *exterminate, wipe out.

foundation. Basis, *base, ground, groundwork.

Ant. Superstructure.

foxy. Wily, tricky, crafty, cunning, *sly, artful.

Ana. Devious, *crooked, oblique: deceitful, *dishonest.

Con. *Straightforward, aboveboard, forthright: candid, open, plain, *frank.

foyer. *Entry, entryway, vestibule, lobby, hall, narthex, anteroom, antechamber.

fracas. *Brawl, broil, melee, row, rumpus, scrap.

Ana. Fray, affray, fight, conflict, combat, *contest: altercation, wrangle, *quarrel, squabble: contention, dissension, strife, *discord.

fraction. Fragment, piece, *part, portion, section, segment, sector, detail, member, division, parcel.

fractious. *Irritable, peevish, snappish, waspish, petulant, pettish, huffy, fretful, querulous.

Ana. *Unruly, refractory, recalcitrant, ungovernable, intractable, willful: perverse, *contrary, froward, restive, wayward.

Con. Complaisant, *amiable, good-natured: docile, tractable, *obedient, amenable, biddable.

fracture, *n.* **Fracture, rupture,** although they agree in meaning the act or an instance of breaking apart, are used in surgery and the physiological sciences as sharply differentiated terms. **Fracture** always implies the breaking of a hard or rigid substance, sometimes cartilage, but commonly bone; as, a *fracture* of the skull or of the shoulder blade. **Rupture** usually implies the breaking of some softer tissue, such as the wall of a blood vessel. In medicine, however, *rupture* often is used specifically to denote *hernia*, or the protrusion of an organ or of a part through some opening in the wall of the cavity in which that organ or part is normally placed; as, an abdominal *rupture*.

fragile. 1 **Fragile, frangible, brittle, crisp, short, friable** agree in meaning inclined to break easily. They are, however, not often interchangeable. **Fragile** (see also WEAK) is applicable to anything which must be handled or treated carefully lest it be broken; as, a *fragile* chair; a *fragile* dish; a *fragile* flower. "I found the skeleton, or, at all events, the larger bones, rendered so *fragile* by the fierce heat they had been subjected to, that they fell to pieces when handled" (*Hudson*). **Frangible** stresses susceptibility to being broken rather than positive weakness or delicacy of material or construction; as, *frangible* stone; to avoid using *frangible* materials in ship construction. **Brittle** implies hardness plus frangibility because of the inflexibility of, or lack of elasticity in, the substance of which a thing is made; it also suggests susceptibility to quick snapping or fracture when subjected to pressure or strain; as, glass is especially *brittle;* as a person ages, his bones grow more *brittle; brittle* sticks of candy. The term is much used figuratively of things that are dangerously inelastic or taut. "He would take no risks with a thing so *brittle* as the Roman polity, on which depended the fate of forty-four millions of men" (*Buchan*). **Crisp** usually suggests a good quality, which makes a thing firm and brittle yet delicate and easily broken or crushed, especially between the teeth; as, *crisp* toast; *crisp* lettuce. In extended use, it implies freshness, briskness, cleanness of cut, incisiveness, or other qualities that suggest the opposite of limpness, languor, slackness, or the like; as, a *crisp* morning; a *crisp* style; a *crisp* answer. **Short** implies a tendency to crumble or break readily, and is applicable to different things; thus, a *short* biscuit (or *short*cake) is rich in butter or other fat and is crisp and crumbly when eaten; *short* mortar is difficult to spread because of oversanding; *short* timber is desiccated wood; *short* (or hot-*short*) steel is brittle when heated beyond a certain point because of an excess of sulphur. **Friable** is applicable to substances that are easily crumbled or pulverized; as, *friable* soil; *friable* sandstone; a *friable* blackboard crayon.

Ant. Tough. — ***Con.*** *Elastic, resilient, flexible: *strong, stout, sturdy, tenacious.

2 Frail, *weak, feeble, decrepit, infirm.

Ana. Impotent, *powerless: delicate, dainty (see CHOICE): evanescent, ephemeral, *transient, transitory.

Ant. Durable.

fragment. Fraction, piece, *part, portion, section, segment, sector, division, detail, member, parcel.

Ana. Remnant, *remainder, relic.

fragrance. Fragrance, perfume, scent, incense, redolence, bouquet are here compared as denoting a sweet or pleasant odor. **Fragrance** usually suggests the odor diffused by flowers or other growing things, though it is applicable to odors that merely suggest the presence of flowers; as, "*fragrance* after showers" (*Milton*); "Flowers laugh before thee on their beds And *fragrance* in thy footing treads" (*Wordsworth*); "through the open doors ...the soft wind...brought in the garden *fragrance*" (*Stark Young*); "A *fragrance* such as never clings To aught save happy living things" (*Millay*). **Perfume** originally applied either to the pleasantly odorous smoke emitted by burning things such as some spices, gums, leaves, or the like (as, "Three April *perfumes* in three hot Junes burn'd Since first I saw you"—*Shak.*), or to some natural or prepared substance which emits a pleasant odor (as, "Take unto thee sweet spices...with pure frankincense...And thou shalt make it a *perfume*... after the art of the apothecary"—*Exodus* xxx. 34-35). Only the latter sense prevails in current use, though the substance called a *perfume* is now usually a preparation in liquid form, also called a **scent** (for full treatment of this term see SMELL) that contains the essence of a fragrant flower or flowers or is a synthetic concoction; as, "Rose like a steam of rich distilled *perfumes*" (*Milton*); a *perfume* redolent of the odor of violets. When applied to an odor rather than to a preparation, *perfume* differs little from *fragrance* except that it usually, when unqualified, suggests a heavier and more redolent odor, or at least a less delicate one, than the latter word; as, "The *perfume* of lilies had overcome the *scent* of books" (*Galsworthy*); "a gigantic rose-tree which clambered over the house...filling the air with the *perfume* of its sweetness" (*L. P. Smith*). **Incense** is now used in place of *perfume* for the agreeably odorous smoke emitted by burning spices, gums, and the like, but since this smoke is closely associated with its ceremonial religious use (as, the church was filled with the odor of *incense*), the term, in the more general sense in which it is here chiefly considered, applies to odors or things comparable to odors that are not only pleasant but grateful to the senses or that for some cause uplift or are mentally or spiritually exalting; as, "The breezy call of *incense*-breathing Morn" (*Gray*); "Grateful the *incense* from the lime-tree flower" (*Keats*); "Love wraps his wings on either side the heart... Absorbing all the *incense* of sweet thoughts So that they pass not to the shrine of sound" (*Tennyson*); "This [prayer] is that *incense* of the heart, Whose fragrance smells to heaven" (*N. Cotton*). **Redolence** now usually implies a different mixture of fragrant, often pungently agreeable, odors; as, the *redolence* of a forest; the *redolence* of a garden in spring. **Bouquet,** as here compared, applies to the distinctive fragrance of a good wine, which is perceptible when one inhales the delicate and agreeable odor; as, "Lifting his glass to his lips, [he] voluptuously inhaled its *bouquet*" (*Lytton*).

Ana. *Smell, scent, odor, aroma.

Ant. Stench, stink.

fragrant. *Odorous, aromatic, redolent, balmy.

Ana. Ambrosial, nectared (see under AMBROSIA): delicious, delectable, *delightful.

Ant. Fetid. — *Con.* *Malodorous, stinking, noisome, putrid, rank.

frail. Fragile, *weak, feeble, infirm, decrepit.

Ana. Slight, slender, tenuous, *thin, slim: puny, *petty: flimsy, sleazy (see LIMP): *powerless, impotent.

Ant. Robust. — *Con.* *Strong, stout, sturdy, stalwart, tough, tenacious: *healthy, sound, hale: *vigorous, lusty.

frailty. *Fault, failing, foible, vice.

Ana. Defect, flaw, *blemish: infirmity, fragility, feebleness, weakness (see corresponding adjectives at WEAK).

framer. *Carpenter, joiner, cabinetmaker.

frame-up. Cabal, intrigue, *plot, machination, conspiracy.

framework. *Structure, skeleton, anatomy.

franchise. *Suffrage, vote, ballot.

frangible. *Fragile, brittle, crisp, short, friable.

frank, *adj.* **Frank, candid, open, plain** come into comparison when they mean showing in speech, looks, and manners the willingness to tell what one feels or thinks. **Frank** (etymologically, free) stresses lack of reserve or of reticence in the expression of one's thoughts or feelings; it therefore usually connotes complete freedom from restraints such as fear, shyness, inarticulateness, secretiveness, and the like. "This, to Anne, was a decided imperfection...She prized the *frank*, the open-hearted, the eager character beyond all others" (*Austen*). "Things were as she had suspected: she had been *frank* in her questions and Polly had been *frank* in her answers" (*Joyce*). "The child who has been treated wisely and kindly has a *frank* look in the eyes, and a fearless demeanour even with strangers" (*B. Russell*). **Candid** (etymologically, white and glistening) is often used interchangeably with *frank*. Among highly discriminating writers and speakers this does not occur, for *candid* implies a fundamental honesty and fairness that make evasion impossible; consequently, in precise use, it suggests a refusal to dodge an issue or to be governed by bias or fear. "I have tried to be as *candid* as possible, to follow out every thought as far as I could without caring where it would lead and without tempering any conclusions out of consideration to either my own sensibilities or those of any one else" (*J. W. Krutch*). "That letter had the cardinal defects of all Cyril's relations with his mother; it was casual, and it was not *candid*. It gave no hint of the nature of the obstacle which had prevented him from coming" (*Bennett*). **Open** implies both frankness and candor but it often suggests more naturalness or artlessness than *frank*, and less conscientiousness than *candid*. "Mr. Elliot was rational, discreet, polished, but he was not *open*. There was never any burst of feeling, any warmth of indignation or delight, at the evil or good of others" (*Austen*). "For the white man to put himself mentally on their level is not more impossible than for these aborigines to be perfectly *open*, as children are, towards the white" (*Hudson*). **Plain** comes closer to *candid* than to *frank*, but it suggests outspokenness, downrightness, and freedom from affectation more than fairness of mind. "I am no orator, as Brutus is; But, as you know me all, a *plain* blunt man" (*Shak.*). "*Plain* truth, dear Murray, needs no flow'rs of speech" (*Pope*). "A *plain* confession, such as leaves no doubt" (*Wordsworth*).

Ana. Ingenuous, naïve, unsophisticated, simple, *natural: *forthright, downright: *straightforward, aboveboard.

Ant. Reticent. — *Con.* *Silent, taciturn, reserved, uncommunicative: furtive, *secret, covert, underhand.

fraud, *n.* **1** *Deception, trickery, chicanery, chicane, double-dealing, subterfuge.

Ana. Duplicity, *deceit, guile, dissimulation: defrauding, swindling, cheating, cozening, overreaching (see CHEAT, *v.*).

2 *Imposture, cheat, sham, fake, humbug, deceit, deception, counterfeit, simulacrum.

Ana. Hoaxing *or* hoax, bamboozling *or* bamboozlement, hoodwinking, duping *or* dupery (see corresponding verbs at DUPE): *trick, ruse, stratagem, maneuver, wile, artifice.

fray, *n.* Affray, fight, conflict, combat, *contest.

Ana. Fracas, broil, *brawl, melee: altercation, wrangle, *quarrel: contention, strife, dissension, *discord.

freak, *n.* *Caprice, whim, whimsey, vagary, crotchet.

Ana. Notion, *idea: *fancy, fantasy, dream, daydream.

free, *v.* **Free, release, liberate, emancipate, manumit, deliver, discharge, enfranchise, affranchise** are here compared as meaning to set loose from that which ties or binds or to make clear of that which encumbers or holds back. **Free** is the ordinary general term interchangeable with many of the succeeding terms: it may be used not only in reference to persons that are in bondage, or in a state of dependence or oppression, or under restraint or constraint (as, to *free* one's slaves; to *free* an oppressed people; to *free* a person from prison or from a charge; to *free* one from the necessity of speaking against a proposal), but also in reference to things that are confined, entangled, encumbered, or the like, and are therefore unfastened, unloosed, disentangled, disengaged, or the like (as, to *free* a squirrel from a trap; to *free* one's hair from a net; "flower-scents, that only night-time *frees*"—*Amy Lowell*). **Release** carries a much stronger implication of loosing or of setting a person or thing loose from something or someone that holds him or it confined, restrained, under obligation, or the like; as, to *release* a prisoner; to *release* a person from a promise; "*Release* me from my bands With the help of your good hands" (*Shak.*); activities that *release* one's stored-up energy; death has *released* him from his sufferings. **Liberate,** a very close synonym of the preceding words, differs from them chiefly in carrying a stronger suggestion of resulting liberty. The term may therefore connote, as do the others, emergence from some more or less disagreeable bondage or restraint (as, to *liberate* all slaves by a proclamation) or it may merely suggest a cutting of any tie, relationship, or connection without regard to the power of another thing or things to restrain or restrict, thereby approaching *separate, disengage,* or *detach* in meaning (as, oxygen is *liberated* when potassium chlorate is heated; an electric current will decompose water, *liberating* hydrogen). "The poet draws life...from the community...: to cut himself off from this source of life is much more likely to cripple than to *liberate* him" (*Day Lewis*). **Emancipate,** originally a legal term meaning to free one person from subjection to another, as a child from subjection to his parent, or a slave from subjection to his master (thereby conferring on him the status of freeman), is still often used historically in this sense. "Little more hope than had the son of an Athenian slave to be *emancipated*" (*Quiller-Couch*). In current use, the term is more frequently found in an extended sense, implying a liberation of someone or something from that which controls or dominates: it usually but not invariably also suggests a freedom by which one's own judgment, or conscience, or intelligence decrees the course to be taken, the principles to be followed, or the like. "If we can imagine the various County Councils of England *emancipated* from the control of Parliament and set free to make their own laws" (*G. L. Dickinson*). "All the philanthropic and humanitarian movements to which the Quakers, now *emancipated* from the notion that all initiative in such matters is an attempt to force the hand of the Almighty, devoted themselves in the nineteenth century" (*Inge*). **Manumit** differs from *emancipate* in its historical sense in always implying liberation from slavery or servitude: it is therefore sometimes preferred as the more definite term. "Darnall...was the son of a white man by one of his slaves, and his father executed certain instruments to *manumit* him" (*Ch. Just. Taney*). "The Church was the great *manumitter* and improver of the condition of the serf" (*J. B. Mozley*). **Deliver** (etymologically, to liberate) is now comparatively rare as a close synonym of *free.* But in all of its many extended senses the idea of freeing is the basic, though not the strongest, implication. It is specifically a synonym of *rescue* (see RESCUE) when it implies release from peril, danger, or other evil: it comes close to *transfer* or *convey* when it implies a disburdening of oneself of something which belongs to another or is intended for him (as, to *deliver* a letter to the addressee; to *deliver* a package to the purchaser), or to *utter* or *pronounce* when it implies a relieving oneself of something one must say or is charged by oneself or another with saying (as, to *deliver* oneself of one's opinions; to *deliver* a message over the telephone; to *deliver* a speech). In idiomatic English, the term implies the disburdening of a woman of offspring at the time of its birth, usually by the aid of a physician or midwife (as, the queen was safely *delivered* of a son and heir), or the freeing of all prisoners confined in a prison (as, to *deliver* a jail). **Discharge,** as here compared (see also DISMISS, 1; PERFORM), implies the release of someone or something that is held in confinement or under restraint or within the bounds of a thing: it may suggest liberation (as, to *discharge* a prisoner) but often it implies an ejection (as, to *discharge* a shot; to *discharge* an arrow), an emission (as, to *discharge* passengers from a train; to *discharge* a cargo; to *discharge* a patient from a hospital), or a pouring forth through an outlet, vent, or the like (as, the smoke is *discharged* through a very large chimney; the stream *discharges* its waters into the Hudson River), or a payment or settlement as of an obligation (as, to *discharge* one's debts). Often *discharge* differs from *release* in carrying a stronger connotation of force or violence. "Many creative writers have a critical activity which is not all *discharged* into their work" (*T. S. Eliot*). "All his accumulated nervous agitation was *discharged* on Maud like a thunderbolt" (*Bennett*). **Enfranchise** once stressed the idea of freeing from servitude, as from a vow, an obligation, or the like: the term is still used in the sense of to free from subjection (as, "The nobles desired...to *enfranchise* themselves...from the power of the King"—*Belloc*) but in its commonest current sense it implies the removal of political disabilities and admission to full political rights, especially as a freeman or as a citizen; as, the slaves were *emancipated* by the proclamation of President Lincoln on January 1, 1863, but were not *enfranchised* until the Fifteenth Amendment went into effect in 1870. **Affranchise,** which is much less common than *enfranchise,* usually implies freeing from servitude, subjection, confinement, or any condition that deprives one of personal or political liberty; as, "Every slave, after fifteen years, should be *affranchised*" (*Landor*).

Con. *Hamper, fetter, manacle, shackle, trammel, hog-tie: *imprison, incarcerate, jail, immure, intern: confine, circumscribe, restrict, *limit: *restrain, curb, inhibit.

free, *adj.* **Free, independent, sovereign, autonomous, autonomic, autarchic** (*or* **autarchical**), **autarkic** (*or* **autarkical**) come into comparison in the sense of not subject to the rule or control of another. The same differences in implications and connotations are found in their corresponding nouns **freedom, independence, sovereignty, autonomy, autarchy, autarky,** when they denote the state or condition of not being subject to external rule or control. **Free** and **freedom** (as here compared: see also FREEDOM, 2) stress the absence of external compulsion or determination and not the absence of restraint. For *free* as applied to a state, a people, a person, the will, and the like, implies self-government, and therefore the right to determine one's own acts, one's own laws and one's own restraints, or to accept or reject those that are proposed from without. "The motive power to realize it [the dream of the habitable earth peaceful under a universal empire] must come from the West, where men could still be both disciplined and *free*" (*Buchan*). "*Freedom* makes man to choose what he likes; that is, makes him *free*" (*Quiller-Couch*). "After all, the boy had a right to choose. Mr. Arvold [the boy's father] believed in perfect *freedom* for the individual, didn't he?" (*M. Austin*). **Independent** and **independence** have for their fundamental implication lack of relatedness to anyone or anything else. When used strictly, *independent* implies that the person or thing so described stands alone. "Words have a meaning *independent* of the pattern in which they are arranged" (*A. Huxley*). When applied to a state or government, it implies not complete detachment from other states or governments and a refusal to have allies or dominions, but a lack of connection with any state or government that has the power to interfere with one's liberty of action; thus, the Thirteen Colonies sacrificed their *independence,* but not their *freedom,* when they joined the federation that became the United States of America. When applied to a person, his acts, opinions, and the like, it implies either a disposition to stand alone and apart from others, or refusal to accept other's judgments, or self-reliance amounting almost to a fault; thus, a person who is *independent* in politics is attached to no political party; one might wish that a person one is trying vainly to help were less *independent.* "An economist should form an *independent* judgment on currency questions, but an ordinary mortal had better follow authority" (*B. Russell*). **Sovereign** (see also DOMINANT) and **sovereignty** stress the absence of a superior power and imply the supremacy within its own domain or sphere of that which is so described or so designated. As applied to a state or government, these words usually involve the ideas both of political independence and of the possession of original and underived power; thus, for many years before the Civil War, it was debated whether the federal government was *sovereign*. "The powers of the general government, it has been said, are delegated by the States, who alone are truly *sovereign* ....It would be difficult to sustain this proposition" (*Ch. Just. Marshall*). "Although it [the government of the United States] is *sovereign* and supreme in its appropriate sphere of action, yet it does not possess all the powers which usually belong to the *sovereignty* of a nation" (*Ch. Just. Taney*). When used in reference to a thing, both words impute to that thing unquestioned supremacy and imply that whereas it acknowledges no master, everything within its sphere of influence is subject to it; as, "noble and most *sovereign* reason" (*Shak.*). "The *sovereignty* of man lieth hid in knowledge; wherein many things are reserved that kings with their treasure cannot buy, nor with their force command" (*Bacon*). **Autonomous** and **autonomy,** in very precise use, imply independence combined with freedom. The terms are much used in philosophy to describe or designate a theoretical or ideal freedom in which the individual is absolutely self-governing and acknowledges no claim of another to interference or control; as, the question is often asked whether an *autonomous* state and an *autonomous* church can exist side by side. "If this pre-eminence and *autonomy* of the spiritual be not granted, it is misleading to use the word God at all" (*Inge*). In political use, the words seldom imply this absolute independence and freedom, for they are employed largely in reference to states which belong to an empire, a federation, or a commonwealth of nations (as used in the designation *British Commonwealth of Nations*). In reference to such states, *autonomy* and *autonomous* commonly imply independence of the central power only in matters pertaining to self-government; they also usually imply recognition of the central governmental sovereignty in certain matters affecting the empire, federation, or commonwealth of nations as a whole, such as its foreign policy. When a state is granted autonomy or becomes autonomous, the terms of such a grant are usually precisely stated. "The Imperial Conference of 1926 defined the Dominions as '*autonomous* Communities within the British Empire, equal in status, in no way subordinate one to another in any aspect of their domestic or foreign affairs, though united by a common allegiance to the Crown, and freely associated as members of the British Commonwealth of Nations'" (*Statesman's Year-Book*, 1939). **Autonomic,** once a close but not frequently employed synonym of *autonomous*, is now chiefly a technical term, used in the biological sciences, to describe movements which originate in the organism and not as a result of external influence, or to designate the nerves or the nervous system (the *autonomic nervous system* as distinguished from the *central nervous system*) controlling such spontaneous or involuntary movements. **Autarchic** and **autarchy** [Gr. *autarchia*, autocracy] originally implied absolute sovereignty or absolute or autocratic rule. They have, however, been confused with **autarkic** and **autarky** [Gr. *autarkeia*, self-sufficiency] and both pairs of words now have acquired the implication of national economic self-sufficiency. Consequently, all four words are used in reference to states or governments that favor isolation through a policy of economic self-sufficiency, as a means of maintaining their independence; as, to convert Germany into an *autarky;* the *autarkic* (or *autarchic*) policies characteristic of dictators.

Ana. Liberated, emancipated, delivered, freed, released, enfranchised (see FREE, *v.*).

Ant. Bond. — ***Con.*** Compelled, coerced, forced, constrained, obliged (see FORCE, *v.*).

freedom. **1** Independence, autonomy, sovereignty, autarky. See under FREE, *adj.*

Ana. Liberation, emancipation, release, delivery, enfranchisement, manumission (see corresponding verbs at FREE): liberty, license (see FREEDOM).

Ant. Bondage. — ***Con.*** *Servitude, slavery.

2 Freedom, liberty, license (*or* **licence**) are here compared as meaning the state or condition of one who can think, believe, or act as he wishes. **Freedom,** as here compared (see also under FREE, *adj.*), is the term of widest application; in philosophy, for example, it often implies a state or condition in which there is not only total absence of restraint but release even from the compulsion of necessity; at the other extreme, in ordinary unthinking use, *freedom* merely implies the absence of any awareness of being restrained, repressed, or hampered in any way: between these two extremes the term may imply the absence of any definite restraint or of compulsion from any particular power or agency; as, "me this unchartered *freedom* tires" (*Wordsworth*); the *freedom* of the press; "he was not affected by her reserve, and talked to her with the same *freedom* as to anybody else" (*Arch. Marshall*). "Who would not say, with Huxley, 'let me be wound up every day like a watch, to go right fatally, and I ask no better *freedom*'" (*W. James*). **Liberty** is often used interchangeably with *freedom*, but in precise speech or writing it often carries one of two implications which are not so marked in the use of *freedom*. The first of these implications is the power to choose what one wishes to do, say, believe, or the like, as distinguished from the state of being uninhibited in doing, thinking, etc.; as, to have the *liberty* (better than *freedom*) to come and go as one pleases; "in totalitarian states there is no *liberty* of expression for writers and no *liberty* of choice for their readers" (*A. Huxley*); "*freedom* in thought, the *liberty* to try and err, the right to be his own man" (*Mencken*). The second of these implications is deliverance or release from restraint or compulsion; as, to set a slave at *liberty* (not *freedom*); the prisoners were willing to fight for their *liberty;* "From bondage freed, At *liberty* to serve as you loved best" (*M. Baring*). **License** often implies the liberty to disobey the rules or regulations imposed on the many, but not necessarily governing all, when a great advantage is to be gained by disobedience; as, poetic *license;* "sometimes, with truly medieval *license*, singing to the sacred music ...songs from the street" (*Pater*); a general must be allowed considerable *license* in the field. More often, however, the term implies an abuse of liberty in the sense of the power to do exactly what one pleases; as, "*Licence* they mean when they cry *Liberty*" (*Milton*); "[The grammarian's] rules are useful....Without them *freedom* might become *licence*" (*H. Ellis*); many persons think that *freedom* of the press and *liberty* of free speech often degenerate into *license*.

Ana. *Exemption, immunity: scope, *range, compass, sweep.

Ant. Necessity. — ***Con.*** Compulsion, constraint, coercion (see corresponding verbs at FORCE).

freethinker. Unbeliever, *atheist, agnostic, deist, infidel.

Ana. *Skeptic, agnostic.

freezing, *adj.* *Cold, frigid, frosty, gelid, icy, glacial, arctic, chilly, cool.

freight, *n.* Cargo, *load, burden, lading.

frenzy *or* **phrenzy.** **1** Delirium, *mania, hysteria.
2 Fury, furor, enthusiasm, *inspiration, afflatus.
Ana. *Ecstasy, rapture, transport.

frequent, *v.* **Frequent, haunt, habituate** come into comparison in the sense of to visit or resort to often and habitually. **Frequent** implies little more than this: it is chiefly used of places, especially places of amusement (as, to *frequent* the cinemas; to *frequent* the lobby of a hotel) but it still is preserved in some idiomatic phrases such as to *frequent* the Sacraments [that is, to go to confession and to Holy Communion frequently]. "Myself when young did eagerly *frequent* Doctor and Saint, and heard great argument" (*FitzGerald*). **Haunt** may imply a continual or pertinacious frequenting (as, "a poor Cavalier knight who *haunted* Whitehall"—*Macaulay;* "*haunting* [shipmasters] with demands for a job"—*Conrad*), but it has so long been associated with the actions of ghosts or specters alleged to frequent places (as, a *haunted* house) that the term now suggests the frequent or persistent coming of thoughts, ideas, fears, or the like, that terrify and upset or obsess the mind; as, "Wordsworth...seems ever *haunted* by the sorrows of mankind" (*Binyon*); "the continual dread of falling into poverty which *haunts* us all at present" (*Shaw*). **Habituate** (see also HABITUATE, 1) is a colloquial Americanism in this sense. It differs little from *frequent* except in its stronger implication of a formed habit; as, boys that *habituate* poolrooms are usually a problem.
Ana. *Resort (to), go (to), turn (to): *infest, overrun.
Con. Shun, avoid, eschew (see ESCAPE).

frequently. *Often, oft, oftentimes.
Ant. Rarely, seldom.

fresh. Novel, *new, new-fashioned, newfangled, modern, modernistic, original, neoteric.
Ana. Gleaming, glistening, sparkling (see FLASH, *v.*): virginal, *youthful: raw, green, crude (see RUDE): naïve, unsophisticated, artless, *natural.
Ant. Stale. — *Con.* *Trite, hackneyed, shopworn, stereotyped, threadbare.

fret. Chafe, gall, *abrade, excoriate.
Ana. *Irritate, exasperate, nettle, aggravate: *annoy, vex, irk.

fretful. Peevish, *irritable, petulant, querulous, fractious, snappish, waspish, pettish, huffy.
Ana. Cross, cranky, touchy, techy, choleric, *irascible: captious, carping, caviling, faultfinding, *critical: *contrary, perverse.
Con. Patient, long-suffering, forbearing, resigned (see corresponding nouns at PATIENCE): *tame, submissive, subdued.

friable. Short, frangible, crisp, brittle, *fragile.
Ana. Crumbling *or* crumbly, disintegrating (see corresponding verbs at DECAY).

friar. *Religious, monk, nun.

friend. **Friend, acquaintance, intimate, confidant** come into comparison when they designate a person, especially a person not related by blood, with whom one is on good and, usually, familiar terms. **Friend,** in its application, ranges from any person who is not hostile or is a well-wisher to any person whose society one seeks or accepts with pleasure because of liking, respect, or affection. **Acquaintance,** in its most inclusive sense, is applied to any person with whom one is on speaking terms. However, when these words are used in contrast, both imply a degree of familiarity; *friend* distinctively connoting close bonds of love and affection and *acquaintance,* comparative infrequency of contact and less close personal interest. "You understand that I am not their *friend.* I am only a holiday *acquaintance*" (*Conrad*). This distinction is commonly but not invariably observed, especially when *acquaintance* is used as a collective plural; as, he has a wide circle of *friends;* he has a large *acquaintance.* "He never speaks much, unless among his intimate *acquaintance*" (*Austen*). **Intimate** adds to *friend* the implications of a depth of affection and a closeness of association that tend to preclude reserve; as, only his *intimates* were aware of his plans. **Confidant** usually designates that intimate who actually is entrusted with one's secrets or is admitted to confidential intercourse.
Ana. Comrade, companion, crony, chum, pal, *associate: ally, colleague, *partner.
Ant. Foe. — *Con.* *Enemy: antagonist, *opponent, adversary: rival, competitor (see corresponding verbs at RIVAL).

friendly. *Amicable, neighborly.
Ana. *Familiar, intimate, close: *loving, affectionate, devoted: loyal, leal, true, steadfast, *faithful.
Ant. Unfriendly: belligerent. — *Con.* Hostile, antagonistic, antipathetic (see corresponding nouns at ENMITY).

friendship. **Friendship, amity, comity, good will** are comparable when they denote the relation (or, in the first three instances, the alliance) existing between persons, communities, states, or the like, that are in accord and in sympathy with each other. **Friendship** is the strongest of these terms in its implications of sentiment in the relation and of closeness of attachment. "The *friendship* between me and you [the Indians with whom he has concluded a treaty] I will not compare to a chain; for that the rains might rust, or the falling tree might break" (*Penn*). Sometimes, as in the illustration just given, it suggests an alliance; at other times it excludes that suggestion. "Peace, commerce, and honest *friendship* with all nations—entangling alliances with none" (*Jefferson*). **Amity** always implies the absence of enmity or discord. Positively, it may imply nothing more than amicable relations (as, the colonists and the Indians seldom lived together in *amity*), or it may suggest reciprocal friendliness. "On his arrival he [the new bishop] found *amity* [between the French priest and the Mexicans] instead of enmity awaiting him. Father Vaillant had already endeared himself to the people" (*Cather*). In current use, the suggestion of a friendly alliance is rare, but it was not uncommon in the past. "The *amity* that wisdom knits not, folly may easily untie" (*Shak.*). "The less we have to do with the *amities* or enmities of Europe, the better" (*Jefferson*). **Comity,** in modern use (see also COURTESY), owing to an etymological confusion between *comitas,* friendliness, and *comes* (pl. *comites*), companion, has come to imply comradeship based either upon an interchange of courtesies or upon a similarity of interests and aims. So strong has this implication become in recent years that the word now often denotes a group bound together by friendship or by common interests. It never implies loss of independence by any member of the group or the transference of sovereignty to the group. "Turkey should...be saved ...and rendered a useful member of the civilised *comity*" (*Daily Telegraph,* 1880). "The more...the merrier, to win their way into the great *comity* [of poets influenced by the troubadours]" (*Quiller-Couch*). "Outside the *comity* of the [Roman] empire, beyond the border provinces and client-kingdoms, lay the unknown lands and the strange peoples" (*Buchan*). **Good will,** as here narrowly considered, derives its chief implication of a benevolent attitude or of reciprocal good feeling largely from the Authorized Version's translation of the Angelic Hymn, "Glory to God in the highest, and on earth peace, *good will* toward men" (*Luke* ii. 14). The term is now often used in international diplomacy to designate a reciprocal friendliness which constitutes an informal bond between nations and works to the advantage of all concerned. "*Good Will* is the mightiest practical force in the universe" (*C. F. Dole*). "To promote the exchange of intellectual ideas and *good-will* between Belgium and America" (*School and Society*).

Ana. Sympathy, affinity, *attraction: sympathy, empathy (see PITY): accord, concord, consonance, *harmony: *alliance, league, coalition, fusion, federation.

Ant. Animosity. — *Con.* *Enmity, hostility, antagonism, antipathy, rancor: *hate, hatred.

fright, *n.* Alarm, consternation, panic, *fear, dread, dismay, terror, horror, trepidation.

Ana. Scaring *or* scare, startling, affrighting, frightening (see corresponding verbs at FRIGHTEN): appalling, horrifying, daunting (see DISMAY, *v.*).

fright, *v.* *Frighten, scare, alarm, terrify, terrorize, startle, affray, affright.

Ana. See those at FRIGHTEN.

frighten. Frighten, fright, scare, alarm, terrify, terrorize, startle, affray, affright mean to strike or to fill with fear or dread. **Frighten** is perhaps the most frequent in use; it is the most inclusive, for it may imply a momentary reaction to a stimulus or a state of mind in which fear or dread prevails. In careful use, however, it commonly implies paralyzing fear, affecting either the body or the will. "The silence of the house...*frightened* Clara" (*S. Anderson*). "In a world too *frightened* to be honest" (*T. S. Eliot*). **Fright** is the older form of **frighten;** it now rarely occurs in speech or nonliterary writing, except in Scotland. "They fled like *frighted* dows [doves]" (*Burns*). In colloquial use **scare** is often equivalent to *frighten;* in the work of discriminating writers, it usually implies fear that causes one to run, shy, or tremble. "Sour visages, enough to *scare* ye" (*Gray*). "A noise did *scare* me from the tomb" (*Shak.*). "Earth shakes beneath them, and heaven roars above; But nothing *scares* them from the course they love" (*Cowper*). **Alarm,** in modern use, nearly always stresses apprehension or anxiety; as, they are *alarmed* for his safety. "The girl was...*alarmed* by the altogether unknown expression in the woman's face" (*Conrad*). In older use, however, it retained its etymological implication of a sharply sudden awakening or a call to be on the alert. "Great crimes *alarm* the conscience, but it sleeps While thoughtful man is plausibly amused" (*Cowper*). **Terrify** emphasizes intensity of fear and agitation; it usually suggests a state of mind in which self-control or self-direction is impossible; as, they were *terrified* out of their wits; the dread of failure *terrified* them. **Terrorize,** in distinction from *terrify,* implies the effect of an intention, and therefore is used in reference to voluntary agents; thus, one may say that gangs *terrorized* (more explicit than *terrified*) the neighborhood by their constant depredations, and that the depredations of the gangs *terrified* (but not *terrorized*) the neighborhood. *Terrorize* often implies coercion or intimidation; as, to *terrorize* a people into submission. **Startle** always implies surprise and a sudden shock that causes one to jump or shrink; occasionally its suggestion of fright is very weak. "One learns in parish work not to start, however much one may be *startled*" (*R. Macaulay*). "Investigations of scientists....sprung on a Public shocked and *startled* by the revelation that facts which they were accustomed to revere were conspicuously at fault" (*Galsworthy*). **Affray** and **affright** are now archaic and poetic, the former, as a rule, coming close to *terrify,* and the latter, to *frighten.*

Ana. Appall, horrify, *dismay, daunt: *intimidate, cow, browbeat, bulldoze: agitate, perturb, upset, disquiet, *discompose.

frightful. Dreadful, *fearful, awful, terrible, terrific, horrible, horrific, shocking, appalling.

Ana. *Ghastly, grisly, gruesome, macabre, grim, lurid: *sinister, baleful, malign.

frigid. Freezing, gelid, icy, glacial, arctic, *cold, cool, chilly, frosty.

Ant. Torrid (*temperature*): amorous (*persons*).

frivolity. Levity, flippancy, light-mindedness, volatility, flightiness, *lightness.

Ana. Trifling, flirting, dallying, coquetting, toying (see TRIFLE, *v.*): play, sport, *fun, jest, game: gaiety, liveliness, vivaciousness, sprightliness (see corresponding adjectives at LIVELY).

Ant. Seriousness, staidness. — *Con.* Sedateness, gravity, solemnity, soberness, earnestness (see corresponding adjectives at SERIOUS).

frolic, *n.* Play, sport, disport, rollick, romp, gambol. See under PLAY, *v.*

Ana. *Fun, jest, game, play, sport: caper, *prank, antic, monkeyshine, dido: levity, *lightness, frivolity.

frolic, *v.* *Play, sport, disport, rollick, romp, gambol.

frolicsome. *Playful, sportive, roguish, waggish, impish, mischievous, wanton.

Ana. *Merry, blithe, jocund, jovial, jolly: mirthful, gleeful, hilarious (see corresponding nouns at MIRTH): *lively, vivacious, sprightly, gay.

front, *n.* Port, presence, *bearing, demeanor, deportment, mien, manner, carriage.

frontage. Frontage, exposure, aspect come into comparison when they mean situation with respect to that which is faced. **Frontage** is capable of being used in reference to anything whose location may be described in terms of that which it faces or fronts; as, a lot with a river *frontage;* a slope with a southern *frontage;* a store with a 100-foot *frontage* on Main Street. **Exposure** is used in reference to anything that is made more or less desirable or is helped or hindered by the point or points of the compass it faces, and the conditions of light or wind to which it is exposed; as, the artist sought a studio with northern *exposure* because of the steadiness of the light; city dwellers often prefer apartments with a southern *exposure;* the house's eastern *exposure* was weatherbeaten. **Aspect** is used commonly in reference to something from which one can get a view or outlook, as a window or a room with windows, a veranda or piazza; like *exposure,* it is used in relation to a point or points of the compass, but it suggests the direction in which one looks rather than the quarter from which light or air comes. " 'What *aspect* do you like for your bedroom?—East?' said the Baronet" (*Meredith*).

frontier. March, border, *boundary.

Ana. *Limit, bound, bourn, confine, end.

frosty. Chilly, *cold, cool, frigid, freezing, gelid, icy, glacial, arctic.

froth, *n.* *Foam, spume, scum, lather, suds, yeast.

Ana. Effervescence, *ebullition, ferment, fermentation: *lightness, levity, frivolity, flippancy.

froward. *Contrary, perverse, balky, restive, wayward.

Ana. *Obstinate, stubborn, mulish, pigheaded, stiffnecked: willful, headstrong, refractory, *unruly, ungovernable, intractable, recalcitrant: contumacious, *insubordinate, rebellious.

Ant. Compliant. — *Con.* Docile, tractable, amenable, *obedient, biddable: acquiescent, resigned (see COMPLIANT).

frown, *v.* **Frown, scowl, glower, lower** (*or* **lour**), **gloom** come into comparison when they mean to put on a dark or malignant countenance or aspect. **Frown** commonly implies a stern face and contracted brows that express displeasure, disapprobation, anger, or contempt; as, "that Stonehenge circle of elderly disapproving Faces—Faces of the Uncles, and Schoolmasters and the Tutors who *frowned* on my youth" (*L. P. Smith*). **Scowl** carries an implication of wrinkled drawn-down brows that express ill humor, sullenness, or discontent; as, "a spinner that would not rebel, nor mutter, nor *scowl*, nor strike for wages?" (*Emerson*). **Glower** (in its earliest sense, now rare except in Scotland, to stare) implies a more direct stare or gaze than *frown* or *scowl* and carries a stronger connotation of anger, contempt, or defiance; as, "The steward...*glowered* at Powell, that new-comer, that ignoramus, that stranger without right or privileges" (*Conrad*); "He...stood *glowering* from a distance at her, as she sat bowed over the child" (*D. H. Lawrence*). **Lower** implies a menacing blackness and sullenness of face or of aspect; the term is used in reference not only to persons but to skies that give promise of a storm; as, "Stand firm, for in his look defiance *lours*" (*Milton*); "wandering from chamber to chamber...all distinguishable by the same *lowering* gloom" (*Beckford*); "Up behind the Sangre de Cristo, gathered great thunderheads, *lowering* as they came, fringed threateningly with light" (*M. Austin*). **Gloom** in earlier use was a close synonym of *lower* (as, "What's he, who with contracted brow, And sullen port, *glooms* downward with his eyes?"—*Congreve*) but in current English carries a much stronger implication of gloominess or dejection, and a much weaker (often nonexistent) suggestion of threatening; as, "They may be wise in not *glooming* over what is inevitable" (*J. B. Cabell*); "Skiddaw [a mountain] *gloomed* solemnly overhead" (*E. Dowden*).

Ant. Smile. — *Con.* *Disapprove, deprecate.

frowzy. Blowzy, *slatternly, dowdy.

Ana. Slovenly, unkempt, sloppy, *slipshod: squalid, *dirty, filthy: *negligent, neglectful, lax, slack, remiss.

Ant. Trim: smart. — *Con.* *Neat, tidy, trig, spick-and-span: *clean, cleanly.

frugal. Thrifty, economical, *sparing.

Ana. *Careful, meticulous: provident, prudent, discreet (see under PRUDENCE): saving, preserving, conserving (see SAVE): parsimonious, cheeseparing, penny-pinching (see STINGY).

Ant. Wasteful. — *Con.* Extravagant (see EXCESSIVE): prodigal, lavish, *profuse.

fruitful. Fecund, prolific, *fertile.

Ana. Reproducing *or* reproductive, propagating, breeding (see corresponding verbs at GENERATE): bearing, producing *or* productive, yielding (see corresponding verbs at BEAR): teeming, abounding (see TEEM): luxuriant, lush, exuberant (see PROFUSE).

Ant. Unfruitful: fruitless. — *Con.* *Sterile, barren, impotent, infertile: *futile, vain, bootless, abortive.

fruitfulness. Prolificacy, fecundity, fertility. See under FERTILE.

fruition. Enjoyment, delectation, *pleasure, delight, joy.

Ana. Realization, actualization, substantiation, materialization (see corresponding verbs at REALIZE): fulfillment, accomplishment (see corresponding verbs at PERFORM): attainment, achievement (see corresponding verbs at REACH): possession, enjoyment (see corresponding verbs at HAVE).

fruitless. *Futile, vain, bootless, abortive.

Ana. Unfruitful, barren, infertile, *sterile: *vain, idle, otiose, nugatory, empty, hollow: frustrated, thwarted, foiled (see FRUSTRATE).

Ant. Fruitful. — *Con.* *Effective, effectual, efficacious, efficient: *fertile, fecund, prolific.

frustrate. Frustrate, thwart, foil, baffle, balk, circumvent, outwit agree in meaning either to defeat a person attempting or hoping to achieve an end or satisfy a desire or, in some cases, to defeat another's desire. To **frustrate** is to render vain or ineffectual all efforts, however feeble or however vigorous, to fulfill one's intention or desire. "If such a failure can change a writer ...from a second-rate poet and novelist into a supreme critical historian...ought we not rather to welcome this *frustration?*" (*L. P. Smith*). "Whatever Nature...purposes to herself, she never suffers any reason, design, or accident to *frustrate*" (*Fielding*). "My good intentions towards you...are continually *frustrated*" (*Cowper*). To **thwart** is to frustrate especially by crossing or running counter to someone or something making headway. "Others had thrust themselves into his life and *thwarted* his purposes" (*G. Eliot*). "Public enforcement of hygienic practices is *thwarted* by a really obstructive neglect of the rules of health by her [France's] peasantry" (*J. A. Hobson*). **Foil** commonly implies repulse or discomfiture that makes further effort difficult or destroys one's inclination to proceed further. "His attempts to replace ambition by love had been as fully *foiled* as his ambition itself" (*Hardy*). To **baffle** is to frustrate especially by confusing or puzzling; to **balk**, by interposing obstacles or hindrances. "Such knotty problems of alleys, such enigmatical entries, and such sphinx's riddles of streets without thoroughfares as must, I conceive, *baffle* the audacity of porters and confound the intellects of hackney coachmen" (*De Quincey*). "I like reading my Bible without being *baffled* by unmeaningnesses" (*Arnold*). "When an affection as intense as that is *balked* in its direct path and repressed it usually, as we know, finds an indirect outlet" (*Van W. Brooks*). "His inclination to dreams, *balked* by the persistent holding of his mind to definite things" (*S. Anderson*). **Circumvent** implies frustration by stratagem; **outwit,** by craft or cunning. "Immigration laws had been growing more and more effective....But...the rejected aliens soon learned a method of *circumventing* them" (*V. Heiser*). "The skill with which she [Elizabeth] had hoodwinked and *outwitted* every statesman in Europe" (*J. R. Green*).

Ana. Negative, counteract, *neutralize: defeat, beat, overcome, *conquer: *forbid, prohibit, inhibit: *prevent, preclude, obviate: *hinder, impede, obstruct, block, bar.

Ant. Fulfill. — *Con.* Effect, accomplish, achieve, *perform: further, forward, promote, *advance: *incite, instigate, abet, foment.

fuddle. Muddle, bemuddle, addle, *confuse.

Ana. & *Ant.* See those at BEFUDDLE.

fugitive, *adj.* Evanescent, transitory, *transient, fleeting, passing, ephemeral, momentary, short-lived.

fulfill *or* **fulfil.** **1** Effect, achieve, accomplish, execute, *perform, discharge.

Ana. *Enforce, implement: compass, attain, *reach, gain: *realize, actualize: finish, complete (see CLOSE).

Ant. Frustrate: fail (in).

2 *Satisfy, meet, answer.

Ana. Equal, approach, *match, touch, rival.

Ant. Fall short (of).

full. Full, complete, plenary, replete are not synonyms in the sense that they are interchangeable with each other, but the last three are interchangeable with the most comprehensive term, *full,* in at least one of its senses. **Full** implies the presence or inclusion of everything that is wanted or required by something, or that can be held, contained, attained, or the like, by it; thus, a *full* year numbers 365 days or, in leap years, 366 days; a *full* basket is one that can hold nothing more; a *full* mind is stocked to the point of overflowing with knowledge or ideas; a *full* moon has reached the height of its development; a *full* stomach is one that can contain no more food with comfort or is completely satisfied; a *full* meal is one lacking in none of the courses (or sometimes in none of the elements) to make a satisfying or balanced meal; a sponge *full* of water has absorbed all the water it can hold. **Complete** comes into comparison and close synonymity with *full* when the latter implies the entirety that is needed to the perfection, consummation, integrity, or realization of a thing; as, *complete* (or *full*) combustion; a *complete* (or *full*) meal; *complete* (or *full*) sovereignty or control. "If you consider the ritual of the Church during the cycle of the year, you have the *complete* drama represented. The Mass is a small drama, having all the unities; but in the Church year you have represented the *full* drama of creation" (*T. S. Eliot*). "The panorama of to-day's events is not an accurate or *complete* picture, for history will supply posterity with much evidence which is hidden from the eyes of contemporaries" (*C. W. Eliot*). Only when *complete* means *completed* (as, the building is now *complete*) is *full* not a synonym of the word. **Plenary** comes into comparison with *full* when *full* implies the absence of all qualification or even suggestion of qualification as to a thing's completeness. *Plenary*, however, heightens the force of *full* in this sense and carries a much stronger suggestion of absoluteness; thus, to give *plenary* powers is to give full power without the slightest qualification; a *plenary* indulgence implies the remission of the entire temporal punishment due for one's sins. "By this word 'miracle' I meant to suggest to you a something like *plenary* inspiration in these...men; an inspiration at once supernatural and so authoritative that it were sacrilege now to alter their text by one jot or tittle" (*Quiller-Couch*). **Replete** (*with*), the more bookish term, as compared with *full* (*of*), heightens the implication of abundant supply, or of being filled to the brim with something; as, "Should a man *full* of talk be justified?" (*Job* xi. 2); "He is quick, unaffected, *replete* with anecdote" (*Hazlitt*); "An anxious captain, who has suddenly got news, *replete* with importance for him" (*H. James*). Often, however, the term implies fullness to satiety or to the point of being surfeited; as, "When he of wine was *replete* at his feast" (*Chaucer*); "Right reading makes a *full* man in a sense even better than Bacon's; not *replete*, but *complete* rather, to the pattern for which Heaven designed him" (*Quiller-Couch*).

Ana. Including *or* inclusive, comprehending *or* comprehensive (see corresponding verbs at INCLUDE): teeming, abounding, superabounding (see TEEM): glutted, cloyed, gorged, surfeited, sated (see SATIATE).

Ant. Empty. — *Con.* Void, vacant, blank (see EMPTY): *bare, barren: stripped, dismantled, divested, denuded (see STRIP).

full-fledged. *Mature, matured, ripe, mellow, adult, grown-up.

Ant. Unfledged: callow. — *Con.* *Proficient, skilled, skillful, expert, adept.

fulsome. **Fulsome, oily, unctuous, oleaginous, sleek, soapy** are here compared as adjectives that mean too obviously extravagant or ingratiating to be accepted as genuine or sincere. **Fulsome** (etymologically, exceedingly full) has passed through an interesting sense development until it now stresses a surfeit of that which in measure is not displeasing, but which in abundance is cloyingly extravagant and offensive. In current use, the term is applied chiefly to praise, flattery, and compliments, with the intent to suggest that they exceed the bounds of good taste and are lacking in truth and sincerity; as, *fulsome* flattery; "He was bedaubing one of those worthies with the most *fulsome* praise" (*Smollett*); "The *fulsome* strains of courtly adulation" (*Edgeworth*); "He could never be made ridiculous, for he was always ready to laugh at himself and to prick the bladder of *fulsome* praise" (*Buchan*). **Oily** and **unctuous** both suggest the smoothness and blandness of oil. The former, as applied to persons and their utterances and acts, carries a strong implication of an offensively ingratiating quality, and sometimes suggests a suavity, a benevolence, a kindliness, or the like, that is assumed as a mask for one's own evil or dubious ends; as, an *oily* scoundrel; *oily* manners; *oily* smugness; "Only *oily* and commonplace evasion" (*Stevenson*). *Unctuous*, on the other hand, suggests the assumption, often in hypocrisy, of the tone or manner of one who is grave, devout, or spiritual; as, the *unctuous* grandiloquence of Dickens's Chadband; "The look [of benevolence] was, perhaps, *unctuous*, rather than spiritual, and had, so to speak, a kind of fleshy effulgence....He...smiled with more *unctuous* benignity than ever" (*N. Hawthorne*); "Mark Twain writes those words with an almost *unctuous* gravity of conviction" (*Van W. Brooks*); "the English...bear their patriotism heavily, *unctuously*, speak solemnly of the white man's burden, and introduce religion into the gay and worldly affair" (*R. Macaulay*). **Oleaginous** is sometimes used in place of *oily* or *unctuous* when pomposity is connoted or a humorous note is desired; as, "[the person] who snuffles the responses with such *oleaginous* sanctimony" (*F. W. Farrar*). **Sleek** (as here compared: see also SLEEK, 1) may suggest the assumption of any of the outward marks that distinguish the suave, the courtly, or the urbane gentleman, but it usually stresses the speciousness of that appearance and often imputes rank hypocrisy to the person who assumes it; as, *sleek* rogues preying upon young girls. "Another [than Lancelot] sinning on such heights with one [Queen Guinevere], The flower of all the west and all the world, Had been the *sleeker* for it" (*Tennyson*). **Soapy** comes close to *unctuous* in its extended sense but it carries almost no suggestion of hypocrisy: rather, it connotes an unduly soft, bland, or ingratiating manner; as, "But why...do people call him [Bishop Wilberforce] 'Soapy Sam'?" (*Pall Mall Gazette*).

Ana. Lavish, *profuse, exuberant: *excessive, extravagant: cloying, satiating, sating (see SATIATE): bombastic, grandiloquent, magniloquent (see RHETORICAL).

fumigate. Disinfect, sanitize, *sterilize.

fun, *n.* **Fun, jest, sport, game, play** come into comparison when they mean anything, such as an activity, an utterance, a form of expression, or the spirit behind any of these, which provides oneself with amusement or is expected or intended to arouse others' smiles or laughter. **Fun,** the ordinary colloquial term of this group, may imply merely amusement, or the engagement of the mind in something that interests one without thought of another end or effect (as, to play football for *fun;* he writes just for the *fun* of it), but it more often implies a natural or inherent capacity for laughing, for provoking laughter, or for finding a cause for laughter in other persons, or in their situations or activities; as, "He used to be full of *fun*. Once we laughed all day together tumbling in the hay" (*Meredith*); "Artemus Ward was all *fun* and sweet reasonableness and profoundest common sense" (*Lucas*); "It will be fine *fun* to see how you'll master your husband and never raise your voice above the singing o' the kettle all the while" (*G. Eliot*); "A couple of boys left to themselves will furnish richer *fun* than any troop of trained comedians" (*Meredith*). **Jest** (as here compared: see also JEST, 1) comes into comparison with *fun* chiefly when used in phrases such as *in jest* (cf. *in fun*), or when used in the larger sense of activities, utterances, or forms of expression not to be taken seriously. But in these instances, *jest* carries a stronger implication of raillery, ridicule, or hoaxing than *fun* usually carries; as, one never can determine whether he is telling these tales of adventure in *jest* or in earnest; he is such a hoaxer that one takes nearly everything that he does or says as *jest*. **Sport** (as here compared: see also under PLAY, *v.*, 1) also comes into comparison with *fun* chiefly in idiomatic phrases such as *in sport* or *to make sport* (cf. *to make fun*), where it suggests not only a desire to arouse laughter, but to make one a butt of one's mirth or a laughingstock; as, "then make *sport* at me" (*Shak.*); the offensive nickname was given to him in *sport;* to find *sport* in his deep embarrassment. **Game** was originally a close synonym of *fun*, but in this sense it is now rare except in the phrase *to make game of*, where it often carries an implication of mischievous or malicious fun; as, "Do they not seek occasion... to ...make a *game* of my calamities?" (*Milton*); "She had all the talents which qualified her... to make *game* of his scruples" (*Macaulay*). But *game*, largely through association with other senses of the word, such as a contest or competition in sports (see *games* under ATHLETICS) or an object of pursuit in a hunt, applies to an activity indulged in or carried on in the spirit of fun or sport (as, "It is an amusing *game*...to waylay leader-writers and tackle them...turn them inside out and show how empty they are"—*R. Macaulay*), or to a person or situation that is made fun of (as, "Their sour aspect, their nasal twang, their stiff posture, their long graces, their Hebrew names...were indeed fair *game* for the laughers"—*Macaulay*). When the phrases *in fun* and *in sport* seem a little too explicit in their connotations, **play,** which implies nothing more than an opposition to the noun *earnest* (especially in the phrase "in *earnest*"), is sometimes substituted for *fun* or *sport;* as, you have no reason to be offended, for the remark was made only in *play*.

Ana. Amusement, diversion, recreation, entertainment (see under AMUSE): merriment, jocundity, blitheness, joviality (see corresponding adjectives at MERRY): *mirth, glee, hilarity, jollity.

function, *n.* **1 Function, office, duty, province** come into comparison when they mean the act, acts, activities, or operations expected of a person or thing by virtue of his or its nature, structure, status, position, or the like. **Function** is the most comprehensive of these terms, capable of referring not only to any living thing or to any organ or member of a living thing, but to anything in nature (such as the sun, the stars, the earth) or in art (such as poetry, painting, music, or an example of one of these), or to anything constructed that serves a definite end or purpose or is intended to perform a certain kind of work; as, to fulfill one's *function* as a mother; the *function* of the stomach is to digest food sufficiently to enable it to pass into the intestines where digestion is completed and absorption takes place; "The *function* of language is twofold: to communicate emotion and to give information" (*A. Huxley*); the *function* of the leaves of a plant; the *function* of criticism; the *function* of a stationary engine; "what after all...is the true *function* of religion?" (*G. L. Dickinson*). **Office** applies usually, but not exclusively, to the function of, or the work to be performed by, a person as a result of his trade, profession, employment, position with relation to others, or the like; in this sense it refers to a service that is expected of one or to a charge that is laid upon one; as, "O, pardon me for bringing these ill news, Since you did leave it for my *office*, sir" (*Shak.*) "to suppose she would shrink...from the *office* of a friend" (*Austen*); "They exercise the *offices* of the judge, the priest, the counsellor" (*Gladstone*). The term was once, and is still occasionally, used in reference to things in a sense very close to that of *function;* as, "the gown which had been let down to hide it [the muddied rim of a petticoat] not doing its *office*" (*Austen*). **Duty** (as here considered: for a more restricted sense, see TASK) applies not only to the tasks the performance of which is expected or required of one by reason of one's occupation or employment (as, the *duties* of a cook; the *duties* of a hotel porter) but to the offices associated with one's status, one's rank, one's calling, and generally regarded as inherent in that status, rank, and calling and as imposing an obligation upon the person so stationed; thus, a man and wife fulfill their biological *function* when they produce children but they must still perform their *duties* as parents in rearing, protecting, and educating those children; the governor regarded it as his *duty* to warn the citizens of the dangers ahead. "It is not only the right, but it is the judicial *duty* of the court, to examine the whole case as presented by the record" (*Ch. Just. Taney*). **Province,** in the sense here considered, is closely related to the sense in which it is discriminated from *field* and other terms (see FIELD, 2), but it is distinguishable from that sense in denoting any function, office, or duty which comes within one's range of jurisdiction, powers, competence, and the like; as, "Nursing does not belong to a man; it is not his *province*" (*Austen*); "It is emphatically the *province* and *duty* of the judicial department to say what the law is" (*Ch. Just. Marshall*).

Ana. End, goal, object, objective, purpose (see INTENTION): business, concern, *affair: *task, job.

2 *Power, faculty.

Ana. *Ability, capacity, capability: action, behavior, operation (see corresponding verbs at ACT).

function, *v.* Operate, work, *act, behave, react.

fundamental, *adj.* **1 Fundamental, basic, basal, underlying, substratal, substrative, radical** come into comparison when they mean forming or affecting the groundwork, roots, or lowest part of something. **Fundamental** is now used chiefly, but not exclusively, in reference to immaterial things or to abstractions, whether they are thought of figuratively as built up on a foundation or as having their origins in roots; as, the *fundamental* rules of poetry; a *fundamental* change in his attitude to life; the *fundamental* rock in a geological formation; "The *fundamental* absurdity of the plot... remains" (*FitzGerald*); "The *fundamental* note [in an oasis] is struck by the palms" (*A. Huxley*). **Basic** is often used interchangeably with *fundamental* when the latter implies reference to a substructure; as, the *fundamental* or *basic* argument. But *basic* is preferred to *fundamental* when the reference is to a definite or concrete base (that is, groundwork, bottom, or starting point); as, the *basic* stone of a pillar; a *basic* wage in the electrical industry; the *basic* speed of an automobile. **Basal** differs from *basic* chiefly in not being used as often in reference to immaterial things and in more often implying reference to the bottom or to the lowest point or regions of a thing; as, "geologising the *basal* parts of the Andes" (*Darwin*); the *basal* plane of a crystal; the *basal* leaves on a stem. **Underlying** may be used to suggest nothing more than extension beneath something else; as, the *underlying* strata; the *underlying* layer of tissue. However, especially when the reference is to something immaterial, the term frequently comes close to *fundamental*, differing from it chiefly in suggesting a depth that removes the thing from one's range of vision or a remoteness that demands study or research on the part of one that would detect it; as, the *underlying* motive for his act; the *underlying* causes of the World War; the *underlying* differences between Communism and Socialism. **Substratal,** and the still rarer **substrative,** often refer to the metaphysical conception of a substratum, or the substance in which the qualities of a thing inhere (as, the *substratal* substance), or to the derived scientific (chiefly biological) conception of a substratum as the substance or base in which something grows, such as a medium used for the cultivation of bacteria or other organisms, or of cells; as, the *substratal* substance in this experiment is gelatin. However, *substratal* and *substrative* are also applied to something which literally underlies an upper layer or stratum; as, *substratal* soil; *substratal* rock. **Radical** (see also LIBERAL, 2) implies reference to the root or origin or ultimate source of a thing; thus, a *radical* change is one that is so thoroughgoing that it affects the fundamental character of the thing involved; a *radical* error touches the very center and source of a thing's life. "Actual differences distinguishing the different races of mankind—differences that may be ascribed to *radical* peculiarities of mind" (*Bridges*).

Ana. *Primary, primal, primordial, prime: *elementary, elemental.

2 *Essential, vital, cardinal.

Ana. Requisite, *needful, necessary, indispensable: paramount, *dominant: principal, capital, foremost, *chief.

Con. *Superficial: *subordinate, secondary.

fundamental, *n.* *Principle, axiom, law, theorem.

Ana. *Element, integrant, constituent, component, factor: ground, basis, foundation, *base, groundwork.

funny. *Laughable, risible, ludicrous, ridiculous, farcical, comic, comical, droll.

Ana. Humorous, *witty, jocose, jocular, facetious: amusing, diverting, entertaining (see AMUSE): grotesque, bizarre, *fantastic, antic.

Con. *Serious, solemn, grave, sober: *melancholy, plaintive, doleful, dolorous, lugubrious.

furbish, *v.* Buff, *polish, shine, burnish.

Ana. *Clean, cleanse: renovate, refurbish, restore, *renew, rejuvenate: revise, reform, amend, rectify (see CORRECT).

furnish. Furnish, equip, outfit, appoint, accouter (*or* **accoutre**), **arm** are comparable when they mean to supply a person, or something used by him, with the adjuncts necessary or appropriate to his daily living or his occupation. **Furnish** stresses the provision of all essentials; thus, one *furnishes* a house when it is supplied with all the necessary conveniences (not parts of its structure) that make it ready for use as a home. **Equip** stresses the provision of things (sometimes a single thing) making for efficiency in action or in use; thus, a poorly *furnished* kitchen may be short in tables or chairs, but a poorly *equipped* kitchen is not adequately provided with the utensils or appliances needed for cooking and other work carried on there; one may *equip* (but not *furnish*) an automobile with four-wheel brakes. **Outfit** stresses provision for a journey, an expedition, or a special kind of work; it is used chiefly with reference to necessary clothes, tools, and the like, and so is narrower in its range of applications than *furnish* and broader than *equip*. "It took several days to *outfit* me for my journey to Washington" (*Cather*). **Appoint** (now somewhat bookish in this sense) suggests complete, or often elegant, furnishings or equipment; as, well-*appointed* drawing rooms. "The Bristol mail is the best *appointed* in the kingdom" (*De Quincey*). **Accouter** stresses provision of dress, array, or personal equipment, esp. for military service; as, soldiers *accoutered* for the conflict. "He... was *accoutred* in a riding dress" (*Dickens*). It often refers to harness or trappings. "As soon as his master was in the saddle, he shook his *accoutrements* and sprang forward" (*G. Moore*). In its specific military sense, the noun *accouterments* is used only of such articles of a soldier's personal outfit as the belt or sword hanger, and excludes clothes and weapons; as, inspection of arms and *accouterments*. **Arm** stresses provision for effective action or operation; it is used chiefly with reference to equipment necessary for offense or defense; as, to *arm* a man of war; *armed* to the teeth; but it may imply any means of preparation for added strength, security, or the like; as, to *arm* the hilt of a sword with a plate; *armed* with rubbers and umbrella.

In their figurative senses, the words in this group retain their respective implications, but refer to mental, moral, or physical qualifications rather than to things; as, a strong heart is an important part of an athlete's *equipment*. "Perception is only part of our mental *outfit*" (*Eddington*). "He *armed* himself with patience, as was needful, having so much to endure" (*C. E. Norton*).

Ana. Endue, endow, *dower: array, apparel, *clothe.

Con. *Strip, dismantle, denude, divest: despoil, spoliate (see RAVAGE).

furor *or* **furore.** Fury, frenzy, enthusiasm, *inspiration, afflatus.

further, *adv. & adj.* *Farther.

further, *v.* Forward, *advance, promote.

Ana. *Help, aid, assist: back, champion, *support, uphold: propagate, *generate, engender: accelerate, *speed, hasten, quicken.

Ant. Hinder: retard. — *Con.* *Frustrate, thwart, foil, balk, baffle, circumvent, outwit: impede, obstruct, bar, block (see HINDER): *prevent, forestall.

furthermore. Moreover, besides, likewise, *also, too.

furtive. Stealthy, clandestine, surreptitious, underhand, underhanded, *secret, covert, privy, backstairs.

Ana. *Sly, cunning, crafty, wily, artful: *cautious, calculating, wary, circumspect: disguised, cloaked, masked (see DISGUISE, *v.*).

Ant. Forthright: brazen. — *Con.* *Straightforward, aboveboard: barefaced, brash, *shameless, impudent.

fury. 1 Rage, ire, *anger, wrath, indignation.

Ana. *Passion: exasperation, irritation, aggravation (see IRRITATE): *acrimony, asperity, acerbity.

2 Furor, frenzy, *inspiration, enthusiasm, afflatus.

fuse, *v.* **1** *Liquefy, melt, dissolve, deliquesce, thaw.

2 Amalgamate, merge, coalesce, blend, mingle, commingle, *mix.

Ana. Consolidate, unify, *compact: *unite, combine, conjoin.

fusion. Coalition, *alliance, league, federation, confederation, confederacy.

fuss, *n.* Pother, ado, flurry, *stir, bustle.

Ana. Agitation, perturbation, disturbance, flustering *or* fluster (see corresponding verbs at DISCOMPOSE): *haste, hurry, speed.

fussy. Finical, particular, pernickety, fastidious, squeamish, *nice.

Ana. Exacting, demanding, requiring (see DEMAND, *v.*): querulous, fretful, *irritable.

fustian, *n.* Rant, rodomontade, *bombast, rhapsody.

fusty. Musty, rancid, *malodorous, putrid, fetid, stinking, noisome, rank.

Ana. *Dirty, squalid, nasty, filthy, foul: slovenly, unkempt, sloppy, *slipshod.

futile. Futile, vain, fruitless, bootless, abortive agree in denoting barren of result. **Futile** and **vain** parallel each other only when they imply failure to realize an immediate aim. "It was equally in *vain*, and he soon wearied of his *futile* vigilance" (*Stevenson*). *Vain* (see VAIN, 1) usually implies little more than simple failure; *futile* may connote the completeness of the failure or the unwisdom of the undertaking. "All literature, art, and science are *vain*...if they do not enable you to be glad" (*Ruskin*). "...the *futility* of Sophia's career....She had grown old and hard in joyless years in order to amass this money which Cyril would spend coldly and ungratefully" (*Bennett*). Though both *vain* and *futile* may be applied to something contemplated but not yet tried, *vain* more often suggests a judgment based on previous experience; *futile*, one based on reasoning from self-evident principles. "But it is *vain* to talk of form and symmetry to the pure expansionist" (*Babbitt*). "It is *futile* to ask which [Shakespeare or Dante] undertook the more difficult job" (*T. S. Eliot*). **Fruitless** is often interchangeable with *vain*. But its literal meaning makes it especially applicable to undertakings that entail long, patient, arduous effort and severe disappointment. "...Whom he had long time sought with *fruitlesse* suit" (*Spenser*). **Bootless**, chiefly poetic, is especially applied to petitions or efforts to obtain relief. "They would not pity me, yet plead I must; And *bootless* unto them" (*Shak.*). **Abortive** implies failure before plans are matured or activities begun; as, an *abortive* conspiracy; an *abortive* attempt to break jail. "He had stirred up the Maronites to attack us...had I not brought up unexpectedly so many Arabs as rendered the scheme *abortive*" (*Scott*).

Ana. *Vain, idle, otiose, nugatory: *ineffective, ineffectual, inefficacious.

Con. Effectual, *effective, efficacious: fruitful (see FERTILE).

G

gab, *v.* *Chat, chatter, patter, prate, prattle, babble, gabble, jabber, gibber.

gabble, *v.* Babble, gab, chatter, *chat, patter, prate, prattle, jabber, gibber.

gad, *v.* *Wander, stray, roam, ramble, rove, range, prowl, gallivant, traipse, meander.

gadget. Contraption, *device, contrivance.

gag, *n.* *Jest, joke, jape, quip, witticism, wisecrack, crack.

gage, *n.*[1] *Pledge, earnest, token, pawn, hostage.

gage, *n.*[2] Variant of GAUGE.

gaggle, *n.* *Flock, herd, drove, pack, bevy, covey, flight, swarm, shoal.

gain, *v.* **1** Win, earn, obtain, procure, secure, acquire, *get.

Ana. Achieve, accomplish, effect (see PERFORM): endeavor, strive, struggle, *attempt, try.

Ant. Forfeit: lose.

2 Compass, *reach, achieve, attain.

Ana. & *Ant.* See those at GAIN, 1.

gainsay. *Deny, contradict, impugn, contravene, negative, traverse.

Ana. Controvert, refute, confute, *disprove: *oppose, combat, resist, withstand.

Ant. Admit (sense 2). — *Con.* *Grant, concede, allow.

gale. *Wind, hurricane, gust, blast, flaw, whirlwind, cyclone, typhoon, waterspout, twister, breeze.

gall, *n.* Effrontery, nerve, cheek, *temerity, hardihood, audacity.

gall, *v.* Chafe, excoriate, fret, *abrade.

Ana. *Injure, hurt, harm, damage.

gallant, *adj.* Courtly, chivalrous, courteous, polite, *civil.

Ana. Attentive, considerate, *thoughtful: *debonair: *spirited, mettlesome, high-spirited: urbane, *suave.

gallantry. 1 *Heroism, valor, prowess.

Ana. Bravery, intrepidity, valorousness, dauntlessness (see corresponding adjectives at BRAVE): *courage, mettle, spirit, resolution.

Ant. Dastardliness. — *Con.* Poltroonery, cravenness, cowardliness *or* cowardice (see corresponding adjectives at COWARDLY).

2 *Courtesy, attention, amenity, comity.

Ana. Chivalrousness *or* chivalry, courtliness (see corresponding adjectives at CIVIL): deference, homage (see HONOR): suavity, urbanity (see corresponding adjectives at SUAVE): address, poise, *tact, savoir-faire.

Con. Boorishness, churlishness, loutishness, clownishness (see corresponding adjectives under BOOR): discourteousness *or* discourtesy, ungraciousness, rudeness (see corresponding adjectives at RUDE).

gallery. 1 *Passage, passageway, corridor, arcade, cloister, ambulatory, aisle, hall, hallway.

2 *Balcony, loggia, veranda, piazza, porch, portico, stoop.

3 *Museum, treasury, thesaurus, archives, library.

gallivant. *Wander, stray, roam, ramble, rove, range, prowl, gad, traipse, meander.

gallop, *v.* *Trot, pace, single-foot, walk, run, canter, lope, rack, amble. See under TROT, *n.*

gallop, *n.* *Trot, pace, single-foot, walk, run, canter, lope, rack, amble.

galvanize. Excite, stimulate, *provoke, quicken, pique.

Ana. Rouse, arouse, rally, *stir, awaken, waken: electrify, *thrill, enthuse: enkindle, kindle, fire, inflame (see LIGHT, *v.*).

gambol, *n.* Frolic, disport, play, sport, rollick, romp. See under PLAY, *v.*

gambol, *v.* Frolic, disport, *play, sport, rollick, romp.

game, *n.* **1** Sport, play, *fun, jest.

Ana. Diversion, amusement, recreation, entertainment (see under AMUSE).

2 In plural form **games.** *Athletics, sports.

Ana. *Contest, conflict.

gamut. *Range, scope, compass, reach, sweep, radius, ken, purview, horizon, orbit.

gangster. *Ruffian, thug, Mohock, apache, desperado.

gaol. Variant of JAIL.

gape, *v.* *Gaze, stare, glare, gloat, peer.

Ana. Regard, admire (see under REGARD, *n.*): look, watch, *see.

Gargantuan. *Enormous, immense, huge, gigantic, giant, gigantean, colossal, titanic, herculean, Cyclopean, Antaean, Brobdingnagian, mammoth, elephantine, vast.

garish. *Gaudy, tawdry, flashy, meretricious.

Ana. Resplendent, gorgeous, *splendid: *showy, ostentatious, pretentious.

Ant. Somber.

garland. *Anthology, florilegium, treasury, thesaurus, corpus, chrestomathy, chapbook.

garnish, *v.* Embellish, beautify, deck, bedeck, *adorn, decorate, ornament.
Ana. Enhance, heighten, *intensify: prank, prink, perk up, doll up (see PREEN).

garrulity *or* **garrulousness.** Talkativeness, loquacity, volubility. See under TALKATIVE.
Ana. *Verbiage: prolixity, verboseness, diffuseness, wordiness (see corresponding adjectives at WORDY): chattering, prating, babbling, jabbering (see CHAT, *v.*).

garrulous. *Talkative, loquacious, voluble.
Ana. Glib, voluble, fluent, *vocal, articulate, eloquent.
Ant. Taciturn. — *Con.* Reserved, reticent, *silent, uncommunicative, close: laconic, terse, *concise: curt, brusque, blunt (see BLUFF).

gasconade, *v.* Vaunt, *boast, brag, crow.

gastronome *or* **gastronomer.** *Epicure, gourmet, gourmand, bon vivant, glutton.

gate. *Door, portal, gateway, postern, doorway.

gateway. Gate, portal, *door, postern, doorway.

gather, *v.* **1 Gather, collect, assemble, congregate** agree in meaning to come or to bring together so as to form a group, a mass, or a unit. The same distinctions in applications and in implications characterize their derivative nouns **gathering, collection, assemblage** (which see) or **assembly, congregation. Gather** is the most widely applicable of these words; it may be used in reference not only to persons and objects but to intangible things; as, a crowd *gathers* wherever there is excitement; to *gather* the boys and girls of the neighborhood for a picnic; leaves *gather* in heaps on windy days; to *gather* the leaves for burning; beads of moisture *gathered* on his brow; to *gather* one's ideas together before planning one's speech. In certain phrases *gather* acquires additional specific connotations; thus, to *gather* flowers or crops implies plucking and culling as well as bringing together; to *gather* a ruffle implies a drawing together or into folds as in shirring; to *gather* one's wits connotes an effort at concentration or at mustering or rallying; in the phrase "pus *gathers* to form an abscess" there is an implication of generation as well as of coming to a head. **Collect** is often used in place of *gather* with no intended difference in meaning; thus, one may say: to *collect* leaves or leaves *collect;* beads of moisture *collected* on his brow. They are not interchangeable, however, whenever the ideas of careful selection or a principle of selection, of orderly arrangement, or of a definitely understood (though not always expressed) end in view are involved; thus, to *collect* butterflies implies a selection of specimens and, usually, their cataloguing; to *collect* books (as in book *collector*) implies a choice of books with regard to some principle such as rarity, beauty of binding, authorship, and the like. There is a subtle difference between to *gather* one's thoughts, which often merely implies previous scattering, and to *collect* one's thoughts, which in precise use implies their organization; there is also a difference between to *gather* money, which may mean merely to accumulate it, and to *collect* money, which usually suggests raising a fund by gifts, subscriptions, and the like. In idiomatic English *collect* and *collection* are often preferred to *gather* and *gathering* when various things are brought together; thus, a jumble or an omnium-gatherum (despite its literal translation) is called a miscellaneous *collection* (not *gathering*); one *collects* (better than *gathers*) an assortment of articles. **Assemble** stresses more emphatically than either *gather* or *collect* a close union of individuals and a conscious or a definite end in their coming or in their being brought together. It is used chiefly (but far from exclusively) in reference to persons who gather together, either of their own will or at the call of another, so as to form a group or body that will unite in action, join in counsel, or the like; as, the democratic rights of free speech and free *assembly.* "They acted upon it [the proposed Constitution of the United States] in the only manner in which they can act safely, effectively, and wisely, on such a subject, by *assembling* in Convention" (*Ch. Just. Marshall*). "Even after a new crew had...been *assembled,* I had qualms about setting forth over the treacherous waters of the China Sea" (*V. Heiser*). In reference to things, *assemble,* in discriminating use, always implies an agent who collects them in order to unite them into a single body or structure, or into a distinct and isolated group; thus, the *assembly* department of an automobile plant is the department in which the workmen build the cars by *assembling* the component parts made in other departments or in other factories; it took twenty years to *assemble* the musical instruments which form this collection. **Congregate** implies a flocking together into a crowd, a huddle, a mass, or the like; as, cattle *congregate* during a storm; to pass laws forbidding persons to *congregate* on the streets. "They [tinted clouds produced in a gas-discharge lamp] are *congregations* of atoms excited and lucent, mingled with free electricity" (*Karl K. Darrow*). **Congregation** is specifically applied to an assembly meeting for religious worship, but it usually retains the suggestion of a crowd that has flocked together.
Ana. *Accumulate, amass, hoard: *heap, pile, stack, mass.
2 *Infer, deduce, conclude, judge.

gathering. Collection, assemblage, assembly, congregation. See under GATHER, *v.*
Ana. *Crowd, throng, press, horde, mob, rout, crush: accumulation (see corresponding verb ACCUMULATE).

gauche. Maladroit, *awkward, clumsy, inept.

gaudy. Gaudy, tawdry, garish, flashy, meretricious come into comparison as meaning vulgar or cheap in its showiness. That is **gaudy** which uses gay colors and conspicuous ornaments or ornamentation lavishly, ostentatiously, and tastelessly; as, "*gaudy* calicoes" (*Shaw*); "False eloquence, like the prismatic glass, Its *gaudy* colors spreads on ev'ry place" (*Pope*). That is **tawdry** which is not only gaudy but cheap. "Beneath the lamp her *tawdry* ribbons glare" (*Gay*). "A fancy...fruitful, yet not wanton, and gay without being *tawdry*" (*Cowper*). "He saw nothing else; the *tawdry* scenery, the soiled cotton velvet and flimsy crumpled satin, the reek of vulgarity, never touched his innocent mind" (*Deland*). That is **garish** which is dazzlingly or offensively bright; as, "Hide me from day's *garish* eye" (*Milton*); "for this week he would produce a bunch [of flowers] as *garish* as a gypsy, all blue and purple and orange, but next week a bunch discreet as a pastel, all rose and gray with a dash of yellow" (*V. Sackville-West*). That is **flashy** which dazzles for a moment but then reveals itself as shallow or vulgar display; as, "Tom Paine was considered for the time as a Tom Fool to him [Godwin], Paley an old woman, Edmund Burke a *flashy* sophist" (*Hazlitt*); "*flashy* make-believe" (*G. Eliot*). That is **meretricious** (literally, having to do with harlots, or prostitutes) which allures by false or deceitful show of worth, value, brilliancy, or the like; as, "The jewels in the crisped hair, the diadem on the polished brow, are thought *meretricious,* theatrical, vulgar" (*Hazlitt*). "The false taste, the showy and *meretricious* element...invading the social life of the period [around 1800] and supplanting the severe elegance, the instinctive grace of the eighteenth century" (*Binyon*). "If a writer's attitude toward his characters and his scene is as vulgar as a showman's, as mercenary as an auctioneer's, vulgar and *meretricious* will his product for ever remain" (*Cather*).

Ana. *Showy, pretentious, ostentatious: vulgar, *coarse, gross: resplendent, gorgeous (see SPLENDID).

Ant. Quiet (*in taste or style*). — *Con.* Modest, *chaste, decent, pure.

gauge *or* **gage,** *n.* *Standard, criterion, yardstick, touchstone.

gaunt. Rawboned, angular, lank, lanky, *lean, spare, scrawny, skinny.

Ana. Cadaverous, wasted, *haggard, worn: *thin, slim, slender, slight.

Con. Portly, plump, *fleshy, fat, stout, corpulent, obese, rotund, chubby.

gay. Vivacious, *lively, sprightly, animated.

Ana. *Merry, blithe, jocund, jovial, jolly: *playful, frolicsome, sportive.

Ant. Grave, sober. — *Con.* *Serious, sedate, staid, solemn, earnest: quiet, *still, silent.

gaze, *v.* **Gaze, gape, stare, glare, peer, gloat** come into comparison as meaning to look at long and attentively, but they vary greatly in their implications of attitude and motive. **Gaze** implies fixed and prolonged attention, especially as in admiration or wonder; as, "And still they *gazed*, and still the wonder grew, That one small head could carry all he knew" (*Goldsmith*); "He *gazed* so long That both his eyes were dazzled" (*Tennyson*). **Gape** adds to *gaze* the implication of stupid and openmouthed wonder or indecision; as, a yokel *gaping* at the sights on his first visit to the city; "The little men [Gurkhas] hitched their kukris well to hand, and *gaped* expectantly at their officers" (*Kipling*). **Stare** implies a fixed and direct gazing at a person or object: it may connote curiosity, astonishment, insolence, or vacant fixedness; as, "Or like stout Cortez when with eagle eyes He *star'd* at the Pacific—and all his men Look'd at each other with a wild surmise— Silent, upon a peak in Darien" (*Keats*); "*staring* at each other as if a bet were depending on the first man who winked" (*G. Eliot*); "She tried not to *stare* at Mr. Scales, but her gaze would not leave him" (*Bennett*). **Glare** adds to *stare* the implication of fierceness or anger; as, "All... with countenance grim *Glared* on him passing" (*Milton*); "Neither Clem nor Lonnie replied. Arch *glared* at them for not answering" (*E. Caldwell*). **Peer** suggests a looking narrowly, especially with or as if with partly closed eyes, or curiously, especially through or from behind something; as, "Mrs. Cary kept *peering* uneasily out of the window at her husband" (*M. Wilkins*); "His pale, near-sighted eyes had always the look of *peering* into distance" (*Cather*). **Gloat** usually implies prolonged or frequent gazing upon something, especially in secret, in earlier use amorously, but now more often with profound, usually malignant or unhallowed, satisfaction; as, a miser *gloating* over his hoard, "To *gaze* and *gloat* with his hungry eye On jewels that gleamed like a glowworm's spark" (*Longfellow*). In more recent use, the implication of malignant satisfaction is often so emphasized that the implication of gazing is obscured or lost; as, "in vengeance *gloating* on another's pain" (*Byron*); "that resolution of Orrin's is chock-full of bad grammar, and King'll *gloat* over that" (*Kipling*).

Ana. Watch, look, *see: observe, survey, contemplate (see SEE): regard, admire (see under REGARD, *n.*).

azetteer. *Dictionary, lexicon, wordbook, glossary, onomasticon, synonymicon.

ear. Tackle, *equipment, paraphernalia, outfit, apparatus, machinery.

Ana. Appurtenances, accessories, adjuncts, appendages (see singular nouns at APPENDAGE): *possessions, belongings, effects, means.

geld. Castrate, *sterilize, asexualize, spay, emasculate, caponize, mutilate.

gelid. Icy, frigid, freezing, *cold, glacial, arctic, cool, chilly, frosty.

gem. Jewel, *stone.

gendarme. Officer, *policeman, constable, bailiff, catchpole, bobby, peeler, copper, cop, bull.

gender. *Sex.

general, *adj.* Generic, *universal, common.

Ana. *Regular, typical, normal, natural.

Con. Specific, *special, particular, individual, concrete: peculiar, distinctive, *characteristic, individual.

generate, *v.* **Generate, engender, breed, beget, get, sire, procreate, propagate, reproduce** come into comparison in the sense of to give life or origin to or to bring into existence by or as by natural processes. **Generate,** which means no more than this, is now used rarely in reference to human beings, seldom in reference to animals or plants (as, mushrooms are not *generated* from seeds), but is the technical term in reference to electricity (as, to *generate* an electric current) and is used commonly in reference to ideas, emotions, passions, moods, conditions, or the like, that have a traceable cause or source; as, "a habit of thought...only to be *generated* by intimate knowledge of good literature" (*B. Russell*); "I do not think religious feeling is ever aroused, except by ideas of objective truth and value; but these ideas are certainly not *generated* by feeling" (*Inge*); "the mood *generated* in me by the intellectual convictions current in my time" (*J. W. Krutch*). **Engender,** like *generate*, is now chiefly found in its extended sense. Literally, however, it refers particularly to the initial step in the process of generation, sometimes on the part of the male parent (as, "When a man...*engenders* his like...it is no miracle"—*Hobbes*), sometimes, but less often, on the part of the female parent (as, "O error, soon conceived, Thou... kill'st the mother that *engender'd* thee!"—*Shak.*); as a result, in extended use, it more often suggests an originating or a sudden or immediate birth than a bringing into fullness of life or being; as, "to hunger for the hope and happiness which...the dance seemed to *engender* within them" (*Hardy*); "a sudden spontaneous illumination...*engendered* in the course of writing a poem" (*Day Lewis*); "the strike, during which three men had been killed and ill-feeling *engendered* in hundreds of silent workers" (*S. Anderson*). **Breed** originally meant, but now rarely means except in dialectal or vulgar use, to bring, as a mother, one's young through the process of development from the time of the fertilization of the seed or egg to the time of birth or hatching. Now, the term often carries a less specific meaning and suggests merely the production of offspring (as, "Mankind will in every country *breed* up to a certain point"—*W. Paley*), sometimes by parental action but even more often by the activity of those who determine the parentage, the time of mating, the number of offspring, and the like (as, specialists who *breed* horses for racing; *breeders* of fine cattle; "the notion of a Government department trying to make out how many different types were necessary, and how many persons of each type, and proceeding to *breed* them by appropriate marriages, is amusing but not practicable"—*Shaw*). Oftentimes, the word adds the implication of nurturing or rearing to that of producing offspring, sometimes so stressing it that there is no reference to the life processes involved in generation; as, he was *bred* in a manner befitting the son of a king; "he was born and *bred* in your house" (*Jowett*); "*bred* and born in a brier patch, Br'er Fox" (*J. C. Harris*). In its extended sense, *breed* usually implies a gradual or continuous process of coming into being: it may specifically suggest a period of latency or quiescence before breaking out; as, "An iniquitous government *breeds* despair in men's souls" (*J. Morley*); "The yoke a man creates for himself by wrong-doing will *breed* hate in the kindliest nature" (*G. Eliot*); "Incessant recurrence without variety *breeds* tedium" (*Lowes*). **Beget,** or **get,** and **sire** imply the act of the male parent: in current use, *beget* is preferred in reference to men and *get* and *sire* in reference to animals, but in earlier use all three were interchangeable; as, "Cowards father cowards and base things *sire* base" (*Shak.*); "He that *begetteth* a fool doeth it to his sorrow" (*Proverbs* xvii. 21); the only lawfully-*begotten* son of the King; "I had rather to adopt a child than *get* it" (*Shak.*); a thoroughbred *sired* by one of the most famous stallions of the breed. Only *beget* has an extended sense derived from this literal meaning. In such use there is very little difference between *beget* and *engender*, both terms often being employed interchangeably without loss. But *beget* tends to stress calling into being, as on the spur of the moment or without any previous preparation or expectation; as, beauty that *begets* wonder and admiration; "stories...spring from the fillip of some suggestion, and one *begets* another" (*Lowes*). **Procreate,** a somewhat formal or literary word, comes close in meaning to *breed* in the sense of to produce offspring. Though sometimes used as a synonym of *beget*, it more often refers to sexual acts involved in a mating and their results in the production of children; as, through this marriage an heir to the throne was *procreated;* "Matrimony....was ordained for the *procreation* of children" (*Marriage Service in Book of Common Prayer*). **Propagate** is now more often used than *procreate*, but it carries implications of preserving and increasing one's kind that are not inherent in *procreate;* also, it is used as frequently of animals and of plants as of men, and may be employed in reference to races, peoples, species, and the like, as well as in reference to individuals; as, plants are *propagated* by seeds, cuttings, division of roots, offsets, and the like; the rabbit *propagates* itself with great rapidity; "Thine ordinance [matrimony], whereby Thou hast provided for the *propagation* of mankind" (*Marriage Service in Manual of Prayers*). In its extended use, *propagate* implies not only giving rise to something or bringing it into existence, but often also a continuation of that existence or the widespread dissemination of the thing that is brought into existence; as, Communists have been successful in *propagating* their ideas; the Society for the *Propagation* of the Gospel in Foreign Parts; " 'Oh! does patience *beget* patience?' said Adrian. 'I was not aware it was a *propagating* virtue' " (*Meredith*). **Reproduce** may be used in reference to any living thing capable of bringing into existence one or more of its kind. The term does not necessarily imply the mating of male and female and consequent generation, for it may suggest an asexual process such as the division of one body into two parts (a process which occurs in the lowest forms of life) or the formation of a protuberance or projection on the parent's body and its development (sometimes separating as in the hydra, sometimes remaining attached, as in the coral). "The tribe was dying out; infant mortality was heavy, and the young couples did not *reproduce* freely,—the life-force seemed low" (*Cather*).

Ana. *Bear, produce, yield: *teem, abound.

generic. General, *universal, common.

Ana. Typical, *regular, normal: specific (see SPECIAL).

Con. Individual, peculiar, distinctive, *characteristic: particular, individual, concrete, *special.

generous. Bountiful, munificent, *liberal, handsome.

Ana. Lavish, prodigal, *profuse, exuberant: benevolent, philanthropic, *charitable, altruistic.

Ant. Stingy. — *Con.* Close, closefisted, niggardly, parsimonious, penurious, miserly, curmudgeonly (see STINGY): *mean, ignoble.

genial. Sociable, affable, *gracious, cordial.

Ana. *Kind, kindly, benign, benignant: friendly, neighborly, *amicable: jocund, jovial, jolly, blithe, *merry: cheerful, happy, *glad.

Ant. Saturnine (*manner, disposition, aspect*): caustic (*remarks, comments, etc.*). — *Con.* Ungracious, discourteous, uncivil, *rude: morose, crabbed, *sullen: ironical, sardonic, *sarcastic, satirical.

genius. Talent, *gift, faculty, aptitude, knack, bent, turn.

Ana. *Ability, capacity, capability: originality (see corresponding adjective at NEW): daemon (see DEMON): *inspiration, afflatus, enthusiasm.

genteel. *Gentle.

Ana. Pretentious, pompous, ostentatious, *showy.

Con. Simple, *natural, unaffected, artless, naïve, unsophisticated, ingenuous.

Gentile, *n.* *Pagan, heathen, paynim, ethnic.

Gentile, *adj.* Pagan, heathen, paynim, ethnic. See under PAGAN, *n.*

gentle, *adj.* **1 Gentle, genteel,** come into comparison as meaning characteristic of or befitting a person of good birth or good breeding. **Gentle,** except when applied to terms such as *blood, birth, extraction,* and *breeding,* or when found in compounds such as *gentle*man, *gentle*woman, and *gentle*folk, is now chiefly historical or archaic in the sense of having (or derived from a family having) inherited high rank or social position. When the adjective is applied to actions, words, manners, a way of living, or the like, the term now usually implies the manifestation of qualities commonly associated with such persons, such as courteousness, chivalrousness, cultivation, refinement, taste, and the like. "Monsieur Defarge bent down on one knee to the child of his old master, and put her hand to his lips. It was a *gentle* action, but not at all *gently* done" (*Dickens*). "A restful, friendly room, fitted to the uses of *gentle* life, covered...with beauty, with the... manners of a life lived with...leisure" (*M. Austin*). **Genteel** came into English from the French *gentil* in the late 16th century, the spelling *gentile* being preferred until the late 17th century. The first implication was that of birth and breeding above that of a commoner; though the term was occasionally applied to persons of noble birth, it soon was associated particularly with the class called the gentry, and especially with persons of leisure, or fashion, or good breeding as distinguished from the masses of common or ill-bred persons; as "After staying long enough...to discover that the crowd was insupportable, and that there was not a *genteel* face to be seen...they hastened away to the Crescent, to breathe the fresh air of better company" (*Austen*); "A well-known and respected widow...of a standing which can only be expressed by the word *genteel*" (*Hardy*). Gradually the term came to imply a more or less affected gentility or an effort to retain the outward marks of gentility under the stress of insufficient means and is now regarded as inelegant, except when used humorously or in the combination *shabby-genteel;* as "*Shabby-genteel* houses, surrounded with deal fences, and things called gardens" (*W. Cobbett*). It occurs, however more often in sly than in broad humor; as, "country o

Bavarian beer not being *genteel* enough for the hotel" (*Thackeray*); "Swaying her rattling skirts with a *genteel* air" (*M. Wilkins*); "Her letter, couched in majestic but most *genteel* phrase, reached him Friday evening" (*Deland*).

Ana. Chivalrous, courtly, gallant, courteous (see CIVIL): *debonair: aristocratic, gentlemanly, patrician (see corresponding nouns at GENTLEMAN).

Ant. Boorish. — ***Con.*** Churlish, loutish, clownish (see under BOOR): *rude, ill-mannered, discourteous, ungracious, impolite, uncivil.

2 *Soft, mild, lenient, bland, balmy.

Ana. *Moderate, temperate: *pleasant, agreeable, grateful, pleasing, welcome: *calm, tranquil, serene, placid, peaceful, halcyon.

Ant. Rough, harsh. — ***Con.*** Vehement, *intense: *powerful, forcible, forceful: stimulating, exciting, provoking *or* provocative (see corresponding verbs at PROVOKE).

gentlefolk. Gentry, *aristocracy, nobility, county, elite, society.

gentleman. **Gentleman, patrician, aristocrat** are synonyms when they denote a wellborn or blue-blooded person. **Gentleman,** in its technical British sense (which is now chiefly historical), implies descent from good family, the right to bear a coat of arms, and social rank just below that of the noble and above that of the yeoman. The term, especially in modern use, has been widely extended in its application and has acquired connotations which have little or nothing to do with lineage or heraldic rights; however, when used specifically with reference to social rank, it still commonly suggests the outward marks of good birth, elegance of person and of manners, and a life of leisure. "A *gentleman* born, master parson; who writes himself 'Armigero,' in any bill, warrant, quittance, or obligation" (*Shak.*). "A *gentleman*...I'll be sworn thou art; Thy tongue, thy face, thy limbs, actions and spirit, Do give thee five-fold blazon" (*Shak.*). "Somebody has said that a king may make a nobleman, but he cannot make a *gentleman*" (*Burke*). **Patrician** derives its implications from its historical applications, but chiefly from its earliest reference to a Roman citizen who belonged to one of the original families of ancient Rome which, after the growth of the plebeian order, kept power and authority in their own hands. The word in modern use always suggests a distinguished ancestry, superior culture, and aloofness from all that is common or vulgar; it is applied chiefly to descendants of the oldest and most influential families when they constitute a social caste, especially one marked by exclusiveness and pride in birth. "The merchant-*patricians* [of Boston], like those of Holland and Flanders, in times gone by, wished to perpetuate their names and glorify their capital not only in the elegance of their mansions but also in churches, parks and public buildings" (*Van W. Brooks*). **Aristocrat** carries fewer suggestions of inbred physical characteristics than *gentleman* or *patrician*, but it suggests a sympathy with the point of view common to them. In historical use, it commonly implies an opposition to *democrat*, and is applicable to a person who believes in government by superior persons or by the class which includes such persons; in general modern use it is commonly applied to a person who by reason of birth, breeding, title, wealth, or the like, is accorded recognition as a member of the highest and, in some countries, the ruling caste. "Men...are naturally divided into two parties: 1. Those who fear and distrust the people, and wish to draw all powers from them into the hands of the higher classes. 2. Those who identify themselves with the people, have confidence in them...and consider them as the most honest and safe...depository of the public interests.... The appellation of *Aristocrats* and Democrats is the true one, expressing the essence of all" (*Jefferson*). "Up to now it had been an essentially *aristocratic* movement—superior, sniffish and anti-democratic" (*Mencken*).

Ant. Boor, churl. — ***Con.*** Lout, clown (see BOOR).

gentry. *Aristocracy, county, gentlefolk, nobility, elite, society.

genuine. *Authentic, bona fide, veritable.

Ana. True, *real, actual: unadulterated, unsophisticated (see affirmative verbs at ADULTERATE): *pure, sheer, absolute: *sincere, unfeigned.

Ant. Counterfeit: fraudulent. — ***Con.*** Simulated, feigned, shammed *or* sham, counterfeited (see corresponding verbs at ASSUME): *false: *fictitious, apocryphal, mythical: factitious, *artificial, ersatz.

geoponic. *Rural, rustic, pastoral, bucolic, georgic, Arcadian, agrestic.

georgic. Bucolic, pastoral, *rural, rustic, Arcadian, agrestic, geoponic.

germ, *n.* **Germ, microbe, bacterium, bacillus, virus, pathogen** require discrimination not because they are synonyms but because all except *pathogen,* in the popular mind, denote one of numerous organisms invisible to the naked eye and responsible for the origin and development of many diseases. **Germ** and **microbe** are the ordinary nonscientific names for such an organism, especially for one that causes disease. *Germ* was first used in the early part of the nineteenth century when scientists were beginning to realize that minute organisms were probably responsible for some diseases; *microbe* came into use after the existence of disease-producing microorganisms had been established. *Bacteria,* the plural of **bacterium,** and the form commonly in use, is often incorrectly employed as though it were the equivalent of *germs* and *microbes.* Actually, it is the scientific designation of a very large group of unicellular microorganisms only some of which are instrumental in producing disease in man, animals, and plants, which are found widely distributed in water, air, soil, living things and dead organic matter, and which have structural and biological characteristics distinguishing them from other unicellular microorganisms such as the protozoa. In addition to the pathogenic, or disease-causing bacteria, there are the saprophytic bacteria which live upon dead or decaying organic matter and which, for the most part, are beneficial in their effects. Through the operation of bacteria such organic matter is converted into plant food. Fermentation, oxidation, and many other natural processes are the result of bacterial activity. **Bacillus** is often employed as though it designates any of the pathogenic bacteria. In correct scientific use, it names one of a genus of bacteria which are rod-shaped as distinguished from those which are globe-shaped (the coccus form, of which the streptococcus is an example) and those which are spiral (the spirillus form, of which the vibrio which causes Asiatic cholera is an example). Shape, and usually, nutritive habits, distinguish these genera, and beneficent as well as pathogenic species are found in all three groups. However, *bacillus* has, owing to differences in scientific description of the shape, been used in the designations of many species, including a large number of pathogenic forms, which are properly classified in other genera. It is possible to speak of the *bacilli* of typhus, diphtheria, tetanus, and the like, though they are not true bacilli, only because in some classifications these bacteria are so designated. But only in loose use is *bacillus* employed as meaning any disease-causing microorganism. **Virus** is, in accurate use, a substance, or poison, which is present in the juices of an organism (person, animal, plant) having an infectious disease and which, when transmitted to or injected into another organism, causes the same disease; thus, vaccine is a preparation containing the *virus* of cowpox in attenuated form. Since this substance is usually so minute that it is invisible even under the finest microscopes and passes through the finest filters known to bacteriologists (so that the term *virus* alone is often used as equivalent to the term *filtrable virus*), its exact nature is not known and it is by some believed to be a microorganism and by others a lifeless molecule. The juice of an animal or plant containing this virus in attenuated or dead form is often also, especially in loose or extended use, called *virus*. "When the doctors inoculate you...they give you an infinitesimally attenuated dose. If they gave you the *virus* at full strength it would overcome your resistance and produce its direct effect" (*Shaw*). The specific scientific term for a disease-producing organism or virus is **pathogen,** but this word has not yet been introduced into general use.

germane *or* **german.** *Relevant, pertinent, material, apposite, applicable, apropos.
Ana. Appropriate, fitting, apt, happy, felicitous (see FIT): akin, analogous, comparable, parallel (see SIMILAR): *related, allied, cognate, kindred.
Ant. Foreign. — *Con.* Alien, extraneous, *extrinsic: incongruous, *inconsonant, incompatible.

germicidal. Antiseptic, bactericidal, disinfectant. See under ANTISEPTIC, *n.*

germicide. Bactericide, *antiseptic, disinfectant, bacteriophage, antitoxin.

Gestalt. Configuration, conformation, figure, *form, shape.

gesticulation. *Gesture.

gesture, *n.* **Gesture, gesticulation** come into comparison as meaning an expressive movement or motion of the body or limbs, or the use of such a movement or motion. **Gesture** is commonly the more inclusive term, for it may imply any such movement or motion intended to express what words cannot or to increase the effectiveness or poignancy of words that are being uttered, or to take the place of words when for some reason or other they are unnecessary or impossible; as, "The right [hand of Niobe] is drawing up her daughter to her; and with that instinctive *gesture*...is encouraging the child to believe that it can give security" (*Shelley*); "he had permitted himself his very first and last *gesture* in all these days, raising a hard-clenched fist above his head" (*Conrad*); "the *gesture* with which he threw away the cigar-end struck her as very distinguished" (*Bennett*). **Gesticulation,** on the other hand, is applicable only when there is implication of unrestrained excitement, or the loss or absence of grace or dignity, or a determined effort to attract attention; as, "His [Poussin's] human figures are sometimes 'o'erinformed' with...feeling. Their actions have too much *gesticulation*" (*Hazlitt*); "making various savage *gesticulations*" (*Livingstone*); the speaker's *gesticulations* caused much amusement among the bystanders.

get. **1 Get, obtain, procure, secure, acquire, gain, win, earn** are often used interchangeably in the sense of to come into the possession of. **Get,** one of the most general words in the English language, outstrips all the others in the number and diversity of its implications and in the range of its applicability. Unlike the others in this group, it does not necessarily presuppose effort or, at least, initiative. One *gets*, or comes into possession of, a thing by various means, as by fetching (go and *get* the book), by derivation or extraction (to *get* gold from ore), by receiving (to *get* a present), or in return for something (to *get* interest on one's money). **Obtain** is closest to *get* in extent of applicability, but it almost always implies activity or, at least, intent or hope, in the one who obtains. It suggests, therefore, the satisfaction of a desire or the attainment of an end worked for, sought for, or prayed for; as, to *obtain* money enough to establish a small business; to *obtain* a victory; to *obtain* mercy or pardon. "Evidence *obtained* and only *obtainable* by a criminal act" (*Justice Holmes*). **Procure** suggests effort directed to the obtaining of something for oneself or for others: it distinctively implies care, management, or contrivance; as, to *procure* supplies at the lowest market prices; he was unable to *procure* milk for the children. "They *procured* the means to get the best education England can give" (*Quiller-Couch*). **Secure** as a synonym of *get* and *obtain* is often attacked by purists. Discriminating writers, however, use it so as to retain its etymological implication of placing beyond danger, especially of loss. In such use, one *secures* that which is difficult to obtain because of competition, rarity, or the like, and fixes it in one's possession or under one's control; as, to *secure* the best seat in a coach; several colleges tried to *secure* Professor F's services; to *secure* the good opinion of the critics. "This style which *secures* its emphasis by always hesitating on the edge of caricature at the right moment" (*T. S. Eliot*). **Acquire,** though it usually presupposes exertion, strongly suggests addition, as by accretion, by natural growth, or as an inevitable result, to what is already possessed. "Jane seemed to me to be increasingly interesting; she was *acquiring* new subtleties, complexities, and comprehensions, and shedding crudities" (*R. Macaulay*). In very precise use, that which is *acquired* is not an immediate objective but an ultimate product or a by-product; thus, one reads good poetry and *acquires* a fine literary taste; a lawyer *obtains* a victory and *acquires* renown; by buying books regularly, he finally *acquired* a library of his own. "A doctrine which has *acquired* a mysterious or sacramental value" (*Inge*). The participial adjective *acquired* is often used with the implication of a contrast; as, *acquired* (opposed to *inherited*) wealth; *acquired* (opposed to *innate, inborn*) ability. **Gain** adds to *obtain* the implications of struggle or competition and of value, especially material value, in the thing gained. "For what is a man profited, if he shall *gain* the whole world, and lose his own soul" (*Matthew* xvi. 26). Sometimes only struggle is implied; as, to *gain* a meager living from the soil; sometimes, there is no suggestion of struggle and the value of the thing gained is stressed. "Unless good sense preserve what beauty *gains*" (*Pope*). **Win,** though often interchangeable with *gain*, can suggest, as *gain* cannot, favoring qualities in the one who wins or favorable circumstances affecting the result; as, faint heart never *won* fair lady; to *win* a prize for the best essays; to *win* a hundred dollars in a lottery. **Earn** definitely implies a correspondence between the effort and that which one gets by effort; it therefore usually suggests compensation. "The high repute Which he through hazard huge must *earn*" (*Milton*).
Ana. Fetch, *bring: extract, elicit, extort, *educe, evoke: *receive, accept: seize, *take, grasp, grab, clutch: effect, accomplish, achieve (see PERFORM): *incur, contract, catch.
Con. *Forgo, eschew, abnegate, sacrifice, forbear.
2 Beget, procreate, sire, *generate, engender, breed, propagate, reproduce.
Ana. See those at BEGET.

ghastly. **Ghastly, grisly, gruesome** (*or* **grewsome**), **macabre, grim, lurid** come into comparison only when they mean horrifying and repellent in appearance or aspect. **Ghastly** suggests the terrifying aspects of death or bloodshed; as, his *ghastly* paleness; "Death Grinned horrible a *ghastly* smile" (*Milton*); "the image of a hideous—of a *ghastly* thing—of the gallows!" (*Poe*). The term is often currently used as a strong intensive for *hideous, horrifying;* as, the growing conviction that the defeat was the result of a *ghastly* and unnecessary blunder. **Grisly,** or in modern usage more commonly **gruesome,** implies an appearance that inspires shuddering or uncanny horror; as, "So spake the *grisly* Terror" (*Milton*); "See the *griesly* texture grow, ('Tis of human entrails made)" (*Gray*); "Look down, and see a *griesly* sight; A vault where the bodies are buried upright!" (*Wordsworth*); the *gruesome* details of a murder; many readers find Keats's *Isabella* too *gruesome* for enjoyment. In current English, *grisly* (sometimes as a variant of, but often by confusion with, *grizzly*) occasionally suggests grayness and unkemptness rather than horribleness; as, "the *grisly* old man at the helm, carrying his craft with strange skill through the turmoil of waters" (*Kinglake*). **Macabre** (taken from the French phrase *danse macabre,* or dance of death, a dance in which Death, the leader, is often represented, as in a painting, as a skeleton drawing living persons or other skeletons to the grave) is used in place of *gruesome* when one wishes to imply preoccupation with the horrors of death; as, a *macabre* painting; a *macabre* tale. **Grim** suggests a fierce and forbidding aspect; as, "So should a murderer look, so dead, so *grim*" (*Shak.*); "with countenance *grim* Glared on him passing" (*Milton*). **Lurid** comes into comparison with *ghastly* as referring to light or color; it suggests either a ghastly pallor or coloring reminiscent of death (as, "Death... pale as yonder wan and hornèd moon, With lips of *lurid* blue"—*Shelley*) or more frequently, in modern usage, a sinister and murky glow; as, "He caught the color of what was passing about him but mixed with a *lurid* and portentous hue" (*N. Hawthorne*); "No *lurid* fire of hell or human passion illumines their scenes" (*C. W. Eliot*). In still looser but even commoner use, *lurid* differs little from *gruesome* except, possibly, in its stronger suggestion of sensationalism; as, reporters who like to give all the *lurid* details of a catastrophe; the detective story may be described as *lurid* rather than as mysterious.

Ana. Deathly, *deadly: frightful, horrible, horrific, dreadful, *fearful, appalling: repellent, *repugnant: repulsive, revolting, loathsome, *offensive.

ghost. Spirit, specter, shade, *apparition, phantasm, phantom, wraith, fetch, revenant, spook, haunt.

giant, *adj.* Gigantic, gigantean, colossal, *enormous, huge, mammoth, elephantine, titanic, herculean, immense, vast, Cyclopean, Antaean, Gargantuan, Brobdingnagian.

gib. Variant of JIB.

gibber, *v.* Prate, chatter, *chat, gab, patter, prattle, babble, gabble, jabber.

gibberish. Gibberish, mummery, hocus-pocus, abracadabra are compared here as terms of contempt applied to that which is in itself unintelligible or is meaningless to the person concerned. They are often used interchangeably without justification, for they are not synonyms. **Gibberish** always suggests language. It is applied, however, to inarticulate but expressive sounds or attempts at speech; as, a baby's or a monkey's *gibberish.* When applied to articulate but incoherent utterance it usually implies a low-grade or disordered intelligence in the speaker. It often means little more than *jargon.* One or more of these implications is carried over when the word is used to express contempt. "I have often warn'd you not to talk the court *gibberish* to me" (*Fielding*). **Mummery,** on the other hand, does not suggest language, but actions uninterpreted by words, as in the old dumb shows. As a term of derogation, however, it is applied chiefly to rites, proceedings, and the like, which, whether or not accompanied by words, appear theatrical and ridiculous, as well as meaningless, to the observer. "Nigel felt, and indeed exhibited, some disgust at this *mummery* [ceremony of his acceptance as a resident of Whitefriars]" (*Scott*). **Hocus-pocus** always suggests jugglery and incantations. Sometimes, in its extended use, the stress is placed upon tricks intended to mystify or confuse, sometimes upon empty but impressive-sounding words. In either case there is the suggestion of conscious attempts to bewilder and mislead. "I'd rip their [hypocritical preachers'] rotten, hollow hearts, An' tell aloud Their jugglin, *hocus-pocus* arts To cheat the crowd!" (*Burns*). **Abracadabra** was originally applied to a mystical figure, an inverted triangle, used as an amulet and formed by repetitions of the word *abracadabra* minus one letter at each successive line until only *a* was left. *Abracadabra* in figurative use is applied chiefly to discourse and implies not only its unintelligibility and formulism, but its complete unfitness for the ends it proposes to achieve. "Psychology is either true knowledge concerning the spiritual nature of man or it is moonshine and *abracadabra*" (*J. M. Murry*).

gibe[1] *or* **jibe,** *v.* *Scoff, jeer, sneer, flout, gird, fleer.

Ana. *Ridicule, deride, mock, taunt, twit, rally.

gibe.[2] Variant of JIBE.

gift, *n.* **1 Gift, present, gratuity, favor** (*or* **favour**), **boon, largess** (*or* **largesse**), **fairing** come into comparison when they denote something (often a thing of value, but not necessarily a material thing) given freely to another for his benefit or pleasure. **Gift** is the most inclusive term but it is not interchangeable with some of the others, for, in itself, apart from the context, the term carries no hint of remuneration for something done or received and excludes all suggestion of return; as, a birthday *gift;* a *gift* to a museum; *gifts* to the poor; to fear the Greeks bearing *gifts;* "Every good *gift* and every perfect *gift* is from above" (*James* i. 17). **Present** is ordinarily applied to something tangible which is offered as a compliment or expression of good will; as, "She used to define a *present,* 'That it was a *gift* to a friend of something he wanted or was fond of, and which could not be easily gotten for money' " (*Swift*); "Flowers and fruits are always fit *presents*" (*Emerson*); "Little odd *presents* of game, fruits, perhaps wine" (*Lamb*). **Gratuity** implies voluntary compensation (usually in money) for some service for which there is no fixed charge or for special attention or service over and beyond that which is normally included in a charge, such as a tip to a porter or a fee to a stewardess; he distributed *gratuities* so generously that he received more attention than any other guest of the hotel. **Favor** (see also FAVOR, 1) applies to anything given or granted to another as a token of one's affection, regard, or partiality, or as an indulgence or concession. The term is often intentionally vague, especially when that which is given is not a concrete thing; as, he said he did not deserve so many *favors* from his party. "Queen's *favours* might be fatal *gifts,* but they were much more fatal to reject than to accept" (*H. Adams*). Concretely, the term applies to various small things, such as a ribbon, a cockade, a lady's glove, or the like, given to a lover or admirer as a token, or some knickknack or other trifle, given to guests at a wedding, a cotillion, or the like. *Favor,* rather than *gift,* is used commonly in requests for anything that can be had only from the person addressed; as, to ask the *favor* of one's presence at a reception; "begging the *favour* of a Copy of his Beautiful Book" (*Meredith*). **Boon** applies to any gift or favor either as petitioned for or prayed for as something much desired or needed, yet not necessarily regarded as a right (as, "High emperor, upon my feeble knee I beg this *boon*, with tears not lightly shed"—*Shak.;* "If you mean to please any people, you must give them the *boon* which they ask"—*Burke;* "I ask justice from you, and no *boon*"—*Sheridan*) or as given gratuitously and bringing with it such benefits or advantages that it is regarded as a blessing or cause for gratitude (as, our forefathers have given us the *boon* of freedom; "The *boon* of free and unbought justice was a *boon* for all"—*J. R. Green;* "Corinth was given certain *boons*, since it was a Julian colony, but Athens...was left to academic decay"—*Buchan*). **Largess** is a grandiloquent term for a bountiful gift, especially of money or of food and drink, or a liberal gratuity; it usually suggests an ostentatious bestowal; as, the newly consecrated king bestowed *largesses* on all the heralds and minstrels; "contrasting his [Antony's] meagre bounty with the *largesse* of Octavius" (*Buchan*). **Fairing,** originally applied to a gift bought at a fair and later to any gift or present, now occurs rarely, although it was common up to the nineteenth century. "Colin...gives her a *fairing* to put in her hair" (*Goldsmith*).

Ana. *Donation, benefaction, contribution, alms.

2 Gift, faculty, aptitude, genius, talent, knack, bent, turn come into comparison when they mean a special ability or a capacity for a definite kind of activity, achievement, or the like. **Gift** applies not only to an ability but also to a quality; it always suggests an origin not easily explainable by natural laws and often implies that the recipient is favored by God, by nature, or by fortune. It is, therefore, precisely applied to any innate ability, capacity, or quality, especially to one not commonly found in men or not possible of acquirement; as, a *gift* of humor; "she has a real *gift* for arranging flowers" (*E. Wharton*). "Men have always reverenced prodigious inborn *gifts*, and always will" (*C. W. Eliot*). "An artist is the sort of artist he is, because he happens to possess certain *gifts*" (*A. Huxley*). **Faculty,** as here considered (see also POWER, 2), applies to both innate and acquired abilities or capacities; it does not in itself apart from the context impute an extraordinary value to that power, but it does usually imply distinction or distinctiveness in its quality and skill or facility in its exercise. "He had not that *faculty* of extracting the essence from a heap of statements" (*Dickens*). "She seemed to have lost her *faculty* of discrimination; her power of easily and graciously keeping everyone in his proper place" (*Cather*). **Aptitude** usually implies a natural liking and taste for some particular activity or pursuit as well as a native capacity for it and the ability to master its details or technique. "There are all sorts of people today who write from all sorts of motives other than a genuine *aptitude* for writing" (*H. Ellis*). "At fourteen education should begin to be more or less specialized, according to the tastes and *aptitudes* of the pupil" (*B. Russell*). **Genius,** when it applies to the ability or capacity, rather than to the person who possesses that ability or capacity, always suggests an inborn gift of an exalted character, or more often, a combination of such gifts. Further than this the implications of the term are various and shifting, for the word is tied up in use with psychological, aesthetic, and critical explanations of the nature of genius. Thus, during the age of romanticism, originality and creative energy working without reference to rule or law were its chief connotations; in modern times these connotations have been weakened as the result of a prevalent conception of genius as "an infinite capacity for taking pains." However, the word often retains its etymological implication of a controlling spirit, and in discriminating use usually denotes an inner driving energy (often thought of as an indwelling spirit or other self) which compels utterance or performance, often, but far from invariably, of a lofty or transcendent quality. "Carlyle is one [of the writers having a distinctive style]—who take no care to put listeners at their ease, but rely rather on native force of *genius* to shock and astound" (*Quiller-Couch*). "That effortless and unconscious victory over Death, which is the ultimate interest of her writing, was the outcome of a *genius* she [Madame de Sévigné] never knew she possessed" (*L. P. Smith*). The word is often employed in current English in the sense of *gift*, usually with a connotation of transcendence or of uniqueness; as, "she made her drawing-room a sort of meeting-place; she had a *genius* for it" (*V. Woolf*). "Mr. G. K. Chesterton has a *genius* for saying new and surprising things about old subjects" (*A. Huxley*). In humorous use, the connotation of transcendence is especially strong, but that of supreme unawareness is also usually evident; as, he has a *genius* for ineptness of remark; "the *genius* for illogicality of the English people" (*Inge*). **Talent** comes very close in its meaning to *gift* when the latter term denotes a native capacity or an innate ability. *Talent*, however, carries the implication, derived from the Scriptural parable of the servants' use of the talents (pieces of money) entrusted them by their master (*Matthew* xxv. 14–30), that the gift is a trust, and that its possessor is required to develop it and put it to profitable use. "It is quite probable that many...who would make the best doctors are too poor to take the course. This involves a deplorable waste of *talent*" (*B. Russell*). "Was he to leave such *talents* lying idle (and that after chafing for eight years to employ them)?" (*Belloc*). This basic implication in *talent* led inevitably to another implication: that the gift is under the control of its possessor because its proper exercise depends on industry and the acquirement of necessary knowledge and skill. When the romantic conception of *genius* became prevalent toward the end of the eighteenth century, the two words were commonly opposed, *genius* then denoting great creative ability, beyond the power of its possessor to control or to exercise at will, yet magnificent in its results, and *talent*, a lesser kind of power, capable of development through study and industry, completely under the control of the will, and tending to facile, agreeable, and effective, but not exalted, performance or utterance. Although in modern psychology and aesthetics these distinctions are seldom enforced, *talent*, when applied to a person's ability, may be derogatory if there is an expressed or implied contrast with *genius*. "What Goethe did really say was 'the greatest *talent*,' not 'the greatest *genius*.' The difference is important, because, while *talent* gives the notion of power in a man's performance, *genius* gives rather the notion of felicity and perfection in it" (*Arnold*). "To achieve conspicuous mundane success in literature, a certain degree of good fortune is almost more important than *genius*, or even than *talent*" (*A. C. Benson*). **Knack** stresses ease and dexterity in performance, though it commonly implies an aptitude; as, "she has, certainly, something of a *knack* at characters" (*Burney*); "an uncommon *knack* in Latin verse" (*C. W. Eliot*). **Bent** usually implies a natural inclination or taste; it often carries the same implications as *aptitude* and is sometimes preferred in modern literary English, owing to the technical use of the latter word in educational psychology. "It doesn't seem to me that you've shown any great *bent* towards a scholastic life" (*Arch. Marshall*). "The *bent* thus revealed for precise observation and classification" (*Babbitt*). **Turn** not only implies a bent, but the actual manifestation of power, and often suggests skill or proficiency. "He had a *turn* for mechanics; had invented a plough in his district, had ordered wheel-barrows from England" (*V. Woolf*).

Ana. Endowment, enduement, dowry (see corresponding verbs at DOWER): *power, faculty, function: *acquirement, attainment, accomplishment, acquisition.

gigantic *or* **gigantean.** Giant, colossal, *enormous, huge, mammoth, elephantine, titanic, Herculean, immense, vast, Cyclopean, Antaean, Gargantuan, Brobdingnagian.

Ana. Prodigious, stupendous, tremendous, *monstrous, monumental.

gingery. Fiery, peppery, *spirited, high-spirited, mettlesome, spunky.

gird, *v.* Sneer, flout, *scoff, jeer, gibe, fleer.

Ana. Deride, mock, taunt, twit, rally, *ridicule.

give. Give, present, donate, bestow, confer, afford. Give is the general term meaning to pass over, deliver, or transmit something which becomes the receiver's to own, to use, to enjoy, or the like. "It is more blessed to *give* than to receive" (*Acts* xx. 35). "*Give* my love to your mother and sisters" (*Keats*). **Present** is more formal or ceremonious. "On Saturday Colonel Bellingham is going to address the lads of the Brigade and *present* them with six drums" (*C. Mackenzie*). "Pray, *present* my respects to Lady Scott" (*Byron*). **Donate,** found chiefly in American use, usually implies publicity attending the giving or a public cause or charity as the recipient of the gift; as, to *donate* a piano to an orphanage. **Bestow** implies the settling of something on one as a gift. "Large gifts have I *bestowed* on learned clerks" (*Shak.*). "What nature wants commodious gold *bestows*" (*Pope*). To **confer** is esp. to give graciously, or as a favor or honor. "The Queen *confers* her titles and degrees" (*Pope*). To **afford,** as here compared, is to give or bestow, esp. as a natural or legitimate consequence of the character of that which gives. "This fine day *affords* us some hope" (*Cowper*). "Do the laws of his country *afford* him a remedy?" (*Ch. Just. Marshall*).

Ana. Award, accord, vouchsafe, *grant, concede: assign, *allot, apportion, allocate: *distribute, dispense, deal, dole.

glabrous. Glossy, *sleek, slick, velvety, silken, silky, satiny.

glacial. Arctic, icy, gelid, frigid, freezing, *cold, frosty, cool, chilly.

glad. Glad, happy, cheerful, lighthearted, joyful, joyous come into comparison as meaning characterized by or expressing the mood, temper, or state of mind of a person who is pleased or delighted with something or with things in general. **Glad** is capable of being used (as opposed to *sorry*) in polite conventional expressions of pleasure or gratification; as, I am *glad* to hear of your recovery; I shall be *glad* to have the opportunity to meet you. In richer use, however, it implies opposition to *sad*, and connotes actual delight and a lift of spirits, if not always elation; as, "Wine that maketh *glad* the heart of man" (*Psalms* civ. 15); "*Glad* did I live and *gladly* die" (*Stevenson*); "A child's kiss Set on thy sighing lips shall make thee *glad*" (*E. B. Browning*). **Happy** may also be used in polite conventional phrases in which its content can hardly be distinguished from that of *glad*. In precise and meaningful use, however, it distinctively implies a sense of contentment and well-being or a realization either of one's good fortune or of the fulfillment of one's desires; as, he will never be *happy* until he finds work which utilizes all his talents. "With the tension of an unachieved task no longer felt...I can say with truth that the last phase of my life has been the *happiest*" (*H. Ellis*). **Cheerful** suggests a strong and, often, a spontaneous flow of good spirits, either as a result of feeling glad or happy or as a result of an equable disposition or of a naturally sanguine temperament. "*Cheerfulness* keeps up a kind of daylight in the mind, and fills it with a steady and perpetual serenity" (*Addison*). "Suicidal thoughts...could not enter the *cheerful*, sanguine, courageous scheme of life, which was in part natural to her and in part slowly built up" (*H. Ellis*). **Lighthearted** stresses freedom from care, worry, and discontent. Since it also implies high spirits, vivacity, or gaiety, it commonly suggests in addition youth or an easygoing and somewhat volatile temperament. "He whistles as he goes, *light-hearted* wretch, Cold and yet *cheerful*" (*Cowper*). "Why, man, I was *light-hearted* in my prime, I am *light-hearted* now; what would you have?" (*Browning*). **Joyful** and **joyous** imply keen gladness or happiness with resulting elation; they are often used as though they were equivalent terms. Among highly discriminating writers, however, *joyful* usually suggests a mood or an emotional reaction to an event or situation and it implies rejoicing; as, "in the day of prosperity be *joyful*" (*Ecclesiastes* vii. 14); "And *joyful* nations join in leagues of peace" (*Pope*); a *joyful* countenance. *Joyous*, on the other hand, applies more to that which by its nature or character is filled with joy or is a cause of joy. "All that ever was *Joyous*, and clear, and fresh, thy music doth surpass" (*Shelley*). "The happy and *joyous* temper, which characterises a fresh and confident faith" (*Inge*).

Ana. Pleased, delighted, gratified, tickled, rejoiced (see PLEASE): *elated, elate, exultant: blithe, jocund, *merry, jolly, jovial: gleeful, mirthful, hilarious (see corresponding nouns at MIRTH).

Ant. Sad. — *Con.* Depressed, dejected, melancholy (see corresponding nouns at SADNESS).

gladden. Delight, rejoice, *please, gratify, tickle, arride, regale.

Ana. *Comfort, console, solace: enliven, animate, *quicken, vivify.

Ant. Sadden. — *Con.* *Depress, weigh down, oppress: vex, irk, *annoy, bother.

glance, *v.* Glint, *flash, gleam, sparkle, glitter, glisten, scintillate, coruscate, glimmer, shimmer, twinkle, glister, spark.

glance, *n.* Glimpse, peep, peek, coup d'oeil, *look, sight, view.

Con. Scrutiny, examination, inspection (see under SCRUTINIZE): contemplation, studying *or* study, consideration (see corresponding verbs at CONSIDER).

glare, *v.* **1** Glow, flare, *blaze, flame.

Ana. *Flash, gleam, glitter, glisten, scintillate, coruscate, sparkle.

2 Stare, peer, gloat, gape, *gaze.

Ana. Glower, lower, scowl, *frown.

glare, *n.* **1** Flare, glow, blaze, flame. See under BLAZE, *v.*

Ana. Effulgence, refulgence, radiance, brilliance (see corresponding adjectives at BRIGHT): glittering *or* glitter, sparkling *or* sparkle, flashing *or* flash (see FLASH, *v.*).

2 Glaze, gloss, sheen, *luster.

glaring, *adj.* *Flagrant, gross, rank.

Ana. *Noticeable, conspicuous, outstanding: obtrusive (see IMPERTINENT): extreme, *excessive, inordinate.

glaze, *n.* Glare, gloss, sheen, *luster.

Ana. Shining *or* shine, polishing *or* polish, burnishing *or* burnish (see POLISH, *v.*).

gleam, *v.* *Flash, glance, glint, sparkle, glitter, glisten, scintillate, coruscate, glimmer, shimmer, twinkle, glister, spark.

glee. *Mirth, jollity, hilarity.
Ana. Delight, joy, *pleasure, enjoyment, delectation: merriment, jocundity, blitheness, joviality (see corresponding adjectives at MERRY): gladness, happiness, cheerfulness, joyfulness, joyousness (see corresponding adjectives at GLAD).
Ant. Gloom. — *Con.* *Sadness, dejection, depression, melancholy, blues, dumps.

gleeman. Bard, minstrel, scop, *poet, versifier, rhymer, rhymester, poetaster, jongleur, troubadour, trouvère, minnesinger, scald.

glib. Fluent, voluble, *vocal, articulate, eloquent.
Ana. Garrulous, loquacious, voluble, *talkative: facile, smooth, effortless, *easy.
Con. Hesitant, hesitating (see corresponding nouns at HESITATION): stammering, stuttering (see STAMMER, *v.*): deliberate, leisurely (see SLOW).

glide, *v.* *Slide, slip, skid, glissade, slither, coast, toboggan.
Ana. Float, *fly, skim, scud, sail, shoot.

glimmer, *v.* Shimmer, glisten, scintillate, *flash, gleam, glance, glint, sparkle, coruscate, twinkle, glister, spark.

glimpse, *n.* Glance, peep, peek, coup d'oeil, *look, sight, view.
Con. Surveying *or* survey, observing *or* observation, contemplating *or* contemplation (see corresponding verbs at SEE): scrutiny, examination, inspection (see under SCRUTINIZE).

glint, *v.* Glance, gleam, *flash, sparkle, glitter, glisten, scintillate, coruscate, glimmer, shimmer, twinkle, glister, spark.

glissade, *v.* Glide, *slide, slip, skid, slither, coast, toboggan.

glisten. Sparkle, glitter, *flash, gleam, glance, glint, scintillate, coruscate, glimmer, shimmer, twinkle, glister, spark.

glister, *v.* Glisten, glitter, *flash, gleam, glance, glint, sparkle, scintillate, coruscate, glimmer, shimmer, twinkle, spark.

glitter, *v.* Glister, glisten, sparkle, spark, *flash, gleam, glance, glint, scintillate, coruscate, glimmer, shimmer, twinkle.

gloat. *Gaze, gape, stare, glare, peer.
Con. Envy, *covet, grudge, begrudge.

globe. *Sphere, orb, ball.

globular *or* **globose, globate, globoid.** Spherical, orbicular, *round, circular, annular, discoid.

gloom, *n.* Dejection, depression, melancholy, melancholia, *sadness, blues, dumps, vapors.
Ana. Despondency, forlornness, hopelessness, despair, desperation (see under DESPONDENT).
Ant. Glee. — *Con.* *Mirth, jollity, hilarity: cheerfulness, gladness, happiness, joyousness, joyfulness (see corresponding adjectives at GLAD).

gloom, *v.* Lower, glower, *frown, scowl.
Con. *Threaten, menace.

gloomy. **1** Murky, obscure, *dark, dim, dusk, dusky, darkling, opaque.
Ant. Brilliant (*with reference to illumination*). — *Con.* *Bright, effulgent, radiant, luminous: illuminated, illumined, lighted, lightened (see ILLUMINATE).
2 Glum, *sullen, morose, saturnine, dour, surly, sulky, crabbed.
Ana. Depressed, weighed down, oppressed (see DEPRESS).
Ant. Cheerful. — *Con.* Joyful, joyous, happy, *glad, lighthearted: *merry, blithe, jocund, jovial.

glorious. *Splendid, resplendent, sublime, superb, gorgeous.
Ana. Radiant, brilliant, effulgent, lustrous (see BRIGHT): transcendent, superlative, surpassing, peerless, *supreme: illustrious, renowned, eminent (see FAMOUS).
Ant. Inglorious.

glory, *n.* **1** Renown, honor, celebrity, *fame, éclat, reputation, repute, notoriety.
Ant. Ignominy, shame. — *Con.* *Disgrace, infamy, dishonor, disrepute, opprobrium, obloquy, odium.
2 *Halo, aureole, nimbus.

gloss, *n.*[1] Sheen, *luster, glaze, glare.
Ana. Burnishing *or* burnish, polishing *or* polish, shining *or* shine (see corresponding verbs at POLISH): sleekness, slickness, glossiness, glabrousness (see corresponding adjectives at SLEEK).

gloss, *n.*[2] Annotation. See under ANNOTATE.
Ana. Commentary, comment, note, *remark, observation.

gloss, *v.* **1** *Obs.* **gloze** *or* **glose.** *Annotate.
Ana. Interpret, construe, *explain, elucidate, expound, explicate.
2 Gloze, *palliate, extenuate, whitewash, whiten.
Ana. *Disguise, cloak, mask, dissemble: rationalize, account for, justify, *explain.

glossary. Wordbook, *dictionary, lexicon, onomasticon, synonymicon, gazetteer.

glossy. *Sleek, slick, glabrous, satiny, silken, velvety.
Ana. Lustrous, *bright, brilliant, lucent, lambent: polished, burnished, furbished, shined (see POLISH, *v.*).

glow, *v.* *Blaze, flame, flare, glare.
Ana. *Burn: inflame, kindle, enkindle, ignite, *light: *illuminate, lighten, illumine, illume.

glow, *n.* Blaze, flame, flare, glare. See under BLAZE, *v.*
Ana. Brightness, brilliance, radiance, effulgence, luminosity (see corresponding adjectives at BRIGHT): fervor, ardor (see PASSION).

glower, *v.* Lower, *frown, scowl, gloom.
Ana. Glare, stare (see GAZE): watch, look (see SEE).
Con. Grin, *smile, smirk.

gloze *or* **glose,** *v.* **1** Obs. variant of GLOSS, *v.*, 1.
2 Gloss, whitewash, *palliate, extenuate, whiten.
Ana. Condone, *excuse: justify, rationalize, *explain, account for: dissemble, cloak, mask, *disguise.

glue, *v.* *Cement, agglutinate.
Ana. *Fasten, attach, fix, affix.

gluey. Glutinous, mucilaginous, gummy, *adhesive, sticky.

glum. Gloomy, morose, *sullen, saturnine, dour, surly, sulky, crabbed.
Ana. *Silent, taciturn, close-lipped, tight-lipped: depressed, weighed down, oppressed (see DEPRESS): scowling, frowning, lowering, glowering, glooming (see FROWN, *v.*).
Ant. Cheerful. — *Con.* Happy, *glad, lighthearted, joyful, joyous.

glut, *v.* Gorge, surcharge, surfeit, sate, cloy, pall, *satiate.

glutinous. Gluey, mucilaginous, gummy, *adhesive, sticky.

glutton. Gourmand, gastronome, gastronomer, bon vivant, gourmet, *epicure.

gluttonous. *Voracious, ravenous, ravening, rapacious.
Ana. Greedy, *covetous, grasping.
Ant. Abstemious. — *Con.* Temperate, *sober: dainty, finical, fussy, fastidious, *nice.

gnarl, *v.* Contort, distort, *deform, warp.
Ana. Twist, bend, *curve.

gnome. Dwarf, goblin, brownie, puck, nix, *fairy, faery, fay, elf, sprite, pixy, shee, leprechaun, banshee.

go. **1** **Go, leave, depart, quit, withdraw, retire, scram, clear out, clear off** are synonymous when they mean to move out of or away from the place where one is. Of these terms, **go** is the most general and the least explicit in its implications: it often is used merely as the opposite of *come;* as, he came here yesterday and *went* this morning before I was up; "*Go,* baffled coward, lest I run upon thee" (*Milton*); he would not let her *go* before he had obtained her promise to sell him the property. **Leave** (see also RELINQUISH; LET, 2) so strongly implies a separation from someone or something that the verb in this sense is more often used transitively than intransitively; in its intransitive use, the term commonly implies a more formal or a more conspicuous act than *go* implies and often but not invariably requires a statement of the means of locomotion; as, he plans to *leave* by the noon train; we shall be sorry to have him *leave* (or *leave* us); do not *leave* the place until I return; her servants always *leave* (or *leave* her) after a few days in her employ. **Depart** (as here considered: see also SWERVE) is rarely transitive except in a few idiomatic phrases (such as, to *depart* this life, i.e., to die): as an intransitive verb it not only carries a far stronger implication of separation from a person, place, or status than *leave* carries, but it is somewhat more formal, or at least less colloquial, especially when it is used as the opposite of *arrive;* as, to *depart* for a trip to Europe; " 'You will not *leave* me yet, Richard?'...He had no thought of *departing*" (*Meredith*); "A goddess of *gone* days, *Departed* long ago" (*Millay*). **Quit** (see also STOP, 1; BEHAVE, 1), like *leave,* is more often a transitive than an intransitive verb and carries a strong implication of separation from a person or thing. Unlike *leave,* however, it stresses a getting free or being rid of that which holds, entangles, burdens, or the like; as, "The distinction [knighthood]....had given him a disgust to his business, and to his residence in a small market town; and, *quitting* them both, he had removed with his family to...Lucas Lodge" (*Austen*); "He *quitted* London to take refuge among the mountains" (*Meredith*); "I was at a show only last week when there was such a tremble [of the walls] that every one *quit*" (*Lucas*). **Withdraw** (for transitive senses see REMOVE, 2), which is a literary rather than a colloquial term, stresses, far more than *quit,* a deliberate removal for reasons that seem justifiable to the person concerned or more acceptable to the reader; the term therefore seldom, if ever, carries, as *quit* often carries, a suggestion of cowardice, weakness, or instability (thus, one *quits* a trying job, but one *withdraws* from an insecure position), and frequently implies a motive such as courtesy, a sense of propriety, a grievance, or the like; as, the women *withdrew* from the room when the men were ready to discuss business; the visitors *withdrew* when the doctor entered; "the perfect lyric is a poem from which the author has *withdrawn* once he has set it in motion" (*Day Lewis*); "a hermit *withdrawn* from a wicked world" (*Conrad*). **Retire** is often used interchangeably with *withdraw,* but it is the preferred term when the removal also implies a renunciation, a relinquishing of a position for good, a retreat, a recession, a recoil, or the like; as, to *retire* from the world into a monastery; "When he dies or *retires,* a new manager must be found" (*Shaw*); "After the Captain's terrible fall...which broke him so that he could no longer build railroads, he and his wife *retired* to the house on the hill" (*Cather*). Often *retire* carries the specific sense of to withdraw to one's bedroom and to one's bed for the night; as, to *retire* early. **Scram** (a slang term) and **clear out** or **clear off** (colloquial terms) imply a leaving in haste and usually in fear or under compulsion; as, the boys *scrammed* when they heard the policeman's step; he ordered all the intruders to *clear out.*

Ana. *Escape, decamp, abscond, flee, fly.

Ant. Come. — ***Con.*** Arrive (see COME): *stay, remain, abide.

2 *Resort, refer, apply, turn.

Con. Avoid, shun, elude, evade, *escape.

goad, *n.* Spur, incentive, inducement, *motive, spring, impulse.

Ana. Impelling *or* impulsion, driving *or* drive (see corresponding verbs at MOVE): urge, lust, passion, *desire.

Ant. Curb.

goal. Objective, object, end, aim, *intention, intent, purpose, design.

Ana. *Limit, bourn, bound, confine, end, term: aspiration, *ambition.

gob. Sailor, seaman, tar, matlow, bluejacket, rating, *mariner.

goblin. Gnome, dwarf, brownie, puck, nix, sprite, pixy, elf, *fairy, faery, fay, shee, leprechaun, banshee.

godless. Ungodly, *irreligious, unreligious, nonreligious.

Ana. Atheistic, agnostic, infidel (see corresponding nouns at ATHEIST).

Godspeed. Farewell, *good-by, adieu, au revoir, auf Wiedersehen, bon voyage, adios.

good, *adj.* **Good, right** come into comparison only in the most general of their senses, when they mean in accordance with one's standard of what is satisfactory. **Good** (as opposed to *bad*) implies full approval or commendation of someone or something in the respect under consideration, such as excellence of workmanship, excellence of condition, beneficial properties, competence, agreeableness, purity, freshness, etc. "And God saw every thing that he had made, and, behold, it was very *good*" (*Genesis* i. 31); *good* food; a very *good* light; foods *good* for the teeth; it is a *good* book for children; *good* news; a *good* neighbor. *Good* (as opposed to *poor*) does not imply hearty approval, but it does not suggest dissatisfaction; it implies that the person or thing so described measures up to a point which is regarded as satisfactory, or possesses the qualities necessary to a thing of its kind; as, a *good* crop; *good* soil; *good,* but not excellent, work; the business for the past year was *good;* a *good* return on an investment; a *good* play. "Our ideas of a *good* time aren't the same, and never will be" (*R. Macaulay*). "Between *good* workmanship and design and that touch of rareness which makes not merely *good* but fine and lovely" (*S. Alexander*). Oftentimes, the difference in meaning between these two senses of *good* is apparent only in the inflection or through the medium of a context. **Right** (see also CORRECT) often implies that the thing so described is fitting, proper, appropriate, or the like, with respect to the circumstances; thus, a book one knows to be *good* may not be the *right* book to give to a person who is unable to understand it; the *right* light for a picture may be quite different from a *good* light for reading; so, she always does the *right* thing at the *right* time. "The scene in Julius Caesar is *right* because the object of our attention is not the speech of Antony...but the effect of his speech upon the mob" (*T. S. Eliot*). *Right* may also imply the absence of anything wrong in the person or thing so described. "God's in his heaven— All's *right* with the world!" (*Browning*). "She didn't think he was quite *right* [that is, mentally sound]" (*C. Morley*).

Ant. Bad: poor.

good-by *or* **good-bye. Good-by** (*or* **good-bye**), **farewell, Godspeed, adieu, adios, au revoir, auf Wiedersehen, bon voyage** are the forms of address in conventional good use at parting or leave-taking. Only **good-by** is frequent in colloquial use; it is the ordinary phrase used by everybody and, except in very discriminating use, without reference to the phrase of which it is historically the contraction, "God be with ye." **Farewell** is now chiefly in literary or elevated use; etymologically, it expresses the wish of one left behind ("fare [thee] well") for the well-being of one who departs from home or host. This implication is not always carried by *farewell;* it is, however, pretty generally maintained in **Godspeed** (literally, "God speed you, or make you fare well"), for that is a conventional form of farewell restricted to those going away. **Adieu,** though still sometimes retaining its French pronunciation and often its French plural, is thoroughly naturalized in literary English. Literally a commendation to God (à Dieu), it, like *good-by,* seldom conveys its original significance. **Adios,** its unnaturalized Spanish equivalent, is not uncommon in the Southwestern states of the United States. **Au revoir** (French for "till I see you again") and its German equivalent **auf Wiedersehen,** are frequent in written English and are often preferred in speech where the wish to renew or extend the acquaintance or the expectation of another meeting is to be expressed. **Bon voyage** (French for "good journey"), like *Godspeed,* is reserved for a farewell to one departing, but unlike the latter term, it implies usually a wish for a pleasant trip, especially one over water or across an ocean.

good humor. *Good nature, good temper.

Ana. Geniality, sociableness, affability, graciousness, cordiality (see corresponding adjectives at GRACIOUS).

good-looking. Comely, pretty, bonny, fair, beauteous, pulchritudinous, handsome, *beautiful, lovely.

Ana. Attractive, alluring, taking, charming (see under ATTRACT): pleasing, *pleasant, agreeable.

good nature. Good nature, good humor, good temper are not always clearly distinguished when they denote an agreeable temperament. **Good nature** implies a disposition, usually a natural and inborn rather than an acquired disposition, to please and be pleased; often, but far from invariably, the term is used depreciatively to imply undue compliance with the wishes of others; as, "...their *good nature,* for they would have been glad to do any little service, such as lend a time-table or impart useful information" (*V. Woolf*); his *good nature* is the reason he is so often imposed upon. **Good humor** implies a mood of ease and cheerfulness, especially as displayed in one's demeanor or in social intercourse; **good temper** differs from *good humor* not only in denoting the habit of mind of one not easily ruffled or provoked but in its lack of implication of qualities such as geniality or sociableness. "He had blue eyes, and an expression of boyish *good-humor,* which, however, did not convey any assurance of *good temper*" (*Shaw*).

Ana. Amiability, complaisance, obligingness (see corresponding adjectives at AMIABLE): kindliness, kindness (see corresponding adjectives at KIND).

good-natured. *Amiable, obliging, complaisant.

Ana. Compliant, acquiescent: *kindly, kind: altruistic, benevolent, *charitable.

Ant. Contrary. — *Con.* Cross, cranky, touchy, techy, *irascible, choleric, splenetic: glum, morose, gloomy, *sullen, surly, crabbed.

goodness. Goodness, virtue, rectitude, morality are the most general terms in English denoting moral excellence. **Goodness** is the most homely of these terms: it suggests an excellence so deeply established that it is often thought of as inherent or innate rather than acquired or instilled. Of all these terms it is the only one applied to God; as, "The Lord God, merciful and gracious, longsuffering, and abundant in *goodness* and truth" (*Exodus* xxxiv. 6). When applied to persons, it usually suggests appealing qualities such as kindness, generosity, helpfulness, deep sympathy, or the like; as, "the need I have of thee thine own *goodness* hath made" (*Shak.*)."Abashed the Devil stood, And felt how awful [awe-inspiring] *goodness* is" (*Milton*); "She has more *goodness* in her little finger than he has in his whole body" (*Swift*). **Virtue,** though often coupled with *goodness* as its close synonym, is distinguishable in the sense here considered (see also EXCELLENCE) as suggesting acquired rather than native moral excellence and, often, a greater consciousness of it as a possession: usually the term implies either close conformity to the moral law or persistent choice of that which is good and the persistent rejection of that which is evil; as, *virtue* is its own reward; "*Virtue* may be assailed, but never hurt, Surprised by unjust force, but not enthralled" (*Milton*); "The highest proof of *virtue* is to possess boundless power without abusing it" (*Macaulay*). *Goodness* and *virtue* also come into comparison in the sense of the characteristic and intrinsic power or property of a thing. Since *virtue* often specifically implies chastity or fidelity in marriage, **rectitude** is frequently employed in its place when moral excellence acquired through obedience to the moral law and self-discipline is implied. But the term differs from *virtue* in often having reference to motives, intentions, and habits and not merely to character, and sometimes also in placing greater stress on uprightness, integrity, probity, and similar stern qualities; as, no one can question the *rectitude* of his purpose; "for various reasons all having to do with the delicate *rectitude* of his nature, Roderick Anthony...was frightened" (*Conrad*). "Society is, after all, a recreation and a delight, and ought to be sought for with pleasurable motives, not with a consciousness of *rectitude* and justice" (*A. C. Benson*). All of the preceding words refer directly or indirectly to the moral excellence involved in character. **Morality,** too, may imply such excellence and therefore come close to *virtue* (both in its general and specific sense) and *rectitude* (as, he cared much for power and influence and little for *morality*): in this sense the term often specifically suggests a moral excellence that arises from fidelity to ethical principles as distinguished from that which arises from obedience to the divine law or the moral laws enforced by religious teachings (as, "Evil must come upon us headlong, if *morality* tries to get on without religion"—*Tennyson*). Often, however, *morality* refers not to character but rather to the principles touching morals or ethics as involved in a book, a work of art, a practice, a law, or the like: in such use the term means either moral excellence or trustworthiness derived from adherence to the principles accepted by the Church, the body of people, the virtuous men of the day and age, or the like, or moral influence as exerted by a thing; as, the *morality* of Flaubert's *Madame Bovary* was questioned soon after the book's publication.

Ana. Righteousness, nobility, virtuousness (see corresponding adjectives at MORAL): *honesty, integrity, probity, honor.

Ant. Badness, evil.

good sense. See SENSE, *n.*, 2.

good temper. Good humor, *good nature.

Ant. Ill temper. — *Con.* *Acrimony, asperity, acerbity: ill will, malignity, spite, malevolence, *malice.

good will. 1 *Favor, countenance.

Ana. Friendliness, neighborliness, amicability (see corresponding adjectives at AMICABLE): *attachment, affection, love: respect, esteem, admiration, *regard.

Ant. Ill will. — *Con.* Malevolence, malignity, spite, *malice.

2 *Friendship, amity, comity.

Ant. Animosity.

gorge, *v.* Surfeit, *satiate, sate, glut, surcharge, cloy, pall.

gorgeous. Resplendent, *splendid, glorious, sublime, superb.

Ana. *Luxurious, sumptuous, opulent: *showy, ostentatious, pretentious.

gory. *Bloody, sanguinary, sanguine, sanguineous.

gossip, *v.* **Gossip, blab, tattle** denote in common to disclose something that one would have done better to keep to oneself. To **gossip** is to communicate or exchange in conversation remarks, often uncomplimentary or damaging and of questionable veracity, about the private affairs of others, especially acquaintances or neighbors; as, to *gossip* about the squabbles of the family next door; *gossip* has it that Smith makes at least fifteen thousand dollars a year. To **blab** is to disclose something that has been confided to one as a secret or to which one is privy. "If he sees cards and actual money passing, he will be sure to *blab,* and it will be all over the town in no time" (*Conrad*). **Tattle** variously is more closely akin to *gossip* or to *blab,* or combines the implications of the two. It suggests irreticent and loquacious gossip, the unsolicited revelation, to one having power of discipline or punishment, of some trivial misdeed on the part of another, or blabbing gossip, as of one in a position of confidence; as, Mary always *tattled* to the teacher when a classmate threw a spitball. "So that no discovery... might be made by any *tattling* amongst the servants" (*T. Hook*).

gourmand. Glutton, gastronome, gastronomer, bon vivant, *epicure, gourmet.

gourmet. *Epicure, bon vivant, gastronome, gastronomer, gourmand, glutton.

govern. Govern, rule come into comparison when they mean to exercise power or authority in controlling or directing another or others, often specifically those persons who comprise a state or nation. **Govern** (etymologically, to steer as a pilot) may imply any kind of power, despotic or constitutional, or any kind of authority, assumed by force, acquired by inheritance or through election, or granted by due processes of law, but it usually connotes as its end the keeping of those (or of that) directed or controlled in a straight course or in smooth operation, where perils are avoided and the good of the individual or of the whole is achieved; as, parents who cannot *govern* their children; "The right divine of kings to *govern* wrong" (*Pope*); to *govern* one's emotions. "Every prince should *govern* as he would desire to be *governed* if he were a subject" (*Temple*). "The [Roman] Senate was more than a modern constitutional monarch, reigning and not *governing;* it had a substantial amount of *governing* to its share" (*Buchan*). "As Matthew Arnold pointed out...educated mankind is *governed* by two passions—one the passion for pure knowledge, the other the passion for being of service or doing good" (*C. W. Eliot*). **Rule** (etymologically, to regulate) was not in early use always as clearly distinguished from *govern* as it is in current good use; as, "Fit to *govern* and to *rule* multitudes" (*Shak.*). Now it often implies the power to lay down the laws which shall determine the action of others or to issue commands which must be obeyed: since the term commonly suggests the exercise of despotic or arbitrary power, it is not used of the person or body that exercises authority over the people in a democracy, or republic, or other constitutional state; thus, "resolved to ruin or to *rule* the state" (*Dryden*); dictators *rule* the German, Italian, and Russian peoples. "It's damnable to have to hurt the people we love—but, after all, we can't let our parents *rule* our lives" (*R. Macaulay*). " 'Are you, sir, the person who serves here?' asked a stranger of a minister whom he met in the streets of Rowley. 'I am, sir, the person who *rules* here,' was the swift and apt response" (*A. Repplier*).

Ana. *Execute, administer: *conduct, direct, control, manage: *restrain, curb, inhibit.

government. Government, administration, usually preceded by *the,* denote in common the persons authorized to administer the laws of a country. **Government** may bear either of two connotations: it may consider these persons abstractly, as anonymous agents vested with certain broad powers by the constitution; as, only the *government* may coin money; or it may place emphasis on the persons who happen to hold office at a given time, particularly on the personal or partisan nature of their specific interpretation and application of the broad powers granted by the constitution. **Administration** is interchangeable with *government* when both bear this latter connotation; *administration* is the commoner term in the United States (where it usually refers to the President and his cabinet), *government* in Great Britain (where it usually refers to the ministry); as, the Coolidge *administration,* the Baldwin *government;* a Republican *administration,* a Liberal *government.* In British usage *government* and *administration* are commonly followed by a plural verb. "The *Government* are not prepared to adopt the course suggested" (*The Times*). "As his Majesty's present *administration* are not immortal, their successors may be inclined to attempt to undo what the present ministers shall have attempted to perform" (*Burke*).

grab, *v.* Grasp, clutch, *take, seize, snatch.

Ana. *Catch, capture, nab, cop.

grace, *n.* **1** *Mercy, clemency, lenity, charity.

Ana. Kindliness, kindness, benignity, benignancy (see corresponding adjectives at KIND): *favor, good will, countenance: tenderness, compassionateness, responsiveness (see corresponding adjectives at TENDER): indulgence, forbearance, leniency (see under FORBEARING).

2 *Elegance, dignity.

Ana. Loveliness, beautifulness *or* beauty, fairness, comeliness (see corresponding adjectives at BEAUTIFUL): suppleness, litheness, lithesomeness, lissomeness (see corresponding adjectives at LIMBER): attractiveness, alluringness *or* allurement, charmingness *or* charm (see corresponding adjectives under ATTRACT).

gracious. Gracious, cordial, affable, genial, sociable are used to describe persons (or by extension, their words or acts) who are markedly pleasant and at ease in social intercourse. **Gracious** implies kindliness and courtesy, especially (but not necessarily) to inferiors. When it carries the latter implication, it more often suggests benignity than condescension. "*Gracious* to everyone, but known to a very few" (*Cather*). "Heartened by her *gracious* reception of a nervous bow" (*Shaw*). **Cordial** stresses warmth and heartiness; as, a *cordial* welcome; a *cordial* handclasp; to be on *cordial* terms. **Affable** implies approachability and readiness to talk in the person conversed with or addressed; when applied to a social superior it sometimes connotes condescending familiarity, but more often a gracious willingness to be friendly. "I don't find...that his wealth has made him arrogant and inaccessible; on the contrary, he takes great pains to appear *affable* and gracious" (*Smollett*). " 'His father was an excellent man'.... 'his son will be just like him—just as *affable* to the poor' " (*Austen*). **Genial** sometimes, especially in loose use, emphasizes cheerfulness and even joviality. In very precise use and in the sense here considered *genial* stresses qualities that make for good cheer among companions, such as warm human sympathy, a fine sense of humor; as, a *genial* host. "He was no fanatic and no ascetic. He was *genial*, social, even convivial" (*G. Smith*). **Sociable,** which is felt to be more colloquial than the others, implies a genuine liking for the companionship of others and readiness to engage in social intercourse even with strangers or inferiors. "His father's *sociability* gave a basis for Joyce's wide and miscellaneous acquaintanceship" (*P. Colum*).

Ana. Obliging, complaisant, *amiable: benignant, benign, kindly, *kind: courteous, courtly, chivalrous (see CIVIL).

Ant. Ungracious. — ***Con.*** Churlish, boorish (see under BOOR): brusque, curt, crusty, blunt, gruff (see BLUFF): surly, crabbed, *sullen.

grade, *n.* Gradient, incline, *slant, inclination, slope, acclivity, declivity.

gradient. Grade, incline, *slant, inclination, slope, acclivity, declivity.

grand, *adj.* **Grand, magnificent, imposing, stately, majestic, august, noble, grandiose** come into comparison when they mean large, handsome, dignified, and impressive. They vary somewhat in the emphasis which they respectively place on these qualities, and they differ somewhat also in their additional implications and connotations. **Grand** emphasizes magnitude or greatness of dimensions; often, however, it is not physical largeness that is implied, but a kind of spiritual, intellectual, or aesthetic greatness that makes the thing so described pre-eminent among its kind. It is distinguishable, however, from all other words meaning very large such as *big, huge,* and *colossal,* by its implications of handsomeness, dignity, and impressiveness; as, the *grand* view from the summit; the *grandest* of Gothic cathedrals; a *grand* production of Parsifal. "The *grand* style arises in poetry, when a noble nature, poetically gifted, treats with simplicity or with severity a serious subject" (*Arnold*). "The castle was considered *grand* by the illiterate; but architects...condemned it as a nondescript mixture of styles in the worst possible taste" (*Shaw*). **Magnificent** also may or may not imply actual physical largeness, but it always suggests an impressive largeness proportionate to the thing's scale, without sacrifice of dignity or violation of the canons of good taste. The term was originally applied to certain rulers, notable for their great deeds, the sumptuousness of their way of living, the munificence of their gifts, or the like; as, Lorenzo de' Medici was known as Lorenzo the *Magnificent*. In current English, it is often applied to ways of living or to the things that contribute to a sumptuous and handsome way of living, such as houses, furnishings, clothes, jewels, and the like. "The drawing-room, which was a truly *magnificent* apartment" (*Bennett*). It is also applicable to many things which at one end of a scale with numerous gradations may be described as plain or insignificant and at the other, as magnificent; as, *magnificent* clothes; a *magnificent* theme; "so ostentatiously *magnificent* a name as Gabriele d'Annunzio" (*H. Ellis*); a *magnificent* performance of *Hamlet*. "Much of Dryden's unique merit consists in his ability to make...the prosaic into the poetic, the trivial into the *magnificent*" (*T. S. Eliot*). **Imposing** stresses impressiveness because of size and dignity or sometimes because of magnificence. "Though tall and heavily built, he was not *imposing* like Moxon-Hughes" (*C. Mackenzie*). "It is between the town and the suburb, that midway habitation which fringes every American city, and which is *imposing* or squalid according to the incomes of suburbanites" (*A. Repplier*). **Stately** usually emphasizes dignity but there is an almost equal stress placed on handsomeness and impressiveness, and there is often an implication of larger than usual size; as, *stately* ships under full sail; "*Stately* dames like queens attended" (*Longfellow*); "solid and *stately* furniture" (*Bennett*). "I like to think of the obscure and yet dignified lives that have been lived in these quaint and *stately* chambers" (*A. C. Benson*). **Majestic** combines the implications of *imposing* and *stately,* but it adds a strong connotation of solemn grandeur. Consequently, it is applicable not only to persons, to buildings, interiors, furniture, and the like, but also to intangible things or to things that produce an aesthetic effect. "Both [Goethe and Schiller in appearance] are *majestic;* but one has the majesty of repose, the other of conflict" (*G. H. Lewes*). "Twilight combined with the scenery of Egdon Heath to evolve a thing *majestic* without severity, impressive without showiness" (*Hardy*). "The full moon shone high in the blue vault, *majestic,* lonely, benign" (*Cather*). **August** implies impressiveness so strongly as to impute to the thing so described a power to inspire awe, veneration, or, in humorous use, abashment and dread. But it also ascribes a lofty or exalted character to that which it qualifies. "So glorious is our nature, so *august*" (*Browning*). "How can you look round at these *august* hills, look up at this divine sky...and then talk like a literary hack...?" (*Shaw*). "No assemblage of academic duennas, however *august*" (*C. E. Montague*). **Noble** (as here compared: see also MORAL) carries no suggestion of a moral quality or of a social status; rather it implies a commanding grandeur, or the power to impress the imagination, emotions, or the intellect as incomparably great or excellent. "Now see that *noble* and most sovereign reason, Like sweet bells jangled, out of tune and harsh" (*Shak.*). "The Vandals of our isle... Have burnt to dust a *nobler* pile Than ever Roman saw!" (*Cowper*). **Grandiose** is sometimes distinguished from *grand, magnificent, imposing* and, less often, from the other words of this group, in implying an almost preposterous pretentiousness or pomposity (as, "the *grandiose* manner of the stage"—*Irving;* a *grandiose* project, impossible of fulfillment with the resources at hand), but it is equally often used by good writers and speakers without derogation to imply a more than usual largeness of plan or scope or a grandeur or majesty exceeding that of life or experience; as, "Things painted by a Rubens... All better, all more *grandiose* than the life" (*Browning*); "they [proposed new religions] yet tend to make us forget what more *grandiose,* noble, or beautiful character properly belongs to religious constructions" (*Arnold*); "[Antony] had inherited Julius's plans for a Parthian campaign, and this *grandiose* dream was always at the back of his mind" (*Buchan*).

Ana. Sumptuous, *luxurious, opulent: sublime, superb, *splendid, gorgeous: monumental, tremendous, stupendous, prodigious (see MONSTROUS).

Con. *Petty, puny, paltry, trivial, trifling, measly.

grandiloquent. Magniloquent, *rhetorical, aureate, flowery, euphuistic, bombastic.

Ana. Grandiose, imposing (see GRAND): *inflated, turgid, tumid.

grandiose. Imposing, stately, *grand, august, magnificent, majestic, noble.

Ana. Ostentatious, pompous, pretentious, *showy: grandiloquent, magniloquent, *rhetorical.

grant, *v.* **1 Grant, concede, vouchsafe, accord, award** denote in common to give as a favor or as a right. One **grants,** usually to an inferior or a subordinate, as an act of justice or indulgence, that which is requested or demanded (sometimes implicitly rather than explicitly) or the request or demand itself; as, the governor *granted* the condemned man a week's respite; he begged the Lord to *grant* him his prayer. "Any political rights which the dominant race might...withhold or *grant* at their pleasure" (*Ch. Just. Taney*). One **concedes** something claimed or expected as a right, prerogative, or possession, when one yields it with reluctance and, usually, in response to some compelling force in the claim or the claimant. "If we mean to conciliate and *concede*, let us see of what nature the concession ought to be" (*Burke*). "As an instrument of mind-training, and even of liberal education, it [science] seems to me to have a far higher value than is usually *conceded* to it by humanists" (*Inge*). One **vouchsafes** something prayed for, begged for, or, in looser use, expected as a courtesy, when one grants it to a person beneath one in dignity or station. It is often found in supplications where it implies humility in the suppliant. "*Vouchsafe*, O Lord: to keep us this day without sin" (*Bk. of Com. Prayer*). In modern use, it is often ironical, usually suggesting absurd condescension; as, he *vouchsafed* no reply to our question. One **accords** to another that which is admittedly his due or in keeping with his character or status. "He treated bishops with the superficial deference that a sergeant-major *accords* to a junior subaltern" (*C. Mackenzie*). "Children ...will readily *accord* to others what others *accord* to them" (*B. Russell*). One **awards** something that is deserved or merited; the word usually implies determination by legal adjudication or by judges in a contest or competition; as, the plaintiff was *awarded* heavy damages; to *award* a prize for the best story. "His [Tiberius's] victory was duly acclaimed by Senate and People; he was given the title of Imperator and *awarded* a triumph" (*Buchan*).

Ana. Bestow, confer, *give, present, donate: *allot, assign, apportion, allocate: cede, yield, surrender, *relinquish.

2 Grant, concede, allow come into comparison when they mean to admit something in question, especially a point or contention of one's opponent in an argument. **Grant** usually implies voluntary acceptance in advance of proof in order to clarify the issues or to center attention on what are regarded as the main issues; as, I *grant* there is no obvious motive; let us take his good will for *granted*. **Concede** implies reluctant acceptance, either before or after proofs have been advanced: it usually suggests the strength of the opponent's contention; as, he was unwilling to *concede* the supremacy of any group. **Allow** implies acceptance, but usually a somewhat qualified acceptance; it often suggests admission on the ground of apparent truth, logical validity, reasonableness, or the like. "Even Wickham had *allowed* him merit as a brother" (*Austen*). "We need not wait for this final reconciliation [of science and religion] to *allow*...that science...is working in the service of one of the ultimate values, unified truth" (*Inge*).

Ana. Admit, *acknowledge: *agree, concur, coincide.

grant, *n.* *Appropriation, subvention, subsidy.

Ana. *Donation, benefaction, contribution.

graph, *n.* *Chart, map.

Ana. Plot, scheme, design, *plan: diagram, outline, *sketch.

graph, *v.* Chart, map. See under CHART, *n.*

Ana. See those at GRAPH, *n.*

graphic. Graphic, vivid, picturesque, pictorial come into comparison only when they mean having or manifesting a quality or character that produces a strong, clear impression, especially a visual impression. All of these words, as here compared, apply particularly, but not exclusively, to works of art, chiefly literary art. That is **graphic** which has the power to evoke a strikingly clear-cut, lifelike picture; the term applies technically to the arts of painting, drawing, engraving, etching, and the like (the *graphic* arts), the object of each of which is to present a picture, but it is also definitely applied to any representation of things, especially in words; as, "A *graphic* description of the face of a young Hindoo at the sight of castor oil" (*Darwin*). That is **vivid** which is so vigorously alive that it is felt, seen, heard, or otherwise apprehended with a sense of its intense reality. The term may apply to that which actually exists and impresses itself with such sharp force on the imagination that the memory retains the sight, sound, or other impression; as, a *vivid* sensation of fear; "he fixed his *vivid* eyes on Archer as he lit another cigarette" (*E. Wharton*). "How sights fix themselves upon the mind! For example, the *vivid* green moss" (*V. Woolf*). The term may also apply to a mental state or process of which one is oneself intensely aware (as, "Ripton awoke...to the *vivid* consciousness of hunger"—*Meredith;* "my sense of right or wrong—of individual responsibility—was more *vivid* than at any other period of my life"—*Hudson;* "those for whom the belief in immortality is most *vivid*"—*J. W. Krutch*) or which defines its content clearly and sharply (as, "a man of wide and *vivid* interests"—*B. Russell;* a *vivid* realization of approaching danger; "all three had kept a *vivid* ...recollection...of what they had seen"—*E. Wharton*). Frequently the term applies to that which represents life or one's imaginative conceptions, such as a picture, or a play, or a story, or to the style, colors, language, situations, and the like, which are involved in such a representation: then the implication is of a power, either in the representation itself or in the means of representation, to evoke clearly defined pictures and to give a strong sense of their distinct quality and of their living force; as, "moving pictures are only less *vivid* than reflections from a mirror" (*Justice Holmes*); "In his odes, with their thunder of place-names, he [Horace] makes *vivid* the territorial immensity of the [Roman] empire" (*Buchan*). "Haydon was an acute observer, and he knew how to tell a story. How *vividly*, for example, he has seen this tea-party at Mrs. Siddons's, how well he has described it!" (*A. Huxley*). That is **picturesque** (still a more or less debatable term) which has, in general, the qualities or the character which one believes essential to a striking or effective picture. Although the term is applicable to a place, a person, a building or other construction, and the like (as, a *picturesque* costume; Scott's Meg Merrilies is a *picturesque* character; a *picturesque* ruin), as well as to a work of graphic, literary, or plastic art (as, a *picturesque* landscape; *picturesque* details), and to a style or manner as in writing or painting (as, "the *picturesque* force of his style"—*N. Hawthorne*), it carries in every use an implication that the thing has been observed and judged by one who has regard for its form, color, atmosphere, striking or unfamiliar detail, sharp contrasts, or the like, rather than for qualities which are not perceptible to the eye or that do not draw the eye because they are lacking in distinctness and charm. Around 1800, *picturesque* often specifically implied a kind of wild, rugged beauty associated with untouched or undisciplined nature; that implication is still not unusual; as, "Wide prospects of startling beauty, rugged mountains, steep gorges, great falls of water—all the things that are supposed to be *picturesque*" (*A. C. Benson*). Still later, the term came to imply a charm arising rather from remoteness, strangeness, quaintness, informality, diversity, or the like; as, "Though the upper part of Durnover was mainly composed of a curious congeries of barns and farmsteads, there was a less *picturesque* side to the parish" (*Hardy*); "The Square is rather *picturesque*, but it's such a poor, poor little thing!"

(*Bennett*); "the most *picturesque* Mediterranean craft, with colored sails and lazy evolutions" (*Brownell*). That is **pictorial** which does present or aims to present a vivid picture of something; thus, the *pictorial* arts are the same as the *graphic* arts, but the emphasis is upon the objective rather than upon the medium; a *pictorial* style of poetry uses words as though they were colors or pigments by which a vivid representation is produced.

Ana. Lucid, perspicuous, *clear: clear-cut, *incisive: telling, convincing, cogent (see VALID).

grasp, *v.* Clutch, grab, seize, *take, snatch.

Ana. *Catch, capture, nab, cop: apprehend, *arrest: *apprehend, comprehend.

grasping. Greedy, avaricious, acquisitive, *covetous.

Ana. Rapacious, ravening, ravenous (see VORACIOUS): extorting *or* extortionate (see corresponding verb at EDUCE).

grateful. 1 Grateful, thankful are sometimes used with little or no distinction, for both mean feeling or expressing one's gratitude. But **grateful** is more commonly employed to express a proper sense of favors received from another person or other persons; as, a *grateful* child; a *grateful* recipient of charity; "the Queen herself, *Grateful* to Prince Geraint for service done" (*Tennyson*). **Thankful** is often employed by preference to express one's acknowledgment of divine favor, or of what is vaguely felt to be providential; as, a common grace before meat is: "For what we are about to receive, make us truly *thankful*." "It was really the Lord's Day, for he made his creatures happy in it, and their hearts were *thankful*" (*Landor*); "I am endlessly *thankful* that I was among the last persons to see the original Rheims intact" (*H. Ellis*).

Ana. Appreciating *or* appreciative, valuing, prizing, cherishing (see corresponding verbs at APPRECIATE): gratified, pleased, delighted (see PLEASE): satisfied, contented (see SATISFY).

Ant. Ungrateful.

2 Agreeable, gratifying, *pleasant, pleasing, welcome.

Ana. Comforting, consoling, solacing (see COMFORT, *v.*): refreshing, restoring *or* restorative, renewing, rejuvenating (see corresponding verbs at RENEW): delicious, *delightful, delectable.

Ant. Obnoxious. — ***Con.*** Distasteful, abhorrent, *repugnant, repellent.

gratify. *Please, delight, rejoice, gladden, tickle, arride, regale.

Ana. Content, *satisfy: *indulge, humor, pamper.

Ant. Anger: offend, affront (*by inattention*): disappoint (*desires, hopes, etc.*).

gratifying. Grateful, agreeable, pleasing, welcome, *pleasant.

Ana. Satisfying, contenting (see SATISFY): delighting, rejoicing, gladdening, regaling (see PLEASE).

Con. Distasteful, obnoxious, invidious, repellent, *repugnant: *offensive, revolting.

gratuitous. *Supererogatory, uncalled-for, wanton.

Ana. *Voluntary, willing: unrecompensed, unrequited, unremunerated *or* irremunerable (see affirmative verbs at PAY): unprovoked, unexcited (see affirmative verbs at PROVOKE): unjustified, unwarranted (see affirmative verbs at JUSTIFY).

gratuity. *Gift, largess, fairing, boon, favor, present.

grave, *adj.* Solemn, sedate, sober, *serious, earnest, staid.

Ana. Austere, stern, ascetic, *severe: saturnine, dour (see SULLEN).

Ant. Gay. — ***Con.*** Light, light-minded, frivolous, flighty, flippant, volatile (see corresponding nouns at LIGHTNESS): *vain, idle, otiose, nugatory, empty, hollow.

graze. Pasture, *feed, nourish.

grease, *n.* Fat, *oil, wax.

grease, *v.* Lubricate, anoint, *oil, inunct, cream, pomade, pomatum.

great. *Large, big.

Ana. *Enormous, immense, huge, mammoth: tremendous, prodigious, stupendous, monumental, *monstrous: eminent, illustrious, distinguished, renowned (see FAMOUS): *supreme, superlative, surpassing, transcendent.

Ant. Little. — ***Con.*** *Small, diminutive: *petty, paltry, puny, trivial, trifling, measly.

greed. *Cupidity, rapacity, avarice.

Ana. Greediness, covetousness, avariciousness, acquisitiveness (see corresponding adjectives at COVETOUS): voraciousness, ravenousness, rapaciousness, gluttonousness *or* gluttony (see corresponding adjectives at VORACIOUS).

Con. Prodigality, lavishness, exuberance (see corresponding adjectives at PROFUSE): bountifulness, munificence, generousness *or* generosity, liberality (see corresponding adjectives at LIBERAL).

greedy. *Covetous, acquisitive, grasping, avaricious.

Ana. Rapacious, ravening, ravenous, *voracious, gluttonous: *stingy, parsimonious, miserly, close, closefisted.

Con. Bountiful, generous, *liberal, munificent: prodigal, lavish, exuberant, *profuse.

green, *adj.* Callow, raw, crude, *rude, rough.

Ant. Experienced: seasoned. — ***Con.*** Full-fledged, grown-up, ripe, matured, *mature: trained, instructed, educated (see TEACH): *proficient, skilled, skillful.

greet. Salute, hail, *address, accost.

greeting. Greeting, salutation, salute are the general terms in English denoting the ceremonial words or acts of one who meets, welcomes, or formally addresses another. **Greeting** is the ordinary term which carries so slight a suggestion of formality that it is seldom if ever used when there is any clear suggestion of inferiority in the one who greets or of superiority in the one who is greeted. On the contrary, the term usually suggests friendliness, or good will, or lack of concern for social or official inequalities. "O, to what purpose dost thou hoard thy words, That thou return'st no *greeting* to thy friends?" (*Shak.*). "Why meet we on the bridge of Time to 'change one *greeting* and to part?" (*R. F. Burton*). **Salutation** applies to any more or less formal phrase, gesture, or ceremonial act whereby one greets another: specifically it applies to phrases such as the conventional "How do you do" or the familiar "Hello," or to the words of a letter with which the writer first directly addresses his correspondent, or to acts such as a kiss, an embrace, a bow, or the like. **Salute** is the only one of these words that applies only to gestures determined by convention or to ceremonial acts: though it now seldom, if ever, applies to a speech, it may be used when to the gesture or act a word or two is added; as, to wave a *salute* to the friends awaiting one's arrival; the presidential *salute* of twenty-one guns; the officer returned his subordinate's *salute*. "Sir Austin bent forward, and put his lips to her forehead. Carola received the *salute* with the stolidity of a naughty doll" (*Meredith*).

gregarious. *Social, co-operative, convivial, companionable, hospitable.

grewsome. Variant of GRUESOME.

gridiron. Field, *arena, circus, lists, ring, cockpit, court, diamond, rink.

grief. *Sorrow, anguish, woe, heartache, dole, regret.

Ana. Mourning, grieving, sorrowing (see GRIEVE):

lamenting *or* lamentation, bewailing, bemoaning, deploring (see LAMENT, *v.*).
Con. Comforting *or* comfort, solacing *or* solace, consolation (see corresponding verbs at COMFORT): elation, exultation (see corresponding adjectives at ELATED).

grievance. Wrong, *injustice, injury, tort.
Ana. Hardship, rigor (see DIFFICULTY): *trial, tribulation, affliction, cross.

grieve. Grieve, mourn, sorrow agree in meaning to feel or express one's sorrow or grief. **Grieve** implies actual mental suffering, whether it is outwardly manifested or not: the term often also connotes the concentration of one's mind on one's loss, trouble, or other cause of distress; as, after so many years, she still *grieves* for her dead child; "he *grieved*, like an honest lad, to see his comrade left to face calamity alone" (*Meredith*). "My days Are passed in work, lest I should *grieve* for her, And undo habits used to earn her praise" (*Amy Lowell*). **Mourn** may or may not imply as much sincerity as *grieve* usually implies, but it usually suggests a specific cause, the death of a relative, friend, sovereign, or the like, and carries a much stronger implication of the outward expression of one's grief, as in weeping, sobbing, lamenting, or the wearing of black garments; as, "Blessed are they that *mourn:* for they shall be comforted" (*Matthew* v. 4); "We wept after her hearse, And yet we *mourn*" (*Shak.*); to fix a period of national *mourning* for a dead sovereign. "*Grieve* for an hour, perhaps, then *mourn* a year, And bear about the mockery of woe To midnight dances, and the public show" (*Pope*). "*Mourn* not for Adonais.—Thou young Dawn Turn all thy dew to splendour, for from thee The spirit thou lamentest is not gone" (*Shelley*). **Sorrow** may imply grieving or mourning, and be used in place of either term when sincere mental distress is implied; in distinctive use, however, it carries a stronger implication of regret or of deep sadness than either of its close synonyms; as, "So send them [Adam and Eve from Eden] forth, though *sorrowing*, yet in peace" (*Milton*); "I desire no man to *sorrow* for me" (*J. Hayward*).
Ana. Suffer, *bear, endure: *lament, bemoan, bewail, deplore: *cry, weep, wail, keen.
Ant. Rejoice.

grill, *v.* **1** Broil, barbecue, roast, *bake.
2 Rack, torment, torture, *afflict, try.

grim. 1 Grim, implacable, relentless, unrelenting, merciless come into comparison in the sense of so inexorable or obdurate as to repel or bar any effort to move one from one's purpose or course. **Grim** (as here compared: see also GHASTLY) usually implies tenacity of purpose and stern determination which show themselves outwardly in a forbidding aspect or in a formidable appearance: the term is applicable not only to persons, their words, acts, looks, etc., but to things which reflect or reveal the grimness of persons; as, *grim* Death; *grim* necessity; "The Florentines...prepared to do *grim* battle for their liberties" (*Mrs. Oliphant*). **Implacable** literally implies the impossibility of placating, pacifying, or appeasing, and is often used in reference to men or to higher beings; as, "In friendship false, *implacable* in hate" (*Dryden*); "He [an African god] is utterly and absolutely *implacable;* no prayers, no human sacrifices can ever for one moment appease His cold, malignant rage" (*L. P. Smith*). However, the term is increasingly used to imply an inflexibly uncompromising character or an incapacity for yielding or making concessions, and, in this sense, it is applicable not only to persons but to things; as, "when the true scholar gets thoroughly to work, his logic is remorseless, his art is *implacable*" (*H. Adams*); "I wanted truth presented to me as it is, arduous and honest and *implacable*" (*H. Ellis*). **Relentless** and **unrelenting** differ mainly in that the former suggests a character and the latter a mood governing action: in their literal use, both imply an absence of pity or of any feeling that would cause one to relent and to restrain through compassion the fury or violence of one's rage, hatred, hostility, vengeance, or the like; as, *relentless* critics; "Woe to thee, rash and *unrelenting* chief!" (*Byron*). Both terms, however, often carry so strong an implication of indefinite duration or of unremitting activity that they are frequently used to describe that which promises not the slightest abatement in severity, violence, intensity, or the like, as long as life or strength lasts; as, a *relentless* pursuit; the *relentless* vigilance of the secret service men; the *unrelenting* fury of a storm; "With unwearied, unscrupulous and *unrelenting* ambition" (*Macaulay*). "Everywhere I went in town, the people knew about them, and said nothing.... I found this final, closed, *relentless* silence everywhere" (*T. Wolfe*). **Merciless** differs from *relentless* and *unrelenting* mainly in stressing an innate capacity for inflicting cruelty without qualms, or an unparalleled fierceness or savagery: otherwise it carries much the same implications; as, a *merciless* whipping or tongue-lashing; "harder than any man could be—quite *merciless*" (*S. Cloete*); "the psychic disease which ravaged Europe as *mercilessly* as the Spanish influenza" (*Day Lewis*).
Ana. Inexorable, obdurate, adamant, *inflexible: inevitable, *certain: *fierce, ferocious, cruel, fell: malignant, malevolent (see MALICIOUS).
Ant. Lenient.
2 *Ghastly, grisly, gruesome, macabre, lurid.
Ana. *Fierce, truculent, savage: repellent, *repugnant: repulsive, revolting, loathsome, *offensive.
Con. Benign, benignant, kindly, *kind.

grin, *v.* *Smile, smirk, simper.
Con. Scowl, *frown, glower, lower, gloom.

grin, *n.* Smile, smirk, simper. See under SMILE, *v.*

grind, *n.* Drudgery, toil, travail, labor, *work, swink.
Ana. Pains, trouble, exertion, *effort.

grisly. *Ghastly, gruesome, macabre, grim, lurid.
Ana. Horrific, *horrible, horrendous, horrid: uncanny, eerie, *weird.

grit, *n.* *Fortitude, pluck, backbone, guts, sand.
Ana. *Courage, resolution, tenacity, mettle, spirit: determination, *decision.
Ant. Faintheartedness. — *Con.* Cowardliness *or* cowardice, pusillanimousness *or* pusillanimity, cravenness, poltroonery, recreancy (see corresponding adjectives at COWARDLY): timorousness, timidity (see corresponding adjectives at TIMID): vacillation, faltering, wavering, hesitation (see corresponding verbs at HESITATE).

groan, *v.* Moan, *sigh, sob.
Ana. Wail, weep, *cry: lament, bemoan, bewail, *deplore.

groan, *n.* Moan, sigh, sob. See under SIGH, *v.*

gross, *adj.* **1** Total, *whole, entire, all.
Ant. Net.
2 Vulgar, *coarse, obscene, ribald.
Ana. Fleshly, *carnal, sensual, animal, animalistic: *material, physical, corporeal: loathsome, *offensive, revolting, repulsive.
Ant. Delicate, dainty: ethereal. — *Con.* Spiritual, divine, *holy: *subtle, subtile.
3 *Flagrant, glaring, rank.
Ana. Extreme, *excessive, inordinate, immoderate, exorbitant: *outrageous, atrocious, monstrous, heinous.

Ant. Petty. — *Con.* Trivial, trifling, paltry (see PETTY).

grotesque. Bizarre, *fantastic, antic.
Ana. Baroque, rococo, flamboyant (see ORNATE): *weird, eerie, uncanny: extravagant, extreme (see EXCESSIVE): preposterous, absurd (see FOOLISH): ludicrous, ridiculous, comical, comic, droll (see LAUGHABLE).

ground, *n.* **1** *Base, basis, foundation, groundwork.
Ana. *Background, backdrop.
2 *Reason, argument, proof.
Ana. *Evidence, testimony: determinant, *cause, antecedent: demonstration, proof, trial, test (see under PROVE).

groundwork. Foundation, basis, ground, *base.
Ant. Superstructure.

grovel. *Wallow, welter, flounder.
Ana. *Fawn, cringe, cower, toady, truckle: crawl, *creep: *abase (oneself), demean (oneself), humble (oneself).
Con. Soar, mount, ascend, *rise: aspire (see AIM).

grown-up. Adult, *mature, matured, full-fledged, ripe, mellow.
Ant. Childish: callow.

grub, *v.* *Dig, delve, spade, excavate, exhume, disinter.

grub, *n.* *Food, victuals, eats, chow, viands, provisions, comestibles, provender, fodder, forage.

grudge, *v.* Begrudge, envy, *covet.
Ana. *Deny: refuse (see DECLINE).

grudge, *n.* *Malice, malevolence, ill will, spite, despite, malignity, spleen.
Ana. Animus, antipathy, animosity, rancor (see ENMITY): *hate, hatred: grievance, *injustice, injury.

gruesome *or* **grewsome.** Macabre, *ghastly, grisly, grim, lurid.
Ana. Daunting, appalling, horrifying (see DISMAY, *v.*): horrendous, horrific, *horrible: baleful, *sinister.

gruff. Crusty, brusque, blunt, curt, *bluff.
Ana. Surly, morose, *sullen, saturnine, crabbed, dour: churlish, boorish (see under BOOR): truculent, *fierce.
Con. *Suave, urbane, bland, smooth: unctuous, oily, sleek, soapy, *fulsome.

guarantee, *n.* **Guarantee, guaranty, surety, security, bond, bail** come into comparison when they mean either something that is given or pledged as assurance of one's responsibility for the payment of a debt, the fulfillment of a promise or obligation, the performance of a duty, or the like, or the person who accepts such responsibility and gives or pledges something by way of assurance. **Guarantee** and **guaranty** generally imply acceptance (often contractual acceptance) of this responsibility for another in case of his default; they may, however, imply an agreement to ensure for another the possession or enjoyment of a right, privilege, prerogative, or the like. The words are often used interchangeably, not only of that which is given as a pledge or of the person making the pledge but also of the contract or promise accepting the responsibility or obligation. In precise use, however, they are often distinguished, *guarantee* being the more correct term for the person and *guaranty* the preferred term for the contract or promise; either word is acceptable as a designation for that which is given or pledged; as, to stand *guarantee* (not *guaranty*); the small nations begged for *guaranties* (not *guarantees*) against invasion; his parents gave a *guaranty* (or *guarantee*) for his good behavior. "He even threatened the King of England with interdict, if, as *guarantee* of the treaty, he should enforce its forfeitures" (*Milman*). "Many laws which it would be vain to ask the Court [Supreme Court of the United States] to overthrow could be shown, easily enough, to transgress a scholastic interpretation of one or another of the great *guaranties* in the Bill of Rights" (*Justice Holmes*). In law, especially when a formal engagement, or guaranty, is entered into, the maker is often called a *guarantor* (see SPONSOR), but *guarantee*, despite its *-ee* ending (for this is not etymologically the suffix *-ee*), is not its correlative, but its synonym. **Surety** and **security** stress provision for the safety of the person who is in a position to lose by the default of another. Both are employable as designating either the person who accepts the responsibility or the money or property turned over to be forfeited in case of default. However, in current use, *surety* is the usual and the preferred term for the person (or corporation) that serves as guarantee or guarantor for another, and *security* for the money, property, or certificates of ownership turned over to a creditor, beneficiary, or obligee, or hypothecated for a loan and forfeitable in the case of one's own or another's default; as, every employee handling money is obliged to find a *surety* (not a *security*); a contractor provides a *surety* (usually an insurance corporation) for his performance of a job according to the terms of the contract, but he gives *security* to the bank that loans him money to begin the job; unsecured debts are those for which no *security* has been given to the creditors. In British and in some American use, *surety* is preferred to *guarantor*. However, in some states of the United States, a distinction is made between the two, *surety* distinctly implying responsibility for immediate payment in case of the principal's default (for fuller treatment see SPONSOR). Though *guarantee* and *surety* usually imply a legal status and documentary proof of that status, they are sometimes used more loosely; as, in you as our partner we have a *guarantee* of our success; "King, you are free! We did but keep you *surety* for our son" (*Tennyson*). **Bond,** on the other hand, implies documentary proof of one's acceptance of an obligation, and a legally binding promise to repay the holder of that document a sum of money due him on one's own account or in case of the default of another for whom one serves as surety. *Bond*, therefore, is used either of the document which is given as a pledge (as, government *bonds;* to give a *bond* as proof of one's suretyship; his word is as good as his *bond*) or for the person or corporation that serves as a legally bound surety (as, to go *bond* for another). "A month before This *bond* expires, I do expect return Of thrice three times the value of this *bond*" (*Shak.*). "The King of England shall be *bond* for him" (*Pepys*). **Bail** implies responsibility for the sure reappearance, at the time prescribed by the court, of a prisoner who has been released from jail pending his trial. The term is applicable (1) to the security given and forfeitable if the prisoner does not return (as, the court asked $5000 as *bail;* the prisoner was not released because the *bail* was not forthcoming); (2) to the person serving as surety and providing the security (as, "Sirrah, call in my sons to be my *bail*"—*Shak.;* his *bail* produced him in court at the appointed time); (3) to the state of being out of prison and in the custody of a surety (as, to admit to *bail;* to be out on *bail*).
Ana. *Pledge, earnest, token, gage: guarantor, surety (see SPONSOR).

guarantor. Surety, *sponsor, patron, backer, angel.
Ana. *Guarantee.

guaranty. *Guarantee, surety, security, bond, bail.
Ana. *Pledge, earnest, token, gage: *contract, covenant, bargain.

guard, *v.* Shield, protect, safeguard, *defend.

Ana. Watch, attend, *tend, mind: convoy, escort, chaperon, conduct, *accompany.

guerdon. Reward, meed, bounty, award, prize, *premium, bonus.

guess, *v.* *Conjecture, surmise.
Ana. Speculate, *think, reason: imagine, fancy (see THINK): gather, *infer, deduce: estimate, reckon (see CALCULATE).

guess, *n.* Conjecture, surmise. See under CONJECTURE, *v.*
Ana. *Hypothesis, theory: belief, *opinion, view.
Ant. Certainty.

guest. *Visitor, caller, visitant.

guide, *v.* **Guide, lead, steer, pilot, engineer** are here compared in the sense of to direct a person or thing in his or its course or to show the way which he or it should follow. **Guide** usually implies assistance either by means of a person with intimate knowledge of the course or way and of all its difficulties and dangers (as, "some heavenly power *guide* us Out of this fearful country"—*Shak.;* "How shall I tread... The dark descent, and who shall *guide* the way?"—*Pope;* "Men Who *guide* the plough"—*Crabbe;* "The teacher, the parent, or the friend can often do much...to *guide* the pupil into an enjoyment of thinking"—*C. W. Eliot*) or by means of a thing, such as a light, the stars, a principle, or a device on a machine, which prevents a person or thing from getting off course or going astray (as, "The fine taste which has *guided* the vast expenditure"—*Disraeli;* "a vehement gloomy being, who had quitted the ways of vulgar men, without light to *guide* him on a better way"—*Hardy*). **Lead** stresses the idea of going in advance of a person (or persons) or of a thing (or things) to show the way and, often, to keep those that follow in order or under control: in this sense the term is used both literally and figuratively; as, a band *led* each division of the procession; the flagship *led* the fleet; "he longed...to *lead* his men on to victory" (*Marryat*); "This influence should rather *lead* than drive" (*C. W. Eliot*). Often, especially in idiomatic phrases, *lead* implies the taking of the initiative, the giving of example, or the assumption of the role of leader, director, or guide; as, in the promotion of free education, the United States has *led* the way; "He... Allured to brighter worlds, and *led* the way" (*Goldsmith*); to *lead* people astray by giving them a bad example; to *lead* one's bride to the altar. **Steer** stresses the guidance of one able to control the mechanism which determines the course or direction, as of a boat, of an automobile, of an airplane, or the like: it carries a stronger implication of governing or maneuvering than any of the preceding terms and is found in figurative as well as in literal use; as, to *steer* a ship safely through a narrow channel; "Fortune brings in some boats that are not *steer'd*" (*Shak.*); "I eagerly desire to *steer* clear of metaphysics" (*Lowes*); the *steering* committee of the House of Representatives. **Pilot** literally implies the assistance of a pilot, a person competent to steer a vessel safely through unknown or difficult waters, as through a long and narrow channel into or out of a port (as, to *pilot* a vessel through Ambrose Channel into New York harbor). In its figurative use, it implies guidance over a course where one may easily lose one's way because of its intricacy or may run afoul of various obstacles or dangers; as, their room steward *piloted* them to the ship's dining room; "We know not where we go, or what sweet dream May *pilot* us through caverns strange and fair Of far and pathless passion" (*Shelley*); "[May] the Saints *Pilot* and prosper all thy wandering out And homeward" (*Tennyson*). **Engineer** literally means to lay out and manage the construction of some great project, such as a tunnel under a river, a huge bridge, or the like (as, a firm of experts was called upon to *engineer* the irrigation project), but in its more common extended sense (originally and still chiefly American) it means to serve as a manager in carrying through something which requires contrivance, maneuvering, or the like; as, to *engineer* a resolution through the House of Representatives; to *engineer* a fraud; "the corner in grain *engineered* by parties in Chicago" (*Jay Gould*); the coup d'état was *engineered* by high-ranking army officers.
Ana. Conduct, convoy, escort, chaperon, *accompany: direct, manage, control, *conduct.
Ant. Misguide. — ***Con.*** Distract, bewilder, perplex, mystify, *puzzle: mislead, delude, beguile, *deceive.

guile, *n.* Duplicity, dissimulation, cunning, *deceit.
Ana. Trickery, double-dealing, chicanery, chicane, *deception: craft, artifice (see ART).
Ant. Ingenuousness: candor.

guilt. *Blame, culpability, fault.
Ana. Sin, crime, *offense: responsibility, answerability, liability (see corresponding adjectives at RESPONSIBLE).
Ant. Innocence: guiltlessness.

guilty. *Blameworthy, culpable.
Ana. *Responsible, answerable, accountable: indicted, impeached, incriminated (see ACCUSE).
Ant. Innocent.

gulf. **Gulf, chasm, abysm, abyss** in literal use agree in denoting a hollow place, of vast width and depth, in the earth. *Gulf* and *chasm*, however, suggest a depth which, though vast, is still measurable; *abysm* and *abyss* suggest immeasurable depth. **Gulf** is the most general term and may properly be used of any wide and deep hollow place. "Slippery cliffs arise Close to deep *gulfs*" (*Bryant*). In its figurative use, *gulf* suggests separation by a great, often unbridgeable, distance. "The broad and deep *gulf* which...divides the living from the dead" (*Inge*). **Chasm** adds the implication of a deep, and sometimes wide, breach in a formerly solid surface; as, the *chasm* of the Grand Canyon, worn by the Colorado River. "The brink of a precipice, of a *chasm* in the earth over two hundred feet deep, the sides sheer cliffs" (*Cather*). In figurative use, *chasm* still stresses a sharp break in continuity. "Those *chasms* of momentary indifference and boredom which gape from time to time between even the most ardent lovers" (*A. Huxley*). **Abysm** and **abyss** are etymological variants, *abysm* being the earlier form. Both originally designated the bottomless gulf or cavity of ancient cosmogonies and both have been applied to hell when thought of as a bottomless pit. Therefore they usually connote not only fathomlessness, but also darkness and horror. *Abysm* now has a somewhat archaic flavor. "When my good stars... Have empty left their orbs, and shot their fires Into the *abysm* of hell" (*Shak.*). Figuratively, *abysm* carries over the idea of a vast and immeasurably deep void. "What seest thou else In the dark backward and *abysm* of time?" (*Shak.*). *Abyss* is the form commonly used in modern times. "The *abyss* of Tartarus, fast secured with iron gates" (*Thirlwall*). Like *abysm*, *abyss* carries over into its figurative use the notion of vast, immeasurable void. "The respectability and prosperity of the propertied and middle classes who grew rich on sweated labor covered an *abyss* of horror" (*Shaw*).

gull, *v.* *Dupe, befool, trick, hoax, hoodwink, bamboozle.
Ana. Delude, beguile, *deceive, mislead, double-cross, betray.

gummy. Mucilaginous, gluey, glutinous, *adhesive, sticky.

gumption. *Sense, common sense, good sense, judgment, wisdom.
Ana. Sagaciousness *or* sagacity, shrewdness, perspica-

ciousness *or* perspicacity, astuteness (see corresponding adjectives at SHREWD).

gunman. Trigger man, finger man, *assassin, cutthroat, bravo.

Ana. *Ruffian, thug, gangster.

gust. *Wind, breeze, blast, flaw, zephyr, gale, hurricane, whirlwind, cyclone, typhoon, tornado, waterspout, twister.

gusto. Relish, zest, *taste, palate.

Ana. Enjoyment, delight, delectation, *pleasure: enthusiasm, fervor, ardor, *passion, zeal.

guts. Grit, pluck, *fortitude, backbone, sand.

Ana. Tenacity, resolution, mettle, spirit, *courage.

guy, *v.* *Banter, chaff, rally, quiz, kid, rag, rib, josh, jolly.

gymnasium. *Academy, seminary, lycée, institute, college.

gymnast. *Athlete.

gyrate. Rotate, revolve, *turn, spin, whirl, wheel, circle, twirl, eddy, swirl, pirouette.

H

habit, *n.* **Habit, habitude, practice, usage, custom, consuetude, use, wont** come into comparison when they mean a way of behaving, proceeding, or the like, that has become fixed by constant repetition. In most cases, also, these words may be used as collective or abstract nouns denoting all habits, usages, customs, or the like, considered as a directing or impelling force. **Habit** refers more often to the way of an individual than to the way of a community or other group; the term applies to any way of acting, thinking, or otherwise behaving, which has become so natural to one through repetition that one does it unconsciously or without premeditation; as, he has formed the *habit* of fingering a coat button when he speaks in public; she has not yet the *habit* of tidying her room before she leaves it; to break a bad *habit;* "*habits* acquired very early feel, in later life, just like instincts; they have the same profound grip" (*B. Russell*); *habit* is one of the strongest aids to successful living. **Habitude** more often suggests a habitual or usual state of mind or attitude than an habitual response to a given stimulus; as, "[She was] from *habitude* very little incommoded by the remarks and ejaculations of Mrs. Allen" (*Austen*); "I think, Pericles, you who are so sincere with me are never quite sincere with others. You have contracted this bad *habitude* from your custom of addressing the people" (*Landor*). **Practice,** as here compared (see also *practice, n.,* under PRACTICE, *v.*), applies to any habit which is by its nature an act or a method which is followed regularly and often by choice; as, it is his *practice* to rise early each morning and take a walk before breakfast; it is the *practice* of this surgeon to give local anesthetics wherever possible. **Usage,** as here compared (see also FORM, 3), applies mainly to a practice that has been so long continued and has been adopted so generally that it serves to guide or determine the action or choice of others; as, it is the *usage* in certain European countries to breakfast on a roll and a cup of coffee; it is difficult to conform to the *usages* of a foreign country; "the... inveterate *usages* of our country, growing out of the prejudice of ages" (*Burke*). Specifically, in reference to the correct meanings of words, proper grammatical constructions, and idiomatic forms, where there is a difference of opinion, *usage* (that is, the long-continued and established practice of the best writers and speakers) is regarded as the determining factor; thus, in ordinary *use* (that is, the way in which the ordinary, or average man uses the term), "nice" means pleasing for one reason or another, but *usage* (often, *the best usage*—that is, the way in which the best writers and speakers use the term) indicates that "nice" correctly means showing or involving the use of discrimination; as, "All senses of all words are founded upon *usage,* and nothing else" (*W. Paley*). **Custom** applies to any habit, any practice, any usage that externally manifests itself and that has come to be associated with an individual or a group by reason of its long continuance, its uniformity of character, and, sometimes, its compulsory nature; as, it is his *custom* to smoke each evening after dinner; the *custom* of the club is to wear full dress for dinner; is it the *custom* in your church for the minister to greet each member of his congregation?; it is not the *custom* to speak from the floor before being recognized by the presiding officer. Both in law and elsewhere, a custom, as an established practice or usage (or as the body of established practices and usages) of a community or of a people has the force of an unwritten law or laws; thus, the English common law is based upon *custom* rather than upon legislation. "The answer, 'It is the *custom,*' is final for the savage, as for the lady of fashion. There is no other reason why they behave in a certain way" (*Inge*). Consequently, *custom,* when used as a collective or abstract noun, commonly implies a force as strong, as binding, and as difficult to escape as that exerted by those who enforce the law of the land. "And *custom* lie upon thee with a weight, Heavy as frost, and deep almost as life" (*Wordsworth*). "Consecrated *custom* may keep Chinese civilisation safe in a state of torpid immobility for five thousand years" (*Inge*). **Consuetude,** a somewhat rare word except in Scottish or learned use, often comes close to *custom* in its abstract sense, but it is sometimes nearer to *usage;* as, "The subjection to, or exemption from, jurisdiction, so completely depended upon *consuetude*" (*Wiseman*); "The word was originally not of English but of European *consuetude*" (*Sir W. Hamilton*). **Use** (which is not to be confused with *usage* as considered earlier in this article, or with *use* in the sense of the act or way of using) commonly denotes an action, manner, rite, practice, or the like, that is customary to an individual or a particular group and distinguishes him or it from others; as, "more haste Than is his *use*" (*Shak.*); the *use* (that is, the particular liturgy used in a church or diocese) of York; "it had been a family *use*...to make a point of saving for him anything which he might possibly eat" (*M. Austin*). **Wont,** in current English, usually applies to a habitual manner, method, or practice distinguishing an individual or group; it not only differs little from *use* except in its narrower range of application, but is often coupled with *use* as a term of equivalent content; as, "The painter followed the religious *use* and *wont* of his time" (*Mrs. Oliphant*); "sad beyond his *wont*" (*Tennyson*); "[Renan] begins after the romantic *wont* by an outburst of sympathy and comprehension for the Parthenon and the Athenians and Pallas Athene" (*Babbitt*).

Ana. Instinct (see under INSTINCTIVE): convention, convenance, usage, *form.

habitat. **Habitat, range, station** are here compared only in their technical biological senses in which they agree in denoting the place in which a given species lives or is found. **Habitat** in strict use refers especially to the kind of environment in which a plant or animal is normally found, such as a desert, seacoast, grassland, marsh, forest, etc. **Range,** on the other hand, applies to the geographical region in which a plant or animal naturally grows or lives and throughout which it is distributed. **Station** may be used in place of *range,* but it is commonly restricted to the exact locality or spot where a given species is found or at which a given specimen has been collected.

habitation. **Habitation, dwelling, residence, abode, domicile, house, home.** The first three are chiefly literary or elevated. "My people shall dwell in a peaceable *habitation,* and in sure *dwellings*" (*Isaiah* xxxii. 18). "And one bare *dwelling;* one *abode,* no more!" (*Wordsworth*). **Habitation** sometimes expresses contrast with the wilderness or with nomadism, and suggests little more than shelter and settled living; as, wandering tribes without a *habitation.* **Dwelling** (the equivalent term *dwelling house* is commoner) and, usually, **residence** emphasize the use of a building for living in, and contrast with buildings used for trade or business. *Residence* suggests a certain degree of pretension or dignity in the building and of permanence in occupancy. **Abode** and **domicile** (the latter, chiefly a legal term), by contrast, convey no suggestions of the character of the dwelling place, but may imply the extremes respectively of transience and permanence; as, one's *abode* (not *domicile*) for the night. A *domicile* is, legally, a residence in which one intends to remain indefinitely and to which, however long absent, one intends to return. A **house** (the most general and neutral term of the group) is a building used, or intended for use, as a dwelling place; a **home** is an occupied dwelling place whose associations evoke in the occupants sentiment and feeling; as, a landlord's *house* is his tenants' *home;* "Without hearts there is no *home*" (*Byron*).

habitual. *Usual, customary, wonted, accustomed.
Ana. Habituated, addicted, familiarized (see HABITUATE): practiced, drilled (see PRACTICE, *v.*): confirmed, *inveterate, chronic, deep-seated, deep-rooted.
Ant. Occasional. — *Con.* *Infrequent, sporadic, rare, uncommon.

habituate. 1 **Habituate, accustom, familiarize, addict** agree in meaning to make used to something. **Habituate,** in strict use, implies the formation of habit through repetition of certain acts; as, by constant practice she *habituated* herself to accurate observation. "To *habituate* ourselves, therefore, to approve...things that are really excellent, is of the highest importance" (*Arnold*). **Accustom** implies adjustment to something by frequent or prolonged experience or by constant exposure; as, to *accustom* oneself to cold; to *accustom* students to severe criticism. To *accustom* oneself to nagging is to become inured to nagging by another person; to *habituate* oneself to nagging is to form the habit of nagging others. This distinction is frequently not observed in loose usage. Sometimes *accustom* also connotes reconciliation by overcoming one's resistance or distaste. "The 'fourteener' [common meter]...which repels readers who have not the patience to *accustom* their ears and nerves to its beat" (*T. S. Eliot*). **Familiarize** presupposes lack of knowledge or of experience with consequent strangeness or constraint, and implies the overcoming of these through close study or association; as, to *familiarize* oneself with one's duties or with the rules of a game; to *familiarize* oneself with a foreign language; to *familiarize* a child with the birds or flowers of a region. **Addict** (now used chiefly in a reflexive construction or in the passive) adds to *habituate* the implication of overindulgence or surrender to inclination; as, *addicted* to study; it very frequently refers to bad habits; as, *addicted* to drink or to stealing. "A man gross...and *addicted* to low company" (*Macaulay*).
Ana. Train, discipline, school (see TEACH): inure, *harden, season, acclimatize, acclimate: *practice, exercise, drill.
2 *Frequent, haunt.
Ana. *Resort, go, turn, apply, refer.
Ant. Shun, avoid (see ESCAPE).

habitude. *Habit, practice, usage, custom, consuetude, use, wont.
Ana. Attitude, stand, *position: *state, condition, situation.
Con. *Mood, humor, temper: *caprice, whim, freak, vagary.

habitué. *Addict, votary, devotee, fiend, fan.

hack *or* **hackney,** *adj.* Hireling, *mercenary, venal.
Ana. Toiling, drudging, grinding, laboring (see corresponding nouns at WORK): hired, employed (see HIRE, *v.*): *mean, abject, sordid.

hackneyed. *Trite, stereotyped, threadbare, shopworn.
Ana. Antiquated, archaic, obsolete, antediluvian, *old: worn, wasted (see HAGGARD): attenuated, diluted (see THIN, *v.*).
Con. Fresh, novel, original, *new.

Hadean. Chthonian, *infernal, Tartarean, Stygian, hellish.

haggard. **Haggard, worn, careworn, pinched, wasted, cadaverous** come into comparison when they mean thin and drawn by or as by worry, fatigue, hunger, illness, or the like. **Haggard** in very precise use implies wildness, such as that of a person driven distraught by fear, anxiety, privation, or the like (as, "whose *haggard* eyes Flash desperation"—*Cowper;* "the strong face to which that *haggard* expression was returning"—*Conrad;* "She stood at the door, *haggard* with rage"—*Joyce*), but in looser use it usually also implies the extreme thinness or gauntness that is normally associated with age but that comes to younger persons who never know physical or mental ease (as, "they grow thin and *haggard* with the constant toil of getting food and warmth"—*S. Anderson*). **Worn** is the better word etymologically for this looser sense of *haggard,* for it definitely implies the attrition of flesh characteristic of senility and induced in younger persons by overwork, worry, exhaustion, prolonged ill-health, and the like; as, "The President... looked somewhat *worn* and anxious, and well he might" (*Dickens*). **Careworn** differs from *worn* chiefly in its implication of a being overburdened with cares and responsibilities that cause anxiety; as, the young mother's *careworn* face; three years of heavy responsibility have changed him to an old *careworn* man. **Pinched** and **wasted** suggest the effects of privation or of a wasting disease; as, the *pinched* faces of poorly nourished children; the *wasted* body of a consumptive. **Cadaverous** is often used in place of *pinched* or *wasted* when there is the intent to suggest the appearance of a cadaver, or corpse: it usually implies a deathly paleness and a falling away of the flesh so that the skeleton is apparent though not visible; as, "He has a *cadaverous* countenance, full of cavities and projections" (*Irving*); "For a queer second I did see us all in that...mirror..., *cadaverous,* palsied" (*L. P. Smith*).
Ana. Gaunt, scrawny, skinny, *lean: fatigued, ex-

hausted, wearied, fagged, jaded (see TIRE, *v.*): wan, pallid, ashen, *pale.

Con. Jaunty, *debonair, perky, cocky: *vigorous, lusty, energetic, strenuous.

hail, *v.* Salute, greet, *address, accost.

halcyon. *Calm, serene, placid, tranquil, peaceful.

hale, *v.* Haul, *pull, draw, drag, tug, tow.

hale, *adj.* Robust, *healthy, sound, wholesome, well.

Ana. Lusty, *vigorous: sturdy, stalwart, *strong, stout: spry, *agile.

Ant. Infirm. — *Con.* *Senile, anile, doddering: feeble, frail, fragile, decrepit, *weak.

hall. **1** *Entry, entryway, vestibule, narthex, foyer, lobby, anteroom, antechamber.

2 Also **hallway.** *Passage, passageway, corridor, gallery, arcade, cloister, aisle, ambulatory.

hallow, *v.* Consecrate, dedicate, *devote.

Con. See those at CONSECRATE.

hallucination. *Delusion, mirage, illusion.

Ana. *Apparition, phantasm, phantom, wraith: fantasy, *fancy, vision, dream, nightmare.

halo, *n.* **Halo, glory, aureole** (*or* **aureola**), **nimbus** come into comparison when they denote an emblem, usually circular or oval in form, used in the artistic representation of a saint or a sacred figure to indicate sanctity or divinity, or, in some cases, sovereignty. **Halo** is the ordinary nontechnical term for the most common emblem of sanctity in religious art, especially in paintings, statues, and stained-glass windows, either a circle or band that surrounds the head of the figure or a disk which forms its background. The other three terms are more common in technical use and richer in their implications. **Glory** is the comprehensive term for any representation of an effulgence of light from the head or from the entire body. It therefore is not restricted to an emblem that resembles a crown; it may be an oval in which the figure is embedded. Usually also it implies representation of rays or of light. **Aureole** was earliest applied to a spiritual crown, or radiance, piously believed to distinguish some of the saints in heaven, and later to the representation of such a crown in religious art. The term is now used by some writers as equivalent to *glory* and as including the halo and the pointed oval (*vesica piscis*) surrounding the entire body. **Nimbus** (L. for *cloud*) originally, in English, designated a luminous cloud surrounding a god or goddess visiting earth; it came to be applied in art to any emblematic representation of divinity, sanctity, or sovereignty surrounding the head of a figure. *Nimbus* is not restricted, as is *halo*, to something round; it also suggests differentiation more than the other words, for a distinctive type of nimbus, especially in medieval art, is the attribute by which the figure can be definitely identified. Thus, a circular disk with a cross is the common form of *nimbus* for Christ; a six-pointed star is the *nimbus* of God the Father in many Greek eikons.

hamper, *v.* **Hamper, trammel, clog, fetter, shackle, manacle, hog-tie** are here compared as meaning to hinder or impede one so that one cannot move, progress, or act freely. **Hamper** is to encumber or embarrass as by an impediment or restraining influence of any sort; as, the long dress *hampered* her freedom of movement; "The view is vigorously urged to-day that rhyme and meter *hamper* the poet's free expression" (*Lowes*). "Never...had she so desired to be spontaneous and unrestrained; never...had she so felt herself *hampered* by her timidity, her self-criticism, her deeply ingrained habit of never letting herself go" (*H. G. Wells*). To **trammel** (literally, to catch in a net) is more specifically to entangle or confine as if enmeshed in a net; as, *trammeled* in his endeavors by the web of intrigue about him; "Their life [that is, of women in ancient Rome] was at once dangerously *trammelled* and dangerously free" (*Buchan*). To **clog** (literally, to attach a clog or weight to a man or animal so as to hinder motion) is to hamper the movement, often the ascent, of someone or something by that which is extraneous, encumbering, useless, or the like; as, "The wings of birds were *clogged* with ice and snow" (*Dryden*); "Man is ever *clogged* with his mortality" (*C. Brontë*); "The Cynic preached abstinence from all common ambitions, rank, possessions, power, the things which *clog* man's feet" (*Buchan*). To **fetter** (literally, to tie the feet with chains so that free or extended movement is impossible) is to confine or restrain so that one's freedom or power to progress is lost; as, "My heels are *fettered*, but my fist is free" (*Milton*); "So free we seem, so *fettered* fast we are!" (*Browning*); "I refused to visit Shelley that I might have my own *unfettered* scope" (*Keats*); "We reverence tradition, but we will not be *fettered* by it" (*Inge*). To **shackle** (literally, to encircle a wrist or ankle with a chain or band attached to something else) and to **manacle** (literally, to put on manacles or handcuffs) differ little in their extended use, both implying such interference with one's freedom that one feels that movement, progress, or action is impossible if the bonds are not broken; as, to *shackle* a slave; he would not be *shackled* in his reasoning by the rules of logic; prisoners are *manacled* when brought to court; "Grief too can *manacle* the mind" (*Lovelace*). **Hog-tie, a** recent colloquialism in the United States (literally, to tie the four feet of a hog, steer, or the like), is now much used as an intensive of *fetter;* the term usually implies inability to move from a place, position, duty, or the like; as, he felt *hog-tied* to his business; industries *hog-tied* by restrictions on imports of raw materials.

Ana. *Hinder, impede, obstruct, block, bar: *embarrass, discomfit: baffle, balk, thwart, foil, *frustrate.

Ant. Assist (*persons*): expedite (*work, projects, etc.*).

hand, *n.* Operative, workman, workingman, laborer, craftsman, handicraftsman, mechanic, artisan, roustabout, *worker.

handicap. Allowance, *advantage, odds, edge.

Ant. (*For common extended sense*) advantage: asset.

handicraft. Craft, art, *trade, profession.

handicraftsman. Craftsman, workman, artisan, mechanic, workingman, laborer, operative, hand, roustabout, *worker.

handle, *v.* **Handle, manipulate, wield, swing, ply** come into comparison as meaning to deal with or manage with or, more often, as if with the hands, especially, but far from exclusively, with the implication of easy, skillful, or dexterous management. **Handle,** in both its literal and extended senses, implies the acquirement of skill sufficient (or, if qualified, in the degree stated) to accomplish one's ends; as, a child can be taught early to *handle* a spoon, but it takes longer to teach him to *handle* a knife and fork; "tools to be *handled* with care" (*T. S. Eliot*); she *handled* the reins superbly; he knows how to *handle* men so as to get what he wants out of them; "Richelieu sent Charnacé out to *handle* that situation" (*Belloc*). **Manipulate,** in both its literal and extended uses, implies dexterity and adroitness in handling. Especially in its literal sense the term suggests mechanical or technical skill; as, he is able to *manipulate* the most delicate scientific apparatus; "The kind of courage required for mountaineering, for *manipulating* an aeroplane, or for managing a small ship in a gale" (*B. Russell*). In its extended sense, the term often specifically implies crafty or artful, sometimes fraudulent, handling for the attainment of one's own ends; as, a small group of men by *manipulating* the convention were able to procure the election of their candidate; it was discovered that by *manipulating* his accounts he had concealed his peculations for years. **Wield** (etymologically, to have mastery over) in its chief current sense implies mastery and vigor in the handling of a tool, a weapon, or other implement; as, he knows how to *wield* an axe; to *wield* a sword; "navvies *wielding* their hammers in the streets" (*H. Ellis*). In slightly figurative use, *wield* may be employed when that which is handled with mastery is an instrument such as a writer's pen, an artist's brush, or a king's scepter, implying not the vigorous movement of the implement itself but its effectiveness as a tool in producing a desired result or as a symbol of power; thus, "to *wield* a scepter" means to exercise sovereign power or to hold sway. "Of Wu Tao-tzŭ it is said that it seemed as if a god possessed him and *wielded* the brush in his hand" (*Binyon*). The term may also take for its object words such as authority, influence, power, and the like, when their masterful exercise is implied; as, a great editorial writer *wields* a tremendous influence over the minds of men; "Her newborn power was *wielded*...by unprincipled and ambitious men" (*De Quincey*). **Swing** may be used in place of *wield* in its literal sense when a flourishing with a sweep is also suggested; as, he *swings* his golf club with great effectiveness. In its extended sense of to handle successfully, often in spite of great difficulties, *swing* is an American colloquialism; as, the corporation was able to *swing* its bond issue; he could not *swing* the business. **Ply** (etymologically, to apply) may be used in place of *handle* or *wield* when great diligence or industry are also suggested; as, "Go *ply* thy needle; meddle not" (*Shak.*); "*plying* patiently the chisel and mallet" (*C. E. Montague*); to *ply* one's oars. The term may also be used when constant and diligent employment, as of a power or faculty, or as at a trade, is also suggested; as, to *ply* one's wit; "the housewife *plied* her own peculiar work" (*Wordsworth*); to *ply* one's trade.

Ana. *Swing, flourish, brandish, wave: *direct, aim, point, level, train, lay.

handpick. Pick, single out, select, *choose, elect, opt, cull, prefer.

handsome. 1 Generous, *liberal, bountiful, munificent.

Ana. Lavish, prodigal, *profuse.

Con. Niggardly, penurious, *stingy, parsimonious: frugal, economical, *sparing, thrifty: *meager, skimpy, scrimpy.

2 *Beautiful, pulchritudinous, beauteous, comely, good-looking, lovely, pretty, bonny, fair.

Ana. Majestic, stately, august, noble (see GRAND): elegant, exquisite (see CHOICE): smart, modish, fashionable, *stylish.

handy. Feat, deft, *dexterous, adroit.

Ana. Adept, skillful, skilled, *proficient: *able, capable, competent.

hang, *v.* **Hang, suspend, sling, dangle** come into comparison as meaning to place a thing, or (of a thing) to be placed so that it is supported (literally or figuratively) at one point or on one side, usually a point or side at the top. **Hang** typically implies a fastening to an elevated point or line so as to allow free motion to, or permit free movement of, that which falls from such a point or line; as, to *hang* the washing on a line; hundreds of plums *hang* from the tree's branches; to *hang* curtains; they *hanged* (in this application, not *hung*) the murderer; carcasses of lamb were *hung* (not *hanged*) in the butcher's window; to *hang* out a flag from a window. In extended and figurative use, *hang* often implies a position or a relation suggestive of hanging, such as that of something poised or seemingly poised in the air (as, "musty [air]... *hung* in all the rooms"—*Joyce;* "just above its [the poplar's] pointed tip, *hung* the hollow, silver winter moon"—*Cather*), or of that which is dependent upon something else (as, "A good deal...*hangs* on the meaning...of this short word"—*T. S. Eliot*), or of that which clings or adheres to something else (as, she *hangs* on his arm; "thereby *hangs* a tale"—*Shak.;* "Most heavily remorse *hangs* at my heart!"—*Shelley*), or the like. **Suspend** for a long time after its first use in the sense of *hang* was regarded as a formal or affected term: it is currently used more often, but it still usually seems more literary or less colloquial than *hang;* as, "Hams, tongues, and flitches of bacon, were *suspended* from the ceiling" (*Irving*); "Others [of the rebels] were *suspended* from the boughs of the oak" (*T. Keightley*). In some cases, *suspend*, especially the past participle *suspended*, is preferred to *hang* (or *hung*) when support from a point or points above suggests flexibility, free motion or movement, or a display of skill; as, hundreds of lamps, each held by a thin chain, were *suspended* from the ceiling; a *suspended* bridge (now usually *suspension* bridge). *Suspend* is also employed more often than *hang* when a floating as in air, or water, or other fluid is suggested (see SUSPENDED); as, "Wasp-like flies barred with yellow *suspended* themselves in the air" (*Jefferies*). **Sling,** in its earliest sense, implied the use of a sling, or a strap, rope, chain, or the like, equipped with hooks or tackle for grasping heavy or bulky articles so that they might be hoisted or lowered with ease. Later, the term came to imply a hanging over the shoulder, or arm, or similar support, for ease in carrying, reaching, or the like; as, to *sling* a basket on one's arm; to *sling* a scaffold from a roof. **Dangle** implies a hanging in such a manner as to swing or sway to and fro; as, to *dangle* one's cane from a finger; the children sat on the high wall, their legs *dangling;* "For all might see the bottle-necks Still *dangling* at his waist" (*Cowper*). Figuratively, *dangle* usually implies dependence on someone, often a loose dependence or connection, in hope of a reward for attentions or services; as, she keeps her suitors *dangling.*

Ana. *Stick, adhere, cling: hover (see FLIT).

hanger-on. *Parasite, sycophant, leech, sponge, favorite, toady, lickspit.

hanker. Yearn, pine, *long, hunger, thirst.

Ana. Crave, *desire, covet, wish, want: aspire, pant, *aim.

hant. Variant of HAUNT.

hap, *n.* *Chance, fortune, luck, accident, hazard.

Ana. *Fate, destiny, lot, portion.

hap, *v.* Archaic and poetic variant of HAPPEN.

haphazard. *Random, chance, chancy, casual, desultory, hit-or-miss, happy-go-lucky.

Ana. *Accidental, fortuitous, casual.

Con. Designed, planned, schemed, plotted (see verbs under PLAN, *n.*): intentional, deliberate, willful, *voluntary.

happen, *v.* **Happen, hap, chance, occur, befall, betide, transpire** come into comparison as synonyms only when they mean to come to pass or to come about. **Happen** is the ordinary and general term; **hap,** the archaic and poetic term, for this sense: both may imply either obvious causation or seeming accident, either design or an absence of design; in its simplest use, either term takes the event, situation, or circumstance as its subject (as, the incident *happened* two weeks ago) but in idiomatic phrases it may take the impersonal *it* or the anticipatory *there* as its subject (as, "it *happened* that at Dante's time thought was orderly and strong and beautiful"—*T. S. Eliot;* "Oft it *haps* that...a feather daunts the brave" (*Scott*); there *happened* to be no visitors that day). In still other idiomatic and largely colloquial phrases, *happen* or *hap* may take a person as the subject, especially when the verb implies a coming upon someone or something, or a coming into a place more or less casually or accidentally, rather than a coming to pass; as, the miners *happened* upon a vein of gold; "I go nowhere on purpose: I *happen* by" (*Frost*); "A maiden fine bedight he *hapt* to love" (*Gay*). **Chance** is closer to *happen* in its idiomatic uses than any of the other words; it is also found occasionally, but somewhat archaically, with the event as the subject; however, it differs from *happen* in uniformly implying absence of design or apparent lack of causation; as, "If a bird's nest *chance* to be before thee" (*Deuteronomy* xxii. 6); "Whenever it *chanced* that the feelings of the people were roused" (*Kinglake*); "things they themselves *chance* to know" (*A. Repplier*). **Occur** (etymologically, to run to meet) always, in very precise use, carries an implication of presenting itself to sight, to consciousness, to one's thoughts, or the like; it is, in general, interchangeable with *happen* only when a definite event, incident, or something that actually takes place is the subject; as, the accident *occurred* (or *happened*) yesterday; the bombing raids on the city *occurred* (or *happened*) early in the war; I do not know what *happened* (better than *occurred*) after I left; "it is necessary for the physicist to arrange the situation so that phenomena shall *occur* [far better than *happen*] in which ...the underlying simplicity will come to light" (*Karl K. Darrow*). Consequently, *occur* is preferable to *happen* in negative expressions when the idea of presentation in the realm of fact is uppermost. "Scientists of the last century...under the sway of a naturalistic optimism which regarded an actual event as...of superior value to an event which did not *occur*" (*Inge*). "This is possible in theory, but, actually, never seemed to *occur*" (*Heiser*). This fundamental implication of presentation to sight, mind, etc., makes it possible to use *occur* where *happen* would be entirely out of place, as when the word suggests a coming to one's mind (as, "That characters deteriorate in time of need possibly did not *occur* to Henchard"—*Hardy*), or a meeting one's eyes or ears, as in print or speech (as, the word seldom *occurs* except in poetry), or a turning up or appearing (as, another instance of this disease may not *occur* for several years; corundum *occurs* in crystals, masses, and grains). **Befall** (etymologically, to fall, as to one's lot) is used in preference to any of the preceding words, especially in poetry or in literary prose, when there is an implication of a superior power determining events or of the lack of human power to foreknow or forestall them; as, "Anxiety lest mischief should *befall* her" (*Wordsworth*). "I hold it true, whate'er *befall* ... 'Tis better to have loved and lost, Than never to have loved at all" (*Tennyson*). **Betide** is a distinctively archaic synonym of *befall;* as, "whatever fortune *betides* you" (*H. Martineau*). It is, however, often used in poetry in wishes or, especially, in curses; as, "Woe *betide* the wandering wight" (*Scott*). **Transpire** is often used in place of *happen* or *occur*, even by some otherwise careful writers (as, among the events which *transpired* during the war); the usage, though not uncommon, has not been accepted by the best authorities. However, it is necessary to distinguish this disapproved sense from the approved sense with which it is frequently confused, that of to leak out, to become known, especially to the public; as, certain events of the war which have recently *transpired*. "Precisely what passed on that occasion never *transpired*" (*L. Strachey*).

happiness. Happiness, felicity, beatitude, blessedness, bliss agree in denoting the enjoyment or pleasurable satisfaction attendant upon well-being of any kind. **Happiness** is the generic term. **Felicity,** denoting intense happiness, usually has more formal or elevated connotations. **Beatitude** is supreme felicity. "To understand by honorable love romance and beauty and *happiness* in the possession of beautiful, refined, delicate, affectionate women" (*Shaw*). "I know no one more entitled by unpretending merit, or better prepared by habitual suffering, to receive and enjoy *felicity*" (*Austen*). "We may fancy in the happy mother's breast a feeling somewhat akin to that angelic *felicity*, that joy which angels feel in heaven for a sinner repentant" (*Thackeray*). "About him all the Sanctities of Heaven Stood thick as stars, and from his sight received *Beatitude* past utterance" (*Milton*). **Blessedness** implies a feeling of being highly favored, especially by the Supreme Being, and often, a deep joy arising from the purest domestic, benevolent, or religious affections; **bliss** adds to *blessedness* a suggestion of exalted or ecstatic felicity; both *blessedness* and *bliss*, like *beatitude*, often refer to the joys of heaven. "Thrice blest whose lives are faithful prayers, Whose loves in higher love endure; What souls possess themselves so pure, Or is there *blessedness* like theirs?" (*Tennyson*). "*Bliss* was it in that dawn to be alive, But to be young was very Heaven!" (*Wordsworth*).

Ana. Contentedness *or* content, satisfiedness *or* satisfaction (see participial adjectives at SATISFY): *pleasure, enjoyment, delight, delectation, joy, fruition.

Ant. Unhappiness. — *Con.* Despondency, despair, desperation, hopelessness, forlornness (see under DESPONDENT): *distress, misery.

happy. 1 Fortunate, *lucky, providential.

Ana. *Accidental, incidental, fortuitous, casual: *favorable, auspicious, propitious, benign: opportune, timely (see SEASONABLE).

Ant. Unhappy.

2 Felicitous, apt, appropriate, fitting, *fit, suitable, meet, proper.

Ana. *Effective, efficacious, efficient, effectual: telling, cogent, convincing (see VALID): pat, *seasonable, well-timed: right, *correct, nice.

Ant. Unhappy.

3 Cheerful, *glad, lighthearted, joyful, joyous.

Ana. Contented, satisfied (see under SATISFY): gratified, delighted, pleased, gladdened, rejoiced (see PLEASE): *elated, elate, exultant.

Ant. Unhappy: disconsolate. — *Con.* Depressed, weighed down, oppressed (see DEPRESS): *despondent, despairing, desperate, forlorn, hopeless.

happy-go-lucky. *Random, haphazard, hit-or-miss, chance, chancy, casual, desultory.

harangue, *n.* Oration, *speech, address, allocution, lecture, prelection, talk, sermon, homily.

Ana. Rant, rodomontade, *bombast.

harass. Harry, *worry, annoy, plague, pester, tease, tantalize.

Ana. *Bait, badger, hound, ride, hector, chevy, heckle: vex, irk, bother (see ANNOY).

Con. *Comfort, solace, console: *relieve, assuage, alleviate.

harbinger. *Forerunner, precursor, herald.

harbor, *n.* **Harbor** (*or* **harbour**), **haven, port** come into comparison because they have at one time or another meant a place where ships may ride secure from storms. **Harbor** (etymologically, shelter or a shelter) now applies to a portion of a sea or other large body of water that is landlocked or is otherwise artificially protected so that ships or other boats may enter it for safety from storms or may be anchored or moored there when not in use; as, two promontories whose points come near together enclose the *harbor;* the great natural *harbor* at Sydney, Australia. **Haven** is now chiefly literary or occurs in names of towns and cities where a natural harbor, such as a bay, an inlet, a river mouth, or the like, exists and where boats may go for safety during a storm; as, Milford *Haven* (in south Wales); "O young Mariner, Down to the *haven,* Call your companions, Launch your vessel" (*Tennyson*). More than the other words here considered, it connotes a refuge or place of quiet in the midst of storms; as, "My...only *haven*...is in the arms of death" (*Carlyle*). **Port,** even in its earliest sense of a place of security for ships, also denoted a place suitable for landing men or goods; as, "to set me safe ashore in the first *port* where we arrived" (*Swift*). Consequently, in literary and extended use, it suggests a destination or goal; as, "Me... Always from *port* withheld, always distressed" (*Cowper*). In modern commercial use, *port* applies to a place, sometimes a harbor, sometimes, especially in place names, a city or town and its harbor, but still more often in the case of the great ports of transatlantic and transpacific shipping, all the approaches, all the inlets, all the docks, wharves, offices, and the like, involved in the business of loading and unloading ships or of embarking and disembarking passengers; as, the *ports* of New York, Cherbourg, and Southampton.

harbor, *v.* **Harbor** (*or* **harbour**), **shelter, entertain, lodge, house, board** come into comparison when they mean, literally or figuratively, to provide a place (especially in one's home, one's quarters, one's confines) where one may be kept for a time. **Harbour,** in its literal sense, usually implies provision of a place of refuge, especially for a person (or sometimes an animal or insect) that is evil or hunted or noxious; as, to *harbor* thieves; cellars that *harbor* rats and cockroaches; "deportation...is simply a refusal by the Government to *harbor* persons whom it does not want" (*Justice Holmes*); "What good is he? Who else will *harbour* him At his age for the little he can do?" (*Frost*). In its extended sense, the term suggests the reception into one's mind of thoughts, wishes, designs, or the like, especially of those that are evil or harmful, and, usually, the dwelling on them. "Nothing is more astonishing to me than that people...should be capable of *harboring* such weak superstition" (*Pope*). "I did not wish him to know that I had suspected him of *harbouring* any sinister designs" (*Hudson*). **Shelter,** far more often than *harbor,* takes for its subject the place or the thing that affords (as distinguished from the person that supplies) protection or a place of retreat; it also distinctively suggests a threat to one's comfort or safety by the elements, by pursuers or attackers, by a bombardment, or the like; the term further suggests, as *harbor* does not, a covering or screening. "In such a season born, when scarce a shed Could be obtained to *shelter* him or me From the bleak air" (*Milton*). "In Craven's Wilds is many a den, To *shelter* persecuted men" (*Wordsworth*). **Entertain,** in its literal sense, implies the giving of hospitality to a person as a guest at one's table or in one's home. The term, in current use and in this sense, often suggests special efforts to provide for his pleasure and comfort which were not implied in earlier use. "Be not forgetful to *entertain* strangers: for thereby some have *entertained* angels unawares" (*Hebrews* xiii. 2). In its extended sense, *entertain,* like *harbor,* implies admission into the mind, and consequent consideration, of ideas, notions, fears, and the like, but unlike *harbor,* the term in itself apart from the context carries no connotations of their good or evil, benign or noxious, character, or of any prolonged dwelling upon them, or even of deep and serious consideration. "It had been Eudora's idea that jealousy had gone out. It wasn't *entertained* by smart people; it was bourgeois" (*M. Austin*). "No proposal having for its object the readmission of Master Byron to the academy could be *entertained*" (*Shaw*). "Her brothers and sister privately *entertained* a theory that their mother was rather a simpleton" (*V. Sackville-West*). **Lodge,** as here compared, implies the supplying or affording a habitation, often a temporary habitation, for a person or, by extension, for a thing; often it suggests provision merely of a place to sleep, and carries no implications of feeding or entertaining; as, Mrs. Brown will *lodge* three of the party for the week end; "Every house was proud to *lodge* a knight" (*Dryden*). In the now fairly rare figurative extension of this sense, *lodge* may imply reception as if of a guest or denizen, not only (like *harbor*) into the mind, but into anything thought of as a receptacle or as a place where a thing may be deposited or imbedded; as, "I well might *lodge* a fear To be again displaced" (*Shak.*); "So fair a form *lodged* not a mind so ill" (*Shak.*); "And that one talent which is death to hide *Lodged* with me useless" (*Milton*). **House** usually implies the shelter of a building with a roof and side walls that affords protection from the inclemencies of the weather; as, he could find no place in the village to *house* his family suitably; "the rich man has fed himself, and dressed himself, and *housed* himself as sumptuously as possible" (*Shaw*); to *house* gardening implements in a shed; to *house* an art collection in the new library building. *House* is somewhat rare in extended use, but it usually implies enclosing or confining in a particular place. "The universal does not attract us until *housed* in an individual" (*Emerson*). **Board** originally meant to provide a person with meals at one's table, or board (as, "We cannot *lodge* and *board* a dozen or fourteen gentlewomen"—*Shak.*). In current use, however, it is distinguished from *lodge* in implying provision of both room and meals for compensation; as, Mrs. Jones *boards* four teachers at her home (or, idiomatically, four teachers *board* at Mrs. Jones's home).

Ana. Foster, cherish, nurture, *nurse: *hide, conceal, secrete: protect, shield (see DEFEND).

Con. *Eject, expel, oust, evict: *banish, exile, deport: *exclude, eliminate, shut out.

hard. **1** Solid, *firm.

Ana. Compact, dense, *close: consolidated, compacted, concentrated (see COMPACT, *v.*): *hardened, indurated, callous.

Ant. Soft. — ***Con.*** Fluid, *liquid: flabby, flaccid, *limp: pliant, pliable, *plastic: flexible, *elastic, supple, resilient, springy.

2 *Alcoholic, spirituous, strong, ardent.

3 **Hard, difficult, arduous** come into comparison when they are applied to tasks for mind or body and mean demanding great toil or effort in reaching the appointed or the desired end. **Hard** is the simpler, blunter, and more general term; it implies the opposite of all that is implied by *easy,* but usually suggests nothing more specific; as, a *hard* lesson; a *hard* job; a *hard* book to understand; "Your easy reading, Sheridan said, is 'damned *hard* writing'" (*C. E. Montague*). **Difficult** commonly implies the presence of obstacles to be surmounted, or of complications to be removed; it therefore suggests the exercise of skill, ingenuity, sagacity, or courage. "[The tutor] Armed for a work too *difficult* for thee; Prepared by taste, by learning, and true worth, To form thy son, to strike his genius forth" (*Cowper*). "Men like fly-fishing, because it is *difficult;* they will not shoot a bird sitting, because it is easy" (*B. Russell*). *Difficult* is more widely applicable than *hard,* because it often means specifically hard to understand (because abstruse, intricate, abstract), or hard to deal with (because thorny, knotty, cumbersome, delicate, exacting), or the like; as, "he [Hegel] is a very *difficult* writer" (*Inge*); "the *difficult* beauty of many passages...of Winter's Tale or Coriolanus" (*S. Alexander*); "I do not propose...to enter upon the *difficult* question of Disestablishment" (*T. S. Eliot*); "it [the quilt pattern] was a *difficult* design and had to be executed exactly right" (*R. Bradford*). **Arduous** stresses the need of laborious effort, of perseverance, and persistent exertion; thus, one may find a task *difficult*, but not *arduous*, because one has no sense of being kept at it against one's inclination; an ascent of a mountain may be *arduous*, but not especially *difficult*.

Ana. *Onerous, burdensome, oppressive, exacting: intricate, knotty, complicated, involved, *complex: exhausting, fatiguing, wearying, tiring (see TIRE, *v.*).

Ant. Easy. — *Con.* Facile, light, simple, effortless (see EASY).

harden. **Harden, inure, season, acclimatize, acclimate** denote in common to make a person or thing proof against hardship, strain, exposure, or the like. All when referred to persons imply a becoming accustomed by time or experience. **Harden** implies habituation that toughens one and makes one insensible of one's own pain or discomfort, or callous and insensitive to others' misery; as, *hardened* to the rigors of arctic exploration. "I could...hear faint echoes of their grief. It was an experience to which I never became *hardened*" (*V. Heiser*). **Inure** usually implies unwilling submission; it suggests a lesser degree of toughening than *harden*, sometimes simply patient endurance; as, *inured* to insult (cf. *hardened* to insult). "The poor, *inured* to drudgery and distress" (*Cowper*). **Season** implies a gradual bringing into mature, sound, efficient condition; it does not, when referred to persons, necessarily imply that what is to be undergone is uncongenial; as, a *seasoned* marathon runner; a *seasoned* actor; *seasoned* lumber. "With much less compass of muscle than his foe, that which he had was more *seasoned*—iron and compact" (*Lytton*). **Acclimatize** and **acclimate** imply adaptation to a new and adverse climate or, by extension, to new and strange surroundings in general. Some writers have distinguished *acclimatize* from *acclimate* by restricting the first to adaptation by human agency, but this distinction is not commonly observed. "A race...well seated in a region, fixed to the soil by agriculture, *acclimatized* by natural selection" (*W. Z. Ripley*). "I have not been long enough at this table to get well *acclimated*" (*Holmes*).

Ana. *Habituate, accustom, familiarize: *adapt, adjust, accommodate.

Ant. Soften. — *Con.* Enervate, emasculate (see UNNERVE): *weaken, debilitate, enfeeble, sap, undermine.

hardened. **Hardened, indurated, callous** agree in meaning grown or become hard. All these terms are synonyms in both their literal and their figurative uses. **Hardened,** however, is, in its literal sense, the most inclusive of these terms because it is applicable to any substance, whether originally fluid or solid, or loose or firm in texture, or elastic or inelastic, that has become solider and firmer and increasingly resistant to efforts to cut, pierce, bend, or the like; as, *hardened* soap; *hardened* lava; *hardened* steel. Consequently, in figurative use, *hardened* usually implies a fixing or setting with loss of flexibility, elasticity, pliancy, susceptibility, impressionableness, or similar qualities; as, *hardened* beliefs; *hardened* distrust; a *hardened* criminal; a *hardened* heart. **Indurated,** which in its literal sense is chiefly in geological and in medical use, usually implies an increase of hardness (especially in something already firm or hard) or compactness, sometimes even suggesting abnormal hardness; as, *indurated* clay; *indurated* sandstone; an *indurated* abscess. In its figurative use, it usually implies excessive hardness or stoniness that repels all efforts to penetrate or to soften; as, "*Indurated* stoic as I am" (*John Adams*); "her husband's *indurated* conscience" (*H. James*). **Callous,** in its earliest and still common sense, implies a hardening and thickening of the skin by constant pressure or friction and a consequent loss of sensibility in the part affected; as, a *callous* spot on the sole of one's foot; a *callous* fingertip. In very precise figurative use, *callous* also implies a loss of sensibility or an insensitiveness that results from constant experience; as, he has grown *callous* to such appeals; he is now *callous* to criticism. "The tiresome and *callous* repetition of old motives which marked the decadence of the classic tradition" (*Binyon*). In current use, *callous* often means unfeeling and carries little implication of the process of hardening; as, a *callous* answer.

Ana. Tempered, annealed (see TEMPER, *v.*): consolidated, compacted, concentrated (see COMPACT, *v.*).

Ant. Softened. — *Con.* Liquefied, melted, thawed, fused (see LIQUEFY): weakened, enfeebled, debilitated (see WEAKEN).

hardihood. *Temerity, audacity, effrontery, nerve, cheek, gall.

Ana. Boldness, intrepidity (see corresponding adjectives at BRAVE): brazenness, impudence, brashness (see corresponding adjectives at SHAMELESS): guts, sand, grit, pluck, *fortitude.

hardly, *adv.* **Hardly, scarcely, barely** are often interchangeable when they mean "just that and no more." In precise use, however, **hardly** suggests difficulty; **scarcely,** scantiness of margin; **barely** (the strongest term) implies that there is nothing to spare; as, he could *hardly* speak; he had *scarcely* gained shelter; he arrived *barely* in time. *Hardly* is the preferred term when the word modified implies ability, capacity, or the like; as, he is *hardly* able to lift this weight. *Scarcely* and *barely,* but not *hardly,* in discriminating use, modify adjectives such as *enough* and *sufficient;* as, there is *scarcely* enough food in the house for one meal; *barely* enough food for dinner.

hardship. Rigor, vicissitude, *difficulty.

Ana. Adversity, *misfortune, mischance: peril, *danger, jeopardy, hazard: *trial, tribulation, affliction: toil, travail, drudgery (see WORK).

Con. Ease, comfort (see REST).

hark. Hearken, *hear, listen, list, attend.

harlequin. *Fool, jester, clown, antic, buffoon, pantaloon, comedian, comic, zany, merry-andrew, stooge.

harm, *n.* Damage, *injury, hurt, mischief.

Ana. Detrimentalness *or* detriment, deleteriousness, perniciousness, noxiousness (see corresponding adjectives at PERNICIOUS): *misfortune, mischance: impairing *or* impairment, marring (see corresponding verbs at INJURE).

Ant. Benefit.

harm, *v.* *Injure, impair, hurt, damage, mar, spoil.

Ana. *Abuse, maltreat, mistreat, misuse: *ruin, dilapidate, wrack: discommode, incommode, molest (see INCONVENIENCE): sap, undermine (see WEAKEN).

Ant. Benefit. — *Con.* *Improve, better, ameliorate: profit, avail, boot, bestead (see BENEFIT): *help, aid, assist.

harmonize. 1 Accord, comport, *agree, correspond, square, conform, tally, jibe.

Ana. Reconcile, adjust, *adapt, accommodate: *match, equal, approach, touch, rival.

Ant. Clash: conflict.

2 Harmonize, tune, attune agree in meaning to bring things which clash or are discordant into accord with each other. **Harmonize** stresses as its end the combination of two or more things so that they go together without loss of individual identities yet constitute a frictionless or pleasing whole; as, to *harmonize* the conflicting colors in a room by an emphasis on blue; "their religion is a mixture of Greek, Latin, and Hebrew elements which refuse to be *harmonised*" (*Inge*). **Tune** implies the adjustment of one thing to another or of several things to each other so that they will conform to each other or work in harmony with each other; thus, to *tune* a piano is to adjust its strings so that the tones produced will conform to a standard pitch or to a predetermined temperament; to *tune* up the instruments of an orchestra is to adjust the instruments so that they will produce harmonious tones; to *tune* up an engine of an automobile is to make all the finer adjustments of its parts necessary to smooth operation. In literary use, *tune* still implies adjustment, as of expression to a mood, or of mood to a situation or need. "For now to sorrow must I *tune* my song" (*Milton*); "a mind well strung and *tuned* To contemplation" (*Cowper*). **Attune** stresses the attainment of aesthetic harmony more than *harmonize* does, and it seldom suggests the idea of mechanical operation or effect often so strong in *tune*. "Riding, walking, gardening, driving about the level Essex lands, she, *attuned* to the soil on which she lived, was happy and serene" (*R. Macaulay*). "How by mastering rhythm, our Prose ...*attuned* itself to rival its twin instrument, Verse" (*Quiller-Couch*).

Ana. Adjust, reconcile (see ADAPT).

harmony. 1 Harmony, consonance, accord, concord all designate the result attained or the effect produced when different things come together without clashing or disagreement. **Harmony,** in its strict etymological sense, denotes the unity, order, and absence of friction produced by the perfect articulation and interrelation of distinct parts in a complex whole. "To heavenliest *harmony* Reduce the seeming chaos" (*Southey*). "The scientific view of the world...seeks to find law, *harmony*, uniformity in nature" (*Inge*). *Harmony*, largely because of its associations with music, often but not necessarily suggests beauty of effect, whether that is achieved by order in a whole or by agreeable blending or arrangement, as of tones, colors, or the like. "A *harmony* of life, a fine balance of all the forces of the human spirit" (*Binyon*). "Like hues and *harmonies* of evening" (*Shelley*). **Consonance,** rather than *harmony*, originally denoted and still often denotes the blending of two or more simultaneous sounds so as to produce an agreeable effect: it is then opposed to *dissonance*. As a rule, it names the fact or the means whereas *harmony* names the result. "Notes in *consonance* constitute *harmony*, as notes in succession constitute melody" (*E. Chambers*). In careful extended application, *consonance* retains these implications of coincidence and concurrence. Sometimes the pleasurable effect is still suggested. "In good poetry there always is this *consonance* of thought and song" (*S. Alexander*). Very often there is no hint of a pleasurable effect but a strong implication of consistency or congruity. "This was an unprecedented act, but it was in *consonance* with Roman tradition" (*Buchan*). **Accord** is often interchangeable with *consonance* without loss; as, it was in *accord* with Roman tradition. However, it can imply, as *consonance* cannot, personal agreement or good will, or, often, absence of ill will or friction. "But here we're a' [all] in ae [one] *accord*" (*Burns*). "For your father's remembrance, be at *accord*" (*Shak.*). Hence, the phrase "with one *accord*" suggests unanimity; as, with one *accord*, they gave a cheer. **Concord,** like *accord*, often stresses agreement between persons, but it is far more positive in its implications, for it suggests peace with amity rather than absence or suppression of ill will. "How comes this gentle *concord* in the world?" (*Shak.*). "Till heart with heart in *concord* beats" (*Wordsworth*). *Concord* also, when applied to sounds, comes close to *harmony* in its implications. However, it seldom (except in a technical sense in music) connotes consonance of tones, but usually the pleasant succession of tones that is the quality of melody. "The man that hath no music in himself, Nor is not moved with *concord* of sweet sounds" (*Shak.*).

Ana. Integration, articulation, concatenation (see corresponding verbs at INTEGRATE): congruousness *or* congruity, consonance, compatibility (see corresponding adjectives at CONSONANT): concurrence, agreement (see corresponding verbs at AGREE).

Ant. Conflict. — ***Con.*** *Discord, strife, contention, variance, dissension: dissonance, discordance (see corresponding adjectives at DISSONANT).

2 *Symmetry, proportion, balance.

Ana. Grace, *elegance, dignity: *unity, integrity.

harry. Harass, *worry, annoy, plague, pester, tease, tantalize.

Ana. Torment, torture, rack, grill, *afflict, try: *trouble, distress: *bait, badger, hound, ride, hector: fret, gall, chafe (see ABRADE).

Con. *Comfort, solace, console: *relieve, assuage, alleviate, allay.

harsh. *Rough, rugged, scabrous, uneven.

Ana. Repellent, *repugnant, distasteful, abhorrent, obnoxious: *coarse, gross: strident, *vociferous, blatant: rigorous, strict, stringent, *rigid.

Ant. Pleasant: mild. — ***Con.*** Pleasing, agreeable, grateful, gratifying (see PLEASANT): *soft, gentle, bland, lenient, balmy.

haste, *n.* **Haste, hurry, speed, expedition, dispatch** (*or* **despatch**) come into comparison as meaning quickness or swiftness in movement or in action. **Haste** in precise use implies quickness or swiftness in persons rather than in machines, vehicles, methods of transportation, or the like; thus, a business that requires *haste* demands that the persons concerned move or act swiftly. "She came in straightway with *haste* unto the king" (*Mark* vi. 25). But *haste* may imply other goads than urgency or pressure for time; it may imply intense eagerness (as, "His tongue, all impatient to speak... Did stumble with *haste*"—*Shak.*), or lack of due reflection and precipitancy in decision (as, "Marry in *haste* and repent at leisure"—*Old Proverb*), or the impulsion of anger (as, "I said in my *haste*, All men are liars"—*Psalms* cxvi. 11). **Hurry,** though often used colloquially in place of *haste* as the simpler term, in precise use carries a stronger implication of confusion, agitation, bustle, or the like (as, "Whoever is in a *hurry*, shows that the thing he is about is too big for him. *Haste* and *hurry* are very different things"—*Chesterfield;* "the incessant *hurry*...of daily life"—*C. W. Eliot*) and more frequently refers to the things which are operated or the actions which are performed with haste than to the persons concerned (thus, *haste* in preparation, but the *hurry* of preparations). Also, *hurry* may imply the state of mind or the need of one who demands haste as well as of the one who makes haste; as, I am in a great *hurry* (not *haste*) for the articles ordered; you need not be in a *hurry* to fill (or make *haste* in filling) my order. **Speed,** as here compared (see also SPEED, *n.*, 2), usually implies mere swiftness or rapidity, primarily in motion or movement, but secondarily in action, performance, or accomplishment. Unlike *haste* and *hurry*, the term, which may be used with propriety in reference to things as well as to persons, carries no connotations of precipitancy, urgency, agitation, or the like, although it may from its original sense carry a suggestion of success; as, "the more *haste* the less [or in some versions, the worse] speed" (*Old Proverb*); "A performance [by flying albatrosses] which had the beauty of *speed* uncontaminated by *haste*" (*Harper's Mag.*); "Many an adult reader with trained habits of attention and concentration will absorb the contents of a book with a *speed*...no child can approach" (*C. W. Eliot*). **Expedition** and **dispatch** imply both speed and efficiency, especially in business or affairs, but *dispatch* carries a stronger suggestion of promptness in bringing matters to a conclusion, and *expedition* more often carries a hint of ease; as, they made their plans with *expedition;* "Sophia put her things on with remarkable *expedition*" (*Bennett*); "Serious business, craving quick *dispatch*" (*Shak.*); "There is nothing more requisite in business than *despatch*" (*Addison*); "To do everything when it ought to be done is the soul of *expedition*" (*Scott*); "The soul of *dispatch* is decision" (*Hazlitt*).

Ana. *Celerity, alacrity, legerity: rapidity, swiftness, quickness, expeditiousness (see corresponding adjectives at FAST): readiness, promptness (see corresponding adjectives at QUICK): agility, briskness (see corresponding adjectives at AGILE).

Ant. Deliberation. — ***Con.*** Slowness, leisureliness, deliberateness, dilatoriness (see corresponding adjectives at SLOW): procrastination, delaying *or* delay, dawdling (see corresponding verbs at DELAY).

hasten. *Speed, accelerate, quicken, hurry, precipitate.

Ant. Delay. — ***Con.*** Retard, slow, slacken, detain (see DELAY): lag, procrastinate, dally, dawdle (see DELAY).

hasty. 1 Speedy, quick, expeditious, rapid, *fast, swift, fleet.

Ana. *Agile, brisk, nimble: hurried, quickened (see SPEED, *v.*).

Con. *Slow, deliberate, dilatory, leisurely, laggard.

2 *Precipitate, headlong, abrupt, impetuous, sudden.

Con. Considered, advised, *deliberate, premeditated, designed, studied.

hate, *v.* **Hate, detest, abhor, abominate, loathe. Hate,** the general term, implies extreme aversion, esp. as coupled with enmity or malice. "She did not *hate* him; she rather despised him, and just suffered him" (*Thackeray*). "Whom we fear more than love, we are not far from *hating*" (*Richardson*). **Detest** connotes violent or intense antipathy or dislike. "The mob is a monster I never could abide....I *detest* the whole of it, as a mass of ignorance, presumption, malice, and brutality" (*Smollett*). "I mortally *detest* cards" (*Fielding*). **Abhor** suggests profound (as it were, shuddering) repugnance. "A woman...waxing too womanly, and swelling from tears and supplications to a scene, [was] of all things *abhorred* by him the most" (*Meredith*). **Abominate** suggests strong detestation, as of something ill-omened or shameful. "The Egyptians...lived only on the fruits of the earth, and *abominated* flesh-eaters" (*Newton*). **Loathe** implies utter disgust or intolerance. "Except when I am listening to their music I *loathe* the whole race; great stupid, brutal, immoral, sentimental savages" (*R. Macaulay*). The same distinctions in implications and connotations are evident in the derivative nouns **hate, hatred** (for a distinction between these terms see HATE, *n.*, 2), **detestation, abhorrence, abomination, loathing,** when they name the feeling of one who hates, detests, etc.

Ana. *Despise, contemn, scorn, disdain: *disapprove, deprecate.

Ant. Love. — ***Con.*** *Like, enjoy, relish, fancy, dote on *or* upon: respect, esteem, admire (see under REGARD, *n.*).

hate, *n.* **1** Hatred, abhorrence, detestation, abomination, loathing. See under HATE, *v.*

Ana. *Antipathy, aversion: animosity, rancor, hostility, *enmity: despite, contempt, scorn, disdain (see under DESPISE).

Ant. Love. — ***Con.*** Affection, *attachment: admiration, respect, esteem, *regard: reverence, veneration (see under REVERE).

2 Hate, hatred are not always interchangeable although they agree in denoting intense, settled dislike for a person or thing that causes one either to avoid him (or it) scrupulously or to be his (or its) bitter enemy. **Hate** is always the preferable term when the emotion is thought of in the abstract as the diametrical opposite of *love*, or when the term is used without reference to particular individuals. "Love you cannot help, and *hate* you cannot help; but contempt is—for you—the sovereign idiocy...!" (*Galsworthy*). "It [the emotion of some satires] is...not really *hate* at all, but spite; and it takes a very remarkable poet, like Pope...to elevate malice into *hate*" (*Day Lewis*). In concrete use, *hate* is seldom found outside of poetry except when contrasted with *love*, also in concrete use; it then always denotes the object of one's hate; as, "the scum of men, the *hate* and scourge of God" (*Marlowe*). "My only love [Juliet] sprung from my only *hate* [the Capulets]!" (*Shak.*). **Hatred** is the preferable term when the emotion referred to is actually experienced and is therefore personal and individual in character; *hate* is definable because men are in agreement concerning its distinguishing marks, but *hatred* escapes exact definition because its implications, other than that of intense dislike, can be gathered only from the context or with reference to its object. Usually it implies in addition one or more emotions such as antipathy, aversion, rancor, vindictiveness, resentment, or fear; as, he had a deep-seated *hatred* of aristocrats; a violent *hatred* of restrictions on his freedom; "a healthy *hatred* of scoundrels" (*Carlyle*). "It was apparent that his [Galsworthy's] special type of satire had its roots not in *hatred* but in sympathy. His wrath was an inverted love" (*Bliss Perry*). "'*Hatred* is the coward's revenge for being intimidated'" (*Shaw*). *Hatred* also is often used in reference to its effect on the one who is hated; in such cases, the nature of the emotion is not stressed, but its power to harm. "He sowed doubtful speeches, and reaped plain, unequivocal *hatred*" (*Lamb*); "Battered by *hatred*, seared by ridicule" (*J. E. Flecker*). In concrete use, *hatred* usually denotes a particular instance, as of obsession by the emotion of hatred or of suffering as a result of another's hatred; as, given to violent *hatreds;* the victim of human *hatreds;* "a family famous for its *hatreds*" (*Disraeli*).

hateful. Hateful, odious, abhorrent, detestable, abominable are sometimes used with little distinction. But **hateful** more frequently applies to that which excites actual hatred; **odious,** to that which is excessively disagreeable, or which awakens offense or repugnance. "Why shouldn't we hate what is *hateful* in people, and scorn what is mean?" (*Thackeray*). "Between these two natures, so antipathetic, so *hateful* to each other, there was depending an unpardonable affront" (*Stevenson*). "Our blind poet, who in his later day stood almost single, uttering *odious* truth" (*Wordsworth*). "There was something more *odious* to him in her friendship than her hatred" (*Thackeray*). That is **abhorrent** which outrages one's sense of what is just, right, honorable, or decent. "She [his wife] was his property....To me it is a view that has always been *abhorrent*" (*Galsworthy*). That is

detestable which deserves scorn or contempt; as, hypocrisy is more *detestable* than shamelessness. "Dancing is nowhere the passion that it is with us; if it were, the French, who dance *detestably*, would perhaps dance better" (*Brownell*). That is **abominable** which is so abhorrent as to deserve execration. "On board ship ready to sail away from this *abominable* world of treacheries, and scorns and envies and lies" (*Conrad*). "All the living conditions were *abominable*" (*Cather*).

Ana. *Antipathetic, unsympathetic, averse: repellent, *repugnant, obnoxious, distasteful.

Ant. Lovable: sympathetic. — *Con.* Congenial, compatible, *consonant: *amiable (sense 1): attractive, alluring, taking, charming (see under ATTRACT).

hatred. 1 *Hate.

Ana. Animosity, *enmity, hostility, rancor: aversion, *antipathy: malevolence, malignity, ill will, despite, *malice: envy, jealousy (see corresponding adjectives at ENVIOUS).

Con. Love, affection, *attachment: sympathy, affinity, *attraction: charity, *mercy, lenity.

2 Hate, abhorrence, detestation, abomination, loathing. See under HATE, *v.*

haughty. *Proud, arrogant, insolent, lordly, overbearing, supercilious, disdainful.

Ana. Aloof, detached, *indifferent: vain, vainglorious, proud (see under PRIDE, *n.*): contemptuous, scornful (see corresponding nouns at DESPISE).

Ant. Lowly. — *Con.* *Humble, modest, meek: obsequious, servile, *subservient.

haul, *v.* Hale, *pull, draw, drag, tug, tow.

Ana. *Move, remove, shift: *lift, raise, hoist, heave, boost, elevate: convey, transport, *carry.

haunt, *v.* *Frequent, habituate.

Ana. *Resort (to), turn (to), go (to): *infest, overrun, beset.

haunt *or* **hant,** *n.* Ghost, spirit, specter, shade, revenant, spook, *apparition, phantasm, phantom, wraith, fetch.

have. 1 **Have, hold, own, possess, enjoy** are here compared as verbs which mean to produce, control, retain, or the like, as one's own. **Have** is the most general term, implying any of a multitude of reasons for regarding the thing had as one's own; as, he *has* considerable property; they *have* five children; we *have* no cow at present; to *have* opinions on a subject; she *has* many friends; they are going to *have* a baby; he *has* no French; we shall *have* some trouble with it. **Hold** implies stronger control over than *have* and usually suggests a grasp upon, an occupancy of, a bond between, or the like; thus, "to *have* friends" implies a mere amicable relationship but "to *hold* one's friends" implies either the reducing of them to subjection or the retaining of their affection; "to *have* an opinion" implies merely the existence of that opinion, whereas "to *hold* an opinion" usually suggests its assertion; so, to *hold* certain securities; to *hold* extensive properties in New York State. "Once did she *hold* the gorgeous East in fee" (*Wordsworth*); "The Breton seized more than he could *hold;* the Norman took less than he would have liked" (*H. Adams*); "the receptive imagination...*holds* fast the visions genius creates" (*C. W. Eliot*). **Own** implies a natural or legal right to hold as one's property and as under one's full control; as, to *own* a house; to *own* some good securities; to *own* several horses. "When a child is old enough, he should...be allowed to *own* books" (*B. Russell*); some parents treat their children as if they *owned* them. **Possess** is preferred in law to *own* as implying one's having full title and right to a particular property, to the exclusion of everyone else; thus, a husband and wife might say that they *own* a piece of land when legally only the husband *possesses* (or has *possession* of) it. In general use, *possess* differs from *own* in being referable to other things than property, such as a characteristic, a quality, a power, a faculty; as, to *possess* contentment; "the States *possessed* the power to exclude or admit them [slaves]" (*Ch. Just. Marshall*); "that astonishingly retentive memory which we *possessed* as little boys" (*Inge*); "the great medicinal value *possessed* by this water" (*V. Heiser*). **Enjoy,** as here compared (see also LIKE), implies the having of something as one's own or for one's use with all its benefits and advantages; in this sense, there is no necessary connotation of pleasure or delight in having or using, but as a matter of fact the word, except in law, often carries a hint if not a definite suggestion of it; as, "During his lifetime he *enjoyed* a distinguished reputation for the excellence of his sermons" (*T. S. Eliot*); "While man *enjoyed*...an unlimited freedom to be wicked" (*H. Adams*); classes that *enjoy* certain rights and privileges. "*Possession*...Act, fact, or condition of a person's having such control of property that he may legally *enjoy* it to the exclusion of all others having no better right than himself" (*Webster's New Int. Dict., 2d Ed.*).

Con. Want, *lack, need.

2 Also **have got.** Must, *ought, should.

haven. *Harbor, port.

Ana. Asylum, refuge, retreat, *shelter, cover.

hazard, *n.* 1 Accident, *chance, fortune, luck, hap.

2 Jeopardy, peril, *danger, risk.

Ana. Possibility, probability, likelihood (see corresponding adjectives at PROBABLE): contingency, exigency, emergency (see JUNCTURE).

hazardous. Precarious, jeopardous, risky, *dangerous, perilous.

Ana. Venturous, venturesome, *adventurous: chancy, chance, haphazard, happy-go-lucky, *random.

Con. Secure, *safe.

haze, *n.* **Haze, mist, fog, smog, brume** agree in denoting an atmospheric condition which deprives the air near the earth of its transparency. **Haze** applies to such a condition as is caused by the diffusion of smoke, dust, or any light vapor through the air in such a way as to impede but not obstruct the vision and to convey no (or practically no) impression of dampness; as, the early morning *haze* on a warm day in autumn; there is *haze* today because the wind carries the smoke from the railroad yards. **Mist** applies to a condition where water is held in suspension in fine particles in the air, floating or slowly falling in minute drops. A **fog** differs from a mist only in its greater density and in its power to cut off the vision. A fog differs from a cloud in being near to the ground. "Not the thin glassy *mist* of twenty minutes ago, but a thick, dense, blinding *fog* that hemmed in like walls of wadding on every side" (*Hugh Walpole*). **Smog** [a blend of *smoke* and *fog*] is a recent American coinage for a fog made heavier and darker by the smoke of an industrial city; as, a Pittsburgh *smog*. **Brume,** a rare poetic term, applies to a fog or heavy mist, especially one that occurs in winter or in the very early spring; as, "The drifting *brume*" (*Longfellow*); "It was an orchard with blossoming trees—that much I could see through the *brume*" (*Buchan*).

In their figurative use, **haze** suggests vagueness or lack of clear definition of thought or feeling (as, "That he [Gilbert Murray as translator] should. blur the Greek lyric to the fluid *haze* of Swinburne"—*T. S. Eliot*); **mist** applies to that which can be only dimly apprehended because of its remoteness (as, "The origin of detergents is...lost in the *mists* of antiquity"—*A. C. Morrison*) or to that which prevents exact knowledge or clear understanding (as, "Times...half shrouded in the *mist* of legend"—*Freeman*); **fog** implies an obscuring of the mental or spiritual vision or of that which can be detected only by such vision (as, the *fog* of ignorance in which so many live; "Life and its few years— A wisp of *fog* betwixt us and the sun"—*L. W. Reese*).

head *or* **headman.** *Chief, leader, chieftain, commander, captain, master.

headlong. *Precipitate, impetuous, abrupt, hasty, sudden.
Ana. Rash, reckless, daring, temerarious, daredevil, foolhardy (see ADVENTUROUS).

headstrong. Ungovernable, *unruly, intractable, refractory, recalcitrant, willful.
Ana. Perverse, *contrary, froward, wayward: stubborn, *obstinate, pigheaded, stiffnecked.
Con. Submissive, *tame, subdued: docile, tractable, amenable, biddable, *obedient.

headway. Pace, *speed, velocity, momentum, impetus.
Ana. Advance, progress (see under ADVANCE, *v.*): *motion, movement.

heal. *Cure, remedy.

healthful. Healthful, healthy, wholesome, salubrious, salutary, hygienic, sanitary come into comparison when they mean conducive or beneficial to the health or soundness of body or mind. **Healthful** is now preferred to **healthy** as the term carrying this sense, but often in the past and to some extent still, the latter word has taken the place of the former even among informed writers and speakers; as, a *healthful* climate (cf. "one of the *healthiest* climates in England"—*Bennett*); *healthful* recreation (cf. "The French boy gets *healthy* recreation" —*Grandgent*); sound sleep is *healthful* (cf. "All mothers wish their children to sleep, because it is...*healthy*"—*B. Russell*). "The second fruit of friendship is *healthful* and sovereign for the understanding" (*Bacon*). Nevertheless, *healthy* is being displaced by *healthful* in this sense (for chief current sense of the former word see HEALTHY, 2). **Wholesome** (see also HEALTHY, 2), as here compared, is not only a more homely word than *healthful* but it carries an even stronger suggestion of a capacity for producing, or of the actual production of, a good effect physically, morally, intellectually, or the like; as, *wholesome* food; to provide *wholesome*, well-balanced meals; books that are *wholesome* reading; the influence of such companions is not *wholesome*. "Mathematics...is a *wholesome* discipline because it requires a high degree of concentration and because it shows so inexorably the difference between right and wrong" (*Grandgent*). **Salubrious** now applies chiefly to climate, air, or the like, that is pleasantly invigorating yet devoid of harshness or extremes. Because the term is now so often used in the advertising of summer and winter resorts, it is falling into disuse among fastidious writers and speakers. "Hail, calm acclivity, *salubrious* spot!" (*Browning*). **Salutary** implies a tonic, corrective, or similarly beneficial effectiveness; often it is applied to that which is in itself unpleasant; as, *salutary* advice; "Idle ladies and gentlemen are treated with *salutary* contempt" (*Shaw*). "The use of force in education should be very rare. But for the conquest of fear it is, I think, sometimes *salutary*" (*B. Russell*). **Hygienic** suggests reference to hygiene, or the science which deals with the means and the rules of promoting physical or mental health, especially of the public. The term therefore commonly implies use of the approved means or obedience to the approved rules because they are conducive to health; as, to instruct children in the *hygienic* care of mouth and teeth; stuffy schoolrooms are not *hygienic*. **Sanitary** implies reference to any or all measures taken or that can be taken to guard against infections or other conditions that promote disease. The term therefore usually implies the promotion of health, especially public health, through interference with causes that bring about disease, epidemics, and the like; as, *sanitary* plumbing; *sanitary* regulations; the *sanitary* care of foods; drainage of swamps and similar *sanitary* measures. In the United States, *sanitary* is sometimes used in place of *healthful* but with a stronger emphasis upon effectiveness. "Solitary communion with Nature does not seem to have been *sanitary* or sweetening in its influence on Thoreau's character" (*J. R. Lowell*).
Ana. *Beneficial, advantageous, profitable: remedying *or* remedial, correcting *or* corrective (see corresponding verbs at CORRECT): helping *or* helpful, aiding (see corresponding verbs at HELP).
Con. Deleterious, detrimental, noxious, *pernicious.

healthy. 1 *Healthful, wholesome, salubrious, salutary, hygienic, sanitary.
Ana. & *Con.* See those at HEALTHFUL.
2 Healthy, sound, wholesome, robust, hale, well agree in meaning having or manifesting health of mind or body or indicative of such health. **Healthy** may imply the possession of full vigor and strength of body or mind or it may merely imply freedom from any signs of disease or other morbid condition; as, a *healthy* body; a *healthy* boy; "during a *healthy* and active life" (*C. W. Eliot*); "I [the physician] went along to keep everybody *healthy*" (*V. Heiser*). Often the term applies not to that which has health but to that which manifests one's health or vigor or serves as a sign of it; as, "he had a *healthy* color in his cheeks" (*Dickens*); she has a *healthy* appetite; "a *healthy* craving for the sap and savour of a more personal, national art" (*Binyon*). **Sound** even more strongly implies the possession of perfect health or the absence of all defects, and therefore suggests not even the slightest sign of disease, morbidity, or the like; as, a *sound* mind in a *sound* body; "The other [man] compact, broad and sturdy of limb...full of *sound* organs functioning vigorously all the time" (*Conrad*); "That child is...much too emotional to be ever really *sound*" (*Conrad*); "His tastes were *healthy*, his wits *sound*" (*R. Macaulay*). **Wholesome** (see also HEALTHFUL) implies a healthiness that impresses others favorably, especially as indicative of a person's physical, mental, and moral soundness, or often more specifically of a person's balance or equilibrium; as, "thankful [for]...his mother, so sane and *wholesome*" (*D. H. Lawrence*); "They [scientific studies] promote... a *wholesome* dislike of sophistry and rhetoric" (*Inge*). **Robust** implies the antithesis of all that is delicate; it usually connotes manifest vigor of health as shown in muscularity, fresh color, a strong voice, an ability to work long and hard, and the like; as, exercise tends to develop *robust* boys and girls; a man of *robust* constitution; he is in *robust* health; to speak in a *robust* voice. **Hale,** which is a close synonym of *sound*, is in current use applied chiefly to elderly or aged persons who not only show no signs of infirmity or senility but manifest qualities of men in their prime; as, he is *hale* and hearty at 85; "Pete Gurney was a lusty cock Turned sixty-three, but bright and *hale*" (*Masefield*). **Well,** which is commoner as a predicative than as an attributive adjective, is more or less a noncommittal term; it merely implies freedom from disease or illness of any sort and so does not necessarily suggest soundness or robustness; as, is your father *well?*; he is always *well;* she has never been a *well* person.
Ana. *Vigorous, lusty, energetic: *strong, sturdy, stalwart, tough, tenacious.

Ant. Unhealthy. — *Con.* *Sick, ill: infirm, frail, feeble, *weak.

heap, *v.* **Heap, pile, stack, shock, cock, mass, bank** come into comparison as verbs when they mean to bring together into a more or less compact group or collection a number of things, and as nouns when they denote the group or collection so assembled. **Heap** is the least definite in its implications; it usually, however, implies a moundlike shape and more or less careless or fortuitous arrangement; it may or may not imply a personal agent, an assemblage of like things, close packing, or a large quantity; as, throw all the discarded clothes into a *heap; heap* the sand in this corner of the lot; the miser gloated over his *heaps* of coins; the wind *heaps* the leaves under the garden wall. **Pile,** in discriminating use, implies the laying of one thing or one layer on top of another in orderly formation; it usually, but not invariably, implies a personal agent, and an assembling of like things or things of approximately the same size or shape; as, to *pile* sheets according to their sizes; a *pile* of silver dollars; to *pile* logs; a *pile* of bricks. **Stack,** like *pile,* implies orderly and compact arrangement and the assembling of like things; it differs from it in almost invariably suggesting personal agency and a particular shape or form and in having a more restricted range of reference. One *stacks* hay, straw, grain in the sheaf, and the like, into a conical or a four-sided, round-cornered formation, the latter usually with a sloping top; one *stacks* firewood when one arranges the pieces neatly into a rectangular pile; one *stacks* arms, when one sets up rifles (now often three), so that they form a pyramid; so, hay*stack* or hay in the *stack;* a *stack* of fagots or lumber. So strongly does *stack* suggest care in arrangement that it carries specific connotations in some of its applications; thus, to *stack* cards is to arrange them secretly for cheating; a *stack* is in Great Britain a measure of stacked coal or firewood equal to four cubic yards. **Shock** and **cock** are the narrowest of these terms. *Shock* is used only of sheaves of grain, as of wheat, rye, or oats, or in the United States stalks of maize, or Indian corn, which are stacked upright with butt ends resting on the ground. "When the frost is on the punkin and the fodder's in the *shock*" (*J. W. Riley*). *Cock* is used with reference to hay, turf, dung, and the like, stacked in a conical pile; as, a *cock* of hay; to *cock* the manure. **Mass** (as here compared: see *mass, n.* under BULK) usually suggests amorphousness; it also implies either a capacity in the things which are brought together for cohering with or adhering to each other so as to form a blended or fused whole or a highly compact or dense agglomerate, or an external process which forces them to cohere or adhere; thus, a pasty substance which is a mixture of various ingredients and is used in making pills, troches, and the like, is called a *mass* by pharmacists; some flowers, like violets, tend to grow in *masses* or to *mass* themselves in growing; to *mass* colors in a painting or in stained-glass windows is to combine the various colors used in any one significant portion of the whole so that though they remain distinct in study of detail they seem to flow into each other and give a unitary effect (often contrasting with that of the other portions) when the painting or window is viewed in perspective. *Mass,* therefore, usually implies integration but it may be a physical, a spiritual, an emotional, an intellectual, or a purely aesthetic integration; as, to *mass* one's arguments; "compounding the American people into one common *mass*" (*Ch. Just. Marshall*). "Dense *masses* of smoke hung amid the darting snakes of fire" (*Meredith*). "A vine, remarkable for its tendency, not to spread and ramble, but to *mass* and mount" (*Cather*). **Bank** (the verb is often followed by *up*) is used chiefly, but not exclusively, in reference to substances which when affected by moisture, freezing, or the like, form or, in extended use, seem to form, into compact masses or which can be massed and shaped; as, to *bank* up the snow on each side of the path; to *bank* up a sand pile; to build a snow *bank;* cloud *banks.* "The wiser heads in Rome, seeing the clouds *banking* in the North, had clamoured for the employment of the ablest of Roman commanders" (*Buchan*).

Ana. *Accumulate, amass, hoard: collect, assemble, *gather.

Con. *Scatter, disperse, dissipate, dispel.

heap, *n.* Pile, stack, shock, cock, mass, bank. See under HEAP, *v.*

Ana. *Aggregate, aggregation, conglomerate, conglomeration: collection, assemblage (see under GATHER).

hear. Hear, hearken, hark, listen, list, attend are here compared as meaning to perceive or apprehend through the ears. *Hear* is both an intransitive and a transitive verb; the others, except in some archaic use, require the addition of *to* (or *unto*) when they take an object. **Hear,** except in extended use, always implies the actual sensation and the response of the auditory nerves to a stimulus; as, he no longer *hears* well; did you *hear* that sound? "Eye hath not seen, nor ear *heard*...the things which God hath prepared for them that love him" (*1 Corinthians* ii. 9). *Hear* may also imply a giving one's ear to something, so that one may be informed, may learn, may judge, may answer fittingly, or the like; in this use, the implication of perception through the auditory sense is often obscured and sometimes lost; as, Judge Blank *heard* the case of Brown vs. Jones; he has not *heard* how his son is getting along; I *hear* that you are going abroad; the Lord *heard* his prayer. **Hearken** and **hark** (usually *hearken to* or *hark to,* except in imperatives), now chiefly literary or poetic terms, imply a voluntary exercise of one's auditory sense. *Hearken* usually also implies compliance or obedience as the end of this act; *hark,* the appreciative or understanding hearing of that to which one gives ear. "*Hearken,* O Israel, unto the statutes" (*Deuteronomy* iv. 1). "Those who possess this inner voice are ready enough to *hearken* to it, and will *hear* no other" (*T. S. Eliot*). "*Hark, hark!* the lark at heaven's gate sings" (*Shak.*). **Listen** is now the common term for the conscious or voluntary effort to hear, especially to hear what is being said; **list** is its archaic form, still frequently found in poetry; as, the recital of his experiences bored her, but she *listened* patiently until the end; "the disease of not *listening,* the malady of not marking" (*Shak.*). "Great Napoleon Stops his horse, and *lists* with delight" (*Emerson*). *Listen,* like *hear* in extended use, does not always imply actual hearing or audition; in such cases it usually connotes either thoughtful consideration or a yielding to an argument, a proposal, an appeal, or the like, whether it has been advanced orally or in writing; as, children should *listen* to their parents' advice; "supposing that the Greeks had *listened* to... proposals...to abolish nude statues" (*H. Ellis*). **Attend** stresses a concentration of the mind in listening; it implies a following with the intelligence as well as with the ears. "My son, *attend* to my words; incline thine ear" (*Proverbs* iv. 20). "We hunted for the lost pistol among the bushes, I with little hope of finding it, while he *attended* to the bird voices, and frequently asked me to stand or lie still" (*Hudson*). Though listening was the original and is still a frequent implication in this sense of *attend,* it has come to be subordinated to the implication of concentration; hence, *attend* may imply close application to any task requiring mental concentration; as, he was not a good bridge player, for he found it hard to *attend* to the game; it is impossible, he says, to *attend* at the same time to driving a car and to a conversation.

hearing. Hearing, audience, audition, although they also agree in meaning the act of listening especially with attention, are here compared only in the sense of a formal opportunity to be heard by a person or persons having authority to question or the power of decision. **Hearing** is not only the general word, but also a technical term. In legal use, it designates a formal listening by a judge or tribunal to the arguments and proofs offered either in interlocutory proceedings or in a preliminary examination in a criminal case; however, only in equity practice is it applicable to a trial. It is also used in government and politics for a formal opportunity offered to citizens to state their views on proposed legislation or administrative action, or to present their objections to assessments on property, or to give evidence in a legislative or other investigation. **Audience** is now more often used of a hearing that is granted as a favor or mark of esteem than of one that can be demanded as a right; therefore, it is used particularly in reference to interviews by appointment granted by a sovereign, a high-ranking ecclesiastic, especially the pope, or a diplomatic representative of high standing. "The French ambassador upon that instant Crav'd *audience;* and the hour, I think, is come To give him *hearing*" (*Shak.*). "I had an *audience*...with the Spanish Minister" (*Disraeli*). **Audition,** which has only recently come into use in this sense, is applicable to a hearing by expert judges of a singer, a musician, a public speaker, an actor, or the like, in order to test the merits of his performance with, usually, a view to his possible employment; as, operatic or radio *auditions.*

hearken. *Hear, hark, listen, list, attend.

heart. *Center, middle, core, hub, nucleus, midst, omphalos, focus.

heartache. *Sorrow, grief, anguish, woe, dole, regret.

heartfelt. *Sincere, hearty, unfeigned, wholehearted, whole-souled.
Ana. Genuine, veritable, *authentic, bona fide: profound, *deep.

hearty. Heartfelt, *sincere, unfeigned, wholehearted, whole-souled.
Ana. Warm, warmhearted, responsive (see TENDER): *deep, profound: exuberant, *profuse.
Ant. Hollow.

heathen, *n.* *Pagan, paynim, ethnic, Gentile.
Ana. Infidel, unbeliever (see ATHEIST).

heathen, *adj.* Pagan, paynim, ethnic, Gentile. See under PAGAN, *n.*

heave, *v.* Raise, *lift, hoist, elevate, boost, rear.

heavenly. *Celestial, empyrean.
Con. Hellish, *infernal: *earthly, earthy, terrestrial, mundane, worldly, mortal, sublunary.

heavy, *adj.* **Heavy, weighty, ponderous, cumbrous, cumbersome, hefty.** That is **heavy,** literally, which is denser and more compact in substance or larger in size or amount than the average of its kind or class and so weighs much more in proportion; as, lead is a *heavy* metal; a *heavy* stone; a *heavy* child for his age; a *heavy* silk; *heavy* bread. Figuratively, that is *heavy* which is charged with something that weighs down the senses or the spirits or that the mind or the body finds difficult to bear or endure; as, "there came through the open door the *heavy* scent of the lilac" (*Wilde*); "there was the crushing sense...of having been put down as a tiresome and *heavy* young man" (*A. C. Benson*); "When a great writer...creates a speech of his own which is too clumsy to be flexible and too *heavy* to be intimate" (*H. Ellis*). Oftentimes, also, *heavy* is applied to the heart, the mind, the body, weighed down with grief, worry, weariness, overwork, or the like; as, "the old minister's heart was often *heavy* in his breast" (*Deland*); "when he was not too *heavy* with fatigue" (*M. Austin*). At other times, the term merely implies a lack of lightness, vivacity, grace, or some other quality which enlivens and stimulates. "Compared with her, other women were *heavy* and dull ...they had not that something in their glance that made one's blood tingle" (*Cather*). That is **weighty,** literally, which is actually and not merely relatively heavy; as, the larger trucks will carry the *weighty* packages; "as *weighty* bodies to the centre tend" (*Pope*). Figuratively, that is *weighty* which is highly important or momentous (as, *weighty* matters of state; *weighty* questions for consideration) or which produces a powerful effect or exerts an impressive influence (as, *weighty* arguments; a *weighty* speech; a *weighty* speaker). "There were also *weighty* reasons of statecraft to influence him" (*Buchan*). That is **ponderous,** literally, which is exceedingly heavy because of its size or its massiveness; as, a *ponderous* shield; a *ponderous* machine; a *ponderous* door. "The sepulchre... Hath oped his *ponderous* and marble jaws" (*Shak.*). That is *ponderous,* figuratively, which is unduly intricate, involved, complicated, labored, or the like; as, "his *ponderous* work on the Fairy Mythology of Europe" (*Meredith*); *ponderous* jests. "I have heard mathematicians groaning over the demonstrations of Kelvin. *Ponderous* and clumsy, they bludgeon the mind into a reluctant assent" (*A. Huxley*). That is **cumbrous** or **cumbersome,** literally, which is so heavy and so bulky that it is difficult to deal with, as in moving or carrying. "The only currency in circulation was of iron, so *cumbrous* that it was impossible to accumulate or conceal it" (*G. L. Dickinson*). "Its space was pretty well occupied with the two beds, and the *cumbrous* furniture that had been bought for a larger house" (*Arch. Marshall*). "The *cumbersome* old table with twisted legs" (*Dickens*). Figuratively, both words are applicable to that which is both ponderous and unwieldy. "He is the Philistine who upholds and aids the heavy, *cumbrous,* blind, mechanical forces of society" (*Wilde*). That is **hefty** (a colloquial term) which one estimates as heavy or weighty, as by holding in one's hands or by measuring with one's eyes; as, a *hefty* chair; she has grown *hefty* since I saw her last.
Ana. Solid, hard, *firm: oppressing *or* oppressive, weighing down *or* upon, depressing (see corresponding verbs at DEPRESS).
Ant. Light.

heckle, *v.* *Bait, badger, hector, chevy, hound, ride.
Ana. Plague, pester, harass, harry, *worry, annoy: disconcert, rattle, faze, discomfit, *embarrass: grill, rack, torment (see AFFLICT).

hectic. Feverish, jittery, *impatient, nervous, unquiet, restless, restive, uneasy, fidgety, skittish, jumpy.
Ana. Hurrying *or* hurried (see corresponding verb at SPEED): hasty, impetuous, *precipitate, headlong: agitated, flustered, flurried (see DISCOMPOSE).
Con. *Calm, serene, tranquil, placid, peaceful.

hector, *v.* *Bait, badger, chevy, heckle, hound, ride.
Ana. Tease, tantalize, plague, pester, *worry: bother, vex, irk, *annoy: fret, chafe, gall (see ABRADE).

heedless. Thoughtless, *careless, inadvertent.
Ana. *Forgetful, oblivious, unmindful: *abstracted, absent, absent-minded, distrait, distraught: frivolous, light-minded, flippant, volatile (see corresponding nouns at LIGHTNESS): remiss, lax, slack, *negligent, neglectful.
Ant. Heedful. — *Con.* Attentive, *thoughtful, considerate: *watchful, vigilant, alert.

heel, *v.* Careen, list, *tip, tilt, cant.
Ana. & *Con.* See those at CAREEN.

hefty. *Heavy, weighty, ponderous, cumbrous, cumbersome.
Ana. & *Ant.* See those at HEAVY.

height. Height, stature, elevation, altitude mean the distance a thing rises above its base, or the level on which it stands, or the vertical distance between a given level taken as a base and a thing that is above it. **Height** may be used with reference to anything that can be so measured, whether high or low by any standard of comparison; as, letters not more than one-twentieth of an inch in *height;* the tree rises to a *height* of one hundred feet; the airplane reached the unprecedented *height* of twelve miles. It may be used interchangeably with any of the other words, but it is not so explicit. **Stature,** except in its figurative sense, is confined to animal bodies, especially to the human body when fully developed; as, he is six feet in *stature;* malnutrition in childhood often prevents a person from reaching his full *stature* in maturity. **Elevation** is applicable chiefly to things which are raised or are thought of as raised; as, an airplane designed to attain an *elevation* (more precise than *height*) of seven miles; the sun reaches its highest *elevation* at noon; Pikes Peak has an *elevation* of 14,108 feet. *Elevation* and **altitude,** however, may suggest determination or reckoning of height by angular measurement; in such cases, although they often connote height so great as to be otherwise incalculable, they are not restricted to what is pre-eminently or even comparatively high; as, the *altitude* of the triangle formed by the ground and shells fired at an *elevation* of 45° varies with the distance covered by the individual shells. Otherwise, *altitude* is applicable only to things which are extremely and not relatively high; as, the *altitude* of Mars; the *altitudes* of the Himalayas.

heighten. Enhance, *intensify, aggravate.
Ana. *Exalt, magnify, aggrandize: elevate, *lift, raise: *improve, better.
Con. Diminish, reduce, lessen, *decrease: *abase, debase, degrade, humble, humiliate.

heinous. *Outrageous, atrocious, monstrous.
Ana. *Flagrant, glaring, gross, rank: nefarious, flagitious, infamous (see VICIOUS).
Ant. Venial. — *Con.* Trivial, trifling, *petty, paltry.

hellish. *Infernal, chthonian, Hadean, Tartarean, Stygian.
Ana. Devilish, diabolical, *fiendish, demoniacal.

Helot. *Serf, slave, bondslave, bondsman, bondman, peon, thrall, villein, vassal.

help, *v.* **1 Help, aid, assist** and their corresponding nouns **help, aid, assistance** are often used with little distinction as meaning (for the verbs) to furnish another person or thing with what is needed, as for the accomplishment of work or the attainment of an end, or (for the nouns) the support so furnished. All usually, but not invariably, imply co-operation or a combination of effort. **Help,** however, carries a stronger implication of advance toward the end or objective than do the others; as, every little *helps;* you are hindering rather than *helping;* a drug that *helps* one to sleep; please *help* me over the fence; the food shortage in Germany *helped* the Allies. **Aid** strongly suggests the need of help or relief and therefore sometimes imputes weakness to the one aided and strength to the one aiding. "But this she knows... That saints will *aid* if men will call" (*Coleridge*). "Cannonballs may *aid* the truth But thought's a weapon stronger; We'll win our battles by its *aid*" (*C. Mackay*). **Assist,** which seldom loses its etymological implication of standing by, distinctively suggests a secondary role in the assistant or a subordinate character in the assistance; thus, a deputy *assists* (better than *aids*) his superior; a good light *assists* the eyes in reading. "Every additional proof that the world is a closely interwoven system... *assists* religious belief" (*Inge*).
Ana. *Support, uphold, back, champion: *benefit, profit, avail, boot, bestead: forward, further, promote, *advance.
Ant. Hinder. — *Con.* Impede, obstruct, block, bar (see HINDER): *frustrate, thwart, foil, baffle, balk: *embarrass, discomfit: harm, hurt, *injure.
2 *Improve, better, ameliorate.
Ana. *Palliate, gloss, extenuate, whitewash, whiten: alleviate, *relieve, mitigate.

help, *n.* Aid, assistance. See under HELP, *v.* 1.
Ana. Co-operation, uniting *or* union (see corresponding verbs at UNITE): supporting *or* support, backing (see corresponding verbs at SUPPORT): *favor, good will, countenance.

helper. *Assistant, coadjutor, adjutant, aide, aide-de-camp.

hence. Consequently, *therefore, then, accordingly, so.

henchman. *Follower, adherent, disciple, partisan, satellite, sectary.

herald, *n.* *Forerunner, harbinger, precursor.

herculean. *Enormous, immense, huge, vast, gigantic, giant, gigantean, colossal, mammoth, elephantine, titanic, Cyclopean, Antaean, Gargantuan, Brobdingnagian.

herd, *n.* *Flock, drove, pack, bevy, covey, gaggle, flight, swarm, shoal, school.

here. *Hither.

hereditary. Congenital, inborn, inherited, *innate, inbred.
Ana. Transmitted, conveyed (see CARRY): *inherent, constitutional, intrinsic, ingrained.

heredity. *Inheritance.

heretic, *n.* **Heretic, schismatic, sectarian, sectary, dissenter, nonconformist** come into comparison as denoting a person who from the point of view of a given or understood church or religious faith is not orthodox in his beliefs. **Heretic** applies to one who teaches and maintains doctrines that are contrary to those which are actually taught by the church or faith to which he belongs or has belonged; as, the precursors of Luther were for the most part regarded as *heretics;* "He drew a circle that shut me out— *Heretic,* rebel, a thing to flout" (*Markham*). **Schismatic** applies to one who (often unjustifiably or contentiously) separates from, or especially provokes division (or schism) in, a church or communion, usually by differing on a minor point or points of doctrine; thus, from the point of view of the Roman Catholic Church, those Eastern Christians who seceded to form the Orthodox Church are *schismatics,* whereas Luther, Calvin, Cranmer, and other leaders of the Reformation, are *heretics;* to the Church of England, the early Puritans and Quakers were *schismatics.* **Sectarian** and **sectary** applied originally, especially in Great Britain, to a member of a heretical or schismatical body, but the former term now applies chiefly to the member of any religious denomination or sect. *Sectary,* which is now chiefly historical, more than *sectarian,* implies membership in a sect that is relatively small and composed of ardent, and often by connotation, narrow-minded and bigoted, partisans; as, the passing of the bill by Parliament was advocated both by churchmen and by *sectarians;* "Collectivist movements within Christianity have proceeded almost entirely from the Anabaptists and other *sectaries*" (*Inge*). **Dissenter** applies to one who separates himself (without the implication of causing a division or break conveyed by *schismatic*) from an established church, specifically from the Church of England; **nonconformist** is ordinarily synonymous with *dissenter*, but the term has been applied in England to men who refused to accept religious doctrines or to follow religious practices that are imposed by the state, or Established, Church; in this sense, many of the 2000 clergymen who refused to subscribe to the Act of Uniformity in 1662 were regarded as *nonconformists;* Roman Catholics in England (as a class) have been held to be *nonconformists* rather than *dissenters*, since they did not accept the Church of England at any time. Nevertheless, the terms are often used interchangeably; as, "Wesley was not a *schismatic*, or even, in the doctrinal sense, a *dissenter*. He desired, not to secede from the Established Church, but to fill it with new life" (*Atlantic Monthly*); "The English and Scotch *Nonconformists* have a great horror of establishments and endowments for religion" (*Arnold*).

Ana. Freethinker, deist, unbeliever (see ATHEIST): *skeptic, agnostic: *renegade, apostate.

heretical. *Heterodox.

heritage. Heritage, inheritance, patrimony, birthright are synonymous terms when they denote something which one receives or is entitled to receive by succession, as from a parent or predecessor. **Heritage** is not only poetical or elevated but it is also the most widely applicable of these words, for it may apply to anything that is passed on not only to one's heir or heirs but to the generation or generations that succeed, as a tradition, a right, a trade, the effect of a cause, or the like; as, "[Livy] made the average Roman realize the grandeur of the past and the magnitude of his *heritage*" (*Buchan*); "our neglect of the magnificent spiritual *heritage* which we possess in our own history and literature" (*Inge*); "But the war had left its *heritage* of poverty..., of disease, of misery, of discontent" (*R. Macaulay*). **Inheritance** strictly applies to that which passes from parent to children, whether it be money, property, traits of character, or the like (as, "My father's blessing, and this little coin Is my *inheritance*"—*Beaumont & Fletcher*); but the term may be used in place of *heritage* when such descent is literally or figuratively implied (as, "A good man leaveth an *inheritance* to his children's children"—*Proverbs* xiii. 22). *Inheritance*, but not *heritage*, may also apply to the fact of inheriting or to the means by which something passes into one's possession; as, to come into possession of a property by *inheritance* (not *heritage*); "the power of regulating the devolution of property by *inheritance* or will upon the death of the owner" (*Justice Holmes*). **Patrimony** applies strictly to the money or property inherited from one's father, but is also used (especially figuratively) in the more general sense of ancestral inheritance; as, "to reave the orphan of his *patrimony*" (*Shak.*); "Content...to leave his *patrimony* not worse but something better than he found it" (*Quiller-Couch*). **Birthright** is now more often used in its extended sense (see RIGHT) than in its original sense of *inheritance*, or the property, goods, privileges, or rank which belong to one by reason of one's birth. But in this sense *birthright* is often more specific than *inheritance*, because it usually applies only to that which belongs to the first-born son by the law of primogeniture; as, "And Jacob said [to his older brother Esau], Sell me this day thy *birthright*. And Esau said, Behold, I am at the point to die: and what profit shall this *birthright* do to me...? and he sold his *birthright* unto Jacob" (*Genesis* xxv. 31–33).

hermaphrodite, hermaphroditic. *Bisexual, androgynous, epicene.

hermit. Eremite, anchorite, *recluse, cenobite.

Con. *Religious, monk, friar, nun: *ascetic, mystic.

heroism. Heroism, valor (*or* **valour**), **prowess, gallantry** are synonymous terms when they mean conspicuous courage or bravery as displayed in conduct or behavior, especially in conflict. **Heroism,** the strongest term, in discriminating use implies superlative, often transcendent, courage or bravery, not only as exhibited by deeds of daring in the presence of danger, as in a battle, a fire, or a wreck at sea, but in carrying through without submitting or yielding an eminently arduous but exalted enterprise, such as an exploration, or in the same spirit fulfilling a superhumanly high purpose where the odds are against one, such as the conquest of self or the institution of a great moral reform. "Acts of *heroism* are in the very essence of them but rare: for if they were common they would not be acts of *heroism*" (*Bentham*). "The characteristic of genuine *heroism* is its persistency. All men have wandering impulses, fits and starts of generosity....The heroic cannot be the common, nor the common the heroic" (*Emerson*). **Valor,** in earlier use, was often applied to the quality of mind, as distinct from the manifestation of that quality in action. "My *valour* is certainly going...I feel it oozing out" (*Sheridan*). In current use commonly, and in past use occasionally, both the possession of a high degree of courage and the exhibition of that quality, especially in fighting, are implied; as, to be awarded a medal for *valor* in action. In contrast with *heroism, valor* implies illustrious rather than superlative courage or bravery; it carries a far weaker implication of a persistent struggle against odds but a stronger one of fearlessness and audacity in conflict with a powerful enemy. "Real *valour* consists not in being insensible to danger, but in being prompt to confront and disarm it" (*Scott*). "Wherever *valour* true is found, True modesty will there abound" (*W. S. Gilbert*). **Prowess,** which is now a literary term in its original sense, differs from *valor* chiefly in its greater emphasis upon brilliant achievements or exploits in arms. "How insignificant a thing...does personal *prowess* appear compared with the fortitude of patience and heroic martyrdom" (*Wordsworth*). "Chevaliers were seldom intellectually brilliant in the mediaeval romans [romances], and even the 'Chansons de Geste' liked better to talk of their *prowess* than of their wit" (*H. Adams*). In current loose use, *prowess* oftentimes loses its basic implication of distinguished skill and bravery in arms and means little more than distinguished skill; as, *prowess* in debating or in athletics. **Gallantry** far more than *valor*, its close synonym, stresses mettle and spirit as well as courage and an almost gay indifference to danger or hardship. "Few augured the possibility that the encounter could terminate well for...the Disinherited Knight, yet his courage and *gallantry* secured the general good wishes of the spectators" (*Scott*).

Ana. Bravery, intrepidity, dauntlessness, doughtiness (see corresponding adjectives at BRAVE): *courage, tenacity, resolution, mettle, spirit: *fortitude, pluck, grit, guts, sand.

hesitancy. *Hesitation.

Ana. Reluctance, averseness, indisposedness *or* indisposition (see corresponding adjectives at DISINCLINED): faltering, wavering, vacillation (see corresponding verbs at HESITATE).

Con. Determination, *decision: resolution, tenacity, spirit, *courage: backbone, pluck, grit, guts, sand, *fortitude.

hesitant. Reluctant, loath, averse, indisposed, *disinclined.

Ana. *Fearful, afraid, apprehensive: diffident, *shy,

bashful: recoiling, flinching, blenching, shrinking (see RECOIL).

Con. *Eager, avid, keen: resolute, steadfast, stanch (see FAITHFUL).

hesitate. **Hesitate, waver, vacillate, falter** agree in meaning to show irresolution or uncertainty. **Hesitate,** the general term, usually implies a pause or other sign of indecision before one makes up one's mind what to do, say, choose, or the like; as, "I have for many months *hesitated* about the propriety of allowing...any part of my narrative to come before the public eye" (*De Quincey*); "When delivering a speech to pour it out in a copious stream, without pausing to take breath or *hesitating* over a word" (*Hudson*). **Waver,** as here compared (see also SWING, 2), implies hesitation after a decision has been reached and so usually connotes weakness or retreat; as, "Let us hold fast...without *wavering*" (*Hebrews* x. 23); the front line which had been advancing rapidly *wavered* under the heavy fire. "You *waver* in your convictions" (*Jefferies*). **Vacillate** implies prolonged hesitation resulting from one's inability to reach a fixed or final decision; the term therefore connotes alternate decision and indecision or a shifting in opinions, choices, or the like. "He may pause, but he must not *hesitate,*—and tremble, but he must not *vacillate*" (*Ruskin*). "He had *vacillated* between various substitutes for Oswald up to the very moment when he named the four upon whom he decided finally" (*H. G. Wells*). **Falter** suggests a wavering in purpose or action that is evident or is made evident in trembling, the breaking of the voice, or other signs of fear or nervousness; as, "with voice That did not *falter* though the heart was moved" (*Wordsworth*); "Neither to change, nor *falter*, nor repent" (*Shelley*); "His eyes did not flinch and his tongue did not *falter*" (*Conrad*).

Ana. Balk, boggle, stick, stickle, scruple, *demur, shy: fluctuate, oscillate (see SWING).

hesitation. **Hesitation, hesitancy** are often used interchangeably as meaning a hesitating. But **hesitation** more commonly applies to the act or fact, or to a sign of hesitating; as, to accept without *hesitation;* "without *hesitation* Flora seized her father round the body and pulled back" (*Conrad*); "She drove without any uncertainty or *hesitation* as to her route" (*Deland*). **Hesitancy,** on the other hand, applies to the feeling or the mood of one who hesitates; as, to feel great *hesitancy* about accepting; she never experiences *hesitancy* when called upon for assistance. "To [Henry] James's intimates...these elaborate *hesitancies*...were like a cobweb bridge flung from his mind to theirs" (*E. Wharton*).

Ana. *Uncertainty, doubt, dubiety, dubiosity, mistrust: procrastination, delaying *or* delay, dawdling (see corresponding verbs at DELAY).

Con. Resolution, spirit, mettle, *courage, tenacity: *confidence, assurance, self-possession, aplomb.

heterodox. **Heterodox, heretical** come into comparison when they mean not in conformity with orthodox beliefs or teachings. That is **heterodox** which is at variance with accepted doctrines (especially religious or scientific doctrines), interpretation (as of the Bible, the Constitution, or the like), or any view regarded as authorized by reason, revelation, tradition, or convention; as, Milton's *heterodox* opinions on divorce and the episcopacy; Darwin's contemporaries were slow in accepting his *heterodox* theory of the origin of species. That is **heretical** which is not only heterodox, but is regarded as erroneous and as destructive of truth; as, "a great Christian society defending itself against *heretical* anarchy from within" (*Belloc*); *heretical* books; the propagation of *heretical* doctrines; Galileo's writings championing the *heterodox* Copernican theory of the solar system were condemned by the Inquisition as *heretical.*

Ant. Orthodox.

heterogeneous. *Miscellaneous, motley, promiscuous, assorted.

Ana. Diverse, disparate, various, divergent, *different: mixed, mingled, commingled (see MIX): multifarious, divers (see MANY).

Ant. Homogeneous. — *Con.* Uniform, identical, alike, akin, analogous, comparable, parallel (see SIMILAR).

hew. Chop, *cut, carve, slit, slash.

Ana. Cleave, rive, split (see TEAR).

hide, *n.* *Skin, pelt, fell, rind, bark, peel.

hide, *v.* **Hide, conceal, screen, secrete, cache, bury, ensconce** agree in meaning to withdraw or to withhold from sight or observation. **Hide** (the general term) and **conceal** are often interchangeable. But *hide* may or may not suggest intent (as, "Let me go, that I may *hide* myself in the field"—*1 Samuel* xx. 5; the snow *hides* all the ground), or a putting into a place out of the range of others' sight (as, to *hide* the money under a mattress; "He *hid* somewhere in his grimy little soul a genuine love for music"—*Kipling*). *Conceal,* on the other hand, more often implies intention (as, "*Hidden* things that had never been *concealed,* that had merely been dropped into forgotten corners and out-of-the-way places, to be found a long while afterward"—*E. M. Roberts*), or effective hiding (as, "Sophia had held that telegram *concealed* in her hand and its information *concealed* in her heart"—*Bennett*), or a refusal to divulge (as, "I am glad to be constrain'd to utter that Which torments me to *conceal*" *Shak.*). **Screen** implies a hiding or concealment of someone (or something) in danger of being seen or known by interposing between him (or it) and others a screen, curtain, or other device which shelters and prevents discovery; as, "Wildeve *screened* himself under a bush and waited" (*Hardy*); "The prominence afforded to them [unemployment and other causes of a depression] helps to *screen* the great fundamental source of trouble, the lack of any conscious equitable government of industry" (*J. A. Hobson*). **Secrete,** as here compared, implies depositing, often by stealth, in a place screened from view or unknown to others; as, to *secrete* smuggled goods in a cave; squirrels *secrete* their winter supply of nuts. **Cache** implies an even more carefully chosen hiding place than *secrete,* for it usually implies protection from thieves, from the elements, and the like: in current use it often suggests secure storage more than concealment; as, the explorers took only enough food and ammunition for the three days' trip, the rest they *cached* in pits dug for that purpose. **Bury** implies a covering with (or in) something that hides or conceals or serves as a hiding place; as, to *bury* one's face in one's hands; "his intention had been to *bury* the incident in his bosom" (*E. Wharton*). **Ensconce,** in earlier use, implied a placing oneself securely in hiding; as, "She shall not see me: I will *ensconce* me behind the arras" (*Shak.*). The term now usually means to establish oneself snugly or comfortably, commonly with no idea of concealment; as, to *ensconce* oneself in an armchair before a cosy fire.

Ana. Cloak, mask, *disguise, dissemble: *suppress, repress.

Con. Expose, parade, flaunt, display, exhibit, *show: emerge, loom, *appear.

high. **High, tall, lofty** agree in meaning above the average in height. **High,** the general term (opposed to *low*), implies marked extension upward; the term is applied chiefly to things which rise from a base or foundation (as, a *high* hill; a *high* building) or are placed at a conspicuous height above a lower level, such as a floor or the ground (as, a *high* ceiling; a *high*-arched bridge). **Tall** (often opposed to *short*) applies to that which rises or grows high as compared with others of its kind, especially when its breadth or diameter is small in proportion to its height; as, a *high* (not *tall*) hill; a *high* (or *tall*) tree; a *tall* (better than *high*) pole; a *tall* (not *high*) man. **Lofty** is often poetical for *high*, but it usually implies even greater and more imposing altitude; as, a *lofty* mountain peak; a *lofty* pinnacle; *lofty* clouds; "the *loftiest* star of unascended heaven" (*Shelley*). *High* alone of these words is used to express degree or intensity; as, *high* speed, *high* power, *high* color, *high* seasoning; cf. a *high* wind, a *high* fever. Figuratively, *high* connotes distinction, elevation, sometimes pride or arrogance; as, "Heaven's *high* King" (*Milton*); "an *high* look and a proud heart" (*Psalms* ci. 5); "She... thought him cold, *High*, self-contain'd, and passionless" (*Tennyson*). "Nobody else could utter those two words as he did, with such gravity and *high* courtesy" (*Cather*). *Lofty* suggests moral grandeur or dignity; as, "exultation... Solemn, serene and *lofty*" (*Shelley*); "That *lofty* musing on the ultimate nature of things which constitutes, for Pascal, 'the whole dignity and business of man'" (*A. Huxley*). The term may also imply (especially as applied to persons) haughtiness or superciliousness; as, she is greatly disliked because of her *lofty* airs. *Tall* is now rarely figurative except in slang or in colloquial use, when it often implies exaggeration or departure from strict truth; as, he is given to *tall* stories or to *tall* talk. In older and now practically obsolete English, *tall* implied qualities not necessarily associated with height, such as comeliness (as, "he was a *tall* proper man"—*Henry More*), deftness (as, a man *tall* of his hands) and doughtiness or sturdiness (as, "The old fellow's spirit is as *tall* and as gallant as ever"—*Irving*).

Ana. Elevated, lifted, raised, reared (see LIFT, *v.*): *deep, profound, abysmal: heightened, enhanced, intensified (see INTENSIFY): increased, augmented (see INCREASE, *v.*).

Ant. Low.

high-spirited. *Spirited, mettlesome, spunky, fiery, peppery, gingery.

Ana. Gallant, chivalrous, courtly, courteous (see CIVIL): audacious, bold, *brave, intrepid.

highway, highroad. Street, avenue, boulevard, *road, roadway, terrace, drive, parkway, thoroughfare, byway, lane, alley, alleyway.

highwayman. Footpad, bandit, *brigand, marauder.

hilarity. Jollity, *mirth, glee.

Ana. Merriment, blitheness, jocundity (see corresponding adjectives at MERRY): cheerfulness, gladness, joyfulness, joyousness, lightheartedness (see corresponding adjectives at GLAD): *fun, play, sport, jest, game.

hind, *adj.* Hinder, rear, *posterior, after, back.

Ant. Fore, front.

hinder, *adj.* Hind, rear, *posterior, after, back.

Ant. Front, fore.

hinder, *v.* **Hinder, impede, obstruct, block, bar, dam** agree in meaning to put obstacles in the way of a person or thing or of his or its action. To **hinder** (etymologically, to put or keep behind) is to check or hold back someone or something in action or about to act, move, start, or the like: the term usually stresses harmful or annoying delay or interference with progress; as, "From your affairs I *hinder* you too long" (*Shak.*); "[the artist's] education is...*hindered* rather than helped by the ordinary processes of society which constitute education for the ordinary man" (*T. S. Eliot*). Sometimes, however, *hinder* definitely implies prevention; as, the rain *hindered* their going. To **impede** (etymologically, to entangle the feet) is to impose upon a person or thing that is moving, in action, in progress, or the like, something that slows him or it up, as by clogging, hampering, or fettering: the term seldom suggests the stopping of movement or progress, but it commonly implies difficulties so great that movement or action are painfully slow or nearly impossible; as, "around their tattooed limbs they often wore coiled brass rings or bands, which in time became so tight that they *impeded* the circulation" (*V. Heiser*); "the teaching of mathematics is... *impeded* by the use of Roman symbols" (*Grandgent*); "He...placed his hand on hers, *impeding* the rapidity of her embroidery needle" (*R. Macaulay*). To **obstruct** is to hinder free or easy passage: it implies interference with something in motion or in progress or obstacles in the path or channel; thus, fallen trees may be said to obstruct the highways, or to obstruct traffic, at various points; so, the recalcitrant senators succeeded in *obstructing* legislation for several days; the tall building *obstructed* the light from the west; the view was *obstructed* by several tall trees. To **block** (or *block up*) is to obstruct so effectively as to close up all means of egress or ingress and to prevent all passage for a time; as, shifting sand *blocked* the entrance to the channel; to *block* a child's ambition by indifference or discouragement. "In these wild places...a snow-storm...does not *block* the King's highways and paralyse traffic as [in] London" (*Jefferies*). To **bar** is to block or to prohibit passage, ingress, or egress; as, "a long freight train...*barred* the passage along the road" (*S. Anderson*); "that route is *barred* to steamers" (*Kipling*). Sometimes the implication of prohibition is so strong that there is no hint of blocking. "The law of arms doth *bar* The use of venom'd shot in war" (*Butler*). To **dam** (often *dam up*) is to obstruct with obstacles that prevent a continued flow, as of water, emotion, or the like, and so provide no outlet or exit; as, fallen trees *dammed* up the brook; "The strait pass was *damm'd* With dead men" (*Shak.*); *dammed*-up emotion.

Ana. *Arrest, check, interrupt: *hamper, fetter, clog, trammel, shackle, manacle, hog-tie: *restrain, inhibit, curb, check, snaffle: baffle, balk, *frustrate.

Ant. Further. — *Con.* *Advance, forward, promote: *speed, accelerate, quicken.

hint, *n.* Occasion, *opportunity, time, chance, break.

hint, *v.* Intimate, insinuate, imply, *suggest.

Ana. Allude, advert, *refer.

Con. Voice, utter, *express, vent: declare, *assert, affirm, aver.

hire, *n.* *Wage, wages, pay, salary, stipend, fee, emolument, screw.

hire, *v.* **1** *Employ.

Con. Fire, discharge, *dismiss, cashier, sack.

2 Hire, let, lease, rent, charter come into comparison when they refer to the taking or engaging of something or the granting the use of something for a stipulated price or rate. Because some of these words are referable only to the act of the owner and some only to the act of the one who engages, and because they vary in their applications, they are not always true synonyms. In very precise use, **hire** and **let** are complementary yet opposite terms, the former meaning to engage the use or occupancy of something at a price or rate, and the latter meaning to grant its use or occupancy for a stipulated return; as, we *hired* the house for the summer after having some difficulty in persuading the owner to *let* it. "Sometimes a family would *hire* them [Norfolk wherries, or barges], more generally a group of young men from the City or from the Universities. They *let* [idiomatic for *were let*] at a good price" (*Arch. Marshall*). Nevertheless *hire*, especially when used of persons or, by implication, their services, may be employed in either sense; as, to *hire* a servant; to *hire* oneself (often with *out*) as a servant; to *hire* workers by the day; men willing to *hire* themselves out at any wage. In most discriminating use, **lease** means to let on a lease, that is, on a contract by which the owner conveys to another for a given term, and usually at a given rate, certain land, buildings, or similar property. "The lands in America [in Colonial days]...are in general not tenanted nor *leased* out to farmers" (*Adam Smith*). In current English, *lease* is often employed in the sense of to hire on a lease, but this use is not approved by all authorities; as, they have *leased* the house from Mr. Blank for three years. Etymologically and in long-continued good use, **rent** implies the payment in money (or payment in kind) for the use of land and the buildings thereon. As long as this idea is stressed, the verb may denote either to hire or to let a property; as, they *rent* their house from the college; the college *rents* these houses only to professors. In American, but rarely if ever in British, use, *rent* (in the sense of either *hire* or *let*) is employed in reference to various commodities; as, to *rent* books from a circulating library; to *rent* an automobile for the summer. **Charter** strictly means to hire (a ship or vessel) by charter party, that is, by a contract similar to a lease whereby the use of a ship is given for a certain time and the safe delivery of its cargo is promised; as, "It was impossible to *charter* a ship for the purpose" (*Irving*). In extended use, *charter* is also used of vehicles, especially public vehicles or similar means of transportation; as, to *charter* a bus or an airplane.

Ana. Secure, obtain, *get, procure: engage, contract, *promise.

hireling, *adj.* *Mercenary, hack, hackney, venal.

Ana. Servile, menial, *subservient: *mean, abject, sordid.

history. History, chronicle, annals, as here compared, agree in meaning a written record of events important in the life or career of a race, a nation, an institution, or the like. A **history** is more than a mere recital of what has occurred; in the modern conception, at least, it requires order and purpose in narration, but not necessarily a strictly chronological order nor a common definitely defined purpose. Usually, also, it is thought of as an interpretation of events especially in their causal relationships. It may exhibit fullness and completeness, or, on the other hand, selection of details, especially when a single aspect is considered or a thesis is to be proved; as, Macaulay's *History* of England; Justin McCarthy's *History* of Our Own Times. A **chronicle** is a recital of events in chronological order without any attempt at interpretation or, usually, literary style; its chief function is to record events; as, the Anglo-Saxon *Chronicle;* Holinshed's *Chronicles* of England, Scotland, and Ireland. **Annals** is not always clearly distinguishable from *chronicle* except in its emphasis upon the progress or succession of events from year to year. The term may or may not imply a discursive treatment or a continued narrative, for some of the ancient annals are merely records of important events in each year of the time covered; thus, the *annals* of the Four Masters, a 17th-century work by Irish scholars, begins with A.M. [anno mundi, or year of the world] 2242 and ends with A.D. 1616. However, in the selection of titles for modern historical works, these distinctions are not always observed, for *chronicle* and *annals* are sometimes chosen as less formal or pretentious than *history* or because *chronicle* stresses narrative quality and *annals* the selection of noteworthy events.

In their extended or figurative senses, only **history** and **annals** are synonymous. Both of these words designate more or less shifting abstractions. *History* usually signifies the known past, or the sum total of events that are remembered because recorded by historians, evidenced by documents, monuments, remains, or the like; as, nothing like this has happened hitherto in the *history* of man. "A land without ruins is a land without memories—a land without memories is a land without *history*" (*A. J. Ryan*). *Annals* most often signifies the sum total of events, with their dates, that have become fixed in the mind because of the momentousness, often tragic momentousness, of those events; as, "The short and simple *annals* of the poor" (*Gray*); "happy the people whose *annals* are blank" (*Carlyle*). **Chronicle,** on the other hand, is often applied to something concrete, as a person or thing that records, relates, or manifests events as they happen. "Good my lord, will you see the players well bestowed?...let them be well used; for they are the abstract and brief *chronicles* of the time:...you were better have a bad epitaph than their ill report while you live" (*Shak.*).

histrionic, *adj.* *Dramatic, theatrical, dramaturgic, melodramatic.

Ana. Acting, playing, impersonating, personating (see ACT, *v.*).

hit, *v.* *Strike, smite, slug, slap, swat, clout, punch, box, cuff.

Ana. *Beat, buffet, pound, pummel, thrash.

hither. Hither, here indicate the point or place where the speaker or writer is. **Hither** was formerly used with verbs of motion (such as *come, bring, send,* etc.); **here,** with verbs of rest (such as *be, live, stay,* etc.). In modern usage *here* has displaced *hither,* except in poetical or elevated style and is now employed after verbs of motion as well as of rest.

hit-or-miss. *Random, haphazard, happy-go-lucky, desultory, casual, chance, chancy.

hoard, *v.* Amass, *accumulate.

Ana. Collect, assemble, *gather: pile, *heap, stack, mass.

Con. Dissipate, disperse, *scatter: *distribute, divide, dispense.

hoax, *v.* Hoodwink, bamboozle, *dupe, gull, befool, trick.

Ana. Delude, mislead, *deceive: *cheat, cozen, overreach, defraud.

hobo, *n.* Tramp, vagrant, *vagabond, truant, bum, stiff, swagman, sundowner.

hocus-pocus. Mummery, *gibberish, abracadabra.

hog-tie. *Hamper, trammel, clog, fetter, shackle, manacle.

Ana. Impede, *hinder, obstruct, block, bar, dam: curb, check, snaffle, *restrain: *tie, bind.

hoist, *v.* *Lift, raise, elevate, boost, heave, rear.

Ana. *Rise, arise, ascend, mount, levitate.

hold, *v.* **1** In form **hold back.** Withhold, reserve, detain, retain, *keep.

Ana. *Restrain, inhibit, curb, check, snaffle: preserve, conserve, *save.

Con. *Relinquish, surrender, abandon, resign, yield.

2 *Contain, accommodate.

Ana. *Carry, bear, convey: *receive, admit, take: house, lodge, *harbor, shelter: *include, comprehend.

3 *Have, own, possess, enjoy.

Ana. Control, direct, manage, *conduct.

hole, *n.* **Hole, hollow, cavity, pocket, void, vacuum** come into comparison only when they mean an open or unfilled space in a thing. **Hole** may apply to an opening in a solid body that is or that suggests a depression or an excavation (as, "Those *holes* Where eyes did once inhabit"—

Shak.; a *hole* in the ground) or to one that passes through the material from surface to surface (as, to look through a *hole* in the wall; a *hole* in a garment). **Hollow,** which etymologically implies opposition to *solid*, strictly suggests an unfilled space within a solid object, usually, but not necessarily, one that has a surface opening; as, a cave is a *hollow* in a rock; a nest in the *hollow* of a tree trunk. The term, however, is often applied to a depression in a surface (as, the ground was not quite smooth, but had many little heights and *hollows*), and specifically to a deep and usually narrow valley, such as a gully or ravine. "I hate the dreadful *hollow* behind the little wood" (*Tennyson*). **Cavity** is a somewhat more learned word than *hollow* with much the same implications as the latter in its strict sense. The words are often used interchangeably, but *cavity* is preferred in scientific and professional use; as, a *cavity* in a tooth; the abdominal *cavity*. **Pocket** is often employed in place of *cavity* for an abnormal or irregular formation, such as a bubblelike one in a substance or a sacklike one in a body; it is particularly referred to one that is a source of danger, especially in possessing the tendency to hold or to collect a foreign substance, such as dirt, air, pus, and the like; as, a pus *pocket* in the lungs; a *pocket* in a casting; an air *pocket* in a pipe supposedly full of liquid interferes with the flow of the latter. "We found many persons at work ...searching for veins and *pockets* of gold" (*B. Taylor*). **Void** applies to any apparently empty space, especially one of marked extent or, figuratively, of conspicuous duration, whether in a thing that is normally continuous (as, *voids* in a wall where the windows and doors are to be) or between things that are normally separate (as, the immense *void* between the earth and the nearest of the planets). "We suffer when we have time to spare and no printed matter with which to plug the *void*" (*A. Huxley*). **Vacuum,** in its strictest sense, applies to space entirely devoid of matter; more commonly, however, it is applied to the space within an enclosed vessel in which by mechanical means the air has been practically (though seldom completely) exhausted. In its figurative use, the term applies to a condition or situation which resembles a true vacuum in its emptiness of all that normally should fill it or exert influence on anyone or anything that remains in it. "You are not asked, as you are by so many novelists, to concern yourself with the fortunes of two or three people who live in a *vacuum*...but with the fortunes of all the sorts and conditions of men who make up the world in which we all live" (*Maugham*). "He felt a sort of emptiness, almost like a *vacuum* in his soul" (*D. H. Lawrence*).

Ana. *Aperture, orifice, interstice: perforation, puncture, bore, prick (see corresponding verbs at PERFORATE): slit, slash, cut (see CUT, *v.*).

holiness. **Holiness, sanctity** are very close synonyms which are often used without distinction to mean either the state or the character of one who is spiritually perfect or of that which is sacred or hallowed. **Holiness** more often implies spiritual perfection, whether intrinsic and essential (as, the *holiness* of the Lord) or acquired by effort (as, the *holiness* of a saint), than it does sacredness, although the latter implication is not uncommon. "And an highway shall be there, and a way, and it shall be called The way of *holiness;* the unclean shall not pass over it" (*Isaiah* xxxv. 8). "*Holiness* becometh thine house, O Lord, for ever" (*Psalms* xciii. 5). **Sanctity** may be used either as denoting saintliness, or the holiness attained by a saint (as, to die in the odor of *sanctity;* "a few of them [bishops] were men of eminent *sanctity*" —*Burke*), or the quality of being sacred, or by law (especially by natural or divine law) immune from violation; as, "the sense of the dignity of human nature is an even more civilized feeling than the sense of the *sanctity* of human life" (*Brownell*); "There is no greater *sanctity* in the right to combine than in the right to make other contracts" (*Justice Holmes*).

Ana. Sacredness, divineness *or* divinity, spirituality, blessedness, religiousness (see corresponding adjectives at HOLY): devoutness *or* devotion, piousness *or* piety (see corresponding adjectives at DEVOUT): *goodness, virtue, rectitude.

hollow, *adj.* Empty, *vain, nugatory, otiose, idle.

Ana.* & *Con. See those at EMPTY, *adj.* 2.

hollow, *n.* Cavity, *hole, pocket, void, vacuum.

Ana. Excavation, digging (see corresponding verbs at DIG): *gulf, chasm, abyss: orifice, *aperture.

holy. **Holy, sacred, divine, spiritual, religious, blessed** are here compared chiefly as epithets applied to persons or things associated with religion or worship and therefore either regarded with special reverence or veneration or thought of as having a character apart from that which is material or secular. Their choice is often a matter of idiom rather than of meaning inherent in the term. **Holy** (for sense of *holy* as full of holiness, see HOLINESS) usually implies some quality or some attribute in the thing itself which makes it either suitable for use in worship or an object of veneration. As the strongest of these terms in its suggestion of a claim upon one's reverence, it is the only one directly applied to the Supreme Being in praise or laudation (as, "*Holy, holy, holy,* Lord God Almighty"—*Revelation* iv. 8): it also forms a part of some titles of the godhead or of a person of the Trinity (as, the *Holy* Trinity; the *Holy* Spirit; the *Holy* Redeemer). It is also applied to some persons or group of persons as a mark of highest reverence or esteem; as, the *Holy* Family (i.e., Mary, Joseph, and Jesus); the *Holy* Father (i.e., the Pope); the *Holy* Synod (i.e., the governing body in some Orthodox churches). The term is variously applied, as in the names of the central Eucharistic service of Christian churches (as, *Holy* Communion; the *Holy* Sacrifice of the Mass), in the names of places and things associated with the life and death of Christ (as, the *Holy* Land; the *Holy* Cross), in the names of material things that are blessed for use in religious services (as, *holy* water; *holy* bread), in the names of days or periods of time set apart for pious observance (as, a *holy* day; *Holy* Week). These illustrate the chief but not the only uses of *holy* as an epithet: in more general use, the word is often chosen when one wishes to impute to that which is so described some inherent character that dissociates it from that which is mundane, material, or transitory, as, "So *holy* and so perfect is my love" (*Shak.*); "All is *holy* where devotion kneels" (*Holmes*). **Sacred** (as here compared: see also SACRED, 2) differs chiefly from *holy* in implying a character given to a thing by blessing, dedication, consecration to religion or worship or to the uses of religion or worship, or by its being devoted wholly to such ends or uses: the term therefore usually suggests an opposition to that which is profane or which exists for profane uses; thus, the vessels used in a Eucharistic service are preferably called *sacred* vessels; the vestments worn in church services are called *sacred* vestments; *sacred* (as opposed to *profane*) history is Biblical history or history dealing with Biblical characters or Biblical events; "*sacred* literature" (as opposed to "*profane* literature") sometimes is equal in its denotation to any or all of the books of the Bible, and sometimes to any or all of the books such as the Bible, the Talmud, the Koran, etc., which are regarded by various religions as sources of revealed truth; so, a *sacred* writing; *Sacred* Writ; *sacred* music; *sacred* and profane love. In more general use, *sacred* applies chiefly to that which one treasures as a thing apart, not to be violated or contaminated by being put to vulgar or low uses or associated with vulgar or low ends. "When they saw all that was *sacred* to them laid waste, the Navajos lost heart. They did not surrender; they simply ceased to fight" (*Cather*). **Divine,** in its oldest and most definite sense, implies either the character of deity or an origin from or an association with deity; thus, "*divine* being" implies both a difference from "human being" and from "angelic being" and the possession of the nature or essence of deity (as, the belief that Christ is both human and *divine*); a *divine* right is one that comes from God; *divine* service is a service having for its end the worship of God. In its weaker senses, *divine* may suggest a supernatural or a superhuman character or origin, or, in hyperbolical use, a perfection that is above that which is found on earth; as, "that mighty orb of song, The *divine* Milton" (*Wordsworth*); "the strains...of *divinest* music" (*F. W. Farrar*); "By what magic was it that this *divine* sweet creature could be allied with that old churl!" (*Meredith*). **Spiritual** implies an opposition in character or in quality to that which is bodily, material, earthy, or mundane: it may suggest incorporeal existence (as, angels are conceived of as *spiritual* beings; the *spiritual* part of man) or independence of that which is physical or sensible (as, a *spiritual* marriage; *spiritual* as opposed to earthly love), or a definite relation to the soul or spirit in its aspiration toward or dependence on God or in its perception of eternal values (as, "the responsibility of human nature, not merely on the moral side, but equally on the *spiritual* side"—*C. Mackenzie;* "The emotion of Morris is not more refined or more *spiritual* [than that of Marvell]; it is merely more vague"—*T. S. Eliot*). *Spiritual* in several legal and theological phrases is more or less equivalent to *ecclesiastical* and in this sense usually implies an opposition to *temporal* or *civil;* thus, in British use, a *spiritual* lord, or lord *spiritual,* is a bishop or archbishop of the Church of England who has a right to sit in the House of Lords; so, the *spiritual* versus the temporal power. **Religious** (for the application of this term to persons, see DEVOUT) implies an opposition to *secular* and a relation of some kind to religion; thus, *religious* history (cf. *sacred* history, above) is the history of a religion or religions; *religious* literature is not the same as sacred literature (see above) but has a character that is determined by religion or by religious belief or feeling; *religious* music, unlike sacred music, is not necessarily suitable for use in services or prayer, for, although it includes sacred music, the term may also apply to music not composed for church use, but animated by feeling or prompted by themes associated with religion. "He stated that his discourses to people were to be sometimes secular, and sometimes *religious,* but never dogmatic" (*Hardy*). "Except for the nominal subjects of the legends, one sees nothing *religious* about them; the medallions, when studied with the binocle, turn out to be less *religious* than decorative" (*H. Adams*). **Blessed,** which etymologically means consecrated, is literally used in the phrase "the *Blessed* Sacrament" (i.e., the Eucharist, or the sacrament which involves the rite of consecration). But that phrase usually also suggests a supremely sacred and love-inspiring character, and it is that connotation rather than the implication of consecration which obtains in the phrases our *Blessed* Lord and the *Blessed* Virgin. In its derived senses, *blessed* means beatified; that is, supremely happy because enjoying the sight of God in heaven (as, the *blessed* spirits in heaven) or, in Roman Catholic usage, so designated because, having gone through the process called *beatification* (the second step toward canonization), one has been adjudged worthy of veneration; as, the *Blessed* Isaac Jogues (now a canonized saint). So, in general use, *blessed* sometimes means worthy of particular veneration, love, or the like. "We have no green vegetables here in winter, and no one seems ever to have heard of that *blessed* plant, the lettuce" (*Cather*).

Ana. Hallowed, consecrated, dedicated (see DEVOTE): adored, worshiped, venerated, reverenced, revered (see REVERE): *devout, pious, religious.

Ant. Unholy. — ***Con.*** *Profane, secular: *impious, blasphemous, sacrilegious, profane.

homage. 1 *Allegiance, fealty.

2 Reverence, deference, obeisance, *honor.

Ana. Worship, adoration, veneration, reverence (see under REVERE): fealty, *fidelity, devotion, loyalty, allegiance: tribute, panegyric, eulogy, *encomium.

home. Domicile, abode, residence, house, dwelling, *habitation.

homily. Sermon, talk, *speech, address, oration, harangue, allocution, lecture, prelection.

homogeneous. Uniform, akin, identical, alike, analogous, comparable, parallel, *similar, like.

Ana. Congruous, compatible, congenial, *consonant: equal, equivalent, *same.

Ant. Heterogeneous. — ***Con.*** Diverse, disparate, various, divergent, *different: multifarious, divers (see MANY).

homunculus, homuncle, homuncule. Manikin, midget, *dwarf, pygmy, runt.

honest. *Upright, just, conscientious, scrupulous, honorable.

Ana. Truthful, veracious (see corresponding nouns at TRUTH): candid, open, plain, *frank: *straightforward, aboveboard, forthright: *fair, equitable, dispassionate, objective.

Ant. Dishonest. — ***Con.*** Mendacious, lying, untruthful, deceitful (see DISHONEST).

honesty. Honesty, honor (*or* **honour**), **integrity, probity** agree in meaning uprightness as evidenced in one's character and actions. **Honesty** implies refusal to lie, steal, defraud, or deceive under any circumstances; as, you can rely on his *honesty;* he is a man of scrupulous *honesty;* "in business matters it [New York in the 1870's] exacted a limpid and impeccable *honesty*" (*E. Wharton*); "this crisis will be surmounted if the Church has the faith and courage, and, above all, the common *honesty,* to face it candidly" (*Inge*). **Honor,** as here compared (see FAME), adds to *honesty* the implication of high-mindedness or a nice sense of allegiance to the standards of one's profession, calling, or position; as, business *honor* is the foundation of trade; "I could not love thee, dear, so much, Lov'd I not *honour* more" (*Lovelace*); "The fourth generation of Ralstons had nothing left in the way of convictions save an acute sense of *honour* in private and business matters" (*E. Wharton*). **Integrity** implies such rectitude that one is incorruptible or incapable of being false to a trust or a responsibility or to one's own standards; as, "his unimpeachable *integrity* as treasurer of a widows' and orphans' fund" (*N. Hawthorne*). "The poet's sense of responsibility to nothing but his own inner voice, is perhaps his only way of preserving poetic *integrity* against the influences of a perverse generation" (*Day Lewis*). **Probity** stresses tried or proved honesty or integrity; as, "That sort of *probity* which such men as Bailey possess" (*Keats*); "as a man of indisputable *probity*...Geake was entrusted with many odd jobs of this kind [collecting rents]" (*Quiller-Couch*).

Ana. Veracity, *truth, verity: uprightness, justness,

conscientiousness, scrupulousness (see corresponding adjectives at UPRIGHT): candidness *or* candor, openness, plainness, frankness (see corresponding adjectives at FRANK): reliability, trustworthiness, dependability (see corresponding adjectives at RELIABLE): rectitude, virtue, *goodness.

Ant. Dishonesty. — *Con.* Untruthfulness, deceitfulness, mendaciousness *or* mendacity (see corresponding adjectives at DISHONEST): guile, duplicity, *deceit.

honor *or* **honour,** *n.* **1** Glory, renown, *fame, celebrity, éclat, reputation, repute, notoriety.

Ana. Esteem, respect, *regard, admiration: reverence, veneration, worship, adoration (see under REVERE): prestige, credit, authority, *influence, weight.

Ant. Dishonour. — *Con.* *Disgrace, disrepute, shame, ignominy, infamy.

2 Honor (*or* **honour**), **homage, reverence, deference, obeisance** are here compared as words meaning respect or esteem shown another as his due or claimed by him as a right. **Honor** may apply to the recognition of one's title to great respect or esteem or to any expression or manifestation of such respect and esteem; as, to hold every good and conscientious man in high *honor;* he declined the *honor* that was offered him. **Homage** (as here considered: see ALLEGIANCE, 1) adds to *honor* implications of accompanying praise or tributes of esteem, especially from those who owe allegiance or service; as, "All these are... Thy gentle ministers, who come to pay Thee *homage,* and acknowledge thee their Lord" (*Milton*). In its extended use, the term carries a stronger implication of a worshipful attitude than *honor* carries; as, "To the poetry of Byron the world has ardently paid *homage*" (*Arnold*); " 'They say I'm handsome.' 'You're lovely, Bella!' She drank in his *homage*" (*Meredith*). **Reverence** (as here considered: see also REVERENCE) implies profound respect mingled with love or devotion; as, "In general those parents have the most *reverence* who deserve it" (*Johnson*); "What a sweet *reverence* is that when a young man...almost chides himself for longing to bring her [his beloved] close to his heart" (*N. Hawthorne*). **Deference** implies such respect for the person or his position, or such reverence for his personality, or such honor for his years or achievements, or the like, that one courteously yields or submits one's own judgment, opinion, or preference to his; as, the arrangements for the flower show were altered out of *deference* to the wishes of the duchess; "A certain *deference,* not to say servility, to the heads of colleges is perhaps necessary to a physician that means to establish himself here" (*Gray*); "a carriage [i.e., a bearing] which, while it indicated *deference* to the court, indicated also habitual self-possession and self-respect" (*Macaulay*); "An attitude of hostility to aristocracy because it was aristocracy, was as incomprehensible to him as an attitude of *deference*" (*Galsworthy*). **Obeisance** implies a show of honor or reverence by some act or gesture that indicates submission, humility, or the like; as, "The Spanish prince was welcomed...by a goodly company of English lords, assembled to pay him their *obeisance*" (*Prescott*). Sometimes, the term is used in place of one of the other words in this group to suggest abject humiliation on the part of the one who pays honor or reverence; as, "a throne to which conquered nations yielded *obeisance*" (*Steele*).

Ana. Recognition, acknowledgment (see corresponding verbs at ACKNOWLEDGE): adulation, *compliment: tribute, panegyric, eulogy, *encomium.

Con. Contempt, disdain, scorn, despite (see under DESPISE).

3 *Honesty, integrity, probity.

Ana. Uprightness, justness, honorableness, scrupulousness, conscientiousness (see corresponding adjectives at UPRIGHT): *truth, veracity: straightforwardness, forthrightness (see corresponding adjectives at STRAIGHTFORWARD): rectitude, virtue (see GOODNESS).

honorable *or* **honourable. 1 Honorable** (*or* **honourable**), **honorary** are sometimes not clearly distinguished. **Honorable** commonly applies to that which is worthy of honor, as in being noble, high-minded, or the like; as, an *honorable* calling; *honorable* service; an *honorable* man. It is also used as a prefix to the names of some persons of distinction, such as members of parliament or of congress, mayors, certain scions of the nobility, and the like (as, *Honorable* T. B. Reed; the *Honorable* Herbert Asquith), and as a merely courteous appellation in speaking of an opponent in a debate, controversy, and the like (as, my *honorable* colleague says...). **Honorary** regularly and *honorable* occasionally apply to that which is conferred, awarded, or given as an honor; as, an *honorary* degree; *honorable* mention; an *honorary* title. *Honorary* (but not *honorable*) is also used before a title of an office, or the like, which is held without emolument or without responsibility for services; as, the *honorary* president of a society.

Ana. Respected, esteemed, admired (see corresponding verbs under REGARD, *n.*): illustrious, eminent, distinguished (see FAMOUS).

2 *Upright, just, scrupulous, conscientious, honest.

Ana. Trustworthy, *reliable, dependable: noble, virtuous, righteous, *moral, ethical.

Ant. Dishonorable.

honorary. *Honorable.

hoodwink, *v.* Hoax, trick, *dupe, gull, befool, bamboozle.

Ana. Delude, *deceive, mislead: cozen, *cheat, overreach: *confuse, muddle, fuddle, befuddle, bemuddle: baffle, outwit, circumvent (see FRUSTRATE).

hop, *v.* *Skip, bound, curvet, lope, lollop, ricochet.

hope, *v.* *Expect, look, look for, await.

Ana. Aspire, *aim, pant: yearn, *long, hunger, thirst, pine: *rely, trust, depend, count, bank, reckon: anticipate, *foresee, foreknow, divine.

Ant. Despair (*of*): despond.

hopeful. Hopeful, optimistic, roseate, rose-colored are here compared as meaning having or showing confidence that the end or outcome will be favorable or for the best. **Hopeful,** which is often used in distinction from *sanguine* (see CONFIDENT) usually implies some ground, often reasonably good grounds, for one's having hope: it therefore typically, but not invariably, suggests confidence in which there is little or no self-deception or which is the result of a realistic consideration of the possibilities; as, "the air of youth, *Hopeful* and cheerful" (*Milton*); "I may (without being too...sanguine) affirm ...that...my affairs were never in so fair and *hopeful* a way" (*Ludlow*); "I am *hopeful* of purification [in politics], but not sanguine" (*J. R. Lowell*). **Optimistic** usually implies a temperamental confidence that all will turn out for the best: unlike *hopeful,* it often, but far from commonly, suggests a failure to consider things closely and realistically or, even, a willingness to be guided by illusions rather than by facts; as, "the *optimistic* or sentimental hypothesis that wickedness always fares ill in the world" (*J. Morley*); "The barren *optimistic* sophistries Of comfortable moles" (*Arnold*). Sometimes, however, the term carries a suggestion not of weakness but of a fundamental faith in the triumph of good or right. "There is a species of discontent which is more fervently *optimistic* than all the cheerfulness the world can boast" (*A. Repplier*). **Roseate** and **rose-colored,** in their figurative senses only, imply the optimism of an aboundingly cheerful temperament which enables such a one to see persons, events, situations, and the like, "through *rose-colored* spectacles," that is, in their most attractive and alluring aspects. The terms definitely imply illusion or delusion and therefore connote an element of falsity, though not necessarily intentional falsity; as, "A persuasive person who could depict the merits of his scheme with *roseate* but delusive eloquence" (*G. Smith*); a *rose-colored* view of the world's future.

Ana. Expecting, hoping, awaiting (see EXPECT): anticipating, foreseeing, divining (see FORESEE): sanguine, sure, *confident, assured.

Ant. Hopeless, despairing. — *Con.* *Despondent, desperate, forlorn: pessimistic, *cynical.

hopeless. Despairing, *despondent, desperate, forlorn.

Ana. Dejected, depressed, melancholy, sad (see corresponding nouns at SADNESS): gloomy, glum, morose (see SULLEN): acquiescent (see COMPLIANT).

Ant. Hopeful. — *Con.* Optimistic, roseate, rose-colored (see HOPEFUL): *confident, assured, sanguine, sure.

hopelessness. Despair, despondency, desperation, forlornness. See under DESPONDENT.

Ana. Dejection, depression, melancholy, gloom (see SADNESS).

Ant. Hopefulness. — *Con.* Optimism (see corresponding adjective at HOPEFUL): *confidence, assurance, aplomb: *courage, spirit, tenacity, resolution.

horde, *n.* **1** *Tribe, sib, clan, sept.

2 Mob, throng, *crowd, crush, press, rout.

horizon. Purview, ken, compass, reach, *range, scope, sweep, radius, orbit, gamut.

Ana. *Limit, bound, confine, term, bourn, end: spread, stretch, amplitude, *expanse.

horrendous. Horrific, *horrible, horrid.

horrible. **1** **Horrible, horrid, horrific, horrendous** agree in meaning inspiring horror or abhorrence. **Horrible** (see also FEARFUL, 2) is the general term for that which inspires horror; as, "some... *horrible* form, Which might deprive your sovereignty of reason" (*Shak.*); "wrongs and shames, *Horrible*, hateful, monstrous, not to be told" (*Tennyson*). **Horrid,** often practically synonymous with *horrible*, sometimes carries a stronger implication of inherent or innate offensiveness or repulsiveness; as, "This emperor ... from Rome retired To Capreae ... with purpose there His *horrid* lusts in private to enjoy" (*Milton*); "some *horrid* beliefs from which...human nature revolts" (*Bagehot*). In modern colloquial usage the word is often weakened to a general term of aversion; as, *horrid* weather; *horrid* little boys. **Horrific** (see also FEARFUL, 2), a somewhat bookish term, stresses the power to horrify; as, "She was a brave narrator..., her voice sinking into a whisper over the supernatural or the *horrific*" (*Stevenson*). **Horrendous** is rarely used except in producing a literary effect, such as the suggestion of extreme frightfulness, an apt rhyme for *tremendous* or *stupendous*, or an onomatopoeic rhythm; as, "Damnings most dreadful...Execrations *horrendous*, Blasphemies *stupendous*" (*E. Hooker*).

Ana. Abhorrent, abominable, detestable, *hateful: *repugnant, repellent, obnoxious: *offensive, repulsive, revolting, loathsome.

Ant. Fascinating. —*Con.* *Pleasant, pleasing, grateful, gratifying: attractive, alluring, charming, enchanting, taking (see under ATTRACT).

2 Horrific, shocking, appalling, *fearful, awful, dreadful, frightful, terrible, terrific.

Ana., Ant., & *Con.* See those at HORRIBLE, 1.

horrid. *Horrible, horrific, horrendous.

Ana. Distasteful, repellent, *repugnant, obnoxious: loathsome, *offensive, revolting, repulsive.

Ant. Delightful. — *Con.* Attractive, alluring, fascinating, taking, charming (see under ATTRACT): *pleasant, pleasing, gratifying, grateful.

horrific. **1** *Horrible, horrid, horrendous.

Ana. Horrifying, appalling, dismaying, daunting (see DISMAY, *v.*): terrorizing, terrifying, frightening, alarming (see FRIGHTEN).

2 Horrible, terrible, terrific, shocking, appalling, *fearful, awful, dreadful, frightful.

Ana. See those at HORRIFIC, 1.

horrify. Daunt, appall, *dismay.

Ana. Agitate, upset, perturb, *discompose: *offend, outrage.

Con. Delight, rejoice, gladden, gratify, *please.

horror. Terror, *fear, dread, fright, alarm, dismay, consternation, panic, trepidation.

Ana. Aversion, *antipathy: repugnance, abhorrence, repellency *or* repulsion, distastefulness *or* distaste (see corresponding adjectives at REPUGNANT): recoiling *or* recoil, flinching, shrinking, blenching (see corresponding verbs at RECOIL).

Ant. Fascination.

hors d'oeuvre. *Appetizer, antipasto, smörgåsbord, apéritif.

horse sense. See SENSE, *n.*, 2.

hospitable. *Social, gregarious, convivial, co-operative, companionable.

Ana. Sociable, *gracious, cordial, genial, affable: generous, *liberal, bountiful: friendly, neighborly, *amicable.

Ant. Inhospitable. — *Con.* Churlish, boorish (see under BOOR): *indifferent, aloof, detached: reserved, taciturn, uncommunicative (see SILENT).

host. *Multitude, army, legion.

hostage. Gage, pawn, *pledge, earnest, token.

Ana. Surety, security, *guarantee, guaranty.

hostility. *Enmity, animosity, antagonism, antipathy, rancor, animus.

Ana. Hatred, *hate: ill will, malevolence, malignity, *malice: aggression, *attack: opposing *or* opposition, combating, resisting *or* resistance (see corresponding verbs at OPPOSE).

Con. *Friendship, amity, comity, good will: forbearance, tolerance, clemency, leniency, indulgence (see under FORBEARING).

hound, *v.* Ride, hector, *bait, badger, heckle, chevy.

Ana. Harry, harass, *worry, annoy: torment, torture, try, *afflict: persecute, oppress, *wrong.

house, *n.* Residence, dwelling, abode, domicile, home, *habitation.

house, *v.* Lodge, board, shelter, *harbor, entertain.

Ana. Accommodate, hold, *contain.

Con. Evict, *eject, oust, expel, dismiss.

hover. *Flit, flutter, flitter, flicker.

Ana. *Hang, suspend: poise, balance (see STABILIZE): float, *fly, skim, sail.

however. *But, still, nevertheless, yet.

howler. Boner, bloomer, floater, *error, mistake, blunder, slip, lapse, faux pas, bull.

hub, *n.* Core, *center, middle, nucleus, heart, focus, midst, omphalos.

hubbub. *Din, uproar, pandemonium, hullabaloo, babel, racket.

hue. Chroma, *color, shade, tint, tinge.

huff, *n.* Dudgeon, pique, resentment, *offense, umbrage.

Ana. Petulance, huffiness, irritability, fractiousness (see corresponding adjectives at IRRITABLE): *anger, indignation, rage, wrath.

huffy. Petulant, pettish, *irritable, fractious, peevish, snappish, waspish, fretful, querulous.
Ana. *Angry, mad, indignant, irate.

huge. *Enormous, gigantic, giant, gigantean, colossal, mammoth, elephantine, immense, vast, titanic, herculean, Cyclopean, Antaean, Gargantuan, Brobdingnagian.
Ana. Stupendous, tremendous, prodigious, monumental, *monstrous: big, great, *large.

hull, *v.* Shell, *husk, shuck.

hullabaloo. *Din, uproar, pandemonium, babel, hubbub, racket.

humane. Humanitarian, *charitable, benevolent, philanthropic, altruistic.
Ana. Compassionate, *tender, warmhearted: gentle, lenient, mild (see SOFT): clement, merciful, tolerant, *forbearing: kindly, *kind, benign, benignant.
Ant. Barbarous, inhuman: atrocious. — *Con.* Savage, cruel, fell (see FIERCE): merciless, relentless, implacable (see GRIM).

humanitarian. Humane, benevolent, philanthropic, *charitable, altruistic.

humanities. *Literature, belles-lettres, letters.

humble, *adj.* **Humble, meek, modest, lowly** are here compared as meaning lacking all signs of pride, self-assertiveness, or the like, either in spirit or in outward show. All are applicable to persons and their attitudes and manners, and all but *meek* may also be applied to homes, occupations, interests, and the like. **Humble** may suggest a virtue that consists in the absence of pride in oneself or in one's achievements and, in religious use, a consciousness of one's weakness and a disposition to ascribe to the Supreme Being any credit for what one is or what one does that is meritorious; as, "God resisteth the proud, but giveth grace unto the *humble*" (*James* iv. 6); "Knowledge is proud that he has learned so much; Wisdom is *humble* that he knows no more" (*Cowper*). In current usage, *humble* often connotes undue self-depreciation or humiliation, sometimes verging on abjectness; as, "She is *humble* to abjectness" (*De Quincey*). As applied to a person's circumstances, *humble* suggests low rank, or poverty, or insignificance; as, a man of *humble* extraction; "a *humble* Mexican family" (*Cather*); "he regarded no task as too *humble* for him to undertake" (*A. Huxley*). **Meek** also, especially in Christian use, may imply a virtue evident not only in the absence of passion or wrath, but in a consistent mildness or gentleness of temper; as, "a *meek* and quiet spirit, which is in the sight of God of great price" (*1 Peter* iii. 4). In current use, however, the term so often additionally suggests spiritlessness or undue submissiveness that even when it is employed without derogation these ideas are often connoted. "Stephen's face grew serious....'I'm sorry I upset you.' Oh, so he was going to be *meek* and Christian! Tony wasn't going to stand that either" (*Arch. Marshall*). "*Meek, humble,* timid persons, who accept things as they are...who are cautious, prudent, and submissive, leave things very much as they find them" (*A. C. Benson*). **Modest** is now often preferred to *humble* in describing a person who takes no credit to himself for what he is or for what he does; the term usually connotes a lack of boastfulness or show of conceit, but it does not necessarily imply, as *humble* often does imply, a deep conviction of one's unworthiness or inferiority. "The model of an eighteenth-century parish priest...just, *modest*...loved and esteemed by all" (*H. Ellis*). As applied to things, such as a home, a position, a price, and the like, *modest* suggests neither extreme lowness nor the opposite, but a reasonable and often unobtrusive medium between extremes; as, to live in *modest* circumstances; "the terms [for a room] were *modest*, but the respectability was prodigious" (*Bennett*). **Lowly** is often indistinguishable from *humble* except in its lack of derogatory connotations such as abjectness, sense of inferiority, or the like; as, "Surely he scorneth the scorners: but he giveth grace unto the *lowly*" (*Proverbs* iii. 34); "Thy heart The *lowliest* duties on herself did lay" (*Wordsworth*).
Ana. Submissive, subdued (see TAME): resigned, acquiescent, *compliant.
Con. *Proud, arrogant, insolent, haughty, lordly, overbearing, disdainful: vain, vainglorious, proud (see under PRIDE, *n.*): pompous, ostentatious, pretentious, *showy.

humble, *v.* Humiliate, *abase, demean, debase, degrade.
Ana. Abash, discomfit, *embarrass: chagrin, mortify (see corresponding adjectives at ASHAMED).
Con. *Exalt, magnify, aggrandize.

humbug, *n.* Fake, sham, *imposture, cheat, fraud, deceit, deception, counterfeit, simulacrum.
Ana. *Pretense, pretension, make-believe, make-belief: *impostor, faker, charlatan, mountebank: hocus-pocus, mummery, *gibberish, abracadabra.

humdrum. *Irksome, tiresome, wearisome, tedious.
Ana. Prosy, *prosaic, matter-of-fact: *stupid, dull.
Ant. Lively. — *Con.* Gay, animated, sprightly, vivacious (see LIVELY): enlivening, quickening, vivifying (see QUICKEN): exciting, stimulating, provoking *or* provocative (see corresponding verbs at PROVOKE).

humid. Moist, damp, *wet, dank.
Con. *Dry, arid.

humiliate. Humble, degrade, debase, demean, *abase.
Ana. Mortify, chagrin (see corresponding adjectives at ASHAMED): confound, bewilder, nonplus (see PUZZLE): *embarrass, discomfit, abash, disconcert, faze, rattle.

humor *or* **humour,** *n.* **1** *Mood, temper, vein.
Ana. *Caprice, freak, whim, whimsey, vagary, crotchet: attitude, *position, stand.
2 *Wit, irony, satire, sarcasm, repartee.

humor *or* **humour,** *v.* *Indulge, pamper, spoil, baby, mollycoddle.
Ana. Gratify, delight, *please, rejoice, gladden, tickle: content, *satisfy.

humorous. *Witty, facetious, jocular, jocose.
Ana. Droll, comic, comical, farcical, funny, *laughable: amusing, diverting, entertaining (see AMUSE).
Con. Grave, *serious, earnest, solemn, sober.

hunger, *v.* Yearn, hanker, pine, thirst, *long.
Ana. Crave, *desire, covet, wish, want.

hurl. Fling, cast, *throw, pitch, toss, sling.
Con. *Catch, capture, nab, cop: grasp, clutch, seize, grab, *take.

hurrah. Huzza, root, cheer, *applaud.

hurricane. Gale, whirlwind, cyclone, typhoon, tornado, waterspout, twister, *wind, breeze, flaw, zephyr, gust, blast.

hurry, *v.* *Speed, quicken, precipitate, hasten.
Ana. Impel, drive, *move.
Ant. Delay. — *Con.* Retard, slow, slacken, detain (see DELAY): procrastinate, lag, loiter, dally, dawdle (see DELAY).

hurry, *n.* *Haste, speed, dispatch, expedition.
Ana. Swiftness, rapidity, expeditiousness, quickness, speediness (see corresponding adjectives at FAST): *celerity, alacrity, legerity: flurry, *stir, bustle, pother, ado.

hurt, *v.* *Injure, harm, damage, impair, mar, spoil.
Ana. *Afflict, torture, torment: *trouble, distress: *wrong, oppress, persecute, aggrieve.

hurt, *n.* *Injury, harm, damage, mischief.

Ana. *Pain, ache, pang, throe, twinge, stitch: *injustice, wrong, tort, grievance.

husbandry. Farming, *agriculture.

husk, *v.* **Husk, hull, shell, shuck** (*or* **shock**) agree in meaning to divest something, especially a vegetable or nut, of its covering or envelope. **Husk** implies the removal of the outer envelope (called *husk* or *husks*), originally of certain grains, seeds, or nuts, but now usually, especially in the United States, of the leafy outer covering of an ear of Indian corn; thus, a *husking* bee is a gathering of the neighbors to help a farmer in *husking* his corn at harvest time. **Hull** originally implied the removal of the pods or similar envelopes of peas, beans, and the like, but in current use, **shell** is more often applied to this process; as, to *shell* peas or Lima beans. *Hull,* on the other hand, is now used to imply the removal of the calyx or leafy circle out of which some berries grow (as, to *hull* strawberries) or the removal of the tough outer covering of a grain of corn, of rice, or the like. *Shell* is applicable not only to vegetables with a pod but also to nuts and to mollusks, or the like, which are covered by a hard shell; as, to *shell* peanuts; to *shell* pecans; to *shell* oysters. **Shuck,** or the dialect form **shock,** is now rarely used except colloquially or locally. It sometimes takes the place of *husk* in reference to Indian corn, but it is usable, where *shell* is the preferred term, to imply the removal of pods, nutshells, and the shells of mollusks; as, to *shuck* corn; to *shuck* chestnuts; to *shuck* oysters. It is also applicable to the removal of anything which suggests an outer envelope; as, to *shuck* off one's clothes before taking a swim.

husky. *Muscular, brawny, sinewy, athletic, burly.
Ana. Stalwart, stout, *strong, sturdy, tough: *powerful, puissant, potent, forceful.

hussy *or* **huzzy.** *Wench, minx, baggage.

huzza. Hurrah, root, cheer, *applaud.

hygienic. Sanitary, *healthful, healthy, wholesome, salubrious, salutary.

hymeneal. Nuptial, marital, connubial, conjugal, *matrimonial.

hymn. Hymn, laud, psalm, canticle, antiphon, anthem, canon are comparable when they mean a sacred song, especially one used in a religious service. **Hymn,** though historically applied to any rhapsodic poem of praise or worship, is in popular (as distinguished from scholarly) English commonly restricted to a song suitable for use in worship, especially one adapted to congregational singing. In this application, it often suggests supplication or thanksgiving as its motive, as well as praise or adoration. **Laud,** a somewhat literary word, means distinctively a hymn of praise. **Psalm** usually, and **canticle** in older liturgical use (especially in the canonical hours), both imply a Biblical source; the former is applied to any of the songs which comprise the Old Testament Book of Psalms, and the latter to other Biblical hymns of praise such as the Magnificat (the response of the Virgin Mary to Elizabeth's salutation: *Luke* i. 46–55) or the Benedicite (the song of the three children in the fiery furnace: *Daniel* iii. 57 ff. *D.V.*). Only the Benedicite is designated a *canticle* in the Book of Common Prayer, but the term is often applied to other Biblical hymns of praise, including some psalms, and to the Te Deum. *Psalm* is sometimes used of any more or less spontaneous hymn (or poem) that represents the outpouring of the heart in praise, in supplication, or the like. "When ye come together, every one of you hath a *psalm,* hath a doctrine, hath a tongue" (*1 Corinthians* xiv. 26). **Antiphon** designates a piece of verse or prose sung responsively as part of a liturgy. **Anthem,** which is etymologically a corrupt form derived from the same root as *antiphon,* no longer implies responsive singing. It is applied to a type of hymn that has a musical setting suitable for choral rather than congregational singing. "To Psalms and Hymns we may aspire, If *Anthems* are too high" (*C. Wesley*). In extended use, it is also applied to any serious or impassioned song of praise or glorification, as of a hero or of one's country; as, the national *anthem.* **Canon** is a technical term of the Orthodox and other Eastern churches, applied to a long liturgical hymn consisting of several parts (often nine), each of which follows the structure of an ode.

hypercritical. Captious, caviling, carping, censorious, faultfinding, *critical.
Ana. Finical, fastidious, fussy, pernickety, squeamish, particular (see NICE).

hypersensitivity, hypersensitiveness. *Susceptibility, allergy, anaphylaxis.

hypochondriac, hypochondriacal. *Melancholic, melancholy, atrabilious.

hypocrisy. Hypocrisy, sanctimony (*or* **sanctimoniousness**), **pharisaism, cant, canting,** as here compared, mean the pretense or affectation of being more virtuous or more religious than one actually is. The same differences in implications and connotations are found in their corresponding adjectives, **hypocritical** (*or, rare,* **hypocritic**), **sanctimonious, pharisaical** (*or* **pharisaic**), **canting. Hypocrisy** and **hypocritical,** the most inclusive of these terms, imply an assumption of goodness, sincerity, piety, or the like, by one who is either not good, sincere, or pious, or is actually corrupt, dishonest, or irreligious. "I thought where all thy circling wiles would end— In feigned religion, smooth *hypocrisy*" (*Milton*). "Be *hypocritical,* be cautious, be Not what you seem but always what you see" (*Byron*). "Archer's New York tolerated *hypocrisy* in private relations; but in business matters it exacted a limpid and impeccable honesty" (*E. Wharton*). "Much of the religiosity which unwise parents delight to observe in their children is...innocent *hypocrisy*" (*Inge*). **Sanctimony** and **sanctimonious,** once terms of approbation implying personal holiness, are now exclusively terms of opprobrium implying an affectation or merely outward pretense of such holiness or of piety; as, he took pleasure in comparing the sanctity of the early Christians with the *sanctimony* of many modern churchgoers; the preacher urged his flock to seek holiness but to take care lest they fall into *sanctimony; sanctimonious* professions of faith. **Pharisaism** (literally, the beliefs and practices of the Pharisees, the strictest sect of ancient Jews, who were insistent on close and unfailing observance of the written law and of traditional ceremonies and rites), and **pharisaical** imply a stern and censorious attitude to the manners and morals of others, or a conviction of one's own moral superiority, or both (cf. *Luke* xviii. 10–14): the term frequently suggests sanctimony or, less often, out-and-out hypocrisy; as, the self-righteousness of many leaders of reform movements had brought upon them and their followers the accusation of *pharisaism;* "Of all the *Pharisaisms* of the day, our Churchgoing seems to me the masterpiece" (*Pusey*); "the assured, the positive, the *Pharisaical* temper, that believes itself to be impregnably in the right and its opponents indubitably in the wrong" (*A. C. Benson*). **Cant** (as here compared: see also JARGON) and **canting** (both noun and adjective) commonly imply the use of religious or pietistic language or phraseology in such a way as to suggest sanctimony or hypocrisy rather than genuine holiness or deep religiousness; often, however, especially in current use, the terms suggest reference not only to such outward indications of sanctimony and hypocrisy, but to the state of mind or the attitude of one who is so pharisaical, or so deeply convinced of his righteousness or holiness, that he is unaware that he is displaying his religion in a mechanical or perfunctory rather than in a sincere manner and in a spirit of arrogance rather than of humility; as, *canting* preachers; a *canting* assumption of one's righteousness. "What he [Byron] called the *cant* of the great middle part of the English nation...revolted him....'Come what may,' are his own words, 'I will never flatter the million's *canting* in any shape' " (*Arnold*). "The whole spiritual atmosphere was saturated with *cant*...an affectation of high principle which had ceased to touch the conduct, and flowed on in...insincere and unreal speech" (*Froude*). "One of those rare artists...who, by virtue of some inward grace, constantly flowing through the intellect, purge the mind of *cant*" (*Van W. Brooks*).

Ana. Dissimulation, duplicity, guile, *deceit: *pretense, pretension, make-believe, make-belief.

hypocritical. Sanctimonious, pharisaical, canting. See under HYPOCRISY.

Ana. Unctuous, oily, sleek, *fulsome: feigned, affected, assumed, simulated, shammed, counterfeited, pretended (see ASSUME).

Con. Genuine, veritable, bona fide, *authentic: *sincere, heartfelt, wholehearted, whole-souled, unfeigned.

hypostatize. Reify, externalize, materialize, incarnate, *realize, actualize, embody, objectify, substantiate, substantialize.

hypothesis. Hypothesis, theory, law are often interchangeable in general use. In the technical senses in which they are here considered, however, they are rigidly discriminated by the scientists and philosophers who employ them precisely. In general, the terms denote an inference from data gathered by observation and experiment that is offered as a formula to explain the abstract and general principle that lies behind them as their cause, their method of operation, their relation to other phenomena, or the like. In such usage, **hypothesis** implies tentativeness in the inference because of insufficient evidence or of the impossibility of obtaining further evidence. In such cases, *hypothesis* applies to a well-founded conjecture that serves as a point of departure for scientific discussion or as a tentative guide for further investigation or as the most reasonable explanation of certain phenomena now available. "A scientist says in effect—'Observation shews that the following facts are true; I find that a certain *hypothesis* as to their origin is consistent with them all' " (*Jeans*). "The resemblance to electric polarization is very close; it is in fact so close that it would not be foolish at all to make the *hypothesis* that the iron contains not only electrons but also tiny corpuscles of some subtle magnetic fluid" (*Karl K. Darrow*). "In the last chapter I proposed the *hypothesis* that a pure poetry exists, employing the term 'lyric' to describe poems which 'consist of poetry and nothing else' " (*Day Lewis*). **Theory,** in general use, often means little more than *hypothesis* or *conjecture* (as, " 'let us sit quiet, and hear the echoes about which you have your *theory*.' 'Not a *theory;* it was a fancy' "—*Dickens;* "In the course of my work in Egypt, I had formulated certain *theories* of my own about plague, and could not reconcile them to the findings of the Commission"—*V. Heiser*), but in the precise technical sense in which it is here considered, it presupposes much more supporting evidence than *hypothesis* does, a much wider range of application, and greater likelihood of truth. It is not always obvious when *hypothesis* and when *theory* should be used, the former being preferred by some scientists as the more modest in its claims, the latter being preferred by others as suggesting such confidence in the reliability of the inference and its supporting evidence as to imply that it deserves acceptance; thus, the Darwinian explanation of the origin of species is regarded by some as a *hypothesis*, but is more often designated as the "*theory* of evolution." "That exact verbal expression of as much as we know of the facts, and no more, which constitutes a perfect scientific *theory*" (*T. H. Huxley*). "In 1905 Einstein crystallised these concepts and *hypotheses* in his *theory* of light-quanta, according to which all radiation consisted of discrete bullet-like units, which he called 'light-quanta' at the time, although we now call them 'photons' " (*Jeans*). "There was also a nascent *theory* of sound waves; and out of it there grew...a tremendous mathematical doctrine of waves which nowadays has almost come to dominate the physics of these times" (*Karl K. Darrow*). **Law** (as here considered: for fuller treatment see PRINCIPLE) emphasizes certainty and proof and therefore applies to a statement of an order or relation in phenomena that has been found to be invariable under the same conditions; as, in philology, Grimm's *law* is a statement of the regular changes which the stops, or mute consonants, of the primitive Indo-European consonant system have undergone in the Teutonic languages. However, since even so-called "laws" are open to disproof or alteration by the discovery of contradictory or additional evidence, the term is often changed in the course of time to *theory;* for example, what has long been known as Newton's *law* of gravitation is currently being revised as a result of Einstein's discoveries and is now designated by careful scientists as Newton's mathematical *theory* of universal gravitation.

Ana. Conjecture, surmise, guess (see under CONJECTURE, *v.*): inference, deduction, conclusion (see under INFER).

hypothetical. Conjectural, *supposed, supposititious, reputed, putative.

Ana. *Theoretical, speculative, academic: *doubtful, dubious, problematical, questionable.

Con. *Certain, inevitable, necessary, apodictic: proved, tested, tried, demonstrated (see PROVE).

hysteria. Delirium, frenzy, *mania.

I

icon *or* **eikon, ikon.** *Image, portrait, simulacrum, effigy, statue, photograph, mask.

iconoclast. *Rebel, insurgent.

icy. Glacial, arctic, gelid, *cold, frosty, frigid, freezing, cool, chilly.

Ant. Fiery.

idea. **Idea, concept, conception, thought, notion, impression** are here compared as meaning something which exists in the mind as a representation of that which it apprehends or comprehends, or as a formulation of an opinion, a plan, a design, or the like. **Idea** is the most comprehensive and widely applicable of these terms: it may be used of an image of something at one time or another actually perceived through the senses, or of something never perceived but visualized from bits of information (as, to describe one's *idea* of a penthouse; his *idea* of heaven does not correspond to that of most persons), or of something that is the clearly or vaguely defined product of fancy, imagination, inventive power, or the like (as, "he...invented a new kind of buoy which was found by the authorities to be excellent in *idea*, but impracticable"—*H. Ellis;* "one of those accepted *ideas*, which are always wrong, that China is and was a country of immovable and unchanging traditions"—*Binyon*); it may denote a mere supposition (as, "I had no *idea* that the law had been so great a slavery"—*Austen*), or a good or practical solution or suggestion (as, "A very clever point that....You are really full of *ideas*"—*Shaw;* "all it [the government] desired was *ideas*"—*V. Heiser*), or a ridiculous or preposterous suggestion (as, "Mr. Elton in love with me! What an *idea!*"—*Austen*). **Concept** applies in logic to the idea of a thing which the mind conceives after knowing many instances of the genus, species, or other category, and which is devoid of all details except those that are typical or generic; as, the *concept* of a horse, a table, a mountain; "the author of 'Mein Kampf' has abolished the whole *concept* of the citizen as we have known it from the days of Pericles" (*D. Thompson*). In more general use, the term applies to any formulated and widely accepted idea of what a thing should be; as, "[prose and verse demand] a different *concept* of what the writer should aim at and what avoid" (*Quiller-Couch*); "We find among the Greeks germinal *concepts* which are a vital part of modern thought" (*Buchan*). **Conception** is often used in place of *concept* in this latter sense; in fact, it is sometimes preferred by those who wish to keep *concept* as a technical term of logic. However, *conception* so strongly suggests the activity of the mental power of conceiving, or of bringing into existence, an idea of something not yet realized or not yet given outward form, that it often implies not only the exercise of the reflective powers but of the imagination as colored by feeling: the term therefore more often applies to a peculiar or an individual idea than to one held by men as a whole or by an entire class, profession, or the like; as, compare Poe's *conception* of poetry as "the rhythmical creation of beauty" with the Aristotelian *conception* of it as the imitation of human actions "according to probability and necessity"; "What I needed was...some clear *conception* of the meaning of existence" (*L. P. Smith*). *Conception* is also, especially in literary and art criticism, the preferred term for the idea or design conceived by the writer or artist in advance of or in company with his giving it expression or form; as, Dante's boldness of *conception;* the dramatist's power to express his *conception* with frankness and daring; "the *conception* comes through the actual execution" (*S. Alexander*). **Thought** applies either to an expressed or to an unexpressed idea, especially one that comes into the mind as a result of meditation, reasoning, or contemplation; as, a penny for your *thoughts;* a child's *thoughts* about God; the book is full of noble *thoughts;* he had not a *thought* of disaster. **Notion** often adds to *idea's* implication of vagueness the suggestion of caprice or whim, or of half-formed or tentative purpose or intention; as, "I had no *notion* that he liked me so very much" (*Austen*); "One never does form a just *idea* of anybody beforehand. One takes up a *notion*, and runs away with it" (*Austen*); "modest, sober, cured of all Her *notions* hyperbolical" (*Cowper*). **Impression,** as here compared (see also IMPRESSION, 1), commonly applies to an idea which comes into the mind as the result of an external stimulus; as, I should like to know your first *impressions* of this book; "Poetry...aims at the transmission...of *impressions*, not facts" (*Lowes*); "Looking out over the steep hills, the first *impression* is of an immense void like the sea" (*Jefferies*).

Ana. *Opinion, view, belief, conviction, sentiment: theory, hypothesis, *law.

ideal, *adj.* *Abstract, transcendent, transcendental.

Ana. Utopian (see AMBITIOUS): surpassing, peerless, *supreme.

Ant. Actual.

ideal, *n.* Pattern, exemplar, *model, example, paradigm, beau ideal, standard, mirror.

Ana. Archetype, *prototype: *truth, verity: perfection, *excellence.

identical, identic. **1** Selfsame, *same, very, equivalent, equal, tantamount.

Ana. Correspondent, correlative, convertible (see RECIPROCAL).

Ant. Diverse. — *Con.* *Different, disparate, divergent: *distinct, separate, several.

2 Alike, like, uniform, parallel, *similar, akin, analogous, comparable, homogeneous.

Ana. Matching, equaling (see MATCH): agreeing, squaring, tallying, jibing, corresponding (see AGREE).

Ant. Different.

identification. *Recognition, apperception, assimilation.

Ana. Perception, *discernment, discrimination, clairvoyance, divination: image, percept, *sensation.

identify. **Identify, incorporate, embody, assimilate** come into comparison when they mean to bring (one or more things) into union with another thing. **Identify** always involves the idea of a union of things that are identical, or the same; it may further imply either an actual union, as by making one thing (sometimes things) the same as another, or merely a theoretical union by mentally apprehending one thing as identical with the other. Thus, a man who *identifies* his interests with those of his neighbors may be said consciously to change his interests so that they are in conformity with those of his neighbors; on the other hand, a man who *identifies* his own enrichment with the impoverishing of others may be said merely to view the two things as identical. This latter use frequently connotes confusion in thought or self-deception. "There is not much difference between *identifying* oneself with the Universe and *identifying* the Universe with oneself" (*T. S. Eliot*). **Incorporate** implies a union of one or more things with another, or of different things, so that when blended, fused, or otherwise united they constitute a uniform substance, a single body, or an integral whole; as, fertilizers should, in general, be *incorporated* with the soil; that which is learned is of no value until it is *incorporated* into one's stock of knowledge; writers often unwittingly *incorporate* the ideas of others in their own work. **Embody** (see also REALIZE, 1) is more restricted in its range of application than *incorporate*, because it can be used only when one or more things are made part of another thing that is a body or independent unit, such as an organized structure, a group, or a system. "Yet so much of these treaties has been *embodied* into the general law of Europe" (*J. Mackintosh*). "He is the greatest artist who has *embodied*, in the sum of his works, the greatest number of the greatest ideas" (*Ruskin*). "It is obvious that those whose wishes and opinions were *embodied* in the [Eighteenth] Amendment meant to stop the whole [liquor] business" (*Justice Holmes*). **Assimilate** (see also ABSORB, 1) falls short of *identify* because it does not always imply the actual fusion or blending, or when self-deception is connoted, the actual confusion, of two things. Like *identify*, however, *assimilate* implies the making of two or more things exactly alike, either actually or in thought; thus, to *assimilate* one's beliefs to those of another is merely to cause the former to become the same as the latter; to *identify* one's beliefs with those of another is to make them one and indistinguishable as well as the same; the prefix "af-" is a form of "ad-" *assimilated* in Latin before "*f*," as in "affectus" for "adfectus." "Our manufacturing class was *assimilated* in no time to the conservative classes" (*H. G. Wells*). "The *assimilation* of men to machines...is hardly likely to give us a just standard of values" (*B. Russell*).

Ana. Fuse, blend, merge (see MIX): *mistake, confuse, confound.

idiom. **1** Dialect, *language, speech, tongue.

Ana. Jargon, patois, cant, argot (see DIALECT).

2 Expression, locution, *phrase, collocation.

idiosyncrasy. *Eccentricity.

Ana. Peculiarity, individuality, distinctiveness *or* distinction, characteristicness *or* characteristic (see corresponding adjectives at CHARACTERISTIC): manner, way, *method, mode: mannerism, affectation, *pose.

idiot. Imbecile, moron, *fool, simpleton, natural.

idle, *adj.* **1** *Vain, nugatory, otiose, empty, hollow.

Ana. Fruitless, bootless, *futile, vain: *ineffective, ineffectual, inefficacious: trivial, paltry, *petty, trifling.

Con. Significant, pregnant, meaningful (see EXPRESSIVE): profitable, *beneficial, advantageous.

2 *Inactive, inert, passive, supine.

Ana. Indolent, fainéant, *lazy, slothful: dawdling, dallying, lagging, procrastinating (see DELAY).

Ant. Busy. — ***Con.*** Industrious, diligent, assiduous, sedulous (see BUSY): employed (see EMPLOY, 2).

idolize. *Adore, worship.

Ana. Dote on *or* upon, love, *like: venerate, *revere, reverence.

Con. *Despise, contemn, scorn, disdain: *hate, abhor, detest, loathe, abominate.

if. **If, provided** are both used to introduce conditional clauses. When merely a condition (that is, a possibility which may or may not be true) is expressed, **if** is the usual conjunction; as, "*If* this counsel...be of men, it will come to nought" (*Acts* v. 38). When the clause which follows names a stipulation or proviso, **provided** is the preferred form; as, "It is not hard to know God, *provided* one will not force oneself to define him" (*Arnold*).

ignite. Kindle, enkindle, *light, fire, inflame.

Ant. Stifle: extinguish.

ignoble. *Mean, sordid, abject.

Ana. *Base, low, vile: churlish, boorish, loutish (see under BOOR): *petty, puny, paltry, measly, trivial: abased, debased, degraded (see ABASE).

Ant. Noble: magnanimous. — ***Con.*** Lofty, *high: sublime, glorious, *splendid: illustrious, eminent, distinguished (see FAMOUS).

ignominy. Infamy, shame, *disgrace, opprobrium, dishonor, disrepute, obloquy, odium, scandal.

Ana. Humiliation, degradation, abasement (see corresponding verbs at ABASE): contempt, scorn, disdain, despite (see under DESPISE): mortification, chagrin (see corresponding adjectives at ASHAMED).

Con. Honor, glory (see FAME): respect, esteem, admiration, *regard.

ignorant. **Ignorant, illiterate, unlettered, uneducated, untaught, untutored, unlearned, nescient** agree in meaning not having knowledge. One is **ignorant** who is without knowledge, whether in general or of some particular thing; as, "a very superficial, *ignorant*, unweighing fellow" (*Shak.*); "the disputants on both sides were *ignorant* of the matter they were disputing about" (*H. Ellis*). One is **illiterate,** in the strict interpretation of that term, who is without the necessary rudiments of education. In the eighteenth century this term often implied ignorance of Latin or Greek; as, "an *illiterate* Portuguese friar, who understood no language but his own" (*Fielding*); "The word *illiterate*, in its common acceptation, means a man who is ignorant of those two languages [Greek and Latin]" (*Chesterfield*). In somewhat later and still current use, *illiterate* often implies a failure to attain a standard set for the educated or cultivated man; as, "You might read all the books in the British Museum (if you could live long enough), and remain an utterly *illiterate*, uneducated person" (*Ruskin*). In current English, both in Great Britain and in America, the term when directly applied to a person usually implies inability to read or write the English language or another language (as, *illiterate* voters); when applied to words or corruptions of words, grammatical constructions, and the like, it implies violation of the principles which govern the usage of educated men or a status far below that of the standard English of the day; thus, most authorities would stigmatize the expression "awful nice" as *illiterate*. The word, however, is often used merely as a contemptuous description of a person, an utterance, a letter, etc., that shows little evidence of education or cultivation (as, his speech is positively *illiterate*), or who shows inability to read and understand. "It is common knowledge that our professional students and candidates for the Ph.D. are *illiterate*. One thing you learn very quickly in teaching students at the loftiest levels of education is that they cannot read" (*R. M. Hutchins*). One is **unlettered** who is without the learning that is to be gained through the knowledge of books. Often it implies mere knowledge of how to read and write, but the absence of facility in both reading and writing (as, *unlettered* peasants); sometimes, however, it implies general ignorance or illiteracy (as, "His [Prince Hal's] addiction was to courses vain, His companies [companions] *unlettr'd*, rude and shallow"—*Shak.*). One is **uneducated, untaught, untutored,** or **unlearned** who either has had no training in the schools or under teachers or whose ignorance, or crudeness, or general lack of intelligence suggests such a lack; none of the words, however, is used with great precision or in a strict sense; as, among *uneducated* men; *untaught* savages; "Lo, the poor Indian! whose *untutor'd* mind Sees God in clouds, or hears him in the wind" (*Pope*); plays which make no appeal to the *unlearned*. **Nescient** seldom applies directly to persons, but rather to their minds, their natures, and the like, or to abstractions such as humanity, or mankind, or nature. In such use the term implies invincible ignorance of all that is not apparent to the senses or apprehensible by the intellect; as, "Most men are not intended to be any wiser than their cocks and bulls—duly scientific of their yard and pasture, peacefully *nescient* of all beyond" (*Ruskin*).

Ana. *Rude, crude, raw, callow, green: simple, ingenuous, unsophisticated, naïve (see NATURAL).

Ant. Cognizant (*of something*): conversant: informed. — *Con.* *Learned, erudite, polymathic, scholarly: conscious, *aware.

ignore. Disregard, overlook, slight, *neglect, omit, forget.

Ana. Blink, *wink (at): evade, elude, *escape, avoid, shun, eschew.

Ant. Heed (*a warning, a sign, a symptom, etc.*): acknowledge (sense 2).

ikon. Variant of ICON.

ilk. Kind, sort, *type, nature, description, character, stripe, kidney.

ill, *adj.* **1** *Bad, evil, wicked, naughty.

Ana. See those at EVIL.

Ant. Good.

2 *Sick.

Ant. Well.

ill, *n.* *Evil, bale.

Ant. Good.

illation. Ratiocination, *inference.

Ana. *Deduction, induction: reasoning, reflection, cogitation, deliberation, speculation, thinking (see corresponding verbs at THINK): *reason, understanding.

illative. Ratiocinative, inferential. See under INFERENCE.

illimitable. Boundless, *infinite, uncircumscribed, eternal, sempiternal.

Ana. Endless, never-ending, *everlasting, interminable.

illiterate, *adj.* Unlettered, uneducated, untaught, *ignorant, untutored, unlearned, nescient.

Ant. Literate. — *Con.* Taught, instructed, educated, schooled (see TEACH).

ill-mannered. *Rude, uncivil, ungracious, impolite, discourteous.

Ana. Boorish, loutish, churlish (see under BOOR).

Ant. Well-bred.

ill-treat. Maltreat, mistreat, *abuse, misuse, outrage.

Ana. *Wrong, oppress, persecute, aggrieve: *injure, harm, hurt.

illuminate, illumine *or* **illume. Illuminate, illumine, illume, light, lighten, enlighten, illustrate** are here compared as meaning literally or figuratively to fill with light or to throw light upon. **Illuminate** implies the use of a bright light or of something comparable to it in such a way that what is dark is made bright or what is complicated, obscure, or vague, is made perfectly clear; as, "The oblique band of sunlight....*illuminated* her as her presence *illuminated* the heath" (*Hardy*); "The greatest truths are perhaps those which being simple in themselves *illuminate* a large and complex body of knowledge" (*S. Alexander*); "He longed...to hear more about the life of which her careless words had given him so *illuminating* a glimpse" (*E. Wharton*). **Illumine** is chiefly, and **illume,** as here compared, is always, literary or poetical for *illuminate;* as, "What in me is dark *illumine*" (*Milton*); "no lurid fire of hell or human passion *illumines* their scenes" (*C. W. Eliot*); "When yond same star... Had made his course to *illume* that part of heaven Where now it burns" (*Shak.*); "The beams yet filter through, *illuming* the wide spaces beneath" (*Hudson*). *Light, lighten,* and *enlighten* carry a stronger implication of providing with light for clear seeing than of throwing a light upon. **Light** is the most consistently literal of these terms, though it often carries a suggestion of brightening the way of one who otherwise might stumble or go astray; as, the room was brilliantly *lighted;* "All our yesterdays have *lighted* fools The way to dusty death" (*Shak.*). "Seas roll to waft me, suns to *light* me rise" (*Pope*); "The old man scratched a match, the spark *Lit* up the keyhole of a door" (*Amy Lowell*). **Lighten,** as here compared, usually implies the presence of something comparable to an inner light or glow that shines outwardly; as, "*Lighten* our darkness, we beseech thee, O Lord" (*Book of Common Prayer*); "*Lighten* my spirit with one clear heavenly ray" (*J. Davies*). In current usage, **enlighten** is rare in the literal sense of *lighten* (as, "The quick smile had *enlightened* [her face]"—*Stevenson*), but it is far more common than *lighten* when filling with intellectual or spiritual light is implied. Sometimes the term implies that one has been supplied with information necessary to the understanding of something (as, "In her simplicity she did not know what it [her mistake] was, till a hint from a nodding acquaintance *enlightened* her"—*Hardy*), sometimes it implies sufficient education and experience to enable one to meet all needs and (especially in the adjective *enlightened*) to remove all traces of superstition, prejudice, or intolerance (as, "the civilized and *enlightened* portions of the world at the time of the Declaration of Independence"—*Ch. Just. Taney;* "What, still there! in this *enlightened* age too, since you [ghosts] have been proved not to exist!"—*Shelley*). **Illustrate** (see also EXEMPLIFY) is now used less often than in the past in a sense approaching that of *illuminate,* but it still occurs in the writings and speech of those learned or sensitive writers who have a fine feeling for the specific quality of words. As compared to *illuminate,* it suggests the shedding of luster rather than of light, embellishment rather than elucidation, distinct exhibition rather than a bringing into view; as, "The poet or philosopher *illustrates* his age and country by the efforts of a single mind" (*Gibbon*); "Narrow of vision but steadfast to principles, they [the American Puritans] fronted life resolutely, honouring and *illustrating* the supreme worth of freedom" (*A. Repplier*).

Ana. *Light, inflame, fire, kindle, enkindle: elucidate, *explain: illustrate, *exemplify.

Ant. Darken, obscure. — *Con.* Complicate, involve (see corresponding adjectives at COMPLEX).

illusion. *Delusion, mirage, hallucination.

Ana. *Imagination, fancy, fantasy, phantasy: *sensation, percept, image.

illusory. *Apparent, seeming, ostensible.

Ana. Chimerical, fanciful, visionary, *imaginary, fantastic: delusory, delusive, *misleading, deceptive.

Ant. Factual: matter-of-fact.

☞ *Do not confuse* illusory *with* delusory.

illustrate. 1 Enlighten, *illuminate, illumine, illume, light, lighten.

Ana. *Adorn, embellish: expose, exhibit, display, *show: *reveal, disclose, discover.

Ant. Dim.

2 *Exemplify.

Ana. Elucidate, interpret, *explain, expound: vivify, enliven (see QUICKEN): demonstrate, manifest, *show.

illustration. Example, *instance, case, sample, specimen.

illustrious. Eminent, distinguished, renowned, noted, celebrated, *famous, famed, notorious.

Ana. Glorious, *splendid, resplendent, sublime: outstanding, signal, striking, conspicuous (see NOTICEABLE).

Ant. Infamous. — *Con.* Ignoble, *mean, abject:

ignominious, disgraceful, shameful, infamous, dishonorable, scandalous (see corresponding nouns at DISGRACE).

ill will. *Malice, malevolence, malignity, spite, despite, spleen, grudge.

Ana. Animosity, antipathy, rancor, animus, hostility, *enmity: *hate, hatred.

Ant. Good will: charity.

image. 1 **Image, simulacrum, effigy, statue, icon** (*or* **eikon** *or* **ikon**), **portrait, photograph, mask** are here compared only as meaning a lifelike representation, especially (but not exclusively) of a living being. **Image** (see also SENSATION, 1), in its earliest English sense, denotes a sculptured, cast, or modeled representation, as of a god, a sacred or saintly person, or the like, especially one intended for the veneration of the people. The term is also applicable to a representation of a person made in wax, clay, or other plastic substance, as for use in a museum, waxworks, or the like, or by a sorcerer who wishes to injure or destroy the person through attack on his image; in such cases, however, **simulacrum** (see also IMPOSTURE) is often used. **Effigy** is now commonly limited to images as sculptured (especially on sepulchral monuments as in medieval cathedrals) or engraved (especially on coins), and to the phrase "to burn (or hang) in *effigy*." In the latter use, *effigy* often implies a crude simulacrum in clothes similar to those worn by the original which serves merely as an object on which is inflicted the sort of punishment (burning or hanging) which he is supposed to deserve; as, in some parts of England, Guy Fawkes is burned in *effigy* each fifth of November. **Statue** applies not only to any image for use in a church but to any sculptured, cast, or modeled representation of the entire figure (as distinguished from a *bust* or *head*) of a living or dead person, set up in a conspicuous (often a public) place as a reminder of a person's virtues or achievements or as a memorial or monument; as, a colossal *statue* of Christ on the peak of a high mountain overlooking the harbor; an equestrian *statue* of Washington. **Icon** specifically designates the type of representation of Christ, the Virgin Mary, or a saint, used in Orthodox churches and homes. Because of a literal interpretation of the Second Commandment ("Thou shalt not make unto thee any graven *image*..."—*Exodus* xx. 4), an icon is never a statue but is a painting, a mosaic, or a bas-relief. "The walls were studded with little *ikons* of saints, each one with its guttering lamp before it" (*Buchan*). **Portrait** always implies pictorial representation, especially of the figure or of the face of a person; it may be used of such a representation as is executed by drawing, photographing, engraving, or, in its now common specific sense, by painting; as, the Gilbert Stuart *portraits* of Washington; the latest *portrait* of the chief justice of the Supreme Court. **Photograph** (except in its extended sense of an exact representation, one devoid of all imaginative additions) applies only to a portrait that is made by means of a camera and sensitive plates or films. **Mask,** as here compared, applies only to a sculptured face (or face and neck) or to a molded copy of a face made in wax or plaster; thus, a death *mask* is a copy made very soon after a person has died, especially a cast or impression taken directly from the face of the dead person.

Ana. *Reproduction, copy, duplicate, facsimile, replica: *form, figure, shape.

2 Percept, *sensation.

Ana. *Idea, concept, impression, conception, notion: fabrication, figment (see FICTION): phantasy, *fancy, fantasy.

imaginable. *Imaginative, imaginal, imaginary.

Ana. Realized *or* realizable, conceived *or* conceivable, imagined, envisaged, envisioned (see corresponding verbs at THINK).

Ant. Unimaginable, unconceivable.

imaginal. *Imaginative, imaginable, imaginary.

imaginary, *adj.* 1 **Imaginary, fanciful, visionary, fantastic** (*or* **fantastical**), **chimerical, quixotic** are synonymous adjectives when they are applied to conceptions (or, in some instances, to the persons who form the conceptions) and mean unreal or unbelievable and out of keeping with things as they are (or conceiving such unreal or unbelievable things). That is **imaginary** which is fictitious and purely the product of an active or, especially, an excited imagination; as, "*Imaginary* ills and fancied tortures" (*Addison*); "those nervous persons who may be terrified by *imaginary* dangers are often courageous in the face of real danger" (*H. Ellis*). That is (or, less often, one is) **fanciful** which (or who) indicates a giving rein to the power of conceiving or producing things that have no real counterpart in nature or in fact. "In Wales he found a cottage perfectly roofed with fern....Had a painter put this in a picture, many would have exclaimed: 'How *fanciful!*'" (*Jefferies*). "Rousseau's *fanciful* image of primitive man, uncontaminated by science or art, undepraved by thought" (*Grandgent*). That is **visionary** which, although it seems real and practical to the one who conceives it, is usually the product of a dream or vision or of an unrestrained imagination and is incapable of realization; as, *visionary* schemes for world conquest; "Goldsmith had long a *visionary* project, that...he would go to Aleppo, in order to acquire a knowledge...of any arts peculiar to the East, and introduce them into Britain" (*Boswell*); "This was a *visionary* scheme...a project far above his skill" (*Swift*). One is *visionary* who is given to such dreams, visions, and fancies, and inspired by the hopes they arouse. "If a man happens not to succeed in such an enquiry, he will be thought weak and *visionary*" (*Burke*). That is **fantastic** (see also FANTASTIC, 2) which is, or now more often, seems, extravagantly fanciful or queer and hence incapable of belief or, sometimes, approval. "In words, as fashions, the same rule will hold; Alike *fantastic*, if too new, or old" (*Pope*). "His strange coming, his strange story, his devotion, his early death and posthumous fame—it was all *fantastic*" (*Cather*). That is **chimerical** which is wildly or fantastically visionary or unreal. "An universal institutional Church is as *chimerical* an idea as an universal Empire" (*Inge*). That is (or one is) **quixotic** which (or who) is motivated by extravagantly chivalrous devotion to visionary ideals; as, "His moral attitude to his fellow creatures was that of one who was...*quixotically* high-minded" (*J. M. Robertson*); "To insist upon clemency in the circumstances would...have required *quixotic* courage" (*Buchan*). "The economic notion that our present population...can live on this island [Great Britain] and produce by their work a real income that will give them a rising standard of comfort and leisure, is utterly *quixotic*" (*J. A. Hobson*).

Ana. *Fictitious, fabulous, mythical, legendary, apocryphal: ideal, transcendent, transcendental, *abstract: utopian (see AMBITIOUS): delusory, delusive (see MISLEADING): illusory, seeming, *apparent.

Ant. Real, actual.

2 *Imaginative, imaginal, imaginable.

imagination. **Imagination, fancy, fantasy, phantasy** are here compared as denoting either the power or the function of the mind by which mental images of things are formed, or the exercise of that power as manifested in poetry or other works of art. The meanings of all of these terms have been greatly influenced by changing psychological and aesthetic theories with the result that in the past they have often carried implications or connotations (sometimes denotations) not observable in their current use. **Imagination** is not only the most inclusive of these terms, but, especially in present aesthetic use, it is the freest from derogatory connotations. As an inclusive term it may apply either to the power of forming images of things once known but now absent (often called the *reproductive imagination*) or to the power of forming images of things never seen (or never seen in their entirety), or actually nonexistent, or incapable of actual existence (often called the *productive, inventive, constructive,* or *creative imagination*). The term in the sense of reproductive imagination suggests the use of memory as well as of the image-making power; as, to recall the past in one's *imagination;* her face haunted his *imagination.* In the sense of productive imagination, it usually suggests either a new combination of elements found in one's experience, or an ability to conceive of that which is seen in fragments or on the surface as a complete, perfected, and integral whole; as, a man of no *imagination* is less likely to feel physical fear; with *imagination* enough to see the possible consequences. "And as *imagination* bodies forth The forms of things unknown, the poet's pen Turns them to shapes and gives to airy nothing A local habitation and a name" (*Shak.*). "It is only through *imagination* that men become aware of what the world might be" (*B. Russell*). "Facts...give us wherewithal to think straight and they stimulate the *imagination;* for *imagination,* like reason, cannot run without the gasoline of knowledge" (*Grandgent*). **Fancy,** a contraction from the earlier *fantasy* or *phantasy* (see also FANCY, 2, for all three words), like its original forms, once denoted what is now called the reproductive imagination. Much earlier in their histories all these words, but especially *fancy* and *fantasy,* denoted a whimsical or fantastic notion, a sense now frequently associated with *fancy* (see FANCY, 2). By gradual intermingling of these ideas *fancy* acquired its now common meaning of the power to conceive and give expression to images that are far removed from reality or that represent purely imaginary things. "She saw, with the creative eye of *fancy,* the streets of that gay bathing-place [Brighton] covered with officers" (*Austen*). "The world which any consciousness inhabits is a world made up in part of experience and in part of *fancy*" (*J. W. Krutch*). In aesthetic use, since the late 18th century the tendency has been to make *imagination* and *fancy* antithetical. *Imagination* is often used to designate the power of representing the real (or that which gives an illusion of reality) in its entirety and organic unity and, usually, in its ideal or universal character; *fancy,* the power of inventing the novel and unreal by recombining the elements found in reality. So interpreted, *imagination* represents men not only in their outward but in their inward life, and produces a Hamlet; *fancy* presents them in alien surroundings, or essentially changed in their natural physical and mental constitution, and produces centaurs and Brobdingnagians. "The *imagination,* or shaping or modifying power; the *fancy,* or the aggregative and associative power" (*Coleridge*). **Fantasy** now takes the place of *fancy* in naming the power of unrestrained (often extravagant or delusive) fancy or its exhibition in art. "[Readers]...live a compensatory life of *fantasy* between the lines of print" (*A. Huxley*). **Phantasy,** as here compared (see FANCY, 2), seldom occurs in modern use except in its technical sense of the image-making power in general.

Ana. Invention, creation (see corresponding verbs at INVENT): conceiving *or* conception, realizing *or* realization (see corresponding verbs at THINK).

imaginative. **Imaginative, imaginal, imaginable, imaginary** are not synonymous adjectives but they are sometimes confused because of their verbal likeness. **Imaginative** applies to that which is the product of the imagination or has a character indicating the exercise or the power of the imagination; thus, *imaginative* writings are often distinguished from historical, expository, argumentative, and similar types of writing; an *imaginative* poet is one whose imagination heightens a thing or brings out its fine and almost imperceptible essence. "It is a common fallacy that a writer...can achieve this poignant quality by improving upon his subject-matter, by using his 'imagination' upon it and twisting it to suit his purpose. The truth is that by such a process (which is not *imaginative* at all!) he can at best produce only a brilliant sham" (*Cather*). **Imaginal,** an old and until recently obsolete word meaning of the imagination or within the conceptive powers of the imagination, has been revived, especially by psychologists, to fill the need for an adjective which refers to the imagination only as a function of the mind (rather than as a creative power), or to images as the mental representations which follow a sensation of any sort; thus, a person belongs to one *imaginal* type rather than to another because of his tendency to have sensory images of a particular kind (visual, tactile, auditory, or the like). **Imaginable** often means little more than *conceivable,* but in careful use, it implies that the thing so qualified can be seen or apprehended in a clear mental image; as, "St. Thomas was perhaps of all the apostles the one most easily *imaginable* in the present" (*C. Mackenzie*). **Imaginary** (for fuller treatment see IMAGINARY, 1) implies existence only in the imagination; as, *imaginary* woes; "*Imaginary* Conversations," a book by Walter Savage Landor giving *imaginary* dialogues and *imaginary* letters between famous persons of long ago.

Ana. Imagining, fancying, realizing, conceiving (see THINK): creative, inventive (see corresponding verbs at INVENT).

Con. *Prosaic, prosy, matter-of-fact.

imagine. Conceive, fancy, realize, envisage, envision, *think.

Ana. *Invent, create: fabricate, form, fashion, shape, *make: *conjecture, surmise, guess.

imbecile. Idiot, moron, *fool, simpleton, natural.

imbibe. *Absorb, assimilate.

Ana. *Receive, take, admit, accept: *soak, saturate, steep, impregnate: *permeate, pervade, penetrate, impenetrate: acquire, obtain, *get.

Ant. Ooze, exude.

imbue. Inoculate, leaven, ingrain, *infuse, suffuse.

Ana. *Inform, inspire, fire, animate: impregnate, saturate, *permeate, pervade.

imitate. *Copy, mimic, ape, mock.

Ana. Impersonate, personate (see ACT, *v.*): simulate, feign, counterfeit (see ASSUME): *caricature, burlesque, parody, travesty.

immature. **Immature, unmatured, unripe, unmellow** (*or* **unmellowed**), **unfledged** agree in meaning not fully developed. Except for this denial of full development, the terms agree in implications and connotations with the affirmative adjectives *mature, matured, ripe, mellow, full-fledged* discriminated at MATURE.

Ana. Crude, callow, green, *rude: *premature, precocious, untimely: childish, *childlike.

Ant. Mature. — *Con.* Matured, ripe, mellow, adult, grown-up, full-fledged (see MATURE, *adj.*).

immediate. *Direct.

Ana. *Nearest, next: intuitive, *instinctive.

Ant. Mediate (*knowledge, relation, operation, etc.*): distant (*relatives, etc.*).

immediately. *Directly, instantly, instantaneously, forthwith, straightway, at once, anon, right away.

immense. Vast, *enormous, huge, gigantic, giant, gigantean, colossal, mammoth, elephantine, titanic, herculean, Cyclopean, Antaean, Gargantuan, Brobdingnagian.

Ana. Tremendous, prodigious, stupendous, *monstrous: *large, big, great.

immerse. *Dip, submerge, duck, souse, dunk.

Ana. Drench, *soak, saturate, sop, impregnate: *infuse, imbue, ingrain: engross, absorb (see MONOPOLIZE).

immigrant, *n.* **1** *Stranger, alien, foreigner, outlander, outsider, émigré.

2 *Emigrant.

immigrate. Emigrate. See under EMIGRANT.

immigration. Emigration. See under EMIGRANT.

imminent. *Impending.

Ana. Threatening, menacing (see THREATEN): likely, *probable, possible: *inevitable, ineluctable, inescapable, unavoidable: expected, awaited (see EXPECT).

Con. *Distant, remote, far-off: *doubtful, dubious, questionable, problematical.

☞ *Do not confuse* imminent *with* immanent.

immobile. *Immovable, immotile, immotive.

Ant. Mobile.

immoderate. Inordinate, *excessive, exorbitant, extreme, extravagant.

Ana. *Profuse, lavish, prodigal, exuberant: superabounding, teeming, overflowing (see TEEM).

Ant. Moderate. — *Con.* Temperate (see MODERATE, *adj.*): restrained, curbed, checked, inhibited (see RESTRAIN): reasonable, *rational.

immoral. **Immoral, unmoral, nonmoral, amoral** may all be defined briefly as not moral, yet they are not often interchangeable and are frequently confused, largely because the implications and connotations of the second element are not the same in each compound, but partly also because the meanings of *unmoral* and *amoral* are still not fully established. **Immoral** describes the opposite extreme of that which is *moral*, or ethically good because in accordance with accepted ethical principles or the dictates of one's conscience; it therefore may be translated as ethically wrong and unjustifiable, or sinful. "How *immoral* to impose it [the oath to support the Constitution] on them [judges], if they were to be used as the...knowing instruments for violating what they swear to support!" (*Ch. Just. Marshall*). *Immoral* is often used narrowly to imply illicit sex relations: then it is equal to *licentious* and *lascivious;* as, *immoral* women; to lead a life of *immorality*. Sometimes *immoral* implies reference not to a code or one's conscience, but to one's judgment of what is right or proper under the circumstances. " 'It is one of the worst and most unintelligent forms of *immorality* for two people who irritate each other to expose themselves to misery and anger by living together' " (*R. Macaulay*). **Unmoral** is probably the most loosely used of these words. The best modern writers tend to restrict it, however, to persons (or sometimes to the acts of such persons) who are not moral in the sense that they cannot, because of age, or imbecility or insanity, distinguish right from wrong; thus, idiots are *unmoral* persons whose acts can neither be described as moral nor immoral. "Reynard, like Gulliver, is...pleasing to the child...children being by nature pitiless and *unmoral*" (*A. Repplier*). Sometimes the word is about equal to *conscienceless*. "She was as inconsequent and *unmoral*, this little, flashing, suffering, pretty creature, as the sparkle of sunshine on a rippling wave" (*Deland*). **Nonmoral** implies that the thing so qualified cannot be described as moral in any sense of that word, for it is neither good nor bad ethically and it does not demand any judgment of its rightness or wrongness; as, breathing, walking, eating, and sleeping are *nonmoral* physical acts. **Amoral** originally carried practically the same meaning as *nonmoral*. Careful modern writers, however, tend to distinguish the two. *Nonmoral* is preferred when the word which is qualified names a thing which is by common consent outside the sphere in which moral distinctions apply; *amoral* is preferred when applied to something not customarily or universally exempted from moral judgments; as, perspective is a *nonmoral* element in the art of painting; the painter contended that his representation of the nude was *amoral*. "To make it appear as though wars were not fought by individuals...but either by impersonal and therefore wholly *non-moral* and impassible forces, or else by personified abstractions" (*A. Huxley*). "To the idea of poetry as exclusive, esoteric, *a-moral*, the private affair of the poet...I should oppose the idea of poetry as catholic, diverse in function, moral, everyone's business" (*Day Lewis*). When applied to persons or their acts, *amoral* diverges in its meaning from *unmoral*, for it implies, not inability to distinguish right and wrong, but indifference to, or neglect of, or even defiance of, moral standards, sometimes because of absence of moral principles, sometimes for the sake of one's ends; as, "*amoral* megalomaniacs" (*Current History*); "she was theoretically anti-social and *amoral*" (*H. G. Wells*). "Bismarck...is without doubt a great man, but some of his great acts were not so much *immoral* as...*a-moral*" (*S. Alexander*).

Ana. *Licentious, lewd, lascivious, libertine, libidinous, lecherous, wanton, lustful: *abandoned, profligate, dissolute, reprobate: obscene, gross, ribald (see COARSE).

Ant. Moral: chaste, pure.

immortal. **Immortal, deathless, undying, unfading, fadeless, amaranthine** agree in meaning not subject to death or decay and, hence, everlasting. With the exception of *immortal*, all of these words are found chiefly in poetic use and are distinguishable especially in their connotations and applications. In its strictest sense, **immortal** implies little more than exemption from liability to death and, therefore, is rarely applied literally to anything other than the soul, or spirit, of man. "Such harmony is in *immortal* souls; But whilst this muddy vesture of decay Doth grossly close it in, we cannot hear it" (*Shak.*). In freer use, *immortal* often equals *eternal* ("*Immortal* gods, I crave no pelf"—*Shak.*); more frequently it keeps close to the strict sense in being applied to something comparable to the soul in that it lives on in fullness of vigor after its maker, possessor, or the like, has died; as, the *immortal* epics of Homer; " 'tis verse that gives *Immortal* youth to mortal maids" (*Landor*). "Oh may I join the choir invisible Of those *immortal* dead who live again In minds made better by their presence" (*G. Eliot*). **Deathless** also implies incapacity for death; in modern use it is seldom applied to the soul but, especially in the work of discriminating writers, to immaterial things that transcend the limitations of mortal existence; as, "Truth's *deathless* voice" (*Shelley*); "Art's *deathless* dreams" (*Shelley*); "Virtue crowned with glory's *deathless* meed" (*Wordsworth*). **Undying** is applied chiefly to emotions or passions marked by such intensity or vitality as to be or to seem incapable of extinction while life lasts; as, *undying* love; *undying* hatred; "a Patriot's heart, warm with *undying* fire" (*Wordsworth*). **Unfading** and **fadeless** often come close to *undying* in meaning, but they connote persistence of brightness or bloom rather than of intensity; as, *unfading* recollections; *fadeless* memories. In so far as they differ, *unfading* usually stresses a fact and *fadeless* an incapacity for decay. "True Charity...Thrives against hope, and in the rudest scene, Storms but enliven its *unfading* green" (*Cowper*). "Love's brightest roses on the scaffold bloom, Mingling with freedom's *fadeless* laurels" (*Shelley*). **Amaranthine,** derived from amaranth, a mythical everlasting flower, is used rarely outside of poetry. Sometimes it stresses deathlessness, sometimes fadelessness, but usually it also connotes richness of beauty; as, "the only *amaranthine* flower on earth is virtue" (*Cowper*); "Iona's Saints...Garlands shall wear of *amaranthine* bloom" (*Wordsworth*).

Ana. *Everlasting, never-ending, endless.

Ant. Mortal. — *Con.* Transitory, fleeting, fugitive, ephemeral, evanescent, *transient.

immotile. Immobile, *immovable, immotive.

immotive. *Immovable, immobile, immotile.

immovable *or* **unmovable. Immovable** (or the less frequent **unmovable), immobile, immotile, immotive** come into comparison when they mean incapable of moving or being moved. Except for this denial of power, the terms otherwise carry the implications and connotations of the affirmative words as discriminated at MOVABLE.

Ant. Movable.

immunity. *Exemption.

Ant. Susceptibility, allergy.

immure. *Imprison, incarcerate, jail, intern.

Ana. Confine, circumscribe, *limit, restrict.

Con. Liberate, *free, release.

impact, *n.* **Impact, impingement, collision, clash, shock, concussion, percussion, jar, jolt, brunt** come into comparison when they mean a forcible or enforced contact between two (sometimes more) things, especially a contact so violent as to affect seriously one or the other or all of the persons or things involved. **Impact,** though it often means this and no more, may be used more generally to imply contact between any two things, one of which at least is driven or impelled in the direction of the other and produces definite impressions on it, though not necessarily a physical impression or one that results in injury; as, the *impact* of a hammer upon a nail; a target constructed to resist the *impact* of a bullet; to live in an age where every mind feels the *impact* of new ideas. "Bashville...seized the door to shut him out; but Cashel forced it back against him, sent him reeling some paces by its *impact*..." (*Shaw*). "It is not electricity which we see, it is the air rendered incandescent by the vehemence of the *impacts* of the electrons against its molecules" (*Karl K. Darrow*). **Impingement** often means little more than *impact,* but distinctively it may imply an even sharper or more forcible impression than *impact* (as, the *impingement* of sound waves on the tympanum, or eardrum) or may carry, as *impact* does not, a suggestion of encroachment (as, the *impingement* of scientific theories upon religious beliefs). **Collision** implies the coming together of two (or, sometimes, more) things (one of which, usually both or all, must be in motion) with such force that both (or all) are more or less damaged or their progress is seriously impeded. "In the path of the revolving stable [to whose roof the narrator clung in a flood] loomed suddenly the house of our neighbor, Mrs. Fenn. To avoid being hurled off by the inevitable *collision,* I leaped into the air at the precise moment of *impact*" (*V. Heiser*). "His uneasiness grew by the recollection of the forty tons of dynamite in the body of the 'Ferndale'; not the sort of cargo one thinks of with equanimity in connexion with a threatened *collision*" (*Conrad*). *Collision* may be used, though such use is somewhat infrequent, when the things which come together so as to seriously affect one another are immaterial rather than physical entities; as, the frequent *collision* of scientific and religious ideas in the nineteenth century; "The *collision* of contrary false principles" (*Warburton*). **Clash** (etymologically, the sharp discordant sounds produced by the impact, often repeated impact, of two or more bodies, especially metallic bodies) is often used in preference to *collision* when two or more things come into contact with one another with such force that noises of crashing and jangling are more apparent than the destruction or ruin wrought; as, the *clash* of swords in battle; "the *clash* of cymbals, and the rolling of drums" (*Macaulay*). *Clash,* also, is used more often of immaterial things, such as beliefs, theories, and ideas, which are irreconcilable, incompatible, etc., and lead to violent conflict, controversy, and the like; as, a *clash* of creeds; "In *Le Misanthrope*...there is...a *clash*...between the high-strung demands of Alceste and the unbending reasonableness of the social standard" (*S. Alexander*). "An appeal to the workers and employers to be good boys and not paralyze the industry of the nation by the *clash* of their quite irreconcilable interests" (*Shaw*). **Shock** denotes the effect, as of shaking, rocking, agitating, stunning, or the like, produced by an impact or collision. As here compared, it may imply a physical, mental, or emotional effect, but in every case it carries a strong suggestion of something that strikes or hits with force and often with violence; as, "He stood the *shock* of a whole host of foes" (*Addison*); "the *shock* Of cataract seas that snap The three-decker's oaken spine" (*Tennyson*); "The soft *shock* Of wizened apples falling ...Upon the hilly rock" (*Millay*); "For strong emotion, however, the *shock* of sudden external stimulus is necessary" (*H. Ellis*). **Concussion** is found more often than *shock* in learned and technical use: it also usually suggests the physical effect produced by the impact of a blow upon, a hitting of, or a collision with something material yet not necessarily solid or substantial; as, "Its [a dress form's] hardness was not that of wood, which responds to *concussion* with living vibration" (*Cather*). In the common phrase "*concussion* of the brain" the term implies a condition of lowered functional activity of the brain resulting from a blow or fall upon the head. **Percussion** implies a more deliberate or intentional striking, knocking, tapping, or the like, for the sake of something produced by the impact of such a stroke, knock, or tap, such as a sound, an explosion, a vibration, or the like; thus, *percussion* instruments in an orchestra are those played by striking, such as a drum, a gong, cymbals, bells, a tambourine, and the like; a *percussion* bullet contains a substance that is exploded by *percussion;* a doctor by *percussion* (that is, by tapping or striking the chest or abdomen) discovers by the sounds produced the condition of a patient's lungs or abdominal organs. **Jar** applies to the painful and disturbing, but not necessarily injurious, shaking suffered as a result of a collision, clash, shock, or concussion; as, the fall gave him a *jar,* but nothing worse; we felt only the *jar* of the earthquake. **Jolt** carries a stronger implication of jerking out of place than of shaking and therefore carries a clearer suggestion of loss or near-loss of balance; as, to receive a *jolt* when the car ran over a hole in the road; the stern criticism gave him the first *jolt* he had ever had. **Brunt** once denoted, and still to a certain extent denotes, the force or shock of something which assails one as with a blow, an attack, or an assault (as, "Bearing the first *brunt* of the enemy's attack"—*Wellington;* "Grindal...bore the whole *brunt* of the queen's displeasure"—*Hallam*). The term now more often denotes either the major part of such a shock or, even more frequently, the chief stress or strain imposed upon one by a crisis, or a situation or condition beyond one's control; as, to bear the *brunt* of his parents' support; the *brunt* of the defense fell on civilians rather than on the trained soldiers.

Ana. Hitting *or* hit, striking *or* stroke, smiting, slapping *or* slap (see corresponding verbs at STRIKE): beating, pounding, buffeting (see BEAT, *v.*).

impair. Damage, mar, *injure, harm, hurt, spoil.

Ana. *Weaken, enfeeble, debilitate, sap, undermine, disable, cripple: *deface, disfigure, disfeature: *deform, distort, contort, warp.

Ant. Improve, amend: repair. — ***Con.*** Better, ameliorate (see IMPROVE).

impalpable. *Imperceptible, insensible, intangible, inappreciable, imponderable.

Ana. Tenuous, rare, slight (see THIN, *adj.*): attenuated, extenuated, rarefied (see THIN, *v.*).

Ant. Palpable. — ***Con.*** *Perceptible, sensible, tangible, appreciable, imponderable.

impart. *Communicate.

Ana. *Share, participate, partake: *distribute, dispense, divide: convey, *transfer: instill, inculcate, *implant: imbue, inoculate, leaven, *infuse.

impartial. *Fair, equitable, unbiased, objective, just, dispassionate, uncolored.

Ana. Disinterested, detached, aloof, *indifferent.

Ant. Partial. — ***Con.*** Influenced, swayed, affected (see AFFECT).

impassable. **Impassable, impenetrable, impervious, impermeable** agree in meaning not admitting passage through. **Impassable** applies chiefly to stretches of land, water, or the like, which cannot be passed over or crossed because of some insuperable difficulty or obstruction; as, the river is *impassable* in the rainy season; the road between here and the city is *impassable* since the storm blew down the trees; "this ocean of snow, which after October is *impassable*" (*Evelyn*); "The gulf is the difference between the angelic and the diabolic temperament. What more *impassable* gulf could you have?" (*Shaw*). **Impenetrable** applies chiefly to that which is so dense or so thick that not even the thinnest shaft (as of light, air, etc.) can find its way through; as, an *impenetrable* fog; *impenetrable* gloom or darkness; "this gentleman was *impenetrable* to ideas" (*P. Colum*); "Professor [Gilbert] Murray has...interposed between Euripides and ourselves a barrier more *impenetrable* than the Greek language" (*T. S. Eliot*). Often, however, *impenetrable* is preferred to *impassable* when implying an exceedingly dense growth that prevents passage; as, an *impenetrable* thicket; an *impenetrable* forest. **Impervious** implies impenetrability but it is used more often in its extended than in its literal sense. Literally, it now applies chiefly to substances or materials whose surfaces have been finished or treated so that they are airtight, watertight, soundproof, or the like; as, "No surface coating has ever been found which is *impervious* to sun, wind and rain" (*C. C. Furnas*). When applied to persons, or their minds or hearts, *impervious* usually implies complete resistance to that which attempts entrance; as, "*Impervious* to threats or prayers or tears" (*Hewlett*); "We become *impervious* to new truth both from habit and from desire" (*B. Russell*); "so soaked with the preserve [i.e., preserving fluid] 'good form' that we are *impervious* to the claims and clamour of that ill-bred creature—life!" (*Galsworthy*). **Impermeable** implies impenetrability (either natural or artificially acquired) by a fluid such as water or gas, and incapacity for becoming soaked or permeated; the term applies chiefly to substances such as some clays which do not absorb water, to cloths treated so as to be rainproof, or to materials which do not admit the passage of air, light, gas, and the like; as, *impermeable* rocks; gas pipes should be made of an *impermeable* metal; *impermeable* roofing.

Ant. Passable.

☞ *Do not confuse* impassable *with* impassible.

impassible. Insensitive, *insensible, anesthetic.

☞ *Do not confuse* impassible *with* impassable *or with* impassive.

impassioned. **Impassioned, passionate, ardent, fervent, fervid, perfervid** agree in meaning actuated by or manifesting intense feeling. **Impassioned,** though applicable to persons, is far more often found in current use in reference to utterance or artistic expression or to the mood or mental state which evokes such utterance or expression. The word usually implies intensity without violence, and feeling of such depth, sincerity, and potency that it passes naturally and inevitably from the person into his expression. "Poetry is the breath and finer spirit of all knowledge; it is the *impassioned* expression which is in the countenance of all Science" (*Wordsworth*). "The letters...are written by this master of *impassioned* recollection in a style so musical, so magical and moving, that the experiences he recounts become our own" (*L. P. Smith*). **Passionate,** on the other hand, always implies vehemence and, often, violence of emotion; when the latter idea is suggested, the word also may connote loss of rational guidance or wasteful diffusion (sometimes even perversion) of emotional power; as, a *passionate* (usually better than *impassioned*) harangue; a *passionate* reformer; *passionate* (not *impassioned*) partisanship. "*Passionate* feeling is desirable, provided it is not destructive" (*B. Russell*). " 'To match mere good, sound reasons, against the *passionate* conclusions of love is a waste of intellect bordering on the absurd' " (*Conrad*). **Ardent** differs from *passionate* largely in its freedom from derogatory implications and in its connotations of qualities suggestive of flame or fire. It is the preferred word when vehemence is implied and the intense feeling expresses itself in eagerness, zeal, enthusiasm, acts of devotion, and the like; as, an *ardent* desire for the truth; an *ardent* supporter of liberal ideas; an *ardent* lover; *ardent* love. "Heredity in man is hardly the simple thing that many of the *ardent* eugenists would have us believe" (*C. C. Furnas*). **Fervent** also implies a quality of fire, but it suggests a fire that glows rather than one that bursts into flame. Hence, though it implies strength and depth of feeling, it more often suggests steadiness than vehemence and inward quiet rather than outward activity. It is applicable chiefly to wishes, prayers, hopes, or the like, that are heartfelt or devout but it is also applied to an emotion (or to a person feeling such an emotion) that is free from turbulence, as of sexual desire or of personal ambitions; as, *fervent* thanks; *fervent* good wishes; a *fervent* Christian; *fervent* prayers. "Jane's feelings, though *fervent*, were little displayed" (*Austen*). "The Gods approve The depth, and not the tumult, of the soul; A *fervent*, not ungovernable, love" (*Wordsworth*). **Fervid,** like *impassioned*, is applied more to moods and expressions than to persons; in contrast to *impassioned*, however, it sometimes suggests more obvious, more warmly expressed, and, often, more spontaneous emotion. "Who could help liking her? her generous nature, her gift for appreciation, her wholehearted, *fervid* enthusiasm?" (*L. P. Smith*). Frequently, it carries a strong suggestion of feverishness which distinguishes it sharply from *fervent*, to which it is etymologically allied; thus, *fervent* thanks suggest the depth and sincerity of the emotion which prompt them; *fervid* thanks suggest profuseness or an overwrought state of mind. "Was it because his *fervid* manner of love-making offended her...?" (*Bennett*). **Perfervid,** however, always carries an implication of too great emotional excitement or of overwrought feelings; it far more than *fervid* casts doubt upon the sincerity of the emotion that is displayed with vehemence. "To court their own discomfiture by love is a common instinct with certain *perfervid* women" (*Hardy*).

Ana. Vehement, *intense: *deep, profound: *sentimental, romantic, maudlin.

Ant. Unimpassioned. — ***Con.*** Dispassionate, uncolored, objective (see FAIR, *adj.*).

impassive. **Impassive, stoic, phlegmatic, apathetic, stolid** denote in common unresponsive, or but slightly responsive, to something that might be expected to excite emotion or interest, or to produce a sensation. The distinctions to be drawn between these adjectives hold true also of their corresponding nouns, **impassivity** *or* **impassiveness, stoicism, phlegm, apathy, stolidity.** One is **impassive** who feels or shows no emotion or sensation, without necessary implication of insusceptibility. "His majestic *impassivity* contrasting with the overt astonishment with which a row of savagely ugly attendant chiefs grinned and gaped" (*Shaw*). "Under their *impassive* exterior they preserve...emotions of burning intensity" (*G. P. Lathrop*). One is **stoic** who is indifferent to pleasure or (esp.) pain; the word frequently suggests unflinching fortitude. "Not only the cataclysm of a world, but also the *stoic* and indomitable temper that endures it" (*Lowes*). **Phlegmatic** implies a temperament or constitution in which emotion is hard to arouse, or, when aroused, is moderate or restrained. "Cold and *phlegmatic* must he be who is not warmed into admiration by the surrounding scenery" (*C. Waterton*). "His fervid manner of love-making offended her English *phlegm*" (*Bennett*). **Apathetic,** in its earliest philosophical use implying "the extinction of the passions by the ascendancy of reason" (*W. Fleming*), now usually implies either a remiss and culpable indifference, or such a preoccupation with a particular depressing emotion (as care, grief, or despair) or bodily pain as makes one insensible to other emotion or pain, and deficient in, or devoid of, the usual human interests. "There is only one alarming aspect of our national debt...the *apathy* and ignorance of the American public with regard to it. The common attitude is...: why should an ordinary citizen add the national debt to his other workaday worries" (*H. Scherman*). "The dull *apathy* of despair" (*Wilde*). "An uncomplaining *apathy* displaced This anguish; and, indifferent to delight, To aim and purpose, he consumed his days, To private interest dead, and public care" (*Wordsworth*). **Stolid** implies heavy, dull, obtuse impassivity or apathy, or utter blankness of countenance mirroring or suggesting such quality; often, specifically, impassive, mechanical, plodding, unquestioning, unresourceful adherence to routine. "*Stolid* Saxon rustics, in whom the temperature of religious zeal was little...above absolute zero" (*A. Huxley*). "The *stolidest* mask ever given to man" (*Meredith*). "[One] who said, 'I won't have any soup, steward, I'll have the fish,' was met by a *stolidly* reproving glance. 'The soup is being served, sir' " (*V. Heiser*).

Ana. *Cool, composed, collected, imperturbable: reserved, taciturn, *silent, reticent: callous, *hardened, indurated: *insensible, insensitive.

Ant. Responsive. — ***Con.*** *Tender, compassionate, sympathetic, warm, warmhearted.

☞ *Do not confuse* impassive *with* impassible.

impassivity *or* **impassiveness.** Apathy, stolidity, phlegm, stoicism. See under IMPASSIVE.

impatient. **Impatient, nervous, nervy, unquiet, restless, restive, uneasy, fidgety, skittish, feverish, hectic, jumpy, jittery** come into comparison only when they mean manifesting signs of unrest or an inability to keep still or quiet. **Impatient** implies an inability to bear delay, opposition, discomfort, undue prolixity, and the like, with composure: it therefore connotes, as a rule, not physical but mental or emotional unrest, and may suggest unrestrained eagerness, extreme irritableness, brusqueness, testiness, intolerance, or the like; as, "So tedious is this day As is the night before some festival To an *impatient* child that hath new robes" (*Shak.*); "Cease your contention, which has been too long; I grow *impatient*" (*Pope*); "When we pursue the ulterior significance of the colours into yet wider regions...I fear the august common sense of the Occident becomes affronted and *impatient*" (*Binyon*). **Nervous** or often, in informal British use, **nervy,** implies unsteadiness of nerves, and a proneness to excitability: the word may suggest any one of various causes, such as disease, or temperament, or anxiety; as, a *nervous* (or *nervy*), fretful woman; "you and I, whose ordinary daily talk maintains its slow or hurried, *nervous* or phlegmatic..., but always pedestrian gait" (*Lowes*); "Becoming more *nervous* as the gloom increased" (*Hudson*). **Unquiet,** though applicable to anything that is not quiet, is commonly used with a strong implication of prolonged or conspicuous agitation or of troubling or disturbing distractions that hinder one's peace of mind or soul or prevent concentration: the word is applicable both to the person and to the thing which troubles him; as, these *unquiet* times; "*Unquiet* meals make ill digestions" (*Shak.*). **Restless** (whose basic term is ultimately a Teutonic word meaning bed, grave, stopping place) usually implies constant and more or less aimless motion or activity: often, specifically, it connotes mental agitation (as, "our heart is *restless*, until it repose in Thee"—*St. Augustine, transl. by Pusey;* "indubitably not happy...*restless* and disquieted, his disquietude sometimes amounting to agony" —*Arnold*), or eagerness to change (as, "He was *restless* and dissatisfied with his life"—*S. Anderson*), or continuous or unceasing movements to and fro or back and forth (as, the *restless* sea; a *restless* crowd; a *restless* drumming on the table with his fingers; "he was as *restless* as a hyena"—*De Quincey*). **Restive** (ultimately from a Latin verb meaning to stay back, withstand, resist) not only has no etymological connection with *restless*, but in its earlier and stricter senses implies an unwillingness to move (see CONTRARY, 2): however, it has so long been confused with *restless* even by good writers that it is now an acceptable, if not a universally approved, synonym. Even in the sense here considered it implies impatience under attempts to restrain, to control, or, especially, to keep attentive, and suggests either inability to keep still or to persist in what one is doing. "He did right to preach to women: men would not have listened to him. As it was, Miss Joy Blewins, and Mrs. M'Murphy, were *restive*" (*Meredith*). "They were all becoming *restive* under the monotonous persistence of the missionary" (*Cather*). "As *restive* and dissatisfied as a party of 7 bridge-players" (*Eddington*). **Uneasy** usually implies restlessness born of anxiety, doubt, uncertainty, or insecurity; as, he is *uneasy* over business conditions; an *uneasy* conscience; an *uneasy* sense that all was not well with his family; "*Uneasy* lies the head that wears a crown" (*Shak.*). "So we come down, *uneasy*, to look, *uneasily* pacing the beach. These are the dykes our fathers made: we have never known a breach" (*Kipling*).

Fidgety implies restless movements resulting from nervousness, boredom, or uneasiness of mind: it usually suggests an inability to keep one's hands, feet, or body still or to settle down to any definite task or occupation; as, toward the end of the day, the pupils become *fidgety;* "He declared if I was *fidgety* he should have no comfort" (*Burney*). **Skittish** (etymologically, capering) applies especially to horses: the term usually implies restiveness, or impatience of restraint, and a dancing backwards and forwards in or as if in a fright; as, they never allowed their daughter to ride a horse known to be *skittish.* The term is applied to persons (or to things that are personified) whose movements or actions suggest those of a skittish horse; in such use, *skittish* may connote extreme liveliness and frivolity (as, a young *skittish* widow), unsteadiness or undependableness (as, "*skittish* fortune" —*Shak.;* "they are...jealous of each other—fearful, timid, *skittish*"—*John Adams*), or extreme coyness (as, "Name not yourself her lover, but her friend. How many *skittish* girls have thus been caught?"—*Dryden*). Both **feverish** and **hectic,** as here considered, imply an underlying and disturbing excitement that makes for restlessness, or incapacity for ease, quiet, or calm. *Feverish* suggests the hotness, rush, or intensity of a high fever; as, "Work...pressed forward with the same *feverish* haste" (*H. Adams*); "his life...broken by *feverish* business trips across the ocean" (*Van W. Brooks*); "the world has become a laboratory where immature and *feverish* minds experiment with unknown forces" (*Buchan*). *Hectic* (literally, feverish, as in a wasting disease), on the other hand, implies an excitement created as by the need of hurry, the pressure of activities, or the like; usually it suggests conditions that exhaust one or rob one of capacity for keeping oneself calm or keeping one's activities under steady control; as, "even Death moves swiftly in *hectic,* high-stepping New York" (*Lucas*); all the students found examination week a *hectic* time; *hectic* preparations for a big dinner. **Jumpy** and **jittery** (both colloquial, somewhat slangy terms) imply extreme nervousness that exhibits itself in tremulous, uncertain movements. *Jumpy,* however, usually suggests a fearful or apprehensive mood, and lack of control over one's temper as well as over one's muscles (as, the refugee children are still *jumpy* though it is now some time since they left England); *jittery* suggests domination not only by fears but by recollections that destroy one's nervous control and impair one's mental stability; as, soldiers still *jittery* from their experiences under heavy fire; "the chief factor in making children *jittery* is *jittery* parents" (*Time*).

Ana. Fretful, querulous, *irritable, snappish, waspish: *eager, anxious, avid, keen: impetuous, *precipitate, headlong, hasty, sudden, abrupt.

Ant. Patient. — *Con.* Composed, imperturbable, unruffled, *cool: *calm, serene, tranquil, placid.

impeach. Indict, incriminate, criminate, *accuse, charge, arraign.

Ana. Condemn, denounce, blame, censure (see CRITICIZE): try, test, *prove.

Con. *Exculpate, vindicate, exonerate, acquit, absolve.

impeccable. **Impeccable, faultless, flawless, errorless** are often used with little distinction in the sense of absolutely correct and beyond criticism. **Impeccable,** in modern usage, usually applies to something with which no fault can be found, or which is irreproachably correct; as, "The only *impeccable* writers are those that never wrote" (*Hazlitt*); "her logical process is *impeccable*" (*Grandgent*); "in *impeccable* sureness of hand he [Okio, the Japanese artist] has scarcely a rival" (*Binyon*). **Faultless** is often used in place of *impeccable* without loss, but it is sometimes preferred when the emphasis is upon the absence of defect or blemish of any kind rather than upon technical correctness; as, "Whoever thinks a *faultless* piece to see, Thinks what ne'er was, nor is, nor e'er shall be" (*Pope*). Its distinctive implication, however, is often that of insipidity or tediousness; as, "Faultily *faultless,* icily regular, splendidly null, Dead perfection, no more" (*Tennyson*). **Flawless** applies especially, but not exclusively, to natural products in which no cracks, blemishes, or the like, can be detected (as, a *flawless* diamond; a *flawless* flower), to character, reputation, or the like, which is admittedly perfect or unblemished (as, to sacrifice one's *flawless* reputation by a single act), to a work of art or its execution (as, a *flawless* lyric; the *flawless* technique of the pianist). **Errorless** usually implies absence of all mistakes, especially of such mistakes as are technically regarded as errors; thus, an *errorless* baseball game may not involve *flawless* playing.

Ana. Inerrant, unerring, *infallible: *correct, accurate, precise, right, nice: *perfect, entire, whole, intact.

Con. *Deficient, defective: *superficial, shallow, uncritical, cursory: culpable, *blameworthy.

impede. *Hinder, obstruct, block, bar, dam.

Ana. Clog, *hamper, fetter, trammel, shackle, manacle, hog-tie: *embarrass, discomfit, disconcert, rattle, faze: thwart, baffle, balk, *frustrate.

Ant. Assist: promote. — *Con.* *Advance, further, forward: *help, aid.

impediment. *Obstacle, obstruction, bar, snag.

Ana. *Difficulty, hardship, rigor, vicissitude: barrier, *bar: handicap (see ADVANTAGE, 1).

Ant. Aid, assistance: advantage (sense 1).

impedimenta. *Baggage, luggage.

impel. Drive, *move, actuate.

Ana. Compel, constrain, *force: *provoke, excite, stimulate: *incite, instigate, foment: goad, spur (see corresponding nouns at MOTIVE).

Ant. Restrain. — *Con.* Curb, check, snaffle, inhibit (see RESTRAIN).

impending. **Impending, imminent** come into comparison as meaning highly likely to occur very soon or without further warning. **Impending** carries a strong implication that the thing which is likely to occur forecasts itself long enough ahead by some ominous or threatening signs as to keep one in suspense; as, an *impending* storm; an *impending* dismissal; not so ill that he was unaware of his *impending* death; "Th' *impending* woe sat heavy on his breast" (*Pope*); "his face...gave me no clue to the character of the *impending* communication" (*Conrad*). **Imminent,** the stronger term, applies to that (especially danger, misfortune, etc.) which threatens to happen immediately, or is on the point of happening; as, "Three times to-day You have defended me from *imminent* death" (*Shak.*); discovery was *imminent;* "The one thing plain was that a new war was *imminent,* and he longed for Brutus and Cassius, now exiles beyond the sea" (*Buchan*).

Ana. *Close, near, nigh: approaching, nearing (see APPROACH, *v.*): likely, *probable: threatening, menacing (see THREATEN).

impenetrable. Impervious, impermeable, *impassable.

Ana. *Close, dense, compact, thick: solid, hard, *firm: compacted, concentrated, consolidated (see COMPACT, *v.*): callous, *hardened, indurated: obdurate, adamant, *inflexible.

Ant. Penetrable. — *Con.* *Soft, mild, gentle, lenient: indulgent, merciful, clement, *forbearing, tolerant.

impenetrate. Interpenetrate, penetrate, *permeate, pervade, impregnate, saturate.

Ana. *Enter, pierce, probe, penetrate: invade, entrench (see TRESPASS): drench, *soak, sog.

imperative. Peremptory, imperious, *masterful, domineering.

Ana. Commanding, ordering, bidding (see COMMAND, *v.*): magisterial, authoritative, *dictatorial, dogmatic, oracular: arbitrary, autocratic, despotic (see ABSOLUTE).

Con. Supplicating *or* supplicatory, entreating, imploring, beseeching, begging (see corresponding verbs at BEG): mild, gentle, lenient, *soft.

imperceptible. Imperceptible, insensible, impalpable, intangible, inappreciable, imponderable come into comparison when they mean incapable of being apprehended by the senses or intellect in form, nature, extent, degree, or the like, even though known to be real or existent. Except for this denial of apprehensibility, these terms carry the same implications and connotations as the affirmative adjectives discriminated at PERCEPTIBLE; as, the *imperceptible* movement of the earth; "he grew into the scheme of things by *insensible* gradations" (*H. G. Wells*); "the almost *impalpable* beauties of style and expression" (*Prescott*); "we shall consider that more subtle and *intangible* thing, the soul which he [Augustus] sought to build up in his people" (*Buchan*); that *inappreciable* particle of an element called an atom; the *imponderable* factors, such as temperament and mental stability, which make or mar a promising career.

Ant. Perceptible.

imperial. *Kingly, regal, royal, queenly, princely.

Ana. Majestic, august, stately, noble, *grand: sovereign, *dominant.

☞ *Do not confuse* imperial *with* imperious.

imperious. Domineering, *masterful, peremptory, imperative.

Ana. *Dictatorial, authoritative, authoritarian, magisterial: despotic, tyrannical, arbitrary, autocratic (see ABSOLUTE): lordly, overbearing (see PROUD).

Ant. Abject. — *Con.* Obsequious, servile, menial, *subservient, slavish: *compliant, acquiescent.

☞ *Do not confuse* imperious *with* imperial.

impermeable. Impervious, impenetrable, *impassable.

Ana. Solid, hard, *firm: *tight.

Con. Absorbing *or* absorbent, imbibing, assimilating *or* assimilative (see corresponding verbs at ABSORB).

impersonate. Personate, play, *act.

Ana. Imitate, mimic, ape, *copy: simulate, counterfeit, feign (see ASSUME): *caricature, burlesque.

impersonator. *Actor, player, mummer, mime, performer, Thespian, trouper.

impertinent. Impertinent, officious, pragmatical (*or* **pragmatic**), **meddlesome, intrusive, obtrusive** come into comparison when they are applied to persons, and their acts and utterances, and mean given to exceeding, or manifesting a disposition to exceed, the bounds of propriety regarding the interposition of oneself in another person's affairs. **Impertinent,** as here compared (it is also the opposite of *pertinent;* see RELEVANT), implies a concerning oneself more or less offensively with things which are another's business or, at least, not in any sense one's own. "I told him of all that had occurred to make my former interference in his affairs absurd and *impertinent*" (*Austen*). "I should have liked to ask the girl for a word which would give my imagination its line. But how was one to venture so far? I can be rough sometimes but I am not naturally *impertinent*" (*Conrad*). **Officious** implies the offering, often well-meant offering, of services, attentions, or assistance that are not needed or that are unwelcome or offensive; as, " 'Twas but the *officious* zeal of a well-meaning creature for my honor" (*Sterne*); "I cannot walk home from office, but some *officious* friend offers his unwelcome courtesies to accompany me" (*Lamb*). **Pragmatical** (*or, less often,* **pragmatic**), now the least common of all the terms here discussed, stresses the disposition to busy oneself fussily, especially in that which is not one's own affair: it also carries a stronger connotation of self-importance or self-assurance than any of the others; as, "like some *pragmatical* old coxcomb represented on the stage" (*Burney*); "Coming to-day in this *pragmatical* way, when nobody sent for you" (*Godwin*); "*Pragmatical* insolence" (*Scott*). **Meddlesome** carries a stronger implication of annoying interference in other people's affairs than any of the preceding terms: it may imply the qualities of character suggested by any of the other words, but it usually also connotes a prying or inquisitive nature; as, a *meddlesome* old woman; the people found the government unduly *meddlesome;* to poke *meddlesomely* into another's affairs. **Intrusive,** as here compared, applies largely to persons, actions, words, and the like, that reveal a disposition to thrust oneself into other people's affairs or society or to be unduly curious about what is not one's concern. "Navajo hospitality is not *intrusive.* Eusabio made the Bishop understand that he was glad to have him there, and let him alone" (*Cather*). **Obtrusive,** as here considered, is applicable like *intrusive* and often carries very similar implications. Distinctively, however, it connotes objectionable actions more than an objectionable disposition, and so stresses a thrusting forward of oneself, as into a position where one can harm more often than help or where one is unduly or improperly conspicuous. "Rebels against a social order that has no genuine need of them and is disposed to tolerate them only when they are not *obtrusive*" (*Mencken*).

Ana. Insinuating, insinuative, ingratiating (see DISARMING): interfering, meddling (see MEDDLE): arrogant, insolent (see PROUD): brazen, impudent, brash, barefaced, *shameless: *offensive, repugnant.

Con. Decent, *decorous, seemly, proper, comme il faut: reserved, reticent, *silent.

imperturbable. Composed, collected, *cool, unruffled, nonchalant.

Ana. Immobile, *immovable: serene, *calm, tranquil, placid: *complacent, self-satisfied, smug.

Ant. Choleric, touchy. — *Con.* Discomfited, disconcerted, rattled, fazed (see EMBARRASS): *irascible, splenetic, testy, techy.

impervious. Impenetrable, impermeable, *impassable.

Ana. Resisting *or* resistant, withstanding, opposing, combating (see corresponding verbs at OPPOSE): *hardened, indurated, callous: obdurate, adamant, adamantine, *inflexible.

Con. Open, exposed, susceptible, sensitive, *liable, prone.

impetuous. Headlong, *precipitate, abrupt, hasty, sudden.

Ana. Impulsive, *spontaneous: vehement, *intense: forceful, forcible, *powerful: violent (see corresponding noun at FORCE): *impatient, restive, feverish, hectic: *impassioned, passionate, fervid, ardent.

Con. *Steady, even, equable: *deliberate, premeditated, considered, advised.

impetus. 1 Momentum, *speed, velocity, pace.

Ana. Energy, force, *power: impelling *or* impulsion, driving, moving (see corresponding verbs at MOVE).

2 *Stimulus, incitement, stimulant.

Ana. Incentive, impulse, spur, goad, *motive, spring.

impingement. *Impact, collision, clash, shock, concussion, percussion, jar, jolt, brunt.

Ana. Hitting *or* hit, striking *or* stroke, smiting (see corresponding verbs at STRIKE): encroachment, entrenchment (see corresponding verbs at TRESPASS): *impression, impress, imprint, stamp, print.

impious. **Impious, profane, blasphemous, sacrilegious** agree in meaning showing marked irreverence for that which is sacred or divine. **Impious** usually implies extreme disrespect for God or the laws of God, or for those endowed with God-given authority, particularly as shown positively in thought or in actions; as, "Against the throne and monarchy of God, Raised *impious* war in Heaven" (*Milton*); "When vice prevails, and *impious* men bear sway, The post of honour is a private station" (*Addison*); "The *impious* challenger of power divine" (*Cowper*). **Profane** (see PROFANE, 1) applies to men and to words and acts that manifest not only impiety but defilement or desecration, sometimes thoughtless, and sometimes intentional, of that which is worthy of highest reverence or respect; as, "Shall I... add a greater sin By prostituting holy things to idols... What act more execrably unclean, *profane?*" (*Milton*); "then [in the Golden Age] speech *profane*, And manners profligate, were rarely found" (*Cowper*); "that such impiety may be utterly banished from these works [the building of St. Paul's Cathedral]...it is ordered that *profane* swearing shall be a sufficient crime to dismiss any labourer" (*Sir C. Wren*). **Blasphemous** adds to *profane* the implication of indignity offered directly or indirectly to the Supreme Being: in very strict use, it implies a conscious or deliberate insult; as, the *blasphemous* rites of devil worshipers; "We have heard him speak *blasphemous* words against Moses, and against God" (*Acts* vi. 11). **Sacrilegious,** in its strictest sense, implies the commission of a sacrilege (see PROFANATION), but in its extended sense, which is now the more common, it implies the defilement of that which is holy or sacred, as by acts of depredation, disrespect, contempt, or the like; as, the *sacrilegious* despoilers of ancient churches; "A most *sacrilegious* breach of trust" (*Bolingbroke*); "She saw that it was a terrible, a *sacrilegious* thing to interfere with another's destiny, to lay the tenderest touch upon any human being's right to love and suffer after his own fashion" (*E. Wharton*).

Ana. Nefarious, iniquitous, flagitious (see VICIOUS): *irreligious, ungodly, godless.

Ant. Pious: reverent. — *Con.* *Holy, sacred, blessed, religious, spiritual, divine.

impish. Roguish, waggish, mischievous, *playful, wanton, frolicsome, sportive.

Ana. *Saucy, pert, arch: naughty, *bad: *sly, cunning, tricky.

implacable. Relentless, unrelenting, merciless, *grim.

Ana. *Inflexible, inexorable, obdurate, adamant: pitiless, ruthless, compassionlesss (see affirmative nouns at PITY).

Con. Yielding, submitting, capitulating (see YIELD): merciful, lenient, clement, *forbearing, indulgent, tolerant.

implant. **Implant, inculcate, instill** (*or* **instil**), **inseminate, infix** are here compared chiefly in their secondary senses, in which they agree in meaning to introduce into the mind. **Implant** (literally, to plant something in or as if in the soil so that it will take root and grow) usually implies teaching, and it stresses the fixedness or permanency of that which has been taught; as, "The teacher, the parent, or the friend can often do much to *implant* this conviction" (*C. W. Eliot*); "The defect in this theory lies in the fact that such a taste [for music], granting it to be elevating, simply cannot be *implanted*" (*Mencken*). **Inculcate** (etymologically, to tread on with the heels) implies persistent or repeated endeavor with the intent to impress firmly on the mind; as, "[she] had sedulously *inculcated* into the mind of her son...maxims of worldly wisdom" (*Edgeworth*); "Skillful, conscientious schoolmistresses whose lives were spent in trying to *inculcate* real knowledge" (*Grandgent*); "whatever happened, Newland would continue to *inculcate* in Dallas the same principles and prejudices which had shaped his parents' lives" (*E. Wharton*). **Instill** carries from its literal meaning (to pour in drop by drop) the implication of a gradual and gentle method of imparting knowledge: it usually suggests either a teaching that extends over a long period of time, as from infancy to adolescence, or a pupil that cannot, because of age, lack of background, or the like, take in at once that which is taught; as, "Those principles my parents *instilled* into my unwary understanding" (*Browne*); "the Viceroy plumed himself on the way in which he had *instilled* notions of reticence into his staff" (*Kipling*); "It would be useless, in early years, to attempt to *instil* a Stoic contempt for death" (*B. Russell*). **Inseminate** (literally, to sow as seed where it will germinate or sprout) usually implies an implanting in many minds, either as one step or as a result of a series of steps, so that the ideas take hold and govern the group, class, community, nation, or the like; as, they did not succeed in *inseminating* radical ideas in the minds of the workers; to uproot old falsities and to *inseminate* new truths. **Infix** (literally, to set one thing firmly or fixedly into another) implies teaching or other process that has for its end the formation of habit or the inculcation of something that will be definitely remembered; as, a teacher is often more successful in *infixing* the illustrative example than the illustrated principle in the minds of his pupils; "The vices which they introduced, and the habits they *infixed*" (*Lamb*).

Ana. *Infuse, imbue, inoculate, ingrain, leaven: impregnate, saturate, impenetrate, penetrate, *permeate, pervade.

implement. **Implement, tool, instrument, appliance, utensil,** as here compared, agree in meaning any relatively simple device by means of which one engaged in a craft, trade, art, profession, or any employment involving mechanical or manual operations, is enabled to accomplish one or more of those operations. Nearly all of these words (the distinct exception is *appliance*) are interchangeable in their general senses, but custom and good usage have greatly restricted them in their specific and most common applications. An **implement,** in general, is anything that is requisite to effecting the end one has in view or to performing the work one undertakes; thus, the *implements* of modern warfare consist of all the weapons necessary to a well-equipped army, navy, and air force. "The sit-down strike, a relatively new *implement* of organized labor" (*Americana Annual*, 1938). In specific use, *implement* is the preferred term when the reference is to a contrivance for tilling the soil, such as a spade, a plow, a harrow, or a cultivator; as, farming *implements;* gardening *implements.* Historically, it is the preferred term for any of the articles which are essential to the performance of a religious service; thus, the *implements* of the Mass include vestments as well as chalice, paten, altar stone, and the like. It is also the preferred term for the various crude devices made from stone, wood, and earth, by primitive peoples, as weapons or for use in digging, carrying, lifting, and the like. A **tool,** in general, is anything that facilitates the accomplishment of the end one has in view; it is therefore something particularly adapted in its nature or by its construction to make possible or relatively easy the work one is doing; as, it is not difficult to keep house when one has the proper *tools;* a scholar needs foreign languages as *tools.* "Comparison and analysis...are the chief *tools* of the critic" (*T. S. Eliot*). In specific use, *tool* is the preferred term when reference is made to any of the implements used by carpenters, mechanics, or other artisans or craftsmen in accomplishing a particular kind of work, such as sawing, boring, piercing, or chipping; thus, a saw, a gimlet, an awl, a chisel, are *tools*. Ordinarily *tool* suggests manipulation by the hand; but some machines for doing work that may be accomplished more slowly by manual labor and tools are called *machine tools* (as, for example, the lathe). An **instrument,** as here compared (see also MEAN, *n.*, 2; PAPER, 1), is, in general, any delicately constructed device by means of which work (not exclusively a mechanical operation) may be accomplished with precision. Many *instruments* are by definition *tools*, but *instrument* is the preferred term among surgeons, dentists, draftsmen, surveyors, artists, and the like, whose technique requires delicate tools and expertness and finesse in their manipulation. Some instruments, however, are not tools, but implements in the larger sense, for they are requisite to the effecting of one's ends, but do not necessarily facilitate any manual operations; thus, a thermometer and a barometer are recording *instruments* essential to the meteorologist; a telescope is an astronomical *instrument;* a piano, a violin, a cello are musical *instruments* by means of which a performer evokes musical sounds. An **appliance** (see also MACHINE) is in general a device which effects work but which is moved by some kind of power (such as hand power, water power, steam, or electricity), usually, but not necessarily, under the guidance of a hand; thus, a dentist's drill may be called an *appliance* when it is attached to a dental engine; in industry, an *appliance* is often distinguished from a *tool*, though they may both do the same kind of work, in that a *tool* is manipulated by hand, and an *appliance* is moved and regulated by machinery. A **utensil** is, in general, anything that is useful in accomplishing the work associated with a domestic or similar establishment, such as cooking, cleaning, and the like; it may be applied to tools used in cookery and other household work, such as eggbeaters, graters, rolling pins, brooms, mops, and the like, but it is most commonly applied to containers, such as pots, pans, pails, jars, especially those which form part of the kitchen, dairy, or bedroom equipment. Consequently, *utensil*, in other than household use, often means a vessel; as, the sacred *utensils* of a church.

Ana. *Machine, engine, apparatus, appliance: contrivance, *device, contraption, gadget.

implement, *v.* *Enforce.

Ana. Effect, fulfill, execute, achieve, accomplish, *perform: *realize, actualize, materialize.

implicate. **1** Imply, involve, *include, comprehend, embrace, subsume.

Ana. Connect, link, associate, relate, *join.

Ant. Dissociate. — *Con.* *Exclude, eliminate, rule out: *extricate, disentangle, untangle.

2 *Involve.

Ana. *Concern, affect: incriminate, criminate (see ACCUSE).

Con. *Exculpate, absolve, acquit, exonerate.

implication. **Implication, inference** are often used, even by careful writers, without a clear sense of their fine distinctions when they specifically refer to something that is hinted at but not explicitly stated. **Implication** applies only to that which is hinted, whether the writer or speaker is aware of it or not, or whether the reader or hearer recognizes it or not. When, however, the reader or hearer recognizes that which is implied and gathers from it its full significance or makes an explicit statement of it, he has drawn or made an **inference;** as, You misunderstood the *implications* of his speech, so that your *inferences* misrepresent his point of view; by *implication* (not *inference*) you argue that this is the only possible solution; by *inference* (not *implication*) from what you leave unsaid, I know you believe this the only possible solution; he did not perceive the *implications* (not *inferences*) of his remark; the *inferences* (not *implications*) to be drawn from his remark are inescapable.

Ana. Hinting *or* hint, suggestion, intimation (see corresponding verbs at SUGGEST): *insinuation, innuendo.

implicit. **Implicit, virtual, constructive** come into comparison only when they mean being such (i.e., the thing expressed by the term qualified) by correct or justifiable inference rather than by direct statement or proof. That is **implicit** (as opposed to *explicit*) which is implied by the words, acts, appearance, character, methods, or the like, of the person or thing concerned, but is not definitely stated or expressed; as, "A good present behavior is an *implicit* repentance for any miscarriage in what is past" (*Spectator*); "the distinction between poetry and drama, which Mr. Archer makes explicit, is *implicit* in the view of Swinburne" (*T. S. Eliot*). That is **virtual** (as opposed to *actual*) which exists in essence or effect but is not actually designated, or recognized, or put forward, or regarded, as such; as, his statement is a *virtual* confession; "But America [i.e., the Colonies] is *virtually* represented. What! does the electric force of *virtual* representation more easily pass over the Atlantic than pervade... Chester and Durham, surrounded by abundance of representation that is actual and palpable?" (*Burke*); "the dictator's constant associate and his *virtual* chief-of-staff" (*Buchan*). That is **constructive** (chiefly a legal term: opposed to *manifest*) which is inferred from a text, from known acts, known conditions, or the like, and which rests therefore on an interpretation of this text, these acts, or these conditions rather than upon direct statement or direct evidence; thus, if the law explicitly gives a governor the right of removal of certain officials, he may claim the right to control and direct their official acts as a *constructive* power; a mere failure to obey the orders of the court may be interpreted by the judge as *constructive* contempt.

Ana. Implied, suggested, intimated, hinted (see SUGGEST): inferred, deduced, gathered (see INFER).

Ant. Explicit. — *Con.* Express, definite, specific (see EXPLICIT): expressed, voiced, uttered (see EXPRESS, *v.*): stated, recited, recounted, described (see RELATE).

implore. Entreat, beseech, supplicate, *beg, importune, adjure, conjure.

Ana. Pray, plead, sue, appeal, petition (see under PRAYER): *ask, request, solicit.

imply. **1** Involve, implicate, comprehend, *include, embrace, subsume.

Ana. Import, *mean, signify, denote: *contain, hold: comprise, consist of (see COMPOSE): convey, *carry, bear.

2 *Suggest, hint, intimate, insinuate.

Ana. Connote, *denote: *presuppose, presume, assume, postulate: betoken, bespeak, *indicate, attest, argue, prove.

Ant. Express. — *Con.* State, *relate: utter, voice, broach (see EXPRESS, *v.*): declare, predicate, affirm, *assert, aver.

3 *Infer.

impolite. Uncivil, discourteous, *rude, ill-mannered, ungracious.

Ana. Churlish, boorish, loutish (see under BOOR): curt, gruff, brusque, blunt (see BLUFF).

Ant. Polite. — *Con.* *Civil, courteous, chivalrous,

gallant: *suave, urbane, diplomatic, politic: *thoughtful, considerate, attentive.

imponderable. Impalpable, *imperceptible, inappreciable, insensible, intangible.

Ant. Ponderable, appreciable. — *Con.* Weighty, consequential, important, significant, momentous (see corresponding nouns at IMPORTANCE).

import, *v.* *Mean, denote, signify.

Ana. *Denote, connote: involve, imply, *include, comprehend: *suggest, imply, intimate, hint: mean, *intend.

import, *n.* **1** Significance, *meaning, sense, acceptation, signification.

Ana. Denotation, connotation (see under DENOTE, 2): interpreting *or* interpretation, construing *or* construction (see corresponding verbs at EXPLAIN): drift, tenor (see TENDENCY): *implication.

2 Significance, *importance, consequence, moment, weight.

Ana. *Worth, value: purpose, intent, design, object, objective (see INTENTION): *emphasis, stress.

importance. **Importance, consequence, moment, weight, significance, import** come into comparison when they denote the quality, or the character, or the state of someone or something that impresses others as of great (sometimes eminent) worth, value, influence, or the like. **Importance,** probably the most inclusive of these terms, implies a judgment of the mind by which superior value, worth, influence, or the like, is ascribed to a person or thing; as, there are no cities of *importance* in this state; he always attaches *importance* to what seem to others trivial events; tradition gives *importance* to the study of the classics; "Hence flowers come to assume [in Oriental art]...an *importance* equal to that of figure-painting with us" (*Binyon*). **Consequence** is often used interchangeably with *importance,* especially in implying superior social rank or distinction (as, men of *importance,* or *consequence*) but among discriminating writers and speakers it usually implies importance because of the thing's possible or probable outcome, effects, results, or the like; as, "Woe betide him, and her too, when it comes to things of *consequence*...if she have not resolution enough to resist idle interference" (*Austen*); "He... was eager to have the Cathedral begun; but whether it was Midi Romanesque or Ohio German in style, seemed to him of little *consequence*" (*Cather*); " 'To marry one of the right people...is of the greatest *consequence* for a happy life' " (*R. Macaulay*); "to cultivate the love of truth, it is of the utmost *consequence* that children should study things as well as words, external nature as well as books" (*C. W. Eliot*). **Moment** implies conspicuous or self-evident consequence; as, "enterprises of great pitch and *moment*" (*Shak.*); "a mistake of no very great *moment*—in fine, a mere slip" (*Barham*); "What was of very high *moment* was his [Montmorency's] first step, the summoning of the Estates of Languedoc" (*Belloc*). **Weight** implies a judgment of the relatively great importance or of the particular moment of the thing under consideration; as, the judge gave great *weight* to the testimony of the accused man; "In such a point of *weight,* so near mine honour" (*Shak.*). "I looked for you at dinner-time; I forget now What for; but then 'twas a matter of more *weight* Than laying siege to a city" (*Millay*). **Significance** and **import** are often used as though they were indistinguishable in meaning from *importance* or *consequence;* actually, they imply a quality or character in a person or thing which ought to mark it as of importance or consequence but which may or may not be recognized; thus, one may miss the *significance* (not the *importance*) of an occurrence; one may recognize the *import* (better than *importance*) of a piece of testimony; so, "a widespread recognition of the *significance* of that achievement" (*H. Ellis*); "the book was invested with a *significance*...which its intrinsic literary and philosophical merits could not justify" (*A. Huxley*); "a fear that the spectator might lose, in the shock of crude sensation, the spiritual *import* of the catastrophe" (*Binyon*).

Ana. Prominence, conspicuousness, saliency (see corresponding adjectives at NOTICEABLE): eminence, illustriousness, distinguishableness *or* distinction (see corresponding adjectives at FAMOUS): seriousness, gravity (see corresponding adjectives at SERIOUS): magnitude, *size, extent.

Ant. Unimportance. — *Con.* Pettiness, triviality, paltriness (see corresponding adjectives at PETTY).

importune. *Beg, entreat, beseech, implore, supplicate, adjure, conjure.

Ana. Tease, pester, plague, harry, *worry: hound, hector, badger (see BAIT): plead, appeal, sue (see under PRAYER).

imposing. Stately, majestic, august, noble, magnificent, *grand, grandiose.

Ana. *Showy, pretentious, ostentatious, pompous: impressive, *moving: regal, imperial (see KINGLY): monumental, stupendous, prodigious (see MONSTROUS).

Ant. Unimposing. — *Con.* *Contemptible, despicable, sorry, cheap, scurvy, pitiable, beggarly.

impost. *Tax, levy, excise, customs, duty, toll, assessment, rate, tariff, tribute, tithe, teind, cess.

impostor. **Impostor, faker, empiric, quack, mountebank, charlatan** come into comparison when they denote a person who makes pretensions to being someone or something that he is not, or of being able to do something he cannot really do. **Impostor** applies especially to one who passes himself off for someone else. "There is an *impostor* abroad, who takes upon him the name of this young gentleman, and would willingly pass for him" (*Addison*). However, the word often serves as a general term for anyone who assumes a title, character, or profession that is not his own. "He [Jesus] stripped the *impostors* in the noonday sun, Showed that they followed all they seemed to shun" (*Cowper*). **Faker** (often confused with *fakir,* a different word, meaning a Moslem mendicant) is a purely colloquial term applicable to one who gives himself the appearance of being what, in character, in profession, or the like, he is not; as, the accused man is not insane, he is merely a clever *faker;* a hypocrite is a moral or religious *faker.* **Empiric** was originally applied to one of an ancient school of physicians who derided medical science and made their personal observations and experience the basis of their medical practice. The term, by extension, now applies to any ignorant and untrained practitioner in medicine, law, or other profession. The term always suggests pretensions to knowledge and skill. "Gordon's efforts to suppress it [slave trade in the Sudan] resembled the palliatives of an *empiric* treating the superficial symptoms of some profound constitutional disease" (*L. Strachey*). **Quack** is the popular and contemptuous term for *empiric,* but it usually carries an even stronger implication of fraud or self-delusion. "Enthusiasm's [religious fanaticism is] past redemption ... Not a' her *quacks* wi' a' their gumption Can ever mend her" (*Burns*). "Dishonesty is the raw material not of *quacks* only, but also, in great part, of dupes" (*Carlyle*). **Mountebank** and **charlatan** were both originally applied to an itinerant quack who mounted a platform and by his tricks and buffoonery attracted a crowd to whom he sold his remedies. In extended use, *mountebank* may or may not suggest quackery, but it always suggests cheap and undignified efforts (such as by buffoonery) to win attention; as, political *mountebanks*. "Our Sabbaths [will be], closed with mummery and buffoon; Preaching and pranks will share the motley scene ... God's worship and the *mountebank* between" (*Cowper*). *Charlatan* now applies to any writer, speaker, preacher, or the like, who covers his ignorance, lack of skill, or the like, by pretentious, flashy, or magniloquent display. "Insolent, pretentious, and given to that reckless innovation for the sake of noise and show which was the essence of the *charlatan*" (*G. Eliot*).

Ana. Cheat, fraud, fake, humbug (see IMPOSTURE): deceiver, beguiler, misleader (see corresponding verbs at DECEIVE).

imposture, *n.* **Imposture, cheat, fraud, sham, fake, humbug, deceit, deception, counterfeit, simulacrum** come into comparison when they mean a thing which pretends to be one thing in its nature, character, or quality, but is really another. **Imposture** applies not only to any object but to any act or practice which is foisted upon or passed off to another as genuine, authentic, or bona fide; as, several of the gallery's paintings reputed to be the work of Rubens and Rembrandt were *impostures;* "the hero is as gross an *imposture* as the heroine" (*Shaw*). **Cheat** applies chiefly to something (sometimes to someone) that wins one's belief in its (or his) genuineness, either because one is deliberately misled or imposed upon by another or is the victim of illusion or delusion. "When I consider life, 'tis all a *cheat*. Yet fool'd with hope, men favour the deceit" (*Dryden*). "What...man ... Shall prove (what argument could never yet) The Bible an *imposture* and a *cheat?*" (*Cowper*). "Hence, pageant history! hence, gilded *cheat!*" (*Keats*). "If I passed myself off on Miss Carew as a gentleman, I should deserve to be exposed as a *cheat*" (*Shaw*). **Fraud** applies to any imposture or impostor that positively reveals perversion of the truth, often criminal perversion, in the claims made for it or for him. "Many persons persisted in believing that his supposed suicide was but another *fraud*" (*J. M'Carthy*). "O fallen nobility that, overawed, Would lisp in honey'd whispers of this monstrous *fraud* [Louis Napoleon]!" (*Tennyson*). "We may take it as undisputed that Swinburne...did something that had not been done before, and that what he did will not turn out to be a *fraud*" (*T. S. Eliot*). The not uncommon term *pious fraud* applies to any imposture for the sake of a good end, especially for the advancement of religion. "The outworn rite, the old abuse, The *pious fraud* transparent grown" (*Whittier*). The term is also commonly applied to a person whose piety or zeal for religion is pretense or hypocrisy. **Sham** applies to any close copy of a thing, especially to one that is more or less obviously a fraudulent imitation. "A strong living Soul in him, and Sincerity there; a Reality, not an artificiality, not a *Sham!*" (*Carlyle*). "He smiled, in his worldliest manner. But the smile was a *sham*" (*Bennett*). **Fake** (a colloquial term) applies either to a person that represents himself as someone he is not or, more often, to a worthless thing that is represented as being something that it is not; *fake* differs from *fraud* in not necessarily implying dishonesty in these representations, for a *fake* may be a joke, or a theatrical device, or the like, or it may be a clear fraud; as, this testimonial is clearly a *fake;* one of the great *fakes* of all time was the Cardiff Giant; actors using *fakes* instead of real swords on the stage. **Humbug** (a colloquial rather than a literary term, much used, however, by good writers) applies to a person, or far less often a thing, that pretends or is pretended to be other, and usually more important, than he or it is, not necessarily because of a desire on the part of the person involved to deceive others, but often because he is self-deceived. "You will take to politics, where you will become...the henchman of ambitious *humbugs*" (*Shaw*). "What *humbugs* we are, who pretend to live for Beauty, and never see the Dawn!" (*L. P. Smith*). **Deceit** and **deception,** as here compared, both apply to something that misleads one or deludes one into taking it for what it is not. *Deceit*, however, usually, but not invariably, suggests the work of a deceiver, or of one (not necessarily a person) that misleads or leads astray the unwary; as, "the *deceits* of the world, the flesh, and the devil" (*Book of Common Prayer*); "Thy painted baits, And poor *deceits*, Are all bestowed on me in vain" (*Wither*). *Deception*, on the other hand, often suggests a quality or character in the thing, which causes one to mistake it or frankly to take it as other than it really is; as, the rising and the setting of the sun are pure *deceptions*. "Sylph was it? or a Bird...? A second darted by;—and lo! Another.... Transient *deception!* a gay freak Of April's mimicries! Those brilliant strangers... Proved last year's leaves, pushed from the spray To frolic on the breeze" (*Wordsworth*). **Counterfeit** commonly applies to a close imitation or copy of a thing, such as a coin, a postage stamp, paper money, a bond or other security, depending upon pictorial devices or engraved designs for assurance of its genuineness: the term usually also implies the passing or circulation of such an imitation as if it were genuine; as, the city is being flooded with *counterfeits* of five-dollar bills. The term is also applicable to any thing or, less often, to any person, that passes for something other than it actually or truly is; as, his newly purchased painting by Raphael was proved to be a clever *counterfeit;* "She had the illusion that she was not really a married woman and a house-mistress, but only a kind of *counterfeit*" (*Bennett*). **Simulacrum** may be used in place of any of the preceding words that do not carry a strong implication of deliberate deception or of intentional imposition. It implies a counterfeiting of something real, but not an attempt to pass off as real; as, "The dead-alive gape, stare, and hue of the lumpish *simulacrums* of a wax show" (*Pall Mall Gazette*). Often, however, the term applies to a person, an object, or an immaterial thing that is what he or it is supposed to be only in external appearance: it suggests lack of substance or of life or, in reference to a person such as a sovereign or ruler, a lack of all the qualities essential to his station; as, "Some spirit of life breathed into their *simulacrum* of a faith" (*Edinburgh Review*); "[George IV] nothing but a coat and a wig and a mask smiling below it—nothing but a great *simulacrum*" (*Thackeray*).

Ana. *Trick, ruse, feint, artifice, wile, stratagem, maneuver.

impotent. **1** *Powerless, impuissant.

Ana. *Ineffective, ineffectual, inefficacious, inefficient: *incapable, incompetent: disabled, crippled, debilitated, enfeebled (see WEAKEN).

Ant. Potent. — ***Con.*** *Powerful, puissant, forceful, forcible: *vigorous, energetic, strenuous: *effective, effectual, efficacious, efficient: *able, capable.

2 *Sterile, barren, unfruitful, infertile.

Ant. Virile.

impoverish. Bankrupt, exhaust, *deplete, drain.

Ant. Enrich. — ***Con.*** Enhance, heighten, *intensify: augment, *increase.

imprecation. *Curse, malediction, malison, anathema.

Ana. Execration, damning, objurgation (see corresponding verbs at EXECRATE): *blasphemy, profanity, swearing.

Ant. Prayer. — ***Con.*** *Blessing, benediction, benison.

impregnable. Inexpugnable, unassailable, invulnerable, *invincible, unconquerable, indomitable.
Ana. *Formidable, redoubtable: secure, *safe: protected, shielded, guarded, safeguarded, defended (see DEFEND).
Con. Exposed, open, *liable, susceptible, subject.

impregnate. 1 Saturate, *permeate, pervade, penetrate, interpenetrate, impenetrate.
Ana. Imbue, inoculate, ingrain, *infuse, suffuse, leaven: *enter, pierce, probe, penetrate.
2 *Soak, saturate, drench, steep, sog, sop, ret, waterlog.
Ana. Immerse, submerge, *dip, souse.

impress, *v.* Touch, strike, *affect, influence, sway.
Ana. *Move, actuate: *thrill, electrify, enthuse: *provoke, excite, stimulate, galvanize, pique.

impress, *n.* *Impression, imprint, print, stamp.
Ana. See those at IMPRESSION, 1.

impression. 1 **Impression, impress, imprint, print, stamp** come into comparison as denoting the visible or otherwise perceptible trace or traces left (either literally or figuratively) by pressure on the surface or ground of something. **Impression** is the most widely applicable of these terms. It may be used with reference to any mark or trace, or any series or combination of marks or traces, which are produced by the physical pressure of one thing on another, as of a seal upon wax, of a foot upon mud, or of inked type or etched plate upon paper; as, in general, the first *impressions* made from an etcher's plate are the most valuable; the printers will make no further *impressions* from the old type; the detectives found a clear *impression* of finger tips on the handle of the door; the dentist said he must get a plaster of Paris *impression* of the jaw and near-by teeth before he could make the denture. But *impression* may also be used of any definite or distinct trace or traces left on the mind, soul, character, or memory by the impact of sensation, experience, or the like; as, the shock has left its *impression* on her nerves; his first *impression* of Paris still remains clear in his memory; the incident made no *impression* on his mind. **Impress** is often used in place of *impression,* especially when the reference is to any clear trace left on the character, the form, the personality, or the like, by some influence; as, his father's uprightness has left a lasting *impress* on his character; he reveals the *impress* of Keats's influence in every poem he writes; "The dusting of the white paper...is a symbol of the sweeping clear from the mind of all accumulated prejudice that it may receive the *impress* of beauty in all its freshness and power" (*Binyon*). **Imprint** carries a strong implication of sharpness, clearness, or permanence in outline. It may be used in reference to any impression left on a plastic substance; as, the *imprint* of a heel in the soil; the children left *imprints* of their feet on the fresh cement of the walk. The term specifically applies to the printed name of the publisher (sometimes, of the printer) and place and date of publication at the foot of a book's title page; as, this book bears the *imprint* of the G. & C. Merriam Company. **Print** is often interchangeable with *imprint* in the general sense of that word, but is more likely to be used when the trace is considered with reference to its retention of every line or characteristic detail of the original; as, the *print* (better than *imprint*) of a finger tip. It is the preferred term in combinations; as, foot*prints* in the sand; finger*prints* left by a burglar; hoof*prints*. **Stamp** applies to an impression produced by or as if by a tool or machine which strikes so hard that it leaves a distinct imprint, often one that serves to authenticate or to approve that which is so imprinted, to indicate its origin, to authorize its passage through the mails, or the like. Hence, in figurative use, *stamp* designates a marked or conspicuous impress which wins almost immediate recognition; as, "We do wish as many sons of this University as may be to carry forth that lifelong *stamp* from her precincts" (*Quiller-Couch*); "These works have the 'classic' *stamp* upon them, and have been to the artists of the Far East what Greek marbles have been to us" (*Binyon*).
Ana. *Trace, vestige, track, rack: mark, token, *sign: *stigma, brand, blot, stain.
2 Notion, thought, *idea, concept, conception.
Ana. Image, percept, *sensation: sentiment, *opinion, view.
Con. Explanation, interpretation, elucidation (see corresponding verbs at EXPLAIN).

impressive. *Moving, effecting, poignant, touching, pathetic.
Ana. Imposing, majestic, august, noble, magnificent, grandiose, *grand: sublime, superb, glorious, *splendid: striking, arresting, remarkable, *noticeable.
Ant. Unimpressive. — *Con.* *Ineffective, ineffectual, inefficacious: *vain, nugatory, empty, hollow, idle, otiose.

imprint, *n.* Print, *impression, impress, stamp.

imprison. **Imprison, incarcerate, jail** (*also* **gaol**), **immure, intern** agree in meaning to confine closely so that escape is impossible or unlikely. The first three words, *imprison, incarcerate, jail* imply a shutting up in or as if in a prison, *imprison* being the general term, *incarcerate* the bookish or journalistic term, and *jail* the ordinary colloquial word. **Imprison,** however, strictly implies seizure and detention in custody; the term therefore is applicable even when the one confined is not in a prison, or jail, or suffering a penalty; as, "*imprisoned* like a fly in amber" (*Inge*); "the tremendous forces *imprisoned* in minute particles of matter" (*Inge*). **Incarcerate** in precise use implies a shutting up in or as if in a prison cell; as, he easily obtained bail and will, in all probability, not be *incarcerated* before his trial. **Jail** (or **gaol** in British official use and in some literary use) is often preferred to *incarcerate* in its literal sense as a simpler and more generally intelligible term; as, to be *jailed* for life. Often, however, *jail,* the verb, following *jail,* the noun, in its present accepted sense connotes imprisonment in a building in which persons are held for short periods, either paying the penalty for minor offenses or for the purpose of awaiting legal proceedings. **Immure** (etymologically, to enclose with walls; later, to enclose within walls) is a literary rather than technical term. When it implies punishment for a crime, especially in the type of romantic fiction known as the "Gothic novel (tale or story)" it may connote burial alive within a wall; usually, however, the term suggests imprisonment in closely confined quarters as a captive, a devotee to duty or religion, or the like; as, "Constance was now *immured* with her father, it being her 'turn' to nurse" (*Bennett*); "a convent of nuns vowed to contemplation, who were *immured* there for life, and never went outside the convent walls" (*L. P. Smith*). **Intern** is chiefly in military or wartime use; it seldom implies incarceration and usually suggests a keeping within prescribed limits (as in a guarded camp) and under severe restraints; as, to *intern* all enemy aliens for the duration of a war; to *intern* all the war refugees entering a neutral country; to *intern* [i.e., keep in port] a ship carrying contraband.
Ana. Confine, circumscribe, restrict, *limit: *restrain, curb, snaffle, check.

impromptu. Unpremeditated, offhand, improvised, *extemporaneous, extempore, extemporary.
Ana. *Spontaneous, impulsive: ready, prompt, *quick, apt.

Con. Considered, premeditated, *deliberate, studied, designed, advised: finished, *consummate.

improper. 1 Inappropriate, unfitting, unsuitable, unmeet, *unfit, inapt, unhappy, infelicitous.

Ana. Wrong, *bad, poor: *amiss, astray: incongruous, *inconsonant.

Ant. Proper. — *Con.* Right, *good: *regular, natural, normal, typical: *due, rightful, condign: legitimate, licit, *lawful, legal.

2 *Indecorous, indecent, unseemly, unbecoming, indelicate.

Ana. Unconventional, unceremonious, informal (see affirmative adjectives at CEREMONIAL): *shameless, brazen, impudent, brash, barefaced: obscene, ribald, *coarse, vulgar, gross.

Ant. Proper. — *Con.* Right, *correct: *decorous, comme il faut, decent, seemly, nice, demure.

impropriety. Barbarism, *solecism.

improve. **Improve, better, help, ameliorate** agree in denoting to mend or correct in part or in some degree. **Improve** (the general term) and **better** (more vigorous and homely) apply both to objects and to states or conditions, not of necessity bad; as, "the faculties of the mind are *improved* by exercise" (*Locke*); "Striving to *better*, oft we mar what's well" (*Shak.*); to *improve* (or *better*) one's circumstances. With a reflexive pronoun, *improve* implies a change for the better within oneself, *better* a change for the better in one's social or financial status. "[She] had from her youth *improved* herself by reading" (*J. Fordyce*). "Girls marry merely to '*better* themselves,' to borrow a significant vulgar phrase" (*M. Wollstonecraft*). To **help** is to improve while still leaving something to be desired; as, a coat of paint would *help* that house. **Ameliorate** is used chiefly in reference to conditions that are hard to bear or that cause suffering, and implies partial relief or changes that make them tolerable. "There is no hope whatever of *ameliorating* his condition" (*Peacock*).

Ana. *Benefit, profit: amend, *correct, rectify, reform, revise: enhance, heighten (see INTENSIFY).

Ant. Impair: worsen. — *Con.* Corrupt, pervert, vitiate, *debase, deprave: *injure, harm, damage, mar.

improvised. Unpremeditated, impromptu, offhand, *extemporaneous, extempore, extemporary.

Ana. & *Con.* See those at IMPROMPTU.

impudent. *Shameless, brazen, barefaced, brash.

Ana. *Impertinent, intrusive, obtrusive, officious, meddlesome: *rude, impolite, discourteous, uncivil, ungracious.

Ant. Respectful. — *Con.* *Shy, modest, diffident, bashful.

impugn. Gainsay, contradict, negative, traverse, *deny, contravene.

Ana. *Attack, assail: refute, rebut, confute, controvert, *disprove.

Ant. Authenticate: advocate. — *Con.* *Confirm, corroborate, substantiate: *support, uphold, back.

impuissant. Impotent, *powerless.

Ana. & *Con.* See those at IMPOTENT, 1.

Ant. Puissant.

impulse, *n.* *Motive, spring, incentive, inducement, spur, goad.

Ana. Impetus, *stimulus, incitement, stimulant: urge, passion, lust, *desire, appetite: moving *or* movement, driving *or* drive, impelling *or* impulsion, actuation (see corresponding verbs at MOVE).

impulsive. *Spontaneous, instinctive, automatic, mechanical.

Ana. Impetuous, *precipitate, headlong, abrupt, sudden, hasty.

Ant. Deliberate (sense 1). — *Con.* *Voluntary, intentional: premeditated, considered, *deliberate, designed: *cautious, circumspect, calculating.

impute. Attribute, *ascribe, assign, refer, credit, accredit, charge.

Ana. Attach, *fasten, affix: *accuse, charge, indict: allege, advance, *adduce: intimate, insinuate, hint (see SUGGEST).

in-. *Un-, a-, non-.

in, *prep.* 1 *At, on.

2 *At, on.

in abeyance. Dormant, quiescent, *latent, potential, abeyant.

Ana. & *Con.* See those at ABEYANT.

inability. **Inability, disability** are sometimes confused because of their verbal likeness. Although both denote a lack of ability to perform a given act or to follow a given trade or profession, they are otherwise clearly distinguished. **Inability** implies lack of power (sometimes an inherent lack) to perform; it may suggest mental deficiency or temperamental unfitness, but more often it suggests lack of means, lack of health, lack of training, or the like; as, "an *inability* to laugh" (*Lucas*); "an *inability* to see" (*A. Huxley*); "the *inability* of the economic system to effect a cure" (*J. A. Hobson*). **Disability** implies the loss or the deprivation of such power, as by accident, illness, disqualification, or the like; the term, therefore, is applicable not only to the resulting inability, but to the injury, the impediment, or whatever it is that makes one unable to do a certain thing, hold a certain office, or the like; as, because of *disabilities*, many of the soldiers could not return to their former occupations when the war ended; to teach new trades to all those suffering from *disabilities;* one may be ineligible to office on account of some legal *disability* such as foreign birth; a judge is under a *disability* of deciding in his own case.

Ana. Incapability, incompetence, unqualifiedness (see corresponding adjectives at INCAPABLE): unfitness, unsuitability (see corresponding adjectives at UNFIT).

Ant. Ability. — *Con.* Capacity, capability (see ABILITY).

inactive. **Inactive, idle, inert, passive, supine** come into comparison when they mean not engaged in work or activity. **Inactive** is applicable to anyone or to anything that for any reason is not in action, in operation, in use, at work, or the like; as, *inactive* machines; delicate children are usually *inactive;* an *inactive* account. **Idle** (see also VAIN, 1) applies chiefly to persons who are without occupation or not busy at the moment, but it is also applicable to their powers, their organs, the implements they use, and the like; as, "Why stand ye here all the day *idle?* They say unto him, Because no man hath hired us" (*Matthew* xx. 6–7); "Though his pen was now *idle*, his tongue was active" (*Macaulay*); "Is a field *idle* when it is fallow?" (*Shaw*). **Inert** as applied to a thing (matter, a substance, a drug, and the like) implies inherent lack of power to set itself in motion or by itself to produce a given or understood effect; as, "[comets] were now shewn to be mere chunks of *inert* matter, driven to describe paths round the sun by exactly the same forces as prescribed the orderly motions of the planets" (*Jeans*); "Commercial fertilizers consist of three to five hundred pounds of available plant food...extended with harmless *inert* materials to make a ton of product" (*A. C. Morrison*). As applied to persons or their activities, *inert* always suggests inherent or habitual indisposition to activity, or extreme difficulty in stimulating or setting in motion; thus, *inert* citizens are not easily aroused to action when evidence of graft or waste of the city's money is presented to them; many students are too *inert* to derive much stimulation from the books they read. "The *inert* Were roused, and lively natures rapt away!" (*Wordsworth*). **Passive** (etymologically, the reverse of *active;* that is, being the thing that is affected by another's action) implies immobility or a lack of a positive reaction when subjected to external driving or impelling forces or to provocation of any sort; as, "the mind is wholly *passive* in the reception of all its simple ideas" (*Locke*); "To sit as a *passive* bucket and be pumped into...can in the long run be exhilarating to no creature" (*Carlyle*); "[Noah Webster] deprecated '... the *passive* reception of everything that comes from a foreign press' " (*H. R. Warfel*). In an extended sense, *passive* often implies submissiveness without action that helps the person or side that attacks or seeks to impose its will (as, *passive* obedience; *passive* resistance) but it still more often implies a failure to be provoked to action or resistance (as, "to be *passive* in calamity is the province of no woman"—*Meredith*). **Supine** implies abject or cowardly inertia or passivity, usually as a result of sloth or indolence; as, it is impossible to remain *supine* when war threatens; "[Antony's] apparent *supineness* as Julius's avenger" (*Buchan*).

Ana. *Latent, quiescent, dormant, abeyant, potential: torpid, comatose, sluggish, *lethargic.

Ant. Active, live. — *Con.* Operative, dynamic (see ACTIVE): *busy, industrious, diligent: employed, used, utilized, applied (see USE, *v.*).

inadvertent. Heedless, *careless, thoughtless.

Con. Conscious, *aware, cognizant, alive, awake: *deliberate, advised, designed, studied: *voluntary, intentional.

inalienable. *Indefeasible.

inane. Banal, wishy-washy, jejune, *insipid, vapid, flat.

Ana. Foolish, silly, fatuous, asinine (see SIMPLE): *vain, idle, empty, hollow, nugatory: vacuous, blank (see EMPTY).

Con. *Expressive, significant, meaningful, pregnant.

inanimate. Lifeless, *dead, defunct, deceased, departed, late.

Ana. Inert, *inactive.

Ant. Animate. — *Con.* *Living, alive, quick.

inappreciable. Imponderable, impalpable, *imperceptible, insensible, intangible.

Ant. Appreciable, ponderable.

inappropriate. Unfitting, unmeet, inapt, improper, unsuitable, *unfit, unhappy, infelicitous.

Ana. Unbecoming, unseemly, *indecorous: incongruous, discordant, *inconsonant.

Ant. Appropriate. — *Con.* Fitting, proper, happy, felicitous, suitable, meet, *fit.

inapt. Unhappy, infelicitous, inappropriate, unfitting, unmeet, unsuitable, improper, *unfit.

Ana. Inept, maladroit, gauche, *awkward, clumsy: banal, flat, jejune, *insipid.

Ant. Apt. — *Con.* Happy, felicitous, appropriate (see FIT): apposite, germane, pertinent, *relevant.

inarticulate. *Dumb, speechless, mute.

Ana. *Silent, taciturn, reserved.

Ant. Articulate. — *Con.* *Vocal, fluent, eloquent, voluble, glib.

inasmuch as. Since, *because, for, as.

inaugurate. **1** Install, induct, invest, *initiate.

Ana. Introduce, admit, *enter.

2 Initiate, start, *begin, commence.

Ana. *Found, establish, institute, organize.

Con. Terminate, end, conclude, *close.

inauspicious. Unpropitious, *ominous, portentous, fateful.

Ana. Threatening, menacing (see THREATEN): *sinister, malign, malefic, baleful.

Ant. Auspicious. — *Con.* *Favorable, propitious, benign: fortunate, *lucky, happy, providential.

inborn. *Innate, congenital, hereditary, inherited, inbred.

Ana. *Inherent, intrinsic, constitutional, essential: natural, normal, *regular, typical: *native, indigenous.

Ant. Acquired.

inbred. *Innate, inborn, congenital, hereditary, inherited.

Ana. Ingrained, *inherent, constitutional, intrinsic: deep-rooted, deep-seated, *inveterate, confirmed, chronic.

Con. Infused, imbued, inoculated (see INFUSE).

incapable, *adj.* **Incapable, incompetent, unqualified** come into comparison when they mean mentally or physically unfit, or unfitted by nature, character, or training to do a given kind of work. Except for this denial of fitness, the terms otherwise correspond to the affirmative adjectives in their attributive use as discriminated at ABLE, especially when their limitations in application and their distinguishing implications are considered.

Ana. Inefficient, *ineffective: disabled, crippled, debilitated (see WEAKEN).

Ant. Capable. — *Con.* Competent, *able, qualified: efficient, *effective.

incarcerate. *Imprison, jail, immure, intern.

Ana. Confine, circumscribe, restrict, *limit.

incarnate, *v.* Embody, hypostatize, materialize, externalize, objectify, substantiate, substantialize, *realize, actualize, reify.

incense, *v.* Enrage, infuriate, *anger, madden.

Ana. Exasperate, *irritate, roil, provoke, nettle, aggravate: *offend, outrage, affront, insult.

Ant. Placate. — *Con.* Appease, mollify, *pacify, propitiate, conciliate.

incense, *n.* Redolence, *fragrance, perfume, scent, bouquet.

Ana. Odor, aroma, *smell.

incentive. Inducement, *motive, spring, spur, goad, impulse.

Ana. *Stimulus, incitement, stimulant, impetus: provoking *or* provocation, excitement, stimulation (see corresponding verbs at PROVOKE): reason, *cause, determinant.

inception. *Origin, source, root, provenance, provenience.

Ana. Beginning, commencement, starting *or* start, initiation, inauguration (see corresponding verbs at BEGIN): rising *or* rise, origination, derivation (see corresponding verbs at SPRING).

Ant. Termination. — *Con.* *End, ending, terminus: completion, finishing, concluding *or* conclusion, closing (see corresponding verbs at CLOSE).

incessant. Continuous, constant, perpetual, *continual, perennial.

Ana. Unceasing, interminable, never-ending, endless, *everlasting: *steady, constant: vexing, irking, annoying, bothering (see ANNOY).

Ant. Intermittent. — *Con.* Periodic, recurrent (see INTERMITTENT).

incest. *Adultery, fornication.

inchoate. Unformed, *formless, amorphous, shapeless, chaotic.

Ana. *Elementary, elemental: beginning, commencing, starting, initiating *or* initial (see corresponding verbs at BEGIN): unfinished, uncompleted *or* incomplete (see

affirmative verbs at CLOSE): *immature, unmatured.
Con. *Perfect, whole, entire, intact: *consummate, finished.

incident, *adj.* *Liable, subject, open, exposed, prone, susceptible, sensitive.
Ana. Typical (*of*), natural (*to*), normal (*in*) (see REGULAR): *characteristic (*of*), peculiar (*to*).

incident, *n.* Episode, event, *occurrence, circumstance.

incidental. *Accidental, casual, fortuitous, contingent, adventitious.
Ana. Incident (see LIABLE): *subordinate, secondary, collateral: associated, related, linked, connected (see JOIN).
Ant. Essential (sense 2). — *Con.* Fundamental, cardinal, vital (see ESSENTIAL).

incisive. **Incisive, trenchant, clear-cut, cutting, biting, crisp** come into comparison when they are applied to utterances, thoughts, style, mentalities, or the like, and mean having or manifesting the qualities associated with sharpness, keenness, and acuteness, especially of mind. **Incisive** usually implies not only qualities in the thing so described which give it the power to penetrate, pierce, or cut through, but also the production of such an effect upon the person or persons impressed; thus, an *incisive* voice, or tone of voice, is one that is not only sharply clear and edged but one that affects the nerves of the ear as though it cuts into them; an *incisive* command is so sharply imperative and direct that it can neither be misunderstood nor disobeyed. "Bismarck's will had not that *incisive,* rapier quality, that quality of highly tempered steel—flexible, unbreakable, of mortal effect, decisive...which had Richelieu's" (*Belloc*). "When finally pushed into a corner, he would be more *incisive,* more deadly, than any man seated four-square and full of importance at a governmental desk" (*V. Sackville-West*). **Trenchant,** literally applied to weapons with an extremely sharp edge or point (as, a *trenchant* spear), in the figurative use in which it is here considered carries a stronger implication than does *incisive* of cutting so as to define differences, categories, or classes with sharpness and perfect clearness or of probing deeply into the inmost nature of a thing so as to reveal that which is hidden or concealed; as, a *trenchant* analysis; "When roused by indignation or moral enthusiasm, how *trenchant* are our reflections!" (*W. James*); "The *trenchant* divisions between right and wrong, honest and dishonest, respectable and the reverse, had left so little scope for the unforeseen" (*E. Wharton*); "No one...was more *trenchant* than he in his criticism of the popular faith" (*G. L. Dickinson*). **Clear-cut** is applied chiefly to that which is the effect of the qualities which make for penetration, incisiveness, trenchancy, or the like: it therefore suggests sharp chiseling, clear definition, or distinct outlines, and the absence of all soft edges, haziness, or confusion in the thing or things so described; as, *clear-cut* features; *clear-cut* utterance; *clear-cut* distinctions; "the demands of Communism are too imperative, too *clear-cut* for the writer who wants only the cessation of mental pain and a private peace in his own time" (*Day Lewis*). **Cutting** is often used in place of *incisive* when a less pleasant or less agreeable quality or effect is to be connoted: the term frequently suggests sarcasm, acrimony, asperity, or the like, that wounds or hurts, but it sometimes carries a hint, at least, of penetrating truthfulness, acute discernment, or of similar mental qualities; as, "Eloquence, smooth and *cutting,* is like a razor whetted with oil" (*Swift*); "He can say the driest, most *cutting* things in the quietest of tones" (*C. Brontë*); " 'I suppose you'd leave me here without money or anything?' she said in a cold, *cutting* voice" (*Bennett*). **Biting,** when it is applied especially to utterances, expressed ideas, style, and the like, suggests a power to grip and deeply impress itself on the mind or memory, as acid bites into an etcher's plate: it therefore often suggests a caustic or mordant quality; as, his *biting* wit; *biting* epigrams; her *biting* words. **Crisp** (as here compared: see also FRAGILE, 1) suggests not only incisiveness but either vigorous terseness of expression or a bracing, invigorating quality; as, "the blithe, *crisp* sentence, decisive as a child's expression of its needs" (*Pater*); "it is a relief to come to a diction that is frequently *crisp,* and *incisive,* and terse" (*Lowes*).
Ana. Terse, succinct, laconic, *concise: poignant, *pungent, piquant.
Con. Prolix, diffuse, verbose, *wordy: *loose, lax, slack: unctuous, *fulsome.

incite. **Incite, instigate, abet, foment** are synonymous terms meaning to spur on to action or to excite into activity. **Incite** stresses stirring up and urging on; frequently, but not necessarily, it implies prompting; as, the riot was *incited* by paid agitators. "It was just like Lady Pinkerton...to have gone round to Hobart *inciting* him to drag Jane from my office" (*R. Macaulay*). **Instigate,** in contrast with *incite,* unequivocally implies prompting and responsibility for the initiation of the action; it also commonly connotes underhandedness and evil intention; as, one may be *incited* (not *instigated*) to the performance of a good act; one may be *incited* or *instigated* to the commission of a crime. "The early persecutions were...*instigated*...by the government as a safety-valve for popular discontent" (*Inge*). **Abet,** in present usage, tends to lose its etymological implication of baiting, or hounding on, and to emphasize its acquired implications (largely through association with *aid* in the legal phrase "aid and abet") of seconding, supporting, and encouraging. "Unthinkingly, I have laid myself open to the charge of aiding and *abetting* the seal-cutter in obtaining money under false pretenses" (*Kipling*). "Mr. Howells...seconded him [Mark Twain] as often as not in these innocuous, infantile ventures, *abetting* him in the production of...plays of an abysmal foolishness" (*Van W. Brooks*). **Foment** stresses persistence in goading. One who *incites* rebellion may provide only the initial stimulus; one who *foments* rebellion keeps the rebellious spirit alive by supplying fresh incitements.
Ana. Stimulate, excite, *provoke, pique, galvanize: arouse, rouse, *stir.
Ant. Restrain. — *Con.* Curb, check, inhibit, snaffle (see RESTRAIN): *frustrate, thwart, foil, circumvent, baffle, balk, outwit.

incitement. *Stimulus, stimulant, impetus.
Ana. Spur, goad, incentive, inducement, impulse, *motive, spring: provoking *or* provocation, excitement, stimulation, piquing (see corresponding verbs at PROVOKE): motivation, activation, actuation (see corresponding verbs at ACTIVATE).
Ant. Restraint: inhibition.

inclination. *Slant, slope, incline, grade, gradient, acclivity, declivity.
Ana. Bending, turning (see CURVE, *v.*): leaning, slanting (see SLANT, *v.*).

incline, *v.* **1** Lean, *slant, slope.
Ana. *Tip, tilt, cant, list, careen, heel: bend, turn, *curve: *swerve, veer, deviate: deflect, *turn.
2 Incline, bias, dispose, predispose come into comparison when they mean to influence one to take a stated or implied attitude to something or to someone, or to have such an attitude as a result of prior influences. **Incline,** literally to lean or bend (see SLANT), implies that the

mind or the feelings have been so affected that one is already leaning toward one of two or more possible conclusions, or projects, or decisions, or objects of affection, or the like. The word never suggests more than the tipping of the balance toward one, and therefore connotes merely a tendency to favor one more than the other or others. "Such considerations are not supposed to be entertained by judges, except as *inclining* them to one of two interpretations" (*Justice Holmes*). "Only a system with order and progress in the heart of it could elaborate itself so perfectly and intricately. There is assuredly much to *incline* us to 'assert Eternal Providence, And justify the ways of God to men'" (*J. A. Thomson*). "On this visit I found Australia generally *inclined* to be inimical" (*V. Heiser*). **Bias** implies a stronger and more settled leaning than *incline* suggests: it usually connotes a prejudice for or against; as, "It would be mortifying to...many ladies could they... understand how little the heart of man is affected by what is costly or new in their attire; how little it is *biassed* by the texture of their muslin" (*Austen*); "she was unfairly *biassed* towards the Liberal party in the state, and too apt to approve of the measures they passed" (*R. Macaulay*). **Dispose** differs from *incline* in stressing the implication of putting one into a frame of mind that is proper or necessary for the end in view or that makes one ready or willing to do something or to take some stand: therefore, it often connotes the sway of one's disposition, mood, temper, or the like; as, his open face *disposes* one to believe him innocent; the depression *disposed* many persons to become more thrifty; "a thinker so little *disposed* to treat the names of these religious philosophers with respect" (*Inge*). **Predispose** differs from *dispose* in implying the existence of the frame of mind, or of the proper disposition, in advance of the opportunity to manifest itself in action; as, circumstances are *predisposing* men to accept principles which they attacked a few years ago; if she is flattered and indulged, she will be *predisposed* to be favorable to him. *Predispose* is also used of a physical tendency or condition which makes one susceptible to a given infection or disease; as, *predisposed* to tuberculosis.

Ana. Influence, *affect, sway: *move, drive, impel.

Ant. Disincline, indispose.

incline, *n.* Inclination, *slant, slope, grade, gradient, acclivity, declivity.

Ana. *Mountain, mount, peak, alp: embankment, bank, dune, terrace, *mound.

include. **Include, comprehend, embrace, involve, imply, implicate, subsume** are not close synonyms, but they come into comparison as meaning basically to contain something within itself as a part or portion of the whole. **Include** suggests that the thing included forms a constituent, component, or subordinate part; as, the genus *Viola includes* the pansy as well as various species of violets; the collection will not *include* any examples of the artist's earliest and inferior paintings; an edition of the Bible which *includes* the Apocrypha; "It would not be argued today that the power to regulate does not *include* the power to prohibit" (*Justice Holmes*). **Comprehend** (etymologically, to grasp) suggests that within the scope or range of the whole under consideration (such as the content of a term, a concept, a conception, a view, or the like) the thing comprehended is held or enclosed even though it may or may not be clearly distinguished or actually distinguishable. "If there be any other commandment, it is briefly *comprehended* in this saying, namely, Thou shalt love thy neighbour as thyself" (*Romans* xiii. 9). "The counsel for the appellee would limit it [the term *commerce*] to traffic, to buying and selling, or the interchange of commodities, and do not admit that it *comprehends* navigation" (*Ch. Just. Marshall*). **Embrace,** as here compared (see also ADOPT), suggests a reaching out to gather the thing embraced within the whole (such as the content of a mind or of a course, a construction or interpretation of a law, etc.); as, "The scene before the reddleman's eyes....*embraced* hillocks, pits, ridges, acclivities, one behind the other" (*Hardy*); "By Baudelaire's time it was no longer necessary for a man to *embrace* such varied interests in order to have the sense of the age" (*T. S. Eliot*); "Whatever disagreement there may be as to the scope of the phrase 'due process of law,' there can be no doubt that it *embraces* the fundamental conception of a fair trial" (*Justice Holmes*). **Involve** (etymologically, to roll up in, or to infold) suggests inclusion by virtue of the nature of the whole, such as by being its natural or inevitable consequence (as, surrender *involves* submission; "It is quite probable that many of those who would make the best doctors are too poor to take the course. This *involves* a deplorable waste of talent"—*B. Russell*), or one of its antecedent conditions (as, "Clerkship did not necessarily *involve* even minor orders"—*Quiller-Couch;* "I should...supply the humanistic elements of education in ways not *involving* a great apparatus of learning" —*B. Russell*), or one of the parts or elements which comprise it by necessity or definition (as, "that fusion of public and private life which was *involved* in the ideal of the Greek citizen"—*G. L. Dickinson*). **Imply** is very close to *involve* in its etymological meaning, for it also connotes a carrying within its folds; however, the term stresses a thing's inclusion not, as *involve* does, by the nature or constitution of the whole, but as something which can be inferred because hinted at (see also SUGGEST, 1; INFER, 2), or because normally or customarily part of its content, especially by definition (as, embrace *implies* a reaching out to gather to oneself or within one's grasp), or because invariably associated with the thing under consideration as its cause or its effect, or as its maker or its product (as, a watch *implies* a watchmaker), or the like. For this reason, *imply* may, in comparison with *involve*, suggest a degree of uncertainty; thus, silence is often said to *imply* consent, but it would be rash to say that it *involves* consent. **Implicate** (etymologically, to intertwine) implies so intimate a connection between things that one is necessarily involved in the other; as, the brain is pathologically *implicated* in a case of insanity; "there was never any idea of domestic comfort...*implicated* in such structures" (*N. Hawthorne*). But this use of *implicate* is now comparatively rare in the verb, unless there is the added connotation of incrimination (for this sense see INVOLVE, 1). **Subsume,** a technical term in logic, philosophy, and the classificatory sciences, implies inclusion within a class or category (as an individual in a species or a species in a genus) or a being comprehended by a principle, proposition, or the like; as, "Absolute generic unity would obtain if there were one summum genus under which all things without exception could be eventually *subsumed*" (*W. James*).

Ana. Comprise, consist of, *compose, constitute: *contain, hold, accommodate.

Ant. Exclude. — *Con.* Eliminate, rule out, debar, disbar, shut out (see EXCLUDE): omit, forget (see NEGLECT, *v.*).

incognito. *Pseudonym, alias, nom de guerre, pen name, nom de plume, allonym.

incommode. Discommode, *inconvenience, trouble, molest.

Ana. *Hinder, impede, obstruct, block: disturb, *discompose: bother, irk, vex, *annoy.

Ant. Accommodate (sense 2). — *Con.* *Oblige, favor: *indulge, humor: *please, gratify.

incomparable. Peerless, *supreme, superlative, transcendent, surpassing, pre-eminent, banner.
Ana. Unrivaled, unmatched, unapproached, unequaled (see affirmative verbs at MATCH).
Con. Ordinary, *common: fair, mediocre, *medium, second-rate, average.

incompatible. Incongruous, *inconsonant, inconsistent, discordant, discrepant, uncongenial, unsympathetic.
Ana. Antagonistic, counter, *adverse: *antipathetic, averse: contrary, contradictory, antithetical, antipodal, *opposite: irreconcilable, unconformable, unadaptable (see affirmative verbs at ADAPT).
Ant. Compatible. — *Con.* Congruous, *consonant, consistent, congenial: harmonizing *or* harmonious, corresponding *or* correspondent, agreeing (see corresponding verbs at AGREE).

incompetent. Unqualified, *incapable.
Ana. Inefficient, *ineffective.
Ant. Competent. — *Con.* *Able, capable, qualified: skilled, *proficient, expert.

incongruous. *Inconsonant, uncongenial, incompatible, inconsistent, discordant, discrepant, unsympathetic.
Ana. Alien, foreign, extraneous (see EXTRINSIC): grotesque, bizarre, *fantastic.
Ant. Congruous. — *Con.* Fitting, suitable, appropriate, meet, *fit: *consonant, compatible, congenial, consistent.

inconsistent. *Inconsonant, incompatible, incongruous, uncongenial, unsympathetic, discordant, discrepant.
Ana. Divergent, disparate, diverse, *different: irreconcilable (see affirmative verb at ADAPT).
Ant. Consistent. — *Con.* *Consonant, compatible, congruous: according *or* accordant, agreeing, tallying, jibing, corresponding *or* correspondent (see corresponding verbs at AGREE).

inconsonant. Inconsonant, inconsistent, incompatible, incongruous, uncongenial, unsympathetic, discordant, discrepant come into comparison as meaning not in agreement with one another or not agreeable one to the other. Except for this denial of reciprocal agreement or agreeableness, the first six words correspond to the affirmative adjectives as discriminated at CONSONANT, especially in regard to their specific implications and their syntactical differences. **Discordant** (see also DISSONANT) is more common than *inconsonant* when applied, in the sense of devoid of harmony, to things coming into contact or comparison with each other; as, *discordant* voices; the *discordant* views of cabinet officers. **Discrepant** is also often preferred to *inconsistent* in attributive use, especially when a wide variance between details of two things that should be alike or consistent is to be suggested; thus, "two *discrepant* accounts of an accident" suggests more obvious differences in details than "their accounts are *inconsistent.*" *Inconsistent* is now usually preferred in predicative use.
Ana. *Dissonant, discordant.
Ant. Consonant. — *Con.* Congruous, compatible, consistent, congenial (see CONSONANT): harmonized *or* harmonious, attuned (see corresponding verbs at HARMONIZE).

inconstant. Inconstant, fickle, capricious, mercurial, unstable come into comparison when they mean lacking or showing lack of firmness or steadiness in purpose, attachment, devotion, or the like. **Inconstant,** now usually applied to persons, though sometimes still applied to things, suggests an inherent or constitutional tendency to change frequently (cf. CHANGEABLE): it commonly implies an incapacity for fixity or steadiness, as in one's affections, aspirations, course, or the like; as, "O, swear not by the moon, the *inconstant* moon, That monthly changes in her circled orb" (*Shak.*); " 'people seldom know what they would be at, young men especially, they are so amazingly changeable and *inconstant*' " (*Austen*). "One of his [Montaigne's] own *inconstant* essays, never true for a page to its proposed subject" (*Pater*). **Fickle** now retains only a hint of its etymological implication of deceitfulness or treacherousness, but its basic implications of instability and unreliability are colored by the suggestion of an incapacity for being true, steadfast, or certain; as, "O fortune, fortune! all men call thee *fickle*" (*Shak.*); "Bitter experience soon taught him that lordly patrons are *fickle* and their favour not to be relied on" (*A. Huxley*); "La, she is *fickle!* How she turns from one face To another face,— and smiles into them all!" (*Millay*). **Capricious** suggests qualities which manifest or seem to manifest a lack of guidance by law, by authority, by reason, or by any power that tends to regularize movements or acts. When used in reference to persons, it suggests guidance by whim, mood, freak, or the like; as, "Louis XIII...a boy of eight at his accession...grows up *capricious,* restricted and cold, hardly normal" (*Belloc*); "he judged her to be *capricious,* and easily wearied of the pleasure of the moment" (*E. Wharton*). When used in reference to things, it implies an irregularity, an uncertainty, or a variableness that seems incompatible with the operation of any law; as, a *capricious* climate; "The *capricious* hues of the sea" (*Lamb*); "the *capricious* uncertain lease on which you and I hold life" (*Quiller-Couch*); "The olive is slow-growing, *capricious* in its yield" (*A. Huxley*). **Mercurial** is a synonym of the other words here discriminated only when it carries a strong implication of resemblance to the metal mercury and its fluctuations when subjected to any external influence. The word, however, is seldom devoid of implications derived from its earlier association with the god Mercury, such as swiftness, eloquence, cleverness, and volatility. Consequently when, as here considered, it applies to persons, their temperaments, their natures, and the like, it usually suggests a pleasing, even if a baffling, variability, an amazing succession of gifts capable of being displayed at will or at need, and various other qualities such as sprightliness, restlessness, flashing wit, elusive charm, and the like; as, "The gay, gallant, *mercurial* Frenchman" (*Disraeli*); "I was ardent in my temperament; quick, *mercurial,* impetuous" (*Irving*); "It seems impossible that her bright and *mercurial* figure is no longer among us, that she will delight us no more with the keen precision and stabbing brilliance of that jewelled brain" (*New Republic*). **Unstable,** which is applicable to persons as well as to things, implies a constitutional incapacity for remaining in a fixed position, mentally or emotionally as well as physically: it suggests, therefore, such fluctuations in behavior as frequent, and often unjustified, changes in occupation or in residence, or sudden and startling changes of faith or of interests; as, "*Unstable* as water, thou shalt not excel" (*Genesis* xlix. 4); "His nature, lamentably *unstable,* was not ignoble" (*Macaulay*).
Ana. *Changeable, changeful, variable, protean, mutable: *faithless, disloyal, false, treacherous, traitorous, perfidious: volatile, frivolous, light, light-minded (see corresponding nouns at LIGHTNESS).
Ant. Constant. — *Con.* *Reliable, dependable, trustworthy, trusty: true, leal, loyal, stanch, steadfast, *faithful.

inconvenience, *v.* **Inconvenience, incommode, discommode, trouble, molest** come into comparison in the sense of to subject one to disturbance or annoyance. **Inconvenience** usually suggests little more than interference with one's plans, one's comfort, one's freedom, or the like: it seldom carries suggestions of more than a temporary or slight disturbance or annoyance; as, I hope the new arrangement will not *inconvenience* you; do not *inconvenience* him by intruding upon him while he is writing; will it *inconvenience* you to send an answer by return mail? **Incommode** and, even more, **discommode** carry a somewhat heightened suggestion of disturbance or annoyance, but still of not so much as to imply actual suffering or injury: rather, they connote some mental agitation such as embarrassment or vexation or more or less disagreeable interference with one's comfort or plans; as, "very little *incommoded* [in reading a book] by the remarks and ejaculations of Mrs. Allen" (*Austen*); "Lucian was soon *incommoded* by the attention his cousin attracted" (*Shaw*); "It could not *discommode* you to receive any of his Grace's visiters or mine" (*Scott*); "Finding herself and the younger children *discommoded* in the boat" (*Galt*). **Trouble** is often used in polite intercourse (especially in requests) in a sense close to that of *inconvenience*, when it suggests even less effort or disturbance; as, may I *trouble* you to pass the salt; will it *trouble* you to drop this letter in the box when you are passing? It is, however, also used to imply serious disturbance or annoyance such as worry, deep concern, great pains, or the like: in this sense and sometimes in the lighter sense, it is frequently a reflexive verb or, in current colloquial use, an intransitive verb taking the place of a reflexive; as, do not *trouble* yourself about our bad fortune; "Men *troubled* themselves about pain and death much as healthy bears did" (*H. Adams*); "An artist who does not *trouble* about the philosophy of things, but just obeys the dim promptings of instinct" (*C. E. Montague*). **Molest** implies extreme disturbance or annoyance, as through meddlesomeness or through hostile or malicious interference with one's rights, one's freedom, one's security, etc.; as, "safe, where no critics damn, no duns *molest*" (*Pope*); "It does not seem...to follow that she intended to persecute or *molest* Protestants" (*A. Lang*); the nurse went wherever called, without fear of being *molested*.

Ana. Disturb, *discompose: interfere, intermeddle, *meddle.

incorporate, *v.* Embody, assimilate, *identify.

Ana. Merge, blend, fuse, coalesce (see MIX): *unite, combine, conjoin: consolidate, unify, *compact.

increase, *v.* **Increase, enlarge, augment, multiply** come into comparison as meaning to become or cause to become greater or more numerous. **Increase,** in discriminating use of the intransitive, always carries the idea of progressive growth; sometimes it means nothing more than this. "And Jesus *increased* in wisdom and stature, and in favour with God and man" (*Luke* ii. 52). Sometimes it implies growth in numbers, as by propagation (as, "He blessed them, saying: *Increase* [*A.V.*, Be fruitful] and multiply, and fill the waters of the sea"—*Genesis* i. 22, *D. V.*), or growth in size, amount, or quantity, as by increments or accretions (as, their salaries *increase* annually by one hundred dollars; his strength will *increase* when his health improves), or growth in intensity, especially by degrees or in proportion to something else (as, the darkness *increases* the further we advance into the forest; "your misery *increase* with your age!"—*Shak.*). In transitive use, *increase* may or may not imply progressive growth; often it so stresses the operation or the effectiveness of a cause, that it loses the connotation of natural or regular progression; as, the trustees *increased* all salaries; a rich diet *increases* one's weight; the depression *increased* his misery; the girl's actions *increased* the observer's suspicions; good teaching *increases* one's desire for knowledge. **Enlarge** stresses expansion or extension so that whatever is affected is greater in some or all of its dimensions or in its size or capacity; as, he *enlarged* his farm by the purchase of one hundred adjoining acres; to *enlarge* a hotel by building a new wing. Figuratively, *enlarge* is applicable in discriminating use only to that which may be thought of as capable of being made larger or smaller in extent or size; thus, one does not *enlarge* one's interests or one's activities, but the field of one's interests, or the scope of one's activities; hence, to *enlarge* the circle of one's acquaintances; to *enlarge* one's capacity for enjoyment. Nevertheless, field, scope, capacity, etc., are sometimes implied. "Its [a constitutional clause's] terms purport to *enlarge*...the powers vested in the government" (*Ch. Just. Marshall*). "*Enlarging* our personality by establishing new affinities and sympathies with our fellow-men, with nature, and with God" (*Inge*). **Augment,** like *increase*, etymologically implies growth; it rarely, however, carries the implication of progressive growth or growth by degrees, which is often so strong in *increase*. It differs from *increase* chiefly in being used in reference to things already well grown, well developed, or the like; thus, when one says "the team's confidence *increases* with every victory" one implies that its confidence was originally not strong; on the other hand, when one says "the team's confidence *augments* with every victory" one implies that its confidence was never weak. Consequently the distinctive implication of *augment* is a growing greater, more numerous, larger, more intense, or the like. "Even an increase of fame served only to *augment* their industry" (*Sir J. Reynolds*). "To fret over unavoidable evils, or *augment* them by anxiety" (*Austen*). **Multiply** commonly implies an increase in number, especially by natural generation; as, the Creator bade his creatures to *multiply* and fill the earth. "Hookworms live a long, long time in the small intestine...but they cannot *multiply* there" (*V. Heiser*). Sometimes, however, the word implies increase in numbers by indefinite repetition of things of the same kind; as, a machine for *multiplying* typewritten copies; if there were space, we might *multiply* illustrative citations.

Ana. *Intensify, aggravate, heighten, enhance: *expand, swell, amplify, dilate, distend, inflate: *extend, lengthen, elongate, prolong, protract.

Ant. Decrease. — *Con.* Diminish, lessen, reduce, abate, dwindle (see DECREASE): *shorten, abridge, abbreviate, curtail, retrench: *contract, condense, shrink, deflate.

incredulity. Disbelief, *unbelief.

Ana. Doubt, dubiety, dubiosity, skepticism, *uncertainty.

Ant. Credulity. — *Con.* Certitude, *certainty, assurance, conviction: positiveness, cocksureness, sureness (see corresponding adjectives at SURE).

increment. Accretion, *addition, accession.

incriminate. Criminate, impeach, indict, *accuse, charge, arraign.

Ana. *Involve, implicate.

Con. *Exculpate, exonerate, absolve, acquit, vindicate.

inculcate. *Implant, instill, inseminate, infix.

Ana. *Infuse, inoculate, imbue, leaven: *teach, instruct, educate: impart, *communicate.

incur. **Incur, contract, catch** come into comparison when they mean to bring upon oneself something, especially something unpleasant, onerous, or injurious. **Incur** (etymologically, to run into) may or may not imply foreknowledge of what is to happen (as, to *incur* a debt; to *incur* criticism) but it usually implies the responsibility of the person or thing for the acts which bring about that which he (or it) incurs; as, to *incur* a serious risk by submitting to an experimental operation; he said he would tell the truth, even if he *incurred* the displeasure of his constituents. **Contract** carries a stronger implication than *incur* of acquirement, but it is equally inexplicit in its lack of clear suggestion as to whether the acquisition derives from intention or accident; as, to *contract* heavy debts; to *contract* a disease; to *contract* bad habits. But *contract* often distinctively implies a meeting between two things that permits either an interchange of qualities (as, "Each from each *contract* new strength and light"—*Pope*) or a transmission of something from one to the other (as, "They say that sherry ought to live for a while in an old brandy-cask, so as to *contract* a certain convincing quality from the cask's genial timbers"—*C. E. Montague*). **Catch,** the least literary and most ordinary of these terms, usually implies infection or something analogous to it; as, to *catch* a contagious disease; to *catch* a heavy cold; "With such immunity [a mind highly resistant to literary suggestion] he is not likely to *catch* harm from the most insinuating book" (*S. M. Crothers*); "religion, in point of fact, is seldom taught at all; it is *caught*, by contact with someone who has it" (*Inge*).

Ana. *Get, obtain, acquire.

Con. *Escape, elude, evade, avoid, shun, eschew: avert, ward off, *prevent.

incurious. Unconcerned, *indifferent, aloof, detached, disinterested.

Ana. Uninterested (see DISINTERESTED): *abstracted, preoccupied, absent, absent-minded, distrait, distraught.

Ant. Curious, inquisitive. — ***Con.*** Prying, snoopy, nosy (see CURIOUS): intrusive, meddlesome, *impertinent: observing *or* observant, remarking, noticing, noting (see corresponding verbs at SEE).

incursion. *Invasion, raid, irruption, inroad.

indebtedness. *Debt, debit, obligation, liability, arrear, arrearage.

indecent. Unseemly, indelicate, improper, *indecorous, unbecoming.

Ana. Obscene, ribald, *coarse, gross, vulgar: lewd, lascivious, *licentious: *immoral: *offensive, revolting, repulsive, repugnant, loathsome.

Ant. Decent. — ***Con.*** *Chaste, pure, modest: virtuous, *moral, ethical.

indecorous. Indecorous, improper, unseemly, indecent, unbecoming, indelicate agree in meaning not in conformity with the accepted standard of what is right or fitting or is regarded as good form. The first four words, *indecorous, improper, unseemly, indecent* are in general the antonyms, or diametrical opposites, of *decorous, proper, seemly, decent* (discriminated at DECOROUS), but the negative terms are often more sharply distinguished from each other than the affirmative terms. That is **indecorous** which transgresses the conventions of polite society or its notions of what constitutes good form or good manners; as, *indecorous* behavior at a funeral; they regarded argument in the drawing room as *indecorous.* That is **improper** which violates propriety, or the standard of what is right, correct, or fitting, determined by those who are the authorities, especially in etiquette, in language, in aesthetics, or in morals; as, "I am sure if I had known it to be *improper* I would not have gone with Mr. Thorpe at all; but I always hoped you would tell me, if you thought I was doing wrong" (*Austen*); "It was most *improper* to intrude the dog into the houses of the people they were calling on" (*Conrad*); "He was telling her a funny story, probably an *improper* one, for it brought out her naughtiest laugh" (*Cather*). That is **unseemly** which is not only indecorous or improper but also offensive to persons of good taste or to strict followers of the conventions; as, to bury the old man with *unseemly* haste; "I consider it very *unseemly* to talk in this loose fashion before young men" (*Cather*); "Maurice disgraced Amy and himself by joining in an *unseemly* fracas with the police" (*R. Macaulay*); "We were in no danger of being betrayed into any *unseemly* manifestations of religious fervour" (*L. P. Smith*). That is **indecent** which is grossly offensive to those who observe the proprieties or, in its present stronger sense, to persons of sound morals or high standards of modesty or propriety; as, "when wine has given *indecent* language birth" (*Cowper*); *indecent* plays; *indecent* behavior; "these dances, though to the eyes of Johnston... 'grossly *indecent*'...are 'danced reverently' " (*H. Ellis*). That is **unbecoming** which does not befit one's character or standing, or is not in accordance with one's own standards; as, "Rosamond never showed any *unbecoming* knowledge" (*G. Eliot*); "The nurse...had a...look in her eye that was *unbecoming* in a menial position" (*H. G. Wells*). That is **indelicate** which verges upon immodesty, or (sometimes) which betrays lack of tact or of refined perceptions; as, "She had visions, so startling that she half repudiated them as *indelicate,* of coarse masculine belongings strewn about in endless litter" (*M. Wilkins*); "Think no more of the matter. It is very *indelicate* for a young lady to dwell on such subjects" (*Deland*).

Ana. Unfitting, inappropriate, unmeet, unsuitable, *unfit: incongruous, *inconsonant: *rude, ill-mannered, uncivil, discourteous, impolite: *coarse, vulgar, gross.

Ant. Decorous. — ***Con.*** Decent, nice, comme il faut, demure (see DECOROUS): ceremonious, formal, conventional (see CEREMONIAL).

indefatigable. Indefatigable, tireless, weariless, untiring, unwearying, unwearied, unflagging carry as their basic meaning not feeling or manifesting fatigue, but they are closer synonyms in their extended sense of capable of prolonged and arduous effort. **Indefatigable** etymologically implies an incapacity for fatigue, but in its actual use it usually suggests persistent and unremitting activity or effort; as, "*indefatigable* fingers" (*E. Wharton*); "The *indefatigable* pursuit of an unattainable perfection" (*L. P. Smith*); "the strenuous, persevering, and absolutely *indefatigable* champion of every victim of oppression" (*J. Morley*). **Tireless** and **weariless** are sometimes employed with little distinction from *indefatigable;* frequently, however, they connote less busyness, and even greater or more remarkable power of continuance; as, the *tireless* sweep of the eagle's flight; "out in the breakers *tirelessly* tossing" (*Whitman*); "Was not [Matthew] Arnold the *tireless* critic of his country and his age, the lifelong arraigner of British limitedness and complacency?" (*C. E. Montague*); "A sturdy Dissenter, a *weariless* promoter of godliness" (*Times Lit. Sup.*). **Untiring** and **unwearying** differ from *tireless* in carrying a stronger implication of uninterrupted activity; often, they specifically suggest an extraordinary ability to go on continuously and without a break (*tireless* and *weariless,* by contrast, often imply repeated returns over a very long course of time); as, an *untiring* (or *unwearying*) search for a lost child; *tireless* (or *weariless*) efforts to attract attention; *untiring* devotion to a cause; the *tireless* reiteration of a call; the *unwearying* pursuit of an ideal. **Unwearied** differs little from *untiring* in its meaning, but it is more often applied directly to the person or thing concerned than to the activity in which he (or it) is engaged; as, "I, so long A worshipper of Nature, hither came *Unwearied* in that service" (*Wordsworth*); "the *unwearied* and disinterested seeker after truth" (*Jowett*). **Unflagging** differs little from *tireless*, for it too stresses a display of power to continue without signs of weariness; but it also suggests no diminution of activity, and it applies to a person's powers rather than to the person himself; as, *unflagging* zeal, interest, attention; "A purpose...which he pursued with *unflagging* energy" (*Froude*).

Ana. Diligent, assiduous, sedulous, industrious, *busy: dogged, pertinacious (see OBSTINATE): energetic, strenuous, *vigorous.

Con. Wearying, tiring (see TIRE, *v.*): lagging, dawdling, procrastinating (see DELAY): indolent, fainéant, slothful, *lazy.

indefeasible *or* **undefeasible.** **Indefeasible** (*or* **undefeasible**), **inalienable** (*or* **unalienable**) come into comparison as meaning belonging to one absolutely and without qualification. That is **indefeasible** of which one cannot be deprived without one's consent (or which, in legal language, cannot be defeated, as by a subsequent condition); that is **inalienable** which one cannot give away or dispose of even if one wishes. Thus, one has an *indefeasible* title to the house which one owns absolutely, but this title may be transferred to another if one wishes to sell the house or deed it to another; under the Constitution of the United States, personal liberty, freedom of speech, etc., are *inalienable* rights. Both words, however, carry so strong an implication of unforfeitableness that they are often employed without clear distinction when the intent is to imply that no superior force can take them away; as, "The great writers...have mostly asserted freedom of conscience as an *indefeasible* right" (*J. S. Mill*); "By the *inalienable* claim of nature Anna belonged to the woman who had brought her into the world" (*Deland*).

indelicate. Indecent, unseemly, improper, *indecorous, unbecoming.

Ana. *Coarse, gross, vulgar, obscene: *rude, rough, crude, callow: lewd, wanton (see LICENTIOUS).

Ant. Delicate, refined. — *Con.* Pure, modest, *chaste, decent.

indemnify. Reimburse, recompense, requite, compensate, remunerate, *pay, repay, satisfy.

indemnity. *Reparation, redress, amends, restitution.

indentation. Indenture, nick, notch, *dent, dint.

indenture. 1 *Contract, bargain, compact, pact, treaty, entente, convention, cartel, covenant, concordat, mise.

2 Indentation, notch, nick, *dent, dint.

indentured. Articled, *bound, bond.

independence. Autonomy, freedom, sovereignty, autarky. See under FREE, *adj.*

Ana. Liberty, *freedom, license: self-reliance, reliance (see corresponding adjectives at RELIANT).

Ant. Dependence. — *Con.* Subordination, subjection (see corresponding adjectives at SUBORDINATE): *servitude, slavery, bondage.

independent. Autonomous, autonomic, *free, sovereign, autarchic, autarkic.

Ana. *Alone, solitary: self-reliant (see RELIANT): self-governed, self-ruled (see primitive verbs at GOVERN).

Ant. Dependent. — *Con.* *Subordinate, subject, tributary: *subservient, servile, slavish: relative, adjective (see DEPENDENT).

indescribable. Inenarrable, *unutterable, inexpressible, ineffable, unspeakable.

indicate. **Indicate, betoken, attest, bespeak, argue, prove** come into comparison when they mean to give evidence of, or to serve as ground for, a valid or reasonable inference. One thing **indicates** another when the former serves as a symptom, a sign, or the like, pointing to the latter as a justifiable or necessary conclusion or, in medicine, as the necessary treatment or remedy; as, the facts revealed by the auditor's investigation *indicate* that the peculations were not confined to one person; such symptoms *indicate* an operation. "The similarity [between a certain trademark and an imitation]...*indicates* nothing except perhaps the poverty of the designer's invention" (*Justice Holmes*). One thing **betokens** another when the former serves as visible or sensible evidence, or more narrowly, as a presage or portent, of the latter; as, "his appearance *betokened* complete security" (*Meredith*); the black clouds *betoken* a storm. "Like a red morn, that ever yet *betoken'd* Wreck to the seaman, tempest to the field" (*Shak.*). One thing **attests** another when the former serves as indisputable evidence of the latter, and has the force (not necessarily the character) of legal testimony, documentary proof, or the like. "The great seal....*attests*...the verity of the presidential signature" (*Ch. Just. Marshall*). "Their success is *attested* by the marvelous exactness with which eclipses are foretold" (*Karl K. Darrow*). One thing **bespeaks** another when the former leads to the inference that it is the outward manifestation of the latter. "To Him whose works *bespeak* his nature" (*Cowper*). "The large abstention from voting in our elections must certainly *bespeak* an indifference not without meaning" (*Frankfurter*). One thing **argues** another when the former gives good reason for belief in the existence, the reality, or the presence of the latter. "His evasion, of course, was the height of insolence, but it *argued* unlimited resource and verve" (*Kipling*). "To the grub under the bark the exquisite fitness of the woodpecker's organism to extract him would certainly *argue* a diabolical designer" (*W. James*). One thing **proves** another when the former serves to demonstrate or manifest the truth of the latter; as, "Your language *proves* you still the child" (*Tennyson*).

Ana. Intimate, hint, *suggest: evince, evidence, demonstrate, manifest, *show: import, signify, denote, *mean.

indict. Incriminate, criminate, impeach, charge, arraign, *accuse.

Ana. Blame, denounce, condemn (see CRITICIZE).

Con. *Exculpate, absolve, exonerate, acquit, vindicate.

indifferent. 1 **Indifferent, unconcerned, incurious, aloof, detached, disinterested** agree in meaning not feeling or showing interest, especially natural or normal interest. **Indifferent** is often used in place of the other and more specific terms. In precise usage, however, it implies neutrality of attitude arising either from a lack of bias, prejudice, or predilection when two or more persons or things are considered, or from a lack of feeling for or against a particular person or thing; as, it is impossible to remain *indifferent* to political parties when great issues are at stake; she was completely *indifferent* to him. "He was...exceedingly difficult to please, not...because he was hypercritical and exacting, but because he was *indifferent*" (*Bennett*). **Unconcerned** implies indifference arising from unconsciousness, insensitiveness, selfishness, or the like, which prevents one from being moved, worried, made solicitous, or otherwise affected. "I stood, 'mid those concussions [of the French Revolution], *unconcerned*, Tranquil almost" (*Wordsworth*). "You think you carry it off very well...but with you it is a sort of bravado, an air of affected *unconcern*" (*Austen*).

Incurious implies indifference arising from a lack of intellectual interest or normal curiosity; it often suggests incapacity because of age, temperament, or state of mind. "Irving and Una had been led, heedless and *incurious*, to each of papa's places of worship in turn" (*R. Macaulay*). **Aloof**, and especially its derivative *aloofness*, stress indifference that is the natural result of feeling apart or at a distance from someone or something, as because of temperamental reserve, a sense of superiority, or an aversion to the inferior. "Young people...tend to become arrogant and hard, ignorant of the problems of adult life, and quite *aloof* from their parents" (*B. Russell*). "It nerved him to break through the awe-inspiring *aloofness* of his captain" (*Conrad*). **Detached** often implies a commendable aloofness which is the result of freedom from prejudices or of selfish concern for one's personal interests. "[The] *detachment* [of the saints], which is emancipation wrought in the soul, and the inevitable efflorescence of the Christian spirit" (*Guiney*). Sometimes it distinctively suggests a point of view or way of looking at persons or things as though they bear no relation to one's own life. "Rome contemplated the spectacle with the *detached*, intelligent amusement of the ...theatre-goer" (*R. Macaulay*). **Disinterested** usually suggests a freedom from thought of personal advantage or interest that permits one to detect the truth, to tell the truth, or to judge truly; as, a *disinterested* observer; a *disinterested* historian (see also DISINTERESTED, 2).

Ana. Impartial, unbiased, dispassionate, *fair: uninterested (see DISINTERESTED): apathetic, *impassive, phlegmatic: *cool, nonchalant.

Ant. Avid. — ***Con.*** *Eager, keen, agog: sympathetic, responsive, compassionate (see TENDER): *antipathetic, unsympathetic, averse.

2 Average, moderate, *medium, middling, fair, mediocre, second-rate.

Ana. Ordinary, *common.

Ant. Choice. — ***Con.*** Exquisite, rare, recherché (see CHOICE): superlative, surpassing, peerless, *supreme.

3 *Neutral, adiaphorous, negative.

indigence. Penury, want, *poverty, destitution, privation.

Ana. Straits, exigency, emergency, pass (see JUNCTURE).

Ant. Affluence, opulence.

indigene, *n.* Native, aborigine, autochthon. See under NATIVE, *adj.*

indigenous. *Native, autochthonous, endemic, aboriginal.

Ant. Naturalized: exotic. — ***Con.*** Foreign, alien, extraneous (see EXTRINSIC).

indignant. *Angry, irate, wrathful, acrimonious, mad.

Ana. Incensed, infuriated, enraged, angered, maddened (see ANGER, *v.*): exasperated, roiled, provoked, nettled (see IRRITATE): roused, aroused, stirred (see STIR).

Con. *Complacent, smug, self-satisfied: *indifferent, unconcerned, aloof.

indignation. Wrath, *anger, ire, rage, fury.

Ana. Resentment, dudgeon, *offense: *passion.

indignity. *Affront, insult.

Ana. Injury, wrong, *injustice, grievance: offending *or* offense, outraging *or* outrage (see corresponding verbs at OFFEND).

indirect. Indirect, circuitous, roundabout come into comparison when they are applied to ways, routes, means, and the like, and agree in meaning not leading by or as if by a straight path to a destination or goal. **Indirect,** in literal use, implies departure from the straight and short line between two points; as, the *indirect* road to the city is the wider and better paved and therefore the speedier. Figuratively, *indirect* implies following a course that is not plain, obvious, explicit, straightforward, or the like; as, *indirect* methods of teaching moral principles; "Jane's mother was making *indirect* but perfectly legitimate inquiries into his prospects" (*M. Austin*); *indirect* taxation; *indirect* evidence. **Circuitous** implies not only indirection, but usually a winding and, because of its length, slow way or course; as, they were forced to take a *circuitous* route on account of the floods; a *circuitous* approach to the house; a *circuitous* method of solving a problem; "Paths... more *circuitous*, but not less sure Duly to reach the point marked out by Heaven" (*Wordsworth*). "And though *circuitous* and obscure The feet of Nemesis how sure!" (*W. Watson*). **Roundabout** may be used interchangeably with *circuitous*, but specifically, in its literal sense, it implies a following of a more or less circular (or semicircular) course from one point to another; the term far more often than *indirect* or *circuitous*, especially in its extended use, implies deliberate, often blameworthy, evasion or avoidance of the direct course or way; as, to take a *roundabout* course to one's destination; a *roundabout* explanation; a *roundabout* process of reasoning; "the *roundabout*, diffident appeal for pity" (*Day Lewis*). "She declared that she would have nothing to do with any *roundabout* ways, but go openly and instantly to law" (*Burney*).

Ana. Devious, oblique, *crooked: *winding, sinuous, tortuous, anfractuous.

Ant. Direct: forthright, straightforward.

indiscriminate. Indiscriminate, wholesale, sweeping come into comparison only when they carry the meaning including all, or nearly all, within the range of choice, operation, or effectiveness. That is **indiscriminate** which does not distinguish that which deserves from that which does not deserve, but gives, treats, selects, includes, or the like, regardless of individual deserts or merits; as, *indiscriminate* charity; *indiscriminate* praise. "The critic does a wrong who brings them under his *indiscriminate* censure" (*Quiller-Couch*). **Wholesale** sometimes (perhaps usually) implies indiscriminateness, but sometimes it carries almost no suggestion of it: invariably, however, it stresses extensiveness, usually suggesting that no person or thing within the range of choice, operation, or effectiveness has escaped; as, the *wholesale* vaccination of a community; the *wholesale* slaughter of a people; "Time for *wholesale* trust" (*Mrs. H. Ward*); "Communism can spread only...as a development of existing economic civilization and not by a sudden *wholesale* overthrow of it" (*Shaw*). **Sweeping** implies a reaching out in, or as if in, a wide circle to draw in everyone or everything within range: it usually carries a stronger suggestion of indiscriminateness than *wholesale* and often specifically implies exceeding the bounds of right, justice, jurisdiction, or the like, or generality rather than a concrete, specific character; as, *sweeping* reforms; *sweeping* accusations; "A *sweeping* and consummate vengeance for the indignity alone should satisfy him" (*Meredith*); "the statute is of a very *sweeping* and general character" (*Justice Holmes*).

Ana. Promiscuous, motley, heterogeneous, assorted, *miscellaneous: uncritical, *superficial, shallow.

Ant. Selective: discriminating.

indispensable. Essential, necessary, requisite, *needful.

Ana. Vital, cardinal, fundamental, *essential.

Ant. Dispensable.

indisposed. *Disinclined, loath, averse, hesitant, reluctant.

Ana. Inimical, hostile, antagonistic, antipathetic (see corresponding nouns at ENMITY).

Ant. Disposed. — ***Con.*** *Eager, avid, keen, anxious:

friendly, *amicable, neighborly: sympathetic, responsive (see TENDER).

individual, *adj.* **1** Particular, specific, *special, especial, concrete, respective.
Ana. *Single, sole, separate, particular.
Ant. General. — *Con.* Generic, *universal, common.
2 Peculiar, distinctive, *characteristic.
Ana. Unique, singular (see STRANGE): *distinct, separate, several.
Ant. Common. — *Con.* Ordinary, familiar, popular (see COMMON).

individuality. Personality, *disposition, temperament, temper, complexion, character.

individually. *Each, apiece, severally, respectively.

indolent. Fainéant, slothful, *lazy.
Ana. *Lethargic, sluggish, comatose: *inactive, inert, idle, passive, supine: *languid, languorous, lackadaisical, listless.
Ant. Industrious. — *Con.* *Busy, diligent, assiduous, sedulous: energetic, strenuous, *vigorous.

indomitable. *Invincible, unconquerable, impregnable, inexpugnable, unassailable, invulnerable.
Ana. Stubborn, dogged, pertinacious (see OBSTINATE): resolute, stanch, steadfast (see FAITHFUL): redoubtable, *formidable: undaunted, dauntless, intrepid, doughty (see BRAVE).

indorse. Variant of ENDORSE.

induce. **Induce, persuade, prevail on** *or* **upon** agree in meaning to move another by arguments, allurements, or the like, to do something or to follow a certain course. **Induce** usually implies an influencing of the reason or judgment of one who is temperamentally opposed or who is convinced that another course or act is better: the term usually suggests that the decision is outwardly at least made by the one induced rather than forced upon him by the one that induces; as, "only those... doctors who were possessed of superior courage and capable of supreme self-sacrifice could be *induced* to continue at the work" (*V. Heiser*); "the object is to *induce* the child to lend of his own free will; so long as authority is required, the end aimed at has not been achieved" (*B. Russell*). **Persuade** implies an appeal to another's feelings or desires rather than to his reason; it may suggest entreaty, coaxing, expostulation, cajoling, or the like, but it usually implies that the one persuaded is more or less won over (sometimes even tricked) by the one that persuades. "Ten o'clock! it was eleven, upon my soul! I counted every stroke. This brother of yours would *persuade* me out of my senses" (*Austen*). "It is not very difficult to *persuade* people to do what they are all longing to do" (*A. Huxley*). **Prevail on** *or* **upon** (sometimes, especially in the past, **prevail with**) may be employed in place of either *induce* or *persuade*, but it usually carries a stronger implication of opposition to be faced or of good arguments to be overcome; as, "He had never before supposed that, could Wickham be *prevailed on* to marry his daughter, it would be done with so little inconvenience to himself as by the present arrangement" (*Austen*); "I will go now and try to *prevail on* my mother to let me stay with you" (*Shaw*).
Ana. *Incite, instigate, abet: *move, actuate, drive, impel: motivate, *activate, actuate.
Con. *Command, order, enjoin, direct, bid, charge: *prescribe, assign, define.

inducement. Incentive, spur, *motive, goad, spring, impulse.
Ana. Temptation, enticement, seduction, luring *or* lure (see corresponding verbs at LURE): *stimulus, incitement, impetus, stimulant.

induct. Inaugurate, install, *initiate, invest.

induction. **1** Prologue, *introduction, prelude, overture, preface, foreword, prolegomenon, proem, exordium, preamble, prolusion, protasis, avant-propos.
2 *Deduction.
Ana. *Inference, illation, ratiocination.

inductive. Deductive. See under DEDUCTION.
Ana. Illative, ratiocinative, inferential (see under INFERENCE).

indulge. **Indulge, pamper, humor** (*or* **humour**), **spoil, baby, mollycoddle** come into comparison when they mean to show undue favor or attention to a person or his desires. **Indulge** implies complaisance or even weakness in gratifying another's wishes or desires, especially those which have no claim to fulfillment or which ought to be kept under control; as, "I would *indulge* her every whim" (*Hardy*); "pasty-faced languid creatures... *indulged* in food and disciplined in play" (*B. Russell*); "When schoolboys were less *indulged* with pocket-money" (*Arch. Marshall*). **Pamper,** which originally implied overfeeding, still carries an implication of inordinate gratification of an appetite or taste, especially for what is luxurious or dainty and, therefore, softening in its physical, mental, or moral effects; as, rich though they were, they refused to *pamper* their children. "He [Socrates] preserved without an effort the supremacy of character and mind over the flesh he neither starved nor *pampered*" (*G. L. Dickinson*). **Humor** stresses either attention to or an easy yielding to whim, caprice, or changing desires; it therefore often suggests accommodation to the moods of another. "Like a froward child, that must be played with and *humored* a little to keep it quiet" (*Temple*). "I hate sending the children to the Great House...their grandmamma...*humours* and *indulges* them to such a degree...that they are sure to come back sick and cross for the rest of the day" (*Austen*). **Spoil** stresses the injurious effect on the character or disposition of one who is indulged, pampered, humored, or otherwise made the recipient of special attention; however, the word is often used to imply attentions that are likely to have this effect. " 'She talks a great deal, sir,' Elizabeth apologized. 'She's our only little girl, and I'm afraid we *spoil* her' " (*Deland*). **Baby** implies excessive attentions, the kind given to those who are unable to care for themselves and need the constant assistance of a mother or nurse; it also carries a strong implication of humoring or pampering; as, she refused to *baby* her children after they were able to care for themselves and attend to their own needs. **Mollycoddle** usually implies babying; it distinctively suggests inordinate attention to another's health or physical comfort or, in extended use, undue efforts to relieve another of strain or hardship. It often also connotes, as the effect or danger of such treatment, effeminateness or infantilism (retarded physical, mental, or emotional development); as, schools where grown boys and girls are *mollycoddled*. "Look here, mother dear: I'm as well as ever I was, and I'm not going to be *mollicoddled* any more" (*M. E. Braddon*).
Ana. Favor, accommodate, *oblige: gratify, *please, regale, arride, delight.
Ant. Discipline (*others*): abstain (*with reference to oneself, one's appetite, etc.*).

indulgence. **1** Forbearance, tolerance, clemency, mercifulness, leniency. See under FORBEARING.
Ana. *Mercy, charity, lenity, grace: kindness, benignancy *or* benignity, benignness, kindliness (see corresponding adjectives at KIND): mildness, gentleness (see corresponding adjectives at SOFT).
Ant. Strictness. — *Con.* Severity, sternness (see

corresponding adjectives at SEVERE): rigorousness, rigidity (see corresponding adjectives at RIGID): harshness (see corresponding adjective at ROUGH).
2 *Pardon, amnesty, absolution.

indulgent. Lenient, *forbearing, tolerant, clement, merciful.
Ana. Humoring, pampering (see INDULGE): forgiving, pardoning, condoning, excusing (see EXCUSE, *v.*): benignant, benign, *kind, kindly: mild, gentle (see SOFT).
Ant. Strict. — *Con.* Stern, *severe: rigorous, stringent (see RIGID): harsh (see ROUGH).

indurated. *Hardened, callous.
Ana. Rigid, *stiff, inflexible: obdurate, adamant, adamantine, inexorable, *inflexible.
Ant. Pliable. — *Con.* *Plastic, pliant, ductile, malleable: flexible, *elastic, supple, resilient.

industrious. Diligent, *busy, assiduous, sedulous.
Ana. *Active, operative, live, dynamic: persevering, persisting *or* persistent (see corresponding verbs at PERSEVERE): *indefatigable, tireless, untiring, unflagging, unwearied.
Ant. Slothful, indolent. — *Con.* Idle, *inactive, inert, supine: *lazy, fainéant: *lethargic, sluggish, torpid.

industry. *Business, trade, commerce, traffic.

inebriate, inebriated, *adj.* *Drunk, drunken, intoxicated, tipsy, tight.

inebriate, *n.* *Drunkard, alcoholic, dipsomaniac, sot, soak, toper, tosspot, tippler.
Ant. Teetotaler.

ineffable. *Unutterable, inexpressible, inenarrable, unspeakable, indescribable.
Ana. *Celestial, heavenly, empyrean, empyreal: ethereal (see AIRY): spiritual, divine, *holy, sacred: transcendent, transcendental, ideal, *abstract.
Con. Expressible, utterable (see corresponding verbs at EXPRESS).

ineffective. Ineffective, ineffectual, inefficient, inefficacious and their less frequent forms in **un-** (**uneffective,** etc.) come into comparison as meaning not producing or incapable of producing a result or results. Except for this denial of production or capacity for production, these adjectives correspond in their applications and implications to the affirmative adjectives as discriminated at EFFECTIVE.
Ana. *Futile, vain, fruitless, bootless, abortive: *vain, nugatory, otiose, idle, empty, hollow: *sterile, barren, unfruitful, infertile.
Ant. Effective. — *Con.* Effectual, efficacious, efficient (see EFFECTIVE): fruitful, *fertile, fecund: forceful, forcible, *powerful, potent.

ineffectual. *Ineffective, inefficacious, inefficient.
Ana. See those at INEFFECTIVE.
Ant. Effectual. — *Con.* *Effective, efficacious, efficient: useful, profitable (see corresponding nouns at USE).

inefficacious. *Ineffective, ineffectual, inefficient.
Ana. *Inactive, inert, idle: *futile, vain, fruitless, bootless, abortive: *powerless, impotent.
Ant. Efficacious. — *Con.* *Powerful, potent, forcible, forceful: cogent, telling (see VALID): *effective, effectual, efficient.

inefficient. *Ineffective, ineffectual, inefficacious.
Ana. Incompetent, unqualified, *incapable: infirm, decrepit, feeble, *weak: indolent, slothful, fainéant, *lazy: remiss, lax, slack, *negligent, neglectful.
Ant. Efficient. — *Con.* Competent, *able, capable, qualified: skillful, skilled, *proficient, expert, adept.

ineluctable. *Inevitable, inescapable, unavoidable.
Ana. Destined, *prescribed, appointed: *certain, inevitable, necessary, apodictic.

Con. Escapable, avoidable, evadable *or* evasible, eludible (see corresponding verbs at ESCAPE): *doubtful, dubious, questionable: possible, *probable.

inenarrable. Indescribable, inexpressible, *unutterable, unspeakable, ineffable.

inept. *Awkward, clumsy, maladroit, gauche.
Ana. Inapt, *unfit, unsuitable, inappropriate: *impertinent, intrusive, obtrusive: *vain, nugatory, idle, empty, hollow, otiose: fatuous, asinine, foolish, silly (see SIMPLE).
Ant. Apt: adept: able (*as a result of nature, training, etc.*).

inerrable. *Infallible, inerrant, unerring.

inerrant. Unerring, *infallible, inerrable.
Ana. *Impeccable, flawless, faultless: accurate, exact, *correct, precise: *reliable, dependable, trustworthy: inevitable, *certain.

inert. *Inactive, passive, idle, supine.
Ana. Lifeless, inanimate, *dead: impotent, *powerless: apathetic, *impassive, phlegmatic, stolid.
Ant. Dynamic: animated. — *Con.* *Active, operative, live: alert, vigilant, *watchful.

inescapable *or* **unescapable.** *Inevitable, ineluctable, unavoidable.
Ana. *Certain, necessary, apodictic: inexorable, *inflexible.
Ant. Escapable.

inevitable. 1 Inevitable, ineluctable, inescapable, unescapable, unavoidable agree in meaning incapable of being shunned or evaded. **Inevitable** (see also CERTAIN) implies that causes are already in operation or that the conditions of one's existence, one's work, one's temperament, or the like, are such that the thing so described is bound to occur; as, "Life is full of perils, but the wise man ignores those that are *inevitable*" (*B. Russell*); "As soon as one lays down a rule...one has to face the *inevitable* exception" (*C. E. Montague*); "She was winding up all sorts of affairs, with the *inevitable* result that she was encountering all sorts of urgent expenses which she was unable to meet" (*H. Ellis*). **Ineluctable** adds to *inevitable* the suggestions that struggle or defiance is futile and that no way out is possible. "Doesn't the very 'seriousness' that we attribute to life mean that *ineluctable* noes and losses form a part of it...?" (*W. James*). "Social tolerance was not dealt in the same measure to men and to women, and neither Delia nor Charlotte had ever wondered why: like all the young women of their class they simply bowed to the *ineluctable*" (*E. Wharton*). **Inescapable** *or* **unescapable** (both forms are common) carries a stronger suggestion than either *inevitable* or *ineluctable* that the person concerned would, if he could, avoid what must be or is convinced of its inexorable character; as, his *inescapable* fate. "[D. H.] Lawrence was always and *unescapably* an artist. Yes, *unescapably* is the word; for there were moments when he wanted to escape from his destiny" (*A. Huxley*). **Unavoidable** carries a weaker implication of necessary occurrence than the other terms, but it does imply that the exercise of foresight or care has not enabled one to escape what has occurred; as, *unavoidable* delays; an *unavoidable* accident.
Ana. *Prescribed, destined, appointed: *certain, necessary, apodictic: determined, settled, decided (see DECIDE): inexorable, *inflexible.
Ant. Evitable. — *Con.* Escapable, avoidable, eludible, evadable *or* evasible (see corresponding verbs at ESCAPE): preventable, avertible (see corresponding verbs at PREVENT).
2 *Certain, necessary, apodictic.

Ana. *Infallible, inerrant, unerring: *perfect, entire, whole: definitive, determinative, decisive, *conclusive.

inexorable. Obdurate, adamant, adamantine, *inflexible.

Ana. *Rigid, rigorous, strict: resolute, steadfast (see FAITHFUL): *immovable, immobile: implacable, unrelenting, relentless, merciless, *grim.

Ant. Exorable. — *Con.* Compassionate, responsive, sympathetic, *tender: merciful, clement, lenient, indulgent, *forbearing.

inexpressible. *Unutterable, ineffable, unspeakable, inenarrable, indescribable.

Ana. *Subtle, subtile: tenuous, rare (see THIN): *infinite, boundless, illimitable.

Ant. Expressible.

inexpugnable. Unassailable, impregnable, *invincible, unconquerable, invulnerable, indomitable.

Ana. Redoubtable, *formidable: uncombatable, irresistible, unopposable (see affirmative verbs at OPPOSE).

Ant. Expugnable. — *Con.* Assailable, attackable, stormable (see corresponding verbs at ATTACK).

infallible. **Infallible, inerrable, inerrant, unerring** come into comparison when they mean incapable, or manifesting incapability, of making mistakes or errors. **Infallible** now occurs in this strict sense chiefly (but not exclusively) in reference to the person, institution, book, or the like, that is accepted as the divinely inspired medium for the revelation of moral or spiritual truth; thus, the pope is held by Roman Catholics to be *infallible* only when he speaks ex cathedra and defines a doctrine or a rule of morals held by the church; so, belief in an *infallible* church, in an *infallible* bible. "No mathematician is *infallible;* he may make mistakes; but he must not hedge" (*Eddington*). **Inerrable** (a literary rather than a colloquial word) is often preferred to *infallible*, its very close synonym, as a more explicit or a less technical term; as, "No man or men on the globe compose a tribunal from whose *inerrable* decision we may not appeal" (*J. Rogers*); "Many speak wisely, some *inerrably*" (*Patmore*). **Inerrant** (also chiefly literary) emphasizes not so much the incapacity for making mistakes or errors as the fact of their absence; as, he is an *inerrant* authority; an *inerrant* account of the battle. **Unerring** implies inerrancy but it stresses, especially in current use, reliability, sureness, exactness, or similar qualities; as, a marksman of *unerring* aim; "an *unerring* eye for [the] fleeting expression of the moral features of character" (*J. R. Lowell*); "A man is *infallible*, whose words are always true; a rule is *infallible*, if it is *unerring* in all its possible applications" (*Newman*); "a man's language is an *unerring* index of his nature" (*Binyon*).

Ana. *Certain, inevitable, necessary, apodictic: *impeccable, flawless, faultless.

Ant. Fallible. — *Con.* Questionable, dubious, *doubtful.

infamous. Nefarious, flagitious, iniquitous, *vicious, villainous, corrupt, degenerate.

Ana. Scandalous, ignominious, disgraceful, disreputable, shameful (see corresponding nouns at DISGRACE).

Ant. Illustrious. — *Con.* Glorious, *splendid, sublime.

infamy. Ignominy, shame, *disgrace, dishonor, disrepute, opprobrium, obloquy, odium, scandal.

Ana. Notoriety (see FAME): degradation, humiliation, debasement, abasement (see ABASE).

Con. Honor, glory, renown, celebrity, *fame, repute: prestige, authority, *influence, credit, weight.

infancy. **Infancy, minority, nonage** are interchangeable terms when they denote the state or period of being under the age established by law for the attainment of one's full civil rights and independence of guardianship. **Infancy,** because of its more familiar general senses, is seldom used in this denotation outside of legal documents and court reports; it is there, however, the preferable term when reference is made to the condition or status of the person who is not of age (that is, the *infant*, or *minor*). "The defendant...pleaded *infancy* at the time of the lease made" (*Sir H. Grimston*). On the other hand, **minority** is widely used in general as well as in legal writing and is the word to be chosen when the period or term of being under age is meant; as, he fell heir to the title during his *minority*. **Nonage** is the equivalent of *infancy* and *minority* in their legal senses, but it is to be distinguished from them in its acquired connotations and by its greater susceptibility to literary and figurative use. Very often, *nonage* suggests immaturity; not infrequently it suggests adolescence and its weaknesses and is thought of, by an etymological confusion, as the opposite of *dotage*, or *senility*. "Nations outgrow their spiritual *nonage*" (*F. W. Farrar*). "Three million such people as can read the Globe with interest are as yet in too crude a state of *nonage* to deserve any regard" (*Emerson*).

Con. *Age, majority.

infatuated, infatuate. **1** *Fond, besotted, insensate.

Ana. Deluded, deceived, beguiled, misled (see DECEIVE): duped, gulled, befooled (see DUPE): foolish, silly, fatuous, asinine (see SIMPLE): stultified (see corresponding verb at STUNT).

Con. Sensible, prudent, sane, judicious, *wise: *rational, reasonable.

2 *Enamored.

infection. **Infection, contagion** are interchangeable without loss only when they denote the matter by which a disease is carried from one person to another. When they denote either the way in which a disease is transmitted or acquired, or the disease itself (though less often in this instance), they preserve, in careful use, the differences in meaning between *infectious* and *contagious* (see INFECTIOUS, 1); as, there will be no risk of *infection* (not *contagion*) if you drink boiled water; there will be no risk of *contagion* (more explicit than *infection*) if you keep out of the sickroom. However, **infection** and **contagion** were both used in the sense of an epidemic disease so long before the discovery of the bacterial origin of what are now called infectious diseases that, except in very precise language, they still often refer to any communicable disease; as, the *infection* (or *contagion*) spread from town to town. "Manila, the only large city until recent years where an imported *infection* has been eradicated" (*V. Heiser*). *Infection* and *contagion* (technical **contagium**) are interchangeable when they denote the matter producing a contagious disease, such as a germ-laden secretion or a virus; as, the air of a sickroom is charged with *contagion*. "There is even a strong possibility that the *infection* [of smallpox] may be carried through the air" (*V. Heiser*). Figuratively, these words are not as close in their meanings as *infectious* and *contagious*, because *infection* rarely loses the implication of corruption so strong in *infect;* as, the ignorant are susceptible to the *infection* of false propaganda; everyone felt the *contagion* of her merriment.

infectious. **1** **Infectious, contagious, communicable, catching,** when applied to diseases, are distinguishable in spite of very close similarities of meaning. *Infectious* and *contagious* are so precisely defined in pathology that they are now rarely confused in general usage. **Infectious** designates any disease resulting from the invasion of the body by rapidly multiplying germs (bacteria, protozoans, and analogous microorganisms) that produce toxins or destroy or injure tissues. **Contagious** designates that type of infectious disease caused by receiving living germs directly from a person afflicted with it or by contact with a secretion of his or some object he has touched. The tendency to use *infectious* more narrowly and only of such diseases as are transmitted through an agent, such as a mosquito or rat, or a source of infection, as a polluted water supply, is not scientifically countenanced. **Communicable,** as here compared, is nearly equivalent to *infectious,* but it emphasizes the transmissibility of the disease rather than the method by which it is acquired. The colloquial **catching** is close in meaning to *contagious,* but it implies even more the dangers of contact.

Of these four terms, *infectious, contagious,* and *catching* are used figuratively. The fine distinctions exhibited in their technical senses are not carried over into the extended senses, with the result that they are nearly exact synonyms meaning rapidly imparted to others; as, *contagious* (or *infectious*) enthusiasm; What a bad temper! I hope it's not *catching.* "Fear is exceedingly *infectious:* children catch it from their elders even when their elders are not aware of having shown it" (*B. Russell*).

Ana. Toxic, mephitic, pestilent, pestilential, virulent, *poisonous.

2 Infectious, infective agree in denoting that infects or tends to infect. **Infectious,** however, is more often restricted to the technical and figurative senses expounded in the preceding article. **Infective,** an older word than *infectious,* was for a time displaced by it, but it has recently been revived, especially in pathology, where it is applied chiefly to matter and means potentially infectious; as, an *infective* secretion; an *infective* wart. Figuratively, it preserves the implication of corruption, strong in *infect* but often absent in *infectious;* as, *infective* doctrines (but, *infectious* laughter).

infective. *Infectious.

Ana. Contaminating, tainting, polluting, defiling (see CONTAMINATE): corrupting, vitiating (see DEBASE): *poisonous, virulent, toxic, mephitic.

Con. Salutary, hygienic, *healthful, wholesome.

infelicitous. Unhappy, inapt, inappropriate, unfitting, *unfit, unsuitable, unmeet, improper.

Ana. Unbecoming, unseemly, *indecorous, improper, indelicate, indecent: inept, maladroit, gauche, *awkward.

Ant. Felicitous. — ***Con.*** Happy, apt, appropriate, fitting (see FIT, *adj.*): apposite, apropos, germane, pertinent, *relevant.

infer. 1 Infer, deduce, conclude, judge, gather come into comparison when they mean to arrive at by reasoning from evidence or from premises. All except *gather* are so clearly differentiated in strict logical use that thoughtful writers and speakers tend to observe these distinctions. The derivative nouns **inference, deduction, conclusion, judgment,** especially as applied to the propositions or mental formulations derived by reasoning, are even more precisely fixed in careful usage. **Infer** implies the drawing of an opinion, a principle, a fact, a probability, or the like, from the evidence presented or the premises accepted. In popular use the term often connotes slightness in the evidence and so comes close to *surmise;* in logic, however, it and **inference** convey no suggestion of weakness or strength. " 'I see motion,' said Thomas [Aquinas]: 'I *infer* a motor!' This reasoning...is...stronger than some more modern *inferences* of science" (*H. Adams*). " 'Oh, well, don't worry. Jane hasn't got any complexes.' From which Gard...*inferred* she thought he [Gard] had" (*M. Austin*). **Deduce,** in nontechnical language, usually means to infer, with added implications of very definite grounds for the inference; in strict logical use, it means to derive an inference from a general principle; that is, to make a **deduction** as opposed to an *induction* (see DEDUCTION, 3). This distinction, an important one to logicians and philosophers, is nearly lost in general use, where *deduce* and *deduction* imply inferences of any kind. "Then the diets [of polished and of unpolished rice] were reversed. The sick group recovered and the well group came down with the disease. It warranted the *deduction* that a diet which included vitamin B was a preventive for beriberi" (*V. Heiser*). "What a man is as an end perishes when he dies; what he produces as a means continues to the end of time. We cannot deny this, but we can deny the consequences *deduced* from it" (*B. Russell*). **Conclude** is often loosely employed as an equivalent of *deduce* in its general sense. Strictly, it means to draw the inference that is the necessary consequence of preceding propositions, whether these propositions be the premises of a syllogism or the members of a series of previously drawn inferences constituting an unbroken chain of reasoning. A **conclusion** is therefore either the third proposition of a syllogism or the final, summarizing proposition in a rational process. In general use, *conclude* and *conclusion* are not always so strictly applied, though they frequently preserve the implication of logical necessity in the inference. "Do not *conclude* that all State activities will be State monopolies" (*Shaw*). "The more one scans the later pages of Mark Twain's history the more one is forced to the *conclusion* that there was something gravely amiss with his inner life" (*Van W. Brooks*). **Judge** and **judgment,** as here compared, are nearly equivalent to *conclude* and *conclusion,* but in their strictest construction they (especially *judgment*) connote careful examination of evidence or critical testing of premises and the fitness of the conclusion for affirmation. "You must have had a charming evening...if I may *judge* from the way you have kept the memory green" (*Conrad*). "An economist should form an independent *judgment* on currency questions, but an ordinary mortal had better follow authority" (*B. Russell*). To **gather** is to conclude, but it connotes reflection (rather than careful reasoning) and the putting of two and two together; as, "thereby he may *gather* The ground of your ill-will" (*Shak.*); "From Thomasin's words and manner he had plainly *gathered* that Wildeve neglected her" (*Hardy*).

☞ *Do not confuse* infer *with* imply.

Ana. Reason, speculate, *think: surmise, *conjecture, guess.

2 Infer, imply are not always as strictly distinguished even by otherwise careful writers and speakers as they are by linguistic authorities, with the result that *infer* is often used where *imply* would be the correct or desirable word. In general, **infer** (for fuller treatment see INFER, 1) means to draw a conclusion from facts, evidence, premises, statements, or the like, by deductive or inductive reasoning (as, Darwin *inferred* an evolutionary process in nature from evidence gathered on voyages over a long period), and **imply** (as here considered; see also SUGGEST, 1; INCLUDE), means to give a ground or the grounds for an inference, as by a hint, an intimation, a significant omission, an act, or the like (as, his words *imply* that he means to leave his family; "praise less claims my gratitude, Than the indulgent insight it *implies*"—*Browning*). The use of *infer* in the sense of to hint at or to intimate (as, by his remarks he *infers* [correctly *implies*] that she is mentally unsound) is still regarded as erroneous. However, in the past *infer* sometimes meant, and still to some extent means, to give grounds for believing (something that is stated) or to permit (something) to be inferred. In such use, a personal subject is to be avoided, for in precise English only that which gives the ground for or permits an inference, or which leads to a given conclusion, can rightly be the subject; as, "This doth *infer* the zeal I had to see him" (*Shak.*); "Consider first that great Or bright *infers* not excellence" (*Milton*); "Matters were by no means so far advanced between the young people as Henchard's jealous grief *inferred*" (*Hardy*). Many good writers of the present prefer *imply* to *infer* in this particular sense.

inference. 1 Deduction, conclusion, judgment. See under INFER.

2 **Inference, illation, ratiocination** come into comparison when they denote the process of arriving at conclusions from data or premises. **Inference,** in colloquial use, often connotes guesswork; in strict logical use, it merely names the process of inferring (see INFER, 1), but does not, as **illation** does, suggest careful reasoning, especially in deduction. **Ratiocination** adds the implication of an extended process or the passing by steps from one inference to another. In present use, it often carries the humorous connotation of tediousness or of logic chopping. The same distinctions in implications are observable in the corresponding adjectives **inferential, illative,** and **ratiocinative.**

Ana. Deduction, conclusion, judgment (see under INFER, 1): reasoning, thinking, speculation, cogitation (see corresponding verbs at THINK): surmise, conjecture (see under CONJECTURE, *v.*).

Con. Intuition, understanding (see REASON): assumption, presumption, presupposition (see under PRESUPPOSE).

3 *Implication.

inferential. Illative, ratiocinative. See under INFERENCE, 2.

Ana. Hypothetical, putative, conjectural, supposititious, *supposed: *theoretical, speculative, academic: *implicit, constructive, virtual.

Con. *Explicit, express, definite, categorical: intuitive, *instinctive: proved, demonstrated, tried, tested (see PROVE).

infernal. **Infernal, chthonian, hellish, Hadean, Tartarean, Stygian** agree in meaning of or characteristic of the abode of the dead. **Infernal,** which is derived from a Latin word meaning subterranean, in its strictest sense denotes of or characteristic of the underworld, or regions inhabited by the earth gods and spirits of the dead. Through confusion of pagan conceptions of the underworld with Jewish and Christian conceptions of hell as the abode of devils and a place of torment for the souls of the damned, *infernal* has acquired connotations of horror, torturing fiends, and unendurable suffering through fire, which nearly always blur and sometimes blot out its etymological implications. When the classical conception of the underworld must be suggested without any admixture of alien connotations, **chthonian,** a learned word, is sometimes used. "From the *infernal* Gods, 'mid shades forlorn" (*Wordsworth*). "The most abhorred fiend in the *infernal* regions is sent to torment me" (*Scott*). **Hellish** comes close to the current meaning of *infernal* but carries so strong an implication of devilishness that it now more nearly approaches *fiendish* in its meaning. "Heavenly love shall outdo *hellish* hate" (*Milton*). "Burned them both with *hellish* mockery" (*Shelley*). **Hadean, Tartarean,** and **Stygian** are used in poetry in place of *infernal,* sometimes without any reference to the conception of Hades, Tartarus, and the Styx in classic mythology. Very frequently, *Hadean* is a loose equivalent for *chthonian, Tartarean* suggests darkness and remoteness, *Stygian* connotes bounds with no outlet for escape, but all three are without fixed content.

Ana. *Fiendish, devilish, diabolical, demoniacal: damnable, accursed, cursed, *execrable: nefarious, flagitious, iniquitous, villainous, *vicious.

Ant. Supernal.

infertile. *Sterile, barren, impotent, unfruitful.

Ana. *Dry, arid: impoverished, exhausted, drained, depleted (see DEPLETE).

Ant. Fertile. — *Con.* Fecund, fruitful, prolific (see FERTILE): producing *or* productive, bearing, yielding (see corresponding verbs at BEAR): reproducing, propagating, breeding, generating (see GENERATE).

infest. **Infest, overrun, beset** come into comparison only when they are used in reference to disagreeable or noxious things and mean to make trouble because of their presence in swarms. To **infest** carries only by suggestion the idea of annoyance or repugnance, because the idiom does not require reference to the person so affected. "And robber-bands *infest* the mountain's foot!" (*Browning*); nevertheless, the term is always derogatory. "To poison vermin that *infest* his plants" (*Cowper*). "The idle rich who at present *infest* the older universities" (*B. Russell*). **Overrun,** as here compared, is often interchangeable with *infest,* especially in the passive. Usually it retains the implications of its literal sense and is, therefore, the precise word when the idea of running or spreading is to be conveyed; as, the cellar is *overrun* with mice; the garden is *overrun* with weeds. **Beset,** which in its primary sense denotes to set or stud, has now more frequently the meaning to trouble through frequency and persistence, and often connotes assailing or attacking; as, he was *beset* by enemies on every side. "She hurried at his words, *beset* with fears" (*Keats*).

Ana. *Frequent, haunt: *teem, swarm, abound, superabound: harass, harry, pester, plague, *worry, annoy.

Ant. Disinfest. — *Con.* *Exterminate, extirpate, eradicate, wipe out: *abolish, annihilate, extinguish, abate.

infidel. Unbeliever, *atheist, freethinker, agnostic, deist.

Ana. Heathen, *pagan, paynim.

infinite. **Infinite, eternal, sempiternal, boundless, illimitable, uncircumscribed** agree in meaning having neither beginning nor end or being without known limits of any sort. **Infinite** (etymologically, without limits of any kind) was in early English use applied chiefly to God and to his attributes: in such applications, it implied immeasurability or an incapacity for being estimated in extent, duration, or in any conceivable respect; as, "Great is our Lord, and of great power: his understanding is *infinite*" (*Psalms* cxlvii. 5); "Great are thy works, Jehovah! *infinite* Thy power! what thought can measure thee, or tongue Relate thee" (*Milton*). In popular mathematical and scientific use, the term usually stresses indeterminateness rather than immeasurability: often it implies that no limits can be set to which a thing does or may extend, or that no point at which it ends can be discerned; thus, the number of positive integers (i.e., numerals) is *infinite* (i.e., no one can set a limit to the number that can be indicated); an *infinite* decimal is one that cannot be brought to a termination, such as a repeating (or recurring) decimal or a circulating decimal. "The total number of stars is supposed, even by those who reject the idea of *infinite* extension, to run into thousands of millions" (*Inge*). In general and looser use, *infinite* usually implies not only exceeding greatness or vastness but indefiniteness or seeming endlessness of extent; as, "Chinese landscape [painting] is certainly pre-eminent...in suggesting *infinite* horizons, the look of mountains...melting away into remote sky" (*Binyon*); "The Truth...is of necessity *infinite* and so is not for any poor finite creature like man" (*Babbitt*). **Eternal,** in its earliest and still prevailing sense, implies neither beginning nor end in time: it is therefore applied chiefly to God, in the sense of being *uncaused* or *uncreated* and *unending;* as, "The *eternal* God is thy refuge" (*Deuteronomy* xxxiii. 27); "*Eternal* Providence" (*Milton*). It is also sometimes applied to things, especially to those regarded as abstractions which are creations of the human and therefore finite mind, for which no beginning is known or under present conditions is discoverable, and for which no end can be foreseen or predicted; as, to argue that matter is *eternal;* the idea that the world is *eternal* is now seldom, if ever, advanced. " 'If space is *infinite* and time *eternal*,' Mark murmured, 'I am in infinity and I am in eternity' " (*C. Mackenzie*). In some thinking, *eternal* applies to that which is independent of, or capable of being thought of without reference to, human and finite concepts such as those of time and space; as, "to think...of heaven as a state rather than a place—a state, too, which is *eternal* in a deeper sense than that of unending time-succession" (*Inge*). Equally common is the use of *eternal* in the sense of *endless* or *everlasting* (see EVERLASTING) when it applies to things which have a known or an acknowledged beginning in time; as, to enter into *eternal* life; those dying unrepentant will suffer *eternal* punishment for their sins. In nonreligious contexts, this sense is frequent in hyperbolical or humorous use (as, "the staircase door opened with its *eternal* creak"—*Bennett*), but it also applies to that which, though it changes in appearance, form, or method, never dies out; as, "The tragedy of *The Changeling* [i.e., 'of the not naturally bad but irresponsible and undeveloped nature, caught in the consequences of its own action'] is an *eternal* tragedy" (*T. S. Eliot*); "Macaulay, who has a special affinity for the *eternal* schoolboy" (*Inge*). **Sempiternal,** a bookish word, is, in origin at least, an intensive of *eternal*, with somewhat greater emphasis upon the continuity of the thing so described (as, "All truth is from the *sempiternal* source Of Light Divine"—*Cowper;* "he did not really believe that infinity was *infinite* or that the *eternal* was also *sempiternal*"—*Shaw*), but, as is often the case with intensives, it is now chiefly a hyperbolical term (as, "Dull dinners...with the *sempiternal* saddle of mutton"—*J. Jekyll*). **Boundless,** except in recent scientific and mathematical use, where it and *infinite* are employed as contrasted terms, implies little more than an apparent lack of restrictions or bounds, or a capacity for extending, expanding, or increasing indefinitely: it often applies to something which so far exceeds in range, measure, or amount what is usual for a thing of its kind that it staggers the human mind; as, *boundless* wealth; *boundless* impudence; "My bounty is as *boundless* as the sea" (*Shak.*); "A *boundless* command of the rhetoric in which the vulgar express hatred and contempt" (*Macaulay*); "When that which drew from out the *boundless* deep Turns again home" (*Tennyson*). In current mathematical and scientific usage, *boundless* refers to a space (as represented by a closed curved line, or a spherical surface, etc., and without regard to its calculable extension or area) which has the property of permitting an object starting from any point in the space and proceeding by one mathematical law to return to the same point without being interrupted; thus, in the Einsteinian conception, physical space is *boundless* but not *infinite*, since a ray of light, assumed to travel along a curve rather than a straight line, can conceivably return to its starting point after an estimated 500 billion years. **Illimitable** also stresses a lack of bounds or limits, and may be used in place of *boundless* (as, "an *illimitable* appetite"—*L. Stephen*), but it is often applied specifically to that (such as a distance) which can usually be measured in extent but which, in the instance noted, exceeds the capacity of human ingenuity or of any human instrument for measurement or determination of extent; as, "The heavens' *illimitable* height" (*Spenser*); the *illimitable* distances between the earth and some of the stars. **Uncircumscribed** implies the lack of a determinable limit in any conceivable direction: it applies to anything that extends or expands or seems to extend or expand in all directions in the manner of radii from the center of a circle; as, *uncircumscribed* freedom; "So arbitrary and *uncircumscribed* a Power" (*Charles I of England*).

Ant. Finite. — ***Con.*** Circumscribed, limited, restricted (see LIMIT, *v.*): *dependent, conditional, contingent, relative, adjective.

infirm. Feeble, decrepit, *weak, frail, fragile.

Ana. Debilitated, disabled, crippled (see WEAKEN): *sick, ill.

Ant. Hale. — ***Con.*** *Strong, sturdy, stalwart, stout: *healthy, robust, sound.

infix. *Implant, inculcate, instill, inseminate.

Ana. *Set, settle, fix, establish, firm: *enter, introduce, admit: ingrain, inoculate, *infuse, imbue.

inflame. Fire, kindle, enkindle, *light, ignite.

Ana. *Inform, inspire, animate: incense, infuriate, enrage (see ANGER, *v.*): exasperate, provoke, aggravate, nettle, *irritate.

Ant. Extinguish (*a fire, a passion*).

inflate. Distend, swell, *expand, amplify, dilate.

Ana. Enlarge, *increase, augment: magnify, aggrandize, *exalt.

Ant. Deflate. — ***Con.*** *Contract, compress, shrink, condense, constrict.

inflated. **Inflated, flatulent, tumid, turgid** are here considered not only in their literal senses but also, and chiefly in their secondary senses, especially as applied to persons, their temperaments, their language, and their style. Literally, all agree in meaning filled with something insubstantial such as air or gas. **Inflated** implies expansion by the introduction of air or gas or something equally lacking in substance to the point where the walls are stretched taut or tension is evident; as, an *inflated* tire; an *inflated* balloon. In its extended use, *inflated* implies a stretching or expanding, often by artificial or questionable means, to a point not justified by reality or truth; thus, currency is said to be *inflated* when the amount in circulation far exceeds the amount normally necessary to meet the demands of trade and commerce; one's ego is said to be *inflated* when one is puffed up with self-confidence and pride not warranted by one's ability or achievements; a style may be described as *inflated* when it is far more pretentious or imposing than its subject matter warrants. **Flatulent,** in literal use, is applied chiefly to persons or their organs affected by a condition (flatulence) where wind or gases generating in the alimentary canal cause distention of stomach or bowels. In its extended use, *flatulent* usually implies emptiness with the appearance of fullness, or a lack of pith or substance; as, "*Flatulent* with fumes of self-applause" (*Young*). "A score or two of poems, each more feeble and more *flatulent* than the last" (*Swinburne*). "To this day he [Emerson] is the victim of gross misrepresentation by enthusiasts who read into him all sorts of *flatulent* bombast" (*Mencken*). **Tumid** implies noticeable enlargement by swelling or bloating, especially as a result of a morbid or abnormal condition; as, "my thighs grow very *tumid*" (*Johnson*); "So high as heaved the *tumid* hills [at the command of the Creator], so low Down sunk a hollow bottom broad and deep, Capacious bed of waters" (*Milton*). In its extended use, *tumid* implies an abnormal or conspicuous increase in volume without a proportionate increase in mass or weight. "To compare, in thy *tumid* pride, with me?" (*Shelley*). "While Shakespeare, using great words on the lowlier subject, contrives to make them appropriate, with Burke, writing on the loftier subject, the same or similar words have become *tumid*" (*Quiller-Couch*). **Turgid** is not always distinguishable from *tumid* in its literal use; however, it is the preferred word when normal distention as distinct from morbid bloating is implied; as, healthy living cells are *turgid;* woody tissue *turgid* with sap. Consequently, in extended use, especially as applied to expression or style, *turgid* often adds to *tumid* the connotation of unrestrained vitality or of undisciplined emotion, especially as manifest in bombast, rant, or rhapsody (see BOMBAST). In general, however, *turgid* is used to describe any style or language that is not measured or restrained and perfectly in keeping with the thought. "The *turgid* speech And stately tone of moralists, who boast, As if, like him of fabulous renown, They...were each An Orpheus, and omnipotent in song" (*Cowper*). "The effects...already...show in French architecture—which is growing repulsive—and in French prose—which is growing *turgid*" (*Belloc*).

Ana. Bombastic, grandiloquent, magniloquent, aureate, flowery, *rhetorical: pompous, pretentious, ostentatious, *showy: rhapsodical, ranting, fustian (see corresponding nouns at BOMBAST): *wordy, verbose, prolix, diffuse.

Ant. Pithy. — ***Con.*** Compendious, *concise, summary, terse, succinct, laconic.

inflection *or* **inflexion.** **Inflection** (*or* **inflexion**), **intonation, accent** are comparable when they designate a particular manner of employing the tones of the voice in speech. **Inflection** implies change in pitch or tone; it often suggests a variation expressive of emotion or sentiment, and, usually, a momentary mood; as, it was not her words, but her *inflection*, that hurt. "A slight *inflection* made one feel that one had received a great compliment" (*Cather*). **Intonation** is often, though not necessarily, individual but it is seldom thought of as the result of a mood; it is applied to the rise and fall in pitch that constitutes what is called "speech melody" and that distinguishes the utterance of one individual or group from another; as, a ministerial *intonation.* "We still write...for the actors, reckon upon their *intonations*, their gestures" (*Quiller-Couch*). "That peculiar and pleasant *intonation* that marks the speech of the Hebridean" (*W. Black*). In some languages (as Chinese), called "tone languages," fixed pitch, or *intonation*, distinguishes the various meanings of single words. In a more specific sense, *intonation* often (as **intone** always) implies reciting or speaking a psalm, prayer, or the like, in a singing voice, usually in monotone. "*Intonation* of that majestic iambic [Greek] verse whose measure would have been obscured by a rapid and conversational delivery" (*G. L. Dickinson*). **Accent** denotes such manner or quality of utterance or tone as may distinguish the speech peculiar to a person, race, district, class, etc.; as, a Southern, a Parisian, or a nasal *accent;* to speak with a refined *accent.* Like the other terms in this group, it often suggests, and sometimes indicates, the speaker's feelings. "A different *accent* was notable in Joseph's voice when he spoke of Azariah" (*G. Moore*).

Ana. Enunciation, pronunciation, articulation (see corresponding verbs at PRONOUNCE).

inflexible. 1 Rigid, *stiff, tense, stark, wooden.

Ana. Hard, solid, *firm: *rigid, rigorous, strict, stringent: tough, tenacious, stout, *strong: immobile, *immovable.

Ant. Flexible. — ***Con.*** *Elastic, resilient, supple, springy: pliable, pliant, *plastic, malleable, ductile: fluid, *liquid.

2 Inflexible, inexorable, obdurate, adamant, adamantine come into comparison when they mean not to be moved from or changed in one's predetermined course or purpose. All are applicable to persons, decisions, laws, and principles; otherwise, they vary in their applications. **Inflexible** usually implies firmly established principles rigidly adhered to; sometimes it connotes resolute steadfastness, sometimes slavish conformity, sometimes mere pigheadedness. "Society's attitude toward drink and dishonesty was still *inflexible*" (*E. Wharton*). "A morality that is rigid and *inflexible* and dead" (*H. Ellis*). **Inexorable,** when applied to persons, stresses deafness to entreaty. "More fierce and more *inexorable* far Than empty tigers or the roaring sea" (*Shak.*). When applied to decisions, rules, laws, and their enforcement, it often connotes relentlessness, ruthlessness, and finality beyond question. "Nature *inexorably* ordains that the human race shall perish of famine if it stops working" (*Shaw*). It is also often applied to that which exists or happens of necessity or which cannot be avoided or evaded; as, the *inexorable* limitations of human nature; *inexorable* destiny. **Obdurate** is applicable chiefly to persons for it now almost invariably implies hardness of heart or insensitiveness to external influences such as divine grace or to appeals for mercy, forgiveness, or assistance. "If when you make your prayers, God should be so *obdurate* as yourselves, How would it fare with your departed souls?" (*Shak.*). **Adamant** and **adamantine** usually imply extraordinary strength of will or impenetrability to temptation or entreaty. "Cromwell's *adamantine* courage was shown on many a field of battle" (*G. Smith*). "When Eve upon the first of men The apple pressed with specious cant, O, what a thousand pities then That Adam was not *Adam-ant*" (*T. Moore*).

Ana. *Rigid, strict, rigorous, stringent: intractable, refractory, headstrong, *unruly, ungovernable: implacable, relentless, unrelenting, *grim: stubborn, *obstinate, dogged, stiff-necked, mulish.

Ant. Flexible. — ***Con.*** *Elastic, resilient, expansive, volatile, buoyant: amenable, tractable, docile, biddable (see OBEDIENT).

influence, *n.* **Influence, authority, prestige, weight, credit** come into comparison when they mean power exerted over the minds or acts of others either without apparent effort or as the result of the qualities, the position, or the reputation of the person or thing that exerts this power. **Influence** etymologically suggests a flowing out, from one thing into another, of something imperceptible or impalpable: this connotation is retained when the word implies the effect or effects which one person or thing insensibly has on another or the ascendancy which one person or thing similarly acquires over another; as, every close friend has some *influence* in shaping one's character or personality; he was not strong enough to resist the *influence* of bad companions; the *influence* of Milton's poetry on Keats has been carefully traced by more than one critic. "We find primitive men thinking that almost everything...can exert *influence* of some sort" (*W. James*). However, in current use, *influence* often loses this implication of insensible or unconscious operation and suggests the conscious use of personal power or, sometimes, of underhanded means to determine the acts of another; in this sense it often follows the verb *use* or one of its synonyms; as, to use undue *influence* over a person making a will; to use one's *influence* in getting a bill through a legislature. **Authority** originally was applied to a preacher, teacher, writer, or the like, or to any of his writings or utterances that had the power to compel belief or to win acceptance. In such cases the word usually imputed great learning, great wisdom, divine inspiration, or the like, to the person or his work. "By turning o'er *authorities,* I have...made familiar To me...the blest infusions That dwell in vegetives, in metals, stones" (*Shak.*). In modern use, *authority* is still applied to the person, book, or the like, that is able to gain such credence or to inspire belief in its authoritativeness; as, do not cite this historian; he is not an *authority.* "An economist should form an independent judgment on currency questions, but an ordinary mortal had better follow *authority*" (*B. Russell*). From this use mainly, but also from its other sense (see POWER, 3), *authority* has come to be applied also to the power resident in any person or thing that is able because of his or its inherent qualities to win the devotion or allegiance of men and to gain (rather than exact) their obedience and belief; as, a book of manifest *authority.* "That personal *authority* [of Augustus], which, far more than any legal or constitutional device, was the true secret of his later power" (*Buchan*). "A doctrine that has acquired *authority* in our own time" (*S. Alexander*). "Some of the new philosophies undermine the *authority* of science, as some of the older systems undermined the *authority* of religion" (*Inge*). **Prestige,** in contrast with *authority,* implies the power to gain ascendancy over the minds of men and to command their admiration for distinguished and superior performance, or for conspicuous excellence in its kind. "Nothing more affects the *prestige* of a power than its dramatic and rapid defeat in the field" (*Belloc*). "Augustus sought to make of it [the Roman Senate] a true colleague and in every way to enhance its *prestige*" (*Buchan*). "The almost magical *prestige* that had belonged to the original humanists" (*A. Huxley*). **Weight** denotes measurable influence, especially in determining the acts of others; as, persons whose judgments have *weight* on the decisions of others. "Mrs. Hawthorne's authoritative air was beginning to have some *weight* with him" (*Arch. Marshall*). "She seemed scarcely of any *weight* beyond a man's need of her youth and her gift of making men comfortable" (*E. M. Roberts*). **Credit** (as here compared: see also BELIEF, 1) denotes influence that arises from one's reputation for inspiring confidence or admiration, or the like. "Buckingham...resolved to employ all his *credit* in order to prevent the marriage" (*Hume*). "As it [the ballet] declined as an art, so also it declined in *credit* and in popularity; it became scarcely respectable even to admire dancing" (*H. Ellis*).

Ana. Driving *or* drive, impelling *or* impulsion, actuation (see corresponding verbs at MOVE): *power, control, dominion, sway, authority: ascendancy, *supremacy: dominance (see corresponding adjective DOMINANT).

influence, *v.* *Affect, sway, impress, touch, strike.

Ana. *Move, actuate, drive, impel: stimulate, *provoke, excite: *stir, arouse, rouse: *incline, dispose, predispose, bias.

inform, *v.* **1 Inform, animate, inspire, fire** are synonyms when they mean to infuse into (a person or thing) a spirit, a principle, an idea, a passion, or the like, that gives (him or it) effective power or an urge to action or activity. Sometimes, especially in the last three words, the idea of driving or actuating is so strong that it becomes their common denotation and the idea of infusion is merely a common connotation. To **inform** is to endow with a form, or formative principle. But in its philosophical earlier sense *inform* implies a concept of form as that element in a thing which makes it what it is generically or specifically (a man, a tree, a horse) as distinguished from the matter in which the form is embodied; in modern literary use, it suggests a concept of form as the active principle of a thing or the spirit or quality that gives it its peculiar, essential, and often abiding, character. "The inspiration of religion passed on to *inform* and subtly to perfume an art [Buddhist art] nominally concerned with the aspects of earth and sky, wild creatures and wild flowers" (*Binyon*). "Everything that is made from without and by dead rules, and does not spring from within through some spirit *informing* it" (*Wilde*). "That which makes Chartres Cathedral...the *Song of Roland,* the Arthurian Legends, great art and unique, is...the peculiar spiritual impulse which *informed* the time" (*R. A. Cram*). To **animate** is to endow with a soul, or a principle of life, or an impulse to action. Although *animate* is often used where *inform* is also possible, it suggests, far more than *inform,* vitality and living energy; as, "religion...which is *animated*...by faith and hope" (*Johnson*). When that which is affected is a person or when motivation of action or transiency of impulse is to be implied, *animate* is the required word; as, he was *animated* (not *informed*) with love for all men; "when the community is *animated* with anger against some heinous offence" (*S. Alexander*); his hatred of restraint *animated* his resistance to authority. To **inspire** is to communicate to a person, as if by breathing in, power or energy in excess of that which he believes to be his own. In its strictest sense, the word usually implies both the operation of a supernatural power or of some inexplicable agency and an effect such as a spiritual illumination, or a quickening of intellectual or imaginative activity, or an exaltation of feeling. "Great artists know or believe that they are *inspired* from something outside themselves" (*S. Alexander*). "That sublimated language used by the finest minds in their *inspired* moments" (*Hudson*). "We climb the mountains for their views and the sense of grandeur they *inspire*" (*Jefferies*). In looser use, *inspire* often implies indirect rather than inexplicable influence, methods, or source, as in imparting knowledge, arousing a feeling, or the like; as, teachers should *inspire* their pupils to work hard; today's editorial on the mayor's policy was certainly *inspired* (that is, it does not represent the editor's views but those of someone in power). To **fire** is to animate or inspire so powerfully that one is inflamed with passion, ardor, enthusiasm, or the like. "Patient of constitutional control...One step beyond the boundary of the laws *Fires* him at once in Freedom's glorious cause" (*Cowper*). "O how they *fire* the heart devout" (*Burns*).

Ana. *Infuse, inoculate, imbue, leaven: instill, *implant, inculcate, inseminate: enlighten, *illuminate: inflame, fire, enkindle, kindle (see LIGHT, *v.*): endue, endow (see DOWER).

Con. Stultify, atrophy, *stunt.

2 Inform, acquaint, apprise, advise, notify, advertise agree in meaning to make one aware or cognizant of something. One **informs** a person *of* something when one imparts knowledge of any sort, but particularly of occurrences or of facts necessary to the understanding of a situation; as, to *inform* a person of his success in a competition; the radio announcer *informed* his audience of the accident ten minutes after it happened. "Fyne told her that I was fully *informed*" (*Conrad*). Also, one *informs* oneself (*of, on, upon, how, why,* etc.) when by study or investigation one gathers the pertinent facts; as, to *inform* oneself why the expedition was a failure. "He must *inform* himself upon Miss Mary Ferris's condition, if he would make himself pleasing to the family" (*Deland*). *Inform,* in a more restricted use, also carries the implication of talebearing or accusation. "I shall not *inform* upon you. It is not my business" (*Wilde*). One **acquaints** a person *with* something when by introducing him to the experience of it or by imparting information concerning it one makes him familiar with it; as, in the first meeting of the class, the teacher *acquainted* his pupils with the program of study. Familiarity is even more strongly implied in the participial adjective *acquainted* than in the finite verb. "A man of sorrows, and *acquainted* with grief" (*Isaiah* liii. 3). One **apprises** a person *of* something when by a message or sign one communicates something which is of interest or importance to him; as, to *apprise* one's employers of one's intention to resign. "I made up my mind to send the waiter to...*apprise* him that I was there" (*M. Austin*). One **advises** a person *of* something when one informs him of something that is important to him, as in making a decision, determining a policy, arranging plans, or the like; as, the president asked to be kept *advised* of changes in public sentiment. Oftentimes, there is a suggestion of forewarning or counsel; as, the passengers were *advised* of the risk before the vessel left New York. One **notifies** a person *of* something when one sends a notice or formal communication concerning a thing requiring his attention; as, to *notify* students of a change in the date of opening college; the court clerk promised to *notify* the witnesses when to appear. In commercial use, *advise* is used in preference to *notify* when information is given by letter, telegram, cable, or the like; as, please *advise* us when the shipment is made. One **advertises** a person *of* or *concerning* something when one gives him information by way of warning or of formal notification. This sense of *advertise*, once common, is now obsolescent. "Let me now add a short hint on the subject of another [event]; of which we have been *advertised* by the same authority" (*Austen*).

Ana. *Communicate, impart: *teach, instruct, school, discipline, educate, train: *warn, forewarn, caution.

information. Lore, learning, *knowledge, science, erudition, scholarship.

Ana. *News, tidings, intelligence, advice.

infraction. *Breach, violation, transgression, infringement, trespass, contravention.

Ana. *Offense, sin, crime, vice, scandal: slip, lapse, faux pas, *error.

Ant. Observance.

infrequent. **Infrequent, uncommon, scarce, rare, occasional, sporadic** are not close synonyms but they come into comparison because they agree in meaning appearing, happening, or met with so seldom as to attract attention or to create a shortage. That is **infrequent** which does not occur often, especially within a given period of time, or which does not recur except at very wide intervals of time or of space; as, tornadoes are *infrequent* in New England; "far from being *infrequent*, the crystalline state is almost universal among solids" (*Karl K. Darrow*); *infrequent* pines dot the forest. "Though it was only a few hundred miles north of Santa Fé, communication with that region was so *infrequent* that news traveled to Santa Fé from Europe more quickly than from Pike's Peak" (*Cather*). That is **uncommon** which does not occur or is not found ordinarily and which therefore is singular, exceptional, or extraordinary; as, smallpox is now *uncommon* in most parts of the United States; "In certain country districts in Europe families of fifteen are not *uncommon* enough to be regarded as extraordinary" (*Shaw*); such muscular strength is *uncommon* among girls. That is **scarce** which at the moment in mind is not easily found or which does not exist or is not produced in sufficient quantities; as, butter is cheap when it is plentiful and dear when it is *scarce;* a bad harvest makes wheat *scarce;* highly skilled mechanics are now *scarce*. That is **rare** (as here compared: see also CHOICE, THIN) of which but few examples, specimens, or instances are found; also, the term often carries the implications of *uncommon*, such as exceptional or extraordinary character; as, *rare* postage stamps; *rare* books and first editions; "A perfect union of wit and judgment is one of the *rarest* things in the world" (*Burke*); "Great men are *scarce* (to use the booksellers' distinction), but great biographers are positively *rare*" (*T. Seccombe*); "I may say again, if only *rare*, how this butterfly would be prized!" (*Jefferies*); "[He]... was reported to give very indifferent wines to the *rare* guests he received in his grim old house" (*E. Wharton*). That is **occasional** which happens or is met with merely now and then. *Occasional* more than any of the preceding terms implies irregularity or nonconformity to any rule or law that might govern occurrences or appearances; as, "This was not an *occasional* outburst of activity; it was Wesley's routine" (*S. M. Crothers*); "Artemus Ward was all fun and sweet reasonableness..., with an *occasional* barb that by its unexpectedness did the more damage" (*Lucas*). That is **sporadic** which has no continuous existence or continuity in its manifestations and which comes into existence or occurs only in rare and, usually, isolated instances; as, *sporadic* cases of an infectious disease; *sporadic* outbursts of opposition to high taxes; *sporadic* occurrences of loan words in the manuscripts of that period; "Humanism and religion are thus, as historical facts, by no means parallel; humanism has been *sporadic*, but Christianity continuous" (*T. S. Eliot*).

Ana. *Exceptional: singular, unique, *strange: *irregular, anomalous, unnatural.

Ant. Frequent. — ***Con.*** *Usual, customary, accustomed: ordinary, *common, familiar.

infringe. Encroach, trench, entrench, *trespass, invade.

Ana. *Intrude, obtrude, butt in, interlope: violate, break, transgress (see corresponding nouns at BREACH).

infringement. *Breach, infraction, violation, trespass, transgression, contravention.

Ana. Encroachment, invading *or* invasion, entrenchment (see corresponding verbs at TRESPASS): intruding *or* intrusion, obtruding *or* obtrusion (see corresponding verbs at INTRUDE).

infuriate. Enrage, incense, *anger, madden.

Ana. Provoke, roil, exasperate, aggravate (see IRRITATE): outrage, insult, affront, *offend.

infuse. **Infuse, suffuse, imbue, ingrain** (*or* **engrain**), **inoculate, leaven** are here compared as meaning to introduce one thing into another so as to change or affect it superficially, extensively, or profoundly. **Infuse** (literally, to pour into), in the sense here considered, refers to the act of an agent or agency that introduces something which gives physical, mental, or spiritual life or vigor, or new significance to the thing (often the person) affected; as, "thou didst smile, *Infused* with a fortitude from heaven, When I... Under my burthen groan'd" (*Shak.*); "He *infused* his own intrepid spirit into the troops" (*Gibbon*); "Unfortunately Okio [a Japanese painter]...was of too cold a temperament to *infuse* a powerful current of life into the old tradition" (*Binyon*). **Suffuse** (etymologically, to pour under) implies an overspreading of a surface by, or a spreading through an extent of, something that gives the thing affected a distinctive or unusual color, aspect, texture, quality, or the like; as, a blush *suffused* her cheek; eyes *suffused* with tears; "when purple light shall next *suffuse* the skies" (*Pope*); "she...pulled the chain of the incandescent mantle....the room was *suffused* with the sickly illumination" (*C. Mackenzie*); "the poetic faculty will, in fact, have to deal—not with an abstract idea,—but with an idea *suffused* and moulded by emotion" (*Day Lewis*). **Imbue** (literally, to saturate, especially with color as in dyeing) implies the introduction of something that enters so deeply and so extensively into the thing's substance or nature that no part is left untouched or unaffected: unlike *infuse*, which it otherwise closely resembles, *imbue* takes as its object the person or thing affected, and not the thing that is introduced; thus, to *infuse* courage into his soldiers; to *imbue* his soldiers with courage; to *infuse* grace into the soul; to *imbue* the soul with grace. "Thy words, with grace divine *Imbued*, bring to their sweetness no satiety" (*Milton*). "[Virgil] has *imbued* every object that he touches, with the light and warmth and color absorbed from its contact with life" (*Lowes*). **Ingrain** (literally, to dye in a fast color, especially before weaving) is now found, in the sense here considered, in the past participle or passive forms only: like *imbue*, it implies an incorporation of something comparable to a pervading dye with the body, substance, or nature of whatever is affected, but unlike *imbue*, it takes for its object (or, when the verb is passive, as its subject) the thing introduced rather than the person or thing affected; as, "Cruelty and jealousy seemed to be *ingrained* in a man who has these vices at all" (*Sir A. Helps*); "The idea of absolute financial probity as the first law of a gentleman's code was...deeply *ingrained* in him" (*E. Wharton*); "The feeling...is so deeply *engrained* in human nature" (*Max Müller*). **Inoculate** (literally, to introduce a disease germ, virus, or the like, so that it produces infection or disease or, more often in current use, serves as a step in producing immunity) in extended use implies imbuing a person with something that acts in the manner of a disease germ. Often, the term implies an introduction of an idea, an emotion, a taste, or the like, by highly surreptitious or artificial means, in order to achieve a desired end: less often, it also implies a similar introduction of something evil and destructive; as, to *inoculate* a group with suspicion of their government; "the theory...that if the great masses of the plain people could be *inoculated* with it [a taste for music] they would cease to herd into the moving-picture theaters" (*Mencken*). **Leaven** (literally, to make dough rise and become light and porous by the introduction of yeast) implies a transforming or tempering of a body, mass, or the like, by the introduction of something which enlivens, elevates, exalts, or, on the other hand, that causes disturbance, agitation, or corruption. "Your glorying *is* not good. Know ye not that a little leaven *leaveneth* the whole lump? Purge out therefore the old leaven, that ye may be a new lump" (*1 Corinthians* v. 6–7). "[The believer] knows that if indeed the spirit of Christ could truly *leaven* the world, the pomps, the glories, the splendours which veil it [religion], would melt like unsubstantial wreaths of smoke" (*A. C. Benson*).

Ana. Impregnate, saturate, impenetrate, *permeate, pervade: *inform, inspire, animate, fire: instill, inculcate, *implant, inseminate, infix.

ingeminate. *Repeat, iterate, reiterate.

ingenious. Cunning, *clever, adroit.

Ana. Inventing *or* inventive, creating *or* creative, discovering (see corresponding verbs at INVENT): *dexterous, feat, handy, deft: skillful, adept, skilled, expert, *proficient.

☞ *Do not confuse* ingenious *with* ingenuous.

ingenuous. *Natural, simple, naïve, unsophisticated, artless.

Ana. Open, *frank, candid, plain: transparent, *clear: *childlike, childish: *straightforward, aboveboard: *sincere, unfeigned.

Ant. Disingenuous: cunning. — ***Con.*** Stealthy, covert, furtive, surreptitious, underhand (see SECRET): wily, artful, crafty, tricky, foxy, *sly.

☞ *Do not confuse* ingenuous *with* ingenious.

ingrain *or* **engrain.** *Infuse, suffuse, imbue, inoculate, leaven.

Ana. Impregnate, saturate, *permeate, pervade, interpenetrate, impenetrate: instill, infix, inculcate, *implant, inseminate: incorporate, embody (see IDENTIFY).

ingrained. *Inherent, constitutional, essential, intrinsic.

Ana. Confirmed, *inveterate, deep-seated, deep-rooted, chronic: infixed, implanted, inseminated (see IMPLANT): imbued, inoculated (see INFUSE).

Con. Shallow, *superficial: external, outward, *outer, exterior, outside: extraneous, *extrinsic, alien, foreign.

ingratiating. *Disarming, insinuating, insinuative.

Ana. Obsequious, *subservient, servile: fawning, truckling, toadying (see FAWN): flattering, complimenting (see corresponding nouns at COMPLIMENT): blandishing, cajoling, wheedling (see COAX).

Ant. Forbidding.

ingredient, *n.* Constituent, component, *element, integrant, factor.

Ana. *Item, detail, particular.

Con. Compound, composite, amalgam, *mixture, admixture, blend.

ingress. *Entrance, entry, entree, access.

Ant. Egress.

inhabitant. **Inhabitant, denizen, resident, citizen** are here compared as meaning one whose home or dwelling place is in a definite location. Of these terms *inhabitant* applies regularly in nonfigurative use to animals as well as persons, and only *denizen* applies also to plants, and sometimes even to words. **Inhabitant,** the least specific word, implies nothing more than an abode in a given place; as, in 1940 the city had 243,718 *inhabitants;* "certain disagreeable *inhabitants* of open impounded water supplies, known as algae" (*A. C. Morrison*). **Denizen** denotes one that belongs by birth or naturalization to a given locality; as, *denizens* of the deep; "winged *denizens* of the crag" (*Scott*); "as if the old *denizens* of the forest had been felled with an axe" (*M. F. Maury*). Originally, though now rarely in literal use, *denizen* denoted one who lives within a country (sometimes a city) as distinguished from a foreigner; later it came sometimes to be applied specifically to a naturalized alien (as, "Charles [I] seemed ambitious of making English *denizens* of every man of genius in Europe"—*I. D'Israeli*). Even when substituted in literary use for *inhabitant, denizen* retains something of its own flavor of belonging to the locality by birth or naturalization; as, "jaded and oversophisticated *denizens* of towns" (*Lowes*). **Resident** is not always clearly distinguished from *inhabitant*, especially when a town or city, as distinguished from a state or country, is in question. Often the term implies nothing more than tenancy of a room, an apartment, a house, or the like, for a considerable length of time; as, the summer *residents* of Bar Harbor. Often, in the case of a person who has several residences or who lives mainly in a place other than the one regarded as his home, the term suggests not permanent inhabitancy but legal recognition of one of these places as his domicile, and as the place where he votes, pays his income taxes, and the like; thus, proof that the multimillionaire was a *resident* of Massachusetts brought several million dollars in inheritance taxes to that state; are the students at this college considered *residents* of the town and entitled to vote in town matters? In reference to a country, *resident* is preferred to *inhabitant* as a designation of an alien living in that country for a time and regarded as subject to certain taxes. "An alien actually present in the United States who is not a mere transient or sojourner is a *resident* of the United States for purposes of the income tax" (*Income Tax Regulations, U. S.*). **Citizen,** as here compared (see also CITIZEN, 2, for discussion of citizen of a country), applies to a resident of a city or town, especially to one of full age who enjoys the right to vote and other privileges; as, to call a mass meeting of *citizens* to protest the proposed legislation.

inherent. **Inherent, ingrained, intrinsic, essential, constitutional** come into comparison as meaning being a part, element, or quality of a thing's internal character or inmost being. That is **inherent** which is so deeply infixed in a thing that it is an element or quality resident in its very nature or essence; as, "certain *inherent* and indestructible qualities of the human mind" (*Wordsworth*); "Is the inferiority of the modern to the ancient languages, as a means of mental discipline, *inherent* in these tongues, or does it arise from causes that can be overcome?" (*Grandgent*); "Too much insistence on the fatalism *inherent* in their religion has reduced them [Arabs] to the condition of static lethargy...in which they now find themselves" (*A. Huxley*). That is **ingrained** (originally, dyed a fast red; now, technically, dyed in the fiber or yarn as distinguished from the woven fabric) which is wrought into the very fiber or texture of a person's being; as, an *ingrained* prejudice; "Attributable rather to the *ingrained* law-abidingness of the [French] people than to the perfection of the Paris police system" (*Brownell*); "her deeply *ingrained* habit of never letting herself go" (*H. G. Wells*). That is **intrinsic** which belongs to or is a property of a thing itself, as considered apart from all the external relations, connections, or conditions that affect its usefulness, value, significance, or the like; as, "When the subject has no *intrinsic* dignity, it must necessarily owe its attractions to artificial embellishments" (*Johnson*); "A fine big bird he [the turkey-cock] is...but there is no *intrinsic* beauty about him" (*Jefferies*); "The knowledge of geographical facts is useful, but without *intrinsic* intellectual value" (*B. Russell*). That is **essential** (see also ESSENTIAL, 2; NEEDFUL) which is an element of a thing's essence and therefore indissolubly involved in its very nature or being; as, "Certain *essential* differences between verse and prose" (*Quiller-Couch*); "that *essential* sweetness of the moor, born of the heather roots and the south-west wind" (*Galsworthy*). That is **constitutional** which is inherent in the physical structure or composition of the body or mind given one by nature; as, a *constitutional* infirmity; his vigor is *constitutional;* "thoughtful ones will assure you that happiness and unhappiness are *constitutional*, and have nothing to do with money" (*Shaw*).

Ana. *Innate, inborn, inbred, congenital: *inner, inward, internal: natural, typical, normal, *regular: integrated *or* integral (see corresponding verb INTEGRATE).

Ant. Adventitious. — *Con.* *Accidental, fortuitous, incidental: extraneous, foreign, alien, *extrinsic.

inheritance. **1** *Heritage, patrimony, birthright.

2 Inheritance, heredity are here compared only as denoting the acquisition of physical or mental characters from one's parents or ancestors. **Inheritance,** as here compared (see HERITAGE), denotes the act or state of receiving or deriving qualities, powers, physical peculiarities, or the like, by transmission from parent to offspring; as, "Instincts...acquired by habit in one generation, and then transmitted by *inheritance* in succeeding generations" (*Darwin*). **Heredity** may be used in place of *inheritance*, but more often it designates the biological law in accordance with which such transmission takes place; as, "These two, *heredity* and environment, are the master influences of the organic world" (*H. Drummond*).

inherited. Hereditary, inborn, inbred, *innate, congenital.

Ana. Transmitted, conveyed (see CARRY): generated, engendered, bred (see GENERATE).

Con. Acquired, gained, obtained, gotten (see GET).

inhibit. **1** *Forbid, prohibit, interdict, ban, enjoin.

Ana. *Prevent, preclude, obviate, avert, ward off: debar, rule out, *exclude: *hinder, impede, obstruct, block, bar.

Ant. Allow. — *Con.* *Let, permit, suffer, leave.

2 *Restrain, curb, check, snaffle, bridle.

Ana. *Suppress, repress: *prevent, forestall: *arrest, check.

Ant. Animate (sense 2): activate (sense 2).

inhuman. Savage, barbarous, *fierce, truculent, ferocious, cruel, fell.

Ana. Pitiless, ruthless (see affirmative nouns at PITY): malign, malignant, *malicious, despiteous: merciless, relentless, unrelenting, implacable, *grim: *fiendish, diabolical, devilish.

Ant. Humane. — *Con.* Benevolent, humanitarian, *charitable, altruistic, philanthropic: compassionate, *tender.

iniquitous. Nefarious, flagitious, *vicious, villainous, infamous, corrupt, degenerate.

Ana. Wicked, evil, ill, *bad: atrocious, heinous, *outrageous, monstrous: ungodly, godless, *irreligious.

Ant. Righteous. — *Con.* Virtuous, *moral, ethical, noble: just, *upright, honorable, honest.

initiate, *v.* **1** *Begin, commence, start, inaugurate.

Ana. *Found, establish, organize, institute.

Ant. Consummate. — *Con.* Effect, fulfill, execute, accomplish, achieve, *perform: *enforce, implement.

2 Initiate, induct, inaugurate, install (*or* **instal**), **invest** agree in meaning to put one through the processes, ceremonies, or other formalities regarded as essential to one's being admitted to one's duties as a member, an official, or the like. **Initiate,** as here compared (see also BEGIN), usually implies admission to some organization, cult, craft, or the like, especially to one requiring indoctrination in its mysteries or mysterious (often pseudo-mysterious) rites or ceremonies in the introduction of new members; as, to *initiate* the newly elected members of a college fraternity; "to *initiate* young people in the elements of physical science" (*T. H. Huxley*); to *initiate* a new reporter into the secrets of successful news gathering. **Induct** may often be used in place of *initiate*, especially when introduction under guidance is also implied; as, to *induct* a person into a new position or into the duties of a new position. But *induct*, as well as **inaugurate, install,** and **invest** may imply a formal or ceremonious endowing of a person with the powers and prerogatives of an office or post; as, to *induct* the new governor of a colony. *Induct* is used technically of clergymen who are put in possession of a benefice or living, or of officials who are established in their office with appropriate rites or ceremonies; as, to *induct* the new rector of a parish; the new superintendent of schools was *inducted* into office at last night's meeting of the board of education. *Inaugurate* (see also BEGIN) usually implies more formal and dignified ceremonies and much more publicity than *induct;* as, to *inaugurate* the president of the United States; to *inaugurate* the new president of the university. *Install* etymologically implies an establishing in a stall or seat; in both literal and figurative use, it implies induction into an office associated with a seat; as, to *install* the officers of a society; to *install* a canon of a cathedral; to *install* a bishop as the archbishop of his new diocese. The term also may be used in reference to persons who are formally or comfortably seated (as, to *install* the guest of honor in the most comfortable of their chairs; to *install* the tottering old lady in a chair by the fireside); it is also the only one of these terms which may be used (in the meaning here discussed) in reference to things as well as to persons (as, to *install* new machinery in a factory; to *install* electric light fixtures). *Invest* (for fuller treatment of this sense see CLOTHE) usually implies a clothing with the robes or other insignia of an office and, by extension, with the powers of that office. It often also implies a ceremony (as, to *invest* a king with his crown) but it may suggest only the addition of powers that come to one on one's induction into a position or office (as, "By the constitution of the United States the president is *invested* with certain important political powers"—*Ch. Just. Marshall*).

Ana. Introduce, admit, *enter.

Con. *Eject, oust, expel, dismiss: *exclude, eliminate, disbar, blackball, shut out: divest, *strip.

initiative. Referendum, *mandate, plebiscite.

injunction. *Command, order, bidding, behest, mandate, dictate.

Ana. Instruction, direction, charging *or* charge (see corresponding verbs at COMMAND): warning (see WARN): precept, rule, regulation, *law, statute, ordinance, canon.

injure. Injure, harm, hurt, damage, impair, mar, spoil agree in meaning to affect someone or something so as to rob it of soundness, strength, or perfection, or to reduce its value, usefulness, or effectiveness. **Injure,** in its earliest and still not uncommon sense, implies the doing of an injustice or the wronging of another as by robbing him of his good name, of a rightful possession, or the like; in this sense, it often suggests intent or knowledge on the part of one that injures; as, "When have I *injured* thee? when done thee wrong?" (*Shak.*); "I would not *injure* him so much as to suppose the truth of it possible" (*Austen*). In later use, the verb came to imply the infliction not of injustice but of anything detrimental to one's appearance, health, success, comfort, or the like; as, a bullet *injured* his eye; "Is it best for you to *injure* your prospects for such a voluptuous, idle woman as that?" (*Hardy*); "Industrialism has been very injurious to art; may it not have *injured* religion also?" (*Inge*). **Harm** often carries a stronger implication of inflicting annoyance, pain, suffering, or loss than *injure;* as, the boy is so gentle that he would not *harm* a fly; the circulation of the rumor greatly *harmed* his business; "For many have been *harmed* by speech, Through thinking, few or none" (*Vaux*); "For none of woman born Shall *harm* Macbeth" (*Shak.*). **Hurt,** a term in wide colloquial use, usually implies the infliction of a wound (figuratively as well as literally), not only to the body or feelings, but to anything capable of sustaining an injury that may or may not be cured or healed; often, it is used where *injure* is also possible; as, he was severely *hurt* by a falling brick; to *hurt* a friend's feelings; "It's damnable to have to *hurt* the people we love" (*R. Macaulay*); "a limitless desire to *hurt* and humiliate" (*H. G. Wells*). **Damage** implies an injury that results in lowered value or involves loss in effectiveness, attractiveness, efficiency, or the like; as, his automobile was *damaged* in a collision; the frost *damaged* the late crops; "her fair skin little *damaged* by time" (*R. Macaulay*). "Whatever psycho-analysts may say, the parental instinct is essentially different from the sex instinct, and is *damaged* by the intrusion of emotions appropriate to sex" (*B. Russell*). **Impair,** though coming close to *damage* in its meaning and often interchangeable with it, more frequently suggests deterioration or diminution as in value, strength, validity, or the like (as, a weak piece of evidence often *impairs* the strength of a good argument; his value as a candidate has been *impaired* by his hysterical attacks on his opponent) or a weakening as of a function or power of functioning (as, his eye was *injured* and his vision *impaired*). "Kindness that left an impression on my heart not yet *impaired*" (*De Quincey*); "Religion, always a principle of energy, in this new people is no way worn out or *impaired*" (*Burke*). **Mar** implies the infliction of an injury that disfigures or maims or involves the loss of a thing's perfection or well-being; as, "I pray you, *mar* no more trees with writing love-songs in their barks" (*Shak.*); "Striving to better, oft we *mar* what's well" (*Shak.*); "Plato asserts that a life of drudgery disfigures the body and *mars* and enervates the soul" (*G. L. Dickinson*). **Spoil,** as here compared (see also DECAY, INDULGE), carries a stronger implication of ruin than *mar,* for it suggests the operation of something that not only induces the impairment of strength, vigor, value, or the like, but also brings about their inevitable destruction; as, "Bitter shame hath *spoil'd* the sweet world's taste" (*Shak.*); "a man who had *spoiled* his constitution with bad living" (*Shaw*); "When a child persistently interferes with other children or *spoils* their pleasures, the obvious punishment is banishment" (*B. Russell*).

Ana. *Deface, disfigure, disfeature: *deform, distort, contort: *afflict, torture, torment: *maim, cripple, mutilate, mangle, batter: *abuse, ill-treat, maltreat, outrage, mistreat, misuse.

Ant. Aid. — ***Con.*** *Help, assist: *benefit, profit, avail, bestead: preserve, conserve, *save.

injury. 1 Injury, hurt, damage, harm, mischief are here compared as denoting the act or the result of doing to a person or thing something that causes loss, pain, or the like. **Injury** is the comprehensive term referable to any act or to any result of that act which involves a violation of a right or of health, freedom, soundness, and the like, or causes a partial or entire loss of something of value; as, an *injury* to one's eyes, to one's feelings, to one's reputation; to forgive an *injury;* an *injury* to a tree, to a watch. "The very essence of civil liberty...consists in the right of every individual to claim the protection of laws, whenever he receives an *injury*" (*Ch. Just. Marshall*). **Hurt** applies literally to a physical injury such as a wound, a lesion, a contusion, or the like, that results from a hit, a stab, or other blow; as, "Get him to bed, and let his *hurt* be look'd to" (*Shak.*). Figuratively, *hurt* applies chiefly to an act or result that involves pain, suffering, or loss; thus, a person whose rights as an heir have been violated may be said to suffer an *injury* but not a *hurt;* a person whose reputation has been damaged by a false rumor has suffered both an *injury* to his business and a *hurt* to his feelings; a dentist in drilling a tooth may cause a *hurt,* but not an *injury.* But *hurt* may also imply, especially in archaic use, a disadvantage; as, "He that sweareth to his own *hurt,* and changeth not" (*Psalms* xv. 4). **Damage** always applies to an injury that involves loss (usually calculable loss) as in property, in value, or in usefulness; as, the fire caused great *damage* to the house; to repair the *damage* done to the cathedral by the bombs. "Deliver Helen, and all *damage* else— As honour, loss of time, travail, expense ... Shall be struck off" (*Shak.*). **Harm** (usually without an article) is referable to any evil that is or may be suffered or sustained to one's injury; often it suggests suffering such as grief, shame, or the like, but this connotation is far from invariable; as, "Do thyself no *harm*" (*Acts* xvi. 28); I meant no *harm;* to put one out of *harm's* way. "Almost every evening he saw Lucy. The inexperienced little wife apprehended no *harm* in his visits" (*Meredith*). **Mischief** carries a far stronger reference to the person or thing that works harm or is capable of inflicting injury; in fact, it applies either to the harm or injury as the work of such an agent or agency (as, "We don't begin to imagine all the *mischief* it [the war] is going to do"—*H. G. Wells;* "That's the *mischief* of the Modernists....They don't claim that the Divine revelation has been supplanted or even added to, but that it has been amplified"—*C. Mackenzie*), or to the person or thing which serves as a cause of harm, vexation, or the like (as, "This power [of erecting such buildings as one pleases on one's own property]...may, we presume, be restrained, if exercised so as to produce a public *mischief*"—*Ch. Just. Marshall*).

Ana. *Distress, suffering, agony, misery: *pain, pang: violation, transgression, trespass, infringement (see BREACH): detriment (see corresponding adjective at PERNICIOUS): *evil, ill, bale.

2 Wrong, tort, *injustice, grievance.

Ana. See those at INJURY, 1.

injustice. **Injustice, injury, wrong, tort, grievance** are comparable, though not strictly synonymous, terms when they denote an act that inflicts undeserved damage, loss, or hardship on a person. **Injustice** is the general term applicable not only to any act which involves unfairness to another or a violation of his rights (as, "class-privileges which make *injustices* easy"—*H. Spencer*) but, as a collective noun, to all acts which come under this description (as, "[Galsworthy] flamed out against *injustice* because he was a lover of justice"—*Bliss Perry*). **Injury,** in this sense chiefly a legal term, applies to any injustice to a person for which the law allows an action to recover compensation or specific property, or both; thus, a person whose payment for services is wrongfully withheld suffers an *injury* in the legal sense of that word. **Wrong** is, in law, a more general term than *injury* for it applies not only to all injuries as just defined (*private wrongs*) but to any misdemeanors or crimes which affect the community (*public wrongs*) and which are punishable according to the criminal code. But in general use, *wrong* differs little from *injustice*, except in carrying a stronger connotation of flagrancy or of seriousness; as, to endure *wrongs* from their oppressors over a long period; "we are... steel to the very back, Yet wrung with *wrongs* more than our backs can bear" (*Shak.*). **Tort** is now almost exclusively a legal term, referable to any injury (as defined in law) except a breach of contract: it therefore always suggests a civil proceeding; as, to bring an action in *tort;* to get a judgment for *tort*. **Grievance,** which is a general rather than a legal term, applies to any circumstance or condition that, in the opinion of those affected, constitutes a wrong or that, in a lighter sense, gives one just grounds for complaint; as, "They sent to the King a statement of their *grievances*" (*T. Keightley*); "In an early state of society any kind of taxation is apt to be looked on as a *grievance*" (*Freeman*).

Ana. Damage, hurt, harm, mischief, *injury: infringement, trespass, transgression, violation, infraction, *breach: unfairness, inequitableness (see affirmative adjectives at FAIR).

Con. *Justice, equity.

innate. **Innate, inborn, inbred, congenital, hereditary, inherited** are not always synonymous terms, but they come into comparison because of their literal meaning: not acquired after birth but derived from one's inheritance or from conditions attending one's birth. *Innate* (the Latin term) and *inborn* (the Anglo-Saxon term) are often used without distinction. But **innate** (opposed to *acquired*) is frequently synonymous, in a broad sense, with *inherent, essential,* or *constitutional,* not only because it may apply to qualities, characters, or elements of an organism, organ, or the like, that are not inherited but belong to it as part of its nature or essence (thus, *innate* ideas are by definition ideas that exist in the mind as a result of its constitution and are therefore found wherever a mind exists), but because it may apply to elements or qualities, such as virtues or defects, which arise out of the very nature or character of a thing that has no life and therefore literally no birth (as, the *innate* defect of this plan; the *innate* tendency of a dictatorship to overreach itself). "I do not believe that a sense of justice is *innate,* but I have been astonished to see how quickly it can be created" (*B. Russell*). On the other hand, **inborn,** which is frequently synonymous with *natural* or *native,* retains more specific reference to that which is actually born in one or is so deep-seated as to seem to have been born in one; the term is therefore usually, but not invariably, applied to qualities or characters that are peculiar or distinctive, sometimes to the type, often to the individual; as, *inborn* aptitudes; his *inborn* ability to sing; an *inborn* love of country life. **Inbred** etymologically implies reference to breeding, or to any of the processes concerned with the generation, nourishment, and rearing of offspring; the term therefore is more readily applied to that which is deeply rooted or ingrained as a result of one's immediate parentage or the circumstances attending one's earliest education or training than to that which is constitutional or merely natural; as, an *inbred* love of freedom; an *inbred* feeling of superiority; "those *inbred* sentiments which are... the true supporters of all liberal and manly morals" (*Burke*). **Congenital,** in current English, applies chiefly to something which dates from the birth of the person, animal, or plant concerned; as, *congenital* hip disease; *congenital* blindness; *congenital* deafness; "the theory that what was acquired habit in the ancestor may become *congenital* tendency in the offspring" (*W. James*). Both **hereditary** and **inherited** apply to that which is the result of heredity; as, a *hereditary,* or an *inherited,* mental defect. *Hereditary,* however, and not *inherited,* applies usually to that which passes to one or is derived through inheritance; as, a *hereditary* office; "several *hereditary* enemies of the Olivares brothers" (*Cather*). In biology, *congenital* and *hereditary* are regarded as synonyms that are, however, clearly distinguishable, for *congenital* implies acquirement (as of a disease or an organic defect) during the development of the fetus in the womb and *hereditary* implies transmission (as of a tendency, a weakness, or the like) from an ancestor through the germ plasm; thus, a birthmark is a *congenital* blemish of the skin; the color of one's hair or of one's eyes is *hereditary.*

Ana. Constitutional, *inherent, intrinsic, essential, ingrained: *instinctive, intuitive: natural, typical, *regular, normal: *native, indigenous.

Ant. Acquired. — ***Con.*** *Accidental, adventitious, incidental, fortuitous: assumed, affected, feigned, simulated (see ASSUME): cultivated, fostered, nurtured (see NURSE).

inner. **Inner, inward, inside, interior, internal, intestine** (*or* **intestinal**) are here compared as adjectives meaning being or placed within something. Although in many cases interchangeable, they are more or less restricted in their applications and therefore clearly distinguished in their implications. **Inner** and, less frequently, **inward** may be used when spatial relations are implied, but *inner* often applies to that which is farther within or nearer the center (as, "[He] thrust them into the *inner* prison" —*Acts* xvi. 24; an *inner* room, the *inner* bark of a tree) and *inward* often applies to that which is hidden within (as, the *inward* organs of the body; the *inward* part of an apple is the core) or to that which moves to a point within (as, *inward* mails; the *inward* curve of a scroll). Both words apply also to that which is mental or spiritual, frequently with the added implication of something intimate, secret, or inaccessible; as, "the sense By which thy *inner* nature was apprised Of outward shows" (*Shelley*); the *inner* life; the *Inner* Light (in Quaker doctrine, a divine and guiding presence in the soul of each person); "Though our outward man perish, yet the *inward* man is renewed day by day" (*2 Corinthians* iv. 16); "that *inward* eye Which is the bliss of solitude" (*Wordsworth*). **Inside** is used chiefly of spatial relations (as, an *inside* seat, the *inside* track) but it may be used with reference to persons who are so placed in their work or who have such contacts that they may be said to be figuratively *inside* a place or group (thus, *inside* work implies a contrast with field or road work; *inside* knowledge of a negotiation implies participation to some extent in that negotiation; so, *inside* employees; to have *inside* information of what is going on in a club). **Interior** and **internal** commonly suggest more abstract or technical, less intimate, relations than *inner* and *inward*. *Interior* frequently implies contrast with the exterior, or outer, limits of the thing itself; thus, the *interior* features of a country are by implication opposed to those of the coast or boundaries; *interior* decoration (as a profession) deals with the decoration and furnishing of the inside of a house or other building rather than with its outside; one's *interior* life is one's life as expressed in thoughts and aspirations rather than in outward activities. *Internal* implies contrast with that which lies beyond or outside of the outer limits of a thing; thus, *internal* evidence of a poem's authorship is gained from a study of the poem itself rather than from outside sources; the *internal* affairs of a country are its domestic, as opposed to its foreign, affairs (but cf. secretary of the *interior*, a cabinet official who has charge of *internal* affairs); *internal* medicine is that branch of medicine dealing with the diagnosis and treatment of diseases affecting the inward organs, such as the heart, lungs, stomach, liver, etc. **Intestine** (or the rarer **intestinal**), as here compared, is a close synonym of *internal*, applicable in current use only to that which may otherwise be described as *domestic* or *civil* (as opposed to *foreign*), with, however, the connotation of an evil or mischievous origin or nature; as, *intestine* difficulties in France were largely responsible for the defeat of that country in **1940**; an *intestine* or *intestinal* (i.e., a civil) war.

Ana. Central, middle, focal, nuclear (see corresponding nouns at CENTER): intimate, close, *familiar: intrinsic, constitutional, essential, *inherent: *instinctive, intuitive: deep-seated, deep-rooted (see INVETERATE).

Ant. Outer. — ***Con.*** Outward, outside, exterior, external (see OUTER).

innuendo. *Insinuation.

Ana. Hinting *or* hint, intimation, suggestion (see corresponding verbs at SUGGEST): *implication, inference: allusion (see corresponding verb at REFER).

inoculate. *Infuse, imbue, ingrain, leaven, suffuse.

Ana. Impregnate, saturate, interpenetrate, impenetrate, *permeate, pervade: introduce, admit, *enter: instill, inculcate, infix, inseminate, *implant.

inordinate. *Excessive, immoderate, exorbitant, extreme, extravagant.

Ana. *Irrational, unreasonable: *supererogatory, wanton, uncalled-for, gratuitous: *superfluous, surplus, extra.

Ant. Ordinate (*rare*): temperate. — ***Con.*** *Moderate: restrained, curbed, checked, inhibited (see RESTRAIN): *due, rightful, condign: *fair, just, equitable.

inquest. Investigation, probe, *inquiry, inquisition, research.

Ana. Examination, inspection, scrutiny, audit (see under SCRUTINIZE): questioning, interrogation, catechizing, examining (see corresponding verbs at ASK).

inquire *or* **enquire.** Query, question, *ask, interrogate, speer, catechize, quiz, examine.

Con. Reply, *answer, respond, rejoin, retort.

inquiry *or* **enquiry.** **Inquiry** (*or* **enquiry**), **inquisition, investigation, inquest, probe, research** are here compared as meaning a search for truth, knowledge, or information. **Inquiry** is the most general of these terms, applicable to any such search regardless of the means (questioning, observation, experimentation, etc.) used or of the end in view; as, a letter of *inquiry;* to address an *inquiry* to the proper authorities; to make *inquiries* about a sick friend; "The passion for pure knowledge is to be gratified only through the scientific method of *inquiry*" (*C. W. Eliot*); "the True, which is the goal of all scientific and all philosophical *inquiry*" (*Inge*); "a primitive but effective police *inquiry*" (*T. S. Eliot*). **Inquisition** ordinarily carries heightened implications of searchingness and of penetration far below the surface to uncover what is concealed or withheld; as, to be subjected to an *inquisition* into one's motives; "the nicest *inquisition* of the microscope" (*Burke*). The term, however, is chiefly applied to a judicial inquiry aiming to unearth facts or conditions to support suspicions, charges, or the like: often, because it is applied historically both to a body of ecclesiastical (or sometimes, civil) officials engaged in ferreting out heretics or heresy, especially in the late Middle Ages and in the Reformation period, and to methods of inquiry pursued by such a body (as, for example, the Spanish *Inquisition*), the term not only in its specific sense but even in its general sense connotes relentless pursuit of a clue or of a suspect, and sometimes merciless and ruthless persecution. "When, as becomes a man who would prepare For such an arduous work, I through myself Make rigorous *inquisition*, the report Is often cheering" (*Wordsworth*). "What shall I do? Cenci must find me here, and I must bear The imperious *inquisition* of his looks As to what brought me hither" (*Shelley*). **Investigation** applies to an inquiry which has for its aim the uncovering of the facts and the establishment of the truth. In very precise use, it implies a systematic tracking down of something that one hopes to discover or needs to know, if true; as, an *investigation* of the causes of the prolonged depression; the bank never employs a clerk or teller without an *investigation* of his habits and record; senatorial committees of *investigation.* **Inquest** is now used rarely, even in a poetic or rhetorical context, in place of *inquiry* or *inquisition*, for it is commonly a legal term applying to an investigation by a jury and judge, and specifically to one conducted by a coroner and jury in order to determine the cause of a death when there is good ground for suspecting other than natural causes; as, when the rumors of murder became rife, the body was exhumed and an *inquest* held. Consequently, in general use, the term usually applies to an investigation that has some of the characteristics of a coroner's inquest, such as the determination of the grounds for an accusation or suspicion; as, "Remembering this [Ben Jonson's creative power], we turn to Mr. Gregory Smith's objection—that Jonson's characters lack the third dimension, have no life out of the theatrical existence in which they appear—and demand an *inquest*" (*T. S. Eliot*). **Probe,** which is chiefly an Americanism in this sense, applies to an investigation that searches deeply and extensively with the intent to detect wrongdoing, if any: it suggests methods of exploration comparable to a surgeon's probing for a bullet, a diseased condition, etc.; as, a legislative *probe* of banking activities. **Research** now applies chiefly to an inquiry or investigation which requires prolonged and careful study, especially of actual conditions or of primary sources of information. In precise use, it is restricted to inquiries or investigations carried on by scientists, historians, and other scholars, especially for the sake of uncovering new knowledge, of getting at the facts when these are not known, or of discovering laws of nature: the popular tendency to use it for any study leading to the writing of a résumé of facts or laws already known is consequently decried. "*Research* has shown and practice has established the futility of the charge that it was a usurpation when this Court undertook to declare an Act of Congress unconstitutional" (*Justice Holmes*). "Scientists who had done distinctive work in leprosy... laid down a set of principles for the guidance of leprosy *research*" (*V. Heiser*).

Ana. Questioning, interrogation, catechizing (see ASK): examination, inspection, scrutiny, audit (see under SCRUTINIZE): grilling (see AFFLICT).

inquisition. Inquest, *inquiry, probe, investigation, research.

Ana. See those at INQUIRY.

inquisitive. *Curious, prying, snoopy, nosy.

Ana. *Impertinent, intrusive, meddlesome: interfering, meddling, intermeddling (see MEDDLE).

Ant. Incurious. — *Con.* *Indifferent, unconcerned, aloof, detached: uninterested, *disinterested.

inroad. *Invasion, incursion, raid, irruption.

Ana. Intrusion, butting in (see corresponding verbs at INTRUDE): encroachment, entrenchment, infringement, trespassing *or* trespass (see corresponding verbs at TRESPASS): *entrance, entry, ingress.

insane. **Insane, mad, crazy, crazed, demented, deranged, lunatic, maniac** (*or* **maniacal**), **wood, non compos mentis** are here compared chiefly in their general or nontechnical senses (for senses of corresponding nouns used technically see INSANITY) and as meaning afflicted by or manifesting unsoundness of mind or an inability to control one's rational processes. **Insane** as applied in medicine, psychiatry, and law to persons, usually implies such unsoundness of mind that one does not recognize one's own condition or is not responsible for one's actions; as, to be adjudged *insane* after a period of observation. In more general use, *insane* implies utter folly or irrationality; the person (or more often, the act or utterance) so described is, by implication, governed by blind passion, senselessness, or the like; as, "Day after day he would seek his dear mistress, pour *insane* hopes, supplications, rhapsodies, raptures, into her ear" (*Thackeray*); "*insane* spite" (*Shaw*); "Now that wars...have become far more horrible and...*insane*" (*Inge*). **Mad** usually implies more frenzy than *insane* and therefore carries a stronger suggestion of wildness, rabidness, raving, or complete loss of self-control; as, "O, let me not be *mad*, not *mad*, sweet heaven! Keep me in temper: I would not be *mad!*" (*Shak.*); "A *mad* pleasure in the prospect of wreaking vengeance on the villain who had laid the trap for him" (*Meredith*); "And then to hear a dead man chatter Is enough to drive one *mad*" (*Tennyson*). **Crazy** (etymologically, broken or shattered) often, especially in its oldest sense, suggests a breakdown, especially a complete mental breakdown, such as may result from illness or old age; as, he has gone *crazy;* "We will bestow you in some better place, Fitter for sickness and for *crazy* age" (*Shak.*). In current use, the term more often suggests a distraught or wild state of mind induced by some intense emotion such as anxiety, grief, joy, desire, excitement, or the like; as, "the lady in the gallery is half *crazy* with anxiety for St. George" (*Shaw*); "Somebody had shot a squirrel and he took on about it as though he had lost a child. I said then he was *crazy*" (*S. Anderson*). As applied to things such as schemes, projects, notions, or the like, *crazy* usually suggests that they are the product of a crackbrained mind; as, "no educated Socialist believes such *crazy* nonsense" (*Shaw*); who would pay such a *crazy* price for a book? **Crazed** is often used in place of **crazy** when a going crazy is implied; as, *crazed* with grief; he seems *crazed* of late. **Demented** and **deranged** are less colloquial than the preceding words and less rich in connotations; both terms, moreover, imply a change from mental soundness to unsoundness, *demented* commonly suggesting signs, such as profound apathy or incoherence in thought, speech, or action, which indicate deterioration of the mental powers (as, there was now no doubt that the sick man was *demented*), *deranged* (cf. *derangement* under ABERRATION, 2) suggesting a loss of mental balance or a state of mental disorder resulting from a functional disturbance of the brain or nervous system (as, he was temporarily *deranged* by the shock). **Lunatic** is usually far wider in its range of application than **maniac.** The former term is approximately the equivalent of *insane,* though it often retains from its earliest sense a suggestion of alternations between irrational and rational states of mind; as, "Persuade him that he hath been *lunatic*" (*Shak.*); "it is easier for an inferior dramatic poet to write poetry when he has a *lunatic* character to speak it, because...he is less tied down to relevance and ordinary sense" (*T. S. Eliot*). *Maniac* comes closer to *mad,* for it commonly (but not invariably) connotes violence, fury, raving, or the like; as, the *maniac* rage of the multitude; "the *maniac* dreamer; cruel ... Is he with fear" (*Shelley*). **Wood** is now obsolete or dialectal for *mad* or *maniac;* as, "Our hoste gan to swear as [if] he were *wood*" (*Chaucer*). **Non compos mentis** (Latin for "not sound of mind") is a legal term which specifies a state, but does not define the particular condition or kind, of mental unsoundness. It, especially in its shortened form *non compos,* is often used colloquially with similar indefiniteness.

Ana. *Irrational, unreasonable: distracted, bewildered (see PUZZLE, *v.*).

Ant. Sane. — *Con.* Sensible, judicious, *wise, sapient, prudent.

insanity. **Insanity, lunacy, psychosis, mania, dementia** are here compared as the leading general terms denoting serious mental disorder. **Insanity** is a technical term of law rather than of medicine, although it has some use in medicine: in neither field is it strictly defined but is used as a general term to cover a wide variety of mental disorders, all of which have in common one characteristic —an unfitting of the afflicted individual to manage his own affairs or perform his social duties. Mental deficiency and delirious conditions are usually but not invariably excluded, the former because inborn and not acquired, the latter because temporary and not long-lasting. Since in law a person's sanity or insanity becomes an issue when he is charged with a crime or when his legal capacity to make a will or contract, to transfer property, or the like, is questioned, proof of insanity is tantamount to proof of his inability to act rationally and to understand the nature of his act and its natural consequences in affecting his rights, obligations, and liabilities. In general use, *insanity* is commonly distinguished from *mental deficiency* and from *neuroses*, and is applied chiefly to disorders involving loss of mind or mental derangement. **Lunacy,** a term derived from the adjective *lunatic*, still carries some suggestion of the implication inherent in the earliest meaning of *lunatic*—that of recurring periods dependent on changes of the moon. In popular use it often applies to a form of insanity that comes occasionally and manifests itself in madness and fury: the term, therefore, often implies spells of lucidity; as, "The terms of our estate may not endure Hazard so near us as doth hourly grow Out of his *lunacies*" (*Shak.*); "It's the tangle of good and badness; It's the *lunacy* linked with sanity Makes up, and mocks, humanity!" (*A. Stringer*). In Great Britain, *lunacy* was originally and still is, to a certain extent, used in place of *insanity* in law, and in practically the same sense as that given for *insanity;* as, a *lunacy* commission. **Psychosis** is the psychiatric term for any mental disease. It is preferred to *insanity* because of its lack of legal connotations, and to *lunacy* because of legal and popular connotations. **Mania** is now used in medicine and psychiatry for one of the spells of excitement or mental derangement that characterize certain mental diseases (for fuller treatment, see MANIA, 2). **Dementia** is also a technical term of psychiatry, implying a sharp contrast with *mental deficiency*, and applicable to any condition or disease that outwardly manifests a marked mental deterioration. It therefore covers practically all mental diseases that involve organic deterioration, not only those manifesting themselves in spells of excitement but those manifesting themselves in apathy, depression, flightiness, split personality (schizophrenia), and the like.

Ana. Alienation, derangement, *aberration: frenzy, delirium, *mania, hysteria.

Ant. Sanity.

inscrutable. *Mysterious, arcane.

Ana. Profound, abysmal, *deep: baffling, balking, thwarting, frustrating, foiling (see FRUSTRATE): hidden, concealed, secreted (see HIDE): enigmatic, cryptic, dark, *obscure, vague: mystifying, perplexing, puzzling (see PUZZLE, *v.*).

Con. Obvious, plain, clear, manifest, *evident, patent.

inseminate. *Implant, inculcate, instill, infix.

Ana. *Introduce, interject, insinuate, insert: impregnate, interpenetrate, impenetrate, saturate, *permeate, pervade: *scatter: *distribute, dispense.

Ant. Uproot. — *Con.* Eradicate, deracinate, extirpate, *exterminate, wipe out.

insensate. Besotted, *fond, infatuated.

Ana. Fatuous, asinine, foolish, silly (see SIMPLE): *stupid, dense, crass, dull, dumb: *irrational, unreasonable.

Con. Sensible, sane, judicious, *wise, prudent, sapient, sage: *rational, reasonable: *intelligent, quick-witted, knowing, alert.

insensible. **1 Insensible, insensitive, impassible, anesthetic** (*or* **anaesthetic**) agree in meaning unresponsive to stimuli or to external influences. **Insensible** usually implies total unresponsiveness, and therefore unawareness or unconsciousness, caused by any of a number of things, such as blunted powers of sensation, obtuseness of mind, apathy, or complete absorption in something else; as, "*insensible* to fatigue, to pleasure, and to pain" (*Macaulay*); so engrossed in his work that he was *insensible* of the flight of time. "Vulgar constitutions ...*insensible* of a thousand things that fret and gall... delicate people" (*Berkeley*). "This Court can be *insensible* neither to the magnitude nor delicacy of this question" (*Ch. Just. Marshall*). **Insensitive,** on the other hand, implies sluggishness in response or less than normal susceptibility; more specifically, it suggests dullness rather than acuteness of sensation or perception, thickness rather than thinness of skin, callousness rather than sympathy or compassion; as, an ear *insensitive* to changes of pitch; "he was *insensitive* to all kinds of discourtesy" (*Joyce*); *insensitive* to the misery of others. "Their genius for prose is a possession which involves an incapacity for poetry, an *insensitiveness* to what is intimately poetic" (*Brownell*). **Impassible,** in its historic and precise sense, implies absence of response because of incapacity for feeling or suffering. Originally derived from theology, where it was applied chiefly to the resurrected body united to its soul after the Last Judgment, the word is now rarely used except as confused with *impassive* or in reference to persons who by discipline have conquered the normal human susceptibility to pain or suffering (as, the Hindu striving for Nirvana renders himself *impassible*), or in reference to things in contrast with persons (or creatures) thought of as beings who through necessity of nature suffer pain or are susceptible to injury. "The language of strategy and politics is designed...to make it appear as though wars were not fought by individuals...but either by impersonal and therefore wholly non-moral and *impassible* forces, or else by personified abstractions" (*A. Huxley*). **Anesthetic** implies a deadening of the mind or senses (literally, by chloroform, ether, or the like; figuratively, by any agency having a similar effect) and, usually, an induced rather than a natural insensitiveness. "The intelligentsia ...neither as *anaesthetic* to ideas as the plutocracy on the one hand nor as much the slaves of emotion as the proletariat on the other" (*Mencken*).

Ana. Obtuse, *dull, blunt: *impassive, apathetic, phlegmatic, stolid, stoic: *hardened, indurated, callous: engrossed, absorbed, *intent, rapt.

Ant. Sensible (*to or of something*). — *Con.* Conscious, *aware, cognizant, alive, awake: impressed, affected, influenced, touched (see AFFECT).

2 *Imperceptible, impalpable, intangible, inappreciable, imponderable.

Ana. Tenuous, rare, slight, slender (see THIN, *adj.*): attenuated, extenuated, diluted, rarefied (see THIN, *v.*): *subtle, subtile.

Ant. Sensible, palpable. — *Con.* *Perceptible, tangible, appreciable, ponderable.

insensitive. *Insensible, impassible, anesthetic.

Ana. *Hardened, indurated, callous: *indifferent, unconcerned, aloof, incurious: *impassive, stoic, apathetic, phlegmatic, stolid.

Ant. Sensitive. — *Con.* Susceptible, subject, prone, open, exposed, *liable: allergic, hypersensitive (see corresponding nouns at SUSCEPTIBILITY): responsive, *tender, compassionate.

insert, *v.* *Introduce, interpolate, intercalate, insinuate, interpose, interject.

Ana. *Intrude, obtrude, interlope: infix, instill, inculcate, *implant: *enter, admit.

Ant. Abstract: extract. — *Con.* Disengage, *detach, prescind: withdraw, *remove, draw.

inside, *adj.* Interior, internal, intestine, *inner, inward.

Ant. Outside. — *Con.* Exterior, external, *outer, outward.

insight. Penetration, acumen, clairvoyance, divination, *discernment, discrimination, perception.

Ana. Intuition, understanding, *reason: comprehension, apprehension (see under APPREHEND): appreciation,

understanding (see corresponding verbs at UNDERSTAND): perspicaciousness, sagacity, shrewdness (see corresponding adjectives at SHREWD).
Ant. Obtuseness.

insinuate. 1 *Introduce, insert, interject, interpolate, intercalate, interpose.
Ana. *Infuse, inoculate, imbue, leaven: instill, inseminate, inculcate, infix, *implant.
2 Intimate, hint, *suggest, imply.
Ana. Allude, advert, *refer: impute, *ascribe.
Con. Voice, utter, *express, vent, air, broach: declare, *assert, affirm, aver, avouch, avow.

insinuating, insinuative. *Disarming, ingratiating.
Ana. Winning, gaining (see GET): oily, unctuous, soapy, sleek, *fulsome: blandishing, wheedling, cajoling (see COAX): politic, bland, diplomatic, smooth, *suave: artful, crafty, cunning, wily, *sly.
Con. *Forthright, downright: candid, *frank.

insinuation. **Insinuation, innuendo** agree in meaning covert suggestion or a covert allusion to something. **Insinuation** applies chiefly to any remark, comment, question, or the like, which conveys or seems to convey a hint or implication, often but not invariably one that is discreditable to the person at whom it is aimed; as, "Had he ever been a spy himself? No, he scorned the base *insinuation*" (*Dickens*); "By tacit agreement they ignored the remarks and *insinuations* of their acquaintances" (*D. H. Lawrence*). **Innuendo** more often applies to the method of covert suggestion than does *insinuation*, and when it applies to a definite instance, it is referable to meaningful smiles, glances, inflections, as well as to remarks; in both cases the term definitely implies a suggestion of something that is injurious to the reputation of the person concerned; as, "I prefer the most disagreeable certainties to hints and *innuendos*" (*Byron*); "in this play Middleton shows his interest...in *innuendo* and double meanings" (*T. S. Eliot*); " 'He—eventually—married her.' There were volumes of *innuendo* in the way the 'eventually' was spaced, and each syllable given its due stress" (*E. Wharton*).
Ana. Hinting *or* hint, implying *or* implication, suggestion, intimation (see corresponding verbs at SUGGEST): *animadversion, aspersion, reflection: imputation, ascription (see corresponding verbs at ASCRIBE): allusion (see corresponding verb at REFER).

insipid. **Insipid, vapid, flat, jejune, banal, wishy-washy, inane** come into comparison when they mean devoid of qualities which give spirit, character, or substance to a thing. That is **insipid** which is without taste, or savor, or pungency, literally or figuratively; it is applied not only to food and drink which are so tasteless as to give no pleasure or stimulation to the palate (as, *insipid* substitutes for coffee; the *insipid* vegetable marrow), but also to persons and their utterances, their ideas, their contributions to art, and the like, which strike one as thin, weak, and characterless and leave one completely indifferent. "You have so much animation, which is exactly what Miss Andrews wants; for I must confess there is something amazingly *insipid* about her" (*Austen*). "Happiness is a wine of the rarest vintage, and seems *insipid* to a vulgar taste" (*L. P. Smith*). "The *insipid* veracity with which Crabbe used to report some of the most trite doings of Nature and of man" (*C. E. Montague*). That is **vapid** which has lost its characteristic taste, savor, or zest, literally or figuratively; it is applied by very discriminating writers only to that which has lost or seems to have lost its freshness, spirit, sparkle, or tang, and is stale, uninteresting, pointless, or the like. "The table beer was sour...the wine *vapid*" (*Smollett*). "The happy and joyous temper, which characterizes a fresh and confident faith, degenerates [when religion is decadent] into moroseness, or into...*vapid* hilarity" (*Inge*). That is **flat** which is so vapid that it seems dead or lifeless. The word is applied chiefly to that out of which all savor, sparkle, zest, or capacity for stimulating interest or pleasure has departed. "How weary, stale, *flat* and unprofitable, Seem to me all the uses of this world" (*Shak.*). "The sonnet became, in the hands of innumerable practitioners, a thing...of artificial sentiment, *flat* as the lees and dregs of wine" (*Lowes*). That is **jejune** which is so devoid of substance or nutritive quality that it cannot satisfy the appetite (as, the *jejune* diet of the very poor); the word is occasionally used with reference to physical hunger, but is far more often employed with reference to the hunger of the mind, or the emotions, or the soul. In discerning use, it often connotes barrenness, aridity, or meagerness, in addition to its basic implications; only in loose use does it imply merely one of these qualities. "Mark...read through the sermon once more. It seemed more *jejune* than ever" (*C. Mackenzie*). "Naturalism is not science, but a *jejune* and self-contradictory philosophy" (*Inge*). That is **banal** which is so commonplace or so trite that it lacks all freshness or power to stimulate or appeal, and strikes one as flat or jejune. It often also carries one or more of various connotations such as vulgarity, tastelessness, pedestrianism, triviality, or platitudinism. "A simple person marvelously protected from vulgarity and the *banal*" (*T. E. Brown*). "Just the sort of *banality*, you know, one does come out with" (*Arnold*). "Mark found that...by attending to his parish duties without making himself too prominent by his enthusiasm or his originality, by preaching sermons of the most perfect *banality*... he could acquit himself satisfactorily in the eyes of the parochial world" (*C. Mackenzie*). That is **wishy-washy** (a somewhat colloquial term) in which the essential or characteristic qualities are so weak or diluted that it strikes one as extremely insipid or vapid; as, weak and *wishy-washy* tea; she is too *wishy-washy* to attract interesting friends. "Baudelaire's notion of beatitude certainly tended to the *wishy-washy*" (*T. S. Eliot*). That is **inane** (literally, void or empty) which is devoid of sense, significance, or point; as, "To us the book seems a very *inane*, tiresome, and purposeless affair" (*Manchester Examiner*); "In order to cover his embarrassment, he made some *inane* remark on the weather" (*Conrad*).
Ana. *Thin, slight, tenuous, rare: *weak, feeble: *tame, subdued: bland, mild, *soft.
Ant. Sapid: zestful. — *Con.* *Pungent, piquant, poignant, racy, spicy: *spirited, high-spirited, mettlesome, spunky, fiery, peppery, gingery: savory, saporous, tasty, *palatable, appetizing: stimulating, exciting, piquing, provoking *or* provocative (see corresponding verbs at PROVOKE).

insolent. Arrogant, overbearing, supercilious, disdainful, haughty, lordly. See PROUD.
Ana. Domineering, *masterful, imperious, peremptory, imperative: pompous, pretentious, ostentatious (see SHOWY): *dictatorial, magisterial: scornful, contemptuous (see corresponding nouns under DESPISE, *v.*).
Ant. Deferential. — *Con.* Submissive (see TAME): courteous, polite, *civil.

insolvency. **Insolvency, bankruptcy, receivership, failure, suspension** are not synonyms, but they are not always clearly distinguished when used to designate one of the situations in which a person, an institution, or a business unable to meet his (or its) financial obligations may find himself (or itself). **Insolvency** is the condition of a person or business that is **insolvent**, that is, unable to meet his or its debts because of insufficient funds or realizable assets; as, the estate was legally declared *insolvent;* unless the members pay their dues immediately, the organization faces *insolvency.* **Bankruptcy** is the state of an insolvent person or business that is **bankrupt;** that is, in the position of having his or its property administered under the law for the benefit of the creditors. Originally, bankruptcy was a state into which a trader who committed or was suspected of committing fraudulent acts was forced on petition of his creditors who wished to protect themselves; in present use, and as a result of changes in legislation in Great Britain and the United States since about the middle of the nineteenth century, it is also a state in which any insolvent person may find himself by his own petition or that of another. In general, the ends of bankruptcy today are to treat all creditors equitably and to effect a legal discharge of the obligations of the debtor. **Receivership,** like *bankruptcy,* implies administration of the property of a person or business under the law. It may or may not imply insolvency, but it always implies that the property is subject to litigation. Such property may be the estate of an incompetent or the assets of a business being liquidated, of a partnership being dissolved, or of a corporation undergoing reorganization, but it is perhaps more commonly the assets of a business which finds itself not necessarily insolvent but in a state of serious financial embarrassment. **Failure** (a popular term) is commonly applied to the discontinuance of a business brought about by insolvency or bankruptcy; **suspension** (also a popular term) to the temporary discontinuance of a business brought about by its insolvency or by its being under receivership.

Ant. Solvency.

inspect. *Scrutinize, examine, scan, audit.

Ana. Survey, view, observe, notice (see SEE): probe, penetrate (see ENTER): inquire, interrogate, question, speer, catechize (see ASK).

inspection. Examination, scrutiny, scanning, audit. See under SCRUTINIZE, *v.*

Ana. Investigation, probe, inquest, *inquiry, inquisition, research: surveillance, *oversight, supervision.

inspiration. Inspiration, enthusiasm, afflatus, fury, furor (*or* **furore**), **frenzy** (*or* **phrenzy**), especially when qualified by *divine* or *poetic,* come into comparison as the commonest terms in English designating the involuntary element in the arts of expression for which the artist holds a power outside himself responsible. The words are often vaguely used even by good writers, and their meanings have been so affected by the dominating theology, philosophy, or opinion of the age, that it is almost impossible to fix them. **Inspiration,** in discriminating use which respects its etymology and its historical development, implies a preternatural enlightening and quickening of the mind, and connotes, especially when used by religious persons, a supernatural influence, such as the Holy Spirit. "Among such men there remains a... belief in what is vaguely called *inspiration.* They know by hard experience that there are days when their ideas flow freely and clearly, and days when they are dammed up damnably" (*Mencken*). Oftentimes, from its use in connection with the authorship of the Scriptures, *inspiration* implies supernatural or supranatural communication of knowledge. "Has the highest aspect of Greek religion ever been better expressed than by Wordsworth himself, to whom...it came by *inspiration* and not from books?" (*Inge*). **Enthusiasm,** a word derived from Greek which is etymologically the equivalent of the Latin word *inspiration,* was used, in the sense here considered, chiefly from the Renaissance to the eighteenth century. It characteristically implies an infusion of the divine power which compels utterance. Consequently, it came to be used not only of poets, but also of preachers, especially of unordained men in some of the new religious sects who felt a call to preaching. From their methods, the term in the 17th and 18th centuries acquired connotations of extravagance, fanaticism, and even lunacy, and so fell into disrepute. "*Inspiration* is a real feeling of the Divine Presence, and *Enthusiasm* a false one" (*Shaftesbury*). **Afflatus,** now a bookish word, in most precise use applies to the inspiring influence rather than to the process or its effects. "The artists and poets who but once in their lives had known the divine *afflatus,* and touched the high level of the best" (*H. James*). In loose use, it, as the preceding terms, often names a quality rather than an influence or an operation. "There must be the *inspiration,* the *enthusiasm,* the *afflatus,* the glow; and they are here in Sidney's tractate" (*Saintsbury*). **Fury, furor,** and **frenzy** all emphasize the emotional excitement that attends artistic creation and the tendency of the artist to be carried out of himself. *Fury* and *furor,* found most often in the phrases "poetic fury or furor" (especially the Latin "furor poeticus") and "divine fury," do not, except in loose or humorous use, imply extreme agitation: they characteristically connote profound ecstasy induced by the poet's vision (or sometimes, conception). "They are so beloved of the Gods, that whatsoever they write, proceeds of a divine *fury*" (*Sidney*). "By turns they felt the glowing Mind, Disturb'd, delighted, rais'd, refin'd....Filled with *Fury,* rapt, inspir'd" (*Collins*). *Frenzy* usually implies agitation rather than rapture, and stresses the imaginative or inventive element in creation more than any of the others. Sometimes it does not even connote an extraneous influence. "The poet's eye, in a fine *frenzy* rolling, Doth glance from heaven to earth, from earth to heaven" (*Shak.*).

Ana. Enlightenment, illumination (see corresponding verbs at ILLUMINATE): *ecstasy, rapture, transport: *revelation, vision, apocalypse, prophecy.

inspire. Animate, *inform, fire.

Ana. Enlighten, *illuminate: quicken, stimulate, excite, galvanize, *provoke: activate, energize, *vitalize: endue, endow (see DOWER).

in spite of. *Notwithstanding, despite.

install. Induct, inaugurate, invest, *initiate.

instance, *n.* **Instance, case, illustration, example, sample, specimen** agree in meaning a concrete thing which has or manifests the qualities, characters, or nature of the type, the class, the group, or the like. **Instance** applies to any individual (person or thing) brought forth in support or disproof of a general statement (as, "He [T. H. Green] claims that great men have ...been determinative of the course of things...in so far as their work was the vehicle of larger forces. His *instance* is Napoleon"—*S. Alexander*) or as a means of indicating the character of a genus, species, or the like (as, this novel is a good *instance* of his best work). **Case** (etymologically, a happening or occurrence), as here considered, applies only to an act, situation, condition, event, or the like, that shows the occurrence or the existence of something which is being considered, studied, investigated, or dealt with, as a whole or in general, or that exhibits it in actual operation; as, to cite *cases* of bribes given as payments for services never performed; students of the effects of poverty now base their conclusions on *cases* actually investigated; there has been no *case* of malaria in this section for three years; the professor cited the *case* of the Jukes family as an *instance* of the relation of heredity to crime, immorality, disease, and pauperism. **Illustration** applies only to an instance or a case adduced or cited as a means of throwing light upon what has been explained or discussed in general terms; as, to give several *illustrations* of the use of a word in a particular sense; Matthew Arnold used Milton's lines "which cost Ceres all that pain To seek her through the world" as an *illustration* of poetry of the highest quality. An **example,** as here compared (see MODEL), is a typical, representative, or illustrative instance or case; as, "If I were asked to define what this gentlemanliness is, I should say that it is only to be defined by *examples*" (*Byron*); it is impossible to study a writer without *examples* of his work. A **sample** (etymologically from the same original as *example*) is a part of a thing itself, designed to show the quality of the whole. "When I deal in wine, cloth, or cheese, I will give *samples*, but of verse never" (*Cowper*). A **specimen** is commonly representative of a class of things rather than of an individual object; but *sample* and *specimen* are often used without distinction; as, a collection of geological or botanical *specimens;* "The subjects being so various, no single passage can in all respects be a *specimen* of the book at large" (*Cowper*).

Ana. Proof, *reason, ground: *evidence: particular, *item, detail.

instant, *n.* **Instant, moment, minute, second, flash, trice, jiffy, twinkling, twinkle, split second** come into comparison when they mean a particular point of time, usually, but not invariably, one of almost imperceptible duration. **Instant** and **moment** are often used interchangeably in this sense (as, the *instant* [or *moment*] he comes, let me know), but *instant* carries so much stronger a suggestion of infinitely small duration that it is better fitted than *moment* for contexts that imply urgency, extreme transiency, inconceivable swiftness, or the like; as, come this *instant;* he was not an *instant* too soon; it passed in an *instant. Moment,* on the other hand, is particularly serviceable when the word or the context carries the implication of a definitely apprehended, even though extremely brief, point of time; as, wait a *moment;* it was the finest *moment* of her life; I haven't had a *moment* to attend to it. "To us....the *moment* 8.17 A.M. means something...very important, if it happens to be the starting time of our daily train. To our ancestors, such an odd eccentric *instant* was without significance—did not even exist" (*A. Huxley*). **Minute** and **second** in technical use apply only to measured fractions of an hour, but in looser use and as here compared, *minute,* even more than *moment,* suggests an appreciable (though extremely short) duration of time, and *second,* quite as much as *instant,* suggests its imperceptible duration; as, "Who buys a *minute's* mirth to wail a week?" (*Shak.*); the train will start in a *minute;* I was gone only a *minute;* please hold this a *second* or two; I'll get it this *second.* **Flash** suggests duration comparable to that of a flash of lightning; the term is therefore often used when incredible speed in movement, action, thought, or the like, is implied; as, "The secret of the poor wretch's death was plain to me in a *flash*" (*Kipling*); "eyes that in a *flash* could pick out a friend...from a throng" (*Cather*). **Trice** (etymologically, a pull or a tug) implies a duration suggestive of, rather than equal to, the time it takes to haul up a sail, or the like. The word is found chiefly in the phrase *in a trice,* which is equivalent to *immediately* or *directly;* as, I'll be there in a *trice.* **Jiffy,** a colloquial term, is now more common than *trice,* which seems literary or affected; as, I'll be there in a *jiffy.* **Twinkling** and **twinkle,** often but not invariably with an added "of the eye," suggest the quickness of a wink or blink; as, "In a moment, in the *twinkling* of an eye...the trumpet shall sound" (*1 Corinthians* xv. 52). **Split second** (literally, the fractional part of a second, usually one tenth of a second; as, the stop watch showed Smith the winner of the race by a *split second*) is a recently adopted phrase which heightens the implication of brevity as expressed by *second;* as, "Mr. Moon stood for one *split second* astonished" (*Chesterton*).

instantaneously. Instantly, immediately, *directly, forthwith, straightway, at once, anon, right away.

instantly. Immediately, instantaneously, *directly, forthwith, straightway, at once, anon, right away.

instigate. *Incite, abet, foment.

Ana. *Activate, actuate, motivate: *suggest, hint, insinuate: plan, plot, scheme (see under PLAN, *n.*).

instill *or* **instil.** Inculcate, *implant, inseminate, infix.

Ana. *Infuse, inoculate, imbue, ingrain, leaven: impregnate, *permeate, saturate, pervade, impenetrate, interpenetrate.

instinct. Intuition (see under INSTINCTIVE).

Ana. Incitement, impetus, *stimulus: impulse, spring, *motive: bent, turn, faculty, aptitude, knack, *gift.

instinctive. 1 Instinctive, intuitive are here compared because, in ordinary usage, they are frequently employed as close synonyms meaning having or manifesting the power to reach a conclusion or to apprehend truth without reasoning. **Instinctive** (for correct senses, see SPONTANEOUS, 1) is applicable only to something which seems to involve knowledge, conclusions, judgments, etc., that come quickly, when that thing is associated with **instinct,** or a tendency innate in the species rather than in the individual (thus, a reaction which is characteristic of man as a species, and which comes whether one wills it or not, or is aware of it or not, may be described as *instinctive*) or, permissively, with something almost as deep and native as instinct, such as inbred habit (as, an *instinctive* avoidance of excess; an *instinctive* comprehension of another's preference for privacy). But the emphasis in both these cases is on the lack of need for willing or thinking rather than, as in **intuitive,** upon the use of a specific power of the intellect, that is, **intuition** (see under REASON, 3), which enables one to reach knowledge or truth immediately, and not mediately as through inference from facts; as, "Women...judge rather by *intuitive* perceptions than by deliberate reasoning" (*Lecky*); "the *intuitive* concepts of space and time which we derive from individual experience" (*Jeans*); "His *intuitive* faculties were constantly cultivated at the expense of the rational process of the mind" (*C. Mackenzie*). But neither term is correctly applied to that which is known by clever guessing, conjecture, or through a "hunch."

Ana. *Innate, inborn, congenital: constitutional, *inherent, ingrained.

Ant. Reasoned.

2 Impulsive, *spontaneous, automatic, mechanical.

Ana. Natural, normal, typical, *regular: habitual, customary, wonted, accustomed, *usual.

Ant. Intentional. — *Con.* *Voluntary, deliberate, willful, willing.

institute, *v.* *Found, establish, organize.

Ana. *Begin, commence, start, initiate, inaugurate: introduce (see ENTER).

Ant. Abrogate. — *Con.* End, terminate, conclude, *close, finish, complete.

institute, *n.* *Academy, seminary, college, lycée, gymnasium.

instruct. 1 *Teach, train, educate, discipline, school.

Ana. Impart, *communicate: *inform, acquaint, apprise: lead, *guide, steer, pilot, engineer: *practice, drill, exercise.

2 Direct, enjoin, bid, *command, order, charge.
Ana. *Prescribe, assign, define.

instrument. 1 *Means, instrumentality, agency, medium, agent, organ, vehicle, channel.
Ana. *Method, system, mode, way, manner, fashion: machinery, apparatus, tackle, gear, *equipment, paraphernalia: *device, contrivance, contraption.
2 Tool, *implement, appliance, utensil.
3 *Paper, document.

instrumentality. *Means, agency, instrument, medium, organ, vehicle, channel.
Ana. *Work, labor, toil: *effort, exertion, trouble, pains: *power, energy, force, might: *action, deed, act.

insubordinate. **Insubordinate, rebellious, mutinous, seditious, factious, contumacious** come into comparison when meaning having or manifesting a spirit of defiance or indifference to constituted authority. **Insubordinate** in careful English is used only in reference to a person whose status is that of a subordinate, such as a member of a force, a crew, a staff, or other organized group under the control of a military or naval officer, a chief, a head, a master, or the like, who is responsible for their service as individuals and their discipline as a group: the term implies disobedience to orders or infraction of rules, in a particular instance or as a habit, and is therefore often used less strictly of one who will not submit to the discipline of a parent, a teacher, or the like; as, *insubordinate* sailors are confined in the warship's brig; the *insubordinate* soldiers will be disciplined; "Lady Blandish was still...decidedly *insubordinate*" (*Meredith*). **Rebellious** implies disaffection and insubordination: it may refer to a state of mind or to a temperamental tendency (as, the undisciplined are often *rebellious* in spirit), but more often it suggests organized resistance (as, *rebellious* troops; the *rebellious* acts of those who participated in the Boston Tea Party). **Mutinous** is a stronger and more derogatory term than *rebellious* (which may imply justifiable resistance) for it suggests the refusal to obey the lawful demands or commands of an officer in charge, especially a military, naval, or ship's officer, with the result that there is no longer discipline and efficiency in the group or, if the mutiny is successful, that a new control is set up; as, the master ordered the *mutinous* sailors put into irons; the *mutinous* members of the crew finally gained the upper hand. *Mutinous* is also frequently applied to passions, winds, waters, and the like, that are exceedingly turbulent or uncontrollable; as, "I have... call'd forth the *mutinous* winds" (*Shak.*); "*Mutinous* passions, and conflicting fears" (*Shelley*). **Seditious** implies treasonable activities and often specifically a stirring up of discontent, or of opposition to or rebellion against the government; as, *seditious* societies; *seditious* writings. "A *seditious* preacher, who inculcated on his audience...the tyranny of artificial distinctions, and the abuses which had arisen" (*Hume*). **Factious** stresses the contentious, perverse, or turbulent provocation of party spirit or a tendency to break up into embittered and irreconcilable factions: only when it implies as a result the destruction of peace in the group as a whole does it suggest indifference to or defiance of constituted authority: very frequently it suggests the opposition of legislative groups or blocs to the government; as, a *factious* race; the government's plan to entertain the proposals for peace aroused the *factious* spirit of the parliament; "*factious* fury" (*Burke*); "Florence...sowing the wind and reaping the whirlwind, wearing her soul out by *factious* struggles" (*Mrs. Oliphant*). **Contumacious** is found chiefly in legal and ecclesiastical use. It implies persistent, willful, or open disobedience of the orders of a court or of one's superiors: often, it specifically suggests contempt of court by a bold refusal to obey a summons or subpoena, or open and stubborn defiance of laws or orders that for one reason or other are seldom disobeyed; as, "On her refusal to appear in person or by her attorney, she was pronounced *contumacious*" (*J. Lingard*). "Magistrates and populace were incensed at a refusal [by Fox the Quaker] of customary marks of courtesy and respect for the laws, which in their eyes was purely *contumacious*" (*Inge*).
Ana. Recalcitrant, refractory, *unruly, ungovernable, intractable.
Con. *Obedient, amenable, docile, tractable, biddable: submissive, subdued, *tame.

insult, *v.* Affront, outrage, *offend.
Ana. Humiliate, humble, debase, degrade, *abase: flout, *scoff, jeer, gird, gibe, fleer, sneer: mock, taunt, deride, *ridicule.
Ant. Honor. — *Con.* Gratify, *please: respect, esteem, admire (see under REGARD, *n.*).

insult, *n.* *Affront, indignity.
Ana. *Abuse, vituperation, invective, obloquy: dishonor, shame, ignominy, opprobrium, *disgrace: insolence, superciliousness, disdainfulness (see corresponding adjectives at PROUD): contempt, despite, scorn, disdain (see under DESPISE).
Con. *Compliment, flattery, adulation: *honor, homage, obeisance, deference, reverence.

insurance. **Insurance, assurance** are both used in reference to the business of guaranteeing compensation for loss or damage by a specified contingent event such as fire, death, shipwreck, and the like. **Insurance** is the common and customary term in the United States and the popular term in British use, not only for any business of this character but for the policies issued and the protection afforded by a company engaging in this business. **Assurance** is not infrequent in British use, especially in the titles of some of the older concerns engaged in the business of insuring lives. Some British writers on this subject regard this latter distinction of importance and use *assurance* for contracts (or the business involving the issuing of such contracts) taking risks on lives, and *insurance* for those guaranteeing indemnification against loss by fire, perils of the sea, war, and the like. Others make a distinction on etymological grounds, for which there is more or less justification in the historical use of these words. By these persons, *assurance* is applied to the business of undertaking risks and to the contracts issued in the course of such a business, *insurance* is applied to the protection sought and paid for by those who hold policies and to the policies they hold; as, one is in the *assurance* business; he wants *insurance* on his furniture; a company sells *assurance;* a person buys *insurance.* This distinction, however, is far from universally accepted.

insure. *Ensure, assure, secure.
Ana. Protect, shield, guard, safeguard (see DEFEND): indemnify, requite, compensate (see PAY, *v.*).

insurgent, *n.* *Rebel, iconoclast.

insurrection. Uprising, revolt, mutiny, *rebellion, revolution, Putsch.

intact. Whole, entire, *perfect.
Ana. Flawless, faultless, *impeccable: complete, replete, *full: *consummate, finished.
Ant. Defective. — *Con.* Impaired, damaged, injured, marred (see INJURE): vitiated, corrupted *or* corrupt (see corresponding verbs under DEBASE).

intangible. Impalpable, *imperceptible, insensible, inappreciable, imponderable.
Ana. Tenuous, rare, slight, slender, *thin: ethereal, *airy, aerial: subtile, *subtle: eluding *or* elusive, evading *or* evasive (see corresponding verbs at ESCAPE).

Ant. Tangible. — ***Con.*** Palpable, *perceptible, sensible, appreciable, ponderable: *material, physical, corporeal.

integrant, *n.* Component, *element, constituent, ingredient, factor.

integrate, *v.* **Integrate, articulate, concatenate** are synonyms only in their extended senses where they mean to join together a number of distinct things so that they move, operate, or function as a unit. The implications of these senses are probably more often found in the participial adjectives **integrated, articulated** (*or* **articulate**), **concatenated,** and in the derived nouns **integration, articulation, concatenation,** than in the finite verbs. **Integrate** [Latin *integer*, a whole] implies that the things combined (parts, elements, factors, details, etc.) are so intimately connected with each other that a perfect whole results. Usually it suggests a complete fusion or coalescence of particulars with loss therefore of their separate identities; as, the *integration* of races in the United States into a single people; in perception, we unconsciously *integrate* a vast number of details into a single visual image. **Articulate** [Latin *articulus*, a joint] also implies as its result a perfect whole, but it differs from *integrate* in implying no loss of identity or of distinctness of the things combined (usually parts, branches, departments, and the like) and in suggesting a connection between them that is found in its perfection in the skeletons of vertebrate animals, and especially in man. For *articulate*, as here considered (in the sense of *joint*, see *articulation* under JOINT, *n.*), implies organization in which each part fits into another in a manner comparable to the fitting into each other of two bones at a movable joint and a structure is built up that functions as a whole yet without loss of flexibility or distinctness in any of its component units or without any conflict between them; as, a perfectly *articulated* system of railroads. "Few people have definitely *articulated* philosophies of their own" (*W. James*). "In four years the principate had scarcely begun that process of *articulation* which was to make it one of the most complex and yet smooth-running systems of government known to history" (*Buchan*). **Concatenate** [Latin *catena*, a chain] suggests neither fusion nor organization, but a linking together of smaller units until figuratively a powerful chain is forged. It implies addition of one thing to another with cumulative effect; as, not one cause brings about war, but a *concatenation* of causes; the *concatenated* circumstantial evidence presented by the prosecutor was sufficient to offset the lack of direct evidence against the defendant. "Henchard...could not help thinking that the *concatenation* of events this evening had produced was the scheme of some sinister intelligence bent on punishing him" (*Hardy*).

Ana. *Unite, combine, conjoin: unify, consolidate, concentrate, *compact: fuse, blend, merge, coalesce (see MIX): organize, systematize (see ORDER).

Ant. Disintegrate. — ***Con.*** Crumble, decompose (see DECAY): dissipate, disperse, *scatter: *analyze, resolve, break down.

integrated. Articulated, concatenated. See under INTEGRATE, *v.*

Ana. Unified, consolidated, concentrated (see COMPACT, *v.*): fused, blended, coalesced, merged (see MIX): whole, entire, intact, *perfect: organized, systematized (see ORDER, *v.*).

Ant. Disintegrated.

integration. Articulation, concatenation. See under INTEGRATE, *v.*

Ana. Unification, consolidation, concentration (see corresponding verbs at COMPACT): integrity, union, *unity, solidarity.

integrity. 1 *Unity, solidarity, union.

Ana. Wholeness, entirety, perfection, intactness (see corresponding adjectives at PERFECT): consummateness (see corresponding adjective at CONSUMMATE): purity, simplicity, absoluteness (see corresponding adjectives at PURE).

2 Probity, *honesty, honor.

Ana. Uprightness, justness, conscientiousness, scrupulousness *or* scrupulosity (see corresponding adjectives at UPRIGHT): rectitude, virtue, *goodness, morality: *truth, veracity, verity.

Ant. Duplicity. — ***Con.*** *Deceit, dissimulation, guile: dishonesty, deceitfulness, mendaciousness *or* mendacity (see corresponding adjectives at DISHONEST).

intellect. *Mind, soul, psyche, brain, brains, intelligence, wit, wits.

Ana. *Reason, understanding, intuition.

intellectual. *Mental, psychic, cerebral, intelligent.

Ant. Carnal. — ***Con.*** *Bodily, physical, corporeal, corporal, somatic: fleshly, animal, animalistic, sensual (see CARNAL).

intelligence. 1 Brain, brains, *mind, intellect, soul, psyche, wit, wits.

Ana. *Sense, judgment, wisdom, gumption: *discernment, penetration, insight, acumen: sagaciousness *or* sagacity, perspicaciousness *or* perspicacity, astuteness, shrewdness (see corresponding adjectives at SHREWD).

2 *News, tidings, advice.

intelligencer. *Emissary, spy, secret-service agent, scout.

intelligent. 1 Intellectual, *mental, cerebral, psychic.

2 Intelligent, clever, alert, quick-witted, bright, smart, knowing, brilliant come into comparison when they mean intellectually keen. **Intelligent** stresses the power to use one's mind successfully when demands are made upon it, as in understanding the new or abstruse, or in meeting and solving problems, especially novel practical problems. "*Intelligent* self-interest should lead to a careful consideration of what the road [that is, railroad] is able to do without ruin" (*Justice Holmes*). "The moral obligation to be *intelligent*" (*J. Erskine*). **Clever** implies native ability or aptness more strongly than *intelligent;* it also emphasizes quickness in apprehension rather than fullness of comprehension, and dexterity or adroitness, rather than soundness, in the mental processes. "The poor girl liked to be thought *clever*, but she hated to be thought bookish" (*H. James*). "He could deal competently with effects, but he was not *clever* at assigning causes" (*M. Sinclair*). Oftentimes the word suggests a contrast with more substantial qualities. "Be good, sweet maid, and let who will be *clever*" (*Kingsley*). "A *clever* boy trains for an examination as he trains for a race; and goes out of training as fast as possible when it is over" (*Inge*). **Alert** stresses quickness in the mental processes, especially in comprehending a situation. Though often applied to persons, it is chiefly used to characterize minds, habits of thought, and the like. "She seemed more feeble in body...but her mind was still *alert*" (*L. P. Smith*). **Quick-witted** also implies quickness in thinking but in addition it suggests promptness in action as in an emergency, or in response, as to a challenge, in conversation or in debate. "We are not a *quick-witted* race; and we have succeeded...by dint of a kind of instinct for improvising the right course of action" (*Inge*). *Bright* and *smart* have a colloquial rather than a literary flavor, and are more often applied to young or promising persons than to those who are proficient or of proved intelligence. **Bright** suggests cleverness that is apparent as in liveness of mind or in liveliness of talk or manner. "I began life unluckily by being the wag and *bright* fellow at school" (*Irving*). **Smart,** too, implies cleverness but it also suggests alertness or quick-wittedness that enables one to get ahead. "I wish I was *smart* enough to invent something and maybe get rich" (*S. Anderson*). "The master said he was the *smartest* lad in the school" (*D. H. Lawrence*). Both words are used ironically, *bright* (less frequently than *smart*) then implying dullness or stupidity and *smart,* pertness, facetiousness, or sometimes trickery or duplicity; as, a *smart* aleck; given to making *smart* retorts. "I am Hector's father, as this *bright* Britisher would have guessed in the course of another hour or two" (*Shaw*). " 'I do not want,' he says, 'to be converted by a *smart* syllogism' " (*Birrell*). "The *smart* work is hidden in the wording of the Monroe doctrine" (*Emporia Gazette*). **Knowing** carries a stronger implication than any of the preceding terms of the possession of the knowledge that is necessary or useful under the circumstances, but it also carries a strong connotation of mental alertness and of ability to deal competently with situations as they arise; as, "My master...was thought the *knowingest* gentleman about court" (*Lytton*); "He is the most *knowing* of all living men" (*Jowett*). Occasionally the term further suggests a less agreeable quality such as sophistication, secretiveness, or the possession of knowledge of others' secrets; as, a *knowing* wink; "I don't quite like this chit. She looks *knowing*" (*Goldsmith*); "A face so mean, so *knowing*" (*Thackeray*). **Brilliant** occurs frequently in current writing and speech when one wishes to add to *intelligent* or to any other of the terms here considered (when used without derogatory connotations) the implication of unusual and outstanding keenness of intellect that manifests itself so openly or effectively as to excite admiration: the term usually suggests an opposition to qualities that characterize one whose mind works more slowly or cautiously; as, a *brilliant* mathematician; "John Todhunter was esteemed a shrewd sensible man—only not *brilliant*" (*Meredith*); "[Prescott's History of] the Reign of Ferdinand and Isabella....was a *brilliant* performance, as any child could see and no scholar was ever to deny" (*Van W. Brooks*).

Ana. *Sharp, keen, acute: *shrewd, sagacious, perspicacious, astute: cunning, ingenious, adroit, *clever.

Ant. Unintelligent. — ***Con.*** Foolish, idiotic, imbecilic, moronic (see corresponding nouns at FOOL): *stupid, dull, dense, crass, dumb: *irrational, unreasonable.

intend. Intend, mean, design, propose, purpose come into comparison when they signify to have in mind as an aim, end, or function. **Intend** implies that the mind is directed to some definite accomplishment or to the achievement of a definite end (as, to *intend* to write a book; "He did not *intend* annexation of Italian land" —*Belloc;* "that He [God] *intended* joy, of a purified and elevated kind, to be the ultimate inheritance of His creatures"—*A. C. Benson*) or is bent upon some person or some thing (such as a thing invented, written, or otherwise produced) serving a certain purpose or use, fulfilling a certain destiny, or the like (as, the younger son is *intended* for the church; "a play, *Intended* for great Theseus' nuptial-day"—*Shak.;* "a strong suspicion that the new instrument with which Einstein has presented the mathematicians is being put to uses for which it was never *intended*"—*Inge*). *Intend* often implies an aim to express a definite idea by a given word or phrase; as, the word, because of its connotations, says more than I *intend;* just what the framers of the constitution *intended* by the phrase "to be twice put in jeopardy" is still a matter of some doubt. "Whenever this word [i.e., "mob"] occurs in our writings, it *intends* persons without virtue or sense, in all stations" (*Fielding*). This sense of *intend* is now more often carried by *mean, signify,* or *denote* (see MEAN, 2). On the other hand, **mean** still often carries a denotation close to that of the usual sense of *intend:* it does not, however, convey so clear an implication of determination to effect one's end as does *intend* and, sometimes, it implies little more than volition or decision; as, he always *means* to work harder (cf. well-*meaning*); he *intends* to succeed. "I don't *mean* to defend Charles' errors, but before I form my judgment of either of them I *intend* to make a trial of their hearts" (*Sheridan*). "He shouldn't have done it, of course; but he was thoughtless. And he *meant* to pay the money back" (*Deland*). **Design** (as here compared: see under PLAN, *n.*) usually stresses forethought and deliberation in arriving at an intention: on the other hand, it carries no suggestion of probable or improbable success; as, "the American people....did not *design* to make their government dependent on the States" (*Ch. Just. Marshall*); "At twelve we met to give an account to one another of what we had done since our last meeting and what we *designed* to do before our next" (*S. M. Crothers*); "the great drive that was apparently *designed* to reach Calais" (*H. G. Wells*). Often, the term also implies scheming or contriving, especially by underhand means (cf. the adjective *designing*), in an attempt to effect what is designed; as, "your father and sister, in their civilities and invitations, were *designing* a match between the heir and the young lady" (*Austen*); "Ah! Friend! to dazzle let the vain *design;* To raise the thought, and touch the heart be thine!" (*Pope*). **Propose** implies a declaration of one's intention or a setting it clearly before oneself or others. It therefore usually connotes clear definition or open avowal; as, what do you *propose* to do when your funds run out? "I *propose* to describe the circumstances under which Richelieu worked when he produced and realised the centralised nation of to-day" (*Belloc*); "The child was not clandestine; she *proposed* returning in the same open way. She also *proposed* telling Mr. King that she would make no more promises" (*Deland*); "What is reached in the end may be better or worse than what was *proposed*" (*W. James*). **Purpose** differs little from *propose* except in carrying a somewhat stronger implication of determination to effect or achieve one's intention, and in occasionally connoting clearer definition in one's own mind; as, "he who has so little knowledge of human nature as to seek happiness by changing anything but his own disposition, will waste his life in fruitless efforts and multiply the griefs which he *purposes* to remove" (*Johnson*); "I *purpose* to write the history of England from the accession of King James the Second" (*Macaulay*).

Ana. *Aim, aspire: *attempt, try, endeavor, strive, essay, assay: plan, design, scheme, plot (see under PLAN, *n.*).

intense. Intense, vehement are often used interchangeably when they mean extreme in degree, pitch, power, fury, or the like; thus, the average writer or speaker sees little difference between *intense* rage and *vehement* rage or between an *intense* prejudice and a *vehement* prejudice. Nevertheless, precise writers and speakers use these words in ways that reveal many differences in implications and applications. **Intense** is preferred when the idea of great depth, as in quality, in reach, in effect, or the like, is to be implied. In such use, *intense* may apply to thought or thoughts, to feeling or emotion, to any activity, or to any outstanding quality or character such as color, brilliancy, tone, or the like; as, *intense* concentration; *intense* hatred; an *intense* red; "the *intense* blue sky" (*L. P. Smith*); *intense* silence; an *intense* friendship; "The *intense*, clear, star-sown vault of heaven" (*Arnold*); "work so *intense* that it takes the last inch out of the workers" (*Shaw*). When the term is applied directly to a person or his mood or temper, it usually carries a suggestion of tenseness as well as of deep feeling, effort, ambition, or the like; as, "the *intense* Dante is *intense* in all things" (*Carlyle*); "He was in such an *intense* mood that humor was entirely barred out" (*M. Wilkins*); "an *intense* and voluble mother, and three blowsy daughters who imitated her" (*E. Wharton*); "One of the inspired moments that come to *intense* natures, working *intensely*, had come to him" (*S. Anderson*). **Vehement** is preferred when a manifestation of abundant energy is to be suggested or where the ardency, violence, or driving force of the thing so described are to be connoted. "Jealousy is cruel as the grave: the coals thereof are coals of fire, which hath a most *vehement* flame" (*Song of Solomon* viii. 6). "He cursed himself like a less scrupulous Job, as a *vehement* man will do when he loses self-respect, the last mental prop under poverty" (*Hardy*). "The most *vehement* scorn of cowardly compromise with things base" (*J. R. Lowell*). "The temper of monists has been so *vehement*, as almost at times to be convulsive" (*W. James*). "Lastly, if *vehement* assertions on the one side have driven me into too *vehement* dissent on the other, I crave pardon" (*Quiller-Couch*).

Ana. Extreme, immoderate, *excessive, inordinate: heightened, intensified, enhanced, aggravated (see INTENSIFY): *impassioned, ardent, fervent, fervid, perfervid, passionate.

Ant. Subdued (*colors, lights, emotions, etc.*).

intensify. **Intensify, aggravate, heighten, enhance** agree in meaning to increase markedly in degree or measure. **Intensify** implies a deepening or strengthening of a thing, or especially of its characteristic quality, until it is noticeably or abnormally deep or strong; as, a clear atmosphere *intensifies* the blue of the sky; frustration only served to *intensify* his desire (or the urgency of his desire). "Historical circumstances of recent years have conspired to *intensify* Nationalism" (*A. Huxley*). "The unknown labyrinth around...seemed to *intensify* his sense of loneliness" (*G. Eliot*). **Aggravate** implies a manifest increase in seriousness or gravity without, however, conveying any suggestion of an approach to an extreme. The word is most often used in reference to something that is evil or unpleasant in itself or because of its qualities; as, false rumors that *aggravate* racial animosities. "Truth and frankness dispel difficulties, but the attempt at repressive moral discipline only *aggravates* them" (*B. Russell*). **Heighten** and **enhance** both imply a lifting or raising; *heighten*, however, tends to imply a lifting above the ordinary, the trite, the commonplace, and a consequent increase in sharpness and poignancy, and *enhance* a lifting above the norm or the average in desirability or attractiveness by the addition of something that increases the value, charm, prestige, or the like, of the thing enhanced; as, a dramatist *heightens* the effect of his scenes by rapidity of the action and he *enhances* his dialogue by the addition of witty repartee. "[Vitality] *heightens* pleasures and diminishes pains" (*B. Russell*). "A painter discards many trivial points of exactness, in order to *heighten* the truthfulness of a few fundamentals" (*C. E. Montague*). "Augustus sought... in every way to *enhance* its [the Roman Senate's] prestige and dignity" (*Buchan*).

Ana. Accentuate, emphasize, stress, accent (see corresponding nouns at EMPHASIS): magnify, aggrandize, *exalt.

Ant. Temper, attemper: mitigate, allay: abate (sense 2). — ***Con.*** *Moderate, qualify: alleviate, lighten, *relieve: reduce, lessen, diminish, *decrease.

intent, *adj.* **Intent, engrossed, absorbed, rapt** agree in meaning having one's mind or attention deeply fixed on something. **Intent** (etymologically, stretched toward) implies that one's mind, one's desires, or one's energies are eagerly bent on something: it therefore suggests the direction of the entire attention to that which engages it; as, "persons whose hearts are wholly bent toward pleasure, or *intent* upon gain" (*Spectator*); "the wise author *intent* on getting at truth" (*Quiller-Couch*); "Those who make poetry are *intent*, and rightly, on moulding it in living forms" (*Lowes*). **Engrossed** implies monopolization of one's attention either by a driving purpose or emotion or an eager interest or by the force or urgency of circumstances beyond one's control; as, "the dramatist *engrossed* in his creative job" (*C. E. Montague*); "alike when one's mind is deeply *engrossed* in congenial work, as well as when one is busy and distracted" (*A. C. Benson*). "These constitutional changes ...were pushed through during and after the war by a group of busybodies who were not too much *engrossed* by the agony of their country to conduct a raging agitation in all parts of England" (*Inge*). **Absorbed** often differs little from *engrossed* in this sense, but in very precise use it commonly carries a stronger suggestion of the power of the thing on which the attention is fixed to capture one's attention and to hold it firmly so that there is difficulty in distracting it; as, "wholly *absorbed* in his preparations for saving souls in the gold camps—blind to everything else" (*Cather*). "Human beings are prone to become *absorbed* in themselves, unable to be interested in what they see and hear or in anything outside their own skins" (*B. Russell*). "Already they had read 'Farthest North.' Imogen, at eight years old, had read it, *absorbed*, breathless, intent, tongue clenched between teeth" (*Macaulay*). **Rapt** implies both extreme intentness and complete absorption, as though one were taken out of oneself or were in an ecstatic trance; as, "*rapt* in adoring contemplation" (*F. W. Farrar*); "He was so *rapt* that nothing else interested him" (*Cather*); "expounded the ultimate meaning of existence to the white, *rapt* faces of Humanity" (*L. P. Smith*). "In open-mouthed wonder the lama turned to this and that, and finally checked in *rapt* attention before a large alto-relief representing a coronation or apotheosis of the Lord Buddha" (*Kipling*).

Ana. Attending *or* attentive, minding, watching (see corresponding verbs at TEND): *abstracted, preoccupied: concentrated (see COMPACT, *v.*): riveted (see SECURE, *v.*).

Ant. Distracted.

intent, *n.* *Intention, purpose, design, aim, end, object, objective, goal.

Ana. *Will, volition, conation: determination, *decision.

Ant. Accident. — ***Con.*** *Chance, hap, luck, fortune, hazard.

intention. **Intention, intent, purpose, design, aim, end, object, objective, goal** agree in meaning that which one proposes to accomplish or to attain by doing or making something, in distinction from that which prompts one (the *motive*), or from the activity itself (the *means*), or from the envisioned outcome (the *effect*). The first four of these words stress the clearly defined will to do or make something. **Intention,** however, often denotes little more than what one has in mind to do or to bring about. "She had not had an *intention* or a thought of going home" (*Dickens*). "Sir, Hell is paved with good *intentions*" (*Johnson*). "She had divined the *intention* behind her mother's tolerance" (*Joyce*). **Intent,** except in the phrase "to all intents and purposes," is chiefly legal; even in general use it suggests clearer formulation and greater deliberateness than *intention*. "To tell a lie...with *intent* to deceive, was a serious offence" (*H. Ellis*). "Behind my look You saw such unmistakable *intent*" (*Millay*). **Purpose** implies more settled determination or more resolution than *intention;* as, to have a *purpose* in life. "The missionary was here for a *purpose*, and he pressed his point" (*Cather*). "There lie youth and irresolution: here manhood and *purpose*" (*Meredith*). **Design** denoting intention is not always clearly distinguishable from *design* denoting plan for it retains the implications of careful ordering of details, of calculation, and sometimes of scheming; as, achieved rather by accident than by *design*. "I had suspected him of harbouring...sinister *designs*" (*Hudson*). "Should he find me here, [he] would discover my name, and perhaps my *designs*, to the rest of the family" (*Goldsmith*). **Aim,** the transitional word of this group of synonyms, implies a clear definition of that which one hopes to effect and a direction of one's efforts or energies to its attainment; thus, one who proposes to make the best of his powers and of his opportunities may be said to have a *purpose* in life: one who has clearly defined the mark he hopes to reach and determines his actions by it may be said to have an *aim* in life. "To [his trust] keeps faithful with a singleness of *aim*" (*Wordsworth*). "Her steadiness and courage in the pursuit of her *aims*" (*J. R. Green*). The last four words of this group, like *aim*, imply that what one does is affected by what one hopes to accomplish or attain. **End** stresses the determination of what one does by the effect one aims to produce or by the condition one hopes to attain; it usually connotes, therefore, the subordination of the activity (the *means*). "In every work regard the writer's *End*, Since none can compass more than they intend" (*Pope*). "The final *end* of Government is not to exert restraint but to do good" (*R. Choate*). "Vision should be a by-product of an activity, not its *end*" (*Day Lewis*). **Object** often equals *end*, but careful writers usually prefer it when the end is determined by a wish or a need rather than by principle or logical necessity; thus, one's *object* in writing is to earn money, but one's *end* is the edification of the reader; the *object* of a satire may be to discredit a person, but the *end* of satire is usually to expose follies or vices. **Objective** strongly implies attainability; it is chiefly applied to an end that is concrete and can be achieved as easily as a destination is reached by travel; as, the immediate *objective* of this project is flood control; its ultimate *objective* is the conservation of water power. **Goal** often evokes the image of one running a race; usually, it implies struggle and endurance of hardships and cessation of effort at attainment. "The Good, which is the *goal* of all moral endeavour" (*Inge*). "In the average man's mind... leisure is...a *goal* to strive for" (*C. C. Furnas*). "Life is real! Life is earnest! And the grave is not its *goal*" (*Longfellow*).

Ana. *Plan, design, scheme, project: desiring *or* desire, wishing *or* wish (see corresponding verbs at DESIRE).

intentional. *Voluntary, deliberate, willful, willing.

Ana. Intended, meant, purposed, proposed (see INTEND): considered, premeditated, advised, studied, designed, *deliberate.

Ant. Instinctive. — ***Con.*** *Accidental, casual, fortuitous: inadvertent, thoughtless, *careless, heedless.

intercalate. Interpolate, insert, *introduce, interpose, interject, insinuate.

intercede. Mediate, intervene, *interpose, interfere.

Ana. Plead, petition, sue, pray (see under PRAYER).

interchange, *v.* *Exchange, bandy, swap.

Ana. Trade, barter (see SELL): transpose, *reverse.

intercourse. **Intercourse, commerce, traffic, dealings, communication, communion, commune, conversation, converse, correspondence** are here compared as meaning the connection established between persons or peoples through any medium that permits interchange such as of information, of opinions, of ideas, of goods, or the like. **Intercourse,** the commonest term of this group, usually means little more than this and requires a qualifying adjective to indicate the things interchanged or the medium permitting interchange; as, business *intercourse;* trade *intercourse;* spiritual *intercourse;* sexual *intercourse;* social *intercourse*. In ordinary use, when employed without qualification, *intercourse* means *social intercourse*, or the normal interchange of ideas, opinions, news, civilities, and the like, between one person or group and another with whom (or which) there are more or less intimate relations; as, "They had no...*intercourse* but what the commonest civility required. Once so much to each other! Now nothing!" (*Austen*); "the truth was, he could not be happy for long without human *intercourse*" (*Cather*); "the keen and animated *intercourse* with its exchange of disputable convictions" (*A. Repplier*). **Commerce,** which etymologically implies the interchange of goods by buying from and selling to each other (for this sense, see BUSINESS, 3), also is used in the more general sense of *intercourse;* as, "*Commerce* with the world has made him wiser" (*Macaulay*). In current use, the word tends to be restricted in its application to intercourse, through the spirit or mind, that involves an interchange of ideas, influences, and the like, without a necessary interchange of words (as, "our repair thither [i.e., to the churches] is especially for...*commerce* to be had between God and us"—*Hooker;* "How is poetry born in us? There is, I think, some *commerce* between the outer and an inner being"—*G. W. Russell*), or, in an evil sense, to illicit sexual intercourse (as, "What say ye to Sir Lancelot...? That *commerce* with the Queen ...is it ... whisper'd in the corner?"—*Tennyson*). **Traffic** (as here considered: see also BUSINESS, 3 & 4) is now somewhat rare in the sense of *intercourse*, but it is still used when connotations derived from the other senses are to be suggested, such as the interchange of goods, especially of tangible or material goods, or a rapid passing to and from the persons or things concerned. "The latter [the Stoic] believed in a World-Soul immanent in man, the former [the Epicurean] held that there was no *traffic* between the human and the divine" (*Buchan*). "This flippant *traffic*...with Clara" (*D. H. Lawrence*). **Dealings** is a more homely and a more suggestive term than *intercourse*, for it usually implies a closer connection, such as one with more familiarity or less formality, or one having for its object mutual or personal gain; as, they said they would have no *dealings* with the new neighbors; they suspected that he was having *dealings* with the enemy. "Being a woman is a terribly difficult trade since it consists principally of *dealings* with men" (*Conrad*). **Communication** is less general than any of the preceding terms because it implies intercourse based upon an interchange of words (spoken, written, cabled, or the like) or meaningful signals of some sort; as, there has been no *communication* with the island since the storm; *communication* even with their nearest neighbors was impossible when they were snowbound; the men in prison had *communication* with each other only by tapping on the wall; the enemy has broken off all *communication* between his prisoners and the outside world. **Communion,** or the poetic form **commune,** usually implies intercourse between those who are close in love or sympathy or in mutual understanding: both terms often suggest rather than imply spiritual intercourse or the absence of words; as, "the consummation of *communion* with God coincides with the final resolution of the sense of estrangement from Him" (*Inge*); "during all these middle years we had been growing closer in *communion*" (*H. Ellis*); "Delia sat down beside her, and their clasped hands lay upon the coverlet. They did not say much...their *communion* had no need of words" (*E. Wharton*); "An austere *commune* with the stars" (*Masefield*). **Conversation** has an archaic sense in which it is a close synonym of *commerce* (as, "contrariety frustrates...all the...peace of wedded *conversation*"—*Milton*) and a use (in the phrase "criminal *conversation*") in which it is equivalent to "sexual intercourse," and **converse** has a poetic sense in which it approaches *communion*, or *commune* (as, "With nature here, high *converse* hold"—*Shenstone*). In current use, however, both terms usually imply a free, and often lively, oral interchange of opinions, comments, news, or the like, between two or more persons: *conversation* often applies specifically to the act of interchanging opinions, etc., in talk, and *converse*, to the ideas, gossip, etc., involved in such conversation; as, the *conversation* went on briskly for an hour; "all useful exchange of *converse* in our daily life" (*Quiller-Couch*). **Correspondence** implies intercourse through an interchange of letters; as, there has been no let-up in their *correspondence* for fifty years; the business was conducted by *correspondence*.

interdict, *n.* *Excommunication, anathema.

interdict, *v.* Ban, inhibit, enjoin, *forbid, prohibit.
Ana. Proscribe (see SENTENCE): debar, rule out, *exclude: *restrain, curb, check, snaffle.
Ant. Sanction. — *Con.* *Let, allow, permit.

interfere. 1 *Interpose, intervene, mediate, intercede.
Ana. Impede, obstruct, block, *hinder, bar.
2 *Meddle, intermeddle, tamper.
Ana. *Intrude, interlope, butt in, obtrude: molest, incommode, discommode, *inconvenience, trouble: thwart, foil, balk, baffle, *frustrate.

interior, *adj.* Inside, internal, *inner, inward, intestine.
Ana. Intimate, *familiar: spiritual (see HOLY): intrinsic, constitutional, *inherent.
Ant. Exterior. — *Con.* *Outer, outward, outside, external: extraneous, foreign, *extrinsic.

interject. *Introduce, interpolate, interpose, insert, intercalate, insinuate.
Ana. *Throw (in), cast (in), toss (in): obtrude, *intrude, interlope, butt in: comment, *remark, animadvert.

interlope. *Intrude, butt in, obtrude.
Ana. *Trespass, encroach, invade, entrench, infringe: interfere, *interpose, intervene.

intermeddle. *Meddle, interfere, tamper.
Ana. *Intrude, obtrude, butt in, interlope: entrench, encroach, *trespass, invade: molest (see INCONVENIENCE).

interminable. Unceasing, never-ending, *everlasting, endless.
Ana. Perpetual, *lasting, perdurable, permanent: incessant, *continual, continuous, constant: eternal, *infinite.
Con. *Intermittent, periodic: stopped, discontinued (see STOP): ended, terminated, closed, finished, completed (see CLOSE, *v.*).

intermit. Suspend, stay, *defer, postpone.
Ana. Interrupt, *arrest, check: *stop, discontinue: abate, reduce, lessen, *decrease.
Con. *Continue, persist: *repeat, iterate, reiterate.

intermittent. **Intermittent, recurrent, periodic, alternate** come into comparison when they mean recurring or reappearing more or less regularly but in interrupted sequence. That is **intermittent** which from time to time is omitted or disappears but always returns; as, an *intermittent* fever or pulse; an *intermittent* correspondence. "In most poets there is an *intermittent* conflict between the poetic self and the rest of the man" (*Day Lewis*). That is **recurrent** which returns or has the habit of returning after omission or disappearance. In contrast, *intermittent* stresses breaks in continuity and *recurrent* stresses repetition; as, *intermittent* attacks of appendicitis; *recurrent* attacks of appendicitis; an *intermittent* noise; a *recurrent* noise. That is **periodic** which is known to be recurrent at more or less fixed intervals over a long period of time and which, therefore, can be fairly accurately forecast; as, *periodic* epidemics; *periodic* appearances of a comet. That is **alternate** which is both intermittent and recurrent, each in turn with something else. When applied to two contrasted or different things, *alternate* implies a succession of one after the other; as, *alternate* smiles and tears; *alternate* work and play; *alternate* stripes of orange and green. When applied to things of the same kind or description that follow each other in serial order, *alternate* means every other one; as, the class meets on *alternate* days of the week, beginning Tuesday; the *alternate* stripes are narrow and white.
Ana. Interrupted, checked, arrested (see ARREST, *v.*): *fitful, spasmodic: sporadic, occasional, *infrequent: discontinuing *or* discontinuous, stopping, quitting (see corresponding verbs at STOP).
Ant. Incessant, continual. — *Con.* Continuous, constant, perpetual (see CONTINUAL): *everlasting, unceasing, never-ending, interminable.

intern, *v.* *Imprison, immure, incarcerate, jail.
Ana. Confine, circumscribe, restrict, *limit: *restrain, curb, check, snaffle: fetter, manacle, shackle, *hamper.
Con. Release, liberate, *free.

internal. Interior, intestine, *inner, inward, inside.
Ana. Intrinsic, constitutional, *inherent, essential.
Ant. External. — *Con.* Exterior, *outer, outward, outside: extraneous, *extrinsic, foreign, alien.

internuncio. Nuncio, legate, *ambassador, minister, envoy.

interpenetrate. Impenetrate, penetrate, *permeate, pervade, impregnate, saturate.
Ana. See those at IMPENETRATE.

interpolate. Insert, intercalate, *introduce, insinuate, interpose, interject.
Ana. *Enter, introduce, admit: *intrude, interlope: *add, superadd, annex, append.
Con. Delete, dele, expunge, *erase, cancel.

interpose. 1 Interject, *introduce, insert, insinuate, interpolate, intercalate.
Ana. *Throw (in), toss (in), cast (in): *intrude, obtrude: *push (in), shove (in), thrust (in).
2 **Interpose, interfere, intervene, mediate, intercede** come into comparison because they all basically mean to come or to go between two persons, two things, or a person and thing. **Interpose** (as here considered: see also INTRODUCE, 2) may be used in place of any of the succeeding words largely because it carries no further implications, except as these are derived from the context, but it is now used intransitively chiefly in reference to persons; as, "I listened...to this dispute, and at length *interposed* once more on the old man's side" (*Hudson*); "Our host...*interposed* and forbade the experiment, pleading at the same time for a change of subject" (*Shaw*). **Interfere** (as here compared: see also MEDDLE) implies a getting in the way of a person or thing as by crossing his or its path or, more often, by creating a condition that hinders his movement, activity, view, or the like, or its free operation or full effectiveness; as, "Parliament *interfered* to protect employers against their labourers" (*Froude*); the atmospheric disturbance *interfered* with radio reception of the speech; "wooden palings that did not *interfere* with a wide view" (*C. Mac-*

kenzie). **Intervene** may be used with reference to anything that interposes itself or is interposed between things as in space or time (as, "There still *intervenes* a narrow space between the last house of London and the ancient Forest Hall"—*Jefferies;* a long period *intervened* between the declaration of war and the beginning of hostilities), or between persons (as, to *intervene* between two persons engaged in a fight; to *intervene* between the warring groups with a plea for conciliation), or between a person and his interests, work, or the like (as, "the trained self-consciousness, which...*intervenes* between the poet's moods and his poetry"—*Day Lewis*). **Mediate** often specifically implies intervention between those who are hostile, antagonistic, or otherwise opposed to each other, for the sake of reconciling them or settling their difficulties; *mediate* usually implies, as *intervene* may or may not imply, an interest in both sides or freedom from bias toward either side; as, in Christian belief, Christ *mediates* between God and the sinner; "Bacon attempted to *mediate* between his friend [the earl of Essex] and the Queen" (*Macaulay*); "Philosophy tries to *mediate* between them [religion, science, art], and the task has so far been beyond its powers" (*Inge*). But *mediate* may also be used abstractly in reference to something that lies between extremes or contradictories and effects either their union or a transition between them; as, "The problem of *mediating* between the two terms [that is, "the shapely" and "the vital" as the dual elements of beauty]...is one that may be solved in innumerable ways" (*Babbitt*). **Intercede** implies intervention on another's (usually an offender's) behalf and the use of one's good offices in imploring mercy or forgiveness for him from the one who has been injured or offended; as, "For each at utter need — True comrade and true foeman— Madonna, *intercede!*" (*Kipling*); the Duchess of Aiguillon *interceded* for Marie de Médicis with Richelieu.

Ana. *Intrude, butt in, interlope: *meddle, intermeddle: interrupt (see ARREST).

interpret. Elucidate, construe, *explain, expound, explicate.

Ana. Illustrate, *exemplify: gloss, *annotate: comment, commentate (see REMARK, *v.*).

Con. Distort, contort, *deform: *misrepresent: *mistake, confuse, confound.

interrogate. Question, catechize, quiz, examine, *ask, query, inquire, speer.

Con. *Answer, reply, respond, rejoin, retort.

interrupt. *Arrest, check.

Ana. Suspend, stay, intermit, *defer, postpone: *intrude, obtrude, interlope, butt in: interfere, *interpose, intervene.

interstice. *Aperture, orifice.

intervene. *Interpose, mediate, intercede, interfere.

Ana. *Separate, part, divide, sever: *intrude, interlope, butt in, obtrude.

intestine, intestinal. Internal, *inner, interior, inside.

Ant. Foreign. — *Con.* External, *outer, exterior, outside, outward: extraneous, alien, *extrinsic.

intimate, *v.* *Suggest, imply, hint, insinuate.

Ana. *Indicate, betoken, attest, bespeak: allude, advert, *refer.

Con. *Express, voice, utter, vent, air: declare, *assert, affirm, aver, avouch: *suppress, repress: conceal, *hide.

intimate, *adj.* *Familiar, close, confidential, chummy, thick.

Ana. *Nearest, next: devoted, fond, affectionate, *loving: *secret, privy: friendly, neighborly (see AMICABLE): companionable, convivial, *social, hospitable, co-operative.

Con. Formal, conventional, ceremonious, *ceremonial: *distant, remote.

intimate, *n.* *Friend, confidant, acquaintance.

Ana. Comrade, companion, crony, pal, chum, buddy, *associate.

Ant. Stranger, outsider.

intimidate. Intimidate, cow, bulldoze, bully, browbeat agree in meaning to frighten one into submission or obedience. **Intimidate** etymologically implies a making timid or fearful, but in current use it often suggests a display of force or the use of coercive measures as the cause of the fear and consequent submission; as, he would not be *intimidated* by vociferous public opposition to his plans; "A musket was, therefore, fired over them, but...they seemed rather to be provoked than *intimidated*" (*Capt. Cook*); "He wasn't lazy, he wasn't a fool, and he meant to be honest; but he was *intimidated* by that miserable sort of departmental life" (*Cather*). **Cow** implies reduction to a state where the spirit is broken or all courage is lost; as, "The lash of that woman...had *cowed* that helpless, gentle, noble spirit" (*Thackeray*); "One night he rescued a young leveret from a stoat, who seemed...inclined to give him battle for its prey until he *cowed* and defeated it with the glare of his electric torch" (*H. G. Wells*). **Bulldoze,** an American colloquialism (used originally of the intimidation of Negro voters, in Louisiana), implies the use of terroristic methods, such as threatening, displaying one's power, and the like, in asserting one's will or authority over others. "If he [President Hayes] has strength of character and tact, the *bulldozers* cannot subdue him....If he gives up Mr. Evarts...the *bulldozers* will subdue his cabinet" (*N. Y. Herald*). **Bully** implies intimidation through overbearing, swaggering threats or insults, but in schoolboy use it usually suggests bulldozing of small boys by those who are larger or more aggressive; as, "suppose the cabman *bullies* you for double fare" (*Shaw*); "I know what you're going to call me...but I am not to be *bullied* by words" (*L. P. Smith*). **Browbeat** implies a cowing through arrogant, scornful, contemptuous, or insolent treatment; as, "He *browbeat* the informers against us, and treated their evidence with ...little favour" (*Fielding*). "Who saw my old kind parents... too much trustful... Cheated, *brow-beaten*, stripped and starved, cast out Into the kennel" (*Browning*).

Ana. Terrorize, terrify, *frighten: hector, hound, ride, chevy, *bait, badger: coerce, *force, compel, constrain, oblige.

Con. *Coax, wheedle, cajole, blandish: persuade, prevail on *or* upon, *induce.

intonation. *Inflection, accent.

intoxicated. *Drunk, drunken, inebriate, inebriated, tipsy, tight.

Ana. Fuddled, befuddled, confused, bemuddled, muddled (see CONFUSE): maudlin, *sentimental.

Con. *Sober, temperate.

intractable. *Unruly, ungovernable, refractory, recalcitrant, willful, headstrong.

Ana. Obstreperous, boisterous (see VOCIFEROUS): contumacious, rebellious, factious, *insubordinate: froward, perverse, *contrary, wayward, balky.

Ant. Tractable. — *Con.* *Obedient, docile, biddable, amenable: *tame, submissive, subdued: *compliant, acquiescent.

intrench. Variant of ENTRENCH.

intrepid. Dauntless, undaunted, valiant, valorous, doughty, bold, audacious, *brave, courageous.

Ana. Daring, venturous, venturesome, *adventurous,

temerarious, daredevil: mettlesome, high-spirited, *spirited, fiery: plucky, gritty (see corresponding nouns at FORTITUDE).

Con. *Cowardly, pusillanimous, craven, poltroon, dastardly: timorous, *timid: *fearful, apprehensive, afraid.

intricate. Complicated, involved, *complex, knotty.

Ana. Perplexing, puzzling, mystifying, bewildering (see PUZZLE, *v.*): tortuous, anfractuous (see WINDING): difficult, *hard, arduous.

Con. *Easy, simple, light, smooth, facile, effortless: obvious, plain, clear, patent, *evident, manifest.

intrigue, *n.* **1** Conspiracy, machination, *plot, complot, cabal, frame-up.

Ana. Scheme, design, *plan: stratagem, maneuver, ruse, artifice, *trick, feint.

2 Liaison, affair, affaire, *amour.

intrinsic. *Inherent, ingrained, constitutional, essential.

Ana. *Inner, inward, internal, interior, inside, intestine: *innate, inborn, inbred, congenital: natural, normal, typical, *regular.

Ant. Extrinsic. — *Con.* *Outer, outward, external, outside, exterior: adventitious, *accidental, incidental: added, annexed, appended, superadded (see ADD): extraneous, alien, foreign (see EXTRINSIC).

introduce. 1 *Enter, admit.

Ana. *Bring (in): induct, install, inaugurate (see INITIATE): instill, inculcate, infix, *implant, inseminate: *infuse, inoculate, imbue.

2 Introduce, insert, insinuate, interpolate, intercalate, interpose, interject are not close synonyms, but they come into comparison when they mean to put something (or someone) in a place among or between other things (or persons). **Introduce** (see also ENTER, 2) implies a bringing forward of someone or something not already in company with the other persons or things, but it also suggests as the aim of such an act the placing of the person or thing in the midst of that group or collection so as to form a part of it; as, to *introduce* a new subject into the conversation; to *introduce* several amendments into a bill before the legislature; to *introduce* some new stanzas into an old hymn. **Insert** implies a setting of a thing in a fixed place between or among other things; thus, to *insert* lace in a garment is to put it between two pieces of the material which forms the garment; to *insert* leaves in a book is to put leaves (usually additional leaves) into their proper places, as by the use of glue; so, to *insert* an egg in a robin's nest; to *insert* additional words in a statement; to *insert* an advertisement in a newspaper. **Insinuate** implies a slow, careful, often gentle or artful, introduction as into or through a narrow or winding passage, by pushing, worming its (or one's) way, or the like; as, the dog liked to *insinuate* his nose into his master's closed hand; to *insinuate* oneself into the good graces of another; trees which *insinuate* their roots into the fissures of near-by rocks; slowly but surely they *insinuated* themselves through the crowd to the edge of the pavement. "Horace...*insinuates* virtue rather by familiar examples than by the severity of precepts" (*Dryden*). **Interpolate** implies the insertion of something that does not belong, as because it is extraneous to the subject under discussion or because it is spurious and not part of the original; as, "It may be well if I *interpolate* here some remarks upon certain errors" (*S. Alexander*); some passages in this manuscript were *interpolated* by copyists. **Intercalate** primarily implies an insertion in the calendar, as of a day or month, but in its extended sense, it implies insertion into a sequence or series, then often also connoting intrusion; as, an *inserted* stanza (implying nothing beyond its introduction); an *intercalated* stanza (suggesting an intrusion into a sequence); an *interpolated* (i. e., spurious) stanza. **Interpose,** as here compared (see also INTERPOSE, 2), differs from *interpolate* mainly in its implication that that which is inserted serves as an obstacle, obstruction, cause of delay, or the like; as, "I ask leave to break the order of my argument and to *interpose* some words" (*Quiller-Couch*); " 'No ye don't!' Father Victor saw Kim edging towards the door, and *interposed* a strong leg" (*Kipling*); "Professor [Gilbert] Murray has simply *interposed* between Euripides and ourselves a barrier more impenetrable than the Greek language" (*T. S. Eliot*). Of all of these words, **interject** carries the strongest implication of abrupt or forced introduction; as, he remained silent for the most part but occasionally *interjected* a question. In current use, the word is often employed in place of *said*, or the like, in introducing a remark, statement, or question that comes more or less as an interruption or addition. " 'I fear we must give him up tonight,' observed Lady Blandish, 'If he said he would come, he will come,' Sir Austin *interjected*" (*Meredith*).

Ant. Withdraw (*something or someone present*): abstract (*something from a file, etc.*). — *Con.* *Remove, draw: *eject, oust, evict: eliminate, *exclude.

introduction. Introduction, prologue, induction, prelude, overture, preface, foreword, prolegomenon, proem, exordium, preamble, prolusion, protasis, avant-propos come into comparison as denoting something that serves as a preliminary or as an antecedent to an extended treatment, development, discussion, or presentation, as in an exposition, a dramatic or musical work, a poem, or the like. In their extended senses many of these terms are interchangeable, but in the special or technical senses in which they are here chiefly considered they tend to be (with a few exceptions) mutually exclusive. **Introduction,** the ordinary term of this group, and the comprehensive one, specifically applies to that part of a discourse, treatise, play, musical composition, or the like, which prepares the reader or auditor for the body of the work, especially by giving him that which is necessary for his understanding of what follows; as, he always writes the body of his treatise first and then adds the *introduction* and conclusion. **Prologue** applies specifically to the initial and distinct part of a poetic or dramatic work that may serve the purposes of an introduction, as by describing the characters or expounding the situations in which they find themselves (as, Chaucer's *Prologue* to the "Canterbury Tales"), or which may be a discourse, preceding the opening of a play, by a character of the play or by an actor who serves as a mouthpiece for the author, and giving a hint of the author's purposes or methods or attempting to attract the auditors' attention to or interest in the play to come (as, the *Prologue* to Shakespeare's "Troilus and Cressida" and to each act of his "King Henry V"). In its extended use, therefore, *prologue* often suggests an act, an event, or the like, that sets the stage or paves the way for a series of exploits, achievements, or the like; as, "this as a *prologue* to her own later dazzling history" (*Hugh Walpole*). In older and now chiefly historical use, **induction** often appears in place of *prologue* (as, the *Induction* to "The Mirror for Magistrates") and sometimes in place of *introduction* (as, "That which he takes for the second argument...is no argument, but an *induction* to those that follow"—*Milton*). **Prelude** (etymologically, a preceding play) applies in its general sense to anything such as a series of events, actions, natural phenomena, or the like, which constitute figuratively a short play or performance, and serve as a sign or indication of, or a preparation for, what is to follow; as, functional changes in glands often serve as a *prelude* to structural changes. "That was the *prelude* to a stormy afternoon" (*H. G. Wells*). As a technical term in music, *prelude* applies sometimes to an opening voluntary in a religious service but more often, and more specifically, to an introductory piece forming a section or a movement, especially of a fugue or a suite but sometimes of an oratorio or of an opera, and serving usually to introduce the theme or chief subject of the work. In this sense, *prelude* applies sometimes to works (not always musical works) which have something of the character of an introductory section or movement, but are so constructed that they have intrinsic and independent value; as, Debussy's "*Prelude* to the Afternoon of a Faun" ["Prélude à l'après-midi d'un faune"]; Wordsworth's poem "The *Prelude*." **Overture** (etymologically, an opening), as here compared (see also OVERTURE, 1), applies to an elaborate orchestral preliminary to an extended musical work such as an opera or oratorio, sometimes but not always serving the functions of a prelude; as, Wagner's *Overture* to "Tannhäuser." Most of the great overtures, though composed as preliminary pieces, have independent musical value. In ecclesiastical use, **preface** still applies to the prayer of exhortation to thanksgiving and of divine praise which opens the important part of a solemn Eucharistic service (such as the canon of the Mass), where the consecration of the bread and wine occurs. In its more common general sense, *preface* applies specifically to a short discourse which is distinct from the literary work which follows (a treatise, a novel, a poem or collection of poems, or the like), which is written usually by the author, but sometimes by an editor or a friend, and which has for its main purpose either to put the reader into the right frame of mind for the understanding or appreciation of the work he is about to read or to supply him with information that may be necessary to his proper understanding or use of it. When, however, a work is preceded by both a preface and an introduction, *preface* is usually applied to the introductory discourse written, and often also signed, by the author, editor, or the like, and *introduction* to the one which is definitely informative rather than personal in its character and usually carries no signature. In extended use *preface* may apply to anything which serves as an introduction or prelude, such as an introductory work on or a more or less tentative treatment of a subject (as, Walter Lippmann's book entitled "A *Preface* to Morals"), or to an act or speech, or series of acts or speeches, which has no other purpose than to prepare the way for what is to follow. "They walked in the rose garden. 'Do you read Utopias?' said Mr. Direck, cutting any *preface*, in the English manner" (*H. G. Wells*). "We fight for lost causes because we know that our defeat and dismay may be the *preface* to our successor's victory" (*T. S. Eliot*). **Foreword** is now often used in place of *preface* to a book, especially by those who wish to suggest simplicity and brevity of treatment, in contrast to the profundity and prolixity associated with some historic prefaces. **Prolegomenon** (often in plural form *prolegomena*) applies either to a preface of a learned work, such as one presenting a philosophy, a new scientific theory, or an exposition of theological doctrine (as, "his *Prolegomenon* to the Polyglot Bible"—*Evelyn*), or now somewhat more often to a preface in the extended sense of an introductory work (as, Thomas Hill Green's "*Prolegomena* to Ethics"). **Proem** is a bookish or literary rather than a technical term, applying usually to the commencement of a discourse, especially to a formal commencement, such as the invocation to a muse in a poem, or to the introductory remarks in a spoken discourse which serve to bring the speaker into touch with his audience. "I seye that first with heigh style he endyteth, Er [ere] he the body of his tale he wryteth, A *proheme* [*proem*]" (*Chaucer*). **Exordium,** a technical term of rhetoric, applies to a formal beginning, especially of an oration but sometimes of a written exposition or argument, in which the speaker or writer makes an approach to his subject by remarks intended to awaken the interest of his auditors or readers and to pave the way for their understanding of what he is to say or for their acceptance of his conclusions. **Preamble** applies to a formal introduction, often only an introductory paragraph, as in a statute, a constitution, a treaty, a deed, or a set of resolutions, which states the grounds, purposes, or the like, of that which follows. Because of its etymological suggestion of ambling before, the term lends itself to humorous use as a designation of a long monotonous preface. "Now, dame... This ["The Wife of Bath's prologue"] is a long *preamble* of a tale" (*Chaucer*). **Prolusion** is a now rare synonym of *prologue:* distinctively it applies to a short literary work (now often called *preface* or *prolegomena*) which sets forth briefly ideas which the author may or may not intend to amplify later; as, "My treatise...was intended but for a *prolusion*" (*Evelyn*). **Protasis,** a now rare highly technical term once much used by rhetoricians dealing with the drama, applies to that part of a play which serves as an introduction to the body of the play (the *epitasis*), or in modern terms, as the exposition (see EXPOSITION, 2). **Avant-propos,** a French phrase not yet naturalized in English, is also rare but is sometimes used by those who prefer it to *proem* for a few introductory remarks, or to *preface* or *foreword*, as a more informal or more ingratiating term.

intrude. **Intrude, obtrude, interlope, butt in** agree in meaning to thrust oneself or something in without invitation or authorization. **Intrude** both transitively and intransitively carries a strong implication of forcing someone or something in without leave, without right, or against the will of others; it often connotes rudeness, officiousness, or invasion of another's property, time, or the like; as, "Enow of such as, for their bellies' sake, Creep, and *intrude*, and climb into the fold!" (*Milton*); " 'Sir,' said I, 'I am afraid that I *intrude* upon you. It is benevolent to allow me to sit and hear you' " (*Boswell*); "This court always had disavowed the right to *intrude* its judgment upon questions of policy or morals" (*Justice Holmes*). **Obtrude** (now chiefly but not exclusively a transitive verb) suggests even more strongly than *intrude* the impropriety, the boldness, or the futility of the act or the disagreeableness of the offense; as, "The former *obtrudes* his attention...; it is so pointed, that it always confuses me, and so public, that it attracts general notice" (*Burney*); "I intended plain prose, but a rhyme *obtruded* itself and I became poetical" (*Cowper*); "The first sin against style as against good manners is to *obtrude* or exploit personality" (*Quiller-Couch*). **Interlope** (etymologically, a back formation from the more common agent noun **interloper**) originally implied the action of an unauthorized trader who trespassed on the rights or charters of others, in this way obtaining advantages or profits belonging rightfully to another. In more recent use, both verb and noun imply an interposition of oneself in a place or position which has an injurious effect on one or both of the persons or things concerned; as, he regarded her new acquaintance as an *interloping* rival for her hand; the independent stores charged the chain stores with *interloping*. **Butt in,** originally American slang, implies an abrupt or offensive intrusion suggestive of the manner in which a horned animal attacks its enemy; in this sense, the term usually suggests absence of ceremony or of a sense of propriety, or of any other sign of good breeding; as, "I've not gone there or written, or anything yet, because I didn't want to *butt in*" (*R. Macaulay*).

Ana. *Trespass, invade, encroach, entrench, infringe: interject, interpose, insinuate, interpolate, intercalate, *introduce: interfere, intervene, *interpose: *meddle, intermeddle, interfere, tamper.

Ant. Stand off. — *Con.* Withdraw, retire (see GO): retreat, *recede.

intrusive. *Impertinent, officious, meddlesome, obtrusive, pragmatical.

Ana. Intruding, butting in, interloping, obtruding (see INTRUDE): inquisitive, prying, snoopy, nosy, *curious: interfering, meddling, intermeddling (see MEDDLE).

Ant. Retiring: unintrusive. — *Con.* Diffident, bashful, modest, coy, *shy.

intrust. Variant of ENTRUST.

intuition. 1 Understanding, *reason.

Ana. Intellect, soul, *mind: clairvoyance, insight, divination, acumen, *discernment.

Ant. Ratiocination. — *Con.* *Inference, illation.

2 Instinct (see under INSTINCTIVE).

intuitive. *Instinctive.

Ana. Immediate, *direct.

Ant. Ratiocinative. — *Con.* Inferential, illative (see under INFERENCE).

inunct. Anoint, lubricate, *oil, grease, cream, pomade, pomatum.

inure. *Harden, season, acclimatize, acclimate.

Ana. Accustom, *habituate, familiarize: *adapt, adjust, accommodate: drill, exercise, *practice: train, school, discipline (see TEACH).

Con. Enervate, emasculate (see UNNERVE): debilitate, enfeeble, *weaken.

invade. Encroach, *trespass, trench, entrench, infringe.

Ana. *Intrude, obtrude, butt in, interlope: *enter, penetrate, pierce, probe: *permeate, pervade, interpenetrate, impenetrate.

invalidate. *Nullify, negate, annul, abrogate.

Ana. Negative, counteract, *neutralize: void, avoid, vacate, quash, *annul.

Ant. Validate. — *Con.* *Enforce, implement: administer, *execute.

invaluable. Priceless, precious, valuable, dear, *costly, expensive.

Ant. Worthless.

invasion. **Invasion, incursion, raid, irruption, inroad** come into comparison not only as military terms, but also in their extended senses and as meaning an entrance effected by force or strategy. **Invasion** strictly implies entrance upon another's territory with hostile intentions, such as conquest, plunder, or use as a basis of operations; as, the Roman *invasion* of Britain; the German *invasion* of Belgium. In nonmilitary use it may imply encroachment, trespass, or any intrusion that involves an aggressive or hostile purpose; as, "She was conscious of an *invasion* of her rights" (*Stevenson*); "the Proletariat will extend its present *invasion* of Parliament until it achieves in effect complete conquest" (*Shaw*). In still looser use, it often implies entrance with, or as if with, a rush by a horde or crowd; as, summer brought with it the usual *invasion* of tourists. **Incursion,** especially in military use, carries a much stronger connotation of suddenness, unexpectedness, or haste than *invasion;* it often also suggests an immediate end and a quick withdrawal when the end is achieved; as, the American colonists were in constant fear of *incursions* by the Indians. In its extended sense, *incursion* applies chiefly to an invasion in large numbers of something dreaded or harmful, undesirable, but not necessarily inimical; as, the peace of the neighborhood was frequently broken by *incursions* of gangs of small boys; "terrible like an *incursion* of wild beasts" (*J. Martineau*). **Raid,** now frequent in military use for a swift, sudden invasion (formerly of cavalry, now more often of air forces) may or may not suggest more preparation, more strategy, and more fury in attack than *incursion,* its close synonym; as, the *raids* in the Shenandoah Valley by Forrest's Confederate cavalry during 1863; nightly bombing *raids* on a city. In international law, however, *raid* is technically applicable only to an incursion of armed forces that are unauthorized or unrecognized by any state into a country that is at peace; thus, an *incursion* of armed persons on one side of a border, or boundary line, into the adjoining country for a predatory or hostile purpose is technically a *raid.* In its extended use, *raid* applies to any sudden descent, such as one by officers of the law upon a gambling resort or a place where liquor or the like is illicitly made or sold, to obtain evidence and arrest offenders (as, to make a *raid* upon a speakeasy), or as by speculators, politicians, etc., for the purpose of making profit, mulcting public moneys, or gaining control of a situation (as, to make a *raid* on the market; to make a *raid* on the Treasury), or, in still looser and somewhat humorous use, by hungry persons in search of food (as, nightly *raids* on the refrigerator). **Irruption** applies to any incursion that implies or suggests a breaking in or similar acts of violence; as, an *irruption* of Goths into Gaul; an *irruption* of schoolboys into a garden. **Inroad** was applied originally to an incursion or raid made by armed horsemen into the territory of another race or nation; as, "Aggressive war, as distinguished from mere plundering *inroads*" (*Freeman*). The term is now applicable to any invasion that involves encroachment or trespass with injurious results; as, activities that make *inroads* upon one's time and one's health; the physician discovered the *inroads* of the disease; "During Silas's absence in the daytime the door had been locked, and there had been no marks of any *inroad* on his return by daylight" (*G. Eliot*).

Ana. Aggression, *attack, offense, offensive: trespass, violation, transgression, infringement, infraction, *breach: intruding *or* intrusion, interloping, butting in, obtruding *or* obtrusion (see corresponding verbs at INTRUDE): encroachment, trenching, entrenchment (see corresponding verbs at TRESPASS).

invective. *Abuse, vituperation, obloquy, scurrility, billingsgate.

Ana. Vilifying *or* vilification, maligning, calumniation, traducing (see corresponding verbs at MALIGN): *animadversion, stricture, aspersion, reflection.

inveigle. Decoy, entice, *lure, tempt, seduce.

Ana. Snare, ensnare, trap, entrap (see CATCH): beguile, mislead, delude, *deceive, betray: cajole, wheedle, blandish, *coax.

invent. **Invent, create, discover** are not genuinely synonymous terms, but they are frequently confused in the sense of to bring into being something new. **Invent** (etymologically, to come upon, or find) in earlier times stressed fabrication of something new through the exercise of the imagination; it therefore was used chiefly in reference to poets and their fictions or plots. "A poet is a maker, as the word signifies: and he who cannot make, that is, *invent,* hath his name for nothing" (*Dryden*). This use, with stress on imagination, is now rare, for the emphasis is more on the fabrication of something new and, often, useful, as a result of study, thought, experiment, or the like; the word therefore often presupposes labor and ingenuity rather than, as in older times, inspiration; as, to *invent* a device for stopping a car quickly; the cotton gin was *invented* by Eli Whitney in 1793; "Socrates was in just as good a position as Benjamin Franklin to *invent* the stove which goes by the latter's name" (*J. W. Krutch*). However, *invent* often stresses the finding, as well as the bringing into being, of something new or hitherto unknown as the result of mental effort. "[Love, as conceived by Plato] was not *invented* but interpreted by Plato" (*G. L. Dickinson*). "She was tired of *inventing* means for making the days and nights pleasant and capriciously variable for others" (*Van Vechten*). **Create** stresses a causing of something to exist; it not only implies previous nonexistence but it often suggests an evoking of something into being out of, or as if out of, nothing, as by fiat, by an act of the will, by inspiration, or the like; as, God *created* the world; the poet *creates* beauty; the law *creates* rights; the king *created* an earldom for his favorite. "To this strange force within him, to this power that *created* his works of art, there was nothing to do but submit" (*A. Huxley*). "I do not believe that a sense of justice is innate, but I have been astonished to see how quickly it can be *created*" (*B. Russell*). **Discover,** as here compared (see also DISCOVER, 2; REVEAL), presupposes the pre-existence of something, and lack of knowledge of it; the term therefore implies the finding of that thing, often as the result of mental or physical effort, as by exploration, investigation, experiment, and the like; as, Columbus *discovered* America; William Harvey *discovered* the circulation of the blood. Hence, in precise use, one *invents* processes or ways of doing something, as well as instruments, tools, implements, or machines, but one *discovers* things which exist but have not yet been known, such as lands, stars, natural laws, and the like. "Newton *invented* the differential and the integral calculus...and *discovered* the laws of motion" (*Karl K. Darrow*).

Ana. Fabricate, fashion, form, shape, forge, *make: imagine, conceive, envision (see THINK): design, project, plan, plot, scheme (see under PLAN, *n.*): produce, turn out (see BEAR).

inventory, *n.* *List, register, schedule, catalogue, table, roll, roster, rota, canon.

invert, *v.* Transpose, *reverse.

Ana. Upset, *overturn, overset, capsize: interchange, *exchange: derange, disarrange (see DISORDER, *v.*).

invest. **1** Vest, robe, apparel, array, *clothe, attire, tire, dress.

2 Induct, install, inaugurate, *initiate.

Ana. Endue, endow (see DOWER): consecrate (see DEVOTE).

Ant. Divest, strip (*of robes, insignia, power, etc.*): unfrock.

investigation. Probe, inquest, inquisition, *inquiry, research.

Ana. Inspection, examination, scrutiny, audit (see under SCRUTINIZE): surveying *or* survey, observing *or* observation (see corresponding verbs at SEE).

inveterate. Inveterate, confirmed, chronic, deep-seated, deep-rooted come into comparison as meaning so firmly established or settled that change is almost impossible. **Inveterate** (etymologically, become old) applies especially to that which has persisted so long and so obstinately that it has become a fixed habit or an almost inalterable custom or tradition; as, "the growing infirmities of age manifest themselves in nothing more strongly, than in an *inveterate* dislike of interruption" (*Lamb*); "The Nonconformist Conscience...[and] its *inveterate* feud against everything that people mean by the word 'beauty'" (*Day Lewis*). When applied to a person, the term implies the formation of an ineradicable habit, attitude, or the like; as, an *inveterate* smoker; "an *inveterate* and formidable foe" (*Peacock*). **Confirmed** applies chiefly to that which has grown stronger or firmer with time until it resists all attack or assault or attempts to uproot it (as, a *confirmed* belief in God; a *confirmed* hatred of a person; "His intense egoism rendered him impatient of all reproof or instruction, and... as a natural consequence, he soon became the victim of *confirmed* mannerisms"—*The Nation*). Like *inveterate*, it may also apply to a person who is such as he is described in the noun by the strengthening or crystallization of a taste, a vice or virtue, an attitude, or the like (as, a *confirmed* bachelor; a *confirmed* drunkard; a *confirmed* invalid; a *confirmed* optimist; "I am a *confirmed* wanderer"—*Disraeli*). **Chronic** also implies long duration, but it applies either to diseases, habits, conditions, and the like, which persist without marked interruption in spite of attempts to alleviate or to cure them, or to the persons who are afflicted or affected by such diseases, habits, or the like; as, "his *chronic* state of mental restlessness" (*G. Eliot*); *chronic* bronchitis; "hysterical with failure and repeated disappointment and *chronic* poverty" (*A. Huxley*); "The working scientist...must steer a middle course between *chronic* indecision and precipitant judgment" (*Eddington*); a *chronic* faultfinder. **Deep-seated** and **deep-rooted** in their figurative senses emphasize rather the extent to which something has entered into the structure or texture of the thing (a person's body or mind, a people's nature, or the like) in which it becomes fixed or embedded; as, "the old, dependent, chaotic, haphazard pioneer instinct of his [Mark Twain's] childhood [was] so *deep-seated*, that... he slipped back into the boy he had been before" (*Van W. Brooks*); "a *deep-rooted* reverence for truth" (*J. Morley*).

Ana. Habituated, accustomed, addicted (see HABITUATE): habitual, customary, *usual: *hardened, indurated: settled, set, fixed, established (see SET): inbred, *innate: persisting *or* persistent, enduring, abiding (see corresponding verbs at CONTINUE).

invidious. Distasteful, obnoxious, *repugnant, repellent, abhorrent.

Ana. *Hateful, odious, abominable, detestable: *offensive, loathsome, revolting, repulsive.

Con. Agreeable, gratifying, grateful, pleasing, *pleasant: attractive, alluring, fascinating (see under ATTRACT): enticing, tempting, seducing *or* seductive (see corresponding verbs at LURE).

invincible. Invincible, unconquerable, indomitable, impregnable, inexpugnable, unassailable, invulnerable come into comparison as meaning proof against attack or assault. A person or thing is **invincible** or **unconquerable** that presents insuperable difficulties to his or its being overcome, resisted, displaced, or the like; *invincible*, however, usually implies a quality or character in the person or thing which makes him or it actually or seemingly incapable of being vanquished; *unconquerable* implies rather the fact of having successfully resisted all attempts at subdual or mastery; as, *invincible* ignorance; "the armed forces, police and military, form a large permanent body wholly subject to that which governs, a weapon which renders that which governs almost *invincible*" (*Belloc*); "He made plan after plan; but each one was discarded because he saw it would encounter *invincible* selfishness, or *invincible* self-sacrifice" (*Deland*); "The story of a noble mind wrestling with *unconquerable* Fate" (*I. D'Israeli*); "the iron face of those men of empire and *unconquerable* will, those Caesars and Napoleons" (*L. P. Smith*). A person, a will, a mind, or the like, is **indomitable** that stubbornly and determinedly resists all attempts to gain mastery over him or it or endures seemingly insuperable difficulties with fortitude until they are overcome; as, *indomitable* courage; an *indomitable* will; *indomitable* energy; "Founding colonies...or exploring in crazy pinnaces the fierce latitudes of the polar seas—they are the same *indomitable* God-fearing men" (*Froude*). A fortress or stronghold (or something analogous) is **impregnable** that is strong enough or sufficiently guarded to repel all attacks or assaults; as, "the Tarpeian rock, her citadel *Impregnable*" (*Milton*). "There was always a traitor in the citadel; and after he (or generally she) had surrendered the keys, what was the use of pretending that it was *impregnable?*" (*E. Wharton*). A thing (sometimes, a person) is **inexpugnable** or **unassailable** either because it is impregnable, or, in very precise use, because it offers no point at which it can be attacked or no occasion or reason (such as a weakness or a defect) for attacking or impugning; as, castles were often built at the tops of craggy mountains in the hope that they might be *inexpugnable;* as long as Great Britain remains *unassailable* by all but air raiders, it cannot be conquered; the *inexpugnable* meekness of a saint; an argument so logical and convincing that it is *unassailable.* A person or thing is **invulnerable** that cannot be wounded or penetrated by any destructive weapon, any piercing instrument, or the like; as, according to legend, Achilles had been rendered *invulnerable* except at one spot when his mother, holding him by the heel, dipped him in the Styx; ironclad warships were once believed to be *invulnerable.* "What was one to do with people like that? How was one to pierce such hidebound complacency? It was *invulnerable* except to the Grace of God" (*C. Mackenzie*).

Ana. *Formidable, redoubtable: dauntless, undaunted, intrepid (see BRAVE).

Con. Conquerable, vanquishable, surmountable, subduable (see corresponding verbs at CONQUER).

inviolable. Inviolate, *sacred, sacrosanct.

Ana. Hallowed, consecrated, dedicated (see DEVOTE): *holy, sacred, blessed, divine, religious: pure, *chaste.

inviolate. Sacrosanct, *sacred, inviolable.

Ant. Violated. — *Con.* Profaned, desecrated (see corresponding nouns at PROFANATION): polluted, defiled (see CONTAMINATE).

invite. **Invite, bid, solicit, court, woo** come into comparison only when they mean to request or encourage a person or a thing to come to one or to fall in with one's plans or desires. **Invite** in its ordinary and usual sense implies a courteous request to go somewhere, do something, give some assistance, or the like, which going, doing, or the like, it is assumed will be agreeable, or at least not disagreeable, to the person invited; as, to *invite* a few friends to dinner; to *invite* an acquaintance to spend the night in one's home; to *invite* an audience to express their opinions. In this sense, the word usually implies providing an opening for those who otherwise might hesitate to go, or do, or give without such a request. Consequently, in its extended sense, *invite* implies providing an opening by any of various means, such as a seductive manner or a challenging statement or policy, that serves as an encouragement or temptation to another to do that to which he feels he has been called; as, to dress so conspicuously as to *invite* unwelcome attentions; "The public press no longer *invites* its readers to sustained thought" (*C. W. Eliot*); "the writer who brings a new revelation is not necessarily called upon to *invite* the execration of the herd" (*H. Ellis*). **Bid** is archaic or dialectal for *invite*, in the sense of to request the presence of as at a feast, a marriage, or other great occasion: the noun *bid* for *invitation* is, however, now not uncommon in colloquial use. "Then saith he to his servants, The wedding is ready, but they which were *bidden* were not worthy. Go ye therefore into the highways, and as many as ye shall find, *bid* to the marriage" (*Matthew* xxii. 8-9). But *bid for* (literally, to offer a price for something up for sale) in extended use sometimes comes close to *invite* in the sense of to provide a tempting opening for something; as, politicians *bidding for* votes by promising lower taxes and higher wages. "In his lifelong passion for getting his name and fame associated with those of other men who were secure of the suffrages of the multitude Mark Twain was almost consciously *bidding for* approval" (*Van W. Brooks*). **Solicit** (as here considered: see also ASK, 2) differs from *invite* in implying urgency rather than courtesy in requesting or encouraging; as, "He... without any indelicate display of regard...was *soliciting* the good opinion of her friends" (*Austen*); "Not only is what is put forward by one person as true open to the judgment of others, but it *solicits* and compels such judgment" (*S. Alexander*). **Court** basically implies an endeavor to win the favor of a person by flattery, attentions, love-making, or the like. Only in its extended sense does it imply a providing of a favorable opportunity by tempting or encouraging something to come to one or to be visited upon one; as, "He kept himself somewhat aloof, seeming to avoid notice rather than to *court* it" (*Arnold*); "so long as a scientific textbook is obsolete in a decade or less, to poetize science is to *court* mortality" (*Lowes*). **Woo** literally implies amorous courting: consequently, in its extended sense, it frequently stresses a drawing to or upon one by allurements, blandishments, or the like; as, "Herodotus in search of a public...found a favourable 'pitch,' as we should say, and *wooed* an audience to him" (*Quiller-Couch*). Nevertheless, the word occasionally is very close to *court* and scarcely distinguishable from it; as, "You... *woo* your own destruction" (*Shak.*).

Ana. *Ask, request, solicit: *lure, tempt, entice, inveigle: excite, *provoke, stimulate.

involve. **1** **Involve, implicate,** as here compared (see also INCLUDE), agree in meaning to bring one (a person or thing) into circumstances or a situation from which one cannot easily free oneself. **Involve** may or may not impute disgrace to the circumstances or situation, but it usually implies complication or entangling and often suggests extreme embarrassment; as, to become *involved* in debt; the war may not end until every nation in Europe is *involved* in it; "The case of a judge *involved* by the exigencies of his office in a strong conflict between public duty and private interest or affection" (*Colvin*); "[he] had been *involved* in some affair that made it uncomfortable for him to return to live in that city" (*S. Anderson*). **Implicate** usually, but not invariably, implies a disgraceful connection or one that casts a reflection on a person's reputation; it may even imply definite proof of association with a crime; as, the detectives discovered that an uncle of the child was *implicated* in its kidnaping; they were unable to *implicate* any of the suspected political leaders in the conspiracy to defraud the city.

Ana. Ensnare, entrap, snare, trap (see CATCH): connect, link, associate, relate (see JOIN): *embarrass: fetter, shackle, *hamper.

Con. *Extricate, disentangle, untangle, disembarrass: disengage, *detach: *free, liberate, release.

2 Comprehend, embrace, *include, imply, implicate, subsume.

Ana. Comprise, *compose, constitute: import, *mean, signify, denote: bespeak, attest, betoken, *indicate, argue, prove.

Con. Eliminate, *exclude, rule out, debar.

involved. Intricate, complicated, knotty, *complex.

Ana. Confused, muddled, bemuddled (see CONFUSE): perplexing, puzzling, bewildering, mystifying (see PUZZLE): difficult, *hard, arduous.

Con. Simple, *easy, facile.

invulnerable. Impregnable, inexpugnable, unassailable, *invincible, unconquerable, indomitable.

Ant. Vulnerable.

inward. *Inner, interior, internal, inside, intestine.

Ana. Inbred, *innate, inborn: ingrained, *inherent, intrinsic, constitutional: intimate, *familiar: objective, sensible, *material: heartfelt, unfeigned, *sincere: impalpable, *imperceptible.

Ant. Outward. — *Con.* *Outer, exterior, external, outside: extraneous, *extrinsic, foreign, alien: spiritual (see corresponding noun at SOUL).

iota. Jot, tittle, whit, *particle, bit, mite, smitch, smidgen, atom.

irascible. **Irascible, choleric, splenetic, testy, techy** (*or* **tetchy**), **touchy, cranky, cross** come into comparison as meaning easily angered or enraged. **Irascible** implies the possession of a fiery or inflammable temper or a disposition to be incensed on the slightest provocation; as, "an English plebeian...coarse, proud, *irascible*, imperious" (*Carlyle*); a peppery and *irascible* old gentleman. **Choleric** implies excitability of temper, unreasonableness in anger and, usually, an impatient and uniformly irritable frame of mind; as, "That in the captain's but a *choleric* word, Which in the soldier is flat blasphemy" (*Shak.*); "Where melancholic men abandon effort, men of the *choleric* type take to kicking and smashing" (*H. G. Wells*). **Splenetic** implies a similar temperament, but one especially given to moroseness and fits of spleen which exhibit themselves in angry, sullen, or intensely peevish moods, words, or acts; as, "More peevish, cross, and *splenetic*, than dog distract or monkey sick" (*Butler*, 1612–1680); "That *splenetic* temper, which seems to grudge brightness to the flames of hell" (*Landor*); "he was not *splenetic:* nay, he proved in the offending volume he could be civil, courteous, chivalrous" (*Meredith*). **Testy** implies irascibility occasioned by small annoyances such as being thwarted, compelled to wait, or the like; as, men who are imperious by nature are inclined to grow more and more *testy* with age; "The *testy* major was in fume To find no hunter standing waiting" (*Masefield*). **Techy** (or now more frequently its derivative **touchy**) suggests readiness to take offense; it often connotes undue irritability or over-sensitiveness; as, "He is *techy* and impatient of contradiction, sore with wounded pride" (*Hazlitt*); "I am not *touchy* under criticism" (*Stevenson*). **Cranky** and **cross** are the most common of these terms in colloquial use, both often meaning little more than difficult to please. In precise use, however, *cranky* carries a strong implication of the possession of set notions, fixed ideas, or unvarying standards, which predispose one to anger or a show of temper when others in their speech, conduct, requests, work, and the like, do not conform to them; as, a *cranky* critic; a *cranky* employer; a *cranky* teacher. *Cross*, on the other hand, implies a being out of sorts, owing to any of numerous causes or conditions; it also implies irascibility or irritability, but only for the duration of one's mood; as, "Sometimes, when I am *cross* and cannot sleep, I engage in angry contests with the Opinions I object to" (*L. P. Smith*); "the attempts to persuade the Intelligent Woman that she is having a glorious treat when she is in fact being...bored and tired out and sent home *cross* and miserable" (*Shaw*).

Ana. *Irritable, fractious, snappish, waspish, huffy, querulous, petulant, peevish: *impatient, restive, jumpy, jittery, nervous: crabbed, surly (see SULLEN).

Con. Good-natured, *amiable, complaisant, obliging: *calm, placid, serene, tranquil.

irate. *Angry, wrathful, mad, indignant, acrimonious.

Ana. Provoked, exasperated, nettled, irritated (see IRRITATE): incensed, infuriated, enraged (see ANGER, *v.*).

Con. Good-humored, good-tempered, good-natured (see corresponding noun phrases at GOOD NATURE): *forbearing, tolerant, clement, lenient, indulgent, merciful.

ire. Rage, fury, *anger, indignation, wrath.

Ana. *Passion: temper, humor, *mood.

irenic, irenical *or* **eirenic, eirenical.** *Pacific, peaceable, peaceful, pacifist, pacifistic.

Ana. Conciliating *or* conciliatory, placating *or* placatory, propitiating *or* propitiatory (see corresponding verbs at PACIFY).

Ant. Acrimonious.

iridescent. Opalescent, opaline, *prismatic.

irk. Vex, *annoy, bother.

Ana. Perturb, disturb, upset, *discompose: discommode, incommode, trouble, *inconvenience, molest: fret, chafe (see ABRADE).

irksome. **Irksome, tiresome, wearisome, tedious, humdrum** agree in meaning burdensome because tiring or boring or both. A person or thing is **irksome** that inspires distaste, reluctance, or impatience, because of its demand for effort not made easy by interest; as, "Mr. Collins...was neither sensible nor agreeable; his society was *irksome*" (*Austen*); "The difficulty of grasping abstract statements made learning very *irksome* to me" (*Symonds*); "Why is it that the study of the past seems *irksome* to the new generation?" (*Grandgent*). A person or thing is **tiresome** that is dull and unenlivening and therefore is either intensely boring or soon productive of fatigue; as, "It is *tiresome* to be funny for a whole evening" (*Scott*); "The second curate was Chator, who was so good as sometimes to be nearly *tiresome*" (*C. Mackenzie*); "We think of rain as *tiresome* and uncomfortable" (*Binyon*); "The importunity of the little boys was *tiresome* when one wanted to be alone" (*A. Huxley*). A person or, especially, a thing is **wearisome** that exhausts one's strength or patience through long-continued or constant call for effort, exertion, attention, and the like, or for tiresome uniformity of character; as, "These high wild hills and rough uneven ways Draws out our miles, and make them *wearisome*" (*Shak.*); "the same *wearisome* round of stereotyped habits" (*Wilde*); "The acquisition of exact knowledge is apt to be *wearisome*, but it is essential to every kind of excellence" (*B. Russell*). A person or thing is **tedious** that is tiresomely monotonous, slow, or prolix; as, "Life is as *tedious* as a twice-told tale Vexing the dull ear of a drowsy man" (*Shak.*). "The prose of the writer who can deliberately make his own personal cadences monotonously audible all the time grows *wearisome;* it affects us as a *tedious* mannerism" (*H. Ellis*). A person or thing is **humdrum** that is continuously commonplace in character, or goes on without variety or variation in a monotonous routine: often, the implication of wearisomeness is obscure or lost; as, "A plain, *humdrum* domestic life, with eight hundred a year, and a small house, full of babies" (*Trollope*); "They regarded their adversaries as *humdrum* people, slaves to routine, enemies to light" (*Arnold*); "For music, so far from showing a *humdrum* and homekeeping spirit, has kept pace with the other arts in its restless striving away from its own centre toward that doubtful periphery where it is on the point of passing over into something else" (*Babbitt*).

Ana. Dull, *stupid: fatiguing, exhausting, fagging, tiring (see TIRE, *v.*).

Ant. Absorbing, engrossing.

ironical, ironic. Satirical, *sarcastic, sardonic.
Ana. Biting, cutting, *incisive, trenchant: *caustic, mordant, mordacious, scathing.

irony. *Wit, satire, sarcasm, humor, repartee.

irrational. Irrational, unreasonable are here compared as meaning not governed or guided by reason. Both terms have been used and very occasionally are still used in the sense of not having the power to reason; as, "Nothing has a greater effect on all plants and *irrational* animals" (*Hume*); "Whilst his fellow-man... Must as the *unreasonable* beast drag on A life of labour" (*Southey*). In current good use, except in technical senses such as in mathematics, both words apply commonly to men, their acts, utterances, feelings, policies, demands, and the like. **Irrational** may imply mental derangement or a temporary loss of mental control (as, the patient was *irrational* during the course of his fever), but, more often, it suggests a lack of control or guidance by the reason, or direct conflict with reason's dictates: it therefore comes close to *absurd, illogical, foolish, preposterous, senseless,* or *fantastic;* as, to be governed by an *irrational* fear; *irrational* beliefs; an *irrational* policy; "his temperamental impulse to energetic practical action...and the reserve, passivity, and isolation which myopia enforced, seemed to him absolutely *irrational*" (*H. Ellis*); "His spirits, which had dropped at her last words, rose with an *irrational* leap" (*E. Wharton*). **Unreasonable,** on the other hand, implies guidance or control by some force, such as self-will, passion, ambition, avarice, or the like, which makes one deficient in judgment or good sense: as applied to one's acts, utterances, demands, etc., it suggests lack of justification by reason: the term therefore comes close to *inequitable, immoderate, excessive, unfair, extravagant,* and the like; as, you will not be so *unreasonable* as to send your child out in this storm; his demands are *unreasonable;* obstinate and *unreasonable* pertinacity; an *unreasonable* price for beef; "he contracted an *unreasonable* aversion towards his son" (*Addison*).
Ana. Absurd, preposterous, *foolish, silly: fatuous, asinine, *simple: crazy, demented, mad, *insane.
Ant. Rational. — ***Con.*** Reasonable (see RATIONAL): *wise, judicious, sage, sapient, prudent, sane, sensible: *logical.

irregular. Irregular, anomalous, unnatural come into comparison when they mean outside the sphere of that which conforms to, or is explainable by, law, rule, custom, or the like. **Irregular** implies failure to conform to a rule, a law, a pattern, especially to one imposed for the sake of uniformity in method, practice, or conduct; thus, an *irregular* marriage is one that does not conform to the regulations of church or state; an *irregular* verse does not correspond to an accepted metrical pattern for its type; guerilla warfare is called *irregular* because it does not accord with the practice of civilized nations or conventional military theory; *irregular* conduct may or may not be morally reprehensible but it defies the code or standard of the community or class. **Anomalous** stresses lack of conformity to what might be expected of a thing (sometimes a person) because of the class or type to which it belongs, the laws which govern its existence, the environment in which it is found, and the like. Sometimes, it specifically implies inconsistency, or a conflict of principles; as, "acts so *anomalous,* in such startling contradiction to all our usual ways and accepted notions of life and its value" (*L. P. Smith*): sometimes it specifically means unclassifiable or indefinable; as, *anomalous* literary works such as Holmes's "Autocrat of the Breakfast Table"; *anomalous* emotions: sometimes it suggests the absence of the character or of the characteristics essential to a thing of its kind; as, "the position of the [Roman] Senate [which had been deprived of its powers by the triumvirate] was no less *anomalous* and impotent" (*Buchan*): sometimes it suggests a contradiction between the professed aims or intentions of a person or institution and the conditions in which that person or institution exists or finds himself (itself) at a given time; as, President Wilson found himself in an *anomalous* position when congress rejected his proposal that the United States enter the League of Nations. **Unnatural** is the strongest of these words in its implication of censure, especially when it implies a violation of natural law, or of principles accepted by all civilized men as based on reason and essential to the well-being of society. In such cases it often specifically connotes moral perversion (as, an *unnatural* practice), or abnormal indifference or cruelty (as, an *unnatural* parent). Sometimes, the word merely means contrary to what is received as *natural,* either because it is not in accordance with the normal course of nature (as, snow in May is *unnatural* in this region), or because it is not in keeping with what one regards as normal, balanced, proper, fitting, or the like, under the circumstances (as, Platonic love is *unnatural;* an *unnatural* appetite for acid foods). "Thy deed, inhuman and *unnatural* Provokes this deluge most *unnatural*" (*Shak.*). "Charles [a child]...was naturally good. *Unnaturally* good might be a better term" (*Deland*).
Ana. Aberrant, *abnormal, atypic: *exceptional: singular, unique, *strange, peculiar, odd, queer.
Ant. Regular. — ***Con.*** Natural, normal, typical (see REGULAR): *usual, customary, wonted, accustomed, habitual: licit, legitimate, legal, *lawful.

irreligious. Irreligious, unreligious, nonreligious, ungodly, godless agree in meaning not religious or not devoted to the ends of religion. **Irreligious** is not only the most common of the negative forms of *religious* but the most clearly defined in meaning, for it implies not merely lack of religion but hostility to religion or courses in opposition to it or in violation of its precepts: it therefore sometimes suggests impiety, immorality, blasphemy, or the like; as, "it is unworthy a religious man to view an *irreligious* one either with alarm or aversion" (*Carlyle*); "*Irreligious* men, whose short prospects are filled with earth, and sense, and mortal life" (*Berkeley*). **Unreligious** commonly implies nothing more than lack of religion: it therefore usually applies to men, their utterances, works, etc., and suggests absence of religion or of religious training or religious ideas; as, "If *unreligious,* let him be at once, Among ten thousand innocents, enrolled A pupil" (*Wordsworth*); "The popular poetry...became...*unreligious*...in some parts *irreligious*" (*Milman*). **Nonreligious** applies not so much to persons as to institutions, activities, projects, themes for art, etc., that are outside the sphere or province of religion or not under the control of any religious body: it therefore comes close in meaning to *secular* (see under PROFANE, 1); as, *nonreligious* education; *nonreligious* charitable societies. **Ungodly** often comes close to *irreligious,* but it carries a stronger suggestion of disobedience to or defiance of the divine law; as, "Blessed is the man that walketh not in the counsel of the *ungodly*" (*Psalms* i. 1); "And if the righteous scarcely be saved, where shall the *ungodly* and the sinner appear?" (*1 Peter* iv. 18); "that *ungodly* custom of swearing" (*Sir C. Wren*). **Godless,** though usually closer to *unreligious* than to *irreligious,* commonly implies atheism or, in some cases, agnosticism: in current use, it often definitely implies rejection of religion; as, *godless* philosophers; teachings.
Ana. *Impious, profane, blasphemous, sacrilegious: *immoral, amoral, unmoral.

Ant. Religious. — *Con.* Pious, *devout.

irritable. **Irritable, fractious, peevish, snappish, waspish, petulant, pettish, huffy, huffish, fretful, querulous** apply to persons or to their moods or dispositions in the sense of manifesting impatience or anger without due or sufficient cause. **Irritable** implies extreme excitability of temperament, often owing to a physical or nervous condition, that makes one exceedingly easy to annoy or difficult to please; as, "Mental work brings on...an *irritable* and nervous disgust" (*Arnold*); "Byron, growing *irritable* and fat in the enervating climate of Italy" (*L. P. Smith*). **Fractious** carries a stronger implication of willfulness or of ungovernableness than *irritable* and although it also implies extreme excitability, it suggests even greater loss of self-control: the term is often applied to animals as well as to persons; as, the teacher found the children unduly *fractious* that day; an extremely *fractious* horse. **Peevish** implies childish irritability and a tendency to give expression to petty complaints or ill-humored trivial criticisms; as, "The town, like a *peevish* child, knows not what it desires" (*Fielding*); "He [Gray] thought that Pope had a good heart, in spite of his *peevish* temper" (*N. Nicholls*); "I have heard some London wits, rather *peevish* at Macaulay's superiority, complain that he occupied too much of the talk" (*Thackeray*). **Snappish** implies irritability, sometimes peevishness that manifests itself in sharp, cutting questions, comments, or the like, that discourage conversation or sociability; as, an extremely unlikable, *snappish* old fellow; the cook found her mistress *snappish* that morning. **Waspish** stresses testiness rather than irritability but it implies a readiness to sting or hurt others without warrant or without sufficient warrant; as, beware of his *waspish* temper; her comments may be amusing but they are always *waspish*. **Petulant** usually suggests the sulkiness of or as of a spoiled child as well as peevishness and capricious impatience; as, "a girl of about nineteen with an impatient and *petulant* expression both in her face and in her shoulders" (*Dickens*); "her quick *petulant* nature" (*Stevenson*); "As he had no means of confuting his nephew, all he could do...was to utter *petulant* remarks on his powerlessness to appear at the dinner-table that day" (*Meredith*). **Pettish** implies sulky or childish ill-humor, as of one who is slighted or offended; as, "a *pettish* ejaculation" (*N. Hawthorne*); "Chivalry is a thing which must be courteously and generously conceded, and must never be *pettishly* claimed" (*A. C. Benson*). **Huffy** (or now less often **huffish**) also implies a tendency to take offense without due cause, but it suggests more of a display of injured pride than *pettish;* as, when he is reproved, he is *huffy* for the rest of the day; "To return...a *huffish* answer" (*Dickens*). **Fretful** implies irritability or peevishness that manifests itself in complaints, or in a complaining tone of voice; as, a *fretful* child; his *fretfulness* that afternoon disturbed the whole family. **Querulous** implies a profound and often habitual discontent that manifests itself in whining complaints or in fretfulness of temper; it often also suggests petulance; as, "her *querulous* and never-ending complaints" (*Gaskell*); "the man himself grew old and *querulous* and hysterical with failure and repeated disappointment and chronic poverty" (*A. Huxley*).

Ana. Cranky, cross, testy, touchy, techy, choleric, splenetic, *irascible.

Ant. Easygoing. — *Con.* *Amiable, good-natured, complaisant, obliging: genial, sociable, affable, cordial, *gracious.

irritate. **Irritate, exasperate, nettle, provoke, aggravate, roil** (*or* **rile**), **peeve** agree in meaning to excite a feeling of angry annoyance in a person. That which **irritates** is something which greatly displeases or offends and evokes a display of feeling ranging from momentary impatience to an outburst of rage. "The chattering crowd, with their rude jokes...*irritated* him sharply" (*S. Anderson*). "Her intensity, which would leave no emotion on a normal plane, *irritated* the youth into a frenzy" (*D. H. Lawrence*). That which **exasperates** arouses bitter or intense irritation as at something unendurable; the word, however, sometimes expresses nothing more than keen vexation or annoyance. "When we turn from Owen's work to Eliot's we turn from...anger to *exasperation*, from wounds to nerves, from the love of living to the will to die" (*Day Lewis*). "Though she could *exasperate* she could never offend" (*H. G. Wells*). That which **nettles** irritates sharply but momentarily and stings or piques more than angers. That which **provokes** awakens strong annoyance or vexation, or (esp. in the form *provoking*) teases or tantalizes. "[This]...must be very *provoking* to the dignity of some dissenting doctors; and to *nettle* them still the more, you in a manner impose upon them the necessity of being silent" (*Cowper*). "He is *provoked* with me for not talking more" (*Burney*). **Aggravate,** as equivalent to *provoke,* has not been accepted by careful writers and is rarely used by them except when it is needed for color or as indicating the quality of the speaker. "It is *aggravating* to have you talking about so small a business" (*Shaw*). That which **roils** (or, colloquially, **riles**) is that which disturbs one's serenity or peace and agitates as well as angers. "That his friends should believe it, was what *roiled* him exceedingly" (*R. North*). That which **peeves** (a colloquial word) excites fretfulness or a tendency to be easily irritated; as, he is easily *peeved* after a restless night.

Ana. *Annoy, vex, irk, bother: incense, *anger, madden, enrage, infuriate: *offend, affront: fret, chafe (see ABRADE).

Con. Appease, mollify, conciliate, propitiate, placate, *pacify: gratify, *please, gladden, delight.

irruption. Incursion, raid, *invasion, inroad.

isolation. *Solitude, seclusion.

Ana. Loneliness, solitariness, loneness, desolateness *or* desolation (see corresponding adjectives at ALONE).

issue, *n.* Outcome, upshot, sequel, *effect, consequence, result, event, aftereffect, aftermath.

Ana. Ending *or* end, termination, concluding *or* conclusion, closing (see corresponding verbs at CLOSE).

Con. *Cause, antecedent, determinant: inception, *origin, source, root.

issue, *v.* Emanate, proceed, flow, derive, originate, *spring, arise, rise, stem.

Ana. Emerge, *appear, loom.

item. **Item, detail, particular** come into comparison as meaning one of the separate and distinct things which constitute a whole. **Item** applies mainly to each thing that is put down in a list, as of things needed, things to be done, things to be seen, etc., or in an account, a record, or an inventory: sometimes, the term applies to the actual thing as apart from the list; as, the bill has ten *items;* "each separate *item* of income" (*J. A. Hobson*); "The dog too went: the most noble-looking *item* in the beggarly assets [of an estate]" (*Conrad*). **Detail** (as here compared: see also PART) applies to each separate thing which enters into the building or construction of something, such as a house, a painting, a narrative, or enters into the performance of a task or job, the pursuit of a career, the living of a life, or the like: often, in this sense, *detail* is contrasted with *structure, outline, design,* and the like; as, "while...labouring indefatigably in the *details* of domestic life on a farm, her outlook was large" (*H. Ellis*); "Alike in its large outlines and its small *details*, Chinese life is always the art of balancing an aesthetic temperament and guarding against its excesses" (*H. Ellis*). Oftentimes, the singular form in this sense is used as a collective noun; as, "The poet's chief aim...is to communicate not the exact *detail* of an experience, but its tone and rhythm" (*Day Lewis*); to formulate a plan (or report an incident) in *detail*. **Particular** often implies a relation to something general or universal (as, "it foolishly derides the universal, saying that it chooses to consider the *particular* as more important"—*Quiller-Couch*), but still more often it implies a relation to any whole the individual units of which are called also *items* or *details*. In this sense, *particular* is often preferred to *item* and *detail* when it stresses smallness and the singleness and concreteness of each item or detail; thus, in law, a bill of *particulars* is a statement of the items of a plaintiff's claim or a defendant's counterclaim; so, I do not care to go into the *particulars* of the agreement; "the moment they bring us down from moral generalities to business *particulars* it becomes plain..." (*Shaw*); "The real question is what is the world...and that can be revealed only by the study of all nature's *particulars*" (*W. James*).

Ana. *Thing, object, article: constituent, component, *element, integrant, factor.

itemized. Detailed, particularized, *circumstantial, minute, particular.

Ant. Summarized.

iterate. *Repeat, reiterate, ingeminate.

itinerant, *adj.* **Itinerant, peripatetic, ambulatory, ambulant, nomadic, vagrant** agree in meaning having no fixed or settled station but moving from place to place. **Itinerant** is applicable chiefly to individuals or to groups whose calling or office requires travel along a circuit or route; as, an *itinerant* player; an *itinerant* merchant. "An advantage *itinerant* preachers have over those who are stationary, the latter cannot well improve their delivery of a sermon by so many rehearsals" (*Franklin*). **Peripatetic** was first used in reference to the followers of Aristotle and the Aristotelian philosophy because Aristotle gave instruction to his disciples while walking in the Lyceum in Athens; it therefore usually is applied to activities carried on while walking or moving about; as, *peripatetic* teaching. "*Peripatetic* habits, favorable to Meditation" (*Carlyle*). When referred to persons, it is often used humorously to imply restlessness or a state of being constantly on the go; as, a very *peripatetic* young lady. **Ambulatory** and the less common **ambulant** sometimes, but not always, retain their etymological implication of walking: in such cases, they are close synonyms of *pedestrian;* as, *ambulatory* exercise; an *ambulatory* journey. More often, however, they imply, as *pedestrian* does not, ability to move about (thus, an *ambulatory*, or *ambulant*, patient is one not confined to bed or to his home) or, when applied to things, a lack of fixity not only in station (as, an *ambulatory* school or church) but in terms (as, the provisions of a will are *ambulatory* until a testator's death). **Nomadic,** though applicable to individuals, is more often used to designate groups or tribes of men who have no fixed place of residence but wander, according to season or food supply or the needs of their means of livelihood, from one place or region to another; thus, the Bedouins are a *nomadic* tribe found in the deserts of Arabia, Syria, and North Africa. **Vagrant,** though it stresses lack of a fixed residence, is applicable rather to individuals such as tramps or hobos than to races or tribes; it also carries implications of shiftlessness, aimlessness, and unsteadiness, not usually found in *nomadic;* as, the great increase in numbers of *vagrant* boys during the depression. "The adventure...of listening to Gallaher's stories and of sharing for a brief space Gallaher's *vagrant*...life" (*Joyce*).

Ana. Wandering, roving, rambling, straying, roaming, ranging (see WANDER): moving, shifting (see MOVE, *v.*).

J

jabber. Jabber, chatter, *chat, gab, patter, prate, prattle, babble, gabble, gibber.

jack, *n.* *Flag, ensign, standard, banner, color, streamer, pennant, pennon.

jade, *v.* Exhaust, fatigue, *tire, weary, fag, tucker.

Ana. Oppress, *depress, weigh (down): enervate, *unnerve, unman, emasculate: sate, *satiate, surfeit, pall, cloy.

Ant. Refresh. — *Con.* *Renew, restore, rejuvenate.

jail *or* **gaol,** *v.* Incarcerate, *imprison, immure, intern.

Ana. Confine, circumscribe, restrict, *limit: shackle, manacle, fetter (see HAMPER).

Con. Release, liberate, *free.

jam, *n.* *Predicament, plight, fix, dilemma, quandary, scrape, pickle.

Ana. *Difficulty, vicissitude: pinch, strait, exigency (see JUNCTURE).

jape, *n.* *Jest, joke, quip, witticism, wisecrack, crack, gag.

jar, *n.* Jolt, *impact, impingement, collision, clash, shock, concussion, percussion, brunt.

Ana. Shaking *or* shake, quaking *or* quake (see corresponding verbs at SHAKE): vibration, fluctuation, swaying *or* sway (see corresponding verbs at SWING): agitation, disturbance, upsetting *or* upset (see corresponding verbs at DISCOMPOSE).

jargon. *Dialect, vernacular, patois, lingo, cant, argot, patter, slang.

Ana. Idiom, speech (see LANGUAGE): abracadabra, *gibberish.

jaunt, *n.* Excursion, *journey, trip, tour, voyage, cruise, expedition, pilgrimage.

jaunty. *Debonair, perky, cocky, chipper.

Ana. Sprightly, *lively, animated: spruce, dapper, dashing, natty (see STYLISH).

Ant. Staid: demure.

jaw, *v.* Upbraid, *scold, rate, berate, tonguelash, bawl out, wig, rail, revile, vituperate.

Ana. Censure, denounce, reprobate, reprehend, *criticize, blame, condemn: *reprove, reproach, chide, reprimand, rebuke.

jealous. *Envious.

Ana. Suspicious, mistrustful (see corresponding nouns at UNCERTAINTY): *doubtful, dubious: vigilant, *watchful, alert: distrusting, mistrusting (see DISTRUST).

jeer, *v.* *Scoff, gibe, fleer, gird, sneer, flout.

Ana. Deride, *ridicule, mock, taunt, twit, rally.

Con. *Fawn, truckle, toady, cringe, cower.

jejune. *Insipid, vapid, flat, wishy-washy, inane, banal.
Ana. *Thin, slight, slim, tenuous: arid, *dry: attenuated, extenuated, diluted, thinned (see THIN, *v.*): *meager, skimpy, exiguous.
Con. Lavish, *profuse, lush, luxuriant, prodigal, exuberant: nutritious, nourishing, sustaining (see corresponding nouns at FOOD).

jeopardous. Perilous, *dangerous, hazardous, risky, precarious.
Ana. Chancy, happy-go-lucky, hit-or-miss, haphazard, *random.
Con. Safe, *secure: defended, protected, shielded, guarded, safeguarded (see DEFEND).

jeopardy. Peril, hazard, risk, *danger.
Ana. Threatening *or* threat, menacing *or* menace (see corresponding verbs at THREATEN): exposure (see EXPOSITION): liability, susceptibility, sensitiveness, openness (see corresponding adjectives at LIABLE): *chance, accident, hap.
Con. Security, safety (see corresponding adjectives at SAFE): immunity, *exemption.

jest, *n.* **1 Jest, joke, jape, quip, witticism, wisecrack, crack, gag** come into comparison when they mean a remark, a comment, a story, or sometimes an act, intended to evoke laughter. **Jest** now seldom retains its older implication of taunting, jeering, or other ill-natured raillery (as, "Might he but set the rabble in a roar, He cared not with what *jest*"—*Cowper*). Although it still may imply raillery, it carries a stronger connotation of lightness or sportiveness and suggests banter, persiflage, or the like; as, "genial table-talk, Or deep dispute, and graceful *jest*" (*Tennyson*). **Joke** applies not only to something that is said but quite as often to an act or incident that is intended to excite uproarious laughter; as, to play a *joke* (usually a *practical joke*) upon a friend. When applied to a remark, comment, or story, it usually suggests a sportive sally designed to promote good humor without wounding the feelings of its object; as, "He takes his chirping pint, and cracks his *joke*" (*Pope*); "We shall have our little *jokes*, like other people" (*Gray*). **Jape,** a word that had become obsolete before Spenser's and Shakespeare's time, was revived by Lamb and others early in the nineteenth century and still occurs occasionally. In earliest use, it denoted a diverting or amusing story or anecdote (as, "Thomas, that *jape* is not worth a mite"—*Chaucer*); in its more modern use it comes nearer to *jest* or *joke;* as, "the coy giggle of the young lady to whom he has imparted his latest merry *jape*" (*Besant*). **Quip** applies especially to a quick, neatly turned jest flung off in banter, raillery, or sarcasm; as, "*Quips* and Cranks and wanton Wiles . . . And Laughter holding both his sides" (*Milton*); "The whole conversation is . . . a hailstorm of short stories, *quips*, and retorts" (*Lever*). **Witticism** is the polite or bookish term, **wisecrack** or **crack** the slang term, for an especially clever or witty retort to a question, comment on a situation, or the like. "There was a current *witticism* . . . that you called her [a frequently divorced and remarried woman] Eudora because it was the only one of her names of the continuity of which you felt at all certain!" (*M. Austin*). "He has a merry tongue which articulates scientific problems with what the contemporaries of his younger days called *witticisms*. His present contemporaries call them *cracks*" (*Time*). "*Wise-crack* dialogue of the wonderful American variety. 'That guy's so crooked the tears run down his back,' was one remark" (*Daily Express*). **Gag** (literally, something thrust into the mouth to prevent an outcry) was originally theatrical slang for an interpolated joke or witticism, or sometimes trick, or other amusing piece of business (as, the performance was lengthened by the numerous *gags* of the comedian); in current use, however, it applies also to any joke, witticism, or the like, forming a part of the script or text (as, to hire an author to write the *gags* for the radio program) or to any amusing remark, anecdote, trick, or the like, intended to make its subject appear ridiculous or ludicrous.
Ana. *Badinage, persiflage, raillery: bantering *or* banter, chaffing *or* chaff, rallying *or* rally, jollying *or* jolly (see corresponding verbs at BANTER): twitting *or* twit, ridiculing *or* ridicule, deriding *or* derision (see corresponding verbs at RIDICULE).
2 *Fun, sport, game, play.
Ana. Diversion, entertainment, amusement (see under AMUSE): joviality, merriment (see corresponding adjectives at MERRY). — *Con.* Seriousness, earnestness, soberness, gravity (see corresponding adjectives at SERIOUS).

jester. *Fool, clown, antic, buffoon, zany, merry-andrew, pantaloon, harlequin, comedian, comic, stooge.

jewel. Gem, *stone.

jib *or* **gib,** *v.* Balk, shy, boggle, stickle, stick, strain, *demur, scruple.

jibe[1] *or* **gibe.** *Agree, harmonize, accord, conform, square, comport, tally, correspond.

jibe.[2] Variant of *gibe* under SCOFF.

jiffy. *Instant, moment, minute, second, flash, trice, twinkling, twinkle, split second.

jittery. Jumpy, nervous, *impatient, unquiet, restless, restive, uneasy, fidgety, skittish, feverish, hectic.
Ana. Unnerved, unmanned (see UNNERVE): perturbed, agitated, disquieted, upset, discomposed (see DISCOMPOSE).
Con. Collected, composed, *cool, imperturbable, nonchalant: serene, placid, *calm, tranquil.

job. 1 *Task, duty, chare, chore, stint, assignment.
Ana. Office, *function, duty, province: business, concern, *affair, matter, thing.
2 *Position, situation, post, place, berth, billet, capacity.
Ana. *Work, employment, occupation, pursuit, métier, business, calling: *trade, craft, handicraft, art, profession.

jocose. Jocular, facetious, humorous, *witty.
Ana. Waggish, sportive, *playful, roguish: comic, comical, *laughable, ludicrous, droll, funny: *merry, jolly, jovial, jocund, blithe.
Con. *Serious, earnest, grave, sober, solemn, sedate, staid.

jocular. Jocose, humorous, facetious, *witty.
Ana. Jovial, jolly, *merry: *playful, sportive: funny, droll, comic, comical, *laughable, ludicrous, ridiculous.
Con. Grave, earnest, solemn, *serious.

jocund. Blithe, *merry, jolly, jovial.
Ana. Joyful, joyous, cheerful, lighthearted, happy, *glad: mirthful, hilarious, gleeful (see corresponding nouns at MIRTH): sportive, *playful, mischievous, wanton.
Con. Gloomy, morose, glum, *sullen, saturnine, dour: sedate, grave, solemn, staid, *serious.

join. Join, combine, unite, connect, link, associate, relate agree in meaning to attach or fasten one thing to another or several things to each other or to become so attached or fastened. **Join** presupposes prior separation or detachment and, therefore, implies a bringing or a coming together into contact or conjunction or, sometimes, an adding of one thing to another; as, to *join* two pieces of wood by dovetailing them; to *join* skirt lengths by seams; to *join* hands; to *join* a man and woman in matrimony; to *join* battle (that is, to come together in conflict); where the Mohawk River *joins* the Hudson; the opponents of the proposal decided to *join* forces. *Join* is the specific term when one becomes a member of a group or enters into the company of others as an equal; as, to *join* a society; to *join* a church; to *join* a group at a reception; to *join* one's ship; to *join* the army. **Combine** adds to *join* the implications of a mingling or blending and of a common purpose or end; it is therefore used of two or more things (often immaterial things) that may lose or seem to lose their identities and become merged in each other; thus, one *combines* (not *joins*) the ingredients for a cake; to *combine* breakfast and lunch in one meal called "brunch"; to *combine* the training of the mind with the training of the body; "a gift for *combining*, for fusing into a single phrase, two or more diverse impressions" (*T. S. Eliot*); "With this quality of temperance was *combined* in Socrates a rare measure of independence and moral courage" (*G. L. Dickinson*). **Unite** may carry the basic implications of either *join* or *combine*, but it differs from each in stressing the oneness of that which results and the loss of signs of separation or division; thus, to *unite* two pieces of wood suggests not so much the way in which they are brought together as the fact that they comprise a new unit; one may *combine* the dry ingredients of a cake, but they will not become *united* until some liquid is added. "Our peace will, like a broken limb *united*, Grow stronger for the breaking" (*Shak.*). "When the ripe colours soften and *unite*, And sweetly melt into just shade and light" (*Pope*). "In France the whole people saw at once what was upon them; the single word *patrie* was enough to *unite* them in a common enthusiasm and stern determination" (*Inge*). **Connect** implies a loose or, at least, an obvious attachment of things to each other and the preservation not only of each thing's identity but also of the evidence of its physical or logical separateness; in this way it is distinguishable from *join* when physical attachment is implied; thus, a wall is built up of bricks *joined* (not *connected*) together by cement; a chain is made by *connecting* a succession of steel links. Often, but not necessarily, *connect* implies an intervening medium which permits joint movement, intercommunication, or the like; as, to *connect* two railway coaches by means of a coupler; to *connect* two islands with a bridge; ligaments serve to *connect* bones at a joint; to break a telephone *connection;* a *connecting* road (that is, a minor road which *connects* two routes or highways). When the idea of logical attachment is uppermost, *connect* usually implies that the ideas, events, or things (sometimes material as well as immaterial) have a bearing on each other, such as of cause and effect or effect and cause, generic likeness, or reference to the same person or thing; as, to see that the two incidents were *connected;* an unclassified flower is one that no botanist has yet been able to *connect* with any known species or genus; the police have now sufficient evidence to *connect* the suspect with the bombing; there is no logical *connection* between the paragraphs of this essay; anything *connected* with Napoloen is of interest to them. *Connect* (especially with a reflexive pronoun or in the passive), when used in reference to organizations or groups, is preferable to *join* when looseness of attachment, impermanence, or subordination is suggested; thus, one who *joins* a firm of brokers becomes, by implication, a partner; one who becomes, or is, *connected* with a firm of brokers is, by implication, an employee. **Link,** with its literal reference to one of the parts of a chain, is usually more emphatic than *connect* in implying firmness of attachment; it is therefore the preferred word when one wishes to preserve the basic implications of *connect* (preservation of each thing's identity and evidence of their separateness) and yet to avoid its common connotations of a weak or severable attachment; thus, to *link* a person with a crime is, by implication, to have ample evidence of his being its agent, or an accomplice, or the like. "Augustus set himself to revive the state religion...as part of his policy of *linking* up past and present, and as an instrument in securing the restoration of the old morality" (*Buchan*). **Associate** primarily implies a joining with another or others in companionship or in effort, usually on terms of equality; as, a group of men *associated* in business. "When bad men combine, good men must *associate*" (*Burke*). "My father's conviction that they were too lowly to *associate* with me, when it was so clear that I was too poor to *associate* with them, may have had some sort of imaginary validity for him; but for me it was snobbish nonsense" (*Shaw*). In its extended use as referred to things, the implication of companionship on equal terms gives way to the implication of a connection in logic or in thought which comes naturally or involuntarily to the mind of the observer because the things traditionally or, in one's experience, commonly, go together, or naturally or rightfully belong together, or for some reason or other have come to be linked together in one's thoughts, one suggesting the other. "For the artist life is always a discipline, and no discipline can be without pain. That is so even of dancing, which of all the arts is most *associated* in the popular mind with pleasure" (*H. Ellis*). "Every gesture and inflection of voice *associated* by tradition with the part" (*Shaw*). "A fir-tree is not a flower, and yet it is *associated* in my mind with primroses" (*Jefferies*). **Relate** implies a connection, or an attempt to show a connection, between two or more persons or things. In reference to persons it implies a connection through a common ancestor or through marriage (see KINSHIP); as, John and James are remotely *related* to each other. In reference to things, or to persons objectively regarded, it implies a logical connection or an attempt to demonstrate a logical connection, such as that of subordination or co-ordination, of cause and effect or vice versa, or the like; as, to *relate* one's misfortunes to events which preceded them; the two circumstances are not *related;* it is the dramatist's business to see the incidents of his play in their true *relations* to each other. "He suffers from an...incapacity to *relate* them [his poetic ideas] with any scheme of values" (*Day Lewis*).

Ana. Conjoin, *unite, combine, co-operate, concur: articulate, concatenate, *integrate: attach, affix, *fasten: knit, *weave: *tie, bind.

Ant. Disjoin: part. — ***Con.*** *Separate, sever, sunder: *detach, disengage: disentangle, untangle, disembarrass (see EXTRICATE).

joiner. *Carpenter, cabinetmaker, framer.

joint, *n.* **Joint, articulation, suture** are comprehensive terms denoting a place or part where two things are united or the mechanism by which they are united. **Joint** is the most inclusive of these terms and is commonly used in reference both to anatomical and mechanical structures. Specifically, it applies to any junction of two bones or cartilages in a vertebrate's body or to the part of the body at which there is such a junction; as, the knee *joint;* the *joint* at the elbow is flexible; he aches in every *joint.* In mechanical structures, it often names a connection made by shaping the ends of two pieces so that they come together at the proper angle, or fit closely into each other, sometimes forming a rigid union (as, a miter *joint*, a dovetail *joint*), at other times forming a union that permits movement (as, a universal *joint*). The term is also applied to a connective device, such as a bent piece joining pipes that meet at right angles (an elbow *joint*) or a layer of some plastic substance which unites bricks, stones, pieces of crockery, etc. (as, a mortar *joint*, a cement *joint*). **Articulation** is chiefly an anatomical term, though it has some extended and figurative use (see ARTICULATE, *v.* 1). In technical anatomical use, *articulation* is applicable to the same parts of the skeleton or body as *joint;* thus, one speaks of rigid or flexible *joints* (or *articulations*); the *joint* (or the *articulation*) at the knee. However, *articulation* in very precise use implies, as *joint* does not, a fitting together or adjustment of the two parts or bones with relation not only to each other but to the entire structure and its function. It is the preferable, but not always the required, word when the mechanism of a joint or the elements entering into its formation are under consideration; as, ball-and-socket structure of a movable *articulation;* various *articulations* are supported by ligaments; the synovial membrane reduces friction at an *articulation*. The word may also denote the process of joining or the adjustment in joining; as, "in the flat bones the *articulations* usually take place at the edges" (*H. Gray*); imperfect *articulation* of the jaw bones. It is used in dentistry chiefly with reference to the adjustment of the teeth and to the way in which their surfaces come together when the jaws are closed normally (as, an orthodontist corrects faults in the *articulation* of the teeth) or to the process by which artificial teeth are shaped and arranged so that they move upon each other properly and naturally; as, badly constructed dentures without proper *articulation*. **Suture** etymologically denotes a seam; it is used therefore of any joint or articulation that suggests a seam or that has been brought about by sewing; thus, the joints of the two parts of a pea pod are called respectively the ventral and dorsal *sutures;* the form of articulation observable in the skull where two flat bones meet in a line is called a *suture*. *Suture* is used in surgery of a seam, especially of one whereby two edges of an incision are brought together so that they may ultimately unite.

joke, *n.* *Jest, jape, quip, witticism, wisecrack, crack, gag.

Ana. *Prank, caper, antic, monkeyshine, dido: *trick, ruse, wile: travesty, parody, burlesque, *caricature: raillery, *badinage, persiflage: jocoseness, jocularity, facetiousness, wittiness, humorousness (see corresponding adjectives at WITTY): *wit, humor, repartee, sarcasm.

jollity. Hilarity, glee, *mirth.

Ana. Merriment, joviality, jocundity, blitheness (see corresponding adjectives at MERRY): sport, disport, play, frolic, rollick, gambol, romp (see under PLAY, *v.*): diversion, amusement, recreation, entertainment (see under AMUSE): *fun, jest, sport, game, play.

Con. Gloom, dejection, depression, melancholy, *sadness: solemnity, gravity, seriousness, earnestness, staidness, sedateness (see corresponding adjectives at SERIOUS).

jolly, *adj.* Jovial, jocund, *merry, blithe.

Ana. Bantering, chaffing, rallying, jollying, joshing (see BANTER, *v.*): jocular, jocose, *witty, humorous, facetious: sportive, *playful, mischievous, wanton, roguish, waggish, frolicsome: gay, *lively, vivacious, animated, sprightly.

Con. Solemn, grave, sedate, staid, *serious, earnest: lugubrious, doleful, dolorous, *melancholy, rueful: morose, gloomy, glum, *sullen, dour, saturnine.

jolly, *v.* *Banter, chaff, rally, quiz, kid, rag, guy, rib, josh.

Ana. Blandish, cajole (see COAX): deride, *ridicule, twit, rally, mock, taunt.

jolt, *n.* Jar, shock, *impact, impingement, collision, clash, concussion, percussion.

Ana. Shaking *or* shake, rocking *or* rock, convulsing *or* convulsion (see corresponding verbs at SHAKE).

jongleur. Bard, minstrel, scop, gleeman, troubadour, trouvère, minnesinger, scald, *poet, versifier, rhymer, rhymester, poetaster.

josh, *v.* *Banter, chaff, rally, quiz, kid, rag, guy, rib, jolly.

jot, *n.* Tittle, iota, *particle, bit, mite, smitch, smidgen, whit, atom.

journal. **Journal, periodical, newspaper, magazine, review, organ** come into comparison as denoting a publication which appears regularly at stated times. Strictly, a **journal** is a publication which is issued daily and gives an account of the events, transactions, etc., of the preceding twenty-four hours. Continued use, however, has made it an acceptable designation of a publication that appears less often, such as a weekly, a monthly, or a quarterly; as, "[The *Hibbert Journal*] appeared every three months and called itself a *journal*" (*C. Mackenzie*). **Periodical** is the strictly correct term for any publication appearing at regular intervals: it applies chiefly to weeklies, biweeklies, monthlies, and quarterlies; as, the *periodicals* are assembled in a special room of the library. **Newspaper** is the usual term for a sheet or group of sheets providing the news of the day and issued, usually, six or seven days of the week: it is called a *journal* only in formal speech or writing, although those whose profession is writing for newspapers are often termed *journalists* and although the language and style believed to be typical of the newspaper is commonly called *journalese*. **Magazine** (etymologically, storehouse) applies chiefly to a periodical, often an illustrated periodical, which offers a number of miscellaneous articles, fiction, poetry, discussions of live questions, descriptive sketches, and the like. **Review** applies to a periodical that specializes in critical writings or in articles commenting on the important events and the significant questions of the day. **Organ,** which specifically means a medium of communication, usually applies to any journal or periodical that serves as a mouthpiece of a political party, a church, a business, an institution, or any organization that desires to give the news concerning it for the benefit of its members or adherents or to present its particular principles, doctrines, accomplishments, aspirations, or the like, authoritatively: as, "Science" is the official *organ* of the American Association for the Advancement of Science.

journey, *n.* **Journey, voyage, tour, trip, jaunt, excursion, cruise, expedition, pilgrimage** come into comparison as meaning travel or a passage from one place to another. **Journey** is the most comprehensive term in literary or more formal colloquial use: it now carries no specific implications of length or shortness, of farness or nearness of destination, of a specific object or purpose, or of the mode of transportation; as, to plan a *journey* to California; to wish one a happy *journey* home; the *journey* to Italy will not take more than two months. "For the Son of man is as a man taking a far *journey*, who left his house, and gave authority to his servants" (*Mark* xiii. 34). **Voyage** was once almost as comprehensive a term as *journey* but in current use it always implies a journey of some length over water (especially a sea or ocean), or in more recent usage, through the air; as, "With a fair sea *voyage*, and a fair land *journey*, you will be soon at his dear side" (*Dickens*); "Packets which ply along the coast, as well as those which make *voyages* between Europe and America" (*Ch. Just. Marshall*). **Tour** applies only to a journey which follows a circuitous course from place to place; usually, the term implies that the journey ends when one reaches one's starting point; as, to set out on a walking *tour;* to make a *tour* of Western Europe; a lecture *tour;* penologists made a *tour* of all the prisons in the state; "My next design was to make a *tour* round the island" (*Defoe*). **Trip,** in strict use, applies to a relatively short journey, especially one for business or pleasure; as, his new position requires frequent *trips* to New York; weekend *trips* by automobile. In looser and colloquial use, the term is often used in place of *journey;* as, to plan a *trip* to Europe. Until approximately the middle of the eighteenth century, **jaunt** applied chiefly, if not exclusively, to a journey or trip that was found fatiguing. "I am a-weary, give me leave awhile: Fie, how my bones ache! What a *jaunt* have I had!" (*Shak.*). In current use, the term carries a stronger implication of casualness and of informality than any of the others, and is therefore often applied to any short trip away from one's home or one's business, especially in pursuit of recreation; as, they are off for a day's *jaunt* to the beach; "glad to see again its...welcoming façade when he returns home from any *jaunt*" (*Lucas*). **Excursion** (etymologically, a setting out or forth), as here compared, applies to a short trip, especially one taken for recreation or as a relief from the routine of daily life; as, "The rural neighbourhood of Sneyd, where they had been making an afternoon *excursion*" (*Bennett*). *Excursion* is the preferred term, especially in railroad and steamship use, for a round trip at reduced rates to any point of interest, such as a resort, or an exposition, or a metropolis. When the excursion involves a voyage of some days or weeks and, often, a sight-seeing tour with frequent stops during which the participants use the ship as their living quarters, **cruise** is the preferred term; as, a Mediterranean *cruise;* the steamship lines are featuring winter *cruises* through the Caribbean Sea; their yacht is off with a party on a *cruise.* **Expedition,** in current use especially, applies only to a journey intended to further a definite purpose; as, "He called this trip frankly a begging *expedition*" (*Cather*); he made a special *expedition* to the city to try to straighten out the difficulty; a group of ships under the command of Admiral Byrd sailed on an exploring *expedition.* In military use, *expedition* either implies the movement of troops especially into a foreign country to wage war (as, Caesar wrote a history of his *expedition* into Gaul) or applies to the body of troops so moved, also called *expeditionary force* (as, the young diplomat accompanied the *expedition* into France as an observer for his country). **Pilgrimage** applies strictly to an expedition to a place hallowed by religious or similar associations; often, but far from invariably, it implies an arduous journey or slow and difficult passage; as, the palmer had just returned from a *pilgrimage* to the Holy Land; Chaucer's "Canterbury Tales" is a collection of stories told by men and women on a *pilgrimage* to the tomb of St. Thomas à Becket at Canterbury; "Rydal Mount [Wordsworth's home] became an object of *pilgrimage*" (*Arnold*).

Of all these words, only *pilgrimage, journey,* and *voyage* are used figuratively denoting the passage through life; as, "Here is my *journey's* end, here is my butt, And very sea-mark of my utmost sail" (*Shak.*); "The days of the years of my *pilgrimage* are an hundred and thirty years" (*Genesis* xlvii. 9); "throes That nature's fragile vessel doth sustain In life's uncertain *voyage*" (*Shak.*).

jovial. Jolly, jocund, *merry, blithe.
Ana. Jocular, jocose, facetious, humorous, *witty: genial, sociable, affable (see GRACIOUS): good-natured, *amiable: bantering, chaffing, jollying, joshing, rallying (see BANTER, *v.*).
Con. Saturnine, dour, morose, gloomy, glum, *sullen: sedate, staid, grave, solemn, *serious.

joy. Delight, *pleasure, enjoyment, delectation, fruition.
Ana. Bliss, beatitude, *happiness, felicity: *ecstasy, rapture, transport: elation, exultation (see corresponding adjectives at ELATED).
Ant. Sorrow (*as emotion*): misery (*as a state of mind*): abomination (*in concrete sense*).

joyful. Joyous, cheerful, happy, *glad, lighthearted.
Ana. Blithe, jocund, *merry, jolly: *elated, elate, exultant: buoyant, effervescent, expansive (see ELASTIC).
Ant. Joyless. — *Con.* *Despondent, despairing, desperate, forlorn, hopeless: depressed, weighed (down), oppressed (see OPPRESS).

joyous. Joyful, happy, *glad, cheerful, lighthearted.
Ana. Blithe, jocund, *merry: exultant, *elated, elate: rapturous, ecstatic, transported (see corresponding nouns at ECSTASY).
Ant. Lugubrious. — *Con.* Dolorous, doleful, *melancholy: *miserable, wretched.

judge, *n.* **Judge, arbiter, arbitrator, referee, umpire** are here compared as denoting a person who makes decisions in questions of justice, merit, taste, skill, performance, or the like. **Judge** implies the assumption or the possession both of superior knowledge, experience, or wisdom, and of the power to determine the truth by weighing critically and impartially the merits of the case. "It doth appear you are a worthy *judge;* You know the law, your exposition Hath been most sound" (*Shak.*). "A man who is no *judge* of law may be a good *judge* of poetry, or eloquence, or of the merits of a painting" (*Dryden*). **Arbiter** stresses authoritativeness of decision and is applied to one, whether or not a professed judge, whose word or example is accepted as final and indisputable. "[Horace] had become the *arbiter* of taste...the persuasive exponent of a reasonable life, the clear, sad thinker who led no man astray" (*A. Repplier*). "They were the *arbiters* of fashion, the Court of last Appeal, and they knew it" (*E. Wharton*). "That 'common consent of mankind' which certain moralists make the *arbiter* in ethics" (*Brownell*). **Arbitrator, referee,** and **umpire** are applied to persons to whom a dispute is referred for decision. *Arbitrator* specifically implies an aim to conciliate disputants by reaching a decision just to all concerned; it is commonly applied, therefore, to each member of a group (usually an odd number) whose selection has been approved by both parties; as, the Governor appointed as *arbitrators* two persons recommended by the striking miners, two recommended by the mineowners, and one person selected by both sides. *Referee* and *umpire* are employed chiefly in courts of law and in sports, but they have some literary use. In American legal use, *referee* is applied to an attorney at law appointed either to determine a case or to report on it to the court which he serves as an officer. It is therefore clearly distinguished from *arbitrator* in the United States. This distinction is not commonly observed in England. *Umpire,* on the other hand, is applied to the person selected to make a final decision when arbitrators have disagreed or are tied. Often, the one who serves actually, but not nominally, as umpire in a group of three, five, or seven arbitrators is the odd member who casts the deciding vote. In literary use, *referee* usually is applied to one to whom disputants have recourse when agreement seems impossible, *umpire* to one who enters in and arbitrarily ends the struggle or dispute. "Clear-sighted, unprejudiced, sagacious...he was the universal *referee*" (*Disraeli*). "Just death, kind *umpire* of men's miseries" (*Shak.*). In sports and games, both *umpire* (much the earlier term in this use) and *referee* are technical terms applied to the official or officials charged with the regulation of a contest, enforcement of rules of the game, making decisions on plays, and the like. In most sports today, either one term or the other is used; thus, these officials in baseball, cricket, tennis are designated *umpires*, the officials in boxing, basketball, ice hockey are designated *referees*. In American football, however, both terms are used, the term *referee* being applied to the official whose decision is final but who is especially judge of matters connected with the progress of the ball, as distinguished from the *umpire*, who is, in general, judge of the acts of the players.

judge, *v.* **1 Judge, adjudge, adjudicate, arbitrate** agree in meaning to pass a decision upon something in dispute or controversy. All of these words imply the existence of a competent legal tribunal or of its equivalent. **Judge** is now more often used intransitively in the sense in which it is here considered; it implies mainly the investigation of evidence on both sides, a comparison of the merits of each case, and a decision as to where the truth lies; as, the court must *judge* between the claimants. **Adjudge** stresses decision by a court either at the end of a trial or during a legal process; as, the evidence was *adjudged* inadmissible; the court *adjudged* the will void; to be *adjudged* bankrupt; the prize was *adjudged* to the captor. **Adjudicate,** on the other hand, stresses formal deliberate determination of an issue by or as by a court; as, the court proceeded to *adjudicate* the rights and interests of the parties. "To obtain an *adjudication* of the supreme court of the United States on the validity of any such rights" (*Ch. Just. Marshall*). "It is useless to reargue a seemingly *adjudicated* case" (*Lowes*). **Arbitrate** implies deliberate determination of a matter in dispute by one or more persons who constitute an extralegal tribunal that may or may not be legally recognized and who are chosen by both sides to the controversy; as, the strikers and the employers finally agreed on a group of three men to *arbitrate* their differences. The decision reached through *arbitration* is not binding unless it is assented to by both parties, or is confirmed by a competent court. On the other hand, the decision reached by an *adjudication* is binding, unless it is reversed by a higher court.
Ana. Determine, *decide, settle, rule.
2 Conclude, deduce, *infer, gather.
Ana. *Prove, demonstrate, try, test.

judgment. 1 Conclusion, deduction, inference. See under INFER.
Ana. Decision, determination, ruling (see corresponding verbs at DECIDE): *opinion, conviction, persuasion, view, belief.
2 *Sense, wisdom, gumption.
Ana. Intelligence, wit, wits, brains, brain, *mind: sagaciousness *or* sagacity, perspicaciousness *or* perspicacity, shrewdness, astuteness (see corresponding adjectives at SHREWD): acumen, *discernment, insight, penetration: *prudence, discretion.

judicial. Judicial, judiciary, juridical (*or* **juridic**), **juristic** (*or* **juristical**) come into comparison because of verbal confusion and because all imply some connection with courts of law. **Judicial,** by far the most common of these adjectives both in legal and in general use, often implies a direct reference to the courts of justice, the judge who presides over a court of justice, or the judges who form such a court; as, a *judicial* decision; a *judicial* duty; a *judicial* proceeding. The term is also used in distinction from *executive, legislative,* etc., when applied to that one of the powers, departments, or functions of the government which is associated with that court (in the United States, the Supreme Court) which gives definitive decisions on questions of law or interprets the constitution or basic law; as, the executive, legislative, and *judicial* branches of the government. When used in an extended sense, as applied especially to a type of mind, of mental activity, of manner, etc., the term suggests likeness to that of a judge, as in detachment or fair-mindedness, or appropriateness to a judge or court of justice, as in orderliness and seriousness of procedure; as, "To a strictly *judicial* mind...the quality of age or of novelty would carry no necessary implication of value" (*Grandgent*). **Judiciary** is sometimes used in place of *judicial,* especially when applied to a department or function of the government. "I like the organization of the government into Legislative, *Judiciary* and Executive" (*Jefferson*). In most use, however, it suggests reference to the courts in general and to the administration of justice as a whole; thus, a *judicial* act is an act involving the exercise of the power vested in a judge or court to hear and determine controversies or to determine a question of right or obligation; a *judiciary* act is a legislative act respecting the establishment or reform of the courts; a *judicial* question is one that requires settlement by a judge or court; a *judiciary* question is one that concerns the jurisdiction or powers of a court or the courts or the administration of justice by the courts. *Judiciary* is the only one of these terms now used as a substantive: so used it is a collective noun for judges as a class or for courts of justice. It may also be used in opposition to *legislature* and *executive* (as a noun). The last two words, *juridical* and *juristic,* imply a connection with the law, especially as it is administered in the courts, rather than with the judges, or those who settle questions of law. Often these terms come close to *legal* in meaning, but in learned use (they seldom occur elsewhere) they are more restricted in significance. Both terms, but especially **juridical,** imply a reference to the law as it appears to learned lawyers and judges—that is, as a highly complex and involved body of principles, statutes, decisions, precedents, and the like, requiring vast knowledge, skill in interpretation, and a keen logical mind in those who put it to use: therefore, the term often means characteristic of, determinable by, or useful to a person with such knowledge and skill; as, *juridical* reasoning; *juridical* evidence; "not Peace to depend on the *juridical* determination of perplexing questions" (*Burke*); "Foreigners in Turkey; Their *Juridical* Status" (title of a book by Philip Marshall Brown). **Juristic** implies rather a reference to the science of law (as, "[Justice] Holmes had struck in 1905 in his dissent in *Lochmer v. N.Y.* the high pitch of American *juristic* thought"—*The New Republic*). It is, however, more often used in another sense in describing a legal person (a *juristic*—less often, a *juridical*—person), that is, a corporation, body, or state which is recognized by the law as a subject of rights and duties in the same manner as a human being.
☞ *Do not confuse* judicial *with* judicious.

judiciary. *Judicial, juridical, juristic.

judicious. *Wise, sage, sapient, prudent, sensible, sane.
Ana. *Rational, reasonable: just, *fair, equitable, dispassionate, objective: sagacious, perspicacious, astute, *shrewd: discreet, prudent (see under PRUDENCE).
Ant. Injudicious: asinine. — *Con.* *Foolish, silly, absurd, preposterous: *stupid, dull, dumb, crass, dense: rash, reckless, foolhardy (see ADVENTUROUS).

jumble, *n.* *Confusion, disorder, chaos, disarray, clutter, pie, snarl, muddle.

jumpy. Jittery, nervous, restless, uneasy, fidgety, *impatient, unquiet, restive, skittish, feverish, hectic.
Ant. Steady.

juncture. Juncture, pass, exigency, emergency, contingency, pinch, strait, straits, crisis agree in denoting a critical or crucial time or state of affairs in the life of a person or institution, the history of a country, or the like. **Juncture** emphasizes the concurrence or convergence of events, especially of events that, when combined, convey a threat of danger or disaster, an intimation of one's duty, or the like; as, "It happened that just at that *juncture* was published a ridiculous book against him" (*Warburton*); "the Church of England is at the present *juncture* the one church upon which the duty of working towards reunion most devolves" (*T. S. Eliot*). **Pass** carries a stronger implication of the state of affairs brought about by a combination of causes than of the time at which their effect is noted; whether qualified or unqualified, the term usually connotes an evil or distressing condition; as, "Have his daughters brought him to this *pass?*" (*Shak.*); matters had come to such a *pass* that security seemed to him more desirable than independence. "Constance, after...reflection on the frightful *pass* to which destiny had brought her, had said that she supposed she would have to manage with a charwoman until Rose's advent" (*Bennett*). **Exigency** (see also NEED) strongly emphasizes the pressure or restrictions of necessity, or the urgency of the demands created by a juncture or pass; as, "[He] had conjured the king...not to insist too nicely upon terms in the present *exigency* of his affairs" (*Ludlow*). "It would have been an unwise attempt to provide, by immutable rules, for *exigencies* which, if foreseen at all, must have been seen dimly, and which can be best provided for as they occur" (*Ch. Just. Marshall*). **Emergency** stresses the suddenness or the unforeseen character of the juncture; the term may or may not imply that what constitutes an emergency has also the quality of an *exigency*, for the latter term is far stronger in its suggestion of extreme difficulty; as, "Of all the public services, that of the navy is the one... which can worst be supplied upon an *emergency*" (*Burke*); "It was a special provision...to meet a present *emergency*, and nothing more" (*Ch. Just. Taney*); "A presence of mind which no *emergency* can perturb" (*C. W. Eliot*). **Contingency** is occasionally used in place of *exigency* or *emergency* as here considered where the occurrence of that which is highly uncertain or no more than remotely possible is stressed; as, "Advantage might be taken of some political *contingency* for a private arrangement" (*Froude*). **Pinch** suggests the quality of *exigency*, but not the same intensity of strain; it is often used when the juncture occurs in personal affairs or is not as severe or as exorbitant in its demands on one's powers of resistance or endurance; as, "men who can do better than their best at a *pinch*" (*T. Hughes*); "This—the great *pinch* of his life" (*N. Hawthorne*). **Strait,** or now more commonly **straits,** applies to a situation from which the person involved finds it difficult to escape, so hampered or fettered is he by some given or implied set of circumstances; as, he was in great *straits* for lack of money; "Take me; I'll serve you better in a *strait*" (*Tennyson*); "This disagreeable companion had, of his own free will, assisted him in the *strait* of the day" (*Dickens*); "He was at a loss what to invent to detain him....He rendered homage to the genius of woman in these *straits*. 'My Aunt,' he thought, 'would have the lie ready' " (*Meredith*). **Crisis** applies to any juncture or pass the outcome of which has or will have a decisive effect and which, therefore, serves as a turning point in a life or a history, or, in medical use, of a disease. The term usually connotes suspense, but it may or may not suggest inherent evil in the situation; as, the pneumonia patient has passed the *crisis* safely; "Tiberius gave one million pounds out of his own pocket to relieve the agrarian *crisis* of A.D. 33" (*Buchan*); "Father finally...brought the matter to a *crisis*. He said, after all, the boy had a right to choose" (*M. Austin*); "this *crisis* will be surmounted if the Church has the faith and courage, and, above all, the common honesty, to face it candidly" (*Inge*).

Ana. *State, posture, situation, condition, status: *predicament, plight, quandary.

junk, *v.* Scrap, *discard, cast, shed, molt, exuviate, slough.

junto. Faction, ring, cabal, bloc, *combination, combine, party.

Ana. Clique, coterie, *set.

juridical *or* **juridic.** Juristic, *judicial, judiciary.

jurisdiction. *Power, authority, control, command, sway, dominion.

Ana. Limits, bounds, confines (see singular nouns at LIMIT): *range, scope, compass, reach: circuit, ambit, periphery (see CIRCUMFERENCE): province, office, *function, duty: domain, territory, province, *field, sphere, bailiwick.

juristic *or* **juristical.** Juridical, *judicial, judiciary.

just, *adj.* **1** *Upright, honorable, conscientious, scrupulous, honest.

Ana. Strict, *rigid: virtuous, righteous, *moral, ethical, noble: *reliable, dependable, tried, trustworthy.

Con. *Crooked, devious, oblique: corrupt, perverted, debauched, depraved (see under DEBASE): *base, low, vile: ignoble, *mean.

2 Equitable, *fair, impartial, unbiased, dispassionate, uncolored, objective.

Ana. Detached, disinterested, aloof (see INDIFFERENT): *due, rightful, condign: *rational, reasonable.

Ant. Unjust.

justice. **Justice, equity** are comparable terms largely because of their legal uses and chiefly because they agree in denoting the act, practice, or obligation of giving or rendering to a person or thing that which is his (or its) due, as in conformity with right, truth, or the dictates of reason. **Justice** is by far the wider-ranging term, for it may apply to an abstraction which represents an ideal (as, "He [Galsworthy] flamed out against injustice because he was a lover of *justice*"—*Bliss Perry*), or to a quality of mind which exhibits adherence to this ideal (as, "Nothing escaped the kind eyes, the far-seeing love, that punished and praised with that calm *justice* which children so keenly appreciate"—*Deland*), or to a quality in a thing which never departs from the truth in the slightest degree (as, "[Pepys] painted a psychological portrait of himself which for its serenely impartial *justice*, its subtle gradations...has all the qualities of the finest Velasquez"—*H. Ellis*), or to the treatment accorded one who has transgressed a law—divine law, natural law, the law of a state, etc.—or who seeks relief when wronged or protection when his rights are threatened (as, "At the present time...there is more danger that criminals will escape *justice* than that they will be subjected to tyranny"—*Justice Holmes*), or to the system of courts of law whereby the rights of an individual or his innocence or guilt are determined in accordance with the laws of the state (as, "In the modern state.... *Justice* and administration are directly connected with whatever governs"—*Belloc*). **Equity** differs from *justice* chiefly in being more restricted in its denotation, for it usually implies a justice that transcends the strict letter of the law and is in keeping with what is reasonable rather than with what is merely legal. It is in this sense that a court of equity is, theoretically at least, distinguished from a court of law. To the former go for adjudication and settlement the unusual cases where abstract justice might not be dealt out according to the limitations of the written law: to the latter go the vast majority of cases where the determination of facts is of first importance and where the law, once the facts are established, provides the treatment to be accorded the person or parties involved. But *equity* in nonlegal use implies a justice based upon a strictly impartial meting out of rewards and punishments, of praise and blame, or the like, all conditions of fair play being respected; as, "The plain confidence of an honest servant in the *equity* of a discerning master" (*Burke*); the union claimed that the lower wages paid to aliens were not in keeping with any principle of *equity*.

justify. 1 Vindicate, defend, *maintain, assert.

Ana. *Prove, demonstrate: *support, uphold, back.

Con. *Disprove, refute, confute.

2 Account for, rationalize, *explain.

Ana. *Excuse, condone: *exculpate, exonerate, absolve, acquit, vindicate: extenuate, gloze, gloss, whitewash, *palliate.

Con. Incriminate, indict, arraign, *accuse: condemn, denounce, blame (see CRITICIZE).

3 **Justify, warrant** are here compared as meaning to afford, as evidence, a circumstance, a situation, a state of affairs, or the like, good grounds for doing, saying, using, or believing something. **Justify** implies the provision of grounds so good that they satisfy one's reason and, often, one's conscience, especially if there is a conflict between what seems necessary and what is morally right; as, "He says that more men are killed by overwork than the importance of this world *justifies*" (*Kipling*); "no consideration on earth *justifies* a parent in telling lies to his child" (*B. Russell*). "I remember a very tender-hearted judge being of opinion that closing a hatch to stop a fire and the destruction of a cargo was *justified* even if it was known that doing so would stifle a man below" (*Justice Holmes*). **Warrant** implies support by authority, precedent, experience, logic, and the like: the term rarely suggests moral grounds; as, "So bred, no wonder if I took the bent that seemed even *warranted* by thy consent" (*Dryden*); "the dimensions are not great, though greater than safe construction *warranted*" (*H. Adams*); "Public danger *warrants* the substitution of the executive process for the judicial process" (*Justice Holmes*); "[The experiment] *warranted* the deduction that a diet which included vitamin B was a preventive for beri-beri" (*V. Heiser*).

Ana. Allow, permit (see LET): sanction (see APPROVE): *authorize.

juvenile. *Youthful, puerile, boyish, virgin, virginal, maiden.

Ana. *Immature, unmatured, unfledged: callow, green, crude (see RUDE).

Ant. Adult: senile. — *Con.* *Mature, matured, grown-up, full-fledged.

juxtaposed. *Adjacent, adjoining, contiguous, abutting, tangent, conterminous.

Ana. *Close, near, nigh.

K

keen, *adj.* 1 *Sharp, acute.

Ana. Piercing, penetrating, probing (see ENTER): *pungent, poignant, piquant: cutting, biting, *incisive, trenchant.

Ant. Blunt. — *Con.* *Dull, obtuse.

2 *Eager, avid, agog, a-tiptoe, athirst, anxious.

Ana. Ardent, fervent, fervid, perfervid (see IMPASSIONED): *intense, vehement: fired, inflamed, enkindled (see LIGHT, *v.*).

Con. Apathetic, *impassive, stolid, phlegmatic: uninterested, *disinterested: listless, *languid: unconcerned, incurious, *indifferent.

keen, *v.* Wail, weep, *cry, whimper, blubber.

Ana. Lament, bewail, bemoan (see DEPLORE): mourn, sorrow, *grieve.

keep, *v.* 1 **Keep, observe, celebrate, solemnize, commemorate** come into comparison only when they mean to pay proper attention or honor to something prescribed, obligatory, or demanded by one's nationality, religion, rank, or the like. They are, however, not close synonyms except in smaller groups because they vary widely in their range of reference or application. *Keep* and *observe* are closely synonymous terms, especially when they imply heed of that which is prescribed or obligatory, but they differ fundamentally in their connotations. **Keep** implies opposition to *break*, and emphasizes the idea of not neglecting or violating; as, to *keep* (not *observe*) a promise; to *keep* (not *observe*) the peace; to *keep* (not *observe*) the commandments. **Observe** carries positive implications, such as punctiliousness in performance of the required acts, rites, and the like, and usually, a spirit of respect or reverence for that which one heeds or honors; when these ideas are definitely to be suggested, *observe* is the precise term, even though *keep* would otherwise be possible; as, few persons *observe* (better than *keep*) the Sabbath in the manner of the early Puritans; they *observe* (better than *keep*) Passover (or Lent) with the utmost strictness; he *observes* (not *keeps*) the letter of the law; the veterans of the World War *observe* Memorial Day. *Celebrate* and *solemnize* are also close synonyms because they may take as their objects not only a day, a season, or an occasion which for religious, political, or other significant reasons is observed with pomp and ceremony, but also a ceremony or rite (usually a religious ceremony or rite) that is marked with unusual dignity and splendor. **Celebrate,** however, except in certain idiomatic phrases (such as, to *celebrate* the Eucharist; to *celebrate* Mass), now suggests demonstrations, often public demonstrations of joy or festivity, such as by singing, shouting, speechmaking, feasting, and the like; as, to *celebrate* Independence Day; to *celebrate* New Year's Eve; to *celebrate* their golden wedding; the family decided to *celebrate* the occasion by a large dinner party. **Solemnize,** on the other hand, now tends to be restricted in its reference to religious ceremonies, especially the ceremonies attending the marriage of a couple; thus, in the Roman Catholic Church, to *solemnize* a marriage is not merely to unite a couple in marriage according to the rite of the church but to follow this ceremony by a nuptial Mass and a special blessing; in the Anglican Communion, the same phrase implies the following in detail of the Form of Solemnization of Marriage in the Book of Common Prayer. In the past, and still on occasion, the term, when used in reference to a time or occasion, suggests greater formality and gravity in observance and greater dignity and splendor of ceremony than *celebrate.* "This blessed day Ever in France shall be kept festival: To *solemnize* this day the glorious sun Stays in his course" (*Shak.*). "We *solemnize* this sorrowing natal day To prove our loyal truth" (*Burns*). **Commemorate** in strict use always implies remembrance; as here compared, it also suggests observances that tend to call to mind what the day, the season, the ceremony, or whatever is celebrated, stands for; thus, one *celebrates* Christmas by religious ceremonies that *commemorate* the birth of Christ; the people of the United States *commemorate* the birth of their independence on the 4th of July; the French people *commemorate* the fall of the Bastille on the 14th of July.

Ana. Regard, respect (see under REGARD, *n.*).

Ant. Break. — *Con.* *Neglect, ignore, forget, disregard, overlook, omit, slight: violate, transgress, contravene, infringe (see corresponding nouns at BREACH).

2 Sometimes **keep back. Keep, keep back, retain, detain, withhold, reserve, hold back,** as here compared, agree in meaning not to let go from one's possession, custody, or control. **Keep** is the most general of these terms, often carrying no further implications; as, *keep* this until I ask for it. When, however, it positively denotes a holding securely in one's possession, custody, or control, *keep* or, often, **keep back,** is synonymous with one or another of the last five words, all of which convey, in general, the same idea but vary in some of their implications. Each one, because of its narrower meaning and greater explicitness, is in some collocations preferable to *keep.* **Retain** implies continued keeping, especially as against threatened seizure or forced loss; as, Germany was unable to *retain* [not *keep*] her colonies after the first World War. "The conception of one who...poor, sickly, and a slave perhaps, or even in prison or on the rack, should nevertheless *retain* unimpaired the dignity of manhood and the freedom of his own soul" (*G. L. Dickinson*). **Detain** (see also ARREST, 2), as well as *keep back,* implies a delay in letting go from one's possession or control, as money when due, or a train or messenger when ready to depart; as, to *detain* a ship in quarantine; to *detain* a suspect for examination. **Withhold,** in some contexts, may be used in place of *detain;* as, to *detain* (or *withhold*) a part of a preferred dividend. In general, however, *withhold* implies restraint in letting go or a refusal to let go. Sometimes it is interchangeable with *keep,* or *keep back,* especially when hindrance is also implied; as, timidity caused him to *withhold* (or *keep back*) the advice he longed to give. Sometimes, *keep* and *withhold* are widely different in meaning; thus, to *withhold* one's promise is to refuse to give one's promise; to *keep* (see KEEP, 1) one's promise is to fulfill that which has been promised. **Reserve** implies either a keeping in store for other or for future use (as, the runner *reserved* some of his energy for the final sprint; to *reserve* some of the milk for the next day's breakfast) or a withholding from present or from others' use, enjoyment, or the like (as, "the force of will which had enabled her to *reserve* the fund intact"—*Bennett;* to *reserve* one's judgment). This term, also, is not invariably interchangeable with *keep;* as, please *reserve* (or *keep*) a room for me; to *reserve* (not *keep*) a part of each month's income. **Hold back** is often used in place of *withhold* or *keep back* and sometimes in place of *detain* and *reserve* when restraint (either self-imposed, or originating in oneself, or imposed by others) in letting go is implied; as, to *hold back* a portion of each week's wages for group insurance; to *hold back* the truth in giving testimony.

Ana. *Save, preserve, conserve: hold, *have, enjoy, possess, own: control, direct, manage, *conduct.

Ant. Relinquish. — *Con.* *Discard, cast, junk: refuse, reject, repudiate, spurn (see DECLINE, *v.*): surrender, abandon, resign, yield (see RELINQUISH).

keep, *n.* *Living, livelihood, subsistence, sustenance, maintenance, support, bread.

ken, *n.* Purview, *range, reach, scope, compass, sweep, gamut, radius, horizon, orbit.

Ana. *Field, sphere, province, domain: view, sight (see LOOK, *n.*, 1).

kibitzer. Onlooker, looker-on, bystander, *spectator, observer, beholder, witness, eyewitness.

kick, *v.* *Object, protest, remonstrate, expostulate.

Ana. *Oppose, combat, resist, withstand: *criticize, denounce, condemn: objurgate, *execrate, curse, damn, anathematize.

kid, *v.* Rally, chaff, *banter, rag, guy, rib, josh, jolly, quiz.

Ana. Tease, plague, pester, harry, *worry.

kidnap. *Abduct.

kidney. Kind, sort, *type, nature, description, character, stripe, ilk.

kill, *v.* **Kill, slay, murder, assassinate, dispatch** (*or* **despatch**), **execute** agree in meaning to deprive of life or to put to death. **Kill** is so general that it merely states the fact and does not, except in special phrases (such as "Thou shalt not *kill*"), suggest human agency and the means of death or the conditions attending the putting to death. Also, the object of the action may be not only a person or a living thing but also an inanimate thing that has qualities suggestive of life; as, the rebels *killed* the king; cancer *killed* the king; grief over the loss of his son *killed* the king; the president *killed* the project when he vetoed the bill making an appropriation for it; to *kill* a friend's love by indifference; the city editor *killed* the story (that is, prevented its publication). "He believed at that time that the League of Nations was going to *kill* war, that the Labour Party were going to *kill* industrial inequity" (*R. Macaulay*). **Slay** implies killing by force or in wantonness; it is rare in spoken English, but it often occurs in written English, sometimes in poetic or elevated writing, at other times in journalese; as, "Though he *slay* me, yet will I trust in him" (*Job* xiii. 15); "He could not *slay* a thing so fair" (*Byron*); "*Slay* not him who gave you life" (*Tennyson*); the gangsters *slew* the man in cold blood; the *slain* man has not yet been identified. In its extended uses, *slay* usually suggests wanton or deliberate destruction or annihilation. "To *slay* The reverence living in the minds of men" (*Shelley*). "Never had she greatly loved before; never would she greatly love again; and the great love she now had she was *slaying*" (*R. Macaulay*). **Murder** definitely implies a motive and, often, premeditation, and imputes to the act a criminal character; it is the exact word to use in reference to one person killing another either in passion or in cold blood; as, Macbeth *murdered* Duncan; Thomas à Becket, archbishop of Canterbury, was *murdered* in his own cathedral. It is sometimes used in place of *kill* as more expressive, or in place of *slay* as more brutally direct and condemnatory, both in literal and extended use. "Glamis hath *murder'd* sleep, and therefore Cawdor Shall sleep no more; Macbeth shall sleep no more" (*Shak.*). "The language of strategy and politics is designed...to make it appear as though wars were not fought by individuals drilled to *murder* one another in cold blood" (*A. Huxley*). **Assassinate** implies murder (especially of an important person) by stealth or treachery, and often by an agent (sometimes a self-appointed agent) or hireling of an opposition. It usually suggests an attempt to get rid of a person who is believed (often fanatically) to be an obstacle to the safety of a tyrant, the welfare of a people, the liberty of a nation, or the success of a design; as, Marat was *assassinated* by Charlotte Corday; at least two attempts were made to *assassinate* William of Orange; the *assassination* of President Lincoln. **Dispatch** also suggests an attempt to get rid of a person by killing him, but it is far more colorless than *assassinate*. It nearly always implies taking direct means of killing, as by shooting or stabbing, and so sometimes connotes expedition or speed in killing, or in ending suffering. "Edmund, I think, is gone, In pity of his misery, to *dispatch* His [Gloucester's] nighted life" (*Shak.*). "And the company shall stone them with stones, and *dispatch* them with their swords" (*Ezekiel* xxiii. 47). Oftentimes, however, it is merely a euphemism for any of the terms of this group when quick killing or a sudden end is implied. "Meanwhile, Hercules has (contrary to the usual belief that Seneca [the dramatist] murders all his victims in full view of the audience) *despatched* Lycus off-stage" (*T. S. Eliot*). **Execute** is the term for putting to death one who has been condemned to such a fate by a legal or military process, or sometimes by summary action of a group; as, to *execute* the convicted assassin by hanging.

kind, *n.* *Type, sort, nature, description, character, stripe, kidney.

kind, *adj.* **Kind, kindly, benign, benignant** agree in meaning having or exhibiting a nature that is gentle, considerate, and inclined to benevolent or beneficent actions. As here compared they are chiefly, but not exclusively, applied to persons and to their acts and utterances. **Kind** and **kindly** both imply possession of qualities appropriate to man as a rational, sensitive, and social being, such as interest in others' welfare, sympathy, humaneness, and the like. The two words are often used interchangeably without loss; as, a *kind* (or *kindly*) person. Nevertheless, especially in current usage, they tend to be distinguished, *kind* implying reference to a disposition to be sympathetic and helpful, and *kindly* to the expression of a benevolent, sympathetic, or helpful nature, mood, or impulse; thus, he has a *kind* (better than *kindly*) heart; he takes a *kindly* (not *kind*) interest in ambitious boys; be *kind* (not *kindly*) to animals; the *kindly* (better than *kind*) ministrations of a nurse; a severe but *kind* (or *kindly*, if the emphasis is on his acts rather than his nature) teacher; *kindly* words of advice. "The *kindest* man, The best-condition'd and unwearied spirit In doing courtesies" (*Shak.*). "Ring in the valiant man and free, The larger heart, the *kindlier* hand!" (*Tennyson*). **Benign** (see also FAVORABLE) and **benignant** stress mildness, serenity, and mercifulness more than do *kind* and *kindly;* they also often imply graciousness and therefore are more frequently applied to superiors than to equals, when they are used to describe persons, their acts, utterances, policies, or the like; as, a *benign* master; "The meek, *benign*, and lacerated face [of the crucified Jesus]" (*Wordsworth*); the *benign* rule of a benevolent despot; a *benignant* influence; "Strange peace and rest fell on me from the presence Of a *benignant* Spirit standing near" (*E. R. Sill*).

Ana. Benevolent, *charitable, humane, altruistic, philanthropic, humanitarian: sympathetic, warm, warmhearted, responsive, *tender, compassionate: clement, lenient, indulgent, merciful, *forbearing, tolerant: *amiable, good-natured, complaisant, obliging.

Ant. Unkind. — ***Con.*** Cruel, inhuman, *fierce, savage, fell: harsh, *rough: *grim, implacable, unrelenting, merciless.

kindle. Enkindle, ignite, fire, inflame, *light.

Ana. *Blaze, flame, flare, glow: *provoke, excite, stimulate: arouse, rouse, *stir: *incite, foment, instigate.

Ant. Smother, stifle.

kindly. Benign, benignant, *kind.

Ana. *Gracious, cordial, genial, affable, sociable: *amiable, good-natured, complaisant, obliging: friendly, neighborly (see AMICABLE): considerate, *thoughtful, attentive.

Ant. Unkindly: acrid (*of temper, attitudes, comments, etc.*). — ***Con.*** Malevolent, malign, *malicious, spiteful.

kindred. *Related, cognate, allied, affiliated.

Ant. Alien.

kingly. **Kingly, regal, royal, queenly, imperial, princely** come into comparison as meaning of, relating to, or befitting one who occupies a throne. **Kingly** (derived from Old English), **regal** (derived from Latin), and **royal** (derived from Old French) are often interchanged, especially when used in reference to a monarch who is called *king* (as, the *kingly, regal*, or *royal* power), but usage shows a preference for *kingly* when the reference is to the personal or ideal character of a king, to his feelings, disposition, aims, actions, or the like (as, *kingly* courtesy; *kingly* condescension; "Leave *kingly* backs to cope with *kingly* cares"—*Cowper*), for *regal* when the reference is to the king's office, or the state or pomp which accompanies the exercise of his powers (as, *regal* ceremonies; *regal* interchanges of courtesies; *regal* functions), and for *royal* when the reference is to persons or things associated with the king either as a person or as a monarch, but not necessarily involving magnificence or display (as, the *royal* family; *royal* rank; the *royal* residences; *royal* domains; a *royal* society is one under the patronage of the king or members of his family). Figuratively, *kingly* carries the strongest implication of dignity and nobility (as, *kingly* pride; *kingly* qualities); *regal*, of magnificence or majestic character (as, a *regal* feast; "*regal* trees"—*Lytton*); *royal*, of superlative excellence (as, a *royal* welcome; to have had a *royal* time; *royal* entertainment). **Queenly** is used in place of *kingly* when the reference is directly to a person who is the female sovereign (in place of a king) or is the consort of a king; as, *queenly* courtesy; *queenly* prerogatives. But when the reference is to the office, the family of the queen, or to anything to which *regal* and *royal* are normally applied, the latter adjectives are used without reference to the sex of the sovereign. **Imperial** suggests reference to a monarch who is called *emperor* or *empress;* as, His *Imperial* Majesty; an *imperial* court; the *imperial* power. In extended use, the term commonly implies a more awe-inspiring quality than *kingly* (as, *imperial* pride; *imperial* condescension), and more pomp and grandeur than *regal* or *royal* (as, *imperial* banquets; *imperial* palaces). **Princely** implies reference to one who is called a *prince* in any sense but especially to one who is so called as the monarch of a principality, or as the heir to a royal throne, or as a male member of the immediate royal family; as, "the representative of the *princely* power" (*S. Austin*); "Among the *princely* houses of Western Europe" (*Freeman*). In its extended use, *princely* often carries a strong implication of sumptuousness (as, "two *princely* temples, rich with painting and many-colored marble"—*Macaulay*), or of opulence or munificence (as, "he had been told to spend his *princely* allowance in a *princely* manner, and to return home with a gallery of masterpieces"—*E. Wharton*).

kinship. **Kinship, affinity, consanguinity, cognation, agnation, enation** are here compared only in their technical senses. All designate family relationship. **Kinship** is the most general, denoting relationship either by blood or by marriage; it also is the richest in connotations, usually suggesting closeness in feeling and in interests. **Affinity** refers to connection by marriage; **consanguinity,** to connection by blood. **Cognation** is equivalent to *consanguinity,* but is rarely used today; **agnation** implies relationship, either, as in Civil law, exclusively through males, or as in English and Scots law, through one's father; **enation** implies relationship on one's mother's side.

knack. Bent, turn, *gift, faculty, aptitude, genius, talent.
Ana. *Ability, capacity, capability: aptness, readiness, quickness (see corresponding adjectives at QUICK): facility, dexterity, ease, *readiness.
Ant. Ineptitude.

knit, *v.* *Weave, crochet, braid, plait, tat.
Ana. *Join, connect, link, unite.

knotty. Intricate, involved, complicated, *complex.

knowing. Alert, bright, smart, *intelligent, clever, quick-witted, brilliant.
Ana. *Shrewd, astute, perspicacious, sagacious: *watchful, vigilant, alert: discerning, observing *or* observant, perceiving *or* perceptive (see corresponding verbs at SEE).
Con. Obtuse, *dull, blunt: dense, crass, *stupid.

knowledge. Knowledge, science, learning, erudition, scholarship, information, lore, as here compared, agree in meaning that which is known or which can be known, usually by an individual but sometimes by human beings in general. **Knowledge** applies not only to any body of facts gathered by study, investigation, observation, or the like, but also to any body of ideas acquired by inference from such facts or accepted on good grounds as truths; as, his *knowledge* is both extensive and accurate; he has no special *knowledge* of conditions abroad. " 'Strength and bustle build up a firm. But judgment and *knowledge* are what keep it established' " (*Hardy*). "The inventor of the radio...had the advantage of accumulated *knowledge*" (*J. W. Krutch*). **Science** (see also ART, 3) was often in the past and is still occasionally employed as a close synonym of *knowledge;* as, "All this new *science* that men lere [teach]" (*Chaucer*). In current use it commonly applies only to the (or a) body of systematized knowledge dealing with facts gathered over a long period and by numerous persons as a result of observation and experiment, and with the general truths, or laws, derived by inference from such facts. The term usually connotes more exactness and more rigorous testing of conclusions than *knowledge* does, and therefore is often used to denote knowledge the certainty of which cannot be questioned. "An osteopath undertakes to be something more than a nurse or masseur, and the difference rests precisely in a claim to greater *science*" (*Justice Holmes*). "Perhaps all the *science* that is not at bottom physical *science* is only pretentious nescience" (*Shaw*). **Learning** specifically applies to knowledge gained by long and close study, not only in the schools or universities, but by individual research and investigation; it may be used of those who are engaged in the study of science, but it is more often employed in reference to those who devote themselves to the study of languages, literature, history, philosophy, or the like; as, "he is a man...of deep *learning*" (*Burney*); "*Learning* is the *knowledge* of that which is not generally known to others" (*Hazlitt*); "Jonson failed as a tragic dramatist...because his genius was for satiric comedy and because of the weight of pedantic *learning* with which he burdened his two tragic failures" (*T. S. Eliot*). **Erudition** carries a stronger implication of the possession of profound or recondite or bookish knowledge than does *learning,* but often the terms are employed as if they were equivalent in meaning; as, "I arrived at Oxford with a stock of *erudition,* that might have puzzled a doctor" (*Gibbon*); "it does not seem to me fitting...that one layman, with no special *erudition* in that subject, should publicly express his views" (*T. S. Eliot*). **Scholarship** implies the possession of the learning characteristic of the trained scholar; the term usually suggests mastery in detail of a given field of study or investigation, the exhibition of such qualities as accuracy and skill in carrying on research intended to extend knowledge in that field, and the display of powers of critical analysis in the interpretation of the material that is gathered; as, *scholarship* is essential to any person who proposes to write a history of any nation, period, or movement; "that this conception [of the relation between art and nature] is Aristotelian, even the essential Greek conception, is no testimony to Shakespeare's *scholarship*" (*H. Ellis*). **Information** may or may not apply to knowledge gained by haphazard methods, for the term carries no specific implication regarding the extent, character, or soundness of that knowledge. The word usually denotes a kind of knowledge that is gathered from other persons or from books and is accepted as truth; often, but not necessarily, with the implication that it has neither been confirmed nor verified; as, useless *information;* his sources of *information* are not always reliable. "I look with sorrow on the habit...of making a considerable part of the education of the place to turn on the art of serving up gobbets of prepared *information* in essays....It is the business of a university to...impart solid *knowledge*" (*F. Harrison*). "The theme-writing high-school student could scarcely be sent there [to Hawthorne's 'Scarlet Letter'] for *information* regarding the manners and dress and interiors of Puritan society" (*Cather*). "What we need [in understanding Dante's mind] is not *information* but *knowledge:* the first step to *knowledge* is to recognize the differences between his form of thought and feeling and ours" (*T. S. Eliot*). **Lore** is sometimes used in poetry in place of *learning,* but more often in current English it applies to a body of special or out-of-the-way knowledge pertaining to a particular subject (such as plant life, the fairies, the habits of birds, etc.) possessed by an individual or by a group, and traditional and anecdotal rather than scientific in its character; as, "the *lore* of bards and sages old" (*Shelley*); "Skill'd in legendary *lore*" (*Goldsmith*); sacred *lore;* folk*lore;* plant *lore.*
Ant. Ignorance.

L

labor *or* **labour,** *n.* **1** *Work, toil, travail, swink, drudgery, grind.

Ana. *Effort, exertion, pains, trouble: endeavor, striving, struggle (see under ATTEMPT, *v.*).

Con. *Rest, repose, relaxation, leisure, ease: recreation, diversion, amusement, entertainment (see under AMUSE): inactivity, idleness, inertness *or* inertia, passiveness (see corresponding adjectives at INACTIVE).

2 Travail, *childbirth, parturition, delivery, accouchement.

laborer. Workingman, workman, *worker, craftsman, handicraftsman, mechanic, artisan, operative, hand, roustabout.

labyrinth. Labyrinth, maze come into comparison when they mean an exceedingly tortuous path or course or a highly complicated arrangement of paths or courses (literal or figurative) which it is difficult or impossible to follow without a means of guidance. **Labyrinth** was originally applied to an enclosure of intricate design constructed by Daedalus for Minos, King of Crete, for confining the Minotaur, from which Theseus was able to escape because he was guided by a clew, or ball of thread, provided by Ariadne, the king's daughter. In its extended use, the term implies structural intricacy, the result of many divergences from a straight course or of many convolutions. It is therefore applied to the bony and membranous part of the internal ear, to portions of the cortex of the kidney, and to other anatomical structures manifesting a similar complexity, as well as to any highly complicated arrangement or design in which involved paths, lines, grooves, and the like, are resorted to for an artistic or utilitarian end; as, "arranged plantations, with...dry and pleasant walks and *labyrinths,* and artificial echoes" (*L. P. Smith*); by means of a *labyrinth* of channels, it was found possible to avoid the flooding of the lowlands. In purely figurative use, *labyrinth* often suggests almost hopeless involvement or extreme difficulty in escaping; as, "he was trying...to find his way through the...*labyrinth* of passion through which he was wandering" (*Wilde*). **Maze** suggests not confusing convolutions but a confusing and bewildering network: it implies so many possibilities or so many false leads that one is bewildered or constantly baffled or frustrated by finding oneself in a blind alley or at a dead end; as, the *maze* at Hampton Court; the older section of the city was a *maze* of streets; lost in the *mazes* of philosophy; "the *maze* of educative forces that have made the child what it is" (*H. Suzzallo*).

lack, *n.* **Lack, absence, privation, defect, want.** All of these words except *absence* often imply deficiency or a falling short, but in their abstract senses, in which they are here compared, they denote the fact or the state of being without something expressed or implied. Because of this dual and confusing use, **lack** usually requires qualification to express totality; as, he shows an entire *lack* of courtesy; complete *lack* of rest for three days. **Absence,** however, is unequivocal; it is therefore usually preferred in careful discourse. "Mark's inward discontent...not so much discontent as *absence* of content, for it was rather a spiritual emptiness" (*C. Mackenzie*). "Absolute liberty is *absence* of restraint" (*H. Adams*). **Privation** (as here compared: see also POVERTY) is chiefly in philosophical use; it is there employed in defining a word, a concept, or an idea expressing a negative state or quality in terms of its opposite, or positive, word, concept, or idea. *Privation* therefore suggests the absence of all the marks, attributes, or characters implied in the positive; as, cold is the *privation* of heat; darkness is the *privation* of light. **Defect,** like *lack,* sometimes connotes inadequacy: as here compared it (and, often, its derivative *defective*) implies the absence in something either of characters alien to its nature or of a quality or an element necessary to its completeness or perfection. "Either sex alone Is half itself, and in true marriage... each fulfills *Defect* in each" (*Tennyson*). "Be mine the privilege to supplement *defect* Give dumbness voice" (*Browning*). **Want** implies either the absence of something essential or indispensable or a deficiency in the supply; as, "For *want* of a nail the shoe is lost, for *want* of a shoe the horse is lost, for *want* of a horse the rider is lost" (*Herbert*); "The battle was over, and, but for *want* of fresh troops, the Afghans would have been wiped off the earth" (*Kipling*); "this *want* of foresight and care" (*Ch. Just. Taney*); "the poet's *want* of taste" (*Quiller-Couch*). *Want* also is applicable to a need that is felt or apprehended by the person or persons concerned and so often comes closer to *desire* or *wish* than to *need;* as, it is difficult to satisfy all his *wants;* he has few *wants.*

Ana. *Need, necessity, exigency: deficiency (see corresponding adjective DEFICIENT): exhaustion, impoverishment, draining, depletion (see corresponding verbs at DEPLETE).

Con. Sufficiency, adequacy, competence (see corresponding adjectives at SUFFICIENT): abundance, ampleness, copiousness, plentifulness, plenteousness *or* plenty (see corresponding adjectives at PLENTIFUL): *excess, superfluity, surplus.

lack, *v.* **Lack, want, need, require** are here compared as meaning to be without something, especially something essential or greatly to be desired. **Lack** may imply either an absence of that something or a shortage in the supply or amount; as, to *lack* a knowledge of French; the house *lacks* a back stairway; the army *lacked* tanks and airplanes as well as rifles; they are not *lacking* in food or comforts; "Good counsellors *lack* no clients" (*Shak.*); "Several establishments *lacked* tenants" (*Bennett*). **Want** frequently but not invariably adds to *lack* the implication of pressing desire or of urgent necessity. The sense here considered is not always clearly distinguishable from the sense (of *want*) as discriminated at DESIRE. For this reason, **need** is often preferred when a clear connotation of urgent necessity is desirable; thus, he cannot get the rest he *needs* [rather than *wants*]; "like an angry hive of bees That *want* their leader" (*Shak.*); the house *wants* painting; those children *want* manners. *Need* usually throws the emphasis on urgent necessity rather than on absence or shortage, though both implications are commonly found; as, that family *needs* food and clothing; the country *needs* the services and support of every citizen; the letter *needs* no reply, but it would be courteous to acknowledge it; "That woman *needs* a lesson, Gideon. She's a public nuisance" (*R. Macaulay*). **Require** (as here compared: see also DEMAND) differs from *need* usually in heightening the implication of urgent necessity (as, "Great acts *require* great means of enterprise"—*Milton;* "the Doctor...*required* a few days of complete rest"—*Dickens*), and sometimes, in suggesting the importunity of urgent desire or craving (as, "Surely it does not *require* a palace to be happy with Mary"—*Irving*).

Con. *Have, hold, possess, own, enjoy.

lackadaisical. Listless, spiritless, enervated, *languid, languishing, languorous.

Ana. *Indifferent, unconcerned, incurious: indolent, slothful, fainéant, *lazy: inert, *inactive, passive, supine, idle: *sentimental, romantic: enervated, emasculated (see UNNERVE).
Con. Energetic, strenuous, *vigorous, lusty: dynamic, live, *active.

laconic. Succinct, terse, *concise, summary, pithy, compendious.
Ana. Curt, brusque (see BLUFF): *brief, short.
Ant. Verbose. — *Con.* *Wordy, prolix, diffuse: loquacious, *talkative, voluble, garrulous.

lacuscular. Lacustrine, *aquatic, fluvial, fluviatile, marine, oceanic, thalassic, neritic, pelagic, abyssal, bathysmal, bathybic.

lacustrine, lacustrian. Lacuscular, *aquatic, fluvial, fluviatile, marine, oceanic, thalassic, neritic, pelagic, abyssal, bathysmal, bathybic.

lade, *v.* *Dip, bail, scoop, ladle, spoon, dish.

lading. Freight, cargo, *load, burden.

ladle, *v.* Scoop, spoon, dish, *dip, lade, bail.

lady. Woman, *female.

ladylike. Feminine, womanly, womanlike, *female, womanish, effeminate.
Ana. *Gentle, genteel: dainty, fastidious, finical, particular, *nice: fashionable, modish, smart, chic, *stylish: *decorous, proper, seemly, comme il faut, demure.

lag. Loiter, dawdle, dally, dillydally, *delay, procrastinate.
Ana. Slow, slacken, retard, *delay: tarry, linger, wait, *stay.
Con. Hurry, hasten, *speed, quicken, accelerate.

lager. *Beer, bock, ale, stout, porter.

laggard, *adj.* Dilatory, *slow, leisurely, deliberate.
Ana. Dawdling, dallying, dillydallying, loitering, delaying, procrastinating (see DELAY): *lethargic, sluggish, comatose: phlegmatic, apathetic, *impassive.
Ant. Prompt, quick. — *Con.* Alert, wide-awake, vigilant, *watchful: *fast, swift, rapid, fleet, speedy, expeditious.

lambent. Beaming, beamy, luminous, *bright, brilliant, radiant, lustrous, effulgent, refulgent, lucent.
Ana. Gleaming, glistening, shimmering, glimmering (see FLASH, *v.*).

lament, *v.* *Deplore, bewail, bemoan.
Ana. Weep, keen, wail, *cry: *grieve, mourn, sorrow.
Ant. Exult: rejoice.

lampoon, *n.* *Libel, skit, squib, pasquinade.

land, *v.* *Alight, light, perch, roost.
Ana. Arrive, *come: *reach, gain, achieve, attain.

landing field. *Airport, airdrome, air field, flying field.

lane. Byway, alley, alleyway, roadway, *road, street, highway, highroad, avenue, boulevard, terrace, drive, parkway, thoroughfare.

language. 1 Language, dialect, tongue, speech, idiom are here compared only as denoting a body or system of words and phrases used by a people, a nation or group of nations, or other considerable community. Among philologists, the distinctions in meaning of some of these terms are still a matter of controversy; it is not the purpose of this article to enter into those debates, but to indicate the meanings that these terms have acquired through usage. **Language** may be employed as a general term for any medium of communication whether it utilizes a body of words, or sounds, gestures, facial expressions, and the like; as, the inarticulate *language* of a baby. However, in the specific sense here considered, the term refers to a body of words that by long use (commonly over a widespread territory) has become the means whereby the ideas or feelings of the individual members of that community are communicated or expressed; specifically, the term suggests more or less fixity in meaning, in pronunciation, in methods of combining words or of making compounds, and the like; it usually, but not invariably, connotes the existence of a standard determined by the usage of the best writers and speakers; as, German is the *language* of Prussians, Bavarians, Saxons, Austrians, some Swiss, and various other peoples; dead *languages* such as Latin and ancient Greek. But *language* is also applied to a body of words and phrases that is peculiar to an art, a science, a profession, a class, and that, however well understood by others of the community, is not generally adopted by them; as, "in economic *language* the 'marginal saver' determines the price" (*J. A. Hobson*). **Dialect,** as here compared (see also DIALECT, 1), is purely a technical term used by philologists in place of *language* to denote specifically one of a number of languages which retain obvious signs of their origin from a common, or root, language, yet each of which is clearly distinguishable not only from the root language but from the other branches by marked differences and an identity of its own; as, Welsh, Irish, and Gaelic are Celtic *dialects;* the perennial controversy as to whether Scottish is a *language* or a *dialect. Tongue* and *speech,* in the sense here considered, both go back for their first use to the early Middle Ages, when by the vast majority of persons languages were recognized through hearing rather than through reading. **Tongue,** however, has not continuously denoted the spoken language. In fact, *tongue* differs from *language* chiefly in its being applicable to a dialect, a patois, an argot (for these terms, see DIALECT, 1) as well as to the fixed or standard form; as, "The *language* her [Sarah O. Jewett's] people speak to each other is a native *tongue.* No writer can invent it" (*Cather*); "There is no poet in any *tongue*—not even in Latin or Greek—who stands so firmly [as Dante] as a model for all poets" (*T. S. Eliot*); "They [immigrants to the United States] came to us speaking many *tongues*—but a single *language,* the universal *language* of human aspiration" (*F. D. Roosevelt*). On the other hand **speech,** with rare exceptions, always means spoken language, or tongue, or, as in modern technical use, the language (under consideration) as it is spoken; as, "People of a strange *speech*" (*Ezekiel* iii. 6); "There are at least two sounds in the Anglo-Saxon which are unknown in our present *speech*" (*W. D. Whitney*). **Idiom,** though a much later addition to the English language than *tongue* or *speech,* also suggests reference to a condition prevalent at the time of its origin (the Renaissance) when every country, sometimes every province or section of a country, had its own peculiar and distinctive tongue; as, "The histories of all our former wars are transmitted to us in our vernacular *idiom*" (*Addison*); "On the spot I read...the classics of the Tuscan *idiom*" (*Gibbon*). In current use, *idiom* applies to the private or peculiar language of a particular writer, class, literary school, or the like; as, "the eminently personal *idiom* of Swinburne" (*T. S. Eliot*); "The mediaeval poetic *idiom* came after a while to seem a jargon" (*Lowes*).
Ana. *Dialect, vernacular, patois, lingo, jargon, cant, argot, patter, slang.

2 Language, vocabulary, phraseology, phrasing, diction, style are associated rather than synonymous terms when they are used as meaning oral or written expression or a quality of such expression that is dependent on the variety, or arrangement, or expressiveness of words. **Language,** as here considered, may apply to any form of verbal expression with reference to the words employed. It may call attention to correctness or lack of correctness in the use of words, to their dignity or their vulgarity, to their fitness or lack of fitness, to their sonority or their stridency, or to any of the qualities which speech or writing may derive from the choice and arrangement of words; as, the "plain *language*" of Quakers; he avoided harsh *language* in dealing with his children; "*Language*, grave and majestic, but of vague and uncertain import" (*Macaulay*). "When I read Shakespeare I am struck with wonder That such trivial people should muse and thunder In such lovely *language*" (*D. H. Lawrence*). **Vocabulary,** when used in reference to verbal expression, calls attention only to the extent or variety of the writer's or speaker's stock of words or to the sources from which such a stock is derived; as, the range of his *vocabulary* of vituperation was unsurpassed; "Little has changed [in modern as distinguished from medieval discussion of fundamental problems] except the *vocabulary* and the method" (*H. Adams*); "In the *vocabulary* of the English Bible sixty per cent [of the words] are native" (*G. P. Marsh*); "people with a dignity of port, an amplitude of back, an emphasis of *vocabulary*" (*L. P. Smith*). **Phraseology** or **phrasing** is sometimes used in place of *vocabulary* when the reader's attention is called especially to its idiomatic or peculiar character (as, eccentricities of *phraseology* [or *phrasing*]), but in very precise use, *phraseology* in particular stresses the grouping (often the conventional grouping) of words as much as their choice; as, one can say in the *phraseology* of the sentimentalist that "one loves nature"; the *phraseology*, rather than the *vocabulary*, of Donne offers difficulty to the inexperienced reader; "Men, according to their habits and professions, have a *phraseology* of their own" (*Burke*); "the gaudiness and inane *phraseology* of many modern writers" (*Wordsworth*). **Diction** calls attention to the choice and arrangement of words with reference to their expression of ideas or emotions. The term is used commonly of the considered language of poetry, literary prose, oratory, or the like, and it usually, therefore, implies selection or arrangement with reference to such ends as impressiveness, elegance, and beauty of sound; as, "In the sure and flawless perfection of his [Milton's] rhythm and *diction* he is as admirable as Vergil or Dante" (*Arnold*); "He was in a high fever while he was writing, and the blood-and-thunder magazine *diction* he adopted did not calm him" (*Kipling*); "The Romantic movement in England destroyed the convention of a specialized poetic *diction*" (*Day Lewis*). In current use, *diction* often applies not only to this quality as shown in orations or public addresses, but to a vocal quality evident in delivery, as in acting, singing, or speaking, which implies effectiveness in elocution, correct pronunciation of words, and pleasant enunciation. Though this sense is often questioned, it is used by some good writers; as, "Notice...the *diction* of French acting. It is the sense and not the sentiment of the verse or prose that is savored by the actor and the audience" (*Brownell*). **Style** (especially, but not exclusively, *literary style*) is a more complex term than any of the preceding words: it is less fixed, not only in its meaning but also in its implications, owing to the fact that the nature and essence of style (in this sense) have long been disputed. Always, however, it denotes a mode or manner of expressing one's thoughts or emotions or imaginative conceptions in words, as distinct from or as distinguishable from the thoughts, emotions, etc., expressed. It is sometimes thought of as a structure and diction peculiar to an age or a literary type and found in each representative work of that time and type; as, the Renaissance epic *style* is based upon that of Vergil; a poem written in the *style* of the ode. It is now more often thought of as a manner of expression which in structure and diction involves artistry but is individual and characteristic of its author; as, "*Style*...is a peculiar recasting and heightening, under a certain condition of spiritual excitement, of what a man has to say, in such a manner as to add dignity and distinction to it" (*Arnold*); "What he believed in was *style*: that is to say, a certain absolute and unique manner of expressing a thing, in all its intensity and color" (*Pater*); "His [Addison's] *style*, with its free unaffected movement, its clear distinctness, its graceful transitions, its delicate harmonies, its appropriateness of tone..., what [is this] but the literary reflection of Addison himself?" (*J. R. Green*); "This then is *Style*. As technically manifested in literature it is the power to touch with ease, grace, precision, any note in the gamut of human thought or emotion" (*Quiller-Couch*).

languid. **Languid, languishing, languorous, lackadaisical, listless, spiritless, enervated** agree in meaning lacking in vim or energy or, when applied to things, the appearance of it. **Languid** usually implies an unwillingness or an inability to exert oneself owing to fatigue, exhaustion, or physical weakness; as, the long illness had left her *languid* and in drooping spirits; the intense heat made everyone too *languid* for play; "Archer was struck by something *languid* and inelastic in her attitude, and wondered if the deadly monotony of their lives had laid its weight on her also" (*E. Wharton*). **Languishing** has been much affected in its meaning, especially in its connotations, by its frequent application to ladies, to lovers, or to expressions and acts of love, and the like, in sentimental novels and poems, particularly of the eighteenth and nineteenth centuries. For this reason, the term now seldom suggests its once common implication of actual physical weakness, such as that which results from a long or severe illness; as, "He was now in so *languishing* a state...that...his death...seemed to be very near" (*Bp. Burnet*). Rather, it connotes either the appearance of delicacy or of indolence, especially of delicacy or indolence once associated with high breeding, or the appearance of faintness, as though one were swooning under the stress of emotion or longing; as, *languishing* Spanish beauties; a *languishing* gaze; a *languishing* embrace. **Languorous,** like *languishing*, now seldom implies debility arising from illness or disease (as, "To wile the length from *languorous* hours, and draw The sting from pain"—*Tennyson*), for it far more often carries a suggestion of languidness and delicacy acquired through soft living, through shrinking from exertion, or through sentimentalism or overindulgence in tender or amorous emotions; as, a *languorous* gait; *languorous* black eyes. "Miss Mitchell [in "Gone with the Wind"] sought out rich words with which to re-create the *languorous*, stilling beauty of the Old South" (*Springfield* [Mass.] *Republican*). **Lackadaisical,** on the other hand, has followed the reverse order in its change of meaning. Once the term carried the present meaning of *languishing* but with a stronger connotation of insipid sentimentality (as, "His [Byron's] utter contempt of all the affectations of literature, from the school-magisterial style to the *lackadaisical*"—*Scott*); it now far more often implies a carefree or indifferent attitude that either forbids exertion or makes for futile, piddling, or halfhearted and indolent efforts; as, "The sheep on the dike were half asleep and chewed *lackadaisically*" (*Atlantic Monthly*); "Our radio propaganda should also be working at full pressure, but there must be a great improvement upon the present *lackadaisical* outlook" (*Springfield* [Mass.] *Republican*). **Listless** may or may not imply physical weakness, but it almost invariably implies either a lack of interest in what is going on around one or in what one is doing, or a languid appearance that may be the result either of boredom or ennui or of fatigue or disease; as, a dull speech makes a *listless* audience; the child has grown thin, white, and *listless* within the past two months. "He was struck by her *listless* attitude: she sat there as if she had nothing else to do" (*E. Wharton*). **Spiritless** implies the loss or the absence of the animation or fire that gives life or dash to a person or to his words, acts, or the like; as, a *spiritless* performance of a play; "rendered *spiritless* by the ill-success of all their endeavours" (*Austen*). **Enervated** implies a destruction of qualities or powers essential to the vigorous exercise of the will and the intellect. Often, but not necessarily, it suggests the influence of luxury or of sloth, but it may imply the operation of other causes, even of those that in themselves are not evil but may have deleterious effects; as, "*enervated* lords...softly lolling in their chariots" (*Arbuthnot & Pope*); a race *enervated* by living so long under a line of benevolent despots; "The *enervated* and sickly habits of the literary class" (*Emerson*).

Ana. *Lethargic, sluggish, comatose, stuporous, torpid: phlegmatic, apathetic, *impassive: inert, *inactive, supine.

Ant. Vivacious: chipper.

languishing. *Languid, languorous, listless, lackadaisical, spiritless, enervated.

Ana. Weakened, enfeebled, debilitated (see WEAKEN): indolent, fainéant (see LAZY): inert, *inactive, supine: *sentimental, romantic: pining, longing, yearning (see LONG, *v.*).

Ant. Thriving, flourishing: unaffected. — *Con.* Robust, *healthy, sound, hale: *vigorous, energetic, lusty: *natural, artless, unsophisticated, naïve.

languor. *Lethargy, lassitude, stupor, torpor, torpidity.

Ana. Exhaustion, fatigue, weariness (see corresponding verbs at TIRE): ennui, doldrums, *tedium: depression, blues, dumps, vapors (see SADNESS).

Ant. Alacrity. — *Con.* *Celerity, legerity: quickness, promptness, readiness (see corresponding adjectives at QUICK): zest, gusto (see TASTE).

languorous. Languishing, *languid, listless, lackadaisical, spiritless, enervated.

Ana. Leisurely, laggard, *slow, dilatory: indolent, slothful, fainéant (see LAZY): passive, inert, *inactive, supine: relaxed, slack, lax, *loose: pampered, indulged (see INDULGE).

Ant. Vigorous (*of persons, moods, etc.*): strenuous (*of times, seasons, etc.*).

lank, lanky. Gaunt, rawboned, *lean, spare, angular, scrawny, skinny.

Ana. *Thin, slim, slender, slight: attenuated, extenuated (see THIN, *v.*).

Ant. Burly. — *Con.* Husky, brawny, *muscular, sinewy: plump, portly, rotund, chubby, *fleshy, stout.

lapse, *n.* **1** Slip, *error, mistake, blunder, faux pas, bull, howler, boner, bloomer, floater.

Ana. *Offense, sin, vice, crime: *fault, failing, frailty, foible: transgression, *breach, violation, trespass.

2 Relapse, backsliding, recidivation, recidivism. See under LAPSE, *v.*

Ana. *Deterioration, decline, declension, decadence, degeneration, devolution: retrograding *or* retrogradation, receding *or* recession (see corresponding verbs at RECEDE): retrogressiveness *or* retrogression, regressiveness *or* regression (see corresponding adjectives at BACKWARD).

Con. Advance, progress (see under ADVANCE, *v.*): *development, evolution.

lapse, *v.* **Lapse, relapse, backslide, recidivate** and their corresponding nouns, **lapse, relapse, backsliding, recidivation** and **recidivism** are comparable when they mean to fall back into a state or condition from which one has raised oneself or has been raised, or the act or state of one who has so fallen back. As distinguished from *decline, degenerate, deteriorate,* and the like, these verbs do not necessarily imply the reversion of a process or development, or the gradual losing and the inevitable loss of strength, power, influence, and the like, but they do distinctively imply a failure to continue without break a course of improvement and a return, often a quickly effected but not irreparable return, to the earlier bad or lower state or condition. Both *lapse* and *relapse* etymologically imply a sliding or slipping, but they are increasingly divergent in their applications and connotations. **Lapse** usually presupposes reformation in manners, morals, or habits, or the acceptance of a high standard of rectitude, accuracy, accomplishment, or the like. It may or may not imply culpability or weakness, for it often suggests merely a sudden failure of the memory, or the influence of habit or tradition, or the pressure of an overwhelming emotion; as, it is easy for the person who has acquired good manners by effort to *lapse* into old ways when he is not on guard; only when she was strongly moved did she *lapse* into the dialect she spoke in her youth; a *lapse* in accuracy; "he had been on the watch for a *lapse* from the straight path" (*Conrad*). When culpability is strongly implied, the word still, in comparison to the other terms in the group, often connotes extenuating circumstances; it is therefore the fitting choice when the context indicates such circumstances; as, he constantly fought his tendency to *lapse* into easy-going ways; the speaker argued that the democratic ideal is too high for men and that democracies ultimately *lapse* into oligarchies or autocracies. "In estimating a man's place in the scale of perfection...the moral judgment, not withholding condemnation of a particular *lapse*, may not condemn the man wholly for it" (*S. Alexander*). **Relapse** presupposes definite improvement or an advance, as toward health or toward a higher physical, moral, or intellectual state, and it implies a complete and often dangerous reversal of direction; thus, one whose improvement in a serious illness has been marked may be said to *relapse*, or suffer a *relapse*, when his condition becomes definitely worse; a reformed thief is said to *relapse* when he returns to his old life. "Augustus... saved the world from disintegration. Without him Rome must have lost her conquests one by one, and seen them *relapse* into barbarism" (*Buchan*). "The Arabs were once the continuators of the Greek tradition; they produced men of science. They have *relapsed*...into pre-scientific fatalism, with its attendant incuriosity and apathy" (*A. Huxley*). **Backslide** and **backsliding** also imply a reversal in direction of one who has been going forward but unlike *relapse*, which is in many ways their close synonym, they are restricted in their reference to moral and religious lapses. They therefore often suggest recreancy or apostasy and the abandonment of a faith or of principles once professed. "Turn, O *backsliding* children, saith the Lord" (*Jeremiah* iii. 14). "Did not I...*backslide* into intemperance and folly" (*Marryat*). **Recidivate** and **recidivation** are now rarely, if ever, used for *relapse* and *backslide* and *backsliding*, although in this use they were once common terms, especially in the seventeenth century. **Recidivism** occurs very frequently today, especially in the social sciences, but it implies a relapse or tendency to relapse, or the habit of relapsing, into criminal practices. It is used more often of former convicts than of reformed criminals, and therefore stresses reversion to a former state rather than a failure to continue in the direction of reformation; as, the statistics of *recidivism* among discharged prisoners are a matter of much concern to penologists.

Ana. Revert, *return: slip, *slide: deteriorate, degenerate, decline (see corresponding nouns at DETERIORATION): *descend: *recede, retrograde.

Con. Progress, *advance: develop, *mature.

larcener. Thief, robber, burglar. See under THEFT.

larceny. *Theft, robbery, burglary.

lard. Suet, tallow, *adipose, marrow.

large. **Large, big, great** agree in meaning above the average of its kind in magnitude, especially physical magnitude. **Large,** however, is preferred when the dimensions, or extent, or capacity, or quantity, or amount is being considered; as, a *large* lot; a *large* hall; a *large* basket; a *large* meal; a *large* allowance. **Big,** on the other hand, is preferred when the emphasis is on bulk, or mass, or weight, or volume; as, a *big* book; a *big* pile; the box is too *big* to carry; a *big* voice. A *large* man is by implication a man who is tall and broad; a *big* man (physically), one who is bulky and heavy. As applied to material objects, **great** has been practically displaced by *large* or *big*. Where *great* is used to denote physical magnitude, it now regularly connotes some impression (as of wonder, surprise, amusement, annoyance) associated with the size; as, a *large* (or *big*) dog; cf. a *great* dog (i.e., a dog whose size is imposing, terrifying, disconcerting, etc.); a *large* (or *big*) head; cf. "the *great* head that seemed so weighted down with thought and study" (*The Nation*); "their classical profiles...their *large* black eyes" (*Byron*); "[She] on the trembling man with *great* eyes gazed" (*W. Morris*). *Great* alone, in literary or good colloquial English, expresses degree; as, *great* kindness, haste; *great* heat. Figuratively, *great* suggests eminence, distinction, or supremacy; *large* suggests breadth, comprehensiveness, generosity; *big* carries over the implication of mass or bulk but often suggests impressiveness or importance rather than solidity or great worth; as, a *great* cathedral, symphony; a *great* general; *large* tolerance, discretion; "that *large* utterance of the early gods" (*Keats*); "I don't know any paper which takes a *larger* and more reasonable view of the war" (*H. Ellis*); the *big* men of the city; *big* talk. "There is something in [Daniel] Webster that reminds me of Victor Hugo. There is the same confusion of what is *big* with what is *great*" (*J. R. Lowell*).

Ana. Vast, immense, *enormous, huge, mammoth, colossal, gigantic: tremendous, prodigious, monumental, stupendous, *monstrous: inordinate, *excessive, exorbitant, extreme, immoderate, extravagant.

Ant. Small. — *Con.* Little, diminutive, tiny, wee, minute (see SMALL): slight, slender, slim, *thin.

largess *or* **largesse.** Boon, *gift, present, gratuity, favor, fairing.

Ana. Benefaction, *donation, contribution: grant, subvention (see APPROPRIATION).

lascivious. Lewd, *licentious, libertine, lustful, libidinous, lecherous, wanton.

Ana. *Immoral, unmoral, amoral: sensual, *carnal, fleshly, animal, animalistic: obscene, gross, *coarse.

Con. *Chaste, pure, modest, decent: virtuous, *moral.

lassitude. Languor, *lethargy, stupor, torpor, torpidity.

Ana. Exhaustion, weariness, fatigue (see corresponding verbs at TIRE): ennui, doldrums, *tedium: dumps, vapors, blues, depression (see SADNESS): impotence, powerlessness (see corresponding adjectives at POWERLESS).

Ant. Vigor. — *Con.* Energy, strength, might, force, *power.

last, *adj.* **Last, latest, final, terminal, concluding, eventual, ultimate, extreme** come into comparison when they mean following all the others, usually in time or order, but sometimes in importance. That is **last** which comes at the end of a series, especially of things of the same kind or class; the term usually implies that no more will follow or have followed (as, the *last* page of a book; their *last* child is now ten years of age; the *last* leaf on a tree), but it may imply that the thing so qualified is or was the most recent or is the closest or nearest with respect to the present or a given time or period (as, his *last* book; their *last* visit to us was in December). In this latter sense **latest** is usually preferred as less ambiguous; thus, "his *latest* book" is clearer than "his *last* book," since the latter wording might suggest the author's ensuing death; the *latest* (or *last*) train on Sunday leaves at 11.45; so, the *latest* (better than *last*) number of a current magazine; the *latest* (better than *last*) news is that all is well. That is **final** which definitely closes a series or process not only because it is the last in order of individuals or details (as, the *final* day of school; the *final* float in the procession; the *final* event on a program) but because it is decisive, conclusive, or the like (as, the judges' decision on all questions in this contest is *final;* the *final* answer to a question; a *final* decree of divorce; "I think he settles many questions...on which a *final* verdict is what we now want"—*FitzGerald*), or has the power of deciding or settling absolutely (as, "this court [the Supreme Court of the United States] is not the *final* authority concerning the laws of New York"—*Justice Holmes*). That is **terminal** which comes at the end of something and marks the limit of its extension, its growth, or its completion as a series or process; as, the *terminal* point of a railroad; the *terminal* bud of a plant; the *terminal* syllable of a word. That is **concluding** which brings something (such as a speech, a book, a program, a celebration) to an end or which marks its finish; as, the *concluding* address was delivered by the chairman; "As the *concluding* words... were uttered" (*Macaulay*). That is **eventual** which is bound to follow as the final effect of causes already in operation or of causes that will be operative if a given or understood contingency occurs; as, "The silent decay and *eventual* overthrow of her natural defences" (*Gladstone*); "It is his object to point out the necessity...for a deliberate and purposive art of eugenics, if we would prevent the *eventual* shipwreck of civilisation" (*H. Ellis*). That is **ultimate,** as here compared (see also ULTIMATE, 2), which is the last, final, or terminal event, element, or the like, in a series or process (as, "the *ultimate* extinction of Herculaneum in August, 79 A.D., was the work of Vesuvius"—*Lucas;* "the *ultimate* stage in a process of descent"—*H. Ellis*), or is the final outcome or end to which a person or thing is moving or working (as, the *ultimate* effect of a drug; "When I think of the earth's refrigeration, and the *ultimate* collapse of our Solar System"—*L. P. Smith*), or is the most remote as in time (either past or future time), or most important in scale of values (as, the *ultimate* effect of a war; that word comes into English from French, but its *ultimate* source is Sanskrit; "*ultimate* issues, primal springs"—*Kipling*). **Extreme** is now rarely synonymous with *last* except in the phrase *Extreme* Unction (i.e., the Sacrament administered to the dying): it comes close to *ultimate* in such phrases as "he has reached the *extreme* limit of his strength."

Ant. First.

last, *v.* Endure, *continue, abide, persist.

Ana. Survive, outlast, *outlive: remain, *stay.

Ant. Fleet.

lasting. **Lasting, permanent, perdurable, durable, stable, perpetual** come into comparison as meaning enduring for so long as to seem fixed or established. **Lasting** usually implies long continuance with no end in sight: in this sense, it may be equivalent to *everlasting* (as, "Who . . . sings His soul and body to their *lasting* rest"—*Shak.;* "to the great and *lasting* injury of the spiritual life"—*Inge*). More often, however, it does not imply endlessness, but rather a surprising capacity to continue indefinitely (as, "matter too soft a *lasting* mark to bear"—*Pope;* "The anger of slow, mild, loving people has a *lasting* quality that mere bad-tempered folk cannot understand"—*Deland*). **Permanent** applies chiefly to things which are not temporary, tentative, transitory, fluctuating, or the like (as other things of the same class may be), but which continue or are likely to continue indefinitely; as, a *permanent* position; a *permanent* arrangement; "the armed force of government was not *permanent* but occasional" (*Belloc*); "the stimulation of violent emotions may leave *permanent* traces on the mind" (*Inge*). **Perdurable** carries even a stronger implication than *lasting* often carries, of endlessness of existence, but the term is so rarely applied to anything thought of as eternal that it suggests endless or apparently endless existence from the point of view of human remembrance or human history; as, "Leaving a name *perdurable* on earth" (*Southey*); "Our literature is going to be our most *perdurable* claim on man's remembrance" (*Quiller-Couch*). **Durable** commonly implies power of resistance to destructive agencies; it usually suggests a capacity for lasting that exceeds that of other things of the same kind or sort; as, a *durable* pavement; *durable* color; "more *durable* than brass" (*Philip Francis*); "many writers have longed for *durable* renown" (*L. P. Smith*). **Stable** literally applies to that which is so firmly or solidly established that it cannot be moved or changed; the term therefore is applicable to things that are lasting or durable because they are deeply rooted, or infixed and not subject or likely to be subject to fluctuations; as, a *stable* foundation; a *stable* form of government; *stable* institutions; *stable* pronunciations; *stable* habits; "the *stable* earth and the changing day" (*G. Eliot*). **Perpetual** (as here compared: see also CONTINUAL) often suggests an approach to *eternal* in implying endlessness or a going on forever. However, it always clearly suggests a beginning in time and is, therefore, never applied to God, the Absolute, or the like. It differs from *permanent* chiefly in stressing an uninterrupted course and in being applied to anything thought of as consecutive or continuous rather than as being limited to a term; thus, one says a *permanent* (not *perpetual*) position; a *permanent* (not *perpetual*) settlement of a problem; *perpetual* (not *permanent*) motion; a *perpetual* (not *permanent*) calendar: so, "a *perpetual* embargo was the annihilation, and not the regulation of commerce" (*Ch. Just. Marshall*).

Ana. Enduring, abiding, persisting *or* persistent, continuing (see corresponding verbs at CONTINUE): *everlasting, endless, unceasing, never-ending: *continual, continuous, incessant, perennial: eternal, sempiternal (see INFINITE).

Ant. Fleeting. — *Con.* Fugitive, passing, evanescent, transitory, *transient, short-lived.

late. 1 *Tardy, behindhand, overdue.

Ana. Delayed, retarded, detained (see DELAY).

Ant. Early: punctual, prompt. — *Con.* Timely, *seasonable, opportune, well-timed.

2 Departed, deceased, defunct, *dead, lifeless, inanimate.

latent. **Latent, dormant, quiescent, potential, abeyant** (*or* **in abeyance**) agree in meaning not now manifesting its existence. **Latent** implies concealment and is applied to that which is present without showing itself; **dormant** usually suggests sleeping and is applied to that which is alive without manifesting activity; as, a *latent* talent; *latent* energy; a *dormant* plant or volcano. "The poet's gift of seeing the *latent* possibilities in everything he touched" (*Lowes*). "Which power can never be exercised by the people themselves, but must be placed in the hands of agents, or lie *dormant*" (*Ch. Just. Marshall*). **Quiescent** emphasizes the cessation of action rather than the presence of energy. "With the increase of their wealth . . . they sank into *quiescent* Tories" (*Meredith*). Sometimes it connotes immobility. "If only we could persuade ourselves to remain *quiescent* when we are happy!" (*Jefferies*). **Potential** is applied to that which does not now exist but which is bound to exist if the present process of coming into being is not arrested. "It [an infant] must from the very first be viewed seriously, as a *potential* adult" (*B. Russell*). **Abeyant** (more often, predicatively, **in abeyance**) always implies a suspension of activity or active existence. "In Mr. Brooke the hereditary strain of Puritan energy was clearly *in abeyance*" (*G. Eliot*). It usually connotes expectancy of revival. "Nothing seemed left . . . of . . . the former Lewis Raycie, save a lurking and *abeyant* fear of Mr. Raycie senior" (*E. Wharton*).

Ana. Hidden, concealed (see HIDE, *v.*): *inactive, inert, idle: unripe, unmatured, unfledged, *immature.

Ant. Patent. — *Con.* *Active, operative, live, dynamic: activated, vitalized, energized (see VITALIZE).

latest. Final, *last, terminal, concluding, eventual, ultimate, extreme.

Ant. Earliest.

lather, *n.* Suds, froth, *foam, spume, scum, yeast.

laud, *n.* *Hymn, psalm, canticle, antiphon, anthem, canon.

laud, *v.* Extol, eulogize, *praise, acclaim.

Ana. Magnify, aggrandize, *exalt: worship, adore, venerate, *revere, reverence: *commend, applaud, compliment.

Ant. Revile. — *Con.* *Decry, depreciate, disparage, belittle: censure, condemn, denounce, blame, *criticize, reprobate, reprehend: *execrate, curse, damn, anathematize, objurgate.

laughable. **Laughable, ludicrous, ridiculous, comic, comical, farcical, risible, droll, funny** come into comparison as meaning provoking or evoking laughter or mirth. **Laughable** is the general term for whatever is fit to provoke laughter; as, modern audiences do not find Shylock a *laughable* character; a *laughable* incident; "[Mrs. Kemble] would have contributed magnificent *laughable* touches . . . to any picture of her peculiarities" (*H. James*). **Ludicrous** applies to that which is laughable because of its absurdity, incongruity, or preposterousness; as, the *ludicrous* mistakes called schoolboy howlers; "[Louis XIII] had friendships, one after another, so violent as to be often *ludicrous*" (*Belloc*); "Some of the best public school teachers in the last century were hot-tempered men whose disciplinary performances were *ludicrous*" (*Inge*). **Ridiculous** applies to that which excites derision because of extreme absurdity, foolishness, contemptibility, or the like; as, "Good manners at the court are as *ridiculous* in the country as the behaviour of the country is most mockable at the court" (*Shak.*); "'Curates, mothers-in-law, British workmen, shopwalkers [are] all recognized as fair sport for the facetious . . . . But it's only the curate that bothers about trying not to be *ridiculous*'" (*C. Mackenzie*). In current English, *comic* and *comical* are becoming distinct in implications and in applications, although they are still to a certain extent interchangeable. **Comic** is usually the more dignified word applicable to anything that partakes of the spirit of comedy, especially of the literary form which aims to present life in a way that does not leave a painful impression and that does evoke smiles or laughter, especially thoughtful laughter, or amused reflection; as, "With minds easy, detached...a great deal of their theology—the amativeness of Zeus for example—must needs seem...*comic*" (*Quiller-Couch*); " 'I quite agree with Juke that it is *comic* to see poor little nonentities like Frank Potter caught in it [Christianity], tangled up in it, and trying to get free and carry on as though it wasn't there' " (*R. Macaulay*). **Comical** applies not so much to the character of that which induces laughter as to the impression it produces upon the observer; commonly, the term suggests unrestrained laughter as its effect. "The abrupt transition of her features from assured pride to *ludicrous* astonishment and alarm was *comical* enough to have sent into wild uncharitable laughter any creature less humane than Constance" (*Bennett*). **Farcical** is often used interchangeably with *comical*, but it is ordinarily the preferred term when that which creates amusement is, like farce (the dramatic form), dependent upon extravagance, nonsense, practical jokes, burlesque, or the like, for the effect it produces; as, " 'Boys are like monkeys...the gravest actors of *farcical* nonsense that the world possesses' " (*Meredith*). **Risible**, which is increasingly rare in this sense, applies only to that which evokes amusement of any sort or degree; as, *risible* manners; *risible* blunders in speech. **Droll** and **funny** usually impute oddity or strangeness to that which makes a thing risible or laughable, but *droll* ordinarily carries a stronger implication of unfamiliarity, quaintness, absurdity, or intentional (though often sly) humorousness (as, "Thackeray's names, though often *ludicrous*, are always happy, and often inimitably *droll*" —*Athenaeum*) and *funny* of queerness or curiousness (as, "the night mail set me down at Marwar Junction, where a *funny* little happy-go-lucky native-managed railway runs to Jodhpore"—*Kipling*). *Funny* is, however, the ordinary colloquial term interchangeable with any other word of the group. "The strangest of all was a portrait of Samuel Povey as an infant in arms. Sophia checked an impulse to laugh at it. But when Constance said: 'Isn't it *funny?*' she did allow herself to laugh" (*Bennett*).

Ana. Amusing, diverting, entertaining (see AMUSE): humorous, *witty, facetious, jocular, jocose.

Con. Solemn, *serious, grave: tedious, tiresome, wearisome, humdrum, *irksome: pathetic, poignant, touching, affecting, *moving, impressive.

lavish. *Profuse, prodigal, luxuriant, lush, exuberant.

Ana. *Liberal, bountiful, generous, munificent, handsome: sumptuous, opulent, *luxurious: *excessive, inordinate, extravagant.

Ant. Sparing. — *Con.* *Meager, scanty, scant: economical, frugal, thrifty (see SPARING): provident, prudent, discreet (see under PRUDENCE): *stingy, niggardly, parsimonious, penurious, miserly.

law. 1 Law, rule, regulation, precept, statute, ordinance, canon are often used interchangeably but with loss of precision. They all designate a principle laid down or accepted as governing conduct, action, or procedure. *Law, rule,* and *precept* are also used as collective nouns to denote a body of laws, rules, or precepts; as, to obey the *law;* to work by *rule;* to teach by *precept. Law* and *precept* are often used abstractly. "The world demanded peace and *law*, not liberties and privileges" (*Buchan*). "The poet's business is not with *precept*" (*Lowes*). **Law** primarily implies imposition by a sovereign authority and the obligation of obedience on the part of those governed. "There was no *law* save that of the strongest" (*Kipling*). In more restricted use, however, it implies a will to maintain peace and justice in the community or group governed and the expression of that will in concrete injunctions or prohibitions. Laws may be written or unwritten: when the latter, they indicate derivation from established custom; when the former, they commonly indicate enactment by a legislative body or power; as, the *laws* of New York State. "The Ten Commandments...were politically useless until an elaborate set of *laws*...had been provided to give effect to them" (*Shaw*). In extended use, *law* may be applied to any principle of guidance that forms part of a code accepted as binding; as, respect for the confidences of patients is a *law* in medical practice. **Rule**, in contrast with *law*, suggests closer relation to individual conduct and method, or a desire for order and discipline in the group. Sometimes it implies restriction, whether prescribed or self-imposed, for the sake of an immediate end, such as unity in action, uniformity in procedure, or conformity to a standard of practice; as, the *rules* of a game; the *rules* of a school; the *rules* of good writing. Sometimes *rule* does not imply prohibition, but suggests a positive way of thinking or acting in order to get desired or concrete results; as, the *rule* of three; a *rule* of thumb. **Regulation** often equals *rule*, but in discriminating use it connotes prescription by authority for the control or management of an organization or system; as, military *regulations; regulations* respecting interstate commerce; factory *regulations*. **Precept**, like *law*, usually implies generality and lack of detail in the statement and an authoritative origin; like *rule*, however, it implies closer reference to individual conduct than to government. "He really was the one child to whom the 'spare-the-rod' *precept* did not apply" (*Deland*). In modern use, *precept* is applied to that which is enjoined by teaching: it often suggests counsel or advice, and is commonly opposed in its abstract use to *practice* or *example*. "By *precept* and by practice he proclaimed the lofty solitude of the individual soul" (*H. Ellis*). *Statute, ordinance,* and *canon* all come under the description of *law*. A **statute** is a written law, formally enacted by a legislative body. An **ordinance**, in American usage, is a local law, especially one enacted by a municipal government. In strict British usage, it is a law that is not an act of Parliament. Historically, *ordinance* has been applied to laws promulgated without the assent of one of the three powers (the Crown, the House of Lords, the House of Commons) whose assent is necessary to such an act; at present it is applied to any law or regulation enacted by a lesser body than Parliament. A **canon**, in strict use, is a law of a church, binding upon all of its members. In extended use, *canon* is applied to such laws of ethics, of society, of criticism, and the like, as have the sanction of accepted authority and are enforced by one's moral, social, or artistic conscience. "Are we witnessing a violent reaction against accepted *canons* of decency in life?" (*Grandgent*).

Ana. Mandate, dictate, *command.

2 *Principle, axiom, fundamental, theorem.

Ana. Necessity, exigency (see NEED, *n.*).

Ant. Chance.

3 *Hypothesis, theory.

4 Statute, act, *bill.

lawful. Lawful, legal, legitimate, licit are synonyms only when they mean permitted, sanctioned, or recognized by law or the law. **Lawful** differs from all the others in implying a reference to law of any sort, such as divine law, natural law, or the law of the land, or such as civil law, common law, or canon law. Consequently, the term often comes close in meaning to *allowable* or *permissible* (as, "All things are *lawful* unto me, but all things are not expedient"—*1 Corinthians* vi. 12) or (now less often) to *justifiable* (as, "Tell me, which knave is *lawful* game, which not? Must great offenders, once escap'd the Crown, Like royal harts, be never more run down?"—*Pope;* "a *lawful* military operation"—*Macaulay*), or *rightful* (as, the *lawful* heir; a *lawful* prize; the *lawful* sovereign). **Legal** implies a reference to the law as it appears on the statute books or is administered in the courts; thus, the *lawful* heir is also the *legal* heir; the *lawful* owner of a piece of property is one whose *legal* right to it is certain; a money-lender is entitled only to *legal* interest (better than *lawful*, for *legal* suggests rates fixed by law for the state or nation) on his loans. *Legal* is used more often in the sense of sanctioned by law, or in conformity with the law, or not contrary to the law, than in the sense of allowable by the terms of the law; as, a *legal* marriage; the *legal* period for the payment of a debt; the capture of the neutral ship carrying contraband was held to be *legal;* the secretary of labor declared that sit-down strikes were not *lawful* (better than *legal*, which implies express recognition of this type of strike). **Legitimate** was originally applied to a child born of legally married parents: it was later also used to describe the person who had legal title to a throne, an inheritance, a property, or the like, especially when a dispute arose; as, the *legitimate* monarch; the *legitimate* heir; the *legitimate* owner. In current use these meanings prevail, but the adjective implies not merely recognition by law but recognition or acceptance by custom, tradition, or the proper authorities, logical admissibility, or the like; thus, a lie may be considered *legitimate* (not *legal* or *lawful*) if a patient's restoration to health depends on it; "Jane's mother was making indirect but perfectly *legitimate* inquiries into his prospects" (*M. Austin*); a *legitimate* conclusion from one's premises; the *legitimate* drama (that is, the historic and long-accepted form of drama in contrast especially with vaudeville and motion pictures). **Licit** usually implies strict conformity to the provisions of the law respecting the way in which something should be performed, carried on, executed, or the like: the term therefore is used especially of that which is regulated by law; thus, a *licit* marriage, from the point of view of canon law, is one in which all prerequisites and all conditions attached to the performance of the ceremony have been attended to; *licit* liquor traffic is such traffic as obeys strictly the terms of the law; since dealings in the stock market have come under the control of the government, many deals once regarded as *lawful* are no longer *licit*.

Ana. Rightful, *due, condign: allowed *or* allowable, permitted *or* permissible (see corresponding verbs at LET): justified *or* justifiable, warranted *or* warrantable (see corresponding verbs at JUSTIFY).

Ant. Unlawful. — ***Con.*** Iniquitous, nefarious, flagitious (see VICIOUS).

lawlessness. *Anarchy, chaos.

Ana. *Discord, strife, dissension, contention, conflict, variance: *confusion, disorder.

Ant. Discipline: order.

lawsuit. *Suit, action, cause, case.

lawyer. Lawyer, counselor, barrister, counsel, advocate, attorney, solicitor, proctor, procurator. Lawyer is the general term designating any person versed in the principles of law and authorized to practice law in the courts or to serve clients in the capacity of legal agent or adviser. *Counselor*, *barrister*, *counsel*, and *advocate* name a lawyer who has acquired the right to plead causes in open court or whose specialty is conducting and arguing court cases. **Counselor** (more fully, **counselor at law**) is the usual designation in the United States for a lawyer who accepts court cases and gives advice on legal problems. The corresponding British term is **barrister,** with, however, special emphasis on court pleading. **Counsel** is used in the United States as the equivalent of *counselor;* it (but not *counselor*) is also used collectively; as, a brilliant array of *counsel*. The term is now used in England chiefly in "King's *Counsel*" (*abbr. K.C.*), formerly the title of a barrister appointed as counsel to the crown on nomination of the lord chancellor, but now the title of a barrister called to the rank of leader. **Advocate** is in its implications the equivalent of *barrister* and *counselor*, but it is used as a designation only in admiralty and in countries in which the legal system is based on Roman law, such as Scotland and France (Fr. *avocat*). *Attorney*, *solicitor*, *proctor*, *procurator* are applied chiefly to a lawyer who serves as a legal agent for clients, transacting their business in specific courts such as probate court. Other powers vary with the law of the state or country. **Attorney** (more fully, **attorney at law**) is now often used in the United States as equivalent to *lawyer*. Strictly, however, it names a legal agent who acts for a client, as in conveying property, settling wills, or defending or prosecuting a case in court; as, the *attorney* for the executors of the will; the State's *attorney*. In England, the term *attorney* has been supplanted by **solicitor,** with, however, emphasis on the transaction of legal business for a client and the preparation of cases for trial. A solicitor may conduct cases only in a few minor courts. **Proctor,** once restricted in application to an attorney practicing in ecclesiastical and admiralty courts, is now in England technically the equivalent of *solicitor*. Actually, however, it is limited as a designation to practitioners in probate and, sometimes in America as well as England, to practitioners in admiralty courts. **Procurator** is to *advocate*, in countries whose legal system is based on Roman law (Fr. *procureur*), as *solicitor* is to *barrister* in England. It is also used of an attorney authorized to practice in courts of canon law.

lax. 1 Relaxed, *loose, slack.

Ana. *Limp, loppy, flabby, flaccid.

Ant. Rigid (sense 2). — ***Con.*** *Firm, solid, hard: tense, taut, *tight: *elastic, resilient, springy.

2 Slack, remiss, *negligent, neglectful.

Ana. *Careless, heedless, thoughtless: *indifferent, unconcerned: *forgetful, unmindful, oblivious.

Ant. Strict, stringent. — ***Con.*** *Severe, stern, austere: *rigid, rigorous: strait, *narrow: conscientious, scrupulous, honest, *upright.

laxative. *Physic, aperient, purgative, cathartic, purge.

lay, *adj.* Secular, temporal, *profane.

Con. Ecclesiastical, clerical (see corresponding nouns at CLERIC): professional (see corresponding noun at TRADE): spiritual, religious, sacred (see HOLY).

lay, *v.* *Direct, aim, point, level, train.

lazy. Lazy, indolent, slothful, fainéant are here compared chiefly as applied to persons, their powers, movements, and the like, but also in some degree to things. All agree in meaning not easily aroused to action or activity. **Lazy** (opposed to *industrious*), especially when applied to persons, suggests a disinclination or aversion to effort or work and usually connotes idleness or dawdling, even when one is supposedly at work; the term is commonly derogatory; as, "Rubbing their sleepy eyes with *lazy* wrists" (*Keats*); "A *lazy* slouching boy, with...big feet trailing *lazily* one after the other, and large *lazy* hands, dawdling from out the tight sleeves" (*Thackeray*); "Una, now twenty-three, grandly beautiful, alternately *lazy* and amazingly energetic" (*R. Macaulay*). **Indolent** (opposed to *energetic*) implies a habitual love of ease and a settled dislike of movement or activity; as,

"The stretching, *indolent* ease that the flesh and the spirit of this creature invariably seemed to move with" (*Wister*); "We were too *lazy*, we were too negligent. We passed our *indolent* days leaving everything to somebody else" (*H. G. Wells*). **Slothful** (opposed to *diligent*) suggests the temper or indolence of one who is inactive when he knows he should be active or who moves or acts with excessive slowness when speed is essential; as, "As the door turneth upon his hinges, so doth the *slothful* upon his bed" (*Proverbs* xxvi. 14); "Be not *slothful*, but followers of them who through faith and patience inherit the promises" (*Hebrews* vi. 12); "You shall not find Patrick Charteris *slothful* in a matter of this importance" (*Scott*). **Fainéant** (the earliest English use of which was in allusion to the Merovingian kings, from the French phrase *rois fainéants*) was a popular term among good writers in the eighteenth and early nineteenth centuries but now occurs infrequently except in the original use: it implies both a slothful temper and a disposition to remain idle in spite of pressure or urgency; as, "the *faineant* aristocrat and apathetic dullard" (*M. Pattison*).

Ana. Inert, idle, *inactive, supine, passive: torpid, comatose, sluggish, *lethargic: *languid, languorous, lackadaisical, listless: slack, remiss, lax, *negligent, neglectful.

lead, *v.* *Guide, pilot, engineer, steer.

Ana. *Conduct, direct, manage, control: *set, fix, establish: *command, order, direct: *induce, persuade, prevail on *or* upon.

Ant. Follow. — ***Con.*** Mislead, delude, *deceive: drive, impel (see MOVE, *v.*): *force, compel, coerce, constrain, oblige.

leader. Head, *chief, chieftain, commander, captain, master.

Ant. Follower. — ***Con.*** Disciple, adherent, henchman, satellite, partisan (see FOLLOWER).

leading, *adj.* *Chief, principal, main, foremost, capital.

Ana. Governing, ruling (see GOVERN): conducting, directing, managing, controlling (see CONDUCT, *v.*): prominent, outstanding (see NOTICEABLE): eminent, distinguished (see FAMOUS): pre-eminent, *supreme, superlative.

Ant. Subordinate.

league. *Alliance, coalition, fusion, confederacy, confederation, federation.

leal. Loyal, true, *faithful, constant, stanch, steadfast, resolute.

Ant. False.

lean, *v.* *Slant, slope, incline.

Ana. Bend, *curve: *turn, deflect, divert, sheer: *tip, tilt, cant, careen, list, heel.

lean, *adj.* **Lean, spare, lank, lanky, gaunt, rawboned, angular, scrawny** (*or* **scranny**), **skinny** agree in meaning thin because of absence of superfluous flesh. **Lean** stresses the lack of fat and therefore of curving contours; as, "*lean* as a greyhound" (*Thackeray*); "a small, *lean*, wiry man With sunk cheeks weathered to a tan" (*Masefield*). **Spare** often suggests abstemiousness or sinewy strength; as, "He had the *spare* form...which became a student" (*G. Eliot*); "he had the *spare*, alert, and jaunty figure that one often finds in army men" (*T. Wolfe*). **Lank** suggests tallness or length as well as leanness; oftentimes also, it implies wasting; as, "Thou art long, and *lank*, and brown" (*Coleridge*); "Meager and *lank* with fasting grown, and nothing left but skin and bone" (*Swift*). **Lanky** adds the suggestions of awkwardness and loose-jointedness; as, a *lanky* youth, all arms and legs. **Gaunt** stresses want of sufficient flesh to conceal the bones; it often connotes overwork or undernourishment. "Her bony visage—*gaunt* and deadly wan" (*Wordsworth*). **Rawboned** often equals *gaunt*, but it is applied particularly to persons of large, ungainly frame and it seldom implies undernourishment; as, "a long, gawky, *rawboned* Yorkshireman" (*Kipling*). **Angular** implies not only absence of curves, but jerkiness or stiffness in movement; as, "Sudden retirement of the *angular* female in oxydated bombazine" (*Holmes*). **Scrawny** (*or* **scranny**) and **skinny** imply extreme thinness without any suggestion of awkwardness, but with a connotation of deficiency of vitality. *Scrawny* is common in the United States, but *scranny* is dialectal in England and in Scotland; as, a *scrawny* dog; *skinny* children.

Ana. Slender, slim, *thin, slight: cadaverous, wasted, pinched, *haggard.

Ant. Fleshy. — ***Con.*** Brawny, *muscular, sinewy, burly, husky: stout, *strong, sturdy, stalwart: plump, portly, rotund, fat, obese, corpulent (see FLESHY).

leaning, *n.* **Leaning, propensity, proclivity, penchant, flair** come into comparison when they mean a strong instinct or liking for something (sometimes someone) that drives or leads one to it. One has a **leaning** *to* or *toward* something when one definitely inclines to attachment to it (as a church, a party, a school of philosophy, etc.) or to follow it as a pursuit, a profession, a course, or the like. *Leaning*, however, indicates only the direction in which one is going or is pulled by the force of attraction; it carries no implication of one's final choice; as, "the king was suspected by many of a *leaning* towards Rome" (*Macaulay*); he had a *leaning* toward the law, but his father urged him to study medicine; he found himself at 21 without a *leaning* toward any particular political party. One has a **propensity** *to, toward* or *for* something when one has an innate or inherent, and often, uncontrollable, longing for it or is driven to it by a natural appetite; as, to study the *propensities* of a group of children; a *propensity* to drink; "such vehement *propensities* as drove Romeo, Antony, Coriolanus, to their doom" (*Bradley*); "the normal romanticism of the human spirit, its *propensity* for fiction, for wonder, adventure" (*Babbitt*). "That *propensity* to caricature which tempts clever writers...to transform into objects of derision the venerated Great" (*L. P. Smith*). One has a **proclivity** *to* or *towards* something or *to do* something when one is prone to it not only by natural inclination but also by habitual indulgence in it or by the peculiarities of one's constitution or temperament; as, kleptomania is a *proclivity* to steal; to curb a *proclivity* to lying. *Proclivity* often implies a tendency toward evil; when it is used without this implication, it still implies a stronger and less controllable urge than any other of the words here considered. "It [the American national genius] is nourished and sustained by ancient traditions and strong racial *proclivities*" (*S. P. Sherman*). One has a **penchant** *for* (occasionally *to* or *to do*) something (or someone), when the latter possesses an irresistible attraction for one or when one has a decided taste for it. "I own I have too strong a *penchant* to the building of hypotheses" (*Franklin*). "She could manage him as she pleased, provided she never let him see her *penchant* for Count Altenberg" (*Edgeworth*). "Never was there so grand a *penchant* for the triste" (*Lytton*). One has a **flair** *for* something when one has an instinct for it comparable to that of a hound on the scent and is drawn or led to it even when it is not easily discoverable or is actually out of sight; as, reporters with a *flair* for news. "That marvellous *flair* [of Leonardo Da Vinci] for detecting vital mechanism in every field" (*H. Ellis*). Often, especially in extended use, *flair* implies acumen or an innate power of discernment and the ability to distinguish the genuine from the counterfeit, the valuable from the valueless, and the like; as, a collector with a *flair* for the genuine antique. "As an editor he had superlative courage, and a *flair* for new writers" (*A. Repplier*). The use of *flair* in the sense of *bent* or *aptitude* or *talent* is now common, but is widely regarded as a misuse of the word; as, she hasn't a *flair* for writing.

Ana. Bias, *predilection, partiality, prepossession, prejudice: inclining *or* inclination, predisposition (see corresponding verbs at INCLINE): bent, turn, aptitude, faculty, *gift.

Ant. Distaste. — *Con.* *Antipathy, aversion: repugnance, abhorrence, repellency *or* repulsion (see corresponding adjectives at REPUGNANT).

learn. Ascertain, *discover, determine, unearth.

learned. Learned, scholarly, erudite, polymathic come into comparison as meaning possessing or manifesting unusually wide and deep knowledge. **Learned** implies the possession of knowledge gained by study and research: in current use, it implies far wider and deeper knowledge than do *educated, cultivated, cultured*, and the like, and is usually applied to those who are the most conspicuous in their class or profession for learning, to associations composed of such men, to books or articles written by them, to periodicals edited by them or publishing articles by them, and the like; as, the *learned* professions; *learned* societies; a *learned* clergyman; *learned* journals. **Scholarly** also implies great learning, but it is applied particularly to persons or to the utterances, ideas, etc., of persons who have attained mastery in a field of study or investigation, who have to a greater or lesser extent advanced knowledge in that field, and who have exhibited consistently high standards in the appraisal of their own and others' discoveries: often, more narrowly, the term implies great care for accuracy or exactness; as, a *scholarly* study of the causes of the war; *scholarly* pursuits. **Erudite,** though often employed as an equivalent of *learned* or *scholarly*, usually implies, in very precise use, a love of learning for its own sake, a taste for that which is out-of-the-way or remote from the interests of the average well-read man, and often, an inordinately wide range of knowledge; as, "the point of view of a profound and *erudite* student, with a deep belief in the efficacy of useless knowledge" (*A. C. Benson*); "That excellent critic, the late Mr. Walkley, was often spoken of as *erudite*, because his charming quotations gave so many readers a feeling of having to do with a man who had all literature at his command" (*C. E. Montague*). **Polymathic,** a rare word, implies wide-ranging encyclopedic knowledge rather than accurate and extensive knowledge within the limits of a given field. "It is sad to think that the day of the great *polymathic* student is at an end; that we may, perhaps, never again see a Scaliger, a Haller, or a Humboldt—men who took the whole field of knowledge for their domain and viewed it as from a pinnacle" (*Osler*).

Ana. Cultivated, cultured (see corresponding nouns at CULTURE): *pedantic, academic, scholastic, bookish: *recondite, abstruse, esoteric.

Con. Illiterate, unlettered, uneducated, unlearned, untutored, *ignorant.

learning. Erudition, scholarship, *knowledge, science, information, lore.

Ana. *Culture, cultivation, breeding, refinement: enlightenment (see corresponding verb at ILLUMINATE): letters, the humanities, *literature, belles-lettres.

lease, *v.* Let, charter, *hire, rent.

leave, *n.* *Permission, sufferance.

Ana. Consenting *or* consent, assenting *or* assent (see corresponding verbs at ASSENT): sanctioning *or* sanction, endorsement, approval (see corresponding verbs at APPROVE): authorization (see corresponding verb at AUTHORIZE).

Con. Refusing *or* refusal, rejecting *or* rejection (see corresponding verbs at DECLINE): forbidding *or* forbiddance, prohibition, interdiction (see corresponding verbs at FORBID).

leave, *v.* **1** *Relinquish, resign, surrender, abandon, yield, cede, waive.

Ana. Forsake, *abandon, desert: *forgo, forbear, sacrifice, abnegate, eschew: *neglect, ignore, forget, omit: *grant, concede, vouchsafe: relegate, *commit, confide, entrust.

2 Depart, quit, *go, withdraw, retire, scram, clear out.

Ana. *Escape, flee, fly, abscond, decamp.

Con. *Come, arrive: *appear, emerge, loom.

3 *Let, allow, permit, suffer.

leaven. *Infuse, imbue, inoculate, ingrain, suffuse.

Ana. Temper, qualify, attemper, *moderate: *inform, animate, inspire: pervade, *permeate, impregnate, saturate: vivify, enliven, *quicken.

leavings. Remains, *remainder, residue, residuum, relics, rest, balance, remnant.

Ana. Fragments, pieces, portions (see singular nouns at PART): discardings *or* discards, scrappings *or* scraps, junkings *or* junk (see corresponding verbs at DISCARD).

lecherous. Libidinous, lascivious, lustful, lewd, wanton, *licentious, libertine.

Ana. Dissolute, *abandoned, reprobate, profligate: degenerate, corrupt (see VICIOUS).

lecture. Address, *speech, oration, harangue, allocution, prelection, talk, sermon, homily.

leech. *Parasite, sponge, sycophant, toady, lickspit, hanger-on, favorite.

left, *adj.* Radical, *liberal, progressive, advanced.

Ant. Right.

legal. Legitimate, licit, *lawful.

Ant. Illegal.

legal tender. *Money, cash, currency, specie, coin, coinage.

legate. *Ambassador, nuncio, internuncio, minister, envoy.

legend. *Myth, saga.

legendary. 1 *Traditional.

Ana. *Doubtful, dubious, questionable: imagined, fancied (see THINK): invented, created (see INVENT).

Ant. Historical. — *Con.* Actual, *real, true: genuine, veritable, bona fide, *authentic.

2 Mythical, apocryphal, fabulous, *fictitious.

Ana., Ant., & Con. See those at LEGENDARY, 1.

legerity. *Celerity, alacrity.

Ana. Nimbleness, agility, briskness, spryness (see corresponding adjectives at AGILE): swiftness, fleetness, rapidity (see corresponding adjectives at FAST): dexterity, ease, *readiness, facility: dispatch, expedition, speed (see HASTE).

Ant. Deliberateness: sluggishness.

legion. Host, army, *multitude.

legitimate. Legal, *lawful, licit.

Ana. Justified *or* justifiable, warranted *or* warrantable (see corresponding verbs at JUSTIFY): *valid, sound, cogent: recognized, acknowledged (see ACKNOWLEDGE): customary, *usual: *regular, normal, typical, natural.

Ant. Illegitimate: arbitrary (*powers, means, etc.*).

leisure. Relaxation, *rest, repose, ease, comfort.

Ant. Toil. — *Con.* *Work, labor, travail, swink, grind, drudgery.

leisurely. Deliberate, *slow, dilatory, laggard.

Ana. Relaxed, slack, lax (see LOOSE): slackened, retarded, delayed (see DELAY): easy, *comfortable, restful, reposeful.

Ant. Hurried: abrupt. — *Con.* Hasty, speedy, quick, *fast, rapid: *precipitate, headlong, impetuous.

leitmotiv *or* **leitmotif.** Motive, theme, *subject, matter, subject matter, argument, topic, text.

lengthen. *Extend, elongate, prolong, protract.

Ana. *Increase, augment: *expand, amplify, distend.

Ant. Shorten. — *Con.* Abridge, abbreviate, curtail (see SHORTEN).

leniency, lenience. Clemency, mercifulness, forbearance, tolerance, indulgence. See under FORBEARING.

Ana. Lenity, clemency, *mercy, charity, grace: kindliness, benignity, benignancy, kindness (see corresponding adjectives at KIND): compassionateness, tenderness (see corresponding adjectives at TENDER).

lenient. 1 *Soft, gentle, mild, bland, balmy.

Ana. Assuaging, alleviating, relieving (see RELIEVE): emollient, demulcent (see corresponding nouns at BALM): grateful, agreeable, welcome, gratifying, pleasing, *pleasant.

Ant. Caustic (*in literal and figurative senses*). — *Con.* Harsh, *rough.

2 Indulgent, merciful, clement, *forbearing, tolerant.

Ana. Forgiving, excusing, condoning, pardoning (see EXCUSE, *v.*): kindly, benign, benignant (see KIND): compassionate, *tender: indulging, pampering, humoring, spoiling, mollycoddling (see INDULGE): lax (see NEGLIGENT).

Ant. Stern: exacting. — *Con.* *Rigid, rigorous, stringent: *severe, austere.

lenity. Clemency, *mercy, charity, grace.

Ana. Leniency, indulgence, clemency, mercifulness, forbearance, tolerance (see under FORBEARING): benignity, benignancy, kindliness, kindness (see corresponding adjectives at KIND): compassionateness *or* compassion, tenderness (see corresponding adjectives at TENDER): benevolence, humaneness, charitableness (see corresponding adjectives at CHARITABLE): laxity (see corresponding adjective at NEGLIGENT).

Ant. Severity. — *Con.* Strictness, rigorousness, rigidity, stringency (see corresponding adjectives at RIGID): sternness, austerity (see corresponding adjectives at SEVERE).

leprechaun. *Fairy, faery, fay, elf, sprite, pixy, gnome, dwarf, goblin, brownie, puck, nix, shee, banshee.

less, *adj.* **Less, lesser, smaller, fewer** approach each other in meaning but are not synonyms and are rarely interchangeable. **Less,** the comparative of *little,* means not as much, especially in degree, value, or amount: its opposite is usually *more;* it applies chiefly to collective nouns or nouns denoting a mass or abstract whole; as, the moon yields *less* light than the sun; John has *less* money than James; please make *less* noise; humility has *less* appeal to men of today than other virtues; books whose value is *less* than half the value of this one. **Lesser,** a word formed by adding the comparative suffix *-er* to the comparative form *less,* means not as great, as important, or as significant as that with which the thing so qualified is compared and implies opposition to *greater* or *major;* as, "God made...the *lesser* light to rule the night" (*Genesis* i. 16); James is a *lesser* person than John in the public estimation; humility is not, in Christian ethics, regarded as a *lesser* virtue; "*lesser* breaches of the law" (*Locke*). In the biological sciences, especially in the names of species, *lesser* implies that the species so designated is distinguished from a very similar one carrying the same name only by its comparative smallness of size; as, the *lesser* celandine; the *lesser* snipe. **Smaller,** the comparative of *small,* means not as large as that with which the thing so qualified is compared in size, dimensions, quantity, or the like; as, the *smaller* of two rooms; give her the *smaller* table for it will take up *less* room; she likes *less* sugar (or a *smaller* quantity of sugar) for her tea than you are giving her. **Fewer,** the comparative of *few,* means not as many and implies a difference in number of individuals or units; the term therefore always modifies a plural noun; as, he has *fewer* pupils than he had last year; give her *fewer* lumps of sugar; no *fewer* [persons] than fifty were present.

Ant. More.

lessen. *Decrease, diminish, reduce, abate, dwindle.

Ana. *Shorten, curtail, retrench, abridge, abbreviate: shrink, *contract: lighten, mitigate, alleviate (see RELIEVE): *thin, dilute, attenuate.

lesser. Smaller, *less, fewer.

Ant. Major.

let. 1 Lease, rent, *hire, charter.

2 Let, allow, permit, suffer, leave agree in denoting to refrain from preventing, or to fail to prevent, or to indicate an intention not to prevent. *Let, allow, permit,* though frequently used with little distinction of meaning, are capable of careful discrimination. **Let** is the most informal; it is always followed by an expressed or elliptical complementary infinitive, whereas *allow* and *permit* may take an object noun of action; as, her mother wouldn't *let* her go; she didn't go because her mother wouldn't *let* her; we do not *allow* (or *permit*) gambling. Sometimes *let* implies failure to prevent through awkwardness, inadvertence, negligence, inaction, etc.; as, the third baseman *let* the ball roll between his feet; "this dismal sketch of the future of countries that *let* themselves become dependent on the labor of other countries" (*Shaw*); and sometimes it implies failure to prevent through lack of power or authority to do so; as, Are you going to *let* him insult you like that? **Allow** and **permit** imply power or authority to prohibit or prevent if that had been deemed the better alternative. But *allow* may imply little more than forbearance of prohibition, whereas *permit* implies express signification of willingness or acquiescence; as, nothing is *permitted,* everything is *allowed;* the sentinel *allowed* the strangers to advance several paces before he stopped them; the sentinel *permitted* the strangers to pass when they had given the countersign. To **suffer** (now somewhat bookish in this sense) is often a mere synonym for *allow* in the narrowest implication of that word; as, "*Suffer* little children to come unto me" (*Luke* xviii. 16); but it may imply indifference or reluctance; as, "The eagle *suffers* little birds to sing" (*Shak.*); "Why do ye not rather *suffer* yourselves to be defrauded?" (*1 Corinthians* vi. 7). **Leave** (as here compared: see also GO, 1; RELINQUISH) may be used with the implication of letting, allowing, or permitting, only when the object as naming the person affected is followed by an infinitive in the active voice, or as naming the thing permitted is followed by an infinitive in the passive voice. In such use, *leave* always carries a comparatively stronger implication of noninterference: often, it also suggests the departure of the person who might interfere; as, to *leave* the young people to follow their own devices; to *leave* the choice of games to be settled by the guests; the defendant's attorney *left* him free to tell his story as he wished; "We must *leave* the children to settle their affairs for themselves" (*R. Macaulay*). When *leave* implies interference, and is followed by an infinitive without *to,* the use in this sense is regarded as questionable or even as illiterate; as, *leave* him be; *leave* him go.

Ana. Sanction, endorse, *approve, accredit, certify: *authorize, license, commission.

Con. *Forbid, prohibit, interdict, enjoin, ban, inhibit:

*hinder, impede, obstruct, block, bar: thwart, *frustrate, foil, circumvent.

lethal. *Deadly, fatal, mortal.

Ana. Destroying *or* destructive (see corresponding verb at DESTROY): killing, slaying (see KILL): *pernicious, baneful, noxious: *poisonous, virulent, venomous, toxic.

Con. Salutary, wholesome, hygienic, *healthful: renewing, restoring *or* restorative (see corresponding verbs at RENEW).

lethargic. **Lethargic, sluggish, torpid, stuporous, comatose** come into comparison when they mean being by constitution or condition physically, and often mentally, inert or inactive. **Lethargic** usually implies a constitutional, but sometimes a temporary or morbid (i.e., induced by disease), state of sleepiness or drowsiness that makes for slowness in reactions, responses, or movements, or for temperamental apathy; as, drugs that induce a *lethargic* condition; "[Nature] allows not such noble faculties to lie *lethargic*" (*Hume*); "Not all the industry of a Hercules will suffice to awaken the *lethargic* brain" (*Mencken*); "But it [a calm succeeding agitation] was no *lethargic* calm; my brain was more active than ever" (*Hudson*). **Sluggish** applies not only to persons, but to anything that by its nature moves, acts, or functions: the term implies conditions which create stagnation, inertia, indolence, or other signs of inability to proceed at a normal or usual pace; as, *sluggish* attention; a *sluggish* liver; a *sluggish* pond; a *sluggish* circulation; a *sluggish* market for securities. "Three years of intensive teaching have conquered the *sluggish* mind" (*A. Repplier*). "'England has become unenterprising and *sluggish* because England has been so prosperous and comfortable'" (*H. G. Wells*). **Torpid** suggests the loss of power of feeling and of exertion: literally it implies the numb or benumbed state of a hibernating animal, but in its more common extended sense it implies a lack of the energy, vim, responsiveness, or the like, that one associates with healthy, vital, active beings; as, "Memory was not so utterly *torpid* in Silas that it could not be wakened by these words" (*G. Eliot*); "still Richard was *torpid;* could not think or move" (*V. Woolf*); "Consecrated custom may keep Chinese civilisation safe in a state of *torpid* immobility for five thousand years" (*Inge*). **Stuporous** also implies marked unresponsiveness but it suggests a mind and heart dulled by drugs, disease, or the like, rather than in a frozen or benumbed state. The term is chiefly used in reference to psychopathological conditions; as, melancholia that manifests itself in a *stuporous* condition; the *stuporous* state of mind of a drug addict. **Comatose** literally suggests a being in the state of profound insensibility called coma that results from a disease such as diabetes or uremia which spreads poisons through the system, or from severe injury, or the like. "The almost *comatose* condition which had first supervened never developed into a fatal diabetic coma" (*H. Ellis*). In extended use, *comatose* implies stuporousness, torpidity, or other manifestations of extreme lethargy; as, "Wailing, stupid, *comatose* creatures" (*Emerson*).

Ana. Inert, idle, *inactive, supine, passive: phlegmatic, stolid, *impassive, apathetic: *languid, languorous, lackadaisical, listless: *slow, dilatory, laggard.

Ant. Energetic, vigorous. — *Con.* Alert, quick-witted, *intelligent: *quick, ready, prompt, apt: responsive (see TENDER): *spirited, gingery, peppery.

lethargy. **Lethargy, languor, lassitude, stupor, torpor, torpidity** come into comparison as meaning physical and mental inertness. **Lethargy** implies a state, marked by an aversion to activity, which has been induced by disease, extreme fatigue or exhaustion, overeating or overdrinking, constant frustration, or the like, and which exhibits itself in drowsiness or apathy; as, "[Arabs] reduced... to the condition of static *lethargy*...in which they now find themselves" (*A. Huxley*). "What means this heaviness that hangs upon me? This *lethargy* that creeps through all my senses? Nature, oppress'd and harrass'd out with care, Sinks down to rest" (*Addison*). **Languor** (cf. LANGUID) in early English use applied chiefly to a condition of weakness, faintness, or delicacy of constitution induced by illness and serving as a bar to exertion or effort. "Make *languor* smile, and smooth the bed of death" (*Pope*). Gradually, however, the term has come to imply an inertia resulting from soft living, from an enervating climate, from amorous emotion, or the like. "Radiant with ardour divine, Beacons of Hope ye appear! *Languor* is not in your heart, Weakness is not in your word, Weariness not on your brow" (*Arnold*). "From the winter's gray despair, From the summer's golden *languor*, Death, the lover of Life, Frees us for ever" (*Henley*). "That stick over which his tall person swayed with fashionable *languor*" (*Mrs. Oliphant*). **Lassitude** implies a physical condition resulting from strain, overwork, poor health, intense worry, or the like, and resulting in listlessness or seediness: it usually connotes an inertia of mind or body which one has not the strength to fight; as, "the results of overstrained energies are feebleness and *lassitude*" (*Borrow*); "She sat for twenty minutes or more ere she could summon resolution to go down to the door, her courage being lowered to zero by her physical *lassitude*" (*Hardy*). **Stupor** implies a state of heaviness when the mind is deadened as by extreme drowsiness, intoxication, narcotic poisoning, the coma of illness, or the like: the term may imply any state from a dreamy trancelike condition to almost complete unconsciousness; as, "there is... something almost narcotic in much mediaeval poetry; one is lulled into a pleasing *stupor*" (*Lowes*); "the sort of animal-like *stupor* in which his father [a confirmed drunkard and idler] had lived" (*S. Anderson*). **Torpor** and **torpidity** suggest a condition approaching that of a hibernating animal which has lost all power of exertion or of feeling: both terms, especially when employed in reference to persons, usually connote suspended animation or the extreme sluggishness and inertness of some forms of insanity: *torpidity*, however, probably more often applies to a physical condition (as, the *torpidity* of a person's liver; the *torpidity* induced by the extreme cold) and *torpor*, to a mental state. "Causes...now acting... to blunt the discriminating powers of the mind, and, unfitting it for all voluntary exertion, to reduce it to a state of almost savage *torpor*" (*Wordsworth*). "A deathlike *torpor* has succeeded to her former intellectual activity" (*Prescott*).

Ana. Sluggishness, comatoseness (see corresponding adjectives at LETHARGIC): indolence, slothfulness *or* sloth, laziness (see corresponding adjectives at LAZY): inertness *or* inertia, inactivity, idleness, passiveness, supineness (see corresponding adjectives at INACTIVE): apathy, phlegm, impassivity (see under IMPASSIVE).

Ant. Vigor. — *Con.* Quickness, readiness, promptness, aptness (see corresponding adjectives at QUICK): alertness, quick-wittedness (see corresponding adjectives at INTELLIGENT).

letter, *n.* **Letter, epistle, missive, note, message, dispatch** (*or* **despatch**), **report, memorandum** come into comparison only when they mean a written or otherwise formulated communication sent by mail, telegraph, messenger, or the like. **Letter** is the ordinary term for any written, typed, or printed communication sent by any means of transmission, but especially by mail, to a person, a company, a body, or the like, regardless of whether it deals with personal or business matters or with affairs of public concern; as, she received a *letter* from her husband yesterday; all *letters* sent out from the belligerent countries are censored; he addressed an open *letter* (i.e., one given out for publication) to his constituents. **Epistle** is now seldom used in place of *letter* except historically in reference to the letters of advice and counsel such as those of the Apostles Peter, Paul, etc., in the New Testament (as, the Second *Epistle* to the Corinthians) and to certain open letters in poetry so called by their authors (as, Pope's "*Epistle* to Dr. Arbuthnot"), or humorously or sarcastically (as, "Samuel's *letter*...was merely the amiable *epistle* of a son-in-law anxious to be a little more than correct"—*Bennett*). **Missive** is now usually a high-flown term for a sealed personal letter, especially one containing private information or expressions of love; as, "Scarce had Ripton plunged his head into the *missive*, than he gave way to violent transports" (*Meredith*). **Note** applies to a very short letter or other communication that is brief and pointed: the term is applicable to any such communication whether it is formal or informal; as, to send a *note* of condolence; to write a *note* of acceptance or of thanks for a gift. In diplomatic usage, *note* is applied to a formal communication sent by one government to another; as, "The Porte...acknowledged the validity of the Latin claims in a formal *note*" (*Kinglake*). **Message** differs from all the preceding terms in being applicable not only to a written, typed, or printed communication but to one that is orally transmitted as over the telephone or by a messenger or servant, or is telegraphed, cabled, radioed, or the like; as, to send a *message* to his mother that he had been called out of town; "But his citizens hated him, and sent a *message* after him, saying, We will not have this man to reign over us" (*Luke* xix. 14). In official, especially governmental, use *message* applies to a formal communication from the head of the state, such as one sent by the president of the United States to Congress, or by a governor to the law-making body of the state; as, President Wilson broke tradition by delivering his *messages* to Congress personally. **Dispatch** applies to any message, especially any brief message, that is sent posthaste as by telegraph, cable, or radiotelegraph: the term is often used specifically for any message sent by such means of transmission; as, to send a *dispatch* asking a hotel to reserve a room. In more technical language, *dispatch* applies to the telegraphed messages sent by an authorized correspondent to a newspaper or news association: it also specifically applies to any important official message, often one in cipher, sent by (or to) the government to (or by) a diplomatic, military, or naval officer in its service. **Report** (for fuller discussion of this sense see ACCOUNT, 3) applies particularly to a communication sent by a diplomat or similar official to his own government, but the term is also applicable to any official communication giving a detailed statement of facts, proceedings, or recommendations; as, the committee on foreign affairs is ready to make a *report* to congress; the school sends a monthly *report* of each student's work to his parents. **Memorandum,** as here compared, is used chiefly in business for an informal communication sent to an executive or employee, conveying instructions, directions, or the like.

2 In plural form **letters.** *Literature, belles-lettres, the humanities.

level, *adj.* **Level, flat, plat, plane, plain, even, smooth, flush** come into comparison chiefly as applied to surfaces and as meaning having a surface such as that of a perfectly calm lake or sea with no part higher than another. That is **level** whose surface, from every point of view, lies on a line corresponding to or parallel with that of the horizon; as, the top of the table is not perfectly *level;* the prairies are vast stretches of nearly *level* land; a plot of ground made *level* by grading. But *level* is also applicable to an adjacent surface lying in exactly the same plane; as, in the spring, the river's surface is often *level* with its banks; to erect buildings whose roofs are *level* with one another. In extended use, *level* implies an equality of parts, or of one thing with another, so that there are no manifest fluctuations, irregularities, differences, or the like; thus, to speak in a *level* voice is to speak without the variations in pitch or voice volume that indicate imperfect self-control; to keep a *level* head is to keep free from distracting excitement; to attempt no work that is not *level* with one's capacities is to avoid work above one's powers or skill. That is **flat** (see also INSIPID) or, in limited dialectal use, **plat,** which is marked by the absence of noticeable curvatures, prominences, or depressions, whether it lies in a horizontal plane or not; as, there is no *flat* ground hereabouts; the *flat* face of a cliff; the sides of a pyramid are all *flat.* But *flat* may apply to anything that lies directly upon or against a flat surface; as, *flat* feet; lay the map *flat* on the table; the chairs have their backs *flat* against the wall; here he is, *flat* on the ground. In figurative use, *flat* applies sometimes to that which is so lacking in variation or variety as to be monotonous (as, a *flat* speech delivered by the new president; a *flat* entertainment) or to that which gives no ground for doubt or for difference in description because direct, pure, complete, or the like (as, a *flat* question; a belief that is *flat* heresy; a *flat* failure) or to that which is fixed or absolutely exact (as, to ask a *flat* price; he ran the race in a *flat* ten seconds). That is **plane** (the geometrical and scientific term) or **plain** (the original but now rare sense of this word) which is flat and, usually, level. *Plain* applies chiefly but not exclusively to the ground; as, "The crooked shall be made straight, and the rough places *plain*" (*Isaiah* xl. 4); "I recovered some strength, so as to be able to walk a little on *plain* ground" (*J. Wesley*). *Plane,* on the other hand, more often applies to angles, curves, figures (such as triangles, rectangles, pentagons, etc.) all points of which lie in the same real or imaginary surface (called a *plane*) so that if any two points be taken within the boundary lines of the angle, curve, or figure, the straight line joining them lies wholly within that surface; thus, *plane* geometry, which deals with *plane* angles, curves, and figures, is distinguished from *solid* geometry; the *plane* sides of a crystal or of a cut and polished emerald. **Even** (see also STEADY) implies a uniformity of all the points, not only of a plane surface but also of a line, so that the surface's flatness or levelness, or the line's straightness, is observable; as, he trimmed the top of the hedge to make it *even;* the hem of your skirt is not *even;* "the frigate was on an *even* keel" (*Marryat*). **Smooth** implies perfect evenness of surface, as though polished, rolled, planed, or otherwise freed even from the slightest traces of roughness or unevenness; as, the *smooth* surface of a rubbed and polished table; a *smooth* lawn; "The tall bamboo and the long moss threw farther shadows... over the *smooth* bayou" (*Stark Young*). **Flush** applies to a surface or to a line that is in the same horizontal or vertical plane, or forms a continuous surface or line, with another surface or line; as, the front of the house is *flush* with the front boundary line; the river's surface is now *flush* with that of its banks; a *flush* panel; in the ordinary printed page, all lines are *flush* except those in

titles or headings or those that are indented for paragraphing.
Ana. Parallel, uniform, like, alike, akin, identical, *similar: *same, equivalent, equal.
Con. Undulating, fluctuating, swaying (see SWING, *v.*): varying, changing (see CHANGE, *v.*).

level, *v.* Point, train, *direct, aim, lay.

levitate. *Rise, arise, ascend, mount, soar, tower, rocket, surge.
Ant. Gravitate, sink.

levity. *Lightness, light-mindedness, frivolity, flippancy, volatility, flightiness.
Ana. Foolishness *or* folly, silliness, absurdity (see corresponding adjectives at FOOLISH): gaiety, liveliness, sprightliness, vivaciousness *or* vivacity (see corresponding adjectives at LIVELY).
Ant. Gravity. — *Con.* Seriousness, soberness *or* sobriety, earnestness, solemnity (see corresponding adjectives at SERIOUS): severity, sternness, austerity, asceticism (see corresponding adjectives at SEVERE).

levy, *n.* *Tax, assessment, rate, excise, impost, customs, duty, toll, tariff, tribute, tithe, teind, cess.

lewd. Lustful, lascivious, libidinous, lecherous, wanton, *licentious, libertine.
Ana. *Immoral, unmoral, amoral: gross, *coarse, obscene: indecent, indelicate (see INDECOROUS).
Ant. Chaste. — *Con.* Decent, pure, modest (see CHASTE): *moral, virtuous: continent, temperate (see SOBER).

lexicon. *Dictionary, wordbook, glossary, onomasticon, gazetteer, synonymicon.

liability. *Debt, indebtedness, obligation, debit, arrear, arrearage.
Ant. Asset (*or plural* assets).

liable. 1 Amenable, answerable, *responsible, accountable.
Ana. Obliged, constrained, compelled (see FORCE, *v.*): bound, tied (see TIE, *v.*).
Con. Exempt, immune (see corresponding nouns at EXEMPTION): *free, independent.

2 Liable, open, exposed, subject, prone, susceptible, sensitive, incident come into comparison when they are used with reference to persons or things, followed by *to* (sometimes *of*), and mean being by nature or situation in a position where something stated or implied may happen. **Liable** (as here considered: see also APT, 2; RESPONSIBLE) is used particularly when the thing one incurs or may incur is the result of one's obligation to authority, of one's state in life, or of submission to forces beyond one's control; as, "one of the most horrible diseases to which mankind is *liable*" (*C. W. Eliot*); "literature is *liable* to obsolescence, not only because language changes and gradually becomes less intelligible, but because the ideas, the interests, the conception of life it expresses, the very form of the thought, the experiences which arouse emotion, all become obsolete" (*R. Aldington*); "Ultimately 32 per cent. of those *liable* to military service joined the forces" (*Inge*). **Open,** literally not closed, covered, or obstructed, as here considered suggests lack of barriers or ease of access; as, "To-night, with his mind *open* to all impressions of romance" (*Arch. Marshall*); "another modern tendency in education...somewhat more *open* to question—I mean the tendency to make education useful rather than ornamental" (*B. Russell*). **Exposed** presupposes the same conditions as *open*, but it is more restricted in application because it implies a position or state of peril or a lack of protection or of resistance; as, the left flank was fully *exposed* to the attack of the enemy; the children were *exposed* to scarlet fever. **Subject** and **prone** (see also PRONE, 2) both suggest greater likelihood of incurring or suffering than *liable* and even less resistance than *exposed*. Etymologically, both connote the position of being under the sway or control of a superior power, but otherwise they differ in implications. *Subject* implies openness for any reason, such as a state in life, a social, economic, or political status, a temperament, a constitution, a nature, etc., to something which must be suffered, borne, undergone, or the like; as, "the French people would have stood permanently weak, open to invasion and *subject* to continual interference" (*Belloc*); "Both were *subject* to constant criticism from men and bodies of men whose minds were as acute and whose learning was as great as their own" (*H. Adams*); "Paul was rather a delicate boy, *subject* to bronchitis" (*D. H. Lawrence*); "the cycles to which all civilisations are *subject*" (*H. Ellis*); "The constitution was strictly an unwritten one, and was avowedly *subject* to revision in the light of new developments" (*Buchan*). *Prone*, on the other hand, usually implies that the person, or less often the thing, concerned is more or less governed by a propensity or predisposition to something pleasant or unpleasant which makes him or it almost certain to incur or to do something when conditions are favorable; as, "You may well warn me against such an evil. Human nature is so *prone* to fall into it!" (*Austen*); "I think that girls are less *prone* than boys to punish oddity by serious physical cruelty" (*B. Russell*); "in those industries that are most *prone* to periods of depression and unemployment" (*J. A. Hobson*); "Our painters are *prone* to acquiesce in the colours of nature as they find them, rather than to use colours expressive of the mood evoked in themselves" (*Binyon*). **Susceptible** carries a stronger implication than any of the preceding terms, with the exception of *prone*, of something in the person's or thing's nature, character, constitution, or temperament that makes him or it unresistant to a thing (often a deleterious thing or a thing that exerts a deleterious influence) or liable to it; as, to be *susceptible* to infection; she was very *susceptible* to criticism: when used attributively, it often implies a readiness to fall in love; as, a very *susceptible* young man. "Wheat tends to be very *susceptible* to smut" (*C. C. Furnas*). "A mind enormously more *susceptible* to tragic impressions than your own" (*C. E. Montague*). "[Mark Twain] who seemed to his friends such a natural-born actor, who was, in childhood, *susceptible* not only to somnambulism but to mesmeric control" (*Van W. Brooks*). Sometimes, however, *susceptible* stresses openness by reason of one's nature, character, or constitution, rather than liability: it is then followed by *of* (the phrase *susceptible of* often being merely equivalent to *admitting*); as, a theory *susceptible* of proof; "That rhythm [of speech under the stress of emotion] is not the rhythm of verse; it is infinitely more varied, less *susceptible* of formulation" (*Lowes*); "Today's pedagogical theory asserts that memory cannot be cultivated: it is inborn, full-grown at the start, and not *susceptible* of increase" (*Grandgent*). **Sensitive** differs from *susceptible* chiefly in implying a physical or emotional condition that predisposes one to certain impressions, certain reactions, or the like; as, "She was too *sensitive* to abuse and calumny" (*Macaulay*); "She discovered that with the clarification of her complexion and the birth of pink cheeks her skin had grown more *sensitive* to the sun's rays" (*Hardy*); "She was extremely *sensitive* to neglect, to disagreeable impressions, to want of intelligence in her surroundings" (*H. Adams*); "The eye is much more *sensitive* to light than the hand or the balance to weight" (*Karl K. Darrow*). **Incident** is not exactly a synonym of the preceding terms, for it applies not to the person or thing that is itself liable or open, but to the thing to which a person or another thing is liable or open. Often, the term means little more than belonging or pertaining to a person or thing as a subordinate feature or as a necessary or usual accompaniment; thus, old persons are *subject* to hardening of the arteries, but hardening of the arteries is *incident* to old age; life is *subject* to change, but change is *incident* to life; "a malady Most *incident* to maids" (*Shak.*); "For I have no doubt that the disease of self-consciousness is *incident* to intelligent youth" (*A. C. Benson*). "The fact that the statute...may bear hard upon some individuals...is no greater infirmity than is *incident* to all law" (*Justice Holmes*).

Ant. Exempt, immune.

3 Likely, *apt.

liaison. Intrigue, *amour, affair, affaire.

libel, *n.* **Libel, skit, squib, lampoon, pasquinade** (*or, now rare,* **pasquin, pasquil**) are here compared as meaning a public and often satirical presentation of faults or weaknesses, especially those of an individual. **Libel** is now the correct legal term for any statement or representation (such as a cartoon), published or circulated without just cause or excuse which tends to expose a person to public contempt, hatred, or ridicule; in earlier and now only historical use, the term applies specifically to a leaflet or handbill publicly circulated or posted in a public place and containing a scurrilous attack, especially on an individual; as, "cheap senseless *libels* were scattered about the city" (*Clarendon*). **Skit** applies to an amusing satire (originally a comment or remark, now often a dramatic sketch or story that may be more humorous or ironical than satirical) of no very great weight or seriousness: the term seldom connotes malice, bitterness, or abusiveness, but it often suggests the infliction of a sting; as, "He did not deserve your *skit* about his 'Finsbury Circus gentility' " (*FitzGerald*); the first of the one-act plays was a *skit*, more or less obviously dealing with the prime minister's attempt to forestall war. **Squib** (originally and still literally a kind of firecracker), as here compared, applies to any short and clever, often more or less malicious, piece of satirical writing that makes its point with a sharp thrust and evokes laughter or amusement; as, "No one was more faithful to his early friends...particularly if they could write a *squib*" (*Disraeli*). **Lampoon** (etymologically, a drinking song), suggests even more virulence and abusiveness than *libel*, and a coarser humor than *skit* or *squib;* as, "a lust to misapply, Make satire a *lampoon*, and fiction, lie" (*Pope*); "On his master at Twyford he had already exercised his poetry in a *lampoon*" (*Johnson*). **Pasquinade** was originally applied to one of the anonymous lampoons attached to a mutilated statue, called Pasquin or Pasquino, in Rome on St. Mark's day; the term now is preferred to *lampoon* when similar circumstances (such as anonymity, public posting, extreme scurrility) are implied; as, "The white walls of the barracks were covered with...*pasquinades* leveled at Cortez" (*Prescott*).

Ana. Scurrility, invective, vituperation, *abuse: burlesque, travesty (see CARICATURE, *n.*).

libel, *v.* Defame, slander, *malign, traduce, asperse, vilify, calumniate.

Ana. Revile, vituperate (see SCOLD): *decry, disparage, derogate from, detract from: caricature, travesty, burlesque (see under CARICATURE, *n.*).

liberal, *adj.* **1 Liberal, generous, bountiful, munificent, handsome** come into comparison when they are applied to a person, or to his deeds, utterances, or the like, and mean showing or revealing a spirit of giving freely and without stint. **Liberal** suggests openhandedness or lack of closeness, meanness, or the like, in the giver, and largeness in the thing that is given; as, to make a *liberal* provision for a son at college; a *liberal* offer for a house; *liberal* in praise. "The magazines, like the newspapers, were *liberal* with their space, but again the results were terribly meagre" (*V. Heiser*). **Generous** usually emphasizes some positive quality of heart or mind that prompts the giver or the gift, such as warmhearted readiness to give, forgetfulness of self, or magnanimity, more than the size or importance of the gift; as, to make a *generous* provision for one's servants in one's will; to reject a friend's *generous* offer of assistance; "a *generous* view of humanity" (*A. C. Benson*). "Mark Twain's boys 'not manly enough nor brave enough' to do a *generous* action where there was a chance that it could get them into trouble?" (*Van W. Brooks*). **Bountiful** suggests lavish or unremitting generosity in providing or giving. "He is a worthy gentleman...as *bountiful* As mines of India" (*Shak.*). "Lady *Bountiful*" (*Farquhar*). "The Governor of all, Himself to all So *bountiful*" (*Cowper*). **Munificent** stresses splendid or princely liberality; as, a *munificent* endowment. "If riches increase, let thy mind hold pace with them; and think it not enough to be *liberal* but *munificent*" (*Browne*). **Handsome,** as here compared, is not applicable to a person (for this use see BEAUTIFUL), but it is often a close synonym of *liberal* (with a suggestion of astonishing largeness) when applied to a gift, an offer, a remuneration, or the like. "In the case of the King and other public dignitaries we have arranged that they shall have *handsome* incomes" (*Shaw*). "They figured on the boards of all the old-established charities, gave *handsomely* to thriving institutions" (*E. Wharton*). On the other hand, it is often a close synonym of *generous*, especially when applied to an act or deed that evokes admiration for its unexpected magnanimity or graciousness. "Through this *handsome* conduct of the dean the dispute was amicably settled" (*J. H. Monk*). " 'I should like you to think of our house as your home, Tony.'... This was *handsome*, if it was meant, and there seemed no reason why it shouldn't be" (*Arch. Marshall*).

Ana. Lavish, prodigal, *profuse, exuberant: benevolent, philanthropic, *charitable.

Ant. Close (sense 5). — ***Con.*** *Stingy, niggardly, closefisted, tight, tightfisted, penurious, miserly, parsimonious: *meager, scanty.

2 Liberal, progressive, advanced, radical, left are used more or less loosely to mean the opposite of *conservative* in opinions, views, and policies. The secondary implications of all these words (with the possible exception of *progressive*) are often determined by the bias of the persons who use them; they may therefore carry connotations of extreme disparagement or of strong approval. **Liberal** implies emancipation from that which binds the mind or will and connotes either indifference to tradition, convention, dogmas, or laws, or the rejection of one or more of these. It therefore may suggest tolerance and broad-mindedness on the one hand, or unorthodoxy, laxness, or even lawlessness, on the other; as, a *liberal* Christian; a *liberal* Democrat; *liberal* liquor legislation. "Some people who themselves hold *liberal* views are willing that their children shall first acquire conventional morals" (*B. Russell*). **Progressive** is commonly a relative term, because it usually implies a comparison with those that are reactionary or backward. "Mentally so *progressive* that they were agitating for schools and the vote" (*V. Heiser*). It implies, therefore, a willingness to forsake past methods or beliefs, but it seldom suggests the espousal of extreme policies; as, a *progressive* business man; a *progressive* political party; *progressive* ideas in education. **Advanced,** on the other hand, is usually applied to men or ideas that are, or are believed to be, ahead of their time. It therefore often implies extreme liberalism or progressiveness and distinctively connotes mental daring. Sometimes, however, it strongly implies adventurousness or foolhardiness and impracticality. "Dr. Ashmore, the new Rector of St. Matthew's, had been chosen because he was very '*advanced*': his sermons were considered bold in thought and novel in language" (*E. Wharton*). **Radical** often is employed in place of *advanced*, but in discriminating use it commonly implies a willingness to root up and destroy the institutions which conserve or propagate the ideas or policies condemned; it is often therefore applied to anarchists, bolshevists, and the like. "*Radical* ideas let loose by the American Revolution, the French Revolution, the revolutionary movements of 1848, have slowly but profoundly affected men's desires and their demands upon government" (*Frankfurter*). **Left** is used chiefly in politics to designate a person, party, view, or policy that is liberal or radical. In current use, it commonly connotes extremeness, and often is preferred to *radical* since so many hitherto radical ideas have been generally accepted.

Ana. Tolerant, *forbearing, indulgent, lenient.

Ant. Authoritarian. — ***Con.*** Strait, *narrow: strict, stringent, *rigid, rigorous: dogmatic, doctrinaire, *dictatorial, oracular.

liberate. Release, *free, emancipate, manumit, deliver, discharge, enfranchise, affranchise.

Ana. Disengage, *detach: *extricate, disentangle, untangle, disencumber, disembarrass: *rescue, redeem, ransom, deliver.

Con. *Imprison, incarcerate, immure, intern: confine, circumscribe, restrict, *limit: *tie, bind: ensnare, snare, entrap, trap (see CATCH).

libertine. *Licentious, lewd, wanton, lustful, lascivious, libidinous, lecherous.

Ana. Debauched, corrupted *or* corrupt (see under DEBASE): *abandoned, dissolute, profligate, reprobate: *immoral, unmoral, amoral.

Ant. Strait-laced. — ***Con.*** *Moral, virtuous, ethical: continent, *sober, temperate: *chaste, decent.

liberty. *Freedom, license.

Ana. Independence, autonomy (see under FREE, *adj.*): *exemption, immunity: liberation, emancipation, enfranchisement, delivery (see corresponding verbs at FREE): scope, *range, compass, sweep.

Ant. Restraint. — ***Con.*** Constraint, compulsion, duress, coercion (see FORCE, *n.*): confinement, restriction, limitation, circumscription (see corresponding verbs at LIMIT).

libidinous. Lecherous, lustful, lascivious, lewd, wanton, libertine, *licentious.

Ana. Sensual, animalistic, animal, *carnal: *immoral: gross, obscene, *coarse: dissolute, *abandoned, profligate, reprobate.

library. *Museum, archives, treasury, thesaurus, gallery.

license *or* **licence,** *n.* Liberty, *freedom.

Ana. *Exemption, immunity: looseness, laxity, slackness, relaxedness *or* relaxation (see corresponding adjectives at LOOSE): privilege, prerogative (see RIGHT).

Ant. Decorum. — ***Con.*** *Obligation, duty: decency, propriety (see DECORUM): restraint, constraint, compulsion (see FORCE): continence, *temperance, sobriety.

license *or* **licence,** *v.* *Authorize, commission, accredit.

Ana. Permit, *let, allow, suffer: *approve, endorse, sanction, certify: empower, *enable.

Ant. Ban. — ***Con.*** Interdict, inhibit, enjoin, prohibit, *forbid: *restrain, curb, check.

licentious. Licentious, libertine, lewd, wanton, lustful, lascivious, libidinous, lecherous are here compared as meaning given to or indicative of immorality in sex relations, or unchaste habits. **Licentious,** literally given to license, or lack of restraint, is now chiefly used in a sense implying disregard of the restraints imposed by any law or custom enforcing chastity: the term stresses looseness of life and of habits rather than the imperiousness of one's desires; as, *licentious* living; *licentious* morals; "a spectre at their *licentious* feasts" (*Dickens*). **Libertine** suggests a more open and a more habitual disregard of moral laws, especially those pertaining to the sex relations of men and women; as, "The frank *libertine* wit of their old stage" (*Gibbon*); he castigated the *libertine* lives of many of his generation. **Lewd** so often retains from earlier and now obsolete senses (cf. "certain *lewd* fellows of the baser sort"—*Acts* xvii. 5) connotations of grossness, vileness, and vulgarity which color its other implications of sensuality, dissoluteness, and unconcern for chastity, that in contrast with the preceding terms it is less often applied to persons, or to the manners, thoughts, and acts of persons, who show breeding, refinement, or gentility in any measure than to those of low station, dull wits, coarse habits, and the like; as, to be seen in the company of *lewd* women; *lewd* songs; *lewd* actions in public. **Wanton** (see also PLAYFUL, SUPEREROGATORY) implies moral irresponsibility, or a disposition or a life manifesting an indifference to moral restraints: it often suggests freedom from restraint comparable to that of animals, thereby connoting lightness, incapacity for faithfulness or seriousness, or a generally unmoral attitude; as, "Let us walk honestly, as in the day; not in rioting and drunkenness, not in chambering and *wantonness*" (*Romans* xiii. 13); "So *wanton*, light and false, my love, are you, I am most faithless when I most am true" (*Millay*). **Lustful** implies the influence or the frequent incitement of desires, especially of strong, and often unlawful, sexual desires; as, a *lustful* passion; a *lustful* man. **Lascivious,** like *lewd*, definitely suggests sensuality, but it carries a clearer implication of an inclination to lustfulness or of a capacity for inciting lust; as, *lascivious* desires; *lascivious* thoughts; *lascivious* glances; *lascivious* dress; "To the *lascivious* pipe and *wanton* song, That charm down fear, they frolic it along" (*Cowper*); arrested and charged with being *lewd* and *lascivious* in speech and behavior. **Libidinous** and **lecherous** are the strongest of all these terms in their implications of deeply ingrained lustfulness and of debauchery. *Libidinous* distinctively suggests a complete surrender to one's sexual desires (as, "A *lewd* youth...advances by degrees into a *libidinous* old man"—*Addison*); *lecherous* clearly implies habitual indulgence of one's lust, the term often being used when any of the others would seem too weak to express one's contempt (as, "Remorseless, treacherous, *lecherous*, kindless villain!"—*Shak.*).

Ana. Profligate, reprobate, dissolute, *abandoned: debauched, depraved, corrupted *or* corrupt (see under DEBASE): lax, *loose, relaxed: *immoral, unmoral, amoral.

Ant. Continent. — ***Con.*** *Chaste, decent, pure: *moral, virtuous: strict, *rigid: austere, ascetic, *severe.

licit. *Lawful, legitimate, legal.

Ana. Permitted, allowed (see LET): sanctioned, approved (see APPROVE): authorized, licensed (see AUTHORIZE): regulated (see ADJUST).

Ant. Illicit. — ***Con.*** Forbidden, prohibited, interdicted, inhibited, banned (see FORBID).

lick, *v.* Beat, defeat, *conquer, vanquish, subdue,

subjugate, reduce, overcome, surmount, overthrow, rout.

lickspittle, lickspit. *Parasite, sycophant, toady, hanger-on, leech, sponge, favorite.

lie, *n.* **Lie, falsehood, untruth, fib, misrepresentation, story** come into comparison when they mean a statement or declaration that does not conform to the truth. **Lie** is usually felt to be a term of extreme opprobrium because it implies a flat and unquestioned contradiction of the truth, and an intent to deceive or mislead. Seldom, except in the expression "white lie" (that is, an untrue statement that is harmless or is insignificant in its content), does the term involve no implication of moral censure. "You told a *lie;* an odious, damned *lie*" (*Shak.*). "People....don't send for him [the minister] every time they make a slight moral slip,—tell a *lie,* for instance, or smuggle a silk dress through the custom-house" (*Holmes*). **Falsehood** is not only less censorious than *lie,* but it is also wider in its range of application. The term may or may not imply sinfulness or criminality, for it applies not only to lies of any degree, but to fictions, such as literary fictions, polite fictions, some legal fictions, and the like. Like *lie,* the term implies known nonconformity to the truth, but unlike *lie,* it does not invariably suggest a desire to pass off as true that which is known to be untrue; as, "'Tis not enough, your counsel still be true; Blunt truths more mischief than nice *falsehoods* do" *Pope*); "Mr. Bulstrode shrank from the direct *falsehood* of denying true statements" (*G. Eliot*); "*Falsehoods* which we spurn to-day Were the truths of long ago" (*Whittier*). **Untruth** is often euphemistic for *lie* or *falsehood* and carries the same implications; as, "'How do those *Signal* people find out things?'....'I don't know,' said Mr. Critchlow. This was an *untruth.* Mr. Critchlow had himself given the information" (*Bennett*). Sometimes, however, *untruth* may apply to an untrue statement made as a result of ignorance or a misconception of the truth; as, so far as he knew he had never told an *untruth;* little children with vivid imaginations seldom know the difference between a truth and an *untruth.* **Fib** is a colloquial, often childishly colloquial, term for an untruth or for a trivial falsehood: it is often applied to one told to save one's own or another's face. "Not that I couldn't tell a downright *fib* if I had to...but a *lie* is to me just as silly a performance when it is about marriage or work as about the law of gravitation" (*M. Austin*). **Misrepresentation** applies to a misleading (usually an intentionally or deliberately misleading) statement which gives an impression that is contrary to the truth: the term implies glossing over defects or weaknesses as in something offered for sale, or placing the emphasis upon details that high-light a character, an occurrence, or a train of events rather than on those that in reality marked it; as, he claimed that the advertisement was a *misrepresentation;* "our guides deceived us with *misrepresentations*" (*Addison*); the biography is full of *misrepresentations.* **Story** is a colloquialism, used chiefly by children or in conversation with children, in place of any of the preceding terms, especially *falsehood, untruth,* and *fib.*

Ana. Prevarication, equivocation, fibbing *or* fib (see corresponding verbs at LIE): mendaciousness *or* mendacity, untruthfulness, dishonesty, deceitfulness (see corresponding adjectives at DISHONEST).

Ant. Truth. — *Con.* Veracity, verity, verisimilitude (see TRUTH).

lie, *v.* **Lie, prevaricate, equivocate, palter, fib** agree in meaning to tell an untruth directly or indirectly. **Lie** is the straightforward word, imputing dishonesty to the speaker; as, I shall tell him to his face that he *lies;* "He *lies,* and he knows he *lies*" (*Johnson*). **Prevaricate** (etymologically, to walk crookedly or deviate from a straight course) is often used in place of *lie* as a more formal term; in strict use, however, it implies evasion of the truth, as by quibbling, dodging the real point, or confusing the issue; as, "Thou dost *prevaricate*...thou wouldst sophistically imply both are unlawful" (*Butler,* 1612–1680); "he could *prevaricate* no longer, and, confessing to the gambling, told her the truth" (*Hardy*); "'Even if it wos so, which I don't say it is'—'Don't *prevaricate,*' said Mr. Lorry" (*Dickens*). **Equivocate** implies saying one thing and meaning another; it usually suggests the use of words that carry more than one sense in the hope that the sense which gives the incorrect impression may be the one accepted by the hearer; as, "You...*equivocate;* For 'real,' as you now the word expound, From solid substance dwindles to a sound" (*Dryden*); "By *equivocating,* hesitating, and giving ambiguous answers, she effected her purpose" (*H. Martineau*). **Palter** implies a playing fast and loose, not only in statements but in dealings; it often specifically implies prevarication, equivocation, or the making of promises one does not intend to keep; as, "And be these juggling fiends no more believ'd That *palter* with us in a double sense" (*Shak.*); "Caroline, don't go back—don't *palter* with us—abide by your own words" (*Edgeworth*); "If you *palter* or double in your answers, I will have thee hung alive in an iron chain" (*Scott*). **Fib** (see also LIE, *n.*) may be used as a euphemism for *lie,* but it more often implies the telling of an untruth that is trivial either in matter or in significance; as, she was given to *fibbing* about her admirers; the child *fibs* when he thinks he can gain his end.

Ana. *Deceive, delude, mislead, beguile.

lifeless. Inanimate, *dead, defunct, deceased, departed, late.

Ana. Inert, *inactive, passive: *stiff, rigid, stark, wooden, inflexible: torpid (see LETHARGIC).

Ant. Living. — *Con.* Alive, quick, animate, animated, vital (see LIVING): *active, operative, dynamic, live.

lift, *v.* **1 Lift, raise, rear, elevate, hoist, heave, boost** are here compared as meaning (literally or figuratively) to move from a lower to a higher place or position. **Lift** often carries an implication of effort exerted to overcome the resistance of weight (as, to *lift* a large stone; to *lift* a pail of water from the ground; to *lift* a child to one's shoulders) but it may be used more or less figuratively of anything that rises high by natural or artificial means or processes (as, the mountains *lift* their peaks in the air; "High *lifted* up were many lofty towers"—*Spenser*) or of anything immaterial that rises or is made to rise as if in spirit, in feeling, in aspiration, or the like (as, "Unto thee, O Lord, do I *lift* up my soul"—*Psalms* lxxxvi. 4; the news *lifted* a weight from his mind; "One memory of the green corn, fresh beneath the sun and wind, will *lift* up the heart from the clods"—*Jefferies*). **Raise** may or may not suggest less effort than *lift,* but it carries a stronger implication of bringing something to the vertical or other high position for which it is fitted by nature, by function, or the like; thus, "to *raise* a pole" is to set it on end but "to *lift* a pole" is to pick it up from the ground; "to *raise* a flag" is to cause it to rise to the top of a flagstaff, but "to *lift* a flag" is to hold it up high enough so that everyone can see it; so, in figurative use, one who gives the care and attention necessary to their production and growth is said to *raise* crops; one who collects the constituent elements and gathers them together is said to *raise* a fund or to *raise* an army. "The most whole-hearted attempt ever made to *raise* the individual to his highest power" (*Day Lewis*). **Rear** is often used in place of *raise,* especially in literary English (as, "the mast we rear"—*Pope;* "the May-pole was *reared*"—*Irving*), and it is the preferred term (except in certain sections, especially the southern United States) when reference is to the bringing up of children (as, to bear five children and to *rear* three of them; cf. born and *raised* in South Carolina). Also, as an intransitive verb it means to raise itself, or in the case of a horse, to raise its forelegs (as, "The...storm-clouds *reared* on high"—*Millay;* "horses, *rearing* and prancing"—*S. Anderson*). **Elevate** may be used in place of *lift* or *raise* in their literal senses but only in certain collocations where it does not seem unduly formal or pretentious (as, "Lord Henry *elevated* his eyebrows"—*Wilde*), but, in general, the word suggests exaltation, uplifting, enhancing, or the like; as, to *elevate* a priest to a bishopric; to *elevate* humanity; to *elevate* one's standards of literary taste. **Hoist** implies raising something heavy aloft, often but not invariably by mechanical means, such as a tackle; as, to *hoist* a cargo into a ship; to *hoist* a sail; *hoist* me up by my arms to the top of the wall. The term is sometimes preferred to *lift* in humorous use. "Mrs. Malins was helped down the front steps by her son and Mr. Browne and, after many manoeuvres, *hoisted* into the cab" (*Joyce*). **Heave** implies a lifting with strain or effort as by impulsion from below (as, a boat *heaved* high by a wave; to *heave* a sigh) or by means of continuous shoveling (as, to *heave* coal). "Nature's way of creating a mountain peak—first the *heaving* up of some blunt monstrous bulk of rumpled rock" (*C. E. Montague*). **Boost**, an American colloquialism verging on slang in its extended uses, implies lifting by means of a push or other help from below (or in extended use, by other than the natural or usual agencies); as, he had to be *boosted* by his companions when he tried to climb the tree; to *boost* prices; friendly critics *boosted* the sales of his books; no matter how depressed he might be, a few cocktails always *boosted* his spirits.

Ana. *Rise, arise, ascend, levitate, mount, soar, tower, rocket, surge: *exalt, magnify, aggrandize: heighten, enhance, *intensify.

Ant. Lower. — ***Con.*** Reduce, lessen, diminish, *decrease: *abase, debase, degrade, demean, humble, humiliate: *depress, weigh (down, on, *or* upon), oppress.

2 Purloin, filch, *steal, pilfer, pinch, snitch, swipe, cop.

light, *v.*[1] **1 Light, kindle, enkindle, ignite, fire, inflame** come into comparison in both their literal and figurative senses because they agree in meaning to set something burning or on fire. **Light** (see also ILLUMINATE), when it takes as its subject the agent or agency, usually implies as the end of the action illumination (as, she *lighted* the lamps), or heating (as, he will *light* a fire in the fireplace), or smoking (as, he *lit* his cigar), or the like. **Kindle,** and now rarely **enkindle**, often, but by no means always, connote difficulty or slowness in setting combustible materials (wood, straw, vegetation, and the like) afire or aflame: it is therefore the preferred word when that which is to burn requires special preparation or does not at once burst into flame; as, using kerosene to *kindle* the damp wood; a carelessly thrown match *kindled* one of the worst forest fires in the state's history; bonfires were *kindled* on the top of every hill. **Ignite** is not only much more common in technical than in popular use, but it also (though to a lesser degree than formerly) manifests a difference in meaning. In technical use, *ignite* sometimes implies heating of a substance until it glows or becomes incandescent (as, when the electric current is turned on, it *ignites* the tungsten filaments in the bulbs) but it more often, especially in recent use, implies the placing of a small flame or spark (often an electric spark) in direct or indirect contact with a substance such as gasoline, fuel oil, or gunpowder so as to produce its combustion; as, to *ignite* the charge in the cylinder of an internal-combustion engine or the charge of powder in a gun. In more popular use, *ignite* varies little from *kindle* except in being more frequently employed in reference to explosives or highly inflammable substances; as, the gas flame *ignited* the gasoline she was using in cleansing a dress. **Fire,** the more colloquial term, and **inflame,** the more literary and, in its literal senses, now unusual, term, both imply blazing (sometimes with color rather than with light) and rapid combustion of that which is burning; as, a lighted match was sufficient to *fire* the haystack; "The turnkey *fired* the little pile, which blazed high and hot" (*Dickens*); "Fire will *inflame* straw" (*F. W. Robertson*).

All of these words are used figuratively as well as literally. **Light,** as here compared, is purely a figure of speech in such use (as, "Each morn my life I *lighted* at her eye"—*Young*); **kindle** and **enkindle** imply an exciting, arousing, or stimulating (as, poems that *kindle* indignation against social wrongs; "real intellectual interest....can be *kindled*...by a master who really loves and believes in his subject"—*Inge;* "In her heart new life was *enkindled*"—*Kingsley*); **ignite** implies a stirring up into activity (as, "flames That low desire *ignites* and feeds"—*J. G. Holland*); **fire** and **inflame** imply an inspiring with strong passion, ardent desire, intense zeal, *fire* usually being chosen when the agent or agency ennables or induces energetic activity; *inflame*, when it merely arouses passion, often ignoble or dangerous passion (as, "The nations of Europe were *fired* with boundless expectation"—*Johnson;* "The subject...had *fired* her imagination"—*Jan Struther;* "*inflamed* with lust"—*Milton;* "nationalistic feeling was never so acutely *inflamed* as it is today"—*A. Huxley*).

2 Lighten, *illuminate, illumine, illume, enlighten, illustrate.

light, *v.*[2] *Alight, land, perch, roost.

light, *adj.* *Easy, simple, facile, effortless, smooth.

Ana. Slight (see THIN): trivial, trifling, *petty, puny.

Ant. Heavy: arduous: burdensome. — ***Con.*** Difficult, *hard: *onerous, oppressive, exacting: rigorous, stringent (see RIGID).

lighten, *v.*[1] *Illuminate, illumine, illume, light, enlighten, illustrate.

Ant. Darken.

lighten, *v.*[2] Alleviate, mitigate, *relieve, assuage, allay.

Ana. Lessen, reduce, diminish, *decrease, abate: *moderate, temper, attemper, qualify: attenuate, extenuate, *thin, dilute.

Con. *Intensify, aggravate, heighten: *increase, augment: magnify, aggrandize (see EXALT): oppress, weigh (down, on, *or* upon), *depress.

lighthearted. Cheerful, happy, *glad, joyful, joyous.

Ana. Buoyant, resilient, volatile, effervescent, expansive (see ELASTIC): blithe, jocund, *merry, jolly: high-spirited, *spirited: gay, sprightly, vivacious, *lively.

Ant. Despondent. — ***Con.*** Sad, depressed, dejected, melancholy (see corresponding nouns at SADNESS): morose, glum, gloomy, *sullen.

lightness, light-mindedness. **Lightness, light-mindedness, levity, frivolity, flippancy, volatility, flightiness** are here compared only as denoting the quality, manner, or attitude of one who is irresponsibly gay or indifferent, especially when seriousness is expected. **Lightness,** as here compared, implies a general lack of weight or seriousness in character, mood, conduct, or speech; the term may further imply instability (as, "There is a *lightness* about the feminine mind—a touch and go"—*G. Eliot*) or freedom from care (as, "Archer looked at her perplexedly, wondering if it were *lightness* or dissimulation that enabled her to touch so easily on the past"—*E. Wharton*) or indifference to the seriousness of a situation (as, "treating with *lightness* what is matter of life and death"—*Arnold*). **Light-mindedness,** even more than *lightness*, suggests a temperamental lack of seriousness or stability; as, society women are often unjustly accused of *light-mindedness.* **Levity** usually suggests more specifically trifling or unseasonable gaiety; as, "her [Queen Elizabeth's] *levity*, her frivolous laughter, her unwomanly jests" (*J. R. Green*); "Molière and his audience were accustomed to regard conjugal infidelity with *levity* when it did not touch themselves" (*S. Alexander*). **Frivolity** adds to *lightness* the implication of empty or idle speech or conduct; the term often carries a strong connotation of triviality or of pettiness (as, "the extraordinary *frivolity* of much which passes for religious interest"—*Inge*) but its most frequent implication is that of such indulgence in meaningless gaieties that serious employments are disregarded (as, "gay without *frivolity*"—*Arnold;* "people...whose idleness and *frivolity* and extravagance set a most corrupting moral example"—*Shaw*). **Flippancy** is especially unbecoming levity or pertness in speaking of or in dealing with serious or sacred things; as, "[Tennyson] was always reverent—hating all *levity* or *flippancy* in thought or language about divine things" (*Duke of Argyll*); "One hardly knows which is the more appalling: the abjectness of the credulity [of those who believe in a First Cause] or the *flippancy* of the scepticism [of those who disbelieve in one]" (*Shaw*). **Volatility** implies such lightness or fickleness of disposition as precludes long or serious dwelling upon any one idea or plan; as, "*Volatility* of character evinces no capabilities for great affections" (*Shelley*). **Flightiness** may imply extreme volatility, often with a suggestion of loss of mental balance (as, his *flightiness* has been noticeable since his severe illness) but it often suggests extreme capriciousness or a gay whimsicality characteristic of one who is not long contented with what he has or does; as, every employer suspected her of *flightiness* after a few days' trial.

Ana. Buoyancy, resiliency, elasticity, effervescence, expansiveness (see corresponding adjectives at ELASTIC): gaiety, liveliness, vivaciousness *or* vivacity (see corresponding adjectives at LIVELY): lightheartedness, cheerfulness (see corresponding adjectives at GLAD).

Ant. Seriousness. — ***Con.*** Graveness *or* gravity, earnestness, soberness, sedateness, staidness (see corresponding adjectives at SERIOUS).

like, *adj.* *Similar, alike, identical, akin, analogous, comparable, parallel, homogeneous, uniform.

Ana. Equivalent, equal, *same, selfsame, identical: cognate, allied, *related.

Ant. Unlike. — ***Con.*** *Different, diverse, divergent, disparate, various: dissimilar, distinct (see corresponding nouns at DISSIMILARITY): discrepant, discordant, *inconsonant, inconsistent.

like, *v.* **Like, love, enjoy, relish, fancy, dote** (*or* **doat**) **on** *or* **upon** are here compared as meaning to be so attracted to a person or thing as to regard him or it with favor. **Like** (opposed to *dislike*), the most general and, especially when unqualified, the most colorless of these words, means merely to regard with distinct favor or without the slightest aversion. Therefore, it is chiefly used in reference to persons or things that are pleasing but evoke no great warmth of feeling or urgency of desire. **Love** (opposed to *hate*) implies not only strong liking but ardent attachment and is therefore used with reference to persons or things that arouse the deeper or higher emotions; as, to *like* one's neighbors; to *love* one's family; to *like* the country; to *love* one's country. "I *like* a church; I *like* a cowl; I *love* a prophet of the soul" (*Emerson*). The habitual use of *love* for *like*, with reference to trivial objects (as, I *love* ice cream), is a vulgarism, but *love* is often used for *like* in humorous hyperbole; as, "old Sarah Battle...*loved* a good game of whist" (*Lamb*). **Enjoy** (opposed to *loathe* or *abhor*) implies a liking or loving that awakens keen delight (sometimes sensuous, sometimes intellectual, delight but often a mingling of the two) and deep satisfaction; as, "even if she had unconsciously *liked* it [life in Paris], she had never *enjoyed* it" (*Bennett*); "We had written our first stories together...and together *enjoyed* the first sweets of success" (*R. Macaulay*); "No one but Molny and the Bishop had ever seemed to *enjoy* the beautiful site of that building,—perhaps no one ever would. But these two had spent many an hour admiring it" (*Cather*). "It is this specific quality, the power of *enjoying* things without being reduced to the need of possessing them, which differentiates the aesthetic instinct from other instincts" (*H. Ellis*). **Relish** implies a liking, or sometimes, an enjoyment, that arises because the thing relished meets one's approval, satisfies one's taste, or gives one personal gratification: except in negative expressions, this verb is slightly archaic in its flavor; as, "his fine taste taught him to *relish* the beauties of Virgil and Cicero" (*Hallam*); "concerts of classical music, which she did not particularly *relish*" (*Shaw*). **Fancy** (see also THINK, 1) implies a liking for something that corresponds to one's imaginative conception (sometimes, one's ideal) of what it should be (as, "I never yet beheld that special face Which I could *fancy* more than any other" —*Shak.;* "He should have yachts, horses, whatever he *fancied*"—*Meredith;* "they did not *fancy* having their demands for a better wage scale confused by the talk of anarchists and socialists"—*S. Anderson*), or for something that appeals to one's taste, one's eye, or the like, especially at the moment (as, while she was ill, she *fancied* only the most delicate of foods). **Dote on** *or* **upon** implies an infatuation or a foolish excessive liking; as, "You *dote on* her that cares not for your love" (*Shak.*). It is, however, often used colloquially in hyperbole; as, she said she *doted on* vanilla caramels.

Ana. Prefer, *choose, select, elect: admire, esteem, respect, regard (see under REGARD, *n.*): *approve, endorse: appreciate, comprehend, *understand.

Ant. Dislike. — ***Con.*** *Hate, abhor, detest, abominate, loathe: *despise, contemn, scorn, disdain.

likely, 1 *Probable, possible.

Ana. Credible, believable, colorable, *plausible: reasonable, *rational.

Ant. Unlikely. — ***Con.*** *Doubtful, dubious, questionable, problematic: *certain, inevitable, necessary.

2 *Apt, liable.

likeness. Likeness, similarity, resemblance, similitude, analogy, affinity are synonymous terms when they denote agreement or correspondence (or an instance of agreement or correspondence) in details of appearance, in qualities, etc., brought out by a comparison of two or more things. **Likeness** commonly implies closer correspondence than **similarity,** which often applies to things which are merely somewhat alike. "Yes, I should have known you anywhere from your *likeness* to your father" (*Arch. Marshall*). "Certain insects escape danger by their *similarity* to plants" (*J. Lubbock*). **Resemblance** suggests especially similarity in appearance or in superficial or external qualities. "It would be as difficult to discover any *resemblance* between the two situations as between the appearance of the persons concerned" (*E. Wharton*). **Similitude,** which is now somewhat infrequent in this sense and widely regarded as bookish, is occasionally preferred to *likeness* or *similarity* when an abstract term is desired. "The law which reconciles *similitude* and *dissimilitude,* the harmony of contrast" (*H. Reed*). **Analogy,** in careful use, always implies comparison of things which are unlike, not only specifically or generically, but often even in substance or essence. In its strictest sense, *analogy* implies likeness or parallelism in relations rather than in appearances or qualities; it is based on assumptions such as that similar causes will produce similar effects or that what is true in one order of existence must be true in another. "Three principal types [of ants] offering a curious *analogy* to... the hunting, pastoral, and agricultural stages in the history of human development" (*J. Lubbock*). "Such senile efforts to penetrate...the mystery of religion... have a real *analogy* to that final effort of the emotionally starved to grasp at love which has been called 'old maid's insanity'" (*H. Ellis*). **Affinity** adds to *resemblance* the implications of a relationship, such as natural kinship, temperamental sympathy, similar experience, or historical influence, which is responsible for the likeness. "In Keats, there are...phrases and paradoxes that have surprising *affinities* with Taoist thought" (*Binyon*). "His face...had a curious *affinity* to the faces of old sailors or fishermen who have lived a simple, practical life in the light of an overmastering tradition" (*Galsworthy*).

Ana. Equivalence, equality, sameness, identicalness *or* identity (see corresponding adjectives at SAME): agreement, conformity, correspondence (see corresponding verbs at AGREE): analogousness, comparableness, homogeneousness *or* homogeneity, uniformity, parallelism (see corresponding adjectives at SIMILAR).

Ant. Unlikeness. — *Con.* *Dissimilarity: difference, divergence, distinction.

likewise. *Also, too, besides, moreover, furthermore.

limb. Bough, branch, *shoot.

limber, *adj.* *Supple, lithe, lithesome, lissome.

Ana. Pliant, pliable, *plastic: flexible, *elastic, resilient, springy.

Con. *Stiff, inflexible, rigid, tense, stark, wooden.

limit, *n.* **Limit, bound, confine, end, term, bourn** (*or* **bourne**) are comparable when they mean an actual or imaginary line beyond which a thing does not or cannot extend. **Limit** is the most inclusive of these terms because it carries no necessary implication of number, that always being suggested by the context; thus, a thing, such as one's strength, the extent of one's authority, the reach of one's arm may be said to have a *limit,* implying one only; another thing, such as a race course, a lifetime, a period of time, and the like, may be said to have its *limits,* but since linear extent and duration are specifically implied, these limits are by implication two in number; so, the *limits* of a room are usually its four walls; the *limits* of a country are its boundaries, their number being dependent on the individual country's geographical location. Also, *limit* may be applied to any line which is fixed by nature or inner necessity, is established by authority, is determined by agreement, or the like; as, within the *limits* of human reason; the *limit* of the fisherman's catch is determined by the state game laws for each of the most desirable kinds of fish; to live within the *limits* of one's income; to determine the *limits* for the treatment of a topic. **Bound** and **confine,** on the other hand, are applicable to only one of the limits that comprise the boundaries (literally or figuratively) of a thing. Both terms are now rarely, if ever, used except in the plural, even when the boundary line is continuous and forms a circle or only one side; the same is true of a bounding surface that forms a sphere; as, within the *bounds* of the earth; to "beat the *bounds*" (an annual but now almost obsolete English ceremony of surveying the boundaries of a parish and marking them at certain points by beating with boughs); the western *confines* of China; within the *confines* of our subject. The distinctions between these two words are not always apparent. Not without exceptions, however, *bounds* usually indicates a point of view from within, and suggests restriction; *confines,* a point of view either from within or without, and suggests enclosure; as, the book passes beyond the *bounds* of decency; "as many as thirty bonfires could be counted within the whole *bounds* of the district" (*Hardy*); to approach, after a long absence, the *confines* (not the *bounds*) of one's own country; to remain within the *confines* of one's estate. **End** (as here compared: see also END, 2; INTENTION) applies usually to one of the two uttermost limits or extremes of a thing; this use is chiefly found in idiomatic phrases (as, to travel to the *ends* of the earth), but it occurs also in reference to either extreme in an ascending or descending scale, or in a series that progresses from one extreme to its diametrical opposite (as, at one *end* of the social scale there is the outcast or the pariah; at the other *end,* the elite). "To sweep away in art all that is...fundamentally ugly, whether by being, at the one *end,* distastefully pretty, or, at the other, hopelessly crude" (*H. Ellis*). **Term** (etymologically, an end or bound) applies to a limit in duration or, sometimes, in extent. "Neither history nor archaeology has yet put a *term* to Roman civilization in London" (*Wm. Page*). **Bourn** (archaic or literary) applies to a limit in space, such as a boundary line ("Oft as in their course They came to the field's *bourn*" —*Cowper*) or to a limit set as an end, goal, or destination ("a prescience of some *bourn,* incalculably distant perhaps, to which we are all moving"—*Hudson*).

Ana. Limitation, restriction, circumscription, confinement (see corresponding verbs at LIMIT): *border, margin, verge, edge, rim, brim, brink: *boundary, border, march, frontier.

limit, *v.* **Limit, restrict, circumscribe, confine** come into comparison when they mean to set or prescribe the bounds for a person or thing. **Limit** usually implies the predetermination of the point in time, in space, in quantity, in capacity, in production, or the like, beyond which the person or thing concerned cannot go or is not permitted to go without suffering a penalty or incurring undesirable consequences; as, to *limit* the speed of automobiles to 45 miles an hour outside of towns and cities; to *limit* the time allowed for the erection of a building to one year from the date of the signing of the contract; laws to *limit* the speed of automobiles on highways; to *limit* the acreage planted with potatoes; to *limit* a day's work to eight hours. "The great point...on these sacred occasions was for each man to strictly *limit* himself to half-a-pint of liquor" (*Hardy*). But *limit* may also be used with reference to a bound or bounds not predetermined but inherent in a situation or in the nature or constitution of a thing (as, he found that small-town life *limited* his opportunities; the poor soil *limited* their means of subsistence), or brought about as desirable by conscious effort or by full choice (as, "medical science knows how to *limit* these evils"—*C. W. Eliot;* to *limit* one's aspirations to the search for the attainable). **Restrict,** in contrast to *limit,* suggests a boundary that encircles and encloses rather than a point that ends: the term therefore often applies to that which can be thought of in the terms of the space, territory, or field that it covers: it often also connotes a narrowing or tightening;

thus, a *restricted* district in a city zoning law is a clearly outlined territory within which only buildings of a certain kind and often of a certain valuation can be erected; so, to *restrict* the powers of a court; to *restrict* the freedom of the press; to *restrict* one's diet on orders from one's physician. "The Bureau was dismembered, its staff dispersed, and its appropriations for research *restricted* almost to the vanishing point" (*V. Heiser*). **Circumscribe** differs from *restrict* in that its implication of an encircling or enclosing boundary is always clear: consequently, it is often preferred to *restrict* when the idea of being kept within too small an extent or range is to be stressed (as, " 'People....think that the emotional range, and the realistic truth, of drama is limited and *circumscribed* by verse' "—*T. S. Eliot*), or when there is the intent to suggest a distinct, complete, but limited whole and its apartness from all that surrounds it (as, "to undertake here to inquire into the degree of its necessity, would be to pass the line which *circumscribes* the judicial department"—*Ch. Just. Marshall;* "The world to which they belonged and for which they worked was strictly *circumscribed* and complete within itself"—*Binyon*). **Confine** may imply limitation, restriction, or circumscription, but it usually emphasizes the bounds which must not or cannot be passed: consequently, it often suggests severe restraint or restraints and carries connotations such as those of cramping, fettering, hampering, bottling up, and the like, which are seldom even hinted at in the other words. "Now I am cabin'd, cribb'd, *confin'd*, bound in To saucy doubts and fears" (*Shak.*). "The distinction between a government with limited and unlimited powers is abolished, if those limits do not *confine* the persons on whom they are imposed" (*Ch. Just. Marshall*). "It is not desirable to *confine* knowledge to whatever can be put into a useful shape for examinations, drawing-rooms, or the still more pretentious modes of publicity" (*T. S. Eliot*). "We are *confined* to our senses for perceiving the world" (*Karl K. Darrow*).

Ana. Define, *prescribe, assign: *restrain, curb, check.

Ant. Widen. — ***Con.*** *Expand, swell, distend: enlarge, *increase: *extend, lengthen, prolong, protract.

limp. **Limp, loppy, flaccid, flabby, flimsy, sleazy** (*or* **sleezy**) agree in meaning wanting firmness in texture, substance, or structure, and therefore unable to keep its shape or in shape. **Limp** applies to that which is devoid of the necessary stiffness or firmness to keep it from drooping or losing its original sturdiness or freshness; as, collars *limp* with perspiration; organdy becomes *limp* when there is excessive humidity; the intense heat has made him *limp;* "[Punch's] body was dangling in a most uncomfortable position, all loose and *limp*, and shapeless" (*Dickens*). **Loppy** applies to that which sags, or hangs limply; as, a dog with *loppy* ears; a *loppy* veil falls from her hat. **Flaccid** implies a loss or want of elasticity or resilience and therefore an incapacity to return to its original shape or condition or to keep a desired shape: the term in literal use applies chiefly, but not exclusively, to flesh and other living tissues; as, *flaccid* muscles; a *flaccid* stem; "Now, in swift collapse, he was as *flaccid* as a sick hound and as disgusting as an aged drunkard" (*Bennett*). In figurative use, the term implies lack of force or energy or substance; as, "the style is...worthless, slipshod, *flaccid*" (*Wilde*); "our *flaccid* culture" (*T. S. Eliot*). **Flabby** applies to that which is so soft that it yields readily to the touch or is easily shaken; as, *flabby* flesh or muscles; *flabby* cheeks. In figurative use, the term implies the loss or lack of that which keeps a thing up or in good sound condition; it often carries suggestions of spinelessness, spiritlessness, lethargy, or the like; as, "the *flabby* pseudo-religions in which the modern world is so prolific" (*J. W. Krutch*); "a few subjects thoroughly taught are infinitely better than a large number of subjects *flabbily* taught" (*A. C. Benson*). **Flimsy** applies to that which by its looseness of structure or insubstantiality of texture cannot hold up under use or strain; as, cheesecloth is *flimsy; flimsy* paper, such as is often used for typewritten copies; "a wooden seat put together with nails—a *flimsy* contrivance" (*Jefferies*). In extended use, the term applies to anything that is so frail or slight as to be without value or endurance; as, a *flimsy* excuse; a *flimsy* moral code. **Sleazy** applies chiefly to flimsy fabrics, but it often differs from *flimsy* in carrying a suggestion of fraud or of carelessness in its manufacture; as, *sleazy* calicoes; *sleazy* silks. In its somewhat rare extended use, the term often emphasizes absence of proper care more than the quality of the work; as, "You shall not conceal the *sleezy*, fraudulent, rotten hours you have slipped into the piece" (*Emerson*).

Ana. *Loose, slack, relaxed, lax: limber, *supple.

Con. *Stiff, rigid, inflexible, stark, wooden, tense: *firm, hard, solid: brittle, crisp (see FRAGILE).

limpid. *Clear, transparent, translucent, lucid, pellucid, diaphanous.

Ana. *Pure, sheer: lucid, perspicuous, *clear.

Ant. Turbid. — ***Con.*** Muddy, roiled, roily (see TURBID): *obscure, vague, dark: opaque, murky, dusky (see DARK).

line, *v.* **Line, align** (*or* **aline**), **range, array** agree in meaning to arrange in a line or in lines. **Line,** or more often **line up,** implies setting in single file or in parallel rows; as, to *line up* prisoners for identification; to *line up* troops for inspection. **Align** stresses the bringing of points or parts that should be in a straight line into correct adjustment or into correspondence; as, to *align* the lenses of a telescope; to *align* the front and rear wheels of an automobile; to *align* type in printing. **Range** stresses orderly or correct disposition, sometimes merely in straight or parallel lines, but more often with the added implication of separation into groups or classes according to some plan or design. "Oaken benches *ranged* In seemly rows" (*Wordsworth*). "Thus useful arms in magazines we place, All *rang'd* in order, and dispos'd with grace" (*Pope*). **Array** implies actual formation in order, especially battle order, and therefore suggests full equipment and readiness for action. "There is a great Field-Marshal, my friend, who *arrays* our battalions; Let us to Providence trust, and abide and work in our stations" (*Clough*).

Figuratively, these words also come into comparison. **Line up** stresses organization for unity or singleness of effort; as, to *line up* the opponents of a measure to achieve its defeat; to *line up* public opinion in favor of a proposal. **Align** is commonly used reflexively in its figurative sense and implies falling into line or into a line-up; as, at the beginning of the World War, France, England, and Belgium *aligned* themselves with Serbia. "So long as the symptoms [of disease] failed to *align* themselves with any known disorder, they were supposed to be amenable to neighbourly advice" (*M. Austin*). **Range,** in precise use, implies putting or falling into a group, such as a class, a party, a rank, or a category: it may suggest alignment but more often it connotes partisanship or alliance, or, when used of things, susceptibility of classification. Consequently it is followed not only by *with*, but by *under, against, around*, and the like. " 'Tis better to be lowly born, And *range* with humble livers in content" (*Shak.*). "The friends my enemies, All *ranged* against me" (*Browning*). **Array** in its figurative sense retains its implication of orderly formation; it sometimes also suggests arrangement in logical or chronological order, or as parts of a design. "These doubts will be *arrayed* before their minds" (*F. W. Farrar*). More often, however, it stresses the impressive or imposing character of an opposition and is followed by *against;* as, several of the best legal minds were *arrayed* against the prosecution.

Ana. Marshal, arrange, *order.

Con. Derange, disarrange, *disorder, disturb: disperse, dissipate, *scatter.

lineage. *Ancestry, pedigree.

linger. Tarry, wait, *stay, remain, abide.

Ana. *Delay, procrastinate, loiter, dawdle, dally, dilly-dally, lag.

Con. Hurry, hasten, precipitate, quicken, accelerate, *speed.

lingo. *Dialect, vernacular, patois, jargon, cant, argot, patter, slang.

link, *v.* Connect, relate, associate, *join, combine, unite.

Ana. Concatenate, articulate, *integrate: *tie, bind.

Ant. Sunder. — *Con.* *Separate, part, sever, divorce.

liquefy. Liquefy, deliquesce, melt, fuse, dissolve, thaw come into comparison as meaning to reduce or to become reduced to a liquid state. **Liquefy,** the general term, is applicable not only to solids but also to gases; as, to *liquefy* oxygen and nitrogen; to *liquefy* a solid mass of ice; jellies *liquefy* if exposed to the air in a warm room. **Deliquesce** (always an intransitive verb) implies a slow and gradual liquefying through exposure to the air and the absorption of moisture from it; as, humid heat causes the small quantities of magnesium chloride and calcium chloride in salt to *deliquesce* and to provide the liquid which compacts the mass. The term is also used in reference to fungi and similar vegetation which show liquefying in their decay; as, "a great display of specimens [of fungi] that presently dried up or *deliquesced* and stank" (*H. G. Wells*). **Melt** in its literal sense implies slow liquefaction, usually but not invariably through heat: the term commonly suggests a softening, a loss of shape, and a running consistency; as, butter *melts* when not stored in a cool place; to *melt* wax or maple sugar. In its frequent extended use, *melt* is applied to masses that are gradually dispersed or grow thinner or more tenuous and finally disappear (as, "the crowd gradually *melted* away"—*Dickens;* "mountains beyond mountains *melting* away into remote sky"—*Binyon*), or to persons, their emotions, or the like, that grow softer, gentler, or more tender (as, "one whose subdued eyes, Albeit unused to the *melting* mood, Drop tears as fast as the Arabian trees Their medicinal gum"—*Shak.;* "in *Romeo and Juliet* the profounder dramatist shows his lovers *melting* into unconsciousness of their isolated selves"—*T. S. Eliot;* "I cannot look up to your face. You *melt* my strength—*A. Lowell*), or to tones, colors, sounds, and the like, that have a liquid quality and merge imperceptibly with others (as, "A purer sapphire *melts* into the sea"—*Tennyson;* "snow-light cadences *Melting* to silence"—*Keats*). **Fuse** (see also MIX), in this sense once applied generally to metals liquefied by intense heat, is now less common in this application than *melt,* especially in its past participial form *molten;* as, "a quantity of silver which had been *fused* in a ladle was allowed to solidify" (*J. Tyndall*). When, however, the union or separation of two things by melting is indicated, *fuse,* often followed by *together* or *apart,* is the preferred term; as, "the strata *fused* together by heat" (*Livingstone*); "as by fierce heat, the chains be *fused* apart" (*B. Taylor*). **Dissolve** carries, as the other terms do not, a strong implication of the disintegration of the solid into its smallest component parts: as here compared, it implies the reduction of a solid to a liquid state by immersing it in another liquid, called a *solvent,* which has the power to reduce it to particles so fine that the solvent and the particles unite and form or seem to form a homogeneous liquid; as, *dissolve* salt in warm water; alcohol is frequently used in pharmacy to *dissolve* drugs; silver that *dissolves* in nitric acid is called silver nitrate. In its extended use, *dissolve* differs little from *melt,* except in its occasional stronger implication of breaking up before disappearance (as, "The cloud-capp'd towers, the gorgeous palaces, The solemn temples, the great globe itself . . . shall *dissolve* And, like this insubstantial pageant faded, Leave not a rack behind"—*Shak.*) or in its suggestion of the use of something comparable to a solvent (as, "Her heart *dissolved* in pity for him"—*Bennett;* relief caused her to *dissolve* in tears). **Thaw** is used only in reference to something that is frozen, as ice or snow, or in extended use, to something equally stiff or rigid, such as a cold heart, a cold disposition, or extreme reserve; as, the midday sun has *thawed* the ice on the roads; "a lady. . .whose very looks would *thaw* a man more frozen than the Alps" (*Shirley*); "A native reserve being *thawed* by this genial consciousness" (*N. Hawthorne*).

Ant. Solidify: vaporize.

liquid, *adj.* **Liquid, fluid** come into comparison both as adjectives meaning composed of particles that move easily and flowingly and change their relative position without any perceptible break in their continuity, and as nouns denoting any substance composed of such particles. Both terms (of either part of speech) imply an opposition to *solid,* but **liquid** is the more restricted in its application, for the term implies the flow characteristic of water and refers only to substances which, like water, have a definite volume but no definite form except such as is given by their container and as is readily lost when there is an upset, an overflow, or the like; as, water, fresh milk, various wines, beers, and liquors, and all other drinkables are *liquids;* oils are found chiefly in a *liquid* state; blood does not remain *liquid* long after removal from the blood vessels. **Fluid,** on the other hand, stresses flowing of any sort, and is applicable not only to all liquids, but also to any gas or gaseous substance which, unlike liquids, has no independent volume or shape; as, *fluid* air; gas is an aeriform *fluid; fluid* blood; *fluid* oils. *Fluid* is often preferred to *liquid* when the substance is highly viscous (as, molasses is a *fluid* substance) or when it represents the form taken by something usually solid but liquefied by melting, dissolving, saturating with water, and the like; as, *fluid* rock; *fluid* wax; mud is *fluid* earth.

Figuratively, **fluid** is opposed to *rigid, fixed, unchangeable;* as, " 'open societies' of which the boundaries are *fluid* or indefinite, such as humanity or even the League of Nations" (*S. Alexander*); "Emotion, formless, chaotic, *fluid* in itself" (*Lowes*); "In London all values and all meanings were *fluid*" (*R. Macaulay*). **Liquid,** on the other hand, often implies an opposition to *harshness* (as, *liquid* tones; "thy *liquid* notes that close the eye of day" —*Milton*) but it sometimes implies transparency or extreme softness or both (as, the air is *liquid* today; "his *liquid* glance"—*E. Wharton;* "with what *liquid* tenderness she turned and looked back"—*Bennett*). In financial circles, where both terms are used, *fluid* implies a floating, and therefore applies to money or funds that are not permanently invested or that are constantly in circulation (as, the *fluid* gold of international trade); *liquid* implies a quality or condition of assets that are in the form of money or are easily convertible into money, and applies not only to cash on hand but to securities, properties, and the like; as, *liquid* assets; *liquid* securities.

Ant. Solid: vaporous.

liquid, *n.* Fluid (see under LIQUID, *adj.*).

Ant. Solid: vapor.

lissome *or* **lissom.** Lithesome, lithe, *supple, limber.

Ana. & *Con.* See those at LITHE.

list, *n.* **List, table, catalogue, schedule, register, roll, roster, rota, canon, inventory** are comparable because they agree in denoting a series of names or of items written down or printed as a memorandum, a record, or a source of information, but, because of wide differences in their range of application, they are not always interchangeable. **List** is now the most comprehensive and the most widely applicable of these terms; it may or may not imply arrangement, such as in alphabetical, chronological, or other methodical order; it may itemize persons, or objects, or facts, or words, or figures, or the like; as, a grocery *list;* a *list* of invited guests; a price *list;* an engagement *list.* **Table** is also widely applicable, but it distinctively implies arrangement in an order that will assist the person who makes use of it in quickly finding the information he desires; consequently, it usually suggests presentation of these items in columns, often, when the items are related or associated with each other, in parallel columns; thus, a *table* of weights may give in the first column an alphabetical list of the weights of all countries and add in the following columns, directly on a line with each of these names, the place in which it is used, its equivalent in American or British weights, and its equivalent in metric weight; so, a *table* of contents of a book; a *table* of logarithms; annuity *tables;* a time*table* of classes or of trains. **Catalogue** was originally, and is still, though now more rarely, applied to any complete list or enumeration of all instances of a kind; as, a *catalogue* of the popes; "In the *catalogue* of the slain the author has followed the example of the greatest ancient poets" (*Addison*). The term is now used more often of an informative descriptive list of all the books in a library, or of those issued by a publisher or sold by a bookseller, or of all the works of art in a museum, or of all the courses given in a university or college, or the like. Because business, educational, and art catalogues often contain other information of value, the term is gradually losing its etymological meaning of *list,* although these catalogues have usually for their main object the presentation of complete lists. **Schedule** was originally applied to a paper annexed to a larger document, such as a will, a lease, a statute, or the like, especially to one giving a list of particulars of a pertinent character which could not be included in the document. "Of which territories, etc. a detailed *list* is given in the accompanying *schedule*" (*Wellington*). Hence, the term is now applied to an itemized statement of particulars, whether it is appended to a bill, statute, or the like, and gives supplementary details (as, *Schedule* D of the tariff bill) or is separate (as, a *schedule* of a bankrupt's debts; a *schedule* of assets and liabilities). Especially in the United States, *schedule* (see also PROGRAM) is applied to a timetable, as of trains, steamships, classes, or, more particularly, of the various operations in a procedure or in the execution of a project; as, the contractor's *schedule* for the erection of the court house was carefully followed. **Register,** in strict use, is applicable only to the official book, parchments, or papers in which are entered from time to time names or items of a specific character, together with pertinent details, for the sake of maintaining a record; as, a *register* of births; a *register* of marriages; a *register* of seamen. Since, however, these entries constitute not only a record but also a list or catalogue, the term often more strongly suggests an official listing or enumeration than a series of entries; as, his name is not in the *register* of voters; "Lloyd's *Register* of British and Foreign Shipping, which is published yearly, is an alphabetical list of vessels ranked in different classes according to their qualifications" (*Young's Naut. Dict.*). "He had ascertained, through the *registers* on the table, that his son-in-law was among the living prisoners" (*Dickens*). **Roll,** originally a piece of parchment or paper which can be rolled up and on which something is inscribed, now is applicable to any list, especially official list, of the names of those who belong to a certain group or force; thus, *the rolls,* in England, designates the official list of solicitors; a muster *roll* includes the names of all the officers and men of a military body or of a ship's company present or accounted for on the day of muster; a class *roll* is a list of all students belonging to a class that is usually called each day in order to keep a record of attendance. **Roster,** which is chiefly but not exclusively a military term, applies strictly to a table containing a roll of officers and men, or sometimes of units, and specifying the order of their rotation in duties, their special assignments, and the like. "You may know the White Hussars by their 'side,' which is greater than that of all the Cavalry Regiments on the *roster*" (*Kipling*). **Rota** is much rarer than *roster,* its close synonym, but it occasionally occurs in Great Britain, especially in reference to schoolboys. "The senior fag who kept the *rota*" (*T. Hughes*). **Canon** (etymologically, a rule or model) applies only to a list or catalogue, now chiefly of writings, but occasionally of persons, that conform to certain requirements; thus, the sacred *canon* is a list of the books of the Bible which are accepted as genuine and inspired Holy Scriptures; the Shakespearean *canon* is a list of the plays and poems which scholars have accepted as written by Shakespeare himself; a canonized saint is one whose name is entered in a *canon,* or list of persons recognized as saints by the Roman Catholic Church. **Inventory** is a catalogue of the goods, chattels, and sometimes, real estate (usually with their estimated worth), found in a person's or a corporation's possession at a given time, such as at the person's death or at the time of a stocktaking; as, the merchant makes an *inventory* of his stock annually on January 15th. In extended use, the term often refers to a list similar in its details to those of a true inventory. "Nothing short of an authentic passion for concrete detail... can give the saving gusto and animation which carry off safely the long *inventories* of utensils and articles of food and attire in Scott and Defoe" (*C. E. Montague*).

list, *v.*[1] Heel, careen, *tip, tilt, cant.

Ana. Incline, lean, *slant, slope.

list, *v.*[2] Listen, hark, *hear, hearken, attend.

listen. List, hark, *hear, hearken, attend.

listless. Spiritless, *languid, languishing, languorous, lackadaisical, enervated.

Ana. Apathetic, *impassive, phlegmatic: heedless, thoughtless, *careless: inert, *inactive, passive, supine, idle.

Ant. Eager. — *Con.* Avid, keen, anxious, agog (see EAGER): alert, *watchful, vigilant: *vigorous, energetic, lusty: *quick, prompt, ready.

lists. *Arena, circus, ring, cockpit, court, field, gridiron, diamond, rink.

literature, *n.* **Literature, belles-lettres, the humanities, letters** are not, strictly speaking, synonymous terms, for they are rarely interchangeable in idiomatic English. Nevertheless, they come into comparison both when they denote a branch of learning or culture concerned primarily with writings that endure or are likely to endure primarily because of their artistic, as distinguished from their informative, values, and when they designate these writings as an aggregate. **Literature** (except when it is used comprehensively of the body of writings on a particular subject; as, the *literature* of medicine) suggests reference to writings that are dominantly imaginative, that emphasize artistry or perfection of form or style, and that give aesthetic pleasure. "The thing that teases the mind over and over for years, and at last gets itself put down rightly on paper—whether little or great, it belongs to *Literature*" (*Sarah O. Jewett*). The term **belles-lettres** stresses absence of utilitarian or informational value more than *literature* does: it is usually restricted in its reference to literary productions that are read or studied (or are capable of being read or studied) as works of art or as sources of aesthetic delight, rather than because of their documentary or human values; thus, a course in *literature* may or may not imply consideration of historical values, but a course in *belles-lettres* implies an emphasis upon appreciation. In some use, *belles-lettres* (and still more the adjective *belletristic*) has acquired connotations of lack of solidity or seriousness, or lack of practical value, and is, as a result, applied to literary works which are more distinguished for their artistry than for their enduring emotional or imaginative appeal. For this reason, *belles-lettres* is preferred to *literature* when interest in artistic qualities is implied. "Why should a spokesman for *belles-lettres*...hesitate to go before a group of 'practical' men and talk to them, unashamed, of the 'utilities' of artistic expression?" (*S. P. Sherman*). **The humanities** is a term which has an inclusive and a restricted meaning. In the former it is referable to all the branches of learning, or the subject matter of such branches, that are concerned with the human, not merely as distinguished from the supernatural or the natural (that is, the world external to man), but especially as referring to the activities, interests, and progress of man, chiefly as they are recorded in the languages and literature of the past. In a somewhat narrower application, the term often designates Greek and Latin (in Scottish universities, Latin only) languages and literature because, during the Renaissance, interest in these subjects drove philosophy and theology from their position of eminence in the curricula of the universities. In present use, however, the term is often applied to those branches of learning or their subject matter which are not classed under the head of science (pure or applied) and are concerned primarily with human culture, especially as it is manifested in the literature or the classics of any people or age. In distinction from *literature* and *belles-lettres*, however, *the humanities* seldom stresses artistic values or appeal; often, in fact, it definitely implies a historical, as distinguished from an aesthetic, interest in literature. "There doe arise three knowledges, Divine Philosophy, Natural Philosophy, and Humane Philosophy, or *Humanitie*" (*Bacon*). "Neither would I have you neglect the *humanities*. I could wish that every one of you...could enjoy in the originals Homer, and Virgil, and Dante, and Rabelais, and Goethe" (*F. Pollock*). **Letters** is chiefly, but not exclusively, found in certain idiomatic phrases where it denotes the pursuit or profession of those who produce literature or are learned in the humanities; as, a man of *letters;* in the republic of *letters* (that is, in the body composed of enlightened and highly cultured men) there should be no such thing as racial prejudice. "He [Ben Jonson] was a literary artist even more than he was a man of *letters*" (*T. S. Eliot*). "It was one of the deepest of his [Richelieu's] concerns...that the State should nourish *letters*" (*Belloc*).

lithe, lithesome. Lissome, *supple, limber.

Ana. Slender, slim, slight, *thin: *lean, spare: pliant, pliable, *plastic: nimble, *agile, brisk, spry: graceful, elegant (see corresponding nouns at ELEGANCE).

Con. Clumsy, maladroit, *awkward, gauche, inept: *stiff, tense, wooden, inflexible.

litigious. Contentious, quarrelsome, *belligerent, bellicose, pugnacious.

Ana. *Aggressive, militant, assertive: fighting, contending, battling, warring (see CONTEND): suing, pleading, petitioning, praying (see under PRAYER).

little. *Small, diminutive, wee, tiny, minute, miniature.

Ana. *Petty, paltry, puny, trivial, trifling: slight, slim, slender, *thin: *meager, scanty, scrimpy, skimpy.

Ant. Big. — *Con.* *Large, great: abundant, ample, *plentiful, plenteous.

littoral. *Shore, coast, beach, strand, bank, ripa, foreshore.

liturgy. Ritual, rite, ceremony, ceremonial, *form, formality.

live, *v.* **1** Exist, *be, subsist.

Ana. Endure, abide, persist, *continue.

2 *Reside, dwell, sojourn, lodge, stay, put up, stop.

live, *adj.* *Active, operative, dynamic.

Ana. *Vigorous, energetic, lusty, strenuous: *powerful, potent, forcible, forceful: *effective, efficacious, effectual, efficient.

Ant. Inactive, inert: dormant (*as a volcano*): defunct (*as an institution, journal, or the like*).

livelihood. *Living, subsistence, sustenance, maintenance, support, keep, bread.

Ana. *Trade, craft, handicraft, art, profession: *wage *or* wages, salary, pay, stipend, fee, emolument.

lively, *adj.* **Lively, animated, vivacious, sprightly, gay** denote in common, keenly alive. **Lively** suggests especially briskness, alertness, or energy; as, they spent an hour in *lively* talk about their respective travels in England and France. "The mate, if *lively*, is soon aloft" (*Scoresby*). **Animated** applies especially to that which is also spirited or bright. "Even the hardest and coldest of his friends...became *animated* when he took her hand, tried to meet the gay challenge in her eyes and to reply cleverly to the droll word of greeting on her lips" (*Cather*). "Johnson was in high spirits...talked with great *animation* and success" (*Boswell*). **Vivacious** and (esp.) **sprightly** suggest greater lightness of spirits or quickness of wit; they are used most commonly of manner or language. "The stuff has sparkle; whatever he [Stevenson] means to convey at the time is being *vivaciously* put; the wordage is...always witty and winning" (*C. E. Montague*). "The *sprightly* Repartees fly about with the Glass" (*T. Brown*). **Gay** implies utter carefreeness and exuberant or overflowing spirits. "Wild with joyful expectation, she had there run backwards and forwards some ten times a-day, with an heart light, *gay*, and independent; looking forward to pleasures untasted and unalloyed, and as free from the apprehension of evil as from the knowledge of it" (*Austen*).

Ana. *Agile, nimble, brisk, spry: buoyant, effervescent, volatile, expansive, resilient, *elastic: *merry, blithe, jocund, jolly: mirthful, gleeful, hilarious (see corresponding nouns at MIRTH).

Ant. Dull. — *Con.* *Lethargic, sluggish, torpid: *languid, lackadaisical, listless, languorous: stolid, apathetic, phlegmatic, *impassive: tedious, *irksome, humdrum.

livid. Ashen, ashy, *pale, pallid, wan.

Ana. *Ghastly, grisly, lurid: murky, gloomy, dusky, opaque (see DARK).

Con. Brilliant, *bright, luminous, radiant, lustrous, effulgent, lucent: *intense, vehement.

living, *n.* **Living, livelihood, subsistence, sustenance, maintenance, support, keep, bread, bread and butter** are not, as here compared, close synonyms, but they come into comparison because they agree in denoting the means, especially the amount of money or goods, required to keep one fed, housed, clothed, and the like. **Living** is the general term for this sense, although it now occurs chiefly in specific idiomatic phrases; as, he works hard but he does not earn a *living* for himself and his family; "I am quite pleased to make my *living* by what I write, but the attempt to write for my *living* would be hopeless" (*H. Ellis*). **Livelihood,** once not clearly distinguishable from *living,* in current use often applies either to the trade, profession, craft, or other form of work by means of which one earns his living (as, "Let each man practise one art which is to be his *livelihood*"—*Jowett;* often the work one does as a diversion in one's youth turns out to be one's *livelihood*) or the wages, salary, or income derived from such work (as, to earn an honest *livelihood;* "Though I must slave for *livelihood*" —*F. P. Adams*). **Subsistence** was also once used as a close synonym of *living,* but in the course of time the term has acquired distinguishing implications so that it now, especially in sociological and economic language, specifically denotes means sufficient merely to maintain life or to enable one to subsist, and implies an amount of money or supply of goods that provides a person or his family with absolute necessities only, such as the simplest type of home and just enough to eat and wear; as, persons on relief are provided only with *subsistence.* This sense is found chiefly in two-word phrases such as *subsistence wage,* a term frequently contrasted with *living wage,* which implies means whereby adequate food, clothes, living quarters, etc., are provided (as, "if the owners will not pay *subsistence wages* the nation must" —*Shaw*), *subsistence level* (as, "a large proportion of British workers near *subsistence level*"—*The Nation*), *subsistence rate* (as, "beyond the bare *subsistence rate*" —*J. A. Hobson*), *subsistence homestead,* a small home with a plot of arable ground provided by the government of the United States at a very low rental to a destitute family that has no other means of support. **Sustenance** etymologically implies a sustaining of life. It is often used in place of *living* when the emphasis is upon the food that is necessary not only to one's existence but to one's well-being; as, he was able to wring only a bare *sustenance* from his farm. But it is also often used to imply all the necessaries of life; as, "It was the fur trade...which gave early *sustenance* and vitality to the great Canadian provinces" (*Irving*). **Maintenance,** as here compared, is more variable in its meanings than the other terms, but most often it denotes either the amount necessary for one's board, lodgings, clothes, and the like, or, as in income tax reports, the amount equivalent to the cost of one's board, lodgings, laundry, and the like, when they form part of one's emolument for services; thus, a husband who has been divorced by his wife is usually required by the court to provide *maintenance* for her and their children; "Enough to give him books, and a moderate *maintainance*" (*Cibber*); how much of this income represents your *maintenance?* **Support,** which in general applies to anything or to anyone that provides a means by which a person or thing is kept up or kept from falling, in the sense here considered applies not only to the amount of money that provides maintenance for others, but to the person who provides the means by which others are maintained; as, his earnings are (or he is) the sole *support* of his family; they look for their *support* to him. **Keep** is a colloquial term often used in place of *maintenance* or *sustenance* (food) and applicable not only to men but to animals such as horses, dogs, and cows; as, the new hired man is not worth his *keep;* the *keep* of a horse is almost equal in cost to that of a man. **Bread,** or **bread and butter,** often takes the place of *living* or *sustenance,* partly as a result of the use of the former in the Lord's Prayer ("Give us this day our daily *bread*) but also because the terms denote the simplest necessities of life; as, to make one's *bread* by one's pen; to earn one's *bread and butter* by intense toil.

living, *adj.* **Living, alive, quick, animate, animated, vital** agree in meaning endowed with or manifesting life. In their primary senses, where *life* means that character or quality which is peculiar to things that are capable of growth, reproduction, and, often, motion, and which is lost by death, they come very close to each other. **Living** and **alive** are opposed to *dead* and, therefore, are applied to organic bodies which have life as distinguished from those from which life has departed; they are distinguishable chiefly by the fact that *alive* follows the noun it modifies either directly or as a predicative adjective; as, among *living* men; among men still *alive;* all *living* things; all things which are *alive.* **Quick** (now archaic in this sense) is sometimes opposed to *inanimate* and sometimes to *dead;* it is applied chiefly to things which have life because it is their nature, as distinguished from those incapable of life; thus, the old English phrase "*quick* goods" is practically equal to the modern *livestock;* a "*quick* fence" is the modern *hedge,* made up of living plants instead of stakes or stones; "*quick* wood" is the opposite of *dead* wood, and therefore signifies the parts of a shrub through which sap still circulates. **Animate** is opposed to *inanimate* and is applied to living organic bodies in contrast to dead organic bodies or, especially, to inorganic bodies having no capacity for life; as, the lowest orders of *animate* things. **Animated** is opposed to *lifeless* or *inert,* and is applied to that which, once devoid of life, becomes alive; as, it is difficult to find out when in the course of evolution inanimate matter became *animated.* **Vital** is opposed to *mechanical,* and is applied chiefly to power, force, energy, motion, or the like, which results naturally from life in distinction from that power, force, etc., which results from purely physical or chemical causes; as, *vital* functions; a *vital,* as opposed to a mechanistic, principle.

When these words are applied to things which have not life in the sense defined, they form other groupings. All, however, stress qualities suggestive of life. **Living** usually suggests continued or continuous existence with no diminution of activity, efficacy, or the like; as, a *living* language; a *living* principle; a *living* force. **Alive** and **vital** are very close in their emphasis on abundance of vigor, on capacity for development, or on powers of endurance; both are applicable to persons as well as to things. "His gigantic gusto, his delight in toil and struggle, his superb *aliveness*" (*Mencken*). "The provisions of the Constitution...are organic living institutions ....Their significance is *vital* not formal; it is to be gathered...by considering their origin and the line of their growth" (*Justice Holmes*). **Alive** and **animated** often imply the presence of living things in great numbers; as, the stream is *alive* with trout; "as *animated* as water under a microscope" (*Hardy*). *Animated,* as here compared (see also LIVELY), usually stresses endowment with qualities suggestive of life, especially motion; as, *animated* pictures; an *animated* doll. "Perhaps no people has ever been stirred by a great idea till that idea was *animated* and made memorable by finding its right expression in rhythmical phrase" (*Binyon*). **Quick** often, and **animate** less rarely, imply newness, freshness, fluidity, or responsiveness. "The *quick* green Of every new leaf on the oldest tree" (*J. Freeman*). "Thine own heart, *quick* and enamoured of love and of light" (*Binyon*).

Ana. Existing, being, subsisting (see BE): *active, live, operative, dynamic.

Ant. Lifeless. — *Con.* *Dead, defunct, deceased, departed, inanimate.

load, *n.* **Load, burden, freight, cargo, lading** are comparable when they mean that which is carried, conveyed, or transported from one place to another, as in a cart, car, or vessel. **Load** is the most comprehensive of these terms, being referable also to that which is carried by man or horse, as on the back, or in bags; as, the peddler carries a heavy *load;* the truckman will deliver a *load* of wood tomorrow; a ship*load* of grain. *Load* is also applicable to the quantity or amount carried, as by a wagon, a truck, or by a freight car; thus, in England, a wagon*load* (with some local exceptions) is forty bushels of wheat or eighty bushels of oats. **Burden** (etymologically, that which is borne) is now used in the sense here considered only in idiomatic phrases; as, a ship of 100 tons *burden* carries a load of 100 tons; a beast of *burden* is an animal used for carrying loads. In current use the term applies figuratively to something that weighs heavily on one's mind or spirit, such as a care or a responsibility; as, "Bear ye another's *burdens*" (*Galatians* vi. 2); he has become a *burden* to his family. **Freight** applies to goods or merchandise of any sort in transit, especially long-distance transit, as by ship, railway train, motor truck, or the like; as, the wrecked truck spilled its *freight* over the road; a *freight* train (that is, a train all of whose cars carry freight). **Cargo** applies specifically to the freight carried by a ship; in current use it frequently is preferred to *freight* when a vessel is the carrier, although often there is no reason why *freight* should not be used; as, a tramp ship carrying a *cargo* of grain (or grain as *freight*); the Italian vessel's *cargo* of wine. In law, *cargo* is inapplicable to a shipload of animals or of persons, but in general use the term is often used humorously of persons, whether carried by boat or by train. "Before a train could get to any villadom with a *cargo* of season-ticket holders it would have to circle about this...woodland" (*H. G. Wells*). **Lading** (now chiefly poetic, except in the commercial phrase "bill of *lading*") applies either to freight or to a cargo.

load, *v.* *Adulterate, weight, sophisticate, doctor, deacon.

loath *or* **loth.** *Disinclined, indisposed, averse, hesitant, reluctant.

Ana. *Adverse, averse: *antipathetic, unsympathetic, averse.

Ant. Anxious. — *Con.* *Eager, keen, avid: desiring *or* desirous, wishing, wanting (see corresponding verbs at DESIRE).

loathe. Abominate, detest, abhor, *hate.

Ana. *Despise, contemn, scorn, disdain: refuse, reject, spurn, repudiate, *decline: *recoil, shrink, flinch, blench, quail.

Ant. Dote on. — *Con.* *Like, love, relish, fancy, enjoy: *desire, crave, wish, want, covet.

loathing. Abhorrence, detestation, abomination, hate, hatred. See under HATE, *v.*

Ana. Aversion, *antipathy: repugnance, repellency *or* repulsion, distaste (see corresponding adjectives at REPUGNANT).

Ant. Tolerance.

loathsome. *Offensive, repulsive, repugnant, revolting.

Ana. Abominable, abhorrent, detestable, odious, *hateful: repellent, *repugnant, distasteful, obnoxious, invidious.

Ant. Engaging, inviting. — *Con.* Attractive, alluring, charming, enchanting, fascinating, bewitching (see under ATTRACT).

lobby, *n.* Foyer, anteroom, antechamber, vestibule, *entry, entryway, hall, narthex.

locality. Locality, district, vicinage, vicinity, neighborhood (*or* **neighbourhood**) come into comparison as denoting a more or less definitely circumscribed place or region, especially from the point of view of those who live in it. **Locality** applies to a region of undefined boundaries, but it usually suggests an area round a center, such as the place where the speaker or writer lives (as, he no longer resides in this *locality*) or a particular place remarkable for some event, some landmark, or the like (as, "the deliverer is to be sought in the *locality* nearest to the chief scene of the invasion"—*Dean Stanley*). **District** usually applies to a locality that has clearly defined boundaries determined by the nation, state, county, or town for administrative, electoral, or other purposes; as, the new representative of the Fifth Congressional *District;* federal judicial *districts;* a police *district;* a postal *district.* In a less specific, but in this instance more pertinent, sense *district* is often applied to a locality with reference to some of its most obvious or clearly defined characteristics rather than to the exact area it covers; as, the agricultural *districts* of the United States; the Lake *District* of England; the mining *district* of Pennsylvania; the business *district,* or the theater *district,* of a city. **Vicinage,** a once common but now increasingly rare word, applies particularly to a group of towns or villages which lie so close together that the entire locality is regarded by the inhabitants and others as a geographical unit; as, the regiment was recruited from this *vicinage;* there is no first-rate doctor in the *vicinage.* The term has come to apply somewhat more vaguely to the territory near to the speaker's or writer's home or to the inhabitants of that territory; as, "the French ladies in my *vicinage*" (*Walpole*); he gained the good will of this *vicinage.* **Vicinity** never loses its basic implication of nearness in this sense but, since it always suggests a distinct point of view, it applies only to the locality that is very near from that point of view; as, there are no ponds in this *vicinity;* the wealthy business men of New York usually have their homes in the *vicinity* of the metropolis. **Neighborhood** usually carries an implied reference to one's neighbors (etymologically, nigh dwellers): in very precise use, therefore, the term is preferred to *vicinity,* which it closely resembles in denotation, when the locality referred to is so near that one knows it and its inhabitants rather well; as, there is no one of that name in this *neighborhood; neighborhood* parties; she is on good terms with the entire *neighborhood.* However, with a growing tendency of the people of one country to think of those inhabiting near-by countries as neighbors, the term is often less restricted in its application than formerly; as, the country must be on guard against the establishment of hostile bases in its *neighborhood.*

Ana. Region, *area, zone, belt, tract: section, sector (see PART): territory, *field, bailiwick, province, sphere, domain.

locomotion. *Motion, movement, move, stir.

locum tenens. *Substitute, supply, alternate, understudy, pinch hitter, double, stand-in.

locution. *Phrase, collocation, idiom, expression.

lodge, *v.* **1** House, board, *harbor, shelter, entertain.

Ana. *Receive, take, accept, admit: accommodate, *contain, hold.

2 *Reside, live, dwell, sojourn, stay, put up, stop.

lodgings. *Room, chambers, quarters, diggings, digs, apartment, flat, tenement.

lofty. *High, tall.

Ana. Elevated, raised, lifted (see LIFT): exalted,

magnified, aggrandized (see EXALT): imposing, stately, august, majestic (see GRAND): sublime, glorious, superb (see SPLENDID).

Con. Lowly, *humble, modest.

loggia. Gallery, *balcony, veranda, piazza, porch, portico, stoop.

logical. **Logical, analytical** (*or* **analytic**), **subtle** (*or* **subtile**) are here considered only as applied to persons, their minds, their mental habits or processes, and as meaning having or showing skill in thinking or reasoning. They are often used interchangeably or without clear distinction, but there are grounds in good usage for employing them with precision. **Logical** may imply the power to think according to the rules of logic and therefore in an orderly fashion; more often, however, it suggests the power to impress others that clearness of thought, soundness of reasoning, and freedom from bias underlie one's arguments, one's decisions, one's policies, and the like. "He had...the *logical* as opposed to the intuitive temper. He distrusted emotion for which he could not find a rational basis" (*C. E. Montague*). **Analytical** stresses the power to simplify either that which is complex or complicated, as by separating it into its constituent parts, or that which is chaotic or confused, by organization that shows the relation of the details to each other and the whole. In derogatory use it sometimes, especially when qualified by *over*, implies a tendency to multiply subdivisions; but in complimentary use, it commonly connotes a power to systematize, clarify, and interpret, as distinguished from the power to create or invent. "The early eighteenth century had arrived at an *over-analytical* dryness of mind" (*Babbitt*). "His [Noah Webster's] mind was *analytical* rather than constructive" (*H. E. Scudder*). **Subtle** (see also SUBTLE, 2) stresses the power to penetrate below the surface and to perceive fine distinctions and delicate, almost imperceptible, relations. Often its use implies a criticism, such as of being hard to follow, because of being overrefined. "John Donne....one of the most *subtle*...intellects that ever, before or since, expressed itself through the medium of verse" (*Lowes*). Usually, however, it connotes extraordinary skill in reasoning or in analysis. "That is a point of view which...would hardly have escaped the *subtle* intellect of the Greeks" (*G. L. Dickinson*). "The actual facts have required for...their interpretation the most *subtle* speculations of modern science" (*Justice Holmes*).

Ana. Cogent, *valid, sound, telling, convincing: *clear, lucid, perspicuous: *rational, reasonable: inferential, illative, ratiocinative (see under INFERENCE).

Ant. Illogical. — *Con.* Intuitive, *instinctive: *irrational, unreasonable: fallacious, sophistical, casuistical (see under FALLACY).

loiter. Dawdle, lag, dally, procrastinate, *delay, dillydally.

Ana. Tarry, linger, wait (see STAY).

Con. Hasten, hurry (see SPEED, *v.*).

lollop, *v.* *Skip, bound, hop, curvet, lope, ricochet.

lone. 1 Lonely, lonesome, *alone, forlorn, lorn, solitary, desolate.

2 *Single, sole, unique, solitary, separate, particular.

lonely. Lonesome, lone, *alone, solitary, forlorn, lorn, desolate.

Ana. Abandoned, deserted, forsaken (see ABANDON): secluded, isolated (see corresponding nouns at SOLITUDE).

Con. Teeming, swarming (see TEEM): frequented, haunted (see FREQUENT): *social, gregarious, convivial.

lonesome. Lonely, lone, *alone, solitary, forlorn, lorn, desolate.

Ana. & *Con.* See those at LONELY.

long, *v.* **Long, yearn, hanker, pine, hunger, thirst** come into comparison as meaning to have a strong and urgent desire for something. One **longs** (with *for* or an infinitive) when one wishes for something with one's whole heart or with great earnestness and, in some cases, strives to gain it so far as lies within one's power; often, however, the word is used when the desire is for that which is exceedingly difficult or impossible to attain; as, "Oh that I might have my request; and that God would grant me the thing that I *long* for!" (*Job* vi. 8); "ever have I *long'd* to slake My thirst for the world's praises" (*Keats*). One **yearns** (with *for, after, towards, to,* or an infinitive) when one regards or desires something with eager, restless, often tender or passionate, longing; as, "But Enoch *yearn'd* to see her face again" (*Tennyson*); "Then with teeming heart I *yearned,* O Angel of the Schools, towards Christ with thee!" (*W. H. Mallock*); "She gazed into his faded blue eyes as if *yearning* to be understood" (*Conrad*). One **hankers** (*for* or *after* something) when one is possessed with or made uneasy by a desire because of the urgency of a physical appetite (as, to *hanker* for strawberries, peaches, and other fresh fruits in the winter time), or because of a passion such as greed, lust, ambition, covetousness, or the like (as, "She ...still *hankered,* with a natural *hankering,* after her money"—*Trollope;* "[Octavian's] *hankering* from the start after the office of tribune"—*Buchan*), or because it is, sometimes only for the time being, beyond one's reach or one's powers (as, "to wean your minds from *hankering* after false Germanic standards"—*Quiller-Couch;* "Too long a siege of the familiar [in poetry]... sets us *hankering* after the strange"—*Lowes*). One **pines** (with *for, after,* or an infinitive) when one languishes or grows weak through longing for something or gives oneself up to fruitless longing for it; as, "We look before and after, And *pine* for what is not" (*Shelley*); "Harry Temple was wise enough to give up *pining* after what he could not get" (*Besant & Rice*). One **hungers,** literally, *for* that which will satisfy his urgent craving for nourishment or for a given kind of food essential to his physical well-being; one **thirsts,** literally, *for* that which will satisfy his urgent need for liquid or drink; as, to *hunger* for fresh vegetables; to *thirst* for cool fresh water. In their extended senses, one *hungers* or *thirsts* (with *for, after,* or an infinitive) when one longs for something with the full force of one's being or works or struggles with all one's powers for something which will satisfy a compelling craving, especially of mind or soul; as, "My soul *thirsteth* for thee" (*Psalms* lxiii. 1); "Blessed are they which do *hunger* and *thirst* after righteousness: for they shall be filled" (*Matthew* v. 6); "She *hungered* for a new environment in which to expand her new powers" (*H. Ellis*). But *thirst* and *hunger* may suggest a driving desire for that which will satisfy one's greed, revenge, etc.; as, to *hunger* for wealth or for power; to *thirst* for blood; to *thirst* to begin the combat.

Ana. Crave, *desire, wish, want, covet: pant, aspire, *aim.

longanimity. *Patience, long-suffering, forbearance, resignation.

Ana. *Fortitude, sand, grit, pluck, backbone: endurance, toleration *or* tolerance (see corresponding verbs at BEAR): submissiveness (see corresponding adjective at TAME).

long-suffering, long-sufferance. *Patience, resignation, forbearance.

Ana. Submissiveness, subduedness (see corresponding adjectives at TAME): meekness, humbleness *or* humility, lowliness (see corresponding adjectives at HUMBLE): *fortitude, grit: endurance, toleration (see corresponding verbs at BEAR).

Con. Impatience, restiveness, uneasiness (see corresponding adjectives at IMPATIENT): irksomeness, wearisomeness, tediousness (see corresponding adjectives at IRKSOME): *tedium, boredom, ennui.

look, *v.* **1** *See, watch.

Ana. *Gaze, gape, stare, glare, peer: *scrutinize, scan, inspect, examine.

2 *Seem, appear.

Ana. *Indicate, betoken, bespeak: *show, manifest, evidence, evince, demonstrate.

3 Also **look for.** *Expect, hope, await.

Ana. *Foresee, foreknow, anticipate, divine.

look, *n.* **1 Look, sight, view, glance, glimpse, peep, peek, coup d'oeil** are here compared as meaning both the act of seeing something and the thing that is seen. **Look** (see also APPEARANCE) implies the direction of one's eyes to a thing or the use of one's power of vision; as, let me have a *look* at the patient; "One dying *look* he upward cast" (*Scott*); he did not vouchsafe her one kind *look.* When applied to the thing seen, the impression produced tends to be stressed; as, judging by the *look* of his rash, he has scarlet fever; "The *look* of his face as he spoke was by no means pleasant" (*Trollope*). **Sight,** on the other hand, so strongly implies reference to the object that is seen that it suggests reception of an image by the visual powers or presentation to the sense of sight rather than a conscious use of that sense. Thus, when the term denotes the act (sometimes the power) of seeing, one takes a look at something which catches his *sight;* one has far *sight* who sees things at a great distance; "The litter is set down stage in full *sight* of the audience" (*Millay*); at first *sight,* he seems unkempt. When the term denotes the thing that is seen, qualifying words or phrases are necessary to suggest its character, appearance, or the effect it produces; as, there is no *sight* in the world equal to it; a goodly *sight;* a disagreeable *sight;* "The earth, and every common *sight*" (*Wordsworth*). **View,** as here compared, especially when it denotes the act of seeing, was once used in place of *look* when a careful looking over or inspection was implied (as, "Surveying Nature with too nice a *view*"—*Dryden*) but this sense prevails in current use only when the term implies the exercise of the mental rather than the physical vision or an attempt to comprehend something beyond the range of the physical vision; as, "bring the buried ages back to *view*" (*Gray*); "The scientific *view* of the world is not indifferent to quality or value. It seeks to find law, harmony, uniformity in nature" (*Inge*). More often, when seeing through the eyes is suggested, *view* takes the place of *sight* in either sense, with, however, a stronger implication of a directed or fixed gaze; as, "Far better scenes than these had blest our *view*" (*Gray*); "Thy dales, and hills, are fading from my *view*" (*Keats*); a house that affords a *view* of the ocean; the *view* from this hill is beautiful; trees that intercept the *view.* **Glance,** in what is probably the earliest of its senses, denotes something which is seen as a sudden flash or gleam, or the presence or movement of which is recognized by a swift sudden flash; as, "With winged expedition Swift as the lightning *glance*" (*Milton*); "Each swords bright *glance,* seem'd summons from their fate" (*Stirling*). It is in this sense that "a *glance* from the eye" is often to be interpreted, especially in older writings (as, "Dart not scornful *glances* from those eyes, To wound thy lord"—*Shak.*); but the transition in sense from the flash that is seen to the quick look that is given to a thing (the chief modern sense) is not clearly marked. "Lift our heads to heaven, And never more abase our sight so low As to vouchsafe one *glance* unto the ground" (*Shak.*). "A *glance* satisfied him of the hopelessness of the struggle" (*J. R. Green*). **Glimpse** (which is etymologically akin to *glimmer* and *glitter*) also in an early (but not necessarily its earliest) sense applied to something seen as a flash or a gleam; as, "No dear *glimpse* of the sun's lovely face, Strikes through the solid darkness of the place" (*Cowley*); "a *glimpse* of the moon showed the dark and huge tower" (*Scott*). This sense is now rare except in poetry, for the word in current usage commonly implies a brief view of a thing or, even more often, as much of it as may be taken in at a glance; as, "I did indeed for a brief evening obtain a *glimpse* of the richness and still beauty of an English harvest" (*Jefferies*); "You remember I had a *glimpse* of him once" (*Conrad*). **Peep** and **peek** are not clearly distinguishable in meaning, but *peep* is generally regarded as more dignified or less childish. When they denote the act of looking, both terms imply an attempt to see what is hidden or concealed, or what can be only furtively watched, as through a hole or a crevice, through half-shut eyes, or the like; as, to take a *peep* (or *peek*) through a keyhole. When, however, they denote something which is seen by peeping or peeking, *peep* seems to be the favored word; as, "You've only seen a *peep* through the curtain" (*H. B. Stowe*); "none of these men has so far written a popular book of *peeps* into the fairyland of Reality" (*T. S. Eliot*). **Coup d'oeil,** a French phrase literally meaning "a stroke of the eye," has often been used in English both in place of *glance* (a quick look) and *glimpse* (what can be seen in a glance); as, "All this you have at one *coup d'œil* in entering the garden" (*Gray*); "The *coup d'œil* of the Brussels opera-house did not strike Mrs. O'Dowd as being so fine as the theatre in Fishamble Street, Dublin" (*Thackeray*).

Ana. Gazing *or* gaze, staring *or* stare (see GAZE): scrutiny, inspection, examination (see under SCRUTINIZE).

2 *Appearance, aspect, semblance.

Ana. *Bearing, demeanor, mien, manner: *posture, attitude, pose: *face, countenance, visage, physiognomy.

looker-on. Onlooker, beholder, *spectator, observer, witness, eyewitness, bystander, kibitzer.

loom, *v.* Emerge, *appear.

Ant. Vanish.

loose, *adj.* **Loose, relaxed, slack, lax** are here compared as meaning not tightly bound, held, restrained, or the like. **Loose** is the widest of these terms in its range of application. It is referable, for example, to persons or things that are free from a usual or a temporary restraint, whether that restraint be a rope, a bond, a fetter, a prison, or the like, or a rule, a principle (especially a moral principle), or a law having for its object the order, discipline, or well-being of the group and the individuals which compose it; as, we found the boat *loose* after the storm; the bull is *loose* in the field; finally he worked his hand *loose;* some sheets of this book are *loose; loose* thinking (i.e., thinking unrestrained by concern for logic or accuracy); *loose* talk (i.e., talk that pays scant attention to the truth of its statements); *loose* principles, *loose* habits, *loose* living (i.e., principles, habits, living which are definitely immoral because opposed to or ungoverned by moral or ethical principles). *Loose* is also applicable to that which is not firmly or tightly held by, attached to, connected with, or fitted to, that which supports or guides, or that which it is intended to cover; as, to drive with *loose* reins; a *loose* belt; a *loose* coat; *loose* joints; a *loose* sense of a word; *loose* skin. Often, the word applies to a substance, fabric, or the like, the particles or filaments of which are not close or compact in arrangement; as, *loose* soil; a *loose* weave or texture. **Relaxed** implies a loss of some tightness, tension, strictness, or rigidity, rather than a freedom from restraint of any kind or even a considerable departure from discipline, fitness, firmness, etc.: not only does it never suggest wildness, lawlessness, or immorality, but it rarely, if ever, suggests anything worse than an easing up, a mitigation, an alleviation of strain, or a softening; as, *relaxed* discipline; a *relaxed* enforcement of law; *relaxed* nerves; "Augustus during these months was suffering from the *relaxed* and surfeited mood which always attends success" (*Buchan*). **Slack** (as here compared: see also NEGLIGENT) comes close to *relaxed* in its limitations and implications, but it stresses lack of firmness or steadiness rather than a release from strain or severity; thus, a *slack* rope is one that is not taut, usually one that is not as taut as is necessary or desirable; a *slack* hold is a weak, unsteady hold. *Slack* is applied both to business, work, or the like, that is subject to periods of lessened activity, and to the periods or seasons when business is dull or work is hard to find; as, "It'll be play to me after I've done my day's work, or any odd bits o' time when the work's *slack*" (*G. Eliot*); the *slack* season for milliners or carpenters. **Lax** (see also NEGLIGENT) usually implies undue relaxation, with consequent loss of the tension, or firmness, or tone essential to health, discipline, proper functioning, or the like; as, *lax* discipline; *lax* morals; "a...*lax* state of the bowels" (*J. M. Good*); "That neither the faculties of the one [the mind] nor of the other [the body] be suffered to grow *lax* or torpid for want of use" (*Johnson*).

Ana. *Limp, flabby, flaccid, flimsy: *free, independent: disengaged, detached (see DETACH): casual, desultory, hit-or-miss, happy-go-lucky, *random, haphazard: *negligent, remiss, lax, slack: *careless, heedless, thoughtless.

Ant. Tight: strict. — *Con.* Taut, tense (see TIGHT): *rigid, stringent, rigorous: precise, exact, *correct: tied, bound (see TIE, *v.*): restrained, curbed, checked, inhibited (see RESTRAIN).

loot, *n.* Booty, plunder, *spoil, pillage, swag, prize.

loot, *v.* *Rob, plunder, rifle, thieve, burglarize.

Ana. Sack, pillage, despoil, *ravage, spoliate, devastate, waste: *steal, pilfer, filch, purloin.

lope, *v.* **1** *Skip, bound, hop, curvet, lollop, ricochet.

2 Trot, pace, single-foot, walk, gallop, run, canter, rack, amble. See under TROT, *n.*

lope, *n.* *Trot, pace, single-foot, walk, gallop, run, canter, rack, amble.

loppy. *Limp, flabby, flaccid, flimsy, sleazy.

Ana. *Loose, relaxed, lax, slack.

Con. *Firm, hard: *stiff, inflexible, rigid, tense, stark: taut, *tight, tense.

loquacious. Garrulous, voluble, *talkative.

Ana. Fluent, *vocal, articulate, glib, eloquent, voluble: chatting *or* chatty, gabbing *or* gabby, chattering, prating, jabbering (see corresponding verbs at CHAT).

Con. Reserved, taciturn, uncommunicative, reticent, *silent: laconic, succinct, terse, *concise: curt, brusque (see BLUFF).

loquacity, loquaciousness. Garrulity, volubility, talkativeness. See under TALKATIVE.

Ana. Chattering *or* chatter, chatting *or* chat, gabbing *or* gab, prating, jabbering (see corresponding verbs at CHAT): fluency, articulateness, glibness, volubleness (see corresponding adjectives at VOCAL): *readiness, ease, facility.

Con. Taciturnity, reservedness *or* reserve, reticence, silence (see corresponding adjectives at SILENT): curtness, brusqueness (see corresponding adjectives at BLUFF).

lordly. Haughty, arrogant, overbearing, *proud, insolent, supercilious, disdainful.

Ana. Pompous, pretentious (see SHOWY): *dictatorial, magisterial, authoritarian: imperious, domineering, *masterful.

Con. Meek, modest, *humble, lowly: submissive, *tame, subdued: gentle, mild (see SOFT): abject, *mean.

Lord's Day. *Sunday, Sabbath.

lore. *Knowledge, science, learning, erudition, scholarship, information.

lorn. Forlorn, lonely, lonesome, lone, *alone, solitary, desolate.

Ana. See those at FORLORN.

lot. Destiny, portion, *fate, doom.

Ana. Fortune, luck, hap, *chance, hazard.

loth. Variant of LOATH.

lour, *v.* Variant of LOWER.

lout, *n.* *Boor, churl, clown, clodhopper, bumpkin.

Con. *Gentleman, patrician, aristocrat.

loutish. Boorish, churlish, clownish. See under BOOR.

Ana. Clumsy, gauche, maladroit, inept, *awkward: burly, brawny, husky, *muscular: *rude, rough, crude, raw, callow, green.

lovable. **Lovable, amiable** come into comparison only when the latter means, as the former invariably means, capable of inspiring affection or liking. **Lovable** is the more positive term, and implies warmth and sincerity of feeling and a definitely personal reaction. "I have never been able to love what was not *lovable* or hate what was not hateful out of deference for some general principle" (*Conrad*). "The wide sympathy with all that is human which is so *loveable* in Chaucer and Shakspere" (*J. R. Green*). **Amiable** (here compared only as applied to persons or things in their effect on another) often, especially in modern use, connotes little more than a definitely pleasant or agreeable (as opposed to a *distasteful* or *forbidding*) impression. "The philosopher Herbert Spencer...had the *amiable* trait in his character of an intense dislike to coercion" (*Shaw*). "Our modern appreciativeness is often only the *amiable* aspect of a fault—an undue tolerance for indeterminate enthusiasms and vapid emotionalism" (*Babbitt*).

Ana. Admired, respected, esteemed (see under REGARD, *n.*): idolized, adored, worshiped (see ADORE): attractive, alluring, charming, enchanting (see under ATTRACT): responsive, sympathetic, warm, warmhearted, *tender.

Ant. Hateful. — *Con.* Detestable, odious, abominable, abhorrent (see HATEFUL): *repugnant, repellent, distasteful, obnoxious.

love, *n.* *Attachment, affection.

Ana. Devotion, piety, *fidelity, allegiance, loyalty: adoration, worship, idolatry (see corresponding verbs at ADORE): *passion, fervor, ardor, enthusiasm, zeal.

Ant. Hate. — *Con.* Aversion, *antipathy: *enmity, hostility, animosity, rancor, animus: hatred, abhorrence, detestation (see under HATE, *v.*).

love, *v.* *Like, enjoy, dote on *or* upon, relish, fancy.

Ana. *Adore, worship, idolize: cherish, treasure, value, prize, *appreciate.

Ant. Hate. — *Con.* Abhor, detest, abominate, loathe (see HATE, *v.*): *despise, contemn, scorn, disdain.

lovely. *Beautiful, fair, comely, pretty, bonny, handsome, beauteous, pulchritudinous, good-looking.

Ana. Alluring, enchanting, charming, taking, attractive (see under ATTRACT): *delightful, delectable: exquisite, delicate, dainty, rare (see CHOICE).

Ant. Unlovely: plain.

loving. **Loving, affectionate, devoted, fond, doting** are comparable when they mean feeling or showing love or strong liking. **Loving** stresses the inward emotion and usually implies sincerity and depth of feeling; as, a *loving* father; *loving* friends. "Looking at it with eyes at once critical and *loving*, as if recalling the glow with which he had created it" (*Galsworthy*). **Affectionate** often stresses demonstrativeness or implies need of expression; as, she is a very *affectionate* child. "He had an *affectionate* heart. He must love somebody" (*Austen*). "His [Augustus's] *affectionate* care for his people was winning him love" (*Buchan*). **Devoted** emphasizes attentiveness, sometimes implying little more than assiduousness, sometimes connoting self-dedication or active loyalty to the person or thing one loves or likes; as, a *devoted* lover; a *devoted* disciple. "I did everything for him that the most *devoted* mother could do" (*Shaw*). **Fond** implies affectionate attachment; in its earlier use it connoted, and still often connotes, foolish tenderness. "A loving husband is a very amiable character. A *fond* one I think is not so" (*J. Wesley*). "Her preoccupation with petty things of no importance whatever was worthy of the finest traditions of *fond* motherhood" (*Bennett*). When *fond* (of) and *devoted* (to) imply a strong predilection or addiction, they are not often clearly distinguished. However, one is *fond* of the theater who welcomes every opportunity to see a play; one is *devoted* to the theater who spends much of his time in seeing plays or in efforts to further the development of the drama. One may be *fond* of the country and yet not go there often, but if one is *devoted* to it, one prefers to spend most of one's time there. **Doting** implies excessive fondness that leads to overindulgence in parents, fatuousness in lovers, or the like. " 'Thou chid'st me oft for loving Rosaline'—'For *doting*, not for loving' " (*Shak.*).

Ana. Amorous, amatory, *erotic: *enamored, infatuated: attentive, considerate, *thoughtful: *impassioned, passionate, ardent, fervent: leal, true, constant, *faithful.

Ant. Unloving. — *Con.* *Indifferent, unconcerned, aloof, detached: *cold, chilly, frigid: *faithless, false.

low. *Base, vile.

Ana. Abject, ignoble, *mean, sordid: *coarse, vulgar, gross, obscene, ribald: *crooked, devious, oblique.

Con. Decent, seemly, proper, *decorous, comme il faut: noble, *moral, ethical: lofty, *high.

lower *or* **lour,** *v.* Glower, *frown, scowl, gloom.

Ana. Glare, stare, peer (see GAZE).

lowly. Meek, *humble, modest.

Ana. Submissive, subdued, *tame: retiring, withdrawing (see GO): reverential, deferential, obeisant (see corresponding nouns at HONOR).

Ant. Pompous. — *Con.* Pretentious, ostentatious, *showy: arrogant, lordly, overbearing, haughty, *proud.

loyal. *Faithful, leal, true, constant, stanch, steadfast, resolute.

Ant. Disloyal. — *Con.* False, *faithless, perfidious, traitorous, treacherous: disaffected, alienated, estranged (see ESTRANGE): rebellious, mutinous, seditious, *insubordinate, factious, contumacious.

loyalty. *Fidelity, allegiance, fealty, devotion, piety.

Ana. Lealness *or* lealty, trueness *or* truth, faithfulness, constancy, stanchness, steadfastness (see corresponding adjectives at FAITHFUL): *attachment, affection, love.

Ant. Disloyalty. — *Con.* Faithlessness, falseness *or* falsity, perfidiousness *or* perfidy, treacherousness *or* treachery, traitorousness (see corresponding adjectives at FAITHLESS).

lubricate. Grease, *oil, anoint, inunct, cream, pomade, pomatum.

lucent. *Bright, brilliant, radiant, luminous, lustrous, effulgent, refulgent, beaming, beamy, lambent.

Ana. Glowing, blazing, flaming (see BLAZE, *v.*): *splendid, resplendent, glorious.

lucid. **1** Pellucid, *clear, transparent, translucent, diaphanous, limpid.

Ana. Luminous, *bright, brilliant, lucent.

Con. Murky, gloomy, opaque, darkling, dusky, *dark: *turbid, muddy.

2 *Clear, perspicuous.

Ana. Distinct, plain, manifest, *evident.

Ant. Obscure, vague, dark. — *Con.* Enigmatic, cryptic, ambiguous, equivocal (see OBSCURE).

luck. Fortune, hap, accident, hazard, *chance.

Ana. Break, chance, occasion, *opportunity: lot, portion, destiny, *fate.

lucky. **Lucky, fortunate, happy, providential** come into comparison when they mean meeting with or producing a favorable outcome or an unforeseen or unpredictable success. **Lucky** implies that the person or persons involved have been favored by chance and that the success has not been the result of merit or merits; as, a *lucky* player; "some *lucky* hit, which took with everybody" (*Locke*); "Said he was a *lucky* fellow not to be sent to school" (*Meredith*); it was a *lucky* day for him when he met the girl who later became his wife. **Fortunate,** although it is often indistinguishable from *lucky* in its implications, is less colloquial and often less suggestive of fortuitousness or of a favorable accident; sometimes, it even carries a hint of a higher power (cf. *fortune*, under CHANCE, *n.*, 1) that watches over one or of a being blessed beyond one's deserts; as, "In friendships I had been most *fortunate*" (*Shelley*); "We are aware, too, that the critical discrimination which comes so hardly to us has in more *fortunate* men flashed in the very heat of creation" (*T. S. Eliot*); "If Wee Willie Winkie took an interest in any one, the *fortunate* man was envied alike by the mess and the rank and file" (*Kipling*). **Happy** (in its original sense, fortuitous) differs from the preceding words, especially in its current use, chiefly in its combining the meaning of *lucky* or *fortunate* with that of its more common sense of being blessed or made glad (see GLAD); thus, a *happy* outcome is not only one that is fortunate but one that makes the person affected feel happy; a *happy* accident by which a rare book is discovered is an accidental event or circumstance that brings to light something that proves a treasure; so, "giving them patience under their sufferings, and a *happy* issue out of all their afflictions" (*Bk. of Com. Prayer*); "Chemists have been more *happy* in finding experiments than the causes of them" (*R. Boyle*). **Providential** often carries an implication of good fortune resulting from the help or interference of Providence; as, a *providential* escape; they declared that the delay, which made them miss the ship that was later torpedoed, was nothing short of *providential*. Often, however, the word carries no trace of this implication and means little more than *lucky* or *fortunate;* as, "It was *providential:* the sisters had made no remark that the Critchlows might not hear" (*Bennett*).

Ana. *Favorable, benign, auspicious, propitious: advantageous, *beneficial, profitable: happy, felicitous, meet (see FIT).

Ant. Unlucky. — *Con.* *Sinister, baleful, malefic, malign.

ludicrous. *Laughable, ridiculous, comic, comical, farcical, risible, droll, funny.

Ana. Absurd, preposterous, *foolish, silly: grotesque, bizarre, antic, *fantastic: amusing, diverting, entertaining (see AMUSE).

Con. Lugubrious, doleful, dolorous, *melancholy: solemn, grave, *serious.

luggage. *Baggage, impedimenta.

lugubrious. Doleful, dolorous, *melancholy, rueful, plaintive.

Ana. Depressing, oppressing *or* oppressive (see corresponding verbs at DEPRESS): sorrowful, woeful (see corresponding nouns at SORROW): gloomy, saturnine, dour, morose, glum, *sullen.

Ant. Joyous: facetious. — *Con.* *Merry, blithe, jocund, jolly, jovial: cheerful, *glad, joyful.

luminous. *Bright, brilliant, radiant, lustrous, effulgent, lucent, refulgent, beaming, beamy, lambent.

Ana. Glowing, blazing, flaming (see BLAZE, *v.*): gleaming, glittering, flashing, scintillating, shimmering (see FLASH, *v.*): resplendent, glorious, *splendid.

Con. Dim, dusky, obscure, murky, gloomy, *dark.

lunacy. *Insanity, psychosis, mania, dementia.

Ana. Alienation, derangement, *aberration: *mania, delirium, frenzy, hysteria.

lunatic, *adj.* *Insane, mad, crazy, crazed, demented, deranged, maniac, wood, non compos mentis.

lure, *n.* **Lure, bait, decoy, snare, trap** come into comparison when they denote something that leads one, literally and originally an animal, figuratively a person, unwittingly or inveigles such an animal or person into a particular place or situation, especially one from which it or he cannot easily escape. **Lure** (originally a device carrying raw meat and resembling a bird, which was employed by falconers in training young hawks for hunting) in extended use suggests something that always attracts and often deceives, yet does not necessarily lead one into evil or into danger. "How many [men] have with a smile made small account Of beauty and her *lures*... on worthier things intent!" (*Milton*). In current extended use, the connotation of deception is growing increasingly rare, and that of drawing power or seductiveness is being heightened; as, "What is this *lure*, this attraction, that cricket exercises" (*Lucas*); "how can they resist...the *lure* of so adventurous, so enchanting an invitation?" (*L. P. Smith*); "the *lure* of the simple life" (*Buchan*). **Bait** (literally a morsel of food tempting to a fish or, by extension, any animal, so placed that if the fish or animal bites, it finds itself hooked, netted, or otherwise caught) in extended use is applied to something, often in itself something relatively insignificant, which is held out as a temptation or as a suggestion of an inviting prospect, in the hope (or with the result) of inveigling another into a desired act, position, or situation; as, shop windows filled with *baits* to shoppers; in spite of her shyness, the girl's beauty was sufficient *bait* to attract many suitors. "But to quote Seneca is not criticism; it is merely to offer *baits* to a possible reader" (*T. S. Eliot*). **Decoy** (originally a pond or pool with a net-covered channel into which ducks or other wild fowl were enticed, but now, in literal use, a wild fowl or the likeness of one which is used to lure other wild fowl into shooting range or into a net) in extended use is applied chiefly to a person, but sometimes to a thing, that leads one to go somewhere or to do something that exposes one to the danger of being detected in crime, of being swindled or robbed, of being found in compromising or in merely unpleasant circumstances, or of being used to further another person's ends; as, marked bills sent through the mails as *decoys* were found in the pocket of one postal employee; pretty young girls were the unconscious *decoys* by means of which she assembled numbers of men at her receptions; the troops were led into ambush by a *decoy*. **Snare** (literally a string with a running noose or a similar inconspicuous device in which a foot or the head of a bird or small animal may be caught and by which it is more and more firmly held the harder the victim tries to extricate itself) in extended use is applicable to any danger one may run into accidentally or unexpectedly or through lack of caution or wariness and from which, once involved, one cannot easily extricate oneself. "The path to bliss abounds with many a *snare*" (*Cowper*). "Thou [God] know'st the *snares* on ev'ry hand, Guide Thou their steps alway" (*Burns*). "Trial by jury itself, instead of being a security to persons who are accused, will be a delusion, a mockery, and a *snare*" (*Baron Denman*). Oftentimes the word implies malevolence or trickery on the part of another who is responsible for the danger. This use is commonly a figurative extension of the literal sense. "She meant to weave me a *snare*... To entangle me when we met, To have her lion roll in a silken net And fawn at a victor's feet" (*Tennyson*). **Trap** (literally a device that shuts with a spring for capturing game or destructive animals, either fatally injuring the animal or causing its mutilation if it escapes) in extended use is, like *snare*, applied to that which is a danger to the unwary or incautious. The two words are often used interchangeably as though they were indistinguishable in meaning; however, *trap* is preferred to *snare* when disastrous effects, or deliberate setting for the purposes of capture, or trickery beyond detection are implied; thus, the army feared a *trap* (not a *snare*), but rather than retreat, they advanced into it; a *trap* (not a *snare*) for speedsters; knowing the examiner's methods, he was certain that there would be a *trap* set for him but he could discover none. "Thou laid'st a *trap* to take my life" (*Shak.*).

lure, *v.* **Lure, entice, inveigle, decoy, tempt, seduce** agree in denoting to draw one into danger, evil, a false position, or the like, by exerting an attracting influence or by practicing deception. **Lure** implies a strong or irresistible, and usually a baleful, attraction. "Good wine *lures* back the winebibber" (*Arnold*). "It was not money that *lured* the adolescent husbandman to the cities, but the gay life" (*Mencken*). To **entice** is to lure artfully and adroitly. "She appeared to be playing with the bird, possibly amusing herself by trying to *entice* it on to her hand" (*Hudson*). To **inveigle** is to entice by beguiling and cajoling. "Many of them are *inveigled* to enlist by drink, or by bounty money" (*A. Tucker*). To **decoy** is to entrap or lead into danger by artifice, especially by false appearances; as, a small body of troops *decoyed* the enemy into action, while the main body lay in ambush. To **tempt** is to exert an attraction so strong that one is inclined to act in defiance of one's conscience or better judgment. "'I am forbidden tea. I mustn't drink it.' She looked at the cup, tremendously *tempted.* She longed for tea. An occasional transgression could not harm her" (*Bennett*). To **seduce** is to lead astray, usually by overcoming scruples, from rectitude, propriety, or duty. "The hideous beast whose craft had *seduced* me into murder" (*Poe*). "That quaintness, into which your admiration of Tacitus sometimes *seduced* you" (*Gibbon*).

Ana. Ensnare, snare, entrap, trap, capture, *catch, bag: bewitch, fascinate, allure, captivate, take, *attract: blandish, wheedle, cajole (see COAX).

Ant. Revolt, repel.

lurid. *Ghastly, grisly, gruesome, macabre, grim.

Ana. Livid, *pale, pallid, wan, ashy, ashen: *sinister, malign, baleful, malefic.

lurk, *v.* **Lurk, couch, skulk** (*or* **sculk**), **slink, sneak** do not carry a common denotation, but they come into comparison because the major implication of each word is furtive action intended to escape the attention of others. To **lurk** is to lie in wait, as in an ambush: the term sometimes implies only a place of concealment (as, "his faithful Tom...with his young master's mare... was *lurking* in a plantation of firs"—*Meredith*) but it often also suggests an evil intention, or quiet, stealthy movements, or a readiness to spring upon a victim (as, "There...ugly treasons *lurk*"—*Shak.*; "in the corners of the old building shadows *lurked*"—*S. Anderson;* "the latent scepticism which *lurks* behind all faith"—*H. Adams*). To **couch** (now archaic in this sense) is to hide oneself from view for any reason but sometimes, like *lurk*, it suggests a malign motive or intention. "There's not a hollow cave or *lurking*-place, No vast obscurity or misty vale, Where bloody murder or detested rape Can *couch* for fear, but I will find them out" (*Shak.*). To **skulk** is usually to move furtively but sometimes to lurk: it carries a stronger implication than any of the preceding words either of a sinister intention or of cowardice or fear; as, "[Adulterers] *skulking* in corners" (*Shak.*); "Gaming and Grub-street *skulk* behind the King" (*Pope*); "Disdainful Anger, pallid Fear, And Shame that *sculks* behind" (*Gray*); to come home late and *skulk* to bed. To **slink** is to move stealthily or slyly in order not to attract attention; as, "like beasts of prey *slinking* about a camp fire" (*Conrad*); "by skirting outhouses and *slinking* under walls, [they] escaped" (*Meredith*); "After a while I *slunk* away out of the great circle of firelight into the thick darkness beyond" (*Hudson*). To **sneak** is to get oneself out of or into a place by slinking, or out of a difficulty or the like by methods that are lacking in straightforwardness or are definitely underhand; as, he *sneaked* out of the house after his parents had gone to bed; "meanly to *sneak* out of difficulties into which they had proudly strutted" (*Burke*).

Ana. *Hide, conceal, secrete: ambush, waylay, *surprise.

Con. *Appear, emerge, loom.

luscious. Delicious, delectable, *delightful.

Ana. Sapid, saporous, flavorsome, toothsome, *palatable, appetizing: grateful, gratifying, pleasing, *pleasant.

Ant. Austere: tasteless.

lush. Luxuriant, *profuse, lavish, prodigal, exuberant.

Ana. Abounding *or* abundant, teeming, swarming, superabounding *or* superabundant (see corresponding verbs at TEEM): sumptuous, opulent, *luxurious.

lust. Concupiscence, *desire, appetite, appetence, passion, urge, yen.

Ana. *Cupidity, greed, avarice, rapacity: yearning, longing, hankering, thirsting *or* thirst, hungering *or* hunger (see corresponding verbs at LONG): craving, coveting (see DESIRE, *v.*): gusto, zest, *taste.

luster *or* **lustre.** **Luster** (*or* **lustre**), **sheen, gloss, glaze, glare** come into comparison when they denote a smooth shining surface that is the natural property of a thing or is given to it by some process such as polishing, burnishing, coating, or the like. **Luster** always implies a shedding of light, often of iridescent light, and always, in very precise use, of reflected light; as, the silvery or satiny *luster* of the finest pearls; the soft *luster* of rubbed and waxed mahogany; "Cut a piece of lead or of zinc, and observe the *lustre* of its fresh surface" (*T. H. Huxley*); "The sun...shining on her...hair...gave it a metallic *lustre*" (*Watts-Dunton*). In literary use, *luster* is often more loosely used to imply radiance or brilliance (see BRIGHT, 1); as, "The sun was shining with uncommon *lustre*" (*Dickens*). **Sheen** suggests more glittering or gleaming than *luster*, and seldom, if ever, connotes iridescence: it is applicable chiefly to highly polished or brightly finished metals (as, "The *sheen* of their spears was like stars on the sea"—*Byron*), to fabrics with a shining surface, such as satin, some alpacas, and the like (as, "the *sheen* of his poplin and velvet"—*Cather*), or to the shiny surface produced on certain fabrics by long wear (as, the *sheen* of his old blue serge suit), or to anything that emits or reflects brilliant or dazzling light (as, "Throned in celestial *sheen*"—*Milton;* the *sheen* of the river under the noonday sun; "the *sheen* of gardenia ...leaves"—*Stark Young*). **Gloss** carries a stronger implication of superficiality than *luster* or *sheen*, and therefore applies chiefly to something that shines through being coated with a shining substance (as, the *gloss* of a newly varnished floor or of freshly blackened shoes) or through being given a bright finish as by polishing, dressing, or the like (as, only very hard woods can be given a *gloss* that lasts more than a few days; the *gloss* on this chintz will wash off). Consequently in extended use, *gloss* often implies speciousness, plausibility, extraneousness, or the like; as, "Beauty is but a... shining *gloss*" (*Shak.*); "National claims can always be given the *gloss* of moral sanction" (*Times Lit. Sup.*). **Glaze** applies particularly to a glasslike coating which provides a glossy surface on earthenware or porcelain, but it is also applicable to other similar coatings, such as one made on cooked meats by pouring over them broth boiled until it forms a gelatinous paste, or on pies, rolls, and the like by various substances such as beaten egg or sirup, or on flat paint by the use of an enamel, or on the ground by rain that freezes on the smooth surface of roads, walks, and the like; as, some chinas have an especially beautiful *glaze;* the bright *glaze* of the candied sweet potatoes; to apply a fresh *glaze* to the surface of an old car; the *glaze* on the sidewalks is very bad this morning. Although *glaze* (or *glazed frost*) is the technical meteorological term for a coating of freezing rain, **glare** is common in general use. The latter term also applies to any surface coating or sheet of clear ice.

Ana. Polishing *or* polish, burnishing *or* burnish, shining *or* shine (see corresponding verbs at POLISH): iridescence, opalescence (see corresponding adjectives at PRISMATIC): brilliancy, radiance, luminosity, effulgence, refulgence (see corresponding adjectives at BRIGHT).

lustful. Lascivious, libidinous, lecherous, wanton, lewd, *licentious, libertine.

Ana. *Carnal, fleshly, sensual, animal, animalistic: *immoral, unmoral, amoral.

Con. Pure, modest, decent, *chaste: *moral, virtuous.

lustration. *Purification, ablution, purgation, catharsis.

lustre. Variant of LUSTER.

lustrous. Luminous, radiant, brilliant, *bright, effulgent, refulgent, beaming, beamy, lambent, lucent.

Ana. Polished, burnished, shining (see POLISH): glorious, resplendent, *splendid: glowing, blazing, flaming (see BLAZE, *v.*).

lusty. *Vigorous, energetic, strenuous, nervous.

Ana. Robust, sound, *healthy, hale: stout, sturdy, *strong, stalwart: husky, brawny, *muscular, sinewy, athletic.

Ant. Effete. — *Con.* *Sick, ill: *weak, infirm, feeble, decrepit.

luxuriant. Lush, exuberant, *profuse, lavish, prodigal.

Ana. Fruitful, fecund, *fertile, prolific: *rank, rampant: abounding *or* abundant, superabounding *or* superabundant, teeming (see corresponding verbs at TEEM).

Con. Barren, *sterile, unfruitful, infertile: *meager, scanty, scrimpy, skimpy: arid, *dry.

☞ *Do not confuse* luxuriant *with* luxurious.

luxurious. **1** Voluptuous, sybaritic, epicurean, *sensuous, sensual.

Ana. Self-indulging *or* self-indulgent, self-pampering (see primitive verbs at INDULGE): languorous, languishing (see LANGUID).

Ant. Ascetic. — *Con.* Austere, stern, *severe: self-denying, self-abnegating (see corresponding nouns at RENUNCIATION).

2 **Luxurious, sumptuous, opulent** come into comparison when they are applied to things and mean ostentatiously or obviously rich and magnificent. That is **luxurious** (as here considered: see also SENSUOUS) which is exceedingly choice and costly; as, her *luxurious* sable coat; the *luxurious* appointments of their drawing room; *luxurious* wines; *luxurious* table linens. That is **sumptuous** which is extravagantly rich, splendid, gorgeous, luxurious, or the like: the word usually suggests a grandeur or magnificence that almost overwhelms the senses; as, "The *sumptuous* life of the Court provided material for some painters" (*Binyon*); "Venice, soon to be known as the most beautiful and *sumptuous* city of Europe" (*H. Ellis*); "the too *sumptuous* note of the entertainment" (*M. Austin*); "for the most *sumptuous* masques in England, Italian managers, engineers and artists were brought over" (*T. S. Eliot*). That is **opulent** (as here considered: see also RICH) which flaunts or seems to flaunt its luxuriousness, or luxuriance, and, in some cases, costliness; as, "[Cleopatra] offered [Antony] the bribe not only of her person but of an *opulent* and glittering eastern throne" (*Buchan*); "The diction of poetry became, with notable exceptions, *opulent*, *sumptuous*, lavish, rather than pointed, terse, concrete" (*Lowes*). "It [the beauty of the countryside] was an ample, rolling *opulent* beauty; Georgian, somehow, with a suggestion of full-bottomed wigs and old port. A trifle oppressive to live with, perhaps" (*Jan Struther*).

Ana. Ostentatious, pretentious, pompous, *showy: magnificent, stately, imposing, majestic, *grand: *costly, expensive, valuable, precious.

Con. Frugal, thrifty, economical, *sparing: *meager, scanty, scant, skimpy, scrimpy, spare, exiguous.

☞ *Do not confuse* luxurious *with* luxuriant.

luxury. *Amenity, pleasance.

Ana. *Pleasure, joy, delight: agreeableness, gratification, gratefulness (see corresponding adjectives at PLEASANT).

Ant. Hardship. — *Con.* *Difficulty, rigor, vicissitude.

lycée. College, gymnasium, *academy, seminary, institute.

lying. Mendacious, untruthful, *dishonest, deceitful.

Ana. *False, wrong: deceptive, *misleading, delusive, delusory.

Ant. Truthtelling. — *Con.* Honest, just, *upright, conscientious, scrupulous, honorable: true, *real, actual: candid, *frank, open, plain: *reliable, dependable, trustworthy.

M

macabre. Gruesome, *ghastly, grisly, grim, lurid.

Ana. Horrifying, daunting, appalling, dismaying (see DISMAY): horrific, horrendous, *horrible, horrid.

macaroni. Buck, spark, dude, élégant, exquisite, coxcomb, beau, *fop, dandy, swell, nob, toff.

machination. Intrigue, conspiracy, *plot, complot, cabal, frame-up.

Ana. *Trick, ruse, stratagem, maneuver, artifice, feint, wile.

machine. **Machine, engine, apparatus, appliance** are here compared as denoting a device (particularly a device involving a more or less complicated mechanism) for doing work that exceeds human capacity or that can be accomplished by human power only with a comparative waste of time and effort. **Machine** and **engine** in their early use in English were applied to any contrivance that evidenced human ingenuity, but *machine* usually suggested a marvel of construction and *engine* a device that exerted force. Although the words were occasionally applied to the same things, they diverged in meaning when *machine* came to denote specifically a vehicle and *engine* a contrivance used in propelling, pulling, pumping, and the like; thus, a sedan chair, a carriage, a coach were called *machines*, and a battering ram, a cannon, a pump, *engines;* as, "You mortal *engines* [cannon], whose rude throats The immortal Jove's dread clamours counterfeit" (*Shak.*); "now that the *machine* [dogcart] is at the gate" (*Barrie*). This distinction is still apparent in current use; we still call certain vehicles (the automobile, the airplane, etc.) *machines* (though not for the same reasons) and that unit in their structure which generates or supplies power, the *engine.* The words, however, are usually distinguished more broadly. A machine is a construction the parts of which are so formed and so connected with each other that it can be set in motion and made to accomplish work, such as shaping or fabricating materials (as a lathe, a sewing machine), hoisting (an elevator, a crane), printing (a printing press), and the like. An engine is a machine also, but in its specific sense, a machine which turns one form of physical force into another and more usable form, such as pressure on a piston or torque on a crankshaft; thus, a turbine of a vessel is an *engine;* the motor of an automobile or a motorboat is usually a gasoline *engine. Engine* is sometimes applied to the machine which combines both the power-developing and the working units; as, a railway *engine;* a fire *engine.* In extended and figurative use, *machine* is usually applied to something that is like a machine, as in organization (complexity of parts, a specific function for each part, ability to move or act only in obedience to an external force or a prime mover; as, a political *machine*) or in its automatism (as, "in short, I have no feelings; I am a mere *machine*"—*Dickens*). In extended use, *engine* is applied rather to the person or thing that supplies the motive power or the driving force than to the thing moved; as, unenlightened public opinion is an *engine* of destruction; "O, for an *engine* to keep back all clocks" (*B. Jonson*). "Wit's an unruly *engine*, wildly striking Sometimes a friend, sometimes the engineer" (*Herbert*). "Never...had the press been turned into an *engine* of such political importance" (*Prescott*). **Apparatus,** as applied to a thing rather than to a collection of things (see EQUIPMENT), is the most general and the least specific in its implications of any of these words. Like the other words, it denotes a more or less complicated mechanism for effecting a given kind of work, but the parts may be either numerous or very few; they may be adjusted to each other either crudely or delicately; as, a radio receiving *apparatus;* the boy rigged up an *apparatus* consisting of an alarm clock and pulleys for closing his bedroom windows on winter mornings; a machine is an *apparatus* for applying mechanical power; "people...in whom the sensory nervous *apparatus* is highly developed" (*H. Ellis*). **Appliance** is often used in place of *apparatus* for a simple, often portable, machine useful in household work, in laboratories, hospitals, and the like, especially when the intent is to indicate that the power for operation can be supplied readily, as by attaching it to an electrical outlet (electrical *appliances*); thus, vacuum cleaners, washing machines, mechanical refrigerators and sterilizers, etc., come under the description of *appliance*, whether the power is supplied by hand, gas, electricity, heat, or the like.

Ana. Contrivance, *device, contraption, gadget: *implement, tool, instrument, utensil, appliance.

machinery. *Equipment, apparatus, paraphernalia, outfit, tackle, gear, matériel.

Ana. *Means, instrument, instrumentality, agency, medium, vehicle, organ, channel, agent: *machine, engine, apparatus, appliance: *device, contrivance, contraption, gadget: *implement, tool, instrument, utensil, appliance.

macrocosm. Cosmos, universe, world, *earth.

mad. 1 *Insane, crazy, crazed, demented, deranged, lunatic, maniac, wood, non compos mentis.

Ana. Frenzied, hysterical, delirious (see corresponding nouns at MANIA): *irrational, unreasonable.

2 *Angry, irate, wrathful, indignant, acrimonious.

Ana. Maddened, incensed, infuriated, enraged (see ANGER, *v.*): inflamed, fired, enkindled (see LIGHT, *v.*).

Con. Collected, composed, *cool, nonchalant, imperturbable.

madden. *Anger, incense, enrage, infuriate.

Ana. Vex, *annoy, irk: exasperate, provoke, roil, aggravate, *irritate.

Con. *Pacify, placate, mollify, appease, propitiate, conciliate: assuage, allay, mitigate, *relieve.

magazine. 1 *Armory, arsenal.

2 *Journal, periodical, review, organ, newspaper.

magic, *n.* **Magic, sorcery, witchcraft, witchery, wizardry, alchemy, thaumaturgy** are allied rather than synonymous in meaning, especially in their literal senses. Figuratively, they are often employed indifferently, without regard to the implications of their primary senses and with little distinction from the most inclusive term, *magic*. **Magic** literally designates any of the arts or the body of arts whose practitioners claim supernatural or occult powers, as in calling spirits to their assistance, in performing miracles, in divining the future, and in fixing the destinies of men. Figuratively, the word denotes a power or influence that produces effects akin to those of magic. Discriminating writers, however, give it specific implications. Most commonly it stresses the power to call forth an image, an emotion, a response, or the like, from, or as if from, a void. "His *magic* was not far to seek,—He was so human!... Where'er He met a stranger, there he left a friend" (*J. R. Lowell*). "The faint significance of [certain] words...for a common dullard, or their evocative *magic* for a Keats" (*C. E. Montague*). Less often it is applied to an art or an artist transcending the natural or explainable. "But Shakespeare's *magic* could not copied be; Within that circle none durst walk but he" (*Dryden*). **Sorcery** is the form of magic practiced by those who use incantations and charms and cast spells in order to work their ends, usually harmful ends. Consequently, in careful figurative use, it suggests an attempt to overpower or enthrall by glamour or artful enchantment. "To fence my ear against thy *sorceries*" (*Milton*). "Virtues pushed to extremes, And *sorceries* of talent misapplied" (*Wordsworth*). **Witchcraft, witchery, wizardry,** in their primary senses, suggest powers derived from evil spirits or the use of human beings as the instruments for the accomplishment of Satanic ends, the only difference being that the first two are chiefly applied to the work of women, and the last to that of men. Figuratively, however, they vary in implications. **Witchcraft** is sometimes indistinguishable from *sorcery*, but it more often suggests guile rather than enchantment and wiles rather than spells. "There is something more than *witchcraft* in them [women], That masters ev'n the wisest of us all" (*Rowe*). **Witchery,** on the other hand, seldom implies either sorcery or guile, and stresses rather a winning grace or an alluring loveliness. "The soft blue sky did never melt Into his heart; he never felt The *witchery* of the soft blue sky!" (*Wordsworth*). **Wizardry** suggests a more virile and compelling power to enchant and, in modern use, usually connotes abnormal skill, talent, or creative power in the person who exerts such an influence; as, the *wizardry* of a Kreisler. "That white-winged legion through whom we had ploughed our way were not, could never be, to me just gulls...; there was the *wizardry* of my past wonder, the enchantment of romance" (*Galsworthy*). **Alchemy** is properly classed as magic only because its practitioners claimed mastery of secret forces in nature and the power to work miracles, such as the changing of base into precious metals. In discriminating figurative use, therefore, it implies transmutation, sometimes transfiguration. "Gilding pale streams with heavenly *alchemy*" (*Shak.*). "By happy *alchemy* of mind They turn to pleasure all they find" (*M. Green*). "The vast majority of those who write verse are unendowed with the assimilating *alchemy* of genius" (*Lowes*). **Thaumaturgy,** which is literally applied to the art of all wonder-workers, especially to that of conjurors or of those who profess the power to work miracles, is in figurative use applied to that which mystifies and dazzles. "The *thaumaturgic* powers, of Virgil, or...of Shakespeare" (*Pater*).

magisterial, magistral. Authoritative, authoritarian, *dictatorial, dogmatic, doctrinaire, oracular.

Ana. *Masterful, domineering, imperious, imperative, peremptory: directing, controlling, conducting, managing (see CONDUCT, *v.*).

magnificent. Imposing, stately, majestic, august, noble, grandiose, *grand.

Ana. *Splendid, resplendent, glorious, sublime, superb: opulent, sumptuous, *luxurious: ostentatious, pretentious, *showy.

Ant. Modest. — *Con.* *Mean, abject, ignoble, sordid: trifling, trivial, *petty, paltry: *humble, meek, lowly.

magnify. *Exalt, aggrandize.

Ana. Extol, *praise, laud, acclaim, eulogize: enlarge, *increase, augment: *expand, amplify, distend, swell, inflate, dilate.

Ant. Minimize, belittle. — *Con.* *Decry, depreciate, detract from, derogate from: reduce, lessen, diminish, *decrease: *contract, shrink, deflate.

magniloquent. Grandiloquent, aureate, flowery, *rhetorical, euphuistic, bombastic.

Ana. Turgid, tumid, *inflated, flatulent: theatrical, histrionic, melodramatic, *dramatic.

magnitude. Volume, *size, extent, dimensions, area.

Ana. Amplitude, *expanse, stretch, spread: *bulk, mass, volume.

maiden, *adj.* *Youthful, juvenile, virgin, virginal, puerile, boyish.

Ant. Experienced.

maim. **Maim, cripple, mutilate, batter, mangle** come into comparison when they mean to injure the body (or the object) so severely as to leave permanent or long-lasting effects. **Maim** implies the loss of a limb or of a member or the destruction of its usefulness by war, accident, the deliberate act of oneself or another, or the like; as, thousands were killed in the three days' battle but tens of thousands were *maimed;* automobiles *maim* large numbers of persons every year; blinded, legless, armless, and other *maimed* men were carried from the wreck. **Cripple** (as here compared: see also WEAKEN) is more restricted than *maim* because strictly it implies the loss of, or the deprivation of the use of, a leg or arm or part of one; as, he is *crippled* as a result of an amputation following blood poisoning; *crippled* by a congenital hip disease. **Mutilate** (for specific sense of this word, see STERILIZE, 1) implies the cutting off or removal of a part essential to completeness, not only of a person but also of a thing, and to his or its perfection, beauty, entirety, fulfillment of function, or the like; as, "like a company of dolls a cruel child has *mutilated,* snapping a foot off here, tearing out a leg here" (*Jefferies*); "Windows...darkened by time and *mutilated* by wilful injury" (*H. Adams*); "The last twelve pages of this codex have been *mutilated* by...a [burning] brand which fell upon the book... destroying many lines of the text" (*Modern Language Notes*). **Batter** and **mangle** do not suggest loss of limb, member, or part, but they do suggest injuries which excessively disfigure the person or thing. *Batter* implies a pounding (literal or figurative) that bruises deeply, deforms, or mutilates; as, he emerged from the fight *battered* and dazed; "The first time he made a helmet, he tested its capacity for resisting blows, and *battered* it out of shape" (*B. Russell*); "[the captain's unworldliness] must have appealed straight to that bruised and *battered* young soul" (*Conrad*). *Mangle,* on the other hand, implies a tearing or hacking, and a covering (literally or figuratively) with deep wounds or lacerations; as, "*Mangled* with ghastly wounds through plate and mail" (*Milton*); "reckless people who have disregarded the warnings and been *mangled* by sharks" (*V. Heiser*).

Ana. Mar, spoil, damage, *injure: *deface, disfigure.

main, *adj.* Principal, leading, *chief, foremost, capital.

Ana. Cardinal, vital, *essential, fundamental: prime, *primary, primal.

Con. *Subordinate, secondary, dependent, subject, collateral.

maintain. **Maintain, assert, defend, vindicate, justify** come into comparison when they mean to uphold as true, right, just, valid, or worthy of notice or acceptance in the face of opposition or indifference. **Maintain** always implies a firmness of conviction. When this implication is the only one, *maintain* usually means to argue in the spirit of one who does not admit any weakness in one's contention. "The artisan, for example, ranks no doubt lower than the professional man; but no one *maintains* that he is a different kind of being" (*G. L. Dickinson*). "There is...a Philosophic Doctrine—...I know that many serious people believe it—which *maintains* that all men, in spite of appearances and pretensions...live alike for Pleasure" (*L. P. Smith*). Often, however, the term additionally implies persistency or insistency in upholding in defiance of all opposition. "Before this Court ought to intervene the case should be of serious magnitude clearly and fully proved, and the principle to be applied should be one which the Court is prepared deliberately to *maintain* against all considerations on the other side" (*Justice Holmes*). **Assert** (see also ASSERT, 1) so strongly implies a determination to make others accept or recognize that which one puts forward as the truth, or as a claim, or as a right, or the like, that it often suggests aggressiveness or obtrusiveness. "The provision of the constitution never has been understood to embrace other contracts, than those which...confer rights which may be *asserted* in a court of justice" (*Ch. Just. Marshall*). But *assert* does not always imply the use of argument to force conviction or recognition. "Any one ...can feel the sustained dignity of the sculptor's work, which is *asserted* with all the emphasis he could put into it" (*H. Adams*). "On the whole New Zealand was lavish with money and attention, and used force only to *assert* her sovereignty" (*V. Heiser*). **Defend** implies a maintaining in the face of attack with the intention of demonstrating the truth, rightness, etc., of what is questioned; thus, one *defends* a thesis who, as a candidate for a high degree, submits himself to examiners who assail the weak or dubious points of his argument. "The independence of the Supreme Court of the United States should be *defended* at all costs" (*Lippmann*). *Defend,* in this sense, does not imply as it so often implies in its more common sense (see DEFEND, 1), that the defender is in a weak or dubious position; however, it seldom suggests as much aggressiveness as does *assert,* and often connotes the aim of an apologist. "I have not adopted my faith in order to *defend* my views of conduct" (*T. S. Eliot*). **Vindicate,** as here compared (see also EXCULPATE), implies an attempt, usually a successful attempt, at defense or assertion. It presupposes that whatever is being defended or asserted has been, or is capable of being, challenged, questioned, denied, contemned, or the like. When the emphasis is on defense, then argument or something which has the force of argument is usually implied, and an aim not only to make one's point but to confute and confound one's opponents is often connoted. "Writers who *vindicated* our hereditary House of Lords against a certain Parliament Act" (*Quiller-Couch*). "We find him [Mark Twain]...*vindicating,* frantically *vindicating,* causes...which he was constrained to consider just" (*Van W. Brooks*). When the emphasis is upon assertion, *vindicate* usually implies an effort to resist triumphantly the force of encroachment or interference, or to overwhelm those who deny or doubt, not so much by argument as by appropriate action. "Arise, and *vindicate* Thy Glory; free thy people from their yoke!" (*Milton*). "The doctrine of Apostolical Succession, which is not held in this form by any other Church in Christendom, gave them the weapon which they wanted, *vindicating* against Rome their title to be Catholic priests" (*Inge*). "What was it that stood in his way? His unfortunate timidity! He wished to *vindicate* himself in some way, to assert his manhood" (*Joyce*). **Justify** (as here compared: see also EXPLAIN, 2; JUSTIFY, 3) implies that the thing concerned can no longer be opposed or ignored, because it has been conclusively shown to be true, valid, proper, or the like, by irrefutable arguments or on inescapable grounds, such as its consequences, its successful operation, or the like. "If the Germans are to *justify* the high claims they make for Lessing as a critic, they must rest them on other grounds than his intellectual originality" (*Babbitt*). "Fate persists in *justifying* the harsh generalizations of Puritan morals" (*Bennett*). "It isn't by the materials you use that your claim to originality will stand *justified* or condemned; it is solely by the thing you do with them" (*Lowes*).

Ana. Affirm, aver, protest, avow, declare, avouch (see ASSERT): *contend, fight, battle, war: persist, *persevere.

Con. *Oppose, combat, resist, withstand: *deny, gainsay, contradict, traverse.

maintenance. Sustenance, support, *living, livelihood, subsistence, keep, bread.

majestic. Stately, august, noble, magnificent, imposing, *grand, grandiose.

Ana. Lofty, *high: sublime, superb, glorious, *splendid, resplendent: monumental, tremendous (see MONSTROUS): *exceptional.

Con. *Mean, abject, sordid, ignoble: lowly, *humble, modest, meek: *ordinary, common.

major-domo. Seneschal, *steward, reeve, bailiff, agent, factor, oeconomus.

majority. *Age.

Ant. Minority. — *Con.* *Infancy, nonage.

make, *v.* **Make, form, shape, fashion, fabricate, manufacture, forge** are synonymous in so far as they mean to cause something to come into being or existence. This is the underlying meaning of **make,** the most general and the most widely applicable of all these terms. *Make* may imply the operation either of an intelligent agent or of a blind agency, and either material or immaterial existence; as, to *make* a chair, a poem, a bargain, a choice, a nest; this factory *makes* bicycles; he is unable to *make* friends; God *made* the world; the spider *makes* webs; the liver *makes* bile; your statements *make* sense. **Form** adds to *make* the implication that the thing brought into being has a definite outline, design, structure, or the like; as, the sculptor *forms* hands with exquisite delicacy; we are ready to *form* a plan; to *form* a federation of states; character is partly *formed* by training. **Shape,** though often interchangeable with *form,* is much more restricted in its application because it characteristically connotes an external agent or agency literally or figuratively impressing a particular form upon something as by molding, beating, carving, cutting, or the like; as, the blacksmith *shapes* (better than *forms*) a horseshoe on his anvil; to *shape* a hat on a block; events that *shaped* (not *formed*) his career; "Every life is a work of art *shaped* by the man who lives it" (*G. L. Dickinson*). **Fashion,** as here compared, means to form, but it implies an intelligent agent (sometimes, a purposeful agency) and more or less inventive power or ingenuity; as, he *fashioned* a table out of an old box; "like the sculptor, who never can *fashion* a hair or a thread in marble" (*C. E. Montague*); legislative committees often *fashion* strange bills out of miscellaneous suggestions. **Fabricate** stresses a making that unites many parts or materials into a whole; it usually connotes either a making according to a standardized pattern (as, to *fabricate* doors, windows, and other parts of a house; cf. *prefabricated* houses), or skillfulness in construction; as, to *fabricate* a good plot for a novel; "a dramatist...who *fabricates* plays so well knit" (*T. S. Eliot*). Very commonly, however, *fabricate* implies a making or inventing of something false as by the exercise of the imagination. "The particulars of that genealogy, embellished with every detail that memory had handed down or fancy *fabricated*" (*Stevenson*). "His feats of legerdemain sounded so improbable that many people considered his experiences *fabricated*" (*V. Heiser*). **Manufacture** emphasizes the making of something (usually something objective) by labor, originally by hand but now more often by machinery. The term is now applied to any making in which raw materials are used and a definite process or series of processes is followed; as, to *manufacture* wool, or cloth, or utensils, or machines, or automobiles. In extended use, *manufacture* often is preferred to any of the preceding words when laboriousness or the knowledge of the mechanics of a process, rather than skill or ingenuity, is connoted; as, to *manufacture* paintings by the dozen; "*manufactured* sensations" (*Brownell*). **Forge** literally suggests the operation of a blacksmith or other smith who heats metal and beats or hammers it into shape; as, to *forge* a horseshoe; to *forge* a chain. In its extended sense, it carries a strong implication of devising, concocting, or the like, by physical or mental effort, so as to give the appearance of truth or reality; as, "The proud have *forged* a lie against me: but I will keep thy precepts with my whole heart" (*Psalms* cxix. 69); "Whate'er I *forge* to feed his brain-sick fits, Do you uphold and maintain in your speeches" (*Shak.*); "however feeling may render plastic the stuff of poetry, the poem, if it be worthy of the name, is *forged* in the brain" (*Lowes*). In specific use, both legal and ordinary, *forge* implies the making of a counterfeit, especially by imitating the handwriting of an original or of a supposed maker; thus, one *forges* a document, such as a will, deed, check, or the like, by making it or by signing it in imitation of another's handwriting or by making alterations in a genuine document by the same means; as, he was able to live luxuriously by *forging* checks until he was apprehended.

Ana. Produce, turn out, yield, *bear: *compose, comprise, constitute, consist of: accomplish, achieve, effect, fulfill (see PERFORM).

make-believe, make-belief. *Pretense, pretension.

maker, *n.* **Maker, creator, author** are here considered only in their most general sense, when they denote one who brings something into being or existence. When written with an initial capital letter, all three terms designate God, or the Supreme Being; without the capital they ascribe similar but not equivalent powers or effects to a person. **Maker** typically implies a close and immediate relationship between the one who makes and the thing that is made. It implies literally or figuratively the handling of the material, and individual or personal responsibility for that which is turned out; hence, in hymns, prayers, and the like, God is usually called "my *Maker*" or "our *Maker*"; *maker* in such terms as king-*maker,* a *maker* of men, a *maker* of phrases, a *maker* of poems, suggests the use of persons, words, ideas, and the like, as instruments by which one brings something into existence through one's own labor or effort. "The sea is his, and he made it: and his hands formed the dry land. O come, let us worship and bow down: let us kneel before the Lord our *maker*" (*Psalms* xcv. 5–6). **Creator,** on the other hand, seldom suggests either literally or figuratively the use or handling of materials; its leading implication is that of bringing into existence what the mind conceives and the will, as the mind's instrument, carries out. As applied to God, the term usually evokes the picture of Creation, as presented in Genesis; the term is used, therefore, rather than *maker,* when his omnipotence and the greatness of his works are stressed. "And touched their golden harps, and hymning praised God and his works; *Creator* him they sung" (*Milton*). In the same way, *creator* is used of a man who brings into being something new, which has form in his mind or imagination before he gives it objective existence. "[The poetic spirit] Doth like an agent of the one great Mind Create, *creator* and receiver both" (*Wordsworth*). "A conservator, call me, if you please, Not a *creator* nor destroyer" (*Browning*). "To...experiment with new ones [forms of art] not as an imitator, but as a *creator*" (*S. Alexander*). **Author** is applied to one who originates and who, therefore, is not only the source, or ultimate source, but the one responsible for a person's or thing's existence. It is applied to God chiefly in the phrase "the *Author* of my being" (this phrase with *author* uncapitalized is sometimes applied to one's begetter, or father), when the reference is to the gift of life or its attendant circumstances. "Then casting up my eyes, thanked the *Author* of my being for the gift of that wild forest, those green mansions where I had found so great a happiness" (*Hudson*). In reference to persons, it is not only applied to a writer (see WRITER) but also to a founder, an inventor, an initiator, or anyone who brings something into existence; as, "the policy of which he was principally the *author*" (*Belloc*); "the gay and bewitching...coquette Célimène who is the *author* of all Alceste's woes" (*S. Alexander*).

makeshift. Shift, expedient, *resource, resort, stopgap, substitute, surrogate.
Ana. *Device, contrivance, contraption, gadget: *means, instrument, agency, instrumentality.

maladroit. Clumsy, gauche, inept, *awkward.
Ant. Adroit. — *Con.* *Dexterous, deft, feat, handy: *clever, cunning, ingenious: skilled, skillful, expert, adept, *proficient: politic, diplomatic, bland, smooth (see SUAVE).

malady. Ailment, affection, *disease, complaint, distemper.

male, *adj.* **Male, masculine, manly, manlike, mannish, manful, virile** agree in meaning of, characteristic of, or like a male of the species, especially of the human species. **Male** (opposed to *female*) applies to animals and plants as well as to human beings, and always indicates sex; as, "a *male* tiger" (*Shak.*); "a *male* tree" (*Gilbert White*); "*male* children" (*Joshua* xvii. 2); a *male* choir. **Masculine** (opposed to *feminine*) is used to distinguish grammatical gender (as, *masculine* nouns and pronouns), but it applies most frequently to physical and mental characteristics (such as vigor, strength, size, etc.) which belong to men rather than to women; as, "he was a big, active, *masculine* creature" (*Deland*); "the *masculine* character lying behind the lofty idealism of Sung painting" (*Binyon*). "His poetry is *masculine*, plain, concentrated, and energetic" (*Landor*). "In antiquity the virtues that were most admired were...those which are distinctively *masculine*. Courage, self-assertion, magnanimity, and above all, patriotism" (*Lecky*). The use of *masculine* instead of *male* in such phrases as "the *masculine* part of the audience" is not regarded with approval. **Manly** (often opposed to *boyish, childish*) commonly suggests the finer qualities of a man, especially courage, frankness, independence, or the physical characters and skills which come with maturity: it is applicable not only to men but to boys (as, a *manly* boy); as, "His big *manly* voice, Turning again toward childish treble" (*Shak.*); "What more *manly* exercise than hunting?" (*Walton*); "It was amusing to watch the *manly* coolness with which the announcement was taken" (*Meredith*). **Manlike** is more apt to suggest characteristically masculine qualities or, especially, foibles; as, *manlike* bluntness; "From long association with men she had learnt a *manlike* reticence" (*H. S. Scott*). Oftentimes *manlike* suggests reference to man in the more general sense of the word and therefore means little more than human, or like human beings; as, hairy *manlike* creatures such as some apes; "*Man-like* is it to fall into sin ... God-like is it all sin to leave" (*Longfellow, transl. from von Logau*). **Mannish** (often contrasted with *womanish* or *effeminate*) applies chiefly to women, their dress, gait, manners, or the like, when they suggest masculinity rather than femininity; as, "A woman impudent and *mannish* grown" (*Shak.*); a *mannish* costume. But sometimes *mannish* (as opposed to *childish*) applies to boys or youths who affect the airs and manners of a mature man; as, "Why must every thing smack of man and *mannish?* Is the world all grown up?" (*Lamb*). **Manful** differs from *manly* chiefly in its greater stress on sturdiness and resoluteness; as, a *manful* struggle; a *manful* effort to gain self-control. **Virile** (a stronger word than *masculine* and opposed to *puerile* or, in specific sense, to *impotent*) suggests qualities belonging to fully developed manhood, such as aggressiveness, masterfulness, forcefulness, and in a specific sense, procreativeness. It differs from *manly* and *manful* in being applied only to mature men or sometimes, in its general sense, to mature women (since it often suggests character rather than sex); as, "more '*virile*'...than his brothers" (*Galsworthy*); "*virile* controversialists" (*Inge*); a *virile* style. "Ye chiefly, *virile* both to think and feel, Deep-chested Chapman and firm-footed Ben" (*J. R. Lowell*).
Ant. Female. — *Con.* Feminine, womanly, womanlike, womanish, ladylike (see FEMALE).

malediction. *Curse, imprecation, malison, anathema.
Ant. Benediction. — *Con.* *Blessing, benison.

malefic. Malign, baleful, *sinister.

malevolence. Ill will, malignity, *malice, spite, despite, spleen, grudge.
Ana. Animosity, rancor, animus, antipathy, antagonism, *enmity, hostility: hate, hatred, detestation, abhorrence, abomination (see under HATE, *v.*).
Ant. Benevolence. — *Con.* Benignity, benignancy, kindliness, kindness (see corresponding adjectives at KIND): good will, *favor, countenance.

malevolent. Malignant, malign, *malicious, spiteful, despiteful, despiteous.
Ana. *Sinister, baleful, malign, malefic.
Ant. Benevolent. — *Con.* Benign, benignant, *kind, kindly: *charitable, humane, altruistic, humanitarian, philanthropic.

malice. **Malice, malevolence, ill will, spite, despite, malignity, spleen, grudge** come into comparison when they denote a feeling or a state of mind which leads one to desire that another or others should suffer pain or injury. **Malice** usually implies a deep-seated and, often, an unjustified or unexplainable desire: it frequently carries an implication of an innate pleasure in doing evil, in inflicting injury, in seeing others suffer, or in wanton destruction; as, "With *malice* toward none; with charity for all...let us...bind up the nation's wounds" (*Lincoln*); "there are people in the world with that degree of ...*malice* in them that they can't bear to allow a good man his merits" (*Shaw*); "Man, with his usual monkey-like *malice*, took pleasure in pulling down what he had built up" (*H. Adams*). Often, however, in current use, it implies mischievousness or impishness rather than a hardened, vindictive nature. "She was clever, witty, brilliant, and sparkling beyond most of her kind; but possessed of many devils of *malice* and mischievousness" (*Kipling*). In law, *malice* applies to the state of mind of one who willfully commits wrong, as in full deliberation (as, *malice aforethought* or *malice prepense*), or out of hatred and a desire to inflict injury on another (as, *malice in fact*), or out of the depravity of one's nature (as, *implied malice*). **Malevolence,** and the more common **ill will,** usually imply a state of mind or a feeling arising out of hatred, enmity, resentment, or the like: neither term carries so strong an implication of an inherently evil or vicious nature as does *malice*, but neither term necessarily suggests less evil or injuriousness in the acts motivated by them. "Let those who have betrayed him by their adulation, insult him with their *malevolence*" (*Burke*). "Irritable, suspicious, and aggressive...constantly regarding himself as the victim of other people's *malevolence*" (*H. Ellis*). "Catherine could not believe it possible that any injury or any misfortune could provoke such *ill-will* against a person...not supposed to be connected with it" (*Austen*). **Spite** implies active malevolence or ill will colored especially by envy or meanness of spirit; as, "contemporary *spites* do not harm true genius" (*A. Lang*). "One feels that the style [of certain satires] has generated the hate. It is, indeed, a little shabby, a little insignificant: not really hate at all, but *spite*" (*Day Lewis*). **Despite** (see also under DESPISE) differs from *spite* chiefly in carrying a strong implication of wounded pride or of contempt or disdain. "Because thou hast...rejoiced in heart with all thy *despite* against the land of Israel...I will...deliver thee for a spoil to the heathen" (*Ezekiel* xxv. 6–7). "If you will imagine a glint of moonlight running up the blade of a rapier, you may know the chill flame of *spite* and *despite* that bickered in her eyes then as she spoke" (*Quiller-Couch*). **Malignity** implies one or more of these states of mind, but it stresses, more than any of the preceding terms, the intensity of the passion and its driving force; as, he could not escape the *malignity* of his enemy; "he is cruel with the cruelty of petrified feeling, to his poor heroine; he pursues her without pity or pause, as with *malignity*" (*Arnold*). **Spleen** implies deep-seated ill will (sometimes, but not necessarily, directed against a particular individual) combined with a choleric temperament: it usually suggests either latent spite or malice and the wish to harm in an outburst of wrath; as, the old man vented his *spleen* on any child at play who unwittingly impeded his progress. "It requires an infinitely smaller psychic effort to expel one's *spleen* in a verbal joke than in a practical joke or a murder" (*Van W. Brooks*). **Grudge** applies to cherished ill will, against an individual, which seeks satisfaction: it usually suggests deep resentment for some real or fancied slight or affront and, often, a determination to get even; as, "I will feed fat the ancient *grudge* I bear him" (*Shak.*); "this same inveterate *grudge*" (*N. Hawthorne*); "Buried at the root of the relations between the sisters was Sophia's *grudge* against Constance for refusing to leave the Square" (*Bennett*); "He held no *grudge* against any of the people who had misused him" (*Cather*).

Ana. Malignancy, malignity, maliciousness, spitefulness (see corresponding adjectives at MALICIOUS): venom, bane, *poison: animosity, animus, rancor, antipathy, *enmity.

Ant. Charity. — *Con.* *Mercy, grace, clemency, lenity: benignity, benignancy, kindness, kindliness (see corresponding adjectives at KIND): *favor, good will, countenance.

malicious. Malicious, malevolent, malignant, malign, spiteful, despiteful, despiteous, dispiteous come into comparison when they mean disposed, as a person, to do or to inflict evil or, as an act, prompted by such a disposition. A person or thing is **malicious** that is motivated or dictated by hatred or spite and, usually, by a desire to inflict injury and suffering and to see another in disgrace or an object of ridicule or contempt; as, "such *malicious* revenge, such injustice, such inhumanity" (*Austen*); "Gunga Dass took a *malicious* pleasure in emphasizing this point and in watching me wince" (*Kipling*). "One...might certainly have supposed that the reason why the square-shouldered, clumsy, high-featured Priscilla wore a dress the fac-simile of her pretty sister's, was either the mistaken vanity of the one, or the *malicious* contrivance of the other in order to set off her own rare beauty" (*G. Eliot*). A person or thing is **malevolent** that evidences ill will or an intent to do evil, or a sinister influence; as, "Captain Tilney must have heard some *malevolent* misrepresentation of her" (*Austen*); "There is no free breath to be drawn within the sphere of so *malevolent* an influence" (*N. Hawthorne*); "[Henry Adams] did not believe, with Wordsworth, that nature is a holy and beneficent thing, or with Blake, that nature is a wicked and *malevolent* thing" (*A. Repplier*). A person or thing is **malignant** that is actuated or characterized by virulent ill will or extreme malevolence (or, when the reference is to a disease or bodily condition, by extreme virulence or infectiousness); as, a *malignant* enemy; "A churel is the peculiarly *malignant* ghost of a woman who has died in child-bed" (*Kipling*); "His cold, *malignant* rage" (*L. P. Smith*); *malignant* diphtheria; a *malignant* tumor or growth. A person or thing is **malign** (see also SINISTER) that harbors violent enmity or ill will or threatens extreme evil or danger: the term, in contrast with *malignant*, carries a stronger implication of potentiality and therefore may or may not suggest certainty of effect; as, "a soul That spurns the crowd's *malign* control" (*H. Gifford*); *malign* influences; a *malign* desire; "Or praise *malignly* arts I cannot reach" (*Pope*); "By Fiends of aspect more *malign*" (*Wordsworth*). **Spiteful** and **despiteful** imply a deep-seated malice or malevolence provoked especially by a desire to get even with others for real or fancied offenses. *Spiteful*, however, carries a stronger implication of meanness or venomousness of temper and refers even more often to utterances than to acts; as, *spiteful* gossip; she has a *spiteful* tongue; "a *spiteful* saying gratifies so many little passions" (*Addison*). "'Well,' said Mr. Potter, who was not *spiteful* to his children, and preferred his wife unruffled, 'We'll let you off this time'" (*R. Macaulay*). *Despiteful*, on the other hand, stresses cherished ill will or deep contempt as well as a desire to injure or get even; as, "the heinous and *despiteful* act Of Satan done in Paradise" (*Milton*); "the great world dark and *despiteful*" (*Kingsley*). **Despiteous,** and the now more common **dispiteous,** though they imply despitefulness, stress mercilessness or lack of all pity or desire to ease the ills of one's victims; as, "Spurring so hot with rage *dispiteous*" (*Spenser*); "The proud, *despiteous* rich man" (*W. Morris*).

Ana. *Poisonous, venomous, virulent, toxic: *pernicious, noxious, baneful, deleterious, detrimental: *envious, jealous: wanton, gratuitous, uncalled-for, *supererogatory.

malign, *adj.* **1** Malignant, *malicious, malevolent, spiteful, despiteful, despiteous.

Ana. Inimical, hostile, rancorous, antipathetic, antagonistic (see corresponding nouns at ENMITY): venomous, virulent, *poisonous, toxic.

Ant. Benign. — *Con.* Benignant, kindly, *kind.

2 *Sinister, baleful, malefic.

Ana. Threatening, menacing (see THREATEN): baneful, noxious, *pernicious, deleterious: disastrous, catastrophic, cataclysmic, calamitous (see corresponding nouns at DISASTER).

Ant. Benign. — *Con.* *Favorable, auspicious, propitious: fortunate, *lucky, providential, happy.

malign, *v.* **Malign, traduce, asperse, vilify, calumniate, defame, slander, libel** agree in meaning to speak evil of for the purpose of injuring and without regard for the truth. **Malign** and **traduce** usually imply persecution; they commonly suggest hatred, violent prejudice, bigotry, or some other equally blinding passion as the motive. *Malign*, however, although it always carries the implication that the person, group, race, or the like, affected is the victim of lies, does not necessarily impute deliberate lying to the speaker or writer; as, the most *maligned* race in history; "gossips had *maligned* the lady" (*Meredith*); whether Machiavelli has been *maligned* by some of his earlier biographers or not is still an open question. *Traduce* carries these implications also but it stresses the resulting ignominy more than *malign;* as, to believe that the English queen called "Bloody Mary" has been *traduced* by historians. "If I am *Traduced* by ignorant tongues... 'Tis but the fate of place, and the rough brake That virtue must go through" (*Shak.*). "Fear of this witch of the East [Cleopatra], shamelessly *traduced* by Octavian's agents, hag-rode the popular mind" (*Buchan*). **Asperse** and **vilify** both imply efforts to destroy a person's good name or reputation. *Asperse* suggests an intent to detract from one's reputation or to lower one in popular esteem by direct accusations or, more often, by subtler methods such as innuendo or spreading reports; as, to cause a run on a bank by *aspersing* its credit; to *asperse* the family of the opposing candidate in an election. "There were foul tongues to *asperse* a Douglas" (*Scott*). *Vilify* implies open methods and an intent to blacken one's good name and to render it ignominious; it usually suggests direct accusation coupled with violent abuse and scurrilous name-calling. "With a malignant insanity, we oppose the measures, and ungratefully *vilify* the persons, of those whose sole object is our own peace and prosperity" (*Burke*). "The soldier of to-day...should not be blamed for falling back. He should be shot or hanged afterward...but he should not be *vilified* in newspapers" (*Kipling*). **Calumniate** imputes malice to the speaker or writer and falsity to his aspersions or accusations, and usually implies that his false and malicious statements have seriously damaged the good name of his victim; as, the verdict of history is that Benedict Arnold was not *calumniated*, but was justly charged with treason. "*Calumniating* and ridiculing the Church which he had deserted" (*Macaulay*). *Defame, slander*, and *libel* are found both in general and in legal use, but their strict legal definitions are more or less affecting their literary meanings. All imply calumniation, but they differ from *calumniate* mainly in their emphasis on the positive damaging effect of the lies. **Defame,** both in legal and in literary use, suggests an actual injury to one's good name or a definite loss of repute or reputation. "*Defaming* and defacing, till she left Not even Lancelot brave nor Galahad clean" (*Tennyson*). "Captain Basil Hall...was publicly accused of being an agent of the British government on a special mission to blacken and *defame* this country" (*Van W. Brooks*). To **slander,** in strict legal use, is to defame orally; in general use, it is not so narrowly employed, but covers both written and printed as well as oral calumniation. It also, more strongly than *defame* or *calumniate*, connotes positive suffering on the part of the victim. "*Slander'd* to death by villains, That dare as well answer a man indeed As I dare take a serpent by the tongue" (*Shak.*). "And she to be coming and *slandering* me, the base little liar! But the tongue is a fire as you know, my dear, the tongue is a fire" (*Tennyson*). **Libel** is chiefly a legal term; in general use its implications are much the same. It implies the printing or writing of that which defames a person or his reputation and the publication or circulation of such printed or written matter; as, Grub Street hacks who made their living by *libeling* famous men; to *libel* a politician by a caricature.

Ana. Detract from, *decry, disparage, depreciate, derogate from: vituperate, revile (see SCOLD): defile, pollute (see CONTAMINATE).

Ant. Defend. — *Con.* Vindicate, justify, *maintain: extol, eulogize, *praise.

malignant. Malign, malevolent, *malicious, spiteful, despiteful, despiteous.

Ana. Virulent, venomous (see POISONOUS): *envious, jealous: baneful, noxious, *pernicious: diabolical, devilish, *fiendish.

Ant. Benignant. — *Con.* Benign, *kind, kindly: benevolent, *charitable, altruistic, humane.

malignity. *Malice, malevolence, ill will, spite, despite, spleen, grudge.

Ana. Rancor, animus, animosity, *enmity, hostility: malignancy, maliciousness, spitefulness (see corresponding adjectives at MALICIOUS): hatred, *hate: vindictiveness, revengefulness, vengefulness (see corresponding adjectives at VINDICTIVE).

Ant. Benignity. — *Con.* Benignancy, kindliness, kindness (see corresponding adjectives at KIND).

malison. Malediction, *curse, imprecation, anathema.

Ant. Benison. — *Con.* *Blessing, benediction.

mall. *Avenue, alley, allée.

malleable. *Plastic, pliable, pliant, ductile, adaptable.

Ana. Tractable, amenable (see OBEDIENT).

Ant. Refractory. — *Con.* Intractable, recalcitrant, ungovernable, *unruly.

malodorous. Malodorous, stinking, fetid (*or* **foetid**), **noisome, putrid, rank, rancid, fusty, musty** come into comparison when they mean emitting an unpleasant smell. **Malodorous** is the general term which is referable to any smell of this character, from one that is manifestly unpleasant to one that is distinctly offensive; as, *malodorous* flowers; *malodorous* foods such as certain cheeses or sauerkraut may be agreeable to the taste. **Stinking,** the colloquial and vulgar term, and **fetid,** the literary, technical, and often, in colloquial use, the preferable term, describe an odor or a thing that emits an odor which is peculiarly offensive: the former more obviously suggests disgusting foulness than the latter; as, a *stinking* dungeon; a *stinking* outhouse; a *fetid* weed; "he detected at once a *fetid* odour, not very strong but highly disagreeable" (*Cather*). **Noisome,** which in an earlier and now rare sense means noxious, is applicable chiefly to that which emits a poisonously or unwholesomely offensive odor; as, "Four sewers emptied into these twenty-five acres of swamp and morass—stagnant, *noisome*, and crawling with huge snakes" (*V. Heiser*). **Putrid** is applicable, in literal use, only to organic matter in such a state of decomposition that it is loathsomely malodorous; as, "a bloated, *putrid, noisome* carcass" (*Burke*). **Rank** (as here considered: see also RANK, 1; FLAGRANT) applies to an odor or to a thing which emits an odor that is exceedingly strong and unpleasing yet not necessarily loathsome; as, the *rank* smell of a sunflower; the air is *rank* with the odor of the flowers of the ailanthus, or tree of heaven; "O, my offence is *rank*, it smells to heaven" (*Shak.*). **Rancid** usually suggests an offensive taste as well as an offensive smell (it may suggest merely one or the other), that is indicative of a loss of freshness: in current use, it applies chiefly to oil, butter, and similar substances that have undergone a chemical change or some decomposition; as, *rancid* bacon; the odor of *rancid* perspiration. **Fusty** and **musty** both suggest lack of ventilation and sunlight, but of the two words *fusty* carries the stronger implication of prolonged uncleanliness or of an accumulation of dust and of dirt, and *musty*, the stronger implication of moldiness, of age, or of the effects of darkness or dampness; as, "the ill-ventilated schoolroom full of boys smelt...*fusty*" (*H. Ellis*); the *musty* odor of a damp cellar; "There was an acrid, *musty* smell; the raw air was close with breathing" (*R. Macaulay*).

Ant. Odorous. — *Con.* Fragrant, aromatic, redolent (see ODOROUS).

maltreat. Mistreat, ill-treat, misuse, *abuse, outrage.

Ana. See those at ILL-TREAT.

mammoth. Colossal, gigantic, giant, gigantean, elephantine, titanic, herculean, *enormous, immense, huge, vast, Cyclopean, Antaean, Gargantuan, Brobdingnagian.

Ana. *Monstrous, monumental, stupendous, tremendous, prodigious: ponderous, weighty, cumbrous, cumbersome (see HEAVY).

manacle, *v.* *Hamper, trammel, clog, fetter, shackle, hog-tie.

Ana. *Hinder, impede, obstruct, bar, block: *tie, bind: *restrain, inhibit, curb, check, snaffle.

manage. 1 *Conduct, control, direct.
Ana. *Govern, rule: *guide, lead, steer, pilot, engineer: *handle, manipulate, wield, swing, ply.
2 **Manage, contrive, afford** are not true synonyms, but they are sometimes used interchangeably in certain expressions especially when preceded by *can* and followed by an infinitive (sometimes only by the object of a suppressed infinitive); as, how can you *manage*, or *contrive*, or *afford* to live so comfortably on your salary?; he could not *manage*, or *contrive*, or *afford* (to take) a vacation this year. In such contexts, **manage** implies discovery of ways and means (these latter often being understood or inferred), such as the necessary funds, the necessary permission, the necessary time; as, you can *manage* to get along: **contrive** adds to *manage* the implication of ingenuity or of scheming; as, she *contrives* to run a home on a small budget: **afford,** originally equivalent to *manage*, now is more often equal to *manage to bear the expense of* or *manage to spare the money for;* as, he can *afford* (to buy) an automobile. *Afford* in this sense takes *can* as an auxiliary; the other words often do not.

mandate, *n.* 1 Dictate, *command, order, injunction, bidding, behest.
Ana. Charging *or* charge, direction, instruction (see corresponding verbs at COMMAND): sanctioning *or* sanction, endorsement, approval (see corresponding verbs at APPROVE).
2 **Mandate, initiative, referendum, plebiscite** agree in meaning a political action or procedure whereby a constituency instructs or gives information of its desires to its legislature or legislators. **Mandate,** the most general of these terms, now applies to any instructions delivered by the people in any way, such as by a general vote or by a choice in an election, that makes their wishes clear not only to their representatives in a legislature but also to those who hold the executive power, or, in an extended sense, to those who represent them in any way or who by the nature of their office or duties are necessarily responsive to the will of the people; as, the president of the United States, re-elected by an enormous majority, declared that he had a *mandate* from the people to continue his policies; "It would almost seem as if the present school of fiction is, to borrow a phrase from French politics, exhausting its *mandate*" (*J. M'Carthy*); "Obviously I have no *mandate* to speak for any one but myself" (*J. W. Krutch*). **Initiative** (usually, *the initiative*) often denotes a right, but when it denotes a procedure, it implies recognition of the right of a group of voters or, more often, of a clearly defined number of voters, to propose a new measure or a constitutional amendment to a legislature. In Switzerland, where the initiative, or right to originate legislation, is vested in the people, a demand by 50,000 voters sends a proposed constitutional amendment directly to the people for approval or rejection. The initiative, both as a right and as a procedure, is legally recognized in many of the states of the United States of America. **Referendum,** which is often coupled with *initiative* (as, in the right of *initiative and referendum*), applies to the practice, adopted by the Swiss and by some states and cities in the United States, of sending measures that have been considered by or proposed to the legislative body to the voters for approval or rejection or for an expression of their wishes. **Plebiscite** strictly applies to a vote of the people (now usually by universal suffrage) on some measure submitted to them by the group or the body having the initiative, as where the referendum is employed. In a still narrower sense, *plebiscite* implies a vote of the population of a territorial unit that testifies to their wishes as to the form of government they will accept, their choice in a proposed merger with either of two nations, or the like.
3 Protectorate, dominion, *possession, dependency, territory, colony.

maneuver *or* **manoeuvre,** *n.* Stratagem, *trick, ruse, artifice, wile, feint.
Ana. *Device, contrivance: expedient, resort, *resource, shift, makeshift: intrigue, machination, *plot.

manful. Virile, mannish, manlike, manly, masculine, *male.
Ana. Sturdy, stout, tenacious, stalwart, tough, *strong: resolute, steadfast, stanch (see FAITHFUL): intrepid, bold, *brave.

mangle. Batter, mutilate, *maim, cripple.
Ana. *Injure, damage, mar, impair: *deface, disfigure: *deform, contort, distort.

mania. 1 *Insanity, lunacy, psychosis, dementia.
Ana. Alienation, derangement, *aberration.
Ant. Lucidity.
2 **Mania, delirium, frenzy** (*or, now rare,* **phrenzy**), **hysteria** are here compared as meaning a state of mind in which the person concerned loses control over his emotions, nerves, or mental processes. **Mania** (see also INSANITY) definitely implies madness or insanity: the term may designate a type of madness in which the patient manifests extreme excitability or, in still stricter use, that phase of manic-depressive insanity in which the patient loses control over his powers of thought, of speech, and of movement through violent excitement or excessive emotion; as, "[George III] suffered a third attack of *mania*" (*Dict. Nat. Biog., Concise Ed.*). **Delirium** implies extreme mental disturbance but not, usually, a prolonged or serious mental illness: rather it applies to a mental condition induced by an abnormally high fever, prolonged alcoholic intoxication (then specifically called *delirium tremens*), a severe injury, or the like, and characterized by raving, hallucinations, and extreme restlessness; as, "a raging fever accompanied with *delirium*" (*Dickens*); by pain reduced to a state approaching *delirium*. But *delirium* also, in loose untechnical use, applies to a state of intense emotional excitement that manifests itself in an individual or in a group and robs him or them of all semblance of self-control; as, he is in a *delirium* of joy; "the *delirium* of popular enthusiasm" (*Lecky*); "The *delirium* of the preceding [parliamentary] session" (*J. Morley*). **Frenzy** (see also INSPIRATION) suggests wilder or more violent agitation or disorder than *delirium* but no less emotional excitement: it is applicable both to a state bordering on a mania (as, "demoniac *phrenzy*"—*Milton;* "An act done in the...*frensy* of despair"—*Freeman*) and to one in which for the time being all self-control is lost (as, "His hands released her...and went up to his white hair, which they tore in a *frenzy*"—*Dickens;* "Her intensity, which would leave no emotion on a normal plane, irritated the youth into a *frenzy*"—*D. H. Lawrence;* "Paris wholly has got to the acme of its *frenzy;* whirled, all ways, by panic madness"—*Carlyle*). **Hysteria** applies strictly to a functional nervous disorder not caused by an organic condition but simulating an organic disease in its symptoms (such as partial losses of memory or of sensation, functional paralyses or contractures of the limbs, loss of appetite, or nausea); as, the paralysis of her lower limbs proved to be the result of *hysteria.* In ordinary, nontechnical language *hysteria* implies extreme emotional excitability that may or may not show itself in swift transitions from laughing to crying; as, "she laughed and cried together...in a *hysteria* which she could not control" (*Bennett*); "they were gradually worked up to complaisance and then to enthusiasm and then to *hysteria* and then to acute *mania*" (*Mencken*).

Ana. Depression, dejection, melancholia, melancholy (see SADNESS): *ecstasy, transport: excitement, provocation (see corresponding verbs at PROVOKE).

maniac, maniacal. *Insane, mad, crazy, crazed, demented, deranged, lunatic, wood, non compos mentis.
Ana. *Irrational, unreasonable.
Con. *Rational, reasonable.

manifest, *adj.* *Evident, patent, distinct, obvious, apparent, palpable, plain, clear.
Ana. Revealed, disclosed, divulged, told (see REVEAL): shown, evidenced, evinced (see SHOW, *v.*): conspicuous, *noticeable, prominent.
Ant. Latent: constructive (see IMPLICIT). — *Con.* *Obscure, vague, enigmatic, cryptic, dark: *implicit, virtual.

manifest, *v.* *Show, evidence, evince, demonstrate.
Ana. Exhibit, display, expose (see SHOW, *v.*): *express, vent, utter, voice: *reveal, discover, disclose, divulge.
Ant. Suggest. — *Con.* Adumbrate, shadow (see SUGGEST).

manifold. Multifold, *many, several, sundry, various, divers, numerous, multifarious.
Ana. Diverse, divergent, disparate, *different, various.

manikin. Midget, *dwarf, pygmy, homunculus, runt.
Ant. Giant.

manipulate. *Handle, wield, swing, ply.
Ana. Flourish, brandish, *swing, wave, thrash.

manlike. Mannish, manful, virile, manly, masculine, *male.
Con. Womanlike, feminine, womanish, ladylike, effeminate, womanly, *female.

manly. Manlike, manful, virile, masculine, mannish, *male.
Ana. *Mature, matured, grown-up, adult, full-fledged: sturdy, *strong, stout, stalwart.
Ant. Unmanly. — *Con.* Effeminate, womanish, feminine, *female: dastardly, *cowardly: boyish, puerile, juvenile, *youthful.

manna. *Ambrosia, nectar, amrita.

manner. **1** *Method, mode, way, fashion, system.
Ana. Custom, usage, use, wont, consuetude, practice, *habit, habitude.
2 Mien, demeanor, *bearing, deportment, carriage, port, présence, front.
Ana. Etiquette, propriety, *decorum, decency, dignity: *form, usage, convention, convenance: *tact, address, poise, savoir-faire.

mannerism. *Pose, air, affectation.
Ana. *Eccentricity, idiosyncrasy: peculiarity, singularity, oddness, queerness (see corresponding adjectives at STRANGE).

mannish. Manlike, virile, masculine, *male, manful, manly.
Ant. Womanish. — *Con.* Womanlike, ladylike, feminine, effeminate, *female.

manoeuvre. Variant of MANEUVER.

manufacture. Fabricate, forge, *make, form, shape, fashion.
Ana. Produce, turn out, yield (see BEAR).

manumit. Emancipate, enfranchise, affranchise, deliver, discharge, *free, release, liberate.
Ant. Enslave.

many. **Many, several, sundry, various, divers, numerous, manifold, multifold, multifarious** come into comparison when they mean consisting of a large number or comprising a large group. **Many,** as here compared, implies a likeness between the individuals or units as in class, category, kind, or sort: except that it vaguely implies more than a few, the term gives no explicit suggestion as to how large the number is; as, *many* persons; *many* teachers; *many* novels; *many* sources of information. **Several** (etymologically, separate), as here compared (see also DISTINCT, 1), is almost as vague as *many* in its implication of number. In law, the term is construed as meaning more than one; thus, the *several* counts of an indictment may be two or more counts. In more general use, it is usually construed as meaning at least three; as, the journey will take *several* days; they saw *several* strangers on the road; there are *several* reasons why you should not go. In highly discriminating use, the term means both more than a few and different each from the other: in such use, *several* is often preceded by a possessive adjective; as, "her *several* thoughts...as signalled by the changes on her face" (*Hardy*); "they [the delegates charged with the ratification of the Constitution of the United States] assembled in their *several* states" (*Ch. Just. Marshall*). **Sundry** (now somewhat archaic except in humorous use) also implies an indefinite number, but it carries regularly a stronger implication of the difference of each from the others than does *several;* as, there are *several* (not *sundry*) eggs left; there are *sundry* (more explicit than *several*) aspects of the problem that have not been considered; he appealed to all and *sundry* persons [i.e., to persons collectively and as individuals] to make the campaign for funds a success; "she differed...in *sundry* important features" (*Quiller-Couch*). **Various** (see also DIFFERENT) is often used loosely as meaning an indefinite number, with a more or less attenuated implication of difference in identity of each from each: this use is often, but not universally, disapproved; as, *various* [*many* would be better here if no implication of severality is intended] persons spoke to me about it. **Divers** also has come to imply a vague number, often meaning little more than *many* or *several,* thereby losing its original strong implication of difference among the individuals (cf. *diverse,* under DIFFERENT); as, he told his story to *divers* persons. "God, who at *sundry* times and in *divers* manners spake in time past unto the fathers by the prophets" (*Hebrews* i. 1). **Numerous** may qualify plural nouns or singular nouns that designate a collection or assembly of units or individuals. In each case the term implies the existence of a noticeably large number of units or individuals; sometimes, in fact, it connotes a crowding or thronging; as, every President has *numerous* letters from *numerous* persons; "I have contracted a *numerous* acquaintance among the best sort of people" (*Steele*); "The commoners who had been summoned...formed a *numerous* assembly" (*Macaulay*). **Manifold** (etymologically, having many folds or laps) usually implies numerousness (or more than twofold, threefold, fourfold, etc.): when it is applied to a singular noun (either a collective noun or one designating an abstraction), it suggests both numerousness and diversity in its forms, features, qualities, characters, applications, aspects, or the like; as, "He hated the Puritan sects with a *manifold* hatred, theological and political, hereditary and personal" (*Macaulay*); when it is applied, as now happens more frequently, to a plural noun, it stresses not only their numerousness, but their variety; as, "to acknowledge and confess our *manifold* sins and wickedness" (*Book of Common Prayer*); "your *manifold* attractions" (*Austen*); "to the Chinese painters this world of nature seemed...[an] effective way of shadowing forth the *manifold* moods of man" (*Binyon*); "the strength of the dramatic lies in its *manifold* implications" (*Day Lewis*). **Multifold** is sometimes used interchangeably with *manifold,* but not wisely, since it carries, especially in precise use, an implication of repeated duplication that is usually lacking in *manifold;* as, a machine for the *multifold* copying of a typed original; "a first essay...composed...amidst *multifold* disappointment" (*T. Maurice*). **Multifarious** adds to the implications of *manifold* that of great diversity and often incongruity in the units, individuals, or elements involved: for this reason it usually qualifies plural nouns, though it may be applied to collective singulars; as, "in many of the *multifarious* activities he undertook" (*H. Ellis*); "the *multifarious* Italian dialects" (*V. Heiser*); "the large desk on which *multifarious* files and papers were ranged" (*Bennett*); the *multifarious* suffering (or sufferings) of the refugees; *manifold* duties may also be *multifarious*.

Ant. Few.

many-sided. *Versatile, all-round.

map, *n.* & *v.* *Chart, graph.

Ana. *Plan, plot, scheme, design: *sketch, outline, diagram.

mar, *v.* *Injure, damage, hurt, harm, impair, spoil.

Ana. *Deface, disfigure: *deform, contort, distort, gnarl, warp: *ruin, wreck.

Con. Embellish, decorate, *adorn, beautify, ornament: *mend, repair, patch: amend, revise, reform, *correct, rectify, emend.

marauder. *Brigand, bandit, highwayman, footpad.

Ana. Ravager, pillager, sacker, despoiler (see corresponding verbs at RAVAGE): robber, plunderer, thief, looter (see corresponding verbs at ROB).

march, *n.* *Boundary, border, frontier.

margin. *Border, verge, edge, rim, brim, brink.

Ana. Bound, end, term, bourn, confine, *limit: penumbra (see SHADE).

marine, *adj.* **1** Oceanic, thalassic, neritic, pelagic, abyssal, bathysmal, bathybic, *aquatic, lacustrine, lacuscular, fluvial, fluviatile.

2 Marine, maritime, nautical, naval are not synonymous terms but they are so interrelated that their proper choice is sometimes a cause of confusion. *Marine* and *maritime* both etymologically and in their use in English imply a connection with the sea. **Marine** is the preferred term when that which is qualified is produced by or is found in the sea or in a body of salt water (for this sense see AQUATIC), or is intended for use at sea (as, a *marine* barometer; a *marine* chronometer), or deals with the sea or with vessels that ply the sea or other large body of water (as, a *marine* painter or painting; *marine* engineering; *marine* insurance). *Marine* also is sometimes used when there is an actual or implied reference to mariners or seamen (as, "At that time the *Marine* Board examinations took place at the St. Katherine's Dock House on Tower Hill"—*Conrad;* the *Marine* Society founded in 1756); the term commonly applies to soldiers who serve at sea (as, the *Marine* Corps of the United States; the Royal *Marine* forces of Great Britain). **Maritime** is the preferred term when the reference is to countries, peoples, and the like, on the borders of a sea (as, the *Maritime* Provinces—i.e., the Canadian provinces of New Brunswick, Nova Scotia, and Prince Edward Island; the *Maritime* Alps; *maritime* states or races), or to the navigation of or commerce on the seas (as, *maritime* pursuits such as fishing or whaling; *maritime* laws or law; *maritime* perils; "In the whole of British genius...I have estimated the *maritime* ancestry as 1.9, less than any other class"—*H. Ellis*). But *maritime* and *marine* are sometimes used interchangeably, especially in reference to law, insurance, and the like. *Nautical* and *naval*, on the other hand, imply a connection with ships and shipping, and therefore only indirectly with the sea. **Nautical,** however, is the preferred and usual term in any application where its etymological relationship to sailors or seamen or the sailing of ships or boats is distinctly implied; as, *nautical* pursuits such as yachting; *nautical* skill; a man of *nautical* interests is never satisfied until he owns some sort of sailboat; *nautical* clothes; "No one rows, very few sail...; Brighton...is the least *nautical* of seaside places" (*Jefferies*). *Nautical* is usually the preferred term when reference to the art or profession of navigation is implied; as, a *nautical* clock; a *nautical* compass; *nautical* tables; *nautical* astronomy; a *nautical* mile. **Naval** (etymologically, pertaining to ships) now usually implies reference to a navy (as distinguished from a merchant marine) as composed not only of ships, but of men, supplies, and armaments; at times, only from the context can a reader be sure whether ship or naval force is referred to; as, *naval* stores; a *naval* architect; a *naval* engagement; the *Naval* Academy at Annapolis; *naval* officers; he belongs to the *naval* reserve.

mariner. Mariner, sailor, seaman, tar, gob, matlow (*properly* **matelot**), **bluejacket, rating** come into comparison as denoting a person engaged in sailing or navigating a vessel. In general use, **mariner** is loosely employed in reference to anyone directly employed in navigation, but in legal use it is the most general of these terms and is applicable to any person, man or woman, whose work in any way contributes to the accomplishment of the vessel's voyage, whether that work be concerned with the vessel's navigation or not; thus, a ship's master, officers, engineers, stewards, and the like, are in this sense *mariners*. *Mariner* is not so common in colloquial use as many of the preceding terms, but it is very common in literary, especially poetic, use; as, "Ye *mariners* of England That guard our native seas" (*Campbell*). **Sailor** still so strongly retains its original implication of concern with the management of boats (sailboats, yachts, etc.) or ships that are impelled by the action of wind upon sails that it is the preferred term whenever this idea is specifically suggested. However, the term is also applied to any person engaged in the actual navigation of a vessel regardless of the power which drives it. In ordinary use, it applies especially to one who in strict language is called a **seaman,** one of the navigating force (sometimes including, sometimes excluding, officers) employed on a vessel. Both in British and in American use, the term *seaman* alone is not applied to apprentices, for the term suggests skill and craft in operation and guidance of a vessel. In technical British use, however, the word is not used in reference to navigating officers or to pilots. **Tar** is a familiar, often poetic, designation of a sailor; **gob,** chiefly in American, and **matlow,** chiefly in British, use are colloquial designations of a sailor belonging to the navy. Neither of the latter terms is applied to an officer, whether commissioned or noncommissioned. **Bluejacket** is commonly applied to an enlisted man, especially a sailor, in the British or American navy: the term originally referred to the distinguishing uniform of such a seaman. In current use, it is often employed in distinguishing a sailor in the navy from a marine, or as a poetic equivalent of *sailor*. **Rating** is specifically British and is applied to any man in the British navy who holds neither a commission nor a warrant, the term being thus equivalent to the technical phrase *enlisted man* in the United States navy.

marital. *Matrimonial, conjugal, connubial, nuptial, hymeneal.

maritime. *Marine, nautical, naval.

mark, *n.* **1** *Sign, symptom, note, token, badge.

Ana. *Stigma, brand, blot, stain: criterion, touchstone, gauge, yardstick, *standard: *trace, vestige, track, rack: stamp, print, imprint, impress, *impression.

2 *Character, symbol, sign, note.
Ana. *Device, contrivance.

marketable. *Vendible, purchasable, salable.

marriage. **Marriage, matrimony, wedlock, wedding, nuptials, spousal** (*or* **spousals**), **espousals** (*or* **espousal**) are not always synonymous nouns but they are closely allied because they all refer directly or indirectly to the act or acts by which a man and woman become husband and wife, or to the state of being husband and wife. **Marriage** is the common term both in literary and colloquial use: it may apply to the rite or ceremony (as, many were present at their *marriage;* a civil *marriage*), but it more often applies to the legal or spiritual relation which is entered upon (as, to be joined in *marriage;* to annul a *marriage*), to the state of being married (as, theirs was a long and happy *marriage*), or to the institution as an abstraction (as, "Nor does he dishonour *marriage* that praises virginity"—*Donne*). In extended use, the term is applicable to any similarly close and intimate union; as, "Let me not to the *marriage* of true minds Admit impediments" (*Shak.*); "the same sort of poetic effect as the Romantics obtained by the *marriage* of fertile words" (*Day Lewis*). **Matrimony** is the preferred term in religious and sometimes in legal use; in the Roman Catholic and the Eastern (including Orthodox and Uniat) churches and in the use of many members of the Anglican Communion, it designates one of the seven sacraments. The term therefore is used with historical correctness in place of *marriage* only when a religious ceremony or sanction is implied; as, to be joined in bonds of holy *matrimony.* In general, the term is applicable to the relationship which exists between husband and wife, and not (although there are literary exceptions) to the ceremony or the state of marriage. "So prays the Church, to consecrate a vow 'The which would endless *matrimony* make' " (*Wordsworth*). **Wedlock,** a term now chiefly in legal or literary use, applies especially to marriage as a legally sanctioned relationship or state; thus, children born out of *wedlock* are children of parents who are not married. "The sacred academy of man's life, Is holy *wedlock* in a happy wife" (*Quarles*). "Grave authors say, and witty poets sing, That honest *wedlock* is a glorious thing" (*Pope*). **Wedding** is the common term both in colloquial and literary use for the ceremony that marks a marriage and the festivities that accompany it; as, a thousand invitations to the *wedding* were sent out. **Nuptials** is a more rhetorical and grandiose term than *wedding;* it also carries a stronger implication of an elaborate religious ceremony. "I don't object to married priests, but I do strongly object to their *nuptials* ....when a priest like Moxon-Hughes...indulges in an immense artistic *wedding,* I feel there is something undignified and almost unpleasant about it" (*C. Mackenzie*). **Spousal,** or more often **spousals,** is an archaic term which stresses the making of the vows of marriage rather than the performance of a ceremony: it is frequently in extended use applied to the mating of birds, beasts, etc.; as, "till the amorous bird of night Sung *spousal,* and bid haste the evening-star" (*Milton*); "with the morrow, the Church blessed the *spousals*" (*Symonds*). **Espousals** (or its somewhat archaic singular **espousal**), as here compared (see also ENGAGEMENT, 1), differs little from *spousals* (or *spousal*) except in its extended application. In the latter use it commonly implies a spiritual union, especially one that is dependent upon a vow, or pledge; as, "Let every act of worship be Like our *espousals,* Lord, to thee" (*J. Wesley*).

marrow. *Adipose, suet, tallow, lard.

marshal, *v.* *Order, arrange, organize, systematize, methodize.
Ana. Array, range, align, *line.
Con. Derange, disarrange, *disorder, disorganize, unsettle, disturb: *scatter, disperse, dissipate.

martial. **Martial, warlike, military** come into comparison not as close synonyms but because they carry as their basic meaning belonging to, suitable to, or characteristic of war. **Martial** distinctively implies reference to war in general, and to its essential and fundamental characteristics: it often specifically suggests the pomp and circumstance of war; as, *martial* music; standing in *martial* array; "the keen *martial* temper of the Yamato race" (*Binyon*). **Warlike,** as a rule, implies reference to war as a reality, its actual causes, its actual methods, its actual effects: it, therefore, applies more often to feelings, acts, activities, etc., that lead to or accompany real war, than to those which suggest its thrilling or stirring qualities; thus, a *warlike* temper suggests bellicosity, or readiness to fight to the bitter end, whereas a *martial* temper suggests dauntlessness, spiritedness, and an eagerness for war; so, *warlike* preparations; a *warlike* race; "tales of *warlike* feats" (*Wordsworth*); "Then peals the *warlike* thunder of the drum" (*Scott*). **Military** suggests war as fought by trained armies under the guidance of trained leaders. It often implies the conduct of war on land rather than on sea (being then opposed to *naval*) and suggests clashing forces, strategic movements, and the like: often, however, it refers to war in general, especially as it has been carried on since armaments have been employed; as, a *military* expedition; *military* tactics; "*Military* glory—that attractive rainbow that rises in showers of blood" (*Lincoln*).
Ana. *Belligerent, bellicose, pugnacious: *aggressive, militant: *spirited, high-spirited, mettlesome.

masculine. *Male, virile, manful, manly, manlike, mannish.
Ana. *Vigorous, energetic, lusty, strenuous: robust, *healthy, sound.
Ant. Feminine. — *Con.* Womanly, ladylike, womanlike, womanish, *female.

mask, *n.* Portrait, photograph, *image, simulacrum, effigy, statue, icon.

mask, *v.* *Disguise, cloak, dissemble.
Ana. Conceal, *hide, secrete, screen: protect, shield, defend, guard, safeguard.
Con. Discover, divulge, disclose, *reveal: expose, exhibit, display, flaunt, *show.

mass, *n.* **1** *Bulk, volume.
Ana. *Aggregate, aggregation, conglomerate, conglomeration: *sum, amount, total, aggregate, whole.
2 Heap, pile, stack, shock, cock, bank. See under HEAP, *v.*
Ana. Accumulation, hoarding *or* hoard, amassment (see corresponding verbs at ACCUMULATE).

mass, *v.* *Heap, pile, stack, shock, cock, bank.
Ana. *Gather, collect, assemble, congregate: *accumulate, amass, hoard: merge, blend, fuse, coalesce (see MIX): consolidate, *compact, unify, concentrate.

massacre, *n.* **Massacre, slaughter, butchery, carnage, pogrom** are comparable only when they mean great, or a great and often wanton, killing of human beings. **Massacre** implies promiscuous and wholesale slaying, especially of those who are not prepared to defend themselves and can make little or no resistance; as, the Indian *massacre* of the inhabitants of Deerfield, Mass., in 1704. "The tyrannous and bloody deed is done, The most arch act of piteous *massacre* That ever yet this land was guilty of" (*Shak.*). **Slaughter,** originally and still a butcher's term for the killing of animals used as food, as here compared suggests extensive and ruthless killing, whether the scene of that killing be a battle, a massacre, a horrible accident, or the like. "The chief...cut his way through the enemy with great *slaughter*" (*Irving*). **Butchery** adds to *slaughter* the implication of exceeding cruelty or of cold-blooded indifference to the sufferings of the victims. "Boasting of his fights, his cruelties and his *butcheries*" (*Kingsley*). "Thus was the *butchery* waged While the sun clomb Heaven's eastern steep" (*Shelley*). **Carnage** is often not easily distinguishable from *slaughter*, except that it sometimes carries additional connotations similar to those of *massacre*, or suggests the heaping up of the bodies of the slain. "A slight resistance was followed by a dreadful *carnage*" (*Gibbon*). "War and all its deeds of *carnage*" (*Whitman*). **Pogrom,** a term borrowed from Russian, applies especially to an organized massacre of helpless people, such as those of a race other than the dominant one, carried on usually with the connivance of officials. It is often applied specifically to such a massacre of the Jews, especially in one of the European countries; as, the *pogroms* at Gomel and Kishinev in Russia in 1903.

Ana. Assassination, murdering *or* murder, slaying, killing (see corresponding verbs at KILL).

massive. **Massive, massy, bulky, monumental, substantial** are synonyms when they mean impressively large and heavy. **Massive** distinctively stresses solidity and strength of construction and usually implies an imposing appearance; as, "Its ceilings...heavy with *massive* beams" (*Dickens*); "I am sure that the Lord Mayor is glad to see again its [the Mansion House's] sombre and *massive* yet welcoming façade when he returns home from any jaunt" (*Lucas*); "a man whose *massive* shoulders and determined cast of features ought to have convinced him that such an enterprise was nothing short of desperate" (*Shaw*). **Massy,** now a literary word, carries a stronger implication of ponderosity than *massive*, but it still usually also implies solidity and strength. "Your swords are now too *massy* for your strengths And will not be uplifted" (*Shak.*). "Hast thou a goblet for dark sparkling wine? That goblet right heavy, and *massy*, and gold?" (*Keats*). **Bulky** stresses size rather than weight, and the excessive amount of space occupied rather than solidity or strength of construction; as, a *bulky* parcel: nevertheless, the word may still connote these underemphasized qualities; as, a *bulky* report. **Monumental,** as here compared, also implies greatness of size, but it distinctively suggests an imposing massiveness. "Me, Goddess, bring To archèd walks of twilight groves, And shadows brown... Of pine, or *monumental* oak" (*Milton*). "The *monumental* fourpost bed has been taken down" (*Daily Telegraph*). "Miss Dyas was a tall red-haired woman of *monumental* build" (*E. Wharton*). **Substantial** stresses solidity and strength of construction as much as *massive*, but it carries a weaker implication of size, and a stronger implication of established quality, worth, and stability than of outwardly imposing appearance; it is therefore applied often to persons of wealth (or substance) as well as to structures; as, the most *substantial* buildings in England today are the old Norman cathedrals; "*substantial* homes, and *substantial* relatives of some sort or other, on whom we could fall back" (*Galsworthy*).

Ana. *Heavy, weighty, ponderous: solid, hard, *firm: immense, *enormous, huge, gigantic, colossal.

massy. *Massive, bulky, monumental, substantial.

Ana. Ponderous, hefty, cumbrous, cumbersome, weighty, *heavy: *large, big, great: solid, *firm, hard.

master, *n.* Captain, *chief, commander, chieftain, head, leader.

masterful. **Masterful, domineering, imperious, peremptory, imperative** are here compared only as they apply to persons, their acts, utterances, demands, and the like, and mean governed by, or manifesting, a strong tendency to impose one's will on another. One is **masterful** who by the strength and virility of his personality is able to enforce his will on others or who deals with affairs commandingly and compellingly; as, "The major was a *masterful* man; and I knew that he would not give orders for nothing" (*Kipling*); "the man had such a *masterful* and magnetic personality...that it was impossible not to take fire at his ardour" (*A. Huxley*). One is **domineering** who tries to enforce his will or to make a show of his power by an overbearing or insolently tyrannical manner; as, "[He] was violent, arbitrary, *domineering*" (*Mrs. H. Ward*); "They are...not courageous, only quarrelsome; not determined, only obstinate; not *masterful*, only *domineering*" (*Shaw*); a *domineering* lady and her abject suitor. One is **imperious** who by temperament or by position is fitted to command or who assumes the air or manner of such a person; the term implies more arrogance than *masterful* and less insolence than *domineering;* as, "this ancient despot—this *imperious* old Louis XIV in a black front and a cap and ribbon" (*Thackeray*); "One could not have passed him on the street without feeling his great physical force and his *imperious* will" (*Cather*). One is **peremptory** who insists, often with curtness, on an immediate response to his commands; the term usually implies authoritativeness and a refusal to brook disobedience or delay or to entertain any objections however valid; as, the general issued a *peremptory* summons; "Candles...borrowed in a rather *peremptory* manner of Monsieur Gabelle" (*Dickens*); "two *peremptory* raps at the door" (*Shaw*). "When we say of...a man that he has a great deal of character, we generally mean that he has disciplined his temperament, his disposition, into strict obedience to the behests of duty; that he has clear and *peremptory* ideas about right and wrong" (*Brownell*). One is **imperative** who is peremptory, or whose actions or words are peremptory, owing to the urgency of the situation rather than because of one's temperament; as, " 'Go back!' cried the old man, with an *imperative* jerk of the head" (*M. Wilkins*); "the doctor had *imperatively* commanded rest" (*Bennett*).

Ana. Magisterial, magistral, *dictatorial, authoritarian, authoritative, oracular, dogmatic, doctrinaire: arbitrary, *absolute, despotic, tyrannical.

☞ *Do not confuse* masterful *with* masterly.

match, *v.* **Match, rival, equal, approach, touch** are often used interchangeably, especially in negative constructions, when they mean to come up to, or nearly up to, the level or standard of something else. One thing **matches** another when it proves to be its mate (rather than its duplicate) in power, strength, beauty, interest, or the like; as, it has been said that no language can *match* French in expressing ideas with clarity and exactness; "the beauty of his person was *matched* by the grace and dignity of his spirit" (*Buchan*). "No mortal builder's most rare device Could *match* this winter palace of ice" (*J. R. Lowell*). One thing **rivals** another when it closely competes with it for superiority or in excellence. "But would you sing, and *rival* Orpheus' strain, The wond'ring forests soon should dance again" (*Pope*). "Work of a beauty certainly not *rivalled* until we come to the Norman builders" (*Quiller-Couch*). One thing **equals** another when it rises to the same level or plane, as in quantity, value, degree, or the like, and there is no question concerning a difference, especially a deficiency. "Such a striking civility...ought to be imitated, though it could not be *equalled*, by some exertion of politeness on their

side" (*Austen*). "No other measure of our work *equals* the sight of the product put to its full uses" (*H. Suzzallo*). One thing **approaches** another when it comes so close to it that it nearly equals or matches it, and the difference, though apparent, is not important. "An adult reader with trained habits of...concentration will absorb the contents of a book with a speed and retentiveness which no child can *approach*" (*C. W. Eliot*). "An unlettered speaker may startle you with his power of giving to the spoken word an urgent aptness that *approaches* the vivid instancy of an involuntary cry" (*C. E. Montague*). One thing **touches** another thing when the former approaches the very high plane or level reached by the latter; as, "not another woman there to *touch* her" (*W. J. Locke*). "Yeats, the last in the aristocratic tradition of poets... none of us can *touch* his later work....He stands, a lesson to us in integrity, demanding from us a complete subjection to the poetry that occupies us" (*Day Lewis*).
Ana. Correspond, harmonize, *agree, conform, square, accord.
Con. Differ from, *differ with: vary, *change, alter, modify.

matelot. Variant of MATLOW.

material, *adj.* **1 Material, physical, corporeal, phenomenal, sensible, objective** are here compared as meaning belonging to, or having a relation to things that belong to, the world of actuality or of things apparent to the senses. **Material** applies to anything that is formed of matter or that relates to things formed of matter: it often implies an opposition to *spiritual*, but it may imply an antithesis to *ideal*, *formal* (i.e., of or pertaining to form as distinguished from matter), *intangible*, *impalpable*, and the like; as, *material* objects; one's *material* possessions; to believe in no other world than the *material* world; "busy with *material* affairs" (*Conrad*); "an appetite for *material* pleasures" (*A. C. Benson*). "The society of Shakespeare and Raleigh and Sir Philip Sydney... would not console them [modern men] for the absence of bath-rooms..., motor-cars, and other *material* comforts of which that age was ignorant" (*B. Russell*). "These poor Christians are not thrifty like our country people at home [France]; they have no veneration for property, no sense of *material* values" (*Cather*). **Physical** (as here compared: see also BODILY) differs from *material* chiefly in suggesting an opposition to *psychical*, *mental*, *metaphysical*, *imaginary*, and, less often, *spiritual*: it applies especially to things perceived by the senses or capable of being dealt with in the same manner as objects of sense, and it usually implies a contrast to things knowable only through thought or intuition or built up by the mind or imagination; thus, the *material* objects and the *physical* objects within one's reach may be exactly the same objects, but *material* suggests their substantial nature and *physical* suggests their susceptibility of perception and identification, or, what is more important in science, of being weighed, measured, or the like. In scientific use, *physical* is also applicable to things which are not objects, but forces, actions, motions, etc., which are operative in nature or in mechanics and which can be measured or calculated, or put to use, even though, strictly speaking, they cannot be handled; as, the *physical* properties of light; the *physical* effect of radiation; a *physical* explanation of a miracle; "Everything *physical* is measurable by weight, motion, and resistance" (*De Quincey*). "With the advent of Einstein's relativity theory it was necessary for the first time to recognize that the *physical* world differed from the ideal [i.e., mentally constructed] world conceived in terms of everyday experience" (*transl. from W. Heisenberg*). **Corporeal** (as here compared: see also BODILY) applies to that which not only has physical existence but also is tangible or can be described as a body; thus, energy in itself has no *corporeal* existence though it is a *physical* power found usually in *corporeal* things. "In a monistic ...sense 'the mind' may be regarded as a living, growing 'structure,' even though it lacks *corporeal* tangibility" (*Science*). **Phenomenal** implies a relation to that which is known or knowable through the senses and experience, as distinguished from that which is knowable only through thought or intuition because it is beyond perception by the senses: the term is chiefly used in philosophy and science when there is an intent to mark the line between that which is actually perceived and that which has been ascertained by the reason, has been accepted by faith, or is theoretical, hypothetical, or the like; as, *phenomenal* reality is often specifically called *actuality*. "*Phenomenal* nature is reduced to an array of events in the four-dimensional continuum" (*Jeans*). **Sensible,** the psychologist's, and often the layman's, term for that which is known or knowable through sense experience, is sometimes opposed to *intelligible* (i.e., knowable through mental processes): it is therefore a general term comprehending *visible*, *audible*, *tangible*, *palpable*, and the like; as, there is no *sensible* movement of the earth; to claim *sensible* evidence of the immortality of the soul. "Is this a dagger which I see before me, The handle toward my hand? Come, let me clutch thee ... Art thou not...*sensible* To feeling as to sight? or art thou but A dagger of the mind, a false creation" (*Shak.*). **Objective** implies the same kind of existence as *phenomenal* and *sensible*, but it stresses the apartness of the thing known through the senses from the person who perceives it through his senses: the term, therefore, implies not only material existence but an existence which exactly corresponds to the image in the mind of the perceiver; as, "The ancient Hebrew...saw the rainbow as an *objective* structure set in the heavens for all men to behold" (*Jeans*); "acosmism, the theory which denies the *objective* existence of the world or universe" (*Inge*).
Ana. *Carnal, fleshly, sensual, animal, animalistic: actual, true, *real: tangible, *perceptible, appreciable, palpable.
Ant. Immaterial.
2 *Relevant, germane, pertinent, apposite, applicable, apropos.
Ana. Important, significant, consequential, momentous (see corresponding nouns at IMPORTANCE): vital, cardinal, *essential, fundamental.
Ant. Immaterial.

materialize. Externalize, objectify, substantiate, incarnate, embody, actualize, *realize, hypostatize, reify.

matériel *or* **material.** *Equipment, apparatus, machinery, paraphernalia, outfit, tackle, gear.

maternal. Motherly, *parental, paternal, fatherly.

matlow *or* **matelot.** *Mariner, sailor, seaman, tar, gob, bluejacket, rating.

matrimonial. Matrimonial, marital, conjugal, connubial, nuptial, hymeneal agree in meaning of, relating to, or characteristic of marriage. **Matrimonial** is the most general term applicable to that which has to do both with matrimony and with marriage in any of its senses (see MARRIAGE); as, *matrimonial* vows; *matrimonial* advances; the *matrimonial* state; *matrimonial* rites; *matrimonial* bliss. **Marital,** though in strict use it implies reference to the husband and his part in marriage (as, *marital* rights; *marital* authority), is often used interchangeably with *matrimonial* (as, *marital* vows; the *marital* relationship; *marital* bliss). *Conjugal* and *connubial* are frequently used interchangeably. More strictly, **conjugal** connotes reference to the persons who are married (as, "They flaunt their *conjugal* felicity in one's face"—*Wilde;* "I count it my good fortune that never once in...my childhood was I the witness of any *conjugal* jar"—*H. Ellis*); **connubial** implies reference to the marriage state (as, "Of my friends who have been least successful in *connubial* contracts"—*Johnson;* to enter the *connubial* state). **Nuptial** has primary reference to the marriage rites or ceremony; as, "the *nuptial* torch" (*Milton*); an ante*nuptial* contract. **Hymeneal** (etymologically, relating to marriage or its god Hymen) is a purely poetic or literary word, suggestive of the splendors of marriage rites and festivities; as, *hymeneal* songs or hymns; "Chorus *Hymeneal*, Or triumphal chaunt, Matched with thine would be all But an empty vaunt" (*Shelley*).

matrimony. *Marriage, wedlock, wedding, nuptials, spousal, espousals.

matter. 1 *Affair, business, concern, thing.
2 *Subject, subject matter, argument, topic, text, theme, motive, leitmotiv.

matter-of-fact. *Prosaic, prosy.
Ana. Stolid, phlegmatic, *impassive: arid, *dry: *downright, forthright.
Con. Fanciful, *imaginary, fantastic, chimerical, quixotic, visionary: ideal, transcendent, transcendental (see ABSTRACT, *adj.*): romantic, *sentimental.

mature, *adj.* **Mature, matured, ripe, mellow, adult, grown-up, full-fledged** are terms that are not often interchangeable, yet are comparable because they bear the same underlying meaning, "fully developed." **Mature,** in its literal use as applied to living things, stresses the completion of development; as applied specifically to persons, sometimes it (or especially its derivative *maturity*) connotes simply the full development of the sexual organs; more often, however, it implies attainment of the prime of life, when the person is at the height of his powers, physically and mentally. "A great writer of the past is known by the delight and stimulus which he gives to *mature* spirits in the present" (*Van W. Brooks*). As applied to things, *mature* usually equals **matured,** which implies the completion of a course, process, or period; thus, a *matured* plan is a fully thought-out plan; a *matured* wine is one that has been allowed to age properly; a *matured* note is one that has reached the date when payment is due. **Ripe,** though it implies maturity, stresses readiness for use or enjoyment; in its literal sense, it is applied chiefly to fruits ready for eating, to grains or vegetables ready for harvesting, to seeds ready for planting. Figuratively, it often connotes merely readiness, or fully preparedness for action, activity, or use. "*Ripe* for exploits and mighty enterprises" (*Shak.*). "To be careful, in teaching history, not to obtrude aspects which are interesting to us until the child is *ripe* for them" (*B. Russell*). Sometimes, however, *ripe* connotes one or more of the characteristics of ripe things, especially ripe fruits, such as ruddiness, plumpness, richness. "His *ripe* cheeks" (*Quiller-Couch*). "Greek sculpture, in its *ripe* perfection" (*Binyon*). **Mellow** stresses either the agreeable qualities associated with ripe or slightly overripe fruits, such as softness, tenderness, sweetness, or the loss of their opposites, the signs of immaturity, hardness, harshness, or bitterness; as, a *mellow* cheese; a *mellow* wine. "The more *mellow* and cheerful outlook of his [Horace's] second book [of satires]" (*Buchan*). The last three words are applied chiefly to persons, their acts, minds, etc., and only by extension to inanimate things. **Adult** is the equivalent of *mature* in its merely physical implications and in its reference to animals; it presupposes, however, a clear line of demarcation, especially when used of human beings. An *adult* person physiologically is one that has passed beyond adolescence; in law, he is one that has attained full age, or his majority. In extended use, *adult* implies the attainment of that point in development where the weaknesses of immaturity or of imperfection are surmounted. "The difference [between Romanticism and Classicism] seems to me rather the difference between the complete and the fragmentary, the *adult* and the immature, the orderly and the chaotic" (*T. S. Eliot*). **Grown-up,** a colloquial equivalent of *adult*, is sometimes used in preference to it when an antithesis to *childish* is needed; as, adults incapable of *grown-up* behavior. **Full-fledged,** literally applied only to birds that can fly freely because of fully developed wings, in its figurative application to persons retains its implication of being enabled, as by training, experience, etc., to go ahead independently in a particular line of work; as, a *full-fledged* lawyer or physician.
Ant. Immature: childish. — *Con.* *Childlike: *youthful, juvenile, boyish, puerile, maiden.

mature, *v.* **Mature, develop, ripen, age** come into comparison when they are used in reference to living, growing things or to anything with latent capacity for betterment, and mean to come or cause to come to the state of being fit for use, enjoyment, or the like. When employed with reference to living things or their specific characters, **mature** stresses fullness of growth and readiness for normal functioning; as, in warm climates human beings *mature* more rapidly than in cold climates: **develop** stresses the unfolding of all that is latent and the attainment of the perfection that is appropriate to the species or is possible to the individual; as, "the kitten's hunting instinct was not yet *developed*" (*B. Russell*): **ripen** emphasizes the approach to or the attainment of the peak of perfection; as, the fruits are now sufficiently *ripened:* **age** equals *mature* only when it is applied to the young; as, hard work *ages* a boy; more often, it implies approach to the period of decline or decay; as, the leaders of the movement are *aging* rapidly.

In their secondary senses, one **matures** that which is incomplete, imperfect, or not fully formed; as, to *mature* a plan; "an art That toiling ages have but just *matured*" (*Cowper*): one **develops** that which is potential, dormant, latent, nebulous, or the like, as by bringing it into being, into effect, into operation, or into open view; as, "the environment fitted to *develop*...a genius at once so subtle and so humane as that of Socrates" (*G. L. Dickinson*); "the sense of fact is something very slow to *develop*" (*T. S. Eliot*): one **ripens** that which is susceptible of improvement, enrichment, or enhancement if given time or subjected to influences favorable to its development; as, to *ripen* cheese by allowing it to stand or by processing it; friendship often *ripens* into love; "[minds that] have not leisure to grow wise....cannot *ripen* properly" (*S. M. Crothers*): one **ages** that which in its fresh or new state lacks a quality or qualities that fit it for use or enjoyment; as, to *age* wine by keeping it in storage; to *age* game by allowing it to hang for a period; to *age* Oriental rugs by subjecting them to hard usage.
Ana. *Harden, inure, season, acclimatize, acclimate: *habituate, accustom, familiarize, addict.

matured. *Mature, ripe, mellow, adult, grown-up, full-fledged.
Ana. Completed, finished (see CLOSE, *v.*): *deliberate, considered, advised, designed, studied, premeditated.
Ant. Unmatured: premature. — *Con.* Crude, green, callow, *rude, rough, raw: *youthful, juvenile, puerile, boyish: childish, *childlike.

maudlin. Mawkish, *sentimental, romantic, soppy, mushy, slushy.
Ana. Confused, muddled, fuddled, addled, bemuddled,

befuddled (see CONFUSE): embarrassed, rattled, fazed, discomfited, disconcerted (see EMBARRASS).

mawkish. Maudlin, *sentimental, romantic, soppy, mushy, slushy.

Ana. Flat, vapid, jejune, *insipid, banal, inane.

maxim. *Saying, saw, adage, proverb, motto, epigram, aphorism, apothegm.

may. *Can.

maze. *Labyrinth.

meager *or* **meagre.** **Meager** (*or* **meagre**), **scanty, scant, skimpy, scrimpy, exiguous, spare, sparse** come into comparison as meaning so small as in amount, number, or size as to fall short of what is normal, necessary, or desirable. **Meager** stresses thinness: as applied to persons or animals, it suggests emaciation (as, "strange straining eyes, and *meagre* form"—*G. Eliot;* "The *meagre* condition of his horse"—*Scott*), but as applied to things in general, it implies the absence of elements, qualities, or numbers necessary to a thing's richness, substance, potency, or the like; as, a *meager* diet; "a simplicity of diction which reflects a *meagre* and barren stock [of words]" (*Lowes*); "The magazines, like the newspapers, were liberal with their space, but again the results were terribly *meagre*" (*V. Heiser*). "An outline in itself is *meagre*, truly, but it does not necessarily suggest a *meagre* thing" (*W. James*). **Scanty** emphasizes insufficiency in amount, quantity, extent, or the like; as, a *scanty* supply of food for the winter; "The book...is not, like some biographical essays with *scanty* material, stuffed out with appreciation and conjecture" (*T. S. Eliot*). "Such a *scanty* portion of light was admitted...that it was difficult, on first coming in, to see anything" (*Dickens*). **Scant** differs from *scanty* in suggesting a falling short, as in amount or quantity, of that which is desired or is desirable rather than in that which is necessary or essential; as, "the work of those hours was miserably *scant*" (*Hardy*); "they were held in *scant* esteem" (*Grandgent*); "*scant* foliage" (*Cather*). **Skimpy** and **scrimpy,** both colloquial words, imply niggardliness as the reason for a thing's insufficiency in size, amount, numbers, or the like; but *skimpy* suggests stinginess that robs a thing of its proper measure, size, or amount (as, *skimpy* curtains; a *skimpy* allowance), and *scrimpy* usually connotes an enforced thrift or the influence of meager resources (as, their meals are pretty *scrimpy* these days; *scrimpy* portions of food). **Exiguous** stresses a smallness in size, amount, extent, capacity, or the like, that is more or less inherent in the thing under consideration and makes it compare unfavorably with other things of its kind; as, "brains too *exiguous* to hold more than half an idea at a time" (*Amer. Speech*); "building ships to supplement his *exiguous* navy" (*Buchan*); "a much larger dominion than the *exiguous* Dalriada" (*Times Lit. Sup.*). **Spare** (as here compared: see also LEAN, SUPERFLUOUS) implies merely a falling short of that which is sufficient: unlike *scanty* and *meager*, it seldom suggests resulting loss or hardship; as, "the powerful frame attenuated by *spare* living" (*Dickens*); *spare* vegetation; a *spare* diet. In the phrase "*spare*ribs (of pork)" the term suggests meagerness of meat: the phrase applies therefore to ribs trimmed of most of their meat. **Sparse** stresses a lack of normal or desirable thickness or density: the term may or may not suggest insufficiency or inadequacy in numbers or in quantity, but it always connotes a thin scattering of the units; as, the *sparse* population of the mountainous district; "*sparse* grey locks" (*Conrad*); "the sound of their *sparse* talk and laughter...was blown over the walls to the ears of Harbinger" (*Galsworthy*). "Now and then she scattered, with regretful *sparseness*, some seeds and crumbs from her parcels" (*M. Wilkins*).

Ana. *Thin, slender, slim, slight, tenuous, rare: thinned, attenuated, extenuated, diluted (see THIN, *v.*): jejune, flat, *insipid, inane: penurious, *stingy, parsimonious.

Ant. Ample: copious.

mean, *v.* **1** *Intend, design, propose, purpose.

Ana. Wish, want, *desire: *aim, aspire, pant.

2 Mean, denote, signify, import are synonymous terms when used in the sense of to convey to the mind a definite idea or interpretation. Not only words or phrases can be said to *mean, denote, signify,* or *import* something, but also anything which admits of interpretation or of being intellectually appraised, such as a poem or an essay or an act of Congress, or such as the behavior of one person to another, or a set of circumstances. These words are commonly employed without distinction, but precision in their use is often possible and desirable. In their general applications (excluding for the moment their reference to words and phrases), **mean** is the most common; it is often far more expressive or poignant than the others when used to connote not only interpretation but also evaluation or appraisal. "That old vague hurt of discovery that he had never *meant* so much to David as David to him" (*M. Austin*). "He can have no idea of what it *means* to be the daughter of Mr. de Barral" (*Conrad*). **Denote,** in its widest application, is distinguished from the others by its taking for its subject things that serve as outward marks or visible indications; **signify,** by its taking for its subject things of a symbolic or representative character; as, his somber expression *denoted* (better than *signified*) a worried mind; the scales in the hands of the figure of Justice *signify* impartiality; the Eucharistic rite *signifies* one thing to Protestants and another to Catholics. *Signify* often suggests distinctiveness or importance; as, events which *signify* little at the time of occurrence often attain significance when the history of that period is written; does it *signify* nothing to you that your father has failed in health recently? **Import** frequently conveys its etymological implication of carrying in, i.e., in this sense, into the mind (as, new ideas *import* little to those not intellectually fitted to receive them), but it frequently comes close to *signify* (as, "What this *imported* I could ill divine"—*Wordsworth*).

In their special use in reference to the interpretation of the content of a term, these words are not always distinguishable. **Mean,** however, is capable of implying reference to the term's full content, that is, to the idea or relation between ideas which it conveys to the mind and the suggestions which it evokes; as, only a philosophically minded person can grasp what "beauty" and "truth" *mean* in Keats's lines " 'Beauty is truth, truth beauty,'—that is all Ye know on earth, and all ye need to know." **Signify** can, as *mean* cannot, suggest symbolic relationship between the term and the idea it conveys; as, the phrase "bread and butter" *signifies* the material needs of life. **Denote** (see also DENOTE, 2) is even more technical, for it implies a logical definition in which the idea named or expressed by a term is clearly marked out and its application or range of application accurately determined; as, "decoration" *denotes* one of three ideas, the act of adorning, or a thing used in adorning, or the results achieved by one who adorns. **Import,** though used with decreasing frequency in relation to terms, is precise in its implications. A term *imports* not what it *denotes*, or bears as a definition, but any or all of the implications involved in its interpretation. "Does it [the word 'necessary'] always *import* an absolute physical necessity...?" (*Ch. Just. Marshall*).

Ana. *Carry, convey, bear, transmit: *denote, connote:

define, assign, *prescribe: *suggest, imply, intimate, hint.

mean, *adj.*[1] **Mean, ignoble, abject, sordid** come into comparison when applied to persons, their behavior, or the conditions in which they live. All then mean so low as to be out of keeping with human dignity or just standards of human life or character. *Mean* and *ignoble* originally implied low birth, the former being applied to persons of the lowest social classes, the latter to persons below the rank of nobles. **Mean** usually suggests repellent antisocial characteristics, such as malevolence or cupidity. It almost invariably connotes small-mindedness. "Those who are tempted by the flesh have usually nothing to fear from avarice or the *meaner* vices. Those who spend their lives battling against *meanness* in any form are usually immune to the flesh" (*C. Mackenzie*). Often *mean* implies conduct or an attitude that is detestable and unworthy of a human being. "Delane... flung him off like a thing too *mean* for human handling" (*E. Wharton*). **Ignoble,** like its opposite *noble,* now usually implies qualities of mind or soul. It frequently comes close to *mean,* except that it seldom connotes small-mindedness. Its distinguishing implication is loss or lack of some essential high quality, such as spiritual elevation, moral dignity, or intellectual excellence. "Die to the little hatreds; die to greed; Die to the old *ignoble* selves we knew" (*A. Noyes*). "...to see how those he has converted distort and debase and make *ignoble* parodies of his teaching" (*A. Huxley*). **Abject,** in its most inclusive sense, means little more than extremely low in station or in degree; as, *abject* persons; an *abject* sinner; occasionally, it is merely an intensive applied to something that is itself low in the scale; as, *abject* poverty. In careful use, however, *abject* retains its etymological implications of being cast down and so variously implies abasement, debasement, or, more narrowly, contemptible servility. "Disgrace not so your king, That he should be so *abject,* base, and poor, To choose for wealth and not for perfect love" (*Shak.*). "Resolved to be a man Who...would live No longer in subjection to the past With *abject* mind" (*Wordsworth*). "How excessively and *abjectly* he [the painter Haydon] enjoys his week-end with Lord Egremont at Petworth!" (*A. Huxley*). **Sordid,** which originally connoted foulness and squalor, now more often suggests repellent dullness or drabness or degrading drudgery. "The slovenly, *sordid* aspect of the towns and country-side" (*Cather*). "The Greek ideal...postulated ...a competence to secure him against *sordid* cares" (*G. L. Dickinson*).

Ana. *Base, low, vile: *contemptible, despicable, sorry, scurvy, cheap, beggarly, pitiable.

mean, *adj.*[2] Average, median, par. See AVERAGE, *n.*

Ant. Extreme.

mean, *n.* **1** *Average, median, norm, par.

2 In plural form **means. Means, instrument, instrumentality, agent, agency, medium, organ, vehicle, channel** agree in denoting a person or thing through or by which work is performed or an end is effected. **Means** (construed as either plural or singular) is the most general of these words; it may be applied not only to persons and to concrete things such as implements, tools, and machines, but also to their actions or operations; it may also be applied to methods, policies, devices, and the like; as, to find ways and *means* to attain one's ambitions; the *means* does not justify the end. "The habit of regarding the labouring class as a mere *means* to the maintenance of the rest" (*G. L. Dickinson*). "The *means* that a portrait-painter should employ to indicate the inner nature and the circumstances of his sitter" (*Binyon*). **Instrument** is commonly applied to persons who merely carry out another's will or intention, often as tools, sometimes as dupes. "He...turned on me... suspecting perhaps that I only wished to make an *instrument* of him" (*Hudson*). "If they [judges] were to be used as the *instruments,* and the knowing *instruments,* for violating what they swear to support" (*Ch. Just. Marshall*). When applied to concrete things, *instrument* often derives connotations from its musical sense, such as susceptibility to manipulation, responsiveness to touch or use, etc. "He knew his brain was now a very uncertain *instrument,* sometimes quite good, sometimes a weary fount of half-formed ideas" (*H. G. Wells*). **Instrumentality** is interchangeable with *means* but not with *instrument* because its chief implication is effective action by, or effective use of, the instrument; as, through the *instrumentality* of the police he was able to locate his relatives; without the *instrumentality* of a free press liberty could not be preserved. **Agent** is applied chiefly to persons and only by extension to things. Originally meaning one who acts or does (still found in certain phrases such as *a free agent, agent noun*), the term now names (when applied to a person) the one who does the work as distinguished from the one who wills, plans, lays down the law, etc. "I often think, Jean, how you were an unconscious *agent* in the hands of Providence when you recalled me from Tucson" (*Cather*). "Ultimately these tattooed devils [the Kalingas]...were turned into effective *agents* for the maintenance of law and order" (*V. Heiser*). When applied to a thing, *agent* names that which effects a desired result or serves as a cause producing a definite effect; as, the cooling *agent* in making ice cream is a mixture of ice and rock salt. **Agency,** like *instrumentality,* is not interchangeable in good use with its allied noun, for it names the activity or operation of the agent or of something used to produce an effect. It is distinguished from *instrumentality* by its implication of causative (as opposed to effective) activity; as, some communicable diseases are transmitted only through the *agency* of vermin, insects, and the like. "Presumptuous thoughts that would assign Mechanic laws to *agency* divine" (*Wordsworth*). **Medium** is far more often applied to things than to persons; it designates anything (usually a substance or material) through which something, usually something intangible, is conveyed from one person or thing to another or given objective form; as, air is the *medium* through which sound and light waves are transmitted; language is the *medium* through which a person communicates his thoughts and feelings; the sculptor's *medium* may be bronze, marble, or other material. An **organ** is a medium that serves as a mouthpiece or spokesman; as, the two newspapers are *organs* of the Republican party. A **vehicle** is a medium that serves to carry (esp. to carry effectively) that which is to be revealed through it; as, the play was an excellent *vehicle* for the genius of Booth. "We must find a new form of verse which shall be as satisfactory a *vehicle* for us as blank verse was for the Elizabethans" (*T. S. Eliot*). A **channel** is a medium that provides either an outlet or a fixed course through which something may flow from one to another; as, the sacraments in Christian doctrine are *channels* of grace; to find the proper *channel* for the distribution of a fund for charity.

Ana. *Method, mode, manner, way, fashion, system: machinery, apparatus, *equipment, paraphernalia.

3 In plural form **means.** Resources, assets, effects, *possessions, belongings.

Ana. *Money, cash, currency: riches, wealthiness, affluence, opulence (see corresponding adjectives at RICH).

meander. Stray, roam, ramble, *wander, rove, range, prowl, gad, gallivant, traipse.

meaning. **Meaning, sense, acceptation, signification, significance, import** come into comparison when they denote the idea which a word, a passage, a facial expression, an action, situation, or the like, conveys to the mind or, less often, is intended to convey to the mind. **Meaning,** the general term, may be used interchangeably with any other of the terms here considered; it is not only applicable to language and to expressions or gestures but also to symbols, works of art, or other things that require interpretation; as, a dictionary gives the *meanings* of words; "if 'human' and the words formed from it can have an exact *meaning*...that *meaning* must refer to those qualities, characteristics, and powers which distinguish the human being" (*J. W. Krutch*). "Understand a plain man in his plain *meaning*" (*Shak.*). **Sense,** as here compared, denotes either the meaning or, more often, one of the specific or particular meanings, of a word or phrase, or sometimes of an allegory (as, some words have as many as twenty-five *senses;* the literal and figurative *senses* of *Pilgrim's Progress;* "Virtue, in the noble *sense* by Greeks and Romans understood"—*Swift*), or, more abstractly, intelligible or apprehensible meaning (as, "[She] speaks things... That carry but half *sense*" —*Shak.;* "In the first authentic edition...the words, I believe, ran, 'and a table of green fields,' which has no *sense*"—*Newman*). **Acceptation** (see also ACCEPTANCE) differs from *sense* (as denoting a meaning of a term) chiefly in its stress upon the actual use of that sense or upon its acceptance by a large number of writers and speakers; as, "It is necessary first, to consider the different *acceptations* of the word Knowledge" (*Locke*); "[Philosophy] in its common...*acceptation*...signifies, the search after wisdom" (*Fielding*). *Signification* and *significance,* as here compared (see *signify* under MEAN, *v.,* 2; *significance* under IMPORTANCE), are often used interchangeably in spite of the fact that they are carefully differentiated in their meanings. **Signification** (a noun derived ultimately from the same stem as *signify*) applies specifically to the established meaning of a term, a symbol, a character, or the like, or to an established sense of a word: it usually implies that when this term, or this symbol, or this character is used that such and such an idea is evoked in the mind of informed persons; as, the *significations* of the characters which serve as Roman numerals; to know the *signification* of each type of halo; a book alleged to give the *significations* of dreams; "I find it very...interesting to know the *signification* of names, and had written to ask him whether Jerusalem meant 'the vision of peace' or 'the foundation of peace' " (*Arnold*). "The counsel for the appellee would limit it [the term 'commerce'] to traffic, to buying and selling, or the interchange of commodities, and do not admit that it comprehends navigation. This would restrict a general term, applicable to many objects, to one of its *significations*" (*Ch. Just. Marshall*). **Significance,** on the other hand, applies specifically to the covert, as distinguished from the established or the ostensible, meaning of something: it may from its other sense (see IMPORTANCE) carry a connotation of weight or moment (a connotation now rarely, if ever, found in *signification*); as, his language is so grandiose that one wonders if his speeches have any *significance;* no one knows for a certainty the *significance* of some early Christian symbols. "For the mathematically illiterate, like myself, these things [Kelvin's demonstrations] are ...mere scribblings, without *significance*" (*A. Huxley*). "Explaining all the minute happenings of the ranch...as though each of them had a special joyous *significance*" (*M. Austin*). **Import** (see also IMPORTANCE), like *significance,* may imply momentousness, but in contrast with that term, and like *signification,* it denotes the idea or the impression conveyed or to be conveyed to the mind by the medium of words, passages, or the like; as, "the plain *import* of the words [of the Constitution] seems to be, that in one class of cases its [the Supreme Court's] jurisdiction is original, and not appellate; in the other it is appellate, and not original" (*Ch. Just. Marshall*); "[He] spoke words in her ear that had an awful *import* to her" (*Meredith*); "Kim gathered the *import* of the next few sentences" (*Kipling*).

Ana. Suggestion, implication, intimation, hinting *or* hint (see corresponding verbs at SUGGEST): denotation, connotation (see under DENOTE).

meaningful. Significant, pregnant, sententious, *expressive, eloquent.

Ana. Important, consequential, momentous, weighty (see corresponding nouns at IMPORTANCE).

Ant. Meaningless.

measly. Paltry, trifling, trivial, puny, *petty, picayunish, picayune.

Ana. *Contemptible, despicable, sorry, scurvy, cheap, beggarly: *stingy, parsimonious, penurious, miserly, curmudgeonly.

mechanic. Workman, workingman, artisan, *worker, operative, hand, laborer, craftsman, handicraftsman, roustabout.

mechanical. Automatic, instinctive, impulsive, *spontaneous.

Ana. Stereotyped, hackneyed, *trite: dull, *stupid, dense, crass, dumb.

Con. Vital, cardinal, *essential, fundamental: *spirited, high-spirited, mettlesome, fiery, spunky, gingery.

meddle. **Meddle, interfere, intermeddle, tamper** come into comparison when they mean to busy or concern oneself with someone or something officiously, impertinently, or the like. One **meddles** *with* or *in* that which is not one's concern or which is strictly the affair or the responsibility of another or of others: the term usually suggests the interposition of oneself without right or without permission or authorization; as, "It would be better if government *meddled* no farther with trade than to protect it" (*Franklin*); "His enemies accused him... of...*meddling* in matters which did not belong to him" (*Newman*); "it is inexpedient to *meddle* with questions of state in a land where men are highly paid to work them out for you" (*Kipling*). One, or sometimes one's act, **interferes** (see also INTERPOSE, 2) *with* someone or something or *in* something when one meddles (intentionally or unintentionally) in such a way as to hinder, frustrate, molest, or otherwise affect seriously and, usually, injuriously; as, to *interfere* in a dispute; "a physicist ...is not *interfering* with nature, any more than an architect is *interfering* with nature when he directs the building of a house" (*Karl K. Darrow*). One **intermeddles** *with* or *in* something when one meddles impertinently and officiously and in such a way as to interfere; as, "The board of control had no right whatsoever to *intermeddle* in the business" (*Burke*). One **tampers** *with* someone or something when one seeks to make unwarranted alterations, to perform meddlesome experiments, or otherwise to exert an improper influence: the term may or may not suggest corruption or clandestine operation; as, "Provided, the farmer said, nobody had been *tampering* with any of his witnesses" (*Meredith*); "the door had not been *tampered* with" (*Wilde*); "Money and sex are forces too unruly for our reason; they can only be controlled by taboos with which we *tamper* at our peril" (*L. P. Smith*).

Ana. *Intrude, obtrude, interlope, butt in: *interpose, interfere, intervene: molest, discommode, incommode, trouble, *inconvenience.

meddlesome. *Impertinent, intrusive, obtrusive, officious, pragmatical.

Ana. Interfering, meddling, intermeddling, tampering (see MEDDLE): prying, snoopy, nosy, inquisitive, *curious.

median, *adj.* Average, mean, par. See under AVERAGE, *n.*

median, *n.* *Average, mean, norm, par.

mediate. Intercede, intervene, *interpose, interfere.

Ana. Arbitrate, *judge, adjudge, adjudicate: conciliate, propitiate (see PACIFY): reconcile, accommodate, *adapt.

medicament. Medicine, *remedy, cure, specific, physic.

medicinal, *n.* *Drug, pharmaceutical, biological, simple.

medicine. *Remedy, cure, medicament, specific, physic.

mediocre. *Medium, middling, second-rate, moderate, average, fair, indifferent.

Ana. Poor, wrong, *bad: *common, ordinary, vulgar.

meditate. *Ponder, muse, ruminate.

Ana. Contemplate, *consider, study, weigh, revolve: reflect, reason, speculate, deliberate, *think, cogitate: examine, inspect, *scrutinize.

meditative. Contemplative, speculative, *thoughtful, reflective, pensive.

Ana. Pondering, musing, ruminating (see PONDER).

medium, *n.* *Means, instrument, instrumentality, agent, agency, organ, vehicle, channel.

medium, *adj.* **Medium, middling, mediocre, second-rate, moderate, average, fair, indifferent** agree in meaning midway, or about midway, between the extremes of a scale of measurement or evaluation. **Medium** usually presupposes use of a scale of measurement or gradation; it may be an instrument such as a meter or gauge, or it may be a mental power of measuring or gauging attained by experience; as, a boy of *medium* height; a book of *medium* size; a *medium* grade of motor oil; a *medium* gray. **Middling** is seldom used when accurate measurement or gradation is implied; it is employed chiefly in estimations of quality, rank, value, or the like, to describe that which is as far removed from the worst or lowest as it is from the best or highest. Although the word has a colloquial flavor and is much used in noncommittal remarks (as, "How is your health?" "Just *middling*, thank you"), good writers often employ it when they wish to describe something as failing to measure up to the best or the first rate yet not meriting disapproval or rejection. "Longinus...has judiciously preferred the sublime genius that sometimes errs, to the *middling* or indifferent one which makes few faults but seldom or never rises to any excellence" (*Dryden*). "Both of the writers lauded highly...contemporaries who were certainly no better than *middling* performers in their several arts" (*C. E. Montague*). In commercial use, *middling* sometimes occurs as a designation for the second of three grades or as a description of quality of offerings on the market; as, *middling* cottons of good staple. **Mediocre** is not only less colloquial than *middling*, but it also tends to be slightly more depreciative; thus, one who describes a moving picture as *middling* implies that it was good, but far from excellent, but one who describes it as *mediocre* gives ground for the inference that it was distinctly less than what one might call good. Consequently, *mediocre* is often modified by an adverb of degree; as, it is a very *mediocre* poem; he has only *mediocre* ability; "My performance is *médiocre* to the last degree" (*Austen*). "A best-seller is the gilded tomb of a *mediocre* talent" (*L. P. Smith*). **Second-rate** etymologically implies a ranking midway between that which is regarded as first-rate and as third-rate; as, a *second-rate* battleship (sometimes called a *second-class* battleship); a *second-rate* power; a *second-rate* college; a *second-rate* football team. This use often suggests reference to size, equipment, etc., and not to excellence. Frequently, however, *second-rate* connotes inferiority and is used interchangeably with *mediocre* (except that it does not logically admit of qualification); as, a *second-rate* singer; a *second-rate* performance. **Moderate,** as here compared (see also MODERATE, 1), stresses limitations (not self-imposed) in quality, intensity, degree, and the like; it implies distance from the extreme or from either of the extremes possible to a thing of its kind; as, *moderate* wealth; a man of *moderate* ability; a *moderate* wind; to attain *moderate* success; an infusion of *moderate* strength. "I was a *moderate* scholar and a competent athlete" (*A. C. Benson*). **Average,** in the extended sense in which the word is here considered (see also under AVERAGE, *n.*), theoretically implies a level at which all things of a given kind, class, category, or the like, would find themselves or would seek, if their inequalities were resolved; as, this is an *average* June day; where can we find the *average* man? Actually, however, the term is applied to that which seems of the common run or is undistinguished either by its superiority or its inferiority, or is not exceptional or outstanding in any way; thus, a man of *average* ability seems to have neither greater nor less ability than that of the ordinary man. "The only one...with whom he cared to probe into things a little deeper than the *average* level of club and chop-house banter" (*E. Wharton*). "There are readers of papers who...like the ordinary, *average* day, with its good human humdrum" (*C. E. Montague*). **Fair** is applied to that which is neither good nor bad, neither excellent nor poor, neither large nor small, or the like, but is slightly above that which is middling and appreciably better than what is average; as, the quality is *fair* to middling; this region has had a *fair* amount of rain; to be in *fair* physical condition; a *fair* theme; he had a *fair* record in school. **Indifferent** is applied to that which it is difficult to rate because it is neither clearly fair nor clearly mediocre, yet is not obviously middling or average; as, to play an *indifferent* game of bridge; all sorts and conditions, good, bad, and *indifferent*. "The tenacity of wrath which made an *indifferent* poet like Lucilius a fairly great satirist" (*A. Repplier*).

Ana. Mean, median, average, par (see under AVERAGE, *n.*): *common, ordinary, vulgar, popular.

meed, *n.* Guerdon, prize, award, reward, *premium, bounty, bonus.

Ana. Recompensing *or* recompense, remuneration, requital, satisfaction (see corresponding verbs at PAY).

meek. Modest, *humble, lowly.

Ana. Gentle, mild (see SOFT): subdued, submissive, *tame: *compliant, acquiescent, resigned: *forbearing, tolerant, lenient: patient, long-suffering (see corresponding nouns at PATIENCE).

Ant. Arrogant. — *Con.* *Proud, lordly, overbearing, haughty: *spirited, high-spirited, mettlesome, spunky: rebellious, contumacious, *insubordinate.

meet, *v.* *Satisfy, fulfill, answer.

Ana. Equal, approach, *match, touch: gratify, *please: content, *satisfy.

Ant. Disappoint.

meet, *adj.* Suitable, proper, *fit, appropriate, fitting, apt, happy, felicitous.

Ana. Adapted, adjusted, accommodated, conformed, reconciled (see ADAPT): right, *good: just, equitable, *fair.

Ant. Unmeet.

melancholia. Melancholy, *sadness, depression, dejection, gloom, blues, dumps, vapors.

melancholic, *adj.* **Melancholic, melancholy, atrabilious** (*or* **atrabiliar**), **hypochondriac** (*or* **hypochondriacal**) agree in meaning gloomy or depressed, especially as a manifestation of one's temperament or state of health. *Melancholic, melancholy,* and *atrabilious* all once implied the presence or excess of "black bile," one of the "humors" which in the Middle Ages and the Renaissance were supposed to determine a man's temperament and physical constitution. In modern use they are distinguished in meaning. **Melancholic** describes a person who is afflicted with or inclined to melancholia. "Mr. Britling in these moods did not perhaps experience the grey and hopeless desolations of the *melancholic,*...but he saw a world that bristled with misfortune and error" (*H. G. Wells*). **Melancholy,** on the other hand, describes a person, or the mood, disposition, acts, or utterances of a person, who is excessively sad or detached in spirit and, usually, averse to that which is cheerful or gay. " 'They say you are a *melancholy* fellow.' 'I am so; I do love it better than laughing' " (*Shak.*). "Prince, 'tis a *melancholy* lay! For youth, for life we both regret! How fair they seem, how far away" (*A. Lang*). **Atrabilious** preserves the implication of a morbid physical condition more strongly than the preceding words; often in modern use it suggests the morose or choleric disposition of the dyspeptic or the predilection for gloom of those who have been subjected to severe strain. "Neither were those [Puritan settlers of New England] plump rosy-gilled Englishmen that came hither, but a hard-faced, *atrabilious,* earnest-eyed race" (*J. R. Lowell*). "Of nervous *atrabiliar* constitution" (*J. Morley*). **Hypochondriac** comes close to *atrabilious* in its suggestion of constitutional gloominess but, in modern use, it also implies a morbid anxiety about one's state of health. "There was a pleasurable illumination in your eye occasionally, a soft excitement in your aspect, which told of no bitter, bilious, *hypochondriac* brooding" (*C. Brontë*).

Ana. *Despondent, despairing, hopeless, forlorn, desperate: pessimistic, misanthropic, *cynical, misogynic.

melancholy, *n.* *Sadness, melancholia, dejection, gloom, depression, blues, dumps, vapors.

Ana. Miserableness *or* misery, wretchedness (see corresponding adjectives at MISERABLE): despondency, despair, hopelessness, forlornness, desperation (see under DESPONDENT): *tedium, boredom, ennui, doldrums.

Ant. Exhilaration. — *Con.* Joy, delight, *pleasure, enjoyment, delectation, fruition: hopefulness, optimism (see corresponding adjectives at HOPEFUL).

melancholy, *adj.* **1** *Melancholic, atrabilious, hypochondriac.

Ana. Morose, gloomy, glum, *sullen, dour, saturnine: depressed, oppressed, weighed down (see DEPRESS): *despondent, despairing, hopeless, forlorn, desperate.

2 Melancholy, dolorous, doleful, lugubrious, rueful, plaintive come into comparison when they mean expressing or exciting sorrow or mourning. All of these words have, to a greater or less extent, weakened from their original meaning, and are often used with a half-humorous connotation. **Melancholy** in earlier use stressed a quality that inspired pensiveness or sad reflection or awakened mournful thoughts or recollections which were not only not necessarily painful or disagreeable, but often agreeable, especially to the poetic or thoughtful mind. "Sweet bird, that shunn'st the noise of folly, Most musical, most *melancholy!*" (*Milton*). "The tender images we love to trace Steal from each year a *melancholy* grace" (*S. Rogers*). In current use, the term frequently applies to that which expresses or excites dejection or depression; as, "his *melancholy* old house on the hill" (*Deland*); "that *melancholy* problem of a money-earning occupation which lay so heavily on my thoughts" (*H. Ellis*). **Dolorous** in nonderogatory use implies sorrow associated with severe physical or mental suffering; as, "crushed in and bruised ...pain Implacable, and many a *dolorous* groan ...ere they could wind Out of such prison" (*Milton*). In current use, the term describes that which is lamentable in its gloom or dismalness, or is exaggeratedly dismal; as, "That *dolorous* aspect of human nature which in comedy is best portrayed by Molière" (*T. S. Eliot*). " 'I dare say you were exceedingly sorry for what you had done.' 'Indeed, Sir,' *dolorously* moaned Berry, 'I were, and am' " (*Meredith*). **Doleful** and **lugubrious** are also frequently applied to that which is exaggeratedly dismal or dreary, but *doleful* connotes (now humorously) a weight of woe (as, a *doleful* and lackadaisical air; a *doleful* ditty) and *lugubrious,* an undue, and often an affected, heaviness or solemnity (as, "They have been crucifying *Othello* into an opera.... The music good, but *lugubrious*"—*Byron;* "Dark funereal barges like my own had flitted by, and the gondoliers had warned each other at every turning with hoarse, *lugubrious* cries"—*Howells*). **Rueful** implies self-pity or regret but in current use it often suggests a quizzical attitude; as, "the woebegone heroes...eyed each other with *rueful* countenances" (*Irving*). "The deacon looked at his manuscript *ruefully.* 'It reads like a Sunday School essay,' he muttered" (*C. Mackenzie*). **Plaintive** applies chiefly to tones, sounds, utterances, rhythms, and the like, that suggest complaint or mourning or that excite pity or compassion; as, the *plaintive* cries of a child; "She sang *plaintively,* the wounded, aggrieved, hurt notes of the nightingale" (*Hewlett*). In poetic use, however, the term often suggests little more than pensive melancholy or expression in a minor key; as, "Perhaps the *plaintive* numbers flow For old, unhappy, far-off things" (*Wordsworth*).

Ana. Pathetic, poignant, *moving, touching: hopeless, forlorn, despairing (see DESPONDENT): pensive, reflective, *thoughtful: discomposing, disquieting, perturbing, disturbing (see DISCOMPOSE).

Con. Happy, *glad, cheerful, joyous, joyful, lighthearted: *lively, vivacious, gay.

melee. Fracas, row, *brawl, broil, rumpus, scrap.

Ana. Altercation, *quarrel, wrangle, squabble: *confusion, disorder.

mellow. Ripe, matured, *mature, adult, grown-up, full-fledged.

Ana. *Tender, warm, sympathetic, responsive, warmhearted.

Ant. Unmellow: green. — *Con.* Raw, crude, callow, *rude, rough.

melodramatic. Histrionic, theatrical, dramaturgic, *dramatic.

Ana. *Showy, pretentious, ostentatious: *sentimental, romantic, maudlin, mawkish.

melody. Melody, air, tune agree in denoting a clearly distinguishable and, often, easily remembered succession of rhythmically ordered tones. **Melody** stresses the sweetness or beauty of sound produced by such an arrangement of tones. "Sweetest *melodies* Are those that are by distance made more sweet" (*Wordsworth*). It also commonly suggests expressiveness or moving power, and a carefully wrought pattern. "Nerve-dissolving *melody*" (*Tennyson*). " 'Tis a rich sobbing melody, with reliefs Full and majestic" (*Keats*). Technically, as applied to complex musical structure, *melody* always implies a contrast to *harmony;* it designates that kind of musical beauty produced by a continuous series of tones in one or more of the voice parts, in distinction from that produced by simultaneously sounded tones in all the voice parts. Strictly, **air** is applied to the dominating melody, usually carried by the upper voice or voices, in a choral, a part song, or the like. Loosely, however, *air* is often applied to any easily remembered succession of tones which identifies a simple musical composition such as a song, a ballad, or a waltz, and which is more commonly and more precisely called **tune**; as, to hum the *tune* (or the *air*) of the Blue Danube. *Tune* is also applied to the musical setting of a ballad, psalm, lyric, and the like (as, a hymn *tune*), and to any simple composition whether unison or harmonized (as, a dance *tune*).

melt. *Liquefy, deliquesce, dissolve, thaw, fuse.

member. *Part, portion, piece, detail, division, section, segment, sector, fraction, fragment, parcel.

Ana. *Element, component, constituent, integrant: branch, limb, *shoot, bough.

memorandum. *Letter, epistle, missive, note, message, dispatch, report.

memory. **Memory, remembrance, recollection, reminiscence, mind, souvenir** are not synonyms in all of their senses, but they are comparable terms since all involve the ideas of remembering and of being remembered. **Memory** applies chiefly to the power or function of remembering that which has been experienced or learned; in this sense, it suggests the power to reproduce images of what is no longer before one, to retain something that has been learned (words, ideas, skills, etc.), and to recognize and identify something previously known; as, he has a remarkably good *memory;* to train the *memory;* "Her *memory*... went slipping back upon the golden days" (*Tennsyon*). In literary use, *memory* often occurs in the sense of that which is remembered either as an aggregate or as a single item. More than any other of the words as used in this sense, *memory* suggests a keeping in mind rather than a bringing back and often, therefore, a treasuring as something intimate or personal; as, "a present moment of comfortable reality was worth a decade of *memories*" (*Hardy*). "It was the merest *memory* now, vague and a little sweet" (*Galsworthy*); "'You must have had a charming evening...if I may judge from the way you have kept the *memory* green'" (*Conrad*). **Remembrance** in current use applies primarily to the act or the process (as distinguished from the faculty, power, or function) of remembering; as, "Think only of the past as its *remembrance* gives you pleasure" (*Austen*); "The *remembrance* of all that made life dear pierced me to the core" (*Hudson*); "He was unpleasantly affected by the *remembrance* of certain passages between them" (*Arch. Marshall*). *Remembrance* also denotes, but now less often than formerly, the state or fact of being remembered or kept in the memory of a person or group of persons; as, to hold one in fond *remembrance;* "moments...that live again in *remembrance*" (*W. W. Gibson*); "our literature is going to be our most perdurable claim on man's *remembrance*" (*Quiller-Couch*). **Recollection** often takes the place of *remembrance* when not only the act or process of remembering is denoted, but also the act or process of bringing back into the mind something which has been forgotten or not thought of for a long period, or which merely is not in one's mind at the time: the term, therefore, often, but far from always, implies an effort to remember; as, he said he must have time for *recollection* if he was to give an accurate account of what happened that day; "Half a word fixed upon or near the spot, is worth a cartload of *recollection*" (*Gray*); "his uneasiness grew by the *recollection* of the forty tons of dynamite in the body of the *Ferndale;* not the sort of cargo one thinks of with equanimity in connexion with a threatened collision" (*Conrad*). But *recollection* is quite as often used of that which is remembered, especially as the result of conscious effort; as, "You ask me to put down a few *recollections* of your father" (*Lecky*); "Vivid indeed is my *recollection* of our halts before shaded homesteads, our protracted and usually successful parleys with lean housewives, hungry for conversation" (*Grandgent*). **Reminiscence** is more colored in its meaning by philosophical and psychological theories (particularly the Platonic theory of reminiscence) than any of the preceding words. For this reason chiefly, although etymologically it means a bringing back to mind, it carries a stronger implication of recovery through retrospection than any of the other terms. Like *remembrance* and *recollection*, it denotes either the act or the process of remembering but it further suggests either the recollection of that which has been long unremembered, especially because it belongs to one's remote past (as, the old man spent hour after hour indulging in *reminiscence;* "after another quarter of an hour of *reminiscence* they had got around to the things that had happened to each of them since they had last met"—*M. Austin*) or, especially in writings marked by Platonism, the recollection of something that belongs to a previous existence (as, "Knows he his origin? can he ascend By *reminiscence* to his earliest date?"—*Cowper*). "I believe that as we lose our powers of *memory* we may increase the power of *reminiscence*, that is, of recalling what we want in small quantities for a short time" (*Jowett*). The term is often used, however, in place of *recollection* in the concrete sense where that which is remembered serves as a contribution to biography, an autobiography, or a history (as, "The *reminiscences* [of my father] kindly contributed by his different friends"—*H. Tennyson*), or is recalled from the past in conversation or in writing by an aging or aged person (as, to enjoy the *reminiscences* of the old veterans), or is a phrase, a passage, a thought, a custom, or the like, that is so like one found in an earlier writer or race as to be regarded as an unconscious imitation or repetition or a survival (as, the young poet's best phrases are *reminiscences* of Keats; *reminiscences* of medieval pageants in modern carnivals). **Mind** (see also MIND, 2) is now found in the sense here considered chiefly in certain idiomatic phrases where it means either the entity as distinct from the function which stores up that which is remembered (as, I shall keep your need in *mind;* out of sight, out of *mind*) or the power to remember (as, time out of *mind*). **Souvenir** (usually thought of as a memento) is now infrequent in the sense of a memory, or that which is remembered, but it still occurs; as, "little tender thoughts of Constance, some flitting *souvenir*... of her mother" (*Bennett*).

Ana. *Mind, intellect, soul, intelligence, brains, wits: remembering, minding, recalling, reminding (see REMEMBER): awareness, consciousness, cognizance (see corresponding adjectives at AWARE).

Ant. Oblivion.

menace, *v.* *Threaten.

Ana. Alarm, terrify, scare, *frighten: *intimidate, cow: presage, portend, forebode, forecast (see FORETELL).

mend, *v.* **Mend, repair, patch, rebuild, remodel** come into comparison when they mean to make something that has been injured or damaged once again fit for use. **Mend,** which is etymologically a shortened form of *amend*, in general implies a freeing from faults or defects or, less often, a making up for a fault, but in its chief current sense it usually specifically suggests a process of making whole or sound something that has been broken, torn, injured by wear or use, or the like. In slightly archaic English, one speaks of *mending* one's manners (or ways), of *mending* one's health, of *mending* a person's reputation, or one uses the old proverb "the least said, the soonest *mended*." In ordinary English, on the other hand, one *mends* a garment when one sews up rents, darns holes, or puts pieces under worn spots; one *mends* a fountain pen when one puts in a new ink sac, provides a new pen point, or the like; so, to *mend* a broken dish or toy; to *mend* a rug; to *mend* a stone wall; the break in his leg never was properly *mended*. **Repair** may often be used in place of *mend* in the sense of making whole or sound again (as, to *mend* [or *repair*] a stone wall), but it is usually preferred to *mend* when complete success is implied and when the thing that is restored to wholeness or soundness is a complex thing that has been partly destroyed, or extensively damaged, or has suffered dilapidation, debilitation, exhaustion, or the like; as, to *repair* a bicycle or automobile; to *repair* the badly burned house before moving back into it; it will cost a huge sum to *repair* the bridge; food is necessary to *repair* the tissues of the body; "there are few moral wrecks which may not be, to all seeming, completely *repaired* in this world" (*C. W. Eliot*); "if economic havoc and maladjustment attributable to the Great War were *repaired*" (*J. A. Hobson*). **Patch** implies a mending of a hole, rent, breach, or weak spot by the insertion or application of a piece of the same or similar material: the term sometimes, but far from always, implies obvious, hurried, careless, or clumsy mending, or a repairing that merely serves a temporary purpose; as, to *patch* trousers; to *patch* a plastered wall; to *patch* shoes; to *patch* a damaged lawn; to *patch* an inner tube. In extended use, *patch*, or frequently *patch up*, implies a making of something out of a great number of pieces, fragments, odds and ends (as, to *patch* a quilt; to *patch up* an account of a battle from stray bits of information; to *patch up* a code of rules for the guidance of a society), or a settling of something that causes disturbance (as, to *patch up* a quarrel), or a restoring something which has been broken or disrupted in a way suggestive of patching (as, to *patch up* a friendship). In current use, especially in industry and business, **rebuild,** which normally means to build again something which has been razed or ruined, is often preferred to *repair* because it implies a thoroughgoing repairing with addition of new parts when necessary that makes a thing like new; as, a *rebuilt* typewriter or automobile. **Remodel** implies repairing with some changes, often extensive changes, in structure or design; as, to *remodel* an old house; to *remodel* a dress.

Ana. *Improve, better, ameliorate, help: emend, remedy, redress, *correct, rectify, reform: *renew, restore, renovate, rejuvenate, refurbish: fix, *adjust, regulate.

mendacious. *Dishonest, lying, untruthful, deceitful.

Ana. *False, wrong: prevaricating, equivocating, paltering, fibbing (see LIE, *v.*).

Ant. Veracious. — *Con.* *Reliable, dependable, trustworthy: honest, *upright, just, scrupulous, conscientious, honorable.

menial. Servile, slavish, *subservient, obsequious.

Ana. Abject, *mean, sordid, ignoble: *base, low, vile: groveling, floundering, wallowing (see WALLOW).

menstruum. *Solvent, dissolvent, resolvent, alkahest.

mental. **Mental, intellectual, psychic, psychical, intelligent, cerebral** agree in meaning of, relating to, or characteristic of that sum total of powers or functions called variously (and in the senses discriminated at MIND, 2) *mind, intellect, soul* (or *psyche*), or *brain*. In general, **mental** applies directly to that which has to do with the mind as a real (though often immaterial) or as a purely theoretical entity; as, one's *mental* life; a *mental* state; *mental* diseases; *mental* processes; *mental* science. **Intellectual** differs from *mental* not only in its reference to the intellect, and therefore to the higher powers of the mind such as the comprehension of the abstract or difficult and the ability to reason, but also because it is directly applicable to persons, their utterances, acts, and qualities (thus, one says an *intellectual* [not a *mental*] person), and because it often carries an implied contrast to *emotional, moral, imaginative,* and the like; as, "a miracle of *intellectual* delicacy like Dr. Newman's" (*Arnold*); "No abstract, *intellectual* plan of life" (*Browning*); "The knowledge of geographical facts is useful, but without intrinsic *intellectual* value" (*B. Russell*). "It was only on her *intellectual* side that Elizabeth touched the England of her day. All its moral aspects were simply dead to her" (*J. R. Green*). "Part of the value of science is *intellectual*. It would be a dull mind that could see the rich variety of natural phenomena without wondering how they are inter-related" (*Jeans*). **Psychic** and **psychical** imply a reference to the soul or psyche, usually, but not invariably, in their psychological senses; often, therefore, they differ from *mental* in not suggesting a physical basis such as the brain or the nerves; thus, a *mental* disease is sometimes, but only in nontechnical language, distinguished from a *psychic* disease in that the former implies a cause which is organic and the latter a cause which cannot be related to the body but which seems to proceed from wrong ideas or attitudes; the term *psychical research* applies to investigations of phenomena that seem contrary to physical laws and suggest mental activity apart from the body. "You keep talking about maladies of the mind and soul. I don't accept the idea of *psychic* diseases analogous to *mental* diseases" (*C. Mackenzie*). "The humorist was a type that pioneer society required in order to maintain its *psychic* equilibrium" (*Van W. Brooks*). **Intelligent,** as here compared (see also INTELLIGENT, 2), is applicable to any person who is endowed with an intellect or reveals intelligence; as, men are *intelligent* beings; the most *intelligent* of his pupils. The term is also applicable to an animal that reveals sagacity or other qualities suggestive of intelligence; as, an *intelligent* spaniel. **Cerebral** implies a reference to brain (either as a physical organ or as mind or intellect) or brains: it is often used in current English when the physical basis of the mental life is stressed or when the particular qualities implied by brains are to be suggested; thus, the "*cerebral* awakening" of a child is a phrase more suggestive of brain activity than "*mental* awakening"; "*cerebral* music" implies the need of definite intellectual activity if the music is to be understood.

mephitic *or* **mephitical.** Toxic, *poisonous, venomous, virulent, pestilent, pestilential, miasmatic.

Ana. *Offensive, loathsome, revolting, repulsive, repugnant: fetid, noisome, putrid, *malodorous: noxious, *pernicious, baneful.

mercantile. *Commercial.

mercenary, *adj.* **Mercenary, hireling, hack, hackney, venal** are not close synonyms but they are comparable because when they are applied to persons, their acts, their services or products, or the like, they agree in meaning actuated or motivated chiefly by a desire for profit. **Mercenary** stresses self-interest (often self-seeking) as the guiding motive: it therefore usually (except when applied to soldiers who serve a foreign power for a wage) applies to persons, services, etc., that should be prompted by altruism or by noble aims or should be characterized by unselfishness or self-forgetfulness; as, "the faithful service of the heart; so rendered and so free from any *mercenary* taint" (*Dickens*); "She had...nothing sordid or *mercenary;* in fact, she never thought of money" (*G. Eliot*). "If a writer's attitude toward his characters and his scene is as vulgar as a showman's, as *mercenary* as an auctioneer's, vulgar and meretricious will his product for ever remain" (*Cather*). **Hireling** suggests the attitude of one who serves for the wage involved or is guided by servile motives: the term usually, especially in its more common opprobrious use, implies a motive no higher than that of the reward promised or foreseen; as, "the factious and *hireling* historians of all ages" (*Raleigh*, d. 1618); "some *hireling* senators" (*Johnson*); "prostituted muse and *hireling* bard" (*Byron*). **Hack** and the original but now rare form **hackney,** as here compared, apply to a person that is hired or offers his services for hire, or to the services, products, or the like, of such a person: the term often, but not invariably, implies previous failure, as in a profession, a low order of ability or of performance, willingness to drudge, and indifference to the nature of the work required; as, a *hack* writer; a *hack* attorney; "the *hack* moralist of the pulpit or the press" (*J. Morley*); "some starved *hackny* sonneteer" (*Pope*); "the *hackney* libellers of the faction" (*R. North*). **Venal** implies purchasability. The term often connotes the use of bribery, and in the sense here considered it nearly always carries a strong implication of corruption or of corruptibility: it is, of all these terms, the most opprobrious; as, *venal* politicians; *venal* voters; the *venal* sale of political offices; a *venal* arrangement whereby certain contractors are favored; "bartering his *venal* wit for sums of gold" (*Dryden*).

Ana. Vendible, purchasable: abject, *mean, sordid, ignoble: *covetous, greedy, acquisitive, grasping, avaricious: debased, corrupt, corrupted, depraved (see under DEBASE).

merciful. Clement, *forbearing, tolerant, lenient, indulgent.

Ana. Compassionate, *tender: benignant, benign, *kind, kindly: forgiving, pardoning, condoning (see EXCUSE, *v.*).

Ant. Merciless. — *Con.* *Grim, implacable, relentless, unrelenting: cruel, fell, inhuman, *fierce.

mercifulness. Clemency, forbearance, tolerance, leniency, indulgence. See under FORBEARING.

Ana. *Mercy, clemency, lenity, charity, grace: compassion, commiseration, *pity, ruth.

*Con.*契Severeness *or* severity, sternness (see corresponding adjectives at SEVERE): rigorousness *or* rigor, rigidity, strictness, stringency (see corresponding adjectives at RIGID).

merciless. Implacable, relentless, unrelenting, *grim.

Ana. Pitiless, ruthless, compassionless (see affirmative nouns at PITY): wanton, uncalled-for, gratuitous (see SUPEREROGATORY): cruel, fell, *fierce: inexorable, obdurate, *inflexible, adamant, adamantine.

Ant. Merciful. — *Con.* Clement, *forbearing, tolerant, lenient, indulgent.

mercurial. *Inconstant, fickle, capricious, unstable.

Ana. Volatile, effervescent, buoyant, expansive, *elastic, resilient: *changeable, changeful, variable, protean, mutable: mobile, *movable: *clever, adroit, cunning, ingenious.

Ant. Saturnine.

mercy. **Mercy, charity, grace, clemency, lenity** are here compared as meaning either the disposition to show compassion or kindness in one's treatment of others, especially of those who offend one and who are in one's power to punish or rebuke, or an instance in which this disposition is manifested. **Mercy** implies compassion so great as to enable one to forbear, even when justice demands punishment, or to give help or comfort even to the lowliest or most undeserving. "Earthly power doth then show likest God's When *mercy* seasons justice" (*Shak.*). "Which now of these three [the priest, the Levite, the Samaritan]...was neighbour unto him that fell among the thieves? And he said, He that shewed *mercy* on him" (*Luke* x. 36–37). **Charity** fundamentally implies a disposition to love all men as brothers; in more modern use, it stresses benevolence and good will, especially as it reveals itself not only in giving generously (for this sense see CHARITY, 2) but in broad understanding of others and in kindly tolerance; as, "with malice toward none, with *charity* for all" (*Lincoln*); "To know the literature of another language...enlarges aesthetic *charity*" (*J. R. Lowell*). "It is far commoner at the University to meet men of great attainments combined with sincere humility and *charity*, for...the most erudite specialist...becomes aware both of the wide diversity of knowledge and of his own limitations as well" (*A. C. Benson*). **Grace,** as here compared, implies a benignant attitude toward those who are dependent on one and a disposition to bestow favors or to make concessions to them. In its theological sense, in reference to the spiritual assistance given men by God, the word still lives; in its general application, it now tends to be somewhat archaic. "To bow and sue for *grace* With suppliant knee" (*Milton*). "Each in his place, by right, not *grace*, Shall rule his heritage" (*Kipling*). " 'Let him sit with me, or he'll grow up a barbarian, with no manners!'...Miss Hannah was...thankful for this *grace* on her brother's part" (*Deland*). **Clemency,** as here compared (see also *clement* under FORBEARING), implies a mild or merciful disposition in one whose duty or function it is to administer justice or to punish offenses. "*Clemency*...is the standing policy of constitutional governments, as severity is of despotism" (*Hallam*). "Off went poor Tom ....to rejoice in the *clemency* that spared his appearance at Sessions" (*Meredith*). **Lenity** differs from *clemency* only in its far greater emphasis on lack of severity. For this reason it often suggests undue gentleness or softness or even at times undue leniency. "What makes robbers bold but too much *lenity?*" (*Shak.*). "If it produces a proper *lenity* to our citizens in captivity, it will have the effect we meant" (*Jefferson*).

Ana. Compassion, ruth, *pity, commiseration: mercifulness, clemency, forbearance, tolerance, leniency, indulgence (see under FORBEARING).

Con. Vengeance, revenge, retribution, reprisal, *retaliation: punishment, chastening, chastisement, disciplining *or* discipline, correction, castigation (see corresponding verbs at PUNISH).

mere. **Mere, bare** are often employed with little or no distinction in the sense of being such as the term qualified states but nothing more. But **mere** is commonly used to emphasize the limitations of a thing, as if it were declared to be "simply what it is and nothing more"; as, he is a *mere* boy (i.e., in no sense an adolescent or man); "it began to rain—not a *mere* hill-shower, but a good, tepid, monsoonish downpour" (*Kipling*); "Is *mere* living... without reference to any intrinsic values, a thing of any worth?" (*Inge*); "There is scarcely any *mere* paint in the Sistine Madonna, but there is plenty of paint" (*C. E. Montague*). **Bare** is stronger, and frequently suggests that the thing just escapes falling short of what it actually is; as, *mere* civility (that is, civility and nothing more); *bare civility* (that is, civility that just escapes being incivility); to be elected by a *bare* majority; "a *bare* subsistence wage" (*Shaw*).

meretricious. *Gaudy, tawdry, garish, flashy.

Ana. *Showy, pretentious, ostentatious: vulgar, *coarse, gross: deceptive, delusive, delusory, *misleading.

☞ *Do not confuse* meretricious *with* meritorious.

merge. Blend, fuse, coalesce, amalgamate, commingle, mingle, *mix.

Ana. Consolidate, concentrate, *compact, unify: *unite, combine, conjoin: *integrate, concatenate, articulate.

merger. *Consolidation, amalgamation.

meridian. Culmination, zenith, apogee, *summit, peak, pinnacle, climax, apex, acme.

merit, *n.* **1** *Due, desert.

Ana. Meed, reward, guerdon (see PREMIUM): *worth, value: earning(s), gaining(s), winning(s) (see corresponding verbs at GET).

2 *Excellence, virtue, perfection.

Ant. Fault: defect.

merry. **Merry, blithe, jocund, jovial, jolly** come into comparison when they mean indicating or manifesting high spirits or lightheartedness in play, laughter, or the like. **Merry** implies a gay, cheerful temper or mood and uninhibited enjoyment of frolic, festivity, or fun of any sort. "A *merrier* man, Within the limit of becoming mirth, I never spent an hour's talk withal" (*Shak.*). "Let us drink and be *merry*, dance, joke, and rejoice" (*T. Jordan*). "For the good are always the *merry*, Save by an evil chance, And the *merry* love the fiddle, And the *merry* love to dance" (*Yeats*). **Blithe** (now chiefly literary except in Scotland) carries an even stronger implication of freshness, buoyancy, and lightheartedness than *merry;* it usually suggests song, leaping, dancing, and the like; as, "The milkmaid singeth *blithe*" (*Milton*); "Knit the *blithe* dance upon the soft green grass" (*Wordsworth*). "See This lovely child, *blithe*, innocent and free, She spends a happy time with little care" (*Shelley*). **Jocund** (once poetical, but now increasingly common in literary prose) heightens the implication of gladness and usually, also, connotes exhilaration of spirits, or elation; as, "A poet could not but be gay, In such a *jocund* company" (*Wordsworth*); "He was...in that *jocund*, new-married mood" (*M. Austin*). **Jovial** connotes especially good fellowship or conviviality. "Those *jovial* meetings of company where the warmth of a social temper is discovered with least reserve" (*Shenstone*); "Gunga Dass....was a *jovial*, full-stomached, portly government servant with a marvelous capacity for making bad puns" (*Kipling*). **Jolly** often suggests higher spirits than *jovial* and an even more manifest attempt to keep others laughing, as by jesting, bantering, playing tricks, and the like. "Whiles the *jolly* Briton...laughs [at the lovelorn Frenchman] from's free lungs" (*Shak.*). "Haste thee, nymph, and bring with thee Jest, and youthful *jollity*, Quips and cranks and wanton wiles" (*Milton*).

Ana. Gay, vivacious, *lively, sprightly, animated: joyful, joyous, cheerful, *glad, happy, lighthearted: mirthful, gleeful, hilarious (see corresponding nouns at MIRTH).

merry-andrew. *Fool, jester, clown, antic, buffoon, zany, pantaloon, harlequin, comedian, comic, stooge.

mesa. *Mountain, mount, peak, alp, volcano.

message. Missive, note, *letter, epistle, dispatch, report, memorandum.

metachronism. *Anachronism, parachronism, prochronism.

metamorphose. *Transform, transmute, convert, transmogrify, transfigure.

Ana. *Change, vary, alter, modify: develop, *mature, age, ripen.

metamorphosis. Transformation, transmutation, conversion, transmogrification, transfiguration. See under TRANSFORM.

Ana. *Change, mutation, alternation, permutation, vicissitude: change, variation, alteration, modification (see under CHANGE, *v.*).

metaphor. Simile, *analogy.

metaphrase. *Translation, version, paraphrase, construe.

meter *or* **metre.** *Rhythm, cadence.

method. **Method, mode, manner, way, fashion, system** are here compared as denoting the means taken or the plan or procedure followed in doing a given kind of work or in achieving a given end. **Method** may denote either an abstraction or a concrete procedure, but in both cases it implies orderly, logical, and effective arrangement, as of one's ideas for an exposition or an argument, or of the steps to be followed in teaching, in investigation, in the treatment of a disease, or in any kind or piece of work: often, also, the term connotes regularity or formality in procedure; as, his teaching is too informal to be said to have *method;* the inductive *method* of reasoning; a new *method* of dealing with relief cases; "the crude *methods* of trial and error" (*H. Suzzallo*); "the *method* of unfolding the course of a plot must in some ways be different in a play meant for acting and in a book meant for reading" (*C. E. Montague*). **Mode,** as here compared (see also FASHION, 2; STATE), is sometimes used interchangeably with *method,* but not wisely, for it seldom implies an orderly or logical arrangement; rather, it denotes an order or course pursued as the result of custom, tradition, personal preference, or the like; as, "The duty of itself being resolved on, the *mode* of doing it may easily be found" (*Jer. Taylor*); an author's peculiar *mode* of expression; the French *mode* of life; "The reasons given ...do not seem very plausible to our *modes* of thought" (*Binyon*). **Manner** (see also BEARING) is often used in place of *mode* where the reference is to a personal or peculiar course or procedure, or to a method, whether pursued by a number of persons or not, that savors of that which is individual or distinctive; as, "Mark the *manner* of his teaching" (*Shak.*); "The mathematician ...is not capable of giving a reason in the same *manner* as the dialectician" (*Jowett*); "his personality has suggested to me an entirely new *manner* in art" (*Wilde*). **Way** (see also WAY, 1) may be used in place of any of the preceding words, not only because it is the most general of all, but because it is a very old word common both in colloquial and in literary speech, and because it is found in many familiar idiomatic expressions, where theoretically *method, mode,* or *manner* might be more explicit, but would actually be less expressive or less poignant; as, religion implies not only a *way* of worship but a *way* of life; "it was the white man's *way* to assert himself in any landscape, to change it, make it over a little...it was the Indian's *way* to pass through a country...and leave no trace" (*Cather*); "the century has brought us not only new things to see but new *ways* of seeing" (*Day Lewis*); "Sally used to answer Robert's letters, sadly and patiently, and with no reproaches;—that was Sally's *way*" (*Deland*). **Fashion,** as here compared, differs from *way* not so much in denotation as in connotation derived in part from its commoner sense of *style* or *vogue* (see FASHION, 2). The term, therefore, often suggests an origin or source that is not so deep or a motivation that is not so abiding as those usually connoted by *way:* oftentimes also, it is the idiomatic term in prepositional phrases introduced by *after* or *in;* as, "He will, after his sour *fashion*, tell you" (*Shak.*); "Subjects serious in themselves, but treated after my *fashion*, non-seriously" (*Lamb*); "I have been faithful to thee, Cynara, after my *fashion*" (*E. Dowson*); "We hear them talking...in different *fashions* under different moods—even as you and I" (*Lowes*). But *fashion* sometimes comes very close to *mode* when it means the way that is characteristic of or peculiar to a group, type, or the like; as, to swim dog *fashion*. **System,** though not uncommon in the sense of a fully developed and often carefully formulated method, runs so easily into the commoner sense of the term (see SYSTEM, 1) that it may often as easily apply to the scheme as to the actual way of doing something; as, "The mind can scarcely conceive a *system* for regulating commerce between nations, which shall exclude all laws concerning navigation" (*Ch. Just. Marshall*); the *system* of classification now preferred by botanists; "The Greek...helped himself by an elaborate *system* of sacrifice and prayer and divination...the object of which was simply to discover and if possible to affect the divine purposes" (*G. L. Dickinson*). As an abstraction, however, meaning orderliness or plan in arrangement or procedure, *system* is often preferred to *method;* as, housekeeping without *system;* he follows no *system* in his reading.

Ana. *Process, procedure, proceeding: classification, alphabetization (see corresponding verbs at ASSORT): disposition, *disposal.

methodical, methodic. *Orderly, systematic, regular.

Ana. Methodized, systematized, organized (see ORDER, *v.*): *careful, meticulous, scrupulous: *logical, analytical.

Ant. Unmethodical: desultory. — ***Con.*** *Random, haphazard, casual, hit-or-miss: *irregular, unnatural: confused, disordered, chaotic, jumbled (see corresponding nouns at CONFUSION).

methodize. Systematize, organize, *order, arrange, marshal.

Ana. Regulate, *adjust: *set, settle, fix, establish.

meticulous. *Careful, scrupulous, punctilious, punctual.

Ana. Fastidious, finical, particular, fussy, pernickety, *nice: accurate, exact, precise, *correct.

métier. Business, pursuit, calling, occupation, employment, *work.

Ana. *Trade, craft, handicraft, art, profession: *work, labor, toil, travail: *vocation, avocation.

metonymy. Metonymy, synecdoche designate two closely related figures of speech in which the name of one thing is given for that of another thing which bears a close relationship to the first thing. **Metonymy** (etymologically, change of name) is the general term for this type of figure of speech; the relationships it may imply are very numerous, but the most common are these: (1) the use of the sign for the thing signified, as in: the pen (which is the instrument of a writer and the sign, therefore, of literary power) is mightier than the sword (the instrument of a soldier, and the sign of military power); (2) the use of that which contains, holds, or the like, for that which it contains, holds, etc., as in: he keeps a good table (i.e., a table well supplied at meals with good food); all the world (i.e., all the people inhabiting the world) loves a lover; the kettle (i.e., the water inside) is boiling; (3) the use of the cause for the effect or of the effect for the cause, as in: to read Dante (i.e., the poems Dante wrote); to have respect for gray hairs (i.e., for age which has gray hairs for one of its effects). **Synecdoche** is a species of metonymy in which: (1) the name of the whole is given for one of its parts, as in: please raise the window (i.e., the lower sash); (2) the name of a part takes the place of the name of the whole, as in: all hands (i.e., all the men employed at manual labor) were put to work; "I descried a sail [i.e., a ship] steering to the South-East" (*Swift*); (3) the name of the material takes the place of the name of the thing made from that material, as in: one of the finest marbles (i.e., sculptures carved out of marble) in the exhibition; to read a paper (i.e., an article written or typed on paper) at a club meeting.

metropolitan, *n.* Archbishop, primate, *bishop, ordinary.

mettle. *Courage, spirit, resolution, tenacity.

Ana. *Fortitude, backbone, sand, grit, pluck, guts: nerve, hardihood, *temerity, audacity: gallantry, valor, *heroism.

mettlesome. *Spirited, high-spirited, spunky, fiery, peppery, gingery.

Ana. Courageous, bold, audacious, intrepid, *brave: *impassioned, passionate, ardent, fervent: restive, *impatient, restless, skittish.

miasmatic *or* **miasmatical, miasmal, miasmic.** *Poisonous, toxic, venomous, virulent, pestilent, pestilential, mephitic.

Ana. Contagious, *infectious, catching: noxious, *pernicious, baneful, deleterious.

microbe. *Germ, bacterium, bacillus, virus, pathogen.

microscopic. Minute, *small, little, diminutive, miniature, petite, wee, tiny, teeny, weeny.

middle, *n.* *Center, midst, core, hub, omphalos, focus, nucleus, heart.

middling. *Medium, mediocre, second-rate, moderate, average, fair, indifferent.

midget, *n.* Manikin, pygmy, *dwarf, homunculus, runt.

midst. Middle, *center, core, hub, omphalos, focus, nucleus, heart.

mien. Demeanor, deportment, *bearing, manner, carriage, port, presence, front.

Ana. Air *or* airs, *pose, affectation, mannerism: aspect, *appearance, semblance, look.

might, *n.* Strength, energy, *power, force, puissance, arm.

Ana. Vigorousness *or* vigor, strenuousness, energeticness, lustiness (see corresponding adjectives at VIGOROUS): potency, powerfulness, forcibleness, forcefulness (see corresponding adjectives at POWERFUL).

mild. Gentle, lenient, bland, *soft, balmy.

Ana. *Forbearing, tolerant, clement, merciful, lenient, indulgent: delicate, dainty, exquisite, *choice: temperate, *moderate: *calm, serene, tranquil, placid.

Ant. Harsh: fierce.

milieu. Environment, setting, *background, mise-en-scène, backdrop.

militant. *Aggressive, assertive, self-assertive, pushing.

Ana. Bellicose, pugnacious, contentious, *belligerent: combating, opposing, antagonizing *or* antagonistic (see corresponding verbs at OPPOSE): fighting, warring, contending, battling (see CONTEND).

Con. *Pacific, pacifist, pacifistic, peaceful, peaceable: acquiescent, resigned, *compliant.

military. *Martial, warlike.

mime. *Actor, player, performer, mummer, Thespian, impersonator, trouper.

mimic. *Copy, imitate, ape, mock.

Ana. Play, impersonate, personate, *act: counterfeit, feign, simulate, sham, pretend, *assume.

mind, *n.* **1** *Memory, remembrance, recollection, reminiscence, souvenir.

2 Mind, intellect, soul, psyche, brain, brains, intelligence, wit, wits are here compared as meaning that sum total of powers (often thought of as a distinct entity) which man regards as the distinctive possession of human beings and by means of which each individual knows and understands both his inner life and the external world and establishes effective relations between them. **Mind,** like all the other terms, has been variously defined. It is commonly contrasted with *body*, or the physical organism, but it is also in other senses contrasted with *heart*, as the seat of the feelings, and with *soul*, as the immortal spirit of man, or with *soul* as equivalent to *heart*, but in all cases, despite a difference in stress on certain qualities, it denotes a complex of powers of which man is conscious and which includes the perceiving, the remembering, the thinking, and less often, the feeling and willing powers or functions. When all these powers are implied, the opposition to *body* is clear (as, a sound *mind* in a sound body; "to keep the body in strength and vigour, so that it may be able to obey and execute the orders of the *mind*"—*Locke*); when the capacity for understanding and reasoning is stressed, the contrast with *heart* or *soul* is implied (as, "The *mind* must have its share in deciding these important matters, not merely the emotions and desires"—*R. Macaulay*); when the exercise of the powers that operate through physical organs (such as the eye, the ear, the brain, the nerves) is suggested, a distinction from *soul*, as spirit, is often connoted (as, "it is a man's own fault, it is from want of use, if his *mind* grows torpid in old age"—*Johnson;* "Insanity is often the logic of an accurate mind overtaxed"—*Holmes;* "And thou shalt love the Lord thy God with all thy heart, and with all thy soul, and with all thy mind, and with all thy strength: this is the first commandment"—*Mark* xii. 30). *Mind* also is usually the preferred term when the reference is to an individual's mental qualities; as, he has a very good *mind;* "The *mind* of Julius [Caesar], so far as we can read it, was the *mind* of a dreamer joined to the temperament of a soldier" (*Buchan*). **Intellect** and *mind* are often used interchangeably by many persons; however, in psychology and in philosophy *intellect* rather than *mind* has been the usual technical term for the knowing and thinking powers and functions (or the entity they suggest). In spite of numerous variations in definitions and a fundamental difference of opinion between schools of thought as to whether the power of intuition or the power to reason is the distinguishing property of *intellect*, the term has in all but loose nontechnical use denoted that entity (or, in many psychologies, that "faculty," of the mind or soul) by which a person attains knowledge, whether through comprehension of that which is taught or through processes of thought whereby the mind moves from that which was previously known to conclusions that represent new knowledge. In many psychologies this "faculty" of the mind is distinguished from two other "faculties"—those of feeling and of will. "We can trace ...in the romanticism of nineteenth-century France this tendency toward a hypertrophy of sensation and an atrophy of ideas, toward a correspondingly expanding sensorium and a diminishing *intellect*" (*Babbitt*). "The emotionalist steeps himself or herself in luxurious feeling and pathetic imagination, which make no severe call upon either the will or the *intellect*" (*Inge*). **Soul,** as here compared (see also SOUL, 2), is still used in some psychologies (but not in those that reject not only the theory of "faculties" but also any other theory that presupposes the existence of an immaterial entity) as the inclusive term for the immaterial entity which is the seat of man's mental, emotional, and volitional life and which therefore is the prime object of psychological study; as, "I thought of my inner existence, that consciousness which is called the *soul*" (*Jefferies*). The term is now seldom used strictly in this sense, being confused not only with the conceptions of soul as spirit and as heart, but with several other ideas that are the result mainly of varying theologies and philosophies. Some modern psychologists and some writers and speakers prefer **psyche** to *soul*, as less susceptible to the addition of extraneous connotations; some psychologists prefer *psyche* as a name for the life of the individual which comprehends not only all the powers and activities attributed by others to the entity called the soul, but also the subconscious life as well; the term, however, is not universally accepted by schools which deny the existence of the soul as an entity. "I would write *psyche* always instead of *soul*, to avoid meanings which have become attached to the word 'soul,' but it is awkward to do so" (*Jefferies*). **Brain** or, especially in colloquial use, **brains** always suggests a reference to the brain as the physical seat of the life of the mind or intellect; however, either term is often preferred to *intellect* (sometimes to *mind*) as denoting the powers (usually clearly manifested powers) of comprehension and of independent (sometimes creative) thought; as, a *brain* that quickly grasps abstruse ideas. "Have I ever even felt inclined to write anything, until my emotions had been unduly excited, my *brain* immoderately stirred, my senses unusually quickened, or my spirit extravagantly roused?" (*Galsworthy*). "They could more than make up for the cost of complying with the very moderate requirements of the Acts by putting a little more *brains* into their work" (*Shaw*). "It requires *brains* and education to follow the argument [of Aquinas that the existence of God is demonstrable]" (*Inge*). **Intelligence** is distinguished from *intellect*, with which it is often confused, by being in general applied to a concrete or individual exhibition of the powers ascribed to the intellect rather than to an abstraction designated as *intellect* or *mind;* as, men are animals endowed with *intellect* (not *intelligence*); the *intelligence* (i.e., the extent to which a man is able to use his intellect) of individuals is now measured by psychologists; he has grown rapidly in *intelligence* (not *intellect*); "it had turned capable men into mere machines doing their work without *intelligence*" (*Shaw*). In current use, *intelligence* often applies specifically to an ability to deal with a new or trying situation competently, to achieve one's ends in spite of difficulties, or the like; as, the situation demands the exercise of great *intelligence;* "He thinks the war could have been prevented with a little *intelligence*" (*R. Macaulay*). **Wit** (see also WIT, 2) and **wits** are often merely homely or colloquial equivalents of *mind;* as, to lose one's *wits;* he is dull in *wit*. Usually, however, the term carries a stronger implication of an inborn power or of native capacity than *mind*, which often suggests training and development: it therefore may imply ability to use the senses quickly and readily, strong common sense, or intelligence that is the result of the active use of these; as, "the untutored natural *wit* of savages" (*Shaw*); "Doctor Stirling arrived in less than ten minutes. Dick Povey had had the *wit* to look for him at the Federation meeting" (*Bennett*); "Every one had to be a jack-of-all-trades, every one had to live by his *wits*" (*Van W. Brooks*).

Ana. *Power, function, faculty: *reason, intuition, understanding: wisdom, judgment, *sense, gumption.

mind, *v.* **1** *Remember, recollect, recall, remind, reminisce, bethink.

2 *Tend, attend, watch.

Con. *Neglect, ignore, disregard, forget, slight.

mingle. *Mix, commingle, blend, merge, coalesce, amalgamate, fuse.

Ana. *Compose, comprise, consist of, constitute: *join, combine, unite, connect: consolidate, *compact, unify, concentrate.

miniature, *adj.* Minute, diminutive, *small, little, wee, tiny, teeny, weeny.

minimize. Depreciate, *decry, belittle, disparage, derogate from, detract from.

Ant. Magnify. — *Con.* Aggrandize, *exalt: extol, eulogize, acclaim, laud, *praise.

minister. Envoy, *ambassador, legate, nuncio, internuncio.

minnesinger. Troubadour, trouvère, scald, jongleur, gleeman, scop, minstrel, bard, *poet, versifier, rhymer, rhymester, poetaster.

minority. *Infancy, nonage.
Ant. Majority. — *Con.* *Age.

minstrel. Bard, scop, gleeman, jongleur, troubadour, trouvère, minnesinger, scald, *poet, versifier, rhymer, rhymester, poetaster.

minute, *n.* *Instant, moment, second, flash, trice, jiffy, twinkling, twinkle, split second.

minute, *adj.* **1** *Small, little, diminutive, miniature, wee, tiny, teeny, weeny.
2 *Circumstantial, particular, particularized, detailed, itemized.
Ana. Meticulous, scrupulous, *careful, punctilious: precise, accurate, exact, right, nice, *correct.
Con. General, *universal: *abstract, ideal: comprehending *or* comprehensive, including *or* inclusive, embracing *or* embracive (see corresponding verbs at INCLUDE).

minx. *Wench, hussy, baggage.

miraculous. *Supernatural, supranatural, preternatural, superhuman.

mirage. Hallucination, *delusion, illusion.

mirror, *n.* *Model, example, pattern, exemplar, paradigm, ideal, beau ideal, standard.

mirth. Mirth, glee, jollity, hilarity come into comparison when they mean the mood or temper of a person or a group of persons manifesting joy or high spirits in laughter, play, or the like. **Mirth** often implies lightness of heart and a love of gaiety; it may, however, imply great amusement or cause for laughter; as, "Darcy was not of a disposition in which happiness overflows in *mirth*" (*Austen*); "Some of them literally throwing themselves down on the ground in convulsions of unholy *mirth*" (*Kipling*). "The glad circle round them yield their soul To festive *mirth*, and wit that knows no gall" (*Thomson*). **Glee** may be used in reference to a group (as, "Merry damsels... So many, and so many, and such *glee*"—*Keats*), but it is far more often employed in reference to an individual who by reason of special circumstances is filled with joy, delight, or happiness, and shows his exultancy by laughter, smiles, cries of joy, and the like. "Full well they laugh'd, with counterfeited *glee*, At all his jokes, for many a joke had he" (*Goldsmith*). But *glee* may express the exultation of one who takes more or less malicious delight in another's misfortunes or predicaments; as, in great *glee* over his friend's embarrassment; ghoulish *glee*. "Charles Critchlow came to the funeral, full of calm, sardonic *glee*.... Though fabulously senile, he had preserved and even improved his faculty for enjoying a catastrophe" (*Bennett*). **Jollity** in the sense here considered, on the other hand, usually implies mirth in a group, especially a merrymaking group. Distinctively, however, it connotes exuberance and lack of constraint and may imply revelry of any kind. "Midnight shout and revelry, Tipsy dance and *jollity*" (*Milton*). "The entertainment was in that stage when bashfulness itself had passed into easy *jollity*, when gentlemen...could...be prevailed on to dance a hornpipe" (*G. Eliot*). **Hilarity** fundamentally implies the exhilaration of spirits as by wine, pleasurable excitement, or the like. "Wine gives not light, gay, ideal *hilarity*, but tumultuous, noisy, clamorous merriment" (*Johnson*). "Through all the works of Chaucer, there reigns a cheerfulness, a manly *hilarity*" (*Coleridge*). Until around 1800, it carried none of the implications of boisterousness or vulgar excess of spirits it now so frequently stresses; as, "coarse and vulgar *hilarity*" (*Thackeray*); the *hilarity* of a New Year's Eve celebration.
Ana. Cheerfulness *or* cheer, lightheartedness, joyfulness, gladness, happiness (see corresponding adjectives at GLAD): joy, *pleasure, delight: merriment, blitheness, jocundity, joviality (see corresponding adjectives at MERRY).
Con. *Sadness, depression, dejection, melancholy, blues, dumps, vapors: *tedium, boredom, ennui.

misanthropic, misanthropical. Pessimistic, misogynic, *cynical.
Ant. Philanthropic. — *Con.* Benevolent, humane, humanitarian, *charitable, altruistic.

miscarriage. *Abortion.

miscellaneous. Miscellaneous, assorted, heterogeneous, motley, promiscuous come into comparison when they mean marked by diversity or variety and are applied to the things that comprise a group, a collection, a mass, or the like, or to a group, collection, or mass. **Miscellaneous** usually implies a mixture of many kinds, showing few, if any, signs of selection, and often suggesting dependence on chance; as, there is always a *miscellaneous* assemblage at the meetings of the association. "Joyce's wide and *miscellaneous* acquaintanceship" (*P. Colum*). "My second boy...received a sort of *miscellaneous* education at home" (*Goldsmith*). **Assorted** in the restricted sense in which it is here considered (see ASSORT), and the derivative noun **assortment,** also imply a mixture, but not a haphazard one; they carry the implications of a selection including every available kind or variety or involving consideration of every taste or every need; as, a box of *assorted* candies; a basket of *assorted* fruits; a skein of *assorted* wools; a carefully *assorted* group; a case containing an *assortment* of tools. **Heterogeneous** is applicable chiefly to masses, groups, and the like, the individuals or the elements of which are necessarily in proximity or close relationship to each other; it suggests not only variety or diversity in the individuals or the elements but also absence of uniformity or unity and little (if any) evidence of fusion; as, "the task of transforming a *heterogeneous* selection of mankind into a homogeneous nation" (*B. Russell*); "the family is *heterogeneous* enough to make quite a good party in itself" (*R. Macaulay*); the *heterogeneous* structure of granite. **Motley,** literally varicolored, in the extended sense here considered adds to *heterogeneous* the suggestion of discordance in the individuals or elements or their striking contrast to each other; as, a *motley* crew; a *motley* gathering from all sections of the city. "One would enquire from whence this *motley* style Did first our Roman purity defile" (*Dryden*). "How *motley* are the qualities that go to make up a human being" (*Maugham*). **Promiscuous** may suggest haphazardness or the appearance of it, but it usually implies selection that is completely devoid of discrimination and that results in disorderly confusion; thus, a *miscellaneous* acquaintanceship may imply a catholicity of taste, but a *promiscuous* acquaintanceship implies an absence of taste and good judgment; from a description of a club's membership as *heterogeneous* one might infer its interesting diversity but from a description of it as *promiscuous* one can infer only a diversity that is distasteful and senseless from the point of view of the speaker or writer. For this reason *promiscuous* is applicable to acts, emotions, and the like, that affect or include in their scope a number of persons or things; in such use it stresses not only lack of discrimi-

nation, but lack of restriction within bounds set by prudence, good sense, sound morals, or the like; thus, *promiscuous* charity is imprudently lavish charity extended without reference to the needs of those helped; *promiscuous* blame suggests stupid indifference as to the persons or things one's censure may affect; *promiscuous* sexual intercourse implies extreme licentiousness.
Ana. Various, diverse, divergent, disparate, *different: multifarious, multifold, manifold, divers, sundry, *many.
Con. *Similar, alike, like, identical, homogeneous, uniform.

mischance. *Misfortune, adversity.
Ana. *Accident, casualty, mishap: *disaster, calamity, catastrophe, cataclysm.

mischief. *Injury, hurt, damage, harm.
Con. Perniciousness, detrimentalness *or* detriment, deleteriousness, noxiousness, banefulness *or* bane (see corresponding adjectives at PERNICIOUS): *evil, ill, bale: impairment, marring, spoiling (see corresponding verbs at INJURE).

mischievous. Wanton, roguish, waggish, impish, *playful, frolicsome, sportive.
Ana. Annoying, bothering *or* bothersome, vexing *or* vexatious, irking *or* irksome (see corresponding verbs at ANNOY): naughty, *bad, evil, ill, wicked: tricky, foxy, artful, *sly.

mise. *Contract, bargain, compact, pact, treaty, entente, convention, cartel, covenant, concordat, indenture.

mise-en-scène. *Background, setting, environment, milieu, backdrop.

miserable, *adj.* **Miserable, wretched** come into comparison because both adjectives are used to describe anything that is deplorably or contemptibly bad or mean, such as a person's state of health or of mind, a state of affairs, a human being with reference to his condition or character, or anything compared with others of its kind or with the average of its kind. A person is **miserable** if in misery or in a state either of extreme or acute distress of body or mind (as, "[Plato] would forbid any novelist to represent a good man as ever *miserable*" —*H. Ellis;* "Gideon has been absolutely *miserable,* and [has] gone about like a man half stunned, ever since it happened"—*R. Macaulay*), or of pitiable poverty or contemptible degradation (as, "a *miserable* creature of a crazed aspect...shattered and made drunk by horror"—*Dickens*). A thing is *miserable* when it is exceedingly mean or paltry, and provocative only of misery in the person affected or of extreme contempt in the observer; as, a *miserable* cold; a *miserable* dinner; "a *miserable* pun" (*Meredith*); "the squalor of mean and *miserable* streets" (*Binyon*). A person is **wretched** who is extremely unhappy or abjectly despondent because of want, grief, oppression, affliction, anxiety, or the like; a thing that pertains closely to the happiness of a person is *wretched* if it produces such dejection or mental suffering; as, "O cruel death! To those you are more kind Than to the *wretched* mortals left behind" (*Waller*). "It was her unhappy lot to be made more *wretched* by the only affection which she could not suspect" (*Conrad*); "She's 'poor Ellen' certainly, because she had the bad luck to make a *wretched* marriage" (*E. Wharton*). A thing, in general, is *wretched* if it is extremely or deplorably bad; as, "a *wretched* French cabaret, smelling vilely" (*Meredith*); *wretched* crops; *wretched* accommodations; "there is nowhere to be seen, perhaps, such *wretched* whist-playing as in French salons" (*Brownell*).
Ana. Forlorn, hopeless, despairing, *despondent: pitiable, piteous, *pitiful: doleful, dolorous, *melancholy.
Ant. Comfortable.

miserly. Penurious, curmudgeonly, parsimonious, niggardly, tight, tightfisted, *stingy, close, closefisted, cheeseparing, penny-pinching.
Ana. Avaricious, greedy, *covetous, grasping: *mean, sordid, abject, ignoble.
Con. Bountiful, munificent, *liberal, generous: benevolent, *charitable, altruistic.

misery. *Distress, suffering, agony, dolor, passion.
Ana. Adversity, *misfortune: affliction, visitation, *trial, tribulation: melancholy, dejection, *sadness, depression.
Ant. Felicity, blessedness. — *Con.* *Happiness, beatitude, bliss: comfort, ease, repose (see REST).

misfortune. **Misfortune, mischance, adversity** agree in denoting bad luck or adverse fortune. They are not always synonymous in their specific denotations, however. All may denote an instance of adverse fortune, though *adversity* is seldom so used except in the plural; as, to suffer a *misfortune* (or *mischance*). "Pray, tell me more of your *adversities*" (*Longfellow*). *Misfortune* and *mischance* only may designate the incident or the conjunction of events that is the cause of a change in fortune, but only *misfortune* and *adversity* may be used to denote the state itself; as, by *misfortune* (or *mischance*), he lost his position; persons who have never endured *misfortune* (or *adversity*). **Misfortune** usually implies physical or mental distress; **mischance** often suggests nothing more than slight inconvenience, but it may be used to imply affliction and even death, without loss of the objectivity in point of view that often distinguishes it from *misfortune.* "I have many désagrémens that surround me; they have not dignity enough to be called *misfortunes,* but they feel heavy on my mind" (*Gray*). " 'The stupid fellow took it [a book] away with him—by *mischance,* I am bound to believe' " (*Meredith*). "They...let downe with Cords...seuerall Messengers (that if one came to *mischance,* another might passe on)" (*Bacon*). **Adversity,** the strongest of the words compared, denotes grave or continued misfortune. "A wretched soul, bruised with *adversity*" (*Shak.*). "In his [Francis Bacon's] *adversity* I ever prayed that God would give him strength" (*B. Jonson*).
Ana. *Disaster, calamity, catastrophe, cataclysm: *accident, casualty, mishap: *trial, tribulation, cross, affliction, visitation.
Ant. Happiness: prosperity. — *Con.* Felicity, bliss, blessedness, beatitude (see HAPPINESS): comfort, ease (see REST): *victory, triumph.

misgiving. Foreboding, presentiment, *apprehension.
Ana. Mistrust, distrust (see under DISTRUST, *v.*): suspicion, doubt, skepticism, *uncertainty: *fear, alarm, dread, fright.

mishap. *Accident, casualty.
Ana. *Misfortune, mischance: *disaster, calamity: *chance, fortune, hap, hazard.

mislay. *Misplace.

mislead. Delude, beguile, *deceive, betray, double-cross.
Ana. Entice, inveigle, *lure, tempt, seduce: *dupe, gull, hoodwink, hoax, bamboozle.

misleading. **Misleading, deceptive, delusive, delusory** agree in meaning having an appearance or character that leads one astray or into error. **Misleading** is the general term applicable to anything which, intentionally or otherwise, leads one away from the right course or direction as in action, conduct, or the apprehension of truth, and, therefore, into confusion or error; as, a *misleading* sign; a *misleading* question; "The bare statement that 'art is useless' is so vague as to be really meaningless, if not inaccurate and *misleading*" (*H. Ellis*).

Deceptive applies chiefly, but not exclusively, to things that by their aspect or appearance give a false impression; the term may or may not imply the intention to deceive; as, *deceptive* solemnity; *deceptive* words; a *deceptive* show of wealth or power. **Delusive** and the less common **delusory** carry a stronger implication than *deceptive* carries of mocking or cheating as well as misleading; as, *delusive* hopes; *delusory* promises; "it is important for this Court [the Supreme Court of the United States] to avoid extracting from the very general language of the Fourteenth Amendment a system of *delusive* exactness" (*Justice Holmes*).

Ana. Fallacious, casuistical, sophistical (see under FALLACY): *false, wrong: confounding, bewildering, distracting, perplexing, puzzling (see PUZZLE, *v.*).

misogynic, misogynical, misogynous. Misanthropic, pessimistic, *cynical.

Con. Benevolent, *charitable, altruistic.

misplace. Misplace, mislay agree in meaning to put in the wrong place. **Misplace** may imply a putting of a thing in another than its usual or customary location (as, to *misplace* a book inadvertently; I have *misplaced* the dish, for it is not here where it belongs), but it more often suggests a setting or fixing of something where it should not be (as, my confidence in him was *misplaced;* she is suffering from *misplaced* affections). "The globe and sceptre in such hands *misplaced*" (*Cowper*). **Mislay** usually implies a misplacing (in the first sense) but stresses a forgetfulness of the place in which the thing has been put; it therefore often means to lose through misplacing; as, to *mislay* a book or an umbrella.

Ana. Displace (see REPLACE): derange, disarrange, *disorder.

misrepresent. Misrepresent, belie agree in meaning to represent in a manner that is contrary to truth. **Misrepresent,** however, commonly implies intent and therefore takes a person or his utterance as its subject when used in the active voice; it often carries a suggestion of deliberate falsification or injustice, but it may suggest bias or prejudice; as, to *misrepresent* a statement, or the value of an article; the account *misrepresents* not only his actions but his motives. **Belie,** on the other hand, implies an impression given that contradicts or is at variance with the fact; it commonly, but not invariably, takes as its subject a thing, such as an appearance, a look, a manner, or the like; as, his brusque manner *belied* his real kindness of heart. "You are an Englishman ...unless your physiognomy *belies* you" (*Kingsley*).

Ana. *Disguise, dissemble, cloak, mask: simulate, counterfeit, feign, *assume.

misrepresentation. *Lie, falsehood, untruth, fib, story.

Ana. Dishonesty, deceitfulness, mendaciousness *or* mendacity (see corresponding adjectives at DISHONEST): sophistication, doctoring, deaconing, loading, weighting, adulteration (see corresponding verbs at ADULTERATE): sophistry, casuistry (see FALLACY).

missionary, *n.* **Missionary, apostle, evangelist, revivalist,** as here compared, denote a person whose work it is to make converts, especially to Christianity. **Missionary** and **apostle** both etymologically imply a being sent, and are used to designate one who comes from outside, usually in response to a commission but sometimes in answer to a call. *Missionary,* in its more common application, denotes either a man or woman, clerical or lay, who is sent by a church or a religious order to work among peoples of no religion or of another religion, usually in a foreign land. In modern use it connotes social as well as religious activities, such as welfare and health work. In extended use *apostle* often denotes a missionary to the heathen who is the first to bring Christianity into a country or to a people; as, John Eliot, *Apostle* of the Indians; St. Augustine, *Apostle* of the English. *Apostle* also is used of a person who initiates a great reform or preaches a new doctrine, often one of a political or intellectual as well as of a moral character; as, Richard Cobden has been called the *Apostle* of Free Trade. "We inevitably think of Rousseau as...the great *apostle* of the original and the spontaneous" (*Babbitt*). *Missionary,* in a frequent but less widespread use, is applied to an ordained preacher who comes from without a parish to stir up religious fervor among the parishioners and to convert backsliders or the unregenerate. In some churches, a preacher whose aims are similar is called an **evangelist,** but the latter term often suggests, in distinction from *missionary,* autonomous action, or lack of a commission from a superior authority, and activities independent of any one church, congregation, or denomination. "John Wesley the humanist enjoyed preaching in such a pleasant place to such pleasant people, while John Wesley the *Evangelist* was performing a stern moral duty" (*S. M. Crothers*). **Revivalist** stresses the aim of reviving faith and often connotes sensational methods of exciting religious fervor; otherwise, its implications are similar to those of *evangelist;* as, Billy Sunday was an outstanding American *revivalist.*

missive. *Letter, epistle, note, message, dispatch, report, memorandum.

mist, *n.* *Haze, fog, smog, brume.

mistake, *v.* **Mistake, confuse, confound** are here compared as meaning to mix up things, as by taking one thing for another. One **mistakes** one thing *for* another when by an error of perception or of thought (often one justified by a disguise), or as a result of a predisposition or a bias, one fails to recognize the thing or to comprehend its real nature and identifies it with something not itself or with something of another nature; as, "on a casual view Saint George [as presented by a mummer] ...might be *mistaken* for his deadly enemy, the Saracen" (*Hardy*); "Kant..., it has been said, *mistook* Duty for a Prussian drill-sergeant" (*H. Ellis*); "the tendency of the rest of us to *mistake* gush for vigour" (*Day Lewis*). One **confuses** one thing with another when one fails to distinguish two things that have similarities or common characteristics or to observe their lines of demarcation; as, "Very possibly some of the cases *confuse* the principles that govern jurisdiction with those that govern merits" (*Justice Holmes*); "far too intellectually keen to *confuse* moral problems with purely aesthetic problems" (*H. Ellis*). One **confounds** things or one thing *with* another when one mixes them up so hopelessly that one cannot detect their differences or distinctions. *Confound* usually carries a stronger connotation of mental bewilderment or of a muddled mind than the preceding words: for this reason, it is often preferred when the differences are more or less obvious to a clearheaded or intelligent person. "Sir Austin...expostulated, contradicted himself, *confounded* his principles, made nonsense of all his theories" (*Meredith*). "Courage must not be *confounded* with brutality. Brutality is pleasure in forcing one's will upon other people; courage is indifference to personal misfortunes" (*B. Russell*). "The temptation to *confound* accumulated knowledge and experience with intrinsic progress is almost irresistible" (*Inge*).

Ana. Addle, muddle, bemuddle, *confuse.

Ant. Recognize.

mistake, *n.* *Error, slip, lapse, blunder, faux pas, bull, howler, boner, bloomer, floater.

Ana. Confusion, confounding, mistaking (see corresponding verbs at MISTAKE): inadvertence (see corresponding adjective at CARELESS): neglecting *or* neglect, omitting *or* omission, disregarding, slighting *or* slight (see corresponding verbs at NEGLECT).

mistreat. Maltreat, ill-treat, misuse, *abuse, outrage.
Ana. See those at ILL-TREAT.

mistrust, *n.* **1** Suspicion, skepticism, doubt, *uncertainty, dubiety, dubiosity.
Ana. Misgiving, presentiment, foreboding, *apprehension.
Ant. Trust: assurance. — *Con.* Confidence, faith, reliance, dependence (see TRUST): *certainty, certitude, conviction.
2 Distrust (see under DISTRUST, *v.*).

mistrust, *v.* *Distrust.
Ana. Apprehend, anticipate, *foresee: alarm, *frighten, scare: appall, *dismay.
Con. *Rely, trust, depend: confide, entrust, relegate, *commit.

misuse, *v.* *Abuse, mistreat, maltreat, ill-treat, outrage.
Ana. Hurt, *injure, harm, damage, impair, mar, spoil: pervert, *debase, corrupt.
Ant. Respect. — *Con.* Esteem, regard (see under REGARD, *n.*): cherish, treasure, prize, *appreciate.

mite. Bit, *particle, smitch, smidgen, whit, atom, iota, jot, tittle.

mitigate. Allay, *relieve, alleviate, lighten, assuage.
Ana. Temper, attemper, *moderate: abate, reduce, lessen, diminish, *decrease: *palliate, extenuate.
Ant. Intensify. — *Con.* Aggravate, heighten, enhance (see INTENSIFY): *increase, augment.

mix. **Mix, mingle, commingle, blend, merge, coalesce, amalgamate, fuse** are synonymous terms when they are used of two or more things and denote to combine or become combined with resulting diffusion or interpenetration of particles, parts, elements, or the like. **Mix,** the most comprehensive of these terms, may or may not imply loss of identities, but even when the elements are distinguishable it suggests a homogeneous character in the product; as, to *mix* salt and pepper or wine and water; to *mix* colors in painting; to *mix* the ingredients of a cake; oil and water do not *mix.* So far as they differ, **mingle,** rather than *mix,* implies that the constituent elements are distinguished in the product; as, *mingled* sensations; "the evil...strangely *mingled* with the good" (*Babbitt*). "*Mingling,* as no other school of dramatists has done, the oratorical, the conversational, the elaborate and the simple" (*T. S. Eliot*). **Commingle** suggests a more intimate, and often a harmonious, union. "*Commingled* with the gloom of imminent war, The shadow of His loss drew like eclipse, Darkening the world" (*Tennyson*). **Blend** originally was the equivalent of *mix* or *mingle.* "A Tale, that *blends* their glory with their shame" (*Pope*). In current use, it implies a mixing of harmonious or compatible things, a union so intimate as to obscure the individuality of the component parts, and a sharing of their qualities by the resultant product; as, *blended* teas. "What delicious *blending*...of thought and diction!" (*T. E. Brown*). "Offshore where sea and skyline *blend* In rain" (*Kipling*). **Merge** still more distinctly implies the loss in the whole of the constituent elements, or the complete absorption of one element in another; as, to *merge* the private in the general good. "Archer often wondered how, after forty years of the closest conjugality, two such *merged* identities ever separated themselves enough for anything as controversial as a talking-over" (*E. Wharton*). **Coalesce** suggests a natural affinity for each other in the things merging and a resulting organic unity. "All these descriptive details do not *coalesce* for us into the distinct image of a living woman" (*Babbitt*). "It is only gradually [for the infant learning how to perceive], through the formation of habits by association, that touch and sight and smell and hearing...*coalesce* in the...notion of an object" (*B. Russell*). **Amalgamate** in very careful use implies a tendency to merge or draw together, largely as a result of contact or association; it therefore suggests an effective or harmonious union rather than a complete merger with loss of identity. "The Indian race....formed no part of the colonial communities, and never *amalgamated* with them" (*Ch. Just. Taney*). "[Rome's] policy of conciliating and *amalgamating* conquered nations" (*A. Repplier*). **Fuse** stresses even more than *blend* and *merge* the loss of identity of each of the component elements, and, more than *coalesce,* the indissolubility of their union. In very precise use, it implies a powerful cause which operates like heat melting and bringing into one mass disparate substances. "The Scotch nation, nobles and commons, ministers and people, wonderfully *fused* together by fiery enthusiasm" (*G. Smith*). "Truth at white heat—the truth of terror and mystery and baleful beauty, *fused* into one flaming impression" (*Lowes*).
Ana. *Join, combine, unite.
Con. *Separate, part, divide, sever, sunder.

mixture. **Mixture, admixture, blend, compound, composite, amalgam** agree in denoting a product formed by the combination of two or more things. **Mixture** is the most inclusive and most widely applicable term; it has, however, many specific applications; thus, a fabric made by interweaving yarns of different colors is a *mixture;* a tobacco in which several varieties are combined to give a particular flavor or quality is a smoking *mixture.* The word often implies miscellaneousness; as, "society" in a small town is very much of a *mixture.* **Admixture** adds to *mixture* the suggestion of the alien character of one or more of the constituent elements; as, a racial stock that is an *admixture;* prosaic verse is an offensive *admixture* to lovers of pure poetry. **Blend,** on the contrary, adds to *mixture* the implication of thorough mingling of (usually, but not invariably) similar or congruous elements or ingredients. Like *admixture,* it implies that the product is not pure, or simple, but, unlike it, it usually suggests harmony or complete integration. "A curious *blend* of humility and irony" (*T. S. Eliot*). "Unorthodox was the *blend* of executive responsibility, legislative power and financial control" (*Buchan*). *Blend* is used in commerce as a name for mixed whiskies, wines, teas, coffees, etc., to indicate that a new product has been formed that combines the flavors, or the like, of several varieties of the same thing and that the products contain no other substance than whisky, wine, etc. **Compound** usually implies the union of two or more distinguishable or analyzable parts, elements, or ingredients. "It was not fear, it was not ardour,—it was a *compound* of both" (*Scott*). "Rare *compound* of oddity, frolic, and fun" (*Goldsmith*). In its technical senses, *compound* is definitely restricted in application. In chemistry, a compound is a distinct substance formed by a union of two or more elements, united in definite proportions by weight and with the same internal arrangement; thus, water is a *compound* of oxygen and hydrogen. As applied to words, a compound is a word or its equivalent which is formed of distinct parts, but has a distinct sense often not inferable from the meanings of its component parts. A compound may be written solid (as, *blackboard*), or hyphenated (as, *long-distance*), or be composed of separate words (as, *all right*). **Composite** is often interchangeable with *compound* in the general sense of the latter, but there is a tendency to prefer the former when the constituent parts are artificially or fortuitously combined; thus, the American people is a *composite* of many races; the English language is a *composite* of Anglo-Saxon, Norman-French, and Celtic and other languages. An **amalgam** is literally a mixture made by adding mercury to a metal for the purpose of softening the latter; as, dentists use *amalgams* of gold and silver for tooth fillings. In its pertinent figurative sense *amalgam* is especially applicable to something plastic or to something that has not hardened into permanent form; as, the American people is as yet only an *amalgam*, not a race. "One's judgment [of a friend's literary work] is inevitably an *amalgam* of impressions of the work and impressions of the man" (*T. S. Eliot*).

Ana. Joining, combining, uniting (see JOIN).

moan, *v.* Groan, *sigh, sob.

Ana. Mourn, *grieve, sorrow: bemoan, bewail, lament, *deplore.

moan, *n.* Groan, sigh, sob. See under SIGH, *v.*

Ana. Crying *or* cry, wailing *or* wail (see corresponding verbs at CRY): lamenting *or* lament, bemoaning, bewailing (see corresponding verbs at DEPLORE).

mob, *n.* *Crowd, throng, press, crush, rout, horde.

Ana. *Multitude, army, host, legion.

mobile. *Movable, motile, motive.

Ana. Fluid, *liquid: *changeable, changeful, protean, variable: *inconstant, unstable, mercurial, fickle, capricious.

Ant. Immobile.

mock, *v.* **1** Taunt, deride, *ridicule, twit, rally.

Ana. Flout, *scoff, jeer, gird, gibe: *caricature, parody, travesty, burlesque.

2 *Copy, imitate, mimic, ape.

Ana. Counterfeit, feign, affect, simulate, *assume.

mode, *n.*[1] **1** *State, condition, situation, posture, status, estate.

2 *Method, manner, way, fashion, system.

Ana. Trend, drift, *tendency, tenor, current: procedure, *process.

mode, *n.*[2] *Fashion, style, vogue, fad, rage, craze, dernier cri, cry.

model, *n.* **Model, example, pattern, exemplar, paradigm, ideal, beau ideal** (*or* **beau idéal**), **standard, mirror** come into comparison when they denote something set or held before one for guidance or imitation in one's conduct or endeavor. **Model** applies to any person or thing set before one for imitation by oneself or another: the term may suggest nothing more; as, art students painting from a *model;* "the child's patient efforts [in learning to write] to imitate the copperplate *model*...set before him" (*H. Ellis*); "Tennyson gave him [J. R. Lowell] the *model* for Sir Launfal" (*Van W. Brooks*). Oftentimes, however, the term applies to a person or thing that is eminently (sometimes, pre-eminently) worthy of imitation; as, "there is no poet in any tongue...who stands so firmly [as Dante] as a *model* for all poets" (*T. S. Eliot*); "[New Zealand's] system of child hygiene has been regarded as a *model* for all to follow" (*V. Heiser*). **Example** applies chiefly to a person (or his acts, conduct, etc.) that for one of a number of reasons is or may be imitated by others: the term usually implies that the person, or the act, or the conduct, for some good reason (such as the person's being in a position of authority, or his conduct being in the limelight, or his act being widely known) is one that is likely to be imitated, whether he (or it) be good or bad, right or wrong; thus, a father should set a good *example* to his children; she always followed the *example* of her mother in her social behavior; a teacher's conduct should never give a bad *example* to his pupils. Sometimes, however, *example* applies to that which is not to be imitated, but which serves rather as a warning; as, to make an *example* of an offender (i.e., by punishing him conspicuously). "Let it profit thee to have heard, By terrible *example*, the reward Of disobedience" (*Milton*). *Example* is also used in a highly abstract sense in antithesis to *precept*, then implying the setting of an example, usually but not necessarily a good example; as, children learn more quickly by *example* than by precept; "the mistake of thinking that all can be done by precept, when...*example* is no less potent a force" (*A. C. Benson*). **Pattern** in its earliest and, to an extent, still current English senses, applies either to the divine archetype (see PROTOTYPE) of a thing or to a carefully worked-out design or plan (such as an architect's drawing) to be followed by a worker or workers in fashioning a thing. "According to an heavenly *pattern*... Which He [the Creator] had fashioned in his wise foresight, He man did make" (*Spenser*). "Almost all the common things we use now...are made by machinery, and are copies of an original *pattern*" (*Jevons*). In the sense in which the word is here considered (see also FIGURE, 2), *pattern* now usually applies to that which is actually worthy of imitation or is accepted as such: it often differs from *model* in suggesting a more clearly worked out design, or a fuller presentation of details, or in connoting fixity or compelling power; as, "A housewife in bed, at table a slattern; For all an *example*, for no one a *pattern*" (*Swift*); "Somewhere there must have been men and women working out our situation...successfully, but the only *example* life afforded us was not of the acceptable *pattern*" (*M. Austin*); "the inexorable conventions that tied things together and bound people down to the old *pattern*" (*E. Wharton*). **Exemplar** often comes closer to *pattern* than to *example* because it usually applies to that which is set before one as worthy of imitation and is, therefore, inherently good; as, "Christ is the... *exemplar* that all preachers ought to follow" (*Latimer*); "To men of letters doubly dear, not for his wit and genius merely, but as an *exemplar* of goodness, probity, and pure life" (*Thackeray*). Sometimes, however, *exemplar* is specifically applied to a person or thing that exhibits a quality, or sums up all the characteristics that distinguish a type, whether that quality or type be in itself good or bad; as, "Sisyphus, the legendary *exemplar* of cunning" (*Thirlwall*); "Stendhal's Julian Sorel...this *exemplar* of ruthless individualism" (*A. Huxley*). **Paradigm,** once a common but now a rare, synonym, except in its technical grammatical sense, of *pattern* and *exemplar*, often specifically implies existence not in the actual world but in the mind and, therefore, suggests a perfection exceeding what is possible in reality (as, "Socrates makes one more attempt to defend the Platonic ideas by representing them as *paradigms*"—*Jowett*). As a technical term in grammar, *paradigm* designates an example of a conjugation or declension showing a word (verb, noun, pronoun, or adjective) in all its inflectional forms and serving as a pattern for all words of the same class or type; as, a *paradigm* for Latin nouns of the second declension. The term in its nontechnical sense has now given way to **ideal** in popular as well as in learned use. But *ideal* in current use often applies to a person or thing that is found in reality as well as to one that is conceived by the mind and that is held before one as embodying or representing the perfection one hopes to realize or attain; as, the boy found his *ideal* in his father; "[Livia] embodied in her life the *ideal* of the Roman matron" (*Buchan*). In some use **beau ideal** (a French phrase now naturalized in English, correctly meaning "ideal beauty" but often incorrectly translated as "the beautiful, or perfect, ideal" is interchanged with *ideal* in this particular sense; as, "the *beau idéal* of young English manhood" (*M. E. Braddon*). Frequently, however, *ideal* is almost indistinguishable from **standard** when it applies not to a person or object that serves as a pattern or exemplar, but to anything such as a rule, a practice, an aim, an established level of excellence, or the like, by which one seeks to maintain a high quality in a product or of performance; as, "The *ideal* of general cultivation has been one of the standards in education" (*C. W. Eliot*); "[Accuracy] is still a noble and inspiring *ideal*. It is the morality of the intellect: it prescribes what it ought to strive for" (*P. B. Ballard*); "Each generation....has its own *ideals* and its own *standards* of judgment" (*S. M. Crothers*). But *standard* is interchangeable with *ideal* only when it applies to that which is the test of perfection or of human perfection (for other sense see STANDARD, 2); as, "the very art...incommensurable with any *standard* except that of pure beauty—I refer of course to the art of music" (*G. L. Dickinson*); "With the spread of impressionism literature has lost *standards* and discipline, and at the same time virility and seriousness" (*Babbitt*). **Mirror,** now archaic in this sense, was once used frequently in literary or complimentary speech for a person (rarely a thing) upon which others could look as a model or pattern of perfection, the term sometimes implying a reflection of celestial perfections; as, "call him bounteous Buckingham, The *mirror* of all courtesy" (*Shak.*); "*Mirror* of grace and Majesty divine" (*Spenser*).

Ana. Archetype, *prototype: criterion, touchstone, gauge, *standard.

moderate, *adj.* **1 Moderate, temperate** are often used interchangeably to denote not excessive in degree, amount, or the like; as, a *moderate* allowance; *temperate* heat. When contrasted, **moderate** often connotes absence or avoidance of excess (opposed to *excessive, immoderate*), and **temperate,** deliberate restraint or restriction (opposed to *intemperate, inordinate*); thus, "a *moderate* drinker" suggests free but far from excessive indulgence in intoxicants, and "a *temperate* drinker" suggests restrained and cautious indulgence; "*moderate* enthusiasm" suggests lukewarmness, "*temperate* enthusiasm" suggests keeping a hold over one's exhibition of feeling; one's anger may be far from *moderate*, yet one's reply may be *temperate*. In precise, especially technical language, *moderate* and *temperate* often denote midway between extremes or designate a point, as in a scale, characterized neither by excess nor by deficiency of something understood. As a rule, when so used they are not interchangeable, for custom or terminology has determined the selection; as, *moderate* temperature; a *moderate* breeze; a *temperate* climate; a *temperate* zone. In this sense both *moderate* and *temperate* have two antonyms, one on the side of deficiency and the other on the side of excess. These antonyms are usually specific and vary according to the application; as, for example: *light* and *strong* (of breezes); *arctic* and *torrid* (of climate); *abstemious* and *gluttonous* (of eating); *mild* and *violent* (of something having force and intensity).

Ana. Ordinary, *common, familiar: gentle, mild, bland, *soft: *sparing, economical.

Ant. Immoderate. — ***Con.*** *Excessive, extreme, inordinate.

2 *Medium, middling, mediocre, second-rate, average, fair, indifferent.

Ana. Decent, *decorous, proper: *steady, even, equable, constant.

moderate, *v.* **Moderate, qualify, temper, attemper** come into comparison when they mean to modify something so as to avoid an extreme or to keep within due bounds. **Moderate** stresses reduction of that which is excessive, but it does not necessarily imply finding the happy mean; as, the sun at midday *moderates* the cold; you must *moderate* your demands if you wish to be listened to. "'*Moderate* your language, old man,' I said; 'remember that you are addressing a superior'" (*Hudson*). **Qualify,** in most discriminating use, emphasizes restriction or more precise definition that brings a thing closer to the truth or facts, or that makes it less general, inclusive, or sweeping, or that gives it a clearly defined quality or character of its own; as, the teacher *qualified* his praise of the theme by the added comment "you can do better"; our admiration of his genius is *qualified* by our disapproval of his character. "It is time to *qualify* the over simple account I have given of the artist's process of creation" (*S. Alexander*). **Temper** strongly implies accommodation to the needs or requirements of the person, the situation, the time, and the like; it may or may not suggest moderation or qualification, but it usually implies the addition of a counterbalancing or mitigating thing; as, "God *tempers* the wind...to the shorn lamb" (*Sterne*); to *temper* justice with mercy. "Fierce for the right, he bore his part In strife with many a valiant foe; But Laughter winged his polished dart, And kindness *tempered* every blow" (*W. Winter*). **Attemper** is a very close synonym of *temper*. It is, however, increasingly rarer in current use and it seldom so strongly implies accommodation or adaptation as does *temper*. It commonly suggests a softening or mitigating rather than a counterbalancing of that which is harsh, strong, or the like. "The shadow of the willow tree...*attempered* the cheery western sunshine" (*N. Hawthorne*).

Ana. Abate, reduce, lessen, diminish, *decrease: mitigate, alleviate, lighten, *relieve: slow, slacken (see DELAY).

Con. *Intensify, aggravate, heighten, enhance: augment, *increase.

modern. Modernistic, *new, novel, new-fashioned, newfangled, neoteric, original, fresh.

Ana. *Contemporary, contemporaneous, coincident, concomitant, concurrent: *prevailing, current, prevalent.

Ant. Antique: ancient.

modernistic. *New, new-fashioned, newfangled, neoteric, novel, modern, original, fresh.

Ant. Antiquated.

modest. 1 *Humble, meek, lowly.

Ana. Retiring, withdrawing (see GO): *moderate, temperate.

Ant. Ambitious. — ***Con.*** *Showy, pretentious, ostentatious, pompous: arrogant, haughty, *proud, overbearing: *shameless, brazen, barefaced, impudent.

2 *Shy, bashful, diffident, coy.

Ana. Reserved, reticent, *silent: shrinking, recoiling (see RECOIL): demure, nice, seemly, proper (see DECOROUS).

3 Decent, *chaste, pure.

Ana. *Moral, virtuous: *decorous, proper, seemly, decent.

Ant. Immodest. — ***Con.*** Indecent, indelicate, *indecorous, unseemly, improper.

modification. 1 Change, alteration, variation. See under CHANGE, *v.*

Ana. Transformation, metamorphosis, conversion, transmogrification (see under TRANSFORM): qualification, tempering (see corresponding verbs at MODERATE).

2 *Variation, adaptation, mutation.

modify. *Change, alter, vary.
Ana. Temper, attemper, *moderate, qualify: *transform, convert, metamorphose, transmogrify.
modish. *Stylish, fashionable, smart, chic, dapper, dashing, spruce, natty, nifty, nobby, posh, toffish, brave, braw.
Ant. Antiquated.
Mohock. Gangster, apache, *ruffian, thug, desperado.
moist. *Wet, damp, humid, dank.
Con. *Dry, arid.
molecule. Atom, *particle, corpuscle.
molest. Trouble, discommode, incommode, *inconvenience.
Ana. Disturb, *discompose, disquiet, perturb: interfere, *meddle, intermeddle, tamper: *intrude, obtrude, butt in: vex, *annoy, irk, bother.
mollify. Appease, placate, *pacify, propitiate, conciliate.
Ana. *Relieve, allay, mitigate, lighten: *moderate, temper, qualify: abate, lessen, reduce, *decrease.
Ant. Exasperate.
mollycoddle, *v.* Humor, pamper, *indulge, spoil, baby.
molt. *Discard, cast, shed, exuviate, slough, scrap, junk.
moment. 1 *Instant, minute, second, flash, trice, jiffy, twinkling, twinkle, split second.
2 *Importance, consequence, significance, import, weight.
Ana. Value, *worth: advantage, profit, avail, *use.
momentary. *Transient, transitory, passing, ephemeral, fugitive, fleeting, evanescent, short-lived.
Ant. Agelong.
momentum. Impetus, *speed, velocity, pace, headway.
monachal. *Monastic, monkish, cenobitic, cenobitical.
monastery. *Cloister, convent, nunnery, abbey, priory.
monastic *or* **monastical.** **Monastic** (*or* **monastical**), **monkish, monachal, cenobitic** (*or* **cenobitical**; *also* **coenobitic, coenobitical**) agree in meaning of, relating to, or characteristic of monks, monasteries, or by extension, any cloistered religious order. **Monastic** is the preferred term by all writers and speakers who have no intent to depreciate or who wish to avoid any suggestion of bias or prejudice, or who wish to convey its implication of asceticism; as, the *monastic* vows of poverty, chastity, and obedience are taken by the religious of many orders, both male and female; "*monastic* strictness" (*Sheridan*); "*monastic* fare" (*Pater*); "there he lived with *monastic* cleanliness and severity" (*Cather*). **Monkish,** a term originating early in the Reformation period and used therefore by many writers and speakers with derogatory intent, still retains such suggestions even when the writer or speaker is unaware of its connotations; the term, therefore, is increasingly avoided as likely to be offensive; as, "the *monkish* stupidity of the times" (*Goldsmith*); "a *monkish*...superstition" (*Shelley*); "*monkish* cloisters" (*Dickens*). **Monachal** was once popular as a variant of *monastic* and *monkish* but is now rare, possibly because it never acquired particular connotations which would distinguish it from the other terms; as, *monachal* institutions or rules. **Cenobitic** suggests reference to the type of life led by monks, especially in distinction from that lived by friars in the Middle Ages or by hermits or anchorites; the term therefore implies living in a cloistered community under the guidance of a superior and may imply reference both to male and female religious; as, "The old *coenobitic* establishments of England" (*Coleridge*); the earliest followers of the religious life did not lead a *cenobitical* life.
monetary. *Financial, pecuniary, fiscal, bursal.
money, *n.* **Money, cash, currency, legal tender, specie, coin, coinage** agree in meaning the pieces of stamped metal or their equivalents issued usually by a government, or by an authority recognized by the government, to serve as a medium of exchange in the country or section under the control of that government. **Money** was originally applied only to the coined gold, silver, copper, or other metal issued by a government or other authority as a medium of exchange. The term now, however, includes what is often called specifically *paper money*, or certificates or notes promising payment in metal money, that are issued by a government, authorized bank, or the like, and pass like coined metal as a medium of exchange. **Cash** applies to ready money; that is, to money actually in hand or in the boxes, safes, vaults, or the like, of an individual or a business or institution; as, the firm's supply of *cash* was very low because the larger part of the day's accumulation had just been deposited in the bank. **Currency** applies to all of the money in circulation, as distinguished from that which is not in circulation for one reason or another. "The first panacea for a mismanaged nation is inflation of the *currency*" (*Hemingway*). **Legal tender** applies specifically to the type of money which the law authorizes a debtor to offer and requires a creditor to receive as payment of money obligations. In the United States, standard silver dollars and treasury notes are legal tender to any amount unless the contrary is stipulated in the contract; subsidiary silver coins, for sums not over $10; minor (nickel or bronze) coins, for not over 25c. In Great Britain, treasury notes are legal tender to any amount, silver coins are legal tender for not over 40s., the farthing for not over 6d., and other bronze coins for not over one shilling. **Specie, coin** (only in a collective sense), and **coinage** apply only to minted or coined money; they therefore imply an opposition to all forms of paper money such as treasury notes, bank notes, and the like; as, payments were demanded in *specie*, or in the *coin* of the realm. "We are far more concerned today with his debasement of the *coinage*" (*Shaw*).
monk. *Religious, friar, nun.
Ana. *Recluse, hermit, eremite, anchorite, cenobite: ecclesiastic, priest, *cleric, clergyman, abbé.
monkeyshine, *n.* *Prank, caper, antic, dido.
monkish. *Monastic, monachal, cenobitic, cenobitical.
monopolize. **Monopolize, engross, absorb, consume. Monopolize,** the general term, means to possess or control exclusively; as, to *monopolize* the year's crop of cotton; a child should not be allowed to *monopolize* the attention of his family. "Every railroad *monopolizes*, in a popular sense, the trade of some area" (*Justice Holmes*). In its earlier use, **engross** implied the purchase of the whole, or nearly the whole, supply (as of a commodity) to control prices; as, edicts were issued against *engrossing* the market. In present use, *engross* may also be referred to any of a number of things which may be monopolized; as, war news *engrossed* their attention; pursuits which *engross* one's entire time. "The transition from government by a landed aristocracy to government by a city aristocracy gradually *engrossing* the land" (*T. S. Eliot*). **Absorb** is frequently interchangeable with *engross*, but it is less often predicated of persons as conscious agents and more often of things that have an inherent capacity for monopolization. "Manual occupations do not engage the mind sufficiently....But composition, especially of verse, *absorbs* it wholly" (*Cowper*). "It is arithmetically impossible for every child to *absorb* the whole time of an adult tutor" (*B. Russell*). **Consume** comes into comparison with *engross* and *absorb* chiefly in an extended sense of each, implying monopolization of one's time, attention, or interest. These senses are not so common in the finite forms as in the participles; as, an *engrossing* pur-

suit; he is *engrossed* in writing a book; sitting in *absorbed* reflection; an *absorbing* interest or book; a *consuming* passion.

Ana. Possess, own, *have, hold: utilize, *use, employ: control, manage (see CONDUCT, *v.*).

monopoly. Monopoly, corner, pool, syndicate, trust, cartel are not, strictly speaking, synonymous terms but they are often confused. **Monopoly** denotes the exclusive control of any service (such as telephone or telegraph service) or traffic (such as transportation of goods and passengers by railroad) or of any commodity (such as wheat or petroleum) in a given market. *Monopoly* may imply exclusive control created by the state, as when a franchise is granted, an invention is patented, or a book is copyrighted. More frequently, however, the term is used to imply the exclusive power to buy or sell a given commodity or service in a given market, now especially when such control has been gained by the purchase of the sources of supply (such as mines) or of the whole or of the major portion of the stock of a given commodity. "In the reign of Edward III [German traders] had a practical *monopoly* of the carrying trade" (*M. Pattison*). Only by extension is *monopoly* used to denote the group or organization having such control. "It might be that when a combination reached a certain size it might have attributed to it more of the character of a *monopoly* merely by virtue of its size than would be attributed to a smaller one" (*Justice Holmes*). A purely temporal or local monopoly of a given commodity or of a given kind of property (such as the shares of a corporation), as on the stock or produce exchange on a selling day, constitutes a **corner,** so called because it puts all those who are determined to buy into a corner, or position where they must pay the price asked; as, the young and daring financier maintained his *corner* on wheat for three days. **Pool** is applicable strictly to a combination of property, or of interests of different persons or companies, by means of which a more or less permanent control or monopoly is acquired. Distinctively, however, *pool* implies a joint undertaking or end which cannot be attained unless the market is managed either by manipulating the prices for a given commodity, security, or the like, or by destroying the effects of competition, as through agreements concerning prices or rates, regulation of outputs, division of earnings, and the like, of each organization concerned. In common law and especially in the United States, pools are held to be illegal, as in restraint of trade. A group of financiers organized to profit by a monopoly was once, especially in or of European countries, called a **syndicate,** but at present the word is used of a group of individuals, firms, or corporations, often banking houses, which organize for a limited time to accomplish a given purpose, frequently to market an issue of bonds for some railroad, steel company, or public utility, which make their profit from the difference between the agreed-upon sum which they advance to the issuing corporation for the bonds, and the fixed sale price at which they market them, which assume responsibility for absorbing themselves any surplus bonds not marketed, and which dissolve as a group when the marketing period is completed. Outside of the field of finance, the use of the term is constantly being extended in its application to any combination, as of newspapers, business concerns, and the like, interested in a common project or enterprise, and now with decreasing frequency implying relation to a monopoly; as, his daily column appeared in a *syndicate* of over one hundred newspapers. **Trust** became prominent in the financial field when clever lawyers adapted the well-known trust provisions so common in wills and testaments to a scheme for inducing stockholders in merged corporations to surrender their rights to "trustees" who would operate the corporations, and to accept, in return for their ownership stock certificates, trust certificates. Several of the larger business interests adopted this method of organization (the Standard Oil *Trust* and the Tobacco *Trust*, for example). Since the trust form of organization was defeated by U. S. Supreme Court decision, the word has been less common in financial use. Both pools and trusts are known in Germany as **cartels:** the term has some American and British use, and is widened in its application to be used of any large combined business unit.

monstrous. 1 Monstrous, prodigious, tremendous, stupendous, monumental are more or less hyperbolical adjectives, especially in their extended senses in which they mean astonishingly impressive. **Monstrous** commonly applies to that which is abnormal, usually in actual or relative size, but often also in shape or character: the term frequently carries suggestions of deformity, extreme ugliness, fabulousness, or the like; as, "the imagination turbid with *monstrous* fancies and misshapen dreams" (*Wilde*); "such *monstrous* feet they had...that he declined...to try on the Glass Slipper" (*Meredith*); " 'my father, upon whose middle age it [the railway] came as a *monstrous* iron innovation' " (*Shaw*); "some ...*monstrous* bulk of rumpled rock" (*C. E. Montague*). **Prodigious** usually implies a marvelousness that exceeds belief; it sometimes applies to that which is entirely out of proportion to that which is the previous or usual best, greatest, largest, or the like; as, the *prodigious* demand for steel in the World War; "a *prodigious* best-seller" (*A. Huxley*); "Men have always reverenced *prodigious* inborn gifts, and always will" (*C. W. Eliot*); "a mind with such *prodigious* capacity of development as Shakespeare's" (*T. S. Eliot*). **Tremendous** (etymologically, that causes trembling or fear), in very discriminating use, comes closer to awe-inspiring, terrifying in its immensity, and the like, than to gigantic or enormous, its common denotations in loose use; as, "A *tremendous* roar arose from the throat of [the mob in the Faubourg] Saint Antoine" (*Dickens*); "How shall we compare the cramped and limited vision of the universe which spread itself to the imagination of mankind in old time with the *tremendous* vistas opened out to us by modern science" (*Inge*); "the spell and *tremendous* incantation of the Thought of Death" (*L. P. Smith*). **Stupendous** in discriminating use implies the power to stun or astound; it is, therefore, most precisely used when it is applied to that which because of its size, its numbers, its complexity, or its greatness, exceeds one's power to describe or explain; as, "All [things] are but parts of one *stupendous* whole, Whose body Nature is, and God the soul" (*Pope*); "a *stupendous* catastrophe that occurred in the constellation Hercules 1300 years ago" (*W. Kaempffert*). **Monumental,** in its extended sense (see also MASSIVE), applies to that which is as conspicuously impressive or as massively framed or constructed as a monument (such as a great cathedral or an impressive memorial); as, a *monumental* literary work; a *monumental* lie. "The *monumental* pomp of age Was with this goodly personage; A stature undepressed in size, Unbent, which rather seemed to rise, In open victory o'er the weight Of seventy years, to loftier height" (*Wordsworth*).

Ana. *Enormous, immense, huge, vast, colossal, mammoth, gigantic.

2 *Outrageous, heinous, atrocious.

Ana. *Flagrant, glaring, gross, rank: *ominous, portentous, fateful: flagitious, nefarious, infamous (see VICIOUS).

monument. *Document, muniment, record, archive.

monumental. 1 *Monstrous, prodigious, tremendous, stupendous.

Ana. Colossal, gigantic, *enormous, mammoth: impressive, *moving.

2 *Massive, massy, bulky, substantial.

Ana. Imposing, stately, majestic, august, magnificent, *grand.

mood. Mood, humor (*or* **humour**), **temper, vein** are here compared as meaning a temporary state or frame of mind in which one emotion or desire or one set of emotions gains the ascendancy. **Mood** (etymologically, mind or feeling) is now the comprehensive term for any such frame of mind, regardless of its particular cause, its particular character, its effect on others, or its length of existence. *Mood* carries a stronger implication of pervasiveness and of compelling power than the other terms; also, it may refer not only to the frame of mind (as, to feel in a *mood* to work; a sullen *mood;* changing *moods*) but to its expression in a literary or artistic work (as, "the language, the stresses, the very structure of the sentences are imposed upon the writer by the special *mood* of the piece"—*Cather*) or to that which is seen, heard, or the like, in such a way as to evoke a mood or to harmonize with one's mood (as, "Only in summer days of highest feather did its [the heath's] *mood* touch the level of gaiety"—*Hardy;* "Our painters are prone to acquiesce in the colours of nature as they find them, rather than to use colours expressive of the *mood* evoked in themselves"—*Binyon*). **Humor,** as here compared (see also WIT, 2), applies chiefly to a mood which is the result of one's peculiar temperament or of one's physical or mental condition at the moment: it is usually preferred to *mood* when the idea of capriciousness, or of whimsicality, or of ability to see the ludicrous, or the like, is to be suggested; as, "I am not in a *humour* to hear you further. Leave me, please" (*Hardy*); "The Baronet seemed in a *humour* for dignified fooling; the lady for serious converse" (*Meredith*); "he surrendered to her *humour*, and went through the form of begging Mumpsy's pardon" (*Meredith*); "The women were horrified or admiring, as their *humour* moved them" (*E. Wharton*). **Temper,** as here compared (see also DISPOSITION, 2), applies to a mood dominated by a single strong emotion, often specifically that of great anger; as, " 'He is in a *temper!*' 'I never knew him So out of patience with them' " (*Millay*). When qualified by an adjective indicating the controlling emotion, *temper* may apply to any humor that manifests itself in a display of feeling; as, "that meekness has done me more harm than the bitterest *temper*" (*Hardy*); "she was evidently now in a gay, frolicsome *temper*" (*Hudson*). **Vein** (see also TOUCH) is often used in the sense of *mood*, or especially of *humor*, but with a stronger implication of transitoriness than *mood* (as, "When the peacock *vein* rises, I strut a Gentleman Commoner"—*Lamb*), and a weaker implication than *humor* of a temperamental or physical cause (as, "The merry *vein* you knew me in, is sunk into a turn of reflection"—*Pope*).

Ana. *Disposition, temper, temperament, character, personality, individuality: *soul, spirit: emotion, *feeling, affection.

moor, *v.* **1** *Secure, anchor, rivet.

Ana. *Tie, bind: attach, *fasten, affix, fix: balance, steady, *stabilize, trim.

2 *Anchor.

moral, *adj.* **Moral, ethical, virtuous, righteous, noble** are synonyms only when they mean conforming to a standard of what is right and good: *moral* and *ethical* also come into comparison as meaning of or relating to the science or theory of right conduct. **Moral** is by far the most comprehensive term of the group: in all of its here pertinent senses it implies a relationship to character or conduct viewed as good or bad or as right or wrong. Sometimes, *moral* implies an opposition only to that which is not related to or concerned with character or conduct viewed as good or bad or as right or wrong; as, *moral* goodness as distinguished from intellectual goodness or spiritual goodness; *moral* value as distinguished from economic value, aesthetic value, and the like. " 'The whole tendency of modern thought...is to extenuate the responsibility of human nature, not merely on the *moral* side, but equally on the spiritual side' " (*C. Mackenzie*). *Moral* also applies to things such as literary works, works of art, philosophies, or to writers, artists, philosophers, etc., concerned with the determination or teaching of principles of right conduct or good living; as, a *moral* tale; *moral* essays; *moral* philosophy or philosophers; paintings that convey a *moral* lesson; "Tragedy...hath been ever held the gravest, *moralest,* and most profitable of all other poems" (*Milton*). The term also applies to men or communities, to acts, to conduct, and the like, in what is probably its chief current sense of conforming to the accepted standard of what is right and good (often, specifically, in sexual conduct) or, in some use, of conforming to the mores, or customs or conventions of a people regarded as binding laws; as, to lead a *moral* life; a man of high *moral* character; the *moral* ideals of the community; fine *moral* citizens; "to increase his respectability in the eyes of *moral* Britain" (*Meredith*); "by no means ascetic, scarcely even, in the narrow sense, a severely *moral* people" (*H. Ellis*); "His nature was purely sensuous, and she strove to make him *moral*, religious" (*D. H. Lawrence*). **Ethical** primarily implies a relationship to ethics, or the branch of philosophy which deals with moral principles, or often, more specifically, with the principles governing ideal human character and with the ideal ends of human action (as, an *ethical* system; an *ethical* code): for this reason, although *ethical* is often used interchangeably with *moral*, it characteristically gives a slightly different impression owing to certain subtle connotations; thus, *ethical* principles may, according to the context of the phrase, convey a strong suggestion of principles derived from a certain school of ethics, or of a formulated code behind them, or of an idealistic quality; an action is often described as *ethical* rather than *moral* when it accords with what the writer or speaker believes to be a higher or finer standard of morality than that which is generally accepted, or when it is in keeping with the code of ethics governing his profession (especially law and medicine); the phrase "an *ethical* person" often differs from the phrase "a *moral* person," in suggesting an assent to ethical principles or an attention to the niceties of ethics or to the ideal ends suggested by a system or code of ethics. "Meanwhile we hear...the *ethical* instinct of mankind asserting itself with splendid courage and patience" (*H. Van Dyke*). "I have always thought it most regrettable that serious and *ethical* thinkers...should go scuttling through space in this undignified manner" (*L. P. Smith*). **Virtuous** implies the possession or manifestation of moral excellence in character: in its most general sense, it implies rectitude, justice, integrity, and all other virtues (especially those which are described as the Christian [or divine] and as the cardinal virtues), but in a narrower sense, especially as applied to women and sometimes to men, it often means little more than chasteness or perfect fidelity in marriage; as, "poor people...whether they be lazy or busy, drunken or sober, *virtuous* or vicious" (*Shaw*); "A man might grind the faces of the poor; but so long as he refrained from caressing his neighbours' wives and daughters, he was regarded as *virtuous*" (*A. Huxley*). " 'Didst thou not kill this king?' 'I grant ye.' . . . 'God grant me too Thou mayst be damned for that wicked deed! O, he was gentle, mild, and *virtuous!*' " (*Shak.*). **Righteous** differs from *virtuous* chiefly in its stronger implication of freedom from guilt or blame; as applied to persons, it often implies justification, especially worthiness of salvation in the theological sense (as, "I came not to call the *righteous*, but sinners to repentance"—*Mark* ii. 17; "What but thy malice moved thee to misdeem Of *righteous* Job"—*Milton*); as applied to acts, conduct, even displays of passion, it usually implies justifiability (as, *righteous* indignation; "a *righteous* occupation"—*Conrad; righteous* conduct). **Noble** (as here compared: see also GRAND) applies to persons, their acts, utterances, careers, and the like, and implies the possession and exhibition of a conspicuously high character. Oftentimes, the word carries no other clear implications and seems little more than a term of high praise implying moral or ethical eminence; as, "This was the *noblest* Roman of them all" (*Shak.*); "a *noble* aim, Faithfully kept, is as a *noble* deed" (*Wordsworth*). At other times, however, the term suggests not only moral eminence but the absence of all taint of anything petty, such as self-seeking, self-interest, concern for the world's standards, or the like: it then often suggests independence, or magnanimity, or high courage, or some other outstanding moral excellence. " 'Better a man without riches, than riches without a man.' 'A *noble* saying—and acted on would yield A *nobler* breed of men and women' " (*Tennyson*). "The disinterested search for truth is certainly one of the highest and *noblest* careers that a man can choose" (*Inge*).

Ana. Right, *good: *upright, honest, just, honorable, scrupulous, conscientious: *chaste, pure, modest, decent: ideal, *abstract.

Con. *Immoral, unmoral, amoral, nonmoral.

morality. *Goodness, virtue, rectitude.

Ana. Integrity, probity, honor, *honesty: *excellence, perfection, virtue, merit.

morally. *Virtually, practically.

mordacious. *Caustic, mordant, acrid, scathing.

Ana. See those at MORDANT.

mordant. *Caustic, mordacious, acrid, scathing.

Ana. *Incisive, trenchant, cutting, biting, clear-cut, crisp: *pungent, poignant, piquant, racy, spicy, snappy: *sharp, keen, acute.

moreover. Besides, furthermore, likewise, *also, too.

moron. Imbecile, idiot, *fool, simpleton, natural.

morose. Glum, gloomy, saturnine, dour, *sullen, surly, sulky, crabbed.

Ana. Splenetic, choleric, *irascible, testy, cranky, cross: peevish, snappish, waspish, petulant, *irritable: brusque, gruff (see BLUFF).

mortal, *adj.* **1** *Deadly, fatal, lethal.

Ana. Destructive (see corresponding verb DESTROY): virulent, venomous, *poisonous: implacable, unrelenting, relentless (see GRIM).

Ant. Venial (*especially of a sin*).

2 *Earthly, terrestrial, terrene, earthy, mundane, worldly, sublunary.

Ant. Immortal (*of things*).

mortified. *Ashamed, chagrined.

Ana. Harassed, harried, worried, annoyed (see WORRY, *v.*): humiliated, humbled, abased (see ABASE): abashed, embarrassed, discomfited (see EMBARRASS).

motherly. *Parental, maternal, fatherly, paternal.

motif, *n.* **1** Device, design, pattern, *figure.

2 Variant of MOTIVE, 2.

motile. *Movable, mobile, motive.

motion, *n.* **Motion, movement, move, locomotion, stir** are here compared as meaning the act or an instance of moving. **Motion** is the preferred term in abstract use for the act or process of moving, without regard to that which moves or is moved: in philosophical and aesthetic use it is an especially comprehensive term, for it may apply to manifestation of change or of changing not only from place to place, but from condition to condition, from step to step in a progression, or the like; as, the laws of *motion;* "this vicissitude of *motion* and rest, which we call life" (*Steele*); "in all the arts the principle of *motion* prevails increasingly over the principle of repose" (*Babbitt*). Ordinarily, however, the term implies visible moving, whether discernible to the naked eye (or other sense) or through a telescope or other instrument; as, the *motion* of the planets; there is no *motion* in the atmosphere; "I was lying. . . injured, and incapable of *motion*" (*Hudson*); the restless *motion* of the sea. **Movement** usually implies definite regulated motion: the term is seldom used to denote an abstraction, although it may be used figuratively to denote a quality of representation in a work of art that suggests motion (as, *movement* is one of the most striking characteristics of the Elgin marbles and of the Winged Victory), or a quality in poetry, drama, or the like, that suggests a definite rate of speed or progression as in the meter, the action, or the like (as, "No one will so well render Homer's swift-flowing *movement* as he who has himself something of the swift-moving spirit of Homer"—*Arnold*). In concrete use, *movement* implies a passage (sometimes self-initiated, sometimes under guidance or compulsion) from place to place, from situation to situation, from condition to condition, or the like; it may, in this sense, be used interchangeably with *motion* in the collective singular or in the plural; as, the *movements* of the planets; the restless *movement* of the sea; the *movement* of troops to the front was then in progress; severe storms hindered the *movement* of trucks carrying supplies; the progress of man is so slow that the *movement* is rarely perceptible. *Movement* also is frequently used for an instance of moving (especially one involving a change of place or position); as, "a *movement* among the ferns attracted Adrian" (*Meredith*); every *movement* of the bird was watched by the cat. **Move** applies chiefly to a definite instance of moving or of making a change in one's location or in the place occupied by something else: usually, the term suggests a clearly defined purpose or goal; as, the detectives are watching his every *move;* the next *move* (in a game of chess) is yours; their next *move* on their tour will be from Dover to Ostend; when the hostess made a *move* from the table all the guests arose and followed her to the drawing room. **Locomotion** was originally used, especially in philosophy, as a more specific term than *motion* because it definitely implied motion from place to place; thus, plants were described as living things incapable of *locomotion* and animals as living things capable of *locomotion.* In modern use, the term suggests travel especially by artificial means, as by boat, train, airplane, or automobile; as, "Every improvement of the means of *locomotion* benefits mankind morally and intellectually" (*Macaulay*). **Stir** applies to any motion or movement (often without an implication of changes of place or condition, or of progress) that involves a disturbance (but not necessarily a displeasing disturbance), especially of that which has been quiet or at rest, but also of that whose motion or movements indicate excitement, bustle, or agitation; as, "not a *stir* of child or mouse" (*Stevenson*); "many persons find *stir*, and *movement*, and the presence of a crowd an agreeable stimulus" (*A. C. Benson*); "It is an age of *stir* and change" (*Galsworthy*).

Ana. Impetus, momentum, *speed, velocity, pace, headway.

motivate. Actuate, *activate.

Ana. Stimulate, quicken, *provoke, excite: arouse, rouse, *stir: inspire, animate, fire, *inform.

motive, *n.* **1 Motive, spring** (*or* **springs**), **impulse, incentive, inducement, spur, goad** come into comparison when they denote a stimulus inciting or prompting a person to act or behave in a definite way. **Motive** applies chiefly to any emotion, such as fear, anger, hatred, love, or the like, or to any desire (such as one for fame, wealth, knowledge, supremacy, revenge, or the like) or to any physical appetite (such as hunger or lust) which operates on the will and definitely moves it to activity. " 'Do you think,' said Sir Austin...'that you can trace every act of his to its *motive?*' " (*Meredith*). "Whenever a man does a thoroughly stupid thing, it is always from the noblest *motives*" (*Wilde*). "I could slay no living thing except from *motives* of hunger" (*Hudson*). "Even where some piece of knowledge is uninteresting in itself, a man can force himself to acquire it if he has an adequate *motive* for doing so" (*B. Russell*). **Spring,** or the more common plural **springs,** is used in place of *motive* without much difference in meaning; among very precise writers and speakers, however, it often refers to the underlying or basic motive which is often not fully recognized even by the person or persons affected and is especially hidden from all but the most penetrating observers. "It is difficult...to come at the true *springs* of action" (*T. Forrest*). "The love of gold was the sordid *spring* of the most brilliant enterprises of the republic" (*C. Merivale*). **Impulse** is a complex term because it has both a general sense and a very specific sense in each of which some important implications run counter to those of the other sense. In both its inclusive and its specific senses, however, *impulse* may or may not imply, as *motive* or *spring* always do imply in very precise use, performance of an act or engagement in an activity; the term stresses impetus, or driving power, rather than its effect; thus, one may check (or restrain, or forgo, or dismiss) an *impulse.* In its more general sense, *impulse* is applicable to any powerful incitement or instigation to activity resulting from the operation or influence of an external agent or agency or arising within oneself as the result of a native propensity, one's peculiarity of temperament, one's intellectual or emotional constitution, or the like. "He was not a man...to yield timidly to the *impulses* of others" (*Prescott*). "This declamation is in its *impulse,* if not in its achievement, Senecan" (*T. S. Eliot*). "Men like the elder Cato, Varro, and the elder Pliny liked to record the curiosities of nature, but they had not the systematizing *impulse,* the restless passion for order, of the Greeks" (*Buchan*). " 'The *impulse* behind the reformation was the *impulse* of the English to express their nationality' " (*C. Mackenzie*). Specifically, however, *impulse* is applicable to a spontaneous, often irrational, and in undisciplined persons usually irresistible, urge to do something. "Dr. Lavendar...said to himself, chuckling, 'If I'd followed my *impulse,* I'd have married them then and there, and made no bones of it' " (*Deland*). "The first *impulse* of a child in a garden is to pick every attractive flower" (*B. Russell*). "Gard suffered an odd *impulse* to get up and kick his chair over; but people don't do those things. He kicked the back log instead" (*M. Austin*). **Incentive** applies chiefly to any cause which incites and encourages action or activity, often, but far from invariably, one for which the person affected is not himself responsible or which does not originate within himself; as, to offer a bonus as an *incentive* to greater speed and efficiency in production; with some pupils praise is not always an *incentive* to study. "Money is not the only *incentive* to work, nor the strongest" (*Shaw*). "The great *incentive* to effort, all through life, is experience of success after initial difficulties" (*B. Russell*). "People...cut off here without the influence of example or emulation, with no *incentive* but some natural yearning for order and security" (*Cather*). **Inducement** is narrower than *incentive,* for it suggests an external influence and often an attempt to entice or allure to action or activity. "The chief *inducements* to serve were the pension and the right of citizenship which awaited a soldier on his discharge" (*Buchan*). **Spur,** literally a pointed implement worn by a horseman at or above his heel and used to prick his horse in urging him on, in its extended use, applies to any impetus to action which not only incites but stimulates the mind and increases its energy and ardor. "Fame is the *spur* that the clear spirit doth raise ... To scorn delights and live laborious days" (*Milton*). "The *spur* which drove me was sharp....I took on added duties, read books not on any prescribed list, and dashed indefatigably from public ward to private pavilion and to clinics in other hospitals" (*V. Heiser*). **Goad,** literally a pointed rod used to prod a beast who moves or works too slowly, in its extended sense applies to any stimulus to action or activity that keeps one going in spite of one's will or desire. "The daily *goad* urging him to the daily toil" (*Macaulay*).

Ana. *Cause, determinant, antecedent, reason: *desire, appetite, urge, passion, lust: *feeling, emotion, passion: purpose, intent, *intention, aim, end.

2 Also **motif.** *Subject, matter, subject matter, argument, topic, text, theme, leitmotiv.

motive, *adj.* *Movable, mobile, motile.

Ana. *Active, operative, dynamic: moving, driving, impelling *or* impulsive (see corresponding verbs at MOVE).

motley. Heterogeneous, *miscellaneous, assorted, promiscuous.

Ana. *Different, diverse, divergent, disparate, various: discrepant, incompatible, uncongenial, incongruous (see INCONSONANT).

Con. Uniform, homogeneous, parallel, akin, alike, identical (see SIMILAR).

motto. Proverb, adage, *saying, saw, maxim, epigram, aphorism, apothegm.

mound. Mound, bank, dune, embankment, terrace, tumulus, barrow are here compared as meaning a mass of earth or of earth and rock forming a small and often impermanent elevation. **Mound** usually implies a heaping or piling up in the shape of a small hill; it is capable of being applied to any built-up elevation of this shape as inconsiderable in size as those raised around the roots of some growing vegetables or as large as those found in regions where winds and waters pile up hillocks of sand or earth; as, the *mounds* over cemetery graves. "The merest grain of sand drifts unseen into a crevice, and by-and-by another; after a while there is a heap; a century and it is a *mound*" (*Jefferies*). **Bank** may be used in place of *mound* but it more often suggests a long, moderately high elevation rising to a ridge or level and sometimes also descending on the other side. Such banks often run alongside a road or are thrown up as a boundary wall or a fortification. "I know a *bank* where the wild thyme blows, Where oxlips and the nodding violet grows" (*Shak.*). "The gate was locked when he climbed up the steps cut in the *bank*" (*C. Mackenzie*). **Dune**

applies to one of several mounds or banks of sand built up by the force of the wind, as on the shore of the sea, of a large lake, in a river valley, or in a desert region; since the shape and size of dunes are at the mercy of winds, the term suggests shifting and impermanence. "Mounds and *dunes* of loose sand which whirled through the air all day in the boisterous spring winds" (*Cather*). An **embankment** is an artificial bank, usually of solid construction, sloping on both sides, and topped with a roadway or path. Most levees and many dikes, ramparts, bulwarks, and the like, are embankments. Strictly, a **terrace** is the level top of a bank or embankment, used for pleasure or for planting; the word, however, in current use commonly suggests not only the leveled top but the entire formation, including its steep or rounded face or faces walled with stone or brick or covered with grass. Terraces are found chiefly on the landscaped grounds of a house or institution where rough or steep natural elevations have been made smooth, even, and easy, or on the sides of hills or mountains (then usually in tiers), where they counteract the harm done by erosion by providing surfaces which retain the soil and are capable of cultivation. **Tumulus** and **barrow** are applied chiefly to one of the sepulchral mounds of earth and rock built by primitive peoples over the graves of their dead, or to any of the small isolated round hills that dot a plain or gently sloping region of a country, and may or may not have been originally sepulchral mounds. "A plain, on which are five earthen *tumuli*, or *barrows*" (*T. Pennant*). "Danish *barrows*" (*Tennyson*).

mount, *n.* *Mountain, peak, alp, volcano, mesa.

mount, *v.* **1** Ascend, soar, *rise, arise, tower, rocket, levitate, surge.
Ant. Drop.
2 *Ascend, climb, scale.
Ant. Dismount.

mountain. Mountain, mount, peak, alp, volcano, mesa. Mountain, the ordinary and inclusive term, varies somewhat in meaning according to locality. In general, it designates an elevation higher and steeper than a hill, rising more or less abruptly from its surrounding country, and standing out conspicuously when viewed from a distance. **Mount** is often used in proper names of mountains; otherwise it is poetic. **Peak,** when applied to a mountain, designates one that rises to a sharp point; it may be isolated or one of a range. **Alp** (usually capitalized), which is chiefly poetic, suggests a towering, dizzy, or unscalable height. "Yet do I sometimes feel a languishment... To sit upon an *Alp* as on a throne, And half forget what world or worldling meant" (*Keats*). **Volcano,** which is strictly applied to a vent in the earth through which hot or molten rock and the like issue, also designates the cone-shaped mountain formed chiefly of this ejected material, and topped, usually, by a crater. **Mesa,** a Spanish term adopted in English, is commonly used in the southwestern part of the United States to designate a flat-topped elevation, usually comparable to a hill in height, but more suggestive of a mountain because of its steep clifflike sides.
Ana. *Height, elevation, altitude.

mountebank, *n.* *Impostor, faker, charlatan, empiric, quack.

mourn. Sorrow, *grieve.
Ana. Lament, bewail, bemoan (see DEPLORE): weep, keen, wail, *cry.
Con. Rejoice, gladden, delight, *please: exult, elate (see corresponding adjectives at ELATED).

movable *or* **moveable. Movable** (*or* **moveable**), **mobile, motile, motive** come into comparison when they mean capable of moving or of being moved. **Movable,** in current use, applies not to that which has independent power of motion, but to that which is not too heavy to be moved by men or machines as by lifting, drawing, pushing, or driving, to another place or position (as, a *movable* steam engine; one's *movable* possessions; "some of these cabins were *moveable,* and were carried on sledges from one part of the common to another"—*Macaulay*), or to that which is not fixed, as in position or date (as, printing from *movable* types; a *movable* attachment for a machine; *movable* feasts such as Easter and Whitsunday). **Mobile** stresses facility or ease in moving or, less often, in being moved. In early use, it described particularly the quality of eyes that could range at will, or of a star that is not fixed: in current use, it often describes the quality of flowing which distinguishes a liquid or fluid from a solid (as, "the *mobile* liquid passes into a compact rigid solid"—*T. H. Huxley*) or which characterizes an electric current or charge (as, "long-lasting circulation of the *mobile* charge, around and around the circuit"—*Karl K. Darrow*) or the character which distinguishes something that moves or is equipped to move quickly and readily, or to go from place to place, from that which is slow-moving or does inside work (as, a *mobile* army; a *mobile* radio unit). But, more commonly, *mobile* describes features, faces, expressions of face, thoughts, and the like, which respond quickly and obviously to changing emotions, mental states, external stimuli, and the like, often at the same time connoting either fickleness or instability, or flexibility and versatility; as, "the gray restless eye, the thin *mobile* lips" (*J. R. Green*); "the *mobile* mirror of his mind" (*Mrs. H. Ward*); "he was no more *mobile* than his countenance" (*Cather*); "You are as *mobile* as the veering air, And all your charms more changeful than the tide" (*Millay*). **Motile** is almost entirely a technical term. In biology it applies to that which is not permanently attached and is free to move about or which has power of spontaneous motion; as, *motile* cells; *motile* spores; *motile* flagella. In psychology the term describes either the type of person in whom the tendency to recall muscular movements prevails, or the kind of images most easily recalled by a person of this type; thus, the *motile* type is distinguished from the *audile* (or ear-minded) or the *visile* (or eye-minded) types. **Motive** implies a moving only in the transitive sense of driving, or causing movement, or impelling to action: the term is now chiefly applied to power, energy, or the like, produced by fuel such as gasoline, by steam, by electricity, or other forces; as, steam is no longer the only *motive* power used in operating railway locomotives; the question of what *motive* power will be best for the new ship has not yet been decided; auto*motive* (that is, mechanically self-propelled) vehicles. Even when the reference is to that which constitutes a motive for action, "*motive* power," "*motive* force," or "*motive* energy" is more likely to be used than, as in the past, "*motive* cause," "*motive* argument," "*motive* principle," or the like. "There was no *motive* power in experience. It was as little of an active cause as conscience itself" (*Wilde*). "As for the dream of the habitable earth peaceful under a universal empire... the *motive* power to realize it must come from the West, where men could still be both disciplined and free" (*Buchan*).
Ana. *Changeable, changeful, variable, mutable.
Ant. Immovable: stationary. — *Con.* Fixed, set, settled, established (see SET, *v.*).

move, *v.* **1 Move, actuate, drive, impel** come into comparison when they mean to set or keep going or in motion. **Move** is so general that the direction or nature of the motion can be gathered only from the context; it may imply an agent or an agency as the mover; as, what power or force *moves* the rotating earth?; the mechanism that *moves* the locomotive; vessels *moved* by wind, steam, or electricity. **Actuate** is far more restricted in its reference than *move*, being used chiefly in connection with machinery and mechanisms; it stresses the communication of power to work or to set in action; as, a turbine is *actuated* by the force of a current of fluid under pressure. **Drive** implies forward and, usually, continuous rather than recurrent motion; it often emphasizes the effect produced, as of speed, violence, or show of power, rather more than the impetus given; as, a ship *driven* by wind and tide; the washing machine is *driven* by electricity; the heart *drives* the blood through the arteries. **Impel,** when used of physical motion, adds to *drive* the implication of great force in the impetus. " 'They *drive* him with their guns—like this!' He imitated the action of a man's being *impelled* forward by the butt-ends of muskets" (*Dickens*).

These words are also synonymous in another sense, when they mean to excite or provoke a person to a given act or action or to given conduct or behavior. **Move** may imply an agent, human or divine, an external influence, or an inner spring or motive, as the mover. "If kingdom *move* thee not, let *move* thee zeal and duty" (*Milton*). "I *moved* the king my master to speak in the behalf of my daughter" (*Shak.*). **Actuate** always presupposes an inner stimulus, such as a desire, a feeling, a motive. "Men of the greatest abilities are most fired with ambition...; mean and narrow minds are the least *actuated* by it" (*Addison*). "It used to be the thing for parents to represent themselves as Olympians, immune from human passions and always *actuated* by pure reason" (*B. Russell*). **Drive** presupposes a compelling force, sometimes outer, sometimes inner, which affects the freedom of the will. "What had I ever done to you that would *drive* you to such a step?" (*M. Austin*). **Impel,** like *actuate*, implies an inner prompting, but it suggests greater urgency in the desire or motive and more headlong action. "A life of adventure...was that to which his nature irresistibly *impelled* him" (*Arnold*). "She was a prey to shoddy, facile emotions...none of which had power to *impel* her to any action" (*R. Macaulay*).

Ana. *Activate, actuate, motivate: *provoke, excite, quicken, stimulate: *induce, persuade, prevail on *or* upon.

2 Move, remove, shift, transfer come into comparison when they mean to change or to cause to change from one place to another. *Move* is by far the most comprehensive of these terms, all of which are general in that they do not in themselves and apart from the context imply any definite kind of agent or agency or any definite means of conveyance or transportation, or give any indication of the extent of distance covered. **Move** is therefore chiefly used when nothing more than the motion or activity involved in a change of place is to be indicated; as, to *move* a table from a corner to the center of the room; to *move* one's family from New York City to Chicago; to *move* a house across the street to a larger lot; he is about to *move* from the city to the country; he will not *move* from that chair until he is called to dinner. **Remove** is only slightly less general than *move*, but the term implies (as *move* seldom, if ever, implies, apart from a statement in the context) that the person or thing that changes or is changed from one place to another is moved from or quits a place which is his or its normal or original location, station, position, occupation, or the like, for one which is new or temporary; as, to *remove* the cover from a platter; to *remove* the dishes from the table. Many persons prefer the more simple *move* to *remove* when a change of habitation or business location is indicated; as, to *move* one's family to one's summer home; to *move* from Chicago to Denver. When the idea of getting rid or eradicating is stressed, *remove* is the preferred term; as, to *remove* a person from office; they *removed* the cause of the epidemic of typhoid fever when they put the typhoid carrier under close surveillance. **Shift** throws so much emphasis on change of location, direction, or the like, that the implications of voluntary or guided motion or activity are seldom apparent: therefore the term is often preferred when unrest or uncertainty or instability is to be suggested; as, the cargo *shifted* in the storm; the wind will *shift* during the night to due east; he *shifts* continually from job to job; to *shift* one's weight from one foot to another; a ne'er-do-well who *shifts* lodgings from week to week. However, *shift* is often used colloquially when a mere change in position is implied; as, give me a hand in *shifting* this bureau; he *shifted* his quid of tobacco to the other side of his mouth before answering. **Transfer** (as here compared: see also TRANSFER, 2) commonly implies a change from hand to hand, or from one mode of conveyance to another, or from one depository to another, or the like: it is often used in a specific sense, especially in the business of transportation; as, a truck will *transfer* our baggage from the railway station to our home; you will need to *transfer* (i.e., move to another train) at Albany; to *transfer* one's animus from one person to another. "There was no way in which he could *transfer* his own memories of European civilization into the [American] Indian mind" (*Cather*).

Ana. Displace, *replace, supplant, supersede: convey, *carry, bear, transport, transmit.

move, *n.* Movement, *motion, locomotion, stir.

Ana. Change, alteration, variation, modification (see under CHANGE, *v.*): transformation, metamorphosis, conversion, transmogrification (see under TRANSFORM).

moveable. Variant of MOVABLE.

movement. *Motion, move, locomotion, stir.

Ana. *Action, act, deed: change, alteration, variation, modification (see under CHANGE, *v.*): activity, operativeness *or* operation, dynamicness *or* dynamism, liveness (see corresponding adjectives at ACTIVE).

moving. Moving, impressive, poignant, affecting, touching, pathetic are synonymous so far as they agree in meaning having the power to excite or the effect of exciting deep and, usually, solemn emotion in the spectator, the reader, or the like. Only *moving*, the most general of these words, can be used in place of any of the others; the rest, though not mutually exclusive in their implications, are in precise use very specific. That is **moving** which stirs one deeply or evokes a strong emotional response, as by thrilling, entrancing, agitating, saddening, or the like; as, a *moving* scene in a play; a *moving* appeal for help. "To my mind the most *moving* ...single line in English poetry" (*Day Lewis*). "Dancing is...the most *moving*, the most beautiful of the arts" (*H. Ellis*). That is **impressive** which imposes itself forcibly on the mind and compels admiration, awe, conviction, or the like. "Scenery...majestic without severity, *impressive* without showiness" (*Hardy*). "Ordinary men cannot produce really *impressive* art-works" (*Shaw*). "I regret that I cannot put into more *impressive* words my belief that...the defendants were deprived of their rights" (*Justice Holmes*). That is **poignant** which produces so painfully sharp an impression that it pierces one's heart or penetrates to the depth of one's being. "It was warm and yet fresh; blindfold, one could have mistaken it for a morning in early May: but this kind of day...had a more *poignant* loveliness in autumn than in spring, because it was a receding footfall, a waning moon" (*Jan Struther*). That is **affecting** which moves one to tears or to some similar manifestation of feeling; as, even the most callous found the play *affecting;* an *affecting* reunion of a mother and her child. That is **touching** which arouses tenderness or compassion or which melts the heart. "A clean sober little maid, with a very *touching* upward look of trust" (*Galsworthy*). "Hers was a perfect little homily...and it ended with *touching* allusions to Pluffles' Mamma and Papa" (*Kipling*). That is **pathetic** which moves one to pity. Sometimes it suggests pity induced by compassion for one in sorrow or distress. "He was a lonely old man....Rather *pathetic!* Tony...felt a quick sympathy with him" (*Arch. Marshall*). "*Pathetic* gropings after the fragments of a shattered faith" (*Day Lewis*). Sometimes it suggests pity mixed with contempt for that which is weak, inadequate, futile, or the like; as, "a *pathetic* confusion of aims" (*Binyon*); *pathetic* attempts at portrait painting.

Ana. Exciting, stimulating, quickening, provoking (see PROVOKE): thrilling, electrifying (see THRILL): stirring, arousing, rousing, awakening, rallying (see STIR).

mucilaginous. Gummy, *adhesive, gluey, glutinous, sticky.

muddle, *v.* *Confuse, bemuddle, addle, fuddle, befuddle.

Ana. *Puzzle, perplex, mystify, bewilder, distract, nonplus, confound, dumfound: faze, rattle, discomfit, *embarrass: fluster, flurry, upset, agitate, *discompose.

Ant. Enlighten.

muddle, *n.* *Confusion, disorder, chaos, disarray, jumble, clutter, pie, snarl.

muddy. *Turbid, roiled, roily.

Ana. Murky, opaque, gloomy, obscure, *dark: confused, muddled, bemuddled, addle (see CONFUSE): *dirty, filthy, foul, nasty, squalid.

Con. *Clear, transparent, translucent, lucid, limpid.

mug, *n.* *Face, countenance, visage, physiognomy, puss.

mulct. *Penalize, fine, amerce, sconce.

Ana. Exact, require, *demand, claim.

mulish. *Obstinate, dogged, stubborn, pertinacious, stiff-necked, pigheaded, bullheaded.

Ana. Headstrong, intractable, recalcitrant, refractory, ungovernable, *unruly: fixed, set, firmed *or* firm (see corresponding verbs at SET).

multifarious. Manifold, multifold, divers, numerous, various, *many, several, sundry.

Ana. Disparate, diverse, divergent, *different: incongruous, incompatible, uncongenial, discrepant, discordant, *inconsonant, inconsistent.

multifold. *Many, several, sundry, various, divers, numerous, manifold, multifarious.

Ana. Reproduced, copied, duplicated (see corresponding nouns at REPRODUCTION): repeated, iterated (see REPEAT).

multiply. *Increase, augment, enlarge.

Ana. Propagate, reproduce, breed, *generate: expand, spread, stretch (see corresponding nouns at EXPANSE).

Con. *Decrease, diminish, lessen, reduce, abate.

multitude. **Multitude, army, host, legion** come into comparison when they mean, both in the singular and plural, a very large number of persons or things. They do not, as *crowd, throng,* etc., necessarily imply assemblage, but all of them are occasionally, or even often, used with that implication. **Multitude** stresses numerousness; always, however, with respect to what is the standard for, or the test of, numerousness in the thing referred to; thus, in "that child always asks a *multitude* of questions" and "I never saw such a *multitude* of books before in one house" *multitude* obviously refers to a much smaller number in the first than in the second illustration. "We must not...expect systematic education to produce *multitudes* of highly cultivated and symmetrically developed persons" (*C. W. Eliot*). When applied to a group of persons taken as a whole, "a multitude" suggests an assemblage of a large number of persons (as, "moved his arms with large pawing gestures, as though he were distributing lay blessings to a kneeling *multitude*"—*E. Wharton*), but "the multitude" suggests the masses of ordinary people or the populace (as, speeches that sway the *multitude;* a book that appeals to the *multitude*). **Army** usually adds to *multitude* the implications of orderly arrangement without a suggestion of crowding, and often, especially in clearly figurative use, a progressive advance without any suggestion of halting or gathering; as, they were served by a vast *army* of waiters; an *army* of locusts. "Brave conquerors,—for so you are, That war against... the huge *army* of the world's desires" (*Shak.*). "We have considered science as a steadily advancing *army* of ascertained facts" (*Inge*). **Host,** like the other terms of this group, has for its primary implication numerousness. It may mean nothing more (as, she has *hosts* of admirers; he knows *hosts* of people) but it may suggest more strongly than any of the other words a concentration in great numbers of the thing referred to: in such cases it usually connotes an impressive or striking array; as, a clear cold night and a *host* of stars in the sky. "I saw a crowd, A *host,* of golden daffodils; Beside the lake, beneath the trees, Fluttering and dancing in the breeze" (*Wordsworth*). **Legion** derives its leading implication of incalculable numbers from Biblical rather than from military sources (in ancient Rome, it denoted the principal unit of an army), and its tendency to be applied to angels, devils, or things thought of as flying to aid or annoy. "Thinkest thou that I cannot now pray to my Father, and he shall presently give me more than twelve *legions* of angels?" (*Matthew* xxvi. 53). "And he [Jesus] asked him [the unclean spirit possessing the man], What is thy name? And he answered, saying, My name is *Legion:* for we are many" (*Mark* v. 9). "*Armies* of angels that soar, *legions* of demons that lurk" (*Browning*).

Ana. Horde, throng, press, mob, crush, *crowd.

mummer. Performer, mime, player, *actor, Thespian, impersonator, trouper.

mummery. *Gibberish, hocus-pocus, abracadabra.

mundane. Worldly, *earthly, earthy, terrestrial, terrene, mortal, sublunary.

Ana. Fleshly, sensual, *carnal, animal, animalistic: secular, temporal, *profane.

Ant. Eternal. — *Con.* *Infinite, sempiternal, boundless: heavenly, *celestial, empyrean.

munificent. Bountiful, *liberal, generous, handsome.

Ana. Benevolent, *charitable, philanthropic, altruistic: *profuse, lavish, prodigal.

muniment. *Document, monument, record, archive.

munitions. *Armament, arms, ordnance, artillery, ammunition.

murder, *v.* *Kill, slay, assassinate, dispatch, execute.

murky. Obscure, gloomy, opaque, *dark, dim, dusk, dusky, darkling.

Ana. *Turbid, muddy, roiled, roily: lowering, glowering, glooming *or* gloomy (see corresponding verbs at FROWN): lurid, grim, *ghastly.

Con. *Bright, brilliant, radiant, effulgent: illuminated, illumined, lightened, enlightened (see ILLUMINATE): *clear, transparent, translucent, lucid.

muscular. Muscular, brawny, sinewy, athletic, burly, husky are here compared as applied to persons in the sense of strong and powerful in build or physique. **Muscular** implies well-developed, but not overdeveloped, muscles and, usually, a stalwart build. "My Eustace might have sat for Hercules; So *muscular* he spread, so broad of breast" (*Tennyson*). "Hard exercise ...built into a strong, *muscular* body what had been a frail and sickly frame" (*W. A. White*). **Brawny** implies the full development of the muscles; although originally it was a close synonym of *fleshy*, it carries no connotation of stoutness but rather suggests the might that is associated with hard flesh and great size. "The muscles of his *brawny* arms Are strong as iron bands" (*Longfellow*). **Sinewy** attributes no less power to the muscles than *brawny* but it suggests greater energy and quickness and it never connotes hugeness. Rather it often implies a leanness, toughness, and litheness that are the result of training or of persistent exercise. Blacksmiths, steelworkers, prize fighters, and the like, are often described as *brawny*, but fencers, runners, acrobats, and the like, more often as *sinewy*. "Worthy fellows; and like to prove most *sinewy* sword-men" (*Shak.*). **Athletic,** as used in any science in which types of physique are studied, is applied to a build characterized by long limbs, well-developed muscles, and a broad chest. In more general use, *athletic* suggests much the same type, though occasionally it does not emphasize largeness of frame as much as muscularity, sinewiness, or vigor of health; as, a tall, *athletic* young man. **Burly** stresses massiveness of build to such an extent that it often carries connotations of corpulence, of coarseness or grossness, and suggests the possession of brute force. "Benson following his *burly* shadow" (*Meredith*). "Tall...*burly*, Quite fearless, built with such a jaw That no man's rule could be his law" (*Masefield*). **Husky** is an American colloquialism implying a powerful athletic build and brawniness; as, the *huskiest* members of a football team are placed on the line. "Good food and leisure and heredity gave me a *husky* build" (*S. E. White*).

Ana. Robust, *healthy, hale, sound: *strong, sturdy, stalwart, stout: *vigorous, lusty.

muse, *v.* *Ponder, meditate, ruminate.

Ana. *Consider, study, contemplate, weigh, revolve, excogitate: reflect, reason, *think.

museum. Museum, library, gallery, archives, treasury, thesaurus are not synonymous terms, but they come into comparison when they mean a place serving as a repository for monuments (see DOCUMENT, 1, for this sense) of the past. **Museum** is the most general of these terms; it usually implies the intention both to preserve and to exhibit for the education of the public. In Great Britain, it is applied chiefly to an institution concerned with the preservation and exhibition of objects of historical or scientific interest (the conspicuous exception is the British Museum), especially such as illustrate the development of human civilization or the evolution of species; thus, the Ashmolean *Museum* at Oxford is a place for the exhibition of objects of antiquarian or archaeological interest. In the United States, the term is applicable not only to institutions of this character, but to those providing for the preservation and exhibition of works of fine art, such as paintings and sculptures. Consequently the term is usually qualified in proper names or in general designations; as, the *Museum* of Fine Arts; the *Museum* of Natural History; an art *museum.* **Library** is applicable to any room, building, or institution which houses a collection of books not for sale but accessible to those persons who are permitted to use them. The great libraries of the world, however, such as the Vatican Library, the National Library (Bibliothèque Nationale) in Paris, the British Museum (chiefly a library), the Library of Congress are vast storehouses of books of all kinds and of all ages, manuscripts, records, documents, files of journals, and the like; they often, in addition, exhibit works of art, but their primary purpose is to preserve works of literature and of reference, and documents in all fields of research, and to make them available to scholars. **Gallery** (often *art gallery*) is used commonly in Great Britain and often in the United States for a room, a suite, or a building housing and exhibiting paintings, works of sculpture, and the like; as, the National *Gallery* (in London). The term is used of a place housing a private as well as a public collection, and (especially in the plural, *galleries*) of a place where works of art are exhibited for sale. **Archives,** when the term designates the place where a collection of old records, old documents, old files, and similar papers are kept, rather than the collection itself (see DOCUMENT, 1), may refer to a building or, as is more common, to a part of a building, as of a library or museum, where the collection is housed; as, the *archives* of the city hall; the *archives* of the department of state; to place a manuscript in the *archives* of the Royal Society. **Treasury,** and occasionally **thesaurus,** are used to designate a room where possessions of historical value or significance are stored. Many of the old English cathedrals have their treasuries where old ecclesiastical utensils, vestments, relics and reliquaries, and the like, are kept and shown to visitors.

mushy. *Sentimental, romantic, mawkish, maudlin, soppy, slushy.

must. *Ought, should, have, have got.

muster. *Summon, call, cite, convoke, convene.

Ana. Collect, congregate, assemble, *gather: marshal, organize, arrange, *order: align, *line, range, array.

musty. Fusty, *malodorous, stinking, fetid, noisome, putrid, rank, rancid.

Ana. *Dirty, filthy, foul, nasty, squalid: sloppy, *slipshod, unkempt, slovenly.

mutable. *Changeable, changeful, variable, protean.

Ana. Unstable, *inconstant, fickle: fluctuating, wavering, swinging, swaying (see SWING).

Ant. Immutable. — *Con.* *Steady, even, constant, uniform, equable: *lasting, permanent, durable, stable.

mutation. 1 *Change, permutation, vicissitude, alternation.

Ana. Shifting *or* shift, moving *or* move, removing *or* remove (see corresponding verbs at MOVE): variation, modification, alteration (see under CHANGE, *v.*).

Con. Stabilizing *or* stability, steadying *or* steadiness, poising *or* poise (see corresponding verbs at STABILIZE): fluctuation, wavering, swinging *or* swing (see corresponding verbs at SWING).

2 *Variation, adaptation, modification.

mute, *adj.* *Dumb, speechless, inarticulate.

mutilate. 1 *Maim, cripple, batter, mangle.

Ana. *Injure, damage, hurt, spoil, mar: disfigure, disfeature, *deface.

2 *Sterilize, asexualize, castrate, spay, emasculate, geld, caponize.

mutinous. Rebellious, seditious, *insubordinate, factious, contumacious.

Ana. Recalcitrant, refractory, intractable, *unruly, ungovernable: disaffected, alienated (see ESTRANGE).

mutiny. *Rebellion, revolution, uprising, revolt, insurrection, Putsch.

Ana. *Sedition, treason: traitorousness, treacherousness, perfidiousness *or* perfidy, faithlessness (see corresponding adjectives at FAITHLESS).

mutual. *Reciprocal, common.
Ana. Shared, participated, partaken (see SHARE): joined *or* joint, united, connected, related, associated (see corresponding verbs at JOIN).

mysterious. **Mysterious, inscrutable, arcane** agree in meaning beyond one's power to discover, understand, or explain. That is **mysterious** which excites wonder, curiosity, or surmise, yet baffles all attempts to explain it. "Extremes in Nature equal ends produce, In Man they join to some *mysterious* use" (*Pope*). "God moves in a *mysterious* way His wonders to perform" (*Cowper*). "The one thing that can make modern life *mysterious* or marvellous to us" (*Wilde*). That is **inscrutable** which defies all one's efforts to examine or investigate it and leaves one with a sense of hopelessness or defeat. " 'Great God, thy judgments are *inscrutable!*' " (*Browning*). "The plaything of an *inscrutable* power, called Fortune" (*Bradley*). The word is often applied to a person whose intentions, motives, mental processes, and the like, are so well concealed that he excites awe or repels advances. "Many fathers feel that, if they are to maintain their authority, they must be a little distant and *inscrutable*" (*A. C. Benson*). "She still held him at a distance by something *inscrutably* aloof in her look and attitude" (*E. Wharton*). In loose use, the word often means little more than *baffling;* as, an *inscrutable* smile. That is **arcane** which is beyond comprehension because known or knowable only to the possessor of the secret (sometimes by implication God, Nature, the Fates, the authorities). The word often comes close to *occult* in meaning, but it stresses the reservation of that which is necessary for comprehension rather than the supranatural or magical character of that which is not understood; thus, one finds many of the poems of Blake *arcane* rather than *occult;* for some *arcane* (not *occult*) reason, grafters are seldom punished.
Ana. Occult, esoteric, *recondite, abstruse: cryptic, enigmatic, ambiguous, equivocal, *obscure: *mystical, mystic, anagogical, cabalistic.

mystery. **Mystery, problem, enigma, riddle, puzzle, conundrum** come into comparison when they denote anything which baffles or perplexes and challenges one's power to solve it. **Mystery** often, especially in theological use, implies the thing's incapacity for comprehension by the human reason. The term is applied specifically to any one of the doctrines of Christianity (such as those of the Trinity and of the Incarnation of Jesus) which have this character, but it is also applicable to any of the facts of the world about us which defy all attempts to explain their cause or nature; as, "this *mystery* of growth and life" (*Jefferies*). "We must be humble, for we are compassed by *mysteries*, and our spiritual faculties are poor and dull" (*Inge*). The term is also used more loosely denoting something which is guarded by secrecy or which is in itself or by design mystifying; as, he always makes a *mystery* of his intentions; the story deals with the *mystery* of a ship that has disappeared; it's a *mystery* to me how he can keep going. **Problem** applies not only to any perplexing question that demands a solution (as, a geometrical *problem*) but also to any person, situation, or the like, that causes perplexity or puts one in a predicament (as, that child is a *problem* to his parents and teachers). "The *problem*...how to find healthy, happy leisure for all the working millions who are now being liberated by machines" (*L. P. Smith*). "The architect [of Coutances Cathedral] has grappled with more *problems* than one need hope to see solved in any single church" (*H. Adams*). **Enigma** (etymologically, a dark saying) applies to that which hides its meaning under obscure or ambiguous allusions so that one can only guess what it signifies; as, a metaphor should not be farfetched, for then it becomes an *enigma;* the ancient oracles usually spoke in *enigmas*. Figuratively, the term applies to that which is inscrutable or beyond the range of unaided understanding; as, "He [Leonardo da Vinci] was an *enigma* to which they [his contemporaries] never secured the key" (*H. Ellis*). **Riddle** applies to any enigma involving paradoxical or contradictory statements, and definitely proposed to be guessed; as, to make up *riddles* for the amusement of her guests; a book of *riddles;* the *riddle* of the Sphinx. Figuratively, the term applies to any problem which is difficult because of its inner contradictions; as, "he tried to read the *riddle* of this girl's future" (*Galsworthy*). "The *riddle* of Actium is not in the details of the fighting but in the minds of the combatants" (*Buchan*). **Puzzle** applies to any problem or enigma which tests one's ingenuity or skill in solution, or which is peculiarly baffling; as, a jigsaw *puzzle;* a crossword *puzzle;* "hoary old *puzzles* of Ethics and Philosophy" (*L. P. Smith*). "There are few things in the world so difficult to explain as real change; it appears to me that most scientists are far from realising the complexity of this metaphysical *puzzle*" (*Inge*). **Conundrum** specifically applies to any riddle phrased as a question the answer to which involves a pun or an equivocal use of words; as, he rightly suspected that the question was a *conundrum;* "I'll make a *conundrum*" (*Austen*). The term is used figuratively in reference to unsolved or unsolvable problems which provoke speculation rather than serious attempts at solution. "Do you think life is long enough to let me speculate on *conundrums* like that?" (*W. Black*).

mystic, *adj.* *Mystical, anagogical, cabalistic.
Ana. Occult, esoteric, *recondite, abstruse: *mysterious, inscrutable: visionary, quixotic, *imaginary.

mystic, *n.* *Ascetic.

mystical. **Mystical, mystic, anagogical** (*or* **anagogic**), **cabalistic** (*or* **cabalistical**) come into comparison when they denote having a meaning or character hidden from all except those who enjoy profound spiritual insight or are spiritually initiated. *Mystical* and *mystic*, though derived from the same root, are often distinguished in use. In general, **mystical** suggests comprehension of something beyond the range of the perceptive or ratiocinative powers; its use therefore often, but not invariably, implies belief in the possibility of such comprehension. Hence, the word variously connotes penetration into sacred mysteries, holiness of life, idealism, detachment from material concerns, ecstatic contemplation, or spiritual rapture; as, the *mystical* experiences of St. Paul; the *mystical* philosophy of Plotinus; *mystical* religions such as Buddhism; the *mystical* poetry of William Blake. "There is something *mystical* in this doctrine, this faith, as of Keats, that 'what the Imagination seizes as Beauty must be Truth' " (*L. P. Smith*). **Mystic,** on the other hand, is often preferred by writers who wish to avoid these implications or to suggest others more in keeping with a rationalistic or skeptical point of view. Therefore *mystic* often imputes to the thing it describes: (1) an occult, esoteric, or visionary character; as, *mystic* ceremonies; the *mystic* symbolism of Blake's poetry; (2) a mysterious, enigmatic, or sometimes nebulous quality; as, "words of *mystic* import" (*Shelley*); "His [Guérin's] expression has ..., more than Keats's, something *mystic*, inward, and profound" (*Arnold*); (3) a connection with magic or the arts of magic; as, *mystic* numbers; "each silver Vase in *mystic* order laid" (*Pope*). Oftentimes its original denotation is completely obscured and it means merely unintelligible, unfathomable, or incomprehensible; as, "the *mystic* gulf from God to man" (*Emerson*). The last two words are used chiefly in reference to allegoristic interpretation of the Scriptures as practiced in the past. **Anagogical** was applied by medieval allegorizers to the deepest underlying sense they found in the Bible (usually, in their computation, the third below the obvious, or literal, meaning), one hidden as a rule from all but men of profound spiritual insight or those taught by such men. "Jerusalem is literally a city of Palestine, allegorically the Church, morally the believing soul, *anagogically* the heavenly Jerusalem" (*Schaff-Herzog*). The word has been used also in reference to a deeply hidden sense apparent only to the mystical-minded in other writings than the Bible, notably the Divine Comedy of Dante. The anagogical sense is sometimes called the *mystical* sense. **Cabalistic,** in its primary meaning, was applied to a secret interpretation of Scriptures (*Cabala*) held to have been revealed to Moses and handed down orally through a line of chosen Jewish rabbis. The system was later committed to writing and was used by medieval magicians, sorcerers, and the like. In loose use it sometimes comes close to *mystic* in its connotations, but commonly it is closer to *occult*.

Ana. Profound, *deep, abysmal: *ultimate, absolute, categorical: spiritual, divine, sacred, *holy: *supernatural, supranatural, miraculous.

mysticism. Asceticism (see under ASCETIC, *n.*).

mystify. Bewilder, perplex, *puzzle, distract, nonplus, confound, dumfound.

Ana. Discomfit, faze, rattle, *embarrass: *discompose, disquiet, perturb, disturb, agitate, upset.

Ant. Enlighten.

myth. 1 Myth, legend, saga come into comparison as meaning a story which has come down from the past, which ostensibly relates a historical event or events, but whose origin has been forgotten or is not clearly traceable. **Myth** (see also ALLEGORY, 2) is often the general designation for this type of story, but in technical use the term specifically implies as a basis for the story an attempt to explain some practice, some belief, some natural phenomenon, some institution, some extraordinary event, or the like. "Whoever that discoverer [of the magnetic power of amber] may have been, someone ought to make a *myth* about him and call him the brother of Prometheus" (*Karl K. Darrow*). Both in technical and general use, *myth* is commonly applied to stories which tell how some god, or divinity, or hero with divine attributes, imparted the arts of life to man (as, the Prometheus *myth;* the Vulcan *myths*) or of how the gods or certain natural phenomena originated (as, the sun-god *myths;* the Jupiter or Zeus *myths*): in this sense, *myth* has a connection with practically all heathen and pagan religious beliefs and rites. The term is sometimes controversially applied to similar stories, especially those of Scriptural origin involving miracles, but, since the word definitely implies lack of factual basis and is often employed still more generally in the sense of an untrue story (as, the story of George Washington and the cherry tree is now regarded as a *myth*), such application is avoided except by those who wish to stress this imputation. **Legend** (etymologically, something to be read) was originally applied to a saint's life or to a collection of such lives of the kind written or compiled in the Middle Ages for the edification of the people. Since these tales put into form without regard for their authenticity all the stories circulated about the saint and his miracles, the term *legend* came to be applied to any story, especially one of a fabulous nature circulated by word of mouth, which is attached to a saint, a hero, a place, a deed, or the like, which purports to be historical, but which, although it has or may seem to have a basis in history, is either incredible or unverifiable; as, the *legend* that King Alfred was the founder of Oxford University; the *legend* of the angels who appeared to the British troops at the battle of Mons; "there was no record or *legend* of any prisoner with those initials" (*Dickens*); "even after he was ailing he performed a feat which became one of the *legends* of the countryside,—killed a robber in a midnight scuffle" (*Cather*). **Saga,** in strict use, applies to a story of a Norse hero or heroes, especially such a story as was written in the Middle Ages (typically in the Icelandic language), and dealt with historical as well as legendary incidents: this written saga was typically in prose and highly conventional in form; as, the Njals' *Saga;* the Volsunga *Saga*. In extended use, *saga* is often employed in place of *myth* or *legend*, especially, but far from exclusively, when their reference to a hero or heroes of northern Europe is implied. In such use, *myth* commonly connotes a connection with ancient Greece, Rome, Egypt, and the like, though it may be used in reference to the American Indians and other aboriginal races: *legend* often suggests a connection with the Middle Ages under Christian domination, and *saga* usually implies a connection with the Scandinavians or Teutons of the Middle Ages who were not yet fully Christianized; as, "When she was about fourteen Joan's imagination passed out of the phase of *myth* and *saga* into the world of romance. The real world drew closer to her" (*H. G. Wells*). But *saga* is often even more loosely used to denote any literary treatment of the exploits (often superhuman exploits) of a hero or group of heroes (as, "had it fallen to Homer to attempt the impossible *saga* of Nelson's pursuit after Villeneuve he would have achieved it triumphantly"—*Quiller-Couch*) or, in present-day use, any novel or series of novels which is a chronicle of persons of a family through several generations (as, Galsworthy's "The Forsyte *Saga*") or of the persons who comprise a community, a class, or the like (as, "With this last visit terminates my *saga* of Gripsholm"—*H. Marryat*).

Ana. *Fiction, fable, fabrication, figment: invention, creation (see corresponding verbs at INVENT).

2 *Allegory, parable, fable, apologue.

mythical. *Fictitious, fabulous, legendary, apocryphal.

Ana. *Imaginary, visionary, fanciful, fantastic: invented, created (see INVENT): *traditional, legendary.

N

nab. *Catch, capture, cop, trap, snare, entrap, ensnare, bag.

Ana. *Take, seize, grasp, clutch, grab, snatch: apprehend, *arrest, detain.

naïve *or* **naive.** Unsophisticated, artless, ingenuous, *natural, simple.

Ana. *Sincere, unfeigned: *spontaneous, impulsive, instinctive: fresh, original (see NEW).

naked. *Bare, nude, bald, barren.

Ana. Revealed, disclosed, discovered (see REVEAL): *evident, manifest, palpable, obvious: uncolored, *colorless: *pure, simple, sheer.

name, *n.* **Name, designation, denomination, appellation, title, style** agree in meaning the word or phrase by which anything is called and by means of which it can be distinguished or identified. **Name** is so general that it can be used of any such word or phrase whether it distinguishes a person or an object, an individual or a class, a particular or a universal, a thing having distinct existence in fact or a thing having distinct existence only in thought; thus, all nouns are *names;* love is the *name* of an emotion; the child's *name* is John Joseph Brown; the *name* of this synagogue is Beth-El. Sometimes *name* is thought of as something apart from the real character of the thing to which it is attached. "What's in a *name?* that which we call a rose By any other *name* would smell as sweet" (*Shak.*). "For sixty years he had been a *name*, not a figure [in the town of Bursley]" (*Bennett*). More often, however, the term connotes identification of the word with the thing or, especially, the person, it names, so that what affects one affects the other. "[Oxford] home of lost causes, and forsaken beliefs, and unpopular *names*, and impossible loyalties!" (*Arnold*). "If I discovered the worst, and it had to be exposed, I must see that Jane's *name* was kept entirely out of it" (*R. Macaulay*). This common feeling of a mutual and almost inevitable relation between the name and the thing named is what distinguishes *name* from *designation, denomination, appellation*, all of which are thought of as given and therefore as having an artificial association with the thing and a utilitarian purpose such as description or identification. A **designation** is a name given primarily for the sake of distinguishing one thing (an individual or a class) from other things of the same general description; as, the French revolutionists changed the traditional *designations* of days and months; as yet no suitable *designation* has been found for this variety of dahlia; Madame Curie chose "polonium" as the *designation* of the newly discovered radioelement in honor of her native Poland. **Denomination** (see also RELIGION) is the name given to a class, to a category, or to a closely knit group of persons; however, the idea of a class name is so deeply rooted in the word that it, in extended use, often means the kind, or species, or group distinguished by a particular name; as, most of George Eliot's works come under the *denomination* of *novel;* a roll of bills containing notes of every *denomination* or no two notes of the same *denomination;* Protestants of all *denominations* attended the religious service. **Appellation** differs from *designation* and *denomination* in precluding the idea (not necessarily the fact) of self-choice; thus, the *designation*, or name formally given to a thing, may be quite different from its *appellation*, or a name by which it is called; as, "Jesuit" is the common *appellation* of a member of the Society of Jesus; in school histories, George Washington is frequently referred to by the *appellation* "Father of his Country." "The government of the United States has been emphatically termed a government of laws, and not of men. It will certainly cease to deserve this high *appellation*, if the laws furnish no remedy for the violation of a vested right" (*Ch. Just. Marshall*). A **title** is either a distinctive name given to a book, a picture, a play, a musical composition, or an honorary appellation coming to a person by virtue of his rank, office, dignity, descent, or the like, or given to him as a mark of respect; as, many modern books have for their *titles* a phrase from one of the poets, such as "If Winter Comes," and "Such Sweet Compulsion." "The head of the state must have a *title*" (*Buchan*). When used without reference to a particular work of art or person, *title* is sometimes preferred to *denomination* because it connotes distinction and dignity. "Any admixture of logical, of 'prose' meaning detracts from the value of a poem, if it does not disqualify it for the *title* of poetry altogether" (*Day Lewis*). When used abstractly in preference to *name* or *designation*, it often connotes the lack of an essential relation between the name and the thing it names. "Things change their *titles*, as our manners turn" (*Pope*). **Style,** which is now not used as commonly as formerly, is applicable chiefly to legal and formal titles, such as the legal name of a firm or corporation, or the complete, formal designation of a royal or other exalted personage as used in documents or in ceremonial address; as, a business incorporated under the *style* of the Globe Manufacturing Co. "Thrones and Imperial Powers, Offspring of Heaven, Ethereal virtues! or these *titles* now Must we [the fallen angels] renounce, and, changing *style*, be called Princes of Hell?" (*Milton*).

name, *v.* *Designate, nominate, elect, appoint.

Ana. *Choose, select, prefer, elect, opt: *declare, announce, publish, advertise.

narcotic. *Anodyne, opiate, nepenthe.

narrate. *Relate, rehearse, recite, recount, describe, state, report.

Ana. Tell, *reveal, disclose, discover: *discourse, expatiate, dilate, descant.

narrative. *Story, tale, anecdote, yarn.

Ana. Chronicle, *account, report, story, version: *fiction, fabrication, figment, fable.

narrow, *adj.* **Narrow, strait** agree in meaning neither broad nor wide, or having little breadth or width for a thing of its kind. **Narrow** is the ordinary term referable not only to that which in measurements is neither broad nor wide (as, a *narrow* corridor; a *narrow* stairway; a *narrow* box; a *narrow* entrance; a *narrow* stream) but to that which is cramped, restricted, or circumscribed in any way (as, "a poor philosopher who holds a view so *narrow* as to exclude forms not to his personal taste"—*Galsworthy;* "if he becomes isolated and self-absorbed, his work becomes *narrow* and mannerised"—*A. C. Benson;* "Many who though in *narrow* circumstances can hardly be called poor"—*Lecky;* "We are left with a *narrow* choice"—*T. S. Eliot*) or to that which (often, a person who) is provincial, sectional, highly partisan, bigoted, or the like (as, *narrow* opinions; a *narrow* mind; "Mr. Broadbent's robust if *narrow* understanding"—*Arch. Marshall;* "to be neither *narrow* nor puritanical"—*Galsworthy*). **Strait,** which is often confused with *straight*, is now chiefly archaic, dialectal, or literary in its historically correct senses. In its earlier and more consistently exact meanings, as well as in present precise

use, the term carries a stronger implication of tightness or closeness than *narrow* and therefore often suggests limits that are only wide enough to admit entrance, passage, or exit by or as if by squeezing through, or that cramp one unmercifully; as, "wide is the gate, and broad is the way, that leadeth to destruction...*Strait* is the gate, and *narrow* is the way, which leadeth unto life, and few there be that find it" (*Matthew* vii. 13–14); "The place where we dwell with thee is too *strait* for us" (*2 Kings* vi. 1); "To me the *straiter* prison, To me the heavier chain" (*Kipling*). In its extended senses, *strait* carries a far stronger implication than *narrow* of a strictness, a rigorousness, or a stringency that imposes severe, often galling or distressing, restraints; as, "after the most *straitest* sect of our religion I lived a Pharisee" (*Acts* xxvi. 5); "takes on him to reform ...some *strait* decrees That lie too heavy on the commonwealth" (*Shak.*); "To make your *strait* circumstances yet *straiter*" (*T. Secker*).
Ana. Limited, restricted, confined (see LIMIT, *v.*): *rigid, rigorous, strict, stringent.
Ant. Broad.

narrows. *Strait, straits, sound, channel, passage.

narthex. Vestibule, foyer, *entry, entryway, hall, lobby, anteroom, antechamber.

nasty. *Dirty, filthy, squalid, foul.
Ana. *Coarse, gross, vulgar, obscene, ribald: tainted, contaminated, polluted, defiled (see CONTAMINATE): indelicate, indecent, unseemly, improper, *indecorous.

nation. *Race, people.

national, *n.* *Citizen, subject.

native, *adj.* **Native, indigenous, endemic, aboriginal, autochthonous** (*or* **autochthonal, autochthonic**). A person or thing is **native** (opposed to *foreign, alien*), or is a **native,** that has had his or its birth or origin in the place or country in question; as, a *native* American; a *native* New Yorker; a *native* tradition. A person or thing is **indigenous** (opposed to *naturalized, exotic*), or is an **indigene,** that is not only native but also has not been introduced into the country, region, or continent indicated; as, Negroes are *indigenous* to (or *indigenes* of) Africa; maize is *indigenous* to North America; the adobe houses of the Aztecs are of *indigenous* American architecture. *Indigenous* is applied usually to species or races rather than to individuals, and often implies reference to a larger area than *native*, as to a country or region characterized by a particular type of climate. A thing is **endemic** (opposed to *exotic*, and, in medicine, to *pandemic*), or is an **endemic,** which not only is indigenous but is also peculiar to (or in the case of a disease, prevalent in) a restricted region because of special conditions favoring its growth or existence; as, the herb edelweiss is *endemic* in the Alps; beriberi is an *endemic* disease in the Orient. A person or thing is **aboriginal,** or is an **aborigine,** that belongs to the earliest known race inhabiting a country, or to the people found there as by colonists and invaders: it usually implies the lack of a predecessor and often connotes a primitive culture; as, Indians are the *aboriginal* Americans; the *aboriginal* Australians (or Australian *aborigines*) are called "blackfellows." *Aboriginal* is more rarely applied to the earliest ascertainable native plants and animals. That is **autochthonous,** or is an **autochthon,** which has its origin in the place in which it is found; as, *autochthonous* rocks. When applied to races of men or their achievements, it implies purity of stock or freedom from all external influences. "As long as the States continue to...be dominated by the poetry of the Old World, and remain unsupplied with *autochthonous* song...so long will they stop short of first-class Nationality" (*Whitman*).
Ant. Alien, foreign.

native, *n.* Indigene, endemic, aborigine, autochthon. See under NATIVE, *adj.*
Ant. Alien, foreigner.

natty. Spruce, dashing, nifty, nobby, dapper, chic, *stylish, fashionable, modish, smart, posh, toffish, brave, braw.

natural, *adj.* **1** *Regular, normal, typical.
Ana. Ordinary, *common, familiar: *usual, customary, habitual, accustomed, wonted.
Ant. Unnatural: artificial: adventitious.
2 Natural, simple, ingenuous, naïve (*or* **naive**), **unsophisticated, artless, unaffected** are synonyms when they are applied to persons, their acts, and their utterances, in the sense of free from pretension or calculation of any sort. **Natural** implies, on the one hand, freedom from every sign of artificiality, effort, constraint, or affectation, and, on the other hand, an ease, a spontaneousness, or a flexibility that suggests nature rather than art: the term often implies opposition to that which is labored, stiff, formal, or the like; as, "set him [a Frenchman] to write poetry, he is limited, artificial, and impotent; set him to write prose, he is free, *natural*, and effective" (*Arnold*); "it is of the essence of such talk that it should be *natural* and attractive, not professional or didactic" (*A. C. Benson*); "She was so friendly and so *natural* that it was nice to talk to her about what was interesting him" (*Arch. Marshall*). **Simple** stresses complete freedom from everything that savors of unconscious as well as conscious duplicity. It usually implies lack of confusion of aims, desires, interests, or the like, and therefore may carry one or the other of connotations as divergent as mental immaturity and intellectual ripeness, as the lack of experience characteristic of the child and the fullness of wisdom characteristic of the sage, as the transparency of those who do not know how to conceal their nature or motives and that of those who have nothing to conceal. "Nothing is more *simple* than greatness; indeed, to be *simple* is to be great" (*Emerson*). "Gard talked....about Marvin and their work together; how *simple* and thorough and understandable the young architect had turned out to be" (*M. Austin*). "She was so *simple* and trustful that I always thought it would be as wicked to hurt her as to hurt a babe in swaddling clothes" (*M. Webb*). **Ingenuous** stresses inability to disguise or to conceal one's thoughts or feelings: it commonly implies frankness or candor, lack of reserve or freedom from dissimulation, often with a hint of childlike simplicity. "'I know myself too weak, Unworthy! Choose a worthier stronger man!'...'Incapable? Qualmish of conscience? Thou *ingenuous* boy'" (*Browning*). "Father had set a dog on him. A less *ingenuous* character would be silent about such passages...but that is not his quality" (*H. G. Wells*). "In some of these letters of [Matthew] Arnold's I seemed to feel glowing—not indeed that *ingenuous* gusto of Dickens [expressing his delight in the financial success of his lectures], but something distantly akin to it" (*C. E. Montague*). **Naïve** implies freedom from all that is artificial, conventional, or acquired; in earliest English use and still often, especially in its derivative noun *naïveté*, it suggests freshness, spontaneity, and genuine expression of a nature untouched by worldly influences and without affectation or artifices; as, by contrast with the poetry of Vergil, that of Homer seems strikingly *naïve;* a delightfully *naïve* personality. In current English it is often a term of derogation. Sometimes, especially in colloquial use, it implies lack of worldly wisdom. "Sophia, the *naïve* ninny, had actually supposed that her walking along a hundred yards of pavement with a god by her side was not going to excite remark!" (*Bennett*). "One does not ask favors,

if it can be avoided, of persons one genuinely respects; one puts such burdens upon the *naïve* and colorless, upon what are called the good-natured" (*Mencken*). Equally often, but chiefly in learned use, it suggests the point of view of the untutored or unenlightened person or of one whose judgments are not corrected by advanced scientific or philosophical knowledge and who therefore supposes that things are what they seem to be. "The *naive* science of an earlier day merely took it for granted that space and time existed in their own right" (*Jeans*). "That *naive* patriotism which leads every race to regard itself as evidently superior to every other" (*J. W. Krutch*). **Unsophisticated** also stresses lack of wisdom, especially worldly wisdom. It does not, however, emphasize native simplicity as strongly as *naïve;* rather, it suggests lack of the experience or training necessary for worldly success or, more specifically, for graceful and adroit social relations. "She's not the type of the moment, not elegant or artificial, too much the *unsophisticated* child of nature" (*R. Macaulay*). **Artless** lays the stress on the absence of design; it suggests naturalness that is the result of indifference to, or unawareness of, the effect or impression one is producing. "Overflowing with... *artless* maternal gratitude" (*Austen*). "Almost every turn in the *artless* little maid's prattle touched a new mood in him" (*Meredith*). "He hated to seem heavy or profound or anything but *artless* and spontaneous to Cecily" (*H. G. Wells*). **Unaffected** centers the attention on the absence of affectation, but in current use it commonly implies both naturalness and simplicity without any hint of childishness, unworldliness, guilelessness, or the like; as, a well-bred, *unaffected* girl. "Very few English people have the art of conversing *unaffectedly* and sincerely before a circle" (*A. C. Benson*).

Ana. *Spontaneous, impulsive, instinctive: ingrained, constitutional, *inherent.

Con. Formal, conventional, ceremonious, *ceremonial: pretentious, ostentatious, pompous, *showy: affected, assumed, counterfeited, feigned (see ASSUME).

natural, *n.* *Fool, idiot, imbecile, moron, simpleton.

nature. *Type, kind, sort, description, character, stripe, kidney, ilk.

Ana. *Structure, anatomy, framework: *disposition, temperament, character, personality: *form, figure, shape, conformation.

naught. *Cipher, zero, nought, aught, ought.

naughty. *Bad, evil, ill, wicked.

Ana. Mischievous, wanton, roguish, impish, waggish (see PLAYFUL): froward, balky, restive, wayward, *contrary, perverse.

nautical. *Marine, maritime, naval.

naval. Nautical, *marine, maritime.

navvy. *Worker, workman, workingman, laborer, craftsman, handicraftsman, mechanic, artisan, hand, operative, roustabout.

near, *adj. & adv.* *Close, nigh, near by.

Ant. Far.

near, *v.* *Approach, approximate.

Ana. Rival, *match, touch, equal.

Con. Vary, *change, alter, modify: differ from, *differ with.

near by. Also **near-by,** *adj. & adv.* *Close, near, nigh.

Ant. Far off.

nearest. **Nearest, next** are both superlative forms of *near,* but they are not always interchangeable. **Nearest** may be used wherever the intent is merely to indicate the highest degree of propinquity in space, time, kinship, or the like; as, the *nearest* house is five miles distant; their *nearest* neighbor lives two miles away; her *nearest* relatives are her father and mother (or her fifth cousins). **Next,** in earlier usage, was often employed in this sense, but in current use, it commonly implies immediate succession (sometimes, but not so often, precedence) in an order, a series, or a sequence; thus, the *next* house is the house just beyond the one in mind in a row or series of houses; their *next* child is the one who comes after the child under consideration in order of birth; the *next* (never *nearest*) best is the second best in a rating or choice; so, the *next* chapter of the story; the *next* day; the *next* time they met; ask the *next* person we meet. But in law one's *nearest* relative or relatives is (or are) one's "*next* of kin"; one's "*next* friend" is the person who has the right, as one's nearest relative or natural guardian, to act without authorization of a court for an infant, a married woman, or any other person who by the law of the state has not full legal capacity to sue or make other legal moves. In ordinary language, "*nearest* of kin" is found as often as "*next* of kin," but "*nearest* friend" applies only to one's most intimate friend.

nearly. **Nearly, almost, approximately, well-nigh** come into comparison when they mean within a little of being, becoming, reaching, or the like. Their differences in meaning are often imperceptible. However, **nearly** is preferable when mere proximity is implied; as, they are *nearly* at the end of their journey; it is *nearly* six o'clock; she was *nearly* hysterical with fright: **almost** is more explicit when the emphasis is on a falling short or a deficiency; as, they had *almost* finished when they were interrupted; she is *almost* out of her mind with grief; the news is *almost* too good to be true: **approximately** is the proper choice when the difference is of no practical importance and a reasonable approach to accuracy is implied; as, there were *approximately* 10,000 present; government meteorologists make *approximately* correct forecasts: **well-nigh** often equals *virtually;* as, they were *well-nigh* lost in the forest; he is *well-nigh* mad.

neat. **Neat, tidy, trim, trig, snug, shipshape, spick-and-span** come into comparison as meaning manifesting care and orderliness. **Neat** (etymologically, shining) through all its variations in senses keeps as its basic implication clearness, such as the clearness from dirt or soil that is manifest chiefly in perfect cleanliness (as, her house is as *neat* as a pin; the cat is perhaps the *neatest* of domestic animals; "He was remarkably *neat* in his dress"—*Johnson*), or the clearness that is indicated in simplicity and freedom from that which clutters, complicates, confuses, or the like, or that indicates orderliness, deftness, or adroitness (as, *neat* workmanship; a *neat* style; "the *neat* craftsman"—*C. E. Montague;* a *neatly* performed operation; *neat* arrangement of arguments; a *neat* retort; *neat* architectural design), or the clearness that means lack of adulteration, dilution, or the like; as, to take his whisky *neat; neat* silk. **Tidy** (etymologically, timely) was in earliest English use often applied to cattle, flocks, crops, and the like, in thriving and satisfactory condition: this sense now occurs mainly in extended applications to things which indicate a more or less flourishing condition; as, a *tidy* farm; he has a *tidy* fortune; he has made a *tidy* success of his venture. *Tidy,* as first applied to a person or his work, seems to have meant little more than satisfactorily pleasing in appearance or quality: in some use it was approximate to *buxom* or *comely* in meaning, but it seems to have been applied chiefly to peasants and especially to servants. Hence, "*tidy* servant" at first meant a satisfactory servant from the points of view of diligence and neatness, but later came to mean one whose diligence showed itself in orderly habits and neat appearance; as, "If thou knowest of any *tidy* lass like thyself, that wanted a place, and could bring a good character" (*Scott*). In current use *tidy*, as distinguished from *neat*, throws the stress on orderliness, careful arrangement, or a place for everything, rather than on cleanliness or simplicity; as, she keeps her house *tidy;* a *tidy* desk; a *tidy* sewing basket; "He objected to cut and trim them [shrubs]. 'For,' said he, 'God made nothing *tidy*'" (*Jefferies*); "When she [an ailing wife] got downstairs, she would find the house *tidy*, but dirty" (*D. H. Lawrence*). **Trim** in current use implies both neatness and tidiness: it stresses, however, smartness or spruceness in appearance such as is given by clean lines, excellent proportions, and the like; as, a *trim* clipper ship; a *trim* figure; "The sward was *trim* as any garden lawn" (*Tennyson*); "His shoes and buckles, too, though plain, were *trim*" (*Dickens*); "a criss-cross of *trim*...paths" (*Lowes*). **Trig** in its older use is not always distinguishable from *trim*, but in its chief current sense it carries a stronger implication of compactness, of neatness, and of jauntiness of appearance, and is more often applicable to persons or their clothes; as, she has a *trig* new tailored suit; a *trig* West Pointer in his new uniform. **Snug**, as here compared, was in earliest use applied to ships, first to those of trim lines, and then to those where everything is in order and properly prepared to weather a gale; as, "The stern is...plain, and *snug*, without much carving" (*Naval Chronicle*); "Soon all was *snug* aloft, and we were again allowed to go below" (*R. H. Dana, Jr.*). In the eighteenth century *snug* was often applied to persons or things that were markedly trim or spruce (as, "He kames his hair, indeed, and gaes right *snug*"—*A. Ramsay*), but this sense now occurs only in dialectal use. In current use it still often implies neatness or tidiness, but it stresses coziness or comfortableness (see *snug* under COMFORTABLE). **Shipshape** is now often used in place of *snug* to describe not only ships where tidiness and trimness prevail but anything which depends for its success or well-being upon habits of tidiness and orderliness; as, his affairs are in *shipshape* condition; "Look to the babes, and till I come again Keep everything *shipshape*" (*Tennyson*). **Spick-and-span,** which stresses the brightness and freshness of that which is new, is applicable also to that which by care and cleanliness has been kept new in appearance or made to look like new; as, *spick-and-span* white shoes; her mother keeps her *spick-and-span* every moment of the day; the kitchen was *spick-and-span; spick-and-span* machinery.

Ana. *Clean, cleanly: fastidious, *nice, dainty, finical: exact, precise, *correct, accurate.

Ant. Filthy. — *Con.* Unkempt, slovenly, *slipshod, sloppy: slack, lax, remiss, *negligent: confused, muddled, bemuddled, addled (see CONFUSE).

neb. Variant of NIB.

necessary. 1 *Needful, requisite, indispensable, essential.

Ana. Compelling *or* compulsory, obliging *or* obligatory, constraining (see corresponding verbs at FORCE): important, significant, momentous (see corresponding nouns at IMPORTANCE): cardinal, vital, *essential, fundamental.

2 *Certain, inevitable, apodictic.

Ana. Unavoidable, inescapable, ineluctable, *inevitable: *infallible, inerrable, inerrant, unerring.

necessity. *Need, exigency.

Ana. Compelling *or* compulsion, constraining *or* constraint, obliging *or* obligation, coercing *or* coercion (see corresponding verbs at FORCE): indispensableness, requisiteness *or* requisition, needfulness (see corresponding adjectives at NEEDFUL).

nectar. *Ambrosia, manna, amrita.

nectared, nectarean, nectareous. Ambrosial (see under AMBROSIA).

need, *n.* **Need, necessity, exigency** come into comparison when they denote a state or condition requiring something as essential or indispensable, or the requirement itself. **Need** implies pressure and urgency arising either from external or internal causes or forces: it may merely suggest the call of an appetite or demand for emotional or intellectual satisfaction (as, he is in *need* of food; the child suffers because of a *need* for affection; he felt the *need* of an education), or it may imply circumstances, such as great poverty, a severe storm, a threat of war, actual hostilities, or the like, that show a lack of or create a demand for something indispensable to the well-being, protection, security, success, or the like, of those concerned (as, to provide food and lodging for those in *need;* the European war has taught Americans the *need* for a two-ocean navy; "So at the threat ye shall summon—so at the *need* ye shall send Men"—*Kipling*). **Necessity,** though often interchanged with *need,* usually carries a far stronger suggestion of an imperative demand or of a compelling cause; as, telephone me in case of *necessity* (i.e., if in very great *need*); "as soon as war is declared, every nation or institution must subordinate all other considerations to the *necessity* of victory" (*Inge*). "When a legal distinction is determined... between night and day, childhood and maturity...a point has to be fixed or a line has to be drawn...to mark where the change takes place. Looked at by itself without regard to the *necessity* behind it, the line or point seems arbitrary" (*Justice Holmes*). Sometimes, however, in order to enforce this implication, *necessity* is qualified by some such term as *compelling;* as, compelling *necessity* drove him to seek financial aid. *Necessity* may also apply to a compelling principle or abstract force inherent in nature or in the constitution of a thing and inevitable in its operation or inescapable in its results; as, there is no logical *necessity* apparent in the conclusions you have reached; physical *necessity* lies behind our need of food and drink; "One of the unhappy *necessities* of human existence is that we have to 'find things out for ourselves'" (*T. S. Eliot*). **Exigency** (see also JUNCTURE) implies the compulsion of necessity (sometimes, but rarely, of an inherent compelling principle), especially as a result of special circumstances, such as a crisis, an emergency, an accident, that imposes upon one severe restrictions, or great stress and strain: in either case, the term emphasizes, more even than either of the preceding words, extreme urgency, demands of a peremptory and exacting character, and difficulties that cannot be easily overcome; as, they were forced by *exigencies* of space (i.e., by circumstances that required inclusion of certain articles or that restricted the number that could be included) to omit several articles; "the various *exigency* of times and occasions" (*Book of Common Prayer*); "figures which are doing nothing in particular...striking an attitude which is dictated not by the inner *necessities* of balance or motion, but by the *exigencies* of the composition" (*Binyon*); "There are two vivid sonnets of Sir Philip Sidney...which deal with the *exigencies* of the poet's problem" (*Lowes*).

Ana. *Stress, strain, pressure: *lack, want, absence, privation, defect: *poverty, indigence, penury, destitution, privation, want.

need, *v.* *Lack, want, require.

Ana. *Demand, require, claim, exact: *long, hanker, pine, yearn, hunger, thirst: crave, covet, *desire, wish.

needful. Needful, necessary, requisite, indispensable, essential come into comparison as meaning urgently required. **Needful,** in current English, carries the weakest suggestion of urgency, but it applies to that which is required to supply a want or to fill a need; as, "And Jesus answered...Martha, Martha, thou art careful and troubled about many things: But one thing is *needful*" (*Luke* x. 41–42); "forts, magazines, arsenals, dock yards, and other *needful* buildings" (*Ch. Just. Taney*); "tradesmen carrying what was *needful* to British ports" (*A. Repplier*). **Necessary** implies more pressing need or urgent constraint but, except where the compulsion of necessity (in the sense of an inherent compelling principle; as, a *necessary* consequence; a *necessary* conclusion) is suggested, the word does not invariably connote that the thing so qualified cannot be done without; as, "His personal return was most required and *necessary*" (*Shak.*); "always finding a more *necessary* article for which a less *necessary* had to be discarded" (*Cather*); "Of all the bitter and heavy things in this sorry old world, the not being *necessary* is the bitterest and heaviest" (*Deland*); "to classify in a science is *necessary* for the purpose of that science: to classify when you come to art is at best an expedient" (*Quiller-Couch*). **Requisite** differs from *necessary* chiefly in being applied to something that is specifically required by the nature of a thing, the end that is in view, the purpose to be fulfilled, and the like; usually, but not invariably, the adjective suggests an imposed requirement rather than an inner need and so suggests constraint from without or, often, from official sources; as, to complete the subjects *requisite* for college entrance; to gather the *requisite* equipment for a summer in camp; "thinking society to be the one thing *requisite* to the young man, he had introduced him to the people he knew" (*Meredith*); "the vigor *requisite* to success" (*Grandgent*). "Holy Scripture containeth all things *necessary* to salvation: so that whatsoever is not read therein, nor may be proved thereby, is not to be required of any man, that it should be believed as an article of the Faith, or be thought *requisite* or *necessary* to salvation" (*Book of Common Prayer*). **Indispensable** not only carries a stronger implication of urgency than the preceding terms, but it also distinctly implies that the thing so qualified cannot be done without, especially if the implied or expressed end is to be attained; as, there is no such thing as an *indispensable* person, though many persons have made themselves virtually *indispensable;* "acquaintance with it [the scientific method of inquiry] has become an *indispensable* element in culture" (*C. W. Eliot*); "Rigid truthfulness in adults towards children is...absolutely *indispensable* if children are not to learn lying" (*B. Russell*). **Essential** (see also ESSENTIAL, 2; INHERENT) is often used in place of *indispensable* as implying no less urgency but as being less extravagant in its suggestions: it usually also implies inherent necessity from the point of view of what a thing is or must be by its very nature or end; as, knowledge of one's subject is *essential* to successful teaching; *essential* raw materials; "You are *essential* to her perfect happiness" (*Dickens*); "the builders must have begun with the central piers and the choir, because the choir was the only *essential* part of the church" (*H. Adams*); "The construction of the pier was desirable for the more convenient repair of warships, but it was not *essential*" (*Justice Holmes*).

Ana. Wanted, needed, required, lacked (see LACK, *v.*): vital, cardinal, *essential, fundamental.

nefarious. Iniquitous, flagitious, infamous, corrupt, degenerate, *vicious, villainous.

Ana. Heinous, *outrageous, atrocious, monstrous: *flagrant, glaring, gross, rank.

negate. *Nullify, annul, abrogate, invalidate.

Ana. Negative, *neutralize, counteract.

negative, *adj.* *Neutral, indifferent, adiaphorous.

Ant. Affirmative.

negative, *v.* **1** *Deny, gainsay, traverse, contradict, impugn, contravene.

2 *Neutralize, counteract.

Ana. *Nullify, negate, annul, abrogate, invalidate.

neglect, *v.* **Neglect, omit, disregard, ignore, overlook, slight, forget** come into comparison as meaning to pass over something without giving it due or sufficient attention. **Neglect** usually implies intentional or unintentional failure to give full or proper attention, especially to something one is doing (such as a task) or should do (such as a duty) or to someone who has a claim upon one's care or attention; as, to *neglect* one's studies because of undue interest in sports; to *neglect* to pay one's debts; "Pardon me for *neglecting* to profit by your advice" (*Austen*); "He asked Mr. Powell with some brusqueness if the chief mate had *neglected* to instruct him that the captain was to be found on the port side" (*Conrad*); to *neglect* one's family; to *neglect* one's personal appearance; "in March the vicar told his curate that he was...*neglecting* Galton for Oaktown" (*C. Mackenzie*). **Omit** implies a leaving out of something which forms a part of a whole (as, to *omit* two stanzas of a hymn; to *omit* a part of one's lecture) or, as it comes more closely into comparison with the other terms in this article, to neglect entirely through oversight, inattention, or absorption, an important detail, opportunity, aspect, or the like. "Nor could I think well of the man who should *omit* an occasion of testifying his respect towards any body connected with the family" (*Austen*). "Constance remembered small possessions of her own which she had *omitted* to remove from the cutting-out room" (*Bennett*). **Disregard** usually, but not invariably, implies voluntary, sometimes deliberate, inattention: the term may or may not imply justifiable neglect; as, to *disregard* petty annoyances; to *disregard* an unimportant piece of evidence; she persists in *disregarding* the wishes of her mother. "The Great War...a hideous business, in which nearly all the humane alleviations of brutal violence, introduced and practised in the days when professional armies fought for a dynasty or for a point of honour, were *disregarded*" (*Inge*). **Ignore** (etymologically, not to know) usually implies either an intention to disregard or a failure to regard something more or less obvious: it may even suggest a deliberate closing of the eyes to that which one does not wish to recognize; as, "to those who agree with me I am uttering commonplaces and to those who disagree I am *ignoring* the necessary foundations of thought" (*Justice Holmes*); "By tacit agreement they *ignored* the remarks and insinuations of their acquaintances" (*D. H. Lawrence*). "The ancients...tried to identify the fundamental element; one philosopher guessed air, another water, yet another fire; the true one [electricity] lay all about them, but they *ignored* its signals" (*Karl K. Darrow*). **Overlook** implies an omission or disregarding, sometimes through intention (often charitable intention) but more often through haste, lack of care, inadvertence, or the like; as, to *overlook* an item in an account. "It is the practice of good nature to *overlook* the faults which have already, by the consequences, punished the delinquent" (*Johnson*). **Slight** may imply neglect, omission, or disregard, but it also usually implies a contemptuous or an arrogant attitude that makes one undervalue a thing's importance, treat a person disdainfully, or be neglectful in performance of a task or duty. "Alas! what boots it with uncessant care To tend the homely, *slighted*, shepherd's trade [figurative for poet's art]" (*Milton*). "Nothing in the service was *slighted*, every phrase and gesture had its full value"

(*Cather*). "'I have been *slighted*, tricked, threatened, insulted, made ill...but I am justified'" (*H. G. Wells*). **Forget,** as here considered, often retains from its chief current sense the implication of losing the memory of something or someone, so that when it implies neglect, it usually carries a suggestion of willful ignoring or of a failure to impress the thing neglected upon one's mind; as, "I shall not be surprised to be *neglected* and *forgot*" (*Nelson*); "Lord God of Hosts, be with us yet, Lest we *forget*—lest we *forget!*" (*Kipling*). "Still, he told Hannah to get the boy better clothes—though he *forgot* to give her any money for the purpose" (*Deland*).

Ant. Cherish. — ***Con.*** *Appreciate, value, prize, treasure: *nurse, nurture, foster, cultivate.

neglect, *n.* *Negligence.

Ana. Neglecting, omitting or omission, disregarding *or* disregard, ignoring, slighting, forgetting, overlooking (see corresponding verbs at NEGLECT).

neglectful. *Negligent, lax, slack, remiss.

Ana. *Careless, heedless, thoughtless.

Ant. Attentive. — ***Con.*** *Thoughtful, considerate.

negligence. Negligence, neglect are not always clearly distinguished in use, even though in current English the lines between them are being drawn with increasing clearness. **Negligence** stresses the quality or fact of being negligent or careless, either as manifested in a lack of care in the performance of a task, a duty, a piece of work, or in the operation or handling of a dangerous machine or mechanism, which requires effort or close attention (as, the amazing *negligence* of some housekeepers; an act of criminal *negligence;* "no one has done more through *negligence* to corrupt the language"—*Byron;* all these themes indicate *negligence*) or as manifested in a temperamental or assumed indifference to small niceties in dress, manners, style, and the like, that gives an impression of casualness, artlessness, or lack of artificiality (as, to affect *negligence* in dress; "Nothing is so modish as an agreeable *negligence*"—*Addison;* "a princely *negligence*"—*Landor*). **Neglect,** on the other hand, applies either to the act or fact of neglecting or of leaving undone (or, very rarely, imperfectly done) something which it is one's business or duty to do (as, convicted of *neglect* of duty; "We made a nice tidy clean up...If I hadn't done it I ought either to have been shot for *neglect* or dismissed for incapacity"—*H. G. Wells;* "In dealing with the infant...there is need of a delicate balance between *neglect* and indulgence"—*B. Russell*) or to the state or fact of being neglected, slighted, ignored, or forgotten (as, "Rescue my poor remains from vile *neglect*"—*Prior;* "a...motive for reading it...[that] ensured poetry against *neglect*"—*Day Lewis*). For these reasons, the phrase "the *negligence* of a person" always refers to a quality of character of the agent, or to its outward manifestation in an act, a piece of work, an accident, or the like: "the *neglect* of a person" refers to the act of one who neglects, slights, ignores, or forgets another, thereby making that person his victim.

Ana. Laxness, slackness, remissness (see corresponding adjectives at NEGLIGENT): indifference, unconcernedness *or* unconcern, incuriousness (see corresponding adjectives at INDIFFERENT).

Ant. Attention: solicitude. — ***Con.*** *Care, concern, anxiety, worry: diligence, assiduity, sedulousness (see corresponding adjectives at BUSY).

negligent. Negligent, neglectful, lax, slack, remiss are here compared chiefly as applied to persons, their ways of working or acting, and the results of their work or activities, and as meaning culpably careless or manifesting such carelessness. **Negligent** implies inattentiveness to that which is one's duty or business with the result that nothing is done or that one's work shows markedly one's indifference and inattention, as in its imperfection, its slovenliness, its incompleteness, or the like; as, "His family knew him to be...a most *negligent* and dilatory correspondent" (*Austen*); "Byron is so *negligent* in his poetical style...so slovenly, slipshod, and infelicitous...so little haunted by the true artist's fine passion for ...words, that he may be described as having for this artistic gift the insensibility of the barbarian" (*Arnold*). **Neglectful** is usually more derogatory or contemptuous than *negligent*, for it carries a stronger connotation of laziness or deliberate and blameworthy inattention; as, parents *neglectful* of their children's health; "A government at once insatiable and *neglectful*" (*James Mill*); a ship's master *neglectful* of discipline. **Lax** (etymologically, loose; see LOOSE) implies want of necessary strictness, severity, or precision; the term applies chiefly to persons who do not satisfy the rigorous demands made upon them by their work or duties, or to any work or any activity performed or carried on without the close attention, constant care, or strict adherence to law or custom that is necessary; as, a *lax* parent; *lax* discipline; *lax* morals; a *lax* interpretation of a law. "When Delia, who came of the *laxer* Lovells, and was naturally inclined to novelty, had first proposed to her husband to dine at six o'clock instead of two, his malleable young face had become...relentless" (*E. Wharton*). **Slack** (see also LOOSE) stresses the want of proper or necessary diligence and expedition as well as of care; the term usually also implies indolence, or sluggishness, or indifference; as, a *slack* servant; "a *slack* workman" (*G. Eliot*); "We keep our wits *slack*" (*H. G. Wells*). When applied to that which is accomplished by a slack worker, the term usually suggests neglect of important details necessary to the completeness, finish, or perfection of the work; as, "A three-quarters figure of admirable design, though of rather *slack* execution" (*J. C. Stobart*). **Remiss** implies culpable carelessness that shows itself in slackness and forgetfulness or in negligence; it is applied chiefly to that which is lax in performance, maintenance, or the like, but it may be applied to a person who is unduly careless or lax in the performance of his duties; as, *remiss* housekeeping; *remiss* discipline; a *remiss* police officer. "It certainly had been very *remiss* of him, as Mayor...to call no meeting ere this" (*Hardy*).

Ana. *Careless, heedless, thoughtless, inadvertent: *indifferent, unconcerned, incurious: *slipshod, slovenly.

Con. *Rigid, strict, rigorous: *thoughtful, considerate, attentive.

negotiate. 1 Parley, treat, *confer, commune, consult, advise.

2 Negotiate, arrange, concert come into comparison when they mean to bring about or accomplish by mutual agreement, especially after discussion or parley. **Negotiate** and **arrange** both imply prior intercommunication of views and wishes and, sometimes, settlement by bargaining or compromise. *Negotiate* is preferred when the dealings are carried on by diplomatic, business, or legal agencies, and *arrange* when they are carried on by private persons or their representatives; as, to *negotiate* a treaty; to *arrange* a marriage; to *negotiate* the Louisiana Purchase; to *arrange* the settlement of a case out of court; to *arrange* a meeting between estranged persons. **Concert,** which is now found chiefly in its participial form **concerted,** usually, but not invariably, implies an agreement to do something in common; it therefore may or may not suggest conspiracy, intrigue, or the like; as, a *concerted* attack. "The old weakness of barbarians, an incapacity for *concerted* action" (*Buchan*). "We began to *concert* measures for his coming on board with secrecy" (*Defoe*).

neighborhood *or* **neighbourhood.** *Locality, district, vicinage, vicinity.

neighborly *or* **neighbourly.** Friendly, *amicable.
Ana. Peaceful, peaceable, *pacific: *social, hospitable, gregarious, co-operative: cordial, sociable, *gracious.
Ant. Unneighborly: ill-disposed. — *Con.* Antagonistic, *adverse.

neophyte. *Novice, novitiate, probationer, postulant, apprentice.

neoteric. *New, novel, modern, modernistic, newfangled, new-fashioned, original, fresh.

nepenthe. *Anodyne, opiate, narcotic.

neritic. *Aquatic, marine, oceanic, thalassic, pelagic, abyssal, bathysmal, bathybic, lacustrine, lacuscular, fluvial, fluviatile.

nerve. Effrontery, *temerity, audacity, hardihood, cheek, gall.
Ana. Boldness, intrepidity (see corresponding adjectives at BRAVE): *fortitude, grit, pluck, sand, guts: foolhardiness, temerariousness, recklessness (see corresponding adjectives at ADVENTUROUS).

nervous. 1 *Vigorous, lusty, energetic, strenuous.
Ana. Forceful, forcible, potent, *powerful: *spirited, mettlesome: virile, manly (see MALE).
2 Also **nervy.** *Impatient, restless, restive, unquiet, uneasy, fidgety, skittish, feverish, hectic, jumpy, jittery.
Ana. Excited *or* excitable, stimulated, provoked *or* provocative (see corresponding verbs at PROVOKE): *inconstant, unstable, mercurial.
Ant. Steady. — *Con.* Constant, even, equable, uniform (see STEADY).

nescient. *Ignorant, illiterate, unlettered, uneducated, untaught, untutored, unlearned.
Ana. *Indifferent, incurious, aloof, unconcerned.
Con. *Aware, conscious, cognizant.

nettle. Provoke, exasperate, *irritate, aggravate, roil, peeve.
Ana. *Annoy, irk, bother, vex: disturb, perturb, agitate, upset, *discompose: fret, chafe, gall (see ABRADE).

network. *System, scheme, organism, economy, complex.

neurologist. **Neurologist, psychiatrist** (*or* **psychiater**), **alienist, psychopathologist** (*or* **psychopathist**), **psychotherapist, psychoanalyst** agree in denoting a specialist (usually a medically trained specialist) in mental disorders. **Neurologist,** the comprehensive term, is applied to any physician skilled in the diagnosis and treatment of diseases of the nervous system, as epilepsy, locomotor ataxia, and chorea (St. Vitus's dance). Only in loose use is the term ever restricted to a specialist in purely mental diseases. *Psychiatrist, alienist, psychopathologist* are interchangeable terms in scientific use, but they stress different implications. All designate a physician who devotes himself to the diagnosis and treatment of diseases affecting the mind, especially, as distinguished from *neurologist,* of those disorders not demonstrably of physical origin, such as neurasthenia, hysteria, and paranoia. **Psychiatrist,** however, usually suggests skill in treatment and in correction of curable disorders; **alienist,** the preferred term in medical jurisprudence, suggests skill in detection of mental derangements or of insanity; **psychopathologist** (*or* **psychopathist**) suggests the psychologist's approach and skill in discovering causes, such as defects of personality, unfavorable environment, and the like, and in describing the nature of the individual case. A **psychotherapist** is a psychiatrist who employs suggestion, hypnosis, re-education, etc., in the treatment of psychic disorders. A **psychoanalyst** is a psychotherapist who proceeds on the assumption that mental difficulties are the result of disturbances below the level of consciousness, who diagnoses these disorders by a study of the individual's emotional and mental life, especially as manifested in dreams, inhibitions, complexes, and the like, and who treats these disorders by revealing their causes to the patient and suggesting means whereby the disturbances may be eliminated and the mental difficulties overcome.

neutral, *adj.* **Neutral, negative, indifferent, adiaphorous** are here compared as meaning lacking decisiveness or distinctiveness in character, quality, action, or effect. **Neutral,** in what is probably its earliest and is still its most common sense, applies to states, governments, parties, or persons who refuse to take sides with either of two (or any of several) contending parties. The term may or may not imply an attitude of impartiality, but it usually implies either indecision or a refraining from positive action for any one of numerous reasons. "The stepfather [of Octavius] was a moderate Pompeian in sympathies, but his family connections kept him *neutral,* and the household was never drawn into the war" (*Buchan*). "Revolutionary verse....makes the *neutral* reader wonder whether it is aimed to win him for the communist or fascist state" (*Day Lewis*). When otherwise applied, as to colors or terms, to a character or personality, to a substance in chemistry, or to an entity in philosophy, or the like, *neutral* implies a quality, an appearance, or a reaction that belongs to neither of two opposites or extremes: the term, therefore, often connotes vagueness, indefiniteness, indecisiveness, ineffectualness, or the like; thus, a *neutral* character is one that reveals neither positive virtues nor positive vices; a chemically *neutral* substance, such as distilled water, is neither acid nor basic; a *neutral* color, such as taupe, is not clearly or positively any definite color, often because it verges on gray. "The artists of the Far East....use positive tints quite sparingly, giving them for foil large spaces of *neutral* tone" (*Binyon*). "[Crabb Robinson's] honest dullness supplied the *neutral* background that genius needs" (*Times Lit. Sup.*). **Negative** carries a far stronger implication than *neutral* of absence of positive or affirmative (cf. AFFIRMATIVE) characteristics or qualities: the term therefore usually implies inaction, ineffectiveness, or a failure to assume a definite or concrete form; as, "the *negative* propaganda of silence" (*A. Huxley*); "the man who falls in love with one of these *negative* young creatures hardly takes the trouble to ask whether she loves him" (*Deland*); "There is certainly a vague and widespread discontent with our present results [in education]; but it is all a *negative* opinion" (*A. C. Benson*). **Indifferent,** as here compared (see also INDIFFERENT, 1; MEDIUM), implies a character or appearance that does not readily define itself or fall into any clearly marked class or category: the term is applicable to things (rarely to persons) which stir up no feeling or elicit no decision as to whether they are good or bad, in accordance with one's principles or not, necessary or unnecessary, pleasant or unpleasant, or the like; as, though they disliked each other, they could converse at length upon *indifferent* subjects; it is *indifferent* to which race the father or the mother belongs; "Either one attitude is better than the other, or else it is *indifferent*" (*T. S. Eliot*); "At Alexandria Hadrian found a money-loving population worshipping Christ and Sarapis almost *indifferently*" (*Inge*). **Adiaphorous** is chiefly a technical term applicable to rites, ceremonies, practices, and the like, which are regarded as indifferent, or as neither necessary nor unnecessary, but often a matter of purely individual concern; thus, fasting is an obligatory practice in some churches, and an *adiaphorous* practice in others.

Con. Biased, disposed, predisposed (see INCLINE, *v.*): positive, *affirmative: *decided, decisive.

neutralize. Neutralize, counteract, negative come into comparison as meaning to render one thing inoperative or ineffective by means of its opposite force, influence, effect, or the like. **Neutralize** often implies either the reduction of opposites to a state of equality, especially in influence, with the result that neither has the power to make way against the other, or the nullification of the active principle in one thing by its combination with something that annuls its effect; as, drugs that *neutralize* each other's beneficial effects; "our esteem for facts has not *neutralized* in us all religiousness" (*W. James*); "That ...is why we call them [the two electricities] 'positive' and 'negative'—because they are capable of annulling or *neutralizing* one another's actions" (*Karl K. Darrow*). **Counteract** may definitely imply, as *neutralize* does not, that either one of the things concerned, the agency or the thing affected, is an evil or harmful force, influence, or effect. The term may imply merely the counterbalancing of that which is evil or harmful by that which is good or beneficial, or conversely (as, "Unless powerfully *counteracted* by all sorts of opposite agencies, [old age] is a miserable...blighter to the genial charity of the human heart"—*De Quincey;* "Perhaps this [knowledge of drunkenness, quarrels, etc.] does them [slum children] no harm, if it is *counteracted* by other influences"—*B. Russell*), or it may imply the operation or the use of forces that destroy or eradicate the evil or harmful thing or make the beneficial effect of a good thing impossible (as, "the spontaneous physiological processes which *counteract* disease before medical science comes into play"—*H. Ellis;* the effect of his preaching was *counteracted* by the looseness of his behavior). **Negative,** as here compared, stresses a rendering futile, useless, of little or no value, or the like, of one thing by another: it may or may not imply destruction, but it usually suggests a frustration of a purpose or a hindrance to the production of an effect; as, the hurricane *negatived* all the labors of the orange growers; their child's contact with all sorts of children in school *negatived* his early training in correct speech.

Ana. Offset, countervail, counterbalance, counterpoise (see COMPENSATE): defeat, overcome, subdue, *conquer.

never-ending. *Everlasting, endless, interminable, unceasing.

Ana. *Lasting, permanent, durable, perdurable, stable: *immortal, deathless, undying, unfading, fadeless, amaranthine: eternal, sempiternal, *infinite.

nevertheless. Still, however, *but, yet.

new, *adj.* **New, novel, new-fashioned, newfangled, modern, neoteric, modernistic, original, fresh** come into comparison when they mean having very recently come into existence or use, or into a connection, a position, a state of being recognized, or the like. A thing is **new** that has never before the time of its advent been known, thought of, manufactured, experienced, or the like, or that is just ready for use, sale, circulation, or the like; as, *new* books; *new* ideas; a *new* washing machine; "No man putteth *new* wine into old bottles" (*Mark* ii. 22); the *new* baby; a *new* way of dressing the hair. A person is *new* if he has just been taken into a military, business, social, or other connection (as, a *new* soldier; a *new* stenographer; three *new* members; the *new* rich), or if he has received his first experience (as, "he was...frightened, being *new* to the sight"—*Dickens*), or if he has been renewed in spirit or in mind (as, "if any man be in Christ, he is a *new* creature"—*2 Corinthians* v. 17). A thing is **novel** which is not only new but so out of the ordinary course as to strike one as strange, unusual, or unfamiliar; as, "*novel* forms of government, like those of Russia and Italy" (*Frankfurter*); "*novel* schemes of salvation" (*L. P. Smith*); "sermons...bold in thought and *novel* in language" (*E. Wharton*). "The assumption that whatever has been customary must be bad, and that anything which is or seems *novel* must be good" (*Grandgent*). "If a man cannot write what is *new*, at least he can write what is *novel*" (*R. Hallet*). A thing is **new-fashioned** which is so different in form, shape, style, or character from that which was previously known that it challenges curiosity or meets more or less general acceptance; as, *new-fashioned* modes of painting; *new-fashioned* hats for women are regarded as absurd by many men. A thing is **newfangled** which strikes one as unnecessarily or as ingeniously novel in its construction, use, or the like: often, however, the term differs little from *new* except in suggesting disparagement; as, *newfangled* toys; *newfangled* theories of art; "a *newfangled* nomenclature" (*Sir W. Hamilton*). A person or thing is **modern** or **neoteric** (a later term than *modern*, common in the 17th century but now rare) that belongs to the present time or is especially characteristic of it: the terms often imply up-to-dateness and novelty, or a contrast with that which has been long accepted and still is the choice of the conservative: in this special sense **modernistic** is now often preferred to *modern;* as, "the *neoteric* fashion of spending a honeymoon on the railway" (*Meredith*); *modern* (or *modernistic*) furniture; *modern* (or *modernistic*) schools of painting. *Modern*, however, is always preferred to *modernistic* when contemporaneousness only is implied; as, "in *modern* art atmosphere counts for so much" (*Wilde*). "This strange disease of *modern* life, with its sick hurry, its divided aims, its heads o'ertaxed, its palsied hearts" (*Arnold*). But *modern* is also applicable to things of more remote origin than any of the other terms; as opposed to *ancient* and *medieval* it usually implies reference to the centuries beginning with the full Renaissance up to the present (as, *modern* languages; *modern* civilizations); often, however, the dividing line between that which is modern and that which is too far distant in time to be called modern has to be supplied by the context; as, the Victorian era gave way to the *modern* age of machinery. "Most *modern* well-to-do Englishmen and Americans, if they were transported by magic into the age of Elizabeth, would wish themselves back in the *modern* world" (*B. Russell*). A person or thing is **original** that produces or that is something new or novel and, at the same time, the first of its kind; as, "That he would be successful in an *original* way, or that he would go to the dogs in an *original* way, seemed equally probable" (*Hardy*); "Poets...who ...construct an *original* speech" (*Day Lewis*); "A wildly daring, *original*...spirit" (*H. Ellis*). A thing (sometimes a person) is **fresh** that is or seems so new that it has not had time to lose the signs of newness, such as a liveliness, energy, brightness, a virginal quality, or the like; as, *fresh* footprints; to receive a *fresh* impetus; to make a *fresh* start; a *fresh* newspaper. "This was a *new* voice falling upon the attentive ears of youth—a *fresh* challenge to its native and impetuous generosity" (*A. Repplier*).

Ant. Old.

newfangled. *New, novel, new-fashioned, neoteric, modernistic, modern, original, fresh.

new-fashioned. *New, novel, newfangled, neoteric, modernistic, modern, original, fresh.

news. **News, tidings, intelligence, advice** (*or* **advices**) are all used to designate a report or the reports of occurrences and conditions not previously known. **News** stresses novelty and freshness of information; as, the gossip was not *news* to her; the letter contained no *news*. Since *news* is specifically applied to the information disseminated through journals shortly after the incidents have occurred, it also often implies distribution, even in its general sense or in some of its derivatives; as, experts in handling *news; news*mongers. **Tidings** is now poetic or bookish; it is often appropriate in literary English when it refers to news orally communicated or disseminated, as by a herald or messenger. "Fear not...I bring you good *tidings* of great joy....For unto you is born this day in the city of David a Saviour" (*Luke* ii. 10–11). **Intelligence** commonly stresses the desirability or the practical value of the information rather than its freshness. "Their visits to Mrs. Philips were now productive of the most interesting *intelligence*" (*Austen*). In specific military use, *intelligence* suggests clandestine methods of gathering information as by a secret service or spies. It is therefore applied not only to the news gathered but to the branch of the service commissioned to gather it. "An enemy superior in numbers, who possessed also the advantage in armament, position, and more accurate *intelligence*" (*Buchan*). In comparison with *intelligence*, which often suggests the gathering of important information, **advice** stresses the transmission of information and implies the immediacy of its value. It, therefore, or its plural **advices**, is often applied to the means by which this information is communicated, such as letters, telegrams, messengers, and the like. "No doubt he [Richelieu] had *advices* that Casale was sufficiently provisioned to last for many months, perhaps a year" (*Belloc*).

newspaper: *Journal, periodical, magazine, review, organ.

next. *Nearest.

nib *or* **neb.** *Bill, beak.

nice. 1 **Nice, dainty, fastidious, finical, finicking, finicky, particular, fussy, squeamish, pernickety** (*or* **pernicketty, pernickity;** *also* **persnickety**) come into comparison when they mean exacting or displaying exacting standards as in selection, judgment, workmanship, or the like. **Nice,** as here considered (see also CORRECT, DECOROUS), implies fineness of discrimination and power to distinguish the very good from that which is merely good: the term connotes rather more of intellectual quality than the other words; as, "an appetite for knowledge too eager to be *nice*" (*Johnson*); "In language one should be *nice* but not difficult" (*J. R. Lowell*); "to attain this union of gravity and simplicity requires the *nicest* art" (*P. E. More*); "he had a *nice* taste in literature and had edited Crashaw and Vaughan with conspicuous taste and much perception" (*C. Mackenzie*). *Nice* is also applicable to questions, problems, and the like, which require such powers of discrimination and subtlety or delicacy in handling if the solution is to be found; as, a *nice* experiment; the situation raises a *nice* question. **Dainty,** in the sense here considered (see also CHOICE), usually implies a tendency to select carefully that which does, or to reject with more or less disdain that which does not, satisfy one's extremely delicate taste or sensibility: it usually connotes chariness or a tendency to pick and choose, especially in eating; as, she has a *dainty* appetite; "No shape but his can please your *dainty* eye" (*Shak.*); "All highly developed forms of utterance are studiously acquired, the 'tough' jargon of the East Side no less than the *dainty* discourse of the Four Hundred" (*Grandgent*). **Fastidious** etymologically implies a strong aversion to that which does not satisfy one's sense of what is right, proper, in good taste, or the like: in its current use, however, it suggests the possession of ethical, artistic, social, or other standards that are so high that they impose a strain upon those who would meet them (as, "It is...an advantage for an author to have two or three *fastidious* readers whom he can imagine sniffing at his pages"—*L. P. Smith*), or that cause suffering to the possessor when they are not satisfied (as, "I am *fastidious* in voices, and I can't endure listening to an imperfect reader"—*G. Eliot;* "The disorder was almost more than his *fastidious* taste could bear"—*Cather*), or that foster extreme care in selection from that which is offered or available (as, "a *fastidious* instinct for the connotations of a phrase"—*Pater;* "Why such a desperate orgy of literature? I thought you were of a more *fastidious* habit—not like Stanley, who insists on reading everything"—*R. Macaulay*). **Finical** (*or the colloquial* **finicking** *or* **finicky**) implies an affected or overnice fastidiousness; as, "His reserve, his delicacy, his distaste for many of the persons and things surrounding him...have produced an impression of Gray as being a man falsely *fastidious, finical*, effeminate" (*Arnold*); "a world of little *finical* observances, and little frail proprieties" (*Stevenson*); a *finicky* taste in dress. **Particular,** as here compared, implies an insistence that all details or circumstances should be exactly as one wishes them or that one's special or peculiar standards must be met. In contrast with *fastidious, particular* may or may not imply what others would call a high standard: the term usually suggests standards which the individual regards as high or exacting; as, a *particular* teacher; she is *particular* about the way steak should be broiled; "I'm going to change it [one engraving on a wall] with that one.... He said the effect would be very much better if they were changed. And his lordship is very *particular*" (*Bennett*). "As she approached, George Adams, who had a *particular* mother, rose, and Niel followed his example" (*Cather*). **Fussy** is applicable not only to fastidious or particular persons and to acts that manifest a disposition to be querulous or fidgety (as, "she was not one of the trivially *fussy* domesticated women"—*H. Ellis;* "In this matter Augustus moved slowly and tactfully. He was no lawyer, and he had not the *fussy* interest of Claudius in the work of the courts"—*Buchan*), but also to things that are so difficult or so complicated that they make a particular person engaged upon them nervous or fidgety (as, a *fussy* piece of work; an extremely *fussy* operation). **Squeamish** etymologically implies a readiness to be nauseated by the sight, taste, smell, or hearing of something disagreeable; as, "the starved stomach is not *squeamish*" (*Hudson*). In its extended use, it implies a disgust for or an aversion to that which does not satisfy one's standards of what is decent, delicate, honest, or nice: it therefore sometimes connotes extreme sensitiveness, or prudishness, or scrupulousness, or the like; as, "such *squeamish* youths as cannot bear to be connected with a little absurdity are not worth a regret" (*Austen*); "trifles magnified into importance by a *squeamish* conscience" (*Macaulay*); "As to the nudities...they might well have startled a not very *squeamish* eye" (*N. Hawthorne*); "Our nerves...are unduly delicate, and our tastes too *squeamish*" (*L. Stephen*). **Pernickety** is a colloquial term which manifests the speaker's (sometimes writer's) annoyance, exasperation, or disgust, excited by persons who are unduly fussy or finical, or by tasks, problems, etc., that are so delicate or complicated that they impose severe strain on one's patience and good temper; as, "The grammarian, the purist, the *pernicketty* stickler for trifles" (*B. Matthews*); "such

confining and *pernickety* work" (*Harper's Mag.*).
Ana. *Wise, judicious, sage, sapient: punctilious, meticulous, scrupulous, *careful: discriminating, discerning, penetrating (see corresponding nouns at DISCERNMENT).
Con. *Coarse, gross, vulgar: crude, callow, green, raw (see RUDE): *negligent, lax, remiss, neglectful, slack.
2 Precise, exact, accurate, *correct, right.
Ana. Strict, *rigid, rigorous, stringent: exquisite, delicate, rare (see CHOICE, *adj.*).
Con. *Random, haphazard, hit-or-miss, happy-go-lucky: *careless, heedless, inadvertent.
3 Proper, seemly, comme il faut, demure, *decorous, decent.
Ana. Fitting, *fit, appropriate, suitable, meet.
☞ Below this level, and not embodying the main tendency of *nice* to express an aversion to or a distaste for anything that does not reach the state of perfection in method, manner, or deportment, lie several other uses which do not meet general approval. In general, it is a term of approval that reveals nothing out of the ordinary or exacts no attention to a high standard; as, a *nice* day; a *nice* letter; a *nice* book; a *nice* dinner.

niche. *Recess, alcove, nook, embrasure, bay, cubicle, carrell, carol.

nick, *n.* *Dent, dint, notch, indentation, indenture.

nifty. Nobby, natty, spruce, *stylish, fashionable, modish, smart, chic, dapper, dashing, posh, toffish, brave, braw.

niggardly. Parsimonious, penurious, miserly, *stingy, close, closefisted, tight, tightfisted, curmudgeonly, cheeseparing, penny-pinching.
Ana. *Covetous, avaricious, grasping, greedy: *sparing, economical, frugal, thrifty: *mean, ignoble.
Ant. Bountiful. — *Con.* *Liberal, generous, munificent, handsome: *profuse, lavish, prodigal.

nigh, *adj. & adv.* *Close, near, near by.
Ant. Far.

nightly. **Nightly, nocturnal** agree in meaning of, belonging to, or occurring at night. **Nightly** is the preferred term when the opposition to *daily* (as connoting daytime) is to be implied; as, the daily and *nightly* visits of his physician; there were both daily and *nightly* raids for several weeks. But *nightly*, whether opposed to *daily* or not, commonly carries so strong an implication of recurrence that the term is interpreted as meaning night after night unless the context clearly indicates reference to a single night or to special nights; as, the doctor made only two *nightly* visits this week; the *nightly* meetings of the general's staff; *nightly* revels; *nightly* prowls; he kept a *nightly* vigil. **Nocturnal** is often literary or somewhat technical, but it applies specifically and without question to things which are so associated with the night that they are thought of as belonging or appropriate to the hours of darkness; thus, *nocturnal* animals or insects (bats, owls, some flies, etc.) are active or evident only during the night; animals of *nocturnal* habits; the *nocturnal* office of a monk (commonly called *matins*) is usually sung between midnight and dawn; *nocturnal* sounds are those one hears only at night and therefore associates with that period. *Nocturnal* is the correct term when the effect of darkness or of moonlight or starlight is implied; as, "the changing beauty of *nocturnal* landscapes" (*Bennett*).
Ant. Daily.

nightmare. Dream, vision, *fancy, fantasy, phantasy, phantasm, daydream.
Ana. *Delusion, hallucination, illusion: threatening *or* threat, menacing *or* menace (see corresponding verbs at THREATEN).

nihilist. *Collectivist, socialist, communist, Bolshevist, anarchist.

nimble. *Agile, brisk, spry.
Ana. Sprightly, *lively, animated: alert, wide-awake, vigilant, *watchful: *supple, limber, lithe.

nimbus. *Halo, glory, aureole.

nix, *fem.* **nixie.** *Fairy, faery, fay, elf, sprite, pixy, gnome, dwarf, goblin, brownie, puck, shee, leprechaun, banshee.

nob. *Fop, dandy, beau, coxcomb, exquisite, élégant, dude, macaroni, buck, spark, swell, toff.

nobby. *Stylish, fashionable, modish, smart, chic, dapper, dashing, spruce, natty, nifty, posh, toffish, brave, braw.

nobility. *Aristocracy, gentry, county, gentlefolk, elite, society.

noble. **1** Stately, majestic, imposing, august, magnificent, *grand, grandiose.
Ana. Glorious, *splendid, resplendent, superb, sublime: illustrious, eminent, distinguished (see FAMOUS).
Ant. Ignoble: cheap. — *Con.* Despicable, *contemptible, sorry, scurvy, beggarly.
2 Virtuous, righteous, *moral, ethical.
Ana. Honorable, *upright, just, honest.
Ant. Base (*of actions, etc.*): atrocious (*of acts, deeds, etc.*).

nocturnal. *Nightly.
Ana. Diurnal.

noise, *n.* *Sound, sonance.
Ana. Discordance, dissonance (see under DISSONANT): *din, uproar, babel, hubbub, racket, pandemonium.

noiseless. Silent, quiet, *still, stilly.
Ana. *Calm, tranquil, serene, placid.
Con. Clamorous, *vociferous, strident, boisterous.

noisome. Fetid, stinking, *malodorous, putrid, rank, rancid, fusty, musty.
Ana. Foul, nasty, squalid, filthy, *dirty: noxious, baneful, *pernicious, deleterious: loathsome, *offensive, revolting.
Ant. Balmy. — *Con.* *Odorous, fragrant, aromatic, redolent.

nomadic. *Itinerant, peripatetic, ambulatory, ambulant, vagrant.

nom de guerre. *Pseudonym, alias, pen name, nom de plume, incognito, allonym.

nom de plume. Pen name, nom de guerre, *pseudonym, alias, incognito, allonym.

nominate. *Designate, name, elect, appoint.
Ana. Propose, *intend, mean, purpose: present, tender, *offer, proffer.

nominee. *Candidate, aspirant, applicant.

non-. *Un-, in-, a-.

nonage. *Infancy, minority.
Ant. Age.

nonchalant. Unruffled, imperturbable, *cool, composed, collected.
Ana. Unconcerned, *indifferent, aloof, detached: lighthearted, cheerful, *glad: *easy, effortless, light, smooth.
Con. Concerned, solicitous, anxious, worried, careful (see under CARE, *n.*).

non compos mentis. *Insane, mad, crazy, crazed, demented, deranged, lunatic, maniac, wood.

nonconformist, *n.* Dissenter, sectary, sectarian, *heretic, schismatic.

nonesuch. *Paragon, sublimation, apotheosis, phoenix, nonpareil.

nonmoral. Unmoral, amoral, *immoral.

nonpareil. *Paragon, sublimation, apotheosis, phoenix, nonesuch.

nonplus. Bewilder, distract, confound, dumfound, mystify, perplex, *puzzle.
Ana. Faze, rattle, *embarrass, discomfit, disconcert: *confuse, muddle, bemuddle: baffle, balk, *frustrate.
nonreligious. Unreligious, *irreligious, ungodly, godless.
Ana. Secular, *profane, lay, temporal.
nonsocial. *Unsocial, asocial, antisocial.
nook. *Recess, alcove, niche, embrasure, bay, cubicle, carrell, carol.
norm. *Average, mean, median, par.
normal. *Regular, typical, natural.
Ana. Ordinary, *common, familiar: *usual, customary, habitual, wonted, accustomed.
Ant. Abnormal: adventitious (sense 2).
nosy *or* **nosey.** *Curious, inquisitive, prying, snoopy.
Ana. Meddlesome, *impertinent, intrusive, obtrusive.
notch, *n.* *Dent, dint, nick, indentation, indenture.
note, *n.* **1** *Sign, mark, token, badge, symptom.
Ana. Indication, betokening, bespeaking, attesting (see corresponding verbs at INDICATE): character, *quality, property, attribute, accident.
2 Mark, sign, symbol, *character.
3 *Remark, observation, comment, commentary, descant, obiter dictum.
Ana. Annotation, gloss (see under ANNOTATE): remembering, reminding *or* reminder, recalling *or* recaller (see corresponding verbs at REMEMBER).
4 *Letter, epistle, missive, message, dispatch, report, memorandum.
note, *v.* Remark, notice, perceive, discern, observe, contemplate, survey, view, *see, behold, descry, espy.
noted. Renowned, celebrated, *famous, famed, distinguished, eminent, illustrious, notorious.
Ana. Conspicuous, outstanding, salient, signal, *noticeable, remarkable.
notice, *v.* Remark, observe, note, perceive, discern, *see, behold, descry, espy, view, survey, contemplate.
Ana. Recognize, *acknowledge: *refer, advert, allude.
Con. Ignore, slight, overlook, disregard, *neglect.
noticeable. Noticeable, remarkable, prominent, outstanding, conspicuous, salient, signal, striking, arresting agree in meaning attracting or compelling notice or attention. **Noticeable** implies that the thing so described does not or cannot escape observation; as, *noticeable* attentions to a lady; a *noticeable* aversion to another's company; *noticeably* crude behavior. **Remarkable** adds to *noticeable* the further implication of inviting comment or of demanding a call to others' attention; it may or may not impute to the thing so described an extraordinary or exceptional character; as, he has made no *remarkable* gain in skill during the last five years; he has a *remarkable* gift for making friends. **Prominent** seldom loses its earliest implication of protuberance or projection above a level or beyond a surface; in literal use it is applied chiefly to things that noticeably protrude from their background; as, a *prominent* nose; "her eyes were...a china blue, rather *prominent* and inexpressive" (*Cather*); a landscape without *prominent* features. In extended use, it is applied to persons or things that stand out so clearly from their surroundings that they are often in evidence, or are generally known or recognized, or are frequently pointed out, or the like; as, the *prominent* persons in a town; the church occupies a *prominent* position; "attending to his parish duties without making himself too *prominent* by his enthusiasm or his originality" (*C. Mackenzie*). **Outstanding,** although it implies prominence, is applicable only to that which rises above or beyond others of the same kind and is remarkable by comparison with them; as, there is no *outstanding* man among the candidates for this office; the new anthology is *outstanding* in its kind in that it gives complete works, not excerpts. **Conspicuous** is applicable chiefly to that which is so obvious or patent that the eye or the mind cannot miss it (as, *conspicuous* merit; *conspicuous* bravery); it is also used to describe that which strikes the eye or the mind (often unpleasantly) through its singularity; as, to wear *conspicuous* clothes; to make oneself *conspicuous* by one's affectations; his supporters are *conspicuous* by their absence. **Salient** stresses emphatic quality and is applied to that which thrusts itself upon one's attention or impresses itself insistently upon the mind; it imputes significance more often than obtrusiveness to the thing so described. "There are days rich in *salient* news and days far from rich in it" (*C. E. Montague*). "The Middle Ages...sacrificed ruthlessly subsidiary qualities to throw into sharp relief the *salient* trait, till Griselda, for example, carried patience beyond the utmost bound of human thought" (*Lowes*). **Signal** suggests such distinction from that which is ordinary or usual that the thing so described is in itself remarkable or memorable; as, the *signal* sacrifice of Sir Robert Scott; a *signal* mark of esteem; *signal* bravery in action. **Striking** is applicable to that which impresses itself powerfully and deeply upon the observer's mind or vision; as, one easily remembers the *striking* scenes in a story; to give a *striking* example of loyalty; a woman of *striking* beauty. **Arresting** adds to *striking* the suggestion of capturing attention or of more than passing interest; as, an *arresting* personality; an *arresting* story. "The slight, steel-coloured figure with steel-coloured hair, was more *arresting* in its immobility than all the vociferations and gestures of the mob" (*Galsworthy*).
Ana. *Evident, manifest, obvious, palpable, patent.
notify. Apprise, advise, acquaint, *inform, advertise.
Ana. Announce, *declare, proclaim, publish, promulgate, broadcast: *reveal, disclose, discover, divulge, tell.
notion. *Idea, concept, conception, thought, impression.
Ana. *Opinion, view, belief, conviction, persuasion, sentiment.
notoriety. Reputation, repute, éclat, *fame, celebrity, renown, honor, glory.
Ana. *Publicity, propaganda, promotion, ballyhoo.
notorious. *Famous, famed, renowned, noted, celebrated, distinguished, eminent, illustrious.
Ana. Conspicuous, *noticeable, remarkable, outstanding, salient: *flagrant, glaring, gross, rank.
notwithstanding. Notwithstanding, in spite of, despite are often interchangeable prepositions. **Notwithstanding,** the least emphatic, merely implies the presence of an obstacle; **in spite of,** the most emphatic, suggests active opposition or strongly adverse considerations to be encountered; **despite** is somewhat lighter in its emphasis than *in spite of* and otherwise is closer to *notwithstanding* than to *in spite of;* as, *notwithstanding* the rain, I shall go; I shall go *in spite of* all your efforts to prevent me; *despite* his assurances, I doubted him.
nought. Naught, aught, ought, *cipher, zero.
nourish. *Feed, pasture, graze.
Ana. *Nurse, nurture, foster, cultivate.
nourishment. Nutriment, sustenance, *food, aliment, pabulum.
Ana. Support, keep, maintenance, sustenance, *living.
novel, *adj.* *New, new-fashioned, newfangled, neoteric, modern, modernistic, original, fresh.
Ana. *Strange, singular, unique, peculiar.
Con. *Usual, customary, habitual: ordinary, *common, familiar.

novel, *n.* **Novel, romance** are here compared as designating a type of prose fiction. In earlier usage, *novel* and *romance* were rather sharply contrasted with reference to subject matter, style, and, sometimes, length. **Novel** then denoted and still to an extent denotes any work of fiction that deals more or less realistically with the life of the present or of the past, that involves its characters in situations arising out of their individual temperaments or out of the clash between opposing temperaments, and that has a definite plot which moves through entanglements to crisis and disentanglements, and finally to a definite and often (but now far from invariably) happy conclusion. This type of prose fiction, which (in England) was first accepted as a serious literary form with the work of Richardson and Fielding in the mid-eighteenth century and attained a high degree of excellence in the mid-nineteenth century in the work of Thackeray, Dickens, and George Eliot, still prevails, though often in the modern form there is greater emphasis on character than on plot and on the inner life than on external action, with the result that what happens before the action begins or what may happen after it ends is more or less of a concern to the author and to the reader. **Romance,** a much older term in English than *novel,* was used in the Middle Ages and Renaissance to denote a type of narrative, in either poetry (the *metrical romance*), or in prose, dealing with the actual or, more often, the legendary exploits of a hero or heroes, such as Arthur and the knights of the Round Table, Charlemagne, Roland, and others. Originally, the term implied an opposition to the classic form of poetic narrative, the epic or heroic poem, typically represented by Homer's *Iliad* and *Odyssey* and Vergil's *Aeneid.* Hence, in the late eighteenth and early nineteenth centuries (when *romance* and *novel* were first contrasted) and still later, *romance* was applied to any relatively long work of prose fiction that deals typically with the past in a romantic as opposed to a realistic manner, that stresses adventure and action rather than character, and that arouses interest chiefly by surprising incidents, wonderful exploits, or glamorous characters and situations. In still later, and still current, use *romance* as distinguished from *novel* often in addition specifically implies the subordination of character to the plot, little concern for the probability or credibility of situations or incidents, marked use of coincidences, and a swift and often thrilling action that moves from situation to situation to a completely satisfactory end; as, the *romances* of Richard Harding Davis and Anthony Hope.

novice, novitiate. Novice, novitiate, apprentice, probationer, postulant, neophyte come into comparison only when applied to one who is a beginner, especially a beginner in a trade, a profession, a career, or a sphere of life. **Novice** and **novitiate** (an old form discountenanced by some persons) may be applied to anyone who comes under this description, since inexperience is their chief distinguishing implication; as, a *novice* in writing. "You are but *novices* in the art of naval resources" (*Burke*). *Novice* is specifically applied to a new member of a religious order who is undergoing training before taking first (usually not the final) vows. **Apprentice** is applicable only to a beginner who is serving under another as his master or teacher. "The breathless, the fructifying adoration of a young *apprentice* in the atelier of some great master of the Renaissance" (*Van W. Brooks*). In such applications it commonly emphasizes subjection to a taskmaster and to discipline rather than inexperience. Although specifically it often denotes a youth who is bound to a master for a number of years to learn a trade (see BOUND, *adj.*), or denotes an enlisted man in the United States Navy (now usually called *apprentice seaman*) who is receiving instruction in seamanship, gunnery, and the rudiments of a general education (at a training station or on board a training ship), it also has wide general use. "You must from your years be a *novice* in affliction, whereas I have served a long *apprenticeship* to misery" (*Fielding*). **Probationer** designates a beginner who is on trial for a period of time and must prove his aptitude for the work or life; as, the most disagreeable tasks in a hospital are often assigned to *probationers* among the nurses. In Scotland, a divinity student who is licensed to preach but has not yet received a call is spoken of as a *probationer.* **Postulant** implies candidacy for admission, as into a religious order; it usually also implies acceptance for a period of probation; hence, *postulant* and *probationer* are sometimes interchanged in literal use. In extended use they are, because of the difference in their fundamental implications, rarely interchanged. "The brevity and vanity of this life, in which we are but *probationers*" (*Richardson*). "Words... often answering to calls too subtile for analysis, are constantly presenting themselves as *postulants* for recognition" (*F. Hall*). **Neophyte** usually suggests initiation, and is applicable to one who is learning the ways, methods, principles, or the like, of something with which he is newly connected, such as an art, a science, a society, a club, or a religious faith; as, "such an encounter usually perplexes the *neophyte* at first" (*M. C. Cooke*). In discriminating use, however, it carries connotations of innocence and youthful eagerness derived from its earliest English association with a newly baptized person or convert to Christianity. "The old philosopher of Monticello was more than pleased with this ardent *neophyte* ....Not since his own years abroad had Jefferson seen such an eager student" (*Van W. Brooks*).

Ana. Beginner, starter, commencer (see corresponding verbs at BEGIN): *amateur, dilettante, dabbler, tyro.

noxious. Baneful, *pernicious, deleterious, detrimental.

Ana. Injurious, hurtful, harmful (see corresponding nouns at INJURY): *poisonous, virulent, venomous, toxic, pestilent, miasmatic: noisome, stinking, fetid, putrid (see MALODOROUS).

Ant. Wholesome, sanitary.

nucleus. *Center, middle, midst, core, hub, omphalos, focus, heart.

nude, *adj.* *Bare, naked, bald, barren.

Ant. Clothed.

nugatory. *Vain, otiose, idle, empty, hollow.

Ana. Worthless, valueless (see affirmative nouns at WORTH): trifling, trivial, *petty, paltry: ineffectual, *ineffective, inefficacious: fruitless, bootless, *futile, vain, abortive.

nullify. Nullify, negate, annul, abrogate, invalidate in their current literary or general senses are often interchangeable without marked loss. All then bear the common denotation to deprive of effective or continued existence. One thing **nullifies** another when the former reduces the latter to nothingness or deprives it of effectiveness, validity, or value. "Each of his [Antony's] virtues...was *nullified* by some rampant vice" (*Buchan*). One thing **negates** another when one cannot coexist with the other or both are mutually destructive; as, our actions often *negate* our principles; death is the *negation* of life. One thing **annuls** another (see also ANNUL) when it neutralizes the effect of the other or deprives it of power to act or work. "That...is why we call them [the two types of electricity] 'positive' and 'negative'—because they are capable of *annulling*...one another's actions" (*Karl K. Darrow*). One thing **abrogates** another (see also ANNUL) when the former effectively dispenses with or abolishes the latter; as, this law *abrogates* the rights of the minority. One thing **invalidates** another when it deprives the latter of its force or legality. *Invalidate* usually implies failure to meet tests of soundness or to conform to imposed conditions; as, a beneficiary under a will cannot witness the will without *invalidating* it. "Let us try to discover how far the facts confirm or *invalidate* this proud claim" (*A. Huxley*).

Ana. *Neutralize, negative, counteract: offset, countervail, counterbalance, *compensate: *limit, restrict, confine.

number, *n.* Quantity, whole, total, aggregate, *sum, amount.

number, *v.* *Count, tell, enumerate.

Ana. *Calculate, compute, estimate, reckon.

numerous. *Many, several, sundry, various, divers, manifold, multifold, multifarious.

Ana. *Large, great, big: abundant, *plentiful, plenteous.

nun. *Religious, monk, friar.

nuncio. Legate, internuncio, *ambassador, minister, envoy.

nunnery. *Cloister, monastery, convent, abbey, priory.

nuptial, *adj.* *Matrimonial, conjugal, connubial, hymeneal, marital.

nuptials. *Marriage, matrimony, wedlock, wedding, spousal, espousals.

nurse, *v.* **Nurse, nurture, foster, cherish, cultivate** come into comparison not so strikingly in their primary as in their secondary senses, but in both cases they agree in meaning to give the care necessary to the growth, development, or continued welfare or existence of someone or something. **Nurse** literally implies close care of and attention to someone unable to care for himself, such as an infant or a sick person, with the idea of helping that one to grow strong and self-sufficient; as, he was slowly *nursed* back to health. In its extended sense, the term implies similar sedulous attentions, such as brooding over or constant provision of sustenance or that which feeds or nourishes, thereby strengthening what was at first weak, or indefinite, or tentative, or the like; as, "the uncle of this young woman...had...long *nursed* the prudent scheme of marrying her to his son" (*Meredith*); "When I would muse in boyhood ... And *nurse* resolves and fancies" (*Housman*); "They sulkily avoid his eye, and *nurse* their wrath in silence" (*Shaw*). **Nurture** stresses the rearing and training, and so the determination of the course the person or, by extension, the thing, will follow; as, "*Nurtured*, as thy mien bespeaks, in high degree" (*Wordsworth*); "By solemn vision, and bright silver dream, His infancy was *nurtured*" (*Shelley*). "Reverence for age and authority, even for law, has disappeared; and in the train of these have gone the virtues they engendered and *nurtured*" (*G. L. Dickinson*). **Foster** (etymologically, to provide a young thing with food and care as, or more often as if, its parent) is now rarely used literally, although this sense occurred frequently in the past; as, "Some say that ravens *foster* forlorn children" (*Shak.*). In its secondary sense, where it implies encouragement or promotion of the growth or increase of something, the term is very common; as, "Age, I find, *fosters* the finer feelings" (*L. P. Smith*); "Everything...had *fostered* in the princess a like conviction" (*H. James*). "The teaching that *fosters* these ends succeeds; the teaching which neglects them fails" (*H. Suzzallo*). "Governments have deliberately *fostered* nationalistic fervour to serve their own political purposes" (*A. Huxley*). **Cherish** stresses loving, protective care, such as that of a nurse or a parent for a child, or of a husband for a wife; as, "to love and to *cherish*, till death do us part" (*Anglican Marriage Service*). In its extended use, it is not always distinguishable from *nurse*, but among discriminating writers and speakers, it still retains its etymological implications of holding dear or as a thing of value, and stresses prizing and preserving rather than brooding over or causing to increase in strength; as, "She still *cherished* a very tender affection for Bingley" (*Austen*); "from the first, separately and together, she and I had *cherished* ideals of freedom and independence...and cast contempt on the narrow self-absorption of domestic love" (*H. Ellis*). "Julius was a bold iconoclast about republican forms which had survived their usefulness; Augustus sought to *cherish* whatever of these forms could be made to work" (*Buchan*). **Cultivate** in its literal sense implies the care and attention given to land in order to increase its fertility or to plants in order to improve their condition. In figurative or extended use, it implies comparable and equally sedulous attentions to the improvement or growth of something desirable; as, "his sense of personal initiative is *cultivated* instead of being diminished" (*B. Russell*). "Determined that his own books should not justify a similar reproach, he *cultivated* his literary gifts with conscientious industry" (*A. Huxley*). "We shall do well to *foster* the studies most conducive to the habits we wish to *cultivate*" (*Grandgent*).

Ana. *Feed, nourish: promote, *advance, further, forward: *indulge, pamper, humor.

nurture, *v.* Foster, *nurse, cherish, cultivate.

Ana. Raise, rear (see LIFT): train, educate, school, discipline (see TEACH): *support, uphold, back.

Con. *Neglect, overlook, disregard, ignore.

nutriment. Nourishment, sustenance, *food, aliment, pabulum.

Ana. Maintenance, support, keep, bread and butter, *living.

O

obdurate. Inexorable, *inflexible, adamant, adamantine.

Ana. *Hardened, indurated, callous: *obstinate, stubborn, mulish, stiff-necked: *immovable, immobile.

Con. *Tender, compassionate: yielding, submitting, succumbing, relenting (see YIELD).

obedient. Obedient, docile, tractable, amenable, biddable are synonyms carrying the common meaning of submissive to the will, guidance, or control of another. Though applied chiefly to persons, they are by extension applicable also to things. **Obedient** implies due compliance with the commands or requests of a person or power whose authority one recognizes or accepts; as, *obedient* to the law; children trained to be *obedient* to their parents. "Exhort servants to be *obedient* unto their own masters" (*Titus* ii. 9). When applied to things, it implies compulsion by a superior force, movement in accordance with natural law, or the like; as, tides *obedient* to the moon. "And floating straight, *obedient* to the stream, Was carried towards Corinth" (*Shak.*). **Docile** implies a responsiveness to teaching, but it stresses either a predisposition to submit to guidance or control, or negatively, an indisposition to resist impositions or to rebel against authority. "That is a question which you must excuse my child from answering. Not, sir, from want of will, for she is *docile* and obedient" (*Hudson*). "Whatever doctrine is best calculated to make the common people *docile* wage slaves" (*Shaw*). **Tractable,** which is nearly as often applied to things as to persons and animals, suggests success or ease in handling or managing. Unlike *docile*, which in many ways it closely resembles, it seldom implies a submissive temperament; thus, a *docile* child is always *tractable*, but a strong-willed child may prove *tractable* when he is wisely guided. "Loving she is, and *tractable*, though wild" (*Wordsworth*). "It [the Roman Senate] became more and more a dignified anachronism, peevish if unskilfully handled, *tractable* under a discreet Princeps" (*Buchan*). "One of the most *tractable* [that is, easily handled]...of the phenomena of the realm of Nature" (*Karl K. Darrow*). **Amenable** stresses a temperamental willingness or readiness to submit; not, however, in the spirit of obedience, but because of a desire to be agreeable, because of openness of mind, or the like. "We were now dealing with the intractable Sinhalese rather than the stupid but *amenable* Tamils" (*V. Heiser*). "Well, Joan had a broad brow; she thought things over; she was *amenable* to ideas" (*H. G. Wells*). "In spite of his usual *amenableness* to such suggestions, the President replied that...he was going" (*E. Roosevelt*). **Biddable** is a more homely word than *docile;* it is used chiefly of children, of servants, and the like. "Theophilus nodded, silently. He was perfectly apathetic....He seemed to be just a silent, *biddable* child" (*Deland*).

Ana. *Compliant, acquiescent, resigned: submissive, subdued, *tame: deferential, obeisant (see corresponding nouns at HONOR).

Ant. Disobedient: contumacious. — ***Con.*** *Insubordinate, rebellious: *contrary, perverse, froward, wayward: recalcitrant, refractory, intractable, *unruly, ungovernable.

obeisance. Deference, homage, *honor, reverence.

Ana. Allegiance, fealty, loyalty, *fidelity: respect, esteem, *regard: veneration, reverence (see under REVERE).

obese. Corpulent, rotund, chubby, *fleshy, fat, stout, portly, plump.

Ant. Scrawny. — ***Con.*** *Lean, spare, angular, rawboned, lank, lanky, gaunt, skinny: *thin, slender, slim, slight.

obiter dictum. *Remark, observation, comment, commentary, note, descant.

object, *v.* **Object, protest, remonstrate, expostulate, kick** come into comparison when they mean to oppose something, such as a course, a procedure, a policy, or a project, especially by making known one's arguments against it. **Object** carries so strong an implication of dislike or aversion that it often is lacking in a clear or definite implication of vocal or other outward opposition: very frequently, however, such a reaction is suggested; as, why do you always *object* to everything he wishes to do for you? "Censorship of drama....[is] welcomed by the overwhelming majority of the public; *objected* to only by such persons as suffer from it" (*Galsworthy*). **Protest** (as here considered: see also ASSERT, 1) implies strong opposition and, usually, the presentation of objections in speech or in writing against the thing to which one objects; as, the residents of the district unanimously *protested* against the granting of the license; "It is against this dualism or pluralism that scientific men...*protest* when they reject the...conception of miracle as the suspension of a lower law by a higher" (*Inge*); "swearing and *protesting* against every delay in the work" (*S. Anderson*). **Remonstrate** implies protestation but it carries so much stronger an implication of an attempt to convince or persuade than *protest* carries that it is often, though not invariably, the preferred term when the objection is to something being done by a child, a friend, or a relative, rather than by an official or an impersonal agent, or when reproof is also implied. "Now and then a well-meaning friend of Sir Austin's ventured to *remonstrate* on the dangerous trial he was making in modelling any new plan of education for a youth" (*Meredith*). "The family 'attention had been drawn to' the article, as people always express it when writing to a paper to *remonstrate* about something in it they haven't liked" (*R. Macaulay*); " 'Father Joseph,' he *remonstrated*, 'you will never be able to take all these things back to Denver' " (*Cather*). **Expostulate** differs little from *remonstrate*, but it usually carries a heightened implication of firm, earnest, but friendly reasoning or insistence on the merits of one's arguments. "The priestly brotherhood... Prompt to persuade, *expostulate*, and warn" (*Cowper*). "I resolved, for Johnny's sake, to *protest*, and that very evening drew Gibbings aside and *expostulated* with him" (*Quiller-Couch*). **Kick,** once in good English use in the sense here discussed, is now a colloquialism: it implies strenuous protestation and, usually, an exhibition of recalcitrancy or defiance; as, "Wherefore *kick* ye at my sacrifice and at mine offering?" (*1 Samuel* ii. 29); when the tax rate was raised for the fourth successive year, everybody *kicked*.

Ana. *Demur, balk, scruple, jib, boggle, shy, stick, stickle: *criticize, denounce, reprobate.

Ant. Acquiesce. — ***Con.*** *Assent, consent, agree, accede.

object, *n.* **1** *Thing, article.

Ana. *Affair, concern, matter, thing: *form, figure, shape, configuration.

2 Objective, goal, end, aim, design, purpose, *intention, intent.

Ana. *Motive, incentive, inducement.

Con. Result, *effect, consequence.

objectify. Externalize, substantiate, substantialize, materialize, incarnate, embody, *realize, actualize, hypostatize, reify.

objective, *adj.* **1** *Material, physical, corporeal, phenomenal, sensible.

Ana. External, outside, *outer, outward: tangible, palpable, *perceptible.

Ant. Subjective.

2 Impartial, unbiased, dispassionate, uncolored, *fair, just, equitable.

Ana. & ***Ant.*** See those at OBJECTIVE, 1.

objective, *n.* Object, end, goal, aim, design, purpose, *intention, intent.

objurgate. *Execrate, curse, damn, ban, anathematize.

Ana. Revile, vituperate (see SCOLD): condemn, denounce, reprobate, *criticize.

Con. Applaud, *commend, compliment.

obligation. 1 Obligation, duty come into comparison as denoting that which a person is bound to do or refrain from doing or for the performance or nonperformance of which he is held responsible. In ordinary usage, **obligation** commonly implies immediate constraint and a specific reference; as, he is under the *obligation* of supporting his aged mother; "Englishmen and women... wholly indifferent to the *obligations* of their faith" (*T. S. Eliot*); "the Ralstons fulfilled their *obligations* as rich and respected citizens" (*E. Wharton*). **Duty,** on the other hand, often suggests less compulsion from immediate

circumstances but a greater impulsion on moral or ethical grounds; thus, a person weighed down by a sense of *duty* is keenly aware of what in general he ought to do; one has a sense of *obligation* only in a particular case and for a particular reason; so, Wordsworth describes *duty* as "the stern daughter of the voice of God"; "The path of *duty* was the way to glory" (*Tennyson*); "The old statesman [Cicero] was now in a sad frame of mind, torn between *duty* and self-interest" (*Buchan*). "In the apprehension of these eternal Values, and in earnest striving to co-operate with the divine will in actualising them, lies the whole *duty* of man" (*Inge*).
Ana. Compulsion, constraint, restraint (see FORCE, *n.*): responsibility, accountability, answerability (see corresponding adjectives at RESPONSIBLE).
2 *Debt, indebtedness, liability, debit, arrear, arrearage.
Ana. Burden, *load: promising *or* promise, engagement, pledging *or* pledge (see corresponding verbs at PROMISE).

oblige. **1** Constrain, coerce, compel, *force.
Ana. *Tie, bind.
2 Oblige, accommodate, favor agree in denoting to gratify a person by doing him a service or courtesy. To **oblige** a person is to make him indebted by doing something that is pleasing to him. "Punch was always anxious to *oblige* everybody" (*Kipling*). "She had given him up to *oblige* others" (*Austen*). It is commonly used in the passive voice as a conventional acknowledgment of small courtesies or offices. "There is an oversight...which I shall be much *obliged* to you to correct" (*Macaulay*). **Accommodate,** when it is used of services, is often interchangeable with *oblige* in the active voice. Sometimes, especially in the participial adjective, it implies gracious compliance; as, an *accommodating* man; sometimes it connotes the intent to be of assistance. "I was willing to *accommodate* you by undertaking to sell the horse" (*G. Eliot*). But *accommodate* often suggests a business transaction rather than an act of kindness, and an obligation to pay or repay. In such use, it commonly implies a loan of money or acceptance as a paying guest (see also CONTAIN); as, the bank *accommodated* him when he provided sufficient security; no hotel in town could *accommodate* the party. To **favor,** by contrast, is to render an attention or a service solicited or unsolicited, out of good will, and commonly, but not necessarily, without imposing any obligation on, or expecting a return from, the person favored; as, to *favor* a person with one's advice; Fortune *favored* him in all his enterprises. Sometimes the implication of partiality is so strong as to obscure that of giving gratification or assistance; as, he always *favored* gifted students. The verb is of more restricted application than the noun, and in ironical use suggests gratuitousness. "The stupidity with which he was *favoured* by nature" (*Austen*).
Ana. Gratify, *please: *benefit, profit, avail: *help, aid, assist: *support, uphold, back.
Ant. Disoblige. — *Con.* *Inconvenience, incommode, discommode, trouble.

obliging. Good-natured, complaisant, *amiable.
Ana. Helping *or* helpful, aiding, assisting (see corresponding verbs at HELP): accommodating, favoring (see OBLIGE): *compliant, acquiescent: *thoughtful, considerate.
Ant. Disobliging: inconsiderate.

oblique. *Crooked, devious.
Ana. *Awry, askance, askew: *indirect, circuitous, roundabout.
Con. *Direct, immediate: *straightforward, forthright: downright, *forthright.

obliterate. Efface, cancel, expunge, *erase, blot out, delete, dele.
Ana. *Abolish, annihilate, extinguish: *destroy, raze: annul, abrogate, negate, invalidate, *nullify.

oblivious. *Forgetful, unmindful.
Ana. Disregarding, ignoring, forgetting, neglecting, overlooking (see NEGLECT, *v.*).
Con. *Aware, conscious, cognizant: *thoughtful, attentive, considerate: alert, vigilant, *watchful.

obloquy. **1** *Abuse, vituperation, invective, scurrility, billingsgate.
Ana. Censuring *or* censure, condemning *or* condemnation, denouncing *or* denunciation, criticizing *or* criticism (see corresponding verbs at CRITICIZE): calumny, *detraction, backbiting, slander, scandal.
2 *Disgrace, dishonor, disrepute, shame, infamy, ignominy, opprobrium, odium, scandal.
Ana. *Stigma, brand, blot, stain: humiliation, humbling, degradation (see corresponding verbs at ABASE).

obnoxious. Distasteful, invidious, abhorrent, *repugnant, repellent.
Ana. *Hateful, odious, detestable, abominable: *offensive, loathsome, repulsive, revolting.
Ant. Grateful.

obscene. Gross, vulgar, ribald, *coarse.
Ana. Indecent, indelicate, *indecorous: lewd, lascivious, wanton, *licentious: foul, nasty, *dirty.
Ant. Decent.

obscurantist. Obscurantist, Philistine, barbarian agree in denoting one inaccessible or opposed to enlightenment. An **obscurantist** is one who is precluded by prejudice (as traditionalism or bigotry) from intellectual candor and open-minded inquiry and who is opposed to the introduction of new and enlightened ideas and methods. "From this class of [Chinese] *obscurantists* who had hitherto resisted all Western innovations there now came young leaders eager to emulate Japan" (*Peace Handbooks*). "You working men complain of the clergy for being bigoted and *obscurantist,* and hating the cause of the people" (*Kingsley*). A **Philistine** is one whose attention is centered on material or worldly things, and is indifferent or blind to whatever makes an appeal only to the mind or soul. The term usually implies obtuseness and insensitiveness. "In their heavy inaccessibility to ideas, their dull respectability, their tedious orthodoxy, their worship of vulgar success, their entire preoccupation with the gross materialistic side of life, and their ridiculous estimate of themselves and their importance, the Jews of Jerusalem in Christ's day were the exact counterpart of the British *Philistine* of our own" (*Wilde*). In the following quotation, Matthew Arnold has assigned to *Philistine* a restriction, and to **barbarian** a sense, that have been adopted by some later writers. "*Philistine* gives the notion of something particularly stiff-necked and perverse in the resistance to light and its children; and therein it specially suits our middle class ....But the aristocratic class...if it does not pursue light, it is not that it perversely cherishes some dismal and illiberal existence in preference to light, but it is lured off from following light by...worldly splendor, security, power, and pleasure....I often, therefore, when I want to distinguish clearly the aristocratic class from the *Philistines* proper, or middle class, name the former, in my own mind, the *Barbarians.*"

obscure, *adj.* **1** Murky, gloomy, opaque, *dark, dim, dusk, dusky, darkling.
Ana. Shady, shadowy, umbrageous (see corresponding nouns at SHADE).
Con. *Clear, lucid: *bright, brilliant, luminous.
2 Obscure, dark, vague, enigmatic, cryptic, ambiguous, equivocal come into comparison when they are applied to

language or expression (sometimes to causes, motives, etc.) and agree in meaning not sufficiently intelligible or clearly understood. That is **obscure** the true meaning of which is hidden or veiled, because of some fault or defect either in the thing itself or in the person who would understand it. "That decorum and orderliness without which all written speech must be ineffective and *obscure*" (*H. Ellis*). "Real and offensive *obscurity* comes merely of inadequate thought embodied in inadequate language" (*Swinburne*). "The mere text of the play will often look scrappy and disjointed and *obscure* to a reader who does not bring to it the special theatrical imagination" (*C. E. Montague*). That is **dark** which is so imperfectly revealed as to be invested with mystery; as, "I will utter *dark* sayings" (*Psalms* lxxviii. 2); "*dark* hints about Richard" (*Meredith*). That is **vague** which is lacking in distinct outlines or in clear definition, either because it is too general or because it is so imperfectly conceived or thought out that it is incapable of clear formulation. "The only objection that can be urged is found within the *vague* contours of the Fifth Amendment, prohibiting the depriving any person of liberty or property without due process of law" (*Justice Holmes*). "We shall never gain power from *vague* discourse about unknown or unassimilated facts" (*Grandgent*). That is **enigmatic** which puzzles, mystifies, and, often, baffles one who would seek its true meaning or significance. "She fell to conjecturing the meaning of Farfrae's *enigmatic* words about not daring to ask her what he fain would" (*Hardy*). "Puzzling out the threats, or the *enigmatic* promises, of a starry sky" (*Pater*). That is **cryptic** which is stated or expressed darkly or enigmatically; the word often implies a definite intention to perplex or to challenge. " 'She's too young to be really young,' she remarked *cryptically*" (*Van Vechten*). "Instead of inventing, they [the great poets] discovered. If that sounds *cryptic*, let us start with a modern instance" (*Lowes*). That is **ambiguous** which admits of more than one interpretation, largely because of the use of a word or words having a dual (or multiple) meaning without giving an indication of which sense is intended. "The title of this chapter is *ambiguous*. It promises a discussion of the end of the world, but it does not say which end" (*Eddington*). "We are here not far from the *ambiguous* doctrine that art is 'expression,' for 'expression' may be too easily confused with 'communication' " (*H. Ellis*). That is **equivocal** which permits a wrong or false impression, thereby admitting uncertainty and confusion or fostering error. As applied to use of words, *equivocal* is distinguishable from *ambiguous* in that it implies the repeated use of a word in different applications in such a way as to convey the impression that the term carries the same implications and connotations in each case; as, the *equivocal* use of "democracy" by persons who apply it to popular governments of widely varying types. In extended use *equivocal* is applied to anything, such as an act or a mode of life, that admits of two possible or plausible interpretations, one of which may be harmful or discreditable; as, *equivocal* conduct; an *equivocal* remark.

Ana. Abstruse, *recondite, occult, esoteric: difficult, *hard: complicated, intricate, involved (see COMPLEX): *mysterious, inscrutable.

Ant. Distinct, obvious: celebrated (*as a person*). — ***Con.*** *Clear, perspicuous, lucid: *evident, manifest, obvious: express, *explicit, definite.

obsequious. *Subservient, servile, slavish, menial.

Ana. Deferential, obeisant (see corresponding nouns at HONOR): *compliant, acquiescent: sycophantic, parasitic, toadyish (see corresponding nouns at TOADY): cringing, fawning, truckling, cowering (see FAWN, *v.*).

Ant. Contumelious.

observance. **Observance, observation,** though ultimately derived from the same root, came into English as different words about two centuries apart. They are not synonyms but are sometimes confused. **Observance,** the older of the two forms, has always retained a close relation to *observe* in the sense of *keep* (see *observe* under KEEP, 1) and, therefore, almost invariably implies a close heeding or following, as of rules, customs, and rites, or in the celebration of prescribed holidays or holydays, or the like. The term may denote either the act of observing or keeping (as, "He was careful in his *observance* of all prescribed religious rites"—*G. L. Dickinson*) or a rule, custom, rite, or the like, that is observed (as, "He set about it in a very orderly manner, with all the *observances*, which he supposed a regular part of the business"—*Austen;* "The beauty of an inherited courtesy of manners, of a thousand little ceremonies flowering out of the most ordinary relations and *observances* of life"—*Binyon*). **Observation,** the later term, is in current use sharply distinguished from *observance*, for it usually bears a close relation to *observe* in the sense of to watch attentively. Except for its specific sense of a comment (see REMARK, *n.*), the term may denote either the act or process of observing (as, the astronomer devotes several hours each clear night to *observation* of the stars; "He [Trollope] was an honest and industrious craftsman with a considerable power of *observation*"—*Maugham*) or the act or fact, or an instance, of being observed (as, "He needs daily exercise in the open air; but he cannot bear *observation*"—*Shaw*).

observation. 1 *Observance.

2 *Remark, comment, commentary, note, descant.

Ana. *Opinion, view, belief: annotation, gloss (see under ANNOTATE): *criticism, critique.

observe. 1 *Keep, celebrate, solemnize, commemorate.

Ana. Respect, esteem, regard (see under REGARD, *n.*): *revere, reverence, venerate.

Ant. Violate. — ***Con.*** *Neglect, ignore, overlook, disregard, slight.

2 Survey, view, contemplate, notice, remark, note, perceive, discern, *see, behold, descry, espy.

Ana. *Scrutinize, examine, scan, inspect.

observer. *Spectator, beholder, looker-on, onlooker, witness, eyewitness, bystander, kibitzer.

obsolete. *Old, antiquated, archaic, antique, ancient, venerable, antediluvian.

Ant. Current.

obstacle. **Obstacle, obstruction, impediment, bar, snag** agree in denoting something which seriously hampers action or progress. **Obstacle,** which is used of both material and immaterial things, applies to any object, condition, situation, or the like, which stands in one's way and must be removed or surmounted if one is to progress or attain one's ends. "Feeling about for the *obstacle* which had flung him down, he discovered that two tufts of heath had been tied together across the path" (*Hardy*). "It is of the very essence of supremacy to remove all *obstacles* to its action within its own sphere" (*Ch. Just. Marshall*). "The new Lord Advocate ...the conqueror of many *obstacles*" (*Stevenson*). **Obstruction** may be used of immaterial things, but such use is often obviously figurative, for the word suggests a blocking of a way or passage; as, the French Maginot Line and the German Westwall proved serious *obstructions* to the movement of troops; an intestinal *obstruction*. "Any phrase repeated too often becomes an *obstruction* to the flow of thought and feeling. It forms a clot" (*S. M.*

Crothers). **Impediment**, which etymologically implies an entangling of the feet, is, in precise use, applied to something (material or immaterial) which serves to hinder or delay action or progress until one is freed from it; as, the refugee's limited knowledge of English was for a long time an *impediment* to his progress in his profession; divorce is often a means of freeing oneself from an *impediment* to another marriage. "I have made my way through more *impediments* Than twenty times your stop" (*Shak.*). "[In commerce] distance of place, difference of speech, are irremovable *impediments*" (*Bagehot*). **Bar** applies to something interposed, as by nature or by man, which serves, either in effect or by intention, to prevent admission or escape as effectually as the bars of a cage or prison. Sometimes the word carries a strong suggestion of prohibition, especially when it applies to a law or condition that restrains; as, under the immigration laws, a criminal record, an infectious disease, and illiteracy are *bars* to admission to the United States; he found his infirmity no *bar* to his success in his profession. "Must I new *bars* to my own joy create?" (*Dryden*). "Who breaks his birth's invidious *bar*... And breasts the blows of circumstance" (*Tennyson*). **Snag**, from its literal application to a stump of a tree with jagged points which lies hidden under water and proves a hazard to boats, is figuratively applied to any obstacle or impediment which is hidden from view and which one encounters as suddenly and as sharply as a boat that strikes a snag; as, they struck many *snags* in the course of their investigation; refugees continually running against some *snags* in the shape of laws affecting aliens.

Ana. Barrier, *bar: hindering *or* hindrance, blocking *or* block (see corresponding verbs at HINDER): opposing *or* opposition, resisting *or* resistance, withstanding (see corresponding verbs at OPPOSE).

obstinate. Obstinate, dogged, stubborn, pertinacious, mulish, stiff-necked, pigheaded, bullheaded come into comparison when they mean fixed or unyielding in one's purpose, course, or the like. **Obstinate** implies persistent adherence, especially against persuasion or attack, to an opinion, purpose, or course: when applied to persons, their ideas, and the like, the term often suggests unreasonableness or perversity rather than steadfastness; as, "They will not be resolute and firm, but perverse and *obstinate*" (*Burke*); "so yielding doubtful points that he can be firm without seeming *obstinate* in essential ones" (*J. R. Lowell*); "There is nothing in the world which can be quite so *obstinate* as a yielding, mild, opinionless girl" (*Deland*). **Dogged** adds the implication of downright and tenacious, sometimes sullen, persistence: usually, also, it connotes great determination or an unwavering purpose; as, "a *dogged* veracity" (*Johnson*); "a *dogged* perseverance" (*Thackeray*); "Men whose hearts insist upon a *dogged* fidelity to some image or cause" (*Hardy*); "his mother's influence was to make him quietly determined, patient, *dogged*, unwearied" (*D. H. Lawrence*). **Stubborn** is often used interchangeably with *obstinate* and *dogged*, for it implies the unyielding adherence of the one and the tenacious determination of the other; more strongly than either of them, however, it carries an implication of a native fixedness of character or of a deeply inrooted quality that makes a person sturdily resistant to attempts to change his purpose, course, or opinion, or that makes a thing highly intractable to those who would work it, treat it, manipulate it, or the like; as, "*stubborn* as a mule" (*Smollett*); "Their furrow oft the *stubborn* glebe has broke" (*Gray*); "Cases which proved *stubborn* to treat and often impossible to cure" (*V. Heiser*); "Poetry whose democracy is tempered by a *stubborn* conviction that democracy thwarts the development of the individual at its peril" (*Lowes*). **Pertinacious** lacks, as compared with *obstinate*, the implication of resistance, and as compared with *stubborn*, the suggestion of inherent quality: it usually implies a chosen course, and stresses its pursuit with "stick-to-itiveness" and, often, with a persistence that is annoying or irksome; as, *pertinacious* as a mosquito; a *pertinacious* beggar. "[Socrates's] originality lay not in any purely speculative views, but in the *pertinacious* curiosity, practical in its origin and aim, with which he attacked and sifted the ethical conceptions of his time" (*G. L. Dickinson*). **Mulish** suggests an obstinacy as characteristic or as unreasonable as that of a mule; as, "a man...intolerably irritable...with a *mulish* determination to make the worst of everything" (*T. S. Eliot*); "A fierce, hot, hard, old, stupid squire ... Small brain, great courage, *mulish* will" (*Masefield*). **Stiff-necked**, more even than *obstinate* or *stubborn*, stresses inflexibility: it often also suggests a haughtiness or arrogance that makes one, like a high-spirited horse incapable of obeying the rein, incapable of respecting the commands, wishes, or suggestions of others; as, the *stiff-necked* father could neither control his children nor win their love when they approached adolescence; "Be ye not *stiffnecked*, as your fathers were, but yield yourselves unto the Lord" (*2 Chronicles* xxx. 8). **Pigheaded** and **bullheaded** (both more colloquial than the other terms of this group) suggest a particularly perverse or stupid kind of obstinacy; therefore they are chiefly terms of severe reproach; *pigheaded*, however, often suggests impenetrability to argument and *bullheaded*, headstrong determination; as, "many of the managing posts will be filled up by *pigheaded* people only because they happen to have the habit of ordering poor people about" (*Shaw*); "their *bull-headed* obstinacy" (*Scott*).

Ana. Headstrong, willful, recalcitrant, *unruly: obdurate, inexorable, *inflexible: resolute, steadfast, stanch (see FAITHFUL).

Ant. Pliant, pliable. — *Con.* *Plastic, malleable, ductile: submitting *or* submissive, yielding, succumbing (see corresponding verbs at YIELD): *compliant, acquiescent.

obstreperous. *Vociferous, clamorous, blatant, strident, boisterous.

Ana. *Unruly, ungovernable, intractable, headstrong, refractory: uproarious, rackety (see corresponding nouns at DIN).

Con. Restrained, curbed, checked (see RESTRAIN): quiet, *still, silent, noiseless.

obstruct. Impede, block, *hinder, bar, dam.

Ana. *Prevent, preclude, obviate, avert: *restrain, check, curb, inhibit.

obstruction. *Obstacle, impediment, bar, snag.

Ana. Hindering *or* hindrance, blocking *or* block (see corresponding verbs at HINDER): arresting *or* arrest, checking *or* check, interruption (see corresponding verbs at ARREST).

Ant. Assistance. — *Con.* Forwarding, furthering, promoting *or* promotion, advancing *or* advancement (see corresponding verbs at ADVANCE).

obtain. *Get, procure, secure, acquire, gain, win, earn.

Ana. Gain, *reach, achieve, attain: effect, fulfill, accomplish, *perform.

obtrude. *Intrude, interlope, butt in.

Ana. *Interpose, interfere, intervene, mediate.

obtrusive. Intrusive, meddlesome, *impertinent, officious, pragmatical.

Ana. Inquisitive, *curious, prying, snoopy, nosy: blatant, strident (see VOCIFEROUS).

Ant. Unobtrusive: shy.

obtuse. *Dull, blunt.

Ana. Insensitive, *insensible, anesthetic, impassible: stolid, phlegmatic, *impassive.

Ant. Acute. — *Con.* *Sharp, keen: sensitive, susceptible, open, exposed (see LIABLE).

obverse, *n.* *Converse, reverse.

obviate. Preclude, *prevent, avert, ward off.

Ana. Evade, elude, avoid, *escape: forestall, anticipate, *prevent: *interpose, interfere, intervene.

obvious. *Evident, manifest, patent, distinct, apparent, palpable, plain, clear.

Ana. Prominent, conspicuous, salient, signal, striking (see NOTICEABLE).

Ant. Obscure: abstruse.

occasion, *n.* **1** *Opportunity, chance, break, time, tide, hint.

Ana. *Juncture, pass: situation, posture, condition, *state: moment, *instant.

2 *Cause, determinant, antecedent, reason.

Ana. Incident, *occurrence, event: *origin, source, inception.

occasional. *Infrequent, uncommon, scarce, rare, sporadic.

Ana. Casual, desultory, *random: incidental, *accidental.

Ant. Customary. — *Con.* *Usual, habitual, accustomed, wonted: constant, *continual, continuous.

occult. Esoteric, *recondite, abstruse.

Ana. *Mysterious, inscrutable, arcane: mystic, cabalistic, *mystical, anagogical.

occupation. Employment, *work, calling, pursuit, métier, business.

occur. *Happen, hap, chance, befall, betide, transpire.

Ana. Rise, arise, *spring, emanate, issue, proceed: *follow, succeed, ensue, supervene.

occurrence. **Occurrence, event, incident, episode, circumstance** agree in denoting something that happens or takes place. **Occurrence** is the general term for that which takes place; as, "Omit All the *occurrences*, whatever chanced, Till Harry's back-return again to France" (*Shak.*); "Such a happy and convenient *occurrence*, the princess's conversion" (*H. G. Wells*). **Event** (which is frequently regarded as arising from an antecedent state of things) is a more or less important or noteworthy occurrence; as, the *events* of the year; the sequence of *events* that followed the declaration of war; her engagement was the *event* of the season; "The course of human *events*" (*The Declaration of Independence*). An **incident** (cf. *incidental* under ACCIDENTAL) is commonly an occurrence of subordinate character or secondary importance, either a mere casual happening having little relation to major events, or an occurrence that merely follows because of them; as, "Her tone implied that bedroom fires were a quite ordinary *incident* of daily life in a place like Bursley" (*Bennett*). "Many American writers have won that honor [an Oxford degree]; it is, in fact, almost a routine *incident* in a distinguished career. In the case of Mark Twain it became a historic *event*" (*Van W. Brooks*). The term may, however, be used of a single event that stands out or is marked off clearly from the other events (as in a story, a play, a history) in its nature or significance; as, the book narrates a series of thrilling *incidents;* "he was delighted and looked upon the *incident* as an adventure" (*S. Anderson*). In current use the term is applied, especially by journalists, to any critical event that provokes a break in diplomatic relations between countries, suggests the possibility of war, or the like; as, the Corfu *incident* (1923) caused the severance of diplomatic relations between Italy and Greece; border *incidents*. **Episode** (see also DIGRESSION) is often used in place of *incident* in the sense of a single or outstanding event, but the term, in precise use, often carries a stronger implication of distinctiveness or apartness from the main course than does *incident;* as, "A pretty little domestic *episode* occurred this morning" (*Meredith*); "Clare would inevitably...come to regard her passion for Oliver Hobart and its tragic sequel as a romantic *episode* of girlhood" (*R. Macaulay*). **Circumstance** is used as a synonym of *incident* only when the latter is thought of as a detail; as, "before closing his door for the night, [he] stood reflecting on the *circumstances* of the preceding hours" (*Hardy*). The word is also occasionally used as a synonym for *event* in its more general sense; as, certain curious *circumstances* in his history.

Ana. Appearance, emergence (see corresponding verbs at APPEAR): *juncture, pass, exigency, emergency, contingency: posture, situation, condition, *state.

oceanic. *Aquatic, marine, thalassic, neritic, pelagic, abyssal, bathysmal, bathybic, lacustrine, lacuscular, fluvial, fluviatile.

odd. Queer, quaint, *strange, singular, unique, peculiar, eccentric, erratic, outlandish, curious.

Ana. Bizarre, grotesque, *fantastic: anomalous, *irregular, unnatural.

Con. *Usual, customary, habitual: ordinary, *common, familiar: normal, *regular, typical, natural.

odds. *Advantage, handicap, allowance, edge.

odious. *Hateful, abhorrent, abominable, detestable.

Ana. *Repugnant, repellent, distasteful, obnoxious: *offensive, loathsome, repulsive, revolting.

odium. Obloquy, opprobrium, ignominy, infamy, *disgrace, dishonor, disrepute, shame, scandal.

Ana. *Hate, hatred: *antipathy, aversion: abhorrence, abomination, detestation, loathing (see under HATE, *v.*).

odor *or* **odour.** *Smell, scent, aroma.

Ana. *Fragrance, perfume, redolence, incense, bouquet, scent.

odorous. **Odorous, fragrant, redolent, aromatic, balmy** agree in meaning emitting and diffusing scent. **Odorous** applies to anything which has a strong, distinctive smell, whether it is pleasant or not; as, *odorous* flowers such as lilies, tuberoses, and narcissuses; *odorous* chemicals are often malodorous; "*odorous* gums from the East" (*Wilde*). **Fragrant** applies to that which has a sweet and agreeable odor, especially to flowers, fruits, beverages, and the like, that through their lingering sweetness of scent give sensuous delight; as, *fragrant* roses; "Where the *fragrant* limes their boughs unite, We met—and we parted forever!" (*J. Crawford*); "perhaps far back...certain Chinese preferred *fragrant* tea to insipid water" (*V. Heiser*). **Redolent** once meant, and still occasionally means, pleasantly odorous; in such use, it applies not only to things that diffuse a scent, but to the scent itself; as, the *redolent* pine; the *redolent* scent of pine. "Every flower and every fruit the *redolent* breath Of the warm seawind ripeneth" (*Tennyson*). In current use, it chiefly applies to a place or thing impregnated with odors, especially with those that are penetrating and delightful. "Dim, shady wood-roads, *redolent* of fern And bayberry" (*Millay*). **Aromatic** is more restricted in its implications than *aroma*, for it usually suggests a certain type of pungent, often fresh, odor of the kind associated with the foliage of balsams, pine, and spruce, the wood of cedar, the dried leaves of lavender, certain spices such as cloves and certain gums such as myrrh. It is therefore often applied to preparations scented with substances

that are aromatic; as, *aromatic* smelling salts; *aromatic* spirit of ammonia. **Balmy** applies chiefly to things which have a delicate and soothing aromatic odor; as, "the *balmy* air of night" (*Poe*). "As *aromatic* plants bestow No spicy fragrance while they grow; But crush'd, or trodden to the ground, Diffuse their *balmy* sweets around" (*Goldsmith*).
Ant. Malodorous: odorless. — *Con.* Stinking, fetid, noisome, putrid, rank, rancid, fusty, musty (see MALODOROUS).

oeconomus. *Steward, reeve, bailiff, agent, factor, seneschal, major-domo.

oecumenical. Variant of ECUMENICAL.

offend. **Offend, outrage, affront, insult** come into comparison when they mean to cause another, especially by one's actions or words, to be deeply vexed or hurt or to take umbrage. One **offends** who, with or without intention, displeases another by hurting his feelings or by violating his sense of what is proper or fitting. "He begged pardon for having displeased her. In a softened tone she declared herself not at all *offended*" (*Austen*). "The majority of women that he meets *offend* him, repel him, disgust him" (*Mencken*). One **outrages** who offends another past endurance, or offends his pride, or his sense of justice or honor, etc. " 'Grief of two years' standing is only a bad habit.' Alice started, *outraged*. Her mother's grief was sacred to her" (*Shaw*). One **affronts** who, either with an intent to offend or with deliberate indifference to civility or courtesy, humiliates or dishonors a person and arouses his deep resentment. "A moral, sensible, and well-bred man Will not *affront* me, and no other can" (*Cowper*). One **insults** who wantonly and insolently offends another so as to cause him humiliation or shame. "You can annoy, you can *insult*, you cannot move me" (*Meredith*).
Ana. *Annoy, vex, irk, bother: exasperate, nettle, *irritate: pique, *provoke, excite: chafe, fret, gall (see ABRADE).

offense *or* **offence.** 1 Offensive, aggression, *attack.
Ana. Assault, *attack, onslaught, onset.
2 **Offense** (*or* **offence**), **resentment, umbrage, pique, dudgeon, huff** come into comparison as denoting a person's emotional reaction to what he regards as a slight, an affront, an insult, or an indignity. **Offense** implies a state of displeasure (often but not necessarily extreme displeasure) or of wounded feelings; as, criticism so tactfully made that they gave no *offense;* he is so sensitive that he takes *offense* at any unintentional or seeming slight. **Resentment** implies more indignation than *offense,* more prolonged dwelling upon what one regards as a personal injury or grievance and, often, more ill will to the person who has offended; as, "It is very difficult to get up *resentment* towards persons whom one has never seen" (*Newman*); "As long as I am free from all *resentment*...I would be able to face the life with much more calm" (*Wilde*); "Westermarck...claims that *resentment* and gratitude (which he calls emotions) are the foundation of moral judgments" (*S. Alexander*). **Umbrage** (currently used chiefly in the phrase "to take umbrage") differs from *offense* in carrying a clearer implication of being slighted or unfairly ignored: the term therefore generally suggests ruffled pride, resentful suspicion of others' motives, or jealousy of those favored; as, "Although the Rector was not inclined to take *umbrage* at the treatment they had received, he showed...that he was quite aware that it was not what might have been considered due to them" (*Arch. Marshall*). Very often, however, *umbrage* is not clearly distinguishable from *offense;* as, "I should be very loath to give the least *umbrage* or *offence* by what I have said" (*Swift*). **Pique** applies to the fit of one who has taken offense or umbrage, but it distinctively suggests a petty cause and a transient mood, and often connotes wounded vanity; as, "When the wanton heroine chooses to...flirt with Sir Harry or the Captain, the hero, in a *pique,* goes off and makes love to somebody else" (*Thackeray*). **Dudgeon** applies chiefly to a fit of angry resentment or of high indignation provoked by opposition to one's views, a refusal of one's request, or the like; as, to go off in high *dudgeon;* "They often parted in deep *dudgeon*" (*Scott*); "You must not be in a *dudgeon* with me" (*Trollope*). **Huff,** like *dudgeon,* applies to a fit of anger, but it comes closer to *pique* in suggesting pettiness of cause and transitoriness; distinctively, it implies petulance and a refusal to have more to do with those who have offended. "At the first hint that we were tired of waiting and that we should like the show to begin, he was off in a *huff*" (*H. James*). "Half of 'em will be disgusted, and go away in a *huff*" (*W. De Morgan*).
Ana. *Affront, insult, indignity: indignation, wrath, *anger.
Con. *Pleasure, delight, joy: gratifying *or* gratification, rejoicing (see corresponding verbs at PLEASE).
3 **Offense** (*or* **offence**), **sin, vice, crime, scandal** are here compared as general terms denoting a more or less serious or conspicuous infraction or transgression of law. **Offense** is the term of widest application, being referable to a violation of any law, including the law of the state, the law of the church, natural law, moral law, the standards of propriety, taste, etc., set up by society or the arts, and the like. It is also applicable to any transgression regardless of its triviality or gravity, or its voluntary or involuntary character, provided it injures or tends to injure the welfare, or well-being, or happiness of others. "O, my *offence* is rank, it smells to heaven; It hath the primal eldest curse upon't, A brother's murder" (*Shak.*). "Punch....was careful not to repeat the *offence,* because Aunty Rosa told him that God had heard every word he had said and was very angry" (*Kipling*). "The greater the number of laws, the greater the number of *offences* against them" (*H. Ellis*). **Sin,** in strict use, applies to an offense against the moral law, especially as laid down in the Ten Commandments and in laws derived from them. Theologically, its essential character is disobedience of the divine will and willful opposition to the law of God: in somewhat wider use, it implies a failure to live up to the moral ideals of one's time or environment or to the moral ideal one has set as the standard of one's own conduct; as, all regarded stealing and lying as *sins;* the *sin* of sacrilege; nonobservance of the Sabbath was the *sin* most abhorred by the settlers of that region; "what constitutes the essence of the tragedy...is the habituation of Beatrice to her *sin*" (*T. S. Eliot*). **Vice** (as here considered: see also FAULT, 1), though frequently applied to any of the offenses that from the theological and religious points of view are called sins, often carries little suggestion of a violation of divine law; rather, it more uniformly imputes to such offenses a character suggestive of moral depravity, corruption, or deep degradation; also, the term less often applies to single acts or single transgressions than to habits, practices, etc., that debase the character of a person or group of persons; as, "Spare then the person, and expose the *vice*" (*Pope*); "Treachery and cruelty, the most pernicious and most odious of all *vices,* seem peculiar to uncivilized ages" (*Hume*). **Crime,** in its earliest and still most common sense, applies to any infraction of law, especially of common law or statute law, that is punishable by the state or by any power that constitutes itself as the guardian of such law: it is not a technical legal term, but it is often used in the courts

and is sometimes defined in penal codes, usually as a general term applicable to any act or omission forbidden by law and punishable upon conviction. In such use the term comprehends many clearly distinguished types of offenses such as a misdemeanor, a felony, treason, and the like; as, "the reason for excluding evidence obtained by violating the Constitution seems to me logically to lead to excluding evidence obtained by a *crime* of the officers of the law" (*Justice Holmes*); "*offenses* against marriage such as adultery, which is a *crime* punishable by death in Papua and only a *sin* in civilized society" (*Social Science Abstracts*). "Human society may punish us for *crimes;* human monitors reprove us for *vices;* but God alone can charge upon us the *sin,* which He alone is able to forgive" (*J. Martineau*). *Crime* and, less often, *sin,* are often applied to offenses that are of exceedingly grave nature; in fact, this implication is often found in *crime,* even in its quasi-legal sense. "I've not been guilty of anything more than an indiscretion....I behaved foolishly, but that's not a *crime*" (*C. Mackenzie*). **Scandal** comes into comparison with these words in the sense here considered because it applies to an offense against any law that is also an offense in another sense of that word—that of an act, a condition, a practice, or the like, which offends the public conscience or which puts a stumbling block in the way of those who should obey the law or should be trained to obey it: unlike the words *sin, vice,* and *crime,* it carries no implication of probable or certain punishment or retribution, but emphasizes the distressing effect it has on others or the discredit it attaches to religion, to morals, etc.; as, "Catholics... could not appear in Protestant assemblies without causing *scandal* to the weaker brethren" (*Froude*); "the man's life is an open *scandal*" (*Cather*); "There is only one way in which we can meet and be together...and that is as friends....I will be party to no *scandal*" (*R. Macaulay*).

Ana. *Injustice, injury, wrong, grievance, tort: *breach, infraction, violation, transgression, trespass, infringement, contravention.

offensive, *adj.* **1** Attacking, aggressive. See under ATTACK, *n.*

Ana. Invasive, incursive, irruptive (see corresponding nouns at INVASION): assaulting, assailing, attacking, bombarding, storming (see ATTACK, *v.*).

2 Offensive, loathsome, repulsive, repugnant, revolting come into comparison as meaning utterly distasteful or repellent. That is **offensive** which subjects one to painful or highly disagreeable sensations. Sometimes the term implies injured feelings as a result of an affront or insult (as, "Olly, though without the tact to perceive when remarks were untimely, was saved by her very simplicity from rendering them *offensive*"—*Hardy*); often, also, the term suggests the evocation of such aversion that endurance involves mental strain or moral distaste (as, "[a situation] far less *offensive* to modern taste than many other situations in Elizabethan drama"—*T. S. Eliot;* "Particularly *offensive* to the ear of the old-fashioned Yankee is...'goodnus' for goodness"—*Grandgent*); most often, it implies a vileness of appearance, odor, or the like, that excites nausea or extreme disgust (as, "[she] lay stretched awkwardly...her head thrown back, her face discoloured, her eyes bulging, her mouth wet and yawning: a sight horribly *offensive*"—*Bennett*). That is **loathsome** which is so foul or obscene that one cannot look upon it, hear it, feel it, or the like, without a sense of deep disgust and abhorrence: often the term is not clearly distinguishable from *offensive* in the sense of disgustingly nauseating, but it is probably applied more often to things which must be endured or cannot be avoided; as, *loathsome* diseases; *loathsome* prison conditions; the *loathsome* details of a battle scene; "a band of *loathsome* fakirs" (*Kipling*). That is **repulsive** which is so ugly in its appearance, or so completely lacking in all that attracts, or allures, or charms, or even challenges interest, that it either drives one away or makes one unwilling to dwell on it; as, "Mary was not so *repulsive* and unsisterly as Elizabeth" (*Austen*); "To Dorothea it [the memory of an aunt's long illness] was all ghastly and *repulsive*" (*Deland*); "Work which is now *repulsive* can be made no irksomer than the general run of necessary labour" (*Shaw*). "In those days all school-books were as *repulsive* as publishers could make them. Their appearance went a long way in discouraging any intimacy with their contents" (*A. Repplier*). That is **repugnant** (in the extreme sense in which it is here considered: see also REPUGNANT, 1) which is highly offensive or loathsome because in direct conflict with one's nature, one's principles, and one's tastes, and irreconcilable with them. "This frightful condition of internal strain and instability [in Europe in 1914] was not set up by human nature: it was, I repeat, intensely *repugnant* to human nature, being a condition of chronic terror that at last became unbearable" (*Shaw*). "The door is not barred and bolted for a solution less *repugnant* to our deepest intuitions than that [determinism] which has hitherto seemed to be forced upon us" (*Eddington*). That is **revolting** which is so extremely offensive, loathsome, repulsive, or repugnant to a person of fine feeling or delicate sensibilities that the sight or thought of it arouses in him a desire or determination to resist or rebel; as, he found horseflesh *revolting;* "to developed sensibilities the facts of war are *revolting* and horrifying" (*A. Huxley*); "There was something *revolting* in having to plead like this" (*Galsworthy*); "*Revolting* cant about the duty of obedience and the wickedness of resistance to law" (*H. Adams*).

Ana. Repellent, *repugnant, abhorrent, distasteful, obnoxious, invidious: *hateful, odious, abominable, detestable.

offensive, *n.* *Attack, aggression, offense.

Ana. Assault, *attack, onslaught, onset.

offer, *v.* **Offer, proffer, tender, present, prefer,** as here compared, agree in meaning to lay, set, or put something before another for acceptance. **Offer,** the most common of these words, implies in its earliest sense a laying before God, or a god, something devoutly hoped to be worthy of his acceptance; as, to *offer* a goat as a sacrifice; to *offer* up one's prayers. In current use, it frequently implies a putting before one something which may be accepted or rejected according to his will or choice; as, "There was a crown *offered* him: and being *offered* him, he put it by" (*Shak.*); "Had he succeeded, he told me, he would have *offered* me the post of sub-editor" (*H. Ellis*). The verb is also used both transitively and intransitively in the sense of to put something before one for consideration, selection, as a way out of a difficulty, or the like; as, to *offer* one's help; to *offer* a suggestion, a remark, a motion, a plan; to *offer* oneself in marriage; the dress department *offers* several new models this week; he *offered* $10,000 for the house; "she appeared...ready to escape...when a way of escape *offered*" (*Hudson*); "We must ask in the end what they have to *offer* in place of what they denounce" (*T. S. Eliot*). The word is often loosely used in the sense of to give something by or as if by handing it to one, with no suggestion of its formal acceptance or possible rejection; as, "When she *offered* him tea, he made it a point to launch a cautious inquiry if she knew Mr. Farfrae" (*Hardy*). **Proffer,** a more formal or literary term than *offer*, differs from it chiefly in more consistently implying a putting or setting before one something that one is at liberty to accept or reject, and in usually suggesting voluntariness, spontaneity, courtesy, or the like, on the part of the agent; as, he *proffered* his arm to a lady having difficulty in crossing a street; "Dorothea...felt that it would be indelicate just then to ask for any information which Casaubon did not *proffer*" (*G. Eliot*); "rejecting the *proffered* assistance of a couple of officious friends" (*Shaw*); "The flavour of social success is delicious, though it is scorned by those to whose lips the cup has not been *proffered*" (*L. P. Smith*). **Tender** (etymologically, to stretch out, or extend) was originally and still is a formal term in legal use, meaning to offer something to the court or to the person or persons concerned, according to the terms of the law, for formal acceptance or approval; as, to *tender* a thousand dollars in full satisfaction of a debt; the defense will *tender* evidence to prove its contention that the defendant has a sound alibi; to *tender* the oath to a justice being sworn into office. In more general use, *tender* differs from *offer* and *proffer* in carrying a stronger connotation of modesty, humility, gentleness, or the like, on the part of the one who makes the offer; as, "My gracious lord, I *tender* you my service" (*Shak.*); to *tender* one's friendship. "I will not dare to discuss that wisdom here. I observe that when the poets preach it we *tender* them our applause" (*Quiller-Couch*). *Tender*, however, is the idiomatic or highly polite term in certain collocations; as, to *tender* one's resignation; to *tender* one's hospitality; to *tender* one's congratulations. **Present**, as here compared (see also GIVE), carries a stronger implication of ceremonious exhibition or of outward show than any of the preceding terms: otherwise it often suggests little more than *offer* in the sense of to lay or put before one for consideration, selection, approval, one's use or pleasure, or the like; as, the butler *presented* the salver to his mistress; the producer will *present* a new play this week; "My last, least offering, I *present* thee now" (*Cowper*); "There is the fatigued Shakespeare...*presented* by Mr. Lytton Strachey; there is the Messianic Shakespeare...*presented* by Mr. Middleton Murry; and there is the ferocious Shakespeare, a furious Samson, *presented* by Mr. Wyndham Lewis" (*T. S. Eliot*). **Prefer**, as here considered (see also CHOOSE), is now archaic or obsolete in the sense of *proffer* or *present* except in some legal use (as, to *prefer* an indictment; to *prefer* a claim): it is, however, found often in the writings of authors between the late sixteenth and the mid-nineteenth centuries; as, "He spake, and to her hand *preferr'd* the bowl" (*Pope*); "I don't *prefer* any claim to being the soul of Romance" (*Dickens*).

Ana. *Give, present, bestow, confer: *adduce, advance: propose, design, purpose, *intend.

Con. Accept, take, *receive: reject, refuse, *decline.

offhand. *Extemporaneous, extempore, extemporary, improvised, impromptu, unpremeditated.

Ana. Casual, desultory, *random: abrupt, hasty, sudden, *precipitate, impetuous: brusque, curt, blunt (see BLUFF).

Con. Studied, advised, considered, *deliberate.

office. **1** *Function, duty, province.

Ana. *Work, métier, business, calling: *task, job, chore, stint.

2 Post, situation, *position, place, job, berth, billet, capacity.

officer. *Policeman, constable, bailiff, catchpole, gendarme, bobby, peeler, copper, cop, bull.

officious. Meddlesome, intrusive, obtrusive, *impertinent, pragmatical.

Ana. Meddling, interfering, intermeddling, tampering (see MEDDLE): annoying, vexing, irking, bothering (see ANNOY): pushing, assertive, *aggressive.

offset. Countervail, balance, *compensate, counterbalance, counterpoise.

Ana. *Neutralize, negative, counteract: *nullify, negate: redeem, reclaim, save, *rescue.

oft. *Often, frequently, oftentimes.

often. **Often, frequently, oft, oftentimes** are ordinarily used with little or no distinction as meaning again and again in more or less close succession. But **often** stresses the number of times a thing occurs, without regard to the interval of recurrence; **frequently** usually stresses repetition, especially at short intervals; as, he came *often;* he called *frequently;* the disease is *often* fatal; "I *frequently* examined the colour of the snow" (*J. Tyndall*); you will *often* find this to be true; unless you write me more *frequently* I shall feel out of touch with you. **Oft** and **oftentimes** differ little from *often; oft,* however, is usually archaic or poetic (as, "*Oft* in the stilly night"—*T. Moore*) and *oftentimes* is occasionally preferred for metrical reasons, or as a more explicit term than *often* in its clear implication of numerous times (as, he will *oftentimes* regret that fit of anger).

oftentimes. *Often, frequently, oft.

oil, *n.* **Oil, fat, wax, grease** are comparable when they denote a substance of smooth, slippery consistency, typically combustible and insoluble in water, but soluble in gasoline (or other petroleum distillates) or, with some limitations, in ether or in alcohol. **Oil** designates any of a large class of such substances that are liquid, or at least easily liquefiable on warming, and that are used variously, as for food, for fuel, and in the preparation of medicines, perfumes, and lubricants. The term is applicable to all substances of this character, whether of animal origin, as cod-liver *oil*, neat's-foot *oil;* vegetable origin, as olive *oil*, wintergreen *oil;* mineral origin, as kerosene *oil*, shale *oil*. Although there are natural oils, such as petroleum and whale oil, many if not most oils are derived by extraction, expression, or distillation. **Fat** commonly designates a substance which, either as a semisolid or liquid, is found both in the animal and vegetable organism as part of its structure or as a constituent of one of its secretions, and is of considerable nutritive value when the organism or secretion is used as food. It is the chief element of adipose tissue and constitutes an important element of the milk of female animals: it is also found in certain seeds, such as nuts, and certain fruits, such as the olive. It is usually separable from the organism or secretion by processes which decompose the latter; thus, butter, an animal *fat*, is obtained by churning cream and leaving buttermilk as a residue; the *fat* of olive, olive oil, is obtained by expression. Chemically, a fat is distinguished from the other substances here differentiated: it is usually a mixture of glyceryl esters of certain acids, such as oleic and stearic acids, that upon saponification yield glycerol. **Wax** was originally applied only to a substance obtained from a secretion of bees and used by them in constructing the honeycomb; besides this specific sense, the term, however, is now also used in the far more comprehensive sense in which it is here considered. Like a fat, a wax is of animal or vegetable origin, but in contrast to the former it is typically a secretion and in its physical properties is less greasy, harder, and more brittle; thus, spermaceti is a *wax* which separates from the oil of a sperm whale; Chinese *wax* is a substance deposited on certain trees by a scale insect that is common in China and India; carnauba *wax* is obtained from a secretion on the leaves of a Brazilian palm tree, called the carnauba.

Also, in contrast to a fat, a wax is not a food, but is used chiefly in the making of candles, ointments, floor polishes, and the like; one of its physical properties is its readiness to blend with a fat or oil, as in most cerates. Chemically also, so called "true waxes" are distinguished from fats by being esters of higher monohydric alcohols. Certain oils, such as sperm oil, which belong to this group chemically, are called by some "liquid waxes." The term *wax* is also applied to a number of substances which resemble waxes physically, but are either chemically fats, such as bayberry wax, or are of mineral origin and chemically diverse, such as the mixture of hydrocarbons known as paraffin wax and the preparation of shellac and Venice turpentine known as sealing wax. **Grease** is a more popular and less clearly defined term than any of the preceding. The most common of its senses in current use, and the best-grounded historically, is that of animal fat which has been melted and become semisolid in cooling; in this use, the term is applicable to the drippings from meat in cooking (as, sausage *grease*), to melted or rendered adipose tissue (as, goose *grease*), and to the more refined rendered fats, such as lard. The term is also used of any substance composed of fat or fats, wax or waxes, mineral oils, soapy materials, and the like, which is in appearance and texture like animal grease and is used as an ointment, lubricant, or cleanser; as, axle *grease;* cup *grease* (a mixture of petroleum oil, lime or soda soap, etc., used in lubricating mechanisms); face *grease* (a colloquial designation of face cream).

oil, *v.* **Oil, grease, lubricate, anoint, inunct, cream, pomade, pomatum** agree in meaning to smear with an oily, fatty, or similar substance, but they vary greatly in their implications of the substance used and the purpose for which it is employed and in their idiomatic applications. One **oils** the parts of a machine or mechanism subject to friction, typically by drops or squirts of a liquid substance, usually but not necessarily a mineral oil. Also, one *oils* a fabric, such as cloth, silk, paper, etc., when one impregnates it with oil so as to make it waterproof. One **greases** a thing when one rubs on or in a thick fatty substance, often, but far from always, an animal fat or oil, for some purpose such as to increase speed by reducing friction (as, to *grease* axles), or as a medicinal application (as, to *grease* the chest with lard and turpentine), or as a preventive of cohesion (as, to *grease* a baking dish). One **lubricates** when one oils, or greases, or provides for the feeding of oil or grease or some similar substance to, contiguous surfaces in a machine or mechanism to make them slippery, thereby reducing friction, eliminating roughness, and preventing cohesion. *Lubricate* stresses the effect intended or produced; *oil* and *grease,* the substance used or the method of its application. One **anoints,** in strict use, only the body or a part of the body, when one smears it with, or rubs into it, an oily or fatty substance for some purpose such as a protection from the sun, an aid in massage, or the like. *Anoint,* however, is now especially employed in reference to ceremonial uses of oil (see ANOINT, 2). The word preferred in medicine when an oil or fatty application is rubbed in so as to be absorbed by the pores, is **inunct,** or its more common derivative noun *inunction.* In the application of oily or fatty cosmetics, especially those which are called creams, **cream** is the customary term. When one uses perfumed unguent (a pomade) or a greasy substance (a pomatum) to smooth and brighten the hair, or to nourish the scalp, **pomade** and **pomatum** are the specific, but not common, terms. "Their hair...was scrupulously *pomatumed* back from their foreheads with a candle" (*Irving*).

oily. Unctuous, oleaginous, *fulsome, sleek, soapy.

Ana. Ingratiating, insinuating, insinuative, *disarming: hypocritical, pharisaical, sanctimonious (see under HYPOCRISY): bland, politic, diplomatic, smooth (see SUAVE).

old. 1 *Aged, elderly, superannuated.

Ana. *Weak, feeble, infirm, decrepit: *senile, anile, doting, doddering.

Ant. Young.

2 Old, ancient, venerable, antique, antiquated, antediluvian, archaic, obsolete all denote having come into existence or use in the more or less distant past. That is **old** (opposed to *young, new:* see AGED) which has lived or existed long, or which has been long in use or has stood for a long time in a particular relation to something; that is **ancient** (opposed esp. to *modern*) which lived, existed, or happened long ago, or which has existed or come down from remote antiquity; as, *old* wine, books, friends; *old* as the hills. "O heavens, if you do love *old* men...if yourselves are *old*" (*Shak.*). "The papers were dull, the news was local and stale, and the war news was all *old*" (*Hemingway*). "From the *ancient* world those giants came" (*Milton*). "Some illustrious line so *ancient* that it has no beginning" (*Gibbon*). But *ancient* and *old* are often interchangeable; as, the *ancient* Romans; the *old* Romans. "It is an *ancient* mariner" (*Coleridge*). "*Old,* unhappy, far-off things, and battles long ago" (*Wordsworth*). **Venerable,** as here compared (cf. *august* under GRAND), suggests the hoariness and dignity of age. "An *old* man...[who] appeared the more *ancient* from his gray locks, that were truly *venerable*" (*Smollett*). "*Venerable* as Anglo-Saxon is, and worthy to be studied as the mother of our vernacular speech" (*Quiller-Couch*). **Antique** applies to that which has come down from ancient (esp. classical) times, or which is in some way related to them or, with regard to furniture and other household articles, to an old-fashioned type characteristic of an earlier period; as, an *antique* highboy or clock that belonged to one's great-grandmother. "Even a Leonardo regretted his failure to recover the *antique* symmetry, but he at least imitated the ancients vitally" (*Babbitt*). "Refreshing our minds with a savour of the *antique,* primeval world and the earliest hopes and victories of mankind" (*Binyon*). That is **antiquated** which has gone out of vogue or fashion, or that has been for some time discredited; the word often implies a slight touch of contempt. "For the purpose of...endowing it [an almost mushroom period] with an *antiquated* air, events can be as powerful as the passage of time" (*Lucas*). "Is it true that *antiquated* legal ideas prevent government from responding effectively to the demands which modern society makes upon it?" (*Frankfurter*). That is **antediluvian,** literally, which existed before the Noachian Flood; by extension, and always contemptuously, which is extremely antiquated. "The whole system of travelling accommodations was barbarous and *antediluvian*" (*De Quincey*). That is **archaic** which has the characteristics of an earlier, sometimes of a primitive, period; with regard to words, specifically, *archaic* implies not in use in ordinary modern language but retained in special context or for special uses, as in Biblical, ecclesiastical, and legal expressions and in poetry (e.g., *belike, certes*). "We visited Medinin, a town so *archaic* and unreal in its architecture that it was difficult to believe that it was actually inhabited by the human race" (*M. Hoffman*). That is **obsolete** which has gone out of use, or which contains what has gone out of use; as, "a...link between *obsolete* forms of life and those which generally prevail" (*Hardy*). "As [a writer's] language grows *obsolete,* his thoughts must grow obscure"

(*Dryden*). "A scientific textbook is *obsolete* in a decade or less" (*Lowes*).

Ana. *Secular, centuried, agelong, diuturnal, aeonian: primitive, primeval, pristine, primal (see PRIMARY).

Ant. New.

oleaginous. Oily, unctuous, *fulsome, sleek, soapy.

Ana. See those at OILY.

oligarchy. **Oligarchy, aristocracy, plutocracy** come into comparison as meaning government by, or a state governed by, the few. The terms are often applied to governments or states that are ostensibly monarchies or democracies, but are, in the opinion of the user, governed by a clique. **Oligarchy** is the most inclusive term referable to any government or state where the power is openly or virtually in the hands of a few men. "The present [1932] government [of Russia], political and economic...is a self-appointed *oligarchy*" (*J. A. Hobson*). **Aristocracy** etymologically suggests the rule of the best citizens, but it seldom retains this implication except when it is used in distinction from *oligarchy* and the latter connotes power seized or held for selfish or corrupt reasons. "An *Oligarchy* is the swerving, or the corruption of an *Aristocracy*" (*Raleigh*, d. 1618). "It ceased to be, in the Greek sense, an *aristocracy;* it became a faction, an *oligarchy*" (*Thirlwall*). Its commonest current implication is power vested in a privileged class, especially in a nobility that is regarded as superior by birth and breeding and that by owning or controlling much of the land exercises direct control over a large portion of the population; in this sense, Great Britain was until recent generations an *aristocracy*. **Plutocracy,** unlike the other terms, is usually, not occasionally, derogatory; as a rule, it implies concentration of power in the hands of the wealthy and in consequence, a withholding of power from those to whom it properly belongs, either the people or their representatives. "It is true that we still have in England the forms of *aristocracy*, but the spirit is that of *plutocracy*, which is quite a different thing" (*B. Russell*). "Democracy has to fight its way out from under *plutocracy*" (*H. G. Wells*).

omen, *n.* Augury, portent, *foretoken, presage, prognostic.

Ana. *Sign, mark, token, badge, note, symptom: divination, clairvoyance (see DISCERNMENT): foreboding, *apprehension, presentiment, misgiving.

ominous. **Ominous, portentous, fateful, inauspicious, unpropitious** come into comparison as basically meaning having a menacing or threatening character or quality. That is **ominous** which has or seems to have the character of an omen, especially of an omen forecasting evil: in current use, however, the term commonly suggests a frightening or alarming quality that bodes no good, but seldom implies inevitable disaster; as, "an *ominous* change had come over nature" (*Hudson*); "my ears were startled by the...uproar of yelling and shouting. It sounded *ominous*, but....I had to go on" (*V. Heiser*). That is **portentous** which has or seems to have the character of a portent, or some prodigy of nature which gives a forewarning of a calamity to come (as, a *portentous* eclipse; a *portentous* comet). In current use *portentous* far less often than *ominous* suggests a threatening character: it usually means little more than prodigious, monstrous, almost frighteningly marvelous, solemn, or the like; as, "His gravity was unusual, *portentous*, and immeasurable" (*Dickens*); "the assertion that children of six are 'mighty prophets, seers blessed,' would...have seemed to him [Plato] *portentous* nonsense" (*Babbitt*); "They all look *portentous;* but they have nothing to say" (*Shaw*). That is **fateful** which has or, more often, seems to have, the quality, character, or importance decreed for it by fate or that suggests inevitable death or calamity; as, the *fateful* conference that brought on war; "The soldier's *fateful* steel" (*J. Barlow*). In present use, however, the term means little more than momentous, appallingly decisive, or the like; as, "A *fateful* evening doth descend upon us" (*Coleridge*); "Lying awake till morning, Delia lived over every detail of the *fateful* day when she had assumed the charge of Charlotte's child" (*E. Wharton*). That is **inauspicious** (see *auspicious* under FAVORABLE) which is or seems to be attended by signs that are distinctly unfavorable; as, an *inauspicious* horoscope. But *inauspicious* now usually means nothing more than unlucky, unfortunate, or unlikely to succeed; as, an *inauspicious* beginning of a great project; an *inauspicious* war. That is **unpropitious** (see *propitious* under FAVORABLE) which carries or seems to carry no sign of favoring one's ends or intentions; as, *unpropitious* omens. In its more common extended sense, the term means merely unfavorable, discouraging, or harmful; as, "sleep and exercise are *unpropitious* to learning" (*Jowett*); his attitude was *unpropitious*, and suggested a refusal.

Ana. *Sinister, baleful, malign, malefic: threatening, menacing (see THREATEN).

omit. *Neglect, disregard, ignore, overlook, slight, forget.

Ana. Cancel, delete, dele, efface, *erase: *exclude, eliminate.

Con. *Remember, recollect, recall: *tend, attend, mind, watch.

omnipotent. **Omnipotent, almighty** are not clearly distinguishable when applied to God and meaning all-powerful. Nevertheless in their extended and, sometimes, humorous applications a distinction between them is apparent. **Omnipotent** implies the power to effect any or all desired ends, as by irresistible power or by overriding all natural laws. "O powerful love! that, in some respects, makes a beast a man, in some other, a man a beast...O *omnipotent* Love!" (*Shak.*). "Was he not alone *omnipotent* On Earth...? tho' dead Does not his spirit... work for me and mine still the same ruin?" (*Shelley*). **Almighty,** on the other hand, usually stresses the power to command, above everything else, awe, worship, obedience, or the like. "My neglect Of his [Cupid's] *almighty* dreadful little might" (*Shak.*). "Insensible of truth's *almighty* charms" (*Cowper*). "Sir Aylmer Aylmer, that *almighty* man, The county God" (*Tennyson*). "The *almighty* dollar, that great object of universal devotion throughout our land" (*Irving*).

omnipresent. **Omnipresent, ubiquitous, ubiquitary** agree in meaning present or existent everywhere. In strict use, they carry this as a literal or absolute meaning, but in loose current English, they are often used hyperbolically. That is **omnipresent** which is present everywhere at the same time: in earlier and strict use, the term was applicable only to the Supreme Being (as, "*omnipresent* Deity"—*Ken*), but in more recent use, especially in a loose or weakened sense, it applies to that which is always present or existent, as in a class or a type wherever it may be found or in an area to which it belongs (as, "a capable agent makes himself *omnipresent*"—*G. Eliot;* "an *omnipresent* sense of social obligation"—*C. W. Eliot*). That is **ubiquitous** (*or, now comparatively rare,* **ubiquitary**) which is found everywhere and, often but not always, at the time or in the region given or implied; as, "electrons being so numerous and so *ubiquitous*" (*Karl K. Darrow*); "The big public services will have to be made practically *ubiquitous*" (*Shaw*). Either term, but especially *ubiquitous*, is applicable to a singular noun naming a type or an individual, often with the humorous implication that one cannot escape him (or it) wherever one goes; as, the *ubiquitous* American tourist; that child is *ubiquitous;* "the sad, *ubiquitous* spinster, left behind...by the stampede of the young men westward" (*Van W. Brooks*). "God is not *ubiquitous,* but *omnipresent,* and never through all eternity can you and I be nearer to Him than we are at this moment" (*L. Abbott*).

omphalos. *Center, middle, midst, core, hub, focus, nucleus, heart.

on. 1 *At, in.

2 *At, in.

onerous. **Onerous, burdensome, oppressive, exacting** come into comparison when they mean imposing severe trouble, labor, or hardships. All of these terms are applicable to a state of life, its duties or obligations, or to conditions imposed upon a person by that life or by another person: *oppressive* and *exacting* are also applicable to persons or agents responsible for these difficulties. **Onerous** stresses laboriousness and heaviness but often also implies irksomeness or distastefulness; as, the *onerous* life of women among savage tribes; *onerous* tasks. " 'What were the conditions?' 'Oh, they were not *onerous:* just to sit at the head of his table now and then' " (*E. Wharton*). **Burdensome** usually implies mental as well as physical strain, but it often emphasizes the former at the expense of the latter; as, he was finding the life of a farmer unduly *burdensome;* a *burdensome* tax; the restrictions grew increasingly *burdensome.* **Oppressive** adds to *burdensome* the implication of extreme harshness or severity; it, therefore, usually connotes the unendurableness of that which is imposed or inflicted (sometimes by nature as well as by man) or cruelty or tyranny in the one responsible for the impositions or inflictions; as, *oppressive* taxes; *oppressive* legislation; *oppressive* heat; *oppressive* rulers. "There are more ways of coercing a man than by pointing a gun at his head. A pacifist society may be unjust and *oppressive*" (*Inge*). **Exacting,** like *oppressive,* implies extreme severity of demands, but otherwise it differs because it commonly suggests rigor, sternness, or extreme fastidiousness rather than tyranny in the one who demands, or the tremendous care or pains required of the one who satisfies these demands; as, an *exacting* employer; an *exacting* teacher; an *exacting* technique; an *exacting* task. "The *exacting* life of the sea has this advantage over the life of the earth, that its claims are simple and cannot be evaded" (*Conrad*).

Ana. *Heavy, weighty, ponderous, cumbrous, cumbersome, hefty: arduous, *hard, difficult.

onlooker. Looker-on, *spectator, observer, beholder, witness, eyewitness, bystander, kibitzer.

only, *adj. & adv.* **Only, alone** are often used interchangeably (though *alone* is not now found in the attributive position), but seldom if ever without a slight change in meaning or emphasis. **Only** is preferable when restriction to that which is specified or asserted is implied and the term is equivalent to *sole* or *solely;* as, I want *only* this book (that is, this book and no more); of all the family *only* John and Helen came (that is, the specified persons and no more). "To distinguish...that which is established because it is right, from that which is right *only* because it is established" (*Johnson*). **Alone** is preferable when the idea of the elimination of all other possibilities is expressed and the term is the equivalent of *exclusive* or, more often, *exclusively;* as, I want this book *alone* (that is, this book and not any of the others); of all the family John *alone* came (that is, John and none of the others). "Man shall not live by bread *alone,* but by every word that proceedeth out of the mouth of God" (*Matthew* iv. 4).

onomasticon. *Dictionary, lexicon, wordbook, glossary, gazetteer, synonymicon.

onset. *Attack, assault, onslaught.

Ana. Aggression, offensive, offense, *attack: storming, bombarding, assailing (see ATTACK, *v.*): *invasion, raid, incursion, irruption.

onslaught. *Attack, assault, onset.

Ana. See those at ONSET.

onward. **Onward, forward, forth** are here compared as meaning in the act of advancing or getting ahead, as in a movement, progression, series, sequence, or the like. They are frequently used with little or no distinction, but **onward** often suggests progress or advance in general toward a definite goal, end, place, or the like; as, "*Onward,* Christian soldiers, Marching as to war" (*Baring-Gould*); "*onward*-looking men" (*Stevenson*). **Forward** (opposed to *backward*) has more specific reference to movement or advance with reference to that which lies before rather than back in place (see *forward* under BEFORE), in time (as, from that time *forward* he took command), or in a succession, such as the incidents of a narrative or the steps of a process (as, "I am got *forward* too fast with my story"—*Franklin*). **Forth** is often interchangeable with *forward* without loss (as, from that day *forth;* go *forth,* brave soldier) but it is the preferred term in certain idiomatic phrases; thus, one says "backward and *forward*" or "back and *forth,*" the latter phrase often implying swifter or more frequent changes than the former (as, back and *forth* her needle flew); one brings *forth* from, or as if from, a place of concealment (as, to bring *forth* a precious jewel), but one brings *forward* something or someone already in plain view (as, bring *forward* your chair).

opalescent, opaline. Iridescent, *prismatic.

opaque. Obscure, dusk, dusky, darkling, *dark, murky, gloomy.

Ana. *Turbid, muddy, roiled, roily: dull, dense, crass (see STUPID).

open, *adj.* **1** Exposed, subject, prone, susceptible, sensitive, *liable, incident.

Ant. Closed.

2 Plain, candid, *frank.

Ana. *Straightforward, aboveboard, forthright: *natural, simple, ingenuous, naïve, unsophisticated: *fair, equitable, impartial.

Ant. Close, close-mouthed, close-lipped: clandestine.

open-air. *Outdoor, plein-air, alfresco.

operate. *Act, behave, work, function, react.

operative, *adj.* *Active, dynamic, live.

Ana. *Effective, effectual, efficacious, efficient: *fertile, fecund, fruitful.

Ant. Abeyant.

operative, *n.* Mechanic, artisan, hand, workman, workingman, *worker, laborer, craftsman, roustabout.

opiate. *Anodyne, narcotic, nepenthe.

opinion. **Opinion, view, belief, conviction, persuasion, sentiment** come into comparison when they mean a more or less clearly formulated idea or judgment which one holds as true. An **opinion** is a more or less carefully thought-out conclusion concerning something that is or may be questioned. The word not only does not exclude the suggestion of consideration of all the evidence and of arguments on both sides, but it sometimes implies such consideration; as, Justice —— presented the minority *opinion* at today's session of the Supreme Court; the critics differ in their *opinion* of the quality of the book; to seek an expert *opinion* on the authenticity of a painting; the attending physician said he would like the *opinion* of a consulting physician. However, the term more consistently suggests (even in the preceding instances) a personal element in the judgment, the possibility of its being in error, and the strong probability that it will be disputed. " 'If you doubt it, ask Stryver, and he'll tell you so.' 'I prefer to form my own *opinion*, without the aid of his' " (*Dickens*). " 'Books...are a public expression of a man's *opinions*, and consequently they are submitted to the world for criticism' " (*A. C. Benson*). A **view** is an opinion more or less colored by the feeling, sentiment, or bias of the individual; as, he was fond of airing his *views* in the public press; this poet's depressing *view* of life; each member was asked to state his *views* on the proposed change in the constitution. A **belief** differs from an opinion or view in that it is not necessarily formulated by the individual who holds it, but may have been proposed to him for acceptance (as in the form of a doctrine, a dogma, a proposition, or an authoritative opinion). The emphasis in *belief* is placed on intellectual assent or assurance of truth. "He [Augustus] possessed from the start...certain guiding ideas derived from Julius [Caesar], a passion for order, a realism about facts, and a *belief* that he possessed a capacity for reconstruction" (*Buchan*). "It might be better not to call this pantheistic creed Naturalism, reserving the name for the *belief* that the whole system of nature is calculable in terms of mathematics and mechanics" (*Inge*). "I have not adopted my faith in order to defend my *views* of conduct, but have modified my *views* of conduct to conform with what seem to me the implications of my *beliefs*" (*T. S. Eliot*). A **conviction** is a belief which one holds firmly and unshakably because one is undisturbed by doubt of its truth. "If any one had asked him the reason of this *conviction* he could not have told them; but *convictions* do not imply reasons" (*Deland*). "The teacher should learn not to take sides [in controversial questions], even if he or she has strong *convictions*" (*B. Russell*). A **persuasion** is usually at once an opinion and a belief. It often implies that one's assurance of its truth is induced by one's feelings or wishes, rather than by argument or evidence. "It was the avowed opinion and *persuasion* of Callimachus...that Homer was very imperfectly understood even in his day" (*Cowper*). " 'Drugs are not much in cases of this sort. Change! That's what's wanted.... It's no use my talking, I know,' added the Doctor. 'On the contrary,' said Sir Austin, 'I am quite of your *persuasion*' " (*Meredith*). **Sentiment,** as here compared (see also FEELING, 2; SENTIMENT, 3), is now rare or literary in this sense except in a few idiomatic phrases (as, those are my *sentiments*), but it was very common between the late seventeenth and the early nineteenth centuries. The term applies to a more or less settled opinion; often, but not necessarily, with reference to something which involves one's feelings or which is formulated so as to suggest the stimulus of emotion; as, "His 'Solomon' had many noble *sentiments* elegantly expressed" (*Johnson*); " 'Had I the command of millions, were I mistress of the whole world, your brother would be my only choice.' This charming *sentiment*...gave Catherine a most pleasing remembrance of all the heroines of her acquaintance" (*Austen*); "There is no expression in the constitution, no *sentiment* delivered by its contemporaneous expounders, which would justify us in making it [a certain exception]" (*Ch. Just. Marshall*).

Ana. Thought, notion, impression, *idea, concept, conception: inference, deduction, conclusion, judgment (see under INFER): deciding *or* decision, determining *or* determination, settling *or* settlement (see corresponding verbs at DECIDE).

opinionated. **Opinionated, opinionative, self-opinionated** agree in meaning having or holding a decided opinion or opinions. **Opinionated** is now the far more common term: it usually implies either great assurance of the rightness of one's opinions or great obstinacy in their maintenance; as, "[A] painter...bold and *opinionated* enough to dare and to dictate" (*Walpole*). "He is not overbearing, or bigoted, or fanatical—that would be putting it too strongly....He seems to put an excessive value on his own opinions. Yes, I have the word —*opinionated*" (*S. M. Crothers*). **Opinionative** is now comparatively rare, but it is still sometimes preferred to *opinionated* when one wishes to suggest the speculative or doctrinaire character (as opposed to the practical value) of a person's opinions, at the same time suggesting dogmatism in their maintenance; as, "Too young to teach, and too *opinionative* to learn" (*Johnson*); "The common female blue [i.e., bluestocking] is intolerable, *opinionative*, and *opinionated*" (*Edgeworth*). **Self-opinionated** carries a stronger implication of conceitedness or of pride in one's opinions than either of these terms but, like *opinionative*, it usually suggests dogmatism in their maintenance; as, he is far too *self-opinionated* to yield to argument.

Ana. *Sure, certain, positive, cocksure: *confident, assured, sanguine, sure.

opinionative. *Opinionated, self-opinionated.

Ana. Doctrinaire, dogmatic, *dictatorial: *sure, certain, positive, cocksure.

opponent. **Opponent, antagonist, adversary** agree in denoting one who expresses or manifests opposition. Unlike *enemy* (in its strict sense), they do not necessarily imply personal animosity or hostility. An **opponent** is one who is on the opposite side in a contest (as an argument, disputation, or election), or in a conflict of opinion; **antagonist** implies sharper opposition, esp. in a struggle or combat for supremacy or control. "The *opponents* and proponents of the bill" (*N. Y. Times*). "Where you find your *antagonist* beginning to grow warm, put an end to the dispute by some genteel badinage" (*Chesterfield*). **Adversary** ranges in connotation from the idea of mere opposition to that of active hostility. "Do as *adversaries* do in law, Strive mightily, but eat and drink as friends" (*Shak.*). "Your *adversary* the devil, as a roaring lion, walketh about, seeking whom he may devour" (*1 Peter* v. 8).

Ana. *Enemy, foe: rival, competitor, emulator (see corresponding verbs at RIVAL).

opportune. *Seasonable, timely, well-timed, pat.

Ana. Happy, felicitous, appropriate, fitting (see FIT, *adj.*): propitious, auspicious, *favorable: ready, prompt, *quick, apt.

Ant. Inopportune.

opportunity. **Opportunity, occasion, chance, break, time, tide, hint** come into comparison when they mean a state of affairs or a juncture of circumstances favorable to some end. **Opportunity** is perhaps the most common of these terms in both colloquial and literary English: it applies to a juncture which provides an opening for doing something, especially something in line with one's inclinations, ambitions, purposes, or desires; as, the suspect had both motive and *opportunity* for the murder; "To keep in the rear of *opportunity* in matters of indulgence is as valuable a habit as to keep abreast of *opportunity* in matters of enterprise" (*Hardy*); "on the whole an infant's desire to learn is so strong that parents need only provide *opportunity*" (*B. Russell*). **Occasion,** as here considered (see also CAUSE, 1), carries the basic denotation characteristic of its leading senses—a definite moment or juncture, but it applies only to a moment that provides an opportunity or, more often in current use, that calls for or prompts action of a definite kind or nature. In its earliest use, *occasion* meant the opportune moment or the opportunity provided by a moment: an occasion therefore was visualized, as an opportunity is now often visualized, as something that comes and goes almost before its presence is realized. This use continues in certain idiomatic phrases; as, he took the *occasion* to satisfy his desire for revenge; "We can escape even now, So we take fleet *occasion* by the hair" (*Shelley*). In current use, *occasion* suggests more strongly than *opportunity* a juncture that provokes or evokes action; as, "With *occasion* she might have been a Charlotte Corday" (*Meredith*); "With great things charged he shall not hold Aloof till great *occasion* rise" (*Kipling*); "So long as a child is with adults, it has no *occasion* for the exercise of a number of...virtues...required by the strong in dealing with the weak" (*B. Russell*). **Chance** applies chiefly to an opportunity that comes seemingly by luck or accident; as, they had no *chance* to escape; he has long hoped for a *chance* of promotion. Sometimes, the word means little more than a fair or a normal opportunity, especially in negative expressions; as, the boy never had a *chance* to make anything of himself. **Break** is slang (chiefly in the United States) for a chance to make good (or to fail), to make profits (or to lose money), to better oneself (or to lower oneself), or the like: ordinarily, the term is qualified by an adjective indicating the kind of chance and suggesting its outcome (as, he has had a bad *break;* that investment was a lucky *break* for him; he has not had a fair *break* in years) but when it is unqualified, the term usually denotes a good, or lucky, break (as, he is still hoping for a *break;* one says that a team "gets the *breaks*" but a good team usually makes its own *breaks*). **Time** and **tide** are archaic or poetic only when used as a phrase denoting a juncture that is well-timed or opportune for the execution of one's end or purpose: *time* especially, and *tide* somewhat, are still used singly in this sense; as, *time* and *tide* wait for no man; "There is a *tide* in the affairs of men, Which, taken at the flood, leads on to fortune" (*Shak.*); this is the *time* to buy stocks: even tomorrow may be too late. **Hint** is now obsolete in the sense of opportunity or occasion, but it was once common, especially in the 17th and 18th centuries; as, "It was my *hint* to speak" (*Shak.*); "To watch the *hints* which conversation offers for the display of their particular attainments" (*Johnson*).

Ana. *Juncture, pass, contingency, emergency: posture, situation, condition, *state.

oppose. **Oppose, combat, resist, withstand, antagonize** are here compared only as transitive verbs and as meaning to set oneself against someone or something. **Oppose** is the most comprehensive of these words; it may imply at one extreme little more than objection and at the other intense hostility and violent warfare. It commonly implies the intent to thwart or frustrate the will of another or to destroy that which actively interferes with one's own rights or security. "After that they did not *oppose* his plan of leaving the house" (*Deland*). "At the town meeting there is always the chronic objector who *opposes* every popular measure" (*S. M. Crothers*). "Or to take arms against a sea of troubles, And by *opposing* end them?" (*Shak.*). **Combat** stresses a struggle for supremacy and an actual conflict with that which one opposes. In modern English the struggle is often mental (as, to *combat* temptation, one's fears, a weakness) and, when external, the conflict is usually with intangibles, such as ideas, forces, or evils, which one would figuratively put to rout. "He would rather *combat* the superstitions of a whole Indian pueblo than the vanity of one white woman" (*Cather*). "How to *combat* diphtheria or appendicitis or tuberculosis" (*C. W. Eliot*). "Certain fallacies, which it is the duty of the better informed members of society to meet and *combat*" (*Grandgent*). **Resist** and **withstand** both presuppose the initiative in opposition on the other side, as by attack, encroachment, or the use of compulsion. *Resist* merely implies acceptance of the challenge and the exercise of counter force; as, it is the duty of every patriot to *resist* invasion. "To attempt to impose it on us...is an act of tyranny, and to be *resisted*" (*Arnold*). "We must firmly *resist* those who wish to make education purely scientific" (*Inge*). *Withstand* often adds to *resist* the suggestion of a successful outcome; it, therefore, usually implies special qualities in the person or group, such as courage, persistence, or superior training; as, only seasoned troops could *withstand* such an attack. "They had been married that afternoon...Jane having *withstood* the pressure of her parents" (*R. Macaulay*). When used of things that are proof against the onslaught of external forces, such as germs, the elements, military attacks, and the like, there is little difference between the two words, *withstand* being slightly more emphatic; as, few trees could *withstand* (or *resist*) the fury of the hurricane; to *resist* (or *withstand*) infection. Both words also are often used without any connotation of threatened danger from the other side but with a strong suggestion of its power to compel by attracting, convincing, or the like; in these cases either the verb or the subject contains a negative or a near negative; as, one cannot (or, few persons can) *withstand* her charm. "Nobody can *resist* the Bay of Naples, or if he can, then all the simple and sensuous delights of this world must turn to bitterness and ashes in his mouth" (*C. Mackenzie*). **Antagonize** implies that one side (usually one's own) has initiated the opposition and has, therefore, invited resistance or hostility. "The Bishop replied that the time was not yet; for the present it was inexpedient to *antagonize* these people" (*Cather*). In current use, the word often means to incite (sometimes unintentionally) ill will or resentment; as, he is unfortunate because his manner *antagonizes* many persons.

Ana. *Contend, cope, fight, battle, war: *attack, assail, assault, storm, bombard: *defend, protect, shield, guard, safeguard.

opposite, *adj.* **Opposite, contradictory, contrary, antithetical** (*or* **antithetic**), **antipodal** (*or* **antipodean**), **antonymous** are comparable chiefly as applied to abstractions and as meaning so far apart as to be or to seem irreconcilable with each other. The same differences in applications and implications are found in their corresponding nouns, **opposite, contradictory, contrary, antithesis, antipodes** (*or* **antipode**), **antonym,** when they mean one of two things which are opposite, contradictory, etc. *Opposite,* as here narrowly considered, is the inclusive term; it may be used interchangeably with any of the others, though few of the latter are interchangeable in precise use. **Opposite** may be used to describe the relation of either of two ideas, terms, statements, qualities, forces, and the like, to the other when they are set against each other so as to bring out sharply the contrast, conflict, or antagonism between them; as, *opposite* views; attraction and repulsion are *opposite* forces. "Democratism, the tendency to level down all superiorities in the name of equality and good fellowship...is the *opposite* fault to the aristocratism...the assumption that the lower classes must remain excluded from intellectual and even from moral excellence" (*Inge*). **Contradictory,** though often used loosely as an equivalent of *opposite,* retains in precise use its fundamental implication of denial, and therefore, especially when it is applied to terms, propositions, and principles, further implies that if one of the two opposites be true, the other must be false, or if one be false, the other must be true. For any words, propositions, or principles that are *contradictory* in this strict sense are mutually exclusive and, therefore, admit no possibilities between; thus, "John is English" and "John is not English" are *contradictory* statements, one of which must be false if the other is true; "alive" and "dead," are *contradictory* terms because they cannot both be truly applied to the same thing, for if the application is admissible one of them must be true and the other false (as, the tree is either alive or dead). **Contrary,** as here compared (see also CONTRARY, 2), is also used both loosely and strictly. As applied to intentions, motives, opinions, and the like, it usually implies extreme divergence with no basis for agreement; as, to take a *contrary* view of the situation; he maintained that the *contrary* was true. In strict use, especially as applied to terms, propositions, and the like, *contrary* implies diametrical opposition, or the greatest conceivable or possible difference between the things opposed. Contraries are "poles apart"; unlike contradictories, both may be false, for they represent extremes and do not mutually exclude every other possibility; thus, "destitute" and "opulent" are *contrary* terms as applicable to a person's circumstances, but they may be inapplicable in a vast number of particular cases for they describe only the extremes; thus, "John is parsimonious" and "John is prodigal" are *contrary* statements, but John in truth may be neither parsimonious nor prodigal, but merely close, or thrifty, or free, or liberal, in the expenditure of money. **Antithetical** and especially **antithesis** (see also COMPARISON) imply an intent to set the thing under consideration against its opposite, usually its diametrical opposite, in order to emphasize its significance or to reveal or define sharply its true nature. Both words are applicable to persons and things regarded objectively as well as to ideas, qualities, terms, and the like. "I could describe...my own particular *antithesis* among bookworms; and no doubt he could, and probably will, describe me" (*J. C. Powys*). "That mystic faith in unseen powers which is the *antithesis* of materialism" (*R. Macaulay*). "The essential interests of men and women are eternally *antithetical*" (*Mencken*). Although **antipodal** and **antipodes** (the latter in this sense is now construed as a singular and preferred to **antipode**) also imply diametrical opposition, they do not suggest an expository purpose but rather an attempt to emphasize the unlikeness and the remoteness from each other of the things contrasted. So strong are these implications that, at times, the things contrasted are only figuratively, not generically, opposites, and the contrast constitutes, in a sense, an inverse simile. "The same insurgent journal [may] print poems as *antipodal* as a slaughter house and a hand-painted fan" (*Lowes*). "*Antipodes* of each other in temper and endowment" (*J. R. Lowell*). **Antonymous** and **antonym** are applicable only to a word or term which is so opposed to another in meaning that it, in effect, negates or nullifies every implication of it. Antonyms (or antonymous words) may be contradictory or contrary terms, as defined, or they may be terms which negate other terms by implying the undoing or reversing of what is denoted by them; thus, "retain" is the contradictory *antonym* of "lose," but "recover" is the latter word's reverse *antonym*. *Antonym* is sometimes applied to terms that are opposite only in the sense of being relative or complementary (as, *husband* and *wife*, *stimulus* and *response*, *question* and *answer*), but this application is not generally regarded as defensible.

Ana. Reverse, *converse: antagonistic, *adverse, counter, counteractive.

Con. Reconciling, conforming, adapting, adjusting (see ADAPT): consistent, compatible, congruous, congenial, *consonant.

opposite, *n.* Contradictory, contrary, antithesis, antipodes, antonym. See under OPPOSITE, *adj.*

oppress. 1 *Depress, weigh (down, on, *or* upon).

Ana. *Abuse, mistreat, maltreat, ill-treat, outrage: *worry, annoy, harass, harry.

2 *Wrong, persecute, aggrieve.

Ana. *Afflict, torment, torture: overcome, subdue, subjugate, reduce, overthrow (see CONQUER).

oppressive. *Onerous, burdensome, exacting.

Ana. Extorting *or* extortionate, extracting (see corresponding verbs at EDUCE): compelling *or* compulsory, coercing *or* coercion, constraining, obliging *or* obligatory (see corresponding verbs at FORCE): despotic, tyrannical, *absolute, arbitrary.

Con. Humane, humanitarian (see CHARITABLE): compassionate, *tender.

opprobrious. *Abusive, vituperative, contumelious, scurrilous, scurrile, scurril.

Ana. Reviling, vituperating, railing, berating (see SCOLD): despiteful, *malicious, malevolent, malign, malignant: *execrable, damnable, accursed.

opprobrium. Obloquy, odium, ignominy, infamy, shame, *disgrace, dishonor, disrepute, scandal.

Ana. *Abuse, invective, vituperation, obloquy, scurrility: censure, denunciation, condemnation, reprehension (see corresponding verbs at CRITICIZE).

Con. Prestige, authority, credit, *influence.

opt, *v.* *Choose, select, elect, pick, cull, handpick, prefer, single out.

Ana. Take, accept, *receive: *adopt, embrace, espouse.

optimistic. *Hopeful, roseate, rose-colored.

Ana. *Confident, sanguine, assured: cheerful, lighthearted, joyous, *glad.

Ant. Pessimistic. — *Con.* *Cynical, misanthropic.

option. *Choice, alternative, preference, selection, election.

Ana. *Right, prerogative, privilege.

opulent. 1 Affluent, wealthy, *rich.

Ana. Lavish, *profuse, prodigal: *showy, pretentious, ostentatious, pompous.

Ant. Destitute: indigent.

2 Sumptuous, *luxurious.

Ana. Luxuriant, lush, exuberant (see PROFUSE): *splendid, resplendent, gorgeous, superb.

opus. *Work, product, production, artifact.

oracular. Doctrinaire, dogmatic, authoritative, *dictatorial, authoritarian, magisterial, magistral.

Ana. *Opinionated, opinionative, self-opinionated: positive, certain, *sure, cocksure.

oral. 1 *Vocal, articulate.

Ant. Written.

2 Oral, verbal are often confused in use. **Oral** (see also VOCAL, 1) always implies utterance and speech: it is correctly applied to that which is delivered, communicated, transacted, carried on, or the like, directly from one to another by word of mouth; as, an *oral* (as opposed to a written) confession, tradition, command; to receive *oral* instructions; *oral* teaching of the deaf (as distinguished from teaching by signs). **Verbal** stresses the use of words: in correct use, it applies indifferently to that which is written or spoken, for it carries no implication of the method of communication; as, *verbal* (i.e., word for word) inspiration of the Bible; *verbal* difficulties caused by ambiguous or equivocal language; "He often loses himself in little trifling distinctions and *verbal* niceties" (*Gray*). The use of *verbal* as a substitute for *oral* does not meet with approval; as, to receive an *oral* (not a *verbal*) invitation to the dinner; an *oral* (not a *verbal*) contract; one gives *oral* (not *verbal*) testimony; one asks for *oral* (not *verbal*) voting.

oration. *Speech, address, harangue, allocution, lecture, prelection, talk, sermon, homily.

oratory. Eloquence, *elocution.

orb. *Sphere, globe, ball.

orbicular, orbiculate. *Round, spherical, globular, orbicular, annular, circular, discoid.

orbit. *Range, reach, scope, compass, sweep, gamut, radius, ken, purview, horizon.

order, *n.* **1** *Association, society, club.

2 *Command, injunction, bidding, behest, mandate, dictate.

Ana. Instruction, direction, charging *or* charge (see corresponding verbs at COMMAND).

order, *v.* **1 Order, arrange, marshal, organize, systematize, methodize** agree in meaning to put (a number of persons or things) in their proper places especially with relation to each other, or to bring about an orderly disposition of the individuals, units, or elements that comprise (a thing). **Order** is now felt to be archaic when the idea of putting in a definite order is to be expressed; it usually implies a straightening out, and may connote either the elimination of friction or confusion, often with resulting peace or harmony, or the imposition of a fixed and rigid discipline; as, to *order* one's affairs in expectation of death; an *ordered* industry. "It was a home strictly *ordered*, and he would have to conform to its *ordering*" (*Arch. Marshall*). "The Greek states...were not well *ordered;* on the contrary, they were always on the verge, or in the act, of civil war" (*G. L. Dickinson*). **Arrange** is now more often used than *order* where the idea of setting in order, that is, in proper sequence, relationship, or adjustment, is uppermost. The word often implies a notion of what is orderly, fit, suitable, or right, and a placing of things in accordance with this notion; as, to *arrange* the furniture in a room; to *arrange* fruit in a dish; to *arrange* the books on a shelf; to *arrange* one's hair in the newest fashion; "these words are *arranged* without art" (*A. Huxley*). Oftentimes, the term implies a determination of the way in which the things are disposed by an end in view and then frequently suggests contrivance, manipulation, maneuvering, or the like; as, we shall *arrange* matters so that you will not be inconvenienced; to *arrange* the details of a conference between the leaders of the factions. "It is necessary for the physicist to *arrange* the experimental conditions so as to evoke phenomena in which the general laws...can be discerned" (*Karl K. Darrow*). **Marshal,** in precise use, usually connotes generalship, for it always implies assemblage and arrangement either for ease or advantage in management, as under stress, or for effectiveness in display or exhibition; as, to *marshal* troops for battle; to *marshal* one's thoughts before making a public address. "*Marshalled* like soldiers in gay company, The tulips stand arrayed" (*Amy Lowell*). "Thanks to Mr. Dawson's erudition and his gift of *marshalling* facts, we begin to have a notion of what it is all about" (*A. Huxley*). **Organize** implies an arrangement in which all persons or things are so related to each other that they work as a unit, each individual having his (or its) proper function, duty, or the like; as, to *organize* a nation for war; to *organize* a new branch of the military service; "Florence Nightingale *organized* the hospital work of the Crimean War" (*Shaw*); to *organize* the supporters of a candidate for the presidency; a colony of ants always reveals *organization.* **Systematize** implies arrangement according to a definite, and therefore predetermined, scheme; thus, one *systematizes* a collection of coins when one arranges them according to some plan of classification; one *systematizes* one's daily work when one reduces it to routine order. **Methodize** differs from *systematize* in suggesting the imposition of orderly procedure rather than of a fixed scheme; thus, one can *methodize* one's work without giving it the character of routine. "Those rules of old discovered, not devis'd, Are Nature still, but Nature *methodiz'd*" (*Pope*). "That art of reasoning...which *methodizes* and facilitates our discourse" (*J. H. Shorthouse*).

Ana. *Adjust, regulate: *line, align, range, array.

2 *Command, bid, enjoin, direct, instruct, charge.

Ana. Prohibit, *forbid, interdict, inhibit, ban.

Con. Permit, allow, *let: license, *authorize, commission.

orderly, *adj.* **Orderly, methodical** (*or* **methodic**), **systematic** (*or* **systematical**), **regular** come into comparison as meaning following closely a set arrangement, design, or pattern. **Orderly** implies observance of due sequence, or proper arrangement, as in the harmonious or careful disposition of persons or things (as, the guests passed in *orderly* lines into the room where the receiving party stood; an *orderly* placing of furniture), as in obedience to the rules of conduct or behavior that guide disciplined persons (as, an *orderly* group of children; an *orderly* assembly of citizens; an *orderly* election), as in keeping a place free from litter or confusion (as, his study is always *orderly;* an *orderly* housekeeper), or, in a less specific sense, as in a scheme, system, or the like, when all details stand in their proper relations, each playing its due part without interfering with that of any of the others (as, "a process calculated to reduce the *orderly* life of our complicated societies to chaos"—*A. Huxley;* "the difference [between classicism and romanticism] seems to me rather the difference between the complete and the fragmentary, the adult and the immature, the *orderly* and the chaotic"—*T. S. Eliot*). **Methodical,** or the now infrequent **methodic,** implies the observance of an order that has been carefully worked out so that the steps to be followed are exactly known or the pattern that is accepted seems logical or inevitable under the circumstances; as, to make a *methodical* search for evidence; to give *methodical* instructions to a new servant; to begin a *methodical* study of the Bible; the *methodic* school of physicians; a *methodical* performance of one's daily duties. *Methodical* rather than *methodic* is referable to persons who use or follow method in the performance of their duties or tasks or who follow the same order or schedule in their daily occupations; as, a *methodical* housekeeper; a *methodical* teacher; to lead a *methodical* life. **Systematic,** or less often **systematical,** comes close to *methodical* in ordinary use: *systematic,* however, is preferred to *methodical* when the emphasis is not upon the order followed but upon the integrity and completeness of the finished thing; thus, *methodical* training suggests training that follows its course according to a predefined sequence or schedule; *systematic* training usually implies training long enough and intensive enough to gain the end or ends in view; an astronomer makes a *systematic* (better than *methodical*) study of the celestial sphere. "A *systematic* course of five lessons a week, extending through at least the three years between fourteen and seventeen years of age" (*C. W. Eliot*). *Systematic,* but not *systematical,* may also be applied to nouns (often, but not necessarily, nouns of action) with the implications of repetition and of a purpose or intention that is reprehensible; as, "Pope

...was a *systematic* appropriator...of other men's thoughts" (*L. Stephen*); to make a *systematic* attack on the doctrines of a church; "trained by success to a sort of *systematic* selfishness" (*Cather*). **Regular** (as here compared: see also REGULAR, 1) implies a steadiness or uniformity as in following a schedule (as, *regular* habits; *regular* meals; *regular* treatments) or in pursuing a course marked by occurrence or recurrence at fixed or stated intervals (as, a *regular* pulse; as *regular* as the ebb and flow of the tides).

Ana. Tidy, *neat, trim, spick-and-span: formal, conventional, ceremonious (see CEREMONIAL): peaceable, *pacific, peaceful.

Ant. Disorderly: chaotic.

ordinance. Canon, precept, *law, rule, regulation, statute.

ordinary, *adj.* *Common, familiar, popular, vulgar.

Ana. *Usual, customary, habitual, wonted, accustomed.

Ant. Extraordinary. — *Con.* *Abnormal, atypic, aberrant: *exceptional: *irregular, unnatural, anomalous.

ordinary, *n.* *Bishop, archbishop, metropolitan, primate.

Ant. Agent (sense 2—*in ecclesiastical use*).

ordnance. *Armament, munitions, arms, artillery, ammunition.

organ. 1 Medium, vehicle, channel, *means, instrument, instrumentality, agent, agency.

2 *Journal, periodical, newspaper, magazine, review.

organism. *System, scheme, economy, network, complex.

organize. 1 Systematize, methodize, *order, arrange, marshal.

Ana. Design, project, plan, scheme (see under PLAN, *n.*): form, fashion, shape, *make.

Ant. Disorganize.

2 Institute, *found, establish.

Ana. *Begin, commence, start, initiate, inaugurate: *adjust, regulate.

oriel. *Window, casement, dormer.

orifice. *Aperture, interstice.

origin. **Origin, source, inception, root, provenance, provenience, prime mover** come into comparison as denoting the point, as represented by an act, an event, a person, a place, a condition, or the like, at which something (such as a process, a growth, a development, a custom, a habit, or an institution) begins its course or its existence. **Origin** applies chiefly to the point at which the thing under consideration has its rise, or to the person or thing from which it is ultimately derived: it often applies specifically to the causes in operation before the thing itself is finally brought into being; as, Charles Darwin's book "On the *Origin* of Species by Means of Natural Selection"; the *origin* of the custom of giving presents at Christmas; the *origin* of Christianity; the *origin* of a phrase. Often, when used in reference to persons, it means little more than ancestry or parentage: it is then used either in the singular or (now more often) the plural; as, "his father was of no great *origin*" (*Belloc*); "[Ramsay MacDonald's] humble *origins* were known" (*H. Ellis*). **Source** (etymologically, a lifting or surging up), in the earliest of its living senses, applies to the point at which waters from a spring or fountain emerge to form the beginning point of a stream or river; as, the *source* of the Hudson River. In extended use, *source* more often than *origin* applies to that which serves as the ultimate beginning of a thing, especially an immaterial or intangible thing: however, since the term is sometimes qualified by words such as *immediate*, *secondary*, etc., which weaken or destroy this implication, it is often in this sense modified by *ultimate*, *fundamental*, *primary*, or the like; as, "an ever-present energy, which is the *source* of all cosmical movement" (*Inge*); "the power of concentrated attention as the fundamental *source* of the prodigious productiveness of great workers" (*C. W. Eliot*); "Theoretically the mob is the repository of all political wisdom and virtue; actually it is the ultimate *source* of all political power" (*Mencken*). *Source* is also applied to the person, book, manuscript, or the like, from which one derives information: in this sense, a primary *source* is a person who has firsthand knowledge, or a work that was written at the time under discussion, especially by one who had firsthand knowledge, or the like; a secondary *source* is a person who has learned the facts from others, or a work which is based upon information gathered from others; as, graduate students in history are discouraged from using secondary *sources*. "When it [news] comes from one of the great news-collecting agencies like the Associated Press, the *source* generally is indicated" (*Justice Holmes*). **Inception** is often preferred to *origin* when the reference is to the actual beginning of an undertaking, a project, an institution, or the like: the term carries a weaker connotation of underlying causes than *origin*, yet does not, as *source* often does, carry any suggestion that the thing so called is the ultimate origin; as, "They joined the League of Nations Union....Stanley did so, at its *inception*, and became, in fact, a speaker on platforms in the cause" (*R. Macaulay*); "The subject may and does change between the *inception* of the work and its completion" (*S. Alexander*). **Root** is often the preferred term when the actual origin of a thing goes back to something very deep and fundamental, and the thing itself is only an outward manifestation of its influence. *Root*, therefore, more often even than *source*, applies to what is regarded as the first, or final, cause of a thing; as, "the love of money is the *root* of all evil" (*1 Timothy* vi. 10); "Faith, the *root* whence only can arise The graces of a life that wins the skies" (*Cowper*). **Provenance** and **provenience** (the form preferred by some writers) are chiefly used by scholars, especially in the fields of history, anthropology, philology, and the like, for the place (sometimes, the race or people) from which a thing is derived, or where (or by whom or among whom) it originated, was invented, was constructed, or the like; as, not to know the *provenance* (or *provenience*) of a legend or custom; antiquities of doubtful *provenance*. "He would have some difficulty in guessing its *provenance*, and naming the race from which it was brought" (*A. Lang*). **Prime mover** has been employed in philosophy, theology, poetry, but is now chiefly used in mechanics as a designation of an ultimate and original source of motion or motive power. In early use it was applied especially to God, as the source of all motion: this application still occurs, but in more modern use, when applied to a personal agent, it usually refers to an inciter or instigator of an action or course; as, "the *prime mover* in the whole matter was Hugh the Great" (*Freeman*). In mechanics, the term applies to the natural or mechanical power which sets a thing moving or in motion: it has been used in reference to wind (as in driving a sailing ship), steam (as in driving a steamship), a waterwheel, a windmill, a steam engine, and the like.

Ana. Beginning, commencement, initiation, starting (see corresponding verbs at BEGIN): derivation, origination, rising *or* rise (see corresponding verbs at SPRING): *ancestry, lineage.

original. *New, fresh, novel, new-fashioned, newfangled, neoteric, modern, modernistic.

Ant. Dependent: banal: trite.

originate. Rise, derive, arise, *spring, flow, issue, emanate, proceed, stem.

Ana. *Begin, commence, start.

ornament. *Adorn, decorate, embellish, beautify, deck, bedeck, garnish.

Ana. Enhance, heighten, *intensify: prink, primp, prank, doll up, perk up, *preen, prune.

ornate. **Ornate, rococo, baroque, flamboyant, florid** come into comparison when they mean elaborately and, often, pretentiously decorated or designed. **Ornate** is applicable to anything heavily adorned or ornamented or conspicuously embellished; as, an *ornate* style of architecture; "in the fiacre were Gerald and a woman. Gerald...was talking eagerly to his *ornate* companion" (*Bennett*). "[Wendell Phillips] introduced the direct and colloquial manner upon the American public platform, as distinguished from the highly elaborated and often *ornate* style which had been established by Edward Everett" (*T. W. Higginson*). **Rococo** was first applied to a certain style of architecture originating in France in the eighteenth century and carried to an extreme in Italy and Germany, and characterized chiefly by the extravagant and often fantastic use of curves. The term therefore implies the ornateness of design characteristic of this style of decoration, especially as evident in architectural details, in furniture, and in mirror and picture frames. It is now used to describe any style that seems to the writer tastelessly or meaninglessly ornate or overadorned, especially by scrolls and the like; as, "That *rococo* seventeenth-century French imitation of the true Renaissance" (*Pater*). **Baroque** was first applied to a style of art and architecture which prevailed from the time of Michelangelo (d. 1564) to nearly the end of the eighteenth century and which emphasized energy in conception, amplitude in design, the use of dynamic contrasts, extremely high relief, and the employment of curved and often contorted forms. "I entered this *Baroque* interior, with its twisted columns and volutes and high-piled, hideous tombs, adorned with skeletons and allegorical figures and angels blowing trumpets" (*L. P. Smith*). In its current extended sense, *baroque* suggests more grotesqueness and extravagance and less fancifulness than *rococo*, although it also implies tasteless ornamentation. "The decorative art of the French does indeed oftener than not lend itself to the *rococo*, though *baroque* it has rarely been" (*Brownell*). **Flamboyant** (etymologically, flaming or wavy like flames) was originally and still is applied to a late style of French Gothic architecture, or more specifically to the tracery in the windows of buildings in that style. The chief characteristic of that tracery is the use of curves that suggest ascending curving flames. In its more general application *flamboyant* suggests not so much ornateness (though it often also connotes that) as excess of color, conspicuous vigor and dash, bold and daring display, or any of numerous qualities that suggest the freedom and brilliancy of flames; as, a *flamboyant* display of courage; "*flamboyant* penmanship" (*E. Dowden*); "the *flamboyant* period of prose" (*Saintsbury*); "they [war-weary people] want...something novel, *flamboyant* and sensational" (*C. E. Montague*); "These...*flamboyant* tricks of virtuosity have gone quite out of fashion" (*Quiller-Couch*). **Florid** implies richness, usually overrichness, in details, shown particularly in the use of color, figures of speech, flourishes, and the like, for their own sake; it implies, therefore, showy and often ostentatious embellishment; as, a *florid* style of poetry; a *florid* musical composition; "The screen was an old one, of gilt Spanish leather, stamped and wrought with a rather *florid* Louis-Quatorze pattern" (*Wilde*); "the public genuinely admired the *florid* and *rococo* forms of Early Victorian art" (*A. C. Benson*).

Ana. Adorned, decorated, ornamented, embellished (see ADORN): flowery, aureate (see RHETORICAL): *luxurious, sumptuous, opulent: *showy, ostentatious.

Ant. Chaste: austere.

oscillate. *Swing, sway, vibrate, fluctuate, pendulate, waver, undulate.

Ana. Vacillate, waver, *hesitate, falter: *shake, tremble, quiver, quaver.

ostensible. *Apparent, seeming, illusory.

Ana. Specious, *plausible, colorable: pretended, assumed, affected, simulated, feigned (see ASSUME).

ostentatious. *Showy, pretentious, pompous.

Ana. Vainglorious, vain, proud (see under PRIDE): flaunting, parading, displaying (see SHOW, *v.*): boasting, bragging, gasconading (see BOAST).

ostracize. *Banish, exile, expatriate, deport, transport, extradite.

otiose. *Vain, nugatory, idle, empty, hollow.

Ana. *Superfluous, supernumerary, surplus: *futile, vain, fruitless, bootless.

ought, *v.* **Ought, should, must have, have got** come into comparison as auxiliary verbs meaning is or are bound (to do, or to forbear, or the like). **Ought** and **should** express the compulsion of obligation, *ought* commonly suggesting duty or moral constraint, *should* suggesting the obligation of fitness, propriety, expediency, and the like; as, "We have left undone those things which we *ought* to have done; And we have done those things which we *ought* not to have done; And there is no health in us" (*Book of Common Prayer*); "The participle for the substantive *should* be very rarely used" (*Jowett*); "The translator of Homer *should* be penetrated by a sense of four qualities of his author" (*Arnold*). But *ought* is often used in the weaker sense conveyed by *should;* as, "The translator of Homer *ought* steadily to keep in mind...what judges he is to try to satisfy" (*Arnold*). **Must** implies the compulsion of necessity, whether physical or moral; it, therefore, carries no suggestion that the decision is left to the agent or the person involved; as, "I did but taste a little...and, lo, I *must* die" (*1 Samuel* xiv. 43); "Duty whispers low, Thou *must*" (*Emerson*); "I suppose a woman *must* have children to love—somebody else's if not her own" (*E. Wharton*). **Have** and, in low colloquial uses, **have got,** are often used in the sense of *must;* with, however, less stress on inescapable necessity and more on the compulsion of obligation, duty, need, or the like; as, he *has* to go to the hospital for an operation; he *had* to leave before the convention ended; "Science has, and will long have to be a divider" (*Arnold*).

ought, *n.* Aught, naught, nought, *cipher, zero.

oust. *Eject, expel, evict, dismiss.

Ana. *Exclude, eliminate, shut out, rule out, debar, disbar: *dismiss, discharge, fire, cashier, sack.

out-and-out. *Outright, unmitigated, arrant.

outcome. *Effect, consequence, result, aftereffect, event, aftermath, issue, upshot, sequel.

Ana. *Fate, lot, portion, destiny: termination, *end.

outdo. Excel, outstrip, transcend, surpass, *exceed.

outdoor. **Outdoor, open-air, plein-air, alfresco** agree in meaning outside a house or building. **Outdoor** usually implies existence or occurrence outside of any building and in the fresh air; as, *outdoor* exercise or games; *outdoor* clothes (that is, clothes not suitable for house wear); an *outdoor* display of goods. Sometimes, however, it is applied to certain activities carried on outside of an institution, especially a hospital, and then approaches *extramural* in meaning; as, *outdoor* relief. **Open-air** invariably implies existence, occurrence, or the like, outside of any building; as, *open-air* meetings; *open-air* concerts; an *open-air* school (that is, a school conducting all or most of its activities out of doors). **Plein-air,** a French term adopted in English as an equivalent of *open-air,* is chiefly applied to certain schools of painters (or their paintings) who carry on their work out of doors and concentrate attention on atmospheric and light effects. **Alfresco** (derived from the Italian *al fresco* "in the fresh [air]"), also is equivalent to *open-air* in denotation. However, it is applied chiefly to meals, entertainments, etc., and so has acquired connotations of informality, rusticity, and the like.

outer. **Outer, outward, outside, external, exterior** are here compared as adjectives meaning being or placed without something. Although in many cases interchangeable, they are more or less restricted in their applications and are therefore clearly distinguished in their implications. **Outer** usually retains its comparative force, then applying to that which is farther out from something described as *inner* (as, the *outer,* as distinguished from the *inner,* court; the *outer* layer of skin is called the epidermis) or is farther than another thing from the center, the body, or the like (as, to shed one's *outer* garments; the *outer* covering of a butternut is removed before the nut is cracked). *Outer* is also applicable to that which is definitely without as opposed to that which is definitely within something, but in this sense the term rarely suggests spatial relations; thus, the *outer* man is the man as known in the flesh and as distinguished from the inner man, that is, the man as he really is in mind and soul; one's *outer* life is that which is observable to one's fellows; the *outer* world is the world as known directly through the senses. **Outward,** less frequently than formerly, may be used of spatial relations: when it is so used it commonly implies motion or direction away from, or the reverse of, that which is *inward;* as, given to *outward* display; *outward* travel from New York City is very heavy over the weekends; the *outward* curve of a convex lens. Like *outer,* the term is sometimes used in contrast with that which is spiritual (as, "Women's self-possession is an *outward* thing; inwardly they flutter"—*Conrad*), but more often it implies existence entirely without the mind or soul; as, "obstinate questionings Of sense and *outward* things" (*Wordsworth*); "Unless the *outward* and visible signs of Our Authority are always before a native he is...incapable...of understanding what authority means" (*Kipling*). **Outside** usually implies a position on or a reference to the outer parts or surface of a thing; as, an *outside* stateroom on a ship; *outside* shutters; the *outside* paint is looking shabby. But *outside,* in extended use, applies especially to a person or thing that is beyond certain implied borders, bounds, or limits; thus, an *outside* influence is one not emanating from the particular society, group, community, or the like, in mind; the *outside* world is the world beyond the scope or interest of a family group, community, set, or the like, or the confines of a town, city, or state; an *outside* broker is one who is not a member of an exchange; *outside* work is work in the field or on the road, in contrast with *inside* work, as in an office, factory, or store. "If it had condemned, Old Chester would not have cared in the very least. It looked down upon the *outside* world" (*Deland*). **External** and **exterior** are often used interchangeably without loss, for both come close in meaning to *outside* (as, the *exterior,* or *external,* appearance of an object; the *exterior,* or *external,* form of a body). But *external* is usually the term preferred when location or situation beyond or away from the thing under consideration is implied (as, "I was often unable to think of *external* things as having *external* existence"—*Wordsworth;* "Our desires and wills are directed to some object *external* to us"—*S. Alexander*), and *exterior* is the term preferred when location or situation on the surface or on the outer limits of a thing is implied (as, the *exterior* slope of a fortification; the *exterior* parts of the human body; "Thou, whose *exterior* semblance doth belie Thy Soul's immensity"—*Wordsworth*). But *external* often comes close to *superficial* in implying mere appearance or semblance that has no relation or little relation to what the thing really is; as, "But under this *external* appearance of ease she was covered with cold beads of sweat" (*E. Wharton*); beauty that is purely *external.*

Ana. *Extrinsic, extraneous, foreign, alien.

Ant. Inner. — ***Con.*** Inward, inside, internal, interior, intestine (see INNER).

outfit, *n.* *Equipment, apparatus, paraphernalia, tackle, machinery, gear, matériel.

outfit, *v.* *Furnish, equip, appoint, accouter, arm.

outlander *or* **uitlander.** *Stranger, foreigner, alien, outsider, immigrant, émigré.

outlandish. *Strange, singular, unique, peculiar, eccentric, erratic, odd, queer, quaint, curious.

Ana. Bizarre, grotesque, *fantastic, antic: alien, foreign, extraneous, *extrinsic.

outlast. *Outlive, survive.

Ana. Endure, persist, abide, *continue: withstand, resist (see OPPOSE).

outline, *n.* **1 Outline, contour, profile, sky line, silhouette** come into comparison as meaning the boundary line or lines which give form or shape to a body, a mass, a figure, or the like. **Outline** refers to a line which marks or seems to mark the edge or limits of a thing; it may apply either to an outer edge (as, "At night, the *outline* of the shore is traced in transparent silver by the moonlight and the flying foam"—*Stevenson*) or to the continuous line (sometimes then *outlines* is preferred) that marks the edge of a body or mass, especially from a given point of view (as, "Clem...looked at the big house. The dark *outline* against the dark sky made him hesitate"—*E. Caldwell;* "[the lighthouse keeper] far from the earth, of which he scarcely distinguishes the *outlines* through the mist"—*H. Ellis*). **Contour** does not fix the attention on an edge or limit, but on the outer lines as related to a thing's shape and as indicative of its grace or lack of grace, its fullness or slenderness, its softness or harshness, or the like; as, "the full and flowing *contour* of the neck" (*Shelley*); "a child, of timid, soft *contours*" (*Hewlett*); "the blurred *contour* of Rainbarrow obstructed the sky" (*Hardy*). Specifically, *contour* applies to lines (*contour lines*) in a map (*contour map*) that indicates the configuration of a country or tract of land. **Profile** in its earliest sense applies to the representation or the appearance of something in outline, especially of a face in side view showing the contour of the head and emphasizing the line from forehead to under the chin; as, "lips lovely in *profile;*—a little too wide and hard...seen in front" (*Ruskin*). Consequently, *profile* is usually the preferred term when a varied and sharply defined outline as seen against a background is implied, although **sky line** may be chosen as more specific when the background is the sky; as, "Its *sky-line* was like the *profile* of a big beast lying down" (*Cather*); the *sky line* of New York City. **Silhouette,** in its earlier and literal sense, applies especially to a kind of portrait of someone or something made by tracing the outline of his (or its) shadow on a wall on paper (or fabric) that is black on one side, by cutting out this figure as drawn, and by mounting it, black side outward. *Silhouette*, therefore, even more than *outline* or *profile*, eliminates all consideration of details such as color, quality, expression, and the like, and implies an outline seen in or as in a shadow; as, from the distance at which we stood and because of the brightness of the sun behind them, we saw the two figures only in *silhouette;* "The *silhouette* made a blue-black stain On the opposite wall" (*Amy Lowell*).

Ana. Figure, *form, shape, conformation, configuration.

2 Sketch, diagram, delineation, draft, tracing, plot, blueprint. See under SKETCH, *v.*

outline, *v.* *Sketch, diagram, delineate, draft, trace, plot, blueprint.

outlive. Outlive, outlast, survive are here compared as meaning to remain in existence longer than another person or thing, or after a given experience. **Outlive** carries a strong implication of a capacity for endurance and is therefore used by preference when competition, struggle, the surmounting of a difficulty, or the like, is also connoted; as, the three brothers lived to be over ninety, but John *outlived* James and Henry; "Not marble, nor the gilded monuments Of princes, shall *outlive* this powerful rhyme" (*Shak.*); to *outlive* one's shame; "The world has *outlived* much, and will *outlive* a great deal more" (*J. R. Lowell*). **Outlast** usually stresses greater length of duration rather than greater capacity for endurance and therefore is employed when comparison is more important than a suggestion of superiority or when the fact of existing longer is more important than the length of time involved; as, "Customs that have long *outlasted* their usefulness" (*Inge*); "The sweet sensations of returning health made me happy for a time; but such sensations seldom *outlast* convalescence" (*Hudson*). But when length of (as distinguished from capacity for) endurance, rather than length of life or existence, is implied, *outlast* is preferred to *outlive;* as, "He could *outlast* horse and outrace hound" (*Masefield*). **Survive** may be used as an intransitive as well as a transitive verb; in general, it suggests merely a living or existing longer than another person or thing, or after some event (sometimes implied rather than expressed) which might bring about his (or its) end; as, the elder sister *survived* the younger; far more infants *survive* after birth than in the days when no prenatal care was given; he is unlikely to *survive* the operation; "No religion can *survive* the judgment of history unless the best minds of its time have collaborated in its construction" (*T. S. Eliot*); "One in a million of these childish talents *survives* puberty" (*A. Huxley*).

Ana. Endure, persist, abide, *continue: surpass, *exceed.

outlook, *n.* *Prospect, anticipation, foretaste.

Ana. Forecasting *or* forecast, predicting *or* prediction, prophesying *or* prophecy, presaging *or* presage (see corresponding verbs at FORETELL): possibility, probability, likelihood (see corresponding adjectives at PROBABLE).

outrage, *v.* **1** *Abuse, misuse, mistreat, maltreat, ill-treat.

Ana. *Wrong, persecute, oppress, aggrieve: corrupt, pervert, vitiate, deprave, *debase.

2 *Offend, affront, insult.

Ana. Vex, *annoy, irk, bother: mortify, chagrin (see corresponding adjectives at ASHAMED).

outrageous. Outrageous, monstrous, heinous, atrocious agree in meaning enormously or flagrantly bad or horrible. That is **outrageous** which violates even the lowest standard of what is right or decent, or exceeds one's power to suffer or tolerate; as, *outrageous* behavior; an *outrageous* practical joke; an *outrageous* cartoon; *outrageous* treatment of prisoners of war. That is **monstrous** which is shockingly wrong, absurd, horrible, or the like, or is inconceivably fantastic, abnormal, or aberrant; as, a *monstrous* falsehood; a *monstrous* conception of morality. " 'It is natural...that you should consider the idea of an isolated or imprisoned manhood something *monstrous*' " (*Meredith*). "The very horror with which men spoke, centuries after...plainly indicates that such a wholesale massacre was exceptional, *monstrous*" (*Quiller-Couch*). That is **heinous** which is so flagrantly bad or so conspicuous for its enormity that it excites hatred or horror; as, treason has always been regarded as a *heinous* crime. "A process...so *heinous* that men might on it spit" (*Chaucer*). "These animal passions are felt most vividly when the community is animated with anger against some *heinous* offence" (*S. Alexander*). That is **atrocious** which excites condemnation for its savagery or barbarity; as, *atrocious* cruelty; "*atrocious* acts which can only take place in a slave country" (*Darwin*). In current loose use, *atrocious* is often used to suggest savage condemnation rather than to impute savagery to the thing so described; as, *atrocious* English; an *atrocious* book.

Ana. *Flagrant, glaring, gross, rank: notorious (see FAMOUS): *excessive, inordinate, immoderate, extreme: flagitious, nefarious, iniquitous, *vicious.

outright, *adj.* **Outright, out-and-out, unmitigated, arrant** are comparable when they are used hyperbolically as meaning just what one (a person or thing) is said to be, without reservation or qualification. They are often used interchangeably as intensives, but there are clear differences in meaning. That is **outright** which has gone to the extreme and can be made neither better nor worse, or which is past recall; as, he is an *outright* fool; you speak *outright* nonsense; an *outright* killing. That is **out-and-out** which is completely as described at all times, or in every part, or from every conceivable point of view; as, an *out-and-out* fraud; an *out-and-out* villain; an *out-and-out* blessing. That is **unmitigated** which is or seems to be beyond the possibility of being lessened, softened, relieved, or the like; as, an *unmitigated* evil; "unrequited affections are in youth *unmitigated* woes" (*L. P. Smith*). That is **arrant** which is all that is implied by the term that follows (usually a term of abuse); as, an *arrant* coward; an *arrant* hypocrite; an *arrant* liar. *Cf.* fistnote at ABSOLUTE.

outside, *adj.* *Outer, outward, external, exterior.

Ana. *Extrinsic, extraneous, alien, foreign.

Ant. Inside. — *Con.* *Inner, inward, internal, interior, intestine.

outsider. *Stranger, foreigner, alien, outlander, immigrant, émigré.

outstanding. Prominent, conspicuous, salient, signal, striking, arresting, remarkable, *noticeable.

Ana. *Exceptional.

Ant. Commonplace. — *Con.* *Common, ordinary, familiar.

outstrip. Outdo, *exceed, surpass, transcend, excel.

outward. *Outer, outside, external, exterior.

Ana. Extraneous, *extrinsic, alien, foreign.

Ant. Inward. — *Con.* *Inner, inside, internal, interior, intestine.

outwit. *Frustrate, thwart, foil, baffle, balk, circumvent.

Ana. Defeat, overcome, surmount (see CONQUER): *prevent, preclude, obviate, avert: overreach, *cheat, defraud.

over. *Above.

Ant. Beneath.

overbearing. Supercilious, disdainful, lordly, arrogant, haughty, *proud, insolent.

Ana. Domineering, *masterful, imperious: scorning *or* scornful, despising *or* despiteful, contemning (see corresponding verbs at DESPISE): autocratic, despotic, tyrannical, *absolute.

Ant. Subservient.

overcome. Surmount, overthrow, subjugate, rout, *conquer, vanquish, defeat, beat, lick, subdue.

Ana. Capture, *catch: outstrip, outdo, *exceed: *suppress, repress.

overdue. *Tardy, behindhand, late.

Ana. Delayed, retarded, detained, slowed, slackened (see DELAY, *v.*): deferred, postponed (see DEFER).

overflow. *Teem, swarm, abound, superabound.

overlay. **Overlay, superpose, superimpose, appliqué** agree in meaning to add one thing to another by placing the former upon or over the latter. **Overlay** usually implies covering with another material or substance, sometimes thinly, as with a wash, glaze, or coat (as, plated silver is often a white metal *overlaid* with silver), sometimes thickly, as by incrusting, veneering, or plastering (as, a brick wall *overlaid* with stucco). In extended use, *overlay* usually implies accretions or additions that conceal or encumber the original thing or smother and stifle whatever there is of life in it. "The ancient world had its own complexities, but it was not, like ours, heavily *overlaid* with the debris of speculative systems" (*Buchan*). "Ages of fierceness have *overlaid* what is naturally kindly in the dispositions of ordinary men and women" (*B. Russell*). **Superpose** and **superimpose** are not always clearly distinguished, especially when they imply a putting of one thing on top of another, thereby extending the height of the original mass; thus, strata are layers of rock successively built up by sedimentary deposits, each layer being *superimposed* (or *superposed*) on the one previously formed. *Superpose*, however, is the preferred term when relative position only is indicated, and *superimpose* when the thing added rests upon or is supported by the original thing; thus, *superposed* columns do not necessarily have the columns of the lower row for their respective bases, but *superimposed* columns do; an overtone is strictly a *superposed* (not a *superimposed*) tone. *Superpose* is also the preferred term among scientists when dealing with light rays, undulations, etc., that occupy the same position without destroying each other or losing their identities; as, "upon the large and general motion of the glacier, smaller motions are *superposed*" (*J. Tyndall*); "originally they [the two bright spots] were *superposed* on each other" (*Karl K. Darrow*). *Superimpose* often, especially in extended use, carries the implications of imposition or the addition of something extraneous and burdensome; as, many a historian *superimposes* his prejudices or private opinions upon his narrative of events. **Appliqué** (a verb derived from the French past participle *appliqué*, which is used in English as an adjective) always implies an intent to ornament and is chiefly used in reference to cut or shaped pieces of a fabric or textile which are pasted, sewn, or otherwise attached to a similar or contrasting fabric or textile so as to form a decorative pattern on the surface of the latter; as, to *appliqué* a satin blouse with wool of the same color; net on which lace motifs are *appliquéd* is called *appliqué* lace. In extended use, *appliqué* always suggests overlaying so as to form a decorative design. "Never taking his eyes off the pine-trees, *appliquéd* against the blue water" (*Cather*).

overlook. Slight, forget, ignore, disregard, *neglect, omit.

overplus. *Excess, superfluity, surplus, surplusage.

overreach. *Cheat, cozen, defraud, swindle.

overrun. *Infest, beset.

overset. *Overturn, upset, capsize, overthrow, subvert.

oversight. **Oversight, supervision, surveillance** not only carry the same meaning etymologically—a watching over—but in their current use come into comparison when they denote the function or duty of watching or guarding for the sake of proper control or direction. **Oversight,** the term of Anglo-Saxon origin, applies to the function or duty not only of one who is called an overseer or an inspector, but of any one whose duty it is to watch the progress of a piece of work so that no defects or imperfections may occur or to superintend the labors or efforts of a force, a staff, or other body of workers; as, each foreman is charged with the *oversight* of the work done in his department; the bishop has *oversight* of the clergy and parishes in his diocese. **Supervision,** the term of Latin origin, carries the strongest implication of authoritative powers, of responsibility, and of superintendence; it therefore usually suggests more rigorous direction or closer management than *oversight;* as, the architect had *supervision* of the construction of the building; the *supervision* of the schools is the duty of the superintendent rather than of the board of education; police *supervision* of traffic is very strict. **Surveillance,** the term of French origin, applies largely to any duty involving a close watch of persons lest they commit misdeeds of offenses against the law or against morals, or suffer untoward accidents; as, the police are maintaining a strict *surveillance* of the suspect; to keep the inmates of a lunatic asylum under *surveillance.*

Ana. Management, direction, controlling *or* control (see corresponding verbs at CONDUCT): inspection, scrutiny, examination (see under SCRUTINIZE).

overthrow, *v.* **1** *Overturn, overset, subvert, upset, capsize.

Ana. *Throw, cast, fling, hurl, toss.

2 Rout, surmount, overcome, vanquish, *conquer, defeat, beat, lick, subdue, subjugate, reduce.

overture, *n.* **1** **Overture, approach, advance, tender, bid** are, in the senses in which they are here considered, words of somewhat indefinite application covering any of a variety of acts or actions by which one person or party tries to gain the good will of another person or party. **Overture,** in careful use, always implies an attempt to begin a relationship. It may designate a formal proposal intended to open negotiations, as for peace, for a marriage between persons of royal blood, or for a merger of corporations. It is, however, often applied to any act or speech that may be construed as a search for an opening for friendship, for reconciliation, for co-operation, or the like. "She was not one of those backward and delicate ladies, who can die rather than make the first *overture* (*Fielding*). " 'You are the new second officer, I believe.' Mr. Powell answered in the affirmative, wondering if this was a friendly *overture*" (*Conrad*). **Approach** often is used in place of *overture* when the latter is felt to be too formal; as, the two girls made timid *approaches* to each other. **Advance** may be applied to any attempt to gain love, friendship, good will, or the like, whether it serve as an overture or as an effort to establish a closer relationship; as, after his *overtures* (more explicit than *advances*) were accepted, no further *advances* (not *overtures*) were made by either for some days. "She tried to make talk, but Hugh answered all her *advances*. . . briefly" (*S. Anderson*). **Tender** in this looser sense, still retains its primary meaning of offer, but it does not necessarily imply specific acts or a formal proposal. Sometimes it suggests little more than a sign or token. " 'He hath, my lord, of late made many *tenders* Of his affection to me.' 'Affection! pooh! you speak like a green girl . . . Do you believe his *tenders*, as you call them?" " (*Shak.*). **Bid,** a less formal word, adds to *advance* the implication of appeal or, sometimes, of invitation: it always requires qualification; as, a *bid* for sympathy; a *bid* for patronage. Like the other words of this group, the specific nature of the act or action can be inferred only from the context; as, the new state's ready acceptance of the Allies' proposal constituted a *bid* for recognition.

Ana. *Proposal, proposition: offering *or* offer, proffering (see corresponding verbs at OFFER).

2 Induction, *introduction, prologue, prelude, preface, foreword, prolegomenon, proem, exordium, preamble, prolusion, protasis, avant-propos.

overturn. Overturn, overset, upset, capsize, overthrow, subvert come into comparison only because they carry a common basic meaning—to cause to fall (sometimes, intransitively, to fall) from its normal or proper position. Otherwise, they vary widely in their applications and implications. **Overturn** is usually the least explicit of these terms in its additional implications: sometimes it implies a turning upside down (as, the boat *overturned* and floated with its keel upwards) but more often it implies a turning on the side so that the thing affected lies flat on the ground (as, to *overturn* a chair by hitting against it); sometimes, especially when the thing affected is a state, an institution, or something which has been built up or become established, the term also implies a breaking down and, consequently, its ruin or destruction; as, "Without *overturning* all existing institutions" (*Edgeworth*); "Long-reverenced titles cast away as weeds; Laws *overturned*" (*Wordsworth*); "When they seek to *overturn* our rights" (*Tennyson*). **Overset,** once a common and close synonym of *overturn*, is now increasingly rare, having given way to **upset** in its literal and, to some extent, in its extended senses. The latter is now the familiar and colloquial term. Both words, however, more than *overturn*, imply a loss of balance, sometimes physical, sometimes mental, often emotional (for this sense of *upset* see DISCOMPOSE), as the result of some external or internal cause or agency; as, "I *overset* my raft" (*Defoe*); "No birds in last year's nests—the winds have torn and *upset* the mossy structures in the bushes" (*Jefferies*); "A man who knew how slight a thing would *overset* the delicate organisation of the mind" (*Dickens*); "a European war lays its blight on whole peoples, deranges their life, *upsets* their standards of judgement" (*C. E. Montague*). But *upset* far more often than *overturn* or *overset* is used to imply the abolition of something established or the demolishing of something built up; as, to *upset* a person's calculations; to *upset* one's plans. "We are bound to be very cautious in coming to the conclusion that the Fourteenth Amendment has *upset* what thus far has been established and accepted for a long time" (*Justice Holmes*). **Capsize** is the specific term meaning to upset or overturn a boat: since, however, it usually suggests a complete overturning, it is sometimes employed in an extended sense to imply a turning, especially a sudden turning, upside down or topsy-turvy, not only physically, but mentally or morally; as, "When I see youth going to *capsize* [morally]...it makes my blood...curdle" (*Besant*). **Overthrow,** as here considered (for most common specific sense see CONQUER), carries a far stronger implication of the exercise of force, violence, or strategy than any of the preceding terms: it therefore often also implies consequent defeat, destruction, or ruin; as, to *overthrow* one's opponent in a combat; to *overthrow* the images in churches; to *overthrow* a government by force; to seek to *overthrow* religion. **Subvert** implies an overturning or overthrowing of something held to be of intrinsic value, such as a form of government, morality, or religion, by undermining its supports or weakening its foundations: often, but not always, it suggests the operation of insidious or corrupting influences; as, "This doctrine would *subvert* the very foundation of all written constitutions" (*Ch. Just. Marshall*); "A...question... whether more harm will be done to morality by weakening or *subverting* established usage than good" (*S. Alexander*); "Representative government...easily may be, and in England has been, used to *subvert* equality and fraternity" (*Brownell*).

Ana. Invert, *reverse, transpose.

own, *v.* **1** Possess, hold, *have, enjoy.

Ana. Control, manage, direct, *conduct: *keep, retain.

2 *Acknowledge, avow, admit, confess.

Ana. Concede, *grant, allow: *reveal, disclose, divulge.

Ant. Disown: repudiate.

oxygenate. *Aerate, ventilate, carbonate.

ozone. *Air, atmosphere, ether.

P

pabulum. *Food, aliment, nutriment, nourishment, sustenance.

pace, *n.* **1** *Trot, single-foot, walk, gallop, run, canter, lope, rack, amble.

2 *Speed, velocity, momentum, impetus, headway.

pace, *v.* Trot, single-foot, walk, gallop, run, canter, lope, rack, amble. See under TROT, *n.*

pacific. Pacific, peaceable, peaceful, irenic (*or* **irenical;** *also* **eirenic, eirenical), pacifist, pacifistic** are sometimes confused because they all involve the idea of affording or promoting peace. But **pacific** applies chiefly to persons, utterances, acts, influences, ideas, and the like, that tend to make peace or to conciliate strife; as, "the old grave *pacific* Quakers" (*John Adams*); the *pacific* counsels of the ambassador; the *pacific* views of the chief arbitrator in a labor dispute. "It must come in the end to the sword —this the most *pacific* and legally-minded had been forced to admit" (*Buchan*). **Peaceable** applies also to persons, their actions, words, etc., but it describes their character or quality as peace-loving, as disposed to avoid strife, or as inclined to keep peace, rather than their aims or tendencies; as, the villagers were a quiet, *peaceable* folk; "Our king the good Simonides....deserves so to be called for his *peaceable* reign and good government" (*Shak.*); "Fox was a pacifist; but his tongue was not always *peaceable*" (*Inge*). **Peaceful** applies especially to a life, a condition or state, a period or age, a country or people, in which peace prevails or there is no strife, but it may apply to anything which manifests peace, especially peace of mind, or provides an opportunity for such peace; as, "And may at last my weary age Find out the *peaceful* hermitage" (*Milton*); the *peaceful* countenance of the old clergyman; to involve *peaceful* countries in war by sudden and unprovoked invasion; "Thou shouldst have seemed a treasure-house divine Of *peaceful* years" (*Wordsworth*). "I am grown *peaceful* as old age to-night" (*Browning*). **Irenic,** a word of relatively recent origin, applies chiefly to theological arguments, views, and the like, that have for their aim the promotion of peace and of bringing members of divergent sects into accord. "Pieper lived to see his synod adopt a very *irenic* attitude towards its former antagonists" (*Dict. Amer. Biog.*). **Pacifist** and **pacifistic,** terms of very recent coinage, apply chiefly to the views, arguments, writings, or the like, of those who call themselves *pacifists*, or opponents of war or the use of military force for any purpose (as, *pacifist* propaganda; *pacifist* doctrines; the *pacifist* attitude to the Second World War), but they may also apply to the spirit or utterances of anyone who conscientiously objects to wars or who would substitute arbitration for conflict in the settlement of any disputes (as, *pacifistic* antagonism to conscription; *pacifistic* labor leaders).

Ana. *Calm, placid, serene, tranquil: conciliating *or* conciliatory, propitiating *or* propitiatory, appeasing, pacifying *or* pacificatory (see corresponding verbs at PACIFY).

Ant. Bellicose. — ***Con.*** *Belligerent, pugnacious, quarrelsome, contentious.

pacifist, pacifistic. *Pacific, peaceable, peaceful, irenic.

pacify. **Pacify, appease, placate, mollify, propitiate, conciliate** agree in meaning to quiet a person or persons when excited or disturbed. **Pacify** presupposes a disturbance of the peace and often, but far from invariably, a state of insurrection or of active hostility; it implies a reduction to order or quiet, but not necessarily a removal of the cause of the outbreak; as, it took time to *pacify* the excited children; troops were sent to *pacify* the rebellious tribes. **Appease** usually presupposes agitation caused by someone or something that makes demands; it therefore may be used in reference to appetites, desires, passions, as well as persons; it implies giving satisfaction, sometimes complete satisfaction, but more often merely a contenting; as, to *appease* one's curiosity or one's hunger. "When he [an orator] has once tasted the blood of popular applause, he is a tiger, nevermore to be *appeased*" (*Grandgent*). "Thoroughly to *appease* his conceit, it would have been necessary to swing open the gates of honour in the Arc and allow his fiacre to pass through" (*Bennett*). In the constructions "to *appease* one's wrath, rage, temper, etc.," or "to *appease* one in a rage," the implication of demands to be satisfied is often obscured though seldom lost; the emphasis, however, is on calming or quieting the excitement by pleasing or gratifying; as, he hoped to *appease* his father by his candor. "He [Antony] had a hasty temper, but it was easily *appeased*" (*Buchan*). **Placate** always presupposes bitterness of feeling, deep resentment, or the like; it implies success in changing ill will into good will or a hostile to a friendly attitude; as, he never attempts to *placate* his enemies. "Nothing ever *placates* them, nothing ever moves to a look of approval that ring of bleak, old, contemptuous Faces" (*L. P. Smith*). **Mollify** presupposes agitation caused by anger, especially rising anger, or by hurt feelings; it implies a softening of one's wrath or a soothing of one's feelings; as, she takes offense easily, but flattery always *mollifies* her. "His careworn look... *mollified* my wife toward him" (*Thackeray*). **Propitiate** presupposes an offense or affront that makes one ill-disposed; it implies a placating, usually for the sake of gaining that person's or group's active or effective good will. "The gods [of the ancient Greeks]...were capricious and often hostile...but at least they had a nature akin to his; if they were angry, they might be *propitiated;* if they were jealous, they might be *appeased*" (*G. L. Dickinson*). "Aunty Rosa, he argued, had the power to beat him....It would be discreet in the future to *propitiate* Aunty Rosa" (*Kipling*). **Conciliate** presupposes an estrangement or an alienation of a person or group; it implies a winning over as by persuasion, arbitration, inducements, or the like, and a settling of differences. "Dr. Lambert...with amazing good nature and tact, has been able to *conciliate* the various Island administrations" (*V. Heiser*). "The natural instinct of man...to *conciliate* and to *propitiate* him [a deity] by all the means in his power, as he would offer gifts to a prince or chief" (*A. C. Benson*).

Ana. Assuage, alleviate, allay, mitigate, *relieve: *moderate, qualify, temper.

Ant. Anger.

pack, *n.* **1** *Bundle, bunch, package, packet, bale, parcel, fardel.

2 *Flock, herd, drove, bevy, covey, gaggle, flight, swarm, shoal.

package, *n.* Packet, *bundle, bunch, bale, parcel, pack, fardel.

packet, *n.* Package, pack, *bundle, bunch, bale, parcel, fardel.

pact. Compact, *contract, bargain, treaty, entente, convention, cartel, covenant, concordat, indenture, mise.

pagan, *n.* **Pagan, heathen, paynim, ethnic, Gentile** come into comparison both as nouns and as adjectives when they mean one (or, as an adjective, of or characteristic of one) that belongs to a religion that is not Christian and often, by implication, not Jewish. **Pagan,** which came into English from the Latin, and **heathen,** which came into Anglo-Saxon from earlier Germanic languages, were both used in this sense by early Christians, and by some later writers dealing with early Christianity, to designate persons who lived in remote sections or away from the centers of civilization and had not yet been converted to Christianity. In the course of time, with the Christianization of these peoples, the words became somewhat, though not always clearly, differentiated in meaning; hence, *pagan* very frequently refers specifically to a follower of the Greek and Roman and similar polytheistic religions of ancient times or of times before the Christianization of Europe and America (as, "The emperor Julian...was perverted from Christianity, and confirmed a *pagan*, by Maximus a magician" —*Defoe;* "It was the words 'descended into Hades' That seemed too *pagan* to our liberal youth"—*R. Frost*) and *heathen*, by contrast, to one who belongs to a race or people unconverted to Christianity, even though that race or people has a religion (often, but not necessarily, a polytheistic religion) of its own (thus, Christian missionaries are sent to convert the *heathens* [not *pagans*]; "To reveal his Son in me, that I might preach him among the *heathen*"—*Galatians* i. 16). In current use, *pagan* more often suggests an attitude to life than a difference in religion: the term variously implies irreligiousness, indifference to things of the spirit, frank delight in material joys or goods, or the like. "The Renascence is, in part, a return towards the *pagan* spirit, in the special sense in which I have been using the word *pagan;* a return towards the life of the senses and the understanding" (*Arnold*). "You will hear the word '*pagan*' flung loosely about for 'irreligious,' or sometimes as meaning joyous, material and comfort-loving, whereas the simple *pagans* walked the earth full of what is called holy awe and that mystic faith in unseen powers which is the antithesis of materialism, and gloomy with apprehension of the visitations of their horrid and vindictive gods" (*R. Macaulay*). **Paynim,** originally a Middle English word meaning *pagandom* and then *pagan*, is now an archaic or historical term, used chiefly in historical novels, for one who from the point of view of the Middle Ages is a heathen: from the crusades on, the term has been specifically applied to one of the chief enemies of the crusaders, a Mohammedan or Saracen; as, "The *Paynim* turban and the Christian crest" (*Byron*). Both **ethnic** (now obsolete as a noun) and **Gentile** (often uncapitalized) etymologically mean a nation or people, but as here considered the terms usually apply to one of any people not converted to the true faith. This is particularly true of *Gentile*, which names, from the point of view of Jews, a non-Jew and, from the point of view of early Christians, as derived from the New Testament, one of any nation yet to be, or in the course of being, Christianized by the apostles and their successors. "But I say that the things which the *Gentiles* sacrifice, they sacrifice to devils, and not to God" (*1 Corinthians* x. 20). "Such boastings as the *Gentiles* use, Or lesser breeds without the Law" (*Kipling*). In nonhistorical use, *ethnic* comes close to *pagan* or *heathen* in meaning (as, "The *Ethnics* do still repute all great trees to be divine"—*Evelyn;* "These are ancient *ethnic* revels Of a faith long since forsaken"—*Longfellow*). *Gentile*, except when used historically in the New Testament sense, now commonly implies an opposition to *Jew*, and applies, as a rule, to a Christian of any denomination; as, Jews and *Gentiles* gathered to honor the great Hebrew divine.

pagan, *adj.* Heathen, paynim, ethnic, Gentile. See under PAGAN, *n.*

pain, *n.* **1 Pain, ache, pang, throe, twinge, stitch** come into comparison when they mean a bodily sensation that causes acute discomfort or suffering. **Pain** may range in its application from a sensation that makes one uneasily aware of some bodily disturbance or injury to a sensation resulting from severe injuries or disease and of agonizing intensity; from a sensation that is purely local to one that affects the entire body; as, a *pain* in the finger; chest *pains;* his face was drawn with *pain*. More specifically, *pain* implies acute and, often, sudden suffering such as might be inflicted by something that pierces, stings, burns, or the like. An **ache** is, commonly, a steady, often a dull, pain; it is especially referable to sensations arising from disorders that may be relieved; as, a back*ache;* a head*ache*. "A fellow that never had the *ache* in his shoulders" (*Shak.*). A **pang** is a sharp, sudden, and, often, transitory pain of great intensity, especially one that recurs in spasms. "*Pangs* have taken hold upon me, as the *pangs* of a woman that travaileth" (*Isaiah* xxi. 3). A **throe** is a pang characteristic of a process, such as that of labor in childbirth. Because of its association with labor it usually designates a violent and convulsive, as well as a recurrent pain; as, in the *throes* of violent retching. "The *throes* of a mortal and painful disorder" (*Scott*). A **twinge** is a momentary shooting or darting pain, especially one causing muscular contraction or twitching; it is sometimes regarded as a premonitory symptom; as, to feel a *twinge* in the region of the heart. **Stitch** differs from *twinge* in suggesting something that runs through a part of a body (usually a muscle) like a piercing needle; as, a *stitch* in the side.

All of these words except the last designate also mental suffering. **Pain** commonly suggests sorrow, as for something lost or unattainable. "An' lea'e us nought but grief an' *pain* For promis'd joy" (*Burns*). **Ache** usually implies suffering that must be endured or longing not likely to be appeased; as, a dull *ache* in her heart; to know the *ache* of loneliness. **Pang** suggests a sudden sharp access of a painful emotion; as, sharp *pangs* of envy, or fear, or remorse. **Throe** presupposes the existence of mental agony and designates one of the recurrent spasms that characterize the state of mind. "Fierce maternal passion...was now bowing her still lower, in the *throes* of a bitter renunciation" (*E. Wharton*). **Twinge** suggests less poignancy than *pang* but often connotes compunction. "*Twinges* of conscience" (*Thackeray*). "Too painfully preoccupied to feel a *twinge* of self-reproach at this undeserved praise" (*G. Eliot*).

Ana. Agony, *distress, suffering, passion: anguish, *sorrow, grief.

2 In plural form **pains.** *Effort, exertion, trouble.

Ana. Labor, toil, travail, *work: industriousness *or* industry, diligence, sedulousness, assiduousness (see corresponding adjectives at BUSY).

pair, *n.* *Couple, brace, yoke.

pal, *n.* Chum, comrade, *associate, companion, crony, buddy.

palatable. Palatable, appetizing, savory (*or* **savoury**), **sapid, saporous, tasty, toothsome, flavorsome, relishing** agree in meaning agreeable or pleasant to the sense of taste. **Palatable** is not emphatic in its implication of pleasantness; therefore it seldom suggests deliciousness and often, on the other hand, implies little more than acceptability; as, to provide *palatable* meals for one's family; plain but *palatable* food. The term is used frequently in extended applications of things which are mentally digested; as, *palatable* advice; the rebuke was not *palatable*. "I'm afraid that my remarks have not been very *palatable*, but I can assure you that they were sincerely meant" (*C. Mackenzie*). **Appetizing** implies a whetting of the appetite; it is applicable to the smell and appearance as well as to the taste of food; as, the *appetizing* odor of a roasting turkey; a convalescent requires *appetizing* meals. In its extended use, the word is applicable to things that stimulate a desire for more or an eagerness to go further; as, an *appetizing* title; an *appetizing* introduction to a subject. **Savory,** also, is applied to foods that have an agreeable odor as well as taste, but it conveys definite implications of piquancy; it is therefore applied to highly seasoned dishes as contrasted with sweet or bland dishes; as, a bland meat like veal needs a *savory* onion or tomato sauce; a *savory* stuffing for the turkey; to prefer a *savory* to a sweet omelet. In its extended application, the word often suggests, especially in contrast to *unsavory*, a stimulating and refreshing as well as agreeable quality. "With *savoury* truth and wholesome common sense: To lead his son... To some not steep, though philosophic height" (*Cowper*). **Sapid** and **saporous** are not in common use today, but they still occasionally occur as opposites of *insipid*, implying a marked taste or flavor, sometimes one merely lacking in flatness or lifelessness, but often one that is distinctly keen or exhilarating; as, roast beef is more *sapid* than roast veal and roast venison more *sapid* than roast beef; vigorous, *sapid* poetry. **Tasty** also implies a marked taste, but it suggests in addition an appetizing quality; as, a *tasty* morsel; a *tasty* dish; a *tasty* filling for a sandwich; a *tasty* cheese. The word, though in good use in the past and still so regarded by some, is now regarded by others as colloquial, and by still others as common; it is therefore avoided in literary use and in elegant speech. **Toothsome** heightens the implication of agreeableness in *palatable* and usually adds also the suggestion of tenderness or of daintiness; as, a *toothsome* steak; a *toothsome* dessert. **Flavorsome** is the more or less colloquial equivalent of *sapid*, though usually it suggests richness rather than sharpness of taste, and often implies fragrance as well as savor; as, *flavorsome* apricots; a *flavorsome* rum sauce. **Relishing** stresses gusto in enjoyment; as, plain fare is *relishing* to a starving man; he found all this praise extremely *relishing*.

Ana. *Delightful, delicious, delectable, luscious: piquant, *pungent, spicy.

Ant. Unpalatable: distasteful.

palate. *Taste, relish, gusto, zest.

pale, *adj.* **1 Pale, pallid, ashen, ashy, wan, livid** agree in meaning devoid of natural or healthy color (as a complexion) or deficient in vividness or intensity of hue (as a specific color). **Pale** is the least rich in implications and connotations of these words; it merely implies relative nearness to white and deficiency in depth and brilliance of coloring; as, his face grew *pale;* the *pale* pink of a rose; the sea is a *pale* green in this light. **Pallid** adds to *pale* the suggestions of deprivation, rather than absence, of color and of an abnormal condition, such as weakness or faintness, or intense weariness; thus, one's cheeks may be naturally *pale* (better than *pallid*); his *pallid* (more expressive than *pale*) face reveals the strain he has been under; "Trembling limbs and *pallid* lips" (*Shelley*); "Its little smoke, in *pallid* moonshine, died" (*Keats*). **Ashen** and **ashy** definitely suggest not only the pale gray color of ashes but often, also, that of the skin in death. A thing described as *ashen* or *ashy* may therefore be said to be deadly or ghastly pale; as, "The skies they were *ashen* and sober" (*Poe*); "the *ashen* hue of age" (*Scott*); "Oft have I seen a timely-parted ghost, Of *ashy* semblance" (*Shak.*); "Mr. Cruncher, who was all in a tremble... with an *ashy* and solemn visage" (*Dickens*). **Wan** suggests the blanching associated with an unhealthy condition or waning vitality; it usually therefore denotes a sickly paleness; as, "the blasted stars looked *wan*" (*Milton*); "her poor *wan* face with its wistful, pitiful little smile" (*Hewlett*). **Livid** basically means leaden-hued; it is chiefly used of things, especially of human faces that under the influence of something that distorts them have lost their normal coloring and have assumed a dull gray tinge; as, he grew *livid* with rage; the *livid* sky before a storm. "In the greenish glass her own face looked far off like the *livid* face of a drowned corpse at the bottom of a pool" (*Conrad*). The word is also applied to various dull or dun colors when the hue is no more than apparent; as, the *livid* red of the sun seen through a heavy fog; the *livid* yellow of a stormy sky. "His trembling lips are *livid* blue" (*Scott*).

Ana. *Ghastly, macabre: cadaverous, *haggard, worn.

2 Pale, anemic (*or* **anaemic**), **bloodless** come into comparison in their extended senses when they are applied to things and mean weak and thin in substance or in vital qualities, as though drained of blood. **Pale** stresses deficiency in qualities necessary to give a thing its true color, or character. Sometimes it connotes lack of vigor, force, or energy; as, "The French... Shake in their fear and with *pale* policy Seek to divert the English purposes" (*Shak.*); more often, especially in modern use, it implies inadequacy or failure to measure up to the requirements of a type or standard. "I choose to wear you [his love] stamped all over me...That *pale* loves may die out of their pretence" (*Browning*). "Even philosophy, unless you count the *pale* work of Boethius —real philosophy had...nearly perished [in the Dark Ages]" (*Quiller-Couch*). "Dropping a *pale* smile on him she drifted away" (*E. Wharton*). **Anemic,** literally used to describe persons whose blood is deficient in the number or quality of red corpuscles, in its extended applications to things implies deficiency in the elements that make for vigor or richness, especially intellectual or spiritual vigor or richness. "That *anaemic* secular conception of the universe as a whole which he [Darwin] seems to have accepted" (*H. Ellis*). "The African negro has...joy of life, love of colour, keen senses, beautiful voice, and ear for music—contributions that...might one day prove a tonic to an *anaemic* and art-less America" (*Zangwill*). **Bloodless** stresses the absence of qualities necessary to life or lifelikeness, such as vitality, warmth, color, etc. "Books are good enough in their own way, but they are a mighty *bloodless* substitute for life" (*Stevenson*).

Ana. *Insipid, wishy-washy, inane, jejune: inadequate, insufficient (see affirmative adjectives at SUFFICIENT): *ineffective, ineffectual.

pall. Cloy, surfeit, *satiate, sate, glut, gorge, surcharge.

palliate. Palliate, extenuate, gloze, gloss, whitewash, whiten come into comparison as meaning to disguise artfully or otherwise give a speciously fine appearance to that which is base, evil, erroneous, or the like. **Palliate,** in strict use, stresses the concealing or cloaking, or the condoning of (or an attempt to conceal, cloak, or condone) the enormity of a crime or offense; as, "Retracing thus his frolics ('tis a name That *palliates* deeds of folly and of shame)" (*Cowper*); "We have not endeavored to conceal or even *palliate* his errors" (*Lockhart*); "We cannot...explain away this deliberate act as due to the garrulity of age, or accept the other excuses with which his admirers have sought to *palliate* it" (*L. P. Smith*). The word is also used in reference to other than moral evils in the sense of to disguise the true nature or extent of so as to soften its bad effects; as, "Minds which are keener and wills which are stronger than the average do not rest in 'quiet desperation' *palliated* by illusion" (*J. W. Krutch*); "When...Sophia observed a fault in the daily conduct of the house, her first impulse was to go to the root of it and cure it, her second was to leave it alone, or to *palliate* it by some superficial remedy" (*Bennett*). **Extenuate** (as here considered: see also THIN) in very precise use refers not only to crimes and offenses but also to one's guilt: the term implies the aim to lessen, as by excuses or the like, the seriousness or magnitude of the crime, offense, or guilt; as, "When you shall these unlucky deeds relate, Speak of me as I am; nothing *extenuate*, Nor set down aught in malice" (*Shak.*); "These, however varnished, however coloured over, however *extenuated* or diminished..., will in the event feel the wrath of God" (*W. Paley*); "he may...have somewhat overpraised the virtues, and too much *extenuated* the faults, of Bolingbroke" (*T. S. Eliot*). But the term is often, even by good writers, used in the sense of to make excuses for; as, "She had never forgiven Cromwell the execution of the martyr Charles; and to *extenuate* the conduct of the great Roundhead captain, was to make Mrs. Doria despise and detest you" (*Meredith*); "The fact that Soranzo is himself a bad lot does not *extenuate* her [his wife's] willingness to ruin him" (*T. S. Eliot*). **Gloze** and **gloss,** usually followed by *over*, imply an aim to veil as by specious comments, by flattering talk, or by any other more or less light dissembling, the true harshness, unpleasantness, or disagreeableness of something: often, the word suggests a representation of that which is actually disagreeable as more or less agreeable or as not distinctly unpleasant; *gloze*, however, is usually more derogatory than *gloss;* as, the explorer has succeeded in *glossing* over the hardships he endured; "With the tongue of flattery *glozing* deeds which God and Truth condemn" (*Whittier*). **Whitewash,** and less often (especially in colloquial or journalistic use) **whiten,** imply an attempt to cover up a crime, a serious defect or fault, a person's guilt, or the like, by some means or other such as a superficial investigation, or a perfunctory trial, or a special report, that leads to a seeming acquittal or exoneration or that gives the person or persons accused an appearance of innocence or blamelessness; as, "A poet and an author will go as far in *whitewashing* a munificent tyrant (*Walpole*); "By selecting the evidence any society may be relatively blackened, and any other society relatively *whitened*" (*H. Spencer*).

Ana. Mitigate, alleviate, lighten (see RELIEVE): condone, *excuse: *moderate, qualify, temper: cloak, mask, *disguise, dissemble.

pallid. *Pale, ashen, ashy, wan, livid.

palpable. **1** *Perceptible, sensible, tangible, appreciable, ponderable.
Ana. *Apparent, ostensible, seeming: believable, credible, colorable, *plausible.
Ant. Insensible.
2 Plain, clear, *evident, apparent, manifest, patent, obvious, distinct.
Ana. *Sure, certain, positive: *noticeable, remarkable, striking, arresting.
Ant. Impalpable. — *Con.* *Doubtful, dubious, questionable, problematical.

palpitate. Beat, throb, *pulsate, pulse.
Ana. Vibrate, oscillate, fluctuate, *swing, sway.

palpitation. Beat, throb, pulsation, pulse. See under PULSATE, *v.*
Ana. Vibration, oscillation, fluctuation, swinging, swaying (see corresponding verbs at SWING).

palsy. *Paralysis, apoplexy, stroke, shock.

palter. *Lie, prevaricate, equivocate, fib.
Ana. Evade, elude, *escape: *trifle, dally.

paltry. Trifling, trivial, *petty, puny, measly, picayunish, picayune.
Ana. *Contemptible, despicable, sorry, scurvy, cheap, beggarly: abject, ignoble, *mean: *base, low, vile.

pamper. *Indulge, humor, spoil, baby, mollycoddle.
Ana. Gratify, tickle, regale, *please: fondle, pet, *caress, dandle.
Ant. Chasten.

pandect. *Compendium, syllabus, digest, survey, sketch, précis, aperçu.

pandemonium. Uproar, *din, hullabaloo, babel, hubbub, racket.

pander. *Cater, purvey.
Ana. Truckle, toady, *fawn, cringe: gratify, tickle, regale, *please.

panegyric. Tribute, eulogy, *encomium, citation.
Ana. Commendation, applauding *or* applause, complimenting *or* compliment (see corresponding verbs at COMMEND): acclaiming *or* acclaim, laudation, praising *or* praise, extolling *or* extollation (see corresponding verbs at PRAISE).

pang. *Pain, ache, throe, twinge, stitch.
Ana. Agony, *distress, suffering: anguish, *sorrow, grief, heartache: torturing *or* torture, tormenting *or* torment (see corresponding verbs at AFFLICT).

panic. Terror, horror, trepidation, consternation, dismay, alarm, fright, dread, *fear.
Ana. Agitation, upsetting *or* upset, perturbation, disquieting *or* disquiet, discomposing *or* discomposure (see corresponding verbs at DISCOMPOSE).
Con. *Confidence, assurance, self-possession, aplomb: *equanimity, composure, sang-froid.

pant. Aspire, *aim.
Ana. Thirst, hunger, *long, yearn, pine: crave, covet, *desire, wish, want.

pantaloon. *Fool, jester, clown, antic, buffoon, zany, merry-andrew, harlequin, comedian, comic, stooge.

paper, *n.* **1 Paper, instrument, document** are here compared in their most general senses as meaning a writing (often typed, sometimes printed) that is of value to its owner or to others who come after him, as a source of information, proof of a right or contention, or the like. **Paper** is the most general term, applicable to any of the letters, deeds, certificates, writs, etc. (*papers,* in general), that are filed away for future use or reference; as, state *papers;* "A peculiar difficulty I have experienced in dealing with Lord Macaulay's private *papers*" (*G. O. Trevelyan*); "it was not until I was forty that my father put into my hands a few old family *papers* which furnished clues to an investigation of my more remote ancestry" (*H. Ellis*). **Instrument** is a legal term applicable only to a paper (such as a deed, a writ, a will, a contract, or the like) that is made and executed according to the terms of the law, as concrete evidence of a transfer of property, the enforcement of a judgment, one's decisions as to who shall inherit one's property, the terms of an agreement, or the like; as, "[The slave's white] father executed certain *instruments* to manumit him" (*Ch. Just. Taney*). **Document,** as here compared (see also DOCUMENT, 1), applies to any legal instrument or to any original or authentic copy of a letter, a record, or other paper that may be used as a source of information, evidence, or proof; as, the *documents* to be used by the prosecution have been put in a very safe place; "Her [Lady Byron's] letters I sent back except those of the quarreling correspondence, and those, being *documents,* are placed in the hands of a third person" (*Byron*).
2 Article, *essay, theme, composition.

par, *n.* Norm, *average, mean, median.

par, *adj.* Mean, median, average. See under AVERAGE, *n.*

parable. *Allegory, myth, fable, apologue.

parachronism. *Anachronism, metachronism, prochronism.

parade, *n.* *Display, array, pomp.
Ana. Showiness, ostentatiousness *or* ostentation, pretentiousness, pompousness (see corresponding adjectives at SHOWY).

parade, *v.* Flaunt, expose, display, exhibit, *show.
Ana. *Reveal, disclose, divulge: *declare, proclaim, publish, advertise: vaunt, *boast, brag, gasconade.
Con. Cloak, mask, *disguise, dissemble.

paradigm. *Model, example, pattern, exemplar, ideal, beau ideal, standard, mirror.

paradox. Paradox, antinomy, anomaly are not synonyms but they all involve the idea of expressing or revealing an inner or inherent contradiction and are therefore not always clearly distinguished or correctly used. A **paradox** is primarily a statement or proposition which contains a contradiction yet which, absurd as it seems to be, may still be true and in accordance with the facts and common sense. "The perfectly bred man is born, not bred, if the *paradox* may be permitted" (*Brownell*). By extension, a *paradox* is a situation which is known to exist, yet which when described or put in words seems incredible because it involves a logical contradiction. "His [Horace's] own phrase of 'golden mediocrity' expresses with some truth the *paradox* of his poetry; in no other poet, ancient or modern, has such studied and unintermitted mediocrity been wrought in pure gold" (*J. W. Mackail*). "The old will perennially become new at the hand of genius. That is the *paradox* of art" (*Lowes*). An **antinomy,** in philosophical use, is a contradiction between two laws, principles, or conclusions, both of which are held on good grounds or are correctly inferred from the same facts or premises; thus the conclusions that every material thing can be explained by mechanical causes and that some material things cannot be explained unless a final cause is postulated, present an *antinomy,* but in the opinion of Kant both can be accepted as rules regulative of experience. In loose general use, the term is often applied to one thing that contradicts another thing and is irreconcilable with it. "Form and expression. . . .should stand toward one another not as clashing *antinomies* but as reconciled opposites" (*Babbitt*). In discriminating general use, how ever, an *antinomy* is an irresolvable conflict (at least in the light of present knowledge) of principles, beliefs, forces, tendencies, aspirations, and the like. "A mind that is not naturally analytical, and conscious of the *antinomies* of existence" (*Amer. Speech*). "Every dogma is but one side of an inevitable *antinomy*" (*H. Cushing*). "In Greek religion...these two tendencies are also in evidence, the one working towards particularism, the other towards a wider Pan-Hellenic unity...the Greeks —like other ancient peoples—failed to solve the *antinomy*" (*Cambridge Ancient History*). An **anomaly** is something that is contrary to what it should be. For example, it may be an exception, or a contradiction to the rule; it may be a freak, a monster, a sport, or a contradiction to the type; it may be an anachronism or solecism, irreconcilable with its surroundings or conditions; it may be an action, a practice, mood, or the like, that is in effect a denial of what one believes or teaches. " 'There is no greater *anomaly* in nature than a bird that cannot fly' " (*Darwin*). "That he [Mark Twain] remained active and buoyant to the end was...sufficient evidence that his philosophical despair was only an *anomaly*, which had no organic part in the structure of his life" (*Van W. Brooks*). "In Egypt Augustus...had...royal authority ...an *anomaly* in the empire" (*Buchan*).

paragon, *n.* **Paragon, sublimation, apotheosis, phoenix** (*or* **phenix**), **nonpareil, nonesuch** are here compared as meaning a person or thing of consummate quality or transcendent excellence in its kind. **Paragon** distinctively implies supremacy and incomparability; as, "An angel! or, if not, An earthly *paragon!*" (*Shak.*); "on His left [hand] sat smiling Beauty's *paragon*" (*Keats*); "Mill's book is a *paragon* of expository writing" (*J. A. Macy*); "Hawaii, a *Paragon* throughout the East" (*V. Heiser*). **Sublimation,** in precise use, stresses the absence (or sometimes, the removal) of all that is gross, impure, or earthy. "We need not trace the evolution of prayer from a half-magical incantation to the *sublimation* of petition in 'Thy will be done' " (*Inge*). In loose use, the word is often thought of as a synonym of *quintessence*. "That... *sublimation* of all dismal sounds, the bark of a fox" (*Hardy*). **Apotheosis** is rarely used with precision or with a consciousness of its historical implications. For this reason it is often indistinguishable from *paragon* or *sublimation;* as, "here all is spotless grace, etherial delicacy...the very *apotheosis* of womanhood" (*Mrs. Jameson*). In very discriminating use, it implies glorification, or such exaltation of a person or thing that he (or it) loses human or earthly character and becomes almost divine or purely ideal; it is therefore correctly applied not only to the product but also to the act of glorification; as, national or racial heroes are often *apotheoses* of the actual men; the *apotheosis* of the state in totalitarian ideology. "Wagner believed that Beethoven's Seventh Symphony...was an *apotheosis* of the dance" (*H. Ellis*). "For some time no more was heard of them; then news came of Ellen's marriage to an immensely rich Polish nobleman of legendary fame....She disappeared in a kind of sulphurous *apotheosis*" (*E. Wharton*). **Phoenix,** in its literal sense a mythical bird which after having lived its allotted years burns itself on a pyre and arises from the ashes with renewed youth and beauty, has acquired in the figurative sense in which it is here considered the implication of uniqueness or rarity or apartness from others. "For goddes love, let not him be a *Phenix*, let him not be alone" (*Latimer*). "Lucian is far more deeply concerned at seeing the *phoenix* of modern culture throw herself away on a man unworthy of her" (*Shaw*). **Nonpareil** and **nonesuch** are now rarer in literary use than they once were. Like *paragon* they imply the absence of a rival in excellence, but they have been debased by their frequent use in names of botanical and other varieties, and in trade names of manufactured articles. "Thou art the best o' the cut-throats: yet he's good That did the like for Fleance: if thou didst it, Thou art the *nonpareil*" (*Shak.*). "The giddy people had cried him up for a *nonesuch*" (*Cotton Mather*).

paragraph. Paragraph, verse, article, clause, plank, count are here compared only as denoting one of the several and individually distinct statements of a discourse or instrument, each of which deals with a particular point or item. **Paragraph** primarily refers to a typographical division, usually indicated by beginning on a new line, and usually by indenting the first word, or by the use of ¶, but it also is applicable to a similar division in writing or typing. In rhetorical use, the term usually implies a number of sentences which comprise a unit that coherently develops a topic or point, especially one of the subordinate topics or points of an essay, an argument, or the like. In more general use, brief, clear, or pointed statement of a single idea rather than its expansion and adequate exposition is stressed; the term is often used where statements follow in serial or numbered order and are neither developed individually nor logically related to each other; as, see *paragraph* 4 of the accompanying instructions; the witty *paragraphs* of a popular columnist. **Verse,** as here considered (see also VERSE, 1), is applied specifically to one of the numbered paragraphs of the Bible, especially as printed in the Authorized and Douay versions; as, Isaiah, chapter v, *verses* 23–25. **Article** may or may not imply paragraph arrangement of each point or item, but it does imply that each is a distinct yet essential member of a whole. In its more common use it is applied to a statement that stands out distinctly, as, for example, one of the stipulations in a contract, or one of the doctrines in a creed, or one of the provisos of a statute; thus, the Thirty-nine *Articles* are the doctrines to which a clergyman of the Anglican Communion subscribes before being admitted to holy orders; the *articles* of the Apostles' Creed are not paragraphs or sentences, but brief phrases naming each of the dogmas professed by those Christians who hold this creed; the *articles* of an indenture, that is, of an agreement by which an apprentice is bound to a master, are the specific terms or conditions of that agreement. However, in some instruments, such as the Constitution of the United States of America, *article* designates one of the larger and more inclusive divisions, comprising many *articles* in the narrower sense. Therefore, one usually speaks of a specific rule, regulation, specification, stipulation of that document, or of other constitutions, as a **clause.** *Clause* is also used more often than *article* in reference to a will, a deed, and a legislative bill, and with little difference in frequency in reference to a contract, a statute, or similar instruments; as, he added two *clauses* to his will before signing it; strike out *clause* 5 of the agreement. **Plank,** originally an Americanism, though now found in British use, is applied only to an article in a program, as something that those who accept that program implicitly agree to carry out if possible. It is chiefly used in designating one of the specific proposals or pledges in the platform of a political party; as, the speaker argued for a platform with *planks* that were both specific and feasible. **Count** is the legal designation for a particular allegation or charge in a declaration or indictment; as, to try the indicted man on two *counts*.

parallel, *adj.* Analogous, comparable, *similar, like, alike, identical, akin, homogeneous, uniform.

Ana. *Same, identical, equal, equivalent: correspondent, correlative (see RECIPROCAL).

parallel, *n.* **1** *Comparison, contrast, antithesis, collation.
Ana. *Likeness, similarity, resemblance, similitude.
Con. *Dissimilarity, unlikeness, difference, divergence.
2 Parallel, counterpart, analogue, correlate are comparable when they denote a person or thing that corresponds in essentials to another person or thing, or closely resembles the latter in the points under consideration. **Parallel,** in very precise use, is the preferred term when the two things compared are so like each other that their lack of divergence suggests two parallel lines: it is therefore used frequently in negative expressions; as, we shall seek in vain a *parallel* for this situation; it is hard to find a *parallel* for this mode of procedure. "None but thyself can be thy *parallel*" (*Pope*). Sometimes, especially when actual comparison is implied, the word suggests that the two things follow a similar course, order, or the like; as, the life of any one dictator offers a close *parallel* to that of any other. **Counterpart,** because it was originally applied to either of the two parts of an indenture, or a document containing an agreement written in duplicate and later divided between the parties, often suggests a complementary, and sometimes an obverse, relationship; as, the two halves of a globe are *counterparts* of each other. More commonly, however, the word implies a duplication, especially in another sphere, or age, or language, or the like; as, several French words such as "distrait" have been anglicized because they had no *counterparts* in English; synthetic chemistry has produced many a drug or perfume that has no *counterpart* in nature. "He saw that there was no mood of the mind that had not its *counterpart* in the sensuous life" (*Wilde*). **Analogue** usually implies a more remote likeness than the preceding words and usually suggests comparison with something familiar and tangible for the sake of clarifying an explanation or enforcing an argument. Like *counterpart,* it often involves reference to something in another sphere, or order, or genus; as, the gill in fishes is an *analogue* of the lung in quadrupeds. "Boileau is the *analogue* of Pope in French literature" (*Hallam*). "Christian progressives...tried to find some warrant for it [their belief in a law of progress] in the New Testament, where its only *analogue* is the apocalyptic Messianism which we find St. Paul and the author of the Fourth Gospel cautiously discarding" (*Inge*). **Correlate** retains its primary implication of correspondence, but does not, as here compared, retain that of a complementary relationship. A thing which is a correlate of another, in the sense under consideration, is what corresponds to it from another point of view or in a different order of viewing; thus, the scientist asks what is the physical *correlate* of the rainbow; the psychologist seeks the *correlate* of thought in the physical events in the cortex of the brain; for the ideas expressed by many words there are no objective *correlates;* affinity is the *correlate* in chemistry of the force the physicist calls attraction.

paralogism. *Fallacy, sophism, sophistry, casuistry.

paralogistic. Fallacious, sophistical, casuistical. See under FALLACY.

paralysis. Paralysis, palsy, apoplexy, stroke, shock are not all synonyms of each other but they are frequently confused by laymen. **Paralysis** designates an effect rather than a cause; it is the term used to denote loss of power to move (*motor paralysis*), or of power of sensation in (*sensory paralysis*), any part of the body; the loss may occur suddenly (as usually in *hemiplegia,* paralysis of one lateral half of the body, or in *paraplegia,* paralysis of the lower half of the body) or it may be progressively effected (as in *creeping paralysis*). **Palsy** is a close synonym of *paralysis,* but in popular use it generally connotes shaking or tremulousness of the muscles in a part or the whole of the body. **Apoplexy,** or its more popular designation **stroke,** names a sudden diminution or loss of consciousness and paralysis, caused either by a cerebral hemorrhage or by a clot or embolus in an artery that prevents the flow of blood into a part of the brain. Paralysis is often the result of apoplexy, but it may also be caused by an injury to the spinal cord or to other nervous tissues, as by disease or by chemical or bacterial poisons. **Shock** is another popular term for *apoplexy,* but its use is not approved by physicians, because the word has a very different denotation in medicine, always indicating a profound depression of the vital processes of the body.

paramount. Preponderant, preponderating, predominant, *dominant, sovereign.
Ana. *Supreme, surpassing, pre-eminent, superlative: capital, foremost, principal, main, leading, *chief.

parapet. Rampart, breastwork, *bulwark, barbette, bastion.

paraphernalia. Apparatus, *equipment, machinery, outfit, tackle, gear, matériel.

paraphrase, *n.* Metaphrase, construe, version, *translation.

parasite, *n.* **Parasite, sycophant, favorite** (*or* **favourite**), **toady, lickspittle** (*or* **lickspit**), **bootlicker** (*or* **bootlick**), **hanger-on, leech, sponge** (*or* **sponger**) are here compared as denoting a person who seeks support and sustenance (usually physical, but sometimes social or intellectual) from another without right or justification. **Parasite** (etymologically, [one] eating beside or at the table of another) applies strictly to one who is fed and, often, clothed by another without giving any services in return; as, "The poorer citizens [of ancient Rome] were little more than *parasites,* fed with free state bread, amused by free state shows" (*Buchan*). It is in a similar sense that *parasite* is used in the biological sciences, when the term denotes an animal or plant that lives on, in, or with, another animal or plant and, usually, preys upon it. In current extended use, *parasite* is often applied to a person who, like a biological parasite, clings close to a person of wealth, power, and influence and derives some great personal advantage from that association (as, "New friends who had faith in her ideas, as well as new *parasites* who hoped to profit by them, gathered around her" —*H. Ellis*), or who is as useless and unnecessary a member of society as the biological parasite is to its host (as, to regard all idle inheritors of wealth as *parasites*). **Sycophant** (originally, an informer or traducer) applies strictly to one who clings close to a person of great wealth, power, or influence, winning his favor by fawning attentions, flattery, and adulation; as, "The young monarch was accompanied by a swarm of courtly *sycophants*" (*Prescott*). "In France, the cleverest boys go to the École Normale Supérieure and do not mix any longer with the average. This plan certainly has advantages. It prevents the intellectuals from having their nerve broken and becoming *sycophants* of the average Philistine" (*B. Russell*). **Favorite,** in the specific sense here considered, applies to a person who is the close associate and intimate friend of a king, a prince, or the like, and who is unduly favored by him; often, the term carries in addition suggestions of parasitism or sycophancy on the part of the favorite, or of the wielding of undue influence by him; as, "like *favourites,* Made proud by princes" (*Shak.*); "[The Roman emperor] Committing to a wicked *favourite* All public cares, and yet of him suspicious" (*Milton*). **Toady** stresses a truckling to the rich, powerful, or influential. It sometimes implies parasitism or sycophancy, but more often suggests the servility and snobbery of a social climber; as, he was a *toady* in the presence of those he regarded as his superiors, and a bully when surrounded by those he thought of as his inferiors. **Lickspittle,** or the less common **lickspit,** and **bootlicker,** or **bootlick** (the latter pair American slang), are extremely contemptuous synonyms of *sycophant* or *toady:* all heighten the suggestion of abject servility in fawning or truckling; as, "Stage-coachmen were... comrades to gentlemen, *lickspittles* to lords" (*J. Hawthorne*); he's not a friend of B—'s: a *bootlicker*—nothing more. **Hanger-on** is a colloquial general term for anyone who wins contempt for his close adherence to another and dependence on him; as, "He is a perpetual *hanger-on:* yet no-body knows how to be without him" (*Swift*); political *hangers-on,* dancing attendance on this party boss or that, trying to obtain sinecures. **Leech** applies to a hanger-on, especially to a parasite, who resembles, both in his close clinging and in his power to bleed for his own advantage, the blood-sucking worms called *leeches;* as, "the spendthrift and the *leech* That sucks him" (*Cowper*). **Sponge** (now a colloquial term), or **sponger,** applies usually to a parasite, but it stresses his laziness, dependence, and greed, and indifference to the discomforts he may be causing; as, "I will do any thing, Nerissa, ere I'll be married to a *sponge*" (*Shak.*); the school club refused to elect to membership any one who they feared might become a *sponger.*

Ana. Fawner, cringer, truckler (see corresponding verbs at FAWN).

parcel, *n.* **1** *Part, portion, piece, detail, member, division, section, segment, sector, fraction, fragment.

2 *Bundle, bunch, pack, package, packet, bale, fardel.

parcel, *v.* *Apportion, portion, ration, prorate.

Ana. *Allot, assign, allocate, apportion: *grant, accord, award.

parch. *Dry, desiccate, dehydrate, bake.

Ana. Sear, scorch, char, *burn: shrivel, wizen, *wither.

pardon, *v.* Forgive, remit, *excuse, condone.

Ana. *Free, release, liberate: *confess, shrive, absolve: acquit, absolve, *exculpate.

Ant. Punish. — *Con.* *Penalize, fine, amerce: discipline, correct, chasten, castigate, chastise (see PUNISH).

pardon, *n.* **Pardon, amnesty, absolution, indulgence** come into comparison in their legal and ecclesiastical senses. **Pardon,** which is the comprehensive term, denotes a release not, as is often mistakenly supposed, from guilt, but from the penalty due for a transgression of secular or spiritual law. Thus, in civil and military affairs, a *pardon* usually implies a release from prison, or from the payment of a fine, or from a sentence of death, and permission to go scot free, though not acquitted. When a pardon is extended to an entire class, such as an insurgent group, or to an entire community, it is called an **amnesty;** as, a general *amnesty* and liberty of conscience were promised to parliament by Charles II in the Declaration of Breda (1660). *Amnesty* often, but not invariably, carries its etymological implication of oblivion, and suggests not only that past offenses will go unpunished, but that they will be forgotten. When, in ecclesiastical use, especially in the use of the Roman Catholic Church, a pardon is extended for sins confessed and atoned for according to the laws of the Church, it is specifically called **absolution** when it implies that the eternal punishment for sin has been remitted in the sacrament of penance, and it is specifically called **indulgence** when it implies that the temporal punishment (that is, punishment by heavy penances or in Purgatory) has in some degree been remitted by the performance of further acts of piety prescribed by the Church. In older English, *pardon* often equalled *indulgence,* but the former is seldom found in this sense today except as a translation of the French *pardon* or in derivatives such as *pardoner* (the medieval church official). The implication of permission to commit sin which *indulgence* acquired in the late sixteenth century was the result of post-Reformation misunderstanding of the doctrine and is not found today in informed usage.

pardonable. *Venial.

pare. Peel, *skin, decorticate, flay.

parental. Parental, motherly, fatherly, maternal, paternal, despite the difference in sex suggested by some of the terms, come into comparison as meaning of, relating to, or characteristic of a parent. **Parental** carries no specific or distinguishing implications and is therefore the ordinary uncolored term; as, *parental* authority; *parental* duties; *parental* rights. **Motherly** and **fatherly** carry implications of qualities of character or of appearance associated in the first case with the typical (or often, ideal) mother, and in the second the typical (or often, ideal) father. *Motherly,* therefore, often suggests tenderness, and comprehension of or sympathy with the natures or difficulties of children (as, "When I see the *motherly* airs of my little daughters when playing with their puppets"—*Addison*), or the mature, often buxom, appearance of a woman who has competently reared many children (as, "a brisk, wholesome, *motherly* body" —*L. Stephen*). *Fatherly* usually suggests affection, protectiveness, wisdom in advising, and the like (as, to take a *fatherly* interest in a group of orphans; to give the departing son a *fatherly* blessing and *fatherly* counsel), or a benign, often a venerable, appearance (as, "See how the tears run down his [Cranmer's] *fatherly* face"—*Tennyson*). **Maternal** and **paternal** often differ little from *parental* except in their definite indication of sex; as, *maternal* (or *paternal*) authority; *paternal* (or *maternal*) love; *maternal* (or *paternal*) responsibility. They are, however, the preferred terms when relationship on or through the mother's or father's side is indicated; as, one's *paternal* grandfather; ancestors on the *maternal* side; one's *maternal* great-aunt. Oftentimes, also, *maternal* and *paternal* are used in place of *motherly* and *fatherly,* especially when that which is qualified bears a relation to the fact or state of motherhood or fatherhood rather than to the concept of the ideal or typical father or mother; as, *paternal* obligations; *maternal* fears; the *maternal* instinct; *paternal* emotions.

parkway. *Road, roadway, highway, highroad, street, avenue, boulevard, terrace, drive, thoroughfare, byway, lane, alley, alleyway.

parley. Treat, negotiate, *confer, commune, consult, advise.

Ana. *Discuss, debate, dispute, argue, agitate: converse, talk, *speak.

parody, *n.* Travesty, *caricature, burlesque.

Ana. Skit, squib, lampoon, *libel.

parody, *v.* Travesty, caricature, burlesque. See under CARICATURE, *n.*

paroxysm. Spasm, convulsion, *fit, attack, access, accession.

parsimonious. Niggardly, penurious, *stingy, close, closefisted, tight, tightfisted, miserly, curmudgeonly, cheeseparing, penny-pinching.

Ana. Avaricious, *covetous, grasping, greedy: *sparing, frugal: *mean, ignoble, sordid, abject.

Ant. Prodigal. — *Con.* *Profuse, lavish: *liberal, munificent, bountiful, generous.

part, *n.* **Part, portion, piece, detail, member, division, section, segment, sector, fraction, fragment, parcel** are here compared as meaning something which is less than the whole but which is either considered as apart from the rest of the whole or is actually separated from it. **Part** is the most comprehensive of these terms: it may be used in place of any of the succeeding words in this group (or even in place of *element, component, constituent,* or the like: see ELEMENT); as, "All are but *parts* of one stupendous whole" (*Pope*); he spent *part* of his life in China; a large *part* of the estate went to the elder son; the cup was broken into three *parts;* " 'The better *part* of valour is discretion' " (*Shak.*). **Portion,** although it denotes a part of a whole, does not always presuppose a compact or integral whole: it may suggest a whole that comprises all of an existing or a possible stock, store, or the like, without any connotation of its assemblage; as, "That best *portion* of a good man's life, His little, nameless, unremembered, acts Of kindness and of love" (*Wordsworth*); "He is a *portion* of the loveliness Which once he made more lovely" (*Shelley*). But *portion* (see also FATE) is preferred to *part* when there is the intent to imply determination of amount or quantity, or assignment or allotment, especially of a share; as, a bride's *portion* (i.e., her dowry); to divide a pie into six equal *portions;* "A *portion* of each day was given to this artistic labour" (*Hudson*); "When the plant was set, a *portion* of water, nicely calculated as to quantity, ran down a pipe and was deposited at the plant roots" (*S. Anderson*). **Piece** applies always to a separate or detached part or portion of a whole; thus, a *piece* of bread is a part of a larger whole, such as a loaf or a slice; a *piece* of cloth may be the length of a bolt (i.e., a given number of yards cut from a web and made into a roll), or a length cut from a bolt, a smaller length left after the larger part of that piece has been used, or a bit that serves as a swatch or sample; so, to break a stick of candy into *pieces;* to ask for a small *piece* of the cake. But *piece* so stresses the implication of independence that the term is often applied to a thing that is relatively complete in itself, and has reference to a whole only as it presupposes a mass from which it was taken, a collection of similar or related things, especially as produced by one person, one machine, one factory, or the like; as, the red-hot *piece* of iron upon the blacksmith's anvil; *pieces* of pottery; each *piece* of furniture has been freshly polished; many factory workers are paid by the *piece* (that is, according to the number of pieces made during a week or day); a *piece* of poetry; his *pieces* (that is, short articles) are frequently published in the newspapers. **Detail** (see also ITEM) applies to a part chiefly when the presupposed whole is a plan or design, or represents the working out of a plan or design: in this sense the term is used mainly, but not exclusively, in the arts of painting, sculpture, and architecture, and often denotes a small but important part or feature; as, to reproduce a *detail* of a painting; the sculptor's students were set to work, each modeling a *detail* of the Venus de Milo; this blueprint shows the *details* of the façade. In military use, *detail* applies to a small detachment (or sometimes, only one person) assigned to a given piece of work or a given duty; as, "No, not combatants—only *Details* guarding the line" (*Kipling*). **Member,** in general, applies to any part that constitutes one of the units of which a body (a human body, an animal or plant body, a metaphorical body, a construction or structure, such as a chair, a table, a bridge, a building, or, far more often in current use, a body of persons who make up a legislature, a staff, an association, or the like) is comprised; therefore, the term, though it usually implies close association with the body under consideration, also usually implies its separability in thought or in fact; thus, the legs, arms, and head are often specifically regarded as *members* of the human body; the saddle seat is a distinctive *member* of a Windsor chair; the flying buttress is an important architectural *member* of most of the great medieval Gothic cathedrals; *members* of Congress; the club has 500 *members;* "Now ye are the body of Christ, and *members* in particular" (*1 Corinthians* xii. 27); "The body of the law is no less encumbered with superfluous *members*" (*Addison*). **Division** and **section** apply to a distinct, often a detached, part formed by or as if by cutting or dividing. The terms are often used interchangeably, but *division* is usually, though not invariably, applied to larger parts than is *section;* thus, in military use, a *division* is ordinarily one of the large parts of an army in which all types of military service are represented, so that in a sense it constitutes a self-contained army, whereas a *section* is a small group led usually by a sergeant and composed typically of a headquarters and two or more squads; in education, especially in the United States, a *division* is a group of allied departments (as, the *divisions* of modern languages and of political sciences), whereas a *section* is one of the groups into which a large class of students taking a course is divided (as, there are twenty *sections* of freshman English). Except in technical use, both terms carry no explicit suggestions as to size, extent, or the like: *division,* however, is more often used abstractly than *section,* which tends to be applied to a conspicuously distinct part of a writing, a people, a territory, or the like; as, "It is improper to speak of these different parts of the chemical industry as *divisions,* for the solidarity of the whole does not permit splitting it" (*A. C. Morrison*); a *section* of a chapter; the eastern *section* of the country; the Constitution is divided into *sections.* **Segment** is often preferred to *section* for a part cut off by natural lines of cleavage or necessitated by the nature of the thing's construction or design; as, a *segment* of an orange; a *segment* of a compound leaf; a *segment* of a flywheel; the *segment* of the globe known as the Torrid Zone. In mathematical use, *segment* is distinguished from *sector* in that *segment* refers to any part of a plane or solid figure cut off from the whole by a line or plane (as, a *segment* of a cylinder; a *segment* of a circle is bounded by an arc and a chord) and **sector** refers to any part of a circle bounded by an arc and two radii (as, to divide a circle into six *sectors*). In more general use, *sector* applies to a section that roughly corresponds to a mathematical sector; thus, a *sector* assigned to a commander of a division in war has arbitrary bounds on sides and rear but a front that is as extensive as the range of its guns. **Fraction** and **fragment** both apply to a part that is disconnected from a whole, especially by breaking; but *fraction,* probably by its confusion with the arithmetical sense of that word, usually suggests a negligible part (as, "only a small *fraction* of mankind is capable of enthusiasm for language, for its own sake"—*Inge;* "some little *fraction*...of your enjoyment of tragedy"—*C. E. Montague*), and *fragment* applies to one of the pieces left, as after eating, use, the course of time, or the like (as, "They took up of the *fragments*...twelve baskets full" —*Matthew* xiv. 20; only a *fragment* of a statue or a poem remains). **Parcel,** as here compared (see also BUNDLE), is now rarely used except in law and in some idiomatic phrases such as *part and parcel.* In law, it means a piece of land (as, to convey several *parcels* of an estate; to purchase a *parcel* of land); in its archaic general sense, *parcel* differs from *part* in its always implying an undetached or undetachable connection with the whole of which it is a part; as, "[no] *parcel* of the world is denied to man's inquiry and invention" (*Bacon*).

Ant. Whole.

part, *v.* Divide, *separate, sever, sunder, divorce.

Ana. *Detach, disengage: apportion, *allot, allocate, assign: *tear, rend, cleave.
Ant. Cleave.[1] — *Con.* Cling, *stick, adhere: *unite, combine, conjoin.

partake. *Share, participate.
Ana. *Separate, part, divide: take, *receive, accept: *have, hold, own, possess, enjoy: *get, obtain, procure, acquire.

partiality. Prepossession, prejudice, bias, *predilection.
Ana. *Favor, good will, countenance: approving *or* approval, endorsing *or* endorsement (see corresponding verbs at APPROVE).
Ant. Impartiality.

participate. *Share, partake.
Ana. *Separate, divide, part: take, *receive, accept: *have, hold, own, possess, enjoy.

particle. 1 **Particle, bit, mite, smitch, smidgen** (*or* **smidge**), **whit, atom, iota, jot, tittle** come into comparison when they mean a very small or insignificant piece or part. **Particle**, which is literally a diminutive of *part*, is used in reference not only to substances which are actually divisible but to those which are only theoretically so because they are intangible or ideal things such as a quality, a state, or a condition; usually it implies an amount within the range of ocular or mental perception; as, a *particle* of matter; he hasn't a *particle* of sense; "a voice from which every *particle* of emotion was painfully excluded" (*Hardy*). **Bit** sometimes retains its etymological suggestion of *bite*, or *mouthful;* as, there isn't a *bit* of food in the house; he hasn't eaten a *bit* today; but, in the sense here considered, it more often suggests the least possible or feasible amount, extent, or degree; as, to own a *bit* of land; he likes it not a *bit;* he is a *bit* of a coward (that is, he has a *bit* of cowardice in his nature). **Mite** (a colloquial term) because of its dual reference to *mite*, the tiniest of insects, and to the coin of insignificant value (the widow's mite of *Luke* xxi. 2), may stress either diminutiveness in size or minuteness in amount; as, a *mite* of a boy; a *mite* of a diamond; he hasn't a *mite* of suspicion; I have a *mite* of fear. **Smitch, smidgen** are dialectal words not distinguishable in meaning from *bit* or *mite*. **Whit** is used chiefly in negative phrases in the sense of the least conceivable amount; as, it matters not a *whit;* he hasn't a *whit* of knowledge of the subject. **Atom**, with its reference to the scientific atom (see PARTICLE, 2), implies an amount or a size beyond the possibility of further diminution; as, not an *atom* of dust escaped her scrutiny; he exhausted himself to the point where not an *atom* of energy remained. **Iota** and its anglicized form **jot** both imply a minuteness suggestive of the character *iota* [ι], the smallest letter of the Greek alphabet; **tittle** implies a minuteness suggestive of a small diacritical mark such as the dot over an *i* or a cedilla under *ç*. In use they are not distinguishable when they mean the smallest or most minute detail; as, he hasn't added a *jot*, an *iota*, or a *tittle* to our knowledge of the subject. "Till heaven and earth pass, one *jot* or one *tittle* shall in no wise pass from the law, till all be fulfilled" (*Matthew* v. 18). *Iota*, however, sometimes denotes an insignificant amount, extent, or degree. "They never depart an *iota* from the authentic formulas of tyranny and usurpation" (*Burke*).

2 **Particle, corpuscle, atom, molecule** are here considered in their commonest current meaning, in chemistry and physics, of a minute (submicroscopic) division of matter. **Particle**, the oldest and most general of these terms, is applied especially to any of certain minute entities which have more specific designations such as *ion, molecule, atom, electron, proton*, and *alpha particle. Particle* is often used to emphasize the idea of indivisibility without change of identity, commonly suggesting the ultimate entities (protons and electrons) of which all matter is now believed to be composed. **Corpuscle** differs from *particle* chiefly in suggesting a discrete material entity that possesses the properties characteristic of typical material bodies. The words, however, are close synonyms. "They [alpha particles] are *corpuscles* endowed with charge, with mass, and with velocity" (*Karl K. Darrow*). "Let us assume that all lighted bodies emit *particles* of light, or *corpuscles*, which, falling on our eyes, create the sensation of light" (*Einstein & Infeld*). "When Huyghens argued with Newton on the subject of the nature of light, he condemned Newton's idea that light consisted of a flight of *corpuscles*, on the ground that material *particles* could not possibly travel as fast as light had just been found to move" (*Sir W. H. Bragg*). According to the common modern concept, an **atom** is the smallest particle of an element that can exist either alone or in combination with smaller particles of the same or of a different element; as, an *atom* of hydrogen or of oxygen. **Molecule** denotes the smallest particle of an element or compound that retains chemical identity with the substance in mass. Molecules are usually composed of two or more atoms, either of the same or of different elements; as, a *molecule* of water is composed of two *atoms* of hydrogen and one *atom* of oxygen. *Atom* is sometimes used loosely in place of *molecule*.

particular, *adj.* 1 *Single, sole, separate, unique, lone, solitary.
Ant. General.
2 Individual, *special, specific, especial, respective, concrete.
Ant. General, universal.
3 Particularized, detailed, itemized, *circumstantial, minute.
Ana. Scrupulous, meticulous, *careful, punctilious.
4 Fussy, squeamish, *nice, dainty, fastidious, finical, pernickety.
Ana. Exacting, demanding, requiring (see DEMAND): strict, *rigid, rigorous.

particular, *n.* *Item, detail.
Ant. Universal: whole: aggregate.

particularized. Particular, detailed, itemized, *circumstantial, minute.
Ana. Accurate, precise, exact, *correct.
Ant. Generalized.

partisan. *Follower, adherent, disciple, sectary, henchman, satellite.
Ana. Supporter, upholder, backer, champion (see under SUPPORT, *v.*): helper, aider *or* aid, assistant (see corresponding verbs at HELP).
Con. Antagonist, *opponent, adversary.

partner. **Partner, copartner, colleague, ally, confederate** agree in denoting an associate. **Partner** implies especially an associate in business, or one of two associates, as in certain games, in a dance, or in marriage. Since *partner* alone implies association, the addition of *co-*, with its implication of association, in **copartner** sometimes adds little or nothing to *partner;* as, *partners*, or *copartners*, in crime. *Copartner*, however, does not tend to be as specialized in application as *partner*, and it often distinctively implies fellow partner; as, "The authority of a *partner* to bind his *co-partners*" (*Encyc. Brit. 11th ed.*), or equality of share; as, "A *copartner* in that sovereignty of the people" (*J. Spence*). **Colleague** implies especially an associate in office or in professional or academic relations. **Ally** and **confederate**, though referable to persons, most frequently denote an associated state or government (for *confederate*, see also ACCOMPLICE). *Ally* suggests a somewhat temporary union for co-operation in war or in affairs of policy or statecraft; *confederate*, a closer union for strength and solidarity. The latter term often implies a central government or, at least, centralized control of the associated states.

Ant. Rival.

parturition. *Childbirth, delivery, labor, travail, accouchement.

party. 1 *Company, band, troop, troupe.

Ana. Clique, *set, coterie, circle: gathering, collection, assembly *or* assemblage, congregation (see under GATHER).

2 *Combination, combine, bloc, faction, ring, cabal, junto.

pasquinade, pasquin, pasquil. Lampoon, squib, skit, *libel.

pass, *n.*[1] Passage, *way, route, course, artery.

pass, *n.*[2] *Juncture, exigency, emergency, contingency, pinch, strait, crisis.

Ana. Situation, condition, *state, posture: plight, *predicament, quandary.

passage. 1 Pass, *way, route, course, artery.

2 Also **passageway. Passage, passageway, corridor, hall, hallway, gallery, arcade, cloister, aisle, ambulatory** come into comparison when they designate a typically long, narrow way connecting parts of a building or affording access to a particular room or section in it. **Passage** (see also WAY, 1) and **passageway** are the comprehensive terms, interchangeable with any of the others. A **corridor** is a passageway flanked on one or both sides by rooms, apartments, compartments (as, in British use, of a train), offices, or the like, or leading from one part of a building to another. **Hall** and **hallway** are in American use applied to a corridor; the former in both British and American use is also applied to a room that serves as an entrance to a house (see ENTRY, 2). A **gallery** (see also BALCONY) is a corridor having a continuous row of windows; it may be a part of the building or a verandalike enclosure. An **arcade** is an arched and covered passageway, usually between rows of shops but, sometimes, between the front of a row of shops and the street or an open court. A **cloister** is a similar structure in a monastery or in a building imitating monastic architecture, but it runs along one or more sides of an open court or patio, and is arcaded or colonnaded on the outer side. An **aisle** is, strictly, not a passageway but a part of a church or other building divided from the central part, or *nave*, by a row of columns or piers. In Gothic and Romanesque churches, aisles flank the nave. Since in many modern churches the nave and the aisles contain two rows of pews each, to which access is given by a narrow passageway, the term has been transferred to the passageway; it is also applied to any similar passage flanked by rows of seats, as in an auditorium, a theater, or, in American use, a train. **Ambulatory** is a passageway through which one may walk; it is specifically applied to the cloister of a monastery, and to the curved passageway (loosely the *aisle*) between the choir of a church and the chapels of an apse.

3 *Strait, straits, sound, channel, narrows.

passing, *adj.* *Transient, transitory, ephemeral, momentary, fugitive, fleeting, evanescent, short-lived.

passing, *n.* *Death, decease, demise.

passion, *n.* 1 Suffering, agony, dolor, *distress, misery.

Ana. *Trial, tribulation, cross, visitation, affliction.

2 *Feeling, emotion, affection, sentiment.

Ana. *Inspiration, enthusiasm, frenzy, furor: *ecstasy, rapture, transport.

3 Lust, concupiscence, appetite, appetence, *desire, urge, yen.

Ana. Craving, coveting (see DESIRE, *v.*): longing, yearning, hungering *or* hunger, thirsting *or* thirst (see corresponding verbs at LONG): panting, aspiring, aiming (see AIM, *v.*).

4 **Passion, fervor** (*or* **fervour**), **ardor** (*or* **ardour**), **enthusiasm, zeal** agree in denoting intense, high-wrought emotion. **Passion,** as here compared, implies an overwhelming or driving emotion; it may be either the most abstract or the most concrete of these terms. It may be used without implication of a specific emotion; thus, a poet without *passion* is a poet incapable of feeling or of displaying vehement, agitating, or soul-stirring emotion; to be in the grip of *passion* is to be swayed by violent emotion; but without a hint from the context the nature of the emotion remains unknown. On the other hand, *passion* may designate intense erotic love, or often, but far from always, lust; as, "The red rose whispers of *passion* And the white rose breathes of love" (*J. B. O'Reilly*): it may designate violent rage; as, she flew into a *passion*. "I am very sorry, good Horatio, That to Laertes I forgot myself... But, sure, the bravery of his grief did put me Into a towering *passion*" (*Shak.*). **Fervor** and **ardor** both imply the kindling of emotion to a high degree of heat, but *fervor* suggests rather a steady glow or burning and *ardor* a restless or leaping flame. *Fervor* is associated therefore with emotions that express themselves in prayer, contemplation, devotion, preaching, in works of art, or the like; *ardor*, with emotions that express themselves in eager longings, zealous efforts, or the like; as, the *fervor* of a nun; the *ardor* of a missionary; to exhort with *fervor;* to dampen one's *ardor*. "The hieratic Buddhist art was to become formal and gradually lose the *fervour* of its inner life" (*Binyon*). "In the prints of Harunobu there is an intense sympathy with youth, with its shyness, its tremulous *ardours*" (*Binyon*). **Enthusiasm** often comes very close to *ardor*, but it differs from the latter chiefly in its emphasis on the rational grounds for the emotion, such as thoroughgoing admiration for a person or thing, conviction of the worthiness of the cause or end, or the like. *Ardor* may suggest aspiration without a clearly envisioned goal, but *enthusiasm*, correctly used, always implies an objective, a cause, an object of devotion, or the like; thus, a teacher may stimulate *ardor* in a pupil without necessarily directing the latter's emotion into a definite channel, but he stimulates *enthusiasm* only when he provides the pupil with something concrete to admire, to follow, to fight for. "He showed in this cause not only the *enthusiasm* of an idealist, but the sagacity of a practical leader" (*Inge*). **Zeal,** which etymologically implies jealousy and emulation, has now lost these connotations, though it still retains a suggestion of a goading or driving passion equivalent to them in power. In current English, that passion is great ardor or enthusiasm for a cause or end. Coupled with this implication is that of energetic and unflagging activity in the service of a cause or in the pursuit of an end; as, "With all the *zeal* Which young and fiery converts feel" (*Byron*); "It took the Franciscan movement about twenty years to lose the *passion* of its early *zeal*" (*A. Huxley*); "[Shaftesbury's] health was further affected by his *zeal* in public affairs as well as his enthusiasm in study" (*H. Ellis*).

Ana. *Ecstasy, rapture, transport: *anger, rage, fury, wrath: eroticism, amorousness (see corresponding adjectives at EROTIC).

passionate. *Impassioned, ardent, fervent, fervid, perfervid.

Ana. *Intense, vehement: impetuous, headlong, *precipitate, abrupt: excited, quickened, stimulated (see PROVOKE).

passive. *Inactive, inert, idle, supine.
Ana. *Impassive, phlegmatic, stolid, apathetic.
Ant. Active. — *Con.* Live, operative, dynamic (see ACTIVE).

pastoral. *Rural, rustic, bucolic, georgic, Arcadian, agrestic, geoponic.

pasture, *v.* Graze, *feed, nourish.

pat, *adj.* *Seasonable, timely, well-timed, opportune.
Ana. Apt, happy, felicitous, appropriate, fitting (see FIT, *adj.*): pertinent, apposite, apropos, applicable (see RELEVANT).

patch, *v.* *Mend, repair, rebuild, remodel.
Ana. Emend, remedy, redress, amend, *correct: fix, *adjust, regulate.

patent. *Evident, manifest, distinct, obvious, apparent, palpable, plain, clear.
Ana. *Noticeable, conspicuous, salient, prominent: *flagrant, glaring, gross, rank.
Ant. Latent. — *Con.* *Imperceptible, insensible, impalpable: hidden, concealed, secreted (see HIDE, *v.*).

paternal. *Parental, fatherly, maternal, motherly.

pathetic. Poignant, affecting, *moving, touching, impressive.
Ana. *Pitiful, piteous, pitiable: plaintive, *melancholy, doleful.
Ant. Comical.

pathogen. *Germ, microbe, bacterium, bacillus, virus.

pathos. **Pathos, poignancy, bathos** are here compared as denoting the quality found in human situations, or especially in works of art or literature, which moves one to pity or sorrow. **Pathos** is the common term in critical and literary use: because of its early and long-continued association with aesthetics it often implies the arousing of emotions which give pleasure rather than pain and it suggests the detachment of an observer rather than personal involvement in the perturbing events or situations; as, "*Pathos* is the luxury of grief; and when it ceases to be other than a keen-edged pleasure it ceases to be *pathos*" (*Patmore*). Often, also, *pathos* implies not so much an effect produced on the person who sees, hears, or reads, as the art, device, or trick employed by the writer, speaker, artist, or other person seeking to produce such an effect; as, "He passed without an effort from the most solemn appeal to the gayest raillery, from the keenest sarcasm to the tenderest *pathos*" (*J. R. Green*); " 'My poor children, what had I ever done to you that would drive you to such a step?' The touch of *pathos* was all that Jane needed to stiffen her" (*M. Austin*). **Poignancy** is now often preferred by literary and art critics to *pathos* because it carries no suggestion of artificiality and centers the attention on the genuineness of the thing's emotional quality and of the emotions it arouses: it also specifically implies a power to pierce the mind or heart so that the reader, hearer, or observer feels with pain as well as with aesthetic pleasure the emotion aroused whether it be pity or sorrow or any other overwhelming emotion; as, "the most famous of the women-poets of Japan, whose verse expresses with peculiar *poignancy* a sense of the glory of beauty and the *pathos* of it" (*Binyon*); "Out of these illustrious atoms [words]...were made all the glow and intensity of... eloquence and the sweet *poignancy* of songs" (*C. E. Montague*). **Bathos** is often applied to a false or pretentious pathos, especially a strained pathos that by its absurdity arouses laughter rather than tears.

patience. **Patience, long-suffering, long-sufferance, longanimity, forbearance, resignation** come into comparison when they mean the power to endure or a capacity for enduring without complaint that which is disagreeable or requires effort. **Patience** stresses calmness or composure, not only under suffering or under provocation, but in awaiting an outcome that seems unduly or inordinately delayed, or in performing a task that makes severe demands upon one's attention; as, "Upon the heat and flame of thy distemper Sprinkle cool *patience*" (*Shak.*); "In your *patience* possess ye your souls" (*Luke* xxi. 19); "Let us run with *patience* the race that is set before us" (*Hebrews* xii. 1); "I shall never lose the habit of giving myself away to you. You've brought it on yourself by your goodness and *patience*" (*C. Mackenzie*). **Long-suffering** (or, now less often, **long-sufferance**) and **longanimity** imply extraordinary patience under provocation or trial. The former is the common term found both in literary and in colloquial use. In colloquial use, it sometimes also suggests undue meekness or submissiveness; as, "It shows much *long-suffering* in you to put up with him, and keep him in your employ" (*Hardy*); "The *long-sufferance* of the army is almost exhausted" (*Washington*). The latter term more often than the former names a virtue, and so is chiefly found in abstract use; as, "in Isaac such simplicity, such *longanimity* in Jacob" (*Hooker*). **Forbearance** (see FORBEARING) adds to *long-suffering* the implication of restraint in the expression of one's feelings or in exacting punishment: it therefore often suggests toleration, for the sake of peace, of something that merits censure or castigation; as, "My lord Kew has acted with great *forbearance*, and under the most brutal provocation" (*Thackeray*). **Resignation** implies a submission to suffering or evil or an acceptance of it because it must be endured or cannot be escaped: it sometimes connotes patience arising from submission to what is believed to be the Divine Will, but often it implies a stoical or fatalistic, rather than a religious, attitude; as, "*Resignation* superadds to *patience* a submissive disposition...; it acknowledges both the power and the right of a superior to afflict" (*T. Cogan*); "In *resignation*...lies... the only serenity possible in this life of struggle and of combat" (*Mrs. H. Ward*); "For a modern American or Englishman, waiting is a psychological torture. An Indian accepts the blank hours with *resignation*" (*A. Huxley*).
Ana. Perseverance, persistence (see corresponding verbs at PERSEVERE): *fortitude, backbone, pluck, grit, sand, guts: *equanimity, composure.
Ant. Impatience.

patois. *Dialect, vernacular, lingo, jargon, cant, argot, patter, slang.

patrician. *Gentleman, aristocrat.

patrimony. *Heritage, inheritance, birthright.

patron. *Sponsor, surety, guarantor, backer, angel.
Ana. Supporter, upholder, champion (see corresponding verbs at SUPPORT): benefactor, contributor (cf. *benefaction, contribution*, at DONATION): protector, defender (see corresponding verbs at DEFEND).
Ant. Client: protegé.

patter, *v.* Chatter, prate, *chat, gab, prattle, babble, gabble, jabber, gibber.

patter, *n.* *Dialect, vernacular, patois, lingo, jargon, cant, argot, slang.

pattern, *n.* **1** Exemplar, example, *model, paradigm, ideal, beau ideal, standard, mirror.
Ana. *Prototype, archetype: *paragon, apotheosis, sublimation.
2 *Figure, design, motif, device.
Ana. *Form, figure, shape, conformation, configuration.

paunch. *Abdomen, belly, stomach.

pawn, *n.* Hostage, gage, *pledge, earnest, token.

pay, *v.* **Pay, compensate, remunerate, satisfy, reimburse,**

indemnify, repay, recompense, requite come into comparison as meaning to give money or an equivalent in return for something. **Pay** is the ordinary term when the giving or furnishing of money to discharge an obligation for services rendered, goods delivered, or the like, is implied; as, to *pay* one's bills promptly; to *pay* one's gardener good wages (or to *pay* good wages to one's gardener); to *pay* a debt contracted by another; to *pay* ten dollars for a hat; "Taxes are what we *pay* for civilized society" (*Justice Holmes*); "owing doesn't mean *paying*, as any butcher or baker or candlestick-maker can tell you" (*Deland*). When, in extended use, *pay* does not imply the actual giving of money, the term is often employed purely as a figure of speech (as, nothing can *pay* him for his pains; he promised to *pay* the offender in his own coin), or it means merely to give as due or deserved (as, to *pay* a compliment), or to give in the hope of a return in kind (as, to *pay* attention to a young woman). **Compensate** is often preferred to *pay* when no legal obligation is implied or no payment for services is expected, because the term stresses a return, usually but not necessarily in money, that is regarded as an equivalent for a service given, for trouble taken, time spent, or the like; as, to *compensate* a waiter for his cheerful willing service; to *compensate* a friend for the time he spent in helping one; to *compensate* a neighbor for taking care of one's pets during the summer. But in this sense *compensate* often does not imply an obligation to another or the passing of money: it often suggests a counterbalancing, as of something unpleasant by something pleasant, or of something lost by something gained; as the beauty of the view *compensated* for the labor of the climb. (See COMPENSATE, 1.) **Remunerate,** like *pay*, usually implies the discharge of an obligation in money and, like *compensate*, usually suggests the giving of an equivalent for services rendered rather than for goods delivered, but unlike both of these terms, it often carries a suggestion, sometimes a mere hint, sometimes a distinct implication, of a reward; as, he promised to *remunerate* the searchers handsomely; "The king *remunerated* them both, the former with an addition of honour, the latter with an accession of estate" (*Fuller*). Both *compensate* and *remunerate* are used in place of *pay* when the latter term is thought of as offensive or indelicate; as, the party always *remunerates* its faithful workers; the lawyer asked for a thousand dollars to *compensate* him for his services. **Satisfy,** as here considered (see also SATISFY, 1 & 3), implies the payment of something that is asked, demanded, or required by the terms of the law or the decree of a court; as, to *satisfy* a claim; to *satisfy* a judgment against one; certain pieces of property must be sold to *satisfy* legacies involving definite sums; he was not able to *satisfy* all his creditors. **Reimburse** implies a return for money that has been expended by oneself in hope of making a profit, or by another, such as one's agent or attorney, in doing one's business; as, the profits of his business did not *reimburse* him for the money he had invested in it; to *reimburse* one's lawyer for certain expenditures; "a promise of *reimbursing*...what the people should give to the king" (*Bolingbroke*); "Nor do I see that [the book] is likely ever to *reimburse* him the charge of printing" (*Lamb*). **Indemnify** implies promised or actual reimbursement for loss as by fire, for injury as by accident, for damage as by war, or the like; as, the insurance policy *indemnifies* him against the loss of his house and its furnishings by fire, flood, or windstorm; the victors in a war usually demand that the conquered enemy *indemnify* them for all the damages suffered in battle or through invasion or raids. **Repay** and **recompense** carry a weaker implication of giving or furnishing money than any of the preceding terms and a stronger implication of returning like for like: both therefore stress the demands of justice even more than the compulsion of an obligation; in fact, they cover the senses expressed colloquially by the verb phrase *pay back*. When the passing of money or of an equivalent is implied, *repay* is preferred when there is a suggestion of giving something back that has been paid out to one (as, to *repay* a loan) and *recompense*, when compensation for voluntary services or for losses or injuries sustained is suggested and a due or adequate return is implied (as, he *recompensed* each person who had given him assistance; he *recompensed* each of the victims for the injuries sustained in the collision for which he was responsible). But *repay* and *recompense* sometimes imply reciprocation of something given, advanced, inflicted, or the like. *Repay* usually implies little more than paying back in kind or amount (as, "*repay* her scorn for scorn"—*Keats;* we never can *repay* your kindness, or *repay* you for your kindness) but it is sometimes used when the return is not that which might be expected but is its diametrical opposite (as, to *repay* love with hate; "*Repaying* incredulity with faith"—*Browning*). *Recompense* often in this extended sense specifically implies a desire to make amends or to atone for a wrong that has been inflicted; as, the governess sought to *recompense* the child for the coldness of his father and mother; "in some part to *recompense* My rash but more unfortunate misdeed" (*Milton*). **Requite** carries a still stronger implication of reciprocation or retaliation than these terms: it may imply a return not of like for like, but of that for which one is striving (as, she did not *requite* his love; "You will *requite* me...by the sight of your ardour for what is noble"—*Quiller-Couch*), or of that which is the antithesis of the hoped-for return (as, "his servility was *requited* with cold contempt"—*Macaulay*). Often, however, it distinctly implies the avenging of a wrong or the satisfaction of a desire for revenge; as, "Drake...had *requited* the wrongs inflicted by the Inquisition on English seamen" (*J. R. Green*).

pay, *n.* *Wage *or* wages, salary, stipend, fee, hire, emolument, screw.
Ana. *Reparation, restitution, indemnity, redress, amends.

paynim, *adj. & n.* Pagan, heathen, ethnic, Gentile. See under PAGAN, *n.*

peaceable. *Pacific, peaceful, pacifist, pacifistic, irenic.
Ana. *Amicable, friendly, neighborly: *amiable, complaisant: *calm, placid, serene, tranquil.
Ant. Contentious: acrimonious. — *Con.* Quarrelsome, bellicose, *belligerent: *martial, warlike.

peaceful. 1 *Calm, tranquil, serene, placid, halcyon.
Ana. *Soft, gentle, mild: *still, stilly, quiet, silent, noiseless.
Ant. Turbulent.
2 *Pacific, peaceable, pacifist, pacifistic, irenic.
Ana. Composed, collected, unruffled, *cool: equable, constant, *steady.
Con. Disturbed, perturbed, disquieted, agitated, upset, discomposed (see DISCOMPOSE).

peak. 1 *Mountain, mount, alp, volcano, mesa.
2 *Summit, pinnacle, climax, apex, acme, culmination, meridian, zenith, apogee.

peculate. *Defalcate, embezzle.
Ana. Appropriate, *arrogate, pre-empt, usurp, confiscate: *steal, pilfer, purloin, filch: *rob, plunder, rifle, loot.

peculation. Defalcation, embezzlement. See under DEFALCATE.

Ana. Appropriation, arrogation, confiscation (see corresponding verbs at ARROGATE): *theft, larceny, robbery.

peculiar. 1 Individual, *characteristic, distinctive.

Ana. *Special, especial, particular, specific: idiosyncratic, eccentric (see corresponding nouns at ECCENTRICITY).

2 Eccentric, odd, queer, *strange, singular, unique, quaint, outlandish, curious.

Ana. Bizarre, grotesque, *fantastic: *abnormal, atypic, aberrant: unusual, uncustomary (see affirmative adjectives at USUAL).

pecuniary. *Financial, monetary, fiscal, bursal.

pedantic. Pedantic, academic (*or* **academical**), **scholastic, bookish** are here compared as terms of derogation applied to thinkers, scholars, and other learned men and their utterances. **Pedantic** often implies ostentatious display of knowledge, didacticism, and stodginess. "Samuel Johnson...a man artificial in phrase and *pedantic* in judgment" (*Quiller-Couch*). It tends, however, to connote undue attention to scholarly minutiae and small interest in significant issues. "A careful attention to words, which in its extreme form becomes *pedantry*" (*H. Ellis*). **Academic** rarely carries implications of disagreeable personal characteristics, but it does stress abstractness, lack of practical experience and interests, and often, the inability to consider a situation realistically. "There is so much bad writing...because writing has been dominated by...the *academic* teachers and critics" (*H. Ellis*). **Scholastic** is less fixed in its implications than the others, for sometimes the allusion is to the medieval Schools (Scholasticism) and sometimes to modern education. As a rule it implies dryness, formalism, adherence to the letter, and, sometimes, subtlety. "It [Sidney's *Arcadia*] is not romantic, but *scholastic;* not poetry, but casuistry" (*Hazlitt*). "Many laws... could be shown...to transgress a *scholastic* interpretation of one or another of the great guaranties in the Bill of Rights" (*Justice Holmes*). **Bookish** often suggests learning derived from books rather than from actualities; sometimes it implies a decided literary or rhetorical quality; as, *bookish* words; *bookish* interests. "Few novelists are less *bookish* than Kipling" (*C. E. Montague*).

Ana. *Learned, polymathic, erudite: *recondite, abstruse.

pedigree. *Ancestry, lineage.

peek, *n.* Peep, glimpse, glance, *look, sight, view, coup d'oeil.

peel, *v.* *Skin, decorticate, pare, flay.

peel, *n.* *Skin, bark, rind, hide, pelt, fell.

peeler. *Policeman, officer, constable, bailiff, catchpole, bobby, copper, cop, bull, gendarme.

peep, *n.* Glance, glimpse, peek, *look, sight, view, coup d'oeil.

Ana. Peering *or* peer, gazing *or* gaze, staring *or* stare (see corresponding verbs at GAZE).

peer, *v.* *Gaze, gape, stare, glare, gloat.

Ana. Peep, glance, glimpse, look (see corresponding nouns at LOOK).

peerless. Surpassing, pre-eminent, *supreme, superlative, transcendent, incomparable, banner.

Ana. Paramount, sovereign, *dominant, predominant: unmatched, unrivaled, unequaled (see affirmative verbs at MATCH).

peeve, *v.* *Irritate, exasperate, nettle, provoke, aggravate, roil.

Ana. Vex, *annoy, irk, bother: chafe, fret, gall (see ABRADE).

peevish. *Irritable, fractious, snappish, waspish, petulant, pettish, huffy, huffish, fretful, querulous.

Ana. Captious, carping, caviling, faultfinding, *critical.

pelagic. *Aquatic, marine, oceanic, thalassic, neritic, abyssal, bathysmal, bathybic, lacustrine, lacuscular, fluvial, fluviatile.

pellucid. *Clear, transparent, translucent, lucid, diaphanous, limpid.

Ana. *Pure, sheer: *bright, brilliant, luminous, radiant.

Con. *Turbid, muddy, roiled, roily.

pelt, *n.* *Skin, hide, fell, rind, bark, peel.

penalize. Penalize, fine, amerce, mulct, sconce agree in meaning to punish by depriving of something. **Penalize** usually presupposes a violation of laws or rules intended to maintain discipline or fair treatment for all: it implies exaction by the authorities of a pecuniary penalty or a forfeiture of an advantage, or, especially in games, the imposition of a handicap; as, to *penalize* late taxpayers by adding five per cent to the amount due; to *penalize* a football team fifteen yards for holding. **Fine** and **amerce** are chiefly found in technical legal use, in reference to court cases, but their implications in extended use are not materially different. They, and their corresponding nouns, **fine** and **amercement,** are distinguishable in that *fine* implies that the amount exacted is, within certain limits, prescribed by the law; *amerce* and *amercement,* that it has been left to the discretion of the judge; as, violators of the municipal parking ordinances may be *fined* from one to ten dollars; the judge *amerced* the offender in the sum of fifty dollars. **Mulct,** as here compared, commonly implies subjection to a superior power which can legally or illegally exact a penalty (usually in money) for a breach of discipline or for failure to comply with its edicts. Sometimes it merely implies a fine or amercement or a withholding of money due; as, nonconformists were *mulcted* for attendance at services of their own communion; the soldier was *mulcted* of his pay for damage to government property. Often the word suggests force; commonly it implies imposition or the exaction of a heavy (sometimes oppressive) penalty; as, the colonizers *mulcted* the natives of their gold whenever the latter showed signs of resistance. **Sconce,** originally in English university (particularly Oxford) use, suggests a petty fine such as the forfeiture of a tankard of ale, for a slight breach of the rules, especially for an infraction of the conventions while dining in hall. "Sir you have *sconced* me two-pence for non-attendance at a lecture not worth a penny" (*Johnson*). In its rare extended use, it comes close to *mulct,* but it seldom suggests imposition or use of force. "This sanctity of tenure, by which the public had been *sconced,* generation after generation" (*Gladstone*).

Ana. *Punish, discipline, correct, chasten.

penchant. *Leaning, propensity, proclivity, flair.

Ana. Bent, turn, talent, knack, *gift: bias, prepossession, *predilection, prejudice.

pendant. Variant of PENNANT.

pendent *or* **pendant.** *Suspended, pendulous.

pendulate. *Swing, sway, oscillate, vibrate, fluctuate, waver, undulate.

pendulous. *Suspended, pendent.

penetrate. 1 *Enter, pierce, probe.

Ana. Invade, entrench, encroach, *trespass: *perforate, puncture, bore, prick.

2 Pervade, interpenetrate, impenetrate, *permeate, impregnate, saturate.

Ana. Insert, insinuate, interpolate, *introduce: *soak, saturate, drench, steep.

penetration. Insight, acumen, *discernment, discrimination, perception, divination, clairvoyance.

Ana. Sharpness, keenness, acuteness (see corresponding

adjectives at SHARP): shrewdness, astuteness, perspicaciousness *or* perspicacity, sagaciousness *or* sagacity (see corresponding adjectives at SHREWD).

penitence. **Penitence, repentance, contrition, attrition, compunction, remorse** agree in denoting sorrow or regret for sin or wrongdoing. **Penitence** implies little more than such sorrow or regret; as, the outward signs of *penitence;* his *penitence* is only skin-deep; he showed his *penitence* in many ways. **Repentance** is richer in its implications, for it also implies a change of heart, an awareness of one's shortcomings morally or spiritually, or of the evil of one's actions or life as a whole. "I came not to call the righteous, but sinners to *repentance*" (*Luke* v. 32). "God of his mercy give You patience to endure, and true *repentance*" (*Shak.*). **Contrition** and **attrition** (see also EROSION) are both theological terms, and as such contrasted; only *contrition* is found in general use. Both imply deep sorrow for sin and the purpose of amendment, but in strict theological use *contrition* implies that one's sorrow arises out of love of God and a realization of one's failure to respond to his graces, and *attrition* (now rare except in learned use) that it arises from a lower motive, such as fear of hell or fear of the loss of heaven. "O may Thy love and pity supply whatsoever has been wanting in the sufficiency of my *contrition*" (*Manual of Prayers*). "Sacramental grace to raise our sorrow from *attrition* to *contrition*" (*Manning*). In general use, *contrition* implies penitence that is manifest in signs of pain or grief. "You must—whether you feel it or no—present an appearance of *contrition*" (*Meredith*). "Sophia thought that, after such a sin, the least Amy could do was to show *contrition*" (*Bennett*). **Compunction** and **remorse** both imply a painful sting of conscience, but *compunction* usually suggests a momentary reaction not only for something done, but also for something being done or to be done, and *remorse* usually suggests prolonged and insistent self-reproach and, often, intense suffering for consequences which cannot be escaped. "A heartless scoundrel who had...abandoned her in her poverty for evermore, with no touch of *compunction*" (*Dickens*). "He [the older child] has to be taught that the junior can be easily hurt by rough handling, and to feel *compunction* when he has wantonly caused tears" (*B. Russell*). "Make thick my blood; Stop up the access and passage to *remorse*, That no compunctious visitings of Nature Shake my fell purpose" (*Shak.*). "O, that the vain *remorse* which must chastise Crimes done, had but as loud a voice to warn, As its keen sting is mortal to avenge!" (*Shelley*).

Ana. Regret, *sorrow, anguish: humiliation, humbling, degradation, debasement (see corresponding verbs at ABASE): *qualm, scruple.

Con. Obdurateness *or* obduracy, inexorableness, adamant (see corresponding adjectives at INFLEXIBLE).

pen name. *Pseudonym, nom de plume, alias, nom de guerre, incognito, allonym.

pennant *or* **pendant.** *Flag, ensign, standard, banner, color, streamer, pennon, jack.

pennon. *Flag, ensign, standard, banner, color, streamer, pennant, jack.

penny-pinching. *Stingy, close, closefisted, tight, tightfisted, niggardly, parsimonious, penurious, miserly, curmudgeonly, cheeseparing.

pensive. *Thoughtful, reflective, speculative, contemplative, meditative.

Ana. Solemn, *serious, earnest, sober, grave: musing, pondering, ruminating (see PONDER).

penumbra. Umbra, adumbration, umbrage, *shade, shadow.

penurious. Parsimonious, niggardly, *stingy, close, closefisted, tight, tightfisted, miserly, curmudgeonly, cheeseparing, penny-pinching.

Ana. Avaricious, grasping, greedy, *covetous: *mercenary, venal: *mean, abject, sordid, ignoble.

penury. *Poverty, indigence, want, destitution, privation.

Ana. *Need, necessity, exigency: pinch, strait, pass, *juncture.

Ant. Luxury.

peon. Bondsman, bondman, *serf, slave, bondslave, thrall, villein, vassal, Helot.

people, *n.* *Race, nation.

peppery. Fiery, gingery, *spirited, high-spirited, mettlesome, spunky.

Ana. Impetuous, headlong, *precipitate, abrupt: *pungent, piquant, spicy, snappy.

perceive. Discern, note, remark, notice, observe, contemplate, *see, behold, descry, espy, view, survey.

Ana. Grasp, seize, *take: *apprehend, comprehend: *enter, penetrate, pierce, probe.

percept. *Sensation, image.

Ana. *Idea, concept, notion: recognition, acknowledgment (see corresponding verbs at ACKNOWLEDGE).

perceptible. **Perceptible, sensible, palpable, tangible, appreciable, ponderable** come into comparison when they mean capable of being apprehended through the senses or intellect as real and existent. **Perceptible** may be used inclusively to describe anything that comes within the range of one's senses and can be recognized in itself or by certain signs; as, *perceptible* sounds; the ship is barely *perceptible* on the horizon; few objects are distinctly *perceptible* in a fog. It may also be used narrowly without qualification by *just, scarcely, barely,* or the like, to describe a thing that just passes the borderline between invisibility and visibility, inaudibility and audibility, and the like; as, a *perceptible* change in her tone; there are *perceptible* differences between *surprise* and *astonish;* a *perceptible* flavor of onions; her remark had no *perceptible* relevance to the topic of conversation. **Sensible** may be used to describe anything which is clearly apprehended through the bodily senses, or which impresses itself strongly on the mind through the medium of sensations. Originally, *sensible* was opposed to *intelligible,* the former meaning apprehensible directly by the senses, and the latter, apprehensible only by the intellect; as, *sensible* versus *intelligible* reality. This opposition is now rare except in some philosophical use, but *sensible* still often applies to that which can be known through the senses; as, "a rich and thronging world of *sensible* things" (*Lowes*); "Our true ideas of *sensible* things do indeed copy them" (*W. James*). In contrast with *perceptible,* however, *sensible* applies to that which is more obvious, even sometimes to that which is patent through its effects or signs; thus, a *sensible* change in tone is one which is immediately recognized; a *sensible* difference in a person's expression is one that is quickly detected. "The direct, *sensible* influence of Protestantism has been to isolate and to individualize" (*Brownell*). Both **palpable** and **tangible** in their primary senses may be used to describe anything which is perceptible through the sense of touch. *Palpable,* however, although it is used of that which is felt by touching with the tips of the fingers (thus, a *palpable* powder is one that feels gritty), as often implies a sensation produced as a sensation sought and therefore may be applied to anything that evokes a response from the tactile nerves in any part of the body; as, there is a *palpable* chill in the air. "Art thou not, fatal vision [of a dagger] *sensible* To feeling as to sight?... I see thee yet, in form as *palpable* As this [dagger] which now I draw" (*Shak.*). "When I hear A lay that once I saw her hand awake, Her form seems floating *palpable*, and near" (*Keats*). *Tangible*, on the other hand, is applied (literally) only to things which may be or are handled or grasped; as, if an infant is not provided with light *tangible* objects, he will play with a sunbeam or shadow; idols are gods or divinities in *tangible* form. In their secondary senses, these two words diverge widely. *Palpable*, in one of its most common meanings, implies a high degree of perceptibility (see EVIDENT); in poetic use, especially when applied to an immaterial thing, it suggests an almost physical awareness of its existence or reality. "What happiness to live When every hour brings *palpable* access Of knowledge" (*Wordsworth*). "In the expiring, diffused twilight...it was the immensity of space made visible—almost *palpable*" (*Conrad*). *Tangible*, in its extended senses, is applied only to things that can be thought of as having real, independent, or objective existence, whether they are apparent to the senses or not, or whether they can be handled or not; thus, *tangible* ideas are those that can be grasped by the mind and made objects of thought; *tangible* advantages are those having a substantial character; *tangible* assets are those that can be appraised with reasonable accuracy, such as equipment, accounts due, and the like, as distinguished from those that are *intangible*, such as good will. **Appreciable** is applied to anything that is large enough to be measured, weighed, valued, or otherwise estimated; thus, a *perceptible* change in the temperature may be so slight a change that it almost, but not quite, escapes notice; a *palpable* change in temperature may still be slight, but it is great enough to make it definitely felt; an *appreciable* change in temperature may also be slight, but its extent is determinable by reference to a thermometer; some said there was no *perceptible* diminution of war hysteria, others declared that the decrease in tension was *palpable*, but still others maintained that months must elapse before any *tangible* effects of the accord became evident and there was *appreciable* relief from strain. **Ponderable** is applicable to that which can be weighed, either physically or mentally. "Something *ponderable* from the outer world—something of which we can say that its weight is so-and so" (*Jeans*). The word tends, however, to be applied to that which is appreciable in terms of weight or significance as distinguished from that which is so intangible as to elude such determination; as, to exert a *ponderable* influence upon the events of his time.

Ana. *Clear, lucid, perspicuous: *noticeable, conspicuous, signal: discerned *or* discernible, noted *or* notable, observed *or* observable (see corresponding verbs at SEE).

Ant. Imperceptible.

perception. Penetration, insight, acumen, *discernment, discrimination, divination, clairvoyance.

Ana. Appreciation, comprehension, understanding (see corresponding verbs at UNDERSTAND): sharpness, keenness, acuteness (see corresponding adjectives at SHARP).

perch, *v.* *Alight, light, land, roost.

percussion. Concussion, clash, shock, *impact, impingement, collision, jar, jolt, brunt.

Ana. Striking, hitting, smiting (see STRIKE): vibration, oscillation, fluctuation (see corresponding verbs at SWING).

perdurable. Durable, permanent, stable, *lasting, perpetual.

Ana. Enduring, abiding, persisting, continuing (see CONTINUE): *everlasting, endless, interminable.

Ant. Fleeting.

peremptory. Imperative, imperious, *masterful, domineering.

Ana. Decisive, *decided: positive, certain (see SURE): *dictatorial, authoritative, dogmatic, oracular.

perennial. Perpetual, incessant, constant, *continual, continuous.

Ana. *Lasting, perpetual, perdurable, stable: *everlasting, unceasing, never-ending.

Ant. Annual (*esp. of plants*).

perfect, *adj.* **Perfect, whole, entire, intact** come into comparison when they mean not deficient, defective, or faulty in any particular. **Perfect** is the usual term to describe such a condition, for it may imply not only the presence of every part, every element, and every quality necessary to a thing in its finished or fully developed state, but the soundness, the proportionateness, and the excellence of each part, element, or quality; as, a *perfect* set of teeth; a *perfect* diamond; a *perfect* tree; a physically *perfect* infant. The term is also applicable where there is no more definite measure or test than correspondence to a very high standard of excellence (as, a *perfect* gentleman; *perfect* coloring; "a *perfect* poem like Lycidas, a *perfect* fiction like Esmond, a *perfect* handling of a theory like Newman's Idea of a University"—*Pater*), or to an archetype, definition, or pattern (as, a *perfect* hexagon; a *perfect* flower [i.e., one that is both staminate and pistillate]; a *perfect* Greek temple), or to any conception that represents an ideal or personal vision of the highest possible of its kind (as, *perfect* virtue; the *perfect* Christian). The term is also used in the loose sense of *absolute* (see fistnote at ABSOLUTE); as, he is a *perfect* fool; that is *perfect* nonsense. **Whole** and **entire** (as here considered: see also WHOLE, 2) are somewhat poetical or elevated, and often reminiscent of Scriptural use. *Whole* usually implies a perfection, especially a moral or physical perfection, that can be sought and attained, or that can be lost and regained: it usually suggests the attainment of or restoration to health, soundness, completeness, or the like; as, "Daughter, be of good comfort; thy faith hath made thee *whole*" (*Matthew* ix. 22); "she [a statue] is just as *whole* as when she left the hands of the sculptor" (*N. Hawthorne*); "We touch Him in life's throng and press, And we are *whole* again" (*Whittier*). *Entire* usually implies a physical, intellectual, moral, or spiritual perfection that derives from the completeness, integrity, soundness, and often the purity (freedom from admixture) of the thing so described: more than *whole*, it suggests a perfection that is unimpaired or without sign of previous imperfection; as, "But let patience have her perfect work, that ye may be *perfect* and *entire*, wanting nothing" (*James* i. 4). "Oh grant me, Phoebus, calm content, Strength unimpaired, a mind *entire*" (*J. Conington*). **Intact** usually implies the retention of the perfection of a thing in its finished, or its natural, or its original state: often it suggests its passage through some experience that might have destroyed its soundness, integrity, or wholeness; as, "That high courage which enabled Fielding...to keep his manly benevolence and love of truth *intact*" (*Thackeray*); "The group was in wonderful preservation: the figure of Bacchus *intact*, that of the young faun lacking only the arm" (*Vernon Lee*); "I am...thankful that I was among the last persons to see the original Rheims *intact*. The cathedral...remains enshrined...in my memory forever" (*H. Ellis*).

Ana. *Pure, absolute, simple, sheer: *consummate, finished, accomplished: *impeccable, flawless, faultless, errorless.

Ant. Imperfect. — *Con.* *Deficient, defective.

perfection. Virtue, merit, *excellence.

Ant. Failing.

perfervid. Fervid, *impassioned, passionate, ardent, fervent.

Ana. *Intense, vehement: heightened, enhanced, intensified (see INTENSIFY).

perfidious. *Faithless, false, disloyal, traitorous, treacherous.

Ana. *Mercenary, venal: disaffected, alienated, estranged (see ESTRANGE): deceitful, *dishonest: perjured, forsworn (see PERJURE).

perforate. **Perforate, puncture, punch, prick, bore, drill** come into comparison as meaning to pierce through so as to leave a hole or holes. **Perforate** is now used mainly with reference to the action of a machine or instrument which makes several holes, usually small round holes in a line or pattern as for ready tearing, for ornamentation of leather and other products, or for marking with a symbol, device, name, or the like; as, to *perforate* a sheet of postage stamps; to *perforate* leather for the tips of shoes; to *perforate* laundry tabs. The word, however, may be used of any hole, or of any holes in a series or group, produced by natural, artificial, or accidental means; as, leaves *perforated* by insects; the bullet *perforated* the breastbone; the soil is *perforated* by worms. **Puncture** suggests the intentional or accidental entrance of a sharp pointed instrument or thing into a tissue, substance, or material; as, to *puncture* the arm with a hypodermic needle; the tire was *punctured* by a sharp tack. "As the rush began, there flashed through my mind a picture of the ignominious fate which awaited me—*punctured* to death by umbrellas" (*V. Heiser*). Since *puncture* in current use is often associated with the sudden release of air from an inflated object, such as a balloon or a pneumatic tire, the word frequently connotes the sudden deflation of something inflated, unduly pretentious, pompous, or the like; as, to *puncture* a scheme; "The effect of Mark Twain's humorous assault on the dignity of General Grant was to reduce him not to the human but to the common level, to *puncture* the reluctant reverence of the groundlings" (*Van W. Brooks*). **Punch** is often used in place of *perforate* or *pierce* when the use of a tool or machine called a *punch* is implied; as, to *punch* holes in a piece of brass; railway conductors are instructed to *punch* the tickets presented them. (But *punch* does not invariably imply perforation or piercing, for the tool or machine may be so constructed as to perform various other operations such as bending, coining, extruding, and the like.) **Prick** implies a piercing with something that has a very sharp fine point, and therefore suggests a very small hole or a superficial wound; as, to *prick* oneself with a needle; to *prick* out a design on a piece of canvas; to *prick* chapel attendance (i.e., to prick the name of each student attending school or college chapel). In figurative use, *prick* usually stresses either the sharp sting that accompanies the pricking of the skin (as, "his conscience had more than once *pricked* him"—*Arch. Marshall*) or the delicacy and clearness of a pattern or design (as, "the design is *pricked* out, so to speak, by the rhymes"—*Lowes*). Both *bore* and *drill* imply the use of a mechanical means in making a hole. But **bore** (etymologically, to plow) stresses the removal of materials and therefore is employed when there is a suggestion of excavation by hand or machinery (as, to *bore* a hole in the ground; to *bore* a tunnel through a mountain), or the use of a rotary tool such as an auger or gimlet (as, to *bore* holes in a plank; the corn borer is the larva of a moth that winters in the stem of Indian corn and *bores* through the ears as it develops), or in machine-shop practice, of the use of a boring tool, that is, a tool designed for the finishing of roughly made holes by enlarging them and by making them exact in size and true with relation to a specified center line (as, to *bore* the barrel of a gun). **Drill** (etymologically, to bore) commonly implies the use of an instrument or machine equipped with a pointed or two-edged tool for boring holes in hard substances such as metal and stone, or in teeth; as, to *drill* a well in rocky ground; to *drill* holes in a steel plate; a dentist *drills* a tooth to remove decayed dental tissue from a cavity. In their figurative, as distinguished from their extended, senses, *bore* and *drill* (see also PRACTICE) carry differing connotations, *bore* suggesting the slow or continuous forcing of a passage through (as, to *bore* one's way through a crowd; "the sound of an aeroplane *bored* ominously into the ears of the crowd"—*V. Woolf*), and *drill*, the forced entrance of something through a succession of efforts, through persistence (often overpersistence), or the like (as, "A normal child has no spite against work until you have *drilled* one into him by some form of dis-education"—*C. E. Montague*).

Ana. *Enter, penetrate, pierce, probe.

perform. **Perform, execute, discharge, accomplish, achieve, effect, fulfill** (*or* **fulfil**) agree in meaning to carry out completely or into effect. **Perform** (sometimes merely a formal synonym for *do*) is more often used with reference to processes than to acts. One *performs* processes that are lengthy, or exacting, or ceremonial in character; as, to *perform* a play; to *perform* a surgical operation; to *perform* the marriage service. "A solemn Sacrifice, *perform'd* in state" (*Pope*). One *performs* acts that are distinguished or striking; as, to *perform* feats of skill or deeds of heroism. When the end rather than the means to the end is stressed, that which is *performed* is usually something undertaken or pledged. "When she promised a thing she was...scrupulous in *performing* it" (*Austen*). One **executes** that which exists in design or intent by bringing it into being or by putting it into effect. "The heads of departments are...political or confidential agents...merely to *execute* the will of the president" (*Ch. Just. Marshall*). "The quilt was Mammy Clo's masterpiece...a difficult design [that] had to be *executed* exactly right" (*R. Bradford*). Sometimes *execute* is used in place of *perform* of a process involving great skill or a highly exacting technique; as, few dancers can *execute* an adagio beautifully. One **discharges** duties or obligations when one has gone through a required round (usually routine) of tasks. "I had *discharged* my confidential duties as secretary...to the general satisfaction" (*De Quincey*). **Accomplish** usually stresses the completion of a process rather than the means by which it is carried out. One *accomplishes* something begun or something which there is reason to expect. "It took us twenty-three days to *accomplish* the return journey" (*Hudson*). "Who but I saw that prophecy *accomplished*? Indeed, I was the instrument" (*Kipling*). Sometimes *accomplish* implies the fruitfulness of effort or the value of the results obtained. "Because of his efforts things are *accomplished*" (*S. Anderson*). "There's very little to be *accomplished* by telling men anything. You have to show them" (*M. Austin*). **Achieve** adds to *accomplish* the implication of conquered difficulties. One *achieves* a work, a task, an enterprise that is of great importance and that makes unusual demands on one's energy, will power, resources, or the like. "The American public schools *achieve*...the task of transforming a heterogeneous selection of mankind into a homogeneous nation" (*B. Russell*). **Effect** implies obstacles to be removed, but, unlike *achieve*, it emphasizes inherent force in the agent rather than personal qualities such as daring and perseverance. Also, it is often predicated of things as well as of persons; as, only two prisoners *effected* their escape. "That short-cutting of emotion which pure poetry can *effect*" (*Day Lewis*). "Taxation as an instrument for *effecting* a more equal distribution of income" (*Shaw*). **Fulfill** is often used without precision where one of the preceding words would better serve the purpose. It is also often used in-

correctly for *fill;* as, "this *fulfills* a want" (where "this *fills* a want" is correct). Its distinctive implication is full realization, as of that which exists potentially or of that which is demanded especially by the nature of a thing; as, an injured organ cannot *fulfill* its natural function; some laws do not *fulfill* the ends for which they were framed; the prophecy was *fulfilled* to the letter. In reflexive use, *fulfill* suggests complete manifestation of powers or complete self-expression. "God *fulfills* himself in many ways" (*Tennyson*). "Life for her was rich with promise. She was to see herself *fulfilled*" (*D. H. Lawrence*).
Ana. *Reach, gain, compass, achieve, attain: finish, complete, conclude (see CLOSE, *v.*).

performer. *Actor, player, mummer, mime, Thespian, impersonator, trouper.

perfume. *Fragrance, scent, bouquet, redolence, incense.
Ana. Odor, scent, aroma, *smell.

periapt. *Fetish, talisman, charm, amulet.

pericope. *Extract, excerpt.

peril. *Danger, jeopardy, hazard, risk.
Ana. Menacing *or* menace, threatening *or* threat (see corresponding verbs at THREATEN): exposure, subjection, openness, liability (see corresponding adjectives at LIABLE).

perilous. *Dangerous, hazardous, jeopardous, risky, precarious.
Ana. Desperate, forlorn, hopeless (see DESPONDENT): chancy, chance, haphazard, *random.

perimeter. *Circumference, periphery, circuit, compass, ambit.

period. **Period, epoch, era, age, aeon** (*or* **eon**) come into comparison when they denote a portion or division of time; *epoch* and *era* also come into comparison when they denote an event regarded as the beginning of a portion or division of time. **Period,** as here compared, is the generic term, designating an extent of time of any length, for whatever purpose delimited; as, to request a one-minute *period* of silence as a tribute to a dead person. "A centenary *period* in the history of man" (*Milman*). An **epoch** is properly the starting point of a new period, esp. as marked by striking or remarkable changes or events. An **era** is a period (often one extending from an *epoch*) characterized esp. by some new order of things. "The reading of this book was an *epoch* in my life, one of the turning points in my mental history" (*J. S. Mill*). "A better intellectual *era* is dawning for the working men" (*Kingsley*). But *epoch* is frequently used with little distinction from the usual sense of *era*, and *era* is sometimes used with little distinction from the proper sense of *epoch*. "Though the *epoch* was one of confusion...the fame of Volta's work spread gradually" (*Karl K. Darrow*). "The landing of this English Governor was an *era* in their lives" (*W. H. Dixon*). **Age** is commonly more specific and definite than *era;* it is frequently used of a period dominated by some central figure or clearly marked feature; as, the *age* of Pericles; the Bronze *Age*. "The French Revolution and its *age*" (*Arnold*). An **aeon** is an immeasurably or indefinitely long period of time. "He [the elephant] has weight Behind him: *aeons* of primeval power Have shaped that pillared bulk" (*W. W. Gibson*). "During the three terrible hours...he had lived centuries of pain, *aeon* upon *aeon* of torture" (*Wilde*).

Certain or all of these terms are used with arbitrary value in geological and archaeological classifications, but usage is far from uniform. In geology the following classification is perhaps more often used than any other: An *era* is one of the five great divisions (Archeozoic, Proterozoic, Paleozoic, Mesozoic, Cenozoic) of geologic time, as determined by the kinds of fossils found in strata; a *period* is a subdivision of an era; an *epoch*, a subdivision of a period. An *age* is a portion of time characterized by its dominant type of life, and is not an integral part of this classification; thus, the *Age* of Reptiles coincides with the Mesozoic *era*, while the *Age* of Fishes coincides with the Devonian *period*.

In archaeology, uniformity appears to exist only in the use of *age* for one of the three great divisions of human culture (Stone, Bronze, Iron), as determined by the kind of implements used. There is considerable confusion in the use of names for subdivisions of these three divisions; thus, the three subdivisions (Eolithic, Paleolithic, Neolithic) of the Stone Age have been called both *periods* and *eras*.

periodic. *Intermittent, recurrent, alternate.
Ana. *Fitful, spasmodic, convulsive: sporadic, occasional (see INFREQUENT).

periodical, *n.* *Journal, magazine, newspaper, review, organ.

peripatetic. *Itinerant, ambulatory, ambulant, nomadic, vagrant.

periphery. *Circumference, perimeter, circuit, compass, ambit.
Ana. *Limit, confine, bound, end: *boundary, border, march, frontier.

periphrasis. *Verbiage, redundancy, tautology, pleonasm, circumlocution.

peristyle. *Colonnade, arcade, arcature, portico.

perjure. **Perjure, forswear** come into comparison only when they mean to violate one's oath, or, when used reflexively, to make a false swearer of oneself. In general literary use, **perjure** is often employed more loosely than in law, where it is a highly technical term meaning to make a willfully false statement of fact (sometimes of an intention to do something) in spite of an oath or a solemn affirmation that one has told the truth or, as a witness in a judicial proceeding, that one will tell only the truth; as, the judge was convinced that the witness had *perjured* himself. In the looser use, *perjure* often implies making a liar of oneself, whether one is under oath or not; as, "When a native begins *perjury* he *perjures* himself thoroughly. He does not boggle over details" (*Kipling*); "He thanked her, with as much enthusiasm as he could muster without actually *perjuring* himself" (*Arch. Marshall*). **Forswear,** as here compared (see also ABJURE), often implies a violation of an oath, promise, or vow (as, "he swore a thing to me on Monday night, which he *forswore* on Tuesday morning"—*Shak.*; "Thou shalt not *forswear* thyself, but shalt perform unto the Lord thine oaths"—*Matthew* v. 33), but it may also suggest untruth to something as sacred as an oath, such as one's principles, one's beliefs, the laws of one's country, or the like (as, "Shelley indignantly refused to '*forswear* his principles' by accepting 'a proposal so insultingly hateful' "—*Arnold*).
Ana. *Deceive, delude, mislead, beguile: *lie, prevaricate.

perk up. *Preen, prune, primp, doll up, prank, prink.

perky. Jaunty, *debonair, cocky, chipper.
Ana. Gay, *lively, animated, sprightly: trim, trig, *neat, tidy.

permanent. *Lasting, perdurable, durable, stable, perpetual.
Ana. Perennial, constant, continuous, *continual.
Ant. Temporary: ad interim (*of persons*).

permeate. **Permeate, pervade, penetrate, interpenetrate, impenetrate, impregnate, saturate** come into comparison when they mean to pass, or to cause to pass, through every part of a thing. **Permeate** may be used in reference to a material or an immaterial thing and implies its diffusion through all the pores or interstices (literal or figurative) of some substance or entity; as, the rain has *permeated* the sand; "[the dealer in red ocher] was not temporarily overlaid with the colour: it *permeated* him" (*Hardy*); "In...the Elizabethan age, English society at large was accessible to ideas, was *permeated* by them" (*Arnold*); "[Japanese color prints] prove at least how deeply the sense of beauty had *permeated* the whole nation" (*Binyon*). **Pervade** (etymologically, to walk through) is a very close synonym of *permeate*, but in current use it distinctively carries a heightened suggestion of diffusion throughout every part or parcel of the whole (or in the case of very extensive wholes, the portion within one's reach), and it is more often used in reference to places, documents, works of art, and the like; as, "a deep And solemn harmony *pervades* The hollow vale from steep to steep" (*Wordsworth*); "a principle which so entirely *pervades* the constitution...as to be incapable of being separated from it" (*Ch. Just. Marshall*); "we cannot usually say that a smell comes from a certain direction, but merely that the air is *pervaded* by a smell" (*Jeans*). **Penetrate,** as here compared (see also ENTER, 1), is preferred to *permeate* or *pervade* when there is the intent also to suggest the entrance of something that goes deeply or profoundly into the essence or nature of a thing, thereby giving it its characteristic quality or efficient force; as, "a whole nation...*penetrated* with an enthusiasm for pure reason, and with an ardent zeal for making its prescriptions triumph" (*Arnold*); "a letter *penetrated* with affection for the old plain edifice and its memories" (*Quiller-Couch*); "[Painters and poets] *penetrated* with such ideas, and with this innate love of suggestion and understatement" (*Binyon*). **Interpenetrate** and the less common **impenetrate** are merely intensives of *penetrate*, often, but not invariably, also implying a more thoroughgoing diffusion; as, chewing promotes the *interpenetrating* of the food with saliva; totalitarian ideas have deeply *impenetrated* the minds of Central European peoples. **Impregnate** often carries a stronger implication of the operation of a causative power (frequently a human agent) than any of the preceding terms: it also suggests a filling of every available part or portion of a whole so that the thing which enters or is entered is diffused throughout the entire substance, structure, work, group, or the like; as, "the water is *impregnated* with magnesia" (*A. Huxley*); "Any judge who has sat with juries knows that...they are extremely likely to be *impregnated* by the environing atmosphere" (*Justice Holmes*); "He is versifying his ideas...not *impregnating* thought with imaginative beauty" (*Lowes*). **Saturate,** as here compared (see also SOAK), implies impregnation to the point where no more of the thing which enters can be taken up or absorbed: the term, therefore, is often used in preference to *permeate* or *pervade* when that which permeates or pervades is highly obvious, deeply ingrained, conspicuously heavy (as an odor), or the like; as, "the unfinished dresses... were often so *saturated* with smoke that he knew she found it a trial to work on them next morning" (*Cather*); "The [French] Revolution awakened it [democracy] into consciousness, imbued it with ideality, *saturated* it with sentiment" (*Brownell*).

Ana. *Infuse, imbue, ingrain: drench, steep, *soak, saturate: *inform, animate, inspire, fire.

permission. **Permission, leave, sufferance** come into comparison when they denote the sanction which enables one to do something that requires the consent of those in authority. **Permission** is the ordinary term except in some conventional phrases: it commonly implies the power or authority to grant or to refuse what is asked; as, to have the owner's *permission* to hunt on this estate; " 'The horses can go in our barn. I'm sure Mr. Forrester would have no objection.' She spoke as if he had asked her *permission*" (*Cather*). **Leave** differs very little from *permission*. It occurs chiefly in conventionally courteous phrases such as "by your *leave*," "to ask *leave*," "give me *leave*," and the like, but it may be used elsewhere in place of *permission;* as, to ask for *leave* (or *permission*) to remove papers from a file. In military, naval, and some official use, possibly by confusion with the verb *leave* in the sense of *depart*, the term implies official permission to absent oneself from one's duties or from one's station for a fixed period of time, or the furlough or absence so permitted; as, to be granted a *leave* (or a *leave of absence*) of thirty days; to be on sick *leave;* after being absent without *leave* for a month, the soldier was arrested as a deserter. **Sufferance** usually implies a neglect or refusal to forbid, and therefore suggests either a tacit permission withdrawable on cause or, more often, merely suffering a person to be present or to do something; as, you are here only on *sufferance* and if you want to stay, you must listen without interrupting; "He comes among us on *sufferance*, like those concert singers whom mamma treats with so much politeness" (*Thackeray*).

Ana. Authorization, commissioning *or* commission, licensing *or* license (see corresponding verbs at AUTHORIZE): letting, allowing (see LET): sanctioning, approval, endorsement (see corresponding verbs at APPROVE).

Ant. Prohibition.

permit, *v.* *Let, allow, suffer, leave.

Ana. *Authorize, license, commission: sanction, endorse, *approve.

Ant. Prohibit, forbid.

permutation. Mutation, *change, vicissitude, alternation.

Ana. Moving *or* move, shifting *or* shift, removing *or* remove (see corresponding verbs at MOVE): transformation, conversion, metamorphosis (see under TRANSFORM).

pernicious. **Pernicious, baneful, noxious, deleterious, detrimental** agree in meaning exceedingly harmful, but they differ as to the kind and extent of harm done. That is either **pernicious** or **baneful** which is irreparably harmful, but *pernicious* is more often applied to things that corrupt or undermine and *baneful* to those that poison or destroy; as, *pernicious* anemia; a *pernicious* influence; a *baneful* mushroom; a *baneful* atmosphere in which to bring up children. "Untrue beliefs work as *perniciously* in the long run as true beliefs work beneficially" (*W. James*). "A propaganda of *pernicious* humbug" (*Shaw*). "The *baneful* notion that there is no such thing as a high, correct standard in intellectual matters" (*Arnold*). That is **noxious** which is harmful, especially to health of body or mind. "A cold *noxious* wind" (*S. Haughton*). "Only when the educator shall have been educated, the air cleared of *noxious* fallacies...will the reign of Humbug come to an end" (*Grandgent*). **Deleterious** is now seriously used chiefly of that which causes harm when taken into the body, as into the digestive or respiratory tract. "Many drugs that seem so good in the first trials prove to have *deleterious* after effects" (*V. Heiser*). "This gas was well known to be *deleterious*" (*J. Phillips*). **Detrimental** is usually followed by a phrase specifying that which sustains injury, harm, etc.; as, restrictive legislation that is *detrimental* to trade. "Paradoxes...*detrimental* to the true course of thought" (*Jowett*).

Ana. Baleful, malign, *sinister, malefic: *poisonous, venomous, toxic, pestilent, miasmatic: injurious, hurtful, harmful, mischievous (see corresponding nouns at INJURY).

Ant. Innocuous.

pernickety, pernicketty, pernickity, *or* **persnickety.** Fastidious, finical, *nice, dainty, particular, fussy, squeamish.

Ana. Exacting, demanding, requiring (see DEMAND): annoyed, vexed, irked (see ANNOY).

perpendicular. *Vertical, plumb.

Ana. *Steep, abrupt, precipitous, sheer.

Ant. Horizontal.

perpetual. 1 *Lasting, permanent, perdurable, durable, stable.

Ana. *Everlasting, endless, unceasing, interminable, never-ending: eternal, sempiternal, *infinite.

2 *Continual, continuous, constant, incessant, perennial.

Ana. Enduring, persisting, abiding, continuing (see CONTINUE): set, settled, fixed, established (see SET, *v.*).

Ant. Transitory, transient.

perplex. *Puzzle, mystify, bewilder, distract, nonplus, confound, dumfound.

Ana. Disturb, perturb, upset, *discompose: baffle, balk, thwart (see FRUSTRATE): astound, amaze, astonish, *surprise.

perquisite. *Right, prerogative, privilege, appanage, birthright.

persecute. Oppress, *wrong, aggrieve.

Ana. *Worry, annoy, harass, harry: torture, torment, rack, grill (see AFFLICT): *bait, badger, hound, ride.

Con. *Indulge, pamper, humor: favor, *oblige, accommodate: *support, uphold, champion, back.

persevere. Persevere, persist come into comparison when used in reference to persons in the sense of to continue in a given course in the face of difficulty or opposition. **Persevere,** in all but rare instances, now implies an admirable quality: it suggests both refusal to be discouraged by failure, doubts, attacks, or the like, and a steadfast or dogged pursuit of an end or an undertaking. "I will *persevere* in my course of loyalty, though the conflict be sore between that and my blood" (*Shak.*). "For, strength to *persevere* and to support, And energy to conquer and repel— These elements of virtue, that declare The native grandeur of the human soul" (*Wordsworth*). Although **persist** (as here compared: see also CONTINUE) may imply a virtue (as, he *persisted* in his inquiries until he brought the truth to light; "a strength of character...which enables him to *persist*"—*S. Alexander*), it more often suggests a disagreeable or annoying quality, for it stresses stubbornness or obstinacy more than courage or patience, and frequently implies opposition to advice, remonstrance, disapproval, one's own conscience, or the like; as, to *persist* in working when ill; "the [abbreviation] '*Mlle*' in which Frenchmen *persist* to the verge of bigotry" (*C. E. Montague*).

Ana. *Continue, abide, endure, last.

Con. Vary, *change, alter: waver, vacillate, falter, *hesitate.

persiflage. *Badinage, raillery.

Ana. Bantering *or* banter, chaffing *or* chaff, rallying *or* rally (see corresponding verbs at BANTER): ridiculing *or* ridicule, twitting, deriding *or* derision (see corresponding verbs at RIDICULE).

persist. 1 *Persevere.

Ant. Desist. — *Con.* Discontinue, cease, *stop, quit.

2 *Continue, last, endure, abide.

Ant. Desist. — *Con.* *Stop, cease, discontinue.

persnickety. Variant of PERNICKETY.

personality. Character, individuality, temperament, *disposition, temper, complexion.

personate. *Act, play, impersonate.

perspicacious. *Shrewd, sagacious, astute.

Ana. *Sharp, keen, acute: penetrating, piercing, probing (see ENTER).

Ant. Dull.

☞ *Do not confuse* perspicacious *with* perspicuous.

perspicuous. *Clear, lucid.

Ana. Manifest, *evident, plain, distinct: *explicit, express, specific, definite.

Con. *Turbid, muddy: inflated, flatulent, tumid, turgid.

☞ *Do not confuse* perspicuous *with* perspicacious.

persuade. *Induce, prevail on *or* upon.

Ana. Influence, *affect, touch, sway, impress: *move, drive, impel, actuate.

Ant. Dissuade. — *Con.* *Restrain, curb, check, inhibit: *hinder, impede, obstruct.

persuasion. 1 Conviction, belief, *opinion, view, sentiment.

Ana. *Predilection, prepossession, bias, partiality, prejudice: tenet, dogma, *doctrine.

2 *Religion, denomination, sect, cult, communion, faith, creed, church.

pert. *Saucy, arch.

Ana. Flippant, frivolous, volatile, light-minded (see corresponding nouns at LIGHTNESS): *impertinent, intrusive: brash, impudent (see SHAMELESS).

Ant. Coy.

pertain. *Bear, relate, appertain, belong, apply.

Ana. Connect, *join, combine, associate.

pertinacious. *Obstinate, stubborn, dogged, mulish, stiff-necked, pigheaded, bullheaded.

Ana. Tenacious, tough, stout, sturdy, *strong: persistent, persevering (see corresponding verbs at PERSEVERE): resolute, steadfast, stanch (see FAITHFUL): headstrong, willful (see UNRULY).

pertinent. *Relevant, germane, material, apposite, applicable, apropos.

Ana. Fitting, apt, happy, felicitous (see FIT): pat, *seasonable, opportune, timely, well-timed.

Ant. Impertinent: foreign.

perturb. Disturb, agitate, upset, *discompose, disquiet, fluster, flurry.

Ana. *Annoy, vex, irk, bother: *confuse, muddle, addle: *confound, nonplus, distract, bewilder, dumfound (see PUZZLE, *v.*).

pervade. *Permeate, penetrate, interpenetrate, impenetrate, impregnate, saturate.

Ana. *Infuse, imbue, ingrain, leaven: *inform, animate, inspire, fire.

perverse. *Contrary, restive, balky, froward, wayward.

Ana. *Unruly, ungovernable, recalcitrant, refractory: *obstinate, stubborn, mulish, pigheaded, stiff-necked: fractious, *irritable, peevish.

pervert, *v.* Deprave, corrupt, *debase, vitiate, debauch.

Ana. *Abuse, misuse, ill-treat, maltreat, mistreat, outrage: contort, distort, warp (see DEFORM).

pervert, *n.* *Renegade, apostate, turncoat, recreant, backslider.

perverted. Corrupted, depraved, debased, vitiated, debauched. See under DEBASE.

Ana. Distorted, contorted, warped (see DEFORM): abused, misused, outraged (see ABUSE).

pessimistic. *Cynical, misanthropic, misogynic.

Ana. Gloomy, morose (see SULLEN): depressed, oppressed, weighed (down) (see DEPRESS).

Ant. Optimistic. — *Con.* Sanguine, *confident, assured.

pester. Plague, tease, tantalize, *worry, annoy, harass, harry.

Ana. *Bait, badger, hector, heckle, chevy: fret, gall, chafe (see ABRADE): perturb, disturb, agitate, upset, *discompose.

pestilent, pestilential. *Poisonous, venomous, virulent, toxic, mephitic, miasmatic, miasmic, miasmal.
Ana. *Infectious, contagious, catching: noxious, *pernicious, baneful, deleterious.
pet, *v.* *Caress, fondle, cuddle, dandle.
Ana. *Indulge, humor, pamper, mollycoddle, baby.
petite. *Small, little, diminutive, wee, tiny, teeny, weeny, minute, microscopic, miniature.
petition, *n.* *Prayer, suit, plea, appeal.
petition, *v.* Pray, sue, plead, appeal. See under PRAYER.
pettish. *Irritable, fractious, peevish, petulant, snappish, waspish, huffy, fretful, querulous.
petty. **Petty, puny, trivial, trifling, paltry, measly, picayunish, picayune** agree in meaning little and insignificant, often contemptibly so. That is **petty** which by comparison with other things the same in kind, but different in size, importance, gravity, moment, and the like, is among the smallest or least important; as, a *petty* officer; a *petty* interest; a *petty* prince; a *petty* infliction. The word often connotes small-mindedness; as, *petty* gossip. "Hunt does one harm by making fine things *petty* and beautiful things hateful" (*Keats*). "We are split up into the *pettiest* possible squirearchy, who...cut down all the trees, level all the old violet banks, and stop up all the footways they can" (*FitzGerald*). That is **puny** which is so small or slight as to seem impotent, feeble, or completely without vitality. "None of your thin, *puny*, yellow, hectic figures, exhausted with abstinence and hard study" (*Smollett*). "One no sooner grasps the bigness of the world's work than one's own effort seems *puny* and contemptible" (*J. R. Green*). That is **trivial** (etymologically, ordinary or common), in highly discriminating use, which seems petty and commonplace and scarcely worthy of special consideration or notice; as, "that strange interest in *trivial* things that we try to develop when things of high import make us afraid" (*Wilde*); "he regarded no task as too humble for him to undertake, nor so *trivial* that it was not worth his while to do it well" (*A. Huxley*). The term is often applied to persons, minds, activities, and the like, which reveal engrossment in trivial affairs or a lack of serious or profound interests; as, "She knew him for a philanderer, a *trivial* taster in love and life" (*R. Macaulay*); "[Lepidus's] *trivial* mind" (*Buchan*); "Massinger had not the personality to create great farce, and he was too serious to invent *trivial* farce" (*T. S. Eliot*). That is **trifling** which is so small as to have little, if any, value or significance; as, "Our ordinary distinctions become so *trifling*, so impalpable" (*N. Hawthorne*); "The tax is *trifling*" (*Burke*); a few *trifling* purchases. That is **paltry** which is ridiculously or contemptibly small in comparison especially to what it should be; as, a *paltry* allowance; "our little ambitions, our *paltry* joys" (*A. C. Benson*). "The *paltry* prize is hardly worth the cost" (*Byron*). That is **measly** which is contemptibly small (as in size, quantity, etc.) or petty; as, a *measly* portion of pie; "[He] ends as a politician—and a rather *measly* one at that" (*W. A. White*). That is **picayunish,** or **picayune,** which is insignificant in its possibilities, accomplishments, or the like (as, a *picayunish* business; a *picayune* legislature), or hopelessly narrow in its (or his) outlook or interests (as, a *picayunish* policy; a *picayune* congressman).
Ana. *Small, little, diminutive, minute.
Ant. Important, momentous: gross.
petulant. *Irritable, fractious, peevish, pettish, snappish, waspish, huffy, fretful, querulous.
Ana. Cross, cranky, touchy, testy (see IRASCIBLE): *impatient, restive, fidgety, skittish.
phage. Variant of BACTERIOPHAGE.
phantasm. 1 *Apparition, phantom, wraith, fetch, ghost, spirit, specter, shade, revenant, spook, haunt.
Ana. *Delusion, illusion, hallucination.
2 *Fancy, fantasy, phantasy, vision, dream, daydream, nightmare.
phantasy. 1 *Fancy, fantasy, phantasm, vision, dream, daydream, nightmare.
2 *Imagination, fancy, fantasy.
phantom. *Apparition, phantasm, wraith, fetch, ghost, spirit, specter, shade, revenant, spook, haunt.
Ana. Simulacrum, counterfeit, deception, *imposture: *delusion, illusion, hallucination.
pharisaical. Hypocritical, sanctimonious, canting. See under HYPOCRISY.
Pharisaism. *Hypocrisy, sanctimony, cant, canting.
pharmaceutical, *n.* *Drug, medicinal, biological, simple.
pharmaceutist. *Druggist, pharmacist, apothecary, chemist.
pharmacist. *Druggist, pharmaceutist, apothecary, chemist.
phase, *n.* **Phase, aspect, side, facet, angle** come into comparison when they denote one of the possible ways in which an object of contemplation may be seen or may be presented. **Phase,** in very careful use, always implies a change in the appearance of a thing without any change in the observer's point of view. From its original denotation as one of the four different shapes which the moon apparently assumes during its waxing and waning (new moon, first quarter, full moon, last quarter) it often suggests a cyclical change in appearance. "The wheel of the world swings through the same *phases*...Summer passed and winter thereafter, and came and passed again" (*Kipling*). In extended but still discriminating use, it is often applied to an outward and passing manifestation of a stage in growth, development, unfolding, or the like; thus, the red fox exhibits color *phases* in which it is known variously as cross fox, silver fox, black fox, etc. "He saw her in the most attractive *phase* of her character" (*Lytton*). "But it [absorption in religion] might be only a *phase*, as Richard said, such as all girls go through" (*V. Woolf*). **Aspect** comes into comparison here in two of its senses. Sometimes it too implies a change in appearance without a shifting in point of view but, unlike *phase*, it usually suggests a superficial change, especially one brought about by unpredictable circumstances; as, every time I look out of the window, the hills present a new *aspect*. At other times (and this is the sense here emphasized) it implies a change in appearance that is traceable to a change in the observer's point of view; as, as a result of long daily walks he came to know every *aspect* of the near-by hills. "The one and only *aspect* of a rich and complex subject which I mean to treat" (*Lowes*). Thus, one who proposes to treat the *phases* of the depression of the nineteen-thirties implies that he intends to consider its stages as they manifested themselves outwardly; one who proposes to treat all *aspects* of that depression implies that he intends to consider it from every possible point of view, such as the political, economic, and sociological. **Side,** though often used interchangeably with *phase* and *aspect*, in precise use retains implications derived from one of its literal senses and is used chiefly in reference to something that may be thought of as having two or more faces and therefore not fully apprehensible unless it or its observer shifts position; as, to see life only on its pleasant *side;* life presented only its tragic *side* to him. "Hitherto I have shown you only one *side*, or rather one *phase*, of her" (*E. Wharton*). "[Do] You who put sophistry to shame, and shout 'There's but a single *side* to man and thing' ...believe 'tis true?" (*Browning*). But *side* differs from *phase* and *aspect* in not

invariably connoting appearance, or referring to physical or intellectual vision; as, to hear both *sides* of a dispute; to read all *sides* in a controversy. "On its theoretic and perceptive *side*, Morality touches Science; on its emotional *side*, poetic Art" (*G. Eliot*). **Facet** differs from *side* in implying a multiplicity of other faces similar to or like it, all small, sharply distinguished, and manifesting the central quality as every facet of a brilliant manifests the radiance of the diamond. "The strength of the lyric lies in the complete statement of a single selected *facet* of experience" (*Day Lewis*). **Angle** denotes that aspect which is observable from a point of view restricted in its scope; as, he knows only one *angle* of his subject; it is necessary to consider all *angles* of the situation.

Ana. *State, condition, situation, posture: *appearance, look, semblance.

phase, *v.* Variant of FAZE.

phenix. Variant of PHOENIX.

phenomenal. *Material, physical, corporeal, sensible, objective.

Ana. Actual, *real.

Ant. Noumenal.

philanthropic. *Charitable, benevolent, humane, humanitarian, altruistic.

Ana. *Liberal, munificent, bountiful, generous: lavish, *profuse, prodigal.

Ant. Misanthropic.

philanthropy. *Charity.

Ant. Misanthropy.

Philistine, *adj.* *Obscurantist, barbarian.

phlegm. **1** Impassivity, stolidity, apathy, stoicism. See under IMPASSIVE.

Ana. Insensibility, insensitiveness, impassibility, anesthesia (see corresponding adjectives at INSENSIBLE).

2 *Equanimity, composure, sang-froid.

Ana. Imperturbability, nonchalance, coolness, collectedness (see corresponding adjectives at COOL): calmness *or* calm, tranquillity, serenity (see corresponding adjectives at CALM).

phlegmatic. *Impassive, stolid, apathetic, stoic.

Ana. *Indifferent, unconcerned, incurious, aloof: cool, chilly, *cold, frigid: sluggish, *lethargic.

phoenix *or* **phenix.** *Paragon, sublimation, apotheosis, nonpareil, nonesuch.

photograph, *n.* Portrait, *image, simulacrum, effigy, statue, icon, mask.

phrase, *n.* **Phrase, collocation, idiom, expression, locution** come into comparison when they mean a group of words which, when taken together, express a single idea or notion and may be used as a part of a sentence. **Phrase,** as here considered, does not apply to the grammatical unit called *phrase* (such as a *prepositional phrase*) but to any group of words which for one reason or another recurs frequently in the language of a people, the writings of an author or school of authors, the speech of a person or a clique of persons, or the like. Sometimes, the word means little more than this (as, "This phrase, *a priori,* is in common most grossly misunderstood"—*Southey*) but, more often, it suggests a given character, such as triteness (as, "To use the *phrase* of all who ever wrote upon the state of Europe, the political horizon is dark indeed"—*Cowper*) or as pithiness or pointedness (as, "I summed up all systems in a *phrase*"—*Wilde;* " 'You don't understand a young philosopher,' said the Baronet. 'A young philosopher's an old fool!' returned Hippias, not thinking that his growl had begotten a *phrase*"—*Meredith*). **Collocation** when applied to a phrase stresses the order and arrangement of words: the term when used independently in this sense or in the phrase *collocation of words* usually suggests an arrangement that has become fixed in a language, a dialect, or in personal use; sometimes, specifically, it names one that has acquired a special significance; as, *collocations* such as "to turn in" or "by the by"; that oft-repeated *collocation* of Caesar's "I came, I saw, I conquered"; "Expressed in French.... Any given *collocation* of words has a significance that is certain" (*Brownell*). **Idiom** (as here considered: see also LANGUAGE, 1) applies to any phrase or collocation which is peculiar to the language in which it occurs either in its grammatical structure or in the meaning which is associated with it but which cannot be derived from it when the words are interpreted literally; thus, "to keep house," "to center round (a person)," "to catch cold," "to strike a bargain," are homely but truly English phrases called *idioms.* **Expression** and **locution** are sometimes used in place of *phrase* when the idea of a way of expressing oneself is uppermost. Although both terms may be applied to phrases that are generally current, they are usually applied to those that are individual. *Expression* is particularly used when accompanied by a characterizing adjective or clause or phrase; as, he is in the habit of using telling *expressions;* that is a very odd *expression;* an *expression* that has gone out of use. *Locution* is somewhat more formal or bookish than *expression* and is therefore often preferred when the reference is to literary rather than colloquial phrases or to phrases that are as peculiar to a language or a group as an idiom; as, a pet *locution* of the author. "Carlyle and Carlylese were to leave their traces. Even the style of Thoreau was to be tinged faintly here and there with the rhythms and *locutions* of a writer whom lesser minds could not resist" (*Van W. Brooks*).

phraseology, phrasing. *Language, vocabulary, diction, style.

phrenzy. Variant of FRENZY.

physic, *n.* **1** *Remedy, cure, medicine, medicament, specific.

2 Physic, laxative, aperient, aperitive, purgative, cathartic, purge agree in meaning a medicine, or the like, used in effecting a cleansing of the bowels. **Physic** is, in current use (see also REMEDY), the general term for anything taken to relieve or to remedy a constipated or costive condition. A **laxative, aperient,** or **aperitive** (see also APPETIZER), is a mild physic the chief purpose of which is to give relief and to effect a loosening or opening of the intestines by the discharge of fecal matter. *Laxative,* however, is generally applied to those physics, such as mineral oil and agar-agar, that increase the tendency to intestinal evacuations, and *aperient* to those, such as some salts, which promote an easy discharge. **Purgative, cathartic,** and **purge** are applied to any physics that produce an evacuation of the contents of the bowels. *Purgative* and *cathartic* are applicable to those physics, such as castor oil and calomel, which are more certain and energetic in their action than laxatives. They are sometimes used in contrast with *purge,* the latter term being applied to a drastic, irritant physic, such as some salts taken in large doses, which causes profuse, repeated, and watery evacuations, or to a drastic enema.

physical. **1** *Bodily, corporeal, corporal, somatic.

Ana. Fleshly, *carnal, sensual, animal, animalistic.

2 *Material, corporeal, phenomenal, sensible, objective.

Ana. Actual, *real, true: elemental, *elementary.

physiognomy. *Face, countenance, visage, mug, puss.

piazza. *Balcony, gallery, loggia, veranda, porch, portico, stoop.

picayunish, picayune. *Petty, trivial, trifling, puny, paltry, measly.

pick, *v.* *Choose, select, elect, opt, cull, hand-pick, prefer, single out.
Ana. *Take, seize, grasp: determine, *decide, settle.
Con. Reject, spurn, refuse, *decline.

picked. *Select, elect, exclusive.

pickle, *n.* *Predicament, plight, dilemma, quandary, scrape, fix, jam.

pictorial. *Graphic, vivid, picturesque.

picturesque. Vivid, *graphic, pictorial.
Ana. Charming, attractive, alluring (see under ATTRACT): conspicuous, salient, striking, arresting (see NOTICEABLE).

pie. *Confusion, disorder, chaos, disarray, jumble, clutter, snarl, muddle.

piece, *n.* *Part, portion, detail, member, division, section, segment, sector, fraction, fragment, parcel.

pier. *Buttress, abutment.

pierce. Penetrate, probe, *enter.
Ana. *Perforate, bore, drill, puncture: rend, *tear, cleave, split, rive.

pietistic. Sanctimonious, pious, *devout, religious.
Ana. Reverencing *or* reverential, venerating, adoring, worshiping (see corresponding verbs at REVERE): fervid, perfervid, ardent, fervent (see IMPASSIONED): *sentimental, maudlin, romantic.

piety. Devotion, *fidelity, allegiance, fealty, loyalty.
Ana. Obedience, docility (see corresponding adjectives at OBEDIENT): fervor, ardor, zeal, enthusiasm, *passion: *holiness, sanctity.
Ant. Impiety.

pigeonhole. *Assort, sort, classify, alphabetize.
Ana. Systematize, methodize, organize, arrange, *order.

pigheaded. *Obstinate, stubborn, mulish, stiff-necked, bullheaded, dogged, pertinacious.
Ana. Headstrong, willful, recalcitrant, refractory (see UNRULY): *contrary, perverse, froward.

pilaster. *Pillar, column.

pile, *n.* **1** Heap, stack, mass, bank, shock, cock. See under HEAP, *v.*
2 *Building, edifice, structure, fabric.

pile, *v.* *Heap, stack, mass, bank, shock, cock.
Ana. *Gather, collect, assemble, congregate: *accumulate, amass, hoard.

pilfer. *Steal, filch, purloin, lift, pinch, snitch, swipe, cop.
Ana. Seize, *take, grasp, grab, snatch: *catch, capture: *rob, rifle, loot, plunder.

pilgrimage. *Journey, voyage, tour, trip, jaunt, excursion, cruise, expedition.

pillage, *n.* *Spoil, plunder, booty, prize, loot, swag.
Ana. *Cupidity, rapacity, avarice, greed: robbery, *theft.

pillage, *v.* *Ravage, devastate, waste, sack, despoil, spoliate.
Ana. Plunder, loot, *rob, rifle: invade, encroach, *trespass: confiscate, *arrogate, appropriate, usurp.

pillar. Pillar, column, pilaster come into comparison as denoting a structure that rises high from a base or foundation and that is slender in comparison with its width, and is typically (though often only apparently) monolithic and decorative. **Pillar** is the general term, for it applies to any such structure whether it stands alone (as, an obelisk is a kind of *pillar;* "But his wife looked back from behind him, and she became a *pillar* of salt"—*Genesis* xix. 26) or is a supporting architectural member of a building or similar structure (as, "Samson took hold of the two middle *pillars* upon which the house stood"—*Judges* xvi. 29; "The building was a spacious theatre, Half round on two main *pillars* vaulted high"—*Milton*). In figurative use, *pillar* usually applies to that which stays or supports (as, "The four *pillars* of government... religion, justice, counsel, treasure"—*Bacon;* "The Classics have...lost their place as a *pillar* of the social and political system"—*T. S. Eliot*), but when the application is to persons (the most common current application) the term usually suggests the character of one who supports, though it may also imply leadership, prominence, or similar qualities (as, he is a *pillar* of the church; "[Mark Twain's] circle of friends had come to include most of the main *pillars* of American society"—*Van W. Brooks*). **Column** in architectural use strictly applies to a supporting pillar that is often, but by no means always, cylindrical and free at every point except its bottom and top. The term commonly also implies three more or less elaborate parts, the base, by which it is attached to the floor, the shaft, often a fluted or channeled cylinder which rises high from the base, and the capital, the uppermost member which crowns the shaft and takes the weight, or its share of the weight, of that which rests on it. By the shape and decoration of these three parts, especially of the shaft and capital, columns are classifiable as belonging to Doric, Ionic, Corinthian, or other styles of architecture. But *column* is also applicable to a monument or memorial fashioned in the manner of an architectural column, but serving usually as a pedestal for the statue of the person who is honored; as, Nelson's *Column* in London. By extension, the term is also applicable to anything that suggests a column as in shape (as, a *column* of smoke) or in use or structure (as, the spinal *column*), or the like. Very generally it is applied to anything that is long and relatively narrow; as, the *columns* of a newspaper page; the well-known writer of a *column* (i.e., of a special article usually taking a newspaper column); a *column* of figures; a *column* of infantry. **Pilaster,** though used with reference to a supporting member of a piece of furniture, is chiefly employed with reference to an architectural member which in function is a pier (see *pier* under BUTTRESS) but which in design and treatment resembles a column. In this latter sense, *pilaster* implies engagement or attachment to a wall and suggests a rectangular rather than cylindrical form.

pilot, *v.* Steer, *guide, lead, engineer.
Ana. Direct, manage, *conduct, control: *handle, manipulate.

pinch, *v.* *Steal, pilfer, filch, purloin, lift, snitch, swipe, cop.

pinch, *n.* *Juncture, pass, exigency, emergency, contingency, strait, crisis.
Ana. *Difficulty, hardship, rigor, vicissitude.

pinched. *Haggard, cadaverous, worn, careworn, wasted.
Ana. Gaunt, scrawny, skinny, angular, rawboned (see LEAN, *adj.*).
Con. *Strong, sturdy, stout, stalwart: robust, *healthy.

pinch hitter. *Substitute, supply, locum tenens, alternate, understudy, double, stand-in.

pine, *v.* *Long, yearn, hanker, hunger, thirst.
Ana. Crave, covet, *desire: languish, enervate (see corresponding adjectives at LANGUID).

pinnacle. *Summit, peak, apex, acme, climax, culmination, meridian, zenith, apogee.

pious. *Devout, religious, pietistic, sanctimonious.
Ana. *Holy, sacred, divine, religious: worshiping, adoring, reverencing, venerating, revering (see REVERE): fervent, ardent, fervid (see IMPASSIONED).
Ant. Impious.

piquant. *Pungent, poignant, racy, spicy, snappy.
Ana. *Incisive, trenchant, cutting, biting, clear-cut.
Ant. Bland. — *Con.* *Insipid, flat, banal, jejune, inane.

pique, *n.* *Offense, resentment, umbrage, dudgeon, huff.
Ana. Annoyance, vexation, irking *or* irk (see corresponding verbs at ANNOY): irritation, exasperation, provocation (see corresponding verbs at IRRITATE).

pique, *v.* **1** *Provoke, excite, stimulate, quicken, galvanize.
Ana. *Stir, rouse, arouse: prick, punch (see PERFORATE): kindle, ignite, inflame (see LIGHT, *v.*).
2 *Pride, plume, preen.

pirouette, *v.* *Turn, revolve, rotate, gyrate, circle, spin, whirl, twirl, wheel, eddy, swirl.

pitch, *v.* Hurl, fling, cast, *throw, toss, sling.
Ana. Heave, *lift, raise, hoist: *move, drive, impel.

piteous. *Pitiful, pitiable.
Ana. Imploring, supplicating, entreating, beseeching (see BEG): *melancholy, doleful, dolorous, plaintive.

pithy. Summary, compendious, *concise, terse, succinct, laconic.
Ana. Sententious, pregnant, meaningful, *expressive: *brief, short.
Con. Flatulent, *inflated, tumid, turgid: prolix, diffuse, *wordy, verbose.

pitiable. 1 Piteous, *pitiful.
Ana. Sad, depressed, dejected, melancholy (see corresponding nouns at SADNESS): forlorn, hopeless, despairing, desperate, *despondent.
2 Despicable, *contemptible, sorry, scurvy, cheap, beggarly.
Ana. *Miserable, wretched: deplorable, lamentable (see corresponding verbs at DEPLORE).

pitiful. Pitiful, piteous, pitiable are synonymous adjectives only when they mean arousing or deserving pity or compassion. Even in this sense they are not always interchangeable. **Pitiful** applies generally to that which actually excites pity or, sometimes, commiseration, because it is felt to be deeply pathetic; as, their distress was *pitiful;* a long line of *pitiful* refugees. "Her face looked pale and extinguished....She struck Archer, of a sudden, as a pathetic and even *pitiful* figure" (*E. Wharton*). **Piteous** implies not so much an effect on the observer, as a character in the thing that excites pity; thus, a cry is *piteous* if it implores or demands attention or pity; it is *pitiful* only if it actually excites pity; one may scorn a *piteous* appeal, but it would be a contradiction in terms to scorn a *pitiful* appeal. "Cashel cast a glance round, half *piteous*, half desperate, like a hunted animal" (*Shaw*). **Pitiable** is preferable (especially in current good use) to *pitiful* when a contemptuous commiseration is implied, but contempt may be weakly or strongly connoted (see also CONTEMPTIBLE). "That *pitiable* husk of a man who a hundred years ago was a familiar figure in its streets, a shadow of his former insolence and splendour" (*Lucas*). Of all these words only *pitiful* is now employed as meaning full of pity or compassion, but even so its use is chiefly archaic or poetic in this sense; as, "Fair maid, be *pitiful* to my great woe" (*Keats*); "tender-hearted, meek and *pitiful*" (*Shelley*).
Ana. Touching, *moving, pathetic, affecting: *tender, compassionate, responsive, sympathetic.
Ant. Cruel.

pittance. *Ration, allowance, dole.

pity, *n.* **Pity, compassion, commiseration, ruth, condolence, sympathy, empathy, bowels** agree in meaning a feeling for the suffering, distress, or unhappiness of another. **Pity** usually implies sorrow or a melting of the heart with tenderness for the one who is suffering or unhappy; as, "The still tears, stealing down that furrow'd cheek, Spoke *pity,* plainer than the tongue can speak" (*Crabbe*); "*pity*...that was for the murderer on the scaffold, as it was for the dying soldier or the martyr on the rack" (*Cather*); "orators by phrases could move crowds to fury or to *pity*" (*Bennett*). Sometimes, however, the term denotes an emotion aroused in the strong or the self-sufficient for the weak or inferior (as, "scornful *pity*"—*Tennyson;* "Bawdiness, which leaves us less with a sense of repugnance for the man who could write it than with a sense of *pity* for the man who could think of nothing better"—*T. S. Eliot*), or for that which is highly regrettable (as, " 'Tis *pity* love should be so contrary"—*Shak.*). **Compassion,** in precise use, usually suggests tender pity that inspires mercy or charity: the term when used not merely as another word for *pity,* but as a word with distinctive values, connotes an urgent desire to aid or to spare; as, "There was a dead man carried out, the only son of his mother, and she was a widow....And when the Lord saw her, he had *compassion* on her" (*Luke* vii. 12–13); "In his *casa* every day was Friday—unless one of his neighbour women cooked a chicken and brought it in to him out of pure *compassion*" (*Cather*); "A great wave of *compassion* had swept away his indifference and impatience" (*E. Wharton*). **Commiseration** carries a strong implication of pity expressed outwardly as in words, tears, cries, or the like: it often also suggests the attitude of one who sees misery and suffers with the person involved in it, but can neither help him nor relieve it; as, "While we look at Samson...we are forced to think of Milton, of his blindness, of his abandonment, with as deep a *commiseration*" (*Landor*); "There was a murmur of *commiseration* as Charles Darnay crossed the room to a grated door" (*Dickens*); "Here was cause for *commiseration:* All his forty years Mrs. Day had dominated her son's life" (*Deland*). **Ruth** (a term of archaic flavor) differs from *compassion* chiefly in implying a change from hardness of heart, anger, indifference, or the like, to merciful pity; as, "Look homeward, Angel, now, and melt with *ruth*" (*Milton*); "is the truth Within your soul? care for your own, or *ruth* For others' sufferings?" (*Shelley*). **Condolence** etymologically and in its earliest, but now less frequent, meaning denotes a grieving with another who has suffered a loss or great misfortune; as, he deserves *condolence* rather than congratulation on his marriage. In current use, the term applies chiefly to such a sentiment formally expressed, or to the note, letter, telegram, or the like, expressing such a sentiment; as, a letter of *condolence;* she sent her personal card to the bereaved parents with "*Condolences*" written upon it; they received *condolences* from as many as two hundred friends. **Sympathy** (etymologically, suffering with) is often used in place of *pity* or *compassion* (as, his plight aroused her *sympathy*) or in place of *condolence* (as, to offer one's *sympathy* to a bereaved friend), but in its precise meaning, it implies a power to enter into another's emotions or experiences, whether of a sorrowful or joyful nature, as by sharing them, by truly understanding them, or by being equally affected by them; as, "a boy goes for *sympathy* and companionship to his mother and sisters, not often to his father" (*A. C. Benson*); "the rebel, as a human type entitled to respect and often to *sympathy*" (*R. E. N. Dodge*); "Amid the various feelings she was aware of arousing, she let me see that *sympathy*, in the sense of a moved understanding, had always been lacking" (*E. Wharton*). "Ah, then that was it! He was a lonely old man, who didn't want to live in constant reminder of happy times past....Tony...felt a quick *sympathy* with him" (*Arch. Marshall*). *Sympathy* is also applicable to anything that engages one's interest, sometimes because one is in agreement with its aims, accomplishments, principles, or tenets, and is attached to it (as, "the stepfather was a moderate Pompeian in *sympathies*"—*Buchan*), but more often because one has the imaginative capacity to enter into it and understand it in its true nature (as, "a creative writer can do his best only with what lies within the range and character of his deepest *sympathies*"—*Cather*). **Empathy** applies to the imaginative power which enables a person, especially an artist, to understand the emotions and experiences of others and to sympathize with them. "The active power of *empathy* which makes the creative artist, or the passive power of *empathy* which makes the appreciator of art" (*Rebecca West*). **Bowels,** which in Scriptural and other use was applied to the seat of compassion much as *heart* is today (as, "And Joseph made haste; for his *bowels* did yearn upon his brother"—*Genesis* xliii. 30), now less often than formerly denotes pity or compassion. "'I am a man that can feel for my neighbours. I have *bowels*—yes I have *bowels*' " (*Lytton*).

Ana. *Sadness, melancholy, dejection, depression: *pathos, poignancy: *charity, mercy, clemency, lenity.

pixy *or* **pixie.** *Fairy, faery, fay, elf, sprite, gnome, dwarf, goblin, brownie, puck, nix, shee, leprechaun, banshee.

placate, *v.* *Pacify, appease, mollify, propitiate, conciliate.

Ant. Enrage. — *Con.* *Anger, infuriate, incense, madden: *stir, arouse, rouse: *provoke, excite, stimulate, pique.

place, *n.* *Position, situation, office, post, job, berth, billet, capacity.

Ana. Employment, occupation, *work, calling, pursuit, métier, business: *function, office, duty, province.

placid. *Calm, tranquil, serene, peaceful, halcyon.

Ana. Imperturbable, nonchalant, *cool, collected, composed: gentle, mild, lenient (see SOFT): *steady, equable, even, constant.

Ant. Choleric (*of persons*): ruffled (*of things*).

plague, *v.* Pester, tease, tantalize, harry, harass, *worry, annoy.

Ana. Gall, fret, chafe (see ABRADE): *bait, badger, hector, hound, ride: torment, *afflict, try.

Con. *Relieve, mitigate, lighten, assuage, alleviate.

plain, *adj.* **1** Plane, flat, *level, even, smooth, flush.

Ant. Solid.

2 Clear, distinct, obvious, *evident, manifest, patent, apparent, palpable.

Ana. *Clear, lucid, perspicuous: *explicit, express, definite, specific, categorical.

Ant. Abstruse.

3 *Frank, candid, open.

Ana. Forthright, *straightforward, aboveboard: blunt, *bluff: *sincere, unfeigned.

plaintive. Dolorous, doleful, *melancholy, lugubrious, rueful.

Ana. Pensive, reflective, meditative, *thoughtful: lamenting, deploring (see DEPLORE): *pitiful, piteous.

plait *or* **pleat** *or* **plat.** *Weave, knit, crochet, braid, tat.

plan, *n.* **Plan, design, plot, scheme, project** come into comparison both as nouns, when they denote a proposed method of doing or making something or of achieving a given end, and as verbs, when they mean to devise such a method. **Plan,** in its widest sense, always implies mental formulation of the method; as, to *plan*, or make *plans* for, a trip to Europe (or for the future of one's children, for a new book, for an expansion of one's business); "While she sat maturing this *plan*" (*Galsworthy*). In a narrower sense, the terms may imply a graphic representation of that method, as by a mechanical drawing, a chart, a sketch, a layout, or the like; as, an architect's set of *plans;* to *plan* a garden. "The basement of St. Katherine's Dock House is vast in extent and confusing in its *plan*" (*Conrad*). **Design** (see also INTENTION) adds to *plan* an emphasis on intention (often artistic, sometimes divine, intention) in the disposition of individual members or details, often thereby suggesting a definite pattern; since it is used frequently in reference to a completed work, it often implies reference to the degree in which order, harmony, or integrity have been achieved in spite of diversity in the parts, or in which there is the beauty that results from unity in variety. "It...like most architecture erected since the Gothic age, was a compilation rather than a *design*" (*Hardy*). "Buildings are not grouped like that by pure accident, though convenience probably had much to do with it. Convenience often dictates very sound *design*" (*Cather*). "A curious woman, whose dresses always looked as if they had been *designed* in a rage" (*Wilde*). **Plot,** as here narrowly considered (see PLOT, *n.*, 2; SKETCH, *v.*), usually connotes a laying out in clearly distinguished and carefully proportioned sections or divisions, and attention to proper placing and due relation of the parts, and to scale. It is now found chiefly in technical use, as in surveying, where it suggests a ground plan (as, to *plot* a tract of land), or as in literature, where it refers to a fundamental design which the action of a drama or narrative follows; as, there is plenty of action in this play, but no *plot.* **Scheme** has nearly lost its early implication of a diagram except in some technical senses where it suggests tabulation more often than outline drawing; as, the rhyme *scheme* of a Shakespearean sonnet. Nevertheless, the word often suggests, more than *plan* does, system and careful choice or ordering of details; as, to work out a *scheme* for the distribution of war refugees. "She seldom *schemed,* but when she did *scheme,* her plans showed...the comprehensive strategy of a general" (*Hardy*). In current use, the terms often connote, singly or in combination, self-delusion, craftiness, or self-seeking on the part of the agent. "He it was *schem'd* the snare thus subtly wrought" (*Browning*). "He doesn't *scheme* and twist things about trying to get the best of some one else" (*S. Anderson*). "A lurking suspicion that our work was...a *scheme* to superimpose American economic control upon ingenuous foreign countries" (*V. Heiser*). **Project** comes close to *scheme* except in its connotations. Sometimes it suggests enterprise; sometimes, imaginative scope or vision; sometimes, mere extensiveness. "Sanguine *schemes,* Ambitious *projects,* pleased me less" (*Wordsworth*). "Such were my *projects* for the city's good" (*Browning*). "I *projected,* and drew up a *plan* for the union" (*Franklin*). "The difference between *scheme* and *project* is best shown in their derivatives **schemer** and **projector,** the former commonly carrying the specific meaning of a deviser of ways and means to attain his own ends, and the latter, of a promoter of grand, often chimerical, schemes.

Ana. *Intention, intent, purpose: *idea, conception, notion: *chart, map, graph: diagram, outline, sketch (see under SKETCH, *v.*).

plan, *v.* Design, plot, scheme, project. See under PLAN, *n.*

Ana. Propose, purpose, *intend: *sketch, outline, diagram, delineate.

plane, *adj.* Plain, flat, *level, even, smooth, flush.

Ant. Solid.

plank. *Paragraph, verse, article, clause, count.

plastic. Plastic, pliable, pliant, ductile, malleable, adaptable are here compared as they are applied to things and to persons regarded as material susceptible of being modified in form or nature. That is **plastic** which has, literally or figuratively, the quality of wax, clay, or plaster, soft enough to be molded or to receive an impression yet capable of hardening into the given form. "The language at the period during which the Bible was being translated into English was in its most *plastic* stage" (*Lowes*). "When children are small we elders in charge are apt to suppose them altogether *plastic*" (*H. G. Wells*). That is **pliable** or **pliant** which has, literally or figuratively, the quality of willow twigs, supple enough to be easily bent or manipulated and therefore yielding without resistance. *Pliable*, in figurative use, usually suggests the imposition of, or submission to, another's will. "I flatter myself that I have some influence over her. She is *pliable*" (*Hardy*). "Assertiveness is [not] the only mannish trait taken on by successful women, nor is *pliability* the only feminine mark they lose" (*M. Austin*). *Pliant*, on the other hand, suggests flexibility rather than obedience. "Art which is alive and *pliant* in the hands of men" (*Quiller-Couch*). That is **ductile** which has the quality of copper and other tensile metals, tenacious enough to be permanently drawn out or extended, or of water and some other fluids that can be made to flow through channels; thus, platinum is the most *ductile* of all metals; the *ductility* of heated asphalt is tested by a machine. In figurative use, *ductile* often approaches *plastic* and *pliant*. Discriminating writers, however, give it connotations directly derived from its literal senses, such as quick responsiveness (as distinguished from submissiveness) to influences that would form, guide, or fashion. "Bingley was endeared to Darcy by the easiness, openness, and *ductility* of his temper" (*Austen*). "Verse...is easier to write than prose....Mr. Shaw would have found his story [Cashel Byron's Profession] still more *ductile* in the metre of Hiawatha" (*Quiller-Couch*). Sometimes fluidity within bounds is connoted. "Smooth, *ductile*, and even, his fancy must flow" (*Cowper*). That is **malleable** which is literally (like most metals) or figuratively capable of being beaten or pressed into shape, especially after being conditioned as by heating. "Tempers...rendered *pliant* and *malleable* in the fiery furnace of domestic tribulation" (*Irving*). "Truth independent; truth that we find merely; truth no longer *malleable* to human need" (*W. James*). That is **adaptable** which is capable of being modified or of modifying itself to suit other conditions, other needs, or other uses. As applied to persons it implies sometimes a pliant, but more often an accommodating, disposition and a readiness to make one's habits, one's opinions, one's wishes, correspond to those of one's present society or environment; as, it is often said that men are less *adaptable* than women.

Ana. Flexible, supple, *elastic, resilient: tractable, amenable (see OBEDIENT).

Con. Rigid, *stiff, inflexible.

plat, *adj.* Dialectal variant of FLAT, *adj.* (sense 1).

plat, *v.* Variant of PLAIT.

platitude. *Commonplace, truism, bromide, cliché.

Ana. Banality, inanity, vapidity, insipidity (see corresponding adjectives at INSIPID): mawkishness, sentimentality (see corresponding adjectives at SENTIMENTAL).

plaudits. *Applause, acclamation, acclaim.

Ana. Cheering, hurrahing, huzzaing (see APPLAUD).

plausible. Plausible, credible, believable, colorable (*or* **colourable**), **specious** come into comparison as meaning capable of impressing the observer, auditor, or reader as truly or genuinely having or possessing the quality or character that is set forth or claimed. A thing (sometimes a person) is **plausible** (etymologically, worthy of applause) that is capable of winning acceptance, approval, belief, or the like, by its (or his) apparent possession of certain qualities which make it (or him) seem pleasing, genuine, or reasonable at first sight or hearing: the word may or may not definitely imply a false outside, or an intention to deceive, or a lack of soundness, but it usually connotes such a possibility, even though it also clearly suggests its (or his) ingratiating or mentally satisfying character; as, a *plausible* argument; a *plausible* rogue. "That is a perfectly intelligible position, and it is *plausible* to the last degree" (*Lowes*). "He was a grey-haired man, with a *plausible* voice and careful manners" (*Joyce*). "A fairly *plausible* case can be made out for expecting that far fewer marriages and families will be broken up under Socialism than at present" (*Shaw*). "Aristotle...while admitting that Plato's scheme has a *plausible* appearance of philanthropy, maintains that it is inapplicable to the facts of human nature" (*G. L. Dickinson*). A thing (less often a person) is **credible** that appeals to another as worthy of belief or of being credited, sometimes because of plausibility, but more often because of its (or his) support by known facts, or by sound reasoning; as, a *credible* explanation; a *credible* witness; "Right reason makes that which they say appear *credible*" (*Hobbes*). "A theory which denies the truth of one of our fundamental convictions about our own minds must have very strong evidence from other quarters to make it *credible*" (*Inge*). A thing that is credible because it comes within the range of possibility or probability, or because it is in accordance with other facts that are known, is **believable**; as, a *believable* plot; a *believable* situation; it is not *believable* that he could commit perjury. A thing is **colorable** which at least on its face or outwardly seems true, just, valid, or the like, or which is capable to some extent of being sustained or justified; as, no *colorable* evidence has as yet been presented in support of this theory; so far as is known he holds no *colorable* title to the estate; "They gathered together many of her maladministrations, for which they might the more *colorably* put her out of office" (*Bp. Burnet*); "Both might *colourably* have pleaded that they were, after all, writing Latin" (*Quiller-Couch*). A thing or, less often, a person is **specious** that is outwardly or apparently attractive, beautiful, valid, sincere, or the like, but that is inwardly or actually the reverse in character. *Specious* is the only one of these terms that, in current use, always clearly implies dissimulation, or fraud, or deceit, or hypocrisy; as, *specious* picturesqueness; *specious* piety; a *specious* rogue; "they sanctified the worse cause with the *specious* pretext of zeal for the furtherance of the best" (*Cowper*); "some writers are...content with a transient notoriety attained by deliberate and *specious* obscurification" (*Day Lewis*); "effusions of fine sentiments about brotherly love that are only a *specious* mask for envy and hatred of riches and success" (*Babbitt*).

Ana. Smooth, bland, politic, diplomatic, *suave: likely, *probable, possible: unctuous, *fulsome, sleek, oily.

play, *v.* **Play, sport, disport, frolic, rollick, romp, gambol** come into comparison as verbs meaning to engage in exercise or other activity as a pleasure or amusement, and as nouns meaning exercise or activities engaged in for the sake of pleasure or amusement. **Play,** the most general of these terms, suggests an opposition to *work:* like its antithesis, it usually implies activity, often vehement activity, of body or mind, but it emphasizes the absence of any end except that of amusement, diversion, recreation, or pure enjoyment; as, children *play* for hours at keeping house; to *play* chess; to *play* tennis; "All work and no *play* makes Jack a dull boy" (*Old Proverb*); "She is weary of dance and *play*" (*Tennyson*). "I never knew what was *play* and what was work. No *play* is interesting to me unless it effects work, and no work is possible to me unless it possesses the amusement of *play*" (*H. Ellis*).

"They had been...transformed from a dejected, downcast, docile, uninterested people, who could not even *play*, into one which was healthy, alert" (*V. Heiser*). **Sport** and the now archaic or poetic original form **disport** suggest a complete release not only from work but from seriousness: the terms imply indulgence in that which cheers, makes merry, or, especially in current use, serves as a pastime; as, "If all the year were *playing* holidays, To *sport* would be as tedious as to work" (*Shak.*); "*Sport* that wrinkled Care derides" (*Milton*); "See the children *sport* upon the shore" (*Wordsworth*); "And by him *sported* on the green His little grandchild Wilhelmine" (*Southey*); "A day for toil, an hour for *sport*" (*Emerson*); "when... my *disports* corrupt and taint my business, Let housewives make a skillet of my helm" (*Shak.*); "We make ourselves fools, to *disport* ourselves" (*Shak.*); "Say, Father Thames, for thou hast seen Full many a sprightly race *Disporting* on thy margent green" (*Gray*). **Frolic** suggests more gaiety, more levity, more spontaneousness than any of the preceding terms: it often is used in reference to the lighthearted, joyous movements of children (or, by extension, of young animals) at play, but it also suggests the pastimes, antics, or pranks of those who have thrown off all care; as, "I come to *frolic* with you, and to cheer Your drooping souls" (*J. Ford & Dekker*); "They sang as blithe as finches sing ... And *frolic* where they list" (*Cowper*); "Those who meet as we have met, In *frolic* and in laughter" (*Praed*); "their sedateness is as comical as their *frolic*" (*Meredith*). **Rollick** (infrequent as a noun: now used chiefly in the form *rollicking*) adds to *frolic* implications of exuberance in gaiety and of reveling and therefore is used especially in reference to youths or young adults; as, "*Rollicking* blades" (*T. Hook*); a party of young folk off for a *rollick;* " 'Q.' appears as a *rollicking* humourist....He *rollicks*, perhaps, a little too laboriously" (*Pall Mall Gazette*). **Romp** suggests the boisterous carefree frolicking of children, of rough boys, and of hoydens: it usually connotes running or racing in play; as, "This careless jade was eternally *romping* with the footman" (*Steele*); "I have been having a *romp* with my godson" (*M. E. Braddon*). **Gambol** suggests the leaping and skipping characteristic of lambs and young children; it comes close to *frolic*, but carries a stronger suggestion of joy in movement; as, "Where be your gibes now? your *gambols?* your songs? your flashes of merriment...?" (*Shak.*); "Their pigmy king, and little fairy queen, In circling dances *gamboll'd* on the green" (*Pope*).

Ana. Divert, entertain, recreate, *amuse: *trifle, toy, dally.

2 *Act, impersonate, personate.

Ana. Feign, simulate, counterfeit, *assume.

play, *n.* **1** Sport, disport, frolic, rollick, romp, gambol. See under PLAY, *v.*, 1.

Ana. Enjoyment, delectation, *pleasure, delight: amusement, diversion, recreation, entertainment (see under AMUSE): *athletics, sports, games.

Ant. Work.

2 *Fun, jest, sport, game.

Ant. Earnest.

player. *Actor, performer, mummer, mime, Thespian, impersonator, trouper.

playful. Playful, frolicsome, sportive, roguish, waggish, impish, mischievous, wanton come into comparison as meaning given to play, jests, or tricks, or indicative of such a disposition or mood. **Playful** stresses either lighthearted gaiety or merriment (as, *playful* children; in a *playful* mood) or a lack of seriousness or earnestness (as, his words were serious, but in his eyes there was a *playful* gleam; the *playful* humor of Cowper's *John Gilpin*). **Frolicsome** not only heightens the implications of *playful:* it carries a stronger suggestion of friskiness or prankishness or irresponsible merriment; as, "Mingled with the more decent holiday-makers there were *frolicsome* apprentices" (*G. Eliot*); "the voice might proceed from a very *frolicsome* and tricksy creature, full of wild fantastic humours, but nothing worse" (*Hudson*). **Sportive** carries a stronger implication of jesting or of levity than either of the preceding words; the term infrequently implies excess of animal spirits, but it usually connotes a desire to evoke or provoke laughter. "Three generations of serious and of *sportive* writers wept and laughed over the venality of the senate" (*Macaulay*). " 'Strength is a God to you: Purity a toy. A pretty one, and you seem to be fond of playing with it,' he added with unaccustomed slyness. The lady listened pleased at the *sportive* malice" (*Meredith*). **Roguish** not only heightens the implications of *sportive*, but it suggests an engaging naughtiness or slyness. "The most bewitching leer with her eyes, the most *roguish* cast" (*Dryden*); " 'I don't think I shall want anything else when we've got a little garden; and I knew Aaron would dig it for us,' she went on with *roguish* triumph" (*G. Eliot*). **Waggish** suggests a less engaging sportiveness than *roguish* and one less delicate in its character: usually also the term carries a stronger suggestion of jocoseness or of jocularity; as, "With all his overbearing roughness there was a strong dash of *waggish* good-humor at bottom" (*Irving*). **Impish** adds to *roguish* a hint of elfish, malicious mockery; as, "teasing...with *impish* laughter half suppressed" (*Hardy*); to take *impish* delight in the falls of other skaters. **Mischievous** in current, and especially American, use combines the implications of *frolicsome* and *impish:* it may also, as formerly, imply the doing of mischief (see *mischief* under INJURY, 1), or the causing of an injury to others; as, "The opinions, principles, and practices, which I thought so very *mischievous*" (*Burke*); often, however, it suggests little more than thoughtless indifference to the possible effects of one's sports, tricks, or practical jokes; as, a garden ruined by *mischievous* boys; the child is as *mischievous* as a monkey; "She... was...waked by Meta, standing over her with a sponge, looking very *mischievous*" (*C. M. Yonge*). **Wanton,** as here compared (see also SUPEREROGATORY, LEWD), is now archaic in the sense of *sportive* or *frolicsome*, but it occurs frequently in the English classics, especially as applied to children and to animals. So used, however, the term commonly retains from its earliest sense an implication of unruliness or lack of discipline and, therefore, suggests a running wild or without restraint. "As flies to *wanton* boys, are we to the gods, They kill us for their sport" (*Shak.*); "*Wanton* as a child, skipping and vain" (*Shak.*). In current use, this original implication is still often stressed, and that of sportiveness is somewhat obscured or even lost; as, "to produce in the child the same respect for the garden that restrains the grown-ups from picking *wantonly*" (*B. Russell*).

Ana. Gay, sprightly, *lively: *merry, blithe, jocund, jolly, jovial: mirthful, gleeful, hilarious (see corresponding nouns at MIRTH).

plea. 1 *Apology, apologia, excuse, pretext, alibi.

Ana. Explanation, justification, rationalization (see corresponding verbs at EXPLAIN): defense, vindication (see corresponding verbs at MAINTAIN).

2 *Prayer, suit, petition, appeal.

Ana. Entreaty, supplication, imploring, beseeching, begging (see corresponding verbs at BEG).

plead, *v.* Pray, sue, petition, appeal. See under PRAYER.

Ana. Entreat, implore, supplicate, beseech, *beg: intercede, mediate, intervene, *interpose.

Con. Bestow, confer, present, *give: *grant, vouchsafe, accord.

pleasance *or* **pleasaunce.** *Amenity, luxury.

pleasant. **Pleasant, pleasing, agreeable, grateful, gratifying, welcome** are comparable when they mean highly acceptable to the mind or the senses. **Pleasant** and **pleasing** are often indistinguishable; however, *pleasant* usually imputes a quality to the object to which it is applied, and *pleasing* suggests merely the effect of the object upon one; as, a *pleasant* answer, a *pleasing* answer; a *pleasant* face, a *pleasing* face. "Your mother...is a very *pleasant* person to live with" (*M. Austin*). "The thought of gazing on life's Evening Star makes of ugly old age a *pleasing* prospect" (*L. P. Smith*). **Agreeable** implies harmony with one's tastes or likings; as, an *agreeable* (cf. a *pleasant*) taste, odor. "If I was obliged to define politeness, I should call it the art of making oneself *agreeable*" (*Smollett*). **Grateful** carries the implications of both *pleasing* and *agreeable;* in addition it stresses the satisfaction or relief afforded the senses or, somewhat less often, the mind. "They...lay down on the clean grass under the *grateful* shade of the tall cottonwoods" (*Cather*). "Only occasional voices from the road outside came to disturb the *grateful* sense of quiet and seclusion" (*A. Marshall*). **Gratifying** is applied chiefly to that which affords mental pleasure to the individual by satisfying his desires, hopes, conscience, or the like; as, the reviews of his book were very *gratifying.* "The *gratifying* feeling that our duty has been done" (*W. S. Gilbert*). **Welcome** even more than *pleasing* stresses the pleasure or satisfaction given by the thing to which it is applied; it often suggests prior need or an answer to one's longings; as, the explorers found fresh fruit and vegetables a *welcome* addition to their diet; the news was most *welcome.*

Ana. Charming, attractive, alluring (see under ATTRACT, *v.*): *soft, gentle, mild, balmy.

Ant. Unpleasant: distasteful: harsh.

please, *v.* **Please, gratify, delight, rejoice, gladden, tickle, arride, regale** agree in meaning to make happy, or to be a cause of happiness. **Please** usually implies an agreement with one's wishes, tastes, or aspirations, and a happiness which ranges from mere content and the absence of any ground for displeasure to actual elation; as, the family was *pleased* with the daughter's marriage; the aim of poetry is to *please;* the suggestion did not *please* him; the promotion *pleased* not only Henry, but all his friends. **Gratify** (cf. *gratifying* under PLEASANT) suggests an even stronger measure of satisfaction than *please* and is invariably positive in its implication of pleasure; as, "he wished to *gratify* his son by these eulogies of Lucy" (*Meredith*); "it *gratifies* us to imagine that...we have reached a point on the road of progress beyond that vouchsafed to our benighted predecessors" (*H. Ellis*). "It *gratified* him to have his wife wear jewels; it meant something to him" (*Cather*). **Delight** stresses the emotional rather than the intellectual quality of the reaction, though the latter is often also implied; it suggests intense, lively pleasure that is not only keenly felt but, usually, vividly expressed in the countenance or in outward actions. "O, flatter me; for love *delights* in praises" (*Shak.*); "Sailors to tell of winds and seas *delight*" (*Gray*); "gazed From the watch-towers of Helvellyn; Awed, *delighted,* and amazed!" (*Wordsworth*); "The soul *delighted* on each accent dwells,— Enraptur'd dwells,—not daring to respire" (*Keats*). **Rejoice** implies a happiness that exceeds bounds, and reveals itself as in smiles, in song, in festivities, in enthusiastic effort, or the like; as, "*Rejoice,* you men of Angiers, ring your bells" (*Shak.*); "*Rejoice* the soul of thy servant: for unto thee, O Lord, do I lift up my soul" (*Psalms* lxxxvi. 4). "Hendrik worked, *rejoicing* in the strength that God had given him, in his skill, in his power, and in his capacity for righteous anger" (*S. Cloete*). **Gladden** sometimes is indistinguishable from *rejoice* except in rarely suggesting excess of emotion and in being usually transitive. "A small pleasantry frankly uttered by a patron, *gladdens* the heart of the dependant" (*Irving*). It often, however, connotes a raising of the spirits, or a cheering or consoling in depression or grief. "Even so thy latent worth will re-appear, *Gladdening* the people's heart from shore to shore" (*Wordsworth*). *Tickle, arride,* and *regale* involve the idea of delight, but they are often less dignified in their connotations. **Tickle** implies pleasurable sensations, such as tingles and thrills, or it suggests an almost physical gratification; as, food that *tickles* the palate. "Something... that thrilled and *tickled* my heart with a feeling partly sensuous and partly spiritual" (*N. Hawthorne*). Sometimes, with reference to physical tickling it suggests provocation of laughter. "The mimic court of justice in the orchard *tickled* him immensely" (*Deland*). **Arride** suggests a delight that is sometimes near derision but always provoked by that which is amusing or engaging. The word is not now common, but is found in the work of some very good writers. "That conceit *arrided* us most...and still tickles our midriff to remember" (*Lamb*). "As he [Stevenson] would have said, it [his writing] *arrides* you; wherever you open him...and read a sentence or two...whatever he means to convey at the time is being vivaciously put" (*C. E. Montague*). **Regale** always connotes huge enjoyment or a feasting upon that which gives pleasure; as, "The sight is pleased, The scent *regaled*" (*Cowper*); "Mr. Sycamore was *regaling* himself with the discomfiture of Lady Charlotte" (*H. G. Wells*).

Ana. *Satisfy, content: elate, exult (see corresponding adjectives at ELATED): beguile, *while, wile.

Ant. Displease: anger: vex.

pleasing. *Pleasant, agreeable, grateful, gratifying, welcome.

Ana. Winning (see GET): ingratiating, *disarming: charming, attractive, alluring, enchanting (see under ATTRACT).

Ant. Displeasing: repellent.

pleasure. **Pleasure, delight, joy, delectation, enjoyment, fruition** are the most general terms in English for the agreeable emotion which accompanies the possession, acquisition, or expectation of that which is good or greatly desired. **Pleasure** so strongly implies a feeling of satisfaction or gratification that it sometimes carries no implication of visible happiness or actual gladness; as, "the first step [in an infant's development]...is to pass beyond mere *pleasures* of sensation, such as food and warmth, to the *pleasure* of social approbation" (*B. Russell*); "It was for him a bitter sort of *pleasure* to have...a new-comer, to whom he could repeat all these matters of grief and suspicion" (*Conrad*). Often, however, the term suggests an excitement or exaltation of the senses or of the mind that implies positive happiness or gladness; as, "When these wild ecstasies shall be matured Into a sober *pleasure*" (*Wordsworth*); a great work of art always gives *pleasure;* "the doctors found out that a man could digest his food best if he ate it with *pleasure* among cheerful friends" (*C. E. Montague*). **Delight** carries a stronger implication of liveliness, intensity, or obviousness in the satisfaction or gratification induced than *pleasure* (though not as strong an implication as in *glee:* see MIRTH); the term, however, often suggests a less stable or enduring emotion than *pleasure;* as, "What *pleasure* the possession of my money could have afforded him I am unable to say; but...as it did give him evident *delight* I was not sorry that I had parted with it so readily"

(*Kipling*); "Deep was the Old Dog's *delight* to hear the praises of his Beauty sounded by such aristocratic lips as the Hon. Peter Brayder's" (*Meredith*). **Joy** is often used in place of *pleasure* and still more often in the place of *delight*. It is the preferred and often the necessary term, however, when a deep-rooted, rapturous emotion is implied, or when the happiness is so great as to be almost painful in its intensity; as, "And all its aching *joys* are now no more, And all its dizzy raptures" (*Wordsworth*); "It expressed her happiness, relieved the pressure of her *joy* at being alive" (*R. Macaulay*); "Glad to be free, proud too...of stepping this famous pavement, *joy* of a kind, cheap, tinselly, if you like, but all the same rapture, flushed their faces" (*V. Woolf*). *Delectation* and *enjoyment* differ in the main from the other words of this group in denoting the state of mind or the sensuous or emotional reactions of one who takes pleasure, delight, or joy in something. But **delectation,** especially in current use, often carries a strong connotation of amusement, diversion, or entertainment that gives occasion for delight; as, her oddities afforded him the utmost *delectation;* to tell many witty stories for the *delectation* of his guests. **Enjoyment**, on the other hand, usually implies an attitude, or a circumstance, or a favorable response to a stimulus that tends to make one gratified or happy; as, "He gave himself up to the vigorous *enjoyment* of his pipe for a silent minute or two" (*Conrad*); "She drank in all the new impressions...joyously; from that moment dated her...*enjoyment* of French ways, and her *delight* in Paris" (*H. Ellis*); "He accepted chance and weather...with a sort of grave *enjoyment*" (*Cather*). **Fruition** is now so often used even by good writers and speakers in the sense of realization or fulfillment that it has become increasingly rare in its earlier and generally approved sense of pleasure in possession or of enjoyment in attainment; as, "If we live by hope let us desire the end and *fruition* of our hope" (*Latimer*); "in love we must deserve nothing, or the fine bloom of *fruition* is gone" (*Meredith*). In extended use, where realization or fulfillment is stressed and there is still some suggestion of accompanying pleasure, the employment of *fruition* is not disapproved (as, "how mature one has to be before learning...that growth is more desirable than *fruition*"—*Lucas*); where realization or fulfillment is stressed and the word implies only the bearing of fruit or the coming to an issue, and carries not the slightest suggestion of accompanying pleasure, the employment of *fruition* is regarded by some as incorrect and by others as loose (as, the *fruition* of his plan; "It [determinism] is rather the *fruition* of a scientific method which had grown up under the shelter of the old causal method"—*Eddington*).

Ana. *Happiness, felicity, bliss: amusement, diversion, recreation, entertainment (see under AMUSE).

Ant. Displeasure: anger: vexation.

pleat. Variant of PLAIT.

plebiscite. *Mandate, initiative, referendum.

pledge, *n.* **Pledge, earnest, token, pawn, hostage, gage,** as here compared, agree in denoting something that is given or held as a sign of another's faith or intention to do what has been promised. **Pledge,** originally and still in some applications a technical legal term, applies in general to anything (often in the past a person) handed over to another as security for the performance of an obligation, payment of a debt, or the like. "In argument and proof of which contract, Bear her this jewel, *pledge* of my affection" (*Shak.*). "They therefore sent seven galleys...as a *pledge* of their loyalty" (*Thirlwall*). **Earnest,** originally the money or other thing of value given by a buyer to a seller to bind a bargain, in its modern extended sense applies to that which serves as a promise or assurance of more to come, or which establishes a strong probability of it; as, *earnest* money. "That holy Spirit... Which is the *earnest* of our inheritance" (*Ephesians* i. 13, 14). "It seemed to him a sort of *earnest* that Providence intended his rescue from worse consequences" (*G. Eliot*). "This zeal for making a nation's ...language...correct and worthy, is...a weighty *earnest* of future power" (*Arnold*). **Token** (see also SIGN, 1) applies to anything given as a guaranty or proof of a person or thing's authority, authenticity, or good faith; as, "Give me some *token* for the surety of it" (*Shak.*); "I do set my bow in the cloud, and it shall be for a *token* of a covenant between me and the earth" (*Genesis* ix. 13). In specific concrete use, *token* is applied to something which serves as a proof of an obligation, a right, a debt, or the like; thus, a coinlike piece of metal sold by a transportation company for use as a ticket is usually called a *token;* coins, notes, and the like, issued by some countries, states, or cities, as currency at a nominal or face value above their real value as metal (or other substance) but redeemable at their face value, are collectively called *tokens*. **Pawn,** originally a close synonym of *pledge* (as, "He must leave behind, for *pawns*, His mother, wife, and son"—*Dryden*), now specifically refers only to an object of more or less value deposited as security for the money loaned on it by another, usually by a person (called a *pawnbroker*) whose business is the loaning of money on such security; as, he left his watch with the broker as a *pawn*. In very precise extended use, *pawn* often carries a suggestion of something held for a time and liable to redemption or withdrawal by the actual owner. "My life I never held but as a *pawn* To wage against thy enemies" (*Shak.*). "I held what I inherited in thee, As *pawn* for that inheritance of freedom Which thou hast sold" (*Shelley*). **Hostage** literally applies to a person handed over to another or kept by another until one's agreement or promise has been fulfilled; as, to hold the king's children as *hostages* for the safe return of the captured barons. In extended use (which is comparatively rare) the term is applicable to anything which serves as an earnest or pledge of something to come. "One who wisely schemed, And *hostage* from the future took In trained thought and lore of book" (*Whittier*). **Gage,** originally the equivalent of *pledge* in the earliest sense of that word, is now archaic in that sense; the term still occurs, however, as a designation for something which is given as a pledge (such as a glove, a cap, or the like) that a person will appear to fight an opponent, to assert a claim, or the like. In this sense, it is found chiefly in the phrase "to throw down (or fling down) the *gage*," which is figuratively to defy or to challenge one to fight.

Ana. *Guarantee, guaranty, security, surety, bond, bail.

pledge, *v.* *Promise, engage, plight, covenant, contract.

Ana. Bind, *tie: *swear, affirm: *commit, consign, confide, entrust.

Ant. Abjure.

plein-air. Open-air, *outdoor, alfresco.

plenary. *Full, complete, replete.

Ant. Limited.

plenteous. *Plentiful, ample, abundant, copious.

Ana. & *Ant.* See those at PLENTIFUL.

plentiful. Plentiful, plenteous, ample, abundant, copious denote in common more than adequate or sufficient yet not in excess. That is **plentiful** or **plenteous** of which there is great or rich supply; *plenteous* is now bookish. "Butter is cheap when it is *plentiful*, and dear when it is scarce" (*Shaw*). "The king made silver and gold...as *plenteous* as stones" (*2 Chronicles* i. 15). That is **ample**

which is generously sufficient to satisfy a definite requirement. "*Ample* apologies indeed for fifteen years of persecution" (*Macaulay*). "Their mother's fortune, though *ample* for her situation in life, could but ill supply the deficiency of his" (*Austen*). That is **abundant** which is very plentiful or of which there is an unusually large supply. "She found the fruit *abundant*" (*Meredith*). "His *abundant* vitality" (*Bennett*). *Abundant* sometimes implies profusion. "*Abundant* beautiful bright tresses" (*Meredith*). That is **copious** which is marked by great abundance; as, a *copious* supply; "A *copious* stream [of words]" (*Hudson*). *Copious* is especially applicable to that which varies in the quantity or number of things produced, yielded, used, or the like. It is, therefore, not always interchangeable with the other words. Thus, one says "a *copious* (or *plentiful*) supply of food" (not "food was *copious*"); "there was a *copious* crop of potatoes this year" (not "potatoes were *copious* this year"). "*Copious* showers" (*Wordsworth*). "Latin he read *copiously* to the end" (*Lowes*). "*Copious* eating and still more *copious* drinking" (*A. Huxley*). In literary use, *copious* often implies profusion of words, or richness of vocabulary, or fullness of information. "Declaimers of a *copious* vein" (*Berkeley*). "French, English, or any other *copious* language" (*Hobbes*). "Be *copious* and distinct, and tell me a great deal of your mind" (*Johnson*).

Ana. Fruitful, prolific (see FERTILE): sumptuous, opulent, *luxurious: *profuse, lavish, prodigal.

Ant. Scanty, scant.

pleonasm. *Verbiage, redundancy, tautology, circumlocution, periphrasis.

pliable. *Plastic, pliant, ductile, malleable, adaptable.

Ana. Lithe, limber, *supple: *elastic, resilient, springy, flexible: *compliant, acquiescent.

Ant. Obstinate.

pliant. *Plastic, pliable, ductile, malleable, adaptable.

Ana. See those at PLIABLE.

plight, *n.* *Predicament, dilemma, quandary, scrape, fix, jam, pickle.

Ana. Situation, condition, *state, posture: *difficulty, rigor, hardship, vicissitude.

plight, *v.* *Promise, engage, pledge, covenant, contract.

plot, *n.* **1** *Plan, design, scheme, project.

Ana. *Chart, map, graph.

2 Plot, intrigue, machination, conspiracy, complot, cabal, frame-up are here compared only as meaning a secret plan devised to entrap or ensnare another or others. **Plot** implies careful planning of details and an intent to accomplish an evil, mischievous, or treacherous end: it may involve one or more devisers and a person, a group, a class, or a people, as the victim; as, the Gunpowder *Plot;* "There is a *plot* against my life, my crown" (*Shak.*); "the *plots* against him Had madden'd tamer men" (*Tennyson*). **Intrigue** implies more complicated scheming or maneuvering than *plot* and the use of petty underhand methods: it more often implies an attempt to gain one's own ends through clandestine means, as in politics, in business, in love, or the like, rather than (as *plot* frequently implies) an attempt to destroy, to betray, to usurp power, or the like; as, "Mr. Swift hath finely described that passion for *intrigue,* that love of secrecy, slander, and lying, which belongs to weak people, hangers-on of weak courts" (*Thackeray*); "The party politicians forgot their good resolutions, and reverted to their familiar *intrigues*" (*H. G. Wells*). **Machination** (commonly in the plural) usually imputes hostility or treachery to the makers; often, also, it suggests craftiness in devising or contriving annoyances, injuries, evils, or the like: if these ideas are to be connoted, it may be applied to a plot, an intrigue, or any of the secret plans named by the words in this group. "Mrs. Morland knew so little of lords and baronets, that she entertained no notion of their general mischievousness, and was wholly unsuspicious of danger to her daughter from their *machinations*" (*Austen*). "Tortured by some black trouble of the soul, and given over to the *machinations* of his deadliest enemy" (*N. Hawthorne*). **Conspiracy** (as here considered: see also under CONNIVE, *v.*) and the archaic term **complot** differ from *plot* chiefly in implying a combination of persons or groups as the devisers and agents and in being applied chiefly to such a plot when it involves treason or great treachery; as, "To lay a *complot* to betray thy foes" (*Shak.*); "Heaven...hath marr'd Their *complots*" (*Southey*); "This is the fifth *conspiracy* hatch'd in France" (*Tennyson*); "'Tis a long devised *Conspiracy:* the whole tribe is involved" (*Browning*). In legal use, where *conspiracy* is a technical term, the word implies the doing of an unlawful act or the use of unlawful means in accomplishing a lawful end; as, "Every contract, combination in the form of trust or otherwise, or *conspiracy* in restraint of trade or commerce among the several States, or with foreign nations" (*First U. S. Antitrust Act*). **Cabal** (as here considered: see also COMBINATION) applies usually to an intrigue in which a group combines to accomplish some end favorable to it but injurious or disastrous to the person or group (often, specifically, the government) affected; as, "The *cabal* against Washington found supporters exclusively in the north" (*G. Bancroft*). **Frame-up,** originally American slang, applies to any plot which involves fraud or a fraudulent end, especially the incrimination of a person as by planting false evidence or by staging a questionable situation in which he will be found and suspected of a crime; as, "Some one put those little glass figures amongst my traps. It was a *frame-up*" (*Agatha Christie*).

Ana. Connivance, collusion (see under CONNIVE): contrivance, *device, contraption: maneuver, stratagem, *trick, ruse, artifice.

3 Sketch, outline, diagram, delineation, draft, tracing, blueprint. See under SKETCH, *v.*

plot, *v.* **1** Plan, design, scheme, project. See under PLAN, *n.*

Ana. Fashion, fabricate, forge, form, shape, *make: conspire, *connive, collude.

2 *Sketch, outline, diagram, delineate, draft, trace, blueprint.

Ana. Create, *invent: *chart, map, graph.

pluck, *n.* *Fortitude, grit, backbone, guts, sand.

Ana. *Courage, spirit, mettle, resolution, tenacity: determination, *decision: hardihood, audacity, *temerity.

plumb, *adj.* *Vertical, perpendicular.

plume, *v.* *Pride, pique, preen.

Ana. *Appreciate, value, prize.

plump. *Fleshy, stout, portly, rotund, chubby, fat, corpulent, obese.

Ant. Cadaverous. — *Con.* *Lean, spare, scrawny, skinny, lank, lanky: *haggard, pinched, wasted.

plunder, *v.* *Rob, rifle, loot, thieve, burglarize.

Ana. Despoil, spoliate, sack, pillage, *ravage: *strip, denude, bare.

plunder, *n.* *Spoil, pillage, booty, prize, loot, swag.

Ana. Robbery, larceny, *theft.

plutocracy. *Oligarchy, aristocracy.

ply, *v.* *Handle, manipulate, wield, swing.

Ana. Exercise, *practice, drill: operate, work, function (see ACT, *v.*): manage, direct, control, *conduct.

pocket, *n.* *Hole, hollow, cavity, void, vacuum.

poet. Poet, versifier, rhymer (*or* **rimer**), **rhymester** (*or*

rimester), poetaster, bard, minstrel, scop, gleeman, jongleur, troubadour, trouvère, minnesinger, scald (*or* **skald**) come into comparison when they denote a composer who uses metrical or rhythmical language as his medium. **Poet,** etymologically a "maker," is used in a generic sense and in several highly specific senses. In its generic sense, it applies to any writer of verse; in its specific senses, it applies only to a composer of verse who manifests certain qualities regarded as essential by the age or time, or by the writer or speaker who uses the term. With all its variations in implications in these specific senses, *poet* usually stresses inventive and imaginative power as the prime essential, sometimes without clear reference to skill in constructing verses. "Every man, that writes in verse is not a *Poet*" (*B. Jonson*). "The *Poet* is chiefly distinguished from other men by a greater promptness to think and feel without immediate external excitement, and a greater power in expressing such thoughts and feelings" (*Wordsworth*). **Versifier** may designate any composer who uses verse as his medium without reference to any quality or qualities thought of as essential to poetry. In contrast to *poet,* however, it usually implies the lack of such a quality or qualities. "A clever *versifier* might have written Cowley's lines; only a *poet* could have made what Dryden made of them" (*T. S. Eliot*). **Rhymer** and **rhymester** came into English use in the seventeenth century when opposition to rhyme, especially in heroic verse, was crystallizing and there was a pronounced distinction between poets who employed blank verse and those who employed rhyme. In earliest use, the terms were often descriptive rather than depreciative; in later use, especially in the age of romanticism when *poet* was regarded as a title to be bestowed rather than claimed, *rhymer* and *rhymester* were often used by poets in speaking of themselves or of their fellow poets. "I am nae *poet,* in a sense, But just a *rhymer* like by chance.... Whene'er my Muse does on me glance, I jingle at her" (*Burns*). "Novelist, realist, *rhymester,* play your part, Paint the mortal shame of nature with the living hues of art" (*Tennyson*). **Poetaster** is, and has always been, a term of contempt applied to versifiers whose work is regarded as unimportant, trashy, inane, or the like. "There are always *poetasters* enough; but of great *poets*...there are never so many as not to leave room for...more" (*J. Hawthorne*). **Bard,** in strict historical use, applies only to one of a class of Celtic poets, especially of Welsh and Irish poets in ancient times, who composed verses such as those praising heroes, chiefs, or warriors, or recounting historical facts or traditions, and who sang or recited them to the accompaniment of the harp or similar musical instrument. In extended use, *bard* is a more or less romantic designation of any poet, especially of one who is closely associated with a particular place (thus, Shakespeare is called the *Bard* of Avon; Burns, the Ayrshire *Bard;* Wordsworth, the *Bard* of Rydal Mount) or one who is thought of as a composer of verse that sings itself or is written to be sung. "Compile in all the lyrical poetry of the last 150 years a list of half a dozen first-class or even second-class *bards* who wrote primarily to be sung" (*Quiller-Couch*). **Minstrel,** in its historical reference, may or may not imply composition of verse; it applied originally to a public entertainer, often a strolling musician and mountebank, who sang songs (sometimes his own) to the accompaniment of a harp or other instrument and performed tricks; later it was robbed of some of its implications of jugglery and buffoonery (except in reference to a black-faced entertainer in a minstrel show) and given some of the more elevated connotations of *poet;* in its extended use it is close to *bard* in its implications but it places less emphasis on professional character and more on natural lyrical power. "O black and unknown *bards* of long ago, How came your lips to touch the sacred fire? How, in your darkness, did you come to know The power and beauty of the *minstrel's* lyre?" (*J. W. Johnson*). **Scop,** an Anglo-Saxon word, was applied to a type of Anglo-Saxon poet similar to the bard; the scop was, however, a minstrel attached to a court, who provided entertainment by the songs and poetic narratives which he composed or adapted and himself delivered. **Gleeman** (a word of Anglo-Saxon origin) and **jongleur** (of Norman-French origin) are now often used in precise writing in place of *minstrel* in its earliest sense but with a more definite implication of the minstrel's race: only in loose and incorrect use are they employed as synonyms of *minstrel* in the sense of poet. **Troubadour** and **trouvère** are often misapplied except by scholars and learned writers and speakers. The terms are not interchangeable. Both designate one of a class of poets who existed between the tenth and the fourteenth centuries chiefly in what is now known as France, but who used distinctly different tongues. *Troubadour* applies to a type of poet-musician found chiefly in Southern France and Northern Italy, frequently a knightly amateur, who composed lyrics (often also the music) in the Provencal tongue, usually of an amatory character and characteristically in a complicated metrical pattern; *trouvère* applies to a type of poet found in Northern France who composed, in the main, metrical romances, long narrative poems dealing with the loves and exploits of heroes, which were recited or sung by jongleurs and others. *Trouvère* therefore comes close to *bard* in some of its implications; however, the two words in their strict historical senses are not interchangeable because they imply widely different backgrounds and are referable respectively only to a highly specialized type of poet. *Troubadour,* in extended use, is often employed in place of *minstrel* (in its extended sense) but improperly, for *troubadour* rightly implies not naturalness but artifice and technical skill in versifying. "I speak after my fancies, for I am a *Troubadour,* you know, and won the violet at Toulouse; but my voice is harsh here [in Normandy], not in tune, a nightingale out of season" (*Tennyson*). **Minnesinger** is correctly applicable only to one of a class of German lyric poets, usually of noble birth, existing at approximately the same time as the troubadours and having much in common with them, especially in their emphasis on love songs and skill in versification. **Scald** applies to a type of ancient Scandinavian poet and relater of historical and traditional events who both composed and recited his verses and who, like the ancient bard, was regarded as a historian and as a preserver of legends. The term is often misapplied, being used in reference to any Teutonic poet comparable to the ancient bard or trouvère.

Ana. *Maker, creator, author: *writer, author, composer.

poetaster. *Poet, versifier, rhymer, rhymester, bard, minstrel, scop, gleeman, jongleur, troubadour, trouvère, minnesinger, scald.

pogrom. *Massacre, slaughter, butchery, carnage.

poignancy. *Pathos, bathos.

poignant. **1** *Pungent, piquant, racy, spicy, snappy.
Ana. Penetrating, piercing, probing (see ENTER): *sharp, keen, acute: *incisive, trenchant, cutting, biting, crisp.
Ant. Dull (*reaction, sensation, etc.*).
2 *Moving, touching, pathetic, impressive, affecting.
Ana. Exciting, stimulating, provoking (see PROVOKE): disturbing, agitating, perturbing (see DISCOMPOSE).

point, *v.* *Direct, aim, level, train, lay.

Ana. Turn, bend (see CURVE, *v.*): *direct, address, devote: steer, pilot, engineer, *guide.

point of view. **Point of view, standpoint, viewpoint, angle, slant** agree in denoting the position or attitude that determines which aspect of an object of contemplation is seen or presented. **Point of view** is the idiomatic English term: **standpoint** and **viewpoint** came into English as the result of efforts to find a one-word term and a less awkward phrasing; as, from the *point of view* of history; from the *standpoint* of history. The substitutes were slow in meeting approval, but both are now generally accepted, although *viewpoint* is still held in disfavor by many persons. *Standpoint* is increasingly frequent in writing (it was once felt as colloquial) and is acquiring connotations which tend to distinguish it from *point of view* and *viewpoint. Point of view* and *viewpoint* may suggest either a physical or mental position; *standpoint* is gradually being restricted to the mental point of view; as, to paint a scene from the *point of view* of one standing on a hillside; to consider totalitarianism from the German *standpoint* (or *point of view*). *Point of view* permits the inference that there are other ways of looking at that which is considered and therefore usually suggests lack of completeness in the vision, or one-sidedness in the views expressed or presented: *standpoint* more often connotes than definitely implies a fixed way of looking, justified by one's fundamental principles, one's wealth of information, or the like, and not necessarily resulting in a limited understanding. "Every intellectual product must be judged from the *point of view* of the age and the people in which it was produced" (*Pater*). "My criticism of what seem to me one-sided views will be better understood if my general *standpoint* is known" (*Inge*). These distinctions, though apparent in recent good use, are not, however, always observed. **Angle** definitely implies one-sidedness or limitations in the scope of one's vision. "Every man of genius sees the world at a different *angle* from his fellows, and there is his tragedy. But it is usually a measurable *angle*" (*H. Ellis*). "In the rhetorical speeches from Shakespeare which have been cited, we have...a new clue to the character, in noting the *angle* from which he views himself" (*T. S. Eliot*). **Slant** (a colloquial term) stresses bias, but it may be the bias derived from temperament, mental habits, or experience rather than from prejudice; as, he always takes a pessimistic *slant* when any proposal for avoiding war is made. "No one sees anything without some personal *slant*" (*Sat. Review of Lit.*). All of these words are synonyms in their extended senses for they agree in meaning one's view (as held or advocated) or views. *Point of view* (or *viewpoint*), however, implies that the view is an opinion or personal judgment; as, to express one's *point of view;* his *point of view* is generally known. *Standpoint* suggests a basic principle or body of principles; as, to question the validity of an opponent's *standpoint.* "We believe the latter *standpoint* to be that generally assumed by the British Empire" (*Sat. Review*). *Slant* and *angle* also, in colloquial usage, signify opinion, but they imply personal bias far more than does *point of view.* "I remember my confusion when an American professor wanted to know my '*slant* on the leadership question' " (*Irish Statesman*).

Ana. *Position, stand, attitude.

poise, *v.* *Stabilize, steady, balance, ballast, trim.

Ana. *Support, uphold, back.

Con. Disturb, agitate, upset (see DISCOMPOSE): *overturn, overset, overthrow, subvert.

poise, *n.* **1** *Balance, equilibrium, equipoise, tension.

Ana. Suspending *or* suspension, hanging (see corresponding verbs at HANG): *equanimity, composure.

2 *Tact, address, savoir-faire.

Ana. Self-possession, aplomb, assurance, *confidence: calmness, tranquillity, serenity (see corresponding adjectives at CALM): grace, dignity, *elegance.

poison, *n.* **Poison, venom, virus, toxin, bane** agree in meaning matter or a substance that when present in an organism or introduced into it chemically produces an injurious or deadly effect. **Poison,** etymologically a potion or drink, acquired its first specific meaning when it was applied to a potion containing a highly noxious ingredient, especially in such a quantity as to prove fatal to the drinker. In its sense development it came to be applied to the deadly ingredient, rather than to the drink containing it, and to be thought of as something that could be introduced into the system not only through the mouth but in other ways; as, killed by a *poison*-barbed arrow; morphine (usually introduced hypodermically) is, in sufficient quantities, a *poison;* carbon monoxide gas, when inhaled, is a deadly *poison.* In still more recent use, the term is applied to any substance, manufactured within an organism, which under certain conditions chemically produces disease or death; as, *poisons* in the blood made up of accumulated substances which should have been eliminated in urine cause uremia. The term *poison* is now the most general of all these words, and is referable to any highly noxious or deadly matter without reference to whether it is swift or slow in action, whether it is of animal, vegetable, or mineral origin, or whether it is introduced into the system or is manufactured within the system. In its secondary sense, *poison* is merely a figurative extension of its literal sense; as, fear uncontrolled is a *poison* that destroys all self-confidence. **Venom** and **virus** had for their earliest meaning a fluid containing a poison secreted by a snake, scorpion, bee, or the like, whenever the creature bites or uses its organ of offense or defense, such as a fang, a sting, or a spine. *Venom* still retains this meaning in precise use, though it is sometimes applied to a poisonous secretion of a plant. "Man spurns the worm, but pauses ere he wake The slumbering *venom* of the folded snake" (*Byron*). *Virus,* on the other hand, has practically lost this meaning, and is more commonly restricted to designating the poison in the juices of a person having an infectious disease (for fuller treatment see GERM). **Toxin** is specifically applied to a poison, or poisonous secretion, that is manufactured in the plant or animal body. A toxin, such as the venom of a snake, may be harmful to others but not to the organism itself; a toxin produced by faulty metabolism, or a lack of balance in the constructive and destructive processes in an organism, is usually exceedingly harmful to the organism. A toxin may also be the product of bacteria, as in tetanus, diphtheria, or botulism, and therefore dangerous to the organism in which it is produced. **Bane** is an old word, now rare except in poetic or deliberately archaic use and in certain combinations such as rats*bane* (rat poison), and hen*bane,* dog*bane,* wolfs*bane* (certain plants containing a poisonous juice supposedly fatal respectively to hens, dogs, etc.). Originally applied to anything that caused destruction or woe or that wrought great harm (a meaning still found in such phrases as "she is the *bane* of his existence"), it came to be specifically applied to any poison that is fatal if not counteracted by an antidote. "My death and life, My *bane* and antidote, are both before me: This [the bane] in a moment brings me to an end; But this [the antidote] informs me I shall never die" (*Addison*).

poisonous. **Poisonous, venomous, virulent, toxic** (*or* **toxical**), **mephitic** (*or* **mephitical**), **pestilent, pestilential, miasmatic** (*or* **miasmatical**), **miasmic, miasmal** come into comparison as meaning having the properties or the effects of poison (see POISON). In its literal sense, **poisonous** always implies that the thing so described will be fatal or exceedingly harmful if introduced into a living organism (usually a human organism) in sufficient quantities as by eating, drinking, inhaling, or the like; as, the most *poisonous* of mushrooms; *poisonous* gases; "[aniline] is also *poisonous* but by proper chemical manipulation it becomes the parent of many beneficent medicines" (*A. C. Morrison*). Figuratively, the term implies extreme noxiousness, or perniciousness, or power to corrode, rankle, corrupt, or the like; as, "You might condemn us As *poisonous* of your honor" (*Shak.*); "What a difference between Pope's little *poisonous* barbs and Dryden's strong invective!" (*Tennyson*); "The sentence was pronounced...in a stifling *poisonous* atmosphere" (*Conrad*). In its literal sense, **venomous** applies not only to reptiles, insects, etc. (such as the snake, scorpion, bee), whose bite or sting introduces or is believed to introduce a deadly venom (see *venom* under POISON) into the organism, and to plants believed to contain a poisonous fluid (as, a *venomous* snake; "a garden of *venomous* plants"—*Marvell*), but also to the bites, stings, or wounds inflicted by venomous creatures (as, a *venomous* snake bite). The adjective is, however, used far more often in its figurative senses, where it implies extreme malevolence (as, "his [Cobbett's] scolding red face and his radical laugh, in which *venomous* hate mingles with a mocking exultation at his enemies' surely approaching downfall"—*Heinrich Heine, transl. by Arnold*), or destructive malignancy (as, "The most innocent intimacies would not have escaped misrepresentation from the *venomous* tongues of Roman society" —*Froude*). Literally, **virulent** implies the destructive or extremely deleterious properties of a virus (in old use, a venom; in current use, the poisonous substance produced in an organism by an infectious disease): it is now applied chiefly to infectious diseases of a particularly malignant or violent form, or, in technical use, to the virus (as defined above) that induces a violent and often fatal attack; as, "poverty produces outbreaks of *virulent* infectious disease...sooner or later" (*Shaw*); one of the most *virulent* types of the pneumococcus. Figuratively, the term applies to that which is particularly violent in its display of an offensive or noxious nature or quality; as, his *virulent* antipathy to foreigners of any kind; "the *virulent* pen of that rascal the Examiner" (*Steele*); "proceedings...dictated by *virulent* hatred" (*G. Eliot*); "the escholtzia, which...I avoided, for its *virulent* orange flowers" (*H. Ellis*). **Toxic** is chiefly in literal use, where it sometimes implies the presence of properties or effects of a toxin, or poisonous secretion manufactured in an animal or vegetable organism (as, a *toxic* condition of the blood; a *toxic* goiter; *toxic* poisoning of the system) or at other times implies only the character or the properties of a poison, and therefore means little more than *poisonous* (as, the *toxic* principle of a certain drug; *toxic* gases; a *toxic* drug). In its rare figurative use, *toxic* often implies insidious and destructive activity, comparable to that of some toxins in the human organism; as, "Arsène Dumont thought that it [civilization] inevitably held within itself a *toxic* principle, a principle by which it is itself in time poisoned" (*H. Ellis*). **Mephitic** is applicable to that which is so offensive to the sense of smell that it is, or often, is believed to be, actually poisonous; as, *mephitic* vapors rising from a swamp; the *mephitic* air of a disused mine; *mephitic* fumes, such as those of chloroform or ether. **Pestilent** and **pestilential** may come close to *poisonous* or, less often, to *virulent* or *toxic* in meaning (as, *pestilent* opium; the *pestilential* fever or, as it is now called, typhus fever), but they are now chiefly used in the extended sense of exceedingly infectious or dangerous to the health, morals, mental integrity, or the like, especially of the group, as distinguished from the individual: *pestilential* is usually preferred when the breeding of a pestilence is implied; as, "While in all other arts it is agreed that a student should be trained only on the best models...there has been with respect to poetry a *pestilent* notion that the young should be gradually led up to excellence through lower degrees of it" (*Bridges*). "So *pestilential*, so infectious a thing is sin, that it scatters the poison of its breath to all the neighbourhood" (*Jer. Taylor*). **Miasmatic, miasmic, miasmal** all imply a reference to *miasma*, or supposedly infectious matter emanating from swamps or jungles or from putrescent substances and floating in the air; as, a *miasmatic* marsh; "The morning mist Is grey and *miasmic*" (*Amy Lowell*); a *miasmal* place. In their now much more common extended use, these words, especially the first two, come close to *pestilential* in implying a power to spread contamination or to poison the minds or souls of the multitude; as, *miasmatic* doctrines; the *miasmic* influence of a certain institution.

Ana. Mortal, fatal, lethal, *deadly: *pernicious, baneful, noxious, deleterious, detrimental.

polemic, polemical. *Controversial, eristic, apologetic.

Ana. Argumentative, disputatious (see corresponding nouns at ARGUMENTATION): contentious, litigious (see BELLIGERENT).

policeman. **Policeman, officer, constable, bailiff, catchpole** (*or* **catchpoll**), **gendarme, bobby, peeler, copper, cop, bull** come into comparison when they denote a member of the police, or the force or body officially charged with the duty of preserving peace and order in the community by preventing violations of the law and by taking into custody persons who are known or are alleged to be guilty of such violations. **Policeman** is the general term referable to a member of any police force, whether civil or military, or, if civil, whether under the jurisdiction of town or city or of a state. The term is referable to such a person regardless of the specific duties to which he is assigned, such as patrolling, detection, or traffic control. **Officer** (except in the phrase *police officer*, which is equivalent to *policeman*) is now used chiefly in the United States in addressing a policeman; as, *Officer*, will you send in a fire alarm? The word was in British use, however, long before *policeman*, and was applied to any official charged with enforcing peace and order and arresting violators of the law. "The thief doth fear each bush an *officer*" (*Shak.*). **Constable,** which seems to have come into use in this sense around 1400, has since then acquired and lost various specific implications owing to historical changes in the system of policing the community. In general, a constable is now either a policeman in a small community such as a village, a parish, or a township, or a special official, often a sheriff's assistant, charged with executing the warrants of judicial officers, such as warrants for arrest, attachment, eviction, and the like. It is also used of a member of a constabulary, or an organized police force serving a county, state, or section of a country. In British use, *constable* is used as a term of address for a policeman. In British, and in rare American use, a **bailiff** is a sheriff's constable and, therefore, a county police officer; **catchpole** is the now contemptuous equivalent of *bailiff* in this sense or, sometimes, of any constable. **Gendarme** is often used by English-speaking persons of a French or other European policeman (properly in France called *agent de police*). In strict French use, a *gendarme* is a soldier, a member of the gendarmerie, or military police. **Bobby** and **peeler**

are both British colloquial equivalents of *policeman*, derived from the name of Sir Robert Peel, who as British home secretary was responsible for acts organizing the Metropolitan Police (of Greater London) and the Irish constabulary. *Bobby* is used, chiefly in England, of any policeman, but especially of uniformed policemen wearing a helmet; *peeler* was originally an Irish designation for a member of the Irish constabulary, a police force organized on military lines; it was later applied to any policeman. **Copper** and **cop** (literally one who cops, or catches) are slang terms common both in the United States and in Great Britain; they often refer to a policeman who is on the lookout for offenders, such as a patrolman or a motorcycle policeman. **Bull** also is a slang term for *policeman* and is often applied specifically to a detective.

polish, *v.* **Polish, burnish, furbish, buff, shine** agree in meaning to smooth or brighten by rubbing. **Polish,** the most common of these words, fundamentally implies friction that removes all roughnesses of surface or gives a crude product a smooth, often a lustrous, finish, or renews the finish of an old product; it may imply the use of a tool, instrument, or machine (such as a file, a brush, or a grinder), or the application, usually in addition, of a gritty powder, a paste, or the like; as, to *polish* marble for a tombstone; to *polish* mahogany; to *polish* glass; to *polish* furniture; to *polish* shoes. "Windowpanes which she had *polished* until they shone like jewels" (*M. Wilkins*). **Burnish** etymologically implies a causing to shine or gleam. As originally, it is still used chiefly in reference to metals, or to objects made of metals, which are rubbed until they become lustrous; as, *burnished* gold; to *burnish* one's shield; to *burnish* brass candlesticks. In present use, the term is also applied to things which shine as though they were burnished; as, "the blue green of the pines...shone in the sun—a *burnished* colour" (*Jefferies*); "Even his hair...seemed like *burnished* bronze in the evening light" (*Shaw*). **Furbish,** which is now used more often in a figurative than in a literal sense, in earliest use implied cleaning of rust from armor, weapons, and the like, by friction; as, "*furbished* the rusty sword again" (*Dryden*). In extended use, it commonly implies freshening up, renovating, or the like, with very little emphasis (if any) on rubbing, brushing, or scouring. "I took it [the play] to make alterations...and *furbished* it up in a day or two" (*Lamb*). **Buff,** originally a tradesman's word, implies polishing with a soft, rough, oil-treated leather (originally of buffalo hide) or with a stick or tool (called a *buffer*) faced with such leather or with chamois, velvet, or the like; as, to *buff* brass; to *buff* knives; to *buff* one's fingernails. **Shine** is often used in place of *polish* when cleansing or brightening are implied; as, to *shine* silver.

Ana. *Renew, restore, refresh, rejuvenate.

Ant. Tarnish.

polite. *Civil, courteous, courtly, gallant, chivalrous.

Ana. *Gentle, genteel: *suave, urbane, diplomatic, politic: *thoughtful, considerate, attentive.

Ant. Impolite.

politic. 1 *Expedient, advisable.

Ana. Practical, *practicable: *possible, feasible, practicable: *shrewd, astute, perspicacious, sagacious.

2 Diplomatic, bland, smooth, *suave, urbane.

Ana. Ingratiating, insinuating, *disarming: unctuous, sleek, oily, *fulsome: *wise, prudent, judicious.

politician. Politician, statesman, politico are synonymous terms only when they denote a person who is versed in or engaged in politics, or the science or art of government. In American use, they are often, though not always, regarded as opposites rather than as interchangeable terms. When used without derogation, **politician,** as distinguished from *statesman*, both in British and American use applies to a person who by training and temperament is able to deal with masses of persons so as to accomplish desirable ends, such as election to a political office (sometimes of oneself, sometimes of one's chosen candidate), or the passage of bills or the acceptance of measures one upholds, or the settlement of especially difficult problems to the satisfaction of one's constituency or of the country as a whole. Usually, *politician* also connotes the power to deal successfully with opposition, especially opposition coming from other political parties. "What makes Burke stand out so splendidly among *politicians* is that he treats politics with his thought and imagination" (*Arnold*). "The loose cog in the wheel happened to be that he [a former unsuccessful mayor of New York City] held a political position and was 1,000 miles away from being a *politician*. He did not know how to handle people and did not know how to deal with them or how to get along with them" (*Alfred E. Smith*). In American, as distinguished from British, use, *politician* is often a highly derogatory or contemptuous term, implying scheming, self-interest, artifice, or intrigue in accomplishing one's ends. "He has ...a loose, shifty expression of face, and one which gives you the impression of a thorough *politician* in the bad sense of the word" (*E. L. Godkin*). "American readers are asked to note that the term '*politician*' is used in the English sense, as meaning 'one engaged in politics,' and has no derogatory application" (Foreword to *International Who's Who*, 1940). **Statesman,** in both American and British use, carries little if any reference to party politics (except that in effusive American use a *politician* is sometimes pronounced a *statesman*), but throws the emphasis upon skill and sagacity in the management of affairs of state, as in the capacity of president or prime minister, a member of Congress or of Parliament, an ambassador, or the like. The term, in contrast to *politician* (sometimes to *demagogue*), is often applied to the highest representatives (either in actuality or in thought) of this type; as, "Unhappily, the republic [the First French Republic] was subject to men who were mere demagogues and in no sense *statesmen*" (*Macaulay*); "Ticknor was a scholar born, as Webster was a *statesman* born" (*Van W. Brooks*); "Men are employed to bring up the name of a *politician* so that he may be called a *statesman*" (*S. Anderson*). **Politico** is sometimes used in Great Britain in place of *politician* in the derogatory sense: in American use, it is sometimes preferred to *politician* when a term devoid of all depreciation is desired, and yet there is no intent to suggest laudable qualities.

politico. *Politician, statesman.

pollute. *Contaminate, defile, taint, attaint.

Ana. *Debase, vitiate, corrupt, deprave, pervert: *abuse, outrage, mistreat: profane, desecrate, blaspheme (see corresponding nouns at PROFANATION).

poltroon. Craven, dastardly, recreant, *cowardly, pusillanimous.

Ana. *Mean, ignoble, abject: *contemptible, despicable, sorry, scurvy.

Ant. Dauntless.

polymathic. *Learned, erudite, scholarly.

pomade, pomatum, *v.* *Oil, grease, lubricate, anoint, inunct, cream.

pomp, *n.* *Display, parade, array.

Ana. Ceremony, ceremonial, liturgy, ritual, formality, *form: ostentatiousness *or* ostentation, pompousness, showiness *or* show (see corresponding adjectives at SHOWY).

pompous. *Showy, ostentatious, pretentious.
Ana. Ceremonious, *ceremonial, solemn, formal: stately, imposing, majestic, grandiose (see GRAND): *splendid, resplendent, glorious, superb: grandiloquent, magniloquent, bombastic (see RHETORICAL).
Ant. Lowly.

ponder. **Ponder, meditate, muse, ruminate** come into comparison chiefly but not exclusively as intransitive verbs meaning to consider or examine something attentively, seriously, and with more or less deliberation. **Ponder,** in highly discriminating use, retains its etymological implication of weighing and usually suggests consideration of a problem from all angles or of a thing in all its relations in order that nothing important will escape one: unlike *weigh* in an allied sense (see CONSIDER, 1), it does not now usually suggest a balancing that leads to a conclusion; as, "Witness this weighty book...so nicely *pondered,* yet so strongly wrought" (*Dryden*); "[Feverel] *pondered* on what his Aunt said. He loved Lady Blandish, and yet he did not wish to see her Lady Feverel" (*Meredith*); "the great Sung master was wont...to...spend the day *pondering* the subjects of his brush by the side of running streams" (*Binyon*). **Meditate** adds to *ponder* an implication of a definite directing or focusing of one's thought: in intransitive use, especially, it more often suggests an effort to understand the thing so considered in all its aspects, relations, or values than an effort to work out a definite problem. "*Meditate* upon these things; give thyself wholly to them" (*1 Timothy* iv. 15). "Empowered by long training, the young priest blotted himself out of his own consciousness and *meditated* upon the anguish of his Lord" (*Cather*). In transitive use, *meditate* implies such deep consideration of a plan, project, or the like, that it approaches *intend* or *purpose* in meaning; as, "are you really serious in *meditating* a dance at Netherfield?" (*Austen*). **Muse** comes close to *meditate* in implying focused attention but it suggests a less intellectual aim: often it implies absorption as in a dream, a fancy, a remembrance, or the like. "Let him...read a certain passage of full poesy or distilled prose, and let him wander with it, and *muse* upon it...and dream upon it" (*Keats*). " 'What an old-fashioned place it seems to be!' said Elizabeth-Jane, while her silent mother *mused* on other things than topography" (*Hardy*). **Ruminate** (etymologically, to chew the cud as a ruminant animal) implies a going over the same problem, the same subject, or the same object of meditation again and again: it may be used in place of any of these words, but it does not carry as strong a suggestion of weighing as *ponder,* of concentrated attention as *meditate,* or of absorption as *muse,* and, on the other hand, it more often implies processes such as reasoning or speculation. "I sit at home and *ruminate* on the qualities of certain little books like this one—little elixirs of perfection, full of subtlety and sadness—which I can read and read again" (*L. P. Smith*). "Behind [Dr. Alexis] Carrel lies forty years of *ruminating* on life, of glimpsing it in its simplest forms through microscopes, of incredibly delicate surgical operations on tissues or organs" (*W. Kaempffert*). *Muse* and *ruminate* are now very rare as transitive verbs.
Ana. Weigh, *consider, revolve, contemplate: reflect, deliberate, speculate, *think, cogitate.

ponderable. Appreciable, *perceptible, sensible, palpable, tangible.
Ana. Important, significant, momentous, weighty, consequential (see corresponding nouns at IMPORTANCE).
Con. Trivial, trifling, *petty, paltry.

ponderous. Cumbrous, cumbersome, *heavy, weighty, hefty.
Ana. *Massive, massy, bulky, substantial: clumsy, *awkward, maladroit: *onerous, burdensome, oppressive, exacting.

pool, *n.* *Monopoly, corner, syndicate, trust, cartel.

poor. *Bad, wrong.
Ana. *Deficient, defective: *petty, puny, trivial, trifling, paltry: *base, low, vile.
Con. *Good, right: satisfying, fulfilling, meeting, answering (see SATISFY).

popular. *Common, ordinary, familiar, vulgar.
Ana. General, *universal, generic, common: accepted, received, admitted (see RECEIVE): prevalent, *prevailing, current.
Ant. Unpopular: esoteric.

porch. Veranda, piazza, portico, stoop, *balcony, gallery, loggia.

port, *n.*[1] *Harbor, haven.

port, *n.*[2] Presence, carriage, front, *bearing, deportment, demeanor, mien, manner.

portal. *Door, gate, doorway, gateway, postern.

portend. Presage, augur, prognosticate, *foretell, predict, forecast, prophesy, forebode.
Ana. Betoken, *indicate, bespeak, attest: signify, import, *mean, denote.

portent. *Foretoken, presage, prognostic, omen, augury.
Ana. Presentiment, foreboding, misgiving, *apprehension: forewarning, warning, cautioning *or* caution (see corresponding verbs at WARN).

portentous. *Ominous, unpropitious, inauspicious, fateful.
Ana. Threatening, menacing (see THREATEN): prodigious, *monstrous: prophesying *or* prophetic, presaging, foreboding, predicting, foretelling (see corresponding verbs at FORETELL).

porter. *Beer, lager, bock, ale, stout.

portico. **1** *Colonnade, arcade, arcature, peristyle.
2 *Balcony, gallery, loggia, veranda, piazza, porch, stoop.

portion, *n.* **1** *Part, piece, detail, member, division, section, segment, sector, fraction, fragment, parcel.
Ana. Quantity, amount (see SUM, *n.*): apportionment, rationing *or* ration (see corresponding verbs at APPORTION): allotment, assignment, allocation (see corresponding verbs at ALLOT).
2 *Fate, destiny, lot, doom.
Ana. Distribution, dispensation, division, dealing (see corresponding verbs at DISTRIBUTE): fortune, hap, *chance, luck.

portion, *v.* *Apportion, parcel, ration, prorate.
Ana. *Allot, assign, allocate: *distribute, dispense, divide, deal.

portly. *Fleshy, stout, plump, rotund, chubby, fat, corpulent, obese.
Ana. Burly, husky, brawny, *muscular.

portrait. Photograph, *image, simulacrum, effigy, statue, icon, mask.

pose, *v.* Posture, attitudinize. See under POSTURE, *n.*
Ana. *Assume, affect, simulate, feign, counterfeit.

pose, *n.* **1 Pose, air** (*or* **airs**), **affectation, mannerism** are synonyms when they mean an adopted rather than a natural way of speaking, behaving, and the like. **Pose** implies an attitude deliberately assumed in order to impress others or to call attention to oneself; it may be applied to opinions, policies, etc., as well as to manners; as, his reticence is just a *pose.* "The literary *pose* which affects to despise literature" (*Arch. Marshall*). "The insurgent attitude has now become a *pose*" (*Grandgent*). **Air,** except in the plural form **airs,** does not always imply assumption, for it often suggests acquirement through environmental influences; as, she has the *air* of a teacher; he spoke with an *air* of authority. Used absolutely, *air* often implies distinction and aristocratic breeding. "Mr. Wickham was...far beyond them all in person, countenance, *air*" (*Austen*). When it and (especially) *airs* definitely imply artificiality and the intent to give a false appearance, they usually also imply a vulgar pretense of breeding, of grandeur, or of superiority; as, to put on *airs*. "Oh! they give themselves such *airs*" (*Austen*). **Affectation** usually designates a specific trick of speech or behavior of one who obviously puts on airs or whose trick impresses others as deliberately assumed and insincere. **Mannerism** designates an acquired peculiarity or eccentricity in speech or behavior; it seldom implies insincerity, but it nearly always connotes habit or potential habit. A *mannerism* consciously assumed becomes thereby also an *affectation;* what begins as an *affectation* may become an unconscious and habitual trick of behavior, and so a *mannerism.*

2 *Posture, attitude.

posh, *adj.* *Stylish, fashionable, modish, smart, chic, dapper, dashing, spruce, natty, nifty, nobby, toffish, brave, braw.

posit. *Presuppose, presume, assume, postulate, premise.

position, *n.* **1** Presupposition, presumption, assumption, postulate, premise. See under PRESUPPOSE.

2 Position, stand, attitude, as here compared, denote a more or less fixed mental point of view or way of regarding something. **Position** and **stand** both imply reference to a question at issue or to a matter about which there is difference of opinion. *Position,* however, is often the milder term, since it, unlike *stand,* seldom connotes aggressiveness or defiance of a widely held or popular opinion; as, he was asked to make known his *position* on disarmament; he took the *stand* that disarmament would not accomplish the ends its proponents had in view. "There is a strong sceptical element in Newman, though he would have been shocked at the developments of his *position* by the Roman Catholic Modernists" (*Inge*). "He...agreed thoroughly with my *stand* that no government or private organization could give health; people had to achieve it by their own efforts" (*V. Heiser*). **Attitude** suggests a personal or, sometimes, a group or communal point of view, especially one that is colored by personal or party feeling, is influenced by one's environment or the fashion of the moment, and is, on the whole, more the product of temperament or of emotion than of thought or conviction; as, a humorous *attitude* to life; the Greek *attitude* to nature; "Eudora's *attitude* of owning your time and interest" (*M. Austin*); a resentful *attitude* to criticism. "Their *attitude* towards truth (that bug-bear of Potterism) was typical; Clare wouldn't see it; Jane saw it perfectly clearly, and would reject it without hesitation if it suited her book" (*R. Macaulay*).

Ana. *Point of view, viewpoint, standpoint, angle, slant.

3 Position, place, situation, office, post, job, berth, billet, capacity are here considered only in the narrow sense of the particular employment in which one is engaged for a salary or wage. **Position** and **place** mean little more than this: they differ little from each other, except that sometimes *position* is preferred where the employment indicates a higher social status or more dignity in the work involved, and *place* when the reference is to a menial employment; as, he has found a *position* as office manager; she has lost her *place* as a cook; there are few good teaching *positions* open at present; the employment agency can provide *places* for several good servants, chauffeurs, and farm hands at once. This distinction, however, is not maintained in good usage: for example, in British use especially, *place* has not entirely lost its earlier denotation of a position in the government, at court, or the like (as, "in my younger years I used many endeavours to get a *place* at Court"—*Addison;* "To glut their insatiable craving for *place*"—*J. Morley*); in university and collegiate use, a placement officer is charged with the work of finding *places* for students leaving college or on vacation. **Situation** (see also STATE) is not always distinguishable from *position* or *place:* it is frequently the preferred term in the classified columns of newspapers (as, *situations* wanted; *situations* vacant), and it sometimes carries a stronger implication of occupancy (or need of an occupant) than *position;* as, to seek a *position* (i.e., an opening or a place in a group, staff, system); to take or obtain a *situation* (i.e., a place one fills) as governess. **Office,** as here considered (see also FUNCTION, 1), applies specifically to a position of trust, authority, or the like, especially in the service of a nation, state, city, or the like, or of a company, corporation, or association: it often implies the selection of its occupant by election, appointment, or the like: it usually also suggests definite duties or functions, tenure, and (though not necessarily) emoluments beyond those given to holders of positions or situations; as, to elect a new man to the *office* of mayor; he holds the *office* of attorney general of the state; appointed to one of the highest *offices* in the country; the directors elected the president of the corporation to the *office* of chairman of their board. **Post,** originally and still applied to the place where a soldier is stationed for sentry or guard duties, in the sense here considered applies to a position, or more often to an office, attended by great responsibility or involving the performance of onerous duties; as, he has been appointed to the *post* of secretary of war; it is rumored that he will give up his *post* at the beginning of the new year. In British use, *post* is now the common term for a place in the teaching profession. **Job, berth, billet** are more or less colloquial terms (the last somewhat more frequent in British than in American use) for *position, situation, office,* or *post. Job* specifically stresses the work involved; as, a teaching *job;* he has a hard *job;* a man is lost when he is without a *job.* The term, once applied chiefly to places involving heavy labor, is now used not only without depreciation, but even with a suggestion of some special significance; as, he is the only man for that *job;* a *job* requiring skill and courage. *Berth* distinctively implies a place (often a small place) in a system, a staff, or a particular service; often, but less clearly than *billet,* it suggests a place to which one has been allotted, assigned, or appointed; as, he has a good *berth* in the civil service; "The men who cling to easy *billets* ashore" (*Harper's Mag.*). **Capacity,** as here considered (see also ABILITY), comes into comparison with the other terms only when it denotes a position or job with reference to the nature of the tasks to be performed or to the qualifications of the person who performs them; as, he is with the firm in the *capacity* of financial adviser; he serves them in the *capacity* of butler, but they call him their houseman.

Ana. *Work, employment, occupation, calling, pursuit, métier, business.

positive. **1** Certain, *sure, cocksure.

Ana. *Confident, assured, sanguine, sure: dogmatic, doctrinaire, oracular, *dictatorial.

Ant. Doubtful.

2 *Affirmative.

Ant. Negative. — *Con.* *Neutral, indifferent: nugatory, *vain, idle, hollow: nullifying, annulling (see NULLIFY).

possess. Own, enjoy, hold, *have.
Ana. Control, manage, direct, *conduct: retain, *keep, reserve, withhold.

possession, *n.* 1 **Possession, dependency, territory, colony, dominion, protectorate, mandate** come into comparison as meaning a country or state that is subject in whole or in part to the rule or control of another state. **Possession,** as here considered, implies occupation and control by the governing state; as, Canada no longer has the status of a *possession* of Great Britain; the insular *possessions* of the great powers. **Dependency** applies to a possession or, sometimes, to a province that is more or less remote from the governing country and that, therefore, does not form a constituent part of it. Usually, a dependency is self-governing in part; thus, the *possessions* of the United States (including the Canal Zone, Puerto Rico, Guam, the Virgin Islands of the United States, American Samoa, and Wake and Midway Islands) are usually called *dependencies.* **Territory** (as here considered: see also FIELD, 2) applies to a portion of a country (specifically of the United States, Canada, and Australia) not yet recognized as a state or province of that country and, therefore, partly self-governing but under the control of the federal government; as, Alaska is a *territory* of the United States; most of the western states of the United States were *territories* before their admission to statehood; the Northwest *Territories* of Canada. **Colony** applies strictly to a company of people transplanted to a distant region for the purpose of settling in it and of founding a state; as, Germany established *colonies* in many parts of the world. As here specifically compared, the term applies to the state they have established, so long as it is subject to the parent government; as, the British *colonies* which after the American Revolution united to form the United States of America; French *colonies* in the West Indies. **Dominion** is now the preferred term in British use for any of the self-governing states which once as colonies or possessions formed part of the British Empire, and which are now regarded as free members of the British Commonwealth of Nations united by a common allegiance to the crown. Not all of these in their official titles use *dominion,* however; thus, the *Dominion* of Canada and the Commonwealth of Australia are *dominions* in this sense. **Protectorate** applies either to a country over which a more highly organized or more powerful country assumes control for the purposes of protecting it from aggression or internal disturbance and of managing its affairs, or to the form of government which it imposes upon the people of such a country; as, "The programme sketched out by Mr. [Cecil] Rhodes, of drawing a continuous chain of British *protectorates* from Cape Colony to the Nile valley" (*C. Oman*). **Mandate** (see also COMMAND) is the term applied to any former German colony or other conquered territory that was assigned by the Treaty of Versailles, 1919, to another nation (mandatary), not as a possession but as a protectorate with power to administer and regulate its affairs, especially for the benefit of the colony or territory; as, German East Africa was one of the *mandates* assigned to Great Britain.

2 In plural form **possessions. Possessions, belongings, effects, means, resources, assets** come into comparison when they mean all the items that taken together constitute a person's or group's property or wealth. *Possessions, belongings, effects* stress ownership; *means, resources, assets* emphasize value, especially pecuniary value. **Possessions** may be applied to the aggregate of things owned, regardless of the individual worth or significance of each thing; thus, one may speak of the *possessions* of an indigent old woman or of the *possessions* of a Rothschild, the former referring to a few articles of furniture and clothing, the latter to extensive properties, enormous invested capital, and the like. **Belongings** is applied commonly to more intimate personal possessions, such as one's clothes, one's goods, one's valuables, or, in extended use, one's family, one's relatives, or one's dependents; as, to gather up one's *belongings* when leaving boarding school; to have insufficient space for one's *belongings.* "I have sent his folk, His kin, all his *belongings,* over-seas" (*Tennyson*). **Effects** is somewhat more inclusive than *belongings,* but usually less so than *possessions.* It is often applied to personal as distinguished from real property, especially when the reference is to the estate of a deceased person; as, he died leaving no *effects* of value; all his *effects* were divided among his relatives before an administrator could be appointed. Sometimes, it is applied to movable articles as distinguished from those that are stationary; as, a sale of household *effects;* all his personal *effects* are in his one trunk. **Means** usually applies to all the money that is available, in the form of revenue from capital, income, or ready money, for expenditure; as, to live beyond one's *means;* a man of small (or large) *means.* This skill shall be taught to the ablest of those who desire it, quite independently of their parents' *means*" (*B. Russell*). **Resources,** on the other hand, is applied to all possessions of any sort that have actual or potential value (often, but not necessarily, money value), and that may be depended upon in case of need or of deficiency. Sometimes, the term comprehends all possessions (tangibles and intangibles) whether they are actually used or are merely available for use; thus, a statement of a company's *resources* is a statement that covers every item that may be regarded as a part of the company's wealth. More often, however, the term refers specifically to possessions held in reserve for emergencies or to sources of supply as yet untapped; as, the natural *resources* of any country are its unmined minerals, unfelled timber, and the like. "Great acumen has been shown in husbanding the *resources* [that is, the funds] of the Memorial" (*V. Heiser*). "Unless men and women are to turn into unthinking mechanisms...they must possess some *resources* [that is, some other interests or skills] outside their particular work" (*Grandgent*). **Assets** both in law and in accounting always implies an opposition to *liabilities* and therefore suggests the possibility of an inequality between the two and a difference between one's ostensible and one's actual wealth. When the term is used in reference to the settlement of the estate of a deceased person or to the legal administration of the property of an insolvent or bankrupt person or concern, the assets include all the possessions of marketable value which may be turned into money to provide for the payment of the liabilities; thus, the *assets* of the estate were sufficient to cover all liabilities, including the decedent's debts and his legacies. When used in reference to general balance sheets of a company or corporation, the term comprehends all items which from one point of view can be called resources having book value. But *assets* is never exactly the same as *resources,* because the latter word does not, as *assets* always does, imply a comparison with *liabilities.*

possible. 1 **Possible, practicable, feasible** come into comparison as meaning capable of being realized. That is **possible** (as here compared: see also PROBABLE) which is not contrary to the nature of things, but which, given the proper conditions, does or may exist or occur; as, "Although he [Plato] still asserts that community of goods would be the ideal institution, he reluctantly abandons it as a basis for a *possible* state" (*G. L. Dickin-*

son); "there will be such [a minority of abnormal persons]...in every *possible* society" (*H. Ellis*). That is **practicable,** such as a plan, project, scheme, or the like, which may be easily or readily effected by the means at hand or under current conditions (as, "the notion of a Government department trying to make out how many different types were necessary, and how many persons of each type, and proceeding to breed them by appropriate marriages, is amusing but not *practicable*"—*Shaw*), or such as a method or way of doing or making something that the thing turned out is, or remains, of practical value (as, "It is admitted to be impossible to distinguish the innocent from the infected product [the filling of comfortables] in any *practicable* way when it is made up into comfortables"—*Justice Holmes*), or such as a newly devised or untried machine, implement, instrument, process, or the like, which is found usable or operable (as, television was finally shown to be not only *possible* but *practicable;* "Hearing Ed Hall berate a farmer who doubted the *practicability* of the machine"—*S. Anderson*). That is **feasible** which is not only highly possible but also to all appearances practicable (with, however, a less definite suggestion of concrete ways and means), and which therefore (especially when applied to a project, plan, scheme, or the like) is or seems to be capable of working out or of being worked out successfully; as, "My cousin...express[ed] a purpose, if the matter could be contrived, of bringing you with her; I was willing to believe that you had...found it *feasible*" (*Cowper*); "I am not here concerned with the question whether such a 'humanistic' civilization as that aimed at by Professor Babbitt is or is not desirable; only with the question whether it is *feasible*" (*T. S. Eliot*); "Was it really *feasible* to offer Anglicanism as a world religion?" (*C. Mackenzie*). Oftentimes, *feasible* specifically implies suitability to an expressed or understood purpose, or appropriateness as a means of accomplishing a given or implied end; as, a northern resort is not *feasible* for some invalids in winter; the suggested plot was not *feasible* for the type of play he wished to write.

Ana. Practical, *practicable: *expedient, advisable.

2 *Probable, likely.

Ana. Credible, believable, colorable, *plausible: potential, dormant, *latent.

post, *n.* *Position, place, situation, office, job, berth, billet, capacity.

posterior, *adj.* **Posterior, rear, hind, hinder, after, back** agree in meaning behind in order of arrangement in space. **Posterior** is the formal or technical term for that which is situated behind (opposed to *anterior*). "To an anatomical eye the *posterior* part of the skull is even more striking than the anterior" (*T. H. Huxley*). **Rear** belongs especially to military usage, but has general application with reference to structures, vehicles, and the like; as, the *rear* ranks of a column; the *rear* guard (cf. to bring up the *rear*); the *rear* wall of a house. **Hind** (opposed to *front, fore*) is used most commonly with reference to related parts, and designates the member or pair which is in the rear; as, the *hind* wheels of a wagon; the *hind* legs of a horse. It has sometimes more general application. "The lower and *hind* part of the body" (*J. Moore*). **Hinder** is equivalent to *hind* or (in nontechnical use) *posterior;* as, "the *hinder* part of the ship" (*Mark* iv. 38); "the *hinder* part of the skull" (*T. H. Huxley*). **After** is usually confined to nautical usage and applies to that which is abaft the midship section, or in the rear part of a vessel, or relatively near to this part; as, the *after* cabin or hatchway. **Back** applies to that which is thought of as behind, remote from, or inferior or subsidiary to, the main or more important part; as, *back* stairs; a *back* door, seat, settlement; cf. the *back*woods.

Ant. Anterior.

postern. Gate, *door, gateway, doorway, portal.

postpone. *Defer, suspend, stay, intermit.

Ana. *Delay, retard, slow, slacken: *adjourn, prorogue.

postulant. *Novice, novitiate, probationer, neophyte, apprentice.

postulate, *n.* Presupposition, presumption, assumption, premise, position. See under PRESUPPOSE.

Ana. *Principle, axiom, theorem, fundamental, law: theory, *hypothesis.

postulate, *v.* *Presuppose, presume, assume, premise, posit.

Ana. Affirm, aver, predicate, *assert.

posture, *n.* **1 Posture, attitude, pose** come into comparison when they denote a position assumed by the body or the disposition of the parts of the body with relation to one another. The same distinctions in implications and connotations mark the uses of the verbs **posture, attitudinize, pose. Posture** applies either to a position that is habitual or characteristic or to one that is consciously or unconsciously determined with reference to the needs or the mood of the moment. In the former case, the word means the way in which one holds oneself and refers to one's physical carriage or bearing; as, her *posture* is excellent; pictures illustrating defects of *posture;* examples of correct *posture.* In the latter case, the word requires qualification (as, a sitting *posture;* a kneeling *posture;* the *posture* of supplication) or the assistance of the context to evoke a picture of how the parts of the body are disposed or to reveal the intention or end. "There's a *posture* for a man to fight in! His weight isn't resting on his legs" (*Shaw*). "Nearly all the opera of the world is so supported. A few rich cads pay the bills, their wives *posture*...in the boxes" (*Mencken*). **Attitude** applies chiefly to a posture that is unconsciously expressive or is intentionally assumed, often as a result of a particular mood or state of mind; as, not only her standing aside from the crowd but also her *attitude* betrayed her intense shyness; like an actor in the silent pictures striking an *attitude* (or *attitudinizing*) in order to register an emotion. "When her wooer turned from her she rested her arms against the mantel-shelf and bowed her face in her hands....he...left the room without her hearing him or changing her *attitude*" (*E. Wharton*). "Uttering platitudes In stained-glass *attitudes*" (*W. S. Gilbert*). **Pose** applies to an attitude or to a position of some part or parts of the body which is assumed for the sake of effect, or which, if unconscious, strikes the observer as effective or as affected; as, the *pose* of a model; to *pose* for a picture. "Assuming a *pose* for inspection at the threshhold of the parlour, [she] would demand of Samuel: 'Shall I do?' " (*Bennett*). "She was very charming at her instrument [the harp]; the *pose* suited her tip-tilted canary head, and her little foot and white arms" (*Cather*). "The lofty *pose* of her head expressed an habitual sense of her own consequence" (*Shaw*).

Ana. *Bearing, carriage, deportment, mien.

2 Situation, *state, condition, mode, status, estate.

Ana. *Position, stand, attitude: readiness, quickness, promptness (see corresponding adjectives at QUICK).

posture, *v.* Attitudinize, pose. See under POSTURE, *n.*

pot. *Bet, wager, stake, blind, ante.

potent. *Powerful, puissant, forceful, forcible.

Ana. *Vigorous, energetic, strenuous, lusty: *effective, efficacious, effectual: *strong, sturdy, tenacious.

Ant. Impotent.

potential. Dormant, *latent, quiescent, abeyant.
Ant. Active, actual.

pother, *n.* Flurry, fuss, ado, *stir, bustle.
Ana. *Haste, hurry, speed, dispatch: agitation, upset, perturbation, disturbance (see corresponding verbs at DISCOMPOSE).
Con. Coolness, collectedness, composure (see corresponding adjectives at COOL).

pouch. *Bag, sack.

pound, *v.* *Beat, pummel, buffet, baste, belabor, thrash, thresh.
Ana. *Strike, hit, smite, slug: batter, mutilate (see MAIM).

poverty. Poverty, indigence, penury, want, destitution, privation are here compared as denoting the state of one who is poor or without enough to live upon. **Poverty,** the most comprehensive of these terms, may imply either the lack of all personal property or possessions (as, the monk's vow of *poverty* prevents him from having anything he may call his own) or it may imply resources so limited that one is deprived of many of the necessities and of all of the comforts of life (as, "in Syria he feathered his nest so successfully that in two years he raised himself from *poverty* to opulence"—*Buchan*). **Indigence** (often opposed to *affluence*) does not suggest dire or absolute poverty, but it always implies reduced or straitened circumstances and therefore usually connotes the endurance of many hardships and the lack of comforts; as, to endure *indigence* in his old age; clothing neat and clean but somewhat threadbare gave evidence of his *indigence;* "The road that leads from competence and peace To *indigence*" (*Cowper*). **Penury** may or may not imply abject poverty but it does suggest such an extreme of need, especially of money, that one is cramped or oppressed by the lack of it; as, "Chill *Penury* repress'd their noble rage" (*Gray*); "she has to take anything she can get in the way of a husband rather than face *penury*" (*Shaw*). But *penury* may imply the semblance of poverty that comes from miserliness or penuriousness (cf. *penurious* under STINGY); as, "Her relatives considered that the *penury* of her table discredited the Mingott name, which had always been associated with good living" (*E. Wharton*). **Want** (see also LACK) and **destitution** both imply an extreme of poverty that leaves one without the means of mere subsistence: both terms, especially the latter, often imply starvation and homelessness or the need of charity; as, he is in great *want;* a small weekly gift that secures a family against *want;* "Here to the homeless child of *want* My door is open still" (*Goldsmith*); "One estate, passing by death from heir to heir three times...in one year (as happens easily during a war) is wiped out by them [death duties], and the heirs reduced from affluence to *destitution*" (*Shaw*). **Privation,** though implying a state that is comparable to the one suggested by *indigence*, does not, as the latter term does, necessarily suggest poverty: although it always implies a condition of being without many of the necessities of existence or an insufficient supply of them, it may connote another cause of such a condition than a lack of money or of possessions of value; as, an explorer must often undergo prolonged *privations;* months of *privation* had made every member of the family look scrawny and ill-nourished.
Ana. Necessity, *need, exigency: strait, pass, pinch (see JUNCTURE).
Ant. Riches.

power, *n.* **1 Power, force, energy, strength, might, puissance, arm** come into comparison when they mean the ability to exert effort as in doing, bearing, resisting, or the like. **Power** is the most general of these terms, and denotes the ability, latent or exerted, inherent or acquired, physical or mental or spiritual, to act or be acted upon, to effect something or to affect or be affected by something; as, the finest machine in the world is useless without a motor to give it *power;* the mechanical *power* of the internal-combustion engine; the king has great *power* over his people; to raise the productive *power* of a body of workers; "the sound of a great flood moving with majesty and *power*" (*Cather*); "What is it...which has made it [the Authorized Version] a factor of such *power* in the development of our speech?" (*Lowes*); "Her pained reserve had no *power* to awe them into decency" (*Conrad*); to give an attorney the *power* to act for one; "hateful to feel their *power* over me when I knew that they were nothing but fancies" (*Hudson*). **Force,** as here compared (see also FORCE, 2), implies the exhibition or the exercise of power: the term usually therefore carries with it a suggestion of actually overcoming resistance, actually setting a thing in motion or accelerating its motion, actually driving a person or thing in the desired direction, or the like; thus, one has the *power* to do something but exerts *force* when he accomplishes it; a wind gathers *force;* "accumulated *force* which drove them as if discharged from a cross-bow" (*Jefferies*); "[the tiller of the soil] deals with a hard and rebellious element not to be conquered mainly by skill...but mainly by *force*" (*H. Ellis*); "He had in fact settled down into a dilettante, having learnt...to scorn the triumphs which he lacked the *force* to win" (*Bennett*). Therefore, *force* is often applied to a person or thing that exerts its power with marked efficacy or efficiency; as, "They believed that the Church was the only *force* which could consolidate the nation" (*Inge*); "Giles Overreach [in Massinger's *New Way to Pay Old Debts*] is essentially a great *force* directed upon small objects" (*T. S. Eliot*); "Art is but the expression of a harmony of life, a fine balance of all the *forces* of the human spirit" (*Binyon*). **Energy** in practically all of its senses implies contrast to *power* in the sense of latent power and denotes either the power that is expended in actual work or the power that is capable of being transformed into work. In the physical sciences, *energy* is an extremely important term and is, in general, thought of as one aspect of matter, of which the other is mass: when matter, regardless of the size or weight of the mass, is in motion, its capacity for work is described as *actual,* or *kinetic, energy;* when its power for work is dependent on its position with reference to other matter, its capacity for work is described as *potential energy;* thus, a machine that is being operated exhibits kinetic *energy;* a projectile so placed that it will reach the target at which it is aimed when it is fired exhibits potential *energy.* In these sciences energy may be mechanical, electrical, molecular, chemical, or the like; as, "the electrical *energy* expended in the circuit is derived from the chemical *energy* of the freshly compounded battery" (*Karl K. Darrow*). In general use, especially as applied to persons, *energy* implies stored-up power releasing itself in work or craving such release; as, "The *power* of poetry is, by a single word...to instil *energy* into the mind, which compels the imagination to produce the picture" (*Coleridge*); "The prodigious *energy* put forth by industry in time of war" (*A. C. Morrison*); "Politics and patriotism afforded practical outlets for Greek *energy*" (*B. Russell*); "It was marvellous...that the *energy* of her spirit could carry through so triumphantly her frail nervous system" (*H. Ellis*). **Strength** applies to the power that resides in a person or thing as a result of qualities or conditions that enable him or it to exert force or to manifest great energy or to resist pressure, strain, stress, attack, or the like. Physically, *strength* implies soundness, as of health, of construction, or the like (as, *strength* of body; the tensile *strength* of a rope; the blasting *strength* of an explosive); mentally and morally, it implies capacity for endurance, resolution, intrepidity, or the like (as, to show *strength* in trial, or temptation, or in danger); when applied to armies, forces, fleets, and the like, it usually implies numbers, equipment, resources, etc. (as, it was impossible to estimate the exact *strength* of the enemy's army; a fleet incomparable in *strength* with any other). *Might, puissance, arm* are more or less rhetorical or poetic words meaning operative or effective power or force. **Might** often suggests great or superhuman power; it is therefore appropriate when the reference is to supernatural beings or supranatural forces or to human power that is so strong that it cannot be gainsaid. "Protect us by thy *might,* Great God, our King" (*S. F. Smith*). "Let us have faith that right makes *might*" (*Lincoln*). "The pride and *might* and vivid strength of things" (*Galsworthy*). **Puissance** is often indistinguishable from *might,* but in very discriminating use it generally also connotes an impressive display of power. "We should advance ourselves To look with forehead bold and big enough Upon the power and *puissance* of the King" (*Shak.*). "Wherefore should not strength and might There... weakest prove Where boldest, though to sight unconquerable? His [Satan's] *puissance*... I mean to try" (*Milton*). **Arm,** which is a figurative extension of *arm,* the upper human limb, is capable of two applications, both implying operative or effective power. Sometimes, it is applicable to the power, or body having authority, that executes, as one's arm executes that which one's mind conceives or one's will directs; thus, the police force is the *arm* of the law; the civil authority was in past times called the secular *arm,* that is, the *arm* of the ecclesiastical authority. *Arm* is also, in military use, applied to one branch of the service; as, the air *arm.* Sometimes it is applicable to the might that shows itself, especially in overcoming an enemy: in these cases, *arm* often seems metaphorical rather than idiomatic English. "Son of man, I have broken the *arm* of Pharaoh king of Egypt" (*Ezekiel* xxx. 21). "To whom is the *arm* of the Lord revealed?" (*Isaiah* liii. 1). "He, whose strong *arm* the Orient could not check, He, who had held the Soldan at his beck" (*Wordsworth*).

Ana. *Ability, capacity, capability: *gift, genius, talent, faculty: qualification, competence (see corresponding adjectives at ABLE).

Ant. Impotence.

2 Power, faculty, function come into comparison only when they mean an ability to act or perform in a given way or a capacity for a particular kind of action or performance. Since, as so defined, all of these terms are used specifically of human beings, they primarily suggest a mental ability or capacity that controls or directs conscious operations of the body or spirit as well as of the mind. **Power,** the comprehensive term of this group, may apply to a capacity for action or performance that does not, or apparently does not, call the mind into play (as, the *power* to digest food; the *power* of reflex movement) but it more frequently applies to an ability or capacity that involves either mental activity or mental receptiveness (as, the *power* to think clearly; the *power* to understand; to lose one's *power* to remember; "to Rima had been given this quickness of mind and *power* to divine distant things"—*Hudson;* the *power* of hearing delicate sounds; "distinguishing in the soul three principles or *powers,* reason, passion, and desire"—*G. L. Dickinson*). **Faculty,** often but far from always, applies to a native or inherent power: in earlier use it applied especially to those powers which were the possession of every normal human being, though not always manifested in the first months of infancy or the earliest years of childhood; as, the *faculty* of hearing; the *faculty* of speech. Still later, the word became a technical term of psychology referable to any one of the three (or more) powers of the human mind (often will, memory, reason), which psychologists discovered by an analysis of the entity called "mind" or "soul"; as, "The understanding and will, are two *faculties* of the mind" (*Locke*); "The truth is that memory and imagination, the two most important human *faculties,* are scarcely cultivated at all" (*Grandgent*). Individual analyses not only resulted in enumerating widely different faculties and in widely differing definitions of faculties called by the same name (such as reason and understanding), but brought out a tendency to regard each faculty as a separate and distinct thing; consequently, the term as applied to one of the enumerable powers of the mind or soul has fallen into disrepute and is avoided in current psychological use. However, *faculty* as meaning generally a distinct, discoverable power of the human mind or soul, and *faculties* as meaning all the powers of the mind which are essential for its successful operation, are both found in good writing, especially nontechnical writing; as, "There has been endless discussion whether we have a distinct *faculty* for the knowledge of God" (*Inge*); "It is the one occasion when violent grief, disturbing his *faculties,* appears in his correspondence" (*Belloc*). In current psychology, **function,** as denoting an activity which can be more or less definitely associated with the brain or the central nervous system or a part of either, is usually preferred to *faculty* and, sometimes, to *power.* "All mental activities, such as seeing, hearing, perceiving, conceiving, imagining, recalling, etc., are termed *functions*" (*Carl Murchison*). Some psychologists distinguish kinds of psychology according to the stress laid upon mental processes as evidences of the existence of faculties (*faculty psychology*) or as activities involving the sense organs, central nervous system, and brain (*functional psychology*).

3 Power, authority, jurisdiction, control, command, sway, dominion are here compared as meaning the right or prerogative of determining, ruling, or governing, or the exercise of that right or prerogative. **Power** even in this specific sense never loses its fundamental implication of ability, but in this case it is a capacity for rule that resides in one by virtue of one's rank, one's office, or even one's character or personality; as, in an absolute monarchy the king has sole *power;* all *power* over life and death was placed in the hands of the general; knowledge is *power.* "It is a strange desire, to seek *power,* and to lose liberty; or to seek *power* over others, and to lose *power* over a man's self" (*Bacon*). *Power* when used with reference to a definite person or body or office commonly connotes divisibility or strict limitation; as, the trustees have *power* of appointment; the charter gives the city *power* to tax sales; he was given *power* of attorney but he never exercised that *power;* there is no division of *power* when a dictator rules. "It is not enough that a statute goes to the verge of constitutional *power.* We must be able to see clearly that it goes beyond that *power*" (*Justice Holmes*). **Authority** is often used interchangeably with *power;* nevertheless, there is an essential difference in meaning. In precise use, *authority* refers to power resident in or exercised by another than oneself; thus, one may have *power* (not *authority*) to determine one's own actions, but a parent or a master or a ruler has the *authority* (or, less precisely, the *power*) to determine the actions of those under him; so, one is obedient to *authority* (not *power*); *authority* (more precise than *power*) is needed to restrain persons from infringing upon the rights of others; the schoolmaster refrained from exercising his *authority* until all attempts at persuasion failed. "The object is to induce the child to lend of his own free will; so long as *authority* is required, the end aimed at has not been achieved" (*B. Russell*). "*Authority* in the religious sphere generally means absolute or infallible *authority*, such as Catholics ascribe to the Church, some Protestants to the Bible, and a few mystics to the Inner Light" (*Inge*). *Power* and *authority*, especially in the plural, often refer to the person or persons who have or hold power or authority as defined. *Powers*, however, usually occurs in the phrase "the *powers* that be" ("The *powers* that be are ordained of God"—*Romans* xiii. 1) and is either somewhat more comprehensive or less explicit in its reference than "the *authorities*," which often means the persons who have authority in the special instance to decide, to punish, or the like; as, he is always in opposition to the *powers* that be; he threatened to report the offense to the *authorities* (in this case, to the police). In still another sense, *authority* often implies a delegation or grant of power or an authorization to speak, act, or the like, in the name of the one having the real power; as, who gave you the *authority* to remove this fence? "Man, proud man Drest in a little brief *authority*" (*Shak.*). **Jurisdiction** implies possession of legal or actual power to determine, to rule, or to govern within definitely assigned limits, and of the authority to so act in all matters that come within the sphere of that power, or in figurative use, of the thing's influence. "The principle of law is too well settled to be disputed, that a court can give no judgment for either party, where it has no *jurisdiction*" (*Ch. Just. Taney*). "This new and populous community must, for the present, the Kansas Bishop wrote, be accounted under Father Latour's *jurisdiction*" (*Cather*). "Demanding from us a complete subjection to the poetry that occupies us, yet never asking of poetry more than lies within its proper *jurisdiction*" (*Day Lewis*). **Control,** as here compared, stresses possession of the authority to restrain or curb and its effective exercise, or of actual power to regulate or keep responsive to one's will not only persons, but things; thus, a teacher who has lost *control* of his class has reached a point where the pupils no longer recognize his authority; a fire has gone beyond *control* when those who are fighting it have lost all power to check it. "To be virtuous [to the ancient Greek] was to act under the *control* of the universal reason which was supposed to dwell in man as man" (*G. L. Dickinson*). "He talked a great deal of a thing called '*control*.' 'When you get ready to start for yourself keep that in mind....Sell stock and borrow money at the bank...but don't give up *control*....That's the way I made my success. I always kept the *control*' " (*S. Anderson*). **Command** implies such control as makes one the master of men, and such authority that obedience to one's order or one's will either inevitably follows or is inexorably enforced; thus, one speaks of the officer in *command* (rather than in *control*) of a regiment or says that a person has *command* of a situation (rather than *control* of it) when he completely dominates it or has all persons or things involved in it under control; so, the president assumes *command* of the army and navy in time of war. "How, in one house, Should many people, under two *commands*, Hold amity?" (*Shak.*). *Command* is also used in reference to things which one has mastered so thoroughly that one encounters no resistance or interference in using, recalling, or controlling them. "His brush did its work with a steady and sure stroke that indicated *command* of his materials" (*Jefferies*). "These passages [of Shakespeare] are comparable to the best bombast of Kyd or Marlowe, with a greater *command* of language and a greater *control* of the emotion" (*T. S. Eliot*). **Sway** tends to be slightly rhetorical because its use in this sense was originally figurative and the word still carries a hint of its etymological implications of swinging or sweeping through an arc or circle; hence, when a word is desired that means power but also connotes extent or scope, and preponderant influence, compelling authority, potency, or the like, *sway* is the proper choice; as, the British Empire has extended its *sway* to every quarter of the earth. "Primal spirits beneath his *sway*" (*Shelley*). "We can escape from Custom's idiot *sway*" (*Cowper*). "The law of compensation rules supreme in art, as it holds *sway* in life" (*Lowes*). **Dominion,** in precise use, imputes sovereignty to the power in question or supremacy to the authority in question; as, the government of the United States has *dominion* over its dependencies, but many of them have the right of self-government. "The powers of the general government, it has been said, are delegated by the States...and must be exercised in subordination to the States, who alone possess supreme *dominion*" (*Ch. Just. Marshall*). "Foreign *dominion* in any shape would soon become hateful" (*Freeman*).

Ana. *Right, privilege, prerogative, birthright: management, direction (see corresponding verbs at CONDUCT): ascendancy, *supremacy.

powerful. Powerful, potent, puissant, forceful, forcible come into comparison as meaning having or manifesting power to effect great or striking results. **Powerful** is applicable only to that which stands out from the rest of its kind as exceeding the others in its display of strength or force, or in its manifestation of energy: it also usually implies an effectiveness that has been proved rather than attributed; as, the most *powerful* ruler of his age; a *powerful* pugilist; a *powerful* fleet; a *powerful* argument that no one could gainsay; a *powerful* cathartic. **Potent,** though it implies powerfulness, is applicable chiefly to that which derives or seems to derive that character from some hidden or latent virtue or quality rather than from an observable or measurable power or force; as, he exercised a *potent* spell over her imagination; a *potent* medicine; "magic *potent* over sun and star" (*Wordsworth*); "How *potent* is this Oriental blood in Napoleon, in Goethe, in Heine, Victor Hugo" (*J. R. Lowell*); "metre with its repetition is a *potent* means of compacting words into the expression of spontaneous life" (*S. Alexander*); "illusions...no longer *potent* because they are no longer really believed" (*J. W. Krutch*). **Puissant,** a bookish word, referring chiefly to persons (usually princes and potentates), to military or naval forces, or to bodies politic, connotes more the outward attributes of power: it commonly suggests a great and abiding strength; as, a *puissant* monarch; a *puissant* commonwealth; a *puissant* army; "Most...mighty, and most *puissant* Caesar" (*Shak.*). "Methinks I see in my mind a noble and *puissant* nation rousing herself like a strong man after sleep, and shaking her invincible locks" (*Milton*). The last two words of the group, though somewhat more restrained in their suggestion of power, nevertheless imply an ability to effect impressive results. **Forceful** stresses the possession or manifestation of force as a quality: it therefore suggests marked vigor or energy or strength, regardless of whether it is being exercised or not. The word is applicable even to that which makes no display of effort or violence, provided it impresses its undoubted force on the observer; as, a *forceful* personality; a *forceful* style; a *forceful* writer; "he relied more on a *forceful* clarity to convince his readers than on the brilliant and exciting ambiguities of propagandist eloquence" (*A. Huxley*). **Forcible,** on the other hand, suggests the actual exertion of power or force: it often implies the use of physical violence in attaining one's ends; as, to make a *forcible* entry into a building; to take *forcible* possession of goods not paid for; to favor *forcible* measures in treating unruly prisoners. There are times, however, when *forceful* falls short because it does not imply aggressiveness, militancy, or decided potency. In such cases, discriminating writers often prefer *forcible;* thus, one might prefer to describe Theodore Roosevelt's personality or a dictator's speech as *forcible* rather than *forceful.*

Ana. *Able, capable, competent: efficacious, effectual, *effective, efficient: *vigorous, energetic, strenuous.

Ant. Powerless: inefficacious.

powerless. **Powerless, impotent, impuissant** agree in meaning unable to effect one's purpose, intention, or end. **Powerless** denotes merely lack of power or efficacy; as, he suddenly found himself *powerless* to move; "*powerless* as an infant" (*De Quincey*); "Argument is *powerless* against either feeling" (*Hardy*); "I hope that the luxuries of this palatial mansion are *powerless* to corrupt your heart" (*Shaw*). **Impotent** (see also STERILE, 1) implies not only powerlessness, but positive weakness or, especially, complete ineffectiveness; as, "An angry little spitfire sea continually sprits and thrashes with *impotent* irascibility" (*Stevenson*); "terrible and *impotent* rage" (*Wilde*); "Fifteen years later one King of England was put to death, an *impotent* victim" (*Belloc*); "Set him [a Frenchman] to write poetry, he is limited, artificial, and *impotent;* set him to write prose, he is free, natural, and effective" (*Arnold*). **Impuissant,** like *puissant* (see under POWERFUL), is a literary term: often it is indistinguishable from *impotent,* but it is sometimes preferred when there is a contrast between the greatness of the attempt and the complete ineffectiveness of the result; as, an *impuissant* man defying fate; to send an *impuissant* army against a puissant invader.

Ana. Inert, *inactive, passive, supine: feeble, *weak, infirm, decrepit.

Ant. Powerful: efficacious. — ***Con.*** *Effective, efficient.

practicable. **1** Feasible, *possible.

Ana. Operating *or* operable, working *or* workable, functioning (see corresponding verbs at ACT).

Ant. Impracticable.

2 Practicable, practical are not synonyms in good current use, but they are sometimes confused when they imply a capacity for being used or turned to account. **Practicable** (see also POSSIBLE, 1) applies chiefly to things which have not been worked out (as a plan, project, scheme, design) or which have been recently devised, invented, constructed, or the like (such as a new machine, a new form of entertainment, a new implement), and about which one of the following questions arises: is it capable of being developed or worked out, or is it likely to prove successful in operation or use; thus, many plans for the eradication of poverty are dismissed as "not *practicable*" (or "*impracticable*"); the possibility of wireless telegraphy was questioned until Marconi demonstrated its *practicability;* no *practicable* winter automobile that operates on runners rather than on wheels has yet been devised. **Practical** applies not only to things (concrete and immaterial) but also, as *practicable* never does, to persons. The term in all of its senses stresses an opposition to that which is *theoretical, speculative, ideal, unrealistic, imaginative,* or the like, and implies a relation to the actual life of man, his daily needs, or the conditions which must be met. When the term also implies a capacity for use, it emphasizes actual usefulness rather than highly probable or merely discovered usableness; thus, the automobile when first invented was not regarded as *practicable* by many persons but as a result of numerous improvements in the course of time it is now regarded as a most *practical* vehicle for pleasure, business, transportation, and the like; "Without his [Faraday's] researches in magnetic electricity we might have missed...those most *practical* machines of our modern life, the dynamo and the telephone" (*H. Ellis*). Hence, *practical* may apply to anything that is such in kind, character, amount, effect, or the like, that it is definitely useful or serviceable in actual life; as, very few students of French gain a *practical* knowledge of it unless they spend at least a year in France; "In everything he undertook he demanded a utilitarian purpose and a *practical* result" (*Buchan*); "These writers cannot confirm any one in the faith; they can merely have the *practical* value of removing prejudices from the minds of those who have not the faith but who might possibly come to it" (*T. S. Eliot*); "With... the real, *practical* kindness of leaving some money for her board...they moved on" (*Deland*).

practical. *Practicable.

practically. *Virtually, morally.

practice *or* **practise,** *v.* **Practice** (*or, as a verb, spelled also* **practise**), **exercise, drill** come into comparison as verbs meaning to perform or cause one to perform an act or series of acts repeatedly, and as nouns denoting such repeated activity or exertion. **Practice** fundamentally implies doing, especially doing habitually or regularly, often in contrast to thinking, believing, and professing, or to theory and precept; as, to *practice* what one preaches; the *practice* of one's religion; to *practice* medicine; the *practice* of one's profession; in theory, every citizen votes but in *practice,* rarely more than half avail themselves of the privilege; "If a thing has been *practiced* for two hundred years by common consent, it will need a strong case for the Fourteenth Amendment to affect it" (*Justice Holmes*). *Practice* also implies a doing over and over again of certain acts for the sake of acquiring proficiency, dexterity, skill, or the like, or in the hope of attaining perfection; as, "*Practice* makes perfect" (*Proverb*); to *practice* on the piano one hour each day; rifle *practice;* "I suppose they teach you to make Latin verses...? That's very good *practice*" (*Arch. Marshall*). **Exercise** fundamentally implies a keeping busy or a setting to work; it usually presupposes the possession of a power or of powers which can be developed or strengthened only by activity, especially repeated activity, or can be manifested only in practice; as, give him plenty of opportunities to *exercise* his intelligence; a wise father avoids the *exercise* of authority except when other means fail; "he had liberality, and he had the means of *exercising* it" (*Austen*); "so long as a child is with adults, it has no occasion for the *exercise* of a number of important virtues, namely, those required by the strong in dealing with the weak" (*B. Russell*); "Will can only be *exercised* in the presence of something which retards or resists it" (*Inge*). Like *practice, exercise* may be used also to imply acts performed repeatedly for the sake of an ulterior end, but *exercise* usually refers either literally or figuratively to those directed to the attainment of health or physical vigor; as, Tom was being *exercised* like a raw recruit; to grow mentally dull through lack of physical *exercise.* "*Exercise* is good for the muscles of mind and to keep it well in hand for work" (*Lowell*). "Poetry is in France an *exercise,* not an expression. It is to real French expression, to prose, what gymnastics and hygiene are to health" (*Brownell*). **Drill** fundamentally connotes an intention to fix physical or mental habits as deeply as though they were bored in by the use of the drill, the tool; in current use, the term stresses repetition, as of military evolutions, of word pronunciations, of grammatical rules, or the like, as a means of training and disciplining the body or mind or of forming correct habits; as, to *drill* troops; a *drill* in arithmetic. "This is a real danger in modern education, owing to the reaction against the old severe *drill*. The mental work involved in the *drill* was good; what was bad was the killing of intellectual interests" (*B. Russell*).

Ana. *Perform, execute, fulfill: *follow, pursue: *repeat, iterate.

practice, *n.* **1** *Habit, habitude, usage, custom, consuetude, use, wont.

Ana. Procedure, *process, proceeding: *method, system, way, fashion, mode, manner.

2 Exercise, drill. See under PRACTICE, *v.*

Ana. *Use, utility, usefulness: usage, *form, convention, convenance: pursuit, calling, *work.

Ant. Theory: precept.

pragmatical, pragmatic. Officious, meddlesome, *impertinent, intrusive, obtrusive.

Ana. *Curious, prying, inquisitive: *busy, assiduous, sedulous: agitated, disturbed, perturbed (see DISCOMPOSE): interfering, interposing, intervening (see INTERPOSE).

praise, *v.* **Praise, laud, acclaim, extol, eulogize** agree in meaning to express approbation or esteem. **Praise** often implies no more than warmly expressed commendation. "What we admire we *praise*, and when we *praise*, Advance it into notice" (*Cowper*). When specifically referred to persons, it frequently suggests the judgment of a superior; as, to *praise* a pupil for his diligence. However, it is also used in reference to God (or a god), or a saint. Then it implies glorification by acts of homage, such as song or prayer. "*Praise* God from whom all blessings flow" (*Ken*). Sometimes it connotes thanksgiving. "Though we have not beef and mutton...yet (God be *praised*) we want them not; our Indian corn answers for all" (*Winthrop*). **Laud** implies very high, sometimes excessive, praise; as, *lauded* to the skies. "Both of the writers *lauded*...contemporaries who were certainly no better than middling performers in their several arts" (*C. E. Montague*). **Acclaim** usually suggests enthusiastic expression of approval, etc., as by loud applause or cheers. "Dr. Welch...was *acclaimed* not only in his own country but throughout the civilized world" (*V. Heiser*). **Extol** retains its etymological implication of lifting up or raising, and suggests praise that exalts or magnifies. "They...*extoll'd* your perfections to the heavens" (*B. Jonson*). It is often used when a contrast between approbation or esteem and their opposites is enforced. "To find Virtue *extolled*, and Vice stigmatized" (*Addison*). "An age must always decry itself and *extol* its forbears" (*Galsworthy*). **Eulogize,** sometimes interchangeable with *extol*, differs from it in implying formality both in the method and in the occasion; very frequently it suggests a set composition or oration (*eulogy*), suitable for a funeral or testimonial. "He *eulogised* constitutional government as immeasurably superior to despotism" (*Lecky*). "*Eulogies* turn into elegies" (*Spenser*).

Ana. *Commend, applaud, compliment: *exalt, magnify, aggrandize.

Ant. Blame. — ***Con.*** Asperse, *malign, traduce, vilify, calumniate, defame, libel: disparage, *decry, detract from, belittle: reprehend, reprobate, censure, denounce, *criticize.

prank, *n.* **Prank, caper, antic, monkeyshine, dido** agree in meaning a playful, often a mischievous, act or trick. **Prank** still carries the strongest implication of devilry of all these words, though now there is little suggestion of malice and greater emphasis upon the practical joke than in the past. "Hear thou...how many fruitless *pranks* This ruffian hath botch'd up" (*Shak.*). "His [Middleton's] comedies...are long-winded; the fathers are heavy fathers, and rant as heavy fathers should; the sons are wild and wanton sons, and perform all the *pranks* to be expected of them" (*T. S. Eliot*). **Caper** still suggests frisking and bounding like a kid; it does not as often in modern use as in the past evoke the image of dancing and leaping (as, "Faith, I can cut a *caper*" *Shak.*), but rather, especially in the plural, the romping and running of children in overflowing spirits and frolicsome mood; as, to find childish *capers* annoying. **Antic** stresses the ludicrousness and grotesqueness of the movements, gestures, and postures, rather than the spirit in which the acts or tricks are performed; as, the *antics* of a clown. Sometimes, however, it suggests "grandstand play"; as, to watch the *antics* of boys climbing poles. "The Casterbridge tradition was that to drive stock...hideous cries, coupled with yahoo *antics*...should be used" (*Hardy*). **Monkeyshine** (a slang term in American use) may be applied to a caper or antic but it usually also implies amusing mimicry or extreme nimbleness in movement. It is a frequent designation of the mischievous tricks and capers of young boys. **Dido** (also slang) adds to *prank* the implications of racket making and often, of malicious mischief; as, to cut up *didos* on Halloween.

Ana. Frolic, gambol, rollick, sport, play (see under PLAY, *v.*): levity, *lightness, frivolity: vagary, *caprice, freak, whim, whimsey.

prank, *v.* *Preen, prune, prink, primp, perk up, doll up.

Ana. *Adorn, ornament, decorate, deck, bedeck, embellish, beautify.

prate. Chatter, *chat, gab, patter, prattle, babble, gabble, jabber, gibber.

prattle. Chatter, patter, prate, gab, *chat, babble, gabble, jabber, gibber.

pray. Plead, petition, appeal, sue. See under PRAYER.

Ana. Supplicate, entreat, beseech, implore, *beg.

prayer. Prayer, suit, plea, petition, appeal and their corresponding intransitive verbs **pray, sue, plead, petition, appeal** agree in meaning an earnest and, usually, a formal request for something (or to make such a request). **Prayer** and **pray** (*for* or *to*) imply that the request is made to a person or body invested with authority or power, or especially to God or a god; the words usually therefore connote humility in approach and often fervor in entreating. "We do *pray* for mercy; And that same *prayer* doth teach us all to render The deeds of mercy" (*Shak.*). In religious use, however, where *prayer* and *pray* always imply an act of worship, they may or may not connote a request or petition. This implication of making a request is retained, however, in the specific legal use of these terms in a court of equity, where formally one *prays* for relief; the *prayer* in a bill in equity is the part that specifies the kind of relief sought. The words are also used in formal petitions or remonstrances to a legislative body. **Suit** and **sue** (*for* or *to*) imply a deferential and formal solicitation, sometimes for help or relief, but often for a favor, a grace, a kindness, and the like. Except in legal use (see SUIT, *n.*, 3) in reference to the addresses of a man (a suitor) to the lady he hopes to marry, and in some idiomatic phrases such as, "to *sue* for peace," the words are somewhat archaic in flavor. "There Kings shall *sue*, and suppliant States be seen Once more to bend before a BRITISH QUEEN" (*Pope*). "Is it that I *sue* not in some form Of scrupulous law, that ye deny my *suit*?" (*Shelley*). **Plea** (see also APOLOGY) and **plead** (*for*) often suggest a court of law, the status of a defendant or of an accused person, and his formal statements in answer to the plaintiff's allegations or the state's charge. *Plea*, especially, has technical senses not here considered. In general use, however, both terms imply argument or urgent entreaty, of which self-justification, a desire for vindication or support, or strong partisanship, is usually the motive; as, to make a *plea* for forgiveness; to *plead* for a more tolerant attitude. "Though justice be thy *plea*, consider this, That, in the course of justice, none of us Should see salvation" (*Shak.*). "I *plead* frankly for the theistic hypothesis as involving fewer difficulties than any other" (*Inge*). **Petition** and its verb **petition** (*for*) imply a formal and specific request, often in writing, presented to the person or body that has power to grant it. In modern use, the words carry little or no connotation of abject humility of entreaty or the like; rather they suggest a right to make a request, as one of the sovereign people or as one who is confident that it will be judged on its merits; as, to *petition* (or send a *petition* to) the legislature to repeal an obnoxious law; to make a *petition* to the court for a new trial. **Appeal** and **appeal** (*for* or *to*) basically imply a call for attention to and favorable consideration of one's plea; as, to *appeal* for mercy; to *appeal* to one's family for help. Often, they additionally connote an insistence on being heard and hence, a change of plea from an inferior to a superior power, such as a higher court or a higher authority, or, in more recent use, the emotions, in an attempt to evoke a favorable response or judgment; as, to *appeal* to the supreme court for a new trial; the court of last *appeal*. "Against the decree of fate there is no *appeal*" (*A. Huxley*). "Mantalinis and Dobbins who pursue women with *appeals* to their pity or jealousy or vanity" (*Shaw*). In current use, the terms often omit the "to" phrase and imply a sympathetic or favorable response or a compelling quality; as, an *appealing* way; the song has a human *appeal*.

Ana. Supplication, entreaty, beseeching, imploring, begging (see BEG): worship, adoration (see under REVERE).

preamble. *Introduction, prologue, induction, prelude, overture, preface, foreword, prolegomenon, proem, exordium, prolusion, protasis, avant-propos.

precarious. *Dangerous, hazardous, perilous, jeopardous, risky.

Ana. *Doubtful, dubious, questionable: distrustful, mistrustful (see corresponding verbs at DISTRUST): chance, chancy, haphazard, *random.

Con. *Safe, secure: *steady, even, equable, constant.

precedence. *Priority.

Ana. Leading *or* lead, guiding *or* guide (see corresponding verbs at GUIDE): antecedence, foregoing (see corresponding adjectives at PRECEDING).

precedent, *adj.* *Preceding, antecedent, foregoing, previous, prior, former, anterior.

preceding, *adj.* **Preceding, antecedent, precedent, foregoing, previous, prior, former, anterior** agree in meaning being before, especially in time or in order of arrangement. **Preceding** (opposed to *succeeding, following*) is restricted to time and place; it usually means immediately before; as, the *preceding* day; the *preceding* clause; events *preceding* the opening of the story. **Antecedent** (opposed to *subsequent, consequent*) usually implies order in time, but unlike *preceding*, it often suggests an indefinite intervening interval; as, events *antecedent* to the opening of the story; Chaucer's poems were written in a period *antecedent* to the Elizabethan Age. Very often, also, the word implies a causal or a logical, as well as a temporal relation; thus, to understand the success of modern dictators we must have a knowledge of *antecedent* conditions (that is, of conditions earlier in time and causative of dictatorships); a conclusion is based on a chain of *antecedent* inferences. **Precedent** often applies to one thing which must precede another thing if the latter is to be valid or become effective; thus, a condition *precedent* in law is a condition that must be fulfilled before an estate can be vested in one or before a right accrues to one. **Foregoing** (opposed to *following*) applies almost exclusively to statements; as, the *foregoing* citations; the *foregoing* argument. **Previous** and **prior** (opposed to *subsequent*) are often used interchangeably, esp. with *to;* as, *previous* to, or *prior* to, a given date. But *prior* sometimes implies greater importance than *previous;* thus, a *previous* obligation suggests merely an obligation entered into earlier in point of time, whereas a *prior* obligation is one which surpasses the other in importance and must be fulfilled in advance of the other (or others). **Former** (opposed to *latter*), even more definitely than *prior*, implies comparison; as, there can be a *former* engagement only when there is also a later one; a *previous* or *prior* engagement may prevent one's making a second. **Anterior** (opposed to *posterior*), also comparative in force, applies to position, usually in space, sometimes in order or time; as, the *anterior* lobe of the brain. "Organization must presuppose life as *anterior* to it" (*Coleridge*).

Ant. Following.

precept. Rule, *law, canon, regulation, statute, ordinance.

Ana. *Principle, fundamental, axiom: *doctrine, tenet, dogma: injunction, behest, bidding (see COMMAND, *n.*).

Ant. Practice: counsel.

precious. *Costly, expensive, dear, valuable, invaluable, priceless.

Ana. *Choice, exquisite, recherché, rare: valued, prized, appreciated, cherished (see APPRECIATE).

precipitate, *adj.* **Precipitate, headlong, abrupt, impetuous, hasty, sudden,** as applied to persons or their acts or behavior, denote, in common, characterized by excessive haste and unexpectedness. **Precipitate** especially stresses lack of due deliberation; sometimes it suggests prematureness, and is therefore especially applicable to decisions or to actions based on decisions. "It was feared by some that she might be *precipitate* in her choice" (*Irving*). **Headlong** throws the emphasis on rashness and lack of forethought; it is used to describe not only persons and their acts, but the qualities exhibited by such persons or in such acts; as, *headlong* folly; *headlong* haste. **Abrupt,** when applied to a person's actions, suggests complete lack of warning, or, sometimes, unceremoniousness; as, an *abrupt* departure; the story came to an *abrupt* end; when applied to manners or words, it usually implies curtness; as, he answered *abruptly;* when applied to style, it retains its etymological implication of a sudden breaking off and connotes sharp changes in thought without any attempts at transition. **Impetuous** implies violence or vehemence; as applied to persons, it often also suggests impulsiveness or, at times, extreme impatience. "You know the *impetuosity* of my brother's temper" (*Fielding*). "No necessity exists for any hurry, except in the brain of that *impetuous* boy" (*Meredith*). **Hasty** stresses quickness of response, and often suggests thoughtlessness and hot temper rather than impulsiveness. "I am known to be a humorous patrician...*hasty* and tinder-like...what I think I utter, and spend my malice in my breath" (*Shak.*). **Sudden,** as here compared, is distinguishable from *sudden* meaning unexpected only by its added implications of extreme hastiness or impetuosity; as, *sudden* in temper; given to *sudden* rages. "Now and then an access of...*sudden* fury...would lay hold on a man or woman" (*Kipling*).

Ana. Headstrong, willful, refractory (see UNRULY).
Ant. Deliberate. — *Con.* Leisurely, *slow.
☞ *Do not confuse* precipitate *with* precipitous.

precipitate, *v.* *Speed, accelerate, quicken, hasten, hurry.
Ana. Drive, impel (see MOVE, *v.*): *force, compel, coerce, constrain.

precipitous. *Steep, abrupt, sheer.
Ana. Soaring, towering, rocketing, ascending, rising (see RISE).
☞ *Do not confuse* precipitous *with* precipitate.

précis. Sketch, aperçu, survey, *compendium, syllabus, digest, pandect.

precise. Exact, accurate, *correct, nice, right.
Ana. Definite, express, *explicit: strict, *rigid, rigorous, stringent.
Ant. Loose. — *Con.* Lax, slack (see LOOSE): *careless, heedless.

preciseness. *Precision.

precision. **Precision, preciseness** agree in denoting the quality or character of that which is precise. **Precision** commonly denotes a quality that is sought for or is attained, usually as a highly desirable thing. When used in reference to language, it implies expression with such exactitude that neither nothing more nor nothing less than what applies to the thing under consideration is said; as, "expressing herself...with incomparable *precision*" (*Arnold*); "to describe with *precision*...the persons to whom this high privilege was given...the word *citizen* was...substituted for...*free inhabitant*" (*Ch. Just. Taney*); "['Rhetoric'] is merely a vague term of abuse for any style that is...so evidently bad or second-rate that we do not recognize the necessity for greater *precision* in the phrases we apply to it" (*T. S. Eliot*). When used in reference to the arts, sciences, and the like, the term usually implies such clearness of definition or such sharpness in distinction or in distinguishing, that there is no confusion as to outlines, boundaries, dividing lines, movements, or the like; as, "However we may disguise it by veiling words we do not and cannot carry out the distinction between legislative and executive action with mathematical *precision*" (*Justice Holmes*). "Taught her to play the piano with the force and *precision* of a crack regiment of cavalry" (*H. G. Wells*). "Acting, singing, and dancing seem to me the best methods of teaching aesthetic *precision*" (*B. Russell*). *Precision* is also used in reference to an instrument, a machine, or a part of a machine, or the like, that must be made with such exactness of measurements that an infinitesimal fraction of an inch would debar it from fulfilling its function; as, instruments of *precision* (or, often, *precision* instruments); "the fabrication of *precision* parts" (*A. C. Morrison*). **Preciseness** is now rarely used in place of *precision*, for it has come to carry so strong an implication of severity, or of strictness, sometimes, overnicety, in the observance of religious laws, the code of one's profession, the proprieties as dictated by one's class or social equals, or the like, that it is depreciative as often as it is laudatory; as, "savoring of Puritanism and overstrict *preciseness*" (*Prynne*); "prejudiced *preciseness*" (*C. M. Yonge*); "the letter.... had the *preciseness* of an Imperial mandate" (*Meredith*); the *preciseness* of his enunciation and diction is almost the only sign of his foreign birth.

preclude. *Prevent, obviate, avert, ward off.
Ana. *Hinder, obstruct, impede, block, bar: *stop, discontinue, quit, cease: *exclude, eliminate, shut out, debar.

precocious. Untimely, forward, *premature, advanced.
Ana. *Immature, unmatured, unripe.
Ant. Backward.

precursor. *Forerunner, harbinger, herald.
Ana. *Sign, mark, token, symptom: antecedent, determinant, *cause, reason.

predicament. **Predicament, dilemma, quandary, plight, scrape, fix, jam, pickle** are here compared as denoting a situation from which one does or can extricate himself only with difficulty. **Predicament,** originally a term of logic denoting the character, status, or classification assigned by a predication, now carries in its chief current sense no implications derived from this meaning, except possibly the implication that the situation constitutes a problem for those who are involved in it. The term may imply lack of freedom to do what one wishes or finds essential for some reason, or it may imply deep perplexity as to ways out of the situation. "Advice... may be of such nature that it will be painful to reject and yet impossible to follow it; and in this *predicament* I conceive myself to be placed" (*Crabbe*). "The *predicament* with which our civilization now finds itself confronted—the problem, namely, how to find healthy, happy leisure for all the working millions who are now being liberated by machines" (*L. P. Smith*). "He explained his own *predicament* in life. 'I got married,' he said. 'Already I have three children'" (*S. Anderson*). **Dilemma** (also originally, and still, a term of logic denoting a choice of alternatives presented by an opponent in argument either of which is extremely damaging to one's case) applies to a situation which constitutes a predicament from which one can escape only by a choice of equally unpleasant or unsatisfactory alternatives; as, the army was confronted with the *dilemma* of capitulating or starving. **Quandary** differs from *dilemma* chiefly in its stress on puzzlement or perplexity; in fact, this implication is often so emphasized that the suggestion of a dilemma, or a choice between alternatives, is lost or obscured; as, he was in a *quandary* as to how he could keep his appointment; "All his *quandaries* terminated in the same catastrophe; a compromise" (*Disraeli*). All the other words now definitely imply a difficulty, often a very disagreeable situation. **Plight** in its earliest use did not carry this suggestion, for it was applicable to a situation of any kind or character, but in current use, even when unqualified, the term commonly suggests an unfortunate, trying, or unhappy situation; as, "the *plight* in which the world finds itself to-day" (*J. A. Hobson*); the *plight* of this poor family is beyond description. "Cayley Drummle in *The Second Mrs. Tanqueray* has it for his main job to size up the pretty *plight* of Tanqueray and his wife and to speculate plausibly about things which they cannot very well say" (*C. E. Montague*). **Scrape** applies to a plight in which one is involved through one's own fault: often, it suggests a being in disgrace or disfavor; as, "I only suspected it to be Bingley from believing him the kind of young man to get into a *scrape* of that sort" (*Austen*); "they're every one of 'em in *scrapes*, and I've got to pay the piper" (*Meredith*). **Fix** and **jam** are colloquial equivalents of *plight*, but *fix* stresses rather the difficulty in extrication, and *jam* stresses the tight place or hopeless involvements in which one finds oneself; as, he will be in a *fix* if he doesn't settle his debts when they are due hereafter; he is in a *jam* financially. **Pickle** applies to a particularly distressing or sorry plight; as, "How camest thou in this *pickle?*" (*Shak.*); "But when I was left ashore in Melbourne I was in a pretty *pickle*. I knew nobody, and I had no money" (*Shaw*).
Ana. *State, situation, condition, posture: pass, pinch, strait, emergency, exigency, *juncture.

predicate, *v.* Affirm, declare, *assert, aver, protest, avouch, avow, warrant.

predict. *Foretell, forecast, prophesy, prognosticate, augur, presage, portend, forebode.

Ana. *Foresee, foreknow, divine: *warn, forewarn, caution: surmise, *conjecture, guess.

predilection. **Predilection, partiality, prepossession, prejudice, bias** agree in meaning an attitude of mind as exhibited in a feeling or idea which predisposes one to make a certain choice or judgment or to take a certain view without full consideration or reflection. **Predilection** always implies a strong liking that results from one's temperament, one's principles, or one's previous experience, and that predisposes one to prefer certain kinds of friends, books, foods, methods, or the like, or to accept a thing without reference to any other test; as, "For great men I have ever had the warmest *predilection*" (*Carlyle*); "a *predilection* for the strange and whimsical" (*Coleridge*). "Out of the mass of words that make up a language every writer uses only a limited number, and even among these has his words of *predilection*" (*H. Ellis*). "The scientist's refusal to believe in a chaotic universe...is [not] based on any personal *predilections*" (*Inge*). **Partiality** implies a disposition to favor a particular person or thing because of some predilection or, more often, because of overweening fondness or passionate partisanship; it commonly connotes unfairness; as, to show *partiality* in appointments to office; there was no evidence of *partiality* in his treatment of his students; "Mr. and Mrs. Musgrove's fond *partiality* for their own daughters' performance, and total indifference to any other person's" (*Austen*). **Prepossession** always implies a fixed idea or conception in the light of which any new person, new idea, new experience, or the like, is judged; as, Bernard Shaw felt that his dramas were unfavorably criticized because they did not conform to the average critic's *prepossession* of what a play should be; to clear the mind of *prepossessions;* "the *prepossessions* of childhood and youth" (*D. Stewart*). **Prejudice** implies a prepossession (unless distinctly stated, an unfavorable one, implying fear, hate, or repugnance) which affects its possessor's treatment or judgment of a person or thing and tends to work to his or its injury or disadvantage; as, racial *prejudice;* to approach a subject without *prejudice;* "*prejudice* is blind" (*Gibbon*); "the phenomena of life and character...set down without fear, favour, or *prejudice*" (*Galsworthy*). "Those who use their reason do not reach the same conclusions as those who obey their *prejudices*" (*Lippmann*). **Bias** implies a lack of balance or distortion in one's judgment owing to the pull of a predilection or a prepossession, or of partiality or prejudice, and a resulting inclination in favor of or against a person or thing; as, histories that reveal a *bias* in favor of certain races; "a well-proportioned mind is one which shows no particular *bias*" (*Hardy*); "it is as well that you be able to allow for my personal *bias*" (*Shaw*).

Ana. *Leaning, propensity, proclivity, flair: bent, turn, knack, aptitude, *gift.

Ant. Aversion.

predispose. Dispose, *incline, bias.

Ana. Influence, sway, *affect, touch, impress, strike.

predominant. *Dominant, paramount, preponderant, preponderating, sovereign.

Ana. Controlling, directing, conducting, managing (see CONDUCT, *v.*): *prevailing, prevalent: *chief, principal, leading, main, foremost.

Con. *Subordinate, secondary, dependent, subject.

pre-eminent. Surpassing, transcendent, superlative, *supreme, peerless, incomparable, banner.

Ana. *Dominant, predominant, paramount: excelling *or* excellent, outdoing, outstripping (see corresponding verbs at EXCEED): *consummate, finished.

pre-empt. *Arrogate, usurp, appropriate, confiscate.

Ana. *Take, seize, grasp, grab: *exclude, eliminate, shut out, debar.

preen, *v.* **1 Preen, prune, prank, prink, primp, perk up, doll up** come into comparison when they mean to spend time and effort in beautifying or adorning oneself. **Preen** and **prune** (which must not be confused with *prune,* meaning to cut off or out that which is superfluous) both originally implied the smoothing of feathers by the beak and referred, therefore, to the motions of a bird: in later use, both were extended in their application to other animals and to human beings who give close attention to details of grooming. *Prune* is currently less often used than *preen* in this sense, with the result that it is sometimes mistakenly regarded as incorrect. "Below them, in their holes in the sandstone, pigeons *preened* themselves and cooed softly" (*D. H. Lawrence*). "Another...with more beard than brain *prunes* his mustaccio" (*B. Jonson*). "Where contemplation *prunes* her ruffled wings" (*Pope*). **Prank** and **prink** both imply a bedecking or adorning, though they often also suggest a preening or beautifying, as with cosmetics: *prank* more often than *prink* is used of places as well as of persons; as, "Mariners *pranked* out in sky-colored suits" (*K. L. Bates*); "The cottage *prankt* with its holly and mistletoe" (*Zangwill*); "To gather kingcups in the yellow mead, And *prink* their hair with daisies" (*Cowper*); "The thousand and one emporiums which patch and *prink* us" (*Galsworthy*). **Primp,** originally a dialectal term, suggests an almost finicky attention to detail and stresses neatness and nicety more than adornment; as, too much time spent in *primping,* too little at work. **Perk up** and **doll up** are colloquial or slang terms. The former specifically implies a freshening of one's appearance, such as by a smartening of one's attire, a new arrangement of one's hair, a removal of old and the application of fresh rouge and powder, or the like: the latter, like *primp,* suggests close attention to detail but it carries a stronger suggestion than *primp* of bedecking and adorning oneself and of attention to finery, to fashion, and to effective grooming.

Ana. *Adorn, decorate, embellish, beautify.

2 Plume, *pride, pique.

Ana. Congratulate, *felicitate.

preface, *n.* *Introduction, prologue, induction, prelude, overture, foreword, prolegomenon, proem, exordium, preamble, prolusion, protasis, avant-propos.

prefer. 1 *Choose, select, elect, opt, pick, cull, hand-pick, single out.

Ana. Accept, *receive, admit, take: *approve, endorse, sanction: favor, *oblige, accommodate.

2 *Offer, proffer, tender, present.

preference. Selection, election, *choice, option, alternative.

Ana. *Predilection, prepossession, partiality: *favor, countenance.

preferment. *Advancement, promotion, elevation.

Ana. Advance, progress (see under ADVANCE, *v.*, 2): rising *or* rise, ascending *or* ascent (see corresponding verbs at RISE).

pregnant. Meaningful, significant, *expressive, eloquent, sententious.

Ana. Weighty, momentous, consequential, significant, important (see corresponding nouns at IMPORTANCE).

prejudice, *n.* Bias, partiality, prepossession, *predilection.

Ana. Predisposition, disposition, inclination (see corresponding verbs at INCLINE): *favor, countenance: *leaning, penchant.

prelection. *Speech, address, oration, harangue, allocution, lecture, talk, sermon, homily.

prelude. *Introduction, prologue, induction, overture, preface, foreword, prolegomenon, proem, exordium, preamble, prolusion, protasis, avant-propos.

premature. **Premature, untimely, forward, advanced, precocious** are not actually synonyms, for they are rarely interchangeable, but they come into comparison when they mean unduly early in coming, happening, developing, or the like. **Premature** applies usually to that which takes place before its due or proper time (as, a *premature* birth; a *premature* announcement) or comes into existence before it is fully grown or developed or ready for presentation (as, a *premature* baby; a *premature* conclusion; a *premature* report), or to actions or persons that manifest overhaste or impatience (as, "I have been a little *premature*, I perceive; I beg your pardon"—*Austen*). **Untimely** usually means little more than unseasonable but when, as frequently happens, it is applied to that which comes or occurs in advance of its due or proper time, it approaches very close to *premature* in meaning: the term, however, applies not so often to that which begins a life, outward existence, or the like, before its proper time, as to that which ends or destroys a life, a season, or a growing or developing thing, before it has run its normal, natural, or allotted course; as, the *untimely* falling of fruit from a tree; the *untimely* death of the son and heir; the *untimely* frosts that brought summer's beauty to an end; "whose harvest...perished by *untimely* blight" (*C. Brontë*). **Forward,** as here compared, applies chiefly to living things, especially to young persons, young animals, young plants, to growing crops, but also sometimes to seasons, that show signs of progress beyond those that are normal or natural for a thing or things of its kind at the time in question; as, an unusually *forward* spring; he is the most *forward* in mental development of their children. In current use, **advanced** tends to supplant *forward* when by comparison with other persons, other growing things, other seasons, etc., of the same kind or class, the person or thing so described is notably ahead of the others; as, the most *advanced* children in the school; "conflict between the economic interests of the *advanced* and backward peoples" (*J. A. Hobson*). **Precocious** strictly implies a premature fruiting or flowering: in current use, however, it is rarely applied to plants, but chiefly to children who show undue signs of intellectual maturity or an unusual forwardness in mental development. "He was *precocious*...and his mixing with natives had taught him some of the more bitter truths of life" (*Kipling*). The term is also applied to qualities, conditions, circumstances, or the like, which properly belong to maturity, but come or belong to one who is otherwise immature or to the person affected by them; as, "The young Marcellus was proving a little difficult, for...his *precocious* dignities were hard for youth to support without arrogance" (*Buchan*); "Shaw is dramatically *precocious*, and poetically less than immature" (*T. S. Eliot*).

Ana. *Immature, unmatured, unripe, unmellow: abortive, fruitless (see FUTILE): *precipitate, hasty, sudden, abrupt.

Ant. Matured.

premeditated. *Deliberate, considered, advised, designed, studied.

Ana. Intended, purposed, meant (see INTEND): *voluntary, intentional, willful.

Ant. Unpremeditated: casual, accidental. — *Con.* *Precipitate, abrupt, headlong, hasty, sudden.

premise *or* **premiss,** *n.* Postulate, position, presupposition, presumption, assumption. See under PRESUPPOSE.

Ana. Ground, *reason: proposition, *proposal.

premise, *v.* Postulate, posit, *presuppose, presume, assume.

premium. **Premium, prize, award, reward, meed, guerdon, bounty, bonus** agree in meaning something which is bestowed upon a person as a recompense for greater effort, superior merit, supremacy in competition, or the like. **Premium,** as here considered, is applied usually to something extra or additional that serves as an incentive to buy, sell, loan, compete, strive, or the like; as, the school offers *premiums* for excellence in certain studies; to pay a *premium* in addition to an hourly wage to workmen who perform a given amount of work in less than the standard time specified; to ask a *premium* as well as interest for a loan; to increase the sales of a manufactured article by giving *premiums*. **Prize** is applied to something (etymologically something of value) which is striven for or, in looser use, which may be won by chance; it is bestowed upon the winner in a contest or competition, or in a lottery; as, bridge *prizes;* a *prize* for the best composition. In literary use, *prize* commonly implies effort, struggle, and uncertainty in the seeking, and often, but not invariably, imputes value or worth to that which is competed for. "Let a man contend to the uttermost For his life's set *prize*, be it what it will!" (*Browning*). "He had embarked early upon that desperate game of which the *prize* was a throne, and the forfeit, life" (*A. Repplier*). **Award** implies both a decision of judges and a bestowal of a prize or an honor; it is therefore often preferred to *prize* when the recipients have not been competitors in the strict sense but have in their work or performances fulfilled the conditions required by those who offer prizes; as, to receive an *award* for civic service; Boy Scout *awards*. *Award* is logically the correct term for the act of awarding a prize or for the decision in a particular competition; as, the judges have inspected the exhibits and will soon make their *awards;* the Rhodes scholarship *awards* will be announced this week. **Reward** strongly involves the idea of recompense for that which is good or meritorious (only ironically for that which is evil); it may be used in reference to a prize or premium only when that has been earned; thus, a winner of a *prize* for the best novel of the year may feel that he has been given a *reward* for intense effort; a *reward* is offered for the return of a lost article (not for its finding); heaven is thought of as the *reward* for a good life and not as its *prize*. "He scorned to take a *reward* for doing what in justice he ought to do" (*Steele*). "The *reward* of one duty is the power to fulfil another" (*G. Eliot*). **Meed** and **guerdon** are close synonyms of *reward*, but they are used only in poetry or rhetorical prose. They are often employed without distinction, but *meed* tends to suggest a reward recognizing merit and proportioned to it, and *guerdon* a prize or honor conferred as a reward. "He must not float upon his watery bier Unwept, and welter to the parching wind, Without the *meed* of some melodious tear" (*Milton*). "The harsh criticism of the coach on the bank, when we rested for a moment to receive our *meed* of praise or blame" (*A. C. Benson*). "Verse, like the laurel, its immortal *meed*, Should be the *guerdon* of a noble deed" (*Cowper*). "take A horse and arms for *guerdon;* choose the best" (*Tennyson*). **Bounty** and **bonus** are applicable chiefly to a sum of money or its equivalent, given as a premium or reward. *Bounty* is usually, but not exclusively, applied to a premium promised by a government or governmental agency as an inducement to enlistment in the army or navy, to emigration to a distant colony, to the destruction of noxious animals or pests, and the like, or as a subsidy to industry; as, the State pays a *bounty* for every wildcat killed; during the Civil War, some men enlisted for the *bounty* and then deserted. *Bonus*, on the other hand, is applied to something given over and above what is regularly received or due as salary, wages, dividends, interest, or the like, either as a reward or encouragement or as a distribution of surplus; as, a soldier's *bonus;* a shareholder's *bonus*. When used in reference to men in the army and navy, *bounty* refers only to the sum of money paid at enlistment, *bonus* to any sum of money, insurance, and the like, granted after discharge.

Ana. *Gift, present, gratuity, favor: enhancement, intensification, heightening (see corresponding verbs at INTENSIFY).

preoccupied. *Abstracted, absent, absent-minded, distrait, distraught.

Ana. *Intent, engrossed, absorbed: *forgetful, oblivious, unmindful.

preponderant, preponderating. *Dominant, predominant, paramount, sovereign.

Ana. *Supreme, pre-eminent, transcendent, surpassing: outstanding, salient, signal (see NOTICEABLE).

prepossession. Partiality, prejudice, bias, *predilection.

Ana. Bent, turn, knack, aptitude, *gift: *leaning, penchant: predisposition, inclination (see corresponding verbs at INCLINE).

preposterous. Absurd, *foolish, silly.

Ana. *Irrational, unreasonable: bizarre, grotesque, *fantastic.

prerequisite. Requisite, *requirement.

Ana. Necessity, *need, exigency.

prerogative. *Right, privilege, perquisite, appanage, birthright.

Ana. Immunity, *exemption: *claim, title: *freedom, license, liberty.

presage, *n.* *Foretoken, prognostic, omen, augury, portent.

Ana. *Sign, symptom, mark, token: forewarning, warning (see WARN).

presage, *v.* Augur, portend, forebode, prognosticate, *foretell, predict, forecast, prophesy.

Ana. *Indicate, betoken, bespeak: signify, import, denote, *mean.

prescind. *Detach, disengage, abstract.

prescribe. **Prescribe, assign, define** come into comparison when they mean to fix arbitrarily or authoritatively for the sake of order or of a clear understanding. **Prescribe** stresses dictation, especially by one in command, and usually implies that the aim is to give explicit directions or clear guidance to those who accept one's authority or are bound to obey one's injunctions; as, the Constitution *prescribes* the conditions under which it may be amended; the Anglican Church *prescribes* the prayers used in its various services; the attending physician *prescribes* the medicines for his patient. "Can he refuse a copy thereof to a person demanding it on the terms *prescribed* by law?" (*Ch. Just. Marshall*). "They were...ready within the time *prescribed* by Austin" (*Meredith*). **Assign,** in the sense here considered (see also ALLOT, ASCRIBE), usually retains from its other senses at least a suggestion of allotment or ascription; it implies arbitrary, but not despotic, determination for the sake of some practical end such as harmony in operation or functioning, the proper distribution of a number of things, or the settlement of a dispute by agreement; as, a committee is responsible for *assigning* the periods for all classes; the city charter *assigns* the duties of each elected official and the limits of his authority; some phoneticians *assign* one value to "a" in "fare," "mare," "dare," etc., and some another. "Ye know the spheres and various tasks *assign'd* By laws eternal to th' aërial kind [sylphs, genii, daemons, etc.]" (*Pope*). **Define** implies an intent to mark boundaries between things so as to prevent confusion, conflict, or overlapping; as, to *define* the jurisdiction of the various courts; the Constitution of the United States *prescribes* the powers of the government, *assigns* the limits to each, and *defines* the functions of each branch.

Ana. *Set, settle, fix, establish: direct, enjoin, instruct, order, *command.

prescribed. **Prescribed, appointed, destined** come more closely into comparison than the verbs from which they are derived, because some of these adjectives have acquired or retained implications not found in the verb. As here compared, they agree in meaning fixed or settled beforehand. **Prescribed** usually implies an authoritative setting of bounds, not primarily to limit or confine others' activities or to restrict others' freedom, but to achieve some end such as uniformity in practice or equipment, or a conservation of time or energy; thus, a *prescribed* form of words commonly constitutes a formula such as a pledge of allegiance, an oath of office, or the like; the *prescribed* prayers for a service are the prayers that are ordered to be said, but they are not necessarily the only ones that are said; the *prescribed* reading for a course represents not the maximum which an energetic student may accomplish, but the minimum which is required of every student in order that all students may have a common ground. **Appointed** may imply prior determination by agreement of those concerned, or it may imply prior determination by a superior power; it stresses a marking out or fixing in a clear and unmistakable fashion, as of a time or place of meeting, a task to be accomplished, a course to be followed, an end to be aspired to, or a limit to be observed; as, "We were all back in our places at the *appointed* hour" (*Galsworthy*); "Eternal Father!... Who bidd'st the mighty ocean deep Its own *appointed* limits keep" (*W. Whiting*). "Neither snow, nor rain, nor heat, nor night stays these couriers from the swift completion of their *appointed* rounds" (inscribed on N. Y. City post office and translated from Herodotus). **Destined** presupposes a decree by an inexorable power such as God or Fate, or, especially in modern use, a relentless human intention; that which is *destined* is, in strict use, that which is inevitable and cannot be escaped. "The day when I must die... My feet shall fall in the *destined* snare Wherever my road may lie" (*D. G. Rossetti*). "You think that you are Ann's suitor: that you are the pursuer and she the pursued.... Fool: it is you who are the pursued, the marked-down quarry, the *destined* prey" (*Shaw*). The word, however, is now often used loosely and without an implication of inevitability; it may, and commonly does, refer to something that has already happened; as, at last we reached our *destined* goal; she first met her *destined* husband when she was sixteen.

Ana. Set, settled, fixed, established (see SET, *v.*): allotted, assigned, apportioned (see ALLOT).

prescription. *Receipt, recipe.

presence. *Bearing, deportment, demeanor, mien, manner, carriage, port, front.

Ana. Personality, individuality (see DISPOSITION): aspect, *appearance, look.

present, *v.* **1** *Give, bestow, confer, donate, afford.

Ana. *Grant, award, accord.

2 *Offer, tender, proffer, prefer.

Ana. Exhibit, display, parade, *show: advance, *adduce, allege, cite.

present, *n.* *Gift, gratuity, favor, boon, largess, fairing.
Ana. Contribution, *donation, benefaction: grant, subvention (see APPROPRIATION).

presentiment. Misgiving, foreboding, *apprehension.
Ana. *Fear, dread, alarm, terror: foretaste, anticipation, *prospect: disquieting *or* disquietude, discomposing *or* discomposure, disturbance, perturbation (see corresponding verbs at DISCOMPOSE).

preserve, *v.* *Save, conserve.
Ana. *Rescue, deliver, redeem, ransom: protect, guard, safeguard (see DEFEND).

preserves. See under SAVE, *v.*

press, *n.* Throng, crush, *crowd, mob, rout, horde.
Ana. *Multitude, army, host, legion.

pressure. *Stress, strain, tension, shear, thrust, torsion.

prestige. *Influence, authority, weight, credit.
Ana. Ascendancy, *supremacy: *power, sway, dominion: reputation, repute, honor, glory, *fame.

presume. *Presuppose, postulate, premise, posit, assume.
Ana. Surmise, *conjecture: deduce, *infer, judge, gather, conclude.

presumption. Presupposition, assumption, postulate, premise, position. See under PRESUPPOSE.
Ana. View, *opinion, conviction, belief: conjecture, surmise (see under CONJECTURE, *v.*).

presuppose. Presuppose, presume, assume, postulate, premise, posit agree in meaning to take something for granted or as true or existent, especially as a basis for action or reasoning. Their corresponding nouns **presupposition, presumption, assumption, postulate, premise** (*or* **premiss), position** when they denote that which is taken for granted or is accepted as true or existent are distinguishable in general by the same implications and connotations as the verbs. **Presuppose** and **presupposition,** the most inclusive of these words, may or may not imply the dubiousness of that which is taken for granted. At the one extreme they may suggest nothing more than a hazy or imperfectly realized belief that something exists, or is true, or the uncritical acceptance of some hypothesis, in either case casting doubt on that which is taken for granted; as, a lecturer who talks above the heads of his listeners *presupposes* too extensive a knowledge on their part; a school of theology that *presupposed* the total depravity of human nature. At the other extreme the terms may be used in reference to something that is taken for granted because it is the logically necessary antecedent of a thing that is known to be true or the truth of which is not presently in question; as, an effect *presupposes* a cause; so deliberate a murder *presupposes* a motive; "belief in the supernatural *presupposes* a belief in natural law" (*Inge*). **Presume** and **presumption** are often loosely used to imply conjecture (as, I *presume* [that is, venture to believe] they are now in London); in precise English, they always carry the implication that whatever is taken for granted is entitled to belief until it is disproved. Therefore one *presumes* only that for which there is justification in experience, or which has been shown to be sound in practice or in theory, or which is the logical inference from such facts as are known; as, "Every man is to be *presumed* innocent till he is proved to be guilty" (*Blackstone*); the fact that a custom is ancient and is still revered creates a *presumption* in its favor. "It cannot be *presumed* that any clause in the constitution is intended to be without effect" (*Ch. Just. Marshall*). **Assume** and **assumption** stress the arbitrary acceptance as true of something which has not yet been proved or demonstrated or about which there is ground for a difference of opinion; as, some debaters weaken their case by *assuming* too much; for the sake of argument, let us *assume* that the accident occurred as is contended. "I know of nothing more false in science or more actively poisonous in politics...than the *assumption* that we belong as a race to the Teutonic family" (*Quiller-Couch*). "I...*assume* that one purpose of the purchase was to suppress competition" (*Justice Holmes*). **Postulate,** either as a verb or as a noun, differs from *assume* or *assumption* only in being far more restricted in its application and more exact in its implications. One can *assume* or make an *assumption* at any point in a course of reasoning, but one *postulates* something or lays down a proposition as a *postulate* only as the groundwork for a single argument, or for a chain of reasoning, or for a system of thought. *Postulate,* therefore, has reference to one of the underlying assumptions, which are accepted as true but acknowledged as indemonstrable and without which thought or action (also artistic representation) is impossible because of the limitations of human knowledge or of human reason (or of art); thus, the ordinary man always *postulates* the reality of time and of space; the dramatist *postulates* certain conventions which it is necessary for the audience to accept; "belief in the uniformity of nature, which is said to be a *postulate* of science" (*B. Russell*); "the prevailing theological system is one which *postulates* the reality of guidance by a personal God" (*A. Huxley*); "the kind of curvature *postulated* by the generalised theory of relativity" (*Jeans*). **Premise** is often used as though it were identical in meaning with *postulate. Premise,* the noun, in logic denotes a proposition, or one of the two propositions in a syllogism, from which an inference is drawn. In looser use, it commonly refers to any proposition which is the starting point in an argument. But a premise is not, even in this loose use, a proposition that is frankly an assumption, as a postulate often is. It may have been previously demonstrated or it may be admitted as true or axiomatic, but it is always advanced as true and not as assumed; as, his listeners could not assent to his conclusion because they doubted the truth of his *premises. Premise,* the verb, which means to lay down as a premise or as premises, usually refers to the broader rather than to the technical meaning of the noun; as, he *premised* his argument on a proposition which all but a few of his readers accept as true. The verb sometimes does not suggest the laying down of a proposition, but a statement of facts, principles, observations, or the like, which the speaker or writer considers fundamental to his argument or essential to laying a proper groundwork. "These observations are *premised* solely for the purpose of rendering more intelligible those which apply more directly to the particular case under consideration" (*Ch. Just. Marshall*). **Posit** and **position** differ from *postulate* chiefly in implying affirmation as a truth; they rule out the implication of an assumption which is often found in *postulate* and substitute that of a declaration of faith or conviction. "Hooker...rests his *positions* on one solid basis, the eternal obligation of natural law" (*Hallam*). "It seems to me an error to say that we have no grounds for *positing* the existence of God outside His relation to ourselves" (*Inge*).
Ana. Surmise, *conjecture, guess: *infer, deduce, gather, judge.

presupposition. Presumption, assumption, postulate, premise, position. See under PRESUPPOSE.
Ana. Surmise, conjecture, guess (see under CONJECTURE, *v.*): inference, deduction, judgment (see under INFER): belief, conviction, *opinion, view.

pretend. *Assume, affect, simulate, feign, counterfeit, sham.

Ana. *Disguise, dissemble, cloak, mask: *deceive, delude, mislead, beguile.

pretense *or* **pretence.** **1** Pretension, *claim, title.

Ana. Plea, pretext, excuse, *apology, apologia: *right, birthright, privilege.

2 Pretense (*or* **pretence**), **pretension, make-believe, make-belief** are here compared only as terms that are sometimes confused, especially when they involve the idea of offering something false or deceptive as real or true. They are seldom synonymous terms because they rarely agree in denotation. **Pretense** may denote false show in general, or the evidence of it; as, she is utterly devoid of *pretense;* there is too much *pretense* in his piety; "the *pretense* that eludes the detection of others and that which deceives the pretender himself" (*Brownell*). The term may also apply to an act that is performed, an appearance that is assumed, or a statement that is made in the hope that it will convince others of the truth or reality of something that is false or unreal; as, "declining to dance before her, on a *pretense* of sickness, when in fact he was in perfect health" (*Cowper*); "No one was deceived by his *pretense* of professional activity" (*E. Wharton*); "rushing away from the discussion on the transparent *pretence* of quieting the dog" (*Conrad*); "my mother's affectionate *pretense* of his being the head of the family" (*M. Austin*). **Pretension,** as here compared (see also CLAIM, AMBITION), is now rarely if ever used in place of *pretense* as a concrete act, appearance, or statement, but it is often used in the sense of false show or the evidence of it, with, however, somewhat differing implications. Where *pretense* in this general sense often implies hypocrisy or intentional deceit, *pretension* suggests rather an unwarranted assumption that one possesses certain desirable qualities or powers, and therefore more often implies overweening conceit or self-deception; as, " 'Oh! how sick I am of theories, and systems, and the *pretensions* of men!...Give me nothing but common-place unpretending people!' " (*Meredith*); "His disdain of affectation and prudery was magnificent. He hated all *pretension* save his own *pretension*" (*Mencken*). **Make-believe,** or the rarer **make-belief,** applies usually to pretense or pretenses that arise not so much out of a desire to give others a false impression as out of a strong or vivid imagination, such as that of children or poets who like to take that which their fancies create as real or as true; as, in children, the love of *make-believe* usually expresses itself in games; in adults, in the reading of fiction or in attendance at the theater. Both terms are occasionally used to denote the acceptance against one's better judgment of that which is manifestly unreal or untrue because of some power in the thing itself or in its accompaniments. "The attitude of our own public towards popular superstitions, half belief and half *make-belief,* is too common among church-goers" (*Inge*).

Ana. Humbug, fake, sham, fraud, deceit, deception, *imposture: affectation, *pose, air, mannerism.

pretension. **1** *Claim, title, pretense.

Ana. *Right, privilege, prerogative: assertion, affirmation, declaration, protestation (see corresponding verbs at ASSERT).

2 *Pretense, make-believe, make-belief.

Ana. *Hypocrisy, sanctimony, cant: dissimulation, duplicity, guile, *deceit.

3 *Ambition, aspiration.

Ana. Hoping *or* hope, expectation (see corresponding verbs at EXPECT): dream, vision, *fancy.

pretentious. **1** *Showy, ostentatious, pompous.

Ana. *Gaudy, garish, flashy: *ornate, flamboyant, florid, baroque, rococo.

Ant. Unpretentious.

2 *Ambitious, utopian.

Ana. Aiming, aspiring, panting (see AIM, *v.*): conspicuous, striking, arresting (see NOTICEABLE).

preternatural. *Supernatural, supranatural, miraculous, superhuman.

Ana. Unnatural, anomalous (see IRREGULAR): *abnormal, atypic: outstanding, remarkable, salient (see NOTICEABLE): *exceptional.

pretext. Excuse, plea, alibi, *apology, apologia.

Ana. Ruse, *trick, maneuver, stratagem: subterfuge, *deception: justification, vindication, defending *or* defense (see corresponding verbs at MAINTAIN).

pretty. Bonny, comely, fair, *beautiful, lovely, handsome, good-looking, beauteous, pulchritudinous.

Ana. Charming, attractive, alluring, taking (see under ATTRACT): dainty, delicate, exquisite (see CHOICE, *adj.*).

prevail. In form **prevail on** *or* **upon.** *Induce, persuade.

Ana. *Move, actuate, drive, impel: influence, *affect, impress, sway.

prevailing. **Prevailing, prevalent, rife, current** come into comparison as meaning general, as in its circulation, acceptance, use, or the like, especially in a given place or at a given time. **Prevailing** applies especially to that which is predominant, or which generally or commonly obtains at the time or in the place indicated (often, the present, where no statement is made); as, the *prevailing* prices for shares of the ten largest industries; the *prevailing* opinion among booksellers; "the *prevailing* tendency to obliterate the dividing lines between all the arts" (*Lowes*); "the *prevailing* fatalism of Islam" (*A. Huxley*). **Prevalent** applies especially to that which is general or very common over a given area or at a given time: the term, however, does not suggest, as *prevailing* usually suggests, a predominance as in frequency, in favor, or the like: rather, it connotes a frequency without necessarily implying that it is the most frequent; thus, the *prevailing* (that is, the most frequently evident or the usual) wind in a section is from the southeast, but southwest winds may, nevertheless, be *prevalent* there; colds and grippe are *prevalent* in northern states during the winter; a widely *prevalent* pronunciation of a word may not necessarily be the *prevailing* pronunciation. **Rife** adds to *prevalent* an implication such as the rapid spread of the thing which is so qualified, or of a great increase in the number of its instances, or merely of commonness or abundance; as, "Rumour is already *rife* here as to Dr. Trefoil's successor" (*Trollope*); "spiritual maladies, so *rife* in our day" (*Carlyle*); "a heresy which is very *rife* just now" (*Inge*); "Legends were *rife* of its [Spain's] extraordinary wealth" (*Buchan*). **Current** (etymologically, running or flowing) applies especially to things such as language, philosophy, etc., that are constantly in process of change or development, or to things such as coins, diseases, etc., that circulate constantly from one person or thing to another; hence, *current* so often describes that which is widespread in its use, adoption, or acceptance at the time in question, that it has come to imply the present if no other time is indicated; thus, *current* English is the English language of the present time; a *current* notion is one that is widely accepted at the moment; banknotes, postage stamps, coins, etc., of the *current* series are those still being printed or minted for circulation or sale; so, *current* fashions; *current* tendencies; a *current* practice. However, when the term applies to periodicals or other things that come out in a series, in installments, or the like, *current* describes the one appearing during the present week, month, or the like, or the latest to appear; as, the *current* issue of a well-known magazine; the *current* installment of a new novel (that is, of a novel appearing serially in a periodical). But *current* is often used in the place of the other words of this group when the time or place is definitely indicated and merely the passing from one person to another is stressed; as, "Shakespeare used the *current* language of his day" (*J. R. Lowell*); "As *current* in her time, the Evangelical creed was simple" (*H. Ellis*); "She had been given, at fourteen, the *current* version of her origin" (*E. Wharton*).

Ana. *Dominant, predominant, preponderant: *common, ordinary, familiar: general, *universal.

prevalent. *Prevailing, rife, current.

Ana. *Common, ordinary, familiar: pervading, impregnating, saturating (see PERMEATE): *usual, wonted, accustomed, customary.

prevaricate. *Lie, equivocate, palter, fib.

Ana. Evade, elude, *escape: *misrepresent, belie.

prevent. 1 **Prevent, anticipate, forestall** are comparable when they carry the meaning to be or get ahead of or to deal with beforehand, with reference especially to a thing's due time, its actual occurrence, the action of another, or the like. **Prevent,** except in deliberately archaic use, no longer carries its etymological meaning of to go or get before. This, however, was one of its common senses until about a century ago and is found in the work of the best writers before the Victorian era. "Oh! run; *prevent* them [the wise men from the East] with thy humble ode, And lay it lowly at his blessed feet; Have thou the honour first thy Lord to greet" (*Milton*). In current use, *prevent* additionally implies frustration, as of an intention or plan, or an averting, as of a threatened evil, or a rendering impossible, as by setting up an obstacle or obstacles. Sometimes the emphasis upon hindrance (see PREVENT, 2) is so strong that the etymological implication is nearly lost, but in the sense here considered (which affects strongly the meaning of the adjective *preventive*), advance provision or preparation against something possible or probable is clearly implied; as, to take measures to *prevent* an epidemic (cf. *preventive* measures, *preventive* medicine). "Who stands safest? tell me, is it he? ...whose *preventing* care In peace provides fit arms against a war?" (*Pope*). **Anticipate** (see also FORESEE) in modern use takes the place of *prevent* when merely getting ahead of another (especially as a precursor or forerunner) is implied. "Most of the great European thinkers of the eighteenth and early nineteenth centuries were in some measure inspired, influenced, or *anticipated* by Shaftesbury" (*H. Ellis*). "The pithy and succinct comparisons that our mediaeval ancestors, *anticipating* the modern Imagists, delighted in" (*Lowes*). Like *prevent, anticipate* sometimes suggests balking another in carrying out an intention or plan; but unlike the former word, it does not imply putting obstacles in the way of its performance or execution, but implies rather its prior performance or execution. "He would probably have died by the hand of the executioner, if the executioner had not been *anticipated* by the populace" (*Macaulay*). Distinctively, the word implies dealing with, using, treating, or the like, in advance of a thing's due time or proper order but it often involves another implication which can be gathered only from the context; as, to *anticipate* a payment on a loan (to make a payment before the date it is due); to *anticipate* one's salary (to spend one's salary before it is earned); to *anticipate* some details in telling a story (to mention details that chronologically should come later in the narrative). **Forestall,** in what is now the less common meaning, carries over from its earliest sense so strong an implication of intercepting that it means merely to stop in its course. "Something you were not in the least prepared to face, something you hurried to *forestall*" (*M. Austin*). In what is generally regarded as most discriminating usage, the word carries only a suggestion of intercepting, or of a meeting halfway, not for the purpose of stopping, but of lessening its force or effectiveness. It thereby implies beforehand action that serves to render a thing (especially something inevitable) powerless to harm, or merely useless; thus, Thackeray's preface to "Pendennis" was an attempt to *forestall* criticism of his naturalism; "to *forestall* public opinion and guide its judgment" (*L. P. Smith*). " 'Posterity will still be explaining me, long after I am dead. Why, then, should I *forestall* their labours?' " (*R. Macaulay*).

Ana. *Frustrate, thwart, foil, baffle, balk: *arrest, check, interrupt: avoid, shun, eschew, evade, *escape.

2 **Prevent, preclude, obviate, avert, ward off** come into comparison when they mean to hinder or stop something that may occur or, in the case of *prevent* and *preclude*, to hinder or stop someone from doing something. **Prevent** usually implies the existence of something which serves as an insurmountable obstacle or an impediment; as, there is no law to *prevent* you from erecting a building on this spot (or, to *prevent* the erection of a building on this spot). "Her indifferent state of health unhappily *prevents* her being in town" (*Austen*). "Small valvular folds directed in such a manner as to permit the exit of fluid from the heart, while they *prevent* its entrance" (*T. H. Huxley*). **Preclude** differs from *prevent* in stressing the existence of some situation or condition or the taking of anticipatory measures that effectually shuts out every possibility of a thing's occurring or of a person's doing something; as, he makes everything so clear that all misunderstanding is *precluded;* death *precluded* him from completing his investigation. "In wishing to put an end to pernicious experiments, I do not mean to *preclude* the fullest inquiry" (*Burke*). **Obviate** usually implies the use of intelligence or forethought; *preclude* also often implies these but sometimes it suggests the operation of chance. The chief distinction between these words when anticipatory measures are implied is that *obviate* usually connotes an attempt to forestall disagreeable eventualities by clearing away obstacles or by disposing of difficulties; as, the use of bills of exchange *obviates* the risk in transporting money from one country to another; prompt payment will *obviate* the necessity of our taking legal action against you. "No care, no art, no organization of society, could *obviate* the inherent incompatibility of individual perfection with the course of nature" (*G. L. Dickinson*). **Avert** and **ward off** differ from the other words of this group in always implying prevention of an approaching or oncoming evil. They suggest therefore immediate and effective measures in the face of what threatens. *Avert,* however, suggests the use of active measures to force back the evil before it is actually encountered; as, to *avert* a catastrophe by prompt action; "the satisfaction of *averting* war" (*J. R. Green*); "it was very doubtful whether the consequences could be *averted* by sealing my lips" (*Shaw*). *Ward off,* on the other hand, implies a close encounter and the use of defensive measures (cf. to *ward off* an opponent's blow or thrust) in order to avoid the evil or to diminish its disastrous effects; as, it is now too late to *ward off* a chill; to *ward off* an infestation of ants. "If we can *ward off* actual war till the crisis in England is over" (*Jefferson*).

Ana. *Hinder, impede, obstruct block, bar, dam: debar, shut out (see EXCLUDE): prohibit, *forbid, interdict, inhibit.

Ant. Permit.

previous. Foregoing, prior, *preceding, antecedent, precedent, former, anterior.

Ant. Subsequent: consequent.

prey, *n.* *Victim, quarry, ravin.

Ana. *Spoil *or* spoils, booty, prize.

price, *n.* **Price, charge, cost, expense,** as here compared, agree in meaning that which is given or asked in payment for a thing, or for services or the like. **Price** and **charge** in their ordinary nontechnical use commonly designate what is asked or demanded—in the case of *price,* especially for goods or commodities; in the case of *charge,* especially for services; as, what is the *price* of this book?; the *price* of meat has risen greatly; the market *price* of wheat; the *charge* for haulage (or porterage); goods delivered free of *charge* within a radius of one hundred miles; there is a small *charge* for registering a deed. In economics, however, *price* does not necessarily refer to a fixed sum of money asked by a seller, but to the quantity or number of units of one thing exchanged in barter or sale for another thing; thus, the normal or natural *price* of a thing, in economics, is theoretically the amount (usually of money) which is proportionate to the amount (also usually of money) that has been spent in its production, not the amount which has been determined by external conditions or the will of the seller. "Labour was the first *price,* the original purchase-money that was paid for all things" (*Adam Smith*). *Charge,* especially in accounting, also applies to that which is imposed on one as a financial burden and with the payment of which one is charged; thus, the fixed *charges* of a business include rentals, taxes, interest, liens, and the like. **Cost** and **expense** in their ordinary nontechnical use commonly apply to what is given or surrendered for something—*cost* often implying somewhat specifically the payment of the price asked, and *expense* often designating the aggregate amount or, in the plural, the aggregate of the amounts, disbursed for something; as, they found the *cost* of the piano made too severe a drain on their resources; the *cost* of provisions; traveling *expenses;* the heavy *expense* of a long illness. In looser use, *cost* sometimes replaces *price,* with, however, a difference in connotation; thus, "What is the *price* of this article?" means "how much do you ask for it?"; "What is the *cost* of this article?" means "how much do you want from me in payment for it?" In highly precise use, *cost* applies to whatever must be given or sacrificed to obtain something, to produce something, or to attain some end, whether it be money, labor, lives, or the like, or whether it is actually given or sacrificed; as, the *price* of this article is below the *cost* of its manufacture; victory will be won only at great *cost* of life; he felt that the *cost* in effort was greater than he could afford. *Expense* also may denote expenditure, especially but not only of money; as, "Fresh news is got only by enterprise and *expense*" (*Justice Holmes*). "A convenient way of producing the maximum amount of 'copy' with the minimum *expense* of intellect" (*Babbitt*).

priceless. Invaluable, precious, *costly, expensive, dear, valuable.

Ana. Cherished, treasured, prized, valued (see APPRECIATE).

prick, *v.* Punch, puncture, *perforate, bore, drill.

Ana. *Enter, pierce, probe, penetrate: *cut, slit, slash.

pride, *n.* **Pride, vanity, vainglory** are here compared as meaning the quality or the feeling of a person who is keenly aware of his excellence or superiority in any way. The same distinctions in implications and connotations are found in their corresponding adjectives **proud, vain, vainglorious. Pride** and **proud** may imply either justified or unjustified self-esteem, in so far as that which one regards as a merit or a superiority is real or is imagined, and as the feeling which governs one manifests itself either in proper self-respect and in abhorrence of that which is beneath one's standards of what is right and good or in inordinate and arrogant conceit: in one interpretation, pride is a sin or vice and the antithesis of humility (as, "Those that walk in *pride* he is able to abase"—*Daniel* iv. 37; "*Proud* she may be in the sense of respecting herself; but *pride* in the sense of contemning others less gifted than herself deserves the two lowest circles of a vulgar woman's Inferno"—*Holmes*); in the other interpretation, pride is either a virtue or a highly pardonable, even commendable, feeling or quality that is the antithesis of shame and that spurs one to equal or better one's best or gives one rightful gratification (as, to take *pride* in one's work; *proud* of one's ancestry, or of one's skill in fencing; "the solemn *pride* that must be yours to have laid so costly a sacrifice [five sons killed in Civil War] upon the altar of freedom"—*Lincoln*). **Vanity** and **vain** imply an excessive desire to win the notice, approval, or praise of others; both connote an interest centered on oneself and often suggest a concentration on things of little or no importance relatively; as, "Old Auchinleck had...not the gay, tail-spreading peacock *vanity* of his son [James Boswell]" (*Carlyle*); "The heart of the *vain* man is lighter than the heart of the *proud*" (*F. Marion Crawford*); "poor Robert looked only at himself; he had nothing but a small and worthless mortification, which was only wounded *vanity*" (*Deland*); "The idea flattered his *vanity,* which had had little to feed on of late" (*Arch. Marshall*). **Vainglory** and **vainglorious** imply excessive pride which manifests itself in boastfulness and arrogant display of one's power, skill, influence, or the like; as, *vainglorious* conquerors; "*vainglorious* boastings" (*Irving*); "It is not *vain-glory* for a man and his [looking] glass to confer in his own chamber" (*Shak.*); "*Vainglory's* a worm which the very best action Will taint, and its soundness eat through" (*C. & M. Lamb*).

Ana. Arrogance, haughtiness, superciliousness, disdainfulness *or* disdain, insolence (see corresponding adjectives at PROUD): complacency, smugness, priggishness (see corresponding adjectives at COMPLACENT): self-esteem, self-love, egotism, egoism, *conceit.

Ant. Humility: shame.

pride, *v.* **Pride, plume, pique, preen** come into comparison as reflexive verbs meaning to congratulate oneself because of something one is, or has, or has done or achieved. **Pride** usually implies a taking credit to oneself on or upon something that redounds to one's honor or gives just cause for pride in oneself; as, to *pride* oneself on one's ancestry, one's ability, one's success, or one's taste. "Mark *prided* himself upon maintaining outwardly a demeanour that showed not the least trace of overstrung nerves" (*C. Mackenzie*). **Plume** adds to *pride* the implication of a display of vanity or of a more obvious exhibition of one's gratification: the term usually, but not invariably, suggests less justification than does *pride;* as, "the Viceroy *plumed* himself on the way in which he had instilled notions of reticence into his staff" (*Kipling*); "Cicero *plumed* himself on flirting with disreputable actresses" (*Buchan*). **Pique,** as here compared (see also PROVOKE, 1), differs from *plume* chiefly in carrying a hint of stirred-up pride or satisfaction: usually the cause of the pride is a special accomplishment; as, "Every Italian or Frenchman of any rank *piques* himself on speaking his own tongue correctly" (*Walpole*); " 'Pride,' observed Mary, who *piqued* herself upon the solidity of her reflections, 'is a very common failing, I believe' " (*Austen*). **Preen** (see also PREEN, 1) is sometimes, but infrequently, used in place of *plume,* with often a slight suggestion of adorning oneself as with one's virtues; as, "he *preened* himself upon his sapience" (*Amy Lowell*).

Ana. *Boast, brag, vaunt, crow, gasconade: congratulate, *felicitate.

priest. Clergyman, *cleric, ecclesiastic, abbé.

priggish. Smug, self-complacent, self-satisfied, *complacent.

Ana. Righteous, ethical, *moral: conceited, egotistic, self-esteeming, self-loving (see corresponding nouns at CONCEIT).

primal. Primordial, primitive, pristine, primeval, *primary, prime.

Ana. *Ultimate, absolute, categorical: original, fresh, *new.

primary. Primary, primal, primordial, primitive, pristine, primeval, prime come into comparison as meaning first as in order, character, importance, or the like. That is **primary** which comes first in the order of development or of progression. Sometimes the term means little more than *initial* (as, the *primary* lesion of a disease); sometimes, however, it acquires the implications of *fundamental, elemental,* or *elementary,* and describes the first part or element as in time or in importance, or one of such parts or elements in a complicated structure, substance, system, or the like (as, the *primary* xylem [woody tissue] of a tree; the *primary* nerves; the *primary* schools; "The raw material of music is sound. Sound is a *primary,* a 'pure' medium....it has no meaning except in a context"—*Day Lewis*): at other times it means *original* in the sense of not derived (as, the *primary* colors; the *primary* qualities of matter; the *primary* cause). But *primary* may convey little or no suggestion of a time order and imply superiority in importance, thereby coming close to *principal;* as, the *primary* object of education; the *primary* end of poetry. "When a lexicographer speaks of the *primary* meaning of a word he means merely that this meaning is the first in point of time, that is, the oldest meaning. Thus, the *primary* meaning of *nice* is 'stupid, foolish.' But the ordinary man quite naturally thinks that the lexicographer means by *primary* something else altogether, namely, the chief or principal meaning of the work so marked" (*Kemp Malone*). That is **primal** (a term found chiefly in poetry or elevated prose) which is primary in the sense of *initial, fundamental,* or *elemental* (as, "the *primal* slip in Paradise"—*Meredith;* "[Some Christians] would say that the idea of sacrifice is a *primal* instinct of human nature"—*A. C. Benson*), or which goes back to the origin or to the beginnings, especially of the human race (as, "It hath the *primal* eldest curse upon't, A brother's murder"—*Shak.;* "the Biblical vocabulary is compact of the *primal* stuff of our common humanity"—*Lowes;* "Ultimate issues, *primal* springs"—*Kipling*). That is **primordial** which serves as the starting point in a course of development or growth or which is the earliest in order or in formation: the term often suggests a rudimentary quality or state; thus, the *primordial* ooze (or slime) is thought of as the substance out of which the earth was formed; a *primordial* cell is in biology a rudimentary cell without a wall; the *primordial* protoplasm; the *primordial* man; the *primordial* elements of matter; the *primordial* leaves of a plant. That is **primitive** which belongs to or is associated with an early stage, often but not necessarily a remote stage, in the development of something, especially of the human race or of a particular people: the term usually carries one or more important additional implications. Often, when used in reference to art or manufacture, it suggests lack of knowledge of modern techniques or conventions, such as of perspective in painting or of modes in mensurable music; as, *primitive* potteries; the *primitive* French and Italian painters; the *primitive* music of a savage tribe; *primitive* design. When used in reference to persons, their ways of living, their instincts, emotions, laws, etc., it usually suggests either a connection with a very rudimentary civilization or a retention of a character or quality associated with such a civilization; as, " 'In *primitive* society the husband is allowed to punish an unfaithful wife with death' " (*Cather*); "a *primitive* but effective police inquiry" (*T. S. Eliot*); "*primitive* laws to protect inheritance, to safeguard property" (*R. Macaulay*); "genuinely *primitive* traits that reveal themselves in the childhood of either the individual or the race" (*Babbitt*). Often, however, the term merely stresses an opposition to that which is highly civilized or sophisticated, and therefore unduly complicated, and suggests naturalness, simplicity, or the like. " 'Life is very *primitive* here...[which means] only going back to something immediate and simple. It's fetching and carrying and getting water and getting food' " (*H. G. Wells*). That is **pristine** which is characteristic of something in its earliest and freshest and newest state or which, less often, characterizes something (such as an institution or race) that has just come into existence; as, "an image of the *pristine* earth" (*Wordsworth*); to revivify the qualities of *pristine* Christianity; restored to its *pristine* freshness or vigor; "its *pristine* ductility vanished forever" (*Lowes*). That is **primeval** in its strict sense which belongs to or is characteristic of the first ages of the earth; as, "For food you must still go to the earth and to the sea, as in *primeval* days" (*Jefferies*); "refreshing our minds with a savour of the...*primeval* world and the earliest hopes and victories of mankind" (*Binyon*). Often, however, the term merely suggests extreme antiquity or the absence of all signs of human trespass or influence; as, *primeval* ages; *primeval* forests. That is **prime** which is the first in rank, degree, dignity, or the like; as, the *prime* minister; "[He] makes his moral being his *prime* care" (*Wordsworth*); our *prime* men of letters; a matter of *prime* importance; tobacco of *prime* quality. *Prime* is often used briefly to imply choiceness or prime quality; as, "*prime* claret" (*Meredith*).

Ana. Initiating *or* initial, beginning, commencing, starting (see corresponding verbs at BEGIN): elemental, *elementary: basic, *fundamental, radical: *chief, leading, principal.

Con. Following, succeeding, ensuing (see FOLLOW): secondary, *subordinate.

primate. Metropolitan, archbishop, *bishop, ordinary.

prime, *adj.* *Primary, primal, primordial, primitive, pristine, primeval.

Ana. *Chief, leading, principal, main: *choice, exquisite, recherché.

prime mover. *Origin, source, provenance, provenience, inception, root.

primeval. Pristine, primitive, primordial, primal, *primary, prime.

Ana. Aboriginal, *native, indigenous, autochthonous: original, *new.

primitive. *Primary, primal, primordial, pristine, primeval, prime.

Ana. *Fundamental, basic, radical: elemental, *elementary: aboriginal, *native.

primordial. Primeval, pristine, primitive, primal, *primary, prime.

primp. Perk up, doll up, prink, prank, *preen, prune.

Ana. Beautify, deck, bedeck, *adorn.

princely. *Kingly, regal, royal, queenly, imperial.

Ana. *Luxurious, sumptuous, opulent: munificent, bountiful, *liberal.

principal, *adj.* *Chief, main, leading, foremost, capital.
Ana. *Dominant, predominant, paramount: vital, cardinal, fundamental, *essential: pre-eminent, *supreme, superlative.

principle. **Principle, axiom, fundamental, law, theorem** come into comparison when they denote a proposition or other formulation stating a fact or a generalization accepted as true and basic. A **principle** is any such generalization, however derived, which provides a basis for reasoning or, more often in modern use, a guide for conduct or procedure. "If there is any *principle* of the Constitution that...imperatively calls for attachment ...it is the *principle* of free thought" (*Justice Holmes*). "They laid down a set of *principles* for the guidance of leprosy research" (*V. Heiser*). *Principle* often implies fixity or, at least, insusceptibility to change; in modern use, however, this is not always clear without qualification. "Your devotee to abstract and eternal *principles*" (*W. James*). An **axiom,** in its historical definition, is a principle not open to dispute because self-evident; as, the geometrical *axiom* that there can be only one straight line between two points. In the older logic, *axioms* were sometimes called "first principles" because they provided the indisputable bases for reasoning. "Time has been consumed in the attempt to demonstrate propositions which may have been thought *axioms*" (*Ch. Just. Marshall*). In modern usage, *axiom* does not connote necessary truth, but universal acceptance as truth; thus, the *axioms* of political economy are the principles all economists accept, no matter how far they diverge in the conclusions they draw from them. A **fundamental** is usually a principle, but sometimes a fact, that is so essential to a philosophy, a religion, a science, or an art that its rejection or disproof would destroy all the conclusions resting upon it; as, the *fundamentals* of Christian belief. A **law,** as here compared, is a principle derived from observation and experiment that states an order or relation of phenomena which, so far as is known, has always held good and which may be expected to hold good under the given conditions; as, the *law* of gravitation; the *laws* of thought. "It is a *law* that no two electrons may occupy the same orbit" (*Eddington*). **Theorem,** a word once important in philosophy, but now chiefly used in the mathematical sciences, is here considered only in its older sense of a proposition that admits of rational proof. It is distinguished from an *axiom* in not being self-evident; and, in general, from a *law* in not being derived by induction. In strict use, it is a proposition not only fully demonstrable but also logically necessary. "Principles at other times are supposed to be certain fundamental *Theorems* in Arts and Sciences, in Religion and Politics" (*Berkeley*).
Ana. Basis, foundation, ground (see BASE): *law, rule, canon, precept: *form, usage, convention.

prink. Prank, *preen, prune, primp, perk up, doll up.
Ana. Beautify, bedeck, deck, garnish, embellish, decorate, ornament, *adorn.

print, *n.* *Impression, impress, imprint, stamp.
Ana. Mark, token, *sign: *trace, vestige.

print, *v.* **Print, publish** are often confused when used with reference to articles, books, journals, or the like. **Print** implies that the article, book, journal, or the like, has been through all the processes of typesetting, proofreading, and striking off which means that it is finally in print; as, this book is *printed* by the Collegiate Press. **Publish** implies that the book, article, or journal in printed and often bound form is issued for sale to the public or is put in general circulation; as, this book has been *published* by the G. & C. Merriam Company; "Sir William Drummond's late book about the Bible—*printed,* but not *published*" (*Byron*); "Moxon told me... that he was about to *print,* but (I think) not to *publish,* those elegiacs on Hallam" (*FitzGerald*); "the indecency of *publishing* intimate letters which were never written to be *published*" (*H. Ellis*). Similar distinctions obtain between the derived nouns **printer** and **publisher** as applied to the person or company that prints and the person or company that publishes. It should be noted, however, that the same person or company may be both printer and publisher, and that the publisher, though usually, is not necessarily, the owner of the copyright of a printed work.

printer. See under PRINT, *v.*

prior. Previous, foregoing, precedent, anterior, former, antecedent, *preceding.
Ana. Ahead, *before, forward.
Con. Behind, *after.

priority. **Priority, precedence** come into comparison when they mean the act, the fact, or, especially, the right of preceding another. When the reference is to the right, both terms usually imply an established or accepted code that determines which shall precede the other. **Priority** is the usual term in law and the sciences and chiefly concerns an order of time: when there is merely a question concerning the time relations of events, the term implies antecedence in occurrence; as, the courts established the *priority* of the wife's death in an accident; the right to inherit a title is dependent mainly on *priority* of birth. When, however, the question concerns a number of things which cannot be taken care of or dealt with all at once (such as debts, cases, etc.) and must be arranged in order of time, *priority* suggests a law, code, or other rule of arrangement that determines the order in which one goes before another; as, "In payment of debts he must observe the rules of *priority*" (*Blackstone*); liens on a property take *priority* in bankruptcy settlements; the "law of *priority*" in biological classification is the principle that the first published name of a genus or species has preference over any one subsequently published; to grant a man-of-war *priority* over several merchantmen seeking to enter a harbor. **Precedence,** though frequent in general use, is, as here considered, chiefly a term of formal etiquette; in this specific sense, it implies an established order as in receiving, greeting, seating, or the like, which gives preference to those who are superior in rank, dignity, or position; as, among ambassadors of equal rank, *precedence* is usually determined by order of seniority, or length of service; when a person has two claims to *precedence,* he is, as a rule, given the *precedence* that belongs to the higher rank. In general use, the term often suggests a prior place, chance, seat, or the like, accorded to one, often but not necessarily because of age, sex, social position, or as a mere courtesy; as, "Smiling blandly and saying, 'After you, ma'am,' to another lady ...who had politely offered the *precedence* at the looking-glass" (*G. Eliot*); "No one lost anything by granting *precedence* to a man so flawlessly urbane" (*A. Repplier*).
Ana. Ordering *or* order, arrangement (see corresponding verbs at ORDER): ascendancy, *supremacy: pre-eminence, transcendence (see corresponding adjectives at SUPREME).

priory. *Cloister, monastery, nunnery, convent, abbey.

prismatic. **Prismatic, iridescent, opalescent, opaline** agree in meaning marked by or displaying a variety of colors. **Prismatic** implies an exhibition of the colors of the spectrum (as when a ray of light is refracted by a prism) or of a rainbow. In its literary use, it merely suggests a brilliant or striking variety of colors; as, "Jeremy Taylor's style is *prismatic.* It unfolds the colours of the rainbow" (*Hazlitt*). "Have you ever observed a hummingbird moving about in an aërial dance among the flowers—a living *prismatic* gem that changes its colour with every change of position?" (*Hudson*). **Iridescent** (etymologically from *iris*, a rainbow), implies a rainbowlike play of shifting colors such as is exhibited by a soap bubble, by mother of pearl, by the plumage of some birds, and the like; as, "The whole texture of his [Chaucer's] mind, though its substance seem plain and grave, shows itself at every turn *iridescent* with poetic feeling like shot silk" (*J. R. Lowell*); "something *iridescent*, like the shining of wet sand" (*A. Repplier*). **Opalescent,** and the somewhat rarer **opaline,** imply both the soft milky quality and the iridescence of an opal; as, "Titian hardly ever paints sunshine, but a certain *opalescent* twilight which has as much of human emotion as of imitative truth in it" (*Ruskin*); "The *opaline* light which comes through these lateral bays [of Auxerre Cathedral], and makes a sort of veil...under the lofty vaulting" (*Viollet-le-Duc, transl. by H. Adams*).

prisoner. Prisoner, captive, convict agree in denoting one who is deprived of his liberty and is held in custody. **Prisoner** is the general term, applicable to anyone covered by this definition, but it is frequently used in a more specific sense, and applied to one who is confined to a prison, or jail; as, *prisoners* of war; to take one *prisoner;* the *prisoners* in the penitentiary. **Captive** implies seizure by force, as in war, conquest, brigandage, and the like; it also often implies bondage or slavery, rather than imprisonment, and sometimes suggests capture for ransom. "He hath brought many *captives* home to Rome, Whose ransoms did the general coffers fill" (*Shak.*). **Convict,** although it literally means a person proved guilty of a crime by a competent tribunal, is more often applied to an imprisoned person serving a long sentence for a crime or felony and wearing the uniform characteristic of his class; as, an escaped *convict;* a chain gang of *convicts*.

pristine. Primeval, primordial, primitive, primal, *primary, prime.
Ana. Original, fresh, *new.

privation. 1 *Lack, absence, defect.
Ana. Negation, nullification, annulling, abrogation (see corresponding verbs at NULLIFY).
2 *Poverty, want, destitution, indigence, penury.
Ana. Depletion, draining, exhaustion, impoverishment (see corresponding verbs at DEPLETE): *need, necessity, exigency: pinch, strait (see JUNCTURE).

privilege. *Right, prerogative, birthright, perquisite, appanage.
Ana. Concession, *allowance: favor, boon (see GIFT): *claim, title.

privy. Underhand, underhanded, surreptitious, backstairs, clandestine, furtive, *secret, covert, stealthy.

prize, *v.* Value, treasure, cherish, *appreciate.
Ana. Esteem, respect, admire, regard (see under REGARD, *n.*): *estimate, evaluate, assess, assay, rate.

prize, *n.*[1] *Spoil, booty, plunder, pillage, loot, swag.

prize, *n.*[2] *Premium, award, reward, meed, guerdon, bounty, bonus.
Ana. Recompensing *or* recompense, requital, compensation (see corresponding verbs at PAY): winning *or* winnings, earning *or* earnings (see corresponding verbs at GET).
Ant. Forfeit.

probable. Probable, possible, likely are here compared only in the sense of uncertain yet such as may be, or may become, true, real, or actual. That is **probable** (etymologically, provable) which has so much evidence in its support or seems so reasonable that it commends itself to the mind as worthy of belief, though not to be accepted as a certainty; thus, the most *probable* conclusion from evidence at hand is the one which the weight of evidence supports even though it does not provide proof; the *probable* thief is the one at whom so much of the evidence points as to give grounds for a presumption that he is guilty; the "*probable* life" of a person, in the language of actuaries, is the period during which one half the persons of a given age at a given time will remain alive according to mortality tables; so, the *probable* cause of a fire; the *probable* author of an anonymous book; the *probable* expenses of a trip; the *probable* origin of a rumor. That is **possible** which is within the powers of performance, attainment, conception, or the like, of an agent or agency, especially a human agent (as, it is now *possible* to cross the Atlantic in an airplane; knowledge *possible* only to God; that we can relieve him is certain, that we can cure him is *possible*), or which is within the widest limits of a person's ability or a thing's capacity as determined by nature, necessity, circumstances, or the like (as, it is not *possible* to carry more than a thousand gallons of gasoline in this airplane; communication with Mars may never be *possible;* "the number of *possible* amusements [for an infant] is small until the child has learned to grasp objects that it sees"—*B. Russell*), or which, though not probable, may happen by chance or is dependent on a contingency or contingencies (as, his election is *possible*, but not *probable;* it is *possible* that she will come this way; "I think that 'so near as to obstruct' means so near as actually to obstruct—and not merely near enough to threaten a *possible* obstruction"—*Justice Holmes*). That is **likely** (see also APT, 2) which to all appearances is that which is alleged, suggested, required, or the like: in contrast with *probable, likely* does not as often or as invariably suggest grounds sufficient to warrant a presumption of truth, but in contrast with *possible*, it usually implies many more chances in favor of its being true; thus, the *probable* murderer is the suspect whose guilt is nearly but not completely established by the evidence; a *possible* murderer is merely one against whom suspicion is directed for some reason (often inadequate reason) or other; the *likely* murderer is the one among the *possible* murderers who, especially from a more or less superficial point of view, has had the strongest motive and the best opportunity to commit the murder, or toward whom the circumstantial evidence most distinctly points as the murderer; so, no *likely* heir to the bachelor millionaire's estate has been mentioned; the *likely* outcome of the war changes from month to month; this hut in the deep woods would be a *likely* rendezvous for gangsters. *Likely* is also often used in the sense of *promising* because of appearances, ability to win favor, and the like; as, a *likely* young man; a *likely* candidate.
Ana. Credible, believable, colorable, *plausible: *reasonable, rational.
Ant. Certain: improbable.

probationer. *Novice, novitiate, apprentice, postulant, neophyte.

probe, *v.* Pierce, penetrate, *enter.
Ana. Examine, inspect, *scrutinize: *prove, try, test.

probe, *n.* Investigation, *inquiry, inquisition, inquest, research.

probity. *Honesty, honor, integrity.
Ana. Uprightness, justness, conscientiousness, scrupulousness (see corresponding adjectives at UPRIGHT): *truth, veracity: rectitude, *goodness, virtue.

problem. *Mystery, enigma, riddle, puzzle, conundrum.
Ana. Perplexity, mystification, bewilderment, distraction (see corresponding verbs at PUZZLE): *predicament, dilemma, plight, quandary.
Ant. Solution.

problematical, problematic. *Doubtful, dubious, questionable.
Ana. Ambiguous, equivocal, *obscure, vague, cryptic, enigmatic: uncertain, suspicious, mistrustful (see corresponding nouns at UNCERTAINTY).

procedure. *Process, proceeding.
Ana. Ordering *or* order, arrangement (see corresponding verbs at ORDER): *method, system, manner, way: conducting *or* conduct, management (see corresponding verbs at CONDUCT).

proceed. Issue, emanate, stem, flow, derive, *spring, arise, rise, originate.
Ana. *Follow, succeed, ensue: *come, arrive.

proceeding, *n.* *Process, procedure.
Ana. *Action, act, deed: *affair, business, concern: operation, functioning, working (see corresponding verbs at ACT).

process, *n.* **Process, procedure, proceeding** come into comparison as denoting the series of actions, operations, motions, and the like, involved in the accomplishment of an end. **Process** is the preferred term when progress from a definite beginning to a definite end is implied and something is thereby made or produced or is changed from one thing into another: the term usually suggests a division of the entire series into steps or stages; as, to describe the *process* of making sugar from sugar cane; the *process* of digestion; a complicated chemical *process;* "perfect knowledge is no mere intellectual *process*" (*Inge*). The idiomatic phrase "in *process*" means in the course of being made, produced, built, constructed, evolved, attained, or the like. "For men in practical life perfection is something far off and still in *process* of achievement" (*W. James*). **Procedure** is the preferred term when the stress is upon the routine method followed, or the routine course to be followed, not only in an industrial, a chemical, a mental, or other distinct process, but in doing anything such as conducting a meeting, a trial, a conference, a business, or the like, performing an experiment or an operation, and prosecuting an investigation or a search; as, to study the rudiments of parliamentary *procedure;* to know laboratory *procedure* better than any other graduate student in chemistry; the young lawyer was frequently embarrassed by his ignorance of correct legal *procedure.* **Proceeding,** a much less definite term than the others of this group, applies not only to the series, actions, or operations directed toward the attainment of an end, but also to any one of such acts or operations: the term throws more stress on the individual or collective acts or operations than on their closely knit relation to each other or on the final end which they have in view: often, the term means little more than an instance, sometimes a course, of conduct or behavior; as, "The law...stepped in to prevent a *proceeding* which it regarded as petty treason to the commonwealth" (*Froude*); to record the *proceedings* of a meeting of a society; "It's the precise habits, the incredible *proceedings* of human insects I like to note and study" (*L. P. Smith*).
Ana. Progress, advance (see under ADVANCE, *v.*): conducting *or* conduct, management, controlling *or* control, direction (see corresponding verbs at CONDUCT): performance, execution, accomplishment, fulfillment (see corresponding verbs at PERFORM).

prochronism. *Anachronism, metachronism, parachronism.

proclaim. *Declare, announce, publish, advertise, promulgate, broadcast.
Ana. *Reveal, disclose, discover, divulge, tell: voice, utter, vent, ventilate (see EXPRESS, *v.*): *inform, apprise, advertise.

proclamation. Declaration, announcement, publication, advertisement, promulgation, broadcasting. See under DECLARE.

proclivity. Propensity, *leaning, penchant, flair.
Ana. Knack, aptitude, *gift, bent, turn: inclination, disposition, predisposition (see corresponding verbs at INCLINE): *predilection, prepossession, prejudice, bias.

procrastinate. *Delay, lag, dawdle, loiter, dally, dillydally.
Ana. *Defer, suspend, stay, postpone: protract, prolong (see EXTEND).
Ant. Hasten, hurry.

procreate. *Generate, engender, beget, get, sire, breed, propagate, reproduce.

proctor. *Lawyer, counselor, barrister, counsel, advocate, attorney, solicitor, procurator.

procurator. *Lawyer, counselor, barrister, counsel, advocate, attorney, solicitor, proctor.

procure. *Get, obtain, secure, acquire, gain, win, earn.
Ana. *Negotiate, arrange, concert: *reach, compass, gain, achieve, attain: *manage, contrive, afford.

prodigal. *Profuse, lavish, exuberant, luxuriant, lush.
Ana. Extravagant, exorbitant, immoderate, *excessive: abundant, *plentiful, plenteous, ample, copious: *supererogatory, uncalled-for, gratuitous.
Ant. Parsimonious: frugal. — *Con.* Niggardly, penurious, *stingy: economical, *sparing, thrifty.

prodigious. *Monstrous, tremendous, stupendous, monumental.
Ana. *Enormous, immense, huge, vast, gigantic, mammoth, colossal: amazing, astounding, flabbergasting (see SURPRISE).

produce, *v.* *Bear, yield, turn out.
Ana. *Generate, breed, propagate: *make, form, shape, fabricate, manufacture: create, *invent.

produce, *n.* *Product, production.

product. 1 *Work, production, opus, artifact.
Ana. Forming *or* form, fabrication, manufacturing *or* manufacture (see corresponding verbs at MAKE): article, object, *thing.

2 Product, production, produce come into comparison only when they denote something produced or brought into being by any process or operation, especially one involving labor or effort. **Product** is the most general of these terms, for it is applicable to anything produced by generation, growth, labor, or thought, or by any industrial, chemical, mental, or other process, or by the operation of causes in no way controllable by man; as, specimens of all the *products* of this factory will be on exhibition in the railway station next week; the factory's entire *product* (that is, total output of manufactured goods) for the past year exceeds that of any two other factories of the same kind; the boy is a finished *product* of a well-known school; the literary *products* of the Age of Reason; soot is usually the *product* of the imperfect combustion of coal or other fuel; "[Man] is the flower and chief of all the *products* of Nature" (*Henry More*). **Production,** in the sense of the thing produced, is generally restricted in its application to human products involving intellectual or artistic labor. Some persons avoid the use of the term as grandiose, but it is the preferred term in theatrical and motion-picture use; thus, a work of sculpture, a philosophical or historical treatise, or a theatrical representation of a play may be described as a *production;* so, the greatest *production* of Hamlet that this country has been privileged to see and hear; "The finest *productions* of Praxiteles or Zeuxis" (*Froude*); Wagner believed Parsifal the climactic *production* of his career. But *production* is also used in a more abstract sense to denote all things (sometimes all things of a specified or implied kind) manufactured or grown to satisfy human wants; as, to limit *production;* an increase of *production* in factories with defense contracts is extremely necessary; the problems of *production* and of distribution. **Produce** is ordinarily a collective noun applied to agricultural as distinguished from industrial products (as, "the meagre *produce* of the land"—*Cowper;* the *produce* exchange [that is, the exchange in which contracts are made involving large-scale sales or purchases of wheat, corn, and other grains, and other agricultural products]); sometimes, however, it is applied especially to vegetables and fruits (as, the farmer sells his *produce* at the public market; a new store for the sale of fresh *produce*).

production. 1 *Work, product, opus, artifact.
Ana. Execution, fulfillment, performance (see corresponding verbs at PERFORM): *effort, exertion.
2 *Product, produce.

proem. *Introduction, prologue, induction, prelude, overture, preface, foreword, prolegomenon, exordium, preamble, prolusion, protasis, avant-propos.

profanation. Profanation, desecration, sacrilege, blasphemy are here compared as meaning a violation or a misuse of something regarded as sacred. **Profanation,** though strongly derogatory, does not impute such baseness to the act or conduct as do the other words. It usually implies an attitude of irreverence or contempt in the offender that leads him to show his feelings in acts or in words that outrage those who hold the place or the thing sacred. The term often specifically suggests bold, vulgar intrusion or irreverent vandalism; as, the *profanation* of a sanctuary by ignorant tourists; "a wall was built round the tomb to protect it from *profanation*" (*Froude*). **Desecration** in strict use carries a strong implication of defilement or pollution, as of churches, temples, sacred vessels, etc., and a consequent loss of a sacred or hallowed character or of ceremonial cleanliness (as, the *desecration* of a cathedral by its use as a barracks by invading troops): sometimes, however, mere deprivation of the sacred character is implied (as, "Various *profanations* of the sabbath...threaten a gradual *desecration* of that holy day"—*B. Porteus*). **Sacrilege** etymologically implies the stealing of sacred objects, such as the vessels used in the solemn Eucharistic service. This sense still obtains, especially in British use; as, "The very books that are used in the worship of God are Sacred. The man who steals them is guilty of *sacrilege*" (*Manning*). The more common sense in ecclesiastical use is that of reception (or sometimes, administration) of a sacrament, especially the Sacrament of Penance or of the Eucharist, under conditions that make one unworthy to receive (or administer) it. "I shall refuse to administer the Sacrament. In your present state of mind, it would be a *sacrilege*" (*Cather*). In more general use, *sacrilege* is applied to any act, situation, or the like, which constitutes an outrageous profanation of something regarded as sacred; as, "To religious minds this scientific inversion of solemn truths seems, and is, *sacrilege*" (*H. Adams*). **Blasphemy,** in loose use (for strict sense see BLASPHEMY, 1), is often employed in place of *sacrilege* in its general and nonecclesiastical sense, usually, however, with the implication of a base perversion of the truth. "This doctrine sounds like *blasphemy* against friendship" (*P. G. Hamerton*).
Ana. Defilement, pollution, contamination (see corresponding verbs at CONTAMINATE): debasement, vitiation, corruption, perversion (see corresponding verbs at DEBASE): violation, transgression, trespass (see BREACH).

profane, *adj.* **1 Profane, secular, lay, temporal** as here compared agree in meaning not dedicated or set apart for religious ends or uses. **Profane** (etymologically, outside the temple), in its strictest sense, implies an opposition to *sacred* (see HOLY): in this sense, it is purely descriptive and not derogatory; thus, *profane* history, as distinguished from *sacred* history, is history dealing with nations or peoples rather than with Biblical events or characters; *profane* literature, as distinguished from *sacred* literature, comprises all literature except the Scriptures, other sacred writings, and sometimes, writings having a definite religious end or use; *profane* love applies to human love as between man and woman, as distinguished from *sacred* love, the love of man for God and of God for man. The term is, however, used more widely to imply an opposition to *holy, religious, spiritual,* and the like; as, "I have observed that *profane* men living in ships, like the holy men gathered together in monasteries, develop traits of profound resemblance" (*Conrad*). **Secular** (etymologically, of the age or time, therefore of the world) usually implies a relation to the world as distinguished from the church, or religion, or the religious life; it may be opposed to *sacred* and come close to *profane* (as, *secular* music; the *secular* drama); it may be opposed to *regular,* in the sense of governed by a monastic rule (thus, a *secular* priest is a priest who does not belong to a religious order; a *regular* priest is one who does); it is most often opposed to *religious* in the sense of belonging to or serving the ends of a religion or church, then coming close to *civil, public,* etc. (as, *secular* schools; *secular* journals; "the *secular* authority—*C. Mackenzie;* "There are peoples in the world who have no *secular* dances, only religious dances"—*H. Ellis*). **Lay** is commonly applied to persons (sometimes to their activities, interests, duties, etc.) that do not belong to the clergy: it, therefore, usually implies an opposition to *clerical* or *ecclesiastical;* as, the *lay*men and *lay*women of the parish; a *lay* preacher; *lay* sermon; *lay* delegates to a diocesan convention. In religious orders, the term is applied to a class of religious who are occupied chiefly with domestic and manual work as distinguished from those who are occupied with liturgical observances, teaching, study, etc.; as, the *lay* brothers in a monastery; the *lay* sisters in a convent. *Lay* is also used loosely in the sense of nonprofessional or of not having a professional source or character; thus, a *lay* opinion on a question of law is merely an opinion delivered by one who is neither a lawyer nor a judge. **Temporal** (as here considered: see also TEMPORARY, 1) implies an opposition to *spiritual* (in the sense of not concerned with material or mundane but with immaterial and eternal ends) and is applied chiefly to sovereigns, rulers, or dignitaries having political authority or civil power; thus, in British use, lords *temporal* are those members of the House of Lords who are not bishops or archbishops (these latter being called lords *spiritual*); the Papacy had no *temporal* power between 1870, the year of the fall of the Papal State, and 1929, the year of the establishment of Vatican City.
Ana. Worldly, mundane, *earthly, terrestrial.
Ant. Sacred. — *Con.* *Holy, divine, religious, spiritual.
2 *Impious, blasphemous, sacrilegious.
Ana. Foul, filthy, *dirty, nasty: ungodly, godless, *irreligious: iniquitous, nefarious, villainous, *vicious.

profanity. *Blasphemy, cursing, swearing.
Ana. Imprecation, *curse, malediction, malison: execration, objurgation, damning (see corresponding verbs at EXECRATE).

profession. Art, handicraft, craft, *trade.

proffer. *Offer, tender, present, prefer.
Ana. Propose, design, *intend: confer, bestow, present, *give.
Con. Reject, spurn, refuse, *decline.

proficient. **Proficient, adept, skilled, skillful, expert** agree in meaning having the knowledge and experience necessary to success in a given line, especially of work or endeavor. All these terms are applied primarily to persons; when applied to things, the implication is that the quality of the person has been attributed to the thing. One is **proficient** who, as a result of training and practice, has acquired competency beyond that of the average. "*Proficient* in the art of self-defence" (*Shaw*). "Jane began to type. It bored her, but she was fairly *proficient* at it" (*R. Macaulay*). One is **adept** who has proficiency, aptitude, and often, cleverness; as, *adept* at legerdemain. "The Oriental is...*adept* in extracting himself plausibly from the most compromising situations" (*V. Heiser*). One is **skilled** who has mastered the details of a trade or handicraft or the technique of an art or profession. *Skilled* may imply aptitude or proficiency; in modern industrial use, however, it simply connotes that one has met a standard set up by employers for a special type of work or job; as, a *skilled* laborer; the *skilled* trades. "By long practice, he was *skilled* in the arts of teaching" (*Gibbon*). One is **skillful** who unites adeptness and dexterity in execution or performance; as, a *skillful* operator of an automobile; a *skillful* teacher; "a *skillful* economy of means" (*Pater*). One is **expert** who has attained extraordinary proficiency or is marvelously adept; as, an *expert* accountant; an *expert* bridge player; *expert* knowledge of engines. "Neither of them was *expert* in the roping of cattle" (*M. Austin*).
Ana. Efficient, effectual, *effective: capable, *able, competent, qualified: finished, accomplished, *consummate: practiced, drilled, exercised (see under PRACTICE, *v.*).
Con. *Awkward, clumsy, maladroit, inept, gauche: *ignorant, untaught.

profile. *Outline, contour, silhouette, sky line.

profit, *n.* *Use, service, advantage, account, avail.
Ana. Reward, award, meed, guerdon (see PREMIUM): gaining *or* gain, winning, earning (see corresponding verbs at GET).

profit, *v.* *Benefit, avail, boot, bestead.
Ana. *Get, gain, win, earn: *advance, progress.

profitable. *Beneficial, advantageous.
Ana. *Favorable, auspicious, propitious: *expedient, advisable, politic.
Con. Detrimental, deleterious (see PERNICIOUS): harming *or* harmful, injurious, hurting *or* hurtful (see corresponding verbs at INJURE).

profligate. Dissolute, reprobate, *abandoned.
Ana. Debauched, corrupted, depraved, debased, perverted (see under DEBASE): degenerate, corrupt, *vicious: *loose, relaxed, slack, lax.

profound. *Deep, abysmal.
Ana. Penetrating, probing, piercing (see ENTER): scrutinizing, inspecting, examining (see SCRUTINIZE).
Ant. Shallow.

profuse. **Profuse, lavish, prodigal, luxuriant, lush, exuberant** come into comparison because they carry as their basic meaning giving out or given out in great abundance. That is **profuse** which seems to pour or be poured forth in abundance, without restraint, or in a stream; as, *profuse* apologies; *profuse* sweating; *profuse* in expenditure; "Pourest thy full heart In *profuse* strains of unpremeditated art" (*Shelley*); "A land where life was great ...and beauty lay *profuse*" (*Browning*). That is **lavish** (etymologically, deluging) which is so exceedingly profuse as to suggest, positively, munificence or extravagance, or negatively, the absence of all stint or measure; as, *lavish* gifts; a *lavish* feast; *lavish* expenditures; "the *lavish* attentions of his mother" (*Meredith*); "Our *lavish* use of a bountiful supply of crude oil" (*A. C. Morrison*); "it is a noble, *lavish* and distinguished work" (*Lucas*). That is **prodigal** which gives or is given so lavishly and so recklessly as to suggest waste or the ultimate exhaustion of resources; as, the *prodigal* son of a wealthy father; "Chary of praise and *prodigal* of counsel" (*Stevenson*); "he had been *prodigal* of the excellencies of his nature...and, like Timon, he became bankrupt, and fell upon bitterness" (*Meredith*). That is **luxuriant** which produces or is produced in great and rich abundance: the term usually connotes not only profusion but gorgeousness or splendor in that which is produced; as, the *luxuriant* growth of nasturtiums; her *luxuriant* hair; the *luxuriant* imagination of Milton; "religion might well flourish quite as *luxuriantly* as it did in former times" (*J. W. Krutch*). That is **lush** which is not only luxuriant, but which has reached the peak of its perfection: the term distinctively connotes richness, fullness of development, or luxuriousness; as, "How *lush* and lusty the grass looks! how green!" (*Shak.*); *lush* tropical forests; "*lush* dinners here, when anybody came, were the climactic experiences of Ouvrard's...soul" (*Hervey Allen*); "The air was knife-keen and as fresh as lettuce ....a far cry from the *lush*...full-blown landscape of the south through which they had set out that morning" (*Jan Struther*). That is **exuberant** (etymologically, prolific or fruitful) which produces or is produced so abundantly or luxuriantly as to suggest exceedingly great vigor, vitality, or creative power; as, an *exuberant* fancy; the *exuberant* genius of Shakespeare; *exuberant* foliage; "to restrain my too *exuberant* gesture" (*M. Austin*). In current use, *exuberant* applies chiefly to persons, their words, emotions, qualities, or the like, that display a vigor or vitality that is almost rampant; as, *exuberant* energy; the child's *exuberant* gaiety.
Ana. Copious, abundant (see PLENTIFUL): *excessive, immoderate, extravagant: *liberal, bountiful, munificent, generous.
Ant. Spare, scanty, scant. — *Con.* *Meager, skimpy, scrimpy, exiguous, sparse.

progenitor. *Ancestor, forefather, forebear.
Ant. Progeny.

prognostic. *Foretoken, presage, omen, augury, portent.
Ana. Indication, betokening, bespeaking (see corresponding verbs at INDICATE): symptom, *sign, mark, token.

prognosticate. *Foretell, predict, forecast, prophesy, augur, presage, portend, forebode.
Ana. *Indicate, betoken, bespeak: *foresee, foreknow, apprehend, divine, anticipate.

program *or* **programme.** **Program** (*or* **programme**), **schedule, timetable, agenda** agree in denoting a formulated plan listing things to be done or to take place, especially in their time order. **Program** is the term of widest meaning. It may refer to a mental plan or to one that is written or printed; it may be applied not only to a plan for a meeting, an entertainment, a service, or the like, but to one made by an individual in ordering his own day or his own future, or to one made by a group that has certain ends in view and proposes their orderly achievement; as, what is your *program* for today?; the *program* of a concert; theater *programs;* the Five-Year Plan was the name given the industrialization *program* of the Soviet Union. **Schedule** stresses the importance of the time element and implies a plan of procedure which establishes not only the chronological order of events or steps but also their time limits; as, the *schedule* for a college year; a *schedule* of production in a factory;

a *schedule* for the erection of a building. *Schedule* is sometimes used, but **timetable** possibly more often, for a tabulated list of regularly recurring events, such as arrivals and departures of trains; as, a *timetable* of tides; a *schedule* of classes. **Agenda** (a plural noun sometimes construed as a singular) is more informal than the others in its implications; it is applied chiefly to an order of business for a meeting.

progress, *n.* **1** Advance (see under ADVANCE, *v.*, 2).
Ana. Improvement, betterment (see corresponding verbs at IMPROVE): headway, impetus (see SPEED, *n.*).
2 Progress, progression are not always clearly distinguished, although in current usage they are more or less sharply differentiated. Both denote movement forward. **Progress** (for fuller treatment see *progress*, n., under ADVANCE, *v.*, 2) usually applies to the movement considered as a whole, stressing the distance covered, the change or changes taking place, the amount of improvement made, or the like; as, we made little *progress* that day; to note the extent of his *progress* during the past year; "delightful never-ending *progress* to perfection" (*Hazlitt*); the daily *progress* of the sun; the history of educational *progress;* the rapid *progress* of a disease. **Progression** (see also SUCCESSION) commonly applies to the movement in itself or in its detail, often implying a continuous series of steps, degrees, or stages toward an objective, but sometimes implying little more than a moving on more or less continuously; as, mode of *progression* (better than *progress*); "That slow *progression* of things, which naturally makes elegance and refinement the last effect of opulence and power" (*Sir J. Reynolds*); "Every generation... adds...its own discoveries in a *progression* to which there seems no limit" (*Peacock*); "the *progression* of sound waves" (*Karl K. Darrow*).

progress, *v.* *Advance.
Ana. *Move, drive, impel: further, forward, promote, *advance: develop, *mature.
Ant. Retrogress.

progression. **1** *Succession, series, sequence, set, suit, suite, chain, train, string.
2 *Progress.

progressive. *Liberal, advanced, radical, left.
Ant. Reactionary.

prohibit. *Forbid, inhibit, enjoin, interdict, ban.
Ana. *Prevent, preclude, obviate: debar, shut out, *exclude: *hinder, impede, obstruct: *restrain, curb, check.
Ant. Permit. — *Con.* *Let, allow, suffer: tolerate, endure, *bear.

project, *v.* Scheme, design, plot, plan. See under PLAN, *n.*
Ana. Propose, purpose, *intend: *sketch, outline, diagram, delineate.

project, *n.* Scheme, design, plot, *plan.
Ana. Sketch, delineation, draft, outline, diagram (see under SKETCH, *v.*): *device, contrivance.

projection. Projection, protrusion, protuberance, bulge come into comparison when they denote something which extends beyond a level or a normal outer surface. **Projection** is applicable to anything that juts out, especially at a sharp angle; as, buttresses are *projections* which serve to support a wall or a building at a point of great strain or pressure. "Machinery set in motion to keep a level smooth...feels the least *projection*, and tries to flatten it out" (*Hearn*). **Protrusion** applies to something which is thrust out or which pushes out, so that it seems more or less of an excrescence or deformity; as, the architect advised them not to spoil the roof line with *protrusions* such as dormer windows. A **protuberance** swells or pushes out, often in rounded rather than angular form; as, the *protuberances* of a potato; he has a *protuberance* on the cheek which has not as yet been diagnosed. "An obvious moral is indeed a heavy *protuberance* which injures the gracefulness of a poem" (*Landor*). A **bulge** is a protuberance or expansion of a surface caused usually by pressure from within or below; as, a *bulge* in a wall; there is a slight *bulge* in the soil before the first stalk of a plant appears.

projector. See under PLAN, *n.*

prolegomenon. *Introduction, prologue, induction, prelude, overture, preface, foreword, proem, exordium, preamble, prolusion, protasis, avant-propos.

prolific. Fruitful, *fertile, fecund.
Ana. Teeming, swarming, abounding, superabounding (see TEEM): generating, breeding, propagating, reproducing *or* reproductive (see corresponding verbs at GENERATE).
Ant. Barren, unfruitful.

prolificacy, prolificity, prolificness. Fruitfulness, fertility, fecundity. See under FERTILE.
Ant. Barrenness, unfruitfulness.

prolix. *Wordy, verbose, diffuse, redundant.
Ana. Tedious, *irksome, tiresome, wearisome: prolonged, protracted (see EXTEND): pleonastic, circumlocutory, redundant, tautological (see corresponding nouns at VERBIAGE)

prologue. *Introduction, induction, prelude, overture, preface, foreword, prolegomenon, proem, exordium, preamble, prolusion, protasis, avant-propos.

prolong. Protract, *extend, lengthen, elongate.
Ana. *Continue, last, persist, endure: *increase, augment, enlarge: *expand, amplify.
Ant. Curtail. — *Con.* *Shorten, abridge, abbreviate, retrench.

prolusion. *Introduction, prologue, induction, prelude, overture, preface, foreword, prolegomenon, proem, exordium, preamble, protasis, avant-propos.

prominent. Remarkable, conspicuous, salient, outstanding, signal, *noticeable, striking, arresting.
Ana. *Chief, leading, main, principal: important, significant (see corresponding nouns at IMPORTANCE).

promiscuous. Heterogeneous, motley, *miscellaneous.
Ana. Mixed, mingled, blended, merged (see MIX): *random, haphazard, desultory, casual: *indiscriminate, wholesale, sweeping: *licentious, lewd, wanton, lascivious.
Con. Discriminating, perceiving, discerning (see corresponding nouns at DISCERNMENT): discreet, prudent, forethoughted (see under PRUDENCE).

promise, *v.* **Promise, engage, pledge, plight, covenant, contract** come into comparison as meaning to give one's word that one will do, make, give, accept, or the like, something stipulated. **Promise,** both as a transitive and as an intransitive verb, implies a giving assurance (usually orally or in writing) but it suggests no further grounds for expectation of the fulfillment of what is promised; as, he is a man of his word, what he *promises* he performs; he *promised* that he would pay his bill within thirty days; he *promised* each child that he would give her a doll for Christmas; to *promise* his daughter in marriage to his old friend's son (cf. his daughter is *promised*); she has *promised* herself a trip to Bermuda in the near future. **Engage,** both as a transitive and as an intransitive verb, implies more binding agreement than *promise.* Although it is usually far from explicit as to the nature of the agreement (sometimes specifically implying an agreement to marry, sometimes an agreement to accept as an employee), nevertheless it implies a promise that is not likely to be broken; as, to *engage* oneself to provide accommodations for four delegates to the convention; an *engaged* couple; to *engage* a secretary; "Mr. Lorry readily *engaged* for that, and the conference was ended" (*Dickens*); "Mrs. Doria *engaged* to go down to the baronet" (*Meredith*); she said she was *engaged* for the next three dances. But *engage* may also imply the securing of a promise from a person, and the use of argument, persuasion, flattery, threats, or the like, in the attaining of that end; as, "Yes, and I hope to *engage* you to be serious likewise" (*Austen*); "Her highness... when I left her, *engaged* me to write to her" (*Lady M. W. Montagu*). **Pledge,** chiefly a transitive verb, may imply either the giving voluntarily of a promise by some act or words that suggest the giving of a solemn assurance, or the provision of a formal guarantee (as, to *pledge* one's honor that one will see that a dying friend's wish is respected; they *pledged* their loyalty to their sovereign as they lifted their wine glasses; "By the second [clause], they *pledge* themselves to maintain and uphold the right of the master"—*Ch. Just. Taney*), or the putting of another or of others under a solemn promise to do, to forbear, or the like (as, to *pledge* a thousand men to temperance; "Austria swarmed with excited and angry men *pledged* to destroy the Church"—*Belloc;* to *pledge* the children to allegiance to the flag). **Plight,** a very old and now archaic word, appears rarely except in certain idiomatic expressions where the entire phrase means to promise solemnly, as in to *plight* one's faith, or one's honor, or one's troth (then implying betrothal, or, as in the words used in some marriage ceremonies, marriage), or one's word; as, he *plighted* his faith that the injustice would be avenged. **Covenant,** more often an intransitive than a transitive verb, implies at least two parties to the promise, each making a solemn agreement with the other or others. "A man cannot grant any thing to his wife, or enter into covenant with her: for...to *covenant* with her, would be only to *covenant* with himself" (*Blackstone*). "The men of Ulster...*covenanted* to defeat the present conspiracy to set up a Home Rule Parliament in Ireland" (*R. Macaulay*). **Contract** (as here considered: see also CONTRACT, 3; INCUR) implies the entry into a solemn, and now usually legally binding, agreement (see CONTRACT, *n.*): it is currently rare with a noun object (as, "We have *contracted* an inviolable amitie...with the aforesaid queene"—*Hakluyt*) but it is not uncommon with *for* or with an infinitive object; as, to *contract* for a large loan; the company has *contracted* to supply the schools of the state with textbooks.

Ana. Agree, consent, *assent, accede: assure, *ensure, insure.

promote. Forward, further, *advance.

Ana. *Help, aid, assist: *speed, quicken, hasten, hurry.

Ant. Impede. — *Con.* *Hinder, obstruct, block, bar.

promotion. 1 *Advancement, preferment, elevation.

Ana. *Progress, progression: exaltation, magnifying, aggrandizement (see corresponding verbs at EXALT).

Ant. Demotion. — *Con.* Degradation, humiliation, debasement (see corresponding verbs at ABASE).

2 *Publicity, propaganda, ballyhoo.

Ana. Advertisement, promulgation, broadcasting (see corresponding verbs at DECLARE).

prompt, *adj.* *Quick, ready, apt.

Ana. Alert, wide-awake, vigilant, *watchful: expeditious, speedy, swift (see FAST): trained, disciplined (see TEACH): *eager, keen, avid.

Con. Remiss, lax, slack (see NEGLIGENT): dilatory, *slow.

promulgate. Proclaim, announce, *declare, publish, advertise, broadcast.

Ana. *Reveal, disclose, divulge, discover: affirm, aver, avow, avouch (see ASSERT): *communicate, impart.

promulgation. Proclamation, declaration, announcement, publication, advertisement, broadcasting. See under DECLARE.

prone. 1 Subject, exposed, open, *liable, susceptible, sensitive, incident.

Ana. Inclined, predisposed, disposed (see INCLINE, *v.*): addicted, habituated, accustomed (see HABITUATE).

2 **Prone, supine, prostrate, recumbent, reclining, couchant, dormant** are here compared as meaning lying upon the ground, floor, or other surface. *Prone* and *supine* as applied to men or animals are contrasted terms which are often incorrectly used. **Prone,** in strict use, implies a posture where the front of the body lies upon or is turned toward the ground: the term is applicable not only to serpents and the like that move along the ground, but to the natural position of most quadrupeds as distinguished from that of man; as, dogs *prone* upon the ground; "a creature who, not *prone* And brute as other creatures, but endued With sanctity of reason, might erect His stature" (*Milton*). The term is also used in reference to men, chiefly as a quasi-adverb, with verbs such as *lie, fall, land,* etc., implying a position with face and abdominal side downward; as, he fell *prone* upon the ground; the doctor ordered him to lie *prone* for the examination. "Then falls, betrayed by shifting shells, and lands *Prone* in the jeering water, and his hands Clutch for support where no support can be" (*Amy Lowell*). **Supine** (see also INACTIVE), on the other hand, implies a lying upon one's back, usually a lying flat upon one's back; as, he always sleeps in a *supine* position; he fell backward and lay *supine* until help came; "jaded people lolling *supine* in carriages" (*Shaw*). **Prostrate,** in its earliest and still frequent sense, implies the posture of one who throws himself forward full length in a prone position as in adoration, submission, humility, surrender, or fear; as, to fall *prostrate* in worship at the most solemn moment of the liturgy; "*Prostrate* in homage, on her face" (*G. Bottomley*). In somewhat extended use *prostrate* is applicable to men or animals in either a prone or a supine position (as, "Quickly stooping I once more drove my weapon to the hilt in his *prostrate* form"—*Hudson*) and to trees and the like which lie full length upon the ground (as, "He clambered over half-visible rocks, fell over *prostrate* trees, sank into deep holes and struggled out"—*Cather*). **Recumbent** applies chiefly to a person or animal lying down in a position suitable for repose or for sleep; the term apart from the context carries no clear suggestion of the posture, and may imply a flat position or one with the head resting against pillows or the like; as, a *recumbent* alabaster figure on the top of a tomb; "Lady Blandish was *recumbent* upon the brown pine-droppings" (*Meredith*); "Rising proudly from her *recumbent* position" (*Lytton*). **Reclining** suggests either a supine position or a leaning back so as to rest against something; often, it is not clearly distinguishable from *recumbent;* as, she spent the afternoon *reclining* on her couch; *reclining* gracefully in a chaise longue. **Couchant** and **dormant** are used in heraldry to describe a lion or other animal on an escutcheon or coat of arms: both imply a prone position of the body but *couchant* applies only to an animal with head raised, and *dormant,* to one with head lowered as in a sleeping position; as, a sable lion *couchant* on an azure ground.

Ana. Flat, *level: groveling, wallowing, weltering (see WALLOW): crawl, *creep.

Ant. Erect.

pronounce. **Pronounce, articulate, enunciate** are here compared in the sense of to form speech sounds. **Pro-**

nounce involves the assignment of sounds to letters, groups of letters (as syllables and words), or to the words in general of a language, and the distribution of syllabic stress in utterances of more than one syllable in languages that do not have level or even stress; as "s" in "his" is *pronounced* "z"; "colonel" has the same *pronunciation* as "kernel"; he considers it incorrect to *pronounce* "adult" with primary accent on the first syllable; that Frenchman *pronounces* English pretty well. To **articulate,** in the broadest sense in which it comes into comparison here, is to break up, by manipulation of the vocal organs, an expiration of breath into distinct parts (syllables or words), a sequence of these constituting intelligible speech. "His agitation was so great that he could not *articulate*" (*Macaulay*). In a very specialized phonetic sense, to *articulate* is to close or narrow the vocal organs in such a manner as to produce a given sound (esp. a consonant) of a given language, more specifically by the adjustment of the tongue, with relation to the palate, at the place where the tongue has, for that sound, its maximum elevation. "In pronouncing the English variety of the sound **t,** the air passage is completely blocked by...raising the tip of the tongue to touch the teeth-ridge....Many foreigners...*articulate* the sound **t** with the tip of the tongue against the upper teeth.... This *articulation* produces a very unnatural effect when used in English" (*D. Jones*). Hence, by a slight extension, *articulate* may also mean to make the manipulations or articulations for the sounds as a whole in one's speech with such care or carelessness that one's speech is distinctly or indistinctly heard. "A public speaker...must *articulate* more carefully than in ordinary conversation: unstressed vowels will have greater importance and be less reduced, consonants will never be slurred over" (*W. Ripman*). To **enunciate** is to be distinct or indistinct in one's speech as a result of careful or careless articulation and of whatever other factors contribute to distinctness or indistinctness (as sonority, lip action, presence or absence of nasal twang, etc.). "Should children be taught to *enunciate* correctly and to have pleasant manners, or are these mere relics of aristocracy?" (*B. Russell*). But *articulate* and *enunciate* are frequently used with little or no distinction of meaning.

proof. 1 Ground, *reason, argument.
Ana. Demonstration, trial, test (see under PROVE): corroboration, confirmation, substantiation, verification (see corresponding verbs at CONFIRM).
2 Demonstration, test, trial. See under PROVE.
Ant. Disproof.

propaganda. *Publicity, promotion, ballyhoo.
Ana. Propagation, engendering, generating (see corresponding verbs at GENERATE): spread, stretch (see EXPANSE): inculcation, instillment, implanting (see corresponding verbs at IMPLANT).

propagate. *Generate, engender, breed, beget, procreate, sire, reproduce.
Ana. *Increase, multiply, augment: *continue, persist: *extend, lengthen, prolong.

propel. *Push, shove, thrust.
Ana. *Move, drive, impel: *force, compel, constrain, oblige.

propensity. *Leaning, proclivity, penchant, flair.
Ana. *Predilection, prejudice, bias, prepossession: *gift, aptitude, bent, turn, knack: predisposition, disposition, inclination (see corresponding verbs at INCLINE).
Ant. Antipathy.

proper. 1 Meet, appropriate, fitting, apt, happy, felicitous, *fit, suitable.
Ana. Congruous, congenial, compatible, *consonant: *correct, nice, right: *due, rightful, condign.
Ant. Improper. — *Con.* Wrong, *false.
2 Seemly, *decorous, decent, nice, comme il faut, demure.
Ana. Formal, conventional, ceremonious, *ceremonial.

property. *Quality, character, attribute, accident.
Ana. Peculiarity, individuality, characteristic (see corresponding adjectives at CHARACTERISTIC).

prophecy. *Revelation, vision, apocalypse.
Ana. Communication, impartation (see corresponding verbs at COMMUNICATE): *inspiration, enthusiasm.

prophesy. Predict, forecast, *foretell, prognosticate, augur, presage, portend, forebode.
Ana. *Foresee, foreknow, divine, apprehend, anticipate.

propinquity. *Proximity.
Ana. Closeness, nearness (see corresponding adjectives at CLOSE): relatedness *or* relationship, kindredness *or* kindred (see corresponding adjectives at RELATED): *kinship, consanguinity.

propitiate. *Pacify, appease, placate, mollify, conciliate.
Ana. Reconcile, conform, adjust, *adapt: *satisfy, content: intercede, mediate (see INTERPOSE).

propitious. Auspicious, *favorable, benign.
Ana. Benignant, *kind, kindly: fortunate, *lucky, providential, happy.
Ant. Unpropitious: adverse. — *Con.* *Sinister, malefic, malign, baleful: *ominous, inauspicious, portentous, fateful.

proportion. *Symmetry, balance, harmony.

proportionable. Proportionate, *proportional, commensurate, commensurable.
Ana. Corresponding, harmonizing, according (see AGREE).

proportional. Proportional, proportionate, proportionable, commensurate, commensurable are not closely synonymous terms, but they are often used without marked distinction because all mean being duly proportioned to something else. *Proportional, proportionate,* and *proportionable* all imply due proportions either to a related thing or things, or of things that are related, as by belonging to the same set, series, design, or construction, or by being the effect of a cause, the response to a stimulus or the like. **Proportional** is the preferred term when several things that are closely related to each other and must be proportioned to each other as in size, amount, number, length, or the like, are under consideration; as, a good architect knows that the dimensions of a building should be *proportional;* the circumferences of all circles are *proportional* to the lengths of their radii; the increase in number of teachers and of schools has not been *proportional* to the increase in the number of pupils; *proportional* representation. *Proportional* may be used, but **proportionate** is more often used, when the term is intended to imply the adjustment (sometimes, but not invariably, the deliberate adjustment) of one thing that bears a reciprocal relationship to another thing, so that both are in keeping with each other or not out of keeping with what is just, fair, due, reasonable, or the like; as, the punishment should be *proportionate* to the crime; the results were not *proportionate* to the exertions of the workers; the return is not *proportionate* to the investment; "Ponderous bodies forced into velocity move with violence *proportionate* to their weight" (*Johnson*); "They rushed into freedom and enjoyment...with an energy *proportional* to their previous restraint" (*G. L. Dickinson*). **Proportionable** is now comparatively rare in use: the term has been and still may be employed in place of either *proportional* or *proportionate,* especially when there is the intent also to imply a capacity, in the thing or things so qualified, for being regarded as observing due proportions or as being properly adjusted to each other; as, they have five married children and a *proportionable* number of grandchildren; "For us to levy power *Proportionable* to the enemy Is all unpossible" (*Shak.*). **Commensurate** and **commensurable** differ from the preceding words chiefly in carrying a stronger implication of equality between things each of which has a measure, a degree, an intensity, or the like, that is dependent on its relation to the other or others (as, his productiveness is *commensurate* with [that is, neither exceeds nor falls short of] his display of energy; "the meagreness of the result was *commensurate* with the crudity of the methods" (*Buchan*). Sometimes both terms, but especially *commensurable*, differ from the other words in implying a common scale of values by which outwardly different things can be shown to be equal or proportionate in some significant way; as, the delight produced by a beautiful lyric and that produced by an equally beautiful movement of a sonata are *commensurable* because both imply the evocation of a mood; two heroes *commensurate* only in distinction, for one was a hero of the battlefield and the other a hero of the moral sphere.

Ana. Adequate, *sufficient, competent: correspondent, correlative, *reciprocal: relative, contingent, *dependent.

proportionate. *Proportional, proportionable, commensurate, commensurable.

Ana. Correspondent, correlative, *reciprocal: adequate, *sufficient, competent.

Ant. Disproportionate.

proposal. **Proposal, proposition,** as here compared, denote something which is proposed to another or others for consideration. Although the dividing lines between the two terms are not always clear-cut, especially in current English, the tendency to distinguish them sharply still prevails in strict usage. **Proposal** usually carries a clear suggestion of the act of proposing; thus, one receives a *proposal*, or entertains a *proposal*, or listens to a *proposal*. It also commonly implies an offer, as of oneself as a would-be husband, or of a given amount of money in return for the transferring of a piece of property or other valuable possession; as, a *proposal* of marriage; to submit a *proposal* to the owner to take care of his grounds for a small weekly wage. "He offered to sweep the floor of the gymnasium then and there. This *proposal* convinced the Skenes" (*Shaw*). But it may imply the suggestion of a scheme, a plan, a project, or the like, which may be accepted or rejected at the will of the person or persons to whom it is proposed; as, "[the Constitution] when it came from their [the framers'] hands, was a mere *proposal*, without obligation, or pretensions to it" (*Ch. Just. Marshall*); "expressing regret that no *proposal* having for its object the readmission of Master Byron to the academy could be entertained" (*Shaw*). **Proposition** in its strictest sense applies to a statement (usually an affirmative statement) that is propounded for discussion, argument, proof, or disproof; as, to demonstrate the truth of a *proposition;* at first sight the *proposition* seemed absurd; "It is a *proposition* too plain to be contested, that the constitution controls any legislative act repugnant to it" (*Ch. Just. Marshall*). The term is also applicable to any implied or expressed principle that is or may be questioned or is regarded from the point of view of its truth or its falsity. " 'What you think about the stars, Padre?' 'The wise men tell us they are worlds, like ours, Jacinto.'...'I think not,' he said in the tone of one who has considered a *proposition* fairly and rejected it. 'I think they are leaders—great spirits' " (*Cather*). *Proposition* has been and to a restricted extent still is used instead of *proposal* in the sense of a proposal made formally that some course of action be followed, some policy be adopted, some honor granted, or the like. In this sense, the term rarely, in strict use, refers to personal or to business affairs; as, "We hold it essential to our success...that the *proposition* of Sir George Clerk should be adopted" (*Bp. S. Wilberforce*); "The medical major at the first post declares it [a certain heroic act] is impossible. He has to sign the *proposition* for the citation" (*Hemingway*). In looser colloquial use, *proposition* is often used where *proposal* is still regarded by authorities as the preferred word; as, if you wish to buy this land, make me a *proposition*.

propose. Purpose, *intend, mean, design.

Ana. *Aim, aspire: plan, plot, scheme, project (see under PLAN, *n.*).

proposition. *Proposal.

propriety. *Decorum, decency, etiquette, dignity.

Ana. Grace, *elegance, dignity: *form, usage, convention, convenance.

prorate. *Apportion, portion, parcel, ration.

prorogue. *Adjourn, dissolve.

Ant. Convoke.

prosaic. **Prosaic, prosy, matter-of-fact** come into comparison as meaning having a plain, practical, unimaginative, unemotional character or quality. **Prosaic,** as here considered, implies an opposition to *poetic* in the extended sense of the latter word. Although the term etymologically suggests the quality of prose, it seldom refers to literary prose, but rather to the ordinary language of men in communicating their wants, their ideas, or their experiences, or in rendering intelligible that which is difficult to understand or make clear; hence, *prosaic* usually implies a commonplace, unexciting quality, and the absence of everything that would stimulate feeling or awaken great interest; as, "To make verse speak the language of prose, without being *prosaic*..., is one of the most arduous tasks a poet can undertake" (*Cowper*); "Let me have none of your *prosaic* curates" (*Gray*); a *prosaic* and humdrum life; "The eighteenth century, from the religious point of view, is a period of rather cold and *prosaic* common sense" (*Inge*). **Prosy,** on the other hand, suggests a relation to *prose*, the verb, rather than to *prose*, the noun, and heightens the implication in the former of turning that which is poetry or interesting prose into dull plain prose, as by paraphrasing or by translating. Consequently, *prosy* stresses extreme dullness or tediousness and usually, but not invariably, implies a tendency to talk or write at length in a boring or uninviting manner; as, *prosy* preachers; a hopelessly *prosy* book; "It is his special comfort to smoke a pipe and be *prosy* with some good-natured fellow, the dullest of his acquaintance" (*Scott*). **Matter-of-fact** stresses a concern for fact or for facts as well as lack of interest in that which is imaginative, speculative, visionary, romantic or ideal; sometimes it connotes accuracy in detail, but often it suggests concern only for the obvious and a neglect of the deeper or spiritual reality; as, a *matter-of-fact* account of his experience in an air raid; a *matter-of-fact* historian; "Mr. Rose had got so dreamy... that he felt...the necessity of turning a little more *matter-of-fact* again" (*W. H. Mallock*); "Faced with this *matter-of-fact* scepticism you are driven into pure metaphysics" (*Shaw*).

Ana. Practical, *practicable: humdrum, tedious, *irksome.

proscribe. *Sentence, condemn, damn, doom, attaint.

proselyte. *Convert.

prospect, *n.* **Prospect, outlook, anticipation, foretaste** are here compared as meaning an advance realization of something to come, especially of something foreseen or expected. *Prospect* and *outlook* both imply a conjuring up of a picture or mental vision of what the future holds in store for one. **Prospect,** however, is chiefly applied to particular events or situations, especially to those of interest to one as an individual and evocative of an emotional response. "The *prospect* of the Netherfield ball was extremely agreeable to every female of the family" (*Austen*). "He had just received a box of new books... and had preferred the *prospect* of a quiet Sunday at home" (*E. Wharton*). "She asked her father if the *prospect* of living always with his daughter and being taken care of by her affection...was such an awful *prospect*" (*Conrad*). **Outlook** suggests an attempt to forecast the future from the point of view of a thinker, such as an economist or a philosopher, or from that of a practical man, as a politician or businessman, who is concerned not only with immediate but remote possibilities, and who demands accuracy in detail and soundness in conclusions; as, the *outlook* for business has been declared favorable. "The *outlook*, domestic and international, was still what those who think in terms of colour call black" (*R. Macaulay*). **Anticipation** usually implies a prospect or outlook, but in addition it involves the implication of advance suffering or enjoyment of that which is envisioned. "Lord Beaconsfield once said that the worst evil one has to endure is the *anticipation* of the calamities that do not happen" (*A. C. Benson*). **Foretaste** also implies advance experience or prior enjoyment or suffering, but it does not necessarily connote (as does *anticipation*) a mental as distinguished from an actual experience. It implies sufficient experience to give one a hint of what is to come, but the experience, or taste, may be actual enjoyment or suffering or a fleeting but poignant anticipation of it. "A trifle of torture to the flesh... While soul is spared such *foretaste* of hell-fire, Is naught" (*Browning*). "Giving me Amid the fretful dwellings of mankind A *foretaste*...of the calm That Nature breathes among the hills and groves" (*Wordsworth*).

Ana. Hoping, expectation (see corresponding verbs at EXPECT): foreseeing *or* foresight, foreknowing *or* foreknowledge, divining *or* divination (see corresponding verbs at FORESEE).

prostrate. *Prone, supine, recumbent, reclining, couchant, dormant.

Ana. Flat, *level: abject (see MEAN).

prosy. *Prosaic, matter-of-fact.

Ana. *Insipid, jejune, banal, inane: *irksome, humdrum, tedious.

protasis. *Introduction, prologue, induction, prelude, overture, preface, foreword, prolegomenon, proem, exordium, preamble, prolusion, avant-propos.

protean. *Changeable, changeful, variable, mutable.

protect. Shield, guard, safeguard, *defend.

Ana. *Save, preserve, conserve: *ensure, insure, assure: shelter, *harbor.

protectorate. *Possession, dependency, territory, colony, dominion, mandate.

protest, *v.* **1** Avouch, avow, affirm, aver, *assert, declare, predicate, warrant.

Ana. *Swear, affirm, asseverate, testify.

2 *Object, remonstrate, expostulate, kick.

Ana. *Oppose, resist, combat: *demur, scruple, balk.

Ant. Agree (sense 1).

prototype. **Prototype, archetype, antitype, ectype** are not all synonyms, but they are often used carelessly or incorrectly because not clearly distinguished. A **prototype** is the original, or the first instance, of something which is imitated or reproduced, with or without changes and improvements, so that its successors follow in series and form a type, or kind of thing; as, the Roman republic is not the *prototype* of modern republics such as the United States of America; it is a question whether Langley's flying machine was the *prototype* of the airplane. An **archetype** is the pattern which serves as the model for all created things of the same kind. It may be ideal, that is, a conception in the mind of the creator; as, according to Plato, the Ideas are the *archetypes*, of which sensible things are only the copies: it may be real, that is, it may have concrete existence, and thus be the pattern for all future things of the same kind. In this latter sense, it is often used interchangeably with *prototype;* discriminating writers, however, distinguish the words, for *prototype* does not preclude the implication of change and progress, but *archetype* in effect does, since it stresses the determining influence of the pattern. "The House of Commons, the *archetype* of all the representative assemblies which now meet" (*Macaulay*). **Antitype** is often misused as though it were a compound of anti- and -type and not, as it actually is, a word directly derived from the Greek. Originally a theological and philosophical term, it is now found frequently in literary use. An antitype is that which corresponds to or gives real existence to something that is prefigured or foreshadowed by a type (that is, in a rare sense of this word, a person or a thing that serves as a symbol or sign of what is to come); thus, in theological use, Christ is the *antitype* of many persons and things in the Old Testament, such as the goat slain in the wilderness, the paschal lamb, and Melchizedek. In literary use, *antitype* often means the person or thing that realizes or gives substantial form to a poet's or artist's conception; as, more than one actual person has been identified as the *antitype* of Wordsworth's "Happy Warrior." An **ectype** (now rare even in philosophical use) is the person or thing that is a copy of an archetype, or a successor of a prototype; thus, the works of the Creator are called *ectypes* in contrast with his designs, or predetermined patterns, the *archetypes*.

Ana. Pattern, *model, example, exemplar.

protract. Prolong, *extend, lengthen, elongate.

Ana. *Delay, retard, slow, slacken: *defer, suspend, stay, postpone.

Ant. Curtail. — *Con.* *Shorten, abridge, abbreviate.

protrusion. *Projection, protuberance, bulge.

protuberance. *Projection, protrusion, bulge.

proud. **1 Proud, arrogant, haughty, lordly, insolent, overbearing, supercilious, disdainful** come into comparison when they mean filled with or exhibiting a sense of one's superiority and scorn for that which is regarded as beneath one. **Proud** does not always imply presumption or suggest assumed rather than genuine superiority; on the contrary, it may be used in praise as well as in derogation, but in all instances it usually connotes a lofty or imposing manner, attitude, or appearance, that may be interpreted as dignified, elevated, spirited, imperious, satisfied, contemptuous, inordinately conceited, or the like, according to the circumstances. "Oh, why should the spirit of mortal be *proud*? Like a swift-flitting meteor, a fast-flying cloud... He passeth from life to his rest in the grave" (*W. Knox*). "A strange shy lovely girl whose face Was sweet with thought and *proud* with race" (*Masefield*). "The high spirit and *proud* resolution of a real aristocracy" (*Inge*). "He has nothing to be ashamed of in you—rather everything to be *proud* of" (*Meredith*). **Arrogant** implies a disposition to claim for oneself, often domineeringly or aggressively, more consideration than is warranted or justly due; as, an *arrogant* nobility was in part responsible for the French Revolution. "In holidays, the atmosphere of home is apt to be dominated by the young people. Consequently they tend to become *arrogant* and hard" (*B. Russell*). **Haughty** implies a strong consciousness of exalted birth, station, or character, and a more or less obvious scorn of those who are beneath one. "Pride goeth before destruction, and an *haughty* spirit before a fall" (*Proverbs* xvi. 18). "There was a deferential manner in the bearing of the men towards her, which those *haughty* creatures accord not save to clever women" (*Meredith*). The last four words of this group are more specific than the preceding terms and refer more to the ways in which arrogance or haughtiness is exhibited than to the temperament or attitude. **Lordly** usually suggests pomposity, strutting, or a display of power or magnificence; as, *lordly* officials; the *lordly* captain of a ship. "See yonder...wight... Who begs a brother of the earth To give him leave to toil; And see his *lordly* fellow-worm The poor petition spurn" (*Burns*). **Insolent** implies both haughtiness and extreme contemptuousness; it carries a stronger implication than the preceding words of a will to insult or affront the person so treated; as, "she could not determine whether the silent contempt of the gentlemen, or the *insolent* smiles of the ladies, were more intolerable" (*Austen*). **Overbearing** suggests a bullying or tyrannical disposition, or intolerable insolence; as, an *overbearing* employer; an *overbearing* snob. "No one had loved Hendrik van der Berg; he had been too strong, too *overbearing* to be loved" (*S. Cloete*). **Supercilious** stresses the superficial aspects of haughtiness, such as a manner intended to repel advances; it refers to one's behavior to others rather than to one's conceit of oneself, though the latter is always implied: often, it suggests not only scorn but also incivility and occasionally covert curiosity. "They have no blood these people. Their voices, their *supercilious* eyes that look you up and down" (*Galsworthy*). "*Supercilious* and *haughty*, they [camels] turn this way and that, like the dowagers of very aristocratic families at a plebeian evening party" (*A. Huxley*). **Disdainful** implies a more passionate scorn for that which is beneath one than does *supercilious:* it as often as not suggests justifiable pride or justifiable scorn. "He [Caesar] makes me [Antony] angry with him; for he seems Proud and *disdainful*, harping on what I am, Not what he knew I was" (*Shak.*). "Don Manuel Chavez...very elegant in velvet and broadcloth, with delicately cut, *disdainful* features,—one had only to see him cross the room...to feel the electric quality under his cold reserve" (*Cather*).

Ana. Contemptuous, scornful, disdainful (see corresponding nouns under DESPISE): pretentious, pompous, ostentatious (see SHOWY): imperious, domineering, *masterful.

Ant. Humble: ashamed.

2 Vain, vainglorious. See under PRIDE, *n.*

Ana. Exalted, magnified, aggrandized (see EXALT): self-satisfied, *complacent, smug: contented, satisfied (see SATISFY).

Ant. Ashamed: humble.

prove. 1 Prove, try, test, demonstrate come into comparison as meaning to establish a given or an implied contention or reach a convincing conclusion by means of evidence, argument, experiment, or any other appropriate means. The same distinctions in implications and connotations are evident in their corresponding nouns **proof, trial, test, demonstration** when they denote the process or the means by which a contention is established or a convincing conclusion is reached. **Prove** and **proof** (as here compared: see also INDICATE; REASON, *n.*, 1) are the most widely useful of these terms, for they are not only employed in reference to contentions and conclusions, but also in reference to persons or things whose strength, genuineness, fitness, or the like, is in question. When used in reference to contentions or to conclusions reached by study, they imply that evidence sufficient in amount and sufficiently reliable in its character has been adduced to bring conviction of the truth of the contentions or conclusions and to make other contentions or other conclusions untenable. "This proposition may or may not be true; at present there is certainly no evidence sufficient to *prove* it true" (*B. Russell*). "The legislation of the different colonies furnishes positive and indisputable *proof* of this fact" (*Ch. Just. Taney*). But *prove* and *proof* when used in reference to persons or things about which there is doubt in some particular imply the settlement of this doubt or the establishing of certainty of his or its strength, genuineness, fitness for use or service, or the like, as by subjecting the thing to an experiment or by giving the person a chance to manifest his quality in experience, or by other means such as assaying, verifying, checking, or the like; as, to *prove* the strength of gunpowder; to *prove* a cannon (cf. *proving* ground); to *prove* useful members of society; to *prove* one's courage in action; to put a man to the *proof;* to demand visible *proof* of one's love; the *proof* of gold; the *proof* of the pudding is in the eating. **Try** and **trial** (as here compared: see also ATTEMPT, *v.*; TRIAL, 2) still carry implications from their earliest senses of to separate (or the separation of) the good from the bad in a person or thing and, therefore, stress not so much the conclusion reached as the process by which the guilt or innocence of a person is definitely proved, or a thing's genuineness or falsity, its worth or worthlessness, its degree of strength, validity, or the like, is definitely established; as, to *try* a person for theft; to *try* a case in court; "The question whether a right has vested or not, is, in its nature, judicial, and must be *tried* by the judicial authority" (*Ch. Just. Marshall*); "A boy does not like to be called a fool, and is usually ready to *try* the question with his fists" (*Meredith*); the *trial* of metal by fire; the medieval *trial* by combat; the new employee is on *trial;* to take a new vacuum cleaner on *trial.* **Test,** both as a verb and as a noun, implies a putting to decisive proof by means of experiment, use, experience, or comparison with a high standard, or through subjection to a thorough examination or trial for the sake of such proof or a determination of the facts; as, "Experience is the surest standard by which to *test* the real tendency of the existing constitution" (*Washington*); the careful scientist subjects every experiment to severe *tests;* to submit to an intelligence *test;* "The first time he [Don Quixote] made a helmet, he *tested* its capacity for resisting blows, and battered it out of shape; next time he did not *test* it but 'deemed' it to be a very good helmet" (*B. Russell*); "how well his writing has stood the *test* of time" (*L. P. Smith*). **Demonstrate** and **demonstration** (as here compared: see also SHOW, *v.*, 2), imply the conclusive proof of a contention or the reaching of a conclusion about which there can be no doubt. In such use, *prove* and *demonstrate* and their corresponding nouns are not distinguishable except in the latter term's emphasis upon the resulting certainty or formality of method; as, "[Lyell] first imagined, and then *demonstrated*, that the geologic agencies are not explosive and cataclysmal, but steady and patient" (*C. W. Eliot*); "The schools knew that their society hung for life on the *demonstration* that God...was a reality" (*H. Adams*). In current use, there is a tendency to distinguish them and to employ *demonstrate* so that it implies scientific certainty based on sensible evidence or clear experiment; as, "these arguments [for the existence of God] are sometimes called *proofs*, though they are not *demonstrations*" (*Inge*).

Ana. Corroborate, verify, substantiate, *confirm: *justify, warrant.
Ant. Disprove.
2 *Indicate, betoken, attest, bespeak, argue.
Ana. Evidence, manifest, evince, *show, demonstrate.
provenance, provenience. *Origin, source, inception, root, prime mover.
Ana. Beginning, commencement, starting (see corresponding verbs at BEGIN).
provender. *Food, fodder, forage, victuals, viands, provisions, comestibles, grub, eats, chow.
proverb. Maxim, adage, motto, *saying, saw, epigram, aphorism, apothegm.
provided. *If.
providence. *Prudence, foresight, forethought, discretion.
Ana. *Care, solicitude, concern: thoughtfulness, consideration (see corresponding adjectives at THOUGHTFUL): frugality, thriftiness, economicalness *or* economy (see corresponding adjectives at SPARING).
Ant. Improvidence.
provident. Prudent, foresighted, forethoughted, discreet. See under PRUDENCE.
Ana. Careful, solicitous, concerned (see under CARE, *n.*): *thoughtful, considerate: *sparing, economical, frugal, thrifty.
Ant. Improvident.
providential. *Lucky, fortunate, happy.
Ana. Benign, auspicious, propitious, *favorable: benignant, kindly, *kind.
province. 1 *Field, domain, sphere, territory, bailiwick.
Ana. *Boundary, border, frontier, march: *limit, confine, bound, end.
2 *Function, office, duty.
Ana. *Work, calling, pursuit, métier, business: *task, duty, job.
provisional. 1 **Provisional, tentative** come into comparison as meaning not final or definitive. That is **provisional** which is adopted only for the time being and will be discarded when the final or definitive form is established or the need of it no longer exists. *Provisional*, therefore, is used to describe something made or devised while its permanent successor is in process of formation or construction (as, a *provisional* government; a *provisional* arrangement) or when proper materials are lacking or there is no time for permanent construction (as, a *provisional* postage stamp; a *provisional* bridge). "The French ministers have taken up this equality of government only *provisionally*, reserving liberty to alter it according to occurrences" (*Bp. J. Hall*). That is **tentative** which is of the nature of a trial or experiment or which serves as a test of a thing's practicability or feasibility; as, to adopt a *tentative* order of procedure; "The awakening of the modern world to consciousness, and its first *tentative*, then fuller, then rapturous expression of it" (*J. R. Lowell*); "It would be folly to treat the first *tentative* results as final" (*Jeans*).
Ana. *Temporary: conditional, *dependent, contingent.
Ant. Definitive.
2 *Temporary, ad interim, acting, supply.
provisions. *Food, victuals, viands, comestibles, provender, fodder, forage, grub, eats, chow.
provoke. 1 **Provoke, excite, stimulate, pique, quicken, galvanize** come into comparison as meaning to rouse one into doing or feeling something, or to call something into existence by so rousing a person or persons. **Provoke** (etymologically, to call forth) stresses a power in the agent or agency sufficient to produce such an effect, but it is often the least explicit of these terms as to the nature or character of that power; it is, therefore, the preferred term when nothing more is to be implied than the effecting of the stated result; as, "It is one of the misfortunes of the law that ideas become encysted in phrases and thereafter for a long time cease to *provoke* further analysis" (*Justice Holmes*); "It is not in...the emotions *provoked* by particular events in his life, that the poet is in any way remarkable or interesting" (*T. S. Eliot*); "What happens when we prolong and intensify the rubbing to such a degree that we *provoke* a spark?" (*Karl K. Darrow*). **Excite** carries so strong an implication of a rousing that stirs up, moves profoundly, serves as a challenge to one's powers, or the like, that the term is often used merely in the sense of to rouse in any of these ways; as, "the ideas which *excited* my own generation" (*G. W. Russell*); "Have I ever even felt inclined to write anything, until my emotions had been unduly *excited*, my brain immoderately stirred?" (*Galsworthy*). Often, however, *excite* adds to these implications those found in *provoke*, and thereby becomes a more explicit or richer word than the latter by suggesting the powerful or stirring nature of the agent or agency and the degree or intensity of the activity stirred up; as, "the curiosity *excited* by his long absence burst forth in...very direct questions" (*Austen*); "no stimulus was omitted to *excite* and inspire the imagination and the sense" (*G. L. Dickinson*). **Stimulate** suggests a provoking or exciting by, or more often, as if by, a prick, a spur, or a goad: sometimes, therefore, it connotes a rousing out of lethargy, indifference, inaction, or inactivity, or a bringing forth into play something that is latent, dormant, or quiescent; as, to *stimulate* the growth of plants by the use of fertilizers; "Mrs. Yeobright, in her anxiety for her niece's future, had mentioned this lover to *stimulate* the zeal of the other" (*Hardy*); "the stupidity of the opposition *stimulated* him, and made him resolute" (*Mencken*); "Memory must be constantly *stimulated* and helped" (*Grandgent*); "I have always believed that it is better to *stimulate* than to correct, to fortify rather than to punish" (*A. C. Benson*). Often, *stimulate* specifically implies excitement or re-excitement of interest, especially of a deep intellectual interest; as, "some subjects, which are remarkably *stimulating* to the mind of the pupil, are neglected, because they are not well adapted for examinations" (*Inge*); advertising designed to *stimulate* the public's waning interest. **Pique**, a term of far more restricted application, suggests provocation or stimulation by or as if by something that pricks or irritates; as, a show of secrecy always *piques* her curiosity; "make a distinct declaration that she is to think no more of you as a possible husband. That will *pique* her into accepting him" (*Hardy*). **Quicken** implies a stimulation of life, vigor, energy, or activity with consequent beneficial results; as, "The mistress which I serve *quickens* what's dead" (*Shak.*); "Some effluence from her *quickened* him" (*Bennett*); there has been a *quickening* of interest in minorities since Hitler came into power. **Galvanize** (etymologically, to treat or revive by the use of electricity) suggests a highly artificial stimulating or quickening, especially of that which is old, or stiff, or dying; as, "He seemed a mere automaton, *galvanized* into moving and speaking" (*Hardy*); "sonnet-cycles are a treasure-trove of conventions, distorted in a mistaken endeavor to *galvanize* them into life, into sheer grotesquerie" (*Lowes*).
Ana. Arouse, rouse, *stir: *thrill, electrify, enthuse: *incite, instigate, foment.
2 *Irritate, exasperate, nettle, aggravate, roil, peeve.
Ana. Affront, *offend, insult, outrage: *anger, incense, madden: agitate, upset, perturb (see DISCOMPOSE).
Ant. Gratify.

prowess. *Heroism, valor, gallantry.
Ana. Bravery, boldness, audacity, intrepidity (see corresponding adjectives at BRAVE): *courage, mettle, spirit: strength, might, puissance, *power.

prowl, *v.* *Wander, stray, roam, ramble, rove, range, gad, gallivant, traipse, meander.

proximity. Proximity, propinquity are often used interchangeably because both denote nearness. **Proximity,** however, in good current use, commonly implies nearness in space: it may be used with reference to either persons or things found in the same vicinity or neighborhood (as, owing to its *proximity* to the sea, the town usually enjoys mild winters; "for centuries and centuries their [swallows'] nests have been placed in the closest *proximity* to man"—*Jefferies;* "affected much as he might have been by the *proximity* of a large dog of doubtful temper"—*Shaw*), or it may be used as an equivalent of *vicinity* or *neighborhood* (as, there was no inn in the *proximity*). **Propinquity** may imply proximity, but it then usually distinctively suggests closeness, sometimes even contact. "We read a book because it happens to be near us and it looks inviting. It is a case where *propinquity* is everything" (*S. M. Crothers*). It is more often used where *proximity* is not possible to imply nearness in relationship, closeness in association, in age, in tastes, or the like, or even closeness in time; as, relations within the fourth degree of *propinquity;* they are both cousins of his, but not in the same degree of *propinquity; propinquity* is a powerful aid in fostering attachments; events in close *propinquity* to each other. "If you can put up with a tumultuous *propinquity* of...football-man—you can travel up and down England at single fare [for the round trip] with a football team while its luck prevails in the Cup" (*Manchester Guardian*).
Ana. Nearness, closeness (see corresponding adjectives at CLOSE): adjacency, contiguousness, juxtaposition (see corresponding adjectives at ADJACENT).
Ant. Distance.

proxy. Deputy, attorney, *agent, factor.

prudence. Prudence, providence, foresight, forethought, discretion come into comparison when they denote a quality that enables a person to choose the wise and sensible course, especially in managing his practical affairs. The same differences in implications and connotations are apparent in the adjectives **prudent, provident, foresighted, forethoughted, discreet** when they mean manifesting such a quality. **Prudence** and **prudent** (see also WISE) are the most comprehensive of these words, for they imply both that one does not act rashly or unadvisedly and that one has foreseen the probable consequences of one's act. Consequently, the terms usually imply caution and circumspection, but may or may not connote selfishness, mercenariness, calculation, or other unpleasant qualities. "One is given reason and common sense and *prudence* that one may use them" (*A. C. Benson*). "That type of person who is conservative from *prudence* but revolutionary in his dreams" (*T. S. Eliot*). "What is the difference in matrimonial affairs, between the mercenary and the *prudent* motive?" (*Austen*). "An old fort...where the Filipinos, although outnumbering their assailants [Moros]..., had judged it more *prudent* to hide than to fight" (*V. Heiser*). **Providence** and **provident** imply thought for the future, especially with reference to its difficulties and its needs and, usually, the provision in advance of that which will then be required. "Early and *provident* fear is the mother of safety" (*Burke*). "The creature who bears His image is intended to exercise *providence*" (*F. D. Maurice*). "I see your [Indian] tribe as a *provident*, rather thoughtful people, who made their livelihood secure by raising crops and fowl" (*Cather*). **Foresight** and **foresighted** stress a power, usually the result of a highly developed intelligence, of seeing what is likely to happen and of being prepared for it. "The more we study the making of the principate, the more we shall be impressed with the grasp and *foresight* of its founder" (*Buchan*). "Incapable of the *foresighted* control and adjustment of action which are the essence of all the higher forms of behavior" (*Wm. McDougall*). **Forethought** and the less frequent **forethoughted** suggest rather due consideration of contingencies. "In choosing the Yankee dialect, I did not act without *forethought*" (*J. R. Lowell*). **Discretion** and **discreet** stress the qualities which make for prudence or compel prudent action, such as good judgment, caution, self-control, and the like. In early use, discretion and valor were thought of as complementary qualities; as, "The better part of valour is *discretion*" (*Shak.*); "You put too much wind to your sail; *discretion* and hardy valour are the twins of honour" (*Beaumont & Fletcher*). In later use, *discretion* and *discreet* often imply the power to restrain oneself when one is tempted to be temerarious, passionate, incensed, loquacious, or the like. "Prudence and *discretion* forbade me to appeal against this decision" (*A. C. Benson*). "I dare say he will be a *discreeter* man all his life, for the foolishness of his first choice" (*Austen*). "He [Octavian] had been marvellously patient and *discreet*" (*Buchan*). "Well, you don't give me away. You are very *discreet*" (*Cather*).
Ana. Caution, circumspection, calculation (see under CAUTIOUS): expediency, advisableness (see corresponding adjectives at EXPEDIENT): frugality, thriftiness *or* thrift (see corresponding adjectives at SPARING).

prudent. 1 Judicious, sensible, sane, *wise, sage, sapient.
Ana. *Intelligent, brilliant, bright, smart, alert: *shrewd, perspicacious, sagacious, astute: disciplined, schooled (see TEACH).
2 Provident, foresighted, forethoughted, discreet. See under PRUDENCE.
Ana. *Cautious, circumspect, calculating, wary: politic, *expedient, advisable: economical, frugal, thrifty, *sparing.
3 Prudent, prudential are sometimes confused in use. **Prudent** applies to persons, their acts, their words, or the like, and implies qualities of mind or character such as caution, circumspection, and thrift (see *prudent* under PRUDENCE), or as wisdom in practical affairs (see WISE); as, a *prudent* man; a *prudent* course; a *prudent* way of life. **Prudential,** on the other hand, applies not to individuals but either to habits, motives, policies, considerations, or the like, which are dictated or prescribed by prudence, especially by forethought, or business sense, practical wisdom, or the like (as, "in a *prudential* light it is certainly a very good match for her"—*Austen;* "A journalist like Andrew Lang lives by quoting. But no *prudential* motive could bring him the gift. It is, at bottom, a present from Nature"—*C. E. Montague*), or to committees, groups, associations, or the like, having charge of practical affairs such as expenditures, or exercising discretionary or advisory powers in regard to these (as, "the *prudential* men," the former designation, especially in New England, of a group of men selected to look after town affairs; a *prudential* investment society; the *prudential* committee of a Congregational church).
Ana. Politic, *expedient, advisable: advising, counseling (see corresponding nouns at ADVICE).

prune, *v.* *Preen, prank, prink, primp, perk up, doll up.

prying. *Curious, inquisitive, snoopy, nosy.
Ana. Meddlesome, officious, *impertinent, intrusive, obtrusive.

psalm. *Hymn, laud, canticle, antiphon, anthem, canon.
pseudepigrapha. *Apocrypha.
pseudonym. **Pseudonym, alias, nom de guerre, pen-name, nom de plume, incognito, allonym** agree in denoting a name other than one's true or legal name. **Pseudonym** usually implies assumption of the fictitious name; it more often suggests a creditable than a discreditable motive for one's attempt to conceal one's identity. **Alias,** in strict legal use, covers not only assumed names, but those ascribed by others; thus, a boy's true name may be John Potter but he is better known by the *alias* John Rhoads (Rhoads being his stepfather's name). In loose use, however, *alias* is associated with offenders against the law and usually connotes an attempt to free oneself, by a change of name, from the onus of a criminal record. **Nom de guerre** (a French phrase adopted in English) is a pseudonym assumed by one who seeks anonymity or freedom of scope, especially, but not invariably, as an adventurer, a critic, a controversialist, or the like; **pen name** or **nom de plume** (not a French formation) is the pseudonym of a writer. **Incognito** (sometimes, colloquially, *incog*), when it denotes a disguise that is a pseudonym or alias, suggests a desire to remain unrecognized or a polite fiction by which one avoids the honors due because of one's rank or eminence; as, the Prince of Wales often traveled under the *incognito* of Baron Chester. **Allonym,** a rarely used word, designates a pseudonym that is the name of another person; it therefore implies not only the intent to deceive but also to shift responsibility for one's acts.
psyche. *Mind, intellect, soul, brain, brains, intelligence, wit, wits.
psychiatrist, psychiater. *Neurologist, alienist, psychopathologist, psychotherapist, psychoanalyst.
psychic, psychical. *Mental, intellectual, intelligent, cerebral.
psychoanalyst. *Neurologist, psychiatrist, alienist, psychopathologist, psychotherapist.
psychopathologist, psychopathist, psychopath. *Neurologist, psychiatrist, alienist, psychotherapist, psychoanalyst.
psychosis. *Insanity, lunacy, mania, dementia.
psychotherapist. *Neurologist, psychiatrist, alienist, psychopathologist, psychoanalyst.
puberty, pubescence. *Youth, adolescence.
public, *n.* *Following, clientele, clientage, audience.
publication. Declaration, announcement, advertisement, proclamation, promulgation, broadcasting. See under DECLARE.
publicity. **Publicity, propaganda, promotion, ballyhoo** are here compared as meaning either a systematic effort to inform the public regarding something or the means or the matter used in such an effort. Each implies a specialized form of advertising. **Publicity,** in the sense here considered, is used often but not exclusively in reference to the activities of and the information disseminated by a person or persons in the employ of individuals, corporations, organizations, associations, institutions, and the like, that seek advertising through more or less indirect means in order to attract attention to themselves, their products, their objectives, or the like, or that wish to provide a source of authoritative information on matters concerning themselves that are of interest to the public; thus, the work of a theatrical press agent and of a public relations counsel is *publicity;* in the first case, for an actor or producer seeking favorable notices in the press; in the second, for a corporation or institution that seeks to control the kind of information regarding itself that is published. "Some of his [Beau Brummell's] carefully planned speeches, always made in the presence of the right listener, are perfect of their kind—their kind being advertisement, or, as we say now, *publicity*" (*Lucas*). **Propaganda** was originally used in English as a short term for the Congregation for the Propagation of the Faith (L. *propaganda de fide*), a department of the Roman Curia having charge of foreign missions or of churches in recently settled countries. Since the Congregation's objectives were the spread and the maintenance of the faith (the Roman Catholic faith), the term came to be applied to the concerted or systematic efforts of any group that tries to convert others or to hold others to its way of thinking, and to the means employed and the matter circulated. In current English the term has both derogatory and underogatory use. In derogatory use it frequently implies publicity sought through objectionable, usually underhand, methods or for a cause that cannot work in the open, and with the intent to win over the gullible or the unwary; as, to attempt to undermine the people's faith in democracy by communistic *propaganda.* "To bring Antony to reason two things were needed. He [Augustus] must acquire an armed following of his own, by lavish expenditure and adroit *propaganda*" (*Buchan*). In nonderogatory use *propaganda* often implies the ends of convincing a prejudiced or ignorant public and of inducing it to accept something it is disposed to reject. Even in this use the word often suggests indirect methods. "The reformers continued their *propaganda* [for Arabic numerals], and now and then made a convert" (*Grandgent*). "Gradually the terror it [a leper colony] caused was lost through our educational *propaganda*" (*V. Heiser*). **Promotion** is specifically applied to the systematic efforts of a business organization to gain advance publicity for a new venture, a new product, a new issue of bonds, or the like, in order to ensure its favorable reception by the public when it is launched; as, a two months' campaign of *promotion* before the new issue of bonds was floated; $50,000 was appropriated for the *promotion* of the company's new line of soups. **Ballyhoo** (originally the commotion caused by barkers of side shows at a circus) is a slang term indiscriminately applied to any kind of advertising, publicity, or promotion which the speaker or writer regards as sensational, insincere, misleading, unduly obtrusive, and the like; as, the candidate's preconvention campaign was attended with too much *ballyhoo;* the company was too conservative to indulge in *ballyhoo* in its advertising.
Ana. Advertisement, publication, announcement, promulgation, broadcasting (see under DECLARE).
publish. **1** *Declare, announce, advertise, proclaim, promulgate, broadcast.
Ana. Divulge, disclose, *reveal, discover: *communicate, impart: vent, ventilate, utter, broach, *express.
2 *Print.
publisher. See under PRINT, *v.*
puck. *Fairy, faery, fay, elf, sprite, pixy, gnome, dwarf, goblin, brownie, nix.
puerile. *Youthful, juvenile, boyish, virgin, virginal, maiden.
Ana. *Immature, unmatured, unripe, unfledged: raw, callow, green, *rude.
Ant. Adult.
puff, *n.* *Criticism, critique, review, blurb.
pugnacious. *Belligerent, bellicose, quarrelsome, contentious, litigious.
Ana. *Aggressive, militant, assertive, self-assertive, pushing.
Ant. Pacific.
puissance. Might, strength, arm, *power, force, energy.

puissant. *Powerful, potent, forceful, forcible.
Ant. Impuissant.

pulchritudinous. Beauteous, good-looking, comely, bonny, pretty, handsome, fair, lovely, *beautiful.

pull, *v.* **Pull, draw, drag, haul, hale, tug, tow,** as here compared, agree in meaning to move in the direction determined by the person or thing that exerts force. **Pull,** the general term, is often accompanied by an adverb or adverbial phrase to indicate the direction; as, two locomotives *pull* the heavy train up the grade; to *pull* a person toward one; to *pull* down goods from a shelf; to *pull* out a drawer; he felt *pulled* this way and that way by duty and by ambition. **Draw** usually but not invariably implies a pulling forward or toward the person or thing that exerts the force; commonly it implies smoother and often gentler motion than *pull;* as, to *draw* a chair to the fireside; the coach was *drawn* by six horses; to *draw* a sled over the snow; to *draw* the curtains; to *draw* lots from an urn. In extended use *draw* often specifically implies a result dependent on a drawing, as by lot (as, to *draw* a prize; to *draw* a jury), or by extracting, steeping, or the like (as, to *draw* a tooth; to *draw* tea), or by an inferring (as, to *draw* a conclusion), or by attracting (as, "the parasol *drew* him like a magnet"—*E. Wharton;* the *drawing* power of a play), or a bringing forth or eliciting from a source of supply (as, to *draw* money from the bank; "a...being from whom we *draw* power and refreshment"—*Day Lewis*). **Drag** implies a pulling slowly and heavily after one (the agent or thing exerting force), as over the ground or a surface; it usually suggests active or passive resistance; as, the horses *dragged* the overturned carriage half a mile; the vessel *dragged* her moorings in the storm; *drag* the laden net to the shore; to *drag* logs to the river. "It was just like Lady Pinkerton...to have gone round to Hobart inciting him to *drag* Jane from my office" (*R. Macaulay*). "The attempt which is now being made to *drag* Anglicanism away from its history and traditions" (*Inge*). **Haul,** in its strictest use, which still prevails in Great Britain, implies a forcible pulling, sometimes a dragging; as, when the hawser fell into the water, there was no means of *hauling* the boat to shore; to *haul* down the sails; "That dangling figure was *hauled* up forty feet above the fountain" (*Dickens*). "Mr. Bennett gasped and doubled up but without relaxing his grasp...silently *hauled* Kim to his own tent" (*Kipling*). In American usage, *haul* often implies transportation, whether, as originally, in a vehicle or conveyance actually hauled by man or animal power or, later, one hauled by a locomotive, or the like, or even, as now, in an automotive vehicle; as, wagons *hauling* loads of wood; motor trucks *hauling* loads of gravel; laden barges were *hauled* through canals by horses walking on the shore; trains that *haul* coal from the mines to the storeyards. **Hale** was formerly often, but is now seldom, used in place of *haul* merely in the sense of pulling forcibly; as, "The rope that *haled* the buckets from the well" (*Tennyson*). When, however, the idea of constraint or compulsion, or of dragging to prison, is involved, either *haul* or *hale* is possible. "Saul...made havock of the church, entering into every house, and *haling* men and women committed them to prison" (*Acts* viii. 3). " 'A pretty thing that would be: the Senior Shipping Master of the Port of London *hauled* up in a police court and fined fifty pounds' " (*Conrad*). "Rather than pay rates to be used in making Roman Catholics or even Anglo-Catholics of little English children, Nonconformist Protestant ratepayers will let themselves be *haled* before the magistrates" (*Shaw*). **Tug** implies a strenuous pulling, but it may or may not suggest actual movement; as, the child *tugged* at his father's hand; to *tug* a car out of the mire with a team of oxen. "There sweat, there strain, *tug* the laborious oar" (*Roscommon*). **Tow** implies pulling or drawing by a rope or chain something which is not using, or is unable to use, its own power; as, to *tow* a ship (by means of a tugboat) into its berth; to *tow* a wrecked automobile to a garage.

pulsate. **Pulsate, pulse, beat, throb, palpitate** agree in meaning to manifest a rhythmical movement such as or similar to that which occurs in the circulatory system when blood is forced along by alternate contractions and distentions of the ventricles of the heart and of the arterial walls. The same distinctions in implications and connotations are to be found in the nouns **pulsation, pulse, beat, throb, palpitation** when they are used of this rhythmical movement or of one distinct step in it. **Pulsate** and **pulsation** carry few specific or distinguishing connotations, but they usually imply regularity, continuity, and vigor in the rhythm whether it is apparent in movements or in sounds; as, when the heart no longer *pulsates*, death occurs; the *pulsation* or *pulsations* of a motor engine. **Pulse** (the verb) is not common in scientific use, *pulsate* being the preferred term. For *pulse* (originally to push or drive) still carries a strong implication of impelled movement; in distinction from *pulsate* it usually also connotes a lively succession of spurts, waves, gushes, or the like; thus, the arteries *pulsate* (not *pulse*) as the blood *pulses* (not *pulsates*) through them. The term, however, is common in literary use, where it sometimes takes as its subject that which flows or moves in this fashion (as the blood) and at other times, that which evidences the rhythmical movement (as the heart or blood vessels); as, the *pulsing* waters of the sea. "It [the vivacity of Chaucer] *pulses* through any book of lyrics printed yesterday" (*Quiller-Couch*). "Eustacia...set inwardly *pulsing* by his words" (*Hardy*). "They move and breathe in an environment that *pulses* and glows" (*Mencken*). On the other hand, **pulse**, the noun, is chiefly a scientific term; even its figurative use is affected by or dependent on the term's meaning in medicine and physiology. In this sense, *pulse* usually denotes the number of pulsations of the arteries in a minute as observed commonly by feeling the radial artery of the wrist; as, a normal *pulse;* a rapid *pulse;* to feel a patient's *pulse. Pulse* often also implies reference to the regularity, vigor, and continuity of the pulsation; as, an intermittent *pulse;* a strong *pulse;* a fluttering *pulse.* "In his eardrums hammers his heavy *pulse*" (*Amy Lowell*). In figurative use *pulse,* when it does not take the place of *pulsation,* commonly is but an extension of the scientific use; as, the group felt the *pulse* of public opinion before they decided to announce their program. "Rome was the heart and *pulse* of the empire...and on its well-being hung the future of the civilized world" (*Buchan*). **Beat** (both verb and noun) is the ordinary nontechnical word often used in place of *pulsate* and *pulsation* and sometimes in place of *pulse.* It stresses, however, rhythmical recurrence of sounds more often than rhythmical and continuous alternation in movement; thus, one hears the *beat* of his heart or tries to still his *beating* heart. It is the preferred designation therefore for something that strikes the ear at regular intervals, such as the tick or ticks of a clock, a stroke or a series of strokes on a drum, and the accented syllable in verse or note in music; as, to hear a watch *beat;* the *beat* of a bird's wing against a windowpane; the *beating* of tom-toms. "[The Negro evangelist] *Beat* on the Bible till he wore it out Starting the jubilee revival shout" (*V. Lindsay*). "The 'fourteener' [a fourteen-syllable verse]...repels readers who have not the patience to accustom their ears and nerves to its *beat*" (*T. S. Eliot*). Both the noun and verb **throb** imply violent,

often painful, pulsation; either is preferred to *pulsate*, or *pulse*, or *beat* (or corresponding nouns), when there is the intent to imply excitement, strain, emotional stress, or the like; as, every nerve in his body *throbbed*. "Here is a captain, let him tell the tale; Your hearts will *throb* and weep to hear him speak" (*Shak.*). "Godfrey felt a great *throb:* there was one terror in his mind at that moment" (*G. Eliot*). **Palpitate** and **palpitation** imply rapid (often abnormally rapid and fluttering) pulsation; in medical use, the term commonly implies overexertion, violent emotion, or a diseased condition; as, to suffer from spells of *palpitation* of the heart. In extended use, however, the words often imply a rapid vibration, quivering, or shaking, without any connotation of something amiss. "Then, delicate and *palpitating* as a silver reed, she stood up in the soft light of the morning" (*Hewlett*).
Ana. Vibrate, fluctuate, waver, oscillate (see SWING): quiver, shudder, quaver, tremble (see SHAKE).

pulsation. Pulse, beat, throb, palpitation. See under PULSATE.

pulse, *n.* Pulsation, beat, throb, palpitation. See under PULSATE.
Ana. *Rhythm, cadence, meter: vibration, fluctuation (see corresponding verbs at SWING).

pulse, *v.* *Pulsate, beat, throb, palpitate.
Ana. *Move, drive, impel: vibrate, fluctuate, oscillate (see SWING).

pummel, *v.* *Beat, pound, buffet, baste, belabor, thrash, thresh.
Ana. *Strike, hit, smite, slug, punch.

punch, *v.* **1** *Strike, hit, smite, slug, slap, swat, clout, box, cuff.
Ana. *Beat, pound, pummel, baste, belabor.
2 *Perforate, puncture, prick, bore, drill.
Ana. Pierce, penetrate, probe, *enter.

punctilious. Punctual, meticulous, scrupulous, *careful.
Ana. Particular, fussy, squeamish, fastidious, *nice: formal, conventional, ceremonious, *ceremonial.

punctual. Punctilious, meticulous, scrupulous, *careful.
Ana. *Quick, prompt, ready: precise, *correct, nice, right.

puncture, *v.* *Perforate, punch, prick, bore, drill.
Ana. Pierce, penetrate (see ENTER): deflate, shrink (see CONTRACT, *v.*).

pungent. **Pungent, piquant, poignant, racy, spicy, snappy** come into comparison when they mean characterized by sharpness, zest, and piercing or gripping power. **Pungent** literally has reference to taste or smell and implies the stinging, pricking, or penetrating quality associated with that which is biting, acrid, caustic, or the like; as, *pungent* ginger ale; the *pungent* odor of ammonia; "a most *pungent* and sickening stench" (*Kipling*). In its figurative sense the word carries implications of great telling power or driving force, or of a capacity for exciting or stimulating keen attention or interest; as, his *pungent* wit; "If you would be *pungent*, be brief; for it is with words as with sunbeams—the more they are condensed, the deeper they burn" (*Southey*); "the *pungent* elegance of Pope" (*Hunt*); "The acidity of the lemon will very aptly figure *pungency* of raillery" (*Johnson*). **Piquant** literally has reference to a taste that is tart or pleasantly pungent to a degree that whets the appetite; as, a *piquant* sauce; a *piquant* flavor. In its figurative sense it applies to that which has an exciting savor or character that lifts it above the usual, or distinguishes it from the ordinary and gives it a zest, charm, or other quality that is peculiarly its own; as, "a little volume of verse...neat, lively, *piquant*" (*Macaulay*); "Often a drop of irony into an indifferent situation renders the whole *piquant*" (*Hardy*); "She made a *piquant*, pretty show, with her thirty years, and her agreeable, slightly roguish face" (*Bennett*). **Poignant** (as here compared: see also MOVING) originally applied either to that which literally cuts or pierces deeply (as, a *poignant* spear) or to that which is pungent to the taste or smell (as, "*poignant* sauce"—*Chaucer;* "the rich, *poignant* perfume"—*N. Hawthorne*). In current use it often applies to emotions that are keenly or deeply felt, or to experiences, words, or the like, that produce such emotions or have the power to pierce one's inmost consciousness; as, *poignant* sorrow; *poignant* memories; "tenderness...so *poignant* that perhaps neither of us knew whether it was joy or pain" (*H. Ellis*); "Which do you think is more *poignant?* Regret for what one has not done or remorse for what one has? I think regret" (*C. Mackenzie*). **Racy** literally has reference to that which has the peculiar character, taste, or piquancy associated with a thing of its kind in its best and, often, its freshest condition; as, *racy* cider; *racy* grapes; the *racy* flavor of some mushrooms. The term is now more often used in an extended sense, implying such qualities as native verve, dash, vitality, or tang, and the absence of all signs of decadence, sophistication, effeteness, or the like; as, "pure 'mother English,' *racy* and fresh with idiomatic graces" (*De Quincey*); "Yorkshire has such families here and there... peculiar, *racy*, vigorous; of good blood and strong brain" (*C. Brontë*); "The free and *racy* spirit of the soil had been banished from its [Barcelona's] amusements leaving a tame vacuity only too familiar at home" (*H. Ellis*). **Spicy** applies literally to that which has the piquant taste of a food seasoned or flavored with or as if with spice or an odor redolent of spice (as, a *spicy* cake; the *spicy* odors emanating from the kitchen), but in the extended sense in which it is here chiefly considered it usually implies the addition of qualities which give the thing affected decided piquancy or a pointed, often sensational, character, or in some use, a touch of smartness, of spiritedness, of scandalousness, or the like (as, *spicy* criticism; a clever *spicy* style; a columnist's *spicy* gossip). **Snappy** applies literally to that which emits shooting sparks or a series of sharp, quick reports (as, a *snappy* fire), but in slangy colloquial use it implies a somewhat comparable show of vitality, animation, smartness, or the like (as, a *snappy* young woman; *snappy* conversation; a *snappy* car).
Ana. *Incisive, trenchant, biting, cutting: penetrating, piercing, probing (see ENTER): exciting, stimulating, provoking *or* provocative (see corresponding verbs at PROVOKE).
Ant. Bland.

punish. **Punish, chastise, castigate, chasten, discipline, correct** agree in meaning to inflict pain, loss, or other suffering upon a person for his sin, crime, or fault. **Punish** implies violation of law, disobedience of authority, or intentional wrongdoing and subjection to the penalty imposed; as, "If ye will not...hearken unto me, then I will *punish* you" (*Leviticus* xxvi. 18); "no misdemeanour should be *punished* more severely than the most atrocious felonies" (*Macaulay*). **Chastise,** in literal use, commonly suggests the infliction of corporal punishment, sometimes in anger, often with a view to reformation or amendment. "My father hath *chastised* you with whips, but I will *chastise* you with scorpions" (*1 Kings* xii. 11); "All-sufficing nature can *chastise* Those who transgress her law" (*Shelley*). **Castigate,** once close to *chastise*, now implies severe, and often public, lashing by tongue or pen rather than by whip or rod, and so suggests painful censure or bitter rebuke. "Mr. Lowell...who courageously patronizes democracy in England, and with equal courage *castigates* it at home" (*Brownell*). **Chasten**

usually implies subjection to affliction or trial greater than is deserved: it therefore suggests as an aim, not punishment, but a testing whereby one may emerge humbled and purified or strengthened. "For whom the Lord loveth he *chasteneth*....If ye endure *chastening*, God dealeth with you as with sons" (*Hebrews* xii. 6-7). **Discipline** (see also TEACH) implies punishment, chastisement, or sometimes chastening, with the intent to subjugate, subdue, or bring under one's control; as, to *discipline* striking students by taking away certain privileges; these children show that they have never been *disciplined*. " 'But can he be *disciplined*...?' 'Oh, there is no question of discipline! He has been a little potentate too long' " (*Cather*). **Correct** implies punishment having for its aim the amendment or reformation of the offender. "His faults lie open to the laws; let them, Not you, *correct* him" (*Shak.*).

Ana. *Penalize, fine, amerce, mulct: *imprison, incarcerate, immure: *avenge, revenge.

Ant. Excuse: pardon. — *Con.* *Exculpate, acquit, exonerate, absolve, vindicate.

puny. *Petty, trivial, trifling, paltry, measly, picayunish, picayune.

Ana. Feeble, *weak, frail, infirm: *small, little, diminutive: slight, tenuous (see THIN, *adj.*).

pupil. *Scholar, student, disciple.

purblind. *Blind, sightless.

purchasable. *Vendible, salable, marketable.

Ana. *Mercenary, venal, hireling.

purchase, *v.* *Buy.

Ana. Hire, *employ: gain, win, earn, *get, obtain, procure, secure.

pure. 1 **Pure, absolute, simple, sheer** are here compared as used in the sciences, the arts, and to a certain extent, in philosophy. They agree in denoting free from everything that is foreign to the true nature or the essential character of the thing specified. **Pure** distinctively suggests freedom from intermixture. When applied to concrete things, it usually implies lack of contamination, adulteration, or pollution; as, *pure* water; a *pure* breed. When applied to an abstraction or to a concrete example of an abstraction, it implies the absence of everything that would obscure the thing in its essence or in its ideal character; as, *pure* poetry (poetry entirely free of prosaic elements); *pure* science (science where knowledge, and not the application of such knowledge, is the end). "This division into Realism and Romance...is the main cleavage in all the Arts; but it is hard to find *pure* examples of either kind" (*Galsworthy*). **Absolute** implies freedom from relation to or dependence on anything else; it is applied chiefly to abstractions such as space, time, and magnitude, viewed independently of experience and considered in their ultimate ideal character. Thus, "*absolute* space," as used in physics, is space conceived of as apart from the things which occupy it, and which limit or determine the ordinary person's notion of it. Because of such use, *absolute* often comes close to *real*, as opposed to *apparent*. "*Absolute* music," in musical theory, is music that depends solely on the distinctive properties of that art, such as tone, harmony, and rhythm, to produce its effects, and avoids, in contrast to "program music," all suggestion or characterization of external things. *Absolute* is applied to substances less often than is *pure*, but both are applied to alcohol: *pure* alcohol retains a modicum of water; *absolute* alcohol is completely dehydrated. **Simple** stresses singleness of character and is distinguished from that which is *compound* or *complex*. In very precise use it connotes homogeneity and incapacity for analysis or further reduction; as, an element is a *simple* substance; "quality" and "relation" are *simple* notions. *Simple*, as applied to abstractions or conceptions, often suggests artificial freedom from complexity, and sometimes also unreality or untruth, when the simplicity is attained by eliminating essential factors. "The world to which your philosophy-professor introduces you is *simple* ...The contradictions of real life are absent from it" (*W. James*). **Sheer,** more than any of these words, tends to lose its significance and to become a mere intensive; as, *sheer* nonsense. However, in precise use, it still implies such a dissociation from everything else that the pure and essential character of the quality (trait, virtue, power, or the like) to which it is applied is clearly displayed. "The 'Ancient Mariner'...is a work of *sheer* imagination" (*Lowes*).

Ana. Elemental, *elementary: *clear, transparent, lucid, limpid: genuine, *authentic.

Ant. Contaminated, polluted: adulterated (*of foods, metals, etc.*): applied (*of science*).

2 *Chaste, modest, decent.

Ana. *Clean, cleanly: virtuous, *moral, ethical.

Ant. Impure: immoral.

purgation. *Purification, catharsis, ablution, lustration.

purgative. *Physic, cathartic, purge, laxative, aperient.

purge, *n.* *Physic, cathartic, purgative, laxative, aperient.

purification. Purification, ablution, lustration, purgation, catharsis are synonyms in their etymological meanings, all of them denoting a cleansing. In their extended and figurative senses they do not lose this common denotation but they diverge so widely in their applications, especially in ceremonial use, that they are seldom interchangeable. **Purification** always implies prior defilement or pollution. It covers a variety of symbolic rites involving washing, particularly in orthodox Jewish practice; in Christian use it refers particularly to the expiation of sin, as through repentance, penance, or sacramental confession. **Ablution,** though literally meaning washing, does not in its liturgical use imply purification but prevention of profanation. To ensure the consumption of all particles of the consecrated bread and wine, the priest performs *ablution* after the Communion of the Mass by rinsing his index finger and thumb and the inside of the chalice and drinking this liquid. "The moving waters at their priestlike task Of pure *ablution* round earth's human shores" (*Keats*). **Lustration,** in strict use, is applicable only to certain purificatory ceremonies of the ancients, especially of the ancient Romans, as the cleansing of the people every five years after the census (the *lustrum*), or of a city after a plague, or of a fleet ready to depart. *Lustration* does not necessarily connote use of water, for fire, air, and other cleansing agents were used. Nor was it restricted to physical cleansing, for it often implied removal of bloodguiltiness. In best figurative use it connotes purification on a large scale. "St. Peter's mind is full of the Deluge as a type of the world's *lustration*" (*F. W. Farrar*). **Purgation** and its Greek equivalent **catharsis** always imply the elimination or discharge of impurities. Both are more often applied to a freeing of the soul or mind from that which interferes with spiritual or mental health than to a ceremony of purification. *Purgation* explicitly suggests the elimination of desires and interests that are sinful or hamper attainment of spiritual perfection. "Its [the soul's] attempts to eliminate by discipline and mortification all that stands in the way of its progress towards union with God constitute *Purgation:* a state of pain and effort" (*E. Underhill*). *Catharsis* was effectually introduced into English in Butcher's translation of Aristotle's description of the effect of tragedy as "through pity and fear effecting a *catharsis* of these emotions." It has come to imply the attainment of emotional balance through actual or vicarious suffering that provides an outlet for disturbing emotions and cleanses them of what is morbid or selfish. "And what a tragic *catharsis* it may prove, a universal purge of evil passion!" (*Yale Review*).

purloin. *Steal, pilfer, filch, lift, pinch, snitch, swipe, cop.
Ana. Abstract, *detach: *rob, plunder, rifle, loot, thieve, burglarize: *defalcate, peculate, embezzle.

purpose, *v.* Propose, design, *intend, mean.
Ana. Meditate, *ponder: weigh, *consider, revolve, contemplate: plan, plot, scheme, project (see under PLAN, *n.*): determine, *decide.

purpose, *n.* *Intention, intent, design, aim, end, object, objective, goal.
Ana. *Ambition, aspiration: proposition, *proposal: determination, *decision: *plan, project, scheme.

pursue. *Follow, chase, trail, tag, tail.
Ana. *Persevere, persist: *practice, exercise: persecute, oppress (see WRONG, *adj.*): hound, ride, *bait, badger.
Con. Flee, fly, *escape: avoid, evade, elude, shun (see ESCAPE).

pursuit. Calling, occupation, employment, *work, métier, business.

purvey. *Cater, pander.
Ana. *Furnish, equip, outfit.

purview. *Range, reach, scope, compass, sweep, gamut, radius, ken, horizon, orbit.

push, *v.* **Push, shove, thrust, propel** come into comparison when they mean to use pressure or force upon a thing so as to make it move ahead or aside. **Push** implies the application of force by a body (often, but not necessarily, a person) already in contact with the body to be moved onward, aside, out of one's way, or the like; as, a boy *pushing* a wheelbarrow along the road; to *push* a door open; to *push* a man over a cliff; an extra locomotive was needed at the rear to *push* the long train up the grade; to *push* the excited children into another room. **Shove** often differs from *push* in carrying a stronger implication of the exercise of muscular strength and of forcing something along a surface such as the ground or a floor; as, the boys *shoved* the heavy chairs and tables from the center of the room up against the walls; it took three men to *shove* the piano into the adjoining room. Often, when muscular exertion is not strongly implied, haste, or roughness, or rudeness in pushing is suggested; as, he *shoved* the paper into his pocket; to *shove* the articles on the desk into a box; to *shove* a person out of one's way; to *shove* the platter across the table. **Thrust,** as here compared, differs from *push,* especially in its chief current senses, in carrying a weaker implication of steadiness or continuousness in the application of force and a stronger suggestion of rapidity in the movement effected or of violence in the force that is used: oftentimes, also, the use of actual physical force is not clearly implied; as, "They...*thrust* him out of the city" (*Luke* iv. 28–29); "Abraham...*thrust* the old man out of his tent" (*Jer. Taylor*); "Mark first that youth who takes the foremost place, And *thrust* his person full into your face" (*Pope*). Often, also, it implies the sudden and forcible pushing of a weapon, implement, or instrument, or of something held in one's hand, so that it enters into the thing at which it is aimed; as, to *thrust* (not *push* or *shove*) a spear into an opponent's breast; to *thrust* a spade into the ground; to *thrust* a bunch of flowers into her hand. **Propel** implies a driving forward or onward by a force or power that imparts motion. In some use, it still implies pressure exerted from outside or behind, usually, but far from invariably, by some power that is not human; as, boats *propelled* by the wind; "the flow of air which *propels* the slow-sailing clouds" (*Lowes*); he grasped him by the collar and *propelled* him toward the door; "she walked—as if she were being *propelled* from the outside, by a force that she neither knew nor could control" (*A. Tate*). It is the preferred term, however, when the use of a mechanical aid (often called a *propeller*), or of some kind of actuating power, such as steam or electrical power, is implied; as, ships *propelled* by steam; a galley *propelled* by fifty oars; automobiles are usually *propelled* by internal-combustion engines.

In their figurative senses, **push** implies a pressing or urging forward, as with insistence, with vigor, with impetuousness, or the like, so that one's end may be gained, one's work may be completed, or one's goal be reached; as, to *push* the war into the enemy's country; to *push* a bill through Congress; to *push* one's theory to an extreme; to *push* oneself too hard in striving to attain one's ends. **Shove** often suggests obtrusiveness or intrusiveness or lack of firmness in making a way for oneself or another; as, to *shove* oneself into society; to *shove* a relative into a high appointive office. **Thrust** implies a forcing upon others of something that is not wanted, desired, or sought for; as, "some have greatness *thrust* upon 'em" (*Shak.*); "Amy had a grievance...because Sophia had recently *thrust* upon her a fresh method of cooking green vegetables" (*Bennett*). **Propel** is sometimes used in place of *impel* when a strong inner urge or appetite is implied as pushing one on to that which one desires; as, wolves at their very doors, *propelled* there by hunger.
Ana. *Move, drive, impel: *force, compel, constrain, oblige.

push, *n.* *Battle, engagement, action.

pushing. *Aggressive, militant, assertive, self-assertive.
Ana. *Vigorous, energetic, strenuous: officious, intrusive, obtrusive (see IMPERTINENT): self-confident, confident, self-assured, assured (see corresponding nouns at CONFIDENCE).

pusillanimous. *Cowardly, poltroon, craven, dastardly, recreant.
Ana. Timorous, *timid: apprehensive, *fearful, afraid: *contemptible, despicable, sorry, scurvy.
Ant. Courageous.

puss, *n.* *Face, countenance, visage, physiognomy, mug.

putative. *Supposed, supposititious, suppositious, reputed, conjectural, hypothetical.
Ana. Alleged, advanced (see ADDUCE): assumed, pretended, simulated (see ASSUME).

putrefy. Rot, decompose, *decay, spoil, disintegrate, crumble.
Ana. Corrupt, vitiate, deprave, *debase: dissolve, deliquesce (see LIQUEFY).

putrid. Fetid, noisome, stinking, *malodorous, rank, rancid, fusty, musty.
Ana. Decomposed, decayed, rotten, putrefied (see DECAY): corrupted, vitiated (see DEBASE).

Putsch. *Rebellion, revolution, uprising, revolt, insurrection, mutiny.

put up. *Reside, live, dwell, sojourn, lodge, stay, stop.

puzzle, *v.* **Puzzle, perplex, mystify, bewilder, distract, nonplus, confound, dumfound** (*or* **dumbfound**) come into comparison when they mean to disturb and baffle mentally or to cause to be so disturbed and baffled. The first three words express various mental reactions to what is intricate, complicated, or involved. **Puzzle** implies such complication or intricacy that the mind finds it exceedingly, often distressingly, difficult to understand or to solve. "A great poet may tax our brains, but he ought not to *puzzle* our wits" (*Birrell*). "Every economic, political, psychological and moral problem that has puzzled civilized men for 2500 years" (*Lippmann*). **Perplex** adds to *puzzle* the implications of worry and uncertainty, especially about reaching a decision on a course of action or the right solution of a personal problem. "Then must you speak Of one that loved not wisely but too well; Of one not easily jealous, but being wrought *Perplex'd* in the extreme" (*Shak.*). "Undaunted still, though wearied and *perplexed*" (*Cowper*). To **mystify** is to perplex, sometimes by playing upon one's credulity, but more often by concealing important facts or factors or by obscuring issues. "When she [Elizabeth] was weary of *mystifying* foreign statesmen, she turned to find fresh sport in *mystifying* her own ministers" (*J. R. Green*). **Bewilder** often implies perplexity, but it stresses a confused state of mind that makes clear thinking practically impossible; as, to be *bewildered* by contradictory statements or orders; "the *bewildering* flux of modern life" (*Day Lewis*). "Do not run to the Socialists or the Capitalists, or to your favorite newspaper, to make up your mind for you: they will only unsettle and *bewilder* you" (*Shaw*). **Distract** implies strong agitation arising from divergent or conflicting considerations or interests; as, "*distracted* between love and duty" (*Byron*). "She seemed nervous and *distracted*, kept glancing over her shoulder, and crushing her handkerchief up in her hands" (*Cather*). The last three words imply less mental disturbance and distress than some of the preceding terms, but they heighten the implication of bafflement and mental confusion. **Nonplus** implies blankness of mind or utter inability to find anything worth saying or doing. "The Problem which *nonplusses* the wisest heads on this Planet, has become quite a familiar companion of mine. What is Reality?" (*L. P. Smith*). **Confound** (see also MISTAKE) implies mental confusion, but it stresses the implication either of mental paralysis or of profound astonishment. "So spake the son of God; and Satan stood A while as mute, *confounded*" (*Milton*). "Language to him is a means of communication with his fellows, and not a fine art cultivated for art's sake. He does not wish to dazzle or *confound* his friends, but only to make himself understood" (*S. M. Crothers*). **Dumfound** (etymologically, to confound so as to strike dumb) in colloquial language tends to replace *confound*. Originally the term came close to *nonplus*, but it carried a stronger connotation of momentary mental paralysis; as, "to cramp and *dumbfound* his opponents" (*Sterne*); "I cannot wriggle out of it; I am *dumbfounded*" (*Darwin*); *dumfounded* by the beauty of the scene; he stood *dumfounded* with astonishment; "He captured the public and *dumbfounded* the critics" (*J. A. Macy*). In current use, *dumfound* often so strongly implies astonishment that it is used in place of *astound*. "I was *dumbfounded* to hear him say that I was on a Quixotic enterprise" (*W. Lawrence*).

Ana. Amaze, astound, flabbergast (see SURPRISE): *confuse, muddle, bemuddle, addle: *embarrass, disconcert, discomfit.

puzzle, *n.* *Mystery, problem, enigma, riddle, conundrum.

pygmy. *Dwarf, midget, manikin, homunculus, runt.

Q

quack, *n.* *Impostor, faker, empiric, mountebank, charlatan.

Ana. Pretender, simulator, counterfeiter, shammer (see corresponding verbs at ASSUME): *deceit, duplicity, dissimulation, cunning, guile.

quail, *v.* *Recoil, shrink, flinch, wince, blench.

Ana. Cower, cringe (see FAWN): falter, waver, vacillate, *hesitate: quake, quaver, tremble, shudder (see SHAKE).

quaint. *Strange, odd, queer, outlandish, curious, peculiar, eccentric, erratic, singular, unique.

Ana. *Fantastic, bizarre, grotesque: droll, funny, *laughable: archaic, antiquated, antique (see OLD).

quake, *v.* *Shake, tremble, totter, quiver, shiver, shudder, quaver, wobble, teeter, shimmy, didder, dither.

Ana. Quail, shrink, *recoil: vibrate, fluctuate, waver (see SWING): falter, vacillate, *hesitate.

qualified. Competent, capable, *able.

Ana. Trained, instructed, disciplined (see TEACH): examined, quizzed, catechized (see ASK): tested, tried, proved (see PROVE).

Ant. Unqualified.

qualify. *Moderate, temper, attemper.

Ana. Modify, vary, alter, *change: *adapt, adjust, conform, accommodate, reconcile.

quality. **Quality, property, character, attribute, accident** are synonymous terms when they denote one of the intelligible marks or indications by means of which a thing may be identified or its constitution be understood. **Quality** is the term of widest application and may designate any of these marks, material or immaterial, individual or generic; as, distinguishing *qualities* of iron are resistance to fracture (tensile strength) and corrosiveness. "There was only one *quality* in a woman that appealed to him—charm" (*Galsworthy*). "The persistent contemporariness that is a *quality* of all good art" (*A. Huxley*). "The man was much greater than the sum of his *qualities*" (*Cather*). A **property** is a quality that is proper to the species or type; it, therefore, belongs to a thing by virtue of that thing's true or essential nature. "Sir Joseph Thomson...pointed out that weight is only an 'apparently' invariable *property* of matter" (*H. Ellis*). "Religion...is never found pure, and it is not at all easy to isolate it in order to learn its *properties*" (*Inge*). A **character** is a peculiar or distinctive quality of a class more often than of an individual. It is not today common in general use but is often found in scientific and philosophical writing with reference to the properties which distinguish a species (hence *specific characters*) from its generic properties; as, wheat and oats have common *properties*, but they are distinguished by certain specific *characters*. An **attribute** is a quality that is ascribed to a thing. In very precise use, it often implies a lack of definite knowledge of the thing in question; thus, one can speak of the *attributes* of God, meaning the qualities men ascribe to him. "Historical personages become invested with romantic *attributes*" (*T. Wright*). Sometimes, especially in law and philosophy, *attribute* denotes a quality that must belong to a thing by reason of its nature. "Mercy is...an *attribute* to God himself" (*Shak.*). "They [the States] possessed it [power to regulate commerce] as an inseparable *attribute* of sovereignty" (*Ch. Just. Marshall*). An **accident** is merely a quality; in philosophical use, however, it often means one of the qualities by which a thing manifests itself, and implies, therefore, a contrast with something deeper; that is, the substance—or the real, but unapparent, nature—of the thing. "Waves [on a Japanese artist's screen] such as these, divested of all *accident* of appearance, in their naked impetus of movement and recoil" (*Binyon*). In general use, however, *accident* usually implies fortuitousness or lack of intrinsic value. "Rhyme is...an *accident* rather than an essential of verse" (*Lowes*).

Ana. Predication, affirmation (see corresponding verbs at ASSERT): peculiarity, individuality, characteristic (see corresponding adjectives at CHARACTERISTIC).

qualm. **Qualm, scruple, compunction, demur** come into comparison when they denote a feeling of doubt or hesitation as to the rightness or wisdom of something one is doing or is about to do. **Qualm** (etymologically, a sudden illness, esp. nausea) implies an uneasy, often a sickening, sensation that one is not following the dictates of his conscience or of his better judgment; as, he is often tempted to lie, but is always deterred by *qualms* of conscience; "how few little girls can squash insects and kill rabbits without a *qualm*" (*R. Macaulay*); "I had *qualms* about setting forth over the treacherous waters of the China Sea, because the skipper had fortified himself with such huge quantities of alcohol" (*V. Heiser*). **Scruple** implies more or less mental disturbance occasioned by doubt of the rightness, the propriety, the fairness, or, sometimes, the outcome of an act: it may or may not imply an overnice conscience or an extremely delicate sense of honor; as, she has no *scruples* about carrying away any of my books; "some craven *scruple* Of thinking too precisely on the event, A thought which, quarter'd, hath but one part wisdom And ever three parts coward" (*Shak.*); "You are fairly safe in keeping your money at a big bank, and need have no *scruple* about availing yourself of its readiness to oblige you" (*Shaw*); "I respect your *scruple*, sir; but in this case I believe true delicacy requires you to do as I ask" (*E. Wharton*). **Compunction** (as here compared: see also PENITENCE) implies a prick or sting of conscience that warns a person that he is about to commit (or is committing) a sin, crime, or, now more often, slight offense, or is about to inflict (or is inflicting) a wrong or injustice; as, he had not the slightest *compunction* in pulling apples from his neighbors' trees; "he...felt little stirrings of *compunction* at getting married without his mother's knowledge" (*M. Austin*). **Demur** stresses hesitation to such an extent that it carries a stronger implication of delay than any of the other terms: it usually suggests, however, a delay caused by objections or irresolution rather than by an awakened conscience or by a scruple or compunction. "His own possessions, safety, life, he would have hazarded for Lucie and her child, without a moment's *demur*" (*Dickens*). "Rather than be brought into court he will pay without *demur*" (*Shaw*).

Ana. Misgiving, *apprehension, foreboding, presentiment: doubt, mistrust, suspicion, *uncertainty.

quandary. *Predicament, dilemma, plight, scrape, fix, jam, pickle.

Ana. *Juncture, pass, exigency, emergency, contingency, crisis: *difficulty, hardship, vicissitude: puzzling *or* puzzle, mystification, perplexity, bewilderment (see corresponding verbs at PUZZLE).

quantity. Amount, *sum, aggregate, total, whole, number.

quarrel, *n.* **Quarrel, wrangle, altercation, squabble, bickering, spat, tiff** agree in denoting a dispute marked by anger or discord on both sides. The same distinctions in implications and connotations are found in their corresponding verbs, **quarrel, wrangle, altercate, squabble, bicker, spat, tiff. Quarrel** usually implies heated verbal contention, but it stresses strained or severed relations which may persist even after verbal strife has ceased; as, to patch up a *quarrel*. "Spectators of our dull domestic *quarrels*" (*Shelley*). "I don't complain of Betsey, or any of her acts, Exceptin' when we've *quarreled*, and told each other facts" (*W. Carleton*). **Wrangle** implies undignified and often futile disputation with noisy insistency on each person's opinion; as, a *wrangle* over a point of law. "Fill'd with... A scorn of *wrangling*, yet a zeal for truth" (*Pope*). **Altercation** and the rare verb **altercate** imply fighting with words as the chief weapons, though blows may also be connoted. "I have an extreme aversion to public *altercation* on philosophic points" (*Franklin*). "Lydia, foreseeing an *altercation*, and alarmed by the threatening aspect of the man, attempted to hurry away" (*Shaw*). **Squabble** stresses childish and unseemly wrangling over a petty matter; it does not necessarily imply anger or bitter feeling; as, children *squabble* over their toys; "*squabbles* with his fellow-faddists" (*L. P. Smith*); "I wish you chaps would not *squabble* over the picture" (*Wilde*). **Bickering** and **bicker** imply constant and petulant verbal sparring or interchanges of cutting remarks; they suggest an irritable mood or mutual antagonism; as, they never come together without *bickering*. "Tho' men may *bicker* with the things they love, They would not make them laughable in all eyes, Not while they loved them" (*Tennyson*). **Spat** (a colloquial or dialectal word) also implies an insignificant cause, but, unlike *squabble* and *bicker*, it suggests an angry outburst and a quick ending without hard feelings. "They was pretty apt to have *spats*" (*H. B. Stowe*). **Tiff** differs from *spat* chiefly in implying a disagreement that manifests itself in ill-humor or temporarily hurt feelings. "Having learned that storms Subside, and teapot-tempests are akin... *Tiffs* End properly in marriage and a dance!" (*Browning*).

Ana. *Brawl, broil, fracas, melee, row, rumpus, scrap: contention, dissension, conflict, variance, strife, *discord.

quarrel, *v.* Wrangle, altercate, squabble, bicker, spat, tiff. See under QUARREL, *n.*

Ana. *Contend, fight, battle, war: dispute, agitate, argue, *discuss.

Con. *Agree, concur, coincide.

quarrelsome. Pugnacious, bellicose, *belligerent, contentious, litigious.

Ana. Opposing, combating *or* combative, resisting (see corresponding verbs at OPPOSE): antagonistic, *adverse, counter: hostile, inimical, antipathetic, rancorous (see corresponding nouns at ENMITY).

quarry. *Victim, prey, ravin.

quarters. *Rooms, lodgings, chambers, diggings, digs, apartment, flat, tenement.

quash. *Annul, abrogate, void, avoid, vacate.

quaver, *v.* *Shake, tremble, shudder, quake, totter, quiver, shiver, wobble, teeter, shimmy, didder, dither.

Ana. Falter, waver, vacillate, *hesitate: vibrate, fluctuate, sway (see SWING).

queenly. Regal, royal, *kingly, imperial, princely.

queer, *adj.* *Strange, odd, erratic, eccentric, peculiar, quaint, outlandish, curious.

Ana. Dubious, *doubtful, questionable: droll, funny, *laughable: bizarre, grotesque, *fantastic.

querulous. Fretful, petulant, pettish, huffy, *irritable, peevish, fractious, snappish, waspish.

Ana. Crying, weeping, wailing, whimpering, blubbering (see CRY, *v.*): touchy, techy, cranky, cross (see IRASCIBLE): lamenting, deploring, bemoaning (see DEPLORE).

query, *v.* *Ask, question, interrogate, inquire, speer, examine, quiz, catechize.

quest. *Adventure, enterprise, emprise.

Ana. Exploit, *feat, achievement.

question, *v.* *Ask, interrogate, query, inquire, examine, quiz, catechize, speer.

Ant. Answer. — *Con.* Reply, respond (see ANSWER, *v.*).

questionable. *Doubtful, dubious, problematical.

Ana. Uncertain, suspicious (see corresponding nouns at UNCERTAINTY): *obscure, vague, equivocal.

Ant. Authoritative: unquestioned.

quick. 1 *Living, alive, animate, animated, vital.

Ant. Dead: arid.

2 Fleet, swift, rapid, *fast, speedy, expeditious, hasty.

Ana. Brisk, nimble, *agile: abrupt, impetuous, *precipitate, headlong.

3 **Quick, prompt, ready, apt** come into comparison when applied to persons, their mental operations, their acts, and their words, and mean having or manifesting the ability to respond without delay or hesitation. **Quick** stresses instancy of response to such an extent that it usually connotes native rather than acquired power; as, *quick* eyes; *quick* in perception, observation, or decision. "He could at that time barely write his own name. Yet one felt in him a *quick* and discriminating intelligence" (*Cather*). Very often, the word suggests marked capacity for learning or for absorbing that which is taught. "And I would teach them all that men are taught; We [women] are twice as *quick!* "(*Tennyson*). "To be fit to direct, to know enough about roads to take the right one, the *quick* ...must be taught according to their *quickness*" (*Grandgent*). **Prompt** also implies instancy of response, but it may or may not imply native quickness. Often it carries a suggestion of training, discipline, or some kind of preparation that fits one for quick response when the occasion demands it; as, *prompt* service; *prompt* eloquence. "Blest Statesman He...who holds his ministry, Resolute, at all hazards, to fulfil Its duties;—*prompt* to move, but firm to wait" (*Wordsworth*). Sometimes the word carries so strong an implication of willingness or eagerness that a lack of normal inhibitions is also suggested. "A low-born, cell-bred, selfish, servile band, *Prompt* or to guard or stab, to saint or damn" (*Pope*). **Ready,** like *prompt*, implies previous training or a strong predisposition as well as instancy of response, but it more often characterizes the person or his powers than his performance or his expression of thought or feeling. It therefore often implies, as *prompt* does not, skill, facility, fluency, ease in attainment, or the like. "Reading maketh a full man, conference a *readye* man" (*Bacon*). "Wherein lies happiness? In that which becks Our *ready* minds to fellowship divine" (*Keats*). "On graduation from the lycée, at seventeen, he [the French boy]....has as plentiful a supply of knowledge, as *ready* and accurate a judgment [as the American A.B. of twenty-two]" (*Grandgent*). The word is often applied to the bodily organ or to the instrument one uses in manifesting his skill, fluency, or the like; as, he has a *ready* tongue; he wields a *ready* pen; a pair of *ready* hands. **Apt,** as here compared (see also FIT; APT, 2), does not throw the emphasis on the quickness of the response though that is involved in its meaning, but on the possession of certain qualities which make for such quickness, such as a high degree of intelligence, a particular talent or gift, or a strong bent. It is therefore preferable to *quick* when the person in mind responds quickly only to particular stimuli or shows a capacity for a definite kind of work; as, she is *apt* at drawing but not at arithmetic; his *aptness* for all studies is unusual; "supple, sinew-corded, *apt* at arms" (*Tennyson*); "at the hands of a little people, few but *apt* in the field" (*Kipling*).

Ana. *Intelligent, clever, smart, quick-witted: deft, feat, adroit, *dexterous: *sharp, acute, keen.

Ant. Sluggish.

quicken, *v.* 1 **Quicken, animate, enliven, vivify** agree in meaning to make alive or lively. Originally, all of them meant literally to impart physical life to that which is devoid of it. "I have seen a medicine That's able to breathe life into a stone, *Quicken* a rock" (*Shak.*). "It told how first Prometheus did create A man, of many parts from beasts deryv'd, And then stole fire from heven to *animate* His worke" (*Spenser*). "When God hath raised this body, he can *enliven* it with the same soul that inhabited it before" (*J. Wesley*). "The great Soul of the Universe...*vivifyeth* all manner of things" (*Rabelais, transl. by Urquhart*). This literal sense is now rare and the words have diverged more or less widely in their implications. **Quicken,** which is found chiefly in poetic and religious use, stresses either the renewal of life, especially of suspended life or growth, or the rousing into fullness of activity that which is inert. Sometimes the rekindled life is physical. "When her [spring's] breath *Quickens*, as now, the withered heath" (*Wordsworth*). More often, however, it is spiritual, intellectual, or imaginative. "It is the Spirit that *quickeneth*...the words that I speak unto you, they are spirit, and they are life" (*John* vi. 63). **Animate** emphasizes the imparting of motion and activity or, especially in modern use, the giving of the appearance of life to that which is mechanical or artificial; as, *animated* cartoons; the *animated* dolls of the puppet theater. "Lely on *animated* canvas stole The sleepy eye, that spoke the melting soul" (*Pope*). **Enliven** suggests a stimulating influence that kindles, exalts, or brightens; it therefore commonly presupposes dullness, depression, torpidity, or the like, in the thing affected; as, "the sun...was wonderfully warm and *enlivening*" (*D. H. Lawrence*). "But soon the feel of the paint on the canvas begins to *enliven* his mind; and the mind thus *quickened* conceives a livelier curiosity about the creature before him" (*C. E. Montague*). **Vivify** sometimes, like *quicken*, implies the renewal of life, and at other times, like *animate*, implies the giving of the appearance of life. In each case, however, it usually also suggests a freshening or energizing effect, and implies vitality more often than activity or motion. "The Russian ballet...illustrates once more the *vivifying* effect of transplantation on the art of Romantic dancing" (*H. Ellis*). "In...the Elizabethan age, English society at large was accessible to ideas, was permeated by them, was *vivified* by them" (*Arnold*). "That Promethean fire, which *animates* the canvass and *vivifies* the marble" (*Sir J. Reynolds*).

Ana. Activate, *vitalize, energize: rouse, arouse, *stir.

Ant. Deaden.

2 Excite, stimulate, *provoke, pique, galvanize.

Ana. *Activate, actuate, motivate: spur, goad, induce (see corresponding nouns at MOTIVE): *incite, foment.

Ant. Arrest.

3 Hasten, hurry, *speed, accelerate, precipitate.

Ant. Slacken.

quick-witted. Clever, bright, smart, *intelligent, alert, knowing, brilliant.

Ana. Ready, prompt, *quick, apt: *sharp, keen, acute: *witty, humorous, facetious.

quiescent. *Latent, dormant, potential, abeyant.

Ana. Quiet, *still, silent: inert, *inactive, passive, supine.

quiet, *adj.* Silent, noiseless, *still, stilly.

Ana. *Calm, serene, placid, tranquil, peaceful.

Ant. Unquiet. — *Con.* *Rough, harsh: disturbed, agitated, upset, disquieted, perturbed (see DISCOMPOSE): *vociferous, clamorous, boisterous, blatant, strident.

quip. *Jest, joke, jape, witticism, wisecrack, crack, gag.

quit. 1 Acquit, comport, deport, demean, conduct, *behave.

Ana. & *Con.* See those at ACQUIT.
2 *Go, leave, depart, withdraw, retire, scram, clear out.
Ana. Forsake, desert, *abandon: *relinquish, surrender, resign: *escape, flee, fly, abscond.
3 *Stop, cease, discontinue, desist.

quiver, *v.* *Shake, shiver, shudder, quaver, totter, tremble, quake, wobble, teeter, shimmy, didder, dither.
Ana. *Pulsate, pulse, beat, throb, palpitate: flutter, flicker, flitter (see FLIT).

quixotic. Chimerical, fantastic, visionary, fanciful, *imaginary.
Ana. *Sentimental, romantic: utopian, *ambitious: ideal, transcendental, *abstract.

quiz, *v.* **1** *Banter, chaff, rally, kid, rag, guy, rib, josh, jolly.
2 *Ask, question, interrogate, examine, catechize, query, inquire, speer.

quote, *v.* **Quote, cite, repeat** are not close synonyms, even though as here compared they agree in meaning to say or write again in identical words something already said or written by another. To **quote** is to reproduce exactly the words of another, usually with credit given to their author; as, "Chaucer's account of himself must be *quoted*, for the delight and sympathy of all true readers" (*Hunt*). More loosely, to *quote* is to refer a statement in general terms to some one as its author, without implying the repetition of precisely the original words; as, Don't *quote* me in this connection. To **cite,** as here compared (see ADDUCE), is to quote an author or a passage as evidence offered in proof of a point or as an authority for one's statement or contention; as, "He persevered in his refusal to *cite* any distinct passages from any writing of mine" (*Newman*). To **repeat** is to reproduce exactly (or sometimes, almost exactly) the words of another, often without indication of or reference to their author; as, the children *repeated* the poem after the teacher; "I will not *repeat* your words, M. du Pallet, outside this cloister" (*H. Adams*). "When an uncopyrighted combination of words is published there is no general right to forbid other people *repeating* them—in other words there is no property in the combination or in the thoughts or facts that the words express" (*Justice Holmes*).
Ana. *Adduce, allege, advance.

quotidian. *Daily, diurnal.

R

race, *n.* **Race, nation, people** are frequently used as though they are interchangeable when they denote one of the great divisions of mankind, each of which is made up of an aggregate of persons who think of themselves, or are thought of, as comprising a distinct unit. In present technical use, the terms are commonly differentiated in meaning but in general, or popular, use they are often employed (justifiably on historical grounds, such as the usage of the best writers of the past) without a clear sense of these distinctions. In the ensuing discrimination, emphasis will be placed upon the current technical rather than upon the passing historical implications in these words. **Race** is chiefly an anthropological and ethnological term; it usually implies a distinct physical type. One race is distinguishable from another by its possession of certain unchanging characters, such as the color of the skin, the form of the hair, and the shape of the skull. The classification of primary races commonly followed today is that of J. F. Blumenbach (though his five races are sometimes reduced to four) into the Caucasian (or white), the Mongolian (or yellow), the Ethiopian (or black), the American (or red), the Malay (or brown). Secondary classifications, as of the Caucasian race, are numerous though not so universally accepted; thus, W. Z. Ripley distinguished three races in Europe (the Teutonic, the Alpine, the Mediterranean) on the basis of comparative stature, coloring (blond or brunet), and the shape of the head. Many other classifications or designations of groups as *races* are popularly received, even when they are still matters of controversy among scientists; they often imply a common origin or place of origin, a common root language, or the like; as, the Nordic *race;* the Aryan *race;* the Semitic *race.* In popular use, however, *race* is still often applied to any clearly defined group thought of as a unit because of a common past, even though remote, a common history, or the like; as, the Anglo-Saxon *race;* the Celtic *race;* the Hebrew *race.* **Nation** is primarily a political term, but it is also common in historical writing and is even more frequent as a literary word with highly figurative connotations. Literally, it signifies the inhabitants, or more narrowly, the citizenry, of a sovereign state, or any body of persons who have been united under one independent government long enough to have acquired a distinct identity. It implies a certain homogeneity in these persons because of common laws, institutions, loyalties, and customs, but it does not necessarily imply, as *race* usually does, a common origin, or a common remote past, or a common physical or mental type. In this sense, it is often contrasted with *state.* "When the state fell to pieces, the *nation* held together" (*J. R. Seeley*). "A State is accidental; it can be made or unmade; but a *nation* is something real which can be neither made nor destroyed" (*J. R. Green*). Figuratively, *nation* often suggests an ideal to be realized, rather than an established entity; it is then, as a rule, personified; as, "a *nation* strong, train'd up in arms" (*Shak.*); "*nations,* like men, have their infancy" (*Bolingbroke*); "until *nations* are generous they will never be wise" (*Irving*); "the *nation's* honor is dearer than the *nation's* comfort" (*W. Wilson*). There still prevails a use of *nation* which is not clearly distinguishable from that of *race* in its popular sense; as, the Gypsy *nation;* "he hates our sacred [Jewish] *nation*" (*Shak.*). **People** is the preferred word in historical and sociological terminology when a body of persons as a whole and as individuals show a consciousness of solidarity and of peculiarity that is not entirely explainable by *race* or *nation.* The term usually designates an aggregate of persons who, irrespective of their individual racial origins or ancestral nationalities, have through close and long-continued association achieved a common culture, common interests and ideals, and a sense of race or kinship. *People* is interchangeable with *nation* only when the terms imply the same background and cover the same range of instances; as, Congress should voice the will of the American *people* (or *nation*); "Englishman" designates one of a *people* (the English *people*): Briton, one of a *nation* (the British *nation*). *People* is usually far weaker in its implication of political unity and far stronger in its implications of cultural and social unity than *nation*. "The Cry of the Little *Peoples* goes up to God in vain, For the world is given over to the cruel sons of Cain" (*R. Le Gallienne*).

rack, *n.*[1] *Trot, pace, single-foot, lope, amble, walk, gallop, run, canter.

rack, *n.*[2] Track, vestige, *trace.
Ana. *Sign, mark, token.

rack, *v.*[1] Trot, pace, single-foot, lope, amble, walk, gallop, run, canter. See under TROT, *n.*

rack, *v.*[2] Torment, torture, grill, try, *afflict.
Ana. Persecute, oppress (see WRONG, *v.*): harry, harass, *worry, annoy.

rack, *v.*[3] Variant of WRACK.

racket. *Din, uproar, pandemonium, hullabaloo, babel, hubbub.

racking. *Excruciating, agonizing.
Ana. Torturing, tormenting, grilling (see AFFLICT): *intense, vehement: *fierce, ferocious, barbarous, savage, cruel, inhuman.

racy. *Pungent, piquant, poignant, spicy, snappy.
Ana. Exciting, stimulating, quickening, provoking *or* provocative (see corresponding verbs at PROVOKE): *spirited, mettlesome, fiery, gingery, peppery.
Con. *Insipid, flat, jejune, banal, inane.

radiant. Brilliant, *bright, luminous, lustrous, effulgent, refulgent, beaming, beamy, lambent, lucent.
Ana. *Splendid, resplendent, glorious, sublime: sparkling, glittering, gleaming, flashing, scintillating (see FLASH, *v.*).

radical, *adj.* **1** *Fundamental, basic, basal, underlying, substratal, substrative.
Ana. Cardinal, *essential, vital: *inherent, intrinsic, constitutional.
Ant. Superficial.
2 Advanced, progressive, *liberal, left.

radius. *Range, reach, scope, compass, sweep, ken, purview, horizon, orbit.

rag, *v.* *Banter, chaff, rally, quiz, kid, guy, rib, josh, jolly.

rage, *n.* **1** *Anger, ire, fury, indignation, wrath.
Ana. *Acrimony, asperity, acerbity: frenzy, *mania, hysteria: agitation, upset, perturbation (see corresponding verbs at DISCOMPOSE).
2 *Fashion, style, mode, vogue, craze, cry, dernier cri, fad.
Ana. *Caprice, freak, vagary, crotchet, whim.

raid, *n.* *Invasion, incursion, irruption, inroad.
Ana. *Attack, assault, onslaught, onset.

rail, *v.* Revile, vituperate, rate, berate, upbraid, *scold, tonguelash, jaw, bawl out, wig.
Ana. Censure, denounce, condemn, reprobate, reprehend, *criticize: reprimand, rebuke, *reprove, reproach.

raillery. *Badinage, persiflage.
Ana. Bantering *or* banter, chaffing *or* chaff, rallying *or* rally (see corresponding verbs at BANTER): sport, *fun, game, jest, play: satire, sarcasm, irony (see WIT).

raiment. Apparel, attire, tire, *clothes, clothing, dress, vesture, array.

raise, *v.* *Lift, elevate, hoist, heave, rear, boost.
Ana. *Rise, ascend, mount, soar: *exalt, magnify, aggrandize: *advance, promote, forward, further.

rally, *v.*[1] *Stir, rouse, arouse, awaken, waken.
Ana. Excite, stimulate, quicken, *provoke: enkindle, fire, inflame (see LIGHT, *v.*): *renew, restore, refresh.

rally, *v.*[2] **1** *Ridicule, deride, mock, taunt, twit.
Ana. *Scoff, jeer, gibe, flout: tease, tantalize, *worry, harass, harry.
2 *Banter, chaff, quiz, kid, rag, guy, rib, josh, jolly.

ramble, *v.* *Wander, stray, roam, rove, range, prowl, gad, gallivant, traipse, meander.

rampant. *Rank.
Ana. Luxuriant, lush, exuberant, *profuse, lavish: immoderate, *excessive, inordinate.
Con. *Moderate, temperate: restrained, curbed, checked (see RESTRAINED).

rampart. *Bulwark, breastwork, parapet, barbette, bastion.

rancid. *Malodorous, stinking, fetid, rank, noisome, putrid, fusty, musty.
Ana. Decomposed, decayed, spoiled (see DECAY): *offensive, loathsome, repulsive.

rancor *or* **rancour.** Antagonism, animosity, animus, antipathy, *enmity, hostility.
Ana. Hate, hatred, detestation, abhorrence, abomination (see under HATE, *v.*): spite, *malice, malevolence, malignity, spleen, grudge.

random. Random, haphazard, chance, chancy, casual, desultory, hit-or-miss, happy-go-lucky come into comparison as meaning having a cause or a character that is determined by accident rather than by design or by method. That is **random** which comes, goes, occurs, is made, or the like, without a fixed or clearly defined aim, purpose, or evidence of method or system or direction: the term, therefore, implies no or little guidance by a governing mind, eye, objective, or the like; as, a *random* shot; a *random* answer to a question; a *random* collection of books; "My choice was as *random* as blindman's buff" (*Burns*); "They will throw out a *random* word in or out of season" (*Lamb*); "He had not heard her divorce spoken of since Janey's first *random* allusion to it" (*E. Wharton*). That is **haphazard** which is done, is made, is used, is said, or the like, without concern or without sufficient concern for its fitness, its effectiveness, its possible ill effects, or the like, and which, therefore, is more or less at the mercy of chance or of natural or logical necessity; as, a *haphazard* policy; *haphazard* methods of teaching French; a *haphazard* arrangement of shrubs and plants in a garden. That is described as **chance** which comes or happens to one or is done or made by one without prearrangement or preawareness or without preparation: the term is applicable not only to things but to persons with whom one comes into contact more or less by accident; as, a *chance* acquaintance; a *chance* meeting with an old friend; a *chance* remark of the stranger whose face seemed familiar led to my identification of him. "He explained that by a charming accident he had disposed of them to a *chance* buyer in Hanbridge, just before starting for Birmingham" (*Bennett*). That is **chancy** (a colloquial term) which is so haphazard that it involves uncertainty and risk, or that its results, actions, etc., cannot be predicted: the term may apply directly or indirectly to persons who are willing to take chances as well as to things that are precarious as a result of their haphazardness; as, "It's the instinct of the English and the Irish...to suspect government and take the risks of the *chancy* way" (*H. G. Wells*); "[The purchase of shares of a company about to undertake a project] is a *chancy* business" (*Shaw*). A person or a thing is **casual** (as here compared: see also ACCIDENTAL) that leaves, or seems to leave, things to chance, and that works, acts, or comes or goes, haphazardly or by chance, or without method or deliberation or other indication of intent or purpose: the term often also suggests offhandedness (as, a *casual* remark; he's a *casual* fellow; his treatment of his friends is *casual*), or lightness or spontaneity (as, "She was constantly referring to dear friends...in a *casual* and familiar way, and there were so many of them that it was long before I could distinguish them"—*H. Ellis*), or lack of definiteness as in terms or intention (as, "their policy was opportunist at home and *casual* abroad"—*Spectator*). "Perhaps the dominant feeling about government today is distrust. The tone of most comment, whether *casual* or deliberate, implies that ineptitude and inadequacy are the chief characteristics of government" (*Frankfurter*). "The *casual* allusion, the *chance* reference to her" (*H. Adams*). That is **desultory** which is not governed by method or system and which therefore jumps or skips from one thing to another. Usually the term implies another quality as a consequence of these, such as irregularity or lack of continuousness or persistence (as, "He had begun, in a *desultory* way, to annotate the diary that Tom had kept on the mesa"—*Cather*), or rambling discursiveness (as, "The book, in short, is *desultory* to the last degree, and discourses in varying moods on a variety of topics"—*Quiller-Couch*), or the absence of a plan or a definite objective (as, "to make reading have a purpose instead of being *desultory*"—*B. Russell*). That is **hit-or-miss** which is so haphazard in its character or operation that one is indifferent as to how it turns out or as to what pattern or arrangement it makes; as, *hit-or-miss* hammering; *hit-or-miss* patchwork; "A *hit-or-miss* policy was pursued by the Department of Justice" (*W. Z. Ripley*). A person is **happy-go-lucky** who leaves everything to chance or who accepts with happiness or indifference whatever comes; a thing is *happy-go-lucky* that is governed by such a disposition; as, a *happy-go-lucky* race; a *happy-go-lucky* way of earning one's living. "A radical pragmatist on the other hand is a *happy-go-lucky*...sort of creature" (*W. James*). "To make Carter think and talk...in the *happy-go-lucky* way of his class" (*Reade*).

Ana. Fortuitous, *accidental, casual: vagrant, vagabond, truant (see corresponding nouns at VAGABOND).

range, *v.* **1** *Line, align, array.

Ana. Arrange, *order, marshal: *assort, sort, classify: *incline, dispose, predispose, bias.

2 *Wander, rove, ramble, roam, stray, prowl, gad, gallivant, traipse, meander.

range, *n.* **1** *Habitat, station.

2 Range, reach, scope, compass, sweep, gamut, radius, ken, purview, horizon, orbit come into comparison when they denote the extent that lies within the powers of something to cover, to grasp, to control, or the like. **Range** often applies to the extent taken in or covered as by the eye (as, there was no human being within my *range* of vision), or by the ear (as, he did not call until he was within the *range* of our hearing), or by the understanding mind (as, to find Kant's philosophy beyond the *range* of one's intellectual powers), or by the feelings (as, "a creative writer can do his best only with what lies within the *range* and character of his deepest sympathies"—*Cather*), or the like (as, he did not fire until they were within *range* of his rifle). Equally often the term applies to the literal or figurative extent determined by a thing's powers, possibilities, capacity, or performances, and the variety of types, gradations, kinds, etc., that it includes; as, some of the greatest tenors have had voices of remarkable *range;* "We may gather a fairly complete idea of the whole *range* of Greek political life" (*G. L. Dickinson*); "A contrivance...to extend the *range* of conversation in mixed company" (*Brownell*). "Monochrome is a starved and lifeless term to express the marvellous *range* and subtlety of tones of which the preparation of black soot known as Chinese ink is capable" (*Binyon*). When the reference is to something stretched out or stretching itself out as an arm, or in the manner of an arm, so as to grasp, to attain, to embrace, or the like, **reach** (sometimes in the plural **reaches**) is the preferred term: usually it denotes that which lies within the limits or at the uttermost boundary of a thing's powers, influence, or capacity; as, "thoughts beyond the *reaches* of our souls" (*Shak.*); "Be sure yourself and your own *reach* to know, How far your genius, taste, and learning go" (*Pope*); "Mrs. Bennet was beyond the *reach* of reason" (*Austen*); "simple virtues...within every man's *reach* (*Irving*); "anything like sustained reasoning was beyond his *reach*" (*L. Stephen*); "Ah, but a man's *reach* should exceed his grasp, Or what's a heaven for?" (*Browning*). **Scope** (as here compared) occurs in two related but, to some extent, contrasted, senses. In one of these it denotes the extent between established or predetermined limits which encompass one on all sides and which for one reason or another cannot be overpassed; as, the subject does not lie within the *scope* of this book; "all matters within the *scope* of your understanding" (*Austen*); "I shall...put on one side all...speculations about the state, its *scope* and limits" (*Frankfurter*). In the other senses here considered, the term denotes room or space for free uncircumscribed activity, growth, expression, or the like; as, a type of education that gives a child *scope* for the development of all his powers; "We cannot offer you any work among poor or humble folk; but...you will find plenty of *scope* here [as a curate], both in the pulpit and in the box [the confessional]" (*C. Mackenzie*). **Compass,** like *range* and *reach*, applies to the utmost extent which can be taken in or reached by or as if by the eye, the arm, the mind, the imagination, or the like; but, like *scope*, it carries an implication of limits that have the character or quality of a circumference. The term therefore may suggest more restriction than *range* or *reach* but more freedom than *scope* in the sense of established limits; as, "To do this is within the *compass* of man's wit" (*Shak.*); "notes of an insect that lie above the *compass* of the human ear" (*Hardy*). **Sweep** differs from *compass* in implying a range that is determined by something that follows or seems to follow a circular or curving course; as, stars beyond the *sweep* of the most powerful telescope; watching for a fish to swim within the *sweep* of one's net; "London...was brought within the *sweep* of Royal extortion" (*J. R. Green*). **Gamut** (literally, a musical scale ascribed to Guido d'Arezzo) in its extended sense applies to a range which represents a graded series of all the notes, tones, varieties, kinds, etc., which lie between the limits of a thing's reach or scope. "We have the entire *gamut* [of people] run by the Southron [i.e., Southerner] describing a dinner party composed...of 'an elegant gentleman from Virginia, a gentleman from Kentucky, a man from Ohio, a fellow from New York, and a galoot from Boston' " (*Brownell*). " 'Only prose can give the full *gamut* of modern feeling' " (*T. S. Eliot*). "Types of light each occupying its particular place in that far-reaching...*gamut* which is called the 'spectrum' " (*Karl K. Darrow*). **Radius** applies to the space (literal or figurative space) encircling a given point and therefore equidistant from it on all sides; as, "an hour's 'bus drive from London and outside the cab *radius*" (*H. G. Wells*); "the individual has a certain definite *range* and *radius* of sympathy" (*Day Lewis*). **Ken** strictly applies to the range of one's knowledge or understanding or vision; as, "above the reach and *ken* of a mortal apprehension" (*South*); "Eventually, after she had drifted out of his *ken*...[she] returned" (*Cather*). "Then felt I like some watcher of the skies When a new planet swims into his *ken*" (*Keats*). **Purview,** though strictly applied to the scope as of a document, a statute, a book, or the like (as, "The statute intended...to include in its *purview* all the circumstances of the consecration of Parker"—*Gladstone*), is now more often used in a sense that is almost identical with that of *ken*. "Blake conceived that it was his vocation to bring this mystical illumination, this vision of reality, within the *purview* of ordinary men" (*E. Underhill*). **Horizon,** in its extended sense, suggests a compass that represents the utmost reaches on all sides of the human mind or soul, especially under given conditions; as, "the *horizon* of the human intellect has widened wonderfully during the past hundred years" (*C. W. Eliot*); "Your *horizon* contracts, your mind's eye is focused upon a small circle of exasperating detail" (*Jan Struther*). **Orbit** is often used in place of *scope* in the sense of circumscribing limits; as, "A small private income...confined us to a much narrower *orbit*" (*Quiller-Couch*); "the *orbit* within which Mr. Murry's discussion moves" (*T. S. Eliot*).

Ana. Extent, area (see SIZE): *field, domain, province, sphere, territory: spread, stretch, *expanse, amplitude.

rank, *adj.* **1 Rank, rampant** are compared as meaning growing or increasing at an immoderate rate. **Rank,** as here considered, applies chiefly to vegetation, though it is sometimes applied to soil, land, and the like, or is used figuratively. The term implies vigorous, luxuriant, often unchecked, growth, sometimes of crops (as, "And, behold, seven ears of corn came up upon one stalk, *rank* and good"—*Genesis* xli. 5), but more often of coarse and unwanted plants, such as weeds or wild shrubs, or undergrowth (as, *rank* growth; *rank* vegetation; *rank* grass). "The even mead [meadow]... all uncorrected, *rank* ...nothing teems But hateful docks, rough thistles, kecksies, burs" (*Shak.*). "Weed your better judgements Of all opinion that grows *rank* in them" (*Shak.*). **Rampant** is far more widely applicable than *rank*, for it implies rapid, often unrestrained or wild, spreading and therefore is frequently applicable not only to that which literally grows but to that which extends or increases by contagion, diffusion, or the like; as, "It grieved him to see ignorance and impiety so *rampant*" (*Fuller*); "that curiosity which is so *rampant*, as a rule, in an Indian village" (*Kipling*); "the person in whose blood stream malaria is *rampant*" (*A. C. Morrison*).

Ana. *Coarse, gross, vulgar: exuberant, *profuse, lavish, luxuriant.

2 Fusty, musty, rancid, *malodorous, stinking, fetid, noisome, putrid.

Ana. Dank, humid (see WET): *offensive, loathsome, repulsive: decomposed, decayed, spoiled (see DECAY).

Ant. Balmy.

3 *Flagrant, glaring, gross.

Ana. Conspicuous, outstanding, *noticeable: foul, filthy, squalid, nasty (see DIRTY): *outrageous, heinous, atrocious, monstrous.

ransom, *v.* *Rescue, deliver, redeem, reclaim, save.

Ana. *Free, release, liberate, emancipate, manumit: *expiate, atone.

rant, *n.* *Bombast, fustian, rodomontade, rhapsody.

Ana. Inflatedness *or* inflation, turgidity, tumidity, flatulence (see corresponding adjectives at INFLATED).

rapacious. Ravening, ravenous, gluttonous, *voracious.

Ana. *Ferocious, fierce: greedy, grasping, *covetous.

rapacity. Greed, *cupidity, avarice.

Ana. Covetousness, avariciousness, greediness, graspingness (see corresponding adjectives at COVETOUS): exaction, demanding *or* demand, claiming *or* claim (see corresponding verbs at DEMAND).

rapid, *adj.* *Fast, swift, fleet, quick, speedy, hasty, expeditious.

Ana. Brisk, nimble, *agile: hurried, quickened (see SPEED, *v.*).

Ant. Deliberate: leisurely.

rapt. Absorbed, engrossed, *intent.

Ana. Ecstatic, transported, rapturous (see corresponding nouns at ECSTASY): enchanted, captivated, fascinated (see ATTRACT).

Con. *Indifferent, unconcerned, incurious: uninterested, *disinterested.

rapture. *Ecstacy, transport.

Ana. Bliss, beatitude, blessedness, felicity, *happiness: elation, exultation (see corresponding adjectives at ELATED).

rare. 1 Tenuous, slight, *thin, slender, slim.

Ana. *Subtle, subtile.

2 Delicate, dainty, exquisite, *choice, elegant, recherché.

Ana. Excelling *or* excellent, transcending *or* transcendent, surpassing (see corresponding verbs at EXCEED): superlative, *supreme, incomparable.

3 Scarce, *infrequent, uncommon, occasional, sporadic.

Ana. *Exceptional: singular, unique, curious, *strange.

Con. *Usual, customary, wonted, accustomed, habitual: *common, ordinary, familiar.

rarefy. *Thin, attenuate, extenuate, dilute.

Ana. Diminish, reduce, lessen, *decrease: *expand, distend, inflate.

rash. Daring, daredevil, reckless, temerarious, foolhardy, *adventurous, venturous, venturesome.

Ana. *Precipitate, abrupt, impetuous, sudden, hasty: desperate, forlorn (see DESPONDENT).

Ant. Calculating. — *Con.* *Cautious, circumspect, wary, chary.

rate, *n.* Levy, assessment, *tax, excise, impost, customs, duty, toll, tariff, tribute, tithe, teind, cess.

rate, *v.*[1] Berate, upbraid, *scold, tonguelash, jaw, bawl out, wig, rail, revile, vituperate.

Ana. *Reprove, reproach, rebuke, reprimand, admonish, chide: censure, condemn, denounce, reprehend, reprobate, *criticize.

rate, *v.*[2] Value, evaluate, appraise, *estimate, assess, assay.

Ana. *Calculate, compute, reckon, estimate: *decide, determine, settle.

ratify. Ratify, confirm are here compared only as meaning to make something legally valid or operative. Both terms presuppose previous action as by a person or body with power of appointing, of legislating, of framing a document such as a constitution, a treaty, or the like, and imply reference therefore only to the act of the person or body (or persons or bodies) endowed with the power to accept or to veto the appointment, bill, constitution, etc. The terms are occasionally interchanged without loss, but **ratify** usually carries a stronger implication of approval than *confirm* and is therefore used by preference when the acceptance of something such as a constitution, a treaty, a course of action, that has been framed or proposed by a committee or a small body is put up to a society, legislature, or nation as a whole for a vote that testifies to its approval; thus, the Constitution of the United States was framed by the Constitutional Convention in 1787 and went into effect in 1788 after it had been *ratified* by eleven states. "The Report of the [Lambeth] Conference is not intended to be an absolute decree on questions of faith and morals; for the matter of that, the opinions expressed have no compulsion until *ratified* by Convocation" (*T. S. Eliot*). **Confirm,** on the other hand, stresses the giving of formal or decisive assent as necessary to a thing's validity: it applies specifically to appointments made by a president, governor, or other top executive, that according to the constitution of a nation or state require the consent of a senate, a legislature, a council, or other body before they are definitely settled and made legally valid; as, "The other executive function of the Senate, that of *confirming* nominations submitted by the President" (*Bryce*); the executive council yesterday refused to *confirm* two of the governor's appointments.

Ana. *Authorize, accredit, license, commission: sanction, *approve, endorse: validate, authenticate (see CONFIRM).

rating. *Mariner, sailor, seaman, tar, gob, matlow, bluejacket.

ratiocination. *Inference, illation.

Ant. Intuition.

ratiocinative. Illative, inferential. See under INFERENCE.

Ant. Intuitive.

ration, *n.* **Ration, allowance, dole, pittance** denote the amount of food, supplies, money, or the like, allotted to an individual. **Ration** always implies apportionment and, often, equal sharing. Specifically, it is applied in military and naval use to the daily supply of provisions given each man, and in stockbreeding to the daily (or periodical) supply of food for each animal. In these uses, it generally implies dietary variety and restricted amounts of each food. When used of a particular food or commodity, as wheat or coal, it implies a shortage in the supply and a limitation on the amount allowed each person; as, the sugar *ration* in 1918 was two teaspoonfuls a day. **Allowance,** though often interchangeable with *ration,* is far wider in its range of application. Both imply restriction in amount, but *allowance* stresses granting rather than sharing and is applicable to money and many other things besides food; as, a daily *allowance* of tobacco for the old pensioners; a schoolboy's weekly *allowance;* the court determines an heir's *allowance* during his minority. **Dole,** especially in modern use, tends to imply a grudging division and needy or, sometimes, grasping recipients; as, "cold charity's unwelcome *dole*" (*Shelley*). "No rich man's largesse may suffice his soul, Nor are the plundered succored by a *dole*" (*E. V. Cooke*). In current British use, *dole* is applied to a payment to unemployed workers, whether in the form of relief or insurance, by the national government. In the United States, it designates commonly the amount given periodically to a person on public relief. **Pittance,** though originally applied to a gift of money to a monastery to supply an additional allowance of food or drink to the monks on specified occasions, and then to the allowance itself, does not in modern use suggest increase, but, rather, scantiness or meagerness. It is now applicable to a ration, an allowance; a dole, a wage, or the like, the context usually making clear the reference. "And gained, by spinning hemp, a *pittance* for herself" (*Wordsworth*). "In England, such a dowry would be a *pittance,* while elsewhere it is a fortune" (*Byron*).

Ana. Apportionment, portioning *or* portion (see corresponding verbs at APPORTION): sharing *or* share, participation, partaking (see corresponding verbs at SHARE).

ration, *v.* *Apportion, portion, prorate, parcel.

Ana. Divide, *distribute, dispense, deal, dole: *share, partake, participate.

rational. **Rational, reasonable** come into comparison when they are applied to men, their acts, utterances, policies, and the like, in the senses of having or manifesting the power to reason or of being in accordance with what reason dictates as right, wise, sensible, or the like. **Rational** is usually the preferred term when one wishes specifically to imply a latent or active power to make inferences from the facts of which one is aware and to draw from such inferences conclusions that enable one to understand the world about him and to relate such knowledge to the attainment of personal and common ends: often, in this use, *rational* is opposed to *emotional, imaginative, animal,* and the like; as, man is a *rational* animal; "we are *rational;* but we are animal too" (*Cowper*); "In Octavian the emotional side was slow to develop, but from the start the *rational* was all-powerful" (*Buchan*); "To cure this habit of mind, it is necessary...to replace fear by *rational* prevision of misfortune" (*B. Russell*). When the term is applied to policies, projects, systems, or to anything already conceived or formulated, *rational* is preferred when justification on grounds that are satisfactory to the reason is specifically implied; as, "the advantages of a *rational* orthography" (*Grandgent*); "States may do a good deal of classifying that it is difficult to believe *rational*" (*Justice Holmes*). **Reasonable** usually carries a much weaker implication than *rational* of the power to reason in general, or of guidance by conclusions drawn by the reasoning powers: on the other hand, it commonly suggests enough guidance by the reason to enable one to avoid mistakes that will lead one into unforeseen difficulties or to make decisions or choices that are practical, sensible, just, or fair. "When I was a child and was told that our dog and our parrot...were not creatures like myself, but were brutal whilst I was *reasonable,* I... quite consciously and intellectually formed the opinion that the distinction was false" (*Shaw*). "If that belief, whether right or wrong, may be held by a *reasonable* man, it seems to me that it may be enforced by law" (*Justice Holmes*). "A *reasonableness,* a refusal to be stampeded into fanaticism, which...though it may be dismissed by some as compromise, will appeal to others as common sense" (*Day Lewis*). "I don't know any paper which takes a larger and more *reasonable* view of the war" (*H. Ellis*). "The formation of *reasonable* habits, of method, of punctuality, is a duty, not from an exalted point of view, but because it makes enormously for the happiness and convenience of every one about us" (*A. C. Benson*).

Ant. Irrational: animal (*of nature*): demented (*of state of mind*): absurd (*of actions, etc.*).

rationalize. *Explain, account for, justify.

rattle. Faze, *embarrass, discomfit, disconcert, abash.

Ana. *Confuse, muddle, bemuddle, addle: agitate, upset, perturb, disturb, fluster, flurry (see DISCOMPOSE): bewilder, distract, perplex (see PUZZLE, *v.*).

ravage. **Ravage, devastate, waste, sack, pillage, despoil, spoliate** come into comparison as meaning to lay waste or bare by plundering, destroying, or other acts of violence. **Ravage** usually implies the cumulative destruction accomplished by successive depredations, invasions, raids, storms, floods, and the like, but it may be employed when only one such act or event or the like achieves a like effect; as, the barbarians *ravaged* Greece and Italy during the first centuries of the Christian era; wolves *ravaged* the countryside during that bitter winter; "the psychic disease which *ravaged* Europe as mercilessly as the Spanish influenza" (*Day Lewis*). "An Indian hunt was never a slaughter. They *ravaged* neither the rivers nor the forest" (*Cather*). **Devastate** and the less common **waste** (*lay waste* being the commoner expression) stress the ruin and desolation which follow any act or series of acts, or event or series of events, which ravage or are in the process of ravaging a place or a country: it suggests demolition, burning, or other means of eradication of buildings, of forests, of crops, and the like; as, "A succession of cruel wars had *devastated* Europe" (*Macaulay*); "Gresham had *devastated* the neighbouring county to get timber for his Royal Exchange" (*H. Ellis*); "He fell suddenly on the Nervii with four legions, seized their cattle, *wasted* their country" (*Froude*). **Sack** strictly suggests the act or acts of a victorious army entering a town or other place that has been captured and stripping it of all its possessions of value by looting or destruction; as, "We *sacked* the city after nine months' siege" (*T. Heywood*); the English monasteries were *sacked* by the invading Danes. In current use, *sack* often means to burglarize so successfully that little of value is left or that all genuinely valuable articles are taken; as, house after house was *sacked* that summer when their owners were away. **Pillage** stresses ruthless plunder, such as is characteristic of an invading or victorious army, but it carries a weaker implication of devastation than *sack* carries; as, "He *pillaged* many Spanish towns, and took rich prizes" (*Fuller*); the soldiers were allowed to *pillage* any town or fields through which they passed. In current nonmilitary use, *pillage* still implies ruthlessness, but it carries a stronger implication of appropriation to oneself of something that belongs to another as by fleecing, plagiarizing, or robbing; as, "humbugged by their doctors, *pillaged* by their tradesmen" (*Shaw*). **Despoil,** like *sack,* implies a stripping of valuables, but it does not so often refer to places such as towns or cities which are ransacked for booty: it is usually the preferred term when a building, such as a church, a palace, an institution, or the like, or the person (or persons) connected with it is (or are) deprived of valuables by force or violence; as, the *despoiling* (or *despoliation*) of the English monasteries in the 16th century. "We are not yet So utterly *despoil'd* but we can spread The friendly board" (*Southey*). "We can endure that He should waste our lands, *Despoil* our temples ...; Such food a Tyrant's appetite demands" (*Wordsworth*). "Kill! crush! *despoil!* Let not a Greek escape!" (*Shelley*). *Despoil* may also imply wanton deprivation of valuable qualities or excellences; as, "*Despoiled* of innocence, of faith, of bliss" (*Milton*). **Spoliate** is more consistently a legal rather than a military term, but it has some general use: in its meaning it comes close to *despoil,* but it is the preferred term when piracy upon neutral ships in time of war is implied or, especially in current general use, when the gaining of spoils by means of exactions, graft, or various venal practices is suggested; as, the Tweed Ring was charged with *spoliating* (or the *spoliation* of) the people of New York City.

Ana. *Destroy, demolish, raze: plunder, loot, *rob: *ruin, wreck, wrack: invade, *trespass, encroach.

ravening. Rapacious, ravenous, gluttonous, *voracious.

Ana. Greedy, acquisitive, grasping, *covetous.

ravenous. Ravening, rapacious, *voracious, gluttonous.

Ana. Grasping, greedy, acquisitive, *covetous: *fierce, ferocious.

ravin *or* **raven** *or* **ravine.** *Victim, prey, quarry.

raw. Crude, callow, green, *rude, rough.

Ana. *Elementary, elemental: *ignorant, untaught, untutored: *immature, unmatured, unripe.

Con. Practiced, exercised, drilled (see PRACTICE, *v.*): seasoned, hardened, inured (see HARDEN): *mature, matured, ripe, adult, grown-up.

rawboned. Gaunt, angular, *lean, lank, lanky, spare, scrawny, skinny.

ray. **Ray, beam** are here compared chiefly in their popular senses as denoting a shaft of light. This conception of light as a shaft is fixed in our language but is not always in keeping with modern scientific views of the nature of light. **Ray** (etymologically akin to *radius*) suggests emanation from a center in the manner of the spokes of a wheel: it is often applied to one of the apparently thin lines of light that seem to extend from a radiant body, such as the sun or a star, or that are flashed by something brilliant, such as steel glittering in the sun; as, the more numerous the facets of a diamond the more numerous the *rays* of light it reflects. In physics, *ray* often implies a particular color (as, a red *ray;* a violet *ray*). **Beam** implies not a line but a long bar (*timber* was the original sense of the term); it suggests therefore a bar made up of a bundle of rays of light; as, the *beam* of an automobile headlight or of a searchlight. "Thither came Uriel, gliding through the even On a sun*beam,* swift as a shooting star" (*Milton*). "Where a sun*beam* enters, every particle of dust becomes visible" (*Ruskin*). A small beam is sometimes called a *ray;* as, a tiny hole in the window shade admitted a *ray* of sunlight into the room. In physics, a beam of white light is split by a prism into rays of light of the various colors of the spectrum. *Ray* is the usual term for implying heat-giving property; thus, *ray* is more often used of the sun than of the moon; as, the *rays* of the sun are more intense in summer than in winter. "How far that little candle throws his *beams!*" (*Shak.*).

raze. Demolish, *destroy.

Ana. Efface, obliterate (see ERASE): eradicate, extirpate (see EXTERMINATE): *ruin, wreck: *abolish, extinguish, annihilate.

reach, *v.* **Reach, gain, compass, achieve, attain** agree in meaning to arrive at a point by effort or work. **Reach** is the most general term, being capable of reference to anything that can be arrived at by exertion of any degree, as a point in space, in time, or in a development, or as a destination, a goal, a position of eminence, or the like; as, they *reached* Chicago that night; after a long discussion they *reached* an understanding; he *reached* success early in life. In extended use, *reach* may be predicated even of inanimate things; as, the hour hand has *reached* two; the depression has *reached* bottom. **Gain** usually implies a struggle to reach a contemplated or desired destination or goal. "At last, the top of the staircase was *gained*" (*Dickens*). "I had *gained* the frontier and slept safe that night" (*Browning*). **Compass** implies efforts to get around difficulties or to transcend limitations; it often connotes skill or craft in management. "A writer who is attempting a higher strain of elevation or pathos than his powers can *compass*" (*C. E. Montague*). "If you can *compass* it, do cure the younger girls of running after the officers" (*Austen*). **Achieve,** in discriminating use, stresses the skill or the endurance, as well as the efforts, involved in reaching an end. "Some are born great, some *achieve* greatness" (*Shak.*). "No government or private organization could give health; people had to *achieve* it" (*V. Heiser*). Often it implies accomplishment of that which is in itself a feat or triumph. "A complete moral unity such as England *achieved*" (*Belloc*). **Attain,** in careful use, connotes more strongly than any of the others the spur of aspiration or ambition; as, his constant efforts to *attain* his ends. It is therefore especially referable to ends beyond the vision, the scope, or the powers of most men. "This indispensable condition of the safety and civilisation of the world is, indeed, very difficult to *attain*" (*J. A. Hobson*). "A fine balance of all the forces of the human spirit such as but once or twice has been *attained* in the world's history" (*Binyon*).

Ana. Effect, fulfill, execute, accomplish, *perform: *get, obtain, procure, secure.

reach, *n.* *Range, scope, compass, sweep, gamut, radius, ken, purview, horizon, orbit.

Ana. Extent, area, magnitude (see SIZE): spread, stretch, *expanse: capacity, capability, *ability.

react. Operate, work, function, *act, behave.

readiness. **Readiness, ease, facility, dexterity** come into comparison when they denote the power of doing something without evidence of effort, or the quality of a work, performance, or the like, which manifests such effortlessness. **Readiness** lays stress on the quickness or promptitude with which anything is done; as, his *readiness* in repartee; "a happy *readiness* of conversation" (*Austen*). **Ease,** which is probably more often used of the quality than of the power, suggests not only a lack of all signs of strain or care, but an absence of signs of hesitation or uncertainty with resulting evenness in performance and, especially in spoken or written discourse, fluency, directness, grace, and simplicity in expression; as, "True *ease* in writing comes from art, not chance" (*Pope*); "*Ease* and strength, effort and weakness, go together" (*Shaw*); "Constance was surprised at the *ease* which he displayed in the conduct of practical affairs" (*Bennett*). **Facility,** though sometimes used in a derogatory sense (as, his fatal *facility* in composition; "His *facility* in language has been fatal only too often to his logic and philosophy"—*J. C. Van Dyke*), more frequently than *ease* expresses the power, proceeding from practice and use, of performing an act or dispatching a task with lightness and address. But *facility* and *ease* are often interchanged; as, "To this admirable precision she [Eugénie de Guérin] joins a lightness of touch, a feminine *ease* and grace, a flowing *facility* which are her own" (*Arnold*); "I loathed algebra at first, although afterwards I had some *facility* in it" (*B. Russell*). **Dexterity** implies both readiness and facility, but it carries a stronger implication than any of the preceding words of previous training or practice and of proficiency or skill; as, "the singular discernment and *dexterity* with which he had directed his whip" (*Austen*); his amazing *dexterity* in argument; "I should train school-children in forms of more or less dangerous *dexterity*, rather than in such things as football" (*B. Russell*).

Ana. Quickness, promptness, aptness (see corresponding adjectives at QUICK): alacrity, *celerity, legerity: fluency, eloquence, volubility (see corresponding adjectives at VOCAL).

Con. *Effort, exertion, pains, trouble.

ready. *Quick, prompt, apt.

Ana. Expert, adept, skilled, skillful, *proficient: *active, live, dynamic.

real. **Real, actual, true,** and their derivative nouns *reality, actuality, truth,* are often used interchangeably without marked loss when they mean correspondent (or that which is correspondent) to all the facts known and knowable; as, the *real,* or the *actual,* or the *true* state of affairs; his *real,* or *actual,* or *true* motive; the *real,* or *actual,* or *true* George Washington. They are also often used interchangeably, even by good writers, but with distinct loss in clearness and precision, when their common implication is merely that of substantial objective existence. **Real,** in this more inclusive sense, implies genuineness, or correspondence between what the thing appears or pretends to be and what it is; as, this is a *real* diamond; the British sovereign has little *real* power; he has a *real* interest in art. "To know the difference between *real* and sham enjoyment" (*Shaw*). **Actual** emphasizes occurrence or manifest existence; it is applied only to that which has emerged into the sphere of action or fact and is, therefore, inapplicable to abstractions; as, *actual* events; give me an *actual* instance of the workings of this law; the *actual* tests of the new airplane are yet to be made. "Sculpture and painting are not...capable of *actual* movement, but they suggest movement" (*Binyon*). "I'm no judge of the feelings of *actual* or prospective parents" (*R. Macaulay*). "The possible way—I am far from asserting it was the *actual* way—in which our legendary Socrates arose" (*H. Ellis*). **True** implies conformity either to that which is real or to that which is actual. If the former is intended, the term presupposes a standard, a pattern, a model, a technical definition, or a type by which that which is true is determined; as, a *true* Christian; the ladybird is not a *true* bug (an insect of the order Hemiptera), but a beetle (an insect of the order Coleoptera); the whale is not a *true* fish, but an animal; "As part of that resurrection...was born a *true* poet, Carducci" (*Quiller-Couch*); "The *true* refinement...that in art...comes only from strength" (*Wilde*). When *true* stresses conformity to that which is actual, it presupposes the test of correspondence to that which exists in nature or to all the facts known and knowable; as, *true* time; to run *true* to type; a *true* story; a *true* version of a story. "The same event can [not] be said to be *true* for faith but untrue for science" (*Inge*). "The language [of poetry]...must often, in liveliness and *truth,* fall short of that which is uttered by men in *real* life, under the *actual* pressure of those passions" (*Wordsworth*).

These words, especially *real* and *true,* are also used by philosophers and philosophical poets, critics, scientists and others in senses which are often at variance with those in ordinary use and which are, consequently, a source of confusion. All still imply substantial objective existence, but only *actual* necessarily implies existence in experience. **Real** is variously defined in philosophy; only two of those senses have come into use by others than philosophers. The older of these senses (often spoken of as the Platonic sense) distinguishes that which is *real* from that which is *phenomenal,* or existent in the world which is known to the senses. *Real* thus often becomes the equivalent of *ideal* when that word suggests, not a hazy conception but a profound intuition of a thing in its perfection. Thus, when a poet speaks of *real* beauty or of *real* justice, he seldom means the beauty that is seen or the justice that is experienced, but rather a beauty or a justice so far beyond that which occurs in the world of experience that it is apprehended only by the intellect or the imagination. "But from these create he [the poet] can Forms more *real* than living man" (*Shelley*). In nonimaginative writing, *real* still retains its implied contrast to *phenomenal* but further implies the fullness of existence knowable only through the intellect. "A hypothesis.... does not attempt to portray the *reality* of nature, but only what we see of nature—the phenomena of nature.... But...science might legitimately progress along the road from phenomena to *reality*" (*Jeans*). In another but not so common use, *real* denotes having existence independently of the mind. This sense derives from the division of modern philosophy into two branches, realism and idealism. The idealists hold that one knows only the images or ideas of things that are in one's mind and not the things in themselves; the realists assert that the things one sees, hears, feels, understands, or the like, are real because they exist in their own right independently of human limitations in knowing them. "If the physical world is an inference, stars and electrons are inferential; if the physical world exists, stars and electrons are *real*" (*Eddington*). **True,** in philosophical and aesthetic use, implies conformity to reality in its perfection or completeness (often distinguished as *ultimate reality*). Its use often imputes falsehood to actuality, which is by implication imperfect, faulty, or incomplete. "Othello, Macbeth, Lear...are not transcripts of reality [here, actual reality]. They are *truer* than if they were" (*Lowes*). "Thomas [one of Barrie's characters] affects me as a lie....Doubtless he was somebody you [Barrie] knew; that leads people so far astray. The actual is not the *true*" (*Stevenson*).

Ana. Being, existing *or* existent, subsisting *or* subsistent (see corresponding verbs at BE): *certain, necessary, inevitable.

Ant. Unreal: apparent (sense 2): imaginary.

realize. Realize, actualize, embody, incarnate, materialize, externalize, objectify, substantiate, substantialize, hypostatize, reify are the chief words in English meaning to give concrete or objective existence to that which has existed either as an abstraction, a conception, or the like, or as a possibility. Except within smaller groups, they are, however, seldom interchangeable, because their implications vary widely and their applications are largely determined by idiom. **Realize** commonly implies emergence into the sphere of actual things, as of that which has been a dream, an ideal, a hope, or a plan; as, the project was never *realized* owing to a lack of funds; he did not *realize* his ambition until he was past middle life. "The ideal of economic efficiency is best *realized* by a machine" (*Grandgent*). The implication of attainment, of achievement, or of fulfillment is at times so strong in *realize* as to obscure or subordinate its fundamental idea. "To achieve a beautiful relation to another human being is to *realise* a part of perfection" (*Binyon*). "However evolution...is effected, a divine purpose is being *realized* in it" (*Inge*). **Actualize,** though sometimes used interchangeably with *realize,* is found chiefly in philosophical or technical writings with the implication of emergence, as of that which has existed only in potentiality, either into fullness or perfection of existence (as, powers of the mind never *actualized*) or into act or action (as, potential energy becomes kinetic energy when it is *actualized* by motion). **Embody** and **incarnate** sometimes imply investment with an outward or visible form of something abstract, as a principle, an idea, a trait, or a quality; as, "The poet cannot *embody* his conceptions so vividly and completely as the painter" (*Binyon*); Dickens *incarnated* hypocrisy in his Uriah Heap. **Materialize** stresses emergence into the sphere of that which is perceptible or tangible and usually presupposes prior vagueness, haziness, or elusiveness. "I had the glimmering of an idea, and endeavoured to *materialize* it in words" (*N. Hawthorne*). *Materialize,* as a transitive verb, is now used chiefly in Spiritualism (as, to *materialize* spirits, or to make them visible). **Externalize** and **objectify** emphasize the projection of that which is subjective, as a thought, an emotion, a desire, so that it takes form apart from the mind. *Externalize* often suggests a conscious or unconscious urge for expression or relief; as, hallucinations are frequently *externalizations* of a fear. "Madness has produced...valuable art...; the artist attempts to rid himself of his abnormality...by *externalizing* it into the work of art" (*Day Lewis*). *Objectify* is more likely to suggest a conscious attempt to overcome the limitations of subjectivity and to contemplate one's own mental processes; as, introspective psychology depends for its data upon the power of the investigator to *objectify* his own sensations, emotions, and thoughts. **Substantiate, substantialize, hypostatize, reify** occur chiefly in philosophical and technical writing. They all imply conversion by the mind of that which is a concept or abstraction into a thing that has real and objective yet not, as a rule, perceptible existence; thus, in the mind of the ordinary person, space and time are *substantialized, hypostatized,* etc., whereas in the view of philosophers and philosophic scientists they are relations.

Ana. Effect, fulfill, execute, accomplish, achieve, *perform.

2 *Think, conceive, imagine, fancy, envisage, envision.

Ana. *Understand, comprehend, appreciate.

rear, *adj.* *Posterior, after, back, hind, hinder.

Ant. Front.

rear, *v.* Raise, *lift, elevate, hoist, heave, boost.

Ana. *Rise, ascend, mount, soar: *nurse, nurture, foster: breed, propagate (see GENERATE).

reason, *n.* **1 Reason, ground, argument, proof** are here compared as meaning a point or series of points offered or capable of being offered in support of something questioned or disputed. **Reason** usually implies the need of justification, either to oneself or another, of some practice, action, opinion, belief, or the like; it is therefore commonly (though not necessarily) personal in its reference; thus, a father asks the *reason* for his son's disobedience; a person gives the *reasons* for his preference. *Reason* is often applied to any motive, consideration, inducement, or the like, which one offers in explanation or defense. "So convenient it is to be a 'reasonable creature,' since it enables one to find or make a *reason* for everything one has in mind to do" (*Franklin*). **Ground** and its plural **grounds** are often used in place of *reason* and *reasons* because they too imply the intent to justify or defend. When, however, the emphasis is on evidence, data, facts, reasoning, etc., rather than on motives or considerations, *ground* is the acceptable word; thus, the *reasons* for a belief may explain why it is held, but the *grounds* for it give evidence of the validity of that belief; a scientist presents the *grounds* (better than *reasons*) for his conclusion. *Ground* also suggests more solid support in fact and therefore greater cogency than *reason;* thus, one may speak of frivolous or trumped-up *reasons* (but not *grounds*); there is *ground* (better than *reason*) for the popular belief in thought transference. "Suppose I have *grounds* to think that he can't take care of himself in a given instance?" (*Conrad*). **Argument** stresses the intent to convince another or to bring him into agreement with one's view or position. Strictly it implies the use of evidence and reasoning in the making and stating of a point in support of one's contention; as, the debaters came well provided with *arguments;* every possible *argument* in favor of the proposal has been advanced, but still the Congress is obdurate. Loosely, however, it often suggests reasoning without reference to fact. "When he was asked to argue the merits of vaccination, he always rejoined that one fact in such cases was worth a thousand *arguments*" (*V. Heiser*). **Proof,** in strict usage, emphasizes not an intent, but an effect: that of conclusive demonstration; therefore, in the sense here considered, a *proof* is any piece of evidence, such as a fact, a document, or the testimony of a witness or expert, or any argument, that evokes a feeling of certainty in those who are to be convinced. "These arguments [for the existence of God] are sometimes called *proofs,* though they are not demonstrations; they are, however, closely inwoven with the texture of rational experience" (*Inge*).

Ana. Explanation, justification, rationalization (see corresponding verbs at EXPLAIN).

2 *Cause, determinant, antecedent, occasion.

Ana. *Motive, incentive, inducement, impulse: basis, foundation, ground (see BASE, *n.*).

3 Reason, intuition, understanding are here compared as terms denoting that power of the intellect by which man arrives at truth or knowledge. Like the terms discriminated at MIND, these words have been variously defined by psychologists and philosophers, with the result that their precise interpretation in literary use often depends upon a knowledge of the author's philosophical or psychological background. **Reason,** though often loosely used as though it were an equivalent of *mind* and *intellect* (see MIND), as here compared (see also

CAUSE, 1; REASON, 1), applies mainly to the thinking power of the intellect; as such it implies a power which works upon facts gained by perception, or upon facts or principles instilled into one's mind by others, and which orders and relates those facts and principles by drawing inferences from them and a conclusion or conclusions from a body of inferences, thereby increasing one's knowledge or reaching a comprehension of that which was formerly vague or obscure. "Those who use their *reason* do not reach the same conclusions as those who obey their prejudices" (*Lippmann*). "Facts have a double value: they give us wherewithal to think straight and they stimulate the imagination; for imagination, like *reason*, cannot run without the gasoline of knowledge" (*Grandgent*). *Reason* often specifically applies to a power of arriving at knowledge which is higher than perception, or the power of gaining knowledge through the medium of the senses, because it starts from the point where perception ends, and yet which is lower than another power (variously named; e.g., "intuition") which enables one to attain knowledge or comprehension of that which is invisible and immaterial without the aid of the senses; as, truths beyond *reason;* "To admit...that *reason* cannot extend into the religious sphere" (*H. Ellis*); Thomas Aquinas believed that the existence of God could be demonstrated by *reason*. Nevertheless, the term is often used in a very general sense to denote the power of arriving at knowledge or truth by logical processes, whether one starts with observed facts, with principles regarded as axioms or necessary postulates, or the like; thus, in Kant's definition "pure *reason*" does not start with facts derived from experience or observation, but with truths derived through the medium of a higher intellectual power. **Intuition** is the most varied in its applications of all these terms, except possibly *understanding:* in all of its senses, however, it implies a power to know immediately and not through the agency of the reason. The term usually also suggests a knowledge that is comparable to that which one gains through seeing or perceiving, but since it frequently implies knowledge of that which is beyond the senses, it may denote a power, higher than reason, which enables the mind to attain immediate knowledge of the supersensible or supernatural. "One in whom persuasion and belief Had ripened into faith, and faith become A passionate *intuition*" (*Wordsworth*). In philosophical, psychological, and aesthetic use the term commonly denotes a power of arriving at truth or knowledge that is different from though not necessarily higher than reason, and may have its basis in perception, in a power akin to that of imagination, in mystical experience, or the like. "He [Shakespeare] seems to have known the world by *intuition*, to have looked through nature at one glance" (*Pope*). "The man of letters does most of his work not by calculation, not by the application of formulas, but by aesthetic *intuition*" (*A. Huxley*). "All great achievements in science, he [Einstein] holds, start from *intuition*" (*H. Ellis*). In its loosest and most generally current sense, *intuition* (cf. *intuitive*, under INSTINCTIVE, 1) implies a gift or an instinct for immediate comprehension of the significance of facts or of a situation. "Do we not really trust these faint lights of *intuition*, because they are lights, more than *reason*, which is often too slow [a counselor] for us to resort to?" (*G. W. Russell*). "With one of her quick leaps of *intuition* she had entered into the other's soul and once more measured its shuddering loneliness" (*E. Wharton*). **Understanding,** in its usual current sense, applies to the power of the intellect to comprehend or grasp whatever is taught or whatever is studied, or the true purport or significance of a term, a situation, or a set of related facts, or what is required of one to meet adequately a situation or exigency; as, "To have a really precise *understanding* of this matter" (*Shaw*); "Knowledge he has gained...but not...*understanding*" (*A. Repplier*). In its philosophical and here pertinent sense, *understanding* applies to a power to see a thing not as an individual but as an instance of the class or species to which it belongs; thus, in theory, one who regards a thing as an individual may recognize it as belonging to a class, but because his emotions or imagination are stimulated may be prevented from seeing it in its underlying or essential character and therefore from having an understanding of it: one who regards a thing from the point of view of *understanding* sees it in its universal and often, by implication, its eternal essence. In this sense, *understanding* (especially as a translation of the German *Verstand*) is often, but not invariably, distinguished from *reason* (especially as a translation of the German *Vernunft*, which usually includes intuition in its higher sense) in that understanding is thought of as the power of the intellect whereby the external objective world becomes orderly and intelligible, and reason, as the power by which one ascends from what is known to new knowledge. "*Understanding* is the entire power of perceiving and conceiving [that is, making concepts], exclusive of the sensibility; the power of dealing with the impressions of sense, and composing them into wholes" (*Coleridge*). "The neoclassicists, by admitting only what is probable to the *understanding*, reduced unduly the rôle of illusion, the element of wonder and surprise" (*Babbitt*).

Ana. *Mind, intellect, intelligence, brain: ratiocination, illation, *inference.

reason, *v.* Reflect, *think, deliberate, speculate, cogitate.

Ana. *Infer, deduce, conclude, judge, gather.

reasonable. *Rational.

Ana. Sensible, sane, prudent, judicious, *wise: *fair, equitable, just.

Ant. Unreasonable.

rebate. *Deduction, abatement, discount.

rebel, *n.* **Rebel, insurgent, iconoclast** come into comparison when they denote a person who rises up against constituted authority or the established order. **Rebel** carries the strongest implication of a refusal to obey or to accept dictation and of actual, often armed, resistance to that which one opposes; the term does not necessarily imply antagonism to the government of a state or church, however, but is comprehensive enough to cover one who defies the authority such as of a law, a tradition, a custom, or the like; as, "all their friends were protesters and *rebels* and seceders" (*H. G. Wells*); "'[Woman is] a tyrant till she's reduced to bondage, and a *rebel* till she's well beaten'" (*Meredith*). "The *rebel*, as a human type entitled to respect and often to sympathy, was not recognized in Europe till the period of the French Revolution....The term *'rebel'* was in itself a term of reproach...till the days of Byron" (*R. E. N. Dodge*). **Insurgent** applies chiefly to a rebel who rises in revolt but who is not regarded by the authorities as having the status of an enemy or belligerent; hence, *rebels* in a colony or dependency of an empire may, from the imperial point of view, be designated as *insurgents*, even though they call themselves *rebels;* as, the colonial forces were found able to cope with the *insurgents* in India. In a more extended sense, *insurgent* applies to any rebel in a political party, a church, a group of artists or writers, or the like, who rises in revolt not so much in an attempt to destroy the organization or institution or its laws or conventions as in the hope of effecting changes or reforms believed to be necessary; as, never were there so many *insurgents* in the dominant political party as at present;

the free verse movement was led by a group of *insurgents.* **Iconoclast** (etymologically, an image breaker, originally one of a party of insurgents in the Eastern Church in the 8th and 9th centuries who opposed the use of icons [see *icon* under IMAGE, 1]) is now applied in an extended sense to any person who violently attacks an established belief, a venerated custom, a highly respected tradition, or the like, as an obstacle to reform or progress or as a mere fetish. " 'I have become a reformer, and, like all reformers, an *iconoclast*....I shatter creeds and demolish idols' " (*Shaw*). "Julius was a bold *iconoclast* about republican forms which had survived their usefulness; Augustus sought to cherish whatever of these forms could be made to work" (*Buchan*).

Ana. *Opponent, antagonist, adversary: assailant, attacker (see ATTACK, *v.*).

rebellion. **Rebellion, revolution, uprising, revolt, insurrection, mutiny, Putsch** come into comparison only when they denote a war or a warlike outbreak against a government or against powers in authority. **Rebellion** in this narrow sense implies open, organized, and usually armed, resistance to constituted authority or to the government in power: the term is usually applied (only after the event) to an instance of such resistance as has failed to overthrow the powers that be; as, Jack Straw's *Rebellion;* the Jacobite *rebellions* of 1715 and 1745. **Revolution,** on the other hand, applies strictly to a rebellion that has been successful to the extent that the old government is overthrown and a new one substituted; as, the French *Revolution;* the American *Revolution.* The term, however, does not invariably imply a war or a warlike outbreak or even a change in government; as, the industrial *revolution* of the nineteenth century; to effect a bloodless *revolution* by a coup d'état. The words are often applied to the same event according to the point of view of the user or sometimes according to the time in which it is used; thus, the American Civil War of 1861–1865 was called the "War of the *Rebellion*" by Northerners, not only during its progress but for a long time after; a *revolution* is often called a *rebellion* by the overthrown government or its supporters until bitterness has faded; thus, the English Civil War (1642–1652) was, after the Restoration (1660), and still sometimes is, called the Great *Rebellion.* **Uprising** is a somewhat general term applicable to any act of violence that indicates a popular desire to defy or overthrow the government: it is often used in reference to a small and ineffective movement among an insurgent class or section of the people but it is applicable also to the first signs of a general or widespread rebellion; as, there was fear of *uprisings* in different parts of the country; "Whenever the whole nation should join together in one sudden and vigorous *uprising*" (*Freeman*). **Revolt** and **insurrection** in strict use apply to an armed uprising which does not attain the extent of a rebellion, either because it is quickly put down or is immediately effective. *Revolt,* however, carries a stronger suggestion of a refusal to accept conditions or continue in allegiance than does *insurrection,* which often suggests a seditious act such as an attempt to seize the governing power or to gain control for one's party. "The Reformation...was no sudden *revolt,* but the culmination of a long agitation for national independence in religious matters" (*Inge*). "Baltazar's tyranny grew little by little, and the Ácoma people were sometimes at the point of *revolt*" (*Cather*). "*Insurrections* of base people are more furious in their beginnings" (*Bacon*). "Excess of obedience is...as bad as *insurrection*" (*Meredith*). **Mutiny** applies chiefly to an insurrection against military or, especially, maritime or naval authority; as, the ship's master feared *mutiny* long before it occurred; the *mutiny* of a regiment made the situation desperate for the invaders. **Putsch,** a Swiss-German term in some use in English, applies to a small popular uprising; as, the Kapp *Putsch* in Germany in 1920; the Munich beer hall *Putsch* of Hitler's supporters in 1923.

Ana. *Sedition, treason: resistance, opposition, combating, withstanding (see corresponding verbs at OPPOSE).

rebellious. *Insubordinate, mutinous, seditious, factious, contumacious.

Ana. Recalcitrant, refractory, intractable, *unruly, ungovernable: estranged, alienated, disaffected (see ESTRANGE).

Ant. Acquiescent, resigned: submissive.

rebound, *v.* **Rebound, reverberate, recoil, resile, repercuss** come into comparison when they mean to spring back, especially after being thrown, stretched, or the like. **Rebound** literally implies a springing back after a collision or impact; as, the ball readily *rebounds* when thrown against a wall. In figurative use, the term implies a springing back, as from one extreme to another or from an abnormal condition to one that is normal; as, his heart *rebounded* with hope. **Reverberate** is now used chiefly in reference to sounds which are forced back in the manner of an echo or series of echoes, but it is still employed with reference to rays of light, flames, or waves of heat which are repelled or reflected from side to side or from one surface to another. "The evening gun thundered from the fortress, and was *reverberated* from the heights" (*N. Hawthorne*). "The far flashing of their starry lances *Reverberates* the dying light of day" (*Shelley*). **Recoil** in its literal use (see also RECOIL, 1) often implies a springing back after being stretched, strained, or depressed; as, the springs of a mattress *recoil* after the pressure has been removed; the gun *recoils* when a shot is fired. This implication is even more often apparent in one of the figurative senses of the verb, where the suggestion of a return to the source or point of origin in the manner of a boomerang is also evident. "That evidence missed the mark at which it was aimed, and *recoiled* on him from whom it proceeded" (*Macaulay*). But *recoil* often implies a springing back in the sense of being forced back by or as if by a blow: it then may or may not connote a retreat, a receding, a reeling, or the like; as, "Ten paces huge He back *recoiled*" (*Milton*); "As deep *recoiling* surges foam below" (*Burns*); "Cashel [in a fight] *recoiled,* wringing his hand to relieve the tingling of his knuckles" (*Shaw*). **Resile** (the least common of these words), like *recoil,* may imply a springing back into the original state or position, but in this sense it is commonly used in reference to resilient bodies or substances and suggests either literally or figuratively a drawing back that is normal or lacking in abruptness; as, to give a tube time to *resile* after it has been stretched; many of the converts to the new religion *resiled* in the course of time. **Repercuss,** which is now rare (its corresponding noun *repercussion* and adjective *repercussive* are common), is a close synonym of *reverberate* and *rebound,* for it implies the return of something moving ahead with great force or, in figurative use, set in motion or operation, back to or toward the starting point. However, it (or especially, the noun or the adjective) distinctively suggests repulsion upon impact and a return with undiminished force, or sometimes even greater force, and often, when persons are involved, with a marked effect upon the one or the ones who initiated the action; as, the waves dashed against the rocks and *repercussed* with a great roar; the attack was violent but its *repercussion* was destructive; few foresaw the inevitable *repercussions* of the Treaty of Versailles.

Ana. Bound, *skip, ricochet.

rebuild. Remodel, *mend, repair, patch.
Ana. *Renew, restore, renovate, refresh.

rebuke. *Reprove, reprimand, admonish, reproach, chide.
Ana. Rate, upbraid, *scold, berate: *criticize, reprehend, reprobate.

rebut. *Disprove, refute, confute, controvert.

recalcitrant. Refractory, intractable, headstrong, willful, *unruly, ungovernable.
Ana. Rebellious, *insubordinate, factious, contumacious: *obstinate, stubborn: resisting, opposing, withstanding, combating *or* combative (see corresponding verbs at OPPOSE).
Ant. Amenable (sense 2).

recall, *v.* Recollect, *remember, remind, reminisce, bethink, mind.
Ana. Evoke, elicit, extract, *educe: *stir, rouse, arouse, waken, awaken.

recant. Retract, *abjure, renounce, forswear.
Ana. Withdraw, remove.

recede. **Recede, retreat, retrograde, retract, back, crawfish** come into comparison when they mean to move or seem to move in the direction that is exactly the opposite of ahead or forward. **Recede** stresses marked and, usually, increasing distance from a given point, line, or position, but it implies movement on the part of that which recedes only when a fixed point of view is indicated or understood; as, the tide is *receding;* until the flood waters *recede,* the extent of the damage will not be known. "While I stood gazing, both the children gradually grew fainter to my view, *receding,* and still *receding*" (*Lamb*). When the point of view is that of a traveler or the distance is in time, not in space, the receding thing is stationary and the point of view changes. In such a case, either a gradual disappearance as from view or consciousness or a change in perspective is implied; as, he stood at the ship's stern watching the shore *recede* from view; "past events as they *recede* appear in truer proportions" (*L. P. Smith*); "the possibility of certain ultimate solutions has rather *receded* than approached as the years went by" (*J. W. Krutch*). When used of persons and their ideas, attitudes, or the like, *recede* (often followed by *from*) suggests departure from a fixed idea, or determined attitude, or a definite stand. "He was far too self-willed to *recede* from a position, especially as it would involve humiliation" (*Hardy*). **Retreat** implies withdrawal from a point or position reached, usually because one is averse to remaining or to advancing further or is for some reason, such as imminent defeat or danger, or obedience to orders, unable to remain or advance; as, after the failure of the first attack, the army *retreated;* "Some...who picture...Religion as *retreating* from one position to another before the victorious advance of science" (*Inge*). "They frequently approached this theme, and always *retreated* from it" (*Meredith*). **Retrograde** implies movement contrary to that which is normal or natural; thus, a planet *retrogrades* when it moves or seems to move from east to west, or in a direction opposite to that of the usual planetary course. The verb is also used to imply the reverse of progress in the development of a species, a race, or an individual. "Some races have been stationary, or even have *retrograded*" (*J. Lubbock*). "In his Latin and Greek he was *retrograding*" (*Meredith*). Occasionally, it is used to imply a going backward in time or an inversion of the chronological order; as, "Our narrative *retrogrades* to a period shortly previous to the incidents last mentioned" (*Scott*). The next two words, *retract* and *back,* are commonly employed as transitive as well as intransitive verbs. **Retract** is used chiefly, but not exclusively, in the biological sciences as the opposite of *protract,* in reference to those parts of an organism which can be thrust forward or drawn backward; as, to *retract* the tongue; to cause a cat's claws to *retract;* "throwing out and *retracting* their left fists like pawing horses" (*Shaw*). **Back,** in this sense, is usually but not invariably a transitive verb, except when followed by *up, out,* or *down,* when it is more often intransitive than transitive. Often it implies retrograde motion; as, to *back* an automobile; the water in a drain *backs up* when a pipe cannot carry it off and it returns to the bowl or sink; to *back out* of a room; a wind *backs* when it shifts to a counterclockwise direction. Often when followed by *out* or *down* it implies a receding, as from a stand or attitude, or a retreating, as from a promise, an engagement, or the like; as, he will never *back down* once his word is given; he is trying to *back out* now that he sees how much work the project entails; the opposition forced the governor to *back down* and to recall his recommendations. **Crawfish** (a colloquialism in the United States) implies reference to the retrograde motion of the crayfish, or crawfish, but it often also carries the implication of cowardly retreat from a position or stand; as, "I *crawfished* as good as I could about ten yards" (*Twain*); he tried to *crawfish* out of it, when he saw how he had blundered in his speech.
Ana. Withdraw, retire, depart (see GO): *rebound, recoil.
Ant. Proceed: advance (sense 2).

receipt, *n.* **1** *Reception.
2 Receipt, recipe, prescription are here compared as meaning a formula or set of directions for the compounding of ingredients especially, but not exclusively, in cookery and medicine. **Receipt,** the oldest of these terms, is now increasingly rare though it is still often employed as a designation of a formula for making a homemade medicine (as, she has an excellent *receipt* for a cough medicine; a *receipt* for a spring tonic that has been followed by the family for several generations), and less often in reference to cookery formulas, the term being gradually displaced in this sense by *recipe.* **Recipe** (etymologically, the Latin imperative meaning *take*) in its earliest use in an English text meant no more than "take" and was used as the initial word (now abbreviated to R or ℞) of a physician's formula for a medicine. Not until the sixteenth century did the term become a noun denoting such a formula, and not until the mid-eighteenth century was it also applied to a cookery receipt. In the former sense, *recipe* is now rare; in the latter sense, for reasons which are not clear, it is generally preferred to *receipt.* The accepted term in both American and British use for the physician's formula is **prescription.** That term is also applied to the medicine which is compounded according to the terms of the formula; as, Doctor Blank gave him three *prescriptions;* he is still taking the *prescription* for bronchitis.

receive. **Receive, accept, admit, take** are synonymous only when they mean to take or let someone or something come into one's possession, one's presence, one's group, one's mind, one's substance, or the like. They are seldom interchangeable except within a narrow range and, even then, rarely without modification of the thought expressed. **Receive** very often implies nothing more than that which has been stated in the common definition: it may be predicated of persons or of things; as, he did not *receive* the news gladly; the barrel *receives* excess rain water. In general, *receive* implies passiveness in the receiver even when the subject is a person and his response is indicated in the context; as, an infant merely *receives* impressions, for he does not understand them (cf. to be *receptive* to new ideas; to be in a *receptive* frame of mind);

soft wax *receives* the impression of anything that touches it. Only when it implies welcoming or recognition does *receive* connote activity in the receiver; as, after some delay, the king *received* the ambassador; the social leaders refused to *receive* the newcomers. "The indifference and hostility with which his earlier work was *received*" (*Day Lewis*). **Accept,** in contrast with *receive,* always implies a measure of mental consent, even of approval. Thus, a person may be *received,* but not necessarily *accepted,* in society; an idea may be *received,* but not *accepted,* by the mind. "In [Dante's] purgatory the torment of flame is deliberately and consciously *accepted* by the penitent" (*T. S. Eliot*). Frequently, *accept* suggests tacit acquiescence rather than active assent or approval. Sometimes, in such cases, it connotes an uncritical attitude. "The man who...*accepted* simply, as a matter of course, the tradition" (*G. L. Dickinson*). Sometimes it implies a surrender to the inevitable. "It is the business of the sensitive artist in life to *accept* his own nature as it is, not to try to force it into another shape" (*A. Huxley*). **Admit** comes into comparison with *receive* only when the agent (the one that lets in) is the one that receives rather than introduces; as, the king *admitted* the ambassador to his presence (cf. the major-domo *admitted* the ambassador to the throne room); the heart *admits* fluid through these apertures (cf. these apertures readily *admit* fluid into the heart). *Admit,* in this restricted sense, is distinguishable from *receive* by slight syntactical differences but chiefly by its strong implications of permission, allowance, or sufferance. Thus, a judge *admits* evidence only after its admissibility has been questioned and he has allowed its entrance. The situation remains the same when the subject is impersonal; as, the archway was wide enough to *admit* ten men abreast. Sometimes these implications are so strong that the idea of receiving is lost; as, this *admits* of no argument. *Admit,* in contrast with *accept,* often adds the implication of concession. Thus, one who *admits* the truth of a contention *accepts* it more or less unwillingly; one can *accept* a proposition without question, but one *admits* it only after one has questioned it. **Take** is a synonym of *receive* only when it suggests no reaching out on one's own part or of one's own initiative to get hold of something (for the usual sense, see TAKE, 1) or when it suggests an offering, presenting, conferring, inflicting, or the like, by another: it then implies merely a letting something be put into one's hands, one's mind, one's possession, one's control, or the like; as, this gift was meant for you: *take* it or leave it as you please; he *takes* whatever fortune sends him; the British showed that they can *take* the German bombing. "What was it that made men follow Oliver Cromwell and *take* at his hands that which they would not receive from any of his contemporaries?" (*S. M. Crothers*). "You don't have to *take* anything from him, or to stand his bad manners" (*Cather*).

Ana. *Enter, penetrate: seize, *take, grasp.

receivership. *Insolvency, bankruptcy, failure, suspension.

reception. **Reception, receipt** agree in meaning a receiving, but they are not now interchangeable, their correct use being dependent upon accepted idiom. **Reception** is now the preferred term when that which is received is a person, especially a caller, a visitor, a guest, or the like: the term may then apply to the act, fashion, or manner of receiving (as, they are now in line, ready for the *reception* of their guests; she gave all her friends a warm *reception*), or the manner of being received (as, "much pleased with the *reception* she had"—*Pepys*), or a ceremonious receiving or entertaining (as, to invite one's circle of friends to a *reception;* to hold a *reception* for the out-of-town delegates and their wives), or an admission or entrance as into a place, a society, a company, or the like (as, the house is ready for the *reception* of its new tenants; to call attention to the *reception* of several new members into the society). When that which is received is a thing, *reception* is employed only when to the idea of receiving is added the idea of admitting into, or as if into, a space or enclosure (as, the tower is large enough for the *reception* of several bells), or of apprehension as by a sense, or by the senses, or by the mind (as, the *reception* [i.e., the hearing of sound transmitted by the radio] is not good tonight; their minds are not ready for the *reception* of such ideas; the proposal met a favorable *reception*). **Receipt** (see also RECEIPT, 2) is now the preferred term when that which is received is a thing given or sent by another and delivered by hand, by mail, by express, or the like, into one's custody or possession: such a thing may be a sum of money, a piece or lot of goods, a letter or other communication, or the like; as, to acknowledge the *receipt* of goods ordered; I am awaiting the *receipt* of a letter before making my decision. *Receipt* is also applied to a signed paper or document testifying to the receipt of money due, of goods ordered, etc.

recess, *n.* **Recess, alcove, nook, niche, embrasure, bay, cubicle, carrell, carol** are comparable only in their architectural senses. **Recess,** the comprehensive term, names any outward, or seemingly outward, projecting space formed by a break in the straight line of a wall. An **alcove** is a recess large enough to contain a bed, or a secretary, or the like. A **nook** is a recess usually formed by something that projects inward and makes a new wall line, such as a chimney, a row of built-in bookcases, or by partitions. A **niche** is a recess in a wall, usually above the floor and below the ceiling, large enough to contain a piece of sculpture or other decorative object. An **embrasure** is a recess formed by an outward projecting window (or windows) or door; a **bay** is a deep embrasure formed by windows arranged in a rectangular, polygonal, or curved line. A **cubicle** may be a very small room, but the term is often applied to an alcove or nook by a window or in an embrasure, for the use of a student or writer. In technical language **carrell** is commonly used when the cubicle is in a library, and **carol** when it is in a monastery.

recherché. Elegant, *choice, exquisite, delicate, dainty, rare.

Ana. Fresh, original, *new, novel: *select, exclusive, picked.

Ant. Banal.

recidivate. *Lapse, relapse, backslide.

Ana. Degenerate, deteriorate, decline (see corresponding nouns at DETERIORATION).

Con. *Improve, better: reform, amend, remedy, redress, *correct.

recidivation, recidivism. Lapse, relapse, backsliding. See under LAPSE, *v.*

Ana. *Deterioration, degeneration, decline, declension, decadence, devolution.

Con. *Reformation, reform.

recipe. *Receipt, prescription.

reciprocal. 1 **Reciprocal, mutual, common** come into comparison as meaning shared, experienced, shown, or the like, by each of the persons or things concerned. **Reciprocal** has for its distinctive implication the return in due measure by each of two sides of that which exists on the other or of that which is offered, given, or manifested by the other. Usually therefore it implies not only a "this for that," but an equivalence in value (though not necessarily in kind) on each side, as of love, hate, understanding, courtesies, concessions, duties, and the like; as, *reciprocal* reproaches; the *reciprocal* obligations of capital and labor; "the *reciprocal* feelings of man and woman towards each other" (*T. S. Eliot*). **Mutual** is often used in place of *reciprocal* when the idea of return or interchange is suggested and that of sharing equally or jointly is stressed; as, *mutual* (or *reciprocal*) affection; *reciprocal* hate (often better than *mutual* in this phrase); *mutual* enthusiasm (often better than *reciprocal* except when there is the intent to imply a giving to and a getting back from each other). But *mutual* only (and not *reciprocal*) is possible when the adjective applies to two persons who entertain reciprocal feelings to each other; as, they are *mutual* friends; *mutual* foes. When there is very little or no suggestion of a reciprocal relation between thoughts, feelings, and the like, and the emphasis is upon the fact that the two persons or things involved entertain the same feelings towards each other, perform the same actions, suffer the same results, or the like, *mutual* is always preferable to *reciprocal*. "They parted at last with *mutual* civility, and possibly a *mutual* desire of never meeting again" (*Austen*). "Even Shelley sometimes mingles poetry and propaganda to their *mutual* disaster" (*Lowes*). Both *reciprocal* and *mutual* are sometimes used, even by good writers, when more than two persons, classes, or things are involved. This use is not generally approved when there is no implication of reciprocity, **common** being the preferred term in such a case; thus, one says "we (two, three, or more persons) are *mutual* friends" (i.e., we are all friends of each other) but they have *common* friends (i.e., each of them has friends who are friends of the other or others) or a *common* friend [though Dickens entitled one of his novels *Our Mutual Friend*]; the members of a group may have a *common* (not *mutual* unless reciprocity is involved) purpose. For *common*, as here compared (see also COMMON, 3; UNIVERSAL, 2), implies a sharing by, or a joint possession of, two or more persons, and differs from *mutual* in not being restricted as to the number involved and in not carrying, when two persons or things are concerned, any suggestion of a reciprocal relation or of an equivalence of feeling, performance, effort, or the like; as, the barons made a *common* cause against the king; "their *common* fund of intellectual interests and curiosities made their talks exhilarating" (*E. Wharton*); husband and wife have a *common* purse.

Ana. Shared, participated, partaken (see SHARE): interchanged, exchanged (see EXCHANGE): balancing, compensating, counterpoising (see COMPENSATE).

2 Reciprocal, correspondent, correlative, complementary, complemental, convertible are not close synonyms, although in some instances they are interchangeable. All, however, agree basically in meaning like, equivalent, or similarly related to each other as in kind, quality, value, or the like. **Reciprocal,** as here compared (see also RECIPROCAL, 1), implies that the likeness or equivalence of two things or of one thing to another rests on the fact of their being returns or a return in kind, value, or quality for that which one side has given to the other; as, the *reciprocal* courtesies manifested in the meeting of the two generals; *reciprocal* attacks in a battle; a treaty providing for *reciprocal* privileges; a teacher hopes for a *reciprocal* interest on the part of his pupils; "believing in the *reciprocal* friendship of the British" (*W. Wilson*). **Correspondent** implies that the likeness or equivalence proceeds from the fact that one answers to the other or conforms to it so that they are fitted to each other, proportionate to or commensurate with each other, or in perfect accord with each other; as, he found the results *correspondent* to his hopes; "an order of things more *correspondent* to the sentiments of our constituents" (*Jefferson*); her ideas of proper housekeeping were not *correspondent* to those of her mother-in-law. *Correspondent* also applies to things which are analogous in position, character, use, and the like, though found in different places, different arts, different plants or animals, or the like; as, *correspondent* organs such as the stomach of a human being and the gizzard of a fowl; the stripes on the blouse are *correspondent* to those on the skirt. **Correlative** implies a close relationship rather than a likeness, but it is applicable chiefly to two things (or one of two things) which cannot exist independently of each other either because one logically implies the other (as, "husband" and "wife," "father" and "son," are *correlative* terms), or one cannot exist without the other (as, "the 'right' of the worker to demand work on reasonable terms, and the *correlative* obligation of the organized community to provide it"—*J. A. Hobson;* the *correlative* rights and duties of every citizen). In somewhat looser, but correct, use, *correlative* may imply nothing more than so close a correspondence or relation between two things that they come naturally, necessarily, or logically together; as, major changes in social conditions and *correlative* changes in human attitudes; "two *correlative* rules: first, that no one shall be allowed to undertake important work without having acquired the necessary skill; secondly, that this skill shall be taught to the ablest of those who desire it" (*B. Russell*). **Complementary** (or less often, **complemental**) also implies a close relationship rather than a likeness: the term carries a strong suggestion that one thing is so necessary to another or to others that without it an entire or perfect whole is not possible; as, "It is important to recognise that these two uses of the surplus are *complementary* and not competitive" (*J. A. Hobson*); "the corpuscular and undulatory concepts of light must be regarded as *complementary* rather than *antithetical*" (*Jeans*); revelation is regarded by many theologians as *complemental* to reason. **Convertible,** in the sense here considered, implies so strong a likeness that the things, though not identical, are virtually interchangeable; as, "The law, and the opinion of the judge, are not always *convertible* terms, or one and the same thing" (*Blackstone*); "truth and beauty [as in Keats's line 'Beauty is truth, truth beauty'] have never been recognised as identical, and...to employ their names as *convertible* terms would lead to no end of confusion" (*Quiller-Couch*).

Ana. Equivalent, identical, *same: related, associated, linked, united (see JOIN).

recite. Rehearse, recount, *relate, narrate, describe, state, report.

Ana. Enumerate, tell, *count, number: detail, itemize, particularize (see corresponding adjectives at CIRCUMSTANTIAL).

reckless. Daring, daredevil, rash, temerarious, foolhardy, venturesome, venturous, *adventurous.

Ana. *Precipitate, sudden, hasty, headlong, impetuous, abrupt: desperate, hopeless (see DESPONDENT).

Ant. Calculating. — ***Con.*** *Cautious, circumspect, wary, chary.

reckon, *v.* **1** *Calculate, compute, estimate.

Ana. Enumerate, *count, number: figure, total, *add, sum, cast, foot.

2 *Consider, regard, account, deem.

Ana. *Think, conceive, imagine, envision: *conjecture, surmise, guess.

3 Count, bank, *rely, trust, depend.

reclaim. Save, ransom, redeem, deliver, *rescue.

Ana. *Renew, restore, renovate: reform, rectify, remedy, *correct, amend.

Ant. Abandon. — ***Con.*** Desert, forsake (see ABANDON).

reclining. Recumbent, *prone, supine, prostrate, couchant, dormant.
Ana. Resting, reposing (see corresponding nouns at REST): leaning, inclining (see SLANT, *v.*).

recluse. Recluse, hermit, eremite, anchorite (*or* **anchoret**), **cenobite** (*or* **coenobite**) are comparable when they designate a person who lives apart from the world to devote himself to prayer, contemplation, and penance. **Recluse** and **hermit** are now also applied to persons who avoid intercourse with men for other than religious motives, but even in their extended senses they retain their original distinguishing implications, for *recluse* stresses retirement from the world into seclusion, and *hermit*, a solitary life lived apart from men and, usually, in a place or under conditions where there is little likelihood of intrusion. *Recluse* is the broader term for it may be applied either to a hermit or to a religious who lives in a cloistered community. In modern Christian use, *hermit* is often applied to a member of one of the very few religious orders, such as the Carthusians, where the monks dwell alone and meet other members of the community only in church and in the refectory on Sundays. **Eremite,** though an archaic variant of *hermit,* is sometimes preferred in modern use because it unequivocally designates a solitary who is under a religious vow. For this reason, its derivative *eremitical* is the preferred adjective, even when *hermit* or *anchorite* is the chosen noun. **Anchorite** and **cenobite** are contrasted terms for the two leading types of recluses in the Eastern and in the Western Church. *Anchorite* designates the type known as *hermit* or *eremite; cenobite,* the type that dwells in a community, esp. a strictly cloistered community, as a monk or nun.

recognition. Recognition, identification, assimilation, apperception come into comparison only when they designate a form of cognition which relates a perception of something new to knowledge already acquired. **Recognition** implies that the thing now seen, heard, or otherwise perceived has been previously seen, heard, or otherwise perceived, if not in itself, then in another instance of the same species or type, and that the mind is aware that the two things are identical or of the same kind. **Identification** implies not only recognition, but a previous knowledge of the name which belongs to the thing as an individual or as a member of a class, and an ability to apply the name correctly. **Assimilation** implies that the mind responds to new facts, new ideas, and the like, by interpreting them in the light of that which is already known, thereby making them also an integral part of one's body of knowledge. **Apperception,** a word of many meanings, but here compared only as used in educational psychology, denotes a method of learning regarded as normal and therefore as a determinant of methods of instruction. The term implies that the mind responds to new facts, ideas, or situations when it can relate them to that which is already known, and that, on the contrary, it rejects, or is incapable of assimilating, that which it is at the time unprepared to receive.

recognize. *Acknowledge.
Ana. Accept, admit, *receive: notice, note, observe, remark (see SEE).

recoil, *v.* **1 Recoil, shrink, flinch, wince, blench, quail** agree in meaning to draw back through fear, faintheartedness, or the like. **Recoil** more than any of the succeeding terms suggests the physical signs of such drawing back or the sensations that accompany it. Often the term implies a start, a movement away, a prolonged hesitation, or the like; as, "She sat down on the bench beside him. He *recoiled*" (*Dickens*); to *recoil* from the sight of the old man's misery. " 'Lord Worthington has been telling us about you,' said Lydia. He *recoiled,* evidently deeply mortified" (*Shaw*). " 'Why shouldn't we go abroad together?'...'Abroad?' murmured Constance, aghast, *recoiling* from the proposition as from a grave danger" (*Bennett*). Often, however, the term suggests an inner or not outwardly apparent shaking or stirring that affects one mentally more than physically; as, his mind *recoils* from the prospect of war; she *recoiled* from the marriage suggested by her parents. "Archer was too intelligent to think that...Ellen Olenska would necessarily *recoil* from everything that reminded her of her past" (*E. Wharton*). **Shrink** implies an instinctive recoil, as from something painful or unpleasant or horrible; it often implies cowardice, but it may imply extreme sensitiveness or scrupulousness. "Guilt and misery *shrink,* by a natural instinct, from public notice" (*De Quincey*). "She *shrank* from the words which would have expressed their mutual consciousness, as she would have *shrunk* from flakes of fire" (*G. Eliot*). "He might have *shrunk* from defending himself at the expense of a frightened, unhappy girl" (*R. Macaulay*). **Flinch,** in precise use, implies a failure in resolution or an inability to overcome one's desire to avoid or evade something that is painful, difficult, or abhorrent; as, he gritted his teeth and did not *flinch* when the knife cut into his flesh. "She read and took notes incessantly, mastering facts with painful laboriousness, but never *flinching* from her self-imposed task" (*Hardy*). "Though the color had heightened in his cheek, he did not *flinch* from his friend's gaze" (*Joyce*). *Flinch* is sometimes used but **wince** is better when, by some involuntary, often slight, physical movement such as starting or recoiling, one manifests his pain, or fear, or acute sensitiveness. "He is as tender as a man without a skin, who cannot bear the slightest touch without *flinching*" (*Smollett*). "His horse stands *wincing* at the flies, giving sharp shivers of his skin" (*Hunt*). "Old Lady Kew's tongue was a dreadful thong which made numbers of people *wince*" (*Thackeray*). "Dinner at the Bronckhorsts' was an infliction....Bronckhorst took a pleasure in saying things that made his wife *wince*" (*Kipling*). **Blench** is often indistinguishable from *flinch;* it often, however, carries a stronger suggestion of faintheartedness or of signs of fear. "This painful, heroic task he undertook, and never *blenched* from its fulfillment" (*Jeffrey*). "That glaring and dazzling influence at which the eyes of eagles have *blenched*" (*Burke*). To **quail** is to shrink coweringly, as from something which strikes terror; as, "There *quails* Count Guido armed to the chattering teeth, Cowers at the steadfast eye and quiet word O' the Canon" (*Browning*); "*quailing* before his ...adversary" (*Shelley*).
Ana. Waver, falter, *hesitate: shy, balk, stick, stickle (see DEMUR).
Ant. Confront: defy.
2 *Rebound, reverberate, recoil, resile, repercuss.
Ana. Retreat, *recede, back, retract: *return, revert.

recollect. *Remember, recall, remind, reminisce, bethink, mind.
Ana. *Stir, rouse, arouse, rally, waken, awaken.

recollection. *Memory, remembrance, reminiscence, mind, souvenir.

recommend. *Commend, compliment, applaud.
Ana. *Approve, endorse, sanction: *praise, extol, acclaim.

recompense, *v.* Requite, reimburse, indemnify, repay, satisfy, remunerate, compensate, *pay.
Ana. Award, accord, vouchsafe, *grant: balance, offset, *compensate.

reconcile. Conform, accommodate, adjust, *adapt.
Ana. Harmonize, accord, square, *agree: *correct, rectify, amend, revise.

recondite. **Recondite, abstruse, occult, esoteric** agree in denoting beyond the power of the average intelligence to grasp or understand. **Recondite** stresses difficulty resulting from the profundity of the subject matter or its remoteness from ordinary human interest. It often implies scholarly research carried beyond the bounds of usefulness. "*Recondite* points of law" (*Maine*). **Abstruse** suggests extreme complexity or abstractness in the material as well as its remoteness from the ordinary range of human experience or interest. "The Hibbert Journal, which was endowed to promote *abstruse* theological discussion" (*C. Mackenzie*). "Astronomers watch the stars and mathematicians make *abstruse* calculations" (*Shaw*). **Occult** implies secret, mysterious knowledge purporting to be attainable only through supernatural or magical agencies and not through human reason; as, the *occult* sciences. Often it implies the operation of agencies beyond the reach of human understanding. "Whether it be from natural predisposition or from some *occult* influence of the time" (*J. R. Lowell*). **Esoteric** implies knowledge imparted only to members of a cult or inner circle of initiates. It, however, is extended in use to describe knowledge in the possession only of adepts, specialists, and the like. "To the idea of poetry as exclusive, *esoteric*, a-moral, the private affair of the poet...I should oppose the idea of poetry as catholic, diverse in function, moral, everyone's business" (*Day Lewis*).

Ana. Scholarly, erudite, polymathic, *learned: *pedantic, scholastic, academic.

record, *n.* *Document, monument, muniment, archive.

recount. Recite, *relate, rehearse, narrate, describe, state, report.

Ana. Enumerate, *count, number, tell: detail, itemize, particularize (see corresponding adjectives at CIRCUMSTANTIAL).

recoup, *v.* Recruit, retrieve, regain, *recover.

Ana. *Compensate, balance, offset, counterpoise.

recover. **Recover, regain, retrieve, recoup, recruit** agree in meaning to get back something that has been let go or lost. **Recover,** the most comprehensive of these terms, may imply a finding or obtaining something material or immaterial that has been lost in any way (as, to *recover* a lost watch; to *recover* one's health; to *recover* one's peace of mind; to *recover* one's balance) or a getting of something in reparation or compensation (as, to *recover* damages in a lawsuit). **Regain,** though often used interchangeably with *recover,* carries a stronger implication of winning back or getting once more in one's possession something of which one has been deprived as by capture, seizure, or by any power natural or human; as, to *regain* a fortress; to *regain* a person's good will; to *regain* one's sight; to *regain* one's freedom. *Regain* also may imply, as *recover* seldom implies, success in reaching again a place or point at which one has been before; as, "in his efforts to *regain* his hotel" (*Meredith*); "the trench allowed the performers, after being thrust down into perdition, to *regain* the green-room unobserved" (*Quiller-Couch*). **Retrieve,** originally and still often a hunting term used in reference to dogs which (in the earlier sense) find or arouse game that has sought cover or which (in the more common sense) seek out and bring back wounded or killed game, in extended use implies a recovering or regaining after assiduous effort or search; as, desperate efforts to *retrieve* lost territory; it now seemed impossible to *retrieve* the foreign trade lost by war; "his desire to *retrieve* his military reputation" (*Belloc*); "marvelling at the silent untiring activity with which her popularity had been *retrieved*" (*E. Wharton*). But *retrieve* sometimes takes for its object words such as *loss, error, failure, disaster,* etc., then implying not recovery but a repair, as by making that which is bad good, or a reparation, as by making up for that which was wrong or unsuccessful by a series of acts which set things right; as, life is not long enough to *retrieve* so many mistakes; "One false step is ne'er *retriev'd*" (*Gray*); "he is to *retrieve* his father's failure, to *recover* the lost gentility of a family that had once been proud" (*Van W. Brooks*). This latter sense of *retrieve* comes out especially in the adjectives *retrievable* and *irretrievable;* as, an *irretrievable* loss. **Recoup** was originally and still is a legal term implying a rightful deduction, as by a defendant from damages sought by a plaintiff in a lawsuit; thus, when a physician sues a former patient for the payment of his fee, the patient may, if he loses his case, and if he has shown the physician's lack of skill, *recoup* some of the damages. In its extended use *recoup* implies recovery or retrieval by some form of compensation or by reimbursing (oneself); as, he was unable to *recoup* his gambling losses by further play; to *recoup* oneself for expenses incurred in giving shelter and care to the victims of an accident; how will he ever *recoup* the amount lost through reckless investments? "Elizabeth had lost her venture; but if she was bold, she might *recoup* herself at Philip's cost" (*Froude*). **Recruit** literally implies growth through fresh additions: in military use it implies an increase through drafting, enlisting, and the like. However, since the term has often been used in the sense of to fill up vacancies in an army or force resulting from casualties (as, "It was his custom to *recruit* his army with conquered people"—*Newton*), it has come to imply a regaining of that which has been lost (such as vigor through illness, or money through extravagance or heavy expenditures) by fresh additions or replenishment of the supply; as, "*recruiting* his strength with a good plain dinner" (*Dickens*); "[the middle class] is continually *recruited* from the capitalist families" (*Shaw*).

Ana. Redeem, reclaim (see RESCUE): *compensate, offset, balance.

recreant, *adj.* *Cowardly, pusillanimous, poltroon, craven, dastardly.

Ana. *Timid, timorous: submissive, *tame, subdued: *mean, abject, ignoble.

recreant, *n.* *Renegade, apostate, turncoat, backslider, pervert.

Ana. Treacherousness *or* treachery, perfidiousness *or* perfidy, traitorousness (see corresponding adjectives at FAITHLESS).

recreate. *Amuse, divert, entertain.

Ana. *Renew, restore, refresh, rejuvenate: enliven, *quicken, animate.

recreation. Amusement, diversion, entertainment. See under AMUSE.

Ana. Relaxation, repose, ease (see REST): play, sport, frolic, rollick (see under PLAY, *v.*): *mirth, jollity, hilarity.

recrudesce. *Return, revert, recur.

Ana. *Renew, renovate, refurbish.

Con. *Suppress, repress: *stop, cease, discontinue.

recrudescence. Return, reversion, recurrence. See under RETURN, *v.*

Ana. Renewal, restoration, refreshment, renovation (see corresponding verbs at RENEW).

Con. Suppression, repression (see corresponding verbs at SUPPRESS).

recruit, *v.* *Recover, regain, retrieve, recoup.

Ana. *Renew, restore, renovate, refresh: repair, *mend, rebuild.

rectify. *Correct, emend, amend, reform, revise, remedy, redress.

Ana. *Improve, better, help, ameliorate: *mend, repair, rebuild: *adjust, regulate, fix.

rectitude. Virtue, *goodness, morality.
Ana. Integrity, probity, *honesty, honor: righteousness, nobility (see corresponding adjectives at MORAL): uprightness, justness, conscientiousness, scrupulousness (see corresponding adjectives at UPRIGHT).

recumbent. *Prone, supine, prostrate, reclining, couchant, dormant.
Ant. Upright, erect.

recur. *Return, revert, recrudesce.
Ana. *Repeat, iterate, reiterate.

recurrence. Return, reversion, recrudescence. See under RETURN, *v.*
Ana. Relapse, recidivation, recidivism (see under LAPSE, *v.*): repeating *or* repetition, iteration (see corresponding verbs at REPEAT).

recurrent. *Intermittent, periodic, alternate.
Ana. Rhythmic, metrical (see corresponding nouns at RHYTHM): returning, reverting, recrudescing (see RETURN): *fitful, spasmodic.

redeem. Deliver, *rescue, ransom, save, reclaim.
Ana. *Free, liberate, release, emancipate, manumit: restore, *renew, renovate: *recover, regain.

redintegrate. *Renew, restore, refresh, rejuvenate, renovate, refurbish.

redolence. *Fragrance, perfume, scent, incense, bouquet.
Ana. Odor, aroma, *smell: balminess, aromaticness *or* aromacity (see corresponding adjectives at ODOROUS).

redolent. Aromatic, balmy, fragrant, *odorous.
Ana. *Pungent, poignant, piquant, racy, spicy: penetrating, piercing (see ENTER).

redoubtable. *Formidable.
Ana. *Fearful, terrible, dreadful, frightful, awful: intrepid, valiant, doughty, valorous, *brave.

redound. *Conduce, contribute, accrue.
Ana. *Help, aid, assist: further, forward, promote, *advance.

redress, *v.* Emend, remedy, amend, *correct, rectify, reform, revise.
Ana. *Relieve, lighten, alleviate, assuage, mitigate, allay: repair, *mend.

redress, *n.* *Reparation, amends, restitution, indemnity.
Ana. Compensation, offsetting, balancing (see COMPENSATE): *retaliation, reprisal, vengeance, retribution.

reduce. 1 *Decrease, lessen, diminish, abate, dwindle.
Ana. *Shorten, abridge, abbreviate, curtail, retrench: *contract, shrink, condense.
Con. *Increase, augment, enlarge, multiply: *extend, lengthen, elongate, prolong, protract: *expand, swell, amplify.
2 *Conquer, vanquish, defeat, subjugate, beat, overcome, lick, subdue, surmount, overthrow, rout.
Ana. *Weaken, cripple, disable, undermine, enfeeble: humble, humiliate, degrade, debase (see ABASE).

redundancy. *Verbiage, tautology, pleonasm, circumlocution, periphrasis.
Ana. Wordiness, verbosity, prolixity, diffuseness (see corresponding adjectives at WORDY): inflatedness *or* inflation, turgidity, tumidity, flatulence (see corresponding adjectives at INFLATED): *bombast, rant, fustian.

redundant. *Wordy, verbose, prolix, diffuse.
Ana. *Superfluous, surplus, supernumerary, extra, spare: repeating or repetitious, iterating, reiterating (see corresponding verbs at REPEAT).
Ant. Concise. — *Con.* Terse, succinct, laconic, pithy, summary (see CONCISE): compact, *close.

reef, *n.* *Shoal, bank, bar.

reeve. *Steward, bailiff, agent, factor, seneschal, majordomo, oeconomus.

refer. 1 Assign, credit, accredit, *ascribe, attribute, impute, charge.
Ana. Associate, relate, connect (see JOIN): *direct, aim, point, lay.
2 *Resort, apply, go, turn.
Ana. Consult, *confer, commune, advise: address, *direct.
3 **Refer, allude, advert** are synonymous when they mean to mention something so as to call or direct attention to it. **Refer,** when unqualified, usually suggests intentional introduction and distinct mention, as by a thing's true name; as, he frequently *referred* to his friends in his letters to us. "Nor do we any longer suppose that we are impertinent in *referring* to the philosopher's personality....For personality is the very stuff of morals" (*H. Ellis*). **Allude,** in correct use, always implies indirect reference, as by a hint, a suggestive phrase, a roundabout or covert method of expression, a figure of speech; it often connotes modesty, timidity, or reticence in the one who alludes. "When Sir Roger...said he was glad to meet me among his relations...I knew he *alluded* to the pictures" (*Spectator*). Sometimes, however, it connotes bias or ill will. "Proposals, which were never called proposals, but always *alluded* to...as innovations" (*C. Mackenzie*). In its strictest etymological sense, *allude* and its derivatives *allusion* and *allusive* imply a play of fancy or a play upon words, especially so as to evoke their emotional, literary, or historical associations. "The works of Bergson, in which pyrotechnical *allusions* are...frequent" (*H. Ellis*). "We need not wonder that ...poets preferred to tell of their emotions and experiences, not directly but *allusively*" (*Binyon*). **Advert** (see ADVERT, 1) is interchangeable with *refer* only in loose use; then the words are scarcely distinguishable in meaning. "I never heard him [Carlyle] *advert* to his works and his fame" (*FitzGerald*).
Ana. *Introduce, insert, interpolate: *quote, cite.

referee, *n.* Umpire, arbiter, *judge, arbitrator.

referendum. Initiative, *mandate, plebiscite.

refinement. *Culture, cultivation, breeding.
Ana. Suavity, urbanity (see corresponding adjectives at SUAVE): courtesy, politeness, civility (see corresponding adjectives at CIVIL): *elegance, grace, dignity.
Ant. Vulgarity.

reflect. *Think, cogitate, reason, speculate, deliberate.
Ana. *Consider, contemplate, study, weigh, revolve: *ponder, muse, meditate, ruminate.

reflection. *Animadversion, stricture, aspersion.
Ana. Imputing *or* imputation, ascribing *or* ascription (see corresponding verbs at ASCRIBE): criticizing *or* criticism, reprehending *or* reprehension, blaming *or* blame (see corresponding verbs at CRITICIZE): *attack, assault, onslaught, onset: disparagement, derogation, depreciation (see corresponding verbs at DECRY).

reflective. *Thoughtful, contemplative, meditative, pensive, speculative.
Ana. Thinking, reasoning, deliberating, cogitating (see THINK): analytical, *logical, subtle.

reform, *v.* *Correct, rectify, emend, amend, remedy, redress, revise.
Ana. *Mend, repair, rebuild: better, *improve, help, ameliorate.

reform, *n.* *Reformation.

reformation. **Reformation, reform** are not always clearly distinguished when they mean a making better or a giving of a new and improved form or character and are, therefore, sometimes interchangeable without loss;

as, the *reformation* (or *reform*) of a criminal; the *reformation* (or *reform*) of society. **Reformation** is, however, the preferred term as a designation of a movement that has brought about many revolutionary amendments or improvements, especially in morals or religious practices; as, the Protestant *Reformation* (often, simply The *Reformation*); the English *Reformation;* the Counter *Reformation*. It is also preferred when the idea of reforming, or of remaking, so as to eradicate defects, is stressed; as, "not directed to the *reformation* of what was ill" (*Belloc*); "Never came *reformation* in a flood, With such a heady currance, scouring faults" (*Shak.*); "It is the moral basis of this *reformation* that I wish to lay" (*J. A. Hobson*). **Reform,** on the other hand, is preferred as a designation of an attempt (whether successful or unsuccessful) to remove abuses, correct corrupt practices, or to make changes for the better in any way; as, to be hostile to all persons advocating *reform;* "Boeotia, choose *reform* or civil war!" (*Shelley*); "a wave of municipal *reform* had passed over it [Barcelona]" (*H. Ellis*). *Reform* also applies, as *reformation* never does apply, to a particular or specific amendment, whether achieved or proposed, as a measure of reform; as, to initiate sweeping *reforms* [not *reformations*] in the government; "a *reform* worthy of a good prince and of a good parliament" (*Macaulay*).

refractory. Recalcitrant, intractable, ungovernable, *unruly, headstrong, willful.
Ana. *Contrary, perverse, froward, wayward: *insubordinate, rebellious, contumacious.
Ant. Malleable: amenable (sense 2).

refrain, *v.* **Refrain, abstain, forbear** agree in meaning to keep or withhold oneself voluntarily from something to which one is moved by desire or impulse. **Refrain** is especially suitable when the checking of a momentary inclination is implied; as, to *refrain* from laughter. At times, to *refrain* from an action implies merely its nonperformance. "He could scarcely resist calling him in to consult. But by sheer self-coercion he *refrained*" (*Hardy*). **Abstain** is more emphatic than *refrain*, because it usually stresses deliberate renunciation or self-denial on principle. "I have...*abstained* from the use of many expressions, in themselves proper and beautiful, but which have been foolishly repeated by bad Poets" (*Wordsworth*). It also applies with greater frequency to the appetites or passions control over which is essential to self-discipline; as, to *abstain* from intoxicating liquors. "*Abstain* from fleshly lusts" (*1 Peter* ii. 11). **Forbear,** as here compared, usually implies self-restraint rather than self-denial, and the exercise of patience or charity. "Few have repented of having *forborne* to speak" (*Johnson*). "Both bear and *forbear*" (*Old Proverb*). In its derivative forms (*forbearance, forbearing*), it implies great patience under provocation or in trial. "I have now put an end to my *forbearance* of him" (*C. Middleton*). "There is a time...For long-*forbearing* clemency to wait" (*Cowper*).
Ana. Check, *arrest, interrupt: *restrain, curb, inhibit.

refresh. *Renew, restore, redintegrate, rejuvenate, renovate, refurbish.
Ana. Enliven, *quicken, animate, vivify: recruit, *recover, regain: recreate, *amuse, divert.
Ant. Jade, addle.

refuge. Asylum, sanctuary, *shelter, cover, retreat, ark.
Ana. Safety, security (see corresponding adjectives at SAFE): stronghold, citadel, *fort, fortress: *harbor, haven, port.

refulgent. Effulgent, luminous, radiant, lustrous, *bright, brilliant, beaming, beamy, lambent, lucent.

refurbish. Renovate, *renew, refresh, restore, rejuvenate, redintegrate.
Ana. *Polish, burnish, furbish, shine, buff.

refuse, *v.* *Decline, reject, repudiate, spurn.
Ana. *Deny, gainsay: balk, baffle, *frustrate, thwart, foil: debar, *exclude, shut out.

refute. Confute, rebut, *disprove, controvert.
Ana. Contradict, impugn, traverse, negative, contravene (see DENY).

regain. *Recover, recruit, recoup, retrieve.
Ana. Gain, *reach, compass, attain, achieve: redeem, reclaim, save (see RESCUE): redintegrate, restore, *renew.

regal. Royal, *kingly, queenly, imperial, princely.
Ana. Majestic, imposing, stately, magnificent, august (see GRAND): *splendid, resplendent, glorious, sublime.

regale. Tickle, arride, gratify, delight, *please, rejoice, gladden.
Ant. Vex.

regard, *v.* **1** Respect, esteem, admire. See under REGARD, *n.*
Ana. *Appreciate, cherish, value, prize, treasure.
Ant. Despise. — *Con.* Contemn, scorn, disdain (see DESPISE): reject, repudiate, spurn (see DECLINE, *v.*).
2 *Consider, account, reckon, deem.
Ana. Rate, *estimate, value, assess, assay.

regard, *n.* **Regard, respect, esteem, admiration,** and their corresponding verbs (**regard, respect, esteem, admire**) agree in denoting a feeling (or to have a feeling) for someone or something which involves recognition of that person's or thing's worth, and some degree of liking. **Regard** is the most colorless as well as the most formal of these words; as, please give him my *regards*. It usually requires qualification to complete its meaning. "She learned to hope that it [the past]...might not cost her Henry's entire *regard*" (*Austen*). "Steve had not been highly *regarded* in his home town" (*S. Anderson*). **Respect** usually implies careful evaluation or estimation of the worth of a person or thing and of the measure of recognition which is due him or it; as, he *respected* their opinions even though he could not agree with them; he held their word in slight *respect*. "One wants to produce in the child the same *respect* for the garden that restrains the grown-ups from picking wantonly" (*B. Russell*). Oftentimes, when the person or thing is rated highly, *respect* implies a show of deference or veneration. "The *respect*, amounting almost to worship, he sometimes saw in the eyes of the people" (*S. Anderson*). Sometimes it suggests observance of that which is proper or fitting; as, to show *respect* for the dead; to *respect* the wishes of one's parents: sometimes it suggests recognition of something as sacred or inviolable; as, to *respect* a person's privacy; to have *respect* for the rights of others. **Esteem** adds to *respect* the implications of a high valuation, a consequent prizing, and of warmth of feeling or attachment. "What things there are Most abject in *regard* and dear in use! What things again most dear in the *esteem* And poor in worth!" (*Shak.*). "In the Renaissance, no Latin author was more highly *esteemed* than Seneca" (*T. S. Eliot*). **Admiration** and **admire,** like *esteem*, imply a recognition of superiority, but they usually connote more enthusiastic appreciation, and sometimes suggest genuine affection. "Miss Welwood, I have long felt the deepest *esteem* for you, and your present courageous attitude in this distressing financial crisis has added *admiration* to *esteem*" (*Deland*). In somewhat looser use, the words stress the personal attractiveness of the object of admiration, and weaken the implication of *esteem*. "What sight...is sadder than the sight of a lady we *admire admiring* a nauseating picture?" (*L. P. Smith*).
Ana. Deference, *honor, homage, reverence: apprecia-

tion, cherishing, prizing, valuing (see corresponding verbs at APPRECIATE).

Ant. Despite. — *Con.* Contempt, scorn, disdain (see under DESPISE).

regarding. *About, concerning, respecting, anent.

region. *Area, tract, zone, belt.

Ana. *Locality, vicinity, district, neighborhood: section, sector, division, *part: *field, territory, province.

register, *n.* *List, table, catalogue, schedule, roll, roster, rota, canon, inventory.

regressive. Retrogressive, retrograde, *backward.

Ant. Progressive.

regret, *n.* *Sorrow, grief, heartache, anguish, woe, dole.

Ana. Compunction, remorse, *penitence, repentance, contrition: *qualm, scruple, demur.

regular, *adj.* **1 Regular, normal, typical, natural** come into comparison when they mean being of the sort or kind that is expected as usual, ordinary, or average. A person, or far more often, a thing, is **regular** (opposed to *irregular*) that conforms to what is the prescribed rule or standard or the established pattern for its kind; as, to undergo the *regular* tests for admission to the army; a *regular* verb; a *regular* meeting of a society; he is a *regular* practitioner (as opposed to a quack). A person or a thing is **normal** (opposed to *abnormal* or *exceptional*) that does not deviate in any marked way from what has been discovered or established as the norm (see *norm* under AVERAGE, *n.*) for one of its kind: in contrast with *regular*, the term carries a stronger implication of conformity within certain prescribed limits or under certain given conditions, and therefore sometimes admits a wide range of difference among the things that may be described as normal for a class or kind; as, *normal* winter weather; he is a perfectly *normal* child physically as well as mentally; his pulse is *normal* for a person of his age. But when applied to persons, *normal* often specifically connotes mental balance or sanity (as, his actions are not those of a *normal* person): on the other hand, it may connote merely an approach to the average in mentality, implying the exclusion of those below or above this average. "Exceptional capacities are not infrequently associated with mental instability, and in such cases it is desirable to adopt methods [of education] which would be bad for the *normal* boy" (*B. Russell*). "The twins, since they had gone to Oxford, never admitted that they cared for any books that *normal* people cared for" (*R. Macaulay*). A person or thing is **typical** (opposed to *individual*) that markedly exhibits the characters or characteristics peculiar to the type, class, species, group, or the like, to which he (or it) belongs, often to the exclusion or the obscuring of any that differentiate him (or it) as a particular member of the type, class, or species; as, a *typical* example of Browning's style; "I would suggest that the most *typical*, as it is probably the oldest of the arts, is the Dance" (*Binyon*); "The political situation in Ceylon was *typical* of that encountered elsewhere in the East" (*V. Heiser*); "only that is good even on this level which pleases the *typical* or *normal* or generic man" (*S. Alexander*); "a *typical* English country town with wide High Street, narrow Market Street, picturesque Market Square" (*C. Mackenzie*). A person or thing is **natural** (as here compared: see also NATURAL, 2) that acts, behaves, operates, or the like, in accordance with the nature or essence of his (or its) kind or constitution or that is normal in or suitable to him (or it) because of that nature or constitution; as, the father is the *natural* protector of his children; the *natural* love of a mother; flesh is the *natural* food of a dog; he died from *natural* causes.

Ana. *Usual, habitual, customary: *common, ordinary, familiar.

Ant. Irregular.

2 *Orderly, methodical, systematic, regular.

Ana. Fixed, set, settled (see SET): constant, even, equable, *steady, uniform.

Ant. Irregular.

regulate. *Adjust, fix.

Ana. *Order, arrange, organize, systematize, methodize: temper, attemper, *moderate: *correct, rectify.

regulation. Rule, *law, precept, statute, ordinance, canon.

Ana. Instruction, direction, bidding (see corresponding verbs at COMMAND): deciding *or* decision, determination, ruling (see corresponding verbs at DECIDE).

rehearse. *Relate, narrate, describe, recite, recount, state, report.

Ana. *Repeat, iterate, reiterate: detail, itemize, particularize (see corresponding adjectives at CIRCUMSTANTIAL).

reify. *Realize, actualize, embody, incarnate, materialize, externalize, objectify, substantiate, substantialize, hypostatize.

reimburse. Indemnify, repay, recompense, requite, compensate, remunerate, satisfy, *pay.

Ana. Recoup, *recover: *compensate, balance, offset.

reiterate. *Repeat, iterate, ingeminate.

reject, *v.* Repudiate, spurn, refuse, *decline.

Ana. *Discard, cast, shed: oust, expel, dismiss, *eject: *exclude, debar, shut out, eliminate.

Ant. Accept: choose, select.

rejoice. Delight, gladden, *please, gratify, tickle, arride, regale.

Ana. Elate, exult (see corresponding adjectives at ELATED).

Ant. Grieve: aggrieve: bewail.

rejoin. *Answer, respond, reply, retort.

Con. Question, interrogate, *ask, inquire, query, catechize, examine.

rejoinder. Answer, response, reply, retort. See under ANSWER, *v.* 1.

Ana. Returning *or* return, reverting *or* reversion (see under RETURN, *v.*): *retaliation, reprisal.

rejuvenate. *Renew, restore, refresh, redintegrate, renovate, refurbish.

relapse, *v.* *Lapse, backslide, recidivate.

Ana. Revert, *return: degenerate, decline, deteriorate (see corresponding nouns at DETERIORATION).

relapse, *n.* Lapse, backsliding, recidivation, recidivism. See under LAPSE, *v.*

Ana. *Reversion, atavism, throwback: degeneration, decline, declension, decadence, *deterioration.

relate, *v.* **1 Relate, rehearse, recite, recount, narrate, describe, state, report** come into comparison when they mean to tell orally or in writing the details or circumstances necessary to others' understanding or knowledge of a real or imagined situation or combination of events. **Relate** implies the giving of an account, usually a detailed or orderly account, of something one has witnessed, experienced, or otherwise directly known; as, to *relate* the story of one's life; to *relate* an experience; "Then Father Junípero and his companion *related* fully their adventure" (*Cather*). **Rehearse** (etymologically, to harrow over again) usually suggests a repetition: it may imply a summary of what is known (as, "let us *rehearse* the few facts known of the inconspicuous life of Thomas Traherne"—*Quiller-Couch*), or a second or third or oft-repeated telling (as, "his mother... proceeded to *rehearse* once more the monstrous tale of the affront inflicted on

Mrs. Lovell Mingott"—*E. Wharton*), or a going over and over in one's mind, or with another person, or in privacy before relating (and, by extension, delivering, performing, presenting, etc.) it to others or to an audience (as, "Mr. Hynes hesitated a little longer....He seemed to be *rehearsing* the piece in his mind"—*Joyce;* "On his way across the Atlantic...he had *rehearsed* this meeting in varying keys"—*H. G. Wells*). **Recite** and, in the sense here considered, the now more common **recount** imply greater particularity of detail than the preceding terms; in fact, the implication of enumeration or of mention of each particular is so strong that both verbs commonly take a plural object; thus, one *relates* an experience, but he *recites* or *recounts* his experiences; so, to *recite* (or *recount*) the events of the day; "she often *recounts* the conversations with which they filled the long, hot days of driving" (*L. P. Smith*). **Narrate** suggests the employment of devices characteristic of the literary narrative, such as plot, excitement of suspense, movement toward a climax, and the like; as, "What verse can sing, what prose *narrate* The butcher deeds of bloody Fate" (*Burns*); "The discovery of Madeira is *narrated* with all the exaggerations of romance" (*Southey*). **Describe** now usually implies emphasis upon details that give the hearers or readers a clear picture or that give not only a visual representation but one that appeals to the other senses. "Bitter sea and glowing light, bright clear air, dry as dry,—that *describes* the place" (*Jefferies*). "It had never occurred to him that a captain's wife could be anything but a woman to be *described* as stout or thin, as jolly or crabbed, but always mature" (*Conrad*). **State** stresses particularity, clearness, and definiteness of detail, and suggests the aim of presenting facts, ideas, feelings, etc., in their naked truth so that they will be distinctly understood or fixed in others' minds. "Swinburne was also a master of words, but Swinburne's words are all suggestions and no denotation....Dryden's words, on the other hand, are precise, they *state* immensely, but their suggestiveness is often nothing" (*T. S. Eliot*). "One should know what one thinks and what one means, and be able to *state* it in clear terms" (*R. Macaulay*). **Report** implies a recounting and narrating, often after investigation, for the information of others, especially the readers of a newspaper; as, to *report* the progress on defense projects to the cabinet; the ambassador to Great Britain is returning to Washington to *report* on the war situation; he was assigned to *report* the murder trial; he must *report* the events of each day to his father and mother when he returns from school.

Ana. Tell, *reveal, disclose, divulge: detail, itemize, particularize (see corresponding adjectives at CIRCUMSTANTIAL).

2 Associate, link, connect, *join, combine, unite.

Ana. Attach, *fasten, fix: refer, assign, credit, impute, *ascribe.

Con. Disengage, *detach, abstract, prescind: divorce, sever, sunder, *separate.

3 *Bear, pertain, appertain, belong, apply.

related. **Related, cognate, kindred, allied, affiliated** come into comparison when they mean connected by, or as by, close family ties. **Related,** when referred to persons, usually implies consanguinity, or a blood connection; sometimes, however, it implies connection by marriage; as, the royal families in Europe are nearly all *related* to each other. When applied to things, *related* suggests some connection, often a close one, the nature of which is to be gathered from the context and which may be, variously, a common origin, a common cause, interdependence, reciprocal action, mutual opposition, etc.; as, *related* species; *related* events; *related* activities; every part of an organism is *related* to the other parts; body and soul are contrasted, but *related*, concepts. **Cognate,** in discriminating use, differs from *related* in being referable only to things that are generically alike or that can be shown to have a common ancestor or source or to be derived from the same root, stock, or the like; as, *cognate* races; *cognate* languages; *cognate* words in various languages, such as "pater," "Vater," "father"; physics and chemistry are *cognate* sciences. **Kindred,** in its primary sense, stresses blood relationship; as, the *kindred* members of a community. In its more common extended sense, it implies likenesses that might be characteristic of a family, such as common interests, tastes, aims, qualities, and the like. When the reference is to persons, congeniality is usually connoted. "He would never be popular...but he might appeal to a little circle of *kindred* minds" (*Joyce*). When applied to things, a more obvious connection or a closer likeness is implied than in *related*. "*Kindred* qualities in two otherwise alien tongues [Hebrew and English]" (*Lowes*). **Allied** more often implies connection by union than by origin, and especially by marriage or by voluntary association. It often connotes a more remote family connection than *related*. "The Raycie blood was...still to be traced in various *allied* families: Kents, Huzzards, Cosbys" (*E. Wharton*). In its extended use it usually stresses the possession of common characters, qualities, aims, effects, and the like, which lead either to union or to inclusion in the same class or category; as, *allied* genera; *allied* physical types; *allied* societies; *allied* diseases. **Affiliated** also stresses connection by union, but in precise use, it implies a dependent relation such as that of a child to a parent. Sometimes it implies the adoption of the weaker by the stronger; as, a small college *affiliated* to a university. Sometimes it connotes a loose union in which the affiliating units retain their independence, but derive support or strength from the main, central, or parent body, or co-operate in its work; as, Monte Cassino and *affiliated* monasteries; the CIO and its *affiliated* unions.

Ana. Associated, connected (see JOIN): *reciprocal, correspondent, correlative, convertible, complementary: akin, identical, alike, analogous (see SIMILAR): *relevant, germane, pertinent.

relative. *Dependent, contingent, conditional, adjective.

Ant. Absolute.

relaxation. *Rest, repose, leisure, ease, comfort.

Ana. Amusement, diversion, recreation (see under AMUSE, *v.*): relieving *or* relief, assuagement, alleviation, mitigation (see corresponding verbs at RELIEVE).

relaxed. *Loose, slack, lax.

Ana. Mitigated, lightened, alleviated, assuaged, relieved (see RELIEVE): flexuous, sinuous (see WINDING): *soft, mild, gentle, lenient.

Ant. Stiff. — *Con.* Strict, *rigid, rigorous, stringent: *severe, stern, austere, ascetic.

release, *v.* *Free, liberate, emancipate, manumit, deliver, discharge, enfranchise, affranchise.

Ana. *Detach, disengage: *exculpate, exonerate, acquit: surrender, resign, yield, *relinquish.

Ant. Detain (*as a prisoner*): check (*as thoughts, feelings, etc.*): oblige (*as a promise, pledge, etc.*).

relegate, *v.* *Commit, entrust, confide, consign.

Ana. Refer, assign, credit, accredit, charge (see ASCRIBE).

relent. *Yield, submit, capitulate, succumb, defer, bow, cave in.

Ana. Comply, acquiesce (see corresponding adjectives

at COMPLIANT): forbear, *refrain, abstain: *abate, subside, wane, ebb.

relentless. Unrelenting, merciless, implacable, *grim.

Ana. Inexorable, obdurate, adamant, *inflexible: strict, stringent, *rigid, rigorous: *fierce, ferocious, cruel, inhuman.

Con. *Soft, lenient, mild, gentle: *tender, compassionate: yielding, submitting *or* submissive (see corresponding verbs at YIELD).

relevant. **Relevant, germane** (*or* **german**), **material, pertinent, apposite, applicable, apropos** (*or, sometimes,* **à propos**) agree in meaning having a relation to or a bearing upon the matter in hand or the present circumstances. That is **relevant** which has any traceable connection, especially logical connection, with the thing under consideration and which has significance in any degree for those who are engaged in such consideration; as, the judge decided that the evidence was *relevant* and therefore admissible. "The controversy between the useful and the ornamental is *relevant* [to a discussion of the ends of education], though not decisive. Should children be taught to enunciate correctly and to have pleasant manners, or are these mere relics of aristocracy?" (*B. Russell*). That is **germane** which is so closely related as in spirit, tone, or quality, to the subject, the matter, the occasion, the issue, or the like, that the fitness or appropriateness of their association is beyond question; as, to enliven his lecture by introducing amusing anecdotes *germane* to his subject; an interesting point but not *germane* to the issue; to rule out all festivities not *germane* to the celebration of Memorial Day. "To a writer happily engaged on his work and excited by it, there may come a curious extension of his ordinary faculties...; *relevant* passages will quote themselves to his mind from books that he scarcely remembers to have ever read; and he suddenly sees *germane* connections where in his ordinary state of mind he would see nothing" (*C. E. Montague*). That is **material** which is so closely related to the matter in hand that it cannot be dispensed with without having an evident effect, especially a harmful effect; as, these facts, though *relevant*, are not *material* to the defendant's case. "Certain passages *material* to his understanding the rest of this important narrative" (*Scott*). That is **pertinent** which is so decisively or significantly relevant that it touches the real point at issue or contributes materially to the understanding of what is under discussion or to the solution of that which is in question. "Be humble and gentle in your conversation; and of few words, I charge you; but always *pertinent* when you speak" (*Penn*). "It is more *pertinent* to observe that it seems to me that logically and rationally a man cannot be said to be more than once in jeopardy in the same cause, however often he may be tried" (*Justice Holmes*). That is **apposite** which is relevant and germane to such a degree that it strikes one both by its pertinency and by its felicitousness; as, an *apposite* illustration. "Judged by standards that have no intelligible *appositeness* when applied to an artist" (*Mencken*). That is **applicable** which may be brought to bear upon or be used fittingly in reference to a particular case, instance, problem, or the like; as, the word "tool" is *applicable* to a plow only when used in a general sense; the principle is not *applicable* to the case in question. "Although... I do not get much help from general propositions in a case of this sort, I cannot forbear quoting what seems to me *applicable* here" (*Justice Holmes*). That is **apropos** (sometimes found in its French form *à propos*) which is both appropriate and opportune; as, a person who is not aware of an undercurrent of feeling may make remarks that are far from *apropos*. "The wit of man could not have found out a conduct more *à propos* in that conjuncture, than what the king used" (*R. North*). When followed by a preposition (in precise use *of*, but often also *to*), it usually suggests relevancy rather than appropriateness or opportuneness; as, "tell you a story *apropos* of two noble instances of fidelity and generosity" (*Walpole*).

Ana. *Related, cognate, allied: fitting, appropriate, proper (see FIT): important, significant, weighty (see corresponding nouns at IMPORTANCE).

Ant. Extraneous. — *Con.* Alien, foreign, *extrinsic.

reliable. **Reliable, dependable, trustworthy, trusty, tried** come into comparison when they are applied to persons, their utterances, views, methods, instruments, or the like, and mean having or manifesting qualities which assure one that he or it merits confidence or trust. A person or thing is **reliable** when one can count upon him or it not to fail in doing what he or it is expected to do competently (as, she is a very *reliable* servant; one of the most *reliable* of our employees; a *reliable* washing machine), or to give or tell the exact truth (as, a *reliable* work of reference; *reliable* testimony). A person or thing is **dependable** to whom (or which) one can go in full confidence that one will get the support or assistance required in time of need or in an emergency; as, to ask a friend to recommend a *dependable* physician; he is the most *dependable* of our friends; a *dependable* source of information. *Dependable* is also used merely as a descriptive term implying a character that admits nothing that is incalculable, or that is the antithesis of that which is fickle, capricious, or the like. "Laura wasn't pretty, but ...healthy-looking and *dependable*" (*M. Austin*). A person, or less often, a thing, is **trustworthy** that merits or has earned one's complete confidence in his (or its) soundness, integrity, veracity, discretion, reliability, or the like; as, a *trustworthy* confidant; a *trustworthy* witness; a *trustworthy* wife. "The most *trustworthy* comment on the text of the Gospels and the Epistles is to be found in the practice of the primitive Christians" (*Macaulay*). A person is **trusty** who has been found by experience to be reliable and trustworthy; as, a *trusty* guide; a *trusty* servant; a *trusty* prisoner (often called a "trusty"). A thing is *trusty* that has been found never to have failed one in need or in an emergency, or that has been found dependable whenever needed; as, "his *trusty* sword" (*Spenser*); "he wrapped the *trusty* garment about him" (*Cather*). A person or thing is **tried** that has demonstrated his (or its) reliability, dependability, trustworthiness, or trustiness again and again; as, a *tried* and true friend; a *tried* remedy; a *tried* soldier; "his *tried* expedients" (*Bagehot*).

Ana. *Safe, secure: *infallible, inerrable, inerrant, unerring: cogent, *valid, sound, convincing, telling.

Ant. Dubious. — *Con.* *Doubtful, problematical, questionable.

reliance. *Trust, confidence, dependence, faith.

Ana. Credence, credit, *belief, faith: assurance, conviction, certitude, *certainty.

reliant. **Reliant, self-reliant** are often contrasted rather than synonymous terms. **Reliant** usually suggests dependence on another (or on others) that is the result either of confidence in his (or their) powers or, more often, of one's own weakness and need of external support; as, a religious man, always *reliant* on the help of God; she is too *reliant* on her husband; "Seem not *reliant*,—loose thy clinging hand" (*B. Taylor*). **Self-reliant,** on the other hand, carries a strong implication of independence and of trust in oneself: however, it suggests courage and backbone more than overweening self-confidence; as, to bring up one's children to be *self-reliant;* "Johnson first taught literary men the lesson of *self-reliance*" (*Jowett*); doles which tend to pauperize even the *self-reliant* poor.

relics. Remains, leavings, *remainder, residue, residuum, rest, balance, remnant.

relieve. **Relieve, alleviate, lighten, assuage, mitigate, allay** agree in meaning to make something tolerable or less grievous. Though they are often used interchangeably, they are clearly distinguishable. **Relieve** implies a lifting of enough of a burden to make it definitely endurable or temporarily forgotten; as, drugs that *relieve* pain; to *relieve* the misery and suffering caused by a disaster. Occasionally *relieve,* when used in the passive, implies a release from anxiety or fear; as, they were greatly *relieved* when her letter came: sometimes, it suggests a break in monotony or in routine. "I've had some trouble to get them together to *relieve* the dullness of your incarceration" (*Meredith*). **Alleviate** stresses the temporary or partial nature of the relief and usually implies a contrast with *cure* and *remedy;* as, oil of cloves will *alleviate* the toothache. "It has always been considered as an *alleviation* of misery not to suffer alone" (*Johnson*). **Lighten** implies reduction in the weight of that which oppresses or depresses; hence it often connotes a cheering or refreshing influence; as, his interest in his work *lightened* his labors. "That blessed mood... In which the heavy and the weary weight Of all this unintelligible world Is *lightened*" (*Wordsworth*). **Assuage** suggests the moderation of violent emotion by influences that soften or mollify or, sometimes, sweeten. "The good gods *assuage* thy wrath" (*Shak.*). "My sorrows I then might *assuage* In the ways of religion and truth" (*Cowper*). **Mitigate** also suggests moderation in the force, violence, or intensity of something painful; it does not, as *assuage* does, imply something endured but something inflicted or likely to inflict pain; as, "to *mitigate* the barbarity of the criminal law" (*Inge*); to *mitigate* the rigors of an explorer's life; to *mitigate* the severity of a winter. **Allay,** though it seldom implies complete release from that which distresses, disquiets, or the like, does suggest an effective calming or quieting; as, the report *allayed* their fears; to *allay* one's thirst; his suspicions were *allayed.* "These...words....were of sobering tendency; they *allayed* agitation; they composed, and consequently must make her happier" (*Austen*).

Ana. *Comfort, console, solace: *moderate, qualify, temper, attemper: diminish, reduce, lessen, *decrease.

Ant. Intensify: embarrass: alarm.

religion. **Religion, denomination, sect, cult, communion, faith, creed, persuasion, church** come into comparison when they denote a system of religious belief and worship or the body of persons who accept such a system. **Religion,** the usual uncolored term, may apply to any system, such as Christianity, which represents the beliefs and worship of all those who accept a given revelation, or to one, such as Anglicanism, which represents the beliefs and practiced worship of a specific body of those who accept the same revelation; as, the great *religions* such as Judaism, Christianity, Buddhism, and Mohammedanism; the Methodist *religion;* the *religion* of the Arabs; the *religion* of the Scribes and Pharisees. **Denomination** strictly applies to a body of people holding common and distinctive religious beliefs and called by a particular name so as to distinguish them from a more inclusive body; as, the various *denominations* of Protestants; the leading Christian *denominations.* **Sect** strictly means a following and was formerly often, but is now rarely, applied to a group of persons who follow a particular philosopher or school of thought or rule of conduct, or the like (as, "For we have found this man [Paul] a pestilent fellow, and a mover of sedition among all the Jews throughout the world, and a ringleader of the *sect* of the Nazarenes"—*Acts* xxiv. 5; "Einstein.... is not even to be included...in that rigid *sect* which asserts that all real science is precise measurement" —*H. Ellis*): rather through a confusion of its true etymology with a false one, *sect* has come to be applied to a group cut off from a larger body, such as that of Christians, or, more specifically, of an established or a parent church, by differences in the interpretation or application of what all regard as the same revelation; thus, one speaks of the Christian *religion* (never *sect*) as comprising all who accept the New Testament as divine revelation, or of the various *sects* (not *religions,* or even *denominations*) into which the seventeenth-century and eighteenth-century Protestant *denominations* were divided. **Cult** is applied either to a form of religious worship followed by a group, often by a group in a nontheistic religion, or to the group which practices such a form of worship; as, "Ever since the close of the Punic War foreigners had been thronging to Rome, bringing with them their foreign *cults*" (*Buchan*); "The romantic error has been...in short, to turn the nature *cult* into a *religion*" (*Babbitt*). **Communion** stresses not difference from others but union in essentials such as of religious belief and discipline: the term applies therefore not only to a large body (as, the Roman Catholic *communion*) but especially to one comprising several smaller bodies or organizations such as national churches (thus, the Anglican *communion* includes all who are united with the Church of England in matters of faith and order) or even several sects of a denomination (as, the Presbyterian *communion*). **Faith** and **creed** apply to any system of belief and worship that is clearly formulated and definitely accepted; as, men of all *faiths* were present; *creeds* are often a cause of division. **Persuasion,** like *sect,* does not invariably imply reference to religious beliefs and worship (as, men of the same political *persuasion*): very commonly, however, it does imply such reference, then carrying suggestions very much like those of *faith;* as, men and women of the Baptist *persuasion.* **Church** is often used colloquially, by Christians, in either of these senses, and with implications that closely relate it to *denomination.* Distinctively, it always suggests a clearly defined character, both as a system of beliefs or as a body of persons, and often carries a stronger connotation of organization than *denomination* carries; as, to what *church* does he belong?; some *churches* that forbade dancing now countenance it.

religious, *adj.* **1** *Devout, pious, pietistic, sanctimonious.

Ana. *Faithful, stanch, steadfast, leal, true: virtuous, righteous, noble, *moral, ethical: *upright, just, honorable, honest.

Ant. Irreligious. — ***Con.*** Ungodly, godless (see IRRELIGIOUS).

2 Spiritual, *holy, sacred, divine, blessed.

Ant. Secular (*of schools, journals, authorities, etc.*): profane (*of music, drama, etc.*).

religious, *n.* **Religious, monk, friar, nun** agree in meaning a member of a religious order all of whose members are bound by the monastic vows of poverty, chastity, and obedience, and who lead, to a greater or lesser extent, a cloistered life. **Religious** is the comprehensive term, applicable either to a man or a woman: it implies a living apart from the world either in a cloistered community formed of members of the same order, or as a hermit (see RECLUSE) under the governance of the superior or superiors of an order. **Monk** is often used, especially in current English, to designate any male religious; strictly, however, the term applies to a member of certain religious orders for men, such as the Benedictine or Cistercian orders, whose members live an ascetic life in a cloistered community, originally, and still commonly, in the same establishment for life, and devote themselves mainly to contemplation and prayer and to liturgical observances, carrying on in the meantime other labors such as, in medieval days, the copying of manuscripts, and in the present day, various scholarly, artistic, scientific, and other employments. **Friar** (etymologically, *brother*) applies strictly to a member of any mendicant order, especially to one of four, the Franciscan (often called *Gray Friars*, because of the original color of their habit), the Dominican (or *Black Friars*), the Carmelite (or *White Friars*), the Augustinian (or *Austin Friars*), under whose original regulations neither personal nor community tenure of property was allowed, whose members lived by alms, and wandered from place to place preaching the Gospel, administering the sacraments, and the like. At the present time, *friar* applies to any member of these four orders or of any order patterned after them, whether he lives as a mendicant or in a cloistered community and whether he serves as a pastor, a curate, a missionary, a preacher, a teacher, or the like. Both *monk* and *friar* in the strict sense of each term are also distinguished from other types of religious, as the *hermit* (see RECLUSE), the *canon regular*, such as a member of the Premonstratensians, who combines the life of the cloister with the charge of a cathedral or collegiate church, the *clerk regular*, such as a member of the Society of Jesus (the Jesuit order) whose members though bound by monastic rules go abroad as ministers of the gospel, and from members of various other congregations, such as the Vincentians, who serve as teachers, hospitalers, missionaries, and the like. **Nun** applies only to a female religious: since there are no terms to distinguish nuns according to the severity of their discipline, the rigor of their cloistered life, and the nature of their duties, the word is generally applied to any member of a religious order of women who wear a habit and devote themselves to prayer and their chosen work.

relinquish. Relinquish, yield, leave, resign, surrender, cede, abandon, waive come into comparison when they mean to let go from one's control or possession or to give up completely. **Relinquish** in itself seldom carries any added implication, but it often acquires color from the words with which it is associated or from the character of the thing given up; as, he was disinclined (or glad) to *relinquish* his command; he *relinquished* his grasp only after a struggle. "He had let something go...: something very precious, that he could not consciously have *relinquished*" (*Cather*). **Yield** adds to *relinquish* the implication of concession or compliance: in some collocations it does not even suggest finality—a prevailing but not always necessary implication in the words of this group—but rather, a giving way as a favor, or as a sign of weakness, or as an indulgence. "*Yield* not thy neck To fortune's yoke, but let thy dauntless mind Still ride in triumph over all mischance" (*Shak.*). **Leave** is often used colloquially in place of *relinquish*, sometimes implying a forsaking (as, "we have *left* all, and have followed thee"—*Mark* x. 28; " 'He has *left* me....Quitted me! Abandoned me!' "—*Bennett*), sometimes a giving up or letting go that may suggest motives or intentions as far apart as sacrifice (as, "the opium eater who cannot *leave* his drug"—*T. Wolfe*) and as neglect (as, "By all ye *leave* or do, The silent, sullen peoples Shall weight your Gods and you"—*Kipling*) and as concession (as, "the constitution *leaves* them [the States] this right in the confidence that they will not abuse it"—*Ch. Just. Marshall*) and as imposition upon others (as, she *leaves* most of the work to her sister). **Resign** emphasizes voluntary or deliberate sacrifice: it usually connotes either renunciation or acceptance of the inevitable. (These connotations are especially strong in *resigned* and *resignation.*) "*Resign* our own and seek our Maker's will" (*Cowper*). "In her face...was that same strange mingling of *resigned* despair and almost eager appeal" (*Galsworthy*). **Surrender**, in precise use, distinctively implies the existence of external compulsion or demand: it commonly suggests submission after a struggle but carries no connotation of submissiveness. "When they saw all that was sacred to them laid waste, the Navajos...did not *surrender;* they simply ceased to fight" (*Cather*). At times, the implication of resistance is blurred and that of conscious sacrifice, as for a greater advantage, is heightened; as, to *surrender* one's right to a portion of an estate for the sake of another member of the family. **Cede** is narrower in its application than *surrender:* as a rule, it suggests juridical pressure, as expressed in a court decision, the findings of arbitrators, or the terms of a treaty, though it may suggest previous negotiation, and is used in reference to the transfer of lands, territory, or the like. **Abandon** (as here compared: see also ABANDON, 1) stresses finality and completeness in relinquishment, especially of intangible things such as hopes, opinions, methods, or schemes. "No, no; you stick to your prejudices, or at any rate don't *abandon* them on my account" (*C. Mackenzie*). **Waive**, like *yield*, does not invariably imply finality and often suggests a concession, but unlike *yield* and the other terms of this group, it seldom implies the compulsion of force or necessity. Its main implication is a refusal to insist on something, such as a right, a claim, one's preference, one's immunity, obedience to a rule, law, or convention, or the like, usually for the sake of courtesy, simplicity, or concentration on that which is relatively more important; as, to *waive* extradition proceedings; to *waive* a jury trial; he *waived* his right to be heard in his own defense; "He *waived* the ceremony of introduction" (*Burney*); "If art can enthrall him, he is willing to *waive* all question of logic or rationality" (*Babbitt*).

All of these words except *relinquish, leave, cede,* and *waive* may be used reflexively in the sense of giving oneself up to someone or something. They retain their distinctive implications in this usage but they show their differences mainly in their indirect objects. One *surrenders oneself* or, now less often, *yields oneself* to a superior power or force, as a conqueror or a court of justice or an overwhelming emotion; one *resigns oneself* to that which is inevitable or inescapable; one *abandons oneself* to an emotion, a mood, an irresistible influence, a temptation, because of loss of self-control or of relaxation of the will; as, the alleged thief *surrendered himself* to the police today; he will never *resign himself* to the thought of death. "Delia...*abandoned herself* to the spell of the moonlit hour" (*E. Wharton*).

Ana. *Abdicate, renounce, resign, demit: *abandon, desert, forsake: *forgo, forbear, abnegate, sacrifice: *discard, shed, cast.

Ant. Keep.

relish, *n.* **1** Savor, tang, flavor, *taste, sapidity, smack. **2** *Taste, palate, gusto, zest.

Ana. Liking, loving, enjoying, relishing (see LIKE): *predilection, partiality, prepossession, prejudice, bias: propensity, *leaning, flair, penchant.

relish, *v.* Fancy, dote on *or* upon, enjoy, *like, love.

Ana. Appreciate, *understand, comprehend: *approve, endorse, sanction.

relishing. *Palatable, appetizing, savory, sapid, saporous, tasty, toothsome, flavorsome.

Ana. Pleasing, gratifying, delighting, rejoicing, tickling, regaling (see PLEASE).
Con. Flat, *insipid, jejune, banal, inane.

reluctant. *Disinclined, indisposed, hesitant, loath, averse.
Ana. *Cautious, circumspect, chary, wary, calculating: *antipathetic, unsympathetic.
Con. Inclined, disposed, predisposed (see INCLINE, *v.*): *eager, avid, keen.

rely. Rely, trust, depend, count, reckon, bank come into comparison (as intransitive verbs) when they mean to have or place full confidence. One **relies** *on* or *upon* someone or something that one believes will never fail in giving or doing what one wishes or expects. *Rely* usually connotes a judgment based on previous experience and, in the case of persons, actual association; as, he *relies* on his father to help him out of any trouble he gets into; he never *relies* on the opinions of others; a physician upon whom all his patients *rely.* "Even in Miss Jekyll's gardens, with all his admiration for them, Britten could be *relied* upon to find some fault or other" (*L. P. Smith*). "Bitter experience soon taught him that lordly patrons are fickle and their favour not to be *relied* on" (*A. Huxley*). "She bored no one who read her [novels], because she could be *relied* on to give them what they hoped to find" (*R. Macaulay*). One **trusts** (often followed by *in* or by *to*) when one is completely assured or wholly confident that another (often the Supreme Being) will not fail one in need. *Trust* stresses unquestioning faith, though it does not rule out experience as an aid to faith. "I will *trust,* and not be afraid" (*Isaiah* xii. 2). "Take short views, hope for the best, and *trust* in God" (*Sydney Smith*). "There is a great Field-Marshal, my friend, who arrays our battalions; Let us to Providence *trust,* and abide and work in our stations" (*Clough*). One **depends** *on* or *upon* someone or something when one, with or without previous experience, rests confidently on him or it for support or assistance. *Depend,* except when followed by *on oneself, upon one's own efforts,* and the like, may connote a lack of self-sufficiency or even weakness; in most cases, however, it implies so strong a belief or so confident an assumption that the hoped-for support or assistance is forthcoming that no provision for the contrary is made. "His diffidence had prevented his *depending* on his own judgment...but his reliance on mine made everything easy" (*Austen*). "The captain of the ship at sea is a remote, inaccessible creature...*depending* on nobody" (*Conrad*). "The man never cared; he was always getting himself into crusades, or feuds, or love, or debt, and *depended* on the woman to get him out" (*H. Adams*). One **counts** or **reckons** (more colloquial than *count*) *on* something when one takes it into one's calculations as certain or assured; the words often imply even more confidence in expectation than *depend,* but they seldom carry the latter's frequent suggestion of possible disaster if one's expectations are not fulfilled; thus, a captain *counts* (not *depends*) on replenishing his fuel supply at certain ports, when making his calculations for a voyage; the party *counts* (not *depends*) on a much larger representation in congress after the next election; he *reckoned* on the train's being late. "I've told her...that she shall always have a special sum set apart for her poor children...; on that she may absolutely *count*" (*E. Wharton*). One **banks** (a colloquialism) *on* something in which one's confidence is so strong that one is willing to place a heavy wager on it in the certainty one cannot lose; as, I'll *bank* on his succeeding in any venture he undertakes; you can *bank* on his honesty.
Ana. Confide, entrust, *commit: *hope, expect, look, look for, await.

remain. *Stay, wait, abide, tarry, linger.
Ant. Depart.

remainder, *n.* **Remainder, residue, residuum, remains, leavings, relics, rest, balance, remnant** come into comparison in the sense of that which is left after the subtraction or removal of a part. **Remainder** is the technical term for the result in the arithmetical process of subtraction (as, subtract 8 from 10 and the *remainder* is 2); it is otherwise a comprehensive term for any things that remain after the others of a collection, assemblage, or the like, have been taken away, or for any persons that remain after the others of the group have departed; as, he spent the *remainder* (that is, the remaining days, months, or years) of his life in seclusion; it took a week to eat up the *remainder* of their Thanksgiving feast; the *remainder* (that is, those who had not gone further) of the party turned homeward; a sale of publisher's *remainders* (that is, unsold copies of various books). **Residue** and **residuum** are often interchanged with *remainder,* but in current use they usually imply whatever may be left of a former whole, often a previously intact whole, after it has been subjected to some process which depletes or diminishes it but does not annihilate it. Both terms, but especially *residue,* have acquired specific meanings; thus, a testator, after making certain bequests and providing for the payment of all his debts and charges, usually leaves the *residue* of his estate to a legatee, or to legatees, of his choice; water after evaporation often leaves a *residue,* as of lime or some other mineral substance; the *residue* of anything destroyed by burning is called ash or ashes. *Residuum* is frequently used in place of *residue,* especially when evaporation, combustion, or the like, is implied; it is often preferred to *residue* when what is left after a process (not only a physical or chemical, but also a mental, process) is such that it cannot be ignored or left out of account, or may have value as a product or significance as a result; thus, the *residuum* of the process by which sugar is extracted from cane is called molasses; there is always a *residuum* of air in the lungs after the most forcible expiration possible; every severe emotional experience leaves its aftereffect, or *residuum.* "One might say that every fine story must leave in the mind of the sensitive reader an intangible *residuum* of pleasure" (*Cather*). **Remains** (the singular form *remain* has given way to the plural) is now chiefly used of that which is left after death, decay, decline, disintegration, or consumption; the term is specifically applied to a corpse, to the unpublished works of a dead author, and to the ruins of an ancient civilization; as, they buried Keats's *remains* in the Protestant cemetery in Rome; to be appointed executor of a friend's literary *remains;* the *remains* of Pompeii; the *remains* of a meal. **Leavings** usually, but not invariably, implies that the valuable or useful parts or things have been culled out and used up or taken away or that what is left has been rejected or discarded. "How like the *leavings* of some vast over-turned scrap-basket" (*Van W. Brooks*). The term is sometimes humorously applied to a rejected suitor. "Truly, she'd have none of Polly's *Leavings;* no, not she!" (*Richardson*). **Relics,** as here compared, is now chiefly found in poetic use in the senses in which *remains* is more commonly employed. It differs from *remains* in connoting a cherishing or treasuring. "Scooped from the sacred earth where his dear *relics* lie" (*Wordsworth*). "The *relics* [that is, the ruins] of a weed-inwoven cot" (*Shelley*). **Rest** is seldom distinguishable from *remainder* (except in the latter's technical arithmetical sense), and the two are commonly used interchangeably without loss. However, it is preferred to *remainder* by discriminating writers and speakers when it means simply the persons or things not previously referred to or mentioned, as in an enumeration or list, and carries no implication of subtraction, deduction, depletion, and the like; as, England, as well as the *rest* of Europe, awaited the effect of the ultimatum with anxiety; only two stories in this book are interesting but the *rest* are uniformly dull. **Balance,** in the sense of *remainder* or *rest,* has never been fully accepted by authorities even in the United States where it is more common than in England. "Presently I began to receive letters asking for the *rest* of it, sometimes for the *balance* of it" (*J. R. Lowell*). In this sense, the term derives from the commercial use of *balance* for the sum in which one side of an account falls short of the other and which must be added in order that the two sides balance, or become equal. In reference to a banking account, *balance* usually is applied only to the amount left after withdrawals and other charges have been deducted from the deposits and accumulated interest (the reverse being called an *overdraft*); in a mercantile charge account, *balance* is usually applied to the amount owed after credits have been deducted from the debits; thus, a *balance* (strictly, a *deposit balance*) in the bank is a sum of money to the depositor's credit; a *balance* of a bill (or more explicitly, a *balance due*) is an amount still owed by the debtor; a *balance* in hand is an amount left when all assets are reckoned after all liabilities have been discharged. **Remnant,** and its increasingly common plural *remnants,* are now applied only to a remainder that is small in size or numbers or that represents only an insignificant part or piece left from a former whole; as, the *remnant* of a once powerful army; a sale of *remnants* of cloth. "The last representative of the original Cardenas y Barrenuevos was supposed to be living in Santa Fé on the *remnants* of the family fortune" (*M. Austin*). "Sleeping bits of woodlands—*remnants* of the great forests in which Tom had worked as a boy" (*S. Anderson*).

remains. Leavings, residue, *remainder, residuum, relics, rest, balance, remnant.

remark, *v.* **1** Notice, note, observe, perceive, discern, *see, behold, descry, espy, view, survey, contemplate.

2 Remark, comment, commentate, animadvert come into comparison in their intransitive senses where they are usually folowed by *on* or *upon.* They agree in meaning to make observations or to pass judgment but they diverge in their implications regarding the motive and the nature of these observations and judgments. **Remark** usually implies little more than a desire to call attention to something; as, a bore *remarks* upon everything he sees. "So I *remarked* upon our Schumann's victories Over the commonplace, how faded phrase grew fine" (*Browning*). **Comment** stresses interpretation, as by bringing out what is not apparent or by adding details that help to clarify; as, the dramatic reader frequently interrupted his performance to *comment* upon a scene. Very frequently, in modern use, the word implies unfavorable interpretation. "The Vicar told his curate...'One or two of the parishioners have *commented* on your passion for Oaktown, and I fancy that you have given a little offence' " (*C. Mackenzie*). **Commentate,** an old word that had been falling into disuse, has recently been revived as a substitute for *comment,* to suggest a purely expository or interpretative intent. The verb is, however, less frequently used than its agent noun, **commentator;** as, radio *commentators* on the news of the day. **Animadvert** implies a turning of one's attention to something for the sake of judging it; as, "Adrian *animadverted* on everybody very sympathetically" (*Meredith*). In modern use, however, this, its basic implication, is often obscured by an emphasis on passing an adverse judgment (see ANIMADVERSION). "You know you have grievously offended him. I wish not to *animadvert* on your conduct" (*Meredith*).

remark, *n.* **Remark, observation, comment, commentary, note, descant, obiter dictum** come into comparison when they denote a brief expression intended to enlighten, clarify, express an opinion, or the like. A **remark** is a more or less casual expression in speech or writing of an opinion or judgment, as of something seen in passing, something read for the first time, something to which one's attention has been called, or the like: the term usually carries no implication of a final or considered judgment; as, "Perhaps...you may now and then amuse yourself with my translation. Should your *remarks* reach me...they shall be all most welcome" (*Cowper*); "Brousson had a genius for remembering the most telltale gestures as well as the most self-revelatory *remarks*...of his master" (*J. W. Krutch*). **Observation** suggests a reasoned judgment based on more or less careful scrutiny of the evidence. "He apparently was impressed by my *observation* that disease had made it largely impossible for Indians to smile" (*V. Heiser*). "In reading over a package of letters from Sarah Orne Jewett, I find this *observation:* 'The thing that teases the mind over and over for years, and at last gets itself put down rightly on paper...belongs to Literature' " (*Cather*). **Comment** applies to a remark or an observation made in criticism, in interpretation, or in elucidation of something; as, the candidate said he would make no *comment* on the suggestion; "Very often she gave him some wise *observation* or discreet *comment* to begin the day with" (*Cather*). "Katherine seldom does much of the talking....She listens, and puts in from time to time some critical *comment* that often extraordinarily clears up any subject one is talking round" (*R. Macaulay*). **Commentary** may be used in place of *comment* for an annotation or gloss of a passage or text. More often, however, it is employed as a collective noun, designating the series of annotations or glosses provided for the elucidation of a text or literary work. **Note** applies chiefly to a written or printed comment, gloss, or the like, on a particular point, such as the historical origin of an idea, the exact meaning of a term, or the source of the writer's information, made either by the reader of an article or book on the margin of a page or by the author to be printed at the bottom of the page (then called a *footnote*) or, with other comments or glosses, in an appendix. "The author...was advised...to subjoin some few explanatory *notes*" (*Gray*). *Note* is also applicable to any brief statement jotted down, such as one of the minutes of a meeting, a memorandum of a point developed or to be developed in a speech, or of a point made by a speaker or lecturer, or the like; as, to make *notes* of what happened at the conference; to preach from *notes.* **Descant** (originally a musical term designating a voice part above the main one or serving as an accompaniment to it) is often used as a synonym of *remark* or *comment* with, however, a stronger suggestion of addition to or variation of the main theme (as, "Neither shall I make any *descant* or reflection thereon"—*Barrow*); very often, also, the term does not imply brevity, but a playing with or upon a thought or subject. "Charlotte Brontë makes no break in the artistry of her *Villette* when she imbeds in it a *descant* on a piece of acting by Rachel" (*C. E. Montague*). **Obiter dictum** (*pl.* **obiter dicta**) is a Latin phrase (meaning literally a word on the way, that is, in passing) applied in law to an incidental opinion delivered by a judge on a matter bearing upon but not material to the case being tried, and therefore having no binding force. In literary use, its connotations have been determined largely by Augustine

Birrell who in his book of informal essays called *Obiter Dicta,* defines it (*obiter dictum*) humorously as "A gratuitous opinion, an individual impertinence which, whether it be wise or foolish, right or wrong, bindeth none, not even the lips that utter it." The term is usually applied to a remark or observation made more or less on the spur of the moment but not intended to be taken as a final opinion or definitive statement.

remarkable. *Noticeable, prominent, outstanding, conspicuous, salient, signal, striking, arresting.

Ana. *Exceptional: important, significant, weighty, momentous (see corresponding nouns at IMPORTANCE): singular, unique, peculiar, *strange.

remedy, *n.* **Remedy, cure, medicine, medicament, specific, physic** come into comparison when they mean something prescribed or taken for the treatment of disease. **Remedy,** the most general of these terms, is applied to any substance or method of treatment that is known to be, or is said to be, effective in contributing to or in bringing about recovery or restoration to health; as, aspirin is a common *remedy* for headache; sunlight and rest are *remedies* for tuberculosis. **Cure** is more positive in its suggestion of restoration to health or of complete recovery than *remedy;* it is therefore avoided in scientific or very precise writing, but it is the common or popular designation for anything (substance, method of treatment, diet, or the like) which is advocated as being, or is widely believed to be, conducive to recovery; as, sunshine and vitamin D are *cures* for rickets; a water *cure;* a faith *cure;* the *cure* for a psychic disorder. **Medicine,** except in extended and more or less humorous use (as, a year's vacation is the only *medicine* I need), is the ordinary term for any substance or preparation (especially one in the form of a pill, a powder, a capsule, a liquid, or the like) which is used in treating a disturbance of the normal functions of the body and taken internally; as, the doctor prescribed a *medicine* to be taken every hour; proprietary *medicines;* a diuretic *medicine. Medicine* is now rarely applied to a substance or preparation used externally, as by applying, rubbing, or spraying. The term generally used by physicians and pharmacists to cover all substances and preparations whether taken internally or applied externally is **medicament;** as, a nasal *medicament* for treating hay fever; a drug is a substance used in the preparation of *medicaments.* **Specific** is applied usually to a drug, sometimes to a medicine, known to be effective in curing a certain disease; thus, quinine is the *specific* for malaria. "Most medicines are alleviative in their action and not definitely curative....A very few actual curatives are known and these are generally classified as *specific,* denoting thereby that they will definitely cure one disease and presumably no other" (*A. C. Morrison*). **Physic,** the archaic equivalent of *medicine,* is now used chiefly in historical romances. "Throw *physic* to the dogs; I'll none of it" (*Shak.*).

remedy, *v.* **1** *Cure, heal.

2 *Correct, rectify, emend, amend, redress, reform, revise.

Ana. *Relieve, assuage, alleviate, lighten, mitigate: restore, *renew, refresh.

Con. *Intensify, aggravate, heighten.

remember. Remember, recollect, recall, remind, reminisce, bethink, mind are not as a group synonymous terms, although they all carry as their basic meaning to put one (often oneself) in mind of something. **Remember,** except in a few idiomatic expressions such as "*remember* me to him" (i.e., put me and my regard for him in his mind) and in older literary use (as, "*Remembering* them the truth of what they themselves know"—*Milton*), now implies a putting oneself in mind of something. The term in current use carries so strong an implication of keeping in one's memory that it often implies no conscious effort or willing; as, he *remembers* every detail of that occurrence as though it happened yesterday; "The average reader of the newspaper or short story reads to forget, not to *remember*" (*C. W. Eliot*); "Years—so many of them that no one *remembered* the exact number" (*R. Bradford*). **Recollect** (which is distinguished from *re-collect* only in pronunciation and in bearing a more specific significance) etymologically presupposes a scattering and implies a gathering of that which has been scattered: it is distinguished from *remember* in presupposing a letting go from rather than a retaining in one's memory and therefore implies a bringing back, sometimes with effort, to one's own mind that which has not been in it for an appreciable period of time; as, "She tried to *recollect* some instance of goodness, some distinguished trait of integrity or benevolence, that might rescue him from the attacks of Mr. Darcy" (*Austen*); "Beasts and babies *remember,* that is, recognize: man alone *recollects*" (*Coleridge*); "certain phrases...which I have often found myself *recollecting* from a distant past" (*Lucas*). When used reflexively, *recollect* usually implies a remembrance of something one has forgotten in one's eagerness, excitement, anger, or the like, such as one's manners or one's real intention (as, "Catherine, *recollecting* herself, grew ashamed of her eagerness"—*Austen;* "He pointed a foot; *recollected* himself; took it back"—*V. Sackville-West*), but it may imply a gathering together of thoughts one wishes to have in mind and a dismissal of all others that are distracting or that weaken one's powers of concentration (as, to *recollect* oneself in prayer). **Recall** often comes close to *recollect* in implying volition or an effort to bring back what has been forgotten, but it differs from *recollect* in suggesting a summons rather than a process of thought; often, also, it connotes a telling of that which is brought back; as, "Let me *recall* a case within my own recent experience" (*Mencken*); "I will permit my memory to *recall* The vision of you, by all my dreams attended" (*Millay*). "'Miss Manette, had you any conversation with the prisoner on that passage across the channel?' 'Yes, sir.' '*Recall* it.' In the midst of a profound stillness, she faintly began" (*Dickens*). But *recall* may imply, as *recollect* does not and as *remember* now rarely does, an agent or an agency other than oneself, in such use always suggesting the awakening or the evocation of a memory; as, "Forty years later Mr. Wilson *recalled* this circumstance to my memory" (*A. Repplier*); "That tree always awakened pleasant memories, *recalling* a garden in the south of France where he used to visit young cousins" (*Cather*). **Remind** is a closer synonym of *recall* than of *remember* (though only within a century has it become quite obsolete in this sense) or of *recollect,* because it implies the evocation of something forgotten or not at the time in one's mind by some compelling power or agent. Often also, it strongly implies a jogging of one's memory. Usually the agent or agency is someone or something external that causes one to remember; as, he *reminded* me of my promise (or, he *recalled* my promise to me); this incident *reminded* him (or *recalled* to his memory) another and similar one. But when the agent is the person who remembers, *remind* is always a reflexive verb, thereby differing from *recall* in another important particular; as, he *reminded* himself (or he *recalled*) that he had made an appointment for eight o'clock; he found it necessary to keep on *reminding* himself that the time was short and the work must be finished according to schedule. **Reminisce** rarely occurs as a transitive verb, but as an intransitive verb it usually implies the process of recollecting or of recalling something. "She could not have *remembered* much of Keats....How do people *remember* anything? How do they *reminisce?*" (*A. Lang*). In current use, *reminisce* implies not only the recollection but the retelling of events or circumstances of one's past life; as, "Well, anyhow, we old fellows can *reminisce*" (*H. Garland*); "he cut me short to *reminisce* of his schoolmates" (*Hervey Allen*). **Bethink**, an archaic and commonly reflexive verb, usually implies recollection or recalling after reflection, or a reminding oneself by thinking back; as, "I have *bethought* me of another fault" (*Shak.*); "To *bethink* themselves how little they may owe to their own merit" (*Sir A. Helps*). **Mind** (as here compared: see also TEND) is chiefly dialectal, though its use obtains in Scotland and Ireland, in the sense of *remember:* the term, however, is often found in literary use where a dialectal word makes for simplicity or atmosphere; as, "I *mind* him coming down the street" (*Tennyson*); "The lads you leave will *mind* you Till Ludlow tower shall fall" (*Housman*); "I can *mind* her well as a nursing mother—a comely woman in her day" (*Quiller-Couch*).

Ant. Forget. — *Con.* Ignore, disregard, *neglect, overlook.

remembrance. *Memory, recollection, reminiscence, mind, souvenir.

Ant. Forgetfulness.

remind. *Remember, recollect, recall, reminisce, bethink, mind.

Ana. *Suggest, intimate, hint, imply.

reminisce. *Remember, recollect, recall, remind, bethink, mind.

reminiscence. *Memory, remembrance, recollection, mind, souvenir.

remiss. Lax, slack, neglectful, *negligent.

Ana. *Careless, heedless, thoughtless: *forgetful, oblivious, unmindful: indolent, slothful, fainéant, *lazy.

Ant. Scrupulous.

remit. **1** Pardon, forgive, *excuse, condone.

Ana. *Exculpate, exonerate, acquit, vindicate, absolve.

2 *Confess, shrive, absolve.

remnant. *Remainder, residue, residuum, remains, leavings, relics, rest, balance.

Ana. *Part, piece, fragment, segment, section: vestige, *trace.

remodel. Rebuild, *mend, repair, patch.

remonstrate. Expostulate, *object, protest, kick.

Ana. *Oppose, combat, resist, withstand: *criticize, denounce, reprobate.

remorse. *Penitence, repentance, contrition, attrition, compunction.

Ana. Regret, *sorrow, grief: *qualm, scruple, compunction, demur.

remote. *Distant, far, faraway, far-off, removed.

Ant. Close.

remove, *v.* **1** *Move, shift, transfer.

Ana. Convey, *carry, bear, transport, transmit: eradicate, extirpate, uproot (see EXTERMINATE).

2 Remove, draw, withdraw come into comparison not as close synonyms, but as transitive verbs that have for their basic and general meaning to move someone or something from or out of its present position (usually without statement of new location). **Remove** (for more specific meaning see MOVE, 2) is the least explicit as well as the most general of these terms. In the sense here considered, apart from its context it seldom suggests the acts or movements involved; therefore, it may be used with reference to persons and to immaterial things as well as to material things; as, to *remove* oneself from observation; to *remove* a cork from a bottle; to *remove* one's shoes; "the scientific view of the world....regards disorder and inexplicable irregularity as a scandal to be *removed* by more patient observation" (*Inge*); the news *removed* a great load from his mind; to *remove* spots from a coat. **Draw** (as here considered: see also PULL) implies removal from its place by or, often, as if by pulling; it is therefore preferred to *remove* when this idea is uppermost; thus, idiomatically one *removes* a tablecloth or *draws* the cloth; to *draw* a cork is more explicit than to *remove* a cork; however, one *removes* (not *draws*) a stain with gasoline; one *draws* (not *removes*) the truth from a reluctant witness at a trial. **Withdraw** is more restricted in its range of application and more clearly defined in its meaning than the other terms. As here compared (see also GO, 1), it implies a taking back or away someone or something that has been placed elsewhere, as by oneself, or by the will of another, or by nature, or the like; as, to *withdraw* one's money from a bank; she decided to *withdraw* her child from the school; "he looked for a moment at Elizabeth, till catching her eye, he *withdrew* his own" (*Austen*). "A favorite ruse of the opium smugglers was to insert a hypodermic needle into an egg, *withdraw* carefully all the albumen and then refill the cavity with opium" (*V. Heiser*). "They also feel that the classification of events as natural or supernatural *withdraws* the natural order from the immediate jurisdiction of God" (*Inge*). *Withdraw* may also specifically imply a recanting of something said or charged; as, to *withdraw* one's remarks with an apology; to *withdraw* an accusation.

Ana. Eliminate, *exclude, debar: *separate, part, divorce, sever, sunder.

removed. Remote, far-off, faraway, far, *distant.

remunerate. *Pay, compensate, satisfy, reimburse, indemnify, repay, recompense, requite.

Ana. Award, accord, vouchsafe, *grant.

rend, *v.* Split, cleave, rive, rip, *tear.

Ana. *Separate, divide, sever, sunder: rupture, fracture (see corresponding nouns at FRACTURE).

rendezvous. Tryst, *engagement, appointment, assignation, date.

renegade *or* **renegado,** *n.* **Renegade** (*or* **renegado**), **apostate, pervert, turncoat, recreant, backslider** are strongly derogatory terms denoting a person who forsakes his faith or party, a cause, or an allegiance, and aligns himself with another. **Renegade,** or its earlier form **renegado,** was originally applied to a Christian who became a Mohammedan. Consequently, it came to mean one who completely denies all he has been brought up to believe by going over to the enemy or the opposition. "Still violent... But most against the party he forsook: For *renegadoes*, who ne'er turn by halves, Are bound in conscience to be double knaves" (*Dryden*). "He was, in the proper sense of the word, a *renegade*, for he had grown into manhood on the Catholic side, and he had abjured his religion wholly for the prospect of gain and power" (*Belloc*). **Apostate** stresses the giving up, either voluntarily or under compulsion, of something one has formerly professed, such as one's religious beliefs, one's principles, etc., and the acceptance of others, usually, by implication, of a less exalted character. *Apostate* therefore usually connotes surrender, but it does not, as *renegade* often does, imply treachery, or hostility to that which is forsaken. **Pervert,** in older English, implied a change in religious faith from one that is regarded as true to another that is held to be false; as, "that notorious *pervert*, Henry of Navarre" (*Thackeray*). In modern English, this sense is dying out, for the term is now applied to one who seeks sexual satisfaction in unnatural and aberrant ways, such as in homosexuality, sadism, or exhibitionism. **Turncoat,** a contemptuous designation, differs from *renegade* and *apostate* chiefly in its implications that profession of faith or allegiance is regarded lightly and that convenience or profit rather than conviction motivates the change. "An' monie mae that I could tell, Wha fain would openly rebel, Forby [besides] *turn-coats* amang oursel" (*Burns*). "An American who went abroad and stayed, without an official excuse... was regarded as a *turncoat*" (*Van W. Brooks*). **Recreant,** like *apostate*, implies a retreat from a stand one has taken, but it stresses cowardice and mean-spiritedness, and usually connotes treachery to the party or cause once supported. **Backslider,** in contrast to the other terms, usually implies a previous conversion and a reversion to the old indifference or the old beliefs; thus, a convert who goes back to his earlier state morally or to his earlier religious affiliation is regarded as a *backslider*.

Ana. *Rebel, insurgent, iconoclast: deserter, forsaker, abandoner (see corresponding verbs at ABANDON): *heretic, schismatic.

Ant. Adherent.

renew. **Renew, restore, refresh, renovate, refurbish, redintegrate, rejuvenate, rejuvenize, rejuvenesce** come into comparison when they mean to give a person or thing that has become old, worn, exhausted, or the like, the qualities or appearance of that which is fresh or new or young. **Renew** is so inclusive a term that it may imply a making something new to replace the old that has died, decayed, disintegrated, or the like (as, each spring the trees *renew* their foliage; "I think I will be extravagant enough to *renew* my entire wardrobe"—*Shaw*), or a remaking so that it seems like new, of a thing which has depleted its vitality or force or has lost its freshness (as, "They that wait upon the Lord shall *renew* their strength"—*Isaiah* xl. 31; "so that thy youth is *renewed* like the eagle's"—*Psalms* ciii. 5; "to *renew* and rebuild civilization, and save the World from suicide"—*T. S. Eliot*), or a making a fresh start (as, to *renew* one's efforts; to *renew* one's offer of assistance). **Restore** definitely implies a return to an original state or to a prime condition, as after depletion, exhaustion, illness, or the like (as, to *restore* one's vigor; to *restore* one's good humor; a long rest *restored* him to health), or after having been marred, injured, or wrecked as by passage of time, use, accident, or assault in war (as, Rheims Cathedral was *restored* after the World War; an attempt to *restore* a picture or mutilated statue), or after the loss of any vital or essential quality or character (as, "If I quench thee, thou flaming minister, I can again thy former light *restore*, Should I repent me"—*Shak.;* "great artists... have never been able to *restore* the scent and the savour and the substance [of French speech] which Villon and Montaigne...could once find within its borders"—*H. Ellis*). **Refresh** often implies the supplying of something necessary to restore lost strength, animation, power, or the like (as, sleep *refreshes* both body and mind; the tired soldiers were *refreshed* after they had partaken of food; a cool, refreshing drink), or to make up for that which has been lost through forgetfulness or disuse or has never been known or used (as, "he made it his business to see Dr. Lavendar, and be *refreshed* as to facts"—*Deland;* "convinced that our nation, in this storehouse of Latin [as the language of the medieval church] to *refresh* and replenish its most sacred thoughts, has enjoyed a continuous blessing"—*Quiller-Couch*). Equally often the term implies the imparting of freshness to something by or as if by cooling, wetting, or allaying thirst: it then usually connotes an enlivening, invigorating, or exhilarating effect; as, "a dew coming after heat *refresheth*" (*Ecclesiasticus* xliii. 22); "the springs... under the earth...break forth to *refresh* and gladden the life of flowers and the life of man" (*Binyon*); "The presence of Helen renewed and *refreshed* him" (*S. Anderson*). **Renovate** and **refurbish** differ from the preceding terms chiefly in being referred almost, but not quite, exclusively to material things and, as a consequence, in not having gathered the finer poetic connotations so often found in *renew, restore,* and *refresh*. *Renovate* is often used in place of *renew* when cleansing, repairing, rebuilding, or the like, is implied; as, to *renovate* both the rooms and the furnishings of an old colonial house; to *renovate* an old automobile by renewing the upholstery and adding new fenders. *Refurbish* (cf. *furbish*, under POLISH) implies the restoration of newness or freshness by or as if by scouring or polishing: it suggests little more than a freshening up of the appearance or the external aspects of a thing (as, to *refurbish* an old table by sandpapering and waxing it), and therefore occasionally is used in depreciation; as, "the true ring [i.e., distinguishing mark] by which, in this *refurbishing* age, a fossilized survival may be known from a spurious reproduction" (*Hardy*); the *refurbishing* of trite thoughts is the sole accomplishment of many would-be poets. **Redintegrate,** a useful term now seldom used, carries a strong implication of a return to original soundness, integrity, or perfection: it is employed especially with reference to things whose wholeness, soundness, or perfection depends chiefly on a spiritual or an organic unity or on the fine adjustment of each part or element to all of the others; as, only a spirit of good will and a passion for justice will *redintegrate* a warring world; to *redintegrate* an empire. **Rejuvenate** (or the less frequent **rejuvenize** or **rejuvenesce**) implies a restoration of youthful vigor, powers, appearance, activities, or the like: sometimes it merely suggests a giving that which is old a youthful aspect; as, a *rejuvenating* operation; "He...had the air of an old bachelor trying to *rejuvenate* himself" (*Irving*); "Outworn themes may be *rejuvenated* by taking on contemporary garb" (*Lowes*).

Ana. *Mend, repair, rebuild, remodel: reform, revise, rectify, *correct.

Con. Exhaust, *deplete, drain, impoverish, bankrupt.

renounce. **1** *Abdicate, resign, demit.

Ana. Sacrifice, abnegate, *forgo, forbear, eschew.

Ant. Arrogate: covet (sense 2): — ***Con.*** Usurp, preempt, appropriate (see ARROGATE).

2 *Abjure, forswear, recant, retract.

Ana. Reject, repudiate, spurn (see DECLINE, *v.*): *forgo, forbear, eschew.

Ant. Confess (sense 1): claim.

renovate. Refurbish, rejuvenate, *renew, restore, refresh, redintegrate.

Ana. *Mend, repair, patch, remodel: *clean, cleanse: *polish, shine, burnish.

renown. *Fame, honor, glory, celebrity, reputation, repute, notoriety, éclat.

Ana. Prestige, authority, *influence, weight, credit.

Con. Contempt, despite, disdain, scorn (see under DESPISE): disrepute, *disgrace, dishonor, obloquy.

renowned. *Famous, famed, noted, celebrated, distinguished, eminent, illustrious, notorious.

Ana. Praised, acclaimed, lauded, extolled (see PRAISE): outstanding, signal, prominent (see NOTICEABLE).

rent, *v.* *Hire, let, lease, charter.

renunciation. **Renunciation, abnegation, self-abnegation, self-denial** agree in meaning voluntary surrender or putting aside of something desired or desirable. **Renunciation** commonly connotes personal sacrifice for a higher end, such as the good of others, or moral discipline, or the attainment of the highest good. "She had learnt the lesson of *renunciation*, and was as familiar with the wreck of each day's wishes as with the diurnal setting of the sun" (*Hardy*). **Abnegation** is scarcely distinguishable from **self-abnegation** in historical use. Modern writers, however, prefer the latter or its equivalent *abnegation of self*. Both words (except the former in rare instances) more often denote a quality of character than an act; both imply a very high degree of unselfishness or a capacity for putting aside all personal interests or desires. "Individuals who are willing to abandon the pleasures of the world for lepers are rare, but, when found, usually exhibit complete *abnegation* of self" (*V. Heiser*). **Self-denial,** unlike *abnegation,* is usually applied to an act or a practice. Though it means denial of oneself, or forbearance from gratifying one's own desires, it does not necessarily connote nobility in the act, its motive, or its end, and is therefore applicable to a larger range of instances than either *abnegation* or *renunciation*. "Her still face, with the mouth closed tight from suffering and disillusion and *self-denial*" (*D. H. Lawrence*).

Ana. Sacrificing *or* sacrifice, forgoing, forbearing, eschewing (see corresponding verbs at FORGO).

repair, *v.* *Mend, patch, rebuild, remodel.

Ana. Remedy, redress, amend, emend, rectify, *correct: *renew, renovate, refurbish, restore.

reparation. Reparation, redress, amends, restitution, indemnity agree in meaning a return for something lost or suffered, usually through the fault of another. **Reparation** commonly implies an attempt to restore things to their normal or sound condition. Though now chiefly applied to recompense for material losses or damages, or reimbursement for repairs (as, war *reparations;* to seek *reparation* from the state for flood damages), it is still frequently applied to atonement for an offense, especially one incurring injury to others; as, to make *reparation* for one's sins. "I am sensible of the scandal I have given by my loose writings, and make what *reparation* I am able" (*Dryden*). **Redress** heightens the implications of a grievance and, therefore, connotes compensation or satisfaction, or even, at times, retaliation or vengeance; as, to seek *redress* in the courts or by the sword. "*Redress* is always to be had against oppression, by punishing the immediate agents" (*Johnson*). "The civil law by which contracts are enforced, and *redress* given for slanders and injuries that are not dealt with by the police" (*Shaw*). "Particular grievances call not only for *redress,* but also for the formulation of universally valid reasons why they should be *redressed*" (*A. Huxley*). **Amends** is as strong as *redress* in its suggestion of due satisfaction but weaker in its implication of a grievance. It often implies a correction or restoration of a just balance. "If I did take the kingdom from your sons, To make *amends,* I'll give it to your daughter" (*Shak.*). "Love, freedom, comrades, surely make *amends* For all these thorns through which we walk to death" (*Masefield*). **Restitution** implies the restoration in kind or in value of that unlawfully taken from one; as, to make *restitution* for a theft or for slander; a *restitution* of civil rights. **Indemnity** is the specific term for money given, as by an insurance company in reparation for losses caused by fire, accident, illness, etc., or as by a defeated country for losses caused by war.

Ana. Expiation, atonement (see under EXPIATE): compensation, remuneration, requital, recompensing *or* recompense (see corresponding verbs at PAY).

repartee. *Wit, humor, irony, sarcasm, satire.

Ana. Retort, rejoinder, response (see under ANSWER, *v.*): *badinage, persiflage, raillery.

repay. *Pay, compensate, remunerate, recompense, requite, satisfy, reimburse, indemnify.

Ana. Balance, offset, *compensate: accord, award (see GRANT, *v.*).

repeat, *v.* **1 Repeat, iterate, reiterate, ingeminate** come into comparison as meaning to say or do again. **Repeat,** the word in ordinary use, may be used in reference not only to what is said or uttered again (as, to *repeat* a command; to *repeat* a request; the teacher *repeated* her question not once but three times) but to what is made, done, presented, performed, or studied again (as, to *repeat* an attempt to swim the river; to *repeat* a step in a process; the Glee Club will *repeat* the concert tomorrow night; they were asked to *repeat* the performance; to *repeat* a lesson; to wish to *repeat* a pleasant experience). *Repeat* sometimes implies a change in the speaker or doer; as, please do not *repeat* what I have told you; the teacher asked the children to *repeat* the verses after her. Although the use of "again" after *repeat* is regarded as redundant, the use of a word or phrase indicating the number of times something is repeated is not always necessarily redundant, for the verb sometimes implies not one time but an indefinite number of times; as, the same figure is *repeated* (or *repeated* ten or twenty times) in the design. **Iterate** in current use commonly implies one repetition after another, especially of something that is said; as, "matter of hardly less surprise and *iterated* talk in the village" (*G. Eliot*). There is very little difference between *iterate* and **reiterate,** except that the former occasionally refers to a second saying, doing, etc., and the latter carries an even more emphatic implication of manifold repetitions: consequently the two words are often used together when insistency is implied (as, "scientific research *iterates* and *reiterates* one moral...the greatness of little things"—*Sat. Review*), though when only one term is desired to make this point, *reiterate* is usually preferred (as, " 'Mother is wonderful.' Over and over, thought Edith, they had *reiterated* that phrase"—*V. Woolf;* "the muffled footsteps of innumerable pilgrims, and the *reiterated* mantra, Nam-Mo, O-mi-to-Fo, which they murmured"—*L. P. Smith*). **Ingeminate** [from a Latin verb meaning to double], a somewhat rare term still occasionally found in the work of good writers, implies reiteration not for the sake of insistency but for special emphasis or impressiveness. It therefore seldom implies indefinite repetition but rather duplication or triplication for the sake of the effect produced. "[Falkland] often, after a deep silence and frequent sighs, would with a shrill and sad accent, *ingeminate* the word, Peace, Peace" (*Clarendon*).

Ana. *Return, recur, revert, recrudesce: rehearse, recite, recount, *relate.

2 *Quote, cite.

repellent *or* **repellant.** *Repugnant, abhorrent, distasteful, obnoxious, invidious.

Ana. *Offensive, loathsome, repulsive, revolting.

Ant. Attractive: pleasing. — *Con.* Alluring, charming, captivating, bewitching (see under ATTRACT): enticing, seductive, tempting, luring (see corresponding verbs at LURE).

repentance. *Penitence, contrition, attrition, remorse, compunction.

Ana. Regret, *sorrow, grief: confessing *or* confession, absolving *or* absolution (see corresponding verbs at CONFESS).

Con. Complacency, self-complacency, self-satisfaction (see corresponding adjectives at COMPLACENT).

repercuss. Reverberate, recoil, *rebound, resile.

replace. Replace, displace, supplant, supersede come into comparison in spite of the fact that they are rarely interchangeable terms, for they sometimes carry the same basic meaning—to put a person or thing out of his or its place or into the place of another. A person **replaces** that which has been lost, destroyed, used up, worn out, dismissed, or the like, either by filling his or its place with another (as, "A broken toy should not be immediately *replaced* if it has been broken by the child's carelessness"—*B. Russell;* to *replace* a servant; "Mr. Baines had decided not to *replace* it [a signboard destroyed by a gale]"—*Bennett*) or by taking and filling the place of another (as, the children opposed their widowed father's remarriage by saying that no woman could *replace* their mother; although he enjoyed marionettes, he declared that they could never *replace* human actors). Also, one *replaces* a thing when he puts it back in its proper or its assigned place (as, to *replace* a book on a shelf; "the guard soon *replaced* his blunderbuss in his arm-chest"—*Dickens*). In contrast, a person or thing **displaces** a thing (sometimes a person) when he or it puts it (or him) out of the place it (or he) has filled, and either takes the place of that which has been dislodged, crowded out, or ousted, or replaces it (or him) by another. This dual implication of putting out of place and of replacing is the chief distinction of *displace* in contrast with *replace;* as, the weight of water *displaced* by a floating body such as a ship is equal to that of the displacing body. However, one of these ideas is sometimes, but far from always, stressed more than the other so that the emphasis is either on ousting (as, "The trustees have power to appoint and *displace* professors, tutors, and other officers"—*Ch. Just. Marshall*) or on replacing (as, "His eyes rested on a large photograph of May Welland, which...had now *displaced* all the other portraits on the table"—*E. Wharton*). In strictest use, a person **supplants** (etymologically, trips up, or overthrows) another when by craft, fraud, treachery, or the like, he dispossesses or ousts the other and takes or usurps his place, possessions, privileges, etc.; as, "you three From Milan did *supplant* good Prospero" (*Shak.*); "to see myself *supplanted* in your friendship by strangers does cut me to the quick, I own" (*Austen*); "eager to succeed Louis and even to *supplant* him" (*Belloc*). But *supplant,* largely as the result of a false etymology, sometimes implies an uprooting and replacing rather than a dispossessing and usurping: in such cases, trickery or treachery is no longer implied; as, his tutor tried to *supplant* his fears by arousing his sense of curiosity; "the Modernists.... don't claim that the Divine revelation has been *supplanted*...but that it has been amplified" (*C. Mackenzie*). A thing, or less often, a person, **supersedes** (etymologically, sits above) another when it (or he) directly or indirectly causes that other to be set aside, abandoned, or rejected as inferior, no longer of use or value, superannuated, obsolete, or the like; as, a new history of the United States which bids fair to *supersede* all others; "Carpets *superseded* the filthy flooring of rushes" (*J. R. Green*); they believe that Christianity because of its perfection can never be *superseded*. "That is the worst of erudition—that the next scholar sucks the few drops of honey that you have accumulated, sets right your blunders, and you are *superseded*" (*A. C. Benson*). A person supersedes another in a position, an office, a rank, or the like, either when, as the one having authority or appointive power, he replaces the present incumbent by another (as, to *supersede* a dishonest public official), or when, as the one who takes the place, he supplants the present occupant or goes ahead of one in line for promotion (as, "His brilliant and impetuous colleague was in both quarters rapidly *superseding* him"—*Lecky*).

Ana. Restore, *renew: *change, alter: *recover, regain, recoup, retrieve.

replete. *Full, complete, plenary.

Ana. Abundant, *plentiful: sated, satiated, surfeited (see SATIATE).

replica. Facsimile, *reproduction, duplicate, copy, carbon copy, transcript.

reply, *v.* *Answer, respond, rejoin, retort.

Con. *Ask, question, interrogate, query, inquire, catechize, examine: *accuse, charge, impeach, indict: salute, greet, *address.

reply, *or, in law,* **replication,** *n.* Answer, response, rejoinder, retort. See under ANSWER, *v.*, 1.

Ana. Acknowledgment, recognition (see corresponding verbs at ACKNOWLEDGE).

Con. Asking, requesting *or* request, solicitation (see corresponding verbs at ASK): accusation, charging *or* charge (see corresponding verbs at ACCUSE): *argument, dispute: *greeting, salute.

report, *v.* *Relate, narrate, describe, state, recite, recount, rehearse.

Ana. *Communicate, impart: *reveal, disclose, discover, tell, divulge.

report, *n.* **1** *Account, story, chronicle, version.

2 Dispatch, message, note, *letter, epistle, missive, memorandum.

repose, *n.* *Rest, relaxation, leisure, ease, comfort.

Ana. Calmness, tranquillity, serenity, placidity, peacefulness (see corresponding adjectives at CALM): refreshment, restoration, renewal, redintegration (see corresponding verbs at RENEW).

Con. *Work, labor, toil, grind, drudgery: *stress, strain: agitation, perturbation, discomposure (see corresponding verbs at DISCOMPOSE).

reposeful. Restful, *comfortable, cozy, snug, easy.

Ana. Tranquil, serene, placid, peaceful, *calm: *still, quiet, silent.

reprehend. *Criticize, censure, reprobate, condemn, denounce, blame.

Ana. *Reprove, rebuke, reprimand, admonish, reproach, chide: *scold, upbraid, berate, rate.

repress. *Suppress.

Ana. *Restrain, curb, check, inhibit: subdue, overcome (see CONQUER).

reprimand, *v.* *Reprove, rebuke, reproach, admonish, chide.

Ana. Upbraid, rate, berate, *scold: censure, denounce, blame, reprehend, reprobate, *criticize.

reprisal. *Retaliation, retribution, revenge, vengeance.

reproach, *v.* Chide, admonish, *reprove, rebuke, reprimand.

Ana. *Criticize, reprehend, censure, reprobate: *warn, forewarn, caution: counsel, advise (see under ADVICE).

reprobate, *adj.* *Abandoned, profligate, dissolute.

Ana. *Vicious, iniquitous, corrupt, degenerate: *blameworthy, guilty, culpable.

Ant. Elect (*in theology*). — *Con.* Righteous, virtuous, *moral, ethical.

reprobate, *v.* Censure, reprehend, *criticize, blame, condemn, denounce.

Ana. *Decry, derogate from, detract from, depreciate, disparage: reject, repudiate, spurn (see DECLINE, *v.*): reprimand, rebuke, *reprove.

reproduce. Propagate, *generate, engender, breed, beget, get, sire, procreate.

Ana. Produce, *bear, yield: multiply (see INCREASE).

reproduction. Reproduction, duplicate, copy, carbon copy (*or* **carbon**), **facsimile, replica, transcript** agree in denoting one thing which closely resembles something that has already been made, produced, written, or the like. **Reproduction** may imply identity in material or substance, in size, and in quality, or it may imply differences, provided that the imitation gives a fairly true likeness of the original; thus, a *reproduction* of an

Elizabethan theater may be on a very small scale; a *reproduction* of a Sheraton chair may be in cherry rather than in the mahogany of the original. A **duplicate** is strictly a double of something else; the word may be used of that which exactly corresponds to, or is the counterpart, of any object whatsoever; as, a *duplicate* of a book, an engraving, a postage stamp, a bill, a piece of furniture; to make out a receipt in *duplicate*. A **copy** is a reproduction of something else, often without the exact correspondence which belongs to a duplicate; as, two antique medals from the same die are *duplicates*, while a modern reproduction of either is a *copy*. However, *copy*, rather than *duplicate* (which properly may be used only when there is but a single reproduction) is applicable to any one of a number of things printed from the same type format, or struck off from the same die, or made in the same mold, or the like; as, a thousand *copies* of a magazine; fifty *copies* of a medal; mimeographed *copies* of a letter; she ordered two dozen *copies* of the photograph. **Carbon copy,** literally a copy of something typed or written made by use of carbon paper, denotes by extension an exact duplicate; as, the best passages in this poem are *carbon copies* of passages found in a poem written a hundred years ago. A **facsimile** is an exact reproduction; it may imply differences as in scale, but it implies strict identity or close imitating in details, material, and the like; as, "The square-shouldered, clumsy, high-featured Priscilla wore a dress the *fac-simile* of her pretty sister's" (*G. Eliot*). "The heavy chandeliers were loaded with flattened brass balls, magnified *fac-similes* of which crowned the uprights of the...massively-framed chairs" (*Shaw*). **Replica,** in strict use, applies only to an exact reproduction of a statue, a painting, a building, or the like, made by the same artist, architect, or artisan; hence, a replica is not always distinguishable from the original, and is thought of as its equal in value; thus, one does not correctly speak of a modern *replica* of the Winged Victory, but of a modern *reproduction;* one may speak of the confusing tendency of some Renaissance artists to make *replicas* of their paintings. However, the word is often used loosely when very close likeness is indicated. "The young girl...was a slim *replica* of her mother" (*E. Wharton*). **Transcript** applies only to a written, typed, printed, or other copy made directly from an original (either handwritten or typed), from shorthand notes, or the like; as, a stenographer's *transcript* of a letter; to ask for a *transcript* of a will.

reprove. **Reprove, rebuke, reprimand, admonish, reproach, chide** agree in meaning to criticize adversely, especially in order to warn or to correct a fault. The same differences in implications are usually found in their corresponding nouns. To **reprove** is to blame or censure, often kindly or without harshness and, usually, in the hope of correcting the fault; **rebuke** implies sharp or stern reproof; **reprimand** suggests reproof that is formal, and often public or official. "Marcus with blushes owns he loves, and Brutus tenderly *reproves*" (*Pope*). "I have not lacked thy mild *reproof*" (*Tennyson*). "He *rebuked* Peter, saying, Get thee behind me, Satan" (*Mark* viii. 33). "The Lord will come with fire...to render his anger with fury, and his *rebuke* with flames of fire" (*Isaiah* lxvi. 15). "A word...which the Duke of Wellington, or Admiral Stopford, would use in *reprimanding* an officer" (*Macaulay*). **Admonish** stresses the implication of warning or counsel. "Count him not as an enemy, but *admonish* him as a brother" (*2 Thessalonians* iii. 15). "Sincere acknowledgments to both my private and public censors for their friendly *admonitions*" (*Coleridge*). **Reproach** and **chide** imply dissatisfaction or displeasure; *reproach* usually connotes criticism or faultfinding; *chide* (which once implied rebuke), in current use, almost invariably implies mild reproof or a slight scolding. "If he came home late, and she *reproached* him, he frowned and turned on her in an overbearing way" (*D. H. Lawrence*). "He *reproached* himself for ascribing motives to other people without taking care first to look at his own" (*C. Mackenzie*). "Approach her [the Queen]: do not fear; She will not *chide* you" (*G. Bottomley*).

Ana. *Criticize, reprehend, censure, reprobate: chasten, correct, discipline, *punish.

repudiate. Spurn, reject, refuse, *decline.

Ana. Renounce, *abjure: *forgo, forbear, eschew, sacrifice.

Ant. Adopt. — ***Con.*** *Acknowledge, own, admit, avow, confess: embrace, espouse (see ADOPT).

repugnant. 1 **Repugnant, repellent** (*or* **repellant**), **abhorrent, distasteful, obnoxious, invidious** are synonyms when they mean so alien or unlikable as to arouse antagonism and aversion. **Repugnant** is applied to that which is incompatible with one's ideas, principles, or tastes, and stirs up resistance and loathing. "Nor was this state of things [slavery] in the least *repugnant* to the Greek mind" (*G. L. Dickinson*). "The bloomless side of life...when he had to face it...wasn't altogether *repugnant*" (*Cather*). **Repellent** is applied to that which drives one away: it usually implies a forbidding or unlovely character in the thing avoided that causes one to back away from it. "The mediocre was *repellent* to them; cant and sentiment made them sick" (*R. Macaulay*). **Abhorrent** tends to merge with its other and more common sense (see HATEFUL), but it is still found applied to that which is incapable of association or existence with something else, and it often implies profound antagonism. "Dictatorial methods *abhorrent* to American ways of thinking" (*Forum*). **Distasteful** is applied to that from which one instinctively shrinks, not because it in itself is unlikable but because it is contrary to one's taste or inclination. "Even the partition of the world into the animate and the inanimate is *distasteful* to science, which dislikes any lines that cannot be crossed" (*Inge*). **Obnoxious** is applied to that which is so highly objectionable, usually on personal grounds, that one cannot endure the sight or presence of it (or, often, him) with equanimity; as, "He would renounce me for a sister, If I encouraged the addresses of a man so *obnoxious* to them all" (*Richardson*); "The Prussian Government, too, during the war, offered a tempting prize for a song to displace 'Heil dir im Siegerkranz,' which had become *obnoxious* because of its close similarity to the British National Anthem" (*Manchester Guardian*). **Invidious** is applied to that which cannot be used (such as a word) or made (such as a distinction) or undertaken (such as a task or project) without arousing or creating ill will, envy, odium, or the like; as, "the *invidious* word usury" (*Hume*); "What I would urge, therefore, is that no *invidious* distinction should be made between the Old Learning and the New" (*J. R. Lowell*). "If the public wants a standardized pronunciation, I have no doubt that some appropriate standard will evolve itself. If there are any who think otherwise, it must be left to them to undertake the *invidious* task of deciding what is to be approved and what is to be condemned" (*D. Jones*).

Ana. Foreign, alien, extraneous, *extrinsic: uncongenial, incompatible, incongruous, *inconsonant: *antipathetic, averse, unsympathetic.

Ant. Congenial.

2 Repulsive, revolting, *offensive, loathsome.

Ana. Odious, *hateful, abominable, detestable: foul, nasty (see DIRTY): vile, *base, low.

repulsive. Repugnant, revolting, *offensive, loathsome.

Ana. Repellent, *repugnant, abhorrent, obnoxious.
Ant. Alluring, captivating.

reputation. Repute, *fame, renown, honor, glory, celebrity, éclat, notoriety.
Ana. Credit, weight, *influence, authority, prestige.

repute, *n.* Reputation, *fame, renown, celebrity, notoriety, éclat, honor, glory.
Ant. Disrepute.

reputed. *Supposed, supposititious, suppositious, putative, conjectural, hypothetical.
Ana. Assumed, presumed (see PRESUPPOSE): *traditional, legendary.

request, *v.* *Ask, solicit.
Ana. *Beg, entreat, beseech, implore, supplicate, importune: appeal, petition, sue, pray (see under PRAYER).

require. 1 Exact, claim, *demand.
Ana. *Prescribe, assign, define: warrant, *justify.
2 *Lack, want, need.

requirement. **Requirement, requisite, prerequisite** agree in denoting something that is regarded as necessary to the success or perfection of a thing. Although **requirement,** the more general term, may be employed in place of *requisite,* in current use it is the customary term when the idea to be conveyed is of something more or less arbitrarily demanded or expected, especially, but not exclusively, by those who lay down conditions as for admission to college, for enlistment in the army or navy, for membership in a church, for entrance into a course, or the like; as, college entrance *requirements;* a list of *requirements* for all campers; "Edward Casaubon was bent on fulfilling unimpeachably all *requirements*" (*G. Eliot*); "My wardrobe had to provide for a wide range in temperature, and social, business, and sport *requirements*" (*V. Heiser*). **Requisite** is the customary term when the stress is on the idea of something that is indispensable to the end in view, or is necessitated by a thing's nature or essence or is otherwise essential and not arbitrarily demanded; as, the prime *requisite* of a good speech is to have something to say that needs to be said; "the first *requisite* of literary or artistic activity, is that it shall be interesting" (*T. S. Eliot*); the *requisites* of our present social economy are capital and labor. **Prerequisite** differs from *requisite* only in a stress on the time when it becomes indispensable: it applies therefore to things which must be known, or accomplished, or acquired as preliminaries to the study of a subject, the doing of a kind of work, or the attainment of any end; as, "he possesses the *prerequisite* of an original poet—a percipience unifying, exact and exhilarating" (*Day Lewis*).

requisite, *adj.* *Needful, necessary, indispensable, essential.
Ana. Compelled *or* compulsory, constrained, obliged *or* obligatory (see corresponding verbs at FORCE): fundamental, *essential, cardinal, vital.

requisite, *n.* *Requirement, prerequisite.

requite. Recompense, repay, compensate, remunerate, *pay, satisfy, reimburse, indemnify.
Ana. Retaliate, revenge (see corresponding nouns at RETALIATION): regain, *recover, retrieve, recoup.

rescue, *v.* **Rescue, deliver, redeem, ransom, reclaim, save** come into comparison as meaning to free a person or thing from that which subjects him or it to confinement, danger of death or destruction, or any serious evil. One **rescues** a person who is in imminent danger such as of death, of capture, or of assault, by prompt or vigorous action (as, "We are beset with thieves; *Rescue* thy mistress"—*Shak.;* to *rescue* the crew of a sinking ship; to *rescue* a child in danger of being run down by an automobile): less often, one *rescues* a thing that is in danger of destruction, or that has been forcibly seized, by freeing it from danger or from its captors (as, "*Rescued* is Orleans from the English"—*Shak.;* "Diamonds that I *rescued* from the tarn"—*Tennyson;* "a main object of his teaching to *rescue* the idea of justice from identification with the special interest of the strong"—*G. L. Dickinson*). One **delivers** a person (rarely, in the sense here considered, a thing) by setting him (or it) free from prison, confinement, suffering, temptation, embarrassment, or the like; as, "Lead us not unto temptation, but *deliver* us from evil" (*Matthew* vi. 13); to *deliver* the prisoners from the Bastille; "to *deliver* mankind from the paralysing grip of determinism" (*Inge*); "the population of Russia had only just been *delivered,* nominally at least, from serfdom" (*H. Ellis*). One **redeems** a person in bondage, in captivity, or from suffering the consequences of his sin, crime, or the like, by paying the price that is demanded for his release. "Ye know that ye were not *redeemed* with corruptible things, as silver and gold.... But with the precious blood of Christ" (*1 Peter* i. 18–19). "Let me *redeem* my brothers both from death" (*Shak.*). Also, one *redeems* a thing from pawn or like condition by paying the amount that is due or is asked for its recovery (as, at last he was able to *redeem* his watch) or from a state of neglect, deterioration, or decay by spending the money or the time necessary to restore it to good condition (as, "a plot of land *redeemed* from the heath, and after long and laborious years brought into cultivation" —*Hardy*). One **ransoms** a person who has been captured, enslaved, kidnaped, or the like, by paying the amount that is demanded by his captor or owner; as, "My son, whom nought can *ransom* or *redeem*" (*Kyd*); "His wife *ransomed* him at a heavy price" (*Freeman*). *Ransom* is often employed in place of *redeem* in religious use, especially in reference to Christ as the Redeemer, when the emphasis is on the price he paid in accepting crucifixion; as, "His brethren, *ransomed* with his own dear life" (*Milton*). One **reclaims** that which has become debased, wild, savage, waste, desert, or the like, by bringing it back to its former state or condition. Specifically, one *reclaims* a person who has wandered from rectitude or has become a sinner, a reprobate, a degenerate, or the like, when one reforms him or restores him to moral, decent ways of life (as, "I fear he is not to be *reclaimed;* there is scarcely a hope that anything in his character or fortunes is reparable now"—*Dickens*), or a thing that has been abandoned or neglected, when one works with it so that, if it is land, it becomes productive or, if it is waste of any sort, it finds a new use or is made to give up what is still usable in it (as, to *reclaim* long-abandoned farms; to *reclaim* discarded wool). One **saves** (as here compared: see also SAVE, 2) a person or thing when one rescues, delivers, redeems, ransoms, or reclaims him (or it) and enables him (or it) not only to be free from the evil that involves or threatens, but to continue in existence, to enjoy security or happiness, to be of future use or service, or the like; as, to *save* a house from flames; to *save* a tree from destruction by parasites; his life was *saved* by an operation; the lifeguard *saved* him from drowning by throwing him a rope; "He cried, saying, Lord, *save* me" (*Matthew* xiv. 30).
Ana. *Free, release, liberate, emancipate, manumit: preserve, conserve (see SAVE): *extricate, disentangle, disembarrass.

research. Investigation, *inquiry, inquisition, inquest, probe.

resemblance. *Likeness, similarity, similitude, analogy, affinity.
Ana. Correspondence, agreement, harmonizing *or*

harmony, conformity (see corresponding verbs at AGREE): *comparison, parallel.
Ant. Difference: distinction.

resentment. *Offense, umbrage, pique, dudgeon, huff.
Ana. Rancor, animus, animosity, antipathy, antagonism (see ENMITY): ill will, spite, *malice, malignity.

reserve, *v.* *Keep, keep back, hold back, retain, withhold, detain.
Ana. *Save, preserve, conserve: appropriate, pre-empt, confiscate, *arrogate.

reserved. *Silent, reticent, uncommunicative, taciturn, secretive, close, close-lipped, closemouthed, tight-lipped.
Ana. Aloof, detached, disinterested (see INDIFFERENT): *shy, diffident, modest, bashful: formal, ceremonious, conventional (see CEREMONIAL).
Ant. Affable: expansive: blatant.

reside. **Reside, live, dwell, sojourn, lodge, stay, put up, stop** agree in meaning to abide in a given place as one's habitation or domicile. **Reside,** the more formal term, and **live,** the word in everyday use, express this idea, often without further implications; as, he *resides* (or *lives*) in New York City. Usually, however, when the term is intended to suggest the fixed, settled, or legal abode of a person or group such as a family, *reside* is the preferred word: when the idea to be emphasized is the spending of one's time in a given place and the carrying on of the normal activities of one's way of life, *live* is usually the better and less formal word; as, the senator *resides* in San Francisco but he *lives* for the better part of the year in Washington. When the reference is not to persons but to things, *reside* is the term to be used when the thing referred to is a quality, an element, a condition, or the like; as, the power of decision *resides* in the electorate; "His peculiar merit as a critic...*resided* in the combination of this personal gusto and curiosity" (*T. S. Eliot*). "When we have in our minds the idea of art as imitation, we are prone to think of beauty as *residing* in particular objects, particular colours" (*Binyon*). When the thing is something concrete and the idea of making one's abode or home is suggested, *live* may be used; as, "They say that sherry ought to *live* for a while in an old brandy-cask, so as to contract a certain convincing quality from the cask's genial timbers" (*C. E. Montague*). **Dwell** is also a close synonym of these words, but it is more frequently employed in elevated or poetic language (as, "She *dwelt* among the untrodden ways Beside the springs of Dove"—*Wordsworth;* "I dreamt that I *dwelt* in marble halls"—*Alfred Bunn*) or, in extended use, it carries a stronger implication of abiding as in thought or in spirit (as, "The bad poet *dwells* partly in a world of objects and partly in a world of words, and he never can get them to fit"—*T. S. Eliot*). **Sojourn** differs from all the preceding terms in usually implying a temporary habitation or abode or a more or less uncertain place or way of living; as, he *sojourns* in Washington while Congress is in session. "For what purpose, it may be asked, was the world created, and immortal spirits sent to *sojourn* in it, if we have no duties except to make our escape from contaminating surroundings?" (*Inge*). **Lodge** (see also HARBOR) also implies an abode for a time or for the time being. When used in reference to persons, it often implies the status of a lodger or a boarder, and not that of one living in his own house or apartment (as, he *lodges* at the Y.M.C.A. when he is in town; he *lodged* at the inn last winter); when used in reference to animals or things, it implies a stowing away in a place for protection or safety (as, to *lodge* money in a bank; to *lodge* the cattle in the barn for the winter). **Stay** is the term commonly used in colloquial language in place of *sojourn* and often of *lodge;* as, he is *staying* at Miami Beach for the winter; whenever he was in Paris he *stayed* at that hotel. **Put up** is also a common colloquial term but it is used only in the sense of *lodge* and commonly suggests the status of a guest in a hotel or in a home; as, where does he *put up* (i.e., in what hotel does he *stay*) when he is in Chicago?; we can *put* you *up* any night you are in town. **Stop,** which is often used in the sense of *stay* (as, he is *stopping* at the Ritz-Carlton), is regarded as a colloquial use of the term which is avoided by very precise writers and speakers.
Ana. Remain, abide (see STAY): *continue, endure.

residence. *Habitation, dwelling, abode, domicile, house, home.

resident, *n.* *Inhabitant, denizen, citizen.

residue. Residuum, remains, leavings, *remainder, relics, rest, balance, remnant.

residuum. Residue, *remainder, remains, leavings, relics, rest, balance, remnant.

resign. **1** Yield, surrender, leave, abandon, *relinquish, cede, waive.
Ana. *Forgo, eschew, sacrifice, forbear, abnegate: *abjure, renounce, forswear.
2 *Abdicate, renounce, demit.

resignation. **1** Compliance, acquiescence. See under COMPLIANT.
Ana. Submitting *or* submission, yielding, deferring *or* deference (see corresponding verbs at YIELD): meekness, modesty, humbleness *or* humility, lowliness (see corresponding adjectives at HUMBLE).
2 *Patience, long-suffering, longanimity, forbearance.
Ana. Endurance, toleration, suffering *or* sufferance (see corresponding verbs at BEAR): *fortitude, backbone, pluck.

resigned. *Compliant, acquiescent.
Ana. Submissive, subdued (see TAME): reconciled, adjusted, adapted, accommodated, conformed (see ADAPT).
Ant. Rebellious.

resile. Recoil, *rebound, reverberate, repercuss.

resilient. **1** *Elastic, springy, flexible, supple.
Ana. Recoiling, resiling, rebounding (see REBOUND): recovering, regaining, retrieving (see RECOVER).
Con. Rigid, *stiff, inflexible, tense.
2 *Elastic, expansive, buoyant, volatile, effervescent.
Ana. Responsive, sympathetic (see TENDER): *spirited, high-spirited, mettlesome.
Ant. Flaccid.

resist. *Oppose, combat, withstand, antagonize.
Ana. Assail, *attack, assault: impugn, gainsay, contravene (see DENY): thwart, baffle, balk, foil, *frustrate.
Ant. Submit: abide.

resolute. Steadfast, stanch, *faithful, true, leal, loyal.
Ana. Determined, decided, resolved (see DECIDE): intrepid, valiant, *brave, courageous: stubborn, *obstinate, pertinacious.

resolution. **1** Analysis, dissection, anatomy, breakdown. See under ANALYZE.
Ana. Separation, division (see corresponding verbs at SEPARATE): elucidation, interpretation, expounding *or* exposition, explaining *or* explanation (see corresponding verbs at EXPLAIN).
2 Mettle, spirit, tenacity, *courage.
Ana. Determination, *decision: pluck, grit, *fortitude, backbone, guts.

resolve. **1** *Analyze, dissect, anatomize, break down.
Ana. *Separate, part, divide: reduce, diminish (see DECREASE): dissolve, melt, fuse (see LIQUEFY).

Ant. Blend.
2 Determine, *decide, settle, rule.
Ana. Purpose, propose, design, *intend, mean: plan, scheme, project (see under PLAN, *n.*).

resolvent. *Solvent, dissolvent, menstruum, alkahest.

resort, *v.* **Resort, refer, apply, go, turn** come into comparison when they carry the meaning to betake oneself or to have recourse when in need of some help or external aid. **Resort** often implies that one has encountered difficulties or has tried ineffectually to surmount them; when it carries the latter implication, it often also connotes an approach to desperation; as, he found he could not get relief, unless he *resorted* to the courts; cf. court of last *resort*. "Most powers conceivably may be exercised beyond the limits allowed by the law....But we do not on that account *resort* to the blunt expedient of taking away the power" (*Justice Holmes*). **Refer** usually suggests a need of authentic information and recourse to someone or something that will supply such information; as, every time he comes across a new word he *refers* to the dictionary; most men *refer* to their own watches when someone reports the time. **Apply** suggests having direct recourse, as in person or by letter, to a person or persons having the power to grant one's request or petition; as, to *apply* to a hospital for aid; to *apply* to the court for relief; a letter of *application* for a post. "[She was] determined, that if he persisted in considering her repeated refusals as flattering encouragement, to *apply* to her father, whose negative might be uttered in such a manner as must be decisive" (*Austen*). **Go** and **turn** are more general, but are often more picturesque or dramatic terms than the words previously considered, for they suggest action or movement; as, the president decided to *go* to the people with his plan for reorganization; there was no one to whom she could *go* (or *turn*) for sympathy; "she had taken fright at our behavior and *turned* to the captain pitifully" (*Conrad*).
Ana. *Direct, address, devote: *use, employ, utilize.

resort, *n.* *Resource, expedient, shift, makeshift, stopgap, substitute, surrogate.
Ana. See those at RESOURCE, 2.

resource. 1 In plural form **resources.** Assets, belongings, effects, *possessions, means.
2 Resource, resort, expedient, shift, makeshift, stopgap, substitute, surrogate come into comparison as denoting something to which one turns for help or assistance in difficulty or need when the usual means, instrument, source of supply, or the like, fails one, is not at hand, or is unknown to one. **Resource** applies to any action, activity, person, method, device, or contrivance upon which one falls back when in need of support, assistance, diversion, or the like; as, he has exhausted every *resource* he can think of; "I must e'en hasten to matters of fact, which is the comfortable *resource* of dull people" (*Shenstone*); "The Japanese designer was debarred by instinct and tradition from using the *resources* of texture and of light and shade" (*Binyon*). **Resort** is now far less often used than *resource* except when qualified by "last" or in the phrase "to have (or make) *resort* to (something)"; as, to have *resort* to a fortune teller; "Mercy, fled to as the last *resort*" (*Cowper*); "Thus the income tax became a ...last *resort*" (*Shaw*). **Expedient** applies to any means, device, contrivance, or the like, which serves often in lieu of the usual or ordinary means, device, etc., but sometimes merely as a means, a device, or a contrivance to accomplish a difficult end immediately, easily, or without waste of time; as, "Everything is brought about... through the medium of the author's reflections, which is the clumsiest of all *expedients*" (*Scott*). "To classify in a science is necessary for the purpose of that science: to classify when you come to art is at the best an *expedient*, useful to some critics and to a multitude of examiners" (*Quiller-Couch*). A **shift** is commonly a tentative or temporary expedient: the term frequently implies evasiveness or trickery; as, "The dear delicious *shifts* I used to be put to, to gain half a minute's conversation with this fellow!" (*Sheridan*). **Makeshift** is even more derogatory than *shift*, for it implies substitution of the inferior for the superior, and often, though far from always, it imputes carelessness, indifference, or laziness to the one who chooses or makes use of it; as, "Not a model clergyman, only a decent *makeshift*" (*G. Eliot*); using oiled paper in their windows as a *makeshift* for glass. **Stopgap** applies to any person or thing that momentarily or temporarily supplies a need, or fills a gap, hole, vacancy, or the like; as, his monograph just published is said to be a *stopgap* until his book is ready to appear; the new appointee said modestly that he was only a *stopgap* and would retire when a better man was available. **Substitute** (as here compared: for its application to persons, see SUBSTITUTE, 2) does not carry as strong a suggestion of an emergency or exigency as the preceding terms do: the word is applicable to anything one chooses, accepts, or prefers, whether rightly or wrongly, rationally or irrationally, in place of the usual or original thing, or which has been invented or devised to take its place or to do its work; as, "Another discovery...was that a *substitute* for milk...could be manufactured from the soya bean" (*V. Heiser*); "Daydreams, in adult life, are recognized as more or less pathological, and as a *substitute* for efforts in the sphere of reality" (*B. Russell*). **Surrogate** is a somewhat learned word for a substitute, often, but far from always, for a synthetic or artificial product designed to replace a natural product that is scarce or comparatively expensive; as, *surrogates* for various foodstuffs, such as butter; "slang is...a facile *surrogate* for thought" (*Lowes*).
Ana. *Device, contrivance, contraption: *invention, creation (see corresponding verbs at INVENT): *method, manner, way, fashion, mode, system.

respect, *v.* Regard, esteem, admire. See under REGARD, *n.*
Ana. Reverence, *revere, venerate: value, prize, cherish, *appreciate.
Ant. Abuse: misuse.

respect, *n.* *Regard, esteem, admiration.
Ana. *Reverence, awe, fear: *honor, homage, deference: veneration, reverence, worship, adoration (see under REVERE).
Ant. Contempt.

respecting. Concerning, regarding, *about, anent.

respective. Individual, particular, *special, especial, specific, concrete.

respectively. *Each, apiece, severally, individually.

resplendent. *Splendid, gorgeous, glorious, sublime, superb.
Ana. Effulgent, refulgent, radiant, brilliant, *bright: blazing, glowing, flaming (see BLAZE, *v.*).

respond. *Answer, reply, rejoin, retort.
Ana. React, behave, *act.
Con. Stimulate, excite, quicken (see PROVOKE).

response. Answer, reply, rejoinder, retort. See under ANSWER, *v.*, 1.

responsible. Responsible, answerable, accountable, amenable, liable are comparable when they mean subject to an authority which may exact redress in case of default. *Responsible*, *answerable*, and *accountable* are etymologically very close, all meaning capable of being called upon to answer, or to make amends, to someone for something. They are, therefore, often used interchangeably. In precise English, however, they are distinguishable largely in their applications. One is **responsible** for the performance of a task or duty, or the fulfillment of an obligation, or the execution of a trust, or the administration of an office, to the person or body that imposes the task, duty, trust, or the like, or delegates the power; as, the Governor is *responsible* to the electorate for the administration of the laws. Sometimes the *to* phrase or the *for* phrase is suppressed but still implied; as, the salesmen are *responsible* to the manager, and the manager is *responsible* to the owner; a teacher is *responsible* for the conduct of pupils in the classroom. "The ideally free individual is *responsible* only to himself" (*H. Adams*). Sometimes, when both phrases are suppressed, *responsible* implies manifest ability to fulfill one's obligations; as, his record shows that he is a *responsible* person. Still narrower meanings are possible when the word is so used that with the aid of the context a sense of one's moral obligations or the power of judgment is connoted. "James arrived at an age when he could be treated as *responsible*" (*Froude*). One is **answerable** (to someone for something) who, because of a moral or legal obligation or because of the acceptance of such an obligation for another, may be called upon to pay the penalty for a violation of the law or a neglect of duty; it usually indicates or implies the existence of a judge or tribunal; as, the father made himself *answerable* to the court for his son's behavior. "Men in business, who are *answerable* with their fortunes for the consequences of their opinions" (*Hazlitt*). One is **accountable** (to someone for something) who because of something entrusted to one is bound to be called upon to render an account of how that trust has been executed. *Accountable* is much more positive than *responsible* or *answerable* in its suggestion of retributive justice in case of default. "We are held *accountable*, and God... will reckon with us roundly for the abuse of what he deems no mean or trivial trust" (*Cowper*). *Amenable* and *liable* especially stress subjection and suggest the contingency rather than the probability or certainty of being called to account. One is **amenable** (to someone or to something) whose acts are subject to the control or the censure of a higher authority, and who, therefore, is not self-governing or absolute in power; as, a despot is *amenable* to no will other than his own. "Is it to be contended that the heads of departments are not *amenable* to the laws of their country?" (*Ch. Just. Marshall*). One (a person or thing) is **liable** that by the terms of the law may be made answerable in case of one's own or another's default; as, a surety is *liable* for the debts of his principal. "The present United States... took nothing by succession from the Confederation. It ...was not *liable* for any of its [the Confederation's] obligations" (*Ch. Just. Taney*). *Liable* does not, however, always imply answerability. It may imply mere contingent obligation; as, every citizen is *liable* for jury duty (or *liable* to be called to serve on a jury).

Ana. Subject, open, exposed (see LIABLE): *reliable, dependable, trustworthy.

responsive. Sympathetic, warm, warmhearted, compassionate, *tender.

Ana. Gentle, mild, lenient (see SOFT): sensible, conscious, alive, awake, *aware: sensitive, susceptible, prone (see LIABLE).

rest, *n.*[1] **Rest, repose, relaxation, leisure, ease, comfort** come into comparison when they mean freedom from toil or strain. **Rest,** the most general of these terms, implies withdrawal from labor or exertion of any kind, and therefore suggests an opposition to the term *work*, but it may imply freedom from activity of any kind: it does not in itself explicitly imply any particular way of spending one's time, but it always suggests as an aim or as a result the overcoming of physical or mental weariness; as, "There the wicked cease from troubling; and there the weary be at *rest*" (*Job* iii. 17); "Sleep on now, and take your *rest*" (*Matthew* xxvi. 45); "Night came, and with it but little *rest*" (*Hardy*). **Repose** implies freedom from motion or movement, and therefore not only suggests physical quiet (often, specifically, the state of sleeping or slumbering), but also mental quiet and freedom from that which disturbs, annoys, agitates, confuses, or the like: the term, therefore, usually suggests tranquillity or peace or the refreshment that comes from complete quiet or rest. "Heavily passed the night. Sleep, or *repose* that deserved the name of sleep, was out of the question" (*Austen*). "Eighteen years of commotion had made the majority of the people ready to buy *repose* at any price" (*Macaulay*). "Walls...that shut out the world and gave *repose* to the spirit" (*Cather*). *Repose* is also used in aesthetics and art criticism for a principle that is opposed usually to that of motion or action: sometimes the term implies a flawless harmony of colors, hues, or tones or a harmonious disposition of parts, so that the whole rests the eye (or ear) and satisfies the mind (as, "The *repose* of classical art, not in sculpture alone, is gone from our ideals"—*S. Alexander*), but at other times it suggests rather the absence of any straining for effect or of any signs of a difference between that which is attempted (or suggested) and that which is achieved (as, "the new tower [of Chartres Cathedral] is a little wanting in *repose* for a tower whose business is to counterpoise the very classic lines of the old one"—*H. Adams*). **Relaxation** may imply rest that comes from diversion or recreation but, in the sense here stressed, it implies either a releasing of the tension that keeps muscles taut and fit for work or the mind keyed up to the processes of clear and prolonged thinking, or a physical and mental slackening that finally induces repose. "[Amusements] catering to those who wish *relaxation* from analysis—to the tired scientist, and the fagged philologist and the weary man of business" (*Babbitt*). "The hours of the day at which people can work under highest tension, the proportion of pressure and *relaxation* conducive to a maximum output" (*Grandgent*). "Now and then came *relaxation* and lassitude, but never release. The war towered over him like a vigilant teacher" (*H. G. Wells*). **Leisure** implies exemption from labor imposed upon one by a trade or profession, by duties, etc.: it may apply to the hours in which one is not engaged in one's daily work, or to the period in which one is on vacation, or to the entire time of a person who is not compelled to earn his living; as, to have little *leisure* for reading; he looked forward to the prospect of a full month of *leisure;* those who lead lives of *leisure*. *Leisure*, therefore, stresses freedom from compulsion, or routine, or continuous work: it usually suggests not freedom from activity but the freedom to determine one's activities. "Labor is doing what we must; *leisure* is doing what we like; *rest* is doing nothing whilst our bodies and minds are recovering from their fatigue" (*Shaw*). "I cannot include under the pleasant name of '*leisure*' those activities that are carried on systematically after business hours. Very soon they become things that *must* be done" (*S. M. Crothers*). **Ease** (see also READINESS) stresses exemption from toil, but it also implies a freedom from that which worries or disturbs and from that which demands physical or mental activity. In contrast to *leisure* it implies rest and repose: in addition it suggests either complete relaxation of mind and body or a state of mind that finds no attraction in work or activity; as, "lasting *ease*, Elysian quiet, without toil or strife" (*Wordsworth*); "all day I sit in idleness, while to and fro About me thy serene, grave servants go; And I am weary of my lonely *ease*" (*Millay*). But *ease* may also imply absence of strain of any sort, especially mental or nervous strain, rather than freedom from toil; as, "She had never been quite at her *ease* with him" (*Dickens*); "an able one...not only devoted, but resourceful and intelligent, one who would be at his *ease* with all sorts of men" (*Cather*). **Comfort** differs from all the other words of this group in carrying little, if any, suggestion of freedom from toil: it applies rather to a state of mind induced by relief from all that strains or inconveniences or causes pain, disquiet, or discontent. Positively it suggests perfect well-being and a feeling of quiet enjoyment or content; as, "[a life] of *ease* and *comfort*" (*Cather*); he had not known *comfort* for many years. "He had bought for himself out of all the wealth streaming through his fingers neither adulation nor love, neither splendour nor *comfort*" (*Conrad*).

Ana. Intermitting *or* intermission, suspending *or* suspension, deferring (see corresponding verbs at DEFER): stillness, quietness *or* quiet, silentness *or* silence (see corresponding adjectives at STILL): calmness *or* calm, tranquillity, serenity (see corresponding adjectives at CALM).

rest, *n.*[2] *Remainder, residue, residuum, remains, leavings, relics, balance, remnant.

Ana. *Excess, superfluity, surplus, surplusage, overplus.

restful. Reposeful, *comfortable, cozy, snug, easy.

Ana. *Soft, gentle, mild, lenient: *still, quiet, silent: placid, peaceful, *calm, serene, tranquil.

restitution. Amends, redress, *reparation, indemnity.

Ana. Repayment, recompense, reimbursement, requital (see corresponding verbs at PAY).

restive. 1 *Contrary, perverse, balky, froward, wayward.

Ana. Intractable, *unruly, ungovernable, refractory: *obstinate, stubborn, mulish, stiff-necked, pigheaded.

2 Restless, *impatient, nervous, unquiet, uneasy, fidgety, skittish, feverish, hectic, jumpy, jittery.

Ana. See those at RESTLESS.

restless. Restive, *impatient, nervous, unquiet, uneasy, fidgety, skittish, feverish, hectic, jumpy, jittery.

Ana. *Fitful, spasmodic: *inconstant, capricious, unstable, fickle: agitated, disquieted, perturbed, discomposed (see DISCOMPOSE).

restorative. **Restorative, alterative, tonic** are synonymous terms in medicine, denoting an agent that tends to restore a person to normal health or vigor. **Restorative** may be used generally, but it is most often applied to a substance, such as smelling salts or adrenalin, that has a rapid action in restoring a person to consciousness, as after fainting, apparent drowning, or the like. **Alterative** is applied to a medicine or treatment prescribed for building up the body, especially after an illness. An *alterative* acts gradually, having a favorable effect upon the general processes of nutrition and repair in the body, but not having a demonstrable effect on any particular organ. Typical *alteratives* are iron, mercury compounds, and cod-liver oil. **Tonic** is applied to an agent, usually a medicine, that gradually restores normal vigor to the body or to one of its organs or parts, weakened, as by disease or overexertion, and impaired in its normal functioning. Certain medicines, such as compounds of iron or arsenic, as well as exercise, cold baths, and other physical agents, are general tonics. Sometimes a tonic has a specific action; thus, strychnine is a nerve *tonic*.

restore. *Renew, refresh, redintegrate, rejuvenate, renovate, refurbish.

Ana. Save, reclaim, redeem, *rescue: reform, revise, amend (see CORRECT, *v.*): *recover, regain, retrieve, recoup, recruit.

restrain. **Restrain, curb, snaffle, check, bridle, inhibit** come into comparison when they mean to hold a person or thing back from doing something or from going too far in doing something. **Restrain,** the most comprehensive of these terms, may imply the intent either to prevent entirely or to keep under control or within bounds, but it usually suggests the operation of some force, authority, or motive that is so strong or compelling that it achieves the desired end. "Pleasant, excited by the strangeness of the occasion, could not be *restrained;* she was bubbling over with information" (*Deland*). "To produce in the child the same respect for the garden that *restrains* the grown-ups from picking wantonly" (*B. Russell*). "A law of 17 B.C. gave a legal position to slaves informally manumitted and made their children free-born, but drastically *restrained* their power to acquire and bequeath property" (*Buchan*). **Curb** suggests the use of a method comparable to that of a curb (i.e., a chain or strap) which, when pulled back by a rider, draws tightly against the lower jaw of a speeding or unruly horse and brings him under control: it therefore differs from *restrain* in implying either a sharp, drastic method that produces its effect immediately (as, "He's often been on the point of blurting out with it, but I've *curbed* him"—*Cather*) or the influence of something that serves to shackle one or to prevent a thing's free or efficient operation (as, "Authority *curbs* the will power of the individual" —*C. W. Eliot;* "The sober scientific method does not stimulate the imagination; it *curbs* it"—*S. M. Crothers*). **Snaffle** suggests a method comparable to the use of a snaffle (a bit which produces a lighter effect than a curb): the term therefore implies a restraint that guides rather than brings one summarily under control; as, "The guilt and terror that thy sins will *snaffle* thee with" (*Bunyan*). **Check** (as here considered: see also ARREST, 1) often implies the use of a method suggestive of a check rein (or check) of a horse's harness which pulls up a horse's head and slows up his speed or holds him still (as, "Alice... soon *checked* her [horse's] speed; and the white horse subsided to a walk"—*Shaw;* "Father Latour *checked* his impetuous vicar"—*Cather*) but it may carry implications derived from other senses of the noun, such as those of delaying or impeding motion or progress (as, "the ship, hauled up so close as to *check* her way"—*Conrad;* "a spot where her footsteps were no longer *checked* by a hedgerow"—*G. Eliot*) or of attacking or defeating some force or influence (as, "endeavour to *check* that little something, bordering on conceit and impertinence, which your lady possesses"—*Austen;* "the ambition of churchmen ...disciplined and *checked* by the broader interests of the Church"—*H. Adams*). **Bridle** (as here compared: see also STRUT) also derives its implications from the use of a part of a horse's harness, in this case the one called a *bridle* and consisting of all the parts of the headgear by means of which a horse is guided or controlled. The verb carries a stronger implication of keeping under one's control by subduing, moderating, or holding in than does *curb* or *check:* it is used chiefly in respect to strong or vehement emotions or desires; as, to *bridle* one's wrath; to *bridle* one's curiosity; he could no longer *bridle* his passion. **Inhibit** (for fuller treatment see FORBID) is a synonym of these terms only in its current psychological and psychiatric sense, where it implies the repression or suppression of certain emotions, desires, thoughts, or the like (see SUPPRESS) by the curbing influence of one's conscience, religious principles, the social conventions of one's class, or the like; as, he blamed his upbringing and its *inhibiting* influence for his failure as a poet.

Ana. *Arrest, check, interrupt: abstain, *refrain, forbear: *hinder, impede, obstruct, block.
Ant. Impel: incite: activate: abandon (*oneself*).

restraint. Constraint, compulsion, *force, coercion, duress, violence.
Ana. Curbing, checking, inhibiting (see RESTRAIN): hindering, impeding, obstructing, blocking (see HINDER).
Ant. Incitement: liberty.

restrict. *Limit, circumscribe, confine.
Ana. Bind, *tie: *contract, shrink: *restrain, curb, check.
Con. *Extend, lengthen: *expand, amplify, swell: enlarge, *increase.

result. Consequence, *effect, aftereffect, event, aftermath, issue, outcome, upshot, sequel.
Ana. Concluding *or* conclusion, ending *or* end, closing *or* close, termination (see corresponding verbs at CLOSE): *product, production.
Con. *Origin, source, root: *cause, determinant, antecedent.

ret. *Soak, saturate, drench, steep, impregnate, sog, sop, waterlog.

retain. *Keep, keep back, detain, withhold, reserve, hold back.
Ana. *Have, hold, own, possess, enjoy: *save, preserve, conserve.
Con. *Discard, shed, cast: *relinquish, surrender, abandon, yield: *abdicate, resign: *abjure, renounce, forswear, recant, retract.

retaliation. **Retaliation, reprisal, revenge, vengeance, retribution** agree in meaning both the act of inflicting or the intent to inflict injury in return for injury, and the injury so inflicted. **Retaliation** implies a return of like for like, commonly but not exclusively a return of evil for evil; as, raid after raid occurred, each in *retaliation* for one perpetrated by the other side; to be so astonished by a blow as to lose the opportunity for *retaliation;* he is never satisfied until he inflicts a *retaliation* for every injury, real or fancied. **Reprisal** applies specifically to an act of retaliation indulged in for the sake of gaining redress of a grievance or of compelling an enemy or antagonist to cease unlawful acts. The term in legal use commonly, but not invariably, implies the seizure of property by force either as a means of getting compensation for one's own injuries or of inflicting punishment: when used in reference to nations, it may or may not imply an act of war; as, in *reprisal* for the blockade of her ports, Germany engaged in a vigorous submarine campaign against British shipping; air raids on Berlin in *reprisal* for German air raids on London; to make *reprisals* on a neighbor's orchard for the stealing of one's fruit by his children. "Lest Mr. Raycie's mysterious faculty of hearing what was said behind his back should bring sudden *reprisals* on the venerable lady" (*E. Wharton*). **Revenge** usually carries a strong implication of vindictiveness or, sometimes, of justifiable anger that is lacking in *retaliation:* the term therefore more often applies to the strong desire or intent to inflict injury than to the fulfillment of that desire or intent (as, "A man that studieth *revenge* keeps his own wounds green"—*Bacon*), or more pointedly implies the gratification of that desire than the actual infliction of injury (as, he had his *revenge;* "*revenge* is sweet"—*Old Proverb;* " 'Tis sweet to love; but when with scorn we meet, *Revenge* supplies the loss with joys as great"—*G. Granville*). **Vengeance** may imply the avenging of a wrong done to oneself or another by measures that punish the offender so that he suffers in the same degree as his victim, but the term is also applicable to the act or acts committed in gratification of one's revenge; as, "*Vengeance* is mine; I will repay, saith the Lord. Therefore if thine enemy hunger, feed him; if he thirst, give him drink" (*Romans* xii. 19–20); "There was a time in my imprisonment, when my desire for *vengeance* was unbearable" (*Dickens*); "The burning of a rick is an act of *vengeance*, and a ploughman out of employ is a vengeful animal" (*Meredith*). **Retribution** also applies chiefly to a punishment inflicted in return, but it carries less suggestion of a grievance on the part of a victim, and a far stronger implication than any of the others of the operation of strict justice: in fact, the word is often qualified by *just, deserved*, or the like, and the punishment is seldom meted out by the victim, but by a higher power. Therefore it commonly implies merited punishment brought upon oneself, usually, though far from always, by an infraction of law, especially of a law or the laws of God or of nature. "He only retained his boozing dyspeptic brother Hippias at Raynham, in order to exhibit to his son the woful *retribution* Nature wreaked upon a life of indulgence" (*Meredith*). "To be left alone And face to face with my own crime, had been Just *retribution*" (*Longfellow*).
Ana. Punishment, disciplining *or* discipline, correcting *or* correction (see corresponding verbs at PUNISH): requital, recompensing *or* recompense, indemnification, repayment (see corresponding verbs at PAY).

retard. *Delay, slow, slacken, detain.
Ana. Reduce, lessen, *decrease: *arrest, check, interrupt: clog, fetter, *hamper: balk, baffle (see FRUSTRATE).
Ant. Accelerate: advance, further.

reticent. *Silent, reserved, uncommunicative, taciturn, secretive, close, close-lipped, close-mouthed, tight-lipped.
Ana. Restrained, inhibited, curbed, checked (see RESTRAIN): discreet, prudent (see under PRUDENCE).
Ant. Frank. — *Con.* Candid, open, plain (see FRANK).

retire. Withdraw, *go, leave, depart, quit, scram, clear out.
Ana. *Recede, retreat: recoil, *rebound, resile: *relinquish, yield, surrender, abandon.

retort, *n.* Rejoinder, answer, reply, response. See under ANSWER, *v.*, 1.

retort, *v.* Rejoin, reply, *answer, respond.
Ana. *Retaliation, reprisal, revenge: repartee (see WIT).

retract. **1** Retrograde, back, *recede, retreat, crawfish.
Ant. Protract.
2 Recant, *abjure, renounce, forswear.
Ana. Eliminate, *exclude, suspend, rule out.

retreat, *n.* *Shelter, cover, refuge, asylum, sanctuary, ark.
Ana. *Harbor, haven, port: safety, security (see corresponding adjectives at SAFE): seclusion, *solitude.

retreat, *v.* *Recede, retrograde, back, retract, crawfish.
Ana. Withdraw, retire, depart, *go: *recoil, shrink, quail.

retrench. Curtail, abridge, *shorten, abbreviate.
Ana. *Decrease, lessen, reduce, diminish.

retribution. Reprisal, vengeance, revenge, *retaliation.
Ana. *Reparation, redress, amends, restitution: visitation, tribulation, *trial, affliction.
Con. *Mercy, clemency, lenity, grace: forgiveness, pardoning *or* pardon, remitting *or* remission (see corresponding verbs at EXCUSE).

retrieve. *Recover, regain, recoup, recruit.
Ana. Amend, remedy, redress, reform (see CORRECT, *v.*): repair, *mend, rebuild.
Ant. Lose.

retrograde, *adj.* *Backward, retrogressive, regressive.
Ana. Reversed, inverted (see REVERSE, *v.*): relapsing, lapsing, backsliding, recidivating (see LAPSE, *v.*).

retrograde, *v.* *Recede, retreat, back, crawfish, retract.
Ana. *Return, revert: *reverse, invert: relapse, *lapse, backslide, recidivate.

retrogressive. Regressive, retrograde, *backward.
Ana. Reversing, inverting (see REVERSE, *v.*): receding, retreating, retrograding (see RECEDE).
Ant. Progressive. — *Con.* Advancing, furthering, forwarding (see ADVANCE, *v.*): improving, bettering (see IMPROVE).

return, *v.* **Return, revert, recur, recrudesce** come into comparison when they mean to go or come back, as to a person, place, or condition. The same distinctions in implications and connotations are evident in their corresponding nouns **return, reversion, recurrence, recrudescence. Return** is the ordinary term of this group: it usually implies either a going back to the place or person from which it started (as, "They *returned* as wolves *return* to cover, satisfied with the slaughter that they had done"—*Kipling;* "White surf rushing in and *returning* immediately"—*Jefferies;* the sickness of a child caused their sudden *return;* there will be no *return* to good health, we fear), or it may imply, especially in the case of the noun, a coming back to the place or condition where it had formerly been or where it belongs in its turn (as, to look forward to the *return* of spring; he was greeted with enthusiasm on his *return* home; he *returns* here tomorrow; we do not expect any *return* of the fever). **Revert** and **reversion** (for specific sense, as applied to a return to an ancestral type or quality, see REVERSION, 2) most frequently imply a going back to a previous, often an original, state or condition, especially after the person or thing has advanced or progressed; as, to *revert* (or a *reversion*) to barbarism; "the conception of a lordly splendid destiny for the human race, to which we are false when we *revert* to wars and other atavistic follies" (*B. Russell*). Both terms, however, are often used when a return after an interruption is implied, as to a previous owner, to a previous topic, to a previous decision, or the like; as, when the lease expires, the property *reverts* to the lessor; to *revert* (or a *reversion*) to a topic previously discussed. "First Mr. Britling thought that he would not pass between these two, then he decided that he would hurry up and do so, then he *reverted* to his former decision" (*H. G. Wells*). The terms may also imply merely a turning back to the next in line, as for a promotion, a scholarship, an office, or the like; as, when Smith found himself unable to accept the fellowship, it *reverted* to the next best candidate. **Recur** and **recurrence** imply a return (sometimes repeated returns at more or less regular intervals) of something that has previously happened, that has previously affected a person or thing, that has previously been in one's mind, that has been previously known or experienced, or the like; as, there will be no *recurrence* of this dream if you clear your mind of fears; "The relapses [into old ways]...*recur* not only from effort to effort in the case of the individual, but from generation to generation in the case of the race" (*Shaw*); "Incessant *recurrence* without variety breeds tedium; the overiterated becomes the monotonous" (*Lowes*); "Lydia, suddenly *recurring* to their former subject, said..." (*Shaw*); "He had forgotten it [a cynical novel he had once read] when confronted by the author, whose face was not marked by cynicism; but it *recurred* to him now" (*Arch. Marshall*). **Recrudesce** and the far more frequent **recrudescence** imply a return to life or activity: usually the terms imply a breaking out again of something that has been repressed, suppressed, kept under control, or the like; as, boils that *recrudesce* from time to time; the *recrudescence* of an epidemic of influenza; "a *recrudescence* of Ferdinand's power" (*Belloc*). "We are not here concerned with the question whether this *recrudescence* of energy that has communicated itself to verse is the death throes of a social order or the birth-pangs of a new one" (*Day Lewis*).
Ana. *Advert, revert: *turn, rotate, revolve: restore, *renew: *recover, regain: reverberate, repercuss, *rebound.

return, *n.* Reversion, recurrence, recrudescence. See under RETURN, *v.*

reveal, *v.* **Reveal, discover, disclose, divulge, tell, betray, bewray** come into comparison when they mean to make known that which has been or should be concealed or is intended to be kept concealed. **Reveal** implies a setting forth or exhibition by or as if by lifting a curtain that veils or obscures. In its earliest and still not uncommon sense, it implies supernatural communication by means of vision, inspiration, or the like, of truths beyond or above the range of human sight or reason; as, "Sacred laws...unto him *revealed* in vision" (*Spenser*); "There is a God in heaven that *revealeth* secrets, and maketh known to the king Nebuchadnezzar what shall be in the latter days" (*Daniel* ii. 28); "in laws divine, Deduced by reason, or to faith *revealed*" (*Wordsworth*); cf. *revealed* religion. But the term may also imply an imparting by a human being such as a seer or a poet whose vision penetrates into that which cannot be seen or understood by the ordinary man (as, "The artist, the man of genius, raises this veil and *reveals* Nature to us"—*H. Ellis;* "he must feel as a man what he *reveals* as a poet"—*Day Lewis*) or as a person in possession of a secret (as, "His mind...vibrating between the wish to *reveal* himself to her [as her father], and the policy of leaving well alone" —*Hardy*). In somewhat less strict, but nevertheless correct use, *reveal* may carry no suggestions of an intentional communication, but rather an affording of signs or other evidence from which the truth may be inferred; as, "The paradox of both distrusting and burdening government *reveals* the lack of a conscious philosophy of politics" (*Frankfurter*). **Discover** (as here compared: see also DISCOVER, 2; INVENT) implies an exposing to view by or as if by uncovering: the term usually suggests that the thing discovered has been hidden from sight or perception, and is not, as often in the case of *reveal*, in itself beyond the range of human vision or comprehension. "Go draw aside the curtains and *discover* The several caskets to this noble prince" (*Shak.*). "It is a test which we may apply to all figure-painters—a test which will often *discover* the secret of unsatisfactory design" (*Binyon*). **Disclose** is more often used in current English than *discover*, which seems slightly archaic in the sense in which it has here been considered; as, "The door opened and *disclosed* Gerald" (*Bennett*); "The stress of passion often *discloses* an aspect of the personality completely ignored till then by its closest intimates" (*Conrad*). More often, however, *disclose* implies the making known of something that has not been announced or has previously been kept secret; as, the court refused to *disclose* its decision before the proper time. "The confessions of St. Austin and Rousseau *disclose* the secrets of the human heart" (*Gibbon*). "The Bishop did not *disclose* his objective, and the Vicar asked no questions" (*Cather*). **Divulge** differs little from *disclose* in this latter sense except in often carrying a suggestion of impropriety or of a breach of confidence (as, "Horace...declares in sober sadness that he would not for all the world get into a boat with a man who had *divulged* the Eleusinian mysteries"—*Cowper*) or in implying more or less publicity (as, "Legally the execution of de Thou was justified, because he knew of the conspiracy and did not *divulge* it"—*Belloc;*

"it seemed to me an occasion to *divulge* my real ideas and hopes for the Commonwealth"—*L. P. Smith*). **Tell** (as here compared: see also COUNT, 1) may come very close to *divulge* in the sense of making known something which should be kept a secret (as, gentlemen never *tell*) but more often, it implies the giving of necessary or helpful information, especially on request or demand (as, to *tell* one's name or one's intentions; "Why didst thou not *tell* me that she was thy wife?"—*Genesis* xii. 18). **Betray** (as here compared: see also DECEIVE) often implies a divulging of a secret, but it carries either a stronger and more obvious suggestion of a breach of faith (as, "[he] had... written no letters that would *betray* the conspiracy he had entered into against Steve"—*S. Anderson*) or of a disclosure, as through signs or appearances, against one's will (as, "Only May Welland *betrayed*, by a heightened colour...a sense of the gravity of the situation"—*E. Wharton;* "Life moves on, through whatever deserts, and one must compose oneself to meet it, never *betraying* one's soul"—*R. Macaulay*). **Bewray,** an archaic term, carries a slighter implication of intentional secrecy than any of the other terms, but it does imply a making known that which was not known or not clearly recognized; as, "Write down thy mind, *bewray* thy meaning so" (*Shak.*); "thy speech *bewrayeth* thee" (*Matthew* xxvi. 73).

Ana. Impart, *communicate: *suggest, adumbrate, shadow: *declare, announce, publish.

Ant. Conceal.

revelation. Revelation, vision, apocalypse, prophecy are here compared in senses derived mainly from their Scriptural uses and employed not only by religious writers but also by poets, critics, and others. In this use they agree in meaning a (or the) disclosure by divine or preternatural means of something not apparent to the senses nor comprehensible by the unaided reason. **Revelation,** in this sense, is often specifically applied to the religious ideas transmitted by writers of books regarded as sacred, or divinely inspired, especially the Bible; by extension, therefore, it has come to mean a body of knowledge distinguishable from that attained by the normal human processes of observation, experiment, and reason; as, the truths of science and the truths of *revelation*. "'Tis *revelation* satisfies all doubts, Explains all mysteries, except her own" (*Cowper*). "*Revelation* differs from natural knowledge, he [Spinoza] says, not by being more divine or more certain than natural knowledge, but by being conveyed in a different way" (*Arnold*). **Vision** implies, as *revelation* does not, a seeing of something not corporeally present; often, especially in mystical and poetic language, it suggests a profound intuition of something not comprehensible to the ordinary or unaided reason; commonly, therefore, it implies the operation of some agent, such as the Holy Spirit, or the gift (or accession) of some inexplicable power not attributable to all men, such as genius, poetic rapture, or the like. *Vision*, however, unlike *revelation*, does not necessarily imply that what is seen or realized is true, or of value to oneself or others. "And some had *visions*, as they stood on chairs, And sang of Jacob, and the golden stairs" (*V. Lindsay*). "Dante's...imagination....is visual in the sense that he lived in an age in which men still saw *visions*.... We have nothing but dreams, and we have forgotten that seeing *visions*—a practice now relegated to the aberrant and uneducated—was once a more significant, interesting, and disciplined kind of dreaming" (*T. S. Eliot*). **Apocalypse** is, in its etymological sense, the equivalent of *revelation;* it is, in the Douay Version, the designation of the New Testament book called *Revelation* in the Authorized Version. It also specifically denotes a type of sacred book (of which the Book of Revelation is an example) usually of unknown or pseudonymous authorship, which was common in Jewish and Christian literature in the centuries immediately preceding and following the birth of Christ and which presented a vision of the future in which the enemies of Israel or of Christianity would be defeated and God's justice and righteousness prevail. In its modern general application, *apocalypse* usually denotes a vision of the future, when all the mysteries of life shall be explained and good shall magnificently triumph over evil. The noun and, still more, its adjective **apocalyptic** (*or* **apocalyptical**) often carry one or more connotations as various as those of a spectacular splendor or magnitude suggestive of the Book of Revelation or, especially in present use, suggestive of wild and extravagant dreams of the visionary or passionate reformer; as, "the *apocalyptic* imagination of Michelangelo" (*N. Y. Times*). "Slowly as out of the heavens, with *apocalyptical* splendors... Sank the broad red sun" (*Longfellow*). "These problems [race problems], which the Austrian monarchy sought to solve by tolerance, do not concern the *apocalyptic* dreamer [Hitler]" (*D. Thompson*). **Prophecy** is now rarely found in its original meaning except in learned use and in some religious use. Its occasional and permissible connotation of the prediction of future events has been emphasized to such an extent that its historical and etymologically correct implications have almost been lost, with the result that the word in older writings is often misinterpreted. *Prophecy* in this strict sense implies a commission to speak for another, especially and commonly for God or a god. It therefore further implies that the prophet has been the recipient of divine communications or revelations, or that he has been granted a vision or visions. "And though I have the gift of *prophecy*, and understand all mysteries, and all knowledge...and have not charity, I am nothing" (*1 Corinthians* xiii. 2). "The word of *prophecy*, those truths divine, Which make that heaven, if thou desire it, thine" (*Cowper*).

Ant. Adumbration.

revenant. *Apparition, phantasm, phantom, wraith, fetch, ghost, spirit, specter, shade, spook, haunt.

revenge, *v.* *Avenge.

Ana. Requite, recompense, repay (see PAY, *v.*): vindicate, defend, justify (see MAINTAIN).

revenge, *n.* Vengeance, *retaliation, retribution, reprisal.

Ana. *Reparation, redress, amends: requital, recompensing *or* recompense, repayment (see corresponding verbs at PAY).

revengeful. *Vindictive, vengeful.

Ana. Implacable, relentless, unrelenting, merciless, *grim: inexorable, obdurate, adamant, *inflexible.

reverberate. Repercuss, *rebound, recoil, resile.

Ana. *Return, revert, recur.

revere. Revere, reverence, venerate, worship, adore agree in meaning to regard with profound respect and honor. All imply a recognition of the exalted character of that which is so respected and honored, but they differ mainly in regard to their objects and to the feelings and acts which they connote. Their differences in implication extend to their corresponding nouns, **reverence** (for both verbs *revere* and *reverence*), **veneration, worship,** and **adoration.** One **reveres** not only persons who are entitled to respect and honor but also things which are associated with such persons; the word commonly connotes tenderness of feeling and deference. "That makes her lov'd at home, *rever'd* abroad" (*Burns*). "Islands and cities which he *revered* as the cradle of civilization" (*Buchan*). "Towards Johnson...his [Boswell's] feeling was not sycophancy, which is the lowest, but *reverence*, which is the highest of human feelings" (*Carlyle*). One **reverences** things more often than persons, especially things, such as laws and customs, which have an intrinsic claim to respect or are commonly regarded as inviolable. "We *reverence* tradition, but we will not be fettered by it" (*Inge*). "Sincerity and simplicity! if I could only say how I *reverence* them" (*A. C. Benson*). One **venerates** persons as well as things that are regarded as holy, sacred, or sacrosanct because of character, associations, or age; as, to *venerate* saints and heroes; to *venerate* the relics of a saint. "For Socrates he [Gray] had an almost religious *veneration*" (*N. Nicholls*). In strictest use, one **worships** only a divine being, God, a god, or a thing deified, when one pays homage by word or ceremonial; as, churches are buildings in which God is *worshiped;* pagans *worship* idols, the sun, and the stars. In somewhat looser, but still correct, use, *worship* implies any kind of veneration that involves the offering of homage or the attribution of an especially exalted character, whether the object is a divine being or not. "There is a difference between admiring a poet and *worshipping* at a shrine" (*A. Repplier*). "In his calm, unexcited way, he *worships* success" (*R. Macaulay*). As here compared (see also ADORE, 2), one **adores,** as one *worships* (in the strictest sense), a divine being. *Worship,* however, usually suggests the group approach, and *adore* the personal approach, to deity. *Adore* therefore commonly implies love and the performance of individual acts of worship, such as obeisance, prostration, prayer, and the like. "And [the devil] said to him [Jesus]: All these will I give thee, if falling down thou wilt *adore* me" (*Matthew* iv. 9 [*D. V.*]). "Quiet as a Nun Breathless with *adoration*" (*Wordsworth*).

Ana. Esteem, respect, regard, admire (see under REGARD, *n.*): cherish, prize, value, treasure, *appreciate.

Ant. Flout.

reverence, *n.* **1** *Honor, homage, deference, obeisance.

Ana. Piety, devotion, fealty, loyalty, *fidelity: esteem, respect, *regard, admiration.

2 Veneration, worship, adoration. See under REVERE.

Ana. Fervor, ardor, zeal, *passion: devoutness, piousness, religiousness (see corresponding adjectives at DEVOUT).

3 Reverence, awe, fear come into comparison only when they denote the emotion inspired by something which arouses one's deep respect or veneration. **Reverence** distinctively implies a recognition of the sacredness or inviolability of the person or thing which stimulates the emotion; as, to have *reverence* for the law; "a profound *reverence* for and fidelity to the truth" (*Mencken*); "Richelieu's *reverence* for the throne was constant" (*Belloc*); "treating him almost with *reverence*" (*D. H. Lawrence*); "Like you, I feel a *reverence* for this place. Wherever humanity has made that hardest of all starts and lifted itself out of mere brutality, is a sacred spot" (*Cather*). **Awe,** in all of its shades of meaning, has for its fundamental implications a sense of being overwhelmed or overcome by a person's or thing's superiority or greatness and either an inability to speak in his (or its) presence or to come near to him (or it). Otherwise, it may suggest any one of several widely different reactions, such as adoration, profound reverence, wonder, terror, submissiveness, abashment, and the like; as, to be filled with *awe;* to stand in *awe* of one's teachers. "My heart standeth in *awe* of thy word" (*Psalms* cxix. 161). "Make me as the poorest vassal is That doth with *awe* and terror kneel to it [the crown as symbol of sovereignty]!" (*Shak.*). "He is a great man of the city, without fear, but with the most abject *awe* of the aristocracy" (*T. S. Eliot*). **Fear** (for the more familiar sense see FEAR, 1) occurs, in the sense here considered, chiefly in religious use; as, to put the *fear* of God in the hearts of men. In this sense, and as referred chiefly to the Supreme Being as its cause, it implies awed recognition of his power and majesty and, usually, reverence for his law. "And [those] walking in the *fear* of the Lord, and in the comfort of the Holy Ghost, were multiplied" (*Acts* ix. 31). "And calm with *fear* of God's divinity" (*Wordsworth*).

reverence, *v.* Venerate, worship, adore, *revere.

Ana. Love, enjoy (see LIKE): esteem, respect, regard, admire (see under REGARD, *n.*).

reverse, *n.* *Converse, obverse.

Ana. Back, rear, posterior (see corresponding adjectives at POSTERIOR): opposite, contrary (see under OPPOSITE, *adj.*).

reverse, *v.* **Reverse, transpose, invert** agree in meaning to change to the contrary or opposite side or position. **Reverse** is the most general of these terms, implying a change to the opposite not only in side or position but also in direction, order, sequence, relation, bearing; thus, to *reverse* a coin is to turn it upside down; to *reverse* a process is to follow the opposite order of sequence; to *reverse* a judgment is to change a previous judgment to another that is contrary to it; to *reverse* a policy is to change a policy so that it will have a contrary trend or induce a distinctly different result; to *reverse* a garment or part of a garment is to turn it inside out; to *reverse* the direction of a locomotive is to make it go backward instead of forward; so, "having his shield *reversed*" (*Scott*); "Half were put on a diet of unpolished rice; half on polished. The latter group came down with beriberi. Then the diets were *reversed*" (*V. Heiser*). **Transpose** implies a change in position, usually by reversing the order of two or more units such as letters or words, or by an exchange of position; as, the printer was instructed to *transpose* the letters *sr* in the word set up as *vesre;* if the term b in the equation a+b=c is *transposed* (i.e., transferred to the other side of the equation) the result obtained is a=c−b. But *transpose* often, especially in grammar, anatomy, and the like, implies merely a change in the natural order or position; as, he frequently *transposes* words for the sake of effect; a *transposed* heart. **Invert** literally implies a change from one side to another chiefly by turning upside down but occasionally, especially in surgery, by turning inside out or outside in; as, to *invert* a tumbler; to *invert* a comma; to *invert* the uterus; the photograph of the pond showed the *inverted* images of the trees on its bank. In its secondary senses it approaches *reverse,* but applies within narrower limits; as, to *invert* the order of words in a sentence; to *invert* the relation of cause and effect; an *inverted* chord. "The custom...to *invert* now and then the order of the class, so as to make the highest and lowest boys change places" (*T. Moore*).

Ana. *Overturn, overset, upset, capsize.

reversion. **1** Return, recurrence, recrudescence. See under RETURN, *v.*

2 Reversion, atavism, throwback come into comparison as meaning return to an ancestral type or an instance of such return. The same distinctions in implications and connotations are evident in the adjectival forms **reversionary** (*or* **reversive**), **atavistic. Reversion** and **reversionary** (occasionally **reversive**) are the technical terms in the biological sciences for any mutation marked by the reappearance of an ancestral character or characters in an individual, or for the organism or the individual that manifests such a mutation. "We could not have told, whether these characters in our domestic breeds were *reversions* or only analogous variations" (*Darwin*). "Similar mutations are paired together [in the illustration]; divergent or *reversionary* individuals are eliminated" (*J. A. Thomson*). **Atavism** and **atavistic** are widely used both in general and in technical English. Their implication of reversion to a remote rather than to an immediate ancestral type is so strong that some biologists use them not as synonyms of *reversion* and *reversionary* but as far more specific terms implying the reappearance of remote, even primitive, characters after a long period of latency. Often, in general use, this connotation of primitiveness carries with it a suggestion of barbarism or degeneration. "Some mysterious *atavism*—some strange recurrence to a primitive past" (*Bagehot*). "Those who had made England what it was had done so by sticking where they were, regardless of their own *atavistic* instincts, which might have led them back to France or Denmark" (*Van W. Brooks*). **Throwback** is preferred to *reversion* or *atavism* by those who seek a picturesque or more colloquial word. It is, however, chiefly applied to the concrete instance, usually being avoided as an abstract term; as, the youngest son could not be explained except as a *throwback* to his pioneering ancestors.

Ana. Relapse, lapse, backsliding, recidivation, recidivism (see corresponding verbs at LAPSE).

reversionary, reversive. Atavistic (see under REVERSION).

revert. 1 *Return, recur, recrudesce.

Ana. *Recede, retreat, retrograde, back: *lapse, relapse, backslide, recidivate.

2 *Advert.

Ana. *Return, recur.

review, *n.* 1 *Criticism, critique, blurb, puff.

2 *Journal, periodical, magazine, organ, newspaper.

revile. Vituperate, rail, berate, rate, upbraid, *scold, tonguelash, jaw, bawl out, wig.

Ana. Vilify, calumniate, *malign, traduce, defame, asperse, slander, libel: *execrate, objurgate, curse.

Ant. Laud. — *Con.* *Praise, extol, eulogize, acclaim.

revise. *Correct, rectify, emend, remedy, redress, amend, reform.

Ana. *Improve, better, ameliorate: *change, alter, modify.

revivalist. *Missionary, evangelist, apostle.

revolt, *n.* Revolution, uprising, insurrection, *rebellion, mutiny, Putsch.

Ana. Insubordination, seditiousness *or* sedition, factiousness, contumaciousness *or* contumacy (see corresponding adjectives at INSUBORDINATE).

revolting. *Offensive, loathsome, repulsive, repugnant.

Ana. *Horrible, horrid, horrific: repellent, distasteful, obnoxious, abhorrent (see REPUGNANT): odious, *hateful, abominable.

revolution. *Rebellion, uprising, revolt, insurrection, mutiny, Putsch.

Ana. Overthrowing *or* overthrow, subverting *or* subversion, upsetting *or* upset, overturning *or* overturn (see corresponding verbs at OVERTURN): change, modification, alteration (see under CHANGE, *v.*).

revolve. 1 Weigh, excogitate, *consider, study, contemplate.

Ana. Reflect, deliberate, speculate, *think, reason, cogitate: *ponder, muse, meditate, ruminate.

2 *Turn, rotate, gyrate, circle, spin, whirl, twirl, wheel, eddy, swirl, pirouette.

Ana. *Swing, sway, oscillate, vibrate.

reward, *n.* *Premium, prize, award, meed, guerdon, bounty, bonus.

rhapsody. *Bombast, rant, fustian, rodomontade.

rhetorical. **Rhetorical, grandiloquent, magniloquent, aureate, flowery, euphuistic, bombastic** are here compared in the sense of emphasizing style, often, but not invariably, at the expense of thought. **Rhetorical** describes any style, discourse, passage, phrase, or word which, however skillfully constructed or chosen and however effective, impresses the reader or hearer as not natural or effortless, but the result of conscious endeavor to produce an effect; as, the *rhetorical* style of Cicero; the *rhetorical* perorations of Daniel Webster. "Burke catches your eye by *rhetorical* inversions" (*Quiller-Couch*). **Grandiloquent** suggests "tall" talking or writing; it is applicable not only to what is spoken but also to what is written and catches an oratorical tone; it frequently implies a pomposity or an attempt at eloquence that not only is out of keeping with the subject but approaches absurdity; as, a *grandiloquent* tribute. "I find in Johnson's books...a measured *grandiloquence*, stepping or rather stalking along in a very solemn way" (*Carlyle*). **Magniloquent** is not always distinguishable from *grandiloquent*, but in discriminating usage it more often suggests boastfulness or extravagance than an overreaching eloquence; as, the *magniloquent* utterances of the drunken Falstaff. "In his public lectures and speeches, to which the students flocked, he [Everett] let his fancy soar....That he was *magniloquent* they did not know. That he was theatrical, they did not care" (*Van W. Brooks*). **Aureate,** which is itself a rhetorical term in favor in the early Renaissance and revived by some modern critics of literature, implies excessive embellishment of style by figures of speech, high-sounding words, and the like; in ordinary language and in reference to writings which have no pretensions to literature the same quality is described by **flowery**; as, the *aureate* prose of the Elizabethans; the *flowery* style of many young, ambitious writers. **Euphuistic** describes the highly rhetorical and aureate style of John Lyly (1554?–1606), author of *Euphues, the Anatomy of Wit* and *Euphues and his England.* In extended use, it more often suggests extreme artificiality and a straining after effects that distract attention from the thought, rather than the affectation of elegance and the excessive use of alliteration, antithesis, similes, and the like, that characterized Lyly's prose, and are implied in *euphuistic* when used in its strict historical sense; as, in *Love's Labour's Lost,* Shakespeare burlesqued many affectations of language in his own time, most of which are now loosely described as *euphuistic.* **Bombastic** (derived from *bombast,* which originally meant cotton wool, or raw cotton, a use of which is for padding) always implies inflation or grandiosity of style. It suggests verbosity and grandiloquence rather than a straining for rhetorical effects. "These lines of Milton's:—Up to a hill anon his steps he reared From whose high top to ken the prospect round ....would be merely *bombastic* if the poet were starting to set forth how So-and-so climbed a hill for the view—just that, and nothing else" (*Quiller-Couch*).

Ana. Eloquent, articulate, *vocal, fluent, voluble, glib: florid, *ornate, flamboyant: *inflated, turgid, tumid, flatulent.

rhymer, rhymester *or* **rimer, rimester.** *Poet, versifier, poetaster, bard, minstrel, scop, gleeman, jongleur, troubadour, trouvère, minnesinger, scald.

rhythm, *n.* **Rhythm, meter** (*or* **metre**), **cadence,** as here compared, agree in meaning the more or less regular rise and fall (in intensity) of sounds that one associates chiefly with poetry and music. **Rhythm,** which of these three terms is the most inclusive and the widest in its range of application, always implies movement and flow as well as an agreeable succession of rising and falling sounds; it may or may not suggest regular alternation of these sounds, but it fundamentally implies the recurrence at fairly regular intervals of the accented or prolonged syllable in poetry or of the heavy beat or the strongly accented note in music, so that no matter how many unaccented or unstressed syllables or notes lie between these, the continuing up and down movement is strongly apparent to the senses. Consequently, *rhythm* is used not only in reference to speech sounds and musical tones ordered with relation to stress and time, but also to dancing, games, natural phenomena, and the like, where a comparable pulsing movement is apparent, and even to the arts of design, where fluctuations in line or pattern suggest a pulsing movement. "The loveliness, like the wavering, lovely *rhythms* of the sea, of W. B. Yeats, took her, as it took her whole generation, by storm" (*R. Macaulay*). "Even the style of Thoreau was to be tinged faintly here and there with the *rhythms* [of Carlyle]" (*Van W. Brooks*). "Every one learned music, dancing, and song. Therefore it is natural for them to regard *rhythm* and grace in all the actions of life" (*H. Ellis*). **Meter** implies the reduction of rhythm to system and measure. Poetry that has meter (in general, this is true of all poetry except free verse) has a definite rhythmical pattern which determines the typical foot (sometimes the arrangement of feet) in each verse and either the number of feet in every verse or, if a stanzaic pattern is implied, in each verse of a stanza; as, the epics of Homer and Vergil are written in the *meter* called dactylic hexameter; the revolt against *meter* in poetry in the late nineteenth and early twentieth centuries; prose may have *rhythm* but not *meter*. In music, *meter* implies the division of the rhythm into measures, all of which are uniform in number of beats or time units, and each of which begins with the heavily accented tone. **Cadence** (etymologically, a falling) is the least clearly fixed in meaning of these words. The term has often been used as though it were equal to *rhythm*, or sometimes to *meter*, especially when the reference is to poetry; as, "golden *cadence* of poesy" (*Shak.*). "Wit will shine Through the harsh *cadence* of a rugged line" (*Dryden*). "Poetry can never again become a popular art until the poet gives himself wholly to 'the *cadence* of consenting feet' " (*H. Read*). In current English, however, the term is gradually being distinguished from *rhythm*, especially as the latter word increasingly stresses flow and movement not as heard but as felt, as associated with measured time and recurrent stress, and as stimulating a muscular response such as in dancing, in beating with one's hand, or in tapping with one's foot. *Cadence* now often stresses the rise and fall of sound or the rhythm as heard (now often in prose as well as in poetry), and as influenced by tone or modulation, choice of words, feeling, and the like; thus, one remembers the *cadence* (not *rhythm*) of a great Miltonic passage long after its phrasing is forgotten; the *rhythm* (not *cadence*) of Browning's "How They Brought the Good News from Ghent to Aix" sets the feet tapping; so, "the phrases and *cadences* of the Prayer Book [Book of Common Prayer]" (*H. Ellis*); "Great music like that of Prospero's speech in *The Tempest* or the *cadence* of Cleopatra's 'Give me my robe' " (*S. Alexander*). "I could hear the *cadence* of his voice and that was all, nothing but the measured rise and fall of syllables" (*J. P. Marquand*).

rib, *v.* *Banter, chaff, rally, quiz, kid, rag, guy, josh, jolly.

ribald. Obscene, gross, *coarse, vulgar.

Ana. *Offensive, loathsome: indecent, indelicate (see INDECOROUS): lewd, lascivious, wanton (see LICENTIOUS): scurrilous, opprobrious (see ABUSIVE).

ribbon. Fillet, band, *strip, stripe.

rich. **Rich, wealthy, affluent, opulent** come into comparison not only as applied to persons but also to things. The last three are close synonyms of *rich*, the general term, but they are far more explicit in their implications and more limited in their range of application. One is **rich** that possesses more than enough to gratify normal desires and needs. *Rich*, therefore, may describe anyone or anything above the normal (a variable quantity or standard) in possessions. When used of persons, without qualification, it implies the possession of money or of property, especially income-producing property; as, a *rich* citizen; a *rich* state. In its extended use, one may be *rich* in friends, or in gifts, or in interests; a soil may be *rich* in nitrogen; a poem may be *rich* in meaning, a career in promise, a flower in fragrance. That is *rich* also which is above the line dividing the cheap from the costly or precious, or dividing the stinted in elements or ingredients from the bountifully supplied, and the like; as, a *rich* fabric; a *rich* tone; a *rich* red; a *rich* soil; a *rich* cake. One is **wealthy** that possesses money, income-producing property, or intrinsically valuable things in great abundance. *Wealthy* is far rarer than *rich* in extended use, and, therefore, usually connotes material possessions. It also far more often than *rich* implies living conditions in keeping with one's income and a commanding position in the community, state, or world; as, power is in the hands of the *wealthy;* the *wealthy* nations of Europe. "She was indeed *rich*, according to the standards of the Square; nay, *wealthy!*" (*Bennett*). One is **affluent** that is prosperous and therefore continually increasing one's material possessions. *Affluent*, though often used to describe persons, groups, nations, etc., is more often applied to their circumstances or to their state; thus, a rich man is in *affluent* circumstances if his income is increasing or, at least, not decreasing; one is reduced from an *affluent* position, or *affluence*, but not from riches or wealth, for only *affluent* implies increase and therefore suggests decrease as its opposite; the days of a nation's *affluence* are over when its natural resources are used up. "Mrs. Manson Mingott had...lived in *affluence* for half a century; but memories of her early straits had made her excessively thrifty" (*E. Wharton*). One is **opulent** that is ostensibly and ostentatiously rich or wealthy; thus, a person in *affluent* circumstances may or may not maintain an *opulent* establishment, for *affluent* suggests the inflow of money and *opulent* lavish expenditure. Hence, *opulent* usually qualifies things that are luxurious, prodigal, expensively splendid, sumptuous, and the like; as, *opulent* decorations; *opulent* entertainment. "The almost bare simplicity of life in his grandfather's house...as compared with the *opulence* of his own home" (*Arch. Marshall*). When applied to persons, *opulent* usually qualifies a specific term which harmonizes with it in implications; as, *opulent* industrialists; an *opulent* aristocracy; the *opulent* Mr. Croesus. Occasionally, *opulent* does not connote display but inexhaustible richness; as, the *opulent* genius of Shakespeare.

Ant. Poor. — *Con.* Destitute, indigent, penurious (see corresponding nouns at POVERTY).

ricochet, *v.* *Skip, bound, hop, curvet, lope, lollop.

riddle, *v.* *Sift, sieve, screen, bolt, winnow.

riddle, *n.* Puzzle, conundrum, enigma, problem, *mystery.

ride, *v.* **1 Ride, drive,** both as verbs (transitive and intransitive) and as nouns, are frequently confused, especially when they involve the idea of moving in a vehicle or conveyance or upon the back of something. The basic meaning of **ride** is a being borne along in or upon something: when this idea is uppermost, it makes little difference who or what controls the animal, the vehicle, or mechanism by which one is borne along; thus, one *rides* a horse, a bicycle, or a motorcycle when, mounted upon it, one controls its operation or movements; a woman seated on a pillion behind the man's saddle may also be said to *ride* the horse, and a person in the rear seat of a tandem bicycle may be said to *ride* the bicycle, but a person in a sidecar of a motorcycle *rides* in the sidecar (not *rides* the motorcycle). Some, however, prefer *ride*, the transitive verb, when the management of the horse and vehicle is also implied, and *ride*, the intransitive verb, when merely the being mounted upon a moving horse or vehicle is suggested; as, when he *rides* his horse his small daughter usually *rides* on it with him. In the case of the noun *ride*, when there is no expressed or implied opposition to *drive*, the term implies the act or fact of being borne along, usually upon the back of a horse, but sometimes upon the seat of a cycle; as, I think I'll take a *ride* for exercise; he is out for a *ride*. The basic meaning of **drive** (see MOVE, 1) is a causing to move in a given direction: the term therefore primarily refers to the action of an agent that controls either the movements of the horse or other beast of burden or the operation of the mechanism which supplies the power whereby a vehicle, conveyance, or the like, is moved; as, only the coachman *drives* the Victoria; the chauffeur *drives* their car at high speed when Mrs. B— is not in the car; to *drive* a locomotive; they haven't an automobile because there is no one in the family who wants to *drive*. In the case of the noun *drive*, when there is no expressed or implied opposition to *ride*, the term usually implies the act or fact of guiding or controlling the operation of a vehicle; as, he asked her to accompany him on a short *drive;* take as many *drives* in the small sleigh as you wish.

Current good use tends to bring about further distinctions between *ride* and *drive*, sometimes as verbs, but more often as nouns, when movement in a vehicle or conveyance of any sort is implied. *Ride* usually suggests movement in a vehicle which is not in any sense under one's control, such as a train, a bus, a trolley car, or a stranger's automobile; as, it is a long *ride* from New York to Chicago; he said he preferred *riding* in a bus to *riding* in a train; will you give me a *ride* to the next town? *Drive* now often suggests movement in a horse-drawn or motor vehicle the course of which is in some way or in some degree under one's control, whether one is the actual driver or an employer, patron, guest, etc., whose wishes the actual driver observes; as, to take a *drive* along the shore of the lake; we are going for a short *drive;* we'll *drive* to the station in a taxi. In these senses, it will be seen, *ride* still stresses a being borne along and *drive* a causing to move in a given direction. But *ride* is less common in British than in American use when applied to movement in a vehicle or conveyance.

2 *Bait, badger, heckle, hector, chevy, hound.

Ana. *Worry, annoy, harass, harry: persecute, oppress (see WRONG, *v.*): torment, torture (see AFFLICT).

ride, *n.* Drive (see under RIDE, *v.*).

Ana. *Journey, tour, trip, excursion, expedition.

ridicule, *v.* **Ridicule, deride, mock, taunt, twit, rally** agree in meaning to make a person or thing the object of one's own or another's laughter. **Ridicule** may or may not involve unkindness or malice, but it usually implies the belittling of the person or persons affected; as, the critics *ridiculed* his play; "the old State religion which Augustine attacks, *ridiculing* the innumerable Roman godlings whose names he perhaps found in Varro" (*Inge*). **Deride** implies a bitter or contemptuous spirit. "All fools have still an itching to *deride*, And fain would be upon the laughing side" (*Pope*). "He took his revenge on the fate that had made him sad by fiercely *deriding* everything" (*A. Huxley*). "There is no temptation so strong for the aesthetic nature, as to *deride*...the art that we have just outgrown" (*A. C. Benson*). **Mock** stresses scornful derision and, usually, implies words or gestures expressive of one's defiance or contempt. "There came forth little children out of the city, and *mocked* him [Elisha], and said unto him, Go up, thou bald head; go up, thou bald head" (*2 Kings* ii. 23). When used in reference to things, *mock* often implies a setting at naught that suggests scorn or derision. "A perishing That *mocks* the gladness of the Spring!" (*Wordsworth*). "An impenetrable mystery that *mocked* investigation" (*G. Eliot*). **Taunt** implies both mockery and reproach; it often connotes jeering insults. "Some words arose between us. At last he *taunted* me beyond endurance, and offered me—characteristically—twenty pounds to strike him" (*Shaw*). **Twit** implies taunting and a casting something up to someone. "I was *twitted*...unmercifully with my mealy complexion" (*Symonds*). "The upper classes ...are not vulgar, in spite of the absence of ideas with which Matthew Arnold *twits* them" (*Inge*). **Rally** stresses raillery, or good-humored ridicule or banter; nevertheless, it often implies an approach to taunting. "Honeycomb...*rallies* me upon a country life" (*Addison*). "They *rally'd* next Vanessa's dress" (*Swift*).

Ana. *Scoff, flout, jeer, gibe: caricature, burlesque, travesty (see under CARICATURE, *n.*).

ridiculous. *Laughable, ludicrous, droll, funny, comic, comical, farcical, risible.

Ana. Absurd, preposterous, *foolish, silly: amusing, diverting, entertaining (see AMUSE): *fantastic, grotesque, bizarre, antic.

rife. *Prevailing, prevalent, current.

Ana. Abundant, *plentiful, copious, ample: *common, ordinary, familiar.

rifle, *v.* Plunder, *rob, loot, thieve, burglarize.

Ana. Despoil, spoliate, *ravage, pillage, sack, devastate: *steal, pilfer, purloin, filch.

right, *adj.* **1** *Good.

Ant. Wrong.

2 *Correct, accurate, exact, precise, nice.

Ana. Fitting, proper, meet (see FIT): *decorous, decent, seemly, comme il faut: true, *real, actual.

Ant. Wrong.

right, *n.* **Right, prerogative, privilege, perquisite, appanage, birthright** come into comparison when they mean something to which a person has a just or legal claim. They differ, however, in their implications both of the nature of the thing claimed and of the grounds of the claim. **Right** is by far the most inclusive term, for it may be used to designate anything such as a power, a condition of existence, or a possession, to which one is entitled by nature or by the principles of morality, or by grant, as by the laws of the land, or by purchase; as, the *right* to life, liberty, and the pursuit of happiness; *rights* in a patent. "We do not lose our *right* to condemn either measures or men because the country is at war" (*Justice Holmes*). "Every person has a *right* to a certain amount of room in the world, and should not be made to feel wicked in standing up for what is due to him" (*B. Russell*). A **prerogative** is a right which belongs to a person (actual or legal) by virtue of being what one is, as in sex, rank, office, character, or the like, and which thereby gives him precedence, superiority, or an advantage over others. "The fundamental fact is that eminent domain is a *prerogative* of the State" (*Justice Holmes*). "To dread no eye, and to suspect no tongue, is the greatest *prerogative* of innocence" (*Johnson*). "Man, whose *prerogative* it is to be in a great degree a creature of his own making" (*Burke*). A **privilege** is a peculiar right, either granted to one as a favor or concession, or belonging to one as a prerogative; *privilege* often but not invariably implies an advantage over others; as, only passengers with Pullman tickets have the *privilege* of using the club car; it is the *privilege* of a few public officials to collect a fee for their services. "Equal *rights* for all, special *privileges* for none" (*Jefferson*). "What men prize most is a *privilege*, even if it be that of chief mourner at a funeral" (*J. R. Lowell*). A **perquisite** is something, usually money or a thing of monetary value, to which one is entitled, especially by custom, as an addition to one's regular revenue, salary, wages, or the like; thus, a registrar of deeds often receives a small salary and the *perquisites* of his office, as the fees received for search of titles, recording transfers of property, and the like; a domestic servant often regards her mistress's cast-off clothing, shoes, and hats as her *perquisite*. "The pillage of a place taken by storm was regarded as the *perquisite* of the soldier" (*Prescott*). **Appanage** is often loosely used as if it meant merely an adjunct or appurtenance. Historically, the word designates the provision made for the support of a younger son of a great family, as by a grant of land or of money, a lucrative office, or the like; since the same territory or office was granted to a younger son in each succeeding generation, it was thought of as belonging to the family and the perquisite of a member of it; by extension, therefore, *appanage* came to denote anything to which one has a claim through custom, through tradition, or through natural necessity, as an adjunct or appurtenance. "Only from that year [1584] was it [the See of Luçon] regarded as an *appanage* of the House [of Richelieu]" (*Belloc*). "The religious supremacy became a kind of *appanage* to the civil sovereignty" (*Milman*). "Beauty, which is the natural *appanage* of happiness" (*Patmore*). **Birthright,** originally applied to the property or possessions which belong to one by right of inheritance (see HERITAGE) is now far more extended in its application. It differs from *right* only in being restricted to a right to which one is entitled by some reason connected with one's nativity, as by being a man, a native-born citizen, a descendant of a particular line, or the like. "We sell our *birthright* whenever we sell our liberty for any price of gold or honor" (*E. P. Whipple*).

Ana. *Claim, title: *freedom, license, liberty.

right away. Straightway, *directly, immediately, instantly, instantaneously, forthwith, at once, anon.

righteous. Virtuous, noble, *moral, ethical.

Ana. *Upright, honest, just, honorable.

Ant. Iniquitous. — *Con.* *Vicious, nefarious, flagitious, corrupt: profligate, dissolute, reprobate, *abandoned.

rightful. *Due, condign.

Ana. *Fair, equitable, just, impartial: *lawful, legal, legitimate.

rigid. **1** *Stiff, inflexible, tense, stark, wooden.

Ana. *Firm, hard, solid: compact, *close: tough, tenacious, *strong.

Ant. Elastic. — *Con.* Resilient, flexible, supple, springy (see ELASTIC).

2 Rigid, rigorous, strict, stringent are often used interchangeably in the sense of extremely severe and stern, especially when applied to laws or imposed conditions or to the persons who enforce them. There are, however, differences in implications and in range of application which give to each adjective its precise shade of meaning. Literally, *rigid* and *rigorous* imply extreme stiffness or utter lack of elasticity or flexibility, *strict* and *stringent* imply tightness so extreme as to permit no looseness, laxity, or latitude. These implications are preserved even in their figurative senses, which are now more common, the literal senses being, in the case of all the words except *rigid* (see also STIFF), now very seldom used. In its literal sense *rigid* implies great, often extreme, resistance to forces that would deform; as, a *rigid* bar; a *rigid* framework. In its figurative senses, in which it is applied less often to persons than to their acts or to the conditions the persons make for themselves or others, it usually suggests uncompromising inflexibility; as, *rigid* laws; *rigid* discipline; "[a] *rigid* Churchman" (*Quiller-Couch*); a *rigid* definition of "morality"; "A *rigid* system, faithfully administered, would be better than a slatternly compromise" (*A. C. Benson*). **Rigorous** is applied to persons, to their acts, to their way of life, and to the natural or artificial conditions under which they live. It commonly implies imposed severities or hardships or the conscientious acceptance of them; thus, a *rigid* rule admits of no change or compromise; a *rigorous* rule imposes exacting or harsh conditions; a *rigorous* enforcement of a law makes the people feel its rigors; a *rigid* enforcement of a law admits of no relaxations in anyone's favor; we can speak of a *rigorous* (not *rigid*) winter; a *rigorous* (usually better than *rigid*) disciplinarian; the *rigorous* (not *rigid*) life of an explorer or a monk. **Strict** is applied chiefly to persons or their acts and denotes showing or demanding undeviating conformity to rules, standards, conditions, or requirements; thus, a *strict* rule or a *strict* teacher demands obedience; a *strict* watch admits no relaxing of vigilance, and *strict* silence no freedom to speak; a *strict* construction of a law is one confined to the letter of that law; so, "the *strictest* obligations of intellectual honesty" (*Inge*); "*Strict* justice, either on earth or in heaven, was the last thing that society cared to face" (*H. Adams*). **Stringent** is to *strict* as *rigorous* is to *rigid*, in that it usually emphasizes the effect or effects rather than the presence of a quality in an agent or his act. Both *stringent* and *rigorous* connote imposition, but the former suggests impositions that limit, curb, or sometimes coerce; thus, a *stringent* rule narrows one's freedom or range of activities; a *stringent* interpretation of the constitution may either be narrower or more restrictive in its effects than the letter of the constitution warrants; poverty may be described as *stringent* when it narrows one's opportunities to satisfy one's aspirations; necessity may be called *stringent* when it forces one to live within bounds or forces one into certain distasteful acts; so, "he endeavours by the most *stringent* regulations to prevent the growth of inequalities of wealth" (*G. L. Dickinson*); "Not until...Rockefeller Foundation aid [was] eagerly sought everywhere...were we able to lay down more and more *stringent* conditions" (*V. Heiser*).

Ana. *Inflexible, inexorable, obdurate, adamant, adamantine: stern, *severe, austere.

Ant. Lax.

rigor *or* **rigour.** *Difficulty, hardship, vicissitude.

Ana. Austerity, severity, sternness (see corresponding adjectives at SEVERE): harshness, roughness (see corresponding adjectives at ROUGH): *trial, tribulation, visitation, affliction.

Ant. Amenity.

rigorous. *Rigid, strict, stringent.

Ana. *Stiff, rigid, inflexible: stern, austere, ascetic, *severe: exacting, *onerous, burdensome, oppressive.

Con. *Easy, facile, light, smooth, effortless.

rile, *v.* Variant of ROIL.

riled, riley. Variants of ROILED, ROILY.

rim. Brim, brink, *border, margin, verge, edge.

rimer *or* **rimester.** Variants of RHYMER, RHYMESTER.

rind. *Skin, bark, peel, hide, pelt, fell.

ring, *n.* **1** *Combination, combine, party, bloc, faction, cabal, junto.

2 *Arena, circus, lists, cockpit, court, field, gridiron, diamond, rink.

rip, *v.* *Tear, rend, split, cleave, rive.

ripa. *Shore, coast, beach, strand, bank, littoral, foreshore.

ripe. *Mature, matured, mellow, adult, grown-up, full-fledged.

Ana. *Seasonable, timely, well-timed: *consummate, finished, accomplished.

Ant. Green: unripe. — *Con.* Raw, *rude, crude, callow: *immature, unmatured, unmellow.

ripen. *Mature, develop, age.

Ana. *Improve, better: enhance, heighten, *intensify: season, inure (see HARDEN).

ripple, *n.* *Wave, undulation, billow, roller, breaker, comber, beachcomber, surge.

rise, *v.* **1** *Spring, arise, originate, derive, flow, issue, emanate, proceed, stem.

Ana. *Appear, emerge, loom.

Ant. Abate (sense 3). — *Con.* Ebb, subside, wane (see ABATE).

2 Rise, arise, ascend, mount, soar, tower, rocket, levitate, surge, as here compared, agree in meaning to move or come up from a lower to a higher level. **Rise** is the comprehensive term interchangeable with all the others, but often at a sacrifice of explicitness or picturesqueness. *Rise* is idiomatic, and therefore the preferred word, when used: (1) in reference to persons, sometimes animals, that erect themselves from a recumbent position, as in bed or after a fall, or from a sitting or kneeling position (as, to *rise* every morning at six; the injured horse was unable to *rise;* the audience *rose* when the national anthem was sung); (2) in reference to certain things that give the impression of coming up into view (as, the sun *rises* at 5:30; the moon will *rise* at eight o'clock) or an object that seems to lift itself up (as, the hills *rise* in the distance); (3) in reference to water or other fluid under the influence of some natural force that sends it upward (as, the river *rises* regularly each spring; the mercury is *rising*) or to any natural phenomenon indicated by such rising of water or other fluid (as, the tide *rises* early tonight; the temperature is *rising*). The word may be used far more widely than these instances indicate, but in these and in closely related figurative applications, *rise* is specifically necessary. "For the first two weeks, or three...the work *rose* about him like a tide" (*M. Austin*). "Now he felt his mother counting the week's money, and her wrath *rising*" (*D. H. Lawrence*). **Arise** (see also SPRING) is not only far narrower in its range of application than *rise,* but it is also generally felt to be rhetorical or poetic. It is still far from uncommon in spoken English in the senses of to get up in the morning after a night's sleep or to rise from the grave, but such usage (especially the former) is regarded as poetic, formal, or archaic. "*Arise, arise;* Awake the snorting citizens with the bell" (*Shak.*). "The temple rends, the rocks burst, the dead *arise*" (*Steele*). **Ascend** and **mount** (for transitive use of both words see ASCEND, 2) carry a much stronger suggestion of continuous or progressive upward movement and of climbing than *rise* and may therefore be used in distinction from the latter word; thus, the sun *rises* at dawn, but it *ascends* from dawn to noon; smoke *rises* from a fire and *ascends* to the tree tops; a lark *rises* from the ground and *mounts* to the skies; a scientist's hopes *rise* at the first indication of his success and *mount* as one experiment after another turns out as expected. "The third day he *rose* again from the dead, He *ascended* into heaven" (Apostles' Creed, *Bk. of Com. Prayer*). **Soar** always, even in its figurative use, suggests the straight upward flight of a bird, especially of one that mounts without flapping of wings; it therefore usually connotes continuous, often swift, ascent into high altitudes, especially into very high altitudes (intellectually, spiritually, aesthetically, or the like). "[The skylark] singing still dost *soar,* and *soaring* ever singest" (*Shelley*). "What would this man? Now upward will he *soar,* And little less than Angel, would be more" (*Pope*). "The *soaring* melody of the rondo in the Waldstein sonata is Beethoven's... transfiguration of the air of a ribald folk-song" (*Lowes*). **Tower** is used more often in reference to things that attain conspicuous height through growth, building up, or the like, than in reference to things that actually move upward; it also frequently connotes extension to a height beyond that of comparable neighboring objects, such as buildings, trees, mountains or, when eminence is suggested, persons; as, the Empire State Building *towers* above all the New York City skyscrapers; Shakespeare *towers* above all the dramatists of his time. "Full thirty foot she *towered* from waterline to rail" (*Kipling*). When the word does imply movement upward, it usually evokes a picture of something shooting up so as to suggest a tower or steeple. "The nimble flames *towered,* nodded, and swooped through the surrounding air" (*Hardy*). **Rocket** suggests the inordinately swift ascent of a projectile, or especially, of the firework of that name; hence, it is used chiefly with reference to things that rise with incredible or extraordinary rapidity, as under the impetus of events; as, with the first hint of a shortage, wheat prices *rocketed* on the market. **Levitate** (opposed to *gravitate*) implies a force that causes a thing to rise through its actual or induced lightness or buoyancy; in general use, the word may be, but seldom is, used of the rising of balloons, kites, and the like; it is associated chiefly with spiritualistic practices (as, the *levitation* of a table at a séance) and with illusory risings of a person or thing. "It is asserted that a man or a woman '*levitated*' to the ceiling, floated about there, and finally sailed out by the window" (*T. Huxley*). **Surge** suggests heaving or spurting upward, as of waves. It is often used with *up* in reference to emotions and thoughts that rise powerfully from the depths of subconsciousness. "All the enthusiasm of old *surged* up to answer this appeal" (*Mrs. Oliphant*). "Things half-guessed, obscurely felt, *surged* up from unsuspected depths in her" (*E. Wharton*). Quite as often, especially with *forward,* it also suggests a rolling movement comparable to that of oncoming waves; as, the troops *surged* forward.

Ana. Climb, *ascend, mount, scale: *increase, enlarge, augment: *lift, raise, elevate.

Ant. Decline: set (*as the sun*).

risible. Droll, funny, *laughable, ludicrous, ridiculous, comic, comical, farcical.

Ana. Amusing, diverting, entertaining (see AMUSE).

risk, *n.* Hazard, *danger, peril, jeopardy.

Ana. *Chance, fortune, luck, accident: exposedness *or* exposure, liableness *or* liability, openness (see corresponding adjectives at LIABLE).

Con. Safety, security (see corresponding adjectives at SAFE): *exemption, immunity.

risky. Precarious, hazardous, *dangerous, perilous, jeopardous.

Ana. *Adventurous, venturous, venturesome: chancy, *random, haphazard, hit-or-miss, happy-go-lucky.

rite. Ritual, liturgy, ceremonial, ceremony, *form, formality.

ritual. Rite, liturgy, ceremonial, ceremony, *form, formality.

rival, *v.* **1 Rival, compete with, vie with, emulate,** as here compared, agree in meaning to strive to equal or surpass another person or his achievements. **Rival** (see also MATCH) now occurs with increasing rareness with reference to the act of a person or persons; it is, however, still preferred when a struggle to win the hand of a particular woman in marriage is implied; as, to *rival* another in love. The term also may be used when an attempt to outdo each other is suggested; as, "a work...which contending sects have *rivalled* each other in approving" (*Heber*). **Compete with** implies a struggle for the same object, the same position or standing, the same reward, or the like; it may or may not connote a desire to master one's opponents or get the better of them; as, the grocer found that in his new location he must *compete with* two businesses already well established; the track teams of the city high schools will *compete with* each other for the cup next Friday; the child was not strong enough physically or mentally to *compete with* other children of his age. **Vie with** carries less suggestion of arduous struggle to hold one's own or to excel than *compete with;* it sometimes suggests the excitement of contest that is a game rather than a combat; as, the men *vied with* one another in paying her attention; the boys *vied with* each other in showing off. "When they died, and their wills became public, it was found that they had *vied with* one another in enriching her" (*Shaw*). Both *compete with* and *vie with* are sometimes shortened into the intransitive verbs *compete* and *vie* when the *with* phrase is clearly understood; as, to *compete* for a trophy; to *vie* for a prize. **Emulate** implies a conscious effort to equal or surpass someone or something by imitation or by using him or it as a model; as, "a simplicity [that of George Herbert's poetry] *emulated* without success by numerous modern poets" (*T. S. Eliot*). "Her companions she loved and admired, but could not *emulate*, for they were wise about things she knew not of" (*R. Macaulay*). "Modern water-colour...when it tries...to *emulate* the force and solidity of oil-painting, only succeeds in sacrificing its own special felicities" (*Binyon*).

Ana. Strive, struggle, try, *attempt: cope, *contend, fight.

2 *Match, equal, approach, touch.

rive, *v.* Cleave, split, rend, *tear, rip.

Ana. Sever, sunder, divide, *separate: *cut, hew, chop.

rivel. *Wither, shrivel, wizen.

rivet, *v.* *Secure, anchor, moor.

Ana. *Fasten, attach, affix, fix: *join, unite, connect, link.

road. Road, roadway, highway, highroad, street, avenue, boulevard, terrace, drive, parkway, thoroughfare, byway, lane, alley, alleyway, as here compared, denote in common a paved or unpaved way over which vehicles, persons, or animals may pass from one point to another. A **road** is a way, generally outside an urban district and primarily for vehicles and horses, between one place and another. A **roadway** is that part of a road over which traffic travels, as distinct from curbs, shoulders, sidewalks, and the like. A **highway** is a main, often much-traveled, road. **Highroad** stresses the idea of freedom from whatever tends to reduce the speed of traffic, as windings, narrowness, ruts, steep grades, etc. A **street**, originally a paved way, is a public way in a city, town, or village, commonly with a footwalk at one or both sides for pedestrians. An **avenue** is a broad street, often planted with trees; the word suggests a certain degree of stateliness, but is often loosely applied. A **boulevard** is a broad avenue decoratively laid out with trees, belts of turf, and often flowers. In the United States the word is frequently used for a principal street on which traffic is so heavy that traffic from a side street may not enter without first coming to a stop. A **terrace,** as here compared, is a street having houses situated along the side or top of rising ground, above the level of the roadway, or a street with a raised belt of turf, planted with trees, shrubs, flowers, etc., running down the middle. A **drive** is either a private vehicle road leading to a residence, or a public street or road, primarily or only for pleasure vehicles, that is a scenic attraction in itself or that affords a prospect of scenery. A **parkway** is a street or road having enough turf, trees, flowers, etc., along the sides or down the middle, or both, to constitute a park. A **thoroughfare** is a public road, street, or avenue open at both ends, and usually heavily traveled. A **byway** is an obscure or unfrequented side road. A **lane** is a narrow unpaved passage or byway, especially between hedges, fences, or walls. An **alley** is a narrow passageway between buildings in a town or city, as distinguished from a public street; in many American cities it is a passageway for vehicles, providing access to the rear of buildings or lots. **Alleyway** places more emphasis than *alley* on high enclosing walls.

roadway. *Road, street, highway, highroad, avenue, boulevard, terrace, drive, parkway, thoroughfare, byway, lane, alley, alleyway.

roam. *Wander, stray, ramble, rove, range, prowl, gad, gallivant, traipse, meander.

roast, *v.* *Bake, broil, grill, barbecue.

rob, *v.* **Rob, plunder, rifle, loot, thieve, burglarize** come into comparison as meaning to despoil a person of possessions or a place of valuables. In strict legal use, **rob** implies the taking of personal property or valuables from another or from a place in a felonious manner, as by the exercise of violence, by the arousing of fear, or by trickery or fraud; as, to *rob* a bank; to *rob* a man of his savings by selling him worthless securities; to *rob* the poor box of a church. In extended use, *rob* implies deprivation by unjust means or by powers beyond one's control; as, to *rob* a person of his good name; the high winds *robbed* the trees of their fruit; a tree *robs* the adjacent soil of moisture and fertility. **Plunder** implies a despoliation by force, as by armies in war, organized gangs, bandits, or the like: it often suggests robbery on an extensive scale or a ravaging or pillaging of a territory; as, travelers through the remote sections of the country were in constant danger of being *plundered;* to *plunder* the warehouses; "*plundering* wrecked ships...was a well-established business in many places on our shores" (*Shaw*). **Rifle,** like *plunder*, usually implies a despoliation of possessions or valuables, but it distinctively stresses a ransacking and therefore usually takes as its object a place, building, treasury, receptacle, or the like: consequently, it may be used in place of *plunder* when the latter idea is to be clearly implied (as, to *rifle* [or *plunder*] a warehouse; to *rifle* a palace; to *rifle* a man's pockets). But the word may also be used when ransacking for the sake of finding something, such as stolen goods or evidence against a person, is the chief implication. "You cannot accuse a man on the Government House List of stealing. And if you *rifle* his room, you are a thief yourself" (*Kipling*). **Loot** differs from *plunder* chiefly in its suggestion of circumstances which explain the despoliation or make it exceedingly reprehensible: it sometimes implies defiance of all laws governing civilized man (as, to *loot* the bodies of those killed in a train wreck; to *loot* the ruins of a bombed building), or desperation as a motive (as, "if we left them to starve they would begin by breaking our windows and end by *looting* our shops and burning our houses"—*Shaw*), but it quite commonly refers to the pillaging of a captured place (as, soldiers *looted* the town after it was captured). *Loot* also is used when venality and graft, rather than acts of violence, are implied; as, a group of officials who *looted* the state treasury. **Thieve** implies a taking of possessions or valuables by stealth: unlike the other terms of this group, the word is used chiefly, but not exclusively, as an intransitive verb, often implying habitual stealing of goods from persons or places; as, he lives by *thieving;* "When a thief *thieves* from a thief, God laughs" (*West Indian Negro Proverb*); "I never did such a thing as *thieve*" (*Dickens*). **Burglarize** implies an act of burglary, or a breaking and entering by night in order to steal; usually, however, it carries, as *burglary* in law does not necessarily carry, an implication that one's purpose has been accomplished; as, the house was *burglarized* while its occupants were asleep.

Ana. *Steal, pilfer, purloin, filch, lift: defraud, swindle, *cheat: despoil, pillage, sack, *ravage: embezzle, *defalcate, peculate.

robber. Larcener, thief, burglar. See under THEFT.

robbery. Larceny, *theft, burglary.

robe, *v.* *Clothe, attire, tire, dress, apparel, array, vest, invest.

robust. *Healthy, sound, wholesome, hale, well.

Ana. *Strong, sturdy, stout, stalwart: athletic, husky, *muscular, sinewy: *vigorous, energetic, lusty.

Ant. Frail, feeble.

rock, *v.* *Shake, agitate, convulse.

Ana. *Swing, sway, undulate, oscillate: totter, quake, tremble (see SHAKE).

rocket, *v.* *Rise, arise, ascend, mount, soar, tower, levitate, surge.

rococo, *adj.* *Ornate, baroque, flamboyant, florid.

rodomontade. *Bombast, rhapsody, rant, fustian.

Ana. Boasting, bragging, vaunting (see BOAST, *v.*): vainglory, vanity, *pride: magniloquence, grandiloquence (see corresponding adjectives at RHETORICAL).

roguish. *Playful, frolicsome, sportive, waggish, impish, mischievous, wanton.

roil *or* **rile.** Provoke, aggravate, nettle, *irritate, exasperate, peeve.

Ana. *Anger, incense, enrage, infuriate, madden: vex, *annoy, irk, bother.

roiled *or* **riled, roily** *or* **riley.** *Turbid, muddy.

roll, *n.* *List, table, catalogue, schedule, register, roster, rota, canon, inventory.

roller. *Wave, undulation, billow, breaker, comber, beachcomber, surge, ripple.

rollick, *v.* Frolic, disport, sport, *play, romp, gambol.

rollick, *n.* Frolic, disport, sport, play, romp, gambol. See under PLAY, *v.*

romance, *n.* *Novel.

romantic, *adj.* *Sentimental, mawkish, maudlin, soppy, mushy, slushy.

Ana. Fanciful, *imaginary, quixotic, fantastic, visionary: invented, created (see INVENT): picturesque, pictorial, vivid, *graphic.

romp, *v.* Frolic, rollick, gambol, disport, sport, *play.

romp, *n.* Frolic, rollick, gambol, disport, sport, play. See under PLAY, *v.*

room, *n.* **1 Room, chamber, apartment** are here compared as used of space in a building, enclosed or set apart by a partition. **Room** is the word in ordinary use. **Chamber** is chiefly elevated or poetical; it is commonly used of a private room, especially of a bedroom on an upper floor. "High in her *chamber* up a tower to the east" (*Tennyson*). "He...hardly ever slept two nights successively in one *chamber*" (*Southey*). **Apartment** is now rare in the sense of a single room. "Her morning-room was an airy *apartment* on the first-floor" (*M. E. Braddon*).

2 In plural form **rooms. Rooms, lodgings, chambers, quarters, diggings, digs, apartment, flat, tenement** denote in common one or more rooms used as a separate residence in a building in which there are other dwellers. A **room** or **rooms** are engaged in a private house or in a dormitory or hotel, usually by a single person; commonly, certain facilities (as the bathroom) are shared; and there is no provision, or very limited provision, for housekeeping. **Lodgings** are a room or rooms rented in a private house. The term is not much used colloquially in the United States. **Chambers** (chiefly British) are rooms for single persons living alone, either in a private house or in a building containing only such rooms. The term is little used in the United States. **Quarters** are usually an assigned place of residence occupied for a precarious term, especially by soldiers, as in a house or in barracks. With a qualifying word, *quarters* may characterize, or appraise the accommodations of, any place of residence; as, bachelor *quarters;* cramped or spacious *quarters*. **Diggings** is colloquial, **digs** slang (both especially British), for any of the preceding terms. An **apartment,** in the United States and Canada, is usually a suite of rooms having complete facilities for private living and housekeeping, in a building composed exclusively of similar suites. Less often the term is applied to a single room, with bath, and without kitchen, especially in the so-called apartment hotels. In England the singular form *apartment* is now rarely used; the plural form *apartments* is a colloquial and somewhat pretentious term for a set of rooms in a private house, hired for short-term occupancy. "The curate's lodgings—*apartments* his landlady would call them" (*M. R. Mitford*). A **flat** is an apartment occupying the whole or a part of one floor, as distinguished, for instance, from the so-called duplex apartment, which has rooms on two floors. Since, however, the rooms of an apartment are commonly all on one floor, this distinction does not often come into play; and in England *flat* is the term in general use for what in the United States is usually called an apartment. In the United States, *flat* is sometimes used as in England, and thus is applied interchangeably with *apartment* to a suite, of any size, the rooms of which are all on one floor; however, it is perhaps more often applied to a suite of rooms, usually with private entrance from the outside, occupying the whole of one floor, or half of one floor and separated from the other suite on the same floor by a corridor, in a building smaller than the largest of apartment houses, and often of less substantial construction and with less elegant appointments. **Tenement** in the United States usually suggests an inferior apartment or flat, especially a crowded one in the slums. But sometimes the word is so devoid of derogatory connotation that one sees in the windows of buildings containing vacant apartments or flats signs reading "Tenement to Let." In England the word is not derogatory, and differs from *flat* in being applicable to a suite on more than one floor, and from *apartments* in implying more permanent tenure. *Tenement* is often also used for *tenement house.*

roost, *v.* Perch, *alight, light, land.

root, *v.* *Applaud, cheer, hurrah, huzza.

root, *n.* *Origin, source, inception, provenance, provenience, prime mover.

Ana. Beginning, commencing *or* commencement, starting *or* start (see corresponding verbs at BEGIN): foundation, basis, ground (see BASE).

roseate. *Hopeful, optimistic, rose-colored.

rose-colored. *Hopeful, optimistic, roseate.

roster. *List, table, catalogue, schedule, register, roll, rota, canon, inventory.

rot, *v.* *Decay, decompose, putrefy, spoil, disintegrate, crumble.

Ana. Corrupt, vitiate, *debase: taint, *contaminate, pollute, defile.

rota. *List, table, catalogue, schedule, register, roll, roster, canon, inventory.

rotate. 1 *Turn, revolve, gyrate, circle, spin, whirl, twirl, wheel, eddy, swirl, pirouette.

2 **Rotate, alternate** are synonyms when they mean to succeed or cause to succeed each other in turn. **Rotate** may be used in reference to two or more persons or things; it implies indefinite repetition of the order of succession. Thus, persons *rotate* in jobs or offices when they periodically interchange their jobs or offices according, usually, to a predetermined scheme; one *rotates* crops who grows different things on the same land in successive seasons in an order calculated to maintain soil fertility or to enrich exhausted soil. **Alternate** differs from *rotate* in being referable only to two persons or things; though it also implies repetition of the order, it does not convey so strong a suggestion of continuity; as, to *alternate* workers on an exhausting job; to *alternate* hot and cold applications in the treatment of a bruise. "The weather *alternated* between blinding sand-storms and brilliant sunlight" (*Cather*).

Ana. Interchange, *exchange, swap, bandy: suceced, *follow, ensue.

rotund. Plump, chubby, portly, stout, *fleshy, fat, corpulent, obese.

Ant. Angular. — ***Con.*** *Lean, spare, lank, lanky, gaunt, rawboned, skinny, scrawny.

rough, *adj.* 1 **Rough, harsh, uneven, rugged, scabrous** come into comparison when they mean not having a smooth or even surface, exterior, texture, or the like. **Rough,** the usual and comprehensive word, applies literally to anything that may be said to have a surface or an exterior which to the sense of touch or the sense of sight is not smooth but is covered with points, bristles, projections, or ridges of any kind or nature; as, *rough* ground; the *rough* surface of a body of water (or, the sea is *rough* today); a *rough* block of stone; the *rough* skin of chapped hands; a *rough* tweed; a *rough,* unshaved face. Often in literal use, when applied to materials and substances employed in the arts and crafts, *rough* means unpolished, unworked, unwrought, etc.; as, a *rough* diamond; *rough* steel; *rough* lumber. By extension, the term also applies to things which impress another than the tactile sense or one's nerves or one's feelings as lacking in smoothness and evenness; as, *rough* words; *rough* winds; *rough* sounds; a *rough* disposition; he has had a *rough* time (for fuller treatment of extended senses, see RUDE). **Harsh** suggests an even more disagreeable sensation or impression than *rough;* when applied to that which is felt with the hand, it implies a surface or texture that is distinctly unpleasant to the tactile nerves (as, a *harsh* fabric; *harsh* cinders; *harsh* sand); when applied to that which is heard, it suggests a rasping, grating quality (as, *harsh* voices; "*harsh* din Broke the fair music"—*Milton*; a *harsh* language); when applied to anything seen, tasted, or the like, it suggests a character or quality that is offensive or repellent to a sensitive person (as, a *harsh* liquor; *harsh* features; a *harsh* combination of colors). Unlike *rough, harsh* in its extended senses seldom implies lack of polish or refinement, but rather it stresses a nature that is unfeeling, cruel, and indifferent to the pain it inflicts (as, a *harsh* critic; a *harsh* parent), or when applied to things, effectiveness in promoting discomforts or in imposing rigors (as, a *harsh* rebuke; a *harsh* climate; a *harsh* sentence). **Uneven** applies not only to surfaces but to lines, and suggests a lack of uniformity in height through all the points of the surface (as, an *uneven* road; an *uneven* floor) or a lack of straightness and the presence of curves or angles (as, an *uneven* edge; an *uneven* hem). In figurative use, it implies a lack of uniformity in excellence, or agreeableness, or the like, in all the parts, as of a life, a performance, a work of art, etc.; as, the artist's brushwork in this painting is *uneven;* the trio's playing of the sonata was *uneven.* **Rugged,** though now chiefly applied to persons so strong and healthy that they can survive great stress and strain, is still frequently employed in the sense of *rough:* in current use, however, it applies chiefly to surfaces marked with ridges, prominences, and the like, such as those which offer obstacles to the traveler, the worker, and the like (as, a *rugged* road up a mountain; "the rice-fields, all clothed in their *rugged* stubble"—*F. Kemble*), or which, as in the case of faces or countenances, are gaunt, seamed, or heavy-featured, and suggest strength or maturity (as, "any resemblance between you, with your *rugged* strong face and your coal-black hair, and this young Adonis"—*Wilde;* "His face had already lost its youthful chubbiness, and was becoming somewhat like William's—*rough*-featured, almost *rugged*"—*D. H. Lawrence*). *Rugged* is also applicable to writing, especially metrical writing, which has not been made smooth, flowing, and agreeable to the ear, sometimes, but not necessarily, through lack of care or skill; as, "the harsh cadence of a *rugged* line" (*Dryden*); "the most *rugged*-seeming of prose dialogue, the kind...that people sometimes praise as 'simply a page torn from the book of life' " (*C. E. Montague*). **Scabrous** applies literally to a surface that is rough to the touch, though not necessarily uneven: in this sense it is a general term including *scaly, scurfy, scabby, thorny, prickly, knobby, knotty,* and the like, when applied to surfaces; as, a *scabrous* leaf; a *scabrous* stem; a *scabrous* hide. In figurative use, *scabrous* applies chiefly to subject matter or to writings and works of art having subject matter that is prickly or thorny, or difficult to treat, often because it is offensive to the tastes or morals of the community; as, "What writer...has spoken more acutely on the somewhat *scabrous,* but none the less important subject of feminine 'temperament'?" (*A. Huxley*).

Ana. Hard, solid, *firm: *coarse, gross: *rank, rampant.

Ant. Smooth.

2 *Rude, crude, raw, callow, green.

Ana. Brusque, crusty, gruff, curt, blunt, *bluff: ungracious, uncivil, discourteous, impolite (see RUDE): *indecorous, unseemly, indecent, indelicate.

Ant. Gentle.

round, *adj.* **Round, spherical, circular, globular** (*or* **globose, globate, globoid**), **orbicular** (*or* **orbiculate**), **annular, discoid** (*or* **discoidal**) are not all synonyms of each other but they are all synonyms of **round,** the comprehensive term, when it means having an edge, or circumference, or outer surface every point of which is equidistant (often, approximately equidistant) from the center. **Spherical** is applied to round bodies or masses, such as balls, globes, drops, bubbles, thought of as figures of solid geometry: **circular** is applied to round flat surfaces, such as cross sections, tops, or bottoms, or to round bodies thought of as figures of plane geometry and having either the shape of a circle, such as rings and hoops, or the shape of a disk, such as plates, lids, etc. **Globular** and its variant forms are less mathematical and more concrete in their connotations than *spherical:* they often suggest merely an approximation to the spherical in shape (as, the earth is *globular* but not actually *spherical*); as, *globular* (or *globose*) berries; *globular* (or *globoid*) grains; *globular* bowls or wine glasses. **Orbicular** may also mean approximately spherical, as are the orbs, or heavenly bodies, as known; the word frequently, however, means approximately circular, as are the orbs, or heavenly bodies, as seen. Thus, the socket of some bones is described as an *orbicular* (that is, globe-shaped) socket, and the muscle which surrounds the eye socket and controls the opening and closing of the eye is describable as an *orbicular* (that is, *circular*) muscle. **Annular** adds to *circular* the implication of being hollow in the center and therefore ring-shaped; as, *annular* markings on trees; an *annular* eclipse of the sun. **Discoid** adds to *circular* the implications of a continuous surface and of flatness; thus, a *discoid* shell is one like the shell of the nautilus, spiral yet having all its coils practically in the same plane.

round, *adv.* Around, *about.

roundabout. *Indirect, circuitous.

Ana. Sinuous, *winding, tortuous, anfractuous, flexuous.

rouse. Arouse, *stir, awaken, rally, waken.

Ana. Enliven, *quicken, animate, vivify: stimulate, excite, *provoke: *incite, foment, instigate.

roustabout. *Worker, workman, workingman, laborer, mechanic, artisan, operative, hand, craftsman, handicraftsman.

rout, *n.* *Crowd, throng, press, crush, mob, horde.

rout, *v.* *Conquer, vanquish, defeat, subdue, subjugate, reduce, overcome, surmount, overthrow, beat, lick.

route, *n.* *Way, course, passage, pass, artery.

rove. *Wander, stray, roam, ramble, range, prowl, gad, gallivant, traipse, meander.

row, *n.* *Brawl, broil, fracas, melee, rumpus, scrap.

Ana. Fight, affray, fray, combat, conflict, *contest: altercation, wrangle, *quarrel, squabble.

royal. Regal, *kingly, queenly, imperial, princely.

Ana. *Splendid, resplendent, glorious, superb: august, majestic, stately, imposing (see GRAND).

rude. 1 **Rude, rough, crude, raw, callow, green** are synonyms when they mean lacking in most or in all of the qualities that make for finish or for perfection in development or in use. **Rude,** which etymologically means unwrought or unformed, is applicable not only to men, to their minds, to their manners, but also to the things they make or do. As applied to men and their minds, it suggests a comparatively low state of culture or a dearth of learning more often than savagery or barbarism, although it may suggest the latter; as, "Like a *rude* and savage man of Ind" (*Shak.*); "His companies [companions] unletter'd, *rude* and shallow" (*Shak.*). "The melody that was at first designed To cheer the *rude* forefathers of mankind" (*Cowper*). As applied to the things which men make or do, *rude* suggests the makers' ignorance of technique or of proper materials, their inexpertness or inexperience, a deficiency of materials, or the like; as, *rude* attempts at verse; *rude* implements; *rude* workmanship; a *rude* hut. "Our father Adam sat under the Tree and scratched with a stick in the mould; And the first *rude* sketch that the world had seen was joy to his mighty heart" (*Kipling*). **Rough,** as here compared (see also ROUGH, 1), is also applicable to men, their manners, and their works and products; it usually suggests more harshness or violence than *rude* and a more culpable ignorance or inexperience. As applied to men and their manners the term usually implies the absence of signs not only of polish and refinement but of gentleness, politeness, and often even civility. It does not, however, necessarily imply boldness, insolence, boorishness, or other unpleasant qualities; as, "A plain, *rough,* honest man, and wise, tho' not learned" (*Addison*); a couple of *rough* fellows appeared at the door; to use *rough* language; a *rough* but hearty welcome. As applied to men's works and products, *rough* suggests more offhandedness, haste, indifference to technique, or the like, than *rude;* it is therefore usually applied to things which are not carefully made, often intentionally, because they suffice for the purpose, or are not yet finished, being in an early stage of a process or development; as, to make a first *rough* draft of his argument; to show a *rough* sketch of the proposed garden; a *rough* guess; a *rough* buffing of cutlery precedes what is called a gloss buffing. **Crude** may be applied to men and their acts, words, products, and the like, but it gets its fundamental implications from its historically earlier application to things which have been untouched by man, as by being unprocessed, unrefined, untreated, and the like, and are as yet, therefore, in their natural state or in an undeveloped state; as, *crude* petroleum; *crude* rubber; *crude* sugar. Consequently, when applied to men, their acts, words, products, and the like, *crude* implies the far remove of that which is so described from that which is perfected, is highly developed, or fully civilized, as by toning down, refining, disciplining, or the like; as, *crude* colors; *crude* methods; *crude* emotions; a *crude* philosophy. "The blank verse of Tennyson...is *cruder* (not 'rougher' or less perfect in technique) than that of half a dozen contemporaries of Shakespeare; *cruder,* because less capable of expressing complicated, subtle, and surprising emotions" (*T. S. Eliot*). "Our ordinary high school pupils, *crude* as they may appear, represent a degree of refinement notably higher than the stage attained by their parents" (*Grandgent*). **Raw,** which in the earliest of its present senses describes the condition of uncooked food, especially of meat, fish, eggs, and vegetables, is often further applied to natural products which are gathered, mined, or otherwise removed from their native places, but are not yet processed or are in the earliest stage of manufacture or processing; thus, *raw* silk names the fiber from the cocoons of the silkworm as it is drawn from them and reeled; *raw* hides are stripped from the carcasses of animals but are not yet tanned or otherwise dressed; *raw* milk is as yet unpasteurized; the *raw* materials from which the miller produces flour are various cereals such as wheat, barley, rye, and the like; "The *raw* material of music is sound" (*Day Lewis*). As applied to men, their minds, their products, and the like, *raw,* far more than *crude,* suggests the elementariness of the untried and the inexperienced; as, *raw* recruits; "to raise ill-armed, half-starved, under-aged, *raw* levies" (*Brownell*); "the *raw* judgment of the multitude" (*De Quincey*). "Over and over again he had seen her take some *raw* youth, twist him, turn him, wake him up; set him going" (*V. Woolf*). **Callow,** originally applied to an unfledged bird, especially one covered with down, is now more often applied to youths or to those who retain the signs of immaturity in manhood. It usually suggests naïveté, simplicity, lack of sophistication, but not so strikingly as does *crude,* and its suggestions of inexperience or present unfitness are not so strong as those of *raw.* "Souls and wits which have never got beyond the *callow* and boarding-school stage" (*Arnold*). "Pluffles was a subaltern in the 'Unmentionables.' He was *callow,* even for a subaltern" (*Kipling*). **Green,** as here compared, derives most of its connotations from *green* as applied to fruit and implying unripeness and unfitness for use. The term often comes pretty close to *raw* when applied to persons and their abilities, because it suggests inexperience and lack of necessary training; as, to employ *green* hands in a factory. Often, however, it additionally connotes simplicity or gullibility. "He has taken me for a *green* country girl, impressed with him because he is from the city and dressed in fine clothes" (*S. Anderson*). But *green* is also used of products (sometimes of the raw materials) of manufacture or processing which are not yet fully seasoned, cured, dried, or the like; as, *green* liquors (not as yet mellowed by age); *green* sugar (not yet perfectly dried); *green* pelts (fresh from the animal); *green* manure (not yet sufficiently rotted).

Ana. Boorish, churlish, clownish, loutish (see under BOOR): rustic, *rural, bucolic: barbarous, savage, *barbarian: primitive, *primary, primeval.

2 Rude, ill-mannered, impolite, discourteous, uncivil, ungracious come into comparison as meaning not observant of the manners or forms required by good breeding. **Rude** suggests lack of delicacy or consideration for the feelings of others: it does not, however, necessarily suggest lack of breeding, for it is applicable to persons of all stations or conditions. It usually stresses impudence, insolence, or a generally insulting manner; as, a *rude* answer; to brush one aside *rudely;* "demanding an explanation of the *rude* familiarity with which Jim had treated him" (*S. Anderson*). **Ill-mannered** is a more general and less explicit term, and it seldom carries a suggestion of an intent to offend or insult, as *rude* usually carries: it is therefore applicable to any person, act, or utterance that shows ignorance of, indifference to, or a disregard of, the proprieties; as, "Our Royal family are getting a little tired of the well-meant, but at the same time *ill-mannered*, homage of well-dressed crowds" (*Daily News*). **Impolite, discourteous,** and **uncivil,** as the negatives of *polite, courteous, civil* (for all three, see CIVIL), respectively imply merely the reverse of the care in observing the proprieties of good or formal society that is suggested by *polite* (as, "The real Smiths might with equal accuracy have been called the poor Smiths, except that Old Chester could not have been so *impolite*" —*Deland*), of the considerate, dignified politeness that is suggested by *courteous*, thereby implying something like rudeness (as, the clergyman was much humiliated by the *discourteous* reply to his appeal), or of the modicum of good manners that is suggested by *civil*, thereby implying an utter disregard of every rule governing social intercourse among civilized persons (as, "No profanity, Señor. We want nothing from you but to get away from your *uncivil* tongue"—*Cather*). **Ungracious** stresses the lack of kindliness, or courtesy, that enables one to keep gracious (see GRACIOUS); as, an *ungracious* refusal; an *ungracious* answer to a *rude* question; "Richard. . . . gave way *ungraciously*. 'There, do as you like' " (*Meredith*).

Ana. Brusque, curt, gruff, crusty (see BLUFF): *impertinent, intrusive, meddlesome: surly, crabbed (see SULLEN).

Ant. Civil: urbane.

rueful. Dolorous, doleful, lugubrious, plaintive, *melancholy.

Ana. Depressed, weighed (down), oppressed (see DEPRESS): piteous, *pitiful: despairing, *despondent, hopeless.

ruffian, *n.* **Ruffian, thug, desperado, gangster, Mohock, apache** agree in denoting a brutal fellow given to wanton violence and to criminal acts such as waylaying, attacking, or murdering his victims. **Ruffian** designates the type, and though it usually distinctively implies rowdyism and marauding, it may be applied to any excessively brutal person who mercilessly inflicts pain or death on others. "Now, ere you sleep, See that your polished arms be primed with care, And drop the nightbolt; *ruffians* are abroad" (*Cowper*). **Thug** usually implies thievery or other definite motive, as well as ruffianry. Originally applied in India to a member of an organization of thieves who waylaid and strangled their victims, the term is now applied, especially in the United States, to a ruffian who knocks out or bludgeons his victim; as, to employ *thugs* to quell a riot. "This dismal place, in almost any other country, would swarm with *thugs*" (*Twain*). **Desperado** less often suggests city streets or crowded centers of population as the field of operations than the plains or the wild and waste regions of a country. It also implies great recklessness in attack; often, but not necessarily, it is applied to an outlaw or hunted criminal who takes no chance of losing his freedom or security. "Jesse James was a two-gun man. . . . He's gone with the buffler [buffalo] an' the *desperadoes*" (*W. R. Benét*). **Gangster,** in current American colloquial use, has acquired implications not originally found in the word; it now implies membership in a band of thieves, racketeers, or the like, controlled by a leader, and the execution of his orders by acts of terrorism and often, wanton murder. **Mohock,** a historical term, was applied to one of a band of ruffians (often aristocrats by birth) who infested the streets of London, especially at night, in the early eighteenth century and attacked and maltreated their victims. **Apache** is applied to a particularly brutal type of ruffian that roves the streets of Paris, especially in the slum districts.

Ana. Robber, thief, larcener, burglar (see under THEFT): *assassin, cutthroat, gunman, bravo.

ruffle, *v.* Bristle, bridle, swagger, *strut.

Ana. Flaunt, parade, display, exhibit, *show.

rugged. *Rough, scabrous, harsh, uneven.

Ana. *Robust, healthy: burly, brawny, husky, *muscular: *rank, rampant: arduous, *hard, difficult.

Ant. Fragile.

ruin, *v.* **Ruin, wreck, wrack** (*or* **rack**), **dilapidate** come into comparison when they mean to subject a person or, more often, a thing to forces that are destructive of soundness, worth, or usefulness. **Ruin** usually suggests a bringing to an end the structural or mental integrity, the value, beauty, or the well-being of something or of someone, as through destructive agencies such as weather, age, neglect, or the like, through partial destruction by fire, flood, collision, or the like, or through loss of something vital to one's happiness or success (such as one's fortune, one's good name, one's chastity); as, the severe windstorm has *ruined* the garden; nearly every one of the old and beautiful churches in the region was *ruined* by bombs; the firm's reputation was *ruined* by rumors spread by envious competitors. "There was in all of them [persons] something *ruined*, lost or broken —some precious and irretrievable quality which had gone out of them and which they never could get back again" (*T. Wolfe*). **Wreck** implies a ruining by or as if by crashing or being shattered. Literally it is used in reference to a ship, a train, an automobile, an airplane, or the like; as, the vessel was *wrecked* on the rocky coast of Maine; only the locomotive of the second train was *wrecked* in the collision. In its extended sense, *wreck* is often used in place of *ruin* when there is an intent to imply that the thing (often an intangible thing such as one's career, one's credit, one's prospects, or the like) is injured past all hope of repair or of reconstruction; as, his health was *wrecked* by his many years of tropical exploration; the party has been *wrecked* by the misdeeds of a few of its leaders; their plans were *wrecked* by the unexpected change in weather. When the pulling down of a building is implied, *wreck* is often preferred to *demolish* or *destroy*, because it does not necessarily carry the suggestion implicit in the latter words of the uselessness of that which is left. **Wrack** (or in dialectal or erroneous use **rack**) is etymologically allied to *wreck*, but it has not followed the same course in the development of its senses and is now rare except in poetic or archaic use where there is the intent to evoke a picture of widespread ruin or to suggest the effect of an overwhelming catastrophe or disaster. "As if the world's wide continent Had fallen in universal ruin *wracked*" (*Shelley*). "The seas. . . With outstretch'd angry arms. . . *Wracking* whole fleets in pride like riven toys" (*F. T. Palgrave*). The verb is now seldom used but the noun *wrack* is not uncommon. **Dilapidate** (etymologically, to scatter like stones) in precise use implies ruin, especially of a building, of developed property, or of one's fortune or financial resources, through neglect or through wastefulness: the term therefore carries, as the other terms do not, a strong implication of culpability. "Nothing... more certainly *dilapidates* their estates...than the surfeits of intemperance" (*Ken*). In British use, the intransitive verb and the noun *dilapidation* often specifically suggest ecclesiastical wastefulness through a failure to keep a church or church property in proper repair and their consequent depreciation in value; as, "The church of Elgin...was...shamefully suffered to *dilapidate* by deliberate robbery and frigid indifference" (*Johnson*); the *Dilapidations* Acts of 1871 and 1872 regulate the recovery of compensation for money spent in repairing churches and ecclesiastical buildings allowed to *dilapidate*. In more general use, *dilapidate* implies a run-down, often a tumble-down, condition and is used commonly in the past-participial form as an adjective; as, "Over the low *dilapidated* wall" (*Browning*); "the dazzling scarlet cloak in which she had first seen Madame Foucault, *dilapidated* now" (*Bennett*).

Ana. *Destroy, demolish, raze: *deface, disfigure: *maim, mutilate, mangle.

rule, *n.* *Law, regulation, precept, statute, ordinance, canon.

Ana. Order, mandate, dictate, *command: *principle, axiom, fundamental: etiquette, *decorum, propriety.

rule, *v.* **1** *Govern.

Ana. *Guide, lead: manage, direct, control, *conduct: *execute, administer.

2 *Decide, determine, settle, resolve.

Ana. Conclude, judge, gather, deduce, *infer.

3 In form **rule out.** Eliminate, debar, *exclude, shut out, suspend, disbar, blackball.

Ana. Bar, block (see HINDER): *prevent, preclude, obviate.

ruminate. Muse, meditate, *ponder.

Ana. *Consider, weigh, revolve, excogitate: reflect, deliberate, speculate, cogitate, *think.

rumpus. *Brawl, broil, fracas, melee, row, scrap.

run, *v.* Gallop, canter, trot, pace, single-foot, walk, lope, rack, amble. See under TROT, *n.*

run, *n.* Gallop, canter, *trot, pace, single-foot, walk, lope, rack, amble.

runt. *Dwarf, pygmy, midget, manikin, homunculus.

rupture, *n.* *Fracture.

rural. Rural, rustic, pastoral, bucolic, georgic, Arcadian, agrestic, geoponic agree in meaning of or characteristic of the country as distinguished from city life. **Rural** is the most comprehensive term; in its widest meaning it implies open country whether uninhabited or sparsely settled; more narrowly it suggests agricultural pursuits or simple community life. In distinction from *rustic*, however, *rural* suggests the pleasant aspects of country life; **rustic** commonly implies a contrast with the refinements of the city or the town, and often connotes rudeness or lack of polish. "He...buried himself in the *rural*, or rather *rustic*, solitude of Buriton" (*Gibbon*). "He had no taste for *rural* loveliness, green fields and vineyards...but he would often have his tongue in his cheek at the simplicity of *rustic* dupes" (*Stevenson*). *Pastoral, bucolic,* and *georgic* all derive some or most of their connotations from the literary treatment of rural life. **Pastoral,** when it does not literally refer to the life of shepherds, suggests either green pastures and grazing sheep or a life primitive in its simplicity or idyllic in its peace and apartness from the world. "To *pastoral* dales, thin-set with modest farms" (*Wordsworth*). "When I thought that a war would arise in defence of the right, That...No more shall...Peace Pipe on her *pastoral* hillock a languid note" (*Tennyson*). **Bucolic,** especially in modern humorous writing, is referred chiefly to persons, their acts, and their words rather than to landscape and, far more strongly than *rustic*, implies loutishness. "The keenest of *bucolic* minds felt a whispering awe at the sight of the gentry" (*G. Eliot*). "A kind of *bucolic* Ben Franklin" (*W. H. Page*). However, *bucolic* is still sometimes used in place of *pastoral* when referring to the type of poetry. **Georgic** is rarer than the others; it usually suggests the life of the farmer rather than of the shepherd; unlike *pastoral* and *bucolic*, it seldom implies idealization or derogation, but rather exact realism. "Here I peruse the Mantuan's *Georgic* strains, And learn the labours of Italian swains" (*Gay*). **Arcadian** stresses simplicity, innocence, and peace. "Those golden times And those *Arcadian* scenes that Maro sings, And Sidney, warbler of poetic prose" (*Cowper*). **Agrestic** and **geoponic** are found only in occasional literary use, the former the equivalent of *rustic*, and the latter, in modern use, approaching *bucolic* or *georgic;* as, "*agrestic* behavior" (*W. Gregory*); "A brown, parchment-hided old man of the *geoponic* or *bucolic* species" (*J. R. Lowell*).

ruse, *n.* *Trick, stratagem, maneuver, artifice, wile, feint.

Ana. Subterfuge, chicane, trickery, *deception: expedient, shift, makeshift, *resource, resort.

rustic. *Rural, pastoral, bucolic, georgic, Arcadian, agrestic, geoponic.

ruth, *n.* Commiseration, compassion, *pity, condolence, sympathy, empathy, bowels.

Ana. *Mercy, grace, charity, clemency, lenity: forbearance, tolerance, indulgence (see under FORBEARING).

S

Sabbath. *Sunday, the Lord's Day.

sack, *v.*[1] Pillage, despoil, spoliate, *ravage, devastate, waste.

Ana. Plunder, *rob, loot, rifle: *destroy, demolish, raze: *strip, bare, denude.

sack, *v.*[2] *Dismiss, discharge, cashier, fire, bounce, drop.

sack, *n.* *Bag, pouch.

sacred. 1 *Holy, divine, blessed, spiritual, religious.

Ana. Dedicated, consecrated, hallowed (see DEVOTE): cherished, treasured, valued (see APPRECIATE).

Ant. Profane. — *Con.* Secular, lay, temporal (see PROFANE).

2 Sacred, sacrosanct, inviolate, inviolable are here compared as meaning having such a character that it is protected by law, custom, tradition, human respect, or the like, against breach, intrusion, defilement, or profanation. **Sacred** (as here compared: for religious use, see also HOLY) implies either a setting apart for a special and, often, exclusive use or end (as, among civilized peoples, property is regarded as *sacred* to its owner; a fund *sacred* to charity; the study was *sacred* to the father of the family) or a special character or quality which makes the person or thing held sacred an object of almost religious veneration or reverence (as, "[Louis XIII] saw that the things which happened increasingly strengthened the Royal Office which was *sacred* to him"—*Belloc;* " 'Grief of two years' standing is only a bad habit.' Alice started, outraged. Her mother's grief was *sacred* to her"—*Shaw*). Although in earlier use **sacrosanct** (etymologically, sacred and holy) was often used seriously of persons or things regarded as not subject to profanation or violation and therefore reverenced with the same awe and respect as is implied by the religious sense of *sacred* (as, "What confederacy can be imagined more noble, more *sacrosanct*, than that between man and wife?"—*L'Estrange;* "Let them establish your fundamental rights by a *sacrosanct* declaration"—*Jefferson*), the term now is either ironical and occasionally slightly derisive or suggests an imputed rather than a genuinely deserved claim for freedom from attack or violation (as, "etymology is after all not *sacrosanct*"—*Karl K. Darrow;* "The one office which he [Augustus] tried to keep *sacrosanct*... was the consulship"—*Buchan*). **Inviolate** and **inviolable** apply to laws, principles, treaties, agreements, institutions, persons, places, objects, etc., that for one reason or another are secure from breach, infringement, attack, intrusion, injury, or the like: they differ from each other chiefly in that *inviolate* suggests the fact of not having been violated, while *inviolable* implies a character which does not permit or which distinctly forbids violation; thus, one holds a vow *inviolable*, but keeps his vow *inviolate;* so, "What seemed *inviolable* barriers are burst asunder in a trice" (*Meredith*); "The Navajos....believed that their old gods dwelt in the fastnesses of that canyon; like their Shiprock, it was an *inviolate* place" (*Cather*).

Ana. Protected, shielded, defended, guarded (see DEFEND): revered, reverenced, venerated (see REVERE).

sacrifice, *v.* Abnegate, forbear, *forgo, eschew.

Ana. Renounce, *abdicate: surrender, yield, resign, *relinquish.

sacrilege. Desecration, *profanation, blasphemy.

Ana. Defilement, pollution (see corresponding verbs at CONTAMINATE): violation, transgression, trespass, *breach: sin, crime, scandal, *offense.

sacrilegious. Blasphemous, *impious, profane.

Ana. Polluting, defiling (see CONTAMINATE): profaning, desecrating (see corresponding nouns at PROFANATION).

sacrosanct. Inviolate, inviolable, *sacred.

Ana. Respected, regarded, esteemed (see corresponding verbs under REGARD, *n.*): revered, venerated, reverenced (see REVERE).

sadness. Sadness, depression, melancholy, melancholia, dejection, gloom, blues, dumps, vapors (*or* **vapours**) are here compared as meaning a state of mind when one is low-spirited, or an attack of low spirits. **Sadness** is the general term: apart from the context it carries no explicit suggestions of the cause of the low spirits or of the extent to which one is deprived of cheerfulness; as, "A feeling of *sadness* and longing That is not akin to pain" (*Longfellow*); "We feel his [Vergil's] underlying *sadness* ...But Rome may have felt more strongly than we do his hopefulness and pride" (*Buchan*); "She was conscious of a profound *sadness* which was not grief" (*Bennett*). **Depression** applies chiefly to a mood in which one feels let down, discouraged, and devoid of vigor (owing to physical, mental, or other causes), or to a state of mind, usually outwardly manifested by brooding, in which one is listless, despondent, sullen, or the like; as, "On some days he was happy, and then his happiness was followed by an odd fit of *depression*" (*S. Anderson*); "Tina's love was a stormy affair, with continual ups and downs of rapture and *depression*" (*E. Wharton*); "Never before, in any mood of *depression*, had she given evidence of suicidal thoughts" (*H. Ellis*). **Melancholy** in earliest use applied, and still sometimes applies, to a settled depression that is temperamental or constitutional, and that at times shows evidences of insanity (as, "*Melancholy* is the nurse of frenzy"—*Shak.*); in current use, this condition is regarded as the result of a mental disease and is called specifically **melancholia** (as, alone and friendless, she fell into a *melancholia*). *Melancholy* now often applies to a not unpleasant or displeasing mood or a mental state characterized by sadness (but not grief or despair), pensiveness, and deep, but not depressing or heavy, seriousness; as, "To lend our hearts and spirits wholly To the influence of mild-minded *melancholy*" (*Tennyson*); "the lively, curious mind, the wit, the gaiety of spirit tinged with a tender *melancholy*" (*Hudson*). "She dwells with Beauty—Beauty that must die ... Ay, in the very temple of delight Veil'd *Melancholy* has her sovran shrine, Though seen of none save him whose... soul shall taste the *sadness* of her might" (*Keats*). **Dejection** suggests especially the mood of one who is downcast, discouraged, or dispirited: the term differs from *depression* chiefly in its suggestion of an external cause and in its more frequent application to a mood than to a prolonged state of mind; as, "It was the last of the regiment's stay in Meryton, and all the young ladies in the neighborhood were drooping apace. The *dejection* was almost universal" (*Austen*); "As high as we have mounted in delight In our *dejection* do we sink as low" (*Wordsworth*). **Gloom** applies rather to the effect produced by melancholy or melancholia, depression, dejection, or extreme sadness on the person afflicted or to the atmosphere which a person of low spirits or a depressing event creates: in its literal sense, the term implies darkness and dullness, and it further connotes lack of all that enlivens or cheers; as, "the leaden *gloom* of one who has lost all that can make life interesting, or even tolerable" (*Hardy*); "constant repinings at the dulness of everything around them threw a real *gloom* over their domestic circle" (*Austen*); "the idea that I am being studied fills me, after the first outburst of laughter, with a deepening *gloom*" (*A. Huxley*). **Blues, dumps, vapors** are all more or less colloquial terms for an attack of low spirits. *Blues* (short for *blue devils*) commonly suggests an acutely depressed or melancholy mood which afflicts one almost as an illness; as, to have the *blues* frequently; she always finds hard work the best cure for the *blues*. *Dumps* suggests deep dejection of spirits (as, "doleful *dumps* the mind oppress"—*Shak.*). **Vapors** (an archaic or historical term) implies a highly nervous state where the sufferer (usually a woman) cannot control tears, has a painful headache, and is acutely depressed or dejected; as, "Sometimes, thro' pride, the sexes change their airs; My lord has *vapours*, and my lady swears" (*Young*).

Ana. *Sorrow, grief, anguish, woe: despondency, despair, hopelessness, forlornness (see under DESPONDENT).

Ant. Gladness.

saecular. Variant of SECULAR.

safe, *adj.* **Safe, secure** come into comparison only when they mean free from danger or apprehension of danger. **Safe** (etymologically, whole, sound) in its earliest and still current sense implies that one has passed through dangers or has run the risk of injury, of being lost (often, in early use, spiritually lost), or the like, without incurring harm or damage; as, they arrived home *safe* and sound after their long journey; she always insists on seeing her children *safe* in their schoolrooms. In its later and now more common senses, *safe* applies to persons or possessions whose situation or position involves neither risk nor exposure to destruction or loss (as, "Let the great world rage! We will stay here *safe* in the quiet dwellings"—*Shelley;* to build shelters where the people might go to be *safe* from falling bombs; he felt that his money was *safe* when it was in a bank), or to things, such as highways, bridges, or vehicles, or such as policies, actions, or courses, that are so constructed or designed that they expose one to few or no risks (as, a *safe* harbor; a *safe* fire escape; a *safe* investment; " 'Tis never *safe* to despise an enemy"—*Defoe*), or to any cautious procedure which keeps one out of danger or free from the risk of making an error or blunder (as, this is as much as it is *safe* to say about the prospects of a cure for cancer; "What know I?...I take refuge...in the *safe* old question of Montaigne"—*C. E. Montague*). **Secure** (etymologically, without care) in its earliest sense, which is now archaic except in a few idiomatic phrases, implies freedom from anxiety or apprehension of danger; as, most people like to feel *secure*. In this sense, the term so often connoted overconfidence that it was frequently contrasted with *safe;* as, "From being anxious or *secure* deliver us" (*Donne*); "Man may *securely* sin, but *safely* never" (*B. Jonson*). The term is now often a synonym of *safe* rather than a counterterm, but it still often stresses freedom from anxiety not as merely a subjective state but as a frame of mind induced by grounds that are good and sufficient. Sometimes the grounds are intellectual and imply sufficient evidence to establish the certainty of something that has been doubted. "Jane should therefore make the most of every half-hour in which she can command his attention. When she is *secure* of him, there will be leisure for falling in love" (*Austen*). Sometimes the grounds are material, such as the existence of sufficient money, the possession or definite expectation of property, a definite means of livelihood, or the like, which enables one to live or make a venture without fear, or the provision of safeguards or protective devices which make a thing safe to use, follow, or the like; as, the offer of a partnership by making his future *secure* also made his marriage possible; now that the foundations were in good repair they regarded the bridge as *secure*. "A provident, rather thoughtful people, who made their livelihood *secure* by raising crops and fowl" (*Cather*). Often, the term suggests not only a freedom from fear of danger, but a position, condition, or situation free from all hazards; as, the poet has made a *secure* place for himself in the history of English poetry. "To the average man, doomed to some banal and sordid drudgery all his life long, they [women] offer the only grand hazard that he ever encounters. Take them away and his existence would be as flat and *secure* as that of a milch cow" (*Mencken*).

Ana. Protected, guarded, shielded (see DEFEND): *reliable, dependable, tried.

Ant. Dangerous. — ***Con.*** Precarious, hazardous, risky, perilous, jeopardous (see DANGEROUS).

safeguard, *v.* Guard, shield, protect, *defend.

Ana. Conserve, preserve, *save: secure, insure, *ensure, assure.

saga. *Myth, legend.

sagacious. Perspicacious, astute, *shrewd.

Ana. *Sharp, keen, acute: penetrating, piercing, probing (see ENTER): *wise, judicious, sage, sapient.

sage, *adj.* *Wise, sapient, judicious, prudent, sensible, sane.

Ana. *Intelligent, knowing, brilliant: *learned, erudite: sagacious, perspicacious (see SHREWD).

sail, *v.* Float, skim, scud, shoot, dart, *fly.

sailor. *Mariner, seaman, tar, gob, matlow, bluejacket, rating.

salable. Marketable, *vendible, purchasable.

Ant. Unsalable.

salary. *Wage, stipend, pay, hire, emolument, fee, screw.

salient. Conspicuous, outstanding, signal, striking, arresting, prominent, remarkable, *noticeable.

Ana. Significant, important, weighty (see corresponding nouns at IMPORTANCE): impressive, *moving: obtrusive, intrusive (see IMPERTINENT).

salubrious. *Healthful, healthy, wholesome, salutary, hygienic, sanitary.

Ana. *Beneficial, advantageous: benign, *favorable.

salutary. Wholesome, *healthful, healthy, salubrious, hygienic, sanitary.

Ana. *Beneficial, advantageous, profitable: restorative, alterative, tonic (see corresponding nouns at RESTORATIVE).

Ant. Deleterious: evil.

salutation. *Greeting, salute.

salute, *v.* *Address, greet, hail, accost.

salute, *n.* *Greeting, salutation.

salve. *Balm, emollient, demulcent.

same, *adj.* **Same, selfsame, very, identical, identic, equivalent, equal, tantamount** come into comparison when they mean either not different from the other or others or not differing from each other. **Same** may imply, and **selfsame** invariably implies, that the things under consideration are one thing, and not two or three different things; as, this is the *same* (or *selfsame*) book that John once owned; their dresses were made from the *same* (or *selfsame*) bolt of cloth; they go to the *same* summer resort year after year. But *same* (not *selfsame*) may be used to imply numerical difference (that is, that the things considered are actually distinct), with otherwise no appreciable difference in quality, kind, appearance, amount, or the like. "[Marlborough] could see a hero perish or a sparrow fall, with the *same* amount of sympathy for either" (*Thackeray*); "Nothing can be as it has been before; Better, so call it, only not the *same*" (*Browning*). **Very,** like *selfsame*, implies no difference in number between the things under consideration; as, you are the *very* man I have been anxious to see; "That is the *very* thing that I was saying" (*Shelley*). **Identical,** in its strictest use (see also SIMILAR), implies either selfsameness (as, I found it at the *identical* spot where I left it; the authors of the anonymous "Waverley" and of the popular "Lady of the Lake" were found to be *identical*) or absolute agreement in all details as of quality, shape, appearance, and the like (as, since the sculptures are *identical* one must be a replica of the other; no two leaves from the same tree are *identical;* twins that are *identical* develop from a single fertilized egg). "All experience shows, that the *same* measures, or measures scarcely distinguishable from each other, may flow from distinct powers; but this does not prove that the powers themselves are *identical*" (*Ch. Just. Marshall*). **Identic** is used chiefly in diplomacy to describe the use of the same form or the following of the same course by two different governments or by one government when dealing with two or more governments; as, the Allies sent *identic* answers to the ultimatum. Things are **equivalent** when they amount to the same thing (particularly when set off against each other), especially in worth, force, significance, or import; as, some heirs received their legacies in cash, some in real estate of *equivalent* value. "Silence is, after all, *equivalent* to a negation" (*Thackeray*). Things

are **equal** when there is no difference in number, amount, magnitude, value, or the like; as, *equal* salaries; *equal* quantities; *equal* merit; to divide in *equal* shares. **Tantamount** is commonly applied to other than material things one of which is in effect equivalent to the other; as, the Democratic nomination in some of the southern states is *tantamount* to election; "Such a movement... would be *tantamount* to a confession of failure" (*Trollope*).
Ana. Alike, like, akin, parallel, uniform (see SIMILAR).
Ant. Different.

sample, *n.* Specimen, example, *instance, case, illustration.
Ana. Piece, *part, portion, segment, fragment.

sanctimonious. 1 Pietistic, religious, *devout, pious.
Ana. See those at SANCTIMONIOUS, 2.
2 Hypocritical, pharisaical, canting. See under HYPOCRISY.
Ana. Affected, feigned, simulated, counterfeited, assumed, pretended (see ASSUME): perfervid, fervid, ardent, fervent (see IMPASSIONED).

sanctimony, sanctimoniousness. *Hypocrisy, pharisaism, cant, canting.
Ana. Pretending *or* pretense, simulation, feigning, counterfeiting, affecting *or* affectation (see corresponding verbs at ASSUME): enthusiasm, zealotry, fanaticism (cf. nouns at ENTHUSIAST).

sanction, *v.* *Approve, endorse, accredit, certify.
Ana. *Authorize, license, commission: confirm, *ratify: *enforce, implement.
Ant. Interdict.

sanctity. *Holiness.

sanctuary. Refuge, asylum, *shelter, cover, retreat, ark.
Ana. Safety, security (see corresponding adjectives at SAFE): protection, shielding *or* shield, guarding *or* guard (see corresponding verbs at DEFEND).

sand, *n.* *Fortitude, grit, backbone, pluck, guts.
Ana. *Courage, mettle, spirit, resolution, tenacity.

sane. *Wise, judicious, prudent, sensible, sage, sapient.
Ana. *Rational, reasonable: right, *good: sound, cogent, convincing (see VALID).
Ant. Insane.

sang-froid. Phlegm, composure, *equanimity.
Ana. Indifference, unconcernedness *or* unconcern, aloofness, detachment (see corresponding adjectives at INDIFFERENT): self-possession, aplomb, self-assurance, assurance, self-confidence, *confidence.

sanguinary. *Bloody, sanguine, sanguineous, gory.

sanguine. 1 Also **sanguineous.** *Bloody, sanguinary, gory.
Ant. Bloodless.
2 Assured, *confident, sure.
Ana. *Hopeful, optimistic: positive, certain, *sure.
Ant. Afraid (sense 2).

sanitary. *Healthful, hygienic, salutary, salubrious, healthy, wholesome.
Ana. Curing *or* curative, healing, remedying (see corresponding verbs at CURE): *effective, efficacious, effectual.
Ant. Noxious.

sanitize. Disinfect, *sterilize, fumigate.

sap, *v.* Undermine, enfeeble, *weaken, debilitate, cripple, disable.
Ana. Drain, *deplete, exhaust, impoverish: *ruin, wreck: *destroy.

sapid, saporous. *Palatable, appetizing, savory, tasty, toothsome, flavorsome, relishing.
Ant. Insipid. — *Con.* Vapid, flat, inane, jejune (see INSIPID): bland, *soft, mild.

sapidity. *Taste, flavor, savor, tang, relish, smack.
Ant. Insipidity.

sapient. Sage, *wise, judicious, prudent, sensible, sane.
Ana. *Learned, erudite, scholarly: sagacious, perspicacious (see SHREWD).

sarcasm. Satire, irony, *wit, humor, repartee.
Ana. Incisiveness, trenchancy, bitingness, cuttingness (see corresponding adjectives at INCISIVE): mockery, taunting, derision (see corresponding verbs at RIDICULE).

sarcastic *or* **sarcastical. Sarcastic** (*or* **sarcastical**), **satirical** (*or* **satiric**), **ironical** (*or* **ironic**), **sardonic** (*or* **sardonical**) come into comparison when they mean having or manifesting bitterness and power to cut or sting. A person, a mood, a remark, or an expression is **sarcastic** (less often **sarcastical**) when he or it manifests an intent to inflict pain on another by deriding him, taunting him, or making him ridiculous, as by backhanded compliments; as, *sarcastic* comments on an actor's performance; "Mr. Bennet was [an] odd...mixture of quick parts, *sarcastic* humour, reserve, and caprice" (*Austen*); "It is not necessary that the right honourable gentleman should *sarcastically* call that time to our recollection" (*Burke*). A person, or his utterance, expression, or spirit is **satirical** (less often **satiric,** this term being applied chiefly to literature or a literary work involving satire) when he or it manifests the intent to censure someone or something by holding him or it up for ridicule and reprobation. "At a later date Erasmus's ecclesiastical and princely friends laughed no less heartily over his *satirical* comments on kings and clerics" (*A. Huxley*). "All this comedy was filled with bitter *satiric* strokes against a certain young lady" (*Thackeray*). Not only a person, or an utterance, mood, or expression, but also a situation or an event may be described as **ironical** or **ironic** when he or it manifests the power to evoke amused, but often startled or unpleasant, reflection on the difference between what is said and what is intended, or between what happens and what was aimed at or what was expected. "Mr. Cruncher had no particular meaning in these sulky corroborations, but made use of them...to express general *ironical* dissatisfaction" (*Dickens*). "How his [Fielding's] *ironic* lightning plays Around a rogue and all his ways!" (*Dobson*). "How exquisitely *ironic* is the entertainment we can derive from our disillusions!" (*L. P. Smith*). "*Ironically* enough, it was Boston and Cambridge that grew to seem provincial, while the local and even parochial Concord mind...proved to be also national" (*Van W. Brooks*). A person or, more often, a person's smile, expression, or words may be described as **sardonic** when he or it manifests scorn, mockery, and derision or sneering malignancy. "A *sardonic* smile, such as Alexander von Humboldt used to have when he contemplated the late King of Prussia's missionary deaconesses" (*Arnold*). "He would sometimes, with *ironic* deference, send to borrow a rod of the Under Master, and then, with *sardonic* grin, observe to one of his upper boys 'how neat and fresh the twigs looked' " (*Lamb*). "The immortal Charles Critchlow came to the funeral, full of calm, *sardonic* glee, and without being asked" (*Bennett*).
Ana. Biting, cutting, trenchant, *incisive: *caustic, scathing, mordant, mordacious.

sardonic *or* **sardonical.** Ironical, satirical, *sarcastic.
Ana. *Bitter, acrid: deriding *or* derisive, mocking, taunting, ridiculing (see corresponding verbs at RIDICULE): *sinister, malign.

sate, *v.* *Satiate, surfeit, cloy, pall, glut, gorge, surcharge.
Ana. *Satisfy, content: *indulge, pamper, humor: gratify, regale, arride (see PLEASE).

satellite. *Follower, adherent, henchman, partisan, disciple, sectary.
Ana. Sycophant, *parasite, favorite, toady, lickspit, hanger-on: devotee, votary, *addict, fan.

satiate. **Satiate, sate, surfeit, cloy, pall, glut, gorge, surcharge** come into comparison chiefly as transitive, but often as intransitive, verbs meaning to fill or become filled to the point of repletion. Both **satiate** and **sate** have been, but are now less often, used in the sense of merely to satisfy completely (as, "I will *satiate* the soul of the priests with fatness"—*Jeremiah* xxxi. 14; "and my soul procure Wherewith to *sate* its malice"—*Shelley*): both terms, but especially *satiate,* now usually imply an overfilling or an overfeeding so that there is no longer any pleasure in that which had once pleased or seemed desirable. "Addison...had himself not above three or four notes in poetry, sweet enough, indeed, like those of a German flute, but such as soon tire and *satiate* the ear" (*Gray*). "The ordinary Roman...*satiated* alike with the fervours of the democrats and the rigidity of the conservatives" (*Buchan*). "I wondered even then if a few common words of explanation, a few sober words of promise, would not have satisfied the crowd, already *sated* with eloquence" (*A. Repplier*). **Surfeit** distinctly implies a feeding or supplying to excess, with consequent nausea or disgust; as, to *surfeit* oneself with sweets; to *surfeit* a person with flattery; "readers *surfeited* with the ...wild overstatements and wild understatements of public dispute" (*C. E. Montague*). "If music be the food of love, play on; Give me excess of it, that, *surfeiting,* The appetite may sicken, and so die" (*Shak.*). **Cloy** stresses the resulting disgust or boredom more than the surfeit which induces them. "Is it [love] not...all oil, all sugar? Zounds! it is enough to *cloy* the sharp-set appetite of a parson" (*Fielding*). "More happy love! More happy, happy love! For ever warm and still to be enjoy'd, For ever panting, and for ever young; All breathing human passion far above, That leaves a heart high-sorrowful and *cloy'd*" (*Keats*). **Pall** differs from *cloy* only in its greater emphasis upon the loss of all power in that with which one is surfeited to challenge one's interest or attention or to whet one's appetite: the term therefore refers rather to things that tend to satiate than to the persons whose appetites or desires have been sated by such things; as, "And *pall* the sense with one continu'd show" (*Addison*); "There anguish does not sting; nor pleasure *pall*" (*Keats*); "Common-sense does *pall* on a husband sometimes" (*Deland*). **Glut,** like *surfeit,* implies excess in feeding or supplying, but it stresses the consequent overloading rather than the extinction of appetite or desire: often, also, it suggests the stimulation of a greed that knows no limits except those imposed upon it by physical necessity; as, "seeming rather *glutted* than *satiated*" (*Goldsmith*); "Some straggling Cossacks from the town...*glutted,* but not *sated,* with blood" (*Jane Porter*). *Glut* may be used also in reference to impersonal things, implying merely an overloading, and carrying no suggestion of greed or satiation; as, the market is *glutted* with industrial bonds; his works *glut* the counters of the book stores. **Gorge** usually implies the stimulation of greed, but it distinctively suggests a glutting to the point almost of choking or bursting: the term therefore often, but far from always, implies the frustration of that greed; as, to *gorge* oneself with chocolate; "Dick fell upon eggs and bacon and *gorged* till he could *gorge* no more" (*Kipling*); "Heaven can *gorge* us with our own desires" (*Defoe*). **Surcharge** often implies a gorging, a glutting, or a surfeiting, but it carries a stronger implication than any of these terms of a consequent weighing down or oppressing. The term, however, is used less often with reference to persons than to things, though it is still frequently employed figuratively in reference to a person's heart or mind; as, a heart *surcharged* with grief; cares that *surcharge* his mind with worry; "till his spirit sank, *Surcharged,* within him" (*Wordsworth*). When the reference is to things, *surcharge* usually implies an excess of something that disturbs the balance, vitality, freshness, or the like, of the thing affected; as, warm air *surcharged* with moisture; his blood is *surcharged* with tetanus toxin.
Ana. *Satisfy, content: pamper, humor, *indulge: gratify, regale, arride (see PLEASE).

satiny, satin. Silky, silken, velvety, glabrous, glossy, *sleek, slick.

satire. Irony, *wit, humor, sarcasm, repartee.
Ana. Raillery, persiflage, *badinage: lampoon, pasquinade, *libel, skit: ridiculing *or* ridicule, deriding *or* derision, taunting (see corresponding verbs at RIDICULE).

satirical *or* **satiric.** Ironical, sardonic, *sarcastic.
Ana. *Pungent, piquant, poignant: ridiculing, deriding *or* derisive, taunting, mocking (see corresponding verbs at RIDICULE): mordant, mordacious, *caustic, scathing.

satisfied. Content (see under SATISFY).
Ana. Gratified, gladdened, pleased (see PLEASE): appeased, pacified (see PACIFY).

satisfy. **1 Satisfy, content** come into comparison as meaning to appease one's desires or longings. The same distinctions in implications are also found in their corresponding adjectives **satisfied** and **content** (*or* **contented**). **Satisfy** implies full appeasement not only of one's desires or longings but also of one's needs, requirements, or the like; as, walks that *satisfy* one's wish for exercise; he was always ready to *satisfy* every one of her desires. "[Bishop Vaillant] was summoned to Rome to explain his complicated finance before the Papal Court,—and he had very hard work to *satisfy* the Cardinals" (*Cather*). **Content** implies appeasement to the point where one is not disquieted or disturbed by a desire for what one does not have, even though every wish is not fully gratified; as, "When I was at home, I was in a better place: but travellers must be *content*" (*Shak.*); "my own garden must *content* me this year" (*Quiller-Couch*). "I was sure ...they would both be...*satisfied* with life, Jane because she would get what she wanted, Clare because she would be *content* with little" (*R. Macaulay*).
Ana. Gratify, gladden, *please: appease, *pacify: *satiate, sate.
Ant. Tantalize.

2 Recompense, compensate, requite, remunerate, repay, *pay, reimburse, indemnify.
Ana. Balance, *compensate, offset.

3 Satisfy, fulfill (*or* **fulfil**), **meet, answer** come into comparison when they mean to measure up to a condition, a need, a claim, a hope, and the like. They are seldom interchangeable, however, without loss of precision or expressiveness or without violation of idiom. **Satisfy,** as here narrowly interpreted, is used chiefly in reference to things (or persons considered impersonally) which are submitted to a test, such as a condition, a requirement, or a hypothesis, and found to be such in constitution or makeup as not to fall short. "There is one condition that a lyric ought to *satisfy;* it ought to pass the test of being read aloud" (*Binyon*). "He will *satisfy* Newman's famous definition of a gentleman as one who never inflicts pain" (*C. E. Montague*). **Fulfill** usually connotes more than adequacy, or richness and fullness of measure; also, that which is *fulfilled* is not determined by something calculable but by something indefinite or immeasurable, as expectations, hopes, desires, needs, and the like; as, a son seldom *fulfills* his father's hopes; the trip *fulfilled* all the claims made for it. **Meet** implies exact agreement with that which is the test or measure, and therefore usually connotes mathematical equivalence; thus, "the new machine *meets* expectations" is slightly more tempered praise than, "the new machine *fulfills* expectations"; the supply *meets* the demand; the estate is not large enough to *meet* the claims against it. **Answer** usually, but not necessarily, implies even more moderation in praise than *meet;* while it does not imply dissatisfaction, it seldom connotes complete content; as, this knife will *answer* the purpose; his rating *answered* his parents' expectations.

Ana. *Prove, test, try, demonstrate: verify, substantiate, corroborate, *confirm: *match, equal, rival, approach, touch.

saturate. **1** *Soak, steep, impregnate, drench, sog, sop, ret, waterlog.

Ana. *Dip, immerse, submerge: *absorb, imbibe, assimilate.

2 Impregnate, interpenetrate, impenetrate, penetrate, *permeate, pervade.

Ana. *Infuse, imbue, ingrain, inoculate: penetrate, pierce, probe (see ENTER).

saturnine. Dour, gloomy, *sullen, glum, morose, surly, sulky, crabbed.

Ana. Grave, *serious, solemn, staid: taciturn, reserved, uncommunicative, *silent.

Ant. Genial: mercurial.

saucy. **Saucy, pert, arch** come into comparison, in spite of widely different implications, when they agree in meaning flippant and bold rather than serious and respectful in one's manner or attitude. **Saucy** originally stressed insolence or impertinence to superiors, especially as shown in offensive speech: in modern use it is not always so strongly derogatory, though it still implies lack of proper respect; as, a *saucy* pupil; a *saucy* retort. Usually it also implies piquancy and levity, with a hint of smartness or of amusing effrontery. "A little *saucy* rose-bud minx can strike Death-damp into the breast of doughty king" (*Browning*). Sometimes it is applied also to birds and small animals on similar grounds; as, "some *saucy* puppies on their hind legs" (*Ruskin*); "a robin, playing among the moss tufts in the live oak, broke into a *saucy* little song" (*R. Bradford*). It is also applicable to troops (regiments, battalions, etc.), to ships, and the like, that present a brave, smart, and more or less pugnacious appearance; as, the *Saucy* Sixth (The Royal Warwickshire Regiment); "Tight and *saucy*—tight and *saucy*, Trim's the ship we hail from" (*W. C. Bennett*). **Pert** implies a saucy freedom that savors of presumption or affectation rather than of insolence. "A *pert* jackanapes, full of college petulance and self-conceit" (*Smollett*). "A little upstart, vulgar being...with all her airs of *pert* pretension" (*Austen*). In some contexts the word carries additional implications found in its other senses, such as of cleverness, sprightliness, or the like. "A little, upright, *pert*, tart, tripping wight" (*Burns*). **Arch** usually implies roguish audacity or mischievous mockery, and often, when applied to women, carries a hint of coquettishness. "Elizabeth...at the first convenient pause, turned to him with an *arch* smile, and said—'You mean to frighten me, Mr. Darcy, by coming in all this state to hear me?' " (*Austen*). " 'Conceive an Island peopled by Women, and but one Man in their Society....Hem!' and the Aphorist looked *arch*. 'What course of treatment might that one Man anticipate at their hands?' " (*Meredith*).

Ana. Flippant, frivolous, volatile, light-minded (see corresponding nouns at LIGHTNESS): intrusive, obtrusive, meddlesome, *impertinent: brash, impudent (see SHAMELESS): piquant, snappy (see PUNGENT).

saunter. **Saunter, stroll, amble** agree in meaning to walk slowly and more or less aimlessly, especially in the open air. **Saunter** suggests a leisurely pace and an idle and carefree mind; as, "*sauntering* about the streets, loitering in a coffeehouse" (*Fielding*). **Stroll** differs from *saunter* chiefly in its implications of an objective, such as sight-seeing, exercise, or the like, pursued without haste and with wandering from one place to another. "Then we *strolled* For half the day thro' stately theatres" (*Tennyson*). "The notables of the town...*stroll* past with the dignity of Roman senators" (*A. Huxley*). **Amble** occasionally conveys the same implications as *saunter* or, sometimes, *stroll*, but it far more often suggests merely an easy, effortless gait comparable to that of an ambling horse. In older use, it usually was applied to dancing, especially to formal step dancing; as, "you jig, you *amble*, and you lisp" (*Shak.*); in modern English, it sometimes connotes slow mincing steps and at other times, a casual, jaunty gait.

savage, *adj.* **1** *Fierce, ferocious, barbarous, inhuman, cruel, fell, truculent.

Ana. Implacable, relentless, unrelenting, merciless, *grim: rapacious, *voracious, ravenous.

Con. Gentle, mild, lenient (see SOFT): humane, benevolent, *charitable.

2 Barbarous, *barbarian, barbaric.

Ana. Primitive, primeval (see PRIMARY): *rough, harsh: untaught, untutored, *ignorant.

Con. *Tame, submissive, subdued: civilized, cultured (see corresponding nouns at CIVILIZATION).

save, *v.* **1** Deliver, redeem, *rescue, ransom, reclaim.

Ana. *Free, release, liberate, emancipate: *defend, protect, shield, guard, safeguard: *recover, retrieve, recoup, recruit.

Ant. Lose: waste: damn (*in theology*).

2 **Save, preserve, conserve** come into comparison as meaning to keep free or secure from injury, decay, destruction, or loss. **Save** may imply measures taken to protect something from danger of loss, injury, or destruction (as, to *save* one's papers by keeping them in a vault; "All I pray is that this young child may be *saved* from him"—*Meredith*) but, more often, it suggests rescue or delivery from a dangerous situation, especially one which means death or destruction; as, to *save* a child from drowning; the house was *saved* from the fire; "The souls I could not *save*" (*Housman*). **Preserve** stresses the idea of resistance to destructive agencies and hence implies the use of means to keep something in existence or intact; as, old records are *preserved* by protecting them from light and moisture; fruits are *preserved* by heating which destroys bacteria and by the addition of sugar; meats are *preserved* by curing or refrigeration; wood is impregnated with creosote to *preserve* it. "Constitutions are intended to *preserve* practical and substantial rights, not to maintain theories" (*Justice Holmes*). **Conserve,** on the other hand, suggests keeping sound and unimpaired, and implies the use of means to prevent change, loss, or depletion; as, a convalescent must *conserve* his energy if he is to make rapid progress; our constitutional rights can be *conserved* only by an intelligent electorate. Consequently, *conserved* fruits (**conserves**) are sometimes (not invariably) distinguished from all other kinds of preserved fruits (**preserves**), as those which are prepared by a process intended to retain the original color, shape, and flavor of the fruits.

Ana. *Have, hold, own, possess, enjoy: *keep, retain, reserve.

Ant. Spend: consume.

savoir-faire. Poise, *tact, address.

Ana. Grace, dignity, *elegance: ease, *readiness, dexterity, facility: self-possession, self-assurance, aplomb, *confidence.
Con. Awkwardness, clumsiness, ineptness, maladroitness, gaucherie (see corresponding adjectives at AWKWARD).

savor *or* **savour,** *n.* **1** *Taste, sapidity, flavor, tang, relish, smack.
2 *Atmosphere, feeling, feel, tone, aura.
Ana. *Quality, property, character, attribute: peculiarity, individuality, characteristic, distinctiveness (see corresponding adjectives at CHARACTERISTIC): *impression, impress, print, stamp.

savory *or* **savoury.** *Palatable, appetizing, sapid, saporous, tasty, toothsome, flavorsome, relishing.
Ant. Bland (*to taste*): acrid (*in taste and smell*).

saw, *n.* *Saying, maxim, adage, proverb, motto, epigram, aphorism, apothegm.

saying. Saying, saw, maxim, adage, proverb, motto, epigram, aphorism, apothegm, agree in denoting a sententious expression of a general truth. A **saying** is a brief current or habitual expression of whatever form. "The *saying* is true, 'The empty vessel makes the greatest sound' " (*Shak.*). A **saw** is an oft-repeated, and now usually ancient, saying. "Full of wise *saws* and modern instances" (*Shak.*). A **maxim** is a rule or precept sanctioned by experience, and relating especially to the practical concerns of life; as, Benjamin Franklin was the author of many *maxims* such as "early to bed and early to rise, Makes a man healthy, wealthy, and wise." "The difference between principles as universal laws, and *maxims* of conduct as prudential rules" (*Crabb Robinson*). An **adage** is a saying given credit by long use and general acceptance. "If there is verity in wine, according to the old *adage*" (*Thackeray*). A **proverb** is an adage couched, usually, in homely and vividly concrete or figurative phrase. "Accused (in the phrase of a homely *proverb*) of being 'penny-wise and pound-foolish' " (*Spectator*). A **motto** is usually a maxim or moral aphorism adopted by a person, a society, or an institution as a guiding principle or as a statement of an aim or ideal. "William of Wykeham's old *motto* that 'Manners makyth Man' " (*Quiller-Couch*). The last three terms, *epigram*, *aphorism*, and *apothegm* commonly imply known authorship and a conscious literary quality. An **epigram** gets its effectiveness from its terseness and a witty turn of phrase; it characteristically presents a paradox or a cleverly pointed antithesis, as in Pope's "The right divine of kings to govern wrong." "What is an *Epigram?* A dwarfish whole, Its body brevity, and wit its soul" (*Coleridge*). An **aphorism** is a pithy epigram that gives food for thought. "When Mark Twain utters such characteristic *aphorisms* as 'Heaven for climate, hell for society' " (*Van W. Brooks*). An **apothegm** is a sharply pointed and often startling aphorism such as Johnson's remark, "Patriotism is the last refuge of a scoundrel."

scabrous. *Rough, harsh, uneven, rugged.
Ant. Glabrous: smooth.

scald *or* **skald,** *n.* *Poet, versifier, rhymer, rhymester, poetaster, bard, minstrel, scop, gleeman, jongleur, troubadour, trouvère, minnesinger.

scale, *n.* More often in plural form, **scales.** *Balance.

scale, *v.* Climb, mount, *ascend.

scan. *Scrutinize, examine, inspect, audit.
Ana. *Consider, study, contemplate: observe, survey, remark, notice (see SEE).

scandal, *n.* **1** *Offense, sin, vice, crime.
Ana. Indignity, insult, *affront: offending *or* offense, outraging *or* outrage (see corresponding verbs at OFFEND): wrong, grievance, injury, *injustice.
2 *Disgrace, dishonor, disrepute, shame, infamy, ignominy, opprobrium, obloquy, odium.
Ana. Reproaching *or* reproach, rebuking *or* rebuke (see corresponding verbs at REPROVE): reflection, stricture (see ANIMADVERSION).
3 *Detraction, calumny, slander, backbiting.
Ana. Gossiping *or* gossip, tattling (see corresponding verbs at GOSSIP): maligning, defaming *or* defamation, traducing (see corresponding verbs at MALIGN).

scanning. Scrutiny, examination, inspection, audit. See under SCRUTINIZE.
Ana. Study, application, *attention, concentration: *oversight, supervision, surveillance: analysis, dissection (see under ANALYZE).

scant. Scanty, skimpy, scrimpy, *meager, exiguous, spare, sparse.
Ana. *Deficient, defective: scarce, rare, *infrequent: insufficient, inadequate (see affirmative adjectives at SUFFICIENT).
Ant. Plentiful: profuse.

scanty. Scant, skimpy, scrimpy, *meager, exiguous, spare, sparse.
Ana. Insufficient, inadequate (see affirmative adjectives at SUFFICIENT): *deficient.
Ant. Ample, plentiful: profuse.

scarce. Rare, uncommon, *infrequent, occasional, sporadic.
Ana. *Deficient: insufficient, inadequate (see affirmative adjectives at SUFFICIENT): curtailed, abridged, shortened (see SHORTEN).
Ant. Abundant.

scarcely. *Hardly, barely.

scare, *v.* Alarm, *frighten, fright, terrify, terrorize, startle, affray, affright.
Ana. Daunt, appall, *dismay: *intimidate, cow, browbeat: astound, amaze, flabbergast, astonish, *surprise.
Ant. Entice.

scathing. *Caustic, mordant, mordacious, acrid.
Ana. Scorching, searing, burning (see BURN): *fierce, ferocious, truculent, savage: *incisive, biting, cutting, trenchant.

scatter. Scatter, disperse, dissipate, dispel come into comparison when they mean to cause a group, mass, assemblage, or the like to separate or break up. **Scatter** may imply the use or operation of force which drives the persons or things in different directions; as, the hurricane *scattered* the ships of the fleet; the heavy assault *scattered* the troops; the wind *scattered* the leaves. On the other hand, *scatter* may imply little more than throwing or casting so that the things thrown will fall where (or as if where) they will; as, to *scatter* pennies; to *scatter* seeds; to *scatter* rugs. **Disperse** usually implies a wider separation of the units than *scatter* and a complete breaking up of the mass or assemblage; as, the rain quickly *dispersed* the crowd; "In a few years, the Bureau was dismembered, its staff *dispersed*" (*V. Heiser*); "A sea where all the ships in the world might be so *dispersed* as that none should see another" (*Cowper*). **Dissipate** suggests definitely the idea of complete disintegration or dissolution, as by evaporation, crumbling, squandering, or the like, and consequent vanishing; thus, the sun *dissipates* (that is, causes to evaporate) the mist; to *dissipate* one's energy in futile efforts; "[the aesthetic instinct] which ...may restrain the excesses of the possessive instinct and *dissipate* the perils which threaten civilisation" (*H. Ellis*); "Denzil had a small patrimony...that he *dissipated* before he left college" (*Meredith*). **Dispel** carries less suggestion of separation of units or particles than any of these words but it stresses a driving away as if by scattering, of that which clouds, confuses, bothers, or the like; as, the rising sun *dispelled* the darkness; to *dispel* doubts. "A blind man whose darkness no street lamp can *dispel*" (*Shaw*). "Truth and frankness *dispel* difficulties" (*B. Russell*).

Ana. *Throw, cast, fling, toss: *distribute, dispense, divide: *discard, shed, cast.

Con. *Accumulate, amass, hoard: collect, *gather, assemble: *compact, concentrate.

scent, *n.* **1** *Smell, odor, aroma.

Ana. Emanation, issuing *or* issue (see corresponding verbs at SPRING).

2 *Fragrance, perfume, incense, redolence, bouquet.

sceptic. Variant of SKEPTIC.

scepticism. Variant of SKEPTICISM.

schedule, *n.* **1** *List, table, catalogue, register, roll, roster, rota, canon, inventory.

2 *Program, timetable, agenda.

scheme, *n.* **1** *Plan, design, plot, project.

Ana. *Proposal, proposition: arrangement, ordering (see corresponding verbs at ORDER): *device, contrivance: expedient, shift, makeshift (see RESOURCE).

2 *System, organism, economy, network, complex.

Ana. Organization, arrangement, ordering (see corresponding verbs at ORDER): whole, total, *sum.

scheme, *v.* Plan, design, plot, project. See under PLAN, *n.*

Ana. Propose, purpose, *intend: *aim, aspire: manipulate, *handle, swing, wield.

schemer. See under PLAN, *n.*

schismatic, *n.* *Heretic, sectarian, dissenter, nonconformist.

scholar. **Scholar, pupil, student, disciple** come into comparison when they denote one who studies under a teacher. **Scholar** stresses enrollment in a school (now especially, except in its specific senses, in an elementary school, a Sunday school, or the like) and therefore tuition and instruction; as, the school has five hundred *scholars;* an opportunity open to all of our *scholars.* But *scholar* is specifically applied to one who is enrolled in a college or university and holds a scholarship, or an allowance that is granted to enable him to prosecute his studies; as, Rhodes *scholars* at Oxford. **Pupil** suggests more strongly than *scholar* the teacher's personal care or oversight; it therefore may be used not only of those in school but of learners studying privately under a teacher; as, he takes *pupils* in subjects required for college entrance; she has ten *pupils* to whom she gives instruction in music; the teacher found her *pupils* exceedingly restless that day. **Student,** though generally applicable to anyone who studies or who loves to study, is, as here considered, the general term for anyone who attends a higher institution of learning such as a technical school; a college, or a university; as, the number of *students* in the college; a college *student; student* life. **Disciple,** largely if not entirely through the influence of the Biblical sense (as, a *disciple* of Jesus [see FOLLOWER]) has never been much used in English in its etymological sense of *pupil.* It occurs occasionally chiefly in reference to ancient times or in humorous use, but even then with some connotation of devoted adherence to the teachings of the master. "The true teacher defends his *pupils* against his own personal influence.... He will have no *disciple*" (*Bronson Alcott*).

scholarly. *Learned, erudite, polymathic.

Ana. Academic, scholastic, *pedantic: abstruse, *recondite: accurate, exact, precise (see CORRECT).

scholarship. Learning, erudition, *knowledge, science, information, lore.

scholastic. Academic, *pedantic, bookish.

Ana. *Conversant, versed: *dry, arid: formal, conventional (see CEREMONIAL).

school, *n.* *Flock, herd, drove, pack, bevy, covey, gaggle, flight, swarm, shoal.

school, *v.* Discipline, train, *teach, instruct, educate.

Ana. *Practice, exercise, drill: *guide, lead: *conduct, control, direct, manage.

science. **1** *Knowledge, learning, erudition, scholarship, information, lore.

2 *Art.

scintillate. *Flash, gleam, glance, glint, sparkle, glitter, glisten, coruscate, glimmer, shimmer, twinkle, glister, spark.

scoff, *v.* **Scoff, jeer, gibe, jibe, fleer, gird, sneer, flout** are here compared as meaning to manifest one's scorn or contempt in derision or mockery. **Scoff** stresses insolence, irreverence, lack of respect, or incredulity as the motives for one's derision or mockery; as, "It is an easy thing to *scoff* at any art or recreation; a little wit mixed with ill nature, confidence, and malice, will do it" (*Walton*); "Fools, who came to *scoff*, remained to pray" (*Goldsmith*); "In jesting mood his comrades heard his tale, And *scoffed* at it" (*Amy Lowell*). **Jeer** carries a stronger implication of derisive laughter and of loud raillery than *scoff:* it usually connotes a coarser and more vulgar or, at least, a less keenly critical attitude than *scoff;* as, "Tindal and Toland, prompt at priests to *jeer*" (*Pope*); "inclined to *jeer* at those slightly older than himself who show any tendency to abandon the—to him—rational preoccupations of childhood" (*J. W. Krutch*). **Gibe** (or less often, in this sense, **jibe**) stresses taunting, often in derisive sarcasm, sometimes in good-natured raillery; as, "you ... with taunts Did *gibe* my missive out of audience" (*Shak.*); "Richardson...is always *gibing* at Fielding" (*L. Stephen*). "After one of her visitations you *gibed* each other good-naturedly over the extent to which you found yourself shifted from the firm ground of reasoned conclusion" (*M. Austin*). **Fleer** throws the emphasis upon derisive grins, grimaces, and laughs rather than on utterances; as, "[They] look like two old maids of honor got into a circle of *fleering* girls and boys" (*Gray*); "the *fleering* rabble" (*Stevenson*); "He listened with a *fleering* mouth to his father's long dogmatic grace before meat" (*J. Hergesheimer*). **Gird** implies an attack marked by scoffing, gibing, or jeering; as, "The subprior was bidden to sing...the 'Elegy of the Rose'; the author *girding* cheerily at the clerkly man's assumed ignorance of such compositions" (*Pater*); "[Matthew Arnold] *girds* at...Herbert Spencer for substituting *Unknowable* for *God;* quite unaware that his own Eternal...comes to exactly the same thing as the Unknowable" (*T. S. Eliot*). **Sneer** carries the strongest implication of cynicism and ill-natured contempt of any of these terms: it often suggests the use of irony or satire the real purport of which is indicated by an insultingly contemptuous facial expression, tone of voice, or manner of phrasing; as, "[the critic] is always *sneering* at the simple joys of the mentally humble" (*C. E. Montague*); " 'People are nowadays so cynical—they *sneer* at everything that makes life worth living' " (*L. P. Smith*). **Flout,** which is more often used transitively than intransitively, may imply any of the actions suggested by the preceding terms, but it carries a heightened implication not only of disdain and contempt but of refusal to heed or of a denial of a thing's truth or power; as, "That bids him *flout* the Law he makes, That bids

him make the Law he *flouts*" (*Kipling*); "no form of Christianity which *flouts* science is in the true line of progress" (*Inge*); "The women pointed and *flouted* at her" (*Besant & Rice*). "It seems incredible that any nation in the world should have *flouted* another nation so contemptuously as Prussia *flouted* us when we tried the unaccustomed rôle of conciliation" (*A. Repplier*).
Ana. *Ridicule, deride, mock, taunt: scorn, disdain, scout, contemn, *despise.

scold, *n.* Shrew, vixen, termagant, *virago, amazon, barge.

scold, *v.* **Scold, upbraid, rate, berate, tonguelash, jaw, bawl out, wig, rail, revile, vituperate** agree in meaning to reprove, reproach, or censure angrily, harshly, and more or less abusively. **Scold,** the term most common in ordinary use, usually implies a rebuking in a mood of irritation or ill temper, with or without sufficient justification; as, his father *scolded* him for staying out late; "[she] began *scolding* one of her daughters. 'Don't keep coughing so, Kitty, for Heaven's sake! Have a little compassion on my nerves'" (*Austen*); "he was harshly and openly anxious about him [his orphaned nephew]. He *scolded* Miss Hannah because he was pale" (*Deland*). **Upbraid,** which is decreasingly found in colloquial speech, in precise use stresses reproaching or censuring on more definite grounds than *scold* does: it, therefore, usually suggests justification or justifiable anger; as, the judge *upbraided* the parents for the petty thieving of their children; "Afterward he [the risen Christ] appeared ...and *upbraided* them with their unbelief and hardness of heart" (*Mark* xvi. 14). "I think he'd meant to *upbraid* me for sneaking off, but he didn't" (*Cather*). **Rate** and the more common **berate** usually imply more or less prolonged, angry, and sometimes abusive, scolding either in censuring or in reprimanding; as, "the voice continued violently *rating* me" (*Hudson*); "Hearing Ed Hall *berate* a farmer who doubted the practicability of the machine" (*S. Anderson*). Fairly close synonyms of *rate* and *berate* are the expressive **tonguelash** (commonly found as a verbal noun in *-ing*) which stresses the punitive effect on the person berated (as, to suffer from a fifteen-minute *tonguelashing*) and the slang terms **jaw, bawl out** (chiefly American), and **wig** (chiefly British), which emphasize the noisy ranting which usually attends a berating (as, "I have been *jawed* for letting you go"—*Marryat;* "You'll get *bawled out* when you pull a boner"—*C. Mathewson;* "a subordinate...who presumably had been severely '*wigged*' by his chief"—*The Times*). **Rail,** normally an intransitive verb, but followed by *at, against,* or rarely, *on* or *upon* when the person or thing berated is named, carries a more definite implication of either abusive or scoffing language than *rate* or *berate;* as, "David sent messengers...to salute our master; and he *railed* on them" (*1 Samuel* xxv. 14); "Enemies... *rail* at him for crimes he is not guilty of" (*Junius*); "Too often *rails* to gratify his spleen" (*Cowper*); "And the couples *railed* at the chant and the frown Of the witch-men lean, and laughed them down" (*V. Lindsay*). **Revile** carries a much stronger implication of abusive, scurrilous language than *rail* does, but little, if any, suggestion of scoffing: often, also, it implies deliberate vilification; as, "they that passed by *reviled* him, wagging their heads" (*Matthew* xxvii. 39); "she roundly abused the tobacco which she was then smoking, *reviled* all Brahmins" (*Kipling*); "Her tenants, who have to earn the money she spends abroad...*revile* her as a fugitive and an absentee" (*Shaw*). **Vituperate** implies more violence in the censure and in the method of attack than does *revile,* but otherwise they are close synonyms; as, "he *vituperated* from the pulpit the vices of the court" (*Froude*); "The last image that crossed his mind was Sir James with his angry face and his trembling hands *vituperating* him" (*Arch. Marshall*).
Ana. Reprehend, reprobate, censure, blame, *criticize: reproach, reprimand, *reprove, rebuke, admonish, chide: *execrate, objurgate.

sconce. *Penalize, fine, amerce, mulct.

scoop, *v.* *Dip, lade, bail, ladle, spoon, dish.

scop, *n.* Bard, minstrel, *poet, versifier, rhymer, rhymester, poetaster, gleeman, jongleur, troubadour, trouvère, minnesinger, scald.

scope. *Range, reach, compass, sweep, gamut, radius, ken, purview, horizon, orbit.
Ana. *Expanse, amplitude, spread, stretch: *field, domain, sphere, territory, province: extent, area, *size.

scorch, *v.* *Burn, char, sear, singe.
Ana. *Wither, shrivel, rivel.

scorn, *n.* Disdain, contempt, despite. See under DESPISE.
Ana. Superciliousness, insolence, disdainfulness (see corresponding adjectives at PROUD): scoffing, flouting, jeering, gibing (see SCOFF): deriding *or* derision, ridiculing *or* ridicule, taunting, mocking *or* mockery (see corresponding verbs at RIDICULE).

scorn, *v.* Disdain, scout, *despise, contemn.
Ana. Repudiate, spurn, reject (see DECLINE, *v.*): flout, *scoff, jeer, gibe: deride, mock, taunt, *ridicule.

Scotch, *adj.* **Scotch, Scottish, Scots** as adjectives meaning of, belonging to, derived from, or characteristic of Scotland or of its people are not always used with fixed differences in implications or applications, but within the past century or less there has been a perceptible movement toward establishing certain differences in good usage. Similar tendencies also show themselves in the employment of these terms as nouns. The oldest form of the adjective in English is *Scottish;* the oldest in Scottish is *Scots* (*Scottis*); *Scotch* dates from about 1570. **Scotch,** though the most recent of these terms, is the one most widely used outside of Scotland, especially in colloquial language. On the whole, the term is now avoided in literary use in England and America except in such phrases or collocations as are generally accepted as idioms indicating origin or use in Scotland (as, *Scotch* whisky; *Scotch* tweeds; a *Scotch* verdict; a *Scotch* mile; a *Scotch* acre) or as proper nouns or as names of species, types, dishes, or the like, having a real or a fancied connection with Scotland (as, *Scotch* Baptist; *Scotch* crocus; *Scotch* whist; *Scotch* dumpling). **Scottish** is now used in Scotland almost to the exclusion of *Scotch* except in the phrases noted or when *Scots* is preferred. In general, the same holds true with reference to precise literary use in England and America, but there is still evident in these countries a tendency to prefer *Scotch* where *Scottish* might seem an affectation or would not be euphonious; as, *Scotch* (rather than *Scottish*) lassies; the children have a *Scotch* (rather than a *Scottish*) nurse. When there is implied a clear opposition to or distinction from *English, Welsh, Irish,* or the like, *Scottish* is the customary term in these countries; as, the *Scottish* Church; the *Scottish* Episcopal Church; the *Scottish* poets; the *Scottish* School (of philosophers); *Scottish* literature; the *Scottish* character. Within a century, more or less, persons of Scottish birth or extraction have increasingly manifested a preference for **Scots** and now incline to use it in place of *Scottish* as well as of *Scotch;* as, "He thought *Scots* games inferior to southern sports" (*Buchan*); a *Scots* mile; *Scots*men (rather than *Scotch*men or *Scottish* men). Elsewhere, especially in England, this preference for *Scots* has been accepted only in certain phrases where the distinction from that which is English is highly important;

thus, a pound *Scots* is distinguished from a pound Sterling; *Scots* law is distinguished from English and Roman law.

The differences in the use of these terms as nouns do not proceed from their use as adjectives. **Scot** is the preferred term for an individual. **Scotch** usually names the people known as *Scotchmen* and *Scotsmen*, but *Scotch* is sometimes applied to the dialect or dialects of English spoken by this people; as, the *Scotch*, according to Professor Ripley, comprise three ethnic types; "which is to say, in plain *Scotch*, the gallows" (*Scott*). **Scottish** may apply to both the language and to the people, but the latter use is now comparatively rare, *Scotch* being the most widely accepted designation of the people. In Scotland *Scots* is preferred to *Scottish* as the name of the language.

Scotch, *n.* Scottish, Scots. See under SCOTCH, *adj.*

Scots, *adj.* *Scotch, Scottish.

Scots, *n.* Scotch, Scottish. See under SCOTCH, *adj.*

Scottish, *adj.* *Scotch, Scots.

Scottish, *n.* Scotch, Scots. See under SCOTCH, *adj.*

scout, *n.* *Emissary, spy, intelligencer, secret-service agent, secret agent.

scout, *v.* Scorn, *despise, contemn, disdain.
Ana. Flout, *scoff, sneer, jeer: deride, taunt, mock, *ridicule.

scowl, *v.* *Frown, glower, lower, gloom.
Ana. Glare, stare, *gaze.

scram. Retire, withdraw, clear out, *go, leave, depart, quit.

scranny. Variant of SCRAWNY.

scrap, *v.* *Discard, junk, cast, shed, molt, exuviate, slough.

scrap, *n.* *Brawl, broil, fracas, melee, row, rumpus.
Ana. *Quarrel, altercation, squabble, wrangle: fight, affray, fray, combat (see CONTEST).

scrape, *n.* *Predicament, dilemma, quandary, plight, fix, jam, pickle.
Ana. *Difficulty, vicissitude: perplexity, bewilderment, distraction (see corresponding verbs at PUZZLE): embarrassment, discomfiture (see correspondings verbs at EMBARRASS).

scrawny *or* **scranny.** Skinny, lank, lanky, *lean, spare, gaunt, rawboned, angular.
Ana. *Thin, slim, slender: *meager, exiguous.
Ant. Brawny: fleshy: obese.

screen, *v.* **1** *Hide, conceal, secrete, cache, bury, ensconce.
Ana. *Defend, protect, shield, guard, safeguard: *disguise, dissemble, cloak, mask.
2 *Sift, sieve, riddle, bolt, winnow.

screw. *Wage, salary, pay, hire, stipend, fee, emolument.

scribe. *Secretary, amanuensis, scrivener, stenographer, typist.

scrimpy. *Meager, scanty, scant, skimpy, exiguous, spare, sparse.
Ana. *Thin, slight, slender, slim: niggardly, *stingy, penurious, parsimonious.

scrivener. Scribe, amanuensis, *secretary, stenographer, typist.

scruple, *n.* Demur, *qualm, compunction.
Ana. *Hesitation, hesitancy: doubt, *uncertainty, suspicion, mistrust: misgiving, *apprehension.

scruple, *v.* *Demur, balk, jib, shy, boggle, stickle, stick, strain.
Ana. *Hesitate, waver, falter, vacillate: *object, protest.

scrupulous. **1** Meticulous, punctilious, punctual, *careful.
Ana. Fastidious, particular, finical, fussy (see NICE): exact, accurate, precise (see CORRECT).
Ant. Remiss.
2 Conscientious, *upright, honest, just, honorable.
Ana. *Moral, ethical, righteous, virtuous, noble: *rigid, rigorous, strict.
Ant. Unscrupulous.

scrutinize. **Scrutinize, scan, inspect, examine, audit** agree in meaning to look at or over critically and searchingly. The same distinctions in implications and connotations are observable in their corresponding nouns **scrutiny, scanning, inspection, examination,** and **audit.** **Scrutinize** and **scrutiny** imply close observation and attention to minute detail. "Utamaro takes a figure from the most ordinary human life—a woman in a draper's shop *scrutinising* a piece of gauze" (*Binyon*). "We have *scrutinized* the case, but cannot say that it shows an infraction of rights under the Constitution of the United States" (*Justice Holmes*). **Scan** and **scanning** are words which have in current use almost lost their historical emphasis on close analytic observation, except with reference to poetic verse and the detection of its metrical structure. In older English it always implied close survey or close study of a thing in order to reveal its design or inward character, or to pass judgment upon it. "The great Architect Did wisely to conceal, and not divulge His secrets, to be *scanned* by them who ought Rather admire" (*Milton*). "Know then thyself, presume not God to *scan;* The proper study of mankind is man" (*Pope*). In current English, *scan* is usually employed in reference to something that is surveyed from point to point; in discriminating use it still implies careful observation or study, but in loose use it sometimes implies the opposite and suggests a cursory glancing from one point to another; thus, to *scan* the newspaper each morning may admit of either interpretation. Only a context can make the implication clear. "The more one *scans* the later pages of Mark Twain's history the more one is forced to the conclusion that there was something gravely amiss with his inner life" (*Van W. Brooks*). **Inspect** and **inspection** in general use often imply little more than a careful observation, but in legal, military, governmental, and industrial use they imply a searching scrutiny for possible errors, defects, flaws, shortcomings, or the like; as, every length of cloth is *inspected* before it leaves the factory; the health department has ruled that cattle on dairy farms be regularly *inspected;* the troops prepared for the daily *inspection;* these guns will not pass *inspection.* Hence, *inspector* now frequently implies an official status or official duties; as, an *inspector* of sanitation; factory *inspectors.* **Examine,** as here compared (see also ASK, 1), and **examination** imply a close scrutiny or investigation to determine the facts about a thing, or the real nature, character, or condition of a thing, or to test a thing's quality, validity, truth, functioning, or the like; as, the critic refused to give an opinion before he had *examined* the painting closely; the doctor sent him to the hospital for a thorough *examination;* they *examined* the house from cellar to attic before deciding to purchase it. "Could it be the intention of those who gave this power, to say that...a case arising under the constitution should be decided without *examining* the instrument under which it arises?" (*Ch. Just. Marshall*). **Audit,** as verb or noun, implies a searching examination of accounts in order to determine their correctness; originally, as the word etymologically implies, such accounts were presented orally, as by a steward to his master, who examined, or *audited* them. The word was retained when examination of books and ledgers was implied; as, an annual *audit* of the tax books; federal and state examiners regularly *audit* the financial records of each bank. In its extended sense, *audit* often carries a suggestion of a final accounting, as at the Last Judgment. "The general day of account and *audit* to be made at the throne of God" (*Udall*). "When it comes to the *audit* before high heaven" (*Lowes*).

Ana. *Consider, study, contemplate, weigh, revolve: *analyze, resolve, dissect, anatomize: penetrate, pierce, probe (see ENTER).

scrutiny. Examination, scanning, inspection, audit. See under SCRUTINIZE.

Ana. Investigation, research, probe, *inquiry, inquisition: surveying *or* survey, observing *or* observation, viewing *or* view (see corresponding verbs at SEE).

scud. Skim, shoot, sail, *fly, dart, float.

sculk. Variant of SKULK.

scum. *Foam, froth, spume, lather, suds, yeast.

scurrilous, scurrile *or* **scurril.** *Abusive, opprobrious, vituperative, contumelious.

Ana. Ribald, obscene, gross, *coarse, vulgar: insulting, outraging, offending *or* offensive (see corresponding verbs at OFFEND): foul, filthy, *dirty.

scurrility. *Abuse, billingsgate, invective, vituperation, obloquy.

Ana. Vilifying *or* vilification, maligning, traducing, calumniation (see corresponding verbs at MALIGN): reviling, berating, upbraiding, rating, scolding (see SCOLD).

scurvy, *adj.* *Contemptible, despicable, pitiable, sorry, cheap, beggarly.

Ana. *Base, low, vile: *mean, abject.

seaman. *Mariner, sailor, tar, gob, matlow, bluejacket, rating.

sear, *v.* *Burn, scorch, char, singe.

season, *v.* *Harden, inure, acclimatize, acclimate.

Ana. *Habituate, accustom, familiarize: train, school, discipline (see TEACH): *practice, exercise, drill: *temper, anneal.

seasonable. **Seasonable, timely, well-timed, opportune, pat** come into comparison when they mean occurring or coming with peculiar appropriateness as to moment, condition, or the like. That is **seasonable** which is perfectly suited to the season or time of year (thus, *seasonable* fruits are those grown out of doors in their natural season; *seasonable* weather is the weather rightly to be expected at that time of year) or, by extension, which fits in perfectly with the needs of the moment, the character of the occasion, or the like (as, "his caution was... *seasonable*, and his advice...*good*"—*Defoe;* "[her] civility in listening to him [a suitor who had previously annoyed others by his attentions] was a *seasonable* relief to them all" (*Austen*). That is **timely** which is not only seasonable but comes or occurs at such a moment as to be of genuine value or service; as, a *timely* book; "To me alone there came a thought of grief: A *timely* utterance gave that thought relief" (*Wordsworth*); "The château is on fire; valuable objects may be saved from the flames by *timely* aid!" (*Dickens*). That is **well-timed** which is so timely as to suggest the appearance (often the actual exercise) of care, forethought, or design; as, "Their *well-timed* and rapid charge decided the conflict" (*Gibbon*); "The question was *well-timed*" (*Buchan*). That is **opportune** which fits directly into a given concurrence of circumstances or which comes, as if by accident, in the nick of time and works to the advantage of those concerned; as, they decided that the moment was not *opportune* for an uprising; the *opportune* death of the dictator prevented the collapse of peace negotiations; Blank's resignation was *opportune* for it gave Doe, who was at the point of desperation, his first chance for advancement. That is **pat** which is not only perfectly adapted to the situation or the moment but which, usually but far from invariably, comes or occurs at the very moment it is needed; as, a *pat* quotation; "Now might I [Hamlet] do it [kill Claudius] *pat*, now he is praying" (*Shak.*); "a story so *pat*, you may think it is coined" (*Cowper*); "[His presence there] had...the air of a miracle...of something pathetically and impossibly appropriate—'*pat*,' as they say in the Five Towns" (*Bennett*).

Ana. Apropos, apposite, pertinent, *relevant: appropriate, happy, felicitous, apt (see FIT): welcome, grateful, gratifying (see PLEASANT).

Ant. Unseasonable.

seclusion. *Solitude, isolation.

Ana. Retirement, withdrawal (see corresponding verbs at GO): separation, parting, severing *or* severance (see corresponding verbs at SEPARATE).

Con. *Intercourse, communication, commerce, dealings, communion.

second, *n.* *Instant, moment, minute, flash, trice, jiffy, twinkling, twinkle, split second.

secondary, *adj.* *Subordinate, dependent, subject, tributary, succursal, collateral.

Ana. *Auxiliary, accessory, subservient, subsidiary, contributory: incidental, *accidental, adventitious.

Ant. Primary.

second-rate. Mediocre, middling, *medium, moderate, average, fair, indifferent.

secret, *adj.* **Secret, covert, stealthy, furtive, clandestine, surreptitious, underhand, underhanded, privy, backstairs** (*or* **backstair**) come into comparison when they mean done, carried on, operated, or the like, so as not to attract attention or observation. **Secret,** the most general of these terms and the widest in its range of application, implies a hiding or concealing or a being hidden or concealed on any grounds or for any motive, good or bad; as, "These...virtues are the hidden beauties of a soul, the *secret* graces which cannot be discovered by a mortal eye" (*Spectator*); "She seized a lamp...and hurried towards the *secret* passage" (*Walpole*); "for eighteen years a *secret* and an unaccused prisoner in the Bastille" (*Dickens*); "from being public and respectable, its [fetishism's] manifestations become *secret*, personal and slightly shameful" (*A. Huxley*). **Covert** applies to something that is done, as it were, under cover, and is not open or avowed; as, "a *covert* glance at her face, as he walked beside her" (*Dickens*); "a mischievous child, with an eye on the face of a *covertly* watching elder" (*H. James*); "How was she, who was as innocent as a child, to know what was the meaning of the *covert* addresses of a villain?" (*Thackeray*); "his *covert* alliance against the House of Austria" (*Belloc*). **Stealthy** usually suggests an intent to elude, to spy upon, or to gain one's ends without attracting attention: it is, therefore, frequently a term either of derogation or of censure, connoting deliberateness and quietness in decoying, entrapping, or otherwise deceiving; as, "murder... with his *stealthy* pace ... towards his design Moves like a ghost" (*Shak.*); "the *stealthy*, prying manner common to the race [of cats]" (*N. Hawthorne*); "a series of gradual and *stealthy* encroachments on the rights of the people" (*Freeman*); the *stealthy* stalking of game or quarry. **Furtive** (etymologically, having the qualities of a thief) agrees with *stealthy* in suggesting an intent to escape observation, but it carries clearer suggestions of cautiousness, watchfulness, or slyness: consequently, the term not only describes movements and acts, but also faces, features, expressions, etc., which reveal these or similar characteristics; as, "The man in black, after a *furtive*

glance, did not look me in the face" (*Borrow*); "small *furtive* eyes" (*G. Eliot*); "They brought in the prosecutrix to give evidence. Pale, self-possessed, dressed in black, and rather comely, neither brazen nor *furtive*...her broad, matter-of-fact face...made on me...an impression of rather stupid honesty" (*Galsworthy*); "It would be possible for them, by breaking the law discreetly, to get all they want without discomfort; but....they...refuse to be the *furtive* evaders of a rule" (*A. Huxley*). **Clandestine** implies concealment, as in working out a plan, and, usually, an evil or illicit end: it commonly suggests stealthy or furtive methods or a fear lest others may know what is occurring; as, *clandestine* meetings; a *clandestine* marriage; "the *clandestine*, insidious, treacherous admirer of Maria Bertram" (*Austen*); "He had kept it to himself as if there were something *clandestine* in the plan, and discovery might prevent its execution" (*E. Wharton*); to carry on a *clandestine* trade in narcotic drugs. **Surreptitious** applies chiefly to stealthy and furtive actions, but also to emotions or desires and to concrete things which are concealed either for fear of their discovery or because one is violating a right, a law, a custom, or the like; as, "There he kept his *surreptitious* quids of tobacco, his pipe, and his small hoards" (*M. Wilkins*); "Over the paling of the garden we might obtain an oblique and *surreptitious* view" (*H. James*); to cherish a *surreptitious* liking for romantic love stories; the *surreptitious* removal of his stock by a merchant about to be forced into bankruptcy. **Underhand** and **underhanded** always carry an implication of fraud, deceit, or unfairness, in addition to that of secrecy in one's dealings or surreptitiousness in one's methods; as, "He had suspected his agent of some *underhand* dealings" (*Austen*); "I say all this to them as to you....I will have nothing *underhand*" (*Byron*); "He did not look quite like a professional gambler, but something smooth and twinkling in his countenance suggested an *underhanded* mode of life" (*Cather*). **Privy** is now archaic or poetic in the sense of *secret, stealthy* or *surreptitious* as in operation or methods (as, "Besides what [sheep] the grim wolf with *privy* paw Daily devours apace"—*Milton;* "That in an alley had a *privy* place"—*Wordsworth*), but the term is still often applied to the person or persons "in the secret," who are therefore, sometimes but far from always, clandestine participators (as, "She was *privy* to these manoeuvres"—*Thackeray;* "The Governments of Savoy, Spain and England were *privy* to what was toward.... Richelieu was to be killed"—*Belloc*). Historically also, the term survives in such designations as "*privy* council," originally a secret council whose members were appointed by the crown as confidential advisers, and as "the king's *privy* purse," the sum of money allotted to the king of England for his private use. **Backstairs** as an adjective carries an allusion to a stairway other than the main stairway, often an inconspicuous flight of stairs by which private, as distinguished from state, visitors ascended to the apartments of the sovereign or lord, or, in smaller residences, one used by servants. The term often suggests the workings of secret or privy influences and sometimes distinctly connotes intrigue (as, "a *backstairs* influence and clandestine government"—*Burke;* "*back-stairs* plots"—*L. Stephen*), but it may suggest little more than surreptitious acts, such as clandestine meetings, eavesdropping, and the like (as, *backstairs* gossip).
Ana. *Mysterious, inscrutable, arcane: puzzling, perplexing, mystifying (see PUZZLE, *v.*): hidden, concealed, secreted, screened (see HIDE).

secretary. **Secretary, amanuensis, scribe, scrivener, stenographer, typist** come into comparison when they designate a person employed by another to do writing or transcribing for him. The distinctions between the words are often in regard to the services actually performed, rather than the skills possessed, by the person. **Secretary** carries many more implications than those expressed in the common denotation. It implies, in addition, a relation of trust between employer and employee, as shown chiefly in handling correspondence of a confidential nature and in being given discretionary power in certain matters such as in making appointments or in permitting interviews. **Amanuensis, scribe** (obsolete in this sense), and **scrivener** were applied to a person who performed the duties of a secretary or of a copyist when handwriting was the means of transcription. The first and the last are now found chiefly in historical writing. **Stenographer** and **typist** primarily suggest the possession of skills; *stenographer* implies the ability to take notes in shorthand from dictation, of speeches, or of what is uttered in court proceedings, conferences, and the like; *typist*, the ability to operate a typewriter. As applied to employees, especially in an office, a stenographer is one who takes dictation in shorthand and transcribes these notes, usually in typewriting; a typist is one who copies written or printed material by means of a typewriter; thus, a *secretary* in a modern office is usually a *stenographer*, but a *typist* does not serve as a *secretary*.

secrete. *Hide, conceal, screen, cache, bury, ensconce.
Ana. Dissemble, cloak, mask, *disguise: *remove, withdraw.

secretive. Close, close-lipped, close-mouthed, tight-lipped, *silent, uncommunicative, taciturn, reticent, reserved.
Ana. *Cautious, circumspect, wary: restrained, inhibited (see RESTRAIN).
Con. *Talkative, loquacious, garrulous, voluble: candid, open, plain, *frank.

secret-service agent, secret agent. *Emissary, spy, scout, intelligencer.

sect. *Religion, denomination, cult, communion, faith, creed, persuasion, church.

sectary. **1** Adherent, *follower, disciple, partisan, henchman, satellite.
Ana. Devotee, votary, *addict, fan.
2 Also **sectarian.** *Heretic, schismatic, dissenter, nonconformist.
Ana. *Enthusiast, zealot, fanatic, bigot.

section, *n.* Sector, segment, division, *part, portion, piece, detail, member, fraction, fragment, parcel.
Ana. District, *locality, vicinity: region, tract, *area, zone, belt: *field, sphere, territory.

sector. Segment, section, division, *part, portion, piece, detail, member, fraction, fragment, parcel.

secular *or* **saecular.** **1** Temporal, lay, *profane.
Ana. Worldly, mundane, *earthly, earthy, terrestrial.
Ant. Religious (*as schools, journals, authorities, etc.*): profane (*as music, drama, etc*): regular (*as priests*).
2 **Secular** (*or* **saecular**), **centuried, agelong, aeonian** (*or* **eonian**), **diuturnal** agree in meaning enduring for or extending over ages or centuries. **Secular,** when applied to Roman games, plays, etc., means occurring once a century; in its far more common extended sense, partly scientific and partly literary, it implies a duration of several centuries; as, the *secular* contraction of the earth's crust; *secular* variations in the orbits of planets. "*Secular* oaks attired—in golden leafage" (*Symonds*). "Mankind outlives *saecular* animosities" (*Stevenson*). **Centuried,** which is not so frequent as *secular*, is not distinguishable from the latter in literary use. "This *centuried* eclipse of woe" (*Byron*). **Agelong** is the familiar word, but its implications of extent of time are vague and fluctuating.

"The *age-long* processes of Nature" (*J. A. Thomson*). **Aeonian** is rare and poetic; like *aeon*, it connotes immeasurable duration. "The sound of streams that swift or slow Draw down *aeonian* hills" (*Tennyson*). **Diuturnal,** also rare but found chiefly in prose, and its derivative *diuturnity*, are sometimes used in distinction from *eternal* and *eternity* to imply a beginning or an end, or both, that coincide with time's beginning or end. "Those things, by which the Peace between us may be preserv'd entire and *diuturnal*" (*Milton*). "I promise myself, if not immortality, yet *diuturnity* of being read" (*Lamb*).

Ana. Enduring, abiding, persisting (see CONTINUE): *lasting, permanent, perpetual, perdurable, stable.

secure, *adj.* *Safe.

Ana. *Firm, solid: protected, shielded, guarded, safeguarded, defended (see DEFEND): certain, positive, *sure: impregnable, unassailable, invulnerable, *invincible.

Ant. Precarious, dangerous.

secure, *v.* **1 Secure, anchor, moor, rivet** in their extended senses are comparable because they mean to fasten or fix firmly or immovably. They are, however, not often interchangeable because of implications derived from their primary senses. One **secures** that which may get lost, or which may escape, or which may permit invasion or intrusion if allowed to remain loose or to work loose; the word usually implies care or protection as the end of the action; as, to *secure* sails (which are being tugged at by winds); to *secure* doors and windows before retiring (to keep out burglars or other intruders). "And if the fly, like my hero, shews a strength that promises to extricate him, how swiftly does she [a spider] ...fling coil after coil about him until he is *secured* for ever!" (*Shaw*). One **anchors** or **moors** something (which in its very nature is unstable or which is subject to tugging or pulling by external forces or influences) to another thing strong enough to hold it down or in place or powerful enough to counterbalance or counteract the opposing forces; as, to *anchor* the cables of a suspension bridge to towers at either end; "*moored* to the rock on two sides, the cabin stood firm" (*J. Tyndall*). *Moor*, in contrast to *anchor*, usually suggests greater steadiness or an even balancing of forces that make for stability; as, a child is *moored* to his home by his need of food, care, security, and affection, but when adolescence comes, he often longs to break his *moorings*. "Why not believe then? Why not yet *anchor* thy frailty there, where man Hath *moor'd* and rested?" (*Tennyson*). One **rivets** one thing to another when one joins things normally or actually separate from each other as closely together as though a rivet or rivets had been driven through them; as, fear *riveted* him to his chair; "Why should I write this down, that's *riveted*, Screw'd to my memory?" (*Shak.*). "The head of the state, in whose name he [Agrippa] insisted that all his victories were won, to *rivet* the loyalty of the army to the civil administration" (*Buchan*).

Ana. Establish, *set, settle, fix: *fasten, attach, affix.

2 *Ensure, insure, assure.

Ana. Protect, *defend, safeguard, guard, shield: preserve, conserve, *save: guarantee, guaranty (see corresponding nouns at GUARANTEE): warrant, *justify.

3 Procure, obtain, *get, acquire, gain, win, earn.

Ana. Seize, *take, grasp: *reach, attain, achieve, gain: *have, hold, own, possess.

security. Surety, guaranty, *guarantee, bond, bail.

Ana. *Pledge, earnest, token, gage.

sedate. Grave, staid, earnest, sober, *serious, solemn.

Ana. Placid, *calm, serene, tranquil: collected, composed, imperturbable (see COOL): *decorous, seemly, proper.

Ant. Flighty.

sedition. **Sedition, treason** come into comparison only when they mean an offense against the state to which or the sovereign to whom one owes allegiance. **Sedition** applies to any conduct that is not manifested in an overt act and that incites commotion and resistance to lawful authority without amounting to an insurrection. **Treason** applies to conduct marked by an overt act or acts that has for its aim the overthrow of the government, the death of the sovereign, betrayal to the enemy, or the like.

Ana. *Rebellion, revolt, revolution, uprising, insurrection, mutiny, Putsch: disaffection, alienation, estrangement (see corresponding verbs at ESTRANGE).

Con. *Fidelity, allegiance, loyalty, fealty.

seditious. Mutinous, rebellious, factious, *insubordinate, contumacious.

Ana. Traitorous, treacherous, perfidious, disloyal, *faithless: disaffected, alienated (see ESTRANGE).

seduce. Tempt, entice, inveigle, *lure, decoy.

Ana. Mislead, beguile, delude, *deceive: corrupt, debauch, deprave, pervert, *debase: bewitch, captivate, allure (see ATTRACT).

sedulous. Assiduous, diligent, industrious, *busy.

Ana. Persevering, persistent (see corresponding verbs at PERSEVERE): untiring, unwearied, *indefatigable, tireless.

see, *v.* **1 See, behold, descry, espy, view, survey, contemplate, observe, notice, remark, note, perceive, discern** come into comparison as meaning to take cognizance of something by physical (sometimes mental) vision. **See,** the most general of these terms, may be used to imply little more than the use of the organs of vision (as, he cannot *see* the crowd, for he is blind) but more commonly it implies a recognition or appreciation of that which is before one's eyes (as, "Having eyes, *see* ye not? and having ears, hear ye not?"—*Mark* viii. 18; "They can *see* a great deal in Paris, but nothing in an English meadow"—*Jefferies*). The term may imply the exercise of other powers than the sense of sight, such as a vivid imagination (as, I can *see* her plainly now, as she looked forty years ago; " 'methinks I *see* my father.' 'Where, my lord?' 'In my mind's eye, Horatio' "—*Shak.*), or mental insight (as, he was the only one who *saw* the truth), or powers of inference (as, though he appeared calm, I could *see* he was inwardly agitated). **Behold** carries a stronger implication of a definite ocular impression and of distinct recognition than *see:* it also suggests looking at that which is seen; as, "When he *beheld* the serpent of brass, he lived" (*Numbers* xxi. 9); "my Country's cliffs I can *behold*" (*Wordsworth*). **Descry** and **espy** imply a seeing in spite of difficulties such as distance, darkness, partial concealment, or the like. *Descry*, however, more often suggests an effort to discover, or a looking out for someone or something; as, "the grass was high in the meadow, and there was no *descrying* her" (*G. Eliot*); "Sir Austin ascended to the roof...and *descried* him hastening to the boathouse by the river-side" (*Meredith*). *Espy* usually implies skill in detection as of that which is small, or not clearly within the range of vision, or is trying to escape detection; as, "the seamen *espied* a rock within half a cable's length of the ship" (*Swift*); "Sir Bors... there, half-hidden by him [Lancelot] stood, Until the King *espied* him" (*Tennyson*). **View** and **survey**, on the contrary, imply the seeing of that which is spread before one or which one can examine steadily or in detail. Both terms as often imply mental consideration as a literal seeing or looking over. *View* usually implies (or requires a statement of) a particular way of looking at a thing, or a particular purpose in considering it; as, to *view* the panorama with delight; to *view* a piece of property that one thinks of buying; to *view* a painting from various angles; "*View* the industry of the country, and *see* how it is affected by inequality of income" (*Shaw*); to *view* a problem in all of its aspects. *Survey*, on the other hand, usually implies a detailed scrutiny or inspection by the eyes or the mind so that one has a picture or idea of it as a whole; as, "The captain *surveyed* him from cap to waistcoat and from waistcoat to leggings for a few moments" (*Hardy*); "Tony...*surveyed* the room at large, examining the various articles of use or beauty... scattered about it" (*Arch. Marshall*); "A man *surveying* Europe to-day discovers this strange anomaly: it is one great culture, yet it is at deadly issue with itself" (*Belloc*). **Contemplate,** in the looser sense in which it is here compared (see CONSIDER, 1, for stricter sense) implies little more than a fixing of the eyes upon something, sometimes in abstraction, but more often in enjoyment or in reference to some end in view; as, "He had a way of looking her over from beneath lowered lids, while he affected to be examining a glove-button or *contemplating* the tip of his shining boot" (*E. Wharton*); "She took great pleasure in *contemplating* the splendour of the gift" (*Bennett*). **Observe** and **notice** both imply a heeding and not passing over: they commonly imply seeing, but may suggest the use of another sense; as, he *observed* (or *noticed*) every detail in the arrangement; did you *notice* (or *observe* the actions of) the man who just passed us?; he *noticed* a peculiar odor. *Observe* differs from *notice*, especially in scientific use, in carrying a stronger implication of directed attention; as, "In order to get fresh light on this subject, I have *observed* my own children carefully" (*B. Russell*); "Lady Slane, keeping an ear pricked to *observe* the movements of the Viceroy and his group" (*V. Woolf*); "things which are always about us...are the easiest to *observe* with accuracy" (*Grandgent*). *Notice*, by contrast, often implies some definite reaction to that which is seen (sometimes heard, felt, or the like), such as making a mental note of it or a remark about it or, if that which is noticed is a person, recognizing him by a salute, a greeting, or the like; as, "By Mrs. Hurst and Miss Bingley they were *noticed* only by a curtsey" (*Austen*); "Who...in his rapt admiration [of a moonlight effect] omitted to *notice*...a whole quarter of the city on fire" (*Binyon*). **Remark** (see also REMARK) and **note** carry an even stronger implication than *notice* of registering mentally one's impression: though either word may or may not suggest a comment upon that which is noticed, *remark* more often than *note* carries that implication (as, "he thought the circumstance of... removing from one carriage into another might be *remarked*"—*Austen;* "I could not help *remarking* the position of her left arm"—*Quiller-Couch*). *Note*, on the other hand, suggests a recording, sometimes by a mental note, but often in writing or in speech (as, "a certain ungraciousness, *noted* in later years by his nearest colleagues"—*H. Ellis;* he carried a map and *noted* every stream and every hill that we passed). **Perceive** carries a stronger implication of the use of the mind in observation than any of the preceding terms. The word basically implies apprehension or obtaining knowledge of a thing, not only through the sense of sight but through any of the senses. It is often used in place of *see* in the literal sense of the latter word, but since it always implies distinct recognition of that which is seen, the words are sometimes used in contrast, especially by psychologists; as, an infant *sees* objects long before it is able to *perceive* them as definite persons or things; "When he drew nearer he *perceived* it to be a spring van, ordinary in shape, but singular in colour" (*Hardy*). In its richer meaning, it not only suggests dependence on other senses than that of sight, but also, usually, keen mental vision or special insight and penetration; as, "disgusted with every person who could not *perceive*...these obvious truths" (*Bennett*); "only an old New Yorker could *perceive* the shade of difference...between being merely a Duke and being the Van der Luydens' Duke" (*E. Wharton*). **Discern,** like *descry*, often implies little more than a making out of something by means of the eyes; as, "At length he *discerned*, a long distance in front of him, a moving spot, which appeared to be a vehicle" (*Hardy*); "sometimes we *discern* the city afar off" (*A. C. Benson*). In its more precise etymological sense, however, the term usually implies the powers of deeply perceiving and of distinguishing or discriminating that which the senses perceive; as, "Ye can *discern* the face of the sky; but can ye not *discern* the signs of the times?" (*Matthew* xvi. 3); "What is false taste but a want of perception to *discern* propriety and distinguish beauty?" (*Goldsmith*); "His grave eyes steadily *discerned* The good in men and what was wise" (*Masefield*).

Ana. *Scrutinize, scan, examine, inspect: pierce, penetrate, probe (see ENTER): *consider, study, contemplate.

2 See, look, watch are here compared chiefly but not exclusively as intransitive verbs and only in their most general senses, as they mean to perceive something by means of the eyes. **See** (see also SEE, 1) stresses the reception of a visual impression or of visual impressions; as, he is now able to *see* clearly; to have the power of *seeing*. **Look** stresses the directing of the eyes to something or the fixing of the eyes on something in order to see it; as, if you will only *look*, you will be able to see what I am doing; he refused to *look* in the mirror the nurse gave him. **Watch** (see also TEND) implies a following of something with one's eyes, so as to observe every movement, every change, any sign of danger, any favorable opportunity, or the like; as, *watch* for a while and tell us what you *see;* to spend the night *watching* a sick friend; to *watch* something as closely as a cat *watches* a mouse.

Ana. *Gaze, gape, stare, glare.

seem. **Seem, look, appear** come into comparison when they mean to be (as stated) in one's view or judgment, but not necessarily in fact. Oftentimes they are used interchangeably with apparently no difference in meaning; as, he *seems* (or *looks*, or *appears*) tired; the students *appear* (or *look*, or *seem*) eager. But even in these phrases, **seem** suggests a personal opinion based on evidence that satisfies the judgment, such as signs easily recognized through one's familiarity with them; **look** implies that the opinion is based on a visual impression; **appear** may convey the same implication as *look*, but it sometimes suggests a distorted impression produced by an optical illusion, a restricted point of view, another's dissembling, or the like; as, nothing *seems* right when one is out of sorts; the city *looks* its worst in March; the setting sun made the spires *appear* ablaze. "His tongue ...could make the worse *appear* The better reason" (*Milton*).

Ana. *Infer, gather, judge, deduce, conclude.

seeming. *Apparent, illusory, ostensible.

Ana. *Plausible, specious, credible: dissembling, disguising, masking, cloaking (see DISGUISE).

seemly. Proper, nice, comme il faut, *decorous, decent, demure.

Ana. Fitting, suitable, appropriate, meet (see FIT): congruous, compatible, congenial, consistent, *consonant.

Ant. Unseemly.

segment. Section, sector, division, *part, portion, piece, detail, member, fraction, fragment, parcel.

seize. *Take, grasp, clutch, snatch, grab.

Ana. *Catch, capture, nab, cop, snare, ensnare, trap, entrap: appropriate, confiscate, usurp, *arrogate.

select, *adj.* **Select, elect, picked, exclusive** come into comparison when they mean marked by a character or quality which distinguishes the person, the thing, or the group of persons or things so qualified from others, as in value, excellence, favor, or the like. **Select** implies that the person (or thing) has been chosen with discrimination in preference to others of the same class or kind; as, the hotel caters to a *select* clientele; "The Milton of poetry is, in his own words again, the man of 'industrious and *select* reading' " (*Arnold*). " 'Christ died for a *select* company that was known to Him, by name, from eternity,' wrote the Reverend Samuel Willard" (*A. Repplier*). *Select* is also often used, with little or no implication of choice or selection, in the sense of *superior* or *exceptional;* as, a *select* audience; "Persecution of that sort which bows down and crushes all but a very few *select* spirits" (*Macaulay*). **Elect** commonly implies careful or discriminating selection, and it carries a stronger implication than *select* of admission to some carefully restricted or inner circle: sometimes, also, it suggests the award of special privileges; as, "*Elect* according to the foreknowledge of God the Father...: Grace unto you, and peace" (*1 Peter* i. 2); "that delicious phantom of being an *elect* spirit...unlike the crowd" (*Kingsley*); "Darwin was one of those *elect* persons in whose subconscious, if not in their conscious, nature is implanted the realisation that 'science is poetry' " (*H. Ellis*). **Picked,** a somewhat more colloquial term than the others here considered, like *select* may or may not imply actual choice: the term commonly, but not invariably, applies to that which is conspicuously superior or above the average though it may suggest little more than the best available; as, a *picked* team; the candidates are all *picked* men; "the *picked* moments of exaltation and vision which great tragedy brings" (*C. E. Montague*). **Exclusive,** in its most general sense, implies a character in a thing that forces or inclines it to rule out that which is not congruous or compatible with it or that which is its opposite or antithesis in constitution or character; thus, mutually *exclusive* colors when mixed in the right proportions form a neutral gray; so, "*exclusive* concepts—animal and vegetable, for instance" (*F. Bowen*); "didacticism and a sense of humor are mutually *exclusive* qualities" (*Lowes*). As here compared and as applied especially to persons, groups, institutions, and the like, *exclusive* implies tendencies or rules which prevent free acceptance or admission or ready sharing of those (or of that) not conforming to imposed standards or not satisfying the requirements of those who are fastidious, snobbish, or otherwise highly critical; as, "a weak, critical, fastidious creature, vain of a little *exclusive* information or of an uncommon knack in Latin verse" (*C. W. Eliot*); "the *exclusive* caste-system of a rigid feudalism" (*Binyon*); "the [British] public school (meaning a very *exclusive* private school malversating public endowments) and the university" (*Shaw*).

Ana. *Choice, exquisite, rare, delicate, dainty, recherché: superlative, surpassing, peerless, *supreme.

Ant. Indiscriminate.

select, *v.* *Choose, elect, handpick, prefer, opt, pick, cull, single out.

Ana. *Assort, sort, classify: discriminate, discern (see corresponding nouns at DISCERNMENT).

Ant. Reject. — ***Con.*** Refuse, repudiate, spurn (see DECLINE, *v.*).

selection. *Choice, preference, election, option, alternative.

Ana. Choosing, culling, picking, handpicking (see CHOOSE): discrimination, *discernment, insight, acumen.

Ant. Rejection.

self-abnegation. *Renunciation, abnegation, self-denial.

Ana. Sacrificing *or* sacrifice, forbearance, forgoing, eschewal (see corresponding verbs at FORGO): surrendering *or* surrender, resignation, abandonment, relinquishment (see corresponding verbs at RELINQUISH).

self-assertive. Assertive, *aggressive, pushing, militant.

Ana. Obtrusive, intrusive, officious, meddlesome, *impertinent: bold, audacious (see BRAVE): positive, certain, *sure, cocksure.

self-assurance. Assurance, *confidence, self-confidence, aplomb, self-possession.

Ana. Coolness, collectedness, imperturbability (see corresponding adjectives at COOL): composure, sangfroid, *equanimity.

Con. Diffidence, shyness, bashfulness, modesty (see corresponding adjectives at SHY).

self-complacent. *Complacent, self-satisfied, smug, priggish.

Ana. & ***Con.*** See those at COMPLACENT.

self-confidence. *Confidence, assurance, self-assurance, self-possession, aplomb.

Ana. Self-reliance, reliance (see corresponding adjectives at RELIANT): composure, *equanimity: sureness, sanguineness (see corresponding adjectives at CONFIDENT).

self-denial. Self-abnegation, abnegation, *renunciation.

Ana. Sacrificing *or* sacrifice, forbearance (see corresponding verbs at FORGO): abstaining, refraining (see REFRAIN): restraining *or* restraint, curbing *or* curb, checking *or* check (see corresponding verbs at RESTRAIN).

self-esteem. Self-love, *conceit, egotism, egoism, amour-propre.

Ana. *Pride, vanity: self-respect, self-regard, self-admiration (see primitive nouns at REGARD).

Ant. Self-distrust.

self-love. Self-esteem, *conceit, egotism, egoism, amour-propre.

Ana. *Pride, vanity, vainglory: complacency, self-complacency, smugness, priggishness (see corresponding adjectives at COMPLACENT).

Ant. Self-forgetfulness.

self-opinionated. *Opinionated, opinionative.

Ana. Dogmatic, *dictatorial, doctrinaire, oracular: certain, positive, *sure, cocksure.

self-possession. *Confidence, self-confidence, assurance, self-assurance, aplomb.

Ana. *Equanimity, composure: coolness, collectedness, imperturbability, nonchalance (see corresponding adjectives at COOL): poise, savoir-faire, *tact.

self-reliant. *Reliant.

selfsame. *Same, very, identical, identic, equivalent, equal, tantamount.

Ana. Alike, like, identical, uniform (see SIMILAR).

Ant. Diverse.

self-satisfied. *Complacent, self-complacent, smug, priggish.

Ana. Satisfied, content (see under SATISFY): conceited, egoistic, egotistic (see corresponding nouns at CONCEIT).

sell, *v.* **Sell, vend, auction, barter, trade** agree in denoting to take part in a transaction in which property is transferred to another for permanent possession, in exchange for something else. To **sell** is to transfer to another for a price, usually to be paid in money. **Vend** applies chiefly to the selling (sometimes the hawking) of small articles. The derivative nouns *vender* and *vendor* are in much more common use than the verb; as, the din was increased by the cries of *venders* in the noisy streets. The term *vending machine* is applied to a slot machine for dispensing small articles (as candy, chewing gum, and cigarettes). The verb *vend* is not used of lands or tenements, but the legal terms *vendor* and *vendee* may be. To **auction** (frequently followed by the adverb *off*) is to sell, usually in the capacity of a licensed and authorized auctioneer, to that person of an assemblage who makes the highest and last of a series of successively increased bids; as, a public sale at which one's household furnishings are *auctioned* off. **Barter** implies an exchange of commodities. "Every possible device for doing without money altogether by *bartering*" (*Shaw*). By extension, *barter* frequently implies to exchange for an unworthy consideration. "Writers...who will not *barter* human rights for the patronage of the great" (*J. Bright*). **Trade** is often synonymous with *barter*, and suggests the exchange of a particular object or objects for another or others; in this use it appears to be chiefly an Americanism; as, to *trade* a city lot for a farm; to *trade* hats; let's *trade* knives.

Ana. *Transfer, convey, deed: consign, *commit, relegate.

semblance. *Appearance, look, aspect.

Ana. *Likeness, similitude, resemblance, analogy, affinity: *pose, affectation, air (*or* airs): *form, figure, shape.

seminary. *Academy, institute, college, lycée, gymnasium.

sempiternal. Eternal, *infinite, boundless, illimitable, uncircumscribed.

Ana. *Everlasting, endless, interminable, unceasing, never-ending: *immortal, deathless, undying: *lasting, perdurable.

senescence. *Age, senility, senilism, dotage.

Ant. Adolescence.

seneschal. *Steward, reeve, bailiff, agent, factor, major-domo.

senile. **Senile, anile, doting, doted, doddering, doddered** agree in meaning having or showing the weaknesses of old age. **Senile** is the all-round word referable to both sexes and implying physical as well as mental decay; as, *senile* imbecility; *senile* diseases. "He either chatters *senilely*, or falls into the long trances of age" (*Kipling*). **Anile** in technical medical use applies to the senility of women; in its somewhat rare literary use, it implies old-womanishness or decadent femininity, but it is seldom employed with reference to persons. "Romanticism... grew *anile* in its premature decrepitude" (*R. A. Vaughan*). **Doting** (see also LOVING) and **doted** (the latter in common use in Scotland) always imply imbecility or weak-mindedness through age: very frequently, *doting* additionally suggests amorous tendencies. "The third mad passion of thy *doting* age" (*Pope*). Both **doddering** and **doddered** (though etymologically of different origin) stress extreme weakness and infirmity of mind and body. "A little old grey-headed man who...had an ancient *doddering* manner" (*M. E. Braddon*). "Auld feckless *doddered* men" (*Stevenson*).

Ana. Old, *aged, elderly, superannuated: *weak, feeble, infirm, decrepit.

Ant. Juvenile: virgin.

senilism. Senescence, senility, *age, dotage.

senility. Dotage, *age, senescence, senilism.

Ana. Infirmity, feebleness, weakness, decrepitude (see corresponding adjectives at WEAK): childishness, childlikeness (see corresponding adjectives at CHILDLIKE): decay, disintegration (see DECAY, *v.*).

sensation. **1** **Sensation, percept, image** are here compared as denoting the experience or process which is the result of the activity of an organ of sense and its closely connected nerve structures. **Sensation,** the most general of these terms, is applicable to any sensory response to a stimulus from without or within the body, whether it enters fully into one's consciousness or not: specifically it means any impression received by any of the organs of sense, such as the eyes, ears, nostrils, taste buds of the tongue, or tactile nerves; as, to feel a *sensation* of chill; to give oneself up to the enjoyment of the *sensations* provided by a perfect spring day; "such a seeming waste of longevity, on a reptile that appears to relish it so little as to squander more than two-thirds of its existence in a joyless stupor, and be lost to all *sensation* for months together" (*Gilbert White*). *Sensation* is also applicable to any feeling that, apparently, neither results from a stimulus nor has immediate connection with an organ of sense, yet is felt acutely and physically; as, "I have owed to them [recollections of a beautiful landscape]... "*sensations* sweet, Felt in the blood, and felt along the heart" (*Wordsworth*). **Percept,** a psychologist's term, differs from *sensation* in being applicable only to a sensation received through an organ of sense and accompanied by the recognition of the object; thus, an infant feels *sensations* before he has *percepts*, that is, sensations that are referable to definite, recognizable things. **Image** (as here compared: see also IMAGE, 1) applies to any sensation that results in a mental representation of the thing seen, the sound heard, the odor smelled, etc., and in the retention of that mental representation in the memory for an appreciable, even a very long, time; as, "After I had looked long at it, and passed on, the *image* of that perfect flower remained...persistently in my mind" (*Hudson*); "I had never spoken to her, except for a few casual words, and yet her....*image* accompanied me even in places the most hostile to romance" (*Joyce*). *Image* also refers to a mental representation that can be evoked in the mind in the absence of the thing represented: in this case, it may apply to a mental representation that is in the memory as a result of previous sense experience or that is a construction of the imagination or fancy out of various bits of sense experience, or as a result of a verbal description; as, "When I recall London, Paris, Rome..., the *image* that first presents itself is the earliest one" (*Grandgent*); "[a poet] thinks in *images*" (*Binyon*); "the other [element of the murder scene in Othello] a succession of efforts to call up before us veracious *images* of a bedroom, a bed, pillows, a lighted candle, a woman asleep, a man speaking to himself" (*C. E. Montague*).

Ana. *Impression, impress, print, stamp: feeling, feel, savor, tone (see ATMOSPHERE): consciousness, awareness (see corresponding adjectives at AWARE).

2 **Sensation, sense, feeling, sensibility** are not close synonyms but they come into comparison when they agree in meaning the power to respond or the capacity for or the act of responding to stimuli, especially physical stimuli. **Sensation,** the most definite of these terms, is referable chiefly to the higher animals provided with organs such as the eyes, ears, nose, tongue, and tactile nerves which receive impressions and transmit them to the central nervous system. In highly technical use, *sensation* often denotes nothing more than the mere seeing, hearing, smelling, etc., and does not imply recognition or comprehension. "The first step, which most children take at the age of about five months, is to pass beyond mere pleasures of *sensation*, such as food and warmth, to the pleasure of social approbation" (*B. Russell*). In nontechnical use, however, the term usually suggests more than mere seeing, hearing, etc., and implies not only recognition but more or less clearly defined intellectual and emotional reactions, such as those of pleasure or pain. It therefore may apply to responses to other than purely physical stimuli. "The *sensation* of finding a command of no avail is to the mind what sitting down upon a suddenly withdrawn chair is to the body" (*Deland*). "There are *sensations* you cannot describe. You may know what causes them but you cannot tell what portions of your mind they affect nor yet, possibly, what parts of your physical entity" (*F. M. Ford*). Although **sense** is applied specifically to any one of the various powers associated with the organs that receive sensations (as, the *sense* of taste; the *sense* of smell) or in the plural (occasionally in the singular), to the combined powers which enable a sentient being to establish relations between itself and that which is external to itself (as, "the sudden, violent shock almost took away my *senses*"—*Hudson;* "my brain immoderately stirred, my *senses* unusually quickened"—*Galsworthy*), it differs from *sensation,* when applied to the power or act of responding to stimuli, in suggesting a less corporeal and a more intellectual reaction, and often a less objective stimulus. In fact, its most emphatic implication in this sense is often that of intense awareness or of full consciousness. "His first consciousness was a *sense* of the light dry wind blowing in through the windows" (*Cather*); "She had no *sense* at all Of any word I said" (*W. H. Davies*); "He had, however, not only knowledge, but something which is much rarer, a *sense* of quality, a taste for perfection" (*L. P. Smith*); "[Augustus] had in his bones the Roman *sense* of the past" (*Buchan*). **Feeling** (as here compared: see also FEELING, 2; ATMOSPHERE, 2) in its most specific meaning denotes the sense that has its end organs in the skin: usually it signifies the sense of touch (as, to have no *feeling* in one's finger tips) but often it is more inclusive and suggests the sense that is aware of changes in temperature, pressure, and the like (as, he knew by *feeling* that it was getting much colder). But *feeling* is also used more broadly to denote a response to a stimulus or a set of stimuli that is a combination of sensation, emotion, and a degree of thought; as, to judge a situation by one's *feelings* rather than by the facts; you know her *feelings* about the vulgarity of these people. Often also, the term denotes not the response, but the power to respond in general or as a characteristic; as, he says that she has no *feeling;* "The delicacy of his *feeling* makes him sensibly touched" (*Hume*). In this latter sense of *feeling,* **sensibility** is often preferred, especially when a keenly impressionable nature and unusually delicate powers of appreciation or its opposite are implied; as, "the extreme *sensibility* to physical suffering which characterises modern civilisation" (*Inge*); "She was a creature of palpitating *sensibility,* with feelings so delicate that they responded to every breath" (*S. M. Crothers*). In the late eighteenth century, especially as a result of the romantic movement in literature and art, sensibility was thought of as an essential of the poet and artist and of the reader, and the observer, not only of works of art, but of nature. Consequently, the term acquired connotations of sentimentalism and of forced or affected emotionalism which still sometimes color the word. Jane Austen humorously satirized this quality in her novel *Sense* [that is, "good sense"] *and Sensibility.* "The nerveless sentimentalist and dreamer, who spends his life in a weltering sea of *sensibility*" (*W. James*).

Ana. Perceptibleness *or* perceptibility, tangibleness *or* tangibility, palpableness *or* palpability, ponderableness *or* ponderability (see corresponding adjectives at PERCEPTIBLE): reaction, action, behavior (see corresponding verbs at ACT): response, answer (see under ANSWER, *v.*).

sense, *n.* **1** *Sensation, feeling, sensibility.

Ana. Awareness, consciousness, cognizance (see corresponding adjectives at AWARE): perception, *discernment, discrimination, penetration.

2 Sense, common sense, good sense, horse sense, gumption, judgment, wisdom are here compared as meaning the quality of mind or character which enables one to make intelligent choices or decisions, or to reach intelligent conclusions. **Sense,** because of its numerous significations, is often, when this meaning is intended, called **common sense, good sense,** or, in American slang, **horse sense.** All four terms imply a capacity—usually a native capacity—for seeing things as they are and without illusion or emotional bias, for making practical choices or decisions that are sane, prudent, fair, and reasonable, and that commend themselves to the normal, or average good mind. " 'Jane is a goose,' said the doctor, irritably. 'Maggy is the only one that has any *sense* in that family' " (*Deland*). "Rich in saving *common-sense*" (*Tennyson*). "*Good sense,* which only is the gift of Heaven" (*Pope*). "He was a plain man...he had what is roughly known as *horse-sense*" (*C. D. Warner*). **Gumption,** a colloquial term, implies sense, but in addition it suggests a capacity to estimate shrewdly or cleverly the possibilities of success or failure, of change for the better or worse, or the like; as, an investor without *gumption* is bound to lose money; he is a dreamer and, what is worse, he hasn't the slightest bit of *gumption;* if the voters have *gumption* they will re-elect the mayor. **Judgment,** as here considered, seldom applies to a native quality, though it usually suggests a foundation in native good sense. But it also suggests intellectual qualities which are usually the result of training or discipline, such as discernment of facts or conditions that are not obvious as well as knowledge of those that are ascertainable, an ability to comprehend the significance of those facts and conditions and to draw correct unbiased conclusions from them. " 'Tis true that strength and bustle build up a firm. But *judgment* and knowledge are what keep it established" (*Hardy*). "The ultimate test of true worth in pleasure, as in everything else, is the trained *judgment* of the good and sensible man" (*G. L. Dickinson*). "Buckingham...was not a man of *judgment* and he allowed personal feeling to influence his action" (*Belloc*). **Wisdom** is of all these terms the one of highest praise. Although it often suggests great soundness of judgment in practical affairs and unusual sagacity (as, "*Common sense* in an uncommon degree is what the world calls *wisdom*"—*Coleridge*), it is also capable of suggesting an ideal quality of mind or character that is the result of a trained judgment exercised not only in practical affairs but in philosophical speculation, of wide experience in life and thought, of great learning, and of deep understanding. "For *wisdom* is better than rubies; and all the things that may be desired are not to be compared to it" (*Proverbs* viii. 11). "*Wisdom* is said to be the funded experience which man has gathered by living; but for so many harvests the crop is still a light one. Knowledge he has gained and power, but not goodness and understanding" (*A. Repplier*).

Ana. *Prudence, foresight, discretion: understanding, comprehension, appreciation (see corresponding verbs at UNDERSTAND): intelligence, brain, brains, wit, wits (see MIND).

3 *Meaning, acceptation, signification, significance, import.

Ana. Denotation, connotation (see under DENOTE).

sensibility. Feeling, sense, *sensation.

Ana. Perception, *discernment, penetration, discrimination, insight, clairvoyance: sensitiveness, susceptibility (see corresponding adjectives at LIABLE): emotion, *feeling, affection: sentimentalism, *sentiment, sentimentality.

sensible. 1 *Material, physical, corporeal, phenomenal, objective.

Ant. Intelligible.

2 *Perceptible, palpable, tangible, appreciable, ponderable.

Ana. Sensational, perceptual, imaginal (see corresponding nouns at SENSATION): obvious, patent, manifest, *evident: *carnal, fleshly, sensual.
Ant. Insensible.
3 *Aware, conscious, cognizant, alive, awake.
Ana. Perceiving, noting, remarking, observing, seeing (see SEE): knowing, *intelligent: understanding, comprehending, appreciating (see UNDERSTAND): sensitive, susceptible (see LIABLE).
Ant. Insensible (of *or* to). — ***Con.*** Impassible, insensitive, anesthetic (see INSENSIBLE).
4 Prudent, sane, judicious, *wise, sage, sapient.
Ana. Sagacious, perspicacious, astute, *shrewd: foresighted, discreet, provident (see under PRUDENCE): reasonable, *rational.
Ant. Absurd, foolish: fatuous, asinine.

sensitive. Susceptible, subject, exposed, open, *liable, prone, incident.
Ana. Impressed, influenced, affected (see AFFECT): predisposed, disposed, inclined (see INCLINE, *v.*).
Ant. Insensitive.

sensual. **1** *Carnal, fleshly, animal, animalistic.
Ana. *Bodily, physical, corporeal, somatic: *coarse, gross, vulgar: lewd, lascivious, lustful, wanton (see LICENTIOUS).
2 *Sensuous, luxurious, voluptuous, sybaritic, epicurean.
Ana. See those at SENSUAL, 1.
☞ *Do not confuse* sensual *with* sensory.

sensuous. **Sensuous, sensual, luxurious, voluptuous, sybaritic, epicurean** come into comparison when they mean having to do with the gratification of the senses or providing pleasure by gratifying the senses. **Sensuous** was first used by Milton as a term descriptive of one thing which deals with sensations or has the power of evoking sensations as opposed to another thing which deals with ideas, and is intellectual in its character (as, "[Poetry is] more simple, *sensuous*, and passionate [than rhetoric]"—*Milton*); however, the word did not gain currency until around 1800 when Coleridge adopted it in preference to *sensual* because, unlike the latter term, it carried no derogatory connotations. **Sensual** (for fuller treatment see CARNAL) now usually implies the gratification of the senses or the indulgence of the appetites through the impulsion of gluttony, lust, or other base motive; *sensuous*, on the contrary, implies the gratification of the senses (less often the indulgence of the appetites) for the sake of the aesthetic pleasure or the delight in beauty of color, sound, form, or the like, that is induced. "Nobody can resist the Bay of Naples, or if he can, then all the simple and *sensuous* delights of this world must turn to bitterness and ashes in his mouth" (*C. Mackenzie*); "Arise and fly The reeling faun, the *sensual* feast" (*Tennyson*); "Chinese painters are not, like the Persians, absorbed in expressing their *sensuous* delight in the wonder and glory of the world" (*Binyon*). As applied to persons or their natures, *sensuous* often carries an implication of indifference to things of the spirit, but it practically never suggests the bestiality so often connoted by *sensual*. "The *sensuous*, self-indulgent nature she [Elizabeth] derived from Anne Boleyn" (*J. R. Green*). "His nature was purely *sensuous*, and she strove to make him moral, religious" (*D. H. Lawrence*). "The young boy's love is a spiritual passion...without any sensory, still less any *sensual*, elements" (*H. Ellis*). **Luxurious** (as here compared in its primary and still current strict sense: for looser sense, see LUXURIOUS, 2) implies indulgence, often self-indulgence in sensual or, now more often, sensuous pleasures. Originally meaning given to luxury (etymologically, lasciviousness or lust), the term has now practically lost its implications of vice and applies rather to pleasures that induce a pleasant languor, delightful ease, or particularly a grateful peace of mind; as, "the emotionalist steeps himself or herself in *luxurious* feeling and pathetic imagination, which make no severe call upon either the will or the intellect" (*Inge*); "sat down to a long, *luxurious* smoke" (*Kipling*); "the music [in a restaurant gives]....a *luxurious* pleasure not to be had from eating a silent meal" (*Justice Holmes*). **Voluptuous** also implies giving oneself up to the pleasures of sense, but it carries a stronger implication of abandonment to such pleasure for its own sake than does *luxurious;* also, it more frequently carries a suggestion of sensual rather than of sensuous enjoyment; as, "fair fallacious looks... Softened with pleasure and *voluptuous* life" (*Milton*); "a temper too indolent to enquire, too bigoted to doubt, a *voluptuous* devotionality allied perhaps to refined aestheticism, but totally alien to the austerity and penetrating sincerity of the Gospel" (*Inge*). **Sybaritic** implies voluptuousness of an overrefined and effeminate sort; usually, it suggests indulgence in the rarest and choicest foods and drinks, amid surroundings calculated to charm and soothe the senses; as, "It was a *Sybaritic* repast, in a magnificent apartment" (*Thackeray*). **Epicurean** (cf. EPICURE) in earliest use of the term commonly implied sensuality and voluptuousness, but now, largely as a result of a truer understanding of the philsophy of the ancient Greek Epicurus (*Epicurean* philosophy), it suggests sensuous rather than sensual delight in the pleasures of eating, drinking, and the like, and a delicate and fastidious rather than a gross taste; as, "Warming their palace kitchens, and from thence their unctuous, and *epicurean* paunches" (*Milton*); "Nothing to mar the sober majesties Of settled, sweet, *Epicurean* life" (*Tennyson*).
Ana. Sensational, imaginal (see corresponding nouns at SENSATION): delicious, delectable, luscious, *delightful: aesthetic, *artistic.
☞ *Do not confuse* sensuous *with* sensory.

sentence, *v.* **Sentence, condemn, damn, doom, attaint, proscribe** are here compared in the sense of to decree the fate or punishment of a person (sometimes, by extension, a thing) that has been adjudged guilty, unworthy, unfit, or the like. **Sentence** originally implied the act of judging, but it is now used only in reference to the determination and pronouncement of punishment (or the like) following an adverse verdict; thus, when a jury renders a verdict of "guilty," it becomes the duty of the judge who has presided at the trial to *sentence* the convicted person; when a person hears the verdict of his physicians that he is afflicted with an incurable disease, he is aware that in their minds he has been *sentenced* to death. **Condemn,** as here compared (see also CRITICIZE), implies both an adverse judgment and a sentence which carries with it a penalty such as forfeiture of one's freedom, one's rights, or one's life (as, Napoleon was *condemned* to exile; cells for *condemned* prisoners), or, in the case of things, a forfeiture of its existence or of some status which has legally protected it from invasion; thus, to *condemn* an old building is legally to decree its destruction; to *condemn* a piece of property is to take it over for the uses of the state, on payment of its appraised value. **Damn,** which is both etymologically and in its historical meanings akin to *condemn*, is now not employed in law. In theological use, it implies the condemnation of the soul to hell or to eternal punishment. "He that believeth and is baptized shall be saved; but he that believeth not shall be *damned*" (*Mark* xvi. 16). In general use, when it carries this implication, it is often employed in curses, imprecations, or expressions of strong disapproval. "I give thee sixpence! I will see thee *damned* first" (*G. Canning*). Otherwise it usually implies a verdict that is destructive or annihilating in its effects. "The reputation of Jonson has been of the most deadly kind....To be universally accepted; to be *damned* by the praise that quenches all desire to read the book...to be read only by historians and antiquaries—this is the most perfect conspiracy of approval" (*T. S. Eliot*). **Doom** adds to *condemn* the implication of a punishment or penalty that cannot be evaded or escaped, because imposed by an inexorable power. "I am thy father's spirit, *Doom'd* for a certain term to walk the night" (*Shak.*). "She [history] execrates indeed The tyranny that *doomed* them to the fire" (*Cowper*). This idea of fate or destiny is so strongly stressed in *doom* that in some cases the implication of an adverse judgment is lost or obscured; as, it was not long before the Poles realized that Warsaw was *doomed* to destruction. "The substance of a scientific paper is incorporated into the general stock of knowledge; but the paper itself is *doomed* to oblivion" (*A. Huxley*). **Attaint,** which is now chiefly in historical use, implies the pronouncement or decree, as in a *bill of attainder*, of the severe punishments formerly imposed for treason or for a felony, usually including death or banishment, forfeiture of estate, corruption of blood (that is, loss of power to receive or to transmit property by inheritance), and the loss of all rights and privileges as a citizen. "In the United States the Constitution provides...that no bill of attainder shall be passed; and...that no attainder of treason (in consequence of a judicial sentence) shall work corruption of blood or forfeiture, except during the life of the person *attainted*" (*Webster's New Int. Dict., 2d Ed.*). **Proscribe,** originally and still in historical use, implies the publication or posting of a decree condemning a person to banishment or death, or announcing his status as an outlaw and the forfeiture of his property or of his civil rights. "A declaration was...signed by all the Powers, which...*proscribed* Napoleon as a public enemy, with whom neither peace nor truce could be concluded" (*Sir A. Alison*). The word now suggests ostracism or interdiction as the result of a judgment by some authoritative or influential body or group; as, dancing was once, but is now rarely, *proscribed* by certain churches. "You..., your rites, your garb *proscribed*, Must yet receive one degradation more" (*Browning*).

Ana. *Judge, adjudge, adjudicate: condemn, denounce, blame (see CRITICIZE): determine, settle, rule, *decide.

Con. Acquit, absolve, vindicate, exonerate, *exculpate.

sententious. Pregnant, meaningful, significant, *expressive, eloquent.

Ana. Formal, conventional, ceremonious (see CEREMONIAL): Pompous, *showy, ostentatious: terse, pithy, compendious (see CONCISE).

sentiment. 1 Emotion, affection, *feeling, passion.

Ana. Thought, impression, notion, *idea: ideal, standard, exemplar (see MODEL).

2 *Opinion, view, belief, conviction, persuasion.

Ana. *Truth, verity: conclusion, judgment (see under INFER).

3 Sentiment, sentimentality, sentimentalism come into comparison when they denote a quality, or a characteristic, that is the product of sensibility (see at SENSATION, 2) and that is manifested chiefly in written or spoken utterances or in works of art. **Sentiment** (as here considered: see also FEELING, 2; OPINION) usually, but not invariably, is employed in a good sense implying qualities such as the power to express or evoke delicacy or tenderness of feeling, idealism, high and ennobling thought, or the like; as, "the charm Of pious *sentiment* diffused afar [by ancient churches]" (*Wordsworth*); "The unbought grace of life...the nurse of manly *sentiment* and heroic enterprise is gone" (*Burke*). Sometimes, but now rarely, the term has been used to suggest artificiality, insincerity, or a striving for effect. "To be with joy perused, By all whom *sentiment* has not abused; Newfangled *sentiment*, the boasted grace Of those who never feel in the right place" (*Cowper*). **Sentimentality** is definitely a derogatory, and often a contemptuous, term for it always implies mawkishness, affectation, or excess of emotion, and sometimes suggests manufactured or falsified emotion or lack of judgment or good sense; as, "His very pity will be cowardly, egotistic,—*sentimentality*, or little better" (*Carlyle*); "[in] the literature of the past century...nearly all its expressions having reference to the country show...a foolish *sentimentality*.... Brooks are always 'purling'; birds always 'warbling' " (*Ruskin*); "that filigree-work of sentiment which we call *sentimentality*" (*J. R. Lowell*). "Modesty we like even before we approve it morally; and kindness and enthusiasm in like manner; but when they become prudishness and *sentimentality*, we withhold our liking" (*S. Alexander*). **Sentimentalism** is often used in place of *sentimentality*, but precise writers prefer the former as a designation for the habit of mind or disposition of the sentimental man, and the latter for the quality as manifested externally, as in one's utterances; as, "the degradation of reasonable sympathy into *sentimentalism*" (*Inge*); "Call it [inability to bear the thought of a wounded animal's suffering]...squeamishness, namby-pamby *sentimentalism*, what you will—it is stronger than oneself!" (*Galsworthy*).

sentimental. Sentimental, romantic, mawkish, maudlin, soppy, mushy, slushy come into comparison when they mean unduly or affectedly emotional. **Sentimental,** although properly the adjective for both *sentiment* and *sentimentality* (see SENTIMENT), usually suggests emotion that does not arise from genuine or natural feeling but is evoked by an external cause, by a particular mood, or by an excess of sensibility, or for the sake of the thrill, or is merely an affectation that is temperamental, the moment's fashion, or designed to achieve a given end (such as in the so-called "*sentimental* drama," to reveal the natural goodness of human nature, or to arouse pity for criminals and scorn for the society that produces them); as, *sentimental* songs; *sentimental* women; "Mr. Sterne [in 'A *Sentimental* Journey'] becomes *sentimental* over a cab, and weeps generous tears over a donkey" (*Thackeray*); "a *sentimental* person, interested in pathetic novels and all unhappy attachments" (*Thackeray*); "We are all for tootling on the *sentimental* flute in literature" (*Stevenson*); "Whisky made him somewhat *sentimental*" (*S. Anderson*). "I hate the whole tribe of *sentimental* men and women who, impelled by the unimaginative fool nature, exalt sexual love above its proper place in the scheme of things" (*R. Macaulay*). **Romantic** implies emotion that has little relation to things as they actually are, but is derived more from one's imagination of what they should be ideally or from one's conceptions of them as formed by literature, art, one's dreams, or the like; as, "I am not *romantic*, you know; I never was. I ask only a comfortable home" (*Austen*); "a pretty little *romantic* girl...who possessed a laudable zeal to know a live poet" (*Scott*); "her first *romantic* admiration of his lofty bearing has worn off" (*Meredith*); "The process of growing from *romantic* boyhood into cynical maturity" (*Shaw*). **Mawkish,** when it implies sentimentality, suggests a kind that creates loathing or disgust because of its insincerity, emotional excess, or other signs of weakness or futility; as, "[Verses] So sweetly *mawkish*, and so smoothly dull" (*Pope*); "I hate a *mawkish* popularity" (*Keats*); "Stale epithets, which, when I only seem to smell their *mawkish* proximity, produce in me a slight feeling of nausea" (*L. P. Smith*). **Maudlin** stresses a lack of balance or self-restraint that shows itself in tears, laments, or other emotional excess: usually also it suggests extreme or contemptible silliness; as, "A *maudlin* Poetess, a rhyming Peer" (*Pope*); "The mob became not only enthusiastic but *maudlin*" (*Disraeli*). The condition is often a result of great indulgence in alcohol; as, "Schreiderling, when he grew *maudlin* at mess, used to talk about 'my poor dear wife' " (*Kipling*). **Soppy** and **mushy** are terms of slangy or colloquial flavor that come close to *mawkish* in their suggestion of distasteful and disgusting sentimentality, but *soppy* (chiefly in British use) often carries a strong suggestion of silliness in showing affection (as, "Don't be *soppy*, Bryn"—*Galsworthy*) and *mushy*, of softness or wishy-washiness (as, "You may . . . be a sharp, cynical sort of person; or you may be a nice, *mushy*, amiable, goodnatured one"—*Shaw*). **Slushy,** which is colloquial in flavor, applies chiefly to spoken or written utterances that are so sentimental or emotionally confused as to seem mere drivel; as, *slushy* stories; a *slushy* speech.

Ana. Emotional, affectionate, feeling, passionate (see corresponding nouns at FEELING): affecting, *moving, pathetic, touching: affected, pretended, counterfeited, feigned, simulated (see AFFECT).

sentimentalism. Sentimentality, *sentiment.

Ana. Sensibility, feeling (see SENSATION).

sentimentality. Sentimentalism, *sentiment.

Ana. Sensibility, feeling (see SENSATION).

separate, *v.* **Separate, part, divide, sever, sunder, divorce** come into comparison when they mean to cause two or more things or parts of a thing that are united or assembled to become disunited, disjoined, or the like, or, when the subject is the thing or things affected, to become so disunited or disjoined. **Separate** implies a putting or keeping apart; it may suggest a scattering or dispersion of units (as, forces that *separate* families; to *separate* the parts of a watch), or a removal of one from the other or others (as, to *separate* a husband from his wife or a mother from her children; to *separate* the wheat from the chaff; to *separate* one's mind from one's work), or the presence of an intervening thing or things (as, the Atlantic *separates* Europe from America; a thousand miles *separate* the two branches of the family). **Part** usually, but not invariably, suggests the separation of two persons or things in close union or association; often also it suggests a complete separation as by death or violence; as, "The Lord do so to me . . . if ought but death *part* thee and me" (*Ruth* i. 17); "To love and to cherish, till death us do *part*" (*Anglican Marriage Service*); to *part* two combatants; "Soon a faint diverging path was reached, where they *parted* company" (*Hardy*). **Divide** commonly stresses the idea of parts, groups, or sections resulting, literally or figuratively, from cutting, breaking, branching, or the like; as, to *divide* a pie into six pieces; to *divide* a stick of candy into two parts; to *divide* the government into the executive, legislative, and judicial branches; "He that will *divide* a minute into a thousand parts" (*Shak.*). *Divide* often, in addition, carries an implication of apportioning or of distributing; as, to *divide* a pie among the family; to *divide* booty or profits; to *divide* one's estate equitably among one's heirs. Often *divide* is used in place of *separate*, especially when mutual antagonism or wide separation is connoted; as, United we stand, *divided* we fall; "the broad and deep gulf which . . . *divides* the living from the dead, the organic from the inorganic" (*Inge*). **Sever** adds the implication of violence (especially by or as if by cutting), and frequently applies to the separation of a part from the whole or of persons or things that are joined in affection, close affinity, natural association, or the like; as, to *sever* a branch from the trunk by one blow of the ax; to *sever* the head from the body; "*Sever'd* from thee, can I survive?" (*Burns*); "The hour is ill Which *severs* those it should unite" (*Shelley*). **Sunder** often implies a violent rending or wrenching apart; as, "Even as a splitted bark, so *sunder* we" (*Shak.*); "We that are *sindered* [*sundered*] in sorrow may meet again in joy" (*Scott*). **Divorce,** etymologically to turn different ways, implies the legal dissolution of a marriage, and thereby the undoing of a union. The term is widely used in an extended sense, implying the separation of two or more things so closely associated that they interact upon each other or work only in union with each other; as, "Its academic tendency to *divorce* form from matter [in poetry]" (*Day Lewis*); "You cannot *divorce* accurate thought from accurate speech" (*Quiller-Couch*). "Our knowledge of the external world cannot be *divorced* from the nature of the appliances with which we have obtained the knowledge" (*Eddington*).

Ana. Cleave, rend, split, rive (see TEAR): *estrange, alienate: disperse, dispel, *scatter: *detach, disengage.

Ant. Combine.

separate, *adj.* **1** *Distinct, several, discrete.

Ana. Diverse, disparate, *different, divergent, various: *free, independent.

2 *Single, solitary, particular, unique, sole, lone.

Ana. *Special, especial, specific, individual: peculiar, distinctive (see CHARACTERISTIC): detached, disengaged (see DETACH).

sept. *Tribe, sib, clan, horde.

sequel. Upshot, outcome, issue, *effect, consequence, result, aftereffect, event, aftermath.

Ana. Termination, *end, ending: conclusion, closing, finishing *or* finish (see corresponding verbs at CLOSE).

sequence. Series, *succession, progression, set, suit, suite, chain, train, string.

Ana. Ordering *or* order, arrangement (see corresponding verbs at ORDER).

sequent, sequential. *Consecutive, successive, serial, discrete.

seraph. Cherub, archangel, *angel.

serene. Tranquil, *calm, peaceful, placid, halcyon.

Ana. *Still, stilly, silent, noiseless, quiet: *cool, collected, composed: smooth, effortless, *easy.

Con. Disturbed, disquieted, agitated, upset (see DISCOMPOSE).

serf. **Serf, slave, bondslave, thrall, villein, vassal, bondman, bondsman, peon, Helot** are often distinguished in their historical senses, but in their extended or looser senses they agree in designating a person who lives in servitude or in bondage to a master or owner. **Serf,** in its strictest sense, applies to a person who is attached to the soil or land and whose ownership passes to the heir when the lord or master dies or to the purchaser when the land is sold. Historically, the term has been applied to all persons coming under this general description whether their ownership implied control over all their movements and interests or only over their services. In extended use, *serf* usually implies merely the inability to free oneself from something that is imposed upon one; as, "the teacher . . ., that *serf* of custom, that subjugated rebel, that feeble, persistent antagonist of the triumphant things that rule him" (*H. G. Wells*). **Slave,** and its poetic and emphatic equivalent **bondslave,** apply to a person who is the absolute property of his (or her) master and disposable in the same manner as any chattel: both terms imply ownership that gives control not only over the services but also over the person and his (or her) actions; they therefore suggest, both in their historical and in their extended senses, privation of freedom and deprivation of all the rights and privileges associated with independence. "Had you rather Caesar were living and die all *slaves*, than that Caesar were dead, to live all free men?" (*Shak.*). "But foul effeminacy held me [Samson] yoked Her [Dalila's] *bond-slave*" (*Milton*). "An adult with whom a child is in constant contact may easily become so dominant in the child's life as to make the child, even in later life, a mental *slave*" (*B. Russell*). **Thrall,** now an archaic or literary term, implies slavery, but not always a condition of servitude. Rather it suggests a being held in bondage, as in chains (more often figurative than literal) or in captivity, and therefore usually connotes the loss of one's liberty or the forfeit of it to a greater power. Unlike *serf* and *slave* the term carries no clear, specific application, though it is often poetically used in place of them; as, "*Slaves* of drink and *thralls* of sleep" (*Shak.*); "Gurth...is the born *thrall* of Cedric" (*Scott*); "La belle Dame sans merci Hath thee in *thrall!*" (*Keats*). **Villein,** largely as a result of shifting applications in its earliest use in feudal times, being applied both to freemen of the lowest social rank, such as are now often called peasants, and to serfs, has not acquired an extended meaning and carries slight connotations of servitude or of bondage. The term, therefore, is chiefly if not exclusively in historical use. **Vassal,** in its strict historical sense, is not a synonym of the preceding words because it applies only to a person who, under the feudal system (or a system comparable to it), holds lands or receives protection on conditions of homage and allegiance to the overlord who grants the land or promises protection in return for the vassal's pledged support and services, especially in war. Consequently, *vassal* is closer to *subject* than to *serf* and implies only such loss of freedom as is voluntarily surrendered. "I dreamt that I dwelt in marble halls With *vassals* and *serfs* by my side" (*Alfred Bunn*). In a looser extended sense, *vassal* is applied to any person or personified thing that is perforce or voluntarily subordinate to another and dependent upon his will: usually it connotes abjectness or complete subjection to another's influence; as, "thy thoughts, low *vassals* to thy state" (*Shak.*); "The man who by sin makes himself Satan's *vassal* may soon be his victim" (*James Hamilton*); "My dear dumb friend [a dog], low lying there, A willing *vassal* at my feet" (*J. G. Holland*). **Bondman** and **bondsman** (also *bondwoman* and *bondswoman* and *bondmaid* [as in *Galatians* iv. 22; *Leviticus* xxv. 44]; also *bondservant* [as in *Leviticus* xxv. 39]) have shown fluctuations in meaning owing largely to differences in interpreting *bond*, that word in earliest use implying the status of a serf and in later use, through confusion with *bond* (a shackle or fetter) and *bound*, that of one who has been forced into thralldom or who has surrendered his freedom. Because of this lack of fixity in meaning the terms are used largely in poetic or rhetorical language where explicitness is not essential; as, "From chieftain's tower to *bondsman's* cot" (*Scott*); "Fields where the *bondman's* toil No more shall trench the soil" (*Bryant*). **Peon,** a term used chiefly in reference to Spanish-American countries, applies strictly to one of a class, such as of Indians or half-breeds in Mexico, who are agricultural and mining laborers, and whose condition, though not legally that of slaves, actually is that of bondage. By extension, the term now often applies to any agricultural laborer who is virtually in servitude for payment of a debt, as a convict laborer, or as a heavily burdened tenant farmer working on shares. **Helot,** historically applicable only to a Spartan whose status was comparable to that of a serf, is often used in an extended sense to mean *slave* or *serf*, but with added connotations of an oppressed condition or of being driven beyond human bounds.

serial, *adj.* *Consecutive, successive, sequent, sequential, discrete.

Ana. Following, ensuing, succeeding (see FOLLOW): continuous, *continual.

series. *Succession, progression, sequence, set, suit, suite, chain, train, string.

serious. Serious, grave, solemn, sedate, staid, sober, earnest come into comparison when applied to persons, their looks, their acts, and the like, and mean not light or frivolous but actually or seemingly weighed down by deep thought, heavy cares, important work, or the like. **Serious** implies absorption in work rather than in play, or concern for that which really matters rather than for that which merely amuses. "The features [of the imaged Virgin Mary]...were *serious* and almost sad under the austere responsibilities of infinite pity and power" (*H. Adams*). "Molière himself has said that if it had not been for this comedy [*Le Menteur*] he himself might have written his lighter comedies but would not have risen to the height of the *serious* comedy of *Le Tartuffe*" (*S. Alexander*). **Grave** implies both seriousness and dignity, but it commonly also implies a somber expression or attitude and the pressure of weighty interests or responsibilities. "A stately speech; Such as *grave* Livers do in Scotland use" (*Wordsworth*). "She had no flights of eloquence, but the slow, *grave*...tones with which she uttered the things that seemed to her the most worth while in life were more impressive than any arts of the orator" (*H. Ellis*). **Solemn** usually heightens the suggestion of impressiveness or awesomeness often implicit in *grave;* as, "the *solemn* splendour of that most wonderful poem, the story of Job" (*Quiller-Couch*); "It was a *solemn* moment, for these were the last words of Augustus to his people" (*Buchan*); the term often lends itself to humorous use when referred directly to persons; as, *solemn* as a judge; "If the word may be used of so *solemn* a personage, he wriggled" (*Conrad*). **Sedate** implies composure and decorous seriousness, as in character or speech; as, "Good sense alone is a *sedate* and quiescent quality" (*Johnson*); "He was...of a *sedate* look, something approaching to gravity" (*Sterne*). **Staid** implies a settled sedateness, often a prim self-restraint, and an even stronger negation of volatility or frivolity than *sedate.* "The side streets here are excessively maiden-lady-like ....The knockers have a very *staid, serious,* nay almost awful, quietness about them" (*Keats*). "The *staid* Roman citizen was repelled by the wild dances and the frenzied paeans" (*Buchan*). **Sober** sometimes stresses seriousness of purpose (as, "if our pupils are to devote *sober* attention to our instruction"—*Grandgent*), but it more often suggests gravity that proceeds from control over or subdual of one's emotions or passions. "Come, pensive Nun, devout and pure, *Sober*, steadfast, and demure" (*Milton*). **Earnest** implies seriousness of purpose as well as sincerity and, often, zealousness and enthusiasm; as, an *earnest* student. "And men are merry at their chores, And children *earnest* at their play" (*Millay*).

Ana. Austere, stern, *severe, ascetic: *thoughtful, reflective, contemplative, meditative: *deep, profound.

sermon. Homily, *speech, address, oration, harangue, talk, allocution, lecture, prelection.

serpentine. *Winding, sinuous, tortuous, flexuous, anfractuous.

Ana. Circuitous, roundabout, *indirect: *crooked, devious.

service, *n.* *Use, advantage, profit, account, avail.

Ana. Usefulness, utility (see USE, *n.*, 2): *worth, value: helping *or* help, aiding *or* aid, assistance (see corresponding verbs at HELP).

servile. *Subservient, menial, slavish, obsequious.

Ana. *Mean, abject, ignoble: fawning, cringing, truckling, cowering (see FAWN).

Ant. Authoritative.

servitude. **Servitude, slavery, bondage** agree in meaning the state of subjection to a master. **Servitude** may refer to the state of a person, or of a class of persons, or of a race, that is bound to obey the will of a master, a lord, or a sovereign, and lacks the freedom to determine his (or their) own acts, laws, conditions of living, and the like. The term is often vague or rhetorical, sometimes implying lack of political freedom, sometimes lack of liberty to do as one pleases. "I am as free as Nature first made man, Ere the base laws of *servitude* began, When wild in woods the noble savage ran" (*Dryden*). In very precise use, however, *servitude* denotes the condition of one who must give service to a master and perform labor for him, either because he has bound himself (see BOND, *adj.*) voluntarily, or because he is a convict (especially one transported to a colony or one sentenced to *penal servitude*, that is, imprisonment with hard labor), a slave, or the like. **Slavery,** in precise use, implies subjection to a master who is the owner of one's person or who may treat one as his property. *Slavery*, historically, does not invariably imply servitude, but that implication is common when the reference is to modern as distinct from ancient times. "Taken by the insolent foe And sold to *slavery*" (*Shak.*). In rhetorical use, *slavery* implies entire loss of personal freedom and subjugation to another. "Is life so dear, or peace so sweet, as to be purchased at the price of chains and *slavery*?" (*P. Henry*). **Bondage,** which is now chiefly a literary or rhetorical term, originally applied to the state of one who was bound as a serf to the soil and who was sold with the land when the latter was conveyed to a new owner. By confusion with bonds, or the chains of a captive prisoner, the word came to apply to any state of subjection from which there is no hope of escape except by breaking one's chains. "What more oft, in nations grown corrupt, And by their vices brought to *servitude*, Than to love *bondage* more than liberty" (*Milton*).

set, *v.* **Set, settle, fix, establish, firm** come into comparison when they mean to cause someone or something to be put securely in position, as in a place, an office, a category, or the like. **Set** (etymologically, to cause to sit) is the most inclusive of these terms, sometimes implying placing in a definite location, especially to do a certain piece of work or to serve a certain purpose (as, to *set* a hen on eggs—but, idiomatically, a *setting* hen, rather than a *sitting* hen; to *set* a light at each window; to *set* out trees; to *set* food on the table; to *set* a child on a horse), sometimes implying a placing under orders in an occupation, a situation, an office, or a sphere of life, or under conditions where something or someone must perform an allotted or prescribed function (as, to *set* a boy to work; to *set* the maids to cleaning house; to *set* proctors to watch the students; to *set* oneself to a disagreeable task), occasionally suggesting a prescribing or ordaining of the object or objects on which the mind, heart, eyes, or the like, concentrates itself (as, to *set* the subject for a debate; to *set* a goal for one's efforts; to *set* one's heart on winning a prize; to *set* duty before pleasure). **Settle** comes close to *set* in its etymological sense but in actual use it carries a much stronger implication of putting a person or thing in a place or condition of stability, rest, or repose, and often a weaker implication of regulative or dictatorial power; as, to *settle* an invalid in an easy chair; to *settle* themselves in their new home; to *settle* one's eyes on a distant view. Often, the word carries an implication of decisive quieting, calming, or ordering of that which is disturbed, upset, unstable, fluctuating, or the like; as, to *settle* a person's nerves; to *settle* one's doubts; the white of an egg will *settle* the coffee; to *settle* one's bedroom each morning after breakfast; "There's nothing will *settle* me but a bullet" (*Swift*). **Fix,** as here compared (see also ADJUST, 1; FASTEN), usually implies more stability and permanence in position, condition, character, and the like, than *set* or even *settle;* as, "his resolution was already *fixed*" (*Buchan*); "truth which the scientist strives to catch and *fix*" (*Lowes*); "his place in the McCoy household had become *fixed*" (*S. Anderson*). "What I have most at heart is, that some method should be thought of for ascertaining and *fixing* our language forever" (*Swift*). "The undifferentiated, inchoate religious sense is thus intensified and *fixed,* to the great and lasting injury of the spiritual life" (*Inge*). **Establish** (see also FOUND), in its earlier and etymological sense, stresses not the putting in place or the bringing into existence so much as the becoming fixed, stable, or immovable, although in some use both ideas are connoted; as, do not transplant a tree once it is *established* (that is, deeply rooted in the soil and growing normally); "When love is *established,* it never occurs to me either to give or to ask any declarations of love" (*H. Ellis*); "American sculptors...whose reputation was already *established*" (*E. Wharton*). "The child initiates new processes of thought and *establishes* new mental habits much more easily than the adult" (*C. W. Eliot*). **Firm,** in the sense under consideration, is now obsolete except in horticultural uses: it implies a setting so securely in place that the thing set quickly establishes itself or cannot easily be uprooted or broken down by the elements or other disturbing forces; as, to *firm* young shoots in the ground. "The stones...were again by the mason's art so levelled and *firm'd,* as they had been formerly" (*Walton*).

Ana. *Implant, infix: *fasten, attach, fix, affix: *prescribe, assign, define.

Con. Eradicate, deracinate, uproot (see EXTERMINATE): *abolish, annihilate, extinguish: displace, supplant, *replace.

set, *n.* **1** Series, sequence, suit, suite, *succession, progression, chain, train, string.

Ana. Collection, gathering, assemblage (see under GATHER).

2 Set, circle, coterie, clique agree in denoting a more or less carefully selected or exclusive group of persons having a common interest. **Set** applies to a comparatively large group, especially of society men and women bound together by common tastes; as, the smart *set;* the fast *set.* "It gives me great pleasure that you and Sellar like *Thyrsis*....The voices I do turn to are the voices of our old *set*" (*Arnold*). **Circle** implies a common center of the group, such as a person or a cause that draws persons to him or it, or a common interest, activity, or occupation; as, "The *circle* of his acquaintance widened" (*Macaulay*); a sewing *circle;* "The work of the younger writers...has even penetrated into academic *circles*" (*Day Lewis*); "[dismissed professors] posturing in radical *circles* as martyrs" (*Mencken*). **Coterie** stresses the notion of selectness or of congeniality within the small circle; **clique** heightens the implication of an often selfish or arrogant exclusiveness; as, "the Tunbridge *coterie*" (*Burney*); "We three formed a little *coterie* within the household" (*Symonds*); "the poetry of revolt is apt to become the poetry of a *coterie*" (*Lowes*); "The best English society—mind, I don't call the London exclusive *clique* the best English society" (*Coleridge*); "To humanize [knowledge], to make it efficient outside the *clique* of the cultivated and learned" (*Arnold*).

setting. *Background, environment, milieu, mise-en-scène, backdrop.

settle. 1 *Set, fix, establish, firm.
Ana. *Secure, anchor, moor, rivet: *pacify, appease, conciliate, propitiate: *order, arrange.
Ant. Unsettle.
2 Determine, *decide, rule, resolve.
Ana. *Judge, adjudge, adjudicate: *close, end, conclude, terminate.

sever. *Separate, sunder, part, divide, divorce.
Ana. Rive, cleave, rend, split (see TEAR): *cut, hew, chop: *detach, disengage.

several. 1 *Distinct, separate, discrete.
Ana. Respective, individual, particular, *special, especial.
2 *Many, sundry, various, divers, numerous, manifold, multifold, multifarious.
Ana. *Single, separate, particular: detached, disengaged (see DETACH).

severally. Individually, respectively, *each, apiece.

severe, *adj.* **Severe, stern, austere, ascetic** are synonyms when they mean given to or manifesting discipline and restraint. **Severe** is applicable not only to persons, their looks, acts, thoughts, and utterances, but also to things for which persons are responsible, such as laws, penalties, judgments, and styles. In all these applications it implies rigorous standards of what is just, right, ethical, beautiful, and the like, and unsparing or exacting adherence to them; it not only excludes even a hint of laxity or indulgence, but it often suggests a preference for that which is hard, plain, or meager; as, to be as *severe* with oneself as with others; a *severe* teacher; a *severe* thinker; *severe* impartiality; *severe* in dress. "So *severe* is French taste and so acute is the French sense for harmony, that in its full flower any fashion is sure to be distinguished more by unity and measure than by caprice" (*Brownell*). Very often, however, the word suggests harshness or even cruelty; as, a *severe* penalty; *severe* discipline; *severe* criticism; a *severe* test of one's endurance. It is then, by extension, referable also to things for which persons are not responsible but which similarly impose pain or acute discomfort; as, a *severe* attack of lumbago; a *severe* winter; a *severe* climate; a *severe* headache. **Stern,** though it often implies severity when applied to persons, their acts, words, etc., stresses inflexibility or inexorability of temper; thus, a *severe* judge may appear kindly though dispassionately just, but a *stern* judge reveals no disposition to be mild or lenient; to be made of *stern* stuff is to have an unyielding will or an extraordinarily resolute character. Consequently, in extended use, *stern* is applied to that which cannot be escaped or evaded (as, *stern* necessity; "the *stern* compulsion of facts"—*Buchan*) or to that which is harsh and forbidding in its appearance or in its external aspects. "The breaking waves dashed high On a *stern* and rock-bound coast" (*Hemans*). "A marble bath that made cleanliness a luxury instead of one of the *sternest* of the virtues, as it seemed at home" (*Shaw*). **Austere** etymologically implies the absence of juiciness and sweetness characteristic of certain fruits, such as the crab apple and sloe plums. It is still occasionally used to describe the taste of some acrid fruits and wines, but it is chiefly applied to persons, their habits, their modes of life, the environments they create, the works of art they produce, and the like. In these latter applications, *austere* has continuously implied the absence of certain qualities comparable (but not similar) to juiciness and sweetness in a fruit, such as feeling, warmth, color, animation, and ornament, and has therefore positively implied dispassionateness, coldness, reserve, barrenness, and the like. "My common conversation I do acknowledge *austere*, my behavior full of rigor" (*Browne*). In more recent use, although these implications are still retained, the word tends also to connote restraint, self-denial, economy of means, and stark simplicity, and to become a term of praise rather than of depreciation. "The *austere* dignity and simplicity of their existence" (*Pater*). "Mathematics, rightly viewed, possesses not only truth, but supreme beauty—a beauty cold and *austere*, like that of sculpture" (*B. Russell*). "He thought of the *austere* shining cleanness of the Arvold place, of the worn domesticity of his mother's house" (*M. Austin*). **Ascetic** etymologically implies laborious and exacting training or discipline. Through its reference to the spiritual exercises and acts of discipline (such as fasting and mortification) characteristic of monastic life in the Middle Ages, it acquired implications of self-denial, abstention from that which is pleasurable, and the courting of that which is painful or disagreeable. In modern use, these latter implications are often stressed to the exclusion of the earlier and fundamental one. "High nature amorous of the good, But touch'd with no *ascetic* gloom" (*Tennyson*). "A people possessed of the epicurean rather than the *ascetic* ideal in morals" (*Brownell*). In other use, the idea of discipline, especially by abstention from that which is pleasurable, or easy, or self-indulgent, for the sake of spiritual or intellectual ends, is emphasized. "For science is *ascetic*. It is a discipline and a control of personal impulse that could arise only in a relatively mature civilization" (*Baker Brownell*). "When *asceticism* is rational, it is a discipline of the mind and body to fit men for the service of an ideal" (*Lippmann*).
Ana. Exacting, oppressive, *onerous, burdensome: *rigid, rigorous, strict, stringent: *hard, difficult, arduous: harsh, rugged, uneven, *rough.
Ant. Tolerant: tender. — *Con.* Lenient, clement, *forbearing, merciful, indulgent: gentle, mild, *soft.

sex, *n.* **Sex, gender** come into comparison because both denote a character by which a thing is describable as masculine or feminine or as neither. **Sex,** however, applies strictly only to living things, especially to animals, but also to plants, which are identified by anatomical and physiological characteristics as male or female, or neither strictly nor clearly one or the other. **Gender,** except in vulgarly colloquial and humorous use or where anatomical or physiological differences are not implied (as, "black divinities of the feminine *gender*"—*Dickens*), is used only with reference to distinctions in words (primarily nouns and pronouns, but also adjectives and participles in inflected languages requiring correspondence between nouns and pronouns and their modifiers) which mark them as masculine, feminine, or neuter. As a rule, in English (the situation is quite different in many other languages) masculine *gender* is a characteristic of a noun or pronoun that refers to a male, feminine *gender*, of one that refers to a female, and neuter *gender*, of one that refers to a sexless thing. Convention, however, prescribes masculine or feminine gender for some sexless things, such as "ship" (feminine gender esp. in poetry).

shackle, *v.* Fetter, clog, trammel, *hamper, manacle, hog-tie.
Ana. *Restrain, curb, check, inhibit: *hinder, impede, obstruct, block, bar: restrict, circumscribe, confine, *limit.
Con. Disencumber, disembarrass, *extricate: release, liberate, *free.

shade, *n.* **1 Shade, shadow, umbrage, umbra, penumbra, adumbration** are here compared as meaning the comparative darkness caused by something which intercepts rays of light. **Shade** carries no implication of a darkness that has a particular form or definite limit, but the term often implies protection from the glare, heat, or other effect of the light that is cut off; as, "the forest, one vast mass Of mingling *shade*" (*Shelley*); "chiaroscuro, by which light reveals [in paintings] the richness of *shade* and *shade* heightens the brightness of light" (*H. Ellis*); "the trees afforded *shade* and shelter" (*Cather*). **Shadow,** on the other hand, usually applies to shade which preserves something of the form of the object which intercepts the light; as, "It [the garden]...has neither arbor, nor alcove, nor other *shade*, except the *shadow* of the house" (*Cowper*); "[he] saw... The *shadow* of some piece of pointed lace, In the Queen's *shadow*, vibrate on the walls" (*Tennyson*); "the shadowless winter, when it is all *shade*, and therefore no *shadow*" (*Jefferies*). Figuratively, *shade* implies darkness or obscurity; *shadow* (so also *shadowy*), insubstantiality or unreality; as, "there no *shade* can last In that deep dawn behind the tomb" (*Tennyson*); " 'Is't real that I see?' 'No, my good lord; 'Tis but the *shadow* of a wife you see, The name and not the thing' " (*Shak.*). **Umbrage,** as here considered, applies chiefly to the shade cast by heavy foliage or trees, though sometimes it refers to the mass of trees or foliage which make for heavy shade; as, "branches... spreading their *umbrage* to the circumference of two hundred and seven feet" (*J. G. Strutt*); "The thrush sings in that *umbrage*" (*L. P. Smith*). **Umbra** now almost entirely, and **penumbra** fundamentally, are astronomical terms. *Umbra* applies to the perfect or complete shadow cast on the sun by the moon or the earth in an eclipse, and *penumbra* to the imperfect or partly illuminated shadow which often outlines or surrounds the umbra. *Umbra* rarely, and *penumbra* often, are used in extended senses, the former implying a complete overshadowing or eclipse, the latter denoting the marginal region or border between that which is clearly one thing or the other or in which the exact differences between one thing or another are so obscure as not to be clearly discernible. "His memory was eclipsed in the *umbra* of a more compelling personality" (*Irvin S. Cobb*). "Physiology having rudely investigated its phenomena upon the same level as other biological processes, it [love] has been stripped of the mystical *penumbra* in whose shadow its transcendental value seemed real, though hid" (*J. W. Krutch*). "The great ordinances of the Constitution do not establish and divide fields of black and white. Even the more specific of them are found to terminate in a *penumbra* shading gradually from one extreme to the other" (*Justice Holmes*). **Adumbration** (literally, a shadowing or a shadow) applies to something that is so faint or obscure a figure, sketch, or outline of something which actually exists or is to come that it serves as the shadow or hint of the latter. "The lugubrious harmony of the spot with his domestic situation was too perfect for him, impatient of effects, scenes, and *adumbrations*" (*Hardy*). "If the Parthenon has value, it is only as an *adumbration* of something higher than itself" (*Babbitt*).

Ana. Darkness, dimness, obscurity (see corresponding adjectives at DARK): *shelter, cover, retreat.

Con. Brightness, brilliancy, radiance, effulgence (see corresponding adjectives at BRIGHT): glare, glow, blaze (see under BLAZE, *v.*).

2 Tint, *color, chroma, hue, tinge.

3 Ghost, spirit, specter, *apparition, phantasm, phantom, wraith, fetch, revenant, spook, haunt.

4 *Touch, suggestion, suspicion, soupçon, tinge, smack, spice, dash, vein, strain, tincture, streak.

Ana. *Trace, vestige: tint, tinge (see COLOR).

shadow, *n.* *Shade, umbrage, umbra, penumbra, adumbration.

Ana. *Form, figure, shape, conformation, configuration: darkness, obscurity, dimness (see corresponding adjectives at DARK): silhouette, contour, *outline.

shadow, *v.* *Suggest, adumbrate.

Ana. *Foretell, forecast, predict, prognosticate: *foresee, foreknow, divine.

Con. *Reveal, disclose, discover, divulge, tell.

shake, *v.* **1 Shake, tremble, quake, totter, quiver, shiver, shudder, quaver, wobble** (*or* **wabble**), **teeter, shimmy, didder, dither** come into comparison as meaning to reveal instability by vibrating, wavering, fluctuating, or the like. **Shake,** the ordinary and the comprehensive term, may imply any kind of instability, especially physical or emotional instability, that reveals itself in any of the particular ways suggested by the succeeding terms; as, to feel the ground *shake* beneath one's feet; he *shook* with fear; his body *shook* with laughter. **Tremble** applies specifically to uncontrollable shaking of the human body, especially when one is agitated or unmanned by fear, dread, ungovernable passion, or the like. "In this awful tempest of sound I *trembled* like a leaf" (*Hudson*). "She stood with her hand on the door-knob, her whole body *trembling*" (*S. Anderson*). "She is so radiant in her pure beauty that the limbs of the young man *tremble*" (*Meredith*). The term may, however, apply to animals and even to things that shake in a manner suggestive of trembling; as, "as though animated by a life of their own, the tails [of fighting cats] twitch and *tremble*" (*A. Huxley*); the bridge *shook*, as if *trembling*, for several hours before it collapsed. **Quake** is now often used in place of *tremble*, but it commonly carries a stronger implication of violent shaking or of extreme agitation; as, "His name was a terror that made the dead *quake* in their graves" (*Ouida*). In very precise speech or writing, the term usually suggests either an internal convulsion such as an earthquake (now more often, something suggestive of one) or something which rocks a person or thing to its foundations; as, "The sounding of the clock in *Venice Preserved*, makes the hearts of the whole audience *quake*" (*Addison*); "And from his [Milton's] touch sweet thunder flowed... And sanguine thrones and impious altars *quaked*, Prisons and citadels" (*Shelley*). **Totter** usually suggests great physical weakness such as that associated with infancy, extreme old age, or disease: it therefore often connotes a shaking that makes movement extremely difficult and uncertain or that forebodes a fall or collapse; as, the mast *tottered* before it fell. "The little calf That's standing by the mother. It's so young, It *totters* when she licks it with her tongue" (*Frost*). "This is the time to fear, When he [the bear] stands up like a tired man, *tottering* near and near" (*Kipling*). **Quiver** suggests a shaking comparable to the vibration of the strings of a musical instrument that is being played: it differs from *tremble* chiefly in being more often applied to things (as, aspen leaves *quiver* in the slightest breeze; the horse's skin *quivers* when he is annoyed by flies) or, when it is used in reference to persons or animals, in carrying a less necessary suggestion of fear or passion and a stronger implication of vibrating nerves (as, the little boy's lips *quivered* as he tried not to cry; his fingers *quivered* in his excitement; "I was *quivering* and tingling from head to foot"—*Kipling;* "eagerness that made their [the dogs'] flanks *quiver*"—*E. M. Roberts*). *Shiver* and *shudder* usually imply a momentary or short-lived quivering, especially of the flesh. **Shiver** typically suggests the effect of extreme cold (as, he came into the house snow-covered and *shivering*), but it may apply to a similar quivering that results from a premonition, a foreboding, or the like (as, "Such thoughts...may make you *shiver* at first"—*C. E. Montague*), or to a sudden, often seeming, quivering of a thing (as, "His heart *shivered*, as a ship *shivers* at the mountainous crash of the waters"—*Bennett;* "When the first star *shivers* and the last wave pales"—*J. E. Flecker*). **Shudder,** on the other hand, usually suggests the effect of that which is horrible or revolting: physically it implies a sudden sharp quivering that for the moment affects the entire body (or mass); as, "When she saw The haggard father's face and reverend beard ...all dabbled with the blood Of his own son [she] *shudder'd*" (*Tennyson*); " 'I am afraid of it,' she answered, *shuddering*" (*Dickens*); "it was one of those illnesses from which we turn away our eyes, *shuddering*" (*Deland*). **Quaver** sometimes implies continuous vibration or fluctuation, especially as an effect of something that disturbs (as, "The breeze...set the flames of the street lamps *quavering*"—*Stevenson*), but this, its earliest implication, is not as often apparent in current use as that of tremulousness (an implication partly derived from the denotation of the noun in music as a shake or trill). Consequently, *quaver* is now used chiefly in regard to voices, utterances, and the like, as affected by weakness or emotion; as, "A reedy, *quavering* voice" (*Conan Doyle*); " 'You will not leave me, dear?' But dread returned, and the words *quavered* as she spoke them" (*Meredith*). The remaining terms are less literary and likely to occur in informal speech or writing. **Wobble** implies an unsteadiness that shows itself in tottering, or in a quivering characteristic of a mass of soft flesh or of a soft jelly, or in a shakiness characteristic of rickety furniture; as, this table *wobbles;* "bumping when she trots, and *wobbling* when she canters" (*Whyte-Melville*); "her chin *wobbled* pathetically" (*Howells*). Often, in extended use, it implies vacillation; as, to *wobble* in one's opinions. **Teeter** implies an unsteadiness that reveals itself in seesawing motions (as, an inebriated man *teetering* as he stands; a spinning top losing its momentum *teeters* before falling; the plank *teetered* beneath his feet). **Shimmy** suggests the shaking of the body from the shoulders down, so as to simulate trembling, which is characteristic of the dance of that name and, therefore, usually suggests vibratory motions of an abnormal nature; as, " 'I often see the walls of my house *shimmying* a bit' " (*Lucas*); the *shimmying* (that is, abnormal vibration) of the front wheels of an automobile. **Didder** and **dither** are now chiefly dialectal terms implying a shaking through fear or excitement. They are often used in place of *tremble, quake, quiver,* or *shiver,* and sometimes imply merely mental confusion or uncertainty rather than a physical shaking.

Ana. Oscillate, fluctuate, vibrate, waver, *swing, sway.

2 Shake, agitate, rock, convulse are comparable when they mean to cause to move to and fro or up and down with more or less violence. **Shake,** the most general of these words, seldom, if ever, in any of its specific senses loses this basic meaning; however, it seldom conveys merely this idea. Very often, its meaning is narrowed but enriched by an implication of the particular intent or purpose of the movement; thus, to *shake* a rug implies an intent to dislodge dust; to *shake* a tree, to bring down its fruit; to *shake* a cocktail, to mix ingredients; to *shake* hands, to greet or to acknowledge an introduction; to *shake* one's fist, to threaten. Even in its extended or figurative use, *shake* commonly implies movement, usually physical movement; as, he was visibly *shaken;* they were unable to *shake* his belief in himself. **Agitate** usually, but not invariably, carries a much stronger implication of tossing or of violent stirring than *shake;* it often also suggests a prolongation of the movement; as, a churn has a dasher or other device for *agitating* cream or milk; the aurora powerfully *agitates* a magnet. "The leaves on the trees were *agitated* as if by a high wind" (*Hudson*). In modern use *agitate,* when the agent is a person, usually carries connotations of excitement or disturbance. "Mr. Thompson *agitated* his eyebrows dreadfully. He was utterly lost" (*Meredith*). **Rock** suggests a swinging or swaying motion; it tends now to lose the implication of lulling derived from its earliest associations with the movement of a cradle and to emphasize those, such as of upheaving, derived from the violent swaying, as of a ship in a storm or of the earth in an earthquake; as, the wind *rocked* the house; the entire city was *rocked* by the explosion. Often, especially in figurative use, *rock* suggests, as *shaking* does not, tottering and peril of falling; as, the stock market was *rocked* by the rumor of war; constant insinuations finally *rocked* his faith in his friend. **Convulse** often implies more violence in, and more frequent repetition of, the motion than any of the others; it also commonly suggests a pulling to and fro or a wrenching, as of the body in a paroxysm or of the earth in seismic disturbances; as, "Lucetta...*convulsed* on the carpet in the paroxysms of an epileptic seizure" (*Hardy*); "Rome was *convulsed* by the disgrace of Julia, his [the Emperor's] daughter and only child" (*Buchan*); they were *convulsed* with laughter.

Ana. *Move, drive, impel: flourish, brandish, *swing, wave: disturb, derange, unsettle, *disorder.

shallow, *adj.* *Superficial, cursory, uncritical.

Ana. Slim, slight, slender, *thin: trivial, trifling, *petty, paltry: empty, hollow, idle, *vain.

sham, *n.* *Imposture, cheat, fake, humbug, fraud, deceit, deception, counterfeit, simulacrum.

Ana. *Pretense, pretension, make-believe, make-belief: *simulation, dissimulation: *trick, ruse, feint, wile.

sham, *v.* Feign, simulate, counterfeit, pretend, *assume, affect.

Ana. *Invent, create: ape, mock, mimic, imitate, *copy.

shame, *n.* *Disgrace, dishonor, disrepute infamy, ignominy, opprobrium, obloquy, odium, scandal.

Ana. Humiliation, degradation, abasement (see corresponding verbs at ABASE): mortification, chagrin (see corresponding adjectives at ASHAMED).

Ant. Glory: pride.

shameless. Shameless, brazen, barefaced, brash, impudent, when applied to persons and their acts in defiance of the moral code or of social decorum, agree in meaning characterized by boldness and a lack of a sense of shame. **Shameless** implies a lack of effective restraints such as modesty, a sense of decency, an active conscience, concern for the respect of others, and the like; as, a *shameless* neglect of her children; *shameless* gossips; *shameless* graft; "a *shameless* sale of peerages" (*J. R. Green*). **Brazen** suggests a heart or conscience as hard as brass; it implies not only complete shamelessness but defiant insolence; as, a *brazen* hussy; at first a furtive, now a *brazen,* thief. "I knew a *brazen* minister of state, Who bore for twice ten years the public hate" (*Swift*). **Barefaced** implies absence of all effort to disguise or to mask one's transgressions: it connotes extreme effrontery; as, a *barefaced* lie; *barefaced* tyranny; *barefaced* inquisitiveness. **Brash** so strongly implies impetuousness that it does not stress shamelessness as clearly as the preceding words; however, it is often used in place of *shameless* when heedlessness and temerity make one indifferent to the calls of conscience, one's sense of decency, and the like; as, a *brash* intrusion on another's privacy; *brash* reporters. "And deeply I repented Of *brash* and boyish crime" (*V. Lindsay*). **Impudent,** as here compared, not only carries all the implications of *shameless* but in addition it implies bold or pert defiance of principles of modesty or decency; as, *impudent* hussies; "Conduct so sordidly unladylike that even the most *impudent* woman would not dare do it openly" (*Shaw*).

Ana. *Abandoned, profligate, dissolute: *hardened, indurated, callous: *vicious, villainous, iniquitous.

Con. Modest, pure, *chaste, decent: *shy, diffident, bashful.

shape, *n.* *Form, figure, conformation, configuration, Gestalt.

Ana. *Outline, contour, profile, silhouette: *appearance, look, aspect, semblance.

shape, *v.* *Make, form, fashion, fabricate, manufacture, forge.

shapeless. *Formless, unformed, chaotic, inchoate, amorphous.

Ana. *Rude, rough, crude.

Ant. Shapely. — ***Con.*** Proportionate, *proportional, commensurate.

share, *v.* **Share, participate, partake** come into comparison only when they mean to have, get, use, exercise, experience, or engage in something in common with another or others. All were once used transitively in this sense, but with the exception of *share*, they are now more often used intransitively than transitively. One **shares,** or, less often, *shares in*, something *with* another when one as the original owner or holder grants the part use, enjoyment, possession, or the like, to the other (as, I shall *share* my room with you if you cannot find another in the hotel; I shall bring a salad to the picnic which I hope to *share* with all) or when one as the receiver accepts the part use, enjoyment, possession, or the like, of something that belongs to or comes from another (as, she asked all to *share* in the salad; I *shared* my sister's room last night when we had a guest; the employees *shared* in the profits; "I deny, in short, that the reader must *share* the beliefs of the poet in order to enjoy the poetry fully"—*T. S. Eliot*). But *share* may also take for its subject a group, and imply a community of possession, enjoyment, or the like; as, "You do not *share* the great earth among you fairly" (*Jefferies*). One **participates,** or in current use *participates in* something, when one has or takes a part or a share in that thing, such as a work, an experience, an enterprise, or the like; as, to *participate* in a discussion; "May I ask you whether your wife *participates* in this undertaking?" (*Meredith*). "The commerce of the United States with foreign nations, is that of the whole United States. Every district has a right to *participate* in it" (*Ch. Just. Marshall*). A person or thing **partakes,** or *partakes of* (sometimes *in*) something, when he or it accepts, takes, or acquires a share of that thing, such as food, drink, a pleasure, a burden, or, often, its essential nature or quality; as, "Your papa invited Mr. R. to *partake* of our lowly fare" (*Dickens*); "We do not only meet to *share* each others' burdens, but to *partake* in each other's joys" (*C. H. Spurgeon*); "Adventurers who were willing to *partake* his fortunes" (*Kinglake*); "As the chief character is internally melodramatic, the story itself ceases to be merely melodramatic, and *partakes* of true drama" (*T. S. Eliot*).

Ana. *Communicate, impart: divide, dispense, *distribute.

sharp. Sharp, keen, acute come into comparison both in their general and extended senses. As used of things, *sharp* (the common word) applies to either an edge or a point; *keen*, esp. to an edge, rarely to a point; *acute* (commonly more or less technical) applies to an angle, tip, or end, formed by lines or edges converging in a sharp point; as, *sharp* (or *keen*) as a razor; *sharp* (not *keen*) as a needle; as *acute* as the vertex of an isosceles triangle. As applied to that which affects the senses, **sharp** often suggests a disagreeably cutting quality; as, *sharp* as vinegar; a *sharp* voice; a *sharp* flash; a *sharp* wind. Frequently, however, it emphasizes distinctness or clearness of definition; as, a *sharp* contrast. "While one notes each of the unnaturally *sharp* and lustrous images it [a searchlight] picks out" (*E. Wharton*). **Keen,** in contrast, suggests a bracing, zestful, or piquant quality. "The wind came *keen* with a tang of frost" (*Masefield*). "Very *keen* is the savour of the roast beef that floats up" (*A. C. Benson*). **Acute** is rare in this application, being applied chiefly to high-pitched tones; as, an *acute* accent. As applied to the senses themselves, *sharp* is used esp. of sight and hearing, *keen*, of sight and smell, *acute*, of hearing; as, *sharp*-sighted; *keen*-sighted; *sharp* ears; his hearing was still *acute;* dogs *keen* of scent. As characterizing pleasures and pains, *sharp* suggests most definitely that which cuts or pierces, *keen* implies intensity, *acute* implies poignancy; as, a *sharp* pain; *keen* zest; *acute* anguish. With reference to persons or personal qualities, *sharp* often implies overcleverness or trickiness; *keen* suggests clearsightedness, quickness, and sometimes shrewdness; *acute* suggests penetration or nicety of discrimination; as, *sharp* practice; a *sharp* customer; a *keen* intellect. "His *keen*, worldly face" (*Dr. J. Brown*). "Rather...an *acute* thinker than a subtle one" (*De Quincey*). "His criticisms are always sensible, never *acute*" (*Landor*).

Ana. *Incisive, trenchant, cutting, biting: mordant, mordacious, *caustic, scathing: piercing, penetrating, probing (see ENTER): tricky, cunning, artful, wily, *sly.

Ant. Dull: blunt.

shear, *n.* *Stress, strain, pressure, tension, thrust, torsion.

shed, *v.* *Discard, cast, molt, exuviate, slough, scrap, junk.

Ana. Remove, shift, transfer (see MOVE): reject, repudiate, spurn (see DECLINE, *v.*).

shee. *Fairy, faery, fay, elf, sprite, pixy, gnome, dwarf, goblin, brownie, puck, nix, leprechaun, banshee.

sheen. *Luster, gloss, glaze, glare.

Ana. Polishing *or* polish, shining *or* shine, burnishing *or* burnish (see corresponding verbs at POLISH): gleaming *or* gleam, glittering *or* glitter, flashing *or* flash (see corresponding verbs at FLASH).

sheer, *adj.* **1** *Pure, simple, absolute.

Ana. *Outright, out-and-out, arrant, unmitigated.

2 Precipitous, abrupt, *steep.

Ana. Perpendicular, *vertical.

sheer, *v.* *Turn, divert, deflect, avert.

shell, *v.* *Husk, hull, shuck.

shelter, *n.* **Shelter, cover, retreat, refuge, asylum, sanctuary, ark** come into comparison when they mean the state or a place in which one is safe or secure from that which threatens or disturbs. **Shelter** usually implies the protection of something that temporarily covers, as a shield, a roof, or any structure that prevents the entrance of that which would harm or annoy; as, to seek *shelter* from an approaching storm; *shelters* must be provided for sheep in winter; "the trees afforded shade and *shelter*" (*Cather*); "Given only a little *shelter*, in the corner of the hedges or under trees and copses they [brambles] retain green leaves till the buds burst again" (*Jefferies*). **Cover** usually implies complete concealment; it is, as here compared, often applied to a shelter of underbrush (or, by extension, to something similarly thick or protective); as, "they returned as wolves return to *cover*" (*Kipling*); "The [pheasant's] eye betrayed it ....the bird..., looking up from its *cover*, was immediately observed" (*Jefferies*); when the storm broke, they rushed to *cover*. **Retreat** stresses retirement, usually voluntary retirement, from danger or annoyance, and escape to a condition or place promising safety, or security or peace. It therefore often suggests remoteness, solitude, quiet, or, in religious use, conditions affording opportunities for prayer and meditation; as, a hermit's *retreat*. "Ah, for some *retreat* Deep in yonder shining Orient, where my life began to beat" (*Tennyson*). **Refuge** also suggests an attempt to escape that which threatens one's peace, safety, happiness, or the like, but it usually implies fleeing, and sometimes also a pursuer, or something, such as a thought or emotion, that harasses; as, to refuse *refuge* to political exiles; the escaped convict found *refuge* in a deserted house. "Our clubs are ...not *refuges* for bored husbands and homeless bachelors" (*Brownell*). "Stoicism is the *refuge* for the individual in an indifferent or hostile world too big for him" (*T. S. Eliot*). **Asylum,** in precise use, adds to *refuge* the implications of exemption from seizure or spoliation, and the finding of a protector, of a place outside the jurisdiction of the law, or the like; as, the embezzler sought *asylum* in a foreign land; France has time after time provided *asylum* for deposed or abdicated monarchs of other countries; "[the United States] *Asylum* of the oppressed of every nation" (*Democratic Platform*, 1856). *Asylum*, which in its Greek original referred specifically to a temple, altar, or statue of a god in or by which a criminal might take refuge, was later applied to Christian churches where, by medieval law, fugitives from an enemy or from the law might find immunity from seizure. **Sanctuary,** however, is the precise term for the Christian asylum; even in modern use and in its extended applications, it stresses the sacredness of the place and its claim to reverence or inviolability; thus, a *sanctuary* for wild life is an area which is exempt from intrusion by hunters, trappers, and the like, or in some cases (then often called *refuge* by distinction), where predatory animals are controlled so that the more desirable forms of life which are their prey may be allowed to flourish. "If thou breathest aught that can attaint the honour of my house, by Saint George! not the altar itself shall be a *sanctuary*" (*Scott*). "It came over Mark to offer him *sanctuary* in the clergy-house, but he realized almost simultaneously...that it would cause a scandal and not benefit the murderer" (*C. Mackenzie*). **Ark** (now usually *ark of refuge*) implies reference to the boat in which Noah and his family were preserved in the Deluge, and usually, therefore, applies to a place, state, an institution, or the like, to which one has recourse when dangers or difficulties overwhelm one. "The United States has been...an *ark* of refuge to the people of Europe" (*J. Bright*). "How simple and charming is her picture of the life of religion which she chose as her *ark* of refuge" (*Arnold*).

Ana. Protection, safeguarding *or* safeguard (see corresponding verbs at DEFEND): *harbor, haven, port.

shelter, *v.* *Harbor, lodge, house, entertain, board.

Ana. *Defend, protect, shield, guard, safeguard: *receive, accept, admit.

shield, *v.* Protect, guard, safeguard, *defend.

Ana. Preserve, conserve, *save: *harbor, shelter, lodge, house.

shift, *v.* *Move, remove, transfer.

Ana. Displace, *replace: *change, alter, vary: veer, *swerve, deviate.

shift, *n.* Makeshift, expedient, *resource, resort, stopgap, substitute, surrogate.

Ana. *Device, contrivance, contraption: ruse, *trick, stratagem, maneuver, wile, feint, artifice.

shimmer, *v.* *Flash, gleam, glance, glint, sparkle, glitter, glisten, scintillate, coruscate, glimmer, twinkle, glister, spark.

shimmy, *v.* *Shake, tremble, quake, totter, quiver, shiver, shudder, quaver, wobble, teeter, didder, dither.

shine, *v.* *Polish, burnish, furbish, buff.

ship, *n.* *Boat, vessel, craft, argosy.

shipshape. *Neat, tidy, trim, trig, snug, spick-and-span.

shiver, *v.* Quiver, shudder, quaver, *shake, tremble, quake, totter, wobble, teeter, shimmy, didder, dither.

shoal, *n.*[1] *Flock, herd, drove, pack, bevy, covey, gaggle, flight, swarm, school.

shoal, *n.*[2] **Shoal, bank, reef, bar** are here compared only as meaning a shallow place caused by an elevation in a sea or large body of water. All of these terms have their ordinary nontechnical senses; the first three, however, are, in recent geographical usage, employed with great precision as technical terms. In ordinary use, **shoal** is applied to any shallow place, especially one that is difficult to navigate (as, "*Shoals* ahead!"; dangerous *shoals* in uncharted waters), **bank** (or often in the plural *banks*) is applied to one that is formed by a sandy, gravelly, or other elevation but is deep enough to make navigation safe for lighter craft such as fishing vessels (the Grand *Bank*, also called the *Banks* of Newfoundland, is a noted fishing ground), **reef,** to one where the rocks protrude from the water (especially at low tide) or lie dangerously close to its surface (as, the *reef*-bound shores of Bermuda; coral *reefs*). Technically, *shoal* is applied to elevations which are not rocky and on which the water is not more than 6 fathoms (or 11 meters) deep, *bank* to a similar elevation on which the water is between 11 and 200 meters deep, and *reef* to a rocky elevation on which the water (at low tide) is 6 fathoms or less in depth. **Bar** carries implications found in many senses of that word, those of length, narrowness, and hindrance. It is applied to a ridge of sand (a sand *bar*), gravel, or the like, piled up at (often across or nearly across) a river's mouth or an entrance to a harbor and obstructing navigation.

shock, *n.*[1] Cock, stack, heap, pile, mass, bank. See under HEAP, *v.*

shock, *n.*[2] **1** Collision, clash, concussion, *impact, impingement, percussion, jar, jolt, brunt.

Ana. *Encounter, skirmish: *attack, assault, onslaught, onset: shaking, rocking, agitation, convulsion (see corresponding verbs at SHAKE).

2 *Paralysis, palsy, apoplexy, stroke.

shock, *v.*[1] Cock, stack, *heap, pile, mass, bank.

shock, *v.*[2] Dialectal variant of SHUCK.

shocking. Appalling, *fearful, awful, dreadful, frightful, terrible, terrific, horrible, horrific.

Ana. *Ghastly, gruesome, lurid, macabre, grisly, grim: odious, abhorrent, abominable, *hateful: *repugnant, repellent, distasteful, obnoxious.

shoot, *v.* *Fly, dart, float, skim, scud, sail.

Ana. *Speed, hasten, hurry, quicken.

shoot, *n.* **Shoot, branch, bough, limb** come into comparison only when they mean one of the members of a shrub or a tree that are outgrowths from the trunk or stem or from its ramifications. The words are not technical botanical terms, but in general use they carry specific and distinctive implications. **Shoot** and **branch** are referable to most plants as well as to shrubs and trees, and both imply development from a bud. *Shoot*, however, stresses actual growing and therefore applies chiefly to any young, undeveloped member. *Branch* suggests a spreading out by dividing and subdividing and applies to any more or less fully developed member, whether it emanates directly from the trunk or stem, or from that outgrowth or one of its subdivisions. **Bough** is now a more literary term than either of the preceding terms. It is not interchangeable with *shoot* for it usually suggests foliage and fruit or flowers. Although it is often used interchangeably with *branch* and is sometimes thought of as a large or main branch, it now carries a comparatively weak implication of ramification and a strong connotation of full seasonal development; thus, good usage seems to indicate that *bough* is preferred when the shrub or tree is in leaf or bloom, and *branch* when the shrub or tree is stripped of foliage or its members are thought of as barren or dead; as, loaded *boughs;* pine *boughs* for Christmas decorations; bare *branches.* "Superfluous *branches* We lop away, that bearing *boughs* may live" (*Shak.*). "In a drear-nighted December, Too happy, happy tree, Thy *branches* ne'er remember Their green felicity" (*Keats*). "I am sick of endless sunshine, sick of blossom-burdened *bough.* Give me back the leafless woodlands where the winds of Springtime range" (*Kipling*). **Limb,** as here compared, is seldom used of shrubs, but only of large trees; it applies commonly only to a large branch that grows directly out of the trunk of a tree or to a member produced by the forking of the trunk; as, "with *limbs* of British oak" (*Cowper*); "The knotty *limbs* of an enormous oak" (*Shelley*).

shopworn. *Trite, hackneyed, stereotyped, threadbare.
Ana. Wasted (see HAGGARD): attenuated, diluted, thinned (see THIN, *v.*): antiquated, obsolete, archaic (see OLD).

shore, *n.* **Shore, coast, beach, strand, bank, littoral, ripa, foreshore** agree in denoting land bordering a body or stream of water. **Shore** is the general word for the land immediately bordering on the sea, a lake, or a large stream. **Coast** denotes the land along the sea only, regarded especially as a boundary. **Beach** applies to the pebbly or sandy shore washed by the sea or a lake; as, a rocky *shore* with here and there a cove with a *beach.* Both *shore* and *beach* denote a place of resort for pleasure or vacation. *Shore,* however, usually indicates proximity to the sea; as, to spend the summer at the *shore. Beach,* on the other hand, suggests a place of resort for swimmers or sun bathers; as, to spend a part of each day at the *beach.* **Strand** is elevated or poetical for *shore* or *beach.* "To this lakeside, as to the holiest *strand* in Europe, pilgrims full of soul were drawn in thousands" (*L. P. Smith*). **Bank** denotes the steep or sloping margin of a stream. **Littoral** is a somewhat formal or pretentious term, occurring especially in geographic, political, and scientific writings, for the whole or an extended, clearly specified portion of the coast of a particular sea or country; it may imply extension farther inland than *coast* implies. "The whole Mediterranean *littoral* is...subject to earthquakes" (*Scribner's*). **Ripa** is still more uncommon, but it is the technical term for the bank of a river, or at least so much of it and of the water which washes it as belongs legally to owners of land bordering on the stream. Its derivative adjective *riparian* is found chiefly in the legal term *riparian rights.* **Foreshore** is applied sometimes to the part of the shore between high and low watermarks, but it is also at other times extended to include the beach.

short. **1** *Brief.
Ana. Decreased, lessened, reduced, diminished (see DECREASE): shortened, abridged, abbreviated, curtailed (see SHORTEN): *concise, terse, laconic.
Ant. Long.
2 Crisp, brittle, friable, *fragile, frangible.

shorten. **Shorten, curtail, abbreviate, abridge, retrench** agree in denoting to reduce in extent, especially by cutting, but they vary so greatly in their idiomatic associations and in some of their implications that they are not always interchangeable. **Shorten** commonly implies reduction in length, either in dimension or duration; as, to *shorten* a road by eliminating curves; to *shorten* one's stay. Also, it is often used more or less figuratively of apparent rather than actual length; as, they *shortened* the journey by telling stories. **Curtail** adds to *shorten* the implication of docking, or of making cuts that impair completeness or cause deprivation; as, the interruption *curtailed* his speech; the outdoor ceremony was *curtailed* because of the storm; *curtailed* rights. **Abbreviate,** except in humorous use, is now said chiefly of words or phrases. It suggests shortening by contraction, omission, or substitution of a symbol, yet in such a way that the brief form comes to stand for the original word or phrase and to convey the same meaning. **Abridge** expresses reduction in compass or scope rather more than in length, but it usually implies the retention of all that is essential, and the relative completeness of that which results; as, to *abridge* a dictionary; all laws *abridge* liberty. "Thus ended her relation, which I have *abridged*" (*Goldsmith*). **Retrench** stresses reduction in extent or costs of something felt to be in excess; as, to *retrench* expenses. "Any *retrenchment* of their generous way of living would be a hardship for her" (*Cather*).
Ana. Reduce, *decrease, lessen, diminish: *contract, shrink, condense.
Ant. Lengthen, elongate: extend.

short-lived. *Transient, transitory, passing, ephemeral, momentary, fugitive, fleeting, evanescent.
Ant. Agelong.

should. *Ought, must, have, have got.

shove, *v.* *Push, thrust, propel.
Ana. *Force, constrain, oblige, compel, coerce: impel, drive, *move.

show, *v.* **1** **Show, manifest, evidence, evince, demonstrate** are synonymous terms when they mean to reveal something outwardly as by a sign or signs or, when the subject of the verb is the sign or signs, to serve to make something outwardly apparent or visible. **Show,** in this sense, as in its other major sense, implies enabling others to see, but in this case that which is revealed can only be inferred from one's acts, words, looks, or the like; as, he never *shows* what he thinks; a lift of the eyebrow and a shrug of the shoulder *show* their displeasure. "Tony...asked a question or two designed to *show* his intelligence" (*Arch. Marshall*). "In this decision he *showed* his capacity for extreme boldness" (*Buchan*). **Manifest** implies a fuller, plainer, and more indubitable revelation than *show.* "In this was *manifested* the love of God toward us, because that God sent his only begotten Son into the world, that we might live through him" (*1 John* iv. 9). "In handwriting the Chinese believe that the inner personality of the writer is directly *manifested*" (*Binyon*). "As technically *manifested* in Literature it [style] is the power to touch with ease, grace, precision, any note in the gamut of human thought or emotion" (*Quiller-Couch*). **Evidence** is often used in place of *show* (as, to *evidence* one's appreciation), but in highly discriminating use it specifically implies that the outward act, utterance, or the like, serves as proof of the existence or the actuality of something not fully proved or in question; as, he argued that their hostility was *evidenced* by certain acts which could be construed as trespasses. "It follows...that if an appointment was to be *evidenced* by any public act, other than the commission, the performance of such public act would create the officer" (*Ch. Just. Marshall*). **Evince,** in earlier use as strong in its implication of proof as *evidence,* is now considerably the weakest of the terms here discriminated. It merely implies some outward marks or tokens, usually of an interest, an emotion, a power, or the like; as, so far as is known, he has *evinced* no interest in the project. "Cashel, bitterly humiliated by his own tears, and exasperated by a certain cold triumph which his captor *evinced* on witnessing them" (*Shaw*). "[In English slang] you see the old temperament of the race still *evincing* itself; still shying away from the long abstract word" (*C. E. Montague*). **Demonstrate** (see also PROVE, 1) is used chiefly in reference to feelings; it ordinarily implies external signs such as effusiveness, enthusiasm, emotional excitement, and the like: the verb is still used in this sense, but these implications come out more strongly in the noun *demonstration* and in the adjective *demonstrative;* as, to *demonstrate* one's approval by loud applause; a popular *demonstration* of loyalty. "Paul was a person who *demonstrated* all his sentiments" (*Thackeray*).

Ana. *Reveal, disclose, discover: present, *offer, proffer, tender.

Con. *Hide, conceal, secrete.

2 Show, exhibit, display, expose, parade, flaunt, as here compared, agree in meaning to present in such a way as to invite notice or attention. One **shows** anything which one enables another or others to see or to look at, as by putting it forward into view intentionally or inadvertently or by taking another where he may see it; as, to *show* one's tongue to the doctor; to *show* one's new home to one's friends; to *show* the city to an out-of-town guest. One **exhibits** anything which one puts forward prominently or openly, either with the express intention or with the result of attracting others' attention or inspection; as, to *exhibit* the museum's collection of Whistler engravings; to *exhibit* articles made by children in a mission school; in many fashionable gown shops, garments are not *exhibited* but are *shown* only to prospective purchasers; to *exhibit* unreasonable fear. "If any crave redress of injustice, they should *exhibit* their petitions in the street" (*Shak.*). One **displays** anything that one spreads out before the view of others or puts in a position where it can be seen to advantage or with great clearness; as, the exhibition of pictures was criticized because the best paintings were not properly *displayed.* "Before a contest begins, the owner brings in his cock and, holding it firmly by the tail, allows it to struggle and strain in order to *display* its fierceness and strength" (*V. Heiser*). "The host took Father Vaillant through his corrals and stables to *show* him his stock. He *exhibited* with peculiar pride two cream-coloured mules, stalled side by side. With his own hand he led them out of the stable, in order to *display* to advantage their handsome coats" (*Cather*). One **exposes** something when one brings it out of hiding or concealment, or from under cover, and shows, exhibits, or displays it consciously or unconsciously. The term sometimes means little more than to exhibit or display. "He...looked me over as if I had been *exposed* for sale" (*Conrad*). "We were reluctant to *expose* those silent and beautiful places [a newly discovered Indian village] to vulgar curiosity" (*Cather*). Oftentimes it means to reveal publicly something (especially something disagreeable) that has been or should be concealed; as, to *expose* one's ignorance. "It was my duty to leave no stone unturned to discover and *expose* the awful truth" (*R. Macaulay*). Very frequently it carries the additional implication of unmasking. "It was...his friends...that he attacks in this terrible story of the passing stranger who took such a vitriolic joy in *exposing* their pretensions and their hypocrisy" (*Van W. Brooks*). One **parades** anything which one displays ostentatiously or arrogantly; as, the pianist was accused of *parading* his technical dexterity; to *parade* one's honesty; "Henry drove so well, so quietly....without *parading* [his skill] to her" (*Austen*). One **flaunts** something when one parades it shamelessly, often boastfully, and offensively. "They *flaunt* their conjugal felicity in one's face" (*Wilde*). "And ye vaunted your fathomless power, and ye *flaunted* your iron pride" (*Kipling*).

Ana. *Indicate, betoken, attest, bespeak, argue, prove: intimate, hint, *suggest.

Ant. Disguise.

show, *n.* *Exhibition, exhibit, exposition, fair.

showy. Showy, pretentious, ostentatious, pompous come into comparison as meaning given to making or presenting, as a thing, an outward display that is, by implication, greater than that which is justifiable. **Showy,** the ordinary term, carries less definite implications than the other words. It always implies an imposing, striking, or impressive appearance: it often also suggests cheapness, inferiority, or poor taste (as, "*showy* brass ware"—*Shaw; showy* furniture; *showy* decorations), or conspicuousness because of largeness, gorgeousness of coloring, or the like (as, a *showy* wallpaper design; *showy* peonies), or overattention to superficial qualities (as, "The *showy* talents, in which the present age prides itself"—*Newman*). **Pretentious** (see also AMBITIOUS, 2) suggests even less warrant for display for it usually implies an appearance that is not justified by the thing's actual value or actual cost or by the person's actual worth, rank, performance, or the like: the term therefore always implies a criticism of the person or thing that is so described. "I'd rather you didn't call me 'sir'....it might give rise to the idea that I had asked you to.... It might appear rather *pretentious*" (*C. Mackenzie*). "He did not, like some more *pretentious*...critics, occupy himself with reviewing and bluepencilling literary reputations already well established" (*T. S. Eliot*). "A brilliant sham, which, like a badly built and *pretentious* house, looks poor and shabby after a few years" (*Cather*). **Ostentatious** stresses vainglorious display or parade, but it does not necessarily imply either showiness or pretentiousness; as, "*ostentatious* public charities" (*Wilde*); "the *ostentatious* simplicity of their dress" (*Macaulay*); "*ostentatious* funerals" (*L. P. Smith*). "Whoever wishes to attain an English style, familiar, but not coarse, and elegant, but not *ostentatious*, must give his days and nights to the volumes of Addison" (*Johnson*). **Pompous** implies showiness or ostentatiousness dictated usually by a love of ceremony or, more often, by a solemn and exaggerated self-importance; as, "this most *pompous* marriage-feast" (*Shak.*); "this *pompous* show Of art" (*Wordsworth*); "I have to laugh when people are *pompous* and absurd" (*R. Macaulay*). "A well-meaning, civil, prosing, *pompous* woman, who thought nothing of consequence but as it related to her own...concerns" (*Austen*).

Ana. *Gaudy, tawdry, garish, flashy, meretricious: resplendent, gorgeous (see SPLENDID): opulent, sumptuous, *luxurious.

shrew. Scold, vixen, termagant, barge, *virago, amazon.

shrewd. Shrewd, sagacious, perspicacious, astute agree in meaning acute in perception and sound judgment, especially in reference to practical affairs. **Shrewd** implies native cleverness, acumen, and an almost uncanny ability to see below the surface; it often also connotes hard-headedness; as, a *shrewd* bargain; a *shrewd* observer; a *shrewd* remark; "[He] is...sensible and *shrewd*, with a considerable fund of humor" (*Smollett*); "the *shrewd* wisdom of an unlettered old woman" (*Pater*). **Sagacious,** originally applied to a dog keen in the scent of his quarry, is now usually referred to men, their decisions, their judgments, their methods of pursuing their ends, and the like: it stresses penetration, discernment, judiciousness, and often, farsightedness. "[Lincoln] the kindly, earnest, brave, foreseeing man, *sagacious*, patient, dreading praise, not blame" (*J. R. Lowell*). "If they have not the same fund of acquired knowledge, [they] are obliged to rely more on individual *sagacity*" (*Hazlitt*). **Perspicacious** originally was applied to physical sight and meant extraordinarily sharp-sighted; it is now applied chiefly to mental sight, or insight, and suggests unusual power to see through and to understand that which is dark, hidden, mysterious, and the like; as, a *perspicacious* reader of character; a *perspicacious* critic. "We must make allowance also for those blind-spots which are found in the most *perspicacious* mortals" (*L. P. Smith*). **Astute** implies a combination of shrewdness and perspicacity and often, in addition, connotes an ability to keep one's counsel or an incapacity for being fooled, especially where one's own interests are concerned; as, "Savages ...are often as...*astute* socially as trained diplomatists" (*W. James*); "The victim of *astuter* sharpers" (*Thackeray*); "The man who can make millions by an *astute* business deal" (*J. A. Hobson*). *Astute*, opprobriously used, heightens the suggestion, sometimes present in *perspicacious*, of artfulness, diplomacy, or craft. It may connote merely shrewd discernment and sagacity.

Ana. Knowing, *intelligent, smart, clever, quick-witted: politic, diplomatic, smooth (see SUAVE): *wise, prudent, sensible, judicious: penetrating, piercing, probing (see ENTER).

shrine. *Altar, tabernacle, chantry.

shrink. 1 *Contract, constrict, compress, condense, deflate.

Ana. *Decrease, reduce, diminish, lessen: *shorten, abridge, retrench, curtail.

Ant. Swell. — *Con.* *Expand, amplify, distend, dilate, inflate.

2 *Recoil, flinch, quail, blench, wince.

Ana. Cringe, cower (see FAWN): retreat, *recede: balk, shy, boggle, scruple, *demur.

shrive. *Confess, absolve, remit.

shrivel. *Wither, rivel, wizen.

Ana. Parch, desiccate, *dry: sear, scorch, *burn.

shuck *or* **shock,** *v.* *Husk, hull, shell.

shudder, *v.* Shiver, quiver, quaver, *shake, tremble, quake, totter, wobble, teeter, shimmy, didder, dither.

shun. Avoid, evade, elude, *escape, eschew.

Ana. *Decline, refuse, reject: balk, shy, scruple, *demur, stick, stickle: scorn, disdain, *despise.

Ant. Habituate.

shut, *v.* *Close.

shut out. Eliminate, *exclude, debar, rule out, blackball, disbar.

Ana. *Prevent, preclude, obviate: *hinder, obstruct, block, bar.

shy, *adj.* **Shy, bashful, diffident, modest, coy** agree in meaning showing disinclination to obtrude oneself in the presence or company of others. **Shy** implies a shrinking, sometimes constitutional, sometimes the result of inexperience, from familiarity or contact with others; shyness usually manifests itself in a certain reserve of manner or in timidity in approaching others. "The savage...is a *shy* person, imbued with the notion that certain things are not to be talked of to strangers" (*Inge*). "They shook hands and opened a conversation instantly; for Constance...had lost all her *shyness* in the shop, and could chatter with anybody" (*Bennett*). **Bashful** implies an instinctive or constitutional shrinking from public notice that usually expresses itself in awkwardness of demeanor, and is especially characteristic of childhood and adolescence; as applied to mature persons, it connotes abnormal or excessive shyness. "My sudden appearance frightened [the children] into *bashfulness*. They remained for a moment playing on their lips with their fingers, and now and then stealing a *shy* glance from under their eyebrows" (*Irving*). "Like Summer rose, The *bashful* maiden's cheek appeared" (*Scott*). **Diffident** implies a distrust, which may or may not be warranted, of one's own ability, opinion, or powers: it gives rise to hesitation in their exercise. "Far better that the task should be entrusted to one who had no *diffidence*, no hesitation, but a sincere confidence in his power of dealing with the difficulties of the situation" (*A. C. Benson*). "The schoolboy's *diffidence*—his unwillingness to hear his own voice attempting the strange tongue—will vanish; a sense of mastery will replace his distrust" (*Grandgent*). **Modest,** without implying (like *diffident*) self-distrust, denotes an absence of all undue confidence in oneself or one's powers. "Bingley has great natural *modesty*, with a stronger dependence on my judgment than on his own" (*Austen*). "My native *modesty* is such, that I have always been shy of assuming the honorable style of Professor, because this is a title I share with so many distinguished men...who adorn it, I feel, much more than I do" (*Arnold*). **Coy** suggests assumed or affected shyness, often with the further implication of coquetry. "I was vexed, and resolved to be even with her by not visiting the wood for some time. A display of indifference on my part would, I hoped, result in making her less *coy* in the future" (*Hudson*).

Ana. *Timid, timorous: wary, chary, *cautious, circumspect.

Ant. Obtrusive.

shy, *v.* Balk, boggle, scruple, *demur, jib, stickle, stick, strain.

Ana. *Recoil, shrink, quail, blench: *hesitate, waver, falter, vacillate.

sib. *Tribe, clan, horde, sept.

sick. Sick, ill, in the sense of not in sound health or afflicted with a bodily disorder, vary in meaning more in England and some other British countries than they do in the United States, where in general there is little difference in their significance. In both literary and colloquial use in the United States and in literary use in other English-speaking countries, **sick** is the ordinary term to describe a person who is ailing, indisposed, suffering from a disease or the like, or the condition of one who is so afflicted; as, he is a very *sick* man; President Wilson's friends were not aware of how *sick* he was; their children are *sick* half of the time. In Great Britain and many parts of the British Empire, *sick*, especially in colloquial use, now usually means nauseated, especially violently nauseated; thus, in the United States, "to feel *sick*" may carry that meaning but it may also mean to have feelings that indicate one is coming down or is down with a disease; in Great Britain it usually means to have sensations that warn one of an approaching vomiting spell. It is this sense which prevails in compounds where *sick* is the second element and the conveyance in which, or medium through which, one travels is the first element; as, train*sick*, car*sick*, air*sick*, sea*sick*. However, in all use, *sick* often implies actual suffering from other causes than disease, and may suggest great unease, desperate boredom, unsatisfied longing, or the like; as, she was *sick* at heart through anxiety; "[To] medicine the *sick* soul to happy sleep" (*Shelley*); "We [became]... heartily *sick* in the ensuing years of its incessant repetition" (*V. Heiser*); "I am a woman, *sick* for passion" (*Amy Lowell*). **Ill** is also used in the United States in place of *sick* in the ordinary sense, but it is more often employed colloquially in phrases such as "*ill* health," where its relation to its earlier sense of bad or evil is clear, than in phrases such as "an *ill* person," "he is *ill* with pneumonia," because of a more or less common feeling that the term is slightly affected. In British use, on the other hand, *ill* is now generally accepted in preference to *sick* in the sense of not being in good health, or of being afflicted with a disease.

Ant. Healthy.

side. *Phase, aspect, facet, angle.

sidereal. *Starry, stellar, astral.

siege, *n.* *Blockade.

sieve, *v.* *Sift, riddle, screen, bolt, winnow.

sift, *v.* **Sift, sieve, riddle, screen, bolt, winnow** agree in meaning to subject to a process whereby the coarser, larger, or heavier parts are separated from those that are finer, smaller, or lighter. **Sift,** and the much rarer **sieve,** in literal use imply a passing of a pulverized or granulated substance, such as flour, sugar, meal, or ashes, through a sieve (typically, a boxlike or basinlike utensil with meshes or holes on the bottom) for the sake of freeing the substance from extraneous matter or from coarser particles or, sometimes, to separate the particles of a compact mass: the terms may suggest that the process is performed either for the sake of what passes through the meshes or for the sake of what does not pass through them; as, *sift* the flour three times before adding it to the other ingredients; he always *sieves* his ashes to extract unburnt coals. But *sift* is also very often employed in an extended sense. Figuratively, it implies a careful testing in a manner suggestive of a passing through a sieve, as by careful scrutiny, examination, analysis, so that the true is distinguished from the false, the important from the unimportant, the relevant from the irrelevant, the valuable from the worthless, and the like; as, to *sift* the mass of evidence; "documents, carefully *sifted* from other papers of less moment" (*J. A. Symonds*); "he [Socrates] attacked and *sifted* the ethical conceptions of his time: 'What is justice?' 'What is piety?' 'What is temperance?' " (*G. L. Dickinson*). **Riddle** and the now more common **screen** also imply passing through a sieve or a screen (a similar apparatus mounted on a frame), but they suggest the use of an apparatus with a coarse enough mesh to separate relatively smaller particles from those that are larger, for any one of several ends; as, to *riddle* sand so as to extract all gravel, shells, and the like; to *riddle* gravel so as to extract all pebbles, cobbles, and the like; to *screen* coal so as to separate it into the sizes known as pea coal, egg coal, stove coal, and the like; to *screen* loam to remove stones, or the like. Both *riddle* and *screen* are also used in place of *sift*, though the tendency is to employ them in reference to coarser substances than flour, sugar, etc. **Bolt** is chiefly a miller's term, used specifically in reference to the process of sifting or screening through a loose-meshed cloth for the sake of eliminating the bran from the flour; as, "to *bolt* the bran From the pure flour" (*Pope*); *unbolted* flour is flour which contains particles of bran. **Winnow** differs from the other words of this group in its literal sense in implying the use of a fan and the separation thereby of the chaff from the valuable or nutritive part of grain; as, "He *winnoweth* barley to night in the threshingfloor" (*Ruth* iii. 2). Like *sift, winnow* is now often used in a figurative sense, implying the elimination by a process such as analysis, selection, or assorting, the results of which suggest a fanning away of the false, the bad, the worthless, or the useless and the leaving of only that which is true, good, or otherwise valuable; as, "*Winnow* from the coming step of time All chaff of custom" (*Keats*). "There is a simplicity of diction which reflects a meagre and barren stock; there is also a simplicity which results from the *winnowing* of a rich abundance" (*Lowes*).

Ana. *Analyze, resolve, dissect: *scrutinize, examine, inspect: *separate, part, divide.

sigh, *v.* **Sigh, sob, moan, groan** are not synonyms, but they come into comparison both as verbs, when they mean literally or figuratively to emit a sound (commonly an inarticulate sound) indicative of mental or physical pain or distress, and as nouns, when they denote such a sound. **Sigh** implies a deep audible respiration that is usually an involuntary expression of grief, intense longing, regret, discouragement, weariness, boredom, or the like; as, "*Sigh* no more, ladies, *sigh* no more, Men were deceivers ever" (*Shak.*); "The young knight *sighed*... and held his peace" (*Scott*); "a *sigh* uttered from the fulness of the heart" (*Hazlitt*); "The old town was better to look at in those days, Father Latour used to tell Bernard with a *sigh*" (*Cather*). **Sob** strictly implies a sound made by a convulsive catching of the breath when one is weeping, or when one is both speaking and crying, or when one is desperately trying to restrain one's tears; the noun, however, more often refers solely to this sound than does the verb, which usually implies accompanying tears and speech; as, " 'Ah!' It was a long, grieving sound, like a *sigh*—almost like a *sob*" (*Dickens*); "The mother.... knelt by his side, and they prayed, and their joint *sobs* shook their bodies, but neither of them shed many tears" (*Meredith*); she *sobbed* out her story; like a child *sobbing* itself to sleep. **Moan** implies a low, prolonged, usually inarticulate sound, especially one that is indicative of intense suffering of mind or body; as, the patient is *moaning* in his sleep; her self-control was so great that she uttered not even a *moan;* "To hear the piteous *moan* that Rutland made" (*Shak.*). The term, however, is often used figuratively in reference to sounds suggestive of pain, complaint, murmuring, or the like; as, the *moan* of the wind; "The *moan* of doves in immemorial elms" (*Tennyson*); "The rain and the wind splashed and gurgled and *moaned* round the house" (*Kipling*). **Groan** implies a heavier sound than *moan* and more often suggests an unbearable weight of suffering or a strong spirit of rebelliousness to pain or discomfort; as, the *groans* of those caught in the wreckage were heard at a distance; the laborers *groaned* when they tried to lift the boulder; "Thy *groans* Did make wolves howl" (*Shak.*); "The whole creation *groaneth* and travaileth in pain together until now" (*Romans* viii. 22). Often, however, in extended use, the term carries no hint of suffering but implies noises similar to groans made by disapproving persons (as, to greet a speaker with *groans*) or by something that moves or swings heavily (as, trees *groaning* in the wind; "the door upon its hinges *groans*" —*Keats*).

Ana. Lament, *deplore, bemoan, bewail: *long, yearn, pine, hunger, thirst.

sigh, *n.* Groan, moan, sob. See under SIGH, *v.*

Ana. Regret, *sorrow, grief.

sight, *n.* *Look, view, glance, glimpse, peep, peek, coup d'oeil.

Ana. *Prospect, outlook: vision, *revelation.

sightless. *Blind, purblind.

sign, *n.* **1 Sign, mark, token, badge, note, symptom** come into comparison when they denote a sensible, usually visible, indication by means of which something not outwardly apparent or obvious is made known or revealed. **Sign** is the most comprehensive of these terms, being referable to a symbol (see also CHARACTER, 1) or a symbolic device or act (as, the mace is the *sign* of authority; to make the *sign* of the cross), to any visible or sensible manifestation of a mood, a mental or physical state, or a quality of character (as, good manners are the *signs* of good breeding; "Suicide is the *sign* of failure, misery, and despair"—*H. Ellis*), to any trace or vestige of someone or something (as, "the *signs* of her fate in a footprint here, a broken twig there, a trinket dropped by the way"—*Conrad*), to any objective evidence that serves as a presage or foretoken (as, *signs* of an early spring; "there are *signs* that poetry is beginning to occupy itself again with the possibilities of sound"—*Day Lewis*), and, concretely, to any placard, board, tablet, or the like, such as one giving the name of a street, one giving route directions, or especially, one placed over or near an entrance and indicating the nature of the business transacted in that place, or giving the proprietor's name (as, *signs* carrying names in electric lights; they were to meet at the *sign* [that is, the inn carrying the *sign*] of the White Horse). **Mark** (see also CHARACTER, 1) is preferred to *sign* in discriminating use when the distinguishing or revealing indication is thought of as something impressed upon a thing or inherently characteristic of it, especially in contrast to something outwardly manifested or displayed; thus, the bitter experience left its *mark* (not *sign*) on his countenance; courtesy is the *mark* (better than *sign*) of a gentleman; the distinguishing *marks* (not *signs*) of Victorian poetry. "What, then, are the *marks* of culture and efficiency?" (*H. Suzzallo*). "It is a great mistake to suppose that assertiveness is the only mannish trait taken on by successful women, nor is pliability the only feminine *mark* they lose" (*M. Austin*). Concretely also, *mark* is applied either (1) to some visible trace left upon a thing, such as a scar or a brand (as, a birth*mark*, the *marks* of smallpox) or a stain, a print, or a track (as, the high-water *mark* is observable on the pier's supports; the *marks* of an army's passage), or (2) to something that is affixed in order to distinguish, identify, or label a particular thing or to indicate its ownership (as, a trade-*mark;* a laundry *mark*). **Token** (see also PLEDGE) is preferred to *sign* and also to *mark* (except in their specific concrete applications) when the sensible indication serves as a proof of, or is given as evidence of the actual existence of, something that has no physical existence; as, how could he doubt her love when he had had so many *tokens* of her affection?; the savages bore gifts as *tokens* of their desire for peace and friendship. "It is a *token* of healthy and gentle characteristics, when women of high thoughts and accomplishments love to sew" (*N. Hawthorne*). **Badge** designates a piece of metal, a ribbon, or the like, carrying an inscription or emblem and worn upon the person as a token of one's membership in a society or as a sign of one's office, employment, or function; as, a policeman's *badge;* each delegate wore a *badge;* a gold watch key is the *badge* of membership in Phi Beta Kappa. In figurative use, *badge* often is employed in place of *sign, mark,* or *token*, when it is thought of in reference to a class, a group, a category of persons, or as a distinctive feature of their dress, their appearance, their character, or the like; "for sufferance is the *badge* of all our tribe" (*Shak.*); "sweet mercy is nobility's true *badge*" (*Shak.*); "to accept the...petticoat...as the *badge* of disenfranchisement" (*R. Macaulay*). **Note** usually means a distinguishing or dominant mark or characteristic; both when it is so close to its earliest sense, a distinctive musical tone, that its use seems almost figurative, and when it is so far removed that only a historical connection with the earlier meaning can be traced, *note* differs from *mark*, its closest synonym, in suggesting something emitted or given out by a thing, rather than something impressed upon that thing. "A fertile oasis possesses a characteristic color scheme of its own....The fundamental *note* is struck by the palms" (*A. Huxley*). "The *note* of sadness...which...poets were to find so much more to their taste than the *note* of gladness" (*H. Adams*). "Genteel poverty...was the *note* of his grandfather's house" (*Arch. Marshall*). *Note* is much used in theology and also in literary and art criticism in place of *mark* for a characteristic that seems to emanate from a thing that strikes one as true, or authentic, and therefore is the test of a similar thing's truth, genuineness, authoritativeness, and the like; as, to claim that the *notes* of the true church are universality and holiness; the grand manner that is the *note* of great poetry. **Symptom** was originally and is still applied to any of the physical or mental changes from the normal which can be interpreted as signs of disease, and which, taken together in a particular case, provide the ground for a diagnosis; as, his *symptoms* indicate typhoid fever; he has all the *symptoms* of incipient tuberculosis. In extended use, it is applicable to any outward indications of an inner change, as in an institution, a state, or the body politic, or to any external phenomenon that may be interpreted as the result of some internal condition, especially a weakness, defect, disturbance, or the like. "Even that...is treated lightly as a foible of the age, and not as a *symptom* of social decay and change" (*T. S. Eliot*). "The belief that a young man's athletic record is a test of his worth is a *symptom* of our general failure to grasp the need of knowledge and thought in mastering the complex modern world" (*B. Russell*).

Ana. Indication, betokening, attesting *or* attestation (see corresponding verbs at INDICATE): manifestation, evidencing *or* evidence, demonstration, showing *or* show (see corresponding verbs at SHOW): intimation, suggestion (see corresponding verbs at SUGGEST).

2 Sign, signal come into comparison when they mean a motion, an action, a gesture, or a word by which a command or wish is expressed or a thought is made known. **Sign** (as here compared: see also SIGN, 1; CHARACTER, 1) is the general term that in itself carries no explicit connotations: it is now used both in reference to the gestures used in conversation with deaf mutes who do not know how to read lips (as, the only communication with the deaf-and-dumb man was by *signs*) and in reference to significant or conventional gestures the object of which is usually given in the context; as, to make a *sign* for silence; to give the accepted *sign* of warning. **Signal** usually applies to a conventional and recognizable sign, given under circumstances which make it clear to the person or persons concerned: often specifically it implies a command, a direction, or a warning; as, "She was startled by a ring at the door, the certain *signal* of a visitor" (*Austen*); "The flying of the first champagne-cork gave the *signal*, and a hum began to spread" (*Meredith*); "At a *signal* given by the train conductor, the engineer climbed into his engine" (*S. Anderson*). *Signal* is also applied to mechanical devices which operate lights, the movement of arms, and the like, at points where a guard, a watchman, a policeman, or the like, might otherwise be necessary; as, traffic *signals;* railroad *signals.*

Ana. *Gesture, gesticulation: *symbol, emblem.

3 Symbol, *character, mark, note.

Ana. *Device, contrivance.

signal, *n.* *Sign.

Ana. *Alarm, alarum, tocsin, alert: *gesture, gesticulation: *motion, movement: *device, contrivance, contraption.

signal, *adj.* Salient, striking, arresting, outstanding,

prominent, remarkable, *noticeable, conspicuous.
Ana. Distinctive, individual, peculiar, *characteristic: distinguished, eminent, illustrious, *famous, renowned.

significance. 1 Signification, import, *meaning, sense, acceptation.
Ana. Denotation, connotation (see under DENOTE): suggestion, implication, intimation (see corresponding verbs at SUGGEST).
2 *Importance, import, consequence, moment, weight.
Ana. *Worth, value: *influence, authority, credit, prestige: merit, *excellence, virtue, perfection.

significant. *Expressive, meaningful, pregnant, eloquent, sententious.
Ana. Cogent, telling, convincing, *valid, sound: forcible, forceful, *powerful: important, momentous, weighty (see corresponding nouns at IMPORTANCE).

signification. Significance, import, *meaning, sense, acceptation.
Ana. Signifying, meaning, denoting (see MEAN, *v.*): denotation, connotation (see under DENOTE, 2).

signify. Import, *mean, denote.
Ana. Convey, *carry, bear: *denote, connote: imply, *suggest.

silent. 1 **Silent, uncommunicative, taciturn, reticent, reserved, secretive, close, close-lipped, closemouthed, tight-lipped** come into comparison when they mean showing restraint or restraints in speaking to or with others. **Silent** and **uncommunicative** often imply a tendency to say no more than is absolutely necessary as a matter of habit (as, "he had had a rather unhappy boyhood; and it made him a *silent* man"—*Conrad;* "a stern, *silent* man, long a widower"—*Cather;* "whose *uncommunicative* heart Will scarce one precious word impart" —*Swift*) or an abstinence from speech on some particular occasion because of caution, the stress of emotion, or the like (as, "We paused... And...hand-in-hand Sat *silent*"—*Tennyson;* the reporters found the president *uncommunicative* when they asked him his opinion of the proposal). **Taciturn** implies a temperamental disinclination to speech: it usually also connotes extreme unsociableness or the nature of one who grudgingly converses when necessary; as, "Benson was...a *taciturn* hater of woman" (*Meredith*); "Always *taciturn,* he now hardly spoke at all" (*S. Cloete*). **Reticent** implies the disposition to keep one's own counsel or the habit or fact of withholding much that might be said, especially under particular circumstances: the term does not usually connote silence but, rather, sparing speech or an indisposition to discuss one's private affairs; as, "All subsequent autobiographies and confessions seem in comparison *reticent,* wanting in detail" (*L. P. Smith*); "He was *reticent* at first, but he presently warmed up" (*Cather*); "Whatever subject the stranger...exhibits an interest in, that they [the aborigines] will be *reticent* about" (*Hudson*). **Reserved** implies reticence, but it also suggests formality, standoffishness, or a temperamental indisposition to the give and take of friendly conversation or familiar intercourse; as, a *reserved* and distant demeanor; "Grave, though with no formal solemnity, *reserved* if not exactly repressed...she was yet a woman of unmistakable force of character" (*H. Ellis*). "There are no people [in France] whom it is 'difficult to know,' who are very '*reserved*' in the presence of strangers, who are particularly '*reticent*' about their own affairs" (*Brownell*). **Secretive** also implies reticence, but it carries a much stronger hint of disparagement than *reticent,* for it suggests an opposition to *frank* or *open* and often connotes an attempt to hide or conceal something that might properly be told; as, a *secretive* public official is the despair of reporters; "These things, contrary to her custom, and even nature—for she was not *secretive*—were most sedulously kept out of sight for a time" (*C. Brontë*). **Close,** as here compared (see also CLOSE, 1 & 2), comes near to *reticent* and *secretive* in its meaning, but it usually denotes a disposition rather than an attitude or manner and, therefore, often suggests taciturnity; as, "He was too *close* to name his circumstances to me" (*Dickens*). **Close-lipped** and **closemouthed** are often used in place of *close,* not only as more picturesque terms but also as carrying a stronger connotation of criticism or censure, or as more clearly implying a refusal to disclose something that another desires to know; as, he is always *closemouthed* about his plans; she proved a good secretary because she was *close-lipped* about all matters of a confidential nature. **Tight-lipped** carries a stronger implication of resolute, but not necessarily temperamental, reticence; as, "Infinite caution, *tight-lipped,* unshakable patience, these must be his rule" (*Buchan*).
Ana. Restrained, curbed, checked, inhibited (see RESTRAIN): discreet, prudent (see under PRUDENCE).
Ant. Talkative. *Con.* *Vocal, articulate, fluent, voluble, glib: loquacious, garrulous (see TALKATIVE).
2 *Still, stilly, quiet, noiseless.
Ana. *Calm, serene, tranquil, placid, peaceful.

silhouette. *Outline, contour, profile, sky line.
Ana. Shadow, *shade, adumbration.

silken, silky. *Sleek, slick, glossy, velvety, glabrous, satiny.
Ana. Lustrous, luminous, beamy, lambent (see BRIGHT): ingratiating, insinuating (see DISARMING).

silly. 1 *Simple, foolish, fatuous, asinine.
Ana. *Irrational, unreasonable: *stupid, dull, dense, crass, dumb: vacuous, *empty.
2 *Foolish, absurd, preposterous.
Ana. Inane, wishy-washy, *insipid: puerile, juvenile (see YOUTHFUL): ridiculous, ludicrous, *laughable.

silt. *Wash, drift, diluvium, alluvium, alluvion.

similar. **Similar, like, alike, identical, akin, analogous, comparable, parallel, homogeneous, uniform,** as here compared, agree in meaning closely resembling each other. Things are **similar** when in appearance or on the surface they are not readily distinguishable or may be mistaken for each other; they are **like** or **alike** when, though distinct, they seem the same either to close or to superficial views; thus, measles and chickenpox are *similar* diseases but they are not *alike* in certain respects; grippe and influenza are so very *like* each other that diagnosticians cannot always distinguish them. Things are **identical** (see also SAME) when there is exact correspondence between them; as, the typed original and carbon copies are *identical.* "Just as among all the myriad faces in the world, there are no two really *alike,* so are there no two *identical* sets of limbs" (*Lucas*). Things are **akin** to each other when in spite of marked differences they reveal essential rather than superficial likenesses. "A...playing off of one image against another, a technical device *akin* to the interlacing of themes in music" (*Day Lewis*). "The movement, which went on in France under the old régime from 1700 to 1789, was ...*akin*...to the movement of the Renascence" (*Arnold*). Things are **analogous** to each other when, in spite of their belonging to different categories or logical groupings, they are susceptible of comparison and exhibit common likenesses; thus, *analogous* words have many implications in common, but they are not true synonyms because they do not carry a common denotation, or are not applicable to the same things or ideas, or diverge in one or more important implications. "Fear and rage are closely *analogous* emotions: the man who feels rage is not possessed of the highest kind of courage"

(*B. Russell*). "You keep talking about maladies of the mind and soul. I don't accept the idea of psychic diseases *analogous* to mental diseases" (*C. Mackenzie*). Things are **comparable** when they bear sufficient likeness to each other in one or more important respects to admit of a useful or fitting comparison, such as one that explains or evaluates them (or one of them in terms of the other) or that helps to make or illustrate a point in an argument; as, the Lincoln Memorial and Grant's Tomb are not *comparable* either in size or in beauty; modern totalitarianism is *comparable* to ancient political absolutism. "Hot corn-bread baked with squash seeds,—an Indian delicacy *comparable* to raisin bread among the whites" (*Cather*). Things are **parallel** that throughout their course, their development, their history, and the like, show marked likenesses; thus, two literary passages are said to be *parallel* when, placed side by side, they reveal likenesses in thought, in structure, in phrasing; two careers may be said to be *parallel* when they can be shown to have followed a similar course. Things are **homogeneous** when they are alike in kind and in character. But *homogeneous* is rarely used in this sense except in reference to the things which form a collection, an aggregate, or the like. "The family is...a unit composed of people of different ages and sexes, with different functions to perform; it is organic, in a way which a collection of *homogeneous* individuals is not" (*B. Russell*). Things are **uniform** that do not vary wherever they occur or are found; as, *uniform* rites; *uniform* naturalization laws; a *uniform* penalty for murder. *Uniform* frequently connotes monotony, or regularity, or slavish adherence. "One could not have believed that...there could be so many *uniform* red hills" (*Cather*). "Patient endurance of sufferings, bold resistance of power, forgiveness of injuries...are seen in beautiful relief over the flat *uniformity* of life" (*R. H. Dana, sr.*).

Ana. *Same, equivalent, equal, identical: correspondent, correlative, complementary, *reciprocal.

Ant. Dissimilar. — ***Con.*** *Different, disparate, diverse: *opposite, contradictory, contrary, antithetical, antonymous.

similarity. *Likeness, resemblance, similitude, analogy, affinity.

Ana. *Comparison, contrast, collation, parallel: agreement, accordance, harmonizing *or* harmony, correspondence (see corresponding verbs at AGREE).

Ant. Dissimilarity.

simile. *Analogy, metaphor.

similitude. *Likeness, similarity, resemblance, analogy, affinity.

Ant. Dissimilitude, dissimilarity.

simper, *v.* *Smile, smirk, grin.

simper, *n.* Smile, smirk, grin. See under SMILE, *v.*

simple, *adj.* **1** *Pure, absolute, sheer.

Ana. Elemental, *elementary: *single, sole.

Ant. Compound: complex.

2 *Easy, facile, light, effortless, smooth.

Ana. Clear, plain, distinct, obvious, *evident, manifest: *clear, lucid, perspicuous.

Ant. Complicated: difficult.

3 *Natural, ingenuous, naïve, unsophisticated, artless.

Ana. *Sincere, unfeigned: *childlike, childish: open, plain, *frank, candid.

Con. Affected, pretended, assumed (see ASSUME): pretentious, ostentatious, *showy, pompous.

4 Simple, foolish, silly, fatuous, asinine come into comparison when they mean actually or apparently deficient in intelligence. **Simple,** when it implies actual deficiency in intelligence, is applied chiefly to persons whose intelligence is that of a little child (*simpletons*) and who are incapable of dealing with any ideas or situations that involve mental effort. It may imply either illiteracy coupled with a lack of native shrewdness, or feeble-mindedness that does not amount to imbecility; as, they have a *simple* son; "Smooth words he had to wheedle *simple* souls" (*Wordsworth*). When used as a term of criticism of normal persons or their acts, it suggests little more than failure to use one's intelligence. "You are fretting about General Tilney, and that is very *simple* of you; for ten to one whether you ever see him again" (*Austen*). **Foolish** (see also FOOLISH, 2), when it implies actual mental deficiency, is usually applied to persons who are technically imbeciles or idiots and who are unable to earn their living or, in some cases, to take care of themselves in any way; as, the social workers found that three of the nine children were *foolish*, and all but two of the others could be described as *simple*. As a term of criticism of normal persons and their acts, it is far stronger than *simple* because it imputes either the appearance of idiocy or imbecility or a want of intelligence or of good judgment that makes one blind to dangers, consequences, etc.; as, he looks and acts *foolish;* "Oh, *foolish* youth! Thou seek'st the greatness that will overwhelm thee!" (*Shak.*). **Silly** is applied to persons who, though not mentally deficient in the psychiatric sense, fail to act as rationally guided beings, either by showing a lack of common sense or ordinary good judgment or by behaving in a manner that makes them ridiculous in the eyes of others. "She was highly rouged, and looked rather quietly and contentedly *silly*" (*Austen*). "There is nothing So *silly* as young girls at just that age" (*Millay*). **Fatuous** does not necessarily or even often imply a pathological lack of intelligence, but it always implies the appearance of it and suggests a combination of foolishness, stupidity, and inanity. It is a term of contempt rather than of impersonal description, and is capable of additional connotations such as fatheadedness, vacuousness, obtuseness, or loss of a sense of proportion. "Do you doubt that the most *fatuous* of the Georges, whichever it was, thought himself Newton's superior?" (*Landor*). "We...looked at each other in a sort of *fatuous* consternation" (*Conrad*). "Prescott...was no *fatuous* optimist" (*Van W. Brooks*). "It would no longer be possible...for a narrow-minded pedagogue like Brunetière...to be greeted as a prophet when he *fatuously* proclaimed what he termed 'the bankruptcy of science'" (*H. Ellis*). "Fond to the point of *fatuity*" (*A. D. Sedgwick*). **Asinine** is also a term of contempt; etymologically it suggests an intelligence comparable to that of an ass, considered the lowest and most stupid of the beasts of burden. As applied to persons, their acts, choices, opinions, and the like, it connotes a despicable failure to exercise intelligence or thinking unworthy of a rational being; as, an *asinine* choice of profession; an *asinine* use of one's leisure time. "What is one to think of a man so *asinine* that he looks for gratitude in this world?" (*Mencken*).

Ana. Childish, *childlike: dull, dense, dumb, *stupid, crass: *ignorant, illiterate, untaught.

Ant. Wise.

simple, *n.* *Drug, medicinal, pharmaceutical, biological.

simpleton. *Fool, moron, imbecile, idiot, natural.

simulacrum. 1 *Image, effigy, statue, icon, portrait, photograph, mask.

2 *Imposture, cheat, fraud, sham, fake, humbug, deceit, deception, counterfeit.

simulate. Feign, counterfeit, sham, pretend, *assume, affect.

Ana. Dissemble, *disguise, cloak, mask: ape, mock, mimic, imitate, *copy.

simulation. **Simulation, dissimulation,** when they denote the pretense of being what one (usually a person, sometimes a thing) is not, are not always clearly distinguished. **Simulation** (cf. *simulate* under ASSUME) is positive, and implies the assumption of a false appearance: it therefore often suggests an attempt to seem other than what one really is; thus, hypocrisy and protective coloration are both forms of *simulation*. **Dissimulation** is negative, and suggests a dissembling, or a concealment of one's true (usually evil) nature or purpose in order to prevent recognition of it. "*Dissimulation*, in the negative; when a man lets fall signs and arguments, that he is not what he is...*Simulation*, in the affirmative; when a man industriously and expressly feigns and pretends to be that he is not" (*Bacon*). "*Simulation* is a pretence of what is not, and *dissimulation* a concealment of what is" (*Tatler*).
Ana. *Pretense, pretension, make-believe, make-belief: *hypocrisy, sanctimony, Pharisaism, cant, canting.

simultaneous. Synchronous, coincident, *contemporary, contemporaneous, coeval, concomitant, concurrent.
Ana. Concurring, coinciding, agreeing (see AGREE).
Con. *Preceding, foregoing, antecedent, previous: following, succeeding, ensuing (see FOLLOW).

sin, *n.* *Offense, vice, crime.
Ana. Transgression, trespass, *breach, violation: *error, lapse, slip: *fault, failing, frailty.

since, *adv.* **Since, ago. Ago** refers to a point in past time; **since,** in strict usage, to the period intervening between such a point and the present; in *ago* the mind is carried back from the present; in *since*, forward from a starting point in the past; as, I met him ten years *ago*, but have seen him only once *since*.

since, *conj.* *Because, for, as, inasmuch as.

sincere. **Sincere, wholehearted, whole-souled, heartfelt, hearty, unfeigned** agree in meaning genuine in feeling or expression or manifesting such genuineness. **Sincere** stresses the absence of hypocrisy, dissimulation, or falsification in any degree: it therefore usually connotes a strict adherence to truth, a revelation of just what one feels, thinks, sees (especially as an artist or poet) and no more, and an unwillingness to embellish, exaggerate, or make pretenses of any sort; as, "in a few cases where a man professes to be destroying with a view to rebuilding...we are not sure whether he is *sincere*" (*B. Russell*); "The loathing with which he [Hitler] describes the sodden Vienna working classes is...so *sincere* that one thinks for a moment that out of it must come a people's rebel" (*D. Thompson*). **Wholehearted** and the American coinage **whole-souled** imply the absence of all reservations and therefore stress not only sincerity, but also earnestness, or devotion, or zealousness, or other quality which suggests that one's whole being is stirred or moved; as, *wholehearted* support; "The most perfect and *whole-hearted* repentance" (*Pusey*); *whole-souled* dislike of totalitarianism; "A bust of Burns...looking ...not so warm and *whole-souled* as his pictures usually do" (*N. Hawthorne*). "Who could help liking her? her generous nature, her gift for appreciation, her *wholehearted*, fervid enthusiasm?" (*L. P. Smith*). **Heartfelt** places the emphasis upon the depth and genuineness of the feeling which finds expression in words, in signs of emotion such as tears, or in acts: it suggests that one's innermost being is stirred or moved and is applied usually to that which might, by contrast, be formally expressed, outwardly indicated, or the like; as, *heartfelt* sympathy; *heartfelt* piety; *heartfelt* interest in the poor and suffering. **Hearty** comes closer to *wholehearted* than to *heartfelt*, but it carries a stronger implication than *wholehearted* of vigor or energy in expression or manifestation, and may connote either simple honesty, great warmth, or exuberance in the display of feeling; as, to receive a *hearty* welcome; a *hearty* laugh; "in the *hearty* tones natural when the words demanded by politeness coincide with those of deepest feeling" (*Hardy*); "He [the social climber] must have a *hearty* taste for exactly the right sports" (*Mencken*). **Unfeigned** is often used in place of *sincere*, especially when the absence of simulation is to be stressed: the term usually emphasizes spontaneousness as well as genuineness (as, "I confess to *unfeigned* delight in the insurgent propaganda"—*Lowes*).
Ana. Candid, open, *frank, plain: honest, honorable, conscientious, scrupulous, *upright: *straightforward, aboveboard, forthright.
Ant. Insincere.

sinewy. *Muscular, athletic, husky, brawny, burly.
Ana. Robust, *healthy, sound: *strong, tough, tenacious, sturdy: nervous, *vigorous, energetic.

singe. Sear, *burn, scorch, char.

single, *adj.* **Single, sole, unique, lone, solitary, separate, particular** are here compared only as meaning one as distinguished from two or more or all others. That is **single** which is not accompanied or supported by, or combined or united with, another; as, a *single* instance may be cited; a *single* woman; a *single* house; "the strength of the lyric lies in the complete statement of a *single* selected facet of experience" (*Day Lewis*). "A painter discards many trivial points of exactness, in order to heighten the truthfulness of a few fundamentals; he makes the sitter...more like himself...than he actually is at any such *single* moment as a photograph might capture" (*C. E. Montague*). That is **sole** which is the only one that exists, that acts, that has power, that is to be considered, or the like; as, he is the *sole* heir; this is his *sole* invention; he is the *sole* deviser of this scheme; your conscience must be the *sole* judge in this case; to acquire the *sole* rights of publication; "his *sole* object was to study the form of his sitter's head in every detail" (*S. Alexander*). That is **unique** (as here compared: see also STRANGE) which is the only one of its kind or character in existence; as, the medal is *unique*, for no duplicates were made; the stamp is held to be *unique* since, so far as is known, no other specimen exists. That is **lone** (as here considered: see also ALONE) which is not only single but also separated or isolated from others of its kind: the use of this word in place of *single* is sometimes humorous, sometimes technical, sometimes poetic; as, a *lone* (humorous for *single*) woman; to play a *lone* hand in euchre (i.e., to play without one's partner); "To sit beneath a fair *lone* beechen tree" (*Keats*). That is **solitary** (as here considered: see also ALONE) which stands by itself, either as the sole instance or as a unique thing; as, the *solitary* sin of an otherwise blameless character; the *solitary* example of absolutism in the world at that moment. That is **separate** (as here compared: see also DISTINCT, 1) which is not only single, but disconnected from or unconnected with any of the others in question; as, "turning over in his thoughts every *separate* second of their hours together" (*E. Wharton*); the growth of the whole proceeds at the same pace as the growth of the *separate* parts. That is **particular** (as here compared: see also SPECIAL; CIRCUMSTANTIAL; NICE, 1) which is the single or numerically distinct instance, member, example, or the like, of the whole or of the class considered or under consideration; as, "a special provision for a known and *particular* territory" (*Ch. Just. Taney*); "Richard...replied that he had an engagement at a *particular* hour, up to which he was her servant" (*Meredith*); "Reality is a succession of concrete and *particular* situations" (*A. Huxley*).

Ana. Individual, particular, *special, especial, specific.
Ant. Accompanied: supported: conjugal.

single, *v.* In form **single out.** Prefer, handpick, *choose, select, elect, opt, pick, cull.
Ana. *Take, seize, grasp, grab: accept, *receive, admit: *decide, determine, settle.

single-foot, *n.* *Trot, pace, walk, gallop, run, canter, lope, rack, amble.

single-foot, *v.* Trot, pace, walk, gallop, run, canter, lope, rack, amble. See under TROT, *n.*

singular. *Strange, unique, peculiar, eccentric, erratic, odd, queer, quaint, outlandish, curious.
Ana. *Different, diverse, divergent, disparate: *exceptional: *abnormal, atypic, aberrant.
Con. Ordinary, *common, familiar: *usual, customary, habitual.

sinister. Sinister, baleful, malign, malefic come into comparison when they mean seriously threatening, portending, or promising evil or disaster, usually imminent or already initiated evil or disaster. **Sinister** (etymologically on or of the left hand or side, and therefore inauspicious or covert) is the most commonly employed of these words and the widest in its range of reference. It may be applied not only to that which is perceptible (as, a *sinister* cloud; a *sinister* look) but to that which is imperceptible (as, a *sinister* influence; a *sinister* intention). In either case, however, *sinister* often expresses a judgment based on experience or on an interpretation of outward signs, and implies on the part of the observer a resulting fear or apprehension of approaching evil or of lurking dangers; thus, a cloud is describable as *sinister* when it has the color, shape, or general character of one that the observer knows by experience precedes a tornado; a person's influence may be interpreted as *sinister* when it is judged in the light of some of its visible effects. "She was about half a mile from her residence when she beheld a *sinister* redness arising from a ravine a little way in advance" (*Hardy*). "That queer, cosmopolitan, rather *sinister* crowd that is to be found around the Marseilles docks" (*R. Macaulay*). "I did not wish him to know that I had suspected him of harbouring any *sinister* designs" (*Hudson*). *Sinister* is also applied to something that works or operates so covertly, insidiously, or obliquitously, that it is likely to find those whose well-being it threatens off guard; as, a *sinister* disease; a *sinister* policy. "The *sinister* power exercised...by the combination in keeping rivals out of the business and ruining those who already were in" (*Justice Holmes*). **Baleful** carries an even stronger suggestion of menace than *sinister* for it implies inevitable suffering, misery, or destruction; often, it imputes perniciousness, noxiousness, hellishness, or the like, to the thing so described. It is applicable to that which works openly and without indirection as well as to that which works occultly or obliquitously; as, "Deceit Contriv'd by art and *baleful* sorcery" (*Shak.*); "Culling their potent herbs and *baleful* drugs" (*Milton*); "The *baleful* simoon sweeps across the entire tract" (*G. Rawlinson*). "The *baleful* horoscope of Abdallah had predicted the downfall of Granada" (*Prescott*). "Watch a pair of cats, crouching on the brink of a fight. *Balefully* the eyes glare" (*A. Huxley*). **Malign,** as here compared (see also MALICIOUS), carries over from its earliest sense a suggestion of an inherently evil or harmful tendency or disposition, even though the term in this sense is characteristically applied to appearances, aspects, forces, influences, and the like, rather than to persons. It still also carries connotations derived from its reference in astrology to the aspects or the influences of the stars, such as that of boding evil or disaster. "A struggle between two forces, the one beneficent, the other *malign*" (*Bryce*). "The spirit of competition, which, according to Rousseau, was one of the earliest of the *malign* fruits of awakening intelligence" (*Grandgent*). "The prickly topic of symbolism, with its *malign* power to set the wise by the ears" (*C. E. Montague*). **Malefic** carries a stronger suggestion of balefulness than does *malign* for it implies both a tendency and an effect; thus, a *malign* influence bodes disaster; a *malefic* influence is putting the threat of disaster into effect; the *malefic* arts of sorcery, witchcraft, and diabolism.
Ana. *Ominous, portentous, fateful, unpropitious, inauspicious: *secret, covert, furtive, underhand, underhanded: *malicious, malignant, malevolent, spiteful.

sinuous. *Winding, flexuous, serpentine, tortuous, anfractuous.
Ana. Labyrinthine, mazy (see corresponding nouns at LABYRINTH): circuitous, roundabout, *indirect: *crooked, devious.

sire, *v.* Beget, get, procreate, *generate, engender, breed, propagate, reproduce.

situation. 1 *State, condition, mode, posture, status, estate.
Ana. *Juncture, pass, crisis, exigency, emergency: *predicament, plight, quandary, dilemma: case, *instance.
2 *Position, place, office, post, job, berth, billet, capacity.
Ana. Employment, occupation, *work, calling, business, pursuit, métier.

size, *n.* **Size, dimensions, area, extent, magnitude, volume** are here compared primarily as terms meaning the amount of space (sometimes time, energy, and the like) used by a thing and determinable by measuring. **Size** is usually referred to things having length, width, and depth (or height); it does not necessarily imply accurate mathematical measurements, but may suggest a mere estimate of these; as, the *size* of this box is 10 inches long, 8 inches wide, and 5 inches deep; these trees are not the right *size;* what is the *size* of the living room? *Size* is also referable to things which cannot be measured in themselves, but can be computed in terms of the number of individuals which comprise them or the amount of space occupied by those individuals; as, in *size,* New York City outranks all other cities. "The mere complexity and *size* of a modern state is against the identification of the man with the citizen" (*G. L. Dickinson*). Since *dimension* means measurement in a single direction, as the line of length, or breadth, or depth, the plural **dimensions,** when used collectively, is a close synonym of *size;* in contrast, however, it usually implies accurate measurements that are known or specified; as, the window frames must be exactly alike in *dimensions;* the *dimensions* of the universe are not calculable; the *dimensions* of the lot are 33 by 100 feet. **Area** is now referable only to things measurable in two dimensions, or length and breadth. It is used chiefly of plane figures or of plane surfaces, such as the ground, a floor, an arena, or the like, and is computed usually in square measure; as, the estate is 200 acres in *area;* the forest fire covered an *area* of ten square miles; the *area* of a rectangle is computed by multiplying its length by its breadth. **Extent** is referable chiefly to things that are measured in one dimension; it may be the length or the breadth, but it is usually thought of as the length; as, the driveway's *extent* is 100 feet; the wings of the airplane are 75 feet in *extent.* However, it is often used as though it were the equivalent of *area.* "The basement of St. Katherine's Dock House is vast in *extent* and confusing in its plan" (*Conrad*). The word is also referable to measured time or

to space measured in terms of time; thus, the duration of a thing is the *extent* of its existence; few lives reach the *extent* of one hundred years. "[In the time of Augustus] Germany was...a nine days' march from north to south, and of incalculable *extent* from west to east" (*Buchan*). **Magnitude,** which is largely a mathematical and scientific term, may be used in reference to size or two-dimensional extent. "A queer little isolated point in time, with no *magnitude*, but only position" (*R. Macaulay*). It may be used also in reference to anything measurable whose exact quantity, extent, or degree may be expressed mathematically in figures; thus, the *magnitude* of a star is indicated by a number that expresses its relative brightness. "An alpha particle bearing a positive charge equal in *magnitude* to twice the electron charge" (*Karl K. Darrow*). **Volume** (see also BULK) is also, as here considered, a scientific term; it is used in reference to anything which can be measured in terms of the cubic inches, feet, yards, etc., it occupies; thus, the *volume* of a solid cylinder is equal to the cubic measure of air it displaces, and that of a hollow one, to the cubic measure of its capacity; two objects that are equal in *volume* may differ greatly in weight; when a thing expands, it increases in *volume*.
Ana. Amplitude, *expanse, spread, stretch: *bulk, mass, volume.

skald, *n.* Variant of SCALD.

skeleton. *Structure, anatomy, framework.

skeptic *or* **sceptic.** **Skeptic** (*or* **sceptic**), **agnostic,** and their derivative nouns **skepticism, agnosticism,** are very close synonyms when they denote a person (or a philosophy) that regards all human knowledge as uncertain or all absolute knowledge as unattainable by the human mind. They are, however, distinguishable in precise, and especially in philosophical, use. **Skeptic** and **skepticism** imply the attitude of the doubter who suspends judgment because he knows the limitations of the human reason. Historically, therefore, these terms have been applied to every type of thinker or philosophy having for his (or its) fundamental assumption the impotency or the inadequacy of the reason; even, by extension, to those teaching that through revelation, inspiration, intuition, or the like, men come to a measure of truth; thus, philosophical idealism is, in the last analysis, a form of *scepticism*. **Agnostic** and **agnosticism,** on the other hand, stress the impossibility of attaining certainty; in general use, they commonly imply the unknowability of that which transcends the human reason, such as the existence of God, the origin of things, and the like; in philosophical use, they imply the impossibility of attaining truth by any means since all knowledge is relative and conditioned by the nature of the human mind.

skepticism *or* **scepticism.** 1 Agnosticism (see under SKEPTIC).
Ant. Faith.
2 *Uncertainty, doubt, dubiety, dubiosity, suspicion, mistrust.
Ana. Disbelief, *unbelief, incredulity: demur, scruple, compunction, *qualm.
Ant. Credulity.

sketch, *n.* 1 Outline, diagram, delineation, draft, tracing, plot, blueprint. See under SKETCH, *v.*
Ana. Design, plot, *plan, scheme, project: *chart, map, graph.
2 Précis, aperçu, *compendium, syllabus, digest, pandect, survey.

sketch, *v.* **Sketch, outline, diagram, delineate, draft** (*or* **draught**), **trace, plot, blueprint** come into comparison when they mean to present or to represent something by or as if by drawing its lines or its features. The same distinctions in implications and connotations are observable in the corresponding nouns **sketch, outline, diagram, delineation, draft** (*or* **draught**), **tracing, plot, blueprint. Sketch** (etymologically akin to *scheme*) may imply a drawing, a painting, a model, or a verbal presentation (as in a description or exposition) of the main lines, features, or points, with the result that a clear, often a vivid, but not a detailed impression or conception of the whole is given; as, "then, in a calm historian's tone, he proceeded to *sketch*...some pictures of the corruption which was rife abroad" (*Joyce*); "This lecture is a humble attempt to *sketch* out a metaphysics of natural science" (*Inge*); a sculptor's *sketch* of his design for a memorial; an artist usually *sketches* his picture before he paints it; "In some of Miss Jewett's earlier books...one can find first *sketches*, first impressions, which later crystallized into almost flawless examples of literary art" (*Cather*). **Outline** differs from *sketch* in suggesting emphasis upon the contours of a thing that is represented or the main points of a thing expounded, and in implying more or less inattention to the details which fill up, amplify, or particularize: the term therefore usually implies a more rigid selection and greater economy in treatment and less consideration for qualities which give pleasure than *sketch* implies and, often, suggests a presentation of a thing as a simplified whole. "When the period came for the reappearance of Mr. Scales [a traveling salesman], Mrs. Baines *outlined* a plan, and when the circular announcing the exact time of his arrival was dropped into the letter-box, she formulated the plan in detail" (*Bennett*). "The detailed study of history should be supplemented by brilliant *outlines*, even if they contained questionable generalizations" (*B. Russell*). **Diagram** implies presentation of something which requires explanation rather than representation or portrayal by means of a graphic design such as a mechanical drawing, a pattern showing arrangement and distribution of parts, a chart, map, graph, or the like; as, to *diagram* (or to make a *diagram* of) the nervous system; to make a *diagram* of a sentence to show its grammatical structure; "He *diagrammed* his route on the table-cloth" (*Cather*). **Delineate** and **delineation** etymologically and in their early and no longer widely current senses came closer to *sketch* and to *outline* than, as they now come, to *describe* and *description* and *depict* and *depiction*. For that reason, though they still retain a strong implication of drawing a thing so as to show its lines or features with great distinctness, they also suggest more attention to the amplifying details and therefore often imply greater fullness or richness in treatment than the preceding words. "His brush did its work with a steady and sure stroke that indicated command of his materials. He could *delineate* whatever he selected with technical skill" (*Jefferies*). "He [a Chinese painter of the fourth century] seems to have preferred the *delineation* of strongly featured heads, men of character and experience" (*Binyon*). "Chaucer's *delineation* of the Prioress" (*Lowes*). **Draft,** especially in its verbal rather than its substantive use, implies the accurate drawing to scale of something, especially of an architect's plan for a building to be constructed or of a design for a vessel, a machine, an engine, or the like; as, young architects usually spend their first years in *drafting* plans rather than in designing buildings. The term, either as verb or noun, may imply the drawing up of a preliminary statement which when corrected, polished, and copied will serve as a final statement (in either case often specifically called *rough draft*); as, "*draft* me a proper letter to send him" (*Shaw*); to make a *draft* of a petition; there is a rough *draft* of the book among his father's papers. **Trace** and **tracing** more often stress the act or the method of outlining or drawing and in themselves carry little implication of a carefully wrought design, pattern, or the like. The words, therefore, are used chiefly in reference to marking out the course of a road, of boundaries, and the like, on paper or on the ground itself, or to the copying of a design (often a drafted design) on a piece of transparent paper placed over it; as, to *trace* the new route to be followed in rebuilding a road; to get a *tracing* of the pattern of a rose window. Sometimes, however, the terms do suggest a pattern or design which involves the use of tracery, or decorative interlacing of lines; as, "deep-set windows, stain'd and *traced*" (*Tennyson*). **Plot** is often used in place of *diagram* or *draft* or, less often, *sketch* when a map, chart, graph, or the like, rather than a design is implied: distinctively it suggests emphasis upon the indicating of points, locations, areas, sections, or the like, so that their relation to each other or the whole is clear; thus, one who diagrammatically represents the condition of business during a given year by means of a graph is said to *plot* a graph or to make a *plot* of the curve of rise (or fall) in business activity; so, to *plot* the course (sometimes the actual, sometimes the probable, courses) of a hurricane; to *plot* a new garden (i.e., to draft a plan showing where shrubs and plants will be placed). **Blueprint,** from its common application to a photograph in white lines on blue paper of a draftsman's mechanical drawing or of an architect's plan, in extended use implies precise and detailed sketching or delineation: it suggests not the act of drawing or drawing up but the effect produced by that which is drawn or drawn up; as, the purpose of this report is to give a *blueprint* of this country's defenses; the book is a *blueprint* of Communist ambitions; "people engaged in the amusing and innocuous pastime of *blueprinting* a new social order" (*The Commonweal*).

Ana. Design, plot, plan, scheme, project (see under PLAN, *n.*): *chart, map, graph.

skid, *v.* *Slide, slip, glide, glissade, slither, coast, toboggan.

skill. *Art, cunning, craft, artifice.

Ana. Proficiency, adeptness, expertness (see corresponding adjectives at PROFICIENT): efficiency, effectiveness (see corresponding adjectives at EFFECTIVE): *readiness, facility, dexterity, ease.

skilled. Skillful, *proficient, adept, expert.

Ana. Apt, ready, *quick, prompt: practiced, exercised, drilled (see PRACTICE, *v.*): competent, qualified, *able, capable.

Ant. Unskilled.

skillful. *Proficient, adept, expert, skilled.

Ana. *Dexterous, adroit, deft, feat: efficient, *effective: *conversant, versed.

Ant. Unskillful. — *Con.* *Awkward, clumsy, inept, maladroit, gauche.

skim. Float, *fly, dart, scud, shoot, sail.

skimpy. Scrimpy, exiguous, *meager, scanty, scant, spare, sparse.

skin, *n.* **Skin, hide, pelt, fell, rind, bark, peel** come into comparison when they denote the outer removable membranous coat which adheres to and protects the softer inner tissues of a body or organism. **Skin,** the most general term, applies especially to the integument, or outer covering, of animals, whether it is as delicate as that which covers the human body or as tough as that which covers a rhinoceros; it is, however, used also of the outer coverings of certain fruits, plants, seeds, and the like, especially when they are very thin and tight; as, the *skin* of an apple; the *skin* of an almond. *Skin* applies to this integument whether it covers the living organism or has been stripped from it when dead. **Hide** applies especially to the tough skin of large wild and domestic animals, such as the rhinoceros or the horse; it is, however, chiefly in commercial use, where it is applied to the raw or undressed skins of heavy cattle, horses, and other large animals, in distinction from those of calves, sheep, goats, and the like, which are commonly described merely as *skins;* thus, tanned and dressed *hides* are made into shoes, traveling bags, and the like; tanned and dressed *skins* are made into gloves, purses, and the like. **Pelt** is applied chiefly to the skin of an animal that is covered with hair, fur, or wool; in commerce, it usually denotes an undressed skin of any of these animals, especially of a furred animal; as, fox *pelts;* sheep *pelts.* It is also applied to the skin of a sheep or goat stripped of wood or hair, and ready for tanning. **Fell** is now chiefly a literary term for *skin, hide,* or *pelt,* but, in some specific use, it denotes an underskin, or thin tough membrane, lying beneath a pelt. **Rind** applies chiefly to the thick, tough, and often inelastic integument which covers certain fruits such as oranges and grapefruit, or the stems and roots of some woody perennial plants (then usually called **bark**). The hardened skin on smoked meats such as bacon, and the hardened crust of molded cheeses, are also called *rinds.* Any skin, rind, or bark, or a portion of it, that is or may be stripped from a fruit is called **peel;** as, to slip on a banana *peel;* candied orange *peel.*

skin, *v.* **Skin, decorticate, peel, pare, flay** come into comparison when they mean to divest something of its skin or thin outer covering. **Skin** is the most general of these terms, being applicable to any animal as well as to any vegetable or fruit that is covered by or as if by a skin; as, to *skin* calves slaughtered for the market; to *skin* the bark off a birch tree. **Decorticate** is applicable when the bark of a tree, the husk of a seed or grain, or the rind of a fruit is removed by stripping; as, "an oak-trunk...felled and *decorticated*" (*M. J. Berkeley*); to *decorticate* wheat. **Peel** and **pare** are frequently confused in use: *peel* is applicable only when the skin or outer covering can be removed by stripping, especially by pulling off; *pare,* when it is cut off, usually with some of the adjoining substance; thus, freshly boiled potatoes can be easily *peeled,* but uncooked ones must be either scraped or *pared;* one speaks usually of *peeling* an orange, because its rind may be stripped by the hand; one speaks usualling of *paring* an apple, since in most varieties the skin is not easily detached from the flesh; one *peels* (not *pares*) a hard-boiled egg. But *pare* may also be used of anything that is cut close, and so is applicable to many things which do not have a skin, rind, or the like; as, to *pare* one's toe nails; to *pare* expenses to a minimum. **Flay,** a very old word meaning to strip the skin off, has been used variously in place of *skin, peel,* and *decorticate,* but in modern as well as in ancient use, it has been applied largely to persons or animals, in the former case often in threats or in descriptions of torture. Consequently, the word in current use is more literary than technical and more figurative than literal, for it usually carries a connotation of torture or of cruel punishment such as scourging; as, he said he would *flay* the man alive if he again caught him prowling around; "The prospect of dying in Newgate, with a back *flayed* and an eye knocked out" (*Macaulay*).

skinny. Scrawny, rawboned, angular, gaunt, lank, lanky, *lean, spare.

Ant. Fleshy.

skip, *v.* **Skip, bound, hop, curvet, lope, lollop, ricochet** agree in meaning to move or advance with successive springs or leaps. The first three words are commonly referable to persons or animals but they may be used in reference to inanimate things. **Skip** suggests quick, light, graceful movement and a continuous alternation of touching a surface and springing clear of it; often also, when referred to living creatures, connoting sportiveness or excess of animal spirits; as, "He maketh them also to *skip* like a calf" (*Psalms* xxix. 6); "Wanton as a child, *skipping*" (*Shak.*). **Bound** implies longer and more vigorous springs than *skip* and carries a stronger suggestion of elasticity and buoyancy of spirit; as, "Like a roe I *bounded* o'er the mountains" (*Wordsworth*); "I saw her *bounding* down the rocky slope like some wild, agile creature" (*Hudson*); the ball struck the earth and *bounded* across the field. **Hop** suggests a less flowing or springy movement than the two preceding words; at times it connotes jerkiness and lack of dignity in movement. It implies a succession of small quick leaps, such as those characteristic of the movement of birds, toads, grasshoppers, and the like; as, "[birds] *hopping* from spray to spray" (*Dryden*); he does not waltz, he *hops;* "The withered leaves all *skip* and *hop*" (*Wordsworth*); often, especially in reference to children, it suggests a jumping on one foot only. **Curvet** may suggest either a leap or, more often, a succession of leaps such as a horse makes when he raises both forelegs at once and as they are falling lifts both hind legs so that for an instant all his legs clear the surface. When not referred to a horse, it usually implies frisking and gamboling or flightiness. "Would you sell or slay your horse For bounding and *curvetting* in his course...?" (*Cowper*). "A gang of merry roistering devils, frisking and *curveting* on a flat rock" (*Irving*). **Lope** evokes a picture of the long easy bounds of a lithe and agile animal such as a wolf or fox on the run; as, "White rabbits went *loping* about the place" (*Twain*); the long, *loping* stride of a mountaineer; every evening at dusk the athletes in training *loped* round and round the track. **Lollop,** on the other hand, implies a clumsy, irregular bounding that suggests heaviness of movement or spiritlessness; as, a *lolloping* mongrel; "they [the verses called 'fourteeners'] had an almost irresistible tendency to degenerate into a kind of *lolloping* amble" (*Saintsbury*). **Ricochet** is referable almost exclusively to things which are thrown, shot, cast, or the like. It suggests a skipping caused by a series of glancing rebounds after the object first strikes a surface; as, to watch the flat stones they threw *ricocheting* (or *skipping*) over the surface of the water (but, to *skip* stones; not, to *ricochet* stones). "The smaller the angle, under which a shot is made to *ricochet*, the longer it will preserve its force and have effect" (*J. M. Spearman*).

skirmish, *n.* *Encounter, brush.
Ana. *Contest, conflict, combat, fight, affray, fray: engagement, action, *battle.

skit. *Libel, squib, lampoon, pasquinade.

skittish. Restless, restive, uneasy, fidgety, *impatient, nervous, unquiet, feverish, hectic, jumpy, jittery.

skulk *or* **sculk.** *Lurk, couch, slink, sneak.
Ana. Secrete, *hide, conceal.
Con. Emerge, *appear, loom.

sky line. Profile, contour, *outline, silhouette.

slack, *adj.* **1** Lax, remiss, *negligent, neglectful.
Ana. *Lazy, indolent, slothful, fainéant: *indifferent, unconcerned, detached, aloof: sluggish, *lethargic.
Con. Diligent, sedulous, industrious, *busy, assiduous: expeditious, quick, *fast.
2 Relaxed, *loose, lax.
Ana. *Weak, feeble, infirm: inert, supine, passive, *inactive: *slow, leisurely, laggard.
Con. *Tight, taut, tense: *steady, constant, uniform, even, equable: *firm, hard.

slacken. *Delay, retard, slow, detain.
Ana. Abate, reduce, lessen, *decrease: *restrain, curb, check, inhibit: *moderate, temper, qualify.
Ant. Quicken.

slander, *n.* Calumny, *detraction, backbiting, scandal.
Ana. Defamation, vilification, aspersion, traducing (see corresponding verbs at MALIGN): *abuse, vituperation, invective, obloquy, scurrility.

slander, *v.* Defame, libel, calumniate, *malign, traduce, asperse, vilify.
Ana. *Decry, depreciate, detract from, derogate from, disparage, belittle: *injure, damage, hurt: *attack, assail.

slang. *Dialect, vernacular, patois, lingo, jargon, cant, argot, patter.

slant, *n.* **1 Slant, inclination, slope, acclivity, declivity, incline, grade, gradient** agree in denoting obliquity or something oblique. *Slant, inclination, slope* are sometimes interchangeable, but are not exact synonyms. **Slant** is divergence (commonly sharp divergence) from the vertical or horizontal. "The *slant* of a ladder that leans against a house" (*Twain*). **Inclination** is any divergence, slight or sharp, from a straight position or a direction taken as normal; as, to correct an *inclination* of the teeth. Commonly, when there is no contrary indication, a bending sidewise (or forward) and downward is implied; as, the *inclination* of a tree; the *inclination* of a magnetic needle. "She answered only by a slight *inclination* of the head" (*Austen*). **Slope** is used especially of surfaces, and commonly implies a gradual slant; as, the *slope* of a meadow, a windshield, a brow. *Slant* sometimes, and *slope* frequently, are used concretely. So used, *slant* requires qualification to complete its meaning; as, *slants* of rain, of sunshine: *slope* denotes ground whose surface forms an angle with the plane of the horizon; as, a green *slope.* A *slope* of ground considered as ascending is an **acclivity;** the same slope considered as descending, a **declivity.** An **incline** is a natural slope or an artificial structure that leads from one level to another, often forming a passageway; as, a town built on an *incline;* an *incline* between two floors in a garage. **Grade** and **gradient** are equivalent terms, the former chiefly in American, the latter in British use. They are used commonly (*grade* almost exclusively) of railroads and highways, and denote, usually, degree of inclination from the horizontal; as, there is a ten per cent *grade* (that is, an ascent or descent of ten feet to every hundred feet of horizontal distance) between the two villages. "The roads of the period [were] steep in *gradient*" (*Hardy*). *Grade* is often used to denote a stretch of a road or railroad that rises or falls from a level; as, there is a heavy *grade* between Albany and Schenectady.
Ana. Tipping, tilting, canting, careening (see TIP): *deviation, deflection, divergence.
2 *Point of view, standpoint, viewpoint, angle.
Ana. Attitude, *position, stand: bias, prejudice, *predilection.

slant, *v.* **Slant, slope, incline, lean** come into comparison when they mean to diverge or cause to diverge from a vertical or horizontal line. **Slant** carries the sharpest and clearest implication of such divergence of any of these terms, but it carries no explicit implication of how great or how little is the divergence: consequently, it is accepted generally as the comprehensive term implying any noticeable physical divergence; as, the tree *slants* to the right; eyes that *slant* inward; rain *slanted* by the wind; "One side of his body seemed to *slant* towards the other, he settled so much more heavily upon one foot" (*M. Wilkins*). **Slope** is often used in place of *slant,* but it is the preferred term when the reference is to a surface, or a side of an elevation, such as a hill, a roof, or the like, and often, but not invariably, where there is an intent to suggest a gradual divergence from a right (i.e., straight and not oblique) line; thus, "the ground *slopes* to the left" usually suggests a lack of steepness; "a *sloping* roof," unless qualified by *sharply, steeply,* or the like, usually implies a gradual slant; so, the road *slopes* downward from this point; "the path that *sloped* from the door" (*M. Wilkins*). **Incline** (as here compared: see also INCLINE, 2) carries a stronger implication of bending or tipping or of being bent or tipped: it is therefore the preferred word not only when human or similar agency is implied, but when that which is bent or tipped is an immaterial thing such as one's will, one's thoughts, one's intentions, or the like; as, "Just as the twig is bent, the tree's *inclin'd*" (*Pope*); to *incline* one's head to the right; the garden terraces *incline* to the south. "There is another theory to which the late Professor Freeman *inclined* (if so sturdy a figure could be said to *incline*)" (*Quiller-Couch*). **Lean** differs from *incline* in carrying either a stronger implication of a definite directing of the inclination by a human agent or by some shaping or molding force (as, to *lean* back in one's chair; since the hurricane most of the trees of the grove *lean* toward the northwest) or of a resting or an intent to rest against a (literal or figurative) support (as, to *lean* against a pillar; she always *leaned* upon her husband when they walked the mountain trails; a child should not be allowed to *lean* too heavily on parents or teachers).

Ana. *Tip, tilt, cant, careen: veer, *swerve, deviate, diverge.

slap, *v.* *Strike, hit, smite, swat, slug, clout, punch, box, cuff.

slash, *v.* Slit, *cut, hew, chop, carve.

Ana. Rive, rend, cleave, split (see TEAR): penetrate, pierce, *enter.

slatternly, *adj.* **Slatternly, dowdy, frowzy, blowzy** are adjectives usually applied to women (rarely, except *frowzy*, to men; often, except *blowzy*, to children regardless of sex) and their appearance, and meaning negligent of neatness, freshness, or smartness in dress and looks. **Slatternly** implies slovenliness and general unkemptness. "It often grieved her to the heart to think...that her mother...should have an appearance...so comfortless, so *slatternly*, so shabby" (*Austen*). **Dowdy** suggests lack of taste, style, or smartness in dress, in the arrangement of one's hair, and the like, and a drabness of color. "A perfect saint amongst women, but so dreadfully *dowdy* that she reminded one of a badly bound hymn-book" (*Wilde*). **Frowzy** implies an offensive lack of neatness suggestive of mustiness, uncleanliness, and the like. "If a fully fed, presentably clothed, decently housed, fairly literate and cultivated and gently mannered family is not better than a half-starved, ragged, *frowsy*, overcrowded one, there is no meaning in words" (*Shaw*). **Blowzy** suggests coarseness, rude healthiness, floridity, and a general appearance of being wind-blown or living much in the open; as, "that blazing, *blowzy* penitent [of Rubens], in yellow satin and glittering hair" (*Thackeray*). "That cheerful-looking lady herself, with a face made *blowsy* by cold and damp" (*G. Eliot*).

Ana. Slovenly, unkempt, sloppy, *slipshod: *dirty, squalid, foul, filthy.

Con. *Neat, tidy, trim, spick-and-span.

slaughter, *n.* *Massacre, butchery, carnage, pogrom.

slave, *n.* *Serf, bondslave, thrall, villein, vassal, bondsman, bondman, peon, Helot.

slavery. *Servitude, bondage.

slavish. Servile, menial, *subservient, obsequious.

Ana. *Mean, abject, ignoble, sordid: *tame, subdued, submissive: *miserable, wretched.

slay. *Kill, murder, assassinate, dispatch, execute.

sleazy *or* **sleezy.** *Limp, flimsy, loppy, flaccid, flabby.

Ana. *Thin, tenuous, slight: *loose, slack.

sleek. 1 Sleek, slick, glossy, velvety, velvet, silken, silky, satiny, satin, glabrous are here compared as meaning having a smooth, bright surface or appearance. That is **sleek,** literally, which is smoothed and brightened by wetting, oiling, brushing, rubbing, polishing, burnishing, or the like: the term usually connotes a smoothness or brightness that is the result of close attention or is an indication, especially when the reference is to a person or animal, of being in excellent physical condition; as, his hair is always *sleek;* "Let me have men about me that are fat: *Sleek*-headed men and such as sleep o' nights" (*Shak.*); "a beautiful panther...so bright of eye, so *sleek* of coat" (*Thackeray*); "the metal felt *sleek* and warm to his touch" (*S. Cloete*); "a child's mind thrills at the touch of fur because it is *sleek*" (*C. E. Montague*). But *sleek* is also applied to the general appearance of a person who is well groomed and well dressed to an extreme, often a vulgar extreme; as, "the *sleek* lords with their plumes and spurs" (*V. Lindsay*); "he was not carelessly dressed. There was something *sleek* about him, something that suggested a well-bred dog" (*S. Anderson*). That is **slick** (now dialectal or colloquial, but much older than *sleek*, which was probably at first a variant form of it) which is sleek or, more often in current use, which is so perfectly finished that the eye can detect no flaw or roughness in the workmanship. Often, in the latter sense, merely a fair outside is suggested. "Everything was to be *slick*, which was Marvin's [the architect's] term of approbation; but not too *slick*, which was his abomination" (*M. Austin*). "In a word, it [the typical novel produced by popular American writers] is marked by a competent *slickness*. This surface gloss, this sophisticated polish, is worrying to an English reader, who is sometimes led astray...under the mistaken impression that the writer really has something to say, since he takes so much trouble to say it neatly" (*Times Lit. Sup.*). In recent somewhat slangy use, *slick* often connotes a slippery or calendered surface; thus, the "*slick* magazines," or "*slicks*," are those that are printed on calendered paper. That is **glossy** which has by nature or art a surface that is exceedingly smooth and shining; as, the *glossy* leaves of the beech tree; "downy peaches and the *glossy* plum" (*Dryden*); "*glossy* as black rocks on a sunny day cased in ice" (*D. Wordsworth*); the table has a waxed, not a *glossy* finish. That is **velvety** (or, less often, **velvet**) which has the extreme softness associated with the surface or appearance of velvet: though the word is often used of things as they appeal to the sense of touch or of sight, or of both (as, a *velvety*, or *velvet*, skin; a *velvety*, or *velvet*, flower), it is also applicable to sounds that caress the ear or to tastes or odors that are delightfully bland (as, even her high notes are *velvety;* the *velvet* touch of a pianist; "the boy reading in his queer, *velvety* bass voice"—*Galsworthy;* a *velvety* sauce). That is **silken** which has the smoothness and luster as well as the softness of silk; as, *silken* hair; "To what green altar... Lead'st thou that heifer lowing at the skies, And all her *silken* flanks with garlands drest" (*Keats*). The term is increasingly used in reference both to things that appeal to other senses than those of touch or sight and to immaterial things that are peculiarly grateful to the spirit or mind; as, a *silken* voice; *silken* slumbers; a *silken* style; *silken* words. **Silky** is sometimes used in place of *silken* (as, "fingers, *silky* and soft"—*Watts-Dunton;* a *silky* wine) but when the reference is to persons, their voices, manners, etc., the word, more often than *silken*, suggests an ingratiating or a specious quality (as, "Mrs. Gibson...petted him in her sweetest, *silkiest* manner"—*Gaskell*). That is **satiny** (or, less often, **satin**) which is not only soft, but smooth and sleek, especially of surface; as, the *satiny* petals of a flower; a *satin* skin. That is **glabrous** (chiefly a biological term) which has a skin or surface devoid of all hairs, down, or the like, so that its smoothness and, sometimes but not always, its gloss is apparent; as, the *glabrous* leaves of some elms; "the escholtzia, which...I avoided, for its virulent-orange flowers and its strange *glabrous* stalks" (*H. Ellis*).

Ana. *Bright, lustrous, brilliant: smooth, even (see LEVEL): polished, burnished (see POLISH, *v.*).

2 *Fulsome, oily, unctuous, oleaginous, soapy.

Ana. Bland, smooth, diplomatic, politic, *suave, urbane: ingratiating, insinuating, *disarming: specious, *plausible.

sleepy. Sleepy, drowsy, somnolent, slumberous (*or* **slumbrous**) come into comparison when they mean affected by a desire to sleep or affecting one by inducing such a desire. **Sleepy,** the ordinary term of this group, applies not only to persons but to things that suggest a resemblance to persons who show a readiness to fall asleep (as, "Away, you rogue, away! I am *sleepy*"—*Shak.;* a *sleepy* town; "the quiet, *sleepy* railroad station at Pickleville"—*S. Anderson*). The term also applies to conditions or to things which incline one to sleep or to dozing or dreaming (as, "the yellow-hammer trills his *sleepy* song in the noonday heat; the drone of the Greenfinch lulls me into dreamy meditations"—*L. P. Smith*). **Drowsy** differs from *sleepy* in carrying a stronger implication of the heaviness or loginess associated with sleepiness than of the actual need of rest; as, to become *drowsy* after a heavy dinner; "A little later, when the sun should burn through the leaves...Mrs. Barkley would grow *drowsy* ...and go off to take a nap" (*Deland*). When applied to things rather than to persons, *drowsy* connotes far more obviously than *sleepy* a soporific power; as, "Not poppy, nor mandragora, Nor all the *drowsy* sirups of the world, Shall ever medicine thee to that sweet sleep Which thou owedst yesterday" (*Shak.*); "And *drowsy* tinklings lull the distant folds [i.e., sheepfolds]" (*Gray*); "The leisurely swishing of the water to leeward was like a *drowsy* comment on her progress" (*Conrad*). **Somnolent** is often used in place of *drowsy*, especially in formal writing; usually, however, it connotes the sluggishness or inertness (as felt or as induced) characteristic of one who is sleepy or drowsy rather than the actual impulse to sleep or doze; as, "a *somnolent* want of interest" (*De Quincey*); "Eustacia waited, her *somnolent* manner covering her inner heat and agitation" (*Hardy*); the *somnolent* pages of a three-volume novel. **Slumberous** is often used, especially in poetry, in the sense of *sleepy*, or *drowsy*, or *somnolent:* when, as occasionally happens, it carries a distinctive connotation, it usually suggests quiescence or the repose of latent powers; as, "I... heard The mountain's *slumberous* voice" (*Shelley*); "*Slumbrous* azure pools clear as the air" (*Ingelow*); "Eustacia's manner was as a rule of a *slumberous* sort, her passions being of the massive rather than the vivacious kind" (*Hardy*).

Ana. *Lethargic, sluggish, comatose, stuporous.

sleezy. Variant of SLEAZY.

slender. *Thin, slim, slight, tenuous, rare.

Ana. *Lean, spare, lanky, skinny: flimsy, flaccid, flabby, *limp: trivial, trifling, *petty, paltry, puny.

slick, *adj.* *Sleek, glossy, velvety, silken, satiny, silky, glabrous.

Ana. Finished, *consummate: flawless, *impeccable, faultless: shallow, *superficial.

slide, *v.* **Slide, slip, glide, skid, glissade, slither, coast, toboggan** come into comparison when they mean to move along easily and smoothly over or as over a surface. **Slide** usually, but not invariably, implies accelerated motion and unintermittent contact with a surface, especially a waxed, icy, or otherwise slippery surface: it is used not only in reference to persons and to moving things such as vehicles, some instruments, and the like (as, boys like to *slide* down banisters; "The fool *slides* o'er the ice that you should break"—*Shak.;* his pen *slid* across the paper), but also, especially in figurative use, with reference to the things (sometimes persons) which pass rapidly before one because of one's own swift and easy motion (as, house after house *slid* by as we neared the city) or which move easily, unobtrusively, gradually, or the like, from one place or condition to another (as, prose that *slides* into poetry; democracies that *slide* into dictatorships; to *slide* one's hand into another's pocket). **Slip** carries a stronger implication than *slide* of a frictionless and unobstructed surface but a weaker suggestion of continued contact: it therefore often suggests involuntary rather than voluntary sliding, sometimes even definitely implying a loss of footing and a fall, often with resulting injury; as, to *slip* on the ice; "he had hurt his elbow through dropping his stick and *slipping* downstairs" (*Bennett*). When only swift, easy motion is implied, *slip* heightens the emphasis upon quietness, stealth, skillfulness, or the like; as, while we were talking, he *slipped* from the house; "I paddled up the river...; I *slipped* past the barges" (*Jefferies*). Things are said to *slip* that pass quickly or without notice, as from one's grasp, one's control, one's memory, or one's observation (as, the book *slipped* from her feeble hands; "[Augustus] saw that Roman morals were *slipping* into a perilous state"—*Buchan;* the details have *slipped* from his mind) or as a result of one's negligence or inattention (as, the bus *slipped* by while they were engrossed in conversation; the tool *slipped* and cut his hand). **Glide** comes closer to *slide* than to *slip* in its stress upon continued smooth, easy, usually silent motion such as is characteristic of some dances, but it may or may not imply unintermittent contact with a surface and, apart from its context, it seldom carries even a slight hint of an element of danger; as, "They *glide*, like phantoms, into the wide hall" (*Keats*); "even the swallows, the restless swallows, *glided* in an effortless way through the busy air" (*Jefferies*). Often, like *slide* and, to a lesser extent, *slip*, *glide* is used in reference to things that apparently move because the observer is in a moving vehicle, boat, or the like; as, "The landward marks have failed, The fog-bank *glides* unguessed" (*Kipling*); "Soft fell the splash of the oars...softly the banks *glided* by" (*Meredith*). **Skid,** in the sense in which it is here considered, goes back to an earlier sense when it was used in reference to a wheel or wheels that moved as if sliding but without rotation, especially as a result of the use of a skid, or kind of brake which retarded the motion of a vehicle descending a steep hill (as, "The horses stopped to breathe again, and the guard got down to *skid* the wheel for the descent"—*Dickens*): in current use, the term is employed especially in regard to bicycles and automobiles, the tires of which on an icy, wet, or dusty road fail to grip the roadway, thereby causing the vehicle to slip obliquely or to the side; as, the car *skidded* on the icy patch and ran into a telegraph pole. In extended use *skid*, like *slip*, usually implies an element of danger or recklessness or a lack of control (often complete control) or grasp; as, he ran fast, occasionally *skidding* on an icy patch, but always quickly recovering his balance. **Glissade,** originally and still a mountaineering term implying a long slide down a slope, especially a snow-covered or ice-covered slope, and now also a dancing term implying a sliding step to one side, carries the major implications of both *slide* and *glide*, but stresses close contact with a surface in a continuous and well-balanced or graceful motion; as, "Kennedy and Cyril...*glissaded* gallantly over the slopes of snow" (*F. W. Farrar*). **Slither,** an old word now used chiefly for its picturesqueness, often implies a sliding down a rocky, pebbly, or other rough slope with noise and clatter (as, "The rest [of the tile] bounced on the roof and then *slithered* down it and off it"—*Masefield*); but in current use it more often suggests a gliding, sliding, sometimes undulating, motion suggestive of a snake's movement (as, "crawling through walls and *slithering* along the ground"—*de Kruif;* "When he and his papers have *slithered* away In the bodies of innumerable worms"—*Amy Lowell*). **Coast** and **toboggan** always connote a sliding downward on or as if on a sled or toboggan, but *coast* in current use often specifically implies the movement downhill of a freewheel bicycle without aid of the pedals, or of an automobile with the motor disengaged (as, the boys walked up the hill with their bicycles, then mounted and *coasted* down the other side; no *coasting* on hills), and *toboggan* suggests a rapid sliding downward or decline which cannot be impeded until the bottom is reached or some obstruction is provided; as, from 1929 to 1933 the prices of securities *tobogganed.*

slight, *adj.* Tenuous, rare, *thin, slender, slim.
Ana. *Imperceptible, imponderable, impalpable, intangible, insensible, inappreciable: trifling, trivial, puny, *petty, paltry: minute, diminutive, wee, little, *small.

slight, *v.* *Neglect, ignore, overlook, disregard, omit, forget.
Ana. Scorn, disdain, contemn, *despise: flout, *scoff.

slim. *Thin, slender, slight, tenuous, rare.
Ana. *Lean, spare, skinny, scrawny: *meager, exiguous, scant, scanty: lithe, lithesome, lissome (see SUPPLE).
Ant. Chubby (*of persons*).

sling, *v.*[1] Hurl, fling, pitch, toss, *throw, cast.
Ana. Heave, hoist, *lift, raise: impel, drive (see MOVE): propel, shove, thrust, *push.

sling, *v.*[2] *Hang, suspend, dangle.

slink. *Lurk, skulk, sneak, couch.

slip, *v.* *Slide, glide, skid, glissade, slither, coast, toboggan.

slip, *n.* Lapse, *error, mistake, blunder, faux pas, bull, howler, boner, bloomer, floater.
Ana. Accident, *chance: inadvertence, carelessness, heedlessness (see corresponding adjectives at CARELESS): *fault, failing, foible, frailty, vice.

slipshod, *adj.* **Slipshod, slovenly, unkempt, sloppy** come into comparison not only when applied to persons and their appearance, but also to their mental and manual processes, performances, or products, and mean conspicuously manifesting negligence or carelessness. **Slipshod** (etymologically, shod in loose, flapping, or down-at-heel shoes) implies an easygoing tolerance of details that are inaccurate, incongruous, lacking in precision, and the like, or indifference to the niceties of technique or to qualities that make for perfection, such as thoroughness, soundness, and fastidiousness; as, a *slipshod* style; a *slipshod* piece of work; a *slipshod* performance of a symphony. "We need not linger over the details of the *slipshod* campaign which followed" (*Buchan*). **Slovenly,** a much stronger term than *slipshod*, implies laziness and disorderliness which is evident throughout and is not merely a matter of detail. The term was formerly used primarily in regard to a person or his appearance, and implied diametrical opposition to *neat* or *tidy;* as, a *slovenly* housekeeper; "his person showed marks of habitual neglect; his dress was *slovenly*" (*G. Eliot*). In somewhat later use, it was applied to processes, technique, workmanship, and the like; as, *slovenly* thinking; "the *slovenly* manner in which the dinner was served" (*Conrad*); "a tendency to think that a fine idea excuses *slovenly* workmanship" (*Amy Lowell*). **Unkempt** (etymologically, uncombed) is applied usually to that which requires to be kept in order, if a favorable impression is to be produced. It implies extreme negligence amounting to neglect; as, *unkempt* hair; an *unkempt* garden; "most of the shops...had become pettifogging little holes, *unkempt*, shabby, poor" (*Bennett*). **Sloppy** (chiefly in colloquial use) implies a general effect of looseness and of spilling over. When applied to a person or his appearance, it usually suggests loose, ill-fitting, unpressed garments, but it often also carries connotations of slovenliness; as, her *sloppy* appearance at breakfast gave offense to her husband. When applied to ideas or their expression, style, manners, or to a work or its workmanship, the word usually suggests a lack of decorous restraint or confinement within proper limits, manifested in incoherency, in emotional abandon (effusiveness or sentimentality), in formlessness, or the like. "The rather *sloppy* Socialism which pervades this document" (*Inge*). "Archer's coherent thinking, his sense of the worth of order and workmanship, his impatience of humbug, *sloppiness*, and gush" (*C. E. Montague*).
Ana. *Negligent, neglectful, slack, lax, remiss: *careless, heedless, inadvertent: *indifferent, unconcerned: *slatternly, dowdy, frowzy, blowzy.
Con. Precise, accurate, exact, *correct: fastidious, finical, *nice.

slit, *v.* Slash, *cut, hew, chop, carve.

slither. *Slide, slip, glide, skid, glissade, coast, toboggan.

slog, *v.* Variant of SLUG.

slope, *v.* *Slant, incline, lean.
Ana. *Tip, tilt, cant, careen: deviate, diverge, veer, *swerve.

slope, *n.* *Slant, inclination, acclivity, declivity, incline, grade, gradient.
Ana. Tipping, turning, canting, careening (see TIP): *mountain, mount, peak, alp: steepness, abruptness, precipitousness (see corresponding adjectives at STEEP).

sloppy. Slovenly, unkempt, *slipshod.
Ana. *Negligent, neglectful, slack, remiss, lax: mawkish, maudlin, soppy, slushy (see SENTIMENTAL): *slatternly, dowdy, frowzy, blowzy.
Con. *Careful, meticulous, scrupulous, punctilious: fastidious, finical, *nice.

slothful. Indolent, fainéant, *lazy.
Ana. *Inactive, inert, supine, passive, idle: slack, remiss, lax, *negligent, neglectful: *slow, leisurely, deliberate, dilatory, laggard.
Ant. Industrious. — *Con.* *Busy, diligent, sedulous, assiduous.

slough, *v.* Exuviate, *discard, cast, shed, molt, scrap, junk.

slovenly. *Slipshod, unkempt, sloppy.
Ana. *Slatternly, dowdy, frowzy, blowzy: *indifferent, unconcerned: *negligent, neglectful, slack, lax, remiss.
Con. *Orderly, methodical: *neat, tidy, trim, spick-and-span.

slow, *adj.* **Slow, dilatory, laggard, deliberate, leisurely** come into comparison as applied chiefly to persons, their movements, their actions, and the like, and agree in meaning taking a longer time than is necessary and, sometimes, desirable. **Slow,** the term that is the widest in its range of application, may also be used in reference to anything (such as a mechanism, a process, or a drug) that is the opposite of quick or fast in its motion, its performance, its operation, or the like. In its varying applications, *slow* often, but far from invariably, suggests a reprehensible or discreditable cause such as stupidity, lethargy, indolence, inaction (as, a *slow* student; his *slow* progress in school; *slow* wits; *slow* movements; he is as *slow* as a snail; to be *slow* in getting results), but it may suggest either extreme care or caution (as, a *slow* but capable worker; to be *slow* to take offense; he is *slow* in making changes), or a tempo that is required by nature, art, or a plan or schedule (as, a *slow* convalescence; a *slow* growth; a *slow* stream; a *slow* movement in music; a *slow* train), or a falling behind because of structural or mechanical defects or other untoward difficulties (as, a *slow* watch; the train is *slow* tonight because of the snowstorm). **Dilatory** is relatively a term of restricted application referable only to persons or to things for which persons are responsible as their actors, performers, creators, or the like, and always implying slowness that is the result of inertness, procrastination, or indifference; as, a *dilatory* correspondent; a *dilatory* servant; "though *dilatory* in undertaking business, he was quick in its execution" (*Austen*); to pursue a *dilatory* policy in providing adequate defense for the country. **Laggard** is even more censorious a term than *dilatory*, for it implies a failure to observe a schedule for arriving, performing, and the like, or to obey a call or demand promptly: it frequently suggests loitering or waste of time; as, *laggard* pupils keep a whole class back; "For Love was *laggard*, O, Love was *slow* to come" (*Millay*). **Deliberate** (as here compared: see also DELIBERATE, 2) applies only to persons, usually directly, but sometimes indirectly, and then applied to things for which a person is responsible: the term suggests absence of hurry or agitation and a slowness that is the result of care, forethought, calculation, self-restraint, or the like; as, *deliberate* enunciation; *deliberate* movements; a *deliberate* performance of a great symphony; "He returned with the same easy, *deliberate* tread" (*Cather*); "She ate her food in the *deliberate*, constrained way, almost as if she recoiled a little from doing anything so publicly" (*D. H. Lawrence*). **Leisurely** also implies a lack of hurry or a slowness that suggests that there is no pressure for time: the term applies not only to persons and their acts but to things that have no relation to persons; as, "breakfast was a *leisurely* meal" (*Arch. Marshall*); to take a *leisurely* journey through Central America; "the *leisurely* swishing of the water to leeward" (*Conrad*).

Ant. Fast.

slow, *v.* Slacken, *delay, retard, detain.

Ana. *Moderate, temper, qualify: reduce, abate, *decrease, lessen.

Ant. Speed. — *Con.* Accelerate, quicken, hasten, hurry (see SPEED, *v.*).

slug *or* **slog,** *v.* *Strike, hit, smite, slap, swat, clout, punch, box, cuff.

sluggish. *Lethargic, torpid, stuporous, comatose.

Ana. Inert, *inactive: indolent, slothful, *lazy: listless, languishing, *languid.

Ant. Brisk: expeditious: quick (*of mind*).

slumberous *or* **slumbrous.** *Sleepy, drowsy, somnolent.

slushy. *Sentimental, mushy, romantic, mawkish, maudlin, soppy.

sly, *adj.* **Sly, cunning, crafty, tricky, foxy, wily, artful** are synonymous when they mean having or showing a disposition to attain one's ends by devious or indirect means. **Sly** implies a lack of candor, which shows itself in secretiveness, in suggestiveness rather than in frankness, in underhandedness, or, often, in a vulgar turn for furtiveness or duplicity in one's dealings with others. "Why, Jane—you never dropt a word of this; you *sly* thing" (*Austen*). "Wrinkled *slyness* and craft pitted against native truth and sagacity" (*N. Hawthorne*). "With knowing leer and words of *sly* import" (*Irving*). **Cunning,** in the sense in which it is here considered (see also CLEVER, 2), stresses the use of intelligence in overreaching or circumventing; nevertheless, it often suggests a low-grade mentality or a perverted sense of morality. "Every man wishes to be wise, and they who cannot be wise are almost always *cunning*" (*Johnson*). "Infants are far more *cunning* than grown-up people are apt to suppose; if they find that crying produces agreeable results, they will cry" (*B. Russell*). "All gods are cruel, bitter, and to be bribed, But women-gods are mean and *cunning* as well" (*G. Bottomley*). **Crafty** also implies a use of intelligence, but it suggests a higher order of mentality than *cunning:* that of one capable of devising stratagems and adroit in deception. "He disappointeth the devices of the *crafty*, so that their hands cannot perform their enterprise" (*Job* v. 12). "As a *crafty* envoy does his country's business by dint of flirting and conviviality" (*C. E. Montague*). **Tricky** usually suggests unscrupulousness and chicanery in dealings with others; in general, it connotes shiftiness and unreliability rather than skill in deception or in maneuvering; as, to fear a *tricky* opponent more than a *crafty* one. "Able men of high character, and not smart, *tricky* men" (*The Nation*). **Foxy** implies shrewdness in dodging discovery or in practicing deceptions so that one may follow one's own devices or achieve one's own ends; it usually connotes experience and is rarely applied to the young or to novices; as, a *foxy* old man; a *foxy* detective. **Wily** stresses an attempt to ensnare or entrap; it commonly implies astuteness or sagacity and, usually, a lack of scruples regarding the means to one's end. "Shun the insidious arts That Rome provides, less dreading from her frown Than from her wily praise" (*Wordsworth*). "The head-master, *wily*, had not confiscated these [forbidden] articles; he had merely informed the parents concerned" (*Bennett*). **Artful** implies insinuating or alluring indirectness of dealing; it usually also connotes sophistication, or coquetry, or designs. "——is a good-natured old easy fool, and has been deceived by the most *artful* of her sex" (*Sterne*). "The Lucases are very *artful* people indeed, sister. They are all for what they can get" (*Austen*).

Ana. Furtive, clandestine, stealthy, covert (see SECRET): devious, oblique, *crooked: astute, *shrewd.

smack, *n.* **1** *Taste, sapidity, flavor, savor, tang, relish. **2** *Touch, suggestion, suspicion, soupçon, tincture, tinge, shade, spice, dash, vein, strain, streak.

small. Small, little, diminutive, petite, wee, tiny, teeny, weeny, minute, microscopic, miniature come into comparison as meaning conspicuously below the average in magnitude, especially physical magnitude. *Small* (opposed to *large*) and *little* (opposed to *big, great*) are often used without distinction. But **small,** more frequently than *little*, applies to things whose magnitude is determined by number, size, capacity, value, significance, and the like; as, a *small* attendance; a *small* boy; a *small* box; a *small* house; *small* coins; a *small* income; a *small* matter. *Small* is also preferred when words like *quantity, amount, size, capacity*, etc., are qualified; as, give me a *small* quantity of flour; they have only a *small* amount of necessary supplies left; the *small* size of the rooms was disappointing. *Small* also applies to intangible and immeasurable things which, however, may be said to be limited in some pertinent or significant way; as, he has a *small* mind; "the *small* arts called womanish" (*Hardy*); "her sadness at the *small* prospect of seeing him again" (*Arch. Marshall*). **Little** is usually more absolute in its implications than *small*, which often connotes less magnitude than that which is ordinary or which is to be expected or is desirable: it is preferred to *small*, therefore, when there is the intent to convey a hint of petiteness, of pettiness, or of insignificance in size, amount, or quantity, extent, or the like; as, to take *little* interest in politics; "A foolish consistency is the hobgoblin of *little* minds" (*Emerson*); "A *little* advocate in snuff-coloured clothes rose on *little* legs, and commenced to read" (*Galsworthy*); "How unsubstantial then appear our hopes and dreams, our *little* ambitions, our paltry joys!" (*A. C. Benson*). *Little* is also preferred in the sense of "a small amount," "a small quantity," "a small extent," and the like; thus, one asks for "a *little* sugar" or "a *small* quantity of sugar"; one says "the garden is *little*" or "of *small* extent." *Little* is also preferred when the context carries a note of tenderness, pathos, or the like; as, a *little* (cf. *small*) child; our *little* (cf. *small*) house; her pathetic *little* smile; "Sleep, my *little* one" (*Tennyson*). **Diminutive** not only carries a stronger implication of divergence from the normal or usual size or scale than *small* or *little*, but it often carries the meaning of extremely (often abnormally) small or little; as, the bedrooms are *small*, but the parlor is *diminutive;* in so hot a climate peach trees will produce only *diminutive* fruits in very *small* quantities; "The horses are so *diminutive* that they might be, with propriety, said to be Lilliputian" (*Cowper*). **Petite,** originally a French word, has been taken over into English in only one of its applications. It is the usual term to describe a trim, well-shaped woman or girl of diminutive size; as, she is *petite* and unusually pretty. **Wee,** a somewhat more homely term than *diminutive*, and found in dialectal use in place of *small* or *little* (as, a *wee* lad; a *wee* drop of whisky), is also often found in standard English; as, "a little *wee* face, with a little yellow beard" (*Shak.*); "*Wee*, modest, crimson-tipped flow'r" (*Burns*). **Tiny** goes even further than *diminutive* or *wee* in suggesting extreme littleness or a smallness out of proportion to most things of its kind or in comparison with all other things; as, "if such *tiny* entities as the cells of the body are to be regarded as having their own life" (*Inge*); "the behavior of the invisible, intangible, inconceivably *tiny* electrons and atoms" (*Karl K. Darrow*). From *tiny* and *wee* come the colloquial variants **teeny** and **weeny,** now found chiefly in childish, playful, or jocose use: these terms occur also in paired or reduplicated forms, as *teeny-weeny*, *teeny-tiny*, as in, "One day this *teeny-tiny* woman put on her *teeny-tiny* bonnet and went out of her *teeny-tiny* house to take a *teeny-tiny* walk" (in the nursery story "The *Teeny-tiny* Woman"); "he gave a *weeny, weeny* yawn" (*Kate D. Wiggin*). **Minute** is often preferred by scientific and other writers who wish to give a more definite implication of extreme smallness or littleness; as, a *minute* animalcule; *minute* grains of sand; "the tremendous forces imprisoned in *minute* particles of matter" (*Inge*). **Microscopic** applies only to that which is so minute that (at least in its literal sense) it is observable only under a microscope; as, *microscopic* organisms. **Miniature** applies to that which is complete in itself but is built, drawn, made, or the like, on a very small scale; as, "It was one of the *miniature* Italian cities...all compact and complete, on the top of a mountain" (*L. P. Smith*); "We may thus picture an atom as a *miniature* solar system" (*Eddington*). In the fine arts, *miniature* applies to a type of painting (a *miniature* painting), which is typically a portrait painted on a small piece of ivory or metal, often brilliantly colored, and executed with nicety and delicacy so as to bring out each detail.

Ana. *Petty, puny, paltry, trifling, trivial.

Ant. Large. — *Con.* Big, great (see LARGE): vast, huge, immense, *enormous.

small arms. See under WEAPON.

smaller. *Less, lesser, fewer.

smart. **1** Bright, knowing, quick-witted, *intelligent, clever, alert.

Ana. *Sharp, keen, acute: *quick, ready, prompt, apt: *shrewd, astute, perspicacious.

Ant. Dull (*of mind*).

2 Modish, fashionable, *stylish, chic, dapper, dashing, spruce, natty, nifty, nobby, posh, toffish, brave, braw.

Ana. Elegant, exquisite (see CHOICE, *adj.*): *finished, consummate.

Ant. Dowdy, frowzy, blowzy.

smell, *n.* **Smell, scent, odor** (*or* **odour**), **aroma** come into comparison when they denote that property of a thing which makes it perceptible to the olfactory sense. **Smell** is not only the most general of these terms, but it is also the most colorless. It is the appropriate word when merely the sensation is indicated, and no hint of its source, quality, or character is necessary. "Our horses... often reared up and snorted violently at *smells* which we could not perceive" (*Landor*). "For tastes and *smells* and sounds and sights" (*Browning*). It is also the preferred term when accompanied by explicitly qualifying words or phrases; as, "the rank *smell* of weeds" (*Shak.*); "the damp earthy *smell*" (*Stevenson*); "a *smell* of marigold and jasmine stronger even than the reek of the dust" (*Kipling*). **Scent** (see also FRAGRANCE), in precise use, always carries the implication of a physical emanation from that which is smelled; thus, all substances that emit effluvia have a *scent;* things that give off effluvia often leave a *scent* after they have disappeared; the path followed by a person or an animal can be detected, especially by hounds that have a superior sense of smell, by tracing his (or its) *scent* or by following a *scent*. *Scent*, therefore, is the precise term to use when the emphasis is on the emanations or exhalations from an external object which reach the olfactory nerves rather than on the impression produced on the olfactory nerves. "The *scent* of the first wood fire upon the keen October air" (*Pater*). "If the air was void of sound, it was full of *scent*" (*Galsworthy*). "The heavy *scent* of damp, funereal flowers" (*Millay*). **Odor** is oftentimes indistinguishable from *scent*, for it too is thought of as something diffused and as something by means of which external objects are identified by the sense of smell. But the words are not always interchangeable, for *odor* usually implies abundance of effluvia (cf. *odorous* and *odoriferous*) and therefore does not suggest, as *scent* often does, the need of a delicate or highly sensitive sense of smell; as, Trixie knows her master by his *scent* (not *odor*); the *odors* (better than *scents*) of the kitchen clung to her clothes. For these reasons, *odor* usually implies general perceptibility and is the preferred word in scientific use, especially when the classification or description of types is attempted. "Science, while recognizing the potency of our sense of smell, has not yet satisfactorily classified and catalogued the many varieties of *odors* that we recognize" (*A. C. Morrison*). "Henning recognizes six outstanding *odors:* spicy, as cloves; flowery, as heliotrope; fruity, as apple; resinous, as turpentine; foul, as rotten egg; scorched, as tar" (*Webster's New Int. Dict., 2d Ed.*). **Aroma** usually adds to *odor* the implication of a penetrating, pervasive, or sometimes, a pungent quality; it may or may not imply delicacy or fragrance, but it seldom connotes unpleasantness; in very discriminating use, it often suggests something to be savored, and therefore may be used of things that appeal both to the sense of smell and taste, or by extension to one's aesthetic sense; as, the *aroma* of fresh coffee; the *aroma* of pines, spruces, and balsams; "the *aroma* of a wood fire is the significant part of a camper's delight" (*A. C. Morrison*); "what a rich *aroma* hangs about this judgment!" (*A. C. Benson*).

Ana. *Fragrance, redolence, perfume, bouquet, incense: savor, flavor (see TASTE).

smidgen *or* **smidge.** *Particle, bit, mite, smitch, whit, atom, iota, jot, tittle.

smile, *v.* **Smile, grin, simper, smirk** come into comparison as verbs meaning to express amusement, pleasure, or the like, by a brightening of the eyes and an upward curving of the corners of the mouth, and as nouns denoting such an expression of amusement, pleasure, or the like. **Smile** is the general term, capable of being qualified so as to suggest malign as well as benign pleasure or amusement; as, to *smile* tenderly or derisively; a sad or a bright *smile;* to *smile* at one's maiden efforts; to wear a set *smile.* **Grin** implies a broad smile that shows the teeth. It still often carries a suggestion of its earlier meaning—to show one's teeth, as a dog or wolf in anger or pain, in its still not infrequent implication of unnaturalness, of bewilderment, senselessness, or the like. "With rash and awkward force the chords [of a lyre] he [an idiot] shakes, And *grins* with wonder at the jar he makes" (*Cowper*). "They could not see the bitter smile Behind the painted *grin* he wore" (*E. R. Sill*). In current use, however, *grin* tends to imply naïve cheerfulness, mirth, or impishness; as, a boyish *grin.* "How cheerfully he seems to *grin,* How neatly spreads his claws, And welcomes little fishes in With gently *smiling* jaws!" (*Carroll*). **Simper** implies a silly, affected, or languishing smile; as, "*simpering* angels, palms, and harps divine" (*Pope*); "Forming his features into a set smile, and affectedly softening his voice, he added with a *simpering* air..." (*Austen*). **Smirk** suggests extreme self-consciousness and evident complacency or conceit; as, "Amilcare talked profusely, *smirked,* grimaced...writhed his hands" (*Hewlett*); "The faintest *smirk* of self-satisfaction alienates the hearer" (*T. E. Brown*).

Ant. Frown.

smile, *n.* Simper, smirk, grin. See under SMILE, *v.*

Ant. Frown.

smirk, *v.* Simper, grin, *smile.

smirk, *n.* Simper, grin, smile. See under SMILE, *v.*

smitch. *Particle, bit, mite, smidgen, whit, atom, iota, jot, tittle.

smite. *Strike, hit, slug, slap, swat, clout, punch, box, cuff.

Ana. *Beat, pummel, buffet: *punish, discipline, correct.

smog. Fog, mist, *haze, brume.

smooth, *adj.* **1** Even, plane, plain, flat, *level, flush.

Ana. *Sleek, slick, glossy, glabrous: polished, burnished (see POLISH).

Ant. Rough. — *Con.* Harsh, uneven, rugged, scabrous (see ROUGH).

2 Effortless, *easy, light, simple, facile.

Ana. Agreeable, *pleasant, pleasing, gratifying, grateful: serene, tranquil, *calm, placid, peaceful.

Ant. Labored. — *Con.* *Hard, difficult, arduous.

3 Bland, diplomatic, politic, *suave, urbane.

Ana. *Disarming, ingratiating, insinuating: polite, courteous, courtly (see CIVIL): oily, unctuous, sleek, *fulsome.

Ant. Bluff. — *Con.* Blunt, brusque, curt, gruff, crusty (see BLUFF).

smörgåsbord. *Appetizer, hors d'oeuvre, antipasto, apéritif.

smug. Self-complacent, self-satisfied, priggish, *complacent.

Ana. Self-respecting, self-esteeming, self-admiring (see primitive verbs under REGARD, *n.*): pharisaical, sanctimonious, hypocritical (see under HYPOCRISY).

snaffle, *v.* Curb, check, bridle, *restrain, inhibit.

Ana. *Guide, lead: control, manage, direct (see CONDUCT, *v.*).

snag, *n.* *Obstacle, obstruction, impediment, bar.

Ana. *Projection, protuberance: *difficulty, hardship, vicissitude: barring *or* bar, blocking *or* block, hindering *or* hindrance (see corresponding verbs at HINDER).

snappish. *Irritable, fractious, peevish, waspish, petulant, pettish, huffy, huffish, fretful, querulous.

Ana. Testy, techy, touchy, cranky, *irascible: surly, crabbed, morose (see SULLEN).

snappy. *Pungent, piquant, poignant, racy, spicy.

Ana. *Sharp, keen, acute: vivacious, *lively, animated: *quick, prompt, ready: smart, dashing, chic, modish (see STYLISH).

snare, *n.* Trap, *lure, bait, decoy.

Ana. *Trick, ruse, stratagem, maneuver, artifice, feint, wile: trickery, *deception, chicanery, chicane, subterfuge.

snare, *v.* Ensnare, trap, entrap, bag, *catch, capture, nab, cop.

Ana. *Lure, entice, inveigle, tempt, seduce, decoy.

snarl, *n.* *Confusion, disorder, chaos, disarray, jumble, clutter, pie, muddle.

Ana. Complexity, complication, intricateness *or* intricacy (see corresponding adjectives at COMPLEX): *difficulty, hardship.

snatch, *v.* Grasp, grab, clutch, seize, *take.

Ana. *Catch, capture, nab, cop: *pull, drag, draw.

sneak, *v.* Slink, skulk, *lurk, couch.

sneer, *v.* *Scoff, jeer, gird, flout, gibe, fleer.

Ana. Deride, taunt, mock, *ridicule: scout, *despise, scorn, disdain.

snitch. *Steal, pilfer, filch, purloin, lift, pinch, swipe, cop.

snoopy. *Curious, inquisitive, prying, nosy.

Ana. Meddlesome, officious, intrusive, *impertinent, obtrusive: interfering, interposing (see INTERPOSE).

snug. **1** Trim, trig, shipshape, *neat, tidy, spick-and-span.

Ana. Compact, *close: *orderly, methodical, systematic.

2 *Comfortable, cozy, easy, restful, reposeful.

Ana. *Safe, secure: *familiar, intimate, close: sheltered, harbored (see HARBOR, *v.*).

so. *Therefore, hence, consequently, then, accordingly.

soak, *v.* **Soak, saturate, drench, steep, impregnate, sog, sop, ret, waterlog** come into comparison when they mean to subject or to be subjected to the influence of water or, especially in figurative use, of something like water, so as to become permeated with it. **Soak** literally suggests immersion in a liquid so that the substance absorbs the moisture and becomes thoroughly wetted, softened, dissolved, or otherwise affected by it; as, to *soak* a sponge in water; the blotter has *soaked* up nearly all the spilled ink; to *soak* out the dirt from soiled clothes; *soak* the tapioca before cooking it. Figuratively, the term implies a comparable immersion of one thing in another so that the latter is taken up by or enters into the very fibers or tissues of the former and becomes a part of it; as, he *soaked* himself in the poetry of the great romanticists; "The shadowy copse was *soaked* in piney sweetness, golden and dim" (*R. Macaulay*); "*Soaked* in the best prejudices and manners of his class" (*Galsworthy*). **Saturate** may or may not imply a soaking: distinctively it stresses absorption as of a liquid or other substance up to a point where no more can be absorbed; thus, the air is said to be *saturated* when it can retain no more moisture in the form of vapor; one's clothes may be described as *saturated* when they are so damp that the addition of further moisture would make them dripping wet; a solution, as of salt or boric acid in water, is said to be *saturated* when the liquid has dissolved as much of the substance as it can retain under the circumstances as of heat, pressure, or the like. Consequently, in its figurative use, *saturate* usually implies a becoming imbued or infused with something in exactly the right measure or in the most useful degree; as, "To a mind not thoroughly *saturated* with the tolerating maxims of the Gospel" (*Burke*); the entire poem is *saturated* with imagination. "*Saturated* with experience of a particular class of materials, an expert intuitively feels whether a newly reported fact is probable or not" (*W. James*). **Drench** literally implies a thorough wetting by pouring water (such as rain) or other liquid; as, "They were in an open buggy and were *drenched* to the skin" (*Cather*). In its extended sense the term, in very precise use, always carries an implication of being soaked or saturated by something that pours or is poured down upon one; as, "The solid mountains shone... *drenched* in empyrean light" (*Wordsworth*); "the new life with which it *drenches* the spirits" (*Shelley*). **Steep** implies a soaking of one thing in another (literally, a liquid); in current use, it commonly suggests the extraction of the essence of one thing so that it becomes part and parcel of the other; thus, one *steeps* tea leaves in boiling water in order to make the beverage tea. In extended use, the acquirement of the qualities of one thing by a process suggestive of such steeping is often implied (as, "epistles...*steeped* in the phraseology of the Greek mysteries"—*Inge;* "language simple and sensuous and *steeped* in the picturesque imagery of what they saw and felt"—*Lowes*), but often the term means little more than to envelop as with the color, light, or the like, shed from or emanated by something else (as, "her tall spars and rigging *steeped* in a bath of red-gold"—*Conrad;* "The world was all *steeped* in sunshine"—*D. H. Lawrence*). **Impregnate,** less than any of these terms, carries a suggestion of soaking in water; otherwise it implies the interpenetration of one thing by another until the former is everywhere imbued with the latter; as, to *impregnate* rubber with sulphur; "When my mind was, as it were, strongly *impregnated* with the Johnsonian aether" (*Boswell*); "this poem, everywhere *impregnated* with original excellence" (*Wordsworth*). **Sog,** a dialectal term, implies a soaked and sodden condition; as, "*sogged* leaves" (*P. Gosse*); *sogged* shoes. **Sop** usually applies to food soaked as in meat juices, wine, or the like (as, to *sop* one's bread in gravy; to serve cake *sopped* in sherry and covered with a soft custard), but it may apply also to anything, such as soil, that is heavily soaked with liquid; as, *sopping* wet clothes; to *sop* one's plants with too much water. **Ret,** now chiefly a technical term, often applies to a soaking or exposure to moisture that is part of a processing of materials or of seasoning or conditioning them; as, to *ret* hemp or flax; to *ret* timber. **Waterlog** suggests a thorough soaking or drenching that renders a thing either useless or too heavy and sodden for floating, cultivating, or the like; as, a *waterlogged* rowboat; to *waterlog* soil by lack of proper drainage.

Ana. *Dip, immerse, submerge: *permeate, pervade, penetrate.

soak, *n.* *Drunkard, inebriate, alcoholic, dipsomaniac, sot, toper, tosspot, tippler.

soapy. Sleek, *fulsome, oily, unctuous, oleaginous.

soar. *Rise, arise, ascend, mount, tower, rocket, levitate, surge.

Ana. *Fly, dart, shoot: aspire, *aim.

sob, *v.* Moan, groan, *sigh.

Ana. Weep, wail, *cry, blubber.

sob, *n.* Moan, groan, sigh. See under SIGH, *v.*

Ana. Weeping, wailing, crying, blubbering (see CRY, *v.*).

sober. 1 Sober, temperate, continent, unimpassioned come into comparison when they mean having or manifesting self-control or the mastery of one's emotions, passions, or appetites. **Sober** etymologically implies freedom from intoxication: this implication is still often found with another, such as that of habitual abstinence from intoxicating liquors or merely of not being drunk at the time in question; as, he is, by reputation, a *sober* man; he was *sober* when he delivered the blow. As here especially considered (see also SERIOUS), *sober* implies a cool head, great composure, especially under strain or excitement, and freedom from passion, prejudice, fear, or the like; as, he was the only one who could keep a *sober* head during the panic; sound, *sober* advice; a man of *sober* judgment. **Temperate** (as here compared: see also MODERATE, 1) implies control over the expression of one's feelings, passions, appetites, or desires, or the restrained exercise of one's rights, powers, or privileges, with the result that one never exceeds the bounds of what is right or proper or decorous; as, "That *sober* freedom out of which there springs Our loyal passion for our *temperate* kings!" (*Tennyson*); "in what *temperate* language Horace clothes his maxims....Not a flourish! Not a gesture!" (*A. Repplier*); "he *temperately* used the privileges of his office" (*Quiller-Couch*). **Continent** carries a stronger implication of deliberate restraint placed upon oneself and upon one's feelings seeking expression, or upon one's desires (especially sexual desires) seeking satisfaction; as, "I pray you, have a *continent* forbearance till the speed of his rage goes slower" (*Shak.*); "My past life Hath been as *continent*, as chaste, as true, As I am now unhappy" (*Shak.*); "Not...a subject of irregular and interrupted impulses of virtue, but a *continent*, persisting, immovable person" (*Emerson*). **Unimpassioned** so stresses the absence of heat, ardor, or fervor, that it often connotes lack of feeling and, therefore, coldness, stiffness, hardness of heart, or the like (as, "[Selfishness] frozen, *unimpassioned*, spiritless, Shunning the light"—*Shelley*), but in very discriminating use, it often implies a subduing of feeling or passion by allowing reason to gain the mastery (as, the *unimpassioned* administration of disciplinary measures; "one who comes...to ask In weighed and measured *unimpassioned* words, A gift, which, if...denied, He must withdraw, content upon his cheek, Despair within his soul"—*Browning*).

Ana. Abstaining, refraining, forbearing (see REFRAIN): forgoing, eschewing, abnegating (see FORGO): *cool, collected, composed: reasonable, *rational.

Ant. Drunk: excited.

2 Grave, *serious, sedate, staid, solemn, earnest.

Ana. *Decorous, decent, demure, proper: *calm, placid, tranquil, serene: dispassionate, impartial, *fair, equitable.

Ant. Gay. — *Con.* Light, frivolous, flippant, light-minded (see corresponding nouns at LIGHTNESS).

sobriety. *Temperance, abstinence, abstemiousness, continence.

Ana. Moderateness, temperateness (see corresponding adjectives at MODERATE): quietness, stillness (see corresponding adjectives at STILL): seriousness, gravity, sedateness (see corresponding adjectives at SERIOUS).

Ant. Drunkenness: excitement.

sociable. *Gracious, cordial, affable, genial.

Ana. *Social, companionable, convivial, gregarious: intimate, *familiar, close: *amiable, obliging, complaisant, good-natured.

Ant. Unsociable.

social, *adj.* **Social, gregarious, co-operative, convivial, companionable, hospitable** are not actually synonymous terms but they invite comparison because they involve, and often stress, the idea of having or manifesting a liking for the company of others. **Social** is now often used in the general sense of having to do with society, that is, society as an organic or organized unit composed of all men or of all in a community in which the individual is but a part of a whole; as, the *social* order; *social* work; *social* service. Consequently, its more specific sense of characterized by or resulting from a mingling with others as one's fellows, companions, or friends, is not always clearly distinguished; as, there are not many opportunities for *social* activities in this town; they have pleasant *social* relations with all the members of their church; "if . . . every one is talking at once it is evidently because of the *social* desire to contribute to the conversation" (*Brownell*). *Social* is now practically obsolete in the older sense of *sociable* (see *sociable* under GRACIOUS); as, "Preserve him *social*, cheerful, and serene" (*Pope*). **Gregarious** implies a desire or an instinct (often called the *herd instinct*) which drives not only persons but animals to associate with others of their kind, and to form communities, colonies, flocks, sets, or other groups: the term connotes a tendency to solidarity and, often, an aversion to solitariness, but it seldom suggests interest in others for any reason such as a friendly attitude, a sense that they are one's fellows, or a belief that union will be to their advantage as well as one's own. "They are not . . . kind, only sentimental; not *social*, only *gregarious;* not considerate, only polite" (*Shaw*). "It might be inferred . . . that I am an inveterately unsociable person; but such is not the case. I am extremely *gregarious* at the right time and place" (*A. C. Benson*). "Impelled by *gregarious* instincts, Peter followed the crowd" (*H. G. Wells*). **Co-operative,** especially as applied to persons, implies the recognition of common ends which serve as the objectives of the group, the community, or society at large and of the need of mutual assistance in the attainment of those ends: the term, therefore, usually suggests helpfulness and a willingness to work for the welfare or well-being of the entire group; as, the new president of the society found that few of the members were *co-operative;* the citizens of Middleburgh were unusually *co-operative;* "With regard to a young English statesman, we want to know two things mainly—his intrinsic value, and his *co-operative* capacity" (*Pall Mall Gazette*). **Convivial,** which etymologically means festive (as, *convivial* occasions), is now more and more often applied to persons and groups that manifest enjoyment of the company of others, especially in festivities where joviality and eating and drinking form the chief, though not necessarily the only, entertainment; as, "the plump *convivial* parson" (*Cowper*); "dinners *convivial* and political" (*Shelley*); "she was a somewhat sombre figure in that *convivial* household" (*Cather*). **Companionable** implies a special fitness by nature or disposition for friendly and intimate association with others. "Thus we lived on unsocially together. More *companionable* . . . were the large crawling, running insects—crickets, beetles, and others" (*Hudson*). **Hospitable** usually implies a disposition to receive and to entertain not only one's friends, but especially strangers: it therefore stresses receptiveness (sometimes mental receptiveness) and generosity more than any of the preceding terms; as, a *hospitable* race; a *hospitable* family; "visits to . . . great *hospitable* houses" (*H. Ellis*); a mind *hospitable* to ideas.

Ana. *Gracious, cordial, sociable, genial, affable: *amicable, neighborly, friendly.

Ant. Unsocial, antisocial, asocial.

socialist. *Collectivist, communist, Bolshevist, nihilist, anarchist.

society. **1** Elite, gentlefolk, *aristocracy, nobility, gentry, county.

2 *Association, order, club.

soft, *adj.* **Soft, bland, mild, gentle, lenient, balmy** come into comparison when they are applied to things with respect to the sensations they evoke, or the impressions they produce, and agree in meaning pleasantly agreeable because devoid of all harshness or roughness. **Soft,** as here compared, is applied chiefly to that which soothes, tranquilizes, or induces a sensation of delicious quiet; as, "As sweet as balm, as *soft* as air, as gentle" (*Shak.*); "A *soft* answer turneth away wrath" (*Proverbs* xv. 1); "And ever, against eating cares, Lap me in *soft* Lydian airs" (*Milton*); "To feel for ever its *soft* fall and swell" (*Keats*). This positive connotation is apparent in the discriminating use of *soft* even when its major implication is the absence or the subduing of some quality such as pungency, vividness, intensity, force, or the like; thus, a *soft* fragrance is lacking in richness but is quietly agreeable and not overpowering; a *soft* color is lacking in vividness, but it is mellow rather than dull; a *soft* voice is lacking in resonance but it is not faint or feeble, but is pleasantly low and without a trace of harshness or stridency. "The far shore of the river's mouth was just *soft* dusk" (*Galsworthy*). "Or the *soft* shock Of wizened apples falling From an old tree" (*Millay*). **Bland,** which was once applied almost exclusively to persons and their manners (see SUAVE), is now increasingly applied to things which in earlier times might be described as *soft.* It has, however, carried over its original connotations of smoothness and suavity into this use, so that it suggests not so much a tranquilizing effect as the absence of anything that might disturb, excite, stimulate, or the like; thus, foods and beverages which are not unpleasant to the taste yet are lacking in pungency, tang, fruitiness, strong savor, and the like, may be described as *bland* (as, a *bland* wine; *bland* fruits such as pears and peaches; a *bland* dessert such as a custard or junket); a *bland* climate is not only free from extremes, but is neither stimulating nor depressing. "That *bland* and composed country-side [was chosen] for the site of the grave [of Matthew Arnold] in preference to the stern Cumberland hills, which the dead had loved too" (*C. E. Montague*). "Full, clear, with something *bland* and suave, each note [of the bell] floated through the air like a globe of silver" (*Cather*). Both **mild** and **gentle** stress moderation; they are applied chiefly to things that are not, as they might be or often are, harsh, rough, strong, violent, unduly stimulating, or irritating, and are therefore pleasant or agreeable by contrast; as, a *mild* cigar; *mild* weather; a *gentle* breeze; a *gentle* heat. However, both words are capable of connoting positively pleasurable sensations, *mild* often being applied to that which induces a feeling of quiet measured beauty or of serenity, *gentle* to that which evokes a mood of placidity or tranquility, or even more often, a sense of restrained power or force. "Some did shed A clear *mild* beam like Hesperus, while the sea Yet glows with fading sunlight" (*Shelley*). "A thick brake, Nested and quiet in a valley *mild*" (*Keats*). "O sleep, O *gentle* sleep, Nature's soft nurse" (*Shak.*). "They are as *gentle* As zephyrs blowing below the violet" (*Shak.*). **Lenient,** as here considered (see also FORBEARING), is applicable chiefly to things that are grateful to the senses or to the mind because they exert an emollient, relaxing, softening, or assuasive influence; as, a *lenient* balm. "And earthly sounds, though sweet and well combined, And *lenient* as soft opiates to the mind" (*Cowper*). "Pangs of grief for *lenient* time too keen" (*Wordsworth*). The word has, in the course of time, however, taken over from its later but more frequent sense a connotation of merciful indulgence or of mitigation of severity, which tends to weaken or destroy its original sense; thus, the common expression "the *lenient* hand of time" originally meant the softening and assuaging influence of time (as, "Time, that on all things lays his *lenient* hand, Yet tames not this [the passion for praise]"—*Pope*), but in current use, it often implies indulgence or kindliness on the part of time (as, the *lenient* hand of time had left no marks upon her brow, for it was as smooth as ivory). **Balmy** also implies a soothing influence on the senses or mind, but above and beyond this it suggests refreshment and sometimes exhilaration. Coupled with one or another of these implications, there is also frequently a suggestion of fragrance, especially the aromatic fragrance of balm-producing trees. "Tired Nature's sweet restorer, *balmy* sleep!" (*Young*). "O *balmy* gales of soul-reviving air!" (*Cowper*). "Sweet sleep, whose dews Are sweeter than the *balmy* tears of even" (*Shelley*).

Ana. Moderated, tempered, attempered (see MODERATE, *v.*): smooth, effortless, *easy: velvety, silken, *sleek, slick: serene, tranquil, *calm, placid, peaceful.

Ant. Hard: stern. — *Con.* *Rough, harsh, uneven, rugged: *intense, vehement.

sog. *Soak, saturate, drench, steep, impregnate, sop, ret, waterlog.

sojourn, *v.* *Reside, lodge, stay, put up, stop, live, dwell.

solace, *v.* *Comfort, console.

Ana. *Relieve, assuage, mitigate, allay, alleviate, lighten: gladden, rejoice, delight, *please, gratify.

sole, *adj.* *Single, unique, solitary, lone, separate, particular.

Ana. Alone, *only: exclusive, picked, *select.

solecism. 1 Solecism, barbarism, impropriety designate in rhetoric a violation of the standard of good use in language. A **solecism** is a construction which violates the rules of syntax, or less precisely the approved idiom; a **barbarism** is an expression not permissible in reputable use because it is etymologically corrupt, or an importation not yet anglicized, or borrowed from cant or jargon, or a smart coinage; an **impropriety** is a word or phrase employed in a sense contrary to good usage; thus, "between you and I" and "he don't" are *solecisms;* "Humans" for "persons," "burgle," and "irregardless" are *barbarisms;* the use of "transpire" in the sense of "happen" is an *impropriety.*

2 *Anachronism.

solemn. 1 *Ceremonial, ceremonious, formal, conventional.

Ana. Liturgical, ritualistic (see corresponding nouns at FORM): *full, complete, plenary: imposing, august, majestic, magnificent (see GRAND).

2 *Serious, grave, sedate, earnest, staid, sober.

Ana. Impressive, *moving: sublime, superb (see SPLENDID): pompous, ostentatious (see SHOWY).

solemnize. Celebrate, observe, *keep, commemorate.

solicit. 1 *Ask, request.

Ana. *Resort, refer, apply, go, turn: *beg, entreat, beseech, implore, supplicate.

2 *Invite, bid, court, woo.

Ana. Importune, adjure, conjure (see BEG): *demand, claim, exact: evoke, elicit, extract, extort, *educe.

solicitor. *Lawyer, attorney, counselor, barrister, counsel, advocate, proctor, procurator.

solicitous. Careful, concerned, anxious, worried. See under CARE, *n.*

Ana. Apprehensive, *fearful, afraid: agitated, disturbed, disquieted, upset (see DISCOMPOSE): uneasy, fidgety, jittery (see IMPATIENT).

Ant. Unmindful: negligent.

solicitude. *Care, concern, anxiety, worry.

Ana. Misgiving, *apprehension, foreboding, presentiment: compunction, *qualm, scruple: *fear, alarm, consternation, dismay.

Ant. Negligence: unmindfulness.

solid. *Firm, hard.

Ana. Compact, *close, dense: consolidated, concentrated, compacted (see COMPACT, *v.*).

Ant. Fluid, liquid.

solidarity. *Unity, union, integrity.

Ana. Consolidation, concentration, unification (see corresponding verbs at COMPACT): co-operation, concurrence, combination (see corresponding verbs at UNITE).

solitary. 1 *Alone, lonely, lonesome, lone, forlorn, lorn, desolate.

Ana. Isolated, secluded (see corresponding nouns at SOLITUDE): retired, withdrawn (see GO): forsaken, deserted, abandoned (see ABANDON).

2 *Single, sole, unique, lone, separate, particular.

Ana. Alone, *only.

solitude. Solitude, isolation, seclusion come into comparison as meaning the state of one that is alone. **Solitude** applies not only to a physical condition where there are no others of one's kind with whom one can associate in any way (as, "O *Solitude!* where are the charms That sages have seen in thy face? . . . I am out of humanity's reach . . . Never hear the sweet music of speech, I start at the sound of my own"—*Cowper*) but more often to the state, physical or mental, of one who by wish or by compulsion is cut off from neighbors, friends, housemates, or the like (as, "my spirits will not bear *solitude.* I must have employment and society"—*Austen;* "that inward eye [imagination] Which is the bliss of *solitude*"—*Wordsworth;* "to have the choice of society and *solitude* alike"—*A. C. Benson*). Sometimes, the term refers entirely to a mental state and comes very close in meaning to *loneliness,* implying a lack of intimate association with, rather than a separation from, others. "Sophia . . . had not been able to escape from the *solitude* imposed by existence in hotels. Since her marriage she had never spoken to a woman in the way of intimacy" (*Bennett*). **Isolation** stresses detachment from others, either because of causes beyond one's control or because of one's own wish. Since the term may refer to communities and to things as well as to individuals, it often suggests a cutting off physically rather than a frame of mind such as loneliness or depression; as, the *isolation* of a country surrounded on all sides by enemies; "the solemn *isolation* of a man against the sea and sky" (*Stevenson*); "the axiom . . . that the artist and man of letters ought not to work in cloistral *isolation,* removed from public affairs" (*Quiller-Couch*); "the one place in the house where he could get *isolation*" (*Cather*). "Whether splendidly isolated or dangerously isolated, I will not now debate; but for my part, I think splendidly isolated, because this *isolation* of England comes from her superiority" (*Laurier*). **Seclusion** implies a shutting away, or a keeping apart of oneself or another, so that one is either inaccessible to others or is accessible only under very difficult conditions. Usually the term connotes a condition such as confinement in an asylum, a prison, or the like, or withdrawal from the world, as to a monastery, or from human companionship, as to a place of retirement or retreat. "The *seclusion* of their life was such that she would hardly be likely to learn the news except through a special messenger" (*Hardy*). "Shaftesbury...a man of fragile physical constitution...was not a childish hypochondriac in *seclusion*, but a man in the world" (*H. Ellis*). "In his youth, Joseph had wished to lead a life of *seclusion* and solitary devotion; but the truth was, he could not be happy for long without human intercourse" (*Cather*).

Ana. Retreat, refuge, asylum (see SHELTER, *n.*): retirement, withdrawal (see corresponding verbs at GO).

solvent. **Solvent, dissolvent, resolvent, menstruum, alkahest** agree in denoting a substance that dissolves, or mixes homogeneously with, another substance. **Solvent,** the most general of these terms, usually denotes a liquid or a solid in a fluid state (as molten metal) that dissolves another liquid, a gas, or, most commonly, a solid; as, water is a *solvent* for salt; ether is a *solvent* for fats; molten iron is a *solvent* for carbon, with which it forms the alloy steel. **Dissolvent** is now practically displaced by *solvent,* except in chemistry and medicine when there is the intent to imply disintegration; as, a *dissolvent* for gallstones; there are few *dissolvents* for gold. **Resolvent,** a nonscientific and comparatively uncommon term, is practically synonymous in meaning with *dissolvent.* **Menstruum** is applied to solvents for solids and today is restricted mostly to use in pharmacy; as, alcohol is the *menstruum* used for many drugs. **Alkahest** is a term originally used by alchemists to denote a hypothetical solvent for all substances.

somatic. *Bodily, physical, corporeal, corporal.

some, *adj.* **Some, any** are comparable when they mean one, not designated, out of a number. In general, **some** emphasizes lack of specification, **any** stresses indifference of choice or lack of limitation; as, "*some* unsuspected isle in far-off seas" (*Browning*); come and see us *some* day; come *any* day that is convenient for you; "and *any* step which in our dance we tread" (*Shelley*).

somnolent. *Sleepy, drowsy, slumberous.

Ana. Sluggish, stuporous, comatose, *lethargic: inert, *inactive, passive, supine.

sonance. *Sound, noise.

soon, *adv.* *Early, beforehand, betimes.

sop. *Soak, saturate, drench, steep, impregnate, sog, ret, waterlog.

sophism. Sophistry, casuistry, *fallacy, paralogism.

sophistical. Fallacious, casuistical, paralogistic. See under FALLACY.

Ant. Valid. — *Con.* Cogent, sound, convincing, telling (see VALID).

sophisticate. *Adulterate, load, weight, doctor, deacon.

sophistry. *Fallacy, sophism, casuistry, paralogism.

Ana. Plausibility, speciousness (see corresponding adjectives at PLAUSIBLE): equivocation, *ambiguity, tergiversation: evading *or* evasion, avoiding *or* avoidance (see corresponding verbs at ESCAPE).

soppy. *Sentimental, romantic, mawkish, maudlin, mushy, slushy.

sorcery. *Magic, witchcraft, witchery, wizardry, alchemy, thaumaturgy.

sordid. *Mean, ignoble, abject.

Ana. *Mercenary, venal: squalid, foul, filthy, nasty, *dirty: *comtemptible, despicable, sorry, scurvy, cheap, beggarly.

sorrow, *n.* **Sorrow, grief, heartache, anguish, woe, dole, regret** agree in the idea of distress of mind. **Sorrow** is the most general term, implying a sense of one's own or another's loss, or a sense of guilt. "When you depart from me, *sorrow* abides and happiness takes his leave" (*Shak.*). **Grief** is poignant sorrow, especially for some definite cause. "*Grief*...of so flood-gate and o'erbearing nature That it engluts and swallows other sorrows" (*Shak.*). **Heartache** is used especially of sorrow that springs from disappointment, as of hope or love, and which gives little or no outward indication; as, the *heartaches* of a would-be author. "The *heart-aching* that is concealed within the glare and tinsel exposed to the audience" (*W. Ballantine*). **Anguish** is excruciating or torturing grief or dread. "*Anguish* so great that human nature is driven by it from cover to cover, seeking refuge and finding none" (*R. Macaulay*). "I had that terrible pain before playing —that *anguish* which is not to be described" (*Paderewski*). **Woe** is deep or inconsolable grief or misery. "Outcast from God...condemned To waste eternal days in *woe*" (*Milton*). **Dole** (archaic or dialectal) is woe vented in weeping, moaning, or wailing. "Let stremes of teares supply the place of sleepe; Let...all that may augment My *doole,* drawe neare!" (*Spenser*). **Regret** seldom implies a sorrow that shows itself in tears, or sobs, or moans; usually it connotes pain of mind such as deep disappointment, fruitless longing, heartache, or spiritual anguish; consequently, the term is applicable within a wide range that begins with the disappointment one feels (sometimes sincerely but sometimes merely as suggested by the language required by convention) in declining an invitation and ends with the pangs of remorse for something done or left undone or of hopeless repining for that which (or for one who) can never be restored; as, to decline an invitation to dinner with *regret;* "Mrs. Manson, with a sigh that might have been either of *regret* or relief" (*E. Wharton*); "Dante's... nostalgia, his bitter *regrets* for past happiness" (*T. S. Eliot*). "But time hath power to soften all *regrets*" (*Wordsworth*).

Ana. Mourning, grieving (see GRIEVE): *distress, suffering, misery, agony: melancholy, dejection, *sadness, depression.

Ant. Joy.

sorrow, *v.* Mourn, *grieve.

Ana. *Cry, weep, wail, keen: sob, moan, groan (see SIGH, *v*).

sorry. Pitiable, *contemptible, despicable, scurvy, cheap, beggarly.

Ana. *Mean, ignoble, sordid, abject: *miserable, wretched: paltry, *petty, trifling, trivial.

sort, *n.* *Type, kind, nature, description, character, stripe, kidney, ilk.

sort, *v.* *Assort, classify, alphabetize, pigeonhole.

Ana. Arrange, methodize, systematize, *order: cull, pick, *choose, select.

sot. *Drunkard, inebriate, alcoholic, dipsomaniac, soak, toper, tosspot, tippler.

soul. 1 *Mind, intellect, psyche, brain, brains, intelligence, wit, wits.

Ana. Powers, faculties, functions (see singular nouns at POWER).

2 Soul, spirit are often convertible terms, especially when they denote an immaterial entity that is distinguishable from and superior to the body with which it is associated during the life of the individual and that, in most religious beliefs, is regarded as immortal, surviving after the death of the body. **Soul** (as here compared: see also MIND, 2) is usually preferred when the emphasis is upon the thing considered as an entity having certain functions, responsibilities, aspects, or a given destiny: **spirit** (as here compared: see also COURAGE, APPARITION) is preferred when the stress is upon the quality, the constitution, the movement, or the activity of that entity; thus, in idiomatic language, one saves one's *soul* (seldom, if ever, *spirit*); one sells one's *soul* (not *spirit*) for money; one prays for the *souls* (not *spirits*) of the dead; one does the right thing for one's *soul's* (not *spirit's*) sake; one lifts up one's *spirit* (rather than *soul*) in prayer; to come close to God in *spirit* (rather than *soul*); a man fervent in *spirit;* "The *spirit* indeed is willing, but the flesh is weak" (*Matthew* xxvi. 41). *Soul,* both in the sense here emphasized and in the extended meanings derived from that sense, usually suggests a relation to or a connection with a body or with a physical or material entity to which it gives life or power; *spirit* in both its restricted and extended senses suggests an opposition (often an antithesis) to that which is physical, corporeal, material, or the like, and, often but not always, a repugnance to the latter; as, it often takes a war to lay bare the *soul* of a people; to obey the *spirit* rather than the letter of a law. "Gibbon's magnificent saying, that the Greek language gave a *soul* to the objects of sense and a body to the abstractions of metaphysics" (*Quiller-Couch*). "Those who believe in the reality of a world of the *spirit*—the poet, the artist, the mystic—are at one in believing that there are other domains than that of physics" (*Jeans*). *Spirit* only, and not *soul,* is used of incorporeal beings such as angels, devils, and the like; as, "I can call *spirits* from the vasty deep" (*Shak.*).

Ant. Body.

sound, *adj.* **1** *Healthy, wholesome, robust, hale, well.

Ana. *Vigorous, lusty, nervous, energetic, strenuous: *strong, sturdy, stalwart, stout: intact, whole, entire, *perfect.

2 *Valid, cogent, convincing, telling.

Ana. *Impeccable, flawless, faultless, errorless: *correct, exact, precise, accurate: *rational, reasonable.

Ant. Fallacious.

sound, *n.*[1] *Strait, straits, channel, passage, narrows.

sound, *n.*[2] **Sound, noise, sonance** are here compared as meaning a sensation or effect produced by the stimulation of the auditory nerves and auditory centers of the brain. **Sound** is the general term, applicable to anything that is heard, regardless of its loudness or softness, its pleasantness or unpleasantness, its meaningfulness, or its meaninglessness. "Lord Valleys...heard a *sound,* rather shrill and tentative, swell into hoarse, high clamour, and suddenly die out" (*Galsworthy*). **Noise** in its earliest English use applied to sounds emanating from many persons and usually suggested a clamor made by mingled outcries or shouts: gradually, however, it came to imply a disagreeably loud or harsh sound of any kind whether made by a single person or thing or an aggregate of persons or things; as, the terrific *noise* of an explosion; he could not endure the *noise* (or *noises*) of the machine shop; "the hell of distracting *noises* made by the carts, the cabs, the carriages" (*W. H. Mallock*). Although the connotations of unpleasantness and discordance still usually distinguish *noise* from *sound,* the former term does not invariably carry that connotation in recent use, for it is often applied to a sound that merely engages the attention. "Yet still the sails made on A pleasant *noise* till noon, A *noise* like of a hidden brook In the leafy month of June" (*Coleridge*). "There was no sound, not one tiny *noise* of water, wind in trees, or man" (*Galsworthy*). **Sonance** is occasionally found in general use in place of *sound* when the stress is on the quality of the sound as heard by the discriminating ear; as, poets who pay little attention to the *sonance* of their verses; "the far-off mellow *sonance* of a cowbell" (*E. Ferber*). In technical phonetic use, the term applies chiefly to the quality of being voiced (i.e., uttered with vibration of the vocal cords); as, vowels, and certain consonants such as b, d, g, z, have *sonance.*

Ant. Silence.

soupçon. Suspicion, suggestion, *touch, tincture, tinge, shade, smack, spice, dash, vein, strain, streak.

sour. Sour, acid, acidulous, tart, dry mean having a taste devoid of sweetness. All but *dry* suggest the taste of lemons, vinegar, or of most unripe fruits. **Sour** is more often applied to that which through fermentation has lost its sweet or neutral taste or, sometimes, smell; it may or may not suggest rancidness; as, *sour* milk, *sour* wine, *sour* bread, *sour* garbage: **acid,** to that which has such a taste in its natural or normal state; as, *acid* fruits, *acid* drinks. **Acidulous** and **tart** are applied, as a rule, to things which may be described as *acid; acidulous* implying a less-than-average degree of acidity; *tart,* a sharp, but often an agreeable, acidulousness or, sometimes, acidity; as, some mineral waters are pleasantly *acidulous;* most cooks prefer *tart* apples for pies and puddings. **Dry** is usually applied to wines which, although without a suspicion of sweetness, are bland and therefore neither definitely acid nor definitely sour.

In their figurative senses, **sour** applies especially to that which is crabbed or morose; **acidulous** and **tart,** to that which is characterized by asperity, pungency, or sharpness; **acid,** partly by allusion to the corrosive powers of some acids, to that which is biting or caustic. "He [Swift] had a countenance *sour* and severe" (*Johnson*). "A *sour,* malignant, envious disposition" (*Burke*). "A *tart* temper never mellows with age" (*Irving*). "I thought I might venture to say that her mother must be very old; she interrupted me *tartly,* and said, no, her mother had been married extremely young" (*Walpole*). " 'Well, if you don't care about it,' he said, with a slightly *acid* inflection, 'I won't ask you every time' " (*Arch. Marshall*). "An intelligent but *acid* weekly paper" (*R. Macaulay*).

Ana. *Bitter, acrid: *sharp, keen: *astringent, constringent: morose, *sullen, glum, crabbed, saturnine, dour.

source. *Origin, root, inception, provenance, provenience, prime mover.

Ana. Beginning, commencement, starting *or* start (see corresponding verbs at BEGIN): *cause, determinant, antecedent.

Ant. Termination: outcome.

souse. *Dip, immerse, submerge, duck, dunk.

Ana. *Soak, steep, saturate, impregnate.

souvenir. Remembrance, recollection, *memory, reminiscence, mind.

sovereign, *adj.* **1** *Dominant, predominant, paramount, preponderant, preponderating.

Ana. *Supreme, transcendent, surpassing: absolute, *ultimate.

2 Independent, *free, autonomous, autonomic, autarchic, autarkic.

Ana. Highest, loftiest (see positive adjectives at HIGH): *chief, principal, foremost: governing, ruling (see GOVERN): commanding, directing (see COMMAND, *v.*).

sovereignty. Independence, freedom, autonomy, autarky, autarchy. See under FREE, *adj.*

Ana. *Supremacy, ascendancy: command, sway, control, dominion, *power, authority.

spacious. Spacious, commodious, capacious, ample come into comparison when they mean much larger in extent than the average. **Spacious** implies great length and breadth, and, sometimes, height: literally, it is applied chiefly to things that have bounds or walls; as, *spacious* rooms; *spacious* gardens. "The whole interior ...a dim, *spacious,* fragrant place, afloat with golden lights" (*Pater*). Figuratively, though it usually implies limits, it suggests largeness, sweep, freedom, or the like, within those limits; as, "the *spacious* times of great Elizabeth" (*Tennyson*). "Fielding lived when days were longer...when summer afternoons were *spacious*"

(*G. Eliot*). **Commodious** carries as its distinctive implications usefulness, serviceableness, and now, particularly, convenience and comfortableness. "My mother's room is very *commodious*, is it not? Large and cheerful looking, and the dressing-closets so well disposed. It always strikes me as the most comfortable apartment in the house" (*Austen*). In older use, the word meant comfortable, convenient, or accommodating, and carried no implication of spaciousness. "We [Adam and Eve after the Fall] need not fear To pass *commodiously* this life, sustained By him [God] with many comforts" (*Milton*). " 'What nature wants, *commodious* Gold bestows' " (*Pope*). **Capacious** stresses the ability to hold, contain, and, sometimes, receive or retain, more than the ordinary thing of its kind; as, *capacious* pockets; a *capacious* cupboard; "the *capacious* soul of Shakspeare" (*Hazlitt*). The word is often used humorously with reference to the size or nature of its contents; as, "a pair of *capacious* shoes" (*Dickens*); "a *capacious* crimson damask armchair" (*Shaw*). "Justice Malam was...regarded...as a man of *capacious* mind, seeing that he could draw much wider conclusions without evidence than could be expected of his neighbours" (*G. Eliot*). **Ample** emphasizes largeness of size or, particularly, expanse. Literally, it suggests fullness, bulk, and the like; as, she held the child beneath the folds of her *ample* cloak; "a lady...of those *ample* architectural proportions that in women who are not Duchesses are described...as stoutness" (*Wilde*). In figurative use, it often suggests freedom to expand, or absence of trammels or limitations. "More pellucid streams, An *ampler* ether, a diviner air" (*Wordsworth*). "The yearning [of romantic composers] for an *ampler* expression" (*Babbitt*).

Ana. Vast, immense, *enormous: *broad, wide, deep: extended or extensive (see EXTEND).

spade, *v.* *Dig, delve, grub, excavate, exhume, disinter.

spare, *adj.* **1** Extra, *superfluous, surplus, supernumerary.

Ana. *Excessive, immoderate, exorbitant, inordinate.

2 *Lean, lank, lanky, skinny, scrawny, gaunt, rawboned, angular.

Ana. *Thin, slender, slim, slight: sinewy, athletic (see MUSCULAR).

Ant. Corpulent. — ***Con.*** Fat, *fleshy, obese, portly, plump.

3 *Meager, exiguous, sparse, scanty, scant, skimpy, scrimpy.

Ana. Economical, *sparing, frugal, thrifty.

Ant. Profuse.

sparing, *adj.* **Sparing, frugal, thrifty, economical** agree in meaning exercising or manifesting careful and unwasteful use of one's money, goods, resources, and the like. **Sparing** connotes abstention or restraint; as, *sparing* in the expenditure of money (or use of words, or in giving praise). "Nor will this *sparing* touch of noble books be any irreverence to their writers" (*Keats*). **Frugal** suggests the absence of all luxury and lavishness, especially in food, ways of living, dress, and the like; positively it implies simplicity, temperance, and often, content. "O'erjoyed was he to find ... She [his wife] had a *frugal* mind" (*Cowper*). "Roman life was a *frugal* thing, *sparing* in food, temperate in drink, modest in clothing, cleanly in habit" (*Buchan*). **Thrifty** implies industry, good management, and prosperity, as well as frugality. "Far into the night the housewife plied her own peculiar work....[Their] light was famous in its neighborhood, and was a public symbol of the life that *thrifty* pair had lived" (*Wordsworth*). "Mrs. Manson Mingott had...lived in affluence for half a century; but memories of her early straits had made her excessively *thrifty*" (*E. Wharton*). **Economical** often is used interchangeably with *thrifty* when the sparing use of money and goods is emphasized; as, an *economical* housekeeper. However, in precise English the word implies more than saving, for its chief implication is prudent management or use to the best advantage, without waste, and it is therefore far more widely applicable than *thrifty*, which refers only to persons or their expenditures; thus, an artist who is *economical* in detail avoids every dispensable detail and makes each one that he selects count to the utmost. "The verse, which nowhere bursts into a flame of poetry, is yet *economical* and tidy, and formed to extract all the dramatic value possible from the situation" (*T. S. Eliot*).

Ana. *Meager, exiguous, spare: *stingy, niggardly, parsimonious, penurious: *moderate, temperate.

Ant. Lavish. — ***Con.*** *Profuse, prodigal, exuberant.

spark, *v.* *Flash, gleam, glance, glint, sparkle, glitter, glisten, scintillate, coruscate, glimmer, shimmer, twinkle, glister.

spark, *n.* *Fop, dandy, beau, coxcomb, exquisite, élégant, dude, macaroni, buck, swell, nob, toff.

sparkle, *v.* *Flash, gleam, glance, glint, glitter, glisten, scintillate, coruscate, glimmer, shimmer, twinkle, glister, spark.

sparse. *Meager, spare, exiguous, scanty, scant, skimpy, scrimpy.

Ana. Scattered, dispersed (see SCATTER): sporadic, occasional, *infrequent, uncommon: *thin, slim, slender.

Ant. Dense. — ***Con.*** *Close, thick, compact.

spasm. Paroxysm, convulsion, *fit, attack, access, accession.

spasmodic. *Fitful, convulsive.

Ana. *Intermittent, alternate, recurrent, periodic: *irregular, unnatural: *abnormal, aberrant, atypic.

Con. *Steady, even, constant, equable, uniform: regular, methodical, *orderly.

spat, *v.* Bicker, squabble, quarrel, wrangle, altercate, tiff. See under QUARREL, *n.*

Ana. Dispute, argue, agitate, debate (see DISCUSS): *differ with, differ from.

Con. *Agree, concur, coincide.

spat, *n.* Bickering, squabble, *quarrel, wrangle, altercation, tiff.

Ana. Dispute, controversy, *argument: contention, variance, *discord.

Con. Agreement, concurrence, coincidence (see corresponding verbs at AGREE).

spatter. *Sprinkle, besprinkle, asperse, bespatter, splash.

spay. Castrate, *sterilize, asexualize, emasculate, mutilate, geld, caponize.

speak. Speak, talk, converse agree in meaning to articulate words so as to express one's thoughts. **Speak** is, in general, the broader term and may refer to utterances of any kind, however coherent or however broken or disconnected, and with or without reference to a hearer or hearers; as, to learn to *speak;* not to be able to *speak* above a whisper; I shall *speak* to him about it; let him *speak* for the organization. **Talk,** on the other hand, usually implies an auditor or auditors and connected colloquy or discourse; as, he left the room because he did not care to *talk;* "We *talk* in the bosom of our family in a way different from that in which we discourse on state occasions" (*Lowes*). But *speak* is also used of relatively weighty or formal speech (often public speech), *talk*, of that which is more or less empty or frivolous; as, "a fool may *talk*, but a wise man *speaks*" (*B. Jonson*); "a good old man, sir; he will be *talking*" (*Shak.*); "Yet there happened in my time one noble speaker who was full of gravity in his *speaking*....No man ever *spake* more neatly, more pressly, more weightily, or suffered less emptiness, less idleness, in what he uttered" (*B. Jonson*). **Converse** implies an interchange in talk of thoughts and opinions; as, "Words learned by rote a parrot may rehearse, But *talking* is not always to *converse*" (*Cowper*); "If we may not then be said to be able to *converse* before we are able to *talk*...so we may be said not to be able to '*talk*' before we are able to *speak*" (*H. James*). "I believe that to write well it is necessary to *converse* a great deal" (*T. S. Eliot*).

Ana. *Pronounce, articulate, enunciate: *stammer, stutter: *discourse, expatiate, dilate, descant.

special, *adj.* **Special, especial, specific, particular, individual, respective, concrete** are not all synonyms of one another, but they are closely related terms because, in spite of wide variations in the denotations of some, they all, in the senses here considered, carry the meaning relating to or belonging to one thing or one class, especially as distinguished from all the others. Both *special* and *especial* imply differences which distinguish the thing so described from others of its kind. At one time or another, these two words have borne the same senses. In current use, however, **special** is the preferred term when the differences give the thing concerned a quality, character, identity, use, or the like, of its own; as, the mistress of the boardinghouse refused to serve *special* food to any of her guests; the baby requires a *special* soap and a *special* powder; to make Sunday a *special* day, devoted to rest and worship; "If the whole of nature is purposive, it is not likely that we can discern *special* purposes operating" (*Inge*); "a *special* aspect of a more general malady" (*Babbitt*). Often, in addition, *special* implies being out of the ordinary or being conspicuously unusual and therefore comes close to *uncommon* or *exceptional;* as, "It's not like ordinary photographs. There's something *special* about it" (*Bennett*); "Wee Willie Winkie betrayed a *special*...interest in Miss Allardyce ....He was trying to discover why Coppy should have kissed her" (*Kipling*). *Special* is also applicable to something added to a schedule, a series, a sequence, or the like, for an exceptional or extraordinary purpose, reason, or occasion; as, *special* trains will be run to Washington for the inauguration; a *special* dividend. **Especial** is the preferred term when there is the intent to convey the idea of pre-eminence or of being such as is described over and above all the others; as, his *especial* friend; a matter of *especial* importance; this has no *especial* reference to any one person. In general, the adverbs observe the same differences in meaning in current good use; as, a *specially* prescribed medicine; a train run *especially* for commuters; the criticism is *especially* deserved in such cases. **Specific,** especially in philosophical, scientific, and critical use suggests an opposition to *generic* and implies a relation to the species as distinguished from the genus or from any more comprehensive category than the one referred to; as, both the common violet and the pansy are violas, but their *specific* differences are more obvious than their *specific* likenesses; the *specific* virtue of a drug; the *specific* remedy for malaria; intellect is the *specific* possession of man as distinguished from the highest animals. In more general but equally good use, *specific* (see also EXPLICIT) implies a relation to one thing as distinguished from all other things that are of the same species or of the same type or that are covered by a general statement; as, he was asked to give a *specific* example to illustrate the failure of the law; a *specific* instance may be described. "Its [a new guide-book's] *specific* charm was simply that it left out all the gush" (*C. E. Montague*). "Where it [vitality] exists, there is pleasure in feeling alive, quite apart from any *specific* pleasant circumstance" (*B. Russell*). In this latter sense of *specific,* **particular** is preferred by some writers and speakers on the ground that the term is clearly opposed to *general,* and that it is a close synonym of *single* (for fuller treatment see SINGLE). The differences between the two words in this sense are not easily discoverable, but *specific* seems to be chosen more often by careful writers and speakers when the ideas of specification or of illustration are involved, and *particular* when the distinctness of the thing as an individual is to be suggested; thus, one is asked to give a *specific* (better than a *particular*) illustration to indicate a word's correct use, but one describes the *particular* (much better than *specific*) varieties of peaches. "We get a sense for *particular* beauties of nature, rather than a sense for Nature herself" (*Binyon*). *Particular* is also often used in the sense of *special* and *especial* (as, "some half-dozen *particular* friends"—*Dickens;* "Would you...say that it is Christian...to force that *particular* kind [of suffering] on others?"—*Galsworthy*). In logic, *particular* is opposed to *universal,* and applies to propositions, judgments, conceptions, and the like, which have reference to a single member or to some members of a class rather than to all; thus, "some men are highly intelligent" is a *particular* proposition, but "all men make mistakes" is a *universal* proposition. Often, in less technical use, *particular* implies an opposition to *general* as well as to *universal;* as, "[Swinburne] uses the most general word, because his emotion is never *particular*" (*T. S. Eliot*); "one is apt to amplify a *particular* judgment into a general opinion" (*C. Mackenzie*). **Individual** unequivocally implies reference to one of the class or group as clearly distinguished from all the others; as, "the aspect of every *individual* stone or brick" (*Conrad*); "a conflict... between *individual* education and mass economic conditionment" (*Day Lewis*); "[immigrants] arriving in such numbers that *individual* physical examination with our meagre staff was out of the question" (*V. Heiser*). **Respective** is here considered not as a close synonym of the preceding words but because it implies reference to each member of a class or to each subdivision of a group as apart from or as distinguished from each of the others: otherwise, it often comes close to *specific* and *particular* in meaning; as, the *respective* powers of the departments of the government; the *respective* users of this medicine will find widely varying reactions. **Concrete** comes very close to *specific* and *particular* in meaning, but it carries a definite implication not found in the other words—that the thing so described either has actual physical existence, or is something that is within one's own experience: it is therefore usually opposed to *abstract* or *general;* thus, a *concrete* noun is one that designates something that has objective existence or that evokes an image of a particular thing (such as *brick, tulip, snow*) and is especially opposed to an *abstract* noun, which names a concept, idea, or other thing which has no tangible existence (as *matter, beauty, progress*), and sometimes, to a *general* noun, which names a class or category and not a particular instance (as *tree, animal, flower*); a *specific* example supports or illustrates a general statement such as a principle, a law, or the like, but a *concrete* example brings that which is abstract or abstruse within the range of one's experience, especially sense experience; a *concrete* illustration illuminates or vivifies or renders tangible the general statement, whereas a *specific* illustration merely exemplifies it; hence, one speaks of a *concrete* (not *specific*) presentation of a philosophy; a *concrete* (not *specific*) exposition; "[Shakespeare] chooses the *concrete* word, in phrase after phrase forcing you to touch and see" (*Quiller-Couch*). "It is a folly and a waste of time to give abstract moral instruction to a child; everything must be *concrete*, and actually demanded by the existing situation" (*B. Russell*).

Ana. Distinctive, peculiar, individual, *characteristic: *exceptional: uncommon, occasional, rare (see INFREQUENT).

Con. *Common, ordinary, familiar: *usual, customary, habitual.

specie. Cash, currency, *money, legal tender, coin, coinage.

specific, *adj.* **1** *Special, especial, particular, individual, respective, concrete.

Ant. Generic.

2 Definite, *explicit, express, categorical.

Ana. Designating, naming (see DESIGNATE): *clear, lucid, perspicuous: precise, exact (see CORRECT, *adj.*).

Ant. Vague.

specific, *n.* *Remedy, cure, medicine, medicament, physic.

specimen. Example, sample, illustration, *instance, case.

specious. *Plausible, believable, colorable, credible.

Ana. *Vain, nugatory, empty, hollow, idle: delusory, delusive, *misleading, deceptive: deceitful, *dishonest, untruthful, mendacious, lying.

spectator. Spectator, observer, beholder, looker-on, onlooker, witness, eyewitness, bystander, kibitzer agree in meaning one who sees or looks upon something. **Spectator** is, in precise use, used in place of *auditor* (or in the plural, of *audience*) for one (or the group) that attends an exhibition, performance, or entertainment that does not involve an appeal to the sense of hearing; thus, one says the *spectators* at a football game, at a prize fight, at a pageant, at a pantomime, at a circus; but the *auditors* or the *audience* at a concert, a lecture, a play. Very often, however, the term is used more broadly to denote one who regards that which is presented to him (whether to his sight, hearing, understanding, or the like) as though he is not a part of it or identified with it in any way or degree. "A speech in a play should never appear to be intended to move us [the audience] as it might conceivably move other characters in the play, for it is essential that we should preserve our position of *spectators*, and observe always from the outside though with complete understanding" (*T. S. Eliot*); "The artist's work in life is full of struggle and toil; it is only the *spectator* of morals who can assume the calm aesthetic attitude" (*H. Ellis*). **Observer** may or may not imply an intent to see, but it usually does suggest, whether one sees by intention or by accident, that one attends closely to details and often keeps a record of them; the term applies therefore chiefly to scientists who gather evidence by carefully noting natural phenomena or the results of experiments, or to military or diplomatic officials who are sent by countries not participating in a war, or in a meeting of representatives from other nations, to watch proceedings closely and to make a report of them; it is also applicable to anyone who has formed similar habits and can be more or less relied upon for accuracy; as, "It is the man of science who speaks, the unprejudiced *observer*, the accepter of facts" (*A. Huxley*); an *observer* for the United States at all assemblies of the League of Nations. "You go about a lot amongst all sorts of people. You are a tolerably honest *observer*" (*Conrad*). **Beholder** now sometimes carries a stronger implication of watching or regarding intently than either of the preceding terms, but in earlier use it meant little more than one who sees; as, "All the *beholders* take his part with weeping" (*Shak.*). In current use, it is often applicable to one who has been privileged to look intently upon a person or thing with the result that one obtains a clear and accurate impression of him or it and is moved by the beauty, power, tenderness, pathos, or the like, of that which is seen; as, "The love deep-seated in the Saviour's face [in da Vinci's *Last Supper*] . . . [does] melt and thaw The heart of the *beholder*" (*Wordsworth*). **Looker-on** and **onlooker** differ from *beholder* chiefly in their suggestions of casualness or detachment and in their definite implication of lack of participation; as, there was a great crowd of *lookers-on* at the fire; the surgeon refused to operate in the presence of *onlookers*. *Onlooker* is sometimes used in place of *spectator* when the distinction between the one who sees and that which he sees is stressed; as, the *onlookers*, not the participants, see most of the game. **Witness** (etymologically, knowledge) is more comprehensive than the preceding terms in the sense here considered, although it denotes one who knows firsthand and therefore is competent to give testimony: the term sometimes, but very far from always, applies to a person who knows because he has seen; as, "No person shall be convicted of treason, unless on the testimony of two *witnesses* to the same overt act" (*Constitution of the United States*); "Standing there, I was *witness* of a little incident that seemed to escape the rest" (*Quiller-Couch*). Since *witness* does not necessarily imply seeing, **eyewitness** is often preferred as more explicitly implying actual sight; as, there were no *eyewitnesses* of the collision. **Bystander** primarily denotes one who stands by when something is happening, sometimes it carries the implications of *onlooker* (as, the policeman took the names of all the *bystanders*), but at other times it suggests little more than presence at a place (as, a *bystander* was injured by the explosion). **Kibitzer** (a colloquial term) specifically applies to one who watches a card game by looking over the shoulders of the players and who annoys them by offering advice: in extended use, it applies to any onlooker who meddles or makes unwelcome suggestions.

specter. Spirit, ghost, *apparition, phantasm, phantom, wraith, fetch, shade, revenant, spook, haunt.

speculate. Reason, reflect, *think, cogitate, deliberate.

Ana. *Ponder, meditate, muse, ruminate: *consider, weigh, revolve, study, contemplate, excogitate.

speculative. 1 Contemplative, meditative, *thoughtful, reflective, pensive.

Ana. Conjecturing *or* conjectural, surmising, guessing (see corresponding verbs at CONJECTURE): pondering, musing, ruminating (see PONDER).

2 *Theoretical, academic.

speech. 1 *Language, tongue, dialect, idiom.

2 Speech, address, oration, harangue, allocution, lecture, prelection, talk, sermon, homily designate a discourse delivered to an audience. A **speech** is any public discourse, prepared or unprepared, which is intended to influence, instruct, or entertain a group of listeners; as, the senator was called upon to make a *speech;* after-dinner *speeches.* **Address** implies formality and, usually, careful preparation; it often connotes distinction in the speaker or gives emphasis to the importance of the speech; as, the commencement *address;* the president is scheduled to deliver three *addresses* on his trip. **Oration** suggests eloquence, rhetorical style, and, usually, a dignified, but sometimes a high-flown or long-winded, appeal to the emotions of a large audience or assembly; as, the Gettysburg *Oration;* a Fourth of July *oration.* **Harangue,** once nearly equivalent to *oration* except for its added implications of vehemence and passion, now commonly retains only these distinctive implications and connotes either length and tediousness of speech or an impassioned appeal to the populace. "If you do not believe that emotion...is the basic social force, listen to the *harangue* of any successful politician" (*C. C. Furnas*). **Allocution** is applied chiefly to a solemn address of exhortation delivered by a leader, as a general to his army, or as now, almost exclusively, by the Pope to a consistory of cardinals. **Lecture,** as its derivation suggests, usually implies reading; it commonly designates a carefully prepared speech on a special topic, intended to give information and instruction to a group of students or studious persons. **Prelection,** a British term with rare American use, designates a lecture, often in the nature of a running commentary on a text, delivered by a university professor to his students. **Talk** implies informality; it may be used to designate either a lecture or an address when the speaker wishes to emphasize his desire to speak directly and simply to his auditors as individuals. **Sermon** and **homily** both commonly imply religious instruction by an ordained preacher and a church congregation as the listeners. *Sermon* usually connotes a theme drawn from a Scriptural text; *homily* suggests practical moral counsel rather than doctrinal discussion. These distinctions are, however, not always observed.

speechless. *Dumb, mute, inarticulate.

speed, *n.* **1** *Haste, hurry, expedition, dispatch.

Ana. *Celerity, legerity, alacrity: fleetness, rapidity, swiftness, quickness (see corresponding adjectives at FAST): velocity, pace, headway (see SPEED).

2 Speed, velocity, momentum, impetus, pace, headway are not all synonyms of one another but they are often confused through misunderstanding or ignorance of their specific distinctions, especially in physics. The first three are terms of Newtonian physics and are in the course of being subjected to changes in their definitions. In general, they mean rate of motion. **Speed** (as here considered: see also HASTE, *n.*) denotes rate of motion that is computed simply by dividing the distance covered by the number of hours, minutes, seconds, or the like, taken; thus, a car that covers 300 miles in 6 hours has an average *speed* of 50 miles an hour. **Velocity** denotes the speed of something that is directed along a given path. Ordinarily, *velocity* suggests rate of motion in a straight line (*linear velocity*) or in an arc or circle (*angular velocity*); as, the *velocity* of a bullet; the *velocity* of a skier; the *velocity* of a wind; the *velocity* of light. **Momentum** is often used loosely in place of *speed* or *velocity*, but in strict technical use it denotes not rate of motion but, rather, quantity of motion as determined by multiplying the mass of a moving body by its velocity; thus, a falling stone gathers *momentum;* the *momentum* of a football kicked by a small boy is far less than that of the same ball kicked by a powerful man; the *momentum* of an iron ball rolling down an inclined plane is greater than that of a cork ball of the same diameter rolling with the same velocity; "As photons are always in motion, we may also speak of the *momentum* of a photon, much as we speak of the *momentum* of a motor car" (*Jeans*). **Impetus** is a popular rather than scientific synonym of *momentum.* Actually, it is a closer synonym of *impulse*, in the sense of the effect of an impelling force, for it retains its etymological implication of a rushing upon or an onset, with the result that it usually suggests great momentum or implies a powerful driving force as the cause of such momentum; as, "Whether the steam...retains sufficient *impetus* to carry it to our shores" (*T. H. Huxley*); the circulating blood receives a new *impetus* when forced into the arteries by the contraction of the ventricles of the heart. **Pace** belongs here not as a scientific term but as a synonym of *speed*, as rate of motion. The term is often used in reference to things that have the speed or suggest the speed of walkers, runners, trotters (often horses), and the like; as, he set the *pace* for his companions on the hike; the *pace* was too slow (or too fast) for the rest of the party. *Pace* is often used figuratively in describing activities, progress, rate of production, and the like; as, to keep *pace* with the times; the factories were asked to increase their *pace.* **Headway** in its earliest sense meant motion forward and was used chiefly in reference to ships. Although this is still the chief implication of the term (as here considered) it usually now denotes the rate of movement ahead, and is used in reference not only to ships but to anything capable of advancing or making progress; as, the sailboat made no *headway* against the wind; to increase the *headway* of a car by using the accelerator.

speed, *v.* **Speed, accelerate, quicken, hasten, hurry, precipitate** agree in denoting to go or make go fast or faster. Though many of these words are used interchangeably without seeming loss, each one carries distinctive implications which can be brought out to advantage in precise use. **Speed** emphasizes rapidity of motion or progress: as a transitive verb it suggests an increase to rapid tempo; as an intransitive verb, a high degree of swiftness; as, to *speed* up an engine; to *speed* up the work in a factory; the bullet *sped* through the air; I *speeded* homewards; arrested for *speeding.* **Accelerate,** in careful use, stresses increase in rate of motion or progress: it does not necessarily imply speed; as, to *accelerate* one's pace; a rich soil *accelerates* the growth of most plants; to *accelerate* the speed of a car. **Quicken** stresses shortening of the time consumed: there is often a suggestion of its original implication of animation or stimulation; as, to *quicken* one's departure or one's steps; exercise *quickens* the pulse; by training, the eye is *quickened.* **Hasten** implies urgent quickness or a quick or premature outcome; as, to *hasten* to a friend's deathbed; worry *hastened* his death. **Hurry,** when employed as an equivalent of *hasten*, is usually colloquial, or at least less literary. However, in standard English it has its own values, then often implying haste that causes confusion or prevents concentrated attention; as, his aim was *hurried* and his shot went wide of the mark. "A second fear... Which madly *hurries* her she knows not whither" (*Shak.*). **Precipitate** (cf. PRECIPITATE, *adj.*) implies impetuousness, suddenness, or abruptness. "Men will not bide their time, but will insist on *precipitating* the march of affairs" (*Buckle*). "Its ruin was *precipitated* by religious persecution" (*J. R. Green*).

Ana. *Advance, forward, further, promote: *adjust, regulate, fix.

speedy. Expeditious, quick, swift, fleet, rapid, *fast, hasty.

Ana. Brisk, nimble, *agile: prompt, *quick, ready.

Ant. Dilatory.

speer *or* **spier.** Inquire, query, interrogate, question, *ask, examine, catechize, quiz.

sphere, *n.* **1 Sphere, globe, orb, ball** agree in denoting a body or mass which actually or apparently has a continuous outer surface all points of which are equidistant from its center. **Sphere** was originally an astronomical term applied in ancient and medieval times to: (1) the apparent outward shell enclosing all space, of which only the half that forms the dome of the heavens and is surrounded at its base by the horizon is visible from any one place; (2) one of several transparent concentric shells (specifically the *celestial spheres* or the *heavenly spheres*) which revolve around the earth, each in its own orbit and each carrying its own celestial body or bodies such as the sun, the moon, or a planet or the fixed stars. The first conception is an inference drawn from ocular observation, the second is the result of a hypothesis framed to account for the observed motion of celestial bodies. Neither conception is held by modern astronomers, but *sphere* is still sometimes applied as in earlier times to a representation, as in a chart, of the apparent boundaries of space on which are indicated the positions and relations of heavenly bodies at a given time, or their movements, as observable from the earth. Both conceptions of *sphere*, but especially the second, have been, and to a degree still are, influential in the poetic use of the word. "Stand still, you ever moving *spheres* of heaven, That time may cease, and midnight never come" (*Marlowe*). "The face of Nature shines, from where earth seems, Far-stretch'd around, to meet the bending *sphere*" (*Thomson*). The belief (promulgated by the Pythagoreans) that the motions of the celestial spheres are so attuned to each other that they produce ethereal music (the "music of the spheres") and exquisite harmonies no longer prevails, but the idea still occurs in poetic imagery. "She with one breath attunes the *spheres*, And also my poor human heart" (*Thoreau*). *Sphere* is also the technical geometrical term for the figure, body, mass, portion of space, or the like, in three dimensions which has, or is conceived of as having, a surface all points of which are equally distant from its center. **Globe** is far more physical in its implications than *sphere*, being commonly applied to something having or believed to have material existence and the shape (often the approximate shape) of a sphere; thus, the earth because of its form is called a *globe* or the *globe;* a celestial body, such as a planet, is sometimes called a *globe* because of its apparent shape and by analogy with the earth; a spherical construction on the outer surface of which is a map of the earth is called a terrestrial *globe*, in distinction from one depicting the configuration of the heavens and called a celestial *globe;* so, at the peak of each spire is a golden *globe;* a hollow glass *globe* for goldfish. **Orb** was once a close, but not a technical, synonym of *sphere* in the sense of one of the celestial spheres; it also was applied to any celestial body; hence, in poetry, where it now chiefly occurs, it is sometimes difficult to determine whether it denotes a celestial sphere or a celestial body; in fact, there is often confusion in these conceptions. "There's not the smallest *orb* which thou behold'st But in his motion like an angel sings" (*Shak.*). "The moon, whose *orb* Through optic glass the Tuscan artist [Galileo] views At evening" (*Milton*). "Vast beams like spokes of some invisible wheel Which whirl as the *orb* whirls, swifter than thought" (*Shelley*). In extended use, *orb* is usually applied to something which is spherical, transparent (or clear), and, sometimes, radiant. "What a hell of witchcraft lies In the small *orb* of one particular tear!" (*Shak.*). " 'Nothing at all, Sir,' the young man replied, meeting him with the full *orbs* of his eyes" (*Meredith*). Specifically *orb* is applied to the sphere surmounted by a cross which forms part of the English king's regalia. In contrast with the vagueness of *orb*, **ball** is usually conspicuously definite in its applications and in its connotations of perfect sphericity. Its chief use is in names of manufactured things that are usually perfect spheres, such as missiles (especially formerly, as cannon *balls*, musket *balls*), objects that are used in games and play, and hit, thrown, kicked, or bounced (as, tennis *ball*, golf *ball*, base*ball*, soccer *ball*, rubber *ball*), and various things to eat, articles of merchandise, and the like, which are shaped to resemble such balls (as, candy *balls*, meat *balls*, *balls* of yarn, soap *balls*). *Ball* is used of natural things chiefly because of their likeness to artificial things called *balls;* as, puff*balls;* the *ball* of the foot; a *ball*-and-socket joint; the eye*ball*.

2 *Field, domain, province, territory, bailiwick.

Ana. Dominion, sway, jurisdiction, control, *power: *range, reach, scope, compass: *function, office, duty, province.

spherical. Globular, orbicular, *round, circular, annular, discoid.

spice. *Touch, suggestion, suspicion, soupçon, tincture, tinge, shade, smack, dash, vein, strain, streak.

spick-and-span. *Neat, tidy, trim, trig, snug, shipshape.

Ana. *Clean, cleanly: fresh, *new.

Ant. Filthy.

spicy. *Pungent, piquant, poignant, racy, snappy.

Ana. *Spirited, high-spirited, gingery, fiery, peppery: aromatic, redolent, balmy, *odorous.

spier. Variant of SPEER.

spin, *v.* *Turn, revolve, rotate, gyrate, circle, whirl, twirl, wheel, eddy, swirl, pirouette.

Ana. *Swing, sway, oscillate, vibrate.

spine. Spine, backbone, vertebrae, chine designate the articulated column of bones (often called the *spinal*, or *vertebral, column*) which is the central and axial feature of the skeleton of human beings and of all vertebrate animals except a few primitive forms in which it remains undeveloped. **Spine** and **backbone** are interchangeable, but *spine* is usually preferred when anatomical structure and functions are under consideration. *Backbone* is not only a more homely term, but it may convey a wrong impression, since the word suggests one long continuous bone rather than a series of small bones. However, it is preferred both in literary and spoken English for something which resembles the spine in being the main support or the mainstay of a structure or organization. "Men from the uplands were soon to be the *backbone* of the legions and to furnish the best auxiliary corps" (*Buchan*). When the emphasis is on resemblance in appearance or position, *spine* is sometimes preferred. "The shock Of cataract seas that snap The three-decker's oaken *spine*" (*Tennyson*). **Vertebrae,** the plural of *vertebra* (the term denoting one of the segments of the spinal column), when preceded by *the*, is found even more often in technical use than *spine*, and is usually preferred to *spine* when the reference is to one of the lower animals. **Chine** is now rarely employed in the sense of *spine*, except in reference to animals whose flesh is used as meat. It, therefore, has come to be referred less often to the spine than to the part of the back which is supported by the spine. In current use, it is applied chiefly to this part of a carcass of beef or other meat, or to a portion of it served as a roast or joint; as, a *chine* of beef.

spirit, *n.* **1** *Soul.

Ana. *Mind, intellect, soul, psyche.

2 Ghost, *apparition, phantasm, phantom, wraith, fetch, specter, shade, revenant, spook, haunt.

3 *Courage, mettle, resolution, tenacity.

Ana. *Fortitude, pluck, grit, backbone, sand, guts: zeal, fervor, ardor, *passion, enthusiasm: energy, strength, might, *power, force.

spirited. Spirited, high-spirited, mettlesome, spunky, fiery, peppery, gingery come into comparison when they mean having or manifesting a high degree of vitality, spirit, and daring. **Spirited** implies not only fullness of life, but ardor, animation, energy, enthusiasm, or other signs of excellent physical, or sometimes mental, health: the term seldom conveys exactly the same implications in any two contexts, but it always carries a suggestion of exaltation, stimulation, or the like; as, "The third [speech] was...very *spirited* and eloquent" (*Gray*); "a fine, lively, *spirited* young man" (*Scott*); "Shaking his head backward, somewhat after the manner of a *spirited* horse" (*G. Eliot*). **High-spirited** is applied as often to horses as to men. It adds to *spirited* a strong suggestion of gallantry, or of difficulty in bringing under control; as, "Too *high-spirited* to be passive instruments in his hand" (*W. Robertson*); "They were *highspirited*, perhaps a little insolent as well as reckless.... 'You look [said Cornwallis to one of them asking for a commission] as if you had come to confer a favour rather than ask for it' " (*H. Ellis*). **Mettlesome** differs little from *high-spirited* except in its tendency to stress fearlessness and vigor more than restiveness; as, "Their force differs from true spirit, as much as a vicious from a *mettlesome* horse" (*Tatler*); "a powerful *mettlesome* young Achilles" (*Thackeray*). **Spunky,** a more colloquial term than those which precede, often implies qualities similar to those suggested by *high-spirited* and *mettlesome*, but it carries a stronger implication of quickness in taking fire and of an incapacity for being downed or daunted: also, the term is far less often applied to persons or animals that are, by implication, thoroughbred; as, a *spunky* upholding of one's ideas; "They are grown again as young and *spunky* as undergraduates" (*Landor*); "He is a *spunky* fellow, and I'll be his second [in a duel]" (*Marryat*). Only in dialectal use and in colloquial use in the United States does *spunky* imply a degree of irascibility. *Fiery*, *peppery*, and *gingery* are used as synonyms of the preceding terms only when one prefers a more concrete term. **Fiery,** suggesting the heat of flame or fire, implies impetuousness, passionateness, or sometimes, irascibility, in addition to spiritedness (as, "A *fiery* soul, which, working out its way, Fretted the pygmy body to decay"—*Dryden;* "the *fiery*, swift, Italian nature of the man"—*Carlyle;* "the nervous and *fiery* animation of the horses"—*Shelley*); **peppery** adds to *spirited* suggestions of a hotness or pungency characteristic of pepper and often distinctively connotes asperity or excitability (as, a *peppery* response; "Master Rickey is a *peppery* young man. Love and war come as natural to him as bread and butter"—*Meredith*); **gingery** carries a heightened suggestion of a zest, spiciness, or snap associated with ginger (as, *gingery* comments on the life of social leaders; a *gingery* young woman; "He learned the high quick *gingery* ways Of thoroughbreds"—*Masefield*).

Ana. Courageous, intrepid, bold, audacious, valiant, *brave: impetuous, *precipitate: *eager, avid, keen: passionate, enthusiastic, zealous, fervent, ardent (see corresponding nouns at PASSION).

Ant. Spiritless.

spiritless. *Languid, languishing, languorous, listless, enervated, lackadaisical.

Ana. *Lethargic, sluggish, comatose, stuporous: dull, *stupid, dense, crass: *tame, subdued, submissive.

Ant. Spirited.

spiritual. *Holy, sacred, divine, religious, blessed.

Ana. *Supernatural, supranatural: *celestial, heavenly.

Ant. Physical: carnal: material: temporal.

spirituous. *Alcoholic, ardent, hard, strong.

spit, *v.* **Spit, expectorate** agree in meaning to eject matter from the mouth. **Spit** is not only the ordinary word for this act, but it is less suggestive than *expectorate* of the source or nature of the matter ejected; as an intransitive verb it usually implies the emission of saliva (as, "When he had thus spoken, he *spat* on the ground, and made clay of the spittle"—*John* ix. 6) but as a transitive verb it may take as its object anything which is expelled from the mouth; as, to *spit* blood; the baby *spat* out his first taste of oatmeal. **Expectorate** (properly a medical term) implies ejection from the lungs or windpipe, especially by coughing; as, to *expectorate* mucus; to *expectorate* blood. The employment of *expectorate* for *spit*, as an intransitive verb, is common as a euphemism.

spite, *n.* Despite, malignity, spleen, grudge, *malice, malevolence, ill will.

Ana. Rancor, animus, antipathy (see ENMITY): vindictiveness. revengefulness *or* revenge, vengefulness *or* vengeance (see corresponding adjectives at VINDICTIVE).

spiteful. Despiteful, despiteous, malignant, *malicious, malevolent, malign.

Ana. Rancorous, antipathetic, antagonistic, hostile (see corresponding nouns at ENMITY): *vindictive, revengeful, vengeful.

splash, *v.* *Sprinkle, besprinkle, asperse, spatter, bespatter.

spleen. Malignity, grudge, spite, despite, *malice, malevolence, ill will.

Ana. Animosity, antipathy, animus, rancor, antagonism (see ENMITY): venom, *poison: *vindictive, revengeful.

splendid. Splendid, resplendent, gorgeous, glorious, sublime, superb come into comparison when they mean having or displaying outstanding or transcendingly impressive qualities. Although, like nearly all English adjectives implying transcendence, they are often used hyperbolically, only their stricter senses are here considered. That is **splendid** (etymologically, shining) which literally or figuratively far outshines the usual or customary as in brilliancy, luster, grandeur, magnificence, or the like, or which impresses the observer by its surpassing brilliancy, luster, grandeur, etc.; as, "a fine—yea even a *splendid* room, of great height, and carved grandeur" (*Galsworthy*); "The outburst of the first crusade was *splendid* even in a military sense, but it was great beyond comparison in its reflection in architecture, ornament, poetry, colour, religion, and philosophy" (*H. Adams*); "the *splendid* efflorescence of genius in Russia during...the last century" (*H. Ellis*). That is **resplendent** which is glowingly or blazingly splendid; as, diplomats *resplendent* in court costume; "On the blue sunny deep, *resplendent* far away" (*Shelley*); "a *resplendent* butterfly" (*Meredith*); "Juliet [of Shakespeare's *Romeo and Juliet*] died, but not before she had shown how great and *resplendent* a thing love could be" (*J. W. Krutch*). That is **gorgeous** which is sumptuously splendid in color or display or colors; as, "The July sun shone over Egdon and fired its crimson heather to scarlet. It was the one season of the year, and the one weather of the season, in which the heath was *gorgeous*" (*Hardy*); "this *gorgeous* combination of all the hues of Paradise" (*H. Adams*). In somewhat less precise use, the term stresses showiness or elaborateness rather than splendor of coloring; as, a *gorgeous* feast; *gorgeous* attire. That is **glorious** which literally or figuratively is radiant with light or beauty or which stands out as eminently worthy of admiration, renown, or distinction; as, "Now is the winter of our discontent Made *glorious* summer by this sun of York" (*Shak.*); "he soon Saw within ken a *glorious* Angel stand ... His back was turned, but not his brightness hid" (*Milton*); "As often happens after a grey daybreak the sun had risen in a warm and *glorious* splendour" (*Conrad*); "this *glorious* vision of manly strength and beauty" (*Shaw*). "The *glorious* company of the Apostles" (*Te Deum*). That is **sublime** which is so elevated or exalted that the mind in contemplating or picturing it cannot reach full comprehension of it and must, in part at least, feel or imagine the vastness of its extent, power, beauty, nobility, or the like. "And I have felt A presence that disturbs me with the joy Of elevated thoughts; a sense *sublime* Of something far more deeply interfused Whose dwelling is the light of setting suns, And the round ocean and the living air" (*Wordsworth*). "The main force of Buddhist art was spent in the creation of *sublime* figures, the images of those enlightened ones who in the clear beam of their purified vision beheld and understood the sorrows, the struggles, the vain angers and hatreds of imperfect mortality" (*Binyon*). "The thunderstorm when it is felt to be *sublime* has lost in part at least the terrors it possesses as a natural event" (*S. Alexander*). That is **superb** which exceeds that which is merely grand, magnificent, sumptuous, splendid, or the like, and reaches the highest conceivable point of grandeur, magnificence, splendor, etc.; as, a *superb* physique; a *superb* wine; a *superb* performance of a symphony; "[Homer] actually does convey Odysseus from Troy to Ithaca, by a ten years' voyage too; he actually has narrated that voyage to us in plain, straightforward words; and, what is more, he actually has made a *superb* epic of it" (*Quiller-Couch*); "*superb* figures, breathing health and strength" (*Binyon*); "he had the *superb* vitality of early youth" (*Cather*).

Ana. Radiant, effulgent, luminous, brilliant, *bright: illustrious, eminent, distinguished (see FAMOUS): excelling *or* excellent, surpassing, transcending *or* transcendent (see corresponding verbs at EXCEED).

splenetic. *Irascible, choleric, testy, techy, touchy, cranky, cross.

Ana. Morose, *sullen, glum, gloomy: *irritable, querulous, peevish, snappish: captious, carping, caviling (see CRITICAL).

split, *v.* Rend, cleave, rive, rip, *tear.

Ana. *Separate, part, divide, sever: *cut, chop, hew.

split second. *Instant, moment, second, minute, flash, trice, jiffy, twinkling, twinkle.

spoil, *v.* **1** *Injure, harm, hurt, damage, impair, mar.

Ana. *Ruin, wreck: *destroy, demolish.

Con. Preserve, conserve, *save: amend, redress, remedy (see CORRECT, *v.*).

2 *Indulge, pamper, humor, baby, mollycoddle.

Ana. *Injure, harm, hurt, damage: favor, accommodate, *oblige: *debase, deprave, vitiate, debauch.

3 *Decay, decompose, rot, putrefy, disintegrate, crumble.

Ana. Corrupt, vitiate (see DEBASE): *ruin, wreck: impair, harm, *injure.

spoil *or* **spoils,** *n.* **Spoil** (*or* **spoils**), **pillage, plunder, booty, prize, loot, swag** come into comparison as nouns meaning that which is taken from another by superior force or craft. **Spoil** in its earliest and fundamental sense applied to the movable property of a defeated enemy, which by the custom of warfare belonged to the victor, and of which he stripped the captured city or place. "Fire the palace, the fort, and the keep— Leave to the foeman no *spoil* at all" (*Kipling*). With changes in methods of warfare *spoil*, and the currently more common **spoils**, came to be applied to any property, territory, or the like, taken over by the conquering forces in actual warfare or demanded by them from the conquered as a condition of making peace. In extended use, *spoils* applies to anything which by custom (often, by suggestion, unethical custom) belongs to the victor; in political use, this is applied chiefly to the appointive public offices and their emoluments which the successful party in an election regards as its peculiar property to be bestowed as its leaders wish. "In America, where in some cases the civil services are still regarded as the *spoils* of office, a new set of officials oust the old ones whenever the Opposition ousts the Government" (*Shaw*). **Pillage** implies more open violence and greater lawlessness and destructiveness in warfare than *spoil*. It suggests invasion and sacking by more or less disorderly troops or by marauding bands. "That robbed all the countrie there about, And brought the *pillage* home" (*Spenser*). **Plunder** also implies open violence, but even in its earliest use it was a more inclusive term than *spoil* or *pillage* because not restricted to warfare. It has consistently implied robbery, whether as incidental to war or as dissociated from it, and has been applied to that which has been seized not only by spoilers, pillagers, sackers, and the like, but by bandits, brigands, highwaymen, and others of the same kind. "He blamed and protested, but joined in the plan [to rob a poor man's orchard]; He shared in the *plunder*, but pitied the man" (*Cowper*). **Booty,** like *plunder*, is applicable to war as well as to that which is seized by robbery or theft. In ordinary nontechnical use, however, *booty* distinctively suggests something to be shared or divided and therefore presupposes the operations of a band. "The German women plundered; the German cooks and intendants plundered; even Mustapha and Mahomet...had a share of the *booty*" (*Thackeray*). In international law, *booty* is technically used in distinction from **prize** (which is now usually a singular noun only), the former referring to spoil taken on land, the latter to spoil (such as a vessel of war) captured on the high seas or in the territorial waters of the enemy. **Loot** may be used in place of *plunder*, *booty*, or *spoils* when a highly derogatory or a highly offensive term is desired. "Drawn into the conflict by a hope of sharing in the *loot* of the Church" (*Belloc*). In current use, the term is also applied specifically to the plunder of those who rob the dead or helpless victims of a catastrophe, or who steal anything left of value in the ruins of buildings wholly or partly destroyed, as by fire, flood, or violent storm; as, prowlers among the ruins in search of *loot:* in general, it is applicable to ill-gotten gains of any sort; as, corrupt officials enriched by the *loot* of years. **Swag** (a slang term) is also often used in place of *plunder*, especially when the latter is thought of as a collection or as a sackful of miscellaneous things gathered by thieves.

Ana. *Theft, robbery, larceny, burglary: acquisitions, acquirements (see singular nouns at ACQUIREMENT).

spoliate. Despoil, *ravage, devastate, waste, sack, pillage.

Ana. *Rob, plunder, rifle, loot: defraud, swindle, *cheat.

sponge, sponger. *Parasite, sycophant, favorite, toady, lickspit, hanger-on, leech.

sponsalia. Espousal, betrothal, affiance, *engagement.

sponsor, *n.* **Sponsor, patron, surety, guarantor, backer, angel** are comparable only when they denote a person who in a greater or less degree accepts responsibility for another, especially for another's venture or undertaking. **Sponsor** usually implies public acceptance of a responsibility and a definite engagement to perform what is promised. In its earlier and still accepted sense, the word implies making a pledge in behalf of another and thereby accepting responsibility for its fulfillment; thus, the *sponsor* of an infant in baptism makes the promises in the child's name and pledges himself to be responsible for the child's religious training if the latter is deprived of his natural guardians. In its later sense, *sponsor* suggests assumption of the role of promoter or supporter; as, the candidate for mayor had no *sponsors;* Senator Blank appeared as *sponsor* for the bill; the utility company was frequently a *sponsor* for a radio program. **Patron** stresses the acceptance of the relation as a protector or benefactor, especially in return for service, honors, or devotion; it often implies, therefore, the obligation to assist, support, or defend; thus, a *patron* of an artist or of a poet was a wealthy or influential person who made the latter his protégé in return for honors paid him; the *patron* of an institution, a cause, a charity, or the like, is one whose generous and regular contributions to its support are publicly recognized. **Surety** and **guarantor** imply answerability for another's debt or performance of duty in case of default, because of prior acceptance of responsibility. The words are often used interchangeably, but in British use, *surety* is the preferred term, and in some states of the United States a distinction is made in law. In such states a surety is answerable immediately on default and without notice; a guarantor is answerable only after ineffectual legal proceedings have been taken against the principal. **Backer**, a somewhat colloquial term, is used chiefly in sports, politics, and theatrical and similar enterprises. It often implies the giving of financial support (but sometimes merely moral support or encouragement), but it carries no implication that responsibility for debts is assumed. "The success of a publication is the success of its editors, and not of its business managers and its '*backers*'" (*B. Hendrick*). **Angel** is a slang and often derogatory term for a financial backer, especially of a theatrical enterprise.

Ana. Supporter *or* support, upholder, champion, advocator *or* advocate (see corresponding verbs at SUPPORT): promoter, furtherer (see corresponding verbs at ADVANCE).

spontaneity. Abandon, *unconstraint.

Ana. Spontaneousness, instinctiveness, impulsiveness (see corresponding adjectives at SPONTANEOUS): extemporaneousness, offhandedness, unpremeditatedness (see corresponding adjectives at EXTEMPORANEOUS): naturalness, simplicity, unsophistication, naïveté, ingenuousness (see corresponding adjectives at NATURAL).

spontaneous. 1 Spontaneous, impulsive, instinctive, automatic, mechanical are here compared only as applied to persons, their movements, acts, utterances, and the like. All agree in meaning acting or activated without apparent thought or deliberation. That is **spontaneous** which is affected or effected by no compulsion (external or internal) of the will and comes about so naturally that it seems unpremeditated as well as unprompted; as, a *spontaneous* burst of applause; a *spontaneous* expression of feeling. "The *spontaneous* wish to learn, which every normal child possesses...should be the driving-force in education" (*B. Russell*). "His choice of [dancing] partners, which seemed so *spontaneous*, was often managed" (*V. Heiser*). That is **impulsive** which is actuated suddenly and impetuously under the stress of the feeling or spirit of the moment and which, in contrast with *spontaneous* seems involuntary and forced by emotion rather than voluntary and natural; as, an *impulsive* act of generosity; "my heart, *impulsive* and wayward" (*Longfellow*). "He made an *impulsive* gesture, and opened his lips; but he dared not speak" (*Deland*). That is **instinctive,** in precise use, which is guided by or is the result of instinct, or a native and unreasoning prompting to actions characteristic of the species (such as nest building by birds) and contributing to its life and well-being. In less precise but not incorrect use, *instinctive*, when referred to human beings, is applied to actions, movements, feelings, thoughts, and the like, which are instantaneous, unwilled, and often, but not always, unconscious, such as reflex movements, habitual actions, temperamental spontaneous responses to stimuli, and the like. "At the teething period, when the point of the tongue *instinctively* seeks the sore gums" (*Grandgent*). "The most prolonged and difficult operations of our minds may yet become instantaneous, or, as we call it, *instinctive*" (*Shaw*). "Puzzled by the effort to reconcile his *instinctive* disgust at human vileness with his equally *instinctive* pity for human frailty" (*E. Wharton*). That is **automatic** or **mechanical** which, at least to outward appearances, seems to engage neither the mind nor the emotions and to suggest the operation of a machine. But *automatic*, like *instinctive*, stresses promptness in the response. It differs from *instinctive*, however, in implying adaptability to changing circumstances and readiness to react or to respond immediately and unvaryingly each time a given situation or stimulus recurs; as, the responses of a well-trained soldier to commands are *automatic;* the school demanded *automatic* obedience of its pupils. "Delia divined in her tone...that obscure opposition which, at the crucial moments of Tina's life, seemed *automatically* to declare itself" (*E. Wharton*). *Mechanical*, on the other hand, stresses the lifeless and, often, the perfunctory character of the response. It does not, as *automatic* often does, suggest perfect discipline which necessitates perfect attention; rather, it suggests a mind dulled by repetition of the act, motion, or the like, and capable only of routine performance. "He would deal you out facts in a dry *mechanical* way as if reading them in a book" (*Hudson*). "Not only is every transaction impersonal, it is *mechanical*" (*Brownell*).

Ana. *Extemporaneous, extempore, impromptu, improvised, offhand, unpremeditated: *natural, simple, ingenuous, unsophisticated.

2 *Automatic, autogenous, endogenous.

spook. *Apparition, phantasm, phantom, wraith, fetch, ghost, spirit, specter, shade, revenant, haunt.

spoon, *v.* Ladle, dish, *dip, lade, bail, scoop.

sporadic. Occasional, rare, scarce, *infrequent, uncommon.

Ana. Scattered, dispersed (see SCATTER): sparse, exiguous, *meager: *adventitious, adventive.

sport, *n.* **1** Play, disport, frolic, rollick, romp, gambol. See under PLAY, *v.*

Ana. Amusement, diversion, recreation, entertainment (see under AMUSE): merriment, jollity (see corresponding adjectives at MERRY).

2 *Fun, jest, game, play.

Ana. *Mirth, glee, hilarity, jollity.

3 In plural form **sports.** *Athletics, games.

sport, *v.* *Play, disport, frolic, rollick, romp, gambol.

Ana. Divert, *amuse, recreate, entertain: *skip, bound, hop.

sportive. *Playful, frolicsome, roguish, waggish, impish, mischievous, wanton.

Ana. Blithe, *merry, jocund, jovial, jolly: mirthful, gleeful, hilarious (see corresponding nouns at MIRTH).

spousal *or* **spousals.** Espousals, *marriage, matrimony, wedlock, wedding, nuptials.

sprain, *n.* *Strain.

sprain, *v.* Strain. See under STRAIN, *n.*

spread, *n.* *Expanse, amplitude, stretch.

Ana. Extent, area, magnitude, *size: *range, reach, scope, compass.

sprightly. *Lively, animated, vivacious, gay.

Ana. Active, live, dynamic: *agile, nimble, brisk, spry: *merry, blithe, jocund.

spring, *v.* **Spring, arise, rise, originate, derive, flow, issue, emanate, proceed, stem** are synonymous verbs when they mean to come up or out of something into existence. **Spring** stresses emergence, but because it usually retains its etymological implication of leaping or bounding it often suggests sudden emergence, and is especially referred to things which come into outward existence only after a period of concealment, as in the ground, a womb, the subconscious, or the like; as, plants *spring* from seed; out of their union *sprung* ten children; thoughts that *spring* up in one's mind. "We take it for granted that our dreams *spring* from below: possibly the quality of our dreams suffers in consequence" (*T. S.*

Eliot). **Arise** emphasizes the fact of coming into existence or into notice more than the conditions attending the event; often it conveys no clear suggestion of a prior state; as, a rumor *arose* and was widely circulated. "And I would that my tongue could utter The thoughts that *arise* in me" (*Tennyson*). When used with *from*, however, it usually implies a causal connection between that which is the object of the preposition and that which is the subject of the verb; in such cases it is synonymous with *result*, though it neither loses nor obscures its primary implication of coming into existence; as, mistakes often *arise* from ignorance; comfort *arose* from the reflection; the mischief *arose* from careless gossip. Sometimes, when the context suggests a cause, the *from* phrase is omitted; as, where there is continued discontent, trouble is certain to *arise*. "The right never existed, and the question whether it has been surrendered, cannot *arise*" (*Ch. Just. Marshall*). **Rise** and *arise*, as here compared (see also under RISE, 2), are often used interchangeably, but current good usage favors *arise* except where, in addition to the implication of beginning, there is, either in the word or the context, a strong suggestion of ascent; thus, new nations *rise* (better than *arise*) only to fall; the rumor *rose* (better than *arose*) and spread like wildfire; mighty forces *rise* from small beginnings. A river is said to *rise* at a certain point (rather than *arise*) because it usually has its source in a spring or fountain. **Originate** suggests a definite source or starting point which may be specified or located; as, the theory of evolution did not *originate* with Darwin; the fire *originated* in the basement; mental complexes often *originate* from repressed or unsatisfied desires. **Derive** also suggests a source, but usually it does not imply, as *originate* always implies, actual inception; rather, it presupposes a prior existence in another form or in another person or thing, and connotes descent, as by inheritance, endowment, transference, deduction, or the like; as, the power of the executive *derives* from the people; our thoughts often *derive* from our wishes. "The principle of symmetry *derives*, I suppose, from contemplation of the human form" (*Binyon*). *Flow*, *issue*, *emanate* in common imply a passing from one thing to another, the former being the source from which the latter is derived. All of these words are colored by their literal meanings. **Flow** suggests passage like water, easily as if from a spring, or abundantly as if from a reservoir; as, "Praise God, from whom all blessings *flow*" (*Ken*); "Is it not clear that from such a welter [of confused interests and powers], any one of many diverse consequences might have *flowed*?" (*Belloc*). **Issue** most frequently suggests emergence into existence, as if from a womb. "Proud deliverance [of a nation] *issuing* out of pain and direful throes" (*Wordsworth*). "How far Arnold is responsible for the birth of Humanism would be difficult to say; we can at least say that it *issues* very naturally from his doctrine" (*T. S. Eliot*). **Emanate** is used largely in reference to immaterial constructions, such as a law, a principle, a power, a system of thought, or the like; it connotes the passage of something impalpable or invisible, and suggests a less obvious causal connection between the source and the thing derived than *flow* or *issue*. "We may certainly say...that they [the arts and sciences] all *emanate* from the same focus" (*H. Ellis*). "The government of the Union...is, emphatically, and truly, a government of the people. In form and in substance it *emanates* from them" (*Ch. Just. Marshall*). **Proceed** stresses place of origin or, sometimes, parentage, derivation, or cause. "By every word that *proceedeth* out of the mouth of God" (*Matthew* iv. 4). "No public benefit which you receive But it *proceeds* or comes from them to you And no way from yourselves" (*Shak.*). **Stem** suggests growth out of, as of a stem from a root or a branch; it is therefore used in reference to things that come into existence through the influence of a predecessor, as a natural outgrowth, or as a subordinate development. "The good portrait painters...*stem* from Rubens" (*F. J. Mather*).

Ana. Emerge, loom, *appear: *come, arrive: *begin, commence, start.

spring, *n.* *Also* **springs.** *Motive, impulse, incentive, inducement, spur, goad.

Ana. *Origin, source, root, inception: *cause, determinant, antecedent: *stimulus, stimulant, incitement, impetus.

springy. *Elastic, resilient, flexible, supple.

Ana. Yielding, submitting (see YIELD): recoiling, rebounding (see REBOUND).

sprinkle, *v.* **Sprinkle, besprinkle, asperse, spatter, bespatter, splash** agree in meaning to scatter a fluid in drops or blobs, or (in the case of *sprinkle* and *besprinkle*) a powdered substance in fine particles, over the surface of something. **Sprinkle** commonly implies the use of the fingers or of some utensil that permits dispersion in fine drops or particles; as, to water plants by *sprinkling* them; to *sprinkle* food with salt; to *sprinkle* sand over an icy walk; cf. a water *sprinkler*, a sugar *sprinkler*, a *sprinkling* can. In extended use, it may be used in reference to anything that is thinly dispersed or lightly strewn; as, his letters are *sprinkled* with hints of dissatisfaction; a broad plain *sprinkled* with a few houses. **Besprinkle** differs from *sprinkle* only in being a somewhat affected literary word and in occurring more often in the extended than in the primary sense. "Sloping banks *besprinkled* with pleasant villas" (*Dickens*). **Asperse** is now rare in its literal sense of *sprinkle;* it and its derivative noun *aspersion* (especially the latter) are found, however, as technical terms referring to the method of baptizing by sprinkling the head in contrast with that by pouring water on the head or by immersion. "Coleridge, his locks *aspersed* with fairy foam" (*W. Watson*). **Spatter,** and its intensive **bespatter,** more often imply accident than intention; they also carry, in contrast to *sprinkle*, suggestions of more force and sound in the scattering, of greater size in the drops, of one's own or another's carelessness, or of a disagreeable effect such as spotting or soiling; as, a passing automobile *spattered* his coat with mud; the rain *spattered* her silk stockings; ink *bespattered* the walls of the schoolroom; they were *bespattered* with paint from head to foot. In extended use, both words may be used in reference to anything that is more or less thickly strewn or scattered; as, "the bare floor *Spattered* with moonlight" (*Amy Lowell*); a speech *bespattered* with tributes. **Splash** always suggests a violent or careless, profuse, and often noisy, spattering; when it implies soiling or staining it usually suggests a daubing or streaking (or the appearance of these) rather than a spotting; as, to *splash* water while bathing; to *splash* coffee into one's saucer; to *splash* a bib with milk; to *splash* a mirror with lather.

Ana. Drench, impregnate (see SOAK): moisten, dampen (see corresponding adjectives at WET): *scatter, disperse, dissipate.

sprite. *Fairy, faery, fay, elf, pixy, gnome, dwarf, goblin, brownie, puck, nix, shee, leprechaun, banshee.

spruce, *adj.* Dashing, dapper, *stylish, fashionable, modish, smart, chic, natty, nifty, nobby, posh, toffish, brave, braw.

Ana. Fussy, finical, fastidious, pernickety (see NICE).

Ant. Blowzy.

spry. *Agile, brisk, nimble.

Ana. *Quick, ready, prompt: *vigorous, energetic, strenuous: hale, *healthy, sound, robust.
Ant. Doddering.

spume. *Foam, froth, scum, lather, suds, yeast.

spunky. *Spirited, high-spirited, mettlesome, fiery, peppery, gingery.
Ana. Dauntless, undaunted, bold (see BRAVE): daring, venturous, venturesome (see ADVENTUROUS): restive, restless, skittish, *impatient.

spur, *n.* Goad, spring, *motive, impulse, incentive, inducement.
Ana. *Stimulus, stimulant, incitement, impetus: activation, actuation, motivation (see corresponding verbs at ACTIVATE): *cause, determinant: provoking *or* provocation, exciting *or* excitement (see corresponding verbs at PROVOKE).

spurn. Reject, repudiate, refuse, *decline.
Ana. Disdain, scorn, scout, *despise, contemn: flout, *scoff, sneer.
Ant. Crave: embrace.

spy, *n.* *Emissary, scout, intelligencer, secret-service agent, secret agent.

squabble, *v.* Quarrel, wrangle, altercate, bicker, spat, tiff. See under QUARREL, *n.*
Ana. *Contend, fight, battle, war: struggle, strive (see ATTEMPT, *v.*): dispute, agitate, argue (see DISCUSS).

squabble, *n.* *Quarrel, wrangle, altercation, bickering, spat, tiff.
Ana. Dispute, controversy, *argument: row, rumpus, scrap, *brawl, broil.

squadron. *Fleet, flotilla, armada.

squalid. *Dirty, nasty, filthy, foul.
Ana. Slovenly, unkempt, sloppy, *slipshod: sordid, abject (see MEAN, *adj.*): *slatternly, frowzy.

square, *v.* *Agree, conform, accord, comport, harmonize, correspond, tally, jibe.
Ana. Equal, *match, approach, touch, rival: balance, offset (see COMPENSATE): concur, coincide (see AGREE).

squat, *adj.* Thickset, *thick, stocky, chunky, stubby, dumpy.
Ant. Lanky.

squeamish. Finical, fussy, pernickety, fastidious, *nice, dainty.
Ana. Exacting, demanding, requiring (see DEMAND): hypercritical, *critical, faultfinding, caviling, captious, carping.

squib. *Libel, skit, lampoon, pasquinade.

squirm. *Writhe, agonize.
Ana. Twist, bend, turn (see CURVE, *v.*): wince, flinch, blench, shrink, *recoil.

stabilize. **Stabilize, steady, poise, balance, ballast, trim** come into comparison when they mean to maintain or cause to maintain position or equilibrium. Despite their agreement in basic meaning, they vary widely in their implications and in their range of application and are seldom interchangeable. **Stabilize** is used chiefly in reference to that which is fluctuating or is subject to fluctuation and which requires either external aids or regulation; as, to *stabilize* the price of wheat by creating a reserve not to be marketed until the demand exceeds the supply; a gyroscope and other devices for *stabilizing* an airplane. "The practical advantage of organised cult and sanctified custom is to *stabilise* valuable results already won" (*Inge*). **Steady** is used chiefly in reference to that which is losing its customary or necessary stability or equilibrium and is rocking, shaking, fluttering, tipping, or the like; as, to *steady* a table by putting a piece of wood under one of its legs; to take medicine to *steady* one's nerves or one's pulse; a child learning to walk *steadies* himself by grasping at any support within his reach. **Poise** is used chiefly in reference to that which maintains its equilibrium perfectly under adverse conditions or in opposition to external forces such as the law of gravitation; it implies a proper distribution of weight (as the result either of advance action or of conditions inherent in the structure or constitution of the person or thing maintaining equilibrium) with reference to the supporting medium (air, water, etc.) or that which supports (the hand, a column, etc.); as, the ballet dancer *poised* on tiptoe for an instant. "As the fowl can keep Absolute stillness, *poised* aloft in air" (*Wordsworth*). In extended use, when employed in reference to the mind or spirit, *poise* implies either acquired control over the faculties or an inner serenity that enables one to remain steady or impervious to disquieting or disturbing influences; as, "Sobriety of thought which *poises* the heart" (*Steele*); "Self-collected, *poised*, and steady" (*Wordsworth*). **Balance** also implies an equilibrium that is the result of the proper distribution of weight, but it carries none of the suggestions of sustained position or equilibrium so strong in *poise;* thus, one *balances* a boat by adjusting its cargo so that there is no excess weight at any one point, and one *balances* a flywheel by removing portions where the weight is excessive or by adding weight in its lighter sections, but in either case the equilibrium may be lost if the cargo shifts or a section of the flywheel alters in weight. Though both *balance* and *poise* imply that the thing affected is steadied, *balance* often carries so strong an implication of uncertain equilibrium that it suggests wavering or rocking. "In a moment of inattention, the child crept to the edge, and was *balanced* on the very verge. To call to it, to touch it, would have insured its destruction" (*Jefferies*). **Ballast** is used in reference to that which needs to be held down because too light, too buoyant, or the like; it implies the addition of something heavy or solid enough to ensure stability; as, to *ballast* a ship with a cargo of metal; to *ballast* a free balloon with bags of sand which may be thrown overboard if further height is desired. *Ballast* is often found in extended use with reference especially to the mind and the moral character that might otherwise suffer from volatility, frivolousness, or unwieldiness. " 'Tis charity must *ballast* the heart" (*H. Hammond*). "Like many other men of high intellectual gifts, Arnold was *ballasted* with a just proportion of...practical wisdom" (*C. E. Montague*). **Trim,** in the sense here considered, is chiefly nautical; it implies proper balancing of a boat or ship so that it sits well on the water or fulfills any of the conditions that make for steadiness in sailing. "They [the small boats] could only be balanced by man and woman, that was the only way they could be *trimmed* on even keel" (*Jefferies*).
Ana. Regulate, *adjust, fix: *set, settle, firm, establish.

stable, *adj.* *Lasting, durable, perdurable, permanent, perpetual.
Ana. Enduring, persisting, abiding (see CONTINUE): secure, *safe: *steady, constant: stanch, steadfast, resolute (see FAITHFUL).
Ant. Unstable: changeable.

stack, *n.* Heap, pile, mass, bank, shock, cock. See under HEAP, *v.*

stack, *v.* *Heap, pile, mass, bank, shock, cock.
Ana. Collect, *gather, assemble: amass, *accumulate, hoard.

staid. Sedate, grave, *serious, sober, earnest.
Ana. *Decorous, decent, demure, seemly: *cool, collected, composed: smug, priggish, self-complacent, *complacent.
Ant. Jaunty.

stain, *n.* *Stigma, blot, brand.
Ana. *Blemish, defect, flaw: mark, *sign, token: *disgrace, dishonor.

stake. *Bet, wager, pot, blind, ante.

stalwart. *Strong, stout, sturdy, tough, tenacious.
Ana. Husky, brawny, *muscular, sinewy, athletic: lusty, nervous, *vigorous: robust, sound, *healthy.

stammer, *v.* **Stammer, stutter** agree in meaning to speak in a faltering, hesitating, or stumbling manner. Although in their earliest senses there was little, if any, recognized difference in their meaning, they tend to be distinguished in current use. **Stammer** now usually implies a cause such as fear, embarrassment, a sudden shock, or the like, which makes one for the time being lose control over his vocal organs and inhibits his power to speak straightforwardly; also, the word suggests interruptions in which one either cannot form sounds or else articulates with great difficulty. "The eloquent tongue forgot its office. Cicero *stammered*, blundered, and sat down" (*Froude*). "She shrank a little at his vehemence, but neither blushed nor *stammered*; answering: 'I see nothing wrong in doing what Mama thinks right, Richard'" (*Meredith*). **Stutter** often, especially in current use, carries a clearer implication of the involuntary repetition of sounds, especially of consonantal or syllabic sounds, than *stammer* does. In some use, it is distinguished on this ground only; as, "No two persons *stutter* alike...A stutterer who stumbles over the initial of 'Peter' may have no trouble with any other *p* in...'Peter Piper's peppers'" (*E. W. Scripture*). More often, however, *stutter*, in distinction from *stammer*, implies a constitutional defect, such as a nervous affliction or a speech defect. Whichever idea is involved, the term usually suggests a habit and not merely, as *stammer* usually suggests, a temporary reaction. "This gentleman has...a small natural infirmity; he *stutters* a little" (*S. Foote*). In nontechnical use the terms are often employed as though they were interchangeable.

stamp, *n.* *Impression, impress, imprint, print.

stanch *or* **staunch.** Steadfast, resolute, constant, leal, true, *faithful.
Ana. Trusty, trustworthy, *reliable, dependable, tried: stout, *strong, tough, tenacious, sturdy, stalwart.
Con. *Inconstant, fickle, mercurial, unstable, capricious.

stand, *v.* Tolerate, brook, *bear, suffer, endure, abide.

stand, *n.* *Position, attitude.
Ana. *Point of view, standpoint, viewpoint, slant, angle.

standard, *n.* **1** *Flag, ensign, banner, color, streamer, pennant, pennon, jack.
2 Standard, criterion, gauge (*or* **gage**), **yardstick, touchstone** come into comparison when they denote the means by which one determines what a thing should be or whether it is correct or approaches perfection. **Standard** (as here compared: see also MODEL, FLAG) applies to any definite rule, principle, or measure set up and established especially by authority as the means of determining quantity, weight, extent, value, or quality (as the, *standard* for the bushel as established by the United States government is a quantity equaling the contents of a measure that holds 77.6274 pounds of distilled water at 39.2° Fahrenheit; during the seventeenth and eighteenth centuries dramatic and epic poetry were governed by *standards* derived from the practice of the ancient Greeks and Romans), or as a means of ascertaining the level reached by a thing, its degree in a scale, or the like (as, "All sorts of dogmatic *standards* have been set up by which to measure the degree of a people's civilisation"—*H. Ellis;* "they say we have no taste; we cannot make art jugs for the mantelpiece, crockery for the bracket, screens for the fire; we cannot even decorate the wall of a room as it should be done. If these are the *standards* by which a sense of art is to be tried, their scorn is to a certain degree just"—*Jefferies*). In a somewhat looser, but correct, sense, *standard* often applies to a model or pattern accepted as the means of determining what is good or admirable (for this sense see MODEL). The two senses are not always carefully distinguished. **Criterion** differs from *standard* in stressing employment as a test. The term applies only to a rule, principle, model, pattern, or the like, which is used in determining how far a person or thing is good or bad, how closely he or it approaches the standard of perfection, or what is his or its true and exact character. In general, a *criterion* is the measure used by a judge or critic of something that is accomplished, a *standard* is the rule or pattern given to one who is to do something or make something for his guidance in attaining some quality or qualities, such as exactness, morality, soundess, or beauty. A *criterion*, strictly speaking, is an aid by means of which a correct judgment is reached; as, to accept the principles of Aristotle's "Poetics" as *criteria* for the drama; "The *criterion* of constitutionality is not whether we believe the law to be for the public good" (*Justice Holmes*); "Darwinism gives us no *criterion* at all whereby we may pronounce one order of beings higher than another" (*Inge*). All of the other terms here discriminated are synonyms only in their extended or figurative senses. **Gauge,** literally either a standard measure or scale of measurement (thus, in many countries, the standard *gauge* in railways, i.e., the standard for distance between rails is 4 feet, 8½ inches) or an instrument or device by means of which is measured the force, quantity, or the like, of something that fluctuates (as, a rain *gauge;* a pressure *gauge*), is now in its extended use more often applied to a definite criterion than to a standard; as, the usual *gauge* of a veteran's disability is his incapacity for manual labor; "There is not in our hands any fixed *gauge* of minds" (*I. Taylor*). **Yardstick,** literally a measuring stick a yard long marked in feet, inches, and subdivisions of an inch, in figurative use denotes a criterion or gauge especially of that which is intangible, immaterial, or incapable of measurement except in terms of something else; as, there is no *yardstick* by which we can determine a man's spiritual greatness; success is not to be measured by the *yardstick* of the dollar; the Tennessee Valley Authority (TVA) proposed the "utilization of Muscle Shoals as a *yardstick* in determining the relative costs of public and private power operation." **Touchstone,** literally a black siliceous stone allied to flint, which was used in testing the purity of gold or silver by the streak left by the latter when rubbed across it, in its far more common figurative sense designates one thing, especially a superior thing, which when applied as a criterion to another thing of the same kind shows up the extent to which the latter approaches it. "There can be no more useful help for discovering what poetry belongs to the class of the truly excellent...than to have always in one's mind lines and expressions of the great masters, and to apply them as a *touchstone* to other poetry" (*Arnold*). "Till experience had given him some *touchstone* by which he could judge the values of that old tragedy" (*Galsworthy*).
Ana. Norm, median, par, mean, *average: rule, *law: *principle, fundamental, axiom: *model, pattern, exemplar, paradigm.
3 Ideal, beau ideal, paradigm, *model, pattern, exemplar, example, mirror.
Ana. See those at STANDARD, 2.

stand-in. *Substitute, supply, understudy, double, locum tenens, alternate, pinch hitter.

standpoint. *Point of view, viewpoint, angle, slant.
Ana. Stand, *position, attitude.

stanza. *Verse.

stare, *v.* *Gaze, gape, glare, peer, gloat.
Ana. Look, watch, *see: glower, lower, scowl, *frown.

stark. *Stiff, rigid, inflexible, tense, wooden.
Ana. Settled, established, fixed, set, firmed (see SET, *v.*).
Con. *Elastic, resilient, springy, flexible, supple: fluid, *liquid.

starry. Starry, stellar, astral, sidereal agree in meaning of, referring to, or suggestive of a star or group of stars. **Starry** is the ordinary nontechnical term, capable of being used in reference to a star or stars in any sense, such as the celestial bodies known as stars, the geometrical figure having five, six, or more points, the conventionalized star, or, less often, the principal actor or actress in a play or motion picture; as, a *starry* night; a *starry* banner; *starry* eyes; "a...revival of 'The Two Orphans' with a *starry* cast" (*B. Mantle*). **Stellar** has the same range of reference as *starry* but, since the connotations of the words are not the same, they are rarely interchangeable: *starry* gathers its connotations of brilliancy, remoteness, beauty, and the like, chiefly from the appearance of the celestial stars to the ordinary observer; *stellar* derives its suggestions chiefly from astrological lore of the stars as influencing all living things and as shaping human destinies, or from astronomical knowledge of the constitution, arrangement, and classification of stars; thus, one may speak of a *stellar*, rather than a *starry*, influence or aspect; of a *stellar*, rather than *starry*, eclipse or nebula. "These soft fires ...shed down Their *stellar* virtue on all kinds that grow On Earth" (*Milton*). "Kapteyn worked nearly alone in the field of *stellar* astronomy" (*G. W. Gray*). *Stellar* is also used more often than *starry* of theatrical or cinematic stars; as, a *stellar* (usually preferred to *starry*) cast. **Astral** is neither a colloquial word nor a technical term of astronomy. It is, however, a technical term in theosophy and similar cults and is not infrequent in literary use, deriving its connotations of spirituality and remoteness from the fleshly largely from mythological and other conceptions of the stars as the abode of celestial spirits or of supersensible beings whose nature and constitution are rarer and finer than those of human beings, or as the abiding places of souls between successive incarnations; as, *astral* spirits. "It was generally felt that the Reverend Archibald Jones and Miss Chetwynd the elder would lift marriage to what would now be termed an *astral* plane" (*Bennett*). **Sidereal,** though often interchangeable with *stellar*, is now used especially in distinction from *solar* as applied to periods of time measured by the rotation of the earth with reference to a given star; thus, the *sidereal* day (determined by reference to Aries) is 3 minutes and 55.91 seconds shorter (as measured in solar time) than the mean solar day.

start, *v.* *Begin, commence, initiate, inaugurate.
Ana. Institute, *found, establish, organize: *enter, penetrate: originate, proceed, *spring.

startle. Scare, alarm, terrify, terrorize, *frighten, fright, affray, affright.
Ana. *Surprise, astonish, astound: rouse, arouse, *stir: electrify, *thrill.

state, *n.* **State, condition, mode, situation, posture, status, estate** are here compared as abstract terms meaning the way in which a person or thing manifests his or its existence or the circumstances under which he or it exists or by which he or it is given a definite character. **State** may be used so generally that it applies merely to a form of existence which has little or no relation to space, time, body, or the like, but which is purely mental, spiritual, or otherwise immaterial; as, "[Dante's Inferno] reminds us that Hell is not a place but a *state*" (*T. S. Eliot*). "These two propensities [a moving forward with eagerness, a looking backward with regret]...can easily be resolved into the same principle. Both spring from our impatience of the *state* in which we actually are" (*Macaulay*). The term may also be used specifically to name the combination of circumstances affecting a person or thing at a given time, or the sum of the relations, qualities, or characteristics involved in his or its existence at the time under consideration; as, the city was then in a *state* of siege; to live fifty years happily in the *state* of matrimony; the present *state* of industry; "She did not have time to understand...the *state* of her feelings" (*Conrad*); his mental *state* is a cause of great concern. "What is called a *state* of society is the simultaneous *state* of all the greater social facts or phenomena" (*J. S. Mill*). **Condition** is interchangeable with *state* only when actual or concrete use, as in circumstances, is implied (as, his mental *condition* is a cause of concern; the present *condition* of the country; "It is a *condition* which confronts us, not a theory"—*G. Cleveland*), but even then it carries a stronger implication than *state* of a relation to the causes or circumstances which produced or are producing the effect, and a weaker suggestion of the duration of that effect; also, *condition* may be used in the plural in the sense of combination of circumstances and of qualities or characteristics, as *state* may not; as, his physical *condition* improved with rest and sufficient exercise; "Under the best *conditions*, a voyage is one of the severest tests to try a man" (*Emerson*); "the incapacity to achieve anything distinctly good or evil is inherent in our earthly *condition*" (*Conrad*). "There is no possible method of compelling a child to feel sympathy or affection; the only possible method is to observe the *conditions* under which these feelings arise spontaneously, and then endeavour to produce the *conditions*" (*B. Russell*). This suggestion of a relation to an external cause or causes is often so strong that the word frequently denotes a circumstance that serves as a causative influence, rather than a combination of circumstances that form a state of being. "Ancient man sought the shelter of trees and banks, of caves and hollows...so the labourers under somewhat the same *conditions* came to the corner where the bushes grew" (*Jefferies*). "Science has to deal...with scores of chemical energies which it knows little about except that they always seem to be constant to the same *conditions*" (*H. Adams*). **Mode** (as here compared: see also METHOD; FASHION, 2), is purely a philosophical term: as such, it is variously defined. In general, however, despite many differences in definition, the term implies an opposition to substance, defined as the underlying reality which can be known only from its external manifestations such as color, form, texture, etc. Hence, *mode* usually applies to this combination of characters by which a substance is manifested in a particular individual; thus, Spinoza calls particular mental states *modes* of mind or thought and particular physical phenomena *modes* of matter or extension. "I used to live entirely for pleasure. I shunned suffering and sorrow of every kind....I resolved to ignore them as far as possible: to treat them...as *modes* of imperfection" (*Wilde*). **Situation** (as here compared: see also POSITION, 3) applies only to a state or condition that represents a combination of definite concrete circumstances or such a conjunction of particular circumstances that the whole has a peculiarly exciting or interesting character; consequently, more than *state* or *condition*, *situation* implies an arrangement of these circumstances not only with reference to each other but also with respect to the character or circumstances of the person or persons involved, so as to make for difficulty or advantage, embarrassment or elation, uncertainty or security, or the like; as, "Such views of life were to some extent the natural begettings of her *situation* upon her nature" (*Hardy*); "What he expected of me was to extricate him from a difficult *situation*" (*Conrad*); "That slender, unrigid erectness, and the fine carriage of head, which always made him seem master of the *situation*" (*Cather*). The term is also applied to any comparably striking and interesting combination of events in a novel, drama, or other narrative, especially one whose outcome involves uncertainty or suspense. "One knows the *situation* in fiction—the desperate girl appealing out of her misery to the Christian priest for help. So many women have this touch of melodrama, this sense of a *situation*" (*R. Macaulay*). "[Wilkie] Collins...was a master of plot and *situation*, of those elements of drama which are most essential to melodrama" (*T. S. Eliot*). **Posture** (as here compared: see POSTURE, 1) was once used in the sense of *condition* when that represented a state into which one was forced by need of preparation for something to come; as, to put a warship in a *posture* of defense; to put a house on the coast in a *posture* to receive a storm; "[Christ] insisted upon a certain...*posture* of the soul as proper to man's reception of this revelation" (*H. P. Liddon*). In current use, the term is often a closer synonym of *situation* than of *condition* and is chiefly found in the phrase "*posture* of affairs"; as, "Eustacia...had become considerably depressed by the *posture* of affairs" (*Hardy*). **Status** is strictly a legal term implying reference to one's state or condition as determined by one's legal capacity or one's legal relations to another or others, as in marriage, in making contracts, in inheriting property, in citizenship, or the like. In this sense, one's status is often determined by one's age, one's sex, one's degree of mental capacity, one's possession of the right to vote, and the like; as, the *status* of imbeciles and of insane persons; her *status* as a widow entitles her to a third of her husband's estate. In more general use, *status* applies to the standing of a person or thing with reference to all other persons or all other things of the same kind, and as determined by rank, social, official, industrial, or other position, popular estimation, or any other similarly determining factor; as, "In some hazy way, he fancied that it was fine and impressive, that it gave him a *status* among men" (*Kipling*); "As adopted by Augustus, it ['princeps'] was a popular appellation...defining a *status* rather than an office" (*Buchan*); "The necessity of readjusting our way of life to Tommy's new *status* of proprietor" (*M. Austin*); "In the opinion of the theologians of the Middle Age the conduct of life had been reduced to the *status* of an exact science" (*J. W. Krutch*). **Estate,** in its older sense of state or condition, now appears in a very few idiomatic phrases; as, he has come recently to man's *estate*.

Ana. *Phase, aspect: plight, *predicament, quandary, dilemma: pass, *juncture, exigency, emergency, crisis.

state, *v.* Report, *relate, rehearse, recite, recount, narrate, describe.

Ana. Expound, *explain, elucidate, interpret: *assert, affirm, declare.

stately. Magnificent, imposing, majestic, august, *grand, noble, grandiose.

Ana. Princely, regal, royal, *kingly, imperial: *splendid, glorious, superb, sublime: sumptuous, opulent, *luxurious.

statement. *Account, bill.

statesman. *Politician, politico.

station, *n.* **1 Station, depot** are here considered only as denoting a regular railway stop for the discharge and taking on of passengers, baggage (Brit., luggage), and freight (Brit., goods), or the building or buildings at such a stop. **Station** has always been the approved term in British use (especially in the phrase "railway *station*") for the stop and for the building or buildings connected with the transportation of passengers and their luggage. It is now often used also of the building or buildings connected with the transportation of goods (a "goods *station*"). *Station* (especially "railroad *station*") is now also the approved term, in the sense given in the binding sentence, in most parts of the United States. Until the end of the nineteenth century **depot** was the more common term and it still prevails in certain sections, though its use is generally discountenanced. *Depot* still occurs in British use as a designation of what is commonly called a "freight station" in the United States.

2 *Habitat, range.

statue. *Image, simulacrum, effigy, icon, portrait, photograph, mask.

stature. *Height, altitude, elevation.

status. Situation, posture, condition, *state, mode, estate.

statute. 1 Ordinance, regulation, *law, rule, precept, canon.

2 *Bill, act, law.

staunch. Variant of STANCH.

stay, *v.* **1 Stay, remain, wait, abide, tarry, linger. Stay,** the most general of these terms, stresses continuance in a place (sometimes, in a specified condition); it often specifically connotes the status of visitor or guest; as, they could not decide whether to *stay* or to go; they went for tea and *stayed* for dinner; she was asked to *stay* a week. **Remain** is often used interchangeably with *stay*, but in precise usage it means to stay behind or to be left after others have gone; as, few *remained* in the building after the alarm was given. "A little Verse my All that shall *remain*" (*Gray*). To **wait** is to stay in expectation or in readiness; as, at his request, no one *waited* for him at the pier; the taxi *waited* one hour while they were shopping. To **abide** is to stay at length and usually connotes either stable residence or patient waiting for an outcome. "She hated the change; she felt like one banished; but here she was forced to *abide*" (*Hardy*). To **tarry** is to stay or rest when it is time to depart or to proceed; as, do not *tarry* if you wish to catch the noon train; some children like to *tarry* on the way to school. **Linger,** like *tarry*, usually implies outstaying one's appointed or allotted time; frequently, however, it also implies either deliberate delay or disinclination to depart. "Strange, that now she was released she should *linger* by him" (*Meredith*).

Ana. *Delay, procrastinate, lag, loiter: *arrest, check, interrupt: *continue, persist.

2 Sojourn, lodge, put up, stop, *reside, live, dwell.

3 *Defer, postpone, suspend, intermit.

Ana. *Delay, retard, slow, slacken, detain: *restrain, check, curb: *hinder, obstruct, impede.

steadfast *or* **stedfast.** Stanch, resolute, constant, leal, true, *faithful, loyal.

Ana. Settled, established, set, fixed (see SET, *v.*): *steady, constant: stable, durable, perdurable, *lasting: enduring, persisting, abiding (see CONTINUE).

Ant. Capricious.

steady, *adj.* **Steady, uniform, even, equable, constant** come into comparison as meaning neither markedly varying nor variable, but much the same throughout its course, its extent, or the like. **Steady** is by far the most widely applicable of these terms; in general, it suggests regularity and lack of deviation, especially in movement, but it may imply such fixity in position or character as to be immovable or unshakable (as, *steady* as a rock; a *steady* pole; a *steady* person). When, however, movement, motion, or direction is implied, the term may connote lack of fluctuation (as, a *steady* market; *steady* prices; a *steady* flame), or lack of nervousness (as, *steady* hands; a *steady* voice), or a constant uninterrupted flow, pursuit, or the like (as, a *steady* stream; a *steady* rain; *steady* work). **Uniform** stresses the sameness or alikeness of all the elements, parts, units, instances, or the like, that comprise a whole, whether that be an aggregate, a series, a combination of all instances, a course, or the like; as, the cells of the human organism are not *uniform* in structure and function; "an *uniform* course of legislation [respecting citizenship]...by the colonies, by the States, and by Congress, running through a period of more than a century" (*Ch. Just. Taney*); the temperature of this region is nearly *uniform;* the symptoms in all cases of the disease are *uniform.* **Even** stresses steadiness more than uniformity; it often connotes a dead level in quality or in character, or the like, which is unvaryingly maintained, or which is incapable of alteration or disturbance; as, her monotonous *even* voice; the *even* flow of his verse. "I mean to...support with an *even* temper, and without any violent transports of mind, a sudden gust of prosperity" (*Fielding*). **Equable** usually implies an inherent quality which makes for invariability, such as uniformity (as, an *equable* movement; an *equable* pulse) or freedom from extremes or sudden marked changes (as, an *equable* climate; an *equable* temper), or by a temperamental calmness (as, "low *equable* tones, curiously in contrast to the strident babble"—*Kipling;* "she won and lost, with the same *equable* sangfroid"—*R. Macaulay*). **Constant** (see also FAITHFUL, CONTINUAL) implies fixity in character, quality, or condition, or persistence in kind or type under the same conditions; as, "The sand is frequently yellow...but this colour is by no means *constant*" (*Lyell*); "throughout nature there runs a *constant* association of cause and effect" (*Inge*); "Science has to deal... with scores of chemical energies which it knows little about except that they always seem to be *constant* to the same conditions" (*H. Adams*).

Ana. Stable, durable, perdurable, perpetual, *lasting: enduring, persisting, continuing (see CONTINUE): stanch, steadfast, resolute, constant (see FAITHFUL): persevering, persisting (see PERSEVERE).

Ant. Unsteady: nervous, jumpy.

steady, *v.* *Stabilize, poise, balance, ballast, trim.

Con. *Shake, rock, agitate, convulse: *tip, tilt, cant, careen.

steal, *v.* **Steal, pilfer, filch, purloin, lift, pinch, snitch, swipe, cop** agree in meaning to take something that belongs to another such as money, valuables, or goods, either without his knowledge or in a manner that eludes his observation. **Steal,** the ordinary and general term of this group, may be used in reference to any act involving taking what belongs to another or what only he has a right to give or grant; as, to *steal* a person's watch; to *steal* a kiss; to *steal* jewels from their hiding place. The term, however, often carries so strong a suggestion of furtiveness or secrecy that it may be used in reference to getting something without the other's leave, or wish, or knowledge, whether that action is culpable or pardonable or works to the other's injury or not; as, he did not know that his money had been *stolen* until he reached the bank; to *steal* a few moments from work; ill health has *stolen* the bloom from her cheeks; "Powell *stole* several glances at him with a curiosity very natural under the circumstances" (*Conrad*). **Pilfer,** once as strong as *plunder* or *rob* (see these words under ROB), now often specifically implies stealing in small amounts or is chosen as a euphemism when *steal* seems too harsh or plainspoken; as, a *pilfering* servant; he refused to employ any small boys because he suspected all of a tendency to *pilfer;* "ladies of unexceptionable position who are caught *pilfering* furs in shops" (*L. P. Smith*). **Filch,** though close to *pilfer* in its implications of petty thievery, carries a more obvious suggestion of the use of surreptitious means or of snatching; as, "Who steals my purse steals trash... But he that *filches* from me my good name Robs me of that which not enriches him And makes me poor indeed" (*Shak.*); "Fain would they *filch* that little food away" (*Dryden*); "fire which Prometheus *filched* for us from Heaven" (*Byron*); the boys were in the habit of *filching* fruit from the peddlers' carts. **Purloin,** though often differing little in meaning from the preceding terms, is preferred by careful writers and speakers when there is an intent to heighten the implication of removal, carrying off, or making away with, for one's own use or purposes. It may also suggest not only theft or robbery, but even despoliation, plagiarism, defalcation, or the like; as, "I hope to quote him is not to *purloin*" (*Dryden*); "The Edict of Restitution...left the original loot, prior to 1552, in the hands of the spoilers. But it proposed that all since *purloined* should be given back" (*Belloc*). **Lift** is often used colloquially in place of *purloin* or, sometimes, of *steal;* as, "Thieves that came to *lift* their cattle" (*A. Ramsay*); "He took to his old courses, and *lifted* a purse here, and a watch there" (*Thackeray*). The word is found also in the intransitive verb *shoplift* (most commonly in the form of the verbal noun *shoplifting*). The other words of the group are all regarded as slang, **pinch,** and **snitch** in their implications coming closest to *filch,* **swipe** (an Americanism) being used in place of any of the others, and **cop** stressing a stealing on the spur of the moment.

Ana. *Rob, plunder, rifle, loot, thieve, burglarize: embezzle, peculate, *defalcate.

stealthy. *Secret, covert, furtive, clandestine, surreptitious, underhand, underhanded, privy, backstairs.

Ana. *Sly, cunning, crafty, artful, tricky, wily: sneaking, slinking, skulking (see LURK).

stedfast. Variant of STEADFAST.

steep, *adj.* **Steep, abrupt, precipitous, sheer** come into comparison when they mean having an incline approaching the perpendicular. The words are here arranged in ascending order of degree of perpendicularity. That is **steep** which has so sharp a slope or pitch that ascent, or, less frequently, descent, is difficult. "A military road, which rises...by an acclivity not dangerously *steep,* but sufficiently laborious" (*Johnson*). "The descent is... infinitely more *steep* than the going up" (*Gray*). That is **abrupt** which adds to *steep* not only the suggestion of a sharper pitch or angle of ascent or descent, but also that of a sudden break in a level. "It is the high land nearest to the shore which falls most *abruptly*" (*Kinglake*). That is **precipitous** (in ordinary usage) which suggests a headlong descent and an abruptness like that of a precipice; as, a *precipitous* height; a *precipitous* descent. "A big black, *precipitous* roof" (*H. James*). That is **sheer** which is perpendicular (or very nearly so) and shows no break in its line. "*Sheer* cliffs that fell from the summit to the plain, more than a thousand feet" (*Cather*).

Ana. Elevated, lifted, raised (see LIFT): lofty, *high.

steep, *v.* *Soak, saturate, impregnate, drench, sog, sop, ret, waterlog.

Ana. *Infuse, imbue, ingrain: penetrate, pierce, probe (see ENTER).

steer, *v.* *Guide, lead, pilot, engineer.

Ana. *Conduct, direct, manage, control: *govern, rule.

stellar. *Starry, sidereal, astral.

stem, *v.* Proceed, issue, emanate, derive, flow, originate, *spring, arise, rise.

stenographer. Typist, *secretary, amanuensis, scribe, scrivener.

stereotyped. *Trite, hackneyed, threadbare, shopworn.

Ana. Conventional, formal (see CEREMONIAL): obsolete, archaic, antiquated (see OLD): used, employed, utilized, applied (see USE).

Ant. Changeful.

sterile. 1 **Sterile, barren, impotent, unfruitful, infertile** are here compared as meaning not having or manifesting the power to produce offspring or, literally or figuratively, to bear fruit. **Sterile,** as here compared, literally implies an inability to reproduce its kind usually because of a defect in either the male or female organism: the term is applicable to a human being or animal (chiefly to a female), to a plant, flower, and the like; as, a *sterile* woman; the "workers" among ants and bees are *sterile;* a *sterile* plant, flower, or fungus. In figurative use, *sterile* is applicable to many things, such as land in which seeds will not take root and grow (as, the *sterile* wastes of a desert), to minds that do not give birth to ideas, and by extension to persons with such minds (as, for a year his imagination had been *sterile;* a *sterile* author), to money which earns no interest (as, *sterile* gold in a safe-deposit box), or to anything which offers persons in particular or in general nothing of value, profit, or use (as, "beneath his fun lurked the *sterile* bitterness of the still young man who has tried and given up"—*E. Wharton*). **Barren** (as here compared: see also BARE, 1) applies especially to a woman who has borne no offspring or who is, or is believed to be, incapable of bearing children; as, "thy cousin Elisabeth, she hath also conceived a son in her old age: and this is the sixth month with her, who was called *barren*" (*Luke* i. 36). Figuratively (except as considered at BARE), the term usually implies a lack of return or issue; as, "a *barren* conquest which brought him no special repute" (*Buchan*); "to prove...that it [Quakerism] leads to no *barren* and self-centred detachment from social life and its problems" (*Inge*). **Impotent** (as here compared: see also POWERLESS) usually applies to the male of the species (especially of the human species) lacking power of procreation: the term is, however, applicable to persons or animals (sometimes plants) of both sexes, especially when considered as mates or as groups of mates; as, "Whole groups of animals and plants are rendered *impotent* by the same unnatural conditions" (*Darwin*). **Unfruitful** is often used in place of *barren,* not only as applied to women or to the female of any species, but as applied to land, vegetation, or efforts of any kind which bear no fruit, in any sense of that word; as, *unfruitful* women; an *unfruitful* tree; *unfruitful* soil; *unfruitful* attempts, suggestions, zeal. **Infertile** is often used in place of *sterile* especially in its literal sense; as, "animals and plants, when removed from their natural conditions, are often rendered in some degree *infertile*" (*Darwin*).

Ana. *Bare, barren, bald, naked: arid, *dry: *meager, exiguous: empty, hollow, nugatory, *vain.

Ant. Fertile: exuberant. — *Con.* Bearing, yielding, producing, turning out (see BEAR): fecund, fruitful, prolific (see FERTILE).

2 **Sterile, aseptic, antiseptic** agree in meaning free from danger of infection or infecting. That is **sterile** which is free from all living microorganisms, including bacteria and their viable spores, and certain fungi; as, distilled water is a *sterile* fluid; instruments rendered *sterile* by heat. That is **aseptic** which involves **asepsis,** or the methods or processes of making or keeping free from microorganisms causing disease. *Aseptic* implies the use of precautions to prevent infection with pathogenic microorganisms. *Aseptic* technique is used in *aseptic* surgery, that is, surgery in which the attempt is made to prevent pathogenic microorganisms from getting to the incision by such measures as having the mouth and nose of the operators covered with masks and the room, instruments, and site of operation thoroughly cleansed and disinfected. That is **antiseptic** (as here compared applied only to surgery) which involves **antisepsis,** or the process of killing or inhibiting the growth and activity of microorganisms by the use of certain substances (antiseptics). In *antiseptic* surgery, emphasis is placed on the destruction of bacteria at the site of the operation rather than on their exclusion by suitable precautionary measures.

sterilize. 1 **Sterilize, asexualize, castrate, spay, emasculate, mutilate, geld, caponize** agree in meaning to render incapable of producing offspring. **Sterilize,** the most general of these terms, is applicable to both human beings and animals, and is used in referring to any incapacitation of the reproductive power. This incapacitation may be accomplished in various ways, as by undue exposure to X rays which kill germ cells, by a surgical operation, such as vasectomy or salpingotomy, which prevents the germ cells from reaching the site where fertilization can occur, or by removal of the gonads. Today *sterilize* often suggests a legalized procedure undertaken to prevent the reproduction of undesirables such as imbeciles and habitual criminals. The term does not imply physical disfigurement. **Asexualize,** a comparatively uncommon term, is sometimes used instead of *sterilize* when the effect, rather than the process, is emphasized. **Castrate,** a narrower term than *sterilize,* strictly means to deprive of the testicles (the male reproductive glands). It is used of both human beings and animals, and usually implies a surgical procedure. By extension, *castrate* has come to mean also to deprive of the ovaries (the female reproductive glands) and therefore is often used in place of **spay,** the specific term for this operation. **Emasculate** is often preferred to *castrate* in the strict sense when the reference is to human beings, and especially when there is the intent to suggest enervation and the loss of virile or masculine qualities. **Mutilate,** usually a term of much wider significance (see MAIM), is often substituted for *castrate,* especially when the intent is to convey strongly the idea of physical disfigurement or violence, or when a euphemism is desired. **Geld,** the oldest term meaning to castrate, is now applied chiefly to domestic animals, especially the horse, and **caponize,** also meaning to castrate, is most commonly applied to the male domestic fowl, or cock, but both are sometimes used humorously of human beings.

Ant. Fertilize.

2 **Sterilize, disinfect, sanitize, fumigate** are not close synonyms, but they come into comparison when they mean to subject to a process or treatment which has for its end the destruction of living organisms, especially microorganisms. **Sterilize** suggests special drastic methods such as the application of intense heat, boiling, the use of strong chemicals, and the like, which have for their end or effect the destruction of all microorganisms whether they are disease-producing or not. The term usually suggests means taken to avoid infection; as, in preparation for an operation, the nurses and physicians *sterilize* not only every instrument, every bandage, or every sponge to be used, but put on garments that have been *sterilized;* to *sterilize* sewage by chlorination. **Dis-**

infect also suggests special methods such as exposure to strong sunlight and fresh air, thorough washing, and the like, which have for their end the destruction of all disease germs: the term usually suggests an intent to free from such germs something that is known or feared to be infected; as, to *disinfect* a room occupied by a patient with scarlet fever; to *disinfect* blankets by washing and by exposure to sunlight; after the epidemic the board of education gave orders that all books should be *disinfected*. **Sanitize,** literally to make sanitary, is often preferred by bacteriologists and public health officials when the reference is to preventive measures affecting the health of a community, such as the treatment of drinking water, air, and the like, and when neither *sterilize* (because it suggests complete destruction of microorganisms and often implies the taking of measures so drastic as to be impossible where human beings are concerned) nor *disinfect* (because it suggests the actual presence of disease germs) exactly fits their needs or makes clear their intention. **Fumigate** is associated with these terms only because fumigation was once the usual method of disinfection. Literally, it implies the use of fumes (smoke, vapor, or gas) that are destructive not only of microorganisms but of pests, such as cockroaches, beetles, and bedbugs.

stern, *adj.* *Severe, austere, ascetic.

Ana. Strict, *rigid, rigorous, stringent: *grim, implacable, unrelenting: *inflexible, inexorable: disciplined, trained, schooled (see TEACH).

Ant. Soft: lenient.

steward, *n.* **Steward, reeve, bailiff, agent, factor, seneschal, major-domo, oeconomus** come into comparison only when they denote a person who serves a lord or master as his deputy in charge of the latter's temporal affairs, especially of those pertaining to the management of his household and of his estate. With the exception of *steward* and *bailiff*, the words are now chiefly historical. **Steward** was originally applied to an official in a great household, such as that of a royal person or a noble, who was responsible for the management of the servants, the provision and dispensation of supplies, and the proper expenditure of the money or funds entrusted to him for that purpose. In the royal household the steward was always a nobleman. In current use, the term in this sense is applied to an official of a club, institution, or hospital, who has equivalent duties. Later, the term was applied to the head manager of a manor or large estate, who transacted all legal and financial business for his lord, who audited accounts, and who was responsible for all arrangements that had to do with maintaining or increasing the income derived from the estate. In present use, *steward* generally implies management of the concerns of a large landholder, such as the supervision of employees, the collection of rents, and the keeping of accounts, but it seldom suggests so complete a delegation of power from lord to deputy as was implied in the earlier senses. However, in all these senses *steward* carries an implication of custodianship or guardianship of goods or moneys which are entrusted to him by his lord or master and for the use of which he must render an accounting in due time. This implication has been so heightened by use of the word in the New Testament, especially in the parable of "the unjust *steward*" (*Luke* xvi. 1–8), in the figurative reference to a bishop as the "*steward* of God" (*Titus* i. 7), and in the designation of all Christians as by obligation "good *stewards* of the manifold grace of God" (*1 Peter* iv. 10), that the word now is frequently applied to anyone who carries a trust such as a great natural gift, the responsibility for public funds, or power over others by reason of his office or personality. "We are Goddes *stewardes* all, noughte of our owne we bare" (*Chatterton*). "A man of business and a vigilant *steward* of the public money" (*Macaulay*). **Reeve,** which is now purely historical in this sense, and **bailiff** were used from the fourteenth to the seventeenth century as nearly identical terms. Both then implied power to enforce law and order in the domain or on the estate of the lord or master, to collect dues and rents from his tenantry, and to see that his dependents performed their allotted services. Both also suggested duties similar to those of a steward of a landowner and landlord. *Reeve*, in this sense, has given way to *bailiff;* the latter has also lost some of its earlier implications, for it now designates an employee whose duties correspond to those of an overseer or superintendent of an estate, and whose chief concern is the land and its profitable use or the husbandry of its resources, and not the management of a household or of its financial affairs as in the case of a steward. This distinction between *steward* and *bailiff* is not always kept perfectly clear, however. **Agent,** or *estate agent*, is now often used for *bailiff*, especially in England; **factor** is the usual Scottish designation. **Seneschal** and **major-domo** carry with them stronger implications of the grandeur and the power, both of the lord and of the official, than do *steward* or *bailiff*. Both imply a position of authority in a great household, royal or noble, the management and direction of the lord's household affairs, his entertainments, and his estate, and recognition as his representative in legal transactions. The difference between the two words is not always clear except that *major-domo* was originally used in reference to other than English (chiefly Italian and Spanish) officials. When the term later became applicable to an English steward (of a household) or a butler, it acquired a humorous connotation, but it still carries its earlier suggestion of a magnificent establishment. **Oeconomus,** which is a Latinized form of *oikonomos*, a Greek word used in the New Testament and commonly translated *steward* in the English versions of the Bible, occurs (now rarely) in ecclesiastical or scholastic use, being applied to the person whose office it is to manage the temporal affairs of a diocese, a college, or a religious order or community.

stick. 1 Stick, adhere, cohere, cling, cleave agree in meaning to be or become closely, firmly, or indissolubly attached. **Stick,** in early use, suggested attachment by infixing or embedding; it now usually implies attachment by affixing; it is when it carries the latter implication that it comes into comparison with the synonyms here discriminated. One thing (often a person) *sticks* to another, or things (often persons) *stick* together when they are literally or figuratively glued together and can be separated only by tearing or forcing apart; as, the stamp *sticks* to the envelope; he *stuck* to (sometimes *at*) his work; his friends *stuck* to (sometimes *by*) him in all his troubles; by *sticking* together they gained their objective. "His sermons... *stick* too closely to the point to be entertaining" (*T. S. Eliot*). When referred to things, **adhere** is usually more formal than *stick;* as, the mud *adhered* to their shoes. It is the idiomatic term, however, when the attachment results from growth of parts normally distinct or separate; as, abdominal tissues sometimes *adhere* after an operation. When referred to persons, *adhere* usually implies deliberate or voluntary acceptance, as of the creed of a church, the platform of a political party, or the doctrines of a philosopher; as, he *adhered* to the traditional scientific views. "The then current fashion, which royal ladies have *adhered* to ever since" (*R. Macaulay*). **Cohere,** in precise use, takes for its subject a collective singular or a plural noun that names things that stick together to produce a mass, a body, or a unified whole; as, the dry ingredients of a cake *cohere* only when liquid is added. "A complete dissolution of the moral principles by which society *coheres*" (*Lecky*). **Cling** now usually implies attachment by hanging on, as by the arms, the roots, the tendrils, or the like; as, to *cling* to a capsized boat; the vine *clings* to the wall; wet clothes *cling* to the body. In figurative use, *cling* often implies dependence or the need of support; as, she *clung* to her father and mother even after her marriage; *clinging* women. At other times, it suggests tenacity in holding on to something possessed, believed, used, or the like; as, to *cling* to the superstitions of one's childhood; to *cling* to a hope. "Cyril *clung* to his old room on his visits" (*Bennett*). **Cleave** is now literary and elevated. It implies closeness and strength of attachment; when applied to persons, it commonly suggests depth of devotion and fidelity in affection. "Therefore shall a man leave his father and his mother, and shall *cleave* unto his wife" (*Genesis* ii. 24). "My tongue *cleave* to my roof within my mouth, Unless a pardon ere I rise or speak" (*Shak.*).

Ana. *Tie, bind: attach, *fasten, affix, fix: infix, *implant.

Con. Sever, sunder, part, divide, *separate: *detach, disengage.

2 Stickle, balk, shy, boggle, *demur, scruple, jib, strain.

stickle, *v.* Balk, shy, boggle, jib, *demur, scruple, stick, strain.

Ana. *Hesitate, vacillate, falter, waver: *object, kick, protest.

sticky. *Adhesive, gluey, glutinous, mucilaginous, gummy.

stiff, *adj.* **Stiff, rigid, inflexible, tense, stark, wooden** come into comparison when they mean so firm, hard, or tough in texture, consistency, or quality as to be impossible or highly difficult to bend or enliven. **Stiff,** the most common word of this group, is applicable where this condition exists in any noticeable degree; literally, it may describe either a desirable or an undesirable quality, because, except in its extended senses, it merely implies a condition and carries neither depreciative nor commendatory connotations; as, an edition of a book with *stiff* covers; he wants a cane that is very *stiff;* to dislike a *stiff* custard; "every gust made a noise like the rattling of dry bones in the *stiff* toddy-palms outside" (*Kipling*). In its extended senses, *stiff,* when applied to persons, their manners, their expression, and the like, usually suggests either extreme formality and coldness (as, he replied with *stiff* condescension; she preferred the easy-going parties of this day to the *stiff* entertainments she had known in her youth) or a lack of ease, grace, or graciousness in dealing with others (as, "Mrs. Hawthorne...seemed to be struggling with her *stiff* reserve to give him comfort"—*Arch. Marshall;* "Brutus had... a hard face, a pedantic style in speech and writing, and a *stiff* ungracious character"—*Buchan*). When applied to something that must be overcome or must be accomplished, the term implies unusual difficulty or the need of great exertion (as, a *stiff* ascent; a *stiff* opposition; a *stiff* examination; a *stiff* task): when applied to something that under particular circumstances or in a particular case has lost its usual or typical pliancy or pliability, *stiff* implies difficulty in using, moving, handling, or the like (as, branches *stiff* with ice; limbs *stiff* with cold; he grew *stiff* with fear). In a variety of other senses, *stiff* implies harshness or extreme severity (as, a *stiff* sentence; a *stiff* penalty) or great strength or violence (as, a *stiff* breeze; a *stiff* dose). **Rigid** (for extended senses see RIGID, 2) implies so high a degree of stiffness that the thing so described cannot be bent or flexed without breaking it; as, an airship with a *rigid* hull; a bridge supported by a series of *rigid* masonry arches; a *rigid* crosspiece; trees too large and *rigid* to withstand the force of a hurricane. **Inflexible** (for extended sense see INFLEXIBLE, 2) in its literal sense differs from *rigid* only in suggesting a lack of limberness or an incapacity for being bent rather than a texture or consistency that resists bending or deforming. Consequently, it is often used when a less precise term is needed and merely an approach to rigidity is suggested; as, an *inflexible* metal; all *inflexible* twigs are rejected by the basket maker; an *inflexible* blade is not desirable in a carving knife. **Tense** (as here compared: see also TIGHT, 1) now infrequently occurs in its literal sense and then usually in reference to muscles, fibers, membranes, and the like, that are stretched so tight or so strained by effort, nervous excitement, or the like, that they have lost their elasticity or flexibility either for the time being or permanently; as, *tense* arteries; *tense* nerves; with muscles as *tense* as those of a tiger about to spring on its prey. **Stark** in the literal sense of *stiff* or, sometimes, of *rigid,* and in many of the extended senses of *stiff,* is now chiefly a dialectal term. However, one still comes across it in the literature of past centuries and occasionally in the work of modern authors who have a feeling for its special values. For the word usually suggests a stiffness that is associated with loss of life, warmth, power, vitality, or fluidity, and therefore often also connotes desolation, barrenness, death, or present valuelessness. Very frequently, both in past and present use, it is accompanied by *stiff* or *rigid;* as, "many a nobleman lies *stark* and *stiff*" (*Shak.*); "We seem to require an elasticity of system...which is in entire contrast with our rather *stark* and *rigid* methods" (*Gladstone*); "The neo-classic theorists...evidently had a faith in law that was too *stark* and literal; in a world of flux...they tried to set up changeless formulae" (*Babbitt*); "now style, the *stark,* bare structure of language, was to her a fetish" (*R. Macaulay*). More often in current use, *stark* is merely an intensive (often an adverb) meaning little more than such as is stated or described without qualification; as, he was *stark* naked; he stood in *stark* terror; "they...wrote *stark* nonsense" (*Quiller-Couch*). **Wooden** comes into comparison with the preceding terms only in its extended sense where it suggests not only the hardness and inflexibility of wood, but its dryness, its lack of suppleness, plasticity, and the like: consequently, the term not only suggests stiffness and lack of life and grace, but often clumsiness, deadness or heaviness of spirit, or the like; as, despite the gaiety of the conversation, no smile lighted his *wooden* countenance; "Kim took a few paces in a *stiff wooden* style" (*Kipling*).

Ana. Tough, tenacious, *strong, stout: *firm, hard, solid: formal, conventional, ceremonious (see CEREMONIAL): frigid, *cold, cool: difficult, *hard, arduous.

Ant. Relaxed: supple.

stiff, *n.* **1** *Body, corpse, carcass, cadaver.

2 *Vagabond, vagrant, tramp, hobo, bum, truant, swagman, sundowner.

stiff-necked. *Obstinate, stubborn, mulish, dogged, pertinacious, pigheaded, bullheaded.

stigma. **Stigma, brand, blot, stain** are synonyms when they denote a mark of shame left on a name, reputation, or character. **Stigma** and **brand** both derive the senses in which they are here considered from their earlier denotation of a scar made on a person to mark him as a criminal, a slave, or the like; in this sense, *stigma* usually, and *brand* always, implied the use of a hot searing iron in inflicting the wound. In its extended sense, *stigma*, though originally and still often implying dishonor or public shame, now usually applies to a mark that is fastened upon a person or thing or is attached to it so as to discredit it and cause it to be frowned upon; as, the son's devotion to public service made the people forget the *stigma* that the father's corruption had fastened on the family name; the label "Slang" is applied as a *stigma* to certain words. "Public feeling was so strongly with Beaumarchais that he paraded his *stigma* as though it had been a mark of honour" (*Macaulay*). "They can attach a social *stigma* to the relief by taking away the pauper's vote" (*Shaw*). *Brand* carries far stronger implications of disgrace and infamy than *stigma;* in very precise use, it often suggests impossibility of removal, social ostracism, and public condemnation; as, he bore the *brand* of Cain (that is, he was a murderer and fugitive). "But for the sorrow and the shame, The *brand* on me and mine, I'll pay you back in leaping flame" (*Kipling*). **Blot** and **stain** in their figurative use imply a blemish that diminishes the honor of a name or a reputation, or that sullies one's reputation for purity or virtue but does not bring either name or reputation into utter disrepute; as, "Thou noteless *blot* on a remembered name!" (*Shelley*); "A *Blot* in the Scutcheon" (the title of one of Browning's poetic tragedies); "To have loved One peerless, without *stain*" (*Tennyson*).

Ana. *Disgrace, dishonor, opprobrium, odium, shame: contamination, tainting *or* taint, defilement, pollution (see corresponding verbs at CONTAMINATE).

still, *adj.* **Still, stilly, quiet, silent, noiseless** come into comparison when they mean making no stir or noise. **Still** applies to that which is motionless or at rest, often with the further implication of hush or absence of sound; sometimes one implication is stressed, sometimes the other, and sometimes both; as, "Ha! no more moving? *Still* as the grave" (*Shak.*); "the wheels of the mail [coach] were no longer within hearing and the night was quite *still* again" (*Dickens*); "that chair, when you arose and passed Out of the room, rocked silently a while Ere it again was *still*" (*Millay*). **Stilly,** which is poetic for *still*, emphasizes the absence of sounds, but it usually implies also the absence of stir or motion; as, "Oft, in the *stilly* night, Ere Slumber's chain has bound me" (*T. Moore*); "In the *stilly* fields, in the *stilly* ways" (*Henley*). **Quiet,** like *still*, may imply absence of perceptible motion or sound, or of both, but it carries stronger suggestions of lack of excitement, agitation, or turbulence, and of deep tranquillity, serenity, restfulness, or repose; as, "Through the green evening *quiet* in the sun" (*Keats*); "the happy *stillness* of dawn....the *quiet* morning air!" (*Meredith*); "A *quiet* town filled with people who lived *quiet* lives and thought *quiet* thoughts" (*S. Anderson*). **Silent** and **noiseless** differ from the other words of this group in being frequently applied to motion, movement, stir, or the like, that is unaccompanied by sound. *Silent* usually carries more positive suggestions of stillness or quietness (as, "the Earth... from West her *silent* course advance[s]"—*Milton;* "A green and *silent* spot, amid the hills, A small and *silent* dell!"—*Coleridge;* "Three mountain-tops, Three *silent* pinnacles of aged snow"—*Tennyson*), whereas *noiseless* usually connotes absence of commotion or of sounds of activity or movement (as, "Along the cool sequester'd vale of life They kept the *noiseless* tenor of their way"—*Gray;* "This quiet sail is as a *noiseless* wing To waft me from distraction"—*Byron*).

Ana. *Calm, tranquil, serene, placid, peaceful: restful, reposeful, *comfortable.

Ant. Stirring: noisy.

still, *conj.* *But, however, nevertheless, yet.

stilly. *Still, quiet, silent, noiseless.

Ana. *Soft, gentle, mild, bland: placid, peaceful, *calm, tranquil, serene.

Con. Agitated, disturbed (see DISCOMPOSE).

stimulant. *Stimulus, incitement, impetus.

Ana. Provocation, excitement, stimulation, quickening, galvanizing (see corresponding verbs at PROVOKE): incentive, spur, goad, *motive.

Ant. Anesthetic: anodyne.

stimulate. Excite, *provoke, quicken, pique, galvanize.

Ana. *Quicken, animate, enliven, vivify: activate, energize, *vitalize: rouse, arouse, *stir, rally, waken, awaken.

Ant. Unnerve: deaden.

stimulus. Stimulus, stimulant, incitement, impetus come into comparison when they mean a force that arouses a person, a group of persons, an animal, an organism, or the like, to activity. **Stimulus** in its earliest and physiological sense applies to anything (substance or agency) that quickens organic action by pricking it into activity; as, a drug that serves as a sedative rather than as a *stimulus* is usually required in the treatment of lung conditions. In later and now more frequent use, the term applies especially to anything that evokes or induces a reaction or response in any living thing, such as a human being, an animal, or a plant, or in any living organ or tissue, such as the heart, the brain, the nervous system, or the muscles. In this sense the term is used chiefly but far from exclusively in psychology, psychophysics, and the biological sciences; as, some parts of the body are more sensitive to *stimuli* than other parts. "In psychology a *stimulus* is any force that arouses the organism or any of its parts to activity. Light is a *stimulus* to the eye, sound to the ear....some [*stimuli*] arise within the organism. Muscular soreness, hunger and thirst are sensations aroused by internal *stimuli*" (*R. S. Woodworth*). "A knowledge of responses, and their relations to *stimuli*, under the simplest conditions of pre-existing activity...is essential in any accurate survey of the whole field of activity; and thus it is that what we may call the '*stimulus*-response psychology'...is of genuine and fundamental importance" (*R. S. Woodworth*). In more general, nontechnical use, *stimulus* applies especially to anything that by pricking or irritating goads or stirs up not only a person or persons, but his (or their) powers into action, activity, endeavor, or the like; as, "No *stimulus* was omitted to excite and inspire the imagination and the sense" (*G. L. Dickinson*); "Many persons find stir, and movement, and the presence of a crowd an agreeable *stimulus*" (*A. C. Benson*); "For strong emotion...the shock of sudden external *stimulus* is necessary" (*H. Ellis*); "A great writer of the past is known by the delight and *stimulus* which he gives to mature spirits in the present" (*Van W. Brooks*). **Stimulant** is still occasionally used in place of *stimulus* in this last and most general sense, and it is the preferred term when it implies the production of effects of, or similar to, those produced by alcoholic liquors, coffee, tea, and certain drugs (often specifically called *stimulants*), such as a seeming increase of vitality and a temporary excitation to activity, often mental activity; as, "Virtuous indignation is a powerful *stimulant*, but a dangerous diet" (*Shaw*); "If they [generalizations about the character and mentality of persons in the past] have value, it is as *stimulants* to make us think about the present" (*A. Huxley*); "Fresh beginnings are excellent *stimulants* to a jaded world, but a defective method of progression" (*Lowes*). **Incitement** differs from *stimulus* in emphasizing a goading, a spurring, or a whipping intended to drive one into moving or acting quickly, rather than the result attained; as, border incidents serving as *incitements* to war; "these things...which God sends us as an *incitement* to proceed with more honour and alacrity" (*Milton*); "Nor could all the *incitements* of its master induce the beast again to move forward" (*Galsworthy*). **Impetus** (as here compared: see also SPEED, 2) usually stresses the stimulation of an increase in the momentum of activity already initiated. "What also gave an unusual *impetus* to the mind of men at this period was the discovery of the New World" (*Hazlitt*); "In estimating the social importance of this movement, we must be careful to discount the temporary...*impetus* it received from the economic slump of this period" (*Day Lewis*). But the term sometimes applies also to a stimulus that initiates action; as, "It is the *impetus* that I ask of you: the will to try" (*Quiller-Couch*).

Ana. Spur, goad, incentive, *motive, inducement: excitement, piquing, provocation (see corresponding verbs at PROVOKE): irritation, nettling (see corresponding verbs at IRRITATE).

stingy. Stingy, close, closefisted, tight, tightfisted, niggardly, parsimonious, penurious, miserly, curmudgeonly, cheeseparing, penny-pinching come into comparison as meaning unwilling (or manifesting unwillingness) to share one's goods with others or to give to another any of one's possessions. **Stingy,** the ordinary colloquial term, implies mainly a lack of generosity: the term is applicable, therefore, whenever there is a suggestion of a mean or illiberal spirit; as, she is sparing in her gifts because she has very little money, but not because she is *stingy*. "If I want anything, he says that it cannot be afforded. I never thought before that he was *stingy*, but I am sure now that he must be a miser at heart" (*Trollope*). **Close** and **closefisted** and the more colloquial **tight** and **tightfisted** usually imply stinginess of nature, but they also ordinarily suggest the power to keep a tight grip upon whatever one has acquired; as, to be *closefisted* in the expenditure of one's money; he is the most *tightfisted* person we have ever met; though very rich, he is so *close* (or *tight*) that we cannot count upon him for a generous contribution. **Niggardly** implies the character of a niggard, or of one who is so stingy and so closefisted that he grudgingly gives the smallest portion or amount possible: the term may refer not only to the giving or spending of money or the giving of material goods but to the provision of anything that would add to the comfort, happiness, well-being, or the like, of oneself or of others; as, "As poor and *niggardly* as it would be to set down no more meat than your company will be sure to eat up" (*Swift*); his *niggardly* allowance for rent and food; "Kant...was unsympathetic and *niggardly* of appreciation" (*H. Ellis*); "literature is so lavish with wealth and titles...the real world is so *niggardly* of these things" (*A. Huxley*). **Parsimonious** stresses frugality, but it also suggests niggardliness: because of this double connotation, the term suggests not a virtue, but a fault or, often, a vice; as, "Having been a spendthrift all his life, he had now become strictly *parsimonious*...and...devoted every energy of his mind to save shillings and pence" (*Trollope*). **Penurious** (etymologically, poverty-stricken: cf. *penury* under POVERTY) in its current use adds to *parsimonious* the suggestion of a niggardliness so great as to give the appearance of extreme poverty or of excessive closefistedness; as, "a grudging master ... a *penurious* niggard of his wealth" (*Milton*); "I had a rich uncle...a *penurious* accumulating curmudgeon" (*Irving*). **Miserly** implies penuriousness but it stresses sordid avariciousness as the motive; as, "her [Elizabeth's] expenditure was *parsimonious* and even *miserly*" (*J. R. Green*); a *miserly* contribution to the community chest. **Curmudgeonly** is a highly contemptuous term implying in its strictest uses both penuriousness and churlishness (as, *curmudgeonly* gifts to a relative in need); often, in current use, it stresses surliness at the expense of the older implication of stinginess (as, a *curmudgeonly* old fellow). **Cheeseparing** and **penny-pinching** suggest frugality and parsimoniousness carried to the extreme (as, the *cheeseparing* guardians of the city's finances; a *penny-pinching* appropriation for relief).

Ana. *Mean, sordid, ignoble: scrimpy, skimpy, *meager: greedy, acquisitive, avaricious, *covetous, grasping: *sparing, economical, frugal, thrifty.

Ant. Generous. — *Con.* *Liberal, bountiful, munificent: *profuse, lavish, prodigal.

stinking. *Malodorous, fetid, noisome, putrid, rank, rancid, fusty, musty.

Ana. Foul, filthy, nasty, *dirty: *offensive, repulsive, revolting.

stint, *n.* *Task, duty, job, chare, chore, assignment.

Ana. Quantity, amount (see SUM): allotment, apportionment (see corresponding verbs at ALLOT): prescribing *or* prescription, assigning (see corresponding verbs at PRESCRIBE): sharing *or* share, participation (see corresponding verbs at SHARE).

stipend. *Wage, salary, fee, emolument, pay, hire, screw.

Ana. Remuneration, compensation, recompensing *or* recompense (see corresponding verbs at PAY).

stir, *v.* **Stir, rouse, arouse, awaken, waken, rally,** as here compared, agree in meaning to drive from quiescence or torpor into activity. **Stir** (often, in this sense, *stir up*) usually presupposes excitement to activity by that which disturbs or agitates and so brings to the surface or into outward expression something which is latent or dormant. "If the...teacher longs to *stir* the sluggish mind of one of her scholars, she must first find out what the sluggishness is due to" (*C. W. Eliot*). "She wants *stirring up*. She's got into a rut" (*Bennett*). Sometimes the word suggests the evoking of rebellion or revolt; as, "There was a flickering of unrest all along the border...partly the *stirring* of powerful tribes" (*Buchan*). More often it implies the evocation of profound, agitating, but usually agreeable, emotion; as, "Imogen, *stirred* to tears by the swinging by of red-coated troops to a band" (*R. Macaulay*); "the recollection of it...*stirred* him past the point of being able to sleep" (*M. Austin*). *Rouse, arouse, awaken, waken* all presuppose a state of rest or repose, often that of sleep. **Rouse** derives its implications from its earliest application to the starting of game from coverts or lairs by the cries of hunters or by beating of bushes and, in precise use, always suggests incitement to activity by startling, frightening, or upsetting. In addition it commonly implies intense or vigorous activity, and often ensuing commotion or turbulence; as, "every tent *roused* by that clamour dread" (*Shelley*); "At the bridge of the lower saltings the cattle gather and blare, *Roused* by the feet of running men, dazed by the lantern glare" (*Kipling*); "Antony...had spoken words which *roused* the mob to fury" (*Buchan*). **Arouse,** though frequently used interchangeably with *rouse*, is so much weaker in its implications that it often means little more than to start into activity (or, sometimes, existence), and conveys no hint of what follows; thus, a noise in the night *arouses* a sleeping soldier if he merely wakes up into consciousness of it, but it *rouses* him when he also makes determined efforts to trace its source, or hastily arms himself, or the like; a fear may be *aroused* (not *roused*) and immediately dispelled; passions are *roused* (not *aroused*) when they are so stirred up that they exert a harmful influence. "The effect of the 'madness' [Hamlet's] is not to lull but to *arouse* the king's suspicion" (*T. S. Eliot*). **Awaken** and **waken,** in literal use, like *arouse*, frequently imply an ending of sleep; in figurative use, they are employed chiefly in reference to mental or spiritual powers or faculties which need only the proper stimulation to be called forth into activity, or to be elicited; as, to *awaken* attention; to *waken* love; the conscience of the nation was *awakened;* "that tree always *awakened* pleasant memories, recalling a garden in the south of France" (*Cather*). **Rally** (see also RIDICULE, BANTER) presupposes a diffusion of forces or a lack of concentration that promotes lethargy or inaction; it therefore implies a gathering together that stirs up or rouses; as, "young Laon's name *Rallied* their secret hopes" (*Shelley*); "he *rallied* his strength for a final blow" (*Prescott*). "As if his memory were impaired... [he] made an effort to *rally* his attention" (*Dickens*).

Ana. Excite, *provoke, stimulate, quicken, galvanize: *incite, foment, instigate: activate, energize, *vitalize: *move, drive, impel, actuate.

stir, *n.* **1** *Motion, movement, move, locomotion.

Ana. Acting *or* activity, working *or* work, behaving *or* behavior, reaction (see corresponding verbs at ACT): change, alteration, variation, modification (see under CHANGE, *v.*).

2 Stir, bustle, flurry, pother, fuss, ado are comparable when they refer to the signs of excitement or hurry that accompany an act, action, or an event. **Stir** suggests brisk or restless movement, and ordinarily implies a crowd. "I hear A busy *stir* of men about the streets" (*Shelley*). "Many persons find *stir*, and movement, and the presence of a crowd an agreeable stimulus" (*A. C. Benson*). **Bustle** adds the implication of a noisy, obtrusive, or self-important display of energy, especially when used in reference to an individual. "She needs the *bustle* of life in a good hotel" (*Bennett*). " 'Tis true that strength and *bustle* build up a firm. But judgment and knowledge are what keep it established" (*Hardy*). **Flurry** stresses nervous agitation and undue haste; as, the time for departure found them all in a *flurry.* **Pother** and **fuss** both imply flurry and fidgety activity; *pother* often distinctively stresses commotion or confusion and *fuss* needless worry or effort; as, he is always in a *pother* about something or other; there is no *fuss* when she entertains. "She could distinctly catch the tramping, martial syllables, 'Vote, vote, vote.'...The *pother*, once begun, continued" (*Bennett*). "God never takes needless trouble. It is only foolish little men...that are fond of *fusses*" (*J. R. Lowell*). **Ado** also suggests fussiness or waste of energy; as, go to work without any more *ado.* It also often implies trouble or difficulty; as, there was much *ado* before their affairs were straightened out.

Ana. Agitation, disturbance, disquieting *or* disquiet (see corresponding verbs at DISCOMPOSE): excitement, stimulation (see corresponding verbs at PROVOKE): *din, uproar, hubbub, pandemonium.

Ant. Tranquillity.

stitch, *n.* *Pain, twinge, ache, pang, throe.

stocky. *Thick, thickset, squat, chunky, stubby, dumpy.

stoic. *Impassive, phlegmatic, apathetic, stolid.

Ana. Detached, aloof, *indifferent, unconcerned: imperturbable, composed, collected, *cool: unassailable, indomitable (see INVINCIBLE): patient, long-suffering, resigned (see corresponding nouns at PATIENCE).

stoicism. Impassivity, phlegm, apathy, stolidity. See under IMPASSIVE.

Ana. *Fortitude, grit, backbone, pluck, guts, sand: detachment, aloofness, indifference, unconcernedness *or* unconcern (see corresponding adjectives at INDIFFERENT).

stolid. *Impassive, phlegmatic, apathetic.

Ana. *Dull, blunt, obtuse: *stupid, dull, dense, crass, dumb: *heavy, ponderous: passive, supine, inert, *inactive.

Ant. Adroit (sense 2).

stolidity. Impassivity, phlegm, apathy, stoicism. See under IMPASSIVE.

Con. Quickness, promptness, readiness, aptness (see corresponding adjectives at QUICK): animation, enlivening, quickening (see corresponding verbs at QUICKEN): *passion, fervor, ardor, zeal, enthusiasm.

stomach. *Abdomen, belly, paunch.

stone, *n.* **Stone, gem, jewel** agree in denoting a particle of hard mineral or similar substance having the beauty of color, radiance, cutting, or the like, that fits it for use as an ornament. **Stone,** as here compared, is the comprehensive term including all particles of mineral origin of this description whether they are classified as *precious stones*, a class including stones of highest value commercially for rarity, beauty, and hardness, such as diamonds, rubies, sapphires, and emeralds, or as *semiprecious stones*, a class including stones of somewhat lower value because less rare or less hard, such as the garnet, amethyst, jade, and tourmaline. **Gem,** in technical as well as in correct ordinary use, applies especially to a precious stone that is cut and polished, and has beauty apart from its setting, or to a pearl that has beauty of form and quality. The term, however, is also applied to any semiprecious stone that is similarly cut and polished or to any exquisitely carved or engraved stone (cameo or intaglio), fit for setting in a ring, brooch, or the like; as, the chalice was adorned with *gems* of great beauty; "the last finish of the *gem* engraver blowing away the last particle of invisible dust" (*W. Pater*). **Jewel** was originally applied to a costly ornament of gold or silver, often richly enameled or set with gems and used as an adornment of the person; in current precise use, the term is more commonly applied to a gem, especially a precious stone or pearl, that is worn on the person and is set in a ring, brooch, earring, necklace, tiara, crown, or the like; as, the crown *jewels* are on display; "the *jewel* That trembles in her ear" (*Tennyson*); *jewels* flashed from her throat, her ears, her breast, and hands.

Figuratively, both *gem* and *jewel* mean a great treasure, but *gem* usually carries a strong implication of intrinsic value because of the thing's perfection in detail, concentrated beauty or worth, or the like (as, the lyric is a *gem;* a *gem* of a drawing by Rembrandt), and *jewel* stresses rather the value of the thing as an asset to its owner or possessor or as a contribution to his worth, strength, effectiveness, or the like (as, "Good name in man and woman, dear my lord, Is the immediate *jewel* of their souls"—*Shak.;* "she is...a *jewel* of a servant" —*Jane W. Carlyle*).

stooge. *Fool, jester, clown, comedian, comic, antic, buffoon, zany, merry-andrew, pantaloon, harlequin.

stoop, *v.* **Stoop, condescend, deign** agree in meaning to descend below the level, as in rank or dignity, where one belongs or thinks he belongs, to do something. **Stoop,** which literally means to bend one's head or back, as in going through a low-ceilinged passageway or a low door, implies a descent not only in rank or dignity but also, and more often, from a relatively high moral plane to a lower one: the term, therefore, often suggests disgraceful or shameful action; as, to *stoop* to fraud; to think that you should *stoop* to lying! Often, the term implies a lowering of one's standards, as of conduct, or a debasement of one's principles or motives for some lower end, such as pecuniary gain; as, "Aspiring to be the leader of a nation of third-rate men, he had to *stoop* to the common level" (*Mencken*); "His ambition was still to paint huge historical pictures; but meanwhile, to keep the pot boiling, he was prepared to *stoop* to a pettier kind of art" (*A. Huxley*); " 'But on the material side, Mr. Archer, if one may *stoop* to consider such things...' " (*E. Wharton*). **Condescend** may imply the stooping of one who is actually exalted in power, rank, or dignity so as to accommodate himself to intercourse with those who are his inferiors: in this sense, the term usually suggests graciousness and courtesy and a waiving of formalities. "Spain's mighty monarch, In gracious clemency, does *condescend*, On these conditions, to become your friend" (*Dryden*). Often, however, the term implies an assumption of superiority and a patronizing manner that tends to offend or affront the person who is regarded as an inferior; as, "No beggar ever felt him *condescend*, No prince presume" (*J. R. Lowell*); "Those who thought they were honoring me by *condescending* to address a few words to me" (*F. W. Robinson*). **Deign** now implies a temperament or frame of mind that makes one haughty, arrogant, contemptuous, or the like, more often than it implies high rank or dignity or high standards of conduct: with this limitation, especially in current English (in older English *deign* was very close to *condescend;* as, "O *deign* to visit our forsaken seats"—*Pope*), it usually means to stoop to that which one believes is scarcely in keeping with one's dignity, or which one vouchsafes with reluctance; therefore the term is most common with *scarcely, hardly*, etc., or in negative constructions; as, "[The] very dog will hardly *deign* to bark at you" (*Arnold*); "Richard marched hastily out of the room and through the garden, never so much as *deigning* a glance at his wistful little guide...wondering a world of fancies about the handsome proud boy" (*Meredith*); "Mr. Critchlow *deigned* no remark" (*Bennett*).

Ana. *Abase, demean, humble: vouchsafe, accord, *grant, concede: favor, accommodate, *oblige.

stoop, *n.* Porch, piazza, veranda, portico, *balcony, gallery, loggia.

stop, *v.* **1 Stop, cease, quit, discontinue, desist** agree in meaning to suspend or cause to suspend activity. **Stop** applies primarily to action or progress, or to that which is thought of as moving or progressing; **cease** applies primarily to states and conditions, or to that which is thought of as being or as having existence; as, a train *stops*, but does not *cease;* the noise it makes both *stops* and *ceases;* one *stops* a car, but *ceases* driving a car; one *stops* work on a book, but *ceases* one's efforts to perfect its style; one's love may *cease*, but scarcely *stop;* "When I have fears that I may *cease* to be" (*Keats*). *Stop* frequently connotes a sudden or definite; *cease*, a gradual, suspension of activity; as, to *stop* a quarrel; to *cease* quarreling; "I gave commands; Then all smiles *stopped* together" (*Browning*); "You hear the grating roar... begin, and *cease*, and then again begin" (*Arnold*). **Quit,** as a synonym for *stop* and *cease* (see also LEAVE, 2), is an Americanism; as, he *quit* coming; to *quit* smoking; the man who does the work of two men before fifty is usually the one who can afford to *quit* (that is, stop working, or retire) at that age. **Discontinue** implies the suspension of some activity, especially one that has become a form of occupation or employment or is a practice or habit; as, to *discontinue* a business (or a friendship, or a correspondence, or a subscription to a journal, or drinking intoxicating liquors); "How do we *discontinue* to be friends?" (*Browning*). **Desist** (which is rarely transitive in current use) usually stresses forbearance or self-restraint as the motive for stopping or ceasing but it may imply the futility of one's efforts; as, to *desist* from further questioning; "An order...requiring such person...to cease and *desist* from the violation of the law so charged" (*U. S. Code, title* 15, §45); "Never ...*desisting* in my efforts to induce the Indians to join me in that...adventure" (*Hudson*). "He had made two attempts to shave but his hand had been so unsteady that he had been obliged to *desist*" (*Joyce*).

Ana. *Arrest, check, interrupt: intermit, suspend, stay, *defer, postpone: *frustrate, thwart, foil, balk, circumvent.

Con. Start, *begin, commence, initiate: *go, depart, leave.

2 Stay, put up, lodge, sojourn, *reside, live, dwell.

stopgap. Makeshift, shift, expedient, *resource, resort, substitute, surrogate.

storm, *v.* Bombard, assault, assail, *attack.

story. 1 *Account, report, chronicle, version.

Ana. *History, chronicle, annals: relation, rehearsing, recital, recounting (see corresponding verbs at RELATE).

2 Story, narrative, tale, anecdote, yarn are alike in denoting a recital of happenings less elaborate than a novel. **Story** is the most general and the familiar word and may in loose use be interchanged with any of the others of the group, except in its generalized sense of legendary lore, as in "And snowy summits old in *story*" (*Tennyson*). A story may be oral or written, actual or fictitious, in prose or in verse, designed to inform or to entertain, but characteristically treats of a connected series of events or incidents, rather than a single incident; as, a fairy *story;* one's life *story;* the *story* of an opera; the *story* of the Crusades; a *story* full of incident. The short story and a newspaper story may treat of but one incident. **Narrative** in its common use is more often factual than imaginative; as, a historical *narrative;* a *narrative* of discovery or adventure: *narrative* is a more formal word than *story*. As a literary composition, *narrative* usually suggests a plot, or causally connected series of motived incidents; thus a chronicle or a diary is not called a *narrative*. **Tale** suggests, in consequence of its historical connection with oral telling, a more leisurely and more loosely organized recital, characteristically treating legendary or imaginary happenings, especially those of ancient times, and may be in verse; as, Oriental *tales;* folk *tales; tales* of the court of King Arthur. *Tale* is a more elevated or poetical word than *story*. **Anecdote,** retaining something of its original sense of an unpublished item, is a brief story of a single detachable incident of curious or humorous interest, often illustrative of a truth or principle or of the character or foibles of a notable person, and generally designed to entertain; as, a pithy *anecdote;* an *anecdote* of Lincoln's boyhood. "During the meal he entertained them with *anecdotes* of his travels" (*Meredith*). **Yarn,** once sailors' slang, now used only in colloquial language, suggests a rambling and rather dubious tale of exciting adventure, marvelous or incredible, ingenious or fanciful, and not always reaching a clear-cut outcome. "Without motive a story is not a novel, but only a *yarn*" (*Caine*).

Ana. Narration, description (see corresponding verbs at RELATE): *fiction, fable, fabrication: *novel, romance.

3 *Lie, falsehood, untruth, fib, misrepresentation.

stout, *adj.* **1** *Strong, sturdy, stalwart, tough, tenacious.

Ana. *Brave, bold, intrepid, valiant, valorous: indomitable, *invincible: resolute, stanch, steadfast (see FAITHFUL): *vigorous, energetic, lusty.

2 *Fleshy, fat, portly, corpulent, obese, plump, rotund, chubby.

Ana. *Thick, thickset, stocky: burly, brawny, husky, *muscular.
Ant. Cadaverous. — *Con.* *Lean, lank, lanky, spare, angular, rawboned, skinny, scrawny.

stout, *n.* *Beer, lager, bock, ale, porter.

straightforward. Straightforward, forthright, aboveboard when applied to persons, their actions, or their methods agree in meaning honest and open. That is **straightforward** which is consistently direct and free from deviations or evasiveness; as, a *straightforward* course; a *straightforward* answer. "He is a man; with clear, *straightforward* ideas, a frank, noble presence" (*Disraeli*). That is **forthright** which has directness like that of a thrust, or goes straight to the point without swerving or hesitating; as, a *forthright* appeal for votes. "His method in dealing with congressmen was direct, generally courteous, and always *forthright*" (*W. A. White*). That is **aboveboard** (in its figurative sense) which is free from all traces of deception or duplicity. *Aboveboard* is commonly used predicatively, and applies more often (though not invariably) to actions or methods than to persons. "One whose life had been so well-ordered, balanced, and *above-board*" (*Galsworthy*). "She's *aboveboard* and a good Christian" (*E. Phillpotts*). *Straightforward, forthright,* and *aboveboard* are also used adverbially with the same implications and connotations as their adjectival forms.
Ana. Honest, *upright, honorable, just: *fair, equitable, impartial: candid, *frank, open, plain.
Ant. Devious: indirect.

straightway. *Directly, immediately, instantly, instantaneously, forthwith, at once, anon, right away.

strain, *v.* **1** Sprain. See under STRAIN, *n.*
2 *Demur, scruple, balk, jib, shy, boggle, stickle, stick.

strain, *n.*[1] Streak, vein, *touch, suggestion, suspicion, soupçon, tincture, tinge, shade, smack, spice, dash.

strain, *n.*[2] **1** *Stress, pressure, tension, shear, thrust, torsion.
2 Strain, sprain are here compared as nouns meaning an injury to a part of the body through overstretching and as verbs meaning to cause or to suffer such an injury to a part of the body. **Strain,** the more general and less technical term, usually implies an injury to a muscle or to the muscles as a result of overuse, overexercise, overexertion, or of overeffort, as in an attempt to regain one's balance or position; thus, high jumpers' *strain* is an injury to the rotator muscles of the thigh such as occurs frequently in high jumpers; eye*strain* is a condition of the eye (especially of the muscles of the eye) involving pain and fatigue such as occurs in those who do close work with their eyes or in those who suffer from uncorrected defects of vision; so, "Charley horse" is a colloquial term for a stiffness resulting from muscular *strain* in the arm or leg, as of an athlete; to *strain* one's back while trying to avoid a fall on a slippery sidewalk. **Sprain,** though sometimes used in place of *strain* in the sense here considered, is commonly a technical term with very definite implications: in its strictest sense it implies an injury to a joint, usually as a result of a wrenching, with stretching or tearing of its ligaments, damage to the synovial membrane, swelling and pain, and disablement of the joint. Sometimes, also, *sprain* implies a rupture of tendons or muscles attached to the joint; as, to *sprain* one's ankle; a severe shoulder *sprain.*

strait, *adj.* *Narrow.
Ana. Limited, restricted, confined (see LIMIT, *v.*): strict, stringent, *rigid, rigorous.
Ant. Wide.

strait, *n.* **1 Strait, straits, sound, channel, passage, narrows** are comparable when they denote a long and comparatively narrow stretch of water connecting two larger bodies. Their meanings in geography are here especially considered, but it should be noted that their use in proper names does not invariably conform to their technical senses. A **strait** (or sometimes, in proper names, **straits**) is relatively short and very narrow; as, the *Strait* of Dover (connecting the English Channel and the North Sea); the *Strait,* or *Straits,* of Gibraltar (connecting the Atlantic Ocean and the Mediterranean Sea). A **sound** is longer and more extensive than a strait; the term is often applied to a long narrow body of water between the mainland and an island or group of islands and therefore at each end opening into the same ocean or sea, or arms of the same ocean or sea; as, Long Island *Sound* (lying between the Connecticut shore and the north shore of Long Island and connecting the East River and the Atlantic Ocean); the Chandeleur *Sound* (lying between the southeast coast of Louisiana and the Chandeleur Islands and opening at both ends into the Gulf of Mexico). Puget Sound in Washington and Pamlico and Albemarle Sound in North Carolina are not true sounds in this technical sense. **Channel** is less frequent than *strait* or *sound* as a technical term in the sense here considered, but when it is so used it denotes a relatively large sound; as, the English *Channel* (between southeastern England and the north coast of France); the Mozambique *Channel* (between the coast of southeastern Africa and Mozambique Island). **Passage** is practically synonymous with *channel,* denoting a connecting body of water wider than a strait; as, Mona *Passage* (between the islands of Hispaniola and Puerto Rico). **Narrows** designates a strait or a contracted part of a body of water; it is especially used of the necklike part of a bottle-shaped harbor; as, the *Narrows* of New York harbor.
2 Pass, exigency, pinch, emergency, *juncture, contingency, crisis.
Ana. *Difficulty, hardship, vicissitude, rigor: perplexity, bewilderment, mystification (see corresponding verbs at PUZZLE): plight, *predicament, fix, quandary.

strand. *Shore, coast, beach, bank, littoral, ripa, foreshore.

strange. Strange, singular, unique, peculiar, eccentric, erratic, odd, queer, quaint, outlandish, curious come into comparison when they mean varying from that which is ordinary, usual, and to be expected. **Strange,** the most comprehensive of these terms, always suggests unfamiliarity; it may apply to that which is foreign, unnatural, inexplicable, new, or the like; as, "Rovers...among *strange* men and *strange* moralities" (*Hardy*); "a *strange* sort of love, to be entirely free from...selfishness" (*Hardy*); "To most of us the art of China and Japan, however much it may attract and impress, is *strange*" (*Binyon*); "He was in one of those *strange* and novel portents, a 'motor-car' " (*H. G. Wells*). **Singular,** in precise use, always implies difference from every other instance of its kind and therefore always implies individuality; as, "lines...of *singular* beauty" (*T. S. Eliot*); "a distinguished and *singular* excellence" (*Mencken*); "a *singular* dog" (*Bennett*). Often, however, the word suggests strangeness that puzzles one or piques one's curiosity; as, " 'Do you prefer reading to cards?' said he; 'that is rather *singular*' " (*Austen*). " 'Tis *singular* that even within the sight Of the high towers of Antioch you could lose Your way" (*Shelley*). **Unique,** in careful usage, implies not only singularity, in its precise sense, but the fact of being unparalleled. Hence, the description of something as "more or most *unique*" is disapproved by all authorities, since only that which is the one thing of its kind can correctly be called *unique;* as, "Personality always contains something *unique*" (*Justice Holmes*).

"He [John Bright] has the almost *unique* distinction of having made speeches which were both effective when delivered and also models of literary eloquence" (*Inge*). **Peculiar,** as here compared (see also CHARACTERISTIC), implies marked or conspicuous distinctiveness in character, quality, or the like; as, "This difference arises... from the *peculiar* character of the Government of the United States" (*Ch. Just. Taney*). "Only subtle and delicate minds... catch the characteristic aroma, the *peculiar* perfume" (*Brownell*); "The nineteenth century had, like every other, limited tastes and *peculiar* fashions" (*T. S. Eliot*). Often, in looser use, *peculiar* is employed where one of the succeeding terms in this article (such as *eccentric* or *queer*) might better be used; as, he is growing very *peculiar;* recent events have provoked the frequent comment: "We live in a very *peculiar* world." **Eccentric** implies divergence from the beaten track; **erratic** adds to *eccentric* a stronger implication of caprice; as, "his [Carlyle's] taste for the *eccentric,* amorphous, and violent in men" (*J. R. Lowell*); "an *eccentric* preference for beginning his dinner... in the late afternoon" (*Cather*); "geniuses are such *erratic* people, and mediocrities so respectable" (*Shaw*); the workings of his mind were *erratic.* **Odd** stresses a departure from the usual, the normal, the regular; it sometimes suggests an element of the fantastic; **queer** even more strongly implies eccentricity and often suggests that the thing so qualified is dubious or questionable; as, "great men whose *odd* habits it would have been glorious piety to endure" (*G. Eliot*); "His tail cocks up in a very *odd* way" (*Barham*); "our sense of the *odd,* the humorous, the grotesque" (*J. R. Lowell*); "Now Elkanah Settle sounds so *queer;* who can expect much from that name?" (*Boswell*); "Alice was not much surprised at this, she was getting so well used to *queer* things happening" (*Carroll*); there is something *queer* about this transaction. **Quaint** implies pleasant, or especially, old-fashioned, oddness; **outlandish,** uncouth or bizarre oddness; as, a *quaint* village, full of half-timbered houses; "the language... *quaint* and old-fashioned" (*Cowper*); an *outlandish* custom. "A *quaint* procession! Old Solomon, in his seedy clothes and long white locks, seemed to be luring that decent company by the magic scream of his fiddle" (*G. Eliot*). "He wore the prophet's robe with a difference. He never let it look *outlandish*" (*C. E. Montague*). **Curious** usually implies extraordinary oddness or a singularity that invites close attention, study, or inquiry. The word is often employed as an equivalent of one or another of the words here considered; as, *curious* things are happening; a *curious* exhibition of feeling. Discriminating writers and speakers, however, give full value to one or both of the connotations of extraordinariness and singularity, and always imply that the thing so described merits notice or investigation; as, *curious* bits of folklore; *curious* customs and habits of speech surviving from an earlier age. "That she had chosen for her afternoon walk the road along which she had returned to Casterbridge three hours earlier... was *curious*—if anything should be called *curious* in concatenations of phenomena wherein each is known to have its accounting cause" (*Hardy*). "My only guiding principle has been that the examples should be *curious,* striking and even, in certain cases, extravagant" (*A. Huxley*).

Ana. *Abnormal, atypic, aberrant: *fantastic, bizarre, grotesque: surprising, astonishing, amazing, flabbergasting (see SURPRISE).

Ant. Familiar.

stranger. **Stranger, foreigner, alien, outlander** (*or* **uitlander**), **outsider, immigrant, émigré** are not synonymous except when they are used narrowly to designate a person who comes into a community from the outside and is not recognized as a member of that community. This is the primary denotation of some of the words, but the secondary sense of the others, especially the last three. **Stranger** and **foreigner** were originally equivalent and applied to one who came from another country (sometimes, especially in dialectal use, from another section) as a resident or visitor. Their differences in implications, however, have led to present distinctions in meaning, *stranger* stressing the person's unfamiliarity with the language and customs and *foreigner* the fact that he speaks a different language, follows different customs, or bears allegiance to another government. "The time came when I was the observant *foreigner,* examining education in France. To tell the truth, I was not a *stranger* to it, having lived in France as a child and again as a youth" (*Grandgent*). **Alien** emphasizes allegiance to another sovereign or government and is opposed to *citizen;* one may be called a *foreigner* after naturalization, but not an *alien.* Figuratively, therefore, *alien* implies exclusion from full privileges or inability to identify oneself with a group. "The older I grow, the more of an *alien* I find myself in the world; I cannot get used to it, cannot believe that it is real" (*L. P. Smith*). "He is anaesthetic to their theological and political enthusiasms. He finds himself an *alien* at their feasts of soul" (*Mencken*). **Outlander** is the term of Anglo-Saxon origin, **uitlander** of Dutch origin, for *foreigner;* they were specifically applied to English residents in the former South African republics of the Transvaal and Orange Free State. In its general sense, *outlander* is preferred to *foreigner* only for a literary or rhetorical reason or because it carries the implications of *outlandish.* "His neighbors were... *outlanders* of that particular type to which... his own fastidiousness found the greatest objection" (*Tarkington*). **Outsider** usually implies nonmembership in a group, clique, caste, or the like, largely because of essential differences in origin, interests, backgrounds, customs, and manners. "An *outsider* like myself feels a strong suspicion that the new instrument with which Einstein has presented the mathematicians is being put to uses for which it was never intended" (*Inge*). **Immigrant** and **émigré** are often used of foreigners who are residents and no longer aliens. The former usually is applied to a foreigner who came searching for subsistence or for a means of earning a living; the latter implies that the foreigner was a fugitive or refugee from his native land. *Émigré* is often specifically applied to a French refugee in England at the time of the French Revolution.

stratagem. *Trick, ruse, maneuver, artifice, wile, feint.

Ana. *Device, contrivance, contraption: expedient, shift, *resource, resort: machination, intrigue, conspiracy, *plot.

stray, *v.* *Wander, roam, ramble, rove, range, prowl, gad, gallivant, traipse, meander.

streak, *n.* Strain, vein, *touch, suggestion, suspicion, soupçon, tincture, tinge, shade, smack, spice, dash.

stream, *n.* *Flow, current, flood, tide, flux.

streamer. Pennant, pennon, banner, *flag, ensign, standard, color.

street. *Road, roadway, highway, highroad, avenue, boulevard, terrace, drive, parkway, thoroughfare, byway, lane, alley, alleyway.

strength. *Power, force, might, energy, puissance, arm.

Ana. Stoutness, sturdiness, toughness, tenaciousness (see corresponding adjectives at STRONG): soundness, healthiness (see corresponding adjectives at HEALTHY): *possessions, means, resources, assets.

strenuous. Energetic, *vigorous, lusty, nervous.

Ana. Virile, manful, manly (see MALE): dynamic, live, *active, operative: *spirited, high-spirited, mettlesome: vehement, *intense.

stress, *n.* **1 Stress, strain, pressure, tension, shear, thrust, torsion** come into comparison in their mechanical senses when they mean the action or effect of force exerted within or upon a body or structure. *Stress* and *strain* are the comprehensive terms of this group: loosely, they are employed as close synonyms in the sense given in the preceding sentence, but in strict technical use, **stress** is applied to the force exerted when one body or part of a body presses upon, pushes against, pulls upon, or tends to stretch, compress, or twist another body or part of a body. Since in natural bodies and in artificial structures such force meets the opposing force of the thing pressed, pushed, pulled, etc., the term *stress* now usually denotes either (1) the reciprocal action of two opposing forces, which are, or should be, balanced so that either one of the bodies or parts supports the other (as, in a balanced structure *stresses* equal each other; the point of *stress* in a Gothic arch) or (2) the cohesive force or molecular resistance set up in one body or part against the force exerted by the opposing body or part (as, "If the external forces acting on the body increase to the extent that the maximum *stress* that can be developed is unable to balance the external forces, the change in form will increase rapidly and the body will break or rupture"—*Kent's Mechanical Engineers' Handbook*). **Strain,** on the other hand, in its strict technical sense, denotes the alteration in size or shape resulting from stress, either as the force exerted by one body or part upon another or as the resistance developed in opposition to an external force. "In boiler construction...the design of the structure itself has been modified to reduce *strains* to a reasonably safe margin below the danger point in day-to-day operation" (*A. C. Morrison*). "Forgings and castings of irregular shape are subject to internal *strains*, which may cause them to fail in service" (*Kent's Mechanical Engineers' Handbook*). All the other terms designate a particular type of stress, and, in some cases, also of strain. **Pressure** commonly applies to a stress which is characterized by a weighing down upon or a pushing against a surface and which, in fluids, is distributed uniformly in all directions: it is usually measurable per unit area of surface affected; as, "the normal atmospheric *pressure* is about 14.7 pounds per square inch" (*Van Nostrand's Scientific Encyclopedia*); blood *pressure* (i.e., the pressure of the blood against the walls of blood vessels); steam *pressure*. **Tension** applies both to the stress exerted and the strain effected by two forces, usually balanced forces, pulling in opposite directions and causing or tending to cause extension. Such stress is measured per unit area of cross section; as, "Such is the *tension* and friction in the warp on the loom that were the threads themselves not properly lubricated and protected from ravelling by sizes the breakage... would offset...the advantage of the machine's more rapid action" (*A. C. Morrison*). **Shear** is applicable either to a stress or to a strain that occurs when a force lying in the plane of one area or section tends to cause it to slide upon a parallel plane or a contiguous section; as, a *shear* in a layer of rock; the *shear* in the center of a column. **Thrust** applies to the pressure exerted by one part of a structure against another, especially when one member exerts a diagonal or horizontal outward pressure against another; as, the *thrust* of a rafter against a supporting wall; the *thrust* of an arch against an abutment. **Torsion** applies to either the strain (or deformation) produced by twisting, or to the stress (or resistance) displayed by a nonrigid body to deformation by twisting, or to both the strain and the stress; as, to measure magnetic attraction and repulsion by the *torsion* of a wire filament.
2 *Emphasis, accent, accentuation.

stretch, *n.* *Expanse, amplitude, spread.
Ana. *Area, tract, region: extent, magnitude, *size.

strict. Stringent, *rigid, rigorous.
Ana. Stern, *severe, austere, ascetic: *inflexible, inexorable: exacting, oppressive, *onerous, burdensome.
Ant. Lax: loose: lenient, indulgent.

stricture. *Animadversion, aspersion, reflection.
Ana. Criticism, censuring *or* censure, condemnation, denouncing *or* denunciation (see corresponding verbs at CRITICIZE).
Ant. Commendation.

strident. Blatant, clamorous, *vociferous, boisterous, obstreperous.
Ana. Harsh, uneven, *rough: discordant, *dissonant.

strife. *Discord, conflict, contention, dissension, variance.
Ana. Combat, conflict, fight, affray, fray (see CONTEST): dispute, controversy, *argument: *brawl, broil, fracas: altercation, wrangle, *quarrel, squabble.
Ant. Peace: accord.

strike, *v.* **1 Strike, hit, smite, slug, slog, slap, swat, clout, punch, box, cuff** come into comparison when they mean to deal or deliver a blow to someone or upon something. **Strike** (as here compared: see also AFFECT, 1), the most general of these terms, usually suggests both the motions of aiming and dealing a blow and the production of the desired effect: in some cases, however, especially when followed by *at* or used intransitively, the term does not necessarily imply the production of the effect intended; as, he *struck* the boy hard several times; he *struck* at his opponent with his fists but the latter neatly eluded him. *Strike* also typically implies the use of one's hand or of a whip, stick, bat, cane, or similar implement; as, she *struck* him in the face before he could finish his sentence; to *strike* a horse with a whip; to *strike* an anvil. Often, also, the term suggests the making of an imprint, an impression, a sound or combination of sounds, or the like, by movements which involve a careful aiming at a definite spot and a touching it with just the force necessary to achieve one's end; as, to *strike* the keys of a piano; to *strike* a chord on a piano; "A line [in a Chinese painting] once *struck* upon the silk was there for ever" (*Binyon*); to *strike* a bell; to *strike* a medal. Otherwise *strike* may be used not only in place of all the other words of this group but in place of a number of others which carry important additional implications such as a repetition of movements and effects (e.g., *pelt, buffet*), a kind of noise produced (e.g., *rap, whack, bang*, etc.), or the like. **Hit** is often used interchangeably with *strike*, but careful writers and speakers prefer it when the stress is upon the impact of the blow or the reaching of the mark aimed at; thus, in precise usage, the archer *hit* (not *struck*) the target; he *hit* (not *struck*) the boy full in the face; so, to *hit* (not *strike*) a nail upon the head; the mark he *hits* (not *strikes*) is seldom the mark he aims at. Also, *hit* may or may not imply the dealing of a blow in the narrower sense of that word (as *strike* typically though not consistently does), for it may suggest the impact of a missile (as, no one was *hit* by the bullets from his revolver) or of a vehicle such as an automobile (as, a driver who *hits* and runs) or, in extended use, the impact of something which affects the mind or the feelings (as, "The disaster to Teddy and Mrs. Teddy *hit* him hard"—*H. G. Wells*). **Smite,** except in some extended use, is largely archaic and rhetorical: even though it seldom suggests a definite spot or mark to be reached, it may be used in place of *strike* or *hit* in either literal or extended senses because it implies both the dealing of a blow and the production of the intended effect. It is often preferred in literary or poetic English when there is the intent to suggest the forcibleness of the effort involved (as, "with the hammer she *smote* Sisera, she *smote* off his head"—*Judges* v. 26), the injuriousness or destructiveness of the effect produced (as, "thou, all-shaking thunder, *Smite* flat the thick rotundity o' the world!"—*Shak.*; "Liberty, *smitten* to death"—*Shelley*), or the prompting of an emotion such as wrath, anguish, or vengeance (as, "I *smite* this bosom with these two hands as I *smite* it now"—*Dickens*). *Smite* is often preferred to *affect* or *impress* (see AFFECT, 1) when there is the intent to suggest an impression or emotional reaction that cuts deep into the heart or soul; as, *smitten* with love, or grief, or remorse. "The madness of the thing he had done *smote* the young man: now first he tasted hard earthy misery" (*Meredith*). **Slug** in colloquial use chiefly in the United States, or **slog** in more restricted British use, implies a hitting heavily or hard, as with a blunt instrument; as, to be waylaid and *slugged* by robbers. **Slap** literally implies a striking with the open hand (as, to *slap* one in the face); **swat** implies a hitting and, usually, a crushing (as, to *swat* flies); **clout,** a colloquial or dialectal term, stresses the delivery of a blow or blows as on the body or head (as, "nurses and mothers and schoolmistresses...*clout* our heads the moment our conclusions differ from theirs"—*Shaw*); **punch** (as here compared: see also PERFORATE) suggests a hitting with or as if with a closed fist (as, he promised to *punch* the boy's nose if he again interfered); **box** implies a hitting with an open hand, especially on the side of one's head (as, to *box* one's ears). **Cuff** differs little from *box* except in connoting more force or violence in the impact; as, "I swear I'll *cuff* you, if you strike again" (*Shak.*).

Ana. *Beat, pummel, buffet, pound, baste, belabor, thrash, thresh.

2 Impress, touch, influence, *affect, sway.

striking. Arresting, signal, salient, conspicuous, outstanding, *noticeable, remarkable, prominent.

Ana. *Effective, effectual, efficacious: telling, convincing, cogent (see VALID): forcible, forceful, *powerful: impressive, *moving.

string, *n.* *Succession, progression, series, sequence, set, suit, suite, chain, train.

stringent. Strict, *rigid, rigorous.

Ana. *Severe, austere, stern: limiting, restricting, circumscribing, confining (see LIMIT, *v.*): restraining, curbing (see RESTRAIN): exacting, oppressive, *onerous: strait, *narrow.

strip, *v.* **Strip, divest, denude, bare, dismantle** agree in meaning to deprive a person or thing of that with which he or it is clothed, furnished, or invested. **Strip** stresses a pulling or tearing off rather than a laying bare, though the latter implication is frequent; it often connotes more or less violent action or complete deprivation; as, to *strip* the bark from a tree (or to *strip* a tree of its bark); he was quickly *stripped* of his clothes; where pasturing cattle *stripped* the ground; to *strip* tobacco (that is, to separate the leaves from the stalk); "dialogue...*stripped* of all removable literary ornament" (*C. E. Montague*); "*Stripped* of its secret, open, stark and bleak" (*Millay*). "Once start *stripping* poetry of what you imagine are inessentials and you will find...the anatomy is made visible but the life will have gone" (*Day Lewis*). **Divest,** in contrast to *strip,* does not suggest violence; it usually implies a taking away of that with which a person or thing has been clothed or equipped, especially as a sign of power, rank, influence, prestige, or the like. In discriminating use, therefore, it often connotes an undoing or a dispossession, or a degrading, or the like; as, to *divest* an officer of all authority; to *divest* a policeman of his badge. "Electricity....is invested with magnetic qualities when it begins to move, *divested* when it stops again" (*Karl K. Darrow*). "Naturalism *divests* life, whether physical or spiritual, of all that separates it from the inanimate and inorganic" (*Inge*). **Denude** implies a stripping or divesting, but in contrast, it always implies a resulting bareness or nakedness; as, the mountainside was *denuded* of trees by the hurricane. "*Stripped* of its vines and *denuded* of its shrubbery, the house would probably have been ugly enough" (*Cather*). "Though the phrase 'love is best' meant to our grandfathers more things than a volume could describe, it is to us...completely *denuded*...[and] only words, words, words" (*J. W. Krutch*). **Bare,** although it suggests a removal of that which covers or clothes, seldom carries implications of violent or complete stripping; in fact, it is chiefly used in idiomatic phrases which imply more than the mere act; thus, to *bare* one's head is to take off one's hat as a sign of respect, reverence, or the like; to *bare* one's sword is to unsheathe it and to have it ready for action; to *bare* one's heart to another is to reveal feelings one has concealed; to *bare* the secrets of the grave is to disclose, often as a result of a discovery of documents, something which had been known only to persons now dead. **Dismantle,** although it etymologically means to divest one of one's cloak, is now used chiefly with reference to the act of stripping a house, a building, a ship, or the like, of its entire equipment and furnishings; as, to *dismantle* a factory or a yacht. "The cottage itself was built of old stones from the long *dismantled* Priory" (*Hardy*).

Ana. Despoil, spoliate, devastate, waste, *ravage: rifle, loot, plunder, *rob.

Ant. Furnish: invest.

strip, *n.* **Strip, stripe, band, ribbon, fillet** come into comparison only when they mean a relatively long and narrow piece or section or something which suggests such a piece or section. **Strip** and **stripe** have probably undergone etymological confusion, since the verb *strip,* which is much older than the noun, stresses pulling or tearing off not only of clothes but also of bark, skin, rind, and the like, and in reference to the last mentioned may carry no suggestion of the shape of the pieces stripped off. The noun *strip,* nevertheless, like *stripe,* implies shape; that is, length and comparative narrowness and approximate uniformity of width. These nouns differ, however, for *strip* commonly suggests separation from a larger piece (as, to tear old linen into *strips* for bandages; to cut a sheet of paper into *strips*) and *stripe* stresses a contrast, as in color, texture, or pattern, between the section of a surface referred to and the sections bordering upon it (as, each white petal had a *stripe* of red; the *stripes* on a tiger's back; gray cloth with alternate *stripes* of blue and red). Thus, when one or more strips of braid have been sewn on a soldier's sleeve to indicate his rank, his length of service, or the like, they are called *stripes.* If actual separation is not implied (that is, cutting, tearing, or breaking apart), *strip* may be employed when the difference between the portion of surface referred to and its neighboring portions is a matter of use, ownership, or the like; as, the *strips* between sidewalk and curb belong to the city; each man on relief was allotted a *strip* of land for raising vegetables. However, *stripe* is used in such cases in preference to *strip* when the division is made evident by a contrast in appearance; as, "Narrow *stripes* of ice separated from each other by parallel moraines" (*J. Tyndall*); *stripes* of cultivated land in various shades of green. **Band,** after it had acquired the denotation of a strip of material, was for four or more centuries used narrowly of a strip employed in binding, confining, encircling, and the like (for synonyms in this sense see BOND, 1). Only in the early nineteenth century did it acquire the meaning in which it is here considered, in which the stress is on shape rather than on use. However, the difference is often a matter of emphasis, for the word when it means a strip or stripe often also connotes either an encircling without a suggestion (or with only a slight suggestion) of confining or uniting, or a horizontal position rather than the vertical position so often (though not necessarily) connoted by *stripe;* as, the lower parts of the sleeves and of the skirt were adorned with *bands* (encircling horizontal stripes) of blue silk; *bands* of colored light in the sky at dawn; at closer range, the mountain showed three *bands*, the lowest green, the middle gray, and the highest white. However, in such words as waist*band*, collar*band*, and the like, the term implies not only an encircling but a staying, supporting, or strengthening. **Ribbon** had for its earliest meaning the one that is still the most common, a narrow woven material with selvage edges, typically one that is fine and firm in texture and is used for ornamental bands, ties, bows, and the like; concretely, a ribbon is a length or strip of such a material. In extended use, *ribbon* is often used in place of *strip* when the strips are very long, very narrow, and very thin, and the material is flexible enough to appear like ribbon or to be handled like ribbon; as, steel *ribbon* for use in springs; *ribbons* of red, green, silver, blue, and gold paper for tying Christmas packages; he handled the *ribbons* (the reins) with great skill; the sails were torn by the hurricane into *ribbons*. "The road was a *ribbon* of moonlight over the purple moor" (*A. Noyes*). **Fillet** had for its earliest meaning in English a ribbon or other band for confining the hair but in its sense development (somewhat influenced by that of the French word *filet*, thread) it has come to be applied to many a thing which is otherwise describable as a strip, a ribbon, or a band, such as a metal strip or ribbon from which coins are punched, a very thin molding, one of certain bands of white matter in the brain, or, more commonly, a long narrow piece of meat or fish without bone, such as a tenderloin of beef or a piece of the flesh of a flatfish such as sole, halibut, flounder, or turbot. In cookery and on menus, a cooked fillet of beef, sole, etc., is often called a *filet* (with the French pronunciation). When *fillet*, the correct English term, is used, there is no justification for the French pronunciation.

stripe, *n.* **1** *Strip, band, ribbon, fillet.

2 Character, description, nature, *type, kind, sort, kidney, ilk.

strive. Struggle, endeavor, *attempt, essay, assay, try.

Ana. Work, labor, toil, travail (see corresponding nouns at WORK): cope, *contend, fight.

striving, *n.* Struggle, endeavor, essay, assay, attempt, try. See under ATTEMPT, *v.*

Ana. *Work, labor, toil, travail: coping, contending (see CONTEND): *contest, conflict, combat, fight.

stroke, *n.* *Paralysis, palsy, apoplexy, shock.

stroll, *v.* *Saunter, amble.

strong. 1 Strong, stout, sturdy, stalwart, tough, tenacious come into comparison in the sense of having or manifesting great power or force as in acting or resisting. They may be used in reference not only to living things, but also to concrete objects and to intangible things. **Strong,** the most inclusive of these terms, fundamentally implies the possession of great physical power, such as results in animals or plants from sound health or great size, or in things that are made or built from sound construction and substantial materials (as, a *strong* constitution; the hammock is not *strong* enough to bear the weight of two persons; a *strong* foundation), but in extended use it may apply to groups whose force is dependent upon numbers, organization, discipline, or the like (as, a *strong* army; "a *strong* majority forced a wavering minority along the road of rectitude"—*A. Repplier*), or to a spiritual or mental power or faculty that acts with force and vigor (as, a *strong* mind; a *strong* will; a *strong* critical instinct), or to some very potent or powerful thing (as, *strong* liquor; a *strong* poison; a *strong* current; a *strong* battery [i.e., one with very high voltage]; "the young husband had spoken *strong* words"—*Meredith*), or to anything, such as color or shadow, emotion or sentiment, that is particularly intense or violent (as, a *strong* purple; the *strong* light of the setting sun; *strong* anger; a *strong* love; a *strong* attachment). **Stout** (as here compared: see also FLESHY) carries a stronger implication than does *strong* of an ability to resist aggression or destructive forces or of an ability to endure hard use, severe pain, alluring temptation, and the like, without giving way. When applied to persons, it often suggests resolution, doggedness, fearlessness, or the like (as, "a *stouter* champion never handled sword"—*Shak.;* "To quell the valour of the *stoutest* heart"—*Cowper*): when applied to things, it usually also suggests solid, substantial construction (as, a *stout* cane; a *stout* ship) or a texture that resists stress or strain (as, a *stout* canvas; a *stout* paper). In fact, the term is generally applicable when the suggestion of power to resist or endure is more emphatic than that of a power to do or to effect. **Sturdy** implies qualities, in inanimate as well as in animate things, that suggest the possession of rugged health: the term carries no suggestion of powers derived from size, intensity, vehemence, or the like, but connotes rather an inner strength such as is derived from healthy vigorous growth, close, solid construction, a determined spirit, or the like, that gives it staying power and stoutness; as, the little fellow has *sturdy* legs; "a square and *sturdy* little urchin" (*N. Hawthorne*); "it is the *sturdiest* of creepers, facing the ferocious winds of the hills, the tremendous rains that blow up from the sea, and bitter frost" (*Jefferies*); "our people are...conspicuous for a *sturdy* independence" (*Inge*); "It seemed to her a fine expression of *sturdy* Boer patriotism, however misguided" (*R. Macaulay*). **Stalwart** etymologically implies firmness of foundation and, therefore, usually implies such strength as is derived from that which is so deeply established or firmly rooted that it is unassailable or impregnable or is completely dependable; as, "William Law...was a *stalwart* Churchman, and showed no sympathy with the sectaries" (*Inge*); "Dryden brings his *stalwart* common sense to bear upon the problem, and clarifies the issue" (*Lowes*); "Octavius had become the sole hope of the republicans, a more *stalwart* hope, for he had got himself a considerable army" (*Buchan*). When applied to persons with reference to their physique or prowess, *stalwart* always suggests great strength, but it usually throws the emphasis upon heroic build or largeness of frame; as, "a *stalwart* man, limbed like the old heroic breeds" (*J. R. Lowell*). **Tough** suggests the strength that comes from a texture or a spirit that is firm and unyielding and effectively resists attempts to destroy, overcome, or the like: it therefore stresses hardiness rather than vigor, resistant elasticity or wiriness rather than hardness or solidity, or a capacity for yielding that is just sufficient to increase rather than to destroy a person's or thing's strength or stoutness; as, a *tough* membrane; *tough* ore; a *tough* opponent; *tough* resistance. **Tenacious** comes very close to *tough* in its most general implications, but it places greater emphasis upon retentiveness of that which has been gained or of adherence to a support, position, idea, or the like. It therefore carries a strong suggestion of holding on, or of maintaining strength in spite of all opposing forces that would dislodge, dispossess, thwart, or weaken in any particular; when applied to substances, materials, and the like, it suggests extraordinary resistance to forces that would break out, or the like (as, "he seemed to hold on to life by a single thread only, but that single thread was very *tenacious*"—*Arnold;* "bold and *tenacious* as the bamboo shooting up through the hard ground of winter"—*Binyon*); when applied to persons it suggests a stubborn hold upon something, such as a possession or an opinion, that defies the efforts of others to break (as, "Italians in possession are probably as *tenacious* of their rights as any one else"—*Lucas;* "if the child is starved of pleasures, he will of course cling *tenaciously* to those that are attainable"—*B. Russell*).

Ana. *Vigorous, energetic, lusty: *powerful, potent, forcible, forceful: robust, sound, *healthy: vehement, *intense.

Ant. Weak.

2 *Alcoholic, spirituous, ardent, hard.

stronghold. Citadel, *fort, fortress, acropolis, fastness.

structure. 1 *Building, edifice, fabric, pile.

2 Structure, anatomy, framework, skeleton are often used interchangeably. **Structure,** however, is by far the richest in implications and the widest, therefore, in its range of application. In general it denotes the formation, arrangement, and articulation of parts in anything built up by nature or art. Oftentimes the word implies reference to everything that enters into the make-up of a particular body, organism, edifice, substance, or the like; thus, a study of the *structure* of a brain involves attention to the two kinds of matter (gray and white) of which it is composed, to the three parts into which it is divided (forebrain, midbrain, hindbrain), to the subdivisions of each of these parts, to the connections and interrelations between all these divisions, and to any peculiarities as in form or arrangement of parts. Sometimes, however, *structure* implies a reference to certain features only, as for example: (1) the parts or elements which distinguish the type or species and not the individual (as, crocodiles and alligators exhibit certain differences in *structure*); (2) the parts or features which are essential or necessary to a thing's existence as distinguished from those that are removable, detachable, etc. (as, in Gothic architecture the pointed arch is part of the *structure* and is not a decorative addition); (3) the parts or features that reveal the underlying design as opposed to those that complete the work or bring it into fullness of being (as, to study the *structure* of Browning's "Ring and the Book"). In current use, some persons, especially some biologists, prefer **anatomy** when the typical structure of an organism or of an organ is indicated; as, the *anatomy* of an ape; the *anatomy* of the heart. *Framework* and *skeleton* are applied to the underlying or supporting structure. **Framework** is used chiefly in reference to an artificial construction which serves merely as a prop or a guide in building, but which is not visible in the completed thing; as, the *framework* of a sofa; the carpenters are now working on the *framework* for the house. **Skeleton** is frequently used in the building trades for a rigid framework, especially one made of steel; it is often used in place of *structure, design, outline,* in reference to literary constructions, sometimes to imply that the design is carefully developed and its parts definitely articulated (as, the *skeleton* of his argument is now finished), but more often, probably, to indicate a sketchy conception of the whole which serves as a starting point (as, he has the *skeleton* of his plot in mind). In either case, it is usually further implied that the writing out in literary form and the elaboration of atmosphere, details, characters, etc., remain to be accomplished.

Ana. Integration, articulation, concatenation (see under INTEGRATE): organization, arrangement (see corresponding verbs at ORDER): *system, organism, scheme, complex.

struggle, *v.* Strive, endeavor, essay, assay, *attempt, try.

Ana. *Contend, cope, fight: compete (*with*), vie (*with*), *rival, emulate: toil, labor, work, travail (see corresponding nouns at WORK).

struggle, *n.* Striving, endeavor, essay, assay, attempt, try. See under ATTEMPT, *v.*

Ana. Toil, labor, *work, travail: *contest, conflict, fight, affray, fray: contending, coping (see CONTEND).

strut, *v.* **Strut, swagger, ruffle, bristle, bridle** come into comparison when they mean to assume an air of dignity or importance. **Strut** implies a pompous or theatrical affectation of dignity, especially as shown in one's gait or by one's bearing in movement. "A poor player That *struts* and frets his hour upon the stage" (*Shak.*). "Dr. Goldsmith...went...*strutting* away, and calling to me with an air of superiority" (*Boswell*). **Swagger** always implies ostentation, a conviction of one's superiority, and, often, an insolent or overbearing gait or manner. "He...scarcely deigned to set a foot to ground, But *swaggered* like a lord about his hall" (*Dryden*). "What a *swaggering* puppy must he take me for" (*Goldsmith*). **Ruffle,** a term that was common before 1700 but obsolete thereafter until the first quarter of the nineteenth century, is still occasionally found. It carries a strong implication of swaggering, but it suggests even more rowdiness, more defiance, and often more absurdly pretentious display. "[He] gets drunk, *ruffles,* and roysters" (*Kingsley*). "He must *ruffle* it in another sort that would walk to court in a nobleman's train" (*Scott*). **Bristle** implies an aggressive manifestation, originally of anger or of zeal, but now often of any emotion or desire that causes one to display conspicuously one's sense of dignity or importance. "All the time he stuck close to her, *bristling* with a small boy's pride of her" (*D. H. Lawrence*). "The bourgeoisie, *bristling* with prejudices and social snobberies" (*R. Macaulay*). **Bridle** usually suggests awareness of a threat to one's dignity or a suspicion of one's unimportance that leads one to toss up one's head, to draw in one's chin, and otherwise to assume a lofty manner. "By her *bridling* up I perceived she expected to be treated hereafter not as Jenny Distaff, but Mrs. Tranquillus" (*Tatler*). "Everything that poses, prances, *bridles,* struts, bedizens, and plumes itself" (*Mrs. H. Ward*).

Ana. Expose, exhibit, flaunt, parade (see SHOW, *v.*).

Con. Cringe, cower, *fawn, truckle: grovel, flounder (see WALLOW).

stubborn. *Obstinate, dogged, pertinacious, mulish, stiff-necked, pigheaded, bullheaded.

Ana. Rebellious, contumacious, *insubordinate: intractable, recalcitrant, refractory (see UNRULY): obdurate, adamant, inexorable, *inflexible: self-opinionated, *opinionated.

Con. Pliable, pliant, adaptable (see PLASTIC): tractable, amenable (see OBEDIENT).

stubby. Chunky, dumpy, stocky, *thick, thickset, squat.

student. *Scholar, pupil, disciple.

studied. *Deliberate, considered, advised, premeditated, designed.

Ana. *Thoughtful, considerate, attentive: intentional, *voluntary, willing, willful.

Con. *Spontaneous, impulsive, instinctive.

study, *n.* Concentration, application, *attention.

Ana. Consideration, contemplation, weighing, revolving (see corresponding verbs at CONSIDER): reflection, thought, speculation (see corresponding verbs at THINK): pondering, musing, meditation, rumination (see corresponding verbs at PONDER).

study, *v.* *Consider, contemplate, weigh, revolve, excogitate.

Ana. *Scrutinize, examine, inspect: *ponder, muse, meditate: *think, reflect, reason, speculate.

stultify. *Stunt, atrophy.

Ana. *Arrest, check, interrupt: *restrain, inhibit, curb: *hinder, impede, obstruct, block, bar.

stunt, *v.* **Stunt, stultify, atrophy** are synonymous terms only in their extended senses in which they are used in reference to men's minds or souls or men's mental or spiritual activities. However, even in their literal senses they have for their basic meaning to arrest the growth and development of someone or something. **Stunt** implies, primarily, a dwarfing as the result of abnormal or unfavorable conditions and a failure to attain full height or size. "So they [trees] slowly come to full growth, until warped, *stunted,* or risen to fair and gracious height, they stand open to all the winds" (*Galsworthy*). When used with reference to mental or spiritual development, the word commonly suggests a blighting or blasting or a cramping and inhibiting. "When by a cold penury, I blast the abilities of a nation, and *stunt* the growth of it's active energies, the ill I may do is beyond all calculation" (*Burke*). "All are victims of circumstances; all have had characters warped in infancy and intelligence *stunted* at school" (*B. Russell*). **Stultify,** originally a legal term meaning to allege or prove to be of unsound mind (especially oneself, in an endeavor to evade responsibility), has gradually extended in significance so that it and its derivative *stultification* now rarely, except in law, imply imbecility or insanity. In its chief current sense, it implies one's subjection to such influences that one's mind deteriorates and loses its power of growth. "Wearing our lives away in dull *stultifying* routine" (*New Freeman*); "Seek to be as others are, *Stultify* the soul" (*V. Lindsay*); "If the real prophet is he who attacks the *stultifying* illusions of mankind..." (*Van W. Brooks*). In modern idiom, not only things may *stultify* persons or their minds, but persons or their acts may *stultify* things which as forms of human activity or expression (such as a movement, a school of thought, a form of art) are capable of indefinite progress or development. Sometimes, little more than a checking of this progress and a rendering nugatory or useless all that has been or is being done are implied. "The blind folly of his servants had *stultified* his efforts" (*M. E. Braddon*). In very discriminating use, however, the word also connotes a destruction of usefulness or effectiveness by making a thing ridiculous or despicable. "We do *stultify* criticism if...we prostrate ourselves indiscriminately before what is good and what is bad" (*Quiller-Couch*). "Common sense demands that we shall begin with non-violence and not run the risk of *stultifying* the whole process of reform by using violence" (*A. Huxley*). **Atrophy** literally implies a wasting away or a shriveling up because of lack of nourishment or disuse. In medicine, *atrophy* (both as verb and noun) usually also implies degeneration, but the latter is often the result of a prior condition that cuts off or greatly diminishes the blood supply to the affected part; as, the muscles of a paralyzed arm gradually become *atrophied.* In extended use, *atrophy* is used chiefly with reference to instincts, natural appetites, powers of the mind or soul, or the like, which disappear or shrink into nothingness because of one's failure to make use of them or to develop them. "It is the trouble we take over our children that elicits the stronger forms of parental affection; in those who avoid this trouble the parental instinct becomes more or less *atrophied*" (*B. Russell*). "The scientific person will become *atrophied* on the mystical side, the mystical person will become *atrophied* on the scientific side" (*H. Ellis*).

Ana. Disable, cripple, sap, undermine, enfeeble, debilitate, *weaken: *arrest, check, interrupt.

stupendous. Tremendous, prodigious, monumental, *monstrous.

Ana. *Enormous, immense, huge, vast, colossal, gigantic: astounding, amazing, astonishing (see SURPRISE).

stupid, *adj.* **Stupid, dull, dense, crass, dumb** agree in meaning conspicuously lacking in intelligence or power to absorb ideas or impressions, or exhibiting such a lack. **Stupid** implies a benumbed or dazed state of mind that is either congenital or the result of intoxication, a shock, illness, or the like: although it seldom is applied to the insane or the imbecile, it often also suggests senselessness; as, "*stupid* with age" (*Shak.*); *stupid* with drink; "he could not stand *stupid* people, especially those who are made *stupid* by education" (*Wilde*). "What force, what fury drove us into saying the *stupid,* intolerant, denunciatory things we said...?" (*L. P. Smith*). **Dull** (see also DULL, 2) suggests slowness or sluggishness of mind that may be constitutional, or the result of lack of mental exercise, or of overwork, or of a physical condition. A person or thing that is *stupid* reveals a deadness or a deadening of the mental powers; a person or thing that is *dull* manifests a lack of mental quickness or alertness or heavy, labored mental processes; thus, constitutionally *dull* pupils progress slowly until they are awakened by good teaching; constitutionally *stupid* pupils are usually subnormal physically or mentally; a *dull* book is so lacking in brightness, liveliness, or other signs of a stimulated mind, that it bores the reader; a *stupid* book exasperates the reader by its fatuousness, inanity, or other signs of mental ineptness; so, all work and no play makes Jack a *dull* boy; "Compared with her, other women were heavy and *dull*" (*Cather*). **Dense** implies a quality of mind suggestive of thickness or solidity (thickheadedness, thickwittedness, stockishness, blockheadedness, etc.) that makes it (the mind) impervious to ideas. It may imply obtuseness or stolidity, or any of various other qualities that reveal lack of perception, sensitiveness, or subtlety; as, the teacher of mathematics thought he had a particularly *dense* group of students; "More virtuous than myself, or more *dense*" (*Lamb*). **Crass** suggests fatness or grossness of substance (fatheadedness, lumpishness, etc.) that makes the mind incapable of delicate mental processes such as analysis, discrimination, evaluation, and the like, or impervious to refined or spiritual ideas; as, *crass* ignorance. "There were many *crass* minds in Middlemarch, whose reflective scales could only weigh things in the lump" (*G. Eliot*). "The *crass* Toryism of Mr. Chauner" (*Bennett*). **Dumb,** as here compared (see also DUMB, 1), is American slang, partly affected by the German *dumm* and partly by the ordinary sense of the English word. As it is a term of contempt, it may be used in place of any of the preceding terms, especially when obtuseness and inarticulateness are also implied.

Ana. Foolish, silly, *simple, fatuous, asinine: sluggish, comatose, stuporous, *lethargic: inert, idle, supine, *inactive: phlegmatic, stolid, *impassive.

Ant. Intelligent.

stupor. Torpor, torpidity, lassitude, *lethargy, languor.

Ana. Phlegm, impassivity, stolidity (see under IMPASSIVE): inertness *or* inertia, passivity, supineness, inactivity, idleness (see corresponding adjectives at

INACTIVE): insensibility, anesthesia (see corresponding adjectives at INSENSIBLE).

stuporous. *Lethargic, torpid, comatose, sluggish.
Ana. *Dull, obtuse: inert, supine, passive, *inactive: enervated, spiritless, listless, lackadaisical, languorous (see LANGUID).

sturdy. Stout, *strong, stalwart, tough, tenacious.
Ana. Sound, robust, *healthy: *vigorous, energetic, lusty: dogged, pertinacious (see OBSTINATE).
Ant. Decrepit.

stutter. *Stammer.

Stygian. *Infernal, chthonian, Hadean, Tartarean, hellish.

style, *n.* **1** Diction, phraseology, phrasing, *language, vocabulary.
Ana. *Taste, zest, gusto, relish: *form, convention, usage, convenance.
2 *Fashion, mode, vogue, fad, rage, craze, dernier cri, cry.
Ana. Modishness, smartness, chicness, spruceness, nattiness, stylishness, fashionableness (see corresponding adjectives at STYLISH).
3 *Name, designation, title, denomination, appellation.

stylish. **Stylish, fashionable, modish, smart, chic, dapper, dashing, spruce, natty, nifty, nobby, posh, toffish, brave, braw** are here compared as meaning presenting a fine, fresh, and more or less splendid or elegant appearance. Most of these terms, as here considered, apply chiefly to persons and stress the effect produced by clothes or by clothes and grooming. *Stylish, fashionable,* and *modish* are applicable not only to persons, but to clothes, as apart from persons, and to several other things. These three terms usually imply a conformity to the currently accepted style or fashion. **Stylish** applies to any person regardless of class or social station: for this reason, the term sometimes suggests pretentiousness or showiness as well as up-to-dateness (as, the Frenchman remarked the *stylish* clothes of American girls; although without much money to spend on clothes, she nevertheless looks *stylish;* "Her air, though it had not all the decided pretension, the resolute *stilishness,* of Miss Thorpe's, had more real elegance" (*Austen*); "But '*stylish*' is of the shop...and belongs to the dialect of milliners' apprentices and waiting-maids alone...in England" (*Lady F. P. Verney*). On the other hand, **fashionable** usually connotes some connection with those who move in society or belong to a world apart from and above that of the ordinary man, and whose approval of that which is new not only in clothes, in furniture, in decorations, and the like, but also in ideas, in books, in writers, in artists, etc., determines the choice of those who would follow them; hence, to say that a costume, a hat, or a type of interior decoration is *fashionable* is not only to say that it is the latest style but that it meets with the approval of those who are regarded as dictators of fashion; as, in those days it was *fashionable* to stroll along the waterfront on Saturday afternoons; "Taste is now the *fashionable* word of the *fashionable* world" (*Chesterfield*); "The *fashionable* disparagement of reason, and exaltation of will, feeling, or instinct" (*Inge*); "My sister...recommended me to read the *fashionable* prophets of the day, Carlyle and Emerson and Ruskin" (*L. P. Smith*). **Modish** differs from *stylish* chiefly in its greater stress on up-to-dateness, or conformity with the very latest style, rather than on the effect produced: it sometimes suggests a step ahead of what is describable as *stylish* or *fashionable* and a daring or startling quality; as, this shop offers only *modish* dresses and suits; "Mr. Pen, Sir William's son, is come back from France....A most *modish* person grown...a fine gentleman" (*Pepys*); "Thomas Moore's...high-flown and *modish* 'Evenings in Greece' " (*T. Walsh*); "Wit of that genuine kind which is free from *modishness*" (*Birrell*). **Smart** often implies extreme modishness in dress and appearance, but, even more often, it retains implications of trimness and neatness derived from an earlier and now comparatively rare sense of the word and connotes a finish or perfection suggestive not only of modishness but of perfect grooming and an awareness of the importance of cut, line, color, accent, or the like; as, she always wears *smart* clothes; she makes a *smart* appearance, whatever the time of day or night. **Chic,** a term taken from the French, but currently carrying implications that are found only in English, is sometimes loosely used as meaning *modish* or *smart:* in discriminating use, however, it does not imply conformity to the latest fashion, but an effectiveness in style not only of dress or millinery, but of any product of art or craftsmanship which suggests the exercise of a knack or skill and the achievement of distinction; thus, a *chic* hat has not only a style of its own but distinction and charm; a *chic* appearance is produced not by slavish attention to the latest fashion nor by an ignoring of it but by original touches or clever adaptations that distinguish one from those who are merely stylish or fashionable. **Dapper** typically applies to men, now usually only to men of small or slight build: it always implies stylishness, but it also commonly connotes trimness, briskness, and fastidious grooming; as, "Guido's *dapper* Archangel" (*N. Hawthorne*); "Cibber, the *smart, dapper* little Frenchified coxcomb" (*L. Stephen*). **Dashing** applies to men and to women or to things which they wear or use: it implies not only stylishness or, more often, modishness, but a bright, shining appearance that enables one to cut a figure in any group or assemblage; as, "She had two *dashing* daughters, who dressed as fine as dragons" (*Irving*); a pair of *dashing* young brokers; a *dashing* carriage and pair. **Spruce** applies most often to men: it suggests an almost affected attention to the details of one's appearance in order that one will look not only stylish but smart and fresh in appearance: it sometimes connotes a finical, almost vulgar, concern for the perfection of every detail; as, "Fastidious Brisk: a neat, *spruce,* affecting courtier, one that wears clothes well, and is in fashion" (*B. Jonson*); "The *spruce* apprentice sets up for a critic" (*Goldsmith*); "Making themselves as *spruce* as bridegrooms...according to the rules of their newly-acquired town experience" (*Hardy*). **Natty** differs from *spruce* in stressing neatness and orderliness slightly more than stylishness; as, "As *natty* a beau, As Bond Street ever saw" (*Shelley*). **Nifty,** which is chiefly American slang, implies approval of that which is stylish or smart; as, that is a *nifty* suit; a *nifty* hat. **Nobby** (originally British slang), **posh** and **toffish** (more recent British slang) come close to *fashionable* in their application to the clothes, manners, possessions, and the like, characteristic of the upper classes or of the world of fashion. *Nobby* suggests reference to the "nobs," or persons of great wealth or distinction (as, it's a *nobby* place; "An outfit... described as 'rather *nobby*' "—*Quiller-Couch*); *posh* implies a character or appearance that is eminently high-class or wins the favor of the exceedingly rich or aristocratic (as, "I'd like to have...a very cozy car, small but frightfully *posh*"—*J. B. Priestley;* "Unfortunately, Prufrock...became *posh*"—*Day Lewis*); *toffish* suggests reference to that which is characteristic of "toffs," "swells," or of dandies (as, you certainly look *toffish* in that new suit). **Brave,** or its Scottish equivalent **braw,** suggests showiness or splendor, as of dress; as, to make a *brave* appearance in his first evening clothes;

"to shew a *braw* new gown" (*Burns*); " 'Ye think yoursell a *braw* fellow...and troth...there's na fault to find wi' the outside' " (*Scott*).
Ana. *New, novel, new-fashioned, newfangled, modernistic: *showy, ostentatious, pretentious, pompous.

styptic. *Astringent, constringent.

suave. **Suave, urbane, diplomatic, bland, smooth, politic** are here compared as applied to persons, their demeanor, and their utterances and as meaning conspicuously and ingratiatingly tactful and well-mannered. Many of these words at times convey so strong a suggestion of insincerity or of a surface manner that their distinctive implications are obscured. It is chiefly in the underogatory use of these words that their essential differences in meaning are apparent. **Suave** suggests qualities that are (or have the appearance of being) acquired through discipline and training and that encourage or are intended to encourage easy and frictionless intercourse with others. Negatively, it suggests the absence of everything that may offend or repel; positively, it suggests qualities such as affability without fulsomeness, politeness without stiffness, persuasiveness without a hint of a desire to force one's opinion on others; as, the *suave* manner of the well-bred Chinese; "what gentle, *suave*, courteous tones!" (*H. H. Jackson*); "a slight disturbance of his ordinary *suave* and well-bred equanimity" (*Lytton*). **Urbane** (etymologically, characteristic of the city as opposed to the country) implies a high degree of cultivation, poise, and wide social experience; it also commonly suggests an ingrained or inbred courtesy which makes for pleasant and agreeable intercourse among all kinds of men, regardless of their social or intellectual standing. "No one lost anything by granting precedence to a man so flawlessly *urbane*" (*A. Repplier*). "That peculiarly Roman *urbanity*—the spirit at once of the grown man as distinguished from children, of the man of the world, and of the gentleman" (*J. W. Mackail*). Since urbanity and an ability to deal with difficult or ticklish situations with great tact are theoretically the qualities of the typical diplomat, the adjective **diplomatic,** when used in reference to nondiplomats, carries these implications, often adding in addition a hint of artfulness in gaining one's own ends; as, a *diplomatic* reply to an aggrieved client; "Gabrielle's busy, active, *diplomatic* managing of the party" (*E. E. Hale*). "I have grown to believe that the one thing worth aiming at is simplicity of heart and life; that one's relations with others should be direct and not *diplomatic*" (*A. C. Benson*). **Bland** is negative as well as positive in its implications, for it usually implies the absence of irritating qualities as strongly as it suggests serenity, mildness, and gentility. Nevertheless, in spite of this vagueness, the term often carries a hint of benignity, or the appearance of it, and usually directly implies an ingratiating pleasantness. "His manners were gentle, complying, and *bland*" (*Goldsmith*); "Mr. Pickwick was...producing a constant succession of the *blandest* and most benevolent smiles" (*Dickens*). "He's simply a distinguished-looking old cleric with a sweet smile and a white tie: he's just honorable and *bland* and as cold as ice" (*Santayana*). **Smooth** differs from *bland* chiefly in being more positive in its implications and in being more consistently derogatory. Sometimes it stresses suavity, often an assumed suavity; as, "The words of his mouth were *smoother* than butter, but war was in his heart" (*Psalms* lv. 21). At other times it carries even a stronger implication of tactfulness and craft than *diplomatic*. "Octavian had replied *smoothly* to Cleopatra's entreaties, for he wished to preserve her alive to grace his triumph" (*Buchan*). **Politic** (as here compared: see also EXPEDIENT) when applied to persons implies both shrewdness and tact: the term usually suggests the ability to gain one's ends or to avoid friction through ingratiating means or diplomatic methods. It varies considerably, however, in its implication of artfulness, sometimes connoting cunning or craft and sometimes little more than just the right degree of suavity; as, "Am I *politic*? am I subtle? am I a Machiavel?" (*Shak.*); "I... Am an attendant lord, one that will do To swell a progress... advise the prince... Deferential, glad to be of use, *Politic*, cautious, and meticulous" (*T. S. Eliot*).
Ana. *Gracious, cordial, affable, genial, sociable: *disarming, ingratiating: courteous, courtly, polite (see CIVIL): *fulsome, unctuous, sleek.
Ant. Bluff.

subdue. Subjugate, reduce, overcome, surmount, overthrow, rout, *conquer, vanquish, defeat, beat, lick.
Ana. Control, manage, direct (see CONDUCT, *v.*): discipline, *punish, correct: foil, thwart, circumvent, *frustrate: *suppress, repress.
Ant. Awaken (sense 2), waken.

subdued. *Tame, submissive.
Ana. Meek, *humble, modest, lowly: *timid, timorous: docile, tractable, amenable (see OBEDIENT).
Ant. Intense: barbaric (*of taste*): bizarre (*of effects*): effervescent (*of character and temperament*).

subject, *adj.* **1** Dependent, *subordinate, secondary, tributary, succursal, collateral.
Ana. *Subservient, servile, slavish: conditional, contingent, *dependent, relative.
Ant. Sovereign, dominant.
2 *Liable, open, exposed, prone, susceptible, sensitive, incident.
Ana. *Apt, likely, liable.
Ant. Exempt.

subject, *n.* **1** *Citizen, national.
Ant. Sovereign.
2 Subject, matter, subject matter, argument, topic, text, theme, motive (*or* **motif**), **leitmotiv** (*or* **leitmotif**), as here compared, mean the basic idea or the principal object of thought or attention in a discourse or artistic composition. **Subject** is the most widely applicable as well as the least definite in denotation of these words. It may be used in reference to any type of discourse or to a work of art of any kind for it implies merely some restriction in one's field of choice and a governing principle determining the selection of one's material and demanding some concentration in the treatment of it; as, she is the chief *subject* of conversation at present; what is the *subject* of his painting?; a writer should stick to his *subject;* your *subject* is too comprehensive to be treated adequately in so short an article. "That *subject* for an angel's song, The hero and the saint!" (*Cowper*). **Matter** and **subject matter** (which is now more frequent) are often used as close synonyms of *subject*. "Hail, Son of God, Saviour of men! Thy name Shall be the copious *matter* of my song" (*Milton*). "Mr. Lytton Strachey... chose, as *subject-matter* of a book four people of whom the world had heard little but good" (*A. Repplier*). As often, however, these terms refer not to the idea, object, situation, or the like, selected for treatment, but to a restricted field or range of material from which one selects the specific subject he intends to treat; thus, the medieval writers of romance or heroic poetry had three *matters* from which to draw situations, characters, and incidents for their narratives: the *matter* of France (the legends of Charlemagne and his companions), the *matter* of Britain (the Arthurian legends), and the *matter* of Rome (the myths and legends of classical antiquity). " 'Alexander's Bridge' was my first novel, and does not

deal with the kind of *subject-matter* in which I now find myself most at home" (*Cather*). An **argument** is the subject, especially the carefully delimited subject, for a particular discourse, such as a poem or a part of a poem, that is planned in advance of execution. "O Spirit... Instruct me, for Thou know'st... That, to the highth of this great *argument* [the idea to be developed in *Paradise Lost*], I may assert Eternal Providence, And justify the ways of God to men" (*Milton*). The word sometimes, but far from always, implies explicit statement of the leading idea or a summarizing of its development; thus, Pope prefaced each epistle of his *Essay on Man* with an *argument* of it. A **topic** is a subject (usually one of general interest) chosen because of its possibilities for individual or original treatment, or for discussion by different persons holding diverse views; as, the students were asked to write an essay on one of the assigned *topics;* "he had exhausted every *topic* of conversation" (*Mrs. Radcliffe*). A **text,** strictly, is a verse or passage, usually from Scripture, chosen as providing or suggesting a subject for a sermon or similar discourse. "The excellency of this *text* is that it will suit any sermon; and of this sermon, that it will suit any *text*" (*Sterne*). In extended use, it is often applied to anything (not necessarily a phrase) that suggests itself as a good starting point for a discourse the subject of which is yet to be defined or which lacks a definite subject. "The maiden Aunt Took this fair day for *text,* and from it preach'd" (*Tennyson*). A **theme** is a subject which one selects for treatment (especially literary or artistic treatment) because of its appeal to oneself or its possible appeal to others. *Theme* is applicable to any idea, proposition, text (or in music, melodic phrase), mood, or the like, which a writer, composer, or artist proposes to develop (as in a poem), to elaborate upon (as in a movement of a symphony), or to illustrate (as in a mural or series of murals), or which can be detected in a completed work as the dominant object of his concern. "Fools are my *theme,* let satire be my song" (*Byron*). "Waterfalls are from very early times a favourite *theme* for the painter" (*Binyon*). "I somehow played the piece [Schumann's *Carnival*]: remarked on each old theme I' the new dress" (*Browning*). *Theme* does not necessarily suggest any clearer definition than *subject* or *topic* (thus, a poet chooses love for his *subject* or *theme;* an essayist has a wide range of *themes* or of *topics* from which to make a choice), but in distinction from them, it invites comparison with the treatment and calls attention to the quality, the form, the design, or the execution of the completed work; thus, an overworked *theme* implies a lack of freshness in the thought, design, or the like; a compelling *theme* suggests force and enthusiasm in its treatment. "To produce a mighty book you must choose a mighty *theme*" (*Melville*). **Motive** is restricted in its reference to works of art in which design or pattern is the important element. In music, it is interchangeable in this sense with *theme,* the leading phrase which is repeated with variations during the course of a composition or movement; in the decorative arts it is the figure which stands out as the salient and dominant feature of the design, and is repeated at appropriate intervals; as, the chief *motif* of the design is the peacock one, much favored by decorative artists. **Leitmotiv** was originally employed in reference to the music dramas of the German composer Wagner. In music, it designates a specific melodic phrase that is associated with a particular person, mood, or situation, and that is repeated each time this person, mood, or situation reappears. The word has considerable extended use, and is often applied to an insistent or recurrent idea that appeals to a reader as the dominant theme of an author or of a work. " 'Fate went its way uncompromisingly to the terrible end.' This is the *leitmotiv* of this interesting, dignified apologia of one of Austria's Elder Statesmen" (*Sat. Review of Lit.*).

subject matter. *Subject, matter, argument, topic, text, theme, motive, leitmotiv.

subjoin. *Add, append, annex, superadd.

Ana. Attach, affix, *fasten: *unite, conjoin, combine.

Con. *Detach, disengage: *separate, part, sever.

subjugate. Subdue, reduce, overcome, surmount, overthrow, rout, *conquer, vanquish, defeat, beat, lick.

Ana. Circumvent, outwit, foil, thwart, *frustrate: compel, coerce, *force.

sublimation. *Paragon, apotheosis, phoenix, nonpareil, nonesuch.

Ana. Ideal, beau ideal, paradigm, exemplar, pattern, *model.

sublime. Glorious, *splendid, superb, resplendent, gorgeous.

Ana. Transcendent, transcendental, ideal, *abstract: divine, spiritual, sacred, *holy: majestic, august, noble, stately (see GRAND).

sublunary. *Earthly, terrestrial, terrene, earthy, mundane, worldly, mortal.

submerge. Immerse, duck, *dip, souse, dunk.

Ana. *Soak, saturate, drench, impregnate.

submission. *Surrender, capitulation.

Ana. Yielding, submitting, succumbing, bowing, caving in (see YIELD): compliance, acquiescence, resignation (see under COMPLIANT).

Ant. Resistance.

submissive. *Tame, subdued.

Ana. Docile, tractable, amenable, biddable, *obedient: meek, lowly, *humble: *subservient, servile, slavish, menial.

Ant. Rebellious.

submit. *Yield, capitulate, succumb, relent, defer, bow, cave in.

Ana. Surrender, abandon, resign, *relinquish: abide, endure, suffer, *bear.

Ant. Resist, withstand.

subordinate, *adj.* **Subordinate, secondary, dependent, subject, tributary, succursal, collateral** come into comparison as meaning placed in or belonging to a class, rank, or status lower than the highest or the first in importance or power. **Subordinate** applies to any person or thing that is beneath another in any way, such as by being under his (or its) authority (as, all officers of an independent army below the rank of general are *subordinate* officers; the house servants are *subordinate* to the butler), or by having a less important or less conspicuous place, position, or status in the scheme of a whole than some other member, part, element, or the like (as, "the relation of dominating to *subordinate* features [of a landscape]"—*Binyon;* "ceremony is *subordinate* in the scheme of life, as colour is in a painting"—*H. Ellis*), or by loss of independence and reduction to a lower or inferior position (as, "at that time considered as a *subordinate* and inferior class of beings...subjugated by the dominant race"—*Ch. Just. Taney;* "Such a step... would tend to make poetry merely a *subordinate* branch of music"—*Day Lewis*). **Secondary** differs from *subordinate* mainly in suggesting a much narrower range of difference, for it implies a position, an importance, or the like, that is just below that which may be described as *primary, main, chief, leading,* or the like; it is therefore never, in precise and discriminating use, applied to a thing which is distant from the highest by two or more steps or degrees; as, "What they actually believe is of *secondary* consequence; the main thing is what they say" (*Mencken*); "The valuation of an object is thus *secondary* to the apprehension of it" (*S. Alexander*). Often, *secondary* is opposed to *original* or *first* (in order of development or derivation) and carries no necessary implication of inferiority in importance; as, the *secondary* meaning of a word. **Dependent** (as here considered: see also DEPENDENT, 1) implies subordination to someone or something, but it also connotes the position or the status of one (person or thing) that hangs on, or leans on, or relies on, the other for support or for the provision of that which is lacking in itself; thus, a *dependent* clause in a sentence is not intelligible apart from the main clause; a *dependent* child is not old enough to support himself and, therefore, must rely upon his parents or guardians. In its commonest use *dependent* implies a loss, through subjugation or through weakness, of one's independence: it therefore frequently stresses powerlessness or debasement more than subordination; as, "England, long *dependent* and degraded, was again a power of the first rank" (*Macaulay*); "countries that let themselves become *dependent* on the labor of other countries and settle down into a comfortable and ladylike parasitism" (*Shaw*). **Subject** definitely implies subordination to a dominant power, but never carries, as *subordinate* sometimes carries, an implication of relative importance within a scheme of the whole: it often tends to suggest the loss of powers which imply a degree of freedom, responsibility, self-discipline, and the like; as, a *subject* race; "aristocracy is out of date, and *subject* populations will no longer obey even the most wise and virtuous rulers" (*B. Russell*). **Tributary** strictly applies to peoples, races, nations, etc., that have been conquered and made subject to another people, race, or nation, and that are forced to pay tribute to their conquerors; in somewhat looser, but correct, use it is often interchangeable with *subject;* as, "no conquering race ever lived or could live ...among a *tributary* one without begetting children on it" (*Quiller-Couch*). In a secondary sense, it is also applicable to anything that has an outlet into another and larger thing of the same kind and thereby yields supplies, accretions, and the like, which increase the size or importance of the latter; as, the *tributary* streams of the Mississippi River; "the lane, receiving two *tributary* lanes from who should say what remote hamlets, widened out with this accession" (*C. Mackenzie*). **Succursal** was originally applied to churches, chapels, and monastic houses dependent on a larger or more important church or monastery: it is now comparatively rare, but applicable to any branch of an institution or a system that serves as a subsidiary or auxiliary of the main institution or system; as, a *succursal* railway; a *succursal* bank; a *succursal* nest (of ants). **Collateral** etymologically implies a being side by side: it still sometimes suggests parallelism or concomitancy, but it no longer implies co-ordination. In the sense here considered, it retains its etymological implication (that of lying beside) but it suggests not equivalence in value, but subordination as through an indirect relation to, or a loose connection with, the other; thus, a *collateral* cause of a war, though by implication operative at the same time as the most important or primary cause, is subordinate to the latter; a *collateral* issue is not the main issue; a *collateral* descendant is not a direct, or lineal, descendant, but one in a different line, as of a brother or sister. "This...being but *collateral* to my work of examining the preface" (*Marvell*). "The limiting of inquiry to the immediate, with total disregard of the *collateral* or circumstantial events" (*Poe*).

Ana. *Auxiliary, subsidiary, subservient, contributory, adjuvant: *accidental, incidental, fortuitous.

Ant. Chief, leading: dominant.

subscribe. Agree, acquiesce, *assent, consent, accede.

Ana. Concur, coincide, *agree: *approve, endorse, sanction: *promise, pledge, covenant.

Ant. Boggle.

subservient. **1** *Auxiliary, subsidiary, contributory, ancillary, adjuvant, accessory.

Ana. *Subordinate, secondary, dependent, subject.

2 Subservient, servile, slavish, menial, obsequious are synonyms only in so far as they agree in meaning manifesting, as a person or his acts, or requiring, as a position or status, extreme compliance or abject obedience. **Subservient,** as here compared (see also AUXILIARY), applies directly or indirectly to those who occupy a subordinate or dependent condition or who manifest the state of mind of one in such a position: the term may imply nothing more or it may connote cringing or truckling; as, "Editors and journalists who express opinions in print that are opposed to the interests of the rich are dismissed and replaced by *subservient* ones" (*Shaw*); "The writers of the North American group...dry, mechanical, timid, *subservient* to the abstract laws that had governed the eighteenth century" (*Van W. Brooks*). **Servile** implies the work or character typical of slaves or servants of low degree or of those whose attitude is that of mean or cringing submission; as, to occupy a *servile* position; *servile* labors; "mean, *servile* compliance" (*Burns*); "to compose a letter which might...convey gratitude without *servile* regret, be guarded without coldness, and honest without resentment" (*Austen*). **Slavish,** which implies the status, work, or attitude of a slave, carries much stronger implications of utter abjectness or debasement and excessively laborious toil than *servile;* as, the *slavish* condition of the migrant workers; "*slavish* harnessed toil" (*Carlyle*); "Fear took hold on me from head to foot—*slavish* superstitious fear" (*Stevenson*). Both *servile* and *slavish* are used of unduly close dependence upon an original or model; as, "It is the business of art, to imitate nature, but not with a *servile* pencil" (*Goldsmith*); "Close [translation], but not so close as to be *servile*" (*Cowper*); a *slavish* devotion to tradition; a *slavish* adherence to rules is usually a sign of pedantry. **Menial** originally came close to *domestic* or *household* in meaning: in later and still current use, it applies to persons who are servants (chiefly household servants) or to their typical employments, offices, and attitude; in current use, it sometimes, but not invariably, connotes sordidness or degradation; as, "Her ladyship was of humble, I have heard even *menial*, station originally" (*Thackeray*); "The nurse...had a sort of unbroken look in her eye that was unbecoming in a *menial* position" (*H. G. Wells*); "Mark Twain...longed to be a cabin boy, to do any *menial* work about the decks in order to serve the majestic boats and their worthy sovereigns" (*Van W. Brooks*). **Obsequious** now less often than in the past applies to persons who are inferiors or to the words, actions, manners, or the like, by which they reveal their sense of inferiority in the presence of their superiors; as, "a duteous and knee-crooking knave ... doting on his own *obsequious* bondage" (*Shak.*); "be civil, but not *obsequious*" (*Meredith*). In current use, it may imply a servile, often a sycophantic, attitude (as, "citizens of all classes who have to be *obsequious* to the rich and insolent to the poor"—*Shaw;* "On the second Saturday evening after he got his new position, the tobacconist, a rather *obsequious* man, called him Mr. Hall"—*S. Anderson*), or extreme attentiveness in service or to the niceties of service (as, an *obsequious* butler; "Following him out, with *obsequious* politeness"—*Dickens*).

Ana. Fawning, cringing, truckling, cowering (see FAWN):

*compliant, acquiescent, resigned: *mean, ignoble, abject.

Ant. Domineering: overbearing.

subside. *Abate, wane, ebb.

Ana. Dwindle, diminish, *decrease.

subsidiary. *Auxiliary, contributory, subservient, ancillary, adjuvant, accessory.

subsidy. Grant, subvention, *appropriation.

subsist. Exist, live, *be.

subsistence. *Living, livelihood, sustenance, maintenance, support, keep, bread, bread and butter.

substantial. *Massive, massy, bulky, monumental.

Ant. Airy, ethereal.

substantialize. Substantiate, hypostatize, reify, *realize, actualize, embody, incarnate, materialize, externalize, objectify.

substantiate. **1** Substantialize, hypostatize, reify, *realize, actualize, embody, incarnate, materialize, externalize, objectify.

2 Verify, corroborate, *confirm, authenticate, validate.

Ana. *Prove, demonstrate, try, test.

substitute, *n.* **1** Surrogate, *resource, resort, expedient, shift, makeshift, stopgap.

Ana. *Device, contrivance, contraption: duplicate, copy, *reproduction.

2 Substitute, supply, locum tenens, alternate, understudy, double, stand-in, pinch hitter designate a person who performs or is prepared to perform the duties of another during the latter's absence or incapacitation. **Substitute** is the general term interchangeable with any of the others; specifically, in the United States, it is often applied to a teacher not appointed to a full-time position but held in reserve for service when needed. A **supply** is a person who actually substitutes for the regular teacher, preacher, or the like. A **locum tenens** is often a substitute for a professional man with a practice or clientele which needs to be cared for while he is away for a length of time: the term is used especially among physicians; it is also applied to clergymen. An **alternate** is one appointed or elected to take the place of another, as a delegate to a convention, a holder of a fellowship, or the like, if the latter should be incapacitated or disqualified when the appointment or election goes into effect. An **understudy** is a reserve actor or actress prepared to take the part of a regular actor or actress (especially of the legitimate theater) on short notice. A **double** is an anonymous actor or actress in motion pictures who substitutes in shots or scenes where the required action is too risky or difficult for the regular player, or whose voice or instrumentation is recorded on the sound track while the photographed player goes through the appropriate motions. A **stand-in** is not, as often thought, an understudy in motion pictures, for his (or her) chief duty is to substitute for a star during times of waiting for lights and camera to come into play. A **pinch hitter** (an American colloquialism derived from the baseball term for one sent in to bat to replace a weak hitter when a hit is particularly needed) is one who substitutes for another in a "pinch," or emergency; it usually connotes competence or ability to rise to the demands of the situation.

substratal, substrative. Underlying, basic, basal, *fundamental, radical.

subsume. *Include, comprehend, embrace, involve, imply, implicate.

subterfuge. Double-dealing, fraud, *deception, trickery, chicanery, chicane.

Ana. Ruse, stratagem, maneuver, artifice, *trick: expedient, shift, makeshift (see RESOURCE): *ambiguity, equivocation, tergiversation.

subtile. *Subtle.

subtle. Also **subtile.** **1** *Logical, analytical.

Ana. Penetrating, piercing, probing (see ENTER): *deep, profound: abstruse, *recondite.

Ant. Dense (*in mind*): blunt (*in speech*).

2 Subtle, subtile are surviving variant spellings of a Middle English word derived from Old French and later corrected by its Modern French equivalent as influenced by the Latin form. Both still basically mean so fine or tenuous in quality or consistency as to be hard to perceive, detect, or recognize. The choice of spelling is often merely a matter of personal preference, but in current use *subtle* is by far the commoner form. When, as now rarely happens, **subtle** is thought of as distinguishable from *subtile,* it is often preferred in the larger sense of being hard to fix, or seize, or describe, or the like; as, "The falsehood is a little more *subtle,* the injury a little more indirect, than in ordinary cases of unfair trade" (*Justice Holmes*); "Indeed, the difference between what is right and what is harmful is very *subtle*" (*B. Russell*); "Generalizations like these elude proof because they are usually based on very *subtle* factors" (*Frankfurter*). It is commonly the preferred term when applied to the mind or a mental power or mental effort, then implying refinement of thought, insight, perception, or the like: often, it means highly analytic; as, a *subtle* mind; a *subtle* analysis; a *subtle* questioner; a *subtle* question; "How *subtle,* how delicate was the vision of the great painters" (*G. Bradford*). When the emphasis is upon craftiness or ingenuity or the like, both words are usable, but *subtle* is preferred occasionally when there is a suggestion of slyness or indirection; as, a *subtle* thief; a *subtle* form of blackmail; "It will be said that it is a very *subtle* and indirect action which I am thus prescribing for criticism" (*Arnold*); "a *subtle* diplomacy and wary tactics would be necessary" (*Bennett*). **Subtile,** on the other hand, in such discriminating use, often carries a connotation of artfulness or of a beguiling quality; as, "*Subtile* Litigation's pliant tongue" (*Burns*); "Hogarth, in one of his pieces of coarse yet *subtile* engraving, has presented a group of occupants of the pit of a theatre, sketched during the performance of some broad comedy or farce" (*E. Dowden*); "spontaneous variety which people who love English know to be one of its most *subtile* charms" (*B. Wendell*). *Subtile* is perhaps more often the preferred term when the implied opposition is to *gross:* then usually it is applied to something physical; as, a *subtile* odor; "he shows us that a 'matter' so infinitely *subtile,* and performing motions as inconceivably quick and fine as those which modern science postulates in her explanations, has no trace of grossness left" (*W. James*).

subvention. Grant, *appropriation, subsidy.

subvert. *Overturn, overthrow, capsize, overset, upset.

Ana. *Ruin, wreck: *destroy, demolish: corrupt, pervert, deprave, *debase.

Ant. Uphold, sustain.

succeed. *Follow, ensue, supervene.

Ana. Displace, supplant, *replace, supersede.

Ant. Precede.

succession. Succession, progression, series, sequence, set, suit, suite, chain, train, string are here compared as meaning a number of things that come together, often to form a larger whole, in some order or in accordance with some plan. **Succession** always implies that the units (often things, sometimes persons) follow each other, especially but not invariably in order of time, or less often of place, and usually without break or interruption; as, a *succession* of disasters; a *succession* of mild winters; "the long and honourable *succession* of Christian Platonists" (*Inge*). "The peculiar method of composition required by the long scrolls which form the masterpieces of this school was especially favourable to animated narrative and a varied *succession* of warlike scenes" (*Binyon*). "Winter...went out suddenly in a blinding storm of snow and a *succession* of quick, hot suns" (*M. Austin*). "Reality is a *succession* of concrete and particular situations" (*A. Huxley*). **Progression** (as here compared: see also PROGRESS, 2) applies to a succession in which there is movement and flow, and often change, so that a pattern is formed or an advance is indicated. The word is not as frequent in general as in technical use; as, history, especially as written, shows a *progression* rather than a *succession* of events. Its chief use is in mathematics and in music; in the former, it denotes a succession of quantities between every two of which there is a particular but an unvarying relation (as, an arithmetical *progression;* a geometrical *progression*); in the latter it denotes a succession of notes or of chords which constitute a melody or a harmony. **Series** applies to a number of things of similar or uniform character that stand in the same relation to each other or achieve the same end: often the term is indistinguishable from *succession*, but the separateness of the units is rather more stressed than the fact that they follow each other; as, a *series* of notes; a *series* of visits; "The long *series* of my woes" (*Pope*); a *series* of payments; a *series* of monographs on the origins of Romanticism; "It all came together in my understanding, as a *series* of experiments do when you begin to see where they are leading" (*Cather*). **Sequence** is more restricted in meaning than *series* for it implies either a closer connection between the things involved, such as a causal or logical connection, a numerical or chronological order, or a settled recurrence in the same order; as, the *sequence* of the seasons; rules governing the *sequence* of tenses; he was dealt a *sequence* of the ten highest hearts; his thoughts flow in logical *sequence*. "Ford, though intermittently, was able to manipulate *sequences* of words in blank verse in a manner which is quite his own" (*T. S. Eliot*). "Plotinus, for example, found the scale of spiritual values reflected in the world of events, not as a *sequence* of ascending values in time, but as degrees of truth and reality" (*Inge*). "The windows of Chartres have no *sequence*, and their charm is in variety, in individuality, and sometimes even in downright hostility to each other" (*H. Adams*). **Set** applies to a number of things similar in character and use that form a group that are used together or serve all the purposes necessary for a given end; consequently, the things that comprise a set usually either complement each other or are parts of a complete whole; as, a *set* of chairs; a *set* of china; a *set* of teeth. *Set* may also apply to a number of persons who form a closely related or unified group because of the same interests, the same social status, or the like (for this sense, see SET, 2). Less often, the term is used in reference to a group of intangible things which must be met or encountered as a whole or as a group; as, "Its author has to cope, not only with technical difficulties that attend every kind of imaginative writing, but also with the special *set* of difficulties that beset writers for the theatre" (*C. E. Montague*). **Suit** and **suite** apply to a set more often than to a succession but they are now used only in special collocations. Both terms originally applied, but only *suite* still applies, to a retinue, as of a ruler, or to a staff, as of a diplomat; now more generally *suit* applies to a group of things which are used together or form a set (as, a *suit* of clothes; a *suit* of armor; a deck of playing cards is composed of four *suits*, spades, clubs, hearts, and diamonds), and *suite* to a group of things which come together in space (as, a *suite* of rooms [i.e., a group which provide necessary living quarters]; a *suite* of biological specimens [i.e., a graded series of specimens exhibiting variation in size, color, etc., within a species]). But one sometimes uses *suite* in preference to *set* in reference to furniture, or jewels, or minerals, or the like. The last three words of the group here compared are all used figuratively. **Chain** applies to a succession or series which forms a logical or causal sequence; as, a *chain* of arguments; a *chain* of effects; "It would be possible to trace a *succession*, though hardly an unbroken *chain*, from Tertullian and the Montanists to George Fox" (*Inge*); "the long *chain* of development which makes the very language of the English Bible what it is" (*Lowes*); "The conclusion to which we have come, depends on a *chain* of principles which it was necessary to preserve unbroken" (*Ch. Just. Marshall*). **Train** applies to a number of persons, animals, or concrete things, or of effects, ideas, etc., that follow as attendants or as consequences (or, sometimes, as in the case of causes, that precede); as, she always has a *train* of admirers; "I invite your highess and your *train* To my poor cell" (*Shak.*); "a *train* of listeners followed him" (*Jowett*); a long *train* of causes; a *train* of ideas; "It was like the aimless talk of a man pursuing a secret *train* of thought far removed from the idle words we so often utter only to keep in touch with our fellow beings" (*Conrad*); "The August afternoon that the little *train* of silent people carried her out of her own door up to the family burying-ground" (*Deland*). **String** applies to a series or succession so uniform in character, size, quality, or the like, that its units are or seem to be strung on a thread: usually there is little implication of chronological, logical, or causal connection; as, a *string* of fish; a *string* of sausages; a *string* of victories; a *string* of boys filing through the trail. Oftentimes in sports the term is used of a group of players rated according to skill or proficiency; as, the first *string* of the football squad; a third-*string* player.

Ana. Consecutiveness, successiveness (see corresponding adjectives at CONSECUTIVE): articulation, concatenation, integration (see under INTEGRATE).

successive. *Consecutive, sequent, sequential, serial, discrete.

Ana. Continuous, *continual, constant, incessant: rotating, alternating (see ROTATE).

succinct. Terse, *concise, laconic, summary, pithy, compendious.

Ana. *Brief, short: compressed, condensed, contracted (see CONTRACT, *v.*): compact, *close: curt, brusque, blunt (see BLUFF).

Ant. Discursive.

succumb. *Yield, submit, capitulate, relent, defer, bow, cave in.

Ana. Surrender, abandon, resign, *relinquish.

succursal. *Subordinate, secondary, dependent, subject, tributary, collateral.

sudden. Hasty, *precipitate, headlong, abrupt, impetuous.

Ana. Quickened, hurried, speeded, accelerated (see SPEED, *v.*): *fast, rapid, swift, fleet, expeditious.

suds. *Foam, froth, spume, lather, scum, yeast.

sue. Pray, plead, petition. See under PRAYER.

Ana. Entreat, beseech, *beg, importune, implore, supplicate: solicit, request, *ask: *demand, claim, exact, require.

suet. *Adipose, marrow, tallow, lard.

suffer. 1 *Bear, endure, abide, tolerate, stand, brook.

Ana. Accept, *receive, admit: *yield, submit, bow.

2 Permit, allow, *let, leave.

sufferance. *Permission, leave.
Ana. Toleration, endurance (see corresponding verbs at BEAR): acquiescence, resignation, compliance (see under COMPLIANT).

suffering. *Distress, misery, agony, dolor, passion.
Ana. Affliction, tribulation, *trial, visitation: adversity, *misfortune: *sorrow, grief, anguish, woe, heartache.

sufficient. **Sufficient, enough, adequate, competent** come into comparison when they mean exactly commensurate to a requirement or the requirements. That is **sufficient** or **enough** which perfectly satisfies a need or desire with nothing wanting or nothing in excess; as, *sufficient* money for a week's vacation; *enough* food for an army; *sufficient* leisure for travel; they never have *enough* work to keep them busy. That is **adequate** which measures up to a just, fair, or, sometimes, inexacting standard of what is requisite; as, *adequate* medical treatment; *adequate* acting; an *adequate* stimulus. "A man can force himself to acquire it [uninteresting knowledge] if he has an *adequate* motive for doing so" (*B. Russell*). That is **competent** which answers all the requirements or is adequately adapted to the end in view; as, *competent* evidence is evidence that meets the legal requirements for proof; a traveler should have at least a *competent* knowledge of French.
Ana. Ample, *plentiful, plenteous, abundant: satisfying, contenting (see SATISFY): fitting, suitable, meet, proper (see FIT).
Ant. Insufficient: deficient.

suffrage, *n.* **Suffrage, franchise, vote, ballot** come into comparison when they mean the right, privilege, or power of expressing one's choice or wish, as in an election or in the determination of policy. They are here considered only in their current uses and with reference exclusively to public or state affairs. **Suffrage** is the preferred term when the emphasis is upon the extent to which this privilege or power is enjoyed in a state or community or upon the kinds of citizens in a representative government who legally exercise this power; the word is frequently modified by a term indicating such extent or restriction; as, universal *suffrage;* the long-fought battle that brought about woman *suffrage* in England, the United States, and other countries; household *suffrage,* or the restriction of the right to vote to male householders, existed in Great Britain from 1867 to 1918. **Franchise** is preferred when the privilege or power is thought of as conferred by the government or as a statutory or legal right; thus, the *franchise* (not *suffrage*) was long withheld from British citizens who were not householders. "Yet some people hesitate to give women the *franchise!* actually, a miserable privilege which any poor fool of a man may exercise" (*Jefferies*). **Vote** is the preferred term when the stress is on the power of each of the individuals on whom the franchise has been conferred to express his choice or opinion in the approved way, thereby aiding in the task of determining the will of the people; as, to have the *vote* (or a *vote*) and not to exercise it is to show oneself unworthy of one's citizenship; a class that has not the *vote* lacks the power to assert its rights; every American citizen has a like *vote* in choosing those who will make the laws. **Ballot,** which specifically implies some secret method of voting (originally by a ball dropped in a box or urn, later by a written or printed slip, now often by a machine which records choices) is the preferred word when the emphasis is on the power to vote freely, effectively, and without coercion, on the expressed will of the majority, or on the ethical use of the vote; as, to keep the *ballot* pure; the *ballot* is the citizens' means of getting the kind of government they want. "Among free men there can be no successful appeal from the *ballot* to the bullet, and... they who take such appeal are sure to lose their case and pay the cost" (*Lincoln*).

suffuse. *Infuse, imbue, ingrain, inoculate, leaven.
Ana. *Introduce, interpose, interject: impregnate, penetrate, pervade (see PERMEATE).

suggest. **1 Suggest, imply, hint, intimate, insinuate** agree in meaning to convey an idea or the thought of something by indirect means. **Suggest** emphasizes a putting into the mind as the result of an association of ideas, an awakening of a desire, an initiating of a train of thought, or the like; as, "in some curious way...his personality has *suggested* to me an entirely new manner in art, an entirely new mode of style" (*Wilde*); the success of "Waverley" *suggested* to Scott that he should devote himself to the writing of novels; the smell of smoke often *suggests* the possibility that the house is on fire. **Imply** (see also INCLUDE; INFER, 2) is in general opposed to *express;* the term stresses a suggesting, or putting into the mind, of an idea, a thought, or a meaning that is involved in a statement, a situation, a word, or the like, and forms a part, but not necessarily an obvious part, of its full signification or significance; as, "the philosophy of Nature which is *implied* in Chinese art" (*Binyon*). "In the Greek view, to be a citizen of a state did not merely *imply* the payment of taxes, and the possession of a vote; it *implied* a direct and active co-operation in all the functions of civil and military life" (*G. L. Dickinson*). "Catullus...was wont to say that if his friends...wished to *imply* that he was a gentleman, they called him a Tiburtine" (*A. Repplier*). Very often the difference between *suggest* and *imply* is not clear, even in good usage, though *suggest* often connotes the necessity of delicate perception and *imply* the need of inference; as, "a competent portraitist knows how to *imply* the profile in the full face" (*A. Huxley*). "The 'sayings' of a community, its proverbs, are its characteristic comment upon life; they *imply* its history, *suggest* its attitude toward the world and its way of accepting life" (*Cather*). **Hint** implies the use of a remote or covert suggestion, often also connoting lack of candor, frankness, or straightforwardness; as, "Willing to wound, and yet afraid to strike, Just *hint* a fault, and hesitate dislike" (*Pope*); "Your father *hinted* that the school wasn't good enough for you with just Howard Merton and us girls" (*M. Austin*). **Intimate,** in modern usage, frequently implies a lighter or more elusive suggestion than *hint,* but it connotes delicacy of approach without lack of candor or frankness. "He said that he had to be prudent or might not be able to say all that he thought, thus *intimating* to his hearers that they might infer that he meant more" (*Justice Holmes*). **Insinuate,** as here compared (see INTRODUCE, 2), is to hint artfully or to convey an unpleasant suggestion in an underhanded manner; as, by his tone and expression, rather than by his words, he *insinuated* that the boy was not to be trusted; "Mrs. Jamieson came now to *insinuate* pretty plainly that she did not wish that the Cranford ladies should call upon her sister-in-law" (*Gaskell*).
Ana. Present, *offer: *infuse, imbue, inoculate, leaven: *advance, further: allude, *refer, advert: connote, *denote.
Ant. Express.

2 Suggest, adumbrate, shadow are synonymous when they are predicated of things that serve indirectly to represent another thing because they evoke a thought, an image, or a conception of it. One thing **suggests** another when it brings to mind something that is not objectively present, immediately apparent, or directly represented. That which *suggests* may be an outward sign which prompts an inference. "A certain well-to-do air about the man *suggested* that he was not poor for his degree" (*Hardy*). It may be a symbol, which calls to mind that which it conventionally represents; as, the fleur-de-lis *suggests* the royal power of France. It may be a fragment which evokes an image of a whole or a concrete detail that gives an inkling of something abstract or incapable of representation. "The curve of the greyhound is not only the line of beauty, but a line which *suggests* motion" (*Jefferies*). It may be a word, a phrase, or the like, that calls up a train of associations and reveals more than it actually denotes. "Phrases flat and precise on the surface yet *suggesting* mystery below" (*Day Lewis*). "The business of words in prose is primarily to state; in poetry, not only to state, but also (and sometimes primarily) to *suggest*" (*Lowes*). One thing **adumbrates** another when the former very faintly or darkly suggests the latter. *Adumbrate,* in precise use, takes as its object only that which is intangible or beyond the reach of human comprehension or imagination. "Both in the vastness and the richness of the visible universe the invisible God is *adumbrated* (*I. Taylor*). "If the Parthenon has value, it is only as an *adumbration* of something higher than itself...of the law of unity, measure, purpose" (*Babbitt*). One thing **shadows** (or *shadows forth*) another when the former represents the latter obscurely as by a symbol or other indirect means. Sometimes, the word comes close to *prefigure* or *foreshadow,* but as a rule, precedence is not implied. "To the Chinese painters this world of nature seemed a more effective way of *shadowing* forth the manifold moods of man than by representing human figures animated by these moods" (*Binyon*).

Suggest and *adumbrate* also come into comparison when they mean something less than to propose or propound. **Suggest** commonly implies tentativeness, but it is sometimes used to convey the impression of courteous deference to the wishes of others. "Father Duchene *suggested*...that the tribe had been exterminated...in their summer camp...across the river" (*Cather*). "I *suggest* that in the interest of clearness this should be called genesis, not evolution" (*Inge*). **Adumbrate** usually implies partial disclosure. "The less than second-rate colleagues...will shamble behind him in whatever proposals he *adumbrates* to his huge majority" (*Contemp. Review*).

Ant. Manifest.

suggestion. *Touch, suspicion, soupçon, tincture, tinge, shade, smack, spice, dash, vein, strain, streak.

suit. 1 Also **suite.** Set, sequence, *succession, progression, series, chain, train, string.

2 *Prayer, plea, petition, appeal.

Ana. Entreaty, importuning *or* importunity, imploring, supplication (see corresponding verbs at BEG): asking, requesting *or* request, soliciting *or* solicitation (see corresponding verbs at ASK).

3 Suit, lawsuit, action, cause, case are all terms used in law to designate proceedings instituted for the sake of demanding justice or enforcing a right. Though often used interchangeably in the sense of *lawsuit,* their differences in etymology and in earlier meanings to a certain extent affect their connotations and their applications. **Suit** stresses the attempt of a complainant through litigation to gain an end such as redress for a wrong, recognition of a claim, or the enforcement of law; it therefore may be used of the proceedings from the time of formal application through the prosecution; as, to win or lose a *suit;* to withdraw a *suit;* a *suit* in equity. **Lawsuit,** in strict use, adds to *suit* the implication of actual trial in court and oftentimes that of judicial decision; it may therefore refer to the entire proceedings; as, the *lawsuit* of Brown versus Jones ended in victory for the defendant. **Action** comes very close to *suit,* but it is relatively colorless and throws the emphasis on actual proceedings rather than on petition; as, to bring an *action* in Circuit Court. In strict legal use, however, it is a proceeding in a court of law which is distinguished from a suit in equity and which has for its end the ascertainment of facts. If the complainant's diagnosis is found correct, then the legal remedy may be applied. **Cause,** more a literary than a legal term, emphasizes the grounds on which one institutes a suit; consequently, like *suit,* it implies the plaintiff's point of view, but it suggests even more strongly his sense of the justice of his demand. "The customary arts of the pleader, the appeal to the sympathies of the public...he rejected as unworthy of himself and of his *cause*" (*G. L. Dickinson*). **Case,** sometimes, has a looser reference to actual proceedings than any of the other terms in this group; then, like *cause,* it implies the grounds of action, but unlike it, from either or both points of view; as, the plaintiff has a good *case;* the defendant's attorney stated his *case.* However, *case* often is applied to the entire proceedings in a lawsuit including the judicial decision; as, one of the famous *cases* in legal history; a study of *cases.*

suitable. *Fit, meet, proper, appropriate, fitting, apt, happy, felicitous.

Ana. *Decorous, decent, seemly, proper, nice, comme il faut: advisable, *expedient, politic: *due, rightful, condign.

Ant. Unsuitable: unbecoming.

sulky. Surly, morose, glum, *sullen, crabbed, saturnine, dour, gloomy.

Ana. Cranky, cross, testy, touchy, techy (see IRASCIBLE): peevish, petulant, fretful, querulous, *irritable.

sullen. Sullen, glum, morose, surly, sulky, crabbed, saturnine, dour, gloomy agree in meaning governed by or manifesting, especially in one's aspect, a forbidding or disagreeable mood or disposition. One is **sullen** who is (often by disposition) gloomy, silent, and ill-humored and who refuses to be sociable, co-operative, or responsive; as, "*Sullenness* does not imply silence, but an ill-natured silence" (*Tatler*); "In a morning I am always *sullen*" (*Byron*); "Sheridan was generally very dull in society, and sat *sullen* and silent" (*Scott*); "he made them go back to the fields immediately after supper and work until midnight. They went in *sullen* silence" (*S. Anderson*). One is **glum** who is dismally silent either because of low spirits or depressing circumstances; as, "as *glum* as an undertaker" (*Thackeray*); "He looked *glum* under scolding" (*G. Eliot*); "When everything smiles, should a beauty look *glum?*" (*Lover*). One is **morose** who is austerely sour or bitter and inclined to glumness; as, "a *morose* ill-conditioned, ill-natured person" (*South*); "should there be any cold-blooded and *morose* mortals who really dislike this book" (*Boswell*); "The *moroseness* of age and infirmity never touched him" (*Arnold*); "she has tempted him to drink again because he is so *morose* when he is sober that she cannot endure living with him" (*Shaw*). One is **surly** who adds churlishness or gruffness of speech and manner to sullenness or moroseness; as, "Mason replied instantly, in a *surly,* nasal tone" (*N. Nicholls*); "*surly* eyes brow-hidden" (*Keats*); "the somewhat *surly* goodness, the hard and unattractive pieties into which she cannot really enter" (*Pater*). One is **sulky** who manifests displeasure, discontent, or resentment by giving way childishly to a fit of peevish sullenness; as, "In his pleasantest and most gracious moods he looked like a *sulky* cockatoo" (*Gaskell*); "We were a precious pair: I *sulky* and obstinate, she changeable and hot-tempered" (*Shaw*). One is **crabbed** who is actually or seemingly ill-natured, harsh, and especially, forbidding. The term often refers to one's aspect and manner of speaking and usually implies a sour or morose disposition or a settled crossness. "She is Ten times more gentle than her father's *crabbed*, And he's composed of harshness" (*Shak.*). "Divine Philosophy! Not harsh and *crabbed*, as dull fools suppose" (*Milton*). "It had never occurred to him that a captain's wife could be anything but a woman to be described as stout or thin, as jolly or *crabbed*, but always mature, and even, in comparison with his own years, frankly old" (*Conrad*). One is **saturnine** or **dour** who presents a heavy or forbidding aspect. *Saturnine*, however, often also implies gloomy taciturnity or bitterness of disposition; as, "a tall, dark, *saturnine* youth, sparing of speech" (*Lamb*); "Sheridan's humor, or rather wit, was always *saturnine*, and sometimes savage; he never laughed" (*Byron*); "*saturnine*, sour-blooded persons" (*G. Eliot*). *Dour* (a word taken from Scottish and North of England use), on the other hand, stresses severity, obstinacy, and grimness and does not always suggest real sourness or bitterness of disposition. "Though the Filipino seldom smiled, he was by no means *dour*. Kindliness was one of his most charming traits" (*V. Heiser*); "in this *dourest*, sorest Age man's eye has looked upon" (*Millay*). One is **gloomy** who is so depressed by events or conditions or so oppressed by melancholy that all signs of cheerfulness or optimism are obscured and one appears sullen, glum, or saturnine as well as low-spirited; as, to take a *gloomy* view of world conditions; when she is *gloomy* she makes everyone unhappy.

Ana. Lowering, glowering, frowning, scowling (see FROWN): spiteful, despiteful, malevolent, *malicious, malign: *cynical, pessimistic.

sum, *n.* **Sum, amount, aggregate, total, whole, number, quantity** come into comparison when they denote a result obtained by putting or taking together all in a given group or mass. **Sum** denotes the result of simple addition, usually of figures, sometimes of particulars; as, the *sum* of two and two: **amount** denotes the result reached by combining all the sums, or weights, or measures that form a whole; as, the *amount* of one's purchases; the *amount* of cotton raised in one year: **aggregate** denotes the result reached by counting distinct individuals or particulars in a group or collection; as, though his errors are individually insignificant, their *aggregate* is so large as to destroy confidence in his accuracy. "It is not true that a social force or effort is the mere *aggregate* of individual forces and efforts" (*J. A. Hobson*). **Total** and **whole** suggest the completeness or inclusiveness of the result; *total* often further implies magnitude in the result, and *whole*, unity in that which is summed up; as, a grand *total* of ten millions; the *whole* is the *sum* of its parts. **Number,** rather than *sum*, is now used for an aggregate of persons or things, to which (except in the case of things in bulk or mass) *amount* should not be applied; as, the *number* present; a fixed *amount* of cotton; but not, a small *amount* of potatoes. **Quantity** in general use is employed chiefly of things which are measured in bulk, even though they can be counted; as, a *quantity* of apples; but not (except colloquially), a *quantity* of soldiers. In technical and scientific use, *quantity* is not limited to an aggregate or bulk, but may be used of anything that is measurable in extent, duration, volume, magnitude, intensity, or value; as, spatial *quantity;* the *quantity* of a vowel; electrical *quantities;* the *quantity* of heat; *quantity* of work performed by a machine.

sum, *v.* *Add, total, figure, cast, foot.

Ana. Compute, *calculate, estimate, reckon: *count, enumerate, number.

summary, *adj.* Pithy, compendious, *concise, terse, succinct, laconic.

Ana. *Brief, short: *quick, prompt, ready, apt: compacted *or* compact, concentrated (see COMPACT, *v.*).

Ant. Circumstantial.

summative. *Cumulative, accumulative, additive.

summit. **Summit, peak, pinnacle, climax, apex, acme, culmination, meridian, zenith, apogee** in their figurative senses agree in meaning the highest point attained or attainable. To a great extent their distinguishing implications and their idiomatic applications are dependent on their primary meaning or, at least, on an earlier literal meaning. *Summit* and *peak* both denote the top of a hill or mountain, but only the latter suggests a range and implies reference to other levels. **Summit** is applied to that which represents the topmost level attainable by effort or to that which is the highest in its type or kind of attainable things; as, the plays of Shakespeare represent the *summit* of achievement in dramatic writing. "If love be the *summit* of all virtue, humility is the foundation" (*Pusey*). **Peak** usually implies a point rather than a level; as, the *peak* of enthusiasm. It is now frequently applied to something that is or can be represented in a graph; used absolutely, it designates the highest point reached in a course or during a stated or implied length of time; as, the *peak* of security prices was in 1929; the *peak* of production in automobiles is usually reached in the spring. **Pinnacle,** with its literal signification of a slender spire tapering to a point, is applied chiefly to that which has reached a dizzy, and, often, insecure height; as, he had reached the *pinnacle* of earthly fame. "A *pinnacle* of happiness" (*Van W. Brooks*). **Climax** has almost completely lost its literal significance of a ladder but it still implies a scale of ascending values. In its pertinent sense it is applied to that which is the highest point in force, in intensity, in interest, or in impressiveness in an ascending movement or series; as, the events of the day had for their *climax* the visit of the governor; writers of fiction generally aim to make the last scene an effective *climax*. The word often, but not necessarily, suggests an end, or close; as, reserve your strongest argument for the *climax* of your speech. **Apex** is the name given to the tip or top of a thing where all ascending lines converge in a sharp point; as, the *apex* of a cone. Figuratively, it is applied to that to which everything in a career, a system of thought, or the like, ascends and in which everything is concentrated. "The Vision of the One forms the *apex* of those systems of philosophical mysticism of which the scheme of Plotinus is the type" (*Inge*). "Commencing with the rudiments of grammar and terminating in the *apex* of the Doctorate" (*Pattison*). **Acme** (literally, a point) is almost invariably applied to that which exhibits the perfection or pure essence of a thing; as, Sir Philip Sidney was the *acme* of courtesy. 'To say 'mither' instead of 'mother' seems to many the *acme* of romance" (*Wilde*). *Culmination, meridian, zenith,* and *apogee* derive their figurative senses from their astronomical meanings. **Culmination** denotes both the movement of a celestial body to its highest point in the heavens and the point so reached; **meridian,** in nontechnical use, designates the position of the sun at midday (in the old astronomy, its *culmination*); **zenith** denotes the point in the heavens directly overhead where the sun will be at its meridian; **apogee** names the point in the orbit of a celestial body when it is farthest from the earth. Hence, in figurative use, *culmination* is applied to that which is the outcome of a movement, a growth, a development, a progress, or the like, and which represents its natural end or attained objective. "This joint effort of church and crown...found its *culmination* under Louis

XIV, when the nobles were definitively conquered by the crown and the Reformation by the church" (*Brownell*). Oftentimes, especially in modern usage, *culmination* suggests a coming to a head, or issue, rather than to a high point. "The Reformation...was...the *culmination* of a long agitation for national independence in religious matters" (*Inge*). *Meridian* is applied to the prime, or period of fullest development or vigor, in the life of a person, a race, an institution, or the like; it not only connotes prior ascent but ensuing decline. "I have touch'd the highest point of all my greatness: And, from that full *meridian* of my glory, I haste now to my setting" (*Shak.*). *Zenith* adds to *meridian* the implications of luster and distinction; as, he had reached the *zenith* of his powers. "The very magnitude of the offence lends to it [regicide] a... terrible distinction. It is the *zenith*...of the headsman's history" (*A. Repplier*). *Apogee*, like *meridian*, is applied to the highest point in a course, a career, a movement; but, unlike *meridian*, it seldom connotes being at the prime or height of glory; as, the French Revolution reached its *apogee* in the Reign of Terror.

summon *or* **summons,** *v.* **Summon** (*or* **summons**), **call, cite, convoke, convene, muster** come into comparison when they mean to demand the presence of a person or persons or, by extension, of things. **Summon** (or its highly colloquial equivalent **summons**) implies the exercise of authority or of power; it therefore usually suggests a mandate, an imperative order or bidding, urgency, or the like; as, the king *summoned* his privy councilors to the palace; to *summon* one's secretary; to *summon* a person to appear in court. "I *summon* your grace to his majesty's parliament" (*Shak.*). "She could *summon* tears and delights as one *summons* servants" (*H. G. Wells*). **Call** (often followed by *up*, *forth*, and the like) is often used in place of *summon*, especially when less formality is implied or the imperativeness of the bidding is not stressed, or when actual shouting is suggested, or the like. It is, however, in general, a more ordinary or more colloquial term than *summon;* as, to *call* men to arms; to *call* witnesses to court; to *call* a servant; the president *called* congress together for an extra session. Often, however, there is a suggestion of an impulsion of God, of Nature, of necessity, or the like; as, the young man felt that he was *called* to the ministry; he felt *called* upon to speak. **Cite** (see also ADDUCE) in earliest use implied a summons to court, either as a principal or as a witness; this sense still prevails (as, he was *cited* for contempt of court), but in England *cite* usually suggests a summoning to an ecclesiastical court. "He hath *cited* me to Rome, for heresy" (*Tennyson*). The word, however, is also found in the sense of *summon*, especially to action. "I think it *cites* us, brother, to the field" (*Shak.*). **Convoke** implies a summons to assemble, especially for legislative or deliberative purposes; as, the king *convoked* parliament. "The Italian government *convoked* great congresses of physicists and engineers" (*Karl K. Darrow*). **Convene** is related to *convoke* as *call* is to *summon;* it is weaker in its suggestions of the exercise of authority and of imperativeness, but otherwise it is often not distinguishable; as, to *convene* the students in the school auditorium; "The Senate was *convened* by the tribunes" (*Froude*). **Muster** implies the summoning of an army or other body of troops or a ship's company for military action, inspection, parade, exercise, or the like. In extended use, it implies the assembling of a number of things that form a collection, a group, or the like, in order that they may be exhibited, displayed, or utilized as a whole. "A daw that had a mind to be sparkish, trick'd himself up with all the gay-feathers he could *muster* together" (*L'Estrange*). "A procession of twenty coaches belonging to public functionaries was *mustered*" (*Macaulay*). *Muster* is used in place of *summon* with *courage, strength*, and the like, as the object, especially when the context implies the previous dissipation of this courage, strength, etc.; as, "*mustering* courage to come to her side" (*G. Eliot*); "At length you have *mustered* heart to visit the old place" (*Dickens*).

Ana. *Command, order, bid, enjoin: evoke, elicit, *educe.

sumptuous. *Luxurious, opulent.

Ana. Magnificent, stately, majestic, *grand: *splendid, resplendent, gorgeous, superb: *showy, ostentatious, pretentious: lavish, prodigal (see PROFUSE).

Sunday. Sunday, Sabbath, the Lord's Day are synonymous terms only in general Christian use. Strictly, **Sunday** is the name of the first day of the week, **Sabbath** is the name of the seventh day of the week in the Jewish calendar, or of a period extending from Friday evening to Saturday evening. This is the time in Jewish and some Christian use that is regarded as the seventh day sanctified by the Creator (*Genesis* ii. 1–3) and enjoined as a day of rest and worship in the fourth (or, in Roman Catholic versions, the third) Commandment. The change of this day to Sunday after Christianity was established was respected by the new churches after the Reformation but *Sabbath* was more and more often employed in reference to Sunday. This use continues especially among evangelical sects of Protestants. **The Lord's Day,** which is a Christian term in use long before the Reformation, always applies to Sunday regarded as the day on which the resurrection of Christ occurred (*Luke* xxiv. 1–6, and *Revelation* i. 10) and as the accepted day of rest and worship. Its use in this sense continued after the Reformation and was adopted by all denominations of Christians that keep Sunday as the Sabbath.

sunder, *v.* Sever, divide, part, *separate, divorce.

Ana. Rend, rive, cleave, split (see TEAR).

Ant. Link.

sundowner. *Vagabond, vagrant, tramp, hobo, truant, bum, stiff, swagman.

sundry. *Many, several, various, divers, numerous, manifold, multifold, multifarious.

Ana. *Different, disparate, diverse, divergent: *distinct, separate: individual, distinctive, peculiar (see CHARACTERISTIC).

superabound. *Team, abound, swarm, overflow.

superadd. Annex, append, subjoin, *add.

Ana. *Fasten, attach, affix.

superannuated. *Aged, old, elderly.

superb. *Splendid, resplendent, glorious, gorgeous, sublime.

Ana. Superlative, transcendent, surpassing, *supreme: sumptuous, *luxurious, opulent: imposing, stately, majestic, magnificent, *grand.

supercilious. Disdainful, overbearing, arrogant, haughty, *proud, lordly, insolent.

Ana. Vain, vainglorious (see under PRIDE): contemptuous, scornful (see corresponding nouns under DESPISE, V.).

supererogatory. Supererogatory, gratuitous, uncalled-for, wanton are not close synonyms, but they come into comparison when they mean given or done freely and without compulsion or provocation or, in derogatory use, without warrant or justification. **Supererogatory** in its strict sense implies a giving above or beyond that which is required or is laid down in the laws or rules; originally, the term referred to acts (such as works of mercy, sacrifices, prayers, etc.) of a member of the Christian church, but later to acts (such as services, attentions, etc.) of a subject, a citizen, an employee, or the like: the word usually suggests a devotion or loyalty that is not satisfied merely with the doing of that which is required, and that finds expression in the performance of additional labors, works, or the like, beyond those expected or demanded; as, *supererogatory* fasts; the *supererogatory* services of representatives in Congress. Sometimes, especially in current use, the term is definitely depreciative in that it does not imply a giving freely over and above that which is required but a giving or adding of something that is not needed and is therefore more or less an embarrassment or encumbrance; as, *supererogatory* apologies; *supererogatory* attentions. **Gratuitous** (etymologically, pleasing) in the somewhat earlier of its leading senses implies a giving voluntarily without expectation of recompense, reward, or compensation; as, many a physician gives his services *gratuitously* to the poor; the *gratuitous* education provided by the public schools of the United States; the college gives some *gratuitous* concerts for the enjoyment of the townspeople. In its other and slightly later sense, the term stresses a giving of something disagreeable, offensive, troublesome, or painful, without provocation; as, a *gratuitous* insult; "a *gratuitous*...imposition of labor" (*Horace Mann*). In slightly looser use, *gratuitous* means little more than **uncalled-for**, which suggests not only a lack of provocation but a lack of need and, therefore, often implies impertinence or absurdity, often logical absurdity; as, "the *gratuitous* assumption that the new must surpass the old" (*Grandgent*); *uncalled-for* interference; *uncalled-for* advice. **Wanton** (as here considered: see also PLAYFUL, LICENTIOUS) also implies want of provocation, but it stresses the absence of any motive except reckless sportiveness or arbitrariness or pure malice; as, a *wanton* attack; *wanton* destruction; "The *wanton* horrors of her bloody play" (*Shelley*); "believing the deed (the burning of a haystack) to have been unprovoked and *wanton*" (*Meredith*); "Tyranny consists in the *wanton* and improper use of strength by the stronger" (*Bryce*).

Ana. *Free, independent, autonomous: *excessive, extreme, exorbitant: *superfluous, supernumerary, extra, spare.

superficial. Superficial, shallow, cursory, uncritical are not all close synonyms but they come into comparison when they mean lacking in depth, solidity, and comprehensiveness. **Superficial,** in the extended senses in which it is here considered, applies chiefly to persons, their minds, their emotions, their attainments, their utterances or writings, and the like, but it is also applicable to things such as circumstances, factors, conditions, qualities, or the like. Despite great variations in the specific meanings in some of these applications, the term usually implies a taking in of or a concern with surface aspects or obvious features, or an avoidance of all but these aspects or features; as, he had time for no more than a *superficial* consideration of the situation; there are only *superficial* likenesses between these books; a *superficial* treatment of a disease; the war effected merely a *superficial* change in human ideals. "The tendency...of prose drama is to emphasize the ephemeral and *superficial;* if we want to get at the permanent and universal we tend to express ourselves in verse" (*T. S. Eliot*). Often, however, the term is definitely depreciative and further implies some quality such as pretense, ostentation, slightness, lack of thoroughness, insignificance, insincerity, and the like; as, *superficial* people; the lecture was very *superficial;* "Our political theory is hopelessly sophomoric and *superficial*" (*Mencken*); "these judgments, how *superficial,* how fragmentary they are!" (*V. Woolf*). **Shallow,** both in its literal and extended senses, implies a lack of depth (as, a *shallow* stream; *shallow* breathing); when applied to persons, their knowledge, their reasoning, or their emotions, it is almost invariably derogatory and differs little from *superficial* used derogatorily except in its freedom from implication of outward show or of apparent, but not genuine, significance; as, he said that the graduates of a given school were *shallow* and frivolous; "Do you suppose this eternal *shallow* cynicism of yours has any real bearing on a nature like hers?" (*Shaw*); "When the ideas become more automatic...we begin to suspect...that they spring from a *shallower* source" (*T. S. Eliot*). **Cursory,** which literally means hasty or hurried, in the extended sense here considered stresses a lack of thoroughness or of care for details rather than a concentration on the obvious: it often also suggests haste, casualness, skipping, or the like; as, even from a *cursory* reading of the book, I judge that it is a very fine piece of work; "[Mrs. Thrale] stands the test of the closest examination, as well and as much to her honor as she does a mere *cursory* view" (*Burney*); "The coffeehouse must not be dismissed with a *cursory* mention" (*Macaulay*). **Uncritical** implies a superficiality or shallowness unbefitting to a critic or sound judge, not only of literature or the arts but of any data, statements, matters, events, and the like, which must be evaluated, related, estimated, or otherwise judged; as, an *uncritical* judgment of a book; her pretentious singing satisfied only the *uncritical* persons in her audience; "Statements...readily accepted by the *uncritical* who believe all they see in print" (*H. Spencer*); "I would not have you so *uncritical* as to blame the Church or its clergy for what happened" (*Quiller-Couch*).

Ant. Radical (sense 1).

superfluity. *Excess, surplus, surplusage, overplus.

Ana. Superabounding *or* superabundance, overflowing *or* overflow, teeming, swarming (see TEEM): exuberance, profusion, lavishness, prodigality (see corresponding adjectives at PROFUSE).

superfluous. Superfluous, surplus, supernumerary, extra, spare come into comparison when they mean above or beyond what is needed or is indispensable. **Superfluous** strictly implies a superabundance or excess that requires elimination or pruning; as, to cut off all the *superfluous* shoots of a shrub; if you prefer a few large flowers, pinch off all *superfluous* buds; "artists...not tempted, as are those who work direct from nature, to transcribe *superfluous* detail because it happens to be before their eyes" (*Binyon*). Sometimes, however, the term either loses its implication of richness of supply or places no emphasis on that idea, and comes to mean little more than *nonessential* or *dispensable,* if circumstances require its sacrifice (as, " 'art, music, literature, and the like—in short..., *superfluous* things' "—*S. P. Sherman*), or *unnecessary, useless,* or *needless* (as, "[Hamlet] is possibly the one [play] on which Shakespeare spent most pains; and yet he has left in it *superfluous* and inconsistent scenes"—*T. S. Eliot;* "Authority, like a good educator, ought to aim at making itself *superfluous*"—*Inge*). **Surplus** applies to what remains over when that which is needed or required for all present purposes has been used; as, there will be no *surplus* wheat this year; each year the *surplus* funds of the institution were invested in government bonds; he still had *surplus* time for which he must find a use, and *surplus* energy which demanded an outlet. **Supernumerary** literally implies an addition to the number that is usual, prescribed, typical, or the like: the term does not necessarily suggest that there is no need or no use for that which exceeds the regular or expected number, though in reference to a physical condition it often implies a departure from the normal; as, a *supernumerary* tooth; a *supernumerary* member of a cast (i.e., one used for mob scenes, etc., and called a *supernumerary*, often shortened in slang use to *super* or *supe*); *supernumerary* ribs; *supernumerary* officers are usually needed by regiments engaged in active warfare. **Extra** is often used colloquially in place of *supernumerary* (as, she always kept an *extra* servant; to buy a few *extra* Christmas presents in case someone has been forgotten), but it may imply not merely an addition in number but in amount (as, to ask *extra* work of each employee during the vacation period), or in quality (as, *extra* beef; *extra* wheat), or in price (as, there is an *extra* charge for coffee). **Spare** is often used in place of *surplus*, but it carries a stronger suggestion of being held in reserve for use, often a special use (as, a *spare* suit of clothes; the *spare* room is the guest room; to carry a *spare* tire for an automobile) or of not having any demands on it for a particular use (as, he never has any *spare* cash; she said she would write the letter when she had *spare* time), or of being easily spared (as, have you a *spare* cigarette on you?).

Ana. *Supererogatory, gratuitous, uncalled-for, wanton: *profuse, lavish, prodigal, exuberant: *excessive, inordinate, extravagant, extreme.

superhuman. Preternatural, miraculous, supranatural, *supernatural.

Ana. Potent, puissant, *powerful, forcible, forceful: herculean, Antaean, Cyclopean, titanic, gigantic (see ENORMOUS).

superimpose. *Overlay, superpose, appliqué.

superlative, *adj.* *Supreme, transcendent, surpassing, peerless, incomparable, pre-eminent, banner.

Ana. *Consummate, finished, accomplished: *splendid, glorious, sublime, superb.

supernatural. Supernatural, supranatural, preternatural, miraculous, superhuman are not, strictly speaking, synonymous terms, but many persons are confused as to the limits of their meanings. **Supernatural** (literally, above the natural) applies to that which belongs to an order of existence transcending that of nature or of the visible and observable universe. The term usually connotes spiritual as opposed to material being and often suggests a divine existence or origin or influence or a participation in some of the attributes of divinity; as, *supernatural* beings; the *supernatural* character of the soul; *supernatural* forces; to attribute one's recovery from a usually mortal illness to a *supernatural* power. **Supranatural** (etymologically, higher than the natural) is a somewhat equivocal term used in place of *supernatural* by some writers and speakers when they wish to describe that which is not apparent to the senses yet seems to be supported by observable effects or to proceed from observable causes. In such use, the word commonly implies a realm of knowledge not yet penetrated by the human mind, rather than another and higher order of existence; as, *supranatural* phenomena such as telepathy and thought transference; parapsychology deals with the *supranatural*. **Preternatural** (etymologically, beyond the range or compass of nature) applies chiefly to that which is not regarded as natural or as in the regular course of nature. Usually, the term means abnormal or strange and inexplicable to an extreme or startling degree; as, "A degree of acumen which appears to the ordinary apprehension *preternatural*" (*Poe*); "the *preternatural* prowess of the hero" (*Emerson*); "the nimble and versatile Athenian wits trained to *preternatural* acuteness by the debates of the law courts and the Assembly" (*G. L. Dickinson*). "I could not see a green parrot sitting silent and motionless amidst the green foliage as they could; I had not their *preternatural* keenness of sight" (*Hudson*). **Miraculous** (etymologically, marvelous or exceedingly wondrous) applies particularly to events or effects in the physical world that are out of the ordinary course of things or that deviate from the known laws of nature. This sense still prevails in ordinary use; as, "The plant, his hope, which he had deemed dead, blossomed with *miraculous* suddenness" (*Bennett*); "For the last two years he was like a flame burning on in *miraculous* disregard of the fact that there was no more fuel to justify its existence" (*A. Huxley*). In its also common religious use, *miraculous* applies to that which is regarded or accepted as performed by divine power or happening as a result of divine intervention; as, the *miraculous* power of Jesus; the *miraculous* transformation of water into wine at the wedding in Cana (*John* ii. 1–11); the *miraculous* cures attributed to a saint. "The *miraculous* interpositions by which it [Christianity] was attested and carried on" (*Bp. Butler*). **Superhuman** (literally, above or beyond human existence or power) is sometimes loosely used in the sense of *supernatural*. However, even in this use it does not carry as clear an implication of divinity as *supernatural* does and may therefore imply angelic, demonic, or similar existence or power; as, "superstitious belief in *superhuman* agency" (*J. B. Mozley*). But *superhuman* is commonly used in a hyperbolical sense meaning exceeding that which is human or usual to human beings. It therefore often means little more than *herculean, extraordinary*, or the like; as, *superhuman* efforts; *superhuman* energy; a *superhuman* feat. "A child of three years old is a better model for a child one year old, both because the things it does are more what the younger child would wish to do, and because its powers do not seem so *superhuman*" (*B. Russell*).

Ana. Divine, spiritual, sacred, *holy, blessed: *infinite, eternal, boundless, illimitable.

supernumerary. Surplus, extra, spare, *superfluous.

superpose. Superimpose, *overlay, appliqué.

supersede. *Replace, displace, supplant.

Ana. Repudiate, spurn, reject (see DECLINE, *v.*): *abandon, desert, forsake: stay, suspend, intermit (see DEFER).

supervene. *Follow, succeed, ensue.

Ana. *Add, append, annex, subjoin, superadd: combine, *unite, conjoin, co-operate.

supervenient. *Adventitious, adventive, advenient.

supervision. *Oversight, surveillance.

Ana. Controlling *or* control, management, direction, conducting *or* conduct (see corresponding verbs at CONDUCT): leading, guiding (see GUIDE).

supine. 1 *Prone, prostrate, recumbent, reclining, couchant, dormant.

2 *Inactive, inert, passive, idle.

Ana. Slothful, *lazy, indolent, fainéant: *lethargic, sluggish, torpid, stuporous: apathetic, *impassive, phlegmatic.

Ant. Alert.

supplant. Displace, *replace, supersede.

Ana. *Eject, oust, dismiss, expel: uproot, eradicate, extirpate, *exterminate.

supple. 1 Flexible, resilient, *elastic, springy.

Ana. Pliable, pliant, *plastic: *soft, gentle, mild.

Ant. Stiff.

2 Supple, limber, lithe, lithesome, lissome (*or* **lissom**) come into comparison especially when applied to bodily movements and mean showing freedom and ease in bending and twisting. **Supple** implies great flexibility of muscles and joints, perfect muscular co-ordination, and rapidity yet smoothness in change of posture or movement; as, the light *supple* spring of a cat from its hiding place. "The Bishop stood watching the flowing, *supple* movements of their arms and shoulders, the sure rhythm of their tiny moccasined feet" (*Cather*). **Limber** also implies great flexibility of muscles and joints, and the power to move quickly or easily, but it carries no clear suggestion of grace or of muscular co-ordination; as, *limber* country boys jumping from rock to rock; showing his *limberness* in a series of somersaults; the *limber* fingers of a pianist. "I could skip Out of my skin, now, like a subtill snake, I am so *limber*" (*B. Jonson*). **Lithe,** once more often used of things that may be gently or softly curved or twisted (as, a *lithe* rope; a *lithe* twig), is now applied chiefly to persons or animals that are slender, supple, nimble, and usually graceful in movements; as, a *lithe* dancer; "They climbed the wall—your lady must be *lithe*" (*Browning*). "We could not use the term [*buxom*] as Milton did, in its original sense of 'bowsome'—that is, '*lithe*, graceful, bending' " (*J. R. Lowell*). **Lithesome** and **lissome** are now chiefly literary or poetical for *lithe;* the former, however, often suggests agility and vigor; the latter, sinuous grace. "The warlike carriage of the men, and their strong, *lithesome*, resolute step" (*Kinglake*). "A robe Of samite without price... clung about her *lissome* limbs" (*Tennyson*).

Ana. Graceful, elegant (see corresponding nouns at ELEGANCE): *easy, smooth, effortless, facile.

supplement, *n.* **1** *Complement.

2 *Appendix, addendum, addenda.

supplement, *v.* Complement. See under COMPLEMENT, *n.*

Ana. *Improve, better: heighten, enhance, aggravate, *intensify.

supplicate. Implore, beseech, entreat, importune, *beg, adjure, conjure.

Ana. Pray, sue, plead, appeal, petition (see under PRAYER): *ask, request, solicit.

supply, *n.* *Substitute, locum tenens, alternate, understudy, pinch hitter, double, stand-in.

supply, *adj.* *Temporary, provisional, ad interim, acting.

support, *v.* **Support, uphold, advocate, back, champion,** and their corresponding agent nouns, **supporter, upholder, advocate, backer, champion,** are comparable when they mean to favor (or one who favors) actively and in some concrete manner a person or thing that meets opposition. **Support** is comparatively colorless. One *supports* a candidate for election whether one merely votes for him or takes a leading part in his campaign; one *supports* a cause whether one merely announces one's stand in favor of it or contributes money and time to furthering its interests. **Uphold** in this extended sense retains its etymological implication of keeping erect, or from falling or breaking down; it is, therefore, commonly but not invariably used in reference to that which exists but is attacked or challenged. "We're fighting... partly to *uphold* decent international principles" (*R. Macaulay*). "Those who *uphold* the ideal of pure poetry" (*Day Lewis*). "A stout *upholder* of tradition and continuity" (*T. S. Eliot*). **Advocate** always implies vocal support, either in speeches or in writings; often, but not necessarily, it connotes urging or pleading. "So now you know... what Socialism is, and why it is *advocated* so widely" (*Shaw*). "The *advocates* of the old classical education have been gallantly fighting a losing battle" (*Inge*). "A courageous and devoted *advocacy* of causes in which the spirit of our religion calls for strenuous opposition to the current principles and practice of the world" (*Inge*). **Back** often implies strong support from the rear to be used whenever assistance is needed to prevent the failure of a person or of his ventures or efforts. Sometimes, it connotes reserve forces or the use of force: sometimes, it implies money reserves or the promise of financial assistance; as, his father said he would *back* him in business. "States, large and small, with... their very practical traders pushing for foreign markets, and their navies and armies to *back* the traders and annex these markets" (*Shaw*). Often, however, *back* derives its implications from its use in betting (esp. in "to *back* a horse") and suggests a willingness to put money on a person's or thing's chance for success. "I *back* you to hold your own against them all" (*E. Wharton*). **Champion** always in discriminating use implies public defense of a person or thing believed to be unjustly attacked or too weak to advocate its own cause. It, therefore, often connotes distinction or gallantry in the one who champions. "Who... *championed* every cause I called my heart's cause, loving as I loved, Hating my hates, spurned falsehood, *championed* truth" (*Browning*).

Ana. *Approve, endorse, sanction: espouse, embrace, *adopt: *defend, protect, shield.

support, *n.* Maintenance, sustenance, *living, livelihood, subsistence, keep, bread.

supporter. Upholder, advocate, backer, champion. See under SUPPORT, *v.*

Ant. Adversary: antagonist.

supposed. **Supposed, supposititious, suppositious, reputed, putative, conjectural, hypothetical** come into comparison as meaning believed or assumed to be true, real, or in accordance with the facts. Both **supposed** and **supposititious** imply that the person or thing so described is assumed to be actual, real, or genuine in the relation indicated. *Supposed*, however, usually implies more grounds for that belief than *supposititious* and it always suggests uncertainty, lack of assurance, or possibility of error; as, Napoleon's *supposed* aversion to cats; "various real and *supposed* meanings" (*Babbitt*); "nobody would have dared to take a seat in that block who had not attained to some eminence, real or *supposed*, among his fellows" (*Arch. Marshall*). *Supposititious*, on the other hand, properly implies spuriousness that is the result of fraud or invention; as, the *supposititious* heir to an estate; "Catherine had read too much not to be perfectly aware of the ease with which a waxen figure might be introduced, and a *supposititious* funeral carried on" (*Austen*). **Suppositious** is less often used in place of *supposititious* than formerly, but it still occurs when a writer or speaker wishes to imply that the belief has the support only of a theory, a postulate, or a hypothesis, and otherwise has no ground in fact. "That on such a hypothetical and *suppositious* basis, the supreme sacrifice of abdication and potential exile of the sovereign should be demanded, finds no support whatsoever in the British constitution" (*Winston S. Churchill*). **Reputed** and **putative** both imply a basis in tradition or in popular belief. The former is now the usual word, the latter being reserved for a few legal expressions; as, a *reputed* millionaire; the *putative* father of a child; the *reputed* owner of an estate; a *putative* marriage (i.e., a marriage which was performed in good faith but is not valid because of canonical or legal impediments). "I have even been in the Musée at Agen, where there are pictures *reputed* to be by Goya" (*Lucas*). "Congleton butterscotch, *reputed* a harmless sweetmeat" (*Bennett*). **Conjectural** implies inference from incomplete or defective evidence. That which is so described is offered as a possibility or likelihood but not as a fact; as, the *conjectural* etymology of a word; *conjectural* emendations in a faulty text; the *conjectural* causes of a depression. **Hypothetical** describes someone or something (a principle, a situation, a question, etc.) that is invented or put forward as possibly true or as likely to be true in the main if not in detail, or as the tentative basis for continuing an argument, an investigation, or the like; as, a *hypothetical* explanation of nebulae; the cross-examining lawyer posed a *hypothetical* question to the expert witness in order to get his opinion concerning the inference to be drawn from facts not yet fully established. "I tried to expound such sentiments to my French visitor—who was a real, flesh-and-blood visitor, and not, like most of his kind, a *hypothetical* foreigner invented to point a moral" (*Grandgent*). "When Nature produces a thunderstorm she is doing on a very great scale what any of us may do on a very small one by rubbing our feet on the carpet in winter weather, and what my *hypothetical* Greek child was doing on an even smaller one when he rubbed the amber with the cloth" (*Karl K. Darrow*).

Ana. Assumed, presumed, presupposed, postulated (see PRESUPPOSE): tentative, *provisional: *doubtful, dubious, questionable: *theoretical, speculative, academic.

Ant. Certain.

supposititious, suppositious. *Supposed, reputed, putative, conjectural, hypothetical.

Ana. Pretended, simulated, feigned, shammed, counterfeited *or* counterfeit (see ASSUME): questionable, dubious, *doubtful: factitious, *artificial.

suppress. **Suppress, repress** are general terms which mean to hold back, by the use of more or less force, someone or something that seeks expression, activity, or other outlet. **Suppress** carries a strong implication of putting down or keeping back completely. It usually implies the exercise of great or oppressive power or even of violence. It often is a synonym of *overpower, crush, abolish, destroy, eliminate, stifle*, and like words, but in each case it often suggests the prompt use of effective methods; as, to *suppress* an insurrection; "before gaming was *suppressed*" (*Goldsmith*); "ungovernable passions... *suppressed* by the very same means which keep the rest of us in order" (*Conrad*); "I...assume that one purpose of the purchase was to *suppress* competition between the two roads" (*Justice Holmes*); "the bishop was purple with *suppressed* wrath" (*S. P. Sherman*). **Repress,** on the other hand, implies little more than a checking, or restraining, sometimes by an external force, sometimes by the power of the will or mind. It often suggests that the thing so held back may break out again or in a different way and so comes close to *inhibit, bridle, curb*, and the like; as, to *repress* one's curiosity; to *repress* one's desire to weep; the parents have *repressed* his interest in birds and butterflies by not allowing him to give vent to his enthusiasm. "His breathing was a little quickened; but he *repressed* all other signs of agitation" (*Dickens*). "The tendencies which Lycurgus had endeavoured to *repress* by external regulation reasserted themselves in his despite" (*G. L. Dickinson*). "When an affection as intense as that is balked in its direct path and *repressed* it usually, as we know, finds an indirect outlet" (*Van W. Brooks*). In psychology, *suppress* is commonly used with reference to desires, instincts, emotions, and the like, which are consciously and forcibly inhibited by the mind from seeking expression or overt activity: *repress* usually suggests an unconscious or subconscious process by which a desire or an impulse that is regarded as unacceptable because of one's religious, moral, or social training is inhibited by a refusal to recognize it or to permit consideration of it, and so is left to operate in the unconscious.

Ana. *Arrest, check, interrupt: extinguish, *abolish, annihilate: *forbid, prohibit, ban: subdue, overcome, surmount, *conquer.

supranatural. *Supernatural, miraculous, preternatural, superhuman.

supremacy. **Supremacy, ascendancy** (*or* **ascendency**) are sometimes confused when they denote the position of being first, as in rank, power, influence. **Supremacy** implies superiority over all others, as in numbers, in quality, in efficiency, or in prestige; thus, a country that seeks naval *supremacy* directs its efforts to the enlarging and strengthening of its navy until no other country can compete with it; that dramatist holds *supremacy* over all other dramatists who is universally regarded as the best and the greatest. "In the Sahara, the automobile has begun to challenge the *supremacy* of the camel" (*A. Huxley*). "Perhaps each great race has just strength enough for one period of literary *supremacy*" (*T. S. Eliot*). **Ascendancy** may or may not imply supremacy, but it always involves the idea of domination or of autocratic power; thus, a country may lose its *ascendancy* over its colonies after it has been deprived of its military and naval *supremacy;* an idea has *ascendancy* over one's imagination when it has the latter completely under its sway. "The whole system of oppression and cruelty by which dominant castes seek to retain their *ascendancy*" (*B. Russell*). "The *ascendancy* which Spain then had in Europe...had been gained by unquestioned superiority in all the arts of policy and of war" (*Macaulay*).

Ana. Pre-eminence, transcendence, superlativeness, peerlessness, incomparability (see corresponding adjectives at SUPREME): *power, authority, dominion, control, sway.

supreme, *adj.* **Supreme, superlative, transcendent, surpassing, pre-eminent, peerless, incomparable, banner** come into comparison when they mean highest in any scale of values. All of these words are capable of being employed with precision, but all of them are frequently used rhetorically or bombastically with resulting loss in definiteness. It is the precise signification of each that is emphasized in this discrimination. **Supreme** is applicable to that which is not only the highest in rank, power, quality, or the like, but has no equals in that status, all others of the same class or kind being inferior in varying degrees; as, the *Supreme* Being; the *Supreme* Court of the United States; Shakespeare is generally regarded as the *supreme* dramatic poet; the *supreme* power in a nation. **Superlative** is applicable to anything which, by comparison with all other things of the same kind or with all other manifestations of the same quality, may be rated as the highest, best, greatest, finest, noblest, or by any adjective (especially, but not necessarily, commendatory adjective) in the superlative degree; *superlative* may admit equals, but it excludes superiors; as, the *superlative* wit of Alexander Pope; the *superlative* genius of Goethe; his *superlative* rudeness. "What makes him a great artist is a high fervour of spirit, which produces a *superlative*, instead of a comparative, clarity of vision" (*Galsworthy*). **Transcendent** and **surpassing** are applicable to anything that goes beyond everything else of its kind or in its quality: both often connote an exceeding even of the superlative, but *transcendent* suggests realization of the ideal, and *surpassing* suggests almost inconceivable attainment; as, the *transcendent* acting of Duse; Cleopatra's reputation for *transcendent* beauty; his *surpassing* skill in surgery; the *surpassing* success of a new book. **Pre-eminent** is applicable to that which goes beyond all others in achieving distinction or eminence; it implies both superlativeness and uniqueness within the limits indicated, but it seldom in precise use carries a suggestion of supremacy or transcendency; as, the *pre-eminent* general in that war; the *pre-eminent* film of the year; the *pre-eminent* example of magnanimity. **Peerless** and **incomparable** both imply the absence of equals but, commonly, *peerless* connotes the absence of superiors, and *incomparable* connotes the impossibility of being equaled; as, a *peerless* performance of "Hamlet";

"Philip Sidney, called the *peerless* one of his age" (*Quiller-Couch*); "the *incomparable* refinement with which he [Harunobu the Japanese artist] has drawn this interior with its two youthful figures" (*Binyon*); "he proceeds to tell the world in a loud voice how *incomparable* the German Empire is" (*Van W. Brooks*). **Banner,** an Americanism, implies such pre-eminence or incomparability that the thing so qualified is worthy of being distinguished by some outward mark, such as a banner; it is more often a term of strong and enthusiastic approbation, rather than of discreet appraisal; as, the *banner* state; a *banner* occasion; the *banner* regiment; a *banner* year for the company or corporation.

Ana. *Chief, foremost, leading, capital: predominant, *dominant, paramount, sovereign.

surcharge. Gorge, surfeit, *satiate, sate, cloy, pall, glut.

Ana. Oppress, *depress, weigh (down).

sure. 1 Assured, *confident, sanguine.

Ana. Relying, trusting, depending, counting, banking (see RELY): inerrant, unerring, *infallible: *safe, secure.

2 **Sure, certain, positive, cocksure** come into comparison when applied to persons, and to their conclusions and opinions, and mean having or manifesting no doubt. *Sure* and *certain* are often interchangeable. But **sure** frequently emphasizes the mere subjective state of assurance; **certain** often suggests more strongly a conviction that is based on definite grounds or on indubitable evidence; as, " 'I know my hour is come.' 'Not so, my lord.' 'Nay, I am *sure* it is' " (*Shak.*); "Be out of hope, of question, of doubt; Be *certain*" (*Shak.*); I felt for a time *sure* of his innocence; I am now *certain* of his guilt. "Moreover...are we so *sure* that the qualities that mark successful climbers—self-assertion, acquisition, emulation—are highly desirable?" (*H. Ellis*). **Positive** often suggests overconfidence or dogmatism, but it always implies conviction or full confidence in the rightness or correctness of one's statement or conclusion. "They felt very *positive*, but were not quite *certain*" (*Coleridge*). "As I can't be *certain*, I won't be *positive*" (*J. R. Lowell*). "An easy and elegant scepticism was the attitude expected of an educated adult: anything might be discussed, but it was a trifle vulgar to reach very *positive* conclusions" (*B. Russell*). **Cocksure** in earlier use came nearer to *certain* than to *sure;* as time goes on, however, it tends to carry an increasingly stronger implication of presumption or overconfidence in positiveness. "They [quoted passages] show how cautious and profound a thinker he [T. H. Huxley] was—how very far from being...[an] arrogant and *cocksure* materialist" (*A. Huxley*). "Certitude is not the test of certainty. We have been *cocksure* of many things that were not so" (*Justice Holmes*).

Ana. Decisive, *decided: self-assured, assured, self-confident (see corresponding nouns at CONFIDENCE): dogmatic, doctrinaire, oracular (see DICTATORIAL).

Ant. Unsure.

surety. 1 Security, bond, *guarantee, guaranty, bail.

Ana. *Pledge, earnest, token, hostage, pawn, gage.

2 Guarantor, *sponsor, backer, patron, angel.

surfeit, *v.* *Satiate, sate, cloy, pall, glut, gorge, surcharge.

Ant. Whet.

surge, *n.* *Wave, undulation, billow, roller, breaker, comber, beachcomber, ripple.

surge, *v.* *Rise, arise, ascend, mount, soar, tower, rocket, levitate.

surly. Morose, glum, *sullen, crabbed, sulky, saturnine, dour, gloomy.

Ana. *Rude, ungracious, ill-mannered, discourteous: boorish, churlish (see under BOOR): snappish, waspish, fractious, *irritable.

Ant. Amiable.— *Con.* *Gracious, cordial, affable, genial.

surmise, *v.* *Conjecture, guess.

Ana. *Infer, gather, judge, deduce, conclude: *think, conceive, fancy, imagine: *consider, regard, deem.

surmise, *n.* Conjecture, guess. See under CONJECTURE, *v.*

Ana. Inference, deduction, conclusion (see under INFER): *hypothesis, theory.

surmount. Overcome, overthrow, rout, *conquer, vanquish, defeat, subdue, subjugate, reduce, beat, lick.

Ana. Surpass, transcend, outdo, outstrip, excel, *exceed.

surpass. Transcend, excel, outdo, outstrip, *exceed.

Ana. Surmount, overcome, beat (see CONQUER).

surpassing. Transcendent, *supreme, superlative, pre-eminent, peerless, incomparable, banner.

Ana. Excelling, outdoing, outstripping (see EXCEED): *consummate, finished, accomplished.

surplus, *n.* *Excess, superfluity, surplusage, overplus.

Ana. *Remainder, residue, residuum.

Ant. Deficiency.

surplus, *adj.* *Superfluous, supernumerary, extra, spare.

Con. *Needful, necessary, requisite, indispensable, essential.

surplusage. Surplus, superfluity, overplus, *excess.

Ana. & *Ant.* See those at SURPLUS, *n.*

surprise, *v.* 1 **Surprise, waylay, ambush** are synonymous terms when they mean to attack unawares. **Surprise** is in military as well as in general use. As a technical term it implies strategy in the disposition and movement of troops and equipment and secrecy in the operations; it may or may not suggest that the attack has been successful. "So we...may beat down Edward's guard And seize himself; I say not, slaughter him, For I intend but only to *surprise* him" (*Shak.*). "An army suddenly attacked within the lines which it had reckoned upon to ward off its enemy is in a military sense *surprised*" (*J. F. Maurice*). In literary use, one may *surprise* a person or something he is concealing by coming on him when he is off guard; as, "tremble like a guilty thing *surprised*" (*Wordsworth*). "I have sometimes *surprised* a tragic shadow in her eyes" (*Cather*). **Waylay** commonly suggests a lying in wait on a road or highway. Sometimes, it implies concealment by the roadside and an evil intent such as robbery or assault; as, he was *waylaid* on his return from the bank: sometimes, especially in current use, it carries no suggestion of hostility or evil intent but implies intercepting a person in his progress and detaining him. "Riding in the park...Carola beheld her intended galloping furiously down the Row, and left her sister Clementina's side to *waylay* him" (*Meredith*). "I am *waylaid* by Beauty....Oh, savage Beauty, suffer me to pass" (*Millay*). **Ambush** in literal use evokes the image of would-be attackers concealed in a thicket; it is often used in reference to guerrilla warfare; as, Colonial traders were in constant danger of being *ambushed* by Indians.

Ana. *Catch, capture, nab, cop: *take, seize, grasp, grab.

2 **Surprise, astonish, astound, amaze, flabbergast** agree in meaning to impress one forcibly because unexpectedly. **Surprise,** as here considered, derives from an older sense still in good use: to come upon another suddenly and with startling effect. The two senses are often confused because both imply a lack of preparation or a reversal of what is anticipated. The older sense commonly takes a personal subject in the active voice; as, her friends planned to *surprise* her on her birthday with a gift: the newer and more common sense commonly takes an impersonal subject; as, their gift greatly *surprised* and pleased her. The difference may also be illustrated by the old story of the lexicographer who, being discovered in an

embarrassing position by his wife, interrupted her reproof beginning "I am *surprised*—" with the retort, "Not you, my dear—I am *surprised;* you are *astonished.*" Modern authorities, however, countenance both uses of *surprise.* In older English, **astonish** always implied a dazing or silencing. "It is the part of men to fear and tremble, When the most mighty gods by tokens send Such dreadful heralds to *astonish* us" (*Shak.*). In modern use it more often means merely to surprise so greatly as to seem incredible. "While still an undergraduate...[he] had *astonished* the scientific world by his acceleration of the metamorphosis of the tadpole" (*C. Mackenzie*). "He...*astonished* his fellows by buying and smoking ten-cent cigars" (*S. Anderson*). **Astound** stresses shock more than *astonish;* in older use, it always implied a stunning or overwhelming emotional effect. "Threatening the world with high *astounding* terms" (*Marlowe*). In modern English, it usually implies so great a difference between what one believes possible and what one discovers to be true that one can find no precedent for it. Thus, a piece of news *surprises* one when it is unexpected; it *astonishes* when one finds it hard to believe; it *astounds* when one cannot account for it by any previous knowledge or experience; thus, the successful laying of the Atlantic cable *astounded* everybody; its later breaks *astonished* no one, but after it was finally in operation, many said that no future human invention could *surprise* them. **Amaze,** though it carries an implication of astonishment, stresses rather bewilderment, perplexity, or wonder. "That he should even speak to her was *amazing!*—but to speak with such civility" (*Austen*). "I have been *amazed* to discover that town-bred people seldom know the points of the compass...cannot find out which side of the house is out of the wind" (*B. Russell*). **Flabbergast** (a colloquial term) is a picturesque and often hyperbolical synonym of *astonish* or *amaze;* it suggests vividly the physical signs of a sudden dumfounding. "They were *flabbergasted* by this involuntary outbreak" (*L. P. Smith*).

Ana. Startle, alarm, scare (see FRIGHTEN): bewilder, nonplus, confound, dumfound (see PUZZLE, *v.*): *embarrass, disconcert, discomfit, rattle, faze.

surrender, *v.* Abandon, resign, *relinquish, yield, leave, cede, waive.

Ana. *Abdicate, renounce: *forgo, forbear, sacrifice, eschew: submit, capitulate, succumb (see YIELD): *commit, consign, confide, entrust.

surrender, *n.* **Surrender, submission, capitulation** come into comparison, especially in their military meanings, when they denote the act of yielding up one's person, one's forces, or one's possessions to another person or power. **Surrender** usually, but not necessarily, implies a state of war, and present domination by a victor or by an admittedly stronger power; in addition it often also implies the immediate cessation of fighting and succeeding overtures leading to a treaty of peace; as, the commander replied that no terms except an unconditional and immediate *surrender* could be accepted. **Submission** often implies surrender, as of an army, its supplies, its fortifications, and the like, but it stresses the acknowledgment of the power or authority of another, and often suggests loss of independence; it is used chiefly of those who rebel or of those whose weak condition leaves them at the mercy of the stronger power or subject to its threats. Consequently, *submission* may or may not imply a previous state of war; in the latter case, it may merely imply a threat of disastrous warfare. "*Submission,* Dauphin! 'tis a mere French word; We English warriors wot not what it means" (*Shak.*). "Declaring my *submission* to your arms" (*Browning*). **Capitulation** also implies surrender, but it suggests a conditional one, on terms agreed upon between the parties or the commanders of the forces concerned. In current use, *surrender* usually implies a yielding to the force or demand of the stronger party; *capitulation* usually implies a request for terms on the part of those who acknowledge their defeat. "In Greece to offer earth and water was the sign of *capitulation*" (*Newman*).

surreptitious. Underhand, underhanded, *secret, covert, stealthy, furtive, clandestine, privy, backstairs.

Ana. Sneaking, slinking, skulking, lurking (see LURK): hidden, concealed, screened (see HIDE).

surrogate. Substitute, shift, makeshift, expedient, *resource, resort, stopgap.

surveillance. *Oversight, supervision.

Ana. Inspection, scrutiny, examination (see under SCRUTINIZE): observation, *observance.

survey, *v.* View, espy, descry, behold, *see, observe, notice, remark, note, perceive, discern.

Ana. *Scrutinize, scan, inspect, examine: *see, look, watch.

survey, *n.* *Compendium, syllabus, digest, pandect, sketch, précis, aperçu.

survive. *Outlive, outlast.

Ana. Endure, *continue, persist, last: withstand, resist, *oppose.

susceptibility. Susceptibility, hypersensitivity (*or* **hypersensitiveness**), **allergy, anaphylaxis** are related but not synonymous terms used in medicine. In strict technical language, *susceptibility* and *hypersensitivity* are distinguished. **Susceptibility** denotes a lack of resistance to a given infectious disease, or to the action of certain bacteria. One who has a *susceptibility* (or is *susceptible*) to a particular infectious disease will contract that disease when the germs causing it get into the body. **Hypersensitivity** (*or* **hypersensitiveness**) denotes an excessive sensitiveness to some agent and is used in reference both to substances, such as strawberries or the pollen of ragweed, and to environmental factors, such as extremes in temperature. **Allergy,** in strict technical use, means altered susceptibility to the action of a particular germ, or altered degree of sensitiveness to a foreign substance, as indicated by the reaction to a second (or subsequent) inoculation with the same germ or by a second (or subsequent) introduction of the same substance into the body. The term was coined to cover cases where there was any difference in an organism's reaction after it had once been affected by a germ, a serum, a poison, or the like, whether that difference was in the direction of increased resistance or of increased susceptibility or sensitiveness, such a difference being regarded as a sign that a constitutional change has been brought about by the prior experience. In nontechnical or loose use, *allergy* usually means increased susceptibility or sensitiveness and is, therefore, often used interchangeably with *susceptibility* and, especially, *hypersensitivity;* thus, a person who has an *allergy* for (or is *allergic* to) feathers may develop asthma after sleeping on a feather pillow. **Anaphylaxis,** another technical term, unequivocally denotes increased sensitiveness, especially to a poisonous protein substance, following its second (or subsequent) introduction into the body; thus, eating eggs produces *anaphylaxis* in some persons inclined to eczema, and the inhalation of the pollen of ragweed, in some persons susceptible to hay fever. *Anaphylaxis* (and not *allergy*) is usually regarded as the opposite of *immunity,* in the sense of immunity as freedom from the bad effects of certain protein substances.

susceptible. Sensitive, subject, exposed, prone, *liable, open, incident.

Ana. Inclined, disposed, predisposed (see INCLINE, *v.*): alive, awake, sensible, conscious (see AWARE).
Ant. Immune.

suspend. 1 Disbar, shut out, *exclude, eliminate, debar, blackball, rule out.
Ana. *Eject, dismiss, oust: *banish, exile, ostracize.
2 Stay, intermit, postpone, *defer.
Ana. *Arrest, check, interrupt: *stop, cease, discontinue: *delay, detain, retard.
3 *Hang, sling, dangle.
Ana. Poise, balance, steady, *stabilize.

suspended. **Suspended, pendent** (*or* **pendant**), **pendulous** agree in meaning hanging or seeming to hang. **Suspended** may suggest a being poised or a being upheld as by buoyancy, or the like (as, "Pure air, free from *suspended* matter"—*Jefferies;* water clouded by *suspended* particles of an undissolved substance), or it may imply a thing's attachment to a point or to points above itself so that it swings freely (as, balls *suspended* from a chandelier; an acrobat *suspended* by one foot from a trapeze) or is held steady in its proper place or position (as, a *suspended* ceiling; a *suspended* [now commonly a *suspension*] bridge). **Pendent** now usually describes that which hangs downward from a support or from one point of attachment: it seldom carries any further implication and so is applicable both to that which is motionless and to that which swings or moves, or is in danger of falling; as, "he shakes From many a twig the *pendent* drops of ice" (*Cowper*); "a trailing creeper with curving leaf and twining tendril, and *pendent* bud and blossom" (*Hudson*); *pendent* rocks on the side of a cliff. The term is also, but now rarely, applied to that which hangs seemingly without support or without sufficient support; as, "To be imprison'd in the viewless winds, And blown with restless violence round about The *pendent* world" (*Shak.*). **Pendulous** adds to *pendent* the specific implication of swaying or swinging, sometimes even carrying a suggestion of actual floating in space; as, a *pendulous* nest; the *pendulous* wattles of an old barnyard rooster; a *pendulous* double chin; "I see him yonder, with his pipe *pendulous* in his hand, and the ashes falling out of it" (*Sterne*); "So blend the turrets and shadows there That all seems *pendulous* in air" (*Poe*).

suspension. *Insolvency, bankruptcy, receivership, failure.

suspicion. 1 Mistrust, *uncertainty, doubt, dubiety, dubiosity, skepticism.
Ana. Misgiving, foreboding, presentiment, *apprehension: distrust, mistrust (see under DISTRUST, *v.*).
2 *Touch, suggestion, soupçon, tincture, tinge, shade, smack, spice, dash, vein, strain, streak.

sustenance. 1 Nourishment, nutriment, *food, aliment, pabulum.
2 Maintenance, support, *living, livelihood, subsistence, keep, bread.

suture, *n.* *Joint, articulation.

swag, *n.* *Spoil, pillage, plunder, loot, booty, prize.

swagger, *v.* *Strut, ruffle, bristle, bridle.
Ana. Flourish, brandish, *swing, wave: brag, *boast, vaunt, crow, gasconade.
Con. Cower, cringe, truckle (see FAWN): shrink, quail, blench, wince (see RECOIL).

swagman *or* **swagsman.** *Vagabond, vagrant, tramp, hobo, truant, bum, stiff, sundowner.

swap, *v.* Interchange, bandy, *exchange.
Ana. Trade, barter (see SELL).

swarm, *n.* *Flock, herd, drove, pack, bevy, covey, gaggle, flight, shoal, school.

swarm, *v.* *Teem, abound, superabound, overflow.

swarthy. *Dusky, tawny.
Ana. *Dark, murky, gloomy, darkling.

swat, *v.* *Strike, hit, smite, slug, slap, clout, punch, box, cuff.
Ana. *Beat, pound, pummel, baste, belabor.

sway, *v.* 1 *Swing, oscillate, fluctuate, pendulate, vibrate, waver, undulate.
Ana. Brandish, flourish, wave, *swing: *shake, rock, agitate, convulse: *tip, tilt, cant, careen.
2 Influence, impress, strike, touch, *affect.
Ana. Control, direct, manage, *conduct: rule, *govern: bias, *incline, dispose, predispose.

sway, *n.* Dominion, control, command, *power, authority.
Ana. *Supremacy, ascendancy: *range, reach, scope, sweep: spread, stretch, amplitude, *expanse: *government, administration.

swear. **Swear, affirm, asseverate, depose, depone, testify** mean to declare solemnly under oath or on one's word of honor that what one says is true. One **swears** (especially before a magistrate or tribunal) when one gives a solemn pledge with an appeal to God or by laying one's hand on a sacred object, such as the Bible, that one speaks or will speak only the truth or that one will do what one promises. One **affirms** before a magistrate or tribunal when one makes a pledge like that of the one who swears and under the same penalties of perjury, but without reference to a sacred person or object, because one's conscience or creed forbids an oath. One **asseverates** when one insists earnestly and emphatically and (especially in current usage) on one's word of honor that what one says is true or what one promises will be carried out. *Asseverate* is often used when the writer wishes to avoid the legal connotations or implications of *swear,* but it is unusual in speech and rare in the first person. " 'I shall repay you, surely!' Madame Foucault *asseverated.* 'I swear!' " (*Bennett*). One **deposes** or **depones** when one makes a statement, such as an affidavit or a deposition, in writing and under oath. One **testifies** when, on a witness stand or in an affidavit or deposition, one communicates information or gives evidence under oath and under penalties of perjury. *Testify* is also found in nonlegal use, where it retains its implication of personal knowledge on the part of the one who testifies. "And we have seen and do *testify* that the Father sent the Son to be the Saviour of the world" (*1 John* iv. 14). "I can *testify* that he [Columbus] becomes interesting before the age of two, at least to children who know the sea" (*B. Russell*).
Ana. Pledge, plight, covenant, engage, *promise.

swearing. *Blasphemy, profanity, cursing.

sweep, *n.* Compass, scope, *range, reach, gamut, radius, ken, purview, horizon, orbit.
Ana. *Expanse, amplitude, spread.

sweeping. *Indiscriminate, wholesale.
Ana. Promiscuous, heterogeneous, motley, *miscellaneous.

swell, *v.* *Expand, amplify, distend, inflate, dilate.
Ana. *Extend, elongate, lengthen: *intensify, heighten, enhance: *increase, augment, enlarge.
Ant. Shrink. — *Con.* *Contract, condense, compress, constrict.

swell, *n.* *Fop, dandy, beau, coxcomb, exquisite, élégant, dude, macaroni, buck, spark, nob, toff.

swerve, *v.* **Swerve, veer, deviate, depart, digress, diverge** agree in meaning to turn aside from a straight line or a defined course. **Swerve** may refer to a turning aside by a person or thing (as, she never *swerved* from the path till she caught sight of her friends on the right; at that point the road *swerves* to the left; "The great roots of a tree *swerve* upward out of the design"—*Binyon*): it may suggest a physical, mental, moral, or spiritual turning aside (as, never to *swerve* from one's duty; "If I be false, or *swerve* a hair from truth"—*Shak.*; "Our affections and passions put frequently a bias...so strong on our judgments as to make them *swerve* from the direction of right reason"—*Bolingbroke*). **Veer** was originally used and still is frequently used in reference to a change in the course of a wind or of a ship; often, in such contexts, it suggests either a frequent turning this way or that or a series of turnings in the same direction, especially (as in modern meteorology) of the wind in a clockwise direction; as, the wind *veered* to the east; "It [the ship] plunged and tacked and *veered*" (*Coleridge*); "The wind had *veered* round, and the Aurora was now able to lay up clear of the island of Maritimo" (*Marryat*). In extended and discriminating use, the term commonly implies a change or series of changes of direction or course under an external influence comparable to the wind (as, "the world's opinion, as usual, *veered* completely round"—*Meredith*) or a turning aside for a tactical reason such as to avoid an undue influence (as, "Imagist poetry...is right in *veering* away from any tinge of archaism in its diction, because it is aiming at an effect with which such diction is inconsistent"—*Lowes*). **Deviate** (etymologically, to go from the way) implies a turning aside from a customary, allotted, or prescribed course: it is commonly used in reference to persons, their minds, their morals, their actions, and the like, with the suggestion of a swerving from that which is the norm, the law, the standard, or the right procedure or course; as, "[Shenstone] never *deviates* from the beaten paths for fear of being lost" (*Gray*); "Critics, who have blamed Mr. Pope for *deviating*...from the simplicity of Homer" (*Goldsmith*); "if he [a workingman] diminishes his speed by a fraction of a second or *deviates* a hair's breadth from the prescribed and never-changing movements of his hands" (*Grandgent*); "From a fundamental sincerity he could not *deviate*" (*T. S. Eliot*). The last three words of this group usually imply a turning aside from a path, course, track, or the like, which still continues. **Depart** stresses the turning away from and leaving an old path, a customary course, an accepted type or standard, or the like: it may further imply a forsaking of the antiquated, conventional, traditional, or the like (as, "[books] which *depart* widely from the usual type"—*Grandgent*), or a deviation from that which is right, true, normal, or the like (as, the account frequently *departs* from the facts as established; "I have not *departed* from thy judgments: for thou hast taught me"—*Psalms* cxix. 102). **Digress,** in its earliest but now practically obsolete sense, was a close synonym of *depart:* in current use it commonly implies a departure from the subject of one's discourse that may be voluntary and, therefore, made with the intent to return (as, let me *digress* for a few minutes to indicate the possible results of this condition), or involuntary, and the outcome of an inability to think coherently or to stick to the point to be developed (as, he *digressed* so often in his speech that he finally lost the thread of his discourse). **Diverge** is often used in the sense of *depart* even by good writers (as, "Let them [professors] *diverge* in the slightest from what is the current official doctrine, and they are turned out of their chairs"—*Mencken*), but when employed with precision and understanding of its etymological implication of turning in different directions, it always suggests a separation of a main, old, or original course or path into two (or more) courses or paths that lead away from each other; as, "They proceeded along the road together till...their paths *diverged*" (*Hardy*); "two roads *diverging* like the branches of a Y" (*Belloc*); rays of light *diverge* as they proceed from the sun.

Ana. *Turn, divert, deflect, sheer, avert: *curve, bend, turn.

swift. *Fast, rapid, fleet, quick, speedy, hasty, expeditious.

Ana. *Easy, effortless, smooth, facile: headlong, *precipitate, sudden.

swindle, *v.* *Cheat, overreach, cozen, defraud.

Ana. Embezzle, *defalcate, peculate: *dupe, gull, bamboozle, hoodwink, trick: *steal, pilfer, purloin, filch.

swing, *v.* **1 Swing, wave, flourish, brandish, thrash** are comparable when they mean to wield or to shake something so that it moves alternately backward and forward or upward and downward or around and around. **Swing** often implies regular oscillations (as, he walked down the street *swinging* his arms; to *swing* a scythe in mowing); it may, however, imply continuous rotatory movements (as, to *swing* a pail over one's head. **Wave** distinctively implies undulating or fluttering motions; it also carries a weaker implication of rhythmical regularity than *swing;* as, to *wave* a flag; to *wave* a handkerchief. The word, moreover, commonly implies something more than the mere act or operation; according to the nature of the thing waved and the way in which it is waved, the term may suggest a signal, an emotion, a greeting, an order, a magical power, or the like. "Then grave Clarissa graceful *wav'd* her fan; Silence ensu'd" (*Pope*); "*waved* my arm to warn them off" (*Tennyson*). "You cannot *wave* a wand over the country and say 'Let there be Socialism': at least nothing will happen if you do" (*Shaw*). **Flourish** implies ostentation, triumph, or bravado in swinging or waving something which one holds in one's hand, such as a weapon, a stick, or a rod; as, a conductor who never *flourishes* his baton; "With their swords *flourished* as if to fight" (*Wordsworth*); "He walked with a gay spring... *flourishing* his cane" (*Bennett*). **Brandish** stresses menace or threat as *flourish* seldom does; otherwise it suggests somewhat similar motions; as, "I shall *brandish* my sword before them" (*Ezekiel* xxxii. 10); "He *brandishes* his pliant length of whip, Resounding oft" (*Cowper*). **Thrash** (see also BEAT, 1) implies a noisy vigorous swinging suggestive of the motions of a flail in threshing grain; as, to *thrash* one's legs in swimming; to *thrash* one's arms on a cold day.

Ana. Parade, flaunt, display, exhibit (see SHOW, *v.*): *shake, tremble, quiver, quaver, quake.

2 Swing, sway, oscillate, vibrate, fluctuate, pendulate, waver, undulate come into comparison when they mean to move or, in some cases less often, to cause to move from one direction to another, usually to and fro, back and forth, or up and down. **Swing** (as here compared: see also SWING, 1) implies movement of that which is attached only at one side or at one end, as by being suspended, hinged, pivoted, or the like: apart from the context the term conveys no definite implication of whether the movement is induced or is automatic, whether it is occasional or constant, or whether it is rhythmical and regular or intermittent and irregular; as, the tavern sign *swings* from a hook above the door; "the red amaryllises...*swung* in heavy clusters" (*Stark Young*); the door *swung* open; to *swing* (i.e., to hang) a thief from the branch of a tree; "*swinging* their dinner pails" (*S. Anderson*); a pendulum *swings* with great regularity. **Sway** implies a swinging motion, especially in a flexible or unsteady object that yields to lack of support or to pressure from one side or another; as, "to hear the *swaying* of the branches of the giant pine" (*Binyon*); "She stood up; she seemed to *sway* a little as she stood" (*M. Austin*); "caravans of camels, *swaying* with their padded feet across the desert" (*L. P. Smith*); a light breeze *swaying* the branches. **Oscillate** also usually implies a swinging motion, but of something suspended so that it moves in the manner of a pendulum: the term usually implies a movement from one side or place, or, in figurative use, from one condition, attitude, or position to another, with more or less regularity. "Move any body, as a pendulum, in one way, and it will continue to *oscillate* in an arch [arc] of the same circle, until the known causes make it rest" (*Burke*). "His adventures were related by himself in a series of letters and diaries, showing how he *oscillated* between wealth and poverty" (*Lucas*). "So, this way and that, *oscillates* the current fashion among uninspired writers" (*C. E. Montague*). In electricity, *oscillate* specifically implies the flow of electric charges alternately in opposite directions; as, an *oscillating* current; an *oscillating* circuit. **Vibrate** carries a stronger implication of shaking than of swinging: although it is still sometimes used in the sense of *oscillate* (as, "The double complex pendulum, when it *vibrates* in one plane"—*Encyc. Brit., 9th ed.*), it more often suggests the rapid pulsations of the string of a musical instrument such as the piano or violin when touched by a hammer or bow (as, "You know that if you strike a note of music, all the octave notes will *vibrate*"—*Manning*). In the physical sciences, *vibrate* implies a periodic motion of the particles of an elastic body or medium in alternately opposite directions from the point of equilibrium; as, the particles of an elastic medium, such as the air, *vibrate* when a wave of sound or light passes through it; a tuning fork *vibrates* when struck; "the electric oscillations in a circuit may cause the electromagnetic *vibration* of a filament" (*Van Nostrand's Scientific Encyclopedia*). In a more extended sense, *vibrate* usually implies a trembling, a quavering, a throbbing, or the like, suggestive of the movements of musical strings when an instrument is being played; as, "Had I waited on the stile, in a few minutes, becoming used to my presence, he [the nightingale] would have made the hawthorn *vibrate*, so powerful in his voice when heard close at hand" (*Jefferies*); "On summer evenings when the air *vibrated* with the song of insects" (*S. Anderson*); "Nerve and bone of that poor man's body *vibrated* to those words" (*H. B. Stowe*). **Fluctuate** etymologically implies a tossing up and down restlessly as the waves of the sea or of something floating on such waves: although this sense still occurs, it is now somewhat rare; as, "the traveller sees Thy [France's] three-striped banner *fluctuate* on the breeze" (*Wordsworth*); "The surface rolls and *fluctuates* to the eye" (*Bryant*). The term is now chiefly used in an extended sense implying constant irregular alternations suggestive of the movement of waves driven by a high wind; as, stock prices that *fluctuate* from day to day; "the old unquiet breast, Which neither deadens into rest, Nor ever feels the fiery glow That whirls the spirit from itself away, But *fluctuates* to and fro" (*Arnold*); "We have no absolute standard left, and are abandoned to subjective and *fluctuating* valuations" (*Inge*). **Pendulate,** a fairly rare word revived in the nineteenth century, is a near synonym of *oscillate* implying a swinging between two extremes, but it often comes closer to *fluctuate* in its strong suggestion of constant change; as, "The ill-starred scoundrel *pendulates* between Heaven and Earth" (*Carlyle*). **Waver,** in the literal sense in which it is here considered (see also HESITATE), carries a stronger implication of unsteadiness or of uncertainty in swinging than does *sway* or *oscillate*, and therefore often, but far from always, connotes movements suggestive of reeling or tottering; as, "Banners and pennons *wavering* with the wind" (*Berners*); "Some stars *waver* irregularly back and forth between fairly well defined limits of brightness" (*P. W. Merrill*). **Undulate** is now more often used than *fluctuate* when a wavelike motion is implied: it is also often used figuratively, seldom suggesting violent changes, but rather the continuous rolling or rippling that is associated with the steady flow of waves; as, "The ripe corn under the *undulating* air *Undulates* like an ocean" (*Shelley*); "The...flame...made the jades *undulate* like green pools" (*Amy Lowell*).

Ana. *Hang, suspend, dangle: *turn, spin, whirl, wheel, revolve, rotate, gyrate.

3 Wield, manipulate, *handle, ply.

Ana. Control, manage, direct, *conduct: *execute, administer.

swink. Travail, labor, toil, *work, drudgery, grind.

swipe, *v.* *Steal, pilfer, filch, purloin, lift, pinch, snitch, cop.

swirl, *v.* Circle, spin, whirl, twirl, wheel, eddy, *turn, revolve, rotate, gyrate, pirouette.

sybaritic. *Sensuous, sensual, luxurious, voluptuous, epicurean.

sycophant. *Parasite, favorite, toady, lickspit, hanger-on, leech, sponge.

Ana. Blandisher, cajoler, wheedler (see corresponding verbs at COAX): fawner, truckler (see corresponding verbs at FAWN).

syllabus. *Compendium, digest, pandect, survey, sketch, précis, aperçu.

Ana. Conspectus, synopsis, epitome, *abridgment, brief, abstract.

symbol. 1 *Creed, confession, catechism.

2 Symbol, emblem, attribute, type are here compared only as meaning a visible thing that stands for or suggests something that is invisible or intangible. *Symbol* and *emblem* are now often used interchangeably, even by good writers; historically, however, they are clearly distinguishable. **Symbol** (L. *symbolus*, token, sign) derives its implications from its earliest application in English to one of the three Christian creeds (especially the Apostles' Creed) which was so called because its recital was the outward evidence of a person's Christianity. Hence, *symbol* came to be referred to anything that serves as an outward sign of something spiritual or immaterial; thus, the cross is to Christians the *symbol* of salvation because of its connection with the Crucifixion; the circle, in medieval thought, was the *symbol* of eternity because it, like eternity, has neither beginning nor end. This close and natural connection between the symbol and that which it makes visible or partly intelligible is not always so strongly implied in modern use; it may be a traditional, conventional, or even an arbitrary association of one thing with another that is suggested; as, a king's crown is the *symbol* of his sovereignty and his scepter the *symbol* of his authority; to many poets the skylark is the *symbol* of aspiration. **Emblem** (L. *emblema*, inlaid ornament) was, especially in the sixteenth and seventeenth centuries, applied to a pictorial representation of some abstraction to which was appended a motto or set of verses, the purpose of the picture and inscription being moral teaching. In its extended use *emblem*, as distinguished from *symbol*, still always implies representation of an abstraction or use in representation; it is applicable chiefly to any pictorial device, sometimes an object, sometimes a combination of objects, found on a shield, a banner, a flag, or the like, and intended to serve as an arbitrary or chosen symbol of the character or history of the family, the nation, the royal line, or the office that has adopted it; thus, the spread eagle, the

usual *emblem* of the United States, is found in its coat of arms and on some of its coins and postage stamps; the *emblem* of Turkey, a crescent and a star, appears on its flag. This historic difference between *symbol* and *emblem* is, however, being lost sight of in current use. *Emblem* is also correctly applied to what is technically known in painting and sculpture as an **attribute,** or some object that is conventionally associated with the representation either of a character, such as a Greek divinity or a Christian saint, or of a personified abstraction, and is the means by which the character or abstraction is identified; thus, in fine art the balance is the *emblem,* or *attribute,* of Justice; the turning wheel, of Fortune; the club, of Hercules; and the spiked wheel, of St. Catherine of Alexandria. **Type,** considered as the correlative to *antitype* (see under PROTOTYPE), is chiefly, but not exclusively, in theological use. It is applied to a person or thing that prefigures or preshadows someone or something to come, and that stands therefore as his or its symbol, or shadow, until the reality appears. In theology, Biblical interpretation, and religious poetry, it usually also implies a divine dispensation whereby the spiritual or immaterial reality is prefigured by a living person, event, experience, or the like; thus, in medieval religious poetry, Jerusalem is the *type* of heaven (the heavenly Jerusalem); in allegorical interpretation of Scriptures, the paschal lamb is the *type* of Christ, the victim on the Cross. "Spiritual wisdom...is unchanging and eternal; it is communicated to us in *types* and shadows dim—in *symbols*—till we grow up into the power of understanding it" (*Inge*).
Ana. *Sign, mark, token, badge: device, motif, design, *figure, pattern.
3 *Character, sign, mark, note.
Ana. *Device, contrivance: diagram, delineation, outline, sketch (see SKETCH, *v.*).

symbolism. *Allegory.

symmetry. Symmetry, proportion, balance, harmony are here compared chiefly, but not exclusively, as used in the arts of design and decoration and as meaning a quality which gives aesthetic pleasure and which depends upon the proper relating of details and parts to each other, as in magnitude, arrangement, or the like, and to the consequent effect produced by the whole. **Symmetry,** in strict use, implies a median line or an axis on either side of which the details correspond in size, form, placing, and the like. Often, it implies the mathematical precision observable in the corresponding halves of a perfect crystal, in a geometrically regular star, in the conventionalized leaf or flower common in decorative design, in the placing of pictures on a wall so that on either side of the median line there are the same number of pictures, and the same pattern followed in their arrangement according to sizes and levels; thus, *symmetry* is the keynote of most formal gardens; the *symmetry* of a Greek temple; in spite of their apparent *symmetry* human bodies are rarely, if ever, perfectly symmetrical. **Proportion,** in strict use, presupposes a scale, a pattern, or a standard which determines the relative size, duration, intensity, or the like, of each of the component details or parts. The term implies a grace or beauty that has nothing to do with a thing's actual magnitude, duration, or intensity, but depends on the measured fitness of every one of its details and the consequent perfection of the whole. "How sour sweet music is, When time is broke and no *proportion* kept!" (*Shak.*). "In small *proportions* we just beauties see, And in short measures life may perfect be" (*B. Jonson*). "We care for size, but inartistically; we care nothing for *proportion,* which is what makes size count" (*Brownell*). **Balance** is sometimes employed as though it were the equivalent of *symmetry;* in discriminating use it implies opposition rather than repetition of details or parts and a massing of different things such as light and shade, sharply contrasted colors, figures, and background, so that each one tends to offset the other or to reduce the other's emphasis without loss of significance on either side. *Balance* implies as its aesthetic effect an inducing of a pleasant satisfaction in the thing's quiet beauty or of a delight in the unified yet varied beauty of the whole. "It is a similar principle of unsymmetrical *balance* which the Taoist artists sought in design. Space therefore, empty space, becomes a positive factor, no longer something not filled and left over, but something exerting an attractive power to the eye, and balancing the attractive power of forms and masses" (*Binyon*). "Every good statue is marked by a certain air of repose; every fine picture exists in a state of stable equilibrium brought about by the *balance* of its masses" (*J. W. Krutch*). **Harmony,** when used specifically in reference to the arts of design and decoration, retains as its leading implication the same idea as is involved in its general sense (see HARMONY, 1), that of beauty resulting from a perfect interrelation of details and their fusion into an agreeable whole. However, in this connection, it often denotes specifically the aesthetic impression produced by something which manifests symmetry, proportion, or balance, or these qualities in combination. "A coloring *harmony* obtained by the aid of a long experience in the effects of light on translucent surfaces" (*Viollet-le-Duc, transl. by H. Adams*). "We hear harmonious tones; but...the pleasure they give us [is] distinct from the pleasures appropriate to the separate tones...it is the pleasure of their relational form which makes us attribute to them and their physical combination a quality which we call *harmony*" (*S. Alexander*).

sympathetic. 1 *Consonant, congenial, congruous, compatible, consistent.
Ana. Agreeing, harmonizing *or* harmonious, accordant, correspondent (see corresponding verbs at AGREE).
2 *Tender, compassionate, warm, warmhearted, responsive.
Ana. Kindly, *kind, benign, benignant: understanding, appreciating, comprehending (see UNDERSTAND).
Ant. Unsympathetic.

sympathy. 1 *Attraction, affinity.
Ana. Reciprocality, correspondence (see corresponding adjectives at RECIPROCAL): *harmony, consonance, accord, concord.
Ant. Antipathy.
2 *Pity, compassion, commiseration, ruth, condolence, empathy, bowels.
Ana. Tenderness, warmheartedness, warmth, responsiveness (see corresponding adjectives at TENDER): kindliness, kindness, benignness, benignancy (see corresponding adjectives at KIND).

symptom. *Sign, mark, token, badge.

synchronous. Coeval, contemporaneous, *contemporary, simultaneous, coincident, concomitant, concurrent.

syndicate, *n.* *Monopoly, corner, pool, trust, cartel.

synecdoche. *Metonymy.

synod. *Convention, convocation, conference, congress, council.

synonymicon. *Dictionary, lexicon, wordbook, glossary, onomasticon, gazetteer.

synopsis. Brief, conspectus, epitome, *abridgment, abstract.

synthetic. *Artificial, ersatz, factitious.

system. 1 System, organism, scheme, economy, network, complex come into comparison when they mean an organized integrated whole made up of diverse but interrelated and interdependent parts or elements. **System** applies both to a natural and to an artificial aggregation, all of whose units, when physical or material, function, operate, or move in unison or in obedience to some form of control or, when immaterial (such as laws, principles, theories, etc.), fit into each other so as to form a distinctive and coherent whole; as, a telegraph *system;* the solar *system;* a stellar *system;* one's bodily *system;* a *system* of railroads; a philosophical *system;* "Kant...sought to mix up aesthetics with his *system*" (*H. Ellis*); "the fault lay not so much in our characters as in the capitalist *system* which we had allowed to dominate our lives" (*Shaw*). **Organism** applies only to a system that has actual life, such as the human body, where the movement, functioning, or development of any part or parts is governed by its (or their) relation to all the other parts, or to one that seems to have life because it is capable of development and therefore of change and of growth; as, "until definite knowledge became available...of the effects of certain substances upon the human *organism*" (*V. Heiser*); "The Church grew, like any other *organism*, by responding to its environment" (*Inge*); "[Augustus] had created a huge and intricate polity, and it must have the articulate life of an *organism* and not the mere functional differentiation of a machine" (*Buchan*). **Scheme** is often used in place of *system* especially when it refers to a system that has been or seems to have been planned in detail and, therefore, to have the character of a great design or construction: often the term is used with a hint of irony or depreciation but equally often it is free from any derogatory suggestions; as, "In our complex *system* [that of the United States of America], presenting the rare and difficult *scheme* of one general government, whose action extends over the whole" (*Ch. Just. Marshall*); "The organization of eighteenth-century French society was hopelessly inefficient...so...that great numbers of individual Frenchmen, unable to fit into the *scheme* of things, suffered acute discomfort" (*A. Huxley*); "a wider Naturalism which will find room for life, mind, and spirit within the *scheme* of nature" (*Inge*). **Economy,** as here considered, applies to a distinctive system of government or of organization, as of a people, a land, a church, or even of the world (the divine *economy*) or of immaterial things, and implies due consideration of the individual conditions and needs of the governed or of the significance of each part or detail in the organization; as, "The principle may operate successfully in the close *economy* of a good family, or even within a small religious community" (*J. A. Hobson*); "Octavius...looked beyond the political conundrum to the economic problems of the land....The Roman *economy* was unbalanced" (*Buchan*); "the field of music is time, that of painting, space. To multiply simultaneous sounds, or to make colors follow one another in single file, is to change their *economy*" (*Babbitt*). **Network** literally applies to any fabric or structure made of threads, cords, wires, etc., crossing each other at intervals: figuratively it applies to any system, especially any physical system, that has a corresponding structure with all its intercrossing threads coming under a central government or control; as, a vast *network* of railroads. **Complex** applies chiefly to any integrated whole that involves a great variety of parts, elements, or factors yet brings them all into relation and unity: though the term has specific senses, such as in psychology (for a complicated system of desires and memories that exerts an influence on one's temperament and behavior), it tends to be used when *system, organism, scheme*, etc., are too rich in implications or connotations for one's purposes; as, "We do know that a certain *complex* of energies can wag its tail and another make syllogisms" (*Justice Holmes*).

Ant. Chaos.

2 *Method, mode, manner, way, fashion.

Ana. *Plan, project, scheme, design: procedure, *process, proceeding.

systematic, systematical. *Orderly, methodical, regular.

Ana. Systematized, organized, ordered, arranged (see ORDER, *v.*): *logical, analytical.

systematize. Organize, methodize, *order, arrange, marshal.

Ana. *Adjust, regulate, fix.

T

tabernacle. *Altar, shrine, chantry.

table, *n.* *List, catalogue, schedule, register, roll, roster, rota, canon, inventory.

taciturn. *Silent, uncommunicative, reserved, reticent, secretive, close, close-lipped, closemouthed, tight-lipped.

Ana. *Dumb, mute, inarticulate: restrained, inhibited, curbed, checked (see RESTRAIN).

Ant. Garrulous: clamorous (*especially of crowds*): convivial (*of habits*).

tackle, *n.* *Equipment, apparatus, machinery, paraphernalia, outfit, gear, matériel.

tact. **Tact, address, poise, savoir-faire** are comparable when they name the skill and grace with which a well-bred person conducts himself in his relations with others. **Tact** stresses skill and grace in one's association with or handling of others, whether one's social equals or not. It implies delicate and sympathetic perception, especially of what is fit, graceful, or considerate under given circumstances. "Of political wisdom...Elizabeth had little or none; but her political *tact* was unerring" (*J. R. Green*). "His Vicar, who had so much *tact* with the natives, so much sympathy with all their short-comings" (*Cather*). "Without the *tact* to perceive when remarks were untimely" (*Hardy*). **Address** stresses dexterity and grace in approach, as in meeting strangers or in coping with new or with difficult situations. It often connotes adroitness and suavity: it commonly implies success in winning favor or in attaining one's ends. "Her *address* in rendering them [her many guests] easy with one another" (*Burney*). "His acute and flexible logic could support, with equal *address*...the adverse sides of every possible question" (*Gibbon*). "He was as reluctant as other men to be found wanting in *address* by a pretty woman" (*Shaw*). **Poise,** in current use, often implies both tact and address; it stresses, however, self-possession or equanimity in meeting embarrassing or upsetting situations. "Charles Francis Adams was singular for mental *poise*...a balance of mind and temper that neither challenged nor avoided notice, nor admitted question of superiority or inferiority" (*H. Adams*). **Savoir-faire,** a French phrase much used in English, stresses worldly or social experience and a knowledge of what is the

T

proper thing to say or do or of how to act under all circumstances. "The inexperience and want of *savoir faire* in high matters of diplomacy of the Emperor and his ministers" (*Charles Greville*). In current use, it often suggests ease and tact even more than breadth of experience. "Girls don't seem to have to pass through it [the difficult age of adolescence] quite as boys do, or their *savoir faire* is instinctive" (*Tarkington*).

Ana. Diplomaticness *or* diplomacy, politicness *or* policy, suavity, urbanity (see corresponding adjectives at SUAVE): *courtesy, amenity, gallantry.

Ant. Awkwardness.

tag, *v.* *Follow, pursue, chase, trail, tail.

tail, *v.* *Follow, pursue, chase, trail, tag.

taint, *v.* *Contaminate, pollute, defile.

Ana. *Debase, deprave, corrupt, vitiate: spoil, decompose, rot, putrefy, *decay: imbue, inoculate, *infuse.

take. 1 **Take, seize, grasp, clutch, snatch, grab** agree in meaning to get hold of by or as if by reaching out the arm, hand, or tentacles. **Take** is not only the most general but also the only colorless term in this group. In literal use, especially with reference to physical things, it may imply nothing more than a movement of the hand to get hold of something (as, to *take* the lamp from the table; to *take* meat from a platter) or it may imply, with reference not only to physical but to immaterial or intangible things, numerous and, often, difficult operations by means of which one gets possession of or control over something (as, to *take* a band of thieves; to *take* a city). Between these two extremes *take* may imply any of numerous methods of getting hold of something; thus, one *takes* a prize who wins it in a competition; one *takes* a cottage who hires the use of it; one *takes* the temperature of a room by observing the thermometer; so, to *take* a bath; to *take* the air; to *take* a rest; to *take* care. **Seize** usually suggests a sudden and forcible taking or getting hold of, and it therefore is interchangeable with *take* only when emphasis is placed upon these qualities; as, to *seize* a flaming lamp and throw it out of the window; the hungry children *seized* the food that was offered them; the policeman *seized* the thief in the act of escaping; the fort was *seized* before its defenders had time to repel the assault; "*seizing* between his teeth the cartilage of the trainer's ear" (*Shaw*). In extended use, especially when the thing seized or the thing seizing is something immaterial or intangible, the term usually suggests a catching of something fleeting or elusive (as, to *seize* an opportunity; to *seize* the attention of the crowd), or the capture of something by force and, usually, surprise (as, to *seize* the throne; "The Breton *seized* more than he could hold; the Norman *took* less than he would have liked"—*H. Adams*), or the understanding of something extremely difficult to apprehend or analyze (as, unless you *seize* this point of view, you will not understand the age which it governed; "The character of Louis XIII is difficult to *seize*, for it comprised qualities hardly ever combined in one man"—*Belloc*), or the overthrowing by force of a mightier power (as, pneumonia *seized* him in his thirty-fifth year; *seized* by a passion beyond his control). **Grasp** literally implies a laying hold of with the hands, teeth, or claws so as to hold firmly (as, the hawk *grasped* the fowl with its talons; "Thy hand is made to *grasp* a palmer's staff"—*Shak.*): figuratively it implies an ability to comprehend fully or adequately something beyond the mental reach of many (sometimes, most or all) men (as, "Chartres [the cathedral] expressed...an emotion, the deepest man ever felt,—the struggle of his own littleness to *grasp* the infinite"—*H. Adams;* "the evil of the corruption and falsification of law, religion, education, and public opinion is so enormous that the minds of ordinary people are unable to *grasp* it"—*Shaw;* cf. "A man's reach should exceed his *grasp*"—*Browning*). **Clutch,** in its literal use, implies more rush, more avidity, and often, especially in intransitive use, less success in getting hold of (especially with the hands or fingers) the thing desired than *grasp;* only when success is implied is a tight hold or a clenching suggested; as, "I gave him all the money in my possession....Gunga Dass *clutched* the coins, and hid them at once in his ragged loin-cloth" (*Kipling*); "He *clutched* Father Joseph's hand with a grip surprisingly strong" (*Cather*); "I...*clutched* desperately at the twigs as I fell" (*Hudson*); "*clutching* at him as he reeled backwards" (*Shaw*). In extended use, the term is almost entirely figurative, usually suggesting a movement of the mind or spirit or emotions that is comparable to that of tentacles; as, "[Prudentius] *clutches* at, rather than *grasps*, the Roman verse tradition" (*Fitzmaurice-Kelly*); "A man was now terribly at the mercy of fate, and *clutched* at any possible safeguard" (*Buchan*); "Can you never like things without *clutching* them as if you wanted to pull the heart out of them?" (*D. H. Lawrence*). **Snatch** carries the strongest implication of a sudden, hurried movement of any of these terms, but it seldom carries as strong a suggestion of the use of force as does its closest synonym, *seize:* rather, it often implies stealth (as, to *snatch* a purse; to *snatch* a kiss), or promptness in rescuing (as, to *snatch* a child from the flames; he was *snatched* from the jaws of death), or rudeness or roughness (as, he *snatched* the book from her hand; "I *snatched* his hat off his head"—*Steele*). Consequently, in figurative use, one *snatches* only what one can get by chance, surreptitiously, by prompt action, or the like; as, to *snatch* gladly any opportunity for rest; to *snatch* a joy in their discomfiture; to *snatch* a free moment for writing a letter. **Grab** commonly implies more rudeness or roughness than *snatch* does at times, and it also usually implies as much force or violence as *seize:* distinctively, it often suggests vulgarity and indifference to the rights of others or to the standards of the community, or a more or less open unscrupulousness in getting what one wants for oneself; as, to *grab* all the food from the table; to *grab* one's hat and run; to *grab* power; to *grab* a franchise.

Ana. *Have, hold, own, possess: *catch, capture, nab, cop: confiscate, appropriate, pre-empt (see ARROGATE).

2 Captivate, enchant, charm, fascinate, bewitch, allure, *attract.

3 **Take, assume** are very close synonyms when they mean to adopt or accept as one's own something not previously belonging to one (a person or thing) by nature or by virtue of one's constitution, character, office, condition, or the like. As here compared, that which is *taken* or *assumed* is rarely a tangible thing, and then usually one that is the sign or symbol of a function, an office, a duty, or a state in life; thus, to *take* the veil is to be invested with the habit of a nun (of which the veil is a conspicuous feature) in a ceremony which includes the pronouncing of vows; to *assume* the toga (*toga virilis*) was, to the Roman youth of fourteen, to invest himself with the plain white toga which was the recognized sign of his attainment of manhood; to *take* the crown; to *assume* the livery of a servant or the robes of office. When that which is taken or assumed is something intangible, the words are usually distinguishable by subtle differences in meaning which are, however, not the same in all collocations. **Take,** especially when the subject of the verb is a thing, often suggests passivity or lack of resistance to external influences in that which *takes;* **assume,** on the other hand, often implies activity or some compelling power in that which *assumes;* thus, a fiber that *takes* a dye absorbs it easily and readily; an insect

that *assumes* the color of the plant on which it feeds has by implication (not necessarily in fact) some means of imitating that color; a pudding *takes* its shape from the mold in which it is chilled; a person's face *assumes* an expression when it reveals what he feels or what he wishes others to think he feels. When a person, rather than a thing, is the subject of the verb, *take* is often more colorless than *assume*, the latter sometimes suggesting arrogation, sometimes deliberate acceptance of a burden, sometimes presumption, or the like; thus, to *assume* charge of another's affairs suggests more initiative than to *take* charge, which may be merely an answer to a request; one *takes* office, but one *assumes* power, sovereignty, jurisdiction; one may *take* the blame when one does not attempt to answer criticism, but one *assumes* the blame only when one removes it from others; an actor *takes* a role in a play, but a dictator *assumes* the role of lawgiver. In these and similar instances *take* may carry the full implications of *assume* by adding to it one of certain prepositions or prepositional phrases; thus, one says either to *assume*, or to *take on*, the pose of a martyr; to *assume*, or to *take upon oneself*, new obligations; to *assume*, or to *take up*, the burdens of office.

Ana. *Adopt, embrace: appropriate, pre-empt (see ARROGATE): *enter, penetrate.

4 *Receive, accept, admit.

Ana. Acquiesce, accede, *assent, consent, subscribe.

5 *Bring, fetch.

Ana. *Carry, convey, bear: deliver (cf. *delivery* at DELIVERANCE).

taking. Captivating, enchanting, charming, fascinating, bewitching, alluring, attractive. See under ATTRACT.

tale. *Story, narrative, anecdote, yarn.

Ana. *Fiction, fable: *myth, legend, saga: *novel, romance.

talent. Genius, *gift, faculty, aptitude, knack, bent, turn.

Ana. Capacity, *ability, capability: *art, skill, craft, cunning: endowment, enduement (see corresponding verbs at DOWER).

talisman. *Fetish, charm, amulet, periapt.

talk, *v.* *Speak, converse.

Ana. *Discuss, dispute, argue: *discourse, expatiate, dilate, descant: *chat, chatter, prate.

talk, *n.* *Speech, address, oration, harangue, allocution, lecture, prelection, sermon, homily.

talkative. **Talkative, loquacious, garrulous, voluble** are here compared chiefly as applied to persons and their moods and as meaning given to talk or talking. The same distinctions in implications and connotations are also seen in their corresponding nouns **talkativeness, loquacity** (*or* **loquaciousness**), **garrulity** (*or* **garrulousness**), and **volubility** (*or* **volubleness**). **Talkative** and **talkativeness**, the least explicit of these terms, may imply nothing more than a readiness to engage in talk or they may suggest fluency and ease in talking or a disposition to enjoy conversation; as, "A *talkative* boy learns French sooner in France than a silent boy" (*Sydney Smith*); "Good-humoured and *talkative*, he preferred any company rather than none" (*Thackeray*); "among them they noticed a beautiful, slim, *talkative* old man, with bright black eyes and snow-white hair" (*L. P. Smith*). **Loquacious** and **loquacity** more commonly imply fluency and ease in speech: they may variously imply qualities as diverse as the power of expressing oneself articulately or eloquently or a disposition to indulge in chattiness or glibness; as, "Your French friend...stuns you with his *loquacity*" (*Smollett*); "to become *loquacious*, or, as it is familiarly called, chatty" (*Scott*); "every glib and *loquacious* hireling who shows strangers about their picture galleries, palaces, and ruins" (*Trench*); "He was not *loquacious:* but, when he was forced to speak in public, his natural eloquence moved the envy of practised rhetoricians" (*Macaulay*). **Garrulous** and **garrulity** imply prosy, tedious, or rambling loquacity and usually suggest much idle talk about trivial things; as, "a fond *garrulous* old man, who loved to indulge his mind in reminiscences of the past" (*Trollope*); "*garrulous* Pepys" (*J. R. Lowell*). "We cannot, therefore, explain away this deliberate act as due to the *garrulity* of age, or accept the other excuses with which his admirers have sought to palliate it" (*L. P. Smith*). **Voluble** (for fuller consideration see VOCAL, 2) and **volubility** suggest a free, easy, and unending loquacity; as, *voluble* Latins gesturing continuously as they talked; "a brilliant, swift, *voluble*, affectionate, and pleasant creature" (*Carlyle*); "He sang of the lark, and it was the lark's *voluble* self" (*Pater*); "for it was not a fault in him to dislike Aunt Charlotte, whose *volubility* must have assorted ill with his customary reserve" (*Arch. Marshall*).

Ana. *Vocal, fluent, articulate, voluble, glib, eloquent: *vociferous, clamorous.

Ant. Silent. — *Con.* Reticent, reserved, uncommunicative, secretive (see SILENT).

talkativeness. Loquacity, garrulity, volubility. See under TALKATIVE.

Ana. Fluency, articulateness, eloquence, volubility, glibness (see corresponding adjectives at VOCAL).

Ant. Silence.

tall. *High, lofty.

Ant. Short.

tallow. *Adipose, marrow, suet, lard.

tally, *v.* *Agree, square, accord, harmonize, correspond, conform, comport, jibe.

Ana. *Match, equal: coincide, concur (see AGREE).

Con. Differ from, *differ with.

tame, *adj.* **Tame, subdued, submissive** come into comparison when they mean rendered docile and tractable or incapable of asserting one's will, either permanently or for the time being. **Tame** implies opposition to *wild* and in its literal sense applies chiefly to animals that have been domesticated and therefore accustomed to control by men (as, *tame* versus wild horses; the *tamest* of *tame* cats): in extended use it also applies to persons (or, less directly, to the acts, words, etc., of persons) whose wills have been broken or who have allowed themselves to be dominated by the will of another (as, the haughty Katharine became *tame* under Petruchio's treatment; "They should expose themselves...to public contempt, on account of their *tame* behaviour"—*Hume;* "The tribunal lately so insolent, became on a sudden strangely *tame*" (*Macaulay*). Often, the term implies little more than a temperamental lack of proper spirit or independence, or undue docility or timidity; as, a *tame* reply; "*tame* acquiescence in tradition and routine" (*Babbitt*). **Subdued,** in its most general sense, implies a toning down with a loss of all vehemence or intensity (as, *subdued* voices; *subdued* colors): as here considered, in reference to persons, their acts, words, characters, etc., it implies complete domination by or subjection to another (or a similar response to circumstances) and a resulting quietness or meekness that suggests a broken will, complete dependence, excessive timorousness, or the like; as, "Our polished manners are a mask we wear, And at the bottom, barbarous still and rude, We are restrained indeed, but not *subdued*" (*Cowper*); "She had a mild, *subdued*, expiring look" (*Crabbe*); "In such a man, so gentle and *subdued* ... A race illustrious for heroic deeds, Humbled, but not degraded, may expire" (*Wordsworth*). **Submissive** implies the state of mind of one who has yielded his will to control by another and who, therefore, unquestioningly or humbly obeys or accepts what is given; as, "In the *submissive* way of one long accustomed to obey under coercion, he ate and drank what they gave him" (*Dickens*); "Meek, humble, timid persons...who are cautious, prudent, and *submissive*, leave things very much as they find them" (*A. C. Benson*); "Mother had no will of her own; all her life long...she had been wholly *submissive*" (*V. Sackville-West*).

Ana. Tractable, amenable, docile, biddable, *obedient: *timid, timorous: pliant, pliable (see PLASTIC).

Ant. Fierce.

tamper. *Meddle, interfere, intermeddle.

Ana. *Interpose, interfere, intervene: molest, trouble, discommode, *inconvenience.

tang. *Taste, sapidity, flavor, savor, relish, smack.

Ana. Pungency, piquancy, raciness (see corresponding adjectives at PUNGENT).

tangent, *adj.* Abutting, adjoining, *adjacent, contiguous, conterminous, juxtaposed.

tangible. Sensible, *perceptible, palpable, appreciable, ponderable.

Ana. *Material, physical, corporeal, objective: actual, *real, true: obvious, *evident, manifest.

Ant. Intangible.

tantalize. Tease, harass, harry, *worry, annoy, plague, pester.

Ana. Vex, *annoy, irk, bother: torment, torture, try, *afflict: *bait, badger.

Ant. Satisfy.

tantamount. *Same, selfsame, very, identical, identic, equivalent, equal.

Ana. Like, alike, uniform, *similar.

tar, *n.* *Mariner, sailor, seaman, gob, matlow, bluejacket, rating.

tardy, *adj.* **Tardy, late, behindhand, overdue** come into comparison when they apply to persons or things that do not arrive or take place at the time set, the time due, or at the expected and usual time. **Tardy** implies a lack of promptness or punctuality or a coming or happening after the proper or appointed moment: it does not, however, necessarily imply slowness in movement but may suggest rather a being delayed by any of a number of other causes; as, the morning of the storm, the number of *tardy* pupils broke all records; the bridge game was delayed by the *tardy* arrival of several guests. **Late** implies an opposition to *early* and usually connotes a failure to come or take place at the time due because of procrastination, slowness of movement, growth, or the like, or the interference of obstacles: it is applied especially to persons or to things that are governed by a schedule; as, to be *late* for work day after day; you are too *late* to get your dinner; even a *late* repentance is better than no repentance at all; the train is very *late* today; spring is very *late* this year. **Behindhand** usually applies either directly or indirectly to persons who are in arrears, as in the payment of debts or in the fulfillment of obligations, or who are not up to the time or the moment as in mental progress, in the acceptance of fashions, or the like; as, to be *behindhand* in the payment of one's room rent; a physician so *behindhand* in his work that when night arrives he has still a large number of calls to make; "A whole class who were *behindhand* with their lessons" (*N. Hawthorne*). **Overdue** is applied to things (or sometimes to persons) that are affected by a person's being markedly late or behindhand: thus, a person is *behindhand* (not *overdue*) in the payment of his rent, but the rent is *overdue* (not *behindhand*) when such a situation occurs; a ship is *overdue* when it is seriously or conspicuously behind its scheduled time of arrival.

Ana. Dilatory, laggard, *slow: delayed, detained, retarded (see DELAY).

Ant. Prompt.

tariff. Customs, duty, toll, impost, excise, *tax, levy, assessment, rate, tribute, tithe, teind, cess.

tarry. *Stay, remain, wait, abide, linger.

Ana. *Delay, procrastinate, lag, loiter, dawdle, dally, dillydally.

tart, *adj.* *Sour, acid, acidulous, dry.

Ana. Piquant, *pungent: *sharp, keen: curt, brusque, blunt (see BLUFF): *irritable, snappish, waspish.

Tartarean. *Infernal, chthonian, Hadean, Stygian, hellish.

task, *n.* **Task, duty, job, chare** (*or* **char**), **chore, stint, assignment** come into comparison when they mean a piece of work which one is asked to do and is expected to accomplish. **Task** distinctively implies imposition by another such as an employer, a parent, or a teacher; as, he was given the *task* of cleaning the cellar; each day every child was asked to perform a special *task*. In extended use, *task* often suggests imposition not by a person, but by the nature or the necessities of one's occupation, one's station in life, one's beliefs, or the like. "But these miracles in the world of art...could be observed and noted and described and classified; and this, in Sainte-Beuve's opinion, was the most important *task* of the critic" (*L. P. Smith*). Sometimes the work to be accomplished is not that of a person but of a thing: then *task* comes very close to *function* in meaning. "Every inch of material, up and down, from crypt to vault...had its *task*, giving support where support was needed, or weight when concentration was felt" (*H. Adams*). Since the word usually connotes difficulty or strain, it is often qualified by *hard*, *difficult*, etc., but seldom in precise use by their opposites; it may even be used without qualification to imply arduousness; as, to make a *task* of writing a letter. **Duty,** as here considered (see also OBLIGATION, 1), may or may not imply a taskmaster but it invariably suggests an obligation to perform and a responsibility for performance; as, the *duties* of a parlormaid usually include waiting on table; the porter was given the *duty* of seeing that doors and windows were locked at night. "He thought that now all the worries were over, that there was nothing before him but *duties*....A most soothing certitude" (*Conrad*). **Job** (see also POSITION, 3), as here considered, carries in itself no implication of imposition nor of obligation; the term is applied to a piece of work (etymologically, a lump) which one is asked to do because of one's occupation, trade, or business but which one is expected to accomplish only if one accepts the opportunity; as, to engage a carpenter for the *job* of paneling a room; householders needing men for small *jobs* were asked to inquire of the welfare department. *Job* is the commonest term for any piece of work which one undertakes voluntarily when offered or enters into on one's own initiative, and which one judges by its appeal to one, or by its degree of difficulty, or by the way in which it is done; as, when you start a *job* stick to it; to make a good *job* of a piece of research; he found polishing the table a disagreeable *job*. "He doesn't believe in parsons standing outside things and only doing soft *jobs*" (*R. Macaulay*). *Chare* and *chore* (the former the usual, but now obsolescent, British form, the latter the usual American form) though they are both colloquial terms for small pieces of work, especially about the house or its environs, are not exact synonyms. **Chare** usually implies household work and denotes a job of cleaning, scrubbing, or the like, given a woman hired by the day or hour (a *charwoman*), or one of the duties of a domestic servant. **Chore,** on the other hand, is applied to one of the routine activities that must be regularly performed by one responsible for a home, for the care of stock, and the like, or by some person given this as a task or duty; as, when Mrs. B finishes her evening *chores*, she usually goes visiting; each child in the family had his daily *chore;* "He made my health a pretext for taking all the heavy *chores*" (*Cather*). *Chore* is often used colloquially without qualification for a difficult or disagreeable, yet necessary, piece of work; as, picking up the pieces of a shattered glass bulb is a *chore. Stint* and *assignment* denote a specific and clearly defined task. But **stint** implies allotment or prescription and suggests that the task is either one's share of a work in which several persons are engaged or the amount of work set for accomplishment within a given period of time; as, each girl in the family had her daily *stint* which she was expected to finish before noon; to work by *stint. Stint*, when used of the amount of work one sets for oneself, often suggests a minimum which must be accomplished within a given time. "Here...I...took to doing 'German Romance' as my daily work, 'ten pages daily' my *stint*" (*Carlyle*). **Assignment** suggests that the task is prescribed in character and limited in amount; it is used chiefly of a specific task set by one in authority, such as a teacher or an editor, often for accomplishment elsewhere than in the classroom, office, or the like. "The photographers had been sent on an *assignment*, and were determined not to return to their papers without pictures" (*V. Heiser*).

Ana. *Function, office, duty, province: *work, labor, toil: employment, occupation, business, métier (see WORK).

taste, *n.* **1 Taste, sapidity, flavor** (*or* **flavour**), **savor** (*or* **savour**), **tang, relish, smack** are here compared as meaning that property of a substance which makes it perceptible to the gustatory sense when it comes into contact with the taste buds of the tongue or, in popular but scientifically incorrect language, with the palate. **Taste** is not only the most inclusive of these terms but it also gives no suggestion of a specific character or quality; as, to be able to distinguish types of oranges by their *taste;* to dislike the *taste* of olives; "only four *tastes*, acid, bitter, salt, and sweet, are fundamental. All others are either combinations or, more commonly, sensations of *taste* modified by smell" (*Webster's New Int. Dict., 2d Ed.*). **Sapidity** implies, far more than *taste*, a decided or highly perceptible sensation; thus, to say that a given meat or food has no *sapidity* is not to say that it has no taste, but that the taste can be described as bland or neutral or not clearly definable; so, because of its *sapidity*, some persons prefer game that is "high" to that which is fresh; fruits lacking in *sapidity*. **Flavor** applies to the property of a thing which is recognized by the co-operation of the olfactory and gustatory senses. The term therefore usually denotes the combination of tastes and smells perceived when eating or drinking a thing. Usually, also, it suggests the blend of tastes and odors that give a substance a distinctive or peculiar character; as, this peach has a peculiarly fine *flavor;* the *flavor* of a fine tea has been described as "a bouquet which can be tasted"; "My stock of provisions had been so long consumed that I had forgotten the *flavour* of pulse and maize and pumpkins and purple and sweet potatoes" (*Hudson*). **Savor** stresses the quality, such as sweetness or bitterness, that is detected by the organs of taste and smell (sometimes of one more than the other). It often implies sensitiveness of palate (strictly, taste buds) or of nose and may refer to the odor of that which is cooking as well as to the flavor of that which is eaten. "Viands of various kinds allure the taste Of choicest sort and *savour*" (*Pope*). "The *savour* of the stew had floated from the cottage into the porch with such appetizing distinctness, that the meat, the onions, the pepper, and the herbs could be severally recognized by his nose" (*Hardy*). "A traveler...described the *savor* of the durian [a tropical fruit] as a 'rich butter-like custard, highly flavored with almonds...but intermingled with it come wafts of *flavor* that call to mind cream cheese, onion sauce, brown sherry, and other incongruities' " (*V. Heiser*). **Tang** applies chiefly to a sharp penetrating savor, flavor, or odor: it usually implies a live, pungent quality; as, to prefer apples with a *tang;* the *tang* of dry champagne; the *tang* of a salt breeze; "Happiness to me is wine, Effervescent, superfine. Full of *tang* and fiery pleasure" (*Amy Lowell*). **Relish** and **smack** are now comparatively rare in this sense; *relish* (see also TASTE, 2) comes close to *savor* and usually suggests enjoyment of the taste (as, "A Laplander or Negro has no notion of the *relish* of wine"—*Hume;* "My first endeavour must be to distinguish the true *taste* of fruits, refine my palate, and establish a just *relish* in the kind"—*Shaftesbury*); *smack* comes close to *flavor* but applies usually to one that is added to or different from the typical flavor of the substance (as, ale with a burnt musty *smack;* there is a good *smack* of pepper in this stew).

Figuratively, these words usually call up one or more suggestions from their literal senses. **Taste** usually denotes a strong impression or a heightened sense of the quality of something; as, the book leaves a bad *taste* in the mouth; "How comfortable is the feeling and *taste* of grace" (*Lyly*). **Flavor** implies a predominant or distinctive quality suggestive of a flavor in its literal sense; as, "The higher heroisms and the old rare *flavors* are passing out of life" (*W. James*); "The passing hour's supporting joys have lost the keen-edged *flavor*" (*Meredith*); "Your words have no longer their old *flavour*" (*Hardy*); "*Flavour*, in fine, is the spirit of the dramatist projected into his work in a state of volatility, so that no one can exactly lay hands on it, here, there, or anywhere" (*Galsworthy*). **Savor** (see also ATMOSPHERE, 2) differs from *flavor* largely in suggesting a stimulating or enlivening character or quality that, like salt, spice, or other seasoning, gives life or pungency to a thing; as, "a Puritanism that still strove to keep in its creed the intense *savor* which had long gone out of its faith" (*J. R. Lowell*); " 'no one treats me like a child now, and the *savour* has gone out of my life' " (*H. Ellis*). **Tang, relish,** and **smack** come still closer to their literal senses. "The language has a *tang* of Shakespeare" (*Gray*). "Yankeeisms...whose salt-sea *flavor* has its own peculiar *tang* in it" (*J. R. Lowell*). "The full *flavor*, the whole *relish* of delight" (*H. W. Beecher*). "Your lordship...hath yet some *smack* of age in you, some *relish* of the saltness of time" (*Shak.*). "The Saxon names of places, with the pleasant, wholesome *smack* of the soil in them" (*Arnold*).

2 Taste, palate, relish, gusto, zest come into comparison when they mean a liking for or an enjoyment of something because of particular qualities that literally afford one's taste buds (or in idiomatic but scientifically inaccurate English, one's palate) a pleasurable sensation, or that figuratively produce comparably pleasant mental or aesthetic impressions. **Taste** (as here compared: see also TASTE, 1), implies a liking that is either natural or acquired: the term is often used to designate any deep-seated or ingrained longing for something that lies behind one's predilection for it, one's bent to it, one's aptitude for it, or any predisposition to enjoy one thing more than another; as, to cultivate a *taste* for olives; he had no *taste* for the law; "Had he discovered in himself a capacity and a *taste* for that sort of thing [arguing, preaching, remonstrating]?" (*Conrad*). More often, *taste* refers to a liking that is based upon an understanding of peculiar excellences, especially aesthetic excellences, and that gives one a more or less discerning appreciation of a thing's (especially, a work of art's) beauty, or perfection of form, design, color, etc., or grace and dignity, and consequently greater enjoyment of it; as, "Their *taste* is exquisite" (*L. P. Smith*); "Without any technical knowledge she had acquired a good *taste* in music" (*H. Ellis*). In this sense *taste* is often so close to another sense of *taste,* namely, the power of correct or discriminating aesthetic judgment, that the two meanings tend to overlap and are sometimes confused. In the first case, however, *taste* is not an abstraction, but a concrete thing referable to an individual or a group of individuals and therefore subject to evaluation as good, bad, indifferent, etc. "We have our *tastes* in painting as in confectionery. Some of us prefer Tintoretto to Rembrandt, as we do chocolate to cocoanut" (*Brownell*). "If he found this room more to his *taste* than any other in the house, either the house or his *taste* must have been deficient" (*Arch. Marshall*). In the latter sense, *taste* is an abstraction used commonly without reference to individuals. Like all abstractions, it is tenuous, variously defined, and not clearly established in meaning. In general, however, it implies a capacity, characteristic of only the finest minds and spirits, for discerning true beauty and the setting up of standards whereby all may be taught to appreciate the beauty they discern: sometimes it denotes the body of standards so set up; as, an education in *taste;* there is no *taste* evident in the decoration of this house; "every author, as far as he is great and at the same time original, has had the task of creating the *taste* by which he is to be enjoyed" (*Wordsworth*). **Palate** (literally, the roof of the mouth, once popularly regarded and still spoken of as the organ of the sense of taste) may be used either literally or figuratively in the sense here considered: a liking dependent upon pleasurable physical sensation may be suggested (as, cooked according to the *palate* of an epicure; a wine taster must have a discriminating *palate*) but the term refers equally, if not more often, to pleasure afforded the mind (as, "Any subject that was not to their *palate,* they...condemn'd"—*Milton;* "I heard a little too much preaching ...and lost my *palate* for it"—*G. Eliot*). **Relish** often suggests a more distinct or a more exciting flavor in the thing that evokes enjoyment or a liking: it usually, however, implies a keener or more personal gratification than *taste;* as, "a man of...a quick *relish* for pleasure" (*Macaulay*); "He walked up-hill...as the rest of the [stage coach] passengers did; not because they had the least *relish* for walking exercise" (*Dickens*); "It [the artist's brain] can go further and build up, always with a passionate *relish* for what it is producing" (*C. E. Montague*). **Gusto** usually implies either the hearty relish with which one sometimes may attack a meal, execute a piece of work (especially a work of art), or go about the performance of any task, duty, or the like, or a quality in the thing which is executed or in the work which is performed that indicates vital or enthusiastic interest, keen delight, and intense imaginative or emotional energy in the doing of it. "[He] argues that the chief contribution of [Theodore Roosevelt]...to American life was the example of his gigantic *gusto,* his delight in toil and struggle, his superb aliveness" (*Mencken*). "[Prescott's] swing and *gusto,* his abundant detail, and the swift excitement of his narrative" (*Times Lit. Sup.*). "This dramatic sense....gives Rostand's characters—Cyrano at least—a *gusto* which is uncommon on the modern stage" (*T. S. Eliot*). **Zest,** like *gusto,* applies either to the spirit in which one approaches something one likes to do, make, encounter, or the like, or the quality imparted to the thing done, made, envisioned, etc., as a result of this spirit. In contrast with *gusto,* it suggests eagerness, avidity, or a perception of a thing's piquancy or peculiar flavor, rather than a hearty appetite indicative of abounding energy. "The Elizabethan theatre had its cause in an ardent *zest* for life and living" (*Arnold*); "No one has painted the riotous merriment of a country fair...with such *zest* as Rubens" (*Binyon*).

Ana. *Predilection, prepossession, partiality: appreciation, understanding, comprehension (see corresponding verbs at UNDERSTAND): inclination, disposition, predisposition (see corresponding verbs at INCLINE): *discernment, discrimination, penetration, insight, acumen.

Ant. Antipathy.

tasty. Savory, sapid, saporous, *palatable, appetizing, toothsome, flavorsome, relishing.

Ant. Bland.

tat, *v.* *Weave, knit, crochet, braid, plait.

tattle. *Gossip, blab.

Ana. Divulge, disclose, betray, *reveal.

taunt, *v.* Mock, deride, *ridicule, twit, rally.

Ana. *Scoff, jeer, gibe, flout: affront, insult, *offend, outrage: scorn, disdain, scout (see DESPISE): chaff, *banter, quiz.

taut. *Tight, tense.

tautology. *Verbiage, redundancy, pleonasm, circumlocution, periphrasis.

tawdry. *Gaudy, garish, flashy, meretricious.

Ana. *Showy, pretentious: vulgar, gross, *coarse: flamboyant, *ornate, florid.

tawney. Variant of TAWNY.

tawny. *Dusky, swarthy.

tax, *n.* **Tax, levy, assessment, rate, excise, impost, customs, duty, tariff, toll, tribute, tithe, teind, cess** come into comparison when they mean a compulsory contribution exacted by some recognized authority or by some superior power chiefly for the purpose of providing revenue. **Tax** is the ordinary comprehensive term for such a contribution when it is imposed on the citizens or inhabitants of a state by the government, is laid upon their property, income, valuables, transactions, and the like, is payable in money, and is usually determinable in amount by some method of proportioning or of distribution of the burden; as, a sales *tax;* an income *tax;* a poll *tax.* **Levy** stresses compulsory raising and collecting; as here compared, it is applied chiefly to special or emergency taxes but it may also be applied to any contribution that is collected by the exercise of legal or constituted authority, or by the exercise of force, as by an invader or conqueror, and that consists of money or of supplies or even of men to serve in the army or navy; as, to propose a capital *levy* upon the people to bear the cost of a war; "the other ancient *levies* were in the nature of a modern land-tax" (*Blackstone*); "domestic debt redemption *levies*...are highly injudicious" (*Shaw*). **Assessment** is applicable to any money levy made on an individual by constituted authority; etymologically it implies a prorating of the amount, but this implication is not invariably conveyed; as, a real-estate tax is an *assessment* upon property; the stockholders' *assessment* to cover bank losses was fifty percent of the par value of their shares; the society levied an *assessment* on its members of one dollar each to pay for the entertainment. **Rate,** which is in British use, is distinctively applied to a tax on property assessed at so much in the pound of valuation, and levied especially for local purposes; thus, *borough rates* in England roughly correspond to *city taxes* in the United States; a *ratepayer* in England is the equivalent of the American *taxpayer* when the latter term, as is usual, implies reference to property owners. An **excise** is a tax levied on the manufacture, sale, use, and consumption of certain commodities, such as liquor, cigarettes, and automobiles, or on the pursuit of various occupations or sports, such as liquor-selling and hunting, that require a license to be legally engaged in. An **impost** in its specific and more common sense is a tax levied on imports; it is also called **customs** (now rarely, if ever, in the singular form, *custom*) or a **duty;** as, to pay the *impost*, or the *customs*, or a heavy *duty*, on diamonds bought in Amsterdam. In general usage, however, *impost* is often more inclusive and refers to any revenue-raising tax laid upon a person indirectly or directly. "In England.... popular language dubs all *imposts* by a non-sovereign body, *rates*, and all *imposts* by a sovereign, or like a colony, quasi-sovereign body, *taxes*, *customs* or *excise*" (*F. Palgrave*). *Customs* was once wider also in its range of application, for it designated any tax levied on goods or merchandise on its way to market, but especially on those being exported from or imported into a country. *Duty*, especially in British use, is a particularly comprehensive term; in general, it includes all taxes known as *customs* and *excises*, and a variety of other taxes on possessions and on certain transactions such as the transfer or succession of property, the legal acknowledgment of deeds and other instruments, or the probate and execution of a will; as, stamp *duties;* death *duties*. **Tariff,** when it designates a tax, specifically means the scheduled duty on an import; as, the *tariff* on raw wool was generally regarded as too high. **Toll,** which now commonly denotes a tax paid for a privilege, such as a right to use a public highway or a bridge, was once so general in its application that it covered any of the various taxes now known as *customs* and *excises*. "When the King raised his *tolls* on foreign merchandise the courts still decided in his favour" (*Belloc*). **Tribute,** as here compared, is now chiefly historical or figurative in its use. Originally it denoted a tax levied upon a people not for their own or their ruler's use but for payment to another government or ruler in acknowledgment of their subjection to or dependence upon it or him. "Millions for defence, but not one cent for *tribute*" (*inscribed on memorial of Charles Cotesworth Pinckney*). **Tithe,** or in Scots use, **teind** (literally a tenth of something) historically designates either a voluntary or a compulsory contribution for religious or charitable uses paid in money or in kind, representing a tenth of the annual increase arising from the profits of one's stock, one's industry, or the like. In British or other ecclesiastical and legal use, it came to mean any tax levied for the support of the church or of its charities. **Cess,** which is chiefly in Irish, but also in Scottish and English dialectal use, is in Ireland the equivalent of *rate*, and in Scotland the equivalent of *land tax*. It always implies assessment (with which it is etymologically associated) and in some extended use connotes extortionate levying of money and supplies for specific purposes.

teach. Teach, instruct, educate, train, discipline, school are here compared as meaning to cause others (or sometimes oneself) to acquire knowledge or skill. **Teach** implies a direct showing to another, with the intent that he will learn; it usually suggests the imparting of information, but in addition, it often also connotes the giving of any help that will be of assistance to the learner in mastering such difficulties as are involved, in putting the new knowledge to use, or in making it a part of his mental or physical equipment; as, the older child is *teaching* the younger one how to read; to *teach* arithmetic; to *teach* the Gospel; to *teach* dancing. "The common notion is that Darwin *teaches* that all history is development towards a goal" (*Inge*). **Instruct** stresses the furnishing, especially the methodical furnishing, of necessary knowledge or skill to a person or persons; as, a reserve officer was sent to *instruct* the boys in military tactics. "Schoolmasters will I keep within my house, Fit to *instruct* her youth" (*Shak.*). "He is wise who can *instruct* us and assist us in the business of daily virtuous living" (*Carlyle*). **Educate,** although it implies or presupposes teaching or instruction as the means, in discriminating use stresses the intention or the result, the bringing out or development of qualities or capacities latent in the individual or regarded as essential to his position in life; as, to determine that his children should be *educated* in the best schools available; schools that *educate* boys for the ministry or priesthood. "In my eyes the question is not what to teach, but how to *Educate*" (*Kingsley*). **Train,** on the other hand, even when it is used as a close synonym of *educate*, almost invariably suggests a distinct end or aim which guides teachers and instructors; it implies, therefore, such subjection of the pupil as will form him or fit him for the state in mind; as, "*Train* up a child in the way he should go" (*Proverbs* xxii. 6); "Universities exist...on the one hand, to *train* men and women for certain professions" (*B. Russell*). In current use, *train* is especially employed in reference to the instruction of persons (sometimes, animals) who must be physically in best condition, mentally proficient, quickly responsive to orders, or the like, for a given occupation or kind of work; as, to subject new recruits to three months' intensive *training;* to *train* dogs to catch hares; to keep members of a football squad in *training* from early September until the end of November. **Discipline,** even more than *train*, implies subordination to a master or subjection to control, often self-control. "Great natural genius's that were never *disciplined* and broken by rules of art" (*Addison*). "He consciously seeks to *discipline* himself in fine thinking and right living" (*H. Ellis*). "One must not let one's thoughts run on like this; one must *discipline* one's mind" (*V. Sackville-West*). **School,** though it is not infrequently found in the sense of *educate* (as, "some of them have been *schooled* at Eton and Harrow"—*Shaw*) and in the sense of *teach* or *instruct* (as, "*Schooled* by my guide, it was not difficult to realise the scene"—*S. C. Hall*), is now chiefly used in the sense of *train* or *discipline*, often, however, with the added implication of enduring that which is hard to bear. "That I can bear. I can *school* myself to worse than that" (*Wilde*). "He had to *school* himself into keeping quiet when Miss Youghal went out riding with some man who tried to flirt with her" (*Kipling*).

Ana. Impart, *communicate: *practice, drill, exercise: inculcate, instill, *implant.

tear, *v.* **Tear, rip, rend, split, cleave, rive** agree in meaning to separate forcibly one part of a continuous material or substance from another, or one object from another with which it is closely and firmly associated. **Tear** implies pulling apart as by main force; it often suggests jagged, rough edges or, literally or figuratively, laceration; as, to *tear* one's coat; to *tear* a piece of paper lengthwise; to *tear* one's skin on a nail; "he took hold of it [a bush] with his powerful hands and *tore* it out by the roots" (*S. Anderson*); so furious that he could *tear* the hair from his head; to *tear* oneself away from one's home; the grief *tears* her heart. **Rip** usually implies a forcible pulling or breaking or cutting apart, sometimes but not always along a line or juncture (such as a seam, a joint, a connection); as, "Macduff was from his mother's womb Untimely *ripp'd*" (*Shak.*); to *rip* one's gloves (or a garment, or a sail); to *rip* the shingles from a roof; to *rip* a nearly healed incision. **Rend** is elevated or poetical; the term not only implies greater violence than *tear* but it either heightens the implication of a lacerating effect or adds that of severing or sundering; as, "Thou... didst *rend* thy clothes" (*2 Chronicles* xxxiv. 27); "*Rend* your heart, and not your garments" (*Joel* ii. 13); "The black volume of clouds...*rent* asunder by flashes of lightning" (*Irving*); "The unborn child from whom I had been *rent*" (*Dickens*); "his pride and vanity had been *rent* by her ultimate rejection" (*H. G. Wells*). **Split** implies a breaking apart or fracture through the entire length or, less commonly, width or depth, especially in the direction of grain or layers; as, the vessel was *split* in two by the collision; to *split* a log with a wedge; great rocks *split* by an earthquake. Figuratively, the term implies force or intensity sufficient to split, as one's heart with grief, one's sides (or body) with laughter, one's head with pain, or the air with noise; as, "Let sorrow *split* my heart, if ever I Did hate thee" (*Shak.*); a *splitting* headache; air-*splitting* outcries. **Cleave** (commonly somewhat rhetorical) emphasizes more strongly than *split* the idea of sundering, especially of hewing asunder. "William de Tracy...struck the final blow, *cleaving* the Archbishop's [Becket's] skull" (*Lucas*). "To *cleave* a creed in sects and cries [packs]" (*Tennyson*). **Rive** is elevated or poetical for *cleave* or *rend;* as, "Blunt wedges *rive* hard knots" (*Shak.*). "All thoughts to *rive* the heart are here, and all are vain" (*Housman*). "Rock of ages, *cleft* for me, Let me hide myself in Thee; Let the water and the blood, From thy *riven* side which flowed, Be of sin the double cure" (*Toplady*).

Ana. Slit, slash, *cut: *pull, drag: damage, *injure, impair.

tease. Tantalize, pester, plague, harass, harry, *worry, annoy.

Ana. *Bait, badger, hector, chevy: importune, adjure, *beg: fret, chafe, gall (see ABRADE).

techy *or* **tetchy.** *Irascible, choleric, splenetic, testy, touchy, cranky, cross.

Ana. & ***Ant.*** See those at TOUCHY.

tedious. *Irksome, tiresome, wearisome, humdrum.

Ana. Burdensome, *onerous, oppressive: fatiguing, exhausting, fagging, jading (see TIRE, *v.*): *slow, dilatory, deliberate.

Ant. Exciting.

tedium. **Tedium, boredom, ennui, doldrums** come into comparison when they denote a state of dissatisfaction and weariness. **Tedium** suggests a repression of energy for lack of a proper or adequate outlet, and dullness or lowness of spirits resulting from irksome inactivity or from the irksome monotony of one's pursuits or surroundings; as, he could not endure the *tedium* of waiting for more than fifteen minutes; since reading and visitors were prohibited, there was nothing to relieve the *tedium* of her weeks in bed (cf. *tedium vitae* [Latin *taedium vitae*], that is, a feeling of the irksome monotony or of the futility of life). "Able boys and girls will go through endless *tedium*...to acquire some coveted knowledge or skill" (*B. Russell*). **Boredom** adds to *tedium* suggestions of listlessness, dreariness, and unrest, resulting either from a lack of interest in one's pursuits or surroundings or from the fact that they now pall or fail to excite interest. "I suppose I shall go on 'existing' till the *boredom* of it becomes too great" (*J. R. Green*). "Evidence... that the natives of that unfortunate archipelago [Melanesia] are dying out principally for the reason that the 'Civilization' forced upon them has deprived them of all interest in life. They are dying from pure *boredom*" (*T. S. Eliot*). **Ennui** stresses profound dissatisfaction, discontent, or weariness of spirit; usually it suggests physical depression, languor, or lassitude, as well as boredom. "That *ennui*, that terrible taedium vitae, that comes on those to whom life denies nothing" (*Wilde*). "The inexhaustible power and activity of his mind leave him [Pascal] no leisure for *ennui*" (*Arnold*). **Doldrums** applies to a mood or fit of ennui, usually suggesting a flagging of energy, an access of dullness, and a depressing letdown physically and mentally; as, after he has finished writing a new book, he is always in the *doldrums*.

Ana. Irksomeness, tediousness, tiresomeness, wearisomeness (see corresponding adjectives at IRKSOME): melancholy, dumps, blues, gloom, vapors (see SADNESS).

teem. **Teem, abound, superabound, swarm, overflow** come into comparison when they denote to be plentifully supplied (*with*) or to be rich (*in*). Though they are often interchangeable, each of these words carries distinctive implications. **Teem** implies productiveness or fecundity; as, the rivers *teem* with fish; his mind *teems* with schemes. In looser use, it often suggests little more than crowding and activity. "Tozeur, which has a railway station and positively *teems* with French officials" (*A. Huxley*). **Abound** implies excess of sufficiency in numbers or amount; usually it stresses profusion. "Distant forests aglow with tropical colours and *abounding* with strange forms of life" (*Jefferies*). It is often used with reference to qualities; as, the young soldiers *abound* in vigor and courage. Unlike all the other words except its intensive **superabound,** it can be predicated of that which exists in abundance as well as of that which possesses in abundance. "Waste, unreason, moral conflict everywhere *abound*" (*J. A. Hobson*). This is especially true of its participial adjective *abounding*. "The life of ultimate simplicity, which brought its own *abounding* satisfaction" (*Arch. Marshall*). **Swarm** in its extended sense implies even more strongly than *teem* motion and thronging. "A market-place *swarming* with buyers and sellers" (*Macaulay*). It is also more capable of suggesting infestation; as, the house *swarmed* with flies. **Overflow** in its figurative sense adds to *abound* the implication of exceeding capacity; as, he *overflows* with good nature; sometimes it suggests glutting; as, the market *overflows* with goods.

Ana. *Bear, produce, yield, turn out: *generate, engender, breed, propagate: multiply, augment, *increase.

teeny. Tiny, little, diminutive, *small, petite, wee, weeny, minute, microscopic, miniature.

teeter, *v.* *Shake, tremble, quake, totter, quiver, shiver, shudder, quaver, wobble, shimmy, didder, dither.

teind, *n.* Tithe, *tax, levy, assessment, rate, excise, impost, customs, duty, toll, tariff, tribute, cess.

tell, *v.* **1** *Count, enumerate, number.

2 Divulge, discover, *reveal, disclose, betray, bewray.

Ana. Impart, *communicate: *relate, rehearse, recite, recount: *inform, acquaint, apprise.

telling. Convincing, cogent, sound, *valid.

Ana. Forceful, forcible, *powerful, potent: *effective, effectual, efficacious: *conclusive, decisive, determinative, definitive.

temerarious. Rash, reckless, foolhardy, daredevil, daring, venturesome, venturous, *adventurous.

Ana. Audacious, bold, intrepid (see BRAVE): *precipitate, headlong, abrupt, impetuous.

Ant. Cautious.

temerity. **Temerity, audacity, hardihood, effrontery, nerve, cheek, gall** are here compared only as meaning conspicuous or flagrant boldness in speech, behavior, action, or the like. **Temerity** usually implies contempt of danger and consequent rashness, but often it suggests, especially when a proposal or project is under discussion, a failure to estimate one's chances of success; as, such *temerity* in attack could be expected only of young and inexperienced leaders; he had the *temerity* to propose to the richest and most popular girl in the town. "Tenth-rate critics and compilers, for whom any violent shock to the public taste would be a *temerity* not to be risked" (*Arnold*). **Audacity** implies either a bold and open disregard of the restraints imposed by prudence, convention, decorum, sound morals, or the like, or undue presumption in making advances; as, *audacity* in dress or in speech; "he had committed the supreme *audacity* of looking into her soul" (*V. Sackville-West*). "'Lew... there's the colonel coming....Let's go and talk to 'im.' Lew nearly fell out of the tree at the *audacity* of the suggestion" (*Kipling*). **Hardihood** stresses firmness of purpose and often additionally implies considered defiance of conventions, decorum, and the like. It may be used without depreciative intent, but it is frequently employed as a term of contempt almost equivalent to impudence; as, it took *hardihood* in Copernicus to deny the current conception that the earth stood still and that the sun and planets revolved about it; he had the *hardihood* to question his mother's motives in her presence. "The reviewers [of *Leonora*, 1903]...were staggered by my *hardihood* in offering a woman of forty as a subject of serious interest to the public" (*Bennett*). **Effrontery** is invariably derogatory; it is used in place of any of the three preceding words when one wishes to impute to another shameless disregard of the laws of courtesy, propriety, fair dealing, or the like, or an arrogant assumption of a privilege. "You had the *effrontery* to pose as the avenger of outraged morality" (*Shaw*). "She had won her way to success by strength of will and hardness of heart, and a kind of haughty *effrontery*" (*E. Wharton*). "Oxford, unable to endure the cool *effrontery* of a Yankee schoolmaster's dabbling in affairs peculiarly English, did not reply [to Noah Webster's suggestion of a combined effort to standardize English spelling]" (*H. R. Warfel*). **Nerve, cheek,** and **gall** are slang terms for *effrontery*, *nerve*, however, often carrying a strong suggestion of hardihood, *cheek* of impudence, and *gall* of outrageous insolence; as, he had the *nerve* to criticize his superiors; his *cheek* makes him objectionable to his superiors; the summer people had the *gall* to treat the residents as their inferiors.

Ana. Rashness, recklessness, foolhardiness, daring, venturesomeness (see corresponding adjectives at ADVENTUROUS): precipitateness, impetuosity, abruptness (see corresponding adjectives at PRECIPITATE): impertinence, intrusiveness, officiousness (see corresponding adjectives at IMPERTINENT).

Ant. Caution.

temper, *v.* **1** *Moderate, qualify, attemper.

Ana. *Adjust, regulate, fix: mitigate, alleviate, lighten, assuage, allay, *relieve: mollify, *pacify, appease.

Ant. Intensify.

2 Temper, anneal, in technical use, agree in meaning to bring glass, steel, copper, or other metal, to the required degree of hardness or toughness by heating and cooling. **Temper** is often used generally in reference to this process, regardless of the specific consistency sought or of the speed of the heating or cooling. In glassmaking, however, it specifically implies a gradual heating and a gradual cooling so that the glass may be rendered less brittle. In steel manufacture, *temper*, strictly, implies merely a gentle reheating of hardened steel to the desired consistency; it is therefore distinguished on the one hand from the prior process of *hardening* by heating and sudden cooling, and on the other from the complete process including hardening and its subsequent tempering; thus, one *tempers* hardened steel intended for razors by reheating it to 450°, and that intended for swords or springs to 570°. **Anneal** stresses the intent to toughen or make less brittle; it implies a subjection to high heat and either a gradual cooling as in the case of glass or steel or a sudden quenching as in the case of copper or brass. *Anneal* in reference to glass usually implies a reduction of brittleness that has resulted from a prior treatment.

temper, *n.* **1** *Mood, humor, vein.

Ana. Mettle, spirit (see COURAGE): emotion, *feeling, affection, passion: attitude, *position, stand.

2 *Disposition, temperament, complexion, character, personality, individuality.

Ana. Constitution, composition (see corresponding verbs at COMPOSE): *state, condition, posture, situation: *quality, property, attribute.

temperament. *Disposition, temper, complexion, character, personality, individuality.

Ana. Composition, constitution (see corresponding verbs at COMPOSE): *mind, soul: nature, kind, *type.

temperance. Temperance, sobriety, abstinence, abstemiousness, continence agree in expressing self-restraint in the gratification of appetites or passions. In its more exact sense, **temperance** implies simply habitual moderation and the exercise of judgment; as, *temperance* in eating and drinking or in any pleasure. "Exaggeration, exaltation, the fanatic spirit, are extremely rare. *Temperance* is the almost universal rule in speech, demeanor, taste, and habits" (*Brownell*). *Temperance* sometimes, but now less frequently, implies teetotalism; as, a *temperance* movement; a *temperance* hotel is one where no intoxicating liquors are sold or served. **Sobriety,** like *temperance*, suggests avoidance of excess, not only, as originally, in drinking but also in thought or action. Often it connotes the idea of seriousness or of avoidance of ostentation; as, *sobriety* of demeanor; *sobriety* in dress. **Abstinence** usually implies voluntary deprivation. "Their poor ancestors, whose life was passed in melancholy *abstinence* from the joys of this beautiful earth" (*Arnold*). "The Cynic preached *abstinence* from all common ambitions, rank, possessions, power, the things which clog man's feet" (*Buchan*). **Abstemiousness** now suggests habitual self-restraint, or moderation or frugality, especially in eating or drinking. "Instances of longevity are chiefly among the *abstemious*" (*Arbuthnot*). "The meal of the Saracen was *abstemious*" (*Scott*). **Continence** emphasizes self-restraint in regard to one's impulses or desires. "He knew what to say, so he knows also when to leave off, a *continence* which is practised by few writers" (*Dryden*). In its specific sense it stresses self-restraint in sexual indulgence. Sometimes it implies chastity or complete abstention; often, when referred to husband and wife, it implies avoidance of undue indulgence. "Chastity is either *abstinence* or *continence*. *Abstinence* is that of virgins or widows; *continence*, of married persons" (*Jer. Taylor*).

Ana. Forgoing, forbearing *or* forbearance, sacrificing *or* sacrifice, eschewal (see corresponding verbs at FORGO): frugality, sparingness, thriftiness (see corresponding adjectives at SPARING): restrained, curbed, checked (see RESTRAIN).

temperate. 1 *Moderate.

Ana. Mild, gentle, lenient, *soft: *steady, even, equable, constant: restrained, curbed, checked (see RESTRAIN).

Ant. Intemperate: inordinate.

2 *Sober, continent, unimpassioned.

Ana. *Sparing, frugal, economical: abstaining, refraining, forbearing (see REFRAIN): dispassionate, just, equitable, *fair.

temporal. 1 *Temporary.
Ana. *Earthly, mundane, worldly, mortal: transitory, *transient, ephemeral, passing.
Ant. Eternal.
2 *Profane, secular, lay.
Ana. *Material, objective, physical, corporeal.
Ant. Spiritual.

temporary. 1 **Temporary, temporal** are sometimes confused in the sense of existing or enduring for a limited time only. **Temporary** (see also TEMPORARY, 2) is the commoner of these terms. It is opposed in meaning to *permanent* and *lasting* and applies equally well to that which serves only an immediate need and to that which endures over a very long space of time but is bound to come to an end; as, a scaffolding is a *temporary* structure; "Like the planet Mercury surrounded by the lustre of sunset, her permanent brilliancy passed without much notice in the *temporary* glory of the situation" (*Hardy*). "But, unfortunately, owing to a recent though quite *temporary* coldness between the Chaplain-General and the Potter press, Mr. Potter's wire-pulling was ineffectual" (*R. Macaulay*). "Where such deep-rooted tendencies as fetishism are concerned, all that reformers can hope to abolish is the *temporary* form, not the biding substance" (*A. Huxley*). **Temporal,** in its stricter use, implies an opposition to *eternal:* it is chiefly used when there is a reference to the difference between things of this life and things of eternity and is found chiefly in idiomatic expressions; thus, *temporal* matters refer to those which are related to life on earth as opposed to those which are related to the future life; "the *temporal* punishment due to sin" usually refers to the punishment for sin endured in one's life and, in Roman Catholic use, also in Purgatory, as opposed to the eternal punishment suffered in Hell. Consequently, *temporal* often implies an opposition to *immaterial* or *spiritual* as well as to *eternal;* as, "we may, therefore, whenever we wish, treat the *temporal* as if it were potentially the eternal" (*W. James*); "it is the only way in which I can think of the relation of the world of becoming to the world of being, of the *temporal* to the eternal" (*Inge*). Often, *temporal* (for this sense, see PROFANE, 1) is used in the sense of being concerned with temporal, or worldly, as opposed to spiritual, or eternal, affairs, matters, or concerns, and is applied to sovereigns, rulers, or others who deal with these affairs, in opposition to those whose concerns are mostly spiritual; as, *temporal* lords (or lords *temporal*); "His sceptre shows the force of *temporal* power, The attribute to awe and majesty" (*Shak.*). Consequently, *temporal* is often used in the sense of *secular, lay,* or *civil* as distinguished from *clerical* or *ecclesiastical,* sometimes with little reference to the time element. "If such *temporal* pride is ridiculous, surely the spiritual is odious and detestable" (*Fielding*). "The court of Madrid, unlike that of Vienna, would have thought more of *temporal* aims than of ecclesiastical" (*Belloc*).
Ana. Transitory, *transient, ephemeral, passing: *brief, short.
Ant. Permanent, lasting.
2 **Temporary, provisional, ad interim, acting, supply** are here compared as applied to a person holding a post for a limited time, to the post held by that person, or to his appointment. **Temporary** merely implies that the post is not held on tenure but may be terminated at the will of those having the appointive power. It is interchangeable with many of the other words but is not so explicit; as, a *temporary* position; *temporary* clerks; a *temporary* appointment. **Provisional** is applied chiefly to a government or to the head (or leading officials) of a government that is set up in a new state, or after a revolution, until a permanent government can be established; as, following the revolution of September, 1930, the *provisional* president of Argentina was José F. Uriburu. **Ad interim** definitely suggests appointment for an intervening period, as between the death or resignation of an incumbent and the appointment or election of his successor; as, an *ad interim* pastor. In the United States it is also applied to an appointment made by the president when the Senate is not in session and confirmation is not possible until after the recess; as, an *ad interim* appointment as ambassador. **Acting** is applied to the person who during a vacancy in an office, or during the absence of the incumbent, assumes temporarily by appointment or by fixed procedure the powers given the person regularly appointed or elected; as, the president of the common council becomes *acting* mayor when the mayor is on vacation. **Supply** implies the performance of duties of another or service as a locum tenens; as, a *supply* pastor; a *supply* teacher.
Ant. Permanent.

tempt. Entice, inveigle, *lure, decoy, seduce.
Ana. Allure, *attract: *invite, solicit, court, woo: *induce, persuade, prevail on *or* upon.

tenacious. Tough, stout, *strong, sturdy, stalwart.
Ana. Dogged, pertinacious, *obstinate, stubborn: resolute, stanch, steadfast, leal, true (see FAITHFUL): persevering, persisting (see PERSEVERE).

tenacity. Resolution, spirit, mettle, *courage.
Ana. Pluck, grit, guts, sand, *fortitude, backbone: *decision, determination: hardihood, audacity, nerve (see TEMERITY).

tend. **Tend, attend, mind, watch** are here compared only as meaning to take charge of or look after someone or something, especially as a duty or in return for a wage, fee, or other remuneration. In general, **tend** is not only more colloquial than *attend,* but it usually suggests a more menial employment and takes for its object something that requires routine or unskilled care as in looking out for accidents, mishaps, signs of danger, or the like, or merely mechanical operation; thus, one who *tends* a lock is employed to work the devices adjusting the level of the water in the canal when a boat approaches; a shepherd is one who *tends* a flock of sheep; a stoker is one who *tends* a furnace (especially on a ship) and supplies it with fuel when needed. "Standard-roses *tended* by her hands" (*Meredith*). *Tend* is used in reference to the care of persons only when a menial or a ministering rather than a professional relationship is implied; as, to employ a girl to *tend* to the children for a few hours each day; sacrificing her leisure to *tend* the sick and helpless poor in their homes. **Attend,** since it seldom loses its earliest implication of turning the mind to, is the appropriate word when the services given are of a professional character, or are the prerogatives of a post that one holds as a mark of honor or merit; as, Dr. White *attended* the governor in his last illness; ladies-in-waiting are ladies of high degree who as members of the royal household *attend* a queen or princess. *Attend to* (*tend to* is dialectal in this sense) often carries not only the idea of looking after or taking charge of, but also the idea either of disposing of the work that is entailed (as, he has *attended to* [not *tended to*] all the letters awaiting answer) or of giving one's full attention to the matter or person concerned; as, *attend* strictly *to* (not *tend* strictly *to*) business; he asked his assistant to *attend to* (not *tend to*) patients coming in between three and four. **Mind** is closer to *tend* than to *attend,* but it usually implies more casual looking after or less close attention to duties; as, a kind neighbor *minds* the children when their mother is away. "The men...were gone to dinner: I stayed to *mind* the furnace" (*Edgeworth*). **Watch** (in its earliest sense, to be or keep awake), as here compared (see also SEE, 2), implies the charge of something or of someone that may be in danger, such as a factory in danger of fire or of burglary or a sick person in danger of a sudden relapse or change for the worse. The term, therefore, always implies need of vigilance and usually suggests the intention of forestalling danger; as, three men were needed to *watch* the factory when the machines were idle; he was so ill that a night nurse was needed to *watch* him as well as care for him. "Wilt thou receive this weighty trust when I am o'er the sea? To *watch* and ward my castle strong, and to protect my land" (*Scott*).

Ana. *Defend, protect, shield, guard, safeguard: *nurse, nurture, foster, cherish, cultivate.

tendency. **Tendency, trend, drift, tenor, current** come into comparison chiefly when they mean a movement or course having a particular direction and character, or the direction and character which such a movement or course takes. **Tendency** usually implies an inherent, or acquired, or given (supplied) inclination in a person or thing that causes him or it to move in a definite direction so long as no one or nothing interferes. Often when used in reference to persons, the word means little more than *leaning, propensity,* or *disposition* (as, "My *tendency* is to unite extremes rather than to go between them"—*H. Ellis;* "he worked to destroy the *tendency* to dreams in himself"—*S. Anderson*) but, even more often, especially when used in reference to groups or communities or their activities, or the course or direction they take with or without consciousness or intent, the term implies a great driving force behind the direction or course taken and an insusceptibility to its being controlled or changed (as, to ask whether the *tendency* of civilization is upward or downward; "the fissiparous *tendency* of Protestantism"—*Inge;* "the whole *tendency* of evolution is towards a diminishing birth-rate"—*H. Ellis;* "the *tendencies* which Lycurgus had endeavoured to repress by external regulation reasserted themselves"—*G. L. Dickinson*). **Trend** is used in its literal sense chiefly in reference to something that follows an irregular or winding course and often means little more than general direction maintained in spite of these irregularities; as, the *trend* of the stream at this point is northerly; the general *trend* of the Atlantic coast line of the United States is from the southwest to the northeast. As here especially considered, *trend* differs from *tendency* in implying a direction subject to change through the interposition of any sufficiently strong force or agency, or a course taken at a given time by something subject to change and fluctuation, or the general direction followed by a changing or fluctuating thing throughout its entire course or within given limits of space or of time; as, to give a talk on the *trend* (or *trends*) of current fiction; the general *trend* of democracy has been from decentralization of power to centralization; he could observe no clear *trend* in the market for securities during the last six weeks. "Aristotle, the most balanced of all the Greek thinkers and the best exponent of the normal *trend* of their ideas" (*G. L. Dickinson*). **Drift** may apply to a tendency the direction or course of which is determined by external influences such as a wind or the movement of flowing water (figuratively more often than literally), a fashion, a state of feeling, or the like (as, "The whole drift of their institution is contrary to that of the wise legislators of all countries"—*Burke;* "programme music...shows most clearly the *drift* of music along with the other arts toward impressionism"—*Babbitt;* "the whole *drift* of our law is toward the absolute prohibition of all ideas that diverge in the slightest from the accepted platitudes"—*Mencken*), but it also may apply to the direction or course taken by something such as speech, writing, teaching, and the like, that has a meaning, a purpose, or an objective which is not definitely stated or made clear but which is to be gathered or inferred by auditors, readers, observers, or the like: in this sense, the word often means *intention, purport,* or *import;* as, "For the *drift* of the Maker is dark, an Isis hid by a veil" (*Tennyson*); few readers failed to catch the *drift* of the new book on the American Revolution; "I see the whole *drift* of your argument" (*Goldsmith*); the *drift* of the book, though not expressly stated, was Communistic. **Tenor** is a very close synonym of *drift* in this latter sense, but it more often refers to utterances or documents, and carries a much stronger implication of clearness of meaning or purport; as, "According to the *tenor* of the charter...the trustees might, without impropriety, appoint a president and other professors from their own body" (*Ch. Just. Marshall*). Both in this sense and in its more common sense of a course or movement having a particular clearly observable direction, *tenor* carries a strong implication of continuity in that course and of absence of fluctuation in its direction; therefore it frequently suggests unaltered, often unalterable, procedure. "Along the cool sequester'd vale of life They kept the noiseless *tenor* of their way" (*Gray*). "Not keep a journal! How are your absent cousins to understand the *tenour* of your life in Bath without one?" (*Austen*). **Current** (literally, the movement or direction of flowing water; as, to row against the *current*) carries a stronger implication than the other words of a movement or course that is clearly defined, though not necessarily unalterable, in its direction and that has the distinct identity as well as the substantial quality of any natural course of running water such as a river; as, "the kind of genius...that makes its way there [in France]...against the *current* of opinion and the whole *drift* of feeling" (*Brownell*); "those who have isolated themselves from all the *currents* of modern thought" (*Inge*); "When...fifteen, he...had an adventure that changed the whole *current* of his life" (*S. Anderson*).

Ana. *Leaning, propensity, penchant, proclivity: inclination, disposition, predisposition (see corresponding verbs at INCLINE): bent, turn, genius, aptitude (see GIFT).

tender, *v.* *Offer, proffer, present, prefer.

Ana. Propose, purpose, design (see INTEND): *suggest, intimate.

tender, *n.* *Overture, approach, advance, bid.

tender, *adj.* **Tender, compassionate, sympathetic, warm, warmhearted, responsive** are here compared in the sense of expressing or expressive of feeling that reveals affectionate interest in another, especially in his joys, sorrows, welfare, or the like. **Tender** implies a sensitiveness to influences that awaken one's softer emotions, such as love (sometimes called, though now chiefly humorously, "the *tender* passion"), affection, pity, or kindliness, and, often, a capacity for expressing such emotions with a delicacy and gentleness that are especially grateful to the person concerned; as, "His mother was very *tender* with him....she saw the effort it was costing" (*D. H. Lawrence*); "there always remained with me, long after I outgrew his [Longfellow's] poems, a *tender* memory for that first friend of wistful and pensive puberty" (*H. Ellis*); "The inflections of their voices, when they were talking to each other very privately, were often *tender*, and these sudden surprising *tendernesses* secretly thrilled both of them" (*Bennett*). **Compassionate** implies a temperament or a disposition that is either easily moved by the sufferings or hardships of another or is quick to show pity with tenderness or mercy; as, "He was quite incapable of any *compassionate* feeling about the boy, or about his fate" (*Dickens*); "Out of the hardships of his boyhood...he had preserved a clean sense of honour and a *compassionate* heart" (*Cather*); "To wax *compassionate* over a bird, and remain hard as flint to a beast, is possible only to humanity" (*A. Repplier*). **Sympathetic** is a much more comprehensive term than *compassionate* for it implies a temperament or a disposition that enables one to enter into the life of another and share not only his sorrows but his joys and his interests, as well as his antipathies, and the like, and to give the other the impression that he is not alone or that he is being fairly and justly understood. "Maud was very *sympathetic*. That was what made Tony like her so much—that she was always interested in what he had to tell her" (*Arch. Marshall*). "Thus a tête-à-tête with a man of similar tastes, who is just and yet *sympathetic*, critical yet appreciative...is a high intellectual pleasure" (*A. C. Benson*). *Sympathetic* is also applicable to attitudes, treatments, and the like, that reveal not only an ability to enter into the lives of others and share their emotions but a capacity for appraising or treating men and their experiences with great fairness and understanding; as, "a penetrating and profoundly *sympathetic* portrayal of the shifting, fluctuating impulses of a woman yielding both against and with her will" (*Lowes*). **Warm** implies a capacity for feeling and expressing love, affection, interest, or the like, with depth, ardor, or fervency: it suggests less softness of feeling or compassion than *tender*, but more heartiness, cordiality, or force. "Captain Harville, though not equalling Captain Wentworth in manners, was a perfect gentleman, unaffected, *warm*, and obliging" (*Austen*). "We common people are all one way or the other—*warm* or cold, passionate or frigid" (*Hardy*). "A wave of genial friendliness flowed from the *warm* silly hearts of Britons towards the conquered foe" (*R. Macaulay*). **Warmhearted** differs little from *warm* in meaning, but it usually carries a stronger implication of generosity, unselfishness, and, often, compassionateness; as, a kind, *warmhearted* woman; "He's of a rash, *warm-hearted* nature, like Esau" (*G. Eliot*); "That's the way I've gone through life. Experience has never put a chill upon my *warm-heartedness*" (*Dickens*). **Responsive** differs from the preceding terms in usually suggesting sensitiveness to another's display of tenderness, compassion, sympathy, warmth, or the like, and a capacity for responding to that emotion: it, therefore, stresses impressionableness, and suggests a reaction, rather than a taking of the initiative; as, the child is always *responsive* to affection; "She took up life, and became alert to the world again, *responsive*, like a ship in full sail, to every wind that blew" (*R. Macaulay*).

Ana. Gentle, lenient, mild, *soft: humane, benevolent, *charitable, altruistic: *pitiful, piteous.

Ant. Callous: severe.

tenement. *Rooms, lodgings, chambers, quarters, apartment, flat, diggings, digs.

tenet. *Doctrine, dogma.

Ana. Belief, conviction, persuasion, view (see OPINION): *principle, fundamental, axiom: *creed, confession.

tenor. Drift, current, trend, *tendency.

Ana. Movement, *motion, move: procedure, proceeding (see PROCESS): *meaning, significance, import.

tense, *adj.* **1** *Tight, taut.

Ana. Strained (see corresponding noun at STRAIN): nervous, unquiet, uneasy, jittery (see IMPATIENT).

2 *Stiff, rigid, inflexible, stark, wooden.

Ana. Tough, tenacious, stout (see STRONG): *firm, hard.

Ant. Expansive. — ***Con.*** *Loose, relaxed, lax, slack: *limp, flaccid, flabby.

tension. **1** *Stress, strain, pressure, shear, thrust, torsion.

2 Equilibrium, equipoise, *balance, poise.

tentative. *Provisional.

Ana. *Temporary, ad interim, acting: testing, trying, demonstrating, proving (see PROVE).

Ant. Definitive.

tenuous. *Thin, rare, slender, slim, slight.

Ana. *Subtle, subtile: ethereal, aerial, *airy.

Ant. Dense.

tergiversation. *Ambiguity, equivocation, amphibology, amphibologism, double-entendre.

term, *n.* **1** End, confine, bound, *limit, bourn.

2 *Word, vocable.

termagant. *Virago, scold, shrew, vixen, barge, amazon.

terminal, *adj.* Final, concluding, *last, latest, eventual, ultimate, extreme.

Ana. Closing, ending, terminating, concluding (see CLOSE).

Ant. Initial.

terminate. End, *close, conclude, finish, complete.

Ana. *Abolish, extinguish, abate: dissolve, prorogue, *adjourn: *stop, cease, discontinue.

termination. *End, ending, terminus.

Ana. Result, issue, outcome (see EFFECT): concluding *or* conclusion, completion, closing *or* close (see corresponding verbs at CLOSE).

Ant. Inception: source.

terminus. *End, termination, ending.

Ant. Starting-point.

terrace. **1** Embankment, bank, *mound, dune, tumulus, barrow.

2 Avenue, boulevard, drive, parkway, *road, roadway, highway, highroad, street, thoroughfare, byway, lane, alley, alleyway.

terrestrial. Also **terrene.** *Earthly, earthy, mundane, worldly, mortal, sublunary.

Ant. Celestial.

terrible. Terrific, frightful, dreadful, *fearful, awful, horrible, horrific, shocking, appalling.

Ana. Frightening, alarming, startling (see FRIGHTEN): agitating, upsetting, disturbing, perturbing (see DISCOMPOSE).

terrific. Terrible, frightful, dreadful, *fearful, horrible, horrific, awful, shocking, appalling.

Ana. Frightening, alarming, terrorizing (see FRIGHTEN): *formidable, redoubtable: agitating, upsetting, disquieting (see DISCOMPOSE).

terrify. *Frighten, fright, scare, alarm, terrorize, startle, affray, affright.

Ana. Agitate, upset, perturb, disquiet (see DISCOMPOSE): *dismay, appall, horrify, daunt: cow, *intimidate, browbeat, bulldoze.

territory. **1** Colony, dependency, *possession, dominion, protectorate, mandate.

2 Domain, province, *field, sphere, bailiwick.

Ana. Region, tract, *area, zone, belt: limits, confines, bounds (see singular nouns at LIMIT).

terror. Panic, consternation, *fear, dread, fright, alarm, dismay, horror, trepidation.

Ana. Apprehensiveness, fearfulness (see corresponding adjectives at FEARFUL): agitation, disquiet, perturbation, upsetting *or* upset (see corresponding verbs at DISCOMPOSE): appalling, daunting, dismaying (see DISMAY).

terrorize. Terrify, *frighten, fright, alarm, scare, startle, affray, affright.

Ana. *Intimidate, cow, bulldoze, browbeat: coerce, compel, *force: drive, impel, *move: agitate, upset (see DISCOMPOSE).

terse. *Concise, succinct, laconic, summary, pithy, compendious.
Ana. *Brief, short: *compact, close: *expressive, sententious, meaningful: *incisive, crisp, clear-cut.
test, *n.* Trial, proof, demonstration. See under PROVE.
Ana. Experiment, *experience: examination, inspection, scrutiny (see under SCRUTINIZE): verification, substantiation, corroboration, confirmation (see corresponding verbs at CONFIRM).
test, *v.* Try, *prove, demonstrate.
Ana. Assay, essay (see ATTEMPT, *v.*): examine, inspect, *scrutinize: experiment, experience (see corresponding nouns at EXPERIENCE): verify, substantiate, *confirm.
testify. *Swear, affirm, asseverate, depose, depone.
Ana. *Certify, attest, witness, vouch for.
testimony. *Evidence, deposition, affidavit.
Ana. Trial, test, proof, demonstration (see under PROVE): witnessing *or* witness, attesting *or* attestation, certifying *or* certification, vouching for (see corresponding verbs at CERTIFY).
testy. *Irascible, choleric, splenetic, techy, touchy, cranky, cross.
Ana. *Irritable, peevish, snappish, waspish: hasty, sudden, impetuous (see PRECIPITATE): captious, carping, caviling, faultfinding (see CRITICAL).
tetchy. Variant of TECHY.
text. Topic, argument, theme, *subject, matter, subject matter, motive, leitmotiv.
thalassic. *Aquatic, marine, oceanic, neritic, pelagic, abyssal, bathysmal, bathybic.
thankful. *Grateful.
Ana. Appreciating *or* appreciative, valuing, prizing, cherishing, treasuring (see corresponding verbs at APPRECIATE): satisfied, content (see under SATISFY).
Ant. Thankless.
that. *Who, which.
thaumaturgy. *Magic, sorcery, witchcraft, witchery, wizardry, alchemy.
thaw, *v.* Melt, dissolve, *liquefy, deliquesce, fuse.
Ant. Freeze.
theatrical, *adj.* *Dramatic, dramaturgic, melodramatic, histrionic.
Ana. *Artificial, factitious: formal, conventional, *ceremonial, ceremonious: affecting, pretending, assuming, simulating, feigning (see ASSUME): *showy, pretentious, pompous, ostentatious.
theft. **Theft, larceny, robbery, burglary** come into comparison as meaning the act or crime of stealing, especially as differentiated in legal use. The same differences in implications and applications are observable in the agent nouns **thief, larcener** (now extremely rare), **robber, burglar,** denoting one who steals. **Theft** and **thief** are the most general and the least technical of these terms: they imply the taking and removing of another's property, usually by stealth or without his knowledge, and always without his consent. The terms are often so broad in current use (even in legal use) that they may include reference to any form of taking another's property without his consent, such as pilfering, purloining, swindling, embezzling, or plagiarizing; as, the *theft* of a fellow-employee's purse; the *theft* of the city's money by grafters; a *thief* removed his watch from his pocket; *thieves* of good plots from recent plays. **Larceny** especially, and **larcener,** when now used, are strict legal terms implying theft in the usual sense but excluding swindling, embezzlement, plagiarizing, etc. The terms always connote an unlawful or felonious act, a removal of another's property from the place where it belongs, and complete possession, even for a moment, by the thief; as, she was seen shoplifting but was not apprehended until she had left the store, so that there would be proof of *larceny;* the servant was found guilty of *larceny. Grand larceny* and *petty,* or *petit, larceny,* though now rare in legal use, are common in ordinary use as indicating respectively a theft of an appreciable (formerly a stated) amount, and a theft of a negligible amount. **Robbery** and **robber** in their strict legal use imply the taking of another's property from his person or in his presence by means of violence or intimidation; as, highway *robbery;* the paymaster was attacked and deprived of his payroll money by armed *robbers.* **Burglary** and **burglar** in all legal use imply a breaking and entering with an intent to commit a felony, usually but not invariably (though almost always in popular use), that of larceny or robbery. In the laws of different states and nations the other details vary, such as the time of occurrence (nighttime often being stipulated) or the actual commission of the felony (the accomplishment of the intent usually being regarded as not relevant); as, the *burglary* of their home was committed during their absence for the evening; she lived in constant fear of *burglars.*
the Lord's Day. See *Lord's Day,* at SUNDAY.
theme. 1 Text, topic, argument, *subject, matter, subject matter, motive, leitmotiv.
2 Composition, paper, *essay, article.
then. *Therefore, hence, consequently, accordingly, so.
theorem. *Principle, axiom, fundamental, law.
☞ *Do not confuse* theorem *with* theory.
theoretical. Theoretical (*or* **theoretic**), **speculative, academic** are here compared as applied to minds, types of reasoning or philosophizing, branches of learning, and the like, and as meaning concerned principally with abstractions and theories, sometimes at the expense of their practical basis or application. **Theoretical** (or, less often, **theoretic**), in its most usual and nonderogatory sense, applies to sciences or other branches of learning which deal with the inferences drawn from observed facts and from the results of experiments and with the laws or theories that explain them. In this sense, the term is often opposed to *applied,* which describes sciences or branches of learning which have to do with the putting of these laws and theories into use, as in mechanics, in industry, or in social reform; as, *theoretical* versus applied chemistry; *theoretical* physics has contributed more to modern invention than human ingenuity; applied ethics is grounded upon *theoretical* ethics. "A purely *theoretical* definition would be that a person is emotionally sensitive when many stimuli produce emotions in him" (*B. Russell*). But *theoretical* often implies a divorce from actuality or reality that either makes one unable to see things as they are or to see them only in the terms of one's ideas or theories about them. In this sense it is opposed to *practical.* "My *theoretical* and his practical knowledge together could not have failed. He should have worked upon my plans" (*Austen*). "Life demands from us that we should be prepossessed in favour of goodness and her sisters. But we must study these practical prepossessions without *theoretical* prepossession" (*S. Alexander*). "Things that had seemed drearily *theoretical,* dry, axiomatic, platitudinal, showed themselves to be great generalisations from a torrent of human effort and mortal endeavour" (*A. C. Benson*). **Speculative** (as here considered: see also THOUGHTFUL, 1) goes further than *theoretical* in suggesting a deep interest in theorizing or in forming theories or hypotheses, and often additionally implies a daring use of the imagination; as, "He is too *speculative* a writer to awaken confidence in his results" (*Sir H. Davy*). Oftentimes, however,

there is very little difference evident in the use of these terms. "He [the Roman] was a great inventor and builder, but in the *speculative* and theoretic side of science he had little interest" (*Buchan*). "This is about as far as *speculative* chemistry will take one in this field; and the rest of the subject is experimental" (*C. C. Furnas*). **Academic** (as here considered: see also PEDANTIC) carries a much stronger implication of a habit of looking at a thing, or things in general, abstractly and without reference to real life or practical concerns. "The *academic* philosophers of ethics, had they possessed virility enough to enter the field of real life, would have realised...that the slavery to rigid formulas which they preached was the death of all high moral responsibility" (*H. Ellis*). "Apart from its *academic* tendency to divorce form from matter, I cannot believe that any such theory of poetry, built on a neurosis, is admirable or adequate" (*Day Lewis*).

Ana. Conjectural, hypothetical (see SUPPOSED): postulated, premised, presupposed (see PRESUPPOSE).

theory. *Hypothesis, law.

Ana. Judgment, conclusion, deduction, inference (see under INFER): postulate, presumption, assumption, presupposition (see under PRESUPPOSE).

Ant. Practice.

☞ *Do not confuse* theory *with* theorem.

there. *Thither.

therefore. Therefore, hence, consequently, then, accordingly, so are here compared as adverbs used as connectives to indicate logical or causal sequence or both. They vary in the degree of closeness of connection suggested, as well as in the kind of sequence implied. **Therefore** and **hence** are employed chiefly in strict reasoning to indicate that what follows is a necessary deduction from what has preceded. *Therefore* commonly introduces a conclusion; as, all men are rational beings, John Jones is a man, *therefore* John Jones is a rational being. *Hence,* though often interchangeable with *therefore,* stresses the importance of that which precedes; as, both statements may be false, but both cannot be true since they are contradictory; *hence,* if A be true, B is false, or if B be true, A is false. **Consequently,** though often used to introduce a deduction, does not always imply necessity in the inference. Rather it suggests good grounds for the conclusion or implies a strong antecedent probability; as, he said he would come; *consequently,* I expect him. It also may indicate that what follows is a result of what precedes; as, he was injured in an accident; *consequently* he has not been at his office in months. **Then,** when used to indicate logical sequence, is employed chiefly in the consequent clause or conclusion in a conditional sentence; as, if A is true, *then* B is false. **Accordingly** usually indicates logical or causal sequence, but connotes naturalness or usualness in that which follows as a consequence rather than necessity or inevitability; as, he said he was hungry; *accordingly* they shared their meager lunch with him. **So** is largely colloquial and often indefinite in its suggestion of which kind of sequence is indicated; as, the day was fine and *so* we set out. The use of *so* (by itself) as a connective rather than as an adverb is discountenanced by good writers.

thesaurus. 1 Treasury, archives, *museum, library, gallery.

2 Treasury, garland, *anthology, florilegium, corpus, chrestomathy, chapbook.

Thespian. *Actor, player, impersonator, trouper, performer, mummer, mime.

thick. 1 Thick, thickset, squat, stocky, chunky, stubby, dumpy vary widely in their range of application but they come into comparison as meaning having, as a three-dimensional thing, a measurement relatively large from one side to another. **Thick,** the most general word of this group, implies an opposition to *thin* and a clear distinction from *long:* since it is never employed in reference to plane figures or to surfaces, it may sometimes be used in place of *deep* or *broad* or *wide* when these terms refer to one of the three dimensions of a more or less solid body, substance, or mass; thus, a *thick* board, a *thick* layer, a *thick* covering of snow, suggest reference to the measurement from the top to the bottom or from the outside to the inside (but, one says a *deep* [not *thick*] body of water; a *thick* [not *deep*] icing; a *deep* [not *thick*] box): a *thick* trunk (of a tree), a *thick* pole, a *thick* body (of a man) suggest a relatively wide diameter for a thing of its height or length. *Thick,* and not *thin,* is used in phrases indicating measurements of this dimension or diameter without imputing thickness or thinness to that which is measured; thus, paper 1/20 of a millimeter *thick* is actually very thin paper; flooring four inches *thick* was used in the factory. The remaining terms of the group apply chiefly to persons, animals, trees, plants, figures, etc., which are describable as *thick* in relation to their height. **Thickset** applies chiefly to human bodies that suggest a square in their proportions and straightness of lines and in compactness of build: it usually implies shortness out of proportion to girth, though *short* is often added to *thickset* in descriptions; as, "he was *thick-set* of figure" (*Wilde*); "too *thickset* For jockeying" (*Masefield*). **Squat** applies more generally than *thickset* and is commonly depreciative: it also definitely implies both extreme shortness and thickness suggestive of a squatting person or animal; as, he was *squat* as an image of Buddha; "the *squat* misshapen figure" (*Wilde*); "the round *squat* turret" (*Browning*). **Stocky** applies to men, animals, plants, and the like: it differs little from *thickset* in its suggestions of a square and compact build, but it carries a strong implication of sturdiness or of capacity for work; as, *stocky* horses fitted for hard work on the farms; *stocky* young trees; "they had no titles of honour among them, but such as denoted some bodily strength or perfection, as such an one the Tall, such an one the *Stocky*" (*Addison*). **Chunky, stubby,** and **dumpy** are colloquial synonyms of *squat* that suggest slightly different images; *chunky* connoting a resemblance to a chunk of something (as, a *chunky* child), *stubby* a resemblance to a stub, as of a tree cut off near the roots or of a pencil worn down to two or three inches and, therefore, often implying an appearance of stunted development in height (as, a *stubby* middle-aged woman), *dumpy* a resemblance to a dump—an English term denoting a thick shapeless piece—and, therefore, often implying bulging outlines (as, a *dumpy* figure).

Ana. *Broad, wide, deep.

Ant. Thin. — *Con.* Slender, slim, slight, tenuous, rare (see THIN, *adj.*): *lean, spare.

2 Compact, *close, dense.

Ana. Condensed, compressed, contracted (see CONTRACT, *v.*): concentrated, compacted (see COMPACT, *v.*).

3 Close, confidential, chummy, *familiar, intimate.

thickset. Stocky, *thick, squat, chunky, stubby, dumpy.

Ana. Bulky, *massive, massy: *fleshy, stout, portly, plump.

thief. Robber, burglar, larcener. See under THEFT.

thieve, *v.* *Rob, plunder, rifle, loot, burglarize.

Ana. Despoil, spoliate, sack, pillage, *ravage: *steal, purloin, pilfer, filch: embezzle, *defalcate, peculate.

thin, *adj.* **Thin, slender, slim, slight, tenuous, rare** come into comparison as a group of adjectives of wide range of application (cf. LEAN, MEAGER) that are in general referable not only to measure in width or amount, but also to quantity or quality, and that agree in meaning not broad, or thick, or abundant, or dense. **Thin** basically implies comparatively little extension between two surfaces of a thing (as, a *thin* layer of cement; a *thin* stratum of rock; a *thin* coin) or the comparatively small diameter of a cylindrical or nearly cylindrical thing in proportion to its height or length (as, a *thin* body; a *thin* trunk of a tree; a *thin* wire). In its extended senses, the term usually implies the lack of flesh or substance or something comparable to flesh and substance that fills out a thing to its normal or usual extent, and gives it fullness, richness, substantiality, compactness, density, or the like; as, a *thin* face; *thin* wine; a *thin* argument; a *thin* forest; *thin* hair; "*thin*, pebbly earth, which was merely the rock pulverized by weather" (*Cather*); "like the air of a mountain top—*thin*, but pure and bracing" (*Inge*); "Would make a sound as *thin* and sweet As trees in country lanes" (*Millay*). **Slender** in the earliest of its senses (and still its leading sense) applies to the bodies of men and of animals, implying leanness or spareness without, however, a suggestion of gauntness or lankiness: in fact, in present usage, it carries also a connotation of gracefulness and, usually, of good proportions; as, a *slender* girl; a *slender* dog; "*Slender* white hands" (*S. Anderson*). *Slender* is preferred to *thin* in describing things of narrow extension when the thinness is an element of beauty; as, a *slender* vase; the *slender* legs of a Sheraton chair; "the pure *slender* lines [in a painting] of water falling from the abrupt wooded crag" (*Binyon*). In its extended use, *slender* is often employed with little distinction from *thin*, but it is often preferred by good writers when quantity or amount rather than quality is stressed; as, "A few attempts had been made...with *slender* success" (*Macaulay*); "being a discreet woman...when her pupils went...[she] packed up her *slender* belongings and sought for employment afresh" (*Kipling*); "With *slender* forces he [Octavian] had to face the formidable Sextus" (*Buchan*); "such a vision [of life] as might come as the result of few or *slender* experiences" (*T. S. Eliot*). **Slim** differs little, or in some use not at all, from *slender* when applied to the figures of persons or animals; it tends, however, to suggest fragility or gauntness rather than grace, and lack of flesh rather than excellent proportions; as, their children are too *slim*. In its extended senses, however, *slim* usually carries a clearer implication of meagerness or scantiness than *slender*, which though it suggests smallness in amount or quantity, implies less commonly than *slim* a falling short of adequacy or sufficiency; thus, *slim* resources are by suggestion more meager than *slender* resources; so, he has a *slim* chance of recovery; his hopes for success are *slim;* there was a *slim* attendance at the meeting. **Slight,** through most of its variations in meaning, carries a more obvious implication of smallness than of thinness: when applied to persons, it seldom suggests height or length, as *slender* usually does or *slim* sometimes does (as, *slight* in figure; a *slight*, middle-aged man); when applied to things, it is often derogatory and usually implies mere appreciableness or a failure to come up to a level of that which is commensurate, adequate, or the like; as, "Away, *slight* man!" (*Shak.*); "a *slight* and transient fancy" (*Arnold*); a *slight* difference; his success was *slight;* "There is... ground to recognise a *slight* intellectual superiority in the upper social class" (*H. Ellis*); "he liked the folksong, because it was a *slight* thing, born of immediate impulse" (*A. Huxley*). **Tenuous** basically implies extreme thinness or absence of perceptible thickness: the term in its literal senses is applied to lines, cords, wires, and other things of great length or height and of minute diameter (as, the most *tenuous* of threads; as *tenuous* as the filament of a spider's web) or to fabrics, textiles, and the like, which are exceedingly sheer or gauzy (as, a *tenuous* film covered the scalded milk; the *tenuous* web of a spider; *tenuous* fabrics such as tulle and chiffon). In its now more common extended senses, *tenuous* often describes something which covers an expanse but lacks density, compactness, solidity, or the like (as, "Some [stars] are extremely dense and compact, others extremely *tenuous*"—*Eddington;* "*tenuous* evening mists"—*Karl K. Darrow*), or something which is so finespun or so fine-drawn as to be exceedingly subtle, abstruse, visionary, or the like (as, "a *tenuous* idealism"—*Binyon;* "poetry...so *tenuous* in thought and feeling that only the most exquisite diction can justify its perpetuation in cold print" —*Grandgent;* "I did not despise the golden, *tenuous* imaginings...starting in my own spirit"—*Galsworthy*). **Rare,** in the sense here compared (see also INFREQUENT, CHOICE), is now uncommon except in reference to air and gases. This is, however, the earliest and basic sense of the term, originally implying a loose arrangement or wide separation of the component particles or units. As applied to air, gases, and the like, it suggests tenuity, or lack of density or compactness; as, he was unaccustomed to the *rare* atmosphere of the high mountains; "Nova Pictoris, which brightened and faded several times... may have encountered now a dense and now a *rare* mass of such dark matter as it plunged on" (*W. Kaempffert*).

Ana. *Lean, spare, lank, lanky, gaunt: *meager, exiguous, scanty: cadaverous, pinched, wasted, *haggard: attenuated, extenuated, diluted (see THIN, *v.*).

Ant. Thick.

thin, *v.* **Thin, attenuate, extenuate, dilute, rarefy. Thin** is the most inclusive of these terms and is interchangeable with any of the others, though not without loss of precision or of specific connotations. Literally, it implies reduction in thickness or in density; figuratively, it implies a diminution of strength, depth, intensity, or the like; thus, a diet of foods which are not flesh or fat builders *thins* the body; one *thins* a forest by removing surplus trees; one *thins* wine by adding water; one's voice *thins* when one raises its pitch; to *thin* paint; constant use *thins* silver; *thinned* ranks of soldiers. **Attenuate,** in literal use, implies thinning by mechanical, chemical, or other processes, such as drawing out, spinning fine, culturing repeatedly (as a strain of bacteria), or the like, or as the effect of conditions which emaciate, such as disease or starvation; as, to *attenuate* wire by drawing it through successively smaller holes; to hammer brass in order to *attenuate* it; a wave of potential or current *attenuates* in magnitude and phase as it travels along a transmission line; to *attenuate* a virus by heating it. "The powerful frame *attenuated* by spare living" (*Dickens*). In figurative use, which is very common, *attenuate* implies the loss of properties that are necessary to a thing's strength, richness, effectiveness, vitality, or the like, and it often connotes overrefining, oversubtilizing, or overemphasis on the opposite. "We may reject and reject till we *attenuate* history into sapless meagerness" (*F. Palgrave*). "If she had had a little more self-control she would have *attenuated* the emotion to nothing by sheer reasoning" (*Hardy*). "Illusions which science can *attenuate* or destroy, but which it is powerless to enrich" (*J. W. Krutch*). **Extenuate,** as here considered (see also PALLIATE), originally meant and still occasionally means to emaciate and exhaust. "Peasants...so *extenuated* by hunger that they could scarcely hold the spade" (*Lecky*). Later it acquired several of the denotations of *thin*, but in its present limited and somewhat learned use it usually suggests a thinning or abridgment in numbers or detail, or a diminution of a thing's importance or significance. " 'The whole tendency of modern thought..., opinion and...manners is to *extenuate* the responsibility of human nature, not merely on the moral side, but equally on the spiritual side' " (*C. Mackenzie*). **Dilute**, both in literal and in figurative use, implies a thinning of that which is concentrated by the addition (in figurative use, sometimes, by the influence) of that which weakens it, neutralizes it, or destroys its vigor or intensity; as, to *dilute* peppermint oil with alcohol; to *dilute* hydrochloric acid with water; the *diluted* romanticism of Leigh Hunt; the pioneer spirit of the early Americans has been *diluted* in their descendants, sometimes manifesting itself as a passion for thrills. "The rough, spontaneous conversation of men they [clergymen] do not hear, but only a mincing and *diluted* speech" (*Emerson*). **Rarefy** implies a thinning in density and usually an expansion in volume or a decrease in weight or pressure; thus, the *rarefied* air of mountainous regions is trying to some persons; water *rarefies* into steam when subjected to high heat; infected tissue at the base of a tooth becomes *rarefied* and translucent. The word occurs frequently in figurative use, chiefly with reference to ideas, emotions, intellectual powers, and the like, sometimes suggesting their spiritualization or refinement and the elimination of all grossness and impurity and sometimes imputing to them a vaporous or tenuous quality. "Plain truths lose much of their weight when they are *rarefied* into subtleties" (*Cudworth*). "Love is a gentle flame that *rarefies* and expands her whole being" (*Hazlitt*).

Ana. Reduce, lessen, diminish, *decrease: *liquefy, melt, dissolve.

Ant. Thicken.

thing. 1 Matter, concern, business, *affair.

2 Thing, object, article are all, as here compared, comprehensive terms applicable to whatever is apprehended as having actual, distinct, and demonstrable existence. They vary, however, in their range of application. **Thing** is the term of widest reference. In its most inclusive sense it does not necessarily imply direct knowledge through the senses and is applicable as well to anything the existence of which is inferred from its signs, its effects, or the like; thus, one thinks of the state, the church, literature, the law as *things* rather than as ideas or abstractions; a friend's affection is a real *thing*; one distinguishes a word from the *thing* it names. More often, however, *thing* refers to whatever is directly apprehended through the senses, especially through the senses of sight and touch; as, name the *things* that are on this table; get rid of all the useless *things* in this house; a blind person recognizes *things* through their shape, texture, smell, taste, sound, and the like. Occasionally, *thing* implies a distinction from *person* (often also animals, sometimes plants); as, to be more interested in *things* than in human beings. Consequently, it may be used in reference to persons when contempt is expressed or derogation intended; as, do you call that *thing* a man? **Object** has for its primary implication externality to the mind (that is, it is outside the subject). In philosophic and scientific use it is applied to something that is put before one as a thing to be seen, observed, contemplated, or the like; thus, a thinker may make an abstraction, such as love, art, or justice, an *object* of thought; a mystic may make the humility of Jesus an *object* of contemplation; modern physicists are concentrating on the atom as an *object* of study. This basic implication of *object* is its chief distinction from *thing* when either word is used to denote something that can be seen or touched, or, less often, tasted, heard, or smelled. For *object* in this, its ordinary sense, is applied chiefly to that which has body, usually substance and shape; as, he groped his way in the darkness with hands outstretched to detect any *objects* in his path; in the glare of the torch they saw moving *objects* in the distance; a skeleton is an unpleasant *object;* the children were allowed to draw only *objects*, not imaginary things. **Article** is by far the most limited in its range of application, being used only of objects that are thought of as members of a group, kind, or class; as, meat is an important *article* of food; *articles* of merchandise are for sale; a chair is an *article* of furniture; *articles* of apparel.

Ana. *Item, detail, particular.

think. 1 Think, conceive, imagine, fancy, realize, envisage, envision are here compared as meaning to form an idea or notion of something in the mind. **Think** (as here considered), the most general and least explicit word of this group, may imply nothing more than the entrance of an idea or notion into one's mind (as, please do not *think* of it) but usually it suggests some consideration or reflection (as, to *think* base thoughts; to *think* one plot better than another; to *think* that a change in occupation is desirable) and often, it implies a conscious mental act such as a recalling or recollection (as, try to *think* how the accident happened), or a bringing of a definite picture or a clear idea into one's mind (as, one cannot *think* infinity; *think* what a sacrifice he has made), or the framing of a purpose or intention (as, to *think* harm to one's enemies; "He...*thought* he would send for his mother; and then he *thought* he would not"—*Hardy*). **Conceive** implies a bringing forth in the mind (in a manner suggestive of conception in the womb) of an idea, a plan, a project, a design, or the like: often, but not invariably, the term suggests the growth and development of that idea as the mind dwells upon it and brings it into being; as, "It was among the ruins of the Capitol that I first *conceived* the idea of a work which has amused and exercised near twenty years of my life" (*Gibbon*); "Naturalism...was in its origin a protest, not against the supernatural in itself, but against a supernatural *conceived* as arbitrary, incoherent, and chaotic" (*Inge*); "When we try to *conceive* the state of mind of primitive man, the first thing that occurs to us is the bewilderment and terror he must have felt in the presence of the powers of nature" (*G. L. Dickinson*). **Imagine** carries a far stronger implication than *conceive* does of visualization, or of definitely imaging a thing; as, one can *conceive*, but scarcely *imagine*, a world of four dimensions; "My main desire has been to make them *conceive*, and, if possible, reproduce sympathetically in their *imagination*, the mental life of their pupil" (*W. James*); "I could *imagine* easily original plots for stories or plays, but never received any impulse to write them" (*G. W. Russell*). **Fancy** (as here compared: see also LIKE) may differ little from *imagine*, but it commonly suggests unreality or a degree of untruth in the idea conceived or the image developed: sometimes it even implies a tendency to cut oneself off from facts and to be governed by one's dreams, desires, or the like; as, "*Fancy* being cooped up in a horrid ship, with...a black wind blowing the masts down, and tearing the sails into long screaming ribands!" (*Wilde*); "She is almost beautiful...and not in any way what you have been led to *fancy*" (*Meredith*). **Realize** (as here compared: see also REALIZE, 1) implies a very vivid conception or imagination of something that does exist or has existed or may exist, but which is not known through the senses or through experience: the term suggests such vividness that the thing conceived

seems actual or true. "As Father Vaillant remarked, at Rome they did not seem to *realize* that it was no easy matter for two missionaries on horseback to keep up with the march of history" (*Cather*). "People say that they cannot *realize* these big numbers. But that is the last thing anyone wants to do with big numbers [of miles in astronomical distances]—to *realize* them" (*Eddington*). **Envisage,** and the much more recent **envision,** imply a conception or imagination actually or potentially so clear or so detailed that one does or can contemplate it as though it were before one; as, "the radicals...demanded changes which they did not clearly *envisage*" (*Buchan*); "*envisaging* the future without fear" (*Bennett*); "His blackest hypochondria had never *envisioned* quite so miserable a catastrophe" (*L. Strachey*).
Ana. *Consider, weigh, revolve, study, contemplate: *understand, comprehend, appreciate: surmise, *conjecture, guess.

2 Think, cogitate, reflect, reason, speculate, deliberate come into comparison chiefly as intransitive verbs meaning to use one's powers of conception, judgment, or inference in regard to any matter or subject which concerns one or interests one. **Think** (as here considered) is the general term implying mental activity for the sake of forming ideas or of reaching conclusions: the term may or may not suggest closeness of application, clearness in the ideas formed, or correctness in the conclusions reached, though when used without qualification it often does suggest the attainment or approximation of these; as, "When I was a child, I spake as a child, I understood as a child, I *thought* as a child: but when I became a man, I put away childish things" (*1 Corinthians* xiii. 11); "colleges are places where at least some men learn to *think*" (*Lippmann*); "I am even prepared to be told that when you paid the price of this book you were paying me to *think* for you" (*Shaw*). **Cogitate** places more stress on the process than upon the results of thinking: it is often used, somewhat humorously or ironically, to suggest the appearance or the atmosphere of profound, but not necessarily valid, thinking. "Still *cogitating* and looking for an explanation in the fire" (*Dickens*). "Mrs. Berry had not *cogitated* long ere she pronounced distinctly and without a shadow of dubiosity: 'My opinion is...'" (*Meredith*). **Reflect** usually implies a turning of one's thoughts back upon or back to something that exists, has occurred, is without explanation, or the like: it implies quiet and serious consideration or study; as, "[he] stood *reflecting* on the circumstances of the preceding hours" (*Hardy*); "All the most important things in his life, [he] sometimes *reflected*, had been determined by chance" (*Cather*); "When...on a calm night I look up at the stars, I *reflect* on the wonders of creation, the unimportance of this planet, and the possible existence of other worlds like ours" (*L. P. Smith*). **Reason** implies consecutive logical thought, beginning with a postulate or postulates, a premise or premises, or definite data or evidence and proceeding through inferences drawn from these to a conclusion or judgment; as, to *reason* about the nature of matter; few can *reason* clearly or consecutively for any length of time; "since, where all is uncertain, we must *reason* from what is probable of human nature" (*Quiller-Couch*); "No man as near death as I was feeling, could, I *reasoned*, be absorbed by such trifles" (*Lucas*). **Speculate** implies the processes of reasoning, but stresses either the uncertainty of the premises or the incompleteness of the data and, therefore, usually imputes a hypothetical or theoretical character to the conclusions reached; "[Tiberius's retirement] was a strange incident in a life of vigorous action, and Rome *speculated* assiduously on the cause" (*Buchan*); "It is interesting to *speculate* whether it is not a misfortune that two of the greatest masters of diction in our language, Milton and Dryden, triumph with a dazzling disregard of the soul" (*T. S. Eliot*). **Deliberate** suggests slow and careful thought or reasoning on the part of an individual or group, especially before announcing a conclusion or decision; as, "Please you, *deliberate* a day or two" (*Shak.*); "The future relations of the two countries could now be *deliberated* on with a hope of settlement" (*Froude*).
Ana. *Ponder, meditate, muse, ruminate: *infer, deduce, conclude, judge.

thirst, *v.* Hunger, pine, yearn, *long, hanker.
Ana. Covet, crave, *desire, wish, want.

thither. Thither, there indicate a point or place away from the one where the speaker or writer is. **Thither** was formerly in common use with verbs of motion (such as *come, bring, send,* etc.); **there** with verbs of rest (such as *be, live, stay,* etc.). In modern usage *there* has displaced *thither* except in poetic or elevated style and is now employed after verbs of motion as well as of rest.

thoroughfare. Highway, highroad, *road, roadway, street, avenue, boulevard, terrace, drive, parkway, byway, lane, alley, alleyway.

though. Though, although, albeit introduce subordinate clauses stating something that is, or may be, true in spite of what is asserted in the main clause. **Though,** the most widely used of these words, is less formal than *although,* which comes close to it in meaning; the clause it introduces may state an established fact or a supposition (either a hypothesis or an admission of possibility or probability); in the former case, the conjunction is usually followed by a verb in the indicative mood, in the latter by one in the subjunctive mood; as, *though* the work has many good points, it is open to severe criticism; let us not defer our trip, *though* it rain tomorrow. "*Though* he slay me, yet will I trust in him" (*Job* xiii. 15). In modern formal writing, **although** is usually preferred to *though* when it introduces an assertion of fact, when the subordinate clause precedes the main clause, and when there is no ellipsis; as, *although* his policy has not yet been fully declared, we have reason to believe that it will be acceptable to all. "*Although* the necessity of renunciation is evidence of the existence of evil, yet Christianity, in preaching it, has shown...wisdom.... The belief that what must be renounced is bad, *though* sometimes false, is far less often false than untamed passion supposes" (*B. Russell*). **Albeit,** though widely regarded as archaic, is often used in good modern prose when the idea of admission of that which seems a contradiction is expressed. "A worthy fellow, *Albeit* he comes on angry purpose now" (*Shak.*).

thought. *Idea, concept, conception, notion, impression.
Ana. *Opinion, view, sentiment, belief, conviction, persuasion.

thoughtful. 1 Thoughtful, reflective, speculative, contemplative, meditative, pensive are here compared as applied to persons, their moods, attitudes, expressions, utterances, and the like, and as meaning characterized by or manifesting the power to engage in thought, especially in concentrated thinking. **Thoughtful** may imply either the act of thinking concentratedly or the disposition to apply oneself to the careful and serious consideration of problems or questions at issue; as, he has a shrewd rather than a *thoughtful* face; "Marlowe—not excepting Shakespeare or Chapman, the most *thoughtful* and philosophical mind, though immature, among the Elizabethan dramatists" (*T. S. Eliot*); "So now you know...why it [socialism] is advocated so widely by *thoughtful* and experienced people in all classes" (*Shaw*). **Reflective** differs from *thoughtful* in its stronger implication of orderly processes of thought, such as analysis, logical reasoning, or the like, and in its suggestion of a definite aim, such as the understanding of a thing's nature or of its relation to other things, or the reaching of a definite conclusion. "Men of *reflective* and analytical habit, eager to rationalize its [plutocracy's] instincts and to bring it into some sort of relationship to the main streams of human thought" (*Mencken*). **Speculative** (etymologically, spying out) implies a tendency or inclination to think about things direct knowledge of which is either impossible or so extremely limited that any conclusions are bound to be uncertain; as, economics is regarded by many persons as a *speculative* science; "*speculative* writing about the state" (*Frankfurter*). Hence, the term often implies theorizing or conjecturing, without consideration of the evidence or with little attention to the evidence; as, "About a thousand practical and positive topics the Frenchman, who speaks from experience and examination, finds our views *speculative* and immature" (*Brownell*). "The philosophical background of Chinese culture has always tended to create *reflective* rather than *speculative* thinkers" (*H. H. Hart*). **Contemplative** carries a much stronger implication than the other words of an attention fixed on the object of one's thoughts: it also may imply as its object something perceivable by the senses, or something abstract yet comprehensible by the human reason (such as the ideas of love, beauty, the state, or the like), or something beyond the power of the unaided human mind to know or comprehend (such as God, the Absolute, the future life); as, "The women were the crowning joy of his *contemplative* mind....Dear demonstrative creatures!" (*Meredith*). "Practical curiosity becomes *contemplative* and examines things for their own sake when ...man...having arrived at the stage of ideas and thought, applies them to the data presented by sensible experience" (*S. Alexander*). *Contemplative*, as opposed to *active*, is also applied to a type of life, to religious orders, to the members of such orders, or to other persons or institutions that have for their chief aims the consideration of that which is abstract, ideal, spiritual, or the like, or reflection upon ideas beyond the range of sensible perception. "The *contemplative* life which is concerned with human feeling and thought and beauty...the *contemplative* life which has God's person and love in Christ for its object" (*Ruskin*). **Meditative** (except in religious use, where it comes very close to *contemplative*, though it there stresses reflection more than fixity of attention) usually implies a tendency to ponder or muse over something, without necessarily implying any intellectual purpose such as understanding a thing or reaching a conclusion regarding it. The term therefore often comes close to *thoughtful*, though it usually implies some consecutive reasoning and sometimes suggests pleasure rather than seriousness in the exercise of thought; as, to indulge in many a *meditative* walk; a *meditative* temperament. "Sympathies... That steal upon the *meditative* mind, And grow with thought" (*Wordsworth*). **Pensive** is not always clearly distinguishable from *meditative*, though at times it carries a far stronger suggestion of dreaminess, of wistfulness, or of melancholy; as, "For oft, when on my couch I lie In vacant or in *pensive* mood" (*Wordsworth*); "silent and *pensive*, idle, restless, slow" (*Byron*); "There always remained with me, long after I outgrew his [Longfellow's] poems, a tender memory for that first friend of wistful and *pensive* puberty" (*H. Ellis*).

Ana. *Serious, earnest, grave, sober: engrossed, absorbed, *intent: *abstracted, preoccupied.

2 Thoughtful, considerate, attentive, as here compared, are applied to persons and their acts in the sense of mindful of the comfort or happiness of another or of others. **Thoughtful** usually implies unselfish concern for others or the capacity for anticipating another's needs; as, an affectionate but not *thoughtful* daughter. "In his *thoughtful* wish of escorting them through the streets of the rough, riotous town" (*Gaskell*). **Considerate** stresses concern for the feeling of others, or thoughtfulness in preventing or in relieving pain, suffering, or the like. "The people try as much as they can do to compensate for our discomforts by their kindness. The French poor people are very *considerate* where they see suffering" (*Meredith*). "They are...not kind, only sentimental; not social, only gregarious; not *considerate*, only polite" (*Shaw*). **Attentive** emphasizes continuous thoughtfulness, or implies repeated acts of kindness or courtesy. "I was never more surprized than by his behaviour to us. It was more than civil; it was really *attentive*" (*Austen*). "There was a very tender feeling between David and Aunt Marian, as he called her. He was almost more *attentive* to her than her own children" (*M. Austin*).

Ana. Solicitous, concerned, careful, anxious (see under CARE): courteous, polite, gallant, chivalrous (see CIVIL).

Ant. Thoughtless.

thoughtless. *Careless, heedless, inadvertent.

Ana. Rash, reckless, foolhardy (see ADVENTUROUS): *indifferent, unconcerned, incurious, aloof: lax, remiss, *negligent.

Ant. Thoughtful.

thrall. *Serf, villein, vassal, slave, bondslave, bondsman, bondman, peon, Helot.

thrash, *v.* **1** Thresh, *beat, pound, pummel, buffet, baste, belabor.

Ana. *Strike, smite, slug, slap: winnow (see SIFT).

2 Flourish, brandish, *swing, wave.

Ana. Wield, manipulate, swing, ply, *handle.

threadbare. Shopworn, *trite, hackneyed, stereotyped.

Ana. Antiquated, obsolete, archaic (see OLD): exhausted, depleted, drained, impoverished (see DEPLETE).

threaten. Threaten, menace agree in meaning to forecast by word, look, or other means, an evil, an injury, or other infliction likely to be visited upon one. **Threaten** basically implies an attempt to dissuade or influence by promising punishment or the infliction of reprisals upon those who disobey an injunction or perform acts objectionable to the speaker. "The magistrates ... Solicited, commanded, *threatened*, urged" (*Milton*). "Another form of lying, which is extremely bad for the young, is to *threaten* punishments you do not mean to inflict" (*B. Russell*). However, the term has been so extended in its meaning that it is now often used without reference to persons who issue such warnings or who promise such penalties and with reference to things, such as events, conditions, or symptoms, which presage or otherwise indicate something, often, but not necessarily, something dire or disturbing, to happen; as, overcast skies that *threaten* rain; disputes which *threaten* a rupture. "The recollection of the forty tons of dynamite in the body of the 'Ferndale'; not the sort of cargo one thinks of with equanimity in connexion with a *threatened* collision" (*Conrad*). "Without invoking the rule of strict construction I think that 'so near as to obstruct' means so near as actually to obstruct—and not merely near enough to *threaten* a possible obstruction" (*Justice Holmes*). **Menace** is a somewhat more literary term than *threaten:* also, it carries a much weaker implication of an attempt to dissuade or influence and a much stronger suggestion of an alarming or a definitely hostile character or aspect; as, he did not actually *threaten* me but his tone was *menacing;* conditions that *menace* our liberty. "Is it not experience which renders a dog apprehensive of pain, when you *menace* him?" (*Locke*). "Her subjects were incited to rebellion; her life was *menaced*" (*Macaulay*).

Ana. *Intimidate, bulldoze, cow, browbeat: forebode, portend, presage, augur (see FORETELL): *warn, forewarn, caution.

thresh, *v.* Thrash, *beat, pound, pummel, buffet, baste, belabor.

Ana. Winnow (see SIFT): *strike, smite.

thrifty. Economical, *sparing, frugal.

Ana. Provident, prudent, foresighted (see under PRUDENCE): saving, preserving, conserving (see SAVE).

Ant. Wasteful.

thrill, *v.* **Thrill, electrify, enthuse** are here compared as meaning to fill a person with emotions that stir or excite one physically and mentally or, less often, to be stirred by such emotions. **Thrill** (etymologically, to pierce) suggests pervasion by emotions that set one's nerves tingling or quivering with pleasure, horror, or the like: commonly it implies an agreeable sensation even when the exciting cause is painful; as, a *thrilling* detective story; he *thrilled* his audience with his stirring appeal for action; I *thrilled* in response to his appeal; "Me mightier transports move and *thrill*" (*Tennyson*); "Why should not mind be able to pass on to mind its *thrilled* sense of a storm or a flower...?" (*C. E. Montague*). **Electrify** differs from *thrill* in suggesting effects comparable to those produced by an electric current that shocks rather than stuns: it implies a sudden, startling, and violent stimulation of the nerves or the mind by a power that for the time being holds one obedient to its will or under its sway; as, "Those heights of courage which *electrify* an army and ensure victory" (*Burke*). "She was not eating anything, she was using up all her vitality to *electrify* these heavy lads into speech" (*Cather*). **Enthuse,** a back formation from *enthusiasm,* has not been accepted by careful writers and speakers: it is often used carelessly or by undiscriminating writers and speakers to imply a stirring of or a being stirred by strong emotions such as ardor, fervor, zeal, and the like; as, to *enthuse* an audience with his suggestions for home defense; the people were not *enthused* over the prospect of war; he was always *enthusing* about the latest play he had seen.

Ana. Excite, stimulate, galvanize, quicken (see PROVOKE): *stir, arouse, rouse, rally: penetrate, pierce, probe (see ENTER): quiver, tremble, shiver (see SHAKE).

throb, *v.* Beat, *pulsate, pulse, palpitate.

throb, *n.* Beat, pulsation, pulse, palpitation. See under PULSATE.

throe. *Pain, ache, pang, twinge, stitch.

throng, *n.* *Crowd, press, crush, mob, rout, horde.

Ana. *Multitude, army, host, legion: assembly, congregation, gathering, collection (see under GATHER).

through. *By, with.

throw, *v.* **Throw, cast, fling, hurl, pitch, toss, sling** are synonymous terms when they mean to cause to move swiftly forward, sideways, upward, or downward by a propulsive movement as of the arm, or by means of a propelling instrument or agency. **Throw,** now the general word, is often, but not always, followed by an adverb such as *off, away, down, up,* etc., to indicate not only the direction of that which is being propelled, but sometimes, especially in idiomatic phrases, its destination or disposal; as, "people who live in glass houses should not *throw* stones" (*Proverb*); "*Throw* physic to the dogs; I'll none of it" (*Shak.*); the fire engine *throws* a long stream of water; this gun *throws* a huge shell; to *throw* away food; to *throw* off one's coat. "The sceptic cannot *throw* his opponent if his own feet are in the air" (*Inge*). **Cast** is often interchangeable with *throw* but in current use it seems somewhat archaic unless that which is thrown is light (as, to *cast* a net; to *cast* dice), and is either directly aimed (as, to *cast* one's line in angling), or scattered more or less carefully (as, to *cast* seed), or is thrown only in a figurative sense (as, to *cast* a black look). "He that is without sin among you, let him first *cast* a stone at her" (*John* viii. 7). "Every tree therefore which bringeth not forth good fruit is hewn down, and *cast* into the fire" (*Luke* iii. 9). **Fling** implies much more violence in throwing or propulsion than either of the preceding words; commonly, it also implies a force gained from strong emotion such as anger, contempt, or enthusiasm. "I would sooner take Empedocles's leap, and *fling* myself into Mount Etna" (*Cowper*). "Then he loathed his own beauty, and, *flinging* the mirror on the floor, crushed it into silver splinters beneath his heel" (*Wilde*). " 'It's no use!' cried Constance, *flinging* away her work" (*Bennett*). **Hurl** stresses driving and impetuous force that makes for speed and distance; as, to *hurl* quoits. "Him the Almighty Power *Hurled* headlong flaming from the ethereal sky" (*Milton*). **Pitch** more than any of the preceding words implies a sense of direction and of a definite aim in throwing; it is the preferred term in some competitive games such as baseball where skill in determining what course the thrown thing will take is important and in some employments, such as farming, where things are thrown to a definite spot; as, to *pitch* a spear; to *pitch* a ball; to *pitch* hay. **Toss** implies light, careless, or more or less aimless throwing; as, "he...*tossed* me some pieces of money" (*Dickens*); "she rested on a log and *tossed* the fresh chips" (*Frost*); the angry bull *tossed* the boy over the wall; to *toss* a coin to decide which should go. The term often also suggests a throwing to and fro or up and down (as, an hour's play in *tossing* a ball; "They...discuss'd a doubt and *tost* it to and fro"—*Tennyson*). **Sling** does not as often, as in earlier English, imply the use of a sling, or an instrument for throwing or hurling missiles such as stones or shot. When it does not, however, it retains its implication of a sudden, violent propulsion and of directness of aim; as, to *sling* snowballs.

Ana. Drive, impel (see MOVE, *v.*): propel, thrust, shove, *push: heave, raise, *lift, boost.

throwback. *Reversion, atavism.

thrust, *v.* *Push, shove, propel.

Ana. *Throw, cast, fling: drive, impel, *move: *enter, penetrate, pierce.

thrust, *n.* *Stress, strain, pressure, tension, shear, torsion.

thug. *Ruffian, desperado, gangster, Mohock, apache.

thwart. Foil, *frustrate, baffle, balk, circumvent, outwit.

Ana. *Hinder, impede, obstruct, block, bar: defeat, overcome, surmount (see CONQUER): check, curb, *restrain: *prevent, forestall, anticipate.

tickle. *Please, regale, arride, gratify, delight, rejoice, gladden.

Ana. Divert, *amuse, entertain: *thrill, electrify.

tide, *n.* **1** Time, *opportunity, occasion, chance, break, hint.

Ana. *Juncture, emergency, exigency, contingency.

2 Flood, *flow, stream, current, flux.

tidings. *News, intelligence, advice.

tidy. *Neat, trim, trig, snug, shipshape, spick-and-span.

Ana. *Orderly, methodical, systematic.

Ant. Untidy. — *Con.* *Slipshod, slovenly, sloppy, unkempt.

tie, *v.* **Tie, bind** agree in meaning to make fast or secure. They are often used interchangeably without marked loss, but since in both their literal and figurative senses they carry fundamentally distinct connotations, greater precision in their use is often possible. **Tie** in its literal sense implies the use of a cord or rope which can be knotted, and the attachment of one thing that may wander or move, by that cord or rope, to another that is stable. "I'll *tie* them [our horses] in the wood" (*Shak.*). **Bind,** on the other hand, implies the use of a band or bond (see BOND, *n.*) and the attachment of two or more things together by means of this band or bond with the result that they are held together firmly or brought into union. "Gather ye together first the tares, and *bind* them in bundles" (*Matthew* xiii. 30). Even when the idea of attachment is not connoted or is very weak, *tie* still implies knotting and *bind* the use of an encircling band (such as a bandage or bandeau) or a bond (such as a chain, manacle, or fetter); as, to *tie* a sash or cravat; to *bind* a sprained ankle; "a fillet *binds* her hair" (*Pope*); to *bind* a person hand and foot. In figurative use, especially when that which is tied or bound is a person, both terms imply a deprivation of liberty and an imposed restraint. *Tie,* however, specifically suggests a being held down by something stronger than oneself and an inability to get away or free oneself; as, to be *tied* to a job; he is *tied* to his bed. *Bind,* on the other hand, either suggests a being held together in a close union, for the sake of strength or mutual support (as, the common danger *bound* all classes together; "And vows of faith each to the other *bind*"—*Shelley*), or a being held down by a bond, such as a pledge, a compact, a duty, an obligation, or by a bond of blood, marriage, or friendship; as, "And vows, that *bind* the will, in silence made" (*Wordsworth*); "That love, which none may *bind,* be free to fill The world" (*Shelley*).

Ana. *Fasten, attach: *secure, rivet, anchor, moor: *join, connect, link.

Ant. Untie.

tie, *n.* *Bond, band.

tiff, *n.* *Quarrel, bickering, spat, squabble, wrangle, altercation.

Ana. Scrap, rumpus, row, *brawl, broil: variance, dissension, contention, *discord.

tiff, *v.* Spat, bicker, quarrel, squabble, wrangle, altercate. See under QUARREL, *n.*

Ana. Dispute, argue (see DISCUSS): differ from, *differ with: *contend, fight.

tight. **1** **Tight, taut, tense** come into comparison especially in their literal senses when they mean drawn or stretched to the point where there is no looseness or slackness. They are often not closely synonymous terms in their extended senses. **Tight** comes closer etymologically to *compact* and *close* than it does to the senses in which it is here chiefly considered, but even in the latter senses it often implies a drawing around or about something in a way that constricts or binds it or a drawing of the edges of something firmly together; as, a *tight* belt; a *tight* coat; *tight* lips; "Tom has eaten...and imbibed coffee, till his little skin is as *tight* as a drum" (*T. Hughes*); "Law should be regarded as an elastic tissue which clothes a growing body. That tissue, that garment, must fit exactly; if it is too *tight* it will split and there will be lawlessness; if it is too loose, it will impede movement" (*Buchan*). When applied to a structure, *tight* more often suggests a drawing together of all parts so that nothing can enter or escape (as, a ship as *tight* [often *watertight*] as a bottle; a *tightly* built house; "if the granary be not *tight,* the grain will leak out almost as fast as it is shoveled in"—*Grandgent*); when applied to a person, it may imply either secretiveness (as, " 'and loose livers sometimes appear to be rather *tight* talkers' "—*R. Macaulay*) or stinginess (see *tight* under STINGY); when applied to a situation, it suggests that those involved in it are cornered or squeezed unmercifully (as, "those who take refuge in gaps find themselves in a *tight* place when the gaps begin to close"—*Inge*). When the emphasis is upon pulling or stretching a cord, a rope, a fabric, or the like, to the point where it can be stretched no more without breaking or without putting undue strain upon its supports, *tight* is often used but **taut** is strictly the more explicit word and therefore to be preferred in this sense; thus, a *tight* cord may be one which ties up a bundle closely and firmly or is stretched to the limit between two points but a *taut* cord is one which is tight only in the second of these senses; so, *taut* as a drumhead; "he is *taut* as one of the hawsers of his own boat" (*Van W. Brooks*); "Her sails are loose, Her tackles hanging, waiting men to seize And haul them *taut*" (*Amy Lowell*). However, *tight* is usually preferred to *taut* in the compound *tightrope* (as, to dance on a *tightrope*). In other than nautical or mechanical use, *taut* often carries a suggestion of strain, especially of nervous strain; as, "the full lips thrust out and *taut,* like the flesh of animals distended by fear or desire" (*Cather*); "in exchanging Wordsworth for Taylor and Johnson, we have relaxed something with the metre, something that the metre kept *taut;* and this something we discover to be the emotional pitch" (*Quiller-Couch*). When there is an implication of tightness or tautness that involves severe physical or, more often, nervous strain or that manifests itself in signs of such strain, **tense** is the preferred term; as, a cat crouched for a spring, with muscles *tense;* "Help him to unbend his too *tense* thought" (*Arnold*); "faces... delicately tinted...under the *tense* silk of parasols" (*H. James*); "Just as a bicycle chain may be too *tight,* so may one's carefulness and conscientiousness be so *tense* as to hinder the running of one's mind" (*W. James*); "Day after day I searched among the ruins and viewed with a *tense* anxiety the hundreds of corpses constantly being carried to the morgues" (*V. Heiser*).

Ana. Strict, stringent (see RIGID): *close, compact: constricted, contracted, compressed, condensed, shrunken (see CONTRACT, *v.*): snug, shipshape (see NEAT).

Ant. Loose.

2 Also **tightfisted.** *Stingy, close, closefisted, niggardly, parsimonious, penurious, miserly, curmudgeonly, cheeseparing, penny-pinching.

Ana. *Mean, ignoble, sordid, abject.

3 Tipsy, intoxicated, *drunk, drunken, inebriate, inebriated.

tight-lipped. *Silent, uncommunicative, taciturn, close, close-lipped, closemouthed, reticent, reserved, secretive.

tilt, *v.* *Tip, cant, careen, heel, list.

Ana. Incline, *slant, slope, lean.

time, *n.* Tide, *opportunity, occasion, chance, break, hint.

Ana. *Juncture, contingency, emergency, exigency.

timely. Well-timed, opportune, *seasonable, pat.

Ana. Appropriate, fitting, meet, proper, suitable (see FIT): fortunate, *lucky, happy, providential.

Ant. Untimely.

timetable. *Program, schedule, agenda.

timid. **Timid, timorous** agree in meaning so fearful and apprehensive as to hesitate or hold back. **Timid** stresses lack of courage and daring and, therefore, usually implies extreme cautiousness and fearfulness of change or of venture into the unknown or uncertain; as, a *timid* investor; *timid* as a deer; "*timid* about making decisions"

(*Cather*); "A *timid* person would rather remain miserable than do anything unusual" (*B. Russell*). **Timorous,** on the other hand, stresses domination by fears and apprehensions: it implies a temporary or habitual frame of mind which causes one to shrink from any action or activity which requires independence, decision, self-assertiveness, or the like; it, therefore, suggests terror rather than extreme caution; as, "Murray, the most *timorous,* as Byron called him, of all God's booksellers" (*Scott*); "in another moment she seemed to have descended from her womanly eminence to helpless and *timorous* girlhood" (*E. Wharton*); "*timorous* and fearful of challenge" (*Mencken*).

Ana. *Fearful, apprehensive, afraid: *cautious, circumspect, calculating, wary, chary: *cowardly, pusillanimous.

Ant. Valiant.

timorous. *Timid.

Ana. *Fearful, apprehensive, afraid: recoiling, shrinking, quailing, blenching (see RECOIL): trembling, quivering, shivering, shuddering (see SHAKE).

Ant. Assured.

tincture, *n.* *Touch, suggestion, tinge, suspicion, soupçon, shade, smack, spice, dash, vein, strain, streak.

tinge, *n.* **1** Tint, shade, hue, *color, chroma.

2 Tinge, *touch, suggestion, shade, suspicion, soupçon, smack, spice, dash, vein, strain, streak.

tint, *n.* Hue, shade, *color, chroma, tinge.

tiny. Minute, miniature, diminutive, wee, *small, little, teeny, weeny.

tip, *v.* **Tip, tilt, cant, careen, heel, list** agree in meaning to cause something to incline from a vertical or horizontal position or to suffer such an inclination. **Tip** now often depends on a succeeding adverb or adverbial phrase to indicate how far this inclination goes or what direction it takes; as, to *tip* over a vase, or a chair; the boat is *tipping* over; to *tip* dirt out of a cart; to *tip* up a mattress; to *tip* one's chair backward. When used without such a word or phrase, the term usually implies either any possible direction or the conventional direction; as, you will *tip* the boat if you all stand on this side; to *tip* one's hat in saluting. **Tilt** etymologically carries a stronger implication of unsteadiness or of tottering than *tip,* but it has lost this connotation in all but one of its senses when it suggests swaying or pitching, as of a ship in rough seas. "The floating vessel... with beaked prow Rode *tilting* o'er the waves" (*Milton*). Otherwise, *tilt* suggests a distinct, and often a permanent, slope or slant; for this reason, although the terms are interchangeable, careful writers and speakers show a preference for *tip* when the reference is to things that are not stationary, and for *tilt* when the reference is to things that are fixed in position; as, the board *tips* slightly; the tree *tilts* to the south. "That *tilted* cobble street, winding down a hill" (*Cather*). **Cant** is also often used in place of *tip* or *tilt,* but it is preferred to either when that which is tipped or tilted is inclined at or near an angle of 90°; thus, a *tipped*-over boat by implication overturns; a *canted* (or *canted*-over) boat by implication (unless corrected by the context) lies on its side. *Cant* sometimes carries so strong a suggestion of throwing or tossing that the term carries little or no implication of tipping or inclining. "What if the wave ebbed with me? Whereas it *cants* you to another crest" (*Browning*). **Careen** and **heel** as transitive verbs are chiefly used in reference to ships that are turned on one side, especially for cleaning and repairing the parts below the water line. Consequently, both verbs, but especially *careen,* often also imply cleaning, caulking, and the like. "Finding a convenient harbor...he unloaded and *careened* his vessels" (*Irving*). As intransitive verbs, they are chiefly used in reference to ships, especially sailing vessels that cant obviously or dangerously because of a strong wind or unbalanced loading. "*Careening* as if never more to right" (*W. Falconer*). "Eight hundred of the brave ... Had made the vessel *heel,* And laid her on her side" (*Cowper*). **List,** which is commonly but not exclusively an intransitive verb, also is a nautical term. It differs from *careen* and *heel* chiefly in suggesting a dangerous loss of balance owing to the shifting of the cargo to one side, the entrance of water into the hold, or the like; as, it was not until they noticed the *listing* of the ship that they discovered that the emergency bulkheads had not been closed.

Ana. Incline, *slant, slope, lean.

tippler. *Drunkard, inebriate, alcoholic, dipsomaniac, sot, soak, toper, tosspot.

tipsy. Intoxicated, inebriate, inebriated, *drunk, drunken, tight.

tire, *v.* **Tire, weary, fatigue, exhaust, jade, fag, tucker** agree in meaning to make, or in some cases to become, disinclined or unable to continue because of loss of strength or endurance. **Tire** is the general and ordinary word and usually implies the draining of one's strength or patience: it may suggest any of several causes, such as overexertion, long continuance at a task, boredom, a sense of futility, or the like, and usually it requires textual amplification to indicate the cause and the degree of the effect. "It *tires* me to death to read how many ways the warrior is like the moon, or the sun, or a rock, or a lion, or the ocean" (*Walpole*). "Music that gentlier on the spirit lies, Than *tired* eyelids upon *tired* eyes" (*Tennyson*). "Then, to the visible embarrassment of his young associates, he suddenly *tired* of it all [fashionable society] and joined the Anglo-Catholic persuasion" (*Day Lewis*); "We shall not fail or falter; we shall not weaken or *tire*" (*Winston S. Churchill*). **Weary** as often suggests an incapacity for enduring more of the same thing or an unwillingness to continue one's effort, one's interest, or the like, as a depletion of that strength or that interest. "The others would never even raise their eyes when this happened, as men too well aware of the futility of their fellows' attempts and *wearied* with their useless repetition" (*Kipling*). "Ah, I am worn out—I am *wearied* out— It is too much—I am but flesh and blood, And I must sleep" (*Millay*). "The Muses are vindictive virgins, and avenge themselves without mercy on those who *weary* of their charms" (*L. P. Smith*). "It did not last, the Crofts' marriage. In the spring of '95, Stanley *wearied* of her husband's infidelities, and could not bear them any more" (*R. Macaulay*). **Fatigue** is stronger than *tire* and implies great lassitude brought on by overstrain or undue effort. It usually implies an incapacity for further strain or effort without untoward effects; as, his physician ordered him to avoid *fatiguing* himself until he had regained his strength. "[My head] is so *fatigued* by breakfast time...I am utterly incapable of sitting down to my desk again" (*Cowper*). "She flung herself upon a sofa, protesting...that she was *fatigued* to death" (*Burney*). **Exhaust** (as here considered: see also DEPLETE) heightens *fatigue's* implications of drained strength or a worn-out condition of mind or of body; as, she is too *exhausted* to sleep; "I am so *exhausted* as not to be able to write" (*Cowper*). **Jade** (etymologically from *jade,* a worn-out horse) implies weariness or fatigue that makes a person (sometimes a thing) lose all freshness and spirit and become dull and languid. The term seldom carries as clear a suggestion of physical or mental overexertion as *fatigue* and often implies even more satiety than *weary:* it is especially useful when the implication of overindul-

gence in something or the overworking of some power is to be conveyed; as, "*jaded* and restless from the dissipations of the day" (*Smollett*); "To the *jaded*...eye it is all dead and common...flatness and disgust" (*W. James*). "I felt a wreck when I met Percy at an early breakfast next morning. He, too, looked *jaded* and strained, and ate hardly any breakfast" (*R. Macaulay*). **Fag,** a familiar and colloquial term, implies work until one droops with weariness or fatigue. "I worked...at correcting manuscript, which *fags* me excessively" (*Scott*). "And man to man with a gasp for breath Said, 'Lord, what a run. I'm *fagged* to death' " (*Masefield*). **Tucker,** usually with *out,* is an American colloquialism that closely approaches *fatigue* or *exhaust* in meaning but usually carries the additional implication of loss of breath; as, the house cleaning *tuckered* her *out;* all *tuckered out* from the long climb.
Ana. Irk, vex, *annoy, bother: *deplete, drain, exhaust, impoverish, bankrupt.

tire, *v.* Attire, *clothe, dress, apparel, array, robe, vest, invest.
Ana., Ant., & *Con.* See those at ATTIRE.

tire, *n.* Attire, *clothes, clothing, dress, apparel, raiment, vesture, array.

tireless. *Indefatigable, weariless, untiring, unwearying, unwearied, unflagging.
Ana. Assiduous, sedulous, diligent, industrious, *busy: energetic, strenuous, *vigorous.

tiresome. *Irksome, wearisome, tedious, humdrum.
Ana. Oppressive, burdensome, *onerous, exacting: fatiguing, exhausting, jading, fagging (see TIRE, *v.*): arduous, *hard, difficult.

tiro. Variant of TYRO.

titanic. *Enormous, immense, huge, vast, gigantic, giant, gigantean, colossal, mammoth, elephantine, herculean, Cyclopean, Antaean, Gargantuan, Brobdingnagian.

tithe, *n.* *Tax, levy, assessment, rate, excise, impost, customs, duty, toll, tariff, tribute, teind, cess.

title, *n.* **1** *Claim, pretension, pretense.
Ana. *Right, privilege, prerogative, birthright: *reason, ground, argument, proof: *due, desert, merit.
2 *Name, designation, denomination, appellation, style.

tittle. *Particle, bit, mite, smitch, smidgen, whit, atom, iota, jot.

toady, *n.* *Parasite, sycophant, favorite, lickspit, hanger-on, leech, sponge.

toady, *v.* *Fawn, truckle, cringe, cower.
Ana. Ingratiate, insinuate (see corresponding adjectives at DISARMING): *follow, tag, trail, tail: blandish, cajole, wheedle (see COAX).

toboggan, *v.* Coast, *slide, slip, glide, skid, glissade, slither.

tocsin. *Alarm, alarum, alert.
Ana. Signal, *sign.

toff. *Fop, dandy, beau, coxcomb, exquisite, élégant, dude, macaroni, buck, spark, swell, nob.

toffish *or* **toffy.** *Stylish, fashionable, modish, smart, chic, dapper, dashing, spruce, brave, braw, natty, nifty, nobby, posh.

toil, *n.* Labor, *work, travail, swink, drudgery, grind.
Ana. *Effort, exertion, pains, trouble: employment, occupation, calling, pursuit, business, métier (see WORK).
Ant. Leisure.

token. **1** *Sign, mark, symptom, badge, note.
Ana. *Symbol, emblem, attribute: *evidence, testimony: indication, proving *or* proof, betokening (see corresponding verbs at INDICATE).
2 *Pledge, earnest, pawn, hostage, gage.
Ana. *Guarantee, guaranty, security, surety.

tolerance. Forbearance, leniency, indulgence, clemency, mercifulness. See under FORBEARING.
Ana. *Mercy, charity, grace, lenity: *patience, long-suffering, longanimity.
Ant. Intolerance: loathing.

tolerant. *Forbearing, lenient, indulgent, clement, merciful.
Ana. *Charitable, benevolent, humane: forgiving, excusing, condoning (see EXCUSE, *v.*).
Ant. Intolerant: severe.

tolerate. Endure, abide, *bear, suffer, stand, brook.
Ana. Accept, *receive: submit, *yield, bow, succumb.

toll, *n.* *Tax, levy, assessment, rate, excise, impost, customs, duty, tariff, tribute, tithe, teind, cess.

tone. *Atmosphere, feeling, feel, savor, aura.
Ana. Peculiarity, individuality, characteristic (see corresponding adjectives at CHARACTERISTIC): *quality, property, character.

tongue. *Language, dialect, speech, idiom.

tonguelash, *v.* Upbraid, rate, berate, *scold, jaw, bawl out, wig, rail, revile, vituperate.

tonic. *Restorative, alterative.

too. *Also, likewise, besides, moreover, furthermore.

tool. *Implement, instrument, appliance, utensil.
Ana. *Device, contrivance, contraption, gadget: *machine, engine, apparatus, appliance: *means, instrument, instrumentality, agent, agency.

tooth, *n.* **Tooth, tusk, fang** literally mean a hard bony appendage, or one of such appendages, borne on the jaws, or in some cases on the wall of the mouth or of the pharynx, of vertebrates and used chiefly in the grasping, the biting, and the mastication of food. **Tooth** is the general term, but it is used so frequently with reference to the appendages on the jaws of human beings and many of the higher vertebrates that it is rarely employed in general colloquial use to designate what is strictly called a *tusk* or *fang.* But it occurs in poetry in this sense; as, "How sharper than a serpent's *tooth* it is To have a thankless child!" (*Shak.*); "Nature, red in *tooth* and claw With ravine" (*Tennyson*). **Tusk** is an elongated and greatly enlarged tooth which is found in certain animals such as the elephant, the walrus, the narwhal, and the wild boar, and which typically projects from the mouth, even when the mouth is closed, and serves as a means of digging up food, or as a weapon or the like. **Fang** is a long, sharp tooth characteristic of carnivorous animals with strong jaws, such as large dogs and wolves, and used chiefly in seizing and rending prey. The term also designates a similarly pointed hollow tooth of some venomous snakes which is folded back in the mouth and erected only when striking. Hence, in extended use, *tooth* usually suggests a thing which eats or destroys (as, the *tooth* of time; "Fell sorrow's *tooth*"—*Shak.*) or denotes a taste or appetite for food such as is described (as, a sweet *tooth*); *tusk* is used contemptuously of abnormally large projecting human teeth (as, when he opened his mouth, he showed two rows of yellow *tusks*); *fang* suggests power to cut, pierce, or poison (as, "the icy *fang*... of the winter's wind"—*Shak.;* "an equivocation which now turned venomously upon him with the full-grown *fang* of a discerned lie"—*G. Eliot*).

toothsome. *Palatable, appetizing, savory, sapid, saporous, tasty, flavorsome, relishing.

toper. *Drunkard, inebriate, alcoholic, dipsomaniac, sot, soak, tosspot, tippler.

topic. *Subject, matter, subject matter, argument, text, theme, motive, leitmotiv.

torment, *v.* Torture, rack, grill, *afflict, try.
Ana. *Worry, annoy, harry, harass, plague, pester:

distress, *trouble: *bait, badger, hector: agonize, *writhe.

tornado. *Wind, gale, hurricane, whirlwind, cyclone, typhoon, waterspout, twister, gust, blast, flaw, zephyr.

torpid. *Lethargic, sluggish, comatose, stuporous.
Ana. Inert, *inactive, idle, passive: phlegmatic, *impassive, stolid.
Ant. Agile.

torpidity. Torpor, stupor, *lethargy, languor, lassitude.
Ana. Inertness, inactivity, idleness, passiveness (see corresponding adjectives at INACTIVE).

torpor. Torpidity, stupor, *lethargy, languor, lassitude.
Ana. Apathy, phlegm, impassivity, stolidity (see under IMPASSIVE): inertness *or* inertia, passiveness, inactivity (see corresponding adjectives at INACTIVE).
Ant. Animation.

torsion. *Stress, strain, pressure, tension, shear, thrust.

tort. Injury, wrong, grievance, *injustice.

tortuous. *Winding, anfractuous, sinuous, serpentine, flexuous.
Ana. *Crooked, devious: labyrinthine, mazy (see corresponding nouns at LABYRINTH): roundabout, circuitous, *indirect.
☞ *Do not confuse* tortuous *with* torturous.

torture, *v.* Rack, torment, grill, *afflict, try.
Ana. *Writhe, agonize: persecute, oppress, *wrong: *distress, trouble: *worry, annoy, harry, harass: *maim, mutilate, mangle.

toss, *v.* Pitch, sling, *throw, cast, fling, hurl.
Ana. Impel, drive (see MOVE, *v.*): thrust, propel (see PUSH, *v.*).

tosspot. *Drunkard, inebriate, alcoholic, dipsomaniac, sot, soak, toper, tippler.

total, *adj.* *Whole, entire, all, gross.
Ana. Complete, *full, plenary: including *or* inclusive, comprehending *or* comprehensive (see corresponding verbs at INCLUDE).

total, *n.* *Sum, aggregate, whole, amount, number, quantity.

total, *v.* *Add, sum, figure, cast, foot.

totalitarian, *adj.* **Totalitarian, authoritarian,** as applied to a government or state, require discrimination, for, although applicable in current use to the same states, they actually carry a different emphasis. **Totalitarian** implies as an objective an undivided state in which all power (political, economic, commercial, cultural, religious, etc.) is vested in the government, and in which the people as a unit sanction and support this government and obey its orders. Practically, it implies toleration of but one political party, the one which supports the government, and the concentration of authority in the hands of one person or group, theoretically the mouthpiece of the people. **Authoritarian** implies a type of governmental organization in which professedly as well as actually all political power is ultimately concentrated in the hands of a leader, or dictator, and not as in democratic countries, in the people or in a representative body. No matter how the various powers vested in the government may be distributed for practical purposes, an *authoritarian* state is so organized that the final and determining authority is its head. Practically, an *authoritarian* government, though professing political power, often extends its control over the economic and cultural life of the people; thus, Italy, with the rise of Mussolini and the Fascists to power in 1922, became an *authoritarian* state; Germany, with the election of Hitler as Chancellor in 1933, became a *totalitarian* state.

totter. *Shake, tremble, quake, quaver, quiver, shiver, shudder, wobble, teeter, shimmy, didder, dither.
Ana. Rock, agitate, *shake, convulse: sway, *swing, fluctuate, oscillate, waver.

touch, *v.* **1** *Affect, influence, impress, strike, sway.
Ana. Arouse, *stir: excite, stimulate, quicken (see PROVOKE): *injure, harm, damage, hurt, impair.
2 Approach, rival, *match, equal.

touch, *n.* **Touch, suggestion, suspicion, soupçon, tincture, tinge, shade, smack, spice, dash, vein, strain, streak** come into comparison not in their literal senses, where they exhibit great divergence in meaning, but in their extended senses when they mean a perceptible trace of something foreign, extraneous, peculiar, or the like. **Touch** often suggests an impression left on someone or something by or as if by contact with another, but in general, it does not hold close to its literal sense and may imply little more than an appreciable trace; as, "In the air was a *touch* of frost" (*Galsworthy*); "He was a very active lad, fair-haired, with a *touch* of the Dane or Norwegian about him" (*D. H. Lawrence*); "heard in Mrs. Hetherington's voice that acid *touch*" (*M. Austin*). **Suggestion** implies an outward sign that is just enough to give one a hint or an inkling of the presence or existence of something; as, his voice conveyed a *suggestion* of fear; blue with a mere *suggestion* of green. **Suspicion** and the French word **soupçon** differ little from *suggestion*, but they tend to imply a fainter trace requiring even more delicate powers of perception or evoking even less certainty; as, tea with a *suspicion* (or *soupçon*) of brandy; add but a *soupçon* of red pepper; "Just a *suspicion*...of saturnine or sarcastic humor" (*A. W. Ward*). **Tincture, tinge,** and **shade** come from the vocabulary of color. *Tincture* and *tinge* usually imply an admixture with something that gives the thing affected a faint cast or appearance suggestive of a lightly suffused coloring; as, "All manners take a *tincture* from our own" (*Pope*); there was not a *tincture* of overconfidence in his bearing; "Endowed them with that Cymric *tinge* to their habits" (*Meredith*); "a subjective *tinge* entered into the nineteenth-century description of nature" (*Jeans*); "Imagist poetry...is right in veering away from any *tinge* of archaism in its diction" (*Lowes*). *Shade* implies enough of a trace to suggest the smallest possible degree of something: it usually derives its implications from the meaning of *shade* as a gradation in the darkening of a color; as, "He smiled; in that smile there was a *shade* of patronage" (*Galsworthy*); " 'I simply couldn't help myself,' he said with a *shade* of sulkiness" (*Arch. Marshall*); "I known my Ellen—haughty, intractable; shall I say, just a *shade* unforgiving?" (*E. Wharton*). **Smack** and **spice** come from the vocabulary of the gustatory sense. *Smack* suggests a trace which is pronounced enough or decided enough for one to savor it; as, "the Saxon names of places, with the pleasant, wholesome *smack* of the soil in them" (*Arnold*). Not only *spice*, but also **dash,** suggests a slight admixture or infusion, especially such as gives zest, relish, or pungency; as, "There was a *spice* of obstinacy about Miss Dale" (*Trollope*); "A king of England should have a *spice* of the devil in his composition" (*Smollett*); "Sévigné...lover of Montaigne and with a *spice* of his free thought and speech" (*FitzGerald*); "He is a man with a *dash* of genius in him" (*Arnold*); "Godwin ...has a *dash* of affectation" (*Lamb*). **Vein** applies to a trace that runs through a person or thing in the manner of a vein (sometimes a blood vessel, sometimes a vein of ore) so that it lies below the substance or character of the thing as a whole and occasionally shows on the surface or crops out; as, "thy humorous *vein*" (*Prior*); "In Swift he discovered an inimitable *vein* of irony" (*Johnson*); "He had always had a *vein* of childish obstinacy" (*M. Wilkins*). **Strain** sometimes denotes an inherited characteristic or group of characteristics, especially one that contrasts sharply with the rest of one's qualities; as, "the balanced play within me of the Oliver *strain*, Wheatley *strain*, Ellis *strain*, Gray *strain*" (*H. Ellis*); "a *strain* of eccentricity, amounting in some cases almost to insanity" (*L. P. Smith*). **Streak,** like *strain*, is applied chiefly to one's character, but it less often implies inheritance and heightens *strain's* suggestion of unexpectedness; as, when you know him better you will find the yellow *streak* in him; "Sometimes I think [she]... has a common *streak* in her" (*Winston Churchill* [*Amer. novelist*]).

Ana. *Trace, vestige: contamination, pollution, defilement, tainting (see corresponding verbs at CONTAMINATE): *impression, impress, imprint, stamp, print.

touching. Affecting, *moving, impressive, poignant, pathetic.

Ana. *Tender, responsive, sympathetic, compassionate: *pitiful, piteous, pitiable.

touchstone. Criterion, *standard, gauge, yardstick.

Ana. Test, proof, trial, demonstration (see under PROVE).

touchy. *Irascible, choleric, splenetic, testy, techy, cranky, cross.

Ana. *Irritable, fractious, snappish, waspish, peevish: captious, caviling, faultfinding, carping (see CRITICAL).

Ant. Imperturbable.

tough. Tenacious, stout, sturdy, *strong, stalwart.

Ana. Resisting *or* resistent, withstanding, opposing (see corresponding verbs at OPPOSE): *firm, hard: intractable, refractory, recalcitrant, headstrong (see UNRULY): dogged, pertinacious, *obstinate, stubborn.

Ant. Fragile.

tour, *n.* *Journey, voyage, trip, cruise, expedition, jaunt, excursion, pilgrimage.

tow, *v.* Tug, haul, hale, *pull, draw, drag.

tower, *v.* Mount, ascend, soar, rocket, *rise, arise, levitate, surge.

toxic *or* **toxical.** *Poisonous, venomous, virulent, mephitic, pestilent, pestilential, miasmatic, miasmic, miasmal.

toxin. *Poison, venom, virus, bane.

toy, *v.* *Trifle, dally, flirt, coquet.

Ana. *Play, sport, disport, frolic: fondle, *caress, pet, cuddle, dandle.

trace, *n.* **Trace, vestige, track, rack** come into comparison as meaning a visible or otherwise sensible sign left by something that has passed or has taken place. **Trace** literally applies (sometimes in the plural, sometimes in the singular) to a line as of footprints or a rut made by someone or something that has left marks of its passage; as, to follow the *traces* of a deer through the snow; the clear *trace* of a sleigh; "When the hounds of spring are on winter's *traces*" (*Swinburne*); "it was the Indian's way to pass through a country...and leave no *trace*" (*Cather*); "the *trace* Of higher tides along the beach" (*Millay*). But the term is more often used without reference to a line, to suggest any mark, material or immaterial, that shows something that has happened or has influenced a person or thing; as, the child carefully removed the *traces* of jam from his mouth; "faint *traces* of the Norfolk dialect...still lingered about her speech" (*Arch. Marshall*); "the stimulation of violent emotions may leave permanent *traces* on the mind" (*Inge*). **Vestige** (etymologically, a footprint) is now practically obsolete in its earliest sense. In extended use, it is preferred to *trace* when the reference is to something that remains or still exists to give evidence of or testimony to the existence of something in the past: it often therefore applies to remains, such as a fragment, a remnant, a relic, or other tangible or sensible reminder of what has gone before; as, "Of this ancient custom no *vestige* remained" (*Gibbon*); "The *vestiges* of some knowledge of Latin still appear...in his sentences" (*The Nation*). "There is, to be sure, keen zest in retracing the *vestiges* of primitive poetry, and in reconstructing, ex pede Herculem, primitive poetry itself" (*Lowes*). "But this space between the stars, which I have called a desert of emptiness, is not entirely empty. There are *vestiges* of matter everywhere" (*Eddington*). **Track** is now used more often than *trace* in the sense of a line of perceptible marks, especially in hunting (when it often means the scent followed by the hounds) and in geology (when it usually means a line of fossilized footprints); as, the hounds are on the *track* of the fox; the *track* of a dinosaur. "He could just discern the marks made by the little feet on the virgin snow, and he followed their *track* to the furze bushes" (*G. Eliot*). **Rack,** as here considered, owes its sense of a faint trace largely to Shakespeare's use in the passage from *The Tempest* (iv. 1, ll. 152–156): "The cloud-capp'd towers, the gorgeous palaces, The solemn temples, the great globe itself, Yea, all which it inherit, shall dissolve And, like this insubstantial pageant faded, Leave not a *rack* behind." Whether Shakespeare referred to *rack* in the sense of a driving mist, or in the dialectal sense of a track, or in the sense of wreckage (as in *rack* and ruin) has not been definitely established, but the term still occurs in the sense of a faint trace and in a phrase very similar to his; as, not a *rack* was left behind by the primitive race known to have lived in that section of the country.

Ana. *Sign, mark, token.

trace, *v.* *Sketch, outline, diagram, delineate, draft, plot, blueprint.

Ana. Copy, duplicate, reproduce (see corresponding nouns at REPRODUCTION): map, *chart, graph.

tracing, *n.* Sketch, outline, diagram, delineation, draft, plot, blueprint. See under SKETCH, *v.*

Ana. *Reproduction, copy, duplicate: *plan, project, scheme, plot, design.

track, *n.* *Trace, vestige, rack.

Ana. Print, stamp, imprint (see IMPRESSION): *sign, mark, token.

tract. *Area, region, zone, belt.

Ana. *Expanse, stretch, spread, amplitude: *locality, district, vicinity: section, sector, *part, portion.

tractable. Amenable, biddable, docile, *obedient.

Ana. Pliant, pliable, *plastic: submissive, subdued (see TAME): *compliant, acquiescent.

Ant. Intractable: unruly. — *Con.* Ungovernable, refractory, headstrong, willful (see UNRULY): stubborn, *obstinate.

trade, *n.* **1 Trade, craft, handicraft, art, profession** are here compared as general terms which designate a type of pursuit followed as an occupation or means of livelihood and requiring technical knowledge and skill. Not all pursuits of this description fall under one of these headings, especially pursuits that belong to fields of endeavor such as commerce, mercantile business, agriculture, and the like. **Trade,** as here compared, is applied chiefly to pursuits involving skilled manual or mechanical labor and the management of machinery or tools; as, the *trade* of a carpenter, of a bricklayer, of a blacksmith; he is a plumber, or a tinsmith, or a machinist by *trade*. **Craft** is not always clearly distinguished from *trade*, but it tends to be used of those pursuits that involve not only manual or mechanical labor but allow more or less freedom for the exercise of taste, skill, ingenuity, and the like: many of the crafts were once or are still carried on inde-

pendently, as in the home; thus, weaving, tailoring, shoemaking are often spoken of as *crafts;* the *craft* of a goldsmith, of a potter, of a cabinetmaker. **Handicraft** differs from *craft* chiefly in excluding all implication of machine work; it not only implies handwork but usually suggests dexterity in manipulation of instruments or of materials; thus, basketmaking, embroidery, lacemaking, bookbinding, and the like, are *handicrafts* when machinery is not employed. **Art** is the least definitely or consistently used of these words; it is found in such phrases as the manual *arts;* the industrial *arts;* the mechanic *arts;* the household *arts;* the decorative *arts;* the fine *arts; arts* and crafts; the practical *arts*, in which it refers sometimes to pursuits (as, workers employed in the industrial *arts*), sometimes to fields of endeavor (as, a school of practical *arts*), and sometimes to the things that are produced by art in any one of the senses considered at ART, 1 (as, an *arts* and crafts exhibition). As a term denoting a pursuit, *art*, when unqualified, usually designates painting (as, his energies are devoted to *art*), but it sometimes is more comprehensive, including sculpture, etching, illustration, and the like. When qualified, *art* is applied usually only to such pursuits as involve an elaborate technique, great skill, definite ends to be achieved, and the exercise of personal judgment or taste; it is often difficult, however, apart from the context, to determine whether the word denotes a pursuit or a technique; as, the *art* of navigation; the *art* of interior decorating; "dancing as an *art*, a profession, an amusement" (*H. Ellis*); "proficient in the *art* of self-defence" (*Shaw*); "literature is an *art* and therefore not to be pondered only, but practiced" (*Quiller-Couch*). **Profession** is, in general, applied only to a pursuit that requires years of study and training before one is ready to follow it as a means of livelihood; the term also often implies that one has undergone certain tests of one's fitness and has won a degree or has given proof of one's qualifications and has been licensed to practice; it often also implies devotion to a higher end than that of personal profit or the earning of a livelihood; as, the *professions* of law, medicine, architecture, and teaching; a clergyman, a nurse, a civil engineer, a dentist by *profession*.
Ana. *Work, employment, occupation, pursuit, métier: job, *position, place, situation.
2 *Business, traffic.
Ana. Selling, bartering, vending (see SELL): buying, purchasing (see BUY): exchanging *or* exchange, interchanging *or* interchange (see corresponding verbs at EXCHANGE).
3 Commerce, *business, industry.

trade, *v.* Barter, *sell, vend, auction.
Ana. *Exchange, interchange, swap, bandy.

traditional. **Traditional, legendary** are often used as though they both implied a lack of historical foundation. Basically, however, **traditional** does not necessarily imply a lack of authenticity, for it stresses the point that the thing so described has been handed down from generation to generation chiefly by word of mouth, without support of original documents or primary sources; as, *traditional* (i.e., unwritten) history; the *traditional* successors of Peter as bishop of Rome; "the unspoiled *traditional* ballad" (*F. J. Child*); "[Augustus's] preservation throughout the provinces of *traditional* worships" (*Buchan*). But since this method of survival usually implies an absence of documentary support, the term now often implies historical uncertainty or even unreliability; as, the *traditional* birthplace of a great poet; "the *traditional* region of the forty days temptation" (*S. C. Bartlett*); "the *traditional* luck of fools for once protected the wise man" (*Karl K. Darrow*). **Legendary** (for further treatment, see FICTITIOUS) etymologically implies reference to a story (a legend) that has been written so that one may read (L. *legere*, to read) it by himself or to others. Since legends were written largely for edification or entertainment, or both, and often dealt with reputed miracles of saints or fabulous exploits of heroes, the authentic character of the incidents was not a matter of concern when legends were a popular form of literature. Consequently, the term has acquired connotations of fabulousness and of mythical basis; as, "Is it [*Beowulf*] entirely mythical and *legendary*, or is there any actual history contained in it?" (*S. Brooke*).

traduce. *Malign, asperse, vilify, calumniate, defame, slander, libel.
Ana. *Decry, detract from, derogate from, depreciate, disparage: revile, vituperate (see SCOLD, *v.*).

traffic, *n.* **1** *Business, commerce, trade, industry.
Ana. Transportation, conveyance, carrying (see corresponding verbs at CARRY).
2 *Business, trade.
Ana. Selling, vending, bartering, trading (see SELL): buying, purchasing (see BUY).
3 *Intercourse, commerce, dealings, communication, communion, commune, conversation, converse, correspondence.
Ana. Familiarity, intimacy, closeness (see corresponding adjectives at FAMILIAR).

trail, *v.* *Follow, pursue, chase, tag, tail.

train, *n.* *Succession, progression, series, sequence, set, suit, suite, chain, string.

train, *v.* **1** *Teach, discipline, school, instruct, educate.
Ana. *Practice, exercise, drill: *habituate, accustom, familiarize: *harden, inure, season.
2 Aim, *direct, point, level, lay.
Ana. *Turn, divert, deflect.

traipse. *Wander, stray, roam, ramble, rove, range, prowl, gad, gallivant, meander.

traitorous. Treacherous, perfidious, *faithless, false, disloyal.
Ana. Recreant, renegade, apostate (see corresponding nouns at RENEGADE): seditious, mutinous, rebellious (see INSUBORDINATE): disaffected, estranged, alienated (see ESTRANGE).

trammel. *Hamper, fetter, shackle, clog, manacle, hog-tie.
Ana. *Hinder, impede, obstruct, block, bar: *restrain, curb, check, inhibit: *limit, restrict, circumscribe, confine.

tramp, tramper. *Vagabond, vagrant, hobo, truant, bum, stiff, swagman, sundowner.

tranquil. Serene, placid, *calm, peaceful, halcyon.
Ana. Quiet, *still, silent, noiseless: *soft, gentle, mild: restful, reposeful, *comfortable: *cool, composed, collected.
Ant. Troubled.

transcend. Surpass, *exceed, excel, outdo, outstrip.
Ana. Surmount, overcome (see CONQUER).

transcendent. **1** Surpassing, superlative, *supreme, peerless, pre-eminent, incomparable, banner.
Ana. *Consummate, finished, accomplished: *perfect, entire, whole, intact.
2 Transcendental, ideal, *abstract.
Ana. Absolute, *ultimate, categorical: *infinite, boundless, eternal.

transcendental. Transcendent, ideal, *abstract.
Ana. *Supernatural, supranatural: categorical, *ultimate.

transcript. Copy, carbon copy, duplicate, *reproduction, facsimile, replica.

transfer, *v.* **1** *Move, remove, shift.

Ana. *Carry, convey, transport, transmit: *commit, consign.

2 Transfer, convey, alienate, alien, deed are here compared chiefly as legal terms meaning to make over property from one owner to another. **Transfer** is the general term; it is applicable when the property is real or personal, and when it is passed from one owner to another by sale, gift, foreclosure, or the like. **Convey** stresses the legalistic aspects of the transfer; it is the precise term when a sealed writing, or deed, plays an essential part in the transfer. It is therefore used chiefly of the transfer of real property and of ships. **Alienate** and the less used **alien** are not always clearly distinguished from *transfer* or *convey;* in strict legal use, however, they imply the passing of a title by the act of the owner as distinguished from its passing by the operation of the law, as in the case of inheritance by descent; thus, entailed property cannot be *alienated. Alienate,* however, may be used when the sale of property is not voluntary but is ordered or enforced by a court, as in foreclosure or in condemnation proceedings. In nonlegal use, *alienate* often implies diversion as by force, or by a sovereign power, an imperative need, or the like. "He pleaded for the resumption by clerics of Church revenues *alienated* into lay hands" (*Belloc*). **Deed** is a popular rather than a legal term, but it is equivalent to *convey.*

transfiguration. Transformation, metamorphosis, transmutation, conversion, transmogrification. See under TRANSFORM.

Ana. Exaltation, magnification (see corresponding verbs at EXALT): enhancing, heightening, intensifying (see INTENSIFY).

transfigure. *Transform, metamorphose, transmute, convert, transmogrify.

Ana. *Exalt, magnify: heighten, enhance, *intensify.

transform. Transform, metamorphose, transmute, convert, transmogrify, transfigure agree in meaning to turn or change one thing into another or different thing. In general, the same differences in implications and connotations are observable in the corresponding nouns **transformation, metamorphosis, transmutation, conversion, transmogrification, transfiguration** (*or, rarely,* **transfigurement**). **Transform** etymologically implies a change in outward form or shape but in its extended use often implies (additionally or singly) a change in character, in nature, in function, or the like; as, to *transform* electrical energy into light or heat; "To Samarcand ...we owe the art of *transforming* linen into paper" (*Newman*); "The placid sunshine...seems to have been *transformed* in a moment into imperious angry fire" (*Pater*); "the task of *transforming* a heterogeneous selection of mankind into a homogeneous nation" (*B. Russell*). "Every phenomenon of nature, night and 'rosy-fingered' dawn, earth and sun, winds, rivers, and seas, sleep and death—all have been *transformed* [by ancient Greek religion] into Divine and conscious agents" (*G. L. Dickinson*). **Metamorphose** is etymologically akin in meaning to *transform.* Actually, however, it carries implications not often present in *transform* such as that of a supernaturally or magically induced change (as, "*metamorphosed* from seemly shape to birds and ugly beasts"—*Gascoigne;* men *metamorphosed* by Circe into swine), or of a change in structure and habits that marks a stage of the development of some forms of animal life (as, the caterpillar is a larva which is finally *metamorphosed* into a butterfly or moth), or of a transformation induced by chemical or other natural agencies (as, rocks *metamorphosed* by heat). In general use, the term carries a much stronger implication than *transform* of an abrupt, startling, or violent change; as, "this kind of passive, plastic nature, where the whole man is *metamorphosed* into an impersonal poetic instrument, is, I believe, rare" (*Day Lewis*); "the friendliness she had formerly evidenced to the United States had been *metamorphosed* into hostility" (*V. Heiser*). "The nerves may be compared to a number of telephone wires transmitting electric currents into a prison-cell, which suitable instruments subsequently *metamorphose* into messages of sound, television, etc." (*Jeans*). **Transmute,** originally not clearly distinguishable from *transform,* was early affected by its use in alchemy in the sense of to turn a base metal (such as lead) into a precious metal (such as gold). Consequently, the term usually suggests an elemental change, especially one involving a metamorphosis of a lower element or thing into a higher one. "If there was an element in her which religion could not perfectly reach, perfectly *transmute,* she groaned over this element in her, she chid it, she made it bow" (*Arnold*). "A simple romantic narrative *transmuted* by sheer glow or beauty into a prose poem" (*Galsworthy*). "Shakespeare, too, was occupied with the struggle—which alone constitutes life for a poet—to *transmute* his personal and private agonies into something rich and strange, something universal and impersonal" (*T. S. Eliot*). "Once people had tasted of Mrs. Struthers's easy Sunday hospitality they were not likely to sit at home remembering that her champagne was *transmuted* Shoe-Polish" (*E. Wharton*). **Convert** carries a slighter suggestion of change in kind, nature, or structure than the preceding terms, but a stronger one of a change in details which fit it for a given use or function or for a new use or function, or in properties or the like; as, to *convert* a passenger liner into an auxiliary cruiser; to *convert* iron into steel; nature *converts* the fallen trunks of trees into coal; "Having conducted their lame guest to a room in the Georgian corridor hastily *converted* to a bedroom" (*Galsworthy*); "any error of judgment upon his part might have *converted* his profit into a loss" (*J. A. Hobson*); "that a new seam of richest material has been opened up and that poets are learning how to *convert* that raw material to their own uses" (*Day Lewis*). **Transmogrify** implies a thoroughgoing metamorphosis; often, a grotesque, bewildering, or sometimes, preposterous one: the term is often used humorously but is increasingly employed without intent to amuse; as, "See Social life and Glee sit down, All joyous and unthinking, Till, quite *transmugrify'd,* they're grown Debauchery and Drinking" (*Burns*). "Shakespeare was a much finer instrument for transformations than any of his contemporaries....The element of Seneca is the most completely absorbed and *transmogrified,* because it was already the most diffused throughout Shakespeare's world" (*T. S. Eliot*). "The classical heroes and heroines were *transmogrified* into mediaeval knights and ladies" (*Lowes*). **Transfigure,** which is strongly influenced by Biblical usage, suggests an exaltation or glorification of the outward appearance; as, "Jesus...was *transfigured* before them: and his face did shine as the sun" (*Matthew* xvii. 1–2); "If she be guilty, 'twill *transform* her To manifest deformity... If innocent, she will become *transfigured* Into an angel" (*Shelley*).

Ana. *Change, alter, modify, vary.

transformation. Metamorphosis, transmutation, conversion, transmogrification, transfiguration. See under TRANSFORM.

Ana. Change, alteration, modification, variation (see under CHANGE, *v.*): evolution, *development.

transgression. Trespass, violation, infraction, *breach, infringement, contravention.

Ana. Encroachment, invasion, entrenchment (see corresponding verbs at TRESPASS): slip, lapse, *error: *offense, sin, vice, crime.

transient, *adj.* **Transient, transitory, passing, ephemeral, momentary, fugitive, fleeting, evanescent, short-lived** come into comparison as meaning lasting or staying only for a short time. *Transient* and *transitory* are often used as if they were interchangeable; but **transient** more frequently applies to that which is actually short in its duration or stay (as, the summer hotel does not take *transient* guests; "*transient* sorrows"—*Wordsworth;* "With one of these friends he had fallen in love,—a slight and *transient* fancy, but which had already called his poetical powers into exercise"—*Arnold*), and **transitory,** like its close synonym **passing,** to that which is by its nature or essence bound to pass or come to an end, sometimes soon, sometimes inevitably (as, "this *transitory* life"—*Bk. of Com. Prayer;* "Wise men will apply their remedies to... the causes of evil which are permanent, not to...the *transitory* modes in which they appear"—*Burke;* a *passing* fancy; "The confounding of the *Passing* with the Permanent"—*A. Austin*). **Ephemeral** etymologically implies existence for a day: in this strict sense it is applied to certain living things; as, *ephemeral* insects; *ephemeral* flowers. In extended use, it implies marked shortness of life or duration, as of influence or appeal; as, many slang expressions are of their very nature *ephemeral;* "the swarm of *ephemeral* sermons which issue from the press" (*Sydney Smith*); "*ephemeral* successes" (*J. R. Lowell*). **Momentary** literally implies the duration of a moment or of an almost incredibly short time; as, "a *momentary* bliss" (*Gray*); "a *momentary* irritation" (*Hardy*). **Fugitive** and **fleeting** apply to that which passes swiftly, and is gone; but *fugitive* carries a stronger implication of a momentary catching or fixing (as, "Oh joy!... That nature yet remembers What was so *fugitive!*"—*Wordsworth;* "All the forms are *fugitive,* but the substances survive"—*Emerson*) and *fleeting,* of the impossibility of holding back or restraining from flight (as, "not merely some *fleeting* fancy of the day, but a constant longing"—*J. R. Lowell;* "[It] clothes our *fleeting* days with an eternal beauty"—*B. F. Westcott*). **Evanescent** implies momentariness, but it stresses quick and complete vanishing, and it usually connotes an extremely delicate, fragile, or intangible quality; as, "*evanescent* visitations of thought and feeling...arising unforeseen and departing unbidden" (*Shelley*); "All was unstable; quivering as leaves, *evanescent* as lightning" (*Hardy*); "It is poetry of the most *evanescent* type, so tenuous in thought and feeling that only the most exquisite diction can justify its perpetuation in cold print" (*Grandgent*). **Short-lived** implies extreme brevity of life or existence; as, *short-lived* fame; their satisfaction was *short-lived;* a *short-lived* plant; a *short-lived* controversy.

Ant. Perpetual. — *Con.* *Lasting, permanent, perdurable, stable, durable.

transitory. *Transient, passing, ephemeral, momentary, fugitive, fleeting, evanescent, short-lived.

Ant. Everlasting: perpetual.

translation. Translation, version, paraphrase, metaphrase, construe are here compared only as denoting a rendering in intelligible language the meaning or sense of a passage or work, or the passage or work that is the product of such a rendering. **Translation** implies a turning from one language into another, or in its extended use, from one medium, or form of expression, into another; as, English *translations* of the Bible; a literal *translation* of the Odyssey is likely to lose the charm of the original; a free *translation* that catches the spirit of the original; "[Great writers'] music is the audible *translation* of emotion" (*H. Ellis*). **Version,** as here compared (see also ACCOUNT, 3), may be used in place of *translation* (as, "The year 1632 saw a complete *version* of the Aeneid by Vicars"—*J. Conington*), but it is much more often used to denote one of the translations of a given work, especially (if without further identification) of the Bible; as, the Authorized, or King James, *Version;* the Douay *Version* is used by English-speaking Roman Catholics; to compare the Butcher-Lang and the George Herbert Palmer *versions* of the Odyssey. **Paraphrase** may apply to a very free translation, the purpose of which is to present clearly the meaning rather than the phrasing of a passage or work (as, "a *translation* must be a *paraphrase* to be readable"—*FitzGerald*): it also may apply to an imitation with enough changes to obscure its indebtedness to an original in another tongue (as, "[Latin] plays which were not *paraphrases* from the Greek"—*Buchan*): commonly, however, the term denotes a free, amplified, and often, interpretative rendering of the sense of a difficult passage in the same language (as, to write a *paraphrase* of Milton's Lycidas; *paraphrases* of the Psalms in the Authorized Version). **Metaphrase** is occasionally used by learned writers to denote a translation that is almost slavishly faithful to the original (what is now often called a *literal translation*) to distinguish it from a *paraphrase,* or free translation; as, "The way I have taken [in a translation of the Aeneid] is not so straight as *metaphrase,* nor so loose as *paraphrase*" (*Dryden*). **Construe** is chiefly an academic term for an exercise in translation which emphasizes close adherence to the grammatical construction of the original and its word-for-word arrangement.

translucent. Lucid, pellucid, diaphanous, limpid, *clear, transparent.

Ana. Luminous, radiant, brilliant, effulgent, *bright: iridescent, opalescent, *prismatic.

transmit. *Carry, bear, convey, transport.

Ana. *Move, remove, shift, transfer: *communicate, impart: propagate, breed, engender, *generate.

transmogrification. Transformation, metamorphosis, transmutation, conversion, transfiguration. See under TRANSFORM.

transmogrify. *Transform, metamorphose, transmute, convert, transfigure.

transmutation. Transformation, metamorphosis, conversion, transmogrification, transfiguration. See under TRANSFORM.

transmute. *Transform, metamorphose, convert, transmogrify, transfigure.

transparent. *Clear, lucid, pellucid, diaphanous, translucent, limpid.

Ant. Opaque. — *Con.* *Turbid, muddy, roiled, roily.

transpire. *Happen, hap, occur, chance, befall, betide.

transport, *v.* **1** *Carry, bear, convey, transmit.

Ana. *Move, remove, shift, transfer: *bring, fetch, take.

2 Deport, *banish, exile, expatriate, ostracize, extradite.

Ana. Expel, *eject, oust.

transport, *n.* *Ecstasy, rapture.

Ana. Enthusiasm, *passion, fervor, ardor: *inspiration, fury, frenzy: bliss, beatitude, blessedness, felicity, *happiness.

transpose. *Reverse, invert.

Ana. *Exchange, interchange, swap: transfer, shift (see MOVE).

trap, *n.* *Lure, bait, decoy, snare.

Ana. Stratagem, ruse, *trick, maneuver, artifice, wile, feint: *ambush, ambuscade: intrigue, machination, *plot, conspiracy.

trap, *v.* Entrap, snare, ensnare, bag, *catch, capture, nab, cop.

Ana. Seize, *take, clutch, grasp: betray, beguile, delude (see DECEIVE).

travail. 1 Labor, *work, swink, toil, drudgery, grind.
Ana. *Effort, exertion, pains, trouble.
2 Labor, *childbirth, parturition, delivery, accouchement.

traverse. *Deny, gainsay, contradict, negative, impugn, contravene.
Ana. Controvert, confute, refute, *disprove, rebut.
Ant. Allege.

travesty, *n.* *Caricature, parody, burlesque.

travesty, *v.* Caricature, parody, burlesque. See under CARICATURE, *n.*
Ana. *Copy, mimic, ape, mock, imitate.

treacherous. Perfidious, traitorous, *faithless, false, disloyal.
Ana. Betraying, deceiving, misleading, double-crossing (see DECEIVE): recreant, dastardly (see COWARDLY): seditious, mutinous, rebellious (see INSUBORDINATE): *dangerous, perilous, jeopardous.

treason. *Sedition.
Ana. Revolution, revolt, *rebellion, uprising, insurrection: betrayal, deceiving *or* deception, double-crossing (see corresponding verbs at DECEIVE): overthrowing *or* overthrow, subverting *or* subversion (see corresponding verbs at OVERTURN).
Ant. Allegiance (sense 2).

treasure, *v.* Prize, value, *appreciate, cherish.
Ana. Esteem, respect, regard, admire (see under REGARD, *n.*): *revere, reverence, venerate: *save, preserve, conserve.

treasury. 1 Thesaurus, *museum, library, gallery, archives.
2 *Anthology, garland, florilegium, thesaurus, corpus, chrestomathy, chapbook.

treat, *v.* Parley, negotiate, *confer, commune, consult, advise.
Ana. *Discuss, dispute, argue, debate: *consider, weigh, revolve, study: *think, reason, deliberate.

treaty. *Contract, bargain, compact, pact, entente, convention, cartel, covenant, concordat, indenture, mise.

tremble. *Shake, quake, quiver, shiver, shudder, quaver, totter, wobble, teeter, shimmy, didder, dither.
Ana. *Thrill, electrify: falter, waver (see HESITATE): quail, shrink, wince (see RECOIL).

tremendous. Stupendous, monumental, prodigious, *monstrous.
Ana. *Enormous, immense, huge, vast, gigantic, colossal: astounding, amazing, flabbergasting (see SURPRISE): terrifying, alarming, startling, frightening (see FRIGHTEN).

trench, *v.* Entrench, encroach, invade, *trespass, infringe.
Ana. See those at ENTRENCH.

trenchant. *Incisive, clear-cut, cutting, biting, crisp.
Ana. Piercing, penetrating, probing (see ENTER): *sharp, keen, acute: *sarcastic, satirical, ironical, sardonic: *caustic, mordant, acrid, scathing: poignant, *pungent, piquant.

trend. *Tendency, drift, tenor, current.
Ana. Movement, *motion, move: inclination, disposition, predisposition (see corresponding verbs at INCLINE): progression, *progress.

trepidation. Horror, terror, panic, consternation, *fear, dread, fright, alarm, dismay.
Ana. Apprehensiveness, fearfulness (see corresponding adjectives at FEARFUL): anxiety, worry, concern, solicitude, *care: awe, *reverence, fear.

trespass, *v.* **Trespass, encroach, trench, entrench** (*or* **intrench**), **infringe, invade** are not close synonyms, for some are intransitive and usually require a preposition such as *on* or *upon*, whereas the others may be used both transitively and intransitively. Nevertheless they come into comparison because they all mean to make inroads upon the property, territory, or rights of another. **Trespass,** which is now almost always an intransitive verb, implies an intrusion, often one that is either an unwarranted and unpardonable or an unlawful and offensive intrusion: it is usually, but not necessarily, followed by *on* or *upon;* as, to warn hunters against *trespassing* on his land; "shall probably *trespass* on your hospitality till the Saturday se'nnight following" (*Austen*); "what is the difference between the legitimate music of verse and the music it attains by *trespassing* on the domain of a sister art?" (*Babbitt*); "It is essential that...an artist should consciously or unconsciously draw a circle beyond which he does not *trespass*" (*T. S. Eliot*). **Encroach** usually implies gradual or stealthy entrance upon another's territory or assumption of another's rights or possessions: the term may imply either the act of persons or the agency of things which by their nature cannot remain within bounds; as, "Impertinence...ever *encroaches* when it is tolerated" (*Burney*); "an ancient manor, deserted as the sea *encroached*" (*Pater*); "There were clumps of perennials in the borders, upon which each year the grass *encroached* more and more" (*Deland*); "The motive of simplicity is to prevent frivolities of fashion from *encroaching* upon our time" (*Inge*); "By excessive demands upon certain incomes or forms of property, a State may injuriously *encroach* upon the true costs of pecuniary incentives necessary to make capital, ability, or labour function with full efficiency" (*J. A. Hobson*). The once more common **trench** and the currently more commonly **entrench** throw less emphasis upon unlawful intrusion and more upon cutting into or digging one's way into what belongs to another, or should be used in another way, or is outside one's sphere, than do the preceding words; as, demands that *entrench* too much upon one's time; questions *trenching* on rudeness; "it does not appear that he *entrenched* upon his own or his mother's private fortune; from now onwards he never seems to have suffered from financial embarrassment" (*Buchan*). **Infringe** implies an encroachment that is a clear breach of the law or violation of the rights of another: the term is used both transitively and intransitively; as, to *infringe* a patent or a copyright; "He was *infringing* upon the liberties of a man who had never done him any injury" (*Edgeworth*); "the physicians whose exclusive distinction seemed *infringed* on" (*G. Eliot*); the statute proposed would *infringe* fundamental principles as they have been understood by the traditions of our people and our law" (*Justice Holmes*). **Invade,** which is more often a transitive than an intransitive verb, implies a definite entrance into the territory or rights of another, usually (but not now always) with hostile intent and with injurious effect; as, to *invade* the enemy's country; the gangrene has *invaded* healthy tissues; "where there is a legal right, there is also a legal remedy by suit, or action at law, whenever that right is *invaded*" (*Blackstone*); a crowd of tourists *invade* the town each week end.
Ana. *Intrude, obtrude, interlope, butt in: interfere, intervene, *interpose.

trespass, *n.* Transgression, violation, infraction, *breach, infringement, contravention.
Ana. Invading *or* invasion, entrenchment, encroachment (see corresponding verbs at TRESPASS): intrusion, obtrusion (see corresponding verbs at INTRUDE): *offense, sin, vice, crime.

trial. 1 Test, proof, demonstration. See under PROVE.

Ana. Experiment, *experience: inspection, examination, scanning, scrutiny (see under SCRUTINIZE): *process, proceeding, procedure.

2 Trial, tribulation, affliction, visitation, cross are comparable only when they denote suffering, misery, or unhappiness regarded as an infliction which cannot be escaped or avoided. **Trial** implies a test of one's patience, self-control, courage, or of one's power to resist temptation. The word is applicable not only to distressing situations or conditions but to persons or things that cause distress or annoyance; as, the *trials* of the colonists are recorded in history; a life free from *trials*, small or great; characters purified and strengthened by *trial;* he has always been a *trial* to his parents. **Tribulation** heightens the emphasis on the suffering or anguish involved in *trial;* even more often than the latter it connotes divinely permitted suffering as a test of virtue. "The just shall...after all their *tribulations* long, See golden days" (*Milton*). **Affliction** stresses the implication of imposed suffering that challenges one's powers of endurance; it may, but more often does not, suggest a relation between one's suffering and one's deserts. "If severe *afflictions* borne With patience merit the reward of peace, Peace ye deserve" (*Wordsworth*). **Visitation** bears to *affliction* the same relation as *tribulation* to *trial;* the former heightens the implications of the latter by stressing the severity of suffering and by suggesting an ordeal; distinctively, however, it often connotes retribution or retributive justice; as, many people regarded the distastrous flood as a *visitation*. "Woe unto them! for their day is come, the time of their *visitation*" (*Jeremiah* l. 27). **Cross** in its applications closely parallels *trial* and *tribulation*, but it differs from them in its implications of suffering accepted and borne for the sake of a larger good rather than as a test of character. "Leaving her... solemnly elate at the recognition of the *cross* on which she must agonize for the happiness of some other soul" (*Deland*). The word often directly alludes to the words of Jesus to the rich young man: "Come, take up the *cross*, and follow me" (*Mark* x. 21), or to his own carrying of the cross up the Mount of Calvary.

Ana. *Distress, suffering, misery, agony: *sorrow, grief, anguish, woe: *misfortune, adversity: *difficulty, hardship, vicissitude, rigor.

tribe, *n.* **Tribe, sib, clan, horde, sept** are here compared both in their general and technical senses as denoting a division of a race or people having a more or less primitive form of government. **Tribe** in its most common sense applies to an aggregate of persons believed to be or believing themselves to be of a common stock and governed more or less strictly by a chief, chieftain, or headman; often, but not invariably, the term suggests a nomadic life or a barbarous rather than a savage or civilized state. Originally, however, *tribe* was applied to one of the definite divisions of a people, such as the twelve *tribes* of Israel, each of which was believed to have been descended from one of the twelve sons of Jacob, or as the divisions of the ancient Romans varying from three to thirty-five in number at different times in the history of ancient Rome. In anthropology *tribe* usually denotes a social group that has been, by tradition, brought together because of their common ancestry, that is united under a chief or headman, and that marries only within the group. In theory, such a group comprises several smaller divisions, each one technically and specifically called a **sib,** or group consisting of all the people who trace their descent unilaterally (i.e., in the male line, or in the female line, only) from a real or supposed ancestor. Both the tribe as a whole and each of the sibs may have a distinct and characteristic form of worship. **Clan** was originally and still is most commonly applied to any of several groups comparable to a tribe in organization or to a sib in its membership, found in the Highlands, and to some extent in the Lowlands, of Scotland. Strictly, a *clan* consists of several families with the same surname that claim descent from a common ancestor, but it may include bondsmen, adopted foreigners, and members of families or subclans bearing different surnames. The head of the clan and the clan itself were usually designated by the surname; as, "the MacGregor" (i.e., the chief) of the MacGregors or of the *clan* MacGregor: cf. "MacGregor of that ilk" (see *ilk*, under TYPE). In sociology and anthropology a clan is closely related to a sib, in that a common name is characteristic, descent is traced in the male or in the female line only, and inbreeding by marriage is not demanded; also, a *clan*, in this sense, designates a division of a tribe, having its own political, religious, and social character and traditions. **Horde** (see also CROWD) suggests even less advance in civilization than *tribe* and, often, a looser organization. It was originally and is still often applied to one of the groups of nomads from Tatary or other parts of Asia that lived an unsettled life moving as a group from one place to another in search of pasturage for their flocks or for purposes of war or plunder; as, the "Golden *Horde*" of Mongol Tatars that overran eastern Europe in the thirteenth century. In sociology and anthropology, the term denotes one of the social groups comparable to a sib or clan that existed before the organization of tribes. **Sept** applies to the Irish equivalent of a clan in ancient and medieval times when Ireland was divided into small states or tribes, each governed by a king. Under their own lords or chiefs, the septs lived a community life, owned territory, and gave allegiance to the tribal king.

tribulation. *Trial, affliction, visitation, cross.

Ana. Oppression, persecution, wronging *or* wrong (see corresponding verbs at WRONG): *sorrow, grief, anguish, woe: *distress, suffering, misery, agony.

Ant. Consolation.

tributary, *adj.* *Subordinate, secondary, dependent, subject, succursal, collateral.

Ana. Conquered, vanquished, subjugated, subdued (see CONQUER): *auxiliary, subsidiary, ancillary, adjuvant, contributory.

tribute, *n.* **1** *Tax, levy, assessment, rate, excise, impost, customs, duty, toll, tariff, tithe, teind, cess.

2 *Encomium, eulogy, panegyric, citation.

trice, *n.* *Instant, moment, minute, second, flash, jiffy, twinkling, twinkle, split second.

trick, *n.* **Trick, ruse, stratagem, maneuver** (*or* **manoeuvre**), **artifice, wile, feint** agree in meaning an act or an expedient whereby one seeks to gain one's ends by indirection and ingenuity and, often, by cunning. **Trick** originally, and still frequently, implies cheating or deceiving and often, base ends. "When love begins to sicken and decay, It useth an enforced ceremony. There are no *tricks* in plain and simple faith" (*Shak.*). "She could not be entirely sure that...he was not after all merely using a *trick* to get rid of her" (*Bennett*). The word may, however, imply nothing more than roguishness or playfulness and be used to designate an antic, a prank, a practical joke, or a harmless hoax; as, the brothers were fond of playing *tricks* on their sisters; the *tricks* of the clowns in a circus. It may also be applied to any dexterous device or contrivance (not necessarily fraudulent) that pleases, persuades, deludes, or evokes surprise or wonder; as, an auctioneer who knows all the *tricks* of his trade; illusion in the theater is often accomplished by *tricks* of lighting. "That idle *trick* of making words jingle which men of Nuflo's class in my country so greatly admire" (*Hudson*). **Ruse** always implies an attempt to give a false impression, as by diverting others' attention from one's real purposes or by making what is untrue seem true. "That story to her mother about having been attacked by ruffians...had been an invention, a *ruse* to account plausibly for his presence on her mother's doorstep!" (*Bennett*). "A favorite *ruse* of the opium smugglers was to insert a hypodermic needle into an egg, withdraw carefully all the albumen and then refill the cavity with opium....the hole was expertly sealed" (*V. Heiser*). **Stratagem** etymologically implies generalship [Greek *stratēgos*, a general]; though commonly applied to a ruse by which an advantage is gained over an enemy as by outwitting or surprising him, it is not restricted to military operations; in extended use, it usually implies a clear objective such as entrapping or circumventing and a more or less elaborate plan for achieving one's end. "A prudent chief not always must display His pow'rs.... But with th' occasion and the place comply, Conceal his force, nay seem sometimes to fly. Those oft are *stratagems* which error seem" (*Pope*). "Some women...are driven to every possible *trick* and *stratagem* to entrap some man into marriage" (*Shaw*). **Maneuver** is also a military term, but it usually suggests tactics or handling and moving of troops or ships for the accomplishment of definite ends (as, peacetime *maneuvers*, or exercises), rather than strategy, the employment of military or naval forces in such a way as to get an advantage over the enemy. In extended use, it commonly implies adroit or dexterous manipulation of persons or things for one's own ends. "The Longbourn party were the last of all the company to depart, and, by a *manoeuvre* of Mrs. Bennet, had to wait for their carriage a quarter of an hour after everybody else was gone" (*Austen*). It may, however, be applied to a single strategic move comparable to one in a game of chess. "Unless indeed, all her talk of flight had been a blind, and her departure no more than a *manoeuvre*" (*E. Wharton*). **Artifice** suggests the employment of invented, manufactured, or mechanical devices or contrivances; it usually connotes ingenuity, but it may or may not connote an intent to deceive or overreach. "The memory of such men [the old bards] must have needed every *artifice* to help it; and the chief *artifice* to their hand was one which also delighted the ears of their listeners. They sang or intoned to the harp" (*Quiller-Couch*). "The *artifices* by which friends endeavor to spare one another's feelings are pretty disloyalties" (*Shaw*). **Wile** usually suggests sorcery, or an attempt to entrap or ensnare by allurements or by false and deceptive appearances. In earliest use, it always connoted slyness and imposture; now it often suggests coquetry or an attempt to charm. "Put on the whole armour of God, that ye may be able to stand against the *wiles* of the devil" (*Ephesians* vi. 11). "He was no longer a mild old man to be worked on by the *wiles* of engaging youth, but a stern-spoken person in high authority" (*Arch. Marshall*). **Feint** literally applies to a fencer's thrust, a boxer's blow, or the like, seemingly directed at one part of the opponent's body, but actually designed to divert his attention and his guards away from the part at which it is really aimed. In extended use, the term commonly implies the employment of a stratagem or maneuver which distracts attention from one's real end thereby leaving another person or other persons unaware of one's actual intention until it is accomplished; as, "I love to think The leaving us was just a *feint*" (*Browning*); his withdrawal from candidacy was actually a *feint* intended to accentuate the demand for his nomination; the regiment's movement toward A—— was a *feint* that caused the removal of a large part of the enemy's forces from B—— where the successful attack was launched.

Ana. *Imposture, deceit, deception, counterfeit, humbug, fake, cheat, fraud: *fun, jest, sport, game, play.

trick, *v.* Gull, befool, hoax, *dupe, hoodwink, bamboozle.

Ana. *Deceive, delude, beguile, mislead: outwit, circumvent (see FRUSTRATE): cajole, wheedle, blandish, *coax.

trickery. *Deception, double-dealing, chicanery, chicane, subterfuge, fraud.

Ana. *Deceit, dissimulation, guile, cunning, duplicity: *imposture, cheat, fraud, sham, fake, humbug, counterfeit.

tricky. Crafty, foxy, cunning, *sly, wily, artful.

Ana. *Crooked, devious, oblique: deceptive, delusive, *misleading, delusory: deceitful, *dishonest.

tried. *Reliable, dependable, trustworthy, trusty.

Ana. Stanch, steadfast, constant, *faithful: proved, demonstrated, tested (see PROVE).

trifle, *v.* **Trifle, toy, dally, flirt, coquet** come into comparison as meaning to deal with a person or thing without seriousness, earnestness, close attention, or purpose. **Trifle** is the most comprehensive term of the group, for it may be used interchangeably with any of the others, implying any of several attitudes such as playfulness, unconcern, indulgent contempt, light amorousness, or the like; as, "To *trifle* agreeably is a secret which schools cannot impart" (*Johnson*); "o'er cold coffee *trifle* with the spoon" (*Pope*); "'I must go instantly to my mother,' she cried; 'I would not on any account *trifle* with her affectionate solicitude'" (*Austen*); "You see what's to be done, and you hear what I say, and you know I'm not going to be *trifled* with any longer" (*Hardy*); "she began to *trifle* with plans of retirement, of playing in Paris, of taking a theatre in London, and other whims" (*Shaw*); "Niel sat writing in the back office, at the long table where he usually worked or *trifled*" (*Cather*). **Toy** implies a dealing with a person or thing in a way that keeps one pleasantly occupied but does not engage one's full attention or evoke any serious intention; as, to *toy* with a young girl's affections; when his mind is concentrated on a problem, his fingers *toy* with his watch chain; he was not hungry and only *toyed* with his food; "There is evidence that Augustus, like Julius, *toyed* with the idea of giving the Assemblies greater power and making them representative of the whole body of citizens in Italy" (*Buchan*). **Dally** (see also DELAY, 2) stresses indulgence in thoughts, plans, or the like, as a pastime or amusement rather than as leading to something definite or serious; as, "For so, to interpose a little ease, Let our frail thoughts *dally* with false surmise" (*Milton*); "I *dally* with my subject because, to myself, the remembrance of these times is profoundly interesting" (*De Quincey*); "Why should my Soul so rejoice in the crimes placarded by the evening papers, and never weary, in the streets of this cathedral city, of *dallying* with images of wrong?" (*L. P. Smith*). **Flirt,** which etymologically implies quick jerky movement, in this, its chief current sense, implies an interest or attention that exists only for the moment and passes quickly to another person or thing; as, she *flirts* with every handsome man she meets; "If he [a poet] is excited by a railway engine, well and good: if he is not, let him leave it alone and stop *flirting* with fashion by faking an emotion" (*Day Lewis*). **Coquet** usually implies a *trifling* in love, such as is characteristic of a flirtatious yet hard-to-catch young woman, but it is also used in reference to things which catch one's interest but with which one will not come fairly to terms; as, "After Gustavus' death there had been formed a new Protestant

League called that of Heilebron. Richelieu was *coquetting* with it" (*Belloc*); "Some of the Modernists have *coquetted* with this philosophy [pragmatism]" (*Inge*).

Ana. Palter, fib, equivocate, prevaricate, *lie: waver, vacillate, falter, *hesitate: dawdle, dillydally (see DELAY).

trifling. Trivial, *petty, puny, paltry, measly, picayunish, picayune.

Ana. Inane, wishy-washy, banal, jejune, vapid, *insipid: *vain, idle, otiose, nugatory, empty, hollow: *venial, pardonable.

trig. Trim, *neat, tidy, spick-and-span, snug, shipshape.

Ana. *Orderly, methodical: spruce, dapper (see STYLISH): *debonair, jaunty.

trigger man. Gunman, assassin, finger man, cutthroat, bravo.

trim, *v.* *Stabilize, steady, poise, balance, ballast.

Ana. *Adjust, regulate, fix: counterbalance, counterpoise, offset, *compensate.

trim, *adj.* *Neat, tidy, trig, snug, shipshape, spick-and-span.

Ana. *Clean, cleanly: compact, *close: *debonair, jaunty, perky, chipper.

Ant. Frowzy.

trip, *n.* *Journey, voyage, tour, excursion, cruise, expedition, jaunt, pilgrimage.

trite. **Trite, hackneyed, stereotyped, threadbare, shopworn** come into comparison when they mean being without freshness or power to evoke attention and interest. That is **trite** (literally, worn by rubbing) which has been spoiled for use by one's long familiarity with it: the term, therefore, imputes lack of novelty, commonplaceness, and often, loss of vital force or power to impress; as, "It is a *trite* but true observation, that examples work more forcibly on the mind than precepts" (*Fielding*); "a dreary expanse of *trite* sentiments and languid words" (*Sydney Smith*); "our most permanent aesthetic satisfaction arises as a rule from things familiar enough to give the pleasure of recognition, yet not so *trite* as to rob us of the other pleasure of surprise" (*Lowes*). That is **hackneyed** (literally worn out in service, as an overworked horse) which has been used so much and so constantly that all its significance has been dulled or all its spirit has been taken out of it. *Hackneyed* is applied especially to words and phrases that once were impressive and full of meaning, but have become vulgarized and almost meaningless in the service of ordinary writers and speakers (cf. *cliché* under COMMONPLACE); as, *hackneyed* expressions such as "the cruel waves," "a clinging vine" (as applied to a woman), "honeyed kisses"; "the *hackneyed* comparison betwixt blank verse and rhyme" (*Smollett*); "language...worn and *hackneyed* out of all sense and meaning" (*Austen*); "the *hackneyed* melancholy of street-music" (*L. P. Smith*). That is **stereotyped** (literally, produced from a stereotype) which falls invariably into the same pattern or form as though made by a mechanical impression rather than invented or contrived for the occasion. The word suggests lack of originality, initiative, or creativeness; as, "the use of old *stereotyped* phrases...to save the trouble of making a new living phrase to suit our meaning" (*H. Ellis*); "The contemporary 'thriller' is in danger of becoming *stereotyped*" (*T. S. Eliot*); "Their [spiders'] cold intelligence, their *stereotyped*, unremitting industry repel me" (*L. P. Smith*). That is **threadbare** (literally, worn, as the fabric of much-used garments, rugs, etc., until the nap or pile is wholly or partly removed) which has been so frequently used or dealt with that all its possibilities have been exhausted and there is no likelihood of awakening further interest in it; as, *threadbare* plots; a *threadbare* theme or subject. That is **shopworn** which is worn and marred by constant handling, as goods in a shop or as things comparable to them: the term suggests a loss of qualities that are necessary to make an appeal to those who can be stimulated only by what is bright, fresh, and new; as, *shopworn* methods of advertising; *shopworn* ideas of decoration.

Ana. *Old, antiquated, archaic, obsolete: banal, flat, jejune, *insipid, vapid: depleted, exhausted, drained, impoverished (see DEPLETE).

Ant. Original: fresh.

triumph, *n.* *Victory, conquest.

Ana. Vanquishing, subjugation, surmounting, overthrowing, routing (see corresponding verbs at CONQUER).

trivial. Trifling, *petty, puny, paltry, measly, picayunish, picayune.

Ana. *Small, little, diminutive: *futile, vain, fruitless, bootless: slight, slim, slender, *thin, tenuous.

Ant. Weighty: momentous.

troop, *n.* Band, troupe, *company, party.

Ana. *Crowd, throng, press: assembly, gathering, collection (see under GATHER): legion, host, army, *multitude.

trot, *v.* Pace, single-foot, walk, gallop, run, canter, lope, rack, amble. See under TROT, *n.*

trot, *n.* **Trot, pace, single-foot, walk, gallop, run, canter, lope, rack, amble** all denote gaits, especially or only of the horse, and are used as nouns or verbs. In the **trot** the legs move in diagonal pairs, and the feet are typically on the ground in the following order: right fore; right fore, left hind; left hind; all feet off ground; left fore; left fore, right hind; right hind; all feet off ground. In the **pace** the legs move in lateral pairs, and the feet are typically on the ground in the following order: right hind; right hind, right fore; all feet off ground; left hind; left hind, left fore; all feet off ground. In the **single-foot** each foot strikes singly, and there are alternately two feet and one foot on the ground, thus: right hind, right fore; right fore; right fore, left hind; left hind; left hind, left fore; left fore; left fore, right hind; right hind. In the **walk** there are alternately three and two feet on the ground, thus: left hind, left fore, right hind; left fore, right hind; left fore, right hind, right fore; right hind, right fore; right hind, right fore, left hind; right fore, left hind; right fore, left hind, left fore; left hind, left fore. The **gallop** is a rapid, springing gait in which the feet are typically on the ground in the following order: left hind; left hind, right hind; right hind; right hind, left fore; left fore; left fore, right fore; right fore; all feet off ground. The **run** is a much-quickened gallop. The **canter** is a galloplike gait in which the bounds or leaps are moderate and easy. The feet are typically on the ground in the following order: right hind; right hind, right fore; right hind, right fore, left hind; right fore, left hind; right fore, left hind, left fore; left hind, left fore; left fore; all feet off ground. The **lope** is an easy canter. The terms **rack** and **amble** are sometimes used interchangeably with *single-foot*, sometimes with *pace*.

troubadour. Trouvère, *poet, versifier, rhymer, rhymester, poetaster, bard, minstrel, scop, gleeman, jongleur, minnesinger, scald.

trouble, *v.* **1 Trouble, distress, ail** come into comparison when they mean to cause one to be uneasy or upset. **Trouble** suggests loss of tranquillity or serenity and implies disturbance of any sort that interferes with one's convenience, comfort, health of body, or peace of mind; as, I shall not *trouble* you to move; the silence *troubled* him. "'Tis not my speeches that you do mislike, But 'tis my presence that doth *trouble* ye" (*Shak.*). "Let not your heart be *troubled:* ye believe in God, believe also in me" (*John* xiv. 1). **Distress** implies subjection to strain or pressure that causes tension, pain, worry, grief, or the like; thus, a cough *distresses* one when it is tight and phlegm is ejected by straining; the formation of gas in the stomach *distresses* one; one is *distressed* in mind when anxiety distracts or crushes one; a person is financially *distressed* when he is in circumstances so straitened that he cannot pay his debts or satisfy his needs. **Ail** implies nothing more than that something has gone wrong, or is the matter, with one. It is found only in impersonal constructions; as, something *ails* the child for he looks feverish; What *ails* him: is he sick or is he worried? Thus, a cough may be said to *trouble* or *distress* a person, but never to *ail* him; a friend's plight may *trouble* or *distress*, but never *ail*, one. However, in colloquial usage, "What *ails* you?" (that is, "What is the matter with you?" or "What troubles you?") often occurs.

Ana. *Discompose, disquiet, disturb, perturb, upset, agitate: vex, irk, *annoy, bother.

2 *Inconvenience, incommode, discommode, molest.

Ana. *Embarrass, discomfit, disconcert, abash: *worry, annoy, plague, pester: perplex, *puzzle, distract.

trouble, *n.* *Effort, exertion, pains.

Ana. Flurry, fuss, ado, *stir, bustle, pother: labor, toil, *work: *difficulty, rigor, vicissitude, hardship.

troupe. Troop, band, *company, party.

trouper. *Actor, player, performer, mummer, mime, Thespian, impersonator.

trouvère. Troubadour, *poet, versifier, rhymer, rhymester, poetaster, bard, minstrel, scop, gleeman, jongleur, minnesinger, scald.

truant, *n.* *Vagabond, vagrant, tramp, hobo, bum, stiff, swagman, sundowner.

truce, *n.* **Truce, armistice** agree in meaning a suspension of hostilities or an agreement to suspend hostilities. **Truce** is more widely applicable than **armistice,** which definitely suggests laying down of arms, and therefore is the technical term for a suspension of fighting between armed forces. *Truce* may be used in reference not only to warfare, but also to a feud, a strike, or a dispute of any kind. *Truce* often suggests the desire for rest or a hope of settlement by parley rather than by combat: as a rule, it connotes a lull in activities or temporary cessation of fighting. "It is not to say that Arnold's work [the fight against Philistinism] was vain if we say that it is to be done again...the combat may have *truces* but never a peace" (*T. S. Eliot*). *Armistice* may or may not imply complete cessation of fighting. According to article 36 of the Hague Peace Convention, an armistice requires mutual agreement of the belligerents to lay down arms, and permits resumption of activities at any time provided the enemy is given warning prescribed by the terms of the agreement; thus, four *armistices* were signed by belligerents in the World War in 1918 (one each with Bulgaria, Turkey, Austria, and Germany), thereby paving the way for the Versailles Treaty which became effective in 1920.

truckle. *Fawn, toady, cringe, cower.

Ana. Defer, succumb, bow, cave in, *yield, submit: *follow, tag, trail, tail.

truculent. *Fierce, ferocious, barbarous, savage, inhuman, cruel, fell.

Ana. Intimidating, cowing, bulldozing, browbeating, bullying (see INTIMIDATE): terrorizing, terrifying, frightening (see FRIGHTEN): threatening, menacing (see THREATEN).

true. 1 *Faithful, loyal, leal, constant, stanch, steadfast, resolute.

Ana. *Reliable, dependable, trustworthy, tried: persevering, persisting (see PERSEVERE): *sincere, wholehearted, whole-souled, unfeigned.

Ant. False (sense 2): fickle.

2 *Real, actual.

Ana. Genuine, *authentic, veritable, bona fide: exact, precise, *correct, right: typical, natural, *regular.

Ant. False.

truism. *Commonplace, platitude, bromide, cliché.

Ana. Triteness, threadbareness (see corresponding adjectives at TRITE): banality, jejuneness, inanity (see corresponding adjectives at INSIPID).

trust, *n.* **1 Trust, confidence, reliance, dependence, faith** come into comparison when they mean the fact of feeling sure or the state of mind of one who feels sure that a person or thing will not fail him. **Trust** implies an absolute and assured resting on that which is its object: it often suggests a basis upon other (not necessarily weaker) grounds than experience or sensible proofs. It is the most frequent term in religious use (as, "O God...in thee is my *trust*"—*Psalms* cxli. 8) but it occurs also in secular use, especially when an intimate knowledge of, or a deep affection for, the person or persons of whom one is assured is implied (as, "He was a gentleman on whom I built An absolute *trust*"—*Shak.*) or when there has been no cause for changing an instinctive or intuitive judgment respecting a person's or thing's reliability (as, he has always gained the *trust* of his associates; he takes every word of his father on *trust*). **Confidence** may or may not imply definite grounds for one's assurances, such as the support of experience or of convincing evidence: when it does, it carries less suggestion of emotional factors than *trust* and a stronger implication of an assurance based upon the evidence of one's senses; as, "those in whom we had no *confidence*, and who reposed no *confidence* in us" (*Burke*); "the note of easy *confidence* that our London had become what Rome had been, the Capital city" (*Quiller-Couch*). When it does not imply such grounds, it usually suggests even less reliable grounds for that feeling than does *trust;* as, "But several expressions in Darwin's writings leave us in no doubt that he shared the *confidence* in progress which, arising from very unscientific sources, dominated the minds of his generation" (*Inge*). **Reliance** implies not only an attitude or feeling, but also an objective expression of it in an act or action; as, he had such *reliance* on the doctor's skill that he allowed himself to be operated upon at once; "His diffidence had prevented his depending on his own judgment in so anxious a case, but his *reliance* on mine made everything easy" (*Austen*); "Mark had written out his Christmas sermon with a good deal of care and an excessive *reliance* on what other preachers had said before him" (*C. Mackenzie*). **Dependence** differs from *reliance* chiefly in suggesting greater subordination of self; as, her *dependence* on her husband must sometimes be an annoyance to him; "Affectionate *dependence* on the Creator" (*T. Erskine*). **Faith** (as here compared: for most common sense, see BELIEF, 1) implies confidence, but it often suggests a degree of credulity or the acceptance of something capable of being proved without considering the evidence or seeking the facts: it, therefore, is often used when the person or thing in which one has faith is open to question or suspicion; as, he has great *faith* in a popular patent medicine; he takes everything the newspapers say on *faith;* it was a long time before he lost *faith* in his doctor's powers.

Ana. Assurance, conviction, certitude, *certainty: *belief, faith, credence, credit.

Ant. Mistrust.

2 *Monopoly, corner, pool, syndicate, cartel.
trust, *v.* *Rely, depend, count, reckon, bank.
Ana. Confide, entrust, *commit, consign: hope, *expect, look.
trustworthy. *Reliable, dependable, trusty, tried.
Ana. *Safe, secure: veracious, truthful (see corresponding nouns at TRUTH): stanch, constant, steadfast, *faithful: honest, *upright, scrupulous.
Ant. Deceitful: dubious.
trusty. Trustworthy, tried, *reliable, dependable.
Ana. *Faithful, stanch, steadfast, constant: *reliant, self-reliant.
truth. **Truth, veracity, verity, verisimilitude** come into comparison as terms denoting an abstraction, often a quality or property of a person or thing that keeps close to the facts or to things as they are, and avoids lies, fictions, misrepresentation, and the like. **Truth** is, in general, such conformity to facts or reality. It may, however, denote an abstraction that is purely an ideal construction (as, to seek the *truth;* to implant the love of *truth*) or is regarded as the final goal of the individual's intellectual endeavor (as, "ye shall know the *truth*, and the *truth* shall make you free"—*John* viii. 32), or it may denote utterances, statements, acts, or feelings (either singly or collectively) that manifest this conformity (as, he always tells the *truth;* since his actions belied his words, they said there was no *truth* in him; "every heart that loves with *truth* is equal to endure"—*Tennyson*). **Veracity** denotes a quality of persons as manifested chiefly in their utterances, or of the utterances themselves: the term implies a rigid respect for truth and accuracy and, also, either habitual adherence to truth or a willingness to face the truth, whatever the cost; as, "to vindicate [Geoffrey's] *veracity* as an historian" (*Pope*); "a man of perfect *veracity* in thought, word, and deed" (*Carlyle*); "It [Tennyson's charm] lay in a great *veracity* of soul" (*Watts-Dunton*); "But his passion for *veracity* always kept him from taking any unfair rhetorical advantages of an opponent" (*A. Huxley*). **Verity,** as here considered, denotes the quality of a thing that is truly what it purports to be or is in full accordance with the facts; as, "I could almost as soon doubt the Gospel *verity* as his *veracity*" (*Coleridge*); "the great seal....attests...the *verity* of the presidential signature" (*Ch. Just. Marshall*). **Verisimilitude** denotes a quality of representations as in art or in literature that convince one of their truth to life either in detail or in their suggestion of universal conditions: often the term implies a conformity not to things as they are actually or momentarily but to things as they are universally and eternally; as, "There is no *verisimilitude* in the characters, but there is *verisimilitude* in the thoughts; they are true to life, and are always passing through our minds" (*Jowett*); "Scott...satisfied himself with seeking *verisimilitude* rather than antiquarian accuracy" (*Sir W. Raleigh* [d. 1922]); "the mathematical picture [of nature] shows a distinct preeminence over the others in that, so far as we know, it depicts the phenomena of nature with complete *verisimilitude*" (*Jeans*); "the more one knows of seventeenth-century England, the more one marvels at its [*Pilgrim's Progress's*] *verisimilitude*" (*Lowes*).
Ana. Exactness, precision, correctness, rightness (see corresponding adjectives at CORRECT): authenticity, genuineness, veritableness (see corresponding adjectives at AUTHENTIC).
Ant. Untruth: lie, falsehood.
try, *v.* **1** Test, *prove, demonstrate.
Ana. *Judge, adjudge, adjudicate: inspect, examine, *scrutinize.
2 *Afflict, torment, torture, rack, grill.
Ana. *Worry, harass, harry, plague, pester: *trouble, distress: irk, vex, bother, *annoy.
3 *Attempt, endeavor, essay, assay, strive, struggle.
Ana. *Aim, aspire: *intend, mean, propose, purpose, design.
try, *n.* Attempt, endeavor, essay, assay, striving, struggle. See under ATTEMPT, *v.*
Ana. *Effort, exertion, trouble, pains: test, trial, proof (see under PROVE).
tryst. Rendezvous, assignation, *engagement, appointment, date.
tucker. Fatigue, exhaust, jade, fag, *tire, weary.
Ana. *Deplete, drain, exhaust, impoverish, bankrupt.
tug, *v.* Tow, hale, haul, drag, *pull, draw.
tumid. *Inflated, flatulent, turgid.
Ana. *Expanded, distended, swollen, dilated: pompous, pretentious, *showy, ostentatious: bombastic, grandiloquent, magniloquent, *rhetorical.
tumor. **Tumor, cancer.** *Tumor* and *cancer* are mutually exclusive terms only in strict medical use. **Tumor** often designates any morbid swelling or mass of tissue, of which there are two kinds: benign (popularly designated simply as a *tumor*) and malignant (formerly designated simply as a *cancer*). In the strict medical sense, a *tumor* is an abnormal growth of tissue that serves no useful purpose in the body. It does not spread to other parts and usually causes difficulty only by pressure or obstruction. Common forms of benign tumors are *adenoma* (of glandlike structure or of glandular origin), *fibroma* (consisting of fibrous tissue), *chondroma* (consisting of cartilage), *lipoma* (consisting of fatty tissue), *myoma* (consisting of muscular tissue), *osteoma* (consisting of bone). A **cancer** is a malignant growth of tissue, usually ulcerating, tending to spread to other parts of the body, and associated with general ill health and progressive emaciation. The term *cancer* is often applied to either of the two forms of malignant growth more specifically denoted by *carcinoma* (a malignant growth originating in epithelial tissue, as in the skin or in the lining of the stomach) or *sarcoma* (a malignant growth derived from nonepithelial tissue, as lymphoid tissue, cartilage, bone, etc.).
tumulus. *Mound, bank, dune, embankment, terrace, barrow.
tune, *n.* *Melody, air.
tune, *v.* *Harmonize, attune.
Ana. *Adjust, regulate, fix: *adapt, accommodate, reconcile, conform.
turbid. **Turbid, muddy, roiled** (*or* **riled**), **roily** (*or* **riley, rily**) agree in meaning not clear or translucent but clouded with sediment or with something like sediment. That is **turbid,** either literally or figuratively, which is stirred up and disturbed so that it is darkened, obscured, confused, or the like; as, the *turbid* water of a river on a stormy day; careless handling of a bottle makes wine *turbid;* "the *turbid* ebb and flow of human misery" (*Arnold*); "the air without had the *turbid* yellow light of sand-storms" (*Cather*); "for already the phrases at least of Nietzsche were trickling into the...*turbid* current of British thought" (*H. G. Wells*). That is **muddy** which is turbid or opaque as a result of being mixed with mud, or with something similarly slimy or heavy, or which is merely mud-colored (as, *muddy* coffee; a *muddy* pond): in figurative use, the term carries a stronger suggestion than *turbid* of a dull, heavy, or muddled character; as, a *muddy* complexion; a *muddy* style; "Dost think I am so *muddy*, so unsettled?" (*Shak.*); " '*Turbid* ecstasy' is surely not...good....*Turbid* rather suits the *muddy* kind of inspiration which London porter confers"

(*Lamb*). That is **roiled or roily** (or in colloquial use in the United States, **riled or riley**) which is turbid and agitated; as, "that which bubbles from a *roiled* mind" (*J. Beaumont*); the motorboat left behind it a wake of *roily* water.

Ana. Obscure, *dark, murky, opaque: *dirty, foul, nasty.

Ant. Clear: limpid.

turgid. Tumid, *inflated, flatulent.

Ana. Expanded, distended, amplified, swollen (see EXPAND): magniloquent, grandiloquent, *rhetorical, bombastic.

turn, *v.* **1 Turn, revolve, rotate, gyrate, circle, spin, whirl, twirl, wheel, eddy, swirl, pirouette** come into comparison when they mean to go or move or, less often, cause to go or move in a circle or circles. **Turn,** the most general of these words, may imply movement in circle after circle or merely in a complete circle or part of a circle: like many other of the verbs in English which have acquired a multitude of senses, it often is followed by an adverb or adverbial phrase; in this instance, by *round, round and round, around,* and the like, but in some contexts these motions are implied by the word itself; as, the wheel *turns* rapidly when the car is going at high speed; to *turn* a spinning wheel; he *turned* when he heard his name; the dressmaker asked her to *turn* slowly so that she could see if the hem was even; the door *turns* on its hinges. **Revolve** always implies a turning either round and round something as a center or upon a pivot; as, the planets *revolve* around the sun; at the entrance is a *revolving* door. Both *turn* and *revolve* may also imply immaterial as well as material movement, but *turn* usually suggests a relation of dependence upon the thing around which the mind or the course of something goes (as, "that task of reconciling the individual and the class with the whole, about which the political history of the world *turns*"—*G. L. Dickinson;* "[Richelieu's] foreign policy...*turned*...upon...the encirclement of France by Spain"—*Belloc*), and *revolve* usually implies either a consideration of it from every angle or an acceptance of it as the center that guides or determines one's course (as, "Only by...experience does it [speculation] find any center to *revolve* round, and so fashion itself into a system"—*Carlyle;* "it is around the *mélange des genres* and allied topics that my main argument *revolves*"—*Babbitt*). **Rotate** (see also ROTATE, 2) implies a revolving but it carries, as *revolve* does not, the suggestion of turning on or as if on an axis; thus, when one says of the earth that it *rotates* one refers to its movement on an axis, but when one says that it *revolves,* unless one adds "on an axis," one suggests its movement around the sun. "The moon presents always the same side to the earth because it *rotates* on its axis and *revolves* round the earth at the same angular rate" (*Webster's New Int. Dict., 2d Ed.*). **Gyrate** may take the place of *revolve* or *rotate* when the stress is upon the optical or other sensible effect rather than upon the character of the movement as a whole, for the term, even when it implies a relation to a center or axis, throws the emphasis upon the circles, spirals, or convolutions described; as, a moth *gyrating* around a flame; "a low cloud of dust raised by the dog *gyrating* madly about" (*Conrad*); a tornado, a whirlwind, and the like, are characterized by winds that *gyrate.* **Circle** is a somewhat less technical term than *gyrate;* it agrees with it in emphasizing the visible aspects, but often differs from it in carrying a weaker or less obvious suggestion of continuity or speed of movement; as, "thrice the equinoctial line He *circled*" (*Milton*); "other planets *circle* other suns" (*Pope*). **Spin** and **whirl** stress the continuance and the speed of gyrations or revolutions: they are often used transitively as well as intransitively and are commonly the preferred terms when the motion is induced by a human agent; as, to *spin* a top; to *whirl* one's arms; to *whirl* a stick. "For bodies which *revolve* or *whirl* or *turn* or *spin,* angular momentum is quite as important as ordinary momentum is for particles which simply shoot along or fly or fall" (*Karl K. Darrow*). "A thick brown fog, *whirled* into eddies by the wind" (*A. Huxley*). **Twirl** may imply a whirling or spinning, especially of something that moves with great lightness and rapidity or turns or twists through many gyrations: often, in transitive use, it implies the use of the fingers; as, drum majors *twirling* their batons; "whirligigs *twirl'd* round by skilful swain" (*Pope*); *twirling* the ends of his mustache. **Wheel** may imply movement in a circle or circles and so come close to *revolve, rotate* or *gyrate,* differing from them only in suggesting a description of a wheel's motion; as, "When the whirlwind's gusts are *wheeling*" (*Scott*); "play Ixion's part...chained and *wheeled*" (*Browning*). But the term also often suggests, especially when applied to flying birds or to a moving army, a turn, often a sudden turn, in a wide sweep; as, the troops, at his command, *wheeled* to the right; "the starlings *wheeled* in a sudden sheer" (*Masefield*). **Eddy** implies rapid gyratory movements, especially of air, wind, and flowing water, or of something in a whirlpool or an eddy of wind: it often specifically suggests movement contrary to the main current; as, "*Eddying* round and round they sink" (*Wordsworth*); "The vapour...*eddying* wildly in the air" (*J. Tyndall*). **Swirl** is often used in place of *eddy* or *whirl,* especially when the force or grace of the circular motion is suggested; as, the *swirling* currents of a river in flood; the *swirling* skirts of a dancer; "Further than ever comet flared or vagrant star-dust *swirled*" (*Kipling*). **Pirouette** in literal use always implies the whirling of a dancer poised on one or both toes: in extended use, it suggests a whirling or rotating on a similarly precarious support; as, a group of *pirouetting* dancers is a lovely sight; "To...*pirouette* at the apex of his loftiest elocution" (*Baring-Gould*).

Ana. *Swing, oscillate, vibrate, fluctuate, pendulate, undulate.

2 Turn, divert, deflect, avert, sheer agree in meaning to change or cause to change course or direction. **Turn** is not only the most comprehensive of these words, but also the widest in its range of application. It may be used in reference to any change in course or direction of something movable, no matter how small or how large an arc is traversed, but it usually requires qualification; as, here the river *turns* slightly to the north; he *turned* the car just in time to avoid a collision; the force of the impact *turned* the boat completely around; she *turned* her head in order to see better. It may also be used in reference to that which figuratively follows a course or proceeds in a definite direction, such as things that manifest a drift, a bent, a tendency, or the like, or persons or things that can respond to an influence; as, to *turn* the conversation to livelier topics; to *turn* public opinion against a person; to *turn* an enemy into a friend. "For the sake of saying something that might *turn* her mother's thoughts" (*Austen*). "In his need his thoughts *turned* to the sea which had given him so much...congenial solitude" (*Conrad*). **Divert,** in discriminating use, is preferred to *turn* when there is an implication of a change in a fixed (but not necessarily straight) or natural course or direction; as, to *divert* a river by providing a new channel; the unfounded belief that a lightning rod is capable of *diverting* lightning from a building it is about to strike. "The Army was so grateful that a line was *diverted* to his tent from the main cable, through which all the news of the world came to him" (*V. Heiser*). When used in reference to a person's thoughts, interests, attention, intentions, and the like, it often presupposes mental concentration, fixity of attention, or resoluteness of purpose; therefore, when an attempt to distract, to dissuade, to sidetrack, or the like, is to be suggested, *divert* is the appropriate word; as, it is hard to *divert* his attention when he is engrossed in study. "Had I spoke with her, I could have well *diverted* her intents" (*Shak.*). "Could France or Rome *divert* our brave designs, With all their brandies or with all their wines?" (*Pope*). **Deflect**, in contrast to *divert*, implies a turning from a straight course or a fixed direction; it is therefore the preferred word when that which turns or is turned normally or rightly follows such a course or keeps such a direction; as, to *deflect* a ray of light by passing it through a prism; to *deflect* a magnetic needle. In its extended use, it is chiefly referred to thoughts, purposes, interests, that pursue a rigid or clearly defined course or direction; consequently the word sometimes connotes deviation, aberration, or the like. "He underwent all those things—but none of them *deflected* his purpose" (*Belloc*). "After all, she had perhaps purposely *deflected* the conversation from her own affairs" (*E. Wharton*). **Avert** implies a turning away from that which is before one physically or mentally; it is used chiefly in reference to something at which one has been looking or of which one has been thinking, and carries commonly a strong implication of avoidance, and often a further suggestion of repugnance; as, to *avert* one's glance from the sight before one. "She avoided looking that way as much as possible, but it was hardly in human nature to keep the eyes *averted* when the door slammed" (*Hardy*). "The last drop of her magnanimity had been spent, and she tried to *avert* her shuddering mind from Charlotte" (*E. Wharton*). **Sheer** was originally, and still is, used in reference to the turning of a boat or ship from its course, especially under the guidance of the helm and in an emergency. It is usually followed by an adverb such as *to, off, away, alongside*, and *up* which indicates the direction of the turn with reference to another vessel, the shore, or the like; as, the yachts *sheered* to so that their captains could speak to each other; to *sheer* off the boat just in time to avoid collision with a rock. In its extended use, the word commonly implies a sudden or conspicuous divergence from a path or course that has been followed. "An age when the interests of popular liberty and of intellectual freedom had *sheered* off from the church" (*J. R. Green*). "They [men] often were interested in me, but I was never in the least conscious of what drew them or caused them to *sheer* away" (*M. Austin*).

Ana. *Swerve, veer, deviate, diverge, digress, depart: *move, shift.

3 *Curve, bend, twist.

Ana. *Swerve, veer: incline, *slant, slope, lean: *reverse, invert, transpose.

4 *Resort, refer, apply, go.

5 In form **turn out.** *Bear, produce, yield.

Ana. *Make, form, fashion, shape, manufacture, fabricate: propagate, breed, *generate, engender.

turn, *n.* *Gift, bent, faculty, aptitude, genius, talent, knack.

Ana. *Inclination, disposition, predisposition, bias: propensity, proclivity, penchant, *leaning, flair.

turncoat. *Renegade, apostate, recreant, backslider, pervert.

Ana. Deserter, forsaker, abandoner (see corresponding verbs at ABANDON).

tusk. *Tooth, fang.

twinge, *n.* *Pain, ache, pang, throe, stitch.

twinkle, *v.* *Flash, gleam, glance, glint, sparkle, glitter, glisten, scintillate, coruscate, glimmer, shimmer, glister, spark.

twinkling, twinkle. *Instant, moment, minute, second, flash, trice, jiffy, split second.

twirl, *v.* *Turn, revolve, rotate, gyrate, circle, spin, whirl, wheel, eddy, swirl, pirouette.

twist, *v.* Turn, bend, *curve.

Ana. Spin, twirl, whirl (see TURN, *v.*): contort, distort, gnarl (see DEFORM).

twister. *Wind, breeze, gale, hurricane, whirlwind, cyclone, typhoon, tornado, waterspout, gust, blast, flaw, zephyr.

twit, *v.* *Ridicule, deride, mock, taunt, rally.

Ana. Reproach, chide, *reprove: reprehend, blame, censure (see CRITICIZE): *scoff, jeer, gibe.

type, *n.* **1** *Symbol, emblem, attribute.

Ana. *Sign, mark, token: intimation, suggestion (see corresponding verbs at SUGGEST, 1): adumbration, shadowing (see corresponding verbs at SUGGEST, 2).

Ant. Antitype.

2 Type, kind, sort, nature, description, character, stripe, kidney, ilk come into comparison when they denote a number or group of persons or of things thought of as a class or category because of the close resemblance of the individuals in some particular way or ways. **Type** is usually the preferred term for such a group when the resemblances are so strong, clearly marked, or obvious that the distinction between that group and related groups cannot be questioned; as, there are at least four *types* of literary prose—narration, description, exposition, and argument; the seedless *type* of orange; the disappearance of the *type* of poem now known as "the popular ballad"; "that most dangerous *type* of critic" (*T. S. Eliot*). **Kind** may be very explicit or very vague in its reference. When explicit, the term usually implies likenesses that are the result of the fact that all the individuals belong to the same genus or species, often the same biological species (as, "He knew no class in flesh and blood. He loved his *kind* [i.e., all men]"—*Masefield;* the dog shunned all save his master and his own *kind* [i.e., either other dogs or dogs of the same species]), sometimes merely the same scientific genus or species (as, rubies, emeralds, sapphires are all minerals of the same *kind* [i.e., corundum]; a rock of this *kind* is rare in this part of the world), sometimes the same logical or other classification (as, "the Auden-Garrett anthology . . . . is outstanding of its *kind*"—*Day Lewis;* "logic works by predicating of the single instance what is true of all its *kind*"—*W. James*). **Sort** is probably more often used than *kind* when the reference is vague, but frequently the two words are coupled or interchanged as if indistinguishable in meaning; as, men of all *sorts* and *kinds;* what *sort* (or *kind*) of mind has he?; I do not like books of this *kind* (or *sort*). *Sort*, however, is preferred when there is a distinct suggestion of disparagement or contempt; as, "Lewd fellows of the baser *sort*" (*Acts* xvii. 5); one does not enjoy that *sort* of person. The other words in this group are all more or less loosely used in place of *kind* and *sort*. In discriminating use, however, **nature** implies inherent or innate rather than superficial likenesses (as, adventures of this *nature;* sins of the same *nature*), **description** implies agreement in all details that may be regarded as part of the description or definition of the type (as, "all embargoes are not of this *description*"—*Ch. Just. Marshall;* "any class or *description* of persons"—*Ch. Just. Taney*), and **character** suggests likenesses in peculiar or distinctive features or qualities (as, few books of this *character* have come to my attention). **Stripe** and **kidney** are somewhat colloquial and usually humorous substitutes for *kind* or *sort*, *stripe* often carrying a reference to affiliations (as, men of the same political [or religious] *stripe*), and *kidney* suggesting resemblances in character or in quality (as, "With persons of his *kidney* a direct question is never very discreet"—*Maugham*). **Ilk,** originally an adjective meaning *same*, derives its substantive sense from its idiomatic and chiefly Scottish use in the phrase *of that ilk*, meaning of the same name, surname, place, or territorial designation. Hence, in loose use, *ilk* is often employed as a loose substitute for any of the words of this group or for more specific terms such as *class*, *breed*, and *family;* as, "bushwhackers of Daws Dillon's *ilk*" (*John Fox, jr.*).

Ana. Exemplar, example, *model, pattern.

typhoon. *Wind, gale, hurricane, whirlwind, cyclone, tornado, waterspout, twister, breeze, gust, blast, flaw, zephyr.

typical. *Regular, natural, normal.

Ana. Generic, general, *universal, common: specific (see SPECIAL).

Ant. Atypical: distinctive.

typist. Stenographer, *secretary, amanuensis, scribe, scrivener.

tyrannical. Also **tyrannous.** Despotic, arbitrary, *absolute, autocratic.

Ana. *Dictatorial, authoritarian, magisterial: *totalitarian, authoritarian: domineering, imperious, *masterful.

tyro *or* **tiro.** *Amateur, dilettante, dabbler.

Ana. *Novice, apprentice, probationer, neophyte.

U

ubiquitous. Less often **ubiquitary.** *Omnipresent.

uitlander. Variant of OUTLANDER.

ulcer. *Abscess, canker, canker sore.

ultimate. 1 Extreme, *last, latest, final, terminal, concluding, eventual.

2 **Ultimate, absolute, categorical** are here compared mainly in their philosophical senses, where, despite great differences in implications, they have in common the meaning: so fundamental as to represent the extreme limit of actual or possible knowledge. That is **ultimate** which represents the utmost limit attained or attainable either by analysis or by synthesis; as, the *ultimate* constituent of matter is not the atom but a particle of electricity. "That lofty musing on the *ultimate* nature of things which constitutes, for Pascal 'the whole dignity and business of man' " (*A. Huxley*). That is **absolute** (see also PURE, 1; ABSOLUTE, 2) which has the character of being above all imperfection because it is not derived but original, not partial but complete, not subject to qualification because unlimited, not dependent on anything else because self-sufficient. That which is *absolute* has, as a rule, ideal existence and always implies an opposite in actuality lacking the marks of absoluteness; as, *absolute* reality as opposed to reality as known; *absolute*, as opposed to finite, knowledge; *absolute*, as opposed to human, justice. *The* (or *an*) *absolute*, therefore, usually designates that one thing which incorporates (or is believed to incorporate) in itself all the marks of absoluteness. "Luther...was led to set up the text of the Bible as a sort of visible *absolute*, a true and perfect touchstone in matters religious" (*Babbitt*). That is **categorical** (see also EXPLICIT) which is so fundamental that human reason cannot go beyond it in a search for generality or universality and which has, therefore, an affirmative, undeniable character. The "*categorical* imperative" of Kant was offered by him as the inescapable moral law (or "imperative") which is undeniable by reason and universal in its application. The *categorical* concepts, or *the categories*, as they are usually called, are the few concepts, such as quantity, quality, and relation, to which all human knowledge can be reduced, for no more general conceptions can be found to include them.

umbra. Penumbra, *shade, shadow, umbrage, adumbration.

umbrage. 1 Shadow, *shade, umbra, penumbra, adumbration.

2 *Offense, resentment, pique, dudgeon, huff.

Ana. Annoyance, vexation, irking (see corresponding verbs at ANNOY): irritation, exasperation, provocation, nettling (see corresponding verbs at IRRITATE): indignation, rage, fury, wrath, *anger, ire.

umpire, *n.* Referee, *judge, arbiter, arbitrator.

un-. **Un-, in-, non-, a-** are the common negative prefixes in English. **Un-** is not only the most frequent, but it is also the freest in use, because it may be prefixed to any English noun, adjective, or adverb capable of having a negative. As a rule, but not without a multitude of exceptions, *un-* suggests mere negation and the compound of which it is a part means nothing more than not that which is expressed by the second element; as, *un*sweetened equals not sweetened; *un*ladylike equals not ladylike. **In-** (or one of its phonetic variations: **il-** before *l;* **im-** before *b, p, m;* **ir-** before *r*) is akin to *un-* etymologically, but it is found commonly in hosts of long-established compounds (often derived directly from the Latin) and is not subject to free use. Few of these compounds are merely negatives of the affirmative element. A very large (if not the larger) number imply diametrical opposition, or contrariness, as well; thus, *in*cautious is far more restricted and pointed in meaning than *un*cautious (or not cautious), for the latter implies merely the failure to use caution and the former implies the presence of caution's extreme opposite—recklessness. Oftentimes, the *in-* compound is the contrary of the second element in a restricted and meaningful sense, the mere negative of the word in any sense being expressed by an *un-* compound; as, *in*artistic (tasteless, banal), *un*artistic (not artistic); *ir*religious (ungodly, profane), *un*religious (not religious). There are times when both the *in-* and the *un-* compounds have acquired a specific meaning and a mere negative is needed. It is in such cases that the **non-** compound adjectives often originate. *Unchristian* has so long meant that which is the contrary of *Christian* in its richer sense that the compound *non-Christian* was formed to distinguish persons and activities that cannot be designated as *Christian* in its most inclusive sense. *Non-* is also used in forming nouns naming all not included under the second element; as, *non-*Turks. **A-** (or **an-** before a vowel or *h*) is combinable only with root words of Greek origin. As a separable prefix, *a-* is freely used in forming negatives only in the sciences, particularly biology, chemistry, and medicine. It is occasionally used to form new general words when there is a feeling that the existent *un-*, *in-*, and *non-* forms are too specific in meaning and do not strongly enough indicate privation, or the absence of all the characters or qualities implied by the affirmative element. *A*moral (see IMMORAL) was coined when it was discovered that *im*moral, *un*moral, and *non*moral did not explicitly deny the presence of all characteristics that would make a person or thing describable as *moral*. *A*social suggests, in contrast with *un*social and *non*social, the privation of all those qualities included under the meaning of *social*.

unalienable. Variant of INALIENABLE.

unassailable. Impregnable, inexpugnable, invulnerable, *invincible, unconquerable, indomitable.
Ana. Stout, sturdy, tenacious, tough, *strong, stalwart.

unavoidable. *Inevitable, ineluctable, inescapable.
Ana. Certain, positive, *sure.

unbecoming. *Indecorous, improper, unseemly, indecent, indelicate.
Ana. Unfitting, inappropriate, unmeet, unsuitable (see UNFIT): inept, *awkward, maladroit, gauche, clumsy.

unbelief. **Unbelief, disbelief, incredulity** come into comparison as meaning the attitude or state of mind of one who does not believe. **Unbelief** stresses the lack or absence of belief, especially, but not always, in religion or in revelation; as, "he...upbraided them with their *unbelief*" (*Mark* xvi. 14); "If thou canst believe, all things are possible to him that believeth. And straightway the father of the child cried out...Lord, I believe; help thou mine *unbelief*" (*Mark* ix. 23–24); "The second of these books would be condemned for heresy, and the first for *unbelief*" (*J. Martineau*). **Disbelief** implies a positive rejection of what is stated or asserted; as, an attitude of general *unbelief*, with reference to a given rumor, may be changed by evidence to one of absolute *disbelief;* "A *disbelief* in ghosts and witches was one of the most prominent characteristics of scepticism in the seventeenth century" (*Lecky*); "Although the latter [Rousseau] was a disbeliever in aristocracy, he never perceived the implications of his *disbelief* where education was concerned" (*B. Russell*). **Incredulity** implies indisposition to believe or, more often, a skeptical frame of mind; as, "the stare of petulant *incredulity*" (*Johnson*); "there is a vulgar *incredulity*, which...finds it easier to doubt than to examine" (*Scott*).
Ana. *Uncertainty, doubt, dubiety, dubiosity, skepticism: agnosticism, skepticism (see under SKEPTIC).
Ant. Belief.

unbeliever. Freethinker, *atheist, agnostic, infidel, deist.
Ana. *Skeptic, agnostic: *pagan, heathen.

unbiased. Impartial, dispassionate, *fair, just, equitable, uncolored, objective.
Ana. *Disinterested, uninterested: detached, aloof (see INDIFFERENT).
Ant. Biased.

uncalled-for. Gratuitous, wanton, *supererogatory.
Ana. *Impertinent, intrusive, officious: *foolish, silly, absurd, preposterous.

uncanny. *Weird, eerie.
Ana. *Strange, singular, erratic, eccentric, odd, queer: *mysterious, inscrutable.

unceasing. *Everlasting, endless, interminable, neverending.

uncertainty. **Uncertainty, doubt, dubiety, dubiosity, skepticism** (*or* **scepticism**), **suspicion, mistrust** are synonymous terms only when they mean a feeling or a state of mind governed by the feeling that one is not sure about someone or something. **Uncertainty** stresses the lack of certainty or certitude, and may, on the one hand, imply a mere falling short of these, or it may, on the other hand, imply so far a removal from them that one is aware that one has grounds only for guessing or surmising; it may imply that one has no conviction regarding the reality, truth, or rightness of something or that one cannot predict the action, the course, or the outcome of someone or something; as, to suffer from *uncertainty* concerning his son's fate; "she drove without any *uncertainty* or hesitation as to her route" (*Deland*); "Unsuccessful propaganda verse...is the result of the poet trying to convince others without having experienced either *uncertainty* or conviction himself" (*Day Lewis*); "Man's *uncertainties* in regard to all the major issues of life" (*A. Huxley*). **Doubt** implies both an uncertainty about the truth or reality of something and an inability to make a decision, often even after study or investigation: frequently, the term implies such a feeling or state of mind in respect to religious beliefs or doctrines formerly accepted without question; as, he never felt a *doubt* of God's existence; "Ten thousand difficulties do not make one *doubt*" (*Newman*); "There lives more faith in honest *doubt*, Believe me, than in half the creeds" (*Tennyson*); "No man likes to have his intelligence or good faith questioned, especially if he has *doubts* about it himself" (*H. Adams*). **Dubiety** comes closer to *uncertainty* than to *doubt*, for it stresses a lack of sureness rather than an inability to reach a decision as to where the truth lies. But it regularly carries, as *uncertainty* does not, a strong implication of wavering or of fluctuations between one conclusion and another; as, faith free from all *dubiety;* "The twilight of *dubiety* never falls upon him" (*Lamb*); "Chilled Martini... Transfixing all *dubiety* within" (*W. R. Benét*). **Dubiosity** is not always clearly distinguishable from *dubiety:* sometimes, however, it suggests not uncertainty, but vagueness, indistinctness, or mental confusion. "Mrs. Berry had not cogitated long ere she pronounced distinctly and without a shadow of *dubiosity:* 'My opinion is ...' " (*Meredith*). **Skepticism** suggests in this, its general sense (see also under SKEPTIC), an unwillingness to believe without demonstration, or an incredulity while any plausible evidence to the contrary exists: it usually refers to a habitual or temperamental state of mind or to a customary reaction to something proposed for belief. "St. Thomas was perhaps of all the apostles the one most easily imaginable in the present, and his sturdy *scepticism* must have been the consolation of many Christian souls" (*C. Mackenzie*). "An easy and elegant *scepticism* was the attitude expected of an educated adult; anything might be discussed, but it was a trifle vulgar to reach very positive conclusions" (*B. Russell*). "[The scientist's] boasted power to foretell and control upon the basis of his hypotheses has been too often vindicated to permit a *skepticism*" (*J. W. Krutch*). **Suspicion** stresses conjecture or apprehension that someone or something is not true, real, or right in any one of the senses of those words or that he or it has worked or is working evil or injury; however, since the term also implies that the conjecture or apprehension is accompanied by uncertainty or doubt, it comes into comparison with the other words of this group. In fact, when it implies a lack of faith in the truth, reality, or rightness of someone or something, it often comes close to *doubt;* as, "seized with unwonted *suspicion* of his own wisdom" (*Meredith*); "if the spiritual faculty is given fair play, and suffered to develop normally, *suspicion*...of it must disappear" (*Inge*); "a stranger...regarded with *suspicion*, if not actual hostility" (*Hudson*). When, on the other hand, it implies a possible but not as yet well-grounded charge or accusation of wrongdoing, the terms have little in com-

UV

mon except an implied uncertainty; as, he had a horrible *suspicion* that the thief was a member of his own family; he felt that he had grounds for his *suspicion* of the company's cashier. **Mistrust** (as here compared: see also DISTRUST) implies doubt that is based upon suspicion and that therefore precludes the possibility of one's having faith, or confidence, or trust in a person or thing; as, "*Mistrust* of good success hath done this deed" (*Shak.*); "Man is only weak through his *mistrust* And want of hope" (*Wordsworth*).

Ant. Certainty. — ***Con.*** Certitude, conviction, assurance (see CERTAINTY).

uncircumscribed. Boundless, illimitable, *infinite, sempiternal, eternal.

Ant. Circumscribed.

uncivil. *Rude, ill-mannered, impolite, discourteous, ungracious.

Ana. Boorish, loutish, churlish (see under BOOR): brusque, blunt, gruff, crusty (see BLUFF).

Ant. Civil.

uncolored. 1 *Colorless, achromatic.

2 Dispassionate, impartial, objective, unbiased, *fair, just, equitable.

uncommon. *Infrequent, scarce, rare, occasional, sporadic.

Ana. *Strange, singular, unique: *exceptional: *choice, exquisite.

Ant. Common.

uncommunicative. *Silent, taciturn, reticent, reserved, secretive, close, close-lipped, closemouthed, tight-lipped.

Ant. Communicative.

unconcerned. *Indifferent, incurious, aloof, detached, disinterested.

Ana. *Cool, collected, composed, nonchalant: apathetic, *impassive, stolid, phlegmatic.

Ant. Concerned. — ***Con.*** Solicitous, anxious, worried, careful (see under CARE).

uncongenial. Unsympathetic, incompatible, *inconsonant, inconsistent, incongruous, discordant, discrepant.

Ana. *Antipathetic, unsympathetic, averse: *repugnant, repellent, abhorrent, obnoxious.

Ant. Congenial. — ***Con.*** Companionable, co-operative, *social: pleasing, *pleasant, agreeable.

unconquerable. *Invincible, indomitable, impregnable, inexpugnable, unassailable, invulnerable.

Ant. Conquerable.

unconstraint. **Unconstraint, abandon, spontaneity** come into comparison when they denote the free and uninhibited expression of one's thoughts or feelings or the quality of mood or style resulting from a free yielding to impulse. **Unconstraint** is the most general term and may be used in place of either of the others, though not without loss of precision in statement. "The old red blood and stainless gentility of great poets will be proved by their *unconstraint*. A heroic person walks at his ease through and out of that custom or precedent or authority that suits him not" (*Whitman*). **Abandon** adds to *unconstraint* the implication either of entire loss of self-control (as, to weep with *abandon*) or of the absence or impotence of any influence hampering free, full, or natural expression of feeling (as, gaiety and *abandon* mark her style). **Spontaneity,** on the other hand, suggests an unstudied naturalness and agreeable freshness of expression or manner; sometimes it connotes lack of deliberation and obedience to the impulse of the moment. "Keats' letters...have a deceptive *spontaneity* which invites the mind to pass over them...without pausing to penetrate below the surface" (*J. M. Murry*).

Ana. Spontaneousness, impulsiveness, instinctiveness (see corresponding adjectives at SPONTANEOUS): naturalness, simplicity, unsophistication, ingenuousness, naïveté (see corresponding adjectives at NATURAL).

uncritical. *Superficial, shallow, cursory.

Ant. Critical. — ***Con.*** Discerning, discriminating, penetrating (see corresponding nouns at DISCERNMENT): comprehending, understanding, appreciating (see UNDERSTAND).

unctuous. *Fulsome, oily, oleaginous, sleek, soapy.

Ana. Ingratiating, insinuating (see DISARMING): bland, politic, smooth, diplomatic (see SUAVE): obsequious (see SUBSERVIENT).

Ant. Brusque.

undaunted. Dauntless, intrepid, *brave, courageous, bold, audacious, valiant, valorous, doughty.

Ana. Resolute, stanch, steadfast (see FAITHFUL): *confident, assured, sanguine, sure.

Ant. Afraid. — ***Con.*** *Fearful, apprehensive: cowed, browbeaten, bullied (see INTIMIDATE).

undefeasible. Variant of INDEFEASIBLE.

under. *Below, beneath, underneath.

underhand, underhanded. *Secret, covert, stealthy, furtive, clandestine, surreptitious, privy, backstairs.

Ana. Deceitful, *dishonest: *crooked, devious, oblique: *sly, cunning, crafty, tricky, wily.

Ant. Aboveboard. — ***Con.*** *Straightforward, forthright: open, plain, *frank, candid.

underlying. Basic, *fundamental, basal, substratal, substrative, radical.

Ana. *Essential, cardinal, vital, fundamental: requisite, indispensable, necessary, *needful.

undermine. *Weaken, enfeeble, debilitate, sap, cripple, disable.

Ana. *Ruin, wreck: *injure, damage, impair: thwart, foil, *frustrate.

Ant. Reinforce.

underneath. *Below, under, beneath.

understand. **Understand, comprehend, appreciate** are synonyms when they mean to have a clear and true idea or conception, or full and exact knowledge, of something. They (especially the first two) are often used interchangeably and seemingly without loss; nevertheless, they are distinguishable by fine sharp differences in meaning in precise use. In general, it may be said that **understand** refers to the result of a mental process or processes (a clear and exact idea or notion, or full knowledge), **comprehend** to the mental process of arriving at such a result; thus, one may come to *understand* a person although one has had difficulty in *comprehending* his motives and his peculiarities; one may be unable to *comprehend* a poem, no matter how clearly one *understands* every sentence in it. " 'You begin to *comprehend* me, do you?' cried he, turning towards her. 'Oh! Yes—I *understand* you perfectly' " (*Austen*). Sometimes the difference is more subtle; *comprehend* implies the mental act of grasping or seizing clearly and fully; *understand*, the power to receive and register a clear and true impression. "That ye, being rooted and grounded in love, may be able to *comprehend* with all saints what is the breadth, and length, and depth, and height; and to know the love of Christ, which passeth knowledge" (*Ephesians* iii. 17–19). "Some men can think of thousands of dollars, others have to think of hundreds. It's all their minds are big enough to *comprehend*" (*S. Anderson*). "And the peace of God, which passeth all *understanding*, shall keep your hearts and minds through Christ Jesus" (*Philippians* iv. 7). "Chartres is so crowded that one must be content to feel what one can, and let the rest go. *Understand*, we cannot!" (*H. Adams*). **Appreciate,** as here considered (see also APPRECIATE, 2), implies a just judg-

ment or the estimation of a thing's true or exact value; therefore, the word is used in reference to persons or things which may be misjudged, as by underestimating or overestimating, or by undervaluing or overvaluing. "You are of an age now to *appreciate* his character" (*Meredith*). "We do not reproach him [Gilbert Murray] for preferring, apparently, Euripides to Aeschylus. But ...he should at least *appreciate* Euripides" (*T. S. Eliot*). "The public opinion which thus magnifies patriotism into a religion is a force of which it is difficult to *appreciate*...the strength" (*Brownell*). "To *appreciate* the gulf...between the ideal and the fact, we have only to contrast such a scheme as that set forth in the 'Republic' of Plato with the following description...of the state of Greece during the Peloponnesian War" (*G. L. Dickinson*).
Ana. Conceive, realize, envision, envisage (see THINK): interpret, elucidate, construe (see EXPLAIN): penetrate, pierce, probe (see ENTER).

understanding. 1 *Reason, intuition.
Ana. Comprehension, apprehension (see under APPREHEND): *discernment, discrimination, insight, penetration: *universal, general, generic.
2 *Agreement, accord.

understudy, *n.* *Substitute, supply, locum tenens, alternate, pinch hitter, double, stand-in.

undulate. Waver, *swing, sway, oscillate, vibrate, fluctuate, pendulate.
Ana. *Pulsate, pulse, beat, throb, palpitate.

undulation. *Wave, ripple, billow, roller, breaker, comber, beachcomber, surge.

undying. *Immortal, deathless, unfading, fadeless, amaranthine.
Ana. *Everlasting, endless, unceasing, never-ending, interminable.

unearth. *Discover, ascertain, determine, learn.
Ana. Exhume, disinter, *dig, delve: expose, exhibit, *show: *reveal, disclose, discover.

uneasy. *Impatient, nervous, unquiet, restless, restive, fidgety, skittish, feverish, hectic, jumpy, jittery.
Ana. Anxious, worried, solicitous, concerned, careful (see under CARE): disturbed, perturbed, agitated, disquieted (see DISCOMPOSE).

uneducated. *Ignorant, illiterate, unlettered, untaught, untutored, unlearned, nescient.
Ana. *Rude, crude, rough, raw, callow, green.
Ant. Educated.

unerring. *Infallible, inerrable, inerrant.
Ana. *Reliable, dependable, trustworthy: *exact, accurate, precise, *correct.

unescapable. Variant of INESCAPABLE.

uneven. *Rough, harsh, rugged, scabrous.
Ant. Even. — *Con.* *Level, flat, plane, smooth: equable, even, uniform, *steady, constant.

unfading. *Immortal, deathless, undying, fadeless, amaranthine.
Ana. *Everlasting, never-ending, endless: *lasting, perdurable, perpetual.

unfeigned. *Sincere, wholehearted, whole-souled, heartfelt, hearty.
Ana. Genuine, veritable, bona fide, *authentic: *natural, simple, naïve: *spontaneous, impulsive.

unfit, *adj.* **Unfit, unsuitable, unmeet, improper, inappropriate, unfitting, inapt, unhappy, infelicitous** come into comparison when they mean not right with respect to what is required or expected under the circumstances or is demanded by the thing's end, use, or function. Except for this denial of rightness, the terms otherwise correspond in applications and in implications to the affirmative adjectives as discriminated at FIT.
Ant. Fit. — *Con.* Adaptable, pliable, malleable (see PLASTIC): *able, capable, competent, qualified.

unfitting. Inappropriate, improper, unmeet, unsuitable, *unfit, inapt, unhappy, infelicitous.
Ana. Unbecoming, unseemly, *indecorous.
Ant. Fitting.

unflagging. Unwearied, unwearying, tireless, untiring, *indefatigable, weariless.
Ana. Persevering, persisting *or* persistent (see corresponding verbs at PERSEVERE): *steady, constant.
Con. Indolent, fainéant, slothful, *lazy.

unfledged. *Immature, unmatured, unripe, unmellow.
Ana. Crude, callow, raw, green, *rude.
Ant. Full-fledged.

unformed. *Formless, shapeless, chaotic, amorphous, inchoate.
Ant. Formed. — *Con.* *Definite, definitive: developed, matured (see MATURE): fashioned, fabricated, manufactured, made (see MAKE).

unfruitful. Barren, *sterile, infertile, impotent.
Ant. Fruitful, prolific. — *Con.* *Fertile, fecund.

ungodly. *Irreligious, godless, unreligious, nonreligious.
Ana. Wicked, evil, ill, *bad: reprobate, *abandoned, profligate: *impious, blasphemous, profane.

ungovernable. *Unruly, intractable, refractory, recalcitrant, willful, headstrong.
Ana. *Contrary, perverse, froward, wayward: contumacious, *insubordinate, rebellious, factious.
Ant. Governable: docile. — *Con.* Submissive, subdued, *tame: tractable, amenable, *obedient.

ungracious. *Rude, ill-mannered, impolite, discourteous, uncivil.
Ana. Churlish, boorish (see under BOOR): brusque, gruff, blunt, curt (see BLUFF).
Ant. Gracious.

unhappy. Infelicitous, inapt, unsuitable, unmeet, improper, inappropriate, unfitting, *unfit.
Ana. Inept, maladroit, gauche, *awkward.
Ant. Happy.

uniform, *adj.* 1 Parallel, homogeneous, *similar, like, alike, identical, akin, analogous, comparable.
Ana. *Same, equivalent, equal.
Ant. Various.
2 *Steady, constant, even, equable.
Ana. Consistent, *consonant, compatible: regular, *orderly.
Ant. Multiform.

unify. Consolidate, concentrate, *compact.
Ana. *Integrate, articulate, concatenate: organize, systematize (see ORDER, *v.*): *unite, combine, conjoin.

unimpassioned. *Sober, temperate, continent.
Ana. *Cool, composed, collected, imperturbable: *calm, serene, placid, tranquil: *impassive, stolid, stoic, phlegmatic.
Ant. Impassioned.

uninterested. *Disinterested.
Ana. *Indifferent, unconcerned, incurious: *forgetful, unmindful, oblivious.
Ant. Interested: curious.

union. *Unity, solidarity, integrity.
Ana. Integration, articulation, concatenation (see under INTEGRATE): *harmony, consonance, accord, concord.

unique. 1 *Single, sole, lone, solitary, separate, particular.
Ana. *Only, alone.
2 Singular, *strange, peculiar, eccentric, erratic, odd, queer, quaint, outlandish, curious.
Ana. *Exceptional: uncommon, rare, *infrequent.

unite. 1 Combine, *join, connect, link, associate, relate.

Ana. *Mix, blend, merge, amalgamate: *weave, knit: *integrate, concatenate, articulate.
Ant. Divide: alienate.
2 **Unite, combine, conjoin, co-operate, concur** come into comparison when they mean to join forces so as to act together or to form a larger unit. **Unite** may suggest either of these ends (as, the thirteen colonies *united* to form what is now known as the United States of America; all parties *united* in signing the petition), but it more commonly suggests the formation of a new or larger unit, as by merging (as, the three churches *united*), or by blending or coalescence (as, "Rise various wreaths [of smoke] that into one *unite*"—*Wordsworth*), or by growing together (as, the inserted bud and the stock *unite* to form a plant which produces a beautiful and hardy rose), or by adhesion or solidification (as, the mixed sand, gravel, and mortar *unite* to form a substance resembling stone). **Combine** is often used interchangeably with *unite*, but it is usually the preferred term when a somewhat looser or more temporary association is to be suggested, or when the distinctness of the parts or their harmonious relations are connoted; as, "So sweet did harp and voice *combine*" (*Dryden*); several citizens *combined* to lead the campaign for the adoption of the city-manager form of government; "Innumerable factors *combine* in the inextricable complexity of our general story" (*Belloc*). **Conjoin,** a much rarer word than the other terms of this group, differs from them either in implying a uniting or combining at a given point in space or time, or in being used especially of things that have come together at a particular point or moment; as, streams which *conjoin* in the valley to form a river; "He may trace the course of these many causes until they *conjoin* in the great revolt of to-day" (*Manchester Examiner*). **Co-operate** implies a combining for the sake of action or mutual support or assistance; as, "It is... difficult to induce a number of free beings to *co-operate* for their mutual benefit" (*Goldsmith*); "Reasonable people are not such a few—let them *co-operate*, if only by recognizing each other's existence" (*Times Lit. Sup.*). **Concur,** as here considered, is used chiefly of things that combine or co-operate by their convergence or coincidence, rather than by intention; as, "All things *concur* to give it a perfection" (*Herbert*); "Two opposite forces *concurred* in bringing about the Council of Nicaea" (*Dean Stanley*); "all these powerful influences *concur* in warning us" (*T. H. Huxley*).
Ana. Mingle, commingle, coalesce, fuse (see MIX): adhere, cohere, *stick, cling, cleave.
Ant. Part.

unity. Unity, solidarity, integrity, union are synonyms only when they denote a combining of all the parts, elements, or individuals into an effective whole, or the property or character of the whole achieved by such a blending. **Unity** is the comprehensive term applicable to wholes formed either of persons or of things: it may, for example, characterize a people, a nation, a church, or any association, or any natural or artificial structure, such as the human body or a cathedral, or any work of art, such as a drama, an epic, a painting, or a bas-relief. In every case, it implies oneness (especially a oneness of that which is varied or diverse rather than uniform in its elements) that is gained by the interdependence of parts or individuals and by the co-operation of all so that each within its proper limits helps in effecting the end of the whole; as, "the indispensable *unity* of a beautiful design" (*S. Alexander*); "[In Korin's] famous picture of the Thirty-six Poets....There is no building up round a centre; *unity* is maintained by a subtle balance of relations" (*Binyon*). *Unity* often implies a oneness of spirit that results in a group of persons when there is harmony and concord; as, "how good...it is for brethren to dwell together in *unity!*" (*Psalms* cxxxiii. 1); "What he [Augustus] sought was *unity* of sentiment, not an unfeatured uniformity, and he attained it" (*Buchan*). **Solidarity** denotes a kind of unity in a group, a class, a community, or the like, which enables it to manifest its strength, express its opinion, or exert its influence both through individuals and through the whole with the force of an undivided mass: it implies unwillingness in individuals or in smaller groups to go counter to the interests, aspirations, or will of the group as a whole; as, "One secret of their power is their mutual good understanding ....They have *solidarity*, or responsibleness, and trust in each other" (*Emerson*); "Instead of national *solidarity* following the war, we have only a revival of Know-Nothingism; one faction of hyphenates tries to exterminate another faction" (*Mencken*). "The Mingotts had not proclaimed their disapproval aloud: their sense of *solidarity* was too strong" (*E. Wharton*). **Integrity** is used chiefly in reference to wholes that have been built up so that each stands as a thing marked by completeness and a unity dependent on the perfection of its parts and their mutual interdependence: the term usually stresses soundness, undividedness, or freedom from impairment of any sort; as, to preserve the *integrity* of the British Empire; a change in the last act of the original play to satisfy those who wish a happy ending has destroyed the drama's *integrity*. **Union** is now found less often in the sense here considered, because of its being the preferred general term for the act of uniting several things to form a whole or for the body or organization which results from such a uniting (as, the *union* of thirteen states to form the United States; the American Civil War was fought to preserve the *Union*). However, the term does, at times, carry the deeper implications of a thorough integration of parts and of their harmonious co-operation; as, "such harmony alone Could hold all Heaven and Earth in happier *union*" (*Milton*); "The *union*, peace and plenty of the kingdom" (*Clarendon*); "thanks to... God, who has restored *union* to my family" (*Scott*).
Ana. Identification, incorporation, embodiment, assimilation (see corresponding verbs at IDENTIFY): co-operation, concurrence, uniting, combining (see corresponding verbs at UNITE): integration, concatenation, articulation (see under INTEGRATE).

universal. 1 Universal, ecumenical (*or* **oecumenical**), **catholic, cosmopolitan, cosmic** come into comparison when they mean world-wide, or in looser use, extremely widespread in extent, range, influence, appeal, use, or the like. **Universal** etymologically implies reference to the whole of some system or body as distinct from the individuals that constitute it; as here compared, it implies reference to the universe visualized either as the entire system of created things (as, "*universal* Nature"—*Milton;* "*universal* as the air"—*S. Rogers;* "Science has become too complex to affirm the existence of *universal* truths"—*H. Adams*) or, more narrowly and far more frequently, as the world, whether that be the earth as a whole or the totality of men, especially civilized men (as, "this *universal* human art"—*H. Ellis;* a *universal* language; "The qualities which produce a man of great eminence in some one direction are often such as might be undesirable if they were *universal*"—*B. Russell*), or merely that portion of either which may loosely be described as the world which the speaker or writer knows or has in mind (as, "no other theory...has won *universal* acceptance"—*Binyon;* "One of those people... whose *universal* popularity always creates a prejudice against him beforehand"—*C. Mackenzie*). **Ecumenical**

etymologically implies a relationship to the inhabited world; it is therefore sometimes used in place of *universal* as more definite and more fixed in its implications; as, "our *oecumenical* commerce" (*W. H. Mallock*); Augustus imposed an *ecumenical* tax. However, *ecumenical* has been used chiefly as a descriptive title of councils which have been convoked from the entire church; thus, of the twenty councils from 325–1870, which are called *ecumenical* councils by the Roman Catholic Church, only the first seven are accepted as *ecumenical* by the Orthodox Church and the first four (without hesitation) by the Anglican Church. The term is used not only by Roman Catholics but by others with reference to persons, councils, and the like, that represent or govern the entire church; as, the patriarch of Constantinople is the *ecumenical* patriarch of all Orthodox churches. **Catholic,** like *universal*, implies a relation to a whole, but unlike the latter term, it has consistently implied a relationship to all men, especially to those who belong to the body of civilized men, or often, of cultivated men. More often in the past than at present, it has stressed universal prevalence (as, a *catholic* law) or universal applicability or usefulness (as, a *catholic* remedy). Its chief implication in current use is lack of exclusiveness as shown in a true comprehensiveness, as in interests, tastes, sympathies, and the like. "Those writers who in every nation go by the name of Classics have [so far] a *catholic* and *ecumenical* character, that what they express is common to the whole race of man" (*Newman*). "[The] tastes and fashions [of the nineteenth century] had no place for Dryden; yet Dryden is one of the tests of a *catholic* appreciation of poetry" (*T. S. Eliot*). **Cosmopolitan** (etymologically, being a citizen of the world) stresses a lack of provincialism with reference not only to locality, section, nation, or the like, but to profession or other sphere of activity. When applied to individuals, their acts, utterances, and the like, it usually connotes opportunities for travel far and wide over the world and often more or less familiarity with many places, many peoples, and many cultures. "The softened *cosmopolitan* teaching of the prophets of the captivity and the rigid national teaching of the instructors of Israel's youth" (*Arnold*). When used, however, in reference to groups, it commonly suggests a mixture of all or of a wide variety of races and carries few suggestions of cultivation, breadth of mind, or the like." That queer, *cosmopolitan*, rather sinister crowd that is to be found around the Marseilles docks" (*R. Macaulay*). **Cosmic** now usually takes the place of *universal* when the reference is to the universe as opposed to or distinguished from the earth; as, *cosmic* order; "of what astral periods and *cosmic* processes am I not the crown, the wonder?" (*L. P. Smith*); "Natural, *cosmic* time, as it is measured out by sun and moon" (*A. Huxley*).

In ecclesiastical usage, both *Catholic* (usually capitalized) and *universal* (as, the *Catholic* Church; the *universal* church) refer to a church conceived of as the church founded by Jesus Christ and established by his apostles and as having for its mission the Christianization of all nations. In general Protestant usage, this church consists of all Christian denominations; in some Anglican and in Orthodox usage, it consists of all churches guided by an episcopate that traces its succession from the Apostles. *Catholic* is the official designation of the church commonly called the Roman Catholic Church in England and in America, which holds itself to be the ancient undivided church. Because of these differences in the application of *Catholic*, *universal* is often used in its place by those who wish to describe the whole body of Christians, or by those who wish to affirm the world-wide spread of their teachings.

Ana. *Earthly, terrestrial, worldly, mundane: *whole, entire, all, total.

2 Universal, general, generic, common are here compared as meaning characteristic of, belonging or relating to, comprehending, or affecting all or the whole. Because the implication of what constitutes all or the whole varies in each word, these terms are seldom used interchangeably by very precise writers and speakers. **Universal,** as here compared, is used chiefly in logic and philosophy; it implies reference to each one of a whole (such as a class, a category, a genus, or the like) without exception; thus, "All men are animals" is a *universal* affirmative proposition, and "no man is omniscient" is a *universal* negative proposition; color is a *universal* attribute of visible objects, but chroma (that is, hue and degree of saturation) is not; the great dramatist deals with particular men in particular situations but in such a way as to suggest *universal* truth; "if we [writers] want to get at the permanent and *universal* we tend to express ourselves in verse" (*T. S. Eliot*). **General** also implies reference to all, not only of a class, category, type, or species, but of a group, section, division, or other more or less loosely combined or associated number of persons or things. *Universal* tends to be used with great strictness in the particular sense here considered (see, however, UNIVERSAL, 1), but *general* often is used to imply reference to nearly all or to most of the group, even though it may be applied more strictly; as, "ethylene has come into *general* but not yet *universal* favor with surgeons" (*A. C. Morrison*); "the ideal of *general* cultivation has been one of the standards in education" (*C. W. Eliot*). As applied to words or terms, *general* strictly implies the word's or term's inclusiveness of every member of the class or group indicated; thus, "man" is a *general* term; "Under the *general* name of 'Egdon Heath' [in *The Return of the Native*]...are united or typified heaths of various real names" (*Hardy*). Oftentimes, however, *general* is more loosely applied to words, language, ideas, notions, and the like, and suggests lack of precision in significance, more or less loose generalization, or a vague range of application; as, "[Swinburne] uses the most *general* word, because his emotion is never particular" (*T. S. Eliot*); " 'Nothing could change Sophia.' And at the back of that notion was a more *general* notion: 'Nothing could change a Baines' " (*Bennett*); "some rather weak cases must fall within any law which is couched in *general* words" (*Justice Holmes*). **Generic** is now used with increasing frequency in place of *general* when a term implying reference to every member of a genus (sometimes, in looser use, of any other scientific or logical category) and the exclusion of all individuating characteristics is needed; thus, a *general* likeness between certain insects may be a likeness that is observable but not clearly distinguished, whereas a *generic* likeness is one that offers proof that they belong to the same genus or that enables a student to assign a hitherto unknown insect to its proper genus; so, "absolute *generic* unity would obtain if there were one summum genus under which all things without exception could be eventually subsumed" (*W. James*); "only that is good...which pleases the typical or normal or *generic* man" (*S. Alexander*). "The women were the crowning joy of his contemplative mind....Dyspepsia would not weaken their poignant outcries, or self-interest check their fainting fits. On the *generic* woman one could calculate" (*Meredith*). **Common,** as here compared (see also COMMON, 3; RECIPROCAL, 1), differs from *general* in implying participation, use, a sharing, or the like, by all members of the class, group, or community of persons (rarely of things) under consideration; as, "a thing...practiced

for two hundred years by *common* consent" (*Justice Holmes*); "crowds...swept along by a *common* animating impulse" (*Binyon*); "our *common* tongue" (*Lowes*).
Ant. Particular.

universe. Cosmos, macrocosm, *earth, world.

unkempt. Slovenly, sloppy, *slipshod.
Ana. Frowzy, *slatternly, blowzy, dowdy: *negligent, neglectful, lax, slack, remiss.

unlearned. *Ignorant, illiterate, unlettered, uneducated, untaught, untutored, nescient.
Ana. Crude, *rude, rough, raw, callow, green.

unlettered. Illiterate, *ignorant, uneducated, untaught, untutored, unlearned, nescient.

unlikeness. *Dissimilarity, difference, divergence, distinction.
Ana. Diversity, *variety: disparity, variousness (see corresponding adjectives at DIFFERENT): discrepancy, discordance, incongruousness, incompatibility, inconsistency, inconsonance (see corresponding adjectives at INCONSONANT).
Ant. Likeness.

unman. *Unnerve, emasculate, enervate.
Ana. Sap, undermine, *weaken, enfeeble, debilitate: *abase, degrade: *deplete, drain, exhaust, impoverish, bankrupt.

unmatured. *Immature, unripe, unmellow, unfledged.
Ant. Matured. — *Con.* *Mature, adult, grown-up.

unmeet. Unsuitable, *unfit, improper, inappropriate, unfitting, inapt, unhappy, infelicitous.
Ana. Unbecoming, unseemly, *indecorous.
Ant. Meet.

unmellow, unmellowed. *Immature, unmatured, unripe, unfledged.
Ant. Mellow, mellowed. — *Con.* Developed, ripened, matured (see MATURE, *v.*).

unmindful. *Forgetful, oblivious.
Ana. Heedless, thoughtless, *careless, inadvertent: *negligent, neglectful, remiss.
Ant. Mindful: solicitous. — *Con.* Careful, concerned, anxious, worried (see under CARE): *thoughtful, considerate, attentive.

unmitigated. *Outright, out-and-out, arrant.

unmoral. *Immoral, amoral, nonmoral.

unmovable. Variant of IMMOVABLE.

unnatural. Anomalous, *irregular.
Ana. *Abnormal, aberrant, atypic: *monstrous, prodigious: *fantastic, grotesque, bizarre.
Ant. Natural.

unnerve. **Unnerve, enervate, unman, emasculate** come into comparison when they mean to deprive of strength or vigor and of the capacity for endurance, overcoming difficulties, or making progress. **Unnerve** implies marked loss of courage, steadiness, self-control, or of power to act or fight, usually, but far from invariably, as a result of some calamity or sudden shock; as, "Government was *unnerved*, confounded, and in a manner suspended" (*Burke*); "That beloved name *unnerved* my arm" (*Arnold*); he was completely *unnerved* by the accident; "The narcotic and *unnerving* property of these stimulants has been thoroughly established" (*Day Lewis*). **Enervate** implies a much more gradual weakening or dissipation of one's strength until one is too feeble to make effort; usually, but not without exceptions, the term implies relaxation, especially of moral fiber, under the influence of luxury, indolence, effeminacy, and the like; as, "those unhappy people whose tender minds a long course of felicity has *enervated*" (*Bolingbroke*); "The people sink into sloth, and luxury, and prostitution... [the kingdom] is *enervated* at home—becomes contemptible abroad" (*Fielding*); "Plato asserts that a life of drudgery disfigures the body and...*enervates* the soul" (*G. L. Dickinson*). **Unman** implies loss of manly fortitude or spirit: it often suggests a shameful reduction to tears, tremors, extreme timidity, or other state regarded as womanish; as, "What, quite *unmann'd* in folly?.... Fie, for shame!" (*Shak.*); "For a moment the overwhelming conviction of it *unmanned* him" (*Prescott*). **Emasculate** (see also STERILIZE, 1) implies a loss of essential or effective power, especially by the removal of something, such as a factor or a condition, which has made for the strength of a person, a group, or the like. "Hellenism....was not destroyed, though it was *emasculated*, by the loss of political freedom" (*Inge*).
Ana. Upset, agitate, perturb (see DISCOMPOSE): bewilder, distract, confound (see PUZZLE, *v.*): *weaken, enfeeble, sap, undermine.

unpremeditated. *Extemporaneous, extempore, extemporary, improvised, impromptu, offhand.
Ant. Premeditated. — *Con.* *Deliberate, considered, designed, studied.

unpropitious. *Ominous, portentous, fateful, inauspicious.
Ana. *Sinister, baleful, malign, malefic: threatening, menacing (see THREATEN): *adverse, antagonistic, counter.
Ant. Propitious.

unqualified. Incompetent, *incapable.
Ana. Disabled, crippled, weakened, debilitated (see WEAKEN): *unfit, unsuitable.
Ant. Qualified. — *Con.* *Able, capable, competent.

unquiet. *Impatient, nervous, restless, restive, uneasy, fidgety, skittish, feverish, hectic, jumpy, jittery.
Ana. Agitated, upset, perturbed, disquieted, disturbed (see DISCOMPOSE): worried, anxious, solicitous, concerned, careful (see under CARE).
Ant. Quiet.

unreasonable. *Irrational.
Ana. Absurd, preposterous, *foolish, silly: *simple, fatuous, asinine: *excessive, immoderate, inordinate.
Ant. Reasonable.

unrelenting. *Grim, implacable, relentless, merciless.
Ana. Inexorable, obdurate, *inflexible, adamant: *stiff, rigid: *severe, stern.
Ant. Forbearing.

unreligious. *Irreligious, ungodly, godless, nonreligious.

unripe. *Immature, unmatured, unmellow, unfledged.
Ana. Crude, raw, green, callow, *rude: *premature, untimely, forward, precocious.
Ant. Ripe. — *Con.* Matured, ripened, developed (see MATURE, *v.*).

unruffled. Imperturbable, nonchalant, *cool, composed, collected.
Ana. *Calm, placid, peaceful, serene, tranquil: poised, balanced (see STABILIZE).
Ant. Ruffled: excited.

unruly. **Unruly, ungovernable, intractable, refractory, recalcitrant, willful** (*or* **wilful**), **headstrong** come into comparison as meaning not submissive to government or control. **Unruly** stresses a lack of discipline or an incapacity for discipline: in addition it often connotes turbulence, disorderliness, waywardness, obstreperousness, or the like; as, *unruly* children; "Whatever my *unruly* tongue may say" (*J. R. Green*); "the *unruly* passions" (*T. S. Eliot*). **Ungovernable** implies either an incapacity for, or an escape from, guidance or control. When applied directly or indirectly to persons, it usually suggests either no previous subjection to restrictions or a state of being unsubdued (as, "The fiercest and most *ungovernable* part of the...population"—*Macaulay*) or the loss of all power to control oneself or to be controlled by others (as, he fell into an *ungovernable* rage; he knew that if he gave rein to his passion, it would become *ungovernable*). When used in reference to things, it usually suggests their incapacity for human direction or control; as, "That... *ungovernable* wonder the wind" (*N. Hawthorne*); "We palpitate between relief when our *ungovernable* vehicle blunders into a happy valley, and despair when we hear the growl of the waves at the foot of the cliffs" (*Shaw*). **Intractable** and **refractory** both imply resistance to all attempts to bring under one's control, management, or direction. When applied to persons, *intractable* suggests an indisposition to guidance or a disposition to resist (as, an *intractable* child; an *intractable* temper; "his rough, *intractable* spirit"—*J. Wesley;* "We were now dealing with the *intractable* Sinhalese rather than the stupid but amenable Tamils"—*V. Heiser*): when applied to things, it suggests a more or less marked incapacity for working, manipulation, treatment, or the like (as, *intractable* soil; an *intractable* metal; "Shakespeare was unable to impose this motive successfully upon the '*intractable*' material of the old play"—*T. S. Eliot*). *Refractory*, on the other hand, often implies active resistance as indicated by manifest disobedience, open protest, or rebelliousness (as, "It becomes my duty to struggle against my *refractory* feelings"—*Burney;* "There is no use in making the *refractory* child feel guilty; it is much more to the purpose to make him feel that he is missing pleasures which the others are enjoying"—*B. Russell*) or, when the reference is to an inanimate thing, a degree of intractability that offers especially great resistance or presents unusual difficulties (as, bricks and other *refractory* [i.e., heat-resistant] substances are used to line furnaces; "Cheerfulness is in ethics what fluorspar is in metallurgy. It is a flux absolutely necessary in dealing with *refractory* moral elements"—*S. M. Crothers*). **Recalcitrant** (etymologically, kicking back) carries an even stronger implication of active and violent resistance or of obstinate rebellion: it usually suggests defiance of another's will, order, authority, or the like; as, "his father became *recalcitrant* and cut off the supplies" (*Stevenson*); "In Russia a minority of devoted Marxists maintain by sheer force such government as is possible in the teeth of an intensely *recalcitrant* peasantry" (*Shaw*). The term is less often applied to things (other than personal traits, feelings, dispositions, etc.) than *intractable* and *refractory* but there is some use when seemingly insuperable difficulties are implied; as, "The atomicity of nature, supposed to be as yet *recalcitrant* to mind" (*S. Alexander*); "He discovers poetry in the most unlikely places and wrings it out of the most *recalcitrant* material" (*Day Lewis*). **Willful** usually implies intractability because of an overweening desire or an obstinate determination to have one's own way and an unwillingness to be guided by those who are wise or experienced; as, "To *willful* men, the injuries that they themselves procure must be their schoolmasters" (*Shak.*); "to confound [will] with its irritable and purposeless counterfeit, *willfulness*" (*J. R. Lowell*); "her bright audacity, her ardor and her *willfulness*" (*Hewlett*); "We know we haven't finality, and so we are open and receptive, rather than *wilful*" (*H. G. Wells*). **Headstrong** implies violent self-will that makes for refractoriness or recalcitrance; as, "a *headstrong,* moody, murmuring race" (*Dryden*); "the *headstrong* passions of Benvenuto Cellini" (*Gibbon*); "They are testy and *headstrong* through an excess of will and bias" (*Emerson*).

Ana. *Insubordinate, rebellious, contumacious: obstreperous, boisterous, strident (see VOCIFEROUS): *contrary, perverse, froward, wayward: fractious, *irritable, snappish, waspish.

Ant. Tractable, docile.

unseemly. *Indecorous, improper, unbecoming, indecent, indelicate.

Ana. Unfitting, unsuitable, inappropriate, unmeet (see UNFIT): incongruous, incompatible, inconsistent, *inconsonant.

Ant. Seemly.

unsettle. *Disorder, derange, disarrange, disorganize, disturb.

Ana. Discommode, incommode, trouble, molest (see INCONVENIENCE): upset, agitate, perturb, *discompose, disquiet.

Ant. Settle.

unsocial. Unsocial, asocial, antisocial, nonsocial agree in meaning not social and therefore, in a sense, opposed to that which is social. **Unsocial** is applied chiefly to persons, their temperaments, acts, motives, etc., and implies a distaste for the society of others or an aversion to companionship or fraternization; as, he is a most *unsocial* person; an *unsocial* disposition. **Asocial** is also applied to persons, but especially to their behavior, their thoughts, their acts, and the like, regarded objectively, as from the psychologist's point of view; it implies a lack of all the qualities which are suggested by the word *social*, especially as opposed to *individual*. In its most frequent sense, that which is *asocial* has no reference to or significance for others, and is therefore, by implication, individualistic, self-centered, egocentric, egoistic, or the like; as, *asocial* types of persons; *asocial* interests; dreaming is an *asocial* act. **Antisocial** is applied chiefly to ideas, movements, acts, books, and the like, which are regarded as harmful to or destructive of society or the social order or institutions such as the state and church; as, anarchists are both *asocial* in their thinking and *antisocial* in their propaganda; *antisocial* theories; *antisocial* conduct. **Nonsocial** is applied only to things which cannot be described as *social* in any sense of the word; as, *nonsocial* questions; *nonsocial* activities; a *nonsocial* club; *nonsocial* diseases.

Ant. Social.

unsophisticated. *Natural, simple, ingenuous, naïve, artless.

Ana. Candid, *frank, open, plain: genuine, bona fide, *authentic: crude, callow, green (see RUDE).

Ant. Sophisticated.

unspeakable. *Unutterable, inexpressible, ineffable, inenarrable, indescribable.

Ana. *Offensive, loathsome, repulsive, revolting: *repugnant, repellent, obnoxious, distasteful: abominable, odious, *hateful, detestable.

unstable. *Inconstant, fickle, capricious, mercurial.

Ana. *Changeable, variable, mutable, protean: volatile, effervescent, buoyant, resilient, *elastic.

Ant. Stable.

unsuitable. *Unfit, unmeet, improper, inappropriate, unfitting, inapt, unhappy, infelicitous.

Ana. Unbecoming, unseemly, *indecorous, indecent: inept, maladroit, *awkward, clumsy, gauche.

Ant. Suitable.

unsympathetic. **1** Uncongenial, discordant, incongruous, incompatible, *inconsonant, inconsistent, discrepant.

Ant. Sympathetic. — ***Con.*** Harmonizing *or* harmonious, accordant, correspondent (see verbs at AGREE).

2 *Antipathetic, averse.

Ana. *Indifferent, unconcerned, incurious, aloof: *hardened, callous, indurated.

Ant. Sympathetic.

untangle. Disentangle, *extricate, disencumber, disembarrass.
Ana. *Free, release, liberate.
Con. *Hamper, fetter, manacle, shackle, trammel.

untaught. *Ignorant, illiterate, unlettered, uneducated, untutored, unlearned, nescient.
Ant. Taught.

untimely. *Premature, forward, advanced, precocious.
Ana. *Immature, unmatured, unripe, unmellow, unfledged.
Ant. Timely. — *Con.* *Seasonable, opportune, well-timed, pat.

untiring. *Indefatigable, tireless, weariless, unwearying, unwearied, unflagging.
Ana. Unceasing, never-ending, interminable, *everlasting: assiduous, sedulous, diligent (see BUSY): persevering, persisting (see PERSEVERE).

untruth. *Lie, falsehood, fib, misrepresentation, story.
Ana. Mendaciousness *or* mendacity, dishonesty, deceitfulness (see corresponding adjectives at DISHONEST): equivocation, tergiversation (see AMBIGUITY).
Ant. Truth. — *Con.* Veracity, verity (see TRUTH): *honesty, integrity, probity, honor.

untruthful. Lying, mendacious, *dishonest, deceitful.
Ana. *False, wrong: *misleading, deceptive, delusive, delusory.
Ant. Truthful. — *Con.* Honest, *upright, scrupulous: veracious (see corresponding noun at TRUTH).

untutored. *Ignorant, illiterate, unlettered, uneducated, untaught, unlearned, nescient.
Ant. Tutored.

unutterable. **Unutterable, inexpressible, unspeakable, ineffable, inenarrable, indescribable** agree in meaning incapable of being told or described. All, with the possible exception of *inenarrable*, are often nothing more than intensives implying an extreme that goes beyond the power of words to express. In their more explicit denotations, **unutterable** implies any of various reasons why the thing so qualified cannot be voiced or spoken, such as the greatness of one's awe (as, "My tongue... Attempts th' *unutterable* Name, But faints"—*I. Watts*), or one's inability to pronounce correctly (as, to find the French word "roi" *unutterable*), or one's aversion to that which is immodest or obscene (as, I cannot repeat what he said, for his language was *unutterable*). **Inexpressible,** on the other hand, usually applies to that which is so delicate, so immaterial, so subtle, or the like, that there are no words to reveal its true or exact nature; as, "speech able to express subtleties...that before seemed *inexpressible*" (*H. Ellis*). **Unspeakable** differs little from *unutterable* in its etymological and explicit meaning; as, "joy *unspeakable* and full of glory" (*1 Peter* i. 8); "a thousand memories... *Unspeakable* for sadness" (*Tennyson*); "the bawdy thoughts that come into one's head —the *unspeakable* words" (*L. P. Smith*). More often, however, especially in current use, *unspeakable* means too unpleasant, disgusting, horrible, or the like, to describe in detail; as, "My nights were *unspeakable*" (*Jane W. Carlyle*); "twisted shapes of lust, *unspeakable*, Abominable" (*Tennyson*); "Twice...in my public transferences from one prison to another have I been shown under conditions of *unspeakable* humiliation to the gaze and mockery of men" (*Wilde*). **Ineffable,** although it is etymologically closer in meaning to *unutterable* than to *inexpressible*, in actual use is a near synonym of the latter word. It carries, however, a stronger suggestion of a character that transcends expression because of its etherealness, its spirituality, its ideality, or other similarly elusive quality; as, "*ineffable* tenderness" (*Meredith*); "the eyes remained distant and serious, as if bent on some *ineffable* vision" (*E. Wharton*); "The mystic sees the *ineffable*, and the psycho-pathologist the *unspeakable*" (*Maugham*). "Who shall say that in this silence, in this hovering wan light, in this air bereft of wings, and of all scent save freshness, there is less of the *ineffable*, less of that before which words are dumb?" (*Galsworthy*). **Inenarrable** (now practically obsolete) and **indescribable** strongly suggest the inability of the writer or speaker to narrate, or describe, or explain the thing so qualified; they therefore usually fail to ascribe a definite quality to the thing itself and are, by comparison with the other terms, vaguer and less effective; as, "That sacred...mystery of the Holy Trinity is...*inenarrable* by any creature" (*M. Davies*); "Various sacred *indescribable* articles were scattered around" (*H. Martineau*).

unwearied. *Indefatigable, tireless, weariless, untiring, unwearying, unflagging.
Ana. Persevering, persisting *or* persistent (see corresponding verbs at PERSEVERE): unceasing, never-ending, interminable (see EVERLASTING): constant, *steady.

unwearying. *Indefatigable, tireless, weariless, untiring, unwearied, unflagging.
Ana. See those at UNTIRING.

upbraid. *Scold, rate, berate, tonguelash, revile, vituperate, jaw, bawl out, wig, rail.
Ana. Reprehend, reprobate, blame, censure, denounce (see CRITICIZE): reproach, reprimand, rebuke, *reprove.

uphold. *Support, advocate, back, champion.
Ana. *Help, aid, assist: defend, vindicate, justify, *maintain: sanction, *approve, endorse.
Ant. Contravene: subvert.

upholder. Supporter, advocate, backer, champion. See under SUPPORT, *v.*

upright, *adj.* **Upright, honest, just, conscientious, scrupulous, honorable** (*or* **honourable**) come into comparison when they are applied to men, their acts, and words and mean having or exhibiting a strict regard for what is morally right. **Upright** implies manifest rectitude and an uncompromising adherence to high moral principles. "So *upright* Quakers please both man and God" (*Pope*). "We shall exult, if they who rule the land, Be men... Wise, *upright*, valiant; not a servile band" (*Wordsworth*). **Honest,** in its current prevailing sense, implies a recognition of and strict adherence to virtues such as truthfulness, candor, respect for others' possessions, sincerity, fairness, and the like; it is far more widely applicable than *upright* which often implies independence of spirit and self-mastery and which is therefore referable chiefly to thoughtful and highly disciplined men. *Honest*, on the other hand, may be used in reference to the ignorant as well as the learned, and to the simple as well as the wise. "The *honest* heart that's free frae a' Intended fraud or guile" (*Burns*). "If we be *honest* with ourselves, we shall be *honest* with each other" (*G. Macdonald*). **Just,** in early English use, described the man who by his faith and works justified himself in the sight of God, or by his strict adherence to moral principles won the admiration of men; the word now occurs in this sense chiefly as a Biblical archaism. "For he maketh his sun to rise on the evil and on the good, and sendeth rain on the *just* and on the unjust" (*Matthew* v. 45). "Cornelius the centurion, a *just* man, and one that feareth God, and of good report among all the nation of the Jews" (*Acts* x. 22). "Some lead a life unblameable and *just*" (*Cowper*). *Conscientious* and *scrupulous* both imply an active moral sense which governs all one's actions. **Conscientious,** however, stresses painstaking efforts to follow that guide at all costs, especially in one's observance of the moral law, or in the

performance of one's duty. "His [Ben Jonson's] whole character...was far too sturdily *conscientious* to allow of any suspicion being cast upon his rectitude" (*A. W. Ward*). "The skillful, *conscientious* schoolmistresses whose lives were spent in trying to inculcate real knowledge" (*Grandgent*). **Scrupulous** (see also CAREFUL, 2), on the other hand, implies either anxiety lest one should not obey strictly the dictates of conscience, or meticulous attention to the morality of the details of conduct, as well as to the morality of one's ends. "He is so very strict and *scrupulous* in his notions....Do not you think it is quite a mistaken point of conscience, when a clergyman sacrifices his health for the sake of duties which may be just as well performed by another person?" (*Austen*). **Honorable** (see also HONORABLE, 1) implies the guidance of a high sense of honor, or of a sense of what one should do in obedience not only to the dictates of conscience but to the demands made upon one by one's social position or one's office, by the code of one's profession, or by the esteem in which one is held. " 'What do you think of me?' 'As of a man faithful and *honourable*' " (*Shak.*). "Did this vile world show many such as thee, Thou perfect, just, and *honourable* man!" (*Shelley*).
Ana. *Moral, ethical, virtuous, righteous: *fair, equitable, impartial: *straightforward, aboveboard.

uprising. *Rebellion, revolution, revolt, insurrection, mutiny, Putsch.
Ana. Fight, combat, conflict, fray (see CONTEST): strife, contention, dissension (see DISCORD): aggression, *attack.

uproar. *Din, pandemonium, hullabaloo, babel, hubbub, racket.
Ana. Strife, contention, dissension, *discord, conflict, variance: *confusion, disorder, chaos: fracas, *brawl, broil, melee.

uproot. Eradicate, deracinate, extirpate, *exterminate, wipe out.
Ana. *Abolish, extinguish, annihilate, abate: supplant, displace, *replace, supersede: subvert, overthrow, *overturn: *destroy, demolish.
Ant. Establish: inseminate.

upset, *v.* **1** *Overturn, overset, capsize, overthrow, subvert.
Ana. Invert, *reverse: *tip, tilt, cant, careen: turn, bend (see CURVE, *v.*).
2 Agitate, perturb, disturb, disquiet, *discompose, fluster, flurry.
Ana. Bewilder, distract, confound (see PUZZLE, *v.*): discomfit, rattle, faze, *embarrass: *unnerve, unman.

upshot. Outcome, issue, result, consequence, *effect, aftereffect, event, aftermath, sequel.
Ana. *End, termination, ending: climax, culmination (see SUMMIT): concluding *or* conclusion, finishing *or* finish, completion (see corresponding verbs at CLOSE).

urbane. *Suave, smooth, diplomatic, bland, politic.
Ana. Courteous, polite, courtly, *civil: poised, balanced (see STABILIZE): cultured, cultivated, refined (see corresponding nouns at CULTURE).
Ant. Rude: clownish: bucolic.

urge, *n.* *Desire, lust, concupiscence, passion, appetite, appetence, yen.
Ana. *Motive, spring, spur, goad, incentive: longing, yearning, pining (see LONG): craving, coveting, desiring (see DESIRE, *v.*).

usage. **1** Practice, custom, consuetude, use, *habit, habitude, wont.
Ana. *Method, mode, manner, way, fashion: procedure, proceeding, *process: guiding *or* guidance, leading *or* lead (see corresponding verbs at GUIDE): *choice, preference.
2 *Form, convention, convenance.
Ana. Formality, ceremony, *form.

use, *v.* **Use, employ, utilize, apply, avail oneself of** as here compared, agree in meaning to deal with something so as to give it a practical value or to make it serviceable to oneself or others. One **uses** a thing (a person only when regarded as a passive object) as a means or instrument to the accomplishment of a purpose or as an aid to the attainment of one's end; the thing may be concrete (as, to *use* a hoe in cultivating; to *use* a dictionary to build up one's vocabulary; to *use* a person as a tool), or it may be abstract (as, to *use* patience in dealing with children; to *use* one's discretion in the investment of a trust fund. "The way to learn to *use* words is to read some good literature often and carefully"—*B. Russell;* "His sense of being *used* rose suddenly above the treacherous sympathy he had begun to feel for her" —*Tarkington*). One **employs** a person or thing that is idle, inactive, not in use, and the like, when one puts him or it to work or finds a profitable use for him or it; as, "She had...*employed* her leisure in reading every book that came in her way" (*Shaw*); "the student crammed full of knowledge which he cannot *employ*" (*Grandgent*). "The life of a man of business who *employs* his own capital, and *employs* it nearly always in the same way, is by no means fully *employed*" (*Quiller-Couch*). Although *use* and *employ* are often interchanged, there is usually, in precise writing, a perceptible difference in meaning: wherever the idea of serving as the means or instrument is uppermost, *use* is the preferred term; wherever the idea of engaging or selecting, of keeping occupied or busy, or of turning to account is uppermost, *employ* is the desirable and often the necessary choice; thus, a writer *uses* words effectively who knows what ones he should *employ* in a given context; a teacher often *uses* his pupils as monitors when he should keep them *employed* in study. One **utilizes** something when one finds a profitable use for it or discovers how to employ it for a practical purpose; as, "he even tried to figure out a way to *utilize* the small limbs cut from the tops of the trees" (*S. Anderson*); "progress is possible only through *utilization* of experience" (*Grandgent*). One **applies** something when one brings it into contact or into relation with something else where it will prove its usefulness or acquire practical value. This implication of making a connection or bringing into contact is strong in all senses of *apply;* it not only affects the construction (thus, one *uses* a gift of money to pay a debt, but one *applies* that money to the payment of a debt), but it often obscures the implication of usefulness (thus, one *uses* a mustard plaster to relieve a chest pain, but one *applies* a mustard plaster to the chest). This implication also distinguishes *apply* from the other words when the idea of usefulness is stressed; thus, one knows how to *employ* words when one reveals his ability to select those words that express his exact meaning, no more and no less; one knows how to *apply* words when one reveals his ability to use them relevantly, that is, in reference to the things or ideas with which they are idiomatically associated; thus, foreigners learning English find difficulty in *applying* certain words and phrases such as "evening dress" and "nightdress," "tool" and "instrument," "bad" and "naughty," and the like. "Our own word 'virtue' is *applied* only to moral qualities; but the Greek word which we so translate should properly be rendered 'excellence,' and includes a reference to the body as well as to the soul" (*G. L. Dickinson*). The implication of a useful or definite end is strongest in *apply* when the word carries the further suggestion of relating that which is general or theoretical to that which is particular, or concrete, for some practical purpose such as identification (as, we can discover if this fabric is woolen by *applying* certain tests such as burning a portion to see if it has a peculiar odor), or clarification of a problem (as, before forming an opinion, the judges must know what laws *apply* to the particular case), or invention (as, rayon, hard rubber, aniline dyes, wireless telegraphy, the radio, the airplane, and other recent inventions and discoveries are all the result of the *application* of the laws of physics and chemistry). Hence, a science when it is concerned chiefly with theory is called a *pure* science, and when it is concerned with the practical application of that theory is called an *applied* science; as, *applied* chemistry; *applied* sociology. "The law does all that is needed when it does all that it can, indicates a policy, *applies* it to all within the lines, and seeks to bring within the lines all similarly situated" (*Justice Holmes*). "It is a test which we may *apply* to all figure-painters—a test which will often discover the secret of unsatisfactory design—if we ask whether the figures are really occupied by what they are doing" (*Binyon*). One **avails oneself of** something (or someone) that is at hand, is offered, is at one's disposal, or the like, when one uses it or him to one's own benefit, advantage, or the like. "I doubt if I should abuse the permission. It is a hundred to one if I should *avail myself of* it four times in a year" (*Dickens*). "Far from resenting such tutelage I am only too glad to *avail myself of* it" (*Shaw*).

Ana. *Handle, manipulate, ply, wield: *practice, exercise.

use, *n.* **1 Use, service, advantage, profit, account, avail** are synonymous when they agree in meaning a useful or valuable end, result, or purpose. Only the first four are used freely, but even they often, as the last two invariably, occur in idiomatic phrases such as, to put or turn to *use, service, advantage,* etc.; of no *use, advantage, account, avail.* **Use** stresses either employment for some purpose or end of practical value (as, to turn every scrap of material to *use*) or the practical value of the end promoted or attained (as, the findings in the investigation were of little *use*). "The vehicles [balloons] can serve no *use* till we can guide them" (*Johnson*). "Sweet are the *uses* of adversity" (*Shak.*). **Service,** though often interchangeable with *use,* is preferable when the reference is to persons or animals or their work or actions; as, "the horse was unfit for *service*" (*Scott*); to render a *service* to a friend. *Service* often implies that the result of one's act or works is beneficial. "I have done the state some *service,* and they know't" (*Shak.*). "To fret myself would have done me no *service*" (*Smollett*). **Advantage** adds to *use* the implication of improvement or enhancement as in value, position, or the like; as, he uses every penny to *advantage;* her beauty proved to be of great *advantage* to her in her stage career. "Constance had never before seen him to such heroic *advantage*" (*Bennett*). "True Wit is Nature to *advantage* dress'd" (*Pope*). **Profit** distinctively implies reward or the rewarding character of that which is attained; only in its extended use does it imply pecuniary gain; as, to work hard but to no *profit.* "He found moral *profit* also in this self-study; for how, he asked, can we correct our vices if we do not know them" (*L. P. Smith*). **Account** is used chiefly in phrases; as, to turn to *account;* of much, little, or no *account.* In loose use, it is interchangeable with *use, advantage,* or *profit;* in discriminating use, however, it suggests calculable value. "A book that turns to *account* the conclusions of other recent German theorists" (*Babbitt*). Sometimes, it is nearly equivalent to *importance.* "Our family...whose honour is of so much *account* to both of us" (*Dickens*). **Avail** so strongly suggests effectualness or effectiveness in the end attained that the negative idiomatic phrases in which it is often found are equivalent to *ineffectual* or *ineffectually;* as, the search was of no *avail;* he labored unceasingly without *avail* to move the rock; he studied hard but to no *avail.*

Ana. Benefit, profit (see corresponding verbs at BENEFIT): value, *worth: *function, office, duty: purpose, *intention, object.

2 Use, usefulness, utility come into comparison when they mean the character or the quality of serving or of being able to serve one's end or purpose. **Use** (as here compared: see also USE, 1; HABIT) is the most general or least explicit of these terms: it usually implies little more than suitability for employment, sometimes for an implied or stated purpose, but often merely for any conceivable purpose; as, she said she would have saved the pieces had they been of any *use;* there is no *use* in becoming angry; I am sure your conclusions will prove to be of great *use.* **Usefulness,** on the other hand, is employed chiefly with reference to definite concrete things that serve or are capable of serving a practical purpose; as, he demonstrated the *usefulness* of his device for stabilizing airplanes; the gadget has no real *usefulness* so far as I can see. **Utility** is preferred to *use* and *usefulness* in scientific, philosophical, and other formal speech or writing. It is, therefore, often regarded as a property or quality that can be measured, decreased and increased, or the like, or that can be viewed as an abstraction; "Does any sound measure either of the *utility* or the needs of various classes of wage-earners determine that a compositor or a plasterer shall receive ...[a weekly wage] three times that of a skilled farm labourer?" (*J. A. Hobson*). "Universities exist for two purposes; on the one hand, to train men and women for certain professions; on the other hand, to pursue learning and research without regard to immediate *utility*" (*B. Russell*).

Ana. Applicability, relevance, pertinence (see corresponding adjectives at RELEVANT): suitability, fitness, appropriateness (see corresponding adjectives at FIT).

3 Wont, practice, usage, custom, consuetude, *habit, habitude.

Ana. *Form, usage: rite, ceremony, formality (see FORM, *n.*).

usefulness. *Use, utility.

Ana. Value, *worth: *excellence, merit.

usual. Usual, customary, habitual, wonted, accustomed are synonymous when they mean familiar through frequent or regular repetition. **Usual** stresses the absence of strangeness, and is applied to whatever is normally expected or happens in the ordinary course of events; as, they paid the *usual* fee; the *usual* meeting of the trustees; open for business as *usual.* "It appeared to him to be the *usual* castle, and he saw nothing unusual in the manner of his reception by the *usual* old lord" (*H. Adams*). "It's *usual* for a woman to find her life in her husband's" (*M. Austin*). **Customary** often implies characteristic or distinguishing quality, and is applied to that which is according to the usual or prevailing practices, conventions, usages, and the like, of a particular individual or, especially, of a particular community. "The *customary* rule on most lines was dinner jackets in the evening" (*V. Heiser*). "We had no idea how men behave when their *customary* way of life is disrupted" (*Lippmann*). Sometimes, invariable or fixed quality is implied. "The assumption that whatever has been *customary* must be bad, and that anything which is or seems novel must be good" (*Grandgent*). **Habitual** implies settled or established practice, and is commonly applied to the acts or qualities of an individual confirmed in a habit; as, his

habitual energy; a *habitual* smile. "A trace of acidity which began, before he left college, to flavour his comments on human affairs, and has since become *habitual* to him" (*Quiller-Couch*). **Wonted,** now regarded as a bookish word, stresses habituation, and is applied to that which is the result of habit or which represents a custom; as, he preserved his *wonted* demeanor; they returned at their *wonted* hour. **Accustomed** is often interchangeable with *wonted* and *customary*, but it is a more familiar word than the first and is weaker in its suggestions of custom and fixity than the second; as, to work with *accustomed* diligence. "Pausing to fling out an arm with some familiar *accustomed* gesture" (*Quiller-Couch*).
Ana. *Regular, natural, normal, typical: *common, ordinary, familiar: prevalent, *prevailing, rife, current.

usurp. *Arrogate, pre-empt, appropriate, confiscate.
Ana. Seize, *take, grab, grasp: *take, assume.
Ant. Abdicate.

utensil. *Implement, tool, instrument, appliance.
Ana. *Device, contrivance, contraption, gadget.

utility. *Use, usefulness.
Ana. Suitability, fitness, appropriateness (see corresponding adjectives at FIT): value, *worth.

utilize. *Use, employ, apply, avail oneself of.
Ana. *Benefit, profit: *handle, manipulate, ply, wield: forward, further, promote, *advance.

utopian. *Ambitious, pretentious.
Ana. Impracticable, unfeasible, impossible (see affirmative adjectives at POSSIBLE): visionary, quixotic, chimerical (see IMAGINARY): ideal, transcendental, *abstract.

utter. *Express, vent, voice, broach, air, ventilate.
Ana. Enunciate, articulate, *pronounce: *reveal, disclose, discover, divulge: *declare, announce, publish, advertise.

V

vacant. *Empty, blank, void, vacuous.
Ana. *Bare, barren: destitute, void, *devoid: idiotic, imbecilic, foolish (see corresponding nouns at FOOL).
Con. *Full, complete, replete.

vacate. *Annul, abrogate, void, avoid, quash.

vacillate. *Hesitate, waver, falter.
Ana. Fluctuate, sway, oscillate (see SWING): *demur, scruple, boggle.

vacuous. *Empty, vacant, blank, void.
Ana. Barren, *bare: inane, wishy-washy, *insipid.
Con. *Full, replete.

vacuum, *n.* Void, cavity, *hole, hollow, pocket.

vagabond, *n.* **Vagabond, vagrant, truant, tramp, tramper, hobo, bum, stiff, swagman** (*or* **swagsman**), **sundowner** are here considered as meaning one given to wandering at will or as a habit. **Vagabond** and **vagrant** came into use in English in the 15th century as terms denoting a person without fixed home or settled occupation, who wandered from place to place, depending for a livelihood on begging or other disreputable and even dishonest practices. Both were derogatory, sometimes abusive, terms. *Vagabond*, the far commoner term in current literary and general use, though still usually derogatory, now often, because of its emphasis (even stronger in the verb than in the noun) on the mere fact of wandering, implies merely a carefree fondness for a roaming life; as, "That young *vagabond* of genius [Rousseau]" (*L. P. Smith*); spending several happy years as a *vagabond* in the capitals of Europe before settling down to a business career in New York; cf. *vagabonding* about the world. From the first, *vagrant* appears to have been the preferred inclusive legal term; as, "If it shall appear ...such man...to have been a *vagrant* and *vagabond* or idle person" (*Laws of England: 1 Edward VI*); "idle and disorderly persons, rogues and *vagabonds*, incorrigible rogues and other *vagrants*" (*5 George IV*). Though still in general use, it is now chiefly a legal term, especially in Great Britain and various states of the United States, applying to a person without fixed or known residence whose habits or acts are such that he or she is likely to become a public menace or a public charge; as, to be arrested as a *vagrant;* the jail is the winter home of many *vagrants*. Even in general use, the term now carries much stronger implications of disreputableness and waywardness than *vagabond*. **Truant**, an older word than the preceding terms, originally carried a weaker suggestion of vagabondage, or roving, but as strong an implication of laziness, idleness, and beggary. In later times, it came to carry as its strongest implication the habit of wandering away from where one ought to be or of loitering when one ought to be elsewhere, especially and now almost exclusively, at school; as, an officer detailed to capture boys who are *truants* from school. "The village master... A man severe he was... I knew him well, and every *truant* knew" (*Goldsmith*). **Tramp** (or the now rare **tramper**) is the ordinary colloquial term for *vagabond* or *vagrant* in the early sense of either word: in general use it applies to any such person whether he moves about in search of work, especially seasonal work, or whether he lives by beggary and thievery. "Whoever, not being under seventeen, a blind person or a person asking charity within his own town, roves about from place to place begging, or living without labor or visible means of support, shall be deemed a *tramp*" (*General Laws of Massachusetts*). **Hobo** and **bum** are slang terms of U. S. origin. The latter applies to a lazy, idle, and often drunken, good-for-nothing, who will not work but habitually sponges on others. The former has not yet acquired fixed meaning. It has been variously distinguished from *tramp*, sometimes in terms of willingness to work, sometimes in terms of methods of travel, the *tramp* being then taken as one who typically tramps the roads, the *hobo* as one who typically rides surreptitiously on freight trains. Perhaps the commonest application of *hobo* is to the migratory worker who roves about following seasonal occupations such as harvesting and crop picking. The following quotations illustrate the lack of general agreement: "The difference between *hoboes, tramps* and '*bums*' was defined at a meeting of the International Brotherhood Welfare Association... *hoboes* are traveling workers, *tramps* are traveling shirkers and *bums* are stationary shirkers" (*Cleveland Plain Dealer*); "the first strict definition [of *hobo*]...was that given by Josiah Flynt....who declared that '*hobo*' is the distinctive name for such a tramp as will not in any case work....Now you are promulgating a directly opposite limitation for '*hobo*.' My conclusion is that '*hobo*' has as yet all the indefiniteness of slang" (*The Nation*); "The word *hobo*...in its more general...sense...is the name now given...to all the human flotsam and jetsam that floats on the outer fringes of society" (*American Mercury*). "In Western parlance a *hobo* is not a *tramp*. A *hobo* is a migratory laborer, who carries his blankets on his back, looking for work. A picturesque Western synonym more accurately describes him—he is often known as a 'blanket *stiff*' " (*World's Work*). The slang term **stiff,** used generically to denote a person, especially a man, has sometimes the implications of *bum* (as, "there are a large number of '*stiffs*' in this town, getting help from all sorts of charities, who...should be made to work"—*Rand Daily Mail*), but, as here considered, applies chiefly to migratory workers and to roustabouts, especially on cattle ships. The term is often qualified; as, cattle *stiff;* harvest *stiff;* working *stiff;* blanket or bindle *stiff* (one who carries with him his own roll of bedding). In Australian slang, the migratory worker who tramps the "bush" looking for work is termed a **swagman** from the fact that he carries on his back or shoulder a long roll of clothing and bedding, variously termed a *swag, drum,* or *bluey* (hence, to "hump bluey," i.e., to carry a swag; to tramp about seeking work). The swagman making a practice of arriving at sundown at a station and asking for food and shelter is called a **sundowner,** a term used also in South Africa with similar application. "*Swagsmen* too, genuine, or only '*sundowners*,'—men who loaf about till sunset, and then come in with the demand for the unrefusable 'rations' " (*F. W. L. Adams*).

Ana. Wanderer, roamer, rover (see corresponding verbs at WANDER).

vagary. *Caprice, freak, whim, whimsey, crotchet.

Ana. *Mood, humor, temper, vein: *fancy, fantasy, dream, daydream: notion, *idea.

vagrant, *n.* *Vagabond, truant, tramp, hobo, bum, stiff, swagman, sundowner.

Ana. Wanderer, roamer, rover (see corresponding verbs at WANDER).

vagrant, *adj.* *Itinerant, peripatetic, ambulatory, ambulant, nomadic.

Ana. Moving, shifting (see MOVE, *v.*): wandering, roaming, roving, rambling, straying, ranging (see WANDER): strolling, sauntering (see SAUNTER).

vague. *Obscure, dark, enigmatic, cryptic, ambiguous, equivocal.

Ana. *Formless, unformed, inchoate, amorphous: *doubtful, dubious: abstruse, *recondite.

Ant. Definite: specific: lucid. — *Con.* *Clear, perspicuous: express, *explicit.

vain. 1 Vain, nugatory, otiose, idle, empty, hollow come into comparison when they mean devoid of worth or significance. That is **vain** (see also FUTILE) which is devoid of all value, either absolutely, because worthless, superfluous, or unprofitable, or relatively, because there are other things which are of infinitely greater value, greater necessity, or greater profitableness; as, "Let no man deceive you with *vain* words" (*Ephesians* v. 6); "*Vain* pleasures of luxurious life, For ever with yourselves at strife" (*Wordsworth*); "Yet...how *vain* it was! All my bitterness and hatred and defiance were...no more than the whisper of a leaf, the light whirr of an insect's wing" (*Hudson*). That is **nugatory** which is trifling or insignificant, or (often) inoperative; as, "representing all titles...as *nugatory* and superfluous" (*Southey*); "limiting the right to pass laws for the execution of the granted powers, to such as are indispensable, and without which the power would be *nugatory*" (*Ch. Just. Marshall*); "The book is so one-sided that as a constructive contribution it is *nugatory*" (*Times Lit. Supplement*). That is **otiose** which has no excuse for being, or serves no purpose, and which, therefore, is usually an encumbrance or a superfluity; as, "mummified customs that have long outlasted their usefulness, and *otiose* dogmas that have long lost their vitality" (*Inge*); "it ought to be comparatively easy to decide...what kinds of criticism are useful and what are *otiose*" (*T. S. Eliot*); "How far Sir Austen Chamberlain would have risen without his father is...an unanswerable and *otiose* question" (*Times Lit. Supplement*). That is **idle** which has no solidity, either being baseless or groundless or being incapable of having any worthwhile effects or result; as, *idle* theorizing; *idle* dreams. "He had often said to me: 'I am not long for this world,' and I had thought his words *idle*. Now I knew they were true" (*Joyce*). "It is *idle* to illustrate further, because to those who agree with me I am uttering commonplaces and to those who disagree I am ignoring the necessary foundations of thought" (*Justice Holmes*). That is **empty** or **hollow** that is destitute of substance or reality and is therefore only apparently or deceivingly sound, real, worthwhile, genuine, sincere, or the like; as, *empty* pleasures; *empty* threats; *empty* promises; a *hollow* victory; *hollow* reasoning; a *hollow* friend.

Ana. Worthless, valueless (see affirmative nouns at WORTH): ineffectual, *ineffective, inefficacious: fruitless, bootless, *futile, abortive.

Con. Effectual, *effective, efficacious.

2 *Futile, fruitless, bootless, abortive.

Ana. *Ineffective, ineffectual, inefficacious: trivial, trifling, puny, *petty, paltry: delusive, delusory, *misleading.

3 Proud, vainglorious. See under PRIDE, *n.*

Ana. Self-satisfied, self-complacent, *complacent, priggish, smug: conceited, egoistic, egotistic (see corresponding nouns at CONCEIT).

Con. *Humble, meek, modest: diffident, *shy, bashful.

vainglorious. Proud, vain. See under PRIDE, *n.*

Ana. Arrogant, haughty, supercilious, disdainful, insolent, *proud: boasting *or* boastful, bragging, vaunting, gasconading (see corresponding verbs at BOAST).

vainglory. *Pride, vanity.

Ana. Pomp, *display, parade: flaunting, parading, exhibition (see corresponding verbs at SHOW): rhapsody, rodomontade, rant, *bombast.

valediction, *n.* **Valediction, valedictory** agree in meaning a farewell, especially a formal farewell. **Valediction** has always been a learned word; as, "Their last *valediction*, thrice uttered by the attendants, was also very solemn" (*Browne*); "A *Valediction* forbidding Mourning" (*Donne*). **Valedictory,** also a learned term, has come into common use in the United States, where it is ordinarily applied to a commencement farewell oration, usually written and delivered by the highest-ranking student of the graduating class; as, to deliver the *valedictory* at a college commencement.

valedictory, *n.* *Valediction.

valiant. Valorous, doughty, *brave, courageous, bold, audacious, dauntless, undaunted, intrepid.

Ana. *Formidable, redoubtable: stout, sturdy, tenacious, stalwart (see STRONG): indomitable, unconquerable, *invincible.

Ant. Timid: dastardly.

valid. Valid, sound, cogent, convincing, telling come into comparison especially when applied directly or indirectly to arguments, reasons, principles, processes of thought, or the like, or the presentation of arguments, principles, ideas, etc., and mean having or manifesting the power to impress themselves on others as right and well-grounded. That is **valid,** in the most general sense of the word, against which no objections can be maintained, because it conforms strictly to the law or regulations, as of the state or the church (as, to hold a *valid* title to a piece of property; a *valid* ordination; a *valid* marriage), or because it is supported or justified by facts and correct reasoning (as, a *valid* argument; *valid* evidence; "universally *valid* principles"—*Inge;* "You might have had to decline that berth for some very *valid* reason. From sheer necessity perhaps"—*Conrad*), or, less often, because it is fully in accordance with claims or promises made for it and is entirely effectual or efficacious (as, a *valid* method of testing intelligence; " 'art for art's sake' is still *valid* in so far as it can be taken as an exhortation to the artist to stick to his job; it never was and never can be *valid* for the spectator, reader or auditor"—*T. S. Eliot*). A person or a thing is **sound** that is free from error or fault in his or its processes of thought and that avoids fallacies, insufficient evidence, hasty conclusions, superficiality, or the like. The term not only suggests flawlessness in reasoning but solidity in the grounds upon which it is based; as, a *sound* thinker; "his assurance that he had never used an argument which he did not believe to be *sound*" (*Inge*); "To admit...that reason cannot extend into the religious sphere is absolutely *sound* so long as we realise that reason has a coördinate right to lay down the rules in its own sphere of intelligence" (*H. Ellis*). That is **cogent** or **convincing** which compels mental assent. But *cogent* stresses a power or force resident in the argument, reasoning, or the like, such as validity or soundness, that makes it conclusive (cf. CONCLUSIVE) and *convincing* suggests a power to overcome doubt, opposition, reluctance to accept, or the like; as, "the remarks of Gibbon [on universities and their degrees] are still...*cogent*" (*R. Aldington*); "there are other ways of making a thing...*convincing*...besides merely appealing to one's logic and sense of fact" (*Babbitt*); "So expressed, the argument does not sound strongly *convincing;* but it is really *cogent*, and the conclusion is *sound*" (*Karl K. Darrow*). That is **telling** which produces at once the desired effect: frequently the term implies the compelling of assent but it seldom suggests soundness or cogency though, in general, it does not deny the existence of these qualities (as, the first speaker for the affirmative used far more *telling* arguments than the second speaker; every point made by the prosecuting attorney was *telling*): as often, however, the term is applied to words, phrases, tones of expression, methods, and the like, which convince, persuade, win admiration, or the like, because of their pertinency, their suitability, or their forcibleness (as, "a *telling* illustration of what Darwin unintentionally did to the minds of his disciples" —*Shaw;* "such *telling* effects of contrast as the Japanese [artists] produced by an empty space"—*Binyon*).

Ana. *Conclusive, determinative, definitive, decisive: *effective, effectual: legal, *lawful, licit: *logical, analytical, subtle.

Ant. Fallacious, sophistical.

validate. *Confirm, authenticate, substantiate, verify, corroborate.

Ana. *Certify, attest, witness, vouch for.

Ant. Invalidate.

valor *or* **valour.** *Heroism, prowess, gallantry.

Ana. *Courage, mettle, tenacity, spirit, resolution: indomitableness, unconquerableness, invincibility (see corresponding adjectives at INVINCIBLE): *fortitude, guts, sand, backbone.

valorous. Valiant, intrepid, *brave, courageous, dauntless, undaunted, bold, audacious, doughty.

Ana. Venturous, venturesome, daring (see ADVENTUROUS): stout, sturdy, tenacious, stalwart, tough, *strong.

valuable, *adj.* Precious, invaluable, priceless, *costly, expensive, dear.

Ana. Estimated, appraised, evaluated (see ESTIMATE): valued, appreciated, prized, treasured (see APPRECIATE): esteemed, admired, respected (see corresponding verbs under REGARD, *n.*).

value, *n.* *Worth.

Ana. *Price, charge, cost, expense: *importance, consequence, significance, weight: *use, usefulness, utility.

value, *v.* **1** *Estimate, appraise, evaluate, rate, assess, assay.

Ana. *Calculate, compute, reckon: *judge, adjudge, adjudicate.

2 Prize, treasure, *appreciate, cherish.

Ana. Esteem, respect, admire (see under REGARD, *n.*): love, enjoy (see LIKE): *revere, reverence, venerate.

vanity. *Pride, vainglory.

Ana. Self-esteem, self-love, *conceit, egotism, egoism, amour-propre: complacency, self-complacency, self-satisfaction, smuggishness, priggishness (see corresponding adjectives at COMPLACENT): show, ostentation, pomp, pretense (see corresponding adjectives at SHOWY).

vanquish. *Conquer, defeat, beat, lick, subdue, subjugate, reduce, overcome, surmount, overthrow, rout.

Ana. *Frustrate, foil, outwit, circumvent: *overturn, subvert.

Con. Surrender, submit, capitulate (see corresponding nouns at SURRENDER): *yield, succumb.

vanquisher. *Victor, conqueror, winner, champion.

vapid. *Insipid, flat, jejune, banal, wishy-washy, inane.

Ana. *Soft, bland, gentle, mild: *tame, subdued, submissive: mawkish, maudlin, soppy, slushy, mushy, *sentimental.

Con. Racy, spicy, *pungent, piquant: trenchant, crisp, *incisive: *expressive, significant, pregnant, meaningful.

vapors *or* **vapours.** *Sadness, depression, melancholy, melancholia, dejection, gloom, blues, dumps.

variable, *adj.* *Changeable, protean, changeful, mutable.

Ana. *Fitful, spasmodic: fickle, mercurial, unstable, *inconstant, capricious: mobile, *movable.

Ant. Constant: equable.

variance. *Discord, contention, dissension, strife, conflict.

Ana. Difference, diversity, divergency, disparateness (see corresponding adjectives at DIFFERENT): separation, division, severing, sundering (see corresponding verbs at SEPARATE): incongruousness, uncongeniality, incompatibility, discordance, discrepancy (see corresponding adjectives at INCONSONANT).

variation. **1** Change, alteration, modification. See under CHANGE, *v.*

Ana. *Variety, diversity: difference, divergence, *dissimilarity: *deviation, deflection, aberration.

2 Variation, adaptation, mutation, modification as used in biology are terms of overlapping meanings and are therefore frequently confused in their applications. **Variation,** the most inclusive of these terms, denotes any divergence in structural or physiological features or peculiarities from those typical of individuals of the same species or from those of parents. **Adaptation** is applied to the process whereby a change or changes in structural or physiological features or peculiarities occur in an organism fitting it for existence under the conditions of its environment. The term suggests both fitness for making and ability to make adjustments. Thus, the thick epidermis and waxy coating of desert plants diminish transpiration and are therefore the results of *adaptation* to a dry environment; the tanning of the skin in human beings is the result of *adaptation* to bright sunlight. **Mutation** designates a sudden variation in which the offspring differs from its parents in some well-marked feature or features that it may in turn transmit to offspring. The cause of such a variation is usually obscure. **Modification** in strict use applies only to a noninheritable variation in an organism that is caused by the influence of its environment, such as the highly developed muscles of an athlete.

variety. **Variety, diversity** come into comparison when they are used in reference to a group, class, or complex whole and denote the state or quality of being composed of different parts, elements, individuals, or the like. **Variety** often implies that the things which differ are fundamentally alike and belong to the same class or category, their differences representing distinctions in individuals or kinds (as, in that family there is great *variety* as well as great similarity in the individuals; there is more *variety* in some species of plants than in others) but it may imply that the things which differ are very far apart in form, character, location, and the like, yet are related because they contribute to the same end or play a part in the formation of the same whole (as, "as the world... Where order in *variety* we see, And where, tho' all things differ, all agree"—*Pope;* "Most workers would prefer some *variety* in their work, but they cannot get it"—*J. A. Hobson*). **Diversity,** on the other hand, though often used interchangeably with *variety,* distinctively stresses the marked difference or divergence of the individuals, parts, or elements, and seldom suggests even a class or categorical likeness; as, the great *diversity* among human beings; Montaigne has said that "the most universal quality is *diversity*"; "when Babel was confounded, and the great confederacy...was split into *diversity* of tongues" (*Cowper*).

Ana. *Dissimilarity, unlikeness, difference, divergence: multifariousness, variousness (see corresponding adjectives at MANY): miscellaneousness *or* miscellany, heterogeneousness *or* heterogeneity, assortedness *or* assortment (see corresponding adjectives at MISCELLANEOUS).

various. 1 *Different, diverse, divergent, disparate.

Ana. *Distinct, separate: distinctive, peculiar, individual (see CHARACTERISTIC): varying, changing (see CHANGE, *v.*).

Ant. Uniform: cognate.

2 *Many, several, sundry, divers, numerous, manifold, multifold, multifarious.

Ana. *Miscellaneous, heterogeneous, assorted.

Con. *Same, identical, equivalent, equal: *similar, alike, like.

vary. *Change, alter, modify.

Ana. Deviate, diverge, digress, depart (see SWERVE): differ with, differ from (see DIFFER): *transform, metamorphose, convert.

vassal. Thrall, *serf, villein, slave, bondslave, bondsman, bondman, peon, Helot.

vast. Immense, *enormous, huge, gigantic, giant, gigantean, colossal, mammoth, elephantine, titanic, herculean, Cyclopean, Antaean, Gargantuan, Brobdingnagian.

Ana. Stupendous, tremendous, prodigious, *monstrous: *large, big, great: *spacious, capacious.

vaunt, *v.* *Boast, brag, crow, gasconade.

Ana. Parade, flaunt, exhibit, display, *show: magnify, aggrandize, *exalt.

veer. *Swerve, deviate, depart, digress, diverge.

Ana. Shift, transfer, *move: *turn, divert, deflect, sheer.

vehement. *Intense.

Ana. *Fierce, truculent, ferocious: furious, frenzied (see corresponding nouns at INSPIRATION): fervid, perfervid, fervent, ardent, *impassioned, passionate: forcible, forceful, *powerful, potent.

vehicle. *Means, instrument, instrumentality, agent, agency, medium, organ, channel.

vein. 1 *Mood, humor, temper.

Ana. *Disposition, temper, complexion, temperament.

2 Strain, streak, *touch, suggestion, suspicion, soupçon, tincture, tinge, shade, smack, spice, dash.

velocity. *Speed, momentum, impetus, pace, headway.

Ana. *Celerity, legerity, alacrity: *haste, hurry, expedition, dispatch.

velvety, velvet. Silken, satiny, glossy, slick, *sleek, glabrous.

venal. *Mercenary, hireling, hack, hackney.

Ana. Corrupt, nefarious, iniquitous, *vicious, infamous, flagitious: sordid, ignoble (see MEAN, *adj.*): purchasable, *vendible, salable.

vend. *Sell, barter, trade, auction.

vendible. **Vendible, purchasable, salable, marketable** come into comparison as meaning such as may be bought or sold. **Vendible,** though the least common, is the most comprehensive of these terms, for it may apply not only to commodities but also to persons, their talents, their honor, and the like, or to offices, privileges, rights, etc. Therefore, according to its application *vendible* may imply a fit condition for sale or of offering for sale (as, all the *vendible* coal produced by a mine; the berries will not be *vendible* for another two weeks), or a venal or corrupt character or use (as, *vendible* votes; *vendible* magistrates; *vendible* women such as prostitutes), or a being put up for sale (often venally or underhandedly) to the highest bidder (as, *vendible* titles; *vendible* honors). **Purchasable** applies only to that which may be bought or purchased: it is often used in reference to things which are rarely offered for sale or of whose existence one is not certain (as, he found to his delight that a first folio of Shakespeare's dramas was *purchasable;* defense needs will soon make some now common articles *unpurchasable;* such a tool as you describe is no longer *purchasable*). In another sense, it applies to things which are not offered for sale, yet may be bought (as, all goods on exhibition are *purchasable;* he admired the duke's pictures and guessed that some might be *purchasable.* In this sense, the term sometimes imputes a corrupt means of gaining what the purchaser desires; as, a *purchasable* office; a *purchasable* contract; *purchasable* privileges. **Salable** now rarely, and **marketable** practically never, implies corruption or venality. Both stress fitness for the market or the satisfaction of the conditions that will render the thing so described as ready for sale or as ready to find a buyer; as, each night the fruit dealer discarded all fruits which were not *salable; marketable* securities; a *salable* house; a useful and *marketable* product.

Ana. *Mercenary, hireling, hack, hackney, venal.

venerable. *Old, ancient, antique, antiquated, archaic, obsolete, antediluvian.

Ana. Venerated, revered, reverenced (see REVERE): *aged, old: *secular, agelong, centuried.

venerate. *Revere, reverence, worship, adore.

Ana. Esteem, respect, admire, regard (see under REGARD, *n.*): cherish, prize, treasure, value, *appreciate.

veneration. Reverence, worship, adoration. See under REVERE, *v.*

Ana. Deference, homage, obeisance, *honor.

vengeance. Revenge, retribution, *retaliation, reprisal.

Ana. Punishment, disciplining *or* discipline, castigation (see corresponding verbs at PUNISH): avenging, revenging (see AVENGE): requital, recompensing *or* recompense, repayment (see corresponding verbs at PAY).

vengeful. *Vindictive, revengeful.

Ana. Rancorous, inimical, hostile, antagonistic (see corresponding nouns at ENMITY): malevolent, spiteful, despiteful, *malicious, malignant.

venial. **Venial, pardonable** come into comparison when applied to faults, sins, errors, and the like, and mean of such a character as not to warrant punishment or the imposition of a penalty. **Venial,** which etymologically comes close to *forgivable,* in most use implies an opposition to *grave, serious, grievous,* and, in theological use, to *mortal* (see *mortal* under DEADLY): consequently, it often means *trifling,* or *not willful,* or *harmless;* as, "those who imagine that the sins, of which a deep sense was upon his mind, were merely such little *venial* trifles as pouring milk into his tea on Good Friday" (*Boswell*); "the *venial* indiscretions of youth" (*Southey*); "because what is therefore *venial* with them is sometimes grave with us and *vice versâ,* it by no means follows that the French notion of what is right and what is wrong is any the less strict, precise, and universally binding than our own" (*Brownell*). **Pardonable** implies that such excuse or justification may be offered for the fault or error that it is not worthy of consideration; as, it is a *pardonable* error in a foreigner but not in a native; *pardonable* pride in his son; "her heart innocent of the most *pardonable* guile" (*Conrad*).

Ana. Heinous: mortal (*in R. C. theology*).

venom. *Poison, toxin, virus, bane.

venomous. *Poisonous, virulent, toxic, mephitic, pestilent, pestilential, miasmatic, miasmic, miasmal.

Ana. Malignant, malign, malevolent (see MALICIOUS): baleful, malefic (see SINISTER): *pernicious, baneful, noxious, deleterious, detrimental.

vent, *v.* *Express, utter, voice, broach, air, ventilate.

Ana. *Reveal, disclose, discover, divulge: *assert, declare, aver, avow.

Ant. Bridle (sense 1). — *Con.* *Restrain, inhibit, check, curb: *suppress, repress.

ventilate. **1** *Aerate, oxygenate, carbonate.

2 *Express, vent, air, utter, voice, broach.

Ana. Expose, exhibit, display, *show: disclose, divulge, discover, *reveal: publish, advertise, broadcast (see DECLARE).

ventral. *Abdominal, anterior.

venturesome. *Adventurous, venturous, daring, daredevil, rash, reckless, temerarious, foolhardy.

Ana. Bold, audacious, intrepid, *brave: stout, sturdy, stalwart (see STRONG).

Con. *Timid, timorous: *cowardly, pusillanimous: *fearful, apprehensive, afraid.

venturous. *Adventurous, venturesome, daring, daredevil, rash, reckless, temerarious, foolhardy.

Ana. & *Con.* See those at VENTURESOME.

veracity. *Truth, verity, verisimilitude.

Ana. Integrity, probity, *honesty, honor.

veranda *or* **verandah.** Porch, piazza, portico, stoop, *balcony, gallery, loggia.

verbal. *Oral.

verbiage. **Verbiage, redundancy, tautology, pleonasm, circumlocution, periphrasis** are here considered chiefly as technical terms of rhetoric denoting a fault of style or a form or mode of expression involving the use of too many words. **Verbiage** may imply delight in words for their own sake, as for their sound, their color, their suggestions, and overindulgence in their use for these reasons: the term, however, more often suggests nothing more than a wordiness that tends to make what is written pointless, meaningless, obscure, or unduly heavy reading; as, "A whole poem of that quality Burns cannot make; the rest, in the *Farewell to Nancy,* is *verbiage*" (*Arnold*); "the almost luscious richness of Aunt Phoebe's imagination, her florid *verbiage,* her note of sensuous defiance" (*H. G. Wells*). **Redundancy** does not in general carry the implications of expansiveness, floridity, or heaviness so often apparent in *verbiage,* because the term strictly implies merely the use of more words than are strictly needed, and therefore usually suggests a fault of style rather than a mode of expression. "You cannot call them [some lines of Jonson's] *'verbiage';* they do not exhibit prolixity or *redundancy* or the other vices in the rhetoric books" (*T. S. Eliot*); "passages in which you might accuse them of almost infantine *redundancy*" (*C. E. Montague*). All the other terms name particular forms of redundancy, or an example illustrative of the particular fault. **Tautology** is needless or useless repetition of the same idea in different words; as, " 'Boldly dare' is *tautology*" (*Gray*); he cautioned his students to beware of such *tautologies* as "visible to the eye" or "audible to the ear." **Pleonasm** denotes a mode of expression in which syntactically unnecessary words are employed (such as "I saw it *with my own eyes*") omission of which would leave one's meaning intact: such expressions are sometimes regarded as pardonable from the point of view of emphasis and are often thought of as figures of speech; as, "It is a *pleonasm,* a figure usual in Scripture, by a multiplicity of expressions to signify one notable thing" (*South*). **Circumlocution** and **periphrasis** (the more bookish term) denote a roundabout or indirect way of saying a thing; as, "Somehow I can't relish that word Hockey. Can't you supply it by a *circumlocution?*" (*Lamb*); "This was not however a question to be asked point-blank, and I could not think of any effective *circumlocution*" (*Conrad*); "He was one of those anomalous practitioners in lower departments of the law who...on prudential reasons...deny themselves all indulgence in the luxury of too delicate a conscience (a *periphrasis* which might be abridged considerably)" (*De Quincey*).

Ana. Wordiness, verboseness, prolixity, diffuseness (see corresponding adjectives at WORDY).

verbose. *Wordy, prolix, diffuse, redundant.

Ana. Grandiloquent, magniloquent, flowery, bombastic (see RHETORICAL): loquacious, voluble, garrulous, *talkative.

Ant. Laconic. — *Con.* *Concise, terse, succinct: compact, *close.

verge, *n.* Edge, rim, brim, brink, *border, margin.

Ana. Bound, *limit, end, confine: *circumference, perimeter, compass.

verify. Corroborate, substantiate, *confirm, authenticate, validate.

Ana. *Prove, test, try, demonstrate: *certify, attest, witness, vouch for: establish, settle (see SET, *v.*).

verisimilitude. *Truth, veracity, verity.

Ana. Agreement, accordance, harmonizing *or* harmony, correspondence (see corresponding verbs at AGREE): *likeness, similitude, resemblance.

veritable. *Authentic, genuine, bona fide.

Ana. Actual, *real, true.

Ant. Factitious.

verity. *Truth, veracity, verisimilitude.

vernacular. *Dialect, patois, lingo, jargon, cant, argot, patter, slang.

versatile. **Versatile, many-sided, all-round** (*or* **all-around**) are synonymous when they mean manifesting skill and ability in many different directions. **Versatile** stresses not only aptitude for many employments but facility in each or in turning from one to another; it therefore usually implies a wide variety of interests or of skills. "Stevenson's spiritual and intellectual virtues have been partly frustrated by one additional virtue—that of artistic dexterity....He suffered from his *versatility*" (*Chesterton*). **Many-sided** is rarely applied to a person or his work except at or after the culmination of his development; it stresses breadth of interests, as well as variety of gifts; as, the *many-sided* genius of Shakespeare. **All-round** implies completeness and symmetry of development as a human being and as an individual; it does not necessarily imply special gifts, nor great attainments, but ability to do oneself credit in every sphere of life, as in business, social life, public life, and the like. The word is also applied to persons who do not specialize in one branch of their chosen trade, profession, or the like; as, an *all-round* athlete.

Ana. Gifted, talented (see corresponding nouns at GIFT): accomplished, finished, *consummate: ready, apt, *quick, prompt.

verse, *n.* **1 Verse, stanza** are frequently used interchangeably as designating a group of lines forming one of the divisions of a poem and typically, but far from invariably, following a fixed metrical (sometimes rhythmical) pattern. The use of **verse** in this sense is often decried not only because the term's earliest meaning in English is one of the metrical or rhythmical lines that comprise a stanza or an otherwise undivided poem, but also because the confusion of terms often makes for ambiguity. In careful technical use, *verse* is invariably employed in the sense of *line;* as, a stanza of eight *verses;* there are fourteen *verses* in a sonnet; the iambic pentameter is the most common *verse* in English poetry. However, there are certain reasons why the use of *verse* in the sense of **stanza** is allowable: this meaning is long established, having been acquired around 1300 from the Old French *vers* which carried the dual denotation: the use of it in reference to a stanza of a song, a ballad, and especially a hymn, is so widespread that *stanza* seems to many persons unduly formal or technical. However, when the construction of a poetic work is under consideration or prosody is the subject of discussion, the technical sense of *verse* is not only preferable but is practically obligatory.

2 *Paragraph, article, clause, plank, count.

versed. *Conversant.

Ana. *Learned, erudite, polymathic: informed, acquainted (see INFORM): intimate, *familiar.

versifier. *Poet, rhymer, rhymester, poetaster, bard, minstrel, scop, gleeman, jongleur, troubadour, trouvère, minnesinger, scald.

version. **1** *Translation, paraphrase, metaphrase, construe.

2 *Account, report, story, chronicle.

versus. *Against, con.

vertebrae. *Spine, backbone, chine.

vertex. *Apex.

vertical. Vertical, perpendicular, plumb agree in meaning situated at right angles to the plane of the horizon, or extending from that plane at such an angle. **Vertical** is applicable in geometry to lines, planes, circles, angles, and the like, irrespective of whether they rise above the horizon or fall below it. However, since the word etymologically suggests a relation to the vertex, or topmost point (see APEX, 1), it is used far more often when the thing so described actually extends upward from the plane of the horizon or from its base or support in such a direction that if its direction line were produced, it would reach the zenith; as, the *vertical* threads in a tapestry; the *vertical* rays of the sun; a *vertical* piston; the *vertical* walls of a room. *Vertical* is, of these terms, the most frequently applied to abstractions and the most common in figurative use; as, *vertical* motion; *vertical* structure (i.e., in music, the structure of a composition in which two or more voices are viewed in respect to their harmonic relations rather than as independent melodies). **Perpendicular** (etymologically, hanging exactly straight, like a plumb line [Lat. *perpendiculum*]) is used as often, if not more often, of lines or planes that are at right angles to a plane that may be described as *horizontal:* in this sense it is often the preferred term in geometry where figures and drawings have little relation in position to the horizon or zenith. Otherwise, *perpendicular* differs from *vertical* in being normally applied to things that are concrete and extend upward or downward from the horizontal or both upward and downward; thus, one looks up or down the *perpendicular* face of a cliff; a *perpendicular* fall of water. Consequently, *perpendicular* is more often used loosely than *vertical* to suggest little more than precipitousness or extreme steepness or, humorously, in the case of human beings, stiffness and straightness of the line of one's back; as, a *perpendicular* ascent or descent; "a stiff *perpendicular* old maid" (*M. R. Mitford*). **Plumb** is largely an artisan's (especially a carpenter's or mason's) term, used particularly in judging the exact verticality or perpendicularity of something by its conformity to the direction of a "plumb line"; as, they found no indication that the wall was not *plumb* (more often, colloquially, *out of plumb*).

Ant. Horizontal.

very. Selfsame, *same, identical, identic, equivalent, equal, tantamount.

vessel. Ship, *boat, craft, argosy.

vest, *v.* Robe, invest, array, apparel, *clothe, attire, tire, dress.

Ant. Divest.

vestibule. *Entry, entryway, hall, narthex, foyer, lobby, anteroom, antechamber.

vestige. *Trace, track, rack.

Ana. Print, imprint, *impression, stamp.

vesture. Apparel, raiment, array, *clothes, clothing, dress, attire, tire.

vex. Irk, *annoy, bother.

Ana. Chafe, fret, gall (see ABRADE): *irritate, exasperate, nettle, provoke.

Ant. Please, regale. — *Con.* *Pacify, appease, mollify, propitiate.

viands. Provisions, comestibles, *food, victuals, provender, fodder, forage, grub, eats, chow.

vibrate. *Swing, sway, oscillate, fluctuate, pendulate, waver, undulate.

Ana. *Pulsate, pulse, beat, throb, palpitate: quiver, quaver, tremble, *shake.

vice. **1** *Fault, failing, frailty, foible.

Ana. Defect, flaw, *blemish: infirmity, weakness (see corresponding adjectives at WEAK).

2 *Offense, sin, crime, scandal.

Ana. Transgression, trespass, violation, *breach, infraction: immorality (see corresponding adjective at IMMORAL): *evil, ill.

Ant. Virtue.

vicinage. Vicinity, neighborhood, district, *locality.

Ana. Section, sector (see PART, *n.*): region, *area.

vicinity. Neighborhood, vicinage, district, *locality.

Ana. Region, *area: section, sector (see PART, *n.*).

vicious. Vicious, villainous, iniquitous, nefarious, flagitious, infamous, corrupt, degenerate are here compared as meaning highly reprehensible or offensive in character, nature, or conduct. **Vicious** in its earliest and still most common sense implies an addition to or a connection with vice or immorality: usually it suggests moral depravity and is the diametrical opposite of *virtuous;* as, to form *vicious* habits; a set of *vicious* women; "We cannot afford to have poor people anyhow, whether they be lazy or busy, drunken or sober, virtuous or *vicious*" (*Shaw*). Often, however, the word implies a particular highly reprehensible quality such as ugliness or violence of temper or deliberate cruelty (as, "The horseman delivered one last *vicious* cut with his whip" —*Kipling;* "He looked at the piece of meat and crust, and suddenly, in a *vicious* spurt of temper, flung it into the fire"—*D. H. Lawrence*), or a debasing (as, "the multiplication of critical books and essays may create... a *vicious* taste for reading about works of art instead of reading the works themselves"—*T. S. Eliot*), or complete vitiation by faults, defects, irremediable conditions, or the like (as, a *vicious* system of financing; a *vicious* style of writing; a *vicious* circle [i.e., a chain of circumstances, or of arguments, or of processes in an illness, in which one thing is logically or necessarily succeeded by a worse or equally bad thing, either in a continuous unending process or with the result of getting back to the point where the succession began and must start again]). **Villainous** is a more condemnatory term than *vicious:* it may suggest any of a number of qualities which can be associated with a villain, a rascal, or a knave, but usually, it is little more than an intensive of *vicious;* as, a *villainous* assault; a *villainous* practice; a *villainous* temper. **Iniquitous** is more fixed in its meaning than the preceding terms for, in discriminating use, it commonly implies the absence of all signs of justice or fairness or a complete indifference to the standards or principles which govern the conduct of civilized or law-abiding men; as, the *iniquitous* disregard of the rights of small nations; the *iniquitous* practices of slave traders; "These ...precedents, they produce as authorities...to justify the most *iniquitous* opinions" (*Swift*). **Nefarious** is often used in place of *iniquitous* when one wishes an even more censorious form of expression. In very strict use, the word implies impiety in its deepest sense, or a breach of laws and traditions which have immemorially been honored, but in ordinary use, it commonly means inconceivably wicked; as, the *nefarious* neglect of their aged parents; "It [love for children] is still far too weak, or our politicians would not dare to sacrifice the life and happiness of innumerable children to their *nefarious* schemes" (*B. Russell*). **Flagitious** and **infamous** both imply shameful and scandalous badness or wickedness, but the former is somewhat less rhetorical and more closely descriptive than the latter; as, "Most people sell their souls, and live with a good conscience on the proceeds. To sell one's soul and not be paid for it...is perhaps in Heaven's eyes a less *flagitious* bargain" (*L. P. Smith*); "forced and *flagitious* bombast" (*T. S. Eliot*); "else, perhaps, I might have been entangled among deeds, Which, now, as *infamous*, I should abhor" (*Wordsworth*); "Alice...would have scouted as *infamous* any suggestion that her parent was more selfish than saintly" (*Shaw*). **Corrupt** (as here considered: see also DEBASE, 1) is applied chiefly to persons in an official capacity or to their acts, then implying a loss or lack of moral integrity or probity that makes one accessible to bribes, or other inducements to go contrary to their sworn duties or obligations; as, *corrupt* judges; a *corrupt* government; "bent only on turning each to his own personal advantage the now *corrupt* machinery of administration and law" (*G. L. Dickinson*). Frequently, however, the term is more generally applied, and suggests degradation or depravity; as, "Charles II came back ...with tastes as *corrupt* as his morals" (*H. Reed*); "humanity they knew to be *corrupt* and incompetent" (*H. Adams*). **Degenerate** stresses a descent and deterioration from an original or earlier high type or condition to one that is very low in the scale morally, intellectually, physically, artistically, or the like. However, it additionally carries so strong an implication of corruption, and so often suggests extreme viciousness that it is generally used to describe that which is especially reprehensible and offensive from the historical point of view or in comparison to other members of its class or other instances of the type; as, a family stock *degenerate* through generations of inbreeding; "What wise and valiant man would seek to free These, thus *degenerate*, by themselves enslaved..?" (*Milton*); "What he has to say is inspired by revolt against the *degenerate* practice of his times" (*Binyon*); "we are solemnly warned that in the hands of modern writers language has fallen into a morbid state. It has become *degenerate*" (*H. Ellis*).

Ana. Debased, depraved, debauched, perverted (see DEBASE): dissolute, profligate, *abandoned, reprobate: lewd, lascivious, wanton, lecherous, libidinous (see LICENTIOUS).

Ant. Virtuous.

vicissitude. **1** *Change, alternation, mutation, permutation.

Ana. Turning, rotation, revolving *or* revolution (see corresponding verbs at TURN): reversal, transposition (see corresponding verbs at REVERSE): *succession, progression, sequence, series: *variety, diversity.

2 *Difficulty, hardship, rigor.

Ana. *Misfortune, mischance, adversity: *trial, tribulation, affliction.

victim. **Victim, prey, quarry, ravin** (*or* **raven** *or* **ravine**) come into comparison when they denote a person or animal killed or injured for the ends of the one who kills or injures. **Victim,** in its earliest sense (which is still found in religious and historical use), applies to a living creature, usually an animal, sometimes a man, that is killed and offered as a sacrifice to God or a god; as, "And thou shalt offer a calf for sin every day for expiation. And thou shalt cleanse the altar when thou hast offered the *victim* of expiation" (*Exodus* xxix. 36 [*Douay Version*]); "Unto the Paschal *Victim* [i.e., Christ] bring, Christians, your thankful offering" (*transl. of Easter Sequence at Mass, Manual of Prayers*). In general use, it applies to one who has been destroyed, ruined, seriously injured, or the like, by some ruthless person or power before which he has been helpless; as, the *victims* of war; the *victims* of a pestilence; "by persistently attacking an institution authors hope to persuade either its supporters or its *victims* to reform it" (*A. Huxley*); "Was the girl born to be a *victim;* to be always disliked and crushed as if she were too fine for this world?" (*Conrad*); "All are *victims* of circumstances; all have had characters warped in infancy and intelligence stunted at school" (*B. Russell*). **Prey** was originally applied to the spoils or booty taken in war or by violence: in current literal use it applies only to animals hunted and killed for food by more powerful carnivorous animals (the beasts of *prey* include lions, tigers, wolves, etc.; birds of *prey* include eagles, hawks, vultures, etc.); as, "The hungry family flew like vultures on their *prey*" (*Johnson*). In its extended sense *prey* applies to a victim of something that seizes or captures or fells in a manner suggestive of the action of a beast or bird of prey; as, "she was a *prey* to shoddy, facile emotions and moods, none of which had power to impel her to any action" (*R. Macaulay*); "people who make solemn talk about art and are the natural *prey* of the artists of *Punch*" (*C. E. Montague*). **Quarry,** in its most common current sense, is a hunting term referable to the victim of a chase, especially, but not exclusively, by hounds or hawks, and may be applied to the animal as pursued as well as the animal as taken and destroyed after pursuit; as, "The startled *quarry* bounds amain, As fast the gallant greyhounds strain" (*Scott*); "With grain in their store-rooms, and mountain sheep and deer for their *quarry*, they rose gradually from the condition of savagery" (*Cather*). In extended use, *quarry* usually applies to a person or thing determined upon as a victim and vigorously and relentlessly pursued. "You think that you are Ann's suitor; that you are the pursuer and she the pursued....Fool: it is you who are the pursued, the marked-down *quarry*, the destined *prey*" (*Shaw*). **Ravin,** in the sense here considered, is now a poetic synonym of *prey*, suggesting more violence in the method of seizure and more cruelty and voracity in the destroying; as, "his deep devouring jaws Wide gaped... Through which into his dark abyss all *ravin* fell" (*Spenser*); "Nature, red in tooth and claw With *ravine*" (*Tennyson*).

victor. Victor, winner, conqueror, champion, vanquisher agree in denoting a person who gains the mastery in a contest, conflict, or competition. **Victor,** the more formal term, and **winner,** the ordinary term, usually stress the fact of defeating one's opponents: *victor* sometimes specifically connotes a triumph or a glorious proof of one's powers. The terms are applicable when the test is one of strength, strategy, skill, or endurance; as, he was the *winner* in the oratorical contest; "[He] march'd a *victor* from the verdant field" (*Pope*); "ever... *victor* at the tilt and tournament" (*Tennyson*); "And he who battles on her [Justice's] side, God, though he were ten times slain, Crowns him *victor* glorified, *Victor* over death and pain" (*Emerson*). **Conqueror** stresses the defeat or subjugation of an enemy or opposing force: the term is seldom used appropriately in friendly competitions such as in baseball, football, debating, or the like (where *winner* is the regular term), for it usually presupposes a warlike struggle or an attempt to crush by getting the upper hand; as, "England never did, nor never shall, Lie at the proud foot of a *conqueror*" (*Shak.*); "In all these things we are more than *conquerors* through him that loved us" (*Romans* viii. 37); "a savage *conqueror* stained in...blood" (*Shelley*). **Champion** (as here compared: see also under SUPPORT, *v.*) applies to the one who gains acknowledged supremacy through a contest or in a field of competition, as in an athletic contest or in a given sport. The term does not apply to a winner of any test, but only of a test in which one meets all of those of highest rank in the field or meets the one who holds the title of champion or one who challenges one's own right to hold that title; as, the *champion* of prizefighters; the World Series each year determines the baseball team which should bear the title of *champion;* world *champions* in various sports are discovered through the Olympic games. **Vanquisher** is often used in place of *conqueror* and, often humorously or somewhat hyperbolically, in place of *victor* or *winner*, when there is an intent to imply an overpowering or an overwhelming or crushing defeat; as, "Sleep, the universal *vanquisher*" (*Sir G. Young*); "But I shall rise victorious, and subdue My *vanquisher*" (*Milton*).

victory. Victory, conquest, triumph come into comparison as meaning the result achieved by one who gains the mastery in a contest or struggle. **Victory,** like *victor* (see VICTOR), implies the winning of a contest or struggle of any sort: it therefore clearly suggests the defeat of one's opponent but nothing more. **Conquest,** on the other hand, like *conqueror* (see under VICTOR), implies not only a victory over enemies, but the subjugation of one's opponents; as, "that dishonest *victory* At Chaeronea" (*Milton*); "'*Victory*,' said Nelson, 'is not a name strong enough for such a scene'; he called it a *conquest*" (*Southey*). Also, *conquest* may be used in reference to things, both material and immaterial, which are brought under one's control so that they may be used in the achievement of one's end or ends; as, "art is essentially a *conquest* of matter by the spirit" (*Binyon*). **Triumph,** in the special sense in which it is here considered, may apply either to a victory or a conquest, but only when that victory is a brilliant or decisive one, or the conquest is overwhelming; as, "His [Wellington's] *triumph* will be sung...far on in summers that we shall not see" (*Tennyson*); "He finds that 'honest and conscientious men are fully justified in hoping that *victory* will be with France and Britain.' But this logical conclusion he develops a step further than we like to go: 'non-combatants should desire the *triumph* of France and England.' *Victory* and *triumph* are not necessarily synonymous.... *triumph* [suggests] a degree of success that clearly implies the full accomplishment of all their ends, good and bad" (*The Commonweal*).

Ana. Winning, gaining (see GET): ascendancy, *supremacy: control, sway, dominion, command, *power, authority.

Ant. Defeat.

victuals. *Food, viands, provisions, comestibles, provender, fodder, forage, grub, eats, chow.

view, *n.* **1** *Look, sight, glance, glimpse, peep, peek, coup d'oeil.

Ana. Scrutiny, scanning, inspection, examination (see under SCRUTINIZE).

2 *Opinion, belief, conviction, persuasion, sentiment.

Ana. *Idea, thought, concept, conception: inference, deduction, conclusion, judgment (see under INFER).

view, *v.* Survey, contemplate, observe, note, remark, notice, perceive, discern, *see, behold, descry, espy.

Ana. Scan, *scrutinize, inspect, examine: *consider, regard, account.

vie with. *Rival, compete with, emulate.

Ana. Cope, *contend, fight: strive, struggle, essay, endeavor (see ATTEMPT, *v.*).

viewpoint. *Point of view, standpoint, angle, slant.

Ana. *Position, stand, attitude: ground, *reason.

vigilant. Alert, wide-awake, *watchful.

Ana. Anxious, agog, keen, avid, *eager: circumspect, wary, chary, *cautious: *quick, ready, prompt: *sharp, keen, acute.

Con. *Negligent, neglectful, lax, slack, remiss: *forgetful, unmindful, oblivious.

vigorous. Vigorous, energetic, strenuous, lusty, nervous come into comparison when they mean having or manifesting great vitality and force. A person or thing is **vigorous** that has or manifests active strength or force and exhibits no signs of a depletion of the powers associated with freshness or robustness of body or mind; as, he was as *vigorous*, seemingly, as a youth half his age; a *vigorous*, fast-growing tree; the *vigorous* mother of a large family; "The remainder [of the poem] is *vigorous*, direct, and enthusiastic" (*Landor*); "Kate was a bold, *vigorous* thinker" (*S. Anderson*). A person or thing is **energetic** that displays abundant force or a capacity for great activity: the term does not necessarily connote the reserve vitality and force that *vigorous* implies and it sometimes even suggests an exertion of effort or a bustling activity that has little to do with inherent physical or mental strength; therefore, the term may be used to suggest compliment or, less often, slight depreciation; as, "to be counted among the strong, and not the merely *energetic*" (*J. R. Lowell*); "this gives employment to able and *energetic* men" (*Shaw*); "received by bustling male assistants very *energetic* and rapid" (*Bennett*); "a less *energetic* expulsion of air from the lungs" (*Grandgent*). A person is **strenuous** that is continuously and zealously energetic: a thing is *strenuous* that makes constant demands on one's vigor, energy, and zeal: in both cases the term implies no flagging of ardor or no avoidance of the arduous; as, Theodore Roosevelt, the exponent of the *strenuous* life, was himself *strenuous*, both in work and play; "to love bondage more than liberty— Bondage with ease than *strenuous* liberty" (*Milton*); "the spirit of our religion calls for *strenuous* opposition to the current principles and practice of the world" (*Inge*). A person or thing is **lusty** that exhibits exuberant vigor or energy; as, "Therefore my age is as a *lusty* winter, Frosty, but kindly" (*Shak.*); "Pete Gurney was a *lusty* cock Turned sixty-three, but bright and hale" (*Masefield*); a *lusty* appetite; "*lusty* disputation" (*Caine*). A person or a thing (such as style or utterance) is **nervous** (in the sense here considered) that displays forcibleness, compactness, and strength that are the results of mental vigor and energy; as, " 'Miss Brontë? A good and *nervous* tho' coarse describer of a narrow landscape' " (*H. Kingsley*). "*Nervous*, idiomatic English" (*W. D. Whitney*); "Tyndale's own diction was singularly simple, energetic, *nervous*, and yet restrained" (*Lowes*).

Ana. Virile, manly, manful (see MALE): *muscular, athletic, sinewy, husky: stout, sturdy, stalwart, *strong, tough.

Ant. Languorous: lethargic.

vile. *Base, low.

Ana. Depraved, corrupted, perverted, debased, debauched (see DEBASE): *coarse, vulgar, obscene, gross: foul, filthy, nasty, *dirty: *mean, abject, sordid: *offensive, repulsive, revolting, loathsome.

vilify. *Malign, traduce, asperse, calumniate, defame, slander, libel.

Ana. *Abuse, outrage, mistreat, misuse: assail, *attack: revile, vituperate, berate (see SCOLD).

Ant. Eulogize.

villainous. *Vicious, iniquitous, nefarious, flagitious, infamous, corrupt, degenerate.

Ana. Debased, depraved, perverted (see DEBASE): atrocious, *outrageous, heinous: dissolute, profligate, *abandoned.

villein. *Serf, thrall, vassal, slave, bondslave, bondsman, bondman, peon, Helot.

vindicate. 1 Justify, defend, *maintain, assert.

Ana. *Support, uphold, advocate: *avenge, revenge: resist, *oppose, combat.

2 Exonerate, *exculpate, absolve, acquit.

Ana. *Disprove, refute, confute: *defend, protect, shield, guard.

Ant. Calumniate.

vindictive. **Vindictive, revengeful, vengeful** are often used interchangeably, for they are close synonyms meaning having or manifesting a disposition to pay one back for a real or fancied wrong. **Vindictive,** however, in good use, commonly places more stress upon the unforgiving nature or temper of the persons involved than upon their actions, and may, therefore, be applied to those who have not, at the moment, any cause for revenge: occasionally, it is little more than an intensive of *spiteful*, *malicious*, *malevolent*, and the like; as, "You have *vindictive* people to deal with, and you have gone too far to be forgiven" (*Burke*); "There was nothing *vindictive* in his nature; but, if revenge came his way, it might as well be good" (*Stevenson*); "The Muses are *vindictive* virgins, and avenge themselves without mercy on those who weary of their charms" (*L. P. Smith*). **Revengeful** and **vengeful,** though applicable to a man's nature, carry a far stronger reference to him as provoked to action or as about to act: *vengeful*, especially, may apply to his hand or arm, his sword, or any agent or weapon used in inflicting vengeance; as, "You know his nature, That he's *revengeful*, and I know his sword Hath a sharp edge" (*Shak.*); "the downcast look of dark and *revengeful* resolve" (*Coleridge*); "The queen incens'd, his services forgot, Leaves him a victim to the *vengeful* Scot" (*Swift*); "The proud oppressors fly the *vengeful* sword" (*Pope*).

Ana. Implacable, unrelenting, relentless, merciless, *grim: spiteful, despiteful, *malicious, malignant, malign.

violation. *Breach, infraction, transgression, trespass, infringement, contravention.

Ana. *Offense, sin, vice, crime, scandal: desecration, *profanation, sacrilege, blasphemy: invading *or* invasion, encroachment, entrenchment (see corresponding verbs at TRESPASS).

violence. *Force, compulsion, coercion, duress, constraint, restraint.

Ana. Vehemence, intensity (see corresponding adjectives at INTENSE): *effort, exertion, pains, trouble: *attack, assault, onslaught, onset.

virago. **Virago, amazon, termagant, scold, shrew, vixen, barge** agree in meaning a woman of pugnacious temperament. *Virago* and *amazon* both suggest masculine or heroic stature and vigor; in earlier use both designated a female warrior. At present **virago** seldom implies heroic qualities, but rather fierceness of temper and a domineering nature. "To arms, to arms! the fierce *Virago* cries, And swift as lightning to the combat flies" (*Pope*). "The lust of power turned some of them into unsexed *viragos*, like Antony's wife Fulvia" (*Buchan*). **Amazon,** though still applied to one of a mythical race of women warriors, also designates an abnormally large and virile woman; it rarely suggests violence of temper. **Termagant,** though now seldom applied to any but a woman, carries over from its original application to a stock character of the medieval drama, a brawling violent Saracen deity, the implications of turbulence, boisterousness, and an uncontrollable temper.

The last four words are all designations of women who inflict their bad temper on others. **Scold** usually implies vulgarity and habitual abusiveness; as, "I know she is an irksome brawling *scold*" (*Shak.*): **shrew,** a bitter tongue and a nagging disposition; as, "those men...who are under the discipline of *shrews* at home" (*Irving*): **vixen,** a quick fiery temper and snappishness or considerable asperity; as, "A woman tropical, intense... She blended in a like degree The *vixen* and the devotee" (*Whittier*): **barge** (an Anglo-Irish word), frequent indulgence in scolding or faultfinding.

virgin, virginal. Maiden, boyish, *youthful, juvenile, puerile.

Ana. *Chaste, pure, modest, decent: fresh, *new.

Ant. Anile, senile.

virile. Manful, manly, *male, masculine, manlike, mannish.

Ant. Effeminate: impotent (*sense* 2).

virtual. *Implicit, constructive.

Ant. Actual.

virtually. **Virtually, practically, morally** are very close synonyms meaning not absolutely or actually, yet so nearly so that the difference is negligible. So close are these words in meaning that they (especially the first two) are often interchanged in ordinary use; discriminating writers, however, retain their historical implications and employ them, therefore, with better effect. **Virtually** implies that the difference is merely that between what a thing is in name or outward seeming and what it is in fact, in essence, in effect, or, sometimes, in potentiality; as, the prime minister is *virtually* the ruler of his country; their father's request is *virtually* a command; the British contended that the American colonies were *virtually* represented. **Practically** implies a difference between what is enough for practical purposes, or from the point of view of use, value, effectiveness, and the like, and what satisfies the requirements formally or absolutely; as, badly spotted fruit is *practically* worthless; the Democratic nomination to a senatorship in some southern states is *practically* an election; a road is *practically* finished when traffic can pass over it freely and without interruptions. **Morally,** although it is less often used than *virtually* and *practically* in phrases such as "*morally* (*virtually* or *practically*) certain," and "*morally* (*virtually* or *practically*) impossible," is the best selection in such collocations. For *morally* implies a difference between what satisfies one's judgment and what is required for proof by law or by logic; as, the jurors were *morally* certain of the defendant's guilt, but owing to a lack of evidence, they were compelled to render a verdict of "not guilty." When *morally* qualifies words such as "impossible," it occurs in a statement of a conviction and is slightly less positive than "absolutely"; as, it is *morally* impossible to accomplish more under the circumstances.

virtue. 1 *Goodness, morality, rectitude.
Ana. Honor, *honesty, integrity, probity: *fidelity, piety, fealty, loyalty: righteousness, nobility, virtuousness (see corresponding adjectives at MORAL).
Ant. Vice.
2 *Excellence, merit, perfection.
Ana. *Worth, value: effectiveness, efficacy, effectualness (see corresponding adjectives at EFFECTIVE): strength, might, *power, force.

virtuoso. 1 Connoisseur, *aesthete, dilettante.
2 *Expert, adept, artist, dab, dabster, artiste, wizard.

virtuous. *Moral, ethical, righteous, noble.
Ana. Pure, *chaste, modest, decent: *upright, just, honorable.
Ant. Vicious.

virulent. *Poisonous, venomous, toxic, mephitic, pestilent, pestilential, miasmatic, miasmic, miasmal.
Ana. *Deadly, mortal, fatal, lethal: *pernicious, noxious, baneful, deleterious: malignant, malign (see MALICIOUS).

virus. 1 *Poison, venom, toxin, bane.
2 *Germ, microbe, bacterium, bacillus, pathogen.

visage. *Face, countenance, physiognomy, mug, puss.

vision. 1 *Revelation, prophecy, apocalypse.
2 *Fancy, fantasy, phantasy, phastasm, dream, daydream, nightmare.
Ana. Illusion, *delusion, hallucination, mirage: *imagination, fancy, fantasy.

visionary, *adj.* *Imaginary, fanciful, fantastic, chimerical, quixotic.
Ana. Romantic, *sentimental, maudlin: utopian, *ambitious, pretentious: ideal, transcendent, transcendental (see ABSTRACT): illusory, seeming, *apparent.

visit, *n.* **Visit, visitation, call** agree in meaning a coming to stay with another, usually for a brief time, as a courtesy, an act of friendship, or a business or professional duty. **Visit** applies not only to any such stay with another for any of the enumerated reasons (as, to pay a *visit* to a friend; to devote an afternoon weekly to *visits;* a physician's bill for *visits;* a welfare worker's *visit*) but also, to a more prolonged stay as a house guest, or in a place where one goes for purposes of rest, entertainment, sightseeing, or the like (as, a week's *visit* in a friend's summer home; to be off for a *visit* to Washington). **Visitation** (as here compared: see also TRIAL, 2) is now chiefly in formal and official use where it is employed in reference to a visit such as to a church, a college, or a ship, made by one who is the superior, the superintendent, the supervisor, the legal inspector, or the like; as, the parochial *visitations* of a bishop; a *visitation* and search of a merchant ship can be made only by an authorized official. Consequently, the term may also be applied to anything that visits one, often by or as by the will of a superior power (as, "Ye gentle *visitations* of calm thought"—*Shelley*), or that is visited upon one and that is, usually, regarded as an affliction (as, "That going to see people may have different effects is shown in our use of the words '*visit*' and '*visitation.*' Whether a *visit* shall seem like a *visitation* depends a good deal on the visitor"—*S. M. Crothers*). **Call** applies only to the briefest possible visit, such as is made upon a person who is not a friend, but with whom one has social or official relations (as, a society woman must give a portion of her time to formal *calls*) or by a person in quest of business or of a business order (as, the morning *call* of the grocer's boy; a baker's *call*). The term, however, may be used in place of *visit* for a short social visit.

visitant. *Visitor, guest, caller.

visitation. 1 *Visit, call.
2 *Trial, tribulation, affliction, cross.
Ana. *Misfortune, mischance, adversity: calamity, catastrophe, *disaster: hardship, vicissitude (see DIFFICULTY).

visitor. **Visitor, visitant, guest, caller** come into comparison as meaning one who visits another or comes to pay a visit. **Visitor** is the general word applicable to anyone who comes under this description (as, there are *visitors* in the drawing room; summer *visitors*). It is, however, specifically applied to one who makes a friendly visit or one who comes in the cause of charity, social service, investigation, and the like; as, to entertain *visitors;* a frequent *visitor* at his friend's house; the *visitor* from the charitable organization found no one at home. **Visitant** now rarely applies to a human visitor. Some ornithologists and others use it in preference to *visitor,* which is also employed in this sense, of a migratory bird that comes only for a short stay in a given region; as, certain warblers are rare *visitants* in this locality. In general, however, the term is applied to a visitor who is or seems to be from another sphere such as heaven or hell; as, a supernatural *visitant;* "At the sound of this the *visitant* returned.... Markheim... thought he bore a likeness to himself: and always, like a lump of living terror, there lay in his bosom the conviction that this thing was not of the earth" (*Stevenson*). As compared with *visitor,* **guest** emphasizes the idea of hospitable entertainment: it applies therefore chiefly, but not invariably, to one who comes as a result of an invitation; as, they had ten *guests* at dinner; house *guests* (i.e., persons to whom one is host for at least overnight, but often longer); we shall have no *guests* until the children are perfectly well. The term "paying *guest,*" or even *guest* alone, is now often used euphemistically in place of *lodger* or *boarder,* especially when social equality, social relations, or the like, is implied; as, the *guests* at a summer hotel. **Caller** is applicable not only to one who comes for a social or business call (see under VISIT) but to anyone regardless of his intentions who seeks entrance to one's home, office, or the like; as, she told her maid that she would not be at home to *callers* that day.

vital. 1 *Living, alive, quick, animate, animated.
Ana. *Vigorous, energetic, lusty: *active, live, dynamic.
2 Fundamental, *essential, cardinal.
Ana. Important, significant, consequential, weighty,

momentous (see corresponding nouns at IMPORTANCE): indispensable, requisite, necessary, *needful.

vitalize. **Vitalize, energize, activate** agree in meaning to arouse to activity or to life something inert, latent, or arrested in its development. **Vitalize** implies restoration of vigor, freshness, or health, and is used chiefly in reference to persons or their powers and to the arts or their subject matter. "The other sisters were interested in Paul too, but the atrophy of years cannot be easily *vitalized*" (*Deland*). "Greek poetry [as translated by Gilbert Murray] will never have the slightest *vitalizing* effect upon English poetry" (*T. S. Eliot*). **Energize** implies the imparting of force, heat, electricity, or of any power that increases capacity for work; as, certain foods such as butter or chocolate have greater *energizing* power than others, such as lean meat; an electro-magnet is *energized* or de-*energized* by simply establishing or stopping the current in the coil. **Activate** stresses the influence of an external agent or influence. It is much used in the applied sciences with reference to any of several processes differing greatly in character but having in common for their aim or effect the production of beneficial activity not inherent in a thing, or undeveloped in it, or inert and requiring contact with some other substance or source of energy; as, to *activate* cod liver oil by exposure to sunlight so that it may have the desired physiological effect; certain enzymes are *activated* only when other enzymes are present. "[Osler] the *activating* spirit of the...Society" (*H. Cushing*).
Ana. Animate, *quicken, enliven, vivify: stimulate, galvanize, excite, *provoke.
Ant. Atrophy.

vitiate. *Debase, deprave, corrupt, pervert, debauch.
Ana. Pollute, defile, taint, *contaminate: degrade, demean, *abase: impair, spoil, *injure, damage: annul, invalidate, *nullify.

vitiated. Debased, depraved, corrupted, debauched, perverted. See under DEBASE.
Ana. Defiled, polluted, contaminated, taint (see CONTAMINATE): impaired, spoiled, injured (see INJURE): invalidated, annulled (see NULLIFY).

vituperate. Revile, berate, rate, upbraid, *scold, tonguelash, jaw, bawl out, wig, rail.
Ana. Condemn, denounce, censure, blame, reprehend, reprobate (see CRITICIZE): vilify, asperse, traduce, *malign, calumniate: *execrate, objurgate.
Con. *Commend, applaud, compliment: *praise, extol, eulogize.

vituperation. *Abuse, invective, obloquy, scurrility, billingsgate.
Ana. *Animadversion, aspersion, stricture, reflection: *attack, assault, onslaught, onset: condemnation, denunciation, censuring *or* censure (see corresponding verbs at CRITICIZE): vilifying *or* vilification, maligning, calumniation (see corresponding verbs at MALIGN).
Ant. Acclaim, praise.

vituperative. *Abusive, opprobrious, contumelious, scurrilous, scurrile, scurril.
Ana. *Coarse, vulgar, gross, obscene: insulting, offending, outraging (see OFFEND): condemning *or* condemnatory, denouncing *or* denunciatory (see corresponding verbs at CRITICIZE).

vivacious. *Lively, animated, gay, sprightly.
Ana. Buoyant, effervescent, volatile (see ELASTIC): *merry, blithe, jocund: frolicsome, sportive, *playful.
Ant. Languid.

vivid. *Graphic, picturesque, pictorial.
Ana. *Sharp, keen, acute: *dramatic, dramaturgic, theatrical: *expressive, eloquent, meaningful: nervous, lusty, *vigorous: *clear, lucid, perspicuous.
Con. *Obscure, vague, enigmatic.

vivify. *Quicken, animate, enliven.
Ana. *Vitalize, energize, activate: *renew, restore, refresh: *stir, rouse, arouse: stimulate, galvanize, excite (see PROVOKE).

vixen. Shrew, scold, termagant, *virago, amazon, barge.

vocable, *n.* *Word, term.

vocabulary. *Language, phraseology, diction, phrasing, style.

vocal. **1** **Vocal, articulate, oral** agree in meaning uttered or having to do with utterance. **Vocal** implies the use of voice, but not necessarily of speech or language; thus, *vocal* sounds are sounds produced by any creature that has *vocal* organs; *vocal* music is contrasted with instrumental music because the musical tones are produced by the voice rather than evoked from a musical instrument. **Articulate** implies the use of distinct intelligible language; thus, speech is the faculty of uttering *articulate* sounds; *articulate* cries are those that are expressed in meaningful words rather than in meaningless sounds; the *articulate* fine arts are often called belles-lettres. "Constance nodded her head in thorough agreement. She did not trouble to go into *articulate* apologies" (*Bennett*). **Oral** implies the use of the mouth rather than the hand (as in writing, typing, or the like) in communicating one's thoughts, wishes, orders, questions, answers, or the like; as, an *oral* examination; an *oral* command; the tradition was handed down *orally*.

2 **Vocal, articulate, fluent, eloquent, voluble, glib** are here considered chiefly as applied to persons or to the expression of their thoughts and feelings, but in some cases as applied to those thoughts and feelings with reference to their capacity for expression. All of these words mean able to express oneself clearly or easily, or manifesting that ability; some of them also mean (when qualifying a thought or feeling) finding an outlet in expression. **Vocal** usually implies responsiveness to a stimulus to expression or freedom and spontaneity in voicing one's ideas or feelings. "Earth's millions daily fed, a world employed In gathering plenty yet to be enjoyed, Till gratitude grew *vocal* in the praise Of God" (*Cowper*). "This instantaneous indignation of the most impulsive and *vocal* of men was diligently concealed for at least six weeks, with reporters camped upon his doorstep day and night" (*Mencken*). **Articulate** is as often applied to thoughts and emotions with reference to their capacity for expression as to persons or their utterances. In either case, it implies the use of language (in speech or writing) which exactly and distinctly reveals or conveys whatever seeks expression; thus, deeply felt emotion is often not *articulate;* only highly *articulate* persons express their deepest emotions. "The deepest intuitions of a race are deposited in its art; no criticism can make these wholly *articulate*" (*Binyon*). "The primitive poet...was used by the community to make its spiritual needs *articulate*" (*Day Lewis*). **Fluent** stresses facility in utterance or in writing, and copiousness in the flow of words; unlike *vocal* and *articulate,* it refers to the manner of the expression, rather than to the matter seeking expression; as, a *fluent* writer or speaker. "It was his gift to be *fluent* on anything or nothing" (*Stevenson*). The word is often used in depreciation or contempt. "She went on a little less *fluently,* of which I was glad. *Fluency* and accuracy are a bad pair. I would rather people stumbled and stammered out their stories than pour them" (*R. Macaulay*). "Politically at the mercy of every bumptious adventurer and *fluent* charlatan" (*Shaw*). **Eloquent** usually implies fluency, but it also suggests the stimulus of powerful emotion and its expression in fervent and moving language; it is rightly applied not only to speakers, but to writers, poets, and even, by extension, to things; as, to be *eloquent* in one's own behalf. "Of all the attempts to describe such [mystical] experiences these barely *articulate*, incoherent exclamations of Pascal—the intellectual, the philosopher, the master of language and style—are, for me, beyond all compare the most *eloquent* and the most realistic" (*Dom. C. Butler*). "Tully [that is, Cicero] was not so *eloquent* as thou, Thou nameless column with the buried base" (*Byron*). **Voluble,** was once not so derogatory in its connotations as it is now; in earlier use it implied not only fluency but an orotund or oratorical style marked by richness and smoothness of utterance. "Aged ears play truant at his tales... So sweet and *voluble* is his discourse" (*Shak.*). "The style of which is certainly not so melodious and *voluble* as that of Dryden's enchanting prose" (*J. Warton*). In current use, *voluble* and **glib** both imply loquacity. *Voluble* suggests a flow of language that is not easily stemmed; as, to indulge in *voluble* explanations; he grew *voluble* when he saw that he was not in danger of arrest. *Glib* implies such facility in utterance as to suggest superficiality or emptiness in that which is said, or slipperiness or untrustworthiness in the speaker; as, a *glib* reply; he has a *glib* tongue. "Only by forgetting their history is it possible to talk *glibly* of the French as unfitted by nature for self-government" (*Brownell*).

Ana. Expressing, voicing, venting (see EXPRESS, *v.*): *expressive, sententious, eloquent.

vocation. **Vocation, avocation** are often confused. **Vocation** denotes one's occupation or the work in which one is regularly employed or engaged, as a business, a profession, or a trade; as, to make an early choice of one's *vocation*. An **avocation** is an occupation in which one engages in one's leisure time or as subsidiary to one's vocation; as, he is a lawyer by *vocation*, but he has found time for *avocations* such as farming and lecturing. In its strict etymological meaning, an *avocation* is something which calls one away from one's ordinary pursuits; as, "interrupted eternally with these petty *avocations*" (*Scott*). This usage, however, is now rare.

vociferous. **Vociferous, clamorous, blatant, strident, boisterous, obstreperous** agree in meaning so loud and noisy, especially vocally, as to compel attention, often unwilling attention. **Vociferous** implies both loud and vehement cries or shouts: it often also suggests a deafening quality; as, "watermen, fishwomen, oysterwomen, and...all the *vociferous* inhabitants of both shores" (*Fielding*); "*vociferous* vindications of their innocence" (*Irving*); *vociferous* protests. **Clamorous** implies insistency as well as vociferousness: it usually suggests a determination to force acceptance of one's ideas, plans, policies, or the like; as, "I will be...more *clamorous* than a parrot against rain" (*Shak.*); "Sleep not, my country: though night is here, afar Your children of the morning are *clamorous* for war" (*J. E. Flecker*); "It was impossible to yield to her *clamorous* demands" (*A. Repplier*). **Blatant** implies a tendency to bellow or be conspicuously, offensively, or vulgarly noisy or clamorous; as, "They were heretics of the *blatant* sort, loud-mouthed and shallow-minded" (*Expositor*); "*Blatant* he bids the world bow down" (*Kipling*); "Building against our *blatant*, restless time An unseen, skilful, medieval wall" (*V. Lindsay*). **Strident** basically implies a harsh and discordant quality characteristic of some noises that are peculiarly disturbing to the auditory nerves: it has, however, so long been applied especially to loud, harsh voices or vocal sounds, that it now applies to anything which, like them, irresistibly and against one's will, forces itself upon one's attention; as, the colors are too *strident;* a *strident* protest against war; "There was no *strident* old voice to bid him do this or that; no orders to obey, no fierce and insane fault-finding" (*Deland*). **Boisterous** in its common current sense retains its etymological implication of roughness and its acquired implication of violence, but it applies usually to persons or things that are also extremely noisy and turbulent, as though let loose from all restraint; as, *boisterous* children; *boisterous* revellers; *boisterous* merriment; "*boisterous* spring winds" (*Cather*). **Obstreperous** in its earliest and still not uncommon sense is closer to *vociferous* and *clamorous* than to *boisterous*, which is now, frequently, its nearer synonym. Its chief distinctive implication is resistance to or defiance of any power or any efforts that have restraint as their aim; as, "the most careless and *obstreperous* merriment" (*Johnson*); to allow children such freedom that they become *obstreperous* at play; "*obstreperous* in her praise" (*Millay*).

Ana. Noisy, sounding (see corresponding nouns at SOUND): vehement, *intense: bewildering, distracting (see PUZZLE, *v.*).

vogue. Mode, *fashion, style, fad, rage, craze, dernier cri, cry.

voice, *v.* *Express, utter, vent, broach, air, ventilate.

Ana. *Reveal, disclose, tell, discover, divulge: *communicate, impart: *speak, talk.

void, *adj.* **1** *Empty, vacant, blank, vacuous.

Ana. Exhausted, depleted, drained (see DEPLETE): *bare, barren: hollow, empty, nugatory, *vain.

2 *Devoid, destitute.

void, *n.* Vacuum, *hole, hollow, cavity, pocket.

Ana. Emptiness, vacancy, vacuity (see corresponding adjectives at EMPTY): abyss, *gulf, abysm.

void, *v.* Avoid, vacate, *annul, abrogate, quash.

volatile. Effervescent, buoyant, expansive, resilient, *elastic.

Ana. Unstable, mercurial, *inconstant, fickle, capricious: light-minded, frivolous, flippant, flighty (see corresponding nouns at LIGHTNESS): variable, *changeable, protean.

volatility. *Lightness, light-mindedness, levity, frivolity, flippancy, flightiness.

Ana. Vivaciousness *or* vivacity, gaiety, liveliness, animation, sprightliness (see corresponding adjectives at LIVELY): unstableness *or* instability, mercurialness, inconstancy (see corresponding adjectives at INCONSTANT): variability, changeableness (see corresponding adjectives at CHANGEABLE).

volcano. *Mountain, mount, peak, alp, mesa.

volition. *Will, conation.

Ana. *Choice, election, option: *decision, determination.

Con. *Force, coercion, compulsion, duress.

volubility. Garrulity, loquacity, talkativeness. See under TALKATIVE.

Ana. Fluency, glibness, eloquence, articulateness (see corresponding adjectives at VOCAL).

voluble. **1** Fluent, glib, eloquent, *vocal, articulate.

Ana. Copious, abundant, *plentiful: *easy, facile, effortless, smooth.

Ant. Stuttering, stammering.

2 Garrulous, loquacious, *talkative.

Ant. Curt.

volume. **1** Magnitude, *size, extent, dimensions, area.

2 *Bulk, mass.

voluntary. **Voluntary, intentional, deliberate, willful** (*or* **wilful**), **willing** are here compared as meaning done, made, brought about, given, or the like, of one's own free will, and not by compulsion or coercion. **Voluntary,** which is the most widely applicable of these terms, often implies not only freedom from constraint, but freedom from the control of any influence that might suggest, prompt, or incite action: it does not necessarily imply that these influences have not been operative, but it usually suggests that the decision is the result of one's free choice; as, a *voluntary* renunciation of one's inheritance; a *voluntary* confession. Often, the term carries another, sometimes a different, implication, such as that of spontaneity (as, *voluntary* contributions; "our *voluntary* service he requires not"—*Milton*), or, especially when the opposition is to *involuntary*, that of subjection to or regulation by the will (as, *voluntary* movements; *voluntary* muscles), or that of prior consideration and clear choice (as, *voluntary* manslaughter), or, in law, that of absence of any legal obligation or compulsion to do, make, etc. (as, *voluntary* bankruptcy), or of any valuable consideration in return for doing, making, etc. (as, a *voluntary* conveyance of property). **Intentional** applies chiefly to acts or processes entered into in order to achieve a desired end or purpose or to the end or purpose so willed or effected: the use of the word eliminates every suggestion of the possibility of accident or inadvertence; as, an *intentional* insult; a characteristic, such as a keen scent, evolved in a dog by *intentional* selection and breeding; "Not one in a thousand...perpetrates any *intentional* damage to fish, fowl, or flowers" (*Jefferies*). **Deliberate** (as here considered: see also DELIBERATE, 2; SLOW) adds the implication of full knowledge or full consciousness of the nature of one's intended act and a decision to go ahead in spite of such knowledge or consciousness; as, a *deliberate* falsehood; a *deliberate* sin; *deliberate* murder; a *deliberate* attempt to ruin a person's good name. **Willful** (as here considered: see also UNRULY) adds to *deliberate* the implications of a refusal to be taught, counseled, or commanded, and of an obstinate determination to follow one's own will or choice in full consciousness of the influences or arguments opposed to the attitude adopted or the action or deed contemplated; as, a *willful* murder; *willful* ignorance; his *willful* abuse of his children; a sin committed *willfully;* "To such perseverance in *wilful* self-deception Elizabeth would make no reply" (*Austen*); "*wilful* blindness to ascertained truth" (*Inge*). **Willing** carries, on the other hand, an implication of one or more characteristics such as agreeableness, openness of mind, absence of reluctance, or the like, that makes one ready or eager, without suggestion or without coercion, to accede to the wishes or instructions of others, or to do something or effect some end pleasing to them; as, "How curious is that instinct which makes each sex, in different ways, the *willing* slave of the other!" (*Jefferies*); *willing* service; a *willing* servant; "Where ears are *willing*, talk tends to be loud and long" (*A. Huxley*).

Ana. Chosen, elected, opted (see CHOOSE): *free, independent, autonomous.

Ant. Involuntary: instinctive (sense 2). — ***Con.*** Compelled, coerced, forced (see FORCE, *v.*).

voluptuous. Luxurious, sybaritic, epicurean, *sensuous, sensual.

Ana. Indulging *or* indulgent, pampering (see corresponding verbs at INDULGE): *luxurious, opulent, sumptuous.

Ant. Ascetic.

voracious. **Voracious, gluttonous, ravenous, ravening, rapacious** agree in meaning excessively greedy. **Voracious** implies the habit of gorging oneself with food or drink, or with anything that satisfies an excessive appetite of any sort; as, a *voracious* eater; the shark is one of the most *voracious* of fishes; a *voracious* reader; "*voracious* birds, that hotly bill and breed, and largely drink" (*Dryden*). **Gluttonous** differs from *voracious* chiefly in its emphasis on greediness in eating and in its common suggestions of delight in food and of eating past need to the point of satiety; as, *gluttonous* persons often are obese; "Though a Norman was not *gluttonous*, he was epicurean" (*Lytton*). **Ravenous** implies excessive hunger and suggests violent or grasping methods of dealing with food or with whatever satisfies one's appetite; as, "He [Dr. Johnson] contracted a habit of eating with *ravenous* greediness....The sight of food affected him as it affects wild beasts and birds of prey" (*Macaulay*); "He had mad hungers that grew more *ravenous* as he fed them" (*Wilde*). **Ravening,** though sometimes employed in place of *ravenous*, often comes closer to **rapacious** in suggesting a violent tendency to seize or appropriate to oneself in the manner of a bird of prey or a predatory animal; as, "Beware of false prophets, which come to you in sheep's clothing, but inwardly they are *ravening* wolves" (*Matthew* vii. 15). *Rapacious* may imply the seizure of food (as, "*Rapacious* animals we hate: Kites, hawks, and wolves, deserve their fate"—*Gay*), but more often it suggests excessive and utterly selfish acquisitiveness or cupidity; as, "the Indians, who, though often *rapacious*, are devoid of avarice" (*Parkman*); "the European nations, arrogant, domineering, and *rapacious*, have done little to recommend the name of Christianity in Asia and Africa" (*Inge*).

Ana. Greedy, grasping, acquisitive, *covetous: satiating, sating, surfeiting, gorging (see SATIATE).

votary. *Addict, devotee, habitué, fiend, fan.

Ana. *Enthusiast, fanatic, zealot, bigot.

vote, *n.* *Suffrage, franchise, ballot.

vouch for. *Certify, attest, witness.

Ana. *Support, uphold: *confirm, substantiate, verify, corroborate.

vouchsafe. *Grant, accord, concede, award.

Ana. *Give, bestow, confer, present: condescend, deign, *stoop: *oblige, accommodate, favor.

voyage, *n.* *Journey, tour, trip, excursion, cruise, expedition, jaunt, pilgrimage.

vulgar. 1 *Common, ordinary, familiar, popular.

Ana. *Universal, general: *prevailing, prevalent, current, rife: *usual, customary: crude, *rude, rough: sordid, ignoble, *mean.

2 *Coarse, gross, obscene, ribald.

Ana. Low, *base, vile: *offensive, loathsome, repulsive, revolting: indelicate, indecent, *indecorous.

W

wabble. Variant of WOBBLE.

wage *or* **wages.** **Wage** *or* **wages, salary, stipend, fee, pay, hire, emolument, screw** are here compared as meaning the price paid a person for his labor or services. **Wage** or **wages** applies chiefly to the amount paid daily or weekly for labor, especially labor that involves more physical than mental effort; as, a gardener's *wages;* a laundress's daily *wage;* the servant was promised good *wages.* **Salary** and **stipend** usually apply to the fixed compensation, commonly paid at longer intervals than wages, for services (often professional) which require training or ability: in general, *stipend* is less common in the United States than *salary* (as, teachers' *salaries;* the *salary* of a bank president) but it is the usual term in England (as, a teacher's *stipend;* "Many a parson has brought up a family on a *stipend* of seventy pounds a year"—*Shaw*). *Stipend,* however, is sometimes used in the United States in place of *salary* for the remuneration of a teacher, especially in a college, of a clergyman, or a magistrate; in Scotland it is used only of the salary of a clergyman. **Fee** applies to the price asked or paid for the services of a physician, lawyer, musician, artist, or the like, when such services are requested or required; as, to pay the surgeon's *fee* for a major operation; a lawyer's retaining *fee;* a pianist's *fee.* **Pay,** which is often general in its sense, may be equivalent especially to *wages* (as in *pay*day, *pay* roll, etc.); more specifically, it is used with reference to soldiers; as, an officer on half *pay.* **Hire** is now archaic in the sense of remuneration for services (as, "The labourer is worthy of his *hire*"—*Luke* x. 7), although it still sometimes applies to the price paid for the use of another's property, money, or the like (as, the house will be let at a *hire* of fifty dollars a month; "[The writer] of promise lends his pen for small *hires*—*Meredith*). **Emolument** is now chiefly bookish or humorous except in the plural, when it often means the financial reward of one's work or office; as, "the *emoluments* of a profession" (*Gibbon*); "A worthier successor wears his dignity and pockets his *emoluments*" (*N. Hawthorne*). **Screw** is British slang for wages or salary, especially the weekly wage of a clerk or shop employee.

Ana. Remuneration, recompensing *or* recompense (see corresponding verbs at PAY).

wager. *Bet, stake, pot, ante, blind.

waggish. Sportive, frolicsome, *playful, impish, mischievous, roguish, wanton.

Ana. Facetious, jocose, jocular, humorous, *witty: jovial, jolly (see MERRY): comic, comical, *laughable, droll, ludicrous, funny.

Con. *Serious, earnest, sober, grave, sedate, staid.

wail, *v.* Weep, *cry, whimper, blubber, keen.

Ana. Mourn, *grieve: lament, bewail, bemoan, *deplore: moan, sob, *sigh, groan.

wait. *Stay, remain, abide, tarry, linger.

Ana. *Delay, loiter.

Con. Depart, leave, *go, withdraw, retire.

waive. Cede, yield, resign, abandon, surrender, *relinquish, leave.

Ana. *Forgo, forbear, sacrifice: concede, *grant, allow.

Con. *Demand, claim, require, exact: assert, *maintain, defend.

wake, *v.* **Wake, awake, waken, awaken** cause difficulty because the principles of choice as indicated by current good use are not widely known or, in all cases, definitely accepted. All four are both transitive and intransitive verbs meaning to come out of or to cause to come out of sleep or, by extension, a condition resembling sleep. The tendency at present is to prefer **wake** and **awake** for the literal sense in intransitive use, especially in speech and in ordinary prose (as, he *awoke* this morning at three; he *wakes* each morning at six o'clock) and **waken** and **awaken** or sometimes *wake up* in transitive use (as, the porter went through the car *awakening* the sleepers; noises loud enough to *waken* or *wake up* the soundest sleeper). In poetry and literary prose, where the choice is often determined by the rhythm, more freedom is exercised. In both their literal and extended use, *awake* often emphasizes the fact of coming to full consciousness, *wake* the process of throwing off sleep or lethargy; thus, one finds it difficult to *wake* (better than *awake*) when one is unduly fatigued; she *awoke* (better than *woke*) suddenly; when her mind *awakes* to the true situation, she will be crushed; the national spirit *woke* slowly but surely. In both literal and extended use, when a rousing or stirring rather than a reviving is implied, *awaken* and *waken* are definitely preferred by good writers (see treatment of these words under STIR).

Ana. Rouse, arouse, *stir.

waken. 1 *Wake, awake, awaken.

Ana. Rouse, arouse, *stir.

2 Awaken, arouse, rouse, *stir, rally.

Ana. Excite, stimulate, quicken, galvanize, *provoke: inflame, enkindle, fire, kindle (see LIGHT): impel, *move, actuate, drive.

Ant. Subdue. — *Con.* *Pacify, mollify, placate.

walk, *n.* *Trot, pace, single-foot, rack, amble, canter, lope, gallop, run.

walk, *v.* Trot, pace, single-foot, rack, amble, canter, lope, gallop, run. See under TROT, *n.*

wallow, *v.* **Wallow, welter, flounder, grovel** are not close synonyms in either their literal or figurative senses, but they come into comparison as implying heavy clumsy movement and, when the reference is to man, a debased, pitiable, or ignoble condition. **Wallow** literally implies a rolling to and fro, as of a pig in the mire or a ship in the trough of a wave; as, "Whenever the animals grew hot and tired, they would lie down and *wallow*" (*V. Heiser*); the boat pitched and rolled and *wallowed* as she slowly made her way. In extended use the term often implies sensual enjoyment and indifference to the defilement or degradation that the condition suggests; as, "The godly...shall not *wallow* in their sins" (*Ecclesiasticus* xxiii. 12); "Little knots of houses where drunken men and women were positively *wallowing* in filth" (*Dickens*). **Welter** is often employed in place of *wallow,* but in precise use it frequently carries a stronger implication of rolling or tossing helplessly or confusedly or at the mercy of the elements or other external forces than the latter term; as, "He must not float upon his watery bier Unwept, and *welter* to the parching wind" (*Milton*); "beneath the *weltering* of the restless tide" (*Shelley*); "The mass of the people were *weltering* in shocking poverty whilst a handful of owners *wallowed* in millions" (*Shaw*). *Welter,* however, may not imply movement when it suggests the position of one who has been killed and lies soaked in blood; as, "They lie—the fifty corpses—*weltering* in their blood" (*D. G. Mitchell*). **Flounder** stresses stumbling or struggling rather than rolling and usually, but not invariably, implies an effort to proceed when one is out of one's element, as a fish out of water, a horse in the mire, or when one does not know the road or the way; as, "they mashed their way through the thick mud, *floundering* and stumbling" (*Dickens*); "they *floundered* on foot some eight miles to a squatter's cabin, rented horses, and completed their journey by starlight" (*Cather*). In its extended use, *flounder* usually implies the confusion of mind and the uncertainty of one who is completely muddled or at a loss but nevertheless proceeds; as, he *floundered* through his speech; "Nature has been *floundering* along for a great many millions of years to get things as they are" (*C. C. Furnas*). **Grovel** (etymologically, to lie flat on one's face) now implies a crawling or wriggling with face close to the ground, as in abject fear, awe, or self-abasement, or as a sign of one's complete humiliation or degradation; as, the terrified slaves *groveled* before their master; "Upon thy belly *grovelling* thou shalt go, And dust shalt eat all the days of thy life" (*Milton*); "Am I to *grovel* in the dust for him to walk over?" (*Dickens*).

Ana. Crawl, *creep: defile, pollute, *contaminate, taint: *debase, debauch, corrupt, deprave, pervert.

Con. Soar, mount, ascend, *rise.

wan. Pallid, *pale, ashen, ashy, livid.

Ana. Blanched, whitened, decolorized (see WHITEN): *languid, languishing, languorous: *haggard, cadaverous, worn.

wander. **Wander, stray, roam, ramble, rove, range, prowl, gad, gallivant, traipse, meander** come into comparison as meaning to move about more or less aimlessly or without a plan from place to place or from point to point. Most of these verbs may imply walking, but very few of them are restricted in their reference to human beings or to any particular means of locomotion. **Wander** implies the absence of a fixed course or more or less indifference to a course that has been fixed or otherwise indicated: the term may imply the movement of a walker (either a human being or an animal) or of any traveler, but it may be used of anything dirigible which is permitted to move aimlessly; as, "wand'ring thoughtful in the silent wood" (*Pope*); two months spent *wandering* in Europe; his eyes *wandered* over the landscape; his thoughts *wander;* she *wandered* frequently from her subject. **Stray** carries an even stronger suggestion of deviation from a fixed, true, or proper course: it therefore often connotes a being lost or a danger of being lost; as, "fallows grey, Where the nibbling flocks do *stray*" (*Milton*); "We have erred, and *strayed* from thy ways like lost sheep" (*Bk. of Com. Prayer*); "Though we stumbled and we *strayed,* We were led by evil counsellors—the Lord shall deal with them!" (*Kipling*). **Roam** carries a stronger suggestion of freedom and of scope than *wander:* it usually carries no implication of a definite object or goal, but it seldom, if ever, suggests futility or fruitlessness and it often connotes delight or enjoyment; as, "'Mid pleasures and palaces though we may *roam,* Be it ever so humble, there's no place like home" (*J. H. Payne*); "Like us, the Libyan wind delights to *roam* at large" (*Arnold*); "Let the winged Fancy *roam*" (*Keats*); "type of the wise who soar, but never *roam*" (*Wordsworth*); "the charm of a quiet watch on deck when one may let one's thoughts *roam* in space and time" (*Conrad*). **Ramble,** in contrast, suggests carelessness in wandering and more or less indifference to one's path or goal: therefore it often specifically implies a straying beyond bounds, or an inattention to details that ought to serve as guides, or especially in extended use, an inability to proceed directly or under proper restrictions; as, children so uncared-for that they were allowed to *ramble* through the city's streets for hours at a time; "A vine, remarkable for its tendency, not to spread and *ramble,* but to mass and mount" (*Cather*); speakers who *ramble* are almost inevitably bores. **Rove** comes close to *roam* in its implication of wandering over extensive territory, but it usually carries a suggestion of zest in the activity, and does not preclude the possibility of a definite end or purpose; as, the invaders *roved* through the country burning and pillaging homes in their pathway; "ravenous beasts freely *roving* up and down the country" (*Fuller*); "To seek thee did I often *rove* Through woods and on the green; And thou wert still a hope, a love; Still longed for, never seen" (*Wordsworth*). **Range** is often used in place of *rove* without loss: it is, however, the preferred term when literal wandering is not implied or when the stress is on the sweep of territory covered rather than on the form of locomotion involved; as, cattle *ranging* the western plains; "Through Nature and through Art she *ranged*" (*Swift*); "Talk...*ranging* the widest horizons" (*Mrs. H. Ward*); "his thoughts always *ranged* far afield" (*Mencken*). **Prowl** implies a stealthy or furtive roving, especially in search of prey or booty. It is used not only of animals but often also of human beings intent on marauding (as, "Now goes the nightly thief *prowling* abroad"—*Cowper;* "Jackals *prowl* around his campfire"—*Mrs. H. Ward*), but it is also applied, usually humorously and with little or no connotation of an evil intention, to persons, especially those of a restless or vagabond temperament, who rove, often singly, through the streets or the fields in a quiet and leisurely manner (as, "If I should *prowl* about the streets a long time, don't be uneasy"—*Dickens*). **Gad, gallivant, traipse,** all colloquial or dialectal terms, imply a wandering or roving by those who ought to be under restrictions, such as servants, boys and girls, persons who have not much strength or money, or the like. *Gad* implies little more than this; as, "her upper house-maid and laundry-maid, instead of being in their business, are *gadding* about the village all day long" (*Austen*); "He disapproved of her *gadding* about by herself" (*Galsworthy*). *Gallivant* adds to *gad* the implication of a search for pleasure or amusement or the use of an opportunity to display one's finery; as, her father refused to allow her to go *gallivanting* around with any of her suitors; young girls dressed in their Sunday best *gallivanting* along the highways. *Traipse* often adds to *gad* the implication of a fatiguing or tiresome or wearing experience; as, a desire for antiques that gives one an excuse for *traipsing* over the country; "sleeping in the kitchen so as not to have to *traipse* downstairs when the raid-warning goes" (*Jan Struther*). **Meander** (etymologically from the name of a Phrygian river, famous for its windings) may be used in reference to persons and animals but it is even more often used in reference to things such as streams, paths, roads, and the like, that follow a course (usually a winding or intricate course) in such a way as to suggest aimless or listless wandering; as, "Rivers that...*meandered* across the vast plains" (*Haggard*); "Across the ceiling *meandered* a long crack" (*Galsworthy*); "the gray gelding *meandered* along through the hills" (*S. Anderson*).

wane. *Abate, subside, ebb.

Ana. *Decrease, dwindle, lessen, diminish.

Ant. Wax. — *Con.* *Increase, augment: mount, soar, tower, surge, *rise.

want, *v.* **1** *Lack, need, require.

Ana. *Demand, claim, exact.

Con. *Have, hold, own, possess, enjoy.

2 *Desire, wish, crave, covet.

Ana. *Long, yearn, hanker, pine, hunger, thirst: aspire, pant, *aim.

Con. Refuse, *decline, reject, repudiate, spurn.

want, *n.* **1** *Lack, absence, privation, defect.

Ana. *Need, necessity, exigency: deficiency (see corresponding adjective at DEFICIENT).

Con. Plentifulness *or* plenty, abundance, copiousness (see corresponding adjectives at PLENTIFUL): sufficiency, adequacy (see corresponding adjectives at SUFFICIENT).
2 Destitution, *poverty, indigence, privation, penury.
Ana. Pinch, strait *or* straits, pass, exigency (see JUNCTURE): meagerness, scantiness, exiguousness (see corresponding adjectives at MEAGER).
Con. Affluence, opulence, riches, wealth (see corresponding adjectives at RICH).

wanton. 1 Sportive, impish, mischievous, *playful, roguish, waggish, frolicsome.
Ana. *Unruly, ungovernable, intractable: daring, reckless, foolhardy (see ADVENTUROUS): gay, *lively, animated, vivacious, sprightly.
Con. Restrained, checked, bridled, inhibited (see RESTRAIN): *serious, grave, sober.
2 *Licentious, libertine, lewd, lustful, lascivious, libidinous, lecherous.
Ana. *Immoral, unmoral, amoral: *abandoned, profligate, dissolute, reprobate.
Ant. Chaste. — *Con.* Pure, modest, decent (see CHASTE): virtuous, *moral.
3 *Supererogatory, uncalled-for, gratuitous.
Ana. *Malicious, malevolent, spiteful: wayward, *contrary, perverse.

war, *v.* Battle, *contend, cope, fight.
Ana. Resist, withstand, combat, *oppose: strive, struggle, endeavor, essay, *attempt.

ward off. Avert, *prevent, preclude, obviate.
Ana. Block, bar, obstruct, impede, *hinder: forestall, anticipate (see PREVENT): *frustrate, balk, thwart, foil.
Ant. Conduce to.

wariness. Chariness, caution, circumspection, calculation. See under CAUTIOUS.
Ana. Alertness, watchfulness (see corresponding adjectives at WATCHFUL): *prudence, discretion, foresight, forethought, providence.
Ant. Foolhardiness: brashness (*of persons*). — *Con.* Carelessness, heedlessness, thoughtlessness, inadvertence (see corresponding adjectives at CARELESS): recklessness, rashness (see corresponding adjectives at ADVENTUROUS).

warlike. *Martial, military.
Ana. Bellicose, *belligerent, pugnacious, contentious: fighting, warring, contending, battling (see CONTEND).
Con. *Pacific, peaceable, peaceful.

warm, *adj.* Warmhearted, sympathetic, *tender, compassionate, responsive.
Ana. *Loving, affectionate: cordial, *gracious, affable: ardent, fervent, passionate (see IMPASSIONED): *sincere, heartfelt, hearty, wholehearted.
Ant. Cool: austere.

warmhearted. Warm, sympathetic, *tender, compassionate, responsive.
Ana. *Loving, affectionate: *kind, kindly, benign, benignant: heartfelt, hearty, wholehearted, *sincere.
Ant. Coldhearted. — *Con.* Austere, *severe, stern: *cold, cool, frosty, frigid.

warn, *v.* **Warn, forewarn, caution** agree in meaning to let one know of approaching or possible danger, risk, or the like. **Warn** is the most comprehensive of these terms; in all of its senses it stresses a timely notification that makes possible the avoidance of any situation whether it be literally dangerous or merely inconvenient to oneself or others; as, to *warn* ships of an approaching hurricane; five minutes before the end of the class period, a bell rings to *warn* teachers and pupils; the steamship company *warned* those who had taken tickets of the advanced sailing. Nevertheless, the word often carries in addition at least one other implication, such as of admonition (as, to *warn* one of the consequences of his folly), or of exhortation (as, "The priestly brotherhood...Prompt to persuade, expostulate, and *warn*"—*Cowper*), or of threats of punishment, reprisal, or the like (as, "I shall not take him at his word about fishing, as he might change his mind another day, and *warn* me off his grounds"—*Austen*). **Forewarn** carries a far stronger implication of advance notification than *warn;* commonly also, it suggests impending, although not imminent danger or peril. "I will arm me, being thus *forewarn'd*" (*Shak.*). "He knew not one *forewarning* pain" (*Wordsworth*). **Caution** commonly emphasizes advice that puts one on one's guard or that suggests precautions; as, to *caution* one against unwarranted expectations; the doctor *cautioned* him against overindulgence in strenuous exercise. "We... while experience *cautions* us in vain, Grasp seeming happiness, and find it pain" (*Cowper*).
Ana. Apprise, *inform, advise, notify: admonish (see REPROVE): advise, counsel (see under ADVICE).

warp, *v.* Distort, contort, *deform, gnarl.
Ana. Twist, bend, turn (see CURVE, *v.*): *injure, damage, impair, mar: *stunt, stultify, atrophy.

warrant, *v.* **1** *Assert, declare, affirm, aver, protest, avouch, avow, predicate.
Ana. State (see RELATE): *maintain, assert: assure, *ensure, insure.
2 *Justify.
Ana. Vindicate, justify (see MAINTAIN): sanction, *approve, endorse: *authorize.

wary. Chary, *cautious, circumspect, calculating.
Ana. Alert, *watchful: prudent, discreet, foresighted, forethoughted, provident (see under PRUDENCE).
Ant. Foolhardy: brash (*of persons*). — *Con.* *Careless, heedless, thoughtless, inadvertent: reckless, rash, venturous, venturesome (see ADVENTUROUS).

wash, *n.* **Wash, drift, diluvium, alluvium, alluvion, silt** agree in denoting a deposit of rock material (sand, gravel, etc.) or soil that has been transported by running water or moving ice. **Wash** is the most general of these terms, denoting any material transported or deposited by water, but in its specific use in geology, it denotes loose surface material of the earth, especially gravel and other rock debris. **Drift,** a more scientific term, denotes wash whose constituent particles may vary in size from particles of soil to boulders, and is often used in phrases that indicate the means by which the material has been transported; as, river *drift;* fluvioglacial *drift.* **Diluvium** was formerly applied in geology to both glacial and fluvioglacial drift because the material was supposed to have been transported by the waters of a deluge. **Alluvium** usually denotes finer material than *wash,* including soil, and often signifies the deposit left by the flooding of land that is not permanently submerged, as on flood plains and deltas. Alluvium is deposited also where streams issue from mountains and lose velocity. **Alluvion** is equivalent in meaning to *alluvium,* but in legal use *alluvion* denotes the material gradually added to land by repeated flooding, the material becoming the property of the owner of the land to which it is added. **Silt** implies wash whose constituent particles are very fine, such as constitutes deposits on river bottoms and beaches. Particles of silt sometimes are so fine that they remain suspended in standing water and are hard to distinguish from particles of clay.

waspish. Snappish, *irritable, fractious, peevish, petulant, pettish, huffy, huffish, fretful, querulous.
Ana. Testy, touchy, cranky, cross, *irascible: *impatient: *contrary, perverse: spiteful, *malicious.

waste, *v.* Devastate, *ravage, sack, pillage, despoil, spoliate.

Ana. Plunder, loot, *rob, rifle: *destroy, demolish: *ruin, wreck.
Ant. Conserve, save.

waste, *n.* **Waste, desert, badlands, wilderness** agree in meaning a tract or region of land not usable for cultivation or, in general, for habitation. **Waste** is the general term applicable to any tract or region which because of the nature of its soil, its topographical features (such as abrupt elevations, continuous swamps or marshes), or its being covered with rocks, thorny vegetation, or the like, defies or repels human attempts to use it for cultivation or habitation; as, "At this...point of its nightly roll into darkness the great and particular glory of the Egdon *waste* began" (*Hardy*); "*Wastes* of sand and thorns" (*C. E. Montague*). **Desert,** etymologically a deserted, uninhabited tract of land, applies especially to a particularly arid region where areas of shifting sand prevail and there is little or no vegetation; as, the *desert* of Sahara; "yon far *desert* dead and brown" (*Joaquin Miller*); the arid region of the southwestern United States is often described as a *desert*. **Badlands** (a plural noun) applies to any barren waste where soft rocks that suffer from continual erosion prevail and hills are steep, furrowed, and often fantastic in form, drainage is labyrinthine, and watercourses are normally dry; as, extensive tracts in southwest South Dakota and northwest Nebraska are *badlands* (geographically, this region is called *the Bad Lands*). **Wilderness** applies to any waste which human beings find not only incapable of cultivation or habitation, but difficult to make their way through for lack of actual or even possible paths or trails. Commonly, however, *wilderness* specifically implies a pathless region thickly covered with trees and underbrush and inhabited only by wild animals; as, "Oh for a lodge in some vast *wilderness*, Some boundless contiguity of shade" (*Cowper*). "O my poor kingdom ... thou wilt be a *wilderness* again, Peopled with wolves" (*Shak.*).

wasted. Pinched, cadaverous, *haggard, worn, careworn.
Ana. Gaunt, scrawny, skinny, angular, rawboned (see LEAN, *adj.*).
Con. Sturdy, *strong, stout, stalwart: robust, *healthy.

watch, *v.* **1** *Tend, mind, attend.
Ana. Guard, protect, shield, safeguard (see DEFEND).
2 Look, *see.
Ana. *Gaze, gape, stare, glare: *scrutinize, scan, inspect, examine.

watchful. **Watchful, vigilant, wide-awake, alert** agree in meaning on the lookout especially for danger or for opportunities. **Watchful** is the general word; as, "the five *watchful* senses" (*Milton*); "like a lion that unheeded lay, Dissembling sleep, and *watchful* to betray" (*Dryden*). **Vigilant** implies keen, courageous, often wary, watchfulness, especially in the cause of the right. "Be sober, be *vigilant;* because your adversary the devil, as a roaring lion, walketh about, seeking whom he may devour" (*1 Peter* v. 8). "We should be eternally *vigilant* against attempts to check the expression of opinions that we loathe" (*Justice Holmes*). **Wide-awake** stresses awareness of opportunities more often than of dangers and implies knowledge of all events or factors affecting the situation. "Merchants who...were...*wide awake* and full of energy" (*H. W. van Loon*). **Alert** stresses readiness or promptness in apprehending and meeting a danger, an opportunity, or an emergency. "Not only watchful in the night, but *alert* in the drowsy afternoon" (*Pater*). "Our wits are much more *alert* when engaged in wrong-doing ...than in a righteous occupation" (*Conrad*).
Ana. *Cautious, wary, chary, circumspect: *quick, ready, prompt.
Con. *Careless, heedless, thoughtless, inadvertent.

waterlog. *Soak, drench, saturate, steep, impregnate, sog, sop, ret.

waterspout. *Wind, gale, hurricane, gust, blast, whirlwind, cyclone, typhoon, tornado, twister, flaw, breeze, zephyr.

wave, *v.* *Swing, flourish, brandish, thrash.
Ana. Wield, swing, manipulate, *handle, ply: undulate, sway, *swing, fluctuate: *shake, quiver, quaver.

wave, *n.* **Wave, undulation, ripple, billow, roller, breaker, comber, beachcomber, surge** come into comparison when they mean one of the ridges or swells that form on the surface of the ocean or other body of water, or something similar in formation. **Wave** is the general word applicable to any such ridge or swell which has a perceptible crest and trough; as, there is not a *wave* on the lake; the wind whipped up the surface into high *waves;* her hair rises and falls in natural *waves*. The term is also used in the physical sciences in reference to each pulse of the advance of something such as light or sound through a medium such as the air; as, light *waves;* heat *waves*. **Undulation** also applies to any wave or wavelike formation wherever found: the term, however, carries a less vivid picture than *wave* for it either denotes an abstraction or tends to suggest a more or less conventionalized pattern; as, "They roamed at large on the *undulations* of Edgon [Heath]" (*Hardy*); "The stream arranges the sand in the shallow in...minute fixed *undulations*" (*Jefferies*). **Ripple** applies to a small wave such as one of those which cover the surface of water passing over shallows or disturbed by a light wind. "A breeze stirred about them and the bay broke up into long oily *undulations*, then into *ripples* tipped with spray" (*E. Wharton*). **Billow** is sometimes used poetically for *wave*, but in careful, nonrhetorical use it applies chiefly to a high upheaving wave such as one of those that often rise on the surface of the deepest parts of the ocean. "Strongly it [the dactylic hexameter] bears us along in swelling and limitless *billows;* Nothing before and nothing behind but the sky and the ocean" (*Coleridge*). "Where the prairies, like seas where the *billows* have rolled, Are broad as the kingdoms and empires of old" (*C. Mackay*). **Roller** applies to one of a series of long heavy waves which are produced by a storm and which hold their shape over a long course to the shore where they usually break with great force and noise; as, "The league-long *roller* thundering on the reef" (*Tennyson*). **Breaker** applies to a heavy wave which breaks into foam or flying spume when the wave dashes against a rock, reef, or the like. "I have loved thee, Ocean!... from a boy I wantoned with thy *breakers*... And trusted to thy *billows* far and near" (*Byron*). **Comber** and **beachcomber** (both Americanisms) apply to a long curling wave or, especially, breaker. The latter term, as its name implies, applies to one breaking near the shore or beach: the former may imply this or a breaking over the side of a ship, on a reef or shoal, or the like; as, a thundering *comber* struck the rail of the ship. **Surge,** which is chiefly poetic or rhetorical in this sense, usually suggests a high-rising billow or roller; as, "All this time the sea was rolling in immense *surges*" (*R. H. Dana, jr.*).

waver, *v.* **1** Fluctuate, oscillate, pendulate, vibrate, *swing, sway, undulate.
Ana. Flicker, flutter, hover, *flit, flitter: quiver, quaver, tremble, *shake.
2 Falter, *hesitate, vacillate.
Ana. Balk, boggle, stickle, scruple, *demur, shy: fluctuate, oscillate (see SWING).

wax, *n.* *Oil, fat, grease.

way, *n.* **1** **Way, route, course, passage, pass, artery** agree in meaning the track or path traversed in going from one place to another. **Way** was originally applied to a road, especially one for riders or conveyances as well as for pedestrians and animals; it now occurs rarely in this specific sense except in combinations such as high*way*, *way*side, and in some idiomatic phrases; as, he lives across the *way;* the parting of the *ways* (that is, the crossroads). The word is now so general and inclusive in meaning that its specific application must be gathered from the context; as, I know the *way* through the forest; this is the *way* to the market; what is the best *way* to Chicago by train? It is also used in combination with words that make its application clear; as, drive*way*, rail*way*, sea*way*, sub*way*. **Route** originally denoted a path taken or trodden by men or animals. Now it is applied to a way, often a circuitous way covering many roads, paths, tracks, or the like, regularly followed by a person in his business or employment (as, a delivery *route;* a postman's *route*) or laid out as the path to be followed by a marching army, a tourist, a vehicle, or the like (as, the *route* to the battlefield; a bus *route;* U. S. *route* 20). **Course,** in its earliest pertinent sense, denoted the line or track followed by someone or something running or advancing, and was used especially of the path followed by a planet through the heavens, or by a ship at sea. The term may imply straightness and directness (as, to keep to one's *course*) but it does not necessarily imply unchangeableness (as, to turn or bend one's *course*): it may suggest a beginning and end (as, he must run his *course;* the *course* of a missile), but sometimes it connotes circular or unending progress, especially in figurative use (as, the *course* of the seasons): it nearly always, especially in its extended senses, implies progress from point to point (as, a *course* of study; the *course* of a plot). As a modern designation, *course* is applied chiefly to a track for racing by men, horses, automobiles, etc. (a race*course*), to the natural or artificial channel of a stream (a water*course*), and to a tract of ground laid out for playing golf (a golf *course*). **Passage** stresses crossing or transit; when specifically applied to a track or path, it denotes one followed in getting from one point to another and involving passing through or over something; as, the search for a Northwest *Passage* to India. "I'll drink to her as long as there is a *passage* in my throat and drink in Illyria" (*Shak.*). "A bridge...a *passage* broad, Smooth, easy, inoffensive, down to Hell" (*Milton*). In current use, however, *passage* is chiefly found in concrete applications; sometimes it designates a narrow lane for pedestrians (as, St. Helen's *Passage* in Oxford); more often, it names a space (such as a corridor or vestibule), forming a common pathway to a particular room, apartment, or office in a building (see article at PASSAGE, 2). "There her women in a mournful throng Stood in the *passage* whispering" (*Keats*). **Pass** is chiefly applied to a passage through or over something that presents an obstacle or serious difficulty, such as a river (specifically a ford, ferry, or bridge; as, the *passes* of the Rhine), or a sand-choked river mouth (specifically, a narrow navigable channel), or, especially, a mountain range (specifically, a notch or defile; as, the Khyber *Pass* between Afghanistan and India). **Artery,** which is literally applied to one of the tubular branching blood vessels which carry blood from the heart to the various parts or organs of the body, is now also applied to one of the great continuous channels of traffic from which branch off many smaller or shorter channels; it is applied sometimes to a great railroad which traverses a continent or goes directly from one large city to another that is far distant as from New York to Chicago, or Chicago to San Francisco; it is also applied to a through highway from which branch other routes (or roads connecting with them) and which permits swift and unimpeded passage over a great distance; as, the northern *artery* out of Boston.

2 *Method, mode, manner, fashion, system.

Ana. Procedure, *process, proceeding: *plan, design, scheme: practice, *habit, habitude, custom, use, usage, wont.

waylay. *Surprise, ambush.

Ana. *Attack, assault, assail: *prevent, forestall.

wayward. Perverse, froward, restive, *contrary, balky.

Ana. *Insubordinate, contumacious, rebellious: refractory, recalcitrant, intractable, headstrong, *unruly: capricious, *inconstant, fickle, unstable.

Con. Amenable, tractable, *obedient: *compliant, acquiescent.

weak. Weak, feeble, frail, fragile, infirm, decrepit agree in meaning not strong enough to bear, resist, or endure strain, pressure, or the like. **Weak** is by far the widest in its range of application, not only being interchangeable with all of the succeeding words, but also capable of being applied where they are not. Fundamentally, it implies deficiency or inferiority in strength; in this case, it may apply not only to the body, but to the will, the mind, the spirit; as, a *weak* man; *weak* woman; a *weak* army; a *weak* plant; a *weak* character; the *weaker* brethren. "The spirit indeed is willing, but the flesh is *weak*" (*Matthew* xxvi. 41). "Thou, though strong in love, art all too *weak* In reason" (*Wordsworth*). Often it implies a lack of power, skill, efficiency, ability to control, or the like; as, a *weak* government; a *weak* team; a *weak* governor; *weak* nerves; a *weak* influence. It may also suggest a defect, a fault, a dilution, or other sign of impairment of a thing's strength; as, *weak* spots in a mechanism; a *weak* tread in a stairway; *weak* tea; *weak* weapons; a *weak* argument. **Feeble** is not only more restricted than *weak* in its range of application, but it also carries a stronger implication of lamentableness or pitiableness in that weakness. It is chiefly, though far from exclusively, applied to human beings and their acts and utterances, then usually implying a manifest lack or impairment of physical, mental, or moral strength; as, a *feeble,* tottering old man; a *feeble* attempt to resist the enemy's advance. "Rigid principles often do for *feeble* minds what stays do for *feeble* bodies" (*Macaulay*). As applied to things, *feeble* implies faintness, indistinctness, impotency, or inadequacy; as, a *feeble* light; a *feeble* sound; a *feeble* stem; "a *feeble* approximation is accepted" (*Grandgent*). **Frail,** when it implies physical (especially human) weakness, suggests not so much the impairment of strength as natural delicacy of constitution or slightness of build; it may even be used without hint of mental or moral weakness. "Steer Harpit came from Rowell Hill, A small, *frail* man, all heart and will" (*Masefield*). "It was marvellous that...the energy of her spirit could carry through so triumphantly her *frail* nervous system and her delicate constitution" (*H. Ellis*). As applied to things, however, the term usually implies liability to failure or destruction if the thing has physical existence (as, to shoot the rapids in a *frail* canoe) or, if immaterial, an incapacity for dealing with forces or powers opposed to it, or tending to destroy it (as, "Beauty, *frail* flow'r that ev'ry season fears"—*Pope*). When *frail* is applied to the will, the conscience, the moral nature of man, it carries an even stronger implication of lack of power to resist than *weak*. "Or, if he prove unkind, (as who can say But being man, and therefore *frail*, he may)" (*Cowper*). **Fragile** (see also FRAGILE, 1) is frequently used in place of *frail*, but it usually carries even a stronger suggestion of certainty or assurance of destruction or of the strength of the powers or forces opposing. "Shaftesbury was, moreover, a man of *fragile* physical constitution, as Kant was; but, unlike Kant, he was...a man in the world, heroically seeking to live a complete and harmonious life" (*H. Ellis*). "She was passionately realising the moment, its fleeting exquisiteness, its still, *fragile* beauty" (*R. Macaulay*). **Infirm** usually implies a loss of strength, especially of physical strength, with consequent instability, unsoundness, or insecurity. As referred to human beings, it often implies illness, or more often, old age; as, "a poor, *infirm*, weak, and despised old man" (*Shak.*). As referred, however, to the tempers, the designs, or the intentions of men, it often implies wavering or serious vacillation. "*Infirm* of purpose! Give me the daggers" (*Shak.*). **Decrepit** is as applicable to things as to persons that are worn out or broken down by use or age. "Such is its misery and wretchedness, that it resembles a man in the last *decrepit* stages of life" (*Fielding*). "Two or three wooden-bottom chairs, exceedingly *decrepit* and *infirm*" (*N. Hawthorne*).

Ana. Debilitated, weakened, enfeebled (see WEAKEN): doddering, *senile, anile, doting: *powerless, impotent, impuissant.

Ant. Strong. — ***Con.*** Stout, sturdy, tough, stalwart, tenacious (see STRONG).

weaken. Weaken, enfeeble, debilitate, undermine, sap, cripple, disable come into comparison when they mean to lose or, commonly, cause to lose, strength, vigor, or energy. **Weaken,** the most general term of this group, most frequently implies loss of the physical strength characteristic of a healthy living thing or any of its organs or the loss of the soundness or stability characteristic of a strong material structure (as, overexercise has *weakened* his heart; unfertilized plants *weaken* and die; the illness has *weakened* him considerably; decay has *weakened* the wooden supports of the bridge), but it may imply a loss of strength in quality or in effective power in anything material or immaterial, as by a natural or forced reduction in resources, numbers, means of support, and the like (as, the regiment was greatly *weakened* by heavy casualties in battle; the growing power of Parliament *weakened* the authority of the sovereign; his losses in the market have noticeably *weakened* his credit), or by a reduction in intensity by dilution, attenuation, or the like (as, to *weaken* wine or tea with water; frequent quarreling has *weakened* their friendship). **Enfeeble** implies a more obvious and a more pitiable condition than *weaken:* it suggests the state of a person greatly weakened by old age or severe or prolonged illness or a state comparable to it, and therefore usually implies helplessness or powerlessness more strongly than *weaken* does; as, he has been so *enfeebled* by illness that he will probably never walk again; a country crushed and *enfeebled* by war. **Debilitate** may be used in place of *enfeeble* but commonly it suggests a somewhat less marked or less prolonged impairment of strength or vitality: the word occurs commonly, but not exclusively, in the participial forms; as, a life of dissipation has *debilitated* him physically and mentally; "her frail nervous system and her delicate constitution, still further *debilitated* by the slow progress of disease" (*H. Ellis*); a *debilitating* climate. **Undermine** and **sap** both literally mean to dig a trench, tunnel, or the like, under a wall, foundation, or area. In the extended sense in which they are here considered, they imply a weakening by something or someone working surreptitiously or insidiously: *sap*, however, has been so colored by the meaning of another word *sap*—meaning to drain a plant or tree of sap, or vital juice—that it may suggest a draining of strength or a caving in or breaking down, or neither exactly the one nor the other; as, her health has been *undermined* by lack of rest and proper food; his strength has been *sapped* by his fierce struggle for success. "Some of the new philosophies *undermine* the authority of science, as some of the older systems *undermined* the authority of religion" (*Inge*). "But sloth had *sapped* the prophet's strength" (*Newman*). "His moral energy is *sapped* by a kind of scepticism" (*E. Dowden*). **Cripple** literally means to maim or mutilate: as here compared, it suggests a deprivation of something comparable to a limb, organ, or other part essential to the retention of one's strength or efficiency; as, "This injury to the ordinary capitalist quite evidently *cripples* business enterprise" (*J. A. Hobson*); "the poet draws life... from the community...and to cut himself off from this source of life is...likely to *cripple*...him" (*Day Lewis*). **Disable** literally means to make unable, but present usage commonly adds to this meaning implications of a crippling or maiming, or of debilitation or enfeeblement that unfits one for all work or for the work for which one has been trained; as, *disabled* soldiers; "Do not let your mind be *disabled* by excessive sympathy" (*Shaw*).

Ana. Enervate, emasculate, *unnerve, unman: impair, *injure, damage: dilute, *thin, attenuate, extenuate.

Ant. Strengthen. — ***Con.*** Energize, *vitalize, activate: *improve, better.

wealthy. *Rich, affluent, opulent.

Ant. Indigent.

wean. *Estrange, alienate, disaffect.

Ana. *Separate, part, divide, sunder, sever, divorce.

Ant. Addict.

weapon. Weapon, arm agree in denoting something used in combat as an instrument of attack or defense. **Weapon** is very general in application for it is applicable to anything that may be used in injuring, destroying, or defeating an enemy or opponent; it may be used in reference to animals as well as to persons, and sometimes even to things; as, a choice of *weapons* for a duel; the cat's main *weapon* is its claws; a display of primitive *weapons* in a museum. "Fight such a fire by rubbing, not by beating. A board is the best *weapon* if you have it" (*Frost*). **Arm** (chiefly in the plural form **arms**) is historically as general in its application as *weapon* when used literally of an instrument of fighting; thus, the call "To *arms!*" was a call to assume all the weapons, including armor, sword, shield, and the like, necessary for warfare, and to fall in line. In modern use, however, *arms* is applied generally to the class of instruments wielded by the arm, such as swords, daggers, bayonets, rifles, carbines, pistols, etc. Of these instruments, swords, daggers, bayonets, and sometimes revolvers and pistols, are also known as *side arms,* because commonly worn at the side or in a belt. Rifles, carbines, and pistols are often distinguished as *firearms.* This latter term, however, is often used more inclusively to comprehend cannon. When it is desired to distinguish rifles, carbines, revolvers, pistols, and all guns of less than one inch in diameter, from heavy firearms, the term *small arms* is used.

weariless. Unwearying, unwearied, tireless, *indefatigable, untiring, unflagging.

Ana. Dogged, pertinacious (see OBSTINATE): assiduous, sedulous, diligent (see BUSY).

Con. Lagging, dawdling, procrastinating (see DELAY): indolent, fainéant, slothful, *lazy.

wearisome. Tiresome, tedious, humdrum, *irksome.

Ana. Fatiguing, exhausting, fagging, tiring (see TIRE, *v.*): dull, *stupid.

Con. Exciting, stimulating, quickening (see PROVOKE).

weary, *v.* *Tire, fatigue, exhaust, jade, fag, tucker.

Ana. Debilitate, enfeeble, *weaken: *depress, oppress, weigh (down).

Con. Energize, *vitalize: animate, *quicken, enliven, vivify.

weave, *v.* **Weave, knit, crochet, braid, plait** (*or* **pleat, plat**), **tat** are here compared as used in reference to the making of fabrics, textiles, wearing apparel, and the like. In this sense they agree in meaning to make such a fabric or textile, or to form such a garment or other article, by interlacing filaments or strands of material. **Weave** usually implies crossing rows of filaments, strands, etc., interlaced into a web, irrespective of method, material, or pattern; as, to *weave* straw; to *weave* baskets; cf., the spider *weaves* its web. Specifically, the term means to interlace warp and weft yarns, by means of a loom, into a textile fabric, the yarns being passed over and under each other according to a predetermined pattern. **Knit** implies the use of a single strand, commonly of yarn, and, in its specific sense, the use of two smooth-pointed needles alternately holding the material and forming a new row of interlacing loops; as, to *knit* a sweater; to *knit* stockings; *knitted* fabrics. **Crochet** specifically differs from *knit* (which covers it as a general term) by implying the use of a single hooked needle and in not necessarily suggesting a building up by successive rows; as, to *crochet* an afghan; to *crochet* lace. **Braid** implies the entwining of three or more strands, as of hair, cord, or cloth strips, by passing one strand over another in such a manner that each strand winds a sinuous course through the ribbonlike or ropelike contexture that is thus produced; as, to *braid* strands of material to make a *braided* rug (that is, a rug made from a lengthy strip that is so braided and then twisted and sewed together to form the shape desired). **Plait** is sometimes identical in meaning with *braid*, but the tendency now is to restrict it to the interlacing of straw or the like, as in hatmaking or basketmaking, whether the method approaches that of braiding or weaving. **Tat** implies the use of a single thread and of one or more shuttles by means of which a series of sliding knots and, usually, loops, is formed in that thread. The drawing up of the thread and the fastening of it in a circle or ring are done by hand.

wedding. *Marriage, matrimony, nuptials, spousal, espousals, wedlock.

wedlock. *Marriage, matrimony, nuptials, spousal, espousals, wedding.

wee. Diminutive, tiny, teeny, weeny, *small, little, minute, microscopic, miniature, petite.

weeny. Tiny, teeny, wee, diminutive, minute, microscopic, miniature, little, *small.

weep. *Cry, wail, keen, whimper, blubber.

Ana. Bewail, bemoan, lament, *deplore: sob, moan, *sigh, groan.

weigh. **1** *Consider, study, contemplate, revolve, excogitate.

Ana. *Ponder, meditate, ruminate, muse: *think, reflect, cogitate, reason, speculate.

2 In form **weigh down, on,** *or* **upon.** *Depress, oppress.

Ana. *Worry, annoy, harass, harry: torment, torture, *afflict, try, rack.

Con. Lighten, *relieve, alleviate, assuage, mitigate, allay.

weight, *n.* **1** Significance, *importance, moment, consequence, import.

Ana. *Worth, value: magnitude, *size, extent: seriousness, gravity (see corresponding adjectives at SERIOUS).

2 *Influence, authority, prestige, credit.

Ana. Effectiveness, efficacy (see corresponding adjectives at EFFECTIVE): *emphasis, stress: powerfulness, potency, forcefulness, forcibleness (see corresponding adjectives at POWERFUL).

weight, *v.* Load, *adulterate, sophisticate, doctor, deacon.

weighty. *Heavy, ponderous, cumbrous, cumbersome, hefty.

Ana. *Onerous, burdensome, oppressive, exacting.

weird. **Weird, eerie** (*or* **eery**), **uncanny** are synonyms only in their derived sense of fearfully and mysteriously strange or fantastic. **Weird,** originally an old English noun meaning fate or destiny, was later applied to one of the Fates, and then to a witch, wizard, or the like, who had powers of divining future events. The transition to an adjective in "the *Weird* Sisters" (in early use the Fates, and in later use, following Shakespeare, witches such as those who warned Macbeth of future events) led to the later sense of unearthly or preternaturally mysterious; as, "When night makes a *weird* sound of its own stillness" (*Shelley*); "*Weird* whispers, bells that rang without a hand" (*Tennyson*). In still more modern use, the term often means little more than strangely or absurdly queer; as, *weird* remarks; "The government sends out *weird* civilians now and again; but McGoggin was the queerest exported for a long time" (*Kipling*). **Eerie,** a word of Scottish origin, does not connote ordinary justifiable or explainable fear, but rather a vague consciousness that unearthly or mysterious, and often malign, powers or influences are at work: the term is chiefly used to create atmosphere rather than to define the character of the thing so described; as, "I there wi' Something did forgather, That pat [put] me in an *eerie* swither [fluster]" (*Burns*); "My people too were scared with *eerie* sounds" (*Tennyson*). **Uncanny,** originally and still a Scottish and North of England term meaning careless or unreliable, has developed in general use an implication of uncomfortable strangeness or of unpleasant mysteriousness that makes it applicable not only to persons or concrete things but to sensations, feelings, thoughts, and the like; as, "to give you the same *uncanny* sensation as when, alone in a room, you think you see something move which ought not to move" (*Bennett*). "The ordinary reader...becomes chilled and daunted in the *eerie* regions to which Poe carries him....Now, the effective vindication of Poe...is that, *weird* and bizarre and abnormal as are the themes he affected, he is essentially a realist in his method....'The Telltale Heart' and....'The Cask of Amontillado' have had a psychological basis in the perversities of a disturbed imagination; hence the *uncanny* fascination of these and other stories of his in a similar taste" (*J. M. Robertson*).

Ana. *Mysterious, inscrutable: *fearful, awful, dreadful, horrific: *strange, odd, queer, curious, peculiar.

welcome, *adj.* *Pleasant, pleasing, agreeable, grateful, gratifying.

Ana. Satisfying, contenting (see SATISFY): congenial, sympathetic (see CONSONANT).

Ant. Unwelcome. — *Con.* Distasteful, *repugnant, repellent, obnoxious.

well, *adj.* *Healthy, sound, wholesome, robust, hale.

Ant. Unwell, ill. — *Con.* Infirm, frail, feeble, *weak.

well-nigh. *Nearly, almost, approximately.

well-timed. Timely, *seasonable, opportune, pat.

Ana. Apt, happy, felicitous, appropriate, fitting (see FIT, *adj.*).

Con. *Premature, untimely: *late, tardy, behindhand.

welter. *Wallow, flounder, grovel.

Ana. Struggle, strive (see ATTEMPT, *v.*).

wench, *n.* **Wench, hussy** (*or* **huzzy**), **minx, baggage** come into comparison when they are used in place of *girl* or *young woman* and with playful or derogatory insinuations. **Wench** is now dialectal in naïve use or archaic in sophisticated use. It is sometimes employed in endearment and sometimes contemptuously (then often implying harlotry) but, commonly in current use, and sometimes in historical use, it suggests the vulgarity and low station of the speaker or imputes them to the person who is so designated. "I am a gentil womman and no *wenche*" (*Chaucer*). "She was both illiterate and vulgar, but the little *wench* had an instinctive knowledge of art and the artist" (*L. Lewisohn*). **Hussy** (etymologically, housewife) was in earliest use applied to a woman or girl not of gentle birth and so acquired various connotations such as rusticity, strength, thrift, rudeness of behavior, and (especially when qualified by *light, bold, brazen*, etc.) questionable morals. In current use, both naïve and sophisticated, it is applied to young women and usually implies rudeness, boldness, impudence, or the like. "A more...impudent *huzzy*, is not to be found in the United States" (*Washington*). "She was a handsome, insolent *hussy*, who mocked at the youth, and yet flushed if he walked along to the station with her as she went home" (*D. H. Lawrence*). **Minx** stresses pertness, sauciness, and mischievousness; it occasionally implies loose morals but more commonly suggests artfulness under the guise of artlessness. "A little saucy rose-bud *minx* can strike Death-damp into the breast of doughty king" (*Browning*). **Baggage** was in earliest use highly derogatory, being applied chiefly to strumpets or prostitutes, especially to those who were camp followers; in more recent use it frequently approaches *minx* in its connotations, though it less often suggests artfulness and sometimes even carries a hint of qualities foreign to *minx*, such as girlishness or lovableness. "A disreputable, daring, laughing, painted French *baggage*" (*Thackeray*). "She has an orphan niece, a pretty, soft-hearted *baggage*" (*Irving*). "Thompson, the solicitor's daughter!....A pretty little *baggage*" (*Meredith*).

wet, *adj.* **Wet, damp, dank, moist, humid** agree in meaning covered or more or less soaked with water or other liquid. **Wet** may be used with no further implications, but it more often specifically implies saturation; as, *wet* clothes; a *wet* sponge; the rain lies in puddles on the *wet* ground. Often, however, the term refers to a surface covered with water or other liquid; as, *wet* pavements; *wet* hands; cheeks *wet* with tears; "grass...*wet* with dew" (*Hemingway*). But *wet* often means merely not dry, or not yet dry, especially when used in reference to paint, ink, or the like, which has been applied to or used on a surface. **Damp** differs from *wet* chiefly in implying a slight or moderate absorption or covering and often in connoting the presence of unpleasant or disagreeable wetness; as, *damp* shoes; the sheets on the bed are *damp;* a *damp* house. However, *damp* usually implies less wetness than that which is commonly suggested by the adjective *wet;* as, give me a *damp* sponge; sheets should be *damp* when they are ironed. **Dank** unequivocally applies only to that which is disagreeably, penetratingly or, from the point of view of health or comfort, dangerously, wet; as, a cold *dank* mist; *dank* forests; *dank* marshes; a *dank* bed; a *dank* cellar. **Moist** often suggests little more than the absence of dryness or a not unpleasant dampness; as, hands *moist* with perspiration; *moist* eyes; *moist* air; *moist* heat. **Humid** is now chiefly used to imply the presence of sensible moisture in the air; as, the *humid* atmosphere of early August; "the *humid* prairie heat, so nourishing to wheat and corn, so exhausting to human beings" (*Cather*); "a firefly...on a *humid* summer's night" (*C. C. Furnas*). It now appears rarely in medical use, *moist* usually being the preferred term; thus, what was once called a *humid* gangrene (as opposed to a *dry* gangrene) is now commonly called a *moist* gangrene.

Ana. Soaked, saturated, drenched, waterlogged (see SOAK, *v.*).

Ant. Dry.

wheedle. Blandish, cajole, *coax.

Ana. Entice, inveigle, *lure, seduce, decoy: ingratiate, insinuate (see corresponding adjectives at DISARMING).

Con. Bully, browbeat, bulldoze, cow, *intimidate.

wheel, *v.* *Turn, revolve, rotate, gyrate, circle, spin, whirl, twirl, swirl, pirouette, eddy.

where. *Whither.

which. *Who, that.

while, *v.* **While, wile, beguile, fleet** come into comparison when they mean to pass time, especially leisure time, without being bored. One **whiles,** or (by confusion with it) **wiles,** *away* a space of time when one causes it to be filled by something pleasant, diverting, or amusing. "They can *while* away an hour very agreeably at a card table" (*Lamb*). "He had tamed every newt and snake and toad... And each one... *Wiled*...his silent time away" (*Shelley*). One **beguiles** not only a space of leisure time but also its tedium or irksomeness when one occupies that time with some agreeable, but not necessarily time-wasting, employment. "And, skilled in legendary lore, the lingering hours *beguiled*" (*Goldsmith*); "Others ...*beguiled* the little tedium of the way with penny papers" (*Hawthorne*). "To *beguile* his enforced leisure, I tried to teach him sundry little tricks" (*Grandgent*). One **fleets** the time when one causes it to pass quickly or imperceptibly: the term, which is comparatively rare in this use, may or may not imply an effort to while time away. "Many young gentlemen...*fleet* the time carelessly" (*Shak.*). "*Fleeting* the quiet hour in observation of his pets" (*G. H. Lewes*).

Ana. Divert, *amuse, entertain.

whim. Freak, *caprice, whimsey, vagary, crotchet.

Ana. Inclination, disposition (see corresponding verbs at INCLINE): *fancy, fantasy, vision, dream: notion, *idea.

whimper, *v.* Weep, *cry, blubber, wail, keen.

whimsey *or* **whimsy.** *Caprice, freak, whim, vagary, crotchet.

Ana. See those at WHIM.

whirl, *v.* Twirl, spin, wheel, swirl, *turn, revolve, rotate, gyrate, circle, pirouette, eddy.

whirlwind. *Wind, gale, hurricane, cyclone, typhoon, tornado, waterspout, twister, breeze, gust, blast, flaw, zephyr.

whit. Mite, smitch, jot, iota, bit, *particle, smidgen, tittle, atom.

whiten, *v.* **1 Whiten, blanch, bleach, decolorize** (*or* **decolorate), etiolate** agree in meaning to change from its original color to white or a near approach to white. To **whiten** is to make white, commonly, though not necessarily, by the application or addition of something from without (as, to *whiten* shoes with pipe clay); to **blanch** is to whiten as by the removal or withdrawal of color or that which gives or develops color (as, to *blanch* almonds by scalding which removes the brown skin; to *blanch* celery by covering the stalks with earth, so as to exclude the sunlight); to **bleach** is to whiten or lighten in color, especially by exposure to sun and air, or by chemical processes (as, to *bleach* linen by spreading it on the grass in the sun; to *bleach* hair by use of peroxide). "The walls...are *whitened* with lime" (*W. Dampier*); "the moon-*blanched* land" (*Arnold*); "a splintered stump *bleached* to a snowy white" (*Cowper*); "There they lay till their bones were *bleached*" (*Tennyson*). **Decolorize** and the rarer **decolorate** imply the deprivation of color as by processes of bleaching or blanching, but they do not carry as strong an implication of whitening as do the previous two words; as, to *decolorize* a colored fabric by the use of chloride of lime. **Etiolate** is a scientific term used in reference chiefly to plants from which sunlight has been excluded, with the result that the natural coloring, or chlorophyll, is not formed; as, *etiolated* plants look sickly; to *blanch* celery is, in scientific language, to *etiolate* it.

Ant. Blacken.

2 Whitewash, gloze, gloss, *palliate, extenuate.

Ana. See those at WHITEWASH.

whitewash, *v.* Whiten, gloze, gloss, *palliate, extenuate.

Ana. *Disguise, cloak, mask, dissemble: condone, *excuse.

whither. Whither, where come into comparison only when they mean the point to which one is moving. **Whither** was formerly the correct adverb to use in this sense, **where** being used with verbs of rest; as, *whither* are you going?; *where* are you staying? *Where* is now used preferably after verbs of motion, except in poetical, elevated, or archaic style.

who. Who, which, that are here compared as relative pronouns. In modern usage **who** refers to persons (less commonly to animals); **which,** to animals or things, but not (in educated use) to persons; **that** may be used of persons, animals, or things. If a relative clause merely conveys an additional or parenthetic idea, *who* or *which* (preceded by a comma) is usually employed: if the relative clause is restrictive or defining, *who* or *which* or *that* may be used, without a preceding comma; as, this gentleman, *who* (not *that*) was here yesterday, desires to see you; the gentleman *who* (or *that*) was here yesterday desires to see you; knock at the first door, *which* you will find open; knock at the first door *that* (or *which*) you find open. In the restrictive use most authorities on grammar and composition prefer *that,* instead of *which* or *who,* except when the relative pronoun follows immediately the demonstrative *that* or is object of a preposition or in the possessive case; but among contemporary writers consistent discrimination between the restrictive *that* and the nonrestrictive *which* or *who* is not common. The preference of some grammatical authorities for *that* instead of *who,* for persons in restrictive clauses, is in present usage mostly unobserved because of the strong tendency to use *who* to express personality.

whole, *adj.* **1** Entire, *perfect, intact.

Ana. Sound, well, *healthy, robust, wholesome: complete, plenary, *full.

Con. *Deficient, defective: impaired, damaged, injured, marred (see INJURE).

2 Whole, entire, total, all, gross are here compared as meaning including each and every part, particle, individual, instance, etc., of, without exception. **Whole** implies that nothing has been omitted, ignored, abated, or the like; as, he devoted his *whole* energy to the task; the *whole* congregation approved the pastor's policy; the *whole* army will be mobilized; the *whole* country was affected. **Entire** may be used in place of *whole* in any of these illustrations; it, however, can, as *whole* cannot, imply actual completeness or perfection from which not only nothing has been taken but to which nothing can be added. "Whom to obey is happiness *entire*" (*Milton*). "He knows that God demands his heart *entire*" (*Cowper*). "Granting *entire* liberty of conscience" (*Macaulay*). **Total** implies that everything without exception has been counted, measured, weighed, or the like; as, the *total* amount gathered in a community-chest campaign; the *total* output of a factory for a particular year. Sometimes, especially when applied to something that is often incomplete, *total* is used as an indication that no reservation is made; as, a *total* eclipse; *total* blindness; a *total* silence. **All,** as here compared, is usually followed by *the* or a possessive pronoun. Sometimes it equals *whole;* as, *all* the city (the *whole* city) was in an uproar: sometimes it comes closer to *entire;* as, *all* their affection (or their *entire* affection) was centered on their children: sometimes it equals *total;* as, *all* their earnings (their *total* or combined earnings) were insufficient for their needs. **Gross** is used, especially in financial statements, in place of *total,* to indicate that deductions, as for costs or expenses, have not yet been made; as, *gross* earnings; *gross* receipts.

Ant. Partial.

whole, *n.* Total, aggregate, *sum, amount, number, quantity.

Ant. Part: constituent: particular. — *Con.* Portion, piece, detail (see PART, *n.*): *item, detail: component, *element, integrant.

wholehearted. Whole-souled, heartfelt, hearty, unfeigned, *sincere.

Ana. Ardent, fervent, *impassioned, passionate: genuine, bona fide, *authentic: earnest, *serious.

wholesale. *Indiscriminate, sweeping.

wholesome. 1 *Healthful, healthy, salubrious, salutary, hygienic, sanitary.

Ant. Noxious. — *Con.* Deleterious, detrimental, *pernicious.

2 Sound, *healthy, robust, hale, well.

Ana. *Strong, sturdy, stalwart, stout.

whole-souled. Wholehearted, heartfelt, hearty, unfeigned, *sincere.

Ana. See those at WHOLEHEARTED.

wicked. Evil, *bad, ill, naughty.

Ana. *Immoral, unmoral, amoral: iniquitous, *vicious, villainous: *abandoned, reprobate, profligate, dissolute.

Con. *Moral, virtuous, righteous, ethical, noble.

wide. *Broad, deep.

Ana. *Spacious, capacious, ample: extended *or* extensive (see corresponding verb at EXTEND).

Ant. Strait. — *Con.* *Narrow: limited, restricted, confined (see LIMIT, *v.*).

wide-awake. *Watchful, vigilant, alert.

Ana. *Aware, alive, awake, conscious, sensible.

wield. Swing, *handle, manipulate, ply.

Ana. *Swing, flourish, brandish, wave: control, direct, manage, *conduct: exercise, drill, *practice.

wig, *v.* Tonguelash, jaw, bawl out, berate, *scold, upbraid, rate, rail, revile, vituperate.

Ana. Reprimand, reproach, rebuke, *reprove, chide.

wilderness. *Waste, desert, badlands.

wile, *n.* Artifice, feint, ruse, maneuver, *trick, stratagem.

Ana. *Deception, fraud, subterfuge, trickery, chicanery, chicane: cunning, *deceit, duplicity, dissimulation, guile.

wile, *v.* *While, beguile, fleet.

Ana. See those at WHILE, *v.*

will, *n.* **Will, volition, conation** are not often interchangeable because they vary greatly in their range of application and because the last two terms are frequently used to designate different steps in the process that is often denoted by *will.* Nevertheless, the terms are frequently confused when they refer to the power or act of making or effecting a choice or decision. **Will** applies not only to this power or act, but also to a psychological entity (once, but now less frequently, called a "faculty") that is the agent of this power, and to the process by which one makes his choice, resolves it into an intention, and puts that intention into effect. In all of these senses *will* may vary greatly in its specific meaning: it may, for example, denote a dominant desire or inclination which determines one's choice (as, "when he was confronted by accidental extinction, he had felt no *will* to resist"—*Cather*), or it may denote a power that derives from one's conception of what is good or right and that tests and accepts or rejects one's desires or inclinations (as, "appetite is the *will's* solicitor, and the *will* is appetite's controller; what we covet according to the one, by the other, we often reject"—*Hooker*). Also, *will* often denotes mainly the determination that is inseparable from action or the effecting of one's decisions (as, "In the government of self, Bismarck's *will* broke down from time to time, as Richelieu's never did; and, after all, the government of self is the supreme test of *will*"—*Belloc*), but it may still be used when frustration or impossibility of action is suggested (as, "spirits disillusioned, who still pathetically preserve the *will* to conquer, even when life no longer presents them with anything worth winning" —*Binyon*). Further, *will* may designate a subjective power, act, process, or the like (as, "luxurious feeling and pathetic imagination, which make no severe call upon ...the *will*"—*Inge*), or an objective force which must be encountered, challenged, obeyed, or the like (as, to submit oneself to the *will* of God; "this method of consulting the popular *will*"—*Bryce*). **Volition,** in contrast to *will*, is a comparatively simple term. In its ordinary and most sharply distinguished sense, it designates merely the act of making a choice or decision: it usually carries an implication of deliberation, but it rarely suggests struggle or determination to put one's decision or choice into effect. Therefore, it is the preferred term when no other implications are desirable or important; as, to surrender one's authority of one's own *volition;* "Our children do not seek school of their own *volition*" (*Grandgent*); "the primal necessity for the faithful is that by an act of the *will*,—not necessarily an emotional act, but an act of pure and definite *volition*,—they should associate themselves with the true and perfect sacrifice" (*A. C. Benson*). **Conation,** which is a technical and not always consistently defined term of psychology, usually implies a striving to get or achieve what is desired or willed. The term may or may not imply a conscious goal: it may suggest clearly directed striving or it may connote the restless aimless strivings which the mind cannot interpret or explain, but it always implies effort rather than choice. "Religion or the desire for the salvation of our souls, 'Art' or the desire for beautification, Science or the search for the reasons of things—these *conations* of the mind...are really three aspects of the same profound impulse" (*H. Ellis*).

Ana. Determination, *decision: *intention, intent, purpose, design: *choice, election, preference: character, *disposition, temper, temperament.

willful *or* **wilful. 1** Deliberate, intentional, *voluntary, willing.

Ana. Determined, decided, resolved (see DECIDE): intended, purposed (see INTEND): *obstinate, stubborn, dogged, pertinacious.

Con. Acquiescent, *compliant: submissive, *tame.

2 Headstrong, intractable, refractory, recalcitrant, *unruly, ungovernable.

Ana. Rebellious, contumacious, factious, *insubordinate: *obstinate, mulish, bullheaded, pigheaded.

Ant. Biddable. — ***Con.*** Tractable, docile, amenable, *obedient.

willing. *Voluntary, intentional, deliberate, willful.

Ana. Prone, open (see LIABLE): inclined, predisposed, disposed (see INCLINE, *v.*).

Ant. Unwilling. — ***Con.*** Reluctant, loath, *disinclined, indisposed, averse.

wily. *Sly, cunning, crafty, tricky, foxy, artful.

Ana. Astute, sagacious, *shrewd: *subtle, subtile: deceitful, cunning (see corresponding nouns at DECEIT).

win. Gain, earn, acquire, *get, obtain, procure, secure.

Ana. Achieve, accomplish, effect (see PERFORM): attain, *reach, compass: *induce, persuade, prevail on *or* upon.

Ant. Lose.

wince. *Recoil, flinch, shrink, blench, quail.

Ana. Cringe, cower (see FAWN): balk, shy, stick, stickle (see DEMUR): squirm, *writhe.

wind, *n.* **Wind, breeze, gale, hurricane, gust, blast, flaw, zephyr, whirlwind, cyclone, typhoon, tornado, waterspout, twister** come into comparison as meaning air naturally in motion. **Wind** is the general term referable to any phenomenon of this sort, whatever its degree of velocity or of force; as, a strong *wind;* there is no *wind* tonight. **Breeze** in general nontechnical use is applied to a relatively light, but fresh wind; as, "The fair *breeze* blew, the white foam flew, The furrow followed free" (*Coleridge*). In meteorology, however, a *breeze* is defined as a wind with a velocity of from 7 to 38 miles an hour. *Breezes* are sometimes further described as *gentle* (8–12 miles an hour), *moderate* (13–18), *fresh* (19–24), *strong* or *stiff* (25–38). **Gale** in ordinary use is applied to a high, destructive wind of considerable velocity and force; technically, the term is sometimes used to cover a strong or stiff breeze, but it is more specifically applied to a wind between 39 and 75 miles an hour. A *whole gale* is described as one having a velocity of 55 to 75 miles an hour. **Hurricane** is popularly applied to any exceedingly violent or devastating windstorm. Its wind velocity in meteorology is usually between 75 and 100 miles an hour (see also under *cyclone*, below). The remaining terms are distinguished on other grounds than those of velocity and force. **Gust, blast, flaw** denote sudden winds of short duration. *Gust* and *blast*, however, may also be applied to one of the bursts or rushes which in alternation with lulls mark the course of many winds. *Gust* suggests a sudden puff of wind; *blast*, a lashing, driving current of wind. "An angry *gust* of wind Puff'd out his torch" (*Tennyson*). "*Blasts* that blow the poplar white, And lash with storm the streaming pane" (*Tennyson*). *Flaw*, which is now rarely used, is applied chiefly to a sudden and quickly passing windstorm; unlike *gust* and *blast*, it never suggests alternation of violence and quiet. **Zephyr** is a poetical term for any very light gentle breeze that delicately touches objects. "Fair laughs the morn, and soft the *zephyr* blows" (*Gray*). The last six terms all imply a rotatory motion of the wind. **Whirlwind** is applied by some meteorologists to any such wind; by others, however, it is restricted in its application to one of limited extent which begins with an inward and upward spiral motion of the lower air and is followed by an outward and upward spiral motion until, usually, there is a progressive motion at all levels. **Cyclone,** on the other hand, is a highly technical term, applicable chiefly to a system of winds that rotate (clockwise in the Southern Hemisphere, counterclockwise in the Northern Hemisphere) about a center of low barometric pressure, and which has in tropical countries a diameter of from 90 to 500 miles and in the temperate zones a diameter that is often as high as 1500 miles. In the tropics, the winds often rotate as rapidly as from 90 to 150 miles an hour and are highly destructive; in temperate regions, their rotation is often as low as from 9 to 15 miles an hour. In the West Indies and in the China Sea, where these cyclones are usually accompanied by rain, thunder, and lightning, and occur in greatest frequency between August and October, they are called *hurricanes;* in the Philippines and also in the China Sea, such a storm is often called a **typhoon.** In the United States, especially in the central Mississippi valley, *cyclone* is often incorrectly used in place of **tornado** for a violent whirling wind which is accompanied by a funnel-shaped cloud and which moves with immeasurable speed in a narrow path over a stretch of territory, often sweeping away everything before it. A **waterspout** is a rapidly rotating funnel-shaped or tubular column of wind, enclosing fresh water, which extends from the under side of an ordinary cumulus or cumulo-nimbus cloud down to a cloud of spray torn up from the surface of the sea or of a large lake. **Twister** is a colloquial term often applied to a tornado, waterspout, or similar windstorm.

winding. **Winding, sinuous, serpentine, tortuous, flexuous, anfractuous** agree in meaning curving first one way and then another. **Winding,** the general and the ordinary term, often implies spiral ascent; as, *winding* stairs; a *winding* mountain road. When applied to things in a horizontal plane, it implies little more than weaving from side to side or in and out through some length, often without apparent plan; as, a *winding* path through a forest; a *winding* cave. "Following the serpent lightning's *winding* track" (*Shelley*). **Sinuous** fundamentally suggests frequent departures from a straight or direct line by curving. "Streams... *Sinuous* or straight, now rapid and now slow" (*Cowper*). In its figurative sense, where it implies moral deviation, this implication remains strong, but in literal use, the word tends to stress the presence of curves in every line, bend, and movement, and the absence of angularity, awkwardness, and the like; as, "the stealthy terror of the *sinuous* pard" (*F. Thompson*); the *sinuous* movements of the leading lady; "gardens bright with *sinuous* rills" (*Coleridge*). **Serpentine** implies curving in a pattern suggested by the smooth and flowing curves of a moving snake; it may or may not imply regularity in the size and shape of the inward and outward curves. "Up the heathy waste, [the road] Mounts, as you see, in mazes *serpentine*" (*Wordsworth*). As applied to a type of compound curve (*serpentine*, as opposed to *oxbow, curve*) or to the front of a bureau or sideboard having such a curve, the word implies that the bulging or convex curve is in the center. **Tortuous,** like *sinuous*, suggests lack of straightness and directness, but in contrast, it stresses the number and intricacy of bendings, twistings, and turnings rather than the constant flow of curves; as, the course of the river became more *tortuous* as we neared its source; "there remained but a *tortuous* defile for carriages down the centre of the street" (*Hardy*). **Flexuous,** a fairly uncommon word except in literary and some scientific use, comes close to *sinuous* in its implications but it stresses the capacity for bending and turning easily and with grace which gives sinuosity of line or movement. "Her lithe body undulating with *flexuous* grace" (*Holmes*). "Man cannot express love...by external signs, so plainly as does a dog, when with...*flexuous* body...he meets his beloved master" (*Darwin*). **Anfractuous,** a learned word, is applied chiefly to passages, crevices, channels, cavities, and the like, which are exceedingly tortuous and complicated; as, *anfractuous* cavities in the ear bone. Figuratively as well as literally, it connotes difficulty in following because of involutions, contortions, and the like; as, "so intricate, so *anfractuous*, so unsearchable are the ways of Providence" (*Henry More*); "among the *anfractuosities* of the human mind...is a superstitious reluctance to sit for a picture" (*Johnson*).

Ana. Curving, bending, turning, twisting (see CURVE, *v.*): circuitous, *indirect, roundabout: *crooked, devious.

Ant. Straight.

window, *n.* **Window, casement, dormer, oriel** agree in meaning an opening in the wall of a building that is usually covered with glass and serves to admit light and air. **Window** is the ordinary general term for the entire structure, including both its framework and the glass or the movable sashes which that framework encloses. "Come to the *window*, sweet is the night air" (*Arnold*). **Casement** properly denotes a window sash attached to one of the upright sides of the frame by hinges; in ordinary use, however, the term is applied to a window or a series of windows (sometimes called *casement* window) with sashes of this character. Oftentimes, however, the word is less definite than this and is poetical in its associations. "Magic *casements*, opening on the foam Of perilous seas, in faery lands forlorn" (*Keats*). **Dormer** (or *dormer window*) denotes a window or a series of windows which stands out from a sloping roof and is typically enclosed by a gable-topped structure. An **oriel** differs from a dormer in projecting from a wall of a building (rather than from a roof) in being at least three-sided (usually either semihexagonal or semisquare in shape), and in being supported by a corbel or bracket (rather than by a rafter as in the case of a dormer). Oriels are often very ornate in design.

wing. Ell, extension, *annex, dependence.

wink, *v.* **Wink, blink** agree in meaning to move one's eyelids. Originally, to **wink** meant to close one's eyes; now it more often means to close and open the eyelids rapidly and usually involuntarily (as, "houses so white that it makes one *wink* to look at them"—*Dickens*) or to close one eye part way as a hint or a command (as, "Asiatics do not *wink* when they have out-manoeuvred the enemy, but...Mahbub Ali...came very near it"—*Kipling*). To **blink** is to wink involuntarily and with eyes nearly shut as if dazzled, or partly blind, or half asleep, or suddenly startled; as, to *blink* when roused from a sound sleep; to *blink* at the report of a gun. "He was... hauled up...*blinking* and tottering...into the blessed sun" (*Stevenson*). Figuratively, *wink* implies connivance, deriving this connotation from the original sense; *blink* (then properly a transitive verb), evasion or shirking; as, to *wink* at neglect of duty; to *blink* the issue.

winner. *Victor, conqueror, champion, vanquisher.

Ant. Loser.

winnow. *Sift, sieve, riddle, screen, bolt.

Ana. *Assort, sort, classify: *separate, divide: select, *choose, single out.

wipe out. *Exterminate, extirpate, eradicate, uproot, deracinate.

Ana. Obliterate, *erase, efface, expunge, blot out: *abolish, extinguish, annihilate: *destroy, demolish.

wisdom. Judgment, *sense, gumption.

Ana. Discretion, *prudence, foresight: judiciousness, sageness, saneness, sapience (see corresponding adjectives at WISE): sagacity, perspicacity, shrewdness (see corresponding adjectives at SHREWD).

Ant. Folly: injudiciousness.

wise, *adj.* **Wise, sage, sapient, judicious, prudent, sensible, sane** come into comparison when they mean having or manifesting the power to recognize the best ends and the best means to attain those ends. One is **wise** who is so discerning in his understanding of persons, conditions, or situations that he knows how to deal with them so as to correct what is wrong in them, how to get the best out of them considering their limitations or difficulties, or how to estimate them fairly and accurately: often also the term implies a wide range of experience or of knowledge or learning, but these implications are found less often in colloquial than in literary English; as, a *wise* teacher never pushes little children too far; "men... temperate, calm, and *wise*" (*Pope*); "knowing himself *wise* in a mad world" (*Meredith*); "it is *wise* to be cautious in condemning views and systems which are now out of fashion" (*Inge*); "a *wiser* and more generous-hearted way to improve the shining hours" (*L. P. Smith*). One is **sage** who is eminently wise, being a philosopher by temperament and experience. The term commonly suggests a habit of profound reflection upon men and events and an ability to reach conclusions of universal as well as immediate value, and has been applied chiefly to persons and utterances that are venerated for their wisdom and good counsel. "What the *sage* poets, taught by the heavenly Muse, Storied of old in high immortal verse" (*Milton*). "For I, who hold *sage* Homer's rule the best" (*Pope*). "The natural crown that *sage* Experience wears" (*Wordsworth*). In somewhat looser use, *sage* often suggests the affectation or the appearance of great wisdom or knowledge, whether the matters concerned be of significance or not; as, "her *sage* plan to make the family feel her worth" (*Meredith*); "the older women seemed to have a kind of secret among themselves, a reason for *sage* smiles and glances" (*V. Sackville-West*). One is **sapient** who (in older and learned use) is sage, in the high sense of the term, or who (in current ironical use) gives the appearance of such sageness; as, "a *sapient*, instructed, shrewdly ascertaining ignorance" (*Pater*). One is **judicious** who is capable of arriving at wise decisions or just conclusions: the term usually suggests the ability to distinguish fact from falsehood and to eliminate all bias, with the result that one's judgments are fair, well-balanced, and levelheaded, as well as sound; as, "I am perfectly indifferent to the judgment of all, except the few who are indeed *judicious*" (*Cowper*); "I really think that, for *wise* men, this is not *judicious*" (*Burke*). "The love of knowledge is not perhaps as insatiable as with us, but it is infinitely more *judicious*" (*Brownell*). One is **prudent** (in the sense here compared: see also under PRUDENCE; PRUDENT, 3) who is so rich in practical wisdom that he is able to keep himself, his passions, and his actions under control and obedient to that which he knows as right and necessary. In this, the earlier and stricter sense of the term, *prudent* implies the use of one's reason in the attainment of the moral virtue that leads to right living, as distinguished from its use in the attainment of knowledge of things which transcend experience; as, "The *prudent* man looketh well to his going" (*Proverbs* xiv. 15); "The *wise* in heart shall be called *prudent*" (*Proverbs* xvi. 21). "Alas! what boots the long laborious quest Of moral *prudence*, sought through good and ill; Or pains abstruse —to elevate the will, And lead us on to that transcendent rest Where every passion shall the sway attest Of Reason" (*Wordsworth*). One is **sensible,** as here compared (see also AWARE, PERCEPTIBLE, MATERIAL), who in word or act does not exceed the dictates of common sense or of good sense: the term suggests a display of intelligence rather than of wisdom, and of natural reasonableness rather than the exercise of the reason; as, "Mr. Collins was not a *sensible* man, and the deficiency of Nature had been but little assisted by education or society" (*Austen*); "To discuss the ultimate career of a child nine years old would not be the act of a *sensible* parent" (*Bennett*); "Whatever he took up he did in the same matter-of-fact *sensible* way; without a touch of imagination, without a spark of brilliancy" (*V. Woolf*). One is **sane** who reveals his healthy-mindedness and levelheadedness in prudent, judicious, or sensible acts and words; as, "*Sane*...persons who are so well balanced that they can adjust themselves to the conditions of every civilization" (*H. Ellis*); "Thankful in his heart and soul that he had his mother, so *sane* and wholesome" (*D. H. Lawrence*).

Ana. Discreet, prudent, foresighted (see under PRUDENCE): *cautious, circumspect, calculating: sagacious, perspicacious, *shrewd, astute: knowing, *intelligent, alert, bright, smart.

Ant. Simple.

wisecrack, *n.* Crack, gag, *jest, joke, jape, quip, witticism.

wish, *v.* *Desire, want, crave, covet.

Ana. *Long, yearn, hanker, pine, hunger, thirst: aspire, pant, *aim: hope, *expect, look for.

Con. Spurn, refuse, *decline, reject, repudiate: scorn, *despise, disdain.

wishy-washy. *Insipid, vapid, flat, jejune, banal, inane.

Ana. Spiritless, enervated, *languid, listless: *weak, feeble: diluted, attenuated, thinned (see THIN, *v.*).

Con. *Spirited, high-spirited, mettlesome, spunky, fiery, peppery, gingery: stimulating, exciting, piquing, provoking (see PROVOKE).

wit, *n.* **1** Wits, intelligence, brain, brains, *mind, intellect, soul, psyche.

Ana. *Reason, intuition, understanding: comprehension, apprehension (see under APPREHEND): sagaciousness *or* sagacity, perspicaciousness *or* perspicacity (see corresponding adjectives at SHREWD).

2 Wit, humor (*or* **humour**), **irony, sarcasm, satire, repartee** are here compared not as close synonyms but as terms designating either a mode of expression or a quality of mind that manifests itself in what one writes or says and that has for its aim (when a mode of expression) or for its effect (when a quality of mind) the arousing of sudden sharp interest that is accompanied by amusement or laughter. **Wit** (etymologically, the power by which one knows, thinks, learns) from the sixteenth century to the eighteenth century denoted intellectual brilliancy and quickness in perception combined with the talent for expressing one's ideas in a sparkling effective manner. In this sense, *wit* may or may not imply the evocation of laughter, but it always suggests a delighting and entertaining; as, "They never meet but there's a skirmish of *wit* between them" (*Shak.*); "Brevity is the soul of *wit*" (*Shak.*); "True *wit* is nature to advantage dress'd, What oft was thought, but ne'er so well express'd" (*Pope*). Gradually, however, the implication of a power to evoke laughter or smiles became definitely associated with the term without any loss of its earlier suggestions of mental acuteness, of swift perception, especially of the incongruous, of verbal felicity, especially as shown in the expression's unexpectedness of turn, and of aptness of application; as, "He is always laughing, for he has an infinite deal of *wit*" (*Addison*); "The sprightly *wit*... the gaiety, That laugh'd down many a summer sun, And kept you up so oft till one" (*Pope*); "If thou hast *wit*, and fun, and fire, And ne'er gude wine did fear" (*Burns*). **Humor** since the early eighteenth century has been contrasted with *wit*, especially as one of two similar yet strikingly different modes of expression manifest in literature. Etymologically, *humor* denotes a fluid; in earliest English use, the term specifically applied to one of the fluids of the body (blood, bile, black bile, phlegm) which in medieval physiology were held to determine by their relative proportions the individual's temperament (as sanguine, choleric, melancholic, or phlegmatic); in later and still current use, *humor* denotes a particular disposition or inclination, especially one marked by eccentricity, oddity, whimsicalness, capriciousness, or the like. It is from this sense that the one here considered derives, for *humor* as a quality expressed in one's written or spoken words seems originally to have been associated with a peculiar disposition that leads one to perceive the ludicrous, the comical, the ridiculous, and to express one's perceptions so as to make others see or feel the same thing. This meaning still prevails; as, he has the gift of *humor;* "she was always saved by her crisp sense of *humour*, her shrewd and mischievous *wit*" (*H. Ellis*). Partly as a result of a revolt against the brittle, unfeeling, often affected, wit of the eighteenth century, but even more as a result of the frequent eighteenth- and nineteenth-century contrasts of the two qualities, wit and humor, especially as evidenced in literary works, *humor* came to imply more human sympathy, more tolerance, more kindliness than *wit*, a deeper sense of the inherent incongruities in human nature and human life, a feeling for the not readily perceived pathos as well as for the not readily perceived absurdness of characters, of situations, of consequences, and the like; hence, writers distinguished the *humor* of Chaucer and Shakespeare from the *wit* of Dryden and Pope; the *wit* of Molière's comedies from the *humor* of Don Quixote. "You expect *wit* from every man of any eminence in the eighteenth century. But of that sympathetic enjoyment of all the manifold contrasts and incongruities of life which we call *humor*, I think Wesley had very little" (*C. T. Winchester*). **Irony** (etymologically, dissimulation) applies chiefly to a way of speaking or writing in which the meaning intended is contrary to that seemingly expressed; as, " 'Of course Constance is always right,' observed Sophia, with ...*irony*" (*Bennett*); "She was assisted by an impetuous girl called Caroline...who by the *irony* of language 'waited' at table" (*C. Mackenzie*). In a more profound use, *irony* applies both to the quality of mind of a person, such as a poet, dramatist, or philosopher, who perceives discrepancies in life and in character (as between the appearance and the reality, or between what is promised and what is fulfilled, or between what is attempted and what is accomplished) and to the form of humor or wit which has for its aim that person's revelation of the mockery implicit in these contradictions; as, "There must be some meaning beneath all this terrible *irony*" (*Shaw*); "The second type [of memorable lines from the poetry of Wilfrid Owen] is...often witty in the seventeenth-century sense, always ironical: it works through a kind of understatement which recalls to us at once the grim and conscious *irony* of those who knew that 'their feet had come to the end of the world' " (*Day Lewis*). **Sarcasm** (derived from a Greek verb meaning to tear flesh like dogs) applies chiefly to a savage, bitter form of humor intended to cut or wound. *Sarcasm* may or may not imply the use of verbal irony (sometimes, in fact, it suggests plain speaking), but it always implies as its aim the intent to make the victim an object of ridicule; as, "In the intercourse of familiar life, he [Swift] indulged his disposition to petulance and *sarcasm*" (*Johnson*); "The arrows of *sarcasm* are barbed with contempt" (*W. Gladden*). **Satire** primarily designates a type of writing the object of which is to hold up vices or follies (especially those of a people, an age, or the like) for ridicule and reprobation. "Jonson's drama is only incidentally *satire*, because it is only incidentally a criticism upon the actual world. It is not *satire* in the way in which the work of Swift or the work of Molière may be called *satire:* that is, it does not find its source in any precise emotional attitude or precise intellectual criticism of the actual world" (*T. S. Eliot*). Only secondarily does the term apply to a quality of mind or a way of looking at men and conditions. "Stamm adores Remson because he [Remson] has no *satire* at all. You have no conception of the terror of such souls in the presence of the barbed glance and the hyena laughter of the humorist" (*Wm. McFee*). **Repartee**, once applied to a witty or clever retort, now applies chiefly to the power or art of answering quickly, pointedly, skillfully, and with wit or humor or, less often, irony or sarcasm. "As for *repartee* in particular, as it is the very soul of conversation, so it is the greatest grace of comedy" (*Dryden*). "I hadn't known Jane spoke so well. She has a clever, coherent way of making her points, and is concise in reply if questioned, quick at *repartee* if heckled" (*R. Macaulay*).

Ana. Quick-wittedness, alertness, brightness, brilliancy, cleverness, smartness, intelligence (see corresponding adjectives at INTELLIGENT): raillery, *badinage, persiflage: pungency, piquancy, poignancy (see corresponding adjectives at PUNGENT).

witchcraft. Wizardry, witchery, sorcery, *magic, alchemy, thaumaturgy.

witchery. *Magic, sorcery, witchcraft, wizardry, alchemy, thaumaturgy.

with. *By, through.

withdraw. 1 *Remove, draw.

Ana. *Separate, part, sever, sunder.

Ant. Introduce: bring.

2 *Go, leave, depart, quit, withdraw, retire, scram, clear out.

Ana. Abscond, decamp, *escape, flee, fly: retreat, *recede.

Con. Arrive, *come.

wither. Wither, shrivel, rivel, wizen come into comparison as meaning to lose or cause to lose freshness and smoothness of appearance. **Wither** implies a loss of vital moisture, such as sap or body fluids, with consequent fading or drying up and ultimate decay or death (as, *withered* leaves, flowers; "[blossoms] which fall before they *wither*"—*Binyon*): the term is often used in an extended sense implying a similar loss of vitality, vigor, animation, or the like; as, "a man, old, wrinkled, faded, *wither'd*" (*Shak.*); "Age cannot *wither* her, nor custom stale Her infinite variety" (*Shak.*); "Art, he [D. H. Lawrence] thought, should flower from an immediate impulse towards self-expression or communication, and should *wither* with the passing of the impulse" (*A. Huxley*). **Shrivel** carries a stronger implication of becoming wrinkled or crinkled or shrunken in size than *wither:* usually also it implies a cause such as a blasting or blighting by or as if by intense heat, or a lack of invigorating influences such as rain or, in extended use, lack of encouragement, stimulation, variety of employments, or the like; as, the leaves *shrivel* in the hot sun; age has *shriveled* her skin; "[The cow's] udder *shrivels* and the milk goes dry" (*Frost*); "When the soul of a youth can be heated above common heat, the vices of passion *shrivel* up" (*Meredith*); "The man whose...practical life [is] *shrivelled* to an insignificant routine" (*H. Ellis*). **Rivel** (which is now rare), like *shrivel*, implies a wrinkling, shrinking, and a blighting, especially by age; as, the peaches are *riveling;* a *riveled* skin. **Wizen**, especially in the past participle, is often preferred to *wither* or *shrivel* when the ideas of shrinking in size, and the wrinkling of the face or other surface, especially through age, lack of nourishment, or the like, are especially stressed; as, a *wizened* old man; the *wizened* face of a poorly nourished boy; "Was there a *wizened* shrub, a starveling bough" (*Browning*).

Ana. *Dry, parch, desiccate: shrink, *contract, constrict.

withhold. Detain, keep back, retain, hold back, reserve, *keep.

Ana. *Restrain, curb, check, bridle, inhibit: refuse, *decline.

Con. Accord, *grant, concede, award, vouchsafe.

withstand. Resist, *oppose, combat, antagonize.
Ana. *Bear, endure, stand, tolerate, suffer: thwart, baffle, balk, foil, *frustrate: assail, *attack, assault.
Con. Submit, *yield, capitulate.

witness, *n.* *Spectator, observer, beholder, looker-on, onlooker, eyewitness, bystander, kibitzer.

witness, *v.* *Certify, attest, witness, vouch for.
Ana. Testify, affirm, *swear, asseverate: subscribe (see ASSENT).

wits. Wit, intelligence, brain, brains, *mind, intellect, soul, psyche.
Ana. See those at WIT, *n.*, 1.

witticism. *Jest, joke, jape, quip, wisecrack, crack, gag.
Ana. *Wit, humor, sarcasm, satire, irony, repartee.

witty, *adj.* **Witty, humorous, facetious, jocular, jocose** come into comparison when they are applied especially to persons and their utterances and mean provoking or intended to provoke laughter, smiles, or the like. **Witty** (cf. WIT) suggests a high degree of cleverness, and quickness in discerning amusing congruities or incongruities; it may connote sparkling pleasantry (especially in repartee), but it often suggests sarcasm or causticity. "A *witty* thing never excited laughter; it pleases only the mind, and never distorts the countenance" (*Chesterfield*). "There's no possibility of being *witty* without a little ill-nature; the malice of a good thing is the barb that makes it stick" (*Sheridan*). "Alan of Lille in the thirteenth century *wittily* said 'Authority has a nose of wax; it can be twisted either way' " (*Inge*). **Humorous** is now a generic term applied to anyone or anything that provokes laughter; as, a *humorous* account of a picnic; a *humorous* lecture; the *humorous* characters of Shakespeare's plays. As opposed to *witty*, however, *humorous* often suggests sensibility rather than intellect, sympathy rather than aloofness in criticism, and sometimes, whimsicality rather than direct insight; thus, Pope is often described as a *witty*, Burns as a *humorous*, poet. "Whose *humorous* vein, strong sense, and simple style May teach the gayest, make the gravest smile" (*Cowper*). "The genius of the Italians is acute...but not subtle; hence, what they think to be *humorous* is merely *witty*" (*Coleridge*). **Facetious,** though originally used without the derogatory connotations it now commonly carries, has always implied mirthfulness or merriment. It now suggests a kind of attempt at wittiness or humorousness that pleases its maker more than others. "Probably the most tedious bore on earth is the man who feels it incumbent upon him always to be *facetious* and to turn everything into a joke" (*J. Fiske*). "A sort of human stratification of which...the body of the orchestra [was] high-brow, the first balcony sentimental and virtuous, the gallery *facetious*" (*M. Austin*). "Curates, mothers-in-law, British workmen, shopwalkers all recognized as fair sport for the *facetious*" (*C. Mackenzie*). **Jocular** also implies a fondness for jesting and joking, but suggests as its motive the desire to make others laugh or to keep them amused. It may or may not imply loquaciousness; it usually suggests a jolly mood or disposition. "His more solemn and stately brother, at whom he laughed in his *jocular* way" (*Thackeray*). "The water-colour lesson enlivened by the *jocular* conversation of the kindly, *humorous* old man was always great fun" (*Conrad*). **Jocose** always suggests waggishness or sportiveness in jesting and joking; it often also carries a strong implication of facetiousness. "Sundry *jocose* proposals that the ladies should sit in the gentlemen's laps" (*Dickens*).
Ana. Amusing, diverting, entertaining (see AMUSE): sparkling, scintillating (see FLASH, *v.*): *caustic, mordant, acrid, scathing: penetrating, piercing, probing (see ENTER).

wizard. *Expert, adept, artist, artiste, virtuoso, dab, dabster.

wizardry. Witchcraft, witchery, sorcery, *magic, alchemy, thaumaturgy.

wizen. *Wither, shrivel, rivel, wizen.
Ana. Shrink, *contract: dwindle, diminish, reduce, *decrease.

wobble *or* **wabble.** Teeter, totter, shimmy, quiver, shiver, shudder, quaver, quake, *shake, tremble, didder, dither.

woe. Grief, anguish, heartache, *sorrow, dole, regret.
Ana. *Distress, suffering, misery, agony, dolor: lamenting, bewailing, bemoaning, deploring (see DEPLORE).
Con. Elation, exultation (see corresponding adjectives at ELATED): *happiness, bliss, felicity.

woman. *Female, lady.

womanish. Womanlike, womanly, ladylike, feminine, *female, effeminate.
Ant. Mannish.

womanlike. Womanly, womanish, ladylike, feminine, *female, effeminate.
Ant. Manlike.

womanly. Womanlike, ladylike, womanish, feminine, *female, effeminate.
Ant. Manly.

wonder, wonderment. Wonder, wonderment, amaze, amazement, admiration are synonymous when they denote the complex emotion aroused by that which is inexplicable, or incomprehensible, and, often, awe-inspiring. **Wonder** and **wonderment** commonly suggest novelty or strangeness in that which excites the emotion, and astonishment or perplexity in the person affected. "And still the *wonder* grew That one small head could carry all he knew" (*Goldsmith*). In its richest use, as in poetry and in criticism, *wonder* often implies rapturous awe. "Nor any power above or under Ever made us mute with *wonder*" (*Shelley*). **Amaze** (chiefly in poetry) and **amazement** stress bewilderment or loss of power to collect one's thoughts; they rarely give any indication of like or dislike for the object exciting the emotion. "Then from *amaze* into delight he fell" (*Keats*). "We seemed stuck to the ground for some time, as if actually petrified with *amazement*" (*Goldsmith*). **Admiration,** which is etymologically close to *wonder*, usually adds the implication of absorbed or ecstatic attention; as, they were lost in *admiration*. "A Kioto painter...who burnt a hole in his roof to admire a moonlight effect, and in his rapt *admiration* omitted to notice that he had set a whole quarter of the city on fire" (*Binyon*).
Ana. Awe, *reverence, fear: astonishment, amazement (see corresponding verbs at SURPRISE): perplexity, puzzlement, bewilderment (see corresponding verbs at PUZZLE).

wont, *n.* *Habit, habitude, practice, usage, custom, consuetude, use.
Ana. Way, manner, fashion (see METHOD).

wonted. Accustomed, customary, habitual, *usual.
Ana. Familiar, *common, ordinary: natural, *regular, normal, typical.

woo, *v.* Court, solicit, *invite, bid.
Ana. Allure, *attract: *lure, entice, seduce: blandish, *coax, cajole, wheedle: pursue, chase, *follow, trail.

wood, *adj.* *Insane, mad, crazy, crazed, demented, deranged, lunatic, maniac, non compos mentis.

wooden. *Stiff, rigid, inflexible, tense, stark.
Ana. *Firm, hard, solid: *heavy, weighty, ponderous: clumsy, *awkward.
Con. Pliant, pliable, *plastic: *supple, limber.

word, *n.* **Word, vocable, term** agree in meaning any

combination of letters capable of being pronounced or written to express the single idea that is by tradition or common consent associated with that combination. **Word** is not only the most commonly used but is the widest in its application and richest in its implications of the units of this group. Its one limitation is that it applies only to a combination of letters or sounds that forms an indivisible whole and that constitutes one of the ultimate units of language. Otherwise it may suggest a concept, designate a person or thing, assert being, mode of being, or a specific action, express a relation or connection, or the like; as, "the law of the land" is a phrase of five *words;* he knew no *words* to express so subtle an idea; purity of style depends on the choice of *words.* **Vocable** denotes a word, but it throws the emphasis upon the word as pronounced or spelled rather than upon its denotation or meaning. "The word *star* therefore has, in our r-slighting speech, two pronunciations, *stah* and *star,* according to what comes after it. So it is, potentially, with every r-tailed *vocable*" (*Grandgent*). "A flat denial of poetic possibilities, in the case of any *vocable,* is liable to disastrous refutation by a triumphant instance of the 'poetizing' (as Goldsmith calls it) of that very *word*" (*Lowes*). **Term** differs from *word* in being applicable not only to words as units of language but to phrases that express a single idea and form therefore one of the units of expression; as, legal *terms* such as "right of way" or "cease and desist." *Term* further differs from *word* in applying only to such words and phrases as have a precisely limited, often technical, use or meaning. It therefore usually implies need of clear definition and of strict adherence to this definition. "As adopted by Augustus, it [the word *princeps*] was a popular appellation, not a *term* of constitutional art, defining a status rather than an office" (*Buchan*). "This *term* ['moral sense'] was long a stumbling-block in the eyes of innocent philosophic critics, too easily befooled by *words*" (*H. Ellis*). "The outlook, domestic and international, was still what those who think in *terms* of colour call black. The Irish question, the Russian question, the Italian-Adriatic question, all the Asiatic questions, remained what those who think in *terms* of angles call acute" (*R. Macaulay*).

Ana. Expression, idiom, *phrase, collocation, locution.

wordbook. *Dictionary, lexicon, glossary, onomasticon, gazetteer, synonymicon.

wordy. **Wordy, verbose, prolix, diffuse, redundant** come into comparison when they are applied to a person's style in writing or speaking, or to a discourse or part of a discourse, and mean using or manifesting the use of more words than are necessary to express the thought. **Wordy** often carries no further implications, though it may suggest garrulousness or loquacity when the reference is to that which is spoken; as, *wordy* arguments; a *wordy* discussion about nothing important; a *wordy* essay. The term is also applicable directly or indirectly to persons as well as to their utterances; as, "a *wordy,* prolegomenous babbler" (*Stevenson*). **Verbose** suggests overabundance of words as a literary fault characteristic especially of a writer or public speaker or of an entire work or speech: it often implies resulting dullness or obscurity of expression, or the author's lack of incisiveness, confusion of ideas, or grandiloquence; as, a *verbose* style; a dull *verbose* narrative; his letters are full of interesting details but they are never *verbose.* **Prolix** implies such attention to minute details as to extend what is written or told beyond all due bounds: the term carries a far stronger implication of tediousness or wearisomeness than *verbose;* as, "these enormously *prolix* harangues" (*Coleridge*); "This, then, was Nuflo's story, told not in Nuflo's manner, which was infinitely *prolix*" (*Hudson*). **Diffuse** usually implies verbosity, but it throws the emphasis upon the lack of compactness and condensation needed for pointedness and for strength of style: consequently it often attributes flabbiness, looseness, or desultoriness to that which is written. "The one can be profuse on occasion; the other is *diffuse* whether he will or no" (*J. R. Lowell*). "Though Seneca is long-winded, he is not *diffuse;* he is capable of great concision" (*T. S. Eliot*). **Redundant** applies chiefly to anything which is superfluous, but as here considered it applies especially to words or phrases which are superfluous because repetitious or unnecessary (as, to cut out all *redundant* words in a poem) or to writers, speakers, and utterances that manifest a tendency to indulge in redundancies (see *redundancy* under VERBIAGE). "The naturally copious and flowing style of the author is generally *redundant*" (*J. Mackintosh*). "She had been, like nearly all very young writers, superfluous of phrase, *redundant*" (*R. Macaulay*).

Ana. *Inflated, turgid, tumid, flatulent: bombastic, *rhetorical: loquacious, garrulous, voluble, *talkative.

Con. Laconic, *concise, terse, succinct, summary, pithy, compendious.

work, *n.* **1 Work, labor** (*or* **labour**), **travail, swink, toil, drudgery, grind** agree in meaning effort or exertion directed to the accomplishment of an end, or the employment or activity which involves such expenditure of effort or exertion. **Work** is the most comprehensive of these terms, for it may imply activity of body, or of mind, or of a machine, or, in its largest sense, of any natural force. It is applicable not only to the exertion, and to the employment which involves such exertion (as, "[to the inspired artist] *work* is what alcohol is to the dipsomaniac"—*C. E. Montague;* to take up one's *work*) but also to that which is accomplished or produced by such exertion (as, this statue is the *work* of a gifted but unknown sculptor; you have done a day's *work* in three hours) and to the material upon which one is employed (as, put your *work* away). **Labor** (see also CHILDBIRTH) differs from *work* not so much in its specific denotations as in its implications: as a rule, it implies human work, and therefore suggests physical or intellectual exertion only: it may suggest more strenuousness than *work,* but this difference is not as common as generally believed; as, "*Labour* is doing what we must; leisure is doing what we like; rest is doing nothing whilst our bodies and minds are recovering from their fatigue" (*Shaw*); "the larger part of the *labour* of an author in composing his work is critical *labour;* the *labour* of sifting, combining, constructing, expunging, correcting, testing" (*T. S. Eliot*); "Sir William Meredith, anticipating the *labors* of Romilly, protested against the barbarity and the inefficacy of a criminal code" (*G. O. Trevelyan*). **Travail** (see also CHILDBIRTH), now largely a bookish or literary word, carries a stronger implication of painful effort or exertion than does *labor:* in fact, that connotation is often so strong that the term tends to denote suffering rather than labor; as, "The sentimentalist escapes the stern *travail* of thought" (*Lowes*); "It breaks his heart... That all his hours of *travail* here for men Seem yet in vain" (*V. Lindsay*). **Swink,** an Old and Middle English term, now archaic or dialectal, is used chiefly when the idea of heavy physical labor is to be suggested: it is now replaced largely by **toil,** when labor that is prolonged and highly fatiguing, but not necessarily physical, is implied. "His tythes payed he ful faire and wel, Bothe of his propre *swink* and his catel" (*Chaucer*); "Who recks of summer sweat and *swink*...?" (*A. Austin*). "Ye stopped your ears to the warning—ye would neither look nor heed— Ye set your leisure before their *toil* and your lusts above their need" (*Kipling*); "For years he led a life of unremitting physical *toil*" (*Buchan*). **Drudgery** implies dull, irksome, and distasteful labor; as, "[Johnson] relieved the *drudgery* of his Dictionary...by taking an active part in the composition of the *Adventurer*" (*Boswell*) [cf. Johnson's definition of a lexicographer as "...a harmless *drudge*"]; "*labor* of the hands...pursued to the verge of *drudgery*" (*Thoreau*). **Grind** applies to labor that one finds toil or drudgery and, also, trying to the nerves or exhausting to mind or body; as, "The long *grind* of teaching the promiscuous and preoccupied young" (*H. James*).

Ana. Exertion, *effort, pains, trouble: *task, duty, job, chore.

Ant. Play.

2 Work, employment, occupation, calling, pursuit, métier, business come into comparison only when they denote the specific kind of labor or activity in which a person engages seriously, especially (but not invariably) as a means of earning a livelihood. **Work** is the most general of these terms, being applicable to any kind of labor, whether physical or intellectual, whether carried on by the hour, day, week, month, or longer period, and whether done for pay or not, and, if the former, whether compensated for by an employer or out of one's fees for services or the profits of one's business; as, to seek *work;* to be out of *work;* his *work* is that of a railroad engineer; he is at *work* on his book or in his office or in his garden. **Employment** may denote the work (or other activity) in which one employs or uses one's time. "She sat quietly down to her book after breakfast, resolving to remain in the same place and the same *employment* till the clock struck one" (*Austen*). As here compared, however, it implies work for which one has been engaged and is being paid for by an employer or master; as, he is unable to find *employment;* his *employment* is that of a bookbinder (or a reporter, or a chauffeur). "I...went from town to town, working when I could get *employment*" (*Goldsmith*). **Occupation,** as here compared, though often used interchangeably with *employment,* is actually more inclusive for it does not necessarily connote service under an employer or master, and may be referred to the work of any kind in which one engages habitually or for which one has been trained; as, he is by *occupation* a teacher (or an editor, or an architect, or a motorman, or a bookbinder, or a shoemaker); she is a stenographer by *occupation,* but is at present unemployed; one loses one's *employment* (not one's *occupation*) but one follows an *occupation* (not an *employment*). "These are the chief questions which a man would ask...whom circumstances allowed to choose his *occupation*" (*Inge*). **Calling** is sometimes used in place of *occupation,* often somewhat euphemistically, with the implication that one has been called to it by God, or by one's nature or special tastes; as, his *calling* is that of a preacher; the learned *callings;* to make one's choice of a *calling.* "Miss Jekyll had received that luckiest of fairy-gifts, a *calling*...something that she loved to do" (*L. P. Smith*). **Pursuit** may also be used in place of *occupation,* but it is still more often found in the sense of the trade, craft, profession, business, or art that is followed, often, but far from exclusively, as a means of earning one's living. "They never have to learn to adjust themselves to people whose tastes and *pursuits* are different from their own" (*B. Russell*). "Though it was supposed to be proper for them to have an *occupation,* the crude fact of money-making was still regarded as derogatory, and the law, being a profession, was accounted a more gentlemanly *pursuit* than business" (*E. Wharton*). **Métier,** originally a French term for trade or craft, or, more generally, work, is much used in English with some of the connotations of the words *calling* and *pursuit;* as, he believed that writing novels was his *métier.* In careful use, however, it often follows its French significance; as, this hairdresser knows his *métier.* **Business** is often used in the sense of *work* or, sometimes, of *occupation;* as, "the *business* of keeping a lunatic asylum" (*Baron Denman*); "I hated, and still hate, the awful *business* of research" (*Bennett*).

Ana. *Trade, craft, handicraft, art, profession.

3 Work, product, production, opus, artifact (*or* **artefact**) come into comparison only when they denote a concrete thing that is made or brought into being by the exertion of effort and the exercise of skill. **Work** is now applied to anything that comes under this general definition, such as something that is manufactured or that is constructed or built, only when used without reference to a particular concrete thing (as, the *work* reveals the workman) or when used with a possessive (as, the cabinetmaker is proud of his *work;* to preserve from destruction every church that is known as Christopher Wren's *work*) or in certain combinations (as, fire*works*, wax*works*). Otherwise it is applied to a thing that results from mental labor, especially, but not always, one involving composition and artistry in execution (in the latter case sometimes specifically called a *work of art*); thus, the *works* of Keats include his poems and, usually, his prefaces; the *works* of Beethoven are his musical compositions; "The Thinker" [a statue] is one of Rodin's *works;* the new history of literature promises to be a monumental *work.* **Product,** as here narrowly considered (for its applications and specific implications see PRODUCT, 2), is applied chiefly to articles of manufacture, whether they are made by hand or with the aid of machinery; as, the factory seeks a market for its *products;* she was unwilling to part with the embroideries and laces that were the *products* of her handiwork. "Synthetic materials impart their special properties to perfumes and flavors and when properly used, increase rather than diminish the value of the *product*" (*A. C. Morrison*). When, as sometimes happens, *product* rather than *work* is used of a poem, novel, statue, or the like, it is often either depreciative in its connotations or definitely noncommittal. "This dull *product* of a scoffer's pen" (*Wordsworth*). "Shall a literary *product* reveal the spirit of its age and be silent as to the spirit of its author!" (*G. Matheson*). **Production** is sometimes used where *work* would be the commoner and the idiomatic term, but it is avoided by many writers or speakers who look upon it as a formal or slightly bombastic word; others, however, prefer it when it is qualified by a superlative; as, the noblest *productions* of literary genius; the finest *productions* of Michelangelo. "So one [Pygmalion] whose story serves at least to show Men loved their own *productions* long ago, Wooed an unfeeling statue [Galatea] for his wife" (*Cowper*). In current use, it is applied to a theatrical or similar performance viewed as the work of a producer or director who is responsible for all the details; as, the recent "Hamlet" was a magnificent *production.* **Opus** (the Latin term for *work*) is applied almost exclusively (except in humorous use) to a musical composition or group of compositions; it is commonly followed by a number designating the order of its publication or, sometimes, execution; as, Beethoven's *opus* 27. **Artifact** is restricted in its application to an artificial as distinguished from a natural product. It usually implies human workmanship, but it is seldom applied to any product except that of primitive men. The term is used largely by archaeologists as a general designation for primitive weapons and implements as well as works of art; as, flints, arrowheads, and other *artifacts* of stone.

Ana. Article, object, *thing: accomplishment, achievement, performance (see corresponding verbs at PERFORM).

work, *v.* Operate, function, *act, behave, react.

worked. **Worked, wrought** come into comparison as past participles of the verb *work.* They are especially distinguished when used adjectivally in the sense of subjected to some treatment or process. **Worked** now applies chiefly to fabrics or materials which are embellished with needlework, engraving, or the like, or to things made from such fabrics or materials: in this sense, the term is often equivalent to *embroidered, chased, engraved,* etc.; as, *worked* canvas for chair seats; *worked* napkins; *worked* initials on a handkerchief; the *worked* case of a watch. **Wrought** is preferred to *worked* when molding or fashioning into shape is implied, though it is often used when any more or less laborious method of refining, polishing, decorating, carving, or the like, is implied; as, "cups of *wrought*...gold" (*Shelley*); "The screen...of gilt Spanish leather, stamped and *wrought* with a rather florid Louis-Quatorze pattern" (*Wilde*); "first drafts [of poems]...*wrought*...down by long labour into their final structure" (*J. W. Mackail*). *Wrought* is also used in opposition to *raw,* or *unprocessed,* and implies that the material so described has been subjected to some process that fits it for industrial or other use; thus, *wrought* silk is silk that has been spun; *wrought* iron (usually contrasted with *cast* iron) is iron that has been so processed that it is tough, yet relatively soft, and therefore malleable.

worker. **Worker, workman, workingman, laborer, navvy, craftsman, handicraftsman, mechanic, artisan, hand, operative, roustabout** come into comparison because they mean, or have meant, or have come to mean, one who earns his living by labor, especially by manual labor. **Worker,** by far the most comprehensive and least specific of these terms, applies to anyone who earns his living by work of hand or brain; as, office *workers;* factory *workers;* unions for all types of *workers.* **Workman** does not, in any of its senses, imply any specific kind of work, but in all but its extended senses it commonly implies manual labor. It may be applied to one engaged to do a specified piece of work or to help in the construction of something requiring many workers: it may also be applied to a skilled or to an unskilled worker. Usually, it has implied opposition to *employer,* or *manager,* or *foreman,* or the like; as, there were 50 *workmen* on the job; he is the most competent *workman* in our employ; they are about to add 200 *workmen* to their force. In extended use, the term is applicable to a worker in any field, whether he works with his hands or with his mind, provided he makes, constructs, invents, or creates something. "High-minded and untiring *workmen,* they have spared no pains to produce a poetry finer than that of any other country in our time" (*Amy Lowell*). **Workingman** is far more restricted in its range of application than *workman,* and is, in spite of varying legal definitions, applied commonly to a wage-earner such as one who at an hourly, daily, or weekly rate pursues a trade (carpentry, masonry, plumbing, etc.), or is employed in a mercantile, manufacturing, or industrial establishment. Consequently, the plural of the term usually applies to a class as distinguished from industrialists, merchants, professional men, and the like. **Laborer,** and its British synonym **navvy,** like the preceding terms, are not always fixed in their application, but they commonly designate one on a construction or excavation job whose work demands strength and physical exertion rather than skill; thus, a bricklayer's *laborer* (usually called *helper* in the United States) carries bricks and mortar and mixes mortar; "the wages of the *navvy* who swings a sledgehammer" (*Shaw*). In general, in American use, loaders, carriers, wheelers, cleaners, diggers, and the like, are classified as *laborers;* as, day *laborers;* farm *laborers.* **Craftsman** and **handicraftsman** strictly apply to one who is a skilled workman in a craft or handicraft (for these terms see TRADE, 1). The terms are now as common in general as in technical use. *Craftsman,* in current use, often applies to a worker who is a competent technician or who is versed in the technique of his art, profession, trade, or the like. It is especially used of artists, writers, playwrights, skilled artificers, and the like; as, "Pope... one of the most consummate *craftsmen* who ever dealt in words" (*Lowes*); "The good *craftsman* constructs his product as perfectly as he can....He becomes an artist in so far as he treats his materials also for themselves" (*S. Alexander*). *Mechanic* and *artisan* in their earliest English senses applied to one of a class of workmen. **Mechanic,** in its older sense, usually applied to one of the class now called *workingmen,* but first suggested employment in manual work and later in a factory or industry requiring operation of machines; as, "An English *mechanic*..., instead of slaving like a native of Bengal for a piece of copper, exacted a shilling a day" (*Macaulay*). In current use, *mechanic* applies specifically to a workman skilled in the repair or adjustment of machines or engines; as, an automobile *mechanic;* an aviator's *mechanic.* **Artisan** is now more often opposed to *artist* (for this sense, see under ARTIST, 1) than employed as a designation of a particular type of workman. When the term is used in the latter sense, however, it commonly applies to one who is skilled in his trade, such as a carpenter, a weaver, a bootmaker, or the like; as, "We pass from the weavers of cloth to a different class of *artisans*" (*Macaulay*). **Hand** is a colloquial term, usually applied to one of a crew, a force, a gang, or the like, of workmen, but sometimes to an owner's or proprietor's helper or assistant; as, a deck *hand;* a farm *hand;* mill *hands;* "My son has lately lost his principal *hand* by death" (*Franklin*). **Operative,** a general term suggestive of modern industrial conditions, applies to any workman employed in a mill, a manufactory, or any industry utilizing machines: it has now nearly displaced the older terms *mill hand, factory hand,* etc.; as, the steel works employ as many as 2000 *operatives.* **Roustabout** (chiefly United States) is often merely another term for *laborer,* but it carries distinguishing implications such as muscular fitness for exceedingly heavy work, roughness, and, often, migratory habits; as, longshoremen and other *roustabouts.*

Ant. Idler.

workingman. Workman, laborer, *worker, navvy, craftsman, handicraftsman, mechanic, artisan, operative, hand, roustabout.

workman. *Worker, workingman, laborer, navvy, craftsman, handicraftsman, mechanic, artisan, operative, hand, roustabout.

world. Universe, *earth, cosmos, macrocosm.

worldly. Mundane, *earthly, terrestrial, terrene, earthy, mortal, sublunary.

Ana. Temporal, *profane, secular: *material, physical, corporeal: *carnal, fleshly, sensual.

Con. *Celestial, heavenly, empyrean: sacred, *holy, spiritual, divine, religious.

worn. *Haggard, careworn, pinched, wasted, cadaverous.

Ana. Exhausted, *tired, wearied, fatigued, fagged, jaded (see TIRE, *v.*): gaunt, scrawny, skinny, *lean.

Con. Refreshed, restored, rejuvenated (see RENEW): *vigorous, lusty, energetic, strenuous.

worried. Anxious, concerned, careful, solicitous. See under CARE, *n.*

Ana. Apprehensive, afraid, *fearful: troubled, distressed (see TROUBLE, *v.*): harassed, harried (see WORRY, *v.*).

Con. Comforted, solaced, consoled (see COMFORT, *v.*).

worry, *v.* **Worry, annoy, harass, harry, plague, pester, tease, tantalize** come into comparison when they mean to torment so as to destroy one's peace of mind or to disturb one acutely. **Worry,** in the sense here considered, retains implications derived from an earlier meaning, to attack repeatedly and savagely by biting or shaking, as a hound killing its quarry. "That dog, that had his teeth before his eyes, To *worry* lambs and lap their gentle blood" (*Shak.*). For it stresses incessant attacking or goading and an intention (sometimes an effect) of driving the victim to desperation or defeat; as, to pursue a policy of *worrying* the enemy. "*Worry* him out till he gives his consent" (*Swift*). "Brother should not war with brother, And *worry* and devour each other" (*Cowper*). The sense of **annoy** here considered is not always clearly distinguishable from its other sense (see ANNOY, 1), the word being sometimes so used that the emphasis is both on the agent's acts or intentions and on the victim's subjective reactions; when, however, the former is stressed, it implies molestation, interference, intrusion, or the like, to the point of becoming a nuisance. "Therefore has he [the father] closely mew'd her up, Because she will not be *annoy'd* with suitors" (*Shak.*). "Wilt thou [Samson] then serve the Philistines with that gift Which was expressly given thee to *annoy* them?" (*Milton*). "Clouds of flies...*annoyed* our horses" (*Borrow*). **Harass** usually implies persecution, especially continued petty persecutions, or burdensome demands, or exactions that drive one to distraction or exhaust one's nervous or mental power. "It is good for boys and girls to know that their father can be *harassed* by worries and their mother worn out by a multiplicity of details" (*B. Russell*). **Harry,** though often used interchangeably with *harass,* more vividly suggests maltreatment and oppression. "In 1903 throughout the Islands death was the one event in a *harried* life that brought tranquillity and peace to its victims" (*V. Heiser*). "How on earth can you rack and *harry* and post a man for his losings, when you...live in the same Station with him?" (*Kipling*). **Plague** implies an affliction or infliction comparable to that of a devastating epidemic disease. Though greatly weakened in its implications in modern use, it still suggests a tormentor and an agonized or suffering victim. "The gods are just, and of our pleasant vices Make instruments to *plague* us" (*Shak.*). "He went away to his regiment two days ago, and I trust I shall never be *plagued* with him again. He is the greatest coxcomb I ever saw" (*Austen*). **Pester** implies the power to annoy past endurance, as by numbers or by repetition of attacks suggestive of the discomforts of an infestation of vermin; as, to be *pestered* by beggars; to *pester* the authorities with complaints. "Adrian...would accept him entirely as he seemed, and not *pester* him...by trying to unlock his heart" (*Meredith*). **Tease** derives its implications from either of two of its earlier literal senses. When it implies repeated attempts to break down one's resistance, by successive appeals, or importunities, it derives its implications from *teasing,* or breaking down the tangles in fibers, as in the combing of wool or flax. "I have not been to the Rooms this age...except...last night with the Hodges's...: they *teased* me into it" (*Austen*). When it implies an attempt to provoke or "get a rise out of one" by raillery or tormenting, it derives its implications from *teasing,* or scratching the surface of cloth by a teasel, to raise a nap. "Not soon provoked, however stung and *teased,* And, if perhaps made angry, soon appeased" (*Cowper*). **Tantalize** stresses the awakening of expectation and then (often wantonly) its frustration. "The mirage...which so *tantalized* the French soldiers in Egypt" (*J. Tyndall*). "Merciful love that *tantalizes* not, One-thoughted, never-wandering, guileless love" (*Keats*).

Ana. Disquiet, disturb, *discompose, perturb, agitate, upset: torment, try, torture (see AFFLICT): oppress, persecute, *wrong, aggrieve.

Con. *Comfort, solace, console.

worry, *n.* Anxiety, concern, *care, solicitude.

Ana. *Apprehension, foreboding, misgiving, presentiment: anguish, woe, heartache (see SORROW): *uncertainty, doubt, mistrust.

Con. *Equanimity, composure, sang-froid: *certainty, assurance, certitude.

worship, *n.* Adoration, veneration, reverence. See under REVERE, *v.*

Ana. *Honor, homage, obeisance: respect, *regard, esteem, admiration.

Con. *Profanation, desecration, sacrilege: execration, cursing (see corresponding verbs at EXECRATE).

worship, *v.* **1** Adore, venerate, *revere, reverence.

Ana. *Exalt, magnify: respect, esteem (see under REGARD, *n.*).

Con. *Execrate, curse: *despise, scorn, disdain, contemn.

2 *Adore, idolize.

Ana. Love, dote on *or* upon (see LIKE): admire, regard (see under REGARD, *n.*).

Con. *Hate, abhor, detest.

worth, *n.* **Worth, value** are close synonyms in more than one of their senses. Both **worth** (originally an Anglo-Saxon word) and **value** (derived from Latin, through Old French) in their earliest and still current senses denote the equivalent, especially in money, but also in goods, services, or the like, that is or may be given or asked in exchange for another thing such as goods, services, money, or the like; as, to determine the *worth* or *value* of a diamond bracelet (or of a tract of land, a building, a stand of timber, or one's services); the *value,* or *worth,* of these gold coins with reference to their purchasing power is greater than their *value,* or *worth,* as bullion; the present *value,* or *worth,* of the dollar in francs; he always gets his money's *worth,* or gets full *value* for his money; to promise to pay in three months one hundred dollars for *value* received (*value* being the idiomatic term in this phrase). When, however, *worth* and *value* mean the quality of being useful, important, excellent in its kind, or highly desirable or meritorious, they do not always come so closely together. For *worth,* far more often than *value,* applies to that which is excellent intrinsically, as by being superior morally, spiritually, intellectually, aesthetically, or the like; as, "Of ancient race by birth, but nobler yet In his own *worth*" (*Dryden*); "*Worth* makes the man, and want of it, the fellow" (*Pope*). "Archer's...coherent thinking, his sense of the *worth* of order and workmanship" (*C. E. Montague*). *Value,* often influenced by *valuation,* applies more frequently than *worth* to the excellence, usefulness, importance, and the like, imputed to a person or thing or to the degree in which that person or thing is regarded as excellent, useful, important, etc., especially in its relation to other things; thus, one gives an inflated *value* (not *worth*) to a certain poem; "there is always a gap between their appreciation of a man's *value* [far better than *worth*] at any moment and his real weight" (*Belloc*). "Nothing in the [church] service was slighted, every phrase and gesture had its full *value*" (*Cather*). *Value* therefore is in current use applied, as *worth* is not, to something, such as a principle, a quality, a condition, a substance, or the like, which is regarded as important, useful, desirable, or of value in any way, sometimes in its relation to other things, sometimes in the degree which seems proper or fitting to it, and sometimes absolutely. "We may call food a *value* for the animal...not because it is pleasant to him, but because it is nutritious and fills his need of life" (*S. Alexander*). "The opinion...widely held, that while science...contemplates a world of facts without *values*, religion contemplates *values* apart from facts" (*Inge*).

Ana. *Excellence, merit, virtue, perfection: *use, usefulness, utility.

wrack *or* **rack,** *v.* *Ruin, wreck, dilapidate.

Ana. *Destroy, demolish, raze: *abolish, extinguish, annihilate.

Con. *Save, preserve, conserve.

wraith. *Apparition, phantasm, phantom, fetch, ghost, spirit, specter, shade, revenant, spook, haunt.

wrangle, *v.* Quarrel, altercate, squabble, bicker, spat, tiff. See under QUARREL, *n.*

Ana. Argue, dispute, debate (see DISCUSS): fight, cope, *contend.

Con. *Agree, concur, coincide.

wrangle, *n.* *Quarrel, altercation, squabble, bickering, spat, tiff.

Ana. *Argument, dispute, controversy: *discord, contention, dissension, conflict.

wrath. Rage, indignation, ire, fury, *anger.

Ana. Resentment, dudgeon, *offense: *acrimony, acerbity, asperity.

wrathful. Irate, indignant, *angry, mad, acrimonious.

Ana. Infuriated, incensed, enraged (see ANGER, *v.*).

Con. *Forbearing, tolerant, clement, lenient, indulgent, merciful.

wreck, *v.* *Ruin, wrack, dilapidate.

Ana. *Destroy, demolish, raze: *injure, damage, impair.

Con. *Save, preserve, conserve.

wretched. *Miserable.

Ana. *Despondent, forlorn, hopeless, despairing: doleful, dolorous, *melancholy: abject, sordid, *mean: pitiable, piteous, *pitiful.

writer. Writer, author, composer come into comparison in their concrete applications to one who gives expression to his ideas or feelings, but they are not, as a rule, synonyms. **Writer** is a comprehensive term applied to anyone whose occupation or chief employment is that of expressing his ideas in words, especially for others to read. As an occupational designation, it implies that one's profession is writing for publication, and it covers novelists, essayists, poets, dramatists, editors, journalists, and the like; as, a free-lance *writer;* news *writers;* a *writers'* club. **Author,** in its comprehensive sense (see MAKER), may be applied to anyone who is known as the producer of a given painting, a given statue, a given musical composition, or the like; as here considered, it is applied only to a person who has written for publication. It differs from *writer* in placing less stress upon the profession and more upon the fact of having written and published a book, an article, or the like, under one's own name or a pen name; thus, one may decide to become a *writer* (better than *author*); the *authors* (better than *writers*) of some well-known books, such as *David Harum*, were not *writers* by profession. *Author*, in this sense, is also distinguished from *reviser, adapter, editor, dramatizer*, and the like, for it always retains its basic implication of originator, or source. **Composer,** like *author*, may be used generally and specifically. But because it emphasizes the bringing together of a number of things so as to form a whole (a composition), it is applied most frequently to those expressions of ideas or feelings achieved by bringing together musical tones, words, colors, etc., so as to form an artistic pattern. It is the specific term for the author of a musical composition (as, the *composer* of the Peer Gynt suite) but, although this is its commonest application, it is also applicable to poets, painters, designers, and others when composition, rather than creation or representation, is the end; as, Shakespeare was not only a dramatist but a *composer* of lyrics.

writhe. Writhe, agonize, squirm are comparable when they mean to twist or turn in physical or mental distress. **Writhe** always carries vivid suggestions of convulsive contortions, as of those of one in the throes of death, in a paroxysm, in an instrument of torture, or in a trap and fruitlessly struggling to escape. When used in reference to physical distress, it commonly also implies excruciating pain. "Childhood and youth and age *writhing* in savage pains" (*Shelley*). When used figuratively, in reference to mental distress, it usually implies a torturing sense of shame, of bafflement, or the like; as, he *writhed* under the questioning of the cross-examiner. "Thus, at every march, the hidden enemy became bolder and the regiment *writhed*...under attacks it could not avenge" (*Kipling*). **Agonize,** a word derived from two sources, sometimes evokes the image of one in the pangs of death, struggling and in anguish; sometimes it evokes the picture of one wrestling, or straining, with might and main to achieve the difficult victory. "Bled, groaned, and *agonized*, and died in vain" (*Cowper*). "Old Chester children were prayed for, and *agonized* over" (*Deland*). As a rule, however, no matter which implication is the stronger, that of anguish or of straining, the one not stressed is at least connoted. "For you doubt, you hope, O men, You fear, you *agonise*, die" (*Browning*). "Pages which cost a week of unremitting and *agonising* labour" (*A. Huxley*). **Squirm** evokes images of a less dignified or a more familiar character; it suggests wriggling or turning as of a worm prodded by a stick. When used of human beings, therefore, it usually does not imply profound distress, but great unease, as in aversion to restraint or discipline, or a shrinking or wincing, as under sarcasm, criticism, or the like. "Sleek-haired subalterns who *squirmed* painfully in their chairs when they came to call" (*Kipling*).

Ana. Twist, bend, turn (see CURVE, *v.*): distort, contort (see DEFORM): wince, blench, flinch, *recoil.

wrong, *adj.* **1** *False.

Ana. Fallacious, sophistical (see under FALLACY): *misleading, deceptive, delusive, delusory.

Ant. Right. — *Con.* *Correct, exact, accurate, precise.

2 *Bad, poor.

Ana. Improper, *unfit, inappropriate, unmeet, unfitting, unsuitable, inapt, unhappy, infelicitous.

Con. Proper, *fit, appropriate, suitable, fitting: *awry, askew: *amiss, astray.

wrong, *n.* *Injustice, injury, tort, grievance.

Ana. Damage, *injury, harm, mischief: violation, infraction, *breach, trespass, transgression: hardship, *difficulty.

wrong, *v.* **Wrong, oppress, persecute, aggrieve** are comparable when they mean to inflict injury upon a person without just cause or in an outrageous manner. One **wrongs** another who injures him by unjustifiably depriving him of his property, his good name, or the like, or by violating something he holds sacred. "Receive us; we have *wronged* no man, we have corrupted no man, we have defrauded no man" (*2 Corinthians* vii. 2).

"Forgive! forgive! much-*wrong'd* Montrose!" (*Burns*). One **oppresses** another who inhumanely lays upon him burdens too heavy to be endured or exacts of him more than he can possibly perform. "How reviving To the spirits of just men long *oppressed*, When God into the hands of their deliverer Puts invincible might" (*Milton*). "The *oppression* of a tyrannous control" (*Cowper*). One **persecutes** another who relentlessly or unremittingly subjects him to annoyance or suffering. "A boy... [with] abnormal mental powers in some direction, combined with poor physique and great nervousness... may be so *persecuted* [by normal boys] as to be driven mad" (*B. Russell*). One **aggrieves** another or, more often, causes him to be (or to feel) *aggrieved*, who by wronging, oppressing, or persecuting him gives him ground for remonstrance; as, several nations were *aggrieved* by the terms of the Treaty of Versailles. "So the bargain stood: They broke it, and he felt himself *aggrieved*" (*Browning*).

Ana. *Abuse, mistreat, maltreat, ill-treat, outrage: *injure, harm, hurt.

wrought. *Worked.

Y

yardstick. *Standard, criterion, gauge, touchstone.

yarn. Tale, *story, narrative, anecdote.

yearly. *Annual, anniversary.

yearn. *Long, pine, hanker, hunger, thirst.

Ana. Crave, *desire, wish, want, covet: aspire, pant, *aim.

yeast. *Foam, froth, spume, scum, lather, suds.

yen. Urge, *desire, appetite, appetence, passion, lust, concupiscence.

yet. *But, however, still, nevertheless.

yield, *v.* **1** Produce, turn out, *bear.

Ana. *Generate, engender, breed, propagate: create, *invent: form, shape, *make, fabricate, fashion.

2 *Relinquish, surrender, cede, abandon, leave, resign, waive.

Ana. *Forgo, forbear, abnegate, eschew, sacrifice: *abdicate, renounce, resign, demit.

Con. *Keep, retain, withhold: appropriate, *arrogate, confiscate.

3 Yield, submit, capitulate, succumb, relent, defer, bow, cave in are synonyms only when they mean to give way to someone or something that one cannot further resist. **Yield** (as here considered: see also RELINQUISH; BEAR, 2) may be used both of persons and of things. When the reference is to a person or persons, the term implies being overcome by force, by argument, by entreaty, or the like (as, to *yield* to persuasion; to *yield* to temptation; he never *yields* except when the matter under discussion is of no significance to him; "The great principle in a contest with a child is: do not *yield* but do not punish"—*B. Russell*); when the reference is to a thing, the word implies elasticity, or lack of firmness, strength, or endurance (sometimes duration) in the thing that gives way (as, "the door suddenly *yielded* to her hand"—*Austen;* "he passed between them [stalks], and they *yielded* on either side"—*Jefferies*). **Submit** carries an even more definite implication of contention or conflict than *yield* and, therefore, suggests more strongly a surrender after resistance to another's will, or because of another thing's strength or inevitableness; as, "All is not lost—the unconquerable will ... And courage never to *submit* or *yield*" (*Milton*); "Catherine..., having no power of getting away, was obliged to give up the point and *submit*" (*Austen*); "the Indian Summer of her heart, which was slow to *submit* to age" (*Stevenson*); "a long diatribe against Pitt for having tamely *submitted* to the rebuffs of the French Directory" (*Quiller-Couch*); "To this strange force within him [D. H. Lawrence], to this power that created his works of art, there was nothing to do but *submit*" (*A. Huxley*). **Capitulate** literally means to surrender on terms definitely agreed upon, but it is often used without reference to opposing military forces: in extended use, it implies submission to a force or power that one has not the strength, or the skill, or the will to overcome; as, "I still pursued, and, about two o'clock this afternoon, she thought fit to *capitulate*" (*Spectator*, 1714); "If...all the proletarians were for Socialism and all the capitalists for Capitalism, Capitalism would have had to *capitulate* to overwhelming numbers long ago" (*Shaw*). **Succumb** carries a stronger implication than any of the preceding terms of weakness or helplessness in the person or thing that gives way, or of strength or irresistibility in the person or, more often, the thing that causes the giving way. The suggestion of sinking under that force or power is usually so strong in *succumb* that the word frequently implies a disastrous outcome such as death, destruction, or subjugation; as, to *succumb* to pneumonia; he does not easily *succumb* to temptation; " 'true passion...must be crushed before it will *succumb*' " (*Meredith*). All of the preceding terms usually imply a giving way on the part of a person (sometimes, a thing) that has not or cannot maintain the upper hand: they, therefore, often imply a weakening of the one that gives way. **Relent,** by contrast, implies a yielding on the part of the one who has the upper hand and who has been exceedingly severe or harsh in his attitude to another person or fixed in his determination to punish, to interfere, to frustrate, or the like. The term, therefore, implies a softening or mollifying that turns him from his previous course; as, "can you hear a good man groan, And not *relent*?" (*Shak.*); "Stern Proserpine *relented*, And gave him back the fair" (*Pope*); "[Had he seen] his sweetheart...crying and shivering....He might have *relented*" (*Deland*). **Defer** implies a yielding or submitting to because of respect or reverence for another or in recognition of another's authority, superior knowledge, or the like; as, "the house, *deferring* to legal right, acquiesced" (*G. Bancroft*); "Everybody must *defer*....a nation must wait upon her decision, a Dean and Chapter truckle to her wishes" (*V. Sackville-West*). **Bow** is a picturesque word, sometimes a close synonym of *defer*, and at other times of *submit:* it usually suggests a yielding through courtesy or through subjugation; as, to *bow* to the inevitable; to *bow* to established authority; "He admired the tribal discipline which made May *bow* to this decision" (*E. Wharton*). **Cave in,** in its figurative sense, is a close synonym of *succumb*, but it often suggests resistance to pressure to the point of exhaustion and collapse; as, "In the end Government *caved in*, and unconditionally agreed to inquiry" (*Punch*).

Ana. Surrender, cede, waive (see RELINQUISH): concede, accord, award, *grant.

yoke. *Couple, pair, brace.

youth. **Youth, adolescence, puberty, pubescence** are sometimes used interchangeably to denote the period in life when one passes from childhood to maturity. **Youth** is the most general of these terms, being applied sometimes to the whole early part of life from childhood or infancy to maturity; as, *youth*, maturity, senility. More often, however, *youth* is applied to the period between the maturing of the sexual organs and the attaining of maturity. *Youth* often connotes the freshness, vigor, inexperience, or impetuosity characteristic of the young. **Adolescence** designates the same period as *youth* in the restricted sense, but it carries a stronger connotation of immaturity. *Adolescence* suggests the awkwardness resulting from the rapid growth during this period and also the mental and emotional instability resulting from the physiological changes. In education, *adolescence* denotes the period from the end of the elementary course to the end of the high-school course. In legal use, *adolescence* designates the period extending from puberty to the attainment of full legal age or majority. (By extension, *youth* and *adolescence* have come to designate an early stage in the development of anything; as, in physical geography, topographic *adolescence* or *youth* is the condition of a district soon after the beginning of erosion by streams.) Strictly, **puberty** designates the age at which the symptoms of the maturing of the sexual organs appear, such as the beard and changed voice in boys and the development of the breasts in girls. In law this age is commonly fixed at fourteen for boys and twelve for girls. In looser use, *puberty* often designates the period covering the earlier years of adolescence. **Pubescence** is sometimes used as equivalent to *puberty* but it is applied only to boys.

Ant. Age (sense 1).

youthful. **Youthful, juvenile, puerile, boyish, virgin, virginal, maiden** come into comparison only when they mean of, pertaining to, or characteristic of, one who is between childhood and adulthood. They are, however, not synonyms; for, although their basic meaning is the same, they are seldom interchangeable, because of widely differing implications and applications. **Youthful** suggests the possession or the appearance of youth, or of a youngness appropriate to youth: it is commonly employed either in a good sense, or in extenuation; as, *youthful* aspirations, *youthful* indiscretions. **Juvenile** often suggests immaturity of mind or body or lack of experience; it is therefore applied especially (but not exclusively) to that which pertains to, or is suited to or designed for, boys and girls in their teens; as, *juvenile* dances; *juvenile* fiction; a *juvenile* performance. **Puerile** is almost exclusively applied to acts, utterances, and the like, which are excusable in a boy or girl or are characteristic of immaturity, but are unpardonable or out of character in an adult: the word is now used chiefly in contemptuous reference to acts or utterances of the mature. "It [vanity] stimulates cowardice in the face of ridicule, and leads infallibly to *puerile* confusions of shadow and substance" (*Brownell*). "What is one to think of a man so asinine that he looks for gratitude in this world, or so *puerilely* egotistical that he enjoys it when found?" (*Mencken*). **Boyish,** though referred commonly to boys, is sometimes used in reference to girls, or their clothes, appearance, qualities, or the like. The term often suggests some of the engaging qualities or the physical attractiveness of normal, vigorous boys; as, a *boyish* smile; *boyish* charm; *boyish* enthusiasm; *boyish* spirit. **Virgin** and **virginal,** though referable usually to girls are, in the extended sense in which they are here compared, applicable also to boys, because they suggest the freshness, the innocence, the purity, and the inexperience that are associated with youthful virginity. "That beautiful mixture of manly courage and *virginal* modesty" (*F. W. Farrar*). "He smiled like a girl, Or like clear winter skies, A *virginal* light Making stars of his eyes" (*V. Lindsay*). **Maiden,** as here compared in its extended sense, carries an even stronger suggestion than *virgin* or *virginal* of youthful lack of experience: it also implies that one's virtue, worth, competence, strength, or the like, has not been tried or tested; as, a maiden speech; his *maiden* effort at authorship.

Ana. *Immature, unmatured, unfledged.

Ant. Aged. — *Con.* *Mature, matured, grown-up, full-fledged.

Z

zany. *Fool, jester, clown, antic, buffoon, merry-andrew, pantaloon, harlequin, comedian, comic, stooge.

zeal. Enthusiasm, fervor, ardor, *passion.

Ana. Energy, force (see POWER): zest, gusto (see TASTE): earnestness, seriousness (see corresponding adjectives at SERIOUS): intensity, vehemence (see corresponding adjectives at INTENSE).

Ant. Apathy. — *Con.* Impassivity, phlegm, stolidity (see corresponding adjectives at IMPASSIVE).

zealot. *Enthusiast, fanatic, bigot.

Ana. Partisan, sectary, adherent, disciple, *follower: devotee, votary (see ADDICT).

zenith. Apogee, culmination, meridian, *summit, peak, pinnacle, climax, apex, acme.

Ant. Nadir.

zephyr. *Wind, breeze, gust, blast, flaw, gale, hurricane, whirlwind, cyclone, typhoon, tornado, waterspout, twister.

zeppelin. *Aerostat, balloon, airship, dirigible, blimp.

zero. *Cipher, naught, nought, aught, ought.

zest. Relish, gusto, *taste, palate.

Ana. Enthusiasm, fervor, ardor, zeal, *passion: spiritedness *or* spirit, high-spiritedness (see corresponding adjectives at SPIRITED): enjoyment, delight, delectation, *pleasure.

zone. Belt, *area, tract, region.

Ana. *Locality, district: section, sector, segment (see PART, *n.*).

LIST OF AUTHORS QUOTED

The entries in italic type in the left-hand column are the actual forms used in citations in the *Vocabulary* of this Dictionary. These entries are arranged in the alphabetical order of surnames or titles. The right-hand column supplies a full identification of each author or source cited. Only readily understood abbreviations (such as Amer. for American and Eng. for English) are used in this column.

Alternative names (such as the pseudonyms of authors cited by their real names or, conversely, the real names of authors cited by their pseudonyms) are cross-entered in the list below wherever their inclusion is of likely value to the consultant. At such cross-entries the name in the left-hand column is enclosed in square brackets and printed in roman type.

As the names of books of the Bible are given in full wherever cited in the *Vocabulary*, these names are omitted from the list below. Unless otherwise stated at the citation itself in the *Vocabulary*, all Biblical quotations are from the Authorized Version (or King James Bible). Quotations from other versions are indicated by the addition of the abbreviations *R. V.* for Revised Version (of 1885), *D. V.* for Douay Version (or Douay Bible).

L. Abbott . . . Lyman Abbott (1835–1922). Amer. clergyman.

L. Abercrombie Lascelles Abercrombie (1881–1938). Eng. poet.

F. P. Adams . Franklin Pierce Adams (1881–). Amer. journalist.

F. W. L. Adams Francis William Lauderdale Adams (1862–93). Brit. novelist in Australia.

H. Adams . . Henry (Brooks) Adams (1838–1918). Amer. historian.

John Adams . John Adams (1735–1826). Second President of the United States.

J. Q. Adams . John Quincy Adams (1767–1848). Sixth President of the United States.

Jos. Q. Adams. Joseph Quincy Adams (1881–). Amer. Shakespearean scholar.

Addison . . . Joseph Addison (1672–1719). Eng. essayist.

[Æ] . . . . . See George William Russell.

Ainsworth . . William Harrison Ainsworth (1805–82). Eng. novelist.

Akenside . . . Mark Akenside (1721–70). Eng. poet.

Bronson Alcott (Amos) Bronson Alcott (1799–1888). Amer. transcendentalist.

R. Aldington . Richard Aldington (1892–). Eng. poet and novelist.

T. B. Aldrich . Thomas Bailey Aldrich (1836–1907). Amer. author and editor.

H. B. Alexander . . . . Hartley Burr Alexander (1873–1939). Amer. philosopher.

S. Alexander . Samuel Alexander (1859–1938). Australian philosopher in England.

Sir A. Alison . Sir Archibald Alison (1792–1867). Scot. historian.

A. V. G. Allen. Alexander Viets Griswold Allen (1841–1908). Amer. clergyman and author.

Grant Allen. . Grant Allen (1848–99). Canadian man of letters.

Hervey Allen . (William) Hervey Allen (1889–). Amer. author.

J. L. Allen . . James Lane Allen (1849–1925). Amer. novelist.

Americana Annual . . . . Amer. yearbook, pub. (1st vol. 1923) by The Encyclopedia Americana Corporation, New York.

American Mercury . . . . Amer. monthly magazine (founded 1924 by Henry Louis Mencken and George Jean Nathan).

Amer. Speech . *American Speech*, Amer. scholarly quarterly (founded 1925 by Louise Pound).

S. Anderson . Sherwood Anderson (1876–1941). Amer. novelist.

[Arblay]. . . Madame d'Arblay. See Frances ("Fanny") Burney, below.

Arbuthnot . . John Arbuthnot (1667–1735). Scot. author and physician.

Duke of Argyll George John Douglas Campbell (1823–1900), 8th Duke of Argyll. Brit. statesman.

Arnold. . . . Matthew Arnold (1822–88). Eng. poet and critic.

Sir E. Arnold . Sir Edwin Arnold (1832–1904). Eng. poet.

Ascham . . . Roger Ascham (1515–68). Eng. scholar.

[Ashburton] . Baron Ashburton. See Alexander Baring, below.

Athenaeum . . Eng. literary and artistic weekly (founded 1828 by James Silk Buckingham; incorporated in *The Nation and Athenaeum* 1921).

Atlantic Monthly . . Amer. monthly magazine (est. 1857).

Atterbury. . . Francis Atterbury (1662–1732). Eng. bishop.

W. H. Auden . Wystan Hugh Auden (1907–). Eng. poet.

Austen. . . . Jane Austen (1775–1817). Eng. novelist.

A. Austin . . Alfred Austin (1835–1913). Eng. poet laureate.

M. Austin . . Mary Hunter Austin (1868–1934). Amer. novelist.

S. Austin. . . Sarah Austin (1793–1867). Eng. translator.

Authorized Version or *A. V.* Authorized Version (or King James Version) of the Bible. See note preceding this list.

Babbitt. . . . Irving Babbitt (1865–1933). Amer. educator and author.

Bacon . . . . Francis Bacon (1561–1626), 1st Baron Verulam. Eng. philosopher, statesman, author.

H. Baerlein. . Henry Baerlein (1875–). Eng. author.

Bagehot . . . Walter Bagehot (1826–77). Eng. economist and author.

J. Baillie. . . Joanna Baillie (1762–1851). Scot. poet.

Baker's Biog. Dict. of Musicians. . . *Baker's Biographical Dictionary of Musicians* (1919 ed., revised by Alfred Remy), pub. by G. Schirmer, N. Y.

A. J. Balfour . Arthur James Balfour (1848–1930), 1st Earl of Balfour. Brit. statesman and essayist.

W. Ballantine. William Ballantine (1812–87). Eng. barrister.

P. B. Ballard . Philip Boswood Ballard (1865–). Brit. educator.

G. Bancroft . . George Bancroft (1800–91). Amer. historian.

J. K. Bangs . John Kendrick Bangs (1862–1922). Amer. humorist.

Barham . . . Richard Harris Barham (1788–1845). Eng. author.

A. Baring . . Alexander Baring (1774–1848). 1st Baron Ashburton. Brit. financier and statesman.

M. Baring . . Maurice Baring (1874–). Eng. journalist and author.

Baring-Gould . Sabine Baring-Gould (1834–1924). Eng. clergyman and author.

J. Barlow . . Joel Barlow (1754–1812). Amer. author and diplomatist.

M. A. Barnes. Margaret Ayer Barnes (1886–). Amer. author.

Barrie . . . . Sir James Matthew Barrie (1860–1937). Scot. novelist and dramatist.

Barrow . . . Isaac Barrow (1630–77). Eng. theologian, mathematician, and classicist.

S. C. Bartlett . Samuel Colcord Bartlett (1817–1898). Amer. clergyman and educator.

K. L. Bates . . Katharine Lee Bates (1859–1929). Amer. poet.

J. W. Beach . Joseph Warren Beach (1880–). Amer. educator and critic.

[Beaconsfield]. Earl of Beaconsfield. See Benjamin Disraeli, below.

Beaumont & Fletcher . . Francis Beaumont (1584–1616) and John Fletcher (1579–1625). Eng. dramatists (in collaboration).

J. Beaumont . Joseph Beaumont (1616–99). Eng. theologian and poet.

Beckford . . . William Beckford (1759–1844). Eng. author.

H. W. Beecher. Henry Ward Beecher (1813–1887). Amer. preacher.

Behn . . . . (Mrs.) Aphra Behn (1640–89). Eng. dramatist and novelist.

Belloc . . . . (Joseph) Hilary (Pierre) Belloc (1870–). Brit. author.

W. R. Benét . William Rose Benét (1886–). Amer. author and poet.

J. Benjamin . Judah Philip Benjamin (1811–1884). Lawyer in U. S. and England.

Bennett . . . (Enoch) Arnold Bennett (1867–1931). Eng. novelist and playwright.

W. C. Bennett. William Cox Bennett (1820–1895). Eng. song writer.

A. C. Benson . Arthur Christopher Benson (1862–1925). Eng. educator and essayist.

E. F. Benson . Edward Frederic Benson (1867–1940). Eng. novelist.

Bentham . . . Jeremy Bentham (1748–1832). Eng. philosopher and jurist.

J. Beresford. . James Beresford (1764–1840). Eng. miscellaneous writer.

Berkeley . . . George Berkeley (1685–1753). Irish bishop and metaphysician.

M. J. Berkeley Miles Joseph Berkeley (1803–1889). Brit. botanist.

Berners . . . John Bourchier (1467–1533), 2d Baron Berners. Eng. politician and author.

Besant — Sir Walter Besant (1836–1901). Eng. author. Cf. James Rice.

Binyon — Laurence Binyon (1869–). Eng. author and connoisseur of Oriental art.

Birrell — Augustine Birrell (1850–1933). Eng. politician and critic.

Bk. of Com. Prayer — = Book of Common Prayer, below.

W. Black — William Black (1841–98). Scot. novelist.

Blackie — John Stuart Blackie (1809–95). Scot. classical scholar.

Blackmore — Richard Doddridge Blackmore (1825–1900). Eng. novelist.

Blackstone — Sir William Blackstone (1723–1780). Eng. jurist.

H. Blair — Hugh Blair (1718–1800). Scot. scholar and preacher.

J. H. Blunt — John Henry Blunt (1823–84). Eng. religious historian.

Bolingbroke — Henry St. John (1678–1751), 1st Viscount Bolingbroke. Eng. statesman.

Book of Common Prayer — The service book of the Anglican Communion (Church of England edition).

Borrow — George (Henry) Borrow (1803–1881). Eng. novelist.

Bosanquet — Bernard Bosanquet (1848–1923). Eng. philosopher.

Boswell — James Boswell (1740–95). Scot. author; biographer of Samuel Johnson.

G. Bottomley — Gordon Bottomley (1874–). Eng. poet and playwright.

F. Bowen — Francis Bowen (1811–90). Amer. philosopher.

C. G. Bowers — Claude Gernade Bowers (1878–). Amer. historian.

R. Boyle — Robert Boyle (1627–91). Brit. physicist and chemist.

M. K. Bradby — (Miss) M. K. Bradby. Contemporary Brit. psychoanalyst.

M. E. Braddon — Mary Elizabeth Braddon (1837–1915). Eng. novelist.

G. Bradford — Gamaliel Bradford (1863–1932). Amer. biographer and essayist.

R. Bradford — Roark Bradford (1896–). Amer. novelist and short-story writer.

Bradley — Andrew Cecil Bradley (1851–1935). Eng. educator and literary critic.

Sir W. H. Bragg — Sir William Henry Bragg (1862–). Brit. scientist.

Bridges — Robert Seymour Bridges (1844–1930). Eng. poet laureate and phonetician.

J. Bright — John Bright (1811–89). Eng. statesman.

C. Brontë — Charlotte Brontë (1816–55). Eng. novelist.

R. Brooke — Rupert Brooke (1887–1915). Eng. poet.

S. Brooke — Stopford Augustus Brooke (1832–1916). Irish clergyman and author.

Van W. Brooks — Van Wyck Brooks (1886–). Amer. author.

Broome — William Broome (1689–1745). Eng. translator.

Brougham — Henry Peter Brougham (1778–1868), Baron Brougham and Vaux. Brit. lawyer, scholar, and statesman.

Dr. J. Brown — John Brown (1810–82). Scot. physician and author.

T. Brown — Thomas Brown (1663–1704). Eng. satirist.

T. E. Brown — Thomas Edward Brown (1830–1897). Anglo-Manx poet.

Browne — Sir Thomas Browne (1605–82). Eng. physician and author.

Brownell — William Crary Brownell (1851–1928). Amer. critic.

B. Brownell — Baker Brownell (1887–). Amer. educator and author.

Browning — Robert Browning (1812–89). Eng. poet.

E. B. Browning — Elizabeth Barrett Browning (1806–61). Eng. poet; wife of preceding.

Bryant — William Cullen Bryant (1794–1878). Amer. poet.

Bryce — James Bryce (1838–1922), Viscount Bryce. Brit. jurist, historian, and statesman.

Buchan — Sir John Buchan (1875–1940), 1st Baron Tweedsmuir. Scot. novelist and historian.

[Buckingham] — 1st Duke of Buckingham. See John Sheffield, below.

Buckle — Henry Thomas Buckle (1821–1862). Eng. historian.

[Bulwer-Lytton] — See Lytton, below.

Alfred Bunn — Alfred Bunn (1796?–1860). Eng. theater manager and song writer.

Bunyan — John Bunyan (1628–88). Eng. evangelist and author.

Burke — Edmund Burke (1729–97). Brit. statesman.

Bp. Burnet — Bishop Gilbert Burnet (1643–1715). Scot. prelate, statesman, and historian.

Burney — Frances ("Fanny") Burney (1752–1840), Madame d'Arblay. Eng. novelist.

Burns — Robert Burns (1759–96). Scot. poet.

J. Burroughs — John Burroughs (1837–1921). Amer. naturalist.

Burton — Robert Burton (1577–1640). Eng. author.

R. F. Burton — Sir Richard Francis Burton (1821–90). Eng. explorer; translator of *Arabian Nights.*

Butcher — Samuel Henry Butcher (1850–1910). Irish classicist.

Butler [1612–80] — Samuel Butler (1612–80). Eng. satirist and poet; author of *Hudibras.*

Bp. Butler — Bishop Joseph Butler (1692–1752). Eng. theologian.

Dom. C. Butler — Edward Cuthbert Butler (1858–1934). Irish Benedictine scholar and author.

S. Butler [19th-cent.] — Samuel Butler (1835–1902). Eng. satirist; author of *The Way of All Flesh.*

Byron — George Gordon Byron (1788–1824), 6th Baron Byron. Eng. poet.

J. B. Cabell — James Branch Cabell (1879–). Amer. author.

G. W. Cable — George Washington Cable (1844–1925). Amer. novelist.

Caine — Sir (Thomas Henry) Hall Caine (1853–1931). Anglo-Manx author.

E. Caldwell — Erskine Caldwell (1902–). Amer. novelist and short-story writer.

Cambridge Ancient History — Twelve-volume series (numerous editors) pub. by Cambridge Univ. Press, Eng., & Macmillan Co., New York (1923–39).

Campbell — Thomas Campbell (1777–1844). Scot. poet.

D. Canfield — Dorothy (properly Dorothea Frances) Canfield (1879–); Mrs. John Redwood Fisher. Amer. novelist.

G. Canning — George Canning (1770–1827). Brit. statesman.

Carew — Thomas Carew (1595?–?1645). Eng. poet.

W. Carleton — William (McKendree) Carleton (1845–1912). Amer. poet.

Carlyle — Thomas Carlyle (1795–1881). Scot. essayist and historian.

Jane W. Carlyle — Jane Baillie Welsh Carlyle (1801–66). Scot. letter writer; wife of preceding.

Carroll — Lewis Carroll, pseudonym of Charles Lutwidge Dodgson (1832–98). Eng. mathematician and writer of stories for children.

Cather — Willa Sibert Cather (1876–). Amer. novelist.

Caxton — William Caxton (1422?–91). Eng. printer.

E. Chambers — Ephraim Chambers (d. 1740). Eng. encyclopedist.

W. E. Channing — William Ellery Channing (1780–1842). Amer. clergyman and author.

Chatham — William Pitt (1708–78), 1st Earl of Chatham. Eng. statesman.

Chatterton — Thomas Chatterton (1752–70). Eng. poet.

Chaucer — Geoffrey Chaucer (1340?–1400). Eng. poet.

Chesterfield — Philip Dormer Stanhope (1694–1773), 4th Earl of Chesterfield. Eng. statesman, diplomat, and letter writer.

Chesterton — Gilbert Keith Chesterton (1874–1936). Eng. essayist and critic.

F. J. Child — Francis James Child (1825–96). Amer. scholar.

G. W. Childs — George William Childs (1829–1894). Amer. newspaperman.

Chilton — Alexander Wheeler Chilton. See Holt & Chilton, below.

R. Choate — Rufus Choate (1799–1859). Amer. jurist.

Christian Century — Amer. religious weekly (est. 1883).

Agatha Christie — Agatha (Mary Clarissa) Christie. Brit. detective-story writer.

C. Churchill — Charles Churchill (1731–64). Eng. poet and satirist.

Winston Churchill [Amer. novelist] — Winston Churchill (1871–). Amer. novelist.

Winston S. Churchill — Winston Leonard Spencer Churchill (1874–). Eng. statesman and writer.

Cibber — Colley Cibber (1671–1757). Eng. dramatist.

Clarendon — Edward Hyde (1609–74), 1st Earl of Clarendon. Eng. statesman and historian.

J. S. Clarke — John Smith Clarke (1885–). Scot. author.

[Clemens] — Samuel Langhorne Clemens. See Mark Twain, below.

G. Cleveland — (Stephen) Grover Cleveland (1837–1908). 22d and 24th President of the United States.

Cleveland Plain Dealer — Cleveland (Ohio) daily newspaper (est. 1841).

S. Cloete — (Edward Fairly) Stuart (Graham) Cloete (1897–). S. African novelist.

Clough — Arthur Hugh Clough (1819–1861). Eng. poet.

Irvin S. Cobb — Irvin Shrewsbury Cobb (1876–). Amer. humorist.

W. Cobbett — William Cobbett (1763–1835). Eng. politician and essayist.

H. T. Cockburn — Henry Thomas Cockburn (1779–1854). Scot. judge.

T. Cogan — Thomas Cogan (1736–1818). Eng. physician and philosopher.

Coke — Sir Edward Coke (1552–1634). Eng. jurist.

Coleridge — Samuel Taylor Coleridge (1772–1834). Eng. poet.

J. Collier — Jeremy Collier (1650–1726). Eng. theologian.

Collins — William Collins (1721–59). Eng. poet.

Wilkie Collins — (William) Wilkie Collins (1824–1889). Eng. novelist.

P. Colum — Padraic Colum (1881–). Irish author.

Colvin — Sir Sidney Colvin (1845–1927). Eng. man of letters.

The Commonweal — Amer. weekly review of current events, literature and art (est. 1924).

Conan Doyle — See Doyle, below.

Congreve — William Congreve (1670–1729). Eng. dramatist.

J. Conington — John Conington (1825–69). Eng. translator.

Conrad — Joseph Conrad (1857–1924). Brit. novelist.

Contemp. Rev. — *The Contemporary Review*, Brit. monthly (founded 1865 by Sir Percy Bunting).

Capt. Cook . . Captain James Cook (1728–1779). Eng. navigator and explorer.

E. V. Cooke . Edmund Vance Cooke (1866–1932). Amer. author and lecturer.

M. C. Cooke . Mordecai Cubitt Cooke (1825–1913). Brit. mycologist.

Cooper. . . . James Fenimore Cooper (1789–1851). Amer. novelist.

J. Cotgrave . . John Cotgrave (fl. 1655). Eng. compiler.

N. Cotton . . Nathaniel Cotton (1705–88). Eng. physician and poet.

Coverdale. . . Miles Coverdale (1488?–1569). Eng. Bible translator.

Cowley. . . . Abraham Cowley (1618–67). Eng. poet.

Cowper. . . . William Cowper (1731–1800). Eng. poet.

Crabbe . . . . George Crabbe (1754–1832). Eng. poet.

[Craik] . . . Dinah Maria Craik. See MULOCK, below.

R. A. Cram. . Ralph Adams Cram (1863–). Amer. architect.

S. Crane . . . Stephen Crane (1871–1900). Amer. novelist.

Crashaw . . . Richard Crashaw (1613?–49). Eng. poet.

F. Marion Crawford. . Francis Marion Crawford (1854–1909). Amer. novelist.

J. Crawford. . Julia Crawford (1800–85). Purported author of *Kathleen Mavourneen.*

S. M. Crothers. Samuel McChord Crothers (1857–1927). Amer. clergyman and essayist.

W. Cruise . . William Cruise (d. 1824). Brit. legal writer.

Cudworth. . . Ralph Cudworth (1617–88). Eng. philosopher.

C. Cullen. . . Countee Cullen (b. 1903). Amer. poet.

Current History . . . Amer. monthly review of current events (est. 1914).

H. Cushing. . Harvey Cushing (1869–1939). Amer. surgeon.

Daily Express. London (Eng.) daily newspaper (est. 1900 by C. Arthur Pearson).

Daily Mail . . London (Eng.) daily newspaper (est. 1896 by Kennedy Jones).

Daily News. . London (Eng.) daily newspaper (est. 1846 by Charles Dickens; in 1930 it absorbed *The Daily Chronicle,* becoming *The News Chronicle*).

Daily Telegraph . . . London (Eng.) daily newspaper (est. 1855 by Joseph Moses Levy as first penny daily in London).

W. Dampier . William Dampier (1652–1715). Eng. navigator.

R. H. Dana, jr. Richard Henry Dana (1815–1882). Amer. sailor and lawyer; author of *Two Years Before the Mast.*

R. H. Dana, sr. Richard Henry Dana (1787–1879). Amer. lawyer and miscellaneous writer.

Karl K. Darrow . . . Karl Kelchner Darrow (1891–). Amer. physicist.

Darwin . . . Charles Robert Darwin (1809–1882). Eng. naturalist.

Davenant. . . Sir William Davenant (1606–1668). Eng. poet and dramatist.

J. Davies. . . Sir John Davies (1569–1626). Eng. jurist and poet.

M. Davies . . Miles, or Myles, Davies (1662–?1715). Brit. bibliographer.

W. H. Davies . William Henry Davies (1871–1940). Brit. poet and author.

Sir H. Davy . Sir Humphry Davy (1778–1829). Eng. scientist.

Defoe . . . . Daniel Defoe (1659?–1731). Eng. novelist.

Dekker. . . . Thomas Dekker (1572?–?1632). Eng. playwright.

de Kruif . . . Paul de Kruif (1890–). Amer. bacteriologist, author.

de la Mare . . Walter de la Mare (1873–). Eng. poet and novelist.

Deland. . . . (Mrs.) Margaretta, or Margaret, Wade Deland (1857–). Amer. novelist.

W. De Morgan William Frend De Morgan (1839–1917). Eng. novelist and artist.

Baron Denman Thomas Denman (1779–1854), 1st Baron Denman. Eng. chief justice and statesman.

De Quincey. . Thomas De Quincey (1785–1859). Eng. author.

C. Dibdin . . Charles Dibdin (1745–1814). Eng. song writer.

Sir A. Dick . Sir Alexander Dick (1703–85). Scot. physician.

Dickens . . . Charles (John Huffam) Dickens (1812–70). Eng. novelist.

G. L. Dickinson . . . Goldsworthy Lowes Dickinson (1862–1932). Eng. essayist.

Dict. Amer. Biog. . . . *Dictionary of American Biography* (20 vols.+1 Index vol.) ed. by Allen Johnson and Dumas Malone, pub. by Charles Scribner's Sons, New York (1928–36).

Dict. Nat. Biog. *Dictionary of National Biography,* edited by Leslie Stephen and (Sir) Sidney Lee, reissue of 1908–09 (in 22 vols.) pub. by Macmillan Co., N. Y.

Dimnet . . . (Abbé) Ernest Dimnet (1869–). French author and educator.

Disraeli . . . Benjamin Disraeli (1804–81), 1st Earl of Beaconsfield. Brit. statesman and novelist.

I. D'Israeli. . Isaac D'Israeli (1766–1848). Eng. miscellaneous writer; father of preceding.

W. H. Dixon . William Hepworth Dixon (1821–79). Eng. historian.

Dobson. . . . (Henry) Austin Dobson (1840–1921). Eng. poet and critic.

R. E. N. Dodge Robert Elkin Neil Dodge (1867–1935). Amer. educator.

C. F. Dole . . Charles Fletcher Dole (1845–1927). Amer. clergyman.

Donne . . . . John Donne (1573–1631). Eng. poet.

Douay Version Douay Version of the Bible. See note preceding this list.

E. Dowden . . Edward Dowden (1843–1913). Irish literary critic.

E. Dowson . . Ernest Christopher Dowson (1867–1900). Eng. poet.

Conan Doyle Sir Arthur Conan Doyle (1859–1930). Brit. author.

Dreiser . . . Theodore Dreiser (1871–). Amer. novelist.

H. Drummond Henry Drummond (1851–97). Scot. writer.

W. Drummond William Drummond (1585–1649). Scot. poet.

Dryden. . . . John Dryden (1631–1700). Eng. poet and playwright.

D. V. . . . . Douay Version of the Bible. See note preceding this list.

Eddington . . Sir Arthur Stanley Eddington (1882–). Eng. physicist and astronomer.

Edgeworth . . Maria Edgeworth (1767–1849). Irish author.

Edinburgh Review . . . . Scot. literary journal (est. 1802 by Francis Jeffrey, Henry Brougham, and Sydney Smith).

John Edwards. John Edwards (1637–1716). Eng. Calvinistic controversialist.

Einstein & Infeld . . . Albert Einstein (1879–), German-born Amer. physicist, in collaboration with Leopold Infeld (1898–), Polish physicist.

C. W. Eliot. . Charles William Eliot (1834–1926). Amer. educator.

G. Eliot . . . George Eliot, pseudonym of Mary Ann Evans (1819–80). Eng. novelist.

T. S. Eliot . . Thomas Stearns Eliot (1888–). Amer. poet and critic in England.

H. Ellis . . . (Henry) Havelock Ellis (1859–1939). Eng. scientist and author.

C. A. Elton. . Sir Charles Abraham Elton (1778–1853). Eng. author and translator.

Emerson . . . Ralph Waldo Emerson (1803–1882). Amer. essayist and philosopher.

Emporia Gazette . . . Emporia (Kansas) newspaper (est. 1890).

Encyc. Brit. . *Encyclopædia Britannica.* The edition cited is specified in each citation.

J. Erskine . . John Erskine (1879–). Amer. educator and author.

T. Erskine . . Thomas Erskine (1788–1870). Scot. Biblical scholar.

Evelyn . . . . John Evelyn (1620–1706). Eng. diarist.

Expositor . . Eng. religious monthly (est. 1875).

W. Falconer . William Falconer (1732–69). Eng. sailor-poet.

Farquhar. . . George Farquhar (1678–1707). Irish dramatist.

F. W. Farrar . Frederic William Farrar (1831–1903). Eng. clergyman, educator, and author.

Wm. Faulkner William Falkner, or Faulkner (1897–). Amer. novelist.

Felltham . . . Owen Felltham, or Feltham (1602?–68). Eng. author.

C. C. Felton . Cornelius Conway Felton (1807–62). Amer. classicist.

E. Ferber. . . Edna Ferber (1887–). Amer. novelist.

Eugene Field . Eugene Field (1850–95). Amer. humorist and poet.

Fielding . . . Henry Fielding (1707–54). Eng. novelist.

G. Finlay. . . George Finlay (1799–1875). Eng. historian.

[D. C. Fisher]. Dorothy Canfield Fisher. See Dorothy CANFIELD, above.

J. Fiske . . . John Fiske (1842–1901). Amer. historian.

FitzGerald . . Edward FitzGerald (1809–83). Eng. poet and translator.

Percy Fitzgerald . . . Percy Hetherington Fitzgerald (1834–1925). Irish author.

Fitzmaurice-Kelly . . . James Fitzmaurice-Kelly (1857–1923). Brit. Hispanist.

J. E. Flecker . (Herman) James Elroy Flecker (1884–1915). Eng. poet.

W. Fleming . William Fleming (1792?–1866). Scot. divine and scholar.

Fletcher . . . John Fletcher. See BEAUMONT & FLETCHER, above.

G. Fletcher . . Giles Fletcher, the younger (1588?–1623). Eng. poet.

A. Flint . . . Austin Flint, sr. (1812–86). Amer. physician and writer.

S. Foote . . . Samuel Foote (1720–77). Eng. dramatist.

F. M. Ford. . Ford Madox Ford, orig. surname Hueffer (1873–1939). Eng. novelist.

J. Ford . . . John Ford (1586?–after 1638). Eng. dramatist.

J. Fordyce . . James Fordyce (1720–96). Scot. clergyman and poet.

T. Forrest . . Thomas Forrest (1729?–?1802). English navigator.

E. M. Forster. Edward Morgan Forster (1879–). Eng. novelist.

Forum . . . . *The Forum,* American magazine of discussion, orig. pub. quarterly, later monthly (1886–1930; merged into *Forum and Century* 1930, into *Current History and Forum* 1940).

H. W. Fowler . Henry Watson Fowler (1858–1933). Eng. lexicographer.

John Fox, jr. . John William Fox (1863–1919). Amer. story writer.

Foxe. . . . . John Foxe (1516–87). Eng. martyrologist.

Philip Francis Philip Francis (1708?–73). Eng. miscellaneous writer; reputed author of *Letters of Junius.* Cf. JUNIUS, below.

Frankfurter. . Felix Frankfurter (1882–). Amer. jurist.

Franklin . . . Benjamin Franklin (1706–90). Amer. philosopher and statesman.

Fraser's Mag. . . *Fraser's Magazine*, founded by William Maginn and Hugh Fraser, pub. (1830–82) in London, Eng.

J. G. Frazer . Sir James George Frazer (1854–1941). Scot. anthropologist.

Freeman . . . Edward Augustus Freeman (1823–92). Eng. historian.

J. Freeman . . John Freeman (1880–1929). Eng. poet.

[M. Freeman]. Mary Eleanor Wilkins Freeman. See Mary Eleanor WILKINS, below.

C. Frohman . Charles Frohman (1860–1915). Amer. theatrical producer.

Frost . . . . Robert Frost (1875–). Amer. poet.

Froude . . . . James Anthony Froude (1818–1894). Eng. historian.

Fuller . . . . Thomas Fuller (1608–61). Eng. clergyman and author.

T. Fuller [1654–1734] Thomas Fuller (1654–1734). Eng. physician.

C. C. Furnas . Clifford Cook Furnas (1900–). Amer. chemist.

Galsworthy . . John Galsworthy (1867–1933). Eng. novelist and playwright.

Galt . . . . . John Galt (1779–1839). Scot. author.

H. Garland . . Hamlin Garland (1860–1940). Amer. novelist.

R. Garnett . . Richard Garnett (1835–1906). Eng. man of letters.

W. L. Garrison William Lloyd Garrison (1805–1879). Amer. abolitionist.

C. Garstin . . Crosbie Alfred Norman Garstin (1887–1930). Brit. author.

Gascoigne . . George Gascoigne (1525?–77). Eng. poet.

Gaskell. . . . (Mrs.) Elizabeth Cleghorn Gaskell (1810–65). Eng. novelist.

Gay . . . . . John Gay (1685–1732). Eng. poet and dramatist.

K. W. Gehrkens Karl Wilson Gehrkens (1882–). Amer. music educator.

Gibbon. . . . Edward Gibbon (1737–94). Eng. historian.

W. W. Gibson. Wilfrid Wilson Gibson (1878?–). Eng. poet.

H. Gifford . . Humphrey Gifford (fl. 1580). Eng. poet.

J. Gilbert. . . Joseph Gilbert (1779–1852). Eng. Congregational clergyman and religious writer.

W. S. Gilbert . Sir William Schwenk Gilbert (1836–1911). Eng. comic opera librettist and writer of humorous verse.

C. P. Gilman . Charlotte Perkins Gilman (1860–1935). Amer. author.

W. Gilpin . . William Gilpin (1724–1804). Eng. divine.

G. Gissing . . George (Robert) Gissing (1857–1903). Eng. novelist.

W. Gladden. . Washington Gladden (1836–1918). Amer. clergyman.

Gladstone. . . William Ewart Gladstone (1809–98). Eng. statesman.

Glanvill . . . Joseph Glanvill (1636–80). Eng. cleric and philosopher.

E. L. Godkin . Edwin Lawrence Godkin (1831–1902). Irish editor.

Godwin . . . William Godwin, the elder (1756–1836). Eng. novelist and philosopher.

Goldsmith . . Oliver Goldsmith (1728–74). Irish novelist, poet, and dramatist.

J. M. Good. . John Mason Good (1764–1827). Eng. physician and scholar.

Gosse . . . . Sir Edmund William Gosse (1849–1928). Eng. poet and critic.

P. Gosse . . . Philip Henry Gosse (1810–88). Brit. zoologist; father of preceding.

Jay Gould . . Jay Gould (1836–92). Amer. capitalist.

Grandgent . . Charles Hall Grandgent (1862–1939). Amer. scholar and educator.

R. Grant . . . Robert Grant (1852–1940). Amer. novelist.

U. S. Grant. . Ulysses Simpson Grant (1822–1885). Amer. general; 18th President of the United States.

G. Granville. . George Granville, or Grenville (1667–1735), Baron Lansdowne. Eng. poet and dramatist.

Gray. . . . . Thomas Gray (1716–71). Eng. poet.

Asa Gray. . . Asa Gray (1810–88). Amer. botanist.

G. W. Gray. . George William Gray (1886–). Amer. scientific writer.

H. Gray . . . Henry Gray (1825–61). Eng. anatomist.

J. R. Green. . John Richard Green (1837–1883). Eng. historian.

M. Green. . . Matthew Green (1696–1737). Eng. poet.

W. Gregory . . William Gregory (1803–58). Scot. chemist.

Charles Greville Charles Cavendish Fulke Greville (1794–1865). Eng. diarist.

Sir H. Grimston . . . Sir Harbottle Grimston (1603–1685). Eng. judge.

Grote . . . . George Grote (1794–1871). Eng. historian.

E. Guest . . . Edgar (Albert) Guest (1881–). Amer. journalist and verse writer.

Guiney. . . . Louise Imogen Guiney (1861–1920). Amer. poet, essayist.

J. Gunther . . John Gunther (1901–). Amer. journalist and author.

A. T. Hadley . Arthur Twining Hadley (1856–1930). Amer. economist and educator.

Haggard . . . Sir Henry Rider Haggard (1856–1925). Eng. author.

Hakluyt . . . Richard Hakluyt (1552?–1616). Eng. cleric and writer on exploration.

E. E. Hale . . Edward Everett Hale (1822–1909). Amer. clergyman.

M. Hale . . . Sir Matthew Hale (1609–76). Eng. jurist and legal writer.

T. C. Haliburton . . . . Thomas Chandler Haliburton (1796–1865). Canadian humorist.

F. Hall . . . Fitzedward Hall (1825–1901). Amer. philologist.

Bp. J. Hall. . Bishop Joseph Hall (1574–1656). Eng. theologian.

S. C. Hall . . Samuel Carter Hall (1800–89). Eng. editor.

Hallam . . . Henry Hallam (1777–1859). Eng. historian.

R. Hallet. . . Richard Matthews Hallet (1887–). Amer. author.

P. G. Hamerton Philip Gilbert Hamerton (1834–1894). Brit. artist and essayist.

A. Hamilton . Alexander Hamilton (1757–1804). Amer. lawyer and statesman.

James Hamilton . . . . James Hamilton (1814–67). Scot. cleric and hymn writer.

Sir W. Hamilton . . . . Sir William Hamilton (1788–1856). Scot. philosopher.

H. Hammond . Henry Hammond (1605–60). Eng. divine.

Hardy . . . . Thomas Hardy (1840–1928). Eng. novelist and poet.

Harper's Mag. *Harper's Magazine*, Amer. monthly (est. 1850, by Harper & Bros., New York).

J. C. Harris . Joel Chandler Harris (1848–1908). Amer. story writer.

F. Harrison . Frederic Harrison (1831–1923). Eng. author.

H. H. Hart. . Henry Hersch Hart (1886–). Amer. Sinologue.

Harte . . . . (Francis) Bret(t) Harte (1836–1902). Amer. short-story writer.

Sir Paul Harvey . . . Sir Henry Paul Harvey (1869–). Brit. compiler, editor of *Oxford Companion to English Literature.*

S. Haughton . Samuel Haughton (1821–97). Irish scientist.

J. Hawthorne. Julian Hawthorne (1846–1934). Amer. author; son of next.

N. Hawthorne. Nathaniel Hawthorne (1804–1864). Amer. novelist.

J. Hayward . Sir John Hayward (1564?–1627). Eng. historian.

C. Hazard . . Caroline Hazard (1856–). Amer. educator.

Hazlitt. . . . William Hazlitt (1778–1830). Eng. miscellaneous writer.

Hearn . . . . Lafcadio Hearn (1850–1904). Author of British parentage, journalist in United States, teacher in Japan, where he became naturalized.

Heber . . . . Reginald Heber (1783–1826). Eng. bishop, hymn writer.

F. H. Hedge . Frederic Henry Hedge (1805–1890). Amer. clergyman and hymn writer.

W. Heisenberg. Werner Heisenberg (1901–). German physicist.

V. Heiser . . Victor George Heiser (1873–). Amer. physician.

Sir A. Helps . Sir Arthur Helps (1813–75). Eng. essayist and historian.

Hemans . . . (Mrs.) Felicia Dorothea Hemans (1793–1835). Eng. poet.

Hemingway. . Ernest Hemingway (1898–). Amer. novelist.

B. Hendrick . Burton Jesse Hendrick (1871–). Amer. biographer.

Henley. . . . William Ernest Henley (1849–1903). Eng. poet and man of letters.

P. Henry. . . Patrick Henry (1736–99). Amer. statesman and orator.

Herbert. . . . George Herbert (1593–1633). Eng. poet.

J. Hergesheimer Joseph Hergesheimer (1880–). Amer. novelist.

Herrick . . . Robert Herrick (1591–1674). Eng. poet.

Hewlett . . . Maurice Henry Hewlett (1861–1923). Eng. novelist.

J. Heywood. . John Heywood (1497?–?1580). Eng. epigrammatist and author of interludes.

T. Heywood . Thomas Heywood (d. 1650?). Eng. dramatist.

T. W. Higginson . . . . Thomas Wentworth Storrow Higginson (1823–1911). Amer. clergyman and author.

Aaron Hill . . Aaron Hill (1685–1750). Eng. dramatist.

Hippocrates. . Hippocrates (c. 460–c. 357 B.C.). Greek physician.

Hobbes. . . . Thomas Hobbes (1588–1679). Eng. philosopher.

J. C. Hobhouse John Cam Hobhouse (1786–1869), Baron Broughton de Gyfford. Eng. statesman.

J. A. Hobson . John Atkinson Hobson (1858–1940). Eng. economist.

R. Hodgson . . Ralph Hodgson (1872?–). Eng. poet.

M. Hoffman . Malvina Hoffman (1887–). Amer. sculptor.

J. G. Holland. Josiah Gilbert Holland (1819–1881). Amer. author, editor.

Holmes . . . Oliver Wendell Holmes, sr. (1809–94). Amer. physician and man of letters.

Justice Holmes Oliver Wendell Holmes, jr. (1841–1935). Associate justice, U. S. Supreme Court.

Holt & Chilton Lucius Hudson Holt (1881–), Amer. educator and lexicographer, and Alexander Wheeler Chilton (1885?–), Amer. army officer and educator.

Hood . . . . Thomas Hood (1799–1845). Eng. poet.

T. Hook . . . Theodore Edward Hook (1788–1841). Eng. novelist.

Hooker. . . . Richard Hooker (1554?–1600). Eng. theologian.

E. Hooker . . Edward Hooker (fl. 1683). Eng. editor.

T. Hope . . . Thomas Hope (1770?–1831). Brit. connoisseur and author.

Housman. . . Alfred Edward Housman (1859–1936). Eng. classical scholar and poet.

Howells . . . William Dean Howells (1837–1920). Amer. novelist and critic.

Hudson . . . William Henry Hudson (1841–1922). Naturalist and author in Argentina and England; of Amer. parentage, later naturalized Brit. subject.

[Hueffer] . . . Ford Madox Hueffer. See Ford Madox FORD, above.

T. Hughes . . Thomas Hughes (1822–96). Eng. author.

Hume . . . . David Hume (1711–76). Scot. historian and philosopher.

Hunt . . . . (James Henry) Leigh Hunt (1784–1859). Eng. poet, essayist, and critic.

R. Hurd . . . Richard Hurd (1720–1808). Eng. bishop and author.

R. M. Hutchins Robert Maynard Hutchins (1899–). Amer. educator.

A. Huxley . . Aldous (Leonard) Huxley (1894–). Eng. novelist and essayist.

T. H. Huxley . Thomas Henry Huxley (1825–1895). Eng. biologist.

Infeld . . . . Leopold Infeld. See EINSTEIN & INFELD, above.

Inge. . . . . William Ralph Inge (1860–). Eng. clergyman and author.

Ingelow . . . (Miss) Jean Ingelow (1820–97). Eng. poet.

Irish Statesman . . . . Weekly journal (pub. Dublin & London 1919–20, 1923–30).

Irving . . . . Washington Irving (1783–1859). Amer. essayist.

H. H. Jackson. Helen (Maria) Hunt Jackson (1830–85). Amer. poet and novelist.

G. P. R. James George Payne Rainsford James (1799–1860). Eng. novelist.

H. James . . Henry James (1843–1916). Amer. novelist.

W. James . . William James (1842–1910). Amer. philosopher.

Mrs. Jameson. (Mrs.) Anna Brownell Jameson (1794–1860). Irish author.

Jay . . . . . John Jay (1745–1829). First chief justice of U. S.

Jeans . . . . Sir James Hopwood Jeans (1877–). Eng. physicist.

Jefferies . . . Richard Jefferies (1848–87). Eng. naturalist and author.

Jefferson . . . Thomas Jefferson (1743–1826). Third President of the United States.

Jeffrey. . . . Francis Jeffrey (1773–1850), Lord Jeffrey. Scot. judge and literary critic.

J. Jekyll . . . Joseph Jekyll (d. 1837). Eng. wit and politician.

J. Jennings. . James Jennings (fl. 1825). Eng. philologist.

Jevons . . . . William Stanley Jevons (1835–1882). Eng. logician and political economist.

Sarah O. Jewett Sarah Orne Jewett (1849–1909). Amer. story writer.

Johnson . . . Samuel Johnson (1709–84). Eng. lexicographer.

J. W. Johnson James Weldon Johnson (1871–1938). Amer. poet.

D. Jones . . . Daniel Jones (1881–). Eng. phonetician.

R. Jones . . . Rufus Matthew Jones (1863–). Amer. educator.

Sir W. Jones . Sir William Jones (1746–94). Eng. Orientalist.

B. Jonson . . Ben (properly Benjamin) Jonson (1573?–1637). Eng. dramatist and poet.

T. Jordan . . Thomas Jordan (1612?–85). Eng. poet.

Jowett . . . . Benjamin Jowett (1817–93). Eng. scholar; translator of Plato.

Joyce . . . . James Joyce (1882–1941). Irish novelist.

Junius. . . . *Letters of Junius* (1769–72): series of political letters attacking persons prominent in British public life. Cf. Philip FRANCIS, above.

W. Kaempffert Waldemar Bernhard Kaempffert (1877–). Amer. writer on science.

Karsten . . . Rafael Karsten (1879–). Finnish anthropologist.

M. Keating. . Maurice Bagenal St. Leger Keating (d. 1835). Brit. author.

Keats . . . . John Keats (1795–1821). Eng. poet.

Keble . . . . John Keble (1792–1866). Eng. clergyman and poet.

T. Keightley . Thomas Keightley (1789–1872). Irish author.

F. Kemble . . Frances Anne ("Fanny") Kemble (1809–93). Eng. actress.

Ken . . . . . Thomas Ken, or Kenn (1637–1711). Eng. bishop and hymn writer.

Kent's Mechanical Engineers' Handbook . Tenth edition (of handbook orig. compiled by William Kent) rewritten by Robert Thurston Kent and a staff of specialists, pub. (1923) by John Wiley & Sons, N. Y.

Kinglake. . . Alexander William Kinglake (1809–91). Eng. historian.

Kingsley . . . Charles Kingsley (1819–75). Eng. clergyman and novelist.

H. Kingsley . Henry Kingsley (1830–76). Eng. novelist; brother of Charles.

Kipling . . . Rudyard Kipling (1865–1936). Eng. short-story writer, poet, and novelist.

Kittredge . . George Lyman Kittredge (1860–1941). Amer. scholar, educator, and author.

Knox . . . . John Knox (1505–72). Scot. divine and leader of Reformation.

V. Knox . . . Vicesimus Knox (1752–1821). Eng. essayist.

W. Knox. . . William Knox (1789–1825). Scot. poet.

J. W. Krutch . Joseph Wood Krutch (1893–). Amer. critic.

Kyd . . . . . Thomas Kyd (1557?–?1595). Eng. dramatist.

Lamb . . . . Charles Lamb (1775–1834). Eng. essayist and critic.

C. & M. Lamb Charles (preceding entry) and his sister Mary Ann Lamb (1764–1847), authors, in collaboration, of *Tales from Shakespeare.*

Landor. . . . Walter Savage Landor (1775–1864). Eng. poet and miscellaneous writer.

A. Lang . . . Andrew Lang (1844–1912). Scot. novelist and poet.

Langland. . . William Langland (1332?–?1400). Supposed name of English poet, author of *Piers Plowman.* Cf. PIERS PLOWMAN, below.

S. Lanier. . . Sidney Lanier (1842–81). Amer. poet.

Lardner . . . Ring (properly Ringgold Wilmer) Lardner (1885–1933). Amer. short-story writer.

G. P. Lathrop. George Parsons Lathrop (1851–1898). Amer. author and poet.

Latimer . . . Hugh Latimer (1485?–1555). Eng. bishop and martyr.

Laurier . . . Sir Wilfrid Laurier (1841–1919). Canadian statesman.

D. H. Lawrence David Herbert Lawrence (1885–1930). Eng. novelist.

W. Lawrence . William Lawrence (1850–1941). Amer. Protestant Episcopal bishop and author.

Law Times . . Eng. weekly law journal (est. 1843).

Lecky . . . . William Edward Hartpole Lecky (1838–1903). Irish historian.

F. Ledwidge . Francis Ledwidge (1891–1917). Irish poet.

Vernon Lee. . Pseudonym of Violet Paget (1856–1935). Brit. miscellaneous writer.

R. Le Gallienne Richard Le Gallienne (1866–). Eng. man of letters.

C. G. Leland . Charles Godfrey Leland (1824–1903). Amer. humorist.

L'Estrange . . Sir Roger L'Estrange (1616–1704). Eng. pamphleteer.

Lever . . . . Charles James Lever (1806–1872). Irish novelist.

G. H. Lewes . George Henry Lewes (1817–1878). Eng. philosophical writer.

Day Lewis . . Cecil Day Lewis (1904–). Eng. poet and author.

Sinc. Lewis. . Sinclair Lewis (1885–). Amer. novelist.

L. Lewisohn . Ludwig Lewisohn (1882–). Amer. author and critic.

H. P. Liddon . Henry Parry Liddon (1829–1890). Eng. clergyman.

Lincoln . . . Abraham Lincoln (1809–65). 16th President of the United States.

J. C. Lincoln . Joseph Crosby Lincoln (1870–). Amer. novelist.

V. Lindsay . . (Nicholas) Vachel Lindsay (1879–1931). Amer. poet.

J. Lingard . . John Lingard (1771–1851). Eng. historian.

Lippmann . . Walter Lippmann (1889–). Amer. editor and author.

Livingstone . . David Livingstone (1813–73). Scot. explorer.

Locke . . . . John Locke (1632–1704). Eng. philosopher.

W. J. Locke . William John Locke (1863–1930). Brit. novelist.

Lockhart . . . John Gibson Lockhart (1794–1854). Scot. biographer.

J. N. Lockyer. Sir Joseph Norman Lockyer (1836–1920). Eng. astronomer.

von Logau . . Baron Friedrich von Logau (1604–55). German poet and epigrammatist.

Longfellow . . Henry Wadsworth Longfellow (1807–82). Amer. poet.

R. Lord . . . Russell Lord (1895–). Amer. author and editor.

Lovelace . . . Richard Lovelace (1618–58). Eng. poet.

Lover . . . . Samuel Lover (1797–1868). Irish novelist.

Amy Lowell. . Amy Lowell (1874–1925). Amer. poet.

J. R. Lowell . James Russell Lowell (1819–1891). Amer. author, poet, and diplomat.

Lowes . . . . John Livingston Lowes (1867–). Amer. educator, scholar, and author.

J. Lubbock . . Sir John Lubbock (1834–1913), 1st Baron Avebury. Eng. banker and naturalist.

Lucas . . . . Edward Verrall Lucas (1868–1938). Eng. essayist, editor, and publisher.

Ludlow. . . . Edmund Ludlow (1617?–92). Eng. regicide and republican leader.

Lyell . . . . Sir Charles Lyell (1797–1875). Brit. geologist.

Lyly. . . . . John Lyly (1554?–1606). Eng. dramatist and author.

Lytton . . . . Edward George Earle Lytton Bulwer-Lytton (1803–73), 1st Baron Lytton. Eng. author and statesman.

Ward McAllister. . . . (Samuel) Ward McAllister (1827–95). Amer. society leader who originated phrase "the 400."

Macaulay . . Thomas Babington Macaulay (1800–59), 1st Baron Macaulay. Eng. historian and essayist.

R. Macaulay . Rose Macaulay (1889?–). Eng. novelist.

J. M'Carthy . Justin M'Carthy (1830–1912). Irish novelist and politician.

McClure's Mag. . . . *McClure's Magazine*, Amer. monthly, founded, edited and published (1893–1929) by Samuel Sidney McClure.

G. Macdonald. George Macdonald (1824–1905). Scot. poet and novelist.

Wm. McDougall . . . . William McDougall (1871–1938). Brit. psychologist.

Wm. McFee . William McFee (1881–). Eng. marine engineer and novelist in U. S.

J. W. Mackail John William Mackail (1859–). Brit. classicist.

C. Mackay . . Charles Mackay (1814–89). Scot. poet.

C. Mackenzie . Compton Mackenzie (1883–). Eng. novelist.

H. Mackenzie. Henry Mackenzie (1745–1831). Scot. novelist.

J. Mackintosh. Sir James Mackintosh (1765–1832). Scot. philosopher.

J. A. Macy. . John Albert Macy (1877–1932). Amer. author.

J. Madison. . James Madison (1751–1836). Fourth President of the United States.

Maine . . . . Sir Henry James Sumner Maine (1822–88). Brit. jurist.

W. H. Mallock William Hurrell Mallock (1849–1923). Eng. philosophical writer.

Kemp Malone. Kemp Malone (1889–). Amer. philologist.

Malory . . . Sir Thomas Malory (fl. 1470). Eng. translator and compiler of *Le Morte d'Arthur.*

Manchester Examiner. . . . Manchester (Eng.) daily newspaper (started as a weekly 1846; pub. daily 1855–94).

Manchester Guardian. . Manchester (Eng.) daily newspaper (started as a weekly 1821; pub. daily since 1855).

B. Mandeville. Bernard Mandeville (1670?–1733). Eng. satirist, of Dutch parentage.

Horace Mann. Horace Mann (1796–1859). Amer. educator.

Manning. . . Henry Edward Manning (1808–1892). Eng. Roman Catholic cardinal.

B. Mantle . . (Robert) Burns Mantle (1873–). Amer. drama critic.

Manual of Prayers . . A Manual of Prayers for the use of the Catholic Laity.

Markham . . (Charles) Edwin Markham (1852–1940). Amer. poet.

Marlowe . . . Christopher Marlowe (1564–1593). Eng. dramatist.

J. P. Marquand . . . John Phillips Marquand (1893–). Amer. novelist.

Marryat . . (Captain) Frederick Marryat (1792–1848). Eng. naval officer and novelist.

H. Marryat. . Horace Marryat (fl. 1860). Eng. author.

G. P. Marsh . George Perkins Marsh (1801–1882). Amer. philologist and diplomat.

Alfred Marshall. . . . Alfred Marshall (1842–1924). Eng. political economist.

Arch. Marshall Archibald Marshall (1866–1934). Eng. novelist.

Ch. Just. Marshall. . . . John Marshall (1755–1835). Chief justice of U. S.

Marston . . . John Marston (1575?–1634). Eng. dramatist.

H. Martineau. Harriet Martineau (1802–76). Eng. novelist and economist.

J. Martineau . James Martineau (1805–1900). Eng. Unitarian divine and writer; brother of preceding.

Marvell . . . Andrew Marvell (1621–78). Eng. poet.

Masefield. . . John Masefield (1875–). Eng. poet laureate.

Massinger . . Philip Massinger (1583–1640). Eng. dramatist.

E. L. Masters. Edgar Lee Masters (1869–). Amer. poet.

Cotton Mather. Cotton Mather (1663–1728). Amer. theologian.

F. J. Mather . Frank Jewett Mather (1868–). Amer. art critic and educator.

G. Matheson . George Matheson (1842–1906). Scot. clergyman and author.

C. Mathewson. Christopher ("Christy") Mathewson (1880–1925). Amer. baseball player.

B. Matthews . (James) Brander Matthews (1852–1929). Amer. educator and author.

Maugham . . (William) Somerset Maugham (1874–). Eng. novelist and dramatist.

F. D. Maurice. (John) Frederick Denison Maurice (1805–72). Eng. religious historian.

J. F. Maurice. Sir John Frederick Maurice (1841–1912). Eng. military writer.

T. Maurice. . Thomas Maurice (1754–1824). Eng. Orientalist.

M. F. Maury . Matthew Fontaine Maury (1806–73). Amer. oceanographer.

Max Müller . Friedrich Max Müller (1823–1900). Brit. philologist.

Melville . . . Herman Melville (1819–91). Amer. novelist.

Mencken . . . Henry Louis Mencken (1880–). Amer. editor, critic.

Meredith . . . George Meredith (1828–1909). Eng. novelist and poet.

C. Merivale. Charles Merivale (1808–93). Eng. clergyman and historian.

J. Merrick . . James Merrick (1720–69). Eng. poet and scholar.

P. W. Merrill. Paul Willard Merrill (1887–). Amer. astronomer.

[Merriman]. . H(enry) Seton Merriman. See Hugh Stowell SCOTT, below.

Michigan Alumnus Quarterly Review. . . Publication of the Alumni Association of the University of Michigan, Ann Arbor, Mich.

W. J. Mickle . William Julius Mickle (1735–1788). Scot. poet.

Middleton . . Thomas Middleton (1570?–1627). Eng. dramatist.

C. Middleton . Conyers Middleton (1683–1750). Eng. clergyman.

H. R. Mill . . Hugh Robert Mill (1861–). Scot. geographer and meteorologist.

James Mill. . James Mill (1773–1836). Scot. utilitarian philosopher.

J. S. Mill . . John Stuart Mill (1806–73). Brit. philosopher and political economist; son of preceding.

Millay. . . . Edna St. Vincent Millay (b. 1892). Amer. poet.

Joaquin Miller Pen name of Cincinnatus Hiner Miller (1841–1913). Amer. poet.

Milman . . . Henry Hart Milman (1791–1868). Eng. religious historian and dramatist.

Milton. . . . John Milton (1608–74). Eng. poet.

D. G. Mitchell. Donald Grant Mitchell (1822–1908). Amer. author.

M. R. Mitford. Mary Russell Mitford (1787–1855). Eng. novelist and dramatist.

Modern Language Notes. Amer. scholarly monthly (est. 1886), pub. Baltimore, Md.

J. H. Monk. . James Henry Monk (1784–1856). Eng. bishop and classicist.

Lady M. W. Montagu . . Lady Mary Wortley Montagu (1689–1762). Eng. letter writer.

C. E. Montague . . Charles Edward Montague (1867–1928). Eng. author.

Montrose. . . James Graham (1612–50), 1st Marquis of Montrose. Scot. soldier and verse writer.

W. V. Moody. William Vaughn Moody (1869–1910). Amer. poet and dramatist.

G. Moore. . . George Moore (1852–1933). Irish novelist.

J. Moore. . . John Moore (1729–1802). Scot. physician and writer.

T. Moore. . . Thomas Moore (1779–1852). Irish poet.

Hannah More. Hannah More (1745–1833). Eng. philanthropist.

Henry More . Henry More (1614–87). Eng. philosopher.

P. E. More. . Paul Elmer More (1864–1937). Amer. editor and critic.

Lloyd Morgan. Conway Lloyd Morgan (1852–1936). Eng. biologist.

Lady S. Morgan . . . Lady Sydney Morgan (1783?–1859). Irish novelist.

C. Morley . . Christopher Darlington Morley (1890–). Amer. novelist.

J. Morley . . John Morley (1838–1923), Viscount Morley of Blackburn. Eng. author and statesman.

W. Morris . . William Morris (1834–1896). Eng. poet and artist.

A. C. Morrison A(braham) Cressy Morrison (1864–). Amer. chemist and author.

Motley. . . . John Lothrop Motley (1814–1877). Amer. historian.

J. B. Mozley . James Bowling Mozley (1813–1878). Eng. theologian.

Müller, Max . See MAX MÜLLER, above.

Mulock . . . (Mrs.) Dinah Maria Craik, nee Mulock (1826–87). Eng. novelist.

Carl Murchison . . . Carl Murchison (1887–). Amer. psychologist.

G. Murray . . (George) Gilbert (Aimé) Murray (1866–). Brit. Greek scholar and author.

J. M. Murry . John Middleton Murry (1889–). Eng. author.

F. W. H. Myers Frederic William Henry Myers (1843–1901). Eng. poet and essayist.

C. Nairne . . Carolina Nairne (1766–1845), Baroness Nairne. Scot. ballad writer.

Nash . . . . Thomas Nash, or Nashe (1567–1601). Eng. pamphleteer and dramatist.

The Nation. . Amer. weekly journal of opinion and comment (est. 1865).

Naval Chronicle . . Eng. naval journal (1799–1818).

Nelson. . . . Horatio Nelson (1758–1805). Viscount Nelson. Eng. admiral.

New Freeman. Amer. weekly journal of opinion (Mar. 1930–May 1931).

Newman . . . John Henry Newman (1801–1890). Eng. Roman Catholic cardinal and author.

New Republic. Amer. weekly journal of opinion (est. 1914).

Newton . . . Sir Isaac Newton (1642–1727). Eng. mathematician and physicist.

J. Newton . . John Newton (1725–1807). Eng. clergyman and hymn writer.

N. Nicholls. . Norton Nicholls (1742?–1809). Eng. clergyman and letter writer.

M. Nicholson . Meredith Nicholson (1866–). Amer. author and diplomat.

Nineteenth Century . . Brit. monthly review (founded 1877 by Sir J. T. Knowles; from 1900 called *The Nineteenth Century and After*).

R. North . . Roger North (1653–1734). Eng. lawyer and historian.

North American Review . Amer. quarterly review (est. 1815).

C. E. Norton . Charles Eliot Norton (1827–1908). Amer. author and educator.

A. Noyes. . . Alfred Noyes (1880–). Eng. poet.

N. Y. Herald Tribune . . New York daily newspaper (est. 1924 by Ogden Reid by merger of *N. Y. Herald,* founded in 1835 by James Gordon Bennet, and *N. Y. Tribune,* founded in 1841 by Horace Greeley).

N. Y. Sun . . New York daily newspaper (founded 1833 by Benjamin H. Day).

N. Y. Times . New York daily newspaper (founded 1851 by Henry J. Raymond).

Mrs. Oliphant. Mrs. Margaret Oliphant (1828–1897). Scot. novelist.

C. Oman . . . Sir Charles William Chadwick Oman (1860–). Eng. historian.

J. B. O'Reilly. John Boyle O'Reilly (1844–90). Irish poet and journalist.

Osler. Sir William Osler (1849–1919). Canadian physician and author.

Otway. Thomas Otway (1652–85). Eng. dramatist.

Ouida. Pen name of Marie Louise de la Ramée (1839–1908). Eng. novelist.

Oxf. E. D. *A New English Dictionary on Historical Principles*, ed. by Sir James A. H. Murray and his successors Henry Bradley, Sir W. A. Craigie, and C. T. Onions, pub. by Oxford Univ. Press (1884–1928; supplement 1933).

Paderewski. Ignacy Jan Paderewski (1860–1941). Polish pianist, composer, and statesman.

W. H. Page. Walter Hines Page (1855–1918). Amer. editor and diplomat.

Wm. Page. William Page (1861–1934). Eng. editor and historian.

H. W. Paget. Henry William Paget (1768–1854), 1st Marquis of Anglesey. Eng. soldier and politician.

[V. Paget]. Violet Paget. See Vernon LEE, above.

T. Paine. Thomas Paine (1737–1809). Amer. political philosopher, of English birth.

W. Paley. William Paley (1743–1805). Eng. clergyman.

F. Palgrave. Sir Francis Palgrave (1788–1861). Eng. historian.

F. T. Palgrave. Francis Turner Palgrave (1824–1897). Eng. poet and critic; son of preceding.

Pall Mall Gazette. London (Eng.) daily newspaper (1865–1923, when it was incorporated in *The Evening Standard*).

G. Parker. Sir Gilbert Parker (1862–1932). Canadian novelist.

Parkman. Francis Parkman (1823–93). Amer. historian.

Pater. Walter Horatio Pater (1839–1894). Eng. critic and humanist.

Patmore. Coventry (Kersey Dighton) Patmore (1823–96). Eng. poet.

M. Pattison. Mark Pattison (1813–84). Eng. scholar and author.

J. H. Payne. John Howard Payne (1791–1852). Amer. playwright.

Peace Handbooks. Series of 25 vols. prepared under direction of Historical Section of (British) Foreign Office (1920; G. W. Prothero general editor).

Peacock. Thomas Love Peacock (1785–1866). Eng. satirical novelist.

G. Peele. George Peele (1558?–?1597). Eng. dramatist.

Penn. William Penn (1644–1718). Eng. Quaker; founder of Pennsylvania.

T. Pennant. Thomas Pennant (1726–98). Brit. naturalist and traveler.

Pepys. Samuel Pepys (1633–1703). Eng. diarist.

Percy. Thomas Percy (1729–1811). Eng. bishop, editor, and antiquarian.

Bliss Perry. Bliss Perry (1860–). Amer. author and educator.

O. H. Perry. Oliver Hazard Perry (1785–1819). Amer. naval officer.

J. Phillips. John Phillips (1800–74). Eng. geologist.

W. Phillips. Wendell Phillips (1811–84). Amer. orator.

E. Phillpotts. Eden Phillpotts (1862–). Eng. novelist.

Piers Plowman *The Vision of Piers Plowman*, Middle English poem (c. 1362). Cf. William LANGLAND, above.

Poe. Edgar Allan Poe (1809–49). Amer. poet and story writer.

F. Pollock. Sir Frederick Pollock (1845–1937). Eng. legal scholar.

Pope. Alexander Pope (1688–1744). Eng. poet.

Jane Porter. Jane Porter (1776–1850). Eng. novelist.

B. Porteus. Beilby Porteus (1731–1808). Eng. bishop.

J. C. Powys. John Cowper Powys (1872–). Eng. author.

Praed. Winthrop Mackworth Praed (1802–39). Eng. poet and politician.

Precepts of Hippocrates. Cf. HIPPOCRATES above.

Prescott William Hickling Prescott (1796–1859). Amer. historian.

J. B. Priestley. John Boynton Priestley (1894–). Eng. novelist and playwright.

Prior. Matthew Prior (1664–1721). Eng. poet and diplomatist.

Prynne. William Prynne (1600–69). Eng. Puritan controversialist.

Publishers' Weekly. Amer. journal of the book-publishing trade (est. 1872).

Punch. London (Eng.) humorous weekly (founded 1840 by Mark Lemon, who was also its first editor, and Henry Mayhew).

Pusey. Edward Bouverie Pusey (1800–1882). Eng. clergyman.

Quarles. Francis Quarles (1592–1644). Eng. poet.

Quiller-Couch. Sir Arthur (Thomas) Quiller-Couch (1863–). Eng. author and educator.

Jos. Quincy. Josiah Quincy (1744–75). Amer. lawyer.

Rabelais. François Rabelais (1494?–1553). French satirist (translated by Sir Thomas Urquhart).

Mrs. Radcliffe. (Mrs.) Ann Radcliffe (1764–1823). Eng. novelist.

Raleigh [d. 1618]. Sir Walter Raleigh (1552?–1618). Eng. courtier, author, and navigator.

Sir W. Raleigh [d. 1922]. Sir Walter Alexander Raleigh (1861–1922). Eng. essayist and biographer.

A. Ramsay. Allan Ramsay (1686–1758). Scot. poet.

J. H. Randall, jr. John Herman Randall, jr. (1899–). Amer. author and educator.

Rand Daily Mail. Johannesburg (S. Africa) daily newspaper.

G. Rawlinson. George Rawlinson (1812–1902). Eng. clergyman, historian.

H. Read. Herbert Read (1893–). Eng. editor, critic, and poet.

Reade. Charles Reade (1814–84). Eng. novelist.

H. Reed. Henry Hope Reed (1808–54). Amer. man of letters.

L. W. Reese. Lizette Woodworth Reese (1856–1935). Amer. poet.

A. Repplier. Agnes Repplier (1858–). Amer. essayist.

Revised Version Revised Version (1885) of the Bible. See note preceding this list.

Sir J. Reynolds Sir Joshua Reynolds (1723–92.) Eng. portrait painter.

Rice. James Rice (1843–82). Eng. novelist; collaborator with Walter Besant (see above).

Richardson. Samuel Richardson (1689–1761). Eng. novelist.

J. W. Riley. James Whitcomb Riley (1849–1916). Amer. poet.

W. Z. Ripley. William Zebina Ripley (1867–1941). Amer. economist and ethnologist.

W. Ripman. Walter Ripman (1869–). Eng. phonetician and philologist.

L. Ritchie. Leitch Ritchie (1800?–65). Scot. novelist.

E. M. Roberts. Elizabeth Madox Roberts (1886–1941). Amer. novelist and poet.

A. Robertson. Alexander Robertson (fl. 1903). Brit. author.

F. W. Robertson. Frederick William Robertson (1816–53). Eng. clergyman.

J. M. Robertson. John Mackinnon Robertson (1856–1933). Brit. author.

W. Robertson. William Robertson (1721–93). Scot. historian.

Crabb Robinson Henry Crabb Robinson (1775–1867). Eng. lawyer and diarist.

Cyril Robinson Cyril Edward Robinson (1884–). Brit. historian.

E. A. Robinson Edwin Arlington Robinson (1869–1935). Amer. poet.

F. W. Robinson. Frederick William Robinson (1830–1901). Eng. novelist.

J. J. Roche. James Jeffrey Roche (1847–1908). Irish-Amer. poet.

J. Rogers. John Rogers (fl. 1839). Brit. anti-Catholic polemicist.

S. Rogers. Samuel Rogers (1763–1855). Eng. poet.

E. Roosevelt. (Anna) Eleanor Roosevelt (1884–). Amer. author; wife of F. D. Roosevelt.

F. D. Roosevelt Franklin Delano Roosevelt (1882–). 32d President of the United States.

Roscommon. Wentworth Dillon (1633?–1685), 4th Earl of Roscommon. Eng. poet and critic.

Rosebery. Archibald Philip Primrose (1847–1929), 5th Earl of Rosebery. Eng. statesman.

C. Rossetti Christina Georgina Rossetti (1830–94). Eng. poet.

D. G. Rossetti. Dante Gabriel Rossetti (1828–1882). Eng. painter and poet.

C. Rourke. Constance Mayfield Rourke (1885–1941). Amer. author.

Rowe. Nicholas Rowe (1674–1718). Eng. poet and dramatist.

Ruskin. John Ruskin (1819–1900). Eng. author and social reformer.

B. Russell. Bertrand (Arthur William) Russell (1872–), 3d Earl Russell. Eng. mathematician and philosopher.

G. W. Russell. George William Russell (1867–1935); pseudonym Æ. Irish poet and painter.

R. V. =REVISED VERSION, above.

A. J. Ryan. Abram Joseph Ryan (1838–86). Amer. Roman Catholic priest and poet.

V. Sackville-West. Victoria Mary Sackville-West (1892–). Eng. novelist.

Saintsbury. George (Edward Bateman) Saintsbury (1845–1933). Eng. critic.

Sandburg. Carl Sandburg (1878–). Amer. poet.

J. E. Sandys. Sir John Edwin Sandys (1844–1922). Brit. Hellenist.

Santayana. George Santayana (1863–). Amer. philosopher, poet, and novelist.

Epes Sargent. Epes Sargent (1813–80). Amer. song writer.

Sat. Review. *Saturday Review*, Eng. weekly (est. as a Liberal organ 1855; amalgamated with *The Spectator* 1931).

Sat. Review of Lit. *Saturday Review of Literature*, Amer. literary weekly (est. 1924).

Schaff-Herzog. *The New Schaff-Herzog Encyclopedia of Religious Knowledge*, editor in chief Samuel Macauley Jackson, pub. (1908; 12 vols.) by Funk & Wagnalls Co., New York.

J. S. Schapiro. Jacob Salwyn Schapiro (1879–). Amer. historian.

H. Scherman Harry Scherman (1887–). Amer. economist.

School and Society. Amer. educational weekly (est. 1915).

O. Schreiner. Olive Schreiner (1855–1920). S. African novelist.

Science. American scientific weekly (est. 1883).

Scoresby. William Scoresby (1760–1829). Eng. arctic navigator.

Scott . . . . Sir Walter Scott (1771–1832). Scot. novelist and poet.

G. G. Scott . . Sir George Gilbert Scott (1811–1878). Brit. architect.

H. S. Scott . . Hugh Stowell Scott (1862–1903); pseudonym H(enry) Seton Merriman. Eng. novelist.

Scribner's . . *Scribner's Magazine,* Amer. monthly (1887–1939).

E. W. Scripture Edward Wheeler Scripture (1864–). Amer. phonetician and speech specialist.

H. E. Scudder. Horace Elisha Scudder (1838–1902). Amer. author.

T. Seccombe . Thomas Seccombe (1866–1923). Eng. critic and biographer.

T. Secker. . . Thomas Secker (1693–1768). Eng. archbishop.

A. D. Sedgwick Anne Douglas Sedgwick (1873–1935), Mrs. Basil de Selincourt. Amer. novelist in England.

A. Seeger. . . Alan Seeger (1888–1916). Amer. poet.

J. R. Seeley. . Sir John Robert Seeley (1834–1895). Eng. historian.

Shaftesbury. . Anthony Ashley Cooper (1671–1713), 3d Earl of Shaftesbury. Eng. philosopher.

Shak. . . . . William Shakespeare (1564–1616). Eng. dramatist and poet.

J. Sharp . . John Sharp (1645–1714). Eng. archbishop.

Shaw . . . . George Bernard Shaw (1856–). Brit. playwright, critic, and author.

J. Sheffield . . John Sheffield (1648–1721), 1st Duke of Buckingham. Eng. miscellaneous writer, poet.

Shelley. . . . Percy Bysshe Shelley (1792–1822). Eng. poet.

Shenstone. . . William Shenstone (1714–63). Eng. poet.

Sheridan . . . Richard Brinsley Sheridan (1751–1816). Irish playwright and politician.

S. P. Sherman. Stuart Pratt Sherman (1881–1926). Amer. educator and literary critic.

Shirley. . . . James Shirley (1596–1666). Eng. dramatist and poet.

J. H. Shorthouse Joseph Henry Shorthouse (1834–1903). Eng. novelist.

Sidney. . . . Sir Philip Sidney (1554–86). Eng. poet, soldier, and statesman.

E. R. Sill . . Edward Rowland Sill (1841–1887). Amer. poet.

M. Sinclair. . May Sinclair (1870?–). Eng. novelist.

Adam Smith . Adam Smith (1723–90). Scot. economist.

Alfred E. Smith Alfred Emanuel Smith (1873–). Amer. politician.

G. Smith . . . Goldwin Smith (1823–1910). Eng. historian and educator.

H. Smith. . . Horace (properly Horatio) Smith (1779–1849). Eng. poet.

J. R. Smith. . Josiah Renick Smith (1851–1914). Amer. educator.

L. P. Smith. . Logan Pearsall Smith (1865–). Amer. miscellaneous writer in England.

Preserved Smith . . . Preserved Smith (1880–1941). Amer. historian.

S. F. Smith. . Samuel Francis Smith (1808–1895). Amer. hymn writer and poet.

Sydney Smith Sydney Smith (1771–1845). Eng. clergyman and wit.

Smollett . . . Tobias (George) Smollett (1721–71). Scot. novelist.

J. C. Snaith . John Collis Snaith (1862?–1936). Eng. novelist.

Social Science Abstracts . Amer. sociological monthly (1929–32).

South . . . . Robert South (1634–1716). Eng. court preacher and author.

Southey . . . Robert Southey (1774–1843). Eng. poet laureate and miscellaneous writer.

J. M. Spearman James Morton Spearman (fl. 1828). Brit. artillerist.

Spectator . . . *The Spectator,* Eng. literary daily conducted by Richard Steele and Joseph Addison (Mar. 1, 1711–Dec. 6, 1712) and by Addison alone (for 80 issues, 1714).

The Spectator . Eng. weekly (founded by Robert S. Rintoul 1828; amalgamated with *The Saturday Review* 1931).

Speed . . . . John Speed (1552–1629). Eng. historian and cartographer.

J. Spence . . James Spence (fl. 1861). Brit. writer on constitutional law.

H. Spencer . . Herbert Spencer (1820–1903). Eng. philosopher.

S. Spender . . Stephen Spender (1909–). Eng. poet.

Spenser . . . Edmund Spenser (1552?–99). Eng. poet.

Springfield [Mass.] Republican . Springfield (Mass.) daily newspaper (est. 1824).

Springfield [Mass.] Union Springfield (Mass.) daily newspaper (est. 1864).

C. H. Spurgeon Charles Haddon Spurgeon (1834–92). Eng. preacher.

Dean Stanley . Arthur Penrhyn Stanley (1815–1881). Eng. clergyman and author; dean of Westminster.

Statesman's Year-Book . Brit. "Statistical and historical annual of the states of the world," pub. London, Eng. (since 1863).

Steele . . . . Sir Richard Steele (1672–1729). Eng. essayist and dramatist.

L. Stephen . . Sir Leslie Stephen (1832–1904). Eng. man of letters.

J. Stephens. . James Stephens (1882–). Irish poet and novelist.

Sterne . . . . Laurence Sterne (1713–68). Eng. clergyman and novelist.

Stevenson. . . Robert Louis Stevenson (1850–1894). Scot. novelist, poet, and playwright.

Stewart . . . Balfour Stewart. See Tait & Stewart, below.

D. Stewart . . Dugald Stewart (1753–1828). Scot. philosopher.

Stirling . . . Sir William Alexander (1567?–1640), Earl of Stirling. Scot. poet and politician.

J. C. Stobart . John Clarke Stobart (1878–1933). Brit. archaeologist.

H. B. Stowe . Harriet Beecher Stowe, nee Harriet Elizabeth Beecher (1811–96). Amer. novelist.

L. Strachey . (Giles) Lytton Strachey (1880–1932). Eng. biographer.

A. Stringer . . Arthur (John Arbuthnot) Stringer (1874–). Canadian novelist and poet.

Jan Struther . Pen name of Joyce Maxtone Graham, nee Anstruther (1901–). Eng. author.

J. G. Strutt. . Jacob George Strutt (fl. 1820–1850). Brit. painter and engraver.

Stubbs . . . . William Stubbs (1825–1901). Eng. bishop and historian.

Surtees. . . . Robert Smith Surtees (1803–1864). Eng. novelist.

Survey Graphic Amer. monthly magazine of opinion (successor in 1912 to *The Survey,* est. 1897).

H. Suzzallo. . Henry Suzzallo (1875–1933). Amer. educator.

Swift . . . . Jonathan Swift (1667–1745). Eng. satirist; dean of St. Patrick's, Dublin.

Swinburne . . Algernon Charles Swinburne (1837–1909). Eng. poet.

Symonds . . . John Addington Symonds (1840–93). English translator and author.

J. M. Synge . John Millington Synge (1871–1909). Irish dramatist.

Tait & Stewart Peter Guthrie Tait (1831–1901) and Balfour Stewart (1828–87). Brit. scientists, coauthors of *The Unseen Universe* (1875).

Ch. Just. Taney Roger Brooke Taney (1777–1864). Chief justice of U. S.

Tarkington . . (Newton) Booth Tarkington (1869–). Amer. novelist.

A. Tate . . . (John Orley) Allen Tate (1899–). Amer. author.

Tatler . . . . Eng. periodical founded by Richard Steele, and conducted by Steele and Joseph Addison (3 times a week; 1709–11).

B. Taylor . . (James) Bayard Taylor (1825–1878). Amer. author and poet.

H. Taylor . . Sir Henry Taylor (1800–86). Eng. poet.

I. Taylor. . . Isaac Taylor (1787–1865). Eng. author, inventor, and artist.

J. & A. Taylor Jane Taylor (1783–1824) and her sister Ann (1782–1866). Eng. nursery-rhyme writers.

Jer. Taylor . . Jeremy Taylor (1613–67). Eng. bishop and author.

Temple. . . . Sir William Temple (1628–99). Eng. politician and author.

E. W. Tennant E. Wyndham Tennant (fl. 1915). Brit. poet.

Tennyson . . Alfred Tennyson (1809–92), 1st Baron Tennyson. Eng. poet laureate.

H. Tennyson . Hallam Tennyson (1852–1928), 2d Baron Tennyson. Eng. author; son of preceding.

Thackeray . . William Makepeace Thackeray (1811–63). Eng. novelist.

Thirlwall. . . Connop Thirlwall (1797–1875). Eng. bishop and historian.

D. Thompson Dorothy Thompson (1894–). Amer. journalist.

F. Thompson . Francis Thompson (1859–1907). Eng. poet and author.

Thomson . . . James Thomson (1700–48). Scot. poet.

J. A. Thomson Sir (John) Arthur Thomson (1861–1933). Scot. biologist.

Thoreau . . . Henry David Thoreau (1817–1862). Amer. author.

Time . . . . Amer. weekly magazine summarizing current news (founded 1923 by Briton Hadden and Henry R. Luce).

The Times . . London (Eng.) daily newspaper (founded 1785 by John Walter as *The Daily Universal Register,* renamed *The Times* 1788).

Times Lit. Sup. *Times Literary Supplement,* London (Eng.) literary weekly (est. 1902).

R. B. Todd . . Robert Bentley Todd (1809–1860). Irish physician.

John Todhunter John Todhunter (1839–1916). British dramatist and poet.

Toplady . . . Augustus Montague Toplady (1740–78). Eng. clergyman and hymn writer.

Tourneur. . . Cyril Tourneur (1575?–1626). Eng. dramatist.

Trench. . . . Richard Chenevix Trench (1807–86). Eng. philologist, poet; archbishop of Dublin.

G. M. Trevelyan George Macaulay Trevelyan (1876–). Eng. historian.

G. O. Trevelyan Sir George Otto Trevelyan (1838–1928). Eng. biographer and historian; father of preceding.

Trollope . . . Anthony Trollope (1815–82). Eng. novelist.

A. Tucker . . Abraham Tucker (1705–74). Eng. philosopher.

Twain . . . . Mark Twain, pseudonym of Samuel Langhorne Clemens (1835–1910). Amer. novelist and humorist.

[Tweedsmuir] . Baron Tweedsmuir. See John Buchan, above.

E. B. Tylor. . Sir Edward Burnett Tylor (1832–1917). Eng. anthropologist.

K. Tynan . . Katharine Tynan (1861–1931); Mrs. H. A. Hinkson. Irish poet and novelist.

J. Tyndall . . John Tyndall (1820–93). Brit. physicist.

Udall Nicholas Udall, or Uvedale (1505–56). Eng. playwright.
E. Underhill Evelyn Underhill (1875–1941), Mrs. Stuart Moore. Eng. writer on mysticism.
U. S. Code Code of the Laws of the United States (1934 ed.).
U. S. Const. Constitution of the United States.
U. S. Daily. *The United States Daily,* Washington (D. C.) daily newspaper (1926–33) edited by David Lawrence.
Urquhart. Sir Thomas Urquhart, or Urchard (1611–60). Scot. translator of Rabelais.
Vanbrugh Sir John Vanbrugh (1664–1726). Eng. dramatist.
H. van Dyke Henry van Dyke (1852–1933). Amer. clergyman, author, and educator.
J. C. Van Dyke John Charles Van Dyke (1856–1932). Amer. art critic and librarian.
H. W. van Loon Hendrik Willem van Loon (1882–). Amer. author of Dutch birth.
Van Nostrand's Scientific Encyclopedia One-vol. encyclopedia (copyright 1938) pub. by D. Van Nostrand Co., New York.
Van Vechten Carl Van Vechten (1880–). Amer. critic and novelist.
R. A. Vaughan Robert Alfred Vaughan (1823–1857). Eng. Congregational clergyman and writer.
Vaux Thomas Vaux (1510–56), 2d Baron Vaux. Eng. poet.
Lady F. P. Verney. Lady Frances Parthenope Verney (d. 1890). Eng. author.
Viollet-le-Duc Eugène Emmanuel Viollet-le-Duc (1814–79). French architect.
von Logau See LOGAU, above.
C. Waldstein Sir Charles Walston, orig. Waldstein (1856–1927). Brit. archaeologist.
Waller Edmund Waller (1606–87). Eng. poet.
Walpole Horace Walpole (1717–97), 4th Earl of Orford. Eng. author.
Hugh Walpole. Sir Hugh Seymour Walpole (1884–1941). Eng. novelist.
T. Walsh. Thomas Walsh (1875–1928). Amer. poet and author.
Walton. Izaak Walton (1593–1683). English ironmonger and writer on angling.
Warburton William Warburton (1698–1779). Eng. bishop, scholar, and author.
A. W. Ward Sir Adolphus William Ward (1837–1924). Eng. historian.
Mrs. H. Ward. Mrs. Humphry Ward, nee Mary Augusta Arnold (1851–1920). Eng. novelist.
W. G. Ward. William George Ward (1812–1882). Eng. Roman Catholic theologian and philosopher.
H. R. Warfel Harry Redcay Warfel (1899–). Amer. educator.
C. D. Warner Charles Dudley Warner (1829–1900). Amer. author.
J. Warton Joseph Warton (1722–1800). Eng. literary critic.
T. Warton Thomas Warton (1728–90). Eng. poet.
Washington. George Washington (1732–99). First President of the United States.
C. Waterton. Charles Waterton (1782–1865). Eng. naturalist and explorer.
R. Watson Richard Watson (1737–1816). Eng. bishop and chemist.
W. Watson Sir William Watson (1858–1935). Eng. poet.
I. Watts Isaac Watts (1674–1748). Eng. clergyman and hymn writer.
Watts-Dunton. Walter Theodore Watts-Dunton (1832–1914). Eng. poet, novelist, and critic.
B. Waugh Benjamin Waugh (1839–1908). Eng. clergyman.
M. Webb. Mary Webb (1881–1927). Eng. novelist and poet.
D. Webster Daniel Webster (1782–1852). Amer. statesman.
J. Webster John Webster (1580?–?1625). Eng. dramatist.
N. Webster Noah Webster (1758–1843). Amer. lexicographer.
Webster's New Int. Dict., 2d Ed. *Webster's New International Dictionary, Second Edition* (copyright 1934), pub. by G. & C. Merriam Co., Springfield, Mass.
Wellington Arthur Wellesley (1769–1852), 1st Duke of Wellington. Brit. soldier.
C. Wells Carolyn Wells. Amer. writer.
H. G. Wells. Herbert George Wells (1866–). Eng. historian and novelist.
B. Wendell Barrett Wendell (1855–1921). Amer. author and educator.
C. Wesley Charles Wesley (1707–88). Eng. clergyman and hymn writer; brother of John.
J. Wesley John Wesley (1703–91). Eng. clergyman; founder of Methodism.
Rebecca West. Pseudonym of Mrs. Henry Maxwell Andrews, nee Cicily Isabel Fairfield (1892–). Eng. novelist.
B. F. Westcott. Brooke Foss Westcott (1825–1901). Eng. bishop and Bible scholar.
Westminster Rev. Westminster Review, Eng. quarterly (1824–1907) founded by Jeremy Bentham and James Mill.
E. Wharton. (Mrs.) Edith Newbold Wharton, nee Jones (1862–1937). Amer. novelist.
Whately Richard Whately (1787–1863). Eng. scholar and author; archbishop of Dublin.
E. J. Whately. Elizabeth Jane Whately (b. 1822). Eng. philanthropist and woman of letters; daughter of preceding.
H. B. Wheatley Henry Benjamin Wheatley (1838–1917). Eng. bibliographer and author.
Whewell William Whewell (1794–1866). Eng. philosopher and mathematician.
E. P. Whipple Edwin Percy Whipple (1819–1886). Amer. essayist and critic.
Gilbert White Gilbert White (1720–93). Eng. clergyman and naturalist.
S. E. White. Stewart Edward White (1873–). Amer. story writer.
W. A. White William Allen White (1868–). Amer. author and newspaper editor.
A. N. Whitehead. Alfred North Whitehead (1861–). Eng. mathematician and philosopher.
P. Whitehead Paul Whitehead (1710–74). Eng. poet and satirist.
W. Whitehead. William Whitehead (1715–85). Eng. poet laureate.
W. Whiting William Whiting (1825–78). Eng. hymn writer.
Whitman. Walt (properly Walter) Whitman (1819–92). Amer. poet.
W. D. Whitney William Dwight Whitney (1827–94). Amer. philologist.
Whittier John Greenleaf Whittier (1807–1892). Amer. poet.
Whyte-Melville George John Whyte-Melville (1821–78). Brit. author.
[Wiclif, Wickliffe] Variants of WYCLIFFE, below.
Kate D. Wiggin (Mrs.) Kate Douglas Wiggin, nee Smith (1856–1923). Amer. author.
Bp. S. Wilberforce. Samuel Wilberforce (1805–73). Eng. bishop and scholar.
Wilde Oscar Fingal O'Flahertie Wills Wilde (1856–1900). Irish poet, playwright, and wit.
T. Wilder Thornton Niven Wilder (1897–). Amer. novelist.
M. Wilkins. Mary Eleanor Wilkins (1852–1930); Mrs. Charles M. Freeman. Amer. novelist.
N. P. Willis Nathaniel Parker Willis (1806–1867). Amer. poet and journalist.
H. H. Wilson Horace Hayman Wilson (1786–1860). Eng. Orientalist.
J. Wilson John Wilson (1627?–96). Eng. playwright.
W. Wilson (Thomas) Woodrow Wilson (1856–1924). 28th President of the United States.
C. T. Winchester Caleb Thomas Winchester (1847–1920). Amer. educator and author.
W. Windham William Windham (1750–1810). Eng. politician.
W. Winter William Winter (1836–1917). Amer. dramatic critic.
Winthrop. John Winthrop, sr. (1588–1649). First governor of Massachusetts Bay Colony.
Wiseman. Nicholas Patrick Stephen Wiseman (1802–65). Cardinal archbishop of Westminster. Eng. author.
Wister Owen Wister (1860–1938). Amer. novelist.
Wither. George Wither, or Withers (1588–1667). Eng. poet.
P. G. Wodehouse Pelham Grenville Wodehouse (1881–). Eng. humorous novelist.
T. Wolfe Thomas (Clayton) Wolfe (1900–1938). Amer. novelist.
Wollaston William Wollaston (1660–1724). Eng. clergyman.
M. Wollstonecraft. Mary Wollstonecraft Godwin (1759–97). Eng. author.
Mrs. H. Wood. Mrs. Henry Wood (1814–87). Eng. novelist.
R. S. Woodworth Robert Sessions Woodworth (1869–). Amer. psychologist.
V. Woolf. Virginia Woolf (1882–1941). Eng. novelist and essayist.
Wordsworth. William Wordsworth (1770–1850). Eng. poet.
D. Wordsworth Dorothy Wordsworth (1771–1855). Eng. diarist; sister of William.
World's Work. Amer. monthly magazine of current history (1900–32, when it was absorbed by *Review of Reviews*).
Wotton. Sir Henry Wotton (1568–1639). Eng. diplomat and poet.
Sir C. Wren Sir Christopher Wren (1632–1723). Eng. architect.
T. Wright. Thomas Wright (1810–77). Eng. antiquary.
Wyatt Sir Thomas Wyatt, or Wyat (1503?–42). Eng. poet.
Wycherley William Wycherley (1640?–1716). Eng. playwright.
Wycliffe John Wycliffe (d. 1384). Eng. Bible translator, and reformer.
H. C. Wyld. Henry Cecil Kennedy Wyld (1870–). Eng. philologist and lexicographer.
Yale Review Amer. literary quarterly (present series est. 1911).
Yeats William Butler Yeats (1865–1939). Irish poet.
C. M. Yonge Charlotte Mary Yonge (1823–1901). Eng. novelist.
Young Edward Young (1683–1765). Eng. poet and dramatist.
Sir G. Young Sir George Young (1837–1930). Eng. translator.
Stark Young Stark Young (1881–). Amer. novelist, poet, and playwright.
Young's Naut. Dict. *Nautical Dictionary,* by Arthur Young (pub. 1846–63).
Zangwill Israel Zangwill (1864–1926). Eng. novelist and playwright.